A COMPLETE CONCORDANCE

TO

SCIENCE AND HEALTH

WITH KEY TO THE SCRIPTURES

TOGETHER WITH AN INDEX TO
THE MARGINAL HEADINGS AND A
LIST OF THE SCRIPTURAL QUOTA-
TIONS CONTAINED IN THAT BOOK AS
FINALLY REVISED BY ITS AUTHOR

MARY BAKER EDDY

Discoverer and Founder of Christian Science and Author
of Science and Health with Key to the Scriptures

Published by the
Trustees under the Will of Mary Baker G. Eddy
BOSTON, U.S.A.

Authorized Literature of
The First Church of Christ, Scientist
in Boston, Massachusetts

PREFACE

For many years there have been calls for a more complete index to "SCIENCE AND HEALTH WITH KEY TO THE SCRIPTURES," and although the index prepared by the late Rev. J. H. Wiggin about the year 1885 was quite large, neither it nor subsequent indices fully met the requirements of the students of our textbook. It finally became apparent that the only satisfactory way to meet this need was to prepare a complete Concordance, which should include all prominent words and phrases which the student may desire to find. I am confident that this work will fully meet his demands.

Following this is a preface prepared by the individual whom I employed as compiler of this Concordance, in which he sets forth his plan of arrangement, with an explanation of abbreviations used in this work.

MARY BAKER EDDY.

PLEASANT VIEW, CONCORD, N.H., May 15, 1903

COMPILER'S PREFACE

THIS Concordance contains every noun, verb, adjective, and adverb in SCIENCE AND HEALTH, together with certain pronouns, prepositions, and conjunctions, which were deemed of sufficient importance to be introduced.

The numbers indicating page and line refer to the word under consideration and not necessarily to the beginning of the line quoted.

The letters preceding the numbers are abbreviations of the chapters where the references are to be found. A * following a page number indicates that the reference is in the quotation in italics at the head of the chapter indicated.

A special feature of the work is to be found in the fact that every noun of frequent occurrence is provided with sub-titles. These sub-titles are arranged in alphabetical order, under their respective nouns, and consist of adjectives or other qualifying words or phrases, preserving in every case the exact phraseology of SCIENCE AND HEALTH. By this method, all that the author of the Christian Science textbook has said on any given subject will be found grouped in one place. For example: the spiritual man is often referred to as the "idea of God." More than twenty references to this subject will be found in the sub-title "idea of" under the principal word "God." The sub-titles also enable those who are familiar with the text to look up passages by means of such words as God, Life, Truth, Love, Mind, matter, error, etc., without searching through several hundred references.

A few adjectives also, such as human, material, mortal, spiritual, etc., are furnished with sub-titles.

Certain words occurring in some places as nouns, are used in other places as verbs or adjectives. For example: the word "healing" is used as a noun, an adjective, and a participle. All such words appearing more than fifty times are classified and grouped under their respective parts of speech. If used less than fifty times in all, these words are not so separated.

Every reference to the author of SCIENCE AND HEALTH will be found under the heading "Eddy, Mrs. Mary Baker."

An index to the Marginal Headings in SCIENCE AND HEALTH will be found in Appendix A.

Every Scriptural quotation is indexed under every important word in it, in the same manner as other words, and is followed by the book, chapter, and verse where it may be found in the Bible. A separate list of all the books, chapters, and verses of the Bible from which quotations have been taken for use in SCIENCE AND HEALTH will be found in Appendix B.

In the hope that this work may be of service to the many thousand students of our beloved textbook, and an incentive to a more profound study of the life-giving Science elucidated therein, and in grateful acknowledgment of the loving wisdom of its Founder and our Leader, which has alone made this book a possibility, the following pages are committed to the public.

THE COMPILER.

PREFACE TO THE NEW EDITION

IN this edition of the Concordance, compiled from the 1908 edition of SCIENCE AND HEALTH, the plan of the original Concordance has been retained in its entirety. In preparing the references great care has been exercised to select the context which would most successfully suggest the entire sentence in which the indexed word occurs, and increased facilities for the topical study of the textbook have been provided in a rearrangement of some of the sub-titles. All references not found in the current edition of SCIENCE AND HEALTH have been omitted; and about five thousand new references have been inserted. Of these nearly sixteen hundred were needed for new words not hitherto indexed; and more than thirty-four hundred were required to index the changes in SCIENCE AND HEALTH which have been made by its author since the first Concordance was printed.

Mrs. Eddy has said: "I have revised SCIENCE AND HEALTH only to give a clearer and fuller expression of its original meaning" (SCIENCE AND HEALTH, 361–21). Some idea of the extent of her recent revisions may be gained from the above figures, which thus serve to enhance an appreciative recognition of the indefatigable labors of our Leader in the interests of humanity.

ALBERT F. CONANT
Compiler.

This edition of the Concordance to SCIENCE AND HEALTH has been compiled from the 1910 edition of the Christian Science textbook as finally revised by its author. It therefore includes the changes and additions made by Mrs. Eddy subsequent to 1908, the date of the former compilation, and agrees with the current editions.

BOSTON, MASSACHUSETTS, January, 1916

LIST OF ABBREVIATIONS

The abbreviations made use of in this Concordance are as follows:—

CHAPTER TITLES IN SCIENCE AND HEALTH

pref. Preface
pr. . . Prayer
a. . . . Atonement and Eucharist
m. . . Marriage
sp. . . Christian Science versus Spiritualism
an. . . Animal Magnetism Unmasked

s. . . . . Science, Theology, Medicine
ph. . . Physiology
f. . . . . Footsteps of Truth
c. . . . . Creation
b. . . . . Science of Being
o. . . . . Some Objections Answered
p. . . . . Christian Science Practice

t. . . . Teaching Christian Science
r. . . . . Recapitulation
k. . . . . Key to the Scriptures
g. . . . . Genesis
ap. . . The Apocalypse
gl. . . Glossary
fr. . . . Fruitage

The words "Christian Science" have been abbreviated in the lines to C. S.

BOOKS OF THE BIBLE

Gen. . . . . Genesis
Exod. . . . . Exodus
Lev. . . . . Leviticus
Deut. . . . . Deuteronomy
I Kings . . . . . . I Kings
Job . . . . Job
Psal. . . . . Psalms
Prov. . . . . Proverbs
Eccl. . . . . Ecclesiastes
Song. . . . . Song of Solomon
Isa. . . . . Isaiah
Jer. . . . . Jeremiah
Lam. . . . . Lamentations

Ezek. . . . . Ezekiel
Dan. . . . . Daniel
Hos. . . . . Hosea
Hab. . . . . Habakkuk
Matt. . . . . Matthew
Mark . . . . Mark
Luke . . . . Luke
John . . . . John
Acts . . . . Acts
Rom. . . . . Romans
I Cor. . . . . . . I Corinthians
II Cor. . . . . . . II Corinthians
Gal. . . . . Galatians

Eph. . . . . Ephesians
Phil. . . . . Philippians
Col. . . . . Colossians
I Thess. . . . . . I Thessalonians
II Thess. . . . . . II Thessalonians
I Tim. . . . . . . I Timothy
II Tim. . . . . . . II Timothy
Heb. . . . . Hebrews
Jas. . . . . James
I Pet. . . . . . . I Peter
II Pet. . . . . . . II Peter
I John . . . . . . I John
Rev. . . . . Revelation

A COMPLETE CONCORDANCE

TO

SCIENCE AND HEALTH

WITH KEY TO THE SCRIPTURES

A

Aaron's
gl 595–13 The Urim and Thummim, . . . on A· breast

abandon
s 129–21 We must a· pharmaceutics, and take up
f 254–21 a· so fast as practical the material,
o 348–23 would it not be well to a· the defence,
p 400–11 and a· their material beliefs.
g 534– 1 Hence she is first to a· the belief in the

abandoned
pref x–18 a· as hopeless by regular medical attendants.
b 304–32 is a· to conjectures, left in the hands of
p 382–30 medicines I had taken only a· me to

abandonment
p 374–31 expels it through the a· of a belief,

abashed
p 439–15 turned from the a· witnesses,
g 532–19 Ashamed before Truth, error shrank a·

abate
ph 196–24 help to a· sickness and to destroy it.
p 373–25 decomposition, or deposit will a·,
406–14 Sin and sickness will a· and seem less real

abatement
f 219–31 but we may look for an a· of these evils ;

Abel (see also **Abel's**)
g 540–26 And A·, he also brought of the — Gen. 4: 4.
540–31 A· takes his offering from the firstlings
541– 7 [Jehovah] had respect unto A·, — Gen. 4: 4.
541–14 Cain rose up against A· his brother, — Gen. 4: 8.
541–20 Where is A· thy brother? — Gen. 4: 9.
gl 579– 8 definition of

Abel's
g 541– 4 Cain seeks A· life, instead of

abetted
p 439–24 You aided and a· Fear and Health-laws.

abeyance
p 405– 6 to hold hatred in a· with kindness,

abide
a 50–16 They must a· in him and he in them,
55–28 that he may a· with you forever." — John 14: 16.
b 274–12 The senses of Spirit a· in Love,
p 381–27 a· by the rule of perpetual harmony,
t 456–19 One must a· in the morale of truth
456–23 understand and a· by the divine Principle
462–14 a· strictly by its rules, heed every statement,
r 495–16 Allow nothing but His likeness to a· in your

abides
b 304–17 produced by its Principle, . . . and a· with it.
p 384–25 fear subsides and the conviction a· that

abideth
b 325– 5 Such a one a· in Life,

abiding
b 289–11 To suppose that sin, . . . revenge, have life a·
327– 1 there is no a· pleasure in evil,
p 390–21 Dismiss it with an a· conviction that
405–24 The a· consciousness of wrong-doing tends
r 495–30 a· steadfastly in wisdom, Truth, and Love.

abiding-place
f 244– 9 goodness would have no a·
b 282–14 straight line finds no a· in a curve,

abilities
s 128–15 the latent a· and possibilities of man.

ability
God-given
ph 182–26 God-given a· to demonstrate Mind's sacred
healing
p 410–29 until the practitioner's healing a· is
t 449–12 registers his healing a· and fitness to teach.
human
a 52–25 speaking of human a· to reflect divine power,
infinite
r 494–17 Jesus demonstrated . . . the infinite a· of Spirit,
lesser
sp 95–14 greater or lesser a· of a Christian Scientist
one's
c 260–15 distrust of one's a· . . . often hampers
your
ph 182– 1 will diminish your a· to become a Scientist,

---

sp 92–24 the a· to make nothing of error will be
s 128–11 a· to exceed their ordinary capacity.
130–22 a· of Spirit to make the body harmonious,
ph 187– 9 attributes to some material god . . . an a·
f 218–18 without faith in God's willingness and a·.
p 393–14 nothing can vitiate the a· and power
404–25 increases his a· to master evil
405–25 wrong-doing tends to destroy the a· to do right.
428–19 We must realize the a· of mental might
g 524–29 Could Spirit . . . give matter a· to sin and suffer?
555–27 or that Truth confers the a· to

able
a 49–23 a·, through Truth, Life, and Love, to triumph
sp 85–10 a· to read the human mind after this manner
93– 1 substantial and a· to control the body?
95– 9 a· to discern the thought of the sick
s 127–27 Science . . . is alone a· to interpret God aright.
137–10 Who or what is it that is a· to do the work,
145– 3 caught its sweet tones, . . . without being a· to
161– 6 a· to nullify the action of the flames,
ph 191–31 Truth is a· to cast out the ills of the flesh.
196–11 "Fear him which is a· to — Matt. 10: 28.
f 217–24 you will be a· to demonstrate this
235–24 physicians should be a· to teach it.
249– 8 no mortal nor material power as a· to destroy.
253–13 there is no cause . . . a· to make you sick
b 304– 8 nor any other creature, shall be a· — Rom. 8: 39.
323– 2 will not be a· to glean . . . without striving
329–16 until one is a· to prevent bad results,
o 343– 9 one might not be a· to say with the apostle,
345–21 Anybody, who is a· to perceive the incongruity
345–22 ought to be a· to discern the distinction
352– 2 did not sufficiently understand God to be a·
359–24 "God is a· to raise you up from sickness ;"
p 385– 3 a· to undergo without sinking fatigues and
387–11 we are a· to rest in Truth, refreshed by
423– 2 and may not be a· to mend the bone,
r 488– 4 a· to banish a severe malady, the cure shows
493–18 Mind must be found . . . a· to destroy all ills.
g 530–11 as a· to feed and clothe man as He doth the
547–12 Agassiz was a· to see in the egg the
555–31 Jesus was a· to present himself unchanged
ap 568– 4 Science is a· to destroy this lie, called evil.

1

ablest

   g 553–10   One of our *a·* naturalists has said :

ablutions

   p 413–12   daily *a·* of an infant are no more natural
   431–29   I practise daily *a·* and perform my

abnormal

   s 120–14   health is normal and disease is *a·*.
   p 423–27   Ossification or any *a·* condition

abnormally

   p 377–13   suddenly weak or *a·* strong,

abode

   b 280– 5   light and harmony which are the *a·* of Spirit,
   292–23   and *a·* not in the truth, because— *John* 8 : 44.

abolish

   m 58–30   nothing can *a·* the cares of marriage.
   f 225–19   *a·* the whipping-post and slave market ;
   225–23   Legally to *a·* unpaid servitude

abolished

   f 224–29   the Soul-inspired motto, "Slavery is *a·*."
   226– 1   African slavery was *a·* in our land.

abolition

   f 225–24   *a·* of mental slavery is a more difficult task.

abomination

   gl 588– 4   "worketh *a·* or maketh a lie." — *Rev.* 21 : 27.

abortive

   t 459–14   Any attempt to . . . must prove *a·*.

abound

   f 202–26   Truth should "much more *a·*." — *Rom.* 5 : 20.
   223–29   sin will much more *a·* as truth urges
   b 320– 4   Metaphors *a·* in the Bible,
   g 512–11   *a·* in the spiritual atmosphere of Mind,

abounds

   f 202–25   Error *a·* where Truth should

about

   pref xi–27   *a·* the year 1867.
   pr 9–28   Then why make long prayers *a·* it
   13–16   before we tell Him . . . *a·* it.
   a 25– 9   went daily *a·* his Father's business.
   33–13   their Master was *a·* to suffer violence
   41–18   *a·* three centuries after the crucifixion.
   41–26   his apostles still went *a·* doing good
   43–29   beliefs *a·* life, substance, and
   52– 1   From early boyhood he was *a·* his
   an 105–26   will be millstones *a·* his neck,
   s 121–26   revolves *a·* the sun once a year,
   125–19   material theories *a·* laws of health
   132–16   their materialistic beliefs *a·* God.
   134–12   and so it came *a·* that human rights
   137–15   the common report *a·* him.
   153–30   loquacious tattling *a·* disease,
   155– 2   forgets all *a·* the accident,
   ph 169– 9   it always came *a·* as I had foretold.
   172– 3   Theorizing *a·* man's development
   176– 7   taking no thought *a·* food
   193–13   In *a·* ten minutes he opened his eyes
   197–12   *a·* moral and spiritual law,
   f 201–16   we shall not hug our tatters close *a·* us.
   202–24   Our beliefs *a·* a Supreme Being
   222–14   Taking less thought *a·* what he should eat
   222–15   *a·* the economy of living
   230–13   so as to bring *a·* certain evil results,
   232– 5   The beliefs we commonly entertain *a·*
   237– 3   On being questioned *a·* it she answered
   237–17   theories or thoughts *a·* sickness.
   237–24   to hear *a·* the fallacy of matter
   238–28   no time for gossip *a·* false law
   c 260–26   by conversation *a·* the body,
   261–14   walking *a·* as actively as the
   b 305–31   The Sadducees reasoned falsely *a·* the
   328– 6   Understanding little *a·* the divine
   328–12   destroys human delusions *a·* Him
   o 352–30   not irrational to tell the truth *a·* ghosts.
   357–18   false notions *a·* the Divine Being
   357–20   wrong notions *a·* God must have
   p 363– 6   which hung loosely *a·* her shoulders,
   372– 6   One theory *a·* this mortal mind is,
   374– 8   I never thought of and knew nothing *a·*,
   389– 6   The less we know or think *a·* hygiene,
   389–16   metaphors *a·* the fount and stream,
   396– 7   a discouraging remark *a·* recovery,
   413–27   *a·* disease, health-laws, and death,
   414–30   is not brought *a·* by divine Love.
   416–27   If they ask *a·* their disease,
   416–29   they think too much *a·* their ailments,
   419–13   with which to move itself *a·*
   424–23   while others are thinking *a·* your patients
   425–32   Discard all notions *a·* lungs,
   t 445–30   Recalling Jefferson's words *a·* slavery,
   g 521–19   *a·* creation in the book of Genesis.
   529– 4   It came *a·*, also, that instruments were
   536–23   hedge *a·* their achievements with thorns.

about

   g 544–17   The first statement *a·* evil,
   548–20   statements now current, *a·* birth and
   553–27   ancient superstition *a·* the creation
   555– 8   not comprehend what you say *a·* error."

above

   pr 11–24   but if we desire holiness *a·* all else, we shall
   16–20   Only as we rise *a·* all material sensuousness
   a 18–18   could conciliate no nature *a·* his own,
   34–25   ascend far *a·* their apprehension.
   35–17   his spiritual and final ascension *a·* matter,
   44–26   a method infinitely *a·* that of human invention.
   46–21   his exaltation *a·* all material conditions ;
   46–28   rose *a·* the physical knowledge of his disciples,
   49–22   is *a·* the reach of human wrath,
   53–12   *a·* and contrary to the world's religious sense.
   sp 74– 8   a sprout which has risen *a·* the soil.
   77–26   The departed would gradually rise *a·* ignorance
   98– 3   elevation of existence *a·* mortal discord
   98–15   *a·* the loosening grasp of creeds,
   99–19   may possess natures *a·* some others
   s 118– 3   an inference far *a·* the merely ecclesiastical
   123–13   Divine Science, rising *a·* physical theories,
   147–20   lifts you high *a·* the perishing fossils
   153–12   highest attenuation . . . rises *a·* matter into
   ph 167– 7   only as we live *a·* corporeal sense
   174– 9   rising *a·* material standpoints,
   189– 6   raises the human thought *a·* the cruder theories
   f 238–29   place the fact *a·* the falsehood,
   240–10   the Principle is *a·* what it reflects,
   246– 8   by no means a material germ rising . . . *a·* his
   c 262–12   rise *a·* the testimony of the material senses,
   262–13   *a·* the mortal to the immortal idea of God.
   266–30   He is *a·* sin or frailty.
   b 269–11   Metaphysics is *a·* physics,
   302–16   always beyond and *a·* the mortal illusion
   307–31   *A·* error's awful din, blackness, and chaos,
   313– 8   With the oil of gladness *a·* thy— *Heb.* 1 : 9.
   318–16   Is the sick man sinful *a·* all others?
   p 365– 9   enable them to rise *a·* the supposed necessity
   373–21   you must rise *a·* both fear and sin.
   379–14   Had he known . . . he would have risen *a·* the
   385– 7   divine law, rising *a·* the human.
   394–16   that he should not try to rise *a·* his
   400–18   By lifting thought *a·* error, or disease,
   405– 3   any man, who is *a·* the lowest type
   407–14   lifting humanity *a·* itself
   437–30   bar of Truth, which ranks *a·* the lower Court
   t 448–12   C. S. rises *a·* the evidence of the
   448–13   but if you have not risen *a·* sin yourself,
   450–19   evil will boast itself *a·* good.
   451–17   If . . . spiritual, they come from *a·*,
   r 471–26   interprets God as *a·* mortal sense.
   493–13   A full answer to the *a·* question
   g 505–15   which were *a·* the firmament :— *Gen.* 1 : 7.
   511–21   and fowl that may fly *a·* the earth— *Gen.* 1 : 20.
   511–29   The fowls, which fly *a·* the earth
   512– 2   aspirations soaring beyond and *a·* corporeality
   520–28   immortal creating thought is from *a·*,
   521– 1   Knowledge of this lifts man *a·* the sod,
   521– 2   *a·* earth and its environments,
   523–11   comes from beneath, not from *a·*.
   531–11   rise *a·* all material and physical sense,
   ap 558–15   it has for you a light *a·* the sun,
   569–18   not struggling to lift their heads *a·* the

Abraham

   b 333–23   *A·*, Jacob, Moses, and the prophets
   333–29   "Before *A·* was, I am ;"— *John* 8 : 58.
   334– 2   and therefore antedated *A·* ;
   t 444–24   part from these opponents as did *A·*
   g 501– *   appeared unto *A·*, unto *Isaac, and* — *Exod.* 6 : 3.
   gl 579–10   definition of

abroad

   a 29– 2   take up arms against error at home and *a·*.

abscess

   f 251– 3   an *a·* should not grow more painful

absence

of law

   p 391–18   Injustice declares the *a·* of law.

of light

   f 215–17   only a mortal sense of the *a·* of light,

of other proofs

   p 363–28   In the *a·* of other proofs, was her grief

of pain

   ph 186–26   If pain is as real as the *a·* of pain,

of solar time

   g 504–18   words which indicate, in the *a·* of solar time,

of something

   ph 186–12   It is nothing, because it is the *a·* of something.

of soul

   b 311–16   sense of temporary loss or *a·* of soul,

of truth

   sp 92–30   when it is merely the *a·* of truth,
   ph 186–11   a negation, because it is the *a·* of truth.

absence

suppositional

f 215–20   the suppositional *a·* of Life, God,

ph 173–14   Spirit's contrary, the *a·* of Spirit.
186–13   because it presupposes the *a·* of God,
f 207–25   errors, which presuppose the *a·* of Truth,
b 282–29   the opposite of God or God's *a·*,
287– 9   We call the *a·* of Truth, *error.*
287–15   how can He be absent or suggest the *a·* of
g 504–31   supposition of the *a·* of Spirit.
555– 2   and that health attends the *a·* of
gl 584–28   the *a·* of substance, life, or intelligence.

absent

pr 14– 3   "*a·* from the body" — II Cor. 5 : 8.
14–21   because the Ego is *a·* from the body,
sp 82– 2   We think of an *a·* friend as easily as
82– 4   It is no more difficult to read the *a·* mind
s 130–32   no longer imagine evil to be . . . and good *a·*?
ph 179– 5   Science can heal the sick, who are *a·* from
f 216–29   *a·* from the body, — II Cor. 5 : 8.
250–21   and the mind seems to be *a·*.
b 287–14   how can He be *a·* or suggest the absence of
p 383–10   *a·* from the body, — II Cor. 5 : 8.
439– 6   Death testified that he was *a·* from
gl 581–25   *a·* from the body, — II Cor. 5 : 8.

absolute

pr 1– 2   *a·* faith that all things are possible to God,
3–16   demands *a·* consecration of thought,
a 41–21   the divine healing of *a·* Science.
sp 72–11   (in *a·* Science) Soul, or God, is the only
s 107– 5   final revelation of the *a·* divine Principle
109– 9   and thus proved *a·* and divine.
109–20   I won my way to *a·* conclusions
116–31   Mind in a finite form is an *a·* impossibility.
142–10   Truth, alone can furnish us with *a·* evidence.
151– 6   erring, finite, human mind has an *a·* need of
ph 177– 5   divine Mind's healing power and *a·* control
f 219– 4   Mind should be, and is, supreme, *a·*, and final.
254–16   During the sensual ages, *a·* C. S. may not
c 262–15   the *a·* centre and circumference of his being.
b 269–21   testimony of the material senses is neither *a·*
274–23   Divine Science is *a·*, and permits no
283–11   Principle is *a·*.
325–15   *a·* meaning of the apostolic words
o 341–17   facts are so *a·* and numerous in support of
344– 2   it claims God as the only *a·* Life and Soul,
p 388–27   food does not affect the *a·* Life of man,
423–26   which ultimately asserts its *a·* supremacy.
t 448–24   pursuit of instructions opposite to *a·* C. S.
454–12   the doctrine of *a·* C. S.,
r 465– 4   *A·* C. S. pervades its statements,
465–12   They refer to one *a·* God.
483–21   The spirit of C. S., if not the *a·* letter.
484– 2   until its *a·* Science is reached.
g 507– 2   the *a·* formations instituted by Mind,
520– 7   The *a·* ideal, man, is no more seen nor
ap 573–28   This is indeed a foretaste of *a·* C. S.

absolutely

pr 14–10   to be *a·* governed by divine Love,
s 123– 9   the most *a·* weak and inharmonious creature
ph 167–29   timid conservatism is *a·* inadmissible.
182–10   for one *a·* destroys the other,
o 355–20   statement that the teachings . . . are "*a·* false,
p 372–14   When man demonstrates C. S. *a·*,
g 549–30   He *a·* drops from his summit,
ap 565–17   will eventually rule . . . imperatively, *a·*,

absoluteness

o 345– 7   When . . . His *a·* is set forth,

absolution

p 364–12   declaring the *a·* of the penitent.

absorb

s 147–15   never . . . can *a·* the whole meaning
g 556–13   C. S. may *a·* the attention of sage and

absorbed

a 52– 7   their senses . . . *a·* the material evidence of sin,
sp 74– 7   the acorn, already *a·* into a sprout
91–16   *A·* in material selfhood we discern . . . but
      faintly
c 259– 1   Man is not *a·* in Deity,
261–10   turns away from the body with such *a·* interest
b 309–31   never *a·* nor limited by its own formations.
331– 7   God would not be reflected but *a·*,

absorption

c 265–11   by no means suggests man's *a·* into Deity

abstinence

f 220–24   Finding his health failing, he gave up his *a·*,

abstract

t 459–24   To mortal sense C. S. seems *a·*,
r 470–11   Divine Science explains the *a·* statement
ap 558–11   To mortal sense Science seems . . . obscure, *a·*,

absurd

m 67–19   The notion . . . is too *a·* for consideration,
f 208–14   *a·* to suppose that matter can both cause and
217– 3   notion of such a possibility is more *a·* than
r 485– 3   *Material sense* is an *a·* phrase,
495– 7   and it would be *a·* to try.
g 550–29   not so hideous and *a·* as the supposition

absurdities

o 354– 3   Are the protests of C. S. . . . *a·*,"
g 551– 1   material senses must father these *a·*,

absurdity

s 163–28   humiliating view of so much *a·*,
r 472–21   and we should have a self-evident *a·*

abundant

ph 188–25   and you have an *a·* or scanty crop

abundantly

g 511–20   Let the waters bring forth *a·* — Gen. 1 : 20.
512– 6   which the waters brought forth *a·*, — Gen. 1 : 21.
548–25   he would have blessed the human race more *a·*.

abuse

ph 175– 9   What an *a·* of natural beauty to say that a rose,
t 446–32   oftentimes subjects you to its *a·*.
455–22   renders any *a·* of the mission an impossibility.
ap 560–22   *A·* of the motives and religion of St. Paul

abused

an 102–27   is much more likely to be *a·* by its possessor,
s 110–22   and its ideas may be temporarily *a·* and
p 410–26   If mental practice is *a·*
430–32   was personally *a·* on those occasions.
432–23   protested that the prisoner had *a·* him,
t 460–19   If Christian healing is *a·* by mere smatterers

abyss

ph 199–26   to walk the rope over Niagara's *a·* of waters,

academic

f 235–12   not so much *a·* education,

academics

ph 195–19   *A·* of the right sort are requisite.

accelerated

ap 569–23   comes back to him at last with *a·* force,

accept

pr 2–28   pouring forth more than we *a·*
a 54–19   would not *a·* his meek interpretation of life
sp 78–13   Then why . . . *a·* them as oracles?
91– 9   difficult for the sinner to *a·* divine Science,
s 130– 6   and therefore they cannot *a·*.
ph 182– 8   Which, then, are we to *a·* as legitimate
f 227–24   *a·* the "glorious liberty of the — Rom. 8 : 21.
231–17   Therefore we *a·* the conclusion that discords
249– 1   Let us *a·* Science, relinquish all theories
254–20   This task God demands us to *a·* lovingly
c 266–12   Love will force you to *a·* what best promotes
b 272–16   teachings which . . . grossness could not *a·*.
p 420–11   if they will only *a·* Truth, they can
r 494–26   Which of these . . . are you ready to *a·*?

acceptable

pr 3–31   In such a case, the only *a·* prayer
a 34– 4   "holy, *a·* unto God," — Rom. 12 : 1.
f 221–21   Hence semi-starvation is not *a·* to wisdom,
b 325–22   holy, *a·* unto God, — Rom. 12 : 1.

acceptance

f 202–12   the perception and *a·* of Truth.
b 330– 7   would meet with immediate and universal *a·*.
o 343–23   meekness and . . . are the conditions of its *a·*,
355–22   ever offered for *a·*,"

accepted

a 39–18   "*Now,*" . . . "is the *a·* time ; — II Cor. 6 : 2.
sp 93– 8   "Behold, *now* is the *a·* time ; — II Cor. 6 : 2.
s 131–24   not *a·* until the hearts of men are made ready
132–20   it has not yet been generally *a·*.
f 248–17   Have you *a·* the mortal model?
b 316– 2   way of salvation to all who *a·* his word.
o 344–20   not included in the commonly *a·* systems ;
p 386– 2   evidence of the senses is not to be *a·*
t 461– 5   C. S. must be *a·* at this period by induction.
r 469–19   claimed no other Mind and *a·* no other,
g 552– 5   was once an *a·* theory.

accepting

s 129–23   look deep into realism instead of *a·* only
o 357– 5   not by *a·*, but by rejecting a lie.

accepts

pr 8–16   If we feel the aspiration, . . . this God *a·* ;
s 148–17   drops the true tone, and *a·* the discord.
g 520–12   thought *a·* the divine infinite calculus.
536–24   Mortal mind *a·* the erroneous,
gl 585–20   human belief before it *a·* sin, sickness,

access

s 128–17   giving mortals *a·* to broader and higher realms.

accident

s 155– 2   Presently the child forgets all about the *a*·,
f 214–29   Neither age nor *a*· can interfere with the
252–26   says : . . . But a touch, an *a*·, the law of
b 304–24   would lose harmony, if time or *a*· robbed
o 342–18   If . . . truth becomes an *a*·.
p 392–29   exercise, heredity, contagion, or *a*·,
397–12   When an *a*· happens, you think or exclaim,
397–15   Your thought is . . . more powerful than the *a*·
r 486– 4   Suppose one *a*· happens to the eye,

accidents

p 402–16   You say that *a*·, injuries, and disease kill man,
424– 5   *A*· are unknown to God,
424–10   Under divine Providence there can be no *a*·,

accommodate

ph 195–29   lowering the intellectual standard to *a*·
b 280–13   to *a*· its finite sense of the divisibility
313–26   To *a*· himself to immature ideas

accompanied

sp 94– 8   with the demonstration which *a*· it,

accompanies

b 287–17   Neither understanding nor truth *a*· error,
g 514–18   Tenderness *a*· all the might imparted by Spirit.

accompaniment

f 249–28   The night-dream has less matter as its *a*·.

accompaniments

sp 78–16   Spiritualism with its material *a*·
b 310– 8   but without material *a*·.

accompany

f 223–21   Spiritual rationality and free thought *a*·
243–11   must always *a*· the letter of Science
p 375– 4   belief that inflammation and pain must *a*·
g 553– 1   and *a*· their descriptions with important

accompanying

ap 573–13   *A*· this scientific consciousness was

accomplish

sp 77– 3   Neither do other mortals *a*· the
96–32   to find means by which to *a*· more evil ;
o 352–31   To *a*· a good result, it is certainly not irrational
p 394– 8   Knowledge that we can *a*· the good
t 448–22   impossible for error, . . . to *a*· the grand results

accomplished

pref vii–26   must declare what the pioneer has *a*·.
a 51–13   but when his earth-mission was *a*·,
b 322–10   in view of the immense work to be *a*·
p 365–16   healing work will be *a*· at one visit,
t 457– 6   than has been *a*· by other books.
r 484– 3   When this is *a*·, neither pride, prejudice,

accomplishes

g 546–28   resides in the good this system *a*·,

accomplishing

pr 1– 7   God's gracious means for *a*·
ap 571– 2   evil's hidden mental ways of *a*· iniquity.

accomplishment

pr 13– 8   striving for the *a*· of all we ask,
p 429– 7   The final demonstration takes time for its *a*·.

accord

m 63–16   marvel why usage should *a*· woman less rights
s 129– 9   be it in *a*· with your preconceptions or
f 202–16   immortal man, in *a*· with the divine Principle
b 314–31   submissive to death as being in supposed *a*·
337– 9   the Son must be in *a*· with the Father,
p 408–16   Can drugs go of their own *a*· to the brain
t 455– 1   auxiliaries to aid in bringing thought into *a*·
g 515–23   moves in *a*· with Him,
515–28   the lips of this likeness move in *a*· with yours.
545–15   and do not *a*· infinity to Deity.

accordance

a 27–11   in strict *a*· with his scientific statement :
36– 8   not in *a*· with God's government,
sp 96–26   shaped his course in *a*· with divine Science
ph 168–22   in *a*· with God's law, the law of Mind.
f 208–12   not in *a*· with the goodness of God's character
231–26   is in *a*· with divine Science.
b 276– 7   in *a*· with the Scriptural command :
p 440–26   in *a*· with the divine statutes,
g 557–25   in *a*· with the first chapter of the
gl 597– 1   in *a*· with Pharisaical notions.

accorded

r 474– 4   reception *a*· to Truth in the early Christian era

according

pr 5–18   giving us strength *a*· to our day.
6–20   To suppose that God forgives or punishes sin *a*·
7–12   "a zeal . . . not *a*· to knowledge" — *Rom.* 10 : 2.
15–8, 9   rewards *a*· to motives, not *a*· to speech.
a 22–19   and receive *a*· to your deserving.
27–32   *a*· to certain assumed material laws.
m 57–31   Marriage is unblest or blest, *a*· to the
sp 77–17   longer or shorter duration *a*· to the tenacity
97– 7   *A*· to human belief, the lightning is fierce

according

an 100– 2   *A*· to the American Cyclopædia,
105–15   courts reasonably pass sentence, *a*· to the
s 108– 3   *A*· to St. Paul, it was "the gift of the — *Eph.* 3 : 7.
110–28   and demonstrated *a*· to Christ's command,
113–23   *A*· to the Scripture, I find that God is true,
127–11   *a*· to the requirements of the context.
131–17   *a*· to the Scriptural saying,
149–31   and demonstrate truth *a*· to Christ.
155– 5   *a*· to this faith will the effect be.
157–16   (*a*· to the narrative in Genesis)
158– 5   the first prescription, *a*· to the "History of
161–25   treating the case *a*· to his physical diagnosis,
ph 168–10   When sick (*a*· to belief) you rush after drugs,
170– 1   and *a*· to belief, poisons the human system.
173–22   Phrenology makes man knavish or honest *a*·
175–22   was not discussed *a*· to Cutter
183– 8   Can the agriculturist, *a*· to belief, produce
183–10   awaiting its germination *a*· to the laws of
188–26   *a*· to the seedlings of fear.
189–16   it is as truly mortal mind, *a*· to its degree,
189–27   *A*· to mortal thought, the development of
199–16   *a*· as they influence them through mortal mind
f 208–28   harmonious or discordant *a*· to the images of
213–28   *a*· as the hand, which sweeps over it,
230–22   *A*· to Holy Writ, the sick are never
233–25   When numbers have been divided *a*· to
236–16   "a· to the pattern showed to thee— *Heb.* 8 : 5.
239– 9   let worth be judged *a*· to wisdom,
242–21   *A*· to the Bible, the facts of being are
245–30   decrepitude is not *a*· to law,
250–17   *a*· to the dream he entertains in sleep.
c 256–20   "doeth *a*· to His will — *Dan.* 4 : 35.
b 284–28   *A*· to C. S., the only real senses of
320–22   for *a*· to that error man is mortal.
327– 3   gaining an affection for good *a*· to Science,
334–22   *a*· to the testimony of the corporeal senses,
337–10   *A*· to divine Science, man is
o 341–15   demonstrated *a*· to a divine given rule,
342–19   a system which works *a*· to the Scriptures
342–30   practising pharmacy or obstetrics *a*· to the
344–16   *a*· to the rules which disclose its merits or
355–15   One, *a*· to the commands of our Master, heals
357–23   *a*· to the vision of St. John in the Apocalypse.
p 362–12   *A*· to the custom of those days,
370–23   *A*· to both medical testimony and
404– 2   judge the case *a*· to C. S.
416–19   and been developed *a*· to it,
423–12   *A*· to Scripture, it searches
423–17   *a*· to the evidence which matter presents.
423–25   *a*· to the law of Mind, which ultimately asserts
425– 7   leading points included (*a*· to belief)
429–23   *a*· to the calculations of natural science.
435–26   *a*· to the law of Spirit, God.
441–12   *A*· to our statute, Material Law is a liar
t 443–11   work out their own salvation *a*· to their
449–23   attracted or repelled *a*· to personal merit
457–16   both sides were beautiful *a*· to their degree ;
r 473–22   test its unerring Science *a*· to his rule,
478– 4   Even *a*· to the teachings of natural science,
490–16   since he is so already, *a*· to C. S.
g 502–19   *a*· to the teachings of C. S.
516– 1   note how true, *a*· to C. S.
519–28   *a*· to the apprehension of divine Science.
520–11   *a*· to the calendar of time.
523–14   *a*· to the best scholars, there are clear evidences
526–29   The name Eden, *a*· to Cruden, means *pleasure*,
528–28   *a*· to this narrative, surgery was first performed
533–17   *A*· to this belief, the rib taken from
543–22   found, *a*· to divine Science, to be the
545– 4   *a*· to the record, material man was
549–13   *A*· to recent lore, successive generations
ap 565–19   This immaculate idea, . . . *a*· to the Revelator,
gl 584– 6   Mind measures time *a*· to the good that is

accordingly

s 152–19   and he recovered *a*·.
p 385–29   and you are thirsty *a*·,

accords

ph 192–18   this teaching *a*· with Science and harmony.

account

all

f 245– 6   became insane and lost all *a*· of time.

continued

g 521–20   but the continued *a*· is mortal and material.

its own

m 65–25   is never desirable on its own *a*·.

scientific

g 523–24   spiritually scientific *a*· of creation,

Scriptural

g 523– 2   perusal of the Scriptural *a*·

second

g 526–24   second biblical *a*· is a picture of error
537–20   second *a*· in Genesis — is to depict the **falsity of**

account
this
g 538–26   This *a·* is given, not of immortal man, but
gl 579– 4   On this *a·* this chapter is added.
your
p 405–16   until you have balanced your *a·* with God.

sp 90– 2   how then can we *a·* for their primal origin?
s 123–31   but not on that *a·* is it less scientific.
b 290– 6   on *a·* of that single experience,
o 357–11   or makes man capable of suffering on *a·* of
p 379–20   not dying on *a·* of the state of her blood,
386–11   not because of the climate, but on *a·* of the
392– 5   broken moral law should be taken into *a·*
396–18   on *a·* of the tenacity of belief in its truth,
g 553–21   theory . . . to *a·* for human origin,

accounted
m 69–27   But they which shall be *a·* worthy — *Luke* 20 : 35.
b 316–26   That man was *a·* a criminal
o 343–31   is often *a·* a heretic.

accounts
a 30– 8   This *a·* for his struggles in Gethsemane
s 139– 5   Scriptures are full of *a·* of the triumph of
g 523–27   *a·* become more . . . closely intertwined

accredited
a 18–10   Jesus acted boldly, against the *a·* evidence
o 358–32   than they have in their own *a·* . . . pastors,

accretion
m 68–27   C. S. presents unfoldment, not *a·* ;

accumulated
p 380–23   evidence of which has *a·* to prove

accumulates
p 399– 8   No gastric gas *a·*, . . . apart from

accurate
sp 92–17   The portrayal is still graphically *a·*,
c 255– 9   afforded no foundation for *a·* views

accurately
sp 84–32   we can know the truth more *a·* than the
s 129– 3   the reasoning of an *a·* stated syllogism
b 283–26   unless its Science be *a·* stated.
o 349–14   conveying the teachings of divine Science *a·*
t 447– 9   incapable of knowing or judging *a·*

accursed
a 25– 8   shed upon "the *a·* tree," — *see Gal.* 3 : 13.
b 338–20   when matter, as that which is *a·*,
338–27   Jehovah declared the ground was *a·* ;

accusation
a 53– 2   latter *a·* was true, but not in their meaning.
f 203– 9   The *a·* of the rabbis,

accusations
a 52–29   The *a·* of the Pharisees were
s 133–25   one of the Jewish *a·* against him
ap 564–10   The author is convinced that the *a·* against

accused
ap 568–16   *a·* them before our God — *Rev.* 12 : 10.

accuser
t 458–25   Neither is he a false *a·*.
ap 568–16   *a·* of our brethren is cast down, — *Rev.* 12 : 10.
568–29   the *a·* is not there, and Love sends forth

accusers
a 50–21   what would his *a·* have said?

accustomed
c 261–13   noted actor was *a·* night after night
t 452– 7   Walking in the light, we are *a·* to
452– 8   eyes *a·* to darkness are pained by the light.

ache
p 393–18   Have no fear that matter can *a·*,

aches
f 212– 3   tooth . . . extracted sometimes *a·* again in belief,

achieved
f 254–17   may not be *a·* prior to the change

achievement
m 63–25   the *a·* of a nobler race for legislation,
ph 199–21   devotion of thought to an honest *a·*
199–22   makes the *a·* possible.
t 456– 2   adverse to its highest hope and *a·*.

achievements
g 536–23   and hedge about their *a·* with thorns.

achieves
t 459– 5   as mortal man *a·* no worldly honors except by

achieving
c 260–13   Science reveals the possibility of *a·*

aching
ph 165–17   distressed stomachs and *a·* heads.
c 261–17   sat *a·* in his chair till his cue was spoken,
b 295– 1   The belief that a severed limb is *a·*

acid
p 401– 9   (as when an alkali is destroying an *a·*,)
422–14   As when an *a·* and alkali meet and

acknowledge
a 20–24   Material belief is slow to *a·*
25– 1   Thomas was forced to *a·* how complete
sp 94–22   but one returned . . . to *a·* the divine Principle
s 151–29   narrow way is to see and *a·* this fact,
ph 166–20   waiting for the hour . . . in which to *a·* Him,
169–30   Whatever teaches man to . . . *a·* other powers
f 228–26   to *a·* any other power is to dishonor God.
239–17   and whom we *a·* and obey as God.
p 400–10   *a·* the supremacy of divine Mind,
425–21   the less we *a·* matter or its laws,
t 450–16   many are reluctant to *a·* that they have yielded ;
461–19   If you commit a crime, should you *a·* to yourself
r 497– 5   We *a·* and adore one supreme and infinite God
497– 6   We *a·* His Son, one Christ ;
497– 9   We *a·* God's forgiveness of sin in the
497–13   We *a·* Jesus' atonement as the
497–16   we *a·* that man is saved through Christ,
497–20   We *a·* that the crucifixion of Jesus
g 551–14   it does not *a·* the method of divine Mind,

acknowledged
pr 4–15   if not *a·* in audible words,
a 31– 4   Jesus *a·* no ties of the flesh.
54– 5   The world *a·* not his righteousness,
f 227– 2   and the rights of man are fully known and *a·*.
233– 9   perfection is seen and *a·* only by degrees.
239–23   Mortal mind is the *a·* seat of human motives.
p 385– 1   power of Mind . . . will be *a·*,
402– 3   branch of its healing which will be last *a·*.
408– 3   not *a·* nor discovered to be error
427–24   Mind, governing all, must be *a·* as supreme
r 492–17   until one is *a·* to be the victor.
ap 572–18   seen and *a·* that matter must disappear.
gl 587– 3   The rights of woman *a·*
588– 6   Divine Science understood and *a·*.

acknowledging
s 157– 9   *a·* that the divine Mind has all power.
r 491–13   only by *a·* the supremacy of Spirit,
g 521–10   *a·* now and forever God's supremacy,

acknowledgment
sp 91–15   but is the *a·* of them.
f 226– 8   asking a fuller *a·* of the rights of man
p 372–28   a just *a·* of Truth and of what it has done for us

acme
ap 577–30   his vision is the *a·* of this Science

Aconitum
s 152–30   Jahr, from *A·* to *Zincum oxydatum,*

acorn
sp 74– 7   the *a·*, already absorbed into a sprout

acquaint
s 107–13   thoughts *a·* themselves intelligently with God.
b 324–12   "*a·* now thyself with Him, — *Job* 22 : 21.
p 403–24   Never . . . and then *a·* your patient with it.

acquaintance
a 24– 4   *A·* with the original texts,
sp 84–14   *A·* with the Science of being enables us

acquainted
p 432– 3   *a·* with the plaintiff, Personal Sense,

acquiescence
a 48–26   Pilate was drawn into *a·* with the demands

acquires
s 158–21   *a·* an educated appetite for strong drink,

acquit
pr 11– 9   The moral law, which has the right to *a·*

across
pref vii– 9   *a·* a night of error should dawn the morning
sp 74–26   There is no bridge *a·* the gulf which divides

act
motive and
p 376–14   more life . . . in one good motive and *a·*
natural
a 44–24   On the contrary, it was a divinely natural *a·*,
not a supernatural
a 44–23   but it was not a supernatural *a·*.
of commending
sp 92–13   represents the serpent in the *a·* of commending
of describing
sp 79– 1   The *a·* of describing disease — its symptoms,
of doing good
f 202–32   in the *a·* of doing good,
of healing
ph 182– 1   The *a·* of healing the sick through divine Mind
of homicide
p 440–13   disobedience to God, or an *a·* of homicide.
of reading
sp 83–31   *a·* of reading mortal mind investigates

act

of yielding
p 413– 3   The *a·* of yielding one's thoughts to the
slain in the
b 290–28   murderer, though slain in the *a·*, does not
wicked
an 104–32   human mind must move the body to a wicked *a·* ?

———

pr 12– 7   making it *a·* more powerfully on the body
s 160– 3   systems of physics *a·* against metaphysics,
  160–24   If muscles can cease to *a·* and become rigid
ph 176– 8   left the stomach and bowels free to *a·*
  185–28   This is because erroneous methods *a·*
f 250– 4   suppose . . . *a·* unintelligence to *a·* like
c 264–11   we must *a·* as possessing all power
b 283– 9   states of mortal mind which *a·*, react,
p 368–25   matter has no consciousness . . . it cannot *a·* ;
  384– 2   Can matter, . . . *a·* without mind?
  394– 9   stimulates the system to *a·* in the direction
  397–25   than when they *a·*, walk, see,
  402–25   believe that they cannot *a·* voluntarily
  424–17   should not *a·* against your influence
  435– 9   an *a·* which should result in good to himself
gl 582– 8   strength, animation, and power to *a·*.

acted

a 18–10   *a·* boldly, against the accredited evidence
  20– 4   *a·* and spake as he was moved, . . . by Spirit.
s 148– 5   *a·* in direct disobedience to them.

acting

a 43–25   *a·* under spiritual law in defiance of matter
m 67–11   *a·* up to his highest understanding,
s 160–23   never capable of *a·* contrary to mental
ph 172–32   *a·* through the five physical senses
  178–18   Mortal mind, *a·* from the basis of sensation
p 397– 2   *a·* beneficially or injuriously on the health,
  417–13   all causation is Mind, *a·* through spiritual law.
  435–12   to punish a man for *a·* justly.
  436– 8   *a·* within the limits of the divine law,
t 452–25   by right talking and wrong *a·*,
  452–28   *A·* from sinful motives destroys your power
r 495–11   life-giving power of Truth *a·* on human belief,

action

all
ph 187–23   divine Mind includes all *a·* and volition,
p 419–20   Mind produces all *a·*.
basis of
s 160– 5   forsake the material for the spiritual basis of *a·*,
being and its
s 151–18   Fear never stopped being and its *a·*.
belief and
f 253–23   you can alter this wrong belief and *a·*
call into
ph 173–32   call into *a·* less faith than Buddhism
cause
s 160–15   and so cause *a·* ; but what does anatomy say
changed the
ph 185– 4   My metaphysical treatment changed the *a·* of
classify
ph 187–25   The human mind tries to classify *a·* as
devoid of
p 399–21   Without this force the body is devoid of *a·*,
diminishes the
p 420–20   It increases or diminishes the *a·*,
discordant
f 239–25   produces every discordant *a·* of the body.
diseased
p 428– 1   no inaction, diseased *a·*, overaction,
divine
an 104–15   which indicates the rightness of all divine *a·*,
effect or
t 463–30   Such seeming medical effect or *a·* is
entire
r 494– 2   and to govern man's entire *a·* ?
error in
f 207– 7   Error of statement leads to error in *a·*.
error of
g 550–15   Error of thought is reflected in error of *a·*.
every
p 407–24   perfect, harmonious in every *a·*.
excited
p 377–23   the morbid or excited *a·* of any organ.
feeling and
p 393–11   and govern its feeling and *a·*.
form, and
b 301– 3   mirror, repeats the color, form, and *a·*
God rests in
g 519–25   God rests in *a·*.
harmonious
b 283– 6   its perpetual and harmonious *a·*.
  420– 3   no metastasis, no stoppage of harmonious *a·*,
r 480–14   Harmonious *a·* proceeds from Spirit, God.
higher plane of
c 256– 2   Advancing to a higher plane of *a·*,
impedes
ph 166– 4   Mind is all that feels, acts, or impedes *a·*.

action

injurious
t 451–28   It is the injurious *a·* of one mortal mind
is erroneous
r 480–15   its *a·* is erroneous and presupposes
is harmonious
f 239–26   If . . . *a·* is harmonious.
latter
ph 187–17   Anatomy allows the mental cause of the latter *a·*,
law of this
p 422–14   explain to them the law of this *a·*.
life or
ph 187–28   body loses all appearance of life or *a·*,
materialistic
ph 187–19   the cause of all materialistic *a·* ?
mental
an 104–15   C. S. goes to the bottom of mental *a·*,
p 401–22   effect . . . is dependent upon mental *a·*.
  404– 1   physician should be familiar with mental *a·*
modus and
f 213– 1   would reverse the immortal modus and *a·*,
muscular
s 152–10   Anatomy describes muscular *a·* as produced
no involuntary
ph 187–22   There is no involuntary *a·*.
normal
f 212–30   The realities of being, its normal *a·*, and
nullify the
s 161– 7   able to nullify the *a·* of the flames,
of a water-wheel
p 399–18   the *a·* of a water-wheel is but a derivative
of divine Principle
s 121–29   imitates the *a·* of divine Principle ;
of error
r 484–22   voluntary or involuntary *a·* of error
of man
f 207–28   The spiritual fact, repeated in the *a·* of man
of mortal mind
ph 176– 2   The *a·* of mortal mind on the body
p 423–28   is as directly the *a·* of mortal mind
of mortal thought
p 399–10   apart from the *a·* of mortal thought,
of Soul
sp 89–23   *a·* of Soul confers a freedom, which explains
of the divine Mind
f 225–28   rooted out through the *a·* of the divine Mind.
of the human mind
pref xi– 3   a phase of the *a·* of the human mind,
f 234–30   the *a·* of the human mind, unseen to the senses.
of the lungs
p 415–20   the *a·* of the lungs, of the bowels,
of the mortal body
s 108–31   the organism and *a·* of the mortal body,
ph 187–20   *a·* of the mortal body is governed by
of the system
p 378– 9   no inflammatory nor torpid *a·* of the system.
  415– 6   quickens or impedes the *a·* of the system,
t 447–14   The recuperative *a·* of the system,
of this Mind
g 519–27   No exhaustion follows the *a·* of this Mind,
of thought
p 384–13   Through this *a·* of thought and its results
of Truth
ph 169–27   Only the *a·* of Truth, Life, and Love can give
  183–18   legitimate and only possible *a·* of Truth
p 386–13   the *a·* of Truth on the minds of mortals,
organic
s 126– 1   through its supposed organic *a·*
  160–10   the organic *a·* and secretion of the viscera.
or stagnation
s 159–27   how much pain or pleasure, *a·* or stagnation,
physical
p 420–27   power over every physical *a·* and condition.
power of
s 157–15   power of *a·* is proportionately increased.
represent the
p 415–23   represent the *a·* of all the organs
reverse this
c 261– 1   Now reverse this *a·*.
ripen into
ph 188– 9   hatred, revenge ripen into *a·*,
salutary
p 414– 6   it yields . . . to the salutary *a·* of truth,
scientific
f 210–14   the scientific *a·* of the divine Mind
speech and
t 454–21   strength and freedom to speech and *a·*.
spring into
gl 597– 9   crime, . . . which was ready to spring into *a·*
thought and
c 265–13   a wider sphere of thought and *a·*,

pref xi– 3   which *a·* in some unexplained way
pr   3–26   *A·* expresses more gratitude than speech.
an 104–17   wrongness of the opposite so-called *a·*,

action

s 136– 6	no intelligence, a·, nor life separate
ph 167–21	can no more unite in a·,
199– 1	If matter were the cause of a·,
199–31	before his power of putting resolve into a·
f 211–17	and this a· shows the nature of
239–25	If a· proceeds from the divine Mind,
p 400–26	The a· of so-called mortal mind must be
401–26	or restore will and a· to cerebrum
419–20	If the a· proceeds from Truth,
r 480–10	Consciousness, as well as a·, is governed by
gl 586– 8	FAN. . . . that which gives a· to thought.

actions

p 393– 5	ignorant of itself, of its own a·,
413–28	these a· convey mental images to

active

b 327–29	Reason is the most a· human faculty.
p 387– 3	Because mortal mind is kept a·, must it pay
387– 8	when we realize that immortal Mind is ever a·,
ap 570– 5	certain a· yet unseen mental agencies

actively

c 261–14	walking about as a· as the youngest member

activities

ph 185–31	material mentality and its suppositional a·.
ap 562–15	yield to the a· of the divine Principle

activity

b 268– 3	With like a· have thought's swift

actor

c 261–12	a noted a· was accustomed
p 399–15	If Mind is the only a·, how can mechanism

acts

pr 12–11	which a· through blind belief,
s 155–22	a· more powerfully . . . in proportion as
162– 6	C. S. a· as an alterative,
ph 166– 4	Mind is all that feels, a·, or impedes action.
187–31	holds in belief a body, through which it a·
f 206– 1	erring, human thought a· injuriously
238– 1	Motives and a· are not rightly valued
251–21	a· upon the so-called human mind
b 273–26	His a· were the demonstration of Science,
p 436–13	Such a· bear their own justification,
r 473–27	his a· of higher importance than his words.
g 520–30	Spirit a· through the Science of Mind,
gl 595–18	limits, in which are summed up all human a·,

actual

pr 14– 7	but the a· demonstration and
s 110– 3	contradict . . . the belief that matter can be a·.
122– 6	the a· reign of harmony on earth.
ph 183–27	casts out all evils . . . with the a· spiritual law,
f 254–23	which determines the outward and a·.
b 281–23	sin and mortality are without a· origin
297–30	has little relation to the a· or divine.
p 387– 4	Who dares to say that a· Mind can
410–12	showing that Truth is the a· life of man ;
r 478–24	this belief is mortal and far from a·.
491– 4	a belief without a· foundation or

actuality

a 52–20	the mighty a· of all-inclusive God, good.
s 130– 9	you can demonstrate the a· of Science.
b 296–16	spiritual sense, and the a· of being.
321–12	In this incident was seen the a· of Science.
r 481–22	then assume . . . because of their admitted a·.
g 502–13	reflection of God and the spiritual a· of man,

actually

p 397– 6	a· injuring those whom we mean to bless.

acute

sp 85–23	Jew and Gentile may have had a· corporeal
s 162–18	in cases of both a· and chronic disease
ph 176–29	Hence decided types of a· disease
f 246–32	A· and chronic beliefs reproduce their own
247– 1	The a· belief of physical life comes on at
p 369–16	Jesus never asked if disease were a· or chronic,
390–28	approaching symptoms of chronic or a· disease,

acuteness

s 128–10	gives them a· and comprehensiveness

Adam *(see also Adam's)*

alias error

g 528–24	A· — alias error — gives them names.

and Eve

sp 92–12	serpent . . . speaking to A· and Eve.

and his progeny

g 532–10	A· and his progeny were cursed, not blessed ;

as in

g 545–31	"As in A· [error] all die, — I Cor. 15 : 22.

called unto

g 532–14	Lord God [Jehovah] called unto A·, — Gen. 3 : 9.

hypnotic state in

g 528–16	inducing a sleep or hypnotic state in A·

innocent as

ph 175–29	They were as innocent as A·, before he

Adam

knew it not

g 532–29	the body had been naked, and A· knew it not ;

like

f 214–11	The material senses, like A·, originate in

name

b 338–14	Divide the name A· into two syllables,
gl 580–21	The name A· represents the false

or error

ph 177–16	A· or error, . . . had the naming of
g 534–13	unfolded the remedy for A·, or error ;

prior to

c 267–10	must have had children prior to A·.

race of

o 345–25	and the sinning race of A·.

where art thou

ph 181–24	"A·, where art thou?"— Gen. 3 : 9.
b 307–32	Truth still calls : "A·, where art thou?
308– 8	demand, "A·, where art thou?"— Gen. 3 : 9.

f 214– 9	A·, represented in the Scriptures as formed
249–23	Mortals are the A· dreamers.
b 338–12	The word A· is from the Hebrew adamah,
338–28	from this ground, or matter, sprang A·,
338–30	it follows that A· was not the ideal man
o 346– 2	such criticism confounds man with A·.
g 506–28	Upon A· devolved the pleasurable task
506–29	A· has not yet appeared in the narrative.
527–23	and brought them unto A·— Gen. 2 : 19.
527–24	whatsoever A· called every living— Gen. 2 : 19.
528– 4	That A· gave the name and nature of animals,
528–10	caused a deep sleep to fall upon A·, — Gen. 2 : 21,
529–30	A·, the synonym for error, stands for a belief
532– 1	Did God . . . create one man unaided, — that is, A·,
533– 4	This had never been bestowed on A·.
533–14	A·, alias mortal error, charges God and woman
533–23	bone and flesh which came from A·
535–19	And unto A· He said, — Gen. 3 : 17.
538–23	And A· knew Eve his wife ;— Gen. 4 : 1.
553–17	A· was created before Eve.
553–18	the maternal egg never brought forth A·.
556–18	the deep sleep which fell upon A·?
ap 560– 4	typical of six thousand years since A·,
gl 579–15	definition of

adamah

b 338–12	word Adam is from the Hebrew a·,

adamant

f 242–17	a· of error, — self-will, self-justification,

Adam-belief

g 556–23	Even so goes on the A·,

Adam-dream

b 282–29	the A·, which is neither Mind nor man,
306–32	parent of all human discord was the A·,

Adamic

g 525– 5	mankind represents the A· race,

Adam's

g 533–18	the rib taken from A· side has grown into
553–19	Eve was formed from A· rib,
554–24	This he said of Judas, one of A· race.

Adams

ph 176– 4	and unmanly A· attributed their own downfall

adaptation

pr 13– 2	Love is impartial and universal in its a·
s 116–11	correct view of C. S. and of its a·

adapted

m 58– 1	intercourse with those a· to elevate it,
an 101–14	had been promised . . . as conclusive, and as a·
s 146–32	comprehensible by and a· to the thought of
b 318–27	and are not a· to elevate mankind.
p 403–22	and this is best a· for healing the sick.
ap 574– 3	The Revelator also takes in another view, a·

add

s 130–19	cannot a· to the contents of a vessel already full.
ph 180–15	invalid may unwittingly a· more fear to
t 462– 6	and a· continually to his store of spiritual

added

a 50– 6	a· to an overwhelming sense of the magnitude
51– 5	This dread a· the drop of gall to his cup.
m 56– 3	Jesus a·: "Suffer it to be so now :— Matt. 3 : 15.
f 237– 5	with laughing eyes, she presently a·,
b 295– 3	a· proof of the unreliability of
o 342–11	to which command was a· the promise
344– 4	It should be a· that this is claimed
p 398– 4	It is a· that "the spirit— Mark 9 : 26.
t 454– 1	It need not be a· that the use of tobacco
gl 579– 4	On this account this chapter is a·.

adding

p 375–18	a· to his patient's mental . . . power,

addition

pr 16–13	whether the last line is not an *a·* to the prayer
s 128–29	The *a·* of two sums in mathematics
b 329–18	To be discouraged, is to resemble a pupil in *a·*,
g 524–24	Is this *a·* to His creation real or unreal?

additional
m 58–14 With *a·* joys, benevolence should grow

address
s 160– 1 should *a·* himself to the work of destroying it

addresses
p 433– 3 *a·* the jury of Mortal Minds.

addressing
a 38–12 He was *a·* his disciples, yet he did not say,
p 400–20 When we remove disease by *a·* the

adds
sp 99– 7 he straightway *a·* : "for it is God— *Phil.* 2 : 13.
g 551–11 but he *a·* that mankind has ascended

adequate
f 234–23 *a·* to the right education of human thought.
c 256–24 No form nor physical combination is *a·* to
p 412–14 It is indeed *a·* to unclasp the hold

adhere
s 112– 9 and *a·* to some particular system of
141– 5 Few understand or *a·* to Jesus' divine
ph 181–23 if you *a·* to error and are afraid to trust
t 459–32 Scientist should understand and *a·* strictly
r 471–24 tried to *a·* to it until she caught the first gleam
495–28 *A·* to the divine Principle of C. S. and follow

adhered
a 54–22 There *a·* to him only a few unpretentious

adherence
m 65–28 permanence and peace in a more spiritual *a·*.
ph 166–23 Failing to recover health through *a·* to
f 222–18 as was believed, only by the strictest *a·* to
p 382–31 *A·* to hygiene was useless.
t 456– 5 Strict *a·* to the divine Principle and

adherents
s 112– 7 become *a·* of the Socratic, the Platonic,
r 497– 3 As *a·* of Truth, we take the inspired Word

adheres
t 448–26 If the student *a·* strictly to the teachings of
462– 3 any student, who *a·* to the divine rules

adhering
p 387–19 By *a·* to the realities of eternal existence,

adhesion
s 124–20 *A·*, cohesion, and attraction are properties of
b 293–15 whose *a·* and cohesion are Life,

adjective
r 466– 2 *Omni* is adopted from the Latin *a·* signifying

adjudged
p 442– 1 There, Man is *a·* innocent of

adjusted
a 40– 8 adjusts the balance as Jesus *a·* it.
ph 168– 4 If the scales are evenly *a·*,

adjustment
b 282–15 a curve finds no *a·* to a straight line.
p 401–29 *a·* of broken bones and dislocations

adjusts
a 40– 8 *a·* the balance as Jesus adjusted it.
t 449– 8 Right *a·* the balance sooner or later.

administer
s 153–20 Now *a·* mentally to your patient
ph 174–26 why treat the body alone and *a·* a dose of
p 424–13 if one doctor should *a·* a drug to counteract

administered
s 153– 9 a teaspoonful of the water *a·* at intervals of
p 416– 6 A hypodermic injection of morphine is *a·*

administers
p 399– 6 Mortal mind prescribes the drug, and *a·* it.

admission
another
b 278–17 requires another *a·*,— namely, that Spirit
p 388–14 and there follows the necessity for another *a·*
proportionate
ph 167– 8 Our proportionate *a·* of the claims of

sp 75–15 not by an *a·* that his body had died
90–24 *a·* to one's self that man is God's own likeness
f 224–25 stands at the door of this age, knocking for *a·*.
b 278–16 The *a·* that there can be material substance
308– 9 is met by the *a·* from the head, heart,
p 394–10 The *a·* that any bodily condition is
t 450–18 but unless this *a·* is made, evil will boast
gl 596–18 only fit preparation for *a·* to the presence

admissions
f 220– 4 Such *a·* ought to open people's eyes
244–28 Such *a·* cast us headlong into darkness
p 394–13 such *a·* are discouraging,

admit

pr 3–17	We *a·* theoretically that God is
a 24–31	his own disciples could not *a·*
26–23	makes us *a·* its Principle to be Love.
39–32	once *a·* that evil confers no pleasure,
an 105– 7	to contradict precedent and to *a·* that
s 120– 2	never understand this while we *a·* that soul is in
130–12	since you *a·* that God is omnipotent ;
143–18	You *a·* that mind influences the body
ph 172–32	When we *a·* that matter (heart, blood,
182–30	To *a·* that sickness is a condition over which
f 202–27	We *a·* that God has almighty power,
237–28	more for them than they are willing to *a·*
244–16	If man were dust . . . we might *a·* the hypothesis
250–31	nor will Science *a·* that happiness is ever the
b 298–22	and *a·* no materialistic beliefs.
339–30	never to *a·* that sin can have intelligence
o 347– 2	Who is ready to *a·* this?
348– 3	Medical theories virtually *a·* the nothingness
353–10	All must *a·* that Christ is
353–20	We must not continue to *a·* the
355–17	declines to *a·* that Christ's religion
357– 1	In common justice, we must *a·* that God
p 368–27, 28	*A·* the existence of matter, and you *a·*
369– 1	is liable to *a·* also the reality of
376–30	To fear and *a·* the power of disease,
388–12	*A·* the common hypothesis that food is
389–13	Our dietetic theories first *a·* that food sustains
393– 2	we *a·* the intruding belief, forgetting
395– 2	They *a·* its reality, whereas they should deny it.
t 461– 5	We *a·* the whole, because a part is proved
461–21	to *a·* that you are sick, renders your case
r 466–17	the point you will most reluctantly *a·*,
469–22	bury the sense of infinitude, when we *a·*
479–27	We *a·* that black is not a color, because
g 530–22	and saying, . . . Only *a·* that I am real,
555–25	We lose our standard . . . when we *a·*

admits
s 148–31 the guidance of a theology which *a·*
ph 174–23 Anatomy *a·* that mind is somewhere in man,
f 202–11 Common opinion *a·* that a man may take cold
229–12 and at the same time *a·* that Spirit is God,
b 283–12 *a·* of no error, but rests upon understanding.
p 401–27 Until the advancing age *a·* the efficacy
g 551–10 Mr. Darwin *a·* this, but he adds that

admitted
f 204–12 The first power is *a·* to be good,
b 270–12 it is generally *a·* that this intelligence is
276–17 If God is *a·* to be the only Mind
p 428–29 and the immortal facts of being are *a·*.
r 471–13 facts of divine Science should be *a·*,
481–22 assume . . . because of their *a·* actuality.

admittedly
ph 187–15 the hand, *a·* moved by the will.

admitting
p 376–29 you cannot check a fever after *a·*
392–25 *A·* only such conclusions as you wish realized
397–10 You cause bodily sufferings . . . by *a·* their
r 469–26 *a·* that God, or good, is omnipresent

admonition
a 25–20 Hence the force of his *a·*,

adopt
sp 99–18 individuals, who *a·* theosophy, spiritualism,
s 112– 9 they *a·* and adhere to some particular
145–14 It matters not what . . . method one may *a·*,
154–32 method for any mother to *a·*
f 248–23 and *a·* into your experience the
p 441–21 recommend that Materia Medica *a·* C. S.
t 452–31 and then should *a·* C. S.,

adopted
an 101–19 This report was *a·* by the Royal Academy
s 164– 7 none can be *a·* as a safe guidance in practice."
f 220–22 clergyman once *a·* a cake of bread and water
221– 1 I knew a person who when quite a child *a·*
p 378–19 hygienic drilling and drugging, *a·* to cure
r 466– 2 *Omni* is *a·* from the Latin adjective
g 553–20 Whatever theory may be *a·* by

adoption
s 141–27 The *a·* of scientific religion and of
c 255– * the *a·*, to wit, the redemption— *Rom.* 8 : 23.

adopts
p 547–29 Inspired thought . . . *a·* the spiritual and

adorable
pr 16–29 *A·* One.

adoration
sp 88–22 and the individual manifests profound *a·*.
p 363– 8 Did he repel her *a·*?

adore
a 26– 1 While we *a·* Jesus, and the heart overflows
s 140– 9 We shall obey and *a·* in proportion
r 497– 5 We acknowledge and *a·* one supreme and

adored
r 472– 2   that God is to be understood, *a·*,

adorned
f 235–17   though *a·* with gems of scholarly attainment,

adornment
m 60–22   passion, frivolous amusements, personal *a·*,

adroitness
g 515– 8   a wise idea, charming in its *a·*,

adult (*see also* **adult's**)
ph 178–13   Perhaps an *a·* has a deformity produced
p 371–14   The *a·*, in bondage to his beliefs,
371–16   the *a·* must be taken out of his darkness,

adulterated
t 457– 4   Other works, . . . have *a·* the Science.
r 482– 3   Human thought has *a·* the meaning

adulterating
t 464–25   *A·* C. S., makes it void.

adulteries
an 100–*   *evil thoughts, murders, a·,— Matt.* 15 : 19.

adulterous
pr 11– 3   When forgiving the *a·* woman he said,
sp 85–25   Jesus knew the generation to be wicked and *a·*,

adultery
m 56–19   "Thou shalt not commit *a·*,"— *Exod.* 20 : 14.
an 106–21   *A·*, fornication, uncleanness,— *Gal.* 5 : 19.
f 252–19   says : . . . I can cheat, lie, commit *a·*, rob,
b 330–30   hypocrisy, slander, hate, theft, *a·*,

adult's
s 130–20   Laboring long to shake the *a·* faith in matter

adults
f 236–25   Children are more tractable than *a·*,
o 352–17   Children, like *a·*, *ought* to fear a reality which

advance
pr 10–20   But the *a·* guard of progress has
a 41– 3   this *a·* beyond matter must
m 61–30   must greatly improve to *a·* mankind.
s 158–28   Homœopathy, a step in *a·* of allopathy,
f 207– 3   proportionately as we *a·* spiritually,
239– 3   lay it upon those who are in *a·* of creeds.
o 361–23   Spiritual ideas unfold as we *a·*.
p 371–24   because this teaching is in *a·* of the age,
412– 3   to *a·* and destroy the human fear of
430– 8   he will *a·* more rapidly towards God,
t 449–14   *a·* in proportion to your honesty and fidelity,
457–23   To pursue other vocations and *a·* rapidly
462–15   heed every statement, and *a·* from the rudiments
g 542–25   to *a·* itself, breaks God's commandments.

advanced
pr 16– 2   must precede this *a·* spiritual understanding.
a 23–18   Faith, *a·* to spiritual understanding,
40– 2   The *a·* thinker and devout Christian,
45–32   Jesus' students, not sufficiently *a·*
sp 76–12   When *a·* to spiritual being and
77–24   with every *a·* stage of existence.
84– 7   When sufficiently *a·* in Science to be
ph 200– 4   Moses *a·* a nation to the worship of God in
f 230– 7   coming of Christ, the *a·* appearing of Truth,
b 324– 2   renders thought receptive of the *a·* idea.
p 391– 8   the incipient or *a·* stages of disease,
t 461– 8   taught only by those who are morally *a·*

advancement
m 56– 5   Jesus' concessions . . . were for the *a·* of
b 326–20   nothing but wrong intention can hinder your *a·*.
p 429–10   in the line of spiritual *a·*.
t 459– 9   Judge not the future *a·* of C. S. by

advances
sp 95–25   Humanity *a·* slowly out of sinning sense

advancing
a 21– 9   If the disciple is *a·* spiritually,
55– 2   The *a·* century, from a deadened sense
m 65–15   struggling against the *a·* spiritual era.
s 134– 2   At every *a·* step, truth is still opposed
c 256– 2   *A·* to a higher plane of action,
p 401–27   Until the *a·* age admits the efficacy
t 452–11   Your *a·* course may provoke envy,
g 513– 6   *A·* spiritual steps in the teeming universe
536– 7   human concepts *a·* and receding,

advantage
a 42– 5   The universal belief in death is of no *a·*.
sp 77–18   Of what *a·*, then, would it be to us,
s 145–16   Scientific healing has this *a·* over other
b 269–18   they have this *a·* over the objects and
279–12   and they have the *a·* of being eternal.
t 443– 2   as to the propriety, *a·*, and consistency of

advantages
p 369–29   of the *a·* of Mind and immortality?

advent
a 30– 5   Born of a woman, Jesus' *a·* in the flesh
43– 7   The *a·* of this understanding is
b 333–16   The *a·* of Jesus of Nazareth marked

adversary
s 161–32   agrees with his "*a·* quickly,"— *Matt.* 5 : 25.
p 390–19   "Agree with thine *a·* quickly,— *Matt.* 5 : 25.
391–23   your *a·* will deliver you to the judge
gl 580–28   definition of
580–28   An *a·* is one who opposes, denies,
581– 2   name . . . in Scripture, the "*a·*."— *I Pet.* 5 : 8.

adverse
p 419–16   Meet every *a·* circumstance as its master.
t 456– 1   to influence mankind *a·* to its highest

adversity
m 64–12   some noble woman, struggling alone with *a·*,
66– 3   Sweet are the uses of *a·* ;

advertisements
ph 179–32   Descriptions of disease . . . and *a·* of quackery

advertises
p 439– 5   and *a·* largely for his employers.

advice
p 394–14   *a·* to a man who is down in the world,
424–19   either by giving antagonistic *a·* or

advise
s 149–19   *a·* our patients to be hopeful and cheerful

advised
f 220–24   and *a·* others never to try dietetics for
t 444–13   Students are *a·* by the author to be

advising
pr 3– 3   not sufficient to warrant him in *a·* God.

advocate
s 154– 2   and certainly we should not be error's *a·*.

advocates
ph 179–12   Every medical method has its *a·*.

advocating
s 153–31   as we would avoid *a·* crime.

Æon
b 335–11   the Logos, the *A·* or Word of God,

aëriform
g 511–23   To mortal mind, the universe is . . . and *a·*.

Æsculapius
s 150–31   The hosts of *A·* are flooding the world
152– 6   endeavored to make this book the *A·* of mind

afar
g 538– 8   the sword of Truth gleams *a·* and indicates

affairs
p 430–31   the superintendence of human *a·*,

affect
pr 16–14   this does not *a·* the meaning of the prayer itself.
a 55– 5   but this does not *a·* the invincible facts.
s 123– 5   Ptolemaic blunder could not *a·* the harmony of
125–24   find that these changes cannot *a·* his crops.
125–32   mortal belief, wholly inadequate to *a·* a man
p 379–23   so-called vital current does not *a·* the
383–13   does not *a·* his happiness, because
388–22   food does not *a·* the absolute Life of man,
395–31   brain-lobes cannot . . . *a·* the functions of
401–25   remove paralysis, *a·* organization,
402–21   and in this way *a·* the body,
408–19   Drugs do not *a·* a corpse,
g 553–31   you may also ask how belief can *a·* a result

affected
b 310–31   sun is not *a·* by the revolution of the earth.
p 380–17   The body is *a·* only with the belief of disease

affection
Christly
p 365–19   If the Scientist has enough Christly *a·* to
flowers of
m 57–25   may uproot the flowers of *a·*, and scatter them
grave of
m 68– 9   Jealousy is the grave of *a·*.
higher
m 65–19   human mind will at length demand a higher *a·*.
human
m 57–22   Human *a·* is not poured forth vainly,
65– 7   If the foundations of human *a·* are consistent
p 364–28   expressed by meekness and human *a·*,
366–12   physician who . . . is deficient in human *a·*,
ineffable
p 364– 8   the higher tribute to such ineffable *a·*,
justice and
gl 592–13   the union of justice and *a·*,
kindly
gl 594–14   SHEM . . . A corporeal mortal ; kindly *a·* ;
links of
m 60– 7   welding indissolubly the links of *a·*.
maternal
m 60–11   maternal *a·* lives on under whatever
mother's
m 60– 8   A mother's *a·* cannot be weaned from
one
f 201– 4   knowing too that one *a·* would be supreme

affection
practical
a 24–27 efficacy of the crucifixion lay in the practical *a·*
promotes
an 103– 1 promotes *a·* and virtue in families
pure
a 54– 3 Out of the amplitude of his pure *a·*,
s 147–29 A pure *a·* takes form in goodness,
gl 589–21 pure *a·* blessing its enemies.
purity and
pr 15–27 purity, and *a·* are constant prayers.
a 36– 1 They, who know not purity and *a·*
spiritual
p 366–17 Not having this spiritual *a·*, the physician
unrequited
a 49–12 sublime courage, and unrequited *a·*?

pr 8–29 learn what is the *a·* and purpose of the heart,
9–20 surrender of all merely material sensation, *a·*,
s 115–26 MORAL. Humanity, honesty, *a·*, compassion,
ph 183–22 demands man's entire obedience, *a·*, and
b 327– 2 and also by gaining an *a·* for good
p 363–32 the mere fact that she was showing her *a·*

affections
and aims
c 265– 6 their *a·* and aims grow spiritual,
centre for the
m 60–18 strength to man, and a centre for the *a·*.
famished
pr 17– 5 *Give us grace for to-day; feed the famished a·;*
her
s 154–24 and her *a·* need better guidance,
his
a 52– 4 His *a·* were pure; theirs were carnal.
human
m 61– 4 good in human *a·* must have ascendency
interests and
m 59–15 hallowing the union of interests and *a·*,
renewal of
gl 582– 9 Renewal of *a·*; self-offering;
sensualist's
f 241– 8 The sensualist's *a·* are as imaginary,
transplant the
c 265–32 transplant the *a·* from sense to Soul,
understanding and
pr 5–18 riches of His love into the understanding and *a·*,
unselfish
p 365–11 but if the unselfish *a·* be lacking,
whole
b 326–10 his whole *a·* on spiritual things,
worldling's
t 459– 8 have nothing in common with the worldling's *a·*,

a 18– * *crucified the flesh with the a· and — Gal.* 5 : 24.
m 57–16 incompetent to meet the demands of the *a·*,
58–23 the centre, though not the boundary, of the *a·*.
ph 182–11 must be supreme in the *a·*.
f 239–17 we must learn where our *a·* are placed
t 451–16 If our hopes and *a·* are spiritual,
gl 587–23 HEART. Mortal feelings, motives, *a·*,
597– 4 The motives and *a·* of a man

affects
pr 12–16 Prayer to a corporeal God *a·* the sick like
s 149–18 remarked . . . "We know that mind *a·* the body
ph 197– 3 *a·* people like a Parisian name for a
f 222– 4 This person learned that food *a·* the body only
p 297–10 a change in either . . . *a·* the physical
p 397– 2 not seeing how mortal mind *a·* the body,
423– 6 oftentimes *a·* a sensitive patient
r 483–11 Moral ignorance or sin *a·* your demonstration,

affiliation
sp 81– 9 maintain their *a·* with mortal flesh;

affinities
ph 191–28 illusive senses may fancy *a·* with their

affinity
ph 191–30 Mind has no *a·* with matter,

affirm
s 140– 4 That God is a corporeal being, nobody can truly
a·.
f 219–14 When this is understood, we shall never *a·*
c 255–15 That God is . . . material, no man should *a·*.
b 274–19 beliefs of mortal mind, which *a·* that life,

affirmation
p 392–11 The physical *a·* of disease should
429–16 mortal mind's *a·* is not true.

affirmations
s 149–30 to understand the *a·* of divine Science,
p 394–20 their denials are better than their *a·*.

affirmative
s 132– 1 an *a·* reply, recounting his works
p 418–20 Truth is *a·*, and confers harmony.
432–19 and Governor Mortality replies in the *a·*.
r 489–21 An *a·* reply would contradict the

affirmed
a 42– 2 whereas priest and rabbi *a·* God to be a
r 483– 2 It may be *a·* that they do not heal,

affirms
f 215–16 but Science *a·* darkness to be
218– 2 that which *a·* weariness, made that weariness.
b 307– 7 Evil still *a·* itself to be mind,
p 429–13 Mortal mind *a·* that mind is subordinate
t 456–10 Whoever *a·* that there is more than
g 549–32 he virtually *a·* that the germ of humanity is

affixed
r 483–13 she *a·* the name "Science" to Christianity,

affixes
ph 184– 7 the penalties it *a·* last so long as the belief

affliction
m 64– 6 visit the fatherless . . . in their *a·*, — *Jas.* 1 : 27.
p 377– 4 *a·* is often the source of joy,
gl 586–13 *a·* purifying and elevating man.

afflictions
a 41– 5 as well as through their sorrows and *a·*.

afflictive
ap 574–29 suffering sense deems wrathful and *a·*,

affluence
a 54– 4 With the *a·* of Truth, he vanquished error.
s 140–11 but rejoicing in the *a·* of our God.

afford
pr 8– 1 A wordy prayer may *a·* a quiet sense of
m 64–16 aid her sympathy and charity would *a·*.
sp 99– 3 ethics, and superstition *a·* no
s 144–10 and *a·* faint gleams of God, or Truth.
f 232– 6 beliefs . . . *a·* no scatheless and permanent
b 268–15 semi-metaphysical systems *a·* no . . . aid
t 443–19 other systems they fancy will *a·* relief.
r 471– 8 corporeal senses, *a·* no indication of the
492–21 Matter can *a·* you no aid.

afforded
c 255– 9 *a·* no foundation for accurate views
258– 5 craving for something . . . holier, than is *a·* by
t 460–28 through the meagre channel *a·* by language

affording
r 473–19 *a·* the proof of Christianity's truth

affords
sp 81–10 this fact *a·* no certainty of everlasting life.
s 112–24 *a·* no foundation upon which to establish
ph 194–31 The light which *a·* us joy gave him a belief of
f 208– 1 suppositional error, which *a·* no proof of God,
o 356– 4 material existence *a·* no evidence of
gl 583–14 Church is that institution, which *a·* proof of

affrighted
p 366–26 sinners should be *a·* by their sinful beliefs;

aflame
p 367– 8 legitimate C. S., *a·* with divine Love.

aforesaid
p 412–30 on the *a·* basis of C. S.

aforethought
p 437– 7 It indicates malice *a·*, a determination to
t 451–27 malpractice arises from ignorance or malice *a·*.

aforetime
pref xi–18 coming now as was promised *a·*,
s 131–22 As *a·*, the spirit of the Christ,
b 271–28 have the opportunity now, as *a·*, to learn

afraid
ph 181–23 if you adhere to error and are *a·* to trust
b 308– 6 mortal belief will be *a·* as it was in the
o 352–16 but you must not be *a·* of them"?
p 410–30 keynote of . . . "Be not *a·*!" — *Mark* 6 : 50.
t 447–30 A sinner is *a·* to cast the first stone.
g 532–15 I was *a·*, because I was naked; — *Gen.* 3 : 10.

African
f 225–32 when *A·* slavery was abolished in our land.
226– 5 The voice of God in behalf of the *A·* slave

after
pref xii– 2 No charters were granted . . . *a·* 1883,
pr 2– 5 goes forth hungering *a·* righteousness
16– 8 one brief prayer, which we name *a·* him
16– 9 "*A·* this manner therefore — Matt.* 6 : 9.
a 21–29 *A·* following the sun for six days,
24–32 *A·* the resurrection, even the unbelieving
27–11 proved by his reappearance *a·* the crucifixion
41–18 lost, about three centuries *a·* the crucifixion.
43– 2 did understand it *a·* his bodily departure.
45–13 Three days *a·* his bodily burial
45–22 saw Jesus *a·* the resurrection
46– 2 until they saw him *a·* his crucifixion
46–14 and *a·* his resurrection he proved
46–20 Jesus' unchanged physical condition *a·*
47– 5 *A·* gaining the true idea of their glorified
m 59–23 *A·* marriage, it is too late to grumble
59–25 exist before this union and continue ever *a·*,

after

m	62–10	those parents should not, in a· years, complain
sp	74– 5	a· having once left it, would be
	85–11	able to read the human mind a· this manner
	85–18	A· the same method, events of great moment
	94–15	belief that the infinite is formed a· the pattern
s	107– *	*preached of me is not a· man.— Gal. 1 : 11.
	109–11	For three years a· my discovery, I sought
	111–26	A· a lengthy examination of my discovery
	131–15	a· the manner of God's appointing,
	137– 4	even by them, until a· the crucifixion,
s	156–21	A· trying this, she informed me that
	159– 2	A· the autopsy, her sister testified that the
ph	168–11	you rush a· drugs, search out the
	180–10	bearing fruit a· its kind.
	195– 2	A· the babbling boy had been taught to speak
f	217–14	know we no man a· the flesh !"— II Cor. 5 : 16.
	221–10	until three hours a· eating.
	222–11	a· he had availed himself of the fact that
	234–22	the weary searcher a· a divine theology,
	236–15	either a· a model odious to herself
c	259–23	and forms its offspring a· human illusions.
	261–13	was accustomed night a· night to go
	265–24	aspiration a· heavenly good comes
b	317–21	a· his resurrection from the grave,
	333–20	both before and a· the Christian era,
o	344– 8	man in His own image and a· His likeness.
p	372–23	Its false supports fail one a· another.
	376–29	you cannot check a fever a· admitting
	427–16	Man is the same a· as before a bone is broken
	429–20	exist a· the body is disintegrated.
	431– 8	going to sleep immediately a· a heavy meal.
	432–21	I was called for, shortly a· the report of
	434– 8	A· much debate and opposition,
	435–30	to judge . . . a· the law,— Acts 23 : 3.
	436– 3	A· betraying him into the hands of your law,
	438– 2	man in our image, a· our likeness ;— Gen. 1 : 26.
r	465– 2	A· much labor and increased spiritual
	469–26	a· admitting that God, or good, is
	475–23	man in our image, a· our likeness ;— Gen. 1 : 26.
	483–13	A· the author's sacred discovery,
	487– 6	before and a· that which is called death.
g	507–13	yielding fruit a· his kind,— Gen. 1 : 11.
	508–10	herb yielding seed a· his kind,— Gen. 1 : 12.
	508–11	seed was in itself, a· his kind :— Gen. 1 : 12.
	512– 6	abundantly, a· their kind,— Gen. 1 : 21.
	512– 6	every winged fowl a· his kind :— Gen. 1 : 21.
	513–15	the living creature a· his kind,— Gen. 1 : 24.
	513–16	and beast of the earth a· his kind :— Gen. 1 : 24.
	513–22	beast of the earth a· his kind,— Gen. 1 : 25.
	513–23	and cattle a· their kind,— Gen. 1 : 25.
	513–24	upon the earth a· his kind :— Gen. 1 : 25.
	515–12	man in our image, a· our likeness :— Gen. 1 : 26.
	516– 9	fashions all things, a· His own likeness.
	523–29	a· which the distinction is not definitely
	524– 7	constantly went a· "strange gods,"— Jer. 5 : 19.
	525–13	And God said, Let us make man a· our mind
	525–14	and God shaped man a· His mind ;
	525–14	a· God's mind shaped He him ;
	543– 2	This error, a· reaching the climax of
	549– 5	supposition that life . . . must decay a· it has
	555–31	present himself unchanged a· the crucifixion.
ap	565–23	A· the stars sang together
	570– 9	as a flood, a· the woman,— Rev. 12 : 15.
gl	584–24, 25	not a· the image and likeness of Spirit, but a·
	595–20	and continues a·, what is termed death,
		(see also **death**)

after-dinner

ph	175–20	selfishness, coddling, and sickly a· talk.

afternoon

ph	193–15	between three and four o'clock in the a·

afterward

s	163– 2	marking Nature with his name, and a· letting

afterwards

pr	6–10	supposition . . . that a· we shall be free to
a	42–24	A· he would show it to them unchanged.
s	110–16	the truth of C. S. was demonstrated.
	132–32	yet a· he seriously questioned
ph	188– 7	but a· it governs the so-called man.
	190– 2	embryonic mortal mind, a· mortal men
	190–16	a· to . . . return to its native nothingness.
	196–29	mental state, which is a· outlined on the body.
	198–13	a· to appear on the body ;
f	230–19	Does wisdom make blunders which must a· be
p	374–27	a· it is resolved into its primitive mortal
	386–30	assertion might a· be proved to you.
	421– 8	a· make known to the patient your motive
t	452–21	and a· we must wash them clean.
g	514– 2	a· recreate persons or things upon its
	528–25	A· he is supposed to become the basis
	531–16	If, . . . mind was a· put into body by
	532– 2	but a· require the union of a soul
	547–21	and a· must either return to Mind or
ap	562– 5	the idea . . . which Jesus a· manifested,

again

pr	5–12	"shall be measured to you a·,"— Luke 6 : 38.
a	31– 6	A· he asked : "Who is my mother,— Matt. 12 : 48.
	31–28	A·, foreseeing the persecution which
	34–24	rise a· in the spiritual realm of reality,
	37– 4	it shall be measured to you a·."— Matt. 7 : 2.
	46–11	and is a· seen casting out evil and
	52–17	To-day, as of old, error and evil a·
	55– 9	gospel of healing is a· preached by the
	55–13	although it is a· ruled out of the synagogue.
sp	71–14	Close your eyes a·, and you may see
	75–16	that his body had died and then lived a·.
	97–29	Christianity is a· demonstrating the Life
s	110–27	and must a· be spiritually discerned,
	132– 5	"Go and show John a·— Matt. 11 : 4.
	152–14	contradicts another over and over a·.
	156–23	but on the third day she a· suffered,
ph	167–16	A·, an error in the premise must appear in
	185– 5	and she never suffered a· from east winds,
	198–18	A·, giving another direction to faith,
f	212– 3	tooth . . . extracted sometimes aches a· in belief,
	232–16	In our age Christianity is a· demonstrating
b	306–15	brought together a· at some uncertain
	310–12	when the earth has a· turned upon its axis.
p	425–26	You will never fear a· except to offend God,
	436–13	Mortal Man should find it a·.
t	444–21	Fear not that he will smite thee a·
r	480–19	A·, God, or good, never made
	489– 3	lobster loses its claw, the claw grows a·.
g	529– 3	not woman a· taken from man.
	556–11	to live a· in renewed forms,
ap	560–17	A·, without a correct sense of its
	570–20	nor a· sink the world into the deep waters of

against

a	18–10	a· the accredited evidence of the senses,
	18–11	a· Pharisaical creeds and practices,
	29– 2	a· error at home and abroad.
	47–10	Judas conspired a· Jesus.
	48–29	a· human rights and divine Love,
	52–18	common cause a· the exponents of truth.
m	57–17	a· the better claims of intellect,
	60–17	becoming a barrier a· vice,
	65–15	struggling a· the advancing spiritual era.
sp	79– 2	Warning people a· death is an error
	97–21	array the most falsities a· themselves,
an	106– 3	to work a· the free course of honesty
	106– 4	to push vainly a· the current
	106–28	a· such there is no law."— Gal. 5 : 23.
s	116–15	nor do they carry the day a· physical enemies,
	118–27	a kingdom necessarily divided a· itself,
	130–17	beliefs which war a· spiritual facts ;
	131–10	enmity a· God."— Rom. 8 : 7.
	133–25	Jewish accusations a· him who
	138– 1	shall not prevail a· it."— Matt. 16 : 18.
	155–15	belief in physics weighs a· the
	155–18	general belief, . . . works a· C. S. ;
	159– 4	protested a· inhaling the ether
	160– 3	act a· metaphysics, and vice versa.
	160–19	Can muscles, bones, blood, and nerves rebel a·
ph	167–20	lusteth a· the Spirit.— Gal. 5 : 17.
	168– 9	belief militates a· your health,
	177–23	a· God, Spirit and Truth.
	182–24	working a· themselves and their prayers
	200–22	the flesh that warreth a· Spirit.
f	234–10	guard a· false beliefs as watchfully as
	234–11	bar our doors a· the approach of
	236–13	either for or a· crime.
	238–11	who can be a· us ?"— Rom. 8 : 31.
	242–19	which wars a· spirituality
	246–19	so many conspiracies a· manhood
	252– 2	divided a· itself,— Mark 3 : 24.
	253–20	no opposition to right endeavors a·
b	269– 2	a house divided a· itself.
	274–22	the flesh wars a· Spirit.
	307–23	weighs a· our course Spiritward.
	339–14	a· the day of wrath.— Rom. 2 : 5.
	339–15	He is joining in a conspiracy a·
	339–16	a· his own awakening to the
o	347– 1	"The flesh lusteth a·— Gal. 5 : 17.
	347– 1	Spirit a· the flesh."— Gal. 5 : 17.
	354– 1	protests of C. S. a· the notion
	354– 5	obey the Scriptures and war a·
	358–16	verdict of Truth a· error,
	358–31	a· whom they have been warned,
p	368– 2	A· the fatal beliefs that error is as real as
	374–18	no argument a· the mental origin of disease.
	380– 9	a· the control of Mind over body,
	380–14	will be turned a· himself.
	380–31	a· Himself, a· Life, health, harmony.
	384–12	enter his protest a· this belief
	388–19	divided a· itself."— Matt. 12 : 25.
	389–18	kingdom divided a· itself.
	391– 2	arrayed a· the supremacy of Spirit.
	391– 8	rise in rebellion a· them.
	392– 9	take antagonistic grounds a·

against
p 394–22 *a·* whom mortals should not contend?
395– 1 The sick . . . argue for suffering, instead of *a·* it.
395–25 while you argue *a·* their reality,
401– 2 and works *a·* itself ;
405–10 army of conspirators *a·* health,
405–12 the arbiter of truth *a·* error.
411– 5 when he argued *a·* it,
412–20 array your mental plea *a·* the
414–18 lest you array the sick *a·* their
p 417–16 When you silence the witness *a·* your plea,
419–31 If it is found necessary to treat *a·*
420–16 when they will not array themselves *a·* it,
424–17 should not act *a·* your influence
425–31 mental protest *a·* the opposite belief
433–11 the evidence of Personal Sense *a·*
434–26 foul conspiracy *a·* the liberty and
436– 6 a witness *a·* Mortal Man
438–12 bearing false witness *a·* Man.
438–17 *a·* the rights and life of man.
439–22 in his struggles *a·* liver-complaint
440–28 I ask that he be forbidden to enter *a·*
441–14 cannot bear witness *a·* Mortal Man,
441–20 in favor of Man and *a·* Matter.
t 445– 3 defend themselves *a·* sin, and to guard *a·* the
446–30 be watched and guarded *a·*.
449– 7 reacts most heavily *a·* one's self.
449–21 understood and guarded *a·*.
452– 1 bar the door of his thought *a·* this
r 481–13 *a·* which wisdom warns man,
489–20 the medium for sinning *a·* God,
g 531–28 since flesh wars *a·* Spirit
534–19 is enmity *a·* God ;— *Rom.* 8 : 7.
541–14 rose up *a·* Abel— *Gen.* 4 : 8.
543–14 *a·* which divine Science is engaged in a
ap 564–10 accusations *a·* Jesus of Nazareth
564–34 the dragon as warring *a·* innocence.
565– 3 inflamed with war *a·* spirituality,
566–26 fought *a·* the dragon ;— *Rev.* 12 : 7.
566–32 *a·* the power of sin, Satan, and
567– 9 *A·* Love, the dragon warreth not long,
567–11 Truth and Love prevail *a·* the dragon
568–31 in our warfare *a·* error,
gl 581–18 a kingdom divided *a·* itself,
584–12 The flesh, warring *a·* Spirit ;

agamogenesis
m 68–18 one individual who believed in *a·* ;
68–25 but I discredit the belief that *a·* applies to

Agassiz
Louis
g 547– 9 Louis *A·*, by his microscopic examination

an 104– 8 *A·*, the celebrated naturalist and author,
g 547–11 *A·* was able to see in the egg the
548–29 *A·* declares . . . "Certain animals,
549–24 In one instance a celebrated naturalist, *A·*,
ap 561– 5 *A·*, through his microscope, saw

age
advance of the
p 371–24 this teaching is in advance of the *a·*,
advancing
p 401–27 Until the advancing *a·* admits the efficacy
anathemas of the
b 315–10 brought upon him the anathemas of the *a·*.
and blight
f 246–31 rather than into *a·* and blight.
and decay
f 247–30 resplendent and eternal over *a·* and decay.
any
b 325–30 When first spoken in any *a·*, Truth,
ensnare the
an 102–22 they ensnare the *a·* into indolence,
every
a 46–10 has spoken . . . in every *a·* and clime.
f 243– 7 can heal the sick in every *a·* and triumph over
r 482–25 to the hungering heart in every *a·*.
exempt from
f 247–14 Immortality, exempt from *a·* or decay,
her
f 245–16 Asked to guess her *a·*, those unacquainted
ignorant
r 474– 8 To the ignorant *a·* in which it first appears,
malice of the
f 215–32 The ignorance and malice of the *a·* would
material
a 36–15 earthly price of spirituality in a material *a·*
sp 98– 9 Christianity is misinterpreted by a material *a·*,
o 350–17 it was difficult in a material *a·* to apprehend
g 546–23 C. S. is dawning upon a material *a·*.
materiality of the
a 31–25 Referring to the materiality of the *a·*,
nor accident
f 214–28 Neither *a·* nor accident can interfere with the
our
f 232–16 In our *a·* Christianity is again demonstrating

age
pictures
f 244–29 Shakespeare's poetry pictures *a·* as infancy,
present
ap 560– 5 has reference to the present *a·*.
seems ready
ph 170–24 The *a·* seems ready to approach this subject,
sensualism of the
m 65–15 in the materialism and sensualism of the *a·*,
tendency of the
s 111–22 calculated to offset the tendency of the *a·* to
that
b 332–30 He expressed the highest type . . . m that *a·*.
this
pref xi–23 to proclaim His Gospel to this *a·*,
an 106–15 Let this *a·*, which sits in judgment on
f 224–24 stands at the door of this *a·*, knocking
b 317– 6 lives most the life of Jesus in this *a·*
p 364–17 indicated by one of the needs of this *a·*.
367–25 the Christ-cure has come to this *a·*
372–10 The Science . . . would be clearer in this *a·*,
t 456–28 Because it is the voice of Truth to this *a·*,
ap 570–22 In this *a·* the earth will help the woman ;
thought of the
s 147– 1 the thought of the *a·* in which we live.
ugliness to
f 246–11 robs youth and gives ugliness to *a·*.
warn the
m 65– 9 Divorces should warn the *a·*

ph 194–23 at the *a·* of seventeen Kaspar was still a
f 236–30 While *a·* is halting between two opinions
245–25 could not *a·* while believing herself young,
247– 3 I have seen *a·* regain two of the
o 353–13 The *a·* has not wholly outlived the sense of
r 473–18 In an *a·* of ecclesiastical despotism,
ap 562–18 lamps in the spiritual heavens of the *a·*,

agencies
ap 570– 5 certain active yet unseen mental *a·*

agency
s 150–22 This human view infringes man's free moral *a·* ;

agent
pref x– 7 They regard the human mind as a healing *a·*,
an 100–10 susceptible to the influence of this *a·*,
101–23 it is not a remedial *a·*,
s 112– 1 the most effective curative *a·*
146–17 Science, the curative *a·* of God,
b 338–19 dust was deemed the *a·* of Deity
p 435–16 the *a·* of those laws is an outlaw,
t 444– 4 suffering is oft the divine *a·* in this

agents
sp 78–27 claimed to be the *a·* of God's government.
s 164– 6 classification of diseases or of therapeutic *a·*,
r 485–26 delineates foreign *a·*, called disease and sin.

ages
all
sp 98–18 It is imperious throughout all *a·*
b 271– 3 Christ's Christianity . . . reappearing in all *a·*,
bygone
s 134– 1 To-day the cry of bygone *a·* is repeated,
future
pref vii–25 Future *a·* must declare what the pioneer
sensual
f 254–16 During the sensual *a·*, absolute C. S. may not

s 118–10 *A·* pass, but this leaven of Truth is
141– 2 theological and ritualistic religion of the *a·*
ph 174–18 are pursuing and will overtake the *a·*,
f 204–20 When will the *a·* understand the Ego,
233– 9 The *a·* must slowly work up to
241–17 error of the *a·* is preaching without practice.
246–17 Never record *a·*.
b 303–15 All the vanity of the *a·* can never
p 380– 5 Truth is the rock of *a·*, the headstone
ap 560–26 not only obscured the light of the *a·*, but

aggravate
p 401–12 This fermentation should not *a·* the

aggravated
p 422– 7 certain moral and physical symptoms seem *a·*,
g 540–12 when the symptoms of evil, illusion, are *a·*,

aggravation
an 105–27 The *a·* of error foretells its doom,
s 156–14 began to fear an *a·* of symptoms
ph 169– 3 Whenever an *a·* of symptoms has occurred

aggregated
f 209–16 *a·* substances composing the earth,

aggression
t 451– 5 They must renounce *a·*, oppression and

aggressive
an 102–17 its *a·* features are coming to the front.

aghast
ap 563– 7 why should we stand *a·* at nothingness?

alcoholic
p 406–28 The depraved appetite for *a·* drinks,

alias
ph 172–20 obtains in mortals, *a·* mortal mind,
p 391– 2 the plea of mortal mind, *a·* matter,
399–10 mortal thought, *a·* mortal mind.
400–14 conscious thought, *a·* the body,
409– 9 Unconscious mortal mind — *a·* matter,
432– 8 from my residence in matter, *a·* brain,
432–27 justice, *a·* nature's so-called law ;
g 528–24 Adam — *a·* error — gives them names.
533–15 Adam, *a· mortal error,* charges God
gl 591–27 suppositional material sense, *a·* the belief that

alienate
b 303–32 declared that nothing could *a·* him from God,

alike
sp 71–27 and structure of spiritualism are *a·* material
s 135–24 and they are *a·* in demonstration.
b 279–25 this belief contradicts *a·* revelation and

alive
a 44–29 *a·,* demonstrating within the narrow tomb
ph 200– 1 through his verse the gods became *a·* in a
f 216– 3 Who shall say that man is *a·* to-day, but
222–18 he had been kept *a·,* as was believed, only by
b 334–27 and, behold, I am *a·* for evermore, — *Rev.* 1 : 18.
p 373– 4 and be more *a·* to His promises.
g 545–32 shall all be made *a·."* — *I Cor.* 15 : 22.

alkali
p 401– 9 (as when an *a·* is destroying an acid),
422–14 As when an acid and *a·* meet and

All
eternal
b 280– 3 not products of the . . . eternal *A·.*
God as
p 397–21 confidence in God as *A·,*
God is
b 339– 7 Since God is *A·,* there is no room for
p 366–29 Life is God and God is *A·.*
g 532–24 God is *A·* and He is Mind
infinite
ap 576– 4 this New Jerusalem, this infinite *A·,*
Mind is
s 109– 2 the proposition that Mind is *A·*
g 508– 3 Mind is *A·* and reproduces all

pr 17–15 *Life, Truth, Love, over all, and A·.*
p 399– 2 therefore good is infinite, is *A·.*

all
pref x–19 Few invalids will turn to God till *a·* physical
xi– 5 *a·* other pathological methods are the fruits of
pr 2–14 for He already knows *a·.*
2–18 is not *a·* that is required.
3– 8 Shall we ask the divine Principle of *a·* goodness
3–28 and yet return thanks to God for *a·* blessings,
4– 8 evidence of our gratitude for *a·* that he has
5–32 seek the destruction of *a·* evil works,
8– 9 full . . . of *a·* uncleanness." — *Matt.* 23 : 27.
9– 5 The test of *a·* prayer lies in the answer to
9–17 with *a·* thy heart, — *Matt.* 22 : 37.
9–18 and with *a·* thy soul, — *Matt.* 22 : 37.
9–18 and with *a·* thy mind" — *Matt.* 22 : 37.
9–20 surrender of *a·* merely material sensation,
9–25 Are you willing to leave *a·* for Christ,
10–25 misapprehension of the source and means of *a·*
11–24 but if we desire holiness above *a·* else,
11–31 will bring us into *a·* Truth.
12–32 *a·* may avail themselves of God as
13– 8 striving for the accomplishment of *a·* we ask,
13–26 divine Principle, Love, the Father of *a·*
16–11 prayer which covers *a·* human needs.
16–19 the first lie and *a·* liars.
16–20 Only as we rise above *a·* material sensuousness
17–14 *For God is infinite, all-power, a· Life,*
17–15 *Life, Truth, Love, over a·,*
a 18–12 refuted *a·* opponents with his healing power.
20–25 The truth is the centre of *a·* religion.
20–32 divine Principle and Science of *a·* healing.
23–31 spiritual understanding and confides in *a·* to God.
24–21 chiefly as providing a ready pardon for *a·*
25–27 *a·* the emotional love . . . will never alone
26– 6 *a·* have the cup of sorrowful effort
26– 8 till *a·* are redeemed through divine Love.
26–29 It was the divine Principle of *a·* real being
28– 9 While respecting *a·* that is good in the Church
31–11 He recognized Spirit, . . . as the Father of *a·*
31–16 resurrection and the life" to *a·* — *John* 11 : 25.
32–18 saying, Drink ye *a·* of it." — *Matt.* 26 : 27.
33– 9 Their Master had explained it *a·* before,
33–17 and said, "Drink ye *a·* of it." — *Matt.* 26 : 27.
33–22 It gives *a·* for Christ, or Truth.

all
a 33–31 Are *a·* who eat bread and drink wine
34– 1 and leave *a·* for the Christ-principle?
34–10 If *a·* who ever partook of the sacrament
34–13 If *a·* who seek his commemoration
34–18 Through *a·* the disciples experienced,
36–12 He was forsaken by *a·* save
37–17 learn to emulate Jesus in *a·* his ways
37–29 "Go ye into *a·* the world, — *Mark* 16 : 15.
38–14 in *a·* time to come.
39–26 divine Principle of *a·* that really exists
42–13 followed by the desertion of *a·* save a few
43– 4 *a·* enabled the disciples to understand
43–29 must triumph over *a·* material beliefs
44–11 *a·* the claims of medicine, surgery,
45–23 the final proof of *a·* that he had taught,
46– 4 the truthfulness of *a·* that he had taught.
46–21 his exaltation above *a·* material conditions ;
46–31 by *a·* they had witnessed and suffered,
49– 8 Were *a·* conspirators save eleven?
49–17 Forsaken by *a·* whom he had blessed,
50–23 Even what they did say, . . . that *a·* evidence of
51–20 was for the salvation of us *a·,*
51–24 in *a·* that he said and did.
52–26 not for their day only but for *a·* time :
53–29 had not conquered *a·* the beliefs of the flesh
54– 8 *A·* must . . . plant themselves in Christ,
55–23 divine healing is throughout *a·* time ;
55–24 whosoever layeth his earthly *a·* on the altar
m 56– 4 to fulfil *a·* righteousness." — *Matt.* 3 : 15.
56–16 Infidelity . . . is the social scourge of *a·* races,
58–14 selfish exaction of *a·* another's time and
59– 5 should wait on *a·* the years of married life.
59– 9 not be required to participate in *a·* the
64–26 Until it is learned that God is the Father of *a·,*
64–31 will ultimately claim its own, — *a·* that really is,
67–23 Grace and Truth are potent beyond *a·* other
69–14 unfolds *a·* creation, confirms the Scriptures,
sp 70–12 The divine Mind maintains *a·* identities,
71– 5 idea, of *a·* reality continues forever ;
71– 6 Principle of *a·,* is not *in* Spirit's formations.
72–10 and in the place of darkness *a·* is light,
75–22 waken . . . out of the belief that *a·* must die,
76– 4 forgets *a·* else and breathes aboard his rapture.
79–27 Science objects to *a·* this, contending for
83–23 Between C. S. and *a·* forms of
84–28 *A·* we correctly know of Spirit comes from God,
86–27 can *a·* be taken from pictorial thought
87– 1 So is it with *a·* material conceptions.
87–23 yet these are *a·* there.
89–19 It possesses of itself *a·* beauty and poetry,
89–22 We are *a·* capable of more than we do.
91– 7 point of departure for *a·* true spiritual growth.
93–22 belief that Spirit is finite . . . has darkened *a·*
   history.
94– 5 includes *a·* that is implied by the
95– 8 in that ratio we know *a·* human need
96–19 *a·* discord will be swallowed up in spiritual
96–23 until *a·* errors of belief yield to understanding.
97–19 until divine Spirit, . . . dominates *a·* matter,
97–27 indicates that *a·* matter will disappear
98–18 It is imperious throughout *a·* ages
an 102– 2 God governs *a·* that is real, harmonious,
104–15 indicates the rightness of *a·* divine action,
s 108– 8 show the falsity of *a·* material things ;
108–22 *a·* real being is in God, the divine Mind,
108–31 mortal, misnamed *mind* produces *a·* the
109–17 Principle of *a·* harmonious Mind-action
110– 2 filling all space, constituting *a·* Science,
110– 6 God's creation, in which *a·* that He has made
113– 2 one divine Principle of *a·* Science ;
113–18 God, Spirit, being *a·,* nothing is matter.
114–23 C. S. explains *a·* cause and effect as mental,
116–16 even to the extinction of *a·* belief in matter,
116–18 They never . . . insist upon the fact that God
   is *a·,*
118–20 In *a·* mortal forms of thought,
119–12 to make Him responsible for *a·* disasters,
124– 2 based on Truth, the Principle of *a·* science.
126– 8 *A·* Science is divine.
126–18 Or shall *a·* that is beyond the cognizance
130– 8 Science, which destroys *a·* discord,
130–12 demonstrated, will destroy *a·* discord,
132–13 divine Principle which brings out *a·* harmony
136–30 they did not comprehend *a·* that he said
138–18 the precedent for *a·* Christianity,
138–27 "Go ye into *a·* the world, — *Mark* 16 : 15.
141– 9 to leave *a·* for Christ.
141–10 *A·* revelation (such is the popular thought !)
141–20 The Bible declares that *a·* believers in
142– 6 modern religions generally omit *a·* but one of
146–29 It lives through *a·* Life, and extends
148–16 Anatomy takes up man at *a·* points materially.
149–26 divine Mind, governs *a·,* not partially but
150–27 doctrine that man's harmony . . . *a·* his earthly
   days,

all

s 151–26   A· that really exists is the divine Mind
  152– 4   takes away a· its supposed sovereignty,
  155– 2   the child forgets a· about the accident,
  155–18   belief, . . . produces a· medical results,
  157–20   If He creates drugs at a·, and designs
  159–31   belief produces disease and a· its symptoms,
  160–22   Unless muscles are self-acting at a· times,
  163–18   war, pestilence, and famine, a· combined."
  164–12   But a· human systems based on
  164–15   a· the mental microbes of sin and a·
ph 166– 2   human mind is a· that can produce pain.
  166– 3   Mind is a· that feels, acts, or impedes action.
  167–14   divine source of a· health and perfection.
  168– 8   Mind, which would otherwise outweigh a· else.
  168–16   a· in consonance with the laws of God,
  170–31   from which a· ills have gone forth,
  172–16   he must have passed through a· the forms
  174–22   belief is a· that enables a drug to cure
  176–21   Should a· cases of organic disease be treated by
  177– 3   it must relinquish a· its errors,
  177– 4   I have demonstrated this beyond a· cavil.
  177–18   had the naming of a· that was material.
  180–12   nor take the ground that a· causation
  181– 1   more potent than a· lower remedies.
  183–26   Truth casts out a· evils and materialistic
  186–18   falsehood should strip evil of a· pretensions.
  187–19   the cause of a· materialistic action?
  187–19   A· voluntary, as well as miscalled *involuntary*,
  187–23   divine Mind includes a· action and
  187–28   material body loses a· appearance of life
  189–18   supposed to furnish the evidence of a· mortal
  189–21   The reverse is the case with a· the formations
  190– 2   a· this while matter is a belief, ignorant of
  192– 6   until we leave a· for Christ.
  192–15   a· that is selfish, wicked, dishonest,
  193–14   and said: . . . My suffering is a· gone."
  194– 6   change in human belief changes a· the physical
  195– 6   A· that he ate, except his black crust,
  195– 8   A· that gives pleasure to our educated senses
  195–22   out of itself, out of a· that is mortal.
f 201– *   *the reproach of a· the mighty — Psal.* 89 : 50.
  201–10   hatred, fear, a· sensuality, yield to
  202–15   Outside of this Science a· is mutable ;
  204– 3   A· forms of error support the false
  204–28   never . . . distinct from God, the a· Mind.
  205– 5   consume with disease,— a· because of their
  205–12   the prolific source of a· suffering?
  205–12   God created a· through Mind,
  205–13   and made a· perfect and eternal.
  206–16   whatever blesses one blesses a·,
206–28, 29   infinite Mind made a· and includes a·.
  208–32   banish a· thoughts of disease and sin
  209– 5   Mind, supreme over a· its formations
  209– 6   and governing them a·,
  209– 7   light of a· its own vast creation ;
  209–21   they a· must give place to the spiritual fact
  209–26   a· the paraphernalia of speculative theories,
  211–17   nature of a· so-called material cause and effect.
  212–25   a· the methods of Mind are not understood,
  214–21   A· material knowledge, like the
  215– 5   with a· the faculties of Mind ;
  219– 3   My method . . . applies to a· bodily ailments,
  220–30   Mortal mind forms a· conditions of the
  222–20   and yet he continued ill a· the while.
  222–30   consult matter not at a·, and eat what
  223– 8   If Spirit is a· . . . what and where is matter?
  225–14   a· history, illustrates the might of Mind,
  225–29   Men and women of a· climes and races
  227–15   we . . . foresee the doom of a· oppression.
  228– 1   in defiance of a· material conditions.
  229– 7   God made a· that was made,
  229–24   a· that He makes is good and will stand
  230–32   the exciting cause of a· suffering,
  238–24   He who leaves a· for Christ forsakes
  239–32   the wise man said, "A· is vanity."— *Eccl.* 1 : 2.
  240– 5   a· point to Mind, the spiritual intelligence
  240–11   a· is one grand concord.
  240–20   until a· wrong work is effaced or rectified.
  241–19   substance of a· devotion is the reflection
  241–26   corner-stone of a· spiritual building is
  241–27   washing the body of a· the impurities of flesh,
  242– 4   time when "they shall a· know Me— *Jer.* 31 : 34.
  244– 7   to derive a· our conceptions of man from
  245– 6   became insane and lost a· account of time.
  246–21   error of . . . limiting a· that is good
  247–18   which transcend a· material sense.
  248–13   We are a· sculptors, working at various forms,
  248–19   Do you not hear from a· mankind of the
  249– 1   Let us accept Science, relinquish a· theories
  252–27   says: . . . for a· my fancied joys are fatal.
  253– 3   perfection of being, imperishable glory,— a· are
  253– 5   include and impart a· bliss,
  253– 7   and give a·, for I am Mind.
  253– 8   substance of a·, because I AM THAT I AM.
c 257–22   Finite mind manifests a· sorts of errors,

all

c 258–15   Mind manifests a· that exists
  259– 4   infinite Mind, the sum of a· substance.
  260– 8   the ideal of a· that is perfect and eternal.
  261– 3   the Principle of a· happiness, harmony,
  262–23   conquering a· that is unlike God.
  263–17   the dust we a· have trod."
  263–20   but one creator, who has created a·.
  264–18   finding in God, good, and needing no other
  264–30   a· the glories of earth and heaven and man.
  267–11   made a· "that was made."— *John* 1 : 3.
b 268– 7   from which may be deduced a· rationality,
  269– 1   These . . . systems are one and a· pantheistic,
  269–26   A· other systems — systems based wholly or
  269–29   theories I combat . . . that a· is matter ;
  271– 3   Christianity . . . reappearing in a· ages,
  271– 4   uniting a· periods in the design of God.
  271–10   Truth, casting out a· inharmony.
  272–29   the divine Principle of a· that represents Him
  272–30   and of a· that really exists.
  273–30   beliefs emit the effects of error at a· times,
  274– 6   and symbolizes a· that is evil
  275–12   the divine Principle of a· that really is.
  275–14   A· substance, intelligence, wisdom, being,
  275–23   a· presence, a· Science.
  275–24   a· is in reality the manifestation of Mind.
  276– 6   a· have one Spirit, God,
  276–12   realization that a· inharmony is unreal
  277– 2   To a· that is unlike unerring . . . Mind,
  277–20   produces a· the ills of flesh,
  278–11   Spirit, God, is infinite, a·.
  278–28   A· that we term sin, sickness, and death
  281–15   supplies a· form and comeliness
  282–23   a· that is material is a . . . mortal thought,
  283– 4   Mind is the source of a· movement,
  283–23   lost to a· who cling to this falsity.
  284–19   answer to a· these questions must forever be
  286– 8   is better than a· burnt offerings.
  286–14   divine Principle, Love, creates and governs a·
  286–17   The Scriptures declare a· that He made to be
  287– 2   belong, with a· that is material and
  287– 4   A· creations of Spirit are eternal ;
  287–16   How can there be more than a·?
  288– 7   will settle a· questions through faith
  290–22   removes a· ignorance and sin.
  291– 5   We know that a· will be changed
  291–14   a· the manifestations of Mind are harmonious
  291–31   divested of a· material error.
  295–12   but infinite Spirit being a·,
  295–25   A· that is called mortal thought is made up of
  296– 7   suffering or Science must destroy a· illusions
  296–17   lose a· satisfaction in error and sin
  302– 7   infinitude . . . of a· identity is thereby
  302– 9   when God is a· and eternally his.
  302–12   this belief is a· that will ever be lost.
  303–14   A· the vanity of the ages can never
  305–24   deflections of matter . . . are a· unlike Spirit,
  306–32   The parent of a· human discord was the
  310– 6   a· might is divine Mind.
  310– 7   seen in a· form, substance, and color,
  310–10   God is His own infinite Mind, and expresses a·.
  311– 5   a· that Mind, God, is, or hath made,
  311– 6   and He made a·.
  311–28   lose a· supposed consciousness or claim
  314– 5   spiritual sense had quenched a· earthly
  315–27   more spiritual than a· other earthly
  316– 2   the way of salvation to a· who accepted
  317–14   that is, not only in a· time, but in a· *ways*
  318– 6   Scriptures declare that God made a·,
  318–10   a· that is material, untrue, selfish, or
  319– 9   sustains man under a· circumstances ;
  320–28   in Him who healeth a· our diseases ;
  325– 3   He . . . loses a· sense of evil,
  325–13   When . . . understood in a· its perfection,
  326– 8   A· nature teaches God's love to man,
  327– 6   a· the sinful appetites of the human mind.
  329– 4   glow in a· the grandeur of universal goodness.
  329– 6   proves the truth of a· that I say of it.
  329–27   their real spiritual source to be a· blessedness,
  330–31   with a· the etceteras that word includes.
  331– 5   Therefore in Spirit a· is harmony, and
  331–16   a· is Life, and there is no death.
  331–21   reflected by a· that is real and eternal
  331–24   Hence a· is Spirit and spiritual.
  333–19   Throughout a· generations both before and
  333–22   has come with . . . power and grace to a·
  333–31   The one Spirit includes a· identities.
  335– 7   Spirit, God, has created a·
  335–20   Spirit is more than a· else.
  336– 7   reflected in a· spiritual individuality
  339– 8   God, Spirit, alone created a·,
  339–25   basis of a· health, sinlessness, and
  340–13   a· that really exists is in and of God,
o 342–10   "Go ye into a· the world,— *Mark* 16 : 15.
  343–14   Jesus strips a· disguise from error,
  347– 7   a· is Life, and death has no dominion.

all

o 349–15 like a· other languages, English is inadequate
349–29 equally true of a· learning, even that which
350– 6 To understand a· our Master's sayings
353–10 A· must admit that Christ is
353–16 A· the real is eternal.
353–20 We must give up the spectral at a· points.
353–22 but we must yield up a· belief in it
354– 7 to leave a· for Christ, Truth?
360– 2 nothing is lost, and a· is won, by
361–14 conflicts not at a· with another of his sayings :
p 363–10 Nor was this a·.
363–21 and so brought home the lesson to a·,
364– 5 lay down his mortal existence in behalf of a·
365– 6 than a· cries of "Lord, Lord !"
367–16 with those hairs a· numbered by the Father.
368– 6 time will prove a· this.
368–27 the source of a· seeming sickness.
369– 2 a· discordant conditions,
369– 5 loses to human sense a· entity
369–10 A· these deeds manifested Jesus' control
371–13 looks for relief in a· ways except the right
372– 9 Science of being, in which a· is divine Mind,
373– 1 If we are Christians on a· moral questions,
373– 9 Under a· modes of pathological treatment,
374–16 we can destroy a· ills which proceed from
375–15 A· unscientific mental practice is erroneous
376–14 than in a· the blood, which ever flowed
377–10 they can be healthy in a· climates,
377–26 cause of a· so-called disease is mental,
379– 7 recognizing a· causation as vested in divine
384–28 a· the evidence before the senses can never
385– 9 and endurance surpassing a· other aids,
385–13 exempts man from a· penalties but those
385–15 a· untoward conditions, *if without sin,*
386–22 Thus it is with a· sorrow, sickness, and
386–25 Error, . . . produces a· the suffering on earth.
388–17 ambiguous nature of a· material health-theories.
390– 2 she said, "My food is a· digested,
390–10 Truth will at length compel us a· to exchange
391–15 Truth, will destroy a· other supposed suffering,
391–31 as a· that is pure, and bearing the fruits
392– 9 take antagonistic grounds against a· that
393– 7 remote, and exciting cause of a· bad effects
393–12 resist a· that is unlike good.
394– 3 to understand that . . . is best of a·,
394–21 assuring him that a· misfortunes
395–12 destroys a· faith in sin and
396– 3 efface from thought a· forms and types of
396–20 wrong side,— a· teaching that the body suffers,
399–28 A· that is real is included in this
400–23 Mortal mind rules a· that is mortal.
403–26 so-called mind produces a· that is unlike
404–10 Lust, malice, and a· sorts of evil are
404–17 The temperance reform, felt a· over our land,
406– 1 The Bible contains the recipe for a· healing.
406–16 a· that is unlike the true likeness disappears.
411–20 procuring cause and foundation of a· sickness
412– 2 The great fact that God lovingly governs a·,
413–22 need not wash his little body a· over each day
415–23 represent the action of a· the organs
417–13 a· causation is Mind, acting through
418– 3 depends on mentally destroying a· belief
418–21 A· metaphysical logic is inspired by this simple
418–22 rule of Truth, which governs a· reality.
418–27 Cast out a· manner of evil.
419– 4 Errors of a· sorts tend in this direction.
419–20 Mind produces a· action.
421– 6 true definition of a· human belief
421–17 God, Spirit, is a·, and there is none beside Him,
425–32 Discard a· notions about lungs, tubercles,
426–23 The relinquishment of a· faith in death
426–32 human concepts . . . are a· that can be destroyed,
427–24 Mind, governing a·, must be acknowledged
427–27 when a· such remedies have failed?
429–27 have faith in a· the sayings of our Master,
430– 1 includes a· the phenomena of existence.
431– 5 During a· this time the prisoner
431–16 a· these assistants resigned to me,
434–24 A· the testimony has been on the side of
436–10 Upon this statute hangs a· the law
438– 5 over a· the power of the enemy :— *Luke* 10 : 19.
439–27 Our higher statutes declare you a·,
441– 1 comprehending and defining a· law
442–10 a· sallowness and debility had disappeared.
t 443–10 a· are privileged to work out their
443–21 with a· longsuffering— *II Tim.* 4 : 2.
444– 3 a· must rise superior to materiality.
447–21 the claims of evil and disease in a· their forms,
451–26 A· mental malpractice arises from ignorance or
454–13 truth which strips a· disguise from error.
454–27 loving care . . . support a· their feeble footsteps,
456–26 so do a· his students and patients.
458– 1 on the same platform as a· other quackery.
459– 6 gain . . . by forsaking a· worldliness.
460– 4 necessary constituents and relations of a·

all

t 460– 5 and it underlies a· metaphysical practice.
460–12 to the material thought a· is material,
r 466– 2 adopted from the Latin adjective signifying a·.
466–26 the outcome of a· man-made beliefs.
468–10 A· is infinite Mind and its infinite
469– 3 which includes in itself a· substance
471– 3 a· that He creates are perfect and eternal,
471–28 gave the spiritual import, . . . of a· that proceeds
472– 7 making it coordinate with a· that is real
472–24 A· reality is in God, and His creation,
472–26 and He makes a· that is made.
473– 1 a· inharmony of mortal mind or body is
473–13 more than a· other men, has presented
474–17 they must a· be from the same source ;
474–26 Truth spares a· that is true.
474–29 while a· that is real is eternal.
475– 2 To Truth there is no error,— a· is Truth.
475– 3 a· is Spirit, divine Principle and its idea.
475–15 compound idea of God, including a· right ideas ;
475–16 generic term for a· that reflects God's image
475–22 reflects spiritually a· that belongs to his Maker.
476–22 outside of a· material selfhood.
479–10 image of mortal thought, . . . is a· that the eye
481–23 origin and governor of a· that Science reveals.
483– 7 Mind transcends a· other power,
483– 8 supersede a· other means in healing.
483–26 to receive aid, . . . from a· thinking persons.
484–23 involuntary action of error in a· its forms ;
484–26 hypotheses involved in a· false theories and
486–23 a· the spiritual senses of man, are eternal.
488–24 Mind alone possesses a· faculties,
488–29 reproduce them in a· their perfection ;
489–13 it breaks a· the commands of the
489–29 Outside the material sense of things, a· is
490–24 destroy a· material sense with immortal
491–12 facts of being, in which a· must end.
492–19 fight it out on this line, if it takes a· summer."
493– 6 A· the evidence of physical sense and a·
493–17 superior to a· the beliefs of the five corporeal
493–18 Mind must be found . . . able to destroy a· ills.
495– 3 A· of Truth is not understood ;
496– 9 We a· must learn that Life is God.
496–19 overlying, and encompassing a· true being.
g 504– 6 A· questions as to the divine creation
505– 9 divine Mind, not matter, creates a· identities,
506–29 task of finding names for a· material things,
507– 7 Spirit names and blesses a·.
507–21 reflect the Mind which includes a·.
507–24 Infinite Mind creates and governs a·,
507–25 divine Principle of a· expresses Science
508– 3 Mind is All and reproduces a·
508– 7 Mind is the Soul of a·.
508– 8 Mind is Life, . . . which governs a·.
509– 1 is discerned to be the Life of a·,
510–11 reflected spiritually by a· who walk in the light
512–22 a· form, color, quality, and quantity,
513–17 classifies, and individualizes a· thoughts,
513–20 continuity of a· individuality
513–26 God creates a· forms of reality.
514–19 Tenderness accompanies a· the might
514–26 the control which Love held over a·,
514–28 A· of God's creatures, moving in the
515–22 family name for a· ideas,
515–22 A· that God imparts moves in accord with
516–13 bathes a· in beauty and light.
517–19 they a· have one Principle and parentage.
518–16 a· having the same Principle, or Father ;
518–21 which shine through a· as the blossom
518–21 A· the varied expressions of God reflect
518–28 Spirit, comprehends and expresses a·,
518–28 a· must therefore be as perfect as the
519– 2 who from a· eternity knoweth His own
519– 8 and a· the host of them.— *Gen.* 2 : 1.
519–24 "we a· come in the unity of— *Eph.* 4 : 13.
519–24 a· His work which He had made.— *Gen.* 2 : 2.
520–13 in which a· sense of error forever disappears
520–23 emphatic declaration that God creates a·
520–29 Because Mind makes a·, there is
521–5, 6 A· that is made is the work of God, and a· is
522– 5 assigns a· might and government to God,
523–12 A· is material myth, instead of
524–23 God is reflected in a· His creation.
526– 8 namely, that a· Life is God.
526–16 God pronounced good a· that He created,
526–17 Scriptures declare that He created a·.
529–28 faith to fight a· claims of evil,
530–11 recognizing God, the Father and Mother of a·,
531– 4 maintained in a· the subsequent forms of belief.
531–11 rise above a· material and physical sense,
532– 4 God makes and governs a·.
532– 5 A· human knowledge and material sense
533–10 an attempt to trace a· human errors
535–23 eat of it a· the days of thy life :— *Gen.* 3 : 17.
536– 9 The divine understanding reigns, is a·,

all

g 538– 3   drive error out of *a·* selfhood.
539–18   the serpent, to grovel beneath *a·* the beasts
540– 6   I the Lord do *a·* these things ;" — *Isa.* 45 : 7.
540–15   that Truth may annihilate *a·* sense of evil
543–13   with *a·* its sin, sickness, and death,
543–25   When Spirit made *a·*, did it leave aught for
544–16   *A·* is under the control of the one Mind,
545–14   errors send falsity into *a·* human doctrines
545–18   Outside of C. S. *a·* is vague and hypothetical,
545–31   "As in Adam [error] *a·* die, — *I Cor.* 15 : 22.
545–32   shall *a·* be made alive." — *I Cor.* 15 : 22.
546–30   Principle which *a·* may understand.
547– 1   one example would authenticate *a·* the others.
547– 3   contains the proof of *a·* here said of C. S.
551–11   through *a·* the lower grades of existence.
551–16   *a·* Science is of God, not of man.
551–20   by which *a·* peculiarities of ancestry,
551–27, 28   *A·* must be Mind, or else *a·* must be matter.
552– 6   geology, and *a·* other material hypotheses
554– 2   even the cause of *a·* that exists,
554–26   *A·* these sayings were to show that
556– 7   destroys forever *a·* belief in
ap 559– 2   open for *a·* to read and understand.
559– 6   the source of *a·* error's visible forms?
560–24   *a·* who have spoken something new
562–12   The twelve tribes of Israel with *a·* mortals,
564–15   Since Jesus must have been tempted in *a·* points,
565– 7   rule *a·* nations with a rod of iron :— *Rev.* 12 : 5.
565–16   God's idea, will eventually rule *a·* nations and
565–23   and *a·* was primeval harmony,
566– 6   so shall the spiritual idea guide *a·* right desires
567– 7   To infinite, ever-present Love, *a·* is Love,
568–31   Self-abnegation, by which we lay down *a·* for
571–15   At *a·* times and under *a·* circumstances,
571–20   higher humanity will unite *a·* interests
573–31   and *a·* tears will be wiped away.
574– 4   weary pilgrim, journeying "uphill *a·* the way."
575–20   must be shut at *a·* by day :— *Rev.* 21 : 25.
577–22   *A·* who are saved must walk in this light.
577–25   *a·* is good, and nothing can enter that
578–16   mercy shall follow me *a·* the days — *Psal.* 23 : 6.
gl 583–21   divine Principle of *a·* that is real and good ;
583–24   God, who made *a·* that was made
587– 7   Life ; Truth ; Love ; *a·* substance ;
588–15   *A·* the objects of God's creation reflect
592–23   the immortality of *a·* that is spiritual.
593–21   demonstrated as supreme over *a·* ;
594–20   *a·* that is good ; God ;
595–18   limits, in which are summed up *a·* human acts,
596–15   reveals Spirit, . . . as the illuminator of *a·*.
fr 600– *   *worthy of the Lord unto a· pleasing,* — *Col.* 1 : 10.
(see also **being, disease, earth, error, evil, existence, good, mankind, men, Mind, others, power, sin, space, things, truth**)

all-absorbing

c 264–27   peace which comes from an *a·* spiritual love.

all-acting

gl 587– 6   *a·*, all-wise, all-loving, and eternal ;

allay

a 44–13   He took no drugs to *a·* inflammation.

allayed

s 159–18   They would either have *a·* her fear

allaying

p 411–27   begin your treatment by *a·* the fear
422– 9   *a·* the tremor which Truth often brings to error

alleged

sp 81–14   Nor is the case improved when *a·* spirits
o 345–32   as is *a·* by one critic.
p 434–28   shows the *a·* crime never to have been
436– 8   on the night of the *a·* offence

allegiance

a 32– 4   soldier was required to swear *a·*
f 226–21   man's birthright of sole *a·* to his Maker

allegorical

ap 564–31   this *a·*, talking serpent typifies mortal mind,
575–16   Taken in its *a·* sense,

allegory

ph 177–15   Scriptural *a·* of the material creation,
b 280–21   The argument of the serpent in the *a·*,
p 430–13   I here present to my readers an *a·*
430–15   an *a·* in which the plea of C. S. heals
g 531– 2   The order of this *a·* — the belief that
532–28   In the *a·* the body had been naked,
533–12   The *a·* shows that the snake-talker utters the
537–20   the purpose of this *a·* — this second account
540–22   Hebrew *a·*, representing error as assuming
544–26   Therefore man, in this *a·*, is neither a

all-embracing

an 102–10   pointing of the needle . . . symbolizes this *a·*

alleviate

an 101–26   If animal magnetism seems to *a·*

alleviates

p 411–31   it *a·* the symptoms of every disease.

alleviating

an 100– 6   as a means of *a·* disease.

all-harmonious

pr 16–27   *Our Father-Mother God, a·,*

all-hearing

pr 7–24   It is the *a·* and all-knowing Mind,

allied

s 121–31   and is *a·* to divine Science as displayed in
g 512–14   their natures are *a·* to God's nature ;

All-in-all
God being
s 142–28   God being *A·*, He made medicine ;
God is
(see **God**)
Mind is
s 109– 5   reveals incontrovertibly that Mind is *A·*,

sp 72–24   derived from God, the infinite *A·*,
an 103–16   God and His idea, the *A·*.
s 127– 4   If God, the *A·*, be the creator
b 275– 7   starting-point . . . is that God, Spirit, is *A·*,
gl 596– 6   makes Him better known as the *A·*,

all-in-all

g 552–17   emerge from this notion of material life as *a·*.

all-inclusive

a 52–21   the mighty actuality of *a·* God, good.
s 116–19   is and must of necessity be, — *a·*.
b 287–14   God being everywhere and *a·*,
331–20   He is *a·*, and is reflected by
g 514– 4   nothing exists beyond the range of *a·* infinity,

all-inclusiveness

o 351–26   the *a·* of harmonious Truth.

all-knowing

pr 7–25   It is the all-hearing and *a·* Mind,
ph 187– 4   how ignorant must they be of the *a·* Mind
r 487–15   Spirit is *a·* ;
gl 587– 5   The great I AM ; the *a·*, all-seeing,

All-loving

pr 2–12   the *A·* does not grant them simply on the

all-loving

gl 587– 6   all-acting, all-wise, *a·*, and eternal ;

all-might

b 319–11   must yield to the *a·* of infinite Spirit.

allness

pr 15–18   we must deny sin and plead God's *a·*.
c 267– 6   The *a·* of Deity is His oneness.
b 328–13   the grand realities of His *a·*.
336–23   *A·* is the measure of the infinite,
o 346–12   to prove the somethingness — yea, the *a·* — of
p 424–25   the oneness and the *a·* of divine Love ;
t 450–21   by understanding . . . the *a·* of God,
r 497–22   even the *a·* of Soul, Spirit,
ap 563–17   the nothingness of evil and the *a·* of God.

allopathic

p 416– 9   Yet any physician — *a·*, homœopathic,

allopathy

s 158–28   Homœopathy, a step in advance of *a·*,
o 344–30   Is it because *a·* and homœopathy are more

allow

a 30–27   to *a·* Soul to hold the control,
c 259–10   higher than their poor thought-models would *a·*,
p 433– 8   urges the jury not to *a·* their judgment to be
r 495–15   *A·* nothing but His likeness to abide

allowed

a 51– 9   but he *a·* men to attempt the
m 62–17   Children should be *a·* to remain children
63–30   woman should be *a·* to collect her own wages,
p 431– 2   *a·* to testify in the case.
434–10   where C. S. is *a·* to appear as counsel
437–15   Spirit not *a·* a hearing ;
437–30   unjust usages were not *a·* at the bar of Truth,

allowing

s 108–12   My conclusions were reached by *a·* the evidence
159–28   how much . . . one form of matter is *a·*

allows

ph 187–16   Anatomy *a·* the mental cause of the
o 343–28   Hence the mistake which *a·* words, rather than
g 549–29   and *a·* matter and material law to usurp

All-power

f 231–10   no lesser power equals the infinite *A·* ;
t 454– 6   The understanding, . . . of the divine *A·*
gl 581– 3   ALMIGHTY. *A·* ; infinity ; omnipotence.

all-power
pr 17–14 *For God is infinite, a·*,
s 130–14 good and its sweet concords have *a·*.
f 203– 4 omnipotence— has *a·*, assigns sure rewards
228–26 Omnipotence has *a·*,
r 466– 3 Hence God combines *a·* or potency,
469–27 after admitting that God, . . . has *a·*,

all-powerful
s 108–23 Life, Truth, and Love are *a·*
t 450– 4 belief . . . in a natural, *a·* devil.

all-presence
b 278–22 Spirit is supreme and *a·*.
r 466– 4 all-science or true knowledge, *a·*.

all-science
r 466– 3 God combines all-power or potency, *a·*

all-seeing
gl 587– 5 The great I AM ; the all-knowing, *a·*,

alludes
b 333–10 *a·* to the spirituality which is taught,
o 342– 1 *a·* to "doubtful disputations."— *Rom.* 14 : 1.

alluring
a 21–28 The company is *a·* and the pleasures exciting.

allusion
g 510–21 There is no Scriptural *a·* to solar light until
510–23 and the *a·* to fluids . . . indicates

All-wise
t 455–23 The *A·* does not bestow

all-wise
gl 587– 6 all-acting, *a·*, all-loving, and eternal ;

almanacs
ph 171– 9 not needing to consult *a·* for the probabilities

almightiness
r 487–29 reality of Life, its *a·* and immortality.

Aimighty (*see also* Almighty's)
s 119– 4 When we . . . we disown the *A·*,
g 501– * *by the name of God A·;— Exod.* 6 : 3.
ap 576–10 the Lord God *A·* and the Lamb— *Rev.* 21 : 22.
gl 581– 3 definition of

almighty
f 202–27 admit that God has *a·* power,
o 348–15 when we ascribe to Him *a·* Life and Love?
357–27 Can Deity be *a·*, if another mighty

Almighty God
f 228–15 assert their freedom in the name of *A· G·*.
p 438–15 I ask your arrest in the name of *A· G·*

Almighty's
f 218–20 why do you substitute drugs for the *A·* power,

almost
f 221–11 in hunger and weakness, *a·* in starvation,
o 350– 2 They think of matter as something and *a·*
p 376– 7 and does its work *a·* self-deceived.
g 502– 3 is so brief that it would *a·* seem,
524–10 the true idea of God seems *a·* lost.
gl 590–17 the word *kurios a·* always has this lower sense,

aloft
p 426–27 hold the banner of Christianity *a·*

alone
pr 6– 4 this divine Principle *a·* reforms the sinner.
11–28 nor can prayer *a·* give us an
a 25–28 will never *a·* make us imitators of him.
26– 2 treading *a·* his loving pathway
49–15 met his earthly fate *a·* with God.
51–22 His purpose in healing was not *a·* to
m 57–20 it cannot exist *a·*, but requires all mankind
60–13 selfishness and impurity *a·* are fleeting,
60–32 Higher enjoyments *a·* can satisfy
64–11 some noble woman, struggling *a·* with
sp 86– 2 to be occasioned by physical contact *a·*,
86–23 Education *a·* determines the difference.
90– 8 earth's motion . . . sustained by Mind *a·*.
92–29 instead of urging the claims of Truth *a·*.
s 117– 4 not one of a series, but one *a·*
117– 9 mortals *a·* do this.
127–10 The terms . . . C. S., or Science *a·*,
127–27 and is *a·* able to interpret God aright.
135– 9 Spiritual evolution *a·* is worthy of
142– 9 Truth, *a·* can furnish us with absolute
147–30 but Science *a·* reveals the divine Principle
157– 9 rests on Mind *a·* as the curative Principle,
ph 173–28 error which the human mind *a·* has created.
174–25 if . . . sick, why treat the body *a·*
182– 2 healing the sick through divine Mind *a·*,
184–21 Mortal mind *a·* suffers,
194–31 a belief formed by education *a·*.
196– 9 Sin *a·* brings death, for sin is the only
199–10 great fact that Mind *a·* enlarges and
f 203–32 for God *a·* is man's life.
212–22 God *a·* makes and clothes the lilies
219–28 not rendering to God the honor due to Him *a·*.
251–14 an error that Christ, Truth, *a·* can destroy.

alone
c 263– 6 Immortal spiritual man *a·* represents the
b 270–26 Truth and Love *a·* can unmake them.
270–29 the fact that the human mind *a·* suffers,
270–30 the divine Mind *a·* heals.
271–17 "Neither pray I for these *a·*,— John* 17 : 20.
272–31 C. S., . . . *a·* reveals the natural, divine
279–28 not two bases of being, . . . but one *a·*,
285– 4 Science of being obtains not *a·* hereafter
292– 4 Divine Science *a·* can compass the heights
308–16 Jacob was *a·* wrestling with error,
339– 8 Spirit, *a·* created all, and called it good.
p 366–19 Love which *a·* confers the healing power.
382– 7 this *a·* would usher in the millennium.
388– 4 a victory which Science *a·* can explain.
391–26 Mortal mind *a·* sentences itself.
400–22 thought *a·* creates the suffering. ·
402– 6 cure, . . . through mental surgery *a·*,
409–20 should be governed by God *a·*.
410–10 "Man shall not live by bread *a·*,— Matt.* 4 : 4.
419– 6 God and His ideas *a·* are real
424–26 to be *a·* with God and the sick when
435– 6 Mortal Mind, which *a·* is capable of sin and
t 456– 8 This *a·* entitles them to the high standing
462–18 self-denial, sincerity, . . . and persistence *a·*
r 483–24 wrestle with material observations *a·*,
488–23 Mind *a·* possesses all faculties,
g 510–18 Love *a·* can impart the limitless idea of
518– 3 himself subordinate *a·* to his Maker.
533–20 more rapidly than he can *a·*.
543–26 Ideas of Truth *a·* are reflected in the
546– 3 this belief *a·* is mortal.
556–15 but the Christian *a·* can fathom it.
gl 595–15 which *a·* can fit us for the office of
596– 1 That which spiritual sense *a·* comprehends,

along
s 129–27 some of the leading illusions *a·* the path
141–11 *a·* the line of scholarly and ecclesiastical
156–22 she could get *a·* two days without globules ;
o 343–31 first . . . to press *a·* the line of gospel-healing,
p 373–28 languidly creeps *a·* its frozen channels,
415–30 whole frame will sink from sight *a·* with
r 490–22 *a·* with the dissolving elements of clay.

aloof
s 109–13 kept *a·* from society, and devoted time

aloud
sp 76– 5 forgets all else and breathes *a·* his rapture.
p 396– 9 avoid speaking *a·* the name of the disease.

Alpine
m 61–17 like tropical flowers born amid *A·* snows.

already
pr 2– 9 to do more than He has *a·* done,
2–14 for He *a·* knows all.
2–25 anything He does not *a·* comprehend?
3– 6 The rule is *a·* established, and it is our task
3–23 really grateful for the good *a·* received?
8–26 do we not *a·* know more of this heart
11–15 if indeed, he has not *a·* suffered sufficiently
m 69– 7 God's children *a·* created will be cognized
sp 74– 7 acorn, *a·* absorbed into a sprout
80–20 when we *a·* know that it is mind-power which
s 108–20 *a·* within the shadow of the death-valley,
112–24 *a·* been stated and proved to be true,
130–20 cannot add to the contents of a vessel *a·* full.
131–15 This Science has come *a·*,
137–12 In his rejection of the answer *a·* given
147–21 perishing fossils of theories *a·* antiquated,
161–28 if it were not *a·* determined by mortal mind.
163–17 it has *a·* destroyed more lives than
ph 168–13 have *a·* brought yourself into the slough of
175– 2 efface the outlines of disease *a·* formulated
180–15 reservoir *a·* overflowing with that emotion.
198– 7 his fear, which has *a·* developed the disease
f 201–13 We cannot fill vessels *a·* full.
206–22 Is God creating anew what He has *a·* created?
229– 2 it is *a·* proved that matter has not destroyed
233–16 *A·* the shadow of His right hand rests upon
c 260–14 to discover what God has *a·* done;
266– 9 this seeming vacuum is *a·* filled
b 274–31 This suppositional partnership is *a·* obsolete,
291– 8 till mortals have *a·* yielded to each lesser call
323–14 must put into practice what we *a·* know.
p 402– 4 the author has *a·* in her possession
416–30 have *a·* heard too much on that subject.
t 459–10 Judge not . . . by the steps *a·* taken,
r 490–16 since he is so *a·*, according to C. S.
492– 7 It is *a·* proved that a knowledge of this,
g 510–22 *a·* divided into evening and morning ;
521–24 presented in the verses *a·* considered,
528– 3 God has *a·* created man, both male and
533–21 is *a·* found in the rapid deterioration
533–31 She has *a·* learned that corporeal sense
ap 572–24 he *a·* saw a new heaven and a new earth.

also

pref	ix– 1	She *a·* began to jot down her thoughts
	xi–23	there came *a·* the charge to plant and
pr	6– 2	"he *a·* will deny us."— *II Tim.* 2 : 12.
	11– 2	specified *a·* the terms of forgiveness.
	14–20	works that I do shall he do *a·* ;— *John* 14 : 12.
a	23–32	Hebrew verb *to believe* means *a·* *to be firm*
	34–20	His resurrection was *a·* their resurrection.
	40–13	opposite is *a·* true, While there's sin there's
	42–31	works that I do shall he do *a·*."— *John* 14 : 12.
	52–28	works that I do shall he do *a·* ;"— *John* 14 : 12.
m	60– 6	The beautiful in character is *a·* the good,
sp	71–16	Thus you learn that these *a·* are images,
	71–18	From dreams *a·* you learn that
	92– 5	*a·* capable of imparting these sensations.
	93– 5	works that I do shall he do *a·*,"— *John* 14 : 12.
	93– 5	*a·* said, "But the hour cometh,— *John* 4 : 23.
an	106–25	as I have *a·* told you in time past,— *Gal.* 5 : 21.
s	112–26	*A·*, if any so-called new school claims to
	117– 1	term *individuality* is *a·* open to objections,
	133– 5	There was *a·* a certain centurion of whose
	135–11	same power which heals sin heals *a·* sickness.
	137–29	"And I say *a·* unto thee,— *Matt.* 16 : 18.
	158– 7	Apollo was *a·* regarded as the sender of
	162–15	*a·* without the false beliefs of a so-called
ph	169–19	*a·* declares that all disease is cured by
	181–29	there will your heart be *a·*."— *Matt.* 6 : 21.
	186–24	If . . . evil is *a·* as immortal.
f	221– 8	His physician *a·* recommended that he
	222– 7	He learned *a·* that mortal mind
	222–13	he *a·* had less faith in the so-called
	243–10	which was *a·* in Christ Jesus"— *Phil.* 2 : 5.
	253–22	*A·*, if you believe yourself diseased,
c	255– *	*not only they, but ourselves a·,*— *Rom.* 8 : 23.
	262–26	there will your heart be *a·*."— *Matt.* 6 : 21.
b	268– *	*a· may have fellowship with*— *I John* 1 : 3.
	271–18	for them *a·* which shall believe — *John* 17 : 20.
	276– 9	which was *a·* in Christ Jesus."— *Phil.* 2 : 5.
	286–29	error must *a·* say, "I am true."
	305– 2	Gender *a·* is a quality, not of God,
	305–19	these *a·* doeth the Son likewise."— *John* 5 : 19.
	320–13	for that he *a·* is flesh,"— *Gen.* 6 : 3.
	325–11	then shall ye *a·* appear— *Col.* 3 : 4.
	326– 5	works that I do shall he do *a·*."— *John* 14 : 12.
	327– 2	and *a·* by gaining an affection for good
	331–14	Scriptures *a·* declare that God is Spirit.
	332– 1	They *a·* indicate the divine Principle
	332– 8	"For we are *a·* His offspring."— *Acts* 17 : 28.
	334–29	and is *a·* a reference to the human sense of
o	341– *	*a· quicken your mortal bodies*— *Rom.* 8 : 11.
	343–17	he *a·* scientifically demonstrates this great fact,
p	364–21	it must be said of them *a·* that they
	366–22	The physician must *a·* watch, lest he
	369– 1	and he is liable to admit *a·* the reality of
	370–26	Hygienic treatment *a·* loses its efficacy.
	372–25	*a·* deny before my Father— *Matt.* 10 : 33.
	373–17	Scriptures *a·* declare, through the exalted
	377–23	You *a·* remove in this way what are termed
	377–28	*a·* a fear that Mind is helpless
	398–25	So *a·* faith, cooperating with a belief
	405–17	that shall he *a·* reap."— *Gal.* 6 : 7.
	414–11	*a·* the fact that truth and love will
	414–24	*a·* that matter neither feels, suffers, nor enjoys.
	416– 1	At last the agony *a·* vanishes.
	426–15	*a·* learning the necessity of working out his
	426–23	and *a·* of the fear of its sting
	429–23	it must *a·* have an ending,
	437– 2	*a·* testified that he was on intimate terms
	439– 2	*A·*, be it known that False Belief,
	441– 5	He *a·* decided that the plaintiff, Personal Sense,
	441–32	speaks of him *a·* as "a murderer— *John* 8 : 44.
	444–18	but let us *a·* be careful always to
	444–20	turn to him the other *a·*."— *Matt.* 5 : 39.
	445– 2	*A·* the teacher must thoroughly fit his students
	451–16	there will his heart be *a·*.
	452–12	but it will *a·* attract respect.
	463– 5	Teacher and student should *a·* be familiar with
r	465–13	They are *a·* intended to express the nature,
	467–16	having that Mind which was *a·* in Christ.
	469– 6	it would *a·* have an ending.
	490–10	From this *a·* comes its powerlessness,
	494–31	It should be said of his followers *a·*,
	496– 1	You will *a·* learn that in Science there is no
	497–25	that Mind to be in us which was *a·* in Christ
g	504–12	This *a·* shows that there is no place where
	510–15	He made the stars *a·*.— *Gen.* 1 : 16.
	512– 9	*a·* by holy thoughts, winged with Love.
	514–22	wolf *a·* shall dwell with the lamb,— *Isa.* 11 : 6.
	515–26	lift a weight, your reflection does this *a·*.
	517– 1	the word for *man* is used *a·* as the synonym
	524– 6	It was *a·* found among the Israelites.
	526– 1	the tree of life *a·*, in the midst of— *Gen.* 2 : 9.
	527–15	that *a·* that material perception,
	529– 4	It came about, *a·*, that instruments were needed
	535–24	thorns *a·* and thistles shall it — *Gen.* 3 : 18.
	537– 2	and take *a·* of the tree of life,— *Gen.* 3 : 22.

also

g	537–14	that shall he *a·* reap."— *Gal.* 6 : 7.
	540–26	And Abel, he *a·* brought of the — *Gen.* 4 : 4.
	548–31	*a·* increase their numbers naturally
	553–31	may *a·* ask how belief can affect a result
	554–22	*a·* said, "Have not I chosen— *John* 6 : 70.
ap	561–11	saw *a·* the spiritual ideal as a woman
	562–24	*A·* the spiritual idea is typified by
	563–16	but he *a·* sees the nothingness of evil
	566–19	we may *a·* offer the prayer which concludes
	568–11	Here, *a·*, the Revelator first exhibits the
	570–28	They should *a·* know the great delusion of
	574– 3	The Revelator *a·* takes in another view,
	574–21	brought *a·* the experience which at last
	576–14	The word *temple a·* means *body*.
gl	579– 6	which is *a·* their original meaning.
	598– 1	Greek word for *wind (pneuma)* is used *a·*

altar

a	55–24	on the *a·* of divine Science,
m	65– 4	May Christ, Truth, be present at every bridal *a·*
t	454–21	Love is priestess at the *a·* of Truth.
gl	596– 7	Paul saw in Athens an *a·* dedicated

alter

f	253–23	you can *a·* this wrong belief and action
b	297– 4	no circumstance can *a·* the situation, until
	382– 8	bathing and rubbing to *a·* the secretions

alterative

s	162– 6	C. S. acts as an *a·*, neutralizing error
f	224– 2	the world feels the *a·* effect of truth
p	371–30	Truth is an *a·* in the entire system,
	420–21	better than any drug, *a·*, or tonic.
	421–22	chemicalization, which is the *a·* effect
	423–11	This corrective is an *a·*, reaching to every part

altered

p	408– 2	This view is not *a·* by the fact that

alternating

b	298–16	This human belief, *a·* between a

alternative

f	221–14	informed him that death was indeed his only *a·*.
p	436–21	You have left Mortal Man no *a·*.

although

a	19–14	*a·* his teaching set households at variance,
	19–28	*A·* is good.
	30– 6	*a·* he was endowed with the Christ,
	55–13	*a·* it is again ruled out of the synagogue.
s	112–10	*A·* these opinions may have occasional gleams
	147–14	*A·* this volume contains the complete
	148–32	*a·* our great Master demonstrated that
	152– 8	*a·* they know not how the work is done.
	158–32	*a·* her physicians insisted that it would be
o	343– 8	*a·*, without this cross-bearing, one might not
p	386–29	you would not have understood him, *a·* the
	430–31	*A·* I have the superintendence of
	431–28	*a·* nothing on my part has occasioned
r	466–17	*a·* . . . it is the most important to understand.
	469–22	when we admit that, *a·* God is infinite,
	471–14	*a·* the evidence as to these facts
	492– 2	*a·* the so-called dreamer is unconscious?
g	523– 6	*A·* presenting the exact opposite of
	546–16	*a·* the material senses can take no cognizance

altitudes

f	215–11	not subordinate to geometric *a·*.

altogether

pr	3–14	the One "*a·* lovely ;"— *Song* 5 : 16.
sp	87–32	or *a·* gone from physical sight
g	538– 1	Love infinitely wise and *a·* lovely,

alway

b	317–14	"Lo, I am with you *a·*,"— *Matt.* 28 : 20.
t	446–22	"Lo, I am with you *a·*,— *Matt.* 28 : 20.

always

pr	4–12	The habitual struggle to be *a·* good
	5–14	but not *a·* in this world.
	7–18	If spiritual sense *a·* guided men,
	7–26	to whom each need of man is *a·* known
	8–21	does not *a·* mean a desire for it.
	10–22	Experience teaches us that we do not *a·* receive
	10–29	it is not *a·* best for us to receive.
	11– 9	*a·* demands restitution before mortals can
	12– 5	no power to gain more . . . than is *a·* at hand.
m	62– 9	to b *a·* fed, rocked, tossed, or talked to,
	66–26	If one is better than the other, as must *a·*
sp	86–16	though we can *a·* feel their influence.
	95– 1	The effect of his Mind was *a·* to heal and
	98–22	For centuries— yea, *a·* — natural science has
an	104–12	Lastly, they say they have *a·* believed it."
s	125– 5	Moral conditions will be found *a·* harmonious
	128–30	must *a·* bring the same result.
	134– 8	and so has come *a·* to mean one who
	134–26	Thou hearest me *a·* ;"— *John* 11 : 42.
	145–22	mystery which godliness *a·* presents to
	145–22	mystery *a·* arising from ignorance of the

always

ph	169– 8	But it a· came about as I had foretold.
	170–20	a· in opposition, never in obedience, to physics.
	184–27	a· breathed with great difficulty when the
	189–30	keeping a· in the direct line of matter,
	200– 9	Life is, a· has been, and ever will be
f	225–12	There is a· some tumult, but there is a
	225–26	a· germinating in new forms of tyranny,
	243–11	must a· accompany the letter of Science
	246–24	is a· beautiful and grand.
c	267–28	"let thy garments be a· white."— Eccl. 9 : 8.
b	277–31	mortal phenomenon, . . . a· erroneous.
	282–24	a· governing itself erroneously.
	284–32	intercommunication is a· from God to
	302–16	is a· beyond and above the mortal illusion
	309–29	so-called life a· ends in death.
	320–13	My spirit shall not a· strive— Gen. 6 : 3.
	326–25	spiritual sense, which is a· right.
	329–23	A· right, its divine Principle never repents,
	334–19	as the Christ has a· done,
	336–17	never was material, but a· spiritual
p	375–26	Consumptive patients a· show . . . courage,
	377– 5	he should rejoice a· in ever-present Love.
	380– 4	Truth is a· the victor.
	392–11	should a· be met with the mental negation.
	402– 1	C. S. is a· the most skilful surgeon,
	411–21	Disease is a· induced by a false sense
	411–27	A· begin your treatment by allaying the fear
	417– 4	A· support their trust in the power of Mind
	425–30	be a· ready with the mental protest against
	426– 6	when she has the high goal a· before her
t	443–10	she a· has felt, that all are privileged to
	444–18	a· to "judge righteous— John 7 : 24.
	448–25	must a· hinder scientific demonstration.
	458–14	Divinity is a· ready.
r	482– 6	proper use of the word soul can a· be
	492–32	would keep truth and error a· at war.
	494–10	Divine Love a· has met and a· will meet
g	508–20	grammars a· recognize a neuter gender,
	518–14	in return, the higher a· protects the lower.
	523–20	Deity therein is a· called Jehovah,
	530–17	myth represents error as a· asserting its
	537–32	God, who is Love a·,
	552–30	matter a· surrenders its claims when
	554– 8	Error is a· error.
ap	575–14	Spiritual teaching must a· be by symbols.
gl	590–17	the word kurios almost a· has

amalgamation

f	207–11	such as the a· of Truth and error
g	550–27	A· is deemed monstrous

amazement

c	263–25	peers from its cloister with a·

ambiguities

s	114–26	disentangles the interlaced a· of being,

ambiguity

o	355– 2	and then the a· will vanish.

ambiguous

p	388–17	a· nature of all material health-theories.

ambition

m	58– 8	Unselfish a·, noble life-motives, and purity,
	61– 8	and give higher aims to a·.
	61–21	What hope of happiness, what noble a·,
t	462–28	It teaches the control of mad a·.

ambush

ap	571–11	Who is telling mankind of the foe in a·?

ameliorate

s	141–28	divine healing will a· sin, sickness, and death.
t	458–22	but Science will a· mortal malice.

Amen

b	268– *	I can do no otherwise; so help me God! A·!
o	343– 1	The people are taught in such cases to say, A·.

amenable

p	434–31	God made Man immortal and a· to Spirit

America

b	320– 6	theologians in Europe and A· agree that

American

f	245–12	Some A· travellers saw her when she was

American Cyclopædia

an	100– 3	According to the A· C·, he regarded this

amid

a	37–14	not a· the smoke of battle is merit seen
m	61–17	like tropical flowers born a· Alpine snows.
	67– 8	Can you steer safely a· the storm?"
sp	95–23	Led by a solitary star a· the darkness,
f	220–12	snowbird sings and soars a· the blasts;
b	306–25	Undisturbed a· the jarring testimony of the

amidst

m	66–17	A· gratitude for conjugal felicity,
	66–18	A· conjugal infelicity, it is well to hope, pray,
ap	563–28	subtlety, winding its way a· all evil,

amiss

pr	10–28	receive not, because ye ask a·,— Jas. 4 : 3.
	10–32	Then "ye ask a·."— Jas. 4 : 3.

among

pref	ix–13	still in circulation a· her first pupils ;
pr	9–26	and so be counted a· sinners?
	16–12	some doubt a· Bible scholars,
a	24–29	The truth had been lived a· men ;
	32– 6	A· the Jews it was an ancient custom
m	56– 8	generation a· human kind.
	65–22	impurity and error are left a· the lees.
	65–26	which was once a fixed fact a· us,
an	101– 9	a· whom were Roux, Bouillaud, and
	106– 8	a· which are self-government, reason,
s	129–28	reformatory mission a· mortals.
	133–16	in captivity a· foreign nations,
	150–10	a permanent dispensation a· men ;
	161–17	a· which are life, liberty, and
ph	196–32	diseases a· the human family.
	200–26	not to know anything a· you,— I Cor. 2 : 2.
	200–28	not to know anything a· you,
f	237–16	C. S., a· their first lessons,
	238– 7	"Come out from a· them,— II Cor. 6 : 17.
	242–23	parted my raiment a·— John 19 : 24.
c	256–21	a· the inhabitants of the earth ; — Dan. 4 : 35.
t	453– 2	a· the examples on the blackboard,
	460–29	her manuscript circulated a· the students.
	463– 2	The material physician gropes a·
g	524– 6	It was also found a· the Israelites,
	535–17	into the heritage of the first born a· men?

Amorites

g	524– 3	in the Moloch of the A·,

amount

ph	175–21	The exact a· of food the stomach could digest

amounts

ph	172– 5	a· to nothing in the right direction and
p	375–31	fear so excessive that it a· to fortitude.
g	551–23	question of the naturalist a· to this :

ample

s	163–26	so a· an exhibition of human invention

amplification

g	501–10	that a· of wonder and glory

amplitude

a	54– 3	Out of the a· of his pure affection,

amputate

ph	172–26	when you a· a limb ;

amputated

f	212– 5	A limb which has been a· has continued

amusement

m	58–20	a wandering desire for incessant a·
	62– 9	create in their babes a desire for incessant a·,
ph	195–30	to meet a frivolous demand for a·

amusements

m	60–22	frivolous a·, personal adornment,

analogous

g	510–25	a· to the suppositional resolving of

analogy

s	110–32	No a· exists between the vague hypotheses of

analyzes

p	433– 3	He a· the offence, reviews the testimony,

anathemas

b	315–10	brought upon him the a· of the age.

Anatomy

p	430–23	Materia Medica, A·, Physiology,
	437–22	Materia Medica, A·, Physiology,

anatomy

admits
ph	174–23	A· admits that mind is somewhere in man,

allows
ph	187–16	A· allows the mental cause of the latter action,

and theology
s	148–13	a· and theology define man as
	148–17	A· and theology reject the divine Principle

declares
ph	173–17	A· declares man to be structural.

describes
s	152–10	A· describes muscular action as

finds
s	160–14	A· finds a necessity for nerves to

learn from
s	160–29	only to learn from a· that muscle is not

mental
t	462–32	Scientist, through understanding mental a·,

nor theology
s	148– 7	Neither a· nor theology has ever

of Christian Science
t	462–25	a· of C. S. teaches when and how to probe the

takes up man
s	148–15	A· takes up man at all points materially.

anatomy
  treatises on
  ph 179–21　Treatises on *a*·, physiology, and health,

————

  s 160–16　what does *a*· say when the cords contract
  160–27　Why then consult *a*· to learn how
  ph 173– 2　we fail to see how *a*· can distinguish
  173–23　*a*·, physiology, phrenology, do not define
  t 462–20　*A*·, when conceived of spiritually, is

ancestors
  m 61–20　the grosser traits of their *a*·.
  ph 175–27　empurpled the plump cheeks of our *a*·,

ancestry
  m 63– 6　The beautiful, good, and pure constitute his *a*·.
  g 551–20　by which all peculiarities of *a*·,

anchor
  a 40–32　the *a*· of hope must be cast beyond the

ancient
  a 32– 3　In *a*· Rome a soldier was required to
  32– 7　Among the Jews it was an *a*· custom
  41–18　No *a*· school of philosophy, *materia medica*,
  43–10　and is now repeating its *a*· history.
  sp 84– 3　The *a*· prophets gained their foresight
  an 105–28　and confirms the *a*· axiom :
  s 126–26　found nothing in *a*· or in modern systems
  139–17　manifest mistakes in the *a*· versions ;
  144–30　It is a question to-day, whether the *a*·
  146– 2　The *a*· Christians were healers.
  146–28　It is as *a*· as "the Ancient of days."— *Dan.* 7 : 9.
  f 243–12　to confirm and repeat the *a*· demonstrations.
  b 319–16　are so many *a*· and modern mythologies.
  o 349– 3　As Paul asked of the unfaithful in *a*· days,
  p 389–24　the *a*· error that there is fraternity between
  r 469–30　*a*· mythology and pagan idolatry.
  483–19　To . . . the *a*· worthies, and to Christ Jesus,
  g 514–31　source of strength to the *a*· worthies.
  516–31　In one of the *a*· languages
  551–32　The *a*· and hypothetical question,
  553–26　supersede the more *a*· superstition
  ap 567–18　That false claim— that *a*· belief,

anciently
  s 142– 4　*A*· the followers of Christ, or Truth,
  c 255– 7　*a*· classified as the higher criticism,
  o 343–25　*A*· those apostles who were

Ancient of days
  s 146–28　It is as ancient as "the *A*· of *d*·."— *Dan.* 7 : 9.

anew
  pr 4–22　will mould and fashion us *a*·,
  a 20–22　saves retracing and traversing *a*· the path
  35– 6　Discerning Christ, Truth, *a*·
  m 66–13　Love propagates *a*· the higher joys
  s 150– 7　Its appearing is the coming *a*· of the gospel of
  f 206–21　Is God creating *a*· what He has already created?
  p 425–26　and Spirit will form you *a*·.
  g 528– 6　cannot be true that man was ordered to create man *a*·

angel
  f 224–26　Will you open or close the door upon this *a*·
  b 308–19　an *a*·, a message from Truth and Love,
  g 521–17　point of a diamond" and the pen of an *a*·.
  ap 558– 3　And I saw another mighty *a*·— *Rev.* 10 : 1.
  558– 9　This *a*· or message which comes from
  559– 1　*a*· had in his hand "a little book,"— *Rev.* 10 : 2.
  561– 8　saw an "*a*· standing in the— *Rev.* 19 : 17.
  574–29　Love can make an *a*· entertained unawares.

angelic
  sp 93–19　may clothe it with *a*· vestments,
  ap 574–18　the seven *a*· vials full of seven plagues,

angel's
  ap 559– 6　The *a*· left foot was upon the earth ;

angels
  confers upon
  b 298–30　Human conjecture confers upon *a*· its own
  His
  o 360–27　And His *a*· He chargeth with— *see Job* 4 : 18.
  his
  ap 566–26　Michael and his *a*· fought— *Rev.* 12 : 7.
  566–27　the dragon fought, and his *a*·,— *Rev.* 12 : 7.
  567–17　his *a*· were cast out with him.— *Rev.* 12 : 9.
  567–26　His *a*·, or messages, are cast out with
  my
  b 299– 7　My *a*· are exalted thoughts,
  seven
  ap 574– 6　came unto me one of the seven *a*·— *Rev.* 21 : 9.
  these
  g 512– 9　These *a*· of His presence, which have the
  ap 567– 3　These *a*· deliver us from the depths.

  m 56– *　*as the a*· of God in heaven.*— *Matt.* 22 : 30.
  64–21　but man would be as the *a*·.
  ph 174–11　*a*· of His presence— the spiritual intuitions

angels
  b 298–25　*A*· are not etherealized human beings,
  298–28　*A*· are pure thoughts from God,
  299–11　*A*· are God's representatives.
  299–17　we entertain "*a*· unawares."— *Heb.* 13 : 2.
  p 372–17　Therefore he will be as the *a*· in heaven.
  r 482–23　*A*· announced to the Wisemen of old
  482–24　and *a*· whisper it, through faith,
  g 501–11　glory which *a*· could only whisper
  548–16　by which men may entertain *a*·,
  ap 566–29　The Old Testament assigns to the *a*·,
  gl 581– 4　definition of

anger
  b 293–25　"The *a*· of the Lord."— *Deut.* 29 : 20.
  gl 595– 4　The idea of Truth ; justice. Revenge ; *a*·.
  597–29　Destruction ; *a*· ; mortal passions.

angry
  p 369–32　to murmur or to be *a*· over sin.

anguish
  ph 195– 6　Every sound convulsed him with *a*·.
  p 386–19　You think that your *a*· is occasioned by your

angular
  f 248–23　*a*· outline and deformity of matter models.

animal
  magnetism
  (*see* **magnetism**)

————

  a 28–32　There is too much *a*· courage in society
  48–23　rebuking resentment or *a*· courage.
  m 61– 5　and the spiritual over the *a*·,
  67–18　notion that *a*· natures can possibly give
  sp 90– 1　or if one *a*· can originate another,
  an 100– 9　*A*· bodies are susceptible to
  100–20　no proof of the existence of the *a*· magnetic
  102– 3　His power is neither *a*· nor human.
  102– 4　Its basis being a belief and this belief *a*·,
  104–20　revenge, malice, are *a*· propensities
  ph 173– 5　farther than his *a*· progenitors.
  179–17　the wild *a*·, . . . sniffs the wind with delight.
  f 222–25　if eating a bit of *a*· flesh could overpower
  252–20　*A*· in propensity, deceitful in sentiment,
  b 298–26　not . . . evolving *a*· qualities in their wings ;
  309–28　to suppose that there can be . . . organic *a*· or
  327–25　the man who has more *a*· than moral courage,
  p 374–30　Mortal mind produces *a*· heat,
  378–12　An *a*· may infuriate another by
  t 450–32　electricity, *a*· nature, and organic life,
  r 490– 5　Human will is an *a*· propensity,
  g 509–20　So-called mineral, vegetable, and *a*· substances
  512–26　confers *a*· names and natures upon its
  529–24　nothing in the *a*· kingdom which represents the
  541–10　the homage bestowed through a gentle *a*·
  548–24　far apart from his material sense of *a*· growth
  ap 563–31　It is the *a*· instinct in mortals,
  564– 4　This malicious *a*· instinct, of which the dragon
  564–26　are typified by a serpent, or *a*· subtlety.
  gl 597–20　mortal belief ; *a*· power.

animality
  ap 569–12　masters his mortal beliefs, *a*·, and hate

animals
  b 277–13　Natural history presents vegetables and *a*·
  g 511–25　*A*· and mortals metaphorically present
  528– 5　Adam gave the name and nature of *a*·,
  531–20　Who will say that minerals, vegetables, and *a*·
  548–30　"Certain *a*·, besides the ordinary
  549– 3　multiplication of certain *a*· takes place
  550– 7　the individuality and identity of *a*·
  554–29　It is the general belief that the lower *a*·
  557– 8　many *a*· suffer no pain in multiplying ;

animate
  ph 189–26　belief of inanimate, and then of *a*· matter.
  f 243–32　Perfection does not *a*· imperfection.
  p 409– 6　its final statement,— *a*· error
  409–19　The *a*· should be governed by God alone.
  g 541– 2　A lamb is a more *a*· form of existence,

animated
  a 26–14　the godliness which *a*· him.
  an 100– 9　the celestial bodies, the earth, and *a*· things.
  t 459–19　Whether *a*· by malice or ignorance,
  g 525– 2　a mortal sinner, *a*· by the breath of God?

animating
  gl 583–20　the *a*· divine Principle of all

animation
  gl 582– 8　life, strength, *a*·, and
  599– 4　ZEAL. The reflected *a*· of Life,

ankylosed
  s 162–21　*a*· joints have been made supple,

annihilate
  an 103–25　they *a*· the fables of mortal mind,
  ph 172–27　and worms *a*· it.
  f 252–27　the law of God, may at any moment *a*·

annihilate

t 451– 1 the errors which Truth must and will *a·*
r 490–21 would, by fair logic, *a·* man
g 540–15 that Truth may *a·* all sense of evil

annihilated

f 246– 1 Mind and its formations can never be *a·*.
b 292–28 man would be *a·*, were it not
310–28 then Spirit, . . . would be *a·*.
r 477–18 Were it otherwise, man would be *a·*.
486–27 If this were not so, man would be speedily *a·*.
493–19 Sickness is a belief, which must be *a·*
g 536–16 governed by corporeality . . . man would be *a·*.

annihilates

b 330–26 delusion of material sense, which Science *a·*.
340–25 *a·* pagan and Christian idolatry,

annihilation

f 243–28 a law of *a·* to everything unlike themselves,
b 278–26 logic which would prove his *a·*.
310–25 If . . . the *a·* of Spirit would be inevitable.
gl 582–22 physical sense put out of sight and hearing ; *a·*.

announce

s 119–13 but to *a·* Him as their source,
p 391–25 Disease has no intelligence to . . . *a·* its name.

announced

b 298–19 When the real is attained, which is *a·* by
p 379– 3 *a·* as partners in the beginning.
r 482–23 Angels *a·* to the Wisemen of old

announcing

p 386–16 blundering despatch, mistakenly *a·*

annoyances

m 59– 9 *a·* and cares of domestic economy,

annually

b 328–20 hundreds of persons die there *a·* from

annul

pr 11–19 not to *a·* the divine sentence
s 139–25 nor *a·* the healing by the prophets,
f 229–28 should not if we could, *a·* the decrees of
b 273–21 God never ordained a material law to *a·*
p 381–29 man's moral right to *a·* an unjust sentence.
384–12 has only to enter his protest . . . in order to *a·*
385–12 though it can never *a·* the law which
389–20 cannot *a·* these regulations by an

annulled

m 59–27 The nuptial vow should never be *a·*,
o 349– 7 our Master *a·* material law
p 382– 1 he *a·* supposed laws of matter,

annuls

b 340–28 *a·* the curse on man,
r 491–13 Spirit, which *a·* the claims of matter,

anodynes

s 143–17 and quiets pain with *a·*.
p 374– 2 *A·*, counter-irritants, and depletion

anoint

p 364–14 wash and *a·* his guest's feet,

anointed

a 42–22 glory which God bestowed on His *a·*,
f 201– * *the footsteps of Thine a·.— Psal.* 89 : 51.
b 313– 4 may be rendered "Jesus the *a·*,"
313– 7 even thy God, hath *a·* thee— *Heb.* 1 : 9.
p 363–28 before she *a·* them with the oil.
gl 597–10 which was ready to . . . crucify God's *a·*.

anointeth

ap 578–14 [LOVE] *a·* my head with oil ;— *see Psal.* 23 : 5.

anointing

p 367–26 through silent utterances, and divine *a·*

anomalous

p 375–29 This state of mind seems *a·* except to the

anon

g 513–10 *a·* the veil is lifted, and the scene shifts

another (see also another's)

pr 1– 4 Regardless of what *a·* may say
12– 9 This, however, is one belief casting out *a·*,
12–28 *a·* who offers the same measure of prayer?
16–19 is but *a·* name for the first lie
a 23–25 *A·* kind of faith understands divine Love
36– 4 simply through translation into *a·* sphere.
37–10 connect one stage with *a·* in the history of
38–18 At *a·* time Jesus prayed, not for the twelve only,
40– 5 *A·* will say: "Go thy way— *Acts* 24 : 25.
55–27 "He shall give you *a·* Comforter,— *John* 14 : 16.
m 58–27 because *a·* supplies her wants.
sp 73– 4 but *a·*, who has died . . . it terms a *spirit*.
73– 8 belief that one man, as spirit, can control *a·*
75–30 pass from one dream to *a·* dream,
88–16 and at *a·* are called spirits.
89– 4 in the belief that *a·* mind is
90– 1 if one animal can originate *a·*,
an 100– 5 exerted by one living organism over *a·*,
104–23 hypnotizer employs one error to destroy *a·*.

another

s 110–10 brought to light *a·* glorious proposition,
112–28 and yet uses *a·* author's discoveries
122–15 optical focus is *a·* proof of the illusion
125–12 As human thought changes from one stage to *a·*
130– 5 One has a farm, *a·* has merchandise,
143–14 human mind uses one error to medicine *a·*.
149– 8 succeeds in one instance fails in *a·*,
152–11 in one instance and not in *a·*,
152–13 in which one statement contradicts *a·*
159–28 allowing *a·* form of matter.
160–20 in one instance and not in *a·*,
ph 176–25 One disease is no more real than *a·*.
187–11 and then impute this result to *a·* illusive
198–18 Again, giving *a·* direction to faith,
f 211–22 transfer of the thoughts . . . to *a·*,
220–21 and thinking it sees *a·* kitten.
221–31 brings with it *a·* lesson,
229–14 declaring Him good in one instance and evil in *a·*,
235– 2 cannot go . . . from one human mind to *a·*,
236–13 Her thoughts form the embryo of *a·*
247– 5 *A·* woman at ninety had new teeth,
250–29 Mortal thoughts chase one *a·* like snowflakes,
b 276– 6 in which one mind is not at war with *a·*,
278–17 requires *a·* admission,— namely,
313– 9 With this agrees *a·* passage
o 348– 9 one disease can be just as much a delusion as *a·*.
357–27 Can Deity be almighty, if *a·* mighty
361–14 conflicts not at all with *a·* of his sayings :
p 372–23 Its false supports fail one after *a·*.
378–13 An animal may infuriate *a·* by
383–31 *a·* medical mistake, resulting from
386–19 *A·* despatch, correcting the mistake,
388–13 there follows the necessity for *a·* admission
' 402–20 We say that one human mind can influence *a·*
418–16 one disease would be as readily destroyed as *a·*.
419–14 or to change itself from one form to *a·*
420– 1 nor go from one part to *a·*, for Truth destroys
424–14 a remedy prescribed by *a·* doctor.
427–13 Death is but *a·* phase of the dream
431–25 *A·* witness takes the stand and testifies :
432– 9 *A·* witness is called for by the
432–20 *A·* witness takes the stand and testifies :
438–19 *A·* witness, equally inadequate, said
t 445– 6 No hypothesis as to the existence of *a·* power
449– 1 to free *a·* from the fetters of disease.
449– 7 The wrong done *a·* reacts most heavily
450– 4 *A·* class, still more unfortunate,
451–29 one mortal mind controlling *a·*
458– 8 *A·* plank in the platform is this,
r 469–27 believe there is *a·* power, named *evil*.
483– 4 exchanging one disease for *a·*.
486– 4 Suppose one accident happens to the eye, *a·*
486–13 and one error will not correct *a·*.
489–20 at *a·* the medium for obeying God?
491–18 awake at one time and asleep at *a·*,
491–20 this belief culminates in *a·* belief,
496– 3 no transfer of evil suggestions . . . to *a·*,
496– 7 to have one Mind, and to love *a·* as
g 504–21 Here we have the explanation of *a·* passage
529– 6 *A·* change will come as to the nature and
530–21 saying, . . . Bow down to me and have *a·* god.
552– 2 *A·* question follows : Who or what produces
554–14 *a·* false claim, that of self-conscious matter,
ap 558– 3 And I saw *a·* mighty angel— *Rev.* 10 : 1.
562–29 And there appeared *a·* wonder— *Rev.* 12 : 3.
570– 6 will finally be shocked into *a·* extreme
570– 7 for one extreme follows *a·*.
572– 6 Love one *a·'"— I John* 3 : 23.
573– 8 while to *a·*, the unillumined human mind,
573–13 *a·* revelation, even the declaration
574– 3 The Revelator also takes in *a·* view,
gl 583–28 one belief preying upon *a·*.
584–14 free from one belief only to be fettered by *a·*,
591– 8 *a·* name for mortal mind ; illusion ;
594–10 claim . . . that there was *a·* power,

another's

a 21– 7 *a·* goodness, suffering, and triumph,
22–26 nor by pinning one's faith . . . to *a·* vicarious
40–14 *A·* suffering cannot lessen our own liability.
m 58–14 selfish exaction of all *a·* time and thoughts.
t 449– 2 manacled, it is hard to break *a·* chains.
g 518–19 seeking his own in *a·* good.

answer (noun)

pr 9– 5 test of all prayer lies in the *a·* to these
136–10 His *a·* to this question the world rejected.
137–12 In his rejection of the *a·* already given
ph 183–10 The *a·* is no, and yet the Scriptures inform us
b 284–19 The *a·* to all these questions must forever be
p 363–21 Jesus approved the *a·*,
399–14 matter can return no *a·* to immortal Mind.
r 465– 9 *A·.*— God is incorporeal, divine,
465–12 *A·.*— They are. They refer to one absolute
465–17 *A·.*— There is not. Principle and its idea
466– 8 *A·.*— To human belief, they are

answer (noun)

r 467– 3	A·.— The first demand of this Science is,
468– 9	A·.— There is no life, truth, . . . in matter.
468–17	A·.— Substance is that which is
468–26	A·.— Life is divine Principle, Mind,
469– 8	A·.— Intelligence is omniscience,
469–13	A·.— Mind is God.
471–23	A·.— The author subscribed to an orthodox
472–14	A·.— Error is a supposition that pleasure
472–24	A·.— All reality is in God and His creation,
475– 6	A·.— Man is not matter;
477–20	A·.— Identity is the reflection of Spirit,
478–16	A·.— No, not if God is true
482–15	A·.— It is, since Christ is . . . the truth
484– 9	A·.— Not one of them is included in it.
485– 1	A·.— If error is necessary to define
485– 2	If error is necessary . . . the a· is yes ;
487–15	A·.— Spirit is all-knowing ;
488–16	A·.— C. S. sustains with immortal proof
493–11	A·.— The method of C. S. Mind-healing
493–13	A full a· to the above question involves
495–27	A·.— Study thoroughly the letter
496–30	A·.— They have not, if by that term

answer (verb)

s 132– 3	the divine power to heal would fully a·
f 223–20	The efforts of error to a· this question
o 342–24	and they a· with rejoicing.
p 440– 5	to a· for his crime.
g 551–24	We a· that it cannot.

answered

pref viii–12	What is Truth, is a· by demonstration,
pr 15–21	Such prayer is a·, in so far as we
a 49– 1	The women at the cross could have a·
sp 86– 3	a·, "The multitude throng thee." — Luke 8 : 45.
86– 6	Repeating his inquiry, he was a· by
f 237– 3	she a· ingenuously, "There is no sensation in
b 305–16	"Then a· Jesus and said — John 5 : 19.
308–29	he straightway a· ; and then his name
p 364–10	Jesus a· by rebuking self-righteousness
374– 9	The author has a· this question
g 504– 7	are a· in this passage,
552– 1	is a·, if the egg produces the parent.

answers

m 67– 9	He a· bravely, but even the dauntless seaman
r 465– 7	chapter sub-title

antagonism

s 145–26	and thus they increase the a· of
145–29	By this a· mortal mind must continually weaken
o 345–30	the main cause of the carnal mind's a·.

antagonistic

sp 83– 9	Nothing is more a· to C. S. than
s 108– 2	a conviction a· to the testimony of the
129–18	pantheism, and infidelity are a· to true
ph 182–15	The hypotheses of mortals are a· to
f 204– 7	a· entities and beings,
204–16	the first and second a· powers,
231–14	but there are no a· powers nor laws,
o 353– 4	physical senses and Science have ever been a·,
356– 2	so a· that the material thought must
p 392– 9	take a· grounds against all that
424–19	either by giving a· advice or
g 522– 5	the other is false, for they are a·.

antecedent

b 299– 5	but which has no physical a· reality
o 356–30	Does subsequent follow its a· ?

antedated

b 334– 2	and therefore a· Abraham ;

Antediluvians

pref viii–21	the reputed longevity of the A·,

anterior

s 146–27	far a· to the period in which Jesus lived.

anthropomorphic

f 224–13	were ready to hail an a· God,
c 257–17	and would say that an a· God, instead of
b 317– 5	and proclaimed an a· God.
337– 1	but not in any a· sense.
o 351–19	a personal devil and an a· God
g 517–3, 4	The word a·, in such a phrase as "an a· God,"

anthropomorphism

g 517– 2	This definition has been weakened by a·,

anti-Christian

ph 169–31	Whatever teaches man to . . . is a·.

anticipating

a 33– 3	a· the hour of their Master's betrayal,
s 132–24	A· this rejection of idealism,
ap 566– 5	and a· the promised joy.

antidote

s 155–29, 30	if drugs are an a· to disease, why lessen the a·?
b 274– 1	Truth and Love a· this mental miasma,
o 346–20	because Truth is error's a·.
r 495–10	and find a sovereign a· for error

antidotes

g 270–28	and a sense of ease a· suffering,

antipathies

s 163–32	the fixed and repulsive a· of nature.

antipode

sp 72–18	not made manifest through matter, the a· of
ph 200–20	suppositional a· of divine infinite Spirit,
f 208–10	It is the very a· of immortal Mind,
215–25	Mortal man is the a· of immortal man
c 257–24	mind in matter to be the a· of Mind.
r 484–23	it is the human a· of divine Science.
gl 580–12	the a· of God, or Spirit ;

antipodes

b 286–27	Transitory thoughts are the a· of
335–30	the suppositional a· of Spirit,
g 544–23	the very a· of immortal and spiritual being.

antiquated

s 147–21	perishing fossils of theories already a·,

antithesis

s 133–19	Judaism was the a· of Christianity,

anvil

ph 199– 2	lift the hammer and strike the a·,

anxiety

gl 586–11	FEAR. Heat ; inflammation ; a· ; ignorance ;

any

pref x–23	personal experience of a· sincere seeker of Truth.
x–25	than that of a· other sanitary method.
pr 7–10	But does it produce a· lasting benefit?
9– 4	the falsehood which does no one a· good.
a 47–32	belief in a· possible material intelligence.
55– 1	if he entertained a· other sense of being
m 67–31	rebuked the suffering from a· such cause
sp 73–11	A· other control or attraction of so-called
73–16	electricity or a· other form of matter,
73–26	mistake to suppose that matter is a· part
76–14	a· more than a tree can return to its seed.
87–24	Do not suppose that a· mental concept is gone
87–27	by friendship or by a· intense feeling
95–11	Error of a· kind cannot hide from the
98–23	has not been considered a part of a· religion,
an 101–31	A· seeming benefit derived from it
103–13	wholly separate from a· half-way
s 112–24	A· theory of C. S., which departs from
112–26	Also, if a· so-called new school claims
115– 6	to make them comprehensible to a· reader,
120–25	A· conclusion pro or con, deduced from
132–10	gave his benediction to a· one who should not
132–23	if it is wrought on a· but a material
145–20	If there is a· mystery in Christian healing,
149–12	If you fail to succeed in a· case, it is because
154– 1	to cherish error in a· form,
154–31	more successful method for a· mother
ph 167–28	impossible to gain control . . . in a· other way
169–22	drug or a· other means toward which
175–12	and dissuade a· sense of fear or fever.
177–23	in a· direction against God,
181–13	when you resort to a· except spiritual means.
181–31	A· hypnotic power you may exercise will
183–23	for a· lesser loyalty.
f 206–25	Can there be a· birth or death for man,
207–21	there can be no effect from a· other cause,
217–26	or a· illusion of physical weariness,
228–26	to acknowledge a· other power is to
230–23	drugs, hygiene, or a· material method.
233– 1	nor opportunity in Science for error of a· sort.
233–29	counter fact relative to a· disease
244– 6	never fearing nor obeying error in a· form.
249–10	A· other theory of Life, or God,
250–22	Now I ask, Is there a· more reality in
252–27	may at a· moment annihilate
253–25	Do not believe in a· supposed necessity for
c 255–17	finiteness, cannot be made the basis of a· true
b 276–18	ceases to be a· opportunity for sin and death.
280– 9	belief can never do justice to Truth in a·
283– 2	belief that there is a· true existence apart from
297–17	only fact concerning a· material concept is,
301–20	belief that man has a· other substance,
302–17	illusion of a· life, substance, . . . in matter.
302–27	not in a· bodily or personal likeness
304– 8	nor depth, nor a· other creature, — Rom. 8 : 39.
315– 7	and laid no claim to a· other.
325–30	When first spoken in a· age, Truth,
328–24	and if they drink a· deadly thing, — Mark 16 : 18.
337– 1	but not in a· anthropomorphic sense.
339– 5	God's pardon, destroying a· one sin,
339–29	divest sin of a· supposed mind or reality,
o 342–14	heal the sick in a· town where they
348– 6	Ought we not, then, to approve a· cure,

any

o 348–18 to have no faith in evil or in a˙ power but God,
350–20 lest at a˙ time they should see— *Matt.* 13 : 15.
352–19 for at a˙ moment they may become
354–13 opponents . . . neither give nor offer a˙ proofs
355–18 a˙ systematic healing power
356–14 not contributing in a˙ way to
356–27 Would a˙ one call it wise and good
359– 3 Let a˙ clergyman try to cure his friends by
p 362– * *if they drink a˙ deadly thing,* — *Mark* 16 : 18.
369–12 or the constructor of a˙ form of existence.
369–31 a˙ more than he is morally saved in or by sin.
372–19 How, then, in Christianity a˙ more than in C. S.,
372–30 If pride, superstition, or a˙ error
375–14 by yielding his mentality to a˙ mental
377–23 the morbid or excited action of a˙ organ.
377–30 Without this . . . . a˙ circumstance is
384–26 consumption, nor a˙ other disease
385–31 A˙ supposed information, coming from
386– 3 a˙ more than it is in the case of sin.
387–23 cannot suffer as the result of a˙ labor of love,
393–20 as the result of a law of a˙ kind,
394–10 admission that a˙ bodily condition
401– 1 A˙ human error is its own enemy,
401–23 could you produce a˙ effect upon the brain
404– 4 a˙ one of the myriad forms of sin,
406–26 Inharmony of a˙ kind involves
410–26 or is used in a˙ way except to
413–30 probable at a˙ time that such ills
413–32 or a˙ other malady, timorously held
414–14 dementia, hatred, or a˙ other discord.
415–14 Opiates do not remove the pain in a˙
416– 8 To him there is no longer a˙ pain.
416– 9 Yet a˙ physician— allopathic, homœopathic,
419– 8 If your patient from a˙ cause suffers a
419–22 mortal mind is liable to a˙ phase of belief
420–21 better than a˙ drug, alterative, or tonic.
423–27 Ossification or a˙ abnormal condition
424–21 divine Mind can remove a˙ obstacle,
425–27 never believe that heart or a˙ portion
426– 1 or disease arising from a˙ circumstance,
429–23 for if Life ever had a˙ beginning,
438– 6 nothing shall by a˙ means— *Luke* 10 : 19.
440–15 what greater justification can a˙ deed
440–29 forbidden to enter . . . a˙ more suits
441– 3 a˙ so-called law, which undertakes to
441– 6 not permitted to enter a˙ suits at the bar of
t 445–17 or limit in a˙ direction of thought
446–31 and the ultimate triumph of a˙ cause.
448–30 nothing short of right-doing has a˙ claim to
455–22 renders a˙ abuse of the mission an
456–16 A˙ dishonesty in your theory and practice
457– 9 never used this newly discovered power in a˙
459–12 A˙ attempt to heal mortals with erring
459–30 than a˙ other healer on the globe.
462– 2 a˙ student, who adheres to the divine rules
464–13 If from an injury or from a˙ cause,
r 479– 4 be uttered by a˙ mother,
479–16 or use a˙ of the physical senses?
483–25 but if a˙ system honors God,
485–32 The notion of a˙ life or intelligence
488–17 the impossibility of a˙ material sense,
489– 8 A˙ hypothesis which supposes life
493–23 just as it removes a˙ other sense of
493–26 A˙ sense of soul in matter is not the
495–19 can destroy a˙ painful sense of,
496–28 Have Christian Scientists a˙ religious creed?
g 507–19 do not yield fruit because of a˙
525– 9 In the Saxon, *mankind, a woman, a˙ one;*
529–14 more subtle than a˙ beast of the— *Gen.* 3 : 1.
542–17 Let a˙ finding him should kill him.— *Gen.* 4 : 15.
550–20 If Life has a˙ starting-point
554– 5 nor are there properly a˙ mortal beings,
554– 8 A˙ statement of life, following from a
554–10 because it is destitute of a˙ knowledge
554–12 destitute of a˙ knowledge of its
ap 564–32 "more subtle than a˙ beast of the— *Gen.* 3 : 1.
566–28 found a˙ more in heaven.— *Rev.* 12 : 8.
gl 584–15 A˙ material evidence of death is false,
(*see also* **man**)

anybody

o 345–21 A˙, who is able to perceive the

anyone

t 461– 1 I do not maintain that a˙ can
ap 560–16 or entertain a false estimate of a˙ whom God

anything

pr 2–24 a˙ He does not already comprehend?
s 164– 7 or a˙ like the truth,
ph 200–25 not to know a˙ among you,— *I Cor.* 2 : 2.
200–28 not to know a˙ among you,
f 232– 1 without Him was not a˙ made— *John* 1 : 3.
b 335–11 "was not a˙ made that was made."— *John* 1 : 3.
o 347– 8 This writer infers that if a˙ needs
p 381–11 cannot in reality suffer from breaking a˙
t 458–11 It is a˙ but scientifically Christian

anything

r 477–24 can never reflect a˙ inferior to Spirit.
480–27 without Him was not a˙ made— *John* 1 : 3.
g 501– * *without Him was not a˙ made— John* 1 : 3.
525–19 was not a˙ made that was made."— *John* 1 : 3.

apace

c 265–17 as if man were a weed growing a˙

apart

a 30–11 Had his origin and birth been wholly a˙
52– 2 His pursuits lay far a˙ from theirs.
sp 87–10 Though bodies are leagues a˙
91–26 postulate of belief . . . something a˙ from God.
s 114–32 A˙ from the usual opposition to
f 213– 8 spiritual facts exist a˙ from this mortal and
228–25 There is no power a˙ from God.
b 270–11 Few deny . . . that intelligence, a˙ from man
283– 3 belief that there is any true existence a˙ from
p 399– 9 a˙ from the action of mortal thought,
r 473– 9 nothing a˙ from Him is present or has power.
480–13 Material sense has its realm a˙ from Science
488–22 a˙ from what belief bestows upon them,
g 544– 2 a creation so wholly a˙ from God's,
548–23 so far a˙ from his material sense
549– 3 takes place a˙ from sexual conditions.

apathy

an 102–22 produce the very a˙ on the subject which
f 249–24 Sleep and a˙ are phases of the
ap 570– 4 The present a˙ as to the tendency of

apehood

g 543–21 May not Darwin be right in thinking that a˙

aphorisms

o 358–14 C. S. is neither made up of contradictory a˙

Aphrodite

g 524– 4 in the Hindoo Vishnu, in the Greek A˙,

Apocalypse

m 56–11 as in the vision of the A˙,
o 357–24 according to the vision of St. John in the A˙.
g 536– 1 In the A˙ it is written :
546–18 Genesis and the A˙ seem more obscure
ap 559–32 The twelfth chapter of the A˙,
561–22 The woman in the A˙ symbolizes
564–24 From Genesis to the A˙, sin, sickness, and
565– 1 In the A˙, when nearing its doom,
568– 5 The twelfth chapter of the A˙ typifies
572– 4 in Genesis and in the A˙,
572–15 furnish the vision of the A˙,
575– 7 This sacred city, described in the A˙

apodictical

s 107– 7 This a˙ Principle points to the revelation

Apollo

s 158– 3 designated A˙ as "the god of medicine."
158– 7 A˙ was also regarded as the sender of disease,
158–13 A˙, who was banished from heaven

apostle (*see also* **apostle's**)

pr 5–29 An a˙ says that the Son of God [Christ]
a 28–29 encountered by prophet, disciple, and a˙,
39–18 "Now," cried the a˙, "is the— *II Cor.* 6 : 2.
sp 99– 7 "Work out your . . . says the a˙,— *Phil.* 2 : 12.
ph 172–21 to which the a˙ refers when he says
b 303–32 the a˙ declared that nothing could alienate
332– 6 As the a˙ expressed it in words which
o 343– 9 one might not be able to say with the a˙,
345–26 a˙ says : "For if a man think himself— *Gal.* 6 : 3.
r 474–29 The a˙ says that the mission of Christ is
g 519–18 till, in the language of the a˙,
ap 577–30 St. John's Revelation as recorded by the great a˙

Apostle James

m 64– 3 taught by the A˙ J˙, when he said :
r 487–25 A˙ J˙ said, "Show me thy faith— *Jas.* 2 : 18.
g 527–12 A˙ J˙ says : "God cannot be tempted— *Jas.* 1 : 13.

Apostle John

p 388– 7 The A˙ J˙ testified to the divine basis of
410–17 A˙ J˙ says : "There is no fear in— *I John* 4 : 18.

Apostle Paul

sp 79–17 A˙ P˙ bade men have the Mind that was
an 103– 2 A˙ P˙ refers to the personification of evil as
p 383– 9 like the A˙ P˙, is "willing rather— *II Cor.* 5 : 8.
g 534–14 and the A˙ P˙ explains this warfare

apostle's

ap 560–23 hid from view the a˙ character,

apostles

Christian
o 349–22 the prophecy concerning the Christian a˙,
floral
f 240– 6 The floral a˙ are hieroglyphs of Deity.
his
a 40–27 follow the example of our Master and his *a*
41–26 Persecuted from city to city, his a˙ still
b 269–23 on the teachings of Jesus, of his a˙,
o 358–17 illustrated by the prophets, by Jesus, by his a˙,

apostles
lesser
a 40–21 lesser *a·* of Truth may endure human brutality
those
o 343–25 Anciently those *a·* who were Jesus' students,
———
s 126–29 and the lives of prophets and *a·*.
f 243–13 the ancient demonstrations of prophets and *a·*.

apostolic
sp 97–30 *a·* work of casting out error and healing the
b 325–15 The absolute meaning of the *a·* words is
o 347–19 namely, *a·*, divine healing?
p 366–14 and we have the *a·* warrant for asking :
t 443–20 may learn the value of the *a·* precept :
451– 3 constant pressure of the *a·* command

apothecary
s 163–10 surgeon, *a·*, man-midwife, chemist,

apparent
a 42– 6 It cannot make Life or Truth *a·*.
f 207– 2 evil becomes more *a·* and obnoxious
251– 3 belief of mortal mind *a·* as an abscess
b 324– 8 Unless the . . . are becoming more *a·*,
o 345–15 at least none which are *a·* to those
359–16 is not *a·* to the material senses,
p 374–11 before it is consciously *a·* on the body,
390– 8 which produces *a·* discord,
428–27 immortality will become more *a·*, as
r 467–12 perfect in proportion as this fact becomes *a·*,
g 505–11 the ideas of Spirit *a·* only as Mind,
543– 7 becomes more beautifully *a·* at error's demise.
552– 8 and as necessarily *a·* to the

apparently
pr 8–10 If a man, though *a·* fervent and prayerful,
12–21 to be *a·* either poisonous or sanative.
s 108–19 When *a·* near the confines of mortal existence,
109–23 gradually and *a·* through divine power.
122–17 sky and tree-tops *a·* join hands,
152–14 Sir Humphry Davy once *a·* cured a case of
b 321–17 when he discovered that what he *a·* saw
p 415–27 Etherization will *a·* cause the body
r 491–25 *a·* with their own separate embodiment.

apparitions
sp 86–14 These may appear to the ignorant to be *a·* ;
86–18 *a·* brought out in dark seances

appeal
a 50– 9 This despairing *a·*, if made to a human parent,
50–12 The *a·* of Jesus was made both to his
ph 182– 5 The demands of God *a·* to thought only ;
b 319–10 the lower *a·* to the general faith in
o 351–32 They might *a·* to Jehovah, but their prayer
p 405–32 and to *a·* to divine sources outside of
440–20 Mortal Man has his *a·* to Spirit, God,
440–30 *a·* to the just and equitable decisions of

appealed
s 136–11 He *a·* to his students :
p 403–11 but matter is *a·* to in the other.

appeals
s 130– 2 is alarmed by constant *a·* to Mind.

appear
pref ix–21 but it did not *a·* in print until 1876,
a 40– 2 Remove error from thought, and it will not *a·* in
m 69– 2 and man, not of the earth earthly . . . will *a·*.
sp 86–13 These may *a·* to the ignorant to be apparitions ;
91–12 the sooner man's great reality will *a·*
97–12 the more its nothingness will *a·*,
s 123– 4 The true idea and Principle of man will then *a·*.
164–17 If you or I should *a·* to die,
ph 167–17 error in the premise must *a·* in the conclusion.
168–28 sensation would not *a·* if the error of belief
191– 6 man in God's likeness will *a·*,
198–13 afterwards to *a·* on the body ;
199–31 before his power . . . . could *a·*.
f 211–11 does not *a·* in the spiritual understanding
211–17 Without mortal mind, the tear could not *a·* ;
216–23 evil would *a·* to be the master of good,
249– 5 Let the "male and female" . . . *a·*.— *Gen.* 1 : 27.
c 264– 3 before the permanent facts . . . *a·*.
b 295–15 and the real sense of being, . . . will *a·*.
297–23 begins to *a·*, and Truth, the ever-present,
312–17 without Love, God, immortality cannot *a·*.
325–11 "When Christ, who is our life, shall *a·*— *Col.* 3 : 4.
325–12 then shall ye also *a·*— *Col.* 3 : 4.
332–24 *a·* to mortals in such a form of humanity
o 341– 7 *a·* contradictory when subjected to such usage.
347–30 The harmonious will *a·* real,
348– 6 making the disease *a·* to be— what it really is
p 378– 2 and causes the two to *a·* conjoined,
390–12 When the first symptoms of disease *a·*,
395–29 it may *a·* in a more alarming form.
410–24 Selfishness does not *a·* in the
417–22 Disease should not *a·* real to the physician,

appear
p 428–10 that the spiritual facts of being may *a·*,
430– 5 immortal manhood, the Christ ideal, will *a·*.
434–10 where C. S. is allowed to *a·* as counsel
434–13 now summoned to *a·* before the bar of Justice
t 450– 6 so depraved that they *a·* to be innocent.
r 476–12 immortals, or the children of God, will *a·*
485– 8 If the unimportant and evil *a·*,
485–12 disease, and death *a·* more and more unreal
488–11 *a·* in our common version to approve
g 502–16 Christian views of the universe *a·*,
506–17 and let the dry land *a·* :— *Gen.* 1 : 9.
506–21 in order that the purpose may *a·*.
507–29 and must ever continue to *a·*
509–27 *a·* in man and the universe
520–12 These days will *a·* as mortality disappears,
537–26 the text is made to *a·* contradictory
550–13 its eternal perfection should *a·* now,
556– 8 Then will the new heaven and new earth *a·*,
ap 573–30 this reality of being will surely *a·* sometime
fr 600– * *whether the tender grape a·,— Song* 7 : 12.

appearance
an 101–27 this *a·* is deceptive, since error cannot
ph 168–26 before the so-called disease made its *a·*
187–28 body loses all *a·* of life or action,
f 215–18 darkness loses the *a·* of reality.
p 416–23 body is no longer the parent, even in *a·*.
432–28 but my *a·* with a message from
r 491–19 sometimes presenting no *a·* of mind,
g 553–22 sure to become the signal for the *a·* of

appearances
s 121–22 Science shows *a·* often to be erroneous,

appeared
s 138–10 his cures, which *a·* miraculous to outsiders.
154–12 symptoms of this disease *a·*,
b 308–20 a message from Truth and Love, *a·* to him
309– 7 The result of Jacob's struggle thus *a·*.
324–20 When the truth first *a·* to him in Science,
334–11 Jesus *a·* as a bodily existence.
p 374– 9 and knew nothing about, until it *a·*
r 477– 1 the perfect man, who *a·* to him
g 501– * *And I a· unto Abraham,— Exod.* 6 : 3.
507– 1 Adam has not yet *a·* in the narrative.
ap 560– 6 And there *a·* a great wonder in— *Rev.* 12 : 1.
562–29 And there *a·* another wonder in— *Rev.* 12 : 3.
gl 597– 5 if only he *a·* unto men to fast.

appearing
Messianic
s 133– 1 questioned the signs of the Messianic *a·*,
———
s 118– 7 foretelling the second *a·* in the flesh
150– 6 Its *a·* is the coming anew of the gospel of
f 224–14 but this was not the manner of truth's *a·*.
224–21 the harbingers of truth's full-orbed *a·*.
230– 7 the advanced *a·* of Truth, which
b 299– 7 *a·* at the door of some sepulchre.
r 482–24 announced to the Wisemen of old this dual *a·*,
g 504–16 The successive *a·* of God's ideas
507–28 Creation is ever *a·*, and must ever continue
507–30 Mortal sense inverts this *a·*
gl 589–25 spiritual understanding of God and man *a·*.

appears
m 69– 9 the real, ideal man *a·* in proportion as
sp 76–31 must be overcome, . . . before immortality *a·*.
92–23 Until the fact concerning error . . . *a·*,
96–18 until their nothingness *a·*,
s 116– 5 and man as God's image *a·*.
ph 187–31 which *a·* to the human mind to live,
f 210–27 and *a·* . . . to make good its claim.
250–24 whatever *a·* to be a mortal man is a
b 271–22 When the Science of Christianity *a·*, it will
281– 5 When one *a·*, the other disappears.
289–18 what *a·* to the senses to be death is but
295–20 through which Truth *a·* most vividly
312– 7 sense-dream vanishes and reality *a·*.
320–20 (however transcendental such a thought *a·*),
o 353–19 until perfection *a·* and reality is reached.
354–32 If the letter of C. S. *a·* inconsistent,
p 415–10 Inflammation never *a·* in a part which
r 474– 9 To the ignorant age in which it first *a·*,
477– 2 where sinning mortal man *a·* to mortals.
477–10 *a·* to be matter and mind united ;
480– 1 When the substance of Spirit *a·*
493– 3 To corporeal sense, the sun *a·* to rise and set,
g 507– 4 feeds and clothes every object, as it *a·*
516– 2 As the reflection of yourself *a·*
542– 5 whenever and wherever it *a·*
gl 595–21 mortal disappears and spiritual perfection *a·*.

appeased
a 22–28 or that divinity is *a·* by human suffering,
22–32 Wrath which is only *a·* is not destroyed,

appellation
b 309– 1 but this *a·* was withheld,

appellative

 c 267–14 the same authority for the *a·* mother,

appertain

 ph 182– 7 what are termed laws of nature, *a·* to matter.

appetite

 s 158–22 acquires an educated *a·* for strong drink,
 f 218–11 and say, "I am malice, lust, *a·*, envy, hate."
 b 327– 4 neither pleasure nor pain, *a·* nor passion,
 p 398–23 *A·* and disease reside in mortal mind,
 406–28 The depraved *a·* for alcoholic drinks,
 r 490– 9 cooperates with *a·* and passion.

appetites

 a 53– 5 so far removed from *a·* and passions
 s 115–21 Evil beliefs, passions and *a·*, fear,
 ph 188– 8 Passion, depraved *a·*, dishonesty,
 f 201–10 false *a·*, hatred, fear, all sensuality,
 b 327– 7 all the sinful *a·* of the human mind.
 p 404– 8 there is no real pleasure in false *a·*.
 g 526–11 The *a·* and passions, sin, sickness,
 536–20 Passions and *a·* must end in pain.

applause

 pr 7–16 may embrace too much love of *a·*

apples

 ph 165– 1 Physiology is one of the *a·* from

applicable

 t 463–27 There is a law of God *a·* to healing,

application

 s 126–22 its *a·* to the treatment of disease
 126–32 If Christendom resists the author's *a·* of the
 147– 4 the sacred rules for its present *a·*
 ph 198–17 by the *a·* of caustic or croton oil,
 b 271–16 Hence the universal *a·* of his saying :
 o 341–13 Sneers at the *a·* of the word *Science*
 p 421–29 or by employing a single material *a·*

applications

 s 118– 4 and formal *a·* of the illustration.

applied

 s 116–25 words *person* and *personal* . . . when *a·* to
 116–28 If the term personality, as *a·* to God,
 127–16 relates especially to Science as *a·* to
 147– 8 and everywhere, when honestly *a·*
 150– 2 Truth, as *a·* through this Christian system
 o 344–32 the word *Spirit* is so commonly *a·* to Deity,
 t 457–30 Let this Principle be *a·* to the cure of disease
 gl 597–26 *a·* to Mind or to one of God's qualities.
 599– 3 You. As *a·* to corporeality, a mortal ;

applies

 a 24– 1 This certainly *a·* to Truth and Love
 m 68–26 I discredit the belief that agamogenesis *a·* to
 sp 93–24 and *a·* exclusively to God.
 f 219– 3 My method of treating fatigue *a·* to

apply

 an 105–17 and no longer *a·* legal rulings wholly to

applying

 f 218–30 that passage is not perverted by *a·* it literally
 p 401–24 by *a·* the drug to either?

appointed

 an 100–15 Under this order a commission was *a·*,
 101– 8 In 1837, a committee of nine persons was *a·*,
 c 261–14 to go upon the stage and sustain his *a·* task,
 b 332–23 He was *a·* to speak God's word
 ap 560–17 whom God has *a·* to voice His word.

appointing

 s 131–15 has come already, after the manner of God's *a·*,
 b 326– 4 it must be in the way of God's *a·*.
 r 483–29 and it does this in the way of His *a·*,

apportion

 g 505–30 human beliefs, which *a·* to themselves a task

appreciable

 a 30–12 Jesus would not have been *a·* to

appreciated

 a 37–14 not . . . seen and *a·* by lookers-on.

appreciating

 m 60–24 calls discord harmony, not *a·* concord.

appreciation

 s 136–22 That a wicked king . . . should have no high *a·*
 b 300– 3 Finite sense has no true *a·* of

apprehend

 a 31–18 following his demonstration so far as we *a·*
 s 140– 9 as we *a·* the divine nature and love Him
 ph 167– 6 We *a·* Life in divine Science only as
 179– 8 the spiritual capacity to *a·* thought
 f 222– 2 as we better *a·* our spiritual existence
 231–28 To fear them is impossible, when you fully *a·*
 b 280–12 belief can neither *a·* nor worship the
 323–13 In order to *a·* more, we must
 o 350–17 difficult in a material age to *a·* spiritual Truth.
 353–32 nor *a·* the reality of Life.
 g 510– 2 How much more should we seek to *a·*

apprehend

 g 545–25 could not *a·* the nature and operation of

apprehended

 a 39–28 This thought is *a·* slowly,
 m 56– 9 is discerned intact, is *a·* and understood,
 sp 91–24 that the spiritual facts may be better *a·*.
 96–29 real objects will be *a·* mentally
 s 110–30 Its Science must be *a·* by as many as believe
 136–29 The disciples *a·* their Master better than
 b 288–11 When the . . . effects of C. S. are fully *a·*,
 p 402–10 Mind and its formations will be *a·*
 g 513–13 reflections of deific power cannot be *a·* until

apprehension

 clear
 t 459– 4 Paul and John had a clear *a·* that,
 deific
 ap 576–29 not yet elevated to deific *a·*
 human
 r 471–30 reduced to human *a·*, she has named C. S.
 of divine Principle
 sp 90–30 through an *a·* of divine Principle.
 of divine Science
 g 519–28 according to the *a·* of divine Science.
 of mortals
 p 368– 7 nearer than ever before to the *a·* of mortals,
 our
 sp 80– 1 in proportion to our *a·* of the truth,
 93–31 This belief tends to becloud our *a·* of the
 quick
 sp 86– 7 His quick *a·* of this mental call
 rejoice in the
 o 354–28 I rejoice in the *a·* of this grand verity.
 rests on the
 t 460– 6 Mind-healing rests on the *a·* of the
 right
 pref vii–19 only guarantee of obedience is a right *a·* of
 t 460–17 to be dealt with through right *a·* of
 scientific
 pr 16–17 This reading strengthens our scientific *a·*
 spiritual
 o 349–28 as thought is educated up to spiritual *a·*.
 g 506–12 calm and exalted thought or spiritual *a·*
 their
 a 34–26 and ascend far above their *a·*.
 g 509– 5 to their *a·* he rose from the grave,
 r 487–10 The *a·* of this gave sight to the blind
 g 548–14 and so aids the *a·* of immortal Truth.
 gl 583–16 to the *a·* of spiritual ideas

approach

 sp 95– 6 We *a·* God, or Life, in proportion to
 ph 170–25 The age seems ready to *a·* this subject,
 f 234–11 as we bar our doors against the *a·* of
 b 278–15 Hence, as we *a·* Spirit and Truth,
 p 374–17 Ignorance of the cause or *a·* of disease
 406–14 seem less real as we *a·* the scientific period,
 t 450–10 open to the *a·* and recognition of Truth.
 r 483–12 hinders its *a·* to the standard in C. S.
 ap 559–24 When you *a·* nearer and nearer to

approached

 p 362–12 this woman (Mary Magdalene, . . . *a·* Jesus.

approaches

 m 67–32 The epoch *a·* when the understanding
 sp 97–14 The nearer a false belief *a·* truth
 p 402– 8 The time *a·* when mortal mind will
 409– 5 and the nearer matter *a·* its final statement,
 r 496–10 Am I living the life that *a·* the supreme good?
 ap 576–30 the word gradually *a·* a higher meaning.

approaching

 a 47–16 A period was *a·* which would reveal
 f 223–22 accompany *a·* Science
 241–29 and are *a·* spiritual Life
 p 390–27 "Agree to disagree" with *a·* symptoms

approbation

 m 59– 5 and mutual attention and *a·*
 b 332– 7 quoted with *a·* from a classic poet :

appropriates

 f 242–27 superstition *a·* no part of the
 t 459– 2 Man then *a·* those things which

approval

 a 42–11 endorsed pre-eminently by the *a·* of God,
 s 132–17 received no aid nor *a·* from other
 p 382– 3 having only human *a·* for their sanction.

approve

 o 348– 5 Ought we not, then, to *a·* any
 r 488–12 Scriptures often appear . . . to *a·* and

approved

 p 363–20 Jesus *a·* the answer, and so brought

approves

 a 22–31 Mercy cancels the debt only when justice *a·*,

approximation

 sp 94–30 An *a·* of this discernment

a priori
r 467–25 *a· p·* reasoning shows material existence to be

apt
p 384–21 are not *a·* to follow exposure ;

arbiter
p 369–12 belief that matter . . . can be the *a·* of life
405–12 the *a·* of truth against error.

arbitrament
g 555– 4 human belief, and not the divine *a·*,

arbutus
g 516–15 The modest *a·* sends her sweet breath

arch
a 40–23 through the triumphal *a·* of Truth and Love.

arches
f 247–25 *a·* the cloud with the bow of beauty,

architect
m 68– 5 learn how Spirit, the great *a·*,

architectural
s 142–11 *a·* skill, making dome and spire

archpriests
r 481– 5 Like the *a·* of yore, man is free

arctic
f 240– 2 *A·* regions, sunny tropics, giant hills,

Arcturus
c 257–21 guideth "*A·* with his sons."— *Job* 38 : 32.

arduous
p 396–16 refutation becomes *a·*, not because the

arena
sp 96–12 material world is even now becoming the *a·*
g 538–20 Until that . . . enters into the *a·*,

Argentum nitratum
s 156– 9 prescribed the fourth attenuation of *A· n·*

argue
p 380–12 as though the defendant should *a·* for the
395– 1 The sick unconsciously *a·* for suffering,
395–25 while you *a·* against their reality,
412–20 *A·* at first mentally, not audibly.

argued
p 411– 5 If the student . . . when he *a·* against it,
435– 5 False Belief has *a·* that the body should die,

argues
g 551– 9 One distinguished naturalist *a·* that

arguing
p 376–23 by both silently and audibly *a·*
g 539–23 *a·* for the Science of creation,

argument
mental
t 454–32 the letter and mental *a·* are only
no
p 374–18 no *a·* against the mental origin of
b 280–21 The *a·* of the serpent in the allegory,
o 343–15 By parable and *a·* he explains the
p 412–18 To heal by *a·*, find the type of
412–22 conform the *a·* so as to destroy the evidence
414–20 The Christian Scientist's *a·* rests on the
434–20 and opens the *a·* for the defence :
g 539–20 In parable and *a·*, this falsity is exposed

arguments
b 268–16 their *a·* are based on the
o 355– 7 proofs are better than mere verbal *a·*
p 367– 7 borrowed speeches, and the doling of *a·*,
411– 9 and needed the *a·* of truth for reminders.
412– 5 You may vary the *a·* to meet the
414– 7 The *a·* to be used in curing insanity
418–17 if *a·* are used to destroy it,
418–23 By the truthful *a·* you employ,

aright
pref vii–19 whom to know *a·* is Life eternal.
pr 15–14 In order to pray *a·*, we must
a 18– 7 He did life's work *a·* not only in
28–18 Not a . . . did the material world measure *a·*.
53–16 The world could not interpret *a·* the
sp 94–26 enabled him to direct those thoughts *a·* ;
s 127–27 and is alone able to interpret God *a·*.
f 254–13 to *begin a·* and to continue the strife
c 256–15 nor can He be understood *a·* through
b 326–16 The purpose and motive to live *a·* can be
r 466–28 Science will declare God *a·*,
490– 6 Hence it cannot govern man *a·*.

arise
sp 80–26 *a·* from the volition of human belief,
88–25 for both *a·* from mortal belief.
94–15 *a·* from the belief that the infinite is
s 145–18 From this fact *a·* its ethical as well as its
f 238–23 Attempts to conciliate society . . . *a·* from
b 301–25 sin, disease, and death *a·* from the
p 398–13 "Damsel, I say unto thee, *a·* !"— *Mark* 5 : 41.

arise
p 421– 3 *a·* from the belief that other portions
t 446– 7 may either *a·* from the alarm of the physician,
g 523– 8 The creations of matter *a·* from a mist
544– 7 Birth, decay, and death *a·* from the
ap 575– 1 *A·* from your false consciousness

arises
pref viii–18 question *a·*, Is there less sickness because of
a 53–20 *a·* from the great distance between
sp 92– 7 From the illusion . . . *a·* the decomposition of
s 120–10 Then the question inevitably *a·* :
154– 3 Disease *a·*, like other mental conditions, from
ph 166–16 From it *a·* the inharmonious body.
f 243–14 *a·* not so much from lack of desire as from
p 433– 2 Judge Medicine *a·*, and with great solemnity
t 451–27 *a·* from ignorance or malice aforethought.
r 490–10 From this cooperation *a·* its evil.

arising
sp 94–20 betrayal, *a·* from sensuality.
s 145–23 the mystery always *a·* from ignorance
p 426– 1 or disease *a·* from any circumstance,

arithmetic
s 129– 4 a properly computed sum in *a·*.

ark
gl 581– 8 definition of
581–13 *a·* indicates temptation overcome

arm
a 24–11 "the *a·* of the Lord" is revealed— *Isa.* 53 : 1.
49–17 No human eye was there to pity, no *a·* to save.
s 160– 9 motion of the *a·* is no more dependent
ph 198–29 Because the muscles of the blacksmith's *a·*
198–32 it does not follow that . . . a less used *a·*
199–13 by reason of the blacksmith's faith . . . his *a·*
p 365–14 to evoke healing from the outstretched *a·*
379–12 warm water was trickling over his *a·*.

armed
a 52–23 which *a·* him with Love.
b 298– 7 cannot destroy Science *a·* with faith,

arms
a 29– 1 Christians must take up *a·* against error
m 61–15 promising children in the *a·* of gross parents,
b 322–28 turn us like tired children to the *a·* of

army
c 256–21 in the *a·* of heaven, and among— *Dan.* 4 : 35.
p 405–10 if you would not cherish an *a·* of conspirators

aroma
ph 191–32 Mind, God, sends forth the *a·* of Spirit,

around
a 32–32 with shadows fast falling *a·* ;
sp 92–11 a serpent coiled *a·* the tree of knowledge
s 163–31 the fleeting vapors *a·* us,
164– 2 the groping of Homer's Cyclops *a·* his cave."
b 310–16 *a·* which circle harmoniously all things
p 363–10 Knowing what those *a·* him were saying

arouse
p 404–22 *A·* the sinner to this new and true view

arouses
ap 559–13 It *a·* the "seven thunders" of evil,— *Rev.* 10 : 3.

arraigned
ap 564–20 spiritual idea was *a·* before the

arraigns
p 440– 4 whom Truth *a·* before the supreme bar

arrange
s 163–31 as impracticable as to *a·* the fleeting vapors

arranges
ph 190–11 and *a·* itself into five so-called senses,

arranging
f 230–12 to suppose Him capable of first *a·*

array
sp 97–21 broadest facts *a·* the most falsities against
ph 176–10 ghastly *a·* of diseases was not paraded
f 224–14 and *a·* His vicegerent with pomp and splendor ;
c 260–28 If we *a·* thought in mortal vestures,
p 412–10 *a·* your mental plea against the physical.
414–18 lest you *a·* the sick against their own interests
420–15 when they will not *a·* themselves against it,

arrayed
p 391– 2 *a·* against the supremacy of Spirit.

arrest
an 105–24 God will *a·* him.
p 431–13 At the time of the *a·* the prisoner
436–15 Prior to the night of his *a·*, the prisoner
436–18 and thus save him from *a·*.
438–15 I ask your *a·* in the name of Almighty God
441–14 neither can Fear *A·* Mortal Man

arrested
p 431–10 *a·* Mortal Man in behalf of the state
t 452– 5 The wrong thought should be *a·*

arrive

s 120– 8   a· at the fundamental facts of being.
f 233–11   before we a· at the demonstration of
c 260– 1   one can no more a· at the
o 359–19   when shall we a· at the goal which
p 406–24   until we a· at the fulness of God's idea,
r 468– 1   Thus we a· at Truth, or intelligence,
g 543–12   a· at the understanding that material life,

arrived

p 432–26   Materia Medica, was present when I a·,

arrogance

f 252–17   Material sense lifts its voice with the a· of
p 367–12   with the a· of rank and display of scholarship,

arsenic

ph 178– 2   a·, the strychnine, or whatever the drug

art

a 44–23   It was a method of surgery beyond material a·,
g 507–26   expresses Science and a· throughout His crea-
      tion,

article

s 145–32   Our Master's first a· of faith propounded to
b 320–11   and in the learned a· on Noah

articulata

g 556– 3   Vertebrata, a·, mollusca, and radiata

articulations

g 501– 4   spiritual import of the Word, in its earliest a·,

artifice

sp 83– 4   a· and delusion claimed that they could equal

artificial

r 489– 7   not with an a· limb, but with the genuine

artist (see also artist's)

sp 86–32   before the a· can convey them to canvas.
ph 198– 9   materialistic doctor, . . . is an a· who outlines
b 310– 1   The a· is not in his painting.
o 360– 4   The other a· replies : "You wrong my

artist's

b 299– 5   save in the a· own observation and
310– 2   picture is the a· thought objectified.

artists

o 359–30   Scientist and an opponent are like two a·.

arts

p 369–24   preventive . . . a· belong emphatically to

ascend

a 34–25   and a· far above their apprehension.
ph 189–24   we constantly a· in infinite being.
f 222– 2   and a· the ladder of life.
p 407–19   a· a degree in the scale of health,

ascended

a 46–16   was not changed until he himself a·,
g 551–11   but he adds that mankind has a·

ascendency

m 61– 4   good in human affections must have a·
67–20   remember that through spiritual a·

ascending

ph 189–30   goes on in an a· scale by evolution,
c 265–27   brightens the a· path of many a heart.
g 508–22   last in the a· order of creation.
509– 6   on the third day of his a· thought,

ascends

g 509–16   rarefaction of thought as it a· higher.

ascension

a 34–28   which has since been called the a·.
46–23   his spiritual and final a· above matter,
46–26   his final demonstration, called the a·,
b 292–31   In his resurrection and a·, Jesus showed
314– 2   and no less material until the a·
334–15   continued until the Master's a·,
g 509–25   periods of spiritual a· are the days

ascertain

s 152–17   to a· the temperature of the patient's body ;
159–25   to a· how much harmony, or health,
f 239–16   To a· our progress, we must learn
b 337–31   you a· that this Science is demonstrably true,
r 495–31   you will soon a· that error cannot destroy error.
g 547– 7   and so a· if the author has given

ascetic

a 53– 3   Jesus was no a·.

ascribe

a 34– 2   why a· this inspiration to a dead rite,
o 348–15   when we a· to Him almighty Life and

ascribes

c 262– 7   but it a· to Him the entire glory.

ashamed

a 21–32   By-and-by, a· of his zigzag course,
g 532–19   A· before Truth, error shrank abashed

Asher

gl 581–15   definition of

Asia Minor

b 324–25   A· M·, Greece, and even in imperial Rome.

aside

a 20–28   "Let us lay a· every weight,— Heb. 12 : 1.
20–30   put a· material self and sense,
44– 2   before the thorns can be laid a· for a crown,
49–31   turned "a· the right of a man— Lam. 3 : 35.
52–15   Herod and Pilate laid a· old feuds
sp 83–18   belief . . . that occasionally Spirit sets a· these
s 141– 8   to set a· even the most cherished beliefs
ph 166–18   Instead of thrusting Him a· in times of
f 237– 8   before her parents would have laid a· their drugs,
b 286–12   Physical causation was put a·
304–31   thrusting a· his divine Principle
338–26   a· from their metaphysical derivation,
p 409–23   to be laid a· for the pure reality.
g 521–30   would set a· the omnipotence of Spirit ;
555–24   and set a· the proper conception of Deity,

ask

pr 1– *   before ye a· Him.— Matt. 6 : 8.
2–23   God is Love. Can we a· Him to be more?
3– 8   Shall we a· the divine Principle of all
6– 9   supposition that we have nothing to do but to a·
6–17   More than this we cannot a·,
7–31   or mean to a· forgiveness at some later day.
8–25   and a· that it may be laid bare before us,
9–28   Then why . . . a· to be Christians, since you
10–23   the blessings we a· for in prayer.
10–26   or we should certainly receive that for which
      we a·.
10–27   The Scriptures say : Ye a·, and— Jas. 4 : 3.
10–27   receive not, because ye a· amiss,— Jas. 4 : 3.
10–29   and for which we a·,
10–31   Do you a· wisdom to be merciful and not
10–32   Then "ye a· amiss."— Jas. 4 : 3.
13– 8   striving for the accomplishment of all we a·,
13–11   we labor for what we a· ;
a 24–22   sinners who a· for it and are willing
m 67– 7   We a· the helmsman : "Do you know your
69–20   Some day the child will a· his parent :
69–23   the child may a·, "Do you teach this death?
ph 177–28   does human belief, you a·, cause this death?
181– 4   one should a·, "Who art thou that
191–18   It should no longer a· of the head,
f 250–22   Now I a·, Is there any more reality in
o 349– 4   rabbis of the present day a· concerning
355–32   Strangely enough, we a· for material theories
p 371–22   No impossible thing do I a· when urging
416–27   If they a· about their disease,
435–34   I a· that the prisoner be restored to
437–18   I a· that the Supreme Court of Spirit reverse
438–15   I a· your arrest in the name of Almighty God
440–28   I a· that he be forbidden to
r 496– 9   A· yourself : Am I living the life that
g 521–18   will naturally a· if there is nothing more
551–17   Naturalists a· : "What can there be, of a
553–31   may also a· how belief can affect a result

asked

a 31– 6   Again he a· : "Who is my mother,— Matt. 12 : 48.
sp 86– 1   Jesus once a·, "Who touched— Luke 8 : 45.
s 132–26   Jesus a·, "When the Son of man— Luke 18 : 8.
ph 195– 3   he a· to be taken back to his dungeon,
f 216–26   Paul a· : What concord hath— II Cor. 6 : 15.
245–15   A· to guess her age, those unacquainted with
b 308–29   was a·, "What is thy name?"— Gen. 32 : 27.
o 349– 3   As Paul a· of the unfaithful
p 369–16   Jesus never a· if disease were acute or chronic,
395–15   Prayers, in which God is not a· to heal
399–29   Our Master a· : "How can one— Matt. 12 : 29
411–13   It is recorded that once Jesus a·
g 539–24   Paul a· : "What communion— II Cor. 6 : 14.

asking

pr 2–31   A· God to be God is a vain repetition.
4–17   Simply a· that we may love God will never
9– 7   Do we love . . . better because of this a·?
9–14   shall never meet this great duty simply by a·
s 135–19   limiting the Holy One of Israel and a·
f 222–30   "a· no question for conscience— I Cor. 10 : 25.
226– 8   a· a fuller acknowledgment of the rights of
p 366–14   we have the apostolic warrant for a· :
g 527–27   and a· a prospective sinner to help

asks

b 281– 9   Science . . . rebukes mortal belief, and a· :
p 432–16   The Judge a· if by doing good to his neighbor,

asleep

sp 95–28   the world is a· in the cradle of infancy,
ph 193–13   the breathing became natural ; he was a·.
b 291–22   As man falleth a·, so shall he awake.
p 416– 8   in twenty minutes the sufferer is quietly a·.
442–31   either when a· or when awake.
r 491–18   awake at one time and a· at another,

aspect

   t 457–17   no good *a·*, either silvern or golden.

aspersion

   p 437– 5   This is a foul *a·* on man's Maker.

aspiration

   pr   8–14   If we feel the *a·*, humility, gratitude,
       16–21   reach the heaven-born *a·* and
   c 265–24   The *a·* after heavenly good comes even before

aspirations

   m 60– 4   Kindred tastes, motives, and *a·*
   c 257–26   to still the desires, to satisfy the *a·*?
   g 512– 1   correspond to *a·* soaring beyond and above

assassin

   p 419–26   the mental *a·*, who, in attempting to rule
   t 445– 4   the attacks of the would-be *mental a·*,

assassins

   s 164–20   or produced by mental *a·*,
   t 447–11   and save the victims of the mental *a·*.

assent

   r 471–11   but yield *a·* to astronomical propositions

assert

   f 228–14   Mortals will some day *a·* their freedom
     253–16   *a·* your prerogative to overcome the belief in
   p 395– 9   *a·* its claims over mortality and disease.

asserting

   sp 79–26   *a·* that Mind controls body and brain.
   p 421–30   like *a·* that the products of eight multiplied by
   g 530–17   myth represents error as always *a·* its

assertion

   sp 80–10   the *a·* that spirit-communications are
     81–11   A man's *a·* that he is immortal no more proves
     81–13   than the opposite *a·*, that he is mortal,
   s 136–26   Hence Herod's *a·*: "John have I — *Luke* 9 : 9·.
     137–21   This *a·* elicited from Jesus the benediction,
   p 383–24   Does his *a·* prove the use of tobacco to be
     386–30   although the correctness of the *a·* might
   t 460–23   superficial and cold *a·*, "Nothing ails you."
   r 478–17   *a·* that there can be pain or

asserts

   ph 166–30   but when Mind at last *a·* its mastery
   f 226–21   birthright of sole allegiance to his Maker *a·*
   b 277–19   Error . . . *a·* that Spirit produces matter
   p 423–26   which ultimately *a·* its absolute supremacy.

assiduously

   f 233–14   the goal of goodness is *a·* earned

assigning

   s 122– 3   *a·* seeming power to sin, sickness,
   f 244–30   instead of *a·* to man the everlasting grandeur

assigns

   s 123– 7   reverses the order of Science and *a·*
   f 203– 4   *a·* sure rewards to righteousness,
   p 400–17   except what mortal mind *a·* to it.
   g 522– 5   The first record *a·* all might and government
   ap 566–29   The Old Testament *a·* to the angels,

assimilate

   pr   4–20   striving to *a·* more of the divine character,
   t 462– 2   Some individuals *a·* truth more readily
   r 466–13   which neither dwell together nor *a·*.

assimilated

   b 272– 4   This sense is *a·* only as we are honest,

assist

   p 432–26   endeavoring to *a·* the prisoner to escape
   g 529– 5   were needed to *a·* the birth of mortals.

assistants

   p 431–16   all these *a·* resigned to me,

associates

   p 377–32   *a·* sickness with certain circumstances
   t 449–19   baneful effect of evil *a·* is less seen than

association

   s 154– 3   like other mental conditions, from *a·*.
     154– 6   this law obtains credit through *a·*,

associations

   sp 87–10   leagues apart and their *a·* forgotten,
     87–11   their *a·* float in the general atmosphere

assume

   sp 96–17   sin, sickness, and death, which *a·* new phases
   s 119– 7   they *a·* that matter is the product of Spirit.
   b 313–15   we may *a·* that the author of this
   o 344– 8   Is it sacrilegious to *a·* that God's likeness
   t 447–32   To *a·* that there are no claims of evil and yet
   r 481–20   Human hypotheses first *a·* the reality of
     481–21   *a·* the necessity of these evils
   g 553–11   "We have no right to *a·* that

assumed

   a 27–32   according to certain *a·* material laws.
   s 145–30   continually weaken its own *a·* power.
   b 326–26   Thought *a·* a nobler outlook,
   r 470– 7   *a·* the loss of spiritual power,

assumes

   p 421–28   not build it up by wishing to see the forms it **a.**

assuming

   g 540–22   representing error as *a·* a divine character,

assumption

   sp 75– 1   truth lays bare the mistaken *a·*
   g 546– 7   this *a·* of error would dethrone the
     552– 9   proof requisite to sustain this *a·*

assurance

   m 69–15   brings the sweet *a·* of no parting,
   ph 176–32   Truth handles . . . contagion with perfect *a·*.
   f 223–15   the *a·* which comes of understanding ;

assurances

   p 387–12   the *a·* of immortality, opposed to mortality.

assure

   p 416–28   *A·* them that they think too much about

assured

   a 38– 2   men are *a·* that this command was
   sp 98– 2   spiritual recompense of the persecuted is *a·*
   o 352–23   should be *a·* that their fears are groundless,
     358–24   Sometimes it is said : "Rest *a·* that

assuredly

   pr 15–30   they *a·* call down infinite blessings.
   m 65–30   will *a·* throw off this evil,

assures

   r 489–32   It *a·* mortals that there is

assuring

   ph 169– 5   *a·* me that danger was over,
   p 394–21   *a·* him that all misfortunes are
   t 447–23   A sinner is not reformed merely by *a·* him

Assyrian

   an 103– 5   Sin was the *A·* moon-god.

astonished

   ap 563– 3   We may well be *a·* at sin,

astonishing

   s 134–19   its *a·* and unequalled success in the

astounded

   m 56– 2   came to him for baptism, John was *a·*.
   s 130–29   *a·* at the vigorous claims of evil
   ap 563– 5   and still more *a·* at hatred,

astray

   b 309–17   If these children should go *a·*,

astrography

   s 121– 5   before he spake, *a·* was chaotic,

astronomer

   sp 84–32   more accurately than the *a·* can read the stars
   s 125–28   The *a·* will no longer look up to the stars,

astronomical

   s 121–28   As thus indicated, *a·* order
     122–32   *A·* science has destroyed the false theory
   f 209–25   mundane formations, *a·* calculations,
   r 471–11   but yield assent to *a·* propositions
     493– 4   but *a·* science contradicts this,

astronomy

   s 119–27   As *a·* reverses the human perception
   ph 188–31   *A·* gives the desired information
     189– 2   willing to leave with *a·* the explanation
     195–16   Through *a·*, natural history, chemistry,
   f 235–16   will reach higher than the heavens of *a·* ;
   r 471–11   of the earth's motions or of the science of *a·*,

astutely

   p 378–26   nor a self-constituted . . . power, which copes *a·*

asunder

   m 56– *   *let not man put a·.— Matt.* 19 : 6.
     60–14   wisdom will ultimately put *a·* what she hath not
   f 226–20   Science rends *a·* these fetters,

asylum

   ph 193–26   threatened with incarceration in an insane *a·*

asylums

   p 408–11   people who are committed to insane *a·*

ate

   a 32–28   Passover, which Jesus *a·* with his disciples
   ph 175–29   before he *a·* the fruit of false knowledge,
     195– 7   All that he *a·*, except his black crust,
     197–21   the simple food our forefathers *a·*
   f 221– 3   he *a·* only bread and vegetables,
     221–24   and he *a·* without suffering,

atheism

   s 139–28   *A·*, pantheism, theosophy, and
   gl 580–27   and then disappeared in the *a·* of matter.

atheistic

   s 139–31   does not follow that the profane or *a·* invalid

Athenians

gl 596– 8   Referring to it, he said to the *A·* :

Athens

gl 596– 7   Paul saw in *A·* an altar dedicated

athirst

ap 570–15   weary wanderers, *a·* in the desert

athlete

ph 172–30   may present more nobility than the . . . *a·*,

atmosphere

damp
 ph 175–26   Damp *a·* and freezing snow empurpled the
earth's
 g 547–12   was able to see in the egg the earth's *a·*,
general
 sp 87–11   float in the general *a·* of human mind.
immoral
 t 452–15   Never breathe an immoral *a·*, unless
of intelligence
 ph 192– 1   aroma of Spirit, the *a·* of intelligence.
of Mind
 g 512–11   abound in the spiritual *a·* of Mind,
of Soul
 gl 587–26   HEAVEN. . . . bliss ; the *a·* of Soul.
of Spirit
 sp 70– 6   can never enter the *a·* of Spirit.
 gl 590– 3   the *a·* of Spirit, where Soul is supreme.
surrounding
 s 128–21   its escape into the surrounding *a·*.
this
 b 273–31   this *a·* . . . cannot be destructive to morals

    ———

a 37–11   cleanse and rarefy the *a·* of material sense
s 125–26   mariner will have dominion over the *a·*
 128–16   It extends the *a·* of thought,
f 220–14   The *a·* of the earth,
 220–14   kinder than the *a·* of mortal mind,
p 386– 9   mortals declare that certain states of the *a·*
 392–21   If you decide that climate or *a·* is unhealthy,
gl 585–19   *a·* of human belief before it accepts sin,

atom

c 263–29   A sensual thought, like an *a·* of dust
gl 583–25   could not create an *a·* . . . the opposite of

atone

a 19– 4   Man cannot exceed divine Love, and so *a·* for

atonement

in the
 a 19–21   has little part in the *a·*,
 24–13   This is having part in the *a·* ;
Jesus'
 a 19–19   will help us to understand Jesus' *a·* for sin
 r 497–13   We acknowledge Jesus' *a·* as the
of Christ
 a 18–13   *a·* of Christ reconciles man to God,
requires
 a 23– 4   The *a·* requires constant self-immolation
views of
 a 24–16   ordinary theological views of *a·* will

a 18– 1   *A·* is the exemplification of man's unity with
 23– 8   The *a·* is a hard problem in theology,

at-one-ment

a 19–22   in the *a·* with God,
 21– 5   This is having our part in the *a·*
 45–20   hath elevated them to possible *a·* with

atrocities

an 105–23   to commit fresh *a·* as opportunity occurs

attach

p 385–10   penalty which our beliefs would *a·* to our best
 440–11   to which you *a·* penalties ;

attached

a 31–13   He *a·* no importance to dead ceremonies.

attaches

s 117– 7   C. S. *a·* no physical nature and significance to

attack

a 27–30   Jesus' persecutors made their strongest *a·* upon
p 379– 1   If disease can *a·* and control the body
 392–16   liable to an *a·* from that source.

attacks

f 236– 8   infuriated *a·* on individuals, who
t 445– 4   to guard against the *a·* of the

attain

pr 9–27   Do you really desire to *a·* this point?
m 57– 3   without it one cannot *a·* the Science of
ph 181–20   till you finally *a·* the understanding of C. S.
f 251–29   corrected before we can *a·* harmony.
 254– 5   or *a·* slowly and yield not to discouragement.
c 262–22   and *a·* the bliss of loving unselfishly,
p 366– 5   and thus *a·* the spiritual freedom which will
g 536–27   Through toil, . . . what do mortals *a·*?

attainable

r 487– 4   never *a·* through death, but gained by

attained

m 60–30   and happiness would be more readily *a·*
s 117–12   the spiritual meaning of which is *a·*
ph 167– 4   If . . . the Science of healing is not *a·*,
 167–27   must be *a·* through the divine Mind.
f 237– 9   mental height their little daughter . . . *a·*.
b 297–16   Thus the reality of being is *a·*
 298–19   When the real is *a·*, which is announced by
o 356– 3   before the spiritual fact is *a·*.

attaining

c 260– 9   human beliefs will be *a·* diviner conceptions,
b 273–14   impossibility of *a·* perfect understanding till

attainment

a 39–28   interval before its *a·* is attended with doubts
m 61– 6   *a·* of this celestial condition would
f 235–17   though adorned with gems of scholarly *a·*,
p 428–11   the great *a·* by means of which
t 455–31   The higher your *a·* in the Science of

attainments

pr 10–15   Spiritual *a·* open the door to a
p 367–29   student's higher *a·* in this line of light.
g 505–27   is not the result of scholarly *a·* ;

attains

pr 2–16   Goodness *a·* the demonstration of

attempt

any
 t 459–12   Any *a·* to heal mortals with erring
every
 ph 186–20   Every *a·* of evil to destroy good
mental
 g 517– 6   mental *a·* to reduce Deity to corporeality.
to purify
 t 452–15   Never . . . unless in the *a·* to purify it.
to trace
 g 533–10   an *a·* to trace all human errors
unwitting
 f 212–11   I have seen an unwitting *a·* to

    ———

a 51– 9   he allowed men to *a·* the destruction of
ph 178–29   may *a·* to unite with it hypnotism,
 182–13   If we *a·* it, we shall presently
 187–26   and suffers from the *a·*.
f 230– 2   Would you *a·* with drugs, or without,
 231– 8   What God cannot do, man need not *a·*
 238–16   when we *a·* to claim the benefits of an
o 357–16   how dare we *a·* to destroy what
p 395–22   and then to *a·* its cure through Mind.
 439–11   manacling . . . in the *a·* to save him.
t 447– 4   no moral right to *a·* to influence the

attempted

o 351–28   in their *a·* worship of the spiritual.
g 513– 3   and is an *a·* infringement on infinity.

attempting

p 419–26   assassin, who, in *a·* to rule mankind,
r 480–18   thus *a·* to separate Mind from God.

attempts

pref ix– 7   *a·* to convey his feeling.
 ix–14   but they are feeble *a·* to state the Principle
f 238–22   *A·* to conciliate society and so gain
c 263–25   and *a·* to pattern the infinite.
b 300– 1   Human logic is awry when it *a·* to
 318–25   *a·* to heal it, with matter.
 329–18   *a·* to solve a problem of Euclid,
t 445– 5   *assassin*, who *a·* to kill morally and
 447– 7   ignorant *a·* to do good may render you

attend

pr 13–22   doubts and fears which *a·* such a belief,
a 31–29   would *a·* the Science of Spirit,
 33–29   the persecutions which *a·* a new and
sp 98– 1   which *a·* a new step in Christianity ;
f 235– 4   doctor infected with smallpox to *a·* you
t 463– 6   To *a·* properly the birth of the new child,
g 549–22   such vague hypotheses as must necessarily *a·*

attendants

pref x–19   abandoned as hopeless by regular medical *a·*.

attended

a 39–29   interval before its attainment is *a·* with doubts
s 133–13   miracles *a·* the successes of the Hebrews ;
 139– 9   Reforms have commonly been *a·* with
f 224– 9   *a·* by life and peace instead of discord and
p 422–23   and *a·* by the same symptoms.
 431– 6   During all this time the prisoner *a·* to

attends

g 555– 2   and that health *a·* the absence of

attention

m 59– 5   mutual *a·* and approbation should
ph 198–14   but to do this requires *a·*.
p 369–17   never recommended *a·* to laws of health,

attention
p 382– 5 If half the *a·* given to hygiene were
396– 8 nor draw *a·* to certain symptoms as
g 556–14 C. S. may absorb the *a·* of sage and
556–25 Ontology receives less *a·* than physiology.

attenuated
s 153– 1 is frequently *a·* to such a degree that
153– 5 the author has a *a· Natrum muriaticum*

attenuation
s 153– 8 with one drop of that *a·* in a goblet of water,
153–11 The highest *a·* of homœopathy
153–21 a high *a·* of truth,
156– 9 the fourth *a·* of *Argentum nitratum*
156–10 occasional doses of a high *a·* of *Sulphuris.*
158–29 mortal mind, of a higher *a·* than the drug,

attest
pr 4–15 *a·* our worthiness to be partakers of
15–24 and let our lives *a·* our sincerity.
s 150–15 to *a·* the reality of the higher mission
ph 193–28 I cannot *a·* the truth of that report,
p 272–24 which really *a·* the divine origin and

attested
sp 80–23 *a·* the control of mortal mind over its

attorney
p 430–22 False Belief is the *a·* for Personal Sense.
437–32 The *a·,* C. S., then read from the
438–23 False Belief, the *a·* for Personal Sense,
440– 8 Mortal Minds were deceived by your *a·,*
441–28 Your *a·,* False Belief, is an impostor,

attract
t 452–12 may provoke envy, but it will also *a·* respect.

attracted
a 21–26 and will be *a·* thitherward.
t 449–23 a mind which is *a·* or repelled according to

attracting
ph 169–12 fosters disease by *a·* the mind to the subject

attraction
m 57–11 *a·* between native qualities will be
sp 73–12 Any other control or *a·* of so-called spirit
an 102– 9 There is but one real *a·,*
102–11 or the *a·* of God, divine Mind.
s 124–20 Adhesion, cohesion, and *a·* are properties of
f 213–13 Material theories partially paralyze this *a·*
213–14 by an opposite *a·* towards the finite,
b 293–15 whose potency is Truth, whose *a·* is Love,
g 536–12 spiritual gravitation and *a·* to one Father,

attractive
p 407– 4 *a·* to no creature except a loathsome worm,
r 491–27 may have an *a·* personality.

attribute
m 62–20 must not *a·* more and more intelligence
s 111–22 tendency of the age to *a·* physical effects to
ph 199–29 the unscientific might *a·* to a lubricating oil.
b 319–30 for instance, to name Love as merely an *a·*

attributed
ph 176– 5 unmanly Adam *a·* their own downfall
b 284–27 the effects commonly *a·* to them

attributes
ph 187– 9 With pagan blindness, it *a·* to
f 210–11 Knowing that Soul and its *a·* were
b 275–16 These are His *a·* the eternal
301– 1 yea, which manifests God's *a·*
r 465–14 The *a·* of God are justice, mercy,
473–11 the ideal Truth . . . . *a·* all power to God.
g 555–13 C. S. *a·* to error neither entity nor power,

attuned
p 411– 8 was not perfectly *a·* to divine Science,

audible
pr 4–15 which, even if not acknowledged in *a·* words,
4–27 *A·* prayer can never do the works of
7– 8 *A·* prayer is impressive!
8–11 Professions and *a·* prayers are like
11–31 Such a desire has little need of *a·* expression.
ap 559– 8 exercised upon visible error and *a·* sin.
gl 594– 9 first *a·* claim that God was not omnipotent

audibly
pr 12–30 because they pray or are prayed for *a·,*
p 376–22 silently and *a·* arguing the true facts
412–11 but by naming it *a·,* you are liable
412–21 at first mentally, not *a·,*
412–30 through the parent's thought, silently or *a·*
417–27 Explain *a·* to your patients, as soon as

audience
pr 15–12 that man may have *a·* with Spirit,

audience-chamber
p 442– 6 resounded throughout the vast *a·*

auditor
p 424–22 you need the ear of your *a·.*

auditory
pr 7–24 The "divine ear" is not an *a·* nerve.
ph 194–10 Destruction of the *a·* nerve and

aught
sp 93–13 nor creates *a·* that can cause evil.
s 120–18 impossible for *a·* but Mind to testify truly
ph 181–25 It is unnecessary to resort to *a·* besides Mind
f 203–14 destroys reliance on *a·* but God,
207–22 no reality in *a·* which does not proceed from
b 284–14 or know *a·* unlike the infinite?
291– 4 *a·* but the destruction of sin,
302– 9 It is impossible that man should lose *a·*
p 391–14 It is error to suffer for *a·* but your own sins.
412– 2 never punishing *a·* but sin,
419–17 lest *a·* unfit for development enter
429– 1 It is a sin to believe that *a·* can overpower
441– 4 which undertakes to punish *a·* but sin,
r 479– 6 On the contrary, if *a·* comes from God,
g 504– 2 never reflected by *a·* but the good.
543–25 did it leave *a·* for matter to create?
553–30 before they think or know *a·* of their origin,
555–25 author of *a·* that can become

augury
m 58–20 a poor *a·* for the happiness of wedlock.

Australia
sp 82–29 When wandering in *A·,* do we look

authentic
ph 194–17 The *a·* history of Kaspar Hauser is

authenticate
g 547– 1 proving of one example would *a·* all

author (*see also* **Eddy, Mrs. Mary Baker**)
called the
pref xi–22 God called the *a·* to proclaim His Gospel
cannot be, the
f 230–16 cannot be, the *a·* of experimental sins.
naturalist and
an 104– 8 Agassiz, the celebrated naturalist and *a·,*
not as the
s 127–17 C. S. reveals God, not as the *a·* of sin, sickness,
not the
sp 89–26 The tree is not the *a·* of itself.
f 231–16 God is not the *a·* of mortal discords.
249–12 Mind is not the *a·* of matter,
o 349–12 God is not the *a·* of sickness.
p 381–16 He is not the *a·* of barbarous codes.
of all things
g 519– 1 eternal Mind, the *a·* of all things,
of the unreal
r 474–28 error, not Truth, is the *a·* of the unreal,
started by the
pref xi–26 Mind-healing was started by the *a·*
the only
a 29–16 perception that God is the only *a·* of man.

b 313–15 we may assume that the *a·* of this
p 390–23 God is no more the *a·* of sickness than
r 474–18 If . . . God must be their *a·.*
480–24 God is not its *a·.*
g 512–30 and claims God as their *a·* ;
538–31 supposes God to be the *a·* of sin and
554–27 is the *a·* of itself, and is simply a falsity
555–25 when we admit that the perfect is the *a·* of
ap 567–27 are cast out with their *a·.*

authorities
a 29–13 tradition that Publius Lentulus wrote to the *a·*

authority
better
p 438– 1 remarking that the Bible was better *a·* than
divine
(*see* **divine**)
my only
s 126–29 The Bible has been my only *a·.*
no
t 447– 3 We have no *a· . . .* to attempt to
of this science
ph 189– 1 yield to the *a·* of this science,
Scriptural
o 342–20 Shall it be denied that . . . has Scriptural *a·?*
ap 573–24 This is Scriptural *a·* for concluding

pr 14–30 speak "as one having *a·.*" — *Matt.* 7 : 29.
a 26–15 gave Jesus *a·* over sin, sickness, and death.
ph 168–18 Are we to believe an *a·* which denies
168–19 an *a·* which Jesus proved to be false
c 267–14 the same *a·* for the appellative mother,
o 357–14 the creativeness and *a·* of Deity,
p 393–10 Exercise this God-given *a·.*
395– 7 should speak to disease as one having *a·*
r 471–12 but yield . . . on the *a·* of natural science.
g 517–11 not as much *a·* for considering

author's (*see* **Eddy, Mrs. Mary Baker**)

authors
c 263– 2 independent workers, personal *a·,* and
p 387–15 If printers and *a·* have the shortest span of

automatic
p 399–16 how can mechanism be *a·*?

autopsy
s 159– 2 After the *a·*, her sister testified that

auxiliaries
t 454–32 letter and mental argument are only human *a·*

auxiliary
pref xii–19 as *a·* to her church.

avail
pr 3– 9 we have only to *a·* ourselves of God's rule
    3–23 Then we shall *a·* ourselves of the blessings we
  12–32 *all* may *a·* themselves of God as
ph 167–18 To have one God and *a·* yourself of the
  183– 2 so-called laws . . . would render Spirit of no *a·*,
p 406–21 We can, and ultimately shall, so rise as to *a·*
g 550–10 Of what *a·* is it to investigate what

availability
f 236–19 *a·* of good as the remedy for every woe.

available
s 143–23 deprives you of the *a·* superiority of
f 237–22 This makes C. S. early *a·*.

availed
f 222–12 *a·* himself of the fact that Mind governs man,

avenue
b 280–22 urges through every *a·* the belief

avenues
b 293–32 The five physical senses are the *a·* and

aver
o 348–29 this I do *a·*, that, as a result of teaching C. S.,
  354– 3 "utter falsities and absurdities," as some *a·*?
  359–11 *a·* that the material senses are indispensable
r 474–20 *a·*, "I am not come to destroy, — *Matt.* 5 : 17.

avers
b 320–20 *a·* that this fact is not forever to be humbled

avert
a 40–20 could not *a·* a felon's fate,

avoid
s 153–30 we shall *a·* loquacious tattling about
  153–31 as we would *a·* advocating crime.
ph 169–14 and by dosing the body in order to *a·* it.
f 230–15 for doing what they could not *a·* doing.
  234–14 *a·* casting pearls before those who
b 329–16 he should *a·* their occasion.
p 396– 5 *A·* talking illness to the patient.
  396– 9 *a·* speaking aloud the name of the disease.

avoidance
g 542–10 The *a·* of justice and the denial of truth
ap 571– 5 necessary to ensure the *a·* of the evil?

await
a 28–30 *a·*, in some form, every pioneer of truth.
m 66–22 It is better to *a·* the logic of events
sp 97– 3 *a·* the certainty of ultimate perfection.

awaited
a 20–20 scourge and the cross *a·* the great Teacher.

awaiting
ph 183– 9 *a·* its germination according to the laws of
p 439–28 *a·* the sentence which General Progress

awaits
m 67–13 the mariner works on and *a·* the issue.
b 291–26 No resurrection from the grave *a·* Mind
  291–28 No final judgment *a·* mortals,

awake
pr 4–22 until we *a·* in His likeness.
sp 75–13 that I may *a·* him out of sleep." — *John* 11 : 11.
  75–31 when we *a·* from earth's sleep to the
ph 190–29 when I *a·*, with Thy likeness. — *Psal.* 17 : 15.
f 249–27 than are the thoughts of mortals when *a·*.
b 291–23 As man falleth asleep, so shall he *a·*.
  323–19 When the sick or the sinning *a·* to realize
p 420–30 tell your patient that he must *a·*.
  442–32 either when asleep or when *a·*.
r 491–18 that matter is *a·* at one time and
  491–28 *a·*, we dream of the pains and pleasures of

awaken
b 291–10 need not fancy that . . . death will *a·* them
  327–30 *a·* the man's dormant sense of moral
g 553– 3 which should *a·* thought to a higher and

awakened
p 417–21 from which the patient needs to be *a·*.
r 493–28 If Jesus *a·* Lazarus from the dream,

awakening
f 230– 4 the *a·* from this mortal dream, or illusion,
  230– 6 This *a·* is the forever coming of Christ,
b 339–16 against his own *a·* to the awful unreality
g 556–29 when that *a·* comes, existence will be

awakenings
sp 82–27 Different dreams and different *a·*

awakens
ph 196– 6 Better the suffering which *a·* mortal mind
o 342–21 C. S. *a·* the sinner, reclaims the

award
pr 5–14 Saints and sinners get their full *a·*,

away
pref vii–17 Contentment with . . . . are crumbling *a·*.
pr 8–22 If we turn *a·* from the poor,
a 21–10 He constantly turns *a·* from material sense,
  22–18 When the smoke of battle clears *a·*,
  27–26 They fell *a·* from grace because they
  35– 5 turned *a·* from material things,
  39–24 material pains and material pleasures to pass *a·*,
  45–17 Christ hath rolled *a·* the stone from
  48– 8 turned forever *a·* from earth to heaven,
sp 87– 8 Though individuals have passed *a·*,
  87–31 which are thousands of miles *a·*
  89–29 had the right to take it *a·*.
  95–29 dreaming *a·* the hours.
s 122–25 To material sense, the severance . . . takes *a·*
  131–23 which taketh *a·* the ceremonies and doctrines
  147–12 centuries had passed *a·* since Jesus practised
  150–16 to take *a·* the sins of the world.
  152– 4 Mind takes *a·* all its supposed sovereignty,
  155– 6 Even when you take *a·* the
ph 168– 7 you take *a·* from Mind,
  172–25 you take *a·* a portion of the
  187–27 If you take *a·* this erring mind,
  191–15 Truth . . . chasing *a·* the darkness of error.
f 201– 8 a new creature, in whom old things pass *a·*
  206–20 and then taking it *a·* by death?
  212–15 take *a·* this so-called mind instead of a piece of
  232–29 so-called pleasures and pains of sense pass *a·*
  237–13 snatches *a·* the good seed before it has
  238–12 To fall *a·* from Truth in times of persecution,
  239– 5 Take *a·* wealth, fame, and social
  241–10 revenge, and so forth, steal *a·* the treasures of
  241–14 Take *a·* the spiritual signification of
  247–11 the beauty of material things passes *a·*,
  250–25 Take *a·* the mortal mind, and matter has no
c 261– 2 Look *a·* from the body into Truth and
  261– 9 If one turns *a·* from the body
  261–24 Breaking *a·* from the mutations of time
  265–31 if they wrench *a·* false pleasurable beliefs
b 268– 8 looking *a·* from matter to Mind
  273–11 and thus tears *a·* the foundations of error.
  276–22 *a·* from materiality to the Principle
  278– 3 Divine metaphysics explains *a·* matter.
  288–16 the tumult dies *a·* in the distance.
  294– 7 loss of one finger would take *a·* some quality
  296–26 foundations which time is wearing *a·*.
  299–29 will melt *a·* the shadow
  312–28 and so turns *a·* from the intelligent and
  323–21 towards Soul and *a·* from material sense,
  323–26 takes *a·* all sin and the delusion that
  323–30 We are either turning *a·* from this utterance,
  334–18 taking *a·* the sins of the world,
o 347–23 If C. S. takes *a·* the popular gods,
p 362–14 and his bare feet *a·* from it.
  365– 3 the heavenly homesick looking *a·* from earth,
  376–10 whom you declare to be wasting *a·*
  376–12 blood never gave life and can never take it *a·*,
  377– 8 come back no better than when they went *a·*.
  401–19 forcing impurities to pass *a·*,
  403–20 sweeps *a·* the gossamer web of mortal illusion.
  416–31 Turn their thoughts *a·* from their bodies
  428–12 sweep *a·* the dream and give place to the true.
  439–10 frightening *a·* Materia Medica, who was then
t 462– 9 If the student goes *a·* to practise
r 479–13 Take *a·* so-called mortal mind, which constitutes
  484– 4 bigotry, nor envy can wash *a·* its foundation,
  493–22 takes *a·* this physical sense of discord,
g 510–12 and turn *a·* from a false material sense.
  521–13 should look *a·* from the opposite supposition
  522– 9 as having broken *a·* from Deity
  536– 4 and the first earth were passed *a·* ; — *Rev.* 21 : 1.
  536– 8 the sea, . . . is represented as having passed *a·*.
  539– 7 as if . . . matter can both give and take *a·*.
  548–11 only as the clouds of corporeal sense roll *a·*,
  556– 9 for the former things will have passed *a·*.
ap 570–10 to be carried *a·* of the flood. — *Rev.* 12 : 15.
  571–31 He takes *a·* mitre and sceptre.
  572–21 and the first earth were passed *a·* ; — *Rev.* 21 : 1.
  573–31 and all tears will be wiped *a·*.
  574–11 carried John *a·* in spirit.

awful
a 48–28 ignorant of the consequences of his *a·* decision
  50– 7 wrung from Jesus' lips the *a·* cry,
s 106– 8 I beheld, as never before, the *a·* unreality
  151–14 the *a·* and oppressive bondage now enforced
f 207– 9 We must learn that evil is the *a·* deception
  223–30 but the *a·* daring of sin destroys sin,
  226–30 I saw before me the *a·* conflict,
b 307–31 Above error's *a·* din, blackness, and chaos,

awful
   b 308– 8 This *a·* demand, "Adam, where—*Gen.* 3 : 9.
      339–16 against his own awakening to the *a·* unreality
   r 472–28 the *a·* fact that unrealities seem real
   g 536–10 The way of error is *a·* to contemplate.
  ap 563–16 beholds its *a·* character ; but he also sees
      566–18 An *a·* guide, in smoke and flame,

awry
   b 300– 1 Human logic is *a·* when it attempts to
   t 451–11 will either . . . or be turned sadly *a·*.

axe
   a 27–18 He laid the *a·* of Science at the root
   b 303–16 Divine Science lays the *a·* at the root of the
   o 358– 1 Is the woodman's *a·*, which destroys a tree's

axiom
  an 105–28 foretells its doom, and confirms the ancient *a·* :

axis
   s 121–27 besides turning daily on its own *a·*.
   b 310–12 when the earth has again turned upon its *a·*.

B

baneful
  ph 181–17 ignorant of the *b·* effects of magnetism,
   p 400–30 Scriptures plainly declare the *b·* influence of
      408–12 *b·* effects of illusion on mortal minds
      418– 1 shield them from the *b·* effects of
   t 449–19 The *b·* effect of evil associates is
   g 525–21 Whatever is valueless or *b·*, He did not make,

banish
   f 208–32 *b·* all thoughts of disease and sin
   o 353–25 grave does not *b·* the ghost of materiality.
   p 381–27 Let us *b·* sickness as an outlaw,
      391– 9 *B·* the belief that you can possibly entertain a
   r 488– 4 When, . . . you are able to *b·* a severe malady,

banished
   s 158–14 Apollo, who was *b·* from heaven

banishes
   s 128–25 should not resist Truth, which *b·* — yea,

banishment
   f 226– 2 the *b·* of a world-wide slavery,

banner
   f 224–28 On its *b·* is the Soul-inspired motto,
      225– 8 time bears onward freedom's *b·*.
   p 426–26 and would enable us to hold the *b·* of
   r 492–32 Victory would perch on neither *b·*.

baptism
   a 35–19 Our *b·* is a purification from all error.
   m 56– 1 When our great Teacher came to him for *b·*,
   f 241–27 The *b·* of Spirit, . . . signifies that
      242– 2 Through repentance, spiritual *b·*, and
  ap 558–17 It brings the *b·* of the Holy Ghost,
      565–20 the fiery *b·* will burn up the chaff of error
  gl 581–23 definition of

Baptist
   (see **John the Baptist**)

Baptist's
   a 53– 4 He did not fast as did the *B·* disciples ;

baptize
   a 18– * for Christ sent me not to *b·*, but—I *Cor.* 1 : 17.
  ap 562– 2 Messiah, who would *b·* with the Holy Ghost,
      565–20 according to the Revelator, . . . will *b·* with fire ;

baptized
   a 20–11 He knew that men can be *b·*, . . . and yet be
      31–19 are *b·* with his purity ;
   b 333–25 which *b·* these seers in the divine nature,

bar
   f 234–11 as watchfully as we *b·* our doors against the
   p 432– 5 whereas Mortal Man, the prisoner at the *b·*,
      434–13 now summoned to appear before the *b·* of Justice
      434–22 The prisoner at the *b·* has been unjustly
      437– 8 At the *b·* of Truth, in the presence of
      437–24 question of expelling C. S. from the *b·*,
      437–30 unjust usages were not allowed at the *b·* of
      440– 5 arraigns before the supreme *b·* of Spirit
      440–26 standing at the *b·* of Truth, and
      441– 6 not permitted to enter any suits at the *b·* of
   t 452– 1 Instruct him how to *b·* the door of his thought

barbarism
  ph 173–31 more fatal to health . . . than are the idols of *b·*

barbarisms
  ph 195–23 It is the tangled *b·* of learning which

barbarity
   a 43–24 Out of reach of the *b·* of his enemies,
  ap 564–16 brutal *b·* of his foes could emanate from

barbarous
   p 381–16 but He is not the author of *b·* codes.

bard
  ph 190–21 Hebrew *b·*, swayed by mortal thoughts,

bare
  pr 8–25 and ask that it may be laid *b·* before us,
  sp 75– 1 This simple truth lays *b·* the mistaken
   p 362–14 and his *b·* feet away from it.
   t 459–15 the *b·* process of mental healing
   g 538–24 she conceived, and *b·* Cain,—*Gen.* 4 : 1.

Baal
  sp 83– 3 the worshippers of *B·* failed to do ;
   g 524– 2 seen in the Phœnician worship of *B·*,

babbling
  ph 195– 2 After the *b·* boy had been taught to speak

babe
  pref vii– 6 the Bethlehem *b·*, the human herald of
  ph 194–25 chattering with no more intelligence than a *b·*
   p 371–21 nor would I keep the suckling a lifelong *b·*.
      413– 6 to meet the simplest needs of the *b·*
   g 556–31 plunged his infant *b·*, only a few hours old,

Babel
  gl 581–17 definition of

babes
   m 62– 8 If parents create in their *b·* a desire for
   s 131–21 hast revealed them unto *b·* :— *Luke* 10 : 21.
   o 354–22 and out of the mouth of *b·* He

Babylonian
   s 161– 8 Hebrew captives, cast into the *B·* furnace ,

back
   a 22–16 go not *b·* to error, nor become a sluggard
  sp 75– 9 from the spiritual sense of existence *b·* into
   s 115–10 when translating material terms *b·* into
      135– 3 Jordan, that thou wast driven *b·* ?—*Psal.* 114 : 5.
  ph 195– 3 he asked to be taken *b·* to his dungeon,
      195–18 thought passes naturally from effect *b·* to
   f 209–22 translation of man and the universe *b·* into
   b 309–20 they were to be brought *b·* through great
      321–10 bade him come *b·* and handle the serpent,
   o 360–19 you will be thrown *b·* and forth,
   p 377– 7 they come *b·* no better than when they went
      378–12 sent it cowering *b·* into the jungle.
      425– 1 or some of his progenitors farther *b·*
   t 450– 8 never fail to stab their benefactor in the *b·*.
   g 543– 1 sinful misconception of Life . . . falls *b·* upon
      557–19 Divine Science rolls *b·* the clouds of error
  ap 569–22 comes *b·* to him at last with accelerated force,

backward
  sp 74–20 a *b·* transformation is impossible in Science.

backwardness
  ap 571– 4 Why this *b·*, since exposure is necessary

bad
   s 156– 3 and what made them good or *b·*
      157–19 If He could create drugs intrinsically *b·*,
   f 202– 9 they would not go on from *b·* to worse,
   c 260–22 evolves *b·* physical and moral conditions.
   b 329–16 Until one is able to prevent *b·* results,
      330–22 Mind is not both good and *b·*,
   p 377–18 that it may not produce blindly its *b·* effects.
      384–24 to destroy the *b·* effects of your belief.
      393– 7 remote, and exciting cause of all *b·* effects
      413–10 good or *b·* effects on the health of children.
   t 446– 2 perhaps communicating his own *b·* morals,
   r 489–32 sometimes good and sometimes *b·*.

bade
  sp 79–18 Paul *b·* men have the Mind that was
   s 117–29 Jesus *b·* his disciples beware of the
   b 321–10 *b·* him come back and handle the serpent,
   o 342–13 He *b·* the seventy disciples, as well as the

badly
  pr 6– 8 Calling on Him to forgive our work *b·* done
   f 237– 2 A little girl, . . . *b·* wounded her finger.

baggage
   g 514–17 They carry the *b·* of stern resolve,

balance
   a 40– 8 Divine Science adjusts the *b·* as
  ph 166–28 The *b·* of power is conceded to be
   f 239– 6 weigh not one jot in the *b·* of God,
   p 392– 7 must be cast out to readjust the *b·*
   t 449– 8 Right adjusts the *b·* sooner or later.

balanced
   m 61–13 better *b·* minds, and sounder constitutions.
   p 405–16 until you have *b·* your account with God.

bald
  sp 99–26 are seen to be a *b·* imposition,

3

Bar-jona, Simon
s 137–22   "Blessed art thou, Simon *B*· :— *Matt.* 16 : 17.
    137–27   called only by his common names, Simon *B*·,

bark
f 254–27   If you launch your *b*· upon the

barometer
s 122–18   The *b*·, — that little prophet of storm and

barrel
s 156– 8   the patient looked like a *b*·.

barren
pr 4– 2   cannot conceal the ingratitude of *b*· lives.
    a 36–11   pour his dear-bought bounty into *b*· lives.
    s 146– 9   Such systems are *b*· of the vitality of
    o 354–15   Surely it is not enough to cleave to *b*· and
    g 537–16   Error tills its own *b*· soil

barrenness
p 366– 8   while his own spiritual *b*· debars him

barrier
m 60–17   becoming a *b*· against vice, a protection to

barriers
c 266–30   does not cross the *b*· of time into

basal
ph 189–29   lower, *b*· portion of the brain,

base
s 162–10   stir the human mind to a change of *b*·,
    p 422–16   changes the material *b*· of thought,
    430– 6   enlarge its borders and strengthen its *b*·

based
pref x–10   A few books, . . . *b*· on this book,
    s 114– 7   unscientific definition of mind is *b*· on
    124– 1   *b*· on Truth, the Principle of all science.
    147– 3   upon which Jesus' healing was *b*·,
    164–12   But all human systems *b*· on
    ph 178–15   and *b*· on Science or the divine Mind,
    191–25   Science of being reveals man . . . as *b*· on
    191–26   sense defines mortal man as *b*· on matter,
    f 209–27   *b*· on the hypothesis of material law or
    249– 1   relinquish all theories *b*· on sense-testimony,
    b 268–16   their arguments are *b*· on the
    269–26   All other systems— systems *b*· wholly or
    273– 9   because they are not *b*· on the divine law.
    274–14   are *b*· on spiritual understanding,
    302–18   This statement is *b*· on fact, not fable.
    304– 3   *b*· on a material sense of things,
    312–23   theories are *b*· on finite premises,
    o 341– 5   are generally *b*· on detached sentences
    341–15   which is *b*· on divine Principle,
    r 484– 1   will never be *b*· on a divine Principle . . . until
    496–18   rule of healing, *b*· upon its divine Principle,
    g 522–27   *b*· on some hypothesis of error,

bases
b 279–28   there are not two *b*· of being, matter and mind,
    340–21   divine Principle . . . *b*· the Science of being,
    p 378–21   represented by two material erroneous *b*·.
    g 551–25   so long as it *b*· creation on materiality.

basic
s 164–21   the truth of its *b*· proposition
    p 405– 1   The *b*· error is mortal mind.
    r 470– 6   the *b*· error of idolatry.

basis
and support
    f 229– 3   but is their *b*· and support.
better
    g 553– 7   Mortal thought must obtain a better *b*·,
boundless
    c 258–15   rising higher and higher from a boundless *b*·.
change our
    p 370–30   change our *b*· from sensation to C. S.,
establish a
    b 335– 6   would . . . establish a *b*· for pantheism.
false
    m 60–26   physical sense, . . . places it on a false *b*·.
    g 523– 3   Because of its false *b*·, the mist of
higher
    t 453–10   and a higher *b*· is thus won ;
impossible
    r 492–31   uniting on some impossible *b*·.
its
    an 102– 4   Its *b*· being a belief and this belief
material
    (*see* **material**)
metaphysical
    b 268– 8   slowly yielding to the idea of a metaphysical *b*·,
mortal
    p 424– 6   and we must leave the mortal *b*· of belief
naturalist's
    g 553–15   Why, then, is the naturalist's *b*· so
no
    sp 84–27   spiritualism has no *b*· upon which to build.
no other
    f 201–19   Christian perfection is won on no other *b*·.

basis
no real
    r 480–23   evil is but an illusion, and it has no real *b*·.
of all health
    b 339–25   *b*· of all health, sinlessness, and
of Christian Science
    a 44–10   He met and mastered on the *b*· of C. S.,
    p 388– 7   John testified to the divine *b*· of C. S.,
    412–30   met . . . on the aforesaid *b*· of C. S.
of evidence
    gl 581–19   on the *b*· of evidence obtained from the
of health
    s 120–22   Truth, which is the only *b*· of health ;
of his spirituality
    o 356–10   controlled . . . on the *b*· of his spirituality.
of immortality
    gl 585–12   Elias. . . . the *b*· of immortality.
of matter
    ph 195–13   We should forsake the *b*· of matter
    b 316–30   resting on the *b*· of matter,
of one God
    ph 183– 4   thus departing from the *b*· of one God,
of operation
    p 423–19   making Mind his *b*· of operation
of physical sense
    s 124–16   but when explained on the *b*· of physical sense
of practice
    t 456–21   So long as matter is the *b*· of practice,
of Science
    ph 182–17   to those who heal the sick on the *b*· of Science.
of sensation
    ph 178–18   Mortal mind, acting from the *b*· of sensation in
of thought
    c 259–14   as the *b*· of thought and demonstration.
of true healing
    ph 192–29   Christianity is the *b*· of true healing.
of true religion
    m 68– 1   understanding . . . will be the *b*· of true religion.
one
    b 269–14   categories of metaphysics rest on one *b*·,
same
    p 383–14   mind and body rest on the same *b*·.
scientific
    sp 71–22   having no scientific *b*· nor origin,
    94–29   Our Master read mortal mind on a scientific *b*·,
    s 138– 9   On this spiritually scientific *b*· Jesus
    p 414–20   on the Christianly scientific *b*· of being.
spiritual
    (*see* **spiritual**)
sure
    t 460– 2   rest his demonstration on this sure *b*·.
this
    pref viii–16   On this *b*· C. S. will have a fair fight.
    s 143–16   On this *b*· it saves from starvation by
    148–23   how from this *b*· of division and discord

    sp 71–27   The *b*· and structure of spiritualism are
    ph 170– 2   Truth is not the *b*· of theogony.
    178–28   Ignorant of the methods and the *b*· of
    f 234–13   on the *b*· of the Golden Rule ;
    244– 5   On their *b*· Jesus demonstrated Life,
    c 255–17   cannot be made the *b*· of any true idea
    o 360–31   on the very *b*· of Jesus' words and works.
    r 478– 7   What *b*· is there for the theory
    482–28   heals the sick on the *b*· of the one Mind or God.
    g 524–20   could a material organization become the *b*· of
    528–25   he is supposed to become the *b*· of the
    539–13   How then has man a *b*· for wrong-doing?
    539–32   the *b*· of his marvellous demonstrations.

bathed
p 363–27   She *b*· his feet with her tears

bathes
g 516–13   Love, . . . *b*· all in beauty and light.

bathing
p 382– 8   Constant *b*· and rubbing to alter the secretions

baths
ph 174– 6   to flannels, to *b*·, diet, exercise, and air?
    f 220– 2   said : . . . I take cold *b*·, in order to overcome

battle
a 22–18   When the smoke of *b*· clears away,
    37–14   not amid the smoke of *b*· is merit seen
    f 254– 7   not until the *b*· between Spirit and flesh
    b 268–12   woman goes forth to *b*· with Goliath.
    292– 2   final trump will sound which will end the *b*·
    r 483–16   Science has called the world to *b*· over this issue

battle-axe
p 389–27   totters to its falling before the *b*· of Science.

battling
f 236–30   While age is . . . *b*· with false beliefs,

bay
pr 5–19   flourish "like a green *b*· tree ;"— *Psal.* 37 : 35.

bayonet

f 225–11   Science, heeding not the pointed b·, marches on.
226–12   not through human warfare, not with b· and

beam

f 205–28   Selfishness tips the b· of human existence
t 455–14   "First cast out the b· out of— Matt. 7 : 5.

beaming

p 442–12   countenance b· with health and happiness.

beams

pref vii– 3   beholds the first faint morning b·,
vii–10   should dawn the morning b·
g 504– 8   solar b· are not yet included in the record

bear

pref xii–24   is joyful to b· consolation to the sorrowing
a 31– 2   Pride and fear are unfit to b· the standard of
s 120–16   nor can the material senses b· reliable
f 201– *   b· in my bosom the reproach— Psal. 89 : 50.
202– 6   If men would bring to b· upon the study of
254–30   Take it up and b· it, for through it you win
b 298–10   spiritual sense can b· witness only to Truth
330– 9   and the letter and the spirit b· witness,
p 411–10   b· witness to the truth,
417–28   Explain . . . as soon as they can b· it,
436–13   Such acts b· their own justification,
441–13   Material Law is a liar who cannot b· witness
t 451–18   they b· as of old the fruits of the Spirit.
ap 561–31   to b· witness of that Light."— John 1 : 8.

beards

g 549–25   and b· the lion of materialism in its den.

beareth

b 272– 7   else it b· not much fruit, for the

bearing

ph 180– 9   the seed within itself b· fruit
f 252–31   Spirit, b· opposite testimony, saith :
b 299–19   a tree, b· the fruits of sin,
p 391–31   and b· the fruits of Spirit.
438–12   and b· false witness against Man.
r 494–28   b· Truth's signet, its lap piled high with
g 518– 6   given you every herb b· seed,— Gen. 1 : 29.

bears

ph 197– 9   which b· the fruit of sin, disease, and
f 207–31   which b· no resemblance to spirituality,
225– 7   time b· onward freedom's banner.
b 271– 1   seed of Truth springs up and b· much fruit.
o 361–29   That which when sown b· immortal fruit,

beast

any
g 529–14   more subtle than any b· of the— Gen. 3 : 1.
ap 564–32   "more subtle than any b· of the— Gen. 3 : 1.
every
g 518– 9   And to every b· of the earth,— Gen. 1 : 30.
527–22   formed every b· of the field,— Gen. 2 : 19.
ferocious
sp 78– 2   the gnarled oak, the ferocious b·,
p 378–14   man's gaze, fastened fearlessly on a ferocious b·,

f 244–24   not a b·, a vegetable, nor a migratory mind.
b 327–14   Sin is the image of the b·
p 378–15   often causes the b· to retreat in terror.
g 513–16   b· of the earth after his kind :— Gen. 1 : 24.
513–22   God made the b· of the earth— Gen. 1 : 25.
542– 9   sets upon error the mark of the b·.
551– 7   the bird is not the product of a b·.
ap 567–27   b· and the false prophets are lust and

beasts

f 244–14   is like the b· and vegetables,
g 539–18   the serpent, to grovel beneath all the b·

beat

f 203–30   sin, sorrow, and death b· in vain.

beatific

c 266–28   he reflects the b· presence,

beatified

b 303–19   b· understanding of the Science of Life.

beatitudes

t 446–25   divine b·, reflect the spiritual light

Beaumont's "Medical Experiments"

ph 175–24   B· "M· E·" did not govern the digestion.

beautifies

g 516–19   b· the landscape, blesses the earth.

beautiful

a 32–25   it was natural and b·.
m 60– 6   The b· in character is also the good,
61–15   often these b· children early droop and die,
63– 5   The b·, good, and pure constitute his ancestry.
sp 74–17   The caterpillar, transformed into a b· insect,
ph 190–15   springing from the soil with b· green blades,
f 240– 8   The stars make night b·,
246–21   and limiting all that is good and b·,
246–24   is always b· and grand.
248– 5   that a friend can ever seem less than b·.

beautiful

f 248– 9   supplying it with b· images of thought
b 276–14   and presents them as b· and immortal.
277–31   mortal phenomenon, . . . sometimes b·,
280– 6   All things b· and harmless are ideas of Mind.
304–20   Harmony in man is as b· as in music,
p 442–14   feet "b· upon the mountains,"— Isa. 52 : 7.
t 457–16   both sides were b· according to their degree ;
r 477–28   when they called a certain b· lake
485–25   its own b· images, but it effaces them
g 527– 3   to make it b· or to cause it to live and grow.
527– 5   but ever b· and complete.
ap 566–12   the b· description which Sir Walter Scott
575–22   "B· for situation, the joy of the. — Psal. 48 : 2.
gl 593– 1   The love of the good and b·,

beautifully

sp 77–24   would grow b· less
g 543– 7   becomes more b· apparent at error's demise.

beauty

all
sp 89–19   It possesses of itself all b· and poetry,
and fragrance
ph 175–11   The joy of its presence, its b· and fragrance,
and goodness
sp 76–23   possessing unlimited divine b· and goodness
b 304– 4   which hide spiritual b· and goodness.
g 503–22   immortal forms of b· and goodness.
and holiness
f 246– 5   unfolds wisdom, b·, and holiness.
bathes all in
g 516–13   bathes all in b· and light.
bow of
f 247–26   arches the cloud with the bow of b·,
demonstrates the
a 26–19   musician demonstrates the b· of the music
goodness and
s 121–13   So we have goodness and b· to gladden the
grace and
c 263–14   when he would outline grace and b·,
grow in
o 341– 7   Scriptures, which grow in b· and consistency
natural
ph 175– 9   an abuse of natural b· to say that a rose,
of holiness
s 135–12   This is "the b· of holiness,"— Psal. 29 : 2.
f 253– 2   The b· of holiness, the perfection of being,
of this text
ap 574–16   b· of this text is, that the sum total of
recipe for
f 247–31   recipe for b· is to have less illusion
secret
pr 15–25   Christians rejoice in secret b· and bounty,
sense of
f 246–14   the transient sense of b· fades,
tremulous with
s 142–13   making dome and spire tremulous with b·,

m 57–15   B·, wealth, or fame is incompetent
f 247–10   B·, as well as truth, is eternal ;
247–10   but the b· of material things passes away,
247–21   B· is a thing of life, which dwells forever in
g 509–26   in which b·, sublimity, purity, and holiness

became

a 34–18   they b· more spiritual and understood better
47– 6   they b· better healers, leaning no longer on
s 111–27   this fact b· evident to me,
ph 193–12   the breathing b· natural ; he was asleep.
200– 1   the gods b· alive in a nation's belief.
f 245– 5   she b· insane and lost all account of time.
b 314–28   the more odious he b· to sinners
316– 1   he b· the way of salvation to all who
321–26   the inward voice b· to him the voice of God,
326–27   and his life b· more spiritual.
o 351– 8   The author b· a member of the orthodox
p 411–17   and straightway b· whole.
t 460–31   the teaching b· clearer, until finally the
g 524–15   and man b· a living soul.— Gen. 2 : 7.
544– 4   In God's creation ideas b· productive,
ap 574–11   It exalted him till he b· conscious of the

because

pref viii–19   b· of these practitioners?
x–20   b· there is so little faith in
pr 5–28   b· he fancies himself forgiven.
9– 6   Do we love our neighbor better b· of
10–27   b· ye ask amiss,— Jas. 4 : 3.
11–20   b· sin brings inevitable suffering.
12–19   b· it has no intelligence.
12–29   If the sick recover b· they
13–25   B· of human ignorance of the
14–20   b· I go unto my— John 14 : 12.
14–21   b· the Ego is absent from the body,
a 21– 3   b· you are a better man.
21– 7   b· of another's goodness,
27–26   They fell away from grace b· they

| | | |

because

  a 28–27 *b·* it is honored by sects and societies,
      29– 9 *b·* then our labor is more needed.
      32– 1 *b·* they have not known — *John* 16 : 3.
      38– 1 *B·* men are assured that
      39–24 unreal, *b·* impossible in Science.
      41–29 *B·* it demanded more than they
      42–21 *B·* of the wondrous glory which
      43–21 rose higher in demonstration *b·* of
      53– 6 *b·* he was their friend ;
      53– 9 *B·* the divine Principle and practice
      53–12 were unknown to the world *b·*
  m 58–27 *b·* another supplies her wants.
      60– 9 *b·* the mother-love includes purity
      60–20 *B·* the education of the higher
      62–31 *B·* mortals believe in material laws
  sp 82–10 *b·* different states of consciousness are
      82–15 *b·* both of us are either unconscious or
      86–15 *b·* it is unusual to see thoughts,
      87–24 *b·* you do not think of it.
      91–10 *l* Science exposes his nothingness ;
      94–10 *b·* he made himself the Son of God.'' — *John* 19 : 7.
      95–20 *b·* even human invention must
      99–16 errs *b·* it is human.
  an 103–13 *b·* Mind-science is of God
  s 117– 1 *b·* an individual may be one of
     117–25 *b·* of opacity to the true light,
     118–28 *b·* these definitions portray law as
     119–23 *b·* it is opposed to the nature of Spirit,
     129– 2 *b·* its logic is as harmonious as the
     133–19 *b·* Judaism engendered the
     134–23 not *b·* this Science is supernatural
     134–24 nor *b·* it is an infraction of
     134–25 *b·* it is the immutable law of God,
     141– 6 *B·* his precepts require the
     144–23 *B·* divine Science wars with so-called
     146– 4 *B·* our systems of religion are governed
     146–18 *B·* truth divests material drugs of
     149–13 it is *b·* you have not demonstrated the
     149–14 *b·* you have not obeyed the rule
     150–32 *b·* they are ignorant that the human mind
     153–25 We weep *b·* others weep, we yawn *b·* they yawn,
     153–26 we have smallpox *b·* others have it ;
     154–14 *b·* no cholera patient had been in that bed.
     157– 4 *b·* its one recognized Principle of healing is
  ph 168–15 *B·* man-made systems insist that
     178– 9 is not dangerous *b·* of its priority
     181–16 you manipulate *b·* you are ignorant of
     184–21 not *b·* a law of matter has been
     184–22 *b·* a law of this so-called mind has been
     185–28 *b·* erroneous methods act on and through
     186–11 *b·* it is the absence of truth.
     186–12 *b·* it is the absence of something.
     186–13 *b·* it presupposes the absence of God,
     198–29 *B·* the muscles of the blacksmith's arm
     199– 6 *B·* nobody believes that mind is producing
     199–12 Not *b·* of muscular exercise,
  f 205– 5 all *b·* of their blindness,
     207– 2 *B·* God is Spirit, evil becomes
     210–21 *B·*, in obedience to the immutable law
     210–30 *B·* immortal sense has no error of sense,
     212– 9 *B·* the memory of pain is more vivid
     212–25 *B·* all the methods of Mind are not
     215– 9 *b·* matter and mortality do not reflect
     215–27 *B·* he understood the superiority and
     216– 1 *b·* of his faith in Soul and his
     227–10 *b·* some public teachers permit
     231–20 To hold yourself superior to sin, *b·*
     236–28 Jesus loved little children *b·* of their
     238–20 *b·* we suffer severely from error.
     243–28 *b·* they declare nothing except God.
     245–21 Years had not made her old, *b·*
     253– 8 *b·* I AM THAT I AM.
  c 263–10 *b·* he has not tasted heaven.
  b 273– 9 *b·* they are not based on the divine law.
     274– 8 not really natural nor scientific, *b·*
     278–29 We define matter as error, *b·* it is the
     289–32 *B·* Life is God, Life must be eternal,
     291–16 immortal, *b·* sin is not there
     292–13 *b·* this so-called mind has no
     292–21 Even *b·* ye cannot — *John* 8 : 43.
     292–24 *b·* there is no truth in — *John* 8 : 44.
     301–14 seems to mortal sense transcendental, *b·*
     302–20 *b·* the Soul, or Mind, of the spiritual man
     302–22 *b·* this real man is governed by
     305–27 *B·* man is the reflection of his
     310–30 *b·* Mind is Spirit, which
     311– 7 Soul is immortal *b·* it is Spirit,
     312– 2 *b·* such so-called knowledge is reversed
     314– 1 no more perfect *b·* of death
     314–23 *B·* of mortals' material and sinful belief,
     316–18 rose higher to human view *b·* of the
     317–16 no less tangible *b·* it is spiritual
     317–17 *b·* his life is not at the mercy of
     329– 7 *B·* you cannot walk on the water

because

  b 329–19 denies the rule of the problem *b·*
    330–23 one Mind only, *b·* there is one God.
    335– 2 no evil in Spirit, *b·* God is Spirit.
    335–20 *B·* Soul is immortal, it does not
  o 341– * *b· I tell you the truth,* — *John* 8 : 45.
    343–21 *b·* meekness and spirituality are
    344– 6 and that this claim is made *b·*
    344–29 Is it *b·* allopathy and homœopathy
    346–20 *b·* Truth is error's antidote.
    346–23 *b·* matter has no sensation,
    348–17 *b·* I desire to have no faith in evil
    349–17 *b·* one is obliged to use material terms
    350–16 often refused to explain his words, *b·*
    351–22 *B·* such starting-points are neither
    352– 1 *b·* they did not sufficiently understand
    352–27 *b·* there are no such things.
    355–27 *b·* . . . are God's immortal keynotes,
    358–21 *b·* there are few who have gained a
    359– 6 Is this *b·* the patients have more faith
    360– 1 *b·* drawn from Truth,
  p 364–30 *b·* much is forgiven them.
    367–30 *B·* Truth is infinite,
    367–31 *B·* Truth is omnipotent
    368–24 *B·* matter has no consciousness
    371–23 *b·* this teaching is in advance
    373– 7 partly *b·* they were willing to
    374– 6 *B·* mortal mind seems to be conscious,
    374–24 your steps are less firm *b·* of your
    375–31 *b·* it is a stage of fear so excessive
    376–18 *B·* the so-called material body
    377–16 *B·* a belief originates unseen,
    379–10 and died *b·* of that belief,
    383–13 *b·* mind and body rest on the
    385–27 *b·* you have partaken of salt fish,
    386–11 not *b·* of the climate, but
    387– 3 *b·* mortal mind is kept active,
    387–13 *b·* they faithfully perform the
    387–16 it is not *b·* they occupy the most
    387–24 but grows stronger *b·* of it.
    388– 6 *b·* it knows less of material law.
    388–24 *B·* sin and sickness are not qualities of
    390– 6 *b·*, to the mortal senses, there is
    390–22 *b·* you know that God is no
    393– 4 *b·* mortal mind is ignorant of itself,
    396–17 not *b·* the testimony of sin . . . is true,
    397–27 *b·* they combine as one.
    401– 1 ''*b·* of their unbelief'' — *Matt.* 13 : 58.
    401– 9 *b·* the truth of being must
    402–27 *b·* their belief is not better instructed
    407–31 *b·* its method of madness is in
    411– 8 *b·* the student was not perfectly attuned
    415– 7 *b·* thought moves quickly or slowly,
    426–30 *b·* matter has no life to surrender.
    433–19 *B·* he has loved his neighbor as himself,
    442– 2 *b·* there are no such laws.
  t 447–23 *b·* there is no sin.
    456–27 *B·* it is the voice of Truth
    456–30 *B·* it was the first book . . . containing
    457– 4 *B·* this book has done more for
    457–15 *b·* each of them could see but one face
    461– 6 *b·* a part is proved and that
    461–13 *b·* Science reverses the evidence before
    461–20 *b·* of the different effects
    464–26 ''The hireling fleeth, *b·* — *John* 10 : 13.
  r 468– 4 *b·* it kills itself.
    468– 5 *b·* error is unlike Truth.
    468– 6 *B·* Soul is immortal,
    469–18 *b·* there is but one God ;
    471–15 *b·* the evidence . . . is fully sustained by
    472–19 Error is unreal *b·* untrue.
    472–30 *b·* they are not of God.
    475–11 *b·* he is spiritual and perfect,
    479–27 *b·* it reflects no light.
    479–29 *b·* it has none of the divine hues.
    481–21 *b·* of their admitted actuality.
    483–22 *B·* the Science of Mind seems to
    485– 8 *b·* of their uselessness or their
    489–25 *b·* matter has no sensation,
  g 501– 3 *b·* the spiritual import of the Word,
    507–19 do not yield fruit *b·* of any
    507–20 *b·* they reflect the Mind which
    517–16 *b·* there is but one God.
    520–25 not *b·* of seed or soil,
    520–25 *b·* growth is the eternal mandate of Mind.
    520–28 *B·* Mind makes all,
    523– 3 *B·* of its false basis, the mist of
    523–17 *b·* the Supreme Being is therein called
    523–19 *b·* Deity therein is always called Jehovah,
    527–20 Evil is unreal *b·* it is a lie,
    529–28 *b·* we know that they are worthless
    532–16 *b·* I was naked ; — *Gen.* 3 : 10.
    535–19 *B·* thou hast hearkened — *Gen.* 3 : 17.
    544–11 man exists *b·* God exists.
    546–19 *b·* they cannot possibly be
    554– 6 *b·* being is immortal, like Deity,

because

g	554–10	b· it is destitute of any knowledge
	555–14	b· error is neither mind nor the
	556–26	B· mortal mind must waken to
	557–10	has its suffering b· it is a false belief.
ap	559–27	b· you must share the hemlock cup
	560–27	B· it has hid from them the true idea
	561– 6	B· of his more spiritual vision,
	567–11	b· the dragon cannot war with them.
	568–22	b· he knoweth that— Rev. 12 : 12.
	571– 5	B· people like you better when
	573–19	B· St. John's corporeal sense of the

beck

a	21–26	the worldly man is at the b· and call of error,

beckons

sp	76– 3	and the hand which b· them,

becloud

sp	93–31	This belief tends to b· our apprehension

beclouds

b	315–17	sin, which b· the spiritual sense of Truth ;

become

pr	7–28	By it we may b· involuntary hypocrites,
	14–12	B· conscious for a single moment that Life
a	22–16	go not back to error, nor b· a sluggard in
m	59– 8	compact which might otherwise b· unbearable
	61–18	b· parents in their turn,
	62–18	should b· men and women only through
	65–31	marriage will b· purer when the scum
sp	73–31	nor the finite b· the channel of the infinite.
	84– 9	men b· seers and prophets
	89– 5	the devotee may b· unwontedly eloquent.
	96– 8	Earth will b· dreary and desolate,
	97–10	the blow of the other will b· harmless.
an	105–19	words of Judge Parmenter . . . will b·
s	112– 7	b· adherents to the Socratic,
	139–26	b· "the head of the corner."— Matt. 21 : 42.
	158–23	until . . . men and women b· loathsome sots.
	160–16	when the cords contract and b· immovable?
	160–20	Can muscles, . . . b· cramped despite the
	160–24	and b· rigid of their own preference,
ph	172–16	in order to b· man.
	182– 1	will diminish your ability to b· a
f	201– 9	"all things are b· new."— II Cor. 5 : 17.
	234– 9	b· more familiar with good than with evil,
	240–23	we must b· dissatisfied with it.
	251– 5	neither should a fever b· more severe
c	264–15	multitudinous objects . . . will b· visible.
b	270–25	They think sickly thoughts, and so b· sick.
	282–20	nor can non-intelligence b· Soul.
	295–22	in order to b· a better transparency for Truth.
	309–12	He was to b· the father of those, who
	311–23	it will b· the law of Life to man,
	321– 9	When, . . . he saw it b· a serpent,
	323–32	Willingness to b· as a little child
	352–19	lose the deific character, and b· less than
o	352–19	at any moment they may b· its helpless victims ;
	354–26	Sin should b· unreal to every one.
	356– 2	material thought must b· spiritualized
p	368– 8	truth will b· still clearer
	369– 6	in that proportion does man b· its master.
	380– 2	b· a fever case, which ends in a belief called
	397–30	b· more manly or womanly.
	409– 7	the more prolific it is likely to b· in sin and
	420–16	ready to b· receptive to the new idea.
	422– 9	the book will b· the physician,
	428–27	man's immortality will b· more apparent,
	431–28	testifies :—. . . I have lost my healthy hue and b·
	432–17	Judge asks if . . . it is possible for man to b·
t	455–32	the more impossible it will b· for
r	467–11	Mankind will b· perfect in proportion as this
g	523–27	The different accounts b· more and more closely
	524–16	Did the . . . infinite Principle b· a finite deity,
	524–20	How then could a material organization b· the
	524–21	How could the non-intelligent b· the medium of
	525– 1	Does Mind, God, enter matter to b· there a
	528– 1	Was it requisite. . .that dust should b· sentient,
	528–25	Afterwards he is supposed to b· the basis of
	530– 2	increases in falsehood and his days b· shorter.
	536–31	the man is b· as one of us,— Gen. 3 : 22.
	537–31	lest man should improve it and b· better ;
	545– 3	the man is b· as one of us."— Gen. 3 : 22.
	547–21	implies that the great First Cause must b·
	550– 8	God cannot b· finite, and be limited
	550– 9	Spirit cannot b· matter, nor can
	552–20	may b· wild with freedom
	553– 9	or . . . harmony will never b· the standard of
	553–32	that theory is sure to b· the signal for
	555–26	of aught that can b· imperfect.
ap	573–26	we can b· conscious, here and now, of
gl	587–17	God . . . cannot b· finite and imperfect.
	590–26	statements of the Scriptures b· clouded

becomes

sp	72–28	The joy of intercourse b· the jest of sin, when
	97– 7	the more impotent error b· as a belief.
	97–11	The more destructive matter b·, the more
	97–16	the riper it b· for destruction.
s	123– 8	reverses the order of Science . . . so that man b·
	128–12	b· more elastic, is capable of greater
	128–20	An odor b· beneficent and agreeable only
	146–11	is made the servant of Science and religion b·
	157–12	the drug b· more like the human mind than
	160– 7	the inanimate drug b· powerless.
	160–12	the heart b· as torpid as the hand.
ph	168–26	man-made systems insist that man b·
	199–13	his arm b· stronger.
f	207– 2	evil b· more apparent and obnoxious
c	263–15	He b· a general mis-creator, who
b	290–26	b· thus only when he reaches perfection.
	291–25	Mind never b· dust.
	297–29	Until belief b· faith, and faith b·
	312– 6	b· nothingness, as the sense-dream vanishes
	319–18	when it b· fairly understood that the
	327–12	and it b· his torment.
o	342–17	then there is no . . . law, and truth b·
p	377–12	Through different states of mind, the body b·
	388–23	and this b· self-evident, when we learn that
	396–16	refutation b· arduous, not because the
	400–15	This task b· easy, if you understand
	400–25	the image which b· visible to the senses.
	420–28	If it b· necessary to startle mortal mind
	424– 2	the child b· a separate, individualized
t	460–19	it b· a tedious mischief-maker.
r	467–12	perfect in proportion as this fact b· apparent,
	480– 4	Where the Spirit of God is, . . . evil b· nothing,
g	513–13	until divine Science b· the interpreter.
	524–10	God b· " a man of war,"— Exod. 15 : 3.
	531– 1	it supposes that . . . matter b· living,
	531– 6	error, . . . that non-intelligence b·
	543– 6	b·. . . . apparent at error's demise.
	544–31	It declares . . . that matter b· spiritual.
ap	565– 2	and b· the great red dragon,

becometh

m	56– 3	it b· us to fulfil all.— Matt. 3 : 15.

becoming

m	60–16	b· a barrier against vice,
sp	96–12	even now b· the arena for conflicting forces.
f	239–18	If divine Love is b· nearer, dearer,
b	297–24	and Truth, . . . is b· understood.
	324– 7	Unless the harmony and immortality of man are b·
p	395–32	would prevent the brain from b· diseased,
	406–32	b· a fool or an object of loathing ;
t	458–24	thus b· a law unto himself.

bed

sp	90–17	The looker-on sees the body in b·,
s	154–11	made to believe that he occupied a b· where
	154–15	because no cholera patient had been in that b·.
	156– 7	and yet, as she lay in her b·, the patient
ph	193– 1	Mr. Clark . . . had been confined to his b· '
p	390–17	nor laid upon a b· of suffering in payment of
	427–26	Called to the b· of death, what material remedy

bedside

ph	193–10	I went to his b·.

Beelzebub

a	28–20	saying : . . . B· is his patron.
	53– 1	casteth out devils through B·,"— Luke 11 : 15.
p	422– 2	Jesus said : "If I by B· cast out— Matt. 12 : 27
ap	564– 2	and cast out devils through B·.

Beethoven

f	213–23	This was even more strikingly true of B·,

befogged

f	205–15	B· in error (the error of believing that

befool

p	440– 6	is taught how to make sleep b· reason

before

pref	ix–23	b· a work on the subject could be
	ix–26	B· writing this work,
	xi–11	b· which sin and disease lose their
pr	1– *	b· ye ask Him.— Matt. 6 : 8.
	1–13	exalted b· they take form in words
	3– 4	Who would stand b· a blackboard, and pray
	6–23	b· he cast it out.
	8–25	that it may be laid bare b· us,
	9–15	b· we can enjoy the fruition
	11–10	demands restitution b· mortals can
	13–15	knows our need b· we tell Him
a	19–30	no other gods b· me,"— Exod. 20 : 3.
	20– 8	kingdom of God b· you."— Matt. 21 : 31.
	20–30	race that is set b· us ;"— Heb. 12 : 1.
	32–29	on the night b· his crucifixion,
	33– 9	Their Master had explained it all b·,
	35–12	They bow b· Christ, Truth,
	36– 5	sufficient suffering, either b· or after
	37– 8	falls only b· the sword of Spirit.

before

a 39–28   the interval *b·* its attainment
41– 2   into which Jesus has passed *b·* us ;
41–23   *b·* it was understood,
43– 4   his material disappearance *b·* their eyes
44– 1   *b·* the thorns can be laid aside
44–19   that he might employ his feet as *b·*.
45–29   same body that he had *b·* his crucifixion,
48–20   was silent *b·* envy and hate.
49–26   priests and rabbis, *b·* whom he
49–31   *b·* the face of the — *Lam.* 3 : 35.
50– 2   a sheep *b·* her shearers — *Isa.* 53 : 7.
50–20   *b·* the evidence of the bodily senses,
m 59–25   understanding should exist *b·* this union
64– 4   undefiled *b·* God — *Jas.* 1 : 27.
sp 76– 1   those who have gone *b·*.
76–31   must be overcome, . . . *b·* immortality appears.
82–20   *b·* the change we call death,
86–32   *b·* the artist can convey them to canvas.
87–31   forms rise *b·* us, which are
89–16   tongue grows mute which *b·* was eloquent.
96– 5   *B·* error is wholly destroyed,
97–27   all matter will disappear *b·* the
an 104–11   they say it has been discovered *b·*.
104–27   leaving the case worse than *b·*
106–24   I tell you *b·*, — *Gal.* 5 : 21.
s 110– 8   I beheld, as never *b·*,
116– 6   *b·* the corporeal human senses,
119–26   the evidence *b·* the senses
121– 4   *b·* he spake, astrography was
125–30   will find his flower *b·* its seed.
129–16   torment us *b·* the time?" — *Matt.* 8 : 29.
131– 7   false evidence *b·* the corporeal senses
137– 5   immaculate Teacher stood *b·* them,
137–26   *B·* this the impetuous disciple had
143–12   *b·* it could be considered as medicine.
161–21   she knelt *b·* a statue of Liberty,
164–14   *b·* all mankind is saved
ph 168–25   *b·* the so-called disease made its
169– 5   *b·* the patient felt the change ;
174–29   holding it *b·* the thought of both
175–29   as innocent as Adam, *b·* he
176– 3   *b·* inquisitive modern Eves took
176–11   was not paraded *b·* the imagination.
180–19   even *b·* they go to work to
181– 2   *B·* deciding that the body, matter, is
185– 7   *B·* this book was published,
187–32   a body like the one it had *b·* death.
191–20   is not mute *b·* non-intelligence,
196–28   and from the image brought *b·* the mind ;
198–15   is formed *b·* one sees a doctor
198–15   *b·* the doctor undertakes to
199–30   fear must have disappeared *b·* the
f 213–30   *B·* human knowledge dipped to its
214– 6   evidence *b·* his material senses,
215–20   flee as phantoms of error *b·* truth
219–18   *b·* it can be made manifest on the body,
222–30   and eat what is set *b·* you,
226–22   I saw *b·* me the sick,
226–29   I saw *b·* me the awful conflict,
233–11   *b·* we arrive at the demonstration of
234–14   avoid casting pearls *b·* those who
234–25   Sin and disease must be thought *b·* they
237– 7   It might have been months or years *b·*
237–13   snatches away the good seed *b·* it
238– 1   not rightly valued *b·* they are understood.
238–27   People with mental work *b·* them
245– 9   she stood daily *b·* the window
247–20   *b·* they are perceived humanly.
248–15   What is the model *b·* mortal mind?
248–21   The world is holding it *b·* your gaze
251– 4   should not grow more painful *b·* it suppurates,
251– 5   neither should a fever become more severe *b·*
251–29   *b·* we can attain harmony.
254– 9   *b·* the spiritual facts of existence are
c 264– 2   *b·* the permanent facts and their
264–14   which *b·* were invisible,
265–25   *b·* we discover what belongs to
b 272– 3   *b·* Truth can be understood.
272–18   your pearls *b·* swine." — *Matt.* 7 : 6.
280–19   no other gods *b·* me !" — *Exod.* 20 : 3.
290– 4   are not in the least understood *b·*
290– 7   as material as *b·* the transition,
297–13   that disappears which *b·* seemed real
303–31   *b·* the material senses yielded to
314–21   presented to her, more than ever *b·*,
317–13   *b·* it hated you ;" — *John* 15 : 18.
317–23   had loved *b·* the tragedy on Calvary.
320–32   in celestial perfection *b·* Elohim,
321– 9   Moses fled *b·* it ;
322– 8   *b·* harmonious and immortal man
322–10   *b·* this recognition of divine Science
324–17   certainly *b·* we can reach the goal
333–19   *b·* and after the Christian era,
333–29   "*B·* Abraham was, — *John* 8 : 58.
334–19   *b·* the human Jesus was incarnate

before

b 340–15   no other gods *b·* me." — *Exod.* 20 : 3.
o 350–26   *b·* the Science of being can be demonstrated.
356– 3   *b·* the spiritual fact is attained.
p 363–27   *b·* she anointed them with the oil.
365–18   like dew *b·* the morning sunshine.
368– 5   Error is a coward *b·* Truth.
368– 7   nearer than ever *b·* to the apprehension
371–17   *b·* he can get rid of the illusive
372–25   shall deny me *b·* men, — *Matt.* 10 : 33.
372–26   deny *b·* my Father — *Matt.* 10 : 33.
374–11   *b·* it is consciously apparent on the
384–29   the evidence *b·* the senses
384–30   *b·* the divine rights of intelligence,
389–26   This belief totters to its falling *b·* the
396–12   *b·* a crisis is passed.
397–32   You will understand . . . better than *b·*.
400– 5   must be held in subjection *b·* its
400–13   *b·* it has taken tangible shape in
415–28   *B·* the thoughts are fully at rest,
417–18   The evidence *b·* the corporeal senses
418–32   flee *b·* the light of Truth.
· 426– 6   when she has the high goal always *b·* her
427–11   *b·* Life can be understood
427–17   the same after as *b·* a bone is broken
429– 8   We look *b·* our feet, and
429–19   If man did not exist *b·* the
429–22   must have lived *b·* birth,
434–13   to appear *b·* the bar of Justice
437– 9   the Judge of our higher tribunal,
437–10   *b·* its jurors, the Spiritual Senses,
440– 5   *b·* the supreme bar of Spirit
440– 7   *b·* sacrificing mortals to their false gods.
441–33   *b·* the tribunal of divine Spirit.
t 452– 5   *b·* it has a chance to manifest itself.
453–14   *b·* he can know others and
461–13   because Science reverses the evidence *b·* the
464–24   ignorance, envy, fall *b·* an honest heart.
r 467– 4   no other gods *b·* me." — *Exod.* 20 : 3.
471– 7   evidence *b·* the five corporeal senses,
480–31   As vapor melts *b·* the sun,
480–32   would vanish *b·* the reality of good.
486–15   the same immediately after death as *b·*.
487– 5   both *b·* and after that which is called death.
492– 3   there should be but one fact *b·* the
k 499– *   *I have set b· thee an* — *Rev.* 3 : 8.
g 509–24   *b·* it was in the earth." — *Gen.* 2 : 5.
515–28   compare man *b·* the mirror to his
520–19   *b·* it was in the earth, — *Gen.* 2 : 5.
520–20   herb of the field *b·* it — *Gen.* 2 : 5.
521–29   opposite of scientific truth as *b·* recorded.
526– 4   *b·* it was in the earth." — *Gen.* 2 : 5.
532–19   *b·* Truth, error shrank abashed
535–13   other creations must go down *b·* C. S.
543–17   evidence *b·* the material senses.
548–12   *b·* Life is spiritually learned.
549– 5   after it has grown to maturity, if not *b·*,
553–17   Adam was created *b·* Eve.
553–29   *b·* they think or know aught of their
556–27   *b·* it cares to solve the problem of
ap 563–25   stood *b·* the woman — *Rev.* 12 : 4.
564–21   *b·* the tribunal of so-called mortal mind,
566–10   moves *b·* them, a pillar of cloud
566–17   Her fathers' God *b·* her moved,
568–17   *b·* our God day and night. — *Rev.* 12 : 10.
568–27   than has ever *b·* reached high heaven,
578–13   prepareth a table *b·* me — *see Psal.* 23 : 5.
gl 579– *   *I have set b· thee an* — *Rev.* 3 : 8.
585–20   human belief *b·* it accepts sin,
593– 5   *b·* the conscious facts of spiritual Truth.
595–14   when he went *b·* Jehovah,
595–19   TIME. . . . that which begins *b·*, and

beforehand

p 396–10   Never say *b·* how much you have to

began

pref viii–28   As early as 1862 she *b·* to write down and
ix– 1   She also *b·* to jot down her thoughts on the
s 133–15   when . . . their demoralization *b·*.
156–14   *b·* to fear an aggravation of symptoms
ph 200– 2   Pagan worship *b·* with muscularity,
f 245–32   The infinite never *b·* nor will it ever end.
249–15   God is the infinite, and infinity never *b·*,
p 429–20   before the material organization *b·*,
g 532–27   error *b·* and will end the dream of matter.
534–26   since the Christian era *b·*.
557–23   as if he *b·* materially right,

begets

ph 169–12   faith in rules of health or in drugs *b·*
g 550–26   A serpent never *b·* a bird,

begin

f 234–19   We must *b·* with this so-called mind and
246–27   and *b·* the demonstration thereof.
252– 8   they *b·* to disappear.
254–13   but to *b·* aright and to continue the strife

begin

c 258–32	and thus b· to comprehend in Science
262–28	To b· rightly is to end rightly.
262–29	Every concept which seems to b· with the
b 275–11	you must b· by reckoning God as the
283– 1	As mortals b· to understand Spirit, they
322–29	Then we b· to learn Life in divine Science.
p 411–27	Always b· your treatment by allaying the
429– 4	We must b·, however, with the more simple
429– 6	and the sooner we b· the better.
r 467–30	we b· with Mind, which must be understood
g 531–26	Does Life b· with Mind or with matter?
549–14	successive generations do not b· with the

beginning

and end

b 282– 8	which has both b· and end.
338– 5	belief— that man . . . has b· and end,
gl 580–22	supposition that Life . . . has b· and end ;

any

p 429–23	for if Life ever had any b·,

from the

sp 89–31	"a murderer from the b·."— John 8 : 44.
ph 186–32	human mind has been an idolater from the b·,
b 268– *	That which was from the b·,— I John 1 : 1.
292–23	a murderer from the b·,— John 8 : 44.
296–31	Mortal belief is a liar from the b·,
p 409–23	are counterfeits from the b·,
441–33	"a murderer from the b·."— John 8 : 44.
r 476–16	They were, from the b· of mortal history,
g 539– 3	"a murderer from the b·."— John 8 : 44.
ap 564–29	From the b· to the end, the serpent
567–26	he must be a lie from the b·.
580–31	a murderer from the b·,— John 8 : 44.

in the

an 103– 9	As in the b·, however, this liberation
s 140–28	In the b· God created man
ph 188– 6	is an unconscious error in the b·,
b 308– 7	belief will be afraid as it was in the b·,
p 379– 3	announced as partners in the b·,
r 479–18	"In the b· God created the— Gen. 1 : 1.
g 502–22	In the b· God created the— Gen. 1 : 1.
531–15	If, in the b·, man's body originated in

its

t 463–15	Its b· will be meek, its growth sturdy,

no

b 307–25	Truth has no b·.
g 502–24	The infinite has no b·.

of the Old Testament

g 501– 2	starts with the b· of the Old Testament,

of the world

s 129–14	not since the b· of the world ;"— Matt. 24 : 21.

of wisdom

p 373–16	fear of the Lord is the b· of wisdom,"— Psal. 111 : 10.

scientific

f 219–31	this scientific b· is in the right direction.

this word

g 502–24	This word b· is employed to signify the only,

to end

s 139– 4	From b· to end, the Scriptures are full of
r 478–24	From b· to end, whatever is mortal
ap 559–21	Read this book from b· to end.

with Genesis

g 502– 1	A second necessity for b· with Genesis is

without

f 253– 6	life, without b· and without end,
b 282– 7	represents the infinite without b· or end ;
333–18	without b· of years or end of days.
p 399–32	without b· with so-called mortal mind,
r 468–27	Life is without b· and without end.
g 521– 5	narrative of being that is without b· or end..
gl 585– 6	which are likewise without b· or end.

b 331– 9	falsely testifies to a b· and an end.
r 469– 1	If Life ever had a b·, it would also have
g 528–19	B· creation with darkness instead of
538–28	As both mortal man and sin have a b·,
550–17	as b· and ending, and with birth, decay,
gl 585–23	Eve. A b· ; mortality ;
592– 4	the belief that life has a b·

beginnings

p 384–14	will prove to himself, by small b·,

begins

m 57–29	and b· to unfold its wings for heaven.
f 216–12	b· at once to destroy the errors of mortal sense
c 262–30	concept which seems to begin with the brain b· falsely.
b 297–23	in which spiritual evidence, . . . b· to appear,
p 410–29	Christian scientific practice b· with
r 476– 3	declares that man b· in dust or as
g 529–31	b· his reign over man somewhat mildly,
539– 3	Error b· by reckoning life as separate
544–31	Error b· with corporeality as the producer
550–11	ends, even as it b·, in nameless nothingness?
gl 595–19	that which b· before, . . . what is termed death,

begotten

c 257–19	"who hath b· the drops of dew,"— Job 38 : 28.
b 282–30	for it is not b· of the Father.
325–24	But he, who is b· of the beliefs of the

beguiled

g 533–28	She says, "The serpent b· me,— Gen. 3 : 13.

beguiles

g 533–14	first voluble lie, which b· the woman

begun

sp 96–22	This mental fermentation has b·,
b 326–18	You have b· at the numeration-table of C. S.,

behalf

pr 12–27	Does Deity interpose in b· of one worshipper,
f 226– 5	The voice of God in b· of the African slave
p 364– 5	to lay down his mortal existence in b· of
389– 3	given in b· of the control of Mind over
431–11	arrested Mortal Man in b· of the state
t 455–13	to use the energies of Mind in your own b·,

behavior

p 441– 8	to give heavy bonds for good b·.

beheaded

s 136–27	"John have I b· : but who is this?"— Luke 9 : 9.

beheld

a 45–23	b· the final proof of all that he had taught,
s 110– 8	Thus it was that I b·, as never before,
c 259–16	then mortals have never b· in man the
b 326–23	Saul of Tarsus b· the way— the Christ, or
326–30	He b· for the first time the true idea of Love,
r 476–32	Jesus b· in Science the perfect man,
478– 5	never b· Spirit or Soul leaving a body or
ap 561– 9	The Revelator b· the spiritual idea
gl 583– 8	some of the ideas of God b· as men,

behest

iii– *	This is Thy high b· :
g 533– 2	Had he lost man's rich inheritance and God's b·,

behests

r 495–29	and follow the b· of God,

behind

pr 7– 2	"Get thee b· me, Satan."— Matt. 16 : 23.
s 138– 4	lay b· Peter's confession of the
b 299– 1	It has b· it no more reality than
o 353–24	those things which are b·."— Phil. 3 : 13.
p 362–15	to come b· the couch
g 542– 6	Though error hides b· a lie

behold

pref vii–11	The Wisemen were led to b· and to follow
a 39–18	b·, now is the day of salvation,"— II Cor. 6 : 2.
sp 93– 7	"B·, now is the accepted time ;— II Cor. 6 : 2.
93– 8	b·, now is the day of salvation,"— II Cor. 6 : 2.
ph 190–28	As for me, I will b· Thy face—Psal. 17 : 15.
f 243–23	"of purer eyes than to b· evil,"— Hab. 1 : 13.
c 264– 5	sometimes b· in the camera of divine Mind,
264–29	we shall b· and understand God's creation,
b 280–19	b· the zeal of belief to establish the
334–27	b·, I am alive for evermore,— Rev. 1 : 18.
o 346–18	"fraught with falsities painful to b·"?
347–13	they would b· the signs of Christ's coming.
347–28	mortals will b· the nothingness of sickness
357– 5	"of purer eyes than to b· evil."— Hab. 1 : 13.
360–26	B·, He putteth no trust in— see Job 4 : 18.
p 438– 5	B·, I give unto you power— Luke 10 : 19.
k 499– *	b·, I have set before thee an open— Rev. 3 : 8.
g 517–21	Who shall b· it?
518– 5	And God said, B·, I have given— Gen. 1 : 29.
518–25	and, b·, it was very good.— Gen. 1 : 31.
525–24	"and, b·, it was very good."— Gen. 1 : 31.
534– 3	and to b· at the sepulchre the risen Saviour,
536–31	B·, the man is become as— Gen. 3 : 22.
545– 3	"B·, the man is become as— Gen. 3 : 22.
ap 562–30	and b· a great red dragon,— Rev. 12 : 3.
574–22	at last lifted the seer to b· the great city,
574–26	and you will b· the soft-winged dove
575– 2	and b· the Lamb's wife,— Love wedded to
gl 579– *	b·, I have set before thee an open— Rev. 3 : 8.
585–11	of whatever the material senses b· ;

beholding

m 65–16	B· the world's lack of Christianity
b 323– 9	B· the infinite tasks of truth,
g 528–22	B· the creations of his own dream
ap 573– 4	b· what the eye cannot see,

beholds

pref vii– 2	wakeful shepherd b· the first
sp 95–26	when he b· the light which heralds
98– 4	prophet of to-day b· in the mental horizon
s 126– 5	when man b· himself God's reflection,
r 479–10	image of mortal thought, . . . is all that the eye b·.
ap 563–16	and b· its awful character ;
571–26	thoughts which he b· in mortal mind.

Being
Divine
pr 3–12 The Divine *B·* must be reflected by man,
o 357–18 false notions about the Divine *B·*
omnipresent
r 466– 1 omniscient, and omnipresent *B·*,
Supreme
sp 93–23 the name of the Supreme *B·*.
s 117– 9 the Supreme *B·* or His manifestation ;
127–18 Supreme *B·*, Mind, exempt from all evil.
f 202–24 Our beliefs about a Supreme *B·* contradict
b 285–22 the Supreme *B·*, or divine Principle,'
g 523–18 the Supreme *B·* is therein called Elohim.
524– 8 They called the Supreme *B·* by the
527–29 Is the Supreme *B·* retrograding,

b 290– 1 Life is the everlasting I ᴀᴍ, the *B·*

being
actuality of
b 296–16 spiritual sense, and the actuality of *b·*.
all
s 131– 5 God, the divine Principle of all *b·*.
f 244– 1 God is good and the fount of all *b·*,
b 302–22 God, the divine Principle of all *b·*,
p 407–23 In Science, all *b·* is eternal,
414–27 God, in whom all *b·* is painless and permanent.
t 460– 7 the nature and essence of all *b·*,
g 528– 1 all *b·* is the reflection of the eternal Mind,
ambiguities of
s 114–27 disentangles the interlaced ambiguities of *b·*,
and Deity
g 554– 6 *b·* and Deity are inseparable.
basis of
p 414–21 rests on the Christianly scientific basis of *b·*.
cannot be lost
f 215– 6 *b·* cannot be lost while God exists.
capacities of
ph 200– 6 illustrated the grand human capacities of *b·*
celestial
a 26–17 to reveal the Science of celestial *b·*,
b 337–18 and perfection is the order of celestial *b·*
charms of
f 247–29 are poor substitutes for the charms of *b·*,
circumference of
f 204– 1 is at once the centre and circumference of *b·*.
circumference of his
c 262–16 the absolute centre and circumference of his *b·*.
coexists with
f 246–12 radiant sun of virtue and truth coexists with *b·*.
conception of
sp 84–24 true conception of *b·* destroys the belief of
s 148–12 instead of from the highest, conception of *b·*.
c 260–12 seen as the only true conception of *b·*.
b 324–29 which is the true conception of *b·*,
concord of
s 129–26 or learn from discord the concord of *b·*?
consciousness of
c 261–28 you will rise to the spiritual consciousness of *b·*,
continuity of
s 123–29 the scientific order and continuity of *b·*.
corporeal
sp 71–31 a corporeal *b·*, a finite form,
s 140– 4 That God is a corporeal *b·*, nobody can truly
b 309– 2 for the messenger was not a corporeal *b·*,
ap 577– 8 God as Father-Mother, not as a corporeal *b·*.
deflection of
g 502–11 This deflection of *b·*, rightly viewed, serves to
demonstration of man's
b 290– 3 Principle, rule, and demonstration of man's *b·*
divine Principle of
g 530– 6 sustained by God, the divine Principle of *b·*.
economy of
p 423–25 Both. . .are now at work in the economy of *b·*
entire
s 151–27 the entire *b·* is found harmonious
eternal
f 232– 8 the claims of harmonious and eternal *b·*
g 521– 3 spiritual harmony and eternal *b·*.
fact of
f 228– 5 if this great fact of *b·* were learned,
249–26 night-dream is sometimes nearer the fact of *b·*
b 285– 5 the great fact of *b·* for time and eternity.
320–18 text declares plainly the spiritual fact of *b·*,
facts of
s 120– 9 arrive at the fundamental facts of *b·*.
147–22 enables you to grasp the spiritual facts of *b·* ;
f 221–18 beliefs of mortals, and not the facts of *b·* ;
242–22 the facts of *b·* are commonly misconstrued,
b 279–18 the immortal facts of *b·* are seen,
293–16 perpetuating the eternal facts of *b·*.
312– 3 reversed by the spiritual facts of *b·*
315–22 enabled him to demonstrate the facts of *b·*,
323– 3 not . . . glean from C. S. the facts of *b·* without
p 370– 4 gather the facts of *b·* from the divine Mind.
428–10 in order that the spiritual facts of *b·* may

being
facts of
p 428–28 and the immortal facts of *b·* are admitted.
r 471– 9 afford no indication of the grand facts of *b·* ;
491–12 cannot connect mortals with the. . . facts of *b·*,
g 546–24 facts of *b·*, . . . shine in the darkness,
ap 574–12 became conscious of the spiritual facts of *b·*
gl 584–16 for it contradicts the spiritual facts of *b·*.
functions of
p 387–14 faithfully perform the natural functions of *b·*.
glorified
b 291–11 not . . . death will awaken them to glorified *b·*.
God's
r 470–24 Man is the expression of God's *b·*.
481– 3 God's *b·* is infinity, freedom, harmony,
happiness of
m 60–26 not discerning the true happiness of *b·*,
b 286– 1 relates most nearly to the happiness of *b·*.
harmonious
m 68–32 the unbroken links of eternal, harmonious *b·*
p 376–24 the true facts in regard to harmonious *b·*,
412–25 Realize . . . the fact of harmonious *b·*,
harmony of
(*see* **harmony**)
his original
sp 97–20 in the likeness of Spirit, his original *b·*.
human
pr 2–20 as one pleads with a human *b·*,
sp 82–27 as it would be between a mole and a human *b·*.
idea of (*see also* **true idea of**)
a 55– 8 the healing Christ and spiritual idea of *b·*.
r 477–17 the immortal idea of *b·*, indestructible
identity of
r 475–17 conscious identity of *b·* as found in Science,
image of His
b 313–22 and an image of His *b·*."—*see* Heb. 1 : 3.
immortal
ph 178–27 understanding of the status of immortal *b·*.
190–18 it never merges into immortal *b·*,
p 420–32 harmonious facts of Soul and immortal *b·*.
individual
p 427– 5 Man's individual *b·* can no more die nor
infinite
ph 189–24 constantly ascend in infinite *b·*.
is eternal
s 122–27 Life goes on unchanged and *b·* is eternal.
is holiness
r 492– 7 *B·* is holiness, harmony, immortality.
is immortal
g 554– 6 because *b·* is immortal, like Deity,
is Spirit
a 29–26 the full recognition that *b·* is Spirit.
is sustained
f 221–22 Science, in which *b·* is sustained by God,
keynote of
f 240–14 and you lose the keynote of *b·*,
law of
ph 186–27 and if so, harmony cannot be the law of *b·*.
r 485–22 by fulfilling the spiritual law of *b·*,
law of his
m 63–11 and Life is the law of his *b·*.
Life and
an 103–31 Life and *b·* are of God.
o 355–13 the harmonious and true sense of Life and *b·*
material
ph 172–11 this supposed chain of material *b·*.
172–15 If man was first a material *b·*,
mysteries of
sp 90–29 improve our time in solving the mysteries of *b·*
narrative of
g 521– 4 inspired record closes its narrative of *b·*
one's
m 60– 2 Science inevitably lifts one's *b·* higher
our
f 208– 6 and move, and have our *b·*."— *Acts* 17 : 28.
c 264–12 in whom we have our *b·*.
o 361–20 and move, and have our *b·*."— *Acts* 17 : 28.
p 381–19 we live, move, and have our *b·* in
g 536–13 and move, and have our *b·*,"— *Acts* 17 : 28.
perfection of
f 253– 2 The beauty of holiness, the perfection of *b·*,
perpetuates
f 235–23 divine Truth which is Life and perpetuates *b·*,
possibilities of
f 203–14 brings out the possibilities of *b·*,
Principle of
pr 6–16 we must understand the divine Principle of *b·*.
a 25–19 demonstrated . . . the Principle of *b·*.
b 286–10 [the divine Principle of *b·*]
gl 579–11 faith in the divine Life and...Principle of *b·*.
Principle of his
f 202–16 in accord with the divine Principle of his *b·*,
problem of
(*see* **problem**)

being
real
a 26–29 It was the divine Principle of all real *b·*
s 108–22 all real *b·* is in God, the divine Mind,
129–22 ontology,—"the science of real *b·*."
p 371–15 no more comprehends his real *b·* than
r 491–22 material man as never the real *b·*.
realism of
s 144–20 and is not a factor in the realism of *b·*.
realities of
f 212–29 The realities of *b·*, its normal action, and
229– 6 but if sin and suffering are realities of *b·*,
c 264–20 Spirit and . . . are the only realities of *b·*.
reality of
    (*see* **reality**)
reality or
g 538–14 is significant of eternal reality or *b·*.
recognition of
ap 573–25 such a recognition of *b·* is, . . . possible
Science of
    (*see* **Science**)
scientific
f 233–12 the demonstration of scientific *b·*,
c 259–12 The Christlike understanding of scientific *b·*
b 271– 2 chain of scientific *b·* reappearing in all ages,
332– 2 indicate the divine Principle of scientific *b·*,
r 494–24 unbroken reality of scientific *b·*.
scientific statement of
r 468– 8 What is the scientific statement of *b·*?
sense of
a 41– 7 into the spiritual sense of *b·*.
55– 1 any other sense of *b·* and religion than theirs?
ph 172–14 only as the false sense of *b·* disappears.
191–13 the spiritual sense of *b·*
c 265–10 This spiritual sense of *b·*, forsaking matter
b 295–14 the real sense of *b·*, perfect and forever intact,
298–24 and to the spiritual sense of *b·*.
309– 5 gave him the spiritual sense of *b·*
r 490–26 ushers in the spiritual sense of *b·*,
g 545–22 entertained a false sense of *b·*.
548–17 true ideas of God, the spiritual sense of *b·*.
550–12 The true sense of *b·* and its eternal perfection
solution of
b 314– 8 Our Master gained the solution of *b·*,
source of
m 63–10 Spirit is his primitive and ultimate source of *b·* ;
f 213–32 the one Mind and true source of *b·*,
spiritual
    (*see* **spiritual**)
star of
pref vii–10 and shine the guiding star of *b·*.
state of
r 476–14 They never had a perfect state of *b·*,
superabundance of
f 201–11 superabundance of *b·* is on the side of God,
true
s 126– 9 never projected the least portion of true *b·*.
129–19 are antagonistic to true *b·*
r 496–19 overlying, and encompassing all true *b·*.
true idea of
b 325– 8 Jesus gave the true idea of *b·*,
o 353–29 true idea of *b·* is spiritual and immortal,
truth of
    (*see* **truth**)
understanding of
f 211–12 in the spiritual understanding of *b·*?
b 330– 2 understanding of *b·* supersedes mere belief.
r 495–22 Let C. S.,. . .support your understanding of *b·*,
universal
g 519– 9 the ideas of God in universal *b·*
verities of
p 397–24 familiar with the great verities of *b·*.
verity of
p 414–26 Keep in mind the verity of *b·*,
r 468– 7 for sin is not the eternal verity of *b·*.
will be recognized
sp 90–12 *b·* will be recognized as spiritual,
will be understood
sp 91–13 his genuine *b·* will be understood.
f 214–16 *b·* will be understood and found to be
your
f 227–29 and defaced the tablet of your *b·*.

sp 76– 6 When *b·* is understood, Life will
76–26 constitutes . . . man, whose *b·* is spiritual.
s 151–18 Fear never stopped *b·* and its action.
f 215– 4 then *b·* and immortality would be lost,
228– 6 nothing inharmonious can enter *b·*,
244–20 If man . . . springs from matter into *b·*,
247–19 *B·* possesses its qualities before they
c 265– 7 must near the broader interpretations of *b·*,
b 275–10 To grasp the reality and order of *b·*
275–14 All substance, intelligence, wisdom, *b·*,
279–28 there are not two bases of *b·*,
292– 5 compass the heights and depths of *b·*
305– 8 Man, . . . reflects the central light of *b·*,

being
o 351–21 especially if we consider Satan as a *b·* coequal
361–18 Father and son, are one in *b·*.
p 416–32 Teach them that their *b·* is sustained by
g 531–14 will recognize his God-given dominion and *b·*.
being (*ppr.*)
pr 3– 1 without *b·* reminded of His province.
a 21–25 *B·* in sympathy with matter,
45–12 *b·* reconciled, we shall be saved— *Rom.* 5 : 10.
m 68– 3 for fear of *b·* thought ridiculous.
sp 72–21 God, good, *b·* ever present, it follows
75–29 the moment when the link . . . is *b·* sundered.
81–18 Man . . . cannot help *b·* immortal,
98–29 and *b·* practical and complete,
an 102– 4 Its basis *b·* a belief and this belief
s 113–18 God, Spirit, *b·* all, nothing is matter.
124– 1 *b·* based on Truth, the Principle of
126–17 Shall Science explain cause and effect as *b·*
142–28 God *b·* All-in-all, He made medicine ; but
145– 2 without *b·* able to explain them.
163–23 we cannot help *b·* disgusted with
ph 168–27 Disease *b·* a belief, a latent illusion
184– 2 The premises *b·* erroneous,
f 203– 7 If God were understood instead of *b·* merely
206–17 Spirit, not matter, *b·* the source of supply.
209– 1 Man, *b·* immortal, has a perfect . . . life.
210–25 What is termed matter, *b·* unintelligent,
222–22 far from *b·* the image and likeness of
230–31 *b·* the remote, predisposing, and
237– 3 On *b·* questioned about it
250–30 not *b·* at the mercy of death,
254– 8 To stop eating, drinking, or *b·* clothed
c 257–13 is very far from *b·* the supposed substance of
b 279–12 and they have the advantage of *b·* eternal.
280–27 *b·* perpetual in His own individuality,
287–14 God *b·* everywhere and all-inclusive,
293–19 the great difference *b·* that electricity is not
295–12 but infinite Spirit *b·* all,
308–22 and Truth, *b·* thereby understood,
313–21 "Who, *b·* a brightness from His— *see Heb.* 1 : 3.
314–31 as *b·* in supposed accord with the
315–30 *b·* conceived by a human mother,
316– 4 The real man *b·* linked by Science to
325– 4 is *b·* ushered into the undying realities of
334–31 Spirit *b·* God, there is but one Spirit,
335–16 Soul and Spirit *b·* one,
337–27 *b·* the opposite of the real or the spiritual
339– 3 *B·* destroyed, sin needs no other
339– 9 evil, *b·* contrary to good,
o 341–14 cannot prevent that from *b·* scientific
p 363–12 they were wondering why, *b·* a prophet,
413–26 that mind *b·* laden with illusions
430–27 evidence for the prosecution *b·* called for,
433– 1 testimony for the plaintiff, . . . *b·* closed,
438– 9 Instead of *b·* a ruler in the Province of
t 455– 7 Hence the necessity of *b·* right yourself
r 472– 9 Sickness, sin, and death, *b·* inharmonious,
477– 7 Soul, *b·* Spirit, is seen in nothing imperfect
479–31 *b·* understood by the things that— *Rom.* 1 : 20.
g 504– 6 questions as to the divine creation *b·*
506– 4 matter, not *b·* the reflection of Spirit,
513–27 So-called mortal mind— *b·* non-existent
516– 3 so you, *b·* spiritual, are the reflection
525–10 the primary sense *b· image, form ;*
544– 6 Mind, instead of matter, *b·* the producer,
557–25 *b·* in accordance with the first chapter of the
ap 562–22 And she *b·* with child cried,— *Rev.* 12 : 2.
567–25 therefore, in his pretence of *b·* a talker,
fr 600– * *b· fruitful in every good work,— Col.* 1 : 10.

beings
all
t 460– 4 necessary constituents and relations of all *b·*,"
corporeal
sp 70–10 supposition that corporeal *b·* are spirits,
entities and
f 204– 8 antagonistic entities and *b·*,
exalted
g 513– 7 lead on to spiritual spheres and exalted *b·*.
human
b 298–25 Angels are not etherealized human *b·*,
inhabited by
sp 91– 3 inhabited by *b·* under the control of supreme
mortal
g 554– 5 nor are there properly any mortal *b·*,
spiritual
c 264–32 universe of Spirit is peopled with spiritual *b·*
upward-soaring
b 299–12 These upward-soaring *b·* never lead towards
Belial
ph 171–24 than between *B·* and Christ.
f 216–26 "What concord hath Christ with *B·*?"—
    II Cor. 6 : 15.
g 539–26 what concord hath Christ with *B·*?"—
    II Cor. 6 : 15.

belied

an 104– 6   and *b·* by wolves in sheep's clothing.

belief

abandonment of a
  p 374–31   expels it through the abandonment of a *b·*,
abandon the
  g 534– 1   Hence she is first to abandon the *b·* in the
according to
  ph 168–10   When sick (according to *b·*)
  170– 1   according to *b·*, poisons the human system.
  183– 8   Can the agriculturist, according to *b·*,
  p 425– 7   the leading points included (according to *b·*)
aches again in
  f 212– 3   sometimes aches again in *b·*,
acute
  f 247– 1   acute *b·* of physical life comes on at a remote
all
  s 116–16   even to the extinction of all *b·* in matter,
  o 353–22   we must yield up all *b·* in it and be wise.
  p 418– 4   depends on mentally destroying all *b·* in
  g 556– 7   destroys forever all *b·* in
ancient
  ap 567–18   That false claim—that ancient *b·*,
another
  r 491–20   this belief culminates in another *b·*,
arise from the
  sp 94–15   arise from the *b·* that the infinite is
  p 421– 4   physical ailments . . . arise from the *b·* that
ask how
  g 553–31   you may also ask how *b·* can affect
banish the
  p 391– 9   Banish the *b·* that you can possibly
basis of
  p 424– 6   and we must leave the mortal basis of *b·*
believer and
  r 487–18   The believer and *b·* are one and are mortal.
bestows
  r 488–22   apart from what *b·* bestows upon them,
better
  p 442–21   changes a belief of sin . . . into a better *b·*,
blind
  pr 12–11   which acts through blind *b·*,
  12–23   The common custom . . . finds help in blind *b·*
  a 34–22   dulness and blind *b·* in God
  sp 83–10   a blind *b·* without understanding,
  s 124– 4   a law of mortal mind, a blind *b·*,
  132–21   blind *b·* shuts the door upon it,
blindness of
  r 486–18   Alas for the blindness of *b·*, which
called death
  p 380– 2   fever case, which ends in a *b·* called death,
change of
  ph 169– 1   change of *b·* from a material to a spiritual
changes in
  pr 12–24   Changes in *b·* may go on indefinitely,
change the
  p 398–27   change the *b·* of disease to a
  r 491– 5   Change the *b·*, and the sensation changes.
chronic
  f 247– 2   is not so disastrous as the chronic *b·*.
cling to a
  f 237–26   They . . . cling to a *b·* in the life and
controlled by
  b 304–28   Controlled by *b·*, instead of understanding,
corporeal
  gl 587–21   HAM (Noah's son).   Corporeal *b·* ;
  589– 1   ISSACHAR (Jacob's son).   A corporeal *b·* ;
coupled with the
  p 389– 2   for the penalty is coupled with the *b·*.
customary
  f 229–17   This customary *b·* is misnamed material law,
darkness of
  ap 569–17   dwellers still in the deep darkness of *b·*.
defined as a
  s 129–11   Pantheism may be defined as a *b·* in the
destroys the
  a 37– 1   which destroys the *b·* called sin
  sp 84–24   true conception of being destroys the *b·* of
destroy the
  p 368–50   can destroy the *b·* in material conditions.
  375–23   Destroy the *b·*, show mortal mind that
  424–29   you must destroy the *b·* in these ills
  r 473– 7   Christ came to destroy the *b·* of sin.
  491– 6   Destroy the *b·*, and the sensation disappears.
destruction of the
  f 219–19   the destruction of the *b·* will be the
disease being a
  ph 168–27   Disease being a *b·*, a latent illusion
doctor's
  ph 198–24   moulded and formed by his doctor's *b·*
doctrine, or
  a 26–28   Our Master taught no mere . . . doctrine, or *b·*.
dream or
  r 491–22   The dream or *b·* goes on,
drive
  f 251– 8   as to drive *b·* into new paths.

belief

educated
  a 39–10   The educated *b·* that Soul is in the body
  r 489– 9   Any hypothesis which . . . is an educated *b·*.
element of the
  r 480– 8   Nerves are an element of the *b·* that
embodied in the
  sp 93–29   this is the error embodied in the *b·* that
erring
  r 472–29   seem real to human, erring *b·*,
erroneous
  ph 184–11   never honoring erroneous *b·* with the
  b 297–12   Erroneous *b·* is destroyed by truth.
  p 389– 5   every erroneous *b·*, or material condition.
  415–16   till it can master an erroneous *b·*.
  420–23   but erroneous *b·*, taken at its best,
  g 541–16   erroneous *b·* that life, substance, and
  544–28   erroneous *b·* reverses understanding and
error of
  (*see* **error**)
error of a
  a 47–32   Jesus realized the utter error of a *b·* in
  g 526–12   error of a *b·* in intelligent matter.
errors of
  sp 96–23   until all errors of *b·* yield to understanding.
  t 450–25   knows that they are errors of *b·*,
evolves, in
  s 108–27   this false sense evolves, in *b·*, a
experiences of
  b 322–26   The sharp experiences of *b·* in the
faith and
  pr 12–18   borrows its power from human faith and *b·*.
false
  sp 97–14   The nearer a false *b·* approaches truth
  an 103–20   the false *b·* that mind is in matter,
  ph 168–14   through just this false *b·*.
  184–17   Whatever is governed by a false *b·*
  194– 8   When one's false *b·* is corrected,
  f 222–32   We must destroy the false *b·* that
  b 283–21   false *b·* as to what really constitutes life
  297–14   seemed real to this false *b·*,
  298– 5   false *b·* silences for a while the voice of
  298– 6   false *b·* cannot destroy Science
  304– 3   It is ignorance and false *b·*,
  o 346–24   hence pain in matter is a false *b·*,
  p 370– 4   turn from the lie of false *b·* to Truth,
  376–22   destroy the patient's false *b·* by
  379–14   he would have risen above the false *b·*.
  383–27   the illusive physical effect of a false *b·*,
  393–30   A false *b·* is both the tempter and the tempted,
  r 480–24   Evil is a false *b·*.
  g 546– 1   false *b·* that spirit is now submerged in
  557–10   human propagation . . . is a false *b·*.
  gl 582– 7   pride ; envy ; fame ; illusion ; a false *b·* ;
finite
  b 280– 9   Finite *b·* can never do justice to Truth
  280–10   Finite *b·* limits all things,
  322–12   that finite *b·* may be prepared to relinquish
  gl 585–24   a finite *b·* concerning life, substance, and
formed by education
  ph 194–30   material sense . . . a *b·* formed by education
forms of
  g 531– 4   in all the subsequent forms of *b·*.
freed from the
  ph 178–24   freed from the *b·* of heredity,
fulfils
  b 297–32   A mortal *b·* fulfils its own conditions.
general
  s 155– 4   it is the law of a general *b·*,
  155–11   When the general *b·* endorses the inanimate
  155–11   This erroneous general *b·*, which
  g 554–29   general *b·* that the lower animals are less sickly
give up the
  b 283– 2   they give up the *b·* that there is
  p 397–28   Give up the *b·* that mind is,
her
  sp 89– 9   Destroy her *b·* in outside aid,
  89–10   The former limits of her *b·* return.
  ph 185– 4   changed the action of her *b·* on the lungs,
  f 245–23   bodily results of her *b·* that she was young
  p 379–21   from her *b·* that blood is destroying her life.
  379–23   her *b·* produces the very results she dreads.
  389–29   In her *b·* . . . had chronic liver-complaint,
his
  ph 197–31   his *b·* in its reality and fatality will harm his
  199–27   His *b·* that he could do it gave
  b 325– 2   loses his *b·* in death.
  o 346–23   there is no reality in his *b·* of pain,
  p 425–21   God is more to a man than his *b·*
human
  (*see* **human**)
illusion of
  r 490–31   Under the mesmeric illusion of *b·*,
improved
  b 296–28   An improved *b·* is one step out of error,

belief

improved
  p 442–19 An improved *b·* cannot retrograde.
in a bodily soul
  c 257– 9 it is the *b·* in a bodily soul and
in a diseased brain
  p 421– 2 insanity implies *b·* in a diseased brain,
in a human doctrine
  b 286– 2 To seek Truth through *b·* in a human doctrine
in a material basis
  b 268– 6 *B·* in a material basis, from which
in a self-made
  b 282–10 a *b·* in a self-made and temporary
in consumption
  p 375–32 *b·* in consumption presents to mortal thought
in death
  (*see* **death**)
in disease
  s 145–12 Christ, Truth, subdues the human *b·* in disease.
  p 377–31 It is latent *b·* in disease, as well as
  414– 2 the foundations of the *b·* in disease
  419– 3 or even create the *b·* in disease.
  r 482–31 mortal mind . . . causes the *b·* in disease.
in error
  b 297–27 A belief in Truth is better than a *b·* in error,
in evil
  g 540– 7 stirring up the *b·* in evil to its utmost,
in feebleness
  f 219–17 for the *b·* in feebleness must obtain in
in illusion
  g 555–32 not the *b·* in illusion or error.
in many gods
  gl 591– 2 mythology,— *b·* in many gods,
in material life
  pr 6–13 until *b·* in material life and sin is destroyed.
  g 533–23 *b·* in material life and intelligence is
in material origins
  f 213–31 into *b·* in material origins
in material suffering
  p 405–30 *B·* in material suffering causes mortals to
in matter
  gl 581–10 understanding . . . destroying *b·* in matter.
in "original sin"
  gl 579–15 a falsity ; the *b·* in "original sin,"
in other gods
  g 535–12 A *b·* in other gods, other creators,
in pain
  s 153–19 The boil simply manifests, . . . a *b·* in pain,
  153–24 that is, its own *b·* in pain.
in sickness
  pr 12– 9 casting out a *b·* in sickness.
  14–15 If suffering from a *b·* in sickness,
  f 218–24 Treat a *b·* in sickness as you would sin,
  b 297–10 a health-belief or a *b·* in sickness
  p 430– 9 *B·* in sickness and death, as certainly as
in sin
  f 219–29 Entire immunity from the *b·* in sin, suffering,
  253–16 overcome the *b·* in sin, disease, or
  253–28 *b·* in sin and death is destroyed
  b 289– 3 *débris* of error, *b·* in sin, sickness, and
  290–16 If the change . . . destroyed the *b·* in sin,
  p 430–10 *b·* in sin, tends to shut out the true sense
  r 497–11 But the *b·* in sin is punished
  gl 584–18 a *b·* in sin, sickness, and death ;
in something
  sp 92–26 is laid on a *b·* in something besides God.
in the experience
  b 291–10 need not fancy that *b·* in the experience of
in their reality
  o 352–27 if *b·* in their reality is destroyed,
in the material origin
  g 549–31 coming down to a *b·* in the material origin of
in the necessity
  f 251–18 a *b·* in the necessity of sickness and death,
in the plagues
  s 133– 9 saved the Israelites from *b·* in the plagues.
in the unknown
  pr 12– 9 a *b·* in the unknown casting out a
intruding
  p 393– 2 we admit the intruding *b·*, forgetting
in Truth
  b 297–26 A *b·* in Truth is better than a belief in error,
involves
  g 526– 9 *B·* involves theories of material hearing,
is changeable
  sp 96–23 *B·* is changeable, but
Jew's
  o 361–11 Thus he virtually unites with the Jew's *b·*
latent
  p 377–31 It is latent *b·* in disease, as well as
leads to
  sp 92–30 leads to *b·* in the superiority of error.
lord of the
  g 518– 2 He is lord of the *b·* in earth and heaven,
lost in the
  t 455–11 If you are yourself lost in the *b·* and fear of

belief

man's
  s 159–30 Ignorant of the fact that a man's *b·* produces
  ph 175–23 A man's *b·* in those days was not so severe upon
material
  (*see* **material**)
matter is a
  ph 190– 3 all this while matter is a *b·*,
melts
  p 442–21 *b·* melts into spiritual understanding,
mere
  a 23–16 Faith, if it be mere *b·*, is as a pendulum
  b 330– 2 understanding of being supersedes mere *b·*.
  r 487–22 Mere *b·* is blindness without Principle
mistaken
  p 377–27 a mistaken *b·* or conviction of the
  g 554–19 Mind sets at naught such a mistaken *b·*.
Mohammedan's
  ph 166–12 Mohammedan's *b·* is a religious delusion ;
mortal
  (*see* **mortal**)
mortal in
  r 486–22 will continue mortal in *b·* and subject to chance
nation's
  ph 200– 2 the gods became alive in a nation's *b·*.
new
  f 251–11 they have but passed the portals of a new *b·*.
no
  a 19–31 Thou shalt have no *b·* of Life as mortal ;
not
  pr 15–29 Practice not profession, understanding not *b·*,
nourishes the
  pr 5–25 If prayer nourishes the *b·* that sin is
of corporeal sense
  sp 77– 5 continues to be a *b·* of corporeal sense
of danger
  p 374–23 You cannot forget the *b·* of danger,
of disease
  ph 178– 8 remote cause or *b·* of disease is not
  p 380–18 The body is affected only with the *b·* of disease
  398–27 change the *b·* of disease to a belief of health.
of grief
  p 386–27 under the influence of the *b·* of grief,
of having died
  sp 74–14 the *b·* of having died and left a material body
of health
  p 398–27 change the belief of disease to a *b·* of health.
of intense pain
  ph 195– 1 gave him a *b·* of intense pain.
of life
  sp 74–10 When here or hereafter the *b·* of life in matter
  89–30 incident shows that the *b·* of life in matter was
  f 203–21 when evil has overtaxed the *b·* of life
  t 450–31 all evil combines in the *b·* of life,
  g 542– 1 The *b·* of life in matter sins
  gl 584–14 until every *b·* of life where Life is not
of material mind
  g 529–30 Adam, . . . stands for a *b·* of material mind.
of mortal mind
  f 229–29 transgression of a *b·* of mortal mind,
  251– 3 So-called *b·* of mortal mind
  b 292–13 Matter is the primitive *b·* of mortal mind,
  p 384–10 this is but a *b·* of mortal mind,
of pain
  f 247–32 to retreat from the *b·* of pain or pleasure
  o 346–23 there is no reality in his *b·* of pain,
  p 416– 3 the *b·* of pain will presently return, unless
  t 464–18 when the *b·* of pain was lulled,
of sickness
  f 229–30 which causes the *b·* of sickness.
of sin
  a 38–27 To those buried in the *b·* of sin and self,
  ph 188– 4 The *b·* of sin, which has grown terrible in
  b 318–14 brought the *b·* of sin and death
  p 442–20 Christ . . . *b·* of sin or sickness into
  r 473– 7 Christ came to destroy the *b·* of sin.
of substance-matter
  b 314– 4 had relinquished the *b·* of substance-matter,
of the disease
  p 377–20 when the *b·* of the disease had gone.
of the eternity
  b 278–23 *b·* of the eternity of matter contradicts
of the flesh
  b 310–22 It is the *b·* of the flesh . . . which sins.
old
  b 281–30 The old *b·* must be cast out
one
  pr 12– 8 This, however, is one *b·* casting out another,
  p 370–16 produces through one *b·*,
  gl 583–28 one *b·* preying upon another.
  584–13 that which frets itself free from one *b·*
one's
  f 234–32 and do no more harm than one's *b·* permits.
only in
  b 328– 8 mortals get·rid of . . . only in *b·*.

belief

only in
  gl 591–15 feels, hears, tastes, and smells only in *b·*.

opposite
  f 205–11 the opposite *b·* is the prolific source of
  b 338– 4 opposite *b·*— that man originates in matter
  p 370–16 it removes through an opposite *b·*,
    385–30 opposite *b·* would produce the opposite result.
    425–31 protest against the opposite *b·* in heredity.
    427– 2 can never change in Science to the opposite *b·*

originates unseen
  p 377–16 Because a *b·* originates unseen, the

palsy is a
  p 375–21 Palsy is a *b·* that matter governs mortals,

pantheistic
  b 279–24 infected with the pantheistic *b·* that

patient's
  ph 198–23 A patient's *b·* is more or less moulded

perpetuates the
  pr 2–20 perpetuates the *b·* in God as humanly

phase of
  p 419–22 mortal mind is liable to any phase of *b·*.

physical
  p 395–27 erroneous . . . to feel these ills in physical *b·*.
    418–26 Include moral as well as physical *b·* in
  gl 582– 4 BENJAMIN . . . A physical *b·* as to life,
    586–18 FLESH. An error of physical *b·* ;

plane of
  sp 75–19 would have stood on the same plane of *b·*

popular
  s 155–21 must mightily outweigh the power of popular *b·*
  b 316–15 and the blindness of popular *b·*,

postulate of
  sp 91–25 The first erroneous postulate of *b·* is,

potent
  g 553–25 this potent *b·* will immediately supersede

proceeds from the
  sp 88–32 When eloquence proceeds from the *b·* that

produces the
  ph 184– 6 *B·* produces the results of belief,

product of
  r 490– 3 Will-power is but a product of *b·*,

relinquish the
  o 357– 9 If mankind would relinquish the *b·* that

removing the
  p 421–14 removing the *b·* that this chemicalization

results of
  ph 184– 6 Belief produces the results of *b·*,

reverse the
  p 408–26 Reverse the *b·*, and the results would be

sensual
  gl 590–11 LEVI . . . A corporeal and sensual *b·* ;

sensuous
  gl 582–24 CANAAN (the son of Ham). A sensuous *b·* ;
    592–27 PHARISEE. Corporeal and sensuous *b·* ;

separated by
  ap 562–13 separated by *b·* from man's divine origin

separate from the
  pr 14–25 Entirely separate from the *b·* and dream of

sickness is a
  r 493–19 Sickness is a *b·*, which must be annihilated

simply a
  sp 71– 3 simply a *b·*, an illusion of material sense.

sinful
  b 314–23 Because of mortals' material and sinful *b·*,

strays into a sense
  b 311–15 *b·* strays into a sense of temporary loss

such
  b 280–11 Such *b·* can neither apprehend nor worship

such a
  pr 13–22 doubts and fears which attend such a *b·*,
  sp 83–11 for such a *b·* hides Truth
  s 155–14 such a *b·* is governed by the majority.
  f 245–24 manifested the influence of such a *b·*.

tenacity of
  p 396–18 on account of the tenacity of *b·* in its truth,

that
  a 41–31 that *b·*, . . . has never made a disciple who
  p 379–11 and died because of that *b·*,
  g 553–32 precedes the development of that *b·*.

that all must die
  sp 75–21 out of the *b·* that all must die,

that another mind
  sp 89– 4 in the *b·* that another mind is speaking

that everything
  g 531– 2 the *b·* that everything springs from dust

that existence
  p 427– 9 The *b·* that existence is contingent on matter

that God
  f 204–30 *b·* that God lives in matter is pantheistic.
  o 357– 9 the *b·* that God makes sickness,

that he dies
  r 486–11 The *b·* that he dies will not establish his

that inflammation
  p 375– 3 the *b·* that inflammation and pain must

belief

that life
  sp 76– 8 the *b·* that life, or mind, was ever in
  f 222–32 *b·* that life and intelligence are in
  b 289– 4 *b·* that life and sensation are in the body
    318–20 error— or *b·* that life is in matter
  r 485–19 The *b·* that life can be in matter
    487–23 The *b·* that life is sentient and
  g 541–16 erroneous *b·* that life, substance, and
  gl 587– 9 Mythology ; a *b·* that life, substance,
    588–17 even the *b·* that life, substance, and
    592– 1 *b·* that life, substance, and intelligence are
    592– 4 the *b·* that life has a beginning

that man
  a 42–19 *b·* that man has existence or mind separate
  sp 91– 5 rid ourselves of the *b·* that man is separated
  b 301–20 The *b·* that man has any other substance,
    320–21 the *b·* that man is flesh and matter,
  p 427– 2 the opposite *b·* that man dies.
  gl 592– 5 *b·* that man is the offspring of mortals ;

that material bodies
  sp 73–19 The *b·* that material bodies return to dust,

that matter
  s 110– 3 contradict forever the *b·* that matter can
  b 289–21 The *b·* that matter has life results,
    294– 9 The *b·* that matter thinks, sees, or feels
    294–10 *b·* that matter enjoys and suffers.
  p 369–11 the *b·* that matter is substance,
    372–10 the *b·* that matter is the medium of man,
    375–21 Palsy is a *b·* that matter governs mortals,
  r 491–17 The *b·* that matter and mind are one,
  g 543–28 The *b·* that matter supports life
  ap 563–11 the *b·* that matter has power of its own,
  gl 586–20 a *b·* that matter has sensation.

that Mind
  b 292– 8 the *b·* that Mind, . . . can be fettered

that mind
  an 103–20 It is the false *b·* that mind is in matter,
  b 298–15 expresses the *b·* that mind is in matter.
    308– 1 the *b·* that mind is in matter,
  p 379–31 through the *b·* that mind is in matter
    397–28 Give up the *b·* that mind is, . . . compressed
  gl 587– 1 a *b·* that mind is outlined and limited ;

that one man
  sp 73– 8 The *b·* that one man, as spirit, can

that pain
  b 303–21 The *b·* that pain and pleasure, . . . mingle

that sensation
  gl 591–27 the *b·* that sensation is in matter,

that Soul
  a 39–10 educated *b·* that Soul is in the body
  b 280–22 the *b·* that Soul is in body,

that Spirit
  sp 93–21 The *b·* that Spirit is finite as well as infinite

that spirit
  sp 73–22 Equally incorrect is the *b·* that spirit is confined
  g 546– 1 *b·* that spirit is now submerged in

that substance
  ap 563– 8 the *b·* that substance, . . . can be material.

that the body governed
  f 226–23 the *b·* that the body governed them,

that the human race
  gl 585–25 *b·* that the human race originated materially

that the universe
  sp 83–16 The *b·* that the universe, including man,

their
  sp 81– 6 their *b·* in mediumship would vanish.
  p 389–23 Their *b·* in material laws and in
    402–27 because their *b·* is not better instructed
  g 536–28 They give up their *b·* in perishable life

this
  sp 80–30 This *b·* rests on the common conviction that
    83–18 this *b·* belittles omnipotent wisdom,
    89–16 the body responds to this *b·*,
    92–27 This *b·* tends to support two opposite powers,
    93–30 This *b·* tends to becloud our apprehension of
  an 102– 4 Its basis being a belief and this *b·* animal,
    103–22 This *b·* has not one quality of Truth.
  s 124– 8 this *b·* mistakes effect for cause
    143–21 Controlled by this *b·*, you continue in the
    153–19 this *b·* is called a boil.
  c 257–10 This *b·* is shallow pantheism.
    258– 7 The insufficiency of this *b·* to supply the
  b 279–25 this *b·* contradicts alike revelation and
    302–12 and this *b·* is all that will ever be lost.
  p 374–20 this *b·* helps rather than hinders disease.
    384–12 has only to enter his protest against this *b·*
    389– 4 control of Mind over this *b·*
    389–26 This *b·* totters to its falling before the
    389–31 symptoms connected with this *b·*.
    423– 2 this *b·* should not be communicated to the
  r 469–28 This *b·* that there is more than one mind
    478–24 this *b·* is mortal and far from actual.
    489– 9 In infancy this *b·* is not equal to guiding the
    489–11 as consciousness develops, this *b·* goes out
    490– 3 this *b·* commits depredations on harmony.

belief

this
r 491–20 this *b·* culminates in another belief,
g 533–17 According to this *b·*, the rib taken from
546– 3 this *b·* alone is mortal.
understanding and
b 288–12 the conflict between . . . understanding and *b·*,
understanding or
b 324–11 understanding or *b·*, Spirit or matter.
unexpressed
p 423– 6 Remember that the unexpressed *b·* oftentimes
universal
a 42– 5 The universal *b·* in death is of no advantage.
s 155–15 The universal *b·* in physics weighs against
unreal
o 353–30 the ghost, some unreal *b·*.
until the
b 297– 2 nothing can change this state, until the *b·* changes.
297– 4 until the *b·* on this subject changes.
whatever the
p 418–17 Whatever the *b·* is, if arguments are used
which breeds
m 62– 7 a *b·* which breeds disease.
which unites
f 229– 9 the *b·* which unites such opposites as
without understanding
sp 83–10 a blind *b·* without understanding,
r 472–18 Error is a *b·* without understanding.
wrong
f 253–23 you can alter this wrong *b·* and action
your
ph 168– 8 Your *b·* militates against your health,
p 384–24 to destroy the bad effects of your *b·*.
385–24 will suffer in proportion to your *b·* and fear.
386–22 your suffering was merely the result of your *b·*.
t 461–17 you should tell your *b·* sometimes,
zeal of
b 280–20 zeal of *b·* to establish the opposite error

m 62– 6 master the *b·* in so-called physical laws,
68–25 the *b·* that agamogenesis applies to the
sp 74–11 error which has held the *b·*
74–12 dissolves with the *b·*,
74–15 *b·* of still living in an organic, material body.
78– 6 How unreasonable is the *b·* that we are
97– 7 the more impotent error becomes as a *b·*.
97–17 The more material the *b·*, the more
an 102– 4 Its basis being a *b·* and this belief animal,
104–24 If he heals sickness through a *b·*,
104–24 and a *b·* originally caused the sickness,
s 129–12 Pantheism . . . a *b·* which Science overthrows.
144–11 The more material a *b·*, the more obstinately
155–13 a *b·* held by a minority,
164–22 mortal thoughts in *b·* rule the materiality
ph 172–19 The *b·* that there is Soul in sense or Life in
184– 7 penalties it affixes last so long as the *b·*
187–30 the human mind still holds in *b·* a body,
189–26 first the *b·* of inanimate, and then of
192– 1 The *b·* that a pulpy substance under the skull
198– 2 has in *b·* more power to harm
f 205–24 a *b·* in many ruling minds hinders man's
212– 5 limb . . . amputated has continued in *b·* to pain
220–26 The *b·* that either fasting or feasting makes
b 279–16 In proportion as the *b·* disappears that life
285–16 The *b·* that a material body is man
286– 5 We must not . . . depend upon *b·* instead of
295– 1 The *b·* that a severed limb is aching in the
297–20 Faith is higher and more spiritual than *b·*.
297–29 Until *b·* becomes faith, and faith becomes
312–11 The *b·* of that mortal that he must die
321–13 Matter was shown to be a *b·* only.
o 346–14 the *b·* that we suffer from the sins of others.
358–26 a *b·* that in the removal of disease
p 380– 3 which *b·* must be finally conquered by
386– 5 *b·* says that you may catch cold
386–12 not because of the climate, but on account of the *b·*.
392–17 You will call it neuralgia, but we call it a *b·*.
398–25 faith, cooperating with a *b·* in the healing
402–32 a *b·* without a real cause.
409–11 The *b·*, that the unconscious substratum
416–13 unless the *b·* which occasions the pain has
418–18 the *b·* must be repudiated,
422–32 the *b·* that he has met his master in
425–20 What if the *b·* is consumption?
t 450– 3 *b·* in a mysterious, supernatural God,
r 467–19 The *b·* that the greater can be in the lesser
487–13 You speak of *b·*. Who or what is it that
488– 7 Hebrew and Greek words often translated *b·*
488–12 appear . . . to approve and endorse *b·*,
491– 4 a *b·* without actual foundation
495–20 *b·* in, that which Life is not.
497–12 punished so long as the *b·* lasts.
g 526– 8 *B·* is less than understanding.
535– 2 The seed . . . of *b·* and of understanding,
gl 579–17 a curse ; a *b·* in intelligent matter,

belief
gl 587–11 the *b·* that infinite Mind is in finite forms ;
592– 6 the *b·* that there can be more than one creator ;
594– 3 the *b·* in more than one God ;

beliefs

all the
a 53–29 had not conquered all the *b·* of the flesh
r 493–17 superior to all the *b·* of the five corporeal senses,
and opinions
gl 590– 5 mortality ; *b·* and opinions ;
begotten of the
b 325–24 begotten of the *b·* of the flesh
carnal
c 263–11 Carnal *b·* defraud us.
changes its
s 125– 2 as mortal mind changes its *b·*.
cherished
s 141– 8 to set aside even the most cherished *b·*
chronic
f 246–32 Acute and chronic *b·* reproduce their own types.
different
sp 74–22 different *b·*, which never blend.
diseased
p 404–10 all sorts of evil are diseased *b·*,
dismal
b 272–27 the dismal *b·* of sin, sickness, and death.
doctrinal
r 496–31 if by that term is meant doctrinal *b·*.
dying
sp 76–18 Suffering, sinning, dying *b·* are unreal.
erroneous
c 267–21 inverted thoughts and erroneous *b·*
evil
s 115–21 Evil *b·*, passions and appetites, fear,
115–25 *Second Degree:* Evil *b·* disappearing.
f 206–32 There are evil *b·*, often called evil spirits ;
c 266–26 evil *b·* which originate in mortals are hell.
false
sp 79–17 Jesus cast out evil spirits, or false *b·*.
99–20 some others who eschew their false *b·*.
s 162–16 false *b·* of a so-called material existence.
ph 171–25 so-called laws of matter are nothing but false *b·*
171–27 These false *b·* are the procuring cause
f 234–10 and guard against false *b·* as watchfully
236–31 or battling with false *b·*,
237–31 they hug false *b·* and suffer the delusive
b 274–21 These false *b·* and their products
278–13 one of the false *b·* of mortals,
327– 6 destroy the false *b·* of pleasure, pain,
p 421– 1 the insane suffer, from false *b·*.
g 556– 5 These false *b·* will disappear,
fatal
p 368–10 Against the fatal *b·* that error is as
former
t 460–30 As former *b·* were gradually expelled
ghostly
o 353–14 not wholly outlived the sense of ghostly *b·*.
held in the
p 413–32 malady, timorously held in the *b·*
his
p 371–15 The adult, in bondage to his *b·*,
his own
p 372–12 bind himself with his own *b·*,
human
(*see* **human**)
inharmonious
f 251–30 Inharmonious *b·*, which rob Mind,
in sickness
p 391– 3 Blot out . . . its *b·* in sickness and sin.
insidious
p 376– 9 hidden, undefined, and insidious *b·*.
man-made
r 466–26 the outcome of all man-made *b·*.
material
(*see* **material**)
materialistic
s 132–16 retained their materialistic *b·* about God.
b 298–22 and admit no materialistic *b·*.
316–28 spiritualizing materialistic *b·*,
mortal
(*see* **mortal**)
of mortal mind
sp 89– 3 shows that the *b·* of mortal mind are loosed.
b 274–19 simply the manifested *b·* of mortal mind,
p 425–14 this is but one of the *b·* of mortal mind.
of the human mind
ph 187–10 *b·* of the human mind rob and enslave it,
opinions and
b 273–30 conflicting mortal opinions and *b·*
opposite
sp 75–29 when the link between their opposite *b·*
other
f 208–32 and of other *b·* included in matter.
our
f 202–24 Our *b·* about a Supreme Being contradict
p 385–10 forestalls the penalty which our *b·* would

beliefs

outgrow their
sp 77–27   Spiritualists would outgrow their *b·*

outgrown
a 28–12   we cannot hold to *b·* outgrown ;

perilous
t 450–27   Who, that has felt the perilous *b·* in

pleasurable
c 265–32   if they wrench away false pleasurable *b·*

present
f 228–17   Dropping their present *b·*, they

remove its
p 421– 8   in order to remove its *b·*,

self-imposed
f 221–18   the self-imposed *b·* of mortals,

sick
p 366–25   The sick are terrified by their sick *b·*,

sinful
a 53–32   Had he shared the sinful *b·* of others,
f 241–32   than for sinful *b·* to enter the kingdom of
p 366–26   sinners should be affrighted by their sinful *b·* ;

stubborn
f 237–10   more stubborn *b·* and theories of parents

their
p 396–23   explain to the sick the power which their *b·*
403– 1   So the sick through their *b·* have

their own
f 226–27   I wished to save from the slavery of their own *b·*

these
sp 79–12   C. S. removes these *b·* and

those
a 54– 1   he would have been less sensitive to those *b·*.

traditional
o 352–24   ghosts are not realities, but traditional *b·*,

unjust
p 440–22   The false and unjust *b·* of your

---

a 43–31   errors growing from such *b·*.
sp 88–14   *B·* proceed from the so-called material senses,
99–26   until the *b·* of material existence are
s 155–10   and the *b·* which are in the majority rule.
f 232– 4   The *b·* we commonly entertain about happiness
o 343–19   that sin, sickness, and death are *b·*
p 425–10   hemorrhage, and decomposition are *b·*,
gl 595–18   thoughts, *b·*, opinions, knowledge ;

believe

pr 1– *   *but shall b· that those things— Mark* 11 : 23.
1– *   *b· that ye receive them,— Mark* 11 : 24.
a 23–27   "Lord, I *b·* ; help thou mine— *Mark* 9 : 24.
23–29   "*B·* . . . and thou shalt be saved !"— *Acts* 16 : 31.
23–32   Hebrew verb *to b·* means also *to be firm*
24–12   He . . . will *b·* our report,
29–13   "The disciples of Jesus *b·* him the Son
38–10   signs shall follow them that *b·* ;— *Mark* 16 : 17.
38–14   but *them*— "them that *b·*"— *Mark* 16 : 17.
38–19   as should *b·* "through their word."— *John* 17: 20.
41–30   enough for them to *b·* in a national Deity ;
52–28   signs shall follow them that *b·*."— *Mark* 16 : 17.
m 62–31   Because mortals *b·* in material laws
sp 71–26   I never could *b·* in spiritualism.
93–10   If we *b·* otherwise, we may be
s 110–30   apprehended by as many as *b·* on Christ
119–26   to *b·* that the earth is in motion
147–15   never *b·* that you can absorb the
150–18   would have one *b·* that both matter and
154–10   A man was made to *b·* that he
ph 168–17   are we to *b·* it?
168–18   Are we to *b·* an authority which denies God's
177–31   In such cases a few persons *b·* the potion
178– 2   *b·* the arsenic, the strychnine, or
186–30   Since it must *b·* in something besides itself,
189– 4   we still *b·* that there is solar light and heat.
f 203–11   We are prone to *b·* either in more than one
203–22   then mortals *b·* that the deathless Principle,
212–21   In legerdemain and . . . mortals *b·*
215–15   We are sometimes led to *b·* that darkness is
218–19   If you do *b·* in God, why do you substitute
218–25   Resist the temptation to *b·* in
222– 6   to *b·* that proper food supplies nutriment
253–18   If you *b·* in and practise wrong knowingly,
253–22   Also, if you *b·* yourself diseased,
253–25   Do not *b·* in any supposed necessity for sin,
c 263– 1   They *b·* themselves to be independent workers,
b 271–18   for them also which shall *b·*— *John* 17: 20.
277–29   Nothing we can say or *b·* regarding
285–32   essential to understand, instead of *b·*,
302–30   though mortal sense would fain have us so *b·*.
311–20   So long as we *b·* that soul can sin
312–18   Mortals try to *b·* without understanding
312–20   Mortals *b·* in a finite personal God ;
318– 1   For him to *b·* in matter was no task,
321–27   if they will not *b·* thee,— *Exod.* 4 : 8.
321–28   will *b·* the voice of the latter sign."— *Exod.* 4 : 8.
328–23   signs shall follow them that *b·*,— *Mark* 16 : 17.
o 341– *   *ye b· me not.— John* 8 : 45.

believe

o 341– *   *why do ye not b· me?— John* 8 : 46.
346–26   when you *b·* that nitrous-oxide gas has
349–32   the opponents of C. S. *b·* substance to be
352–26   should be told not to *b·* in ghosts,
359–27   signs shall follow them that *b·* ;— *Mark* 16 : 17.
p 362– *   *signs shall follow them that b· :— Mark* 16 : 17.
368–32   Once let the mental physician *b·* in the
372–20   How, then, . . . can we *b·* in the reality and
380–28   Nothing is more disheartening than to *b·* that
381–23   or you will never *b·* that you are quite free
384–22   but if you *b·* in laws of matter
392–15   If you *b·* in inflamed and weak nerves,
395–24   to *b·* in the real existence of a tumor,
402–25   operator would make his subjects *b·* that they
425– 4   You will have humors, just so long as you *b·*
425–27   you will never *b·* that heart . . . can destroy
428–32   It is a sin to *b·* that aught can overpower
429–25   Do you *b·* this?
t 461– 2   but I do *b·* that the real man is immortal
461–16   If you *b·* that you are sick,
463–29   sick are not healed by . . . drugs, as they *b·*
r 469–27   still *b·* there is another power,
474–21   Is it possible, then, to *b·* that the
487–16   Matter cannot *b·*, and Mind understands.
487–17   The body cannot *b·*.
488– 9   the English verb *b·* ;
494– 5   infidelity to *b·* that so great a work
g 540–23   is to teach mortals never to *b·* a lie.

believed

pr 6–29   It is *b·* by many that a certain magistrate,
a 43– 6   Heretofore they had only *b·* ;
44–28   His disciples *b·* Jesus to be dead
45–26   for they *b·* his body to be dead.
53–13   Mortals *b·* in God as humanly mighty,
m 68–16   one individual who *b·* in agamogenesis ;
sp 75–17   Had Jesus *b·* that Lazarus had
95–25   Is the wise man of to-day *b·*,
an 104–12   Lastly, they say they have always *b·* it."
s 133–11   and straightway *b·* that they were healed
136–18   some of the people *b·* that Jesus was a
154–22   Then it is *b·* that exposure to the
ph 199–25   Had Blondin *b·* it impossible
f 203– 7   understood instead of being merely *b·*,
222–18   had been kept alive, as was *b·*, only by
b 305–32   Pharisees, who *b·* error to be as immortal as
328–26   It were well had Christendom *b·*
339–27   Mind must be not merely *b·*,
o 348–28   would not be *b·* for an indefinite
359– 9   I as a Christian Scientist *b·* in the Holy Spirit,
p 371– 9   are *b·* to be here without their consent
403– 9   it is *b·* that the misfortune is a material effect.
409–16   conscious mortal mind is *b·* to be superior
425– 2   His parents . . . have so *b·*.
r 492–29   The conservative theory, long *b·*, is
g 545–22   They *b·* in the existence of matter,
gl 596–12   The rabbins *b·* that the stones in

believer

r 487–18   The *b·* and belief are one and are mortal.

believers

s 141–20   The Bible declares that all *b·* are

believes

a 38–12   Who *b·* him?
39–31   so long as he *b·* in the pleasures of sin?
sp 80–29   *b·* that this wonder emanates from spirits
86–29   Mortal mind sees what it *b·*
86–30   as certainly as it *b·* what it sees.
89–14   If one *b·* that he cannot be an orator without
ph 166– 8   Mohammedan *b·* in a pilgrimage to Mecca
166– 9   The popular doctor *b·* in his prescription,
166–10   pharmacist *b·* in the power of his drugs
171–17   man *b·* himself to be combined matter and
171–18   He *b·* that Spirit is sifted through matter,
199– 6   nobody *b·* that mind is producing such a
f 250–10   Spirit . . . never *b·*, but knows ;
c 263–15   mis-creator, who *b·* he is a semi-god.
b 294–28   inebriate *b·* that there is pleasure in
294–29   thief *b·* that he gains something by stealing,
o 360–32   The Jew *b·* that the Messiah or Christ
361– 1   the Christian *b·* that Christ is God.
361– 6   The Jew who *b·* in the First Commandment
361– 9   Christian who *b·* in the First Commandment
p 375–10   *b·* that matter, not mind, has helped him.
377– 1   If your patient *b·* in taking cold,
402–19   manifests only what mortal mind *b·*,
422–30   he *b·* that something stronger than Mind
427– 7   If man *b·* in death now, he
r 487–14   Who or what is it that *b·*?
g 517–15   The world *b·* in many persons ;

believeth

pr 14–19   "He that *b·* on me,— *John* 14 : 12.
a 22–27   Whosoever *b·* that wrath is righteous
42–30   "He that *b·* on me,— *John* 14 : 12.
52–27   "He that *b·* on me,— *John* 14 : 12.

believeth
- *sp*   93– 4   "He that *b·* on me,— *John* 14 : 12.
- *ph* 170–11   "Whosoever liveth and *b·* in me— *John* 11 : 26.
- *b* 315– 1   "Whosoever liveth and *b·* in me— *John* 11 : 26.
-   324–32   "He that *b·* in me — *see John* 11 : 26.
-   326– 4   "He that *b·* on me,— *John* 14 : 12.

believing
- *m*   69– 6   can never . . . while *b·* that man is a creator.
- *sp*   89– 6   *b·* that somebody else possesses her tongue
- *s* 134–29   There is divine authority for *b·* in the
-   156–11   *B·* then somewhat in the ordinary theories
- *ph* 187– 1   *b·* in more than the one Mind.
- *f* 205– 7   When will the error of *b·* that there is
-   205–15   the error of *b·* that matter can
-   218–14   *b·* that the body can be sick independently
-   245– 6   *B·* that she was still living in the same hour
-   245–25   She could not age while *b·* herself young,
- *b* 290–29   no more spiritual for *b·* that his body died
- *p* 385–23   Saying this and *b·* it,
-   388– 9   Idolaters, *b·* in more than one mind,
-   397–11   by *b·* them to be real and continuous.
- *r* 487–16   this precludes the need of *b·*.
- *gl* 582– 1   definition of

belittle
- *c* 255–11   to *b·* Deity with human conceptions.
- *g* 536–22   Their narrow limits *b·* their gratifications,

belittles
- *sp*   83–19   this belief *b·* omnipotent wisdom,

belly
- *ap* 559–18   it shall make thy *b·* bitter,— *Rev.* 10 : 9.

belong
- *s* 112– 7   forfeit their claims to *b·* to its school,
-   123–25   did not specially *b·* to a dispensation now ended,
-   124–21   They *b·* to divine Principle, and support the
-   124–29   they *b·* wholly to divine Mind,
-   130–25   such as they *b·* to the heavenly kingdom.
- *ph* 192–17   Moral and spiritual might *b·* to Spirit,
- *f* 207–24   disease, and death *b·* not to the Science of being.
- *b* 275–15   immortality, cause, and effect *b·* to God.
-   286–32   and *b·* not to the divine Mind.
-   287– 2   but *b·*, . . . to the nothingness of error,
- *p* 369–24   preventive and curative) arts *b·* emphatically to
- *r* 472–10   nor *b·* to His government.
-   476–19   the facts which *b·* to immortal man.

belonged
- *b* 333– 5   *b·* to him in common with other Hebrew

belonging
- *sp*   73–25   the sensations *b·* to the body.
- *g* 529–11   *b·* to no lesser parent.
-   551–21   all peculiarities of ancestry, *b·* to either sex,

belongs
- *a*   28–25   To suppose that persecution . . . *b·* to the past,
- *s* 144–14   Human will *b·* to the so-called
- *f* 230– 1   If sickness is real, it *b·* to immortality ;
- *c* 258–27   To him *b·* eternal Life.
-   265–26   even before we discover what *b·* to wisdom
- *r* 475–22   reflects spiritually all that *b·* to his Maker.
-   490–11   since all power *b·* to God, good.
- *ap* 572–10   *b·* not to His children,

beloved
- *a*   23– 6   That God's wrath should be vented upon His *b·*
-   36–13   forsaken by all save John, the *b·* disciple,
- *b* 319–32   meaning by that what the *b·* disciple meant
- *ap* 566–15   When Israel, the Lord of the *b·*,
-   576– 9   describing this holy city, the *b·* Disciple writes :

bench
- *p* 430–26   and Judge Medicine is on the *b·*.

beneath
- *a*   36–14   in silent woe *b·* the shadow of his cross.
-   55–16   gathering *b·* its wings the sick and sinning.
- *b* 280–11   would compress Mind, which is infinite, *b·* a
-   281–18   supposed to exist in matter or *b·* a skull bone
-   313–24   He plunged *b·* the material surface of things,
- *t* 451–17   they come from above, not from *b·*,
- *g* 516–13   The grass *b·* our feet silently exclaims,
-   520–28   creating thought is from above, not from *b·*.
-   523–11   In error everything comes from *b·*,
-   539–18   to grovel *b·* all the beasts of the field.

benediction
- *a*   44– 2   laid aside for a crown, the *b·* follow,
-   48–11   fell in holy *b·* on the grass of Gethsemane,
- *s* 132–10   In other words, he gave his *b·*
-   137–22   This assertion elicited from Jesus the *b·*,

benedictions
- *b* 317–11   blessed *b·* rest upon Jesus' followers :

benefactions
- *pr*   3–22   for a liberal outpouring of *b·*.

benefactor
- *t* 450– 8   they never fail to stab their *b·* in the back.

beneficent
- *s* 128–20   An odor becomes *b·* and agreeable
- *p* 394–31   till they feel its *b·* influence.

beneficial
- *pr* 12– 5   The *b·* effect of such prayer for the sick
- *s* 156– 3   what made them . . . *b·* or injurious?
- *p* 367–27   increase the *b·* effects of Christianity.

beneficially
- *p* 397– 2   acting *b·* or injuriously on the health,

benefit
  any lasting
- *pr*   7–10   But does it produce any lasting *b·*?

  any seeming
- *an* 101–31   Any seeming *b·* derived from it is

  great
- *ap* 570–27   the great *b·* which Mind has wrought.

  to man
- *r* 471–22   Are doctrines and creeds a *b·* to man?

- *pr*   2– 2   or to *b·* those who hear us,
-   11– 6   this may be no moral *b·* to the criminal,
- *s* 151–12   enlarged power it confers to *b·* the race
- *ph* 185–26   may seem for a time to *b·* the sick,
- *f* 238– 3   wait till those whom you would *b·* are ready
- *p* 392–12   Whatever *b·* is produced on the body,
-   395–16   Prayers, in which . . . do not *b·* the sick.
- *t* 447– 5   except it be to *b·* them.
-   449–10   than for you to *b·* yourself by injuring others.
- *ap* 567–20   either to *b·* or to injure men

benefited
- *pr*   2– 4   Are we *b·* by praying?
- *b* 324–30   if . . . you cannot be *b·* by what I say.
- *p* 375–14   No person is *b·* by yielding his
- *t* 443–15   and think they can be *b·* by
-   463–32   said to the author, "The world is *b·* by you,

benefiting
- *ap* 571–10   for the sake of doing right and *b·* our race.

benefits
- *s* 149–28   Whatever guides thought spiritually *b·*
- *f* 238–17   when we attempt to claim the *b·* of
-   245– 2   *b·* of destroying that illusion, are illustrated
- *p* 372–31   prevents the honest recognition of *b·* received,

benevolence
- *m*   58–15   With additional joys, *b·* should grow more
- *p* 433–21   guilty of *b·* in the first degree,

benighted
- *pref* vii– 7   would make plain to *b·* understanding

benign
- *p* 365– 7   The *b·* thought of Jesus,
-   440–34   the Chief Justice . . . with *b·* and imposing

Benjamin
- *gl* 582– 4   definition of

Benjamin Franklin
- *an* 100–15   *B· F·* was one of the commissioners.

bereft
- *p* 374–21   body, when *b·* of mortal mind, at first cools,

Berna, Monsieur
- *an* 101–14   facts which had been promised by Monsieur *B·*

beset
- *a*   20–29   sin which doth so easily *b·* us,— *Heb.* 12 : 1.
-   22–15   If your endeavors are *b·* by fearful odds,
- *s* 152–12   Such errors *b·* every material theory,

besets
- *p* 426–21   destroy the great fear that *b·* mortal existence.

beside
- *p* 414–22   none else *b·* Him."— *Deut.* 4 : 35.
-   421–17   and that there is none *b·* Him.
-   435–19   Watching *b·* the couch of pain
- *g* 514–13   *b·* the still waters."— *Psal.* 23 : 2.
- *ap* 578– 7   *b·* the still waters.— *Psal.* 23 : 2.

besides
- *sp*   92–27   a belief in something *b·* God.
- *s* 121–26   *b·* turning daily on its own axis.
- *ph* 181–25   unnecessary to resort to aught *b·*
-   186–31   Since it must believe in something *b·* itself,
- *g* 548–31   *b·* the ordinary process of generation,

besottedness
- *b* 322–19   cannot make the inebriate leave his *b·*, until

besought
- *s* 158– 2   pagan priests, who *b·* the gods to heal the
- *p* 395–15   but is *b·* to take the patient to Himself,

best
- *pref* viii–15   confers the most health and makes the *b·* men.
- *pr* 10–30   it is not always *b·* for us to receive.
-   11– 6   at *b·*, it only saves the criminal from
-   11–32   It is *b·* expressed in thought and in life.
- *a*   52–16   putting to shame and death the *b·* man that
-   52–19   "man of sorrows" *b·* understood— *Isa.* 53 : 3.

best

sp	81– 7	At the very b· and on its own theories,
s	111–20	for the b· essay on Natural Science,
	125– 2	What is now considered the b· condition for
ph	170–15	The b· interpreter of man's needs said :
	176–20	while divine Mind is its b· friend.
f	201– 1	The b· sermon ever preached is
c	259– 7	was b· expressed in Christ Jesus,
	266–12	to accept what b· promotes your growth.
b	317– 7	Whosoever . . . declares b· the power of C. S.,
o	360–29	the Galilean Prophet, the b· Christian on earth,
p	364– 2	rightfully regarded as the b· man that ever
	383– 8	takes the b· care of his body when he
	385–10	penalty which our beliefs would attach to our b·
	394– 3	is b· of all, for this understanding is
	403–22	and this is b· adapted for healing the sick.
	416–28	tell them only what is b· for them to know.
	420–23	erroneous belief, taken at its b·, is not
	439–31	We send our b· detectives to whatever
g	523–15	according to the b· scholars, there are
	556–16	to him who understands b· the divine Life.

bestial

b	293–22	wind, wave, lightning, fire, b· ferocity

bestow

pr	2–10	nor can the infinite do less than b· all good,
a	25–27	and all the emotional love we can b· on him,
	25–31	our Master worked and suffered to b·
	36–23	as for this world to b· on the righteous their
	48–15	Truth and Love b· few palms until
f	202– 7	half the faith they b· upon the so-called pains
t	455–23	does not b· His highest trusts upon the

bestowals

pr	13– 3	universal in its adaptation and b·.

bestowed

a	42–22	glory which God b· on His anointed,
	55– 7	than the later centuries have b· upon
ph	200– 6	capacities of being b· by immortal Mind.
p	387–28	protecting power b· on man by
	393–14	the ability and power divinely b· on man.
g	533– 3	This had never been b· on Adam.
	541– 9	the homage b· through a gentle animal

bestows

pr	6– 6	God is not separate from the wisdom He b·.
	11–17	Truth b· no pardon upon error,
	14–19	Hence the hope of the promise Jesus b· :
b	275–19	no good is, but the good God b·.
r	488–22	apart from what belief b· upon them,
g	555–26	when we admit . . . that God b· the power to
ap	573– 8	that consciousness which God b·,

Bethlehem

pref	vii– 6	the B· babe, the human herald of

betoken

sp	82–27	different awakenings b· a differing

betray

c	266–13	Friends will b· and enemies will slander,
g	542– 8	Truth causes sin to b· itself, and

betrayal

a	33– 4	anticipating the hour of their Master's b·,
	47–11	hatred towards that just man effected his b·.
	47–23	and so he plotted the b· of Jesus
sp	94–19	evoked denial, ingratitude, and b·,

betrayed

p	439–25	You b· Mortal Man, meanwhile declaring

betrayer

a	43–14	the treason and suicide of his b·,
	47–19	placed a gulf between Jesus and his b·,

betraying

p	436– 3	After b· him into the hands of your law,

betrays

ph	192–25	b· its weakness and falls, never to rise.
t	456–16	dishonesty in your theory and practice b· a
r	485– 6	which ever b· mortals into sickness, sin, and
ap	560–30	b· at once a greater ignorance

better

pr	2– 2	Do we pray to make ourselves b·
	4–18	but the longing to be b· and holier,
	5–26	and that man is made b· merely by
	7–20	a higher experience and a b· life
	9– 6	Do we love our neighbor b· because of this
	9– 9	prayed for something b·, though we give no
a	21– 4	can finally say, . . . because you are a b· man.
	25–16	Jesus presented the ideal of God b· than
	34–19	and understood b· what the Master had taught.
	47– 6	they became b· healers, leaning no longer on
	47–23	world generally loves a lie b· than Truth ;
m	57–17	should never weigh against the b· claims of
	61–12	b· balanced minds, and sounder constitutions.
	63– 2	would never think that flannel was b· for
	66–22	It is b· to await the logic of events
	66–25	If one is b· than the other, as must always
sp	91–23	that the spiritual facts may be b· apprehended.

better

sp	94–25	this insight b· enabled him to direct
s	114–18	if a b· word or phrase could be suggested, it
	136–29	apprehended their Master b· than did others ;
	154–25	her affections need b· guidance,
	154–31	The b· and more successful method
	155–32	is it safe to say that the less . . . the b·?
	157–32	Mankind is the b· for this spiritual and
ph	168–31	which will be b· understood hereafter,
	175– 5	there will be b· constitutions and less disease.
	186–29, 30	If mortal mind knew how to be b·, it would be b·.
	194– 7	and determines a case for b· or for worse.
	196– 6	B· the suffering which awakens
	198–12	It is b· to prevent disease from forming
f	210–16	a b· understanding of Soul and salvation.
	220– 8	Instinct is b· than misguided reason,
	220–27	belief that either fasting or feasting makes men b·
	222– 1	as we b· apprehend our spiritual existence
	224– 5	we shall b· understand the Science
	235– 4	B· suffer a doctor infected with smallpox to
	239– 9	and we get b· views of humanity.
c	258– 5	unsatisfied human craving for something b·,
	260–16	and to bring out b· and higher results,
b	285–21	the b· understanding that Science gives
	286– 8	is b· than all burnt offerings.
	295–22	become a b· transparency for Truth.
	297–26	Some thoughts are b· than others.
	297–26	belief in Truth is b· than a belief in error.
	315– 5	His b· understanding of God was a rebuke to
	323–24	contemplation of something b· than disease or
	333–14	but Christ Jesus b· signifies the Godlike.
o	355– 6	proofs are b· than mere verbal arguments
p	367– 5	b· than hecatombs of gushing theories,
	370– 1	To be . . . whole, man must be b· spiritually
	375– 9	proves this when his patient says, "I am b·,"
	377– 7	they come back no b· than when they went
	383–25	Does his assertion prove . . . man to be the b·
	389–11	the b· results of Mind's opposite evidence.
	394– 1	to be hopeful is still b· ;
	394–19	their denials are b· than their affirmations.
	397–31	understand yourself and your Maker b·
	401–28	it is b· for Christian Scientists to leave
	402–27	their belief is not b· instructed by
	404–32	unless it makes him b· mentally,
	405–22	b· to be exposed to every plague on earth than
	407–18	he will get the b· of that desire,
	420–21	b· than any drug, alterative, or tonic.
	425–23	Consciousness constructs a b· body when
	429– 6	and the sooner we begin the b·.
	438– 1	was b· authority than Blackstone :
	442–21	changes a belief of sin or . . . into a b· belief,
t	452–15	B· is the frugal intellectual repast
r	466–30	making mankind b· physically, morally, and
	473–23	a b· understanding of God
	485–16	come naturally into Spirit through b· health
	486–17	If . . . then death is not an enemy but a b·
	489– 1	less mind there is manifested in matter the b·.
g	537–31	lest man should improve it and become b· ;
	553– 7	Mortal thought must obtain a b· basis,
	554–21	Jesus defined this . . . b· than we can,
	557–15	the less a mortal knows of sin, . . . the b·
ap	560–25	all who have spoken something new and b·
	571– 6	Because people like you b· when you
gl	583– 2	whose b· originals are God's thoughts,
	596– 5	makes Him b· known as the All-in-all,

between

pr	16– 5	distinguishes b· Truth that is sinless and
a	22– 3	b· sin and the hope of forgiveness,
	23–16	swinging b· nothing and something,
	30–10	mediator, or way-shower, b· God and
	30–23	difference b· the offspring of Soul and
	34–29	contrast b· our Lord's last supper and
	36–16	distance b· Christianity and sensualism
	47–17	distance b· Judas and his Master.
	47–19	a gulf b· Jesus and his betrayer,
	53–21	distance b· the individual and Truth.
m	57–12	The attraction b· native qualities will
	63–12	establishes very unfair differences b·
sp	73–32	b· so-called material existence and
	74–13	b· persons in such opposite dreams
	75–28	the link b· their opposite beliefs
	81– 2	b· the so-called dead and the living,
	82–23	Communion b· them and ourselves would
	82–26	b· a mole and a human being.
	83– 2	B· C. S. and all forms of
	83–24	impassable as that b· Dives and Lazarus.
an	100– 8	"There exists a mutual influence b· the
s	110–32	No analogy exists b· the vague hypotheses
	126–15	b· C. S. on the one hand and
	141– 1	This indicates the distance b· the
	143–14	Driven to choose b· two difficulties,
	145– 9	not b· material methods, but b·
	145–28	the warfare b· Spirit and the flesh
ph	171–23	No more sympathy exists b· the flesh and

between
ph 171–24	than *b·* Belial and Christ.
173– 2	*b·* humanity and the brute,
193–15	It was *b·* three and four o'clock
f 202– 3	unity which exists *b·* God and man
236–30	While age is halting *b·* two opinions
240–31	how to divide *b·* sense and Soul.
244– 8	is seen *b·* the cradle and the grave,
246– 2	swinging *b·* evil and good,
254– 7	not until the battle *b·* Spirit and flesh is
b 273–12	the enmity *b·* Science and the senses,
288– 3	suppositional warfare *b·* truth and error
288– 4	the mental conflict *b·* the evidence of
288– 6	this warfare *b·* the Spirit and flesh
288–11	the conflict *b·* truth and error,
293– 5	forms no link *b·* matter and Mind,
294–19	*b·* immortal man, representing Spirit, and
298–16	This human belief, alternating *b·* a
312–27	divides faith and understanding *b·*
315–31	the mediator *b·* Spirit and the flesh,
315–32	*b·* Truth and error.
316–13	warfare *b·* this spiritual idea and
316–14	*b·* spiritual clear-sightedness and
332–16	one mediator *b·* God and men,— *I Tim.* 2 : 5.
333– 1	*b·* God and man in His image.
338–24	would impose *b·* man and his creator.
o 345–21	incongruity *b·* God's idea and
345–24	*b·* God's man, made in His image, and
356–18	*b·* error and Truth, *b·* flesh and Spirit.
360–20	swinging *b·* the real and the unreal.
p 389–25	*b·* pain and pleasure, good and evil,
403– 2	*b·* voluntary and involuntary mesmerism
t 444–26	*b·* me and thee, and *b·* my herdmen — *Gen.* 13 : 8.
457–14	led to a quarrel *b·* two knights
462–10	dividing his interests *b·* God and
g 505–21	line of demarcation *b·* the real and
506– 2	*b·* the false and the true.
523–10	which God erects *b·* the true and false.
534– 9	put enmity *b·* thee and— *Gen.* 3 : 15.
534–10	*b·* thy seed and her seed ;— *Gen.* 3 : 15.
534–14	Apostle Paul explains this warfare *b·* the
538– 8	distance *b·* Truth and error,
538– 9	*b·* the material and spiritual,
ap 567–12	conflict *b·* the flesh and Spirit.
gl 586–16	*b·* Truth and error, *b·* Spirit and

beware
s 117–29	Jesus bade his disciples *b·* of the
ph 196–14	The command was a warning to *b·*, not of Rome,
p 382–11	*b·* of making clean merely the outside of

beyond
pr 13– 5	In public prayer we often go *b·* our
13– 6	*b·* the honest standpoint of fervent desire.
27– 2	was intended to prove *b·* a question
41– 1	hope must be cast *b·* the veil of matter
41– 3	this advance *b·* matter must come
44–22	It was a method of surgery *b·* material art,
46–24	and progressive state *b·* the grave.
a 50–26	was terrible *b·* human conception.
m 67–23	Grace and Truth are potent *b·* all
sp 98–15	*B·* the frail premises of human beliefs,
s 116–18	matter is nothing *b·* an image in mortal mind.
125– 7	Neither . . . nor overaction is *b·* God's control ;
126–19	*b·* the cognizance of the material senses
127– 8	there can be nothing *b·* illimitable divinity.
151– 6	has an absolute need of something *b·* itself
156–29	the next stately step *b·* homœopathy.
ph 177– 4	I have demonstrated this *b·* all cavil.
187–10	it attributes to . . . an ability *b·* itself.
194–19	It proves *b·* a doubt that education
f 213–22	He was a musician *b·* what the world knew.
241–15	One's aim, a point *b·* faith, should be
c 264– 7	Mortals must look *b·* fading, finite forms,
b 284–25	*b·* the cognizance of these senses,
298–18	never reaches *b·* the boundary of the
302–16	is always *b·* and above the mortal illusion
306– 6	and demonstrated this *b·* cavil.
312–24	which cannot penetrate *b·* matter.
328–32	reaching *b·* the pale of a single period
p 388–26	it would be foolish to venture *b·* our
394–10	admission that any bodily condition is *b·* the
409–30	and expect to find *b·* the grave
413– 5	A single requirement, *b·* what is necessary
426–25	would raise the standard of health . . . far *b·* its
429– 9	we look *b·* a single step in the line of
g 512– 1	aspirations soaring *b·* and above corporeality
514– 4	nothing exists *b·* the range of

bias
p 381– 3	the *b·* of education enforces this slavery.

Bible
pref viii–30	the *B·* was her sole teacher ;
pr 16–12	some doubt among *B·* scholars, whether the
a 24– 8	make the *B·* the chart of life,
39–13	The *B·* calls death an enemy,

Bible
m 58–32	"She that is married . . . says the *B·* ;" — *I Cor.* 7 : 34.
sp 99– 5	is what the *B·* demands.
an 104–10	First, people say it conflicts with the *B·*.
s 110–14	the *B·* was my only textbook.
126–29	The *B·* has been my only authority.
131–11	The central fact of the *B·* is the
140– 5	The *B·* represents Him as saying :
141–20	The *B·* declares that all believers are
146–23	derives its sanction from the *B·*,
161– 7	nullify the . . . flames, as in the *B·* case of
f 241–13	The *B·* teaches transformation of the
242–21	According to the *B·*, the facts of being
c 263–17	He might say in *B·* language :
b 319–22	the original language of the *B·*
319–24	the spiritual meaning of the *B·*,
320– 4	Metaphors abound in the *B·*,
328–18	Our missionaries carry the *B·* to India,
335–10	as the *B·* declares, without the Logos, the
o 342– 9	in the face of *B·* history and in defiance
344–32	In the *B·* the word *Spirit* is so commonly
p 406– 1	The *B·* contains the recipe for all healing.
435–29	To him I might say, in *B·* language,
437–33	read from the supreme statute-book, the *B·*,
438– 1	remarking that the *B·* was better authority
441– 3	explained from his statute-book, the *B·*,
r 480–26	The *B·* declares : "All things were — *John* 1 : 3.
497– 4	we take the inspired Word of the *B·* as our
g 537–22	Subsequent *B·* revelation is coordinate with
546–22	for they contain the deep divinity of the *B·*.
ap 572– 4	both the first and last books of the *B·*,
577–31	the acme of this Science as the *B·* reveals it.
gl 579– 5	the metaphysical interpretation of *B·* terms,

biblical
g 526–24	This second *b·* account is a

bicuspids
f 247– 6	incisors, cuspids, *b·*, and one molar.

bid
p 363–14	the woman's immoral status and *b·* her depart,
394–20	Will you *b·* a man let evils overcome him,

bidden
s 130– 4	When all men are *b·* to the feast,
160–18	or has it *b·* them to be impotent?
b 307–28	nor *b·* to obey material laws which

bidding
b 321–14	The serpent, evil, under wisdom's *b·*, was

bids
pr 5– 8	Temptation *b·* us repeat the offence,
a 29– 8	It *b·* us work the more earnestly in times of

big
pref vii– 2	to-day is *b·* with blessings.

bigot
a 52–30	The *b·*, the debauchee, the hypocrite,

bigoted
a 48– 2	staves of *b·* ignorance smote him sorely.
p 366–21	swallow the camels of *b·* pedantry.

bigotry
t 450– 1	whose *b·* and conceit twist every fact
464–23	weapons of *b·*, ignorance, envy, fall
r 484– 3	neither pride, prejudice, *b·*, nor envy, can
gl 597–13	tore from *b·* and superstition their coverings,

Bill of Rights
s 161–14	harmony with our Constitution and *B·* of *R·*,

billows
f 240– 4	giant hills, winged winds, mighty *b·*,

bind
a 44–16	*b·* up the wounded side and lacerated feet,
f 229–16	to *b·* mortals to sickness, sin, and death.
p 366–31	we must first learn to *b·* up the broken-hearted.
372–12	*b·* himself with his own beliefs,
399–31	first *b·* the strong man?"— *Matt.* 12 : 29.

binds
sp 96– 2	unwillingness . . . *b·* Christendom with chains.
f 225– 1	What is it that *b·* man with iron shackles
ap 575–31	which *b·* human society into solemn union ;

biographical
pref viii–25	*b·* sketch, narrating experiences which

bird
s 121–11	*b·* and blossom were glad in God's . . . sunshine,
c 261–28	even as the *b·* which has burst from the egg
g 550–26	A serpent never begets a *b·*,
551– 7	the *b·* is not the product of a beast.
552– 1	question, Which is first, the egg or the *b·*?

birth
any
f 206–25	Can there be any *b·* or death for man,

as untimely
c 265–16	senses represent *b·* as untimely

birth

before
p 429–22 If . . . we must have lived before *b*·,
human
ph 190–14 Human *b*·, growth, maturity, and decay
new
t 463–17 When this new *b*· takes place,
g 548–15 This is the new *b*· going on hourly,
origin and
a 30–11 Had his origin and *b*· been wholly apart
prior to his
ph 178–14 produced prior to his *b*· by the fright
spiritual
t 463–12 this idea . . . in the travail of spiritual *b*·.
time-tables of
f 246–18 Time-tables of *b*· and death are

---

ph 185–13 They have their *b*· in mortal mind,
191–12 even to the *b*· of a new-old idea,
f 244–13 Man undergoing *b*·, maturity, and decay
244–24 He has neither *b*· nor death.
b 288–25 spiritual real man has no *b*·,
302–11 the *b*·, sin, sickness, and death of
305–28 not subject to *b*·, growth, maturity, decay.
t 463–7 To attend properly the *b*· of the new child,
463–9 that the *b*· will be natural and safe.
g 529–5 instruments . . . assist the *b*· of mortals.
539–31 Science of creation, so conspicuous in the *b*· of
544–7 *B*·, decay, and death arise from the
548–20 statements now current, about *b*· and
549–14 not begin with the *b*· of new individuals,
550–18 as beginning and ending, and with *b*·, decay,
ap 562–23 travailing in *b*·, and— *Rev.* 12 : 2.
562–27 joy that the *b*· goes on ;

birthright
f 226–20 man's *b*· of sole allegiance to his Maker
g 518–1 His *b*· is dominion, not subjection.

birth-throes
g 557–6 Mind controls the *b*· in the lower realms

bit
f 222–25 if eating a *b*· of animal flesh could
237–6 "Mamma, my finger is not a *b*· sore."

bite
g 534–27 The serpent, material sense, will *b*· the heel
ap 563–20 that he may *b*· the heel of truth

bites
f 216–7 Error *b*· the heel of truth, but cannot kill

bitter
a 32–12 The cup shows forth his *b*· experience,
b 287–13 sweet water and *b*·?"— *Jas.* 3 : 11.
t 455–30 cannot send forth both sweet waters and *b*·.
r 489–23 fountain sendeth not forth sweet waters and *b*·.
ap 559–18 and it shall make thy belly *b*·, — *Rev.* 10 : 9.
559–23 murmur not . . . if you find its digestion *b*·,
559–28 share the hemlock cup and eat the *b*· herbs ;

bitterness
a 43–22 because of the cup of *b*· he drank.
54–21 His earthly cup of *b*· was drained
s 139–13 wisely to stem the tide of sectarian *b*·,

black
ph 195–7 All that he ate, except his *b*· crust,
r 479–27 We admit that *b*· is not a color,

blackboard
pr 3–4 Who would stand before a *b*·, and
t 453–2 among the examples on the *b*·,

blackness
b 307–31 Above error's awful din, *b*·, and chaos,

blacksmith's
ph 198–29 Because the muscles of the *b*· arm
199–13 but by reason of the *b*· faith in

Blackstone
p 438–2 the Bible was better authority than *B*· :

blade
sp 70–12 from a *b*· of grass to a star,
ph 191–21 By its own volition, not a *b*· of grass springs

blades
ph 190–15 grass . . . with beautiful green *b*·,

blameworthy
p 414–30 whereas imperfection is *b*·,

blanches
p 433–14 His sallow face *b*· with fear,

blandly
t 450–7 while looking you *b*· in the face,

blank
c 266–7 Would existence . . . be to you a *b*·?

blanket
ph 179–17 that he will take cold without his *b*·,

blasphemer
sp 94–27 what would be said . . . of an infidel *b*·

blasphemes
sp 88–23 Excite the opposite development, and he *b*·.

blasphemies
an 100– * thefts, false witness, *b*· :— *Matt.* 15 : 19.

blast
t 451–32 malpractice tends to *b*· moral sense,

blasts
m 57–25 The wintry *b*· of earth may uproot the
f 220–12 snowbird sings and soars amid the *b*· ;

blaze
b 296–15 and they must go out under the *b*· of Truth,

blazons
f 247–26 *b*· the night with starry gems,

bleeding
pr 10–2 even though with *b*· footsteps,
a 41–9 though it be with *b*· footprints,
p 379–10 fancied himself *b*· to death,
379–13 Had he known his sense of *b*· was an

blend
m 58–7 they should be concordant in order to *b*·
59–13 their sympathies should *b*· in sweet confidence
sp 74–23 different beliefs, which never *b*·.
gl 588–14 numbers which never *b*· with each other,

blending
b 308–11 a *b*· of false claims, false pleasure,
316–22 Christ illustrates that *b*· with God,
g 552–25 *b*· tints of leaf and flower show the

blends
c 263–7 When mortal man *b*· his thoughts of

bless
pr 9–12 and *b*· them that curse us ;
13–17 God will *b*· it, and we shall incur less
a 30–29 Only in this way can we *b*· our enemies,
50–11 to sustain and *b*· so faithful a son.
m 60–29 infinite resources with which to *b*· mankind,
c 263–14 injuring those whom he would *b*·.
p 397–7 actually injuring those whom we mean to *b*·.
t 453–19 You uncover sin, . . . in order to *b*· the

blessed
pr 2–6 is *b*· of our Father,
32–15 Jesus took bread, and *b*· it— *Matt.* 26 : 26.
36–2 in the *b*· company of Truth and Love
40–31 nature of Christianity is peaceful and *b*·,
49–18 Forsaken by all whom he had *b*·,
s 132–9 And *b*· is he, whosoever— *Matt.* 11 : 6.
137–22 "*B*· art thou, Simon Bar-jona :— *Matt.* 16 : 17.
c 267–28 "*B*· is the man that endureth— *Jas.* 1 : 12.
b 317–11 *b*· benedictions rest upon Jesus' followers :
324–5 "*B*· are the pure in heart :— *Matt.* 5 : 8.
338–29 notwithstanding God had *b*· the earth
338–31 not the ideal man for whom the earth was *b*·,
o 341–9 "*B*· are the pure in heart :— *Matt.* 5 : 8.
g 512–17 And God *b*· them, saying,— *Gen.* 1 : 22.
517–25 And God *b*· them, and— *Gen.* 1 : 28.
518–17 *b*· is that man who seeth his brother's need
532–10 Adam and his progeny were cursed, not *b*· ;
537–28 *b*· the earth and gave it to man
548–25 would have *b*· the human race more
ap 558– * *B*· is he that readeth, and— *Rev.* 1 : 3.
571–8 requires the spirit of our *b*· Master
573–18 but as the *b*· child of God.

blessedness
pr 2–30 the source of all existence and *b*·.
10–25 the source and means of all goodness and *b*·,
c 264–25 Spiritual living and *b*· are the only
b 329–27 their real spiritual source to be all *b*·,

blesses
pr 8–23 the reward of Him who *b*· the poor.
a 30–18 which *b*· even those that curse it.
33–23 It *b*· its enemies, heals the sick,
sp 78–28 Spirit *b*· man, but man
an 103–8 *b*· the whole human family.
f 206–16 we find that whatever *b*· one *b*· all,
234–5 *b*· the human family with crumbs of comfort
g 507–6 Spirit names and *b*· all.
512–20 Spirit *b*· the multiplication of its own
516–19 beautifies the landscape, *b*· the earth.
517–30 Divine Love *b*· its own ideas,

blessing
pr 3–10 in order to receive His *b*·,
a 20–17 returning *b*· for cursing, he taught mortals
50–17 be shorn of its mighty *b*· for the human race.
f 238–3 wait till those . . . are ready for the *b*·,
r 488–6 you receive the *b*· of Truth.
g 545–20 yet this opposite, . . . impudently demands a *b*·.
ap 570–23 Those ready for the *b*· you impart
gl 589–21 pure affection *b*· its enemies.

blessings
all
 pr 3–28 yet return thanks to God for all b·,
great
 a 25–30 else we are not improving the great b·
infinite
 pr 15–30 and they assuredly call down infinite b·.
 b 325– 8 which results in infinite b· to mortals.
our
 pr 3–32 put the finger on the lips and remember our b·.
spiritual
 a 53–17 spiritual b· which might flow from such
 g 512–15 spiritual b·, thus typified, are the

 pref vii– 2 to-day is big with b·.
 pr 3–24 shall avail ourselves of the b· we have,
 4–14 are made manifest in the b· they bring,
 4–14 b· which, even if not acknowledged in
 10–23 we do not always receive the b· we ask for
 c 266–16 the foregoing prophecy and its b·.
 o 343–11 and the blind look up to C. S. with b·,
 r 489–16 channel to man of divine b·
 gl 597– 7 long petitions for b· upon material methods,

blest
 iii– * And I am b· !
 m 57–31 Marriage is unblest or b·, according to

blight
 f 246–31 rather than into age and b·.

blighted
 sp 77–29 a state resembling that of b· buds,
 78– 1 The decaying flower, the b· bud,

blighting
 f 236–22 b· the buddings of self-government.

blind
 pref xi–20 And recovering of sight to the b·,— Luke 4 : 18.
 pr 12– 7 through a b· faith in God.
 13–30 b· to the reality of man's existence,
 a 23–28 expresses the helplessness of a b· faith ;
 27– 4 how that the b· see,— Luke 7 : 22.
 s 124–11 In a word, human belief is a b· conclusion
 132– 6 the b· receive their sight— Matt. 11 : 5.
 ph 167– 4 If we rise no higher than b· faith,
 183–28 the law which gives sight to the b·,
 192–11 a b· miscalled force, the offspring of will
 194–12 if mortal mind says, "I am deaf and b·,"
 196– 2 It is but a b· force.
 f 210–13 gave sight to the b·, hearing to the deaf,
 223–18 "If the b· lead the b·,— Matt. 15 : 14.
 226–25 The lame, the deaf, the dumb, the b·,
 b 316–31 b· to the possibilities of Spirit
 324–21 was made b·, and his blindness was felt ;
 337– 3 b· mortals do lose sight of spiritual
 o 342–25 the lame to walk, and the b· to see.
 343–11 The sick, the halt, and the b· look up to C. S.
 350–15 Unless the works are . . . the words are b·.
 p 391– 7 Instead of b· and calm submission
 398–27 a b· faith removes bodily ailments for a season,
 439–18 the b· Hypnotism, and the masked
 t 444– 2 these very failures may open their b· eyes.
 459–17 putting a sharp knife into the hands of a b· man
 r 487–11 apprehension of this gave sight to the b·
 490– 8 Will— b·, stubborn, and headlong
 g 536–19 The b· leading the b·, both would fall.
 gl 582– 2 not a faltering nor a b· faith,
 599– 5 B· enthusiasm ; mortal will.
 (see also **belief**)

blinded
 f 223–17 but more are b· by their old illusions,

blindly
 b 305–32 not so b· as the Pharisees,
 p 377–18 that it may not produce b· its bad effects.

blindness
mortal
 p 374–13 This mortal b· and its sharp consequences
pagan
 ph 187– 8 With pagan b·, it attributes to

 ph 194–11 not necessary to ensure deafness and b· ;
 f 205– 5 all because of their b·,
 c 263–30 A sensual thought, . . . is dense b·
 b 316–15 between spiritual clear-sightedness and the b·
 324–22 Paul was made blind, and his b· was felt ;
 t 448– 2 B· and self-righteousness cling fast to
 448–15 upon your b· to evil or upon the
 r 486–18 Alas for the b· of belief, which
 486–29 then palsy, b·, and deafness would
 487– 1 Mere belief is b· without Principle

bliss
all
 f 253– 5 include and impart all b·,
attain the
 c 262–22 and attain the b· of loving unselfishly,

bliss
boundless
 r 481– 4 freedom, harmony, and boundless b·.
eternal
 ap 577–10 there is no impediment to eternal b·,
spiritual
 gl 582–15 a sense of Soul, which has spiritual b·

 a 36– 2 never find b· . . . simply through translation
 39–12 out of mortality into immortality and b·.
 ph 175–32 "Where ignorance is b·, 't is folly to be wise,"
 f 203–25 not a stepping-stone to Life, immortality, and b·.
 b 328– 1 the grandeur and b· of a spiritual sense,
 337– 7 Sensualism is not b·, but bondage.
 ap 574–15 the spiritual outpouring of b· and glory,
 gl 587–26 spirituality ; b·; the atmosphere of Soul.

blister
 ph 198–17 by a counter-irritant,— perhaps by a b·,

Blondin
 ph 199–25 Had B· believed it impossible to walk the rope

blood
all the
 p 376–14 than in all the b·, which ever flowed through
and nerves
 s 160–19 Can muscles, bones, b·, and nerves rebel
bayonet and
 f 226–12 won, . . . not with bayonet and b·,
brother's
 g 541–28 The voice of thy brother's b·— Gen. 4 : 10.
consumption of the
 p 376–11 with consumption of the b·,
drink his
 a 25–11 they truly eat his flesh and drink his b·,
essence of
 a 25– 3 The spiritual essence of b· is sacrifice.
flesh and
 a 25–10 His true flesh and b· were his Life ;
 s 137–23 flesh and b· hath not revealed it— Matt. 16 : 17.
 b 321– 4 "Flesh and b· cannot inherit the— I Cor. 15 : 50.
 r 478–29 conferred not with flesh and b·."— Gal. 1 : 16.
her
 p 379–15 inspecting the hue of her b· ·
 379–21 not dying on account of the state of her b·,
his
 a 30–16 by man shall his b· be shed."— Gen. 9 : 6.
 p 379–18 when not a drop of his b· was shed.
human
 a 25– 6 than can be expressed by our sense of human b·.
humor in the
 p 424–32 may tell you that he has a humor in the b·,
man's
 a 30–15 "Whoso sheddeth man's b·,— Gen. 9 : 6.
material
 a 25– 6 The material b· of Jesus was no more efficacious
of the Lamb
 ap 568–18 by the b· of the Lamb,— Rev. 12 : 11.
of the martyrs
 a 37– 5 "The b· of the martyrs is the seed of
passage of the
 ph 187–14 opening and closing for the passage of the b·,
rushes madly
 p 373–27 When the b· rushes madly through the veins
shared the
 a 33–28 Have you shared the b· of the New Covenant,
went down in
 f 225–20 but oppression neither went down in b·,

 s 143–19 but you conclude that the stomach, b·,
 151–19 b·, heart, . . . have nothing to do with Life,
 ph 172–23 Brain, heart, b·, . . . the material structure?
 172–32 (heart, b·, brain, acting through the
 f 220–31 controls the stomach, bones, lungs, heart, b·,
 b 308–10 the head, heart, stomach, b·, nerves,
 p 372– 8 can form b·, flesh, and bones.
 376–11 should be told that b· never gave life
 379–21 her belief that b· is destroying her life.
 408–20 does not distribute drugs through the b·,
 r 475– 7 brain, b·, bones, and other material elements.

bloodshed
 sp 94–14 Tyranny, intolerance, and b·, wherever found,
 s 139–10 Reforms have commonly been attended with b·

blossom
 m 62–23 The divine Mind, which forms the bud and b·,
 s 121–11 bird and b· were glad
 g 518–21 as the b· shines through the bud.
 gl 596–27 maketh the valley to bud and b· as the rose.

blot
 p 391– 3 B· out the images of mortal thought

blots
 p 437– 6 It b· the fair escutcheon of omnipotence.

blow
  sp 97–10   the flight of one and the *b·* of the other
  f 201–15   Then, when the winds of God *b·*,
  g 535–10   Divine Science deals its chief *b·* at
bloweth
  gl 598– 3   *b·* where it listeth. — *John* 3 : 8.
blue
  f 220– 9   violet lifts her *b·* eye to greet the early spring.
blunder
  s 123– 5   Ptolemaic *b·* could not affect the harmony of
  g 549– 7   a *b·* which will finally give place to
blundering
  p 386–16   A *b·* despatch, mistakenly announcing
blunders
  f 230–19   Does wisdom make *b·*
bluntly
  pref x–12   *b·* and honestly given the text of Truth.
blush
  sp 92–25   We should *b·* to call that real which
Board of Health
  p 432–22   by the officer of the *B· of H·*,
  432–28   with a message from the *B· of H·*
boast
  t 450–18   evil will *b·* itself above good.
bodies
  animal
    an 100– 9   Animal *b·* are susceptible to the influence of
  celestial
    an 100– 9   celestial *b·*, the earth, and animated things.
    s 123– 1   theory as to the relations of the celestial *b·*,
    f 209–20   and revolutions of the celestial *b·*,
    g 509–13   creates no other than heavenly or celestial *b·*,
  material
    sp 73–19   The belief that material *b·* return to dust,
  minds and
    s 110–26   power of C. S. to heal mortal minds and *b·*.
    f 210–15   action of . . . Mind on human minds and *b·*
    p 408–13   effects of illusion on mortal minds and *b·*.
  mortal
    sp 92– 8   decomposition of mortal *b·* in what is termed
    o 341– *   *shall also quicken your mortal b·* — *Rom.* 8 : 11.
  organic
    sp 74– 4   must be free from organic *b·* ;
  our
    c 261–31   We should forget our *b·* in remembering good
  our own
    p 402–22   we rarely remember that we govern our own *b·*.
  spiritual
    sp 73–20   belief that . . . rise up as spiritual *b·*
  terrestrial
    s 123– 3   the greater error as to our terrestrial *b·*.
  their
    sp 90–21   yet their *b·* stay in one place.
    p 396–23   which their beliefs exercise over their *b·*.
    409–15   knowing how to govern their *b·*.
    416–31   Turn their thoughts away from their *b·*
  their own
    ph 199–15   Mortals develop their own *b·*
    f 228–16   Then they will control their own *b·*
  these
    g 551–18   transmitted through these *b·* called eggs,
  unseen
    p 429–17   with *b·* unseen by those who think that
  your
    b 325–22   "Present your *b·* a living— *Rom.* 12 : 1.

  sp 87–10   Though *b·* are leagues apart
  87–22   the *b·* which lie buried in its sands :

bodiless
  s 116–22   God is not *corporeal*, but *incorporeal*, . . . *b·*.
bodily
  a 43– 2   they did understand it after his *b·* departure.
  45–13   Three days after his *b·* burial
  50–20   before the evidence of the *b·* senses,
  sp 76–24   without a single *b·* pleasure or pain,
  80– 5   for the support of *b·* endurance.
  s 136– 8   divine power to save men both *b·* and spiritually.
  161–24   ordinary practitioner, examining *b·* symptoms,
  ph 166–19   thrusting Him aside in times of *b·* trouble,
  172– 1   which he has through the *b·* senses,
  f 217–10   unnatural mental and *b·* conditions,
  219– 3   applies to all *b·* ailments,
  228–21   we shall never depend on *b·* conditions,
  245–23   The *b·* results of her belief that she was young
  c 257– 9   belief in a *b·* soul and a material mind,
  b 302–27   not in any *b·* or personal likeness
  334–12   Jesus appeared as a *b·* existence.
  p 368–20   That Life is not contingent on *b·* conditions
  382–32   The ailment was not *b·*, but mental,
  387–32   to defend himself, . . . from *b·* suffering.
  389– 9   Matter does not inform you of *b·* derangements ;

bodily
  p 392– 4   To cure a *b·* ailment, every broken moral law
         should
  392–26   conclusions as you wish realized in *b·* results,
  394–10   The admission that any *b·* condition
  397– 9   You cause *b·* sufferings and increase them
  398–28   faith removes *b·* ailments for a season,
  413–20   I insist on *b·* cleanliness within and without.
  416– 1   as if it were a separate *b·* member.
  t 448– 5   Evil which obtains in the *b·* senses,
Body
  p 432–11   I am Mortality, Governor of the Province of *B·*,
  437– 1   Nerve, testified that he was a ruler of *B·*,
  438–10   Instead of being a ruler in the Province of *B·*,
  439– 7   absent from the Province of *B·*,
body
  absent from the
    pr 14– 4   are not "absent from the *b·*" — *II Cor.* 5 : 8.
    14–22   because the Ego is absent from the *b·*,
    f 216–29   to be absent from the *b·*, — *II Cor.* 5 : 8.
    p 383–10   to be absent from the *b·*, — *II Cor.* 5 : 8.
    gl 581–25   to be absent from the *b·*, — *II Cor.* 5 : 8.
  action of the
    f 239–25   and produces every discordant action of the *b·*.
  affects the
    s 149–18   "We know that mind affects the *b·*
    f 222– 4   learned that food affects the *b·* only as
    p 397– 2   not seeing how mortal mind affects the *b·*,
  affect the
    p 402–21   and in this way affect the *b·*,
  and mind
    ph 190– 5   producing mortals, both *b·* and mind ;
    b 302– 3   The material *b·* and mind are temporal,
  and Soul
    r 477–19   *Question.* — What are *b·* and Soul?
  apparent on the
    p 374–12   before it is consciously apparent on the *b·*,
  appearance in the
    ph 168–26   made its appearance in the *b·*.
  argued that the
    p 435– 5   False Belief has argued that the *b·* should
  as matter
    f 214–31   evident that the *b·* as matter has no sensation
  belief that the
    f 226–23   in the belief that the *b·* governed them,
  believing that the
    f 218–15   believing that the *b·* can be sick independently
  better
    p 425–23   Consciousness constructs a better *b·* when
  brain or
    p 401–24   produce any effect upon the brain or *b·*
  brings to the
    s 162– 4   C. S. brings to the *b·* the sunlight of Truth,
  buried the
    sp 75–19   plane of belief as those who buried the *b·*,
  bury the
    p 429–18   unseen by those who think that they bury the *b·*.
  called man
    sp 81–21   give to the worms the *b·* called man,
    ph 190–13   and the bulk of a *b·*, called man.
  called the
    b 313–29   Jesus called the *b·*, which by
  cannot believe
    r 487–17   The *b·* cannot believe.
  cannot be saved
    sp 98– 7   *B·* cannot be saved except through Mind.
  cannot die
    p 426–30   Man is immortal, and the *b·* cannot die,
  cannot suffer
    p 392–32   then the *b·* cannot suffer from them.
  cause the
    p 415–27   will apparently cause the *b·* to disappear.
  clean
    p 383– 3   We need a clean *b·* and a clean mind,
  coming from the
    p 385–31   coming from the *b·* or from inert matter
  complaint from the
    p 391–29   contradict every complaint from the *b·*,
  concerning the
    f 219–15   never affirm concerning the *b·* what we
  condition of the
    f 217–17   conquered a diseased condition of the *b·* through
    p 408–30   that condition of the *b·* which we call sensation
  control over the
    ph 166– 7   thus the conscious control over the *b·* is lost.
    p 406–27   a loss of control over the *b·*.
  controls the
    p 400– 1   mind, which directly controls the *b·*
  control the
    sp 93– 2   recognize Soul as . . . able to control the *b·*
    p 379– 1   If disease can attack and control the *b·*
  conversation about the
    c 260–26   by conversation about the *b·*,
  corresponds with
    p 412–26   until the *b·* corresponds with the

body

corrupt
  p 404– 9 A corrupt mind is manifested in a corrupt b·.
dead
  s 113– 7 the letter is but the dead b· of Science,
  p 416–21 only in mortal mind, as the dead b· proves ;
derangement of the
  p 423–28 abnormal condition or derangement of the b·
detach sense from the
  c 261–21 Detach sense from the b·, or matter,
divine
  ap 559–25 when you eat the divine b· of
dosing the
  ph 169–14 and by dosing the b· in order to avoid it.
effects on the
  o 350–25 known by its effects on the b·
  p 370–20 very direct and marked effects on the b·.
    374– 5 Hatred and its effects on the b· are removed
effects upon the
  ph 176–10 seen in its glorious effects upon the b·.
effect upon the
  p 398–21 and produces a new effect upon the b·.
even in
  p 404–31 nor Mind can help him . . . even in b·, unless
experiences no pain
  c 261–10 the b· experiences no pain.
explanation of
  ph 200– 9 wise not to undertake the explanation of b·.
expose the
  p 386– 5 Expose the b· to certain temperatures,
feeds the
  f 248– 8 Immortal Mind feeds the b· with
fettered by the
  b 292–10 belief that Mind, . . . can be fettered by the b·,
finite
  b 309–25 impossible for . . . Soul to be in a finite b·
flee from
  p 405–31 to flee from b· to Spirit,
foe of the
  ph 176–20 Mortal mind is the worst foe of the b·,
functions of the
  p 373–22 expressed . . . in the functions of the b·.
governed by the
  c 257–10 belief in . . . a soul governed by the b·
governing the
  p 370– 8 proves that fear is governing the b·.
government of the
  ph 167–27 scientific government of the b· must be attained
    182–18 Mind's government of the b· must supersede
  t 462–30 It urges the government of the b·
governs the
  s 111–28 Mind governs the b·, not partially but wholly.
    162–13 the fact that Mind governs the b·,
  ph 180–14 Ignorant that the human mind governs the b·,
govern the
  f 251–15 learn how mankind govern the b·,
    251–18 should learn whether they govern the b·
greater than
  f 223–12 Soul is Spirit, and Spirit is greater than b·.
guillotined
  p 427–17 bone is broken or the b· guillotined.
had been naked
  g 532–28 In the allegory the b· had been naked,
healer of the
  b 326–15 healer of mortal mind is the healer of the b·.
heal the
  s 146–14 even the might of Mind — to heal the b·
  p 399–32 In other words : How can I heal the b·, without
his
  a 45–26 for they believed his b· to be dead.
    46–15 his b· was not changed until he
    53–25 Jesus bore our sins in his b·.
  sp 75–16 not by an admission that his b· had died
    75–18 that Lazarus had lived or died in his b·,
  ph 188–16 the dreamer thinks that his b· is material
  f 216–17 his b· is in submission to everlasting Life
  b 290–29 no more spiritual for believing that his b· died
    290–31 His b· is as material as his mind, and *vice versa*.
    314–13 When Jesus spoke of reproducing his b·,
    314–16 their material temple instead of his b·.
    320–31 if disease and worms destroyed his b·, yet
  p 383– 8 takes the best care of his b· when he
    388– 9 when dire inflictions failed to destroy his b·.
    414– 1 held in the beliefs concerning his b·.
    416–22 mortal has resigned his b· to dust,
  r 486–14 his b· was the same immediately after death
his own
  s 150–28 doctrine . . . then thrust out of his own b·
human
  m 62–24 will care for the human b·, even as it
  s 125– 4 now considered . . . health in the human b·
  t 458–13 trying to sustain the human b·
imaged on the
  p 379–31 the fever-picture, . . . imaged on the b·
improves under
  p 370– 5 The b· improves under the same regimen

body

indifference to the
  f 216– 2 his faith in Soul and his indifference to the b·.
influences the
  s 143–18 You admit that mind influences the b·
inharmonious
  ph 166–16 From it arises the inharmonious b·.
innocent
  p 437–16 the helpless innocent b· tortured,
instead of
  f 223– 5 illusion that he lives in b· instead of in Soul,
  b 315– 8 He knew that the Ego was Mind instead of b·
  p 419–17 Observe mind instead of b·,
  g 536–15 governed . . . by b· instead of by Soul,
intact in
  r 492– 1 the dream leaves mortal man intact in b·
is affected
  p 380–17 b· is affected only with the belief of disease
is controlled
  pr 14–17 when the b· is controlled by spiritual Life,
is devoid
  p 399–21 Without this force the b· is devoid of action,
is disintegrated
  p 429–20 after the b· is disintegrated.
is not controlled
  s 143–24 b· is not controlled scientifically by a
is not first
  f 207–15 B· is not first and Soul last,
is the substratum
  p 371– 2 The b· is the substratum of mortal mind,
its own
  ph 196– 5 power of mortal mind over its own b·
justice to the
  p 434–32 Denying justice to the b·,
keeping the
  p 413–18 only for the purpose of keeping the b· clean.
keep the
  p 383–19 mind must be clean to keep the b· in proper
leaving a
  r 478– 6 has never beheld Spirit or Soul leaving a b·
lies listless
  f 250–20 To the observer, the b· lies listless,
light of the
  p 393–25 "the light of the b· is the eye,"— *Matt.* 6 : 22.
limited
  b 284– 7 would seem to spring from a limited b· ;
    335–18 never . . . in a limited mind or a limited b·.
little
  p 413–22 need not wash his little b· all over each day
look away from the
  c 261– 2 Look away from the b· into Truth and Love,
lost from the
  r 491–24 memory and consciousness are lost from the b·,
makes . . . tributary
  s 119–31 C. S. . . . makes b· tributary to Mind.
making the
  a 34– 4 making the b· "holy, acceptable— *Rom.* 12 : 1.
manifestation in the
  s 154– 8 and its consequent manifestation in the b·.
manifest on the
  f 219–18 before it can be made manifest on the b·,
  r 493–22 It is fear made manifest on the b·.
man's
  f 216–28 When you say, "Man's b· is material,"
  g 531–15 If, in the beginning, man's b· originated in
masters of the
  f 228–23 but we shall be masters of the b·,
mastery of the
  p 406–30 destroyed only by Mind's mastery of the b·.
material
  (see **material***)*
Mind and
  b 285–13 Spirit and matter, Mind and b·,
mind and
  s 149–29 benefits mind and b·.
    151– 1 ignorant that the human mind and b· are myths.
    157–27 but they leave both mind and b· worse
    157–29 the entire corporeality, — namely, mind and b·,
    158–12 truth which heals both mind and b·.
  ph 169– 1 process which mortal mind and b· undergo
    177– 8 Mortal mind and b· are one.
  b 293– 9 This so-called mind and b· is the
    316–10 manifest . . . upon the human mind and b·,
  p 383– 3 because mind and b· rest on the same basis.
    388–32 the harmonious functions of mind and b·,
    405–15 will be executed upon mortal mind, and b·.
    406– 9 healing of mortals, both mind and b·.
    409– 4 *Mortal mind* and b· combine as one,
Mind controls
  sp 79–28 asserting that Mind controls b· and brain.
mind or
  p 365–31 unchristian practitioner is not giving to mind
                          or b·
  r 473– 1 inharmony of mortal mind or b· is illusion,

body

Mind over
- *ph* 169–16 understood the control of Mind over *b·*,
- *p* 380–10 against the control of Mind over *b·*,

mortal
- (*see* **mortal**)

mortality of the
- *ph* 191–27 infers the mortality of the *b·*.

move the
- *a* 104–32 human mind must move the *b·* to a wicked act

my
- *a* 32–17 Take, eat ; this is my *b·*.— *Matt.* 26 : 26
- *p* 374– 9 until it appeared on my *b·* ?''
- 383– 5 One says : "I take good care of my *b·*.''

no heed to the
- *p* 400–21 giving no heed to the *b·*,

not in
- *pr* 13–32 not cognizant of life in Soul, not in *b·*.

not in the
- *r* 467–17 Science reveals Spirit, Soul, as not in the *b·*,

outlined on the
- *ph* 196–30 which is afterwards outlined on the *b·*.

outline on the
- *r* 485–25 If thought yields . . . it cannot outline on the *b·*

outside the
- *g* 510–17 representation of Soul outside the *b·*,

over the
- *ph* 167–28 to gain control over the *b·*
- 194– 9 Truth sends a report of health over the *b·*.
- *f* 217–26 learn the power of Mind over the *b·*
- 218–16 no jurisdiction over the *b·*.
- *p* 382–27 supporting the power of Mind over the *b·*
- 417–29 control which Mind holds over the *b·*.

parted from the
- *p* 401–22 If the mind were parted from the *b·*,

pass from the
- *p* 375– 2 Heat would pass from the *b·* as painlessly as

patient's
- *s* 152–17 to ascertain the temperature of the patient's *b·* ;

physical
- *s* 124–32 The elements and functions of the physical *b·*

poor
- *p* 383–30 pinching and pounding the poor *b·*,

portion of the
- *p* 425–28 or any portion of the *b·*

portions of the
- *p* 421– 4 belief that other portions of the *b·*

possible for the
- *sp* 90–12 will be found to be equally possible for the *b·*.

produced on the
- *p* 392–13 Whatever benefit is produced on the *b·*,

puts the
- *p* 399– 7 and puts the *b·* through certain motions.

reach the
- *ph* 170–15 and reach the *b·* through Mind.

reconstruct the
- *p* 422–19 changes . . . serve·to reconstruct the *b·*.

redemption of our
- *c* 255– * to wit, the redemption of our *b·*.— *Rom.* 8 : 23.

relieve the
- *s* 157–26 quiet mortal mind, and so relieve the *b·* ;

rendered pure
- *p* 383– 3 a *b·* rendered pure by Mind

responds
- *sp* 89–15 the *b·* responds to this belief,

results upon the
- *p* 384–13 and its results upon the *b·*,

same
- *a* 45–32 He presented the same *b·* that he had before

says of the
- *f* 218– 5 what the human mind says of the *b·*,

sees the
- *sp* 90–17 The looker-on sees the *b·* in bed,

sensationless
- *b* 280–26 man has a sensationless *b·* ;

senses and the
- *b* 317–21 testimony of the material senses and the *b·*,

sensibly with the
- *pr* 14– 1 If we are sensibly with the *b·*

sensuous
- *f* 203–19 We imagine that Mind can be . . . in a sensuous *b·*.

sick
- *c* 260–20 sick *b·* is evolved from sick thoughts.

slave to the
- *gl* 582–27 and would make mortal mind a slave to the *b·*.

solid
- *f* 242–15 Self-love is more opaque than a solid *b·*.

Soul and
- *s* 114–25 It lifts the veil of mystery from Soul and *b·*,
- 119–30 reverses the seeming relation of Soul and *b·*
- 122–30 make the same mistake regarding Soul and *b·*

soul and
- *s* 123– 6 as does the error relating to soul and *b·*,
- *ph* 196–11 able to destroy both soul and *b·* — *Matt.* 10 : 28.
- *b* 338– 6 belief . . . that he is both soul and *b·*,

body

steers the
- *p* 426– 4 divine power, which steers the *b·* into health.

stimulus of the
- *p* 420–22 Mind is the natural stimulus of the *b·*,

stimulus to the
- *p* 420–19 It imparts a healthy stimulus to the *b·*,

superimposed upon the
- *p* 425–11 images . . . superimposed upon the *b·* ;

sustain the
- *p* 417– 5 power of Mind to sustain the *b·*.

teaching that the
- *p* 396–21 all teaching that the *b·* suffers,

temple also means
- *ap* 576–15 The word *temple* also means *b·*.

temple, or
- *p* 428–13 establish in truth the temple, or *b·*,

termed the
- *p* 409–12 substratum of mortal mind, termed the *b·*,

that
- *sp* 72– 5 that *b·* would disappear to mortal sense,
- 73–25 belief . . . sensations belonging to that *b·*.
- 90–18 but the supposed inhabitant of that *b·*
- *ph* 188–17 thinks . . . the suffering is in that *b·*.
- *r* 478–18 That *b·* is most harmonious in which the

this
- *ph* 187–32 This *b·* is put off only as
- *f* 208–27 A mortal man possesses this *b·*,
- *p* 368–22 when we learn that life and man survive this *b·*.

this temple
- *a* 27–12 " Destroy this temple [*b·*], — *John* 2 : 19.
- *r* 494– 2 " Destroy this temple [*b·*], — *John* 2 : 19.

transformation of the
- *f* 241–13 transformation of the *b·* by the renewal of

treat the
- *ph* 174–25 Then, if . . . sick, why treat the *b·* alone

triumph over
- *a* 42–16 the proof of his final triumph over *b·*

triumph over the
- *f* 242– 8 and the final triumph over the *b·*.

washing the
- *f* 241–27 washing the *b·* of all the impurities of flesh,

when bereft
- *p* 374–26 *b·*, when bereft of mortal mind, at first cools,

when the
- *p* 391–18 When the *b·* is supposed to say, "I am sick,"

whole
- *f* 219–12 makes the whole *b·* "sick, — *Isa.* 1 : 5.

will reflect
- *b* 324– 9 the *b·* will reflect what governs it,

will then utter
- *pr* 14–14 the *b·* will then utter no complaints.

would respond
- *p* 411– 5 the *b·* would respond more quickly,

your
- *m* 62–14 less thought "for your *b·* what ye— *Matt.* 6 : 25.
- *sp* 79–24 says : . . . Your *b·* is weak, and it must be
- *ph* 165– * nor yet for your *b·*, what ye— *Matt.* 6 : 25.
- *f* 208–30 You embrace your *b·* in your thought,
- 227–28 crippled your capacities, enfeebled your *b·*,
- *p* 393–11 Take possession of your *b·*,
- 393–21 Your *b·* would suffer no more from tension

- *pr* 12– 7 making it act more powerfully on the *b·*
- *a* 39–10 The educated belief that Soul is in the *b·*
- 42–24 Let men think they had killed the *b·* !
- *sp* 89–29 Cain . . . concluded that if life was in the *b·*,
- *an* 105–12 Can you separate the mentality from the *b·*
- *s* 107–16 false consciousness that life inheres in the *b·*,
- 120– 2 never . . . while we admit that soul is in *b·*
- 122–31 They insist that soul is in *b·*
- 130–22 ability of Spirit to make the *b·* harmonious,
- 151– 3 this one factor they represent to be *b·*,
- 152– 7 Æsculapius of mind as well as of *b·*,
- 160–12 When this so-called mind quits the *b·*,
- 164–23 miscalled life in the *b·* or in matter.
- *ph* 165– * and the *b·* than raiment? — *Matt.* 6 : 25.
- 174–27 Why declare that the *b·* is diseased,
- 176– 2 The action of mortal mind on the *b·*
- 177–10 Matter, or *b·*, is but a false concept
- 177–13 the *b·* is a sensuous, human concept.
- 179–14 the *b·* then seems to require such treatment.
- 180– 3 it should be taught to do the *b·* no harm
- 181– 3 Before deciding that the *b·*, matter,
- 187–30 the human mind still holds in belief a *b·*,
- 187–32 a *b·* like the one it had before death.
- 189–10 to explain the effect of mortal mind on the *b·*,
- 194–21 mortal mind manifests itself in the *b·*
- 198–14 afterwards to appear on the *b·* ;
- *f* 204–31 The error, which says that Soul is in *b·*,
- 206– 9 both upon the *b·* and through it.
- 209– 3 belief which makes the *b·* discordant
- 211– 7 The sensations of the *b·* must either be the
- 211–26 then, when the *b·* is dematerialized,
- 216–15 understanding makes the *b·* harmonious ;
- 217–20 When mentality gives rest to the *b·*,

body

f 218– 3	the *b·* is as material as the wheel.
218– 5	the *b·*, like the inanimate wheel,
218– 9	The *b·* is supposed to say, "I am ill."
219–16	We shall not call the *b·* weak,
223–12	If Spirit were once within the *b·*,
240–13	to be governed by matter or Soul in *b·*,
248– 1	belief of pain or pleasure in the *b·*
253–24	without hindrance from the *b·*.
c 260–31	If we look to the *b·* for pleasure, we find pain ;
261– 9	If one turns away from the *b·*
b 280–23	the belief that Soul is in *b·*,
288–23	Soul is sinless, not to be found in the *b·* ;
289– 5	belief that life and sensation are in the *b·*
291– 3	that the so-called death of the *b·*
293– 8	substratum is named matter or *b·* ;
297– 6	this testimony manifests itself on the *b·*
302–28	the *b·* presents no proper likeness of divinity,
308–11	looking for happiness and life in the *b·*,
313–31	and the *b·* no more perfect because of death
314–18	the *b·*, which they laid in a sepulchre,
318–32	The *b·* does not include soul,
323–22	removes thought from the *b·*, and elevates
325– 6	life obtained not of the *b·* incapable of
329–14	not tarry in the storm if the *b·* is freezing,
337– 3	as material sensation, or a soul in the *b·*,
p 375– 5	the separation of heat from the *b·*.
375–22	belief that matter . . . can paralyze the *b·*,
376–17	If the *b·* is material, it cannot, . . . suffer
377–12	Through different states of mind, the *b·*
379–28	pictures drawn on the *b·* by a mortal mind.
380–32	Every law of . . . the *b·*, supposed to govern,
382–11	no thought . . . for the *b·*."— *Luke* 12 : 22.
383– 7	influence of the divine Mind on the *b·*
386–14	corresponding effects of Truth on the *b·*,
388–10	thought that they could kill the *b·* with matter,
391–12	prevent the development of pain in the *b·*.
393– 4	The *b·* seems to be self-acting, only because
396–29	never giving the *b·* life and sensation.
399–12	mortal mind sends its despatches over its *b·*,
400–14	before it has taken tangible shape in . . . the *b·*,
400–23	We see in the *b·* the images of this mind,
400–31	baneful influence of sinful thought on the *b·*.
411–26	is imaged forth on the *b·*.
416–17	even as the *b·*, which has
416–22	*b·* is no longer the parent, even in
425–14	If the *b·* is diseased, this is but one of the
429–14	affirms that mind is subordinate to the *b·*,
429–14	affirms . . . that the *b·* is dying,
431–11	in behalf of the state (namely, the *b·*)
432– 8	my residence in matter, *alias* brain, to *b·*.
435– 3	Has the *b·* . . . committed a criminal deed?
435– 7	The *b·* committed no offence.
r 476– 7	Error will cease to claim that soul is in *b·*,
478–13	Who can see a soul in the *b·* ?
485–20	belief that life can be in matter or soul in *b·*,
g 531–16	If . . . mind was afterwards put into *b·*
ap 576–20	with "no temple [*b·*] therein"— *Rev.* 21 : 22.
gl 595– 7	TEMPLE. *B·* ; the idea of Life, substance,

boil

s 153–16	You say a *b·* is painful ;
153–17	The *b·* simply manifests, . . . a belief in pain,
153–20	and this belief is called a *b·*.
153–21	and it will soon cure the *b·*.

boiling

f 243– 5	which delivered men from the *b·* oil,

boldly

a 18–10	Jesus acted *b·*, against the accredited evidence

bondage

continued

f 227–12	ignorance . . . the foundation of continued *b·*

human

f 227– 8	law of the divine Mind must end human *b·*,

land of

ap 566–16	Out of the land of *b·* came,

oppressive

s 151–15	oppressive *b·* now enforced by false theories,

out of

ap 559–30	prefigured this perilous passage out of *b·*

ph 191–17	from self-imposed materiality and *b·*.
f 225–30	are still in *b·* to material sense,
226–29	hold the children of Israel in *b·*.
227–22	Escape from the *b·* of sickness, sin, and
b 337– 7	Sensualism is not bliss, but *b·*.
p 368–13	hope of freedom from the *b·* of sickness
371–14	The adult, in *b·* to his beliefs,

bonds

b 284– 9	It can never be in *b·*,
p 372–12	and then call his *b·* material and
434–29	not proved "worthy of death, or of *b·*."— *Acts* 23 : 29.
441– 8	to give heavy *b·* for good behavior.

bone

ph 193– 5	said the *b·* was carious for several inches.
193– 7	the evidence of this condition of the *b·*.
b 280–11	would compress Mind, . . . beneath a skull *b·*.
281–19	mind supposed to exist . . . beneath a skull *b·*
p 402–19	whether it be a broken *b·*, disease, or sin.
423– 2	and may not be able to mend the *b·*,
423–32	The so-called substance of *b·* is formed first by
427–17	Man is the same after as before a *b·* is broken
g 533–22	the rapid deterioration of the *b·* and flesh

bone-disease

p 422–22	Let us suppose two parallel cases of *b·*,

bones

broken

p 401–29	adjustment of broken *b·* and dislocations
402– 6	broken *b·*, dislocated joints, and

carious

s 162– 9	restores carious *b·* to soundness.
162–22	carious *b·* have been restored to healthy

flesh and

a 45–27	"Spirit hath not flesh and *b·*,— *Luke* 24 : 39.
b 313–30	Jesus called . . . "flesh and *b·*."— *Luke* 24 : 39.
o 352– 7	a mortal and material belief of flesh and *b·*,
p 372– 8	One theory about . . . blood, flesh, and *b·*.

muscles and

sp 84–21	nor upon muscles and *b·* for locomotion,

nerves nor

f 219–11	Not muscles, nerves, nor *b·*,

s 143–19	the stomach, blood, nerves, *b·*,
160–19	Can muscles, *b·*, blood, and nerves rebel
ph 172–23	Brain, heart, blood, *b·*, etc.,
173–19	measuring human strength by *b·* and sinews,
f 216–16	makes the nerves, *b·*, brain, etc., servants,
220–31	controls the stomach, *b·*, lungs, heart,
p 423–29	*B·* have only the substance of thought
424– 4	and its own thoughts of *b·*.
r 475– 7	made up of brain, blood, *b·*, and

Book

p 441–31	is recorded in our *B·* of books as a liar.

book

little

ap 558– 6	he had in his hand a little *b·* open :— *Rev.* 10 : 2.
559– 1	angel had in his hand "a little *b·*,"— *Rev.* 10 : 2.
559–17	"Go and take the little *b·*.— *Rev.* 10 : 8.

of Ecclesiastes

b 340– 4	This text in the *b·* of Ecclesiastes

of Genesis

g 502– 9	Spiritually followed, the *b·* of Genesis is
521–19	about creation in the *b·* of Genesis.
523–16	in the early part of the *b·* of Genesis.

of Hebrews

ap 575–12	as we read in the *b·* of Hebrews ;

of Job

b 321– 2	as may be seen by studying the *b·* of Job.

of Revelation

ap 558– 1	in the tenth chapter of his *b·* of Revelation :

perusal of the

t 446– 9	Perseverance in the perusal of the *b·*

same

ap 559– 2	Did this same *b·* contain the revelation of

this

pref x–10	books, however, which are based on this *b·*
xii–21	she had never read this *b·* throughout
an 104– 5	it will be seen why the author of this *b·*
s 110–18	contained in this *b·*, SCIENCE AND HEALTH ;
110–20	This *b·* may be distorted by shallow criticism
129–32	in the system taught in this *b·*,
138–32	It is his theology in this *b·*
147–17	never . . . by a simple *perusal* of this *b·*.
152– 6	endeavored to make this *b·* the Æsculapius of
ph 185– 7	Before this *b·* was published,
b 330– 3	Until the author of this *b·* learned the
p 422– 5	If the reader of this *b·* observes a great stir
t 446– 7	sometimes seem worse while reading this *b·*,
457– 3	borrowed from this *b·* without giving it credit,
457– 4	this *b·* has done more for teacher and
g 546–27	the system stated in this *b·*
547– 4	If one of the statements in this *b·* is true,
ap 559–20	Read this *b·* from beginning to end.

pref vii–22	A *b·* introduces new thoughts,
s 147–17	The *b·* needs to be *studied*,
p 422– 8	Continue to read, and the *b·* will become
t 456–30	Because it was the first *b·* known,

booked

p 382–19	A patient thoroughly *b·* in medical theories

books

pref x– 4	Various *b·* on mental healing have
x– 9	A few *b·*, however, which are based on
sp 88–30	it is said to be a gift . . . obtained from *b·*
ph 176–12	There were fewer *b·* on digestion
185– 7	other *b·* were in circulation, which discussed
196–20	Such *b·* as will rule disease out of mortal mind,

books
p 441–31 is recorded in our Book of b· as a liar.
t 457– 6 than has been accomplished by other b·.
ap 572– 3 in both the first and last b· of the Bible,

borders
p 430– 6 Faith should enlarge its b·

bore
a 20–14 Jesus b· our infirmities ;
50–30 The real cross, which Jesus b· up the hill of grief,
53–25 Jesus b· our sins in his body.
p 363– 1 She b· an alabaster jar

born
a 30– 5 B· of a woman, Jesus' advent in the flesh
m 57–19 Happiness is spiritual, b· of Truth and Love.
61–17 like tropical flowers b· amid Alpine snows.
s 109–26 "Unto us a child is b·, — Isa. 9: 6.
f 227–17 Paul said, "I was free b·." — Acts 22: 28.
250–10 which is never b· and never dies.
c 258–27 Never b· and never dying,
b 274–10 Ideas, on the contrary, are b· of Spirit,
295–32 error theorizes that spirit is b· of matter
296– 4 Progress is b· of experience.
332– 9 Jesus was b· of Mary.
t 463–14 conceived and b· of Truth and Love,
463–18 the C. S. infant is b· of the Spirit, b· of God,
g 529– 3 that man should be b· of woman,
535–17 the heritage of the first b· among men
552–15 "Man that is b· of a woman — Job 14: 1.
557–20 lifts the curtain on man as never b·
ap 563–26 her child as soon as it was b·. — Rev. 12: 4.
gl 598– 4 every one that is b· of the Spirit — John 3: 8.

borne
a 33–10 had b· this bread from house to house,
s 109–24 When a new spiritual idea is b· to earth,
p 383–18 could not be b· by the refined.

borrow
a 21–32 would b· the passport of some wiser pilgrim,

borrowed
s 112–12 b· from that truly divine Science
c 267–22 Thought is b· from a higher source
p 367– 6 better than . . . stereotyped b· speeches,
t 457– 3 b· from this book without giving it credit,
g 511– 2 and radiates their b· light,

borrows
pr 12–17 b· its power from human faith and belief.
ap 562– 9 the universe b· its reflected light,

bosom
a 29–27 dwelt forever an idea in the b· of God,
sp 87–22 of the tall ships that float on its b·,
f 201– * how I do bear in my b· — Psal. 89: 50.
b 321–21 when Moses first put his hand into his b·
334– 5 Christ, dwells forever in the b· of the Father,
ap 569–22 sin, which one has made his b· companion,

Boston
pref xi–29 Massachusetts Metaphysical College in B·,
an 105–19 these words of Judge Parmenter of B·

Boston Herald
an 102–24 an extract from the B· H· :

botanic
p 416–10 allopathic, homœopathic, b·, eclectic

botanist
s 155– 8 The chemist, the b·, the druggist,
ap 560–19 The b· must know the genus

both
pref viii– 9 physics teach that b· Spirit and matter
viii–13 by healing b· disease and sin ;
a 18– 5 His mission was b· individual and collective.
23–10 eventually b· sin and suffering will fall
24–26 Then we must differ from them b·.
39–24 b· are unreal, because impossible in Science.
50–12 The appeal of Jesus was made b· to
m 57–10 B· sexes should be loving, pure, tender,
59– 3 enduring obligations on b· sides.
59–32 it never would, if b· husband and wife were
60–10 purity and constancy, b· of which are immortal.
sp 73– 9 b· the individuality and the Science of man,
77– 7 b· here and hereafter,
80–21 mind-power which moves b· table and hand.
80–31 b· visibly and invisibly,
82–15 because b· of us are either unconscious or
85–23 B· Jew and Gentile may have had
85–30 great Teacher knew b· cause and effect,
88–25 for b· arise from mortal belief.
91–27 erroneous postulate is, that man is b·
91–29 erroneous postulate is, that mind is b·
99– 8 worketh in you b· to will and — Phil. 2: 13.
an 103–11 a knowledge of b· good and evil,
103–21 false belief that mind is . . . b· evil and good ;
104– 4 are b· comprehended, as they will be
s 113–22 B· are not, cannot be, true.
114– 1 Usage classes b· evil and good together

both
114– 8 and calls mind b· human and divine.
126–18 as being b· natural and spiritual?
128–31 If b· the major and the minor propositions
136– 5 and heal b· the sick and the sinning.
136– 8 power to save men b· bodily and spiritually.
148–12 B· anatomy and theology define
148–13 define man as b· physical and mental,
150–19 would have one believe that b· matter and
157–27 but they leave b· mind and body worse
157–31 Science b· neutralizes error and destroys it.
158–11 truth which heals b· mind and body.
162–18 in cases of b· acute and chronic disease
ph 167–15 If God made man b· good and evil,
170–28 or as b· material and spiritual,
174–29 the thought of b· physician and patient?
177– 9 b· must be destroyed by immortal Mind.
180– 1 are b· prolific sources of sickness.
182– 9 We cannot obey b· physiology and Spirit,
186–26 If pain is as real as . . . b· must be immortal ;
188–15 In b· the waking and the sleeping dream,
190– 5 producing mortals, b· body and mind ;
196–11 able to destroy b· soul and body — Matt. 10: 28.
f 206– 8 b· upon the body and through it.
208–14 absurd to suppose that matter can b· cause and
216–20 to suppose that man, . . . is b· matter and Spirit,
216–20 to suppose that man, . . . b· good and evil.
218–12 What renders b· sin and sickness difficult of
223–18 b· shall fall into the ditch." — Matt. 15: 14.
229–11 calls b· the offspring of spirit,
234–15 robbing b· themselves and others.
b 270– 6 hence b· cannot be real.
281– 7 presupposes man to be b· mind and matter.
282– 8 the finite, which has b· beginning and end.
283–15 They speak of b· Truth and error as mind,
287– 6 supposes man to be b· mental and material.
287–29 b· good and evil.
293–11 b· strata, mortal mind and
294– 6 If man is b· mind and matter,
303–13 b· spiritually and materially,
303–13 or by b· God and man,
303–15 can never make b· these contraries true.
307–21 as b· good and evil,
320– 7 Scriptures have b· a spiritual and literal
320–10 must rest upon b· the literal and moral ;"
330–22 Mind is not b· good and bad,
330–25 The notion that b· evil and good
333–19 b· before and after the Christian era,
338– 5 belief . . . that he is b· soul and body,
338– 6 b· good and evil, b· spiritual and material
o 346–30 We cannot serve b· God and mammon
350–12 b· of which must be understood.
355–24 misapprehension b· of the divine Principle and
360– 5 those which are b· mental and material.
360–15 B· you cannot have.
p 366–28 calm in the presence of b· sin and disease,
368– 6 B· truth and error have come nearer
370–17 but it uses the same medicine in b· cases.
370–23 According to b· medical testimony and
372–20 can we believe in the reality and power of b·
373–21 you must rise above b· fear and sin.
376–22 by b· silently and audibly arguing the
378–14 and b· will fight for nothing.
379– 2 for b· are errors,
393–30 false belief is b· the tempter and the tempted,
395–10 same Principle cures b· sin and sickness.
396– 3 b· for one's own sake and for that of the patient.
399–12 so-called mind is b· the service and message
402–30 cannot produce b· disorder and order.
403–12 b· have their origin in the human mind,
404–27 B· cures require the same method
405–15 B· will be manacled until the last farthing is
406– 3 Sin and sickness are b· healed by the same
406– 9 healing of mortals, b· mind and body.
420–17 Truth overcomes b· disease and sin
421–32 are b· forty, and that their combined sum
422–22 cases of bone-disease, b· similarly produced
423–15 as b· his foe and his remedy.
423–24 B· Science and consciousness are now at work
427– 7 for b· are immortal.
t 450–23 heals them b· by understanding God's power
454–18 the true incentive in b· healing and teaching.
455–30 cannot send forth b· sweet waters and bitter.
456–23 you must b· understand and abide by the
457–12 we cannot scientifically b· cure and
457–15 b· sides were beautiful
458– 7 b· a mental and a material standpoint.
461–23 B· sin and sickness are error,
462–30 b· in health and in sickness.
r 482– 4 hypothesis that soul is b· an evil and a good
482– 6 b· before and after that which is called death.
g 504– 6 b· spiritual and material
512–23 are mental, b· primarily and secondarily,
513– 1 b· this mortal mentality, so-called, and its
524–19 Mind had made man, b· male and female.
528– 3 already created man, b· male and female

both

g 529–10   *b·* man and woman proceed from God
531– 7   error, . . . that mind and soul are *b·* right and
531–27   Certainly not by *b·,* since
536–19   The blind leading the blind, *b·* would fall.
538–27   As *b·* mortal man and sin have a
539– 6   as if . . . matter can *b·* give and take away.
542–21   *b·* for what it is and for what it does.
551– 1   *b·* the material senses and their reports are
555–21   as if man were the offspring of *b·* Mind and
555–22   of *b·* Deity and humanity.
ap 561– 3   destroys *b·* faith in evil and the
572– 3   in *b·* the first and last books of the Bible,
577–25   *b·* within and without,
gl 587–10   belief that . . . are *b·* mental and material ;
588–18   belief that . . . are *b·* mental and material.
598– 5   the original word is the same in *b·* cases,

bottles

s 114–21   poured into the old *b·* of the letter.
b 281–27   does not put new wine into old *b·,*

bottom

an 104–13   C. S. goes to the *b·* of mental action,
ph 184– 9   probing the trouble to the *b·,*

Bouillaud

an 101– 9   among whom were Roux, *B·,* and Cloquet,

bound

pr 6–24   he said that Satan had *b·* her,
sp 77– 4   Neither do other mortals . . . at a single *b·.*
f 227–27   The illusion . . . has *b·* you,
r 495–10   "whom Satan hath *b·,*" — *Luke* 13 : 16.
495–12   opens the prison doors to such as are *b·,*
ap 559–10   to the globe's remotest *b·.*

boundary

m 58–22   the centre, though not the *b·,* of the affections.
sp 97–15   without passing the *b·* where,
b 298–18   never reaches beyond the *b·* of the
ap 577–12   This spiritual, holy habitation has no *b·*

bounded

sp 84–19   Mind is infinite, not *b·* by corporeality,
c 256–13   The everlasting I AM is not *b·* nor
b 301–32   Immortality is not *b·* by mortality.

bounding

f 237– 4   *B·* off with laughing eyes,

boundless

a 22–24   *b·* freedom, and sinless sense,
c 258–15   higher and higher from a *b·* basis.
b 323–11   until *b·* thought walks enraptured,
r 481– 4   freedom, harmony, and *b·* bliss.

bounds

g 550– 8   cannot . . . be limited within material *b·.*

bounty

pr 15–25   Christians rejoice in secret beauty and *b·,*
a 36–11   pour his dear-bought *b·* into barren lives.

bow

a 35–12   They *b·* before Christ, Truth,
ph 174– 5   that man should *b·* down to a flesh-brush,
f 214–18   We *b·* down to matter, . . . like the pagan
247–26   arches the cloud with the *b·* of beauty,
g 530–21   saying, . . . *B·* down to me and

bowed

a 32–13   he *b·* in holy submission to the divine decree.
36–13   a few women who *b·* in silent woe
gl 508–11   "He *b·* his head, — *John* 19 : 30.

bowels

ph 176– 8   left the stomach and *b·* free to act
179–28   to move the *b·,* or to produce sleep
p 413– 7   Mind regulates the condition of the stomach, *b·,*
415–21   the action of the lungs, of the *b·,*

box

ph 170–30   is the Pandora *b·,* from which

boy

ph 193– 2   caused by a fall . . . when quite a *b·.*
195– 2   After the babbling *b·* had been taught to
p 398– 2   as when he said to the epileptic *b·,*

boyhood

a 52– 1   From early *b·* he was about his
ph 193–23   ever since the injury was received in *b·.*

boys

b 333– 6   in common with other Hebrew *b·* and men,
p 379–16   think of the experiment of those Oxford *b·,*

Brahman

p 362–11   the household of a high-caste *B·,*

brain

and nerves
s 122–12   sections of matter, such as *b·* and nerves,
p 290–11   manifested through *b·* and nerves, is false.
and viscera
p 415–24   including *b·* and viscera.
body and
sp 79–28   Mind controls body and *b·.*

brain

called
ph 185–29   material stratum of the human mind, called *b·,*
can give no idea
ph 191– 1   The *b·* can give no idea of God's man.
congestion of the
p 408–23   as would congestion of the *b·,*
consult your
ph 165–18   Then you consult your *b·* in order to
diseased
p 421– 3   insanity implies belief in a diseased *b·,*
effect upon the
p 401–23   could you produce any effect upon the *b·* or
is not mind
p 372– 1   Remember, *b·* is not mind.
named
b 295–26   The theoretical mind is matter, named *b·,*
or matter
c 259–24   *B·* or matter never formed a human concept.
portions of the
g 531– 3   It is well that the upper portions of the *b·*
prevent the
p 395–31   would prevent the *b·* from becoming diseased,
proceeding from the
sp 88–12   proceeding from the *b·* or from matter,
size of a
ph 190–12   presently measure mind by the size of a *b·*
size of the
ph 165– 7   To measure . . . by the size of the *b·*
softened
p 387– 4   must it pay the penalty in a softened *b·* ?
substratum of
p 408–29   thought in the corporeal substratum of *b·*
your
sp 79–24   says : . . . Your *b·* is overtaxed,

s 127–20   nerves, *b·,* stomach, lungs, and so forth,
151–19   The blood, heart, lungs, *b·,* etc.,
ph 172–23   *B·,* heart, blood, . . . the material structure?
172–32   heart, blood, *b·,* acting through the
189–16   it is as truly mortal mind, . . . as is the material *b·*
189–29   the lower, basal portion of the *b·,*
190– 7   neither . . . is found in *b·* or elsewhere in
f 211– 1   If *b·,* nerves, stomach, are intelligent,
216–16   it makes . . . bones, *b·,* etc., servants,
c 262–29   Every concept which seems to begin with the *b·*
b 294–13   saying : . . . Nerves feel. *B·* thinks and sins.
p 408–17   Can drugs go of their own accord to the *b·*
408–25   with the mind than is the *b·.*
409– 6   animate error called nerves, *b·,* mind,
409– 9   mortal mind — *alias* matter, *b·*
414–10   impossibility that matter, *b·,* can control
432– 8   for I convey messages from . . . *b·,* to body.
r 475– 7   Man is not matter ; he is not made up of *b·,*
478–14   Does *b·* think, and do nerves feel,
gl 587–13   theories that hold mind . . . existing in *b·,*

brain-lobes

p 395–30   The knowledge that *b·* cannot kill
r 478–22   and *b·* cannot think

brainology

ph 171–10   not needing to study *b·*
b 295–28   *B·* teaches that mortals are created to suffer

brake

a 32–16   *b·* it, and gave it to the disciples, — *Matt.* 26 : 26.

branch

p 402– 2   surgery is the *b·* of its healing which
t 462–24   This *b·* of study is indispensable

brave

s 120–32   chained the limbs of the *b·* old navigator,
144– 7   when dawns the sun's *b·* light.

bravely

m 67– 9   He answers *b·,* but even the dauntless

brazen

s 133–11   The Israelites looked upon the *b·* serpent,

breach

s 112–30   inculcates a *b·* of that divine commandment
p 382–18   "more honored in the *b·* than the observance,"

bread

and vegetables
f 221– 3   he ate only *b·* and vegetables,
breaking of
a 46– 7   and by the breaking of *b·.*
daily
pr 17– 4   Give us this day our daily *b·* ; — *Matt.* 6 : 11.
diet of
f 220–22   clergyman once adopted a diet of *b·* and water
Jesus took
a 32–15   Jesus took *b·,* and blessed it. — *Matt.* 26 : 26.
of Life
f 222–10   feeds thought with the *b·* of Life.
our
a 35–26   Our *b·,* "which cometh down — *John* 6 : 33.

bread

slice of

f 221– 7   only a thin slice of *b·* without water.

their

a 33– 6   Their *b·* indeed came down from heaven.

this

a 31–23   "As often as ye eat this *b·*,— *I Cor.* 11 : 26.
     33–10   this *b·* was feeding and sustaining them.
     33–11   They had borne this *b·* from house to house,

use of

a 32–21   lost, if . . . confined to the use of *b·* and wine.

------

a 31–19   we drink of his cup, partake of his *b·*,
   32–23   yet Jesus prayed and gave them *b·*.
   33–32   Are all who eat *b·* and drink wine
m 68–20   when casting my *b·* upon the waters,
p 410–10   "Man shall not live by *b· alone*,— *Matt.* 4 : 4.
g 535–26   sweat of thy face shalt thou eat *b·*,— *Gen.* 3 : 19.

breadth

g 520– 3   The depth, *b·*, height, might, majesty,

break

a 39–25   To *b·* this earthly spell, mortals must
   41–12   cannot forever *b·* the Golden Rule
f 225–18   potent to *b·* despotic fetters
   234–29   to look with desire . . . was to *b·* a moral precept.
   239– 7   *B·* up cliques. level wealth with honesty,
p 412–17   must *b·* the dream of the material senses.
   420–28   to *b·* its dream of suffering,
t 448–27   ventures not to *b·* its rules,
   449– 2   With . . . wrists manacled, it is hard to *b·*
ap 569–15   Alas for those who *b·* faith with divine Science

breakage

p 402–15   no *b·* nor dislocation can really occur.

breaketh

b 308–24   "Let me go, for the day *b·* ;"— *Gen.* 32 : 26.

breakfast

a 34–30   his last spiritual *b·* with his disciples

breaking

a 33–11   *b·* (explaining) it to others,
   46– 7   and by the *b·* of bread.
sp 96–15   The *b·* up of material beliefs
c 261–24   *B·* away from the mutations of time and sense,
o 349– 5   "Through *b·* the law,— *Rom.* 2 : 23.
p 363– 3   *B·* the sealed jar, that perfumed Jesus' feet
   381–11   cannot in reality suffer from *b·* anything

breaks

f 241– 6   Sin *b·* in upon them,
b 301–21   belief . . . *b·* the First Commandment,
p 396–20   It *b·* the dream of disease
r 489–13   it *b·* all the commands of the
   494–23   *b·* their illusion with the unbroken reality of
g 542–25   to advance itself, *b·* God's commandments.

breast

gl 595–14   which were to be on Aaron's *b·*

breast-plate

gl 596–12   the *b·* of the high-priest

breath

pr 2– 8   God is not moved by the *b·* of praise
s 120–30   When Columbus gave freer *b·* to the globe,
ph 175–13   and the *b·* of new-mown hay
   184–30   Her *b·* came gently.
   192–15   the devouring flame, the tempest's *b·*.
f 225–21   nor did the *b·* of freedom come from
g 516–15   sends her sweet *b·* to heaven.
   524–15   into his nostrils the *b·* of life ;— *Gen.* 2 : 7.
   525– 2   animated by the *b·* of God?

breathe

t 452–14   Never *b·* an immoral atmosphere, unless

breathed

ph 184–28   always *b·* with great difficulty when
g 524–14   and *b·* into his nostrils— *Gen.* 2 : 7.
gl 598–14   common statement, "He *b·* his last."

breathes

sp 76– 4   forgets all else and *b·* aloud his rapture.
g 548– 3   and *b·* through the sacred pages

breathing

ph 185– 2   her difficulty in *b·* had gone.
   193–12   and the *b·* became natural ;
f 225–17   *b·* the omnipotence of divine justice,

breeds

m 62– 7   master the belief . . . which *b·* disease.

brethren

a 31– 7   and who are my *b·*,"— *Matt.* 12 : 48.
s 107– *   *But I certify you*, *b·*, *that*— *Gal.* 1 : 11.
   137–17   Simon replied for his *b·*,
t 444– 8   their *b·* upon whom they may call,
   444–27   for we be *b·*."— *Gen.* 13 : 8.
   444–30   are discordant and ofttimes false *b·*.
r 470– 2   the whole family of man would be *b·* ;
ap 568–16   accuser of our *b·* is cast down,— *Rev.* 12 : 10.

bridal

m 65– 3   May Christ, Truth, be present at every *b·* altar
f 238–13   From out the *b·* chamber of wisdom

bride

m 58–24   Said the peasant *b·* to her lover :
g 548– 1   Spirit and the *b·* say, Come !— *Rev.* 22 : 17.
ap 561–12   a *b·* coming down from heaven,
   561–13   "the *b·*" and "the Lamb"— *see Rev.* 21 : 9.
   574– 8   I will show thee the *b·*,— *Rev.* 21 : 9.
gl 582–14   definition of

bridegroom

gl 582–17   definition of

bridge

sp 74–26   There is no *b·* across the gulf which
gl 598–26   would *b·* over with life discerned spiritually

brief

pr 16– 7   taught his disciples one *b·* prayer,
a 42–12   his *b·* triumphal entry into Jerusalem
ph 194– 3   Reviewing this *b·* experience,
f 206–20   for the *b·* space of a few years
b 334– 9   Jesus, whose earthly career was *b·*.
p 433–16   A *b·* consultation ensues,
r 496–31   a *b·* exposition of the important points,
g 502– 3   real prelude of the older Scriptures is so *b·*
   521– 7   We leave this *b·*, glorious history
ap 565–14   had a *b·* history in the earthly

briefly

g 547–17   *B·*, this is Darwin's theory,

bright

a 34–31   in the *b·* morning hours at the joyful meeting
s 121–11   earth and heaven were *b·*,
f 246–15   dawn . . . with *b·* and imperishable glories.
ap 558–12   but a *b·* promise crowns its brow

brightens

c 265–27   *b·* the ascending path of many a heart.
g 516–18   *b·* the flower, beautifies the landscape,

brighter

a 32–26   refresh his heart with *b·*, with spiritual views.
r 496–13   *b·* "unto the perfect day."— *Prov.* 4 : 18.

brightness

s 139–11   even when the end has been *b·* and peace ;
b 313–10   "the *b·* of His [God's] glory,— *Heb.* 1 : 3.
   313–21   "Who, being a *b·* from His glory,— *see Heb.* 1 : 3.
ap 565– 5   loathing the *b·* of divine glory.

brim

pr 5–16   Ingratitude and persecution filled it to the *b·* ;

bring

pr 2–16   but it tends to *b·* us into harmony with it.
   2–29   The unspoken desire does *b·* us nearer the
   4–14   are made manifest in the blessings they *b·*,
   4–25   and patience must *b·* experience.
   11–21   Petitions *b·* to mortals only the results of
   11–30   will *b·* us into all Truth.
a 34–16   they will *b·* in the millennium.
sp 97–22   they *b·* error from under cover.
s 128–30   addition of two sums . . . must always *b·*
f 202– 6   If men would *b·* to bear upon the
   212–19   *b·* the rose into contact with the olfactory
   230– 5   will *b·* us into health, holiness, and
   230–13   so as to *b·* about certain evil results,
c 260–16   and to *b·* out better and higher results,
   261– 5   you will *b·* these into your experience
b 300–10   will *b·* to light the true reflection of God
o 351–16   cannot *b·* out the practical proof . . . while
p 374– 4   but the truth of being, . . . will *b·* relief.
   386–18   same grief that the friend's real death would *b·*.
   392– 3   Only while . . . remains can it *b·* forth death.
   400–27   to *b·* out the harmony of being.
   405–29   penalties you incur and the ills they *b·*.
   422–15   meet and *b·* out a third quality,
   424– 9   to change the . . . and thus *b·* out harmony.
r 483–22   seems to *b·* into dishonor the ordinary scientific
   492–12   and *b·* immortality to light.
g 504–24   The rays of infinite Truth, . . . *b·* light
   507–11   Let the earth *b·* forth grass,— *Gen.* 1 : 11.
   511–19   Let the waters *b·* forth— *Gen.* 1 : 20.
   513–14   Let the earth *b·* forth— *Gen.* 1 : 24.
   535– 8   in sorrow thou shalt *b·* forth— *Gen.* 3 : 16.
   535–24   thistles shall it *b·* forth to thee ;— *Gen.* 3 : 18.
   550–27   nor does a lion *b·* forth a lamb.
   557–18   "In sorrow thou shalt *b·* forth— *Gen.* 3 : 16.
ap 570– 2   will *b·* the hour when the people will chain,

bringeth

c 257–20   *b·* "forth Mazzaroth in his season,"— *Job* 38 : 32.
p 442–15   as of one "that *b·* good tidings."— *Isa.* 52 : 7.

bringing

a 35–23   by *b·* forth the fruits of Love,
m 57–13   *b·* sweet seasons of renewal
f 210–14   *b·* to light the scientific action of
   249– 6   *b·* us into newness of life
o 360–15   You are *b·* out your own ideal.

bringing

p 435–12   b· joy instead of grief,
t 454–32   auxiliaries to aid in b· thought into accord
g 529– 1   b· forth fruit of its own kind,
540– 8   when b· it to the surface and
ap 561–15   God and his Christ, b· harmony to earth.
gl 589–17   and b· to light man's immortality.

brings

pr 11–11   Broken law b· penalty . . . to compel this
11–20   because sin b· inevitable suffering.
a 37– 2   Does not Science show that sin b· suffering
37–13   Consciousness of right-doing b· its own reward ;
m 69–15   b· the sweet assurance of no parting,
sp 72–13   Truth . . . b· to light immortality.
77– 6   Error b· its own self-destruction
s 132–13   divine Principle which b· out all harmony.
157–29   b· out the proof that Life is continuous
162– 4   C. S. b· to the body the sunlight of Truth,
ph 169–24   mortal mind, not matter, which b· to the sick
196– 9   Sin alone b· death, for sin is the only
f 203–13   Spiritual perception b· out the possibilities of
206–27   He destroys them, and b· to light immortality.
221–31   b· with it another lesson,
224–28   Truth b· the elements of liberty.
224–30   power of God b· deliverance to the
248–11   which each day b· to a nearer tomb.
b 272–10   spiritual sense of the Scriptures b· out the
276–12   b· objects and thoughts into human view
293–29   C. S. b· to light Truth and its supremacy,
305–26   destroys all error and b· immortality to light.
336–28   Science of being . . . b· immortality to light.
338– 2   b· to light the only living and true God
o 348–23   while complaining of the suffering disease b·,
p 401–18   b· sin and sickness to the surface,
404– 7   suffering which his submission to such habits b·,
404–19   cuts down every tree that b· not forth good fruit.
407–27   b· the divine Mind, Life not death,
422–10   tremor which Truth often b· to error
t 446–27   exercise of will b· on a hypnotic state,
r 487–31   b· out the enduring and harmonious phases
496–14   what the understanding of God b· to man.
g 530– 6   The earth, . . . b· forth food for man's use.
540–31   b· a material offering to God.
555– 4   b· the physical organism under the yoke of
ap 558–17   It b· the baptism of the Holy Ghost,
gl 596– 4   but C. S. b· God much nearer to man,

brink

f 235–22   To the tremblers on the b· of death,

broad

t 451–13   "wide is the gate, and b· is — Matt. 7 : 13.

broadcast

m 65–13   b· powers of evil so conspicuous to-day
ph 197–18   departments of knowledge now b· in the earth,

broaden

f 235–32   their listeners will . . . b· their concepts.

broadening

c 258–14   developing itself, b· and rising

broader

s 128–17   access to b· and higher realms.
c 265– 7   must near the b· interpretations of being,

broadest

sp 97–21   b· facts array the most falsities against
s 111–30   submitted . . . to the b· practical tests.
147– 8   submitted to the b· practical test,

broken

pr 11–10   B· law brings penalty
a 38– 8   b· by the demands of divine Science.
m 66– 7   a b· reed, which pierces the heart.
ph 184–25   what is termed a fatally b· physical law.
p 364–27   by their genuine repentance, by their b· hearts,
384–25   that you have b· no law,
385–26   not the penalty for having b· a law of
392– 4   b· moral law should be taken into account
401–29   adjustment of b· bones and dislocations
402– 6   b· bones, dislocated joints, and
402–19   whether it be a b· bone, disease, or sin.
427–17   the same after as before a bone is b·
t 447– 1   heavenly law is b· by trespassing upon
g 522– 9   as having b· away from Deity
ap 563–14   belief . . . the Ten Commandments can be b·.

broken-hearted

p 366–31   must first learn to bind up the b·.

bronchial

ph 175–28   the refinement of inflamed b· tubes.

brood

f 234–18   b· of evils which infest it would be cleared out.

brother (see also brother's)

c 267–15   as for that of b· and sister.
267–17   my b·, and sister, and mother." — Matt. 12 : 50.
p 366–15   "He that loveth not his b· — I John 4 : 20.

brother

g 541–14   rose up against Abel his b·, — Gen. 4 : 8.
541–20   Where is Abel thy b· ? — Gen. 4 : 9.
541–26   the human duty of man towards his b·.

brotherhood

b 340–24   constitutes the b· of man ;
r 467–12   true b· of man will be established.
470– 3   b· of man would consist of Love and
g 518–16   The rich in spirit help the poor in one grand b·,
541–17   ruptures the life and b· of man

brother's

t 455–16   mote out of thy b· eye." — Matt. 7 : 5.
g 518–18   seeth his b· need and supplieth it,
541– 4   Jealous of his b· gift,
541–21   Am I my b· keeper? — Gen. 4 : 9.
541–28   The voice of thy b· blood — Gen. 4 : 10.

brought

a 19–15   b· to material beliefs not peace,
29–22   b· forth her child by the revelation of Truth,
44–25   divinity b· to humanity the understanding
50– 1   b· as a lamb to the slaughter, — Isa. 53 : 7.
m 61–10   every mountain of selfishness be b· low,
65–29   mental chemicalization, which has b·
sp 86–18   apparitions b· out in dark seances
an 100– 1   b· into notice by Mesmer in Germany
s 110– 9   equipollence of God b· to light
115– 7   C. S. as b· forth in my discovery.
121–30   thus b· nearer the spiritual fact,
136– 7   Despite the persecution this b· upon him,
148– 1   When his students b· to him a case
159– 7   The case was b· to trial.
164–27   then shall be b· to pass the saying — I Cor. 15 : 54.
ph 168–13   b· yourself into the slough of disease
196–28   from the image b· before the mind ;
f 240–29   until all error is finally b· into subjection
b 268– 1   In the material world, thought has b· to light
292–30   connection with his God, which Jesus b· to light.
303–12   spiritually conceived and b· forth ;
306–15   to be b· together again at some . . . time
309–20   to be b· back through great tribulation,
315–10   b· upon him the anathemas of the age.
318–14   b· the belief of sin and death
335–24   Life as immortality b· to light.
ɔ 351–32   their prayer b· down no proof that it was heard,
p 363–21   and so b· home the lesson to all,
388–20   which is "b· to desolation." — Matt. 12 : 25.
414–30   unreal, and is not b· about by divine Love.
426–28   Sin b· death, and death will disappear with
428–22   The great spiritual fact must be b· out
429– 2   this Life must be b· to light
436–18   But they b· with them Fear,
r 476–17   "conceived in sin and b· forth in iniquity."
496–26   then shall be b· to pass the saying — I Cor. 15 : 54.
g 505–28   it is the reality of all things b· to light.
508– 9   the earth b· forth grass, — Gen. 1 : 12.
512– 5   which the waters b· forth — Gen. 1 : 21.
527–23   and b· them unto Adam — Gen. 2 : 19.
528–13   and b· her unto the man. — Gen. 2 : 22.
532– 7   when eating its first fruits b· death?
538–21   b· into view only as the unreal
540–25   Cain b· of the fruit of the — Gen. 4 : 3.
540–27   b· of the firstlings of his flock, — Gen. 4 : 4.
548–27   Modern discoveries have b· to light
551–21   b· down from generation to generation?"
553–18   the maternal egg never b· forth Adam.
ap 565– 6   And she b· forth a man child, — Rev. 12 : 5.
569–31   b· forth the man child. — Rev. 12 : 13.
574–21   b· also the experience which at last
gl 582–23   immortality b· to light.

brow

ph 193– 9   The dew of death was on his b·.
f 245–15   youth sat gently on cheek and b·.
t 451– 6   with the crown of Love upon her b·,
ap 558–12   a bright promise crowns its b·.

bruise

g 534–11   it shall b· thy head, — Gen. 3 : 15.
534–11   and thou shalt b· his heel. — Gen. 3 : 15.
534–29   the woman, this idea, will b· the head of

bruised

pref xi–21   To set at liberty them that are b·. — Luke 4 : 18.

bruises

f 216– 8   Truth b· the head of error

brusque

p 365– 1   and the b· business visitor

brutal

a 43–13   The malignity of b· persecutors,
p 405– 2   Hatred inflames the b· propensities.
ap 564–16   b· barbarity of his foes could emanate from

brutality

a 40–22   lesser apostles of Truth may endure human b·

brute
m 63– 7 His origin is not, . . . in b· instinct,
ph 173– 3 distinguish between humanity and the b·,
b 277–16 nor the man by the b·.

bud
m 62–23 which forms the b· and blossom,
68–24 perpetuation of the floral species by b· or
sp 78– 1 The decaying flower, the blighted b·,
g 518–21 as the blossom shines through the b·.
gl 596–26 maketh the valley to b· and blossom as the rose.
fr 600– * *and the pomegranates b· forth.*— *Song 7 : 12.*

Buddhism
ph 173–32 call into action less faith than B·

budding
p 413–28 convey . . . to children's b· thoughts,

buddings
f 236–22 blighting the b· of self-government.

buds
sp 77–29 a state resembling that of blighted b·,
ph 191–22 not a spray b· within the vale,
g 549–12 sometimes through eggs, sometimes through b·,

buffeting
t 460–22 b· them with the . . . cold assertion,

build
sp 84–27 spiritualism has no basis upon which to b·.
s 137–31 I will b· my church ;— *Matt. 16 : 18.*
f 201– 7 We cannot b· safely on false foundations.
235– 3 if virtue and truth b· a strong defence.
p 421–27 you should not b· it up by
t 450– 9 A third class of thinkers b· with solid masonry.

builder
b 314–14 knowing, as he did, that Mind was the b·,
p 428–13 "whose b· and maker is God."— *Heb. 11 : 10.*
428–17 the eternal b·, the everlasting Father,
ap 575–10 b· and maker of this New Jerusalem is God,

builders
s 139–26 stone which the b· rejected"— *Matt. 21 : 42.*

building
f 241–26 corner-stone of all spiritual b· is purity.

builds
sp 83–11 hides Truth and b· on error.
ph 177–11 so-called mind b· its own superstructure,
gl 581–19 The higher false knowledge b·

built
a 35–20 Our church is b· on the divine Principle, Love.
s 127–31 in so far as this is b· on the false hypotheses
138–15 the foundation on which Jesus b·.
f 226–14 God has b· a higher platform of human rights,
226–15 and He has b· it on diviner claims.
b 269–28 not houses b· on the rock.
t 454– 8 path which leads to the house b· without hands
r 484– 4 for it is b· upon the rock, Christ.

bulk
ph 190–12 and the b· of a body, called man.

bullet
o 358– 2 Can a leaden b· deprive a man of Life,

bundle
s 149– 6 a b· of speculative human theories?

buoyant
s 109–16 search was sweet, calm, and b· with hope,

buoys
a 24– 9 the b· and healing currents of Truth

burden
a 50–26 The b· of that hour was terrible

burial
a 35– 8 or the b· of mind in matter,
45–13 Three days after his bodily b·
f 232–30 unquestionably signs of the b· of error
gl 582–21 definition of

buried
a 38–26 To those b· in the belief of sin and self,
sp 75–19 same plane . . . as those who b· the body,
87 –23 the bodies which lie b· in its sands :
b 299– 8 has b· its fondest earthly hopes.
p 429–15 affirms . . . that it must be b·

buries
g 537–16 and b· itself in the ground,

burlesque
sp 92–18 a b· of God's man

burn
a 46– 6 by the words, which made their hearts b·
ap 565–20 fiery baptism will b· up the chaff of error

burned
s 134–11 the followers of Christ were b·, crucified, and
161– 3 You say, "*I have b· my finger.*"
g 535– 4 the one to be b·, the other to be garnered

burning
ap 566–24 A b· and a shining light !

burns
s 161– 5 mortal mind, and not matter, b· it.

burnt
b 286– 8 is better than all b· offerings.

burst
c 261–29 even as the bird which has b· from the egg
b 288–15 lightnings and thunderbolts of error may b·

bursting
f 252–28 Like b· lava, I expand but to my own despair,

bury
o 355–11 let the dead b· their dead."— *Matt. 8 : 22.*
p 367– 2 nor b· the *morale* of C. S.
429–18 unseen by those who think that they b· the
r 469–21 We b· the sense of infinitude, when we admit

business
Father's
a 25– 9 as he went daily about his Father's b·.
52– 1 he was about his "Father's b·."— *Luke 2 : 49.*
neighbor's
m 64–13 never well to interfere with your neighbor's b·."
_____
m 63–30 enter into b· agreements, hold real estate,
s 128– 7 b· men and cultured scholars
p 365– 1 the cook, and the brusque b· visitor

busy
ph 180– 6 when he sees his would-be healers b·,

buyer
p 439– 3 False Belief, . . . is a b· for this firm.

by-and-by
a 21–31 B·, ashamed of his zigzag course,

bygone
s 134– 1 To-day the cry of b· ages is repeated,

byways
s 158–19 the b· of this wilderness world,

C

Cæsar
a 20– 1 He rendered "unto C·— *Matt. 22 : 21.*
g 540–17 Science renders "unto C·— *Matt. 22 : 21.*

Cæsar's
a 20– 2 the things which are C· ;— *Matt. 22 : 21.*
g 540–18 the things which are C· ;— *Matt. 22 : 21.*

Cain (*see also* **Cain's**)
sp 89–27 C· . . . concluded that if life was in the body,
g 538–24 she conceived, and bare C·,— *Gen. 4 : 1.*
540–25 C· brought of the fruit— *Gen. 4 : 3.*
540–28 C· is the type of mortal and material man,
541– 4 Jealous . . . C· seeks Abel's life,
541– 7 but unto C·, and to his offering,— *Gen. 4 : 5.*
541–14 C· rose up against Abel— *Gen. 4 : 8.*
541–19 the Lord [Jehovah] said unto C·,— *Gen. 4 : 9.*
542–15 Therefore whosoever slayeth C·,— *Gen. 4 : 15.*
542–17 set a mark upon C·,— *Gen. 4 : 15.*
542–27 C· went out from the presence— *Gen. 4 : 16.*

Cain's
g 541– 3 more . . . than does C· fruit.
541–10 than for the worship expressed by C· fruit?

calamities
f 223–28 Marvels, c·, and sin will much more abound
r 486–32 these c· often drive mortals to seek and

calculate
sp 85– 1 read the stars or c· an eclipse.
s 162–32 "it is impossible to c· the mischief which
b 319– 5 To c· one's life-prospects from a

calculated
s 111–21 an essay c· to offset the tendency of the age

calculations
f 209–26 mundane formations, astronomical c·,
p 429–24 even according to the c· of natural science.

calculus
f 209–29 swallowed up in the infinite c· of Spirit.
g 520–15 and thought accepts the divine infinite c·.

calendar
a 20– 9 Jesus' history made a new c·,
g 520–11 according to the c· of time.

calendars
f 246– 5 Life and its faculties are not measured by c·.

calf
g 514–24   And the *c·* and the young lion,— *Isa.* 11 : 6.
California
  a 21–16   while I am *en route* for *C·*,
call
last
  b 291– 7   but this last *c·* of wisdom cannot come till
lesser
  b 291– 8   till mortals have . . . yielded to each lesser *c·*
mental
  sp 86– 8   His quick apprehension of this mental *c·*
midnight
  p 365– 6   preparing their helpers for the "midnight *c·*,"
of error
  a 21–26   worldly man is at the beck and *c·* of error,

  pr 15–30   they assuredly *c·* down infinite blessings.
  a 20– 9   which we *c·* the Christian era ;
  31– 4   "*C·* no man your father upon— *Matt.* 23 : 9.
  40– 7   I will *c·* for thee."— *Acts* 24 : 25.
  sp 82–20   as before the change we *c·* death,
  87–13   The Scotch *c·* such vision "second sight,"
  92–25   We should blush to *c·* that real which
  98–25   multitudes consider that which they *c· science*
  s 157–14   the substratum . . . which we *c·* matter ;
  ph 172– 9   if man passes through what we *c·* death
  173–27   and so continue to *c·* upon matter
  173–32   *c·* into action less faith than Buddhism
  189–15   We *c·* the body material ; but
  f 219–16   We shall not *c·* the body weak,
  b 285– 4   not alone hereafter in what men *c·* Paradise,
  287– 9   We *c·* the absence of Truth, *error.*
  307–12   It says : . . . put spirit into what I *c·* matter,
  o 356–20   Would any one *c·* it wise and good
  p 372– 4   What you *c·* matter was originally
  372–12   and then *c·* his bonds material and
  373–28   When . . . we *c·* these conditions disease.
  392–16, 11   You will *c·* it neuralgia, but we *c·* it a belief.
  408–30   condition of the body which we *c·* sensation
  411–14   a disease which moderns would *c·* dementia.
  412–10   may *c·* the disease by name when you mentally
  416–16   The material body, which you *c· me,*
  420– 6   they should early *c·* an experienced
  t 444– 9   their brethren upon whom they may *c·*,
  464–16   the sufferer could *c·* a surgeon,
  r 479–16   Does that which we *c·* dead ever see
  g 504–27   Did infinite Mind create matter, and *c·* it
  515–29   *C·* the mirror divine Science,
  515–30   and *c·* man the reflection.
  527–24   to see what he would *c·* them :— *Gen.* 2 : 19.
  549–20   including those which we *c·* human.
  555–20   and *c·* this sham unity *man,*

called
  pref xi–22   When God *c·* the author to proclaim His Gospel
  a 27–25   "Many are *c·*, but few are— *Matt.* 22 : 14.
  34–28   which has since been *c·* the ascension,
  37– 1   which destroys the belief *c·* sin
  44–20   Could it be *c·* supernatural for the
  45–25   disciples at first *c·* him a spirit, ghost,
  46–26   his final demonstration, *c·* the ascension,
  52–31   *c·* Jesus a glutton and a wine-bibber.
  sp 75–26   one possible moment, when . . . those *c·* dead,
  80–24   over its lower substratum, *c·* matter.
  81–22   give to the worms the body *c·* man,
  84–26   material personalities *c·* spirits,
  86– 5   mortal mind, whose touch *c·* for aid.
  88–17   and at another are *c·* spirits.
  90– 6   the imaginary line *c·* the equator
  an 101–30   animal magnetism, recently *c·* hypnotism,
  s 108–24   the opposite of Truth,— *c·* error,
  109–27   his name shall be *c·* Wonderful."— *Isa.* 9 : 6.
  110– 9   I beheld, . . . the awful unreality *c·* evil.
  126–19   Or shall all that . . . be *c·* supernatural,
  127–30   C. S. eschews what is *c·* natural science,
  135–14   and when Truth casts out the evil *c·* disease,
  137–26   the impetuous disciple had been *c·*
  139– 7   by what men *c·* miracles.
  143–10   The divine Mind never *c·* matter *medicine,*
  153–19   and this belief is *c·* a boil.
  162–23   restored what is *c·* the lost substance of lungs,
  162–26   as surely as it heals what is *c·* functional,
  ph 168–21   in defiance of what is *c·* material law,
  185–29   material stratum of the human mind, *c·* brain,
  190– 8   human belief *c·* mortal man
  190–13   and the bulk of a body, *c·* man.
  192–32   I was *c·* to visit Mr. Clark in Lynn,
  199–28   belief . . . gave his thought-forces, *c·* muscles,
  f 204–13   an intelligence or Mind *c·* God.
  204–15   cannot therefore be mind, though so *c·*.
  206–32   There are evil beliefs, often *c·* evil spirits ;
  213– 2   supposition of reality is *c·* a deceiver,
  245– 4   the London medical magazine *c·* The Lancet.
  250–14   and that one is *c·* man ;
  254–17   prior to the change *c·* death,
  b 274– 7   *Natural science,* as it is commonly *c·*,

called
  b 274–26   The conventional firm, *c·* matter and mind,
  281–14   The one Ego, the one Mind or Spirit *c·* God,
  285–10   the *unlikeness c·* sin, sickness, and
  290–16   If the change *c· death* destroyed the
  293– 9   the more ethereal is *c·* mind.
  293–10   the illusion *c·* a mortal,
  293–25   The manifestations of evil, . . . are *c·*
  295–25   All that is *c·* mortal thought
  302–26   infinite Principle, *c·* Person or God.
  309–10   He was no longer *c·* Jacob, but Israel,
  309–15   were to be *c·* the children of Israel,
  313–29   Jesus *c·* the body, which by spiritual power
  319–11   material means (*c·* nature)
  331–27   constitute the triune Person *c·* God,
  339– 8   Spirit, alone created all, and *c·* it good.
  o 343–18   proving by what are wrongly *c·* miracles,
  p 362–12   (Mary Magdalene, as she has since been *c·*)
  374–13   state of mortal mind, though it is *c·* matter.
  380– 2   which ends in a belief *c·* death,
  398– 1   Sometimes Jesus *c·* a disease by name,
  398–11   synagogue ruler's daughter, whom they *c·* dead
  409– 6   animate error *c·* nerves, brain, mind,
  411– 4   If the student silently *c·* the disease by
  411–24   The mental state is *c·* a material state.
  414–14   whether it is *c·* dementia, hatred,
  427–26   *C·* to the bed of death, what material remedy
  430–27   The evidence for the prosecution being *c·*
  431– 1   must remain silent until *c·* for at this trial,
  431–20   The next witness is *c·* :
  432– 9   Another witness is *c·* for by the
  432–21   I was *c·* for, shortly after the
  436–19   result which they were *c·* to prevent.
  437–20   False Belief, *c·* C. S. to order
  t 447–10   heal the sick when *c·* upon for aid,
  r 469–16   opposite of infinite Mind— *c· devil*
  477–28   when they *c·* a certain beautiful lake
  478–28   and *c·* me by His grace,— *Gal.* 1 : 15.
  482–16   Jesus *c·* himself "the Son of man,"— *Matt.* 9 : 6.
  483–16   Science has *c·* the world to battle
  485–27   delineates foreign agents, *c·* disease and sin.
  487– 6   both before and after that which is *c·* death.
  g 504– 3   God *c·* the light Day,— *Gen.* 1 : 5.
  504– 4   and the darkness He *c·* Night.— *Gen.* 1 : 5.
  506– 8   God *c·* the firmament Heaven.— *Gen.* 1 : 8.
  506–22   God *c·* the dry land Earth ;— *Gen.* 1 : 10.
  506–23   the waters *c·* He Seas : — *Gen.* 1 : 10.
  508– 1   human or material belief, *c·* mortal man.
  520–10   The numerals of infinity, *c· seven days,*
  522–13   *c·* life and intelligence in matter.
  523–17   One is *c·* the Elohistic,
  523–18   Supreme Being is therein *c·* Elohim.
  523–19   The other document is *c·* the Jehovistic,
  523–20   Deity therein is always *c·* Jehovah,
  523–26   the creator is *c·* Jehovah, or the Lord.
  524– 7   *c·* the Supreme Being by the national name of
  524–17   that He should now be *c·* Jehovah?
  527–24   Adam *c·* every living creature,— *Gen.* 2 : 19.
  532–13   Lord God [Jehovah] *c·* unto Adam,— *Gen.* 3 : 9.
  534–16   material intelligence *c· energy*
  535–30   God *c·* the dry land Earth ;— *Gen.* 1 : 10.
  536– 1   the waters *c·* He Seas."— *Gen.* 1 : 10.
  551– 5   cannot produce its opposite . . . *c·* matter.
  551–18   transmitted through these bodies *c·* eggs,
  ap 567–15   that old serpent, *c·* the devil,— *Rev.* 12 : 9.
  568– 5   Science is able to destroy this lie, *c·* evil.
  572–24   stage in human experience *c·* death,
  gl 580–17   the opposite of Love, *c·* hate ;
  580–18   usurper of Spirit's creation, *c·* . . . matter ;
  586–10   the divine Principle, commonly *c·* God.

calling
  pr 6– 7   *C·* on Him to forgive our work
  a 31– 9   no record of his *c·* any man by the name of
  s 148–20   *c·* that *man* which is not the counterpart,
  154– 6   *c·* up the fear that creates the image of disease
  ph 175–16   If a random thought, *c·* itself dyspepsia,
  f 251–31   beliefs, which rob Mind, *c·* it matter,
  b 283–30   by *c·* a curve a straight line
  p 422– 1   and then *c·* the process mathematics.
  491– 9   thd latter *c·* itself right.
  g 528–23   and *c·* them real and God-given,
  528–26   *c·* them *mankind,* — that is, a kind of man.
  532–20   the divine voice *c·* out to the corporeal senses.

calls
  a 39–13   The Bible *c·* death an enemy,
  m 60–24   An ill-attuned ear *c·* discord harmony,
  sp 73– 3   Spiritualism *c·* one person, . . . *material,*
  s 114– 2   *c·* sick and sinful humanity *mortal mind,*
  114– 8   and *c· mind* both human and divine.
  124–27   Human knowledge *c·* them forces of matter ;
  ph 170– 4   The discord which *c·* for material methods
  187–29   this so-called mind then *c·* itself dead ;
  f 229–11   *c·* both the offspring of spirit,
  b 287–18   Evil *c·* itself something, when it is nothing.
  307–32   the voice of Truth still *c·* :

calls

b 311–28   They are only what mortal belief *c·* them.
   312– 4   That which material sense *c·* intangible,
p 399–18   manages it, and then *c·* it material.
g 507–30   inverts this appearing and *c·* ideas material.

calm

sp 99–23   The *c·*, strong currents of true spirituality,
s 109–15   *c·*, and buoyant with hope,
ph 198– 5   The patient may seem *c·* under it, but he is not.
f 248– 1   unchanging *c·* and glorious freedom of
o 358–15   It presents the *c·* and clear verdict of Truth
p 366–27   *c·* in the presence of both sin and disease,
   391– 7   Instead of blind and *c·* submission to
   393–32   It is well to be *c·* in sickness ;
   415–25   *c·* and instruct mortal mind with immortal
   421–21   *C·* the excitement sometimes induced
r 495–18   nor doubt overshadow your . . . *c·* trust,
g 506–11   The *c·* and exalted thought or

calmly

a 41– 8   The God-inspired walk *c·* on

calomel

ph 198– 1   harm his patients even more than his *c·*

Calvary

a 30– 9   his struggles in Gethsemane and on *C·*,
b 317–23   whom they had loved before the tragedy on *C·*.
ap 575–31   Cross of *C·*, which binds human society

cambric

p 379–15   the hue of her blood on a *c·* handkerchief,

came

pref vii– 5   yet it traversed the night, and *c·* where,
   ix–12   she "lisped in numbers, for the numbers *c·*."
   ix–31   she *c·* at length to its solution ;
   xi–23   *c·* also the charge to plant and water His
pr 5–29   *c·* to "destroy the *works* of the— *I John* 3 : 8.
   6–26   He *c·* teaching and showing men how to
a 27–29   the essential religion he *c·* to establish
   30–19   Christ Jesus *c·* to rebuke rabbinical error
   33– 7   Their bread indeed *c·* down from heaven.
   47–28   each one *c·* to a violent death except
m 56– 1   When our great Teacher *c·* to him for baptism,
s 108– 1   Whence *c·* to me this heavenly conviction,
   109–23   The revelation . . . *c·* to me gradually
   131–17   "He *c·* unto his own,— *John* 1 : 11.
   134–12   it *c·* about that human rights were
   135–16   "it *c·* to pass, when the devil was— *Luke* 11 : 14.
ph 169– 8   But it always *c·* about as I had foretold.
   184–30   Her breath *c·* gently.
f 214– 2   they *c·* as sound to the primitive prophets.
   214–13   They go out as they *c·* in,
   224–27   as he *c·* of old to the patriarch at noonday
b 319–22   The divine Science . . . *c·* through inspiration,
p 362– 7   A "strange woman" *c·* in.— *Prov.* 23 : 27.
   364–21   spiritual purgation which *c·* through the
   389–28   case of convulsions, . . . *c·* under my
   398– 5   rent him sore and *c·* out of him,— *Mark* 9 : 26.
   439– 7   when a message *c·* from False Belief,
   439–23   You *c·* to his rescue, only to
r 473– 7   Christ *c·* to destroy the belief of sin.
   474–18   Jesus *c·* to destroy sin, sickness, and death ;
g 529– 2   there *c·* a suggestion of change in the
   529– 4   It *c·* about, also, that instruments were
   533–22   which *c·* from Adam to form Eve.
ap 566–16   Out of the land of bondage *c·*,
   572–26   Through what sense *c·* this vision to St. John?
   574– 6   *c·* unto me one of the seven angels— *Rev.* 21 : 9.

camel

f 241–31   "easier for a *c·* to go through the— *Matt.* 19 : 24.
t 449– 9   "easier for a *c·* to go through the— *Matt.* 19 : 24.

camels

s 140–15   straining out gnats and swallowing *c·*.
f 202– 2   straining out gnats and swallowing *c·*.
p 366–20   while they swallow the *c·* of bigoted pedantry.

camera

c 264– 6   we sometimes behold in the *c·* of
b 305– 5   A picture in the *c·* . . . is not the original,

campaign

r 492–17   Discussing his *c·*, General Grant said :

Canaan

gl 582–24   definition of

cancel

pr 5–22   not to be used as a confessional to *c·* sin.

cancelled

pr 5–26   If prayer nourishes the belief that sin is *c·*,

cancels

a 22–31   Mercy *c·* the debt only when justice approves.
o 361– 3   *c·* the disagreement, and settles the
p 404–15   and reformation *c·* the crime.

cancer

p 390–28   whether it is *c·*, consumption, or smallpox.
   395–25   a tumor, a *c·*, or decayed lungs,

cannibal

f 214–25   spread their table with *c·* tidbits

cannon's

f 225–21   nor did . . . freedom come from the *c·* mouth.

canon

p 382–18   so-called law of matter a *c·* "more honored

canvas

sp 86–32   before the artist can convey them to *c·*.

capabilities

b 312–25   A personal sense of God and of man's *c·*
   322– 9   is obtained and his *c·* revealed.

capable

sp 89–22   We are all *c·* of more than we do.
   92– 5   *c·* of experiencing pleasure and pain
   92– 6   *c·* of imparting these sensations.
s 128–13   is *c·* of greater endurance,
   160–23   never *c·* of acting contrary to
ph 174– 7   Nothing save divine power is *c·* of
   179– 2   the sudden cures of which it is *c·* ;
   182– 8   *c·* of producing the highest human good?
f 206–10   Will-power is *c·* of all evil.
   230–12   to suppose Him *c·* of
o 355–27   Without this . . . no one is *c·* of impartial or
   357– 3   for doing what He created man *c·* of
   357–11   or makes man *c·* of suffering
p 393–13   God has made man *c·* of this,
   432– 5   whereas Mortal Man, . . . is *c·* of falsehood.
   435– 6   Mortal Mind, which alone is *c·* of sin
r 480–20   never made man *c·* of sin.
   480–22   seems to make men *c·* of wrong-doing.
   481–15   declaring . . . good and evil to be *c·* of
g 532–23   Is Mind *c·* of error as well as of truth,

capacious

p 425–29   If you have sound and *c·* lungs

capacities

sp 94–31   union with the infinite *c·* of the one Mind.
ph 200– 6   and illustrated the grand human *c·*
f 202–22   the finity of error and the infinite *c·* of Truth,
   227–28   crippled your *c·*, enfeebled your body,
c 258–22   The human *c·* are enlarged and perfected
t 445– 8   Unfold the latent energies and *c·*

capacity

sp 85– 3   which demonstrates the *c·* of Soul,
s 128–11   ability to exceed their ordinary *c·*.
ph 165– 6   To measure intellectual *c·* by
   179– 8   the spiritual *c·* to apprehend thought
f 209–31   a conscious, constant *c·* to understand God.
   223– 4   fetters of man's finite *c·* are forged by
o 357– 8   Truth creates neither a lie, a *c·* to lie, nor a liar.
r 475–31   nor can God, . . . engender the *c·* or freedom to
g 519–12   Human *c·* is slow to discern and to grasp

capitalization

b 319–31   by special and proper *c·*

captive

f 224–30   power of God brings deliverance to the *c·*.
p 434– 1   open wide these prison doors and set the *c·* free.
r 495–13   sets the *c·* free physically and morally.

captives

pref xi–19   deliverance to the *c·* [of sense],— *Luke* 4 : 18.
s 161– 8   Bible case of the three young Hebrew *c·*,

captivity

s 133–15   Even in *c·* among foreign nations,
f 227–20   but evil and error lead into *c·*.

cardinal

a 52–22   These were the two *c·* points of Mind-healing,
ap 577–13   but its four *c·* points are :

care

best
p 383– 8   Scientist takes the best *c·* of his body when he
God's
m 66–11   Trials are proofs of God's *c·*.
good
p 383– 5   One says : "I take good *c·* of my body."
His
gl 589–11   man is His idea, the child of His *c·*.
loving
t 454–27   Let your loving *c·* and counsel support all their
omnipotent
f 231–25   To fear sin is to . . . distrust His omnipotent *c·*.
unselfish
m 59–17   Tender words and unselfish *c·*

pr 9–29   since you do not *c·* to tread in the footsteps of
m 62–23   divine Mind, . . . will *c·* for the human body,
ph 188–20   sickness and *c·*, are traced upon mortals
b 272–13   the *c·* our Master took not to impart to dull ears

career
　devious
　　s 164– 1　said : . . . Dark and perplexed, our devious *c·*
　earthly
　　a 30–23　throughout the whole earthly *c·* of Jesus,
　　b 334– 8　the fleshly Jesus, whose earthly *c·* was brief.
　glorious
　　a 32–32　in the twilight of a glorious *c·*
　his
　　a 51– 4　the sublimest influence of his *c·*.
　sacred
　　a 37–20　would gladly have turned his sacred *c·* into
　sinless
　　a 26–24　the precious import of our Master s sinless *c·*
　that
　　a 37–22　take up the more practical import of that *c·* !

　　a 40–19　If a *c·* so great and good as that of Jesus

careful
　s 153–29　we shall be more *c·* of our mental conditions,
　ph 196–12　A *c·* study of this text shows
　t 444–18　be *c·* always to "judge righteous— *John* 7 : 24.

careless
　s 110–21　or by *c·* or malicious students,
　p 364–32　Did the *c·* doctor, the nurse, the cook,

care-lined
　f 245–14　She had no *c·* face,

cares
　m 58–30　but nothing can abolish the *c·* of marriage.
　　59–10　the annoyances and *c·* of domestic economy.
　sp 78–25　not in the medley where matter *c·* for matter,
　g 556–27　before it *c·* to solve the problem of being,

careth
　m 58–31　"She that is married *c·* — *I Cor.* 7 : 34.
　t 464–27　and *c·* not for the sheep."— *John* 10 : 13.

caring
　p 413–21　but in *c·* for an infant
　t 445–29　and *c·* only for the fees.

carious
　s 162– 9　restores *c·* bones to soundness.
　　162–22　*c·* bones have been restored to healthy
　ph 193– 5　said the bone was *c·* for several inches.

carnal
　a 52– 5　His affections were pure ; theirs were *c·*.
　an 105– 6　over the *c·* or mortal mind,
　s 131–10　"The *c·* mind is enmity— *Rom.* 8 : 7.
　c 263–11　*C·* beliefs defraud us.
　b 292–27　This *c·* material mentality, misnamed *mind*,
　　311– 3　What we term mortal mind or *c·* mind,
　　315–13　Their *c·* minds were at enmity with it.
　o 345–29　enrages the *c·* mind and is the main cause of
　　345–30　cause of the *c·* mind's antagonism.
　p 395–11　overcomes faith in a *c·* mind,
　g 534–18　"The *c·* mind is enmity— *Rom.* 8 : 7.

carnivorous
　p 514–20　The individuality created by God is not *c·*,

carpet
　s 154–29　thinks she has hurt her face by falling on the *c·*,

carried
　s 133–22　*c·* out in special theories
　ph 171–19　sifted through matter, *c·* on a nerve,
　b 314–25　*c·* the problem of being,
　p 387– 7　that intellectual labor has been *c·*
　ap 570–10　to be *c·* away of the flood.— *Rev.* 12 : 15.
　　574–11　ministry of Truth, . . . *c·* John away in spirit.

carries
　sp 90–18　*c·* it through the air and over the ocean.
　s 153–27　mortal mind, . . . contains and *c·* the infection.
　f 204–10　(mortal man) who *c·* out the delusions
　　241– 7　and *c·* off their fleeting joys.
　b 294– 5　*c·* within itself the seeds of all error.

carry
　pr 10–17　One of the forms of worship in Thibet is to *c·*
　s 116–15　nor do they *c·* the day against physical enemies,
　ph 176–26　can *c·* its ill-effects no farther than
　f 243–21　Neither . . . can *c·* on such telegraphy ;
　b 328–18　Our missionaries *c·* the Bible to India,
　g 514–17　They *c·* the baggage of stern resolve,

carve
　f 248–28　*c·* them out in grand and noble lives.

carves
　b 299– 2　when he *c·* his "Statue of Liberty,"

case
　any
　　s 149–13　If you fail to succeed in any *c·*, it is because
　belief in the
　　ph 198–24　formed by his doctor's belief in the *c·*,
　Bible
　　s 161– 7　as in the Bible *c·* of the three young Hebrew

case
　chronic
　　ph 178–16　that chronic *c·* is not difficult to cure.
　cope with the
　　p 423–22　strong, instead of weak, to cope with the *c·* ;
　determines a
　　ph 194– 7　determines a *c·* for better or for worse.
　difficult
　　t 449–18　than it does to heal the most difficult *c·*.
　either
　　sp 73– 1　In either *c·*, one does not support the other.
　　ph 170–29　but in either *c·* dependent upon his
　　181–18　In either *c·* you must improve your mental
　every
　　an 105–13　Mortal mind, . . . is the criminal in every *c·* ;
　　s 149– 5　more excellent way is divine Science in every *c·*.
　　p 415– 3　Mind in every *c·* is the eternal God,
　factor in the
　　s 151– 2　as if there was but one factor in the *c·* ;
　fever
　　p 380– 2　a fever *c·*, which ends in a belief called
　governs the
　　p 422–31　he believes that . . . matter— governs the *c·*.
　his
　　ph 194–30　His *c·* proves material sense to be but
　his own
　　t 464–18·　he could handle his own *c·*
　hopeless
　　ph 196–25　Many a hopeless *c·* of disease is induced by a
　however obstinate the
　　p 414– 5　However obstinate the *c·*, it yields more readily
　individual
　　p 408– 9　cannot, . . . shield the individual *c·*
　injures the
　　p 403–29　improves or injures the *c·* in proportion
　judge the
　　p 404– 1　in order to judge the *c·* according to C. S.
　leaving the
　　an 104–27　leaving the *c·* worse than before it was grasped
　mental
　　p 430–17　Suppose a mental *c·* to be on trial,
　nature of a
　　p 403–28　The human mind determines the nature of a *c·*,
　of convulsions
　　p 389–28　A *c·* of convulsions, produced by
　of dropsy
　　s 156– 5　A *c·* of dropsy, given up by the faculty,
　of paralysis
　　s 152–15　apparently cured a *c·* of paralysis simply by
　of sickness
　　p 386– 3　not to be accepted in the *c·* of sickness,
　of sin
　　p 386– 4　any more than it is in the *c·* of sin.
　of temptation
　　p 441– 7　and in *c·* of temptation, to give heavy bonds
　one
　　p 403–11　is employed to remove the illusion in one *c·*,
　　422–24　A surgeon is employed in one *c·*,
　one side of the
　　f 238–26　listening only to one side of the *c·*.
　particular
　　ph 178– 2　though they know nothing of this particular *c·*
　plead the
　　p 412– 4　plead the *c·* scientifically for Truth.
　renders your
　　t 461–22　to admit that . . . renders your *c·* less curable,
　reverse the
　　p 392–24　Reverse the *c·*.
　single
　　s 155–21　in order to heal a single *c·* of disease.
　such a
　　pr 3–30　In such a *c·*, the only acceptable prayer is
　symptoms of the
　　p 412– 6　to meet the . . . symptoms of the *c·* you treat,
　take the
　　t 458–14　the divine Mind is ready to take the *c·*.
　terrible
　　s 156– 6　It was a terrible *c·*.
　testimony in the
　　p 434–27　The only valid testimony in the *c·*
　this
　　pr 10–30　In this *c·* infinite Love will not grant the
　　p 435–29　what jurisdiction had his Honor, . . . in this *c·* ?
　treating the
　　s 161–25　treating the *c·* according to his physical diag-
　　　　　　nosis,
　your own
　　p 384–23　if . . . you are not fit to conduct your own *c·*

　　m 66–26　as must always be the *c·*,
　　　68–20　I have named her *c·* to individuals,
　　sp 81–14　Nor is the *c·* improved when alleged spirits
　　　81–23　in the *c·* of man as truly as
　　　81–24　in the *c·* of numbers and of music,
　　an 104–25　it is a *c·* of the greater error overcoming the
　　　135–31　as must be the *c·* in the cycles of

case
s	148– 1	When his students brought to him a c·
	159– 7	The c· was brought to trial.
ph	189–21	The reverse is the c· with all the formations of
	193–30	and what his physician said of the c·,
p	396–11	Never say . . . how much you have to contend
		with in a c·,
	401–19	as is the c· with a fermenting fluid.
	412–28	If the c· is that of a young child or an infant,
	420–20	or diminishes . . . as the c· may require,
	422–13	If such be the c·, explain to them the
	425– 6	If the c· to be mentally treated is consumption,
	431– 2	would be allowed to testify in the c·.
	433–15	The c· is given to the jury.
	434–15	the c· for Mortal Man *versus* Personal Sense
	434–24	Mortal Man has had no proper counsel in the c·.
	436–27	Judge Medicine sat in judgment on the c·,
	438–21	the facts in the c· show that this fear is a

cases
all
ph	176–21	Should all c· of organic disease be treated by

both
p	370–17	but it uses the same medicine in both c·,
gl	598– 6	the original word is the same in both c·,

certain
m	56– 5	Jesus' concessions (in certain c·)

majority of
m	60–19	This, however, in a majority of c·,
r	482– 2	gives the exact meaning in a majority of c·.

most
s	140– 2	more than it is needed in most c· ;

other
r	482– 8	In other c·, use the word *sense*,

parallel
p	422–22	suppose two parallel c· of bone-disease,

same
o	359– 5	Yet Scientists will take the same c·,

such
s	177–31	In such c· a few persons believe the potion
o	343– 1	The people are taught in such c· to say, Amen.
p	394–32	faith is not the healer in such c·.
	433–11	The jury must regard in such c· only the
t	443–18	should give up such c·,
	446–10	has generally completely healed such c·.

these
pref	x–17	These c· for the most part have been

well-authenticated
pref	x–16	thousands of well-authenticated c· of healing,

s	162–18	in c· of both acute and chronic disease
ph	176–23	c· of hysteria, hypochondria, and
p	430–17	as c· are tried in court.

cast
pr	1– *	*and be thou c· into the sea ;— Mark* 11 : 23.
	6–23	uncovered and rebuked sin before he c· it out.
a	35– 5	and c· their net on the right side.
	41– 1	hope must be c· beyond the veil of matter
s	161– 8	captives, c· into the Babylonian furnace ;
ph	168– 6	Whatever influence you c· on the side of matter,
f	242–24	for my vesture they did c· lots."— *John* 19 : 24.
	244–28	Such admissions c· us headlong into darkness
b	271–26	or to c· them on the right side for Truth,
	272–17	neither c· ye your pearls before — *Matt.* 7 : 6.
	321– 8	When, led by wisdom to c· down his rod,
p	362– *	*Why art thou c· down,— Psal.* 42 : 11.
	366– 4	first c· moral evils out of himself
	366– 6	enable him to c· physical evils out of his patient;
	422– 3	by whom do your children c· them out?"—*Matt.*
		12 : 27.
	431–11	arrested Mortal Man . . . and c· him into
	441–15	nor can Disease c· him into prison.
t	447–30	A sinner is afraid to c· the first stone.
	460–32	shadow of old errors was no longer c· upon
r	494–31	should be said . . . they c· fear and all evil
ap	563–24	and did c· them to the earth :— *Rev.* 12 : 4.
	567–23	The words "c· unto the earth"— *Rev.* 12 : 13.
	568–16	accuser of our brethren is c· down,— *Rev.* 12 : 10.
	569–30	saw that he was c· unto the earth,— *Rev.* 12 : 13.

cast out
pr	7– 5	when he c· out devils and healed the sick
a	34–15	heal the sick, c· out evils,
	41–32	c· out evils and heal the sick.
	49– 4	healed the sick, c· out evil,
	51–31	c· out evil, and raise the dead.
m	56–12	the corporeal sense of creation was c· out,
sp	79–17	Jesus c· out evil spirits, or false beliefs.
s	130–18	beliefs must be denied and c· out
	135–15	When Christ c· out the devil of dumbness,
	136– 4	a divine Principle, which would c· out error
	137– 2	c· out evil, raise the dead ;
	138–11	diseases were c· out neither by corporeality,
	138–22	easier for Christianity to c· out sickness than
ph	170–20	Jesus healed the sick and c· out error,
	185–22	Jesus c· out evil and healed the sick,
	188–27	must be uprooted and c· out.

cast out
ph	191–31	Truth is able to c· out the ills of the flesh.
b	281–31	The old belief must be c· out
	322– 1	to heal the sick, and c· out evils
o	342–12	should c· out evils and heal the sick.
	348–12	delusions, were c· out and the dumb spake.
p	362– *	*In my name shall they c· out devils :—Mark* 16 : 17.
	392– 6	must be c· out to readjust the balance for God.
	411–16	Thereupon Jesus c· out the evil,
	418–27	C· out all manner of evil.
	422– 3	"If I by Beelzebub c· out devils,— *Matt.* 12 : 27.
	442–10	Divine Love had c· out fear.
t	445–23	hatred, and revenge are c· out by the
	455–14	"First c· out the beam — *Matt.* 7 : 5.
	455–15	shalt thou see clearly to c· out— *Matt.* 7 : 5.
	462– 5	c· out error, heal the sick,
r	494–30	Our Master c· out devils (evils) and healed the
ap	564– 1	and c· out devils through Beelzebub.
	567–14	And the great dragon was c· out,— *Rev.* 12 : 9.
	567–16	he was c· out into the earth,— *Rev.* 12 : 9.
	567–17	his angels were c· out with him.— *Rev.* 12 : 9.
	567–22	and it is c· out by Christ, Truth,
	567–27	His angels, . . . are c· out with their author.
	570– 8	c· out of his mouth water— *Rev.* 12 : 15.
	570–12	the dragon c· out of his mouth.— *Rev.* 12 : 16.

casteth
a	52–32	"He c· out devils through— *Luke* 11 : 15.
ph	180–24	influence of divine Love which c· out fear.
p	373–18	"perfect Love c· out fear."— *I John* 4 : 18.
	406–10	"Perfect Love c· out fear."— *I John* 4 : 18.
	410–19	perfect Love c· out fear.— *I John* 4 : 18.

casting
pr	12– 8	This, however, is one belief c· out **another**,
	12– 9	a belief in the unknown c· out a
a	33– 8	healing the sick and c· out error.
	34– 3	by c· out error and making the
	35–24	c· out error and healing the sick.
	41–15	c· out error and healing the sick,
	42–30	by c· out error, healing the sick,
	46–11	again seen c· out evil and healing the sick.
m	68–20	when c· my bread upon the waters,
sp	97–31	apostolic work of c· out error and healing the
s	135–29	c· out error and healing the sick,
	136–13	c· out evils and healing the sick?
	138–13	c· out the errors of mortal mind.
ph	182– 2	The act . . . of c· out error with Truth,
	184– 9	finding and c· out by denial the error
f	210– 8	c· out evils, and destroying death,
	234–14	avoid c· pearls before those who trample them
b	271–10	Truth, c· out all inharmony.
	316–28	healing the sick, c· out evils,
	332–15	healing the sick and c· out evils,
o	347–17	healing the sick, and c· out evils.
p	392– 7	C· out evil and fear enables
r	482–16	the truth c· out all error.
gl	583– 8	c· out error and healing the sick ;
	583–18	c· out devils, or error, and healing the sick.

casts
pr	14–28	understanding c· out error and heals the sick,
a	25–15	c· out error, and triumphs over death.
	33–24	c· out error, raises the dead from trespasses
s	135–13	when Truth heals the sick, it c· out evils,
	135–14	and when Truth c· out the evil called disease,
	143– 3	Christ c· out evils and heals the sick.
ph	183–26	Truth c· out all evils and
	189–17	above the cruder theories . . . and c· out a fear.
f	230– 8	which c· out error and heals the sick.
b	275–32	It c· out error and heals the sick.
	282– 1	Truth c· out evils and heals the sick.
o	350–11	Truth c· out error and heals the sick.
t	448–10	and c· thee down from the pinnacle.
r	472– 3	c· out suppositional error and heals the sick.
	473–30	which heals the sick and c· out error,
	482–26	Sickness is part of the error which Truth c· out.
	495– 2	Truth c· out error now as surely as it did
	497–11	spiritual understanding that c· out evil

catalepsy
f	217–11	even of c· and hysteria ;

cataleptic
s	128–24	waking him from a c· nightmare,

cataplasms
s	158–16	Drugs, c·, and whiskey are

cataract
ph	192–14	It is the headlong c·, the devouring flame,

catarrh
f	220– 4	have continual colds, c·, and cough."
	220–10	he has no c· from wet feet,
	220–15	leaves c· to the latter.
p	386– 6	belief says that you may catch cold and have c· ·
	386– 9	c·, fever, rheumatism, or consumption,

catch
f 205–16	we can c· clear glimpses of God only as
o 349–26	Mortal thought does not at once c· the higher
p 386– 6	belief says that you may c· cold
427–32	will waken . . . to c· this trumpet-word

catches
s 145– 2	natural musician c· the tones of harmony,

categories
b 269–13	c· of metaphysics rest on one basis,

caterpillar
sp 74–17	The c·, transformed into a beautiful insect,

Catholic
f 238– 9	Losing her crucifix, the Roman C· girl said,

cattle
f 222–25	and over the c·,"— Gen. 1 : 26.
r 475–25	and over the c·,— Gen. 1 : 26.
g 513–15	c·, and creeping thing,— Gen. 1 : 24.
513–23	and c· after their kind,— Gen. 1 : 25.
514–16	"the c· upon a thousand hills."— Psal. 50 : 10.
515–14	and over the c·,— Gen. 1 : 26.

caught
s 145– 1	or whether they c· its sweet tones,
154–13	had not c· the cholera by material contact,
ph 171– 2	mankind has c· their moral contagion.
b 304–22	If mortals c· harmony through
333–24	c· glorious glimpses of the Messiah, or Christ,
r 471–25	until she c· the first gleam of that which
477–26	Indians c· some glimpses of the underlying
ap 565– 8	c· up unto God, and to His throne.— Rev. 12 : 5.
565–27	and to be c· up unto God,

causation
all
ph 180–12	nor take the ground that all c· is
p 379– 7	recognizing all c· as vested in divine Mind.
417–13	all c· is Mind, acting through spiritual law.

mental
p 423– 9	Scientist, . . . commences with mental c·,

physical
b 286–12	Physical c· was put aside

spiritual
ph 170–22	Spiritual c· is the one question
170–23	spiritual c· relates to human progress.

f 208–25	Mind, not matter, is c·.
230–12	arranging law and c· so as to
g 552– 7	material hypotheses deal with c· as

causative
ph 195–12	whether it is mortal mind . . . that is c·.

Cause
g 547–20	evolution implies that the great First C· must

cause (noun)
and cure
f 220– 6	to look in other directions for c· and cure.

and effect
sp 83–31	from which c· and effect are interpreted.
85–30	The great Teacher knew both c· and effect,
s 114–23	C. S. explains all c· and effect as mental,
126–17	Shall Science explain c· and effect as being
161–30	looked as deeply for c· and effect into
f 211–19	nature of all so-called material c· and effect.
b 275–15	immortality, c·, and effect belong to God.
p 370– 9	law of c· and effect, or like producing like.
374–25	and ignorance of mental c· and effect.
g 556–20	In sleep, c· and effect are mere illusions.

any
p 419– 8	If your patient from any c· suffers a relapse,
t 446–31	will prevent . . . the ultimate triumph of any c·.
464–13	If from an injury or from any c·,

any other
f 207–21	there can be no effect from any other c·,

common
a 52–18	error and evil again make common c·

divine
b 286–24	they lack a divine c·.

exciting
ph 178–11	predisposing cause and the exciting c· are
f 230–32	the exciting c· of all suffering,
p 393– 7	remote, and exciting c· of all bad effects

from effect to
r 467–24	We reason imperfectly from effect to c·,

main
o 345–30	the main c· of the carnal mind's antagonism.

material
f 211–18	nature of all so-called material c·
p 416–11	will tell you that the troublesome material c·

meet the
p 419– 9	meet the c· mentally and courageously,

mental
s 157– 2	C. S. deals wholly with the mental c·
ph 187–17	Anatomy allows the mental c· of the latter
p 374–25	ignorance of mental c· and effect.

cause (noun)
no
f 253–12	you see there is no c· . . . able to
p 386–23	learn at length that there is no c· for grief,

of disease
ph 174–30	should understand that the c· of disease
f 230–32	c· of disease must be obliterated
p 370–21	since mortal mind must be the c· of disease
t 445–26	is the c· of disease rather than its cure.
463– 1	deals with the real c· of disease.

one primal
f 207–20	There is but one primal c·.

only
f 207–23	this great and only c·.
c 262–30	Divine Mind is the only c·
b 286–24	and since God, Spirit, is the only c·,
p 415– 2	Immortal Mind is the only c· ;

or approach
p 374–17	Ignorance of the c· or approach of disease

or effect
m 67–32	from any such c· or effect.
f 207–18	amalgamation of Truth and error in c· or effect

predisposing
ph 178–11	predisposing c· and the exciting cause are

procuring
ph 171–27	the procuring c· of all sin and disease.
p 411–20	procuring c· and foundation of all sickness

real
p 402–32	a belief without a real c·.
t 463– 1	deals with the real c· of disease.

remote
ph 178– 8	The remote c· or belief of disease

seeks
b 279–31	Pantheism . . . seeks c· in effect,

shows the
a 53–19	Science shows the c· of the shock

spiritual
s 111–23	rather than to a final spiritual c·,
b 268– 5	to the spiritual c· of those lower things
313–26	and found the spiritual c·.

their
p 421–24	sometimes explain the symptoms and their c·

to effect
r 467–29	Reasoning from c· to effect

universal
b 331–19	divine Principle, Love, the universal c·,

without
p 386–28	had said, . . . "Your sorrow is without c·,"

without a
ap 564–28	"They hated me without a c·."— John 15 : 25.

s 124– 9	this belief mistakes effect for c·
ph 187–19	the c· of all materialistic action?
189–10	though the c· be unseen,
195–18	thought passes naturally from effect back to c·.
198–32	If matter were the c· of action,
c 262–31	C· does not exist in matter,
b 268– 9	looking . . . to Mind as the c· of every effect.
313–17	and the c· given for the exaltation of Jesus,
o 357–28	if another mighty and self-creative c· exists
p 377–22	and you remove the c· of all disease
377–26	The c· of all so-called disease is mental,
393–32	the sin and the sinner, the disease and its c·.
415– 3	disease is neither a c· nor an effect.
422–11	Patients, unfamiliar with the c· of this
r 480–17	would make matter the c· as well as the effect
g 554– 2	even the c· of all that exists,

cause (verb)
pr 6–11	To c· suffering as the result of sin,
sp 93–14	nor creates aught that can c· evil.
s 160–15	to convey the mandate of mind . . . and so c·
ph 165–16	You say that . . . c· distressed stomachs and
175–14	to fancy that the perfume of clover . . . can c·
177–28	does human belief, you ask, c· this death?
f 206–30	God does not c· man to sin, to be sick, or to die.
208–15	to suppose that matter can both c· and cure
230–18	no more . . . than goodness can c· evil
b 318–13	We must c· the error to cease
p 370–13	by using the same drug which might c· the
374– 7	say : "How can my mind c· a disease I never
397– 9	You c· bodily sufferings and increase them by
403– 5	should and does c· the perpetrator to suffer,
414–10	impossibility that matter, . . . can suffer or c·
415–27	apparently c· the body to disappear.
419–12	nor fear has the power to c· disease or a relapse.
t 457–13	cannot . . . both cure and c· disease
463–18	can c· the mother no more suffering.
g 527– 3	to make it beautiful or to c· it to live and grow.
ap 570–10	that he might c· her to—Rev. 12 : 15.

caused
a 46–18	Jesus c· him to examine the nail-prints and the
49– 4	and c· the disciples to say to their Master :
51–29	c· the selfish materialist to hate him ;
m 64– 1	c· by the selfishness and inhumanity of man.
68–21	it may have c· the good to ponder

5

caused

an 104–24 and a belief originally c· the sickness,
s 164–18 c· by a majority of human beliefs
ph 183–24 first c· the condemnation of man to till the
193– 1 c· by a fall upon a wooden spike
b 312–13 you say that matter has c· his death.
p 377–15 A sudden joy or grief has c· what is termed
379–17 Oxford boys, who c· the death of a man,
399– 5 can matter cure what matter has c·?
411–19 Jesus c· the evil to be self-seen
r 484–19 are really c· by the faith in them
g 520–21 had not c· it to rain — Gen. 2 : 5.
528–10 c· a deep sleep to fall upon Adam, — Gen. 2 : 21.

causeless

p 386–32 that lamentation is needless and c·.

causes

pr 12–20 It is a mortal belief, . . . which c· a drug to
a 22– 7 This c· them, even as drowning men,
39–10 c· mortals to regard death as a friend,
m 68–23 salutary c· sometimes incur these effects.
sp 93–13 Good never c· evil,
s 111–23 to attribute physical effects to physical c·
139– 1 c· the wicked to "forsake his way, — Isa. 55 : 7.
142–17 c· the left to let go its grasp
ph 170–19 what then c· it? Not divine law,
188–23 What c· disease cannot cure it.
198–20 c· a vigorous reaction upon itself,
f 208– 7 this seeming power, . . . which c· disease
211–25 If . . . organism c· the eyes to see
229–23 If God c· man to be sick,
229–30 which c· the belief of sickness.
b 278–20 it would follow that there are two eternal c·,
318– 7 senses are saying that matter c· disease
o 342–25 It c· the deaf to hear,
344–12 understood . . . that error c· disease,
p 377– 3 If grief c· suffering, convince the sufferer that
378– 1 and c· the two to appear conjoined,
378–15 often c· the beast to retreat in terror.
379– 5 where the ordinary physician looks for c·.
387–25 mortal mind, . . . c· all things discordant.
399– 4 but if the material body c· disease,
401– 8 If faith in the truth . . . c· chemicalization
405–30 Belief in material suffering c· mortals to
t 449– 3 A little leaven c· the whole mass to ferment.
458–32 Christianity c· men to turn naturally from
r 482–31 but c· the belief in disease.
g 517–30 c· them to multiply, — to manifest His power.
542– 8 Truth c· sin to betray itself,
550–19 and c· our standard to trail in the dust.

causeth

s 140–26 c· no evil, disease, nor death.

causing

a 22– 4 selfishness and . . . c· constant retrogression,
sp 93–15 does not create a mind susceptible of c· evil,
p 415–18 c· a pale or flushed cheek.
422–17 c· it to depend less on material evidence.
g 520–31 never c· man to till the ground,

caustic

ph 198–17 by the application of c· or croton oil,

caution

gl 586–12 ignorance ; error ; desire ; c·.

cave

s 164– 2 groping of Homer's Cyclops around his c·."

caverns

sp 87–20 ignorant of the gems within its c·,

cave's

a 45– 1 great stone must be rolled from the c· mouth ;

cavil

ph 177– 4 I have demonstrated this beyond all c·.
b 306– 6 and demonstrated this beyond c·.

cavity

f 247– 9 upper and lower teeth without a decaying c·.

cease

s 126– 5 for mortality will c· when man beholds
140–16 only as we c· to worship materially.
160–24 If muscles can c· to act and become rigid
f 204–32 must unsay it and c· from such utterances,
216– 5 Here theories c·, and Science unveils the
219– 2 and the mortal dream will forever c·.
228–12 It will c· when man enters into his heritage
234–21 or sin and sickness will never c·.
c 262–20 supposed pain and pleasure of matter c· to
b 288–14 conflict between truth and error, . . . will c·,
290–24 sin and error . . . do not c· at that moment,
318–14 We must cause the error to c·
327–13 way to escape the misery of sin is to c· sinning.
o 346–14 only as we c· to manifest evil or the belief that
p 370–28 and then they c· to improve.
391–16 will c· in proportion as the sin ceases.
418–14 sickness, sin, and death should c· through C. S.
r 467–12 as this fact becomes apparent, war will c·
476– 7 Error will c· to claim that soul is in body,

ceased

s 160–17 Has mortal mind c· speaking to them,

ceaseless

b 322–27 disappointments and c· woes,

ceases

m 57–28 until it c· to sigh over the world
68–31 Proportionately as human generation c·,
sp 97–16 without passing the boundary where, . . . it c·
b 276–18 c· to be any opportunity for sin and death.
o 346–20 If a dream c·, it is self-destroyed,
p 391–16 will cease in proportion as the sin c·.
r 468–29 One c· in proportion as the other is recognized.

ceasing

pr 15–21 We must "pray without c·." — I Thess. 5 : 17.

celebrate

a 35–14 They c· their Lord's victory over death,

celebrated

an 104– 8 Agassiz, the c· naturalist and author,
g 549–24 In one instance a c· naturalist, Agassiz,

celestial

a 26–17 to reveal the Science of c· being,
m 61– 7 The attainment of this c· condition would
an 60– 8 c· bodies, the earth, and animated things.
s 123– 1 theory as to the relations of the c· bodies,
f 209–19 distances, and revolutions of the c· bodies,
c 267–25 all error disappears in c· Truth.
b 298–26 Angels . . . are c· visitants,
299–29 and reveal the c· peaks.
320–32 stand in c· perfection before Elohim,
337–17 perfection is the order of c· being
g 509–13 Spirit creates no other than . . . c· bodies,
509–14 stellar universe is no more c· than our earth.
ap 572–29 terrestrial or c·, material or spiritual?

cell

ph 191–23 not a flower starts from its cloistered c·.
p 433–27 The prisoner is then remanded to his c·

cell-division

m 68–24 perpetuation of the floral species by bud or c

cement

m 57– 1 Chastity is the c· of civilization
ap 571–19 The c· of a higher humanity will

censure

pr 3–29 the sharp c· our Master pronounces on
9– 3 The wrong lies in unmerited c·,

central

s 121–25 The sun is the c· stillness,
131–10 The c· fact of the Bible is the
f 209– 6 the c· sun of its own systems of ideas,
224–16 Of old the cross was truth's c· sign,
238–31 The cross is the c· emblem of history.
b 305– 7 Man, . . . reflects the c· light of being,
310–15 God, . . . as the c· Life and intelligence
t 454–30 the c· point of C. S.

centre

a 20–25 The truth is the c· of all religion.
m 58–22 c·, though not the boundary, of the affections.
60–18 Marriage . . . a c· for the affections.
f 204– 1 God is at once the c· and circumference of being.
c 262–15 absolute c· and circumference of his being.

centred

o 351–27 Israelites c· their thoughts on the material

centuries

ago
a 46– 8 which identified Jesus thus c· ago,
sp 82– 5 Chaucer wrote c· ago,
93– 2 Remember Jesus, who nearly nineteen c· ago
s 138–26 to-day as readily as it was proved c· ago.
f 224–12 C· ago religionists were ready to hail an
r 487–11 gave . . . hearing to the deaf c· ago,
495– 3 as surely as it did nineteen c· ago.

coming
b 321–30 And so it was in the coming c·,

labor of
m 67–27 does not put to silence the labor of c·.

later
a 55– 7 no more injustice than the later c· have

three
a 41–18 lost, about three c· after the crucifixion.

pref viii–17 Sickness has been combated for c· by doctors
a 55–15 immortal idea is sweeping down the c·,
sp 98–22 For c· — yea, during — natural science
s 147–11 though c· had passed away since
f 224–11 In the record of nineteen c·,
b 328–16 For c· it has been dormant,

centurion

s 133– 5 There was also a certain c· of whose faith

century

a 55– 2 advancing c·, . . . to-day subjects to
s 134–20 and unequalled success in the first c·.
147– 6 Late in the nineteenth c· I demonstrated

century

b 333–17 marked the first c· of the Christian era,
o 355–19 systematic healing power since the first C·.
p 383–22 eating or smoking poison for half a c·,
ap 560– 2 in connection with the nineteenth c·.

cerebellum

p 401–26 or restore will . . . to cerebrum and c·?

cerebro-spinal

ph 175– 7 c· meningitis, hay-fever, and rose-cold?

cerebrum

p 401–26 or restore will and action to c· and

ceremonies

a 31–14 He attached no importance to dead c·.
m 64– 9 seems on most occasions to be the master of c·,
s 131–23 which taketh away the c· and doctrines
135–27 was not a creed, nor a system of c·,
f 228–32 excel the influence of their dead faith and c·.
gl 597– 3 consisted mostly of rites and c·.

ceremony

s 152–18 sick man supposed this c· was intended to

certain

pref ix–10 As a c· poet says of himself,
ix–12 C· essays written at that early date
pr 6–29 It is believed by many that a c· magistrate,
a 27–32 to kill him according to c· assumed
m 56– 4 Jesus' concessions (in c· cases)
57– 6 through c· elements of the feminine,
sp 81– 8 can only prove that c· individuals
91–22 C· erroneous postulates should be
s 122–11 so-called senses . . . ordain c· sections of
133– 5 There was also a c· centurion of whose faith
154– 4 a law of mortal mind that c· diseases
161–16 "Man is endowed by his Maker with c·
ph 177– 6 as c· as the evidence of my own existence.
179–13 preference of mortal mind for a c· method
f 228– 3 c· idiosyncrasies of mortal mind
230–13 to bring about c· evil results,
251– 7 Fright is so great at c· stages of
o 349–28 To a c· extent this is equally true of
p 362– 2 was once the honored guest of a c· Pharisee,
370–11 which might be produced by a c· drug,
375–22 making c· portions of it motionless.
378– 1 associates sickness with c· circumstances
379– 9 on whom c· English students experimented,
386– 5 Expose the body to c· temperatures.
386– 9 So long as mortals declare that c· states of
396– 8 nor draw attention to c· symptoms
399– 3 You say that c· material combinations
399– 8 and puts the body through c· motions.
400–32 recorded that in c· localities he did not
417–30 by c· fears and false conclusions,
418– 9 unerring, and c· effect of divine Science.
422– 6 and c· moral and physical symptoms seem
422–27 and renders them fatal at c· points,
424–20 While it is c· that the divine Mind can
430–29 I was present on c· nights
437–33 c· extracts on the Rights of Man,
t 443–16 c· ordinary physical methods of
449–24 C· minds meet only to separate
459–30 treats disease with more c· results
r 477–28 when they called a c· beautiful lake
478– 9 and by a c· class of persons,
484–17 C· results, supposed to proceed from drugs,
g 509– 7 presented to them the c· sense of eternal Life.
548–30 "C· animals, besides the ordinary
549– 3 the multiplication of c· animals
ap 569–14 in a sweet and c· sense that God is Love.
570– 5 c· active yet unseen mental agencies
gl 581–21 the more c· is the downfall of its structure.

certainly

pr 10–26 or we should c· receive that for which we ask.
a 24– 1 This c· applies to Truth and Love
m 63–28 c· the wronged, and perchance impoverished,
sp 80–28 produces table-tipping as c· as table-setting,
86–30 as c· as it believes what it sees.
90–31 c· shall know this when man reflects God.
an 101–16 c· not conclusive in favor of the doctrine of
s 154– 1 and c· we should not be error's advocate.
ph 170– 8 Christian ideas c· present
177– 2 as c· as it produces hysteria, and
f 233– 7 demands of us only what we can c· fulfil.
b 324–17 c· before we can reach the goal of Spirit,
o 352–31 c· not irrational to tell the truth about ghosts.
353–11 omnipotent Truth c· does destroy error.
p 363–31 c· there was encouragement in
393–26 he c· means that light depends upon Mind,
430–10 Belief in sickness . . . as c· as belief in sin,
r 483–20 God c· revealed the spirit of C. S.,
g 531–27 C· not by both, since flesh wars against Spirit

certainty

sp 81–11 this fact affords no c· of everlasting life.
97– 4 cheerfully await the c· of ultimate perfection.
s 108–13 to multiply with mathematical c·

certainty

f 245–19 a Franklin might work with more c·
p 389–14 then discuss the c· that food can kill man.
r 496–17 enables you to demonstrate, with scientific c·,

certify

s 107– * But I c· you, brethren,— Gal. 1: 11.

cessation

ap 573–27 a c· of death, sorrow, and pain.

chafed

p 383–16 symbolized, and not c·, by its surroundings ;

chaff

b 269– 6 Jesus' demonstrations sift the c· from the wheat,
r 466–28 to separate the c· from the wheat.
ap 565–21 fiery baptism will burn up the c· of error

chain

ph 172–11 this supposed c· of material being.
172–12 divine Science reveals the eternal c·
b 271– 2 the c· of scientific being reappearing
ap 570– 2 people will c·, with fetters of some sort,

chained

s 120–31 c· the limbs of the brave old navigator,
p 380–16 Gazing at a c· lion, crouched for a spring,

chains

sp 96– 3 unwillingness . . . binds Christendom with c·.
p 380–19 ignorant of the truth which c· disease.
t 449– 2 manacled, it is hard to break another's c·.

chair

c 261–17 and sat aching in his c· till his cue was spoken,

Chaldean Wisemen

s 121– 7 The C· W· read in the stars the fate of

challenge

b 268–10 Materialistic hypotheses c· metaphysics

challenges

s 162– 3 agrees only with health and c· disease.

chamber

f 238–14 From out the bridal c· of wisdom

chambers

b 299– 6 artist's own observation and "c· of imagery."
p 365–26 finds its way into the c· of disease

chance

m 58–29 Wealth may obviate . . . the c· for ill-nature
ph 176– 9 and gave the gospel a c· to be seen
p 424– 8 in order to change the notion of c·
t 452– 6 before it has a c· to manifest itself.
r 486–22 subject to c· and change.

chances

sp 77–30 where the c· of the departed for improvement
p 394–25 material means the only refuge from fatal c·?

change (noun)

accomplish the
sp 77– 3 Neither do other mortals accomplish the c·
another
g 529– 7 Another c· will come as to
as radical
a 24–17 a c· as radical as that which has come
before the
sp 82–20 as before the c· we call death,
called death
f 254–17 may not be achieved prior to the c· called death,
b 290–16 If the c· called *death* destroyed the
chance and
r 486–22 mortal in belief and subject to chance and c·.
great
a 24–17 views of atonement will undergo a great c·,
needed
b 291–25 and growth shall effect the needed c·.
of air
f 219–27 impute their recovery to c· of air or diet,
of base
s 162–10 stir the human mind to a c· of base,
of belief
ph 169– 1 c· of belief from a material to a spiritual basis.
subject to
b 297–18 but subject to c· and dissolution.
suggestion of
g 529– 2 a suggestion of c· in the *modus operandi*,
this
p 431–29 nothing on my part has occasioned this c·.
what produces the
p 398–18 What produces the c·?

a 34–27 c· which has since been called the ascension.
ph 169– 6 before the patient felt the c· ;
194– 6 A c· in human belief changes all the
b 297– 9 a c· in either a health-belief or
t 446– 7 the c· may either arise from the

change (verb)

pr 2–15 Prayer cannot c· the Science of being,
2–26 Do we expect to c· perfection?
11–27 Prayer cannot c· the unalterable Truth,

change (verb)

s 125– 1	physical body and of the physical world will c·
125–25	"As a vesture shalt Thou c·— *Psal.* 102 : 26.
f 240–11	C· this statement, suppose Mind to be
253–19	you can at once c· your course
c 260–19	Mortals must c· their ideals
b 281–32	which is to c· our standpoint,
297– 1	nothing can c· this state, until
297–12	C· the evidence, and that disappears which
307–11	It says : . . . Truth shall c· sides
o 359–13	must c· the human concept of life,
p 370–30	naturally and genuinely c· our basis
375– 7	C· the mental state, and the
398–26	c· the belief of disease to a belief of health.
419–13	or to c· itself from one form to another.
419–32	disease or its symptoms cannot c· forms,
424– 8	in order to c· the notion of chance
427– 1	this fact can never c· in Science to
r 481–11	contradictions . . . do not c· the unseen Truth,
491– 5	C· the belief, and the sensation changes.
g 522–32	Does the unerring Principle . . . c· or repent?
544–10	Matter cannot c· the eternal fact

changeable

sp 96–24	Belief is c·,
g 537–29	and divine Love, . . . is represented as c·.

changeableness

s 140–24	wrath, repentance, and human c·.

changed

pref x– 2	she would not have them c·.
a 35– 4	they c· their methods,
46–15	proved . . . that his body was not c·
sp 96– 9	seedtime and harvest (though in c· forms),
s 125– 8	normal and natural to c· mortal thought,
125–25	and they shall be c·."— *Psal.* 102 : 26.
162–19	Secretions have been c·,
ph 185– 1	The wind had not c·,
185– 3	My metaphysical treatment c· the action of
193–10	In a few moments his face c· ;
b 291– 6	We know that all will be c·
308–30	then his name was c· to Israel,
309– 9	This c· the man.
326–26	Then the man was c·.
p 373–32	when by mental means the circulation is c·,
411–17	and the insane man was c·
416–14	unless the belief . . . has meanwhile been c·.
432–29	but my appearance . . . c· the purpose
g 529– 6	suggestive obstetrics has c·.
531–23	Has man . . . c· the method of his Maker?
548–21	will be c· with the progress of information."

changeless

sp 96–24	spiritual understanding is c·.

changes

pr 12–24	C· in belief may go on indefinitely,
s 118–23	c· the whole of mortal thought,
118–24	as yeast c· the chemical properties of meal.
125– 1	as mortal mind c· its beliefs.
125–12	As human thought c· from one stage to
125–21	with c· of time and tide, cold and heat,
125–23	will find that these c· cannot affect his crops.
153– 3	or c· one of the symptoms of disease.
162– 7	It c· the secretions, expels humors,
ph 194– 6	A change in human belief c· all the physical
f 224– 6	the Science which governs these c·,
238– 4	Science is working c· in personal character
b 297– 2	until the belief c·.
297– 5	until the belief on this subject c·.
310–32	These c· are the mutations of material sense,
319–28	A misplaced word c· the sense
322– 3	When understanding c· the standpoints
p 398–29	hypnotism c· such ills into new and
422–16	c· the material base of thought,
422–18	These c· which go on in mortal mind
442–20	Christ c· a belief of sin or of sickness
r 491– 5	Change the belief, and the sensation c·.
g 543– 6	it is the idea of Truth and c· not,

changeth

s 140–26	divine Love, which c· not and
b 310–18	Soul c· not.
g 515– 9	the power which c· the serpent into a staff.

changing

sp 78– 4	the c· deflections of mortal mind ;
79– 6	by c· the patient's thoughts regarding death.
c 255– 1	Eternal Truth is c· the universe.
255– 5	c· chaos into order
b 279– 1	the erring, c·, and dying,
321–32	by c· water into wine,
r 494–26	the mortal testimony, c·, dying, unreal.
g 511–17	The c· glow and full effulgence

channel

sp 73–31	nor can the finite become the c· of the infinite.
t 460–28	through the meagre c· afforded by language
r 489–16	How then can this sense be the God-given c·
gl 593–14	River. C· of thought.

channels

s 108–32	set my thoughts to work in new c·,
f 205–26	and leads human thought into opposite c·
b 276–21	is turned into new and healthy c·,
p 373–28	languidly creeps along its frozen c·,
g 506–19	gathers unformed thoughts into their proper c·,

chaos

c 255– 5	changing c· into order
b 307–31	Above error's awful din, blackness, and c·,
p 372– 6	likened by Milton to "c· and old night."
r 479–23	Darkness and c· are the imaginary opposites of
ap 570–21	the deep waters of c· and old night.

chaotic

s 121– 5	and before he spake, astrography was c·,

Chapman, Dr.

s 163–19	Dr. C·, . . . in a published essay said :

chapter

first

b 313– 6	said of him in the first c· of Hebrews :
g 502–13	as given in the first c· of Genesis.
505– 3	have no record in the first c· of Genesis.
521– 8	(as stated in the first c· of Genesis)
523–22	Throughout the first c· of Genesis
526– 7	contradicts the teaching of the first c·,
535–29	In the first c· of Genesis we read :
537–10	In the first c· of Genesis,
537–24	recorded in the first c· of Genesis.
557–26	the first c· of the Old Testament,
ap 561–29	In the first c· of the Fourth Gospel
gl 590–21	not used in the first c· of Genesis,

last

s 117–11	in the last c· of Mark's Gospel
b 272–11	referred to in the last c· of Mark's Gospel.

previous

r 493–12	is touched upon in a previous c·

same

b 313– 9	another passage in the same c·,
gl 598– 7	as in other passages in this same c·

second

g 521–26	second c· of Genesis contains a statement
522–25	latter part of the second c· of Genesis,
526–15	the second c· of Genesis.

seventh

p 362– 1	in the seventh c· of Luke's Gospel

tenth

ap 558– 1	in the tenth c· of his book of Revelation :

third

gl 598– 2	John's Gospel, the third c·, where we read :

this

r 465– 1	This c· is from the first edition of
gl 579– 4	On this account this c· is added.

twelfth

ap 559–32	The twelfth c· of the Apocalypse,
568– 5	The twelfth c· of the Apocalypse typifies

twelve

g 523–28	to the end of c· twelve,

g 523–26	fourth verse of c· two to c· five,
gl 585–15	Error. See c· on Recapitulation, page 472.
588–26	See c· on Recapitulation, page 469.
590–14	Life. See c· on Recapitulation, page 468.
593– 3	Principle. See c· on Recapitulation, page 465.
594–18	Souls. See c· on Recapitulation, page 466.
594–25	Substance. See c· on Recapitulation, page 468.

chapters

ap 568– 7	following c· depict the fatal effects
gl 590–23	introduced in the second and following c·,

character

apostle's

ap 560–23	hid from view the apostle's c·,

awful

ap 563–16	and beholds its awful c· ;

beautiful in

m 60– 6	The beautiful in c· is also the good,

Christian

b 291– 9	in the growth of Christian c·.

deific

b 336–22	lose the deific c·, and become less than God.

divine

pr 4–21	to assimilate more of the divine c·,
g 540–23	representing error as assuming a divine c·,

elevate

r 492–11	will purify and elevate c·.

finite in

sp 71–29	limited and finite in c· and quality.

God's

f 208–12	not in accordance with the goodness of God's c·.
b 283–22	detracts from God's c· and nature,

his

a 53– 9	was the very opposite of his c·.

human

ap 565–22	melting and purifying even the gold of human c·.

individual

t 449–24	a good detective of individual c·.

character

infinite
c 257–28 or Mind would lose its infinite c·

lovely
m 68–17 she was unmarried, a lovely c·,

no
p 400–17 disease . . . has no c· nor type,

nurseries of
f 235–10 Nurseries of c· should be strongly garrisoned

of Judas
c 260– 5 while holding in thought the c· of Judas.

of Mind
s 142–31 the nature and c· of Mind, God.

origin and
g 539–17 this lie as to man's origin and c·

perception of
s 128– 9 enlarges their perception of c·,

personal
f 238– 4 Science is working changes in personal c·

straightforward
ph 168– 1 fair seeming for straightforward c·,

this
pref xii– 3 hers was the only College of this c·

pr 8– 7 indexes which do not correspond with their c·.
a 28–15 Neither the origin, the c·, nor the work
m 67–19 notion that animal natures . . . give force to c·
b 313–14 is, in the Greek Testament, c·.
o 357–18 false notions about the Divine Being and c·

characteristic

s 152–31 the general symptoms, the c· signs,
b 305–12 Gender also is a quality, . . . a c· of
ap 566–30 Michael's c· is spiritual strength.

characteristics

sp 95–18 and is one of the special c· thereof.
g 512–12 consequently reproduce their own c·.

characterized

sp 76–17 c· by the divine Spirit as idea, not matter.
s 112–21 c· in the epistle to the Hebrews.

characters

f 235–18 will degrade the c· it should inform and elevate.
gl 588–13 unchanged forever in their individual c·,

charge

pref xi–23 the c· to plant and water His vineyard.
m 61–25 more solemn c·, than the culture of your
o 355– 3 The c· of inconsistency
p 398– 3 I c· thee, come out of him,— Mark 9 : 25.
441– 9 He concluded his c· thus :
g 512–11 angels of His presence, which have the holiest c·,
ap 564– 7 to c· the innocent with the crime.

charged

a 49–19 c· with the grandest trust of heaven,
p 430–18 c· with having committed liver-complaint.
436–27 and substantially c· the jury, . . . to find

charges

f 220–19 and then c· them to something else,
b 307–16 Error c· its lie to Truth
p 438–16 on three distinct c· of crime,
g 533–15 c· God and woman with his own dereliction,
ap 564– 3 evil still c· the spiritual idea with

chargeth

o 360–27 His angels He c· with frailty.— see Job 4 : 18.

charitable

o 354–31 opponents of divine Science must be c·, if
t 444–13 Students are advised . . . to be c· and kind,

charity

pref xii–23 In the spirit of Christ's c·,
pr 4–19 are like c· in one respect,
m 64–15 aid her sympathy and c· would afford.
b 270–23 Meekness and c· have divine authority.
p 405– 8 to conquer . . . revenge with c·,
t 447–12 Ignorance, subtlety, or false c·
gl 592–25 OIL. Consecration ; c· ; gentleness ;

charming

g 515– 7 a wise idea, c· in its adroitness,

charms

f 247–23 reflects the c· of His goodness
247–29 poor substitutes for the c· of being,

chart

a 24– 8 and make the Bible the c· of life,

charter

pref xii–18 She retained her c·, and as its President,

chartered

pref xi–31 enabled her to get this institution c·

charters

pref xii– 1 No c· were granted . . . after 1883,

chase

f 250–29 Mortal thoughts c· one another like snowflakes,

chasing

ph 191–15 c· away the darkness of error,

chastened

a 35– 2 hearts c· and pride rebuked.
f 241– 4 he who refuses obedience to God, is c· by Love.

chasteneth

f 241– 1 "Whom the Lord loveth He c·."— Heb. 12 : 6.

chastisements

b 323– 6 Through the wholesome c· of Love,

chastity

m 57– 1 C· is the cement of civilization
b 272–21 it is c· and purity, in contrast with the
p 405– 7 to conquer lust with c·,

chattering

ph 194–25 a mental infant, crying and c·

Chaucer

sp 82– 5 C· wrote centuries ago,

cheat

f 252–19 c·, lie, commit adultery, rob, murder,
b 298–20 joy is no longer a trembler, nor is hope a c·.

cheats

g 536–22 Their supposed joys are c·.

check

sp 97– 2 those who discern C. S. will hold crime in c·.
f 203– 2 as though evil could . . . c· the reward
b 283– 5 and there is no inertia to retard or c·
p 376–28 inquire when it will be safe to c· a fever.
376–29 you cannot c· a fever after admitting

checked

ph 165–13 has not c· sickness.

cheek

f 245–15 youth sat gently on c· and brow.
p 415–19 causing a pale or flushed c·.
t 444–20 shall smite thee on thy right c·,— Matt. 5 : 39.

cheeks

ph 175–27 empurpled the plump c· of our ancestors,

cheer

m 59–13 blend in sweet confidence and c·,

cheerful

s 149–20 advise our patients to be hopeful and c·
p 395–19 The nurse should be c·, orderly,

cheerfully

sp 97– 3 c· await the certainty of ultimate perfection.

chemical

s 118–24 as yeast changes the c· properties of meal.

chemicalization

mental
m 65–29 The mental c·, which has brought
ph 169– 4 has occurred through mental c·,
p 401–18 Mental c· brings sin and sickness to the surface,
t 453– 8 Mental c· follows the explanation of Truth,

moral
sp 96–21 Moral error will vanish in a moral c·.
g 540–11 In moral c·, when the symptoms of evil,

this
p 421–15 by removing the belief that this c· produces

ph 168–31 Here let a word be noticed . . . c·.
168–32 By c· I mean the process which mortal mind
p 401– 8 If faith in the truth of being, . . . causes c·
401–16 What I term c· is the upheaval produced
421–21 Calm the excitement sometimes induced by c·,

chemist

s 155– 8 The c·, the botanist, the druggist,
163–10 surgeon, apothecary, man-midwife, c·,

chemistry

ph 195–17 astronomy, natural history, c·, music,
p 422–16 mental and moral c· changes the

Chemosh

g 524– 3 in the Moabitish god C·,

cherish

pr 13–16 If we c· the desire honestly and silently
m 68– 7 c· nothing which hinders our highest selfhood.
s 153–32 our society should ever tempt us to c· error
p 405–10 if you would not c· an army of conspirators

cherished

s 141– 8 to set aside even the most c· beliefs
b 330– 5 c· sanguine hopes that C. S. would meet with
p 411–25 Whatever is c· in mortal mind

cherishing

p 401– 4 c· evil passions and malicious purposes,

cherub

g 538– 5 Truth places the c· wisdom at the gate

Cherubims

g 537– 6 He placed at the east . . . C·,— Gen. 3 : 24.

chewing

p 407– 4 c· a leaf naturally attractive to no

chide

o 347–32   which they c· us for naming nothing

chief

b 288–20   The c· stones in the temple of C. S.
o 349–13   The c· difficulty . . . lies in this,
t 458– 2   The c· plank in this platform is the doctrine
g 535–10   Divine Science deals its c· blow at the

Chief Justice

p 440–33   the C· J· of the Supreme Court,

chiefly

a 24–21   c· as providing a ready pardon for
p 401–31   mental healer confines himself c· to
g 501– 3   c· because the spiritual import of the Word,

child (see also child's; Eddy, Mrs. Mary Baker)

at prayer
s 119–20   or prostrates in death the c· at prayer,
being with
ap 562–22   And she being with c· cried,— Rev. 12 : 2.
every
a 37–23   duty and privilege of every c·, man, and
her
a 29–22   brought forth her c· by the revelation of Truth,
m 60– 9   affection cannot be weaned from her c·,
s 154–19   govern her c· more than the child's mind
154–25   not a Christian Scientist, . . . who says to her c·:
154–30   moaning more childishly than her c·,
f 206–19   giving the mother her c·
o 352–12   Would a mother say to her c·,
ap 563–26   to devour her c· as soon as,— Rev. 12 : 4.
565– 8   her c· was caught up unto God,— Rev. 12 : 5.
inspire the
m 61–21   what noble ambition, can inspire the c·
is born
s 109–26   "Unto us a c· is born,— Isa. 9 : 6.
is exposed
s 154–16   If a c· is exposed to contagion or infection,
little
b 323–32   Willingness to become as a little c·
p 382–23   the kingdom of God as a little c·,— Luke 18 : 17.
g 514–25   And a little c· shall lead them.— Isa. 11 : 6.
male
ap 565–10   Herod decreed the death of every male c·
new
t 463– 7   To attend properly the birth of the new c·,
of God
b 288–32   man's real existence as a c· of God
ap 573–18   but as the blessed c· of God.
of His care
gl 589–10   man is His idea, the c· of His care.
parent and
p 416–20   This materialism of parent and c· is
quite a
f 221– 1   I knew a person who when quite a c·
until the
g 557– 1   until the c· could remain under water
young
ph 191–11   "where the young c· was,"— Matt. 2 : 9.
p 412–28   If the case is that of a young c· or an infant,

pref ix– 3   A c· drinks in the outward world
m 62– 6   with which the c· can meet and master
69–20   Some day the c· will ask his parent :
69–23   the c· may ask, "Do you teach that
s 154–17   and says, "My c· will be sick."
155– 1   the c· forgets all about the accident,
p 371–16   no more comprehends . . . than does the c· ;
413–31   A c· may have worms, if you say so,
424– 2   the c· becomes a separate, . . . mortal mind,
r 479– 1   If a c· is the offspring of physical sense
479– 2   If . . . the c· must have a material,

childhood

o 359–22   In c·, she often listened with joy to

childhood's

f 221–27   feeling c· hunger

childish

o 352–22   watering the very roots of c· timidity,

childishly

s 154–30   moaning more c· than her child,

childless

b 306–12   and the Father would be c·,— no Father.

children (see also children's)

beautiful
m 61–16   often these beautiful c· early droop and die,
bring forth
g 535– 8   in sorrow thou shalt bring forth c· ;— Gen. 3 : 16.
557–18   thou shalt bring forth c·."— Gen. 3 : 16.
education of
m 62– 4   The entire education of c· should be
God's
m 69– 7   God's c· already created will be cognized
b 303– 5   Multiplication of God's c· comes from
t 444–28   Immortals, or God's c· in divine Science,
r 476–28   When speaking of God's c·,

children

health of
p 413–11   good or bad effects on the health of c·.
her
m 63–32   and own her c· free from interference.
b 317–11   "wisdom is justified of her c·."— Matt. 11 : 19.
His
ap 572–10   belongs not to His c·,
His eternal
g 529–11   and are His eternal c·,
in knowledge
m 62–17   should be allowed to remain c· in knowledge,
little
s 130–24   our Master's love for little c·,
f 236–28   Jesus loved little c· because of
of divine Love
g 529–22   to tempt the c· of divine Love?
of earth
b 309–14   c· of earth who followed his example
of God
f 227–25   liberty of the c· of God,"— Rom. 8 : 21.
r 470–16   The c· of God have but one Mind.
476–12   immortals, or the c· of God, will appear
476–13   Mortals are not fallen c· of God.
ap 572– 8   In Science we are c· of God ;
of Israel
f 226–29   hold the c· of Israel in bondage.
b 309–16   were to be called the c· of Israel,
ap 566– 1   As the c· of Israel were guided
gl 583– 5   definition of
of men
s 107– 9   delivering the c· of men from every ill
148– 9   men of men, or the "c· of men,"— Psal. 14 : 2.
p 409–22   imperfect so-called "c· of men"— Psal. 14 : 2.
t 444–29   but mortals, or the "c· of men"— Psal. 14 : 2.
r 476–28   God's children, not the c· of men,
of the wicked one
r 476– 2   They are the c· of the wicked one,
produced on
p 371– 6   similar to that produced on c·
promising
m 61–14   promising c· in the arms of gross parents,
should be allowed
m 62–16   C· should be allowed to remain
should be assured
o 352–22   c· should be assured that
should be taught
f 237–15   C· should be taught the Truth-cure,
should be told
o 352–26   c· should be told not to believe in ghosts,
should obey
f 236–21   C· should obey their parents ;
temperature of
p 413– 8   the temperature of c· and of men,
their
f 236–23   Parents should teach their c· . . . the truths of
g 557– 4   learn how to develop their c· properly
these
b 309–17   If these c· should go astray,
tired
b 322–28   turn us like tired c· to the arms of divine Love.
transmitted to
m 61–28   Nothing unworthy . . . should be transmitted
        to c·.
your
f 237–19   keep out of the minds of your c·
p 422– 3   by whom do your c· cast— Matt. 12 : 27.

m 69–26   "The c· of this world marry,— Luke 20 : 34.
r 230–25   soothing syrups to put c· to sleep,
236–25   C· are more tractable than adults,
c 267–10   forever Father must have had c· prior to Adam.
o 352–17   C·, . . . ought to fear a reality which can harm
p 371–11   As frightened c· look everywhere for the
414– 2   and thus are c· educated into discord.
gl 582–28   definition of

children's

m 62–11   their c· fretfulness or frivolity,
f 211–20   the c· teeth are set on edge."— Ezek. 18 : 2.
o 352–20   instead of increasing c· fears
p 413–28   these actions convey. . . . to c· budding thoughts,

child's

pref x– 1   the memorials of a c· growth,
s 154–19   more than the c· mind governs itself,

chill

p 378–28   to c· harmony with a long and cold night of

chilled

p 431–26   dry, hot, and c· by turns

chills

c 256–26   it c· the spirit of Christianity.
p 366–10   mental penury c· his faith and understanding.
375– 6   C· and heat are often the form in which
375– 7   and the c· and fever disappear.
384–17   followed by c·, dry cough, influenza,

chiseling

f 248–14　moulding and c· thought.

chloroform

c 261–19　as if he had inhaled c·,

choice

p 409–19　except through fear or c·.

choke

f 237–11　often c· the good seed in the minds of
p 405– 9　C· these errors in their early stages,

cholera

s 154–11　where a c· patient had died.
154–14　had not caught the c· by material contact,
154–14　no c· patient had been in that bed.

choose

a 30–30　We cannot c· for ourselves,
s 143–14　Driven to c· between two difficulties,
r 481– 1　How important, then, to c· good

chords

b 304–25　To be master of c· and discords,

chose

a 47–13　He c· his time, when the
48–18　and c· not the world's means of defence.

chosen

a 27–26　"Many are called, but few are c·."— Matt. 22 : 14.
g 554–23　"Have not I c· you twelve,— John 6 : 70.

Christ (see also Christ's)

also in
r 467–16　having that Mind which was also in C·.
atonement of
a 18–13　atonement of C· reconciles man to God,
Belial and
ph 171–24　than between Belial and C·.
believe on
s 110–31　apprehended by as many as believe on C·
bow before
a 35–12　They bow before C·, Truth, to receive more of
came to destroy
r 473– 6　C· came to destroy the belief of sin.
cast out by
ap 567–22　cast out by C·, Truth, the spiritual idea,
cast out the devil
s 135–15　When C· cast out the devil of dumbness,
casts out evils
s 143– 3　C· casts out evils and heals the sick.
coming of
f 230– 7　This awakening is the forever coming of C·,
consecration to
a 28–10　one's consecration to C· is more on the
deathless
a 28–13　the divine Principle of the deathless C·,
demonstrated
b 332–19　Jesus demonstrated C· ;
demonstrate the
b 285–30　how to demonstrate the C·, Truth,
destroyed by
pr 5–24　Sin is forgiven only as it is destroyed by C·,
discerning
a 35– 6　Discerning C·, Truth, anew on the shore of
divine idea or
b 334– 2　but that the divine idea or C· was and is so
divine Principle of
a 18–14　for the divine Principle of C· is God,
divinity of the
a 25–31　The divinity of the C· was made manifest in the
doctrines of
s 134–16　how can they illustrate the doctrines of C·
dwells forever
b 334– 4　C·, dwells forever in the bosom of the Father,
dwelt forever
a 29–26　The C· dwelt forever an idea in the
endowed with the
a 30– 7　although he was endowed with the C·,
eternal
a 38–23　The eternal C·, . . . never suffered.
b 334–14　the eternal C· and the corporeal Jesus
eternity of the
b 334–29　a mystical statement of the eternity of the C·,
even
a 19– 5　Even C· cannot reconcile Truth to error,
even so in
g 545–31　even so in C· [Truth] shall all be— I Cor. 15 : 22.
faith in the
s 134– 9　The new faith in the C·, Truth, so roused the
follow
a 27–28　those who profess to follow C·
b 326– 3　If we wish to follow C·, Truth, it must be
p 434– 7　Others say, . . . let us follow C·."
followers of
pr 5–15　The followers of C· drank his cup.
s 134–11　the followers of C· were burned, crucified,
142– 4　Anciently the followers of C·, or Truth,
following
ph 179– 3　and following C· in the daily life.

Christ

fulness of
g 519–21　the stature of the fulness oi C·"?— Eph. 4 : 13.
gain the
b 326–13　if we would gain the C· as our only Saviour.
God's idea
ap 565–16　for C·, God's idea, will eventually rule
had come
a 27– 2　intended to prove . . . that the C· had come:
hath rolled away
a 45–17　C· hath rolled away the stone from the door
heart of
ap 568–28　and nearer to the great heart of C· ;
herald of
pref vii– 7　the human herald of C·, Truth,
hid with
b 325–18　"hid with C· in God,"— Col. 3 : 3.
t 445–14　"hid with C· in God,"— Col. 3 : 3.
His
ap 561–15　God and His C·, bringing harmony to earth.
568–15　and the power of His C· :— Rev. 12 : 10.
if we deny
pr 6– 2　The Scriptures say, that if we deny C·,
illustrates
b 316–21　C· illustrates that blending with God,
332–32　Thus it is that C· illustrates the coincidence,
inseparable from
r 482–21　He was inseparable from C·, the Messiah,
invisible
b 334–10　The invisible C· was imperceptible
is the divine idea
b 332–19　he proved that C· is the divine idea of God
r 473–16　Jesus is the human man, and C· is the divine
idea ;
is the ideal
r 473–10　C· is the ideal Truth,
is the true idea
b 332– 9　C· is the true idea voicing good,
is "the way
o 353–10　admit that C· is "the way,— John 14 : 6.
r 482–15　It is, since C· is "the way"— John 14 : 6.
is Truth
a 18–15　C· is Truth, which reaches no higher than
is without beginning
b 333–17　the C· is without beginning of years
Jesus the
b 313– 2　The term Christ Jesus, or Jesus the C·
333–14　name of our Master, . . . was Jesus the C· ;
r 473–17　hence the duality of Jesus the C·.
law of
ph 182–32　law of C·, or Truth, makes all things possible
p 434– 6　"The law of C· supersedes our laws ;
learned through
sp 84–29　and is learned through C· and C. S.
leave all for
pr 9–25　Are you willing to leave all for C·,
s 141– 9　that is, . . . to leave all for C·.
ph 192– 6　not . . . Scientists until we leave all for C·.
o 354– 7　to enable them to leave all for C·, Truth?
leaves all for
f 238–24　He who leaves all for C·
life of
s 149–14　have not demonstrated the life of C·,
like
f 249–18　Life is, like C·, "the same— Heb. 13 : 8.
living
a 31–15　It is the living C·, the practical Truth,
manifestation of
s 141–24　Neither can this manifestation of C· be
merits of
f 202–12　redeemed through the merits of C·,
Messiah or
b 333–24　glorious glimpses of the Messiah, or C·,
o 361– 1　The Jew believes that the Messiah or C·
gl 594–16　Son. The Son of God, the Messiah or C·.
Mind of
pref ix–19　still . . . waiting for the Mind of C·.
mission of
r 474–30　The apostle says that the mission of C· is
nothing left but
f 238–10　said, "I have nothing left but C·."
one
r 497– 6　we acknowledge His Son, one C· ;
or Truth
a 33–23　It gives all for C·, or Truth.
34–15　cast out evils, and preach C·, or Truth,
s 135–30　not merely in the name of C·, or Truth,
142– 4　Anciently the followers of C·, or Truth,
ph 182–32　law of C·, or Truth, makes all things possible
b 289–14　C·, or Truth, overcame . . . death
326–23　Saul . . . beheld the way— the C·, or Truth
p 391–14　C·, or Truth, will destroy all other
r 485–21　mortal error which C·, or Truth, destroys
plainly declared
b 320– 2　C· plainly declared, "I am the way,— John 14 : 6.

Christh

Christ

plant themselves in
a 54– 9   All must sooner or later plant themselves in *C·*,
presence of
o 351–14   the living, palpitating presence of *C·*,
presents
b 316–20   *C·* presents the indestructible man,
profess to follow
a 27–28   Why do those who profess to follow *C·* reject
raiment of
c 267–27   glistering,'' like the raiment of *C·*.— *Luke* 9 : 29.
raised up
o 341– *   *He that raised up C· from the dead*— *Rom.* 8 : 11.
receive
b 333–23   to all prepared to receive *C·*, Truth.
regarded
b 313–16   regarded *C·* as the Son of God,
represented
b 316–12   Jesus represented *C·*, the true idea of God.
ruling of the
s 141–22   do not now, understand this ruling of the *C·* ;
says
b 286–11   for *C·* says, "I am the way."— *John* 14 : 6.
Science of
a 55–18   when man shall recognize the Science of *C·*
s 118– 2   the spiritual leaven signifies the Science of *C·*
spirit of
t 462– 5   and imbibes the spirit of *C·*,
spirit of the
s 131–23   As aforetime, the spirit of the *C·*,
the healing
a 55– 8   the healing *C·* and spiritual idea of being.
the way through
ph 171– 5   even the way through *C·*, Truth,
t 444–17   be faithful in pointing the way through *C·*,
this
a 26–12   This *C·*, or divinity of the man Jesus,
Thou art the
s 137–18   "Thou art the *C·*,— *Matt.* 16 : 16.
to find
b 316– 6   lose sight of mortal selfhood to find *C·*,
understanding of
sp 76–28   the final understanding of *C·* in divine Science.
unveiled the
a 38–25   He unveiled the *C·*, the spiritual idea of
we need
a 39– 7   We need "*C·*, and him crucified."— *I Cor.* 2 : 2.
what concord hath
f 216–26   "What concord hath *C·* with— *II Cor.* 6 : 15.
g 539–26   what concord hath *C·* with— *II Cor.* 6 : 15.
will command
ap 570–25   and *C·* will command the wave.

pr 5–29   An apostle says that the Son of God [*C·*] came
a 18– *   *For C· sent me not to baptize,*— *I Cor.* 1 : 17.
18–17   *C·*, Truth, could conciliate no nature above his
26–10   The *C·* was the Spirit which Jesus implied
34– 5   If *C·*, Truth, has come to us in demonstration,
49–21   He was to prove that the *C·* is not subject
m 65– 3   May *C·*, Truth, be present at every bridal altar
sp 79–18   bade men have the Mind that was in the *C·*.
85–14   is not this the *C·* ?"— *John* 4 : 29.
s 107– *   *but by the revelation of Jesus C·*.— *Gal.* 1 : 12.
107– 1   In the year 1866, I discovered the *C·* Science
118– 8   second appearing in the flesh of the *C·*,
127– 9   The terms . . . *C·* Science or C. S.,
132–30   with the truest conception of the *C·* ?
133– 4   "Is not this the *C·* ?"— *John* 4 : 29.
137–20   *C·*, the spirit of God, of Truth, Life, and Love,
142– 8   seek the undivided garment, the whole *C·*,
142– 9   *C·*, Truth, alone can furnish us with
145–12   as immortal Mind through *C·*, Truth,
149–31   and demonstrate truth according to *C·*.
ph 200–26   Jesus *C·*, and him crucified."— *I Cor.* 2 : 2.
200–28   Jesus *C·*, and him glorified.
f 231– 1   must be obliterated through *C·*
242– 9   and *C·* in divine Science shows us this way.
251–13   is an error that *C·*, Truth, alone can destroy.
b 268– *   *and with His Son Jesus C·*.— *I John* 1 : 3.
270–23   It has nothing in *C·*.
c 286–10   *C·*, Life, Truth, Love;
290–21   shall be unrighteous still, until . . . *C·*, Truth,
316– 7   *C·*, Truth, was demonstrated through Jesus
324–27   "If *C·* [Truth] be not risen,— *I Cor.* 15 : 14.
325–10   *C·*, who is our life, shall appear— *Col.* 3 : 4.
331–30   *C·* the spiritual idea of sonship ;
332–11   The *C·* is incorporeal, spiritual,
333– 3   word *C·* is not properly a synonym for Jesus,
333– 8   *C·* is not a name so much as the divine title of
333– 9   *C·* expresses God's spiritual, eternal nature.
333–20   the *C·*, as the spiritual idea,
333–26   The divine image, idea, or *C·* was, is, and
334–17   while the spiritual self, or *C·*, continues
334–19   taking away the sins of the world, as the *C·*
337–10   in conformity with *C·*,

Christ

b 337–18   demonstrates Life in *C·*, Life's spiritual ideal.
o 347–14   *C·*, as the spiritual or true idea of God,
347–24   it is *C·*, Truth, who destroys these
361– 2   the Christian believes that *C·* is God.
361– 4   *C·*, as the true spiritual idea, is the ideal of
361–12   Jesus *C·* is not God, as Jesus himself declared,
p 364–26   do they show their regard for Truth, or *C·*,
367–10   This is what is meant by seeking Truth, *C·*,
391– 5   delivered to the judgment of Truth, *C·*,
410– 9   the only true God, and Jesus *C·*,— *John* 17 : 3.
428–25   sooner or later, through *C·* and C. S.,
430– 5   immortal manhood, the *C·* ideal, will appear.
433–31   Ah ! but *C·*, Truth, the spirit of Life
442–20   *C·* changes a belief of sin or of sickness
442–22   *C·*, Truth, gives mortals temporary food
r 473–13   *C·*, the true idea of God,
484– 5   for it is built upon the rock, *C·*.
493–29   the *C·* could improve on a false sense.
496–16   *C·*, which enables you to demonstrate,
497–16   we acknowledge that man is saved through *C·*,
g 540– 1   *C·* is the offspring of Spirit,
ap 568–31   by which we lay down all for Truth, or *C·*,
575–18   the Word, *C·*, Christianity, and divine Science ;
577–15   second, the *C·*, the spiritual idea of God ;
gl 583–10   definition of
    (*see also* **Messiah, Saviour, Son**)

Christ-cure
p 367–24   The infinite Truth of the *C·* has come
t 456–17   gross ignorance of the method of the *C·*.

Christ-element
b 288–29   The *C·* in the Messiah made him the

Christendom
sp 96– 2   unwillingness . . . binds *C·* with chains.
s 126–32   If *C·* resists the author's application
b 328–26   It were well had *C·* believed and
o 343–23   *C·* generally demands so much less.

Christ-example
s 138–21   to follow the *C·*, and to heal the sick

Christ-healing
a 44–25   the understanding of the *C·*
s 136– 2   a spiritual foundation of *C·*.

Christian (*see also* **Christian's**)
pr 7–23   ventilation of fervent sentiments never makes
    a *C·*.
a 40– 3   The advanced thinker and devout *C·*,
s 138–25   The *C·* can prove this to-day
148–22   tries to explain how to make this man a *C·*,
f 203–11   to the *C·* the only true spirit is Godlike.
238– 9   enables one to be *C·*.
o 353– 7   How can a *C·*, . . . think of the latter as real
360–29   the Galilean Prophet, the best *C·* on earth,
360–30   while to-day, Jew and *C·* can unite in
361– 1   the *C·* believes that Christ is God.
361– 9   *C·* who believes in the First Commandment
g 556–15   but the *C·* alone can fathom it.

Christian (adj.)
apostles
o 349–22   the prophecy concerning the *C·* apostles,
character
b 291– 9   each lesser call in the growth of *C·* character.
churches
s 131–13   Must C. S. come through the *C·* churches
conversion
f 217– 7   Paul's peculiar *C·* conversion and experience,
demand
a 37–32   Why has this *C·* demand so little inspiration
m 66–22   if there is no *C·* demand for it.
demonstration
s 141– 4   requisite for *C·* demonstration.
duties
a 31–12   First in the list of *C·* duties,
effort
a 38– 1   to stir mankind to *C·* effort?
encouragement
p 367– 3   *C·* encouragement of an invalid,
era
    (*see* **era**)
evidence
r 487–19   *C·* evidence is founded on Science
experience
a 29– 7   *C·* experience teaches faith in the right
explanations
r 490–23   scientifically *C·* explanations of the
healing
    (*see* **healing**)
history
b 328–15   has sadly disappeared from *C·* history.
ap 577–17   the Christ-idea in *C·* history ;
ideas
ph 170– 8   *C·* ideas certainly present . . . the Principle
idolatry
b 340–26   annihilates pagan and *C·* idolatry,

Christian (adj.)

martyr
a 28–22 Remember, thou *C·* martyr,
martyrs
p 388– 1 The *C·* martyrs were prophets of C. S.
marvels
r 474–11 *C·* marvels . . . will be misunderstood
meaning
g 506–27 the scientifically *C·* meaning of the text.
metaphysics
s 155–16 high and mighty truths of *C·* metaphysics.
Mind-healing
sp 98–16 demonstration of *C·* Mind-healing stands
opponents
o 354–12 On the other hand, the *C·* opponents of C. S.
perfection
f 201–18 *C·* perfection is won on no other basis.
power
f 233– 2 rather than professions of *C·* power.
record
g 531–30 the scientifically *C·* record of man
scientific practice
p 410–29 *C·* scientific practice begins with
Scientist
(*see* **Scientist**)
Scientists
(*see* **Scientists**)
sentiment
pr 7–16 to induce or encourage *C·* sentiment.
sermons
o 345– 8 *C·* sermons will heal the sick.
service
p 436–11 Giving a cup of cold water . . . is a *C·* service.
state
p 403–21 The most *C·* state is one of rectitude and
system
s 150– 2 this *C·* system of healing disease.
thought
pref x–26 unbiased *C·* thought is soonest touched
views
g 502–16 scientifically *C·* views of the universe

sp 94– 6 *C·* and scientific statement of personality
　 98–32 is not ecclesiastical but *C·*.
s 112–15 and are not scientifically *C·*.
o 354–31 must be charitable, if they would be *C·*.
p 365–21 then he is *C·* enough to practise
t 458–11 It is anything but scientifically *C·* to
　 459–29 the *C·* and scientific expounder

Christian Church
a 41–16 in the *C·* *C·* this demonstration of

Christianity (*see also* **Christianity's**)

all
s 138–18 precedent for all *C·*, theology, and healing.
antithesis of
s 133–19 Judaism was the antithesis of *C·*,
banner of
p 426–27 would enable us to hold the banner of *C·* aloft
causes men
t 458–32 *C·* causes men to turn naturally from
Christ's
b 271– 2 Christ's *C·* is the chain of scientific being
demonstration of
f 228–31 when they saw the demonstration of *C·*
easier for
s 138–22 It is easier for *C·* to cast out sickness than sin,
effects of
p 367–27 and increase the beneficial effects of *C·*.
El Dorado of
pr 9–21 This is the El Dorado of *C·*.
element of
s 146– 3 Why has this element of *C·* been lost?
b 328–17 a lost element of *C·*.
o 347–18 restoring an essential element of *C·*,
faith in
s 127– 2 she will not therefore lose faith in *C·*,
gains
f 238–24 forsakes popularity and gains *C·*.
history of
p 387–27 The history of *C·* furnishes sublime proofs
is not false
f 232–13 *C·* is not false,
is the basis
ph 192–29 *C·* is the basis of true healing.
lack of
m 65–17 Beholding the world's lack of *C·*
left out of
a 55–13 curative mission, . . . cannot be left out of *C·*,
love of
f 235–32 Love of *C·*, rather than love of popularity,
measured
s 142– 5 measured *C·* by its power over sickness, sin,
more
r 487– 7 more *C·* in seeing and hearing spiritually

Christianity

must be Science
s 135–21 It has been said, . . . that *C·* must be Science,
nature of
a 40–31 The nature of *C·* is peaceful and blessed,
new step in
sp 98– 1 persecutions which attend a new step in *C·* ;
not proceed from
sp 88–24 These effects, however, do not proceed from *C·*,
opponents of
s 134–10 roused the hatred of the opponents of *C·*,
our
ph 167–10 our health, our longevity, and our *C·*.
perceive
b 322– 6 perceive *C·*, or Truth, in its divine Principle.
popular
m 67–26 the limited demonstration of popular *C·*
practical
f 224–22 A higher and more practical *C·*,
o 341– 4 from a theoretical to a practical *C·*.
practice of
r 473–19 introduced the teaching and practice of *C·*,
preaching
b 324–24 healing the sick and preaching *C·*
primitive
m 64– 9 master of ceremonies, ruling out primitive *C·*,
proof of
(*see* **proof**)
pure
b 329– 2 healing elements of pure *C·* will be
reappearance of the
sp 98– 5 reappearance of the *C·* which heals the sick
robs
s 134–18 robs *C·* of the very element, which gave
Science and
f 231–13 If God makes sin, . . . Science and *C·* are helpless ;
p 371–26 Mankind will improve through Science and *C·*.
Science must be
s 135–22 and Science must be *C·*,
Science of
(*see* **Science**)
Science to
s 127– 1 application of the word Science to *C·*,
o 341–13 the application of the word *Science* to *C·*
r 483–14 she affixed the name "Science" to *C·*,
soul of
s 140–17 Spiritual devoutness is the soul of *C·*.
spirit of
c 256–27 it chills the spirit of *C·*.
statement in
f 207– 6 every scientific statement in *C·* has its proof.
support of
o 342– 4 are summoned to the support of *C·*,
true
o 359–18 True *C·* is to be honored wherever found,
will demonstrate
r 466–29 *C·* will demonstrate this declaration

a 28–26 and that *C·* to-day is at peace with the world
　 36–16 moral distance between *C·* and sensualism
sp 97–29 *C·* is again demonstrating the Life that is
　 98–23 *C·* not excepted.
s 127– 1 nor will *C·* lose its hold upon her.
　 133–25 planted *C·* on the foundation of Spirit,
　 135–26 *C·* as Jesus taught it was not a creed,
f 224–12 sects many but not enough *C·*.
　 232–16 In our age *C·* is again demonstrating
b 274–13 *C·* and the Science which expounds it
o 342–16 If *C·* is not scientific,
　 353–31 Mortal beliefs can neither demonstrate *C·*
　 358–22 the great import to *C·* of those works
p 372–18 C. S. and *C·* are one.
　 372–19 How, then, in *C·* any more than in C. S.,
　 373– 2 the physical exemption which *C·* includes,
t 451– 6 *C·*, with the crown of Love upon her brow,
　 462–17 *C·*, and persistence alone win the prize,
　 464–21 In founding a pathological system of *C·*,
r 483–32 *C·* will never be based on a divine . . . until
ap 575–18 the Word, Christ, *C·*, and divine Science ;
　 577–16 *C·*, which is the outcome of the divine Principle

Christianity's
a 39– 3 until *C·* last triumph.
r 473–20 the proof of *C·* truth and love ;

Christianization
pr 1– 8 the *C·* and health of mankind.
b 272–19 It is the spiritualization of thought and *C·*

Christianly
o 353– 1 *C·* scientific real is the sensuous unreal.
　 355– 3 *C·* scientific methods of dealing with sin
p 414–20 rests on the *C·* scientific basis of being.
　 421–25 It is no more *C·* scientific to see disease
t 448–16 A dishonest position is far from *C·* scientific.
　 458–23 The *C·* scientific man reflects the divine law,
g 546–27 system stated in this book is *C·* scientific
ap 572– 5 *C·* and scientifically reduced to its native

Christian's

o	361– 8	Thus the Jew unites with the C· doctrine

Christians

pr	9–28	Then why . . . ask to be C·, since
	15–25	C· rejoice in secret beauty and bounty,
a	21– 6	C· do not continue to labor . . . because of
	29– 1	C· must take up arms against error
	33–27	C·, are you drinking his cup?
	37–21	May the C· of to-day take up the
	37–25	C· claim to be his followers,
s	138–18	C· are under as direct orders now,
	146– 2	The ancient C· were healers.
f	242–31	and require of C· the proof which he gave,
b	326–28	wrong that he had done in persecuting C·,
o	354– 4	Why then do C· try to obey the Scriptures
p	373– 1	If we are C· on all moral questions,

Christian Science

(see Science)

Christian Science Journal

pref	xii–12	sole editor and publisher of the C· S· J·,

Christian Scientist

(see Scientist)

Christian Scientist Association

pref	xii– 9	President of the first C· S· A·,

Christian Scientists

(see Scientists)

Christ-idea

s	112–21	divine Principle of healing and the C·
b	316–17	The C·, . . . rose higher to human view
ap	570–19	to drown the C·?
	577–17	the C· in Christian history ;

Christ Jesus

pref	vii– 8	the way of salvation through C· J·,
a	30–19	C· J· came to rebuke rabbinical error
ph	180–29	as taught and demonstrated by C· J·.
f	235–26	C· J·, the true idea of spiritual power.
	243–10	which was also in C· J·"— Phil. 2 : 5.
	244–11	law of the Spirit of life in C· J·— Rom. 8 : 2.
c	259– 7	The divine nature was best expressed in C· J·,
b	270–31	The life of C· J· was not miraculous,
	276– 9	which was also in C· J·."— Phil. 2 : 5.
	313– 2	The term C· J·, or Jesus the Christ
	315–16	God's spiritual idea as presented by C· J·.
	332–17	one mediator . . . the man C· J·."— I Tim. 2 : 5.
	332–29	incarnate in the good and pure C· J·.
	333–12	life of which C· J· was the embodiment.
	333–14	but C· J· better signifies the Godlike.
	338–32	The ideal man was . . . known as C· J·
o	350– 9	grow into that stature of manhood in C· J·
p	381–31	C· J· overruled the error which would impose
r	483–20	the ancient worthies, and to C· J·,
	497–15	man's unity with God through C· J·,
	497–25	which was also in C· J· ;

Christlike

s	138–20	to be C·, to possess the Christ-spirit,
	146–12	and religion becomes C·.
c	259–11	The C· understanding of scientific being

Christliness

o	342–26	Who would be the first to disown the C· of

Christly

f	242–28	restores every part of the C· garment
p	365–19	If the Scientist has enough C· affection

Christ-man

b	316–17	the C·, rose higher to human view

Christ-power

s	134–15	Devoid of the C·,
	150–16	C· to take away the sins of the world.

Christ-principle

a	34– 2	and leave all for the C·?

Christ's

pref	xi–23	In the spirit of C· charity,
a	18– *	they that are C· have crucified— Gal. 5 : 24.
	19– 1	C· purpose to reconcile man to God,
	22– 6	Waking to C· demand, mortals experience
	22– 9	through C· precious love these efforts are
	55–24	drinketh of C· cup now,
sp	95–26	the light which heralds C· eternal dawn
	98–19	C· revelation of Truth, of Life, and of Love,
	98–27	Mystery does not enshroud C· teachings,
s	110–29	and demonstrated according to C· command,
f	226–13	but through C· divine Science.
	234– 6	crumbs of comfort from C· table,
	236– 9	attacks on . . . who reiterate C· teachings
b	271– 1	C· Christianity is the chain of scientific being
	315–12	hid from their sense C· sonship with God.
o	347–14	they would behold the signs of C· coming.
	355–17	declines to admit that C· religion has
p	410–30	C· keynote of harmony,
	436–11	Giving a cup of cold water in C· name,
t	458–29	C· way is the only one by which mortals are

Christ's

ap	569–12	He that touches the hem of C· robe
	570–17	Give them a cup of cold water in C· name,
gl	583– 9	CHILDREN OF ISRAEL. . . . . C· offspring.

Christ-spirit

s	138–20	to be Christlike, to possess the C·,
	141–16	the C· which governed the corporeal Jesus.

chronic

s	162–18	in cases of both acute and c· disease
ph	176–30	the less distinct type and c· form of disease.
	178–16	that c· case is not difficult to cure.
f	246–32	Acute and c· beliefs reproduce their own types.
	247– 2	and is not so disastrous as the c· belief.
p	369–17	Jesus never asked if disease were acute or c·,
	373– 9	to lift a student out of a c· sin.
	389–30	In her belief the woman had c· liver-complaint,
	390–28	approaching symptoms of c· or acute disease,

chronicles

g	522– 8	second record c· man as mutable and

chronological

f	246–17	C· data are no part of the vast forever.

chronologically

s	143–28	If Mind was first c·, is first potentially,

chrysalis

b	297–21	It is a c· state of human thought,

Church

a	28– 9	While respecting all that is good in the C·
	37– 6	blood of the martyrs is the seed of the C·."
	41–16	in the Christian C· this demonstration of
o	351– 9	a member of the orthodox Congregational C·
gl	583–12	definition of
	583–14	The C· is that institution, which affords proof

church

her

pref	xii–20	as auxiliary to her c·.

his

s	136– 1	Jesus established his c· and

my

s	137–32	upon . . . I will build my c· ;— Matt. 16 : 18.

our

a	35–20	Our c· is built on the divine Principle,

this

a	35–21	We can unite with this c· only as

f	224–20	opposition from c·, state laws, and the press,
o	351–11	prayers of her devout parents and the c· ;

Church Councils

s	139–15	The decisions by vote of C· C·

church-dome

g	516–17	The sunlight glints from the c·,

churches

s	131–14	Must C. S. come through the Christian c·
	131–16	but the c· seem not ready to receive it,
f	235– 7	and the readers in c·

church-members

o	358–29	Is it likely that c· have more faith in

Church of Christ, Scientist

pref	xii– 8	pastor of the first established C· of C·, S· ;

circle

m	58–20	amusement outside the home c·
b	282– 5	a c· or sphere and a straight line.
	282– 6	The c· represents the infinite
	310–16	around which c· harmoniously all things

circulated

t	460–29	by her manuscript c· among the students.

circulation

pref	ix–13	are still in c· among her first pupils ;
	ix–25	copies were, however, in friendly c·.
ph	185– 8	other books were in c·, which discussed
p	373–32	when by mental means the c· is changed,
	415–18	It either retards the c· or quickens it,

circumference

f	204– 1	is at once the centre and c· of being.
c	262–15	the absolute centre and c· of his being.

circumscribe

m	61– 1	We cannot c· happiness within the

circumscribed

pr	2–21	perpetuates the belief in God as humanly c·,
b	284– 5	if the infinite could be c· within the finite,
g	550– 1	a c· and non-intelligent egg.

circumstance

m	61–14	If some fortuitous c· places
f	250–32	nor . . . that happiness is ever the sport of c·.
b	297– 3	no c· can alter the situation, until
p	377–30	any c· is of itself powerless to produce
	378– 6	and meet every c· with truth.
	419–16	Meet every adverse c· as its master.
	426– 1	or disease arising from any c·,
ap	574–28	c·, which your suffering sense deems

circumstances

- *pr* 5– 7   we are placed under the stress of *c*.
- *m* 66–28   patience salutary under such *c*,
- *s* 147– 9   under *c* where demonstration was
- *b* 319– 9   sustains man under all *c* ;
- *p* 378– 1   which associates sickness with certain *c*
- 412–12   liable under some *c* to impress it
- 440–14   under stress of *c*,
- *t* 443– 5   under ordinary *c* a resort to
- 448– 8   Under such *c*, to say that there is no evil,
- *g* 553–12   have grown or been formed under *c* which
- *ap* 571–15   under all *c*, overcome evil with good.

citation

- *s* 137–14   their *c* of the common report about him.

cited

- *sp* 79– 5   Thousands of instances could be *c*
- *o* 358–19   Why are the words . . . more frequently *c*

cities

- *b* 300– 6   which makes trees and *c* seem to be

citizen

- *p* 438–11   Nerve was an insubordinate *c*,

citizens

- *f* 227–24   *C* of the world, accept the

city

great
- *ap* 574–22   lifted the seer to behold the great *c*,

heavenly
- *ap* 576– 3   This heavenly *c*, ... this New Jerusalem,
- 577–24   their honors within the heavenly *c*.

holy
- *ap* 576– 8   describing this holy *c*, the beloved Disciple

of Lynn
- *s* 158–31   A woman in the *c* of Lynn, Massachusetts,

of our God
- *ap* 558– *   *to be praised in the c of our God,— Psal. 48 : 1.*
- 577–19   This *c* of our God has no need of sun

of the Spirit
- *ap* 575–25   It is indeed a *c* of the Spirit,

our
- *ap* 575–18   The four sides of our *c* are

sacred
- *ap* 575– 7   This sacred *c*, described in the Apocalypse

- *a* 41–26   Persecuted from *c* to *c*, his apostles
- *s* 149–32   there is hardly a *c*, village, or hamlet,
- *p* 367–20   A *c* that is set on an hill— *Matt. 5 : 14.*
- *t* 459–19   in the crowded streets of a *c*.
- *ap* 574–15   the *c* which "lieth foursquare."— *Rev. 21 :16.*
- 575–12   "a *c* which hath foundations."— *Heb. 11 : 10.*
- 575–17   the description of the *c* as foursquare
- 575–21   This *c* is wholly spiritual, as its four sides
- 575–24   the *c* of the great King."— *Psal. 48 : 2.*
- 577–26   and nothing can enter that *c*, which

civil

- *pr* 7– 1   The only *c* sentence which he had for error
- *m* 63–12   *C* law establishes very unfair differences
- *b* 340–27   whatever is wrong in social, *c*, criminal,

civilization

- *m* 57– 1   Chastity is the cement of *c*
- 63–14   *c* mitigates it in some measure.
- 63–17   than does either C. S. or *c*.
- *ph* 173–30   idols of *c* are far more fatal to health
- 173–32   idols of *c* call into action less faith
- 174– 4   Is *c* only a higher form of idolatry,

civilized

- *ph* 174– 2   as consciously as do *c* practitioners

civilly

- *gl* 587– 4   rights of woman acknowledged morally, *c*,

clad

- *b* 320–32   still *c* in material flesh,
- *t* 463–15   The new idea, . . . is *c* in white garments.
- *ap* 561–26   The spiritual idea is *c* with the radiance of
- 571–18   *C* in the panoply of Love,

claim

any
- *t* 448–30   nothing short of right-doing has any *c* to

audible
- *gl* 594– 9   first audible *c* that God was not omnipotent

false
- *f* 233–13   false *c* of error continues its delusions
- *g* 523– 4   mist of obscurity . . . deepens the false *c*,
- 523– 8   arise from a mist or false *c*,
- 554–14   as he grows up into another false *c*,
- *ap* 564–22   the false *c* of mind in matter
- 567–18   That false *c*— that ancient belief,

first
- *gl* 594– 5   the first *c* that there is an opposite of Spirit,
- 594– 7   the first *c* that sin, sickness, and death

his
- *s* 131–30   established his *c* to the Messiahship.

claim

its
- *f* 210–28   and appears to itself to make good its *c*.
- *g* 513– 2   this mortal mentality, so-called, and its *c*,

knowing the
- *t* 450–29   Knowing the *c* of animal magnetism,

of sin
- *p* 390–20   Suffer no *c* of sin or of sickness to grow
- *t* 447–24   To put down the *c* of sin, you must detect it,
- 461–27   must first see the *c* of sin, and then destroy it.

strong
- *s* 130–26   If thought is startled at the strong *c* of Science

this
- *o* 344– 6   this *c* is made because the Scriptures say

unreality of the
- *b* 285–11   The unreality of the *c* that a mortal

usurps
- *g* 513– 2   the *c* usurps the deific prerogatives

- *a* 37–26   Christians *c* to be his followers,
- *m* 64–30   Spirit will ultimately *c* its own,
- *ph* 186–23   If we . . . discord has as lasting a *c* upon us
- *f* 238–16   when we attempt to *c* the benefits of an
- *b* 283–16   They *c* that to be life which is but the
- 311–29   lose all supposed consciousness or *c* to life
- 312–19   Mortals *c* that death is inevitable ;
- 315– 7   and laid no *c* to any other.
- 329–25   maintains the *c* of Truth by quenching error.
- *r* 476– 7   Error will cease to *c* that soul is in body,
- 478– 8   except the *c* of mortal belief?

claimants

- *s* 164–11   more scientific than are false *c*

claimed

- *a* 28– 1   Pharisees *c* to know and to teach the divine will,
- *sp* 78–26   *c* to be the agents of God's government.
- 83– 4   *c* that they could equal the work of wisdom.
- *s* 136– 5   He *c* no . . . action, nor life separate from God.
- *o* 344– 4   should be added that this is *c* to represent
- *r* 469–19   and if mortals *c* no other Mind

claiming

- *b* 330–29   nothing *c* to be something,
- *p* 436–32   *C* to protect Mortal Man
- *ap* 567–19   *c* that there is intelligence in matter
- *gl* 591–25   Nothing *c* to be something,

claims

assert it
- *p* 395– 9   assert its *c* over mortality and disease.

better
- *m* 57–17   the better *c* of intellect, goodness, and virtue.

confirms its
- *sp* 94–17   The progress of truth confirms its *c*,

diviner
- *f* 226–15   He has built it on diviner *c*.

false
- *pr* 7– 7   deprives material sense of its false *c*.
- *b* 273–27   the false *c* of material sense or law.
- 308–12   a blending of false *c*,
- 357–23   They are false *c*, which will eventually
- *p* 438–12   putting in false *c* to office
- *g* 538–16   the false *c* that misrepresent God, good.

forfeit their
- *s* 112– 6   forfeit their *c* to belong to its school,

of Christian Science
- *p* 371–23   when urging the *c* of C. S. ;

of evil
- *s* 130–29   astounded at the vigorous *c* of evil
- *t* 447–20   Expose and denounce the *c* of evil
- 448– 1   To assume that there are no *c* of evil
- *g* 529–28   have faith to fight all *c* of evil,

of God
- *a* 23–20   and establishes the *c* of God.

of good
- *ph* 167– 8   Our proportionate admission of the *c* of good

of matter
- *f* 242– 6   Denial of the *c* of matter
- *r* 491–14   which annuls the *c* of matter,

of medicine
- *a* 44–11   all the *c* of medicine, surgery, and hygiene.

of mortality
- *ph* 182– 6   the *c* of mortality, . . . appertain to matter.

of mortal mind
- *an* 103– 6   The destruction of the *c* of mortal mind

of Truth
- *sp* 92–28   instead of urging the *c* of Truth alone.

parental
- *m* 63–20   property, and parental *c* of the two sexes.

resisted
- *f* 223–30   as truth urges upon mortals its resisted *c* ;

surrenders its
- *g* 552–30   matter always surrenders its *c* when

these
- *f* 226–15   These *c* are not made through code or creed,

claims

your

t 455–10   and support your *c·* by demonstration.

---

s 112–27   if any so-called new school *c·* to be C. S.,
148–25   *c·* to rule man by material law,
151–31   mortal mind *c·* to govern every organ
ph 171– 1   Matter, which . . . *c·* to be a creator, is a fiction,
193–25   his physician *c·* to have cured him,
f 227– 6   the *c·* of the enslaving senses must be denied
232– 7   the *c·* of harmonious and eternal being
b 273– 1   Matter and its *c·* of sin, sickness, and death
o 344– 1   it *c·* God as the only absolute Life and Soul,
g 512–29   and *c·* God as their author ;
523– 7   the lie *c·* to be truth.
529–28   have faith to fight all *c·* of evil,

clairvoyance

sp 85– 2   This Mind-reading is the opposite of *c·*.
95–16   This kind of mind-reading is not *c·*,

clairvoyant

sp 87–17   to read the human mind, but not as a *c·*.
an 101–11   the phenomena exhibited by a reputed *c·*.

clamor

b 327–15   rushes forth to *c·* with midnight and tempest.

clap

f 220–10   The leaves *c·* their hands

Clark, Mr.

ph 192–32   I was called to visit Mr. *C·* in Lynn,
193– 8   Mr. *C·* lay with his eyes fixed and sightless.

class

s 151– 9   philanthropy of the higher *c·* of physicians.
161–30   if this old *c·* of philanthropists looked
164– 9   the cultured *c·* of medical practitioners
b 290–14   To the spiritual *c·*, relates the Scripture :
t 450– 1   There is a large *c·* of thinkers whose
450– 5   Another *c·*, still more unfortunate, are
450– 8   A third *c·* of thinkers build with solid masonry.
454–25   at the close of a *c·* term,
r 478–10   and by a certain *c·* of persons,

class-book

r 465– 2   the author's *c·*, copyrighted in 1870.

classes

s 114– 1   Usage *c·* both evil and good together
g 549–10   are supposed to have, as *c·*,

classic

sp 82– 6   What is *c·* study, but discernment
b 332– 7   quoted with approbation from a *c·* poet :

classification

s 124–31   so restores them to their rightful home and *c·*.
127– 6   everything entitled to a *c·* as truth,
164– 5   "No systematic or theoretical *c·* of diseases
p 407–31   Sin is spared from this *c·*, only because

classified

c 255– 7   anciently *c·* as the higher criticism,
r 473– 6   are to be *c·* as effects of error.
g 556– 4   mortal and material concepts *c·*,

classifies

f 213– 7   and then *c·* it materially.
g 513–17   Spirit diversifies, *c·*, and individualizes

classify

an 106–17   *c·* all others as did St. Paul
ph 187–24   The human mind tries to *c·* action
r 483– 5   We *c·* disease as error,
495– 8   *c·* sickness and error as our Master did,
ap 560–20   in order to *c·* it correctly.

clauses

o 341– 5   generally based on detached sentences or *c·*

claw

r 489– 2   When the unthinking lobster loses its *c·*,
489– 2   the *c·* grows again.
489– 7   would be replaced as readily as the lobster's *c·*,

clay

ph 173– 7   supposition, . . . the potter is subject to the *c·*,
f 243–16   The *c·* cannot reply to the potter.
b 310– 9   The potter is not in the *c·* ;
310– 9   else the *c·* would have power over the potter.
r 490–23   along with the dissolving elements of *c·*.

clean

p 382–12   beware of making *c·* merely the outside
383– 3   We need a *c·* body and a *c·* mind,
383–19   This shows that the mind must be *c·*
413–18   only for the purpose of keeping the body *c·*,
t 452–22   and afterwards we must wash them *c·*.

cleanliness

p 413–16   "*C·* is next to godliness,"
413–20   I insist on bodily *c·* within and without.

cleanse

a 25– 7   no more efficacious to *c·* from sin
37–11   *c·* and rarefy the atmosphere of material sense

cleansed

a 27– 5   the lame walk, the lepers are *c·*, — *Luke* 7 : 22.
s 132– 7   the lame walk, the lepers are *c·*, — *Matt.* 11 : 5.
133–32   Creeds and rituals have not *c·* their hands

clear

a 50–11   who could withhold a *c·* token of his presence
m 65–21   until we get at last the *c·* straining of truth,
an 104–31   Is it *not c·* that the human mind must
ph 182–16   *c·* to those who heal the sick on the basis of
f 205–16   we can catch *c·* glimpses of God only as
b 325–20   Paul had a *c·* sense of the demands of Truth
o 358–15   It presents the calm and *c·* verdict of Truth
p 388–28   a *c·* comprehension of the living Spirit.
398– 6   *c·* evidence that the malady was not material.
418– 8   and a *c·* perception of the unchanging,
418–12   It must be *c·* to you that sickness
t 444–31   The teacher must make *c·* to students
459– 4   Paul and John had a *c·* apprehension that,
r 495–17   Let neither fear nor doubt overshadow your *c·* sense
g 523–15   *c·* evidences of two distinct documents

cleared

f 234–18   brood of evils which infest it would be *c·* out.
b 288–16   may burst and flash till the cloud is *c·*

clearer

a 55–12   in a *c·* light than mere words can possibly do,
s 121–20   rebuked by *c·* views of the everlasting facts,
f 239– 7   Take away wealth, . . . and we get *c·* views
c 262–14   These *c·*, higher views inspire the Godlike man
b 313–20   The passage is made even *c·* in
o 361–22   to give a *c·* and fuller expression
p 368– 8   truth will become still *c·*
372– 9   Science of being, . . . would be *c·* in this age,
t 460–31   the teaching became *c·*, until
g 501– 7   whereas the New Testament narratives are *c·*
504–19   spiritually *c·* views of Him,
553– 5   This *c·* consciousness must precede an
ap 568–28   rises *c·* and nearer to the great heart of Christ ;

clearest

g 517–13   Love imparts the *c·* idea of Deity.

clearly

b 275–21   shows *c·* that all is Mind,
t 455–15   then shalt thou see *c·* — *Matt.* 7 : 5.
r 479–31   invisible things . . . are *c·* seen, — *Rom.* 1 : 20.
ap 568–32   This rule *c·* interprets God as divine Principle,

clearness

p 380–26   this evidence will gather momentum and *c·*,

clears

a 22–18   When the smoke of battle *c·* away,

clear-sightedness

b 316–14   between spiritual *c·* and the blindness of

cleave

o 354–15   Surely it is not enough to *c·* to barren and

clergy

a 20–12   partake of the Eucharist, support the *c·*,
o 348–10   It is a pity that the medical faculty and *c·*

clergyman

f 220–22   A *c·* once adopted a diet of bread and water
o 359– 3   Let any *c·* try to cure his friends by their faith

clergymen

f 235–28   *C·*, occupying the watchtowers of the world,

clerical

f 236– 1   should stimulate *c·* labor and progress.

climate

p 377–10   when their fear of *c·* is exterminated.
386–11   not because of the *c·*, but on account of the
392–21   If you decide that *c·* or atmosphere is unhealthy,
394–24   unless it can be aided by a drug or *c·*?

climates

p 377– 6   Invalids flee to tropical *c·*
377–10   prove that they can be healthy in all *c·*,

climax

b 322– 7   This must be the *c·*
g 543– 2   error, after reaching the *c·* of suffering,

climb

b 326– 7   must not try to *c·* the hill of Science by
g 514– 8   In humility they *c·* the heights of holiness.

clime

a 46–10   has spoken . . . in every age and *c·*.

climes

f 225–29   Men and women of all *c·* and races

cling

f 237–26   *c·* to a belief in the life and intelligence of
c 263– 9   *c·* to earth because he has not tasted heaven.
266–11   even if you *c·* to a sense of personal joys,
b 283–23   lost to all who *c·* to this falsity.
328– 9   and must therefore *c·* to mortals until,
t 448– 2   Blindness and self-righteousness *c·* fast to
r 495–14   *c·* steadfastly to God and His idea.

clings
    s 146–15 Scholasticism *c·* for salvation to the person,
clip
    pr 4–31 creeds *c·* the strong pinions of love,
cliques
    f 239– 8 Break up *c·*, level wealth with honesty,
cloaked
    gl 597– 8 but *c·* the crime, latent in thought,
clock
    o 360–19 Like a pendulum in a *c·*,
cloister
    c 263–25 peers from its *c·* with amazement
cloistered
    ph 191–23 not a flower starts from its *c·* cell.
Cloquet
    an 101– 9 among whom were Roux, Bouillaud, and *C·*,
close
    pr 15–15 must *c·* the lips and silence the material senses.
    a 32–31 a sad supper taken at the *c·* of day,
    sp 71–10 *C·* your eyes, and you may dream that you
    71–14 *C·* your eyes again, and you may see
    87–30 *c·* the eyes, and forms rise before us,
    f 201–16 we shall not hug our tatters *c·* about us.
    224–25 Will you open or *c·* the door upon this
    p 431–18 getting Mortal Man into *c·* confinement
    t 454–25 at the *c·* of a class term,
    ap 564–29 The serpent is . . . *c·* upon the heel of harmony.
closed
    pref xii–14 She *c·* her College, October 29, 1889,
    pr 15– 5 *C·* to error, it is open to Truth,
    15–11 the door of the erring senses must be *c·*.
    a 33– 1 and this supper *c·* forever Jesus' ritualism
    46–27 which *c·* the earthly record of Jesus,
    ph 165– 4 *c·* the eyes of mortals to man's God-given
    171– 7 gates of Paradise which human beliefs have *c·*,
    193–12 The eyelids *c·* gently and
    o 350–20 and their eyes they have *c·* ; — *Matt.* 13 : 15.
    p 433– 2 testimony for the plaintiff, . . . being *c·*,
    440–33 Here the counsel for the defence *c·*,
    r 491–03 belief goes on, whether our eyes are *c·* or open.
    g 528–11 and *c·* up the flesh instead — *Gen.* 2 : 21.
closely
    m 57–27 serves to unite thought more *c·* to God,
    sp 97– 5 In reality, the more *c·* error simulates truth
    g 523–28 become more and more *c·* intertwined
closes
    m 69–11 neither *c·* man's continuity nor his sense of
    s 144–26 pride, or prejudice *c·* the door
    g 521– 4 Here the inspired record *c·* its narrative
    ap 577–29 *c·* with St. John's Revelation
closet
    pr 14–31 enter into thy *c·*, — *Matt.* 6 : 6.
    15– 3 The *c·* typifies the sanctuary of Spirit,
    15–15 to pray aright, we must enter into the *c·*
closing
    ph 187–13 opening and *c·* for the passage of the blood,
clothe
    pr 4–32 and *c·* religion in human forms.
    sp 93–19 human faith may *c·* it with angelic vestments,
    g 530–11 as able to feed and *c·* man as He doth the lilies.
clothed
    f 254– 9 To stop eating, drinking, or being *c·* materially
    p 442–25 and man is . . . and fed spiritually.
    ap 558– 4 *c·* with a cloud : — *Rev.* 10 : 1.
    558– 9 This angel . . . *c·* with a cloud, prefigures
    560– 7 a woman *c·* with the sun, — *Rev.* 12 : 1.
    561–11 the spiritual ideal as a woman *c·* in light,
clothes
    m 62–24 even as it *c·* the lily ;
    s 146–19 truth . . . *c·* Spirit with supremacy.
    f 212–23 God alone makes and *c·* the lilies of the field,
    g 507– 4 Spirit duly feeds and *c·* every object,
clothing
    an 104– 7 belied by wolves in sheep's *c·*.
    p 442–23 Truth, gives mortals temporary food and *c·*
    ap 567–29 These wolves in sheep's *c·* are detected
cloud
    f 210–21 as a sunbeam penetrates the *c·*.
    247–26 arches the *c·* with the bow of beauty,
    b 288–16 may burst and flash till the *c·* is cleared
    295–23 like a *c·* melting into thin vapor,
    298– 4 As a *c·* hides the sun it cannot extinguish,
    ap 558– 4 clothed with a *c·* : — *Rev.* 10 : 1.
    558–10 This angel . . . clothed with a *c·*, prefigures
    566–10 a pillar of *c·* by day and of fire by night,
clouded
    gl 590–26 statements of the Scriptures become *c·*

clouds
  gathering
    g 547–13 the gathering *c·*, the moon and stars,
  murky
    s 122–21 in the midst of murky *c·* and drenching rain.
  varying
    b 311– 1 the varying *c·* of mortal belief,
    —
    m 67– 4 the *c·* lower, the wind shrieks
    s 122–17 On the eye's retina, . . . *c·* and ocean meet
    f 245–21 coaxed the enamoured lightning from the *c·*.
    o 354–20 which are like *c·* without rain.
    g 548– 9 when *c·* cover the sun's face !
    548–11 seen only as the *c·* of corporeal sense roll away.
    557–19 Divine Science rolls back the *c·* of error
clover
    ph 175–13 profane to fancy that the perfume of *c·*
coalesce
    s 143–32 may try to make Mind and drugs *c·*,
coalition
    f 218–10 The reports of sickness may form a *c·* with
coated
    p 379–26 The quickened pulse, *c·* tongue, febrile heat,
Coated Tongue
    p 431–21 I am *C· T·*. I am covered with a
coaxed
    f 245–20 *c·* the enamoured lightning from the clouds.
coddling
    ph 175–20 people had less time for selfishness, *c·*,
code
    f 226–16 These claims are not made through *c·* or creed,
codes
    ph 183– 3 and demand obedience to materialistic *c·*,
    f 226–18 Human *c·*, scholastic theology,
    234–21 The present *c·* of human systems disappoint
    b 340–27 civil, criminal, political, and religious *c·* ;
    p 381–16 but He is not the author of barbarous *c·*.
coequal
    o 351–21 if we consider Satan as a being *c·* in power
coeternal
    b 336–11 coexistent and *c·* with that Mind.
coexist
    c 267–12 man and the spiritual universe *c·* with
    b 270– 1 theory, . . . that Mind and matter *c·*
    279–13 Spirit and matter can neither *c·* nor cooperate,
    336–30 God and man *c·* and are eternal.
    r 471–16 the evidence that God and man *c·*
coexistence
    b 269– 3 supposed *c·* of Mind and matter
coexistent
    m 69– 1 not of the earth earthly but *c·* with God,
    b 336–11 *c·* and coeternal with that Mind.
    r 478– 1 for man is *c·* with God.
    g 516–21 Man . . . as *c·* and eternal with God
    520– 9 Principle and its idea, man, are *c·*
    557–21 as never dying, but as *c·* with his creator.
    gl 581–11 God and man *c·* and eternal ;
coexists
    s 120– 5 and man *c·* with and reflects Soul,
    f 246–12 sun of virtue and truth *c·* with being.
    c 266–31 but he *c·* with God and the universe.
coffee
    sp 80– 3 A cup of *c·* or tea is not the equal of truth,
    p 406–29 tobacco, tea, *c·*, opium,
cognizable
    sp 86–28 as readily as from objects *c·* by the senses.
cognizance
  beyond the
    s 126–19 beyond the *c·* of the material senses
    b 284–25 beyond the *c·* of these senses,
  cannot take
    g 543–10 corporeal senses cannot take *c·* of Spirit.
  has no
    b 292–14 this so-called mind has no *c·* of Spirit.
  have no
    c 258–21 so-called senses have no *c·* of either
  of good or evil
    ph 171–32 error . . . that the *c·* of good or evil,
  take
    an 105–16 When our laws eventually take *c·* of
  taken no
    f 245–22 she had taken no *c·* of passing time
  take no
    sp 72– 2 of which corporeal sense can take no *c·*.
    75– 7 or the material senses could take no *c·* of
    ph 191– 2 It can take no *c·* of Mind.
    b 273– 4 physical senses can take no *c·* of God
    r 479–15 and matter can take no *c·* of matter.

cognizance
take no
r 488–21 corporeal senses can take no c· of spiritual
g 531–29 the corporeal senses can take no c· of Spirit.
546–17 the material senses can take no c· of Spirit
takes no
gl 591–14 that of which immortal Mind takes no c· ;

cognizant
pr 13–32 is not c· of life in Soul,
sp 88– 6 The mind may even be c· of a present flavor
b 276–11 consciousness is c· only of the things of God.
285– 1 cannot be c· of good or of evil,

cognize
o 359–17 c· only that which is the opposite of Spirit.

cognized
m 69– 8 God's children already created will be c·
sp 75– 4 the existence c· by the physical senses,
b 311–26 The objects c· by the physical senses

cognizes
b 306–24 which c· Life as permanent.

cohesion
s 124–20 c·, and attraction are properties of Mind.
b 293–16 whose adhesion and c· are Life,

coiled
sp 92–11 a serpent c· around the tree of knowledge.

coincide
sp 80–13 but I cannot c· with their views.
93–10 Divine logic and revelation c·.
ph 167–21 can no more unite . . . than good can c· with
g 522–23 convince reason and c· with revelation

coincidence
ph 194– 4 I cannot fail to discern the c· of
b 332–32 illustrates the c·, or spiritual agreement,
ap 561–16 John saw the human and divine c·,
561–23 illustrates the c· of God and man

coincides
o 358– 9 C. S., understood, c· with the Scriptures,

cold
and heat
s 125–22 c· and heat, latitude and longitude.
effects of
ph 184–19 We say man suffers from the effects of c·,
heat and
p 374–26 Heat and c· are products of mortal mind.
matter cannot take
p 377– 2 convince him that matter cannot take c·,
this
f 202–32 Common opinion admits . . . that this c· may

pref vii–16 and the c· conventionality of materialism
s 113– 8 is but the dead body of Science, — pulseless, c·,
ph 179–16 that he will take c· without his blanket,
195– 5 Outside of dismal darkness and c· silence
f 202–31 Common opinion admits that a man may take c·
220– 2 We hear it said : . . . I take c· baths,
220– 3 to overcome a predisposition to take c· ;
224–19 C· disdain, stubborn resistance,
p 377– 1 If your patient believes in taking c·,
378–18 a long and c· night of discord.
384– 9 though they expose him to fatigue, c·, heat,
386– 6 belief says that you may catch c· and
429–11 corpse, deserted by thought, is c· and decays,
436–11 Giving a cup of c· water in Christ's name,
t 460–22 c· assertion, "Nothing ails you."
ap 570–17 Give them a cup of c· water in Christ's name,

coldness
gl 593–18 Rock. . . . . C· and stubbornness.

colds
f 220– 3 We hear it said : . . . I have continual c·,
220–16 C·, coughs, and contagion are engendered solely

collapse
s 124–27 Withdraw them, and creation must c·.
f 209–10 The world would c· without Mind,

collect
m 63–30 should be allowed to c· her own wages,

collective
a 18– 6 His mission was both individual and c·.

collectively
m 58–10 constitute individually and c·

College
pref xii– 3 hers was the only C· of this character
xii– 7 were taught by the author in this C·.
xii–14 She closed her C·, October 29, 1889,
xii–19 reopened the C· in 1899

colleges
pref xi–30 a law relative to c· having been passed,

color
f 247–24 in expression, form, outline, and c·.
b 301– 3 mirror, repeats the c·, form, and action
310– 7 seen in all form, substance, and c·,
338–13 signifying the *red c· of the ground*,
r 479–27 We admit that black is not a c·,
g 512–22 From . . . the one Mind emanate all form, c·,

Colossians
b 325–10 In C· (iii. 4) Paul writes :

Columbus
s 120–30 When C· gave freer breath to the globe,

combat
b 268–11 challenge metaphysics to meet in final c·.
269–29 The theories I c· are these :
p 396–25 to c· their erroneous sense,

combated
pref viii–17 Sickness has been c· for centuries

combination
c 256–24 No form nor physical c· is adequate to
p 399– 9 not a secretion nor c· can operate, apart from

combinations
p 399– 3 You say that certain material c· produce

combine
b 275–13 Spirit, Life, Truth, Love, c· as one,
288– 9 Superstition and understanding can never c·.
p 397–28 because they c· as one.
409– 4 *Mortal mind* and body c· as one,

combined
pr 1– 6 Prayer, watching, and working, c· with
s 163–18 war, pestilence, and famine, all c·."
ph 171–18 believes himself to be c· matter and Spirit.
p 421–32 and that their c· sum is fifty,

combines
t 450–30 all evil c· in the belief of life, . . . in matter,
r 466– 3 Hence God c· all-power or potency,

combustion
s 161–10 might produce spontaneous c·.

come
pref vii–13 The time for thinkers has c·.
x–29 or discerning the truth, c· not to the light
pr 1– * shall c· to pass ; — *Mark* 11 : 23.
8– 4 little hope for those who c· only spasmodically
12–23 should c· from the enlightened understanding.
13– 4 c· ye to the waters." — *Isa.* 55 : 1.
16–30 Thy kingdom c·. — *Matt.* 6 : 10.
16–31 *Thy kingdom is c·*;
a 18– * *until the kingdom of God shall c·.* — *Luke* 22 : 18.
22–13 "Occupy till I c· !" — *Luke* 19 : 13.
24–18 change as radical as that which has c· over
27– 3 intended to prove . . . that the Christ had c· :
31–24 show the Lord's death till he c·." — *I Cor.* 11 : 26.
34– 5 Truth has c· to the understanding
34– 6 If Christ, Truth, has c· to us in demonstration,
38–14 in all time to c·.
40–29 has c· so generally to mean public worship
41– 3 must c· through the joys and triumphs of the
m 56–10 and His kingdom is c·
sp 80– 6 A communication purporting to c· from the
85–12 "C·, see a man, which — *John* 4 : 29.
86–11 Opposites c· from contrary directions,
90– 5 from which loaf or fish could c·?
90–28 recognition of Spirit must finally c·,
92–32 Do you say the time has not yet c·
an 100–19 we have c· to the unanimous conclusions
s 112–18 with this infinitude c· spiritual rules,
125–21 The seasons will c· and go
129–16 c· hither to torment us — *Matt.* 8 : 29.
130– 5 bidden to the feast, the excuses c·,
131–13 Must C. S. c· through the Christian churches
131–14 This Science has c· already,
131–31 "Art thou he that should c·," — *Matt.* 11 : 3.
133– 2 "Art thou he that should c·?" — *Matt.* 11 : 3.
134– 8 and so has c· always to mean
141–10 revelation (such is the popular thought !) must c·
144– 2 Why should we . . . since no good can c· of it?
ph 173–26 Human reason and religion c· slowly to the
182–27 Pleas for drugs and laws of health c· from
192– 7 They c· from the hearing of the ear,
f 212– 8 Why need pain, ... c· to this mortal sense?
223–32 until "He c· whose right it is." — *Ezek.* 21 : 27.
225–21 nor did the breath of freedom c· from the
238– 6 " C· out from among them, — *II Cor.* 6 : 17.
238–14 there will c· the warning,
c 266– 7 Then the time will c· when
b 280– 6 only reflections of good can c·.
283–10 which act, react, and then c· to a stop.
285–17 time has c· for a finite . . . to give place
291– 8 last call of wisdom cannot c· till
304– 7 nor things present, nor things to c·, — *Rom.* 8 : 38.
321–10 bade him c· back and handle the serpent,
321–27 " It shall c· to pass, — *Exod.* 4 : 8.
322–11 before this recognition of divine Science can c·

come

b 324–30 if the idea . . . . c· not to your thought,
333–21 has c· with some measure of power and grace
o 361– 1 Jew believes that . . . Christ has not yet c· ;
361– 8 God is c· and is present now and forever.
p 362–15 to c· behind the couch and reach his feet.
367–24 Truth of the Christ-cure calls to this age
368– 6 Both truth and error have c· nearer than ever
368–15 When we c· to have more faith in the truth
376– 8 diseases deemed dangerous sometimes c· from
377– 7 they c· back no better than when they went
393– 1 issues of pain or pleasure must c· through
398– 3 I charge thee, c· out of him,— Mark 9 : 25.
398–30 The Science of Mind must c· to the rescue,
411– 1 thing which I greatly feared is c·— Job 3 : 25.
t 451– 3 to c· out from the material world
451–17 they c· from above, not from beneath,
r 474–20 "I am not c· to destroy,— Matt. 5 : 17.
478–11 to go into the house or to c· out of it,
485–15 c· naturally into Spirit through better health
g 501– 7 and c· nearer the heart.
519–18 "we all c· in the unity of the faith,— Eph. 4 : 13.
529– 7 Another change will c· as to the
543–10 They cannot c· into His presence,
548– 1 The Spirit and the bride say, C·!— Rev. 22 : 17.
556–17 c· from the deep sleep which
556–22 Oblivion and dreams, not realities, c· with sleep.
ap 558– 3 mighty angel c· down from heaven,— Rev. 10 : 1.
567– 4 Truth and Love c· nearer in the hour of woe,
568–14 Now is c· salvation, and strength,— Rev. 12 : 10.
568–22 the devil is c· down unto you,— Rev. 12 : 12.
574– 8 C· hither, I will show thee— Rev. 21 : 9.
575– 1 thought gently whispers : "C· hither!
gl 585–13 "Elias truly shall first c·— Matt. 17 : 11.
585–18 a type of the glory which is to c· ;

comeliness

f 247–19 C· and grace are independent of matter.
b 281–15 supplies all form and c·

comes

pr 5– 8 and woe c· in return for what is done.
a 42– 8 c· in darkness and disappears with the light.
sp 75– 2 assumption that man dies . . . but c· to life as
76–32 recognition of Spirit . . . c· not suddenly
84–28 All we correctly know of Spirit c· from God,
85– 5 This Soul-sense c· to the human mind when
s 112–16 c· one Principle and its infinite idea,
113– 5 but its spirit c· only in small degrees.
115– 3 through which the understanding . . . c·,
118–32 the natural order of heaven c· down to earth.
ph 174–31 its cure c· from the immortal divine
178–20 this so-called mind, from which c· all evil,
188–28 When darkness c· over the earth,
189–25 From mortal mind c· the reproduction of the
f 202–19 when God's kingdom c· on earth ;
223–16 the assurance which c· of understanding ;
230– 9 salvation which c· through God,
238–26 Justice often c· too late to secure a verdict.
239–27 If it c· from erring mortal mind,
247– 1 acute belief of physical life c· on at a remote
250–12 a ray of light which c· from the sun,
c 264–27 which c· from an all-absorbing spiritual love.
265–25 The aspiration after heavenly good c·
266–10 When this hour of development c·,
b 280–16 belief c· to have "gods many— I Cor. 8 : 5.
289– 1 real existence as a child of God c· to light.
290–12 Hence Truth c· to destroy this error
291–29 judgment-day of wisdom c· hourly
303– 6 c· from no power of propagation in
318–19 beliefs, from which c· so much suffering,
327– 1 Reform c· by understanding that
339–24 gives place to . . . and God's kingdom c·
o 347–15 Christ, . . . c· now as of old,
358–25 c· through rousing within the sick
p 382–16 the devotee . . . who c· to teach the
387–21 supposition that death c· in obedience to the
434– 2 on the wings of divine Love, there c· a despatch:
r 466–27 Science of Christianity c· with fan in hand
473–10 that c· to heal sickness and sin
479– 6 On the contrary, if aught c· from God,
483– 1 Then c· the question,
490–10 From this also c· its powerlessness,
g 523–11 In error everything c· from beneath,
529–21 Whence c· a talking, lying serpent
556–29 but when that awakening c·,
ap 558– 9 message which c· from God,
569–22 c· back to him at last with accelerated force,
gl 583–10 c· to the flesh to destroy incarnate error.

comet

s 121–15 is as the wandering c· or the desolate star

cometh

pref vii– 3 ere c· the full radiance of a risen day.
a 31–26 "The hour c·, and now is,— John 4 : 23.
31–31 yea, the time c·,— John 16 : 2.
35–26 "which c· down from heaven,"— John 6 : 33.

cometh

m 64–18 the time c· of which Jesus spake,
sp 78–29 cannot "tell whence it c·."— John 3 : 8.
93– 6 "But the hour c·, and now is,— John 4 : 23.
s 132–27 "When the Son of man c·,— Luke 18 : 8.
f 224–26 who c· in the quiet of meekness,
225– 1 Whence c· it?
b 286– 9 Master said, "No man c· unto— John 14 : 6.
325–26 time c· when the spiritual origin of man,
g 550– 3 If this be so, whence c· Life, or Mind,
ap 575– 4 Then c· the marriage feast,
575– 8 and c· "down from God,— Rev. 21 : 2.

comfort

an 101–29 Discomfort under error is preferable to c·.
ph 197– 6 costs many a man his earthly days of c·.
f 234– 6 crumbs of c· from Christ's table,
ap 578–12 [LOVE'S] rod and [LOVE'S] staff they c· me.— Psal. 23 : 4.

comforted

a 33–12 and now it c· themselves.
sp 78–30 By it the sick are healed, the sorrowing are c·,

Comforter

a 55–28 "He shall give you another C·,— John 14 : 16.
55–29 This C· I understand to be Divine Science.
s 123–22 through the teachings of the C·,
127–29 the C· which leadeth into all truth.
b 271–20 Our Master said, "But the C·— John 14 : 26.
331–31 divine Science or the Holy C·.
332–21 the Holy Ghost, or C·, revealing the
r 497– 7 the Holy Ghost or divine C· ;

comforts

gl 582–12 that which c·, consoles, and supports.

coming

pref xi–18 c· now as was promised aforetime,
a 52–14 word concerning the c· Prince of Peace.
sp 83– 7 good and evil elements now c· to the surface.
an 102–17 its aggressive features are c· to the front.
s 132–11 such effects, c· from divine Mind,
150– 7 Its appearing is the c· anew of the gospel of
150– 8 This c·, as was promised by the Master,
f 215–17 at the c· of which darkness loses the
230– 7 This awakening is the forever c· of Christ,
245–10 before the window watching for her lover's c·.
b 321–29 And so it was in the c· centuries,
o 347–14 would behold the signs of Christ's c·.
p 385–21 Any supposed information, c· from the body
g 549–31 c· down to a belief in the material origin of
ap 561–12 the spiritual ideal . . . c· down from heaven,
561–32 John the Baptist prophesied the c· of the
574–13 c· down from God, out of heaven,"— Rev. 21 : 2.

command

apostolic
t 451– 3 the constant pressure of the apostolic c·
Christ's
s 110–29 demonstrated according to Christ's c·,
direct
o 342–10 in defiance of the direct c· of Jesus,
first
b 280–18 as Jehovah's first c· of the Ten :
follow the
f 228–20 If we follow the c· of our Master,
God's
g 530– 6 The earth, at God's c·, brings forth food
Scriptural
f 238– 6 To obey the Scriptural c·,
b 276– 8 in accordance with the Scriptural c· :
single
g 524–18 With a single c·, Mind had made man,
spiritual
ph 168–19 spiritual c· relating to perfection,
this
pr 9–19 This c· includes much,
a 38– 2 Because men are assured that this c·

ph 196–14 The c· was a warning to beware,
f 225– 9 c· their sentinels not to let truth pass
o 342–11 to which c· was added the promise
p 403–14 You c· the situation if you understand
r 467– 5 Therefore the c· means this :
ap 570–25 and Christ will c· the wave.

commanded

a 37–27 do they follow him in the way that he c·?
m 67–22 and c· even the winds and waves
g 527– 6 And the Lord God [Jehovah] c·— Gen. 2 : 16.
533– 7 whereof I c· thee— Gen. 3 : 11.
535–21 which I c· thee, saying,— Gen. 3 : 17.

commandest

p 435–30 and c· . . . to be smitten— Acts 23 : 3.

commanding

p 439– 7 c· him to take part in the homicide.
442–11 His form was erect and c·,

Commandment

m 69–21 "Do you keep the First C·?
b 301–22 not spiritual and breaks the First C·,
  340–16 The First C· is my favorite text.
  340–21 The divine Principle of the First C·
o 361– 6 The Jew who believes in the First C·
  361–10 The Christian who believes in the First C·

commandment

a 19–29 Jesus urged the c·,
m 56–18 c·, "Thou shalt not commit — Exod. 20 : 14.
s 112–30 inculcates a breach of that divine c·
b 308– 4 art thou . . . keeping His c·?"

Commandments

ap 563–13 belief that . . . the Ten C· can be broken.

commandments

pr 4– 5 To keep the c· of our Master
  4–11 "If ye love me, keep my c·." — John 14 : 15.
a 25–20 "If ye love me, keep my c·." — John 14 : 15.
f 241–22 "If ye love me, keep my c·." — John 14 : 15.
b 340– 8 Fear God, and keep His c· : — Eccl. 12 : 13.
  340–11 love God and keep His c· :
g 542–26 to advance itself, breaks God's c·.

commands

a 20–26 It c· sure entrance into the realm of Love.
  26– 6 if we follow his c· faithfully ;
  37–27 Hear these imperative c· :
f 222–28 contrary to His c·.
o 355–16 according to the c· of our Master,
p 405– 5 C. S. c· man to master the propensities,
r 489–14 it breaks all the c· of the Mosaic Decalogue

commemorate

a 32– 5 Eucharist does not c· a Roman soldier's oath,
  35–12 the morning meal which Christian Scientists c·.

commemorated

a 33–31 can you then say that you have c· Jesus
  34–11 If all . . . had really c· the sufferings of Jesus

commemoration

a 34– 6 no other c· is requisite,
  34–13 If all who seek his c· through material symbols

commences

ph 189–29 c· in the lower, basal portion of the brain,
p 423– 9 c· with mental causation,
  430–20 patient feels ill, ruminates, and the trial c·.

commend

t 457–25 some learners c· diet and hygiene.

commendation

p 365–20 such c· as the Magdalen gained from Jesus,

commended

a 35–28 draught our Master drank and c· to his
p 434–32 that court c· man's immortal Spirit

commending

sp 92–14 serpent in the act of c· to

comment

pr 8–12 what must be the c· upon him?
  8–14 there would be no occasion for c·.
a 55– 3 subjects to unchristian c· and usage
g 523– 2 of the Scriptural account now under c·.

commercialism

ph 195–28 Literary c· is lowering the intellectual

commingle

ph 198–26 His thoughts and his patient's c·,
f 211– 3 if . . . Truth and error, c·
b 281– 4 Spirit and matter no more c· than light and
  296–24 When the evidence . . . seems to c·,
r 492–22 The notion that mind and matter c·
g 539–20 false to say that Truth and error c·

commingling

r 481–15 declaring . . . good and evil to be capable of c·.

commission

a 54–13 In witness of his divine c·,
an 100–14 Under this order a c· was appointed,
  100–16 This c· reported to the government
  104–30 as well as the c· of a crime.
p 433–22 this has led him into the c· of the

Commissioner

p 432– 2 the State C·.

commissioners

an 100–15 Benjamin Franklin was one of the c·.

commissions

t 455–24 When He c· a messenger,

commit

m 56–18 "Thou shalt not c· adultery," — Exod. 20 : 14.
an 105– 2 The hands, without . . . could not c· a murder.
  105–10 Can matter c· a crime?
  105–23 to c· fresh atrocities as opportunity occurs
f 252–19 cheat, lie, c· adultery, rob, murder,
o 356–25 Does divine Love c· a fraud on humanity
p 406–17 moral man has no fear that he will c· a murder,
  432– 7 I knew the prisoner would c· it,

commit

  436–30 deeds which the divine law compels man to c·.
t 461–18 If you c· a crime, should you acknowledge

commits

pref xii–26 she c· these pages to honest seekers for Truth.
r 490– 4 this belief c· depredations on harmony.

committed

s 161–22 "Liberty, what crimes are c· in thy name!"
p 408–11 people who are c· to insane asylums
  430–18 is charged with having c· liver-complaint.
  431– 8 At last he c· liver-complaint,
  434–28 shows the alleged crime never to have been c·
  435– 4 Has the body or has Mortal Mind c· a
  435– 7 The body c· no offence.
  435–14 If liver-complaint was c· by trampling on

committee

an 101– 8 a c· of nine persons was appointed,

committing

p 436–17 to prevent his c· liver-complaint,
t 459–14 C· the bare process of mental healing to

common

pr 12–22 c· custom of praying for the recovery
a 52–18 make c· cause against the exponents of truth.
sp 80–30 This belief rests on the c· conviction that
  92–17 for the c· conception of mortal man
an 101–17 nothing in c· with either physiology or
  106– 2 to drop from the platform of c· manhood
s 137–14 implied in their citation of the c· report
  137–27 had been called only by his c· names,
  153– 5 Natrum muriaticum (c· table-salt)
f 202–31 C· opinion admits that a man may take cold
b 294– 2 These senses indicate the c· human belief,
  333– 5 in c· with other Hebrew boys and men,
o 342–30 according to the c· theories,
  357– 1 In c· justice, we must admit that God
p 363– 3 which is in such c· use in the East.
  363–17 were released . . . by their c· creditor.
 365–11, 12 and c· sense and c· humanity are
  383–32 c· notion that health depends on inert matter
  388–12 Admit the c· hypothesis
  407–32 in consonance with c· mortal belief.
t 459– 7 Then he will have nothing in c· with
r 488–12 Scriptures often appear in our c· version
g 523–20 or Lord God, as our c· version translates it.
  540– 9 reducing it to its c· denominator.
gl 598–14 the phrase is equivalent to our c· statement,

commonly

s 116–24 As the words . . . are c· and ignorantly
  139– 9 Reforms have c· been attended with bloodshed
ph 183–20 mortals c· recognize as law that which hides
f 232– 4 The beliefs we c· entertain about happiness
  242–22 the facts of being are c· misconstrued,
  243–13 That those wonders are not more c· repeated
b 274– 7 Natural science, as it is c· called,
  284–26 by the effects c· attributed to them.
  310–18 We are c· taught that there is a human soul
  319–11 material means (c· called nature)
  333– 4 though it is c· so used.
o 344–20 are not included in the c· accepted systems;
  344–32 the word Spirit is so c· applied to Deity,
gl 586–10 the divine Principle, c· called God.

Common Version

b 313–13 "express image" in the C· V· — Heb. 1 : 3.

Commonwealth

pref xi–29 under the seal of the C·,

commotion

p 422–11 Patients, unfamiliar with the cause of this c·

commune

a 35–13 and silently to c· with the divine Principle,
sp 73–29 mistake to suppose that . . . can c· together.
  74–31 so-called dead and living cannot c· together,
  75–26 one possible moment, when those . . . can c·
  76–13 can no longer c· with matter;
  84–15 to c· more largely with the divine Mind,

communed

sp 73–15 If Spirit, or God, c· . . . through electricity

communicable

sp 72–25 but evil is neither c· nor scientific
  72–29 when evil and suffering are c·.
  74– 3 To be on c· terms with Spirit,

communicate

sp 78–22 How then can it c· with man through
  82–14 we do not c· with the dreamer by our side

communicated

f 212– 2 is not c· through a nerve.
  213–18 as c· through the senses of Soul
p 423– 3 this belief should not be c· to the patient,

communicates

sp 85–31 truth c· itself but never imparts error.

communicating

i 446– 2 perhaps c· his own bad morals,

communication
　　sp　73–32　There is no c· between so-called material
　　　78–12　even were c· possible
　　　80– 6　A c· purporting to come from

communications
　　sp　77–22　Even if c· from spirits to mortal consciousness
　　　77–23　such c· would grow beautifully less
　　　78–13　C· gathered from ignorance are pernicious

communicator
　　sp　72–30　divine law is the c· of truth,
　　　81–32　deceased person, supposed to be the c·,

communicators
　　sp　72– 9　So-called *spirits* are but corporeal c·.

communing
　　sp　78– 8　belief . . . that at the same time we are c· with

communion
　　a　30– 1　Mary's self-conscious c· with God.
　　　35–25　Our Eucharist is spiritual c· with the one God.
　　sp　72– 7　condition precedent to c· with Spirit
　　　74–13　No correspondence nor c· can exist between
　　　82–23　C· . . . would be prevented by this difference.
　　g　539–24　"What c· hath light with— *II Cor. 6:* 14.

community
　　an　103– 2　in families and therefore in the c·.
　　t　446– 3　a c· unprepared for self-defence.
　　　456– 9　which most of them hold in the c·,

commute
　　p　378– 5　will enable you to c· this self-sentence,

compact
　　m　59– 7　compromises will often maintain a c·

companion
　　ap　569–22　The sin, which one has made his bosom c·,

companionship
　　a　21–24　and our c· may continue.
　　m　60– 5　formation of a happy and permanent c·.

company
　　a　21–28　c· is alluring and the pleasures exciting.
　　　36– 2　in the blessed c· of Truth and Love
　　m　66–27　the other pre-eminently needs good c·.
　　c　261–15　actively as the youngest member of the c·.

compare
　　g　515–28　Now c· man before the mirror

comparison
　　c　256–17　in c· with the sublime question,
　　b　297–25　Human thoughts have their degrees of c·.

comparative
　　pref　ix–29　her c· ignorance of the stupendous

compass
　　f　233–19　c· the destruction of sin and sickness
　　b　292– 5　Divine Science alone can c· the heights

compassed
　　b　302– 1　Soul is not c· by finiteness.

compassion
　　s　115–26　MORAL. Humanity, honesty, affection, c·,

compassionately
　　p　363– 9　He regarded her c·.
　　　365–22　and deal with his patients c· ;

compel
　　pr　11–11　in order to c· this progress.
　　p　390–10　Truth will at length c· us all to exchange the
　　　440–23　human mental legislators c· them to

compelled
　　s　159– 5　she was c· by her physicians to take it.
　　p　436–25　they were c· to let him be taken

compels
　　p　436–30　deeds which the divine law c· man to commit.

compensated
　　s　163–27　if it were not more than c· by

compensation
　　ap　574–19　has full c· in the law of Love.
　　gl　581–15　Hope and faith ; spiritual c· ;

compilation
　　f　241–15　that c· can do no more for mortals

complain
　　m　62–11　those parents should not, in after years, c·
　　　62–30　and produce the ills of which we c·.

complaining
　　o　348–22　while c· of the suffering disease brings,
　　p　395–17　An ill-tempered, c·, or deceitful person

complaint
　　f　221–15　without a vestige of the old c·.
　　p　391–29　Mentally contradict every c·

complaints
　　pr　14–15　the body will then utter no c·.
　　f　237–31　would rid them of their c·,

complete
　　pref　ix–15　and are not c· nor satisfactory expositions
　　a　25– 1　Thomas was forced to acknowledge how c·
　　sp　98–28　not . . . fragmentary, but practical and c· ;
　　　98–29　and being practical and c·,
　　s　147–14　this volume contains the c· Science of
　　o　353–15　eternity, immortality, c· reality.
　　p　417–28　the c· control which Mind holds over the
　　t　457–27　which they mean to c· with Mind,
　　g　519– 9　the ideas of God in universal being are c·
　　　527– 5　but ever beautiful and c·.

completed
　　a　41–15　c· his earthly mission ;
　　ap　562– 5　Revelator c· this figure with woman,

completely
　　s　137–13　Jesus c· eschewed the narrow opinion
　　t　446–10　has generally c· healed such cases.

completeness
　　m　57– 5　Union of . . . qualities constitutes c·.

complex
　　p　393–27　not upon the c· humors, lenses, muscles,

compliance
　　p　433– 7　In c· with a stern duty, his Honor,

complicated
　　an　102–20　weaving webs more c· and subtle.
　　g　549–19　the most c· corporeal structures,

complication
　　p　389–31　suffering from a c· of symptoms

component
　　a　28–16　Not a single c· part of his nature
　　g　550–18　decay and dissolution as its c· stages

composed
　　r　478–25　is c· of material human beliefs
　　g　551–19　c· of the simplest material elements,

composing
　　f　209–17　aggregated substances c· the earth,

compositions
　　pref　viii–30　but these c· were crude,

compound
　　r　468–23　universe, . . . is a c· idea,
　　　475–14　He is the c· idea of God,
　　g　507–18　multiplication of the c· idea man.
　　gl　585– 8　to spiritual sense, it is a c· idea.
　　　591– 5　MAN. The c· idea of infinite Spirit ;

compounded
　　f　209–16　c· minerals or aggregated substances
　　ap　577– 7　this c· spiritual individuality reflects

comprehend
　　pr　2–25　anything He does not already c·?
　　sp　98–11　which the material senses cannot c·,
　　s　136–14　for how could such a sinner c·
　　　136–30　but they did not c· all that he said
　　ph　187– 3　mortals do not c· even mortal existence,
　　f　210– 1　the language which human thought can c·.
　　c　258–32　and thus begin to c· in Science
　　b　301– 5　Few persons c· what C. S. means by
　　g　555– 8　said . . . I do not c· what you say about error."

comprehended
　　an　104– 4　When C. S. and animal magnetism are both c·,
　　s　141–24　Neither can this manifestation . . . be c·, until
　　　149– 9　These states are not c·,
　　ph　167– 5　and Soul-existence, . . . is not c·.
　　b　303– 9　and are c· in and formed by Spirit,
　　　325–31　the darkness c· it not."— *John* 1: 5.
　　o　350–13　Unless the works are c· which his
　　g　520– 8　is no more seen nor c· by mortals,

comprehending
　　f　219–25　not c· the Principle of the cure,
　　p　441– 1　c· and defining all law and evidence,
　　g　546–25　though the darkness, c· them not,

comprehends
　　o　347–21　which the darkness c· not.
　　p　369– 8　and c· the theology of Jesus
　　　371–15　no more c· his real being than
　　r　481– 8　Through spiritual sense only, man c· . . . Deity.
　　g　518–27　divine Principle, or Spirit, c· and expresses
　　gl　596– 1　That which spiritual sense alone c·,

comprehensible
　　s　115– 6　to make them c· to any reader,
　　　146–32　to a form c· by and adapted to

comprehension
　　p　388–28　and a clear c· of the living Spirit.
　　t　462– 1　requisite for a thorough c· of C. S.
　　r　488–24　Mind alone possesses . . . perception, and c·.

comprehensiveness
　　s　128–10　gives them acuteness and c·

compress
　　　280–10　limits all things, and would c· Mind,

compressed
 c 256–13 nor *c·* within the narrow limits of
 p 397–29 Give up the belief that mind is, . . . *c·* within
comprised
 s 127– 7 *c·* in a knowledge or understanding of God,
 b 286–31 Sin, sickness, and death are *c·* in
compromise
 t 443– 6 those, who make such a *c·*,
compromised
 pref x–11 The author has not *c·* conscience
compromises
 m 59– 7 Mutual *c·* will often maintain a compact
computed
 s 129– 4 or of a properly *c·* sum in arithmetic
con
 s 120–25 Any conclusion *pro* or *c·*,
 129– 9 be the fable *pro* or *c·*,—
conceal
 pr 4– 1 we cannot *c·* the ingratitude of barren lives.
 t 447–13 false charity does not forever *c·* error;
 g 542–10 disposition to excuse guilt or to *c·* it
concealed
 g 542– 7 error cannot forever be *c·*.
concealment
 gl 596–28 VEIL. A cover; *c·*; hiding; hypocrisy.
conceals
 b 256– 1 false sense . . . *c·* scientific demonstration.
concede
 ph 186–22 If we *c·* the same reality to discord as to
conceded
 ph 166–28 balance of power is *c·* to be with matter by
 c 267– 8 It is generally *c·* that God is Father,
 p 396–15 is not a difficult task in view of the *c·* falsity
conceding
 p 394– 5 By *c·* power to discord,
conceit
 t 450– 2 whose bigotry and *c·* twist every fact
 ap 571–27 Thus he rebukes the *c·* of sin,
conceive
 b 318– 2 for him to *c·* of the substantiality of Spirit
 331–23 to *c·* of such omnipresence and individuality
conceived
 a 29–17 Virgin-mother *c·* this idea of God,
 f 211–30 be *c·* of as immortal.
 b 303–11 is spiritually *c·* and brought forth;
 303–12 statement that man is *c·* and evolved
 315–30 being *c·* by a human mother,
 t 462–20 Anatomy, when *c·* of spiritually, is
 463–14 *c·* and born of Truth and Love,
 r 476–16 "*c·* in sin and brought forth in iniquity."
 g 538–24 and she *c·*, and bare Cain,—*Gen.* 4: 1.
 540–28 mortal and material man, *c·* in sin
 545– 6 never had been divinely *c·*.
conceives
 f 213– 6 Mortal mind *c·* of something as
conceiving
 g 513–19 are as eternal as the Mind *c·* them;
 gl 582–14 *c·* man in the idea of God;
concept
 corporeal
  gl 589–16 JESUS. The highest human corporeal *c·*
 every
  c 262–29 Every *c·* which seems to begin with the brain
 false
  ph 177–10 Matter, or body, is but a false *c·*
 human
  (*see* **human**)
 Jewish
  ap 576–28 The term Lord, . . . expresses the Jewish *c·*,
 material
  b 297–17 only fact concerning any material *c·* is,
  334–16 material *c·*, or Jesus, disappeared,
 mental
  sp 87–24 Do not suppose that any mental *c·* is gone
  p 376–19 the so-called material body is a mental *c·*
 perfect
  t 454–23 and form the perfect *c·*.
 true
  sp 87–25 The true *c·* is never lost.
 unreal
  an 102– 7 an unreal *c·* of the so-called mortal mind.
 your
  o 346–27 in your *c·*, the tooth, the operation,
conception
 common
  sp 92–17 the common *c·* of mortal man
 divine
  b 315–25 The divine *c·* of Jesus pointed to this
 faint
  a 47– 3 gave them a faint *c·* of the Life which
 false
  b 281–20 false *c·* as to man and Mind.
  285–16 is a false *c·* of man.

conception
 finite
  c 258– 2 A mortal, corporeal, or finite *c·* of God
  b 285–18 time has come for a finite *c·* . . . to give place
 highest
  s 148–12 instead of from the highest, *c·* of being.
  b 327– 9 Evil is sometimes a man's highest *c·* of right,
 his
  f 248–13 in order to perfect his *c·*.
  b 299– 3 embodies his *c·* of an unseen quality
 human
  a 50–27 The burden . . . was terrible beyond human *c·*.
  ph 185–14 puts forth a human *c·* in the name of Science
  g 505– 7 by which human *c·*, material sense,
 Mary's
  b 332–26 Mary's *c·* of him was spiritual,
 material
  f 213– 9 apart from this mortal and material *c·*.
  g 536–24 erroneous, material *c·* of life and joy,
 mental
  p 403–31 mental *c·* and development of disease
 of God
  s 133–29 Jewish *c·* of God, as Yawah,
  ph 185–19 rests on the *c·* of God as the only Life,
 of mortal mind
  b 274– 4 *c·* of mortal mind, the offspring of sense,
 proper
  g 555–24 and set aside the proper *c·* of Deity,
 thy
  g 535– 7 thy sorrow and thy *c·* :— *Gen.* 3: 16.
 true
  sp 84–24 true *c·* of being destroys the belief of
  c 258–23 gains the true *c·* of man and God.
  260– 2 the true *c·* or understanding of man,
  260–12 as the only true *c·* of being.
  b 324–29 which is the true *c·* of being,
  t 456–14 separates himself from the true *c·* of C. S.
 truest
  s 132–29 or endow him with the truest *c·* of the Christ ?
 unconfined
  b 323–11 *c·* unconfined is winged to reach the divine

conceptions
 diviner
  c 260–10 human beliefs will be attaining diviner *c·*,
 erroneous
  s 116–26 confused and erroneous *c·* of divinity
 finite
  g 545– 1 through mortal and finite *c·*.
 higher
  f 247–17 reflecting those higher *c·* of loveliness
 human
  c 255–12 to belittle Deity with human *c·*.
  257–16 material senses and human *c·* would
 material
  sp 87– 1 So is it with all material *c·*.
  t 463– 9 detach mortal thought from its material *c·*,
 our
  pr 3–17 How empty are our *c·* of Deity !
  f 244– 7 If we were to derive all our *c·*
 spiritual
  o 349–16 inadequate to the expression of spiritual *c·*

  c 260– 7 The *c·* of mortal, erring thought

concepts
 m 62–26 thrusting in the laws of erring, human *c·*.
 f 235–32 and broaden their *c·*.
 239–24 It forms material *c·* and
 c 256–15 nor can He be understood . . . through mortal *c·*.
 259–30 demands spiritual thoughts, divine *c·*,
 264– 1 the fleeting *c·* of the human mind.
 p 426–31 human *c·* named matter, death, disease,
 g 516–31 genders are human *c·*.
 531–13 exchanging human *c·* for the divine
 536– 7 as a symbol of tempest-tossed human *c·*
 556– 4 mortal and material *c·* classified,

concern
 sp 84–16 foretell events which *c·* the universal

concerned
 s 121–25 so far as our solar system is *c·*,

concerning
 a 47–14 people were in doubt *c·* Jesus' teachings.
 52–14 word *c·* the coming Prince of Peace.
 sp 89–13 Scriptural word *c·* a man,
 92–22 Until the fact *c·* error . . . appears,
 s 133–22 *c·* God, man, sanitary methods, and
 f 205– 6 their false sense *c·* God and man.
 219–14 never affirm *c·* the body what we do not wish
 220–28 *c·* which God said.
 b 297–17 The only fact *c·* any material concept is,
 o 349– 4 rabbis of the present day ask *c·* our healing
 349–22 the prophecy *c·* the Christian apostles,
 p 383–27 confirming the Scriptural conclusion *c·* a man,
 412– 7 *c·* the truth which you think or speak,

concerning

p 413–32 held in the beliefs c· his body.
t 448– 9 tell the truth c· the lie.
r 481–16 c· this "tree of the knowledge— *Gen.* 2 : 17.
494–25 Which of these two theories c· man
g 524–25 or is it a lie c· man and God?
gl 585–24 a finite belief c· life, substance, and

concession

sp 84–25 for without the c· of material personalities

concessions

a 33– 1 closed forever Jesus' ritualism or c· to matter.
m 56– 4 Jesus' c· . . . to material methods were
p 398– 7 the c· which Jesus was willing to make
t 456–18 Science makes no c· to persons or

conciliate

a 18–18 Christ, . . . could c· no nature above his own,
f 238–22 Attempts to c· society and so gain

conclude

s 143–19 but you c· that the stomach, blood, nerves,
f 217– 4 than to c· that individual musical tones
p 387– 6 we c· that intellectual labor
r 467–24 We reason imperfectly . . . when we c· that

concluded

sp 89–28 Cain very naturally c· that if life
f 222–26 c· that God never made a dyspeptic,
p 441– 9 He c· his charge thus :

concludes

ap 566–19 we may also offer the prayer which c· the

concluding

ap 573–24 This is Scriptural authority for c·

conclusion

any
s 120–25 Any c· *pro* or *con*, deduced from supposed
blind
s 124–11 In a word, human belief is a blind c·
fair
g 555– 3 A fair c· from this might be,
false
g 525–27 the false c· of the material senses.
no other
sp 109–10 This proof once seen, no other c· can be reached.
premise or
s 129– 6 can tolerate no error in premise or c·.
scientific
b 279–26 A logical and scientific c· is reached
Scriptural
p 383–27 the Scriptural c· concerning a man,
this
p 425– 2 Mortal mind, not matter, induces this c·

s 128–32 c·, if properly drawn, cannot be false.
ph 167–17 error in the premise must appear in the c·.
f 231–17 Therefore we accept the c· that discords
b 277–28 error in the premise leads to errors in the c·
278–24 and leads to the c· that if man is
279– 6 The doom of matter establishes the c·
316–16 which led to the c· that the
340– 7 "Let us hear the c· of the whole— *Eccl.* 12 : 13.
340– 9 Let us hear the c· of the whole matter :
o 347–10 the c· would be that there is nothing
433– 6 His c· is, that laws of nature render

conclusions

absolute
s 109–21 and I won my way to absolute c·
doctrines and
g 545–14 into all human doctrines and c·,
false
s 121–22 deluded the judgment and induced false c·.
f 204– 3 All forms of error support the false c·
p 417–30 by certain fears and false c·,
his
403–30 truth or error which influences his c·.
human
b 298– 1 are the vague realities of human c·.
logical
b 270–10 are scientific and logical c· reached.
my
s 108–12 My c· were reached by allowing the
one's
c 259–32 Deducing one's c· as to man from
our
p 397– 5 By not perceiving . . . we are misled in our c·
spiritual
b 300– 2 it attempts to draw correct spiritual c·
such
p 392–25 Admitting only such c· as you wish
their own
p 418– 2 the baneful effects of their own c·.
unanimous
an 100–19 we have come to the unanimous c·

sp 84– 2 nor with the c· of mortal beliefs.
ph 184– 2 premises being erroneous, the c· are wrong.

conclusions

b 269–13 does not enter into metaphysical premises or c·.
338–10 premises and c· of material and mortal
g 547–10 strengthens the thinker's c· as to the

conclusive

an 101–14 promised by Monsieur Berna . . . as c·,
101–16 are certainly not c· in favor of the **doctrine**
s 159– 8 The evidence was found to be c·,

conclusively

s 108–16 proves c· that three times three
123–11 The verity of Mind shows c·
f 204– 6 that mortal error is as c· mental

concomitant

r 484–28 *Question.* — Is materiality the c·

concomitants

ph 196–16 sin, and death are not c· of Life or Truth.

concord

pref viii– 7 and gives sweet c· to sound.
m 60–25 calls discord harmony, not appreciating c·.
s 129–25 Can we . . . learn from discord the c· of being?
148–23 c· and unity of Spirit and His likeness.
f 216–26 "What c· hath Christ with— *II Cor.* 6 : 15.
240–11 In the order of Science, . . . all is one grand c·.
t 453– 4 when he distinguishes c· from discord.
g 539–25 what c· hath Christ with— *II Cor.* 6 : 15.

concordant

m 58– 6 they should be c· in order to blend properly.

concords

s 130–14 good and its sweet c· have all-power.

concur

b 319–14 Spirit and matter neither c· in man nor in

condemn

pr 11– 9 which has the right to acquit or c·,
o 341– 1 strictures on this volume would c·
p 433–23 which material laws c· as homicide.
435–33 If they c· him not, neither shall
435–34 neither shall Judge Medicine c· him ;
437– 7 a determination to c· Man
t 444–19 and never to c· rashly.
g 522–31 Does the creator c· His own creation?

condemnation

sp 85–28 never spared hypocrisy the sternest c·.
ph 183–12 error, first caused the c· of man
f 232–24 sealed God's c· of sin, sickness, and death.
g 545– 7 The c· of mortals to till the ground

condemnations

o 342– 5 unqualified c· of scientific Mind-healing,

condemned

a 43–22 Human law had c· him,
s 144–15 belongs to the . . . senses, and its use is to be c·.
p 436–26 taken into custody, tried, and c·.
440– 2 when it c· Mortal Man on the ground of
t 443– 9 at times severely c· by some Scientists,
459–10 c· for failing to take the first step.
g 539–16 God c· this lie as to man's origin

condemning

g 539–17 by c· its symbol, the serpent,

condemns

s 132–22 and c· the cure of the sick and sinning if it
t 448– 6 but which the heart c·, has no foundation ;
g 532–11 c· material man and remands him to dust.

condition

abnormal
p 423–27 Ossification or any abnormal c·
action and
p 420–27 power over every physical action and c·.
best
s 125– 2 What is now considered the best c·
bodily
p 394–10 The admission that any bodily c·
celestial
m 61– 7 The attainment of this celestial c·
diseased
ph 193–22 The diseased c· had continued there
f 217–17 have once conquered a diseased c·
earthly
a 30– 6 partook partly of Mary's earthly c·,
elastic
s 161– 1 the supple and elastic c· of the healthy limb,
material
sp 74– 5 and their return to a material c·,
p 389– 5 and every erroneous belief, or material c·.
410–15 The more difficult seems the material c·
mental
ph 181–19 you must improve your mental c·
p 397– 8 Suffering is no less a mental c· than
moral
s 139–32 The moral c· of such a man demands
natural
b 321–23 restored his hand to its natural c·

condition

negative
ph 173–15 to pass through a negative *c·* would be
of matter
s 120–15 Health is not a *c·* of matter, but of Mind ;
b 321–20 and not a *c·* of matter,
p 371– 1 to discover the *c·* of matter,
of mortality
f 215–23 Every quality and *c·* of mortality is lost,
old
sp 74–12 and never returns to the old *c·*.
original
sp 74– 7 the restoration to its original *c·* of the
our own
o 348–24 by so doing our own *c·* can be improved
physical
a 46–20 Jesus' unchanged physical *c·* after what
b 297–10 change in . . . affects the physical *c·*,
p 411–25 cherished in mortal mind as the physical *c·*
primitive
f 244–17 hypothesis that he returns . . . to his primitive *c·* ;
proper
p 383–20 must be clean to keep the body in proper *c·*.
quality or
f 230– 3 to destroy a quality or *c·* of Truth?
b 299– 4 his conception of an unseen quality or *c·*,
regulates the
p 413– 7 Mind regulates the *c·* of the stomach,
sinless
o 344– 5 sinless *c·* of man in divine Science,
source and
ph 181– 2 God, is the source and *c·* of all existence
spiritual
t 460–27 to impart, . . . from her own spiritual *c·*,
subjective
ph 189–32 matter is the subjective *c·* of mortal mind.
superinduced
sp 89–15 without study or a superinduced *c·*,
that
f 217–18 that *c·* never recurs,
p 408–29 that *c·* of the body which we call sensation
their
f 211– 2 if they talk to us, tell us their *c·*,
p 394–23 Will you tell the sick that their *c·* is hopeless,
this
ph 193– 7 the evidence of this *c·* of the bone.
o 349–21 Out of this *c·* grew the prophecy
p 371–19 the only way out of this *c·*.

———

sp 72– 6 A *c·* precedent to communion with Spirit
ph 182–30 To admit that sickness is a *c·* over which
188–14 recognizes his *c·* to be wholly a state of
p 392–27 When the *c·* is present which you say induces

conditional

r 486–19 belief, which makes harmony *c·* upon death

conditions

all
f 220–30 Mortal mind forms all *c·* of the mortal body,
bodily
f 217–10 unnatural mental and bodily *c·*,
228–22 never depend on bodily *c·*, structure, or
p 368–20 That Life is not contingent on bodily *c·*
can make no
s 120–12 No ! for matter can make no *c·* for man.
discordant
p 369– 2 he is liable to admit also . . . discordant *c·*,
diseased
p 403– 2 induced their own diseased *c·*.
excited
p 417–10 there will be no reaction from . . . excited *c·*.
false
p 368–26 and these false *c·* are the source of
healthy
s 162–22 carious bones have been restored to healthy *c·*.
its own
b 297–32 A mortal belief fulfils its own *c·*.
p 422–26 holding that matter forms its own *c·*
material
(*see* **material**)
mental
s 153–29 we shall be more careful of our mental *c·*,
154– 3 Disease arises, like other mental *c·*,
159–12 Is it skilful . . . to take no heed of mental *c·*
moral
s 125– 5 Moral *c·* will be found always harmonious
c 260–23 evolves bad physical and moral *c·*.
normal
p 412–26 corresponds with the normal *c·* of health
of matter
s 162–15 faculties of Spirit exist without the *c·* of matter
of sin
g 556–10 Mortal belief infolds the *c·* of sin.
opposite
sp 74–27 the gulf which divides two such opposite *c·*

conditions

physical
sp 77– 8 mortal mind creates its own physical *c·*.
s 150–27 physical *c·* all his earthly days,
these
p 373–29 we call these *c·* disease.
unsuitable
t 455– 5 unsuitable *c·* for healing the sick.
untoward
p 385–16 and all untoward *c·*, *if without sin,*
ways and
b 317–15 not only in all time, but in *all ways* and *c·*.

———

o 343–22 the *c·* of its acceptance,
p 368–26 its *c·* are illusions,
413– 4 contemplation of physical wants or *c·*
413– 5 induces those very *c·*.
g 549– 3 takes place apart from sexual *c·*.

conduct

p 384–23 if . . . you are not fit to *c·* your own case

confer

m 61– 2 The senses *c·* no real enjoyment.
s 132–28 Did the doctrines . . . *c·* healing power

conferred

r 478–29 I *c·* not with flesh — *Gal.* 1 : 16.
gl 581– 1 the name often *c·* upon him in Scripture,

confers

pref viii–14 Christian healing *c·* the most health and
a 40– 1 once admit that evil *c·* no pleasure,
sp 89–23 influence or action of Soul *c·* a freedom,
s 151–11 the enlarged power it *c·* to benefit the race
157–24 Erring mortal mind *c·* the power
f 217– 2 through the understanding which Science *c·*
c 265–12 but *c·* upon man enlarged individuality,
b 298–30 Human conjecture *c·* upon angels its own forms
p 366–19 Love which alone *c·* the healing power.
404–23 show him that sin *c·* no pleasure,
418–20 Truth is affirmative, and *c·* harmony.
g 512–26 *c·* animal names and natures upon its
555–27 or that Truth *c·* the ability to

confess

pr 8–24 We *c·* to having a very wicked heart
p 374–18 You *c·* to ignorance of the future
g 533–27 finds woman the first to *c·* her fault.

confesseth

t 448–18 whoso *c·* and forsaketh them — *Prov.* 28 : 13.

confession

s 138– 4 Peter's *c·* of the true Messiah.

confessional

pr 5–22 Prayer is not to be used as a *c·*

confidence

m 58–18 the sweet interchange of *c·* and love ;
59–13 their sympathies should blend in sweet *c·*
68–10 The presence of mistrust, where *c·* is due,
s 155– 7 individual *c·* in the drug,
p 368– 3 The *c·* inspired by Science lies in the fact
397–21 in exact proportion to your . . . *c·* in God
t 443– 7 tends to deter those, . . . from entire *c·* in

confident

s 132– 2 *c·* that this exhibition of the divine power

confides

a 23–31 and *c·* all to God.

confine

m 58–17 jealousy, which would *c·* a wife or a husband

confined

a 32–21 if the sacrament is *c·* to the use of bread and
sp 73–22 incorrect is the belief that spirit is *c·*
ph 193– 1 *c·* to his bed six months with hip-disease,
f 214– 5 If Enoch's perception had been *c·* to the
b 331– 1 Life is no more *c·* to the forms
p 390–16 and then you will not be *c·* to a sick-room
429–32 That statement is not *c·* to spiritual life,
r 467–23 Spirit, Soul, is not *c·* in man,
g 508–19 The word is not *c·* to sexuality,

confinement

p 431–18 getting Mortal Man into close *c·*

confines

s 108–19 When apparently near the *c·* of
p 401–31 *c·* himself chiefly to mental reconstruction

confirm

ph 199–22 Exceptions only *c·* this rule,
f 243–12 in order to *c·* and repeat the
p 432–24 was required to *c·* his testimony.

confirmation

r 488– 2 result of our teachings is their sufficient *c·*.

confirmed

a 54–27 and history has *c·* the prediction.
sp 94–18 our Master *c·* his words by his works.
s 131–26 The mission of Jesus *c·* prophecy,
gl 581– 1 This view of Satan is *c·* by the

confirming
   p 383–27 *c·* the Scriptural conclusion concerning a man,

confirms
   pr 6–32 language of our Master *c·* this description.
   m 69–14 unfolds all creation, *c·* the Scriptures,
   sp 94–17 The progress of truth *c·* its claims,
   an 105–28 and *c·* the ancient axiom :
   s 120–28 *c·* that testimony as legitimate
   p 370–13 This *c·* my theory that

conflict
   m 69–19 and not *c·* with the scientific sense of God's
   sp 96–31 During this final *c·*, wicked minds will
   f 226–30 I saw before me the awful *c·*,
   b 288– 4 the mental *c·* between the evidence of the
   288–11 the *c·* between truth and error,
   ap 567–12 Thus endeth the *c·* between the

conflicting
   sp 96–13 even now becoming the arena for *c·* forces.
   b 273–29 *c·* mortal opinions and beliefs
   o 355–14 relative value of the two *c·* theories
   t 447– 7 *c·* selfish motives, and ignorant attempts

conflicts
   an 104–10 First, people say it *c·* with the Bible.
   o 361–14 This declaration of Jesus, understood, *c·* not

conform
   p 412–22 *c·* the argument so as to destroy the evidence
   t 445– 1 Scientist must *c·* to God's requirements.

conformity
   b 337– 9 in *c·* with Christ.

confounded
   o 358– 6 Such doctrines are "confusion worse *c·*."
   gl 597–25 hence it should not be *c·* with the

confounds
   o 346– 1 I regret that such criticism *c· man* with Adam.

confronts
   t 452–13 When error *c·* you, withhold not the rebuke

confused
   s 116–26 *c·* and erroneous conceptions of divinity
   g 506–25 the human concept and divine idea seem *c·*

confusion
   b 304–28 liable to be misapprehended and lost in *c·*.
   o 358– 5 Such doctrines are "*c·* worse confounded."
   gl 581–21 higher false knowledge builds . . . the more *c·*

congestion
   p 408–23 as perceptibly as would *c·* of the brain,

congestive
   p 384–18 *c·* symptoms in the lungs, or hints of

congratulate
   t 448–13 do not *c·* yourself upon your

congregate
   gl 595– 9 superstructure, where mortals *c·* for worship.

Congregational Church
   o 351– 8 author became a member of the orthodox *C· C·*

conjectural
   ph 176–21 weigh down mankind with . . . *c·* evils.
   f 229–20 law of mortal mind, *c·* and speculative,

conjecture
   b 298–30 Human *c·* confers upon angels its own forms
   330–17 knowledge of it is left either to human *c·* or

conjectured
   f 245–16 *c·* that she must be under twenty.

conjectures
   b 304–32 So man, . . . is abandoned to *c·*,
   g 504–26 human doctrines, hypotheses, and vague *c·*

conjoin
   m 57– 9 These different elements *c·* naturally

conjoined
   p 378– 2 and causes the two to appear *c·*,

conjugal
   m 65–29 has brought *c·* infidelity to the surface,
   66–17 Amidst gratitude for *c·* felicity,
   66–18 Amidst *c·* infelicity, it is well to hope,

conjure
   p 403–23 Never *c·* up some new discovery from

connate
   pref viii–20 the response deducible from two *c·* facts,

connect
   a 37– 9 human links which *c·* one stage with another
   r 491–11 Matter cannot *c·* mortals with the true origin

connected
   s 145–20 Indeed, its . . . effects are indissolubly *c·*.
   p 389–31 complication of symptoms *c·* with this belief.
   408–25 less intimately *c·* with the mind than

connection
   sp 98–25 that which they call *science* has no proper *c·* with
   ph 178–10 *c·* of past mortal thoughts with present.
   b 292–30 real man's indissoluble *c·* with his God,
   o 350–28 that life-link forming the *c·* through which
   ap 560– 1 in *c·* with the nineteenth century.

conquer
   b 317–20 enables him to *c·* sin, disease, and
   324–16 in which we must *c·* sin, sickness, and death,
   339–31 You *c·* error by denying its verity.
   p 393– 9 and can *c·* sickness, sin, and death.
   394–26 Is there no divine permission to *c·* discord
   405– 7 to *c·* lust with chastity,
   419–28 you must *c·* your own fears

conquered
   a 53–29 he had not *c·* all the beliefs of the flesh
   f 217–16 When you have once *c·* a diseased condition
   231– 4 Unless an ill is rightly met . . . the ill is never *c·*.
   b 309– 8 He had *c·* material error with
   p 380– 3 must be finally *c·* by eternal Life.
   400– 6 This error *c·*, we can despoil
   405–27 You are *c·* by the moral penalties you incur
   407– 7 is *c·* only by a mighty struggle.
   425–24 when faith in matter has been *c·*.
   ap 564–16 met and *c·* sin in every form.

conquering
   f 253–14 I hope that you are *c·* this false sense.
   c 262–23 and *c·* all that is unlike God.

conquers
   p 378–26 and finally *c·* it.

conquest
   p 418– 2 Show them that the *c·* over sickness,
   ap 568–26 What shall we say of the mighty *c·* over all sin?

conscience
   pref x–11 The author has not compromised *c·*
   a 28–11 In *c·*, we cannot hold to beliefs outgrown ;
   an 106– 9 self-government, reason, and *c·*,
   f 222–31 "asking no question for *c·* sake."—*I Cor.* 10 : 25.
   p 405–23 to endure the cumulative effects of a guilty *c·*.

conscientious
   pr 12–13 prayers were deep and *c·* protests of Truth,
   s 163– 8 said : "I declare my *c·* opinion,
   t 451–19 every *c·* teacher of the Science of Mind-healing,

conscientiously
   o 343–30 Whoever is the first meekly and *c·*

conscious
   pr 14–12 Become *c·* for a single moment that
   sp 82–19 and were in as *c·* a state of existence
   s 125–13 of *c·* pain and painlessness,
   ph 166– 6 thus the *c·* control over the body is lost.
   f 209–31 a *c·*, constant capacity to understand God.
   213–25 Mental melodies . . . supersede *c·* sound.
   250– 9 which never errs. and is ever *c·* ;
   b 302– 6 *c·* infinitude of existence and of all identity
   p 374– 6 Because mortal mind seems to be *c·*,
   379–29 images, . . . frighten *c·* thought.
   390–32 Rise in the *c·* strength of the spirit of Truth
   400–14 before it has taken tangible shape in *c·* thought,
   409–13 independently of this so-called *c·* mind,
   409–16 *c·* mortal mind is believed to be superior
   423–24 the stimulus of courage and *c·* power.
   435– 6 would console *c·* Mortal Mind,
   r 475–16 *c·* identity of being as found in Science,
   484–14 the *c·* and unconscious thoughts of mortals.
   g 521– 2 above earth . . . to *c·* spiritual harmony
   ap 569– 8 when we are *c·* of the supremacy of Truth,
   573–26 can become *c·*, here and now, of a cessation of
   574–12 It exalted him till he became *c·* of the
   gl 593– 5 the *c·* facts of spiritual Truth.

consciously
   sp 87– 6 to be individually and *c·* present.
   ph 174– 2 as *c·* as do civilized practitioners by their
   199–18 whether this development is produced *c·* or
   b 308–15 talked with God as *c·* as man talks with man.
   p 374–11 before it is *c·* apparent on the body,
   403– 4 voluntary mesmerism is induced *c·*
   ap 576–24 man possesses this recognition of harmony *c·*

consciousness
abiding
   p 405–24 The abiding *c·* of wrong-doing
corporeal
   m 67–27 Spiritual, not corporeal, *c·* is needed.
develops
   r 489–10 and as *c·* develops, this belief goes out,
differing
   sp 82–28 Different dreams . . . betoken a differing *c·*.
disappear from
   o 347–29 and sickness will disappear from *c·*.
divine
   g 531–13 exchanging human concepts for the divine *c·*,
   gl 598–23 One moment of divine *c·*,

consigns
 sp 77–28 Spiritism *c·* the so-called dead to a
 g 542–24 To envy's own hell, justice *c·* the lie
consist
 f 233– 3 These proofs *c·* solely in the destruction of sin,
 r 470– 3 brotherhood of man would *c·* of Love and Truth,
consisted
 gl 597– 3 Judaic religion *c·* mostly of rites and
consistency
 f 242–26 one web of *c·* without seam or rent.
 o 341– 7 grow in beauty and *c·* from one grand root,
    354–18 *C·* is seen in example more than in precept.
 t 443– 3 as to the propriety, advantage, and *c·* of
consistent
 pr 9–32 *C·* prayer is the desire to do right.
 m 65– 7 If the foundations of human affection are *c·*
 f 254– 2 Individuals are *c·* who, watching and
 t 458–27 honest and *c·* in following the leadings of
 g 547–16 Darwin's theory . . . is more *c·* than most
consistently
 pr 9–10 by living *c·* with our prayer?
consisteth
 g 544– 9 Life *c·* not of the things which a man eateth.
consisting
 f 221– 7 this meal *c·* of only a thin slice of bread
consists
 s 123–19 The revelation *c·* of two parts :
 ph 184– 8 remedy *c·* in probing the trouble to the bottom
 b 323– 3 This strife *c·* in the endeavor to forsake error
 t 462–21 and *c·* in the dissection of thoughts
 g 503– 1 *c·* of the unfolding of spiritual ideas
consolation
 pref xii–25 and is joyful to bear *c·* to the sorrowing
console
 p 435– 6 Reverend Theology would *c·*
 ap 574– 4 adapted to *c·* the weary pilgrim,
consoles
 gl 582–12 that which comforts, *c·*, and supports
consolidation
 ph 185–30 which is but a mortal *c·* of
consoling
 pr 7–29 and *c·* ourselves in the midst of
consonance
 ph 168–16 all in *c·* with the laws of God,
 p 407–12 is in *c·* with common mortal belief.
consonant
 g 501–13 is *c·* with ever-present Love.
conspicuous
 m 65–13 broadcast powers of evil so *c·* to-day
 g 539–31 so *c·* in the birth of Jesus,
conspiracies
 f 246–19 *c·* against manhood and womanhood.
conspiracy
 b 339–15 He is joining in a *c·* against himself,
 p 434–26 we shall unearth this foul *c·*
    438–16 *c·* against the rights and life of man.
conspirators
 a 49– 8 Were all *c·* save eleven?
 p 405–10 if you would not cherish an army of *c·*
conspired
 a 47–10 Judas *c·* against Jesus.
constancy
 m 60– 9 mother-love includes purity and *c·*,
 r 488–10 understanding, trust, *c·*, firmness.
 gl 582– 1 BELIEVING. Firmness and *c·* ;
constant
 pr 15–27 purity, and affection are *c·* prayers.
 a 22– 4 sensuality causing *c·* retrogression,
    23– 5 The atonement requires *c·* self-immolation
    24– 1 *to believe* means also *to be firm* or *to be c·*.
 m 58– 1 To happify existence by *c·* intercourse
 s 130– 1 petty intellect is alarmed by *c·* appeals to Mind.
 f 209–31 conscious, *c·* capacity to understand God.
 p 382– 8 *C·* bathing and rubbing to alter the
    385–15 *C·* toil, deprivations, exposures, and
 t 451– 2 the *c·* pressure of the apostolic command
constantly
 a 21–10 He *c·* turns away from material sense,
 ph 189–23 we *c·* ascend in infinite being.
 f 235–14 uplifting thoughts . . . *c·* imparted to pupils,
 p 403–16 Mortal mind is *c·* producing on mortal body
    413–25 *c·* directing the mind to such signs,
 t 453–11 with some . . . symptoms *c·* reappear.
 r 492–14 New thoughts are *c·* obtaining the floor.
 g 524– 6 *c·* went after "strange gods."— *Jer.* 5 : 19.
    548–32 increase their numbers naturally and *c·*
 gl 598– 8 our Master had *c·* to employ words of

consternation
 p 434– 3 *C·* fills the prison-yard.
constituent
 f 209–17 relations which *c·* masses hold to each other,
constituents
 m 58– 9 these *c·* of thought, mingling,
 t 460– 4 the necessary *c·* and relations of all beings,''
constitute
 a 53–26 mortal errors which *c·* the material body,
 m 58– 9 *c·* individually and collectively true happiness,
    63– 6 The beautiful, good, and pure *c·* his ancestry.
 b 274–21 false beliefs and their products *c·* the flesh,
    331–26 Life, Truth, and Love *c·* the triune
 p 430–24 Greed and Ingratitude, *c·* the jury.
 r 470– 5 unity of Principle and spiritual power which *c·*
    488–14 Do the five corporeal senses *c·* man?
 g 503– 9 divine Principle and idea *c·* spiritual harmony,
    516– 5 Life, intelligence, Truth, and Love, which *c·*
constituted
 f 229–15 mortal belief has *c·* itself a law
 p 437–27 judicial proceedings of a regularly *c·* court.
 r 466– 9 personalities *c·* of mind and matter,
constitutes
 m 57– 4 Union of the . . . qualities *c·* completeness.
 sp 76–25 *c·* the only veritable, indestructible man,
    85– 7 Such intuitions reveal whatever *c·* and
 ph 172– 1 *c·* his happiness or misery.
    173– 1 When we admit that matter . . . *c·* man,
    183– 5 To suppose that God *c·* laws of inharmony
    194–19 education *c·* this so-called mind,
 b 283–21 false belief as to what really *c·* life
    289– 6 overcome by the understanding of what *c·* man
    297– 9 the understanding of what *c·* health ;
    301–13 *c·* the only real and eternal entity.
    305–15 *c·* the underlying reality of reflection.
    316–21 whom Spirit creates, *c·*, and governs.
    340–23 *c·* the brotherhood of man ;
 r 479–14 which *c·* matter's supposed selfhood,
 g 527–16 *c·* evil and mortal knowledge.
 ap 560–14 *c·* the kingdom of heaven in man.
constituting
 s 110– 2 filling all space, *c·* all Science,
 p 388–19 *c·* a "kingdom divided against— *Matt.* 12 : 25.
    393–28 iris and pupil, *c·* the visual organism.
Constitution
 s 161–14 in harmony with our *C·* and Bill of Rights,
constitutions
 m 61–13 better balanced minds, and sounder *c·*.
 ph 175– 6 there will be better *c·* and less disease.
    197–26 Many of the effeminate *c·* of our time
constructing
 g 522–27 supposedly cooperating with matter in *c·*
construction
 r 489–27 no organic *c·* can give it hearing
constructor
 p 369–12 or the *c·* of any form of existence.
constructs
 p 399–17 It *c·* a machine, manages it,
    402–14 mortal mind *c·* the mortal body
    425–23 Consciousness *c·* a better body when
 gl 580–29 not one who *c·* and sustains reality
construe
 a 30–30 though they may not so *c·* our words.
construed
 p 436–31 *c·* obedience to the law of divine Love as
consult
 a 21–17 We have separate time-tables to *c·*,
 s 160–27 Why then *c·* anatomy to learn
 ph 165–18 Then you *c·* your brain in order to
    171– 9 not needing to *c·* almanacs for the
 f 222–29 *c·* matter not at all,
consultation
 p 433–16 A brief *c·* ensues,
consulted
 s 159–14 as if matter were the only factor to be *c·*?
 t 443– 1 When the discoverer of C. S. is *c·*
consulting
 s 163–22 "*C·* the records of our science,
 f 222–15 *c·* the stomach less about the
consume
 pr 10–28 that ye may *c·* it upon your lusts."— *Jas.* 4 : 3.
 f 205– 4 drop with drunkenness, *c·* with disease,
 p 425–19 and know that there is nothing to *c·*,
consuming
 f 252–30 shine with the resplendency of *c·* fire.
 ap 558–19 described by John the Baptist as *c·* error.

continuity

m 69–11 neither closes man's *c* nor his sense of
s 123–29 the scientific order and *c* of being.
124–25 Spirit is the life, substance, and *c* of
f 246–50 loveliness, freshness, and *c*,
b 325–14 understood in all its perfection, *c*, and might,
g 513–20 existence and *c* . . . remain in God,

continuous

s 157–30 proof that Life is *c* and harmonious.
p 397–12 by believing them to be real and *c*.

contract

m 58–12 Never *c* the horizon of a worthy outlook
s 160–16 when the cords *c* and become immovable?

contracted

s 160–31 Is a stiff joint or a *c* muscle

contradict

an 105– 7 would be to *c* precedent
s 110– 2 *c* forever the belief that
118–29 Therefore they *c* the divine decrees
122– 5 great facts of Life, . . . *c* their false witnesses,
149–22 The logic is lame, and facts *c* it.
f 202–24 *c* the practice growing out of them.
232–14 but religions which *c* its Principle are false.
b 277–22 suppositions *c* even the order of material
o 358– 6 If two statements directly *c* each other
p 389–22 Materialists *c* their own statements.
391–29 Mentally *c* every complaint from the body,
407–21 If delusion says, "I have lost my memory," *c* it.
r 489–21 An affirmative reply would *c* the Scripture,

contradicting

b 297–22 *c* the testimony of material sense,
298–13 Spiritual sense, *c* the material senses,
gl 596–26 C. S., *c* sense, maketh the valley to bud

contradiction

s 163–28 so much absurdity, *c*, and falsehood.
c 257–31 phrase *infinite form* involves a *c* of terms.
r 472–17 Error is the *c* of Truth.
g 504–28 and the *c* of Spirit is matter,
526–23 in *c* of the first creation?
545–26 Hence the seeming *c* in that Scripture,

contradictions

s 129– 2 So in C. S. there are no discords nor *c*,
b 289–26 spiritual fact and the . . . are *c* ;
335–31 and must be *c* of reality.
r 481– 9 The various *c* of the Science of Mind

contradictory

o 341– 8 appear *c* when subjected to such usage.
345–14 in this volume of mine there are no *c*
358– 8 Is Science thus *c* ?
358–13 C. S. is neither made up of *c* aphorisms
r 492–15 These two *c* theories
g 537–27 made to appear *c* in some places,
546– 9 Is C. S. *c* ?

contradicts

sp 93–18 Whatever *c* the real nature of the divine
s 119–25 one finds that it *c* the evidence before the senses
152–13 in which one statement *c* another
ph 170–11 not only *c* human systems, but points to
178–20 but this so-called mind, . . . *c* itself,
f 213– 1 Whoever *c* this mortal mind supposition
b 278–23 *c* the demonstration of life as Spirit,
279–25 *c* alike revelation and right reasoning.
281– 8 Divine Science *c* the corporeal senses,
287– 7 Divine Science *c* this postulate
303–14 but the statement . . . *c* this
o 345–11 mind which *c* itself neither knows itself nor
353– 8 Truth which *c* the evidence of error,
r 485– 5 Whatever *c* this statement is the false sense,
493– 4 science *c* this, and explains the solar system
g 526– 7 *c* the teaching of the first chapter,
529–26 and should rejoice that evil, . . . *c* itself
538–20 Until that which *c* the truth of being
gl 584–16 for it *c* the spiritual facts of being.

contradistinction

s 114– 5 in *c* to the divine Mind, or Truth
p 418– 1 Stick to the truth of being in *c* to the error
g 522– 1 it is the false history in *c* to the true.
538–22 the unreal in *c* to the real and eternal.

contraries

b 303–15 can never make both these *c* true.
p 372–21 and hope to succeed with *c* ?
r 466–11 contrasting pairs of terms represent *c*,

contrarieties

s 163–29 To harmonize the *c* of medical doctrines is

contrariwise

s 130–28 ought we not, *c*, to be astounded at the

contrary

pref xi– 4 On the *c*, C. S. rationally explains
a 21–20 On the *c*, if my friends pursue my course,
44–24 On the *c*, it was a divinely natural act,
53–13 above and *c* to the world's religious sense.

contrary

sp 71–31 a theory *c* to C. S.
83–21 It is *c* to C. S. to suppose that life
86–11 Opposites come from *c* directions,
s 123–32 On the *c*, C. S. is pre-eminently scientific,
129–10 with your preconceptions or utterly *c* to them.
150–21 and *c* to the law of divine Mind.
160–23 never capable of acting *c* to mental direction.
ph 172–18 On the *c*, man is the image and likeness of
173–14 Matter is Spirit's *c*,
183– 7 however much is said to the *c*.
f 222–28 *c* to His commands.
230–11 It would be *c* to our highest ideas of God
b 270– 5 One is *c* to the other
273– 2 claims of sin, sickness, and death are *c* to God,
274– 9 Ideas, on the *c*, are born of Spirit,
275–30 *c* to the one Spirit.
339– 9 evil, being *c* to good, is unreal,
o 349– 8 annulled material law by healing *c* to it.
p 431– 3 Notwithstanding my rules to the *c*,
434– 4 Some exclaim, "It is *c* to law and justice."
435–31 to be smitten *c* to the law?"— *Acts* 23 : 3.
441–29 a verdict *c* to law and gospel.
t 456– 3 but *c* to its spirit or rules,
r 479– 5 On the *c*, if aught comes from God,

contrast

a 34–29 What a *c* between our Lord's last supper and
b 272–20 in *c* with the results of the ghastly farce
272–22 in *c* with the downward tendencies and

contrasting

r 466–10 these *c* pairs of terms represent

contrasts

f 252–15 *c* strikingly with the testimony of Spirit.

contributing

o 356–13 not *c* in any way to each other's happiness

contribution

gl 595–22 TITHE. *C* ; tenth part ; homage ;

contrition

p 364– 9 or the *c* of the Magdalen?

control (noun)

absolute
ph 177– 6 divine Mind's healing power and absolute *c*
attested the
sp 80–23 attested the *c* of mortal mind over its
complete
p 417–28 the complete *c* which Mind holds over the body.
conscious
ph 166– 6 thus the conscious *c* over the body is lost.
despotic
an 102–27 It implies the exercise of despotic *c*,
divine
pr 9–23 recognizes only the divine *c* of Spirit,
p 400–28 Without divine *c* there is discord,
God's
s 125– 7 Neither . . . is beyond God's *c* ;
his
a 25–22 Though demonstrating his *c* over sin and
r 482–21 enabled Jesus to demonstrate his *c* over matter.
hypnotic
p 402–31 the person under hypnotic *c*
Jesus'
p 369–11 All these deeds manifested Jesus' *c*
loss of
p 406–27 a loss of *c* over the body.
Mind's
ph 171–12 Mind's *c* over the universe, including man,
no
s 151–22 it has no *c* over God's man.
ph 182–31 To admit that . . . God has no *c*,
normal
p 406–30 normal *c* is gained through divine strength
other
sp 73–12 Any other *c* or attraction of so-called spirit
took
p 431–23 hypnotized the prisoner and took *c* of his mind,

a 30–27 allow Soul to hold the *c*, we shall loathe sin
sp 91– 3 beings under the *c* of supreme wisdom?
ph 167–28 impossible to gain *c* over the body in any
169–16 If we understood the *c* of Mind over body,
f 217–22 as you understand the *c* which Mind has over
217–24 will be able to demonstrate this *c*.
b 322– 5 gain the reality of Life, the *c* of Soul over sense,
p 380–10 we virtually contend against the *c* of Mind
389– 4 it will be given in behalf of the *c* of Mind
394–11 that any bodily condition is beyond the *c*
429– 5 the more simple demonstrations of *c*,
t 462–28 It teaches the *c* of mad ambition.
g 514–26 Understanding the *c* which Love held
544–16 under the *c* of the one Mind,

control (verb)
  sp 73– 8   belief that one man, as spirit, can *c·* another
     74–19   nor . . . return to fraternize with or *c·* the worm.
     93– 1   as substantial and able to *c·* the body?
  f 228–15   Then they will *c·* their own bodies
     228–23   and form and *c·* it with Truth.
     234–26   You must *c·* evil thoughts
     234–27   or they will *c·* you in the second.
  p 375–13   while the hypnotist . . . in order to *c·* him.
     377–29   and incompetent to *c·* it.
     378– 7   Disease is less than mind, and Mind can *c·* it.
     379– 1   If disease can attack and *c·* the body
     392–26   you will *c·* yourself harmoniously,
     414–10   impossibility that matter, brain, can *c·*
  r 485–29   as much as nerves *c·* sensation

controlled
  pr 14–17   *c·* by spiritual Life, Truth, and Love.
  sp 73–15   communed with mortals or *c·* them
     84– 9   *c·* not by demons, spirits, or demigods,
  s 125–18   man cannot be *c·* by sin or death,
     136–19   believed that Jesus was a medium, *c·* by
     136–25   Herod doubted if Jesus was *c·* by the
     143–20   *C·* by this belief, you continue in the old routine.
     143–24   body is not *c·* scientifically by a negative mind.
  ph 178– 5   *c·* by the majority of opinions,
     184–16   *C·* by the divine intelligence,
  b 292–10   belief that . . . Life be *c·* by death.
     303– 4   *c·* by Mind, the Principle
     304–16   Harmony is produced by its Principle, is *c·* by it
     304–28   *C·* by belief, instead of understanding,
     318–30   as numbers are *c·* and proved by
  o 356– 9   and *c·* sickness, sin, and death
  r 485–28   heathen gods of mythology *c·* war . . . as much as

controlling
  m 63– 3   never think that flannel was better . . . than the *c·*
  p 379– 6   jurisdiction of the world is in Mind, *c·* every
  t 451–28   action of one mortal mind *c·* another
  gl 583–27   so-called mortal mind *c·* mortal mind ;

controls
  sp 73–11   God *c·* man, and God is the only Spirit.
     79–28   asserting that Mind *c·* body and brain.
  s 121–24   simple rule that the greater *c·* the lesser.
     145–17   that in it Truth *c·* error.
  f 220–31   *c·* the stomach, bones, lungs, heart,
  b 319–19   Mind *c·* man and man has no Mind but God.
  p 400– 1   mortal mind, which directly *c·* the body?
  g 557– 6   Mind *c·* the birth-throes in the lower

convenient
  a 40– 6   when I have a *c·* season — *Acts* 24 : 25.
  sp 72–19   Error is not a *c·* sieve through which

convening
  pref xii–10   Christian Scientist Association, *c·* monthly ;

conventional
  b 274–25   The *c·* firm, called matter and mind,

conventionality
  pref vii–16   and the cold *c·* of materialism

conversation
  a 21– 2   overcoming error in your daily walk and *c·*,
  c 260–26   by *c·* about the body,

conversing
  p 424–24   thinking about your patients or *c·* with them,

conversion
  f 217– 7   Paul's peculiar Christian *c·* and experience,

convert
  b 272– 1   how shall they preach, *c·*, and heal multitudes,
  p 365–27   *c·* into a den of thieves the temple

converted
  a 38–30   and be *c·*, and I might heal you.
  o 350–22   should be *c·*, and I should heal — *Matt.* 13 : 15.

convey
  pref ix– 7   stammeringly attempts to *c·* his feeling.
  sp 86–32   before the artist can *c·* them to canvas.
  s 160–14   to *c·* the mandate of mind to muscle
  f 212–26   the lips or hands . . . in order to *c·* thought,
     212–27   we say . . . the undulations of the air *c·* sound,
  p 413–28   these actions *c·* mental images to
     432– 7   *c·* messages from my residence in matter,

conveyed
  f 243–19   If this information is *c·*,
  r 488– 8   *c·* by the English verb *believe ;*

conveying
  o 349–13   The chief difficulty in *c·* the teachings

conveys
  f 214–15   *c·* the impressions of Mind to man,
     243–19   mortal mind *c·* it.
  b 340– 4   This text . . . *c·* the C. S. thought,
  p 421– 5   *c·* the true definition of all human belief in

conviction
  abiding
    p 390–21   Dismiss it with an abiding *c·* that it
  common
    sp 80–30   common *c·* that mind and matter cooperate
  deep-lying
    pref xii–15   with a deep-lying *c·* that the next two years
  heavenly
    s 108– 1   Whence came to me this heavenly *c·*,
  honest
    p 418– 7   Plead with an honest *c·* of truth
  solid
    t 460–16   is more than fancy ; it is solid *c·*.

  sp 90–25   This *c·* shuts the door on death,
  s 108– 1   a *c·* antagonistic to the testimony of the
  p 377–27   *c·* of the necessity and power of
     384–25   When the fear subsides and the *c·* abides
     404–19   This *c·*, that there is no real pleasure in sin,

convictions
  pr 13– 5   In public prayer we often go beyond our *c·*,
  s 134– 8   one who suffers for his *c·*.
  r 494–18   helping . . . human sense to flee from its own *c·*

convince
  a 46–17   To *c·* Thomas of this, Jesus caused him
  an 101–22   *c·* her that it is not a remedial agent,
  b 327–27   *c·* the mortal of his mistake
  p 377– 1   mentally *c·* him that matter cannot take cold,
     377– 3   If grief causes suffering, *c·* the sufferer that
  g 522–23   *c·* reason and coincide with revelation

convinced
  pref x–27   soonest touched by Truth, and *c·* of it.
  a 35– 2   *C·* of the fruitlessness of their toil
     46– 3   This *c·* them of the truthfulness of
  f 240–25   *c·* of the error that is to be overcome.
  o 346–22   When a sufferer is *c·* that
  ap 564–10   The author is *c·* that the accusations

convinceth
  o 341– *   *Which of you c· me of sin? — John* 8 : 46.

convincing
  a 43–11   Jesus' last proof was the highest, the most *c·*,
  p 404– 7   *c·* him that there is no real pleasure in

convivial
  a 32–10   wine, used on *c·* occasions and in Jewish rites,

convulsed
  ph 195– 6   Every sound *c·* him with anguish.

convulses
  sp 80–25   It is mortal mind which *c·* its
  f 223–14   The question, . . . *c·* the world.

convulsions
  p 389–28   A case of *c·*, produced by

cook
  p 364–32   Did the careless doctor, the nurse, the *c·*,

cools
  p 374–27   body, when bereft of mortal mind, at first *c·*,

cooperate
  sp 80–31   belief . . . that mind and matter *c·*
  b 270– 2   theory, . . . that Mind and matter coexist and *c·*.
     279–13   Spirit and matter can neither coexist nor *c·*,

cooperates
  r 490– 9   Will . . . *c·* with appetite and passion.

cooperating
  p 398–25   So also faith, *c·* with a belief in
  g 522–26   Spirit as supposedly *c·* with matter

cooperation
  s 144– 4   needs no *c·* from lower powers,
  o 348–16   I deny His *c·* with evil,
  r 490–10   From this *c·* arises its evil.

coordinate
  sp 84– 1   Science is immortal and *c·* neither with
  r 468– 2   never can be *c·* with human illusions.
     472– 7   making it *c·* with all that is real
  g 537–22   *c·* with the Science of creation

copartnership
  b 274–28   destroy the imaginary *c·*,
  o 356–17   There is neither a present nor an eternal *c·*

cope
  p 423–22   has rendered himself strong, . . . to *c·* with

Copernicus
  s 121– 4   *C·* mapped out the stellar system,

copes
  p 378–26   Sickness is not a . . . power, which *c·* astutely

copies
  pref ix–25   *c·* were, however, in friendly circulation.

copious
  pref ix–27   she made *c·* notes of Scriptural exposition,

copy
  sp 87– 2   They *c·* or reproduce them, even when

copyist
　pr 16–13　addition to the prayer by a later *c·* ;
copyrighted
　pref ix–20　Her first pamphlet on C. S. was *c·* in 1870 ;
　r 465– 2　the author's class-book, *c·* in 1870.
corals
　sp 87–21　the sea is ignorant . . . of the *c·* ,
cords
　s 142–20　The strong *c·* of scientific demonstration,
　160–16　what does anatomy say when the *c·* contract
　r 474– 7　worse *c·* than those which cut the flesh.
Corinthians
　b 321– 3　As Paul says, in his first epistle to the *C·* ,
corner
　s 139–27　become "the head of the *c·*."— *Matt.* 21 : 42.
　p 380– 6　Truth is the rock of ages, the headstone of the *c·* ,
corner-stone
　f 241–26　*c·* of all spiritual building is purity.
corporeal
　pr 12–16　Prayer to a *c·* God affects the sick like
　13–20　If we pray to God as a *c·* person,
　13–26　is represented as a *c·* creator ;
　14– 2　If we . . . regard omnipotence as a *c·* ,
　m 67–27　Spiritual, not *c·* , consciousness is needed.
　sp 70–10　The supposition that *c·* beings are spirits,
　71–31　a *c·* being, a finite form,
　72– 9　So-called *spirits* are but *c·* communicators.
　74–28　and the physical, or *c·* .
　76–16　Neither will man seem to be *c·* ,
　s 116– 6　the evidence before the *c·* human senses,
　116–21　God is not *c·* , but *incorporeal*,
　116–22　Mortals are *c·* , but God is incorporeal.
　140– 4　That God is a *c·* being, nobody can truly affirm.
　141–16　the Christ-spirit which governed the *c·* Jesus.
　144–21　Truth, and not *c·* will, is the divine power
　ph 167– 1　Should we implore a *c·* God to heal
　c 255–14　That God is *c·* or material, no man should
　258– 1　A mortal, *c·* , or finite conception of God
　b 284– 6　If God were limited . . . God would be *c·* ,
　285–23　By interpreting God as a *c·* Saviour
　309– 2　the messenger was not a *c·* being,
　312–14　People go into ecstasies over the sense of a *c·*
　328– 2　silences the material or *c·* .
　332–17　The *c·* man Jesus was human.
　334– 3　not that the *c·* Jesus was one with the
　334–14　the eternal Christ and the *c·* Jesus
　p 402– 9　forsake its *c·* , structural, and material basis,
　408–28　in the *c·* substratum of brain
　t 443– 5　a resort to faith in *c·* means
　453–19　You uncover sin, . . . to bless the *c·* man ;
　g 549–19　the most complicated *c·* structures,
　550–16　contemplation of existence as material and *c·*
　ap 561–20　material and *c·* selfhood disappear,
　577– 8　God as Father-Mother, not as a *c·* being.
　gl 587–21　HAM (Noah's son). *C·* belief ;
　589– 1　ISSACHAR (Jacob's son). A *c·* belief ;
　589–16　JESUS. The highest human *c·* concept
　589–23　JUDAH. A *c·* material belief
　590–11　LEVI (Jacob's son). A *c·* and sensual belief ;
　591– 1　physical sense of God as finite and *c·* .
　592–27　PHARISEE. *C·* and sensuous belief ;
　　　　(see also **mortal, sense, senses**)
corporealities
　sp 71–28　Its spirits are so many *c·* ,
corporeality
　above
　　g 512– 2　aspirations soaring beyond and above *c·*
　applied to
　　gl 599– 3　YOU. As applied to *c·* , a mortal ; finity.
　entire
　　s 157–28　C. S. impresses the entire *c·* ,
　governed by
　　g 536–15　governed by *c·* instead of divine Principle,
　groundwork of
　　sp 84– 6　a groundwork of *c·* and human belief.
　inability of
　　r 494–16　Jesus demonstrated the inability of *c·* ,
　no
　　b 305– 8　there is no *c·* in the mirrored form,
　nor mind
　　gl 584–17　error ; neither *c·* nor mind ;
　not bounded by
　　sp 84–20　Mind is infinite, not bounded by *c·* ,

　s 138–12　diseases were cast out neither by *c·* , . . . nor
　140–11　warring no more over the *c·* .
　ph 192– 8　from *c·* instead of from Principle,
　b 284–10　nor be fully manifested through *c·* .
　g 517– 7　mortally mental attempt to reduce Deity to *c·* .
　544–32　Error begins with *c·* as the producer
　gl 582–21　*C·* and physical sense put out of sight and
　593–12　REUBEN (Jacob's son). *C·* ; sensuality ;
　594–22　SPIRITS. Mortal beliefs ; *c·* ;

corporeally
　s 148–10　as created *c·* instead of spiritually
corpse
　b 312– 8　The senses regard a *c·* , not as man,
　p 408–19　Drugs do not affect a *c·* ,
　429–11　*c·* , deserted by thought, is cold and decays,
correct
　m 60–27　Science will *c·* the discord,
　s 116–11　A *c·* view of C. S.
　128–32　If both . . . are *c·* , the conclusion, if properly
　ph 167– 7　only as we live above corporeal sense and *c·* it.
　180–22　to *c·* this turbulent element of mortal mind
　f 206–30　Mind does not make mistakes and . . . *c·* them.
　219– 7　and then say the product is *c·* .
　235– 9　their learning or their *c·* reading.
　c 264–13　As mortals gain more *c·* views of God
　b 284–17　*c·* testimony as to spiritual life, truth, and
　300– 2　it attempts to draw *c·* spiritual conclusions
　o 355–27　capable of impartial or *c·* criticism,
　361–24　must be *c·* in order to be Science
　p 408–14　supposition that we can *c·* insanity by
　425–24　*C·* material belief by spiritual
　t 453– 1　to distinguish the *c·* from the incorrect
　r 477– 3　this *c·* view of man healed the sick.
　486–13　and one error will not *c·* another.
　492–13　a statement proved to be good must be *c·* .
　494–20　serves to *c·* the errors of corporeal sense ;
　g 547– 8　given you the *c·* interpretation of Scripture.
　ap 560–18　without a *c·* sense of its highest visible idea,
corrected
　pr 11–14　never pardons our sins . . . till they are *c·*
　ph 194– 8　When one's false belief is *c·* ,
　f 251–29　Ignorance must be seen and *c·*
　b 298–11　until this sense is *c·* by C. S.
correcting
　p 386–20　*c·* the mistake, heals your grief,
corrective
　p 423–10　This *c·* is an alterative,
correctly
　sp 84–28　All we *c·* know of Spirit comes from God,
　o 347–10　Had he stated his syllogism *c·* ,
　t 449–17　to teach this subject properly and *c·*
　ap 560–21　in order to classify it *c·* .
correctness
　a 50–23　and that all evidence of their *c·*
　p 386–29　although the *c·* of the assertion
corrects
　pref viii– 7　science of music *c·* false tones and gives
　pr 6– 3　Divine Love *c·* and governs man.
　s 121–23　and *c·* these errors by the simple rule that
　f 233–22　the spiritual idea which *c·* and destroys them.
　c 259–28　*c·* error with truth and demands
　b 294–31　The Science of Mind *c·* such mistakes,
correlated
　b 276–10　Man and his Maker are *c·* in divine Science,
　288– 1　the *c·* statement, that *error*, . . . *is unreal.*
correlation
　ap 561–14　the *c·* of divine Principle and spiritual idea,
correlative
　b 316–31　blind to the possibilities of Spirit and its *c·* truth.
correspond
　pr 8– 6　indexes which do not *c·* with their character.
　s 158–13　history of material medicine may *c·* with
　294– 1　physical senses . . . *c·* with error.
　b 365–23　the result will *c·* with the spiritual intent.
　g 512– 1　*c·* to aspirations soaring beyond and above
correspondence
　sp 74–13　No *c·* nor communion can exist between
　b 271– 3　maintaining its obvious *c·* with
corresponding
　a 23–22　words *c·* thereto have these two definitions,
　p 386–14　and the *c·* effects of Truth on the body,
corresponds
　p 412–26　until the body *c·* with the
　g 509– 1　This period *c·* to the resurrection,
　517– 9　The ideal man *c·* to creation,
　517–10　The ideal woman *c·* to Life and to Love.
　552–14　Human experience . . . *c·* with that of Job,
corroborative
　g 549– 1　This discovery is *c·* of the Science of Mind,
corrupt
　f 204–20　Judging them by their fruits, they are *c·* .
　241– 6　"where moth and rust doth *c·* ."— *Matt.* 6 : 19.
　p 404– 9　A *c·* mind is manifested in a *c·* body.
corruptible
　s 164–25　"When this *c·* shall have— *I Cor.* 15 : 54.
　r 496–24　"when this *c·* shall have— *I Cor.* 15 : 54.

cost
 ph 197– 8 But the price does not exceed the original *c·*.
costly
 p 363– 2 *c·* and fragrant oil,— sandal oil perhaps,
costs
 ph 197– 6 *c·* many a man his earthly days of comfort.
couch
 o 342–22 from the *c·* of pain the helpless invalid.
 p 362–13 he reclined on a *c·*
 363– 1 to come behind the *c·* and reach his feet.
 435–19 Watching beside the *c·* of pain
cough
 f 220– 4 continual colds, catarrh, and *c·*."
 p 384–17 followed by chills, dry *c·*, influenza,
coughs
 f 220–16 Colds, *c·*, and contagion are engendered
Councils
 s 139–15 The decisions by vote of Church *C·*
counsel (*see also* **counsel's**)
 his
 p 442– 9 We noticed, as he shook hands with his *c·*,
 Master's
 t 443–12 our motto should be the Master's *c·*,
 no proper
 p 434–24 Mortal Man has had no proper *c·* in the case.
 opposing
 p 437–20 Here the opposing *c·*, False Belief, called
 profound
 ap 572– 8 simple and profound *c·* of the inspired writer.

 p 434–10 where C. S. is allowed to appear as *c·*
 434–16 Mortal Man's *c·* regards the prisoner
 439– 3 the *c·* for the plaintiff, Personal Sense,
 440– 4 machinations of the *c·*, False Belief,
 440–33 Here the *c·* for the defence closed,
 t 454–27 Let your loving care and *c·* support all their
counsellor
 p 435– 4 *C·* False Belief has argued that
counsel's
 p 434–17 The *c·* earnest, solemn eyes,
counted
 pr 9–26 for Truth, and so be *c·* among sinners?
countenance
 p 362– * *Who is the health of my c·— Psal. 42 : 11.*
 442–12 his *c·* beaming with health and happiness.
counter
 f 233–28 The *c·* fact relative to any disease
counteract
 p 424–13 if one doctor should administer a drug to *c·*
counteracting
 gl 581– 6 purity, and immortality, *c·* all evil,
counteracts
 p 414– 7 salutary action of truth, which *c·* error.
counterfeit
 s 148–21 but the *c·*, of God's man.
 b 285– 9 man's *c·*, the inverted likeness,
 293–24 manifestations of evil, which *c·* divine justice,
 gl 580–16 Life's *c·*, which ultimates in death ;
counterfeits
 c 267–22 beliefs must be *c·* of Truth.
 b 286–26 They are but *c·* of the spiritual
 293–13 so-called gases and forces are *c·* of
 293–17 *c·* the true essence of spirituality
 337–23 poor *c·* of the invisible universe and
 p 409–22 are *c·* from the beginning,
 r 476– 1 Mortals are the *c·* of immortals.
 gl 583– 1 *c·* of creation, whose better originals are
counter-irritant
 ph 198–16 undertakes to dispel it by a *c·*,
counter-irritants
 p 374– 2 Anodynes, *c·*, and depletion
counterpart
 s 148–20 calling that *man* which is not the *c·*,
counterpoise
 p 368– 3 Evil is but the *c·* of nothingness.
countless
 g 503–17 reflecting Him in *c·* spiritual forms.
 517–18 God has *c·* ideas, and they all have
country
 f 225–14 The history of our *c·*, like all history,
counts
 p 426– 7 than when she *c·* her footsteps
coupled
 pr 11–29 prayer, *c·* with a fervent habitual desire
 p 389– 1 for the penalty is *c·* with the belief.
 gl 590–18 unless specially *c·* with the name God.

courage
 animal
 a 28–32 There is too much animal *c·* in society
 48–23 thus rebuking resentment or animal *c·*.
 moral
 a 29– 1 and not sufficient moral *c·*.
 b 327–23 Moral *c·* is requisite to meet the wrong
 327–26 man who has more animal than moral *c·*,
 p 404–24 this knowledge strengthens his moral *c·*
 g 514–10 Moral *c·* is "the lion of the tribe— *Rev. 5 : 5.*
 gl 592–11 MOSES. A corporeal mortal ; moral *c·* ;
 more
 p 417– 6 Never tell the sick that they have more *c·* than
 sublime
 a 49–11 his divine patience, sublime *c·*,
 their
 p 417– 8 their strength is in proportion to their *c·*.

 m 57– 7 while the feminine mind gains *c·* and strength
 sp 97–23 It requires *c·* to utter truth ;
 p 375–27 always show great hopefulness and *c·*,
 423–23 the stimulus of *c·* and conscious power.
courageously
 p 419– 9 meet the cause mentally and *c·*,
course
 advancing
 t 452–11 Your advancing *c·* may provoke envy,
 free
 an 106– 4 to work against the free *c·* of honesty
 his
 a 21–14 till at last he finishes his *c·* with joy.
 sp 96–26 he who has shaped his *c·* in accordance
 t 458–26 The Christian Scientist wisely shapes his *c·*,
 its
 p 376–30 after admitting that it must have its *c·*.
 my
 a 21–21 On the contrary, if my friends pursue my *c·*,
 only
 p 392– 8 The only *c·* is to take antagonistic grounds
 our
 b 307–23 and so weighs against our *c·* Spiritward.
 such a
 t 453–27 for such a *c·* increases fear,
 their
 a 29– 5 until they have finished their *c·*.
 ph 174–19 rebuking in their *c·* all error
 true
 p 419– 4 Your true *c·* is to destroy the foe,
 your
 m 67– 8 "Do you know your *c·*?
 f 253–19 you can at once change your *c·*
 zigzag
 a 21–32 By-and-by, ashamed of his zigzag *c·*, he would

 s 119– 2 of *c·* we cannot really endow matter with
 t 443– 8 While a *c·* of medical study is
 gl 593–15 RIVER. . . . it typifies the *c·* of Truth ;
court
 m 58–26 a wife ought not to *c·* vulgar extravagance or
 p 430–18 case to be on trial, as cases are tried in *c·*,
 434–30 the lower *c·* has sentenced Mortal Man to die,
 434–32 Denying justice to the body, that *c·* commended
 436–33 that *c·* pronounced a sentence of death
 437–21 called C. S. to order for contempt of *c·*.
 437–27 proceedings of a regularly constituted *c·*.
courtesy
 p 364–15 a special sign of Oriental *c·*.
Court of Error
 p 432– 9 Another witness is called for by the *C· of E·*
 434–12 who were at the previous *C· of E·*,
 436–30 the *C· of E·* construed obedience to the
 437–17 the terrible records of your *C· of E·*,
 437–31 bar of Truth, which ranks above the lower
 C· of E·.
 441–18 the decrees of the *C· of E·* in favor of Matter,
 441–27 Your personal jurors in the *C· of E·*
Court of Material Error
 p 440–29 suits to be tried at the *C· of M· E·*.
Court of Spirit
 p 434– 9 permission is obtained for a trial in the *C· of S·*,
 437–10 our higher tribunal, the Supreme *C· of S·*,
 437–18 I ask that the Supreme *C· of S·* reverse this
 437–28 But Judge Justice of the Supreme *C· of S·*
Court of Truth
 p 438–26 When the *C· of T·* summoned Furred Tongue
court-room
 p 430–24 The *c·* is filled with interested spectators,
courts
 an 104–29 *c·* recognize evidence to prove the motive
 105– 3 *C·* and juries judge and sentence mortals
 105–12 the body over which *c·* hold jurisdiction?
 105–14 *c·* reasonably pass sentence, according to

covenant
- *m* 56–15 Infidelity to the marriage *c·* is the
- 64–30 ensure the stability of the marriage *c·*.
- *c* 255–11 Mortal man has made a *c·* with his eyes

cover
- *pr* 8–19 they "*c·* the multitude of sins."— *I Pet.* 4: 8.
- *sp* 97–22 they bring error from under *c·*.
- *g* 548–10 when clouds *c·* the sun's face !
- *gl* 596–28 VEIL. A *c·*; concealment; hiding; hypocrisy.

covered
- *pr* 8–17 "there is nothing *c·* that shall— *Matt.* 10: 26.
- *p* 431–21 I am Coated Tongue. I am *c·* with a

covereth
- *p* 448–17 "He that *c·* his sins shall not— *Prov.* 28: 13.

covering
- *p* 413–14 *c·* it with dirt in order to make it thrive
- *t* 446–30 C· iniquity will prevent prosperity

coverings
- *f* 241–11 Stripped of its *c·*, what a mocking
- *gl* 597–14 tore from bigotry and superstition their *c·*,

covers
- *pr* 16–11 gave that prayer which *c·* all human needs.
- *f* 247–27 and *c·* earth with loveliness.
- *p* 421–16 great fact which *c·* the whole ground,

covetous
- *m* 64–14 debarred by a *c·* domestic tyrant

coward
- *p* 368– 5 Error is a *c·* before Truth.

cowering
- *p* 378–12 sent it *c·* back into the jungle.

cradle
- *sp* 95–29 the world is asleep in the *c·* of infancy,
- *f* 244– 8 is seen between the *c·* and the grave,

cradled
- *pref* vii– 6 in *c·* obscurity, lay the Bethlehem babe,

craftiness
- *an* 103– 5 defines it as dishonesty and *c·*.

cramped
- *s* 160–20 become *c·* despite the mental protest?

cranium
- *sp* 92– 9 Mind is not an entity within the *c·*
- *ph* 173–23 according to the development of the *c·*;

craving
- *c* 258– 4 unsatisfied human *c·* for something better,

cravings
- *m* 60–32 Higher enjoyments alone can satisfy the *c·*
- *s* 108–13 immortal *c·*, "the price of learning love,"
- *g* 501–17 more native to their immortal *c·*

craze
- *p* 408– 8 general *c·* cannot, in a scientific diagnosis,

create
- *m* 62– 8 If parents *c·* in their babes a desire for
- *sp* 93–15 Good does not *c·* a mind susceptible of
- *s* 151– 4 could not possibly *c·* a remedy outside of itself,
- 157–18 If He could *c·* thugs intrinsically bad, then
- *ph* 177–21 and *c·* the so-called laws of the flesh,
- *f* 203– 6 shows that matter can neither . . . *c·* nor
- 204–24 the notion that they can *c·*
- 251–32 imprison themselves in what they *c·*.
- *c* 263– 4 would not or could not *c·*.
- 263–10 producing evil when he would *c·* good,
- *b* 278– 2 nothing in Spirit out of which to *c·* matter.
- 279–14 and one can no more *c·* the other
- 279–15 than Truth can *c·* error, or *vice versa.*
- 287–12 Did God, Truth, *c·* error? No !
- *o* 356–21 is it possible for Him to *c·* man subject to
- 356–24 Does God *c·* a material man out of Himself,
- 356–28 to *c·* the primitive, and then punish its
- 357–31 can Life, or God, dwell in evil and *c·* it?
- *p* 419– 3 hate will perpetuate or even *c·* the
- *g* 504–27 Did infinite Mind *c·* matter, and call it *light?*
- 522–21 represented as entering matter in order to *c·*
- 526–23 Did He *c·* this fruit-bearer of sin
- 528– 6 cannot be true that man was ordered to *c·*
- 528–17 and thereby *c·* woman;
- 532– 1 Did God at first *c·* one man unaided,
- 532– 3 in order to *c·* the rest of the human family?
- 540– 5 "I make peace, and *c·* evil. — *Isa.* 45: 7.
- 543–26 did it leave aught for matter to *c·*?
- 544–15 No mortal mind has the might or right . . . to *c·* or
- *gl* 579–12 the purpose of Love to *c·* trust in good,
- 583–25 could not *c·* . . . an element the opposite of

created
- *m* 68– 6 we shall learn how Spirit, . . . has *c·* men and
- 69– 7 God's children already *c·* will be cognized
- *s* 125–10 the prior states which human belief *c·* and
- 140–29 In the beginning God *c·* man in His,
- 148– 8 described man as *c·* by Spirit,

created
- *s* 148–10 as *c·* corporeally instead of spiritually
- 161– 6 Holy inspiration has *c·* states of mind which
- *ph* 173–29 the error which the human mind alone has *c·*.
- *f* 205–12 God *c·* all through Mind,
- 206–22 Is God creating anew what He has already *c·*?
- 252–12 the eternal verity, man *c·* by and of Spirit,
- *c* 256– 6 All things are *c·* spiritually.
- 263–20 but one creator, who has *c·* all.
- *b* 279– 9 Matter is neither *c·* by Mind nor
- 294–27 God *c·* man.
- 295–12 immortals, *c·* in God's own image ;
- 295–29 Brainology teaches that mortals are *c·* to suffer
- 306–30 God's man, spiritually *c·*, is not material
- 307–27 Man was not *c·* from a material basis,
- 335– 7 Spirit, God, has *c·* all
- 335– 8 Spirit never *c·* matter.
- 339– 8 Spirit, alone *c·* all, and called it good.
- *o* 344– 7 God has *c·* man in His own image
- 357– 2 for doing what He *c·* man capable of doing,
- *r* 479–18 "In the beginning God *c·* the— *Gen.* 1: 1.
- *g* 502–22 In the beginning God *c·* the— *Gen.* 1: 1.
- 507–23 Mind and the universe *c·* by God.
- 512– 4 And God *c·* great whales, — *Gen.* 1: 21.
- 514–20 individuality *c·* by God is not carnivorous,
- 516–24 So God *c·* man— *Gen.* 1: 27.
- 516–25 in the image of God *c·* He him ; — *Gen.* 1: 27.
- 516–26 male and female *c·* He them, — *Gen.* 1: 27.
- 520–17 when they were *c·*, — *Gen.* 2: 4.
- 521–14 supposition that man is *c·* materially,
- 526–16 God pronounced good all that He *c·*,
- 526–17 and the Scriptures declare that He *c·* all.
- 528– 3 record declares that God has already *c·* man,
- 531–31 *c·* by Mind in the image and likeness of God
- 536–16 C· by flesh instead of by Spirit,
- 543–24 man, whom God *c·* with a word,
- 545–10 Man, *c·* by God, was given dominion
- 553–17 Adam was *c·* before Eve.
- *gl* 580–14 image and likeness of what God has not *c·*,
- 580–26 supposition . . . creator entered what He *c·*,
- 581–12 spiritual realities of all things are *c·* by Him
- 584–22 self-made or *c·* by a tribal god

creates
- *m* 69–22 If the father replies, "God *c·* man through
- 69–24 "Do you teach that Spirit *c·* materially,
- *sp* 77– 8 mortal mind *c·* its own physical conditions.
- 93–13 nor *c·* aught that can cause evil.
- *s* 122– 2 and so *c·* a reign of discord,
- 154– 7 calling up the fear that *c·* the image of disease
- 157–20 If He *c·* drugs at all
- *ph* 173– 7 supposition, that Spirit is within what it *c·*
- 179–13 *c·* a demand for that method,
- 187– 6 so-called material sense *c·* its own forms of
- *c* 257–12 Mind *c·* His own likeness in ideas,
- *b* 280– 7 Mind *c·* and multiplies them,
- 286–14 divine Principle, Love, *c·* and governs all
- 295– 5 God *c·* and governs the universe,
- 316–20 man, whom Spirit *c·*, constitutes, and governs.
- 331– 7 If He dwelt within what He *c·*,
- *o* 357– 8 Truth *c·* neither a lie, a capacity to lie, nor a liar.
- *p* 400–22 we prove that thought alone *c·* the suffering.
- *r* 471– 3 all that He *c·* are perfect and eternal,
- 472–25 That which He *c·* is good,
- *g* 503–23 Mind *c·* no element nor symbol of discord and
- 503–24 God *c·* neither erring thought, mortal life,
- 505– 9 divine Mind, not matter, *c·* all identities,
- 507–24 Infinite Mind *c·* and governs all,
- 509–13 Spirit *c·* no other than heavenly
- 513–26 God *c·* all forms of reality.
- 520–23 God *c·* all through Mind, not through matter,
- 523–25 it is Elohim (God) who *c·*.
- 538–19 in which God *c·* the heavens, earth, and man.
- 540– 2 Spirit *c·* neither a wicked nor a mortal man,
- 546– 5 If Mind, God, *c·* error,
- *gl* 582–18 *c·* man as His own spiritual idea,

creating
- *f* 206–21 Is God *c·* anew what He has already created?
- 231–15 *c·* and governing man through perpetual
- 249– 5 "male and female" of God's *c·* — *Gen.* 1: 27.
- *b* 338–19 was deemed the agent of Deity in *c·* man,
- *g* 515– 6 serpent of God's *c·* is neither subtle nor
- 520–27 the immortal *c·* thought is from above,
- 534– 5 to manifest the deathless man of God's *c·*.
- *gl* 591–26 mythology ; error *c·* other errors ;

creation
account of
- *g* 523–24 the spiritually scientific account of *c·*,
accurate views of
- *c* 255– 9 accurate views of *c·* by the divine Mind.
all
- *m* 69–14 unfolds all *c·*, confirms the Scriptures,
basis of the
- *g* 528–26 supposed to become the basis of the *c·* of
consciousness of
- *c* 263–31 scientific eternal consciousness of *c·*.

creation

corresponds to
g 517– 9 The ideal man corresponds to *c*,
counterfeits of
gl 583– 1 Sensual and mortal beliefs ; counterfeits of *c*,
divine
(see divine)
divine Principle of
g 546–10 Is the divine Principle of *c* misstated?
existence and
gl 580–11 opposed to . . . spiritual existence and *c* ;
fact of
r 471–20 spirituality . . . is the only fact of *c*.
g 529–10 usher in . . . the glorious fact of *c*,
facts of
g 539–28 power to expound the facts of *c*,
544–19 The facts of *c*, as previously recorded,
first
g 526–24 in contradiction of the first *c*?
God's
m 69– 6 Mortals can never understand God's *c* while
69–19 not conflict with the scientific sense of God's *c*.
s 110– 5 the radiant reality of God's *c*,
157–16 If drugs are part of God's *c*,
c 260–11 the immortal and perfect model of God's *c*
262–10 the nature and quality of God's *c*
264–30 we shall behold and understand God's *c*,
b 307–23 seems . . . a part of God's *c*,
g 519–13 slow to discern and to grasp God's *c*
544– 3 In God's *c* ideas became productive,
ap 577–11 the perfectibility of God's *c*.
gl 588–16 All the objects of God's *c* reflect one Mind,
590–12 denial of the fulness of God's *c* ;
His
f 231–29 and know that they are no part of His *c*.
r 472–24 All reality is in God and His *c*,
g 502– 8 inverted images of the creator and His *c*.
507–27 expresses Science and art throughout His *c*,
516– 5 are reflected by His *c* ;
523– 6 declares . . . that error can improve His *c*.
524–24 yet God is reflected in all His *c*.
524–24 Is this addition to His *c* real or unreal?
554–20 defined this opposite of God and His *c*
gl 579–17 opposite of good,— of God and His *c* ;
His own
g 522–31 Does the creator condemn His own *c*?
527–19 the tree of death to His own *c*?
illustration of
b 315–26 and presented an illustration of *c*.
line of
g 557–12 as the line of *c* rises towards spiritual man,
man, and
r 489–30 wrong sense of God, man, and *c* is *non-sense*,
material
ph 177–15 Scriptural allegory of the material *c*,
g 522–24 declaring this material *c* false.
544– 1 record of a material *c* which followed the
material view of
g 521–25 opposite error, a material view of *c*.
method of
ap 568–10 first the true method of *c* is set forth
Mind's
g 509–26 the days and seasons of Mind's *c*,
new
c 263–21 Whatever seems to be a new *c*, is but
not
c 263–28 mortal sense of persons and things is not *c*.
objects of
c 264–14 multitudinous objects of *c*, which before
of the world
r 479–31 from the *c* of the world,— *Rom.* 1 : 20.
one
g 502–29 There is but one creator and one *c*.
order of
g 508–23 in the ascending order of *c*.
record of
g 504– 9 not yet included in the record of *c*,
521–15 turn our gaze to the spiritual record of *c*,
526– 3 previous and more scientific record of *c*
reflects the
b 305–14 though he reflects the *c* of Mind,
Science of
g 509–29 Knowing the Science of *c*,
537–23 Science of *c* recorded in the first chapter
539–23 arguing for the Science of *c*,
539–30 The Science of *c*, . . . inspired his wisest
scientific
g 545–21 translators of this record of scientific *c*
sense of
m 56–11 the corporeal sense of *c* was cast out,
Spirit's
gl 580–18 the usurper of Spirit's *c*,
spiritual
(see spiritual)
theories of
c 255– 7 The mythological human theories of *c*,

creation

theory of
g 547–11 conclusions as to the scientific theory of *c*.
this
g 502–29 This *c* consists of the unfolding of spiritual
truth of
sp 93–17 and not the truth of *c*.
c 263– 6 spiritual man alone represents the truth of *c*.
vast
f 209– 7 the life and light of all its own vast *c* ;
whole
c 255– * *we know that the whole c groaneth*— *Rom.* 8 : 22.
would simulate
b 281–25 out of which error would simulate *c*

s 124–27 Withdraw them, and *c* must collapse.
c 256–32 *c* is the infinite . . . idea emanating from this
b 321–20 leprosy was a *c* of mortal mind
g 504–15 a revelation instead of a *c*
507– 8 and *c* would be full of nameless offspring,
507–28 *C* is ever appearing,
521–19 if there is nothing more about *c* in the book of
527–26 the lie represents God as repeating *c*,
528–19 Beginning *c* with darkness instead of light,
537–11 *C* is there represented as spiritual,
539–20 false to say that Truth and error commingle in *c*.
542– 2 a *c* so wholly apart from God's,
551–25 so long as it bases *c* on materiality.
553–27 superstition about the *c* from dust
554–18 the *c* of whatever is sinful and mortal ;
555–22 *C* rests on a spiritual basis.

creations

crude
c 264– 3 The crude *c* of mortal thought
His
ph 187– 5 ignorant . . . of the all-knowing Mind and of His *c*.
b 331– 6 Life is Mind, the creator reflected in His *c*.
gl 580– 4 the opposite of Spirit and His *c* ;
innumerable
r 479–23 the only facts are Spirit and its innumerable *c*.
of God
f 205– 8 error . . . that sin, sickness, and death are *c* of God,
c 266– 1 Soul, where the *c* of God are good,
of matter
b 287– 5 but *c* of matter must return to dust.
g 523– 7 The *c* of matter arise from a mist
of Spirit
b 286–25 temporal and material are not then *c* of Spirit.
287– 4 All *c* of Spirit are eternal ;
of Truth
b 287– 4 error, which simulates the *c* of Truth.
other
g 535–18 belief in . . . other *c* must go down
Spirit's
g 525– 4 not the validity of Spirit or Spirit's *c*.

c 263– 4 The *c* of mortal mind are material.
g 528–23 Beholding the *c* of his own dream
543–23 the *c* of erroneous thought, not of

creative

sp 71– 8 God, the *c*, governing. infinite Principle
89–25 Matter is neither intelligent nor *c*.
b 302–32 is but the reflection of the *c* power
317– 3 usurped the throne of the *c* divine Principle,
r 475–21 no life, intelligence, nor *c* power of his own,
g 502–27 *c* Principle — Life, Truth, and Love — is God.
507–15 universe of Spirit reflects the *c* power
513–21 God, who is the divinely *c* Principle thereof.
531–23 Has man sought out other *c* inventions,
549–29 forsakes Spirit as the divine origin of *c* Truth,
556–19 Sleep is darkness, but God's *c* mandate was,
gl 582–19 God is the only *c* power.

creativeness

o 357–14 the *c* and authority of Deity,

creator

but one
m 69–14 to understand that there is but one *c*,
c 263–20 There can be but one *c*, who has created all.
g 502–29 There is but one *c* and one creation.
coexistent with his
g 557–21 as never dying, but as coexistent with his *c*.
corporeal
pr 13–27 Father of all is represented as a corporeal *c* ;
grand
s 143–26 Mind is the grand *c*,
infinite Mind is the
c 256–32 Infinite Mind is the *c*,
inseparable from his
r 491–16 man . . . inseparable from his *c*.
is called
g 523–26 the *c* is called Jehovah, or the Lord.

creator

man and his
b 338–25　would impose between man and his *c*·.
not a
c 259–26　Vibration is not intelligence ; hence it is not a *c*·.
b 305–14　The verity that God's image is not a *c*·,
not the
f 207– 8　God is not the *c*· of an evil mind.
of ideas
f 249–12　the *c*· of ideas is not the creator of illusions.
of illusions
f 249–13　the creator of ideas is not the creator of illusions.
of man
r 470–21　God is the *c*· of man,
one
o 356–32　Then there must have been more than one *c*·,
gl 592– 7　belief that there can be more than one *c*· ;
prerogative of his
g 530–10　presuming not on the prerogative of his *c*·,
substance and
c 257– 7　theory that Spirit is not the only substance and *c*·
the only
a 31–10　He recognized Spirit, God, as the only *c*·,
b 331–19　the universal cause, the only *c*·,
wisdom of the
b 273–24　and impugn the wisdom of the *c*·.

m 69– 7　never . . . while believing that man is a *c*·.
69–21　Do you have one God and *c*·,
69–22　or is man a *c*·?"
s 119– 9　to leave the *c*· out of His own universe ;
119–11　and regard God as the *c*· of matter,
127– 4　the *c*· of the spiritual universe,
ph 171– 1　Matter, which . . . claims to be a *c*·, is a fiction,
c 256– 7　Mind, not matter, is the *c*·.
b 277–10　and error has no *c*·.
278– 1　Is Spirit the source or *c*· of matter?
303–24　belief that . . . man . . . is himself a *c*·,
331– 5　Life is Mind, the *c*· reflected in
g 502– 7　inverted images of the *c*· and His creation.
507–22　implies a mortal mind and man a *c*·.
508– 6　substance of . . . a flower is God, the *c*· of it.
514– 6　in which and of which God is the sole *c*·.
522–31　Does the *c*· condemn His own creation?
531–17　If, . . . afterwards put into body by the *c*·,
533–12　as if He were the *c*· of evil.
gl 579– 9　surrendering to the *c*· the early fruits of
580–26　supposition that . . . *c*· entered what He created,
583–20　definition of

creators
g 535–12　A belief in other gods, other *c*·,

creature

any other
b 304– 8　nor any other *c*·,— *Rom.* 8 : 39.
every
a 37–30　preach the gospel to every *c*· !"— *Mark* 16 : 15.
s 138–28　preach the gospel to every *c*· !— *Mark* 16 : 15.
p 418–28　"Preach the gospel to every *c*·."— *Mark* 16 : 15.
inharmonious
s 123– 9　weak and inharmonious *c*· in the universe.
living
g 512– 5　and every living *c*· that moveth,— *Gen.* 1 : 21.
513–15　bring forth the living *c*· after his— *Gen.* 1 : 24.
527–25　whatsoever Adam called every living *c*·,— *Gen.* 2 : 19.
moving
g 511–20　moving *c*· that hath life,— *Gen.* 1 : 20.
new
f 201– 8　Truth makes a new *c*·,

b 299–31　If man were solely a *c*· of the
p 407– 4　attractive to no *c*· except a loathsome

creatures
b 298–32　human *c*· with suggestive feathers ;
g 514–28　All of God's *c*·, . . . are harmless,
549– 9　C· of lower forms of organism

credit
pr 8–32　do we listen . . . and *c*· what is said?
s 112–29　without giving that author proper *c*·,
154– 6　this law obtains *c*· through association,
p 417– 3　Give sick people *c*· for sometimes knowing
t 457– 3　borrowed from this book without giving it *c*·,

creditor
p 363–18　released . . . by their common *c*·.

credits
a 27–23　Tradition *c*· him with two or three hundred
g 528–15　Here falsity, error, *c*· Truth, God, with

credulity
p 370–27　fails at length to inspire the *c*· of the sick,

credulous
f 212–21　In legerdemain and *c*· frenzy,

creed

highest
r 471–29　her highest *c*· has been divine Science,
orthodox
r 471–24　The author subscribed to an orthodox *c*·
religious
r 496–29　Have Christian Scientists any religious *c*·?

s 135–27　Christianity as Jesus taught it was not a *c*·,
f 226–16　These claims are not made through code or *c*·,
234– 2　as ritualism and *c*· hamper spirituality.
o 351–12　spiritual sense of the *c*· was discerned
t 450– 2　Their *c*· teaches belief in a
458–21　ritualism and *c*· are summoned to give place

creeds
pr 4–31　Long prayers, superstition, and *c*·
a 18–11　against Pharisaical *c*· and practices,
sp 98–12　C·, doctrines, and human hypotheses
98–16　above the loosening grasp of *c*·,
s 133–32　C· and rituals have not cleansed their
f 239– 4　those who are in advance of *c*·.
r 471–22　Are doctrines and *c*· a benefit to man?

creepeth
r 475–27　that *c*· upon the earth."— *Gen.* 1 : 26.
g 513–24　everything that *c*· upon the earth— *Gen.* 1 : 25.
515–15　that *c*· upon the earth.— *Gen.* 1 : 26.
518–10　everything that *c*· upon the earth,— *Gen.* 1 : 30.

creeping
r 475–26　over every *c*· thing— *Gen.* 1 : 26.
g 513–15　cattle, and *c*· thing,— *Gen.* 1 : 24.
515– 4　*c*· over lofty summits,
515–14　over every *c*· thing— *Gen.* 1 : 26.

creeps
p 373–28　languidly *c*· along its frozen channels,

cried
a 39–18　"Now," *c*· the apostle,— *II Cor.* 6 : 2.
p 398– 5　*c*·, and rent him sore— *Mark* 9 : 26.
ap 562–22　And she being with child *c*·,— *Rev.* 12 : 2.

cries
pr 13– 3　It is the open fount which *c*·,
f 227–22　C. S. raises the standard of liberty and *c*· :
p 365– 6　than all *c*· of "Lord, Lord !"

crieth
g 541–28　*c*· unto Me from the ground.— *Gen.* 4 : 10.

crime

advocating
s 153–31　as we would avoid advocating *c*·.
alleged
p 434–28　alleged *c*· never to have been committed.
cloaked the
gl 597– 8　but cloaked the *c*·, latent in thought,
diminish
m 61– 8　would improve our progeny, diminish *c*·,
invoke
g 542–12　tend to perpetuate sin, invoke *c*·,
looms of
a 102–18　The looms of *c*·, hidden in the dark
mental
an 105–17　laws eventually take cognizance of mental *c*·
second
p 433–23　led him into the commission of the second *c*·,
this
an 106–14　incurs the divine penalty due this *c*·.
p 433–24　For this *c*· Mortal Man is sentenced

sp 97– 1　will hold *c*· in check.
an 104–30　motive as well as the commission of a *c*·.
105– 4　in order to restrain *c*·,
105–10　Can matter commit a *c*·?
105–14　and human law rightly estimates *c*·,
f 236–13　strongest educator, either for or against *c*·.
p 404–15　as . . . reformation cancels the *c*·.
432– 6　I was witness to the *c*· of liver-complaint.
432–22　shortly after the report of the *c*·,
438–16　on three distinct charges of *c*·,
438–20　on the night of the *c*·
440– 5　Truth arraigns . . . to answer for his *c*·.
440–25　render obedience to these laws punishable as *c*·.
t 461–19　If you commit a *c*·, should you acknowledge
ap 564– 7　to charge the innocent with the *c*·.
564–23　its own *c*· of defying immortal Mind.

crimes
a 40–16　*c*· of his implacable enemies less criminal?
s 161–22　"Liberty, what *c*· are committed in thy name !"
p 440–10　Good deeds are transformed into *c*·,

criminal
pr 11– 6　this may be no moral benefit to the *c*·,
11– 7　it only saves the *c*· from one form of
a 40–16　crimes of his implacable enemies less *c*·?
an 102–23　apathy on the subject which the *c*· desires.
105–13　Mortal mind, not matter, is the *c*·
106– 1　*c*· misuse of human will-power,

criminal

ph 198– 4 as a *c·* hears his death-sentence.
b 316–26 That man was accounted a *c·*
340–27 *c·*, political, and religious codes ;
p 431– 9 which I considered *c·*, inasmuch as
432–14 treated as a *c·* and punished with death.
435– 4 or has Mortal Mind committed a *c·* deed?
437– 5 He also testified that . . . Man . . . was a *c·*.
437–15 Soul a *c·* though recommended to
t 461–20 acknowledge to yourself that you are a *c·*?
ap 564–12 instigated by the *c·* instinct

cripple

ph 172–29 the unfortunate *c·* may present more
b 294–14 saying : . . . Injury can *c·* and matter can kill
t 460–21 it starts a petty crossfire over every *c·*

crippled

f 227–28 *c·* your capacities, enfeebled your body,

cripples

t 448–10 Evasion of Truth *c·* integrity,

crisis

p 396–12 growing worse before a *c·* is passed.
421–11 If a *c·* occurs in your treatment,
t 446– 8 or it may mark the *c·* of the disease.

critic

o 346– 1 as is alleged by one *c·*.
347– 3 It is said by one *c·*, that to verify this

criticising

o 345–10 It is sometimes said, in *c·* C. S.,

criticism

s 110–20 This book may be distorted by shallow *c·*
c 255– 7 anciently classified as the higher *c·*,
o 346– 1 such *c·* confounds *man* with Adam.
355–27 capable of impartial or correct *c·*,

criticisms

o 341– 4 These *c·* are generally based on

critics

o 347–12 *C·* should consider that the so-called mortal man
347–31 *c·* will then see that error is indeed the

crop

ph 183– 9 Can the agriculturist, . . . produce a *c·* without
188–25 you have an abundant or scanty *c·*

crops

s 125–24 these changes cannot affect his *c·*.

cross

cup is the
a 35–27 Our cup is the *c·*.
foot of the
a 42–14 sadly followed him to the foot of the *c·*.
gallows and the
s 134–13 hallowed by the gallows and the *c·*.
his
a 34– 1 willing truly to drink his cup, take his *c·*,
36–14 beneath the shadow of his *c·*.
manger and the
s 142–15 In vain do the manger and the *c·* tell their
material
a 50–32 Not the spear nor the material *c·*
on the
a 49–28 mocked him on the *c·*, saying derisively,
real
a 50–30 The real *c·*, which Jesus bore up the hill of grief,
scourge and the
a 20–20 scourge and the *c·* awaited the great Teacher.
take up the
pr 15–19 We must resolve to take up the *c·*,
a 34–14 If all who seek . . . will take up the *c·*,
taking up the
ph 179– 3 this can be done only by taking up the *c·*
women at the
a 49– 1 The women at the *c·* could have answered

pr 9–15 There is a *c·* to be taken up
f 224–16 Of old the *c·* was truth's central sign,
238–31 The *c·* is the central emblem of history.
254–30 Your good will be evil spoken of. This is the *c·*.
c 266–30 He does not *c·* the barriers of time
b 294–14 saying : . . . The stomach can make a man *c·*.

cross-bearing

a 36–28 toil, sacrifice, *c·*, multiplied trials,
o 343– 8 without this *c·*, one might not

crossfire

t 460–21 it starts a petty *c·* over every cripple

Cross of Calvary

ap 575–31 *C·* of *C·*, which binds human society

cross-questioning

g 533–26 Truth, *c·* man as to his

croton oil

ph 198–18 by the application of caustic or *c· o·*,

crouched

p 380–16 Gazing at a chained lion, *c·* for a spring,

crowded

t 459–19 turning him loose in the *c·* streets of a city.

crown

a 29– 6 they will have the *c·* of rejoicing.
44– 2 before the thorns can be laid aside for a *c·*,
s 116–14 They never *c·* the power of Mind as the Messiah,
f 254–31 for through it you win and wear the *c·*.
c 267–30 he shall receive the *c·* of life, — *Jas.* 1 : 12.
t 451– 6 with the *c·* of Love upon her brow,
ap 560– 8 upon her head a *c·* of twelve stars. — *Rev.* 12 : 1.
562–16 These are the stars in the *c·* of rejoicing.
565–13 and deprive Herod of his *c·*.

crowned

a 22– 9 these efforts are *c·* with success.
45– 4 *c·* with the glory of a sublime success,
s 141–12 as kings are *c·* from a royal dynasty.
141–18 Its only *c·* head is immortal sovereignty.
f 243– 8 It *c·* the demonstrations of Jesus
ap 562–11 The spiritual idea is *c·* with twelve stars.

crowning

s 117–22 his mighty, *c·*, unparalleled, and

crowns

ap 558–12 but a bright promise *c·* its brow.
562–31 and seven *c·* upon his heads. — *Rev.* 12 : 3.

crucified

a 18– * have *c·* the flesh — *Gal.* 5 : 24.
28– 6 he would not have been *c·*.
39– 7 We need "Christ, and him *c·*." — *I Cor.* 2 : 2.
43–18 which Jesus taught, and for which he was *c·*,
s 134–11 burned, *c·*, and otherwise persecuted ;
ph 200–26 Jesus Christ, and him *c·*." — *I Cor.* 2 : 2.
b 334–30 a reference to the human sense of Jesus *c·*,

crucifix

f 238– 9 Losing her *c·*, the Roman Catholic girl said,

crucifixion

a 24–20 Does erudite theology regard the *c·* of Jesus
24–27 The efficacy of the *c·* lay in the
27–11 proved by his reappearance after the *c·*
32–29 on the night before his *c·*,
41–18 lost, about three centuries after the *c·*.
45–29 the same body that he had before his *c·*,
46– 2 until they saw him after his *c·*
s 137– 5 not spiritually discerned, . . . until after the *c·*,
b 316–18 rose higher to human view because of the *c·*,
317–29 proof that he was unchanged by the *c·*.
r 497–20 the *c·* of Jesus and his resurrection
g 555–31 able to present himself unchanged after the *c·*,
ap 564–11 author is convinced that . . . even his *c·*

crucify

sp 94– 9, 10 said : "*C·* him, *c·* him — *John* 19 : 6.
s 134– 2 the cry . . . is repeated, "*C·* him !" — *John* 19 : 6.
gl 597– 9 to spring into action and *c·* God's anointed.

crucifying

b 316–17 by *c·* the flesh.

crude

pref viii–31 but these compositions were *c·*,
f 224– 4 As the *c·* footprints of the past disappear
c 264– 3 The *c·* creations of mortal thought
g 502–14 thus the *c·* forms of human thought

Cruden

g 526–29 The name Eden, according to *C·*,

cruder

ph 189– 6 raises the human thought above the *c·* theories

cruel

b 290–30 and learning that his *c·* mind died not.

cruelty

a 51–25 pride, envy, *c·*, and vengeance,

crumbling

pref vii–16 and the cold conventionality . . . are *c·* away.

crumbs

f 234– 6 with *c·* of comfort from Christ's table,

crusade

f 226– 7 the voice of the herald of this new *c·*

crush

p 407–10 they *c·* out happiness, health, and manhood.

crust

ph 195– 7 All that he ate, except his black *c·*,

cry

a 50– 8 wrung from Jesus' lips the awful *c·*,
51– 1 wrung from his faithful lips the plaintive *c·*,
s 129–15 and earth will echo the *c·*,
134– 1 To-day the *c·* of bygone ages is repeated,
ph 194–29 And with no language but a *c·*.
p 442– 7 and there resounded . . . the *c·*, Not guilty.
ap 559–17 Then will a voice from harmony *c·* :

crying
  m 64– 1 Want of uniform justice is a *c·* evil
  ph 194–24 a mental infant, *c·* and chattering
  194–27 An infant *c·* in the night,
  194–28 An infant *c·* for the light,
  f 208–19 voice of one *c·* in the wilderness"— *Matt.* 3: 3.

cue
  c 261–17 sat aching in his chair till his *c·* was spoken,

culminate
  g 549–21 Here these material researches *c·*

culminates
  r 491–20 this belief *c·* in another belief,

culminating
  s 155– 4 law of a general belief, *c·* in individual faith,
  gl 597–10 martyrdom of Jesus was the *c·* sin of Pharisaism.

culmination
  p 380–27 reaches its *c·* of scientific statement and

cultivated
  b 271–14 the result of their *c·* spiritual understanding

cultivating
  ph 197–16 We should master fear, instead of *c·* it.

cultivation
  g 527– 5 Man is God's reflection, needing no *c·*,

culture
  m 61–25 a more solemn charge, than the *c·* of your
  sp 95–12 Whoever reaches this point of moral *c·*
  f 235–13 spiritual *c·*, which lifts one higher.

cultured
  s 128– 7 business men and *c·* scholars
  164– 9 the *c·* class of medical practitioners
  c 255– 8 *c·* scholars in Rome and in Greece,

cultus
  s 133–23 sanitary methods, and a religious *c·*.

cumulative
  p 405–23 the *c·* effects of a guilty conscience.

cup
  Christ's
  a 55–25 drinketh of Christ's *c·* now,
  drink this
  a 31–23 and drink this *c·*,— *I Cor.* 11: 26.
  earthly
  a ʼ54–21 His earthly *c·* of bitterness was drained
  hemlock
  ap 559–28 you must share the hemlock *c·*
  his
  pr 5–15 The followers of Christ drank his *c·*.
  10– 9 and are willing to drink his *c·*,
  a 31–19 we drink of his *c·*, partake of his bread,
  33–14 drain to the dregs his *c·* of sorrow.
  33–27 Christians, are you drinking his *c·*?
  33–31 have commemorated Jesus in his *c·*?
  34– 1 willing truly to drink his *c·*,
  34–12 and drunk of his *c·*,
  51– 5 This dread added the drop of gall to his *c·*.
  54–27 those who followed him should drink of his *c·*,
  Jesus'
  pr 10– 6 If good enough to profit by Jesus' *c·*
  Master's
  b 317– 8 will drink of his Master's *c·*.
  my
  ap 578–14 my *c·* runneth over.— *Psal.* 23: 5.
  of bitterness
  a 43–21 because of the *c·* of bitterness he drank.
  of coffee
  sp 80– 3 A *c·* of coffee or tea is not the equal of truth,
  of cold water
  p 436–11 Giving a *c·* of cold water in Christ's name,
  ap 570–17 Give them a *c·* of cold water in Christ's name,
  of our Lord
  a 32–11 nor was the wine, used . . . the *c·* of our Lord.
  of wine
  a 32– 8 to pass each guest a *c·* of wine.
  our
  a 35–27 Our *c·* is the cross.
  same
  a 48–13 when he drinks from the same *c·*,

  a 26– 7 all have the *c·* of sorrowful effort to drink
  32–11 The *c·* shows forth his bitter experience,
  32–12 the *c·* which he prayed might pass from him,
  32–17 took the *c·*, and gave thanks,— *Matt.* 26: 27.
  53– 7 hence the *c·* he drank.
  m 67– 1 The *c·* our Father hath given,

cups
  b 322–20 Then he turns from his *c·*,

curable
  t 461–22 renders your case less *c·*,

curative
  a 55–11 that *c·* mission, . . . cannot be left out
  s 112– 1 the most effective *c·* agent in medical practice.
  145–15 or reliance on some other minor *c·*.

curative
  s 146–17 Science, the *c·* agent of God,
  152–29 skeptical as to material *c·* methods.
  156– 1 If drugs possess . . . intelligent *c·* qualities,
  157– 9 rests on Mind alone as the *c·* Principle,
  p 369–24 (that is, the preventive and *c·*) arts

cure (noun)
  any
  o 348– 6 Ought we not, then, to approve any *c·*, which
  cause and
  f 220– 7 to look in other directions for cause and *c·*.
  effecting a
  t 460–21 Instead of scientifically effecting a *c·*,
  its
  ph 174–31 and its *c·* comes from the immortal divine Mind.
  p 395–23 and then to attempt its *c·* through Mind.
  t 445–26 and is the cause of disease rather than its *c·*.
  of disease
  pref xi– 4 results in the *c·* of disease.
  s 147– 4 its present application to the *c·* of disease.
  149– 3 as far outweighs drugs in the *c·* of disease
  t 457–31 Let this Principle be applied to the *c·* of disease
  of sin
  s 149– 4 as in the *c·* of sin.
  of the sick
  s 132–22 and condemns the *c·* of the sick and sinning if it
  b 285–22 and resort to matter . . . for the *c·* of the sick.
  Principle of the
  f 219–26 not comprehending the Principle of the *c·*,
  radical
  p 398–31 come to the rescue, to work a radical *c·*.

  f 218–13 What renders . . . sickness difficult of *c·* is,
  222–29 In seeking a *c·* for dyspepsia
  p 370–15 faith in the drug is the sole factor in the *c·*.
  402– 5 well-authenticated records of the *c·*,
  t 457–13 cannot . . . both *c·* and cause disease
  457–27 intending thereby to initiate the *c·*
  r 488– 4 the *c·* shows that you understand this

cure (verb)
  an 101–26 seems to alleviate or to *c·* disease,
  s 149–21 remarked . . . mind can never *c·* organic
  151–22 human mind has no power to kill or to *c·*,
  153–21 and it will soon *c·* the boil.
  161–27 the very disease he is trying to *c·*,
  ph 174–22 belief is all that enables a drug to *c·*
  178–17 that chronic case is not difficult to *c·*.
  180–31 dissolve a tumor, or *c·* organic disease,
  188–24 What causes disease cannot *c·* it.
  197–23 would not *c·* dyspepsia at this period.
  f 208–15 to suppose that matter can both cause and *c·*
  221– 2 adopted the Graham system to *c·* dyspepsia.
  233–29 The counter fact . . . is required to *c·* it.
  o 359– 3 Let any clergyman try to *c·* his friends by
  p 366– 3 to *c·* his patient, the metaphysician must
  373– 5 easier to *c·* the most malignant disease than
  373– 6 easier . . . than it is to *c·* sin.
  375–25 and you *c·* the palsy.
  377– 8 Then is the time to *c·* them through C. S.,
  378–20 drilling and drugging, adopted to *c·* matter,
  392– 4 To *c·* a bodily ailment,
  399– 5 can matter *c·* what matter has caused?
  412–16 To prevent disease or to *c·* it,
  417–24 since it is demonstrable that the way to *c·*
  417–31 divine Mind can *c·* by opposite thoughts.
  424–28 To prevent or *c·* scrofula

cured
  m 68–19 and a Christian Scientist *c·* her.
  s 149–23 author has of what is termed organic disease
  149–24 as readily as she has *c·* purely functional disease,
  152–15 once apparently *c·* a case of paralysis
  153–10 *c·* a patient sinking in the last stage of typhoid
  156–27 employing no other means, and she was *c·*.
  ph 169–19 all disease is *c·* by divine Mind.
  181–27 if they are *c·*, they generally know it
  184–27 A woman, whom I *c·* of consumption,
  193–25 his physician claims to have *c·* him,
  o 355–30 and evidenced by the sick who are *c·*
  p 373–19 The fear occasioned by ignorance can be *c·*;
  383– 1 was *c·* when I learned my way in C. S."
  389–32 I *c·* her in a few minutes.
  398–10 Often he gave no name to the distemper he *c·*.
  400– 4 and therefore the disease is thoroughly *c·*.

cures
  s 109–18 *c·* were produced in primitive Christian healing
  138–10 explained his *c·*, which appeared miraculous
  ph 179– 1 perform the sudden *c·* of which it is capable:
  f 208– 8 which causes disease and *c·* it?
  o 344–29 while C. S. *c·* its hundred
  359– 5 will take the same cases, and *c·* will follow.
  p 395–10 The same Principle *c·* both sin and sickness.
  404–27 Both *c·* require the same method
  g 546–29 for it *c·* on a divine demonstrable Principle

curing
p 414– 8   The arguments to be used in *c·* insanity

current
sp 97– 9   and the electric *c·* swift,
an 106– 5   push vainly against the *c·* running heavenward.
p 379–22   The so-called vital *c·* does not affect
g 548–20   many general statements now *c·*,

currents
a 24– 9   healing *c·* of Truth are pointed out.
sp 99–23   The calm, strong *c·* of true spirituality,
ph 185–10   discussed . . . the earth's magnetic *c·*

curse
pr 9–13   and bless them that *c·* us ;
a 30–18   Love, which blesses even those that *c·* it.
b 340–28   equalizes the sexes ; annuls the *c·* on man,
g 557–17   the *c·* will be removed which says to woman,
gl 579–17   ADAM. Error ; . . . a *c·* ;

cursed
g 532–10   Adam and his progeny were *c·*,
535–22   *c·* is the ground for thy sake ;— *Gen.* 3 : 17.
541–29   And now art thou *c·* from the earth.— *Gen.* 4 : 11.

curses
g 524–27   for God presently *c·* the ground.

cursing
a 20–17   returning blessing for *c·*, he taught mortals

curtain
g 557–20   and lifts the *c·* on man as never born

curve
b 282–14   finds no abiding-place in a *c·*,
282–15   a *c·* finds no adjustment to a straight line.
282–22   Even though they seem to touch, one is still a *c·*
283–30   by calling a *c·* a straight line

cuspids
f 247– 6   incisors, *c·*, bicuspids, and one molar.

custody
p 436–25   compelled to let him be taken into *c·*,
439–13   Health-officer had Mortal Man in *c·*,

custom
pr 12–22   The common *c·* of praying for the recovery of
a 32– 7   Among the Jews it was an ancient *c·*
ph 176– 7   The primitive *c·* of taking no thought about
f 247–12   *C·*, education, and fashion form the
p 362–13   According to the *c·* of those days,

customary
f 229–17   This *c·* belief is misnamed material law,
p 363– 6   as was *c·* with women of her grade.

cut
pref vii–24   and to *c·* the rough granite.
a 27–19   to *c·* down the false doctrine of pantheism,
s 141– 7   *c·* off the right hand and pluck out the right
f 212–11   a finger which had been *c·* off for months.
r 474– 8   worse cords than those which *c·* the flesh.

cuticle
p 382–10   or to remove unhealthy exhalations from the *c·*

cuts
p 404–18   *c·* down every tree that brings not forth

Cutter
ph 170– 8   Did Jesus . . . less than Graham or *C·* ?
175–22   was not discussed according to *C·*

cutting
f 224–19   modern lash is less material . . . but it is equally as *c·*.

cycles
s 135–31   as must be the case in the *c·* of divine light.
b 319–13   the infinite *c·* of eternal existence,

Cyclops
s 164– 2   the groping of Homer's *C·* around his cave."

D

daily
pr 4–19   expressed in *d·* watchfulness and in
17– 4   Give us this day our *d·* bread ;— *Matt.* 6 : 11.
a 21– 1   If Truth is overcoming error in your *d·* walk
25– 9   as he went *d·* about his Father's business.
40–30   public worship instead of *d·* deeds.
s 121–27   besides turning *d·* on its own axis.
ph 179– 3   and following Christ in the *d·* life.
f 220– 1   We hear it said : "I exercise *d·* in the open air.
245– 9   she stood *d·* before the window watching
b 272–20   It is the . . . Christianization of *d·* life,
283–28   We must . . . live it in *d·* life ;
o 350– 4   or as very far removed from *d·* experience.
p 413–12   *d·* ablutions of an infant are no more natural
413–19   without scrubbing the whole surface *d·*.
431– 6   the prisoner attended to his *d·* labors,
431–29   testifies : . . . I practise *d·* ablutions
g 557– 1   and repeated this operation *d·*,

dam
b 338–15   it reads, a *d·*, or obstruction.
338–21   Here a *d·* is not a mere play upon words ;

damnation
s 150–25   predestination of souls to *d·* or salvation.

damned
a 38– 6   doctrine . . . few to be saved, while the rest are *d·* ;

damp
ph 175–26   *D·* atmosphere and freezing snow

damsel
p 398–12   "*D·*, I say unto thee, arise !"— *Mark* 5 : 41.

Dan
gl 583–26   definition of

dance
f 250–28   Upon this stage . . . goes on the *d·* of mortal mind.

danger
belief of
p 374–23   You cannot forget the belief of *d·*,
disease and
p 411–29   their exemption from disease and *d·*.
great
t 445–27   great *d·* in teaching Mind-healing indiscriminately,
hopeless
p 375–28   when they are supposed to be in hopeless *d·*
humanity sees
p 371–12   sick humanity sees *d·* in every direction,
seen the
ap 571–14   unfaithful stewards who have seen the *d·*

pr 7–27   The *d·* from prayer is that it may

danger
s 135–17   *d·* of repeating the offence of the Jews
ph 169– 5   mental signs, assuring me that *d·* was over,
p 381– 9   you say that there is *d·*.
381– 9   This fear is the *d·* and induces

dangerous
s 147–32   Jesus never spoke of disease as *d·*
ph 178– 9   is not *d·* because of its priority
b 228– 9   we shall have no *d·* inheritances,
b 299–22   judge the knowledge . . . to be untrue and *d·*,
p 376– 8   diseases deemed *d·* sometimes come from the
t 445–10   Teach the *d·* possibility of dwarfing the
446–17   or his demonstration is protracted, *d·*,
456– 4   is most *d·* quackery.

Daniel
g 514–27   *D·* felt safe in the lions' den,

dare
o 357–14   how *d·* we attempt to destroy what He

dares
p 387– 4   Who *d·* to say that actual Mind can be overworked?
r 489–19   Who *d·* to say that the senses of man
493–30   Who *d·* to doubt this consummate test
g 531–21   Who *d·* to say either that God is in

daring
f 223–30   but the awful *d·* of sin destroys sin,

dark
a 35– 3   the fruitlessness of their toil in the *d·*
47–25   His *d·* plot fell to the ground,
sp 86–18   apparitions brought out in *d·* seances
an 102–18   hidden in the *d·* recesses of mortal thought,
s 163–32   said : . . . *D·* and perplexed, our devious career
ph 200– 1   When Homer sang . . . Olympus was *d·*,
c 263– 9   he will no longer grope in the *d·*
p 371– 7   telling ghost-stories in the *d·*.
403–24   *d·* forebodings regarding disease
418–31   *d·* images of mortal thought,
428– 4   resolves the *d·* visions of material sense
g 502– 6   the light over the *d·*,
ap 558–12   seems at first obscure, abstract, and *d·* ;
559–12   It is heard in the desert and in *d·* places of fear.
566– 2   *d·* ebbing and flowing tides of human fear,
gl 596–23   Though the way is *d·* in mortal sense,

darkened
sp 93–22   belief that Spirit is finite . . . has *d·* all history

darkening
s 139–21   *d·* to some extent the inspired pages.

darkest
sp 96–11   "The *d·* hour precedes the dawn."

day

and night
ap 568–17   before our God *d·* and night.— *Rev.* 12 : 10.

close of
a 32–31   a sad supper taken at the close of *d·*,

each
a 21–13   gain a little each *d·* in the right direction,
f 248–11   which each *d·* brings to a nearer tomb.
p 413–23   need not wash his little body all over each *d·*

every
sp 70– 1   Every *d·* is a mystery.
f 233– 1   Every *d·* makes its demands upon us
c 261–16   he hobbled every *d·* to the theatre,
p 413–14   taking a fish out of water every *d·*

fifth
g 513– 5   and the morning were the fifth *d·*.— *Gen.* 1 : 23.

first
g 504– 5   and the morning were the first *d·*.— *Gen.* 1 : 5.
gl 584– 3   and the morning were the first *d·*."— *Gen.* 1 : 5.

fourth
g 511–16   and the morning were the fourth *d·*.— *Gen.* 1 : 19.

future
s 150–24   and will be to all others at some future *d·*,

gala
f 252–23   says: . . . make my short span of life one gala *d·*.

God's
gl 584– 7   This unfolding is God's *d·*,

happy
a 55–17   My weary hope tries to realize that happy *d·*,

its
sp 95–21   even human invention must have its *d·*,

later
pr 7–32   or mean to ask forgiveness at some later *d·*.

next
ph 193–18   The next *d·* I saw him in the yard.

of salvation
a 39–19   now is the *d·* of salvation,"— *II Cor.* 6 : 2.
sp 93– 8   now is the *d·* of salvation,"— *II Cor.* 6 : 2.

of Spirit
g 505– 1   No . . . planetary revolutions form the *d·* of Spirit.

of wrath
b 339–15   "wrath against the *d·* of wrath."— *Rom.* 2 : 5.

one
s 156–20   she would give up her medicine for one *d·*,
g 504–22   "one *d·* is with the Lord as— *II Pet.* 3 : 8.
gl 598–21   "One *d·* is with the Lord as— *II Pet.* 3 : 8.

orb of
ph 188–31   The human eye knows not where the orb of *d·* is,
189–12   when the orb of *d·* disappears,

our
pr 5–18   giving us strength according to our *d·*.

perfect
p 388–29   In that perfect *d·* of understanding,
r 496–13   brighter "unto the perfect *d·*."— *Prov.* 4 : 18.
ap 562–20   shines "unto the perfect *d·*"— *Prov.* 4 : 18.

present
o 349– 4   the rabbis of the present *d·* ask

risen
pref vii– 4   ere cometh the full radiance of a risen *d·*.

second
g 506– 9   and the morning were the second *d·*.— *Gen.* 1 : 8.

seventh
g 519–22   And on the seventh *d·* God ended His— *Gen.* 2 : 2.
519–24   He rested on the seventh *d·*— *Gen.* 2 : 2.

sixth
g 518–26   and the morning were the sixth *d·*.— *Gen.* 1 : 31.

some
m 69–20   Some *d·* the child will ask his parent :
f 228–14   Mortals will some *d·* assert their freedom

suppositional
g 533–25   but error has its suppositional *d·*

that
sp 95–21   we want that *d·* to be succeeded by C. S.,
b 292– 3   "but of that *d·* and hour,— *Matt.* 24 : 36.

their
a 52–26   speaking not for their *d·* only
c 264– 2   They have their *d·* before the permanent facts

third
s 156–23   but on the third *d·* she again suffered,
g 508–27   and the morning were the third *d·*.— *Gen.* 1 : 13.
509– 6   he rose from the grave,— on the third *d·*

this
pr 17– 4   Give us this *d·* our daily bread ;— *Matt.* 6 : 11.

s 116–15   nor do they carry the *d·* against physical
ph 174–13   the *d·* is at hand"— *Rom.* 13 : 12.
197–10   "In the *d·* that thou eatest— *Gen.* 2 : 17.
b 308–24   "Let me go, for the *d·* breaketh :"— *Gen.* 32 : 26.
310–11   *D·* may decline and shadows fall,
r 481–18   "In the *d·* that thou eatest— *Gen.* 2 : 17.
g 509–10   to divide the *d·* from the night ;— *Gen.* 1 : 14.
510–14   the greater light to rule the *d·*,— *Gen.* 1 : 16.
511– 9   and to rule over the *d·*— *Gen.* 1 : 18.
520–17   in the *d·* that the Lord God— *Gen.* 2 : 4.
527– 9   in the *d·* that thou eatest— *Gen.* 2 : 17.

day

g 530–14   in the *d·* ye eat thereof,— *Gen.* 3 : 5.
532– 8   "In the *d·* that thou eatest— *Gen.* 2 : 17.
543–31   "In the *d·* that the Lord God— *Gen.* 2 : 4.
ap 566–10   a pillar of cloud by *d·* and of fire by night,
575–20   shall not be shut at all by *d·* :— *Rev.* 21 : 25.
gl 584– 1   definition of

day-dreams
sp 88– 1   In our *d·* we can recall

Day of Pentecost
a 47– 9   an overwhelming power as on the *D· of P·*.

days *(see also* **days'**)

ancient
o 349– 3   As Paul asked of the unfaithful in ancient *d·*,

Ancient of
s 146–29   as ancient as "the Ancient of *d·*."— *Dan.* 7 : 9.

and seasons
g 509–25   the *d·* and seasons of Mind's creation,

and years
g 509–11   and for *d·*, and years.— *Gen.* 1 : 14.

earthly
s 150–27   by physical conditions all his earthly *d·*,
ph 197– 6   costs many a man his earthly *d·* of comfort.

few
g 536–21   "of few *d·*, and full of trouble."— *Job* 14 : 1.
552–15   of few *d·*, and full of trouble."— *Job* 14 : 1.

his
ph 190–23   As for man, his *d·* are as grass :— *Psal.* 103 : 15.
r 476–24   "As for man, his *d·* are as grass :— *Psal.* 103 : 15.
g 530– 1   increases in falsehood and his *d·* become

latter
sp 83– 9   in order to escape the error of these latter *d·*.
b 320–31   yet in the latter *d·* he should stand

length of
b 283–25   demonstrated in length of *d·*,

of my life
ap 578–16   follow me all the *d·* of my life ;— *Psal.* 23 : 6.

our
p 409–29   We cannot spend our *d·* here in ignorance of
r 487–28   lengthens our *d·* by strengthening our trust

seven
g 520–10   The numerals of infinity, called *seven d·*,

six
a 21–30   After following the sun for six *d·*,

these
g 520–12   These *d·* will appear as mortality disappears,

those
s 107–18   the prospect of those *d·* in which we must say,
129–13   In those *d·* there will be
ph 175–23   man's belief in those *d·* was not so severe upon
p 362–23   According to the custom of those *d·*,
ap 562– 1   John saw in those *d·* the spiritual idea

three
a 27–13   in three *d·* I [Spirit] will raise it up."— *John* 2 : 19.
45–13   Three *d·* after his bodily burial he
b 314–15   in three *d·* I will raise it up,"— *John* 2 : 19.
r 494– 3   in three *d·* I [Mind] will— *John* 2 : 19.

two
s 156–22   she could get along two *d·* without globules ;
f 202–17   The *d·* of our pilgrimage will multiply
b 333–18   without beginning of years or end of *d·*.
g 535–23   all the *d·* of thy life :— *Gen.* 3 : 17.

days'
a 44– 7   His three *d·* work in the sepulchre

daystar
pref vii–11   follow this *d·* of divine Science,

dead

are raised
a 27– 5   the deaf hear, the *d·* are raised,— *Luke* 7 : 22.
s 132– 7   the deaf hear, the *d·* are raised— *Matt.* 11 : 5.

Lazarus from the
s 134–27   and he raised Lazarus from the *d·*,

raised the
m 67–22   raised the *d·*, and commanded even the winds
b 273–26   healed the sick, and raised the *d·*

raises the
a 33–24   raises the *d·* from trespasses and sins,

raise the
a 51–32   cast out evil, and raise the *d·*.
s 137– 3   cast out evil, raise the *d·* ;
b 329– 8   Because you cannot . . . raise the *d·*,

raising the
a 43– 1   healing the sick, and raising the *d·*,
b 316–29   casting out evils, . . . and raising the *d·*,
p 369– 9   raising the *d·*, and walking over the wave.
430– 3   healing the dying and raising the *d·*.

so-called
sp 74–30   so-called *d·* and living cannot commune
75– 3   The so-called *d·*, in order to reappear
75– 7   could take no cognizance of the so-called *d·*.
77–28   Spiritism consigns the so-called *d·* to a
81– 2   between the so-called *d·* and the living,

a 23–15   "Faith without works is *d·*."— *Jas.* 2 : 26.

dead

a	31–14	He attached no importance to *d·* ceremonies.
	34– 3	Then why ascribe this inspiration to a *d·* rite,
	44–28	His disciples believed Jesus to be *d·* while he
	45–26	for they believed his body to be *d·*.
m	69–29	and the resurrection from the *d·*, — *Luke* 20 : 35.
sp	75–26	those living on the earth and those called *d·*,
s	113– 7	Without this, the letter is but the *d·* body
	136–17	These prophets were considered *d·*,
	164–18	we should not be *d·*.
ph	187–29	this so-called mind then calls itself *d·* ;
f	216– 3	Who shall say that man . . . may be *d·* to-morrow?
	228–31	excel the influence of their *d·* faith and
	251–10	(1) that they are not *d·* ;
b	295–30	It further teaches that when man is *d·*,
	312– 9	People say, "Man is *d·* ;"
	316–29	those *d·* in trespasses and sins,
	334–26	I am he that liveth, and was *d·* — *Rev.* 1 : 18.
o	341– *	*raised up Jesus from the d·* — *Rom.* 8 : 11.
	341– *	*He that raised up Christ from the d·* — *Rom.* 8 : 11.
	355–10, 11	let the *d·* bury their *d·*." — *Matt.* 8 : 22.
p	369–27	Unscientific methods are finding their *d·* level.
	398– 6	and he was as one *d·*," — *Mark* 9 : 26.
	398–11	synagogue ruler's daughter, whom they called *d·*
	398–12	"she is not *d·*, but sleepeth," — *Luke* 8 : 52.
	416–21	only in mortal mind, as the *d·* body proves ;
	427–32	its own material declaration, "I am *d·*,"
	433–25	sentenced to be tortured until he is *d·*.
r	479–16	Does that which we call *d·* ever see,

deadened

a	55– 2	from a *d·* sense of the invisible God,

deadly

b	328–24	if they drink any *d·* thing, — *Mark* 16 : 18.
p	362– *	*if they drink any d· thing,* — *Mark* 16 : 18.
t	458–20	Sin makes *d·* thrusts at the Christian Scientist

deadness

p	399–21	this *d·* shows that so-called mortal life

deaf

a	27– 5	the *d·* hear, the dead are raised, — *Luke* 7 : 22.
s	132– 7	*d·* hear, the dead are raised — *Matt.* 11 : 5.
ph	183–26	hearing to the *d·*, voice to the dumb,
	194–12	if mortal mind says, "I am *d·* and blind,"
f	210–13	hearing to the *d·*, feet to the lame,
	213–24	Beethoven, who was so long hopelessly *d·*.
	226–25	The lame, the *d·*, the dumb, the blind,
o	342–25	causes the *d·* to hear, the lame to walk,
p	398– 2	"Thou dumb and *d·* spirit, — *Mark* 9 : 25.
t	444–23	If . . . medical schools turn a *d·* ear to
r	487–11	gave . . . hearing to the *d·* centuries ago,

deafness

ph	194–11	not necessary to ensure *d·* and blindness ;
r	486–29	then palsy, blindness, and *d·* would

deal

s	148–19	and *d·* — the one wholly, the other primarily
p	365–22	and *d·* with his patients compassionately ;
g	552– 7	hypotheses *d·* with causation as contingent on

dealer

p	438–28	is not an importer or *d·* in fur,

dealing

o	349–18	in *d·* with spiritual ideas.
	355– 4	methods of *d·* with sin and disease
t	446– 3	and in this way *d·* pitilessly with

deals

s	157– 2	C. S. *d·* wholly with the mental cause
p	423–15	The matter-physician *d·* with matter
t	463– 1	discerns and *d·* with the real cause of disease.
g	535–10	Divine Science *d·* its chief blow at the

dealt

b	329– 3	will be fairly *d·* with ; they will be sought and
t	460–17	*d·* with through right apprehension of

dear

pr	9–30	in the footsteps of our *d·* Master?
a	34–24	for soon their *d·* Master would rise
f	253– 9	I hope, *d·* reader, I am leading you into
o	360–13	*D·* reader, which mind-picture or
p	366– 1	sense of the *d·* Father's loving-kindness.
g	547– 6	You can prove for yourself, *d·* reader,
ap	573–29	Take heart, *d·* sufferer, for this reality
	574–25	Think of this, *d·* reader, for it will

dear-bought

a	36–11	that he might pour his *d·* bounty into
	54–11	liberally pour his *d·* treasures

dearer

f	239–19	If divine Love is becoming nearer, *d·*,

dearest

m	58–21	Home is the *d·* spot on earth,

Death

p	432–21	I am *D·*. I was called for,
	439– 6	*D·* testified that he was absent
p	439– 9	At this request *D·* repaired to the spot
	439–22	his struggles against liver-complaint and *D·*.
	440–10	a verdict delivering Mortal Man to *D·*.

death

after

a	24–24	only for the presentation, after *d·*,
	35–16	his probation in the flesh after *d·*,
	36– 6	sufficient suffering, either before or after *d·*,
sp	81– 9	a continued existence after *d·*
b	291–24	so shall he be after *d·*, until
p	409–28	will not depend on it after *d·*.
	429–21	If we live after *d·* and are immortal,
r	486–15	body was the same immediately after *d·*

and finiteness

r	469– 5	*D·* and finiteness are unknown to Life.

and matter

r	486–19	conditional upon *d·* and matter,

and mortality

b	295–31	resurrected from *d·* and mortality.

and the grave

a	39–14	Jesus overcame *d·* and the grave
	45– 7	in his victory over *d·* and the grave.
	49–24	over sin, sickness, *d·*, and the grave.
s	137– 6	sickness, sin, disease, *d·*, and the grave.

an enemy

a	39–13	The Bible calls *d·* an enemy,

announcing the

p	386–17	mistakenly announcing the *d·* of a friend,

because of

b	314– 1	no more perfect because of *d·*

bed of

p	427–26	Called to the bed of *d·*, what material

before

ph	187–32	a body like the one it had before *d·*.

belief called

p	380– 3	which ends in a belief called *d·*,

belief in

a	42– 5	The universal belief in *d·* is of no advantage.
b	289–22	law of mortal mind, in a belief in *d·*.
	325– 2	he who perceives . . . loses his belief in *d·*.
p	426–11	If the belief in *d·* were obliterated,
	430– 8	When man gives up his belief in *d·*,

birth and

f	246–18	Time-tables of birth and *d·* are so many

birth nor

f	244–24	He has neither birth nor *d·*.

birth or

f	206–25	Can there be any birth or *d·* for man,

bleeding to

p	379–10	fancied himself bleeding to *d·*,

bring forth

p	392– 3	Only while . . . sin remains can it bring forth *d·*.

brink of

f	235–22	To the tremblers on the brink of *d·*,

brought

p	426–28	Sin brought *d·*, and death will disappear with
g	532– 7	when eating its first fruits brought *d·* ?

called

f	254–17	prior to the change called *d·*,
b	290–16	If the change called *d·* destroyed the belief
r	487– 6	both before and after that which is called *d·*.
ap	572–24	stage in human experience called *d·*,

can never

sp	76–29	*D·* can never hasten this state of

caused the

p	379–17	Oxford boys, who caused the *d·* of a man,

cessation of

ap	573–27	conscious, here and now, of a cessation of *d·*,

decay, and

g	544– 7	Birth, decay, and *d·* arise from the

decreed the

ap	565–10	Herod decreed the *d·* of every male child

deny

s	113–19	Life, God, omnipotent good, deny *d·*,

despair and

p	433–15	a look of despair and *d·* settles upon it.

destroyed by his

a	50–24	and that all evidence . . . was destroyed by his *d·*.

destroying

f	210– 8	casting out evils, and destroying *d·*,

dew of

ph	193– 9	The dew of *d·* was on his brow.

discord and

s	124–10	and holding fast to discord and *d·*.
f	224–10	life and peace instead of discord and *d·*.

disease and

(see **disease**)

disease, nor

s	140–27	causeth no evil, disease, nor *d·*.
p	368–22	disease, nor *d·* can be spiritual,

disease, sin, and

sp	78– 3	like the discords of disease, sin, and *d·*,
b	275–29	such as matter, disease, sin, and *d·*,
p	412–15	and to destroy disease, sin, and *d·*.

death

dream of
p 427–29 dream of *d·* must be mastered by Mind
429–17 Mortals waken from the dream of *d·*
end in
b 331– 5 subject to their limitations and would end in *d·*.
ends in
b 307–16 false sense of an existence which ends in *d·*.
309–29 such so-called life always ends in *d·*.
error and
a 44– 1 must seal the victory over error and *d·*,
g 539–10 such as evil, matter, error, and *d·*?
evidence of
gl 584–15 Any material evidence of *d·* is false,
experience of
b 291–10 belief in the experience of *d·*
faith in
p 426–23 The relinquishment of all faith in *d·*
fear of
gl 596–25 destroy . . . the fear of *d·*,
foundations of
ph 171–16 destroying the foundations of *d·*.
frighten into
sp 79– 4 error that tends to frighten into *d·*
has no dominion
o 347– 7 all is Life, and *d·* has no dominion.
hastening to
sp 78– 7 belief that we are . . . hastening to *d·*,
health-laws, and
p 413–27 illusions about disease, health-laws, and *d·*,
ignominy and
an 105–27 down to the depths of ignominy and *d·*.
illusion of
f 251– 9 In the illusion of *d·*, mortals wake to the
r 493–29 awakened Lazarus from the dream, illusion, of *d·*,
instantaneous
p 377–16 has caused what is termed instantaneous *d·*.
instant of
b 290–24 which possess us at the instant of *d·*
instead of
f 253–30 which is the law of Life instead of *d·*,
p 435–14 and life instead of *d·*.
interval of
gl 598–27 would bridge over . . . the interval of *d·*,
is not the result
r 486–12 *D·* is not the result of Truth
is swallowed up
s 164–28 *D·* is swallowed up in victory"— *I Cor.* 15 : 54.
r 496–27 *D·* is swallowed up in victory."— *I Cor.* 15 : 54.
is the illusion
p 428– 3 Life is real, and *d·* is the illusion.
Jesus'
a 24–23 Does spiritualism find Jesus' *d·* necessary
Jesus overcame
a 39–14 Jesus overcame *d·* and the grave
life and
(see **life**)
Life destroys
b 339– 2 Divine Life destroys *d·*,
Life over
p 406–23 Life over *d·*, and good over evil,
master of
b 316–19 proved that Truth was the master of *d·*.
matter and
b 289–29 Matter and *d·* are mortal illusions.
must be overcome
sp 76–30 for *d·* must be overcome, not submitted to,
never see
sp 70– * *he shall never see d·.— John* 8 : 51.
f 217–13 he shall never see *d·* !"— *John* 8 : 51.
p 428– 8 he shall never see *d·*."— *John* 8 : 51.
429–32 he shall never see *d·*."— *John* 8 : 51.
438– 7 he shall never see *d·.— John* 8 : 51.
no
b 288–26 no birth, no material life, and no *d·*.
331–16 all is Life, and there is no *d·*.
p 387– 2 and know that there is no *d·*.
426–13 understanding obtained that there is no *d·*,
428– 1 "There is no *d·*, no inaction,
429– 3 by the understanding that there is no *d·*,
no partnership with
f 243–27 Life has no partnership with *d·*.
no reality in
p 427– 9 learning that there is no reality in *d·*,
not
r 485–18 Not *d·*, but the understanding of Life,
not subject to
sp 74– 2 spiritual life which is not subject to *d·*.
b 288–25 that Life is not subject to *d·* ;
not the
b 271–24 the eternal life, not the *d·* of Jesus,
296–11 not the *d·* of organic matter,
of these errors
b 290–25 but endure until the *d·* of these errors.
overcome
p 427–18 If man is never to overcome *d·*, why do the

death

overcomes
b 289–15 Truth, overcame and still overcomes *d·*
315–24 heals sickness, and overcomes *d·*.
persecuted unto
s 134– 6 were so often persecuted unto *d·*,
physical
an 101–25 lead to moral and to physical *d·*.
power of
r 473–15 and destroying the power of *d·*.
power over
a 26–25 and of his demonstration of power over *d·*,
punishable with
p 431–10 this offence is deemed punishable with *d·*.
punished with
p 432–15 treated as a criminal and punished with *d·*.
regarding
sp 79– 6 changing the patient's thoughts regarding *d·*.
resort to
b 306– 4 and then resort to *d·* to reproduce
resulted in the
o 342–32 if their treatment resulted in the *d·* of a patient.
resulting in
gl 591–10 MATTER. . . . life resulting in *d·*,
second
sp 77–12 "the second *d·* hath no power."— *Rev.* 20 : 6.
b 290–14 the second *d·* hath no power."— *Rev.* 20 : 6.
seemed to be
a 46–21 unchanged . . . after what seemed to be *d·*
[seeming]
a 45–11 by the [seeming] *d·* of His Son,— *Rom.* 5 : 10.
sentence of
p 433–19 the solemn sentence of *d·* upon the prisoner.
436– 3 for which Mortal Man is under sentence of *d·*.
436–33 pronounced a sentence of *d·* for doing right.
shadow of
ap 578–11 valley of the shadow of *d·*,— *Psal.* 23 : 4.
gl 596–22 valley of the shadow of *d·*,— *Psal.* 23 : 4.
shall not see
b 325– 1 "He . . . shall not see *d·*."— *see John* 11 : 26.
shame and
a 52–16 putting to shame and *d·* the best man that
shuts the door on
sp 90–26 This conviction shuts the door on *d·*,
sickness and
(see **sickness**)
sickness, sin, and
(see **sickness**)
sickness, sin, nor
p 381–18 In . . . Love there is no sickness, sin, nor *d·*,
sickness, sin, or
t 463–23 manifested in forms of sickness, sin, or *d·*
sin and
(see **sin**)
sin, disease, and
(see **sin**)
sin, disease, or
f 253–17 overcome the belief in sin, disease, or *d·*,
253–26 Do not believe in . . . sin, disease, or *d·*,
p 380– 9 the demands of sin, disease, or *d·*,
sin or
s 125–19 cannot be controlled by sin or *d·*,
sin, sickness, and
(see **sin**)
sin, sickness, nor
ap 567– 8 there is no error, no sin, sickness, nor *d·*.
sin, sickness, or
r 472–27 the only reality of sin, sickness, or *d·* is
gl 585–21 before it accepts sin, sickness, or *d·* ;
so-called
b 291– 3 suppositions. . .that the so-called *d·* of the body
sorrow and
f 203–30 waves of sin, sorrow, and *d·* beat in vain.
spiritual
b 310–24 and spiritual *d·* is oblivion.
sting of
r 496–20 "The sting of *d·* is sin ;— *I Cor.* 15 : 56.
stung to
ap 569–26 The dragon is at last stung to *d·*
submissive to
b 314–31 submissive to *d·* as being in supposed accord
suffering, and
f 219–30 from the belief in sin, suffering, and *d·*
supposed
gl 598–11 In the record of Jesus' supposed *d·*, we read :
supposition that
p 387–21 supposition that *d·* comes in obedience to
termed
sp 92– 8 decomposition . . . in what is termed *d·*.
b 290– 4 before what is termed *d·* overtakes mortals,
gl 595–20 continues after, what is termed *d·*, until
this
ph 177–28 does human belief, you ask, cause this *d·*?
b 312– 9 but this *d·* is the departure of a mortal's mind,
tree of
g 527–18 the tree of *d·* to His own creation?

death

triumphing over
f 232–19   healing the sick and triumphing over *d·*.

triumph over
a 54–16   and triumph over *d·* through Mind,

triumphs over
a 25–16   casts out error, and triumphs over *d·*.
    31–22   the divine Principle which triumphs over *d·*.

ultimates in
gl 580–17   Life's counterfeit, which ultimates in *d·* ;

until
m 68–12   "until *d·* do us part."

unto the
ap 568–19   loved not their lives unto the *d·*.— *Rev.* 12 : 11.

vanish in
g 555–30   which seemed to vanish in *d·*.

victory over
a 35–15   They celebrate their Lord's victory over *d·*,
   45– 7   in his victory over *d·* and the grave.
p 427–21   shall obtain the victory over *d·* in proportion

violent
a 47–29   each one came to a violent *d·* except

warning people against
sp 79– 3   Warning people against *d·* is an error

was occasioned
s 159– 9   *d·* was occasioned, not by the ether,

we call
sp 82–20   as before the change we call *d·*,
ph 172– 9   if man passes through what we call *d·*

we find
c 260–32   If we look to the body . . . for Life, we find *d·* ;

will be found
a 42– 6   *D·* will be found at length to be a

will be obsolete
sp 90–13   and *d·* will be obsolete,

will disappear
p 426–28   *d·* will disappear with the disappearance of sin

will occur
sp 77– 9   *D·* will occur on the next plane of existence

a 31–24   the Lord's *d·* till he come."— *I Cor.* 11 : 26.
   39–11   causes mortals to regard *d·* as a friend,
   39–15   To him, therefore, *d·* was not the threshold
   47–29   except St. John, of whose *d·* we have no record.
sp 73–23   belief that spirit . . . is freed by *d·*,
   90–14   some insist that *d·* is the necessary prelude to
s 108–25   called error, sin, sickness, disease, *d·*,
  113–20   sin, evil, . . . deny good, omnipotent God,
  115–24   hatred, revenge, sin, sickness, disease, *d·*.
  119–20   or prostrates in *d·* the child at prayer,
  151–17   Mortal belief says that *d·* has
ph 172–10   and *d·* is the Rubicon of spirituality?
  186–25   If *d·* is as real as Life, immortality is a myth.
  196– 9   Sin alone brings *d·*, for sin is the only
f 202–20   true way leads to Life instead of to *d·*,
  203–24   *D·* is not a stepping-stone to Life,
  206–21   and then taking it away by *d·*?
  216–25   while health would seem the exception, *d·* the
  219– 1   sorrow, sin, *d·*, will be unknown,
  221–13   informed him that *d·* was indeed his only
  239–28   it is discordant and ends in sin, sickness, *d·*.
  244–19   If man flickers out in *d·*
  250–31   reveals Life as not being at the mercy of *d·*,
  251–24   the healer of sin, disease, *d·*,
c 265–16   The senses represent . . . *d·* as irresistible,
b 289–18   what appears to the senses to be *d·* is but
  291–23   As *d·* findeth mortal man, so shall he be . . . until
  292–10   belief that . . . Life be controlled by *d·*,
  296–10   The *d·* of a false material sense and of sin,
  304– 6   "Neither *d·*, nor life,— *Rom.* 8 : 38.
  304–14   can never produce mind nor life result in *d·*.
  306– 3   They would first make life result in *d·*,
  306– 5   taught them how *d·* was to be overcome
  312–13   you say that matter has caused his *d·*.
  312–19   Mortals claim that *d·* is inevitable ;
o 360–28   the Jews put to *d·* the Galilean Prophet,
p 386–18   same grief that the friend's real *d·* would bring.
  407–27   and brings . . . Life not *d·*, into
  409–31   *D·* will not make us harmonious and immortal
  426–18   are not saved from sin or sickness by *d·*,
  426–31   human concepts named matter, *d·*, disease,
  427– 7   If man believes in *d·* now, he must disbelieve
          in it
  427–13   *D·* is but another phase of the dream
  427–19   that shall be destroyed is *d·*"— *I Cor.* 15 : 26.
  433–30   to prepare the frightened sense . . . for *d·*.
  434–29   not proved "worthy of *d·*, or— *Acts* 26 : 31.
r 481–14   declaring existence to be at the mercy of *d·*,
  486–15   If *d·* restores sight, sound, and strength
  486–17   If . . . then *d·* is not an enemy
  487– 4   never attainable through *d·*, but gained by
g 522–30   Does Life, Truth, and Love produce *d·*,
gl 584– 9   definition of
  588– 2   revenge ; sin ; sickness ; *d·* ;
  591–11   Matter. Mythology ; . . . *d·* in life ;

death

gl 592–10   Mortal Mind. . . . sin ; sickness ; *d·*.
  595– 6   Tares. . . . sin ; sickness ; disease ; *d·*.

deathless

a 28–13   the divine Principle of the *d·* Christ,
  44– 9   He proved Life to be *d·*
m 69–16   and of man *d·* and perfect
sp 72– 6   would disappear to mortal sense, would be *d·*.
f 203–22   that the *d·* Principle, or Soul,
c 266–29   Man is *d·*, spiritual.
b 335–32   The Ego is *d·* and limitless,
p 427– 9   since the truth of being is *d·*.
r 487– 3   Life is *d·*.   Life is the origin and
  487–28   trust in the *d·* reality of Life,
g 509– 3   the *d·* Life, or Mind,
  534– 5   to manifest the *d·* man of God's creating.

death-pallor

ph 193–11   its *d·* gave place to a natural hue.

death-process

b 289–20   to . . . the real universe there is no *d·*.

death-sentence

ph 198– 4   as a criminal hears his *d·*.

death-valley

s 108–20   within the shadow of the *d·*,

debarred

m 64–14   A wife is sometimes *d·*
p 362– 7   Heedless of the fact that she was *d·*

debars

p 366– 8   *d·* him from giving drink to the thirsty

debased

f 235–16   while the *d·* and unscrupulous mind,
b 318–10   all that is material, untrue, selfish, or *d·*.

debate

p 434– 8   After much *d·* and opposition,

debauched

s 136–21   That a wicked king and *d·* husband

debauchee

a 52–30   The bigot, the *d·*, the hypocrite,

debility

p 442–10   all sallowness and *d·* had disappeared.

débris

b 289– 2   can never rise from the temporal *d·* . . . until

debt

pr 4– 7   our proper *d·* to him and the only worthy
a 22–31   Mercy cancels the *d·* only when justice
  23– 4   One sacrifice, . . . is insufficient to pay the *d·*
p 363–24   Why did he thus summarize her *d·*

debtors

pr 17– 6   as we forgive our *d·*.— *Matt.* 6 : 12.
p 363–16   He described two *d·*, one for a large sum

debts

pr 11– 2   "Forgive us our *d·*,"— *Matt.* 6 : 12.
  17– 6   And forgive us our *d·*,— *Matt.* 6 : 12.

decadence

f 244–30   pictures age as . . . helplessness and *d·*,

Decalogue

s 112–31   commandment in the Hebrew *D·*,
r 489–14   it breaks all the commands of the Mosaic *D·*

decapitates

c 266– 3   sword of Science, with which Truth *d·* error,

decay

age and
f 247–30   shining resplendent and eternal over age and *d·*.

age or
f 247–14   Immortality, exempt from age or *d·*,

and death
g 544– 7   Birth, *d·*, and death arise from the

and dissolution
g 550–18   *d·*, and dissolution as its component stages

discord and
b 280– 2   Symbols and elements of discord and *d·*
r 468–18   eternal and incapable of discord and *d·*.
g 503–24   creates no element nor symbol of discord and *d·*.

laws of
f 244–14   beasts and vegetables,— subject to laws of *d·*.

maturity, and
s 124–18   represented as subject to growth, maturity, and
          d·,
ph 190–14   Human birth, growth, maturity, and *d·*
f 244–13   Man undergoing birth, maturity, and *d·*

maturity, nor
b 310–31   neither growth, maturity, nor *d·* in Soul.

not subject to
ph 200–13   and not subject to *d·* and dust.

m 66–13   when these *d·*, Love propagates anew the
  68–11   and scatters love's petals to *d·*.
b 305–28   not subject to birth, growth, maturity, *d·*,
  318–12   and doom all things to *d·*,

decay

g 549– 5 germinates in eggs and must *d·*
551–30 the material seed must *d·*

decayed

p 395–25 a tumor, a cancer, or *d·* lungs,

decaying

sp 78– 1 The *d·* flower, the blighted bud,
f 247– 9 upper and lower teeth without a *d·* cavity.

decays

b 323–18 the one unused talent *d·* and is lost.
p 429–11 corpse, deserted by thought, is cold and *d·*,

decease

s 164–18 The seeming *d·*, caused by a

deceased

sp 81–32 somebody, . . . must have known the *d·*
s 159– 3 her sister testified that the *d·* protested

deceit

s 115–22 pride, envy, *d·*, hatred, revenge,
p 405– 8 and to overcome *d·* with honesty.
t 448–31 To talk the right and live the wrong is foolish *d·*,

deceitful

f 252–21 Animal in propensity, *d·* in sentiment,
p 395– 4 the testimony of the *d·* senses,
395–17 *d·* person should not be a nurse.

deceive

pr 8–16 it is wise not to try to *d·* ourselves
c 266–23 material sense, . . . would *d·* the very elect.

deceived

f 213– 3 or is said to be *d·*.
b 339–17 awful unreality by which he has been *d·*.
p 440– 8 *d·* by your attorney, False Belief,
t 451–26 subtle degree of evil, *d·* and deceiving.

deceiver

f 213– 3 Whoever contradicts this . . . is called a *d·*,

deceiveth

o 345–27 he *d·* himself."— *Gal.* 6 : 3.
ap 567–15 *d·* the whole world :— *Rev.* 12 : 9.

deceiving

t 451–26 subtle degree of evil, deceived and *d·*.

deception

m 59–25 for *d·* is fatal to happiness.
f 207– 9 evil is the awful *d·* and unreality of existence.

deceptive

an 101–27 this appearance is *d·*, since

decide

a 50– 3 Who shall *d·* what truth and love are?
ph 195–11 The point for each one to *d·* is,
p 392–21 If you *d·* that climate . . . is unhealthy,
t 463–21 To *d·* quickly as to the proper treatment of

decided

ph 176–29 Hence *d·* types of acute disease
f 221– 5 he *d·* that his diet should be more rigid,
p 374– 1 which mortal mind has *d·* upon as essential
432–29 he *d·* at once that the prisoner should die.
441– 5 He also *d·* that the plaintiff, Personal Sense,
t 453–12 I have never witnessed so *d·* effects from

decides

p 385–20 Mind *d·* whether or not the flesh shall
418–19 and to whatever *d·* its type and symptoms.
435–24 *d·* what penalty is due for the sin,
441–19 Spirit *d·* in favor of Man and against Matter.
441–25 Supreme Bench *d·* in favor of intelligence,

deciding

ph 181– 2 Before *d·* that the body, matter, is disordered,

decision

a 48–29 his awful *d·* against human rights and
f 216–22 If the *d·* were left to the corporeal senses,
p 380–13 *d·* which the defendant knows will be
389– 2 If this *d·* be left to C. S.,
437–19 I ask that the Supreme Court . . . reverse this *d·*.

decisions

s 139–15 The *d·* by vote of Church Councils
b 304–26 Left to the *d·* of material sense,
p 392–22 Your *d·* will master you,
440–30 the just and equitable *d·* of divine Spirit

Declaration

an 106– 6 C. S. has its *D·* of Independence.
s 161–16 that immortal sentiment of the *D·*,

declaration

o 361–13 This *d·* of Jesus, understood, conflicts not
p 363–22 that remarkable *d·* to the woman,
427–31 Thought will waken from its own material *d·*,
r 466–29 Christianity will demonstrate this *d·*
478– 9 What would be thought of the *d·* that a
g 520–23 Here is the emphatic *d·* that God creates all
526– 6 This opposite *d·*, . . . contradicts the
538–30 Eve's *d·*, "I have gotten a man — *Gen.* 4 : 1.
ap 573–14 even the *d·* from heaven, supreme harmony,

declare

pref vii–25 Future ages must *d·* what the pioneer has
a 50– 3 "Who shall *d·* his generation?"— *Isa.* 53 : 8.
m 69–24 or do you *d·* that Spirit is infinite,
s 163– 8 said : "I *d·* my conscientious opinion,
ph 174–26 Why *d·* that the body is diseased,
181–14 It is foolish to *d·* that you
f 243–29 because they *d·* nothing except God.
b 268– * *d· we unto you,*— *I John* 1 : 3.
286–17 The Scriptures *d·* all that He made to be good,
287–21 Scriptures *d·* that man was made in God's
307– 9 It says : . . . I *d·* that God makes evil minds
318– 6 Scriptures *d·* that God made all,
320–30 as if Job intended to *d·*
330–19 God is what the Scriptures *d·* Him to be,
331–14 Scriptures also *d·* that God is Spirit.
p 373–17 Scriptures also *d·*, through the exalted thought
376–10 invalid, whom you *d·* to be wasting away
381–18 Scriptures *d·* that we live, move, and
386– 8 So long as mortals *d·* that certain states of the
391–25 Disease has no intelligence to *d·* itself
397–17 *D·* that you are not hurt and understand . . . why,
397–22 which the Scriptures *d·* Him to be.
400–30 Scriptures plainly *d·* the baneful influence of
439–27 Our higher statutes *d·* you all,
r 466–28 Science will *d·* God aright,
g 519–17 How shall we *d·* Him, till,
525–25 The corporeal senses *d·* otherwise ;
526–17 the Scriptures *d·* that He created all.
539–16 Scriptures *d·* that God condemned this lie
546–11 Has God no Science to *d·* Mind,
ap 569–24 Scriptures *d·* that evil is temporal,
gl 596– 9 Him *d·* I unto you."— *Acts* 17 : 23.

declared

m 64–19 when he *d·* that in the resurrection
s 133– 6 centurion of whose faith Jesus himself *d·*,
137–19 The Messiah is what thou hast *d·*,
162–32 He *d·* that "it is impossible to calculate the
163– 5 *d·* himself "sick of learned quackery."
ph 165– 2 Evil *d·* that eating this fruit would
f 234–28 Jesus *d·* that to look with desire on
b 280–17 Moses *d·* as Jehovah's first command
303–32 *d·* that nothing could alienate him from God,
320– 3 Christ plainly *d·*, "I am the way,— *John* 14 : 6.
338–27 Jehovah *d·* the ground was accursed ;
o 352– 5 Our Master *d·* that his material body
361–13 Jesus Christ is not God, as Jesus himself *d·*,
p 437–25 They *d·* that C. S. was overthrowing
g 522–16 this state of things is *d·* to be temporary
525–17 In the Gospel of John, it is *d·* that

declares

s 124–28 *d·* that they belong wholly to divine Mind,
141–20 The Bible *d·* that all believers are
151–26 must be put off, as St. Paul *d·*.
ph 169–19 *d·* that all disease is cured by divine Mind.
173–17 Anatomy *d·* man to be structural.
f 220– 9 Instinct is better . . . as even nature *d·*.
b 307– 7 *d·* that there is more than one intelligence
317– 7 Whosoever . . . *d·* best the power of C. S.,
320–17 Here the original text *d·* plainly the
335–10 for, as the Bible *d·*, without the Logos,
o 347– 4 C. S. *d·* that whatever is mortal or discordant
p 391–17 Injustice *d·* the absence of law.
393–25 When Jesus *d·* that "the light of— *Matt.* 6 : 22.
414–21 *d·*, "The Lord He is God— *Deut.* 4 : 35.
414–23 C. S. *d·* that Mind is substance,
429–12 Science *d·* that man is subject to Mind.
r 475– 1 Scripture *d·* that there is "no night— *Rev.* 22 : 5.
476– 3 which *d·* that man begins in dust or
477–12 *d·* the corporeal senses to be . . . illusions.
480–26 Bible *d·* : "All things were made by— *John* 1 : 3.
485– 4 *d·* that Mind, not matter, sees, hears, feels,
g 507–23 The scientific divine creation *d·*
522–29 Scripture . . . *d·* God's work to be finished.
523– 4 and finally *d·* that God knows error
526– 4 more scientific record of creation *d·*
528– 2 the record *d·* that God has already created man,
544–29 It *d·* mind to be in and of matter,
548–29 Agassiz *d·* . . . "Certain animals,
551–28 error *d·* that the material seed must

declaring

a 19–12 *d·* precisely what would destroy sickness,
ph 180–18 by *d·* disease to be a fixed fact,
f 206–23 *d·* that His work was *finished*,
229–13 *d·* Him good in one instance and evil in another.
o 352–20 increasing children's fears by *d·* ghosts to be
p 364–11 and *d·* the absolution of the penitent.
439–26 meanwhile *d·* Disease to be God's servant
t 447–28 by *d·* there is no sickness,
r 481–14 *d·* existence to be at the mercy of death,
g 522–24 *d·* this material creation false,
528–21 and *d·* what great things error has done.

decline

b 310–11 Day may *d·* and shadows fall,

declines
o 355–17 popular religion, *d·* to admit that
declining
f 246–13 Manhood is . . . undimmed by a *d·* sun.
decomposed
p 429–15 affirms . . . that it must be buried and *d·*
decomposition
sp 92– 7 the *d·* of mortal bodies in what is termed death.
p 373–24 The inflammation, *d·*, or deposit will abate,
425–10 tubercles, hemorrhage, and *d·* are beliefs,
r 488–26 not at the mercy of organization and *d·*,
decree
a 32–14 he bowed in holy submission to the divine *d·*.
p 440–20 You cannot trample upon the *d·* of the
decreed
f 221–19 He learned . . . that God never *d·* disease,
ap 565–10 Herod *d·* the death of every male child
decrees
s 118–30 they contradict the divine *d·*
f 229–28 should not if we could, annul the *d·* of
p 381– 3 Ignorant of . . . we submit to unjust *d·*,
435–11 The law of our Supreme Court *d·* that
441–18 the *d·* of the Court of Error in favor of Matter,
decrepitude
f 245–30 plain that *d·* is not according to law,
decries
o 342– 8 He that *d·* this Science
dedicated
gl 596– 7 *d·* "to the unknown God." — *Acts* 17 : 23.
deduced
s 120–25 Any conclusion *pro* or *con*, *d·* from
b 268– 7 from which may be *d·* all rationality,
274– 8 *d·* from the evidence of the material senses.
deducible
pref viii–20 the response *d·* from two connate facts,
deducing
c 259–32 *D·* one's conclusions as to man
deductions
b 273– 7 *D·* from material hypotheses are not scientific.
g 553–16 why are his *d·* generally material?
deed
any
p 440–15 what greater justification can any *d·* have,
criminal
p 435– 4 Has the body . . . committed a criminal *d·*?
good
p 435–15 trampling on Laws of Health, this was a good *d·*,
436–12 Laying down his life for a good *d·*,
Jesus'
a 45– 8 Jesus' *d·* was for the enlightenment of men
my
o 343– 3 and for proving my word by my *d·*
thought and
a 19–18 every good thought and *d·*, will help us
gl 595–16 holiness and purification of thought and *d·*,
word or
m 59–21 how slight a word or *d·* may renew the
f 205–19 some word or *d·* which indicates the true idea,

a 31–17 to all who follow him in *d·*.
f 203–16 man the image of his Maker in *d·* and in truth.
deeds
best
p 385–11 penalty which our beliefs would attach to our best *d·*.
daily
a 40–30 public worship instead of daily *d·*.
good
pr 4– 5 patience, meekness, love, and good *d·*.
a 41–27 his apostles still went about doing good *d·*,
p 435–12 but good *d·* are immortal, bringing joy
436– 2 he was an eye-witness to the good *d·*
440–10 Good *d·* are transformed into crimes,
his
a 26–26 proved by his *d·* that C. S. destroys sickness,
c 262– 8 the old man with his *d·*," — *Col.* 3 : 9.
b 296– 9 The old man with his *d·* must be put off.
o 350–12 His words were the offspring of his *d·*,
of kindness
p 384– 8 for honest labor, or for *d·* of kindness,
of violence
an 105– 4 to prevent *d·* of violence or to punish them.
our
o 354–21 If our words fail to express our *d·*,
these
p 369–10 All these *d·* manifested Jesus' control
the very
p 436–29 the very *d·* which the divine law compels
wicked
b 314–12 material views were the parents of their wicked *d·*.

deeds
without
o 354–19 Inconsistency is shown by words without *d·*,

pr 1–14 before they take form in words and in *d·*.
o 354–10 find their immortality in *d·*,
p 430– 4 must put off itself with its *d·*,
deem
b 283–19 and *d·* this the manifestation of the one Life,
p 441–10 plea of False Belief we *d·* unworthy of
deemed
s 158–10 This was *d·* progress in medicine ;
b 338–19 dust was *d·* the agent of Deity
p 376– 8 diseases *d·* dangerous sometimes come from
431–10 this offence is *d·* punishable with death.
g 525–28 death must be *d·* as devoid of reality
550–27 Amalgamation is *d·* monstrous
deems
ap 574–29 which your suffering sense *d·* wrathful
deep
pr 12–13 *d·* and conscientious protests of Truth,
s 125–27 dominion over the atmosphere and the great *d·*,
129–22 We must look *d·* into realism
ph 184–30 The inspirations were *d·* and natural.
b 307– 1 the Adam-dream, the *d·* sleep,
338–18 upon the face of the *d·*," — *Gen.* 1 : 2.
r 479–20 upon the face of the *d·*." — *Gen.* 1 : 2.
g 503– 7 upon the face of the *d·*. — *Gen.* 1 : 2.
528–10 caused a *d·* sleep to fall upon Adam, — *Gen.* 2 : 21.
546–21 for they contain the *d·* divinity of the Bible.
556–18 the *d·* sleep which fell upon Adam?
ap 569–17 are dwellers still in the *d·* darkness of belief.
570–21 the *d·* waters of chaos and old night.
deepen
sp 99–25 spirituality, . . . must *d·* human experience,
deepens
g 523– 4 mist of obscurity . . . *d·* the false claim,
deeper
b 329–29 the *d·* the error into which mortal mind
deeply
pr 7–10 Looking *d·* into these things, we find
s 161–30 looked as *d·* for cause and effect
t 453–28 impresses more *d·* the wrong mind-picture.
deep-lying
pref xii–15 with a *d·* conviction that the next two years
defaced
f 227–28 and *d·* the tablet of your being.
defeat
s 122– 5 great facts of Life, . . . *d·* this triad of errors,
f 239–13 success in error is *d·* in Truth.
o 357–32 Can matter . . . *d·* omnipotence?
p 390–31 to *d·* the passage of an inhuman law.
422–32 This mental state invites *d·*.
t 446–18 A wrong motive involves *d·*.
defeats
a 39–29 attended with doubts and *d·* as well as triumphs.
defence
a 48–18 and chose not the world's means of *d·*.
f 235– 3 if virtue and truth build a strong *d·*.
o 348–23 would it not be well to abandon the *d·*,
p 434–21 and opens the argument for the *d·* :
440–33 Here the counsel for the *d·* closed,
defend
p 377–29 a fear that Mind is helpless to *d·* the
387–31 faith and understanding whereby to *d·* himself,
t 445– 2 students to *d·* themselves against sin,
451–22 in order to *d·* himself from the influence of
defendant
p 380–12 as though the *d·* should argue for the plaintiff
380–13 decision which the *d·* knows will be
430–21 Mortal Man is the *d·*.
defending
o 348–21 *d·* the supposed rights of disease,
defiance
a 43–25 acting under spiritual law in *d·* of matter
ph 168–21 in *d·* of what is called material law,
f 228– 1 and in *d·* of all material conditions,
o 342– 9 and in *d·* of the direct command of Jesus,
deficiency
p 388–16 a *d·* or an excess, a quality or a quantity.
deficient
p 366–13 is *d·* in human affection,
defies
an 105– 9 *d·* justice and is recommended to mercy.
defile
an 100– * *the things which d· a man.* — *Matt.* 15 : 20.
defileth
ap 577–26 "*d·*, . . . or maketh a lie." — *Rev.* 21 : 27.

define

sp 81–25 so-called laws of matter, which *d·* man as
s 148–13 anatomy and theology *d·* man as
ph 173–24 physiology, phrenology, do not *d·* the
b 278–29 We *d·* matter as error, because it is the
318– 5 Corporeal senses *d·* diseases as realities ;
r 485– 1 If error is necessary to *d·* or to reveal
gl 596– 3 Paganism and agnosticism may *d·* Deity as

defined

a 54– 3 Out of . . . his pure affection, he *d·* Love.
s 117–30 which he *d·* as human doctrines.
129–11 Pantheism may be *d·* as a belief in the
p 408–12 distinctly *d·* instances of the baneful
t 460– 3 Ontology is *d·* as "the science of
g 507– 7 Without natures particularly *d·*,
517– 6 may be *d·* as a mortally mental attempt
554–20 Jesus *d·* this opposite of God and His creation

defines

an 103– 4 *d·* it as dishonesty and craftiness.
ph 191–25 Physical sense *d·* mortal man as based on matter,
f 208– 2 Material sense *d·* all things materially,
p 410– 5 *d·* everlasting life as a present knowledge of
r 488–17 *d·* these so-called senses as *mortal beliefs*,

defining

p 441– 1 comprehending and *d·* all law and evidence,

definite

pref ix– 8 the tongue voices the more *d·* thought,
s 147–26 but he left no *d·* rule for
f 206–22 The Scriptures are *d·* on this point,
p 410–20 Here is a *d·* and inspired proclamation of C. S.

definitely

g 523–29 after which the distinction is not *d·* traceable.

definition

s 114– 6 spiritually unscientific *d·* of mind
c 257– 3 then all is Mind ; and this *d·* is scientific.
b 270–20 establish the *d·* of omnipotence,
302–14 Continuing our *d·* of *man*,
338–25 The dissection and *d·* of words,
p 421– 6 the true *d·* of all human belief in ill-health,
g 517– 2 *d·* has been weakened by anthropomorphism,
gl 579– 2 material *d·* of a Scriptural word

definitions

a 23–22 two *d·*, *trustfulness* and *trustworthiness*.
s 118–26 The *d·* of material law, as given
118–28 these *d·* portray law as physical,

deflection

g 502–11 This *d·* of being, rightly viewed,

deflections

sp 78– 4 changing *d·* of mortal mind ;
b 305–20 the *d·* of matter as opposed to the Science of

deformed

s 160–25 If muscles can cease to act . . . be *d·* or
p 418–30 tubercles, inflammation, pain, *d·* joints,

deformity

ph 178–13 Perhaps an adult has a *d·*
f 244– 2 He does not produce moral or physical *d·* ;
244– 2 therefore such *d·* is not real,
248–24 the angular outline and *d·* of matter models.
c 263–13 forming *d·* when he would outline grace

defraud

c 263–11 Carnal beliefs *d·* us.

defrauds

r 489–13 Corporeal sense *d·* and lies ;

defying

ap 564–23 uncover its own crime of *d·* immortal

degenerating

g 545– 5 material man was fast *d·*

degrade

f 235–18 will *d·* the characters it should inform

degree

first
s 115–20 *First D· :* Depravity.
p 433–17 "Guilty of liver-complaint in the first *d·*."
433–21 guilty of benevolence in the first *d·*,
highest
s 163–16 are in the highest *d·* uncertain ;
ap 564–18 the highest *d·* of human depravity.
limited
b 313–28 was possessed only in a limited *d·*
second
s 115–25 *Second D· :* Evil beliefs disappearing.
small
r 492– 8 knowledge of this, even in small *d·*,
some
a 37–24 It is possible, . . . to follow in some *d·*
subtle
t 451–26 especially any subtle *d·* of evil,
sufficient
t 454–14 He, who understands in a sufficient *d·*

degree

their
t 457–16 both sides were beautiful according to their *d·* ;
third
s 116– 1 *Third D· :* Understanding.
116– 4 In the third *d·* mortal mind disappears,

s 153– 1 frequently attenuated to such a *d·* that
ph 189–16 it is as truly mortal mind, according to its *d·*,
b 337–10 man is in a *d·* as perfect as
p 407–19 and ascend a *d·* in the scale of health,
t 454– 6 The understanding, even in a *d·*,

degrees

pref ix–31 *d·* by which she came at length to its solution ;
s 113– 5 but its spirit comes only in small *d·*.
f 233– 9 is seen and acknowledged only by *d·*.
b 297–25 Human thoughts have their *d·* of comparison.
327–31 by *d·* he will learn the nothingness of the
p 407–30 All sin is insanity in different *d·*.

deific

b 334–24 but undying in the *d·* Mind.
336–22 else God would . . . lose the *d·* character,
r 482– 7 where the *d·* meaning is required.
g 513– 2 for the claim usurps the *d·* prerogatives
513–12 the motions and reflections of *d·* power
514– 1 could not by simulating *d·* power
ap 576–29 not yet elevated to *d·* apprehension

deify

f 251–31 and *d·* their own notions,

deities

g 524– 5 and in a thousand other so-called *d·*.

Deity

allness of
c 267– 6 The allness of *D·* is His oneness.
a national
a 41–31 enough for them to believe in a national *D·* ;
and humanity
g 555–22 of both *D·* and humanity.
applied to
s 116–26 *person* and *personal* . . . when applied to *D·*,
o 345– 1 word *Spirit* is so commonly applied to *D·*,
authority of
o 357–14 the creativeness and authority of *D·*,
being and
g 554– 7 being and *D·* are inseparable.
conception of
g 555–24 and set aside the proper conception of *D·*,
conceptions of
pr 3–17 How empty are our conceptions of *D·* !
constitute
g 516– 5 Truth, and Love, which constitute *D·*,
define
gl 596– 3 Paganism and agnosticism may define *D·* as
explains
g 545– 1 Error . . . explains *D·* through mortal and
faith in
s 146– 7 faith in drugs the fashion, rather than faith in *D·*.
hieroglyphs of
f 240– 7 The floral apostles are hieroglyphs of *D·*.
humanization of
g 517– 3 anthropomorphism, or a humanization of *D·*.
human sense of
ap 576–31 human sense of *D·* yields to the divine sense,
idea of
b 339–21 has yielded to a more spiritual idea of *D·*,
g 517–14 for Love imparts the clearest idea of *D·*.
loves
r 481– 9 Through . . . man comprehends and loves *D·*.
misconceptions of
sp 94–13 the misconceptions of *D·* there prevalent.
name for
b 232– 4 Father-Mother is the name for *D·*,
perfection of
g 546– 8 error would dethrone the perfection of *D·*.
seal of
g 511–11 divine Science, which is the seal of *D·*
signifies
r 466–20 Soul or Spirit signifies *D·* and nothing else.
Spirit, or
gl 588–23 if used with reference to Spirit, or *D·*.
spiritual sense of
ap 578– 3 the incorporeal or spiritual sense of *D·* :
was satisfied
g 519– 3 *D·* was satisfied with His work.
wholeness of
r 465–14 the nature, essence, and wholeness of *D·*.

pr 12–27 Does *D·* interpose in behalf of one worshipper,
s 111–15 physical hypotheses as to *D·*,
c 255–12 to belittle *D·* with human conceptions.
259– 1 Man is not absorbed in *D·*,
263– 3 originators of something which *D·* would not
265–11 by no means suggests man's absorption into *D·*

Deity
b 284–15 Can *D·* be known through the material senses?
338–19 matter or dust was deemed the agent of *D·*
o 351–21 if we consider Satan . . . coequal in power with *D·*,
357–27 Can *D·* be almighty, if another mighty and
r 470–27 and consequently a time when *D·* was
475–20 has not a single quality underived from *D·* ;
g 517– 7 attempt to reduce *D·* to corporeality.
522– 9 as having broken away from *D·*
523–19 because *D·* therein is always called Jehovah,
531– 3 springs from dust instead of from *D·*
545–15 and do not accord infinity to *D·*.
550–24 An egg is an impossible enclosure for *D·*.
554– 6 because being is immortal, like *D·*,
gl 591–19 *D·*, which outlines but is not outlined.

deity
ph 186–31 it enthrones matter as *d·*.
g 524–17 Did the . . . infinite Principle become a finite *d·*,

delay
p 407– 9 Every hour of *d·* makes the struggle more
434– 2 "*D·* the execution ; the prisoner is not guilty."

delicious
r 491– 2 A *d·* perfume will seem intolerable.

delight
ph 179–18 the wild animal, . . . sniffs the wind with *d·*.
g 526–30 The name Eden, . . . means *pleasure*, *d·*.

delineate
f 208–30 should *d·* upon it thoughts of health,

delineates
b 310– 3 fancies that it *d·* thought on matter,
r 485–26 *d·* foreign agents, called disease and sin.

delineations
ph 198–11 and then fills in his *d·* with

deliver
pr 16–15 In the phrase, "*D·* us from evil,"— *Matt. 6 : 13.*
16–16 "*D·* us from the evil one."
17– 8 but *d·* us from evil ;— *Matt. 6 : 13.*
a 22–20 Love is not hasty to *d·* us from temptation,
s 151–14 Even this . . . would ultimately *d·* mankind
p 391–23 your adversary will *d·* you to the judge
405–11 They will *d·* you to the judge,
405–13 The judge will *d·* you to justice,
ap 567– 3 These angels *d·* us from the depths.

deliverance
pref xi–19 *d·* to the captives [of sense],— *Luke 4 : 18.*
a 22–23 Final *d·* from error, whereby we
f 224–30 power of God brings *d·* to the captive.

delivered
m 67–28 Man *d·* from sin, disease, and death
ph 165– * *d· them from their destructions.*— *Psal. 107 : 20.*
f 243– 5 which *d·* men from the boiling oil,
p 391– 4 Then, when thou art *d·* to the judgment
ap 562–22 and pained to be *d·.*— *Rev. 12 : 2.*
562–25 waiting to be *d·* of her sweet promise ;
563–26 which was ready to be *d·*,— *Rev. 12 : 4.*

deliverer
f 226–32 trusting Truth, the strong *d·*,
b 308–32 Then Jacob questioned his *d·*,

delivereth
pr 17–10 *but d· us from sin, disease, and death.*

delivering
s 107– 9 *d·* the children of men from every ill
p 440– 9 a verdict *d·* Mortal Man to Death.

delivers
p 404–32 and so *d·* him from his destroyers.

deluded
s 121–21 *d·* the judgment and induced false conclusions

delusion
artifice and
sp 83– 4 artifice and *d·* claimed that they could equal
first
gl 594– 7 the first *d·* that error exists as fact ;
give up the
ph 191– 4 As mortals give up the *d·* that
great
ap 570–28 should also know the great *d·* of mortal mind,
of material sense
b 330–26 a *d·* of material sense,
of suffering
ph 184–24 by destroying the *d·* of suffering
pure
ap 567–21 That false claim . . . is pure *d·*, the red dragon ;
religious
ph 166–13 Mohammedan's belief is a religious *d·* ;

b 301–24 *D·*, sin, disease, and death arise from
307– 1 *d·* that life and intelligence proceeded from
319– 1 The *d·* that there is life in matter
323–26 the *d·* that there are other minds,

delusion
o 348– 9 one disease can be just as much a *d·* as another.
p 407–21 If *d·* says, "I have lost my memory,"
gl 593–12 *d·* ; mortality ; error.

delusions
f 204–10 carries out the *d·* of sin, sickness, and death.
233–14 error continues its *d·* until
b 328–12 the Science which destroys human *d·*
o 348–12 *d·*, were cast out and the dumb spake.

delusive
sp 70– 3 cannot inform us what is real and what is *d·*,
f 237–32 hug false beliefs and suffer the *d·* consequences.
249–11 Any other theory . . . is *d·* and mythological.

demand
awful
b 308– 8 This awful *d·*, . . . is met by the admission
Christian
a 37–32 Why has this Christian *d·* so little inspiration
m 66–22 if there is no Christian *d·* for it.
Christ's
a 22– 6 Waking to Christ's *d·*, mortals experience
divine
f 253–32 divine *d·*, "Be ye therefore— *Matt. 5 : 48.*
b 329–23 Science is a divine *d·*, not a human.
eternal
gl 595–11 the eternal *d·* of divine Science.
first
r 467– 3 The first *d·* of this Science is,
frivolous
ph 195–30 to meet a frivolous *d·* for amusement
its
ph 199–11 by reason of its *d·* for and supply of power.
moral
sp 92–23 Until . . . the moral *d·* will not be met,
no
p 435–22 no *d·*, human or divine, renders it just to
perpetual
c 255– 4 the perpetual *d·* of Truth and Love,
spiritual
p 385– 8 spiritual *d·*, ____ supplies energy and endurance

a 22–11 the *d·* of Life and Love,
m 65–18 human mind will at length *d·* a higher affection.
s 152–32 signs, which *d·* different remedies ;
ph 179–13 creates a *d·* for that method,
183– 3 *d·* obedience to materialistic codes,
b 308– 7 hide from the *d·*, "Where art thou?" — *Gen. 3 : 9.*
p 386– 7 no such result occurs without mind to *d·* it
g 524–30 and eventually ejected at the *d·* of matter?

demanded
a 41–29 *d·* more than they were willing to practise.
p 390–18 the last penalty *d·* by error.

demanding
f 226– 9 *d·* that the fetters of sin, sickness, and

demands
acquiescence with the
a 48–27 acquiescence with the *d·* of Jesus' enemies.
different
m 59–12 the different *d·* of their united spheres,
eternal
ph 184–13 the only legitimate and eternal *d·* on man,
he uttered the
b 314–27 he uttered the *d·* of its divine Principle,
its
f 233– 1 Every day makes its *d·* upon us
its own
r 489–14 to meet its own *d·*.
meet the
m 57–16 fame is incompetent to meet the *d·* of the
c 257–25 to meet the *d·* of human want and woe,
of Christian Science
b 327–17 the strict *d·* of C. S. seem peremptory ;
of divine Science
a 38– 8 is broken by the *d·* of divine Science.
f 241– 2 the *d·* of divine Science
of God
s 129–32 the *d·* of God must be met.
ph 182– 5 The *d·* of God appeal to thought only ;
of Truth
ph 170–14 The *d·* of Truth are spiritual,
b 325–20 Paul had a clear sense of the *d·* of Truth
t 450–13 They do not . . . whine over the *d·* of Truth,
spiritual
r 483–10 not be ignorant of the moral and spiritual *d·*

pr 3–15 *d·* absolute consecration of thought, energy, and
11– 9 The moral law, . . . always *d·* restitution
a 23–30 *d·* self-reliant trustworthiness,
40–25 *d·* that all men should follow the example
sp 99– 5 to escape from sin, is what the Bible *d·*.
s 139–32 *d·* the remedy of Truth
ph 183–21 rightly *d·* man's entire obedience,
f 233– 6 *d·* of us only what we can certainly fulfil.
254–20 This task God *d·* us to accept lovingly

demands

c	256–19	Who is it that *d·* our obedience?
	259–29	*d·* spiritual thoughts, divine concepts,
	261–32	Good *d·* of man every hour,
o	343–23	Christendom generally *d·* so much less.
p	380– 8	indulging the *d·* of sin, disease, or death,
r	467– 1	What are the *d·* of the Science of
g	532–30	but now error *d·* that *mind* shall
	545–20	impudently *d·* a blessing.
gl	592–15	justice *d·* penalties under the law.

demarcation

b	294–19	The lines of *d·* between
g	505–21	Understanding is the line of *d·*
gl	586–16	line of *d·* between Truth and error,

dematerialization

f	211–29	only through *d·* and spiritualization

dematerialized

f	211–27	then, when the body is *d·*, these faculties

dementia

b	330–31	*d·*, insanity, inanity, devil,
p	411–14	a disease which moderns would call *d·*.
	414–14	*d·*, hatred, or any other discord.
	423–29	as directly the action of mortal mind as is *d·*

demerit

t	449–23	according to personal merit or *d·*,

demerits

o	344–16	rules which disclose its merits or *d·*,

demigods

sp	84–10	controlled not by demons, spirits, or *d·*,

demise

g	543– 7	more beautifully apparent at error's *d·*.

demon

p	411–15	*d·*, or evil, replied that his name was Legion.

demons

sp	84–10	controlled not by *d·*, spirits, or demigods,

demonstrable

sp	99– 3	ethics, and superstition afford no *d·*
an	106–16	sanction only such methods as are *d·*
s	108– 6	unfolding to me the *d·* fact that
	111– 2	and the *d·* truths of C. S. ;
	112– 4	C. S. is *d·*.
ph	171–15	Mind's control over the universe, . . . is *d·*
b	323–15	Truth is *d·* when understood,
o	344–12	the opponents of a *d·* Science
p	417–23	it is *d·* that the way to cure the patient
r	487–20	is founded on Science or *d·* Truth,
g	546–29	it cures on a divine *d·* Principle

demonstrably

s	134–21	The true Logos is *d·* C. S.,
b	337–31	you ascertain that this Science is *d·* true,

demonstrate

a	19–24	Those who cannot *d·*, at least in part,
	25–25	that they might *d·* this power as he did
	30– 3	and could *d·* the Science of Love
	51–22	to *d·* his divine Principle.
sp	98–14	much less can they *d·* it.
s	111–13	its rules *d·* its Science.
	130– 8	when you can *d·* the actuality of Science.
	141–23	they cannot *d·* God's healing power.
	147– 2	This system enables the learner to *d·*
	149–31	dismiss superstition, and *d·* truth
	150–14	these signs are only to *d·* its divine origin,
	162–28	to *d·* the higher rule.
ph	182–26	ability to *d·* Mind's sacred power.
f	217–24	you will be able to *d·* this control.
	254–18	not the power to *d·* what we do not
b	274–12	and they *d·* Truth and Life.
	283–29	unless we so do, we can no more *d·*
	285–30	will seek to learn, . . . how to *d·* the Christ,
	315–22	enabled him to *d·* the facts of being,
o	352– 2	to *d·* His power to heal,
	353–31	Mortal beliefs can neither *d·* Christianity nor
	355–25	a consequent inability to *d·* this Science.
p	429–26	and do not *d·* the facts it involves.
t	447–32	to know it, he must *d·* his statement.
	452–26	Such a practice does not *d·* the Science
	456–20	or he cannot *d·* the divine Principle.
	460–12	is the one most difficult to understand and *d·*,
	462– 5	any student, . . . can *d·* C. S.,
	462–13	Whoever would *d·* the healing of C. S.
r	466–29	Christianity will *d·* this declaration
	482–22	enabled Jesus to *d·* his control over matter.
	493–15	enables the healer to *d·* . . . the Principle
	496–17	enables you to *d·*, with scientific certainty,
g	539–28	more than human power to . . . *d·* the one Mind

demonstrated

pref	ix–23	this Science must be *d·* by healing,
a	18– 3	taught and *d·* man's oneness with the Father,
	24–28	affection and goodness it *d·* for mankind.
	25–18	he *d·* more spiritually than all others
	30–22	*d·* throughout the whole earthly career of Jesus,

demonstrated

a	41–20	or *d·* the divine healing of absolute Science.
	44– 4	and the supremacy of Spirit be *d·*.
	45– 6	Our Master fully and finally *d·* divine Science
	54– 2	he *d·* the divine Life.
sp	77–11	Then, and not until then, will it be *d·*
	93– 3	Jesus, who . . . *d·* the power of Spirit
s	109– 8	its divine Principle is *d·* by healing the sick
	110–17	afterwards the truth of C. S. was *d·*.
	110–24	will forever remain to be discerned and *d·*.
	110–25	Jesus *d·* the power of C. S.
	110–28	spiritually discerned, taught, and *d·*
	115– 7	any reader, who has not personally *d·* C. S.
	126–24	I have *d·* through Mind the effects of Truth
	130–11	if Science, when understood and *d·*, will
	146–24	the divine origin of Science is *d·*
	147– 6	I *d·* the divine rules of C. S.
	149– 1	our great Master *d·* that Truth could save
	149–13	because you have not *d·* the life of Christ,
	150– 4	the healing power of Truth is widely *d·*
ph	177– 4	I have *d·* this beyond all cavil.
	180–29	as taught and *d·* by Christ Jesus.
	184–23	I have *d·* this as a rule of divine Science
	193–32	It has been *d·* to me that Life is God
f	201– 2	*d·* by the destruction of sin, sickness, and
	230–10	the divine Principle, Love, as *d·* by Jesus.
	244– 5	On their basis Jesus *d·* Life,
b	271–15	the divine Science, which their Master *d·*
	272–31	C. S., as *d·* by Jesus,
	274–16	Jesus *d·* this great verity.
	283–25	practically *d·* in length of days,
	289– 1	Truth *d·* is eternal life.
	306– 6	and *d·* this beyond cavil.
	316– 8	Christ, Truth, was *d·* through Jesus
	321–19	It was scientifically *d·* that leprosy
	321–30	the Science of being was *d·* by Jesus,
	323–16	good is not understood until *d·*.
	325–29	Science . . . will be understood and *d·*.
	330–10	infallibility of divine metaphysics will be *d·*.
	332–19	Jesus *d·* Christ ;
	333–12	*d·* in the life of which Christ Jesus was
o	341–15	*d·* according to a divine given rule,
	346–11	its nothingness is not saved, but must be *d·*
	350–26	before the Science of being can be *d·*.
	360–30	for the truth he spoke and *d·*,
p	369– 9	*d·* in healing the sick, raising the dead,
	406– 8	the power of God is understood and *d·*
	430– 2	Jesus *d·* this, healing the dying
r	472– 3	God is to be understood, adored, and *d·* ;
	494–11	to imagine that Jesus *d·* . . . only for a
	494–16	Jesus *d·* the inability of corporeality,
	495– 5	hence its healing power is not fully *d·*.
	497–17	as *d·* by the Galilean Prophet
g	547– 2	statement of C. S., if *d·* by healing,
ap	559–15	Then is the power of Truth *d·*,
	564–19	Until the majesty of Truth should be *d·*
	572–13	this divine Principle, understood and *d·*,
gl	593–21	understood and *d·* as supreme over all ;

demonstrates

a	26–19	musician *d·* the beauty of the music
	42–25	This *d·* that in C. S. the true man
sp	85– 3	which *d·* the capacity of Soul,
an	103–14	is of God and *d·* the divine Principle,
s	147–31	divine Principle of goodness and *d·* its rules.
b	294–31	Truth *d·* the falsity of error.
	306– 7	Life *d·* Life.
	337–14	C. S. *d·* that none but the pure in heart
	337–18	*d·* Life in Christ, Life's spiritual ideal.
	339–12	Science *d·* the unreality of evil,
	340–17	my favorite text. It *d·* C. S.
	340–22	by which man *d·* health, holiness, and life
o	343–17	he also scientifically *d·* this great fact,
	351– 4	divine Principle which *d·* C. S.,
p	372–14	When man *d·* C. S. absolutely,
	375–11	*d·* that divine Mind heals,
	405–20	*d·* the government of God,
g	505–23	and *d·* the divine sense,

demonstrating

pr	5– 2	keeps him from *d·* his power over error.
a	25–22	Though *d·* his control over sin and disease,
	29–23	*d·* God as the Father of men.
	43–23	but he was *d·* divine Science.
	44–29	*d·* within the narrow tomb the power of Spirit
sp	97–29	Christianity is again *d·* the Life that
s	117–17	and *d·* Life and Truth in himself
	137– 1	teaching and *d·* the truth of being.
	147–27	but he left no definite rule for *d·* this
f	224–22	*d·* justice and meeting the needs of mortals
	232–16	Christianity is again *d·* the power of
	254–14	to *begin* aright and to continue the strife of *d·*
b	314– 8	*d·* the existence of but one Mind
	315–32	Explaining and *d·* the way of divine Science,
o	351–25	*d·* the all-inclusiveness of harmonious Truth.
t	456–12	Principle and method of *d·* C. S.
	456–32	it gave the first rules for *d·* this Science,

demonstrating

r 492–28 d· harmony and immortality.
496–11 d· the healing power of Truth and Love?
g 519–14 d· its spiritual origin.

demonstration

actual
pr 14– 7 the actual d· and understanding of Life
alike in
s 135–25 and they are alike in d·.
and spiritual understanding
o 355–27 d· and spiritual understanding are. . .keynotes,
answered by
pref viii–13 question, What is Truth, is answered by d·,
begin the
f 246–28 We should find this out, and begin the d·
Christian
s 141– 4 More . . . is requisite for Christian d·.
earlier
s 150–11 now, as in the time of its earlier d·,
fatal to its
s 129–19 and fatal to its d· ;
final
a 43–17 final d· of the truth which Jesus taught,
46–26 his final d·, called the ascension,
48–30 hastening the final d· of what life is
53–30 nor had he risen to his final d·
p 429– 6 final d· takes time for its accomplishment.
ground of
a 28–11 is more on the ground of d· than
higher in
a 43–21 Jesus rose higher in d· because of
highest
a 50–15 Had . . . Love forsaken him in his highest d·?
his
a 26–31 his d· of power over death.
31–18 following his d· so far as we apprehend it,
b 309–13 followed his d· of the power of Spirit
312–31 and his d· of divine Principle
314–25 The higher his d· of divine Science
t 446–16 or his d· is protracted, dangerous, and
460– 1 and rest his d· on this sure basis.
instead of
b 286– 5 and so depend upon belief instead of d·,
o 342– 2 proof and d·, instead of opinion
its
s 111–27 and its d· in healing the sick,
f 241–30 approaching spiritual Life and its d·.
r 483–17 to battle over this issue and its d·,
ap 561–18 divinity embracing humanity in Life and its d·,
judgment and
t 455–19 may be mistaken in judgment and d·,
lesser
s 108–14 and the lesser d· to prove the greater,
limited
m 67–25 the limited d· of popular Christianity
mar the
s 139–24 could neither . . . mar the d· of Jesus, nor
my
s 109– 1 led up to my d· of the proposition
of Christian healing
f 238–32 lodestar in the d· of Christian healing,
of Christianity
f 228–30 when they saw the d· of Christianity
of Christian Science
t 445– 7 to hinder the d· of C. S.
of divine Love
s 135–28 but it was the d· of divine Love
f 241–20 the reflection and d· of divine Love,
of divine power
a 27– 7 Tell John what the d· of divine power is,
of divine Principle
b 312–31 and his d· of divine Principle
of divine Science
b 314–25 The higher his d· of divine Science
gl 583–17 and the d· of divine Science,
of eternal Life
b 279–20 d· of eternal Life and Truth and Love.
of healing
a 41–17 this d· of healing was early lost,
of life
a 45–19 through the revelation and d· of life in God,
f 214– 7 nor been guided into the d· of life eternal,
b 278–24 the d· of life as Spirit,
of power
pr 10–11 the unction of Spirit in d· of power
a 26–25 and of his d· of power over death.
of Science
b 273–27 His acts were the d· of Science,
of scientific being
f 233–11 the d· of scientific being,
of Spirit
pr 14– 5 in the d· of Spirit.
of the divine nature
pr 4–23 through d· of the divine nature ;
of the facts
p 428– 3 A d· of the facts of Soul in Jesus' way

demonstration

of this Science
t 457–23 and advance rapidly in the d· of this Science,
of Truth
pr 2–17 Goodness attains the d· of Truth.
a 37–24 the d· of Truth and Life, of health and holiness.
s 135–30 not merely in the name . . . but in d· of Truth,
t 445–12 spiritual understanding and d· of Truth
possible
t 456–15 separates himself . . . from its possible d·.
present
s 123–24 The proof, by present d·, that the
proof and
o 342– 2 The hour has struck when proof and d·,
reason, and
s 109–21 through divine revelation, reason, and d·.
rules for the
s 113– 2 rules for the d· of this divine Principle.
Science and
f 243– 2 the Science and d· of spiritual good
scientific
sp 99–28 the scientific d· of divine Spirit
s 142–21 The strong cords of scientific d·,
b 326– 2 A false sense . . . conceals scientific d·.
p 376–32 to paralyze mental and scientific d·.
t 448–25 must always hinder scientific d·.
Scientist's
t 457–29 The Scientist's d· rests on one Principle,
subject to
o 361–25 must be correct . . . and subject to d·.
teaching and
b 270–18 nature of the teaching and d· of God,
their
a 26– 8 in proportion to their d· of his love,
s 112–18 spiritual rules, laws, and their d·,
this
pref viii–14 this d· shows that Christian healing
a 41–17 this d· of healing was early lost,
o 346–17 How then can this d· be
thought and
c 259–14 the basis of thought and d·.
your
t 456–24 and abide by the divine Principle of your d·.
r 483–11 Moral ignorance or sin affects your d·,
zenith of
ap 565–26 impelled the idea to rise to the zenith of d·,

pr 16– 3 The highest prayer . . . is d·.
a 25–13 Jesus taught the way of Life by d·,
34– 6 If Christ, Truth, has come to us in d·,
34– 7 for d· is Immanuel, or God with us,
sp 94– 8 with the d· which accompanied it,
98–16 d· of Christian Mind-healing stands
s 147– 9 under circumstances where d· was
147–18 the d· of the rules of scientific healing
f 226–16 in d· of "on earth peace, — Luke 2 : 14.
239– 1 the d· by which sin and sickness are destroyed.
b 270–19 the d· which was to destroy sin,
274–25 establishing it by d·.
290– 3 If the Principle, rule, and d· of man's being
329–13 We must prove our faith by d·.
t 455–10 and support your claims by d·.
r 473–26 Jesus established what he said by d·,
gl 592–12 a type of moral law and the d· thereof ;

demonstrations

ancient
f 243–12 the ancient d· of prophets and apostles.
his
c 266–24 his d·, which dominate the flesh.
Jesus'
f 210– 6 are set forth in Jesus' d·,
b 269– 5 Jesus' d· sift the chaff from the wheat,
marvellous
g 540– 1 and was the basis of his marvellous d·.
natural
s 131–28 natural d· of the divine power,
of Jesus
s 122– 9 practically exposed . . . by the d· of Jesus ;
f 243– 8 It crowned the d· of Jesus with
simple
p 429– 5 We must begin, . . . with the more simple d·

a 47– 2 discernment of Jesus' teachings and
s 126–28 the teachings and d· of our great Master
131–28 d· which were not understood.
g 549– 8 give place to higher theories and d·.

demonstratively

o 358–10 sustains logically and d· every point

demonstrator

a 42–15 The resurrection of the great d·
48–19 great d· of Truth and Love was silent
49–14 The meek d· of good,
b 329–10 Be thankful that Jesus, who was the true d· of

demoralization

s 133–15 when they departed from . . . their d· began.

demoralized

p 407–25 the perfect model . . . instead of its *d·* opposite.

demoralizes

g 533–14 beguiles the woman and *d·* the man.

den

p 365–28 convert into a *d·* of thieves
g 514–27 Daniel felt safe in the lions' *d·*,
549–26 and beards the lion of materialism in its *d·*.

denial

evoked
sp 94–19 His healing-power evoked *d·*, ingratitude,
of Truth
p 372–27 In C. S., a *d·* of Truth is fatal,
g 542–11 The avoidance of justice and the *d·* of truth tend

sp 91–17 *d·* of material selfhood aids the discernment
s 134–17 *D·* of the possibility of Christian healing
ph 184– 9 casting out by *d·* the error of belief
f 205–29 *D·* of the oneness of Mind
242– 6 *D·* of the claims of matter is a great step
gl 590–12 *d·* of the fulness of God's creation ;

denials

s 113–22 Which of the *d·* in proposition four is true?
p 394–19 their *d·* are better than their affirmations.

denied

s 130–18 these material beliefs must be *d·* and cast out
f 227– 6 claims of the enslaving senses must be *d·*
o 342–18 Shall it be *d·* that a system which
r 479–28 So evil should be *d·* identity or power,

denies

s 120–23 and thus Science *d·* all disease,
ph 168–18 Are we to believe an authority which *d·*
b 318–22 The Science of Mind *d·* the error of
329–19 and *d·* the rule of the problem
r 492–25 Science of Mind, which *d·* this notion.
gl 580–28 An adversary is one who opposes, *d·*, disputes,

denominated

pref viii–27 the discovery of the system that she *d·* C. S.

denomination

o 360–31 can unite in doctrine and *d·*

denominator

g 540– 9 reducing it to its common *d·*, nothingness.

denounce

t 447–20 Expose and *d·* the claims of evil and disease

dense

c 263–30 A sensual thought, . . . is *d·* blindness

denunciation

o 341–18 misrepresentation and *d·* cannot overthrow it.

denunciations

o 342–31 no *d·* would follow them, even if
g 522–22 God's glowing *d·* of man when not found in

deny

pr 6– 2 The Scriptures say, that if we *d·* Christ,
6– 2 "he also will *d·* us."— *II Tim.* 2 : 12.
15–18 we must *d·* sin and plead God's allness.
a 54–32 Would they not *d·* him even the rights of
s 111–10 some may *d·* its right to the name of Science.
113–19 Life, God, omnipotent good, *d·* death, evil,
113–20 Disease, sin, evil, death, *d·* good,
132–11 any one who should not *d·* that
ph 189– 8 mortals should no more *d·* the power of C. S.
189–11 than they should *d·* the existence of the sunlight
f 232–11 prevalent theories practically *d·* this,
b 270–10 Few *d·* the hypothesis that
309–22 led to *d·* material sense, or mind in matter,
o 348–16 I *d·* His cooperation with evil,
354– 8 Why do they use this phraseology, and yet *d·* C. S.,
357–15 to *d·* that God made man evil
p 368–29 *D·* the existence of matter, and
371–25 we should not *d·* our need of its spiritual
372–25 "Whosoever shall *d·* me— *Matt.* 10 : 33.
372–26 him will I also *d·* before my— *Matt.* 10 : 33.
380–10 and *d·* the power of Mind to heal.
390– 4 We cannot *d·* that Life is self-sustained,
390– 5 never *d·* the everlasting harmony of Soul,
395– 2 They admit . . . whereas they should *d·* it
412–11 call the disease by name when you mentally *d·* it ;
t 450–32 who will *d·* that these are the errors which
453– 1 You do not *d·* the mathematician's right
g 546–26 though the darkness, . . . may *d·* their reality.

denying

a 53–23 weep over the warning, instead of *d·* the truth
s 122–19 *d·* the testimony of the senses,
ph 182–25 by . . . *d·* man's God-given ability to
b 339–32 You conquer error by *d·* its verity.
o 342– 7 the sad effects on the sick of *d·* Truth.
p 390–25 divine authority for *d·* that necessity
434–32 *D·* justice to the body,

depart

a 41– 6 we must *d·* from material sense
s 112– 5 Those who *d·* from this method
o 352–28 terror of ghosts will *d·* and health be restored.
p 363–14 detect the woman's immoral status and bid her *d·*,
r 475–29 The real man cannot *d·* from holiness,

departed

sp 72–25 may flow from the *d·* to mortals ;
77–19 Of what advantage, . . . to us, or to the *d·*,
77–25 The *d·* would gradually rise above ignorance
77–30 chances of the *d·* for improvement
78– 9 If the *d·* are in rapport with mortality,
82– 9 If spiritual life has been won by the *d·*,
82–18 even if our *d·* friends were near us
88–31 said to be . . . received from . . . *d·* spirits.
88–32 the belief that a *d·* spirit is speaking,
s 133–14 but when they *d·* from the true idea,
b 321–11 handle the serpent, and then Moses' fear *d·*,

departing

sp 75–32 the *d·* may hear the glad welcome of
76– 1 The ones *d·* may whisper this vision,
s 111– 8 though *d·* from the realm of the physical,
ph 183– 3 thus *d·* from the basis of one God,
t 457–24 *D·* from C. S., some learners commend diet and

department

t 462–19 as they usually do in every *d·* of life.

departments

ph 197–17 *d·* of knowledge now broadcast in the earth,

departs

s 112–23 Any theory of C. S., which *d·* from
142–30 *d·* from the nature and character of Mind,
g 547– 5 not one *d·* from the stated system and rule.

departure

a 43– 2 they did understand it after his bodily *d·*.
sp 91– 7 great point of *d·* for all true spiritual growth.
f 213–11 Every step towards goodness is a *d·* from
b 312–10 death is the *d·* of a mortal's mind,
312–12 belief of that mortal . . . occasioned his *d·* ;

depend

a 44–14 He did not *d·* upon food or pure air
ph 168–12 and *d·* upon them to heal you,
181–18 not sufficiently spiritual to *d·* on Spirit.
f 228–21 we shall never *d·* on bodily conditions,
b 286– 5 and so *d·* upon belief instead of
p 409–28 will not *d·* on it after death.
422–17 causing it to *d·* less on material evidence.
ap 569–27 periods of torture . . . must *d·* upon sin's obduracy.

dependence

s 152–23 Every material *d·* had failed her
c 262– 2 Consecration to good does not lessen man's *d·*

dependency

b 335– 5 would reduce God to *d·* on matter,

dependent

sp 84–20 not *d·* upon the ear and eye for sound or sight
89–18 Mind is not necessarily *d·* upon
s 160– 9 motion of the arm is no more *d·* upon
ph 170–29 but in either case *d·* upon his
b 292–17 so-called life of mortals is *d·* on matter.
311– 3 *d·* on matter for manifestation,
p 401–21 medicine is *d·* upon mental action.
r 489–17 How can man, . . . be *d·* on material means
g 509– 3 *d·* upon no material organization.

depending

b 314–29 those who, *d·* on doctrines and material laws

depends

sp 81–28 man's immortality *d·* upon that of God,
95–15 *d·* upon his genuine spirituality.
ph 192–22 Your influence for good *d·* upon
b 296–20 *d·* upon the tenacity of error.
p 383–32 notion that health *d·* on inert matter
393–26 certainly means that light *d·* upon Mind,
409–27 no right to say that life *d·* on matter
418– 3 *d·* on mentally destroying all belief in

depict

c 260– 4 or the painter can *d·* the form and face of Jesus,
g 537–20 this second account . . . is to *d·* the falsity of
ap 568– 8 The following chapters *d·* the fatal effects of

depicts

b 319– 3 Science *d·* disease as error,
ap 571–25 In significant figures he *d·* the thoughts

depleted

p 416–25 the mental process by which they are *d·*,

depletion

p 374– 2 Anodynes, counter-irritants, and *d·*

deplorably

s 143– 8 The sick are more *d·* lost than the sinning, if

deplore

ph 195–24 barbarisms of learning which we *d·*,

deport
- *m* 67–13   Thus should we *d·* ourselves on the
- *ph* 180–11   Physicians should not *d·* themselves as if

deposed
- *p* 436– 2   *d·* that he was an eye-witness

deposit
- *m* 63–31   allowed to . . . hold real estate, *d·* funds,
- *p* 373–25   decomposition, or *d·* will abate,

depraved
- *s* 115–22   *d·* will, self-justification, pride, envy,
- *ph* 188– 8   Passion, *d·* appetites, dishonesty,
- *p* 406–28   The *d·* appetite for alcoholic drinks,
- *t* 450– 5   so *d·* that they appear to be innocent.

depraving
- *f* 226– 4   under more subtle and *d·* forms.

depravity
- *s* 115–20   *First Degree: D·*.
- *ph* 195–27   impossible ideals, and specimens of *d·*,
- *ap* 564–18   the highest degree of human *d·*.

depredations
- *r* 490– 4   this belief commits *d·* on harmony.

depress
- *p* 394– 6   majority of doctors *d·* mental energy,

depressed
- *p* 420–18   The fact . . . reassures *d·* hope.

depressing
- *s* 109–16   The search was sweet, . . . not selfish nor *d·*.
- *p* 384– 3   relieve our minds from the *d·* thought

depression
- *gl* 596–20   VALLEY. *D·* ; meekness ; darkness.

deprivations
- *ph* 172–31   teaching us by his very *d·*,
- *p* 385–15   Constant toil, *d·*, exposures, and

deprive
- *o* 358– 2   Can a leaden bullet *d·* a man of Life,
- *ap* 565–12   and *d·* Herod of his crown.

deprived
- *sp* 98–29   are not *d·* of their essential vitality.
- *f* 215–13   is never for an instant *d·* of the light and
- *b* 304–10   Love cannot be *d·* of its manifestation,
- *p* 403–19   *d·* of its imaginary powers by Truth,
-    435–35   liberty of which he has been unjustly *d·*.
-    440–32   the rights of which he has been *d·*.
- *r* 490–13   mortals are more or less *d·* of Truth.

deprives
- *pr* 7– 6   *d·* material sense of its false claims.
- *s* 143–22   *d·* you of the available superiority of divine

depth
- *b* 304– 7   nor height, nor *d·*,— *Rom.* 8 : 39.
- *g* 520– 3   The *d·*, breadth, height, might, majesty,

depths
- *an* 105–27   down to the *d·* of ignominy and death.
- *f* 213–30   Before human knowledge dipped to its *d·*
- *b* 292– 5   compass the heights and *d·* of being
- *ap* 567– 3   These angels deliver us from the *d·*.

De Quincey
- *s* 113–14   *De Q·* says mathematics has not a

derange
- *p* 414–10   impossibility that matter, brain, can . . . *d·* mind,

deranged
- *p* 421– 4   belief that other portions . . . are *d·*.

derangement
- *p* 421– 4   *D·*, . . . is a word which conveys the
-    423–27   abnormal condition or *d·* of the body

derangements
- *p* 389– 9   Matter does not inform you of bodily *d·* ;

dereliction
- *g* 533–16   charges God and woman with his own *d·*,

derisively
- *a* 49–29   mocked him on the cross, saying *d·*,

derivation
- *b* 338–26   aside from their metaphysical *d·*,

derivative
- *o* 356–29   to create the primitive, and then punish its *d·* ?
- *p* 399–19   is but a *d·* from, and continuation of,

derivatives
- *sp* 93–25   The modifying *d·* of the word *spirit*

derive
- *f* 244– 7   If we were to *d·* all our conceptions of man
- *p* 408–21   *d·* a supposed effect on intelligence

derived
- *a* 18–18   *d·* from the eternal Love.
-    32– 6   our English word *sacrament* is *d·* from
-    44–21   in his proof of man's truly *d·* power
- *sp* 72–23   In Science, individual good *d·* from God,
-    88–28   the possibilities *d·* from divine Mind,

derived
- *an* 101–31   Any seeming benefit *d·* from it is
- *s* 143–27   no power except that which is *d·* from Mind.
- *o* 354–16   *d·* from the traditions of the elders
-    358–28   power, *d·* from the Holy Ghost.''
- *p* 385– 6   support which they *d·* from the divine law,
- *g* 517– 5   is *d·* from two Greek words,
-    539–12   possesses nothing which he has not *d·* from God.

derives
- *s* 146–23   Divine Science *d·* its sanction from the Bible,

descending
- *ap* 574–27   soft-winged dove *d·* upon you.

descent
- *a* 43– 8   is what is meant by the *d·* of the Holy Ghost,
- *s* 141–12   line of scholarly and ecclesiastical *d·*,

describe
- *pref* ix– 6   yet he cannot *d·* the world.
- *g* 552–32   Naturalists *d·* the origin of mortal and

described
- *sp* 79–20   He never *d·* disease, . . . but he healed disease.
-    87– 9   remains to be discerned, *d·*, and transmitted.
- *s* 148– 7   Neither anatomy nor theology has ever *d·*
- *ph* 197– 5   A minutely *d·* disease costs many a man his
- *p* 363–15   *d·* two debtors, one for a large sum and
- *g* 529–25   the species *d·*,— a talking serpent,
- *ap* 558–18   whose flames of Truth were prophetically *d·*
-    564–12   instigated by the criminal instinct here *d·*.
-    575– 7   This sacred city, *d·* in the Apocalypse

describes
- *sp* 95–27   when he beholds . . . and *d·* its effulgence?
- *s* 152–10   Anatomy *d·* muscular action as
- *b* 279– 3   A New Testament writer plainly *d·* faith,
- *g* 551–12   *d·* the gradations of human belief,
- *ap* 574–15   which he *d·* as the city which

describing
- *sp* 79– 1   The act of *d·* disease
- *ap* 576– 8   further *d·* this holy city,

description
- *pr* 6–32   strong language of our Master confirms this *d·*.
- *ph* 170–28   The *d·* of man as purely physical, or
-    194–26   and realizing Tennyson's *d·* :
- *ap* 566–12   If we remember the beautiful *d·*
-    575–13   The *d·* is metaphoric.
-    575–16   *d·* of the city as foursquare has a profound

descriptions
- *ph* 179–32   *D·* of disease given by physicians
-    196–23   forcible *d·* and medical details,
-    197– 1   and by printing long *d·* which
- *g* 553– 2   and accompany their *d·* with

desert
- *ap* 559–12   heard in the *d·* and in dark places of fear.
-    566– 5   through the great *d·* of human hopes,
-    570–15   weary wanderers, athirst in the *d·*

deserted
- *p* 429–11   The corpse, *d·* by thought, is cold

desertion
- *a* 42–13   followed by the *d·* of all save a few friends,
-    47–27   The disciples' *d·* of their Master
-    50– 5   last supreme moment of mockery, *d·*,

deserts
- *m* 63–28   If a dissolute husband *d·* his wife,

deserves
- *f* 251–26   nothing is left which *d·* to perish or

deserving
- *a* 22–20   and receive according to your *d·*.
- *b* 296–31   a liar from the beginning, not *d·* power.

design
- *a* 35–30   The *d·* of Love is to reform the sinner.
- *b* 271– 4   uniting all periods in the *d·* of God.

designate
- *s* 114–17   to *d·* that which has no real existence.
-    123–17   to *d·* the scientific system of divine healing.
- *ap* 571–13   *d·* those as unfaithful stewards who

designated
- *s* 158– 3   *d·* Apollo as ''the god of medicine.''

designates
- *t* 454–19   inspires, illumines, *d·*, and leads the way.

designed
- *f* 233–30   *d·* to rebuke and destroy error.

designs
- *s* 157–20   If He . . . . *d·* them for medical use,
- *gl* 583–28   error, working out the *d·* of error ;

desirable
- *pref* x–31   but sound morals are most *d·*.
- *a* 27–23   but only eleven left a *d·* historic record.
- *m* 65–25   never *d·* on its own account.
- *p* 426– 9   When the destination is *d·*,

desire

cherish the
pr 13–16 If we cherish the *d·* honestly and

energy, and
pr 3–16 consecration of thought, energy, and *d·*.

fervent
pr 4– 3 prayer of fervent *d·* for growth in grace,
13– 6 beyond the honest standpoint of fervent *d·*.

for holiness
pr 11–22 a *d·* for holiness is requisite

habitual
pr 11–30 prayer, coupled with a fervent habitual *d·*

heart's
sp 88– 3 the poet Tennyson expressed the heart's *d·*,

humble
t 448– 5 the Publican's wail . . . won his humble *d·*.

lack of
f 243–15 arises not so much from lack of *d·*

look with
f 234–28 Jesus declared that to look with *d·* on

no
t 445–14 there will be no *d·* for other healing methods.

such a
pr 11–31 Such a *d·* has little need of audible expression.

that
p 407–18 and he will get the better of that *d·*,

thy
g 535– 8 thy *d·* shall be to thy husband,— *Gen.* 3 : 16.

to do right
pr 9–32 Consistent prayer is the *d·* to do right.

unspoken
pr 2–28 The unspoken *d·* does bring us nearer the

wandering
m 58–19 a wandering *d·* for incessant amusement

wrong
p 407–17 Let the slave of wrong *d·* learn the

pr 1– * *What things soever ye d· — Mark* 11 : 24.
1–11 *D·* is prayer ; and no loss can occur
2– 5 the *d·* which goes forth hungering after
8–22 does not always mean a *d·* for it.
9–26 Do you really *d·* to attain this point?
10– 1 Prayer means that we *d·* to
10–29 That which we *d·* and for which we ask,
11–24 but if we *d·* holiness above all else,
m 62– 8 If parents create in their babes a *d·*
c 261–12 Under the strong impulse of a *d·* to perform
b 322–32 easier to *d·* Truth than to rid one's self of
o 348– 1 and which we *d·* neither to honor nor to fear.
348–17 I *d·* to have no faith in evil or in
p 398–21 and the *d·* for strong drink is gone.
426–20 It will master either a *d·* to die or a dread of
gl 586–12 ignorance ; error ; *d·* ; caution.

desired

s 136–28 No wonder Herod *d·* to see the new Teacher.
ph 188–32 Astronomy gives the *d·* information
c 260–16 distrust of one's ability to gain the goodness *d·*
g 530–23 saying, . . . more to be *d·* than Truth,

desires

our
pr 1–12 no loss can occur from trusting God with our *d·*,
13–12 public expression of our *d·* increase them?
15–22 in so far as we put our *d·* into practice.

purer
p 407–15 lifting humanity above itself into purer *d·*,

real
pr 10– 4 leave our real *d·* to be rewarded by Him.

right
ap 566– 6 the spiritual idea guide all right *d·*

stronger
c 265–24 gained stronger *d·* for spiritual joy?

pr 7–29 uttering *d·* which are not real
sp 73–21 with material sensations and *d·*,
an 102–23 apathy on the subject which the criminal *d·*.
c 257–26 to still the *d·*, to satisfy the aspirations?
t 458–16 the author *d·* to keep it out of C. S.

desolate

sp 96– 8 Earth will become dreary and *d·*,
s 121–15 as the wandering comet or the *d·* star

desolation

p 388–20 which is "brought to *d·*."— *Matt.* 12 : 25.
gl 599– 8 Emptiness ; unfaithfulness ; *d·*.

despair

pr 8– 3 We never need to *d·* of an honest heart ;
ph 170–31 all ills have gone forth, especially *d·*.
174–26 administer a dose of *d·* to the mind?
f 252–29 says : . . . I expand but to my own *d·*,
p 376– 4 latent fear and the *d·* of recovery
382–31 hopeless suffering and *d·*.
433–14 a look of *d·* and death settles upon it.

despaired

b 321– 6 *d·* of making the people understand

despairing

a 50– 9 This *d·* appeal, if made to a
ph 166–24 the *d·* invalid often drops them,
p 379–14 Let the *d·* invalid, . . . think of the experiment

despairingly

p 389–32 One instant she spoke *d·* of herself.

despatch

p 386–16 A blundering *d·*, mistakenly announcing
386–20 Another *d·*, correcting the mistake,
434– 2 on the wings of divine Love, there comes a *d·* :

despatches

p 399–11 mortal mind sends its *d·* over its body,

despise

ph 182–14 "hold to the one, and *d·* the— *Matt.* 6 : 24.
r 490–19 *D·* not prophesyings."— *I Thess.* 5 : 20.

despised

a 20–16 "*D·* and rejected of men,"— *Isa.* 53 : 3.
52–13 "*D·* and rejected of men,"— *Isa.* 53 : 3.

despite

sp 81–24 *d·* the so-called laws of matter,
82–14 *d·* his physical proximity, because both of us
s 136– 6 *D·* the persecution this brought
160–21 and become cramped *d·* the mental protest?
r 474–24 *D·* the hallowing influence of Truth

despoil

p 400– 7 we can *d·* "the strong man"— *Matt.* 12 : 29.

despoils

an 102–32 C. S. *d·* the kingdom of evil,

despondent

p 431–24 took control of his mind, making him *d·*.

despotic

an 102–27 It implies the exercise of *d·* control,
f 225–18 potent to break *d·* fetters
225–25 *d·* tendencies, inherent in mortal mind

despotism

an 102–31 Its so-called *d·* is but a phase of
p 375–15 yielding his mentality to any mental *d·*
r 473–18 In an age of ecclesiastical *d·*,
gl 590–13 LEVI (Jacob's son). . . . ecclesiastical *d·*

destination

p 426– 8 When the *d·* is desirable,

destiny

c 266– 5 man's higher individuality and *d·*.
b 281–10 whence its origin and what its *d·*?

destitute

b 275–25 human theories are *d·* of Science.
p 437–12 *d·* of intelligence and truth
g 554–10 *d·* of any knowledge of the so-called
554–11 *d·* of any knowledge of its origin

destroy

pr 5–30 "*d·* the *works* of the devil."— *I John* 3 : 8.
6–27 how to *d·* sin, sickness, and death.
16– 5 and must *d·* sin and death.
a 19–13 declaring precisely what would *d·* sickness,
27–12 "*D·* this temple [body],— *John* 2 : 19.
53–27 and could *d·* those errors ;
sp 73–30 This error Science will *d·*.
78–17 would *d·* the supremacy of Spirit.
81–27 cannot *d·* the divine Principle of Science.
85–12 and discern the error you would *d·*.
89– 9 *D·* her belief in outside aid,
an 104–23 hypnotizer employs one error to *d·* another.
105–29 "Whom the gods would *d·*," they first
s 118–11 It must *d·* the entire mass of error,
123– 2 will surely *d·* the greater error
130–12 and demonstrated, will *d·* all discord,
139– 3 theology which the impious sought to *d·*.
146– 8 By trusting matter to *d·* its own discord,
ph 181–12 You weaken or *d·* your power
186–19 The only power of evil is to *d·* itself.
186–20 It can never *d·* one iota of good.
186–21 Every attempt of evil to *d·* good is a failure,
196–11 able to *d·* both soul and body— *Matt.* 10 : 28.
196–24 help to abate sickness and to *d·* it.
f 203– 6 matter can neither . . . create nor *d·*.
216–13 begins at once to *d·* the errors
217–27 and so *d·* this illusion,
222–32 We must *d·* the false belief that
230– 3 Would you attempt . . . to *d·* a quality
231–19 beliefs which divine Truth and Love *d·*.
232–20 or that they could *d·* human life ;
233–30 designed to rebuke and *d·* error.
249– 8 no mortal nor material power as able to *d·*.
251–14 an error that Christ, Truth, alone can *d·*.
b 270–20 *d·* sin, sickness, and death,
274–28 *d·* the imaginary copartnership,
290–12 Hence Truth comes to *d·* this error
296– 7 suffering or Science must *d·* all illusions
298– 6 belief cannot *d·* Science armed with faith,
299–25 which cannot *d·* the right reflection.

destroy

b 303–18	Science will eventually *d·* this illusion
314–14	and said, "*D·* this temple, — *John* 2 : 19.
327– 6	Mind can and does *d·* the false beliefs of
o 343–20	illusive errors — which he could and did *d·*.
353–12	omnipotent Truth certainly does *d·* error.
357–15	how dare we attempt to *d·* what
p 374–16	can *d·* all ills which proceed from mortal mind.
376–22	*d·* the patient's false belief
376–26	*D·* fear, and you end fever.
378–10	Remove the error, and you *d·* its effects.
378–18	exercised over mortal beliefs to *d·* them ;
384–24	or to *d·* the bad effects of your belief.
388– 8	when dire inflictions failed to *d·* his body.
388–15	admission . . . that food has power to *d·*
388–21	If food was prepared by Jesus . . . it cannot *d·*
390–14	Let your higher sense of justice *d·* the
391–14	Truth, will *d·* all other supposed suffering,
394– 2	Truth can *d·* its seeming reality,
398–21	*d·* the illusion of pleasure in intoxication,
400–19	contending persistently for truth, you *d·* error.
404– 5	*d·* these errors with the truth of being,
404–11	*d·* them only by destroying the wicked motives
405–19	This is sin's necessity, — to *d·* itself.
405–25	tends to *d·* the ability to do right.
408–17	*d·* the so-called inflammation of
412– 3	and *d·* the human fear of sickness.
412–15	to unclasp the hold and to *d·* disease,
412–22	so as to *d·* the evidence of disease.
414–13	*d·* all error, whether it is called
417–17	you *d·* the evidence, for the disease disappears.
418–17	if arguments are used to *d·* it,
418–27	in your efforts to *d·* error.
419– 5	Your true course is to *d·* the foe,
421–26	If you would *d·* the sense of disease,
423–10	the truth of being, to *d·* the error.
425–17	can never *d·* God, who is man's Life.
425–28	will never believe that heart . . . can *d·* you.
426–17	learned that disease cannot *d·* life,
426–21	*d·* the great fear that besets mortal existence.
428–19	mortal sense cannot impair nor mortal belief *d·*.
t 447–19	truth and . . . understanding, which *d·* disease.
450–19	errors of belief, which Truth can and will *d·*.
461–27	first see the claim of sin, and then *d·* it.
r 474– 2	*d·* all error, evil, disease, and death.
474–19	Jesus came to *d·* sin, sickness,
474–20	"I am not come to *d·*, but to— *Matt.* 5 : 17.
474–22	the evils which Jesus lived to *d·*
474–30	"*d·* the works of the devil."— *I John* 3 : 8.
490–24	*d·* all material sense with immortal testimony.
492–11	progress will finally *d·* all error,
493–18	and able to *d·* all ills.
494– 2	"*D·* this temple [body], — *John* 2 : 19.
495– 7	If sickness is true . . . you cannot *d·*
495–19	can *d·* any painful sense of, or belief in,
496– 1	will soon ascertain that error cannot *d·* error.
g 529– 8	will *d·* the *dream* of existence,
534–28	will struggle to *d·* the spiritual idea of Love ;
542–19	Let Truth uncover and *d·* error
544–15	No mortal mind has the might . . . to *d·*.
545–10	so improve material belief . . . as to *d·*
548–14	helps error to *d·* error,
ap 568– 4	Science is able to *d·* this lie, called evil.
575– 4	this revelation will *d·* forever the
gl 583–11	comes to the flesh to *d·* incarnate error.
596–24	*d·* the unrest of mortal thought,
	(*see also* **belief**)

destroyed

pr 5–24	Sin is forgiven only as it is *d·* by Christ,
6–14	belief in material life and sin is *d·*.
a 23– 1	Wrath which is only appeased is not *d·*,
27–16	The I . . . is not in matter to be *d·*.
39– 9	We must have trials . . . until all error is *d·*.
50–24	was *d·* by his death.
sp 73–18	If . . . omnipresent Spirit would be *d·*.
76–10	and the belief . . . is *d·* by Mind-science.
81– 4	this latter evidence is *d·* by Mind-science.
96– 6	Before error is wholly *d·*,
97–15	having been *d·* by divine Love,
s 122–32	Astronomical science has *d·* the false theory
131– 6	When once *d·* by divine Science,
163–17	except, indeed, that it has already *d·*
ph 168–29	if the error of belief was met and *d·*
177– 9	both must be *d·* by immortal Mind.
f 203–21	overtaxed the belief . . . and *d·* it,
210– 9	last enemy that shall be *d·*," — *I Cor.* 15 : 26.
229– 3	proved that matter has not *d·* them,
231– 5	not *d·* in the mind of mortals, but seem
233– 5	by the power of Spirit, as Jesus *d·* them.
239– 1	by which sin and sickness are *d·*.
253–28	The belief in sin and death is *d·* by the
c 267– 1	Every object in material thought will be *d·*,
b 274–29	formed only to be *d·* in a manner . . . unknown.
290–16	If the change called *death d·* the belief
292– 1	When the last mortal fault is *d·*,

destroyed

b 294–17	*d·* by Truth through spiritual sense
297–12	Erroneous belief is *d·* by truth.
311–13	Evil is *d·* by the sense of good.
320–31	if disease and worms *d·* his body,
321–14	serpent, . . . was *d·* through understanding
328– 9	These errors are not thus really *d·*,
338– 8	error which must be *d·* by Truth.
339– 3	Being *d·*, sin needs no other form of forgiveness.
340–29	leaves nothing that can . . . be punished or *d·*.
o 352–28	If belief in their reality is *d·*,
p 369–21	man has not two lives, one to be *d·*
379–32	is *d·* through Science,
381–13	The so-called laws of mortal belief are *d·* by
389–11	pseudo-mental testimony can be *d·* only by
400– 2	When disease is once *d·*
400–27	must be *d·* by the divine Mind
406–29	*d·* only by Mind's mastery of the body.
411–19	caused the evil to be self-seen and so *d·*.
411–22	false sense mentally entertained, not *d·*.
418–16	one disease would be as readily *d·* as another.
421–20	and when the fear is *d·*,
426–32	The human concepts . . . are all that can be *d·*.
427–19	last enemy that shall be *d·* — *I Cor.* 15 : 26.
t 452–32	the wrong power would be *d·*.
461–30	you will not feel it, and it is *d·*.
r 488–30	but they cannot be disturbed nor *d·*,
gl 593–22	sin, sickness, and death *d·*.

destroyer

a 48–14	exalting ordeal of sin's revenge on its *d·*?
p 435–16	a *d·* of Mortal Man's liberty

destroyers

p 405– 1	and so delivers him from his *d·*.

destroying

pr 6–12	is the means of *d·* sin.
10–13	overcoming . . . and thus *d·* all error.
a 40–12	God's method of *d·* sin.
s 157– 3	mental cause in judging and *d·* disease.
160– 1	should address himself to the work of *d·* it
ph 171–16	and *d·* the foundations of death.
184–24	by *d·* the delusion of suffering
f 210– 8	casting out evils, and *d·* death,
241–21	healing sickness and *d·*
245– 2	the benefits of *d·* that illusion,
248–10	and *d·* the woes of sense
b 316–11	healing sickness and *d·*
332–15	*d·* sin, disease, and death.
339– 5	Does not God's pardon, *d·* any one sin,
p 368–19	healing the sick and *d·* error.
369– 2	and this hinders his *d·*
379–22	her belief that blood is *d·* her life.
401– 8	which you impart mentally while *d·* error,
401– 9	(as when an alkali is *d·* an acid),
401–17	*d·* erroneous mortal belief.
404–11	*d·* the wicked motives which produce them.
418– 3	*d·* all belief in material pleasure or pain.
422–10	which Truth often brings to error when *d·* it.
t 446–14	*d·* his own power to heal and his own health.
461–23	to recognize your sin, aids in *d·* it.
463–23	is the first step towards *d·* error.
r 473–14	and *d·* the power of death.
ap 565–26	*d·* sin, sickness, and death,
gl 581–10	understanding of Spirit, *d·* belief in matter.
589–17	*d·* error and bringing to light man's

destroys

pr 15–13	divine Principle, Love, which *d·* all error.
a 23–10	an error of sinful sense which Truth *d·*,
26–26	He proved by his deeds that C. S. *d·* sickness,
36–32	the law of righteousness which *d·* the
sp 72–10	As light *d·* darkness
72–12	Truth *d·* mortality, and brings
84–24	the belief of spiritualism at its very
91–19	*d·* the erroneous knowledge gained from
98– 6	Christianity which heals the sick and *d·* error,
s 128–25	*d·* with the higher testimony of Spirit
130– 8	divine Science, which *d·* all discord,
143– 1	Truth *d·* only what is untrue.
157–31	Science both neutralizes error and *d·* it.
ph 171–29	The opposite truth, . . . *d·* sin, sickness,
172–26	If . . . the surgeon *d·* manhood,
182–10	for one absolutely *d·* the other,
186– 5	C. S. *d·* material beliefs
f 203–14	*d·* reliance on matter but God,
206–27	*d·* them, and brings to light immortality.
216– 8	Truth . . . *d·* error.
223–30	but the awful daring of sin *d·* sin,
231– 4	If God *d·* not sin, sickness, and death, they
233–22	the spiritual idea which corrects and *d·* them.
243–31	They are inharmonies which Truth *d·*.
252–10	understanding of Truth which *d·* error,
b 275–27	It *d·* the false evidence that misleads
276–26	The latter *d·* the former.
286–30	But by this saying error, the lie, *d·* itself.
288–31	*d·* what mortals seem to have learned

8

destroys

   b 289–16 a mortal belief, or error, which Truth *d·*
   292– 8 only as it *d·* all error and
   293– 6 material mindlessness, ... *d·* itself.
   299–24 Truth never *d·* God's idea.
   305–26 *d·* all error and brings immortality to light.
   315–23 spiritual Truth *d·* material error,
   323–27 The true idea of God . . . *d·* mortality.
   328–11 *d·* human delusions about Him
   339– 2 Divine Life *d·* death, Truth *d·* error,
   339– 3 and Love *d·* hate.
   o 346–15 Disbelief in error *d·* error,
   347–24 Christ, Truth, who *d·* these evils,
   350–30 Soul rebukes sense, and Truth *d·* error.
   358– 1 axe, which *d·* a tree's so-called life,
   p 395–12 faith in God *d·* all faith in sin
   420– 1 nor go from one part to another, for Truth *d·*
   422–20 Thus C. S., . . . *d·* sin and death.
   t 452–14 withhold not the . . . explanation which *d·* error.
   452–28 Acting from sinful motives *d·* your power
   454– 6 *d·* fear, and plants the feet in the true path,
   r 472–11 His law, rightly understood, *d·* them.
   474–31 Truth *d·* falsity and error,
   483–18 heals the sick, *d·* error, and
   485–22 error which Christ, or Truth, *d·*
   g 556– 7 *d·* forever all belief in intelligent matter.
   ap 561– 3 *d·* both faith in evil and the

destructible

   o 360– 7 renders these ideals imperfect and *d·* ;

destruction

  attempt the
   a 51– 9 to attempt the *d·* of the mortal body
  element of
   ph 196–10 sin is the only element of *d·*.
  error's
   o 357–12 and error's *d·* ensured ;
  final
   b 339– 6 and involve the final *d·* of all sin?
  of all evil works
   pr 5–31 seek the *d·* of all evil works,
  of error
   sp 91–13 The *d·* of error is by no means the
   b 272–26 triumphs of C. S. are recorded in the *d·* of error
   329–26 pardon of divine mercy is the *d·* of error.
   r 474–24 hallowing influence of Truth in the *d·* of error,
   ap 559–16 made manifest in the *d·* of error.
  of evil
   a 53–24 sacrifice which goodness makes for the *d·* of evil.
  of sin
   pr 5–20 the *d·* of sin through suffering.
   f 201– 2 the *d·* of sin, sickness, and death.
   233– 3 proofs . . . in the *d·* of sin, sickness, and
   233–19 compass the *d·* of sin and sickness
   b 291– 4 aught but the *d·* of sin,
   339– 1 *d·* of sin is the divine method of pardon.
   r 497–10 God's forgiveness of sin in the *d·* of sin
  pangs for
   b 296–20 how long they will suffer the pangs of *d·*,
  ripe for
   ap 565– 4 against spirituality, and ripe for *d·*.
  that wasteth
   m 56–17 *d·* that wasteth at noonday." — *Psal.* 91 : 6.

   sp 91–14 is by no means the *d·* of Truth or Life,
   97–17 the riper it becomes for *d·*.
   an 103– 5 The *d·* of the claims of mortal mind
   ph 173–16 For positive Spirit to . . . would be Spirit's *d·*.
   194–10 *D·* of the auditory nerve
   f 219–19 *d·* of the belief will be the removal of its effects.
   t 451–13 the way, that leadeth to *d·*, — *Matt.* 7 : 13.
   gl 586–13 remorse ; lust ; hatred ; *d·* ;
   597–29 *D·* ; anger ; mortal passions.

destructions

   ph 165– * delivered them from their *d·*. — *Psal.* 107 : 20.

destructive

   sp 93–17 *D·* electricity is not the offspring of
   97–11 The more *d·* matter becomes,
   f 210–32 it is without a *d·* element.
   b 273–31 atmosphere of mortal mind cannot be *d·*
   t 445–25 The human will . . . is *d·* to health,
   g 545–17 false view, *d·* to existence and happiness.

desultory

   o 354–15 to cleave to barren and *d·* dogmas,

detach

   c 261–21 *D·* sense from the body, or matter,
   t 463– 8 you should so *d·* mortal thought from its

detached

   o 341– 5 criticisms are generally based on *d·* sentences

detail

   pref x–14 or treat in full *d·* so infinite a theme.

details

   ph 196–23 forcible descriptions and medical *d·*,

detect

   p 363–13 *d·* the woman's . . . status and bid her depart
   363–26 did his insight *d·* this unspoken moral uprising
   t 447–25 To put down the claim of sin, you must *d·* it

detected

   c 267–20 more than is *d·* upon the surface,
   ap 567–29 *d·* and killed by innocence, the Lamb of Love

detection

   f 252–20 elude *d·* by smooth-tongued villainy.

detective

   t 449–24 a good *d·* of individual character.

detectives

   p 439–31 We send our best *d·* to whatever locality

deter

   t 443– 6 tends to *d·* those, who make such a

deterioration

   g 533–22 the rapid *d·* of the bone and flesh

determination

   a 28– 6 *d·* to hold Spirit in the grasp of matter
   p 437– 7 It indicates . . . a *d·* to condemn Man

determine

   ph 173– 3 or *d·* when man is really *man*

determined

   s 161–28 even if it were not already *d·* by mortal mind.
   ph 200–25 "For I *d·* not to know — *I Cor.* 2 : 2.
   200–27 I am *d·* not to know

determines

   sp 86–23 Education alone *d·* the difference.
   ph 167– 8 *d·* the harmony of our existence,
   186– 7 the thoroughness of this work *d·* health.
   194– 7 and *d·* a case for better or for worse.
   f 254–22 the spiritual which *d·* the outward and actual.
   p 403–27 The human mind *d·* the nature of a case,
   g 508–13 God *d·* the gender of His own ideas.

dethrone

   p 378–23 to dispute the empire of Mind or to *d·*
   g 546– 7 would *d·* the perfection of Deity.

dethrones

   s 148–25 Physiology exalts matter, *d·* Mind, and

detracts

   b 283–22 so *d·* from God's character and nature,

detrimental

   t 446–28 *d·* to health and integrity of thought.

develop

   pref viii– 4 To *d·* the full might of this Science,
   ph 199–15 Mortals *d·* their own bodies
   g 557– 4 learn how to *d·* their children properly

developed

   a 29–29 though at first faintly *d·*.
   an 105–22 Whoever uses his *d·* mental powers like an
   ph 198– 7 which has already *d·* the disease
   198–30 muscles of the blacksmith's arm are strongly *d·*,
   p 416–19 and been *d·* according to it,
   g 550– 9 nor can Spirit be *d·* through its opposite.

developing

   c 258–13 forever *d·* itself, broadening and
   p 381– 5 or that some disease is *d·* in the system,

development

  explanation and
   an 102–26 not . . . an easy explanation and *d·*.
  greater
   sp 82–32 hastening to a greater *d·* of power,
  hour of
   c 266–10 When this hour of *d·* comes,
  man's
   ph 172– 3 Theorizing about man's *d·* from
  of disease
   p 400–15 and you prevent the *d·* of disease.
   403–31 mental conception and *d·* of disease
  of pain
   p 391–12 you can prevent the *d·* of pain in the body.
  opposite
   sp 88–22 Excite the opposite *d·*, and he blasphemes.
  precedes the
   g 553–32 which precedes the *d·* of that belief.
  spiritual
   m 66–11 Spiritual *d·* germinates not from
   g 547–27 not in material history but in spiritual *d·*.
  this
   ph 199–17 whether this *d·* is produced consciously or
   g 530– 2 In this *d·*, the immortal, spiritual law

   ph 173–23 according to the *d·* of the cranium ;
   189–28 the *d·* of embryonic mortal mind
   f 244–31 everlasting grandeur and immortality of *d·*,
   p 392–19 liable to the *d·* of that thought
   419–17 lest aught unfit for *d·* enter thought.
   gl 588– 7 the *d·* of eternal Life, Truth, and Love.

develops

s 128–15   *d·* the latent abilities . . . of man.
r 489–11   as consciousness *d·*, this belief goes out,

deviations

g 502– 7   mortal *d·* and inverted images

devil

cast out the
s 135–15   When Christ cast out the *d·* of dumbness,
flesh, and the
o 354– 5   "the world, the flesh, and the *d·*"
hast a
sp 70– *   *Now we know that thou hast a d·.— John 8 : 52.*
is come down
ap 568–20   the *d·* is come down unto you,— *Rev.* 12 : 12.
knoweth
ap 569–23   for the *d·* knoweth his time is short.
or evil
r 469–16   *d·* or evil— is not Mind,
ap 563–19   serpent, whose name is *d·* or evil,
personal
o 351–19   a personal *d·* and an anthropomorphic God
works of the
pr 5–30   "destroy the *works* of the *d·*."— *I John* 3 : 8.
r 474–31   "destroy the works of the *d·*."— *I John* 3 : 8.

s 135–16   when the *d·* was gone out,— *Luke* 11 : 14.
b 292–22   Ye are of your father, the *d·*— *John* 8 : 44.
330–31   dementia, insanity, inanity, *d·*,
t 450– 4   belief . . . in a natural, all-powerful *d·*.
g 539– 2   In the words of Jesus, it (evil, *d·*) is
554–23   and one of you is a *d·*?''— *John* 6 : 70.
554–25   Jesus never intimated that God made a *d·*,
554–26   "Ye are of your father, the *d·*."— *John* 8 : 44.
ap 567–15   that old serpent, called the *d·*,— *Rev.* 12 : 9.
567–19   that old serpent whose name is *d·* (evil),
gl 580–30   Jesus said of the *d·*, "He was— *John* 8 : 44.
584–17   definition of

devils

pr 7– 5   he cast out *d·* and healed the sick and sinning.
a 49– 5   "Even the *d·* are subject unto us— *Luke* 10 : 17.
52–32   "He casteth out *d·* through— *Luke* 11 : 15.
o 348–12   when *d·*, delusions, were cast out
p 362– *   *In my name shall they cast out d· :—Mark* 16 : 17.
422– 3   "If I by Beelzebub cast out *d·*,— *Matt.* 12 : 27.
r 494–30   Our Master cast out *d·* (evils) and healed the
ap 564– 1   and cast out *d·* through Beelzebub.
gl 583–18   casting out *d·*, or error, and healing the sick.

devious

s 164– 1   said : . . . our *d·* career resembles

devised

s 142– 2   the old systems, *d·* for subduing them,
ph 183–14   nor *d·* a law to perpetuate error.

devoid

s 134–15   *D·* of the Christ-power,
p 399–21   Without this force the body is *d·* of action,
r 480– 9   whereas matter is *d·* of sensation.
g 525–29   as *d·* of reality as they are of good,
549–22   false systems, . . . are *d·* of metaphysics.

devolved

g 506–28   Upon Adam *d·* the pleasurable task

devote

f 237–25   They *d·* themselves a little longer to their

devoted

s 109–14   *d·* time and energies to discovering a
gl 582– 6   so-called mortal mind, *d·* to matter ;

devotee

sp 89– 5   the *d·* may become unwontedly eloquent.
p 382–15   than is the *d·* of supposed hygienic law,

devotion

a 49– 2   They knew what had inspired their *d·*,
ph 199–21   *d·* of thought to an honest achievement
f 241–19   The substance of all *d·* is

devour

ap 563–26   for to *d·* her child as soon as— *Rev.* 12 : 4.
564– 1   which would impel them to *d·* each other

devouring

ph 192–14   It is the headlong cataract, the *d·* flame,
b 329–15   nor should he remain in the *d·* flames.

devout

pr 4–29   silent prayer, watchfulness, and *d·* obedience
7–21   with more *d·* self-abnegation and purity.
40– 3   The advanced thinker and *d·* Christian,
o 351–11   as did the prayers of her *d·* parents
p 367–14   from the summit of *d·* consecration,

devoutness

s 140–17   Spiritual *d·* is the soul of Christianity.

dew

ph 193– 9   The *d·* of death was on his brow.
c 257–20   hath begotten the drops of *d·*,''— *Job* 38 : 28.
p 365–18   like *d·* before the morning sunshine.

diagnosis

s 157– 1   Homœopathy . . . in its *d·* of disease.
161–26   treating the case according to his physical *d·*,
p 370–20   A physical *d·* of disease
408– 9   this general craze cannot, in a scientific *d·*,
t 463– 3   under influences not embraced in his *d·*,

diametrically

o 352– 8   the Jews took a *d·* opposite view.

diamond

g 521–16   the point of a *d·*'' and the pen of an angel.

diapason

ap 559–14   to utter the full *d·* of secret tones.

diathesis

p 424–32   a humor in the blood, a scrofulous *d·*.

dictate

f 228–23   we shall be masters of the body, *d·* its terms,
p 409–10   matter, . . . cannot *d·* terms to consciousness

dictated

s 158– 4   supposed to have *d·* the first prescription,

Dictionary, Smith's Bible

b 320– 8   In Smith's Bible *D·* it is said :

dictum

t 444– 6   is the *d·* of Scripture.

did

a 18– 6   He *d·* life's work aright
25–26   demonstrate this power as he *d·*
26– 2   gratitude for what he *d·* for mortals,
30–16   Not so *d·* Jesus, the new executor
51–20   only through doing the works which he *d·*
51–24   in all that he said and *d·*,
53– 3   as *d·* the Baptist's disciples ;
55– 6   Perhaps the early Christian era *d·*
sp 79–19   Jesus *d·* his own work
83– 3   What the prophets of Jehovah *d·*,
85–13   all things that ever I *d· :— John* 4 : 29.
86– 4   Jesus knew, as others *d·* not,
an 106–18   classify all others as *d·* St. Paul
s 136–30   apprehended their Master better than *d·* others ;
136–31   *d·* not comprehend all that he said and *d·*,
139– 7   so *d·* Joshua, Elijah, and Elisha.
141–21   outsiders *d·* not then, and do not now,
152–16   This he *d·* merely to ascertain the
156–17   I *d·* so, and she continued to gain.
ph 168–20   He *d·* the will of the Father.
193–18   and take supper with his family. He *d·* so.
193–29   but what I saw and *d·* for that man,
f 232–17   demonstrating . . . as it *d·* over nineteen hundred
b 314–13   knowing, as he *d·*, that Mind was the builder,
328–19   explain it practically, as Jesus *d·*,
329–11   Be thankful that Jesus, . . . *d·* these things,
o 351–10   as *d·* the prayers of her devout parents
359–10   while they, the patients, *d·* not.
p 364–28   show their regard . . . as *d·* this woman?
400–32   in certain localities he *d·* not many
t 444–24   part from these opponents as *d·* Abraham
r 494– 3   and he *d·* this for tired humanity's reassurance.
495– 3   as surely as it *d·* nineteen centuries ago.
495– 8   classify sickness and error as our Master *d·*,

die

m 61–16   often these beautiful children early droop and *d·*,
sp 75–22   waken . . . out of the belief that all must *d·*,
94–10   by our law he ought to *d·*,— *John* 19 : 7.
s 164–17   If you or I should appear to *d·*,
164–19   human beliefs that man must *d·*,
ph 170–11   believeth in me shall never *d·*,"— *John* 11 : 26.
197–10.   thou shalt surely *d·*.''— *Gen.* 2 : 17.
f 206–31   does not cause man to sin, to be sick, or to *d·*.
210–26   cannot say, "I suffer, I *d·*, I am sick,
221–12   and finally made up his mind to *d·*,
b 277– 3   "Thou shalt surely *d·* ;"— *Gen.* 2 : 17.
289–23   So man, tree, and flower are supposed to *d·* ;
295–29   teaches that mortals are created to . . . *d·*.
310–23   If Soul sinned, Soul would *d·*.
312–12   The belief of that mortal that he must *d·*
315– 2   believeth in me shall never *d·*."— *John* 11 : 26.
328–20   *d·* there annually from serpent-bites
p 375– 1   mortal mind, not matter, which says, "I *d·*."
381–15   types of disease, with which mortals *d·*.
387–13   Our thinkers do not *d·* early because they
406–25   no more fear that we shall be sick and *d·*,
426–20   It will master either a desire to *d·* or a dread
426–30   Man is immortal, and the body cannot *d·*,
427– 6   Man's individual being can no more *d·* nor
432–30   he decided at once that the prisoner should *d·*.
434–31   lower court has sentenced Mortal Man to *d·*,
435– 5   argued that the body should *d·*,
435–12   whosoever *sinneth* shall *d·* ;
435–18   Laws of Health should be sentenced to *d·*.
436–29   His Honor sentenced Mortal Man to *d·*
r 481–19   thou shalt surely *d·*."— *Gen.* 2 : 17.
486– 6   To *d·*, that he may regain these senses?

die

g 527–10 thou shalt surely *d*.— *Gen.* 2 : 17.
529–20 neither shall ye touch it, lest ye *d*.— *Gen.* 3 : 3.
530–14 Ye shall not surely *d* :— *Gen.* 3 : 4.
532– 9 thou shalt surely *d*,"— *Gen.* 2 : 17.
545–31 "As in Adam [error] all *d*,— *I Cor.* 15 : 22.
gl 580–20 saith, "Thou shalt surely *d*."— *Gen.* 2 : 17.

died

a 46– 3 until they . . . learned that he had not *d*.
sp 73– 4 but another, who has *d*. to-day
74–15 belief of having *d*. and left a material body
75–15 the understanding that Lazarus had never *d*,
75–16 not by an admission that his body had *d*.
75–17 Had Jesus believed that Lazarus had . . . *d*.
75–24 those who have thought they *d*.,
s 154–11 a bed where a cholera patient had *d*.
154–13 the symptoms . . . appeared, and the man *d*.
158–32 was etherized and *d* in consequence,
159–20 sequel proved that this Lynn woman *d* from
b 290–29 believing that his body *d*.
290–30 learning that his cruel mind *d*. not.
p 379–10 fancied himself bleeding to death, and *d*.
382–26 wrote to me : "I should have *d*., but for the

dies

sp 75– 2 mistaken assumption that man *d*. as matter
ph 168–16 becomes sick and useless, suffers and *d*.,
177–26 swallowed through mistake, and the patient *d*.
f 202–17 God, neither sins, suffers, nor *d*.
204– 2 It is evil that *d*. ; good *d*. not.
250–11 which is never born and never *d*.
b 275– 1 Matter has no life to lose, and Spirit never *d*.
285– 8 material personality which suffers, sins, and *d*. ?
288–16 the tumult *d*. away in the distance.
o 349–11 neither Life nor man *d*., and that God is not the
p 374–29 Nothing that lives ever *d*., and *vice versa.*
427– 2 the opposite belief that man *d*.
r 486–11 In reality man never *d*.
486–11 The belief that he *d*. will not establish his
491–21 another belief, that man *d*.
g 543– 5 not the real man, who *d*.
556–11 *d*. to live again in renewed forms,

diet

ph 174– 6 to baths, *d*., exercise, and air?
197–23 Their *d*. would not cure dyspepsia at this
f 219–28 and impute their recovery to . . . *d*.,
220–22 once adopted a *d*. of bread and water
221– 5 decided that his *d*. should be more rigid,
t 457–25 some learners commend *d*. and hygiene.

dietetic

p 389–13 *d*. theories first admit that food sustains

dietetics

f 220–25 never to try *d*. for growth in grace.

differ

a 24–26 Then we must *d*. from them both.
b 273– 8 They *d*. from real Science because they
t 461–20 Your responses should *d*. because
r 488– 8 words often translated *belief d*. somewhat

difference

a 30–23 showing the *d*. between the offspring
sp 82–24 would be prevented by this *d*.
86–23 Education alone determines the *d*.
b 293–19 *d*. being that electricity is not
p 403– 2 *d*. between voluntary and involuntary
421– 2 The only *d*. is, that insanity implies

differences

m 63–12 Civil law establishes very unfair *d*.

different

a 21–18 separate time-tables to consult, *d*. routes
m 57– 9 These *d*. elements conjoin naturally
58– 6 Tones of the human mind may be *d*.,
59–12 *d*. demands of their united spheres,
sp 74–22 *d*. beliefs, which never blend.
82–10 *d*. states of consciousness are involved,
82–12 cannot exist in two *d*. states of consciousness
82–16 through *d*. mazes of consciousness.
82–21 their state of consciousness must be *d*.
82–27 *D*. dreams and *d*. awakenings
s 139–18 the thirty thousand *d*. readings in the
149– 8 the *d*. mental states of the patient.
152–32 symptoms, . . . which demand *d*. remedies ;
161–32 upon *d*. terms than does the metaphysician ;
163–24 hypotheses obtruded upon us at *d*. times.
b 293– 7 are but *d*. strata of human belief.
p 377–12 Through *d*. states of mind,
407–30 All sin is insanity in *d*. degrees.
408–27 and the results would be perceptibly *d*.
t 461–21 because of the *d*. effects they produce.
r 493– 5 the solar system as working on a *d*. plan.
g 523–27 The *d*. accounts become more and
525– 8 the term *man* in *d*. languages.
546–31 a thousand *d*. examples of one rule,
549–10 three *d*. methods of reproduction

different

g 552–27 The intermixture of *d*. species,
ap 566–30 assigns to the angels, . . . *d*. offices.
gl 598– 6 yet it has received *d*. translations,

differing

sp 82–28 betoken a *d*. consciousness.
t 444–14 towards *d*. forms of religion and medicine,
444–15 those who hold these *d*. opinions.

differs

s 123–30 C. S. *d*. from material science,

difficult

sp 82– 3 It is no more *d*. to read the absent mind
86–22 why is it more *d*. to see a thought than
91– 9 *d*. for the sinner to accept divine Science,
s 147–32 Jesus never spoke of disease as . . . *d*. to heal.
ph 178–17 that chronic case is not *d*. to cure.
f 218–13 renders both sin and sickness *d*. of cure
225–25 abolition of mental slavery is a more *d*. task.
b 318– 4 but for him to conceive of . . . was more *d*.
o 350–17 *d*. in a material age to apprehend spiritual
p 382–20 more *d*. to heal through Mind than one who
396–15 not a *d*. task in view of the conceded falsity
398–32 changes such ills into new and more *d*. forms
410–15 The more *d*. seems the material condition
424–22 *d*. to make yourself heard mentally while
426– 6 finds the path less *d*. when she
t 448–32 Fettered by sin yourself, it is *d*. to
449–18 than it does to heal the most *d*. case.
452– 2 a task not *d*., when one understands
460–11 the one most *d*. to understand and
462–16 There is nothing *d*. nor toilsome in this task,

difficulties

m 60–11 maternal affection lives on under whatever *d*.
63–22 without encouraging *d*. of greater magnitude,
s 143–14 Driven to choose between two *d*.,
149–21 remarked . . . mind can never cure organic *d*."
p 377–25 organic diseases as readily as functional *d*.,
394–16 that he should not try to rise above his *d*.

difficulty

s 115– 5 and the consequent *d*. of so expressing
115– 9 The great *d*. is to give the right impression,
ph 184–28 breathed with great *d*. when the wind was
185– 1 so her *d*. in breathing had gone.
185– 3 The wind had not produced the *d*.
o 348– 8 Here is the *d*. : it is not generally
349–13 chief *d*. in conveying the teachings of
p 403– 8 the *d*. is a material illusion,
427–22 great *d*. lies in ignorance of what God is.

diffusive

m 58–16 benevolence should grow more *d*.

dig

sp 79–10 *d*. up every seed of error's sowing.

digest

ph 175–21 The exact amount of food the stomach could *d*.

digested

sp 84–31 If . . . thoroughly learned and properly *d*.,
p 390– 2 she said, "My food is all *d*.,

digestible

ph 197–25 and the most *d*. food in the stomach,

digestion

ph 175–25 "Medical Experiments" did not govern the *d*.
176–12 There were fewer books on *d*.
ap 559–23 if you find its *d*. bitter.

dignified

s 118–21 In all mortal forms of thought, dust is *d*. as

dignify

s 149–27 predicting disease does not *d*. therapeutics.

dignity

s 158–17 stupid substitutes for the *d*. and potency
f 236– 7 emolument rather than the *d*. of God's laws,
g 527–30 and is man giving up his *d*. ?

dilemma

s 119– 8 To seize the first horn of this *d*.
119–11 while to grasp the other horn of the *d*.

diligence

g 514–15 *d*., promptness, and perseverance

dim

s 147–23 hitherto unattained and seemingly *d*.
g 513– 8 To material sense, this divine universe is *d*.

diminish

m 61– 8 *d*. crime, and give higher aims to ambition.
ph 181–32 will *d*. your ability to become a Scientist,
f 202–18 The days . . . will multiply instead of *d*.,
248–31 sin, disease, and death will *d*.
c 262– 3 Neither does consecration *d*. man's obligations
p 410–28 will *d*., until the practitioner's

diminished

s 155–29 homœopathy, and . . . have *d*. drugging ;

diminishes
- *sp* 96–28 As material knowledge *d·* and
- *s* 155–25 Homœopathy *d·* the drug,
- *p* 415–20 thought increases or *d·* the secretions,
- 420–20 It increases or *d·* the action, as the case may
- 423– 4 this fear greatly *d·* the tendency towards a

diminishing
- *f* 224– 1 and the power of sin *d·*,

dimly
- *s* 117–26 human reason *d·* reflects and

din
- *b* 307–31 Above error's awful *d·*, blackness, and chaos,

dipped
- *f* 213–30 Before human knowledge *d·* to its depths

dire
- *ph* 196– 4 can save him from the *d·* effects of knowledge.
- *p* 388– 8 *d·* inflictions failed to destroy his body.

direct
- *sp* 94–25 enabled him to *d·* those thoughts aright ;
- *an* 105– 1 The hands, without mortal mind to *d·* them,
- *s* 138–19 under as *d·* orders now, as they were then,
- 148– 5 but acted in *d·* disobedience to them.
- *ph* 189–31 keeping always in the *d·* line of matter,
- *f* 228– 1 by healing in *d·* opposition to them
- 235– 8 selected with as *d·* reference to their morals
- 249–31 He is the *d·* opposite of material sensation,
- *b* 273–26 in *d·* opposition to material laws.
- 284–17 which receive no *d·* evidence of Spirit,
- *o* 342– 9 in defiance of the *d·* command of Jesus,
- *p* 370–19 produce very *d·* and marked effects on
- *t* 457–20 no excellence without labor in a *d·* line.

directed
- *ph* 169–23 towards which human faith or endeavor is *d·*.
- *p* 378–30 if such a power could be divinely *d·*,
- *r* 494–19 Reason, rightly *d·*, serves to correct

directing
- *p* 413–25 constantly *d·* the mind to such signs,

direction
another
- *ph* 198–19 Again, giving another *d·* to faith,
any
- *ph* 177–23 in any *d·* against God,
- *b* 280– 9 can never do justice to Truth in any *d·*.
- *t* 445–17 or limit in any *d·* of thought the omnipresence
- 457– 9 this newly discovered power in any *d·*
every
- *p* 371–13 sick humanity sees danger in every *d·*,
- 406–21 to avail ourselves in every *d·*
- *t* 458–18 sword of Truth must turn in every *d·*
mental
- *s* 160–24 never capable of acting contrary to mental *d·*.
of mortal mind
- *s* 160–10 no more dependent upon the *d·* of mortal mind,
opposite
- *ph* 195–10 those very senses, trained in an opposite *d·*.
- *p* 388–14 another admission in the opposite *d·*,
right
- *a* 21–13 gain a little each day in the right *d·*,
- 21–31 imagine himself drifting in the right *d·*.
- *ph* 172– 5 amounts to nothing in the right *d·*
- *f* 219–32 this scientific beginning is in the right *d·*.
- 248–26 we must first turn our gaze in the right *d·*,
- *p* 401– 3 it does nothing in the right *d·* and
this
- *p* 419– 4 Errors of all sorts tend in this *d·*.
unerring
- *p* 424– 9 the proper sense of God's unerring *d·*
whichever
- *p* 392–23 Your decisions . . . whichever *d·* they take.

- *m* 64– 3 in the *d·* taught by the Apostle James,
- *p* 394– 9 to act in the *d·* which Mind points out.
- *t* 451–15 walks in the *d·* towards which he looks,

directions
- *sp* 86–11 Opposites come from contrary *d·*,
- *f* 220– 6 to look in other *d·* for cause and cure.
- *b* 329– 9 great might of divine Science in these *d·*.

directly
- *ph* 177–29 as *d·* as if the poison had been
- 187–15 as *d·* as does the hand,
- 192–31 receives *d·* the divine power.
- *f* 220–32 as *d·* as the volition or will moves the hand.
- *b* 311–19 *d·* opposite to the immortal reality of being.
- *o* 358– 6 If two statements *d·* contradict each other
- *p* 397–11 as *d·* as you enhance your joys by
- 400– 1 mortal mind, which *d·* controls the body
- 423–28 as *d·* the action of mortal mind as is dementia
- *g* 533–11 to trace all human errors *d·* or indirectly

directs
- *s* 160–26 as they please or as disease *d·*,
- *f* 254–11 seek Truth righteously, He *d·* our path.

dirt
- *p* 383–14 To the mind equally gross, *d·* gives no uneasiness.
- 413–14 and covering it with *d·* in order to
- 413–21 I am not patient with a speck of *d·* ;
- *gl* 595–24 Uncleanliness. Impure thoughts ; error ; sin ; *d·*.

disable
- *p* 378–27 never endowed matter with power to *d·* Life

disabled
- *p* 373–25 the *d·* organ will resume its healthy functions.

disabuse
- *s* 130–15 would *d·* the human mind of material beliefs

disagree
- *p* 390–27 "Agree to *d·*" with approaching symptoms

disagreement
- *o* 361– 3 cancels the *d·*, and settles the question.

disappear
- *pref* xi–12 and *d·* as naturally and as
- *a* 34–27 he would *d·* to material sense
- *sp* 72– 6 that body would *d·* to mortal sense,
- 97–27 will *d·* before the supremacy of Spirit.
- *f* 203–29 should *d·* on the shore of time ;
- 211–21 Sympathy with error should *d·*.
- 224– 4 As the crude footprints of the past *d·*
- 228–10 and fleshly ills will *d·*.
- 248–32 will diminish until they finally *d·*.
- 252– 8 human beliefs . . . begin to *d·*.
- *b* 295–14 mortal consciousness will at last . . . *d·*,
- 319–18 Mystery, miracle, sin, and death will *d·*
- 324– 3 and joy to see them *d·*,
- *o* 347–29 and sickness will *d·* from consciousness.
- 353–18 All things will continue to *d·*, until
- 357–23 are false claims, which will eventually *d·*,
- *p* 375– 8 and the chills and fever *d·*.
- 395–14 sin, disease, and death will *d·*.
- 415–27 will apparently cause the body to *d·*.
- 425–13 Then these ills will *d·*.
- 426–28 death will *d·* with the disappearance of sin.
- 427– 6 can no more die nor *d·* in unconsciousness
- 442–22 and sin, disease, and death *d·*.
- *r* 476–11 Mortals will *d·*, and immortals, . . . will appear
- 476–18 Sin, sickness, and death must *d·*
- 480–30 understood as nothingness, they would *d·*.
- 485– 8 soon to *d·* because of their uselessness
- *g* 509–28 appear in man and the universe never to *d·*.
- 556– 6 These false beliefs will *d·*, when the
- *ap* 561–21 material and corporeal selfhood *d·*,
- 572–18 seen and acknowledged that matter must *d·*.
- *gl* 584– 4 The objects of time and sense *d·*

disappearance
- *a* 43– 3 his material *d·* before their eyes
- *p* 426–29 death will disappear with the *d·* of sin.
- *gl* 593– 4 *d·* of material sense

disappeared
- *ph* 199–30 His fear must have *d·* before his
- *b* 328–15 has sadly *d·* from Christian history.
- 334–16 material concept, or Jesus, *d·*,
- *p* 436– 5 the Health-agent *d·*,
- 438–27 he *d·* and was never heard of more.
- 442–10 all sallowness and debility had *d·*,
- *gl* 580–27 and then *d·* in the atheism of matter.

disappearing
- *an* 102–16 mild forms of animal magnetism are *d·*,
- *s* 115–25 *Second Degree :* Evil beliefs *d·*.
- *gl* 589–24 material belief progressing and *d·* ;
- 590–24 is *d·* from the recorder's thought,

disappears
- *a* 42– 8 comes in darkness and *d·* with the light.
- *m* 69–10 as the false and material *d·*.
- *sp* 89–10 Destroy her belief . . . and her eloquence *d·*.
- 97–13 its mortal zenith in illusion and forever *d·*.
- *s* 116– 4 In the third degree mortal mind *d·*,
- 131– 7 false evidence before the corporeal senses *d·*.
- 155–27 the potency . . . increases as the drug *d·*.
- 156–30 matter *d·* from the remedy entirely,
- *ph* 172–14 only as the false sense of being *d·*.
- 189–12 existence of the sunlight when the orb of day *d·*,
- 190–18 This mortal seeming . . . finally *d·*,
- *f* 207– 4 until it *d·* from our lives.
- 222– 1 this phantasm of mortal mind *d·*
- 230–27 We think that we are healed when a disease *d·*,
- 251–26 improves mankind until error *d·*,
- 252–11 until the entire mortal, material error finally *d·*,
- *c* 264–21 Matter *d·* under the microscope of Spirit.
- 267–25 in which all error *d·* in celestial Truth.
- *b* 274–32 matter, . . . in the light of divine metaphysics, *d·*,
- 279–16 In proportion as the belief *d·* that life
- 281– 5 When one appears, the other *d·*.
- 293– 1 mortality *d·* in presence of the reality.
- 297–13 that *d·* which before seemed real

disappears
p 368–23   material belief in them *d·*
   368–31   When fear *d·*, the foundation of disease is gone.
   406–13   Then error *d·*.   Sin and sickness will abate
   406–16   all that is unlike the true likeness *d·*.
   417–17   you destroy the evidence, for the disease *d·*.
   442–24   material, transformed with the ideal, *d·*,
r 491– 6   Destroy the belief, and the sensation *d·*.
g 520–12   These days will appear as mortality *d·*,
   520–14   in which all sense of error forever *d·*
gl 595–21   mortal *d·* and spiritual perfection appears.
   597–18   in which a material sense of things *d·*,

disappoint
f 234–22   The present codes of human systems *d·*

disappointed
f 245– 5   *D·* in love in her early years,
t 452–25   and you will be *d·*.

disappointments
m 57–31   *d·* it involves or the hopes it fulfils.
b 322–27   as well as our *d·* and ceaseless woes,

disarm
ph 178–25   and we *d·* sin of its imaginary power

disarmed
b 290–31   until evil is *d·* by good.

disarms
p 394–11   *d·* man, prevents him from helping himself,

disarrangement
p 421– 5   *d·*, is a word which conveys the true definition

disasters
s 119–12   to make Him responsible for all *d·*,

disastrous
f 247– 2   is not so *d·* as the chronic belief.

disbelief
a 29– 7   faith in the right and *d·* in the wrong.
o 346–15   *D·* in error destroys error,
p 397–20   in exact proportion to your *d·* in physics,

disbelieve
p 427– 8   If man believes in death now, he must *d·* in it
t 453– 3   You do not . . . *d·* the musician when he

disbelieving
a 50–27   The distrust of mortal minds, *d·* the purpose

discard
f 213–32   which *d·* the one Mind and true source of
p 425–32   *D·* all notions about lungs, tubercles,

discern
a 22–18   you will *d·* the good you have done,
sp 84–23   by which we *d·* man's nature and existence.
   85–11   and *d·* the error you would destroy.
   85–21   ye can *d·* the face of the sky ; — *Matt.* 16 : 3.
   85–22   not *d·* the signs of the times?" — *Matt.* 16 : 3.
   91–16   Absorbed in material selfhood we *d·* . . . faintly
   95– 9   able to *d·* the thought of the sick
   95–14   to *d·* thought scientifically, depends upon
   97– 1   those who *d·* C. S. will hold crime in check.
ph 194– 3   I cannot fail to *d·* the coincidence of
f 233–17   Ye who can *d·* the face of the sky,
   233–19   how much more should ye *d·* the sign
c 258–31   you can *d·* the heart of divinity,
b 310–30   which material sense cannot *d·*.
   315–13   They could not *d·* his spiritual existence.
o 345–23   ought to be able to *d·* the distinction
t 455–27   if he is taught of God to *d·* it.
g 509–31   can *d·* the face of the sky ; — *Matt.* 16 : 3.
   510– 1   not *d·* the signs of the times?" — *Matt.* 16 : 3.
   510– 4   To *d·* the rhythm of Spirit and to be holy,
   519–12   Human capacity is slow to *d·* and to grasp
   534– 2   and to *d·* spiritual creation.

discerned
m 56– 9   Until the spiritual creation is *d·* intact,
   65– 6   spiritual and eternal existence may be *d·*.
   68–32   the unbroken links . . . will be spiritually *d·* ;
sp 85–17   In like manner he *d·* disease
   87– 9   to be *d·*, described, and transmitted.
   98–12   which can only be spiritually *d·*.
s 110–23   forever remain to be *d·* and demonstrated.
   110–27   and must again be spiritually *d·*,
   137– 4   not spiritually *d·*, even by them, until
ph 168–24   I have *d·* disease in the human mind,
f 210– 5   Principle and proof of Christianity are *d·* by
b 275–31   Truth, spiritually *d·*, is scientifically
   302– 7   thereby *d·* and remains unchanged.
   330–15   nor . . . can be *d·* by the material senses.
o 351–12   spiritual sense of the creed was *d·*
t 461–10   nor is it *d·* from the standpoint of
g 509– 2   Spirit is *d·* to be the Life of all,
   512–24   *d·* only through the spiritual senses.
gl 585–10   with which can be *d·* the spiritual fact
   598–27   bridge over with life *d·* spiritually

discernible
sp 76–27   a perfection *d·* only by those who

discerning
pref x–28   or *d·* the truth, come not to the light
a 35– 6   *D·* Christ, Truth, anew on the shore
m 60–25   not *d·* the true happiness of being,
s 143–22   never *d·* how this deprives you
f 227–14   *D·* the rights of man, we cannot

discernment
a 47– 1   *d·* of Jesus' teachings and
sp 82– 6   *d·* of the minds of Homer and Virgil,
   91–18   aids the *d·* of man's spiritual and
   94–30   An approximation of this *d·*
ph 171– 4   Through *d·* of the spiritual opposite
o 346–16   and leads to the *d·* of Truth.
g 505–20   Spiritual sense is the *d·* of spiritual good.
ap 561– 4   leads to the *d·* of the divine idea.
gl 586– 3   EYES.   Spiritual *d·*,

discerns
t 462–32   *d·* and deals with the real cause of disease.

discharge
ph 193–20   The *d·* from the sore stopped,
r 478–19   *d·* of the natural functions is least noticeable

Disciple
ap 576– 9   the beloved *D·* writes:

disciple   (*see also* **Eddy, Mrs. Mary Baker**)
beloved
a 36–13   the beloved *d·*, and a few women
b 319–32   what the beloved *d·* meant in one of his
doubting
b 317–30   To this dull and doubting *d·* Jesus remained
impetuous
s 137–26   Before this the impetuous *d·* had
mightiest
a 48–12   shall the humblest or mightiest *d·* murmur
Simon the
p 362– 4   though he was quite unlike Simon the *d·*.

a 21– 9   If the *d·* is advancing spiritually,
   28–29   encountered by prophet, *d·*, and apostle,
   41–32   belief, . . . never made a *d·* who could cast ou
s 141– 6   Because his precepts require the *d·* to
b 271–11   In Latin the word rendered *d·* signifies
   324–19   Paul was not at first a *d·* of Jesus

disciples   (*see also* **disciples'**)
Baptist's
a 53– 4   He did not fast as did the Baptist's *d·* ;
his
pr 16– 7   Our Master taught his *d·* one brief prayer,
a 32–28   The Passover, which Jesus ate with his *d·*
   34–30   his last spiritual breakfast with his *d·*
   38–13   He was addressing his *d·*, yet he did not say,
   42–28   Jesus had taught his *d·* the Science of
   44–28   His *d·* believed Jesus to be dead while he
   45–14   after his bodily burial he talked with his *d·*.
   45–24   Even his *d·* at first called him a spirit,
   46–28   above the physical knowledge of his *d·*,
   52–26   prophetically said to his *d·*,
sp 86– 3   his *d·* answered, "The multitude— *Luke* 8 : 45
s 117–29   Jesus bade his *d·* beware of the leaven of
   132–31   once pointed his *d·* to Jesus as
b 271– 7   Jesus instructed his *d·* whereby to heal the sick
   313–28   only in a limited degree even by his *d·*,
   317–21   presented himself to his *d·* after his
p 367–18   of which Jesus spoke to his *d·*,
   388–21   If food was prepared by Jesus for his *d·*,
his immediate
b 328–29   Had it been given only to his immediate *d·*,
his own
a 24–31   his own *d·* could not admit such an
its
o 349–20   this sense must be gained by its *d·*
of Jesus
a 29–13   "The *d·* of Jesus believe him the Son of God.'
other
a 27–24   credits him with two or three hundred other *d·*
seventy
o 342–13   He bade the seventy *d·*, as well as

a 32–16   brake it, and gave it to the *d·*, — *Matt.* 26 : 26.
   32–21   The *d·* had eaten, yet Jesus prayed and
   34–18   Through all the *d·* experienced,
   43– 5   all enabled the *d·* to understand
   49– 4   and caused the *d·* to say to their Master :
sp 86–10   more spiritual susceptibility than the *d·*.
s 136–24   what the *d·* did not fully understand?
   136–29   The *d·* apprehended their Master better

disciples'
a 35– 1   and his *d·* grief into repentance,
   47–27   The *d·* desertion of their Master
sp 86– 8   The *d·* misconception of it uncovered

discipline
m 66–28   Xantippe a *d·* for his philosophy.

disciplined
   f 202–10 until *d·* by the prison and the scaffold ;
disclose
   o 344–16 rules which *d·* its merits or demerits,
   t 447–13 evil will in time *d·* and punish itself.
discloses
   f 202–21 experience *d·* the finity of error
discolored
   p 385–21 *d·*, painful, swollen, and inflamed.
discomfiture
   ph 169– 7 to his *d·*, when he was incredulous.
discomfort
   a 53–16 The world could not interpret aright the *d·*
       53–18 which might flow from such *d·*.
   an 101–28 *D·* under error is preferable to comfort.
discontented
   b 305– 2 A *d·*, discordant mortal is no more a *man* than
   ap 559–27 do not be surprised nor *d·* because you must
discord
  accepts the
    s 148–17 drops the true tone, and accepts the *d·*.
  all
    sp 96–20 all *d·* will be swallowed up in spiritual Truth.
    s 130– 8 divine Science, which destroys all *d·*,
     130–12 Science, . . . will destroy all *d·*,
    r 481–23 human verdicts are the procurers of all *d·*.
  and death
    s 124–10 limiting Life and holding fast to *d·* and death.
    f 224–10 life and peace instead of *d·* and death.
  and decay
    b 280– 2 Symbols and elements of *d·* and decay
    r 468–18 eternal and incapable of *d·* and decay.
    g 503–24 no element nor symbol of *d·* and decay.
  and dismay
    sp 96–13 On one side there will be *d·* and dismay ;
  and mortality
    b 338– 7 terminates in *d·* and mortality,
  any other
    p 414–14 dementia, hatred, or any other *d·*.
  apparent
    p 390– 8 ignorance . . . which produces apparent *d·*,
  calls
    m 60–24 An ill-attuned ear calls *d·* harmony,
  can never establish
    o 356– 7 *D·* can never establish the facts of harmony.
  conceding power to
    p 394– 5 By conceding power to *d·*,
  continual
    f 240–14 and there is continual *d·*.
  division and
    s 148–23 how from this basis of division and *d·*
  educated into
    p 414– 3 and thus are children educated into *d·*.
  error and
    p 423–21 superior to error and *d·*,
  fearful
    m 65–11 The union of the sexes suffers fearful *d·*.
  forsake
    p 400–10 only as they forsake *d·*,
  human
    b 306–32 parent of all human *d·* was the Adam-dream,
  instead of
    f 224–10 life and peace instead of *d·* and death.
     253–30 law of . . . harmony instead of *d·*,
  is the nothingness
    b 276–26 *D·* is the *nothingness* named error.
  is unnatural
    b 304–21 and *d·* is unnatural, unreal.
  is unreal
    b 276–15 *D·* is unreal and mortal.
    p 414–23 harmony is universal, and *d·* is unreal.
  its own
    s 146– 8 By trusting matter to destroy its own *d·*,
  learn from
    s 129–25 or learn from *d·* the concord of being?
  marvel at
    ap 563– 1 Human sense may well marvel at *d·*,
  mortal
    sp 98– 3 the elevation of existence above mortal *d·*
    c 262–27 foundation of mortal *d·* is a false sense
  night of
    p 378–28 chill harmony with a . . . night of *d·*.
  no
    b 331–16 in Spirit . . . there can be no *d·* ;
  no rule of
    f 219–20 Science includes no rule of *d·*,
  of every kind
    p 394–26 conquer *d·* of every kind with harmony,
  of every name
    o 355–11 Let *d·* of every name and nature
  opposite
    f 207–30 the opposite *d·*, . . . is not real.

discord
  or harmony
    f 213–28 discoursing either *d·* or harmony
  overcomes
    s 134–22 natural law of harmony which overcomes *d·*,
  physical sense of
    r 493–23 takes away this physical sense of *d·*,
  produce
    m 58– 5 Ill-arranged notes produce *d·*.
  reign of
    s 122– 2 and so creates a reign of *d·*,
  seeming
    p 390– 7 to the mortal senses, there is seeming *d·*
  silence
    r 495–23 and silence *d·* with harmony.
  the unreal
    ap 563– 2 harmony is the real and *d·* the unreal.
  the unreality
    o 352– 3 to make . . . *d·* the unreality.
  will correct the
    m 60–27 Science will correct the *d·*,
        ———
    ph 170– 4 The *d·* which calls for material methods
     186–23 If we concede the same reality to *d·* as to
     186–23 If . . . *d·* has as lasting a claim
    f 228–18 and *d·* as the material unreality.
    c 255– 5 and *d·* into the music of the spheres.
    b 305– 2 subjected to material sense which is *d·*.
     305– 3 mortal is no more a *man* than *d·* is music.
    o 351–24 proves the nothingness of error, *d·*,
    p 368–12 beliefs . . . that *d·* is as normal as harmony,
     379–32 belief that . . . *d·* is as real as harmony,
     400–28 Without divine control there is *d·*,
    t 453– 4 when he distinguishes concord from *d·*.
discordant
   ph 184–18 Whatever is governed by a false belief is *d·*
   f 208–28 and he makes it harmonious or *d·*
    209– 3 mortal belief which makes the body *d·*
    213–15 towards the finite, temporary, and *d·*.
    239–25 produces every *d·* action of the body.
    239–27 it is *d·* and ends in sin, sickness, death.
   b 305– 3 *d·* mortal is no more a *man* than
    318–17 so far as he is *d·*, he is not the image of God.
    337–13 while error is mortal and *d·*.
   o 347– 5 whatever is mortal or *d·* has no origin,
   p 369– 2 to admit also the reality of all *d·* conditions,
    387–26 which causes all things *d·*.
   t 444–30 mortals, . . . are *d·* and ofttimes
discords
   pref viii– 5 *d·* of corporeal sense must yield to
   sp 78– 2 like the *d·* of disease, sin, and death,
   s 129– 2 So in C. S. there are no *d·*
    155–22 to offset the *d·* of matter and the ills of flesh,
   ph 183– 5 *d·* have no support from nature or divine law,
   f 231–16 God is not the author of mortal *d·*.
    231–17 *d·* have only a fabulous existence,
   b 304–25 To be master of chords and *d·*,
discount
   pr 5–10 there is no *d·* in the law of justice
discourage
   p 424–18 such opinions as may alarm or *d·*,
discouraged
   s 130– 2 *d·* over its slight spiritual prospects.
   b 329–17 To be *d·*, is to resemble a
discouragement
   f 254– 6 or attain slowly and yield not to *d·*.
discouraging
   p 394–13 such admissions are *d·*,
    396– 7 Never startle with a *d·* remark
   t 447–18 without frightening or *d·* the patient
discoursing
   f 213–27 *d·* either discord or harmony
discover
   s 129– 7 *d·* it by reversing the material fable,
   c 260–14 at work to *d·* what God has already done ;
    265–25 we *d·* what belongs to wisdom and Love.
   p 369–15 in order to *d·* some means of healing.
    370–32 to *d·* the condition of matter,
   t 462–22 to *d·* their quality, quantity, and origin.
   g 548– 5 we *d·* man in the image and likeness of God.
discoverable
   sp 87– 4 lost to . . . the mind in which they are *d·*.
discovered
   pref viii–31 the first steps of a child in the newly *d·*
   an 104–11 Next, they say it has been *d·* before.
   s 107– 1 In the year 1866, I *d·* the Christ Science
    126–23 just as I have *d·* them.
    147–28 This rule remained to be *d·* in C. S.
   b 321–17 when he *d·* that what he apparently saw
   p 408– 4 nor *d·* to be error by many who are sick.
   t 457– 8 this newly *d·* power in any direction

discoverer of Christian Science
(see **Eddy, Mrs. Mary Baker**)
discoveries
  s 112–28 and yet uses another author's d·
  g 548–27 Modern d· have brought to light important
discovering
  s 109–14 devoted . . . energies to d· a positive rule.
discovers
  g 549–24 d· the pathway leading to divine Science,
discovery
  author's
    pref vii–27 Since the author's d· of the might of
  his
    s 121– 2 if his d· had undermined the
  my
    s 107– 3 and named my d· C. S.
    108–30 My d·, that erring, mortal, misnamed *mind*
    109–11 For three years after my d·,
    111–26 After a lengthy examination of my d·
    115– 8 as brought forth in my d·.
  new
    p 403–23 Never conjure up some new d·
  of the system
    pref viii–26 d· of the system that she denominated C. S.
  sacred
    r 483–13 After the author's sacred d·,
  spiritual
    p 380–22 Many years ago the author made a spiritual d·,
  this
    s 153–13 This d· leads to more light.
    g 549– 1 This d· is corroborative of the Science
    549– 2 this d· shows that the multiplication of

    s 123–20 d· of this divine Science of Mind-healing,
    c 263–21 the d· of some distant idea of Truth ;
    p 411– 3 My first d· in the student's practice
discredit
  m 68–25 I d· the belief that agamogenesis applies to
discrimination
  m 63–19 d· as to the person, property, and
discuss
  p 389–14 then d· the certainty that food can kill man.
discussed
  ph 175–22 was not d· according to Cutter
  185– 8 which d· "mental medicine" and "mind-cure,"
discussing
  f 237–16 kept from d· or entertaining theories or
  r 492–17 D· his campaign, General Grant said :
disdain
  f 224–19 Cold d·, stubborn resistance,
Disease
  p 439–26 meanwhile declaring D· to be God's servant
  439–32 reported to be haunted by D·,
  439–33 they learn that D· was never there,
  441–15 nor can D· cast him into prison.
disease
  acute
    ph 176–29 Hence decided types of acute d·
    p 390–28 approaching symptoms of chronic or acute d·,
  advanced stages of
    p 391– 8 the incipient or advanced stages of d·,
  affirmation of
    p 392–11 physical affirmation of d· should always
  agrees with the
    s 162– 2 the matter-physician agrees with the d·,
  all
    s 120–23 and thus Science denies all d·, heals the sick,
    ph 169–18 not only reveals the origin of all d·
    169–19 declares that all d· is cured by divine Mind.
    176–25 All d· is the result of education,
    f 218–32 all d·, pain, weakness, weariness,
    p 377–22 you remove the cause of all d·
    392– 6 Fear, which is an element of all d·,
  alleviating
    an 100– 6 as a means of alleviating d·.
  and death
    s 116–17 belief in matter, evil, d·, and death,
    ph 176–15 d· and death, will lose their foothold.
    f 207–23 d·, and death belong not to the Science of
    215–19 So sin and sorrow, d· and death,
    c 260–21 d·, and death proceed from fear.
    p 401– 6 but it engenders d· and death.
    414– 2 foundations of the belief in d· and death,
    t 450–20 enlisted to lessen evil, d·, and death ;
    r 474– 3 destroy all error, evil, d·, and death.
    g 547–32 lifts humanity out of d· and death
  and its cause
    p 393–32 the sin and the sinner, the d· and its cause.
  and mortality
    g 557–15 the less a mortal knows of sin, d·, and mortality,

disease
  and sin
    pref viii–13 by healing both d· and sin ;
    f 208–32 banish all thoughts of d· and sin
    p 420–17 Truth overcomes both d· and sin
    r 485–27 and delineates foreign agents, called d· and sin.
  antidote to
    s 155–30 if drugs are an antidote to d·, why lessen the
  any
    f 233–29 The counter fact relative to any d·
  any other
    p 384–27 rheumatism, consumption, nor any other d·
  appetite and
    p 398–23 Appetite and d· reside in mortal mind,
  approach of
    p 374–17 Ignorance of the cause or approach of d·
  arises
    s 154– 3 D· arises, like other mental conditions,
  being a belief
    ph 168–26 D· being a belief, a latent illusion
  belief in
    (see **belief**)
  belief of
    ph 178– 9 The remote cause or belief of d· is not
    p 380–18 body is affected only with the belief of d·
    398–27 and change the belief of d· to a belief of health.
  belief of the
    p 377–20 when the belief of the d· had gone.
  belief produces
    s 159–30 belief produces d· and all its symptoms,
  breeds
    m 62– 7 master the belief . . . which breeds d·.
  called a
    p 398– 1 Sometimes Jesus called a d· by name,
  called the
    p 411– 4 student silently called the d· by name,
  call the
    p 412–10 call the d· by name when you mentally deny it ;
  case of
    s 155–21 in order to heal a single case of d·.
    ph 196–25 Many a hopeless case of d· is induced by
  cause a
    p 374– 7 the sick say : "How can my mind cause a d·
  cause of
    (see **cause**)
  causes
    ph 188–24 What causes d· cannot cure it.
    f 208– 7 What then is this . . . which causes d·
    b 318– 8 senses are saying that matter causes d·
    o 344–12 understood . . . that error causes d·,
    p 399– 4 but if the material body causes d·,
  chains
    p 380–19 mind ignorant of the truth which chains d·.
  challenges
    s 162– 3 agrees only with health and challenges d·.
  chambers of
    p 365–26 finds its way into the chambers of d·
  chronic
    s 162–18 in cases of both acute and chronic d·
  chronic form of
    ph 176–31 less distinct type and chronic form of d·.
  classify
    r 483– 5 We classify d· as error,
  consume with
    f 205– 4 drop with drunkenness, consume with d·,
  consumption, or
    p 426– 1 notions about . . . consumption, or d·
  crisis of the
    t 446– 8 or it may mark the crisis of the d·.
  crop of
    ph 188–25 an abundant or scanty crop of d·,
  cure
    an 101–26 seems to alleviate or to cure d·,
    f 208–15 absurd to suppose that matter can . . . cure d·,
  cure of
    pref xi– 4 results in the cure of d·.
    s 147– 5 its present application to the cure of d·.
    149– 3 far outweighs drugs in the cure of d·
    t 457–31 Let this Principle be applied to the cure of d·
  declaring
    ph 180–18 by declaring d· to be a fixed fact,
  depicts
    b 319– 3 Science depicts d· as error,
  describing
    sp 79– 1 The act of describing d· . . . is not scientific.
  descriptions of
    ph 179–32 Descriptions of d· given by physicians
  destroy
    p 412–15 and to destroy d·, sin, and death.
    t 447–20 truth and . . . which destroy d·.
  destroying
    s 157– 3 in judging and destroying d·.
  destroys
    p 420– 1 nor go from one part to another, for Truth destroys d·.

disease

developed the
  ph 198– 7 his fear, which has already developed the *d·*

development of
  p 400–15 you prevent the development of *d·*.
  403–31 mental conception and development of *d·*

diagnosis of
  s 157– 1 Homœopathy . . . in its diagnosis of *d·*.
  p 370–20 A physical diagnosis of *d·* . . . tends to

disappears
  f 230–27 We think that we are healed when a *d·* disappears,
  p 417–17 you destroy the evidence, for the *d·* disappears.

discords of
  sp 78– 2 like the discords of *d·*, sin, and death,

disquisitions on
  p 371– 5 Disquisitions on *d·* have a mental effect

dread
  b 321–23 white as snow with the dread *d·*,

dream of
  p 396–30 It breaks the dream of *d·*

eradicate the
  ph 180–20 before they go to work to eradicate the *d·*

error and
  pr 5–32 all evil works, error and *d·* included.

error, or
  p 400–18 By lifting thought above error, or *d·*, and

every
  p 400–16 if you understand that every *d·* is an error,
  411–32 it alleviates the symptoms of every *d·*.

evidence of
  p 412–23 so as to destroy the evidence of *d·*.

evil and
  t 447–21 Expose . . . the claims of evil and *d·*

evil called
  s 135–14 and when Truth casts out the evil called *d·*,

exemption from
  p 411–29 their exemption from *d·* and danger.

expels the
  s 153– 3 it is not the drug which expels the *d·*

explanation of
  p 374–10 The author . . . in her explanation of *d·*

fastens
  p 395–28 fastens *d·* on the patient,

fear of
  ph 169–13 by exciting fear of *d·*,
  188–27 Sin and the fear of *d·* must be uprooted
  197–31 should suppress his fear of *d·*,
  p 373–14 The fear of *d·* and the love of sin are
  377–32 fear of *d·*, which associates sickness with
  400– 3 the fear of *d·* is gone, and therefore
  t 455–11 lost in the belief and fear of *d·* or sin,

fear of the
  ph 196–28 but from the fear of the *d·*

feelings or
  p 396– 6 inquiries relative to feelings or *d·*.

fetters of
  t 449– 1 to free another from the fetters of *d·*.

forms of
  p 398–29 more difficult forms of *d·*.

fosters
  ph 169–12 faith . . . in drugs begets and fosters *d·*

foundation of
  p 368–31 When fear disappears, the foundation of *d·* is gone.
  t 453–27 increases fear, the foundation of *d·*,

functional
  s 149–24 as readily as she has cured purely functional *d·*,

God never decreed
  f 221–19 that God never decreed *d·*,

has no intelligence
  p 378– 3 *D·* has no intelligence.
  391–24 *D·* has no intelligence to declare itself
  419–10 *D·* has no intelligence with which to move

heal
  pref x–21 His disposition and power to heal *d·*.
  f 202–29 and yet we rely on . . . to heal *d·*, as if

healed
  sp 79–22 He never described . . . but he healed *d·*.
  p 386–13 healed *d·* through the action of Truth.

healing
  s 150– 3 through this Christian system of healing *d·*.

heals
  t 445–24 cast out by the divine Mind which heals *d·*.

health or
  s 120–27 matter's supposed consciousness of health or *d·*,

he discerned
  sp 85–17 In like manner he discerned *d·*

hinders
  p 374–21 this belief helps rather than hinders *d·*.

holds
  p 395–27 Mental practice, which holds *d·* as a

illusions about
  p 413–27 illusions about *d·*, health-laws, and death,

disease

image of
  s 154– 7 the fear that creates the image of *d·*
  p 400–12 Eradicate the image of *d·* from the

images of
  ph 175– 1 We should prevent the images of *d·* from
  197– 2 which mirror images of *d·* distinctly in thought.

imbecility or
  ph 197–15 removed from imbecility or *d·*.

incipient stages of
  p 390–30 Meet the incipient stages of *d·* with

increase
  s 159–32 is liable to increase *d·* with his own mind,

induce
  p 370–22 physical diagnosis . . . tends to induce *d·*.
  417–30 Show them how mortal mind seems to induce *d·*

induces
  p 392–28 the condition . . . which you say induces *d·*,

injuries, and
  p 402–17 You say that accidents, injuries, and *d·* kill

insist that
  p 409– 3 insist that *d·* is formed by mortal mind

is abnormal
  s 120–14 health is normal and *d·* is abnormal.

is an experience
  r 493–20 *D·* is an experience of so-called mortal mind.

is an image
  p 411–23 *D·* is an image of thought externalized.

is expressed
  p 373–21 *D·* is expressed not so much by the lips as in

is less than mind
  p 378– 7 *D·* is less than mind, and Mind can control it.

is mental
  b 270–28 *d·* is mental, not material.
  p 377–26 cause of all so-called *d·* is mental,

is unreal
  f 229–32 the truth that *d·* is *unreal*.

itself
  p 419–11 Neither *d·* itself, sin, nor fear has the power

leads to
  s 120–29 confirms that testimony . . . and so leads to *d·*.

less
  ph 175– 6 there will be better constitutions and less *d·*.
  g 554–32 This would indicate that there is less *d·*

less for the
  p 421–12 treat the patient less for the *d·* and

load with
  ph 176–17 Human fear of miasma would load with *d·*

malignant
  p 373– 6 It is easier to cure the most malignant *d·* than

method of treating
  o 344–26 to investigate this method of treating *d·*?

methods of treating
  o 344–19 There are various methods of treating *d·*,

minutely described
  ph 197– 5 A minutely described *d·* costs many

mortality and
  p 395–10 its claims over mortality and *d·*.

name of a
  p 411–13 once Jesus asked the name of a *d·*,

name of the
  p 396–10 avoid speaking aloud the name of the *d·*.

never described
  sp 79–21 He never described *d·*,

never spoke of
  s 147–32 Jesus never spoke of *d·* as dangerous

no hereditary
  p 412–32 knows that there can be no hereditary *d·*,

nor death
  s 140–27 causeth no evil, *d·*, nor death.
  p 368–22 Neither evil, *d·*, nor death can be

not aggravate the
  p 401–12 This fermentation should not aggravate the *d·*.

one
  ph 176–24 One *d·* is no more real than another.
  o 348– 9 one *d·* can be just as much a delusion as another.
  p 418–15 one *d·* would be as readily destroyed as another.
  r 483– 4 exchanging one *d·* for another.

organic
  s 149–23 The author has cured what is termed organic *d·*
  162–25 C. S. heals organic *d·* as surely
  ph 176–21 Should all cases of organic *d·* be treated by
  177– 1 Human mind produces what is termed organic *d·*
  180–32 dissolve a tumor, or cure organic *d·*,
  p 428–30 The author has healed hopeless organic *d·*,

origin of
  p 374–18 no argument against the mental origin of *d·*.

origin of all
  ph 169–18 reveals the origin of all *d·* as mental,

or its symptoms
  p 419–32 *d·* or its symptoms cannot change forms,

or sin
  b 323–24 contemplation of something better than *d·* or sin.
  p 402–19 whether it be a broken bone, *d·*, or sin.
  t 455–11 the belief and fear of *d·* or sin,

disease

outlines of
  ph 175– 2   we should efface the outlines of *d·*
pain or
  p 421–15   belief that . . . produces pain or *d·*.
physical
  s 150–14   the metaphysical healing of physical *d·* ;
power of
  p 376–31   To fear and admit the power of *d·*,
predicting
  s 149–27   predicting *d·* does not dignify therapeutics.
prevent
  ph 170–18   If there are material laws which prevent *d·*,
  198–12   It is better to prevent *d·* from forming in
  p 412–16   To prevent *d·* or to cure it,
preventing
  s 147–28   this Principle of healing and preventing *d·*.
produce
  p 399– 4   You say . . . material combinations produce *d·* ;
produces
  f 208–16   absurd to suppose that . . . God, produces *d·*
  b 270–27   If a sense of *d·* produces suffering
pulmonary
  m 63– 2   for warding off pulmonary *d·*
  f 203– 1   that this cold may produce fatal pulmonary *d·* ;
  p 392–20   in the form of what is termed pulmonary *d·*,
question of
  p 406–18   he should be as fearless on the question of *d·*.
regarding
  p 403–24   Never conjure up . . . forebodings regarding *d·*
  432–13   says : . . . there is a statute regarding *d·*,
relative to
  ph 198–10   who outlines his thought relative to *d·*,
removal of
  o 358–27   in the removal of *d·*
remove
  p 400–20   When we remove *d·* by addressing the
render
  p 433– 6   that laws of nature render *d·*
reports
  p 409–13   belief, that . . . body, suffers and reports *d·*
resist
  p 420–11   they can resist *d·* and ward it off,
says to
  s 144–22   says to *d·*, "Peace, be still." — *Mark* 4 : 39.
sender of
  s 158– 8   Apollo was also regarded as the sender of *d·*,
sense of
  b 270–27   If a sense of *d·* produces suffering
  p 421–27   If you would destroy the sense of *d·*,
should not implant
  ph 180–17   Doctors should not implant *d·* in the thoughts
sickness and
  ph 179–23   the promoters of sickness and *d·*.
sin and
  (*see* **sin**)
sin, and death
  sp 78– 2   like the discords of *d·*, sin, and death,
  b 275–29   so-called powers, such as. . .*d·*, sin, and death,
  p 412–15   and to destroy *d·*, sin, and death.
sin, . . . and death
  (*see* **sin**)
sin or
  p 396–17   not because the testimony of sin or *d·* is true,
sin, . . . or death
  f 253–16   overcome the belief in sin, *d·*, or death.
  253–25   supposed necessity for sin, *d·*, or death,
  p 380– 9   the demands of sin, *d·*, or death,
slough of
  ph 168–13   already brought yourself into the slough of *d·*
so-called
  ph 168–26   before the so-called *d·* made its appearance
  p 377–26   cause of all so-called *d·* is mental,
soil of
  ph 188–24   The soil of *d·* is mortal mind,
some
  p 381– 5   or that some *d·* is developing
speak to
  p 395– 7   speak to *d·* as one having authority over it,
subject to
  s 150–19   believe that both . . . are subject to *d·*,
suffering and
  f 221–17   He learned that suffering and *d·* were the
supposed
  p 418–19   the negation must extend to the supposed *d·*
supposed rights of
  o 348–22   defending the supposed rights of *d·*,
symptoms of
  s 153– 4   or changes one of the symptoms of *d·*.
  p 390–12   When the first symptoms of *d·* appear,
  398–18   are known to relieve the symptoms of *d·*.
system of treating
  s 111–30   my metaphysical system of treating *d·*
tattling about
  s 153–31   we shall avoid loquacious tattling about *d·*,

disease

their
  p 416–27   If they ask about their *d·*,
the very
  s 161–27   would naturally induce the very *d·*
this
  s 154–12   Immediately the symptoms of this *d·* appeared,
  ph 174–27   Why . . . picture this *d·* to the mind,
  p 425– 8   leading points included . . . in this *d·*.
thought of
  ph 198–15   The thought of *d·* is formed before
  p 396– 2   never hold in mind the thought of *d·*,
thoughts of
  ph 196–21   so efface the images and thoughts of *d·*,
  f 208–32   banish all thoughts of *d·* and sin
to see
  p 421–25   It is no more Christianly scientific to see *d·*
transmission of
  f 228– 3   The transmission of *d·* or of certain
treatment of
  pref viii– 1   in the treatment of *d·* as well as of sin,
  s 126–23   its application to the treatment of *d·*
  157–22   and recommend them for the treatment of *d·* ?
  p 369– 4   is unfitted for the successful treatment of *d·*.
treats
  b 318–24   Medical science treats *d·* as though
  t 459–30   treats *d·* with more certain results
types of
  p 381–15   cannot legislate the times, . . . and types of *d·*,
  396– 3   all forms and types of *d·*,
unreal
  p 417–24   the way to cure . . . is to make *d·* unreal
unreality of
  p 417–26   understand the unreality of *d·* in Science.
  t 461–29   to prove . . . the error or unreality of *d·*,
unsee the
  t 461–29   you must mentally unsee the *d·* ;
weariness and
  ph 183–16   supposed laws which result in weariness and *d·*
what is termed
  ph 188– 3   What is termed *d·* does not exist.
when treating
  p 424–27   well to be alone with . . . when treating *d·*.
will vanish
  p 365–17   *d·* will vanish into its native nothingness
yoke of
  g 555– 5   physical organism under the yoke of *d·*.
you overcome
  p 392– 2   it is through divine Mind that you overcome *d·*.

———

  s 108–25   called error, sin, sickness, *d·*, death,
  113–20   omnipotent good, deny death, evil, sin, *d·*.
  113–20   *D·*, sin, evil, death, deny good, omnipotent God,
  115–23   hatred, revenge, sin, sickness, *d·*, death.
  137– 6   the victor over sickness, sin, *d·*, death,
  159–21   and not from the *d·* or the operation.
  160–26   If muscles can cease to act . . . as *d·* directs,
  162–24   I have restored . . . where *d·* was organic.
  ph 168–24   I have discerned *d·* in the human mind,
  169–10   *d·* has a mental, mortal origin,
  176–26   *d·* can carry its ill-effects no farther than
  196–20   Such books as will rule *d·* out of mortal mind,
  f 230–18   no more . . . than . . . and health occasion *d·*.
  251–24   the healer of sin, *d·*, death.
  b 318–24   as though *d·* were real,
  318–25   If *d·* is right it is wrong to heal it.
  320–30   even if *d·* and worms destroyed his body,
  o 345–32   not . . . to "educate the idea of God, or treat it for *d·*."
  348– 4   even while treating them as *d·* ;
  348– 6   making the *d·* appear to be . . . an illusion?
  348–22   complaining of the suffering *d·* brings,
  353– 2   Sin, *d·*, whatever seems real to
  p 368–28   mortality (and therefore *d·*)
  369–15   never . . . made a reality of *d·*
  369–16   Jesus never asked if *d·* were acute
  371–30   and health instead of *d·*.
  373–11   the sick recover more rapidly from *d·* than
  373–29   we call these conditions *d·*,
  378–22   *D·* is not an intelligence to dispute
  379– 1   If *d·* can attack and control the body
  395–21   It is mental quackery to make *d·* a reality
  400– 2   When *d·* is once destroyed
  400– 3   therefore the *d·* is thoroughly cured.
  409– 2   "But if *d·* obtains in matter, why do you insist
  411–14   a *d·* which moderns would call *dementia*.
  411–21   *D·* is always induced by a false sense
  412–21   Argue . . . that the patient has no *d·*,
  415– 2   *d·* is neither a cause nor an effect.
  417–21   *D·* should not appear real to the physician,
  419–12   Neither . . . has the power to cause *d·* or a
  419–14   If *d·* moves, mind, not matter, moves it ;
  420–25   they can meet *d·* fearlessly, if
  421–18   There is *no d·*.
  426–17   *d·* cannot destroy life,

disease
- p 426–31 human concepts named matter, death, *d·*,
- 432–14 he upon whose person *d·* is found
- t 457–13 cannot . . . both cure and cause *d·*
- gl 595– 5 Mortality ; error ; sin ; sickness ; *d·* ;

disease-beliefs
- p 409– 7 the more prolific it is likely to become in sin and *d·*.

diseased
- s 164–15 and all *d·* thought-germs are exterminated.
- ph 174–27 Why declare that the body is *d·*,
- 193–21 The *d·* condition had continued there ever since
- f 209– 3 belief which makes the body discordant and *d·*
- 217–17 When you have once conquered a *d·* condition
- 237–20 either sinful or *d·* thoughts.
- 243–18 dizzy, *d·*, consumptive, or lame.
- 253–22 Also, if you believe yourself *d·*,
- p 376–24 representing man as healthy instead of *d·*,
- 395–32 would prevent the brain from becoming *d·*,
- 403– 2 induced their own *d·* conditions.
- 404–10 malice, and all sorts of evil are *d·* beliefs,
- 421– 2 insanity implies belief in a *d·* brain,
- 425–14 If the body is *d·*, this is but one of the
- 428– 1 no inaction, *d·* action, overaction, nor
- 432–17 become *d·*, transgress the laws, and
- r 487–31 This Principle makes whole the *d·*,

diseases
array of
- ph 176–11 A ghastly array of *d·* was not paraded
certain
- s 154– 5 Since it is a law of mortal mind that certain *d·*
classification of
- s 164– 5 "No systematic . . . classification of *d·*
define
- b 318– 5 Corporeal senses define *d·* as realities ;
hereditary
- p 424–29 scrofula and other so-called hereditary *d·*,
most
- p 414– 6 it yields more readily than do most *d·* to the
organic
- p 377–24 You also remove. . .what are termed organic *d·*
other
- p 376– 2 more terrifying than that of most other *d·*.
- 414– 9 The arguments . . . are the same as in other *d·* :
our
- b 320–29 hope in Him who healeth all our *d·* ;
violence of
- pref viii–23 increased violence of *d·* since the flood.
worst of
- p 396– 1 a moral offence is indeed the worst of *d·*.

- s 138–11 He showed that *d·* were cast out
- 150–32 are flooding the world with *d·*,
- ph 165–13 *D·* have multiplied, since man-made material
- 196–32 sorrows and *d·* among the human family.
- 197– 1 It does this by giving names to *d·*
- p 376– 7 *d·* deemed dangerous sometimes come from
- t 453–26 nor give names to *d·*,

disentangles
- s 114–26 *d·* the interlaced ambiguities of being,

disgrace
- s 120–32 *d·* and starvation stared him in the face ;

disguise
- f 254–26 What is there to strip off error's *d·* ?
- o 343–14 Jesus strips all *d·* from error,
- t 454–13 the great truth which strips all *d·* from error.
- r 472–29 until God strips off their *d·*.

disgusted
- s 163–23 we cannot help being *d·* with the

disgusting
- p 407– 5 Puffing the obnoxious fumes . . . is at least *d·*.

disheartening
- p 380–28 Nothing is more *d·* than to believe

dishonest
- ph 192–16 all that is selfish, wicked, *d·*, and impure.
- f 252–18 and says : I am wholly *d·*,
- t 448–16 A *d·* position is far from Christianly

dishonestly
- s 130– 7 It is vain to speak *d·* of

dishonesty
- an 103– 4 further defines it as *d·* and craftiness.
- 104–19 *d·*, sensuality, falsehood, revenge,
- ph 188– 9 Passion, depraved appetites, *d·*, envy,
- b 330–29 *d·*, selfishness, envy, hypocrisy,
- p 404–29 envy, *d·*, fear, . . . make a man sick,
- t 453–16 *D·* is human weakness,
- 456–16 Any *d·* in your theory and practice
- 464–28 Neither *d·* nor ignorance ever founded,

dishonor
- f 228–26 to acknowledge any other power is to *d·* God.
- r 483–22 Science of Mind seems to bring into *d·* the

dishonorest
- o 349– 6 breaking the law, *d·* thou God?"— *Rom.* 2 : 23.

dishonors
- ph 183–30 If C. S. *d·* human belief,

disinclined
- f 218–14 sinner, *d·* to self-correction,

disintegrated
- p 429–20 he could not exist after the body is *d·*.

dislocated
- p 402– 6 broken bones, *d·* joints, and spinal vertebræ.

dislocation
- p 402–15 no breakage nor *d·* can really occur.
- 408–22 *d·* of the tarsal joint would produce

dislocations
- p 401–30 the adjustment of broken bones and *d·*

dismal
- ph 195– 5 Outside of *d·* darkness and cold silence
- b 272–27 the *d·* beliefs of sin, sickness, and death.

dismay
- sp 96–14 On one side there will be discord and *d·* ;

dismiss
- s 149–30 *d·* superstition, and demonstrate truth
- p 390–21 *D·* it with an abiding conviction
- t 454–27 Do not *d·* students at the close of a

dismissal
- f 218–25 Treat a belief in sickness . . . with sudden *d··*

disobedience
- a 19–27 If living in *d·* to Him, we ought to feel no
- s 148– 6 but acted in direct *d·* to them.
- f 227–31 *d·* to which would have made man ill,
- p 436–31 construed . . . as *d·* to the law of Life.
- 440– 3 on the ground of hygienic *d·*,
- 440–12 *d·* to the so-called laws of Matter
- 440–13 *d·* to God, or an act of homicide.

disobey
- p 372–16 nor *d·* the law of God.
- r 483–10 you must not be ignorant of . . . nor *d·*

disobeyed
- ph 184–23 a law of this so-called mind has been *d·*.
- p 385–27 a law of mortal mind which you have *d·*.

disorder
- s 135– 7 The miracle introduces no *d·*,
- ph 184–10 belief which produces a mortal *d·*,
- p 402–30 Science cannot produce both *d·* and order.
- 404–14 you can remove this *d·* as God's law is
- 415–25 To remove the error producing *d·*, you must

disordered
- ph 181– 3 Before deciding that the body, matter, is *d·*,
- p 408–18 the so-called inflammation of *d·* functions,

disown
- s 119– 4 When we endow matter. . .we *d·* the Almighty,
- o 342–26 Who would be the first to *d·* the Christliness of

dispel
- ph 198–16 and before the doctor undertakes to *d·* it

dispelling
- b 332–13 *d·* the illusions of the senses ;

dispels
- sp 80–15 Science *d·* mystery and explains
- b 283– 1 Truth is the light which *d·* error.

dispensation
- s 123–26 did not specially belong to a *d·* now ended,
- 150–10 for its establishment as a permanent *d·*
- b 270–16 hence their foresight of the new *d·* of Truth.

dispensed
- p 389– 1 the food or this thought must be *d·* with,

disperse
- f 205–17 catch clear glimpses of God only as the mists *d·*,

display
- m 60–23 personal adornment, *d·*, and pride,
- b 317–32 Nothing but a *d·* of matter
- p 367–12 the arrogance of rank and *d·* of scholarship,

displayed
- s 121– 9 *d·* upon the empyrean,
- 121–31 *d·* in the . . . government of the universe.
- 163–25 Nowhere is the imagination *d·* to a greater
- p 378–31 less wisdom than we usually find *d·* in

displeasure
- g 542– 2 It incurs divine *d·*, and it would kill Jesus
- ap 571– 9 to tell a man his faults, and so risk human *d·*

disport
- g 514– 7 infinite ideas run and *d·* themselves.

disposal
- b 304–19 is not, therefore, at the *d·* of physical sense.
- 305– 1 placed at the *d·* of illusions,

disposes
- r 473– 4 The Science of Mind *d·* of all evil.

disposition

pref x–21 so little faith in His *d·* and power to heal
m 59–24 to grumble over incompatibility of *d·*.
s 130– 2 The licentious *d·* is discouraged
b 324– 3 this *d·* helps to precipitate the
g 542– 9 the *d·* to excuse guilt . . . is punished.

dispossesses

p 375–12 *d·* the patient of his individuality

disprove

s 164–20 does not in the least *d·* C. S. ;

disputations

o 342– 1 Paul alludes to "doubtful *d·*."— *Rom.* 14 : 1.

dispute

p 378–22 Disease is not an intelligence to *d·* the
390–12 *d·* the testimony of the material senses
r 490– 2 but the grand truths of C. S. *d·* this error.
492–16 will *d·* the ground, until one is

disputed

f 227– 4 and that, even as oppressive laws are *d·*

disputes

gl 580–29 An adversary is one who opposes, denies, *d·*,

disputing

g 539–22 *D·* these points with the Pharisees

disquieted

p 362– * *And why art thou d· within me?* — *Psal.* 42 : 11.

disquisitions

p 371– 5 *D·* on disease have a mental effect similar to
387–20 instead of reading *d·* on the

disregard

m 64–27 Let not mortals permit a *d·* of law
f 210–10 his *d·* of matter and its so-called laws.

disregarded

f 227–32 Jesus would not have *d·* those laws
p 365–12 if . . . common sense and common humanity
are *d·*,

disregarding

t 445–28 thus *d·* the morals of the student

disrobe

f 201–14 Let us *d·* error.

dissatisfied

f 240–23 we must become *d·* with it.

dissection

b 338–25 The *d·* and definition of words,
t 462–21 and consists in the *d·* of thoughts

disseminating

an 100–10 *d·* itself through the substance of the

dissent

s 155–12 individual *d·* or faith, unless it rests on Science,

dissimulation

r 483–31 fulfil one's mission without timidity or *d·*,

dissipates

sp 79–30 It *d·* fatigue in doing good.
p 375– 2 as painlessly as gas *d·* into the air

dissolute

m 63–28 If a *d·* husband deserts his wife,

dissolution

b 290–18 If . . . happiness would be won at the moment
of *d·*,
297–18 but subject to change and *d·*.
g 550–18 birth, decay, and *d·* as its component stages

dissolve

ph 180–31 To reduce inflammation, *d·* a tumor,
f 242–16 *d·* with the universal solvent of Love

dissolves

sp 74–11 the error which has held the belief *d·*
s 162– 8 *d·* tumors, relaxes rigid muscles,

dissolving

f 224– 5 disappear from the *d·* paths
r 490–22 along with the *d·* elements of clay.

dissuade

ph 175–12 and *d·* any sense of fear or fever.

distance

focal
b 301–27 supposed standpoint outside the focal *d·* of
great
a 53–21 the great *d·* between the individual and Truth.
infinite
a 47–17 the infinite *d·* between Judas and his Master.
g 538– 8 the infinite *d·* between Truth and error,
moral
a 36–16 moral *d·* between Christianity and sensualism
not
f 209–15 Nearness, not *d·*, lends enchantment
spiritual
a 47–20 this spiritual *d·* inflamed Judas' envy.

an 105–30 The *d·* from ordinary medical practice to C. S. is

distance

s 141– 1 This indicates the *d·* between the
b 288–17 the tumult dies away in the *d·*.

distances

f 209–19 *d·*, and revolutions of the celestial bodies,

distant

a 24–15 The time is not *d·* when the
sp 82– 1 it is as easy to read *d·* thoughts as near.
an 104– 4 comprehended, as they will be at no *d·* date,
c 263–22 the discovery of some *d·* idea of Truth ;
g 513– 9 To . . . sense, this divine universe is dim and *d·*,

distemper

p 398–10 Often he gave no name to the *d·* he cured.

distinct

sp 70–13 divine Mind maintains all identities, . . . as *d·*
ph 176–30 the less *d·* type and chronic form of disease.
f 204–28 never . . . has a mind of his own, *d·* from God,
214– 2 the impressions from Truth were as *d·* as sound,
217– 9 prove Mind to be scientifically *d·* from matter,
b 306–22 not more *d·* nor real to the material senses
335– 3 theory, that Spirit is *d·* from matter
p 438–16 on three *d·* charges of crime, to wit :
g 523–15 clear evidences of two *d·* documents

distinction

s 116–27 and its *d·* from humanity.
o 345–23 ought to be able to discern the *d·*
523–29 after which the *d·* is not definitely traceable.

distinctive

ap 560– 4 the *d·* feature has reference to

distinctly

sp 83–30 are *d·* opposite standpoints,
ph 197– 2 which mirror images of disease *d·* in thought.
b 314–26 and the more *d·* he uttered the demands of
p 396–26 Keep *d·* in thought that man is
408–11 so many *d·* defined instances of the
415–32 leaving the pain standing forth as *d·* as

distinguish

ph 173– 2 we fail to see how anatomy can *d·*
t 453– 1 to *d·* the correct from the incorrect

distinguished

sp 88– 9 How are veritable ideas to be *d·*
b 320– 5 *d·* theologians in Europe and America
g 551– 9 One *d·* naturalist argues that

distinguishes

pr 16– 5 It *d·* between Truth . . . and the falsity of
t 453– 3 when he *d·* concord from discord.

distinguishing

g 506– 1 *d·* between the false and the true.

distorted

s 110–20 This book may be *d·* by shallow criticism
b 322–22 incurred through the pains of *d·* sense.

distressed

ph 165–17 *d·* stomachs and aching heads.

distribute

p 408–20 Truth does not *d·* drugs through the blood,

distrust

a 50–27 *d·* of mortal minds, disbelieving the purpose
f 231–25 and *d·* His omnipotent care.
234– 3 If we trust matter, we *d·* Spirit.
c 260–15 *d·* of one's ability to gain the goodness
o 351– 3 When we lose faith . . . we *d·* the divine

distrusted

t 459–22 when the latter is *d·* and thwarted

disturb

f 254–25 what is there to *d·* the waters?

disturbance

p 421–13 the mental *d·* or fermentation,

disturbances

sp 96–18 These *d·* will continue until the end of error,

disturbed

p 379–29 The images, held in this *d·* mind,
400–20 by addressing the *d·* mind,
421– 6 human belief in ill-health, or *d·* harmony.
r 488–29 but they cannot be *d·* nor destroyed,

disturbs

p 388–31 If mortals think that food *d·* the

ditch

f 223–19 both shall fall into the *d·*." — *Matt.* 15 : 14.

diurnal

s 121–17 The earth's *d·* rotation is invisible

diverged

a 21–19 Our paths have *d·* at the very outset,

diversifies

g 513–17 Spirit *d·*, classifies, and individualizes

Dives

sp 83–25 as impassable as that between *D·* and Lazarus.

divest
   sp 90– 8   *D·* yourself of the thought that
   b 339–29   to *d·* sin of any supposed mind or reality,
   p 428– 8   To *d·* thought of false trusts

divested
   b 291–30   by which mortal man is *d·* of all material error.

divests
   s 146–18   *d·* material drugs of their imaginary power,

divide
   f 240–31   how to *d·* between sense and Soul.
   250– 1   run into error when we *d·* Soul into souls,
   b 280–14   seeks to *d·* the one Spirit into persons and
   338–14   *D·* the name Adam into two syllables,
   g 505– 5   and let it *d·* the waters from— *Gen.* 1 : 6.
   509–10   to *d·* the day from the night ;— *Gen.* 1 : 14.
   511– 9   *d·* the light from the darkness :— *Gen.* 1 : 18.

divided
   s 118–27   a kingdom necessarily *d·* against itself,
   f 233–25   When numbers have been *d·* according to
   252– 2   "If a kingdom be *d·* against— *Mark* 3 : 24.
   b 269– 2   Pandemonium, a house *d·* against itself.
   294–24   represented as *d·* into intelligent gods.
   o 354–27   It is in itself inconsistent, a *d·* kingdom.
   p 388–19   "kingdom *d·* against itself,"— *Matt.* 12 : 25.
   389–17   and the kingdom *d·* against itself.
   g 503–27   *d·* the light from the darkness.— *Gen.* 1 : 4.
   505–13   *d·* the waters which were under— *Gen.* 1 : 7.
   510–22   already *d·* into evening and morning ;
   gl 581–17   kingdom *d·* against itself, which cannot stand ;

divides
   sp 74–26   There is no bridge across the gulf which *d·*
   b 312–27   It *d·* faith and understanding

dividing
   t 462–10   *d·* his interests between God and mammon

Divine
Being
   pr 3–12   The *D·* Being must be reflected by man,
   o 357–18   false notions about the *D·* Being
Love
   p 439–29   sentence which . . . *D·* Love will pronounce.
Science
   a 55–29   This Comforter I understand to be *D·* Science.
   s 127– 9   The terms *D·* Science, Spiritual Science,

   sp 99–16   C. S. is unerring and *D·* ;
   f 205–32   When we fully understand our relation to the *D·*,

divine
action
   an 104–15   indicates the rightness of all *d·* action,
agent
   t 444– 4   suffering is oft the *d·* agent in this elevation.
aid
   o 354– 6   Why do they invoke the *d·* aid to enable them to
All-power
   t 454– 6   The understanding, . . . of the *d·* All-power
anointing
   p 367–26   through silent utterances and *d·* anointing
arbitrament
   g 555– 4   human belief, and not the *d·* arbitrament,
authority
   sp 76–21   man is immortal and lives by *d·* authority.
   s 134–29   There is *d·* authority for believing in the
   b 270–23   Meekness and charity have *d·* authority.
   o 354–28   Its supposed realism has no *d·* authority,
   p 381–30   a sentence never inflicted by *d·* authority.
   382– 2   lacking *d·* authority and having only
   390–25   have *d·* authority for denying that necessity
basis
   p 388– 7   Apostle John testified to the *d·* basis of C. S.,
beatitudes
   t 446–25   Not human platitudes, but *d·* beatitudes,
beauty
   sp 76–23   possessing unlimited *d·* beauty and goodness
blessings
   r 489–16   channel to man of *d·* blessings
body
   ap 559–25   when you eat the *d·* body of this Principle,
cause
   b 286–24   they lack a *d·* cause.
character
   pr 4–21   to assimilate more of the *d·* character,
   g 540–23   error as assuming a *d·* character,
coincidence
   ap 561–16   John saw the human and *d·* coincidence,
Comforter
   r 497– 7   the Holy Ghost or *d·* Comforter ;
commandment
   s 112–30   inculcates a breach of that *d·* commandment
commission
   a 54–13   In witness of his *d·* commission,
conception
   b 315–25   The *d·* conception of Jesus pointed to

divine
concepts
   c 259–29   demands spiritual thoughts, *d·* concepts,
consciousness
   q 531–13   human concepts for the *d·* consciousness.
   gl 598–23   One moment of *d·* consciousness, or the
control
   pr 9–23   recognizes only the *d·* control of Spirit,
   p 400–28   Without *d·* control there is discord,
creation
   g 504– 6   All questions as to the *d·* creation
   507–22   The scientific *d·* creation declares
   514– 2   could not . . . invert the *d·* creation,
   521–23   The Science and truth of the *d·* creation
   525– 6   a human, not a *d·*, creation.
decree
   a 32–14   bowed in holy submission to the *d·* decree.
decrees
   s 118–30   they contradict the *d·* decrees
demand
   f 253–32   *d·* demand, "Be ye therefore— *Matt.* 5 : 48.
   b 329–23   Science is a *d·* demand, not a human.
displeasure
   g 542– 2   incurs *d·* displeasure, and it would kill Jesus
ear
   pr 7–23   The "*d·* ear" is not an auditory nerve.
economy
   b 327–21   place nor power in the human or the *d·* economy.
Ego
   b 336– 6   The *d·* Ego, or individuality, is reflected
energies
   ph 186– 4   filling it with the *d·* energies of Truth.
energy
   f 249– 6   Let us feel the *d·* energy of Spirit,
   t 445–21   the unlabored motion of the *d·* energy
Esse
   sp 93–19   contradicts the real nature of the *d·* Esse,
Exemplar
   pr 5–31   We should follow our *d·* Exemplar,
force
   s 134–19   the very element, which gave it *d·* force
glory
   b 323–12   is winged to reach the *d·* glory.
   ap 565– 5   loathing the brightness of *d·* glory.
good
   f 203–31   *d·* good, does not kill a man in order to
goodness
   m 66–15   unfolds new views of *d·* goodness and love.
government
   f 225– 3   is opposed to the *d·* government.
healing
   a 41–20   the *d·* healing of absolute Science.
   55–22   The time for the reappearing of the *d·* healing
   s 123–17   the scientific system of *d·* healing.
   141–27   The adoption of . . . *d·* healing will
   c 259–12   understanding of . . . *d·* healing includes
   o 347–19   namely, apostolic, *d·* healing?
heights
   b 325–26   the *d·* heights of our Lord.
   ap 566–11   Science . . . leading to *d·* heights.
help
   p 393– 3   through *d·* help we can forbid this entrance.
   t 453–17   Dishonesty . . . which forfeits *d·* help.
hues
   r 479–29   because it has none of the *d·* hues.
idea
   sp 88–18   To love one's neighbor as one's self, is a *d·* idea ;
   b 332–20   Christ is the *d·* idea of God
   334– 1   the *d·* idea or Christ was and is so
   t 463– 7   birth of the new child, or *d·* idea,
   r 470–22   the *d·* idea or reflection, man,
   473–16   Jesus is the human man, and Christ is the *d·* idea;
   482–21   the *d·* idea of God outside the flesh.
   g 506–25   Here the human concept and *d·* idea seem
   507–31   misinterpreted, the *d·* idea seems to fall
   ap 560–29   ignorant of the *d·* idea he taught.
   560–30   Ignorance of the *d·* idea betrays at once
   561– 4   leads to the discernment of the *d·* idea.
   561–25   as the divine Principle and *d·* idea.
   gl 589–17   JESUS. . . . corporeal concept of the *d·* idea,
ideal
   s 119–20   is not the *d·* ideal of omnipresent Love.
image
   f 205–19   perceive the *d·* image in some word or deed
   c 258–17   man as the true *d·* image and likeness,
   b 301–17   man is the *d·* image and likeness,
   332–12   yea, the *d·* image and likeness,
   333–26   The *d·* image, idea, or Christ
individuality
   b 303– 8   reflect the one *d·* individuality
influence
   pref xi–11   a *d·* influence ever present in
   f 236–16   or through *d·* influence,
intelligence
   ph 184–16   Controlled by the *d·* intelligence,

divine

Justice

p 437– 9   in the presence of *d·* Justice,

justice

an 105–24   *D·* justice will manacle him.
f 225–18   breathing the omnipotence of *d·* justice,
b 293–25   manifestations of evil, which counterfeit *d·* justice,

law

a   30–17   Not so did Jesus, . . . present the *d·* law of Love,
sp   72–30   *d·* law is the communicator of truth,
s 108– 5   It was the *d·* law of Life and Love,
  134–25   nor because it is an infraction of *d·* law,
ph 170–19   Not *d·* law, for Jesus healed the sick
  183– 6   discords have no support from nature or *d·* law,
f 205–22   the *d·* law of loving our neighbor as ourselves
  227–27   The illusion of material sense, not *d·* law,
b 273– 9   because they are not based on the *d·* law.
p 372–13   and then . . . name them *d·* law.
  385– 7   the *d·* law, rising above the human.
  436– 9   acting within the limits of the *d·* law,
  436–29   deeds which the *d·* law compels man to commit.
  440–19   in obedience to *d·* law?
t 445–15   You render the *d·* law of healing obscure
  458–24   Christianly scientific man reflects the *d·* law,
  459–29   (that is, the student . . . of the *d·* law)
g 522–32   Does the unerring Principle of *d·* law change
  540– 7   the prophet referred to *d·* law

laws

s 107– 2   the Christ Science or *d·* laws of Life,

Life

pr   10–16   a higher understanding of the *d·* Life.
  14–26   Life *d·*, revealing spiritual understanding
a   25–11   and they . . . who partake of that *d·* Life.
  54– 2   he demonstrated the *d·* Life.
s 138– 6   It was now evident to Peter that *d·* Life,
b 331– 1   God is *d·* Life, and Life is
  339– 2   *D·* Life destroys death,
g 538–12   a figure of *d·* Life and Love,
  556–16   to him who understands best the *d·* Life.
gl 579–10   ABRAHAM. Fidelity ; faith in the *d·* Life
  596–23   *d·* Life and Love illumine it,

light

s 135–32   as must be the case in the cycles of *d·* light.
t 457– 7   Since the *d·* light of C. S. first dawned

likeness

b 300–22   and of man as reflecting the *d·* likeness.
o 356–23   man who is made in the *d·* likeness
r 491–16   establishes man forever in the *d·* likeness,

logic

sp   72–21   it follows in *d·* logic that evil,
  93–10   *D·* logic and revelation coincide.

Love

pr   6– 3   *D·* Love corrects and governs man.
  14–11   to be absolutely governed by *d·* Love,
a   19– 4   Man cannot exceed *d·* Love,
  19–10   by the law of Spirit, — the law of *d·* Love.
  23–25   understands *d·* Love and how to
  26– 9   till all are redeemed through *d·* Love.
  38–26   the Christ, the spiritual idea of *d·* Love.
  40–25   *d·* Love, demands that all men should
  43–14   were overruled by *d·* Love
  48–29   decision against human rights and *d·* Love,
  54–17   highest proof he could have offered of *d·* Love.
  55–20   and the healing power of the *d·* Love
sp   97–15   having been destroyed by *d·* Love,
  98– 3   above mortal discord and in the gift of *d·* Love.
s 135–29   demonstration of *d·* Love casting out error
  140–26   The C. S. God is universal, eternal, *d·* Love,
ph 180–23   influence of *d·* Love which casteth out fear.
f 218–23   turning in time of need to God, *d·* Love,
  224–31   No power can withstand *d·* Love.
  239–18   If *d·* Love is becoming nearer, dearer,
  240– 1   Nature voices natural, . . . law and *d·* Love,
  241–20   reflection and demonstration of *d·* Love,
  243– 4   The *d·* Love, which made harmless the
c 256–18   What is infinite Mind or *d·* Love?
  257–18   *d·* Love, — is the father of the rain,
  266– 9   seeming vacuum is already filled with *d·* Love.
b 285–24   not as the saving Principle, or *d·* Love,
  288– 8   faith in and the understanding of *d·* Love.
  304–10   *d·* Love cannot be deprived of its manifestation,
  309– 3   incorporeal impartation of *d·* Love to man,
  322–29   turn us like tired children to the arms of *d·* Love.
  325–18   with Truth in *d·* Love,
  337– 8   harmonize with his Principle, *d·* Love ;
  340–12   *D·* Love is infinite.
o 356–25   Does *d·* Love commit a fraud on humanity
p 363–24   Why did he thus summarize his debt to *d·* Love?
  365–15   reaches his patient through *d·* Love.
  367– 9   parodies on . . . C. S., aflame with *d·* Love.
  375–20   restoring him physically through *d·* Love.
  411–10   If Spirit or the power of *d·* Love bear witness
  412–14   power of C. S. and *d·* Love is omnipotent.
  414–30   unreal, and is not brought about by *d·* Love.
  417– 2   health, peace, and harmony in God, *d·* Love.

divine

Love

p 420–26   *d·* Love gives them all power over
  424–25   the oneness and the allness of *d·* Love ;
  434– 1   Swift on the wings of *d·* Love, there comes
  436–31   construed obedience to the law of *d·* Love
  442–12   *D·* Love had cast out fear.
t 454–22   Wait patiently for *d·* Love to move upon
r 494–10   *D·* Love always has met and always will
  494–14   in every hour, *d·* Love supplies all good.
g 517–30   *D·* Love blesses its own ideas,
  529–22   serpent to tempt the children of *d·* Love?
  537–27   *d·* Love, which blessed the earth
ap 560–12   great miracle, to human sense, is *d·* Love,
  574–10   this message from *d·* Love, carried John
  578– 5   [*D· LOVE*] is my shepherd ;— *Psal.* 23 : 1.

manifestation

gl 583–10   CHRIST. The *d·* manifestation of God,

mercy

b 329–26   The pardon of *d·* mercy is the destruction of
g 542–12   jeopardize self-control, and mock *d·* mercy.

message

b 332–10   the *d·* message from God to men

messages

ap 566–29   assigns to the angels, God's *d·* messages,

metaphysics

s 111–11   The Principle of *d·* metaphysics is God ;
  111–12   the practice of *d·* metaphysics is the
  111–14   *D·* metaphysics reverses perverted and
  112–32   God is the Principle of *d·* metaphysics.
  113– 9   fundamental propositions of *d·* metaphysics
  113–26   *d·* metaphysics of C. S., like the method in
  146–31   *D·* metaphysics is now reduced to a system,
ph 192–29   in the understanding of *d·* metaphysics.
f 217–21   the problem of being in *d·* metaphysics ;
b 274–32   in the light of *d·* metaphysics,
  275–20   *D·* metaphysics, as revealed to
  278– 3   *D·* metaphysics explains away matter.
  330– 9   the infallibility of *d·* metaphysics will be
p 374–11   show our need of *d·* metaphysics.
  397–20   your fidelity to *d·* metaphysics,
t 459–32   rules of *d·* metaphysics as laid down
g 549– 6   shown by *d·* metaphysics to be a mistake,

method

f 240–29   The *d·* method of paying sin's wages
b 339– 1   The destruction of sin is the *d·* method
ap 568– 6   typifies the *d·* method of warfare in Science,

Mind

pr   1–10   are not unknown to the *d·* Mind.
  2–19   The mere habit of pleading with the *d·* Mind,
a   36–20   *d·* Mind is the immortal law of justice
m   62–22   The *d·* Mind, which forms the bud
  68–29   an impartation of the *d·* Mind to man
sp   70–12   The *d·* Mind maintains all identities,
  83– 1   whether it is the human mind or the *d·* Mind
  84–11   prerogative of the ever-present, *d·* Mind,
  84–15   to commune more largely with the *d·* Mind,
  85– 6   when the latter yields to the *d·* Mind.
  88–11   Ideas are emanations from the *d·* Mind.
  88–28   It shows the possibilities derived from *d·* Mind,
an 102–11   or the attraction of God, *d·* Mind.
  104–15   as the emanation of *d·* Mind,
  104–19   The medicine of Science is *d·* Mind ;
s 108–10   for the *d·* Mind cannot suffer.
  108–22   all real being is in God, the *d·* Mind,
  109– 5   the only realities are the *d·* Mind and idea.
  111– 5   the human mind, to be opposed to the *d·* Mind,
  114– 5   in contradistinction to the *d·* Mind,
  124–29   they belong wholly to *d·* Mind.
  127–24   all truth proceeds from the *d·* Mind.
  127–27   Science is an emanation of *d·* Mind,
  128– 2   the might of *d·* Mind.
  132–11   such effects, coming from *d·* Mind, prove
  140– 8   we know Him as *d·* Mind, as Life,
  143–10   The *d·* Mind never called matter *medicine*,
  143–23   the available superiority of *d·* Mind.
  149–25   with no power but the *d·* Mind.
  149–26   Since God, *d·* Mind, governs all,
  150–21   contrary to the law of *d·* Mind.
  151–21   the real man is governed by the *d·* Mind.
  151–23   The *d·* Mind that made man maintains His
  151–26   All that really exists is the *d·* Mind and its
  152– 3   The immortal *d·* Mind takes away all its
  153–14   the *d·* Mind is the healer
  157–10   acknowledging that the *d·* Mind has all power.
  158–17   the dignity and potency of *d·* Mind
  160– 2   through the power of the *d·* Mind.
  162–11   may yield to the harmony of the *d·* Mind.
ph 166–26   invalid's faith in the *d·* Mind is less than in
  167–27   must be attained through the *d·* Mind.
  169–20   all disease is cured by *d·* Mind.
  169–30   other powers than the *d·* Mind, is anti-Christian.
  174–32   and its cure comes from the immortal *d·* Mind.
  176–14   human mind gives place to the *d·* Mind.
  176–20   while *d·* Mind is its best friend.
  178–15   based on Science or the *d·* Mind,

divine

Mid

ph.	178–22	yield to the eternal Truth, or the *d·* Mind,
	180–29	found in the Science of *d·* Mind as taught
	182– 2	healing the sick through *d·* Mind alone,
	182–22	Mortals entreat the *d·* Mind to heal
	183–21	*D·* Mind rightly demands man's entire
	187–22	The *d·* Mind includes all action and volition,
	189–22	all the formations of the immortal *d·* Mind.
	194– 4	the spiritual idea of man with the *d·* Mind.
f	204–26	the image or reflection of *d·* Mind ;
	209– 8	and man is tributary to *d·* Mind.
	210–15	scientific action of *d·* Mind on human
	216–17	governed by the law of *d·* Mind,
	218–16	believing . . . that the *d·* Mind has no
	219–13	whereas *d·* Mind heals.
	225–28	rooted out through the action of the *d·* Mind.
	227– 7	law of the *d·* Mind must end human bondage,
	229–30	not of a law of matter nor of *d·* Mind,
	236–10	*d·* Mind heals sickness as well as sin
	239–26	If action proceeds from the *d·* Mind,
	251–20	understanding that the *d·* Mind makes perfect,
	251–23	find the *d·* Mind to be the only Mind,
c	255–10	views of creation by the *d·* Mind
	259–28	are transmitted by the *d·* Mind
	262–30	*D·* Mind is the only cause or Principle
	264– 6	sometimes behold in the camera of *d·* Mind,
	267– 5	They are in and of Spirit, *d·* Mind,
b	269–14	rest on one basis, the *d·* Mind.
	270–18	demonstration of God, *d·* Mind,
	270–30	the *d·* Mind alone heals.
	284–29	are spiritual, emanating from *d·* Mind.
	286–32	belong not to the *d·* Mind.
	293–14	counterfeits of the spiritual forces of *d·* Mind,
	307–25	The *d·* Mind is the Soul of man,
	310– 6	but all might is of *d·* Mind.
	318– 8	saying . . . the *d·* Mind cannot or will not
	319–19	understood that the *d·* Mind controls man
	327– 5	*d·* Mind can and does destroy the false beliefs
	331–13	except the *d·* Mind and His ideas.
p	366–17	lacks faith in the *d·* Mind.
	370– 5	gather the facts of being from the *d·* Mind.
	372– 9	Science of being, in which all is *d·* Mind,
	375–12	Scientist demonstrates that *d·* Mind heals,
	379– 8	all causation as vested in *d·* Mind.
	380–24	the *d·* Mind produces in man health,
	383– 7	exalting influence of the *d·* Mind on the body
	392– 1	you master fear and sin through *d·* Mind ;
	392– 2	through *d·* Mind that you overcome disease.
	393–16	firm in your understanding that the *d·* Mind
	396–32	not by matter nor by the *d·* Mind.
	400–10	acknowledge the supremacy of *d·* Mind,
	400–27	must be destroyed by the *d·* Mind
	403–13	and can be healed only by the *d·* Mind.
	407–27	brings the *d·* Mind, Life not death,
	417–31	and how *d·* Mind can cure by opposite thoughts.
	424–21	the *d·* Mind can remove any obstacle,
	430–14	allegory illustrative of the law of *d·* Mind
	441–26	no law outside of *d·* Mind can punish
t	445–23	hatred, and revenge are cast out by the *d·* Mind
	452–27	the Science by which *d·* Mind heals the sick.
	458–13	the *d·* Mind is ready to take the case.
	458–27	consistent in following the leadings of *d·* Mind.
	459–13	resting on the omnipotence of *d·* Mind,
	460– 7	on the *d·* Mind and Love's essential qualities.
r	469– 4	Life is *d·* Mind.
	470–29	his perfect Principle, the *d·* Mind.
	471–29	import, . . . of all that proceeds from the *d·* Mind.
	484–16	Drugs . . . oppose the supremacy of the *d·* Mind.
	493–20	belief, which willingly by the *d·* Mind.
	493–31	willingness of *d·* Mind to hold man forever intact
g	503–20	Immortal and *d·* Mind presents the idea of God :
	505– 9	The *d·* Mind, . . . creates all identities.
	508– 2	only as the *d·* Mind is All and reproduces all
	508–15	the pure thought emanating from *d·* Mind.
	511– 5	The *d·* Mind supports the sublimity,
	519–26	can never impoverish the *d·* Mind.
	546– 6	If . . . error must exist in the *d·* Mind,
	551–14	does not acknowledge the method of *d·* Mind,
ap	570–31	the power of good resident in *d·* Mind,
	577–21	and *d·* Mind is its own interpreter.

name

r	483–30	through the *d·* name and nature.

nature

pr	4–24	through demonstration of the *d·* nature ;
a	26–13	his *d·* nature, the godliness which
sp	83–14	manifestation of power is from the *d·* nature
s	140–10	as we apprehend the *d·* nature
ph	179–11	but reflecting the *d·* nature.
c	259– 7	*d·* nature was best expressed in Christ Jesus,
b	333–25	the *d·* nature, the essence of Love.
g	509–27	purity, and holiness— yea, the *d·* nature
	524–31	lose therein the *d·* nature and omnipotence?

order

a	20–21	well knowing that to obey the *d·* order

divine

order

sp	73–17	the *d·* order and the Science of
an	106–12	when the *d·* order is interfered with,
r	471– 2	but holds the *d·* order or spiritual law,
g	531–17	If, . . . why is not this *d·* order still maintained

origin

s	146–22	practically prove its *d·* origin and efficacy.
	146–24	*d·* origin of Science is demonstrated through
	150–15	these signs are only to demonstrate its *d·* origin,
b	272–24	*d·* origin and operation of C. S.
	298–23	Spiritual ideas lead up to their *d·* origin,
g	539–27	The *d·* origin of Jesus gave him more than
	549–28	forsakes Spirit as the *d·* origin of
ap	562–13	separated by belief from man's *d·* origin

pardon

a	40–11	This is my sense of *d·* pardon,

patience

a	49–11	privations, sacrifices, his *d·* patience,

penalty

an	106–13	incurs the *d·* penalty due this crime.

perfection

r	470–25	did not express the *d·* perfection,

permission

p	378–29	Such a power, without the *d·* permission, is
	394–25	Is there no *d·* permission to conquer discord

possibilities

b	326– 1	A false sense . . . hides the *d·* possibilities,

power

a	27– 7	Tell John what the demonstration of *d·* power
	49–28	had given the highest proofs of *d·* power,
	52–25	human ability to reflect *d·* power,
s	109–23	gradually and apparently through *d·* power.
	131–28	natural demonstrations of the *d·* power,
	132– 3	exhibition of the *d·* power to heal
	135–10	alone is worthy of the exercise of *d·* power.
	136– 7	he used his *d·* power to save men
	144–21	Truth, . . . is the *d·* power which says to disease,
ph	169–26	except by means of the *d·* power.
	170–32	which takes *d·* power into its own hands
	174– 6	Nothing save *d·* power is capable of
	192–31	receives directly the *d·* power.
f	227–11	an ignorance of *d·* power,
b	309–19	thus losing the *d·* power which heals the sick
	316–27	could prove God's *d·* power by healing
	320–26	gives a profound idea of the *d·* power to heal
p	426– 3	*d·* power, which steers the body into health.
r	494–12	Jesus demonstrated the *d·* power to heal
g	519–13	grasp God's creation and the *d·* power
	534–15	the idea of *d·* power, which Jesus presented,
	541–23	At first it usurps *d·* power.

powers

f	249– 9	subject to the *d·* "powers that be."— *Rom.* 13 : 1.

precepts

s	141– 5	Few understand or adhere to Jesus' *d·* precepts
b	276– 4	When the *d·* precepts are understood,

presence

pr	12– 4	no power to gain more of the *d·* presence than

Principle

pref	viii– 4	live in obedience to its *d·* Principle.
	x–22	The *d·* Principle of healing is proved
	xi–10	*d·* Principle, before which sin and disease
pr	3– 8	Shall we ask the *d·* Principle
	6– 4	*d·* Principle alone reforms the sinner.
	6–16	we must understand the *d·* Principle of being.
	11–12	*d·* Principle never pardons our sins . . . till
	12–20	not *d·* Principle or Love, which causes a
	13–25	human ignorance of the *d·* Principle,
	15–12	*d·* Principle, Love, which destroys all error.
a	18–14	*d·* Principle of Christ is God,
	19– 8	Love, the *d·* Principle of Jesus' teachings,
	19–25	*d·* Principle of the teachings and practice
	20–31	seek the *d·* Principle and Science
	25–14	understand how this *d·* Principle heals
	25–26	understand its *d·* Principle.
	26–29	It was the *d·* Principle of all real being
	28–13	by understanding more of the *d·* Principle
	29–27	*d·* Principle of the man Jesus,
	30– 3	demonstrate the Science . . . or *d·* Principle.
	31–21	*d·* Principle which triumphs over death.
	35–14	commune with the *d·* Principle, Love.
	35–20	Our church is built on the *d·* Principle, Love.
	39–26	*d·* Principle of all that really exists
	45–21	at-one-ment with . . . his *d·* Principle,
	47– 7	leaning . . . on the *d·* Principle of their work.
	50–13	appeal . . . was made both to his *d·* Principle,
	51–23	but to demonstrate his *d·* Principle.
	51–26	aimed at the *d·* Principle, Love,
	53– 9	the *d·* Principle and practice of Jesus
sp	71– 6	*d·* Principle of all, is not *in* Spirit's
	72– 3	The *d·* Principle of man speaks through
	79–14	resting on *d·* Principle, . . . in its revelation of
	81–22	producing, governing, *d·* Principle lives on,
	81–27	cannot destroy the *d·* Principle of Science.
	83–28	gains the *d·* Principle and explanation of
	84–28	All . . . comes from God, *d·* Principle,

divine

Principle

sp	90–30	through an apprehension of *d·* Principle.
	91– 6	obey only the *d·* Principle, Life and Love.
	94–22	acknowledge the *d·* Principle which had healed
	99– 3	afford no demonstrable *d·* Principle by which
an	103–14	is of God and demonstrates the *d·* Principle,
s	107– 6	revelation of the absolute *d·* Principle
	109– 8	until its *d·* Principle is demonstrated
	112–21	the *d·* Principle of healing and the Christ-idea
	113– 1	can be but one *d·* Principle of all Science ;
	113– 3	rules for the demonstration of this *d·* Principle.
	115–13	GOD : *D·* Principle, Life, Truth, Love, Soul,
	117–20	inadequate to interpret the *d·* Principle
	120–20	the *d·* Principle of Science, reversing the
	121–29	imitates the action of *d·* Principle,
	123–27	illustrated an ever-operative *d·* Principle.
	124–15	interpreted by Science from its *d·* Principle,
	124–21	They belong to *d·* Principle, and support the
	127–18	C. S. reveals God, . . . as *d·* Principle,
	130–10	in perfect harmony with God, *d·* Principle,
	131– 5	in harmony with God, the *d·* Principle
	132–12	*d·* Principle which brings out all harmony.
	133–16	*d·* Principle wrought wonders for the people
	136– 3	his religion had a *d·* Principle,
	141–15	followed the understanding of the *d·* Principle
	141–25	until its *d·* Principle is scientifically
	146–16	to the person, instead of to the *d·* Principle,
	147– 2	to demonstrate the *d·* Principle,
	147–25	taught the generalities of its *d·* Principle
	147–30	Science alone reveals the *d·* Principle
	148–18	Anatomy and theology reject the *d·* Principle
	162–27	a fuller understanding of the *d·* Principle
ph	167– 3	should we understand the . . . *d·* Principle
	171–14	Jesus illustrated the *d·* Principle
	191– 9	*d·* Principle of man dawns upon human thought,
	195–14	metaphysical Science and its *d·* Principle
f	202–16	in accord with the *d·* Principle of his being,
	207–14	perfect Father, or the *d·* Principle of man.
	230– 9	the *d·* Principle, Love, as demonstrated by
	232–17	demonstrating the power of *d·* Principle,
c	256– 7	Love, the *d·* Principle, is the Father and
b	270–13	is the eternal Mind or *d·* Principle,
	272–28	The *d·* Principle of the universe must
	272–29	God is the *d·* Principle of all
	272–32	reveals the natural, *d·* Principle of Science.
	273– 6	without the *d·* Principle of divine Science.
	275– 9	God is Love, and therefore He is *d·* Principle.
	275–11	the *d·* Principle of all that really is.
	275–17	the infinite *d·* Principle, Love.
	281–12	perfect Mind, Spirit, *d·* Principle.
	283–24	The *d·* Principle, or Life, cannot be
	283–27	We must receive the *d·* Principle
	285–22	the Supreme Being, or *d·* Principle,
	285–30	seek to learn, . . . from the *d·* Principle, God,
	286–10	[the *d·* Principle of being]
	286–14	He knew that the *d·* Principle, Love, creates
	299–14	guide to the *d·* Principle of all good,
	302–21	God, the *d·* Principle of all being,
	303– 1	the creative power of the *d·* Principle
	303–30	nor separated from its *d·* Principle.
	304–17	*D·* Principle is the Life of man.
	304–31	So man, . . . thrusting aside his *d·* Principle
	305–10	his *d·* Principle, not in a mortal body.
	305–25	Love, the *d·* Principle that obtains in
	306–27	the immutable, harmonious, *d·* Principle,
	312–31	and his demonstration of *d·* Principle
	314–27	uttered the demands of its *d·* Principle,
	316–22	blending with God, his *d·* Principle,
	317– 3	the throne of the creative *d·* Principle,
	318–29	In Science man is governed by God, *d·* Principle,
	319– 8	Having faith in the *d·* Principle of health
	322– 7	perceive Christianity, . . . in its *d·* Principle.
	322–12	turn our thoughts towards *d·* Principle,
	328– 6	Understanding little about the *d·* Principle
	329–24	its *d·* Principle never repents,
	330–20	Spirit is *d·* Principle,
	330–20	*d·* Principle is Love,
	331–18	He is *d·* Principle, Love, the universal
	331–27	that is, the triply *d·* Principle, Love.
	332– 1	indicate the *d·* Principle of scientific being,
	332–21	revealing the *d·* Principle, Love,
	333–27	inseparable from the *d·* Principle, God.
	335–25	Mind is the *d·* Principle, Love,
	336–25	God, the *d·* Principle of man,
	340–20	The *d·* Principle of the First Commandment
o	341–15	that . . . which is based on *d·* Principle,
	345–18	can heal the sick on the *d·* Principle of
	351– 4	the *d·* Principle which demonstrates C. S.,
	355–24	the *d·* Principle and practice of C. S.
p	390– 8	ignorance of God, the *d·* Principle,
	406– 4	tree is typical of man's *d·* Principle,
	419–27	tramples upon the *d·* Principle
t	445–22	hiding the *d·* Principle of harmony,
	456– 5	Strict adherence to the *d·* Principle and
	456–20	or he cannot demonstrate the *d·* Principle.

divine

Principle

t	456–24	the *d·* Principle of your demonstration.
	458–12	to think of aiding the *d·* Principle of healing
	464–22	has labored to expound *d·* Principle,
r	466–30	this declaration and its *d·* Principle.
	468–26	Life is *d·* Principle, Mind, Soul, Spirit.
	470–21	the *d·* Principle of man remaining perfect,
	470–32	The relations of . . . *d·* Principle and idea,
	473–23	God as *d·* Principle, Love,
	475– 3	all is Spirit, *d·* Principle and its idea.
	476– 5	inseparable as *d·* Principle and idea.
	481–28	Soul is the *d·* Principle of man
	484– 1	based on a *d·* Principle and so found to be
	490–17	reduce to practice the real man's *d·* Principle,
	495–28	Adhere to the *d·* Principle of C. S.
	496–18	based upon its *d·* Principle, Love,
g	503– 9	The *d·* Principle and idea constitute
	507–16	the creative power of the *d·* Principle,
	507–25	This *d·* Principle of all expresses Science
	512– 3	incorporeal and *d·* Principle, Love.
	515–29	Now compare man . . . to his *d·* Principle, God.
	518–27	The *d·* Principle, or Spirit, comprehends
	518–29	be as perfect as the *d·* Principle is perfect.
	524–11	the *d·* Principle to be lived and loved.
	530– 5	sustained by God, the *d·* Principle of being.
	536–15	by corporeality instead of *d·* Principle,
	544–32	Error begins with . . . instead of *d·* Principle,
	546– 9	Is the *d·* Principle of creation misstated?
ap	559–24	When you approach . . . this *d·* Principle,
	560–19	without . . . we can never understand the *d·* Principle.
	560–31	a greater ignorance of the *d·* Principle
	561–14	*d·* Principle and spiritual idea,
	561–24	as the *d·* Principle and divine idea.
	562–15	yield to the activities of the *d·* Principle
	565–27	be found in its *d·* Principle.
	567–10	he is killed by the *d·* Principle.
	569– 1	This rule clearly interprets God as *d·* Principle,
	572–13	this *d·* Principle, understood and demonstrated,
	573–15	the *d·* Principle of harmony, is ever with men,
	577–16	which is the outcome of the *d·* Principle,
gl	582–18	God, the *d·* Principle, creates man
	583–13	rests upon and proceeds from *d·* Principle.
	583–21	*d·*Principle of all that is real and good ;
	586– 9	the *d·* Principle, commonly called God.
	587–26	HEAVEN. . . . government by *d·* Principle ;
	588– 9	I, or EGO. *D·* Principle ; Spirit ;
	588–11	There is but one I, or Us, but one *d·* Principle,
	588–20	incorporeal and eternal Mind ; *d·* Principle ;
	589– 9	God is the *d·* Principle of all existence,
	591–16	the only Spirit, Soul, *d·* Principle,
	591–18	not that which is *in* man, but the *d·* Principle,
	594–19	Divine substance ; Mind ; *d·* Principle ;
	595–25	UNGODLINESS. Opposition to the *d·* Principle

proof

f	215–22	With its *d·* proof, Science reverses the

Providence

p	424–10	Under *d·* Providence there can be no accidents,

purpose

sp	83–27	The latter is a revelation of *d·* purpose

reality

sp	95–22	to be succeeded by C. S., by *d·* reality.

record

s	139–21	material sense stole into the *d·* record,

reflection

c	259–18	true likeness cannot be lost in *d·* reflection.

remedy

b	326– 7	and find the *d·* remedy for every ill,

revelation

s	109–21	*d·* revelation, reason, and demonstration.
ap	561–20	In *d·* revelation, . . . the spiritual idea is

right

f	227–26	be free ! This is your *d·* right.

rights

f	253–10	into the understanding of your *d·* rights,
p	384–31	quail before the *d·* rights of intelligence,

rock

b	297–28	no mortal testimony is founded on the *d·* rock.

rules

s	147– 6	the *d·* rules of C. S.
t	462– 3	any student, who adheres to the *d·* rules

Science

(*see* **Science**)

sense

g	505–24	the *d·* sense, giving the spiritual proof
ap	576–31	human sense of Deity yields to the *d·* sense,

sentence

pr	11–19	not to annul the *d·* sentence

service

a	40–28	It is sad that the phrase *d· service* has

sonship

b	316– 7	and to recognize the *d·* sonship.

source

ph	167–14	the *d·* source of all health and perfection.
	189–23	They proceed from the *d·* source ;

divine
sources
p 405-32 appeal to d· sources outside of themselves.
sovereign
g 523-31 the d· sovereign of the Hebrew people,
Spirit
a 29-24 The Holy Ghost, or d· Spirit, overshadowed the
30- 7 endowed with the Christ, the d· Spirit,
46- 7 The d· Spirit, which identified Jesus thus
sp 76-17 characterized by the d· Spirit as idea,
97-18 until d· Spirit, supreme in its domain,
99-28 the scientific demonstration of d· Spirit
s 125-18 When subordinate to the d· Spirit,
138-13 nor by hygiene, but by the d· Spirit,
148-28 it ignores the d· Spirit as unable
p 412-17 power of . . . d· Spirit, must break the dream
440-30 the just and equitable decisions of d· Spirit
442- 1 before the tribunal of d· Spirit.
g 516-29 God made man . . . to reflect the d· Spirit.
522-15 opposed to the supremacy of d· Spirit ;
532-11 this indicates that the d· Spirit, or Father,
state
b 291-14 a d· state of Mind in which all
statutes
ph 184-14 enforcing obedience through d· statutes.
p 440-26 in accordance with the d· statutes,
strength
p 406-31 normal control is gained through d· strength
student
s 117-16 As a d· student he unfolded God to man,
substance
b 300-28 reflects and expresses the d· substance
r 468-24 reflecting the d· substance of Spirit.
gl 594-19 SPIRIT. D· substance ; Mind ;
theology
f 234-22 the weary searcher after a d· theology,
r 469-29 as pernicious to d· theology as
thought
s 118-14 means of d· thought, which include
g 514-15 figurative transmission from the d· thought
title
b 333- 8 not a name so much as the d· title of
Truth
pr 4- 1 While the heart is far from d· Truth
a 18- 2 whereby man reflects d· Truth, Life, and Love.
26-14 D· Truth, Life, and Love gave Jesus authority
an 106-11 governed by his Maker, d· Truth and Love.
ph 180-32 I have found d· Truth more potent than
f 231-18 mortal beliefs which d· Truth and Love destroy.
235-23 d· Truth which is Life and perpetuates being,
o 350-24 D· Truth must be known by its effects
p 388- 3 uplifting and consecrating power of d· Truth,
t 453-29 the d· Truth that makes man free.
459-27 Guided by d· Truth and not guesswork,
r 472- 3 d· Truth casts out suppositional error and heals
understanding
g 536- 8 The d· understanding reigns, is all,
universe
g 513- 8 To material sense, this d· universe is dim
utterance
s 127-28 It is a d· utterance,— the Comforter
vesture
f 242-27 appropriates no part of the d· vesture,
voice
g 532-20 error shrank abashed from the d· voice
way
c 266-19 Universal Love is the d· way in C. S.
will
a 28- 1 Pharisees claimed to know and to teach the d· will,
r 474-22 real or the offspring of the d· will?
wisdom
m 66-20 wait patiently on d· wisdom to point out
p 386-24 d· wisdom will then be understood.
Word
r 480-27 were made by Him [the d· Word] ;— John 1 : 3.

---

pr 12-12 the d· healing Principle as manifested in
a 33-19 human element in him struggled with the d·,
43-27 The d· must overcome the human at every point.
51- 8 identity in the likeness of the d· ;
53-14 as humanly mighty, rather than as d·,
sp 98-32 not human but d·, not physical but
99-15 that which is spiritual and d·,
s 109- 9 and thus proved absolute and d·.
114- 9 and calls mind both human and d·.
126- 8 All Science is d·.
142-17 causes the left to let go its grasp on the d·.
147-11 Truth had lost none of its d· and healing
ph 177- 5 The evidence of d· Mind's healing power
200-20 suppositional antipode of d· infinite Spirit,
f 213-29 hand, which sweeps over it, is human or d·.
b 269-22 testimony of . . . neither absolute nor d·.
275-19 no life is Life but the d· ;
277-25 the opposite of the real is not d·,
287-10 In Science, Truth is d·,

divine
b 297-31 has little relation to the actual or d·.
301-12 He reflects the d·,
302-25 He is therefore the d·, infinite
305-30 mortal dreams are of human origin, not d·.
312-29 the intelligent and d· healing Principle
335-18 Spirit is eternal, d·.
335-28 immutable, immortal, d·, eternal.
o 341-16 according to a d· given rule,
p 396-23 Give them d· and wholesome understanding,
435-22 no demand, human or d·, renders it just
442- 3 our Government is d·.
t 445-17 when you weigh the human in the scale with the d·,
462-23 Are thoughts d· or human?
r 465- 9 God is incorporeal, d·,
473-31 Jesus proved the Principle, . . . to be d·.
483- 6 and this Mind must be d·, not human.
492-27 the Principle of this Science is d·,
497-14 the evidence of d·, efficacious Love,
g 520-14 accepts the d· infinite calculus.
524-16 Did the d· and infinite Principle become a
542-21 let human justice pattern the d·.
546-29 for it cures on a d· demonstrable Principle
554- 4 God, who is its d· immortal Principle.
gl 586-24 the human yielding to the d· ;
590- 6 hypotheses ; that which is not d·
592-16 MOTHER. God ; d· and eternal Principle ;

divinely
pr 10- 8 Until we are thus d· qualified
a 23- 7 d· unnatural. Such a theory is man-made.
42- 1 Jesus' life proved, d· and scientifically,
44-24 On the contrary, it was a d· natural act,
sp 84-17 to be d· inspired,— yea, to reach the
s 145- 3 So d· imbued were they with the spirit of
152-26 by which mortals are d· driven to a
b 313- 5 Jesus the God-crowned or the d· royal man,
p 378-30 if such a power could be d· directed,
393-14 the ability and power d· bestowed
g 513-21 the d· creative Principle thereof.
545- 6 and never had been d· conceived.
ap 577- 9 In this d· united spiritual consciousness,
gl 591-21 MIRACLE. That which is d· natural, but

diviner
s 107-12 are inspired with a d· nature and essence ;
f 226-15 He has built it on d· claims.
c 260-10 beliefs will be attaining d· conceptions,
b 285-20 give place to a d· sense of intelligence
p 369- 7 He enters into a d· sense of the facts,
g 548-23 Had the naturalist, . . . gained the d· side
ap 563- 2 to a d· sense, harmony is the real

diving
c 262-10 d· into the shallows of mortal belief.

divinity
conceptions of
s 116-26 confused and erroneous conceptions of d·
deep
g 546-22 they contain the deep d· of the Bible.
essence of
g 537- 9 knowledge of evil was never the essence of d·
gleams of
s 112-12 opinions may have occasional gleams of d·,
illimitable
s 127- 8 there can be nothing beyond illimitable d·.
likeness of
b 302-29 the body presents no proper likeness of d·,
one
ap 571-21 will unite all interests in the one d·.
raindrops of
b 288-17 the raindrops of d· refresh the earth.

a 22-28 believeth . . . that d· is appeased by
25-31 The d· of the Christ was made manifest in
26-13 This Christ, or d· of the man Jesus,
44-24 d· brought to humanity the understanding
s 116- 9 may be to us what d· really is
132-19 from doctrines of physics or of d· ;
c 258-32 you can discern the heart of d·,
b 281-16 reflects reality and d· in individual
306-10 If . . . there would be no d· reflected.
332-30 He expressed the highest type of d·,
t 458-14 D· is always ready.
g 522-10 Existence, separate from d·, . . . impossible.
ap 561-17 in the man Jesus, as d· embracing humanity

divisibility
b 280-13 finite sense of the d· of Soul

division
s 148-23 from this basis of d· and discord
r 478- 1 But there is, there can be, no such d·,

divisor
gl 598-30 mortal thought, the d· of which is the solar year.

9

divorce

m 59–29 but the frequency of d· shows
b 306–14 and then are separated as by a law of d·

divorced

s 155– 7 have not yet d· the drug from the general faith.
r 477–31 man, d· from Spirit, would lose his entity.

divorces

m 65– 8 D· should warn the age of some

dizzy

f 243–17 do not inform us that they are d·,

do

pr 2– 1 D· we pray to make ourselves better
2– 8 to d· more than He has already done,
2– 9 nor can the infinite d· less than
2–11 We can d· more for ourselves by
3– 1 He who is immutably right will d· right
3– 8 Shall we ask the divine Principle . . . to d· His
4–27 Audible prayer can never d· the works of
6– 9 supposition that we have nothing to d· but
8– 6 which d· not correspond with their character.
8–32 D· we not rather give thanks that
9– 6 D· we love our neighbor better because of this
9– 7 D· we pursue the old selfishness,
9–26 D· you really desire to attain this point?
9–32 Consistent prayer is the desire to d· right.
10–22 we d· not always receive the blessings we ask for
10–31 D· you ask wisdom to be merciful
11–25 We must be willing to d· this,
11–30 desire to know and d· the will of God,
13–13 D· we gain the omnipotent ear sooner by
14–20 works that I d· shall he d· also ;— John 14 : 12.
a 18– 8 to show them how to d· theirs,
18– 8 but not to d· it for them
19–24 enables man to d· the will of wisdom.
21– 6 Christians d· not continue to
25–29 We must go and d· likewise,
27–28 Why d· those who profess to follow Christ
31– 8 they who d· the will of his Father.
32– 1 these things will they d· unto you,— John 16 : 3.
42–31 works that I d· shall he d· also."— John 14 : 12.
48–31 what the true knowledge of God can d·
51–21 which he did and taught others to d·.
52–27 works that I d· shall he d· also ;"— John 14 : 12.
55–12 clearer light than mere words can possibly d·,
m 59– 1 and this is the pleasantest thing to d·.
62–15 will d· much more for the health of
sp 82– 2 as we d· of one present.
83– 3 the worshippers of Baal failed to d· ;
85– 8 enabling one to d· good,
89–22 We are all capable of more than we d·.
93– 5 works that I d· shall he d· also,"— John 14 : 12.
95–13 cannot injure others, and must d· them good.
99– 8 both to will and to d· of His— Phil. 2 : 13.
an 103–32 In C. S., man can d· no harm,
106–25 they which d· such things— Gal. 5 : 21.
s 109–29 If any man will d· His will,— John 7 : 17.
117– 9 mortals alone d· this.
119– 2 that is, when we d· so in our theories,
135–20 What cannot God d·?
137–10 what is it that is able to d· the work,
141–22 did not then, and d· not now, understand
141–29 Let our pulpits d· justice to C. S.
144– 2 Why should we wish to make them d· so,
151–20 brain, etc., have nothing to d· with Life,
161–15 they will d· less violence to that immortal
ph 166–21 He can d· all things for us in sickness
169–32 The good that a poisonous drug seems to d·
174– 2 as consciously as d· civilized practitioners
174– 8 doing so much for man as he can d· for himself.
180– 3 should be taught to d· the body no harm
180–18 as they so frequently d·, by declaring
192–23 The good you d· and embody gives you
198–14 but to d· this requires attention.
199–27 His belief that he could d· it gave
f 214–21 more than they d· a spiritual God.
231– 8 What God cannot d·, man need not attempt.
234–31 d· no more harm than one's belief permits.
237–27 and expect this error to d· more for them
237–29 the only living and true God can d·.
241–15 can d· no more for mortals than
249–19 nothing to d· with Life.
253–19 change your course and d· right.
c 263–18 "The good that I would, I d· not :— Rom. 7 : 19.
263–19 evil which I would not, that I d·."— Rom. 7 : 19.
267–16 whosoever shall d· the will of— Matt. 12 : 50.
b 268– * Here I stand. I can d· no otherwise ;
280– 9 Finite belief can never d· justice to
283–28 unless we so d·, we can no more demonstrate
292–23 lusts of your father ye will d·.— John 8 : 44.
305–17 Son can d· nothing of himself,— John 5 : 19.
305–18 what he seeth the Father d· :— John 5 : 19.
322–23 A man who likes to d· wrong
326– 5 works that I d· shall he d· also."— John 14 : 12.
o 346–32 what frail mortals are trying to d·?

do

o 349–27 can d· so only as thought is educated
357– 4 and knew from the outset that man would d·.
359–32 When others see them as I d·,
p 364–14 his rich entertainer had neglected to d·,
365– 4 this knowledge would d· much more
370–25 and d· no more for the patient.
371–28 father to the fact that Mind can d· it ;
379– 2 If disease can attack . . . sin can d· the same,
383– 6 To d· this, the pure and exalting influence
385–17 Whatever it is your duty to d·,
385–18 you can d· without harm to yourself.
389–10 it is supposed to d· so.
402–26 handle themselves as they should d·.
403–18 and it will continue to d· so, until
405–25 tends to destroy the ability to d· right.
414– 6 yields more readily than d· most diseases
417–25 To d· this, the physician must
420– 7 If they are unwilling to d· this
435–21 that they should d· unto you,"
442– 4 "Shall not the Judge . . . d· right?"— Gen. 18 : 25.
t 447– 8 ignorant attempts to d· good may render you
448–16 the good you know and d· not.
448–29 It is C. S. to d· right,
454–26 feeling that you have no more to d· for them.
456–26 and so d· all his students and patients.
460–27 to d· this orally through the meagre channel
462–18 as they usually d· in every
464– 9 not take her place, even if willing so to d·.
r 497–26 to d· unto others as we would have them d·
g 530–20 saying, . . . I can d· what God has not done
539–14 the propensity or power to d· evil?
540– 6 I the Lord d· all these things ;"— Isa. 45 : 7.

doctor (see also **doctor's**)

another
p 424–14 a remedy prescribed by another d·.
faith of the
p 398–19 It is the faith of the d·
materialistic
ph 198– 9 The materialistic d·, though humane,
one
p 424–13 if one d· should administer a drug to
popular
ph 166– 9 popular d· believes in his prescription,

s 155– 9 the d·, and the nurse equip the medicine with
ph 193– 8 The d· went out.
197–31 The d· should suppress his fear
198–15 is formed before one sees a d·
198–16 before the d· undertakes to dispel it
198–24 even though the d· says nothing to support
f 235– 4 Better suffer a d· infected with smallpox
p 364–32 Did the careless d·, the nurse, the cook,

doctored

o 347– 8 infers that if anything needs to be d·,
347–11 there is nothing left to be d·.

doctoring

p 365–10 physical thought-taking and d· ;

doctor's

ph 166–13 the d· and pharmacist's is a medical
197–30 The d· mind reaches that of his patient.
198– 4 A patient hears the d· verdict
198–24 moulded and formed by his d· belief

doctors

pref viii–17 by d· using material remedies ;
ph 180–17 D· should not implant disease in the
198–27 importance that d· be Christian Scientists.
f 221–12 having exhausted the skill of the d·,
p 394– 6 majority of d· depress mental energy,
417– 4 sometimes knowing more than their d·.

doctrinal

a 37–20 into a mutilated d· platform.
s 132–23 on any but a material and a d· theory.
o 361– 3 C. S. intervenes, explains these d· points,
r 496–31 if by that term is meant d· beliefs.

doctrine

Christian's
o 361– 8 Thus the Jew unites with the Christian's d·
erroneous
g 526–20 erroneous d· that the knowledge of evil
false
a 27–20 to cut down the false d· of pantheism,
forms of
a 20– 3 He at last paid no homage to forms of d·
his
s 132– 2 his works instead of referring to his d·,
human
b 286– 2 To seek Truth through belief in a human d·
my
s 109–28 "My d· is not mine, but His— John 7 : 16.
old
a 38– 5 than the old d· of foreordination,
one
a 23–12 "He that taketh one d·, firm in faith,

doctrine
rejected
s 150–25 rejected *d·* of the predestination of

a 26–28 Our Master taught no mere theory, *d·*,
an 101–16 not conclusive in favor of the *d·*
s 109–30 he shall know of the *d·*, — *John* 7 : 17.
150–26 The *d·* that man's harmony is governed by
150–29 *d·* of the superiority of matter
b 279–22 Every system of human philosophy, *d·*,
304– 9 This is the *d·* of C. S. :
o 360–31 Jew and Christian can unite in *d·*
t 443–22 all longsuffering and *d·*." — *II Tim.* 4 : 2.
454–12 is the *d·* of absolute C. S.,
458– 3 The chief plank in this platform is the *d·*

doctrines
and creeds
r 471–22 Are *d·* and creeds a benefit to man?
human
s 117–31 which he defined as human *d·*.
g 504–25 a thousand years of human *d·*,
545–14 errors send falsity into all human *d·*
man-made
a 38– 8 lethargy of mortals, produced by man-made *d·*,
s 134–14 Man-made *d·* are waning.
medical
s 163–30 To harmonize the contrarieties of medical *d·*
of Christ
s 134–16 how can they illustrate the *d·* of Christ
of John
s 132–28 Did the *d·* of John the Baptist confer
of men
s 131–24 taketh away the ceremonies and *d·* of men,
of physics
s 132–18 from *d·* of physics or of divinity ;
old
o 360–12 my old *d·* or human opinions."
such
o 358– 5 Such *d·* are "confusion worse confounded."
varied
b 319–15 varied *d·* and theories which presuppose

pref vii–14 Truth, independent of *d·* . . . knocks at the
sp 98–12 Creeds, *d·*, and human hypotheses
b 314–29 to those who, depending on *d·*
gl 590– 6 human theories, *d·*, hypotheses ;

document
g 523–19 The other *d·* is called the Jehovistic,

documents
g 523–16 evidences of two distinct *d·*

does
pr 9– 4 the falsehood which *d·* no one any good.
12–18 The drug *d·* nothing, because it has no
a 26–17 to prove what God is and what He *d·* for man.
m 63–17 than *d·* either C. S. or civilization.
s 123– 6 as *d·* the error relating to soul and
162– 1 but upon different terms than *d·* the
ph 187–15 as directly as *d·* the hand,
196–32 It *d·* this by giving names to diseases
f 212–23 and this He *d·* by means of Mind,
218– 1 Mortal mind *d·* the false talking,
b 335–20 Soul . . . *d·* not exist in mortality.
o 342– 8 decries this Science *d·* it presumptuously,
356–30 follow its antecedent? It *d·*.
p 366–28 knowing, as he *d·*, that Life is God
371–16 no more comprehends . . . than *d·* the child ;
373–11 than *d·* the sinner from his sin.
376– 7 and *d·* its work almost self-deceived.
379–22 The so-called vital current *d·* not affect
387–19 That man . . . who *d·* the most good.
401– 3 it *d·* nothing in the right direction
413– 9 Mind regulates . . . and matter *d·* not.
t 449– 4 A grain of C. S. *d·* wonders for mortals,
449–17 than it *d·* to heal the most difficult case.
456–22 Truth *d·* the work,
458–24 He *d·* violence to no man.
r 483–28 it *d·* this in the way of His appointing,
g 515–26 lift a weight, your reflection *d·* this also.
541– 3 more nearly resembles . . . than *d·* Cain's
542–22 penalty, both for what it is and for what it *d·*.
550–27 nor *d·* a lion bring forth a lamb.
551–13 but it *d·* not acknowledge the method
gl 585–23 that which *d·* not last forever ;

doest
c 256–23 What *d·* Thou?" — *Dan.* 4 : 35.

doeth
a 31–32 think that he *d·* God service ; — *John* 16 : 2.
c 256–20 "*d·* according to His will — *Dan.* 4 : 35.
b 305–18 what things soever He *d·*, — *John* 5 : 19.
305–19 these also *d·* the Son likewise." — *John* 5 : 19.

dogma
ph 195–24 the mere *d·*, the speculative theory,
f 244–28 cast us headlong into darkness and *d·*.
o 342– 3 demonstration, instead of opinion and *d·*,

dogmas
o 354–16 to cleave to barren and desultory *d·*,

dogs
b 272–17 not that which is holy unto the *d·*, — *Matt.* 7 : 6.

doing
a 22–14 and "be not weary in well *d·*." — *II Thess.* 3 : 13.
36–29 in return for our efforts at well *d·*.
41–27 apostles still went about *d·* good deeds,
51–20 only through *d·* the works which he did
55–21 what it has done and is *d·* for mankind.
sp 79–30 need "not be weary in well *d·*." — *Gal.* 6 : 9.
79–30 It dissipates fatigue in *d·* good.
s 155–12 inanimate drug as *d·* this or that,
158–28 Homœopathy, . . . is *d·* this.
ph 165– 4 Instead of so *d·*, it closed the eyes of mortals
174– 7 Nothing save divine power is capable of *d·*
181–26 that you are *d·* something for them,
f 202–32 in the act of *d·* good,
203– 2 and check the reward for *d·* good.
230–15 for *d·* what they could not avoid *d·*.
254–15 demonstrating the great problem . . . is *d·* much.
c 266–20 sinner makes his own hell by *d·* evil,
266–21 and the saint his own heaven by *d·* right.
o 348–24 by so *d·* our own condition can be improved
357–2, 3 God never punishes man for *d·* right,
p 384– 7 supposition . . . that God punishes man for *d·* good,
387–22
410–27 to promote right thinking and *d·*,
432–16 The Judge asks if by *d·* good to his neighbor,
435–20 *d·* "unto others as ye would that they should
436–34 pronounced a sentence of death for *d·* right.
t 448–31 *d·* one's self the most harm.
449– 6 in order to continue in well *d·*.
r 483–29 by *d·* many wonderful works
g 527–27 but *d·* so materially, not spiritually,
ap 563–28 but *d·* this in the name of good.
571– 9 *d·* right and benefiting our race.

doleful
f 203–28 and of fearful and *d·* dying

doling
p 367– 7 and the *d·* of arguments,

dolorous
g 552–12 no member of this *d·* and fatal triad.

domain
sp 80–17 *d·* of reason into the realm of mysticism.
97–18 until divine Spirit, supreme in its *d·*,

dome
s 142–12 making *d·* and spire tremulous with beauty,

domestic
m 59–10 annoyances and cares of *d·* economy,
64–14 debarred by a covetous *d·* tyrant

dominant
ap 559– 4 *d·* power of which was upon the sea,

dominate
c 266–25 his demonstrations, which *d·* the flesh.
t 446–16 Good must *d·* in the thoughts of the healer,

dominates
sp 97–19 until divine Spirit, . . . *d·* all matter,

dominion
and power
s 143–30 give to Mind the glory, honor, *d·*, and power
God-given
ph 165– 5 man's God-given *d·* over the earth.
f 228–13 God-given *d·* over the material senses.
p 381–21 will sooner grasp man's God-given *d·*.
g 531–14 recognize his God-given *d·* and being.
its
r 485–24 If thought yields its *d·* to other powers,
over all the earth
an 102–14 has *d·* over all the earth
f 202–22 God gives man *d·* over all the earth.
b 316–23 gives man *d·* over all the earth.
g 516–20 reflects God's *d·* over all the earth.
531–32 and having *d·* over all the earth.
533– 2 God's behest, *d·* over all the earth?
over all things
b 307–26 gives man *d·* over all things.
over error
p 380–21 and prove man's *d·* over error.
over the atmosphere
s 125–26 mariner will have *d·* over the atmosphere
over the fish
f 222–23 "*d·* over the fish of the sea, — *Gen.* 1 : 26.
r 475–42 *d·* over the fish of the sea, — *Gen.* 1 : 26.
g 515–12 *d·* over the fish of the sea, — *Gen.* 1 : 26.
517–27 *d·* over the fish of the sea, — *Gen.* 1 : 28.
over the whole earth
pr 14–27 man's *d·* over the whole earth.
g 545–11 was given *d·* over the whole earth.

dominion

over the works
ph 200–14   d· over the works of Thy hands.— *Psal.* 8: 6.

---

f 238–22   and so gain d· over mankind,
o 347– 7   all is Life, and death has no d·.
p 438– 4   and let them have d·.— *Gen.* 1: 26.
g 515–21   "Let *them* have d·."— *Gen.* 1: 26.
518– 1   His birthright is d·, not subjection.

done

pr   1– 8   whatever has been successfully d· for the
   2– 9   to do more than He has already d·,
   3– 9   His work is d·,
   4– 9   our gratitude for all that he has d·.
   5– 9   woe comes in return for what is d·.
   6– 8   badly d· or left undone,
   9–14   simply by asking that it may be d·.
   17– 1   Thy will be d· in earth, as it is — *Matt.* 6: 10.
a   22–19   you will discern the good you have d·,
   33–20   "Not my will, but Thine, be d· !"— *Luke* 22 : 42.
   38–18   otherwise the healing could not have been d·
   44– 3   "Well d·, good and faithful— *Matt.* 25 : 23.
   55–20   what it has d· and is doing for mankind.
sp   85–29   "These ought ye to have d·,— *Matt.* 23 : 23.
s 152– 8   although they know not how the work is d·.
   163– 1   mischief which Hippocrates has d·,
   164–14   Much yet remains to be said and d·
ph 179– 2   can be d· only by taking up the cross
   187–18   We say,"My hand hath d· it."
   199–27   he could never have d· it.
f 202– 5   God's will must be universally d·.
   209–23   In proportion as this is d·, man and the
c 260–15   to discover what God has already d· ;
   266–18   This is d· through self-abnegation,
b 326–28   He learned the wrong that he had d·
   334–19   as the Christ has always d·,
p 364–13   He even said that this poor woman had d·
   372–29   acknowledgment of Truth and of what it has d·
   373–13   if the teaching is faithfully d·.
t 449– 7   The wrong d· another reacts most heavily
   457– 5   this book has d· more for teacher and student,
r 483–32   to be well d·, the work must be d· unselfishly.
   494– 6   that so great a work as the Messiah's was d·
g 528–22   declaring what great things error has d·.
   530–21   saying, . . . I can do what God has not d·
   557–27   Mind, spake and it was d·.

doom

foresee the
f 227–15   cannot fail to foresee the d· of all oppression.
foreshadows its
ap 571–27   rebukes . . . sin, and foreshadows its d·.
foretells its
an 105–28   The aggravation of error foretells its d·,
moral
p 405–27   hastening on to physical and moral d·.
nearing its
ap 565– 1   when nearing its d·, this evil increases
of matter
b 279– 6   d· of matter establishes the conclusion
precipitates his
m   67–16   precipitates his d· or sunshine gladdens

a   40–14   While there's sin there's d·.
f 241– 6   Mortality is their d·.
b 318–11   They would . . . d· all things to decay.

doomed

g 551–31   the resulting germ is d· to the same routine.

dooms

g 535–11   It d· idolatry.

door

bar the
t 452– 1   Instruct him how to bar the d· of his thought
closes the
s 144–26   Ignorance, pride, or prejudice closes the d·
close the
f 224–25   Will you open or close the d· upon this angel
of this age
f 224–24   stands at the d· of this age, knocking
of thought
p 392–24   Stand porter at the d· of thought.
open
k 499– *   *I have set before thee an open d·,— Rev.* 3 : 8.
gl 579– *   *I have set before thee an open d·,— Rev.* 3 : 8.
opened the
sp   99–11   has opened the d· of the human understanding.
open the
pr   10–15   Spiritual attainments open the d· to a
shuts the
sp   90–26   This conviction shuts the d· on death,
s 132–22   blind belief shuts the d· upon it,
shut the
pr   15–15   enter into the closet and shut the d·.
s 142–14   they . . . shut the d· on progress.

door

shut thy
pr   14–32   when thou hast shut thy d·,— *Matt.* 6 : 6.
some other
sp   99–12   None may pick the lock nor enter by some **other** d·.

---

pr   15– 4   the d· of which shuts out sinful sense
   15–10   the d· of the erring senses must be closed.
a   45–17   hath rolled away the stone from the d·
b 299– 7   appearing at the d· of some sepulchre,

doors

pr   10–19   stop at the d· to earn a penny by
f 234–11   as watchfully as we bar our d· against
p 366–30   If we would open their prison d· for the sick,
   433–32   can open wide those prison d·
r 495–12   opens the prison d· to such as are bound,

dormant

b 327–30   man's d· sense of moral obligation,
   328–16   For centuries it has been d·,
gl 583–16   rousing the d· understanding

dose

ph 174–26   and administer a d· of despair to the
   177–25   If a d· of poison is swallowed through mistake,

doses

s 156–10   d· of a high attenuation of *Sulphuris.*

dosing

ph 169–13   and by d· the body in order to avoid it.

dost

pr   9–17   D· thou "love the Lord thy God — *Matt.* 22 : 37.

double

gl 590–21   This d· term is not used in the first chapter

doubly

o 343– 7   This makes it d· unfair to impugn

doubt

pr   1– *   *and shall not d· in his heart,— Mark* 11 : 23.
   16–11   some d· among Bible scholars, whether
   47–14   were in d· concerning Jesus' teachings.
sp   80–12   I entertain no d· of the humanity
   82– 8   of whose personal existence we may be in d· ?
s 130– 9   unwise to d· if reality is in perfect harmony
   130–30   astounded at the vigorous claims of evil and d·
ph 189–12   or d· that the sun will reappear.
   194–19   It proves beyond a d· that education
f 231–24   To fear sin is . . . to d· His government
p 429–26   This is why you d· the statement
t 445– 7   No hypothesis . . . should interpose a d· or
r 493–30   Who dares to d· this consummate test
   495–17   Let neither fear nor d· overshadow
g 537–19   No one can reasonably d· that the purpose
   551–25   Darkness and d· encompass thought, so long as
gl 592–21   NIGHT. Darkness ; d· ; fear.
   597–16   WILDERNESS. Loneliness ; d· ; darkness.

doubted

s 136–25   But even Herod d· if Jesus was controlled by

doubtful

o 342– 1   alludes to "d· disputations."— *Rom.* 14 : 1.

doubting

b 317–29   To this dull and d· disciple
t 455– 4   a faltering and d· trust in Truth

doubts

pr   13–21   d· and fears which attend such a belief,
a   39–29   d· and defeats as well as triumphs.
s 130–27   If thought is startled at the . . . and d· the
p 422–28   d· as to the ultimate outcome of the injury.

dove

ap 574–27   and you will behold the soft-winged d·
gl 584–26   definition of

down

pref viii–28   As early as 1862 she began to write d·
   ix– 1   She also began to jot d· her thoughts
pr   6–28   "[It] is hewn d·."— *Matt.* 7 : 19.
   15–30   they assuredly call d· infinite blessings.
a   27–20   cut d· the false doctrine of pantheism,
   31–20   we shall rest, sit d· with him,
   33– 7   Their bread indeed came d· from heaven.
   35–26   "which cometh d· from heaven,"— *John* 6 : 33.
   41–25   sat d· at the right hand of the Father.
   51– 7   power to lay d· a human sense of life
   55–15   Truth's immortal idea is sweeping d· the
an 105–26   d· to the depths of ignominy and death.
s 118–32   natural order of heaven comes d· to earth.
ph 174– 5   idolatry, that man should bow d· to a
   176–18   weigh d· mankind with superimposed
   178– 4   for it is set d· as a poison by
f 214–18   We bow d· to matter, . . . like the pagan
   223–22   Spiritual rationality . . . cannot be put d·.
   225–20   oppression neither went d· in blood, nor
c 266–17   Thus He teaches mortals to lay d· their
b 301–29   inverted . . . with everything turned upside **d·**.
   319–27   who only wrote d· what an inspired

down

b 321– 8 led by wisdom to cast d· his rod,
o 351–32 brought d· no proof that it was heard.
p 362– * *Why art thou cast d·, O my soul— Psal. 42 : 11.*
364– 5 to lay d· his mortal existence in behalf
394–15 advice to a man who is d· in the world,
404–18 cuts d· every tree that brings not forth
436–12 Laying d· his life for a good deed,
t 447–24 To put d· the claim of sin, you must
448–10 and casts thee d· from the pinnacle.
460– 1 metaphysics as laid d· in this work,
462–15 and advance from the rudiments laid d·.
r 470–19 Has God taken d· His own standard,
g 514–23 leopard shall lie d· with the kid ;— *Isa.* 11 : 6.
530–21 saying, through the material senses : . . . Bow
d· to me
535–13 A belief in other gods, . . . must go d·
547–22 or go d· into dust and nothingness,
549–31 coming d· to a belief in the material origin
551–21 brought d· from generation to generation?"
ap 558– 3 angel come d· from heaven,— *Rev.* 10 : 1.
561–12 a bride coming d· from heaven,
568–16 accuser of our brethren is cast d·,— *Rev.* 12 : 10.
568–22 the devil is come d· unto you,— *Rev.* 12 : 12.
568–31 by which we lay d· all for Truth,
574–13 "New Jerusalem, coming d· from— *Rev.* 21 : 2.
575– 8 "d· from God, out of heaven,"— *Rev.* 21 : 2.
577–23 will lay d· their honors within the
578– 6 to lie d· in green pastures :— *Psal.* 23 : 2.

downfall

ph 176– 5 unmanly Adams attributed their own d·
gl 581–21 more certain is the d· of its structure.

downward

b 272–22 in contrast with the d· tendencies and

Dragon, Red

gl 593– 7 definition of

dragon

against the
ap 567–11 Truth and Love prevail against the d·
cannot war
ap 567–11 the d· cannot war with them.
cast out
ap 570–12 the d· cast out of his mouth.— *Rev.* 12 : 16.
fought
ap 566–27 d· fought, and his angels,— *Rev.* 12 : 7.
fought against the
ap 566–26 his angels fought against the d· ;— *Rev.* 12 : 7.
great
ap 567–14 the great d· was cast out,— *Rev.* 12 : 9.
horns of the
ap 563–11 The ten horns of the d· typify the belief
old
ap 570–18 What if the old d· should send forth
red
ap 562–30 and behold a great red d·,— *Rev.* 12 : 3.
563– 8 The great red d· symbolizes a lie,
565– 2 and becomes the great red d·,
567–21 false claim . . . is pure delusion, the red d· ;
show the
ap 567–24 show the d· to be nothingness,
stood before the
ap 563–25 and the d· stood before the woman— *Rev.* 12 : 4.
this
ap 563–10 This d· stands for the sum total of human error.
warreth not long
ap 567– 9 Against Love, the d· warreth not long,

ap 564– 5 animal instinct, of which the d· is the type,
564–14 the d· as warring against innocence.
569–25 The d· is at last stung to death by his own
569–29 And when the d· saw that he was— *Rev.* 12 : 13.

drain

a 33–14 and d· to the dregs his cup of sorrow.

drained

a 54–21 cup of bitterness was d· to the dregs.

drank

pr 5–15 The followers of Christ d· his cup.
a 35–28 draught our Master d· and commended
43–22 because of the cup of bitterness he d·.
52– 5 His senses d· in the spiritual evidence
53– 7 hence the cup he d·.
f 221– 3 d· nothing but water.

draught

pref ix– 4 A child drinks . . . and rejoices in the d·.
a 35–28 d· our Master drank and commended
p 384–16 If exposure to a d· of air while in a

draughts

f 234– 1 Spiritual d· heal,

draw

b 300– 2 it attempts to d· correct spiritual conclusions
p 396– 8 nor d· attention to certain symptoms as

drawn

a 48–26 Pilate was d· into acquiescence with the
s 117–24 Evidence d· from the five physical senses
129– 1 conclusion, if properly d·, cannot be false.
f 247–16 models of spiritual sense, d· by perfect Mind
b 274–11 not mere inferences d· from material premises.
o 360– 1 real and eternal because d· from Truth,
p 379–27 pictures d· on the body by a
379–30 the fever-picture, d· by millions of mortals

draws

sp 96–25 As this consummation d· nearer,

dread

a 51– 5 This d· added the drop of gall to his cup.
b 321–22 white as snow with the d· disease,
p 426–20 master either a desire to die or a d· of the grave,

dreads

p 379–24 her belief produces the very results she d·.
415– 9 looks upon some object which he d·.

dream

according to the
f 250–17 according to the d· he entertains in sleep.
another
sp 75–30 we pass from one dream to another d·,
ceases
o 346–20 If a d· ceases, it is self-destroyed,
dreamer and
g 530–28 therefore the dreamer and d· are one,
erroneous
f 223–26 startle . . . thought from its erroneous d·
fleshly
ph 196– 7 awakens mortal mind from its fleshly d·,
has no reality
g 530–26 The d· has no reality, no intelligence,
his own
g 528–23 Beholding the creations of his own d·
illusion or
r 490–30 oblivion, nothingness, or an illusion or d·.
leaves mortal man
r 492– 1 when the d· leaves mortal man intact in body
mortal
(*see* **mortal**)
of death
p 427–29 The d· of death must be mastered by Mind
429–17 Mortals waken from the d· of death
of disease
p 396–30 It breaks the d· of disease to understand that
of existence
g 529– 8 destroy the d· of existence, reinstate reality,
of material life
sp 77–13 period required for this d· of material life,
of material living
pr 14–25 separate from the . . . d· of material living,
of matter
g 532–27 error began and will end the d· of matter.
of mortal existence
f 250–23 in the waking d· of mortal existence
of pain
ph 188–11 Mortal existence is a d· of pain and
of sin
ph 188–12 a d· of sin, sickness, and death ;
of suffering
p 420–29 to break its d· of suffering,
one
sp 75–30 we pass from one d· to another dream,
or belief
r 491–22 The d· or belief goes on, whether our eyes are
phase of the
p 427–13 Death is but another phase of the d· that
phases of the
f 249–24 Sleep and apathy are phases of the d· that
pleasure of a
ph 188–19 produced physically by the pleasure of a d·.
sickness is a
p 417–20 To the C. S. healer, sickness is a d·
sleeping
ph 188–15 In both the waking and the sleeping d·,
f 250–23 any more reality in . . . than in the sleeping d· ?
r 494–22 as the experiences of the sleeping d· seem real
temporal
p 412–24 and that sickness is a temporal d·.
that matter
o 347–26 The d· that matter and error are something
this
sp 77–13 this d· of material life, embracing its
ph 196– 8 which tend to perpetuate this d·.
r 491–31 that this d· . . . may not be mortal man?
vanishes
f 250–18 When that d· vanishes, the mortal finds

m 62–16 will do much more . . . than you d·.
sp 71–10 Close your eyes, and you may d· that you
ph 188–13 is like the d· we have in sleep,
f 250– 6 Mortal existence is a d· ;
p 412–17 break the d· of the material senses.
r 491–28 awake, we d· of the pains and pleasures

dream
r 493–28 awakened Lazarus from the *d*·,
g 528– 7 this supposition was a *d*·, a myth.
556–24 of which mortal and material life is the *d*·.

dreamed
f 249–20 You say, "I *d*· last night."

dreamer
sp 82–14 not communicate with the *d*· by our side
ph 188–16 the *d*· thinks that his body is material
b 322–21 as the startled *d*· who wakens from an
r 491–31 this dream — rather than the *d*·
492– 2 the so-called *d*· is unconscious?
g 530–28 therefore the *d*· and dream are one,

dreamers
f 249–23 Mortals are the Adam *d*·.

dreaming
sp 95–29 in the cradle of infancy, *d*· away the hours.

dream-land
g 543–11 and must dwell in *d*·, until mortals

dream-narrative
g 530–26 The history of error is a *d*·.

dreams
different
sp 82–27 Different *d*· and different awakenings betoken
mortal
b 305–29 These mortal *d*· are of human origin,
opposite
sp 74–14 between persons in such opposite *d*· as
our
sp 82–16 unconscious or are wandering in our *d*·
f 212– 1 We suffer or enjoy in our *d*·,

sp 71–18 From *d*· also you learn that
90–16 In *d*· we fly to Europe and meet a
f 249–22 and His likeness never *d*·.
250– 8 Spirit is the Ego which never *d*·,
p 386– 1 an illusion of mortal mind, — one of its *d*·.
397–26 when they . . . enjoy, or suffer in *d*·.
g 505– 2 mortal mind, sleep, *d*·, sin,
556–22 Oblivion and *d*·, not realities, come with sleep.

dream-sensations
f 250–19 experiencing none of these *d*·.

dream-shadows
p 418–31 pain, deformed joints, are waking *d*·,

dreamy
sp 88– 1 and this not in *d*· sleep.

dreary
sp 96– 8 Earth will become *d*· and desolate,

dregs
a 33–14 drain to the *d*· his cup of sorrow.
54–22 cup of bitterness was drained to the *d*·.

drenching
s 122–21 midst of murky clouds and *d*· rain.

dress
ph 193–17 I told him to rise, *d*· himself, and take supper
g 526–27 into the garden of Eden, to *d*· it — Gen. 2 : 15.
527– 2 God could not put Mind into matter . . . to *d*· it

drew
b 321–22 and *d*· it forth white as snow
ap 563–23 And his tail *d*· the third part — Rev. 12 : 4.

drift
pref x–12 has not compromised . . . to suit the general *d*·
f 205–25 man's normal *d*· towards the one Mind,
250–30 like snowflakes, and *d*· to the ground.

drifting
a 21–31 if he can only imagine himself *d*· in the

drilling
p 378–19 *d*· and drugging, adopted to cure matter,

drink
pr 10– 9 Until we are . . . willing to *d*· his cup,
a 18– * *I will not d· of the fruit of* — Luke 22 : 18.
25–11 they truly eat his flesh and *d*· his blood,
26– 7 all have the cup of sorrowful effort to *d*·
31–18 we *d*· of his cup, partake of his bread,
31–23 and *d*· this cup, — I Cor. 11 : 26.
32–18 *D*· ye all of it." — Matt. 26 : 27.
33–17 "*D*· ye all of it." — Matt. 26 : 27.
33–32 Are all who eat bread and *d*· wine in memory
34– 1 Are all . . . willing truly to *d*· his cup,
54–27 those who followed him should *d*· of his cup,
m 62–14 or what ye shall *d*·" ; — Matt. 6 : 25.
67– 2 shall we not *d*· it and learn the lessons
s 158–22 acquires an educated appetite for strong *d*·,
ph 165– * or what ye shall *d*· ; — Matt. 6 : 25.
170–17 or what ye shall *d*·." — Matt. 6 : 25.
f 222–15 less thought about what he should eat or *d*·,
b 317– 8 will *d*· of his Master's cup.
328–24 and if they *d*· any deadly thing, — Mark 16 : 18.
p 362– * *and if they d· any deadly thing,* — Mark 16 : 18.

drink
p 366– 8 debars him from giving *d*· to the thirsty
398–22 and the desire for strong *d*· is gone.
431– 5 the prisoner gave him *d*·.
g 530– 9 or what ye shall *d*·," — Matt. 6 : 25.
ap 570–16 waiting and watching for rest and *d*·.

drinketh
a 55–24 *d*· of Christ's cup now,

drinking
a 33–27 Christians, are you *d*· his cup?
f 254– 8 To stop eating, *d*·, or being clothed

drinks
pref ix– 3 child *d*· in the outward world through the eyes
a 48–12 when he *d*· from the same cup,
p 406–28 The depraved appetite for alcoholic *d*·,
t 454– 2 the use of tobacco or intoxicating *d*· is not

drive
f 251– 8 to *d*· belief into new paths.
o 357–31 Can matter *d*· Life, Spirit, hence, and so defeat
r 487– 1 these calamities often *d*· mortals to seek
g 538– 3 *d*· error out of all selfhood.

driven
s 135– 3 Jordan, that thou wast *d*· back? — Psal. 114 : 5.
143–14 *D*· to choose between two difficulties,
152–26 mortals are divinely *d*· to a spiritual source

droop
m 61–16 often these beautiful children early *d*· and die,

drooping
m 58– 3 or else joy's *d*· wings trail in dust.

drop
a 51– 5 This dread added the *d*· of gall to his cup.
an 106– 2 to *d*· from the platform of common manhood
s 153– 8 and yet, with one *d*· of that attenuation
f 205– 4 stumble with lameness, *d*· with drunkenness,
c 255– 2 *d*· off their mental swaddling-clothes,
262–21 They will then *d*· the false estimate of life
o 361–16 As a *d*· of water is one with the ocean,
p 379–17 when not a *d*· of his blood was shed.

dropped
f 222–20 Now he *d*· drugs and material hygiene,
b 296– 5 the mortal is *d*· for the immortal.

dropping
f 228–17 *D*· their present beliefs, they will recognize

drops
s 148–16 *d*· the true tone, and accepts the discord.
ph 166–24 the despairing invalid often *d*· them,
c 257–20 "who hath begotten the *d*· of dew," — Job 38 : 28.
g 520–27 Mortal thought *d*· into the ground,
549–31 He absolutely *d*· from his summit,

dropsy
s 156– 5 A case of *d*·, . . . fell into my hands.

dross
m 66–32 furnace separates the gold from the *d*·

drove
g 537– 5 So He *d*· out the man : — Gen. 3 : 24.

drown
ap 570–19 a new flood to *d*· the Christ-idea?
570–20 He can neither *d*· your voice with its roar,

drowning
a 22– 7 This causes them, even as *d*· men,
ap 569–19 to lift their heads above the *d*· wave.

drug (see also drug's)
administer a
p 294–13 if one doctor should administer a *d*· to
any
p 420–21 better than any *d*·, alterative, or tonic.
applying the
p 401–24 by applying the *d*· to either?
causes a
pr 12–21 which causes a *d*· to be apparently
certain
p 370–11 might be produced by a certain *d*·,
confidence in the
s 155– 7 take away the individual confidence in the *d*·,
diminishes the
s 155–26 Homœopathy diminishes the *d*·,
disappears
s 155–27 the potency . . . increases as the *d*· disappears.
divorced the
s 155– 7 you have not yet divorced the *d*· from
does nothing
pr 12–18 The *d*· does nothing, because it has no
enables a
ph 174–22 belief is all that enables a *d*· to
exterminates the
s 157– 8 C. S. exterminates the *d*·,
faith in the
p 370–14 faith in the *d*· is the sole factor in the cure.

drug

inanimate
s 155–12 When the general belief endorses the inanimate *d·*
160– 7 the inanimate *d·* becomes powerless.
b 312–30 and so turns . . . to the inanimate *d·*.
like a
pr 12–17 affects the sick like a *d·*,
may eventually lose
p 370–24 a *d·* may eventually lose its supposed power
mentalizes a
s 157–11 Homœopathy mentalizes a *d·*
no efficacy in a
s 153–15 learned . . . that there is no efficacy in a *d·*.
poisonous
ph 169–32 good that a poisonous *d·* seems to do is evil,
prescribes the
p 399– 6 Mortal mind prescribes the *d·*, and
rely on a
f 202–28 yet we rely on a *d·* . . . to heal disease,
same
p 370–12 are removed by using the same *d·*
whatever the
ph 178– 3 the strychnine, or whatever the *d·* used,

s 152–32 but the *d·* is frequently attenuated
153– 2 it is not the *d·* which expels the disease
157–12 *d·* becomes more like the human mind
157–24 the power which the *d·* seems to possess.
158–30 of a higher attenuation than the *d·*,
163–11 man-midwife, chemist, druggist, or *d·*
ph 169–22 however much we trust a *d·*
p 394–24 unless it can be aided by a *d·*
401–25 Would the *d·* remove paralysis,

drugging

s 155–29 homœopathy, and . . have diminished *d·* ;
p 378–19 hygienic drilling and *d·*, adopted to

druggist

s 155– 9 The chemist, the botanist, the *d·*,
163–11 chemist, *d·*, or drug on the face of the earth,

drug's

s 157–14 and the *d·* power of action is

drugs

and hygiene
ph 167–12 *D·* and hygiene cannot successfully usurp
r 484–15 *D·* and hygiene oppose the supremacy of the
and inert matter
r 484–17 *D·* and inert matter are unconscious, mindless.
does not distribute
p 408–20 Truth does not distribute *d·* through the blood,
does not employ
s 143– 5 God does not employ *d·* or hygiene,
do not affect
p 408–19 *D·* do not affect a corpse,
faith in
s 145–14 whether faith in *d·*, trust in hygiene,
146– 7 have rendered faith in *d·* the fashion,
ph 181–30 If you have more faith in *d·* than in Truth,
giving
p 413–24 Giving *d·* to infants, noticing every symptom
hygiene and
f 222–19 the strictest adherence to hygiene and *d·*,
inanimate
an 106– 1 from the use of inanimate *d·* to the
lose their
s 160– 5 *d·* lose their healing force, for they have no
material
s 146–18 truth divests material *d·* of their
matter or
t 463–29 are not healed by inanimate matter or *d·*,
Mind and
s 143–32 may try to make Mind and *d·* coalesce,
mineral
s 158– 9 from image-gods to vegetable and mineral *d·*
never gave
p 369–18 never gave *d·*, never prayed to know if
never taught that
f 232–19 Jesus never taught that *d·*, food, air,
outweighs
s 149– 3 Mind as far outweighs *d·* in the cure of
physician prescribes
ph 198–19 the physician prescribes *d·*, until the
pleas for
ph 182–27 Pleas for *d·* and laws of health come from
prescribed no
s 148– 4 prescribed no *d·*, urged no obedience to
rush after
ph 168–11 When sick (according to belief) you rush after *d·*,
substitute
f 218–20 why do you substitute *d·* for the
substitutes
s 146–13 Material medicine substitutes *d·* for the
their
f 237– 8 before her parents would have laid aside their *d·*,

drugs

through
o 345– 6 and work through *d·* to heal the sick?
took no
a 44–13 He took no *d·* to allay inflammation.
use of
sp 79– 8 more sanitary than the use of *d·*,
s 155– 3 When the sick recover by the use of *d·*,
with
f 230– 2 Would you attempt with *d·*, or without,
without
ph 185–23 not only without *d·*, but without hypnotism,

s 155–29 but if *d·* are an antidote to disease,
155–30 If *d·* are good things, is it safe to
155–32 If *d·* possess intrinsic virtues or
156– 2 Who named *d·*, and what made them good
157–16 If *d·* are part of God's creation,
157–18 then *d·* cannot be poisonous.
157–19 If He could create *d·* intrinsically bad,
157–20 If He creates *d·* at all . . . why did Jesus not
158–16 *D·*, cataplasms, and whiskey are
ph 166–11 believes in the power of his *d·*
166–27 less than in *d·*, air, and exercise,
169–11 faith in rules of health or in *d·* begets
f 222–20 he dropped *d·* and material hygiene,
230–23 never really healed by *d·*, hygiene,
251–16 faith in hygiene, in *d·*, or in will-power.
p 408–16 Can *d·* go of their own accord to the brain
t 463–26 nor did he use *d·*.
r 483– 1 Then comes the question, how do *d·*,
484–18 results, supposed to proceed from *d·*,

drug-systems

s 158–25 *D·* are quitting their hold on matter

drunk

a 34–11 If all who ever partook of . . . and *d·* of his cup,
p 406–32 There is no enjoyment in getting *d·*,

drunkard

b 322–17 The *d·* thinks he enjoys drunkenness,

drunkenness

an 106–23 *d·*, revellings and such like :— *Gal.* 5 : 21.
f 205– 4 drop with *d·*, consume with disease,
b 322–18 The drunkard thinks he enjoys *d·*,

dry

p 379–26 coated tongue, febrile heat, *d·* skin,
384–17 followed by chills, *d·* cough, influenza,
431–26 I am Sallow Skin. I have been *d·*, hot,
r 491– 1 swimming when he is on *d·* land.
g 506–16 and let the *d·* land appear :— *Gen.* 1 : 9.
506–22 And God called the *d·* land Earth ;— *Gen.* 1 : 10.
507– 1 In metaphor, the *d·* land illustrates
535–30 And God called the *d·* land Earth ;— *Gen.* 1 : 10.
557– 4 develop their children properly on *d·* land.

dual

b 334–12 This *d·* personality of the unseen and the seen,
r 482–24 Angels announced . . . this *d·* appearing,

duality

r 473–16 hence the *d·* of Jesus the Christ.

due

pr 6– 1 We cannot escape the penalty *d·* for sin.
a 36– 7 To remit the penalty *d·* for sin, would be
41–13 he cannot forever . . . escape the penalty *d·*.
m 68–10 mistrust, where confidence is *d·*,
sp 88–27 It is *d·* to inspiration rather than to
an 101– 2 are *d·* to manipulations,
106–14 incurs the divine penalty *d·* this crime.
s 143–30 everlastingly *d·* its holy name.
151– 8 Great respect is *d·* the motives and
162–29 With *d·* respect for the faculty,
ph 184–32 She looked and saw that it pointed *d·* east.
f 219–28 not rendering to God the honor *d·* to Him
b 338–32 The ideal man was revealed in *d·* time,
o 341–12 Proof is essential to a *d·* estimate of this subject.
355–23 wholly *d·* to a misapprehension
p 385–14 from all penalties but those *d·* for wrong-doing.
396–19 *d·* to the force of education
435–25 decides what penalty is *d·* for the sin,
436–24 from the penalty they considered justly *d·*,

dull

b 272–14 not to impart to *d·* ears and gross hearts the
317–29 To this *d·* and doubting disciple
o 350–19 and their ears are *d·* of hearing,— *Matt.* 13 : 15.

dulness

a 34–22 raise themselves and others from spiritual *d·*
b 272–15 which *d·* and grossness could not accept.

duly

g 507– 3 Spirit *d·* feeds and clothes every object,

dumb

a 50– 2 sheep before her shearers is *d·*,— *Isa.* 53 : 7.
s 135–17 "it came to pass,. . .the *d·* spake." — *Luke* 11 : 14.
ph 183–29 voice to the *d·*, feet to the lame.
f 226–25 The lame, the deaf, the *d·*, the blind,

dumb

- o 342–23 It speaks to the *d·* the words of Truth,
- 348–13 when devils, . . . were cast out and the *d·* spake.
- p 398– 2 "Thou *d·* and deaf spirit, — *Mark* 9 : 25.

dumbness

- s 135–16 When Christ cast out the devil of *d·*,

dungeon

- ph 194–22 Incarcerated in a *d·*, where neither sight nor
- 195– 3 he asked to be taken back to his *d·*,

duodecillions

- s 108–17 three times three *d·* must be nine *d·*,

duplicity

- gl 589– 4 JACOB. A corporeal mortal embracing *d·*,

duration

- sp 77–17 will be of longer or shorter *d·*

during

- pref ix–28 This was *d·* the years 1867 and 1868.
- xii– 6 *D·* seven years over four thousand students
- pr 9– 2 *D·* many years the author has been most grateful
- a 47–31 *D·* his night of gloom and glory
- sp 96–31 *D·* this final conflict, wicked minds will
- an 101–10 which tested *d·* several sessions
- s 107– 4 graciously preparing me *d·* many
- f 254–16 *D·* the sensual ages, absolute C. S.
- b 306– 9 *d·* that moment there would be no
- p 431– 5 *D·* all this time the prisoner attended to

dust

and nothingness
- g 547–22 or go down into *d·* and nothingness.
atom of
- c 263–29 like an atom of *d·* thrown into the
decay and
- ph 200–13 and not subject to decay and *d·*.
decomposed into
- p 429–16 buried and decomposed into *d·* ;
dust to
- s 126– 3 The problem of nothingness, or "dust to *d·*,"
- ap 567–25 show the dragon to be nothingness, dust to *d·* ;
- gl 580– 1 "dust to *d·* ;" red sandstone ; nothingness ;
ephemeral
- c 267– 4 start not from matter or ephemeral *d·*.
fall into
- an 103–28 singe their own wings and fall into *d·*.
formed from
- f 214–10 represented in the Scriptures as formed from *d·*,
- b 281–26 through a man formed from *d·*.
ground and
- g 537–17 since ground and *d·* stand for nothingness.
injected into
- g 524–30 Is Spirit, God, injected into *d·*,
matter or
- ph 172–18 If . . . he is a portion of matter, or *d·*.
- b 338–19 matter or *d·* was deemed the agent of Deity
non-intelligent
- g 531–16 If, . . . body originated in non-intelligent *d·*,
primarily
- g 543–20 who shall say that he is not primarily *d·* ?
remands him to
- g 532–12 condemns material man and remands him to *d·*.
returning to
- g 522–17 this man to be mortal, — *d·* returning to *d·*.
returns to
- b 277– 4 the Scripture says that *d·* returns to *d·*.
- g 543– 3 error, . . . yields to Truth and returns to *d·* ;
return to
- sp 73–19 The belief that material bodies return to *d·*,
- f 214–12 originate in matter and return to *d·*,
- b 278–26 originated in matter and must return to *d·*,
- 287– 5 but creations of matter must return to *d·*,
- g 536–29 the mortal and material return to *d·*,
trail in
- m 58– 4 or else joy's drooping wings trail in *d·*.
trail in the
- g 550–20 causes our standard to trail in the *d·*.
turns hope to
- c 263–16 His "touch turns hope to *d·*,

———

- s 118–20 In all mortal forms of thought, *d·* is
- f 244–15 If man were *d·* in his earliest stage
- c 263–16 the *d·* we all have trod."
- b 291–25 Mind never becomes *d·*.
- 296– 1 error . . . man has a resurrection from *d·* ;
- 338–13 *red color of the ground, d·, nothingness.*
- p 416–22 has resigned his body to *d·*,
- r 476– 3 declares that man begins in *d·*
- 485–20 belief . . . that man springs from *d·*
- g 524–14 formed man of the *d·* of the ground, — *Gen.* 2 : 7.
- 524–31 Does Spirit enter *d·*, and lose therein the
- 528– 1 Was it requisite . . . that *d·* should become
- 531– 3 the belief that everything springs from *d·*

dust

- g 535–27 *d·* thou art, and unto *d·* — *Gen.* 3 : 19.
- 545–29 "*D·* [nothingness] thou art, — *Gen.* 3 : 19.
- 545–29 unto *d·* [nothingness] shalt thou— *Gen.* 3 : 19.
- 552–24 is not in egg nor in *d·*.
- 553–27 superstition about the creation from *d·*
- gl 584–28 definition of
- 585–27 belief . . . that man started first from *d·*,

duties

- a 31–12 First in the list of Christian *d·*, he taught

duty

- pr 9–14 we shall never meet this great *d·* simply by
- a 37–22 it is the *d·* and privilege of every
- m 67–12 firm at the post of *d·*, the mariner works on
- b 340– 6 especially when the word *d·*, which is not in the
- 340– 9 for this is the whole *d·* of man." — *Eccl.* 12 : 13.
- p 385–17 Whatever it is your *d·* to do, you can do
- 433– 7 In compliance with a stern *d·*, his Honor,
- r 496– 6 in C. S. the first *d·* is to obey God,
- g 541–26 Now it repudiates even the human *d·* of man

dwarfing

- t 445–11 *d·* the spiritual understanding

dwell

- sp 82–23 nor are they in the mental realm in which we *d·*.
- b 284–14 Can the infinite *d·* in the finite
- o 341– * *But if the spirit . . . d· in you,* — *Rom.* 8 : 11.
- 357–30 if so, can Life, or God, *d·* in evil
- r 466–12 which neither *d·* together nor
- 474–32 light and darkness cannot *d·* together.
- 478–21 How can intelligence *d·* in matter
- g 510– 3 more . . . than to *d·* on the objects of sense !
- 514–22 wolf also shall *d·* with the lamb, — *Isa.* 11 : 6.
- 534–22 that the spirit of God *d·* in you." — *Rom.* 8 : 9.
- 543–11 must *d·* in dream-land, until mortals
- 550–31 originate the impure . . . and *d·* in it.
- ap 568–20 heavens, and ye that *d·* in them. — *Rev.* 12 : 12.
- 578–17 and I will *d·* in the house— *Psal.* 23 : 6.

dweller

- b 301–31 an unsubstantial *d·* in material forms,

dwellers

- ap 569–16 *d·* still in the deep darkness of belief.

dwelleth

- o 341– * *by His spirit that d· in you.* — *Rom.* 8 : 11.

dwelling

- a 23–13 has the Holy Ghost *d·* in him."
- sp 78–31 the invisible good *d·* in eternal Science.
- b 308– 1 Art thou *d·* in the belief that mind is
- 311–14 false estimates of soul as *d·* in sense
- 311–15 and of mind as *d·* in matter,
- o 349–24 while *d·* on a material plane,
- g 503–28 God, Spirit, *d·* in infinite light and

dwelling-places

- s 142–24 meet *d·* for the Most High.

dwells

- f 247–22 which *d·* forever in the eternal Mind
- b 284– 2 It is not rational to say that Mind . . . *d·* in
- 334– 5 Christ, *d·* forever in the bosom of the Father,
- g 514– 9 Mind, joyous in strength, *d·* in the realm of Mind.
- gl 580–24 supposition . . . Soul *d·* in material sense ;

dwelt

- a 29–26 The Christ *d·* forever an idea
- b 331– 6 If He *d·* within what He creates,
- g 542–28 and *d·* in the land of Nod. — *Gen.* 4 : 16.

dying

- a 42–20 existence . . . separate from God is a *d·* error.
- sp 76–18 Suffering, sinning, *d·* beliefs are unreal.
- 78–11 mortal, sinning, suffering, and *d·*.
- ph 193– 4 physician, who said that the patient was *d·*.
- f 203–28 and of fearful and doleful *d·*
- c 258–28 Never born and never *d·*,
- 259–11 presented man as fallen, sick, sinning, and *d·*.
- b 279– 1 the erring, changing, and *d·*,
- 292–11 A sinful, sick, and *d·* mortal is not
- p 368–17 more faith in living than in *d·*.
- 373– 7 The author has raised up the *d·*,
- 379–20 not *d·* on account of the state of her blood,
- 428–31 and raised the *d·* to life and health
- 429–15 Mortal mind affirms . . . that the body is *d·*,
- 430– 2 healing the *d·* and raising the dead.
- 441–16 refuses to recognize Man as sick or *d·*,
- r 494–27 mortal testimony, changing, *d·*, unreal.
- g 556–13 is not to be gained by *d·*.
- 557–21 man as never born and as never *d·*,

dynasties

- ap 577–23 Mighty potentates and *d·* will lay down

dynasty

- s 141–13 as kings are crowned from a royal *d·*,
- 141–17 For this Principle there is no *d·*,

dyspepsia
　ph 175– 7　In old times who ever heard of *d*·,
　　175–16　If a random thought, calling itself *d*·,
　　197–23　Their diet would not cure *d*· at this period.
　f 221– 2　adopted the Graham system to cure *d*·.
　　221– 4　His *d*· increasing, he decided that his diet
　　222–29　In seeking a cure for *d*·

each
　pr 7–25　to whom *e*· need of man is always known
　a 21–13　gain a little *e*· day in the right direction,
　　32– 8　to pass *e*· guest a cup of wine.
　　47–28　*e*· one came to a violent death except St. John,
　m 59– 4　most tender solicitude for *e*· other's happiness,
　　59–13　*e*· partner sustaining the other,
　　66–14　*E*· succesive stage of experience unfolds new
　sp 88–10　By learning the origin of *e*·.
　ph 195–11　The point for *e*· one to decide is,
　f 246–25　*E*· succeeding year unfolds wisdom,
　　248–10　which *e*· day brings to a nearer tomb.
　b 291– 8　*e*· lesser call in the growth of Christian
　o 356–14　not contributing in any way to *e*· other's
　p 413–22　need not wash his little body all over *e*· day
　t 457–15　*e*· of them could see but one face of it,
　g 502–18　*e*· text is followed by its spiritual
　　506–13　forming *e*· successive stage of progress.

each other
　a 21–20　little opportunity to help *e*· other
　m 57– 9　conjoin naturally with *e*· other,
　f 209–18　which constituent masses hold to *e*· other,
　b 278–21　warring forever with *e*· other ;
　o 358– 7　If two statements directly contradict *e*· other
　ap 564– 1　which would impel them to devour *e*· other
　gl 588–14　numbers which never blend with *e*· other,

ear
　and eye
　sp 84–20　not dependent upon the *e*· and eye
　deaf
　t 444–23　a deaf *e*· to the teachings of C. S.,
　divine
　pr 7–24　The "divine *e*·" is not an auditory nerve.
　gain the
　pr 15–29　gain the *e*· and right hand of omnipotence
　hath not heard
　s 117–14　*E*· hath not heard, nor hath lip spoken, the
　heard
　c 255–18　Eye hath not seen Spirit, nor hath *e*· heard His
　t 459– 3　"eye hath not seen nor *e*· heard." — *I Cor. 2 : 9.*
　hearing of the
　ph 192– 8　They come from the hearing of the *e*·,
　c 262–18　by the hearing of the *e*· : — *Job 42 : 5.*
　ill-attuned
　m 60–24　An ill-attuned *e*· calls discord harmony,
　need the
　p 424–22　you need the *e*· of your auditor.
　omnipotent
　pr 13–13　Do we gain the omnipotent *e*· sooner by words
　through the
　b 284–23　through the eye nor hear it through the *e*·,
　trieth words
　s 115– 8　"The *e*· trieth words, — *Job 34 : 3.*
　whispered into the
　p 374– 4　whispered into the *e*· of mortal mind,

　pr 14– 2　material person, whose *e*· we would gain,
　f 213–17　The *e*· does not really hear.
　r 486– 5　accident happens . . . to the *e*·,

earlier
　s 150–11　as in the time of its *e*· demonstration,

earliest
　a 45–22　They who *e*· saw Jesus after the resurrection
　f 236–24　should teach their children at the *e*·
　　244–15　If man were dust in his *e*· stage
　g 501– 4　the Word, in its *e*· articulations,

early
　pref viii–28　As *e*· as 1862 she began to write down
　　ix–12　Certain essays written at that *e*· date
　a 41–17　this demonstration of healing was *e*· lost,
　　52– 1　From *e*· boyhood he was about his
　　55– 6　Perhaps the *e*· Christian era
　m 61–16　often these beautiful children *e*· droop
　f 220–10　lifts her blue eye to greet the *e*· spring.
　　237–22　This makes C. S. *e*· available.
　　245– 5　Disappointed in love in her *e*· years,
　o 351– 9　became a member . . . in *e*· years.
　　359–21　*e*· received her religious education.
　p 387–13　Our thinkers do not die *e*· because they
　　405– 9　Choke these errors in their *e*· stages,
　　420– 6　they should *e*· call an experienced

dyspeptic
　f 222–22　He learned that a *d*· was very far from
　　222–27　finally concluded that God never made a *d*·,

dyspeptics
　ph 197–26　With rules of health . . . there would still be *d*·

E

early
　r 471–24　subscribed to an orthodox creed in *e*· youth,
　　474– 4　accorded to Truth in the *e*· Christian era
　g 523–16　in the *e*· part of the book of Genesis.
　gl 579– 9　surrendering to the creator the *e*· fruits
　fr 600– *　*Let us get up e· to the vineyards : — Song 7 : 12.*

earn
　pr 10–19　and stop at the doors to *e*· a penny

earned
　f 233–15　goal of goodness is assiduously *e*·

earnest
　pr 15–17　In the quiet sanctuary of *e*· longings,
　a 21–12　If honest, he will be in *e*· from the start,
　b 299–16　By giving *e*· heed to these spiritual guides
　　309–13　those, who through *e*· striving followed
　　317–27　to Soul, for an *e*· of immortality,
　p 434–17　*e*·, solemn eyes, kindling with hope

earnestly
　a 29– 8　It bids us work the more *e*· in times of
　sp 82–32　it is wise *e*· to consider whether it is the
　r 476–31　Learn this, O mortal, and *e*· seek the

ears
　a 38–29　and having *e*· ye hear not ;
　f 211–26　the eyes to see and the *e*· to hear,
　b 272–14　not to impart to dull *e*· and gross hearts
　o 350–19　and their *e*· are dull of hearing, — *Matt. 13 : 15.*
　　350–21　and hear with their *e*·, — *Matt. 13 : 15.*
　gl 585– 1　definition of
　　585– 4　"Having *e*·, hear ye not?" — *Mark 8 : 18.*

Earth
　g 506–22　And God called the dry land *E*· ; — *Gen. 1 : 10.*
　　535–30　"And God called the dry land *E*· ; — *Gen. 1 : 10.*

earth (*see also* **earth's**)
　above
　g 521– 2　above the sod, above *e*· and its environments,
　above the
　g 511–21　fowl that may fly above the *e*· — *Gen. 1 : 20.*
　　511–29　fowls which fly above the *e*· in the open
　all the
　an 102–14　has dominion over all the *e*· and its hosts.
　f 202–23　gives man dominion over all the *e*·.
　b 316–23　which gives man dominion over all the *e*·.
　p 442– 4　Judge of all the *e*· do right?" — *Gen. 18 : 25.*
　r 475–26　the cattle, and over all the *e*·, — *Gen. 1 : 26.*
　g 515–14　the cattle, and over all the *e*·, — *Gen. 1 : 26.*
　　516–21　and reflects God's dominion over all the *e*·.
　　518– 7　upon the face of all the *e*·, — *Gen. 1 : 29.*
　　531–32　and having dominion over all the *e*·.
　　533– 3　Had he lost . . . dominion over all the *e*·?
　and heaven
　s 121–10　*e*· and heaven were bright,
　c 264–30　all the glories of *e*· and heaven and
　g 518– 2　lord of the belief in *e*· and heaven,
　and man
　g 538–19　God creates the heavens, *e*·, and man.
　and the heavens
　g 520–18　made the *e*· and the heavens, — *Gen. 2 : 4.*
　　543–31　made the *e*· and the heavens," — *Gen. 2 : 4.*
　at God's command
　g 530– 6　The *e*·, at God's command, brings forth food
　atmosphere of the
　f 220–14　The atmosphere of the *e*·, kinder than
　away from
　p 365– 3　the heavenly homesick looking away from *e*·,
　beast of the
　g 513–16　beast of the *e*· after his kind : — *Gen. 1 : 24.*
　　513–22　beast of the *e*· after his kind, — *Gen. 1 : 25.*
　　518– 9　And to every beast of the *e*·, — *Gen. 1 : 30.*
　blasts of
　m 57–25　The wintry blasts of *e*· may uproot the
　blessed the
　b 338–29　notwithstanding God had blessed the *e*·
　g 537–28　which blessed the *e*· and gave it to man
　blesses the
　g 516–19　beautifies the landscape, blesses the *e*·.
　borne to
　s 109–24　When a new spiritual idea is borne to *e*·,
　broadcast in the
　ph 197–18　knowledge now broadcast in the *e*·,
　brought forth
　g 508– 9　And the *e*· brought forth grass, — *Gen. 1 : 12.*

earth

cast unto the
ap 567–24   The words "cast unto the *e*·"— *Rev.* 12 : 13.
    569–30   saw that he was cast unto the *e*·,— *Rev.* 12 : 13.
children of
b 309–15   the children of *e*· who followed his example
cling to
c 263–10   cling to *e*· because he has not tasted heaven.
composing the
f 209–17   aggregated substances composing the *e*·,
covers
f 247–27   and covers *e*· with loveliness.
dearest spot on
m 58–22   Home is the dearest spot on *e*·,
dominion over the
ph 165– 5   man's God-given dominion over the *e*·.
down to
s 118–32   natural order of heaven comes down to *e*·.
every plague on
p 405–22   better to be exposed to every plague on *e*·
face of the
s 163–11   druggist, or drug on the face of the *e*·,
faith on the
s 132–27   shall he find faith on the *e*·?"— *Luke* 18 / 8.
first
g 536– 3   the first heaven and the first *e*·— *Rev.* 21 : 1.
ap 572–21   the first heaven and the first *e*·— *Rev.* 21 : 1.
from
a 48– 8   turned forever away from *e*· to heaven,
from the
g 521–21   went up a mist from the *e*·,— *Gen.* 2 : 6.
    541–29   now art thou cursed from the *e*·— *Gen.* 4 : 11.
    546–18   went up a mist from the *e*·."— *Gen.* 2 : 6.
glories of
c 264–30   all the glories of *e*· and heaven and man.
harmony on
s 122– 7   the actual reign of harmony on *e*·.
harmony to
sp 72–31   communicator of . . . harmony to *e*· and
ap 561–15   God and His Christ, bringing harmony to *e*·.
has no repayment
sp 97–32   *E*· has no repayment for the persecutions
heaven and
    (*see* heaven)
heaven and the
r 479–19   created the heaven and the *e*·— *Gen.* 1 : 1.
g 502–23   created the heaven and the *e*·— *Gen.* 1 : 1.
heaven on
s 110–12   establishment of the kingdom of heaven on *e*·.
ph 174–20   proclaiming the kingdom of heaven on *e*·.
heavens and
ap 573– 7   heavens and *e*· to one human consciousness,
    573–20   John's corporeal sense of the heavens and *e*·
heavens and the
g 519– 7   heavens and the *e*· were finished,— *Gen.* 2 : 1.
helped the woman
ap 570–10   And the *e*· helped the woman,— *Rev.* 12 : 16.
inhabitant of the
b 317–31   the Master remained an inhabitant of the *e*·.
inhabitants of the
·*c* 256–22   the inhabitants of the *e*· ;— *Dan.* 4 : 35.
inhabiters of the
ap 568–21   inhabiters of the *e*· and of the sea !— *Rev.* 12 : 12.
inherit the
g 516–15   "The meek shall inherit the *e*·."— *Psal.* 37 : 11.
instead of the
s 121–19   instead of the *e*· from west to east.
in the
g 509–24   before it was in the *e*·."— *Gen.* 2 : 5.
    520–19   before it was in the *e*·,— *Gen.* 2 : 5.
    526– 5   before it was in the *e*·."— *Gen.* 2 : 5.
launched the
s 124–23   which launched the *e*· in its orbit
let the
g 507–11   Let the *e*· bring forth grass,— *Gen.* 1 : 11.
    513–14   Let the *e*· bring forth the living— *Gen.* 1 : 24.
material
c 264– 1   the mortal body and material *e*·, are the
melted
sp 97–26   uttered His voice, the *e*· melted."— *Psal.* 46 : 6.
multiply in the
g 512–19   let fowl multiply in the *e*·.— *Gen.* 1 : 22.
new
sp 91– 2   "a new heaven and a new *e*·."— *Rev.* 21 : 1.
g 536– 2   a new heaven and a new *e*· :— *Rev.* 21 : 1.
    556– 8   Then will the new heaven and new *e*· appear,
ap 572–20   a new heaven and a new *e*· :— *Rev.* 21 : 1.
    572–25   he already saw a new heaven and a new *e*·,
    572–29   Were this new heaven and new *e*· terrestrial
    573–22   he could see the new heaven and new *e*·,
opened her mouth
ap 570–11   and the *e*· opened her mouth,— *Rev.* 12 : 16.
our
g 509–14   stellar universe is no more celestial than our *e*·.
    548– 9   How little light or heat reach our *e*· when

earth

over the
ph 188–28   When darkness comes over the *c*·,
    189– 3   explanation of the sun's influence over the *e*·.
pilgrim on
f 254–31   Pilgrim on *e*·, thy home is heaven ;
received the harmony
a 54– 6   *e*· received the harmony his . . . example
refresh the
b 288–18   Then the raindrops of divinity refresh the *e*·.
replenish the
g 511– 5   "multiply and replenish the *e*·."— *Gen.* 1 : 28.
    517–26   multiply, and replenish the *e*·,— *Gen.* 1 : 28.
return to
a 24–25   as a proof that spirits can return to *e*·?
sp 73– 5   and supposedly will return to *e*· to-morrow,
revolution of the
b 310–13   not affected by the revolution of the *e*·.
revolves
s 121–26   the *e*· revolves about the sun once a year,
salt of the
p 367–19   "Ye are the salt of the *e*·."— *Matt.* 5 : 13.
suffering on
p 386–25   Error, . . . produces all the suffering on *e*·.
sufferings upon
s 158–15   and endured great sufferings upon *e*·.
taint of
m 66–14   joys of Spirit, which have no taint of *e*·.
thou
s 135– 5   Tremble, thou *e*·, at the— *Psal.* 114 : 7.
to believe that the
s 119–26   to believe that the *e*· is in motion
Truth on
b 281– 3   enter into the kingdom of Truth on *e*·
upon the
a 31– 5   no man your father upon the *e*· :— *Matt.* 23 : 9.
r 475–27   that creepeth upon the *e*·."— *Gen.* 1 : 26.
g 507–13   seed is in itself, upon the *e*· :— *Gen.* 1 : 11.
    510– 7   to give light upon the *e*· :— *Gen.* 1 : 15.
    511– 8   to give light upon the *e*·,— *Gen.* 1 : 17.
    513–24   that creepeth upon the *e*·— *Gen.* 1 : 25.
    515–15   that creepeth upon the *e*·— *Gen.* 1 : 26.
    517–29   that moveth upon the *e*·— *Gen.* 1 : 28.
    518–10   that creepeth upon the *e*·,— *Gen.* 1 : 30.
    520–21   not caused it to rain upon the *e*·,— *Gen.* 2 : 5.
ap 559– 7   The angel's left foot was upon the *e*· ;
was blessed
b 338–31   not the ideal man for whom the *e*· was blessed.
was without form
r 479–19   the *e*· was without form,— *Gen.* 1 : 2.
g 503– 6   the *e*· was without form,— *Gen.* 1 : 2.
whole
pr 14–28   man's dominion over the whole *e*·.
ph 191–14   Thus the whole *e*· will be transformed by
g 545–11   was given dominion over the whole *e*·.
ap 575–23   the joy of the whole *e*·,— *Psal.* 48 : 2.
will become dreary
sp 96– 7   *E*· will become dreary and desolate,
will echo
s 129–15   and *e*· will echo the cry,
will help the woman
ap 570–22   In this age the *e*· will help the woman ;

pr 17– 1   Thy will be done in *e*·,— *Matt.* 6 : 10.
    17– 2   *as in heaven, so on e*·,
a 54–30   glorified man were physically on *e*· to-day,
m 69– 1   and man, not of the *e*· earthly
sp 72–28   nor the medium through which truth passes to *e*·.
    75–26   those living on the *e*·
an 100– 9   celestial bodies, the *e*·, and animated things.
s 150– 7   "on *e*· peace, good-will toward— *Luke* 2 : 14.
    226–17   "on *e*· peace, good-will toward— *Luke* 2 : 14.
    310–12   when the *e*· has again turned upon its axis.
    339–25   "in *e*·, as it is in heaven."— *Matt.* 6 : 10.
o 360–29   the Galilean Prophet, the best Christian on *e*·,
    361–27   is the higher hope on *e*·,
r 493– 3   and the *e*· to stand still ;
g 520–17   of the heavens and of the *e*·— *Gen.* 2 : 4.
    522–20   as the life-giving principle of the *e*·.
    538–11   The sun, giving light and heat to the *e*·,
    548–12   *E*· has little light or joy for mortals before
    552– 4   That the *e*· was hatched from the
ap 558– 8   and his left foot on the *e*·— *Rev.* 10 : 2.
    563–24   and did cast them to the *e*·— *Rev.* 12 : 4.
    567–16   he was cast out into the *e*·,— *Rev.* 12 : 9.
gl 585– 5   definition of
    585– 7   To material sense, *e*· is matter ;

earthly

pr 10– 7   to profit by Jesus' cup of *e*· sorrows,
a 30– 6   partook partly of Mary's *e*· condition,
    30–23   throughout the whole *e*· career of Jesus,
    36–12   What was his *e*· reward?
    36–14   *e*· price of spirituality in a material age
    39–25   To break this *e*· spell,

earthly

a	41–16	completed his *e·* mission ;
	46–27	which closed the *e·* record of Jesus,
	47–28	in his last *e·* struggle
	49–15	met his *e·* fate alone with God.
	52–24	The highest *e·* representative of God,
	54–21	His *e·* cup of bitterness was drained to the
	55–23	whosoever layeth his *e·* all on the altar
m	69– 1	and man, not of the earth *e·*
sp	72–26	A sinning, *e·* mortal is not the reality of
s	150–27	The doctrine that . . . all his *e·* days,
ph	197– 6	costs many a man his *e·* days of comfort.
f	202–20	*e·* experience discloses the finity of error
c	265–27	The loss of *e·* hopes and pleasures
b	299– 9	buried its fondest *e·* hopes.
	314– 5	spiritual sense had quenched all *e·* yearnings.
	315–28	more spiritual than all other *e·* personalities.
	334– 8	fleshly Jesus, whose *e·* career was brief.
p	387–15	If . . . authors have the shortest span of *e·*
ap	565–14	a brief history in the *e·* life of our Master ;

earth-mission

a	51–13	but when his *e·* was accomplished,

earthquake

b	293–22	expressed in *e·*, wind, wave,

earth's

a	37–10	They are *e·* luminaries, which serve to
sp	75–31	from *e·* sleep to the grand verities of Life,
	90– 6	The *e·* orbit and the imaginary line called
	90– 7	*e·* motion and position are sustained by Mind
s	121–17	The *e·* diurnal rotation is invisible
ph	185–10	the *e·* magnetic currents
r	471–10	the *e·* motions or of the science of astronomy,
	486– 9	*E·* preparatory school must be improved
g	510–20	Geology has never explained the *e·* formations;
	547–12	able to see in the egg the *e·* atmosphere,

earthward

b	272–23	*e·* gravitation of sensualism and impurity,

ease

m	58–27	a wife ought not to court . . . stupid *e·*,
f	220–13	procures a summer residence with more *e·* than
b	270–28	and a sense of *e·* antidotes suffering,

easier

s	138–22	*e·* for Christianity to cast out sickness than
f	241–31	"*e·* for a camel to go through— *Matt.* 19 : 24.
b	322–31	It is *e·* to desire Truth than to
p	373– 5	It is *e·* to cure the most malignant disease than
	373–12	Healing is *e·* than teaching,
t	449– 9	"*e·* for a camel to go through— *Matt.* 19 : 24.

easiest

pr	5– 4	Sorrow for wrong-doing is . . . the very *e·* step.

easily

a	20–29	the sin which doth so *e·* beset us,— *Heb.* 12 : 1.
sp	82– 2	We think of an absent friend as *e·* as
	94–24	Our Master *e·* read the thoughts of mankind,

East

p	363– 3	which is in such common use in the *E·*.

east

a	21–30	he turns *e·* on the seventh, satisfied if
s	121–18	the sun seems to move from *e·* to west,
	121–19	instead of the earth from west to *e·*
ph	184–29	when the wind was from the *e·*.
	184–32	She looked and saw that it pointed due *e·*.
	185– 5	she never suffered again from *e·* winds,
g	537– 5	He placed at the *e·* of the garden— *Gen.* 3 : 24.

eastern

sp	94–12	The *e·* empires and nations owe their

eastward

ap	575–27	*e·*, to the star seen by the Wisemen

easy

sp	82– 1	as *e·* to read distant thoughts as near.
an	102–25	not lending itself to an *e·* explanation
f	236–31	youth makes *e·* and rapid strides towards Truth.
p	362–15	It was therefore *e·* for the Magdalen
	400–15	This task becomes *e·*, if you understand

eat

a	25–10	they truly *e·* his flesh and drink his blood,
	31–22	"As often as ye *e·* this bread,— *I Cor.* 11 : 26.
	32–17	Take, *e·* ; this is my body.— *Matt.* 26 : 26.
	33–32	Are all who *e·* bread and drink wine in memory
m	58–24	"Two *e·* no more together
	58–25	than they *e·* separately."
	62–13	what ye shall *e·*, or what ye shall— *Matt.* 6 : 25.
ph	165– *	*what ye shall e·, or what ye shall— Matt. 6 : 25.*
	170–16	what ye shall *e·*, or what ye shall— *Matt.* 6 : 25.
f	220–29	"Thou shalt not *e·* of it."— *Gen.* 2 : 17.
	222–15	less thought about what he should *e·* or drink,
	222–30	and *e·* what is set before you,
p	388–30	we shall neither *e·* to live nor live to *e·*.
	390– 3	and I should like something more to *e·*."
g	527– 8	thou mayest freely *e·* :— *Gen.* 2 : 16.
	527– 9	thou shalt not *e·* of it :— *Gen.* 2 : 17.

eat

g	529–16	Ye shall not *e·* of every tree— *Gen.* 3 : 1.
	529–17	We may *e·* of the fruit of— *Gen.* 3 : 2.
	529–19	Ye shall not *e·* of it, — *Gen.* 3 : 3.
	530– 9	what ye shall *e·*, or what ye shall— *Matt.* 6 : 25.
	530–15	in the day ye *e·* thereof,— *Gen.* 3 : 5.
	533– 7	that thou shouldst not *e·* ?— *Gen.* 3 : 11.
	533– 9	she gave me of the tree, and I did *e·*.— *Gen.* 3 : 12.
	533–29	beguiled me, and I did *e·* ;"— *Gen.* 3 : 13.
	535–22	Thou shalt not *e·* of it :— *Gen.* 3 : 17.
	535–23	in sorrow shalt thou *e·* of it— *Gen.* 3 : 17.
	535–25	and thou shalt *e·* the herb— *Gen.* 3 : 18.
	535–26	shalt thou *e·* bread,— *Gen.* 3 : 19.
	537– 2	and *e·*, and live forever ;— *Gen.* 3 : 22.
ap	559–17	Take it, and *e·* it up ;— *Rev.* 10 : 9.
	559–25	when you *e·* the divine body
	559–28	share the hemlock cup and *e·* the bitter herbs ;

eaten

a	32–22	The disciples had *e·*,
f	211–20	"the fathers have *e·* sour grapes, — *Ezek.* 18 : 2.
g	533– 6	Hast thou *e·* of the tree,— *Gen.* 3 : 11.
	535–21	and hast *e·* of the tree— *Gen.* 3 : 17.

eaters

sp	90–20	Opium and hashish *e·* mentally travel far

eatest

ph	197–10	"In the day that thou *e·* thereof— *Gen.* 2 : 17.
r	481–19	"In the day that thou *e·* thereof— *Gen.* 2 : 17.
g	527–10	in the day that thou *e·* thereof— *Gen.* 2 : 17.
	532– 8	"In the day that thou *e·* thereof— *Gen.* 2 : 17.

eateth

g	544–10	consisteth not of the things which a man *e·*.

eating

a	32–15	"As they were *e·*, Jesus took— *Matt.* 26 : 26.
ph	165– 2	Evil declared that *e·* this fruit
f	221–10	until three hours after *e·*.
	222–25	if *e·* a bit of animal flesh could overpower him.
	254– 8	To stop *e·*, drinking, or being clothed
p	383–21	*e·* or smoking poison for half a century,
	388–27	foolish to stop *e·* until we gain perfection
g	532– 7	when *e·* its first fruits brought death?

ebbing

ap	566– 2	dark *e·* and flowing tides of human fear,

Ecclesiastes

b	291–20	So we read in *E·*.
	340– 4	This text in the book of *E·*

ecclesiastical

sp	98–32	The way . . . is not *e·* but Christian,
s	118– 4	far above the merely *e·*
	141–11	along the line of scholarly and *e·* descent,
	141–17	For this Principle there is . . . no *e·* monopoly.
t	444–22	If *e·* sects or medical schools turn
r	473–18	In an age of *e·* despotism.
gl	590–13	LEVI (Jacob's son). . . . . *e·* despotism.

echo

s	126–11	and interpreted in its own way the *e·* of Spirit,
	129–15	and earth will *e·* the cry,
c	262–18	Mortals will *e·* Job's thought,

echoing

f	226– 6	voice of God . . . was still *e·* in our land,

eclectic

p	416–10	allopathic, homœopathic, botanic, *e·*

eclipse

sp	85– 1	read the stars or calculate an *e·*.

economy

m	59–10	the annoyances and cares of domestic *e·*,
	59–11	nor . . . be expected to understand political *e·*.
ph	170– 7	Did Jesus understand the *e·* of man less
f	222–19	consulting the stomach less about the *e·* of
	228–22	bodily conditions, structure, or *e·*,
b	327–21	in the human or the divine *e·*.
p	423–25	now at work in the *e·* of being

ecstasies

b	312–14	People go into *e·* over the sense of a

ecstasy

pr	7–17	sensation, not Soul, produces material *e·*
	14– 7	is to have, not mere emotional *e·* or faith,

ecstatic

pr	7–19	there would grow out of *e·* moments

Eddy, Mrs. Mary Baker

pref	xii–27	MARY BAKER EDDY

author

pref	ix–10	So was it with the *a·*.
	x–11	The *a·* has not compromised conscience
	xi–22	When God called the *a·* to
	xi–26	first school of C. S. . . . was started by the *a·*
	xii– 7	four thousand students were taught by the *a·*
pr	9– 2	During many years the *a·* has been most grateful
an	104– 5	will be seen why the *a·* of this book has
s	112–29	without giving that *a·* proper credit,

Eddy, Mrs. Mary Baker

author

s 114– 2	a· calls sick and sinful humanity *mortal mind,*
114–31	what is termed by the a· *mortal mind.*
123–17	The term C. S. was introduced by the a·
130–23	a· has often remembered our Master's love
149–22	a· has cured what is termed organic disease
150–23	it is as evidently erroneous to the a·,
152– 5	The a· has endeavored to make this book the
153– 5	The a· has attenuated *Natrum muriaticum*
162–17	a· has restored health in cases of
c 266–15	The a· has experienced the foregoing
b 330– 3	Until the a· . . . learned the vastness of C. S.,
o 351– 8	The a· became a member of the orthodox
p 373– 6	The a· has raised up the dying,
374– 9	The a· has answered this question
377–19	a· never knew a patient who did not
380–22	years ago the a· made a spiritual discovery,
386–12	The a· has in too many instances
394–17	Experience has proved to the a· the fallacy
402– 4	it is but just to say that the a· has already
428–30	The a· has healed hopeless organic disease,
t 444–13	Students are advised by the a· to be
445–31	the a· trembles whenever she sees a
446–11	Whoever practises the Science the a· teaches,
453– 5	a· understands what she is saying.
457– 8	Since the divine light . . . dawned upon the a·,
458–16	a· desires to keep it out of C. S.
460–25	When . . . was a fresh revelation to the a·,
463–32	It has been said to the a·,
464– 4	Could her friends know how little time the a·
464–22	the a· has labored to expound
r 471–24	a· subscribed to an orthodox creed in early
g 546–21	To the a·, they are transparent,
547– 7	so ascertain if the a· has given you the correct
ap 564–10	The a· is convinced that the accusations

author's

pref vii–27	Since the a· discovery of the
viii–24	In the a· work, RETROSPECTION AND
an 101–21	The a· own observations of the workings of
s 112–28	and yet uses another a· discoveries
126–32	If Christendom resists the a· application
129–30	a· small estimate of the pleasures of the table.
152–21	The a· medical researches and experiments
t 446– 5	thorough perusal of the a· publications
452–24	simply by repeating the a· words,
r 465– 1	from the first edition of the a· class-book,
483–13	After the a· sacred discovery,
g 556–28	hence the a· experience ;

child

pref viii–31	the first steps of a c· in the newly

disciple

pref ix–17	finds herself a willing d· at the heavenly gate,

discoverer of Christian Science

o 359–20	the d· of C. S. early received
p 426– 5	The d· of C. S. finds the path less difficult
t 443– 1	When the d· of C. S. is consulted by
g 555– 6	An inquirer once said to the d· of C. S. :

editor

pref xii–12	sole e· and publisher of the C. S. Journal,

her

pref viii– 1	h· system has been fully tested
viii–26	experiences which led h·, in the year 1866, to
viii–29	the results of h· Scriptural study,
viii–30	the Bible was h· sole teacher ;
ix– 1	She also began to jot down h· thoughts
ix–13	still in circulation among h· first pupils ;
ix–20	H· first pamphlet on C. S. was copyrighted
ix–29	h· comparative ignorance of the stupendous
x–16	she and h· students have proved
x–17	proved the worth of h· teaching.
x–27	Only those quarrel with h· method who
x–28	do not understand h· meaning,
xi–31	enabled h· to get this institution chartered
xii–11	publisher of h· own works ;
xii–14	She closed h· College, October 29, 1889,
xii–16	conviction that the next two years of h· life
xii–18	She retained h· charter,
xii–20	as auxiliary to h· church.
xii–22	in order to elucidate h· idealism.
an 101–22	convince h· that it is not a remedial agent,
s 127– 1	or questions h· use of the word Science,
127– 4	nor will Christianity lose its hold upon h·.
152–22	prepared h· thought for the metaphysics of
152–24	material dependence had failed h· in h· search
152–28	H· experiments in homœopathy
152–28	had made h· skeptical as to
o 351–10	h· own prayers failed to heal h·
351–11	as did the prayers of h· devout parents
359–11	early received h· religious education.
359–23	falling from the lips of h· saintly mother,
p 374–10	The author . . . in h· explanation of disease
402– 4	the author has already in h· possession
402– 5	records of the cure, by herself and h· students
426– 6	when she has the high goal always before h·

Eddy, Mrs. Mary Baker

her

p 426– 7	than when she counts h· footsteps
t 443– 2	consulted by h· followers as to the
457–10	H· prime object, since entering this field
460–26	impart, . . . from h· own spiritual condition,
460–29	by h· manuscript circulated among the students.
460–30	beliefs were gradually expelled from h· thought,
464– 5	Could h· friends know how little time
464– 5	except through h· laborious publications,
464– 9	Others could not take h· place,
464–10	She therefore remains unseen at h· post,
r 471–29	Since then h· highest creed has been

hers

pref xii– 3	h· was the only College of this character

herself

pref ix–17	she still finds h· a willing disciple
p 402– 5	records of the cure, by h· and her students
464– 5	in which to make h· outwardly known

I am blest

iii– *	And I am blest !

I am leading

f 253– 9	I hope, dear reader, I am leading you

I am not patient with

p 413–21	I am not patient with a speck of dirt ;

I as a Christian Scientist

o 359– 8	I as a Christian Scientist believed in the

I ask

f 250–22	Now I ask, Is there any more reality in the
p 371–22	No impossible thing do I ask

I began

s 156–13	Believing then somewhat in . . . I began to

I beheld

s 110– 8	Thus it was that I beheld, as never before,

I cannot attest

ph 193–28	I cannot attest the truth of that report,

I cannot coincide

sp 80–13	but I cannot coincide with their views.

I cannot fail to

ph 194– 3	I cannot fail to discern the coincidence

I combat

b 269–29	The theories I combat are these :

I cured

ph 184–27	A woman, whom I cured of consumption,
p 389–31	I cured her in a few minutes.

I demonstrated

s 147– 6	I demonstrated the divine rules of C. S.

I deny

o 348–16	I deny His cooperation with evil,

I desire

o 348–17	I desire to have no faith in evil

I did so

s 156–18	I did so, and she continued to gain.

I discovered

s 107– 1	In the year 1866, I discovered the Christ Science

I discredit

m 68–25	I discredit the belief that agamogenesis

I do aver

o 348–29	I do aver, that, as a result of teaching C. S.,

I do believe

t 461– 2	but I do believe that the real man is immortal

I do not maintain

t 461– 1	I do not maintain that anyone can

I entertain no

sp 80–12	I entertain no doubt of the humanity

I find

s 111– 3	I find the will, . . . opposed to the divine Mind
113–24	I find that God is true,

I had foretold

ph 169– 9	But it always came about as I had foretold.

I have been informed

ph 193–24	Since his recovery I have been informed that

I have demonstrated

s 126–24	I have demonstrated . . . the effects of Truth
ph 177– 4	I have demonstrated this beyond all cavil.
184–23	I have demonstrated this as a rule

I have discerned

ph 168–24	I have discerned disease in the human mind,

I have discovered

s 126–23	just as I have discovered them.

I have found

s 126–26	I have found nothing in ancient or in
ph 180–32	I have found divine Truth more potent

I have had

s 126–30	I have had no other guide

I have healed

o 359– 7	I have healed infidels

I have made

f 233–27	tests I have made of the effects of truth

I have named

m 68–19	I have named her case to individuals,

I have narrated

ph 193–30	occurred just as I have narrated.

I have never supposed

o 348–26	I have never supposed the world would

Eddy, Mrs. Mary Baker

I have never witnessed
  t 453–11 *I* have never witnessed so decided effects from
I have not seen
  ph 193–19 Since then *I* have not seen him,
I have restored
  s 162–22 *I* have restored what is called the
I have revised
  o 361–21 *I* have revised SCIENCE and HEALTH only to
I have said
  ph 169– 6 and *I* have said to the patient,
I have seen
  ph 169– 4 *I* have seen the mental signs,
  f 212–10 *I* have seen an unwitting attempt
  247– 3 *I* have seen age regain two of the elements
I have set forth
  s 126–22 *I* have set forth C. S.
I here present
  p 430–13 *I* here present to my readers an allegory
I hope
  f 253– 9 *I* hope, dear reader, I am leading you into
  253–11 *I* hope that you are conquering this false
I insist
  p 413–20 *I* insist on bodily cleanliness
I keep
  p 371–21 nor would *I* keep the suckling a
I kindly quote
  s 162–29 *I* kindly quote from Dr. Benjamin Rush,
I knew
  s 109–16 *I* knew the Principle of all harmonious
  f 221– 1 *I* knew a person who when quite a child
  247– 4 A woman of eighty-five, whom *I* knew,
I learned
  s 108–21 *I* learned these truths in divine Science :
  ph 194–14 (as *I* learned in metaphysics)
I long to see
  p 367–27 *I* long to see the consummation of my hope,
I love
  sp 99–21 *I* love mankind, and shall continue
I mean
  ph 168–32 By chemicalization *I* mean the process
I met
  ph 193– 3 On entering the house *I* met his physician,
I must know
  s 109–19 but *I* must know the Science of
I name
  ph 169–10 *I* name these facts to show that
  f 210–23 *I* name it mortal.
I never could
  sp 71–25 *I* never could believe in spiritualism.
I never knew
  m 68–16 *I* never knew more than one individual who
I prescribed
  s 156– 8 *I* prescribed the fourth attenuation of
I pressed on
  f 226–31 but *I* pressed on through faith in God,
I regret
  o 346– 1 *I* regret that such criticism confounds
I rejoice
  o 354–28 *I* rejoice in the apprehension of this grand
I rescued
  p 382–24 One whom *I* rescued from seeming. . .oblivion,
I sat
  ph 184–29 *I* sat silently by her side a few moments.
I saw
  ph 193–18 The next day *I* saw him in the yard.
  193–29 what *I* saw and did for that man,
  f 226–22 *I* saw before me the sick,
  226–29 *I* saw before me the awful conflict,
  227– 3 *I* saw that the law of mortal belief
I say
  b 329– 7 proves the truth of all that *I* say of it.
I say with Paul
  f 216–28 *I* say with Paul : Be "willing — *II Cor.* 5 : 8.
I should appear
  s 164–17 If you or *I* should appear to die,
I sought
  s 109–11 *I* sought the solution of this problem
I speak
  pr 1– 5 *I* speak from experience.
I submitted
  s 111–29 *I* submitted my metaphysical system
I term
  p 401–16 What *I* term *chemicalization* is the upheaval
I then
  o 343– 1 Shall *I* then be smitten for healing
I then requested
  ph 184–31 *I* then requested her to look at the
I therefore
  b 269–22 *I* therefore plant myself unreservedly on the
I told
  ph 193–17 *I* told him to rise, dress himself,

Eddy, Mrs. Mary Baker

I understand
  pr 16–24 let me give what *I* understand to be the
  a 40–11 which *I* understand to mean God's method
  55–29 This Comforter *I* understand to be Divine
        Science.
I was called
  ph 192–32 *I* was called to visit Mr. Clark
I went
  ph 193– 9 *I* went to his bedside.
I wished
  f 226–26 *I* wished to save from the slavery of
I won my way
  s 109–20 *I* won my way to absolute conclusions
I would not transform
  p 371–20 *I* would not transform the infant at once into
me
  pr 16–24 let *m·* give what I understand to be the
  s 107– 4 God had been graciously preparing *m·*
  108– 1 Whence came to *m·* this heavenly conviction,
  108– 5 unfolding to *m·* the demonstrable fact that
  109–23 revelation of Truth . . . came to *m·* gradually
  110–18 No human pen nor tongue taught *m·* the Science
  111–28 this fact became evident to *m·*,
  113–10 in the four following, to *m·*, *self-evident*
  156–17 It then occurred to *m·* to give her
  156–21 After trying this, she informed *m·* that
  156–26 and receiving occasional visits from *m·*,
  ph 169– 5 assuring *m·* that danger was over,
  177– 6 is to *m·* as certain as the
  193–32 It has been demonstrated to *m·*
  f 226–22 I saw before *m·* the sick,
  226–30 I saw before *m·* the awful conflict,
  226–32 to guide *m·* into the land of C. S.,
  p 382–25 One whom I rescued . . . wrote to *m·* :
messenger
  t 455–24 When He commissions a *m·*, it is one who
mine
  o 345–14 but in this volume of *m·* there are no
my
  iii– * OH ! Thou hast heard *m·* prayer ;
  a 40–10 This is *m·* sense of divine pardon,
  55–16 *M·* weary hope tries to realize
  m 68–20 when casting *m·* bread upon the waters,
  sp 99–20 *m·* contest is not with the individual,
  s 108–12 *M·* conclusions were reached by
  108–30 *M·* discovery, that erring, mortal . . . *mind*
  108–32 set *m·* thoughts to work in new channels,
  109– 1 and led up to *m·* demonstration of the
  109–11 For three years after *m·* discovery,
  109–20 I won *m·* way to absolute conclusions
  110–14 the Bible was *m·* only textbook.
  111–26 After a lengthy examination of *m·* discovery
  111–29 I submitted *m·* metaphysical system
  115– 8 C. S. as brought forth in *m·* discovery.
  126–27 nothing . . . on which to found *m·* own, except
  126–29 The Bible has been *m·* only authority.
  156– 6 A case of dropsy, . . . fell into *m·* hands.
  ph 177– 6 as certain as the evidence of *m·* own existence.
  185– 3 *M·* metaphysical treatment changed the
  f 219– 2 *M·* method of treating fatigue applies
  237– 1 little girl, . . . listened to *m·* explanations,
  b 299– 7 *M·* angels are exalted thoughts,
  340–16 The First Commandment is *m·* favorite text.
  o 343– 3 and for proving *m·* word by *m·* deed
  p 367–28 I long to see the consummation of *m·* hope,
  370–14 This confirms *m·* theory that faith in the drug
  389–29 case of convulsions, . . . under *m·* observation.
  411– 3 *M·* first discovery in the student's practice
  t 456–25 requires *m·* work SCIENCE AND HEALTH
myself
  b 269–22 I therefore plant *m·* unreservedly on the
one
  t 455–21 *o·* who has grown into such a fitness for it
  455–25 When He commissions a messenger, it is *o·* who
pastor
  pref xii– 8 *p·* of the first established Church of Christ,
President
  pref xii– 9 *P·* of the first Christian Scientist Association,
  xii–19 and as its *P·*, reopened the College
publisher
  pref xii–10 *p·* of her own works ;
  xii–12 sole editor and *p·* of the C. S. Journal,
she
  pref viii–27 the system that *s·* denominated C. S.
  viii–28 As early as 1862 *s·* began to write
  ix– 1 *S·* also began to jot down her thoughts on the
  ix–11 *s·* "lisped in numbers, for the numbers came."
  ix–17 *s·* still finds herself a willing disciple
  ix–22 *s·* had learned that this Science must
  ix–26 *s·* made copious notes of Scriptural exposition,
  ix–31 *s·* came at length to its solution ;
  ix–32 *s·* values them as a parent may treasure the
  x– 2 and *s·* would not have them changed.
  x–13 *S·* has made no effort to embellish,
  x–16 *s·* and her students have proved

Eddy, Mrs. Mary Baker

she
pref xi–28　In 1881, s· opened the . . . College
　　xii– 8　Meanwhile s· was pastor of the
　　xii–13　S· closed her College, October 29, 1889,
　　xii–18　S· retained her charter,
　　xii–20　s· had never read this book throughout
　　xii–26　s· commits these pages to honest seekers
　s 127– 2　s· will not therefore lose faith in
　　127–10　The terms . . . s· employs interchangeably,
　　149–23　as readily as s· has cured purely functional
　　152–24　and s· can now understand why,
　　153–10　s· has cured a patient sinking in the last stage
　b 330– 5　s· cherished sanguine hopes
　o 351– 9　s· learned that her own prayers
　　359–22　In childhood, s· often listened with joy
　　359–25　s· pondered the meaning of that Scripture
　　359–26　that Scripture s· so often quotes :
　p 373– 8　while s· has struggled long, and
　　426– 6　when s· has the high goal always before her
　　426– 7　than when s· counts her footsteps
　t 443– 4　s· tries to show them that
　　443– 9　s· feels, as s· always has felt, that all are
　　445–32　the author trembles whenever s· sees a
　　453– 5　author understands what s· is saying.
　　457– 8　s· has never used this newly discovered power in
　　457– 9　never used . . . in any direction which s·
　　460–25　s· had to impart, while teaching its grand facts,
　　460–27　and s· had to do this orally
　　464– 8　would understand why s· is so secluded.
　　464–10　S· therefore remains unseen at her post,
　r 465– 3　s· revised that treatise for this volume
　　471–24　until s· caught the first gleam of this
　　471–31　which, . . . s· has named C. S.
　　483–13　s· affixed the name "Science" to Christianity,

writer's
　ap 577–28　The w· present feeble sense of C. S.

you
　p 382–26　but for the glorious Principle y· teach,
　t 464– 1　"The world is benefited by y·,
　　464– 2　it feels your influence without seeing y·.
　　464– 2　Why do y· not make yourself more widely
　　　　　　　known?"
　g 555– 8　I do not comprehend what y· say about error."

your
　t 464– 1　it feels y· influence without seeing you.
　g 555– 7　"I like y· explanations of truth,

yourself
　t 464– 2　Why do you not make y· more widely known?"

Eden

　m 68–11　mistrust, . . . withers the flowers of E·
　ph 176–18　would load with disease the air of E·,
　g 526–27　put him into the garden of E·,— Gen. 2 : 15.
　　526–26　name E·, according to Cruden, means pleasure,
　　526–30　In this text E· stands for the mortal, . . . body.
　　537– 4　forth from the garden of E·,— Gen. 3 : 23.
　　537– 6　at the east of the garden of E·— Gen. 3 : 24.

edge

　f 211–21　the children's teeth are set on e·."— Ezek. 18 : 2.
　p 374–22　walking in darkness on the e· of a precipice.

Edinburgh

　f 208–17　John Young of E· writes :

edition

　pref x– 3　The first e· of S<small>CIENCE AND</small> H<small>EALTH</small> was
　r 465– 1　This chapter is from the first e· of

editor

　(see **Eddy, Mrs. Mary Baker**)

educate

　m 69–17　If Christian Scientists e· their own offspring
　　69–18　they can e· others spiritually
　ph 179–15　You can even e· a healthy horse so far
　o 345–31　not . . . to "e· the idea of God,

educated

　a 39–10　e· belief that Soul is in the body
　s 158–22　acquires an e· appetite for strong drink,
　ph 195– 8　All that gives pleasure to our e· senses
　c 260–24　Selfishness and sensualism are e· in
　o 349–27　as thought is e· up to spiritual apprehension.
　p 414– 2　and thus are children e· into discord.
　r 484–20　false human consciousness is e· to feel.
　　489– 9　hypothesis which supposes . . . is an e· belief.

education

academic
　f 235–12　it is not so much academic e·,
bias of
　p 381– 3　the bias of e· enforces this slavery.
entire
　m 62– 4　The entire e· of children should be
force of
　p 396–19　due to the force of e·
formed by
　ph 194–31　a belief formed by e· alone.

education

religious
　o 359–22　early received her religious e·.
right
　f 234–23　adequate to the right e· of human thought.
this
　c 260–27　this e· is at the expense of spiritual growth.

　m 60–20　the e· of the higher nature is neglected,
　sp 86–23　E· alone determines the difference.
　ph 176–26　All disease is the result of e·,
　　194–19　e· constitutes this so-called mind,
　f 247–12　e·, and fashion form the transient standards of

educational

　sp 89–18　not necessarily dependent upon e· processes.
　f 226–27　the e· systems of the Pharaohs,

educator

　f 236–12　A mother is the strongest e·,

efface

　ph 175– 2　we should e· the outlines of disease
　　196–21　e· the images and thoughts of disease,
　b 318– 3　to know that nothing can e· Mind
　　318–15　would e· the pure sense of omnipotence.
　p 396– 2　e· from thought all forms and types of
　　396–25　e· the images of sickness from mortal mind.

effaced

　f 240–20　until all wrong work is e· or rectified.
　b 327–14　to be e· by the sweat of agony.
　g 543– 5　The image of Spirit cannot be e·,

effaces

　r 485–26　e· them and delineates foreign agents,

effect

alterative
　f 224– 2　the world feels the alterative e· of truth
　p 421–22　alterative e· produced by Truth upon error,
any
　p 401–23　If . . . could you produce any e· upon the brain
appear in
　a 40– 2　and it will not appear in e·.
baneful
　t 449–19　The baneful e· of evil associates is
beneficial
　pr 12– 5　The beneficial e· of such prayer for the sick
cause or
　(see **cause**)
cause or
　m 67–32　from any such cause or e·.
　f 207–18　amalgamation of Truth and error in cause or e·.
cause to
　r 467–29　Reasoning from cause to e· in the Science
certain
　p 418– 9　unerring, and certain e· of divine Science.
every
　b 268– 9　Mind as the cause of every e·.
　p 379– 7　controlling every e· and recognizing all
healing
　s 141–14　the healing e· followed the understanding
　　152– 9　Truth has a healing e·, even when
its
　p 404– 1　familiar with mental action and its e·
material
　p 403– 9　believed that the misfortune is a material e·.
medical
　t 463–30　Such seeming medical e· or action is
mental
　p 371– 5　Disquisitions on disease have a mental e·
mistakes
　s 124– 8　this belief mistakes e· for cause
new
　p 398–20　and produces a new e· upon the body.
no
　f 207–21　there can be no e· from any other cause,
　p 408–29　unconscious thought . . . produces no e·,
none
　f 232–23　never tried to make of none e· the sentence
of illusion
　an 101–31　In no instance . . . other than the e· of illusion.
of mortal mind
　ph 189–10　explain the e· of mortal mind on the body,
　c 261– 8　The e· of mortal mind on health and happiness
of this Science
　s 162– 9　The e· of this Science is to stir the
only
　p 401–21　The only e· produced by medicine is
physical
　p 383–26　prove the illusive physical e· of a false belief,
produce the
　f 211–15　produce the e· seen in the lachrymal gland?
same
　t 458– 9　will finally have the same e· as
seeks cause in
　b 279–31　Pantheism, . . . seeks cause in e·,
supposed
　p 408–21　derive a supposed e· on intelligence

effect
 whatever
  o 358–25 it is said : "Rest assured that whatever *e·*

  sp 95– 1 The *e·* of his Mind was always to heal
  an 101–29 In no instance is the *e·* of animal magnetism,
  s 155– 5 according to this faith will the *e·* be.
  ph 179–30 may erelong reap the *e·* of this mistake.
  195–18 passes naturally from *e·* back to cause.
  b 291–24 until probation and growth shall *e·* the
  p 370–15 The *e·*, which mortal mind produces through
  415– 3 disease is neither a cause nor an *e·*.
  r 467–24 We reason imperfectly from *e·* to cause,
  467–25 when we conclude that matter is the *e·* of Spirit ;
  480–17 would make matter the cause as well as the *e·*

effected
  a 47–11 hatred towards that just man *e·* his betrayal.
  o 348– 6 any cure, which is *e·* by making the
  p 413–18 *e·* without scrubbing the whole surface daily.

effecting
  t 460–20 Instead of scientifically *e·* a cure,

effective
  s 112– 1 most *e·* curative agent in medical practice.

effects
 bad
  p 377–18 that it may not produce blindly its bad *e·*.
  384–24 or to destroy the bad *e·* of your belief.
  393– 7 remote, and exciting cause of all bad *e·*
  413–10 good or bad *e·* on the health of children.
 baneful
  ph 181–17 ignorant of the baneful *e·* of magnetism,
  p 408–12 baneful *e·* of illusion on mortal minds
  418– 1 the baneful *e·* of their own conclusions.
 beneficial
  p 367–27 increase the beneficial *e·* of Christianity.
 cumulative
  p 405–23 the cumulative *e·* of a guilty conscience.
 decided
  t 453–12 I have never witnessed so decided *e·* from
 different
  t 461–21 because of the different *e·* they produce.
 dire
  ph 196– 4 save him from the dire *e·* of knowledge.
 elevating
  s 146–21 elevating *e·* practically prove its divine origin
 fatal
  p 384–22 if you believe in laws of matter and their fatal *e·*
  ap 568– 8 the fatal *e·* of trying to meet error with error.
 glorious
  ph 176–10 in its glorious *e·* upon the body.
 good
  p 397–19 good *e·* to be in exact proportion to your
 healing
  p 398–26 belief in the healing *e·* of time and
 its
  an 101–23 its *e·* upon those who practise it,
  f 219–20 will be the removal of its *e·*.
  b 283– 8 Matter and its *e·* — sin, sickness, and
  290–13 and its *e·*, — sickness, sin, and death.
  316–10 manifest by its *e·* upon the human mind and
  o 350–25 known by its *e·* on the body
  p 374– 5 Hatred and its *e·* on the body
  378–10 Remove the error, and you destroy its *e·*.
  404–13 while its *e·* still remain on the individual,
  g 540–15 uncovers so-called sin and its *e·*,
 material
  sp 78–22 communicate with man through . . . material *e·*?
 of Christian Science
  b 288–10 When the . . . *e·* of C. S. are fully apprehended,
  323–28 *e·* of C. S. are not so much seen as felt.
 of error
  an 101–28 error cannot remove the *e·* of error.
  b 273–30 beliefs emit the *e·* of error at all times,
  r 473– 6 are to be classified as *e·* of error.
  g 537–21 the falsity of error and the *e·* of error.
 of fear
  p 373–20 to remove the *e·* of fear produced by sin,
 of medicine
  s 163–15 Professor in London, said : "The *e·* of medicine
 of sin
  gl 588– 3 HELL. . . . self-imposed agony ; *e·* of sin ;
 of Truth
  s 126–24 the *e·* of Truth on the health, longevity,
  p 386–14 the corresponding *e·* of Truth on the
 of truth
  f 233–27 scientific tests I have made of the *e·* of truth
 only
  p 379– 5 Christian Scientist finds only *e·*, where the
 on the body
  o 350–25 known by its *e·* on the body
  p 370–19 produce very direct and marked *e·* on the body.
  374– 5 Hatred and its *e·* on the body are removed

effects
 physical
  (see **physical**)
 qualities and
  ph 177–21 qualities and *e·* of what is termed matter,
 sad
  o 342– 7 the sad *e·* on the sick of denying Truth.
 such
  s 132–11 any one who should not deny that such *e·*,
 suffers from the
  ph 184–19 We say man suffers from the *e·* of cold,
 their
  f 217–16 are superior to others, is seen by their *e·*.
  p 409– 1 errors it includes and of their *e·*.
 these
  m 68–23 salutary causes sometimes incur these *e·*.
  sp 88–23 These *e·*, however, do not proceed from
 those
  p 386–10 those *e·* will follow, — not because of the climate
 violent
  an 101– 1 that the violent *e·*, which are observed

  sp 78–31 These are the *e·* of one universal God,
  s 156–21 give up her medicine for one day, and risk the *e·*.
  159–21 died from *e·* produced by mortal mind,
  ph 181–22 satisfied with good words instead of *e·*,
  b 284–26 the *e·* commonly attributed to them.

effectual
  pr 11–18 but wipes it out in the most *e·* manner.
  s 108– 4 *e·* working of His power." — *Eph.* 3 : 7.
  140– 2 *e·* in the treatment of moral ailments.
  p 372–29 acknowledgment of Truth . . . is an *e·* help.

effeminate
  ph 197–26 Many of the *e·* constitutions of our time

efficacious
  a 25– 7 The material blood of Jesus was no more *e·*
  r 497–14 the evidence of divine, *e·* Love,

efficaciously
  t 456–21 *e·* treated by the metaphysical process.

efficacy
 admits the
  p 401–27 Until the advancing age admits the *e·*
 aid its
  a 19–20 understand Jesus' atonement for sin and aid its *e·* ;
 healing
  s 147–11 had lost none of its divine and healing *e·*,
 loses its
  p 370–26 Hygienic treatment also loses its *e·*.
 no
  pr 12–17 has no *e·* of its own but borrows
  s 153–15 and that there is no *e·* in a drug.
 origin and
  s 146–22 practically prove its divine origin and *e·*.
 test its
  o 344–15 until the enemies of C. S. test its *e·*

  a 24–27 The *e·* of the crucifixion lay in the
  25– 3 The *e·* of Jesus' spiritual offering is
  s 158–17 divine Mind and its *e·* to heal.

efficient
  f 233–31 Why should truth not be *e·* in sickness,
  p 376–21 Therefore the *e·* remedy is to destroy the

effort
  pref x–13 She has made no *e·* to embellish,
  a 19–17 every *e·* for reform, every good thought
  22–27 pinning one's faith . . . to another's vicarious *e·*.
  26– 7 all have the cup of sorrowful *e·* to drink
  38– 1 to stir mankind to Christian *e·*?
  ph 166– 5 the healing *e·* is made on the wrong side,
  c 262–25 even as light emits light without *e·* ;
  b 329–20 because he fails in his first *e·*.
  g 554–17 The first *e·* of error has been and is to

efforts
 our
  a 36–29 in return for our *e·* at well doing.
  c 262–11 reverse our feeble flutterings — our *e·* to
 their
  ph 180– 6 faith in their *e·* is somewhat helpful
  t 456–10 reputation experimentally justified by their *e·*
 these
  pref ix–29 These *e·* show . . . . the degrees by which
  a 22– 9 these *e·* are crowned with success.
 vigorous
  a 22– 8 to make vigorous *e·* to save themselves ;
 your
  p 418–26 in your *e·* to destroy error.

  f 223–20 The *e·* of error to answer this question

effulgence
  sp 95–27 he beholds the light . . . and describes its *e·*
  g 504–26 vague conjectures emit no such *e·*.
  511–17 The changing glow and full *e·* of

egg

maternal
g 553–18   the maternal *e·* never brought forth Adam.

non-intelligent
g 550– 2   a circumscribed and non-intelligent *e·*.

nor in dust
g 552–24   redeeming power, . . . is not in *e·* nor in dust.

nucleus, or
g 549–16   with the formation of the nucleus, or *e·*,

of night
g 552– 5   That the earth was hatched from the "*e·* of night"

parent of the
g 552– 4   Who or what produces the parent of the *e·*?

c 261–29   even as the bird which has burst from the *e·*
r 485–20   belief . . . man springs from dust or from an *e·*,
g 543–19   If man is material and originates in an *e·*,
543–25   Did man, whom God created . . . originate in an *e·*?
547–12   able to see in the *e·* the earth's atmosphere,
550–23   An *e·* is an impossible enclosure for Deity.
552– 1   Which is first, the *e·* or the bird?
552– 1   is answered, if the *e·* produces the parent.
552–14   mortal life, which starts from an *e·*,
ap 561– 6   Agassiz, . . . saw the sun in an *e·*
gl 585–28   second from a rib, and third from an *e·*.

eggs

g 549– 4   The supposition that life germinates in *e·*
549–12   sometimes through *e·*, sometimes through buds,
551–10   naturalist argues that mortals spring from *e·*
551–18   transmitted through these bodies called *e·*,

Ego

but one
f 249–32   and there is but one *E·*.

divine
b 336– 6   The divine *E·*, or individuality, is reflected

eternal
b 314– 6   Thus he found the eternal *E·*, and proved that

is deathless
b 335–32   The *E·* is deathless and limitless,

is Mind
f 216–11   The understanding that the *E·* is Mind,

one
b 281–14   The one *E·*, the one Mind or Spirit called God,

understand the
f 204–21   When will the ages understand the *E·*,

pr 14–21   [because the *E·* is absent from the body,
sp 70– 9   the *E·* and the Father are inseparable.
f 250– 7   Spirit is the *E·* which never dreams,
250–11   Spiritual man is the likeness of this *E·*.
b 281– 9   What is the *E·*, whence its origin
306–11   The *E·* would be unexpressed,
315– 7   He knew that the *E·* was Mind instead of
p 368–25   Because matter has no consciousness or *E·*,
gl 588– 9   definition of
588–21   I AM. . . . divine Principle ; the only *E·*.

Ego-God

b 281–11   Ego-man is the reflection of the *E·* ;

Ego-man

b 281–11   *E·* is the reflection of the Ego-God ;
281–11   *E·* is the image and likeness of

egotism

t 452–17   than the luxury of learning with *e·* and vice.

egotists

c 263– 1   Mortals are *e·*.

egregious

o 355–22   the most *e·* fallacies ever offered

Egypt

s 133– 8   In *E·*, it was Mind which saved the Israelites
ph 185–16   the necromancers of *E·* strove to emulate
f 221–27   he thought of the flesh-pots of *E·*,

eight

p 421–31   asserting that the products of *e·* multiplied by

eighty-five

f 247– 4   A woman of *e·*, . . . had a return of sight.

either

pr 12–21   drug to be apparently *e·* poisonous or sanative
a 36– 5   suffering, *e·* before or after death,
m 61–22   propensities that must *e·* be overcome or
63–17   less rights than does *e·* C. S. or civilization.
sp 73– 1   In *e·* case, one does not support the other.
77–20   the illusion *e·* of a soul inert or of a
82–15   because both of us are *e·* unconscious or
83–22   to suppose that life is *e·* material or
86–19   *e·* involve feats by tricksters, or
93–11   *e·* our logic is at fault or
an 101–18   nothing in common with *e·* physiology or
103–23   It is *e·* ignorant or malicious,

either

s 119– 6   They *e·* presuppose the self-evolution
153–14   From it may be learned that *e·*
159–17   They would *e·* have allayed her fear or
ph 168– 5   removal of a single weight from *e·* scale
170–29   but in *e·* case dependent upon his
171– 9   *e·* of his life or of the weather,
181–18   In *e·* case you must improve your
f 203–17   We are prone to believe *e·* in more than one
211– 7   The sensations of the body must *e·* be
213– 6   conceives of something as *e·* liquid or solid,
213–28   discoursing *e·* discord or harmony
220–26   The belief that *e·* fasting or feasting makes
232– 7   no scatheless and permanent evidence of *e·*.
236–12   strongest educator, *e·* for or against crime.
236–15   *e·* after a model odious to herself or
237–20   keep out . . . *e·* sinful or diseased thoughts.
240–24   sooner or later, *e·* by suffering or by Science,
249–13   *E·* there is no omnipotence, or omnipotence is
c 258–21   so-called senses have no cognizance of *e·*
b 291–27   for the grave has no power over *e·*.
296– 6   *E·* here or hereafter, suffering or Science must
297–10   a change in *e·* a health-belief or a
323–30   We are *e·* turning away from this utterance, or
324–16   conquer sin, sickness, and death, *e·* here or
330–17   knowledge of it is left *e·* to human conjecture or
o 353– 9   *e·* in the form of sickness or of sin?
360–16   This ideal is *e·* temporal or eternal.
360–17   *E·* Spirit or matter is your model.
p 384– 2   Can matter, . . . *e·* feel or act without
385–32   coming from . . . as if *e·* were intelligent,
388–32   *e·* the food or this thought must be
390–24   no law of His to support the necessity *e·* of sin or
401–24   by applying the drug to *e·*?
415–17   *e·* retards the circulation or quickens it,
423– 3   not to be communicated to the patient, *e·* verbally or
424–18   *e·* by giving antagonistic advice or
426–20   master *e·* a desire to die or a dread of the grave
442–31   *e·* when asleep or when awake.
t 446– 7   may *e·* arise from the alarm of the physician, or
451– 9   will *e·* make shipwreck of their faith or
451–29   *e·* with a mistaken or a wicked purpose.
457–18   there is no good aspect, *e·* silvern or golden.
r 488–19   cannot be true *e·* of man or of his
490–29   Sleep shows material sense as *e·* oblivion,
g 508–18   does not necessarily refer *e·* to masculinity or
531–21   Who dares to say *e·* that God is in matter or
547–21   must *e·* return to Mind or
551– 3   *E·* Mind produces, or it is produced.
551–21   peculiarities of ancestry, belonging to *e·* sex,
ap 567–20   claiming that there is intelligence in matter *e·*

ejected

g 524–30   and eventually *e·* at the demand of matter?

ejection

sp 97– 2   They will aid in the *e·* of error.
ph 171–20   exposed to *e·* by the operation of

elaborate

pref x–14   She has made no effort to embellish, *e·*,

elaborated

s 141–14   Jesus *e·* the fact that the healing effect

elastic

s 128–13   becomes more *e·*, is capable of greater
161– 1   supple and *e·* condition of the healthy limb,

elasticity

ph 198–20   until the *e·* of mortal thought haply causes a

elders

a 41–28   The truth taught by Jesus, the *e·* scoffed at.
o 354–16   derived from the traditions of the *e·*

El Dorado

pr 9–21   This is the *E· D·* of Christianity.
ap 559–30   into the *E· D·* of faith and hope.

elect

c 266–23   material sense, . . . would deceive the very *e·*.

election

a 38– 5   old doctrine of . . . the *e·* of a few to be saved,

elective

m 63–20   If the *e·* franchise for women will remedy

electric

sp 78–22   through *e·*, material effects?
97– 9   and the *e·* current swift,
p 393–23   or the *e·* wire which you stretch,

electricity

destructive
sp 93–17   Destructive *e·* is not the offspring of

hypnotism and
sp 78–26   hypnotism and *e·* are claimed to be

spirits and
sp 80–29   believes that . . . emanates from spirits and *e·*.

trust in
ph 181– 9   When you manipulate patients, you trust in *e·*

electricity
wires nor
   sp 78–19 Spirit needs no wires nor *e·* in order to

—

   sp 73–16 through *e·* or any other form of matter,
   ph 178–30 may attempt to unite with it hypnotism, . . . *e·*;
   b 293– 3 *E·* is not a vital fluid,
   293–17 *E·* is the sharp surplus of materiality
   293–19 *e·* is not intelligent,
   t 450–32 *e·*, animal nature, and organic life,

element
destructive
   f 210–32 it is without a destructive *e·*.
essential
   o 347–18 restoring an essential *e·* of Christianity,
fleshly
   b 332–31 Into the real and ideal man the fleshly *e·* cannot
grossest
   ap 565– 9 Led on by the grossest *e·* of mortal mind,
human
   a 33–18 When the human *e·* in him struggled with
lost
   b 328–17 has been dormant, a lost *e·* of Christianity.
mental
   s 157– 5 whole force of the mental *e·* is employed
native
   p 383–15 It is the native *e·* of such a mind,
no
   b 311– 7 it is Spirit, which has no *e·* of self-destruction.
   g 503–23 no *e·* nor symbol of discord and decay.
no material
   ph 191– 7 will include in that likeness no material *e·*.
of error
   t 463–12 has not a single *e·* of error,
of evil
   g 539–11 God could never impart an *e·* of evil,
of progress
   f 233– 5 This is an *e·* of progress,
only
   ph 196– 9 for sin is the only *e·* of destruction.
swinish
   b 272– 8 the swinish *e·* in human nature uproots it.
the very
   s 134–19 robs Christianity of the very *e·*, which
this
   s 146– 3 Why has this *e·* of Christianity been lost?
turbulent
   ph 180–23 they should try to correct this turbulent *e·*

   b 310–24 Sin is the *e·* of self-destruction,
   p 392– 6 Fear, which is an *e·* of all disease,
   413–16 more vigorously in its own *e·*.
   r 480– 8 Nerves are an *e·* of the belief
   gl 583–25 not create an atom or an *e·* the opposite of

elementary
   p 372– 5 error in solution, *e·* mortal mind,
   p 559– 5 upon the sea, — upon *e·*, latent error,

elements
certain
   m 57– 6 through certain *e·* of the feminine,
different
   m 57– 9 These different *e·* conjoin naturally
dissolving
   r 490–22 along with the dissolving *e·* of clay.
evil
   sp 83– 7 evil *e·* now coming to the surface.
healing
   b 329– 2 the healing *e·* of pure Christianity will be
infinite
   g 512–21 From the infinite *e·* of the one Mind
material
   b 284–25 Even the more subtile and misnamed material *e·*
   r 475– 7 blood, bones, and other material *e·*.
   g 551–20 composed of the simplest material *e·*,
mortal
   p 374–29 is resolved into its primitive mortal *e·*.
primal
   ap 559–26 partaking of the nature, or primal *e·*, of Truth
symbols and
   b 280– 2 Symbols and *e·* of discord

—

   s 124–32 The *e·* and functions of the physical body
   f 224–28 Truth brings the *e·* of liberty.
   247– 3 two of the *e·* it had lost, sight and teeth.
   b 309–18 not in *e·* which are not spiritual,
   r 479–25 and they are the *e·* of nothingness.
   481–24 Sin has the *e·* of self-destruction.
   g 507– 3 while *water* symbolizes the *e·* of Mind.

elevate
   m 58– 2 intercourse with those adapted to *e·* it,
   f 235–18 will degrade the characters it should . . . *e·*.
   b 318–27 and are not adapted to *e·* mankind.
   r 492–11 will purify and *e·* character.

elevated
   a 45–20 hath *e·* them to possible at-one-ment
   ap 576–28 Jewish concept, not yet *e·* to deific apprehension
elevates
   b 323–22 *e·* even mortal mind to the contemplation
elevating
   m 57–24 enlarging, purifying, and *e·* it.
   s 146–21 *e·* effects practically prove its divine origin
   o 341– 3 *e·* them from a theoretical to a practical
   gl 583–15 and is found *e·* the race,
   586–14 FIRE. . . . affliction purifying and *e·* man.
elevation
   pr 7– 9 it gives momentary solemnity and *e·* to thought.
   m 63–24 the *e·* of society in general
   sp 98– 2 the *e·* of existence above mortal discord
   p 426–25 health and morals far beyond its present *e·*,
   t 444– 4 suffering is oft the divine agent in this *e·*.
eleven
   a 27–23 but only *e·* left a desirable historic record.
   49– 8 Were all conspirators save *e·*?
Elias
   s 136–15 some, *E·*; and others, Jeremias, — *Matt.* 16 : 14.
   136–19 controlled by the spirit of John or of *E·*.
   ap 562– 3 As *E·* presented the idea of the fatherhood
   gl 585– 9 definition of
   585–13 "*E·* truly shall first come and — *Matt.* 17 : 11.
elicited
   s 137–21 This assertion *e·* from Jesus the benediction,
Elijah
   s 139– 7 so did Joshua, *E·*, and Elisha.
eliminate
   o 348–18 Is it not well to *e·* from so-called mortal mind
eliminated
   b 273–15 till the errors of sense are *e·*.
Elisha
   s 139– 8 so did Joshua, Elijah, and *E·*.
Elohim
   b 320–32 stand in celestial perfection before *E·*,
   g 515–16 The eternal *E·* includes the
   515–17 The name *E·* is in the plural,
   523–18 the Supreme Being is therein called *E·*.
   523–25 it is *E·* (God) who creates.
   gl 591– 4 one Spirit, or intelligence, named *E·*, or God.
Elohistic
   g 523–17 One is called the *E·*, because
   538–18 no record in the *E·* introduction of Genesis,
Eloi, Eloi, lama sabachthani
   a 51– 1 the plaintive cry, "*E·*, *E·*, *l· s·*?" — *Mark* 15 : 34.
elongated
   s 162–21 shortened limbs have been *e·*,
eloquence
   sp 88–26 *E·* re-echoes the strains of Truth and Love.
   88–31 When *e·* proceeds from the belief that a
   89– 9 Destroy her belief in . . . and her *e·* disappears.
eloquent
   sp 89– 5 the devotee may become unwontedly *e·*.
   89–17 the tongue grows mute which before was *e·*.
else
   pr 3–12 reflected by man, — *e·* man is not the image
   11–24 if we desire holiness above all *e·*,
   a 25–29 *e·* we are not improving the great blessings
   m 58– 3 or *e·* joy's drooping wings trail in dust.
   sp 76– 4 forgets all *e·* and breathes aloud his rapture.
   89– 7 believing that somebody *e·* possesses her tongue
   s 109–13 searched the Scriptures and read little *e·*,
   119– 7 or *e·* they assume that matter is the product of
   135–22 *e·* one or the other is false and useless ;
   143– 6 *e·* Jesus would have recommended and
   ph 168– 8 which would otherwise outweigh all *e·*.
   182–28 or *e·* from ignorance of C. S. and its
   197–31 *e·* his belief in its reality and fatality will
   f 205– 1 *e·* God will continue to be hidden from
   206– 5 *e·* it will misguide the judgment
   208–18 "God is the father of mind, and of nothing *e·*."
   220–19 and then charges them to something *e·*,
   c 263–22 *e·* it is a new multiplication or self-division
   b 272– 7 *e·* it beareth not much fruit,
   289– 9 He is little *e·* than the expression of error.
   310– 9 *e·* the clay would have power over the potter.
   331–22 reflected by . . . and by nothing *e·*.
   335–20 for Spirit is more than all *e·*
   336–21 *e·* God would be manifestly finite,
   p 414–22 there is none *e·* beside Him." — *Deut.* 4 : 35.
   435–26 For naught *e·* can he be punished,
   r 466–20 Soul or Spirit signifies Deity and nothing *e·*.
   478–26 of material human beliefs and of nothing *e·*.
   481– 3 tributary to God, Spirit, and to nothing *e·*.
   g 551–28 All must be Mind, or *e·* all must be matter.

elsewhere
ph 190– 7   neither . . . is found in brain or *e·* in matter
     195– 4   said that he should never be happy *e·*.
b 277– 3   and *e·* the Scripture says that
gl 598– 7   and *e·* in the New Testament.

elucidate
pref xii–21   in order to *e·* her idealism.
r 465– 5   to *e·* scientific metaphysics.

elucidates
gl 579– 3   often *e·* the meaning of the inspired

elucidation
o 349–18   The *e·* of C. S. lies in its spiritual sense,

elude
f 252–19   and says: . . . I *e·* detection by smooth-tongued
p 440– 1   he could not possibly *e·* their search.

emanate
f 229– 7   whence did they *e·*?
     236– 2   Truth should *e·* from the pulpit,
b 273– 2   contrary to God, and cannot *e·* from Him.
g 512–22   From . . . Mind *e·* all form, color,
ap 564–17   barbarity of his foes could *e·* from

emanates
sp 80–29   believes that this wonder *e·* from spirits
g 504– 1   from which *e·* the true idea,

emanating
s 118–15   *e·* from the invisible and infinite power
c 257– 1   infinite image or idea *e·* from this Mind.
b 284–29   spiritual, *e·* from divine Mind.
g 508–15   the pure thought *e·* from divine Mind.

emanation
an 104–15   as the *e·* of divine Mind,
s 127–26   Science is an *e·* of divine Mind,
g 519– 5   the *e·*, of His infinite self-containment

emanations
sp 88–11   Ideas are *e·* from the divine Mind.
b 336–16   They are the *e·* of Him who is Life,

emancipate
r 223–23   They will *e·* humanity, and supplant

emancipated
g 546– 2   at some future time to be *e·* from it,

emasculation
b 271– 5   Neither *e·*, illusion, nor insubordination

embellish
pref x–14   She has made no effort to *e·*,

embellishments
f 247–28   *e·* of the person are poor substitutes

emblem
f 238–31   The cross is the central *e·* of history.

embodied
sp 93–29   this is the error *e·* in the belief that
p 372–11   belief . . . that man can enter his own *e·*

embodies
b 299– 3   which *e·* his conception of an unseen quality

embodiment
r 225–16   proportionate to its *e·* of right thinking.
b 333–13   the life of which Christ Jesus was the *e·*.
o 350–27   Hence its *e·* in the incarnate Jesus,
r 491–25   apparently with their own separate *e·*.
ap 563–15   lifts the veil from this *e·* of all evil,

embody
ph 192–23   good you do and *e·* gives you the only power

embrace
pr 7–15   may *e·* too much love of applause
f 208–29   You *e·* your body in your thought,·
c 258– 2   finite conception of God cannot *e·* the

embraced
t 463– 3   under influences not *e·* in his diagnosis,
g 503– 2   which are *e·* in the infinite Mind

embracing
sp 77–14   *e·* its so-called pleasures and pains,
f 208–10   *e·* sin, sickness, and death
ap 561–17   in the man Jesus, as divinity *e·* humanity
gl 589– 4   A corporeal mortal *e·* duplicity.

embryo
f 236–13   Her thoughts form the *e·* of another
r 476– 4   declares that man begins . . . as a material *e·*.
gl 583– 2   God's thoughts, not in *e·*, but in maturity ;

embryology
g 550–25   *E·* supplies no instance of one species
     553– 1   in the various forms of *e·*,

embryonic
ph 188– 6   an *e·* thought without motive ;
     189–28   the development of *e·* mortal mind,
     190– 1   formation of so-called *e·* mortal mind,
     190– 8   This *e·* and materialistic human belief
g 547–14   the germinating speck of so-called *e·* life

embryonic
g 548–29   facts in regard to so-called *e·* life.
     550–22   If Life is God, . . . then Life is not *e·*,
ap 561– 6   at a point of so-called *e·* life.

emeralds
sp 87–19   The mine knows naught of the *e·* within

emerge
r 485–14   *E·* gently from matter into Spirit.
g 549–17   one or more individualities subsequently *e·* ;
     552–16   Mortals must *e·* from this notion

emergence
g 553–25   as the point of *e·* for the human race,

emergency
p 406– 5   which is equal to every *e·*,

emerging
s 148–11   as *e·* from the lowest, instead of from

emigrant
p 383–12   A hint may be taken from the *e·*,

emit
b 273–30   beliefs *e·* the effects of error at all times,
g 504–26   vague conjectures *e·* no such effulgence.

emits
c 262–25   even as light *e·* light without effort ;

Emmaus
a 46– 5   In the walk to *E·*, Jesus was known

emolument
f 236– 6   *e·* . . . which many leaders seek?

emotion
pr 7–18   produces material ecstasy and *e·*.
ph 180–16   reservoir already overflowing with that *e·*.

emotional
pr 14– 7   is to have, not mere *e·* ecstasy or faith,
a 25–27   all the *e·* love we can bestow on him, will never

emphasize
g 516–27   To *e·* this momentous thought,

emphasizes
s 116–20   C. S. strongly *e·* the thought that

emphatic
g 520–23   Here is the *e·* declaration that God

emphatically
p 369–24   preventive and curative) arts belong *e·* to C. S.

empire
p 378–22   not an intelligence to dispute the *e·* of Mind

empires
pref vii–20   Though *e·* fall, "the Lord shall— *Exod.* 15 : 18.
sp 94–12   The eastern *e·* and nations owe their
s 121– 8   the fate of *e·* and the fortunes of men.

employ
a 44–18   that he might *e·* his feet as before.
s 143– 5   God does not *e·* drugs or hygiene,
     157–21   why did Jesus not *e·* them
ph 181–11   and for that reason, you *e·* matter
f 218–21   and *e·* means which lead only into
     235–19   Physicians, whom the sick *e·* in their
p 390–31   as a legislator would *e·* to defeat the passage of
     418–23   By the truthful arguments you *e·*,
gl 598– 9   to *e·* words of material significance

employed
an 102–28   abused by its possessor, than otherwise *e·*,
s 112– 1   proved itself, whenever scientifically *e·*,
     116–25   are commonly and ignorantly *e·*,
     143– 7   else Jesus would have . . . *e·* them
     156– 7   Tapping had been *e·*, and yet,
     157– 5   whole force of the mental element is *e·*
ph 186– 8   under whatever name . . . they are *e·* ;
o 349–25   material terms must be generally *e·*.
p 403–10   The human mind is *e·* to remove the illusion
     422–24   A surgeon is *e·* in one case,
g 502–25   word *beginning* is *e·* to signify *the only*,
gl 590–15   this term is sometimes *e·* as a title,

employers
p 439– 5   advertises largely for his *e·*.

employing
s 156–26   *e·* no other means, and she was cured.
p 421–29   or by *e·* a single material application

employs
an 104–23   The hypnotizer *e·* one error to destroy
s 127–10   The terms . . . C. S., or Science alone, she *e·*

empowers
ph 199–10   and *e·* man through its mandate,

emptied
f 201–14   They must first be *e·*.

emptiness
gl 599– 7   *E·* ; unfaithfulness ; desolation.

empty
  pr 3–17 How *e·* are our conceptions of Deity !
  a 54–11 *e·* or sin-filled human storehouses,
  f 234–20 and *e·* it of sin and sickness,
emptying
  ph 186– 2 *e·* his thought of the false stimulus
empurpled
  ph 175–26 *e·* the plump cheeks of our ancestors,
empyrean
  s 121–10 was to them displayed upon the *e·*,
emulate
  a 37–16 learn to *e·* him in *all* his ways
  ph 185–17 strove to *e·* the wonders wrought by Moses.
  g 515– 2 enables its possessor to *e·* the example of
emulations
  an 106–22 hatred, variance, *e·*, wrath,— *Gal. 5 : 20.*
enable
  pr 4–29 watchfulness, and devout obedience *e·* us to
  17– 2 *E· us to know,* — as in heaven, so on earth,
  a 42–29 He was here to *e·* them to test his
  o 354– 6 to *e·* them to leave all for Christ,
  p 365– 9 *e·* them to rise above the supposed necessity
  366– 5 *e·* him to cast physical evils out of his patient ;
  378– 5 *e·* you to commute this self-sentence,
  426–26 would *e·* us to hold the banner of Christianity
enabled
  pref xi–30 *e·* her to get this institution chartered
  a 24–30 *e·* their Master to triumph over the grave,
  28–14 *e·* to heal the sick and to triumph over sin.
  30– 9 this *e·* him to be the mediator,
  35– 7 *e·* to rise somewhat from mortal sensuousness,
  43– 4 *e·* the disciples to understand what Jesus
  51–30 which *e·* Jesus to heal the sick,
  54–24 it *e·* them to understand the Nazarene
  sp 94–25 *e·* him to direct those thoughts aright ;
  b 315–21 *e·* him to demonstrate the facts of being,
  324–23 *e·* him to follow the example and teachings
  r 482–22 *e·* Jesus to demonstrate his control over matter.
  g 534– 3 This hereafter *e·* woman to be the
  534– 5 This *e·* woman to be first to interpret
enables
  pr 3–11 *e·* us to work out our own salvation.
  10–14 It is striving that *e·* us to enter.
  a 19–23 and *e·* man to do the will of wisdom.
  sp 84–14 Acquaintance with the Science of being *e·*
  87–15 Science *e·* one to read the human mind,
  87–17 It *e·* one to heal through Mind,
  s 147– 1 This system *e·* the learner to demonstrate
  147–21 and *e·* you to grasp the spiritual facts
  ph 174–22 belief is all that *e·* a drug to cure
  f 238– 8 *e·* one to be Christian.
  b 317–19 and *e·* him to conquer sin,
  o 350– 9 *e·* them to interpret his spiritual meaning.
  p 392– 8 *e·* truth to outweigh error.
  r 493–14 *e·* the healer to demonstrate . . . the Principle
  496–16 *e·* you to demonstrate, with scientific certainty,
  g 515– 1 *e·* its possessor to emulate the example of Jesus.
enabling
  sp 85– 8 *e·* one to do good, but not evil.
enact
  p 440–23 beliefs . . . compel them to *e·* wicked laws of
enactment
  p 384–11 belief of mortal mind, not an *e·* of wisdom,
enactments
  p 381–20 Think less of the *e·* of mortal mind,
enamoured
  f 245–20 coaxed the *e·* lightning from the clouds.
enchantment
  f 209–15 Nearness, not distance, lends *e·* to this view.
enclosure
  g 550–23 An egg is an impossible *e·* for Deity.
encompass
  g 551–25 Darkness and doubt *e·* thought, so long as
encompassing
  r 496–19 overlying, and *e·* all true being.
  gl 585–16 Divine Science *e·* the universe and man ;
  597–29 God's spiritual government, *e·* all things.
encounter
  f 254–28 If you launch your bark . . . you will *e·* storms.
encountered
  a 28–29 The trials *e·* by prophet, disciple, and
encourage
  pr 7–16 to induce or *e·* Christian sentiment.
  p 396–11 nor *e·* in the patient's thought the
encouragement
  b 339–11 sinner can receive no *e·* from the
  p 363–31 there was *e·* in the mere fact that
  367– 4 tender word and Christian *e·* of an invalid,

encourages
  b 320–28 and *e·* mortals to hope in Him
encouraging
  m 63–22 without *e·* difficulties of greater
end (noun)
  beginning and
  b 282– 8 the finite, which has both beginning and *e·*.
  338– 5 belief — that man . . . has beginning and *e·*,
  gl 580–22 supposition that Life . . . has beginning and *e·* ;
  beginning or
  b 282– 7 represents the infinite without beginning or *e·* ;
  g 521– 5 narrative of being that is without beginning
    or *e·*.
  gl 585– 6 which are likewise without beginning or *e·*.
  beginning to
  s 139– 4 From beginning to *e·*, the Scriptures
  r 478–25 From beginning to *e·*, whatever is mortal
  ap 559–21 Read this book from beginning to *e·*.
  no
  ap 565–15 there shall be no *e·*," — *Luke* 1 : 33.
  of error
  sp 95–19 We welcome . . . the *e·* of error,
  96–19 disturbances will continue until the *e·* of error,
  their
  pr 5–20 the Psalmist could see their *e·*,
  this
  pr 5– 6 To this *e·* we are placed under the
  a 22–12 for to this *e·* God worketh with you.
  until the
  sp 96–19 disturbances will continue until the *e·* of error,
  g 533–25 and multiplies until the *e·* thereof.
  unto the
  sp 96–10 will continue unto the *e·*,
  t 446–23 even unto the *e·* of the world." — *Matt.* 28 : 20.
  without
  f 253– 6 life, without beginning and without *e·*,
  r 468–27 Life is without beginning and without *e·*.

  sp 96–27 he . . . will endure to the *e·*.
  s 139–10 even when the *e·* has been brightness
  f 212–11 attempt to scratch the *e·* of a finger which
  c 259–30 to the *e·* that they may produce harmonious
  b 331–10 testifies to a beginning and an *e·*.
  333–18 without beginning of years or *e·* of days.
  p 401–11 to the *e·* of producing a higher
  r 484–26 thus putting an *e·* to the hypotheses
  g 501–14 which subserve the *e·* of natural good,
  523–28 intertwined to the *e·* of chapter twelve,
  538–29 they must consequently have an *e·*,
  ap 564–30 From the beginning to the *e·*, the serpent
  569–20 What must the *e·* be?
  gl 592– 5 a beginning and therefore an *e·* ;
end (verb)
  f 214–27 when a wound on the retina may *e·* the
  227– 8 law of the divine Mind must *e·* human bondage,
  245–32 infinite never began nor will it ever *e·*.
  249–15 infinity never began, will never *e·*,
  c 262–28 To begin rightly is to *e·* rightly.
  b 292– 2 will *e·* the battle of Truth with error
  331– 5 subject to their limitations and would *e·* in death.
  p 376–27 Destroy fear, and you *e·* fever.
  427–15 Nothing can . . . *e·* the existence of man
  r 491–12 facts of being, in which all must *e·*.
  g 532–27 error began and will *e·* the dream of matter.
  536–20 Passions and appetites must *e·* in pain.
endeavor
  sp 96–31 wicked minds will *e·* to find means
  ph 169–23 towards which human faith or *e·* is directed.
  b 323– 4 This strife consists in the *e·* to forsake error
  p 368–14 has little inspiration to nerve *e·*.
endeavored
  a 27–31 *e·* to hold him at the mercy of matter
  s 152– 5 author has *e·* to make this book the Æsculapius
    of
endeavoring
  f 246– 7 and *e·* to reach Spirit
  p 426– 8 in *e·* to reach it.
  432–26 *e·* to assist the prisoner to escape
endeavors
  a 22–15 If your *e·* are beset by fearful odds,
  f 253–20 right *e·* against sin or sickness,
  p 426–14 Man should renew his energies and *e·*,
ended
  s 123–26 not specially belong to a dispensation now *e·*,
  g 519–22 God *e·* His work which — *Gen.* 2 : 2.
endeth
  ap 567–12 Thus *e·* the conflict between the flesh and
ending
  p 429–23 it must also have an *e·*,
  r 469– 6 it would also have an *e·*.
  g 550–17 as beginning and *e·*, and with birth, decay, and

enjoined
　a 55– 4　the idea of Christian healing *e·* by Jesus ;
　p 441– 7　but be *e·* to keep perpetual silence,
　t 463–25　He never *e·* obedience to the laws of nature,

enjoy
　pr 9–15　before we can *e·* the fruition of our hope
　ph 176–28　human mind, . . . is supposed to feel, suffer, *e·*.
　181– 7　Matter, which can neither suffer nor *e·*,
　f 212– 1　We suffer or *e·* in our dreams,
　246–22　would *e·* more than threescore years and ten
　250–16　A mortal may be weary or pained, *e·* or suffer,
　p 397–26　walk, see, hear, *e·*, or suffer in dreams.

enjoyed
　f 221–25　but he never *e·* his food as he had

enjoyment
　m 61– 3　The senses confer no real *e·*.
　p 397– 8　Suffering is no less a mental condition than is *e·*.
　406–32　There is no *e·* in getting drunk,

enjoyments
　m 60–32　Higher *e·* alone can satisfy the cravings

enjoys
　b 294–10　belief that matter *e·* and suffers.
　322–17　drunkard thinks he *e·* drunkenness,
　p 414–25　matter neither feels, suffers, nor *e·*.
　gl 582–16　has spiritual bliss and *e·* but cannot suffer.

enlarge
　ph 199– 3　might be thought true that hammering would *e·*
　p 430– 6　Faith should *e·* its borders

enlarged
　a 46–32　they were roused to an *e·* understanding
　s 151–11　and were in possession of the *e·* power
　c 258–22　The human capacities are *e·* and perfected
　265– 5　treasures of Truth and Love are *e·*.
　265–12　but confers upon man *e·* individuality,
　g 557–13　towards *e·* understanding and intelligence ;

enlarges
　s 128– 9　*e·* their perception of character,
　ph 199–10　Mind alone *e·* and empowers man

enlarging
　m 57–23　Love enriches the nature, *e·*,

enlighten
　pr 2– 3　Do we pray . . . to *e·* the infinite
　g 510– 9　Truth and Love *e·* the understanding,

enlightened
　pr 12–24　help should come from the *e·* understanding.
　15–31　Trustworthiness is the foundation of *e·* faith.

enlightening
　g 538–12　*e·* and sustaining the universe.

enlightenment
　a 45– 8　Jesus' deed was for the *e·* of men
　t 462– 7　understanding, potency, *e·*, and success.
　g 556–17　Did . . . the *e·* of the race come from the

enlisted
　ph 168– 9　when it ought to be *e·* on the side of health.
　t 450–19　Christian Scientist has *e·* to lessen evil,

enmity
　s 131–10　carnal mind is *e·* against God." — *Rom.* 8 : 7.
　b 273–12　Hence the *e·* between Science and the senses,
　315–14　Their carnal minds were at *e·* with it.
　g 534– 9　I will put *e·* between thee and — *Gen.* 3 : 15.
　534–19　carnal mind is *e·* against God ; — *Rom.* 8 : 7.

Enoch's
　f 214– 5　If *E·* perception had been confined to the

enough
　pr 10– 6　If good *e·* to profit by Jesus' cup
　a 28–22　it is *e·* if thou art found worthy to unloose the
　41–30　It was *e·* for them to believe in a national Deity ;
　f 224–12　sects many but not *e·* Christianity.
　o 345–16　well *e·* to pass judgment upon them.
　354–15　Surely it is not *e·* to cleave to
　355–32　Strangely *e·*, we ask for material
　p 365–19　If the Scientist has *e·* Christly affection to
　365–21　Christian *e·* to practise scientifically
　g 520– 5　That is *e·* !

enrages
　o 345–29　*e·* the carnal mind and is the main cause

enraptured
　f 246–15　should dawn upon the *e·* sense
　b 323–11　until boundless thought walks *e·*,

enrich
　sp 79–32　neither does withholding *e·* us.

enriches
　m 57–23　Love *e·* the nature, enlarging, purifying,
　o 361–29　*e·* mankind only when it is understood,

en route
　a 21–15　to Europe, while I am *e· r·* for California,

enshroud
　sp 98–27　Mystery does not *e·* Christ's teachings,

enslave
　ph 187–11　beliefs of the human mind rob and *e·* it,

enslavement
　f 228–11　The *e·* of man is not legitimate.
　p 373–15　are the sources of man's *e·*.
　407– 6　Man's *e·* to the most relentless masters

enslaves
　f 225– 2　Whatever *e·* man is opposed to the

enslaving
　f 227– 6　claims of the *e·* senses must be denied

ensnare
　an 102–21　they *e·* the age into indolence,

ensue
　m 65–20　There will *e·* a fermentation over this

ensues
　p 433–16　A brief consultation *e·*, and the jury
　gl 581–21　confusion *e·*, and the more certain is the

ensuing
　p 397–19　you will find the *e·* good effects to be

ensure
　m 64–29　*e·* the stability of the marriage covenant.
　ph 194–11　are not necessary to *e·* deafness
　ap 571– 5　necessary to *e·* the avoidance of the evil

ensured
　o 357–13　and error's destruction *e·* ;

ensures
　c 260–17　and *e·* failure at the outset.

entangled
　f 227–27　bound you, *e·* your free limbs,

enter
　pr 10–15　It is striving that enables us to *e·*.
　14–31　*e·* into thy closet, — *Matt.* 6 : 6.
　15– 9　To *e·* into the heart of prayer,
　15–14　we must *e·* into the closet and shut the door.
　a 21–10　he is striving to *e·* in.
　40–22　rejoicing to *e·* into fellowship with him
　40–32　but in order to *e·* into the kingdom,
　m 63–30　*e·* into business agreements, hold real estate,
　66–10　Through great tribulation we *e·* the kingdom.
　sp 70– 6　can never *e·* the atmosphere of Spirit.
　99–12　None may pick the lock nor *e·* by some other
　f 228– 6　nothing inharmonious can *e·* being,
　238–15　to *e·* unlawfully into the labors of others.
　241–32　than for sinful beliefs to *e·* the kingdom of
　b 269–12　matter does not *e·* into metaphysical premises
　281– 2　by which we *e·* into the kingdom of Truth
　332–32　Into the . . . ideal man the fleshly element
　　　　　cannot *e·*.
　336–20　A portion of God could not *e·* man ;
　p 372–11　belief . . . that man can *e·* his own embodied
　382–23　shall in no wise *e·* therein." — *Luke* 18 : 17.
　384–11　and man has only to *e·* his protest
　398– 3　and *e·* no more into him." — *Mark* 9 : 25.
　399–29　"How can one *e·* into a — *Matt.* 12 : 29.
　419–18　lest aught unfit for development *e·* thought.
　440–28　forbidden to *e·* against Mortal Man
　441– 6　not permitted to *e·* any suits at the bar of Soul,
　t 451–12　strive, to *e·* the narrow path of Life,
　r 481– 6　free "to *e·* into the holiest," — *Heb.* 10 : 19.
　g 524–31　Does Spirit *e·* dust, and lose therein
　525– 1　Does Mind, God, *e·* matter
　544–30　to *e·* man's nostrils so that
　ap 577–26　nothing can *e·* that city, which

entered
　m 59– 1　Matrimony should never be *e·* into without
　sp 76–11　understood that Spirit never *e·* matter
　gl 580–26　supposition . . . creator *e·* what He created,

entering
　ph 193– 2　On *e·* the house I met his physician,
　t 457–11　Her prime object, since *e·* this field of labor,
　r 478– 6　never beheld Spirit . . . leaving a body or *e·* it.
　g 522–20　Spirit is represented as *e·* matter

enters
　f 228–12　It will cease when man *e·* into his heritage
　b 277–28　in every statement into which it *e·*.
　336– 2　Mind never *e·* the finite.
　336– 4　Good never *e·* into evil,
　p 369– 7　He *e·* into a diviner sense of the facts,
　442–16　Neither animal magnetism nor hypnotism *e·*
　g 503–12　No supposition of error *e·* there.
　529–22　or into the metaphor only as evil.
　530–31　*Second*, it supposes that mind *e·* matter,
　538–20　Until that . . . *e·* into the arena,
　gl 580–11　supposition . . . that the infinite *e·* the

entertain
　sp 80–12　I *e·* no doubt of the humanity and
　f 214–18　We bow down to matter, and *e·* finite thoughts
　232– 5　beliefs we commonly *e·* about happiness
　b 299–17　and we *e·* "angels unawares." — *Heb.* 13 : 2.

entertain

p 391–10 Banish the belief that you can possibly e· a
418–24 spirit of Truth and Love which you e·,
g 548–16 by which men may e· angels,
ap 560–16 or e· a false estimate of anyone whom

entertained

a 54–32 if he e· any other sense of being
p 411–22 always induced by a false sense mentally e·,
g 545–22 The translators . . . e· a false sense of being.
ap 574–30 an angel e· unawares.

entertainer

p 364–13 had done what his rich e· had neglected to do,

entertaining

f 237–17 kept from discussing or e· theories
b 280–31 The only excuse for e· human opinions

entertains

f 250–17 according to the dream he e· in sleep.
p 422–27 e· fears and doubts as to the ultimate

enthroned

f 252–25 and says : . . . I am e· in the gorgeousness of
c 266–26 infinite Mind e· is heaven.
b 306–26 Science, still e·, is unfolding to mortals
t 454–10 hate has . . . no kingdom. Love is e·.

enthrones

ph 186–31 it e· matter as deity.
p 394–12 and e· matter through error.
t 446–21 To understand God . . . e· faith in Truth,
ap 571–32 He e· pure and undefiled religion,

enthusiasm

gl 599– 5 Zeal. . . . Blind e· ; mortal will.

entire

m 62– 4 The e· education of children should be
s 118–11 It must destroy the e· mass of error,
151–27 e· being is found harmonious
157–28 C. S. impresses the e· corporeality,
ph 183–21 man's e· obedience, affection, and strength.
f 219–29 E· immunity from the belief in sin,
244–21 If . . . God is without His e· manifestation,
252–11 e· mortal, material error finally disappears,
c 262– 7 ascribes to Him the e· glory.
b 277–17 throughout the e· round of nature.
p 371–31 Truth is an alterative in the e· system,
384–32 over the e· functions and organs of the
408– 7 throughout the e· round of the material senses,
t 443– 7 e· confidence in omnipotent Mind
461– 7 illustrates and proves the e· Principle.
r 494– 1 and to govern man's e· action?
496– 5 and governs the e· universe.
g 502– 4 preponderance of unreality in the e·
537–12 represented as spiritual, e·, and good.

entirely

pr 14–25 E· separate from the belief and dream of
s 156–30 matter disappears from the remedy e·,
o 353– 6 testimony of the physical senses yields e·
g 545–16 material theory, which is e· a false view,

entireness

b 293–30 the e· of God, good, and the nothingness of evil.

entities

f 204– 8 antagonistic e· and beings,

entitled

a 42–10 Though e· to the homage of the world
s 127– 6 e· to a classification as truth,
ph 183–31 the one Mind only is e· to honor.
b 312–32 richly endowed him and e· him to
r 493–12 in a previous chapter e· C. S. Practice.

entitles

t 456– 8 This alone e· them to the high standing

entity

all
p 369– 5 loses to human sense all e· as man,
eternal
b 301–13 constitutes the only real and eternal e·.
lose his
r 477–31 man, divorced from Spirit, would lose his e·.
man's
o 356– 6 sickness, and death do not prove man's e·
no real
f 250– 7 mortal existence has no real e·,
g 506– 4 Therefore matter, . . . has no real e·.
nor power
g 555–13 C. S. attributes to error neither e· nor power,
real
ph 186–17 It says : "I am a real e·,
without
r 470–28 If . . . Deity was unexpressed — that is, without e·.

sp 92– 9 Mind is not an e· within the cranium
o 359–12 to man's existence or e·,
p 399–25 This misnamed mind is not an e·.

entrance

a 20–26 It commands sure e· into the realm of Love.
p 393– 3 through divine help we can forbid this e·.

entreat

ph 182–22 Mortals e· the divine Mind to heal the sick,

entry

a 42–12 his brief triumphal e· into Jerusalem

enumerates

s 152–30 Jahr, . . . e· the general symptoms,

enunciator

g 524–22 How could . . . error be the e· of Truth?

environment

sp 87– 8 their mental e· remains

environments

c 258–10 which must escape from its e·
g 521– 2 lifts man above the sod, above earth and its e·,

Envy

p 430–23 Hypnotism, E·, Greed and Ingratitude,

envy (see also envy's)

and hate
a 48–21 was silent before e· and hate.
t 462–27 selfishness, malice, e·, and hate.
bigotry, nor
r 484– 4 neither pride, prejudice, bigotry, nor e·
or jealousy
m 64– 8 Pride, e·, or jealousy seems on most occasions

a 47–20 this spiritual distance inflamed Judas' e·.
51–25 motives of his persecutors were pride, e·,
s 115–22 pride, e·, deceit, hatred, revenge,
ph 188– 9 dishonesty, e·, hatred, revenge
f 218–11 malice, lust, appetite, e·, hate."
241– 3 incurs the hostility of e· ;
241– 9 Falsehood, e·, hypocrisy, malice, hate,
b 289–10 To suppose that sin, lust, hatred, e·,
330–30 dishonesty, selfishness, e·, hypocrisy,
p 404–29 e·, dishonesty, fear, . . . make a man sick,
407– 7 passion, selfishness, e·, hatred,
419– 2 Lurking error, lust, e·, revenge, malice, or
t 445–22 Self-seeking, e·, passion, pride, hatred,
452–12 Your advancing course may provoke e·,
464–24 weapons of bigotry, ignorance, e·, fall
ap 564–25 death, e·, hatred, and revenge, — all evil,
gl 582– 6 pride ; e· ; fame ; illusion ;
589– 2 e· ; hatred ; selfishness ; self-will ; lust.
589–14 sensuality ; e· ; oppression ; tyranny.
593– 8 animal magnetism ; e· ; revenge.

envyings

an 106–23 e·, murders, drunkenness, — Gal. 5 : 21.

envy's

g 542–24 To e· own hell, justice consigns the

ephemeral

c 267– 4 offspring of God start not from matter or e· dust.
r 485– 9 e· views of error ought to be obliterated

epileptic

p 398– 2 as when he said to the e· boy,

epistle

an 106–18 in his great e· to the Galatians,
s 112–22 characterized in the e· to the Hebrews.
b 313–16 the author of this remarkable e·
321– 3 Paul says, in his first e· to the Corinthians,
g 534–18 Paul says in his e· to the Romans :

epistles

b 319–32 what the beloved disciple meant in one of his e·

epizoötic

ph 179–18 The e· is a humanly evolved ailment,

epoch

m 67–32 The e· approaches when the understanding

equal

m 67–10 nautical science is not e· to the Science of
sp 80– 3 A cup of coffee or tea is not the e· of truth,
83– 4 artifice and delusion claimed that they could e
s 117– 5 one alone and without an e·.
133–24 made "himself e· with God," — John 5 : 18.
b 314– 9 but one Mind without a second or e·.
368–11 beliefs . . . that evil is e· in power to good
406– 5 is e· to every emergency,
418–10 if your fidelity is half e· to the
r 489– 9 In infancy this belief is not e· to
ap 560–23 made him e· to his great mission.
574–23 the four e· sides of which were heaven-bestowed

equalizes

b 340–28 e· the sexes ; annuls the curse on man,

equalling

s 108–16 three multiplied by three, e· nine,

equally
sp 73–21   E· incorrect is the belief that spirit
   90–11   will be found to be e· possible for the body
ph 167–24   or to expect to work e· with Spirit and matter,
f 211–11   Is it not e· true that matter does not
  221–21   and it is e· far from Science,
  224–18   is less material . . . but it is e· as cutting.
  231–26   To hold yourself superior to . . . is e· wise,
o 349–29   To a certain extent this is e· true of all
p 383–14   To the mind e· gross, dirt gives no uneasiness.
  424–15   It is e· important in metaphysical practice
  438–19   Another witness, e· inadequate, said

equals
f 231–9   no lesser power e· the infinite All-power ;

equator
sp 90–7   the imaginary line called the e·

equip
s 155–9   e· the medicine with their faith,

equipoise
s 124–22   support the e· of that thought-force,

equipollence
s 110–9   The e· of God brought to light another

equipped
b 328–15   man's power, when he is e· by God,

equitable
p 440–30   just and e· decisions of divine Spirit

equity
p 435–24   Supreme Judge in e· decides what penalty

equivalent
pr 6–13   will furnish more than its e· of pain,
gl 598–13   e· to our common statement,

equivalents
g 525–7   some of the e· of the term *man*

era
Christian
a 20–9   which we call the Christian e· ;
  55–6   Perhaps the early Christian e· did Jesus
s 138–17   Jesus established in the Christian e·
  139–8   The Christian e· was ushered in with
b 333–17   marked the first century of the Christian e·,
  333–20   both before and after the Christian e·,
r 474–5   accorded to Truth in the early Christian e·
g 534–26   since the Christian e· began.
new
a 43–18   opened a new e· for the world.
spiritual
m 65–16   struggling against the advancing spiritual e·.

eradicate
s 142–1   and it will e· sickness and sin
ph 180–20   even before they go to work to e· the disease
p 400–12   E· the image of disease from the

eradicated
t 446–32   Ignorance of the error to be e·

erase
sp 81–20   E· the figures which express number,
b 290–2   was and is and shall be, whom nothing can e·.

ere
pref vii–3   e· cometh the full radiance of a

erect
p 442–11   His form was e· and commanding,

erected
s 161–21   a statue of Liberty, e· near the guillotine :

erects
g 523–10   which God e· between the true and false.

erelong
ph 179–30   may e· reap the effect of this mistake.
  192–25   which e· betrays its weakness and falls,

err
b 272–9   "Ye do e·, not knowing the— *Matt.* 22 : 29.
g 555–27   or . . . confers the ability to e·.

erring
pr 15–10   the door of the e· senses must be closed.
m 62–26   the laws of e·, human concepts.
s 108–30   My discovery, that e·, mortal, . . . *mind*
  151–5   e·, finite, human mind has an absolute need
  157–23   E· mortal mind confers the power which
ph 166–15   The e· human mind is inharmonious
  186–7   E· human mind-forces can work only evil
  187–27   If you take away this e· mind,
  188–1   only as the mortal, e· mind yields to God,
  192–11   E· power is a material belief,
f 202–29   senseless matter or e· mortal mind
  206–8   e·, human thought acts injuriously
  211–22   the thoughts of one e· mind
  239–27   If it comes from e· mortal mind,
  253–12   outside of e·, mortal, material sense
c 260–7   The conceptions of mortal, e· thought
b 279–1   the e·, changing, and dying,

erring
t 447–6   you must not forget that e· human opinions,
  459–12   Any attempt to heal mortals with e·
r 472–28   seem real to human, e· belief,
  477–13   corporeal senses to be mortal and e· illusions.
  494–17   thus helping e· human sense to flee from
g 503–24   God creates neither e· thought, mortal life,
  505–30   The mortal, e·, and finite are human beliefs,
gl 587–14   supposititious minds, . . . e· and mortal ;

erroneous
sp 71–22   spiritualism will be found mainly e·,
  91–19   and destroys the e· knowledge
  91–22   Certain e· postulates should be
s 112–29   is e·, for it inculcates a breach of
  116–26   confused and e· conceptions of divinity
  121–23   Science shows appearances often to be e·,
  150–23   it is as evidently e· to the author,
  155–16   e· general belief, which sustains medicine
ph 177–16   e· theory of life and intelligence in matter,
  184–2   The premises being e·, the conclusions
  185–26   E· mental practice may seem
  185–28   because e· methods act on and through the
f 204–18   Such theories are evidently e·.
  223–26   slumbering thought from its e· dream
c 267–21   inverted thoughts and e· beliefs
b 277–32   sometimes beautiful, always e·.
o 352–24   traditional beliefs, e· and man-made.
p 372–2   mortal body is only an e· mortal belief
  375–16   unscientific mental practice is e·
  378–20   represented by two material e· bases.
  395–23   It is no less e· to believe in the
  396–25   with which to combat their e· sense,
  401–17   Truth is destroying e· mortal belief.
r 472–21   absurdity— namely, e· *truth*.
  478–18   The assertion that there can be . . . is e·.
  480–15   Inharmony has no Principle ; its action is e·
  487–24   The belief that life is sentient . . . is e·.
g 522–18   In this e· theory, matter takes the place of
  526–20   e· doctrine that the knowledge of evil is
  536–24   Mortal mind accepts the e·,
  543–23   creations of e· thought, not of matter.
  554–9   following from a misconception of life, is e·,
gl 588–17   whatever reflects not this one Mind, is . . . e·,
    (*see also* **belief, postulate**)

erroneously
b 274–17   what we e· term the five physical
  282–25   mortal thought, always governing itself e·.

Error (*see also* **Error's**)
Court of
    (*see* **Court**)

———

p 438–24   Personal Sense, who is in partnership with E·
  438–31   the firm of Personal Sense, E·, & Co.,

error (*see also* **error's**)
abounds
f 202–25   E· abounds where Truth should
above
p 400–18   By lifting thought above e·, or disease,
accompanies
b 287–17   Neither . . . nor truth accompanies e·,
action of
r 484–22   the voluntary or involuntary action of e·
Adam— *alias*
g 528–24   Adam— *alias* e·— gives them names.
adamant of
f 242–18   the adamant of e·,— self-will,
Adam or
ph 177–16   Adam or e·, . . . had the naming of
g 534–13   unfolded the remedy for Adam, or e· ;
adhere to
ph 181–24   if you adhere to e· and are afraid to trust
against
a 29–2   take up arms against e· at home and abroad.
aggravation of
an 105–27   The aggravation of e· foretells its doom,
all
pr 10–13   and thus destroying all e·.
  15–13   divine Principle, Love, which destroys all e·.
a 35–19   Our baptism is a purification from all e·.
  39–5   He overcame the world, the flesh, and all e·,
  39–9   until all e· is destroyed.
s 132–25   salvation from all e·, physical and mental,
ph 174–19   rebuking in their course all e·
f 227–3   the law of mortal belief included all e·,
  240–28   until all e· is finally brought into
  251–23   leads the human mind to relinquish all e·,
c 267–25   all e· disappears in celestial Truth.
b 292–8   only as it destroys all e·
  294–5   carries within itself the seeds of all e·.
  303–19   through the self-destruction of all e·
  305–26   destroys all e· and brings immortality to light.
p 414–13   destroy all e·, whether it is called
r 474–2   destroy all e·, evil, disease, and death.

error

all
  r 482–16   the truth casting out all *e·*.
  492–12   Thus progress will finally destroy all *e·*,
  g 543–17   All *e·* proceeds from the evidence before the
  545–28   Truth has but one reply to all *e·*,

ancient
  p 389–24   the ancient *e·* that there is fraternity between

and death
  g 539–10   such as evil, matter, *e·*, and death?

and discord
  p 423–21   superior to *e·* and discord,

and disease
  pr 5–32   destruction of all evil works, *e·* and disease

and evil
  a 52–17   *e·* and evil again make common cause
  b 272–26   in the destruction of *e·* and evil,

and hatred
  g 522–30   produce death, *e·*, and hatred?

and mortality
  b 292– 3   the battle of Truth with *e·* and mortality ;

and sin
  b 296–17   lose all satisfaction in *e·* and sin

and Truth
  o 356–13   as the two opposites, — as *e·* and Truth,
  356–18   between *e·* and Truth, between flesh and Spirit.

animate
  p 409– 6   its final statement, — animate *e·*

antidote for
  r 495–10   and find a sovereign antidote for *e·*

any
  p 372–30   If pride, superstition, or any *e·*

assumption of
  g 546– 7   this assumption of *e·* would dethrone the

attributes to
  g 555–13   C. S. attributes to *e·* neither entity nor power,

back to
  a 22–16   go not back to *e·*, nor become a sluggard in the

basic
  p 405– 1   The basic *e·* is mortal mind.
  r 470– 6   was the basic *e·* of idolatry.

befogged in
  f 205–15   Befogged in *e·* (the error of believing that

begins
  g 539– 3   *E·* begins by reckoning life as separate
  544–31   *E·* begins with corporeality as the producer

belief in
  b 297–27   belief in Truth is better than a belief in *e·*,

belief, or
  b 289–16   a mortal belief, or *e·*, which Truth destroys
  gl 589–20   Truth rebuking mortal belief, or *e·*,

beliefs that
  p 368–10   Against the fatal beliefs that *e·* is as real

believed
  b 306– 1   believed *e·* to be as immortal as Truth.

bites the heel
  f 216– 7   *E·* bites the heel of truth, but cannot kill truth.

brings to
  p 422–10   tremor which Truth often brings to *e·*

builds on
  sp 83–11   belief hides Truth and builds on *e·*.

burial of
  f 232–30   unquestionable signs of the burial of *e·*

called
  s 108–24   that the opposite of Truth, — called *e·*,

call of
  a 21–26   the worldly man is at the beck and call of *e·*,

cannot produce
  p 420– 8   *e·* cannot produce this unnatural reluctance.

cannot remove
  an 101–27   *e·* cannot remove the effects of error.

cannot support
  r 481–27   since Truth cannot support *e·*.

capable of
  g 532–23   Is Mind capable of *e·* as well as of truth,

casting out
  a 33– 8   healing the sick and casting out *e·*.
  34– 4   instead of showing, by casting out *e·*
  35–24   casting out *e·* and healing the sick.
  41–15   casting out *e·* and healing the sick,
  43– 1   must understand . . . by casting out *e·*,
  sp 97–31   apostolic work of casting out *e·* and healing
  s 135–29   casting out *e·* and healing the sick,
  ph 182– 3   The act of . . . casting out *e·* with Truth, shows
  gl 583– 9   casting out *e·* and healing the sick ;

cast out
  s 136– 4   divine Principle, which would cast out *e·*
  ph 170–20   Jesus healed the sick and cast out *e·*,
  t 462– 6   can demonstrate C. S., cast out *e·*,

casts out
  pr 14–29   This understanding casts out *e·*
  a 25–15   casts out *e·*, and triumphs over death.
  33–24   casts out *e·*, raises the dead from trespasses
  f 230– 8   casts out *e·* and heals the sick.
  b 275–32   It casts out *e·* and heals the sick.

error

casts out
  o 350–11   Truth casts out *e·* and heals the sick.
  r 473–30   which heals the sick and casts out *e·*,
  495– 2   Truth casts out *e·* now as surely as

causes disease
  o 344–12   understood . . . that *e·* causes disease,

chaff of
  ap 555–21   fiery baptism will burn up the chaff of *e·*

charges its lie
  b 307–16   *E·* charges its lie to Truth

claim of
  f 233–13   false claim of *e·* continues its delusions

closed to
  pr 15– 6   Closed to *e·*, it is open to Truth,

clouds of
  g 557–19   Divine Science rolls back the clouds of *e·*

conquer
  b 339–31   You conquer *e·* by denying its verity.

conquered
  p 400– 6   This *e·* conquered, we can despoil

consuming
  ap 558–19   prophetically described . . . as consuming *e·*.

contaminated by
  b 287–32   Truth cannot be contaminated by *e·*.

convinced of the
  f 240–25   convinced of the *e·* that is to be overcome.

corrects
  c 259–29   which corrects *e·* with truth

correspond with
  b 294– 1   physical senses . . . correspond with *e·*.

counteracts
  p 414– 7   salutary action of truth, which counteracts *e·*.

create
  b 279–15   no more . . . than Truth can create *e·*,
  287–12   Did God, Truth, create *e·*?

creates
  g 546– 6   If Mind, God, creates *e·*, that . . . would

darkness of
  ph 191–15   chasing away the darkness of *e·*.

débris of
  b 289– 3   temporal *débris* of *e·*, belief in sin, sickness,

deliverance from
  a 22–23   Final deliverance from *e·*,

delusion that
  gl 594– 7   first delusion that *e·* exists as fact ;

demanded by
  p 390–18   the last penalty demanded by *e·*.

demands
  g 532–29   *e·* demands that *mind* shall see and feel through

designs of
  gl 583–28   DAN . . . error, working out the designs of *e·* ;

destroy
  f 233–30   is designed to rebuke and destroy *e·*.
  o 353–12   omnipotent Truth certainly does destroy *e·*.
  p 400–19   lifting thought above . . . you destroy *e·*.
  418–27   in your efforts to destroy *e·*.
  r 496– 1   error cannot destroy *e·*.
  g 542–19   Let Truth uncover and destroy *e·*
  548–14   Every agony of . . . helps error to destroy *e·*,

destroying
  p 368–19   healing the sick and destroying *e·*.
  401– 8   If . . . destroying *e·*, causes chemicalization
  t 463–24   first step towards destroying *e·*.
  gl 589–17   rebuking and destroying *e·* and bringing

destroys
  sp 98– 6   which heals the sick and destroys *e·*,
  f 216– 8   Truth . . . destroys *e·*.
  252–10   understanding of Truth which destroys *e·*,
  b 339– 3   Truth destroys *e·*, and Love destroys hate.
  o 346–15   Disbelief in error destroys *e·*,
  350–30   Soul rebukes sense, and Truth destroys *e·*.
  t 452–14   the explanation which destroys *e·*.
  r 483–18   heals the sick, destroys *e·*,

destroy the
  p 423–10   the truth of being, to destroy the *e·*.

destruction of
  (see **destruction**)

devils, or
  gl 583–18   thereby casting out devils, or *e·*,

disappears
  f 251–26   improves mankind until *e·* disappears,
  c 267–25   *e·* disappears in celestial Truth.
  p 406–13   Then *e·* disappears. Sin and sickness will abate

disbelief in
  o 346–15   Disbelief in *e·* destroys error,

discern the
  sp 85–11   and discern the *e·* you would destroy.

discomfort under
  an 101–28   Discomfort under *e·* is preferable to comfort.

disease as
  b 319– 3   Science depicts disease as *e·*,
  r 483– 5   We classify disease as *e·*,

disease is an
  p 400–16   if you understand that every disease is an *e·*,

error

dispels
  b 283– 1 Truth is the light which dispels *e·*.
dominion over
  p 380–21 and prove man's dominion over *e·*.
drive
  g 538– 3 drive *e·* out of all selfhood.
dying
  a 42–20 belief . . . separate from God is a dying *e·*.
effects of
  an 101–28 error cannot remove the effects of *e·*.
  b 273–30 beliefs emit the effects of *e·* at all times,
  r 473– 6 are to be classified as effects of *e·*.
  g 537–21 to depict . . . the effects of *e·*.
effort of
  g 554–17 first effort of *e·* has been and is to impute
efforts of
  f 223–27 The efforts of *e·* to answer this question
ejection of
  sp 97– 2 They will aid in the ejection of *e·*.
element of
  t 463–12 has not a single element of *e·*,
end of
  sp 95–20 We welcome . . . the end of *e·*,
  96–19 disturbances will continue until the end of *e·*,
escape the
  sp 83– 8 to escape the *e·* of these latter days.
every form of
  p 418–29 Speak the truth to every form of *e·*.
evidence of
  o 353– 8 Truth which contradicts the evidence of *e·*,
evil and
  f 227–19 evil and *e·* lead into captivity.
evil or
  r 489–25 the only source of evil or *e·*.
evolved by
  g 523– 4 the mist of obscurity evolved by *e·*
excision of
  t 462–25 indispensable to the excision of *e·*.
excludes itself
  g 537–14 *E·* excludes itself from harmony.
experience of
  f 237–18 To prevent the experience of *e·*
expression of
  b 289– 9 He is little else than the expression of *e·*.
exterminator of
  r 469–13 The exterminator of *e·* is
face of
  g 503–13 saith to the darkness upon the face of *e·*,
fact concerning
  sp 92–22 Until the fact concerning *e·* . . . appears,
falls
  a 37– 8 *e·* falls only before the sword of Spirit.
falsity and
  r 474–31 Truth destroys falsity and *e·*,
falsity of
  b 294–32 Truth demonstrates the falsity of *e·*.
  g 537–21 to depict the falsity of *e·*
fatal
  b 303–24 The belief that . . . is a fatal *e·*.
fear of
  p 380–21 Truth can prevent the fear of *e·*,
felt the power
  a 20–19 when *e·* felt the power of Truth,
finity of
  f 202–21 earthly experience discloses the finity of *e·*
forms of
  f 204– 3 All forms of *e·* support the false conclusions
  c 264–24 proved them to be forms of *e·*.
forsake
  b 323– 4 in the endeavor to forsake *e·*
foundations of
  b 273–12 tears away the foundations of *e·*.
  o 357–12 the foundations of *e·* would be sapped
from . . . to Truth
  p 370–31 from *e·* to Truth, from matter to Spirit.
from . . . to truth
  sp 77– 3 the change from *e·* to truth
fundamental
  m 65– 9 some fundamental *e·* in the marriage state.
  ph 171–31 fundamental *e·* lies in the supposition
give up
  b 330– 1 in proportion as mortals give up *e·*
greater
  an 104–25 the greater *e·* overcoming the lesser.
  104–26 greater *e·* thereafter occupies the ground,
  s 123– 2 will surely destroy the greater *e·*
greater than
  f 223–10 Remember that truth is greater than *e·*,
growth of
  ph 188–22 Sickness is a growth of *e·*,
guilt and
  ap 568– 1 Innocence and Truth overcome guilt and *e·*.
has no creator
  b 277–10 and *e·* has no creator.

error

has no foothold
  b 282–18 *e·* has no foothold in Truth.
· head of
  f 216– 8 Truth bruises the head of *e·*
helps
  g 548–14 helps *e·* to destroy error,
he vanquished
  a 54– 5 With the affluence of Truth, he vanquished *e·*.
hides
  g 542– 5 *e·* hides behind a lie and excuses guilt,
his
  b 308–21 smote the sinew, or strength, of his *e·*,
  308–26 perceiving his *e·* and his need of help,
history of
  g 521–29 history of *e·* or matter, if veritable, would
  522–13 the history of *e·* in its externalized forms,
  525–26 if we give the same heed to the history of *e·*
  530–26 The history of *e·* is a dream-narrative.
human
  b 294– 1 the avenues and instruments of human *e·*,
  p 401– 2 Any human *e·* is its own enemy,
  ap 563–10 dragon stands for the sum total of human *e·*.
husbandman of
  ph 180– 2 mortal mind is the husbandman of *e·*,
hypothesis of
  g 522–28 is based on some hypothesis of *e·*,
ignorance of the
  t 446–31 Ignorance of the *e·* to be eradicated
illusion of
  g 538–16 is significant of the illusion of *e·*,
illusion or
  g 556– 1 and not the belief in illusion or *e·*.
impossible for
  t 448–22 well knowing it to be impossible for *e·*, evil,
impotence of
  t 454– 5 which illustrates the impotence of *e·*.
impotent
  sp 97– 7 the more impotent *e·* becomes as a belief.
  g 555–18 Only impotent *e·* would seek to unite
impurity and
  m 65–22 impurity and *e·* are left among the lees.
in action
  f 207– 7 Error of statement leads to *e·* in action.
incarnate
  gl 583–11 comes to the flesh to destroy incarnate *e·*.
infers from
  b 282–32 rule of inversion infers from *e·* its opposite,
in solution
  p 372– 4 matter was originally *e·* in solution,
in the premise
  ph 167–16 an *e·* in the premise must appear in the
  b 277–27 This *e·* in the premise leads to errors in
involves
  b 301– 8 but his sense of substance involves *e·*
involving
  b 286–23 temporal thoughts are human, involving *e·*,
is a coward
  p 368– 4 *E·* is a coward before Truth.
is always
  g 554– 8 *E·* is always *e·*.   It is *no thing*.
is a supposition
  r 472–14 *E·* is a supposition that pleasure and pain,
is false
  b 287–22 *E·* is false, mortal belief ;
is limited
  r 466–14 Truth is limitless ; *e·* is limited.
is mortal
  b 337–12 while *e·* is mortal and discordant.
  r 466–13 Truth is immortal ; *e·* is mortal.
is non-intelligent
  r 466–14 *e·* is non-intelligent.
is nothing
  o 346–10 we need to understand that *e·* *is* nothing,
is not real
  f 251– 1 *E·* is not real, hence it is not
is not true
  t 461–25 *e·* is not true, hence it is unreal.
is opposed
  p 406–20 *E·* is opposed to Life.
is reduced
  sp 91–11 *e·* is reduced to its native nothingness,
is self-destroyed
  p 368– 8 still clearer as *e·* is self-destroyed.
is unlike Truth
  r 468– 5 because *e·* is unlike Truth.
is unreal
  c 265–21 the *e·* is unreal and obsolete.
  p 368– 4 in the fact that Truth is real and *e·* is unreal.
  r 466–15 Truth is real, and *e·* is unreal.
  472–18 *E·* is unreal because untrue.
its
  sp 97–18 the more obvious its *e·*,
  s 144–12 the more obstinately tenacious its *e·* ;
  ph 197–29 belief loses some portion of its *e·*.
  b 322–13 belief may be prepared to relinquish its *e·*.

error

knowledge of
f 252– 9   A knowledge of *e·* and of its operations
g 533–27   cross-questioning man as to his knowledge of *e·*,
latent
ap 559– 5   upon elementary, latent *e·*,
leading
p 377–21   Remove the leading *e·* or governing fear
learned from
b 288–32   what mortals seem to have learned from *e·*,
level of
ph 173– 9   supposition, . . . Truth is reduced to the level of *e·*,
love rebuking
gl 594–15   love rebuking *e·* ; reproof of sensualism.
lurking
p 419– 2   Lurking *e·*, lust, envy, revenge, malice,
made up of
b 295–25   mortal thought is made up of *e·*.
make nothing of
sp 92–24   the ability to make nothing of *e·* will be
manifestation of the
g 532–26   Fear was the first manifestation of the *e·*
mass of
s 118–11   It must destroy the entire mass of *e·*,
material
f 252–11   mortal, material *e·* finally disappears,
b 291–31   mortal man is divested of all material *e·*.
309– 8   He had conquered material *e·* with the
315–23   spiritual Truth destroys material *e·*,
matter and
ph 181–31   will incline you to the side of matter and *e·*.
o 347–26   dream that matter and *e·* are something
matter as
b 278–29   We define matter as *e·*, because it is the
matter or
s 145–27   towards other forms of matter or *e·*,
f 206– 3   no consciousness of the existence of matter or *e·*.
methods of
t 451–25   may perceive the nature and methods of *e·*
mirage of
f 244– 3   is not real, but is illusion, the mirage of *e·*.
mortal
    (*see* **mortal**)
motive-power of
gl 597–20   WILL. The motive-power of *e·* ;
much
b 295–21   lost much materiality — much *e·*
must be mortal
r 468– 5   If Truth is immortal, *e·* must be mortal,
named
b 276–27   the *nothingness* named *e·*.
r 471– 6   The unlikeness of Truth, — named *e·*,
gl 594– 2   the opposite of Truth, named *e·* ;
nature of
g 555– 9   This is the nature of *e·*.
neutralizes
s 157–31   Science both neutralizes *e·* and destroys it.
neutralizing
s 162– 6   alterative, neutralizing *e·* with Truth.
never imparts
sp 85–32   truth communicates itself but never imparts *e·*.
never made
ph 183–14   Truth never made *e·* necessary,
night of
pref vii– 9   till across a night of *e·*
no
s 129– 5   can tolerate no *e·* in premise or conclusion.
131– 3   There is no *e·* in Science,
f 210–31   immortal sense has no *e·* of sense,
b 278– 8   even as in Truth there is no *e·*,
283–12   It admits of no *e·*, but rests upon
t 450–29   Who, . . . can say that there is no *e·* of belief?
r 475– 2   To Truth there is no *e·*, — all is Truth.
ap 567– 8   there is no *e·*, no sin, sickness, nor death.
no consciousness of
f 243–25   Truth has no consciousness of *e·*.
no home in
b 282–18   Truth has no home in *e·*,
nor obeying
f 244– 6   never fearing nor obeying *e·* in any form.
no sense of
f 210–31   it has no sense of *e·* ;
not
p 420– 3   Truth not *e·*, Love not hate, . . . governs man.
not contaminated by
b 304–20   Truth is not contaminated by *e·*.
nothingness of
    (*see* **nothingness**)
not Truth
p 386–25   *E·*, not Truth, produces all the suffering
r 474–27   *e·*, not Truth, is the author of the unreal,
now simulates
g 528–20   *e·* now simulates the work of Truth,
of action
g 550–15   Error of thought is reflected in *e·* of action.

error

of any kind
sp 95–11   *E·* of any kind cannot hide from the law of God.
of any sort
f 232–32   nor opportunity in Science for *e·* of any sort.
of belief
ph 168–28   if the *e·* of belief was met and destroyed
184–10   casting out by denial the *e·* of belief
f 208– 8   What is it but an *e·* of belief,
t 450–29   Who, . . . can say that there is no *e·* of belief?
r 486–21   So long as this *e·* of belief remains,
of believing
f 205– 7   When will the *e·* of believing that there is
205–15   *e·* of believing that matter can be intelligent
offspring of
gl 589– 2   A corporeal belief ; the offspring of *e·* ;
of measuring
f 246–20   Except for the *e·* of measuring and limiting
of mortal belief
a 20–14   he knew the *e·* of mortal belief,
of physical belief
gl 586–18   FLESH. An *e·* of physical belief ;
of sensation
b 318–22   denies the *e·* of sensation in matter,
of statement
f 207– 6   *E·* of statement leads to error in action.
b 277–26   Matter is an *e·* of statement.
of the ages
f 241–17   *e·* of the ages is preaching without practice.
of thought
g 550–15   *E·* of thought is reflected in error of action.
one
an 104–23   hypnotizer employs one *e·* to destroy another.
s 143–13   the human mind uses one *e·* to
r 486–13   one *e·* will not correct another.
only
gl 585–21   the only *e·* of which is limitation ;
oppose
s 145–25   Other methods undertake to oppose *e·* with
opposing
sp 93–16   evil is the opposing *e·* and not the truth
opposite
b 280–20   the opposite *e·* of many minds.
g 521–25   now the opposite *e·*, . . . is to be set forth.
or unreality
t 461–26   the *e·* or unreality of sin,
461–28   the *e·* or unreality of disease,
out of
b 296–28   An improved belief is one step out of *e·*,
outweigh
p 392– 8   enables truth to outweigh *e·*.
overcoming
a 21– 1   If Truth is overcoming *e·* in your daily walk
an 104–25   the greater *e·* overcoming the lesser.
overruled the
p 381–31   Christ Jesus overruled the *e·* which would
pantheistic
b 307– 3   This pantheistic *e·*, or so-called *serpent*,
partakes of its own
b 307–19   Thus *e·* partakes of its own nature
part of the
r 482–26   Sickness is part of the *e·* which Truth casts out.
part with
p 430– 4   Mortal mind must part with *e·*,
phantoms of
f 215–20   and flee as phantoms of *e·* before truth
picture of
g 526–25   second biblical account is a picture of *e·*
pierces the
f 210–20   Truth pierces the *e·* of mortality
policy of
t 452–23   take no risks in the policy of *e·*.
power over
pr 5– 2   from demonstrating his power over *e·*.
practical
t 452– 4   Incorrect reasoning leads to practical *e·*.
proves that
b 338– 9   proves that *e·* has been ingrafted into the
quenching
b 329–25   maintains the claim of Truth by quenching *e·*.
rabbinical
a 30–20   Christ Jesus came to rebuke rabbinical *e·*
reap the
t 462–12   he will inevitably reap the *e·* he sows.
rejection of
a 20–15   [the rejection of *e·*]
relies
b 277–19   *E·* relies upon a reversal of this order,
relinquish its
b 322–13   belief may be prepared to relinquish its *e·*.
relinquishment of
pr 7– 6   relinquishment of *e·* deprives material sense
remedy for
s 143– 1   Truth is God's remedy for *e·* of every kind,
remove
a 40– 1   Remove *e·* from thought,

error

remove the
- *ph* 173–28   to remove the *e·* which the human mind
- *p* 378–10   Remove the *e·*, and you destroy its effects.
- 415–25   To remove the *e·* producing disorder,

repeats
- *a* 28–28   *E·* repeats itself.

replies
- *g* 554–16   *E·* replies, "God made you."

representing
- *g* 540–22   representing *e·* as assuming a divine character,

representing the
- *b* 294–20   representing the *e·* that life and intelligence

represents
- *g* 530–17   myth represents *e·* as always asserting its
- 546–13   represents *e·* as starting from an idea of good

reversed
- *b* 319– 4   *e·* reversed as subserving the facts

reverse of
- *p* 442–18   but the reverse of *e·* is true.

run into
- *f* 250– 1   We run into *e·* when we divide Soul into souls,

says
- *p* 478–23   *E·* says, "I am man ;"

sea of
- *ap* 569–18   They are in the surging sea of *e·*,

seed of
- *g* 535– 2   The seed of Truth and the seed of *e·*,

self-destroying
- *gl* 581–17   BABEL. Self-destroying *e·* ;

self-destruction
- *b* 293–27   they show the self-destruction of *e·*

self-evident
- *b* 309–27   It is a self-evident *e·* to suppose that there

sense of
- *g* 520–14   in which all sense of *e·* forever disappears

serpents of
- *gl* 587–15   the serpents of *e·*, which say,

seven seals of
- *ap* 572–15   open the seven seals of *e·* with Truth,

should not seem
- *s* 131– 1   *e·* should not seem so real as truth.

shrank abashed
- *g* 532–19   Ashamed before Truth, *e·* shrank abashed

sickness and
- *r* 495– 8   classify sickness and *e·* as our Master did,

side of
- *f* 205–29   Selfishness tips the beam . . . towards the side of *e·*,

signet of
- *gl* 593–23   SEAL. The signet of *e·* revealed by Truth.

simulates truth
- *sp* 97– 5   the more closely *e·* simulates truth

sin and
- *b* 290–23   sin and *e·* which possess us at the instant of

sin, or
- *ph* 183–11   Scriptures inform us that sin, or *e·*,

soweth the wind
- *f* 210–24   *E·* soweth the wind

standpoint of
- *g* 545–24   From that standpoint of *e·*, they could not

state of
- *b* 311–17   This state of *e·* is the mortal dream of life

states of
- *gl* 592– 7   idolatry ; the subjective states of *e·* ;

still the
- *f* 214–13   still the *e·*, not the truth of being.

stronger
- *an* 104–28   before it was grasped by the stronger *e·*.

submission to
- *ph* 183–24   Submission to *e·* superinduces loss of power.

such an
- *pr* 5–23   Such an *e·* would impede true religion.

suffering is an
- *a* 23– 9   suffering is an *e·* of sinful sense

suffer severely from
- *f* 238–21   because we suffer severely from *e·*.

supplant
- *r* 495–22   understanding will supplant *e·* with Truth,

suppose
- *f* 250– 2   and suppose *e·* to be mind,

supposed reality of
- *gl* 596–21   and the supposed reality of *e·*.

supposes man
- *b* 287– 6   *E·* supposes man to be both mental and material.

suppositional
- *f* 208– 1   obtained from suppositional *e·*,
- *r* 472– 4   casts out suppositional *e·* and heals

supposition of
- *g* 503–11   No supposition of *e·* enters there.

surface of
- *f* 254–24   If you venture upon the quiet surface of *e·*

sympathy with
- *f* 211–21   Sympathy with *e·* should disappear.
- 254–25   and are in sympathy with *e·*,

error

synonym for
- *g* 529–30   Adam, the synonym for *e·*, stands for a

tenacity of
- *sp* 77–18   according to the tenacity of *e·*.
- *b* 296–21   depends upon the tenacity of *e·*.

termed
- *gl* 580–16   the opposer of Truth, termed *e·* ;

term for
- *an* 103–19   hypnotism is the specific term for *e·*,

testimony of
- *r* 481–14   forbidden fruit . . . is the testimony of *e·*,

that
- *b* 320–22   according to that *e·* man is mortal.
- *g* 546– 6   that *e·* must exist in the

their
- *b* 320–16   [or, in their *e·* they are]
- *p* 405–31   causes mortals to retreat from their *e·*,

theorizes
- *b* 295–31   *e·* theorizes that spirit is born of matter

this
- *a* 42–20   This *e·* Jesus met with divine Science
- *sp* 73–29   This *e·* Science will destroy.
- *f* 237–27   and expect this *e·* to do more for them than
- *b* 277–27   This *e·* in the premise leads to errors in
- 280–16   Through this *e·*, human belief comes to have
- 290–12   Hence Truth comes to destroy this *e·*
- 295–11   to escape from the mortality of this *e·*.
- 307–14   This *e·* has proved itself to be error.
- *p* 400– 6   This *e·* conquered, we can despoil
- *r* 470– 7   This *e·* assumed the loss of
- 486–21   So long as this *e·* of belief remains,
- 490– 2   grand truths of C. S. dispute this *e·*.
- *g* 526–12   sickness, and death, follow in the train of this *e·*
- 543– 2   This *e·*, . . . yields to Truth

this is the
- *sp* 93–29   and this is the *e·* embodied in the belief
- *g* 531– 5   This is the *e·*,— that mortal man

thunderbolts of
- *b* 288–15   lightnings and thunderbolts of *e·* may burst

treated
- *t* 463–24   Our Master treated *e·* through Mind.

treated as
- *p* 425–12   they should be treated as *e·*

treatment of
- *t* 463–21   as to the proper treatment of *e·*

Truth against
- *o* 358–16   calm and clear verdict of Truth against *e·*,

truth against
- *p* 405–12   the arbiter of truth against *e·*.

Truth and
-   (*see* **Truth**)

truth and
-   (*see* **truth**)

Truth controls
- *s* 145–17   in it Truth controls *e·*.

Truth decapitates
- *c* 266– 3   sword . . . with which Truth decapitates *e·*,

Truth destroys
- *b* 339– 3   Truth destroys *e·*, and Love destroys hate.
- *o* 350–30   Soul rebukes sense, and Truth destroys *e·*.

Truth or
- *f* 211– 5   say whether Truth or *e·* is the greater?
- *b* 324–10   whether it be Truth or *e·*,

truth or
- *p* 403–30   in proportion to the truth or *e·* which

Truth over
- *s* 111–13   the power of Truth over *e·* ;
- *p* 378–17   represents the power of Truth over *e·*,
- 406–22   the supremacy of Truth over *e·*,
- *r* 484–25   Science . . . over material sense, and Truth over *e·*,

truth regarding
- *t* 461–25   The truth regarding *e·* is, that

Truth upon
- *p* 421–23   alterative effect produced by Truth upon *e·*,

trying to meet
- *ap* 568– 8   fatal effects of trying to meet *e·* with error.

type of
- *gl* 593–17   foaming, and dashing, it is a type of *e·*.

unconscious
- *ph* 188– 6   is an unconscious *e·* in the beginning,

uncover
- *sp* 92–21   Uncover *e·*, and it turns the lie upon you.

unnatural as
- *s* 131– 1   Truth should not seem so . . . unnatural as *e·*,

unveils
- *g* 542– 8   Truth, through her eternal laws, unveils *e·*.

utter
- *a* 47–32   Jesus realized the utter *e·* of a belief in any

victory over
- *a* 44– 1   Truth and Life must seal the victory over *e·*

views of
- *r* 485–10   ephemeral views of *e·* ought to be obliterated

visible
- *ap* 559– 8   exercised upon visible *e·* and audible sin.

error
voluntary
   r 491– 8 made up of involuntary and voluntary e·,
warfare against
   ap 568–32 in our warfare against e·,
wars with
   s 144–24 even as Truth wars with e·,
waves of
   t 455– 9 in order to walk over the waves of e·
way of
   g 536–10 The way of e· is awful to contemplate.
way to extract
   f 201–17 The way to extract e· from mortal mind
we find
   c 260–32 If we look to the body . . . for Truth, we find e· ;
we treat
   o 346–19 We treat e· through the understanding of Truth,
what is
   r 472–13 *Question.*— What is e·?
which impedes
   pr 2–21 an e· which impedes spiritual growth.
which prevents
   p 409–14 the e· which prevents mortals from knowing
wilful
   p 369–30 No man is physically healed in wilful e·
will cease
   r 476– 7 E· will cease to claim that soul is in body,
will never save
   a 24– 2 Firmness in e· will never save from sin,
will not expel
   r 482–27 E· will not expel e·.
world of
   pr 13–30 world of e· is ignorant of the world of Truth,
would establish
   ap 568– 2 ever since e· would establish material belief,
would simulate
   b 281–25 out of which e· would simulate creation
wrestled with
   gl 583– 7 who, having wrestled with e·, sin, and
wrestling with
   b 308–16 Jacob was *alone*, wrestling with e·,
yields
   b 329–31 till e· yields to Truth.

---

  pr 7– 1 The only civil sentence which he had for e·
      11–17 Truth bestows no pardon upon e·,
  a 19– 5 cannot reconcile Truth to e·,
      30–25 between the offspring . . . of Truth and of e·.
      36– 7 would be for Truth to pardon e·.
      52–12 foresight of the reception e· would give him.
  sp 72–19 E· is not a convenient sieve
      74–11 the e· which has held the belief dissolves
      77– 6 E· brings its own self-destruction
      79– 3 Warning people against death is an e· that
      92–29 The mistake of thinking that e· can be real,
      92–31 leads to belief in the superiority of e·.
      96– 5 Before e· is wholly destroyed, there will be
      97–22 they bring e· from under cover.
      97–24 the louder will e· scream,
  s 123– 6 the e· relating to soul and body,
      126– 2 E· will be no longer used in stating truth.
      145–25 Other methods . . . oppose error with e·,
      154– 1 Neither . . . should ever tempt us to cherish e·
  ph 183–15 nor devised a law to perpetuate e·.
      188–23 E· rehearses e·.
      191–30 Truth never mingles with e·.
  f 201–14 Let us disrobe e·.
      204–31 The e·, which says that Soul is in body,
      231–13 If . . . truth results in e·, then
      239–12 success in e· is defeat in Truth.
      245– 1 The e· of thinking that we are growing old,
      251–13 Sickness, as well as sin, is an e·
  b 269–10 The first is e· ; the latter is truth.
      281– 7 E· presupposes man to be both mind and
      282–26 E· is the so-called intelligence of mortal mind.
      286–29 e· must also say, "I am true."
      286–30 e·, the lie, destroys itself.
      287– 9 We call the absence of Truth, e·.
      287–18 nor is e· the offshoot of Mind.
      287–25 The supposition that . . . is an e·.
      288– 2 e·, *Truth's unlikeness, is unreal.*
      291–31 As for spiritual e· there is none.
      294–11 This mortal belief, misnamed *man*, is e·,
      299–26 Corporeal sense, or e·, may seem to hide Truth,
      307– 5 that is, I will make e· as
      307–14 This error has proved itself to be e·.
      318–14 We must cause the e· to cease
      318–20 as the e· . . . yields to the reality of
      322–32 than to rid one's self of e·.
      329–29 e· into which mortal mind is plunged,
      338– 8 the e· which must be destroyed by Truth.
      338–22 it stands for obstruction, e·,
  o 343–14 Jesus strips all disguise from e·,
      347– 1 Is it e· which is restoring us
      347–31 These critics will then see that e· is
      351–17 while e· seems as potent and real

error
  o 353–22 When we learn that e· is not real.
  p 367–30 e· should be known as nothing.
      367–32 e·, Truth's opposite, has no might.
      368–16 more faith in the truth of being than . . . in e·,
      369–32 It is e· even to murmur
      391–13 It is e· to suffer for aught but your own sins.
      392– 5 taken into account and the e· be rebuked.
      394–12 enthrones matter through e·.
      398– 5 spirit [e·] cried, and rent him— *Mark* 9 : 26.
      401–11 truth of being must transform the e·
      402–22 The e·, mesmerism— or hypnotism,
      406–19 Resist evil— e· of every sort— and it will
      408– 1 Every sort of sickness is e·,
      408– 4 nor discovered to be e·
      418– 6 in contradistinction to the e· that life,
  t 447–13 false charity does not forever conceal e· ;
      450–13 They do not incline longingly to e·,
      452–12 When e· confronts you, withhold not the rebuke
      454–13 truth which strips all disguise from e·,
      454–15 points out to his student e· as well as truth,
      458– 9 Another plank in the platform is this, that e·
      461–24 Both sin and sickness are e·,
      463–22 whether e· is manifested in forms of
  r 467–20 belief that the greater can be in the lesser is an e·
      469–17 evil— is not Mind, is not Truth, but e·,
      472–16 E· is neither Mind nor one of Mind's faculties.
      472–17 E· is the contradiction of Truth.
      472–18 E· is a belief without understanding.
      472–20 If e· were true, its truth would be e·,
      473– 5 Truth, God, is not the father of e·.
      474–25 must e· still be immortal?
      476– 6 E·, urged to its final limits, is
      483–14 affixed . . . the name "e·" to corporeal sense,
      485– 1 If e· is necessary to define or to reveal
      486–13 Death is not the result of Truth but of e·,
      496– 1 soon ascertain that e· cannot destroy error.
  g 523– 5 and finally declares that God knows e·
      523– 5 and that e· can improve His creation.
      523–11 In e· everything comes from beneath,
      524–22 How could . . . e· be the enunciator of Truth?
      528–15 Here falsity, e·, credits Truth, God, with
      528–22 and declaring what great things e· has done.
      532–27 e· began and will end the dream of matter.
      533–24 but e· has its suppositional day
      537–16 E· tills its own barren soil
      542– 6 e· cannot forever be concealed.
      542– 9 sets upon e· the mark of the beast.
      545–15 E· tills the whole ground
      545–31 "As in Adam [e·] all die,— *I Cor.* 15 : 22.
      548– 3 C. S. separates e· from truth,
      551–29 e· declares that the material seed must
      555– 8 not comprehend what you say about e·."
      555–11 E· would have itself received as mind,
      555–14 e· is neither mind nor the outcome of Mind.
  ap 568– 8 fatal effects of trying to meet error with e·.
  gl 579–10 ADAM. E· ; a falsity ;
      582– 7 e· masquerading as the possessor of life,
      582–25 the e· which would make man mortal
      583–27 e·, working out the designs of error ;
      584–17 DEVIL. Evil ; a lie ; e· ;
      585–15 definition of
      585–25 e· ; the belief that the human race
      586–11 ignorance ; e· ; desire ; caution.
      588– 1 Mortal belief ; e· ; lust ; remorse ; hatred ;
      591–26 e· creating other errors ;
      593– 6 PURSE. Laying up treasures in matter ; e·.
      593– 7 RED DRAGON. E· ; fear ; inflammation ;
      593–13 sensuality ; delusion ; mortality ; e·.
      595– 5 TARES. Mortality ; e· ; sin ; sickness ;
      595–19 beliefs, opinions, knowledge ; matter ; e· ;
      595–24 Impure thoughts ; e· ; sin ; dirt.
      598–17 E· ; fornication ; temptation ; passion.

Error's
  p 438–24 and smuggles E· goods into market
error's
  sp 79–10 dig up every seed of e· sowing.
  s 154– 1 we should not be e· advocate.
  f 254–26 What is there to strip off e· disguise?
  b 307–31 Above e· awful din, blackness, and chaos,
  o 346–20 because Truth is e· antidote.
      357–12 and e· destruction ensured.
  g 543– 7 more beautifully apparent at e· demise.
  ap 559– 5 the source of all e· visible forms
      564– 3 e· own nature and methods.

errors
all its
  ph 177– 3 it must relinquish all its e·,
all sorts of
  c 257–22 Finite mind manifests all sorts of e·,
both are
  p 379– 3 both are e·, announced as partners
casting out the
  s 138–13 casting out the e· of mortal mind.

errors
correct the
   r 494–20 serves to correct the *e·* of corporeal sense ;
destroy the
   f 216–13 begins at once to destroy the *e·* of mortal sense
destroy those
   a 53–27 He knew . . . and could destroy those *e·* ;
fevers are
   p 379–25 Fevers are *e·* of various types.
fundamental
   g 545–13 Such fundamental *e·* send falsity into all
history of the
   an 101– 5 in the history of the *e·* of the human mind,
human
   g 533–10 Here there is an attempt to trace all human *e·*
ignorant of the
   p 408–32 ignorant of the *e·* it includes
illusive
   o 343–19 illusive *e·* — which he could and did destroy.
leads to
   b 277–27 This error in the premise leads to *e·* in
mortal
   a 53–26 mortal *e·* which constitute the material body,
multitudinous
   a 43–30 and the multitudinous *e·* growing from
of all sorts
   p 419– 3 *E·* of all sorts tend in this direction.
of belief
   sp 96–23 until all *e·* of belief yield to
   t 450–25 knows that they are *e·* of belief,
offending
   p 392–31 Exclude from mortal mind the offending *e·* ;
of sense
   f 240–27 In trying to undo the *e·* of sense
   b 273–14 till the *e·* of sense are eliminated.
   p 406–11 The Science of being unveils the *e·* of sense,
old
   t 460–32 finally the shadow of old *e·* was no longer cast
other
   gl 591–27 mythology ; error creating other *e·* ;
such
   s 152–11 Such *e·* beset every material theory,
these
   s 121–23 and corrects these *e·* by the simple rule that
   f 232–21 nor did he illustrate these *e·* by his practice.
   b 290–25 but endure until the death of these *e·*.
   328– 8 These *e·* are not thus really destroyed,
   o 356–21 as He is of experiencing these *e·*.
   p 404– 5 meet and destroy these *e·* with the truth
   405– 9 Choke these *e·* in their early stages,
triad of
   s 122– 5 facts of Life, . . . defeat this triad of *e·*,
   o 356–22 subject to this triad of *e·*,

   a 30–26 If we have triumphed sufficiently over the *e·*
   f 207–25 They are the *e·*, which presuppose
   c 267–24 by reversal, serve as waymarks to the
   b 294–17 even the *e·* that are destroyed by Truth
   t 451– 1 the *e·* which Truth must and will annihilate
   gl 594–24 the opposites of God ; *e·* ; hallucinations.

errs
   sp 99–16 the human sense of things *e·*
   f 250– 9 which never *e·*, and is ever conscious ;
   t 456–12 greatly *e·*, ignorantly or intentionally,

erudite
   a 24–20 Does *e·* theology regard the crucifixion

erudition
   sp 88–27 It is due to inspiration rather than to *e·*.

escape
   pr 6– 1 We cannot *e·* the penalty due for sin.
   a 36– 7 *E·* from punishment is not in accordance with
   41–12 cannot forever break the Golden Rule and *e·* the
   48–13 or even wish, to *e·* the exalting ordeal
   sp 83– 8 to *e·* the error of these latter days,
   99– 4 divine Principle by which mortals can *e·*
   99– 5 to *e·* from sin, is what the Bible demands.
   an 103– 7 by which man can *e·* from sin
   s 128–21 its *e·* into the surrounding atmosphere.
   151–16 from which multitudes would gladly *e·*.
   f 227–22 *E·* from the bondage of sickness, sin, and
   c 258–10 which must *e·* from its environments
   b 295–10 in order to *e·* from the mortality
   316– 3 mortals may learn how to *e·* from evil.
   327–12 way to *e·* the misery of sin is to cease sinning.
   p 432–26 endeavoring to assist the prisoner to *e·*
   ap 571–12 *E·* from evil, and designate those as unfaithful

escaped
   an 105–22 Whoever uses his . . . powers like an *e·* felon

escapes
   s 128–13 *e·* . . . from itself, and requires less repose.
   f 203–23 then mortals believe that . . . Soul, *e·* from

eschew
   sp 99–20 some others who *e·* their false beliefs.
eschewed
   s 137–13 Jesus completely *e·* the narrow opinion
eschews
   s 112–13 divine Science which *e·* man-made systems,
   127–30 C. S. *e·* what is called natural science,
escutcheon
   p 437– 6 It blots the fair *e·* of omnipotence.
esoteric
   an 101–32 proportional to one's faith in *e·* magic.
Esoteric Magic
   p 441–22 Hypnotism, Oriental Witchcraft, and *E· M·*
especially
   s 117–21 miracles (marvels) wrought by Jesus and *e·*
   127–15 term C. S. relates *e·* to
   ph 170–31 all ills have gone forth, *e·* despair.
   b 340– 5 conveys the C. S. thought, *e·* when the
   o 348–24 *e·* when by so doing our own condition
   351–20 *e·* if we consider Satan as a
   p 362– 8 *e·* under the stern rules of rabbinical law,
   363–11 those around him . . . *e·* his host,
   414– 4 treatment of insanity is *e·* interesting.
   418–23 *e·* by the spirit of Truth and Love
   t 444–32 the Science of healing, *e·* its ethics,
   451–25 *e·* any subtle degree of evil,
   g 554–31 *e·* those of the human form.
Esquimaux
   sp 82–29 do we look for help to the *E·*
   ph 174– 1 *E·* restore health by incantations
essay
   s 111–20 for the best *e·* on Natural Science,
   111–21 an *e·* calculated to offset the tendency
   163–21 Dr. Chapman, . . . in a published *e·* said :
essays
   pref ix–12 Certain *e·* written at that early date
Esse
   sp 93–19 the real nature of the divine *E·*,
essence
nature and
   s 107–12 inspired with a diviner nature and *e·* ;
   b 270– 6 in its very nature and *e·* ;
   t 460– 7 the nature and *e·* of all being,
of divinity
   g 537– 9 was never the *e·* of divinity
of Love
   b 333–25 in the divine nature, the *e·* of Love.
of this Science
   b 271–23 Sermon on the Mount is the *e·* of this Science,
real
   b 292–32 mortal man is not the real *e·* of manhood,
resembles its
   sp 97– 6 resembles its *e·*, mortal mind,
same in
   b 331–29 same in *e·*, though multiform in office :
spiritual
   a 25– 3 The spiritual *e·* of blood is sacrifice.
true
   b 293–18 counterfeits the true *e·* of spirituality or

   r 465–13 the nature, *e·*, and wholeness of Deity.
essential
   a 27–29 the *e·* religion he came to establish
   sp 98–30 they are not deprived of their *e·* vitality.
   s 117–10 God's *e·* language is spoken of
   b 285–32 It is *e·* to understand, instead of believe,
   331–32 the threefold, *e·* nature of the infinite.
   o 341–12 Proof is *e·* to a due estimate of this subject.
   347–18 restoring an *e·* element of Christianity,
   349–10 Two *e·* points of C. S. are,
   p 374– 1 mortal mind has decided upon as *e·* for health.
   t 460– 8 the divine Mind and Love's *e·* qualities.
   g 553–13 *e·* to their maintenance and reproduction,
establish
   a 27–29 the essential religion he came to *e·*
   s 108– 9 *e·* the truism that the only sufferer is
   112–25 affords no foundation upon which to *e·* a
   ph 189– 9 the power of C. S. to *e·* harmony
   196–18 no relation to God wherewith to *e·*
   f 203– 8 this understanding would *e·* health.
   b 270–20 *e·* the definition of omnipotence.
   280–20 But behold the zeal of belief to *e·*
   335– 5 would . . . *e·* a basis for pantheism.
   o 356– 7 Discord can never *e·* the facts of harmony.
   p 373–22 *E·* the scientific sense of being,
   414–11 truth and love will *e·* a healthy state,
   428–13 Thus we may *e·* in truth the temple, or body,
   t 464– 7 to *e·* the stately operations of C. S.,
   r 486–11 The belief that he dies will not *e·* his
   ap 568– 3 ever since error would *e·* material belief,

established

pref xii– 4	which had been *e·* in the United States,
xii– 8	pastor of the first *e·* Church of Christ, Scientist ;
pr 3– 6	The rule is already *e·*, and it is our task
a 20–10	but he *e·* no ritualistic worship.
24– 5	(*e·* by hierarchies, and instigated
s 131–30	*e·* his claim to the Messiahship.
136– 1	Jesus *e·* his church and maintained
138–17	Jesus *e·* in the Christian era the
162–24	healthy organizations have been *e·*
c 255– *	*Thy throne is e· of old :— Psal.* 93 : 2.
o 348–11	Jesus *e·* this foundational fact,
p 384–28	In Science this is an *e·* fact
r 467–13	true brotherhood of man will be *e·*.
473–26	Jesus *e·* what he said by demonstration,

establishes

a 23–19	and *e·* the claims of God.
m 63–12	civil law *e·* very unfair differences
b 279– 6	The doom of matter *e·* the conclusion
r 491–15	*e·* man forever in the divine likeness,

establishing

s 135– 8	*e·* the Science of God's unchangeable law.
b 274–24	*e·* it by demonstration.

establishment

s 110–11	the *e·* of the kingdom of heaven on earth.
150– 9	for its *e·* as a permanent dispensation

estate

c 258–30	impossible . . . to fall from his high *e·*.
g 514–21	the millennial *e·* pictured by Isaiah :
548– 7	man has never lost his spiritual *e·*

esteemed

a 49–32	*e·* Jesus as "stricken, smitten— *Isa.* 53 : 4.

estimate

s 129–31	small *e·* of the pleasures of the table.
c 262–21	will then drop the false *e·* of life and
o 341–12	Proof is essential to a due *e·* of this subject.
360– 3	all is won, by a right *e·* of what is real."
ap 560–16	or entertain a false *e·* of anyone whom

estimates

an 105–14	and human law rightly *e·* crime,
b 311–14	false *e·* of soul as dwelling in sense

estimation

a 47–24	in order to raise himself in popular *e·*.

etceteras

b 330–32	with all the *e·* that word includes.

eternal

and harmonious

b 320–18	man's *e·* and harmonious existence as image,

and real

b 300–13	temporal and unreal never touch the *e·* and real.
r 494–27	The other is the *e·* and real evidence,

as God

g 554– 3	universe, inclusive of man, is as *e·* as God,

as the Mind

g 513–18	as *e·* as the Mind conceiving them ;

being

f 232– 8	the claims of harmonious and *e·* being
g 521– 3	conscious spiritual harmony and *e·* being.

being is

s 122–27	Life goes on unchanged and being is *e·*.
p 407–23	In Science, all being is *e·*, spiritual,

bliss

ap 577–10	no impediment to *e·* bliss,

builder

p 428–16	the *e·* builder, the everlasting Father,

causes

b 278–20	it would follow that there are two *e·* causes,

chain

ph 172–12	divine Science reveals the *e·* chain

children

g 529–11	His *e·* children, belonging to

Christ

a 38–23	The *e·* Christ, . . . never suffered.
b 334–14	the *e·* Christ and the corporeal Jesus

coexistent and

g 516–22	Man . . . as coexistent and *e·* with God
520–10	Principle and . . . are coexistent and *e·*.
gl 581–11	God and man coexistent and *e·* ;

consciousness

c 263–30	a scientific *e·* consciousness of creation.

copartnership

o 356–17	neither a present nor an *e·* copartnership

dawn

sp 95–26	the light which heralds Christ's *e·* dawn

demand

gl 595–11	the *e·* demand of divine Science.

demands

ph 184–13	the only legitimate and *e·* demands

distinct and

sp 70–13	maintains all identities, . . . as distinct and *e·*.

Ego

b 314– 6	Thus he found the *e·* Ego,

eternal

Elohim

g 515–16	The *e·* Elohim includes the

entity

b 301–13	constitutes the only real and *e·* entity.

ever present and

b 306–29	Life and the universe, ever present and *e·*.

existence

m 65– 6	spiritual and *e·* existence may be discerned.
b 319–13	the infinite cycles of *e·* existence,
p 387–20	adhering to the realities of *e·* existence,

fact

g 544–10	Matter cannot change the *e·* fact

facts

b 293–16	Life, perpetuating the *e·* facts

Father-Mother

b 335–26	nothing unlike the *e·* Father-Mother, God.

God

p 415– 4	Mind in every case is the *e·* God,

good

f 213–14	attraction towards infinite and *e·* good
b 340–19	have no other spirit or mind but God, *e·* good,
ap 561– 2	which works out the ends of *e·* good

good and

b 269–20	this advantage . . . they are good and *e·*.

harmonious and

sp 88–14	Ideas are spiritual, harmonious, and *e·*.
an 102– 2	all that is real, harmonious, and *e·*,
s 114–29	man, is spiritual, harmonious, and *e·*.
151–28	is found harmonious and *e·*.
ph 184–17	man is harmonious and *e·*.
f 209–24	the universe will be found harmonious and *e·*.
232– 8	the claims of harmonious and *e·* being
b 336–26	are inseparable, harmonious, and *e·*.
r 472– 8	that which is harmonious and *e·*.
472–25	All reality is . . . harmonious and *e·*.

harmony

(*see* **harmony**)

history

r 471– 5	unchanged in its *e·* history.

honors

a 39– 4	He won *e·* honors.

indestructible and

a 51–14	his spiritual life, indestructible and *e·*,
p 402–13	Man is indestructible and *e·*.
r 477–17	immortal idea of being, indestructible and *e·*.

individuality

sp 91–19	man's spiritual and *e·* individuality,
b 282– 9	self-existent and *e·* individuality or Mind ;

interpretation

t 461–14	the *e·* interpretation of God and man.

in the heavens

t 454– 9	"*e·* in the heavens."— *II Cor.* 5 : 1.

law

p 385–11	Let us remember that the *e·* law of right,

laws

g 542– 7	Truth, through her *e·* laws, unveils error.

Life

(*see* **Life**)

life

(*see* **life**)

Life is

f 246–27	Life is *e·*. We should find this out,

likeness

f 246– 5	are the *e·* likeness of their Maker.
p 395– 5	immortality and *e·* likeness to God.

Love

a 19– 1	derived from the *e·* Love

man

a 29–32	Spirit is harmonious and man *e·*.
ph 191– 6	this *e·* man will include in that likeness
b 311–31	the spiritual, *e·* man is not touched by

mandate

g 520–26	growth is the *e·* mandate of Mind.

manifestations

b 275–16	the *e·* manifestations of the infinite divine

man is

g 538–30	the sinless, real man is *e·*.

means

t 444–10	right use of temporary and *e·* means.

Mind

(*see* **Mind**)

nature

b 333– 9	Christ expresses God's spiritual, *e·* nature.

noon

f 246–12	Manhood is its *e·* noon,

not

b 279– 9	and is therefore not *e·*.
ap 569–25	Scriptures declare that evil is temporal, not *e·*.

order

b 334–18	exist in the *e·* order of divine Science,

perfect and

m 69–16	and of man . . . perfect and *e·*.
f 205–13	and made all perfect and *e·*.
c 260– 8	the ideal of all that is perfect and *e·*.

eternal

perfect and
b 280– 3   not products of the . . . perfect, and *e· All.*
286–21   God's thoughts are perfect and *e·,*
292–12   not the likeness of God, the perfect and *e·.*
r 471– 4   all that He creates are perfect and *e·,*
gl 583–22   that which is perfect and *e· ;*

perfection
g 550–13   The true sense of being and its *e·* perfection

Principle
b 299–32   If . . . he would have no *e·* Principle
312–20   man's *e·* Principle is ever-present Life.
gl 579–11   faith in the divine Life and in the *e·* Principle
592–16   Mother. God ; divine and *e·* Principle ;

pure and
r 467–15   man is the likeness of God, pure and *e·,*

quality
r 469– 9   It is the primal and *e·* quality of

real and
  (see **real**)

real is
o 353–16   All the real is *e·.*
r 474–29   while all that is real is *e·.*

realities
sp 78– 5   they are not the *e·* realities of Mind.

reality
g 538–14   significant of *e·* reality or being.

reflection
b 296– 3   man is the spiritual, *e·* reflection of God.

resplendent and
f 247–29   shining resplendent and *e·* over age and decay.

Science
sp 78–32   the invisible good dwelling in *e·* Science.
s 150– 5   demonstrated as an immanent, *e·* Science,
c 258–29   under the government of God in *e·* Science,

scientific nor
b 297–18   it is neither scientific nor *e·,*

self-existent and
b 278–18   self-creative, self-existent, and *e·.*
282– 9   self-existent and *e·* individuality or Mind ;
g 555–18   God, the self-existent and *e·.*

sinless and
b 304–15   The perfect man . . . is sinless and *e·.*

spiritual and
m 65– 6   spiritual and *e·* existence may be discerned.
sp 91–19   man's spiritual and *e·* individuality,
ph 190–19   immortal man, spiritual and *e·,* is found to be
c 264– 7   mental picture is spiritual and *e·.*
b 286–26   but counterfeits of the spiritual and *e·.*
302– 4   the real man is spiritual and *e·.*
335–14   Things spiritual and *e·* are substantial.
336–18   Immortal man is . . . always spiritual and *e·.*
337–28   the opposite of the real or the spiritual and *e·.*
o 356– 1   in support of spiritual and *e·* truths,
p 410– 2   heed to C. S., which is spiritual and *e·,*

substance
b 299–25   *e·* substance, which cannot destroy the
301–11   and reflects the *e·* substance, or Spirit,

temporal or
o 360–17   This ideal is either temporal or *e·.*

things
b 337–24   E· things (verities) are God's thoughts

Truth
  (see **Truth**)

truth
b 303–14   statement . . . contradicts this *e·* truth.

unchangeable and
s 120– 4   Spirit, is God, unchangeable and *e·* ;

unfallen and
r 476–30   man in God's image is unfallen and *e·.*

unfolding
b 335–23   we gain the *e·* unfolding of Life

verities
s 110– 9   These *e·* verities reveal primeval existence
r 476–13   the only and *e·* verities of man.

verity
f 252–12   the *e·* verity, man created by
b 296– 2   whereas Science unfolds the *e·* verity,
r 468– 7   sin is not the *e·* verity of being.
480–28   This is the *e·* verity of divine Science.
g 502–25   *e·* verity and unity of God and man,

wonder
g 503–15   Hence the *e·* wonder,

pr 13–29   ignorant . . . of man's *e·* incorporeal existence.
m 68–31   the unbroken links of *e·,* harmonious being
s 115–16   spiritual idea, individual, perfect, *e·.*
140–25   C. S. God is universal, *e·,* divine Love,
145–23   ignorance of the laws of *e·* and unerring Mind.
ph 173–20   Man is spiritual, individual, and *e·* ;
f 247–10   Beauty, as well as truth, is *e·* ;
c 267– 2   the spiritual idea, . . . is *e·.*
267– 8   God is Father, *e·,* self-created, infinite.
b 275– 5   This shows that matter . . . is not *e·.*
278–32   Spirit is substantial and *e·.*

eternal

b 279–12   and they have the advantage of being *e·.*
287– 5   All creations of Spirit are *e·* ;
290– 1   Because Life is God, Life must be *e·,*
334– 1   not that the human Jesus was or is *e·,*
335–18   Spirit is *e·,* divine.
335–28   immutable, immortal, divine, *e·.*
335–29   Nothing unspiritual can be real, . . . or *e·.*
336– 5   never . . . the *e·* into the temporal,
336–30   God and man coexist and are *e·.*
r 468–17   *Answer.*— Substance is that which is *e·*
475–18   the reflection of God, . . . and therefore is *e·* ;
486–20   spiritual senses of man, are *e·.*
gl 580–22   false supposition that Life is not *e·,*
587– 6   all-acting, all-wise, all-loving, and *e·* ;
590– 2   the realm of unerring, *e·,* and

eternality

s 123–28   indicates the *e·* of the scientific order

eternally

s 118–11   *e·* glorified in man's spiritual freedom.
143–29   If Mind was . . . and must be first *e·,*
f 240–17   revolutions of the universe of Mind go on *e·.*
b 302– 9   when God is all and *e·* his.
r 495–19   life harmonious— as Life *e·* is

eternity

all
g 519– 2   from all *e·* knoweth His own ideas.

belief of the
b 278–23   The belief of the *e·* of matter

foretaste of
gl 598–24   spiritual understanding . . . a foretaste of *e·.*

glory of
g 502–17   illuminating time with the glory of *e·.*

heaven and
g 503–10   spiritual harmony,— heaven and *e·.*

no part of
r 468–29   and time is no part of *e·.*

seal of
a 44– 8   His three days' work. . .set the seal of *e·* on time.

statement of the
b 334–29   statement of the *e·* of the Christ,

time and
b 285– 6   the great fact of being for time and *e·.*

type of
gl 585– 5   a type of *e·* and immortality,

will reveal
g 520–13   and they will reveal *e·,* newness of Life,

work of
pr 3–15   to understand God is the work of *e·,*

o 353–15   Time has not yet reached *e·,*
r 468–28   *E·,* . . . expresses the thought of Life,
469– 1   *e·* is forever infinite.
g 517–22   Even *e·* can never reveal the whole of God,
gl 599– 1   *E·* is God's measurement of

ether

s 159– 2   a needed surgical operation without the *e·.*
159– 4   protested against inhaling the *e·*
159– 9   occasioned, not by the *e·,* but by fear
159–19   would have performed the operation without *e·.*

ethereal

f 249–30   makes its mundane flights quite *e·.*
b 293– 9   the more *e·* is called mind.

etherealized

b 298–25   Angels are not *e·* human beings,
gl 598–15   was indeed air, an *e·* form of matter,

etherization

p 415–27   *E·* will apparently cause the body to

etherized

s 158–32   A woman in the city of Lynn, . . . was *e·*

ethical

s 145–18   From this fact arise its *e·* as well as its
145–19   its *e·* and physical effects are
ph 185–24   the reverse of *e·* and pathological Truth-power.
p 429–30   not understood generally by our *e·* instructors.

ethics

sp 99– 2   *e·,* and superstition afford no demonstrable
o 348–30   *e·* and temperance have received an impulse,
t 444–32   the Science of healing, especially its *e·,*
464–29   a scientific system of *e·.*

Eucharist

a 20–11   partake of the *E·,* support the clergy,
32– 9   But the *E·* does not commemorate a
35–25   Our *E·* is spiritual communion with

Euclid

b 329–18   who attempts to solve a problem of *E·,*

Euphrates

gl 585–16   definition of

Europe

a	21–15	If my friends are going to E·,
sp	74–25	that we are in E· when we are in
	90–16	In dreams we fly to E· and meet a
b	320– 6	distinguished theologians in E· and America

evade

| f | 230–24 | These merely e· the question. |

evangel

| b | 308–24 | Then said the spiritual e· : |
| ap | 559–20 | Mortals, obey the heavenly e·. |

Evangelist's

| f | 231–31 | planted on the E· statement that |

evangelized

| f | 254–19 | But the human self must be e·. |

evaporates

| p | 375– 3 | as painlessly as gas . . . when it e· |
| q | 557–16 | When the mist of mortal mind e·, |

evasion

| t | 448–10 | E· of Truth cripples integrity, |

Eve (see also Eve's)

sp	92–12	serpent . . . speaking to Adam and E·.
g	533–23	which came from Adam to form E·.
	538–23	And Adam knew E· his wife ;— Gen. 4 : 1.
	553–17	Adam was created before E·.
	553–19	E· was formed from Adam's rib,
gl	585–23	definition of

even

pref	viii– 6	e· as the science of music
pr	4–14	blessings which, e· if not acknowledged in
	9–19	e· the surrender of all merely material
	10– 2	e· though with bleeding footsteps,
	13–14	E· if prayer is sincere,
a	19– 5	E· Christ cannot reconcile Truth to error,
	20– 1	there is one Life,— e· God, good.
	20–18	e· the nature of God ;
	22– 7	causes them, e· as drowning men,
	24–32	After the resurrection, e· . . . Thomas
	28– 3	E· many of his students stood in his way.
	28–18	E· his righteousness and purity
	30–18	which blesses e· those that curse it.
	37–28	e· as your Father which is in — Matt. 5 : 48.
	38– 4	e· more pernicious than the old doctrine of
	43– 1	e· as they did understand it
	45–24	E· his disciples at first called him a spirit,
	46–16	or, in other words, rose e· higher
	47– 1	e· to the spiritual interpretation to
	48–13	or e· wish, to escape the exalting ordeal
	49– 5	"E· the devils are subject— Luke 10 : 17.
	50–21	E· what they did say,— that Jesus' teachings
	54–32	Would they not deny him e· the
m	57–22	e· though it meet no return.
	62–24	e· as it clothes the lily ;
	65–23	fermentation e· of fluids is not pleasant.
	67– 9	but e· the dauntless seaman
	67–22	commanded e· the winds and waves
sp	77–22	E· if communications from spirits to
	78–12	e· were communication possible
	80–22	E· planchette— the French toy
	82–18	e· if our departed friends were near us
	87– 3	e· when they are lost to the memory of
	88– 6	The mind may e· be cognizant of a
	95–20	e· human invention must have its day,
	96–12	This material world is e· now becoming
	97–16	it ceases to be e· an illusion,
	98–24	E· now multitudes consider that which they call
s	111–15	e· as the explanation of optics rejects
	113–11	E· if reversed, these propositions will
	116–16	e· to the extinction of all belief in matter,
	126– 6	e· as man sees his reflection in a glass.
	131–21	e· so, Father, for so it seemed — Luke 10 : 21.
	133–15	E· in captivity among foreign nations,
	136–25	But e· Herod doubted if Jesus
	137– 4	not spiritually discerned, e· by them,
	139–10	e· when the end has been brightness
	141– 8	to set aside e· the most cherished beliefs
	144– 4	e· if these so-called powers are real.
	144–24	e· as Truth wars with error,
	146–14	e· the might of Mind
	146–21	e· when its elevating effects
	147–11	e· though centuries had passed away
	150–29	e· the doctrine of the superiority of matter
	151–13	E· this one reform in medicine
	152– 9	e· when not fully understood.
	155– 6	E· when you take away the individual confidence
	161–28	e· if it were not already determined
ph	171– 5	e· the way through Christ, Truth,
	177–26	e· though physician and patient are
	177–28	E· so, and ye deify as if
	179–15	You can e· educate a healthy horse so far
	180–19	e· before they go to work to eradicate
	185–16	e· as the necromancers of Egypt
	187– 3	mortals do not comprehend e· mortal existence,
	191–12	e· to the birth of a new-old idea,

even

ph	193– 6	He e· showed me the probe,
	197–32	will harm his patients e· more than
	198–24	e· though the doctor says nothing
f	213–23	e· more strikingly true of Beethoven,
	215–29	E· the faith of his philosophy spurned
	216–32	and have but one Mind, e· God ;
	217–11	e· of catalepsy and hysteria ;
	220– 8	Instinct is better . . . as e· nature declares.
	227– 4	e· as oppressive laws are disputed
	233–12	not e· "the Son but the Father ;"— Mark 13 : 32.
	234– 2	e· as ritualism and creed hamper
	244–29	E· Shakespeare's poetry pictures age as
	252– 7	When false human beliefs learn e· a little
c	255– *	e· we ourselves groan— Rom. 8 : 23.
	259–20	e· as your Father which is in — Matt. 5 : 48.
	261–28	e· as the bird which has burst from the egg
	262–25	e· as light emits light without effort ;
	263– 2	and e· privileged originators
	265–25	e· before we discover what belongs to wisdom
	266–10	e· if you cling to a sense of personal joys,
	267–27	E· in this world, therefore,
b	276–20	e· as our Father in heaven is perfect,
	277–22	contradict e· the order of material so-called
	278– 7	e· as in Truth there is no error,
	282–21	E· though they seem to touch,
	284–24	e· the more subtile and misnamed
	291–30	e· the judgment by which mortal man
	292–21	E· because ye cannot hear my — John 8 : 43.
	294–17	e· the errors that are destroyed by
	301– 1	e· as the human likeness
	302–20	e· as the Father is perfect,
	302–31	E· in C. S., reproduction
	309–23	e· as the gospel teaches.
	311–23	e· the higher law of Soul,
	313– 7	e· thy God, hath anointed thee— Heb. 1 : 9.
	313–20	e· clearer in the translation of the
	313–28	only in a limited degree e· by his disciples,
	318– 6	e· while the corporeal senses are saying
	320–18	e· man's eternal and harmonious existence
	320–30	e· if disease and worms destroyed his body,
	323–23	and elevates e· mortal mind to the
	324–25	Asia Minor, Greece, and e· in imperial Rome.
	334–19	e· before the human Jesus was incarnate
	336–10	e· the infinite expression of infinite Mind,
	338–22	e· the supposed separation of
o	341– 6	E· the Scriptures, . . . appear contradictory when
	342–31	e· if their treatment resulted in the
	348– 4	e· while treating them as disease ;
	349–29	all learning, e· that which is wholly material.
	357–15	or e· to deny that God made
	359–11	E· though you aver that the
	361–17	e· so God and man, Father and son,
p	364–12	He e· said that this poor woman
	368–12	e· the hope of freedom from the
	369–32	It is error e· to murmur
	375–27	e· when they are supposed to be in hopeless
	378– 2	e· as poetry and music are reproduced
	397–29	belief that mind is, e· temporarily,
	398–27	E· a blind faith removes
	400–24	e· as in optics we see painted on the retina
	400–31	E· our Master felt this.
	404–31	e· in body, unless it makes him better mentally,
	407–15	e· into spiritual power and good-will to man.
	414–22	e· so, harmony is universal,
	416–17	e· as the body, . . . is material.
	416–23	no longer the parent, e· in appearance.
	419– 3	hate will perpetuate or e· create the
	427– 3	e· the law of the spirit of Truth,
	429–23	e· according to the calculations of
	440–13	E· penal law holds homicide, . . . to be
t	446–22	e· unto the end of the world."— Matt. 28 : 20.
	454– 6	The understanding, e· in a degree,
	457–26	They e· practise these, intending
	464– 9	could not take her place, e· if willing so to do.
r	470– 1	With one Father, e· God,
	471– 9	e· as these so-called senses receive no
	478– 4	E· according to the teachings of natural science,
	478–12	nor were they e· visible through the windows?
	485–23	in which man is perfect, e· as the
	486– 7	E· then he must gain spiritual understanding
	491–29	e· though he does not understand C. S.,
	492– 8	a knowledge of this, e· in small degree,
	494–21	e· as the experiences of the sleeping dream
	496–22	e· with the spiritual law which says
	497–22	e· the allness of Soul, Spirit,
g	502–14	E· thus the crude forms of human thought
	506–20	e· as He opens the petals of a
	509–18	e· as nebulæ indicate the immensity of
	517–22	E· eternity can never reveal the whole of God,
	520– 1	sweetest rest, e· from a human standpoint,
	541–12	e· the human concept of Love
	541–25	Now it repudiates e· the human duty
	542– 9	E· the disposition to excuse guilt
	544–17	under the control of the one Mind, e· God.
	545–31	e· so in Christ— I Cor. 15 : 22.

even

g	549–27	e· this great observer mistakes nature,
	550–11	ends, e· as it begins, in nameless nothingness?
	550–13	should appear now, e· as it will hereafter.
	552– 8	e· where the proof requisite to sustain this
	554– 2	e· the cause of all that exists,
	556–22	E· so goes on the Adam-belief,
ap	564– 6	to kill . . . e· their fellow-mortals,
	564–11	and e· his crucifixion
	565–22	purifying e· the gold of human character.
	573–14	e· the declaration from heaven,
	577– 1	e· as the material sense of personality
gl	588–13	e· as numbers which never blend
	588–17	e· the belief that life, substance, and

evening
and morning
g	510–22	already divided into e· and morning ;

and the morning
g	504– 4	e· and the morning were the first — Gen. 1 : 5.
	506– 9	e· and the morning were the second — Gen. 1 : 8.
	508–26	e· and the morning were the third — Gen. 1 : 13.
	511–15	e· and the morning were the fourth — Gen. 1 : 19.
	513– 4	e· and the morning were the fifth — Gen. 1 : 23.
	518–25	e· and the morning were the sixth — Gen. 1 : 31.
gl	584– 3	e· and the morning were the sixth — Gen. 1 : 5.

gl	586– 1	definition of

evenings
g	504–17	taking place on so many e· and *mornings*,

evenly
ph	168– 4	If the scales are e· adjusted,

event
a	24–31	could not admit such an e· to be possible.
	45–24	misconstrued that e·.

events
m	60–12	From the logic of e· we learn that
	66–23	It is better to await the logic of e·
sp	84–16	to foresee and foretell e· which concern the
	85–18	e· of great moment were foretold by the

eventually
a	23–10	e· both sin and suffering will fall at the feet of
an	105–16	When our laws e· take cognizance of
f	244–17	hypothesis that he returns e· to his
b	303–18	will e· destroy this illusion
o	357–23	false claims, which will e· disappear,
p	370–24	a drug may e· lose its supposed power
r	492–23	must e· submit to the Science of Mind,
g	524–30	and e· ejected at the demand of matter?
ap	565–16	will e· rule all nations and peoples
	569–20	must e· expiate their sin through suffering.

ever
pref	xl–17	e· present in human consciousness
pr	5– 9	So it will e· be, till we learn that
a	34–10	If all who e· partook of the sacrament
	41–20	No ancient school . . . e· taught or
	52–16	the best man that e· trod the globe.
m	59–25	before this union and continue e· after,
sp	71–30	presupposes Spirit, which is e· infinite,
	72–21	God, good, being e· present, it follows
	76– 9	belief that life, . . . was e· in a finite form,
	85–13	told me all things that e· I did :— *John* 4 : 29.
	91– 2	Have you e· pictured this heaven and
s	118–10	this leaven of Truth is e· at work.
	129– 5	Truth is e· truthful,
	148– 7	Neither anatomy nor theology has e· described
	153–32	Neither sympathy nor society should e· tempt
	164– 6	e· yet promulgated, is true,
ph	175– 7	In old times who e· heard of dyspepsia,
	193–22	e· since the injury was received in boyhood.
	200–10	Life is, . . . and e· will be independent of
	200–17	the real man was, is, and e· shall be perfect,
f	201– 1	The best sermon e· preached is
	219–21	"The wish," . . . "is e· father to the thought."
	245–32	infinite never began nor will it e· end.
	248– 4	One marvels that a friend can e· seem less
	250– 9	which never errs, and is e· conscious ;
	250–32	nor . . . e· the sport of circumstance.
c	260–32	by the thoughts e· recurring to one's self,
b	277– 1	but matter is e· non-intelligent
	300–21	the realization of God as e· present
	302–13	this belief is all that will e· be lost.
	306–28	Life and the universe, e· present
	313–24	Jesus . . . was the most scientific man that e·
	314–21	presented to her, more than e· before,
	333–27	and e· will be inseparable from the
o	353– 4	senses and Science have e· been antagonistic,
	355–22	e· offered for acceptance,"
p	364– 2	the best man that e· trod this planet.
	368– 7	truth and error have come nearer than e·
	374–29	Nothing that lives e· dies,
	376–14	than in all the blood, which e· flowed
	384–27	neither . . . will e· result from exposure to the
	387– 8	immortal Mind is e· active,

ever
p	429–22	for if Life e· had any beginning,
t	444– 7	If Christian Scientists e· fail to receive
	464–28	Neither dishonesty nor ignorance e· founded,
r	469– 6	If Life e· had a beginning,
	470– 9	the loss of Love as e· present and
	470–24	If there e· was a moment when
	470–30	If man e· existed without this
	471–18	God is infinite, therefore e· present,
	478–10	when no such persons were e· seen to go into
	479–16	Does that which we call dead e· see, hear,
	485– 6	which e· betrays mortals into sickness, sin, and
g	507–28	Creation is e· appearing,
	507–28	and must e· continue to appear
	527– 5	but e· beautiful and complete.
	531– 9	as if hope were e· prophesying thus :
	534–26	than there has e· been since the
ap	568– 1	E· since the foundation of the world,
	568– 2	e· since error would establish material belief,
	568–27	A louder song, sweeter than has e· before
	572–14	can e· furnish the vision of the Apocalypse,
	573–16	the divine Principle of harmony, is e· with men,
	578–18	in the house . . . of [LOVE] for e·.— *Psal.* 23 : 6.

ever-agitated
f	254–27	the e· but healthful waters of truth,

everlasting
a	23–11	will fall at the feet of e· Love.
	33–15	With the great glory of an e· victory
	45– 4	sublime success, an e· victory.
sp	81–11	this fact affords no certainty of e· life.
	99–27	sin, disease, and death give e· place to
s	121–20	clearer views of the e· facts,
	121–31	the e· government of the universe.
f	216–18	in submission to e· Life and Truth and Love.
	244–31	e· grandeur and immortality of development,
c	255– *	*Thou art from e·. — Psal.* 93 : 2.
	256–13	The e· I AM is not bounded nor
b	286–27	are the antipodes of e· Truth,
	290– 1	the e· I AM, the Being who was and is
p	390– 5	should never deny the e· harmony of Soul,
	410– 5	defines e· life as a present knowledge of
	428–17	the eternal builder, the e· Father,
r	489–10	yields to the reality of e· Life.
g	556–12	life e· is not to be gained by dying.
ap	568–30	Love sends forth her primal and e· strain.
gl	594–20	God ; that only which is perfect, e·,

everlastingly
s	143–30	power e· due its holy name.

evermore
b	334–27	and, behold, I am alive for e·,— *Rev.* 1 : 18.

ever-operative
s	123–27	they illustrated an e· divine Principle.

ever-presence
s	107– 8	e·, delivering the children of men
ap	567– 2	the e· of ministering Love.

ever-present
pr	16–31	*Thy kingdom is come ; Thou art e·.*
a	52– 9	the e· rebuke of his perfection and purity.
sp	84–11	prerogative of the divine Mind,
s	108–23	Truth, and Love are all-powerful and e· ;
	130–32	no longer imagine evil to be e·
ph	180–25	the e· Mind who understands all things,
f	218–23	divine Love, who is an e· help
c	256–11	rather than the one e· I AM.
b	297–24	and Truth, the e·, is becoming understood.
	312–20	man's eternal Principle is e· Life.
p	377– 5	he should rejoice always in e· Love.
r	496– 4	this e· omnipotent Mind is reflected
g	501–13	is consonant with e· Love.
	503–14	light of e· Love illumines the universe.
	504–14	fill immensity and are e·.
ap	567– 7	To infinite, e· Love, all is Love,

every
pr	6–12	E· supposed pleasure in sin
	13– 4	"Ho, e· one that thirsteth,— *Isa.* 55 : 1.
a	19–17	E· pang of repentance and suffering,
	19–17	e· effort for reform,
	19–18	e· good thought and deed,
	20–28	"Let us lay aside e· weight,— *Heb.* 12 : 1.
	23–19	Spirit, which rebukes sin of e· kind
	28–31	await, in some form, e· pioneer of truth.
	30–28	loathe sin and rebuke it under e· mask.
	37–23	privilege of e· child, man, and woman,
	37–30	preach the gospel to e· creature !"— *Mark* 16 : 15.
	43–27	divine must overcome the human at e· point.
	45– 2	but Jesus vanquished e· material obstacle,
	45– 2	overcame e· law of matter,
	46–10	spoken . . . in e· age and clime.
m	61– 9	E· valley of sin must be exalted,
	61– 9	and e· mountain of selfishness be brought low,
	65– 3	May Christ, Truth, be present at e· bridal altar
sp	70– 1	E· day is a mystery.
	77–24	less with e· advanced stage of existence.

every

sp	79–10	and dig up *e·* seed of error's sowing.
	98–20	for *e·* man to understand and to practise.
an	102–19	*e·* hour weaving webs more complicated
	104– 9	"E· great scientific truth goes through three
	105–13	Mortal mind, . . . is the criminal in *e·* case ;
s	107–10	delivering the children of men from *e·* ill
	113–24	"but *e·* [mortal] man a liar."— *Rom.* 3 : 4.
	122–22	instances . . . which *e·* thinker can recall
	134– 2	At *e·* advancing step,
	138–27	Our Master said to *e·* follower :
	138–28	preach the gospel to *e·* creature !— *Mark* 16 : 15.
	143– 1	Truth is God's remedy for error of *e·* kind,
	144–28	*e·* man will be his own physician,
	148–14	*e·* function, formation, and manifestation.
	149– 5	more excellent way is divine Science in *e·* case.
	151–20	E· function of the real man is governed by the
	151–31	mortal mind claims to govern *e·* organ
	152–12	Such errors beset *e·* material theory,
	152–23	E· material dependence had failed her
	158–25	Evidences of progress . . . greet us on *e·* hand.
	162–13	not in one instance, but in *e·* instance.
ph	179–12	E· medical method has its advocates.
	186–15	E· mortal must learn that there is neither
	186–20	E· attempt of evil to destroy good
	188–13	*e·* one recognizes his condition to be
	194–13	E· theory opposed to this fact
	195– 6	E· sound convulsed him with anguish.
	197– 4	E· one hastens to get it.
f	207– 5	*e·* scientific statement in Christianity has
	208– 9	a law of mortal mind, wrong in *e·* sense,
	213–11	E· step towards goodness is a departure from
	215–23	E· quality and condition of mortality
	224– 2	feels the . . . effect of truth through *e·* pore.
	224– 7	E· sensuous pleasure or pain is self-destroyed
	233– 1	E· day makes its demands upon us
	236–20	availability of good as the remedy for *e·* woe.
	239–24	produces *e·* discordant action of the body.
	242–28	while inspiration restores *e·* part of the
	243– 7	can heal the sick in *e·* age
c	261–16	he hobbled *e·* day to the theatre,
	261–32	Good demands of man *e·* hour,
	262–28	E· concept which seems to begin with the brain
	267– 1	E· object in material thought
b	268– 9	Mind as the cause of *e·* effect.
	277–28	*e·* statement into which it enters.
	279–22	E· system of human philosophy,
	280–22	urges through *e·* avenue the belief
	299–14	*e·* real individuality, image, or
	307–21	*e·* sin or supposed material pain
	323– 4	the endeavor to forsake error of *e·* kind
	326– 7	and find the divine remedy for *e·* ill,
o	354–26	Sin should become unreal to *e·* one.
	355–11	Let discord of *e·* name and nature
	358–11	and sustains . . . *e·* point it presents.
p	370– 1	To be *e·* whit whole,
	371–13	sick humanity sees danger in *e·* direction,
	371–32	and can make it "*e·* whit whole."— *John* 7 : 23.
	378– 6	and meet *e·* circumstance with truth.
	379– 7	Mind, controlling *e·* effect
	380–32	E· law of matter or the body,
	389– 4	*e·* erroneous belief, or material condition.
	391–29	Mentally contradict *e·* complaint
	392– 4	*e·* broken moral law should be taken into account
	394–26	conquer discord of *e·* kind with harmony,
	400–16	understand that *e·* disease is an error,
	405–22	better to be exposed to *e·* plague on earth
	406– 5	equal to *e·* emergency,
	406–19	Resist evil — error of *e·* sort
	406–21	to avail ourselves in *e·* direction
	407– 8	E· hour of delay makes the
	407–24	perfect, harmonious in *e·* action.
	408– 1	E· sort of sickness is error,
	410–10	*e·* word that proceedeth out of — *Matt.* 4 : 4.
	410–14	E· trial of our faith in God makes us
	411–31	alleviates the symptoms of *e·* disease.
	413–14	taking a fish out of water *e·* day
	413–24	noticing *e·* symptom of flatulency,
	415– 3	Mind in *e·* case is the eternal God,
	418–28	"Preach the gospel to *e·* — *Mark* 16 : 15.
	418–29	Speak the truth to *e·* form of error.
	419–16	Meet *e·* adverse circumstance as its master.
	420–26	*e·* physical action and condition.
	423–11	reaching to *e·* part of the human system.
	431– 4	prisoner watched with the sick *e·* night
t	448–19	Try to leave on *e·* student's mind
	450– 2	twist *e·* fact to suit themselves.
	451–19	E· Christian Scientist, *e·* conscientious teacher
	451–25	nature and methods of error of *e·* sort,
	458–13	sword of Truth must turn in *e·* direction
	460–21	starts a petty crossfire over *e·* cripple
	462–14	abide strictly by its rules, heed *e·* statement,
	462–18	as they . . . do in *e·* department of life.
	463– 2	phenomena, which fluctuate *e·* instant
r	471–21	but *e·* [material] man a liar."— *Rom.* 3 : 4.

every

r	475–26	and over *e·* creeping thing — *Gen.* 1 : 26.
	482–25	to the hungering heart in *e·* age.
	486– 5	until *e·* corporeal sense is quenched.
	494–10	and always will meet *e·* human need.
	494–14	in *e·* hour, divine Love supplies all good.
g	507– 4	Spirit duly feeds and clothes *e·* object,
	512– 4	*e·* living creature that moveth,— *Gen.* 1 : 21.
	512– 6	*e·* winged fowl after his kind :— *Gen.* 1 : 21.
	515–14	and over *e·* creeping thing — *Gen.* 1 : 26.
	517–28	and over *e·* living thing— *Gen.* 1 : 28.
	518– 6	*e·* herb bearing seed,— *Gen.* 1 : 29.
	518– 8	And to *e·* beast of the earth,— *Gen.* 1 : 30.
	518– 9	and to *e·* fowl of the air,— *Gen.* 1 : 30.
	518–11	I have given *e·* green herb— *Gen.* 1 : 30.
	520–19	and *e·* plant of the field— *Gen.* 2 : 5.
	520–19	and *e·* herb of the field— *Gen.* 2 : 5.
	526– 4	"*e·* plant of the field— *Gen.* 2 : 5.
	527–20	Evil is . . . false in *e·* statement.
	527–22	formed *e·* beast of the field,— *Gen.* 2 : 19.
	527–22	and *e·* fowl of the air ;— *Gen.* 2 : 19.
	527–24	Adam called *e·* living creature,— *Gen.* 2 : 19.
	533–24	belief . . . is growing worse at *e·* step,
	537– 7	sword which turned *e·* way,— *Gen.* 3 : 24.
	542– 1	The belief of life in matter sins at *e·* step.
	547– 4	*e·* one must be true, for not one departs from
	548–13	E· agony of mortal error helps error to
ap	564–16	met and conquered sin in *e·* form.
	565–10	decreed the death of *e·* male child
	569– 3	E· mortal at some period,
gl	584–14	*e·* belief of life where Life is not yields to
	598– 4	So is *e·* one that is born of the— *John* 3 : 8.
fr	600– *	being fruitful in *e·* good work,— *Col.* 1 : 10.

(see also **tree**)

everything

belief fhat

g	531– 2	the belief that *e·* springs from dust

God saw

g	518–24	And God saw *e·* that He had made,— *Gen.* 1 : 31.

good in

ph	176–13	"sermons in stones, and good in *e·*."

He saw

g	525–23	He saw *e·* which He had made,

opposition to

s	114–32	the usual opposition to *e·* new,

relating to God

s	127–13	stand for *e·* relating to God,

sacrifice

pr	11–25	we shall sacrifice *e·* for it.

that creepeth

g	513–23	and *e·* that creepeth upon— *Gen.* 1 : 25.
	518–10	and to *e·* that creepeth— *Gen.* 1 : 30.

s	127– 5	*e·* entitled to a classification as truth,
f	243–28	annihilation to *e·* unlike themselves,
b	269–32	The first theory, that matter is *e·*,
	270– 3	(1) that *e·* is matter ; (2) that *e·* is Mind.
	301–28	with *e·* turned upside down.
	331–16	E· in God's universe expresses Him.
g	523–11	In error *e·* comes from beneath,
	525–20	E· good or worthy, God made.

everywhere

	iii– *	Thou here, and *e·*.
s	147– 8	*e·*, when honestly applied
f	223– 8	If Spirit is *all* and is *e·*,
b	287–14	God being *e·* and all-inclusive,
o	361– 5	now and forever, here and *e·*.
p	371–11	As frightened children look *e·* for the
r	473– 8	God is *e·*, and nothing apart from Him is present
g	516– 8	shall see this true likeness and reflection *e·*.

Eve's

g	538–30	E· declaration, "I have gotten— *Gen.* 4 : 1.

Eves

ph	176– 3	modern E· took up the study of medical works

evidence

absolute

s	142–10	Truth, alone can furnish us with absolute *e·*.

according to the

p	423–17	according to the *e·* which matter presents.

accredited

a	18–10	against the accredited *e·* of the senses,

all

a	50–23	and that all *e·* of their correctness

all the

p	384–28	all the *e·* before the senses can never overrule.

basis of

gl	581–19	on the basis of *e·* obtained from the

change the

b	297–13	Change the *e·*, and that disappears

Christian

r	487–19	Christian *e·* is founded on Science

evidence

clear
  p 398– 6   clear *e·* that the malady was not material.
contradicts the
  s 119–26   contradicts the *e·* before the senses
  o 353– 8   which contradicts the *e·* of error,
destroy the
  p 412–22   conform the argument so as to destroy the *e·*
  417–17   you destroy the *e·*, for the disease disappears.
false
  s 120–24   heals the sick, overthrows false *e·*,
  131– 6   false *e·* before the corporeal senses disappears.
  f 252–15   The false *e·* of material sense contrasts
  b 275–27   It destroys the false *e·* that misleads
  287–29   false *e·* will finally yield to Truth,
  p 420–31   Turn his gaze from the false *e·* of the senses
feasible
  o 345–20   the only feasible *e·* that one does understand
full
  a 42–17   and gave full *e·* of divine Science,
furnish the
  ph 189–17   is supposed to furnish the *e·* of
immediate
  ph 188–29   physical senses have no immediate *e·* of
immortal
  a 29–31   immortal *e·* that Spirit is harmonious
latter
  sp 81– 4   this latter *e·* is destroyed by Mind-science.
law and
  p 441– 1   comprehending and defining all law and *e·*,
material
  a 52– 7   the material *e·* of sin, sickness, and death.
  p 422–18   causing it to depend less on material *e·*.
  gl 584–15   Any material *e·* of death is false,
no
  pr 9– 9   though we give no *e·* of the sincerity of
  o 356– 4   material existence affords no *e·* of spiritual
no direct
  b 284–17   which receive no direct *e·* of Spirit,
not so much
  sp 81– 1   There is not so much *e·* to prove
of matter
  s 128–26   the so-called *e·* of matter.
of Personal Sense
  p 433–11   *e·* of Personal Sense against Mortal Man.
of Spirit
  b 296–23   When the *e·* of Spirit and matter,
of the material senses
  b 274– 9   deduced from the *e·* of the material senses.
of the physical senses
  s 114– 7   based on the *e·* of the physical senses,
  122– 1   *e·* of the physical senses often reverses
of the senses
  a 18–10   against the accredited *e·* of the senses,
  p 386– 2   the *e·* of the senses is not to be accepted
  420–31   Turn his gaze from the false *e·* of the senses
of the spiritual senses
  b 288– 4   the *e·* of the spiritual senses
of things
  r 468–21   the *e·* of things not seen." — *Heb.* 11 : 1.
of this condition
  ph 193– 7   *e·* of this condition of the bone.
of this revelation
  s 108–12   allowing the *e·* of this revelation to multiply
only
  f 207–32   The only *e·* of this inversion is
permanent
  f 232– 6   no scatheless and permanent *e·* of either.
real
  r 494–27   The other is the eternal and real *e·*,
recognize
  an 104–29   Our courts recognize *e·* to prove the
reverses the
  s 116– 5   Science so reverses the *e·* before the
  f 215–22   reverses the *e·* of material sense.
  t 461–13   because Science reverses the *e·* before the
rises above the
  t 448–12   rises above the *e·* of the corporeal senses ;
scientific
  p 380–23   scientific *e·* of which has accumulated
sensible
  s 109– 7   not, . . . seen to be supported by sensible *e·*,
spiritual
  a 52– 6   drank in the spiritual *e·* of health,
  b 297–22   spiritual *e·*, contradicting the testimony of
  gl 585– 9   spiritual *e·* opposed to material sense ;
stronger
  pr 7– 2   stronger *e·* that Jesus' reproof was pointed
  o 353– 7   having the stronger *e·* of Truth
sufficient
  p 363–29   was her grief sufficient *e·* to warrant
this
  p 380–26   this *e·* will gather momentum
to the senses
  p 370–10   furnishes the *e·* to the senses,

evidence

worthy
  pr 4– 8   the only worthy *e·* of our gratitude
  a 23–18   Faith, . . . is the *e·* gained from Spirit,
  42–18   *e·* so important to mortals.
  50–20   before the *e·* of the bodily senses,
  s 117–24   *E·* drawn from the five physical senses
  159– 7   The *e·* was found to be conclusive,
  164–21   rather does it *e·* the truth of
  ph 177– 5   The *e·* of divine Mind's healing power
  177– 6   as certain as the *e·* of my own existence.
  f 214– 5   *e·* before his material senses,
  b 303–30   When the *e·* before the material senses yielded
  o 359–14   The *e·* of the existence of Spirit,
  p 380– 8   Contending for the *e·* or indulging the
  389–12   better results of Mind's opposite *e·*.
  417–18   The *e·* before the corporeal senses
  428–26   The *e·* of man's immortality will become
  430–27   *e·* for the prosecution being called for,
  r 471– 7   *e·* before the five corporeal senses,
  471–14   the *e·* as to these facts is not supported by
  471–16   the *e·* that God and man coexist
  478– 3   What *e·* of Soul or of immortality
  493– 6   All the *e·* of physical sense
  497–13   the *e·* of divine, efficacious Love,
  g 543–17   All error proceeds from the *e·* before the
  gl 590– 4   *E·* obtained from the five corporeal senses;

evidenced
  o 355–29   and *e·* by the sick who are cured

evidences
  s 158–24   *E·* of progress and of spiritualization
  c 264–25   the only *e·*, by which we can recognize
  b 289–17   destroys with the spiritual *e·* of Life;
  p 395– 8   master the false *e·* of the corporeal senses
  428– 9   false trusts and material *e·*
  g 523–15   clear *e·* of two distinct documents

evident
  m 68–25   perpetuation of the floral species by bud . . .
              is *e·*
  sp 82– 1   must have known the deceased . . . is *e·*,
  s 111–27   became *e·* to me, — that Mind governs
  138– 6   It was now *e·* to Peter that divine Life,
  f 214–30   *e·* that the body as matter has no sensation
  o 345– 4   As it is *e·* that the likeness of Spirit cannot

evidently
  s 150–23   and it is as *e·* erroneous to the author,
  f 204–18   Such theories are *e·* erroneous.
  o 352– 6   *e·* considering it a mortal and material belief

evil (*see also* **evil's**)

all
  s 127–19   Supreme Being, Mind, exempt from all *e·*.
  ph 178–20   this so-called mind, from which comes all *e·*,
  f 206–10   Will-power is capable of all *e·*.
  t 450–30   claim of animal magnetism, that all *e·*
  r 473– 4   The Science of Mind disposes of all *e·*.
  494–32   they cast fear and all *e·* out of themselves
  ap 563–16   lifts the veil from this embodiment of all *e·*,
  563–28   winding its way amidst all *e·*,
  564–25   hatred, and revenge, — all *e·*, — are typified
  gl 581– 6   counteracting all *e·*, sensuality, and
all manner of
  p 418–27   Cast out all manner of *e·*.
all sorts of
  p 404–10   Lust, malice, and all sorts of *e·*
and error
  f 227–19   but *e·* and error lead into captivity.
and fear
  p 392– 7   Casting out *e·* and fear enables
and good
  sp 91–29   postulate is, that mind is both *e·* and good ;
  an 103–21   belief that mind is . . . both *e·* and good ;
  s 114– 1   Usage classes both *e·* and good together
  f 246– 2   not a pendulum, swinging between *e·* and good,
  b 330–25   The notion that both *e·* and good are real
and hate
  t 448–22   impossible for error, *e·*, and hate to accomplish
and materiality
  b 277–11   *e·* and materiality are unreal
and matter
  b 277– 9   *e·* and matter, are mortal error,
and suffering
  sp 72–29   when *e·* and suffering are communicable.
ascendency over the
  m 61– 5   must have ascendency over the *e·*
attempt of
  ph 186–20   Every attempt of *e·* to destroy good is a failure,
avoidance of the
  ap 571– 5   necessary to ensure the avoidance of the *e·*
becomes more apparent
  f 207– 2   *e·* becomes more apparent and obnoxious
becomes nothing
  r 480– 4   *e·* becomes nothing, — the opposite of

evil

behold
f 243–23 "of purer eyes than to behold *e·*,"— *Hab.* 1 : 13.
o 357– 5 "of purer eyes than to behold *e·*."— *Hab.* 1 : 13.

belief in
g 540– 7 stirring up the belief in *e·* to its utmost,

blindness to
t 448–15 upon your blindness to *e·*

calls itself
b 287–18 *E·* calls itself something, when it is nothing.

cannot be
sp 91–30 whereas the real Mind cannot be *e·*

can only seem
r 470–14 *e·* can only seem to be real by giving reality to

casting out
a 46–11 again seen casting out *e·* and healing the sick.
p 392– 7 Casting out *e·* and fear enables

cast out
a 49– 4 healed the sick, cast out *e·*,
51–31 enabled Jesus to heal the sick, cast out *e·*,
s 137– 2 heal the sick, cast out *e·*, raise the dead ;
ph 185–22 Jesus cast out *e·* and healed the sick,

cast out the
p 411–16 Thereupon Jesus cast out the *e·*,

casts out
r 497–11 understanding that casts out *e·* as unreal.

casts out the
s 135–14 when Truth casts out the *e·* called disease,

causing
sp 93–16 not create a mind susceptible of causing *e·*,

cease to manifest
o 346–14 only as we cease to manifest *e·*

claims of
s 130–30 astounded at the vigorous claims of *e·*
t 447–21 Expose and denounce the claims of *e·*
448– 1 To assume that there are no claims of *e·*
g 529–28 faith to fight all claims of *e·*,

coincide with
ph 167–22 no more . . . than good can coincide with *e·*.

confers no pleasure
a 40– 1 once admit that *e·* confers no pleasure,

constitutes
g 527–17 constitutes *e·* and mortal knowledge.

create
g 540– 5 "I make peace, and create *e·*·"— *Isa.* 45 : 7.

crying
m 64– 1 Want of uniform justice is a crying *e·*

declared
ph 165– 2 *E·* declared that eating this fruit would open

degree of
t 451–26 subtle degree of *e·*, deceived and deceiving.

deliver us from
pr 16–15 "Deliver us from *e·*,"— *Matt.* 6 : 13.
17– 9 deliver us from *e·* ;— *Matt.* 6 : 13.

demon, or
p 411–15 demon, or *e·*, replied that his name was Legion.

destruction of
a 53–24 sacrifice . . . for the destruction of *e·*.

devil or
r 469–16 *devil* or *e·* — is not Mind, is not Truth,
ap 563–19 that old serpent, whose name is devil or *e·*,

element of
g 539–11 God could never impart an element of *e·*,

error and
a 52–17 error and *e·* again make common cause
b 272–26 recorded in the destruction of error and *e·*,

escape from
b 316– 3 may learn how to escape from *e·*.
ap 571–12 Escape from *e·*, and designate those as

flesh, and
pr 10–13 overcoming the world, the flesh, and *e·*,

foreshadowing
sp 84– 5 not by foreshadowing *e·* and mistaking fact

foundation of
sp 92–26 The foundation of *e·* is laid on a belief in

from good to
sp 77– 2 said : "I cannot turn at once from good to *e·*."

good and
(*see* good)

good or
ph 172– 1 and that the cognizance of good or *e·*,
f 205–16 believing that matter can be . . . good or *e·*),
240–18 Mortals move onward towards good or *e·*
b 340– 1 their imaginary power for good or *e·*,

good over
p 406–23 Life over death, and good over *e·*,

has no history
g 538–21 *e·* has no history,

has no power
p 398–32 *E·* has no power, no intelligence,

has no reality
sp 71– 2 *E·* has no reality.

has tried
ap 568– 3 *e·* has tried to slay the Lamb ;

evil

inventions of
ap 563– 7 showing its horns in the many inventions of *e·*

is a negation
ph 186–11 *E·* is a negation, because it is the absence of

is but an illusion
r 480–23 Hence, *e·* is but an illusion,

is destroyed
b 311–13 *E·* is destroyed by the sense of good.

is nothing
b 330–27 *E·* is nothing, no thing, mind, nor power.

is not Mind
f 207– 8 Indeed, *e·* is not Mind.
r 469–16 *e·* — is not Mind, is not Truth,

is not mind
p 398–32 fact remains that *e·* is not mind.

is not power
an 102–30 Mankind must learn that *e·* is not power.
ph 192–24 *E·* is not power.

is not supreme
f 207–10 *E·* is not supreme ; good is not helpless ;

is self-assertive
ph 186–17 *E·* is self-assertive.

is sometimes
b 327– 9 *E·* is sometimes a man's highest conception

is temporal
ap 569–25 *e·* is temporal, not eternal.

is unreal
t 447–31 He may say, as a subterfuge, that *e·* is unreal
g 527–19 *E·* is unreal because it is a lie,

its
r 490–10 From this cooperation arises its *e·*.

knowledge of
g 526–21 erroneous doctrine that the knowledge of *e·* is
527–14 a knowledge of *e·* would make man mortal.
537– 9 knowledge of *e·* was never the essence of

lapse into
r 470–17 How can good lapse into *e·*,

lessen
t 450–20 has enlisted to lessen *e·*,

lie, called
ap 568– 5 Science is able to destroy this lie, called *e·*.

manifestations of
b 293–24 manifestations of *e·*, which counterfeit divine

master
p 404–25 increases his ability to master *e·*

matter and
gl 583–23 CREATOR. . . . the opposite of matter and *e·*,

matter, or
sp 92–16 knowledge gained from matter, or *e·*,
gl 594– 6 claim that there is . . . matter, or *e·* ;

medium of
sp 91–31 Mind cannot be evil nor the medium of *e·*,

mention of
g 526–14 first mention of *e·* is in the legendary

named
r 469–28 believe there is another power, named *e·*.
gl 594–10 claim . . . there was another power, named *e·*

never causes
sp 93–13 Good never causes *e·*,

never enters into
b 336– 4 Good never enters into *e·*,

never produce
b 304–13 good can never produce *e·* ;

no
s 140–27 Love, . . . causeth no *e·*, disease, nor
f 207– 1 for there is no *e·* in Spirit.
210–30 immortal sense includes no *e·* nor pestilence.
b 278– 8 in Truth there is no error, and in good no *e·*.
335– 2 There is no *e·* in Spirit, because God is Spirit,
t 448– 8 Under such circumstances, to say that there is
no *e·*,
453–22 thanks God that there is no *e·*, yet serves evil
ap 578–11 I will fear no *e·* :— *Psal.* 23 : 4.
gl 596–22 I will fear no *e·*."— *Psal.* 23 : 4.

no longer imagine
s 130–32 no longer imagine *e·* to be ever-present

nothingness of
b 269– 8 the unreality, the nothingness, of *e·*.
293–31 entireness of God, good, and the nothingness
of *e·*.
ap 563–17 but he also sees the nothingness of *e·*

not supported by
r 471–15 evidence . . . is not supported by *e·*,

one
pr 16–19 one *e·*, is but another name for
r 476– 2 children of the wicked one, or the one *e·*,

only
ph 186– 8 Erring human mind-forces can work only *e·*

only as
g 529–23 enters into the metaphor only as *e·*.

or matter
t 454–11 *e·* or matter has neither intelligence nor power,

overcome
ap 571–16 under all circumstances, overcome *e·* with

evil

parent of
 r 480–25 The supposititious parent of *e·* is a lie.
personification of
 an 103– 3 Paul refers to the personification of *e·* as
personified
 o 357– 7 Jesus said of personified *e·*, that it was
point out the
 ap 571– 1 they are not so willing to point out the *e·*
produces
 s 144–19 It produces *e·* continually,
 f 231–12 If God makes sin, if good produces *e·*,
producing
 c 263–12 producing *e·* when he would create good,
 o 343–16 impossibility of good producing *e·* ;
prolific of
 t 457–17 mental malpractice, prolific of *e·*,
remedy the
 m 63–21 If . . . franchise for women will remedy the *e·*
repetition of
 sp 73–14 known by its fruit, — the repetition of *e·*.
represents
 b 282–10 the straight line represents *e·*,
resist
 p 406–19 Resist *e·* — error of every sort
resisting
 t 446–24 Resisting *e·*, you overcome it
sense of
 b 325– 3 He . . . loses all sense of *e·*,
 g 540–15 that Truth may annihilate all sense of *e·*
serves
 t 453–22 yet serves *e·* in the name of good.
shalt not know
 a 19–32 thou shalt not know *e·*, for there is one Life,
sin, and
 b 315– 8 matter, sin, and *e·* were not Mind ;
source of
 r 489–24 The corporeal senses are the only source of *e·*
statement about
 g 544–17 The first statement about *e·*,
still charges
 ap 564– 3 *e·* still charges the spiritual idea with
symptoms of
 g 540–12 when the symptoms of *e·*, illusion, are aggra-
    vated,
tempted with
 g 527–13 "God cannot be tempted with *e·*,— *Jas.* 1 : 13
this
 m 65–31 will assuredly throw off this *e·*,
 ap 565– 2 nearing its doom, this *e·* increases
to accomplish more
 sp 96–32 wicked minds will endeavor . . . to accomplish
    more *e·* ;
unimportant and
 r 485– 8 If the unimportant and *e·* appear,
unreality called
 s 110– 9 the awful unreality called *e·*.
unreality of
 f 205–21 the nothingness and unreality of *e·*.
 b 339–12 Science demonstrates the unreality of *e·*,
 339–19 Only those, . . . understand the unreality of *e·*.
victory over
 ap 571–18 the occasion for a victory over *e·*.
will boast
 t 450–18 unless . . . *e·* will boast itself above good.
would appear
 f 216–22 *e·* would appear to be the master of good,
would vanish
 r 480–31 *e·* would vanish before the reality of good.

 pr 5–27 If prayer nourishes the . . . prayer is an *e·*.
 a 42–27 governed by God — by good, not *e·* — and is
 m 65–13 powers of *e·* so conspicuous to-day
 68–22 and the *e·* to hatch their silly innuendoes
 sp 72–22 *e·*, the suppositional opposite of good,
 72–25 *e·* is neither communicable nor scientific.
 76–10 belief . . . in a finite form, or good in *e·*,
 93–14 nor creates aught that can cause *e·*.
 93–16 *e·* is the opposing error and not the truth
 an 102–32 C. S. despoils the kingdom of *e·*,
 103–17 *E·* is a suppositional lie.
 103–21 false belief . . . that *e·* is as real as good
 104–17 *e·*, occultism, necromancy, mesmerism,
 105– 9 *e·*, which is the real outlaw,
 s 113–19 deny death, *e·*, sin, disease.
 113–20 *e·*, death, deny good, omnipotent God, Life.
 114– 5 human mind and *e·* in contradistinction to
 116–17 extinction of all belief in matter, *e·*,
 119–22 *e·* should be regarded as unnatural.
 ph 167– 8 admission of the claims of good or of *e·*
 169–32 good that a poisonous drug seems to do is *e·*,
 186–16 there is neither power nor reality in *e·*.
 186–18 should strip *e·* of all pretensions.
 186–19 The only power of *e·* is to destroy itself.
 186–24 If *e·* is as real as good, *e·* is also as

evil

 f 203– 1 as though *e·* could overbear the law of Love,
 203–20 when *e·* has overtaxed the belief of life
 204– 1 It is *e·* that dies ; good dies not.
 204–13 *e·*, is the unlikeness of good.
 204–32 The error, which says . . . good is in *e·*,
 207– 9 *e·* is the awful deception and unreality
 207–15 nor is *e·* mightier than good.
 229–13 declaring Him good in one instance and *e·* in
 230–18 no more . . . than goodness can cause *e·*
 234–10 more familiar with good than with *e·*,
 236–22 insubordination is an *e·*,
 244–24 He does not pass . . . from *e·* to good,
 244–27 He does not pass . . . from good to *e·*.
 c 263–18 the *e·* which I would not, *that I do.*" — *Rom.* 7 : 19.
 266–20 sinner makes his own hell by doing *e·*,
 266–22 material sense, aiding *e·* with *e·*,
 b 277– 7 Good cannot result in *e·*.
 277–21 asserts . . . that good is the origin of *e·*.
 285– 2 cannot be cognizant of good or of *e·*,
 288–22 that Life is God, good, and not *e·* ;
 290–31 no purer until *e·* is disarmed by good.
 292–15 To mortal mind, . . . *e·* is real.
 292–22 of your father, the devil [*e·*], — *John* 8 : 44.
 307– 7 *E·* still affirms itself to be mind,
 308– 2 Art thou dwelling in the belief . . . that *e·* is
    mind,
 311– 6 Hence *e·* is not made and is not real.
 321–13 The serpent, *e·*, under wisdom's bidding, was
 327– 2 there is no abiding pleasure in *e·*,
 327–20 *e·* has in reality neither place nor power
 339– 9 *e·*, being contrary to good, is unreal,
 o 348–16 I deny His cooperation with *e·*,
 348–17 I desire to have no faith in *e·*
 356–25 Does *e·* proceed from good?
 357–16 deny that God made man evil and made *e·* good
 357–30 can Life, or God, dwell in *e·*
 p 367–32 *E·* is but the counterpoise of nothingness.
 368–11 beliefs . . . that *e·* is equal in power to good
 368–22 Neither *e·*, disease, nor death can be
 404–12 If the *e·* is over in the repentant mortal mind,
 411–19 Jesus caused the *e·* to be self-seen
 t 447–13 *e·* will in time disclose and punish itself.
 448– 5 *E·* which obtains in the bodily senses,
 448– 7 if *e·* is uncondemned, it is undenied
 448– 8 Under such circumstances, to say . . . is an *e·*
 452– 3 *e·* has in reality no power.
 r 469–22 when we admit that, . . . *e·* has a place
 469–23 *e·* can have no place, where
 470–13 *e·*, the unlikeness of God, is unreal.
 474– 3 destroy all error, *e·*, disease, and death.
 474–26 If *e·* is real, Truth must make it so ;
 479–28 *e·* should be denied identity or power,
 480–21 the opposite of good — that is, *e·*
 480–23 *E·* is a false belief.
 g 501–18 the history of perpetual *e·*.
 526–22 Was *e·* instituted through God, Love?
 527–19 Has *e·* the reality of good?
 529–26 should rejoice that *e·*, . . . contradicts itself
 532–23 Is Mind capable . . . of *e·* as well as of good,
 533–12 as if He were the creator of *e·*.
 537–10 *e·* has no local habitation nor
 538–21 *e·* is brought into view only as the unreal
 539– 2 In the words of Jesus, it (*e·*, devil) is
 539– 9 such as *e·*, matter, error, and death
 540–13 may think . . . the Lord hath wrought an *e·* ;
 555–20 error would seek to unite . . . good with *e·*,
 ap 559–13 the "seven thunders" of *e·*, — *Rev.* 10 : 3.
 561– 3 destroys both faith in *e·* and
 561– 4 and the practice of *e·*,
 567–19 serpent whose name is devil (*e·*),
 gl 579–16 *e·* ; the opposite of good, — of God
 584–17 DEVIL. *E·* ; a lie ; error ;

evil (adj., adv.)

 pr 4–25 goodness will "be *e·* spoken of," — *Rom.* 14 : 16.
 5–32 seek the destruction of all *e·* works,
 sp 70–11 that there are good and *e·* spirits, is a mistake.
 79–17 Jesus cast out *e·* spirits, or false beliefs.
 83– 6 incredible good and *e·* elements
 85– 9 enabling one to do good, but not *e·*.
 an 100– * *out of the heart proceed e· thoughts,*—*Matt.* 15 : 19.
 s 115–21 *E·* beliefs, passions and appetites, fear,
 115–25 *Second Degree: E·* beliefs disappearing.
 f 206–23 There are *e·* beliefs, often called *e·* spirits ;
 207– 8 God is not the creator of an *e·* mind.
 229–24 If . . . its opposite, health, must be *e·*,
 230–13 so as to bring about certain *e·* results,
 234–26 You must control *e·* thoughts in the
 234–31 *E·* thoughts and aims reach no farther and
 234–32 *E·* thoughts, lusts, and malicious purposes
 254–29 Your good will "be *e·* spoken of.
 c 266–26 *e·* beliefs which originate in mortals are hell.
 b 274– 6 symbolizes all that is *e·* and perishable.
 307–10 It says : . . . God makes *e·* minds and *e·* spirits,
 o 357–16 deny that God made man *e·*

evil (adj., adv.)

p	401– 5	cherishing e· passions and malicious purposes,
	405– 3	The indulgence of e· motives and aims
	413– 1	and cannot transmit good or e· intelligence
t	449–19	The baneful effect of e· associates
	449–20	The inoculation of e· human thoughts
	458– 4	one good and the other e·,
r	482– 4	hypothesis that soul is both an e· and a good
	496– 2	there is no transfer of e· suggestions
g	533–18	the rib . . . has grown into an e· mind,
	539–14	the propensity or power to do e·?
ap	563–13	and that by means of an e· mind in matter
gl	594–22	Mortal beliefs; corporeality; e· minds;

evil-doer

ph	186–22	aids in peremptorily punishing the e·.

evil one

pr	16–16	"Deliver us from the e· o·."
	16–18	C. S. teaches us that "the e· o·,"

evil's

ap	571– 2	expose e· hidden mental ways of

evils
all

ph	183–26	Truth casts out all e· and

brood of

f	234–18	the brood of e· which infest it

casting out

s	136–14	casting out e· and healing the sick
f	210– 8	casting out e·, and destroying death,
b	316–28	healing the sick, casting out e·,
	332–15	healing the sick and casting out e·,
o	347–17	healing the sick, and casting out e·.

cast out

a	34–15	cast out e·, and preach Christ, or Truth,
	41–32	cast out e· and heal the sick.
b	322– 1	to heal the sick and cast out e·
o	342–12	students should cast out e· and heal the sick.

casts out

s	135–13	when Truth heals the sick, it casts out e·,
	143– 3	Christ casts out e· and heals the sick.
b	282– 1	Truth casts out e· and heals the sick.

conjectural

ph	176–19	superimposed and conjectural e·.

moral

p	366– 4	must first cast moral e· out of himself

physical

p	366– 6	cast physical e· out of his patient;

these

f	207– 1	but these e· are not Spirit,
	219–31	may look for an abatement of these e·;
o	347–25	it is Christ, Truth, who destroys these e·,
r	481–21	hypotheses . . . assume the necessity of these e·

p	394–20	Will you bid a man let e· overcome him,
r	474–21	Is it possible, then, to believe that the e·
	494–30	Our Master cast out devils (e·)

evince

o	355– 7	prayers which e· no spiritual power to heal.

evoke

p	365–13	with which to e· healing from the

evoked

sp	94–19	His healing-power e· denial, ingratitude,

evolution

s	135– 9	Spiritual e· alone is worthy of
ph	189–30	e·, keeping always in the direct line of matter,
g	547–16	Darwin's theory of e· from a material basis
	547–20	Material e· implies that the great First Cause
	551–12	E· describes the gradations of human belief,

evolve

sp	86–13	Mortals e· images of thought.
b	335–19	Nothing but Spirit, Soul, can e· Life,
g	524–28	Could Spirit e· its opposite, matter,

evolved

m	69– 3	man and the universe are e· from Spirit,
sp	86–20	e· involuntarily by mortal mind.
ph	179–19	The epizoötic is a humanly e· ailment,
c	260–20	A sick body is e· from sick thoughts.
b	303–13	statement that man is conceived and e·
r	475–30	nor can God, by whom man is e·,
g	523– 3	the mist of obscurity e· by error
	532–17	e· through material sense,
	544–22	these gods must be e· from materiality
	545–13	the theory of man as e· from Mind.

evolves

sp	71–16	images, which mortal mind holds and e·
s	108–27	e·, in belief, a subjective state
c	260–22	e· bad physical and moral conditions.
b	295– 7	filled with spiritual ideas, which He e·,
r	468– 1	intelligence, which e· its own unerring idea

evolving

b	298–25	e· animal qualities in their wings;

exact

s	113–13	showing mathematically their e· relation
	161– 4	an e· statement, more e· than you suppose;
ph	175–20	The e· amount of food the stomach could digest
b	295–27	The theoretical mind is . . . the e· opposite
p	397–19	in e· proportion to your disbelief in physics,
r	482– 1	gives the e· meaning in a majority of cases.
g	521–28	which is the e· opposite of scientific truth
	523– 6	Although presenting the e· opposite of Truth,

exaction

m	58–13	the selfish e· of all another's time

exactly

o	350– 5	C. S. takes e· the opposite view.

exaggerated

ph	195–26	Novels, remarkable only for their e· pictures,

exalt

c	266–14	until the lesson is sufficient to e· you;
t	464–20	not to e· personality.

exaltation

a	46–21	was followed by his e· above all
	46–22	and this e· explained his ascension,
b	313–17	the cause given for the e· of Jesus,
	314– 2	(his further spiritual e·),
gl	581–14	temptation overcome and followed by e·.

exalted

pr	1–13	that they may be moulded and e·
a	38–16	right hand of the Lord is e·."— Psal. 118 : 16.
m	61– 9	Every valley of sin must be e·,
f	203–12	This thought incites to a more e· worship
b	299– 7	My angels are e· thoughts,
p	363–13	wondering why, being a prophet, the e· guest
	373–17	through the e· thought of John,
g	506–11	e· thought or spiritual apprehension
	513– 7	lead on to spiritual spheres and e· beings.
ap	574–11	It e· him till he became conscious of the
gl	598–25	This e· view, obtained and retained

exalting

a	48–13	e· ordeal of sin's revenge on its destroyer
p	383– 6	the pure and e· influence of the divine Mind

exalts

s	148–25	Physiology e· matter, dethrones Mind,

examination

s	111–26	After a lengthy e· of my discovery
ph	196–26	induced by a single post mortem e·,
p	438–26	summoned Furred Tongue for e·,
g	547– 9	microscopic e· of a vulture's ovum,

examine

pr	8–28	We should e· ourselves and
a	46–18	caused him to e· the nail-prints and the
s	159–24	They e· the lungs, tongue, and pulse
p	370–32	Physicians e· the pulse, tongue, lungs,

examined

c	267–19	e· in the light of divine Science,
b	274–31	e· in the light of divine metaphysics,

examining

s	161–24	ordinary practitioner, e· bodily symptoms,

example
consummate

a	51–19	His consummate e· was for the

emulate the

g	515– 2	to emulate the e· of Jesus.

following the

ph	192–28	following the e· of our Master

follow the

a	40–26	all men should follow the e· of our Master
b	324–23	to follow the e· and teachings of Jesus,

glorified

a	54– 7	the harmony his glorified e· introduced.

great

g	555–28	Our great e·, Jesus, could restore
ap	577–19	forever interprets this great e·

his

pr	4– 7	To keep the commandments. . . and follow his e·,
	9–30	If unwilling to follow his e·,
a	54–20	They would not accept . . . nor follow his e·.
b	309–15	the children of earth who followed his e·
	329–11	and left his e· for us.
r	473–21	but to reach his e· and to test its

Jesus'

pr	4–30	enable us to follow Jesus' e·.
r	494– 7	God, who needed no help from Jesus' e·

Master's

o	349– 9	We propose to follow the Master's e·.

one

g	546–32	proving of one e· would authenticate

teaching and

a	54– 8	Who is ready to follow his teaching and e·?

this

s	161–13	If her sister States follow this e·

a	37–24	to follow . . . the e· of the Master
s	113–28	For e· : There is no pain in Truth,

EXAMPLE   167   EXERCISE

example
f 236–10   in support of his proof by e·
b 320–25   For e·, the text, "In my flesh — *Job.* 19 : 26.
o 354–18   Consistency is seen in e· more than in

examples
o 343–29   which allows words, . . . to follow such e· !
t 453– 2   among the e· on the blackboard,
g 546–32   a thousand different e· of one rule,

exceed
a 19– 4   Man cannot e· divine Love,
s 128–11   ability to e· their ordinary capacity.
ph 197– 7   But the price does not e· the original cost.

excel
f 228–31   e· the influence of their dead faith and

excellence
f 249– 4   producing His own models of e·.
t 457–20   no e· without labor in a direct line.

excellent
s 149– 4   The more e· way is divine Science
o 360–22   as given in the e· translation of the

except
a 47–29   each one came to a violent death e· St. John,
sp 98– 8   Body cannot be saved e· through Mind.
s 126–27   e· the teachings and demonstrations of
143–27   no power e· that which is derived from
149–10   they are left without explanation e· in C. S.
163–16   e·, indeed, that it has already destroyed
ph 169–20   There can be no healing e· by this Mind,
169–26   sick are never really healed e· by means of the
181–13   when you resort to any e· spiritual means.
195– 7   All that he ate, e· his black crust,
f 243–29   they declare nothing e· God.
246–20   E· for the error of measuring
b 271–32   e· they be sent?"— *Rom.* 10 : 15.
272– 2   how shall they preach· . . . e· the people hear?
331–13   nothing possesses reality . . . e· the divine Mind
331–24   e· as infinite Spirit or Mind.
o 360– 5   replies : . . . I have no mind-ideals e· those which
p 371–13   looks for relief in all ways e· the right one.
375–29   seems anomalous e· to the expert in C. S.
381–11   e· a moral or spiritual law.
399–30   e· he first bind the strong man?"— *Matt.* 12 : 29.
400–17   e· what mortal mind assigns to it.
407– 5   no creature e· a loathsome worm,
409–18   e· through fear or choice.
410–26   in any way e· to promote right thinking
425–26   You will never fear again e· to offend God,
t 447– 5   e· it be to benefit them.
453–25   e· that you must not tell the patient that he is
459– 5   achieves no worldly honors e· by sacrifice,
464– 5   e· through her laborious publications,
r 473–31   Few, however, e· his students
478– 7   e· the claim of mortal belief?
ap 564–17   e· the highest degree of human depravity.

excepted
sp 98–24   not . . . a part of any religion, Christianity not e·.

exception
f 216–25   health would seem the e·,
t 457–19   C. S. is not an e· to the general rule,

exceptions
ph 199–22   E· only confirm this rule,

excess
p 388–16   through a deficiency or an e·,

excessive
p 375–31   fear so e· that it amounts to fortitude.

exchange
o 360– 7   replies : . . . yet I would not e·
p 390–10   to e· the pleasures and pains of sense for the

exchanges
b 269–15   e· the objects of sense for the

exchanging
r 483– 4   e· one disease for another.
g 531–11   e· it for spiritual perception,
531–12   e· human concepts for the divine consciousness.

excision
t 462–25   indispensable to the e· of error.

excite
sp 88–20   E· the organ of veneration or religious faith,
88–22   E· the opposite development, and he

excited
p 377–23   the morbid or e· action of any organ.
415– 1   Inflammation is fear, an e· state of mortals
417–10   no reaction . . . from e· conditions.

excitement
an 101– 3   or to the e· of the imagination
p 421–21   Calm the e· sometimes induced by

exciting
a 21–29   The company is alluring and the pleasures e·.
ph 169–13   by e· fear of disease, and by dosing the body
178–11   predisposing cause and the e· cause are mental.
f 230–32   the e· cause of all suffering,
p 393– 7   remote, and e· cause of all bad effects

exclaim
p 397–13   you think or e·, "I am hurt !"
434– 4   Some e·, "It is contrary to law

exclaims
g 516–14   grass beneath our feet silently e·,

exclude
ph 170– 9   certainly present what human theories e·
p 392–31   E· from mortal mind the offending errors ;

excluded
f 237–21   should be e· on the same principle
g 543–16   are never e· by falsity.

excludes
s 123–13   e· matter, resolves *things* into *thoughts,*
ph 185–20   e· the human mind as a spiritual factor
g 537–14   Error e· itself from harmony.

exclusively
sp 93–24   It means quantity . . . and applies e· to God.

excuse
b 280–30   The only e· for entertaining human opinions,
g 542–10   Even the disposition to e· guilt or to

excuses
s 130– 4   bidden to the feast, the e· come.
g 542– 6   hides behind a lie and e· guilt,

executed
p 405–14   will be e· upon mortal mind and body.
441–23   e· at the hands of our sheriff, Progress.

execution
p 434– 2   there comes a despatch : "Delay the e· ;

executioner
p 385–13   the law which makes sin its own e·,

executor
a 30–17   Not so did Jesus, the new e· for God,
p 439–27   and the righteous e· of His laws.

Exegesis
g 502–21   chapter sub-title

exegesis
g 502–18   In the following e·, each text is

Exemplar
pr   5–31   We should follow our divine E·,
p 395– 6   Like the great E·, the healer should
ap 577–19   this great example and the great E·.

exemplification
a 18– 1   the e· of man's unity with God,
35–16   its e· of human probation, and

exempt
s 127–18   Mind, e· from all evil.
f 247–14   Immortality, e· from age or decay,

exemption
p 373– 2   physical e· which Christianity includes,
411–28   their e· from disease and danger.

exempts
p 385–13   e· man from all penalties but those due

exercise
air, and
ph 166–27   less than in drugs, air, and e·,
f 232–19   Jesus never taught that drugs, food, air, and e·
and air
ph 174– 6   to flannels, to baths, diet, e·, and air?
faith in
ph 199–13   the blacksmith's faith in e·,
muscular
ph 199–12   Not because of muscular e·, but
of despotic control
an 102–26   It implies the e· of despotic control,
of divine power
s 135– 9   worthy of the e· of divine power.
of faith
ph 170– 5   result of the e· of faith in material
of will
t 446–27   e· of will brings on a hypnotic state,
perpetual
r 487– 9   the perpetual e· of the Mind-faculties
plans the
p 399– 7   Mortal mind plans the e·,

sp 75–22   can then e· Jesus' spiritual power
ph 165– 7   To measure . . . strength by the e· of muscle,
181–32   Any hypnotic power you may e· will diminish
198–31   does not follow that e· has produced this
199– 5   trip-hammer is not increased in size by e·.
f 206–12   while the e· of the sentiments
220– 1   We hear it said : "I e· daily

exercise

p 392–28 whether it be air, *e·*, heredity, contagion,
393–10 *E·* this God-given authority.
396–23 power which their beliefs *e·* over their
435–19 in the *e·* of a love that
t 455–13 if, . . . you can *e·* little or no power for

exercised

m 64– 3 Our forefathers *e·* their faith in the
f 206– 4 *e·* only in subordination to Truth ;
o 355–18 has *e·* any systematic healing power
p 378–18 *e·* over mortal beliefs to destroy them ;
ap 559– 7 *e·* upon visible error and audible sin.

exerted

an 100– 4 so-called force, which he said could be *e·*

exhalations

p 382– 9 or to remove unhealthy *e·* from the

exhausted

f 221–12 having *e·* the skill of the doctors,
p 416–12 when the soporific influence of the opium is *e·*,

exhaustion

g 519–27 No *e·* follows the action of this Mind,

exhibit

s 120–19 or to *e·* the real status of man.

exhibited

an 101–11 phenomena *e·* by a reputed clairvoyant.

exhibiting

p 404– 6 *e·* to the wrong-doer the suffering which

exhibition

s 132– 3 *e·* of the divine power to heal
150– 6 Science, instead of a phenomenal *e·*.
163–26 so ample an *e·* of human invention

exhibits

ap 568–11 first *e·* the true warfare and then the false.

exhort

t 443–21 "Reprove, rebuke, *e·* — *II Tim.* 4 : 2.

exist

m 57–20 It is unselfish ; therefore it cannot *e·* alone,
59–25 A mutual understanding should *e·*
sp 70–15 Does life or soul *e·* in the thing formed?
74–13 No correspondence nor communion can *e·* between
82–12 cannot *e·* in two different states of
s 153–22 The fact that pain cannot *e·* where
162–14 indestructible faculties of Spirit *e·* without
ph 188– 3 What is termed disease does not *e·*.
f 213– 8 Immortal and spiritual facts *e·* apart from
c 262–31 Cause does not *e·* in matter, in mortal mind,
b 281–18 The mind supposed to *e·* in matter
310– 4 Did it *e·* prior to thought?
319–10 presuppose life and intelligence to *e·* in
327– 5 neither . . . *e·* in or of matter,
334–17 continues to *e·* in the eternal order
335–21 Soul . . . does not *e·* in mortality.
337–25 as they *e·* in the spiritual realm of the real.
o 352–14 Would a mother say . . . They *e·*, and are to be feared ;
p 429–19 If man did not *e·* before the material
429–20 If . . . he could not *e·* after the body
t 461– 1 I do not maintain that anyone can *e·* in the
r 488–30 since they *e·* in immortal Mind, not in matter.
g 546– 6 If . . . error must *e·* in the divine Mind,
gl 581–13 the spiritual realities . . . *e·* forever.

existed

b 302–15 harmonious and immortal man has *e·* forever,
r 470–30 If man ever *e·* without this perfect Principle

existence

all
pr 2–29 the source of all *e·* and blessedness.
ph 181– 2 God, is the source and condition of all *e·*
b 280–27 God, the Soul of man and of all *e·*,
gl 588–12 Mind, governing all *e·* ;
589–10 God is the divine Principle of all *e·*,
and continuity
g 513–19 *e·*, and continuity of all individuality
and happiness
g 545–17 destructive to *e·* and happiness.
and intelligence
g 510–17 giving *e·* and intelligence to the universe.
and utility
an 100–18 "In regard to the *e·* and utility of
belief that
p 427–10 belief that *e·* is contingent on matter
bodily
b 334–12 Jesus appeared as a bodily *e·*.
chain of
ph 172–12 Science reveals the eternal chain of *e·*
consciousness of
p 428–24 must hold forever the consciousness of *e·*,
consecrate
p 428–15 We should consecrate *e·*,

existence

contemplation of
g 550–16 contemplation of *e·* as material
continued
sp 81– 9 a continued *e·* after death
continues to be
sp 77– 5 *E·* continues to be a belief . . . until
declaring
r 481–14 declaring *e·* to be at the mercy of death,
demonstrating the
b 314– 9 demonstrating the *e·* of but one Mind
deny the
ph 189–11 than they should deny the *e·* of the sunlight
p 368–29 Deny the *e·* of matter, and you can
dream of
g 529– 8 will destroy the *dream* of *e·*,
dream that
p 427–13 the dream that *e·* can be material.
earthly
p 387–15 the shortest span of earthly *e·*,
elevation of
sp 98– 2 the elevation of *e·* above mortal discord
eternal
m 65– 6 spiritual and eternal *e·* may be discerned.
b 319–13 the infinite cycles of eternal *e·*,
p 387–20 By adhering to the realities of eternal *e·*,
evidence of the
o 359–15 The evidence of the *e·* of Spirit,
fabulous
f 231–18 discords have only a fabulous *e·*,
facts of
sp 95–31 Material sense does not unfold the facts of *e·* ;
f 254– 9 before the spiritual facts of *e·* are gained
g 552–11 spiritual scientific facts of *e·* include no
gl 597–19 spiritual sense unfolds the great facts of *e·*.
form of
p 369–13 or the constructor of any form of *e·*.
g 541– 2 A lamb is a more animate form of *e·*,
grades of
g 551–12 through all the lower grades of *e·*.
happiness and
o 356–14 each other's happiness and *e·*.
p 407–20 the scale of health, happiness, and *e·*.
r 487– 2 find a higher sense of happiness and *e·*.
harmonious
b 320–19 man's eternal and harmonious *e·* as image,
harmony of our
ph 167– 9 determines the harmony of our *e·*,
has no real
s 114–17 to designate that which has no real *e·*.
b 287–23 it is illusion, . . . and it has no real *e·*.
gl 584–11 Matter has no life, hence it has no real *e·*.
human
ph 190–22 saddening strains on human *e·* :
f 205–28 Selfishness tips the beam of human *e·*
ignorant of the
g 512–30 albeit God is ignorant of the *e·* of both
immortal
g 514– 1 not within the range of immortal *e·*
incorporeal
pr 13–29 man's eternal incorporeal *e·*.
infantile
g 554–13 unconscious of his fœtal and infantile *e·* ;
infinitude of
b 302– 7 conscious infinitude of *e·* and of all identity
inimical to
p 389–21 cannot . . . be inimical to *e·*.
intelligent
sp 73–27 any part of the reality of intelligent *e·*,
life or
b 311–29 lose all . . . claim to life or *e·*,
manifestation of
g 555–29 individualized manifestation of *e·*,
man's
pr 13–31 blind to the reality of man's *e·*,
b 306–20 Science proves man's *e·* to be intact.
o 352– 9 spirituality, was the reality of man's *e·*,
359–12 you aver that . . . are indispensable to man's *e·*
r 470–31 If . . . then man's *e·* was a myth.
material
(see **material**)
misapprehension of
ph 191– 9 is found to be a misapprehension of *e·*,
mortal
(see **mortal**)
my own
ph 177– 7 certain as the evidence of my own *e·*.
nature and
sp 84–23 by which we discern man's nature and *e·*.
necessity of
ap 560–13 the grand necessity of *e·* is to gain the
no other
b 310–28 Spirit, which has no other *e·*,
r 492– 5 In reality there is no other *e·*,
no proof of the
an 100–20 no proof of the *e·* of the animal magnetic

existence

nor realness
o 347– 5 has no origin, *e*·, nor realness.
not the fact, of
s 127–20 matter is the falsity, not the fact, of *e*· ;
of man
p 427–15 Nothing can . . . end the *e*· of man in Science.
origin or
b 287– 1 They are without a real origin or *e*·.
g 554–12 of its origin or *e*·.
or mind
a 42–19 belief that man has *e*· or mind separate
personal
sp 82– 7 of whose personal *e*· we may be in doubt?
phenomena of
p 430– 2 includes all the phenomena of *e*·.
plane of
sp 77– 9 Death will occur on the next plane of *e*·
ap 573– 3 The Revelator was on our plane of *e*·,
planes of
f 226– 3 found on higher planes of *e*·
primeval
s 110– 4 These eternal verities reveal primeval *e*·
Principle of
c 262–31 the only cause or Principle of *e*·.
real
b 288–32 man's real *e*· as a child of God
317–32 Nothing but . . . could make *e*· real to Thomas.
p 395–24 to believe in the real *e*· of a tumor,
reality nor
b 331–12 nothing possesses reality nor *e*· except
reality of
f 215– 9 Mortals are unacquainted with the reality of *e*·,
reflected in
g 516–10 Life is reflected in *e*·,
rightful
b 281–24 without actual origin or rightful *e*·.
scale of
b 290– 6 no higher spiritually in the scale of *e*·
sense of
sp 75– 9 from the spiritual sense of *e*·
s 122–28 Temporal life is a false sense of *e*·.
g 539– 1 This false sense of *e*· is fratricidal.
ap 566– 8 from a material sense of *e*· to the
spiritual
(*see* **spiritual**)
stage of
sp 77–25 less with every advanced stage of *e*·.
f 244–15 If man were dust in his earliest stage of *e*·,
250–28 Upon this stage of *e*· goes on the dance of
state of
(*see* **state**)
states of
sp 74–32 they are in separate states of *e*·,
still in the
sp 75– 4 still in the *e*· cognized by the physical senses,
supposed
s 126– 1 its supposed organic action or supposed *e*·.
r 470– 5 supposed *e*· of more than one mind
sustain
b 274– 2 and thus invigorate and sustain *e*·.
thoughts of
c 263– 7 blends his thoughts of *e*· with
to happify
m 58– 1 To happify *e*· by constant intercourse with
true
c 264–26 by which we can recognize true *e*·
b 283– 2 belief that there is any true *e*· apart from God.
unreality of
f 207–10 evil is the awful deception and unreality of *e*·.
verities of
g 543–15 great verities of *e*· are never excluded by
views of
f 246–29 shape our views of *e*· into loveliness,
world's
pref ix– 5 He is as sure of the world's *e*· as
your own
p 374–20 and incapacity to preserve your own *e*·,

ph 175–30 of the *e*· of tubercles and troches,
f 206– 3 no consciousness of the *e*· of matter or error.
215–25 antipode of immortal man in origin, in *e*·, and
216–24 would appear . . . to be the rule of *e*·,
c 266– 6 Would *e*· without personal friends be
b 307–15 transient, false sense of an *e*· which
p 368–27 Admit the *e*· of matter, and
425–16 matter never sustained *e*·
t 445– 6 No hypothesis as to the *e*· of another power
g 522–10 E·, separate from divinity, . . . impossible.
545–23 They believed in the *e*· of matter,
556–29 *e*· will be on a new standpoint.

existent

s 120–22 reveals man as harmoniously *e*· in Truth,
b 302–18 illusion of any life, . . . as *e*· in matter
308–18 a mortal sense of life, . . . as *e*· in matter
311–18 mortal dream of life . . . as *e*· in matter,
r 472–15 supposition that pleasure and pain, . . . are *e*· in

existing

gl 587–13 theories that hold mind to be . . . *e*· in brain,

exists

a 39–26 divine Principle of all that really *e*·
m 64–29 a worse state of society than now *e*·.
an 100– 8 propositions . . . "There *e*· a mutual influence
s 110–32 No analogy *e*· between the vague hypotheses
151–26 All that really *e*· is the divine Mind
ph 171–23 No more sympathy *e*· between the flesh and
177– 8 Neither *e*· without the other,
188–31 knows not where the orb of day is, nor if it *e*·.
f 202– 3 The scientific unity which *e*· between
215– 6 being cannot be lost while God *e*·.
253–28 for no such law *e*·.
c 258–15 Mind manifests all that *e*·
b 271– 6 Neither . . . *e*· in divine Science.
272–30 the divine Principle . . . of all that really *e*·.
278–13 *e*· only in a suppositious . . . consciousness.
311–10 Sin *e*· . . . only so long as the
340–13 all that really *e*· is in and of God,
o 357–28 if another mighty and self-creative cause *e*·
g 514– 4 nothing *e*· beyond the range of . . . infinity,
520– 7 can repeat only an infinitesimal part of what *e*·.
531–22 Who dares to say . . . that matter *e*· without
544–11 fact that man *e*· because God *e*·.
554– 2 even the cause of all that *e*·,
gl 592– 8 that which neither *e*· in Science nor
504– 7 the first delusion that error *e*· as fact ;

exit

s 117–22 and triumphant *e*· from the flesh.

expand

f 252–28 and says : . . . Like bursting lava, I *e*·
c 264–17 this understanding will *e*· into

expands

c 255– 3 thought *e*· into expression.

expansive

ph 195–20 study, and original thought are *e*·
c 265–14 confers upon man . . . a more *e*· love,

expect

pr 2–26 Do we *e*· to change perfection?
ph 167–23 or to *e*· to work equally with Spirit and matter,
f 219–10 and then *e*· that the result will be harmony.
237–27 and *e*· this error to do more for them than
p 409–30 cannot . . . *e*· to find beyond the grave a
t 452–23 E· to heal simply by . . . and you will be disappointed.

expectation

c 260–26 and by the *e*· of perpetual pleasure or pain
p 363–30 sufficient evidence to warrant the *e*·
396–12 nor encourage . . . the *e*· of growing worse
426– 9 *e*· speeds our progress.

expected

m 59–10 nor should woman be *e*· to understand political

expecting

a 21– 6 not . . . to labor and pray, *e*· because of
ph 177–27 though physician and patient are *e*· favorable

expedients

t 443–22 If the sick find these material *e*· unsatisfactory,

expel

r 482–27 Error will not *e*· error.

expelled

o 346–29 Material beliefs must be *e*·
t 460–30 As former beliefs were gradually *e*·

expelling

p 437–24 rose to the question of *e*· C. S. from the bar,

expels

s 153– 3 it is not the drug which *e*· the disease
162– 7 It changes the secretions, *e*· humors,
p 374–31 then *e*· it through the abandonment of a belief,

expense

c 260–28 this education is at the *e*· of spiritual growth.

experience

author's
g 556–28 hence the author's *e*· ;
bitter
a 32–12 The cup shows forth his bitter *e*·,
brief
ph 194– 3 Reviewing this brief *e*·,
Christian
a 29– 7 Christian *e*· teaches faith in the right
daily
o 350– 4 or as very far removed from daily *e*·.
earthly
f 202–21 earthly *e*· discloses the finity of error
fruits of
gl 579– 9 surrendering to the creator the early fruits of *e*·.
higher
pr 7–20 a higher *e*· and a better life

experience
human
 sp 99–25 spirituality, . . . must deepen human *e·*,
 g 552–13 Human *e·* in mortal life,
 ap 572–24 transitional stage in human *e·* called death,
individual
 a 26– 5 yet Jesus spares us not one individual *e·*,
 p 370–24 medical testimony and individual *e·*,
in practice
 t 461–32 student's spiritual growth and *e·* in practice
my
 o 360– 4 other artist replies : "You wrong my *e·*.
of death
 b 291–10 belief in the *e·* of death
of error
 f 237–18 To prevent the *e·* of error and its sufferings,
personal
 pref x–23 in the personal *e·* of any sincere seeker
single
 b 290– 7 on account of that single *e·*,
speak from
 pr 1– 5 I speak from *e·*.
stage of
 m 66–15 Each successive stage of *e·* unfolds new views
teaches us
 pr 10–22 E· teaches us that we do not always
your
 f 248–23 and adopt into your *e·* the angular
 c 261– 6 and you will bring these into your *e·*

 pr 4–26 and patience must bring *e·*.
 a 22– 7 Waking to Christ's demand, mortals *e·* suffering.
 36– 2 They, who know not purity and affection by *e·*,
 39–22 now is the time in which to *e·* that salvation
 m 65– 1 E· should be the school of virtue.
 s 122–21 E· is full of instances of similar illusions,
 f 217– 8 Paul's peculiar Christian conversion and *e·*,
 238–17 an *e·* we have not made our own,
 240–31 learning from *e·* how to divide between
 b 296– 4 Progress is born of *e·*.
 p 394–17 E· has proved to the author the
 421–26 than it is to *e·* it.
 t 443–14 If patients fail to *e·* the
 r 493–20 Disease is an *e·* of so-called mortal mind.
 ap 574–21 brought also the *e·* which
experienced
 a 34–18 Through all the disciples *e·*,
 38–21 Jesus *e·* few of the pleasures
 f 213–20 Mozart *e·* more than he expressed.
 c 266–15 The author has *e·* the foregoing prophecy
 p 385–16 can be *e·* without suffering.
 420– 6 should early call an *e·* Christian Scientist
experiences
 pref viii–26 *e·* which led her, in the year 1866,
 s 108– 7 human *e·* show the falsity of all material things ;
 c 261–11 If one turns away from . . . the body *e·* no pain.
 b 322–26 The sharp *e·* of belief in the
 r 494–21 as the *e·* of the sleeping dream seem real
experiencing
 sp 92– 5 is not only capable of *e·*
 f 250–19 *e·* none of these dream-sensations.
 o 356–20 as He is of *e·* these errors.
experiment
 an 101– 6 an important *e·* upon the power of
 p 379–18 think of the *e·* of those Oxford boys,
experimental
 f 230–16 cannot be, the author of *e·* sins.
experimentally
 t 456– 9 reputation *e·* justified by their efforts.
experimented
 p 379– 9 A felon, on whom certain English students *e·*,
Experiments, Beaumont's Medical
 ph 175–24 Beaumont's "Medical *E·*" did not govern the
experiments
 s 152–21 The author's medical researches and *e·*
 152–28 Her *e·* in homœopathy had made her skeptical
 162–12 E· have favored the fact that Mind governs
expert
 p 375–29 seems anomalous except to the *e·* in C. S.
expiate
 ap 569–20 eventually *e·* their sin through suffering.
explain
 a 27–17 Jesus' parables *e·* Life as never mingling with
 sp 83– 6 Science only can *e·* the incredible good
 s 126–17 Shall Science *e·* cause and effect
 145– 3 sweet tones, . . . without being able to *e·* them.
 148–22 Then theology tries to *e·* how to make
 ph 189– 9 to *e·* the effect of mortal mind.
 200– 8 Whoever is incompetent to *e·* Soul
 b 328–19 can it be said that they *e·* it practically,
 o 350–16 The Master often refused to *e·* his words,
 p 388– 4 a victory which Science alone can *e·*.

explain
 p 396–22 At the right time *e·* to the sick the
 414–15 *e·* C. S. to them, but not too soon,
 417–27 E· audibly to your patients,
 421–23 sometimes *e·* the symptoms and their cause
 422–13 *e·* to them the law of this action.
 438–29 we have heard Materia Medica *e·* how
 r 487–22 without Principle from which to *e·* the
 490–28 Sleep and mesmerism *e·* the mythical nature
 493– 9 Question.— Will you *e·* sickness
 g 510–20 it cannot *e·* them.
explained
 a 33– 9 Their Master had *e·* it all before,
 46–22 and this exaltation *e·* his ascension,
 s 124–16 but when *e·* on the basis of physical sense
 131–26 *e·* the so-called miracles of olden time
 138–10 On this spiritually scientific basis Jesus *e·*
 b 334–28 [Science has *e·* me]."
 o 350–14 Unless the works . . . which his words *e·*,
 350–31 the Word was materially *e·*,
 p 420–14 This fact of C. S. should be *e·* to invalids when
 441– 2 *e·* from his statute-book, the Bible,
 g 501–15 *e·* by that Love for whose rest the
 510–20 Geology has never *e·* the earth's formations ;
explaining
 a 33–11 *breaking* (*e·*) it to others,
 b 292–19 E· the origin of material man
 315–32 E· and demonstrating the way
explains
 pref xi– 5 C. S. rationally *e·* that all other
 sp 80–16 and *e·* extraordinary phenomena ;
 89–23 *e·* the phenomena of improvisation
 s 114–23 C. S. *e·* all cause and effect as mental,
 148– 8 The former *e·* the man of *men*,
 b 278– 3 Divine metaphysics *e·* away matter.
 o 343–15 *e·* the impossibility of good producing evil ;
 361– 2 Here C. S. intervenes, *e·* these
 p 433– 5 *e·* the law relating to liver-complaint.
 r 470–11 Divine Science *e·* the abstract statement
 493– 5 science contradicts this, and *e·* the
 g 511– 3 and so *e·* the Scripture phrase,
 522–11 Science *e·* as impossible.
 534–14 and the Apostle Paul *e·* this warfare
 545– 1 Error . . . *e·* Deity through mortal and finite
explanation
easy
 an 102–26 not lending itself to an easy *e·*
her
 p 374–10 in her *e·* of disease as originating in
of body
 ph 200– 9 would be wise not to undertake the *e·* of body.
of optics
 s 111–15 even as the *e·* of optics rejects the
Principle and
 sp 83–28 gains the divine Principle and *e·* of all things.
scientific
 a 23– 9 but its scientific *e·* is, that
this
 ph 173–18 Physiology continues this *e·*,
 b 302– 6 not lost, but found through this *e·* ;
without
 s 149–10 they are left without *e·* except in C. S.
your
 f 237–29 Impatient at your *e·*,

 ph 189– 2 the *e·* of the sun's influence over the earth.
 p 385– 5 *e·* lies in the support which they derived from
 414–17 until your patients are prepared for the *e·*,
 t 452–13 withhold not the rebuke or the *e·* which destroys
 453– 9 chemicalization follows the *e·* of Truth,
 g 504–21 Here we have the *e·* of another passage
explanations
 f 237– 1 had occasionally listened to my *e·*,
 r 482–13 Is it important to understand these *e·*
 490–23 The scientifically Christian *e·* of the
 g 555– 7 said . . . "I like your *e·* of truth,
explication
 sp 83–16 since Science is an *e·* of nature.
 g 501– 6 often seems so smothered . . . as to require *e·* ;
exploiting
 t 457–31 without *e·* other means.
explored
 s 121– 6 the heavenly fields were incorrectly *e·*.
exploring
 a 26– 4 in speechless agony *e·* the way for us,
exponent
 a 49– 9 Had they forgotten the great *e·* of God?
exponents
 a 52–18 common cause against the *e·* of truth.

expose

p 384– 8	though they *e·* him to fatigue, cold, heat,
386– 5	E· the body to certain temperatures, and
t 447–20	E· and denounce the claims of evil
ap 571– 2	*e·* evil's hidden mental ways of

exposed

s 122– 8	*e·* nineteen hundred years ago
154–16	If a child is *e·* to contagion or infection,
ph 171–19	*e·* to ejection by the operation of
p 405–22	better to be *e·* to every plague on earth
g 539–21	this falsity is *e·* by our Master

exposes

sp 91–10	because Science *e·* his nothingness ;

exposition

pref ix–27	she made copious notes of Scriptural *e·*,
r 496–31	The following is a brief *e·* of

expositions

pref ix–16	not complete nor satisfactory *e·* of Truth.

exposure

s 154–22	Then it is believed that *e·* to the contagion
p 384–16	If *e·* to a draught of air while in a
384–21	such symptoms are not apt to follow *e·* ;
384–27	nor any other disease will ever result from *e·*
ap 571– 4	Why this backwardness, since *e·* is necessary

exposures

p 385– 4	have been able to undergo . . . fatigues and *e·*
385–15	Constant toil, deprivations, *e·*,

expound

t 464–22	has labored to *e·* divine Principle,
g 539–28	gave him more than human power to *e·*

expounder

t 459–29	the Christian and scientific *e·*

expounds

b 274–14	Christianity and the Science which *e·* it

express

pr 4–10	is not of itself sufficient to *e·* loyal and
8–15	gratitude, and love which our words *e·*,
sp 81–20	Erase the figures which *e·* number,
98–13	human hypotheses do not *e·* C. S. ;
f 223– 7	Matter does not *e·* Spirit.
b 313–11	and the *e·* [expressed] image— *Heb.* 1 : 3.
313–12	the phrase "*e·* image" — *Heb.* 1 : 3.
331–32	*e·* in divine Science the threefold,
332–30	highest type . . . which a fleshly form could *e·*
336–24	and nothing less can *e·* God.
o 354–21	If our words fail to *e·* our deeds,
r 465–13	also intended to *e·* the nature, essence,
470–25	If there ever was a moment when man did not *e·*
470–26	then there was a moment when man did not *e·*

expressed

pr 4– 4	*e·* in patience, meekness, love, and
4–19	*e·* in daily watchfulness and in striving
11–32	It is best *e·* in thought and in life.
a 25– 5	infinitely greater than can be *e·* by our
sp 72–17	Perfection is not *e·* through imperfection.
88– 2	for which the poet Tennyson *e·*
s 111– 5	as *e·* through divine Science.
119–18	spiritual and is not *e·* in matter.
ph 178–22	divine Mind, *e·* in Science.
f 210– 1	Its ideas are *e·* only in
213–20	Mozart experienced more than he *e·*.
c 259– 7	divine nature was best *e·* in Christ Jesus,
b 293–21	fury of mortal mind — *e·* in earthquake,
304–30	music is, must be, imperfectly *e·*.
313–11	and the express [*e·*] image— *Heb.* 1 : 3.
332– 5	As the apostle *e·* it in words which
332–29	He *e·* the highest type of divinity,
p 264–27	*e·* by meekness and human affection,
373–21	Disease is *e·* not so much by the lips as in
392–15	must be *e·* mentally,
423– 7	more strongly than the *e·* thought.
r 471–28	the spiritual import, *e·* through Science,
g 508–16	The feminine gender is not yet *e·*
519–10	are complete and forever *e·*,
520– 3	Unfathomable Mind is *e·*.
541–10	the worship *e·* by Cain's fruit?

expresses

pr 3–26	Action *e·* more gratitude than speech.
a 23–28	*e·* the helplessness of a blind faith ;
38–16	It *e·* spiritual power ;
f 208–26	A material body only *e·* a material and
c 258–13	God *e·* in man the infinite idea
b 298–15	Material sense *e·* the belief that
300–28	reflects and *e·* the divine substance
310–10	God is His own infinite Mind, and *e·* all.
331–17	Everything in God's universe *e·* Him.
333– 9	Christ *e·* God's spiritual, eternal nature.
p 376–21	only what that so-called mind *e·*.
r 467–31	understood through the idea which *e·* it
468–28	Eternity, not time, *e·* the thought of Life,
477–30	Separated from man, who *e·* Soul, Spirit would
484–13	The physical universe *e·* the conscious

expresses

g 507–26	This divine Principle of all *e·* Science
518–27	Spirit, comprehends and *e·* all,
ap 576–27	The term Lord, . . . *e·* the Jewish concept,

expressing

sp 89–20	beauty and poetry, and the power of *e·* them.
s 114–19	in *e·* the new tongue we must
115– 5	difficulty of so *e·* metaphysical ideas
p 424–17	*e·* such opinions as may alarm
g 507– 5	tenderly *e·* the fatherhood and

expression

audible

pr 11–32	Such a desire has little need of audible *e·*.

fervency of

pr 8–21	with whatever fervency of *e·*

fuller

o 361–22	to give a clearer and fuller *e·*

infinite

b 336–10	even the infinite *e·* of infinite Mind,

of Soul

r 477–26	Man is the *e·* of Soul.

of Spirit

r 484–30	the understanding and *e·* of Spirit?

perfect

gl 591–19	of whom man is the full and perfect *e·* ;

public

pr 13–12	Can the mere public *e·* of our desires

verbal

pr 3–25	Gratitude is much more than a verbal *e·* of

sp 86–26	peculiarities of *e·*, recollected sentences,
f 210–19	The *e· mortal mind* is really a solecism,
247–23	reflects the charms of His goodness in *e·*,
c 255– 3	thought expands into *e·*.
b 289– 9	He is little else than the *e·* of error.
o 349–16	English is inadequate to the *e·* of
r 470–23	Man is the *e·* of God's being.

expressions

g 518–22	All the varied *e·* of God

expressive

b 320– 5	names are often *e·* of spiritual ideas.

extend

p 418–18	negation must *e·* to the supposed disease

extended

a 43–20	perpetuated and *e·* it.

extends

s 128–16	It *e·* the atmosphere of thought,
146–29	and *e·* throughout all space.
b 328–31	purpose of his great life-work *e·* through time

extent

s 139–22	darkening to some *e·* the inspired pages.
163–25	Nowhere is . . . displayed to a greater *e·* ;
o 349–28	To a certain *e·* this is equally

exterminated

s 164–16	diseased thought-germs are *e·*.
p 377–11	when their fear of climate is *e·*.

exterminates

s 157– 8	C. S. *e·* the drug, and rests on Mind

extermination

g 543–15	is engaged in a warfare of *e·*.

exterminator

r 469–13	The *e·* of error is the great truth

externalized

o 360–13	which mind-picture or *e·* thought
p 411–23	an image of thought *e·*.
g 512–30	*e·*, yet subjective, states of faith and
522–13	gives the history of error in its *e·* forms,

externals

pr 8– 8	such *e·* are spoken of by Jesus as

extinct

sp 74–11	When . . . the belief of life in matter is *e·*,
b 309–30	Life is never for a moment *e·*.

extinction

s 116–16	even to the *e·* of all belief in matter,

extinguish

b 298– 5	As a cloud hides the sun it cannot *e·*,

extinguished

a 51–18	no more . . . than God could be *e·*.

extinguishes

r 474–32	Light *e·* the darkness,

extract

an 102–24	an *e·* from the Boston Herald :
f 201–17	The way to *e·* error from mortal mind is to

extracted

f 212– 3	tooth . . . *e·* sometimes aches again in belief,

extracts

p 437–33	certain *e·* on the Rights of Man,

extraordinary
 sp 80–16 dispels mystery and explains *e·* phenomena ;
extravagance
 m 58–26 a wife ought not to court vulgar *e·*
extreme
 ap 570– 6 shocked into another *e·* mortal mood,
 570– 7 for one *e·* follows another.
extremity
 ph 166–25 in his *e·* and only as a last resort,
 c 266–14 "man's *e·* is God's opportunity."
eye (*see also* **eye's**)
 beholds
  r 479–10 An image . . . is all that the *e·* beholds.
 blue
  f 220– 9 The violet lifts her blue *e·* to greet the
 brother's
  t 455–16 mote out of thy brother's *e·*."— *Matt.* 7 : 5.
 ear and
  sp 84–20 not dependent upon the ear and *e·* for
 guided by the
  p 429– 8 When walking, we are guided by the *e·*.
 hath not seen
  ph 179– 7 Immortal Mind heals what *e·* hath not seen ;
  c 255–18 *E·* hath not seen Spirit, nor hath ear heard
  t 459– 2 "*e·* hath not seen nor ear heard."— *I Cor.* 2 : 9.
  g 554– 1 reveals what "*e·* hath not seen,"— *I Cor.* 2 : 9.
 human
  a 49–16 No human *e·* was there to pity,
  ph 188–30 The human *e·* knows not where the orb of day is,
 mine
  c 262–18 but now mine *e·* seeth Thee."— *Job.* 42 : 5.
 of a needle
  f 241–31 to go through the *e·* of a needle,"— *Matt.* 19 : 24.
  t 449–10 to go through the *e·* of a needle,"— *Matt.* 19 : 24.
 physical
  s 121–18 is invisible to the physical *e·*,
 right
  s 141– 7 cut off the right hand and pluck out the right *e·*,
 testimony of the
  s 121–21 false testimony of the *e·* deluded the
 thine own
  t 455–15 the beam out of thine own *e·* ;— *Matt.* 7 : 5.
 through the
  b 284–22 They can neither see Spirit through the *e·* nor
 twinkling of an
  b 291– 6 "in the twinkling of an *e·*,"— *I Cor.* 15 : 52.

  a 30–15 "An *e·* for an *e·*,"— *Matt.* 5 : 38.
  b 330–13 *E·* hath neither seen God nor His image
  p 378–11 By looking a tiger fearlessly in the *e·*,
  378–13 may infuriate another by looking it in the *e·*,
  393–26 "the light of the body is the *e·*,"— *Matt.* 6 : 22.
  r 486– 4 Suppose one accident happens to the *e·*,
  ap 573– 4 while yet beholding what the *e·* cannot see,
eyelids
 ph 193–11 *e·* closed gently and the breathing became
eye's
 s 122–16 On the *e·* retina, sky and tree-tops

eyes
 blind
  t 444– 2 these very failures may open their blind *e·*.
 causes the
  f 211–25 If . . . material organism causes the *e·* to see
 close the
  sp 87–30 We have but to close the *e·*, and forms rise
 close your
  sp 71–10 Close your *e·*, and you may dream that you
  71–14 Close your *e·* again, and you may
 having
  a 38–28 Having *e·* ye see not,
  gl 586– 6 "Having *e·*, see ye not?"— *Mark* 8 : 18.
 his
  ph 193– 8 Mr. Clark lay with his *e·* fixed and sightless.
  193–13 In about ten minutes he opened his *e·*
  195– 1 His *e·* were inflamed by the light.
  f 221–23 These truths, opening his *e·*,
  c 255–11 Mortal man has made a covenant with his *e·*
 laughing
  f 237– 5 Bounding off with laughing *e·*, she presently
 man's
  ph 165– 3 declared . . . this fruit would open man's *e·*
 mortal
  b 334–20 Jesus was incarnate to mortal *e·*.
 of purer
  f 243–22 "of purer *e·* than to behold evil,"— *Hab.* 1 : 13.
  o 357– 4 "of purer *e·* than to behold evil."— *Hab.* 1 : 13.
 opened the
  a 49– 3 opened the *e·* of their understanding,
 open the
  t 451–24 obligated to open the *e·* of his students
  ap 570–30 willing to open the *e·* of the people to the
 our
  b 268– * *which we have seen with our e·,*— *I John* 1 : 1.
  r 491–22 goes on, whether our *e·* are closed or open.
 people's
  f 220– 5 Such admissions ought to open people's *e·*
 solemn
  p 434–18 earnest, solemn *e·*, kindling with hope
 their
  a 43– 4 his material disappearance before their *e·*
  o 350–19 and their *e·* they have closed ;— *Matt.* 13 : 15.
  350–21 they should see with their *e·*,— *Matt.* 13 : 15.
 through the
  pref ix– 4 drinks in the outward world through the *e·*
 your
  g 530–15 then your *e·* shall be opened ;— *Gen.* 3 : 5.
  530–20 and saying, . . . "I can open your *e·*.
  ap 574–26 it will lift the sackcloth from your *e·*,

  sp 76– 3 at Niagara, with *e·* open only to that wonder,
  ph 165– 4 it closed the *e·* of mortals
  189– 3 If the *e·* see no sun for a week, we still
  t 452– 8 *e·* accustomed to darkness are pained by
  g 530–23 saying, . . . more pleasant to the *e·*
  gl 586– 3 definition of
eye-witness
 p 436– 2 he was an *e·* to the good deeds

F

fable
 s 129– 8 by reversing the material *f·*,
  129– 9 be the *f·* pro or con,
 b 302–19 This statement is based on fact, not *f·*.
 p 408– 7 a universal insanity . . . mistakes *f·* for fact
 g 544–18 suggestion of more than the one Mind,— is in the *f·*
 gl 586– 7 FAN. Separator of *f·* from fact ;
fables
 an 103–26 they annihilate the *f·* of mortal mind,
fabulous
 f 231–18 discords have only a *f·* existence,
face
 before the
  a 49–31 before the *f·* of the Most High,"— *Lam.* 3 : 35.
 her
  s 154–29 little one, who thinks she has hurt her *f·*
 his
  ph 193–10 In a few moments his *f·* changed ;
  ap 558– 5 and his *f·* was as it were the sun,— *Rev.* 10 : 1.
 My
  s 140– 6 "Thou canst not see My *f·* ;— *Exod.* 33 : 20.
 name the
  sp 76– 2 name the *f·* that smiles on them
 of Jesus
  c 260– 5 or the painter can depict the form and *f·* of Jesus,
 of the sky
  sp 85–21 can discern the *f·* of the sky ;— *Matt.* 16 : 3.
  f 233–17 Ye who can discern the *f·* of the sky,
  g 509–31 can discern the *f·* of the sky ;— *Matt.* 16 : 3.

face
 one
  t 457–15 each of them could see but one *f·* of it,
 pallid
  p 415–17 Note how thought makes the *f·* pallid.
 sallow
  p 433–14 His sallow *f·* blanches with fear,
 sun's
  g 548–10 when clouds cover the sun's *f·* !
 Thy
  ph 190–28 As for me, I will behold Thy *f·*— *Psal.* 17 : 15.
 thy
  g 535–25 in the sweat of thy *f·* shalt thou— *Gen.* 3 : 19.
 whole
  g 521–22 the whole *f·* of the ground.— *Gen.* 2 : 6.

  pr 8– 5 *f·* to *f·* with their wickedness
  s 121– 1 and starvation stared him in the *f·* ;
  163–11 druggist, or drug on the *f·* of the earth,
  f 245–14 She had no care-lined *f·*,
  c 263–29 thrown into the *f·* of spiritual immensity,
  b 305– 5 a *f·* reflected in the mirror is not the original,
  338–18 upon the *f·* of the deep,"— *Gen.* 1 : 2.
  o 342– 9 presumptuously, in the *f·* of Bible history
  t 450– 7 while looking you blandly in the *f·*,
  r 479–20 upon the *f·* of the deep.— *Gen.* 1 : 2.
  g 503– 7 upon the *f·* of the deep.— *Gen.* 1 : 2.
  503– 8 moved upon the *f·* of the waters.— *Gen.* 1 : 2.
  503–13 saith to the darkness upon the *f·* of error,
  518– 6 upon the *f·* of all the earth,— *Gen.* 1 : 29.
  ap 558–14 When you look it fairly in the *f·*,

faces
p 439–16 in the perturbed f· of these worthies,
gl 596–29 The Jewish women wore veils over their f·

facilitate
p 421–10 showing him that it was to f· recovery.

fac-similes
sp 86–25 Portraits, landscape-paintings, f· of

fact
awful
r 472–28 the awful f· that unrealities seem real
based on
b 302–18 This statement is based on f·, not fable.
central
s 131–10 The central f· of the Bible is the
concerning error
sp 92–22 Until the f· concerning error— namely,
counter
f 233–28 The counter f· relative to any disease
demonstrable
s 108– 6 unfolding to me the demonstrable f· that
elaborated the
s 141–14 Jesus elaborated the f· that the healing effect
established
p 384–28 In Science this is an established f·
eternal
g 544–10 Matter cannot change the eternal f·
every
t 450– 2 twist every f· to suit themselves.
figure or in
b 282–13 Mind and . . . never unite in figure or in f·.
fixed
m 65–26 Matrimony, which was once a fixed f· among us,
ph 180–19 by declaring disease to be a fixed f·,
foundational
o 348–12 Jesus established this foundational f·,
glorious
g 529– 9 usher in Science and the glorious f· of creation,
great
s 109– 6 This great f· is not, however, seen to be
137–17 and his reply set forth a great f· :
ph 199– 9 Hence the great f· that Mind alone
f 228– 4 impossible if this great f· of being were learned,
b 285– 5 the great f· of being for time and eternity.
339–26 the great f· that God is the only Mind ;
o 343–18 scientifically demonstrates this great f·,
p 398–32 The great f· remains that
412– 1 The great f· that God lovingly governs all,
421–16 great f· which covers the whole ground,
430–12 When will mankind wake to this great f·
harmony is the
p 412–23 Mentally insist that harmony is the f·,
heedless of the
p 362– 7 Heedless of the f· that she was debarred
ignorant of the
s 159–30 Ignorant of the f· that a man's belief produces
illustrates the
p 402–24 mesmerism . . . illustrates the f· just stated.
immortal
b 327– 4 Science, which reveals the immortal f·
in metaphysics
s 154– 9 This f· in metaphysics is illustrated by
in Science
ap 573– 6 This testimony . . . sustains the f· in Science,
knowledge of the
ph 199–19 of less importance than a knowledge of the f·.
matter of
r 486–32 as a matter of f·, these calamities often
mere
p 363–32 there was encouragement in the mere f·
mistaking
sp 84– 5 not by foreshadowing evil and mistaking f·
of being
f 228– 4 if this great f· of being were learned,
249–26 is sometimes nearer the f· of being than
b 285– 5 the great f· of being for time and eternity.
320–18 declares plainly the spiritual f· of being,
one
r 492– 3 should be but one f· before the thought,
one more
an 101– 5 one more f· to be recorded in the history of
only
b 297–17 The only f· concerning any material concept is,
r 471–20 spirituality of the universe is the only f·
remains
s 164–23 the forever f· remains paramount
b 289–23 the f· remains, that God's universe is
scientific
m 69– 2 The scientific f· that man and the universe
f 207–27 The spiritual reality is the scientific f·
b 295–13 will at last yield to the scientific f·
spiritual
(see **spiritual**)
such a
s 152–19 Such a f· illustrates our theories.

fact
this
sp 81–10 this f· affords no certainty of
s 111–27 this f· became evident to me,
134–32 This f· at present seems more mysterious than
145–17 From this f· arise its ethical as well as
151–29 acknowledge this f·, yield to this power,
154– 9 This f· in metaphysics is illustrated by
ph 194–14 theory opposed to this f· . . . would presuppose
f 207– 5 This f· proves our position,
320–21 avers that this f· is not forever to be humbled
p 420–13 This f· of C. S. should be explained to invalids
427– 1 If it is true that man lives, this f· can never
r 467–11 in proportion as this f· becomes apparent,
whereas the
pref viii–10 whereas the f· is that Spirit is good and real,
f 211–28 whereas the f· is that only through

———

sp 73– 6 The f· is that neither the one nor the other
s 116–17 They never . . . insist upon the f· that God is all,
127–20 It teaches that matter is the falsity, not the f·,
143– 2 Hence the f· that, to-day, as yesterday, Christ
153–22 The f· that pain cannot exist where there is no
154–13 f· was, that he had not caught the cholera by
162–12 Experiments have favored the f· that Mind
f 222–12 availed himself of the f· that Mind governs
238–29 To reconstruct timid justice and place the f·
b 270–29 Hence the f· that the human mind
289–14 The f· that the Christ, or Truth, overcame
339–11 can receive no encouragement from the f·
p 368– 3 confidence inspired by Science lies in the f·
368–29 has a foundation in f·.
371– 1 when in f· all is Mind.
371–28 father to the f· that Mind can do it ;
374–12 is in f· the objective state of mortal mind,
388–22 The f· is, food does not affect the absolute
408– 2 This view is not altered by the f· that
408– 7 mistakes fable for f· throughout the entire
412–25 Realize the presence of health and the f·
414–11 the f· that truth and love will establish a
420–17 f· that Truth overcomes both disease and
r 486– 1 matter is without foundation in f·,
gl 586– 7 FAN. Separator of fable from f· ;
594– 7 the first delusion that error exists as f· ;

factor
pref x– 8 this mind is not a f· in the Principle of C. S.
s 109– 2 as the leading f· in Mind-science.
144–20 is not a f· in the realism of being.
151– 2 as if there was but one f· in the case ;
151– 3 but this one f· they represent to be body,
159–14 as if matter were the only f· to be consulted
ph 185–21 excludes the human mind as a spiritual f·
p 370–14 faith in the drug is the sole f· in the cure.

factors
r 492–30 theory, . . . is that there are two f·,

facts
broadest
sp 97–21 The broadest f· array the most falsities
connate
pref viii–21 the response deducible from two connate f·,
conscious
gl 593– 5 the conscious f· of spiritual Truth.
demonstrate the
p 429–27 and do not demonstrate the f· it involves.
eternal
b 293–16 perpetuating the eternal f·
everlasting
s 121–20 rebuked by clearer views of the everlasting f·,
fundamental
s 120– 9 arrive at the fundamental f· of being.
grand
f 244– 4 Divine Science reveals these grand f·.
t 460–26 she had to impart, while teaching its grand f·,
r 471– 9 afford no indication of the grand f· of being ;
great
s 122– 4 the great f· of Life, rightly understood,
gl 597–19 spiritual sense unfolds the great f· of
immortal
b 279–17 the immortal f· of being are seen,
p 428–28 the immortal f· of being are admitted.
important
g 548–28 important f· in regard to so-called embryonic
invincible
a 55– 5 but this does not affect the invincible f·.
maintain the
p 417–11 Maintain the f· of C. S.,— that Spirit is God,
of being
(see **being**)
of creation
g 539–28 power to expound the f· of creation,
544–19 The f· of creation, as previously recorded,
of divine Science
r 471–13 f· of divine Science should be admitted,

facts
of existence
  sp 95–30 does not unfold the *f·* of existence ;
  g 552–11 spiritual scientific *f·* of existence
  gl 597–19 unfolds the great *f·* of existence.
of harmony
  o 356– 7 Discord can never establish the *f·* of harmony.
of Mind
  b 268–18 as well as on the *f·* of Mind.
  283–10 They are not *f·* of Mind.
of Science
  g 516– 7 subordinate . . . to the *f·* of Science,
of Soul
  p 420–31 the harmonious *f·* of Soul and immortal being.
  428– 4 demonstration of the *f·* of Soul in Jesus' way
of Spirit
  f 215–10 matter and mortality do not reflect the *f·* of Spirit.
  b 281–30 as we grasp the *f·* of Spirit.
only
  r 479–22 the only *f·* are Spirit and its innumerable
permanent
  c 264– 2 before the permanent *f·* . . . appear.
primal
  sp 87–15 for it presents primal *f·* to mortal mind.
spiritual
  (*see* **spiritual**)
subserving the
  b 319– 4 error reversed as subserving the *f·*
these
  s 139–20 these *f·* show how a mortal and material sense
  ph 169–10 I name these *f·* to show that disease has
  r 471–14 the evidence as to these *f·* is not
true
  p 376–23 true *f·* in regard to harmonious being,
two
  f 251–10 mortals wake to the knowledge of two *f·* :

  an 101–13 "The *f·* which had been promised by
  s 149–22 The logic is lame, and *f·* contradict it.
  f 237–23 Some invalids are unwilling to know the *f·*
  o 341–17 The *f·* are so absolute and numerous
  343– 8 unfair to impugn and misrepresent the *f·*,
  p 369– 8 He enters into a diviner sense of the *f·*,
  438–21 the *f·* in the case show that this fur
  r 476–19 the *f·* which belong to immortal man.
  496–22 belief, at war with the *f·* of immortal Life,
faculties
  s 162–14 The indestructible *f·* of Spirit exist without
  f 211–27 then, when the body is dematerialized, these *f·*
  211–30 these *f·* be conceived of as immortal.
  214–32 there is no oblivion for Soul and its *f·*.
  215– 5 with all the *f·* of Mind ;
  246– 4 Life and its *f·* are not measured by
  r 472–17 Error is neither Mind nor one of Mind's *f·*.
  488–24 Mind alone possesses all *f·*,
faculty
  an 100–13 ordered the medical *f·* of Paris to
  s 156– 5 A case of dropsy, given up by the *f·*,
  162–29 With due respect for the *f·*,
  b 327–29 Reason is the most active human *f·*.
  o 348–10 It is a pity that the medical *f·* and clergy
  p 407–22 No *f·* of Mind is lost.
  r 490– 5 Human will is . . . not a *f·* of Soul.
  g 528–31 this may be a useful hint to the medical *f·*.
fade
  sp 81–19 grass seemeth to wither and the flower to *f·*,
fades
  f 246–14 the transient sense of beauty *f·*,
fading
  s 150–30 the doctrine of . . . is *f·* out.
  f 247–11 *f·* and fleeting as mortal belief.
  c 263–32 The *f·* forms of matter,
  264– 7 Mortals must look beyond *f·*, finite forms,
  o 357–22 wrong notions . . . are *f·* out.
fail
  s 149–12 If you *f·* to succeed in any case, it is because
  ph 173– 1 we *f·* to see how anatomy can
  194– 3 I cannot *f·* to discern the coincidence
  f 227–14 cannot *f·* to foresee the doom of all oppression.
  o 354–21 If our words *f·* to express our deeds,
  p 372–22 Its false supports *f·* one after another.
  t 443–14 If patients *f·* to experience the
  444– 7 If Christian Scientists ever *f·* to receive
  448–28 he cannot *f·* of success in healing.
  450– 8 never *f·* to stab their benefactor in the back.
  455–12 and if, knowing the remedy, you *f·* to use the
  ap 569–15 and *f·* to strangle the serpent of sin
failed
  pref x–20 till all physical supports have *f·*,
  a 45–14 persecutors had *f·* to hide immortal Truth
  sp 83– 3 the worshippers of Baal *f·* to do ;
  s 148– 2 brought to him a case they had *f·* to heal,

failed
  s 152–24 Every material dependence had *f·* her
  o 351–10 learned that her own prayers *f·* to heal her
  p 388– 8 when dire inflictions *f·* to destroy his body.
  427–27 when all such remedies have *f·*
  t 464–15 and the Scientists had *f·* to relieve him,
failing
  ph 166–23 *F·* to recover health through adherence to
  f 220–23 Finding his health *f·*, he gave up his
  t 459–10 lest you yourself be condemned for *f·* to
fails
  s 148–27 When physiology *f·* to give health or life
  149– 8 succeeds in one instance *f·* in another,
  157– 3 It succeeds where homœopathy *f·*,
  b 329–19 because he *f·* in his first effort.
  p 370–27 Quackery likewise *f·* at length to
failure
  ph 186–21 Every attempt of evil to destroy good is a *f·*,
  199–23 *f·* is occasioned by a too feeble faith.
  c 260–17 distrust . . . ensures *f·* at the outset.
failures
  f 240–19 past *f·* will be repeated until all wrong work is
  t 444– 2 these very *f·* may open their blind eyes.
fain
  b 302–29 mortal sense would *f·* have us so believe.
faint
  pref vii– 3 beholds the first *f·* morning beams,
  a 47– 3 a *f·* conception of the Life which is God.
  s 144–10 and afford *f·* gleams of God, or Truth.
  f 218–29 they shall walk, and not *f·*." — *Isa.* 40 : 31.
  219–12 "sick, and the whole heart *f·* ;" — *Isa.* 1 : 5.
  254– 4 walk, and not *f·*," — *Isa.* 40 : 31.
faintly
  a 29–29 though at first *f·* developed.
  sp 91–17 and reflect but *f·* the substance of Life or
  ap 577–32 one word shows, though *f·*, the light which C. S.
fair
  pref viii–16 On this basis C. S. will have a *f·* fight.
  s 122–20 barometer, . . . points to *f·* weather in
  141–30 Let it have *f·* representation by the press.
  ph 167–32 *f·* seeming for straightforward character,
  191–22 not a leaf unfolds its *f·* outlines,
  p 437– 6 It blots the *f·* escutcheon of omnipotence.
  r 490–21 would, by *f·* logic, annihilate man
  g 555– 3 A *f·* conclusion from this might be,
  ap 575–25 a city of the Spirit, *f·*, royal, and square.
fairly
  f 231– 3 Unless an ill is rightly met and *f·* overcome
  240–28 one must pay fully and *f·* the
  b 319–19 when it becomes *f·* understood that the divine
  329– 2 elements of pure Christianity will be *f·*
  t 457–10 never . . . fears to have *f·* understood.
  ap 558–14 When you look it *f·* in the face,
fairness
  f 248– 9 feeds the body with supernal freshness and *f·*,
faith
absolute
  pr 1– 2 absolute *f·* that all things are possible to God,
all
  p 395–12 destroys all *f·* in sin and in
  426–23 The relinquishment of all *f·* in death
and belief
  pr 12–18 borrows its power from human *f·* and belief.
and piety
  sp 98–26 no proper connection with *f·* and piety.
and understanding
  s 107–13 fresh pinions are given to *f·* and understanding,
  b 312–27 It divides *f·* and understanding between
  p 366–10 mental penury chills his *f·* and understanding.
  387–30 gives man *f·* and understanding whereby to
armed with
  b 298– 7 Science armed with *f·*, hope, and fruition.
article of
  s 145–32 Our Master's first article of *f·* propounded to
blacksmith's
  ph 199–13 but by reason of the blacksmith's *f·* in
blind
  pr 12– 8 through a blind *f·* in God.
  a 23–28 expresses the helplessness of a blind *f·* ;
  ph 167– 4 If we rise no higher than blind *f·*,
  p 398–28 blind *f·* removes bodily ailments for a season,
  gl 582– 2 not a faltering nor a blind *f·*, but the
break
  ap 569–15 Alas for those who break *f·* with divine Science
dawn in
  b 298– 3 They dawn in *f·* and glow full-orbed
dead
  f 228–32 influence of their dead *f·* and ceremonies.
describes
  b 279– 4 New Testament writer plainly describes *f·*,
dissent or
  s 155–12 individual dissent or *f·*, unless it rests on

faith

ecstasy or
  pr 14– 7 is to have, not mere emotional ecstasy or *f·*,
El Dorado of
  ap 559–30 out of bondage into the El Dorado of *f·* and
enlightened
  pr 15–31 the foundation of enlightened *f·*.
feeble
  ph 199–24 failure is occasioned by a too feeble *f·*.
fetter
  f 226–19 fetter *f·* and spiritual understanding.
firm in
  a 23–13 said : "He that taketh one doctrine, firm in *f·*,
general
  a 155– 8 not yet divorced the drug from the general *f·*.
  b 319–10 lower appeal to the general *f·*
great
  s 133– 7 "I have not found so great *f·*, — *Matt.* 8 : 10.
half the
  f 202– 7 half the *f·* they bestow upon the
his
  s 146– 1 he proved his *f·* by his works.
  ph 180– 6 his *f·* in their efforts is somewhat helpful
  f 216– 1 his *f·* in Soul and his indifference to the body.
  p 366–10 mental penury chills his *f·*
hope and
  pr 9–16 enjoy the fruition of our hope and *f·*.
  a 45–18 from the door of human hope and *f·*,
  gl 581–15 ASHER (Jacob's son). Hope and *f·* ;
  584–27 DOVE. . . . purity and peace ; hope and *f·*.
human
  (*see* **human**)
implicit
  a 25–26 Implicit *f·* in the Teacher and all the
in a carnal mind
  p 395–11 Science overcomes *f·* in a carnal mind,
in Deity
  s 146– 7 faith in drugs the fashion, rather than *f·* in Deity.
individual
  s 155– 4 general belief, culminating in individual *f·*,
in drugs
  s 145–14 whether *f·* in drugs, trust in hygiene,
  146– 7 have rendered *f·* in drugs the fashion,
  ph 181–30 If you have more *f·* in drugs than in Truth,
in God
  (*see* **God**)
in hygiene
  f 251–16 whether through *f·* in hygiene,
in matter
  pref xi– 7 the fruits of human *f·* in matter,
  s 130–21 Laboring long to shake the adult's *f·* in matter
  146– 6 The first idolatry was *f·* in matter.
  ph 170– 6 *f·* in matter instead of in Spirit.
  p 425–24 when *f·* in matter has been conquered.
inspires
  g 547–32 which lifts humanity . . . and inspires *f·*.
in the divine Principle
  b 319– 7 Having *f·* in the divine Principle
in the drug
  p 370–14 *f·* in the drug is the sole factor in the cure.
in the right
  a 29– 7 Christian experience teaches *f·* in the right
in the truth
  p 368–15 When we come to have more *f·* in the truth
  401– 7 If *f·* in the truth of being, which you impart
in Truth
  b 286– 7 gives full *f·* in Truth,
  t 446–21 strengthens hope, enthrones *f·* in Truth,
invalid's
  ph 166–26 The invalid's *f·* in the divine Mind
in words
  f 210– 1 superiority of faith by works over *f·* in words.
is higher
  b 297–20 *F·* is higher and more spiritual than belief.
John's
  s 133– 3 Was John's *f·* greater than that of the
keep the
  a 29– 5 If they keep the *f·*, they will have the
kept the
  a 21– 3 I have kept the *f·*," — *II Tim.* 4 : 7.
lacks
  p 366–17 physician lacks *f·* in the divine Mind
less
  ph 173–32 call into action less *f·* than Buddhism
  f 222–13 he also had less *f·* in the so-called pleasures
little
  pref x–21 because there is so little *f·* in His
  p 394–30 the sick usually have little *f·* in it till they
living
  b 308– 3 art thou in the living *f·* that there is
lose
  s 127– 2 she will not therefore lose *f·* in Christianity.
  o 351– 3 When we lose *f·* in God's power to heal,
material
  ph 180–21 through the material *f·* which they inspire.

faith

more
  sp 89– 6 Having more *f·* in others than in herself,
  ph 181–30 If you have more *f·* in drugs than in Truth,
  o 358–29 Is it likely that church-members have more *f·* in
  359– 6 Is this because the patients have more *f·* in
  p 368–15 When we come to have more *f·* in the truth
  368–16 more *f·* in Spirit than in matter,
  368–16 more *f·* in living than in dying,
  368–17 more *f·* in God than in man,
  373– 3 we must have more *f·* in God on this subject
my
  o 343– 5 show thee my *f·* by my works." — *Jas.* 2 : 18.
  r 487–26 show thee my *f·* by my works." — *Jas.* 2 : 18.
new
  s 134– 9 The new *f·* in the Christ, Truth,
no
  ph 169–17 we should put no *f·* in material means.
  o 348–17 I desire to have no *f·* in evil or
  r 486– 2 you can have no *f·* in falsehood when
one kind of
  a 23–24 One kind of *f·* trusts one's welfare to others.
one's
  a 22–26 nor by pinning one's *f·* without works
  an 101–32 proportional to one's *f·* in esoteric magic.
our
  b 329–13 We must prove our *f·* by demonstration.
  340– 2 until we lose our *f·* in them
  p 410–14 Every trial of our *f·* in God makes us stronger.
  410–17 the stronger should be our *f·*
point beyond
  f 241–23 One's aim, a point beyond *f·*, should be
prayer of
  pr 12– 1 "The prayer of *f·* shall save — *Jas.* 5 : 15.
religious
  sp 88–21 Excite the organ of veneration or religious *f·*,
  s 139–12 reform in religious *f·* will teach men
resort to
  t 443– 5 a resort to *f·* in corporeal means
shall he find
  s 132–27 shall he find *f·* on the earth?" — *Luke* 18 : 8.
significance of
  r 488–10 they have more the significance of *f·*,
stepping-stone to
  pref vii–18 no longer the stepping-stone to *f·*.
strong
  ap 567– 5 strong *f·* or spiritual strength wrestles
superiority of
  f 209–32 It shows the superiority of *f·* by works
that
  o 359– 4 Will that *f·* heal them?
their
  a 49– 3 inspired their devotion, winged their *f·*,
  m 64– 3 Our forefathers exercised their *f·*
  s 155–10 equip the medicine with their *f·*,
  o 359– 4 try to cure his friends by their *f·* in him.
  t 451–10 will either make shipwreck of their *f·* or
this
  s 155– 5 according to this *f·* will the effect be.
  ph 181–30 this *f·* will incline you to the side of
  r 487–30 This *f·* relies upon an understood Principle.
thy
  o 343– 4 "Show me thy *f·* without thy — *Jas.* 2 : 18.
  r 487–25 "Show me thy *f·* without thy — *Jas.* 2 : 18.
to uplift
  r 497–21 served to uplift *f·* to
unflinching
  p 426–27 with unflinching *f·* in God,
unity of the
  g 519–19 come in the unity of the *f·*, — *Eph.* 4 : 13.
uplifting
  s 109–19 Christian healing by holy, uplifting *f·* ;
without works
  a 22–26 nor by pinning one's *f·* without works
  23–15 "*F·* without works is dead." — *Jas.* 2 : 26.

---

  pref xi– 7 *f·* in the workings, not of Spirit, but
  pr 11–22 only the results of mortals' own *f·*.
  16– 3 The highest prayer is not one of *f·* merely ;
  a 23–16 *F·*, if it be mere belief, is as a pendulum
  23–17 *F·*, advanced to spiritual understanding,
  23–21 *f·* and the words corresponding thereto
  23–25 Another kind of *f·* understands divine Love
  sp 86– 7 he was answered by the *f·* of a sick woman.
  an 106–28 gentleness, goodness, *f·*, — *Gal.* 5 : 22.
  s 115–27 compassion, hope, *f·*, meekness, temperance.
  125–14 changes . . . from *f·* to understanding,
  133– 6 also a certain centurion of whose *f·*
  160– 7 Unsupported by the *f·* reposed in it,
  ph 169–11 in rules of health or in drugs begets
  169–14 The *f·* reposed in these things should find
  170– 5 the exercise of *f·* in material modes,
  198–19 giving another direction to *f·*, the physician
  f 206–12 hope, *f·*, love — is the prayer of the righteous
  215–29 Even the *f·* of his philosophy spurned

faith

f	218–18	if you are without f· in God's willingness
b	288– 7	settle all questions through f· in
	297–29	Until belief becomes f·, and f· becomes
	298–14	involves intuition, hope, f·, understanding,
	312–26	limits f· and hinders spiritual
p	382–14	more receptive of spiritual power and of f·
	394–32	shows that f· is not the healer in such cases.
	395–20	punctual, patient, full of f·,
	398–19	It is the f· of the doctor and the
	398–25	So also f·, cooperating with a belief in
	424–30	f· in the possibility of their transmission.
	429–27	We must have f· in all the sayings of our Master,
	430– 6	F· should enlarge its borders
r	482–25	angels whisper it, through f·, to the hungering
	484–19	are really caused by the f· in them
g	512–16	externalized, yet subjective, states of f·
	529–28	f· to fight all claims of evil,
ap	561– 3	destroys both f· in evil and the practice
gl	579–10	f· in the divine Life and in the eternal Principle

faithful

a	44– 3	"Well done, good and f· servant,"—Matt. 25: 23.
	49–18	this f· sentinel of God at the highest post
	50–12	to sustain and bless so f· a son.
	50–32	wrung from his f· lips the plaintive cry,
c	267–30	when he is tried, [proved f·],—Jas. 1: 12.
b	314–20	but the f· Mary saw him,
	323–17	"f· over a few things,"—Matt. 25: 21.
t	444–16	Let us be f· in pointing the way
ap	569– 6	"Thou hast been f· over a few"—Matt. 25: 23.

faithfully

a	26– 6	if we follow his commands f·;
p	373–12	if the teaching is f· done.
	387–13	do not die early because they f· perform the

faithfulness

a	34–26	As the reward for his f·, he would disappear to
f	225– 6	the fewness and f· of its followers.

faithless

s	148– 2	"O f· generation,"—Mark 9: 19.

fall

pref	vii–20	Though empires f·, "the Lord shall—Exod. 15 :18.
a	23–11	will f· at the feet of everlasting Love.
an	103–28	singe their own wings and f· into dust.
ph	193– 2	caused by f· upon a wooden spike
f	223–18	both shall f· into the ditch."—Matt. 15: 14.
	227– 1	into the land of C. S., where fetters f·
	238–12	To f· away from Truth in times of persecution,
c	258–29	it were impossible for man, . . . to f· from his
b	282–24	Whatever indicates the f· of man
	310–11	Day may decline and shadows f·,
p	380– 4	Sickness and sin f· by their own weight.
	380– 6	on whomsoever it shall f·,—Matt. 21: 44.
	441–11	now and forever, f· into oblivion,
t	463– 4	he may stumble and f· in the darkness.
	464–24	weapons of bigotry, . . . f· before an
g	507–31	misinterpreted, the divine idea seems to f·
	528–10	a deep sleep to f· upon Adam,—Gen. 2: 21.
	536–19	The blind leading the blind, both would f·.

fallacies

o	355–22	and the most egregious f· ever offered

fallacy

f	237–24	the f· of matter and its supposed laws.
p	394–17	the f· of material systems in general,
r	466–24	have perpetuated the f· that intelligence,

fallen

c	259–10	thoughts which presented man as f·,
r	470–20	Has God taken down His . . . and has man f· ?
	476–13	Mortals are not f· children of God.

falleth

b	291–19	"In the place where the tree f·,—Eccl. 11: 3.
	291–22	As man f· asleep, so shall he awake.

falling

a	32–32	with shadows fast f· around ;
s	154–29	thinks she has hurt her face by f·
o	359–23	f· from the lips of her saintly mother,
p	389–26	This belief totters to its f·
t	449–12	Man's moral mercury, rising or f·,

falls

a	37– 8	error f· only before the sword of Spirit.
ph	192–26	betrays its weakness and f·, never to rise.
f	249–29	It f· short of the skies, but makes its
b	291–22	"As the tree f·, so it must lie."
g	543– 1	f· back upon itself.

false

pref	viii– 7	as the science of music corrects f· tones
a	27–20	to cut down the f· doctrine of pantheism,
	50–23	they did say,— that Jesus' teachings were f·,
m	60–26	physical sense, . . . places it on a f· basis.
	62–29	f· views of life hide eternal harmony,
	68– 7	We ought to weary of the fleeting and f·
	69–10	as the f· and material disappears.

false

sp	70– 5	Whatever is f· or sinful can never enter
	94–12	owe their f· government to the misconceptions
	99–21	not with the individual, but with the f· system.
an	100– *	thefts, f· witness, blasphemies :— Matt. 15: 19.
s	107–15	Feeling so perpetually the f· consciousness
	108–25	testimony of f· material sense,
	121–22	deluded the . . . and induced f· conclusions.
	122– 5	contradict their f· witnesses, and reveal
	123– 1	science has destroyed the f· theory
	127–31	f· hypotheses that matter is its own lawgiver,
	128–28	not upon the judgment of f· sensation.
	129– 1	conclusion, if properly drawn, cannot be f·.
	135–23	else one or the other is f· and useless ;
	151–15	bondage now enforced by f· theories,
	164–11	more scientific than are f· claimants
ph	168–20	authority which Jesus proved to be f·
	175–30	before he ate the fruit of f· knowledge,
	177–10	body, is but a f· concept of mortal mind.
	180– 3	and to uproot its f· sowing.
	186– 2	by emptying his thought of the f· stimulus
	192– 5	quit our reliance upon that which is f·
	196– 7	f· pleasures which tend to perpetuate this
f	201– 7	We cannot build safely on f· foundations.
	201–10	f· appetites, hatred, fear, all sensuality,
	204– 3	All forms of error support the f· conclusions
	204–23	F· and self-assertive theories have given
	218– 1	Mortal mind does the f· talking,
	229–21	f· law should be trampled under foot.
	232–14	Christianity is not f·,
	232–15	religions which contradict its Principle are f·.
	238–28	no time for gossip about f· law or testimony.
	242– 3	their material beliefs and f· individuality.
	252– 7	When f· human beliefs learn even a little
c	262–21	They will then drop the f· estimate of life
	265–32	if they wrench away f· pleasurable beliefs
b	278– 9	a f· supposition, the notion that there is
	281–19	f· conception as to man and Mind.
	281–29	Our f· views of matter perish
	285–16	is a f· conception of man.
	287–22	Error is f·, mortal belief ;
	290–12	That Life or Mind is finite . . . is f·.
	293–12	both strata, . . . are f· representatives of man.
	296–11	The death of a f· material sense
	308–12	f· pleasure, pain, sin, sickness, and death."
	308–18	matter with its f· pleasures and pains,
	311–14	f· estimates of soul as dwelling in sense
	315–11	The opposite and f· views of the people
	324– 2	Gladness to leave the f· landmarks
o	355–21	"absolutely f·, and the most egregious fallacies
	357–17	f· notions about the Divine Being
	357–21	must have originated in a f· supposition,
	358– 7	one is true, the other must be f·.
p	368–26	these f· conditions are the source of all seeming
	372–22	Its f· supports fail one after another.
	380–11	This f· method is as though the defendant
	389–15	This f· reasoning is rebuked
	390–14	the f· process of mortal opinions
	395– 8	leaving Soul to master the f· evidences
	403–17	producing . . . the results of f· opinions ;
	404– 8	there is no real pleasure in f· appetites.
	417–30	by certain fears and f· conclusions,
	428– 9	To divest thought of f· trusts
	428–12	we shall sweep away the f·
	437–13	Nerve, . . . to be a f· witness.
	438–12	and bearing f· witness against Man.
	440– 7	before sacrificing mortals to their f· gods.
	440–22	The f· and unjust beliefs of your
t	444–30	are discordant and ofttimes f· brethren.
	447–12	Ignorance, subtlety, or f· charity
	458–25	Neither is he a f· accuser.
	459–20	a f· practitioner will work mischief,
r	484–19	f· human consciousness is educated to feel.
	484–26	involved in all f· theories and practices.
	489–25	C. S. shows them to be f·,
g	506– 2	distinguishing between the f· and the true.
	510–12	turn away from a f· material sense.
	522– 1	f· history in contradistinction to the true.
	522– 4	If one is true, the other is f·,
	522–24	in declaring this material creation f·.
	523– 3	Because of its f· basis, the mist of
	523–10	which God erects between the true and f·.
	525–22	favors the f· conclusion of the
	527–20	it is a lie,—f· in every statement.
	539–19	It is f· to say that Truth and error commingle
	545–17	a f· view, destructive to existence
	545–19	this opposite, in its f· view of God and man,
	549–22	as must necessarily attend f· systems,
ap	560–16	a f· estimate of anyone whom God has appointed
	567–28	The beast and the f· prophets are lust and
	568–11	first the true method . . . and then the f·.
	568–12	exhibits the true warfare and then the f·.
	575– 1	Arise from your f· consciousness
gl	580–21	The name Adam represents the f· supposition
	581–19	The higher f· knowledge builds

false

gl 584–16 Any material evidence of death is *f·*,
588–17 whatever reflects not this one Mind, is *f·*
597–12 It revealed the *f·* foundations
(*see also* **belief, beliefs, claim, claims, evidence, sense, testimony**)

False Belief

p 430–21 *F· B·* is the attorney for Personal Sense.
435– 4 Counsellor *F· B·* has argued that
437–20 Here the opposing counsel, *F· B·*,
438–22 a foreign substance, imported by *F· B·*,
439– 2 *F· B·*, the counsel for the plaintiff,
439– 7 when a message came from *F· B·*.
440– 4 machinations of the counsel, *F· B·*,
440– 8 deceived by your attorney, *F· B·*,
441–10 The plea of *F· B·* we deem unworthy
441–11 Let what *F· B·* utters, . . . fall into oblivion,
441–28 Your attorney, *F· B·*, is an impostor,

falsehood

capable of
p 432– 5 the prisoner at the bar, is capable of *f·*.
no faith in
r 486– 2 you can have no faith in *f·*

pr 9– 4 the *f·* which does no one any good.
an 104–20 sensuality, *f·*, revenge, malice,
s 163–29 so much absurdity, contradiction, and *f·*.
ph 186–18 This *f·* should strip evil of all pretensions.
f 238–30 and place the fact above the *f·*,
241– 9 *F·*, envy, hypocrisy, malice,
t 450– 6 They utter a *f·*, while looking you blandly
g 530– 1 increases in *f·* and his days become shorter.

falsehood's

r 486– 3 when you have learned *f·* true nature.

falsely

c 262–30 which seems to begin with the brain begins *f·*.
b 305–31 The Sadducees reasoned *f·* about the
331– 9 *f·* testifies to a beginning and an
p 372–24 *f·* parading in the vestments of law.

falsities

sp 78– 3 They are the *f·* of sense,
97–21 The broadest facts array the most *f·*
b 307–20 partakes of its own nature and utters its own *f·*.
o 346–18 "fraught with *f·* painful to behold"?
354– 3 "utter *f·* and absurdities,"

falsity

and illusion
g 554–28 and is simply a *f·* and illusion.
conceded
p 396–15 not a difficult task in view of the conceded *f·*
matter is the
s 127–19 It teaches that matter is the *f·*,
of error
b 294–32 Truth demonstrates the *f·* of error.
of material belief
c 258– 8 proves the *f·* of material belief.
send
g 545–14 errors send *f·* into all human doctrines
their own
f 252– 8 learn even a little of their own *f·*,
this
b 283–24 lost to all who cling to this *f·*.
301–30 This *f·* presupposes soul to be an
g 539–21 this *f·* is exposed by our Master

pr 16– 6 Truth that is sinless and the *f·* of sinful sense.
s 108– 7 experiences show the *f·* of all material things ;
f 253–15 Knowing the *f·* of so-called material sense,
b 317– 4 insisted on the might of matter, the force of *f·*,
t 464–26 *F·* has no foundation.
r 474–31 Truth destroys *f·* and error,
g 522– 3 proves the *f·* of the second.
528–15 Here *f·*, error, credits Truth, God, with
537–21 to depict the *f·* of error
543–16 are never excluded by *f·*.
gl 579–15 a *f·* ; the belief in "original sin,"

faltering

t 455– 4 a *f·* and doubting trust in Truth
gl 582– 1 not a *f·* nor a blind faith, but the perception

fame

m 57–15 Beauty, wealth, or *f·* is incompetent to meet
f 239– 5 Take away wealth, *f·*, and social organizations,
gl 582– 6 pride ; envy ; *f·* ; illusion ; a false belief ;

familiar

sp 70– * *them that have f· spirits,*— *Isa.* 8 : 19.
89–12 This *f·* instance reaffirms the
f 234– 9 become more *f·* with good than with evil,
b 320–11 the *f·* text, Genesis vi. 3,
p 397–23 To heal the sick, one must be *f·* with
403–32 *f·* with mental action and its effect
t 463– 5 should also be *f·* with the obstetrics
ap 576–15 was *f·* with Jesus' use of this word,

families

an 103– 1 promotes affection and virtue in *f·*

family

harmonious
t 444–29 God's children . . . are one harmonious *f·* ;
his
ph 193–18 dress himself, and take supper with his *f·*.
human
(*see* **human**)
universal
ap 577– 4 one Father with His universal *f·*,
whole
r 470– 1 the whole *f·* of man would be brethren ;
your
p 392–18 If you think that . . . is hereditary in your *f·*,

g 515–21 Man is the *f·* name for all ideas,

famine

sp 96–16 may seem to be *f·* and pestilence,
s 163–18 war, pestilence, and *f·*, all combined."

famished

pr 17– 5 *feed the f· affections ;*

famous

s 161–20 the words of the *f·* Madame Roland,
162–30 I kindly quote from Dr. Benjamin Rush, the *f·*
g 548–18 of the origin of mortals, a *f·* naturalist says :

fan

r 466–27 Science of Christianity comes with *f·* in hand
gl 586– 7 definition of

fancied

f 252–28 and says : . . . all my *f·* joys are fatal.
p 379–10 *f·* himself bleeding to death,

fancies

pr 5–28 because he *f·* himself forgiven.
b 310– 2 The human belief *f·* that it delineates

fancy

s 136–20 This ghostly *f·* was repeated by Herod
ph 175–13 profane to *f·* that the perfume of clover
191–28 illusive senses may *f·* affinities with
b 291–10 Mortals need not *f·* that belief in the
299– 1 suggestive feathers ; but this is only *f·*.
t 443–19 other systems they *f·* will afford relief.
460–16 Sickness is more than *f·* ;

far

pr 3–32 While the heart is *f·* from divine Truth
10– 2 walk in the light so *f·* as we receive it,
15–22 in so *f·* as we put our desires into practice.
a 31–18 so *f·* as we apprehend it,
34–25 ascend *f·* above their apprehension.
52– 2 His pursuits lay *f·* apart from theirs.
53– 4 so *f·* removed from appetites and passions
sp 79–21 so *f·* as can be learned from the Gospels,
90–21 mentally travel *f·* and work wonders,
s 118– 3 an inference *f·* above the merely
121–25 so *f·* as our solar system is concerned,
124–24 "Thus *f·* and no farther."
127–31 in so *f·* as this is built on the false
146–27 *f·* anterior to the period in which Jesus lived.
149– 3 Mind as *f·* outweighs drugs in the cure of
ph 173–30 The idols of civilization are *f·* more fatal
174–12 "the night is *f·* spent,— *Rom.* 13 : 12.
179–16 educate a healthy horse so *f·* in physiology
f 221–10 and it is equally *f·* from Science,
222–22 He learned that a dyspeptic was very *f·* from
222–23 *f·* from having "dominion— *Gen.* 1 : 26.
229– 9 Not *f·* removed from infidelity is the belief
257–13 the substance of an idea is very *f·* from
b 300– 9 So *f·* as the scientific statement as to
318–17 so *f·* as he is discordant, he is not the image
o 350– 4 very *f·* removed from daily experience.
354–23 The night of materiality is *f·* spent,
p 387– 7 has been carried sufficiently *f·* ;
426–25 *f·* beyond its present elevation,
t 448–16 A dishonest position is *f·* from Christianly
r 478–24 this belief is mortal and *f·* from actual.
g 548–23 so *f·* apart from his material sense of

farce

b 272–20 the ghastly *f·* of material existence ;

farm

s 130– 5 One has a *f·*, another has merchandise,

far-off

sp 90–16 we fly to Europe and meet a *f·* friend.

farther

pr 5–19 looking *f·*, the Psalmist could see their end,
6–18 higher we cannot look, *f·* we cannot go.
s 124–24 "Thus far and no *f·*."
ph 173– 4 or determine when man . . . has progressed *f·*
176–27 can carry its ill-effects no *f·* than
197–14 the *f·* mortals will be removed from imbecility
f 234–31 reach no *f·* and do no more harm than
p 425– 1 or some of his progenitors *f·* back

farthing

pr 5–11 "the uttermost *f.*." — *Matt.* 5 : 26.
f 240–28 one must pay fully and fairly the utmost *f.*,
p 390–17 in payment of the last *f.*,
405–15 will be manacled until the last *f.* is paid,

fashion

pr 4–21 will mould and *f.* us anew,
m 68–4 They are slaves to *f.*, pride, and sense.
s 146–7 have rendered faith in drugs the *f.*,
f 247–12 Custom, education, and *f.* form the

fashionable

o 344–30 more *f.* and less spiritual?

fashions

g 516–9 God *f.* all things, after His own

fast

a 32–32 with shadows *f.* falling around ;
53–3 He did not *f.* as did the Baptist's disciples ;
s 124–10 and holding *f.* to discord and death.
f 254–21 abandon so *f.* as practical the material,
p 392–14 thought should be held *f.* to this ideal.
t 448–3 Blindness and . . . cling *f.* to iniquity.
464–20 hold *f.* that which is good." — *I Thess.* 5 : 21.
g 545–5 material man was *f.* degenerating
gl 597–5 if only he appeared unto men to *f.*.

fasten

p 439–23 to *f.* upon him an offence

fastened

p 378–14 *f.* fearlessly on a ferocious beast,

fastens

p 395–28 *f.* disease on the patient,

fasting

f 220–26 The belief that either *f.* or feasting makes
221–20 never ordained a law that *f.* should be

fat

g 540–27 his flock, and of the *f.* thereof. — *Gen.* 4 : 4.

fatal

pr 7–32 Hypocrisy is *f.* to religion.
m 59–26 for deception is *f.* to happiness.
59–30 *f.* mistakes are undermining its foundations.
s 129–19 and *f.* to its demonstration ;
ph 173–30 The idols of civilization are far more *f.*
f 203–1 admits . . . that this cold may produce *f.*
252–28 and says : . . . all my fancied joys are *f.*.
b 286–6 this is *f.* to a knowledge of Science.
303–24 The belief that . . . is a *f.* error.
p 368–10 *f.* beliefs that error is as real as Truth,
372–27 a denial of Truth is *f.*,
384–22 if you believe in laws of matter and their *f.*
394–25 Are material means the only refuge from *f.*
422–27 holding that matter . . . renders them *f.*
g 552–12 no member of this dolorous and *f.* triad.
ap 560–26 but has been *f.* to the persecutors.
568–8 *f.* effects of trying to meet error with error.

fatality

sp 79–2 its symptoms, locality, and *f.*
ph 197–32 his belief in its reality and *f.* will harm

fatally

ph 184–25 termed a *f.* broken physical law.

fate

a 40–21 could not avert a felon's *f.*,
49–15 met his earthly *f.* alone with God.
s 121–2 but sterner still would have been his *f.*, if
121–7 read in the stars the *f.* of empires
ph 176–5 attributed their own downfall and the *f.* of

Father (*see also* Father's)

and Mother
c 256–7 the *F.* and Mother of the universe,
g 530–11 recognizing God, the *F.* and Mother of all,
and son
o 361–18 *F.* and son, are one in being.
bosom of the
b 334–5 dwells forever in the bosom of the *F.*,
cometh unto the
b 286–9 "No man cometh unto the *F.* — *John* 14 : 6.
Ego and the
sp 70–9 the Ego and the *F.* are inseparable.
everlasting
p 428–17 the eternal builder, the everlasting *F.*,
God and the
m 64–5 undefiled before God and the *F.*, — *Jas.* 1 : 27.
God as the
a 29–23 demonstrating God as the *F.* of men.
God is his
m 63–10 God is his *F.*, and Life is the law of his being.
heavenly
a 40–25 Our heavenly *F.*, divine Love, demands that
p 387–29 bestowed on man by his heavenly *F.*,

Father

his
a 30–3 his *F.* or divine Principle.
31–8 they who do the will of his *F.*.
m 63–10 God is his *F.*, and Life is the law of his being.
p 410–6 knowledge of his *F.* and of himself,
in secret
pr 15–7 The *F.* in secret is unseen to the
inspired by the
s 133–27 taught as he was inspired by the *F.*
is perfect
b 302–20 man as perfect, even as the *F.* is perfect,
my
pr 14–21 because I go unto my *F.*," — *John* 14 : 12.
a 26–12 "I and my *F.* are one." — *John* 10 : 30.
sp 79–20 "My *F.* worketh hitherto, — *John* 5 : 17.
s 137–24 my *F.* which is in heaven ;" — *Matt.* 16 : 17.
c 267–16 the will of my *F.* which is in — *Matt.* 12 : 50.
b 315–3 "I and my *F.* are one," — *John* 10 : 30.
333–29 "I and my *F.* are one ;" — *John* 10 : 30.
333–30 "My *F.* is greater than I." — *John* 14 : 28.
o 361–15 "I and my *F.* are one," — *John* 10 : 30.
p 372–26 before my *F.* which is in heaven." — *Matt.* 10 : 33.
not known the
a 32–1 they have not known the *F.* — *John* 16 : 3.
numbered by the
p 367–16 with those hairs all numbered by the *F.*.
of all
pr 13–26 the *F.* of all is represented as a corporeal
m 64–26 Until it is learned that God is the *F.* of all,
a 31–11 the only creator, and therefore as the *F.* of al
our
pr 2–6 the desire . . . is blessed of our *F.*,
13–11 our *F.*, who seeth in secret, will reward
16–26 Our *F.* which art in heaven, — *Matt.* 6 : 9.
m 67–1 The cup our *F.* hath given,
b 276–20 even as our *F.* in heaven is perfect,
the perfect
f 207–14 the perfect *F.*, or the divine Principle of man.
will of the
ph 168–21 He did the will of the *F.*.
with the
a 18–4 demonstrated man's oneness with the *F.*,
b 334–4 not that the corporeal Jesus was one with the *F.*,
337–9 the Son must be in accord with the *F.*,
worship the
a 31–27 shall worship the *F.* in spirit — *John* 4 : 23.
sp 93–7 shall worship the *F.* in spirit — *John* 4 : 23.
s 140–21 shall worship the *F.* in spirit — *John* 4 : 23.
your
pr 1–* *Your F. knoweth what things ye* — *Matt.* 6 : 8.
a 31–5 one is your *F.*, which is in heaven." — *Matt.* 23 : 9.
37–28 your *F.* which is in heaven — *Matt.* 5 : 48.
c 259–20 your *F.* which is in heaven — *Matt.* 5 : 48.
b 326–21 your *F.* will open the way.

———

pr 14–32 pray to thy *F.* which is in secret ; — *Matt.* 6 : 6.
15–1 and thy *F.*, which seeth in secret, — *Matt.* 6 : 6.
a 41–25 then sat down at the right hand of the *F.*.
sp 77–16 neither the Son, but the *F.*." — *Mark* 13 : 32.
s 131–19 "I thank Thee, O *F.*, Lord of — *Luke* 10 : 21.
131–22 even so, *F.*, for so it seemed good — *Luke* 10 : 21.
f 233–13 not even "the Son but the *F.* ;" — *Mark* 13 : 32.
c 257–14 Hence the *F.* Mind is not the father of matter.
267–8 It is generally conceded that God is *F.*,
267–9 If this is so, the forever *F.* must have
b 268–* *our fellowship is with the F.*, — *I John* 1 : 3.
282–31 for it is not begotten of the *F.*.
305–18 but what he seeth the *F.* do : — *John* 5 : 19.
306–11, 12 and the *F.* would be childless, — no *F.*.
314–6 proved that he and the *F.* were inseparable
325–17 found, in His likeness, perfect as the *F.*,
334–6 not that the *F.* is greater than Spirit,
o 357–29 Has the *F.* "Life in Himself," — *John* 5 : 26.
r 467–10 all men have one Mind, one God and *F.*,
470–1 With one *F.*, even God, the whole family of man
485–23 "*F.* which is in heaven — *Matt.* 5 : 48.
g 518–17 all having the same Principle, or *F.* ;
532–11 the divine Spirit, or *F.*, condemns material man
536–12 gravitation and attraction to one *F.*,
ap 569–2 Life, represented by the *F.* ;
577–3 as one *F.* with His universal family,
gl 586–9 definition of

father

name of
a 31–10 no record of his calling any man by the name of *f.*
not the
sp 89–27 and man is not the *f.* of man.
c 257–15 the Father Mind is not the *f.* of matter.
r 473–5 Truth, God, is not the *f.* of error.
of mind
f 208–17 John Young, . . . writes: "God is the *f.* of mind,
of mythology
b 294–23 belief in them to be the *f.* of mythology,

ather

primeval
g 553–28 or from the rib of our primeval *f·*.

your
a 31– 5 "Call no man your *f·* upon— *Matt.* 23 : 9.
b 292–22 Ye are of your *f·*, the devil— *John* 8 : 44.
292–22 the lusts of your *f·* ye will do.— *John* 8 : 44.
g 554–26 "Ye are of your *f·*, the devil."— *John* 8 : 44.

---

a 50–10 would impugn the justice and love of a *f·* who
m 69–22 If the *f·* replies, "God creates man through
f 219–21 "is ever *f·* to the thought."
c 257–19 divine Love,— is the *f·* of the rain,
b 292–26 a liar, and the *f·* of it."— *John* 8 : 44.
309–12 He was to become the *f·* of those, who
o 357– 8 "a liar, and the *f·* of it."— *John* 8 : 44.
p 371–27 is *f·* to the fact that Mind can do it ;
g 533–30 "Neither man nor God shall *f·* my fault."
551– 1 the material senses must *f·* these
554–22 "He is a liar, and the *f·* of it."— *John* 8 : 44.
556–31 It is related that a *f·* plunged his infant
gl 580–31 he is a liar and the *f·* of it."— *John* 8 : 44.

atherhood
g 507– 5 the *f·* and motherhood of God.
519–11 the *f·* and motherhood of Love.
ap 562– 4 As Elias presented the idea of the *f·* of God,

atherless
m 64– 5 To visit the *f·* and widows— *Jas.* 1 : 27.

ʼather-Mother
pr 16–27 Our *F·* God, all-harmonious,
b 331–30 God the *F·* ; Christ the spiritual idea
332– 4 *F·* is the name for Deity,
335–26 nothing unlike the eternal *F·*, God.
g 516–23 the infinite *F·* God.
ap 577– 2 reflects God as *F·*, not as a

ʼather's
a 25– 9 as he went daily about his *F·* business.
52– 1 he was about his "*F·* business."— *Luke* 2 : 49.
p 366– 2 sense of the dear *F·* loving-kindness.
442–27 it is your *F·* good pleasure— *Luke* 12 : 32.

athers
f 211–19 "the *f·* have eaten sour grapes,— *Ezek.* 18 : 2.

athers'
ap 566–17 Her *f·* God before her moved,

athom
c 262– 9 We cannot *f·* the nature and quality of
g 519–17 What can *f·* infinity !
556–15 the Christian alone can *f·* it.

atigue
sp 79–30 It dissipates *f·* in doing good.
ph 165–16 You say that indigestion, *f·*, sleeplessness,
184–19 We say man suffers from the effects of . . . *f·*.
f 217–20 the next toil will *f·* you less,
217–25 scientific and permanent remedy for *f·*
218–30 applying it literally to moments of *f·*,
219– 3 My method of treating *f·* applies to
p 384– 8 though they expose him to *f·*, cold, heat,

atigued
f 218– 3 You do not say a wheel is *f·* ;

atigues
f 217–29 You say, "Toil *f·* me."
p 385– 4 undergo without sinking *f·* and exposures

atling
g 514–24 young lion, and the *f·* together ;— *Isa.* 11 : 6.

ault
pr 8–31 If a friend informs us of a *f·*,
sp 93–12 otherwise, . . . our logic is at *f·*
b 292– 1 When the last mortal *f·* is destroyed,
g 533–27 finds woman the first to confess her *f·*.
533–30 "Neither man nor God shall father my *f·*."

aults
ap 571– 9 to tell a man his *f·*, and so risk

avor
a 36–17 preclude C. S. from finding *f·* with the
an 101–16 not conclusive in *f·* of the doctrine of
p 380–13 in *f·* of a decision which the defendant
441–18 decrees of the Court of Error in *f·* of Matter,
441–19 Spirit decides in *f·* of Man
441–25 The Supreme Bench decides in *f·* of
t 458– 7 This theory is supposed to *f·*

avorable
ph 177–27 physician and patient are expecting *f·*
p 422– 8 these indications are *f·*.
422–12 ignorant that it is a *f·* omen,
423– 5 tendency towards a *f·* result.

avored
s 162–12 Experiments have *f·* the fact that

avorite
s 121– 2 if his discovery had undermined the *f·*
b 340–16 The First Commandment is my *f·* text.

favors
g 525–27 *f·* the false conclusion of the

Fear
p 436–18 they brought with them *F·*, the sheriff,
436–20 It was *F·* who handcuffed Mortal Man
439–24 You aided and abetted *F·*
441–14 neither can *F·* arrest Mortal Man

fear (noun)

and sin
p 373–21 you must rise above both *f·* and sin.
392– 1 you master *f·* and sin through divine

and trembling
a 23–26 with *f·* and trembling."— *Phil.* 2 : 12.
sp 99– 6 with *f·* and trembling,"— *Phil.* 2 : 12.
p 442–26 with *f·* and trembling :"— *Phil.* 2 : 12.

belief and
p 385–25 will suffer in proportion to your belief and *f·*.
t 455–11 lost in the belief and *f·* of disease

blanches with
p 433–14 His sallow face blanches with *f·*,

calling up the
s 154– 6 calling up the *f·* that creates the

casteth out
ph 180–24 divine Love which casteth out *f·*.
p 373–18 "perfect Love casteth out *f·*."— *I John* 4 : 18.
406–10 "Perfect Love casteth out *f·*."— *I John* 4 : 18.
410–19 perfect Love casteth out *f·*.— *I John* 4 : 18.

cast out
p 442–13 Divine Love had cast out *f·*.

darkness induces
p 371–14 Darkness induces *f·*.

dark places of
ap 559–12 heard in the desert and in dark places of *f·*.

destroy
p 376–26 Destroy *f·*, and you end fever.

destroys
t 454– 7 destroys *f·*, and plants the feet in the true

disappears
p 368–31 When *f·* disappears, the foundation of

doubt or
t 445– 7 No hypothesis . . . should interpose a doubt or *f·*

effects of
p 373–20 the effects of *f·* produced by sin,
380–15 The physical effects of *f·* illustrate

evil and
p 392– 7 Casting out evil and *f·* enables

exciting
ph 169–13 by exciting *f·* of disease, and by dosing the body

fruits of
g 532–18 the immediate fruits of *f·* and shame.

governing
p 377–21 Remove the leading error or governing *f·*

great
p 426–21 and thus destroy the great *f·* that besets

her
s 159–18 They would either have allayed her *f·* or

his
ph 197–31 should suppress his *f·* of disease,
198– 6 his *f·*, which has already developed the
199–30 His *f·* must have disappeared before his
p 405–18 good man finally can overcome his *f·* of
423– 2 The belief . . . increases his *f·* ;
436–23 and be punished for his *f·*.

hope and
b 298–17 hope and *f·*, life and death,

human
ph 176–17 Human *f·* of miasma would load with disease
p 412– 3 and destroy the human *f·* of sickness.
ap 563– 5 We may well be perplexed at human *f·* ;
566– 3 dark ebbing and flowing tides of human *f·*,

ignorance or
ph 188–23 springing from mortal ignorance or *f·*.

increases
t 453–27 for such a course increases *f·*,

inflammation is
p 414–32 Inflammation is *f·*, an excited state

latent
p 376– 4 the latent *f·* and the despair of recovery

made manifest
r 493–21 It is *f·* made manifest on the body.

master
ph 197–16 We should master *f·*, instead of cultivating
p 392– 1 you master *f·* and sin through divine

more
ph 180–15 may unwittingly add more *f·* to the

mortal
p 377–27 disease is mental, a mortal *f·*,

Moses'
b 321–11 and then Moses' *f·* departed.
321–25 God had lessened Moses' *f·*

no
p 393–18 Have no *f·* that matter can ache,
406–17 has no *f·* that he will commit a murder,
410–18 "There is no *f·* in Love,— *I John* 4 : 18.

fear (noun)
  nor doubt
    r 495–17 Let neither *f·* nor doubt overshadow
  of climate
    p 377–10 when their *f·* of climate is exterminated.
  of consequences
    b 322–24 only through *f·* of consequences
  of death
    gl 596–25 destroy . . . the *f·* of death,
  of disease
    (*see* **disease**)
  of error
    p 380–20 power of Truth can prevent the *f·* of error,
  of its sting
    p 426–24 and also of the *f·* of its sting
  of patients
    p 411–27 by allaying the *f·* of patients.
  of punishment
    b 327–22 *F·* of punishment never made man truly honest.
  of the disease
    ph 196–27 induced . . . from the *f·* of the disease
  of the Lord
    p 373–15 "The *f·* of the Lord is the— *Psal.* 111 : 10.
  or fever
    ph 175–12 and dissuade any sense of *f·* or fever.
  or sin
    p 392– 3 Only while *f·* or sin remains can it
  patient's
    ph 168–25 and recognized the patient's *f·* of it,
  pride and
    a 31– 1 Pride and *f·* are unfit to bear the standard of
  proceed from
    c 260–22 disease, and death proceed from *f·*.
  removing the
    p 411–32 If you succeed in wholly removing the *f·*,
  seedlings of
    ph 188–26 according to the seedlings of *f·*.
  stage of
    p 375–31 a stage of *f·* so excessive that it amounts to
  this
    p 381– 9 This *f·* is the danger
       423– 4 this *f·* greatly diminishes the tendency
  will soothe
    p 398–26 will soothe *f·* and change the belief of disease to
  your
    p 374–24 your steps are less firm because of your *f·*,

    m 68– 3 for *f·* of being thought ridiculous.
    s 115–21 Evil beliefs, passions and appetites, *f·*,
      125–14 changes . . . from *f·* to hope
      151–18 *F·* never stopped being and its action.
      159– 9 not by the ether, but by *f·* of inhaling it.
    ph 180–22 Instead of furnishing thought with *f·*,
      189– 7 and casts out a *f·*.
    f 201–10 false appetites, hatred, *f·*, all sensuality,
      209– 4 in proportion as ignorance, *f·*, or
      222–27 while *f·*, hygiene, physiology, and physics
      230–26 satisfy mortal belief, and quiet *f·*.
    b 327– 6 destroy the false beliefs of pleasure, pain, or *f·*
    o 352–13 sick in consequence of the *f·* :
      352–30 no longer seeming worthy of *f·* or honor.
    p 370– 8 proves that *f·* is governing the body.
      373–19 The *f·* occasioned by ignorance can be cured ;
      377–28 also a *f·* that Mind is helpless
      384–24 the *f·* subsides and the conviction abides
      391–32 *F·* is the fountain of sickness,
      392– 5 *F·*, which is an element of all disease,
      404–29 envy, dishonesty, *f·*, . . . make a man sick,
      409–19 never yields to the weaker, except through *f·* or
      411–21 foundation of all sickness is *f·*, ignorance, or
      419–11 Neither disease itself, sin, nor *f·* has the power
      421–20 when the *f·* is destroyed, the inflammation
    t 445–19 C. S. silences human will, quiets *f·*
    r 494–31 they cast *f·* and all evil out of
    g 532–26 *F·* was the first manifestation of the error of
    gl 586–11 definition of
      586–13 *F·* ; remorse ; lust ; hatred ; destruction ;
      592–21 Night. Darkness ; doubt ; *f·*.
      593– 7 Red Dragon. Error ; *f·* ; inflammation ;

fear (verb)
    s 156–14 to *f·* an aggravation of symptoms from
    ph 196–11 "*F·* him which is able to— *Matt.* 10 : 28.
    f 214–20 to *f·* . . . what they consider a material body
      231–22 To *f·* sin is to misunderstand the power of Love
      231–27 To *f·* them is impossible, when you
    b 340– 7 *F·* God, and keep His— *Eccl.* 12 : 13.
    o 348– 2 and which we desire neither to honor nor to *f·*.
      352–17 Children, like adults, *ought* to *f·* a
    p 376–30 To *f·* and admit the power of disease,
      406–25 and no more *f·* that we shall be sick
      419–25 Never *f·* the mental malpractitioner,
      425–26 You will never *f·* again except to offend God,
      436–22 He must obey your law, *f·* its consequences,
      442–27 "*F·* not, little flock ;— *Luke* 12 : 32.
    t 444–21 *F·* not that he will smite thee again
      452–10 you should not *f·* to put on the new.

fear (verb)
    ap 570–18 and never *f·* the consequences.
      578–11 I will *f·* no evil :— *Psal.* 23 : 4.
    gl 596–22 I will *f·* no evil."— *Psal.* 23 : 4.
feared
    f 215–28 Socrates *f·* not the hemlock poison.
    o 352–15 Would a mother say . . . They exist, and are
        to be *f·* ;
    p 411– 1 "The thing which I greatly *f·* — *Job* 3 : 25.
      413–31 may be reproduced in the very ailments *f·*.
feareth
    p 410–19 He that *f·* is not made perfect— *I John* 4 : 18
fearful
    pr 6–31 left this record : "His rebuke is *f·*."
    a 22–15 If your endeavors are beset by *f·* odds,
    m 65–11 The union of the sexes suffers *f·* discord.
    f 203–28 of *f·* and doleful dying
    p 415–15 render mortal mind temporarily less *f·*,
fearing
    f 244– 6 never *f·* nor obeying error in any form.
fearless
    p 406–18 should be as *f·* on the question of disease.
    g 514–11 Free and *f·* it roams in the forest.
fearlessly
    p 378–11 By looking a tiger *f·* in the eye,
      378–15 man's gaze, fastened *f·* on a ferocious beast,
      420–25 Tell the sick that they can meet disease *f·*, if
fears
  certain
    p 417–30 seems to induce disease by certain *f·*
  children's
    o 352–20 but instead of increasing children's *f·*
  doubts and
    pr 13–22 doubts and *f·* which attend such a belief,
  entertains
    p 422–27 entertains *f·* and doubts as to the ultimate
  her own
    s 154–18 The law of mortal mind and her own *f·*
  his
    p 367– 5 patience with his *f·* and the removal of them
  mental
    ph 199–20 latent mental *f·* are subdued by him.

    ph 187– 8 and then worships and *f·* them.
    o 352–23 assured that their *f·* are groundless,
    p 392–30 shut out these unhealthy thoughts and *f·*.
      419–29 you must conquer your own *f·*
    t 457– 9 never . . . in any direction which she *f·*
feasible
    m 63–23 A *f·* as well as rational means of improvement
    o 345–19 practical proof is the only *f·* evidence
feast
    a 32– 8 ancient custom for the master of a *f·*
    s 130– 4 When all men are bidden to the *f·*,
    ap 575– 4 Then cometh the marriage *f·*,
feasting
    f 220–26 The belief that either fasting or *f·*
feathers
    b 299– 1 with suggestive *f·* ; but this is only fancy.
feats
    sp 86–19 either involve *f·* by tricksters, or
    ph 199–19 The *f·* of the gymnast prove that
feature
    ap 560– 4 the distinctive *f·* has reference to
features
    an 102–17 its aggressive *f·* are coming to the front.
febrile
    p 379–26 coated tongue, *f·* heat, dry skin,
fed
    a 33– 5 heavenly manna, which of old had *f·*
    m 62– 9 to be always *f·*, rocked, tossed, or talked to,
    b 273–25 *f·* the multitude, healed the sick,
    p 442–25 until . . . man is clothed and *f·* spiritually.
feeble
    pref ix–14 *f·* attempts to state the Principle
    ph 199–23 failure is occasioned by a too *f·* faith.
    c 262–11 We must reverse our *f·* flutterings
    t 454–27 loving care and counsel support all their *f·*
    ap 577–28 The writer's present *f·* sense of C. S.
feebleness
    f 219–17 for the belief in *f·* must
feebly
    s 117–27 dimly reflects and *f·* transmits Jesus' works
feed
    pr 17– 5 *f·* the famished affections;
    g 530–11 as able to *f·* and clothe man
feeding
    a 33–10 this bread was *f·* and sustaining them.
    f 234– 7 *f·* the hungry and giving living waters

feeds

f 222– 9	and *f·* thought with the bread of Life.
248– 8	Mind *f·* the body with supernal
g 507– 4	Spirit duly *f·* and clothes every object,

feel

pr 8–14	If we *f·* the aspiration, humility, gratitude,
a 19–27	in disobedience . . . we ought to *f·* no security,
sp 86–16	though we can always *f·* their influence.
86–22	more difficult to see a thought than to *f·* one?
s 153–23	where there is no mortal mind to *f·* it
ph 176–28	The human mind, not matter, is supposed to *f·*,
193–14	and said : "I *f·* like a new man.
f 211– 2	if they . . . report how they *f·*,
249– 6	Let us *f·* the divine energy of Spirit,
c 264–26	and *f·* the unspeakable peace which comes
b 284–23	nor can they *f·*, taste, or smell Spirit.
294–13	error, saying : . . . Nerves *f·*. Brain thinks
o 346–25	Do you *f·* the pain of tooth-pulling, when you
p 376–26	impossible for matter to suffer, to *f·* pain
384– 2	Can matter, . . . either *f·* or act without
394–31	till they *f·* its beneficent influence.
395–26	to *f·* these ills in physical belief.
t 461–30	unsee the disease ; then you will not *f·* it,
r 478–14	Does brain think, and do nerves *f·*,
479–11	Matter cannot see, *f·*, hear, taste,
479–12	cannot *f·* itself, see itself, nor understand
479–16	see, hear, *f·*, or use any of the
484–20	human consciousness is educated to *f·*.
g 532–30	error demands that *mind* shall . . . *f·* through matter,

feeling

pref ix– 8	attempts to convey his *f·*.
sp 86–21	is no less a quality of physical sense than *f·*.
87–27	by friendship or by any intense *f·*
s 107–15	*F·* so perpetually the false consciousness
f 221–27	childhood's hunger and undisciplined by
p 393–11	and govern its *f·* and action.
t 454–26	Do not dismiss students . . . *f·* that you

feelings

p 396– 6	Make no unnecessary inquiries relative to *f·*
gl 587–23	HEART. Mortal *f·*, motives, affections,

feels

sp 86–30	It *f·*, hears, and sees its own thoughts.
ph 166– 3	Mind is all that *f·*, acts, or impedes action.
f 224– 2	the world *f·* the alterative effect of truth
b 294– 9	The belief that matter thinks, sees, or *f·*
p 401–14	and mortal mind only *f·* and sees materially.
414–25	matter neither *f·*, suffers, nor enjoys.
430–19	The patient *f·* ill, ruminates,
t 443– 9	she *f·*, as she always has felt, that all
451–23	He *f·* morally obligated to open the eyes of
464– 1	*f·* your influence without seeing you.
r 467–28	Matter neither sees, hears, nor *f·*.
485– 5	Science declares that Mind, . . . sees, hears, *f·*,
gl 591–15	*f·*, hears, tastes, and smells only in belief.

fees

t 445–29	danger in . . . caring only for the *f·*.

feet

bare

p 362–14	and his bare *f·* away from it.

guest's

p 364–14	wash and anoint his guest's *f·*,

his

a 44–19	that he might employ his *f·* as before.
p 363– 1	to come behind the couch and reach his *f·*.
363–27	She bathed his *f·* with her tears
442–14	his *f·* "beautiful upon the—*Isa.* 52 : 7.
ap 558– 5	and his *f·* as pillars of fire :—*Rev.* 10 : 1.
	(*see also sub-title* **under his**)

its

ap 558–16	Its *f·* are pillars of fire, foundations of Truth

Jesus'

p 363– 4	she perfumed Jesus' *f·* with the oil,

lacerated

a 44–17	bind up the wounded side and lacerated *f·*,

Master's

a 28–24	to unloose the sandals of thy Master's *f·* !

of everlasting Love

a 23–11	will fall at the *f·* of everlasting Love.

our

f 224– 7	and shall plant our *f·* on firmer ground.
p 429– 8	We look before our *f·*,
g 516–14	The grass beneath our *f·* silently exclaims,

patient's

f 235–25	the patient's *f·* may be planted on the rock

to the lame

ph 183–29	voice to the dumb, *f·* to the lame.
f 210–13	hearing to the deaf, *f·* to the lame,

under her

ap 560– 8	and the moon under her *f·*,— *Rev.* 12 : 1.
561–27	and matter is put under her *f·*.
562– 7	The moon is under her *f·*.

feet

under his

ph 200–15	hast put all things under his *f·*."— *Psal.* 8 : 6.
f 230–21	and can man put that law under his *f·*

under the

ph 182–22	puts matter under the *f·* of Mind.

wet

f 220–12	he has no catarrh from wet *f·*,

t 454– 7	and plants the *f·* in the true path,

felicity

m 66–17	Amidst gratitude for conjugal *f·*,

fell

a 27–26	They *f·* away from grace because
47–25	His dark plot *f·* to the ground,
47–26	and the traitor *f·* with it.
48–10	Remembering the sweat of agony which *f·*
s 133–10	and manna *f·* from the sky.
156– 5	A case of dropsy, . . . *f·* into my hands.
g 556–18	the deep sleep which *f·* upon Adam?
557–23	but immediately *f·* into mental sin ;

fellow-being

p 366–12	physician who lacks sympathy for his *f·*

fellow-beings

pr 13–16	before we tell Him or our *f·* about it.

fellow-countrymen

g 509–31	Jesus rebuked the material thought of his *f·* :

fellow-man

s 128–23	If one would not quarrel with his *f·*
p 435– 8	in obedience to higher law, helped his *f·*,
440–18	for ministering to the wants of his *f·*

fellow-men

t 447– 9	or judging accurately the need of your *f·*.

fellow-mortals

ap 564– 6	incites mortals to kill . . . even their *f·*,

Fellow of the Royal College of Physicians

s 164– 3	*F·* of the *R· C·* of *P·*, London,

fellows

b 313– 8	oil of gladness above thy *f·*.— *Heb.* 1 : 9.

fellowship

pr 8– 7	They hold secret *f·* with sin,
a 40–23	rejoicing to enter into *f·* with him
b 268– *	may have *f·* with us :— *I John* 1 : 3.
268– *	our *f·* is with the Father,— *I John* 1 : 3.
276– 5	unfold the foundation of *f·*,

felon

an 105–23	like an escaped *f·* to commit fresh atrocities
p 379– 9	A *f·*, on whom certain English students

felon's

a 40–21	If a career so great . . . could not avert a *f·* fate,

felt

a 20–19	and when error *f·* the power of Truth,
52– 9	Their imperfections and impurity *f·* the
53–28	but at the time when Jesus *f·* our infirmities,
sp 88–19	can never be seen, *f·*, nor understood through
ph 169– 6	before the patient *f·* the change ;
c 265–23	Who that has *f·* the loss of human peace
b 323–29	The effects of C. S. are not so much seen as *f·*.
324–22	was made blind, and his blindness was *f·* ;
p 395–22	to hold it as something seen and *f·*
400–31	Even our Master *f·* this.
t 443–10	she always has *f·*, that all are privileged to
449–20	baneful effect . . . is less seen than *f·*.
450–27	Who, that has *f·* the perilous beliefs in
g 514–27	Daniel *f·* safe in the lions' den,

female

f 249– 5	"male and *f·*" of God's creating— *Gen.* 1 : 27.
g 508–21	a neuter gender, neither male nor *f·*.
508–22	Mind . . . names the *f·* gender last
508–24	The . . . individual idea, be it male or *f·*,
516–25	male and *f·* created He them.— *Gen.* 1 : 27.
524–19	Mind had made man, both male and *f·*.
525–16	and He shaped them male and *f·*.
528– 4	has already created man, both male and *f·*
ap 577– 5	presents the unity of male and *f·*

feminine

m 57– 4	Union of the masculine and *f·* qualities
57– 7	through certain elements of the *f·*,
57– 7	the *f·* mind gains courage and strength
64–24	masculine wisdom and *f·* love,
g 508–16	*f·* gender is not yet expressed in the text.
511–28	taking form in masculine, *f·*, or neuter gender.
516–30	Masculine, *f·*, and neuter genders
517–13	as we have for considering Him *f·*,

femininity

g 508–19	does not necessarily refer to either . . . or *f·*.

ferment

t 449– 3	A little leaven causes the whole mass to *f·*.

fermentation
 m 65–20 There will ensue a *f·* over this
  65–23 The *f·* even of fluids is not pleasant.
 sp 96–22 This mental *f·* has begun,
 p 401–12 This *f·* should not aggravate the disease,
  421–13 more for the mental disturbance or *f·*,

fermenting
 p 401–20 as is the case with a *f·* fluid.

ferocious
 sp 78–2 the blighted bud, the gnarled oak, the *f·* beast,
 p 378–15 fastened fearlessly on a *f·* beast,

ferocity
 b 293–22 lightning, fire, bestial *f·*

fervency
 pr 8–21 Praying for humility with whatever *f·*

fervent
 pr 2–12 We can do more for ourselves by humble *f·*
  4–3 the prayer of *f·* desire for growth in grace,
  7–22 A self-satisfied ventilation of *f·* sentiments
  8–10 If a man, though apparently *f·* and prayerful,
  11–29 prayer, coupled with a *f·* habitual desire
  13–6 beyond the honest standpoint of *f·* desire.
 ap 565–21 with the *f·* heat of Truth and Love,

fervor
 sp 89–24 and the *f·* of untutored lips.

festive
 f 240–4 *f·* flowers, and glorious heavens,

festivity
 p 362–6 as if to interrupt the scene of Oriental *f·*.

fetter
 f 226–19 material medicine and hygiene, *f·* faith

fettered
 sp 77–21 a so-called mind *f·* to matter.
 b 292–9 belief that Mind, . . . can be *f·* by the body,
 t 448–32 *F·* by sin yourself, it is difficult to
 gl 584–13 free from one belief only to be *f·* by another,

fetterless
 sp 84–17 yea, to reach the range of *f·* Mind.

fetters
 f 223–4 the *f·* of man's finite capacity are forged by
  225–19 potent to break despotic *f·*
  226–10 demanding that the *f·* of sin, sickness,
  226–20 Science rends asunder these *f·*,
  227–1 to guide me into the land of C. S., where *f·* fall
  249–29 It throws off some material *f·*
 t 449–1 to free another from the *f·* of disease.
 ap 570–2 the people will chain, with *f·* of some sort,

feuds
 a 52–15 Herod and Pilate laid aside old *f·* in order to

fever
chills and
 p 375–8 Change the . . . and the chills and *f·* disappear.
fear or
 ph 175–12 and dissuade any sense of fear or *f·*.
typhoid
 s 153–11 patient sinking in the last stage of typhoid *f·*.
you end
 p 376–27 Destroy fear, and you end *f·*.

 f 251–5 neither should a *f·* become more severe
 p 375–6 often the form in which *f·* manifests itself.
  376–18 cannot, for that very reason, suffer with a *f·*.
  376–28 when it will be safe to check a *f·*.
  376–29 in Science you cannot check a *f·* after admitting
  380–2 a *f·* case, which ends in a belief called
  386–10 catarrh, *f·*, rheumatism, or consumption,

fever-picture
 p 379–30 the *f·*, drawn by millions of mortals

fevers
 p 379–25 *F·* are errors of various types.

few
 pref ix–6 He finds a *f·* words, and with these he
  x–9 A *f·* books, however, which are based on this
  x–19 *F·* invalids will turn to God till all
 a 21–3 "Many are called, but *f·* are.— Matt. 22 : 14.
  36–13 He was forsaken by all save . . . a *f·* women
  38–6 old doctrine . . . the election of a *f·* to be saved,
  38–21 Jesus experienced *f·* of the pleasures of the
  42–13 the desertion of all save a *f·* friends.
  48–15 Truth and Love bestow *f·* palms until
  54–22 adhered to him only a *f·* unpretentious friends,
 s 141–4 *F·* understand or adhere to Jesus' divine
 ph 177–31 In such cases a *f·* persons believe the potion
  184–29 I sat silently by her side a *f·* moments.
  193–10 In a *f·* moments his face changed ;
  195–3 babbling boy . . . taught to speak a *f·* words,
 f 206–20 for the brief space of a *f·* years
  225–17 A *f·* immortal sentences, breathing the omnipotence of
 b 270–10 *F·* deny the hypothesis that

few
 b 301–5 *F·* persons comprehend what C. S. means by
  323–17 If "faithful over a *f·* things,"— Matt. 25 : 21.
 o 358–21 *f·* who have gained a true knowledge of
 p 389–32 I cured her in a *f·* minutes.
 t 450–15 *F·* yield without a struggle,
 r 473–31 *F·*, however, except his students understood
 g 536–21 "of *f·* days, and full of trouble."— Job 14 : 1.
  552–15 of *f·* days, and full of trouble."— Job 14 : 1.
  556–32 plunged his infant babe, only a *f·* hours old,
 ap 569–6 faithful over a *f·* things,— Matt. 25 : 23.

fewer
 ph 175–4 When there are *f·* prescriptions,
  176–12 There were *f·* books on digestion

fewness
 f 225–5 the *f·* and faithfulness of its followers.

fibres
 r 488–23 Nerves have no more sensation, . . . than the *f·*

fiction
 sp 84–5 foreshadowing evil and mistaking fact for *f·*,
 ph 171–1 Matter, which . . . claims to be a creator, is a *f·*,
  195–25 the speculative theory, the nauseous *f·*.

fidelity
 a 49–13 gratify his last . . . yearning with one sign of *f·* ?
 sp 95–7 our *f·* to Truth and Love ;
 p 397–20 and your *f·* to divine metaphysics,
  418–10 if your *f·* is half equal to the truth of
 t 449–15 in proportion to your honesty and *f·*,
 gl 579–10 ABRAHAM.　*F·* ; faith in the divine Life

field
beast of the
 g 527–22 formed every beast of the *f·*,— Gen. 2 : 19.
  529–14 more subtle than any beast of the *f·* — Gen. 3 : 1.
 ap 565–1 "more subtle than any beast of the *f·*." — Gen. 3 : 1.
beasts of the
 g 539–19 to grovel beneath all the beasts of the *f·*.
flower of the
 ph 190–24 As a flower of the *f·*, so he— Psal. 103 : 15.
 r 476–25 as a flower of the *f·*, so he— Psal. 103 : 15.
herb of the
 g 520–20 herb of the *f·* before it grew :— Gen. 2 : 5.
  535–25 thou shalt eat the herb of the *f·* :— Gen. 3 : 18.
leave the
 p 419–5 leave the *f·* to God, Life, Truth, and Love,
lilies of the
 f 212–23 makes and clothes the lilies of the *f·*,
open
 g 514–13 Undisturbed it lies in the open *f·*, or rests in
plant of the
 g 509–24 the "plant of the *f·* before it— Gen. 2 : 5.
  520–19 every plant of the *f·* before it— Gen. 2 : 5.
  526–4 "every plant of the *f·* before it— Gen. 2 : 5.
this
 t 457–11 since entering this *f·* of labor,

fields
 s 121–5 the heavenly *f·* were incorrectly explored.

fierce
 sp 97–8 According to human belief, the lightning is *f·*

fiery
 s 133–17 in the *f·* furnace and in kings' palaces.
 f 243–6 from the *f·* furnace, from the jaws of the lion,
 ap 565–20 *f·* baptism will burn up the chaff of error

fifth
 sp 92–3 *f·* erroneous postulate is, that matter holds
 g 513–5 and the morning were the *f·* day.— Gen. 1 : 23.

fifty
 p 422–1 and that their combined sum is *f·*,

fight
 pref viii–16 On this basis C. S. will have a fair *f·*.
 a 21–3 "I have fought a good *f·* — II Tim. 4 : 7.
 f 225–8 The powers of this world will *f·*, and
 b 309–12 a soldier of God, who had fought a good *f·*.
 p 378–14 and both will *f·* for nothing.
 r 492–18 "I propose to *f·* it out on this line,
  492–20 You must *f·* it out on this line.
 g 529–28 faith to *f·* all claims of evil,

fighting
 f 216–10 On which side are we *f·* ?

fights
 ap 567–1 He leads the hosts . . . and *f·* the holy wars.

figs
 b 276–31 grapes from thorns nor *f·* from thistles.

figurative
 g 514–14 In the *f·* transmission from the divine thought

figuratively
 b 299–18 is *f·* represented in Scripture as a tree,

FIGURE   183   FINGERS

figure

b 282–13	never unite in *f·* or in fact.
g 529–26	evil, by whatever *f·* presented,
538–11	The sun, . . . is a *f·* of divine Life and Love,
ap 562– 6	completed this *f·* with woman, typifying the

figured

b 282– 4	are *f·* by two geometrical symbols,

figures

sp 81–20	Erase the *f·* which express number,
ap 571–25	In significant *f·* he depicts the thoughts which

fill

ph 195–27	*f·* our young readers with wrong tastes and
f 201–13	We cannot *f·* vessels already full.
g 504–13	Truth, Life, and Love *f·* immensity
512–18	and *f·* the waters in the seas — *Gen.* 1 : 22.
520– 4	majesty, and glory of infinite Love *f·* all space.

filled

pref x– 6	*f·* with plagiarisms from SCIENCE AND HEALTH.
pr 5–16	Ingratitude and persecution *f·* it to the brim ;
c 266– 9	but this seeming vacuum is already *f·*
b 295– 6	The universe is *f·* with spiritual ideas,
315–15	Their thoughts were *f·* with mortal error,
p 430–25	court-room is *f·* with interested spectators,
r 469–24	where all space is *f·* with God.

filling

s 110– 2	Spirit possessing all power, *f·* all space,
ph 186– 3	*f·* it with the divine energies of Truth.

fills

ph 190– 9	*f·* itself with thoughts of pain and pleasure,
198–11	*f·* in his delineations with sketches from
b 331–22	He *f·* all space, and it is impossible to
p 434– 3	Consternation *f·* the prison-yard.

filth

p 383–12	whose *f·* does not affect his happiness,

final

a 22–23	*F·* deliverance from error, whereby we
35–17	spiritual and *f·* ascension above matter,
42–16	proof of his *f·* triumph over body and
43–17	*f·* demonstration of the truth which Jesus
45–23	*f·* proof of all that he had taught,
46–26	In his *f·* demonstration, called the
48–30	hastening the *f·* demonstration of what life is
53–30	nor had he risen to his *f·* demonstration
sp 76–28	those who have the *f·* understanding of Christ
96–10	until the *f·* spiritualization of all things.
96–31	During this *f·* conflict, wicked minds
s 107– 5	for the reception of this *f·* revelation of the
111–23	rather than to a *f·* spiritual cause,
128– 1	material conditions, and that these are *f·*
ph 188–10	from shame and woe to their *f·* punishment,
f 219– 5	Mind should be, and is, supreme, . . . and *f·*.
242– 7	and the *f·* triumph over the body.
b 268– 2	challenge metaphysics to meet in *f·* combat,
268–10	In this *f·* struggle for supremacy,
288–10	When the *f·* physical and moral effects of C. S.
291–28	No *f·* judgment awaits mortals,
292– 1	then the *f·* trump will sound
339– 6	and involve the *f·* destruction of all sin?
p 409– 5	the nearer matter approaches its *f·* statement,
429– 6	The *f·* demonstration takes time for its
r 476– 9	Error, urged to its *f·* limits, is
g 506– 7	and makes Truth *f·*.

finally

a 21– 2	can *f·* say, "I have fought a— *II Tim.* 4 : 7.
45– 6	Our Master fully and *f·* demonstrated
sp 90–28	recognition of Spirit must *f·* come,
96– 4	Love will *f·* mark the hour of harmony,
s 125–31	will *f·* be proved nothing more than
156–19	*F·* she said that she would give up her
ph 178–21	must *f·* yield to the eternal Truth,
181–19	till you *f·* attain the understanding of C. S.
190–18	This mortal seeming . . . *f·* disappears,
f 221–11	and *f·* made up his mind to die,
222–26	*f·* concluded that God never made a dyspeptic,
240–28	error is *f·* brought into subjection
248–32	will diminish until they *f·* disappear.
252–11	entire mortal, material error *f·* disappears,
c 260–11	God's creation will *f·* be seen as the
264– 4	must *f·* give place to the glorious forms which
b 287–29	false evidence will *f·* yield
310– 6	Thought will *f·* be understood and seen
p 371– 3	this so-called mind must *f·* yield to the
378–26	and *f·* conquers it.
380– 3	death, which belief must be *f·* conquered by
405–18	The good man *f·* can overcome his fear of
t 458– 9	that error will *f·* have the same effect as
460–31	*f·* the shadow of old errors was no longer cast
r 476–17	Mortality is *f·* swallowed up in immortality.
492–11	Thus progress will *f·* destroy all error,
g 523– 4	and *f·* declares that God knows error
549– 7	a blunder which will *f·* give place to
ap 565–17	imperatively, absolutely, *f·*
570– 5	will *f·* be shocked into another extreme

find

pr 7–11	Looking deeply into these things, we *f·* that
14–16	you will *f·* yourself suddenly well.
a 22– 2	thinking with the aid of this to *f·* and follow the
24–23	Does spiritualism *f·* Jesus' death necessary
36– 2	can never *f·* bliss in the blessed company of
m 65–27	*f·* permanence and peace in a more spiritual
sp 83– 7	Mortals must *f·* refuge in Truth
96–32	wicked minds will endeavor to *f·* means
s 111– 3	I *f·* the will, or sensuous reason of the
113–24	According to the Scripture, I *f·* that God is
124– 9	seeks to *f·* life and intelligence in matter,
125–23	agriculturist will *f·* that these changes cannot
125–30	florist will *f·* his flower before its seed.
132–27	shall he *f·* faith on the earth?"— *Luke* 18 : 8.
ph 169–15	should *f·* stronger supports and a higher home.
171– 8	and will *f·* himself unfallen, upright, pure,
f 206–15	we *f·* that whatever blesses one blesses all,
232–29	we *f·* unquestionable signs of the burial of error
241–23	One's aim, . . . should be to *f·* the footsteps of
246–27	Life is eternal. We should *f·* this out,
251–23	to *f·* the divine Mind to be the only Mind,
c 260–31	If we look to the body for pleasure, we *f·* pain ;
260–32	for Life, we *f·* death ; for Truth, we *f·* error ;
261– 1	for Spirit, we *f·* its opposite, matter.
262–11	efforts to *f·* life and truth in matter
b 316– 6	lose sight of mortal selfhood to *f·* Christ,
322–31	"Canst thou by searching *f·* out — *Job.* 11 : 7.
326– 6	and *f·* the divine remedy for every ill,
o 354– 9	words of divine Science *f·* their immortality in
360– 2	they will *f·* that nothing is lost,
p 378–31	less wisdom than we usually *f·* displayed in
397–18	and you will *f·* the ensuing good effects to be
409–30	cannot . . . expect to *f·* beyond the grave a
411–31	will *f·* that it alleviates the symptoms
412–18	*f·* the type of the ailment, get its name,
416–13	will *f·* himself in the same pain, unless
417– 1	and that they *f·* health, peace, and
426– 2	will *f·* that mortal mind, when instructed
436– 7	Your Supreme Court must *f·* the prisoner
436–13	Mortal Man should *f·* it again.
436–28	charged the jury, . . . to *f·* the prisoner guilty.
t 443–22	If the sick *f·* these material expedients
444–11	Step by step will those who trust Him *f·*
r 487– 1	*f·* a higher sense of happiness and existence.
491–15	*f·* the indissoluble spiritual link which
495–10	and *f·* a sovereign antidote for error
g 551–27	"Canst thou by searching *f·* out — *Job.* 11 : 7.
ap 559–23	murmur not . . . if you *f·* its digestion bitter.

findeth

b 291–23	As death *f·* mortal man, so shall he be after

finding

a 36–17	from *f·* favor with the worldly-minded.
ph 184– 9	*f·* and casting out by denial the error
f 220–23	*F·* his health failing, he gave up his
235– 2	cannot go forth, . . . *f·* unsuspected lodgment,
c 264–18	*f·* all in God, good, and needing no other
b 308–11	*f·* only an illusion, a blending of false claims,
322–23	likes to do wrong — *f·* pleasure in it
327– 8	malice, *f·* pleasure in revenge !
p 365– 7	*f·* utterance in such words as
369–27	Unscientific methods are *f·* their
g 506–28	task of *f·* names for all material things,
542–17	lest any *f·* him should kill him.— *Gen.* 4 : 15.

finds

pref ix– 6	He *f·* a few words, and with these he
ix–17	she still *f·* herself a willing disciple at
pr 12–23	The common custom . . . *f·* help in blind belief,
m 59–15	in which the heart *f·* peace and home.
69– 8	only as man *f·* the truth of being.
s 119–25	viewing the sunrise, one *f·* that it contradicts
160–14	Anatomy *f·* a necessity for nerves
f 250–18	*f·* himself experiencing none of these
b 282–14	straight line *f·* no abiding-place in a curve,
282–15	a curve *f·* no adjustment to a straight line.
322–14	Man's wisdom *f·* no satisfaction in sin,
p 365–25	If . . . inhumanity, or vice *f·* its way into the
379– 4	The Christian Scientist *f·* only effects, where
426– 5	The discoverer of C. S. *f·* the path less
g 533–27	*f·* woman the first to confess her fault.

finger

pr 3–31	put the *f·* on the lips and remember our
s 161– 3	You say, "*I* have burned my *f·*."
f 212–11	attempt to scratch the end of a *f·* which
237– 2	A little girl, . . . badly wounded her *f·*.
237– 6	"Mamma, my *f·* is not a bit sore."
b 294– 6	the loss of one *f·* would take away

finger-posts

f 242–30	The *f·* of divine Science show the way

fingers

b 299– 9	With white *f·* they point upward to a
p 401–30	to the *f·* of a surgeon,

finished

a 29– 4   until they have *f·* their course.
f 206–23   declaring that His work was *f·*,
g 519– 8   the heavens and the earth were *f·*,— *Gen.* 2 : 1.
   522–19   the Scripture . . . declares God's work to be *f·*.

finishes

a 21–14   till at last he *f·* his course with joy.

finite

sp 71–29   limited and *f·* in character and quality.
   73–22   belief that spirit is confined in a *f·*,
   73–31   nor can the *f·* become the channel of the infinite.
   76– 7   as neither material nor *f·*, but as infinite,
   93–21   belief that Spirit is *f·* as well as infinite
   93–28   *F·* spirit would be mortal,
   93–30   belief that the infinite can be . . . in the *f·*.
s 133–21   It was a *f·* and material system,
   151– 5   erring, *f·*, human mind has an absolute need of
f 213–15   towards the *f·*, temporary, and discordant.
   214–18   and entertain *f·* thoughts of God
   223– 4   the fetters of man's *f·* capacity are forged by
   223–13   If . . . Spirit would be *f·*,
c 256– 1   The *f·* must yield to the infinite.
   256–25   A *f·* and material sense of God leads to
   256–31   originating from a *f·* or material source
   256–32   must be limited and *f·*.
   257–22   *F·* mind manifests all sorts of errors,
   257–24   Who hath found *f·* life or love sufficient
   257–32   *F·* man cannot be the image and likeness of
   258– 2   A mortal, corporeal, or *f·* conception of God
   264– 8   Mortals must look beyond fading, *f·* forms,
b 280– 9   *F·* belief can never do justice to Truth
   280–10   *F·* belief limits all things,
   280–24   and that infinite Spirit, and Life, is in *f·* forms.
   281–28   does not put . . . the infinite into the *f·*.
   282– 8   the *f·*, which has both beginning and end.
   284– 5   if the infinite could be circumscribed within the *f·*,
   284–14   Can the infinite dwell in the *f·*
   285–18   The time has come for a *f·* . . . to give place
   286– 4   through the *f·*, mutable, and mortal,
   290–10   That Life or Mind is *f·* and physical . . . is false.
   309–25   impossible for . . . Soul to be in a *f·* body
   312–21   Mortals believe in a *f·* personal God ;
   312–23   theories are based on *f·* premises,
   312–28   matter and Spirit, the *f·* and the infinite,
   322–12   that *f·* belief may be prepared to relinquish
   335–22   for Spirit is not *f·*.
   336– 2   Mind never enters the *f·*.
   336–22   else God would be manifestly *f·*,
   339–22   until the *f·* gives place to the infinite,
o 343– 6   Is not *f·* mind ignorant of God's method?
r 466–21   There is no *f·* soul nor spirit.
   468–30   Time is *f·* ; eternity is forever infinite.
g 505–30   mortal, erring, and *f·* are human beliefs,
   524–16   Did the divine . . . become a *f·* deity,
   545– 1   through mortal and *f·* conceptions.
   550– 8   God cannot become *f·*, and be limited
   553–23   appearance of its method in *f·* forms
gl 580– 7   a so-called *f·* mind, producing other minds,
   580–23   supposition . . . that the infinite enters the *f·*,
   585–24   a *f·* belief concerning life, substance, and
   587– 2   GHOST. . . . a supposition that spirit is *f·*.
   587–12   belief that infinite Mind is in *f·* forms ;
   587–18   and cannot become *f·* and imperfect.
   591– 1   a physical sense of God as *f·* and corporeal.
   (see also **form, sense)**

finiteness

c 255–16   physical *f·*, cannot be made the basis of
   256–29   *F·* cannot present the idea or the vastness of
b 284– 2   not rational to say that Mind . . . dwells in *f·*,
   302– 1   Soul is not compassed by *f·*.
r 469– 5   Death and *f·* are unknown to Life.
gl 580– 1   a belief in intelligent matter, *f·*, and mortality ;

finity

f 202–21   earthly experience discloses the *f·* of error
   229– 8   Mind signifies God,— infinity, not *f·*.
gl 585–22   *f·* ; the opposite of infinity.
   594– 5   the first lie of limitation ; *f·* ;
   599– 3   As applied to corporeality, a mortal ; *f·*.

fire

sp 72–32   As readily can you mingle *f·* and frost as
f 252–30   with the resplendency of consuming *f·*.
b 293–22   wind, wave, lightning, *f·*, bestial ferocity
t 457–21   One cannot scatter his *f·*, and
ap 558– 6   and his feet as pillars of *f·* :— *Rev.* 10 : 1.
   558–16   Its feet are pillars of *f·*, foundations of
   565–20   This immaculate idea, . . . will baptize with *f·* ;
   566–10   a pillar of cloud by day and of *f·* by night,
gl 586–13   definition of

firm

a 23–13   "He that taketh one doctrine, *f·* in faith,
   23–32   Hebrew verb *to believe* means also *to be f·*
m 67–12   *f·* at the post of duty, the mariner works on
s 138– 8   a *f·* foundation in the realm of harmony.

firm

b 274–25   The conventional *f·*, called matter and mind,
p 374–24   your steps are less *f·* because of your fear,
   393–16   Be *f·* in your understanding that the
   438–31   the *f·* of Personal Sense, Error, & Co.,
   439– 4   Personal Sense, is a buyer for this *f·*.

firmament

above the
g 505–15   waters which were above the *f·* :— *Gen.* 1 : 7.
God called the
g 506– 8   God called the *f·* Heaven.— *Gen.* 1 : 8.
God made the
g 505–13   And God made the *f·*,— *Gen.* 1 : 7.
of the heaven
g 509–10   lights in the *f·* of the heaven,— *Gen.* 1 : 14.
   510– 6   lights in the *f·* of the heaven,— *Gen.* 1 : 15.
   511– 7   set them in the *f·* of the heaven,— *Gen.* 1 : 17.
open
g 511–21   in the open *f·* of heaven.— *Gen.* 1 : 20.
   511–29   fly above the earth in the open *f·*
or understanding
g 523– 9   and not from the *f·*, or understanding,
under the
g 505–14   waters which were under the *f·*— *Gen.* 1 : 7.

g 505– 4   God said, Let there be a *f·*— *Gen.* 1 : 6.
   505– 8   Spiritual understanding, . . . is the *f·*.
gl 586–15   definition of

firmer

f 224– 7   and shall plant our feet on *f·* ground.

firmly

s 147–19   demonstration of the rules . . . will plant you *f·*
t 454–28   until your students tread *f·* in the straight and

firmness

a 24– 2   *F·* in error will never save from sin, disease,
r 488–11   understanding, trust, constancy, *f·*.
gl 582– 1   BELIEVING. *F·* and constancy ;

first

pref vii– 3   beholds the *f·* faint morning beams,
   viii–31   *f·* steps of a child in the newly discovered
   ix–13   still in circulation among her *f·* pupils ;
   ix–20   Her *f·* pamphlet on C. S. was
   x– 3   The *f·* edition of SCIENCE AND HEALTH was
   xi–25   The *f·* school of C. S. Mind-healing
   xii– 5   the United States, where C. S. was *f·* introduced.
   xii– 8   the *f·* established Church of Christ, Scientist ;
   xii– 9   the *f·* Christian Scientist Association,
   xii–13   the *f·* periodical issued by Christian Scientists.
pr 16–19   is but another name for the *f·* lie
a 29–29   though at *f·* faintly developed.
   31–12   *F·* in the list of Christian duties, he taught
   40– 9   *f·* removing the sin which incurs the penalty.
   45–25   Even his disciples, at *f·* called him a spirit,
m 62–32   this does not make materiality *f·*
sp 87–14   when really it is *f·* sight instead of
   91–25   The *f·* erroneous postulate of belief is,
   92–14   commending to our *f·* parents the knowledge of
an 100– 1   Mesmerism . . . was *f·* brought into notice by
   104–10   *F·*, people say it conflicts with the Bible.
   105–29   "Whom the gods would destroy, they *f·*
s 115–20   *F· Degree:* Depravity.
   116– 8   "The last shall be *f·*, and the *f·* last,"— *Matt.* 20 : 16.
   116–12   includes vastly more than is at *f·* seen.
   119– 8   To seize the *f·* horn of this dilemma
   134–20   its astonishing . . . success in the *f·* century.
   142– 9   the whole Christ, as our *f·* proof of Christianity,
   142–26   Which was *f·*, Mind or medicine?
   142–27   If Mind was *f·* and self-existent,
   142–28   Mind, . . . must have been the *f·* medicine.
   143–28   was *f·* chronologically, is *f·* potentially,
   143–29   and must be *f·* eternally,
   145–32   Our Master's *f·* article of faith propounded to
   146– 5   The *f·* idolatry was faith in matter.
   158– 5   He was supposed to have dictated the *f·*
   163– 1   *f·* marking Nature with his name,
ph 166–28   or he would have resorted to Mind *f·*.
   172–15   If man was *f·* a material being,
   177–13   from *f·* to last, the body is a
   183–11   sin, or error, *f·* caused the condemnation of
   189–26   *f·* the belief of inanimate, and then of
f 201–13   They must *f·* be emptied.
   204–12   The *f·* power is admitted to be good,
   204–16   a supposed mixture of the *f·* and second
   207–15   Body is not *f·* and Soul last,
   225– 5   You may know when *f·* Truth leads by
   230–12   to suppose Him capable of *f·* arranging
   234–26   control evil thoughts in the *f·* instance,
   237–16   taught . . . C. S., among their *f·* lessons,
   248–25   must *f·* turn our gaze in the right direction,
b 269– 3   From *f·* to last the supposed coexistence of
   269–10   The *f·* is error ; the latter is truth.
   269–32   The *f·* theory, that matter is everything,
   280–18   Jehovah's *f·* command of the Ten :

first

b	286–12	Physical causation was put aside from $f\cdot$ to
	306– 3	They would $f\cdot$ make life result in death,
	321– 3	Paul says, in his $f\cdot$ epistle to the
	321–21	when Moses $f\cdot$ put his hand into his bosom
	321–28	to the voice of the $f\cdot$ sign, — *Exod.* 4 : 8.
	324–19	Paul was not at $f\cdot$ a disciple of Jesus
	324–20	When the truth $f\cdot$ appeared to him in Science,
	325–30	When $f\cdot$ spoken in any age, Truth,
	326–31	He beheld for the $f\cdot$ time the true idea of Love,
	329–19	because he fails in his $f\cdot$ effort.
	333–17	the $f\cdot$ century of the Christian era,
	334–26	"I am the $f\cdot$ and the last :— *Rev.* 1 : 17.
o	342–26	Who would be the $f\cdot$ to disown the Christliness
	343–30	$f\cdot$ . . . to press along the line of gospel-healing,
	355–18	any . . . healing power since the $f\cdot$ century.
p	366– 4	must $f\cdot$ cast moral evils out of himself
	366–31	we must $f\cdot$ learn to bind up the broken-hearted.
	374–27	body, when bereft of mortal mind, at $f\cdot$ cools,
	389–13	Our dietetic theories $f\cdot$ admit that food sustains
	390–12	When the $f\cdot$ symptoms of disease appear,
	399–30	$f\cdot$ bind the strong man?" — *Matt.* 12 : 29.
	403– 7	In the $f\cdot$ instance it is understood
	411– 3	My $f\cdot$ discovery in the student's practice
	412–20	Argue at $f\cdot$ mentally, not audibly,
	423–32	so-called substance of bone is formed $f\cdot$ by
	427–28	but it should have been his $f\cdot$ and only resort.
	433–17	"Guilty of liver-complaint in the $f\cdot$ degree."
	433–21	guilty of benevolence in the $f\cdot$ degree,
t	447–30	A sinner is afraid to cast the $f\cdot$ stone.
	449–22	The $f\cdot$ impression, made on a mind which
	455–14	"F∙ cast out the beam out of — *Matt.* 7 : 5.
	456–27	F∙ : Because it is the voice of Truth
	456–30	*Second* : Because it was the $f\cdot$ book
	456–32	Hence it gave the $f\cdot$ rules for
	457– 7	Since the divine light of C. S. $f\cdot$ dawned
	459–11	condemned for failing to take the $f\cdot$ step.
	461–27	you must $f\cdot$ see the claim of sin,
	463–23	the $f\cdot$ step towards destroying error.
r	465– 1	This chapter is from the $f\cdot$ edition of
	466–17	although $f\cdot$ and last it is the most
	467– 3	The $f\cdot$ demand of this Science is,
	471–25	until she caught the $f\cdot$ gleam of that which
	474– 8	To the ignorant age in which it $f\cdot$ appears,
	481–20	Human hypotheses $f\cdot$ assume the reality of
	496– 6	in C. S. the $f\cdot$ duty is to obey God,
g	503–21	$f\cdot$, in light ; *second*, in reflection ;
	504– 5	and the morning were the $f\cdot$ day. — *Gen.* 1 : 5.
	522– 3	The Science of the $f\cdot$ record proves the
	522– 5	The $f\cdot$ record assigns all might and
	526–14	$f\cdot$ mention of evil is in the legendary
	526–24	in contradiction of the $f\cdot$ creation?
	528–18	This is the $f\cdot$ record of magnetism.
	528–28	surgery was $f\cdot$ performed mentally
	529– 5	The $f\cdot$ system of suggestive obstetrics has
	530–29	F∙, this narrative supposes that
	532– 1	Did God at $f\cdot$ create one man unaided,
	532– 7	when eating its $f\cdot$ fruits brought death?
	532–26	Fear was the $f\cdot$ manifestation of the error of
	532–31	The $f\cdot$ impression material man had of himself
	533–13	the snake-talker utters the $f\cdot$ voluble lie,
	533–27	finds woman the $f\cdot$ to confess her fault.
	534– 1	Hence she is $f\cdot$ to abandon the belief
	534– 6	enabled woman to be $f\cdot$ to interpret the
	535–17	the heritage of the $f\cdot$ born among men
	536– 3	the $f\cdot$ heaven and the $f\cdot$ earth — *Rev.* 21 : 1.
	541–22	At $f\cdot$ it usurps divine power.
	541–24	It is supposed to say in the $f\cdot$ instance,
	544–17	The $f\cdot$ statement about evil,
	544–17	the $f\cdot$ suggestion of more than the one Mind,
	551– 4	If Mind is $f\cdot$, it cannot produce its opposite
	551– 5	If matter is $f\cdot$, it cannot produce Mind.
	551–32	Which is $f\cdot$, the egg or the bird?
	553–14	or important to their origin and $f\cdot$
	554–17	$f\cdot$ effort of error has been and is
ap	558–11	To mortal sense Science seems at $f\cdot$ obscure,
	559–22	It will be indeed sweet at its $f\cdot$ taste,
	565–18	represented $f\cdot$ by man and,. . .last by woman,
	568–10	$f\cdot$ the true method of creation is set forth
	568–11	the Revelator $f\cdot$ exhibits the true warfare
	572– 3	in both the $f\cdot$ and last books of the Bible,
	572–20, 21	the $f\cdot$ heaven and the $f\cdot$ earth — *Rev.* 21 : 1.
	577–13	$f\cdot$, the Word of Life, Truth, and Love ;
gl	580– 2	nothingness ; the $f\cdot$ god of mythology ;
	584– 3	and the morning were the $f\cdot$ day." — *Gen.* 1 : 5.
	585–13	"Elias truly shall $f\cdot$ come and — *Matt.* 17 : 11.
	585–27	$f\cdot$ from dust, second from a rib,
	594– 3	the $f\cdot$ statement of mythology and idolatry ;
	594– 4	animal magnetism ; the $f\cdot$ lie of limitation ;
	594– 5	$f\cdot$ claim that there is an opposite of Spirit,
	594– 6	$f\cdot$ delusion that error exists as fact ;
	594– 7	$f\cdot$ claim that sin, sickness, and death are
	594– 8	$f\cdot$ audible claim that God was not omnipotent
		(*see also* **chapter**)

First Cause

g	547–20	evolution implies that the great F∙ C∙

First Commandment

m	69–20	"Do you keep the F∙ C∙?
b	301–22	is not spiritual and breaks the F∙ C∙,
	340–16	The F∙ C∙ is my favorite text.
	340–21	The divine Principle of the F∙ C∙
o	361– 6	The Jew who believes in the F∙ C∙
	361–10	The Christian who believes in the F∙ C∙

firstfruits

c	255– *	*which have the $f\cdot$ of the Spirit,* — *Rom.* 8 : 23.

firstlings

g	540–27	Abel, he also brought of the $f\cdot$ — *Gen.* 4 : 4.
	541– 1	Abel takes his offering from the $f\cdot$ of the

fish

of the sea

s	125–27	$f\cdot$ of the sea and the fowls of the air.
f	222–24	"dominion over the $f\cdot$ of the sea, — *Gen.* 1 : 26.
r	475–24	dominion over the $f\cdot$ of the sea, — *Gen.* 1 : 26.
g	515–13	dominion over the $f\cdot$ of the sea, — *Gen.* 1 : 26.
	517–27	dominion over the $f\cdot$ of the sea, — *Gen.* 1 : 28.

salt

p	385–28	because you have partaken of salt $f\cdot$,

sp	90– 5	from which loaf or $f\cdot$ could come?
p	413–13	taking $f\cdot$ out of water every day
g	557– 3	moving and playing without harm, like a $f\cdot$.

fishes

sp	90– 3	How were the loaves and $f\cdot$ multiplied
f	206–17	as Jesus showed with the loaves and the $f\cdot$,
	367–11	not "for the loaves and $f\cdot$," — *see John* 6 : 26.

fists

ph	192–18	who holds the "wind in His $f\cdot$;" — *Prov.* 30 : 4.

fit

p	384–23	if . . . you are not $f\cdot$ to conduct your own case
	420–15	when they are in a $f\cdot$ mood to receive it,
t	445– 2	teacher must thoroughly $f\cdot$ his students
gl	595–15	alone can $f\cdot$ us for the office of spiritual teaching.
	596–17	the only $f\cdot$ preparation for admission to the

fitness

pr	15–32	Without a $f\cdot$ for holiness, we cannot receive
t	449–12	registers his healing ability and $f\cdot$ to teach.
	455–22	one who has grown into such a $f\cdot$ for it as

fitted

pr	3–24	and thus be $f\cdot$ to receive more.

five

s	117–24	Evidence drawn from the $f\cdot$ physical senses
ph	173– 1	brain, acting through the $f\cdot$ physical senses
	190–11	and arranges itself into $f\cdot$ so-called senses,
	200–22	in other words the $f\cdot$ senses,
b	274– 4	knowledge gained from the $f\cdot$ senses
	274–17	what we erroneously term the $f\cdot$ physical senses
	287–27	$f\cdot$ material senses testify to truth and error
	293–32	The $f\cdot$ physical senses are the avenues and
p	421–31	asserting that the products of eight multiplied
		by $f\cdot$,
r	471– 7	the evidence before the $f\cdot$ corporeal senses,
	477– 9	To the $f\cdot$ corporeal senses, man appears to be
	486–28	If the $f\cdot$ corporeal senses were the medium
	488–14	Do the $f\cdot$ corporeal senses constitute man?
	493–18	all the beliefs of the $f\cdot$ corporeal senses,
g	523–26	fourth verse of chapter two to chapter $f\cdot$,
	526–10	involves theories of . . . termed the $f\cdot$ senses.
	532– 6	gained from the $f\cdot$ corporeal senses.
	532–31	through matter, the $f\cdot$ senses.
	543– 9	$f\cdot$ corporeal senses cannot take cognizance of
gl	581–20	obtained from the $f\cdot$ corporeal senses,
	589–13	obtained from the $f\cdot$ corporeal senses ;
	590– 4	obtained from the $f\cdot$ corporeal senses ;

fix

p	414–15	To $f\cdot$ truth steadfastly in your

fixed

m	65–26	Matrimony, which was once a $f\cdot$ fact
	69– 3	as $f\cdot$ in divine Science as is the proof that
sp	83–22	great gulf is $f\cdot$, as impassable as that between
s	113– 2	there must be $f\cdot$ rules for the demonstration of
	128–27	It rests on $f\cdot$ Principle
	163–32	or to reconcile the $f\cdot$ and repulsive antipathies
ph	180–19	by declaring disease to be a $f\cdot$ fact,
	193– 8	Mr. Clark lay with his eyes $f\cdot$ and sightless.
f	233–25	divided according to a $f\cdot$ rule,

fixedness

b	330– 4	the $f\cdot$ of mortal illusions,

fixing

c	261–27	F∙ your gaze on the realities supernal,

fixity

a	23–17	between nothing and something, having no $f\cdot$.

flame

ph	192–14	It is the headlong cataract, the devouring $f\cdot$,
ap	566–18	An awful guide, in smoke and $f\cdot$,

flames

s 161– 7	able to nullify the action of the f,
b 329–15	nor should he remain in the devouring f.
g 504–10	not from the sun nor from volcanic f,
ap 558–18	f of Truth were prophetically described

flaming

g 537– 6 a f sword which turned every way, — *Gen.* 3 : 24.

flannel

m 63– 2 You would never think that f was

flannels

ph 174– 5 to f, to baths, diet, exercise, and air?

flash

b 288–15 burst and f till the cloud is cleared

flashing

p 439–16 his words f as lightning

flatteries

f 238– 8 this frown, more than f,

flatulency

p 413–25 noticing every symptom of f,

flavor

sp 88– 6 mind may even be cognizant of a present f

fled

b 321– 9	When, ... he saw it become a serpent, Moses f
ap 565–29	woman f into the wilderness, — *Rev.* 12 : 6.

fleddest

s 135– 2 O thou sea, that thou f ? — *Psal.* 114 : 5.

flee

f 215–20	f as phantoms of error before truth and
p 377– 6	Invalids f to tropical climates
405–31	causes mortals . . . to f from body to
406–19	Resist evil . . . and it will f from you.
418–32	dark images . . . which f before the light of
r 494–18	thus helping erring human sense to f from

flees

b 310–11 darkness f when the earth has again

fleeth

t 464–26 "The hireling f, because he is an — *John* 10 : 13.

fleeting

m 60–13	selfishness and impurity alone are f,
66–18	it is well to remember how f are human joys.
68– 7	We ought to weary of the f and false
s 163–31	as to arrange the f vapors around us,
f 241– 7	Sin . . . carries off their f joys.
247–11	fading and f as mortal belief.
c 264– 1	f concepts of the human mind.

flesh

advent in the
  a 30– 5 Born of a woman, Jesus' advent in the f

and all error
  a 39– 5 He overcame the world, the f, and all error,

and blood
a 25–10	His true f and blood were his Life ;
s 137–23	f and blood hath not revealed it — *Matt.* 16 : 17.
b 321– 4	"F and blood cannot inherit the — *I Cor.* 15 : 50.
r 478–29	conferred not with f and blood." — *Gal.* 1 : 16.

and bones
a 45–27	"Spirit hath not f and bones, — *Luke* 24 : 39.
b 313–30	Jesus called the body, . . . "f and bones." — *Luke* 24 : 39.
o 352– 7	mortal and material belief of f and bones,
p 372– 8	can form blood, f, and bones.

and evil
  pr 10–13 overcoming the world, the f, and evil,

and matter
  b 320–22 the belief that man is f and matter,

and Spirit
ph 167–20	The f and Spirit can no more unite
171–23	No more . . . between the f and Spirit
o 356–12	spoke of f and Spirit as the two opposites,
356–18	between error and Truth, between f and Spirit.
ap 567–12	endeth the conflict between the f and Spirit.

and the devil
  o 354– 5 "the world, the f, and the devil"

animal
  f 222–25 if eating a bit of animal f could overpower

belief of the
  b 310–22 It is the belief of the f and of

beliefs of the
a 53–29	he had not conquered all the beliefs of the f
b 325–25	But he, who is begotten of the beliefs of the f

bone and
  g 533–22 rapid deterioration of the bone and f which

comes to the
  gl 583–11 comes to the f to destroy incarnate error.

constitute the
  b 274–21 beliefs and their products constitute the f,

crucified the
  a 18– * *crucified the f with the affections and* — *Gal.* 5 : 24.

crucifying the
  b 316–17 conclusion that . . . by crucifying the f.

flesh

cut the
  r 474– 8 worse cords than those which cut the f.

dominate the
  c 266–25 his demonstrations, which dominate the f.

exit from the
  s 117–23 and triumphant exit from the f.

ills of
s 155–23	the discords of matter and the ills of f,
b 277–21	produces all the ills of f,

ills of the
ph 191–32	able to cast out the ills of the f.
b 320–27	divine power to heal the ills of the f,
gl 581–16	the ills of the f rebuked.

impurities of
  f 241–28 washing the body of all the impurities of f,

in my
  b 320–25 "In my f shall I see God," — *Job* 19 : 26.

let not the
  a 33–20 Let not the f, but the Spirit, be represented

lust of the
f 223– 3	shall not fulfil the lust of the f." — *Gal.* 5 : 16.
gl 584–20	hypnotism ; the lust of the f,

manifest in
  b 334–15 the corporeal Jesus manifest in f,

material
  b 321– 1 still clad in material f,

matter, or the
  a 35–17 final ascension above matter, or the f,

mortal
  sp 81–10 their affiliation with mortal f ;

not in the
  g 534–22 But ye are not in the f, — *Rom.* 8 : 9.

not the offspring of
  b 289–31 Man is not the offspring of f, but of Spirit,

offspring of the
  gl 594–17 The son of man, the offspring of the f.

opposed to
  s 114– 4 meaning . . . the f opposed to Spirit,

outside the
  r 482–22 the divine idea of God outside the f.

overcome the
  b 289– 7 Then Spirit will have overcome the f.

piece of the
  f 212–16 this so-called mind instead of a piece of the f,

pierced his
  a 50–30 sharper than the thorns which pierced his f.

probation in the
  a 35–15 his probation in the f after death,

Spirit against the
  o 347– 2 and the Spirit against the f." — *Gal.* 5 : 17.

Spirit and
f 254– 7	until the battle between Spirit and f is fought
b 288– 7	and this warfare between the Spirit and f
g 530–25	Thus Spirit and f war.

Spirit and the
s 145–28	warfare between Spirit and the f goes on.
b 315–31	the mediator between Spirit and the f,

Spirit over the
  b 316– 9 to prove the power of Spirit over the f,

strength and
  f 222–17 he recovered strength and f rapidly.

warfare with the
  b 324–11 It is a warfare with the f,

Word was made
  o 350–24 "The Word was made f." — *John* 1 : 14.

works of the
  an 106–20 the works of the f are manifest, — *Gal.* 5 : 19.

wound the
  p 385–19 If you sprain the muscles or wound the f,

---

a 25–11	they truly eat his f . . . who partake of
31– 4	Jesus acknowledged no ties of the f.
s 107–10	from every ill "that f is heir to."
118– 7	second appearing in the f of the Christ,
ph 167–20	The "f lusteth against the Spirit." — *Gal.* 5 : 17.
177–22	create the so-called laws of the f,
200–22	the f that warreth against Spirit.
f 217–14	know we no man after the f !" — *II Cor.* 5 : 16.
235–25	when the soul is willing and the f weak,
244–10	the worms would rob him of the f
253–31	of Spirit instead of the f.
b 274–22	and the f wars against Spirit.
310–21	If Soul could sin, Spirit, Soul, would be f
311–10	All sin is of the f.
316–30	satisfied with the f, resting on the basis
320–13	with man, for that he also is f," — *Gen.* 6 : 3.
320–17	they are [or, in their error they are] but f."
o 347– 1	"The f lusteth against the Spirit, — *Gal.* 5 : 17.
356–15	the f profiteth nothing." — *John* 6 : 63.
p 385–21	Mind decides whether or not the f shall
t 461– 1	not . . . exist in the f without food
g 528–11	closed up the f instead thereof ; — *Gen.* 2 : 21.
531–27	since f wars against Spirit

flesh
 g 534–21 they that are in the *f·* cannot— *Rom.* 8 : 8.
 536–16 Created by *f·* instead of by Spirit,
 gl 584–12 The *f·*, warring against Spirit ;
 586–18 definition of

flesh-brush
 ph 174– 5 that man should bow down to a *f·*,

fleshliness
 c 266–17 teaches mortals to lay down their *f·*

fleshly
 pref xi– 8 not of Spirit, but of the *f·* mind
 m 57–27 severance of *f·* ties serves to unite thought
 s 155–24 less weight into the material or *f·* scale
 ph 196– 7 awakens mortal mind from its *f·* dream,
 f 222– 9 whereas Truth regenerates this *f·* mind
 228– 9 and *f·* ills will disappear.
 314– 3 waited until the mortal or *f·* sense
 317–30 remained a *f·* reality, so long as
 332–30 highest type . . . which a *f·* form could express
 332–31 Into the . . . ideal man the *f·* element cannot
 334– 8 infinitely greater, than the *f·* Jesus,

flesh-pots
 f 221–26 he thought of the *f·* of Egypt,

flexibility
 ph 199–28 gave his . . . muscles, their *f·*

flickers
 f 244–19 If man *f·* out in death or

flight
 sp 97–10 yet in C. S. the *f·* of one and the blow of the
 c 261–30 and preens its wings for a skyward *f·*.

flights
 f 249–30 but makes its mundane *f·* quite ethereal.

flimsy
 an 103–26 whose *f·* and gaudy pretensions,

float
 sp 87–11 *f·* in the general atmosphere of
 87–22 of the tall ships that *f·* on its bosom,

flock
 p 442–27 "Fear not, little *f·* ;— *Luke* 12 : 32.
 g 540–27 brought of the firstlings of his *f·*,— *Gen.* 4 : 4.
 541– 1 offering from the firstlings of the *f·*.

flocks
 m 61–26 stock to increase your *f·* and herds?

flood
 pref viii–23 increased violence of diseases since the *f·*.
 ap 570– 9 cast out of his mouth water as a *f·*,— *Rev.* 12 : 15.
 570–10 to be carried away of the *f·*.— *Rev.* 12 : 15.
 570–12 swallowed up the *f·* which the— *Rev.* 12 : 16.
 570–19 What if the old dragon should send forth a new *f·*

flooding
 s 150–31 hosts of Æsculapius are *f·* the world

flood-tides
 f 201–18 pour in truth through *f·* of Love.

floor
 r 492–14 New thoughts are constantly obtaining the *f·*.

floral
 m 68–24 The perpetuation of the *f·* species by bud or
 f 240– 6 The *f·* apostles are hieroglyphs of Deity.

florist
 s 125–30 the *f·* will find his flower before its seed.

flour
 sp 90– 1 and wheat to produce *f·*,

flourish
 pr 5–19 *f·* "like a green bay tree ;"— *Psal.* 37 : 35.
 fr 600– * let us see if the vine *f·*,— *Song* 7 : 12.

flourisheth
 ph 190–24 a flower of the field, so he *f·*.— *Psal.* 103 : 15.
 r 476–25 a flower of the field, so he *f·*.— *Psal.* 103 : 15.

flow
 a 53–18 spiritual blessings which might *f·* from
 sp 72–24 individual good . . . may *f·* from the departed

flowed
 s 133– 9 In the wilderness, streams *f·* from the rock,
 p 376–15 than in all the blood, which ever *f·* through

flower
brightens the
 g 516–19 brightens the *f·*, beautifies the landscape,
decaying
 sp 78– 1 The decaying *f·*, the blighted bud,
his
 s 125–30 the florist will find his *f·* before its seed.
leaf and
 g 552–25 The blending tints of leaf and *f·*
new-blown
 p 413–23 in order to keep it sweet as the new-blown *f·*.

flower
tree, and
 b 289–23 So man, tree, and *f·* are supposed to die ;
  ————
 sp 71–11 you may dream that you see a *f·*.
 71–12 the *f·* is a product of the so-called mind,
 81–19 seemeth to wither and the *f·* to fade,
 ph 190–24 As a *f·* of the field, so he— *Psal.* 103 : 15.
 191–23 not a *f·* starts from its cloistered cell.
 c 265–18 or a *f·* withered by the sun
 t 459– 1 as the *f·* turns from darkness to light.
 r 476–25 as a *f·* of the field,— *Psal.* 103 : 15.
 g 508– 6 substance of a thought, a seed, or a *f·*

flowers
 a 22–25 is not reached through paths of *f·*
 m 57–25 may uproot the *f·* of affection,
 61–17 like tropical *f·* born amid Alpine snows.
 68–10 mistrust, . . . withers the *f·* of Eden
 f 212–22 credulous frenzy, . . . spirits produce the *f·*.
 240– 4 festive *f·*, and glorious heavens,

flowery
 a 41–11 hypocrite may have a *f·* pathway here, but

flowing
 a 25– 8 than when it was *f·* in his veins
 r 487–20 Truth, *f·* from immortal Mind,
 ap 566– 2 the dark ebbing and *f·* tides of human fear,
 gl 589– 8 spiritual peace, *f·* from the understanding

flows
 s 139–13 sectarian bitterness, whenever it *f·* inward.
 g 552–22 From a material source *f·* no remedy for

fluctuate
 t 463– 2 among phenomena, which *f·* every instant

fluid
 an 101– 1 no proof . . . of the animal magnetic *f·* ;
 b 293– 3 Electricity is not a vital *f·*,
 338–16 This suggests the thought of something *f·*,
 p 401–13 should be as painless to man as to a *f·*,
 401–20 as is the case with a fermenting *f·*.

fluids
 m 65–23 The fermentation even of *f·* is not pleasant.
 g 510–23 and the allusion to *f·*
 510–24 by the resolving of *f·* into solids,

flushed
 p 415–19 causing a pale or *f·* cheek.

flutterings
 c 262–11 We must reverse our feeble *f·*

fly
 sp 90–16 In dreams we *f·* to Europe
 g 511–21 fowl that may *f·* above the earth— *Gen.* 1 : 20.
 511–29 The fowls, which *f·* above the earth

flying
 b 298–27 *f·* on spiritual, not material, pinions.

foam
 f 203–27 The *f·* and fury of illegitimate living

foaming
 gl 593–16 *f·*, and dashing, it is a type of error.

focal
 b 301–27 supposed standpoint outside the *f·* distance

focus
 s 122–15 The optical *f·* is another proof of the
 g 504–24 when gathered into the *f·* of ideas,

foe
 ph 176–19 Mortal mind is the worst *f·* of the body,
 p 419– 5 Your true course is to destroy the *f·*,
 423–15 as both his *f·* and his remedy.
 ap 571–11 Who is telling mankind of the *f·* in ambush?
 571–12 Is the informer one who sees the *f·* ?

foes
 a 44– 6 the tomb gave Jesus a refuge from his *f·*,
 ap 564–17 The brutal barbarity of his *f·*

fœtal
 g 553–20 from Adam's rib, not from a *f·* ovum.
 554–13 unconscious of his *f·* and infantile existence ;

fœtus
 m 62– 2 The *f·* must be kept mentally pure

follow
 pref vii–11 The Wisemen were led to behold and to *f·*
 pr 4– 6 and *f·* his example, is our proper debt to him
 4–30 enable us to *f·* Jesus' example.
 5–31 We should *f·* our divine Exemplar,
 9–30 If unwilling to *f·* his example,
 a 22– 2 to find and *f·* the right road.
 26– 6 if we *f·* his commands faithfully ;
 27–28 Why do those who profess to *f·* Christ
 31–16 to all who *f·* him in deed.
 37–23 It is possible, . . . to *f·* in some degree
 37–26 do they *f·* him in the way that he commanded?
 38–10 "These signs shall *f·* them that— *Mark* 16 : 17.

follow

a	38–13	he did not say, "These signs shall *f· you*,"
	40–26	should *f·* the example of our Master
	44– 2	laid aside for a crown, the benediction *f·*,
	52–28	"These signs shall *f·* them that — *Mark* 16 : 17.
	54– 8	Who is ready to *f·* his teaching and example?
	54–20	would not accept . . . nor *f·* his example.
sp	82–18	In like manner it would *f·*, even if our
	96– 5	spiritualization will *f·*, for Love is Spirit.
s	138–21	to *f·* the Christ-example, and to heal the sick
	139–30	it does not *f·* that the profane or atheistic
	151–30	yield to this power, and *f·* the leadings of
	161–13	If her sister States *f·* this example
ph	198–30	does not *f·* that exercise has produced this
f	227–22	and cries: "*F·* me!
	228–20	If we *f·* the command of our Master,
	248–22	are liable to *f·* those lower patterns,
c	266–24	Mortals must *f·* Jesus' sayings and
b	278–20	From this it would *f·* that there are
	324–23	spiritual light soon enabled him to *f·* the
	326– 3	If we wish to *f·* Christ, Truth, it must be
	328–22	"These signs shall *f·* them that — *Mark* 16 : 17.
o	342–31	no denunciations would *f·* them, even if
	343–29	mistake which allows words, . . . to *f·* such
	345– 5	does it not *f·* that God cannot be in His
	349– 8	We propose to *f·* the Master's example.
	355–10	"*F·* me; and let the dead bury — *Matt.* 8 : 22.
	356–30	Does subsequent *f·* its antecedent?
	359– 5	will take the same cases, and cures will *f·*.
	359–26	"And these signs shall *f·* them — *Mark* 16 : 17.
p	362– *	*And these signs shall f· them* — *Mark* 16 : 17.
	384–21	such symptoms are not apt to *f·* exposure;
	386–11	effects will *f·*, . . . on account of the belief.
	434– 6	law of Christ supersedes *our* laws; let us *f·*
r	495–29	and *f·* the behests of God,
g	526–12	sickness, and death, *f·* in the train of this error
ap	578–16	goodness and mercy shall *f·* me — *Psal.* 23 : 6.
gl	591– 2	From this *f·* idolatry and mythology,
	594–12	SHEEP. . . . those who *f·* their leader.

followed

a	42–13	was *f·* by the desertion of all save a few
	42–14	who sadly *f·* him to the foot of the cross.
	46–21	was *f·* by his exaltation above all
	54–26	He said that those who *f·* him should
s	141–15	*f·* the understanding of the divine Principle
b	309–13	those, who through earnest striving *f·* his
	309–15	the children of earth who *f·* his example
p	384–17	by chills, dry cough, influenza,
g	502– 9	Spiritually *f·*, the book of Genesis is the
	502–18	*f·* by its spiritual interpretation
	524– 1	The idolatry which *f·* this material
	544– 1	record of material creation which *f·* the
ap	575–20	who *f·* it to the manger of Jesus ;
gl	581–14	temptation overcome and *f·* by exaltation.

follower

s	138–27	Our Master said to every *f·* :

followers

her

t	443– 2	consulted by her *f·* as to the

his

a	31–12	he taught his *f·* the healing power of
	33– 3	His *f·*, sorrowful and silent,
	35–29	draught our Master . . . commended to his *f·*.
	37–26	Christians claim to be his *f·*,
	39– 2	Such indignities . . . his *f·* will endure until
s	136– 3	He taught his *f·* that his religion
o	350– 8	his *f·* must grow into that stature
r	494–31	It should be said of his *f·* also,

its

f	225– 6	by the fewness and faithfulness of its *f·*.

Jesus'

b	317–12	benedictions rest upon Jesus' *f·* :
	324–20	but a persecutor of Jesus' *f·*.

of Christ

pr	5–15	The *f·* of Christ drank his cup.
s	134–10	the *f·* of Christ were burned, crucified, and
	142– 4	Anciently the *f·* of Christ, or Truth,

persecuted

a	33– 6	the persecuted *f·* of Truth.

professed

a	37–16	When will Jesus' professed *f·* learn to

a	38– 3	a select number of *f·*.

following

pr	10–11	and "with signs *f·*." — *Mark* 16 : 20.
a	21–29	After *f·* the sun for six days,
	31–17	*f·* his demonstration so far as we
an	102–23	The *f·* is an extract from the Boston Herald :
s	110–13	In *f·* these leadings of scientific
	110–29	with "signs *f·*." — *Mark* 16 : 20.
	113–10	are summarized in the four *f·*,
	117–13	attained through "signs *f·*." — *Mark* 16 : 20.
	154– 9	fact in metaphysics is illustrated by the *f·*

following

ph	179– 3	*f·* Christ in the daily life.
	192–27	*f·* the example of our Master
b	270– 2	One only of the *f·* statements can be true :
	288–21	are to be found in the *f·* postulates :
	329– 1	of a single period or of a limited *f·*.
	330– 8	When the *f·* platform is understood
p	363–21	*f·* it with that remarkable declaration
t	458–27	honest and consistent in *f·* the leadings of
r	470–12	the *f·* self-evident proposition :
	496–31	The *f·* is a brief exposition of
g	502–18	In the *f·* exegesis, each text is
	525– 7	The *f·* are some of the equivalents of
	525–12	*f·* translation is from the Icelandic :
	554– 9	*f·* from a misconception of life,
ap	568– 7	*f·* chapters depict the fatal effects of
	577–32	In the *f·* Psalm one word shows,
gl	590–23	introduced in the second and *f·* chapters,

follows

sp	72–21	God, good, being ever present, it *f·*
	80– 7	communication purporting to . . . reads as *f·* :
	81–29	and *f·* as a necessary consequence
an	100– 7	His propositions were as *f·* :
	100–17	reported to the government as *f·* :
	101–12	Their report stated the results as *f·* :
	106–19	when he wrote as *f·* :
s	128– 6	From this it *f·* that business men
	130–13	for from this premise it *f·* that
b	320–14	quoted as *f·*, from the original Hebrew כ
	331–12	From this it *f·* that nothing possesses
	338–30	From this is *f·* that Adam was not the
o	353–29	from this it *f·* that whatever is laid off is
p	388–13	there *f·* the necessity for another admission
t	449–31	and unless this result *f·*, the teacher is
	453– 8	chemicalization *f·* the explanation of Truth,
g	516–29	It *f·* that *man* is a generic term.
	519–27	No exhaustion *f·* the action of this Mind,
	552– 3	Another question *f·* : Who or what
ap	568– 9	narrative *f·* the order used in Genesis.
	570– 7	for one extreme *f·* another.

folly

ph	175–32	"Where ignorance is bliss, 't is *f·* to be wise,"
p	426–15	and see the *f·* of hypocrisy,

fondest

b	299– 9	has buried its *f·* earthly hopes.

food

amount of

ph	175–21	exact amount of *f·* the stomach could digest

and clothing

p	442–23	Truth, gives mortals temporary *f·* and clothing

and raiment

t	461– 2	without *f·* and raiment ;

brings forth

g	530– 7	earth, at God's command, brings forth *f·*

digestible

ph	197–25	and the most digestible *f·* in the stomach,

good for

g	526– 1	pleasant to the sight, and good for *f·* ; — *Gen.* 2 : 9.

my

p	390– 2	she said, "My *f·* is all digested, and

partaking of

p	431– 6	partaking of *f·* at irregular intervals,

proper

f	222– 6	one of which is to believe that proper *f·*

simple

ph	197–21	told that the simple *f·* our forefathers ate

a	44–14	He did not depend upon *f·* or pure air
ph	176– 8	custom of taking no thought about *f·*
	195–16	furnishes *f·* for thought.
f	221–25	but he never enjoyed his *f·* as he
	221–29	understanding, that neither *f·* nor
	222– 4	This person learned that *f·*
	222–11	*F·* had less power to help or to hurt
	232–19	Jesus never taught that drugs, *f·*,
p	388–12	Admit the common hypothesis that *f·*
	388–15	another admission . . . that *f·* has power
	388–20	If *f·* was prepared by Jesus for his
	388–22	The fact is, *f·* does not affect the absolute
	388–31	If mortals think that *f·* disturbs
	388–32	either the *f·* or this thought must be
	389– 8	mortal mind, which reports *f·* as undigested.
	389–13	theories first admit that *f·* sustains
	389–14	theories . . . discuss the certainty that *f·* can
	389–19	If God has, . . . instituted laws that *f·*
	389–21	cannot annul . . . by an opposite law that *f·*
	413– 8	regulates the condition of the . . . bowels, and *f·*,

fool

p	407– 1	becoming a *f·* or an object of loathing ;

foolish

a	32–23	This would have been *f·* in a literal sense ;
ph	181–14	It is *f·* to declare that you
f	202– 1	*f·* as straining out gnats and swallowing camels.
	238–25	Society is a *f·* juror, listening only to one side

foolish

p 388–26 but it would be f· to venture beyond our
388–27 f· to stop eating until we gain perfection
t 448–31 To talk the right and live the wrong is f· deceit,

foot

a 42–14 who sadly followed him to the f· of the cross.
s 113–14 not a f· to stand upon which is not purely
161–11 put their f· on a proposed tyrannical law,
f 229–22 should be trampled under f·.
234–15 those who trample them under f·,
ap 558– 7 his right f· upon the sea,— Rev. 10 : 2.
558– 7 and his left f· on the earth.— Rev. 10 : 2.
559– 4 "right f·" or dominant power— Rev. 10 : 2.
559– 6 The angel's left f· was upon the earth ;

foothold

ph 176–16 disease and death, will lose their f·.
b 282–18 and error has no f· in Truth.
g 535– 1 has given the understanding a f· in C. S.

footing

m 65–26 must lose its present slippery f·,

footprints

a 41– 9 walk calmly on though it be with bleeding f·,
f 224– 4 As the crude f· of the past disappear

footsteps

bleeding
pr 10– 3 even though with bleeding f·,
her
p 426– 7 than when she counts her f·
human
f 254– 1 the human f· leading to perfection
of thought
ph 174– 9 The f· of thought, rising above
of Truth
ph 192–27 We walk in the f· of Truth and Love
f 241–24 should be to find the f· of Truth,
tread in the
pr 9–29 since you do not care to tread in the f·

———

f 201– * the f· of Thine anointed.— Psal. 89 : 51.
t 454–28 care and counsel support all their feeble f·,

forbade

a 48–22 Jesus f· him, thus rebuking resentment

forbearance

t 444–21 Fear not that he will smite thee again for thy f·.

Forbes, Sir John

s 164– 3 Sir John F·, M.D., F.R.S.,

forbid

p 393– 3 forgetting that . . . we can f· this entrance.

forbidden

f 234–28 to look with desire on f· objects
p 440–28 I ask that he be f· to enter
r 481–12 f· fruit of knowledge, . . . is the testimony of
g 528–31 when the f· fruit was bringing forth

forbore

a 19–12 The Master f· not to speak the whole truth,

force

accelerated
ap 569–23 comes back to him at last with accelerated f·,
blind
ph 196– 2 It is but a blind f·.
divine
s 134–19 the very element, which gave it divine f·
healing
s 160– 5 drugs lose their healing f·,
physical
r 484–15 Physical f· and mortal mind are one.
whole
s 157– 5 the whole f· of the mental element is
without this
p 399–20 Without this f· the body is devoid of action,

———

a 25–20 Hence the f· of his admonition,
m 67–18 notion that animal natures . . . give f· to character
sp 80–15 It is mysticism which gives spiritualism its f·.
an 100– 4 he regarded this so-called f·, which he said
ph 192–11 a material mind, a blind miscalled f·,
c 266–12 Love will f· you to accept what best promotes
b 317– 4 insisted on the might of matter, the f· of falsity,
p 396–19 due to the f· of education
g 555– 1 in proportion as the f· of mortal mind is less

forced

a 25– 1 unbelieving Thomas was f· to acknowledge
s 159– 6 Her hands were held, and she was f· into

forceps

o 346–28 the operation, and the f· are unchanged.

forces

sp 96–13 becoming the arena for conflicting f·.
s 124–26 We tread on f·.
124–28 Human knowledge calls them f· of matter ;
b 293–13 The material so-called gases and f·
293–14 counterfeits of the spiritual f· of divine Mind,
ap 559–14 stirs their latent f· to utter the

forcible

pr 7– 5 showing the necessity for such f· utterance,
ph 196–22 f· descriptions and medical details,

forcing

p 401–19 f· impurities to pass away,

forebodings

p 403–24 Never conjure up some new discovery from dark f·

forefathers

m 64– 2 Our f· exercised their faith
ph 175–17 had tried to tyrannize over our f·,
197–17 It was the ignorance of our f·
197–21 We are told that the simple food our f· ate

foregoing

f 245–28 One instance like the f· proves
c 266–16 The author has experienced the f· prophecy

forehead

g 555–10 The mark of ignorance is on its f·,

foreign

s 133–16 Even in captivity among f· nations,
p 438–22 show that this fur is a f· substance,
r 485–26 and delineates f· agents, called disease and sin.

foreknowledge

a 41–23 but this f· hindered him not.

foremost

s 144– 3 If Mind is f· and superior, let us rely

foreordination

a 38– 5 more pernicious than the old doctrine of f·,

foresaw

a 41–22 Jesus f· the reception C. S. would have
s 139–25 f· that "the stone which the— Matt. 21 : 42.

foresee

sp 84–15 to f· and foretell events which
f 227–14 we cannot fail to f· the doom of all oppression.

foreseeing

a 31–28 f· the persecution which would attend the

foreshadowed

b 288–13 f· by the prophets and inaugurated by Jesus,
322–16 necromancy of yesterday f· the mesmerism

foreshadowing

sp 84– 4 not by f· evil and mistaking fact for

foreshadows

f 223–31 and f· the triumph of truth.
ap 571–27 rebukes the conceit of sin, and f· its doom.

foresight

a 52–12 prophet's f· of the reception error would give
sp 84– 3 ancient prophets gained their f· from
b 270–15 hence their f· of the new dispensation

forest

g 514–12 Free and fearless it roams in the f·.

forestalls

p 385– 9 f· the penalty which our beliefs would attach to

foretaste

ap 573–28 This is indeed a f· of absolute C. S.
gl 598–24 understanding of Life and Love, is a f· of

foretell

sp 84–16 f· events which concern the universal welfare,

foretelling

s 118– 7 f· the second appearing in the flesh of

foretells

sp 95–23 Midnight f· the dawn.
an 105–28 The aggravation of error f· its doom,

foretold

sp 85–19 events of great moment were f· by the
85–24 the Magi of old f· the Messiahship of Truth.
ph 169– 9 But it always came about as I had f·.

forever

at peace
f 215– 1 Spirit's senses . . . are f· at peace.
cease
f 219– 2 and the mortal dream will f· cease.
Christ dwelt
a 29–26 The Christ dwelt f· an idea in the bosom
closed
a 33– 1 and this supper closed f· Jesus' ritualism
continue
c 267– 5 They are in and of Spirit, . . . and so f· continue.
continues
sp 71– 5 identity, or idea, of all reality continues f· ;

forever

contradict
s 110– 3 contradict f· the belief that

destroys
s 128–25 f· destroys with the higher testimony of Spirit
g 556– 7 destroys f· all belief in intelligent matter.

disappears
sp 97–13 its mortal zenith in illusion and f· disappears.
g 520–14 in which all sense of error f· disappears

dwells
f 247–22 Beauty . . . dwells f· in the eternal Mind
b 334– 5 Christ, dwells f· in the bosom of the Father,

exist
gl 581–13 are created by Him and exist f·.

expressed
g 519–10 ideas of God . . . are complete and f· expressed,

intact
b 295–15 the real sense of being, perfect and f· intact,
r 481–12 Truth, which remains f· intact.
493–31 f· intact in his perfect state,

lost
b 331– 8 and the Science of being would be f· lost

man has existed
b 302–15 harmonious and immortal man has existed f·,

near
gl 596– 6 better known as the All-in-all, f· near.

not
b 320–15 said, My spirit shall not f· rule
320–21 this fact is not f· to be humbled by

now and
sp 92–10 not an entity . . . sinning now and f·.
o 361– 5 the ideal of God now and f·,
361– 9 God is come and is present now and f·.
p 441–11 Let what False Belief utters, now and f·,
g 521–10 joyfully acknowledging now and f·

opposed
g 530– 4 f· opposed to mortal, material sense.

permanent
b 290–18 happiness would be . . . f· permanent ;

reflected
g 503– 3 in the infinite Mind and f· reflected.

remain
s 110–23 the Science and truth therein will f· remain
f 208–24 which cannot be lost nor remain f· unseen.

silenced
sp 97–25 inarticulate sound is f· silenced in oblivion.

silences
s 124–13 which immortal Spirit silences f·.

the same
a 51–15 his spiritual life, . . . was found f· the same.

to-day and
(see **to-day**)

unchanged
gl 588–13 unchanged f· in their individual characters,

unlimited
b 288–28 f· unlimited by the mortal senses.

vast
f 246–18 Chronological data are no part of the vast f·.
c 266–31 into the vast f· of Life,
r 479–21 In the vast f·, in the Science and truth of

warring
b 278–20 warring f· with each other ;

will destroy
ap 575– 5 will destroy f· the physical plagues

will stand
f 229–25 all that He makes is good and will stand f·.

pref vii–21 "the Lord shall reign f·." — Exod. 15 : 18.
pr 17–13 the power, and the glory, f·. — Matt. 6 : 13.
a 41–12 cannot f· break the Golden Rule and escape the
48– 8 turned f· away from earth to heaven,
55–28 that he may abide with you f·." — John 14 : 16.
m 58–17 which would confine . . . f· within four walls,
64–32 the voices of physical sense will be f· hushed.
s 164–21 the f· fact remains paramount
210–11 Soul and its attributes were f· manifested
230– 6 This awakening is the f· coming of Christ,
c 258–13 the infinite idea f· developing itself,
267– 9 If this is so, the f· Father must have
b 284–19 The answer to all these questions must f· be
336–12 He has been f· in the eternal Mind,
o 343–12 Truth will not be f· hidden by
p 428–24 We must hold f· the consciousness of
441–16 f· in the image and likeness of his Maker.
t 447–12 subtlety, or false charity does not f· conceal
r 469– 1 Time is finite ; eternity is f· infinite.
471–17 Man is, and f· has been, God's reflection.
491–16 establishes man f· in the divine likeness,
g 515–16 eternal Elohim includes the f· universe.
516–22 Man and woman . . . f· reflect,
537– 2 eat, and live f· ; — Gen. 3 : 22.
542– 6 error cannot f· be concealed.
556–12 only to go out at last f· ;
gl 585–24 that which does not last f· ;

forfeit
s 112– 6 f· their claims to belong to its school,

forfeits
t 453–17 Dishonesty is human weakness, which f·

forgave
p 363–20 "He to whom he f· most." — Luke 7 : 43.

forged
f 223– 4 the fetters of man's finite capacity are f· by

forget
c 261–10 with such absorbed interest as to f· it,
261–31 We should f· our bodies in remembering good
b 309–17 and f· that Life is God, good,
p 374–23 You cannot f· the belief of danger,
t 447– 6 In mental practice you must not f· that

forgets
sp 76– 4 f· all else and breathes aloud his rapture.
s 155– 1 Presently the child f· all about the accident,

forgetting
sp 89– 3 F· her ignorance in the belief that
ph 165–19 your remedy lies in f· the whole thing ;
o 353–23 'f· those things which— Phil. 3 : 13.
p 393– 2 f· that through divine help we can forbid

forgive
pr 6– 7 Calling on Him to f· our work badly done
11– 2 Jesus' prayer, "F· us our debts," — Matt. 6 : 12.
17– 6 f· us our debts, as we f· our— Matt. 6 : 12.

forgiven
pr 5–23 Sin is f· only as it is destroyed
5–28 because he fancies himself f·.
a 24–22 and are willing to be f· ?
f 202– 1 supposing that sin can be f· when
p 363–23 "Thy sins are f·." — Luke 7 : 48.
364–31 because much is f· them.

forgiveness
pr 7–31 or mean to ask f· at some later day.
11– 3 specified also the terms of f·.
a 22– 4 Vibrating . . . between sin and the hope of f·,
b 339– 4 Being destroyed, sin needs no other form of f·.
r 497– 9 We acknowledge God's f· of sin in the

forgives
pr 6–19 To suppose that God f· or punishes sin according

forgiving
pr 11– 3 When f· the adulterous woman he said,

forgotten
a 49– 8 Had they f· the great exponent of God?
sp 87–10 leagues apart and their associations f·,

form (noun)

alarming
p 395–29 may appear in a more alarming f·.

all
b 281–15 supplies all f· and comeliness
310– 7 seen in all f·, substance, and color,
g 512–22 all f·, color, quality, and quantity,

and action
b 301– 3 repeats the color, f·, and action

and face
c 260– 4 or the painter can depict the f· and face of Jesus,

animate
g 541– 2 A lamb is a more animate f· of existence,

another
s 159–28 allowing another f· of matter.

any
s 154– 1 to cherish error in any f·,
f 244– 6 never fearing nor obeying error in any f·.
p 369–13 or the constructor of any f· of existence.

any other
sp 73–16 electricity or any other f· of matter,

chronic
ph 176–31 less distinct type and chronic f· of disease.

etherealized
gl 598–15 was indeed air, an etherealized f· of matter,

every
p 418–29 Speak the truth to every f· of error.
ap 564–16 Jesus . . . met and conquered sin in every f·.

finite
sp 71– 8 infinite Principle outside of finite f·,
71–31 a corporeal being, a finite f·,
76– 9 belief that life, or mind, was ever in a finite f·,
s 116–30 An infinite Mind in a finite f· is an
c 257–27 Infinite Mind cannot be limited to a finite f·,
g 527– 2 God could not put . . . Spirit into finite f·

fleshly
b 332–30 highest type of divinity, which a fleshly f· could

higher
ph 174– 4 Is civilization only a higher f· of idolatry,

his
p 442–11 His f· was erect and commanding,

human
c 255–16 The human f·, or physical finiteness, cannot
b 315–29 Wearing in part a human f·
g 554–31 especially those of the human f·.

form (noun)

infinite
  c 257–30 It would require an infinite *f·* to contain
  257–31 phrase *infinite f·* involves a contradiction
limited
  s 133–20 limited *f·* of a national or tribal religion.
malicious
  an 103–24 malicious *f·* of hypnotism ultimates in
man and
  g 517– 6 two Greek words, signifying *man* and *f·*,
material
  c 258– 9 Man is more than a material *f·* with a mind
  b 280–26 instead of possessing a sentient material *f·*,
  293– 4 least material *f·* of illusive consciousness,
mirrored
  b 305– 9 As there is no corporeality in the mirrored *f·*,
new
  sp 74– 9 has a new *f·* and state of existence.
no
  a 26–31 His proof of Christianity was no *f·* or system
  c 256–24 No *f·* nor physical combination is adequate
no other
  b 339– 4 sin needs no other *f·* of forgiveness.
of matter
  (*see* **matter**)
one
  pr 11– 7 it only saves the criminal from one *f·* of
  s 145–26 they increase the antagonism of one *f·*
  159–28 how much . . . one *f·* of matter is
  p 419–14 or to change itself from one *f·* to another.
precise
  c 256–16 precise *f·* of God must be of small importance
serpentine
  ap 563–27 The serpentine *f·* stands for subtlety,
some
  a 28–31 await, in some *f·*, every pioneer of truth.
taking
  ph 175– 1 prevent the images of disease from taking *f·*
  g 511–28 taking *f·* in masculine, feminine, or neuter
without
  s 126– 5 mortal mind will be without *f·* and void,
  r 479–19 And the earth was without *f·*,— *Gen. 1:2.*
  g 503– 6 And the earth was without *f·*,— *Gen. 1:2.*

  pr 1–13 exalted before they take *f·* in words
  s 119–15 in the *f·* and under the name of natural law.
  146–32 to a *f·* comprehensible by and adapted to
  147–29 A pure affection takes *f·* in goodness,
  f 247–23 in expression, *f·*, outline, and color.
  c 261–22 which is only a *f·* of human belief,
  b 332–25 appear to mortals in such a *f·*
  o 353– 9 either in the *f·* of sickness or of sin?
  p 367– 1 under the napkin of its *f·*,
  375– 6 often the *f·* in which fever manifests itself.
  392–19 in the *f·* of what is termed pulmonary disease,
  g 525–10 the primary sense being *image, f·*;

form (verb)
  m 62– 5 such as to *f·* habits of obedience
  ph 170– 3 Modes of matter *f·* neither a moral nor a
  172–10 Spirit can *f·* no real link in this supposed
  f 218–10 The reports of sickness may *f·* a coalition with
  228–22 and *f·* and control it with Truth.
  236–13 *f·* the embryo of another mortal mind,
  247–13 *f·* the transient standards of mortals.
  248–26 We must *f·* perfect models in thought
  p 372– 7 can *f·* blood, flesh, and bones.
  425–25 and Spirit will *f·* you anew.
  t 454–23 and *f·* the perfect concept.
  g 505– 1 No solar rays . . . *f·* the day of Spirit.
  533–23 bone and flesh which came from Adam to *f·*

formal
  s 118– 4 above the merely ecclesiastical and *f·*

formalism
  c 256–26 material sense of God leads to *f·*

formation
  m 60– 5 *f·* of a happy and permanent companionship.
  61–29 *f·* of mortals must greatly improve
  sp 71–13 a *f·* of thought rather than of matter.
  s 148–15 for every function, *f·*, and manifestation.
  ph 190– 1 the *f·* of so-called embryonic mortal mind,
  g 510–23 indicates a supposed *f·* of matter
  527–30 Was it requisite for the *f·* of man
  549–15 with the *f·* of the nucleus, or egg,

formations
  all the
  ph 189–22 The reverse is the case with all the *f·* of
  earth's
  g 510–20 Geology has never explained the earth's *f·*;
  harmonious
  ph 198–22 a picture of healthy and harmonious *f·*.

formations
  its
  f 209– 5 Mind, supreme over all its *f·*
  246– 1 Mind and its *f·* can never be annihilated.
  c 264–20 Spirit and its *f·* are the only realities
  p 402–10 its *f·* will be apprehended in Science,
  g 557–25 proclaims the Science of Mind and its *f·*
  its own
  b 309–32 never absorbed nor limited by its own *f·*.
  mundane
  f 209–25 Material substances or mundane *f·*,
  not in Spirit's
  sp 71– 7 divine Principle of all, is not *in* Spirit's *f·*.

  g 507– 2 the absolute *f·* instituted by Mind,

formed
  sp 70–16 Does life or soul exist in the thing *f·*?
  86–31 Pictures are mentally *f·* before the artist can
  94–15 belief that the infinite is *f·* after the pattern
  ph 194–30 a belief *f·* by education alone.
  198–15 thought of disease is *f·* before
  198–23 moulded and *f·* by his doctor's belief
  200–12 man is the idea of God, not *f·* materially
  f 214– 9 represented in the Scriptures as *f·* from
  c 259–25 Brain . . . never *f·* a human concept.
  b 274–26 firm, called matter and mind, God never *f·*.
  274–29 *f·* only to be destroyed
  281–25 through a man *f·* from dust.
  303– 9 *f·* by Spirit, not by material sensation.
  303–17 illusion that life, or mind, is *f·* by
  p 396–31 understand that sickness is *f·* by the human mind,
  409– 3 why do you insist that disease is *f·* by
  423–32 so-called substance of bone is *f·* first by the
  g 524–13 *f·* man of the dust of the ground,— *Gen. 2:7.*
  527–22 *f·* every beast of the field,— *Gen. 2:19.*
  553–12 *f·* under circumstances which
  553–19 Eve was *f·* from Adam's rib,
  553–29 You may say that mortals are *f·* before they

former
  sp 89–10 The *f·* limits of her belief return.
  s 148– 8 The *f·* explains the men of *men*,
  156–13 her *f·* physician had prescribed these remedies,
  ph 187–17 of the latter action, but not of the *f·*.
  f 237–21 excluded on the same principle as the *f·*.
  b 276–26 The latter destroys the *f·*.
  t 460–29 As *f·* beliefs were gradually expelled
  g 556– 8 for the *f·* things will have passed away.
  ap 573– 1 They could not be the *f·*,

formidable
  b 317–19 more real, more *f·* in truth,

forming
  ph 198–13 to prevent disease from *f·* in mortal mind
  c 263–13 *f·* deformity when he would outline grace
  o 350–28 Jesus,— that life-link *f·* the connection
  g 506–13 *f·* each successive stage of progress.

forms (noun)
  all
  sp 83–23 Between C. S. and all *f·* of superstition
  f 204– 3 All *f·* of error support the false conclusions
  p 396– 3 efface from thought all *f·* and types of disease,
  g 513–26 God creates all *f·* of reality.
  cannot change
  p 419–32 disease or its symptoms cannot change *f·*,
  changed
  sp 96– 9 seedtime and harvest (though in changed *f·*),
  crude
  g 502–14 Even thus the crude *f·* of human thought
  depraving
  f 226– 4 under more subtle and depraving *f·*.
  differing
  t 444–14 not only towards differing *f·* of religion
  difficult
  p 398–29 changes such ills into new and more difficult *f·*
  externalized
  g 522–13 history of error in its externalized *f·*,
  finite
  c 264– 8 Mortals must look beyond fading, finite *f·*,
  b 280–24 belief that . . . . Life, is in finite *f·*.
  g 553–23 appearance of its method in finite *f·*
  gl 587–12 belief that infinite Mind is in finite *f·*;
  glorious
  c 264– 5 must finally give place to the glorious *f·*
  hideous
  f 248–19 vicious sculptors and hideous *f·*.
  human
  pr 4–32 and clothe religion in human *f·*.
  immortal
  g 503–32 immortal *f·* of beauty and goodness.
  in all their
  t 447–21 evil and disease in all their *f·*,
  individual
  g 512–13 Their individual *f·* we know not,

forms (noun)

its
r 484–23   action of error in all its *f·* ;

lower
g 549– 9   Creatures of lower *f·* of organism are

material
b 301–31   presupposes soul . . . in material *f·*,

mild
an 102–16   The mild *f·* of animal magnetism are

modes and
p 406– 8   in place of modes and *f·*,

multifarious
r 477–21   in multifarious *f·* of the living Principle,

myriad
b 306–21   The myriad *f·* of mortal thought,
p 404– 4   servant of any one of the myriad *f·* of sin,

new
f 225–27   always germinating in new *f·* of tyranny,
g 541–22   Here the serpentine lie invents new *f·*.

of doctrine
a 20– 3   He at last paid no homage to *f·* of doctrine

of error
f 204– 3   All *f·* of error support the false conclusions
c 264–24   who proved them to be *f·* of error.

of matter
s 145–27   towards other *f·* of matter or error,
ph 172–16   must have passed through all the *f·* of matter
c 263–32   fading *f·* of matter, the mortal body

of Mind
b 303– 3   reflection, . . . of the multitudinous *f·* of Mind
g 505–10   they are *f·* of Mind, the ideas of Spirit
507–17   reproduces the multitudinous *f·* of Mind

of sickness
t 463–22   whether error is manifested in *f·* of sickness,

of sin
o 348–20   will show itself in *f·* of sin, sickness, and
p 404– 4   servant of any one of the myriad *f·* of sin,

of thought
s 118–20   In all mortal *f·* of thought, dust is
ph 187– 7   material sense creates its own *f·* of thought,
b 298–31   confers upon angels its own *f·* of thought,

of worship
pr 10–17   One of the *f·* of worship in Thibet

physical
c 262–32   Cause does not exist . . . in physical *f·*.

qualities, and
ph 177–19   indicated matter's properties, qualities, and *f·*.

renewed
g 556–11   dies to live again in renewed *f·*,

severest
s 162–19   chronic disease in their severest *f·*.

Soul-created
b 306–23   than are the Soul-created *f·* to spiritual sense,

spiritual
g 503–17   reflecting Him in countless spiritual *f·*.

subsequent
g 531– 4   maintained in all the subsequent *f·* of belief.

various
f 248–14   We are all sculptors, working at various *f·*,
g 553– 1   in the various *f·* of embryology,

visible
ap 559– 6   the source of all error's visible *f·* ?

———

sp 71– 9   outside of finite form, which *f·* only reflect.
87–30   close the eyes, and *f·* rise before us,
b 331– 2   Life is no more confined to the *f·* which reflect
p 421–28   should not build it up by wishing to see the *f·*

forms (verb)

m 62–22   divine Mind, which *f·* the bud and blossom,
f 216–32   this Mind *f·* its own likeness.
220–30   *f·* all conditions of the mortal body,
239–24   It *f·* material concepts and
c 259–22   *f·* its offspring after human illusions.
b 293– 5   *f·* no link between matter and Mind,
337–11   as perfect as the Mind that *f·* him.
p 422–26   holding that matter *f·* its own conditions
423–30   the substance of thought which *f·* them.
g 509–16   God *f·* and peoples the universe.
511– 1   This Mind *f·* ideas, its own images,
515– 9   subject to the Mind which *f·* them,
550– 5   God is the Life, or intelligence, which *f·* and

formulated
s 144– 8   mortal beliefs *f·* in human philosophy,
ph 175– 2   efface the outlines of disease already *f·*

fornication
an 106–21   Adultery, *f·*, uncleanness,— *Gal. 5 : 19.*
gl 598–17   Error ; *f·* ; temptation ; passion.

fornications
an 100– *   *murders, adulteries, f·,— Matt. 15 : 19.*

forsake
s 130–31   no longer think it . . . unnatural to *f·* it,
139– 1   causes the wicked to "*f·* his way,— *Isa. 55 : 7.*
160– 4   When mortals *f·* the material for the
ph 195–13   We should *f·* the basis of matter

forsake
f 239–14   "Let the wicked *f·* his way,— *Isa. 55 : 7.*
b 290–28   The murderer, . . . does not thereby *f·* sin.
323– 4   strife consists in the endeavor to *f·*
326–12   We must *f·* the foundation of
339–18   Only those, who repent of sin and *f·* the
p 370– 2   we must *f·* the mortal sense of things,
400–10   only as they *f·* discord,
402– 8   mortal mind will *f·* its corporeal, structural,

forsaken
a 36–12   He was *f·* by all save
49–17   F· by all whom he had blessed,
50– 8   "My God, why hast Thou *f·* me?"— *Mark 15 : 34.*
50–14   Had Life, Truth, and Love *f·* him
f 202– 1   supposing that sin . . . when it is not *f·*,

forsakes
f 238–24   *f·* popularity and gains Christianity.
g 549–28   this great observer mistakes nature, *f·* Spirit

forsaketh
t 448–18   whoso confesseth and *f·* them— *Prov. 28 : 13.*

forsaking
c 265–10   This scientific sense of being, *f·* matter for
p 393– 2   like a watchman *f·* his post,
t 459– 6   gain heavenly riches by *f·* all worldliness.

forth
pr 2– 5   the desire which goes *f·* hungering after
2–28   which is pouring *f·* more than we accept?
15–19   and go *f·* with honest hearts to work
a 27–22   Jesus sent *f·* seventy students at one time,
29–22   brought *f·* her child by the revelation of Truth,
32–12   The cup shows *f·* his bitter experience,
35–23   by bringing *f·* the fruits of Love,
45– 3   and stepped *f·* from his gloomy resting-place,
49– 7   Where were the seventy whom Jesus sent *f·*?
m 57–22   Human affection is not poured *f·* vainly,
s 115– 7   C. S. as brought *f·* in my discovery.
126–13   nor sent *f·* a positive sound.
126–22   I have set *f·* C. S. and its application to
127–21   nerves, brain, stomach, lungs, and so *f·*,
137–17   and his reply set *f·* a great fact :
ph 170–31   from which all ills have gone *f·*,
185–14   puts *f·* a human conception in the name of
191–32   Mind, God, sends *f·* the aroma of Spirit,
196–31   The press unwittingly sends *f·* many sorrows
f 210– 6   They are set *f·* in Jesus' demonstrations,
235– 1   cannot go *f·*, like wandering pollen,
239–30   The perfect Mind sends *f·* perfection,
239–31   Imperfect mortal mind sends *f·* its own
241–10   hypocrisy, malice, hate, revenge, and so *f·*,
c 257–20   bringeth "*f·* Mazzaroth in his— *Job 38 : 32.*
b 268–12   woman goes *f·* to battle with Goliath.
287–13   "Doth a fountain send *f·* at the— *Jas. 3 : 11.*
303–12   is spiritually conceived and brought *f·*;
321–22   drew it *f·* white as snow with the dread disease,
327–15   rushes *f·* to clamor with midnight and tempest.
o 345– 8   When . . . His absoluteness is set *f·*,
360–20   Like a pendulum . . . you will be thrown back
       and *f·*,
p 392– 3   Only while . . . sin remains can it bring *f·* death.
398–14   "Stretch *f·* thine hand,"— *Matt. 12 : 13.*
404–19   every tree that brings not *f·* good fruit.
404–29   envy, dishonesty, fear, and so *f·*,
411–26   Whatever is cherished . . . is imaged *f·* on the
       body.
415–31   leaving the pain standing *f·* as distinctly as
440–24   wicked laws of sickness and so *f·*,
442–14   Mortal Man, no longer sick . . . walked *f·*,
t 455–29   the same fountain cannot send *f·* both
r 476–17   "conceived in sin and brought *f·* in iniquity."
489–23   sendeth not *f·* sweet waters and bitter.
g 507–11   Let the earth bring *f·* grass,— *Gen. 1 : 11.*
508– 9   And the earth brought *f·* grass,— *Gen. 1 : 12.*
511–19   Let the waters bring *f·*— *Gen. 1 : 20.*
512– 5   which the waters brought *f·*— *Gen. 1 : 21.*
512–29   this so-called mind puts *f·* its own qualities,
513–14   Let the earth bring *f·*— *Gen. 1 : 24.*
521–26   a material view of creation, is to be set *f·*.
529– 1   bringing *f·* fruit of its own kind,
530– 7   The earth, at God's command, brings *f·* food
535– 8   in sorrow thou shalt bring *f·*— *Gen. 3 : 16.*
535–24   thistles shall it bring *f·*— *Gen. 3 : 18.*
537– 1   lest he put *f·* his hand,— *Gen. 3 : 22.*
537– 3   sent him *f·* from the garden— *Gen. 3 : 23.*
g 550–27   nor does a lion bring *f·* a lamb.
553–18   the maternal egg never brought *f·* Adam.
557–18   "In sorrow thou shalt bring *f·*— *Gen. 3 : 16.*
ap 565– 6   And she brought *f·* a man child,— *Rev. 12 : 5.*
568–10   first the true method of creation is set *f·*
568–29   Love sends *f·* her primal and everlasting strain.
569–31   which brought *f·* the man child.— *Rev. 12 : 13.*
570–19   What if the old dragon should send *f·* a new
574–21   which poured *f·* hatred and torment,
fr 600– *   *and the pomegranates bud f·.— Song 7 : 12.*

forthwith
  ph 182–23 and *f·* shut out the aid of Mind

fortitude
  ph 198– 6 His *f·* may sustain him, but his fear,
  p 375–32 fear so excessive that it amounts to *f·*.

fortuitous
  m 61–14 If some *f·* circumstance places

fortunes
  s 121– 8 the fate of empires and the *f·* of men.

forty
  p 421–32 asserting that the products . . . are both *f·*,

fossils
  s 147–21 the perishing *f·* of theories already antiquated,

fosters
  ph 169–12 *f·* disease by attracting the mind to the
  g 555–32 Truth *f·* the idea of Truth,

fought
  a 21– 2 "I have *f·* a good fight— *II Tim.* 4 : 7.
  f 254– 7 not until the battle between Spirit and flesh is *f·*
  b 309–11 a soldier of God, who had *f·* a good fight.
  ap 566–26 Michael and his angels *f·* — *Rev.* 12 : 7.
  566–27 the dragon *f·*, and his angels, — *Rev.* 12 : 7.

foul
  p 431–21 covered with a *f·* fur,
  434–26 we shall unearth this *f·* conspiracy against the
  437– 5 *f·* aspersion on man's Maker.
  438–20 a garment of *f·* fur was spread over him

found
  pref viii– 2 fully tested and has not been *f·* wanting ;
  viii–25 may be *f·* a biographical sketch, narrating
  pr 7– 3 is *f·* in his own words,
  a 28–23 if thou art *f·* worthy to unloose the sandals
  30–32 In meekness and might, he was *f·* preaching
  42– 7 Death will be *f·* at length to be a mortal dream,
  51–15 his spiritual life, . . . was *f·* forever the same.
  m 66–31 It never leaves us where it *f·*
  sp 71–22 spiritualism will be *f·* mainly erroneous,
  90–11 will be *f·* to be equally possible for the body.
  94–14 intolerance, and bloodshed, wherever *f·*,
  97–19 and man is *f·* in the likeness of Spirit,
  s 113–12 these propositions will be *f·* to agree in
  125– 4 may no longer be *f·* indispensable to health.
  125– 5 Moral conditions will be *f·* always harmonious
  125– 8 man will be *f·* normal and natural
  126–26 I have *f·* nothing in ancient or in modern
  126–27 nothing . . . on which to *f·* my own, except
  128– 7 have *f·* that C. S. enhances their
  133– 6 "I have not *f·* so great faith, — *Matt.* 8 : 10.
  150– 1 hardly a . . . hamlet, in which are not to be *f·*
  151–27 the entire being is *f·* harmonious
  159– 8 The evidence was *f·* to be conclusive,
  ph 166–31 *f·* to be harmonious and immortal.
  179–10 as man is *f·*, . . . reflecting the divine nature.
  180–28 The only way to this living Truth, . . . is *f·* in
  180–32 I have *f·* divine Truth more potent than
  188– 2 and man is *f·* in His image.
  190– 7 and yet neither . . . is *f·* in brain
  190–19 immortal man, . . . is *f·* to be the real man.
  191– 8 theoretical life-basis is *f·* to be a
  195– 5 Outside of dismal darkness . . . he *f·* no peace.
  196– 3 but he has not yet *f·* it true that
  f 209–24 man and the universe will be *f·* harmonious
  214–16 will be understood and *f·* to be harmonious.
  226– 3 a world-wide slavery, *f·* on higher planes
  232– 8 Security . . . is *f·* only in divine Science.
  c 257–24 Who hath *f·* finite life or love sufficient
  b 276– 4 "I have *f·* a ransom." — *Job* 33 : 24.
  288–21 are to be *f·* in the following postulates :
  288–23 Soul is sinless, not to be *f·* in the body ;
  291–17 man is *f·* having no righteousness of his own,
  297–16 and man *f·* to be immortal.
  302– 2 Principle is not to be *f·* in fragmentary ideas.
  302– 5 The identity of the real man is not lost, but *f·*
  307–14 Its life is *f·* to be not Life, but only a transient,
  312– 5 is *f·* to be substance.
  313–25 He . . . *f·* the spiritual cause.
  314– 5 Thus he *f·* the eternal Ego,
  325–14 then shall man be *f·* in God's image.
  325–16 Then shall man be *f·*, in His likeness,
  o 344– 9 God's likeness is not *f·* in matter,
  359–18 Christianity is to be honored wherever *f·*,
  p 419–31 If it is *f·* necessary to treat against relapse,
  432–14 he upon whose person disease is *f·* shall be
  r 475–17 conscious identity of being as *f·* in Science,
  481–31 *f·* that it is the sense of sin which is lost,
  484– 1 and so *f·* to be unerring,
  489– 4 it would be *f·* that the senses of Mind are
  493–17 Mind must be *f·* superior to all the beliefs
  g 522–22 denunciations of man when not *f·* in His image,
  524– 6 It was also *f·* among the Israelites,
  533–21 *f·* in the rapid deterioration of the
  543–22 Minerals and vegetables are *f·*,

found
  ap 565–27 be *f·* in its divine Principle.
  566–28 neither was their place *f·* any more— *Rev.* 12 : 8.
  gl 580–12 are *f·* to be the antipode of God,
  583–15 The Church . . . is *f·* elevating the race,

foundation
cause and
  p 411–20 procuring cause and *f·* of all sickness
firm
  s 138– 8 a firm *f·* in the realm of harmony.
its
  r 484– 4 nor envy can wash away its *f·*,
no
  s 112–25 affords no *f·* upon which to establish
  c 255– 9 they afforded no *f·* for
  t 448– 6 Evil . . . which the heart condemns, has no *f·* ;
  464–26 Falsity has no *f·*.
no scientific
  an 102– 1 Animal magnetism has no scientific *f·*,
of disease
  p 368–31 When fear disappears, the *f·* of disease is gone.
  t 453–27 such a course increases fear, the *f·* of disease,
of evil
  sp 92–26 The *f·* of evil is laid on a belief
of Spirit
  s 133–26 planted Christianity on the *f·* of Spirit,
spiritual
  s 136– 2 a spiritual *f·* of Christ-healing.
  gl 593–18 Rock. Spiritual *f·* ; Truth.
  599– 6 Zion. Spiritual *f·* and superstructure ;
without
  sp 93–20 Whatever contradicts the . . . is without *f·*.
  r 486– 1 is without *f·* in fact,
without actual
  r 491– 4 shows it to be a belief without actual *f·*

  pr 15–31 the *f·* of enlightened faith.
  s 138–14 the *f·* on which Jesus built.
  f 227–12 the *f·* of continued bondage
  c 262–27 The *f·* of mortal discord is a false sense
  b 276– 5 they unfold the *f·* of fellowship,
  287–23 without spiritual identity or *f·*,
  317– 2 "secret from the *f·* of the— *Matt.* 13 : 35.
  326–12 forsake the *f·* of material systems,
  334–21 slain from the *f·* of the world," — *Rev.* 13 : 8.
  p 368–29 has a *f·* in fact.
  ap 568– 2 Ever since the *f·* of the world,

foundational
  o 348–12 Jesus established this *f·* fact,

foundations
false
  f 201– 7 We cannot build safely on false *f·*.
  gl 597–12 It revealed the false *f·* and
its
  m 59–31 fatal mistakes are undermining its *f·*.
  s 124– 6 When . . . its *f·* are gone.
material
  g 535–11 supposed material *f·* of life and intelligence.
no
  p 415– 5 Sin, disease, and death have no *f·* in Truth.
of death
  ph 171–16 and destroying the *f·* of death.
of error
  b 273–11 thus tears away the *f·* of error.
  o 357–12 the *f·* of error would be sapped
of Truth
  ap 558–16 Its feet are pillars of fire, *f·* of Truth and Love.
other
  b 269–25 Other *f·* there are none.

  m 65– 7 If the *f·* of human affection
  b 296–25 *f·* which time is wearing away.
  p 414– 1 the *f·* of the belief in disease and death,
  g 539– 5 thus sapping the *f·* of immortality,
  ap 575–12 "a city which hath *f·*." — *Heb.* 11 : 10.

founded
  s 127–32 hypotheses . . . that law is *f·* on material
  163– 8 *f·* on long observation and reflection,
  b 297–27 no mortal testimony is *f·* on the divine rock.
  t 464–28 Neither dishonesty nor ignorance ever *f·*,
  r 487–19 Christian evidence is *f·* on Science

founding
  s 138– 2 Jesus purposed *f·* his society,
  t 464–21 in *f·* a pathological system of Christianity,

fount
  pr 2–27 Shall we plead for more at the open *f·*,
  13– 3 It is the open *f·* which cries,
  f 239–29 opposite sources never mingle in *f·* or stream.
  244– 1 God is good and the *f·* of all being,
  p 389–16 the metaphors about the *f·* and stream,

fountain
　a 18–17　The *f·* can rise no higher than its source.
　ph 190–30　For with Thee is the *f·* of life;— *Psal.* 36 : 9.
　b 287–12　"Doth a *f·* send forth—*Jas.* 3 : 11.
　p 391–32　Fear is the *f·* of sickness,
　t 455–29　the same *f·* cannot send forth both
　r 489–22　same *f·* sendeth not forth sweet waters and

four
　pref xii–16　During seven years over *f·* thousand students
　m 58–17　which would confine. . .forever within *f·* walls,
　s 113–10　*f·* following, to me, *self-evident* propositions.
　113–22　Which of the denials in proposition *f·* is true?
　ph 193–15　between three and *f·* o'clock in the afternoon
　ap 574–23　city, the *f·* equal sides of which were
　575–18　The *f·* sides of our city are
　575–21　wholly spiritual, as its *f·* sides indicate.
　577–13　its *f·* cardinal points are :

foursquare
　ap 574–16　city which "lieth *f·*."— *Rev.* 21 : 16.
　575– 8　as one that "lieth *f·*"— *Rev.* 21 : 16.
　575–17　description of the city as *f·* has a profound

fourth
　sp 91–32　The *f·* erroneous postulate is,
　s 156– 9　the *f·* attenuation of *Argentum nitratum*
　g 511–16　and the morning were the *f·* day.— *Gen.* 1 : 19.
　523–25　From the *f·* verse of chapter two
　ap 577–17　*f·*, C. S., which to-day and forever interprets

Fourth Gospel
　ap 561–30　In the first chapter of the *F· G·* it is written,

fowl
　of the air
　f 222–24　and over the *f·* of the air,— *Gen.* 1 : 26.
　r 475–25　and over the *f·* of the air,— *Gen.* 1 : 26.
　g 515–13　and over the *f·* of the air,— *Gen.* 1 : 26.
　517–28　and over the *f·* of the air,— *Gen.* 1 : 28.
　518– 9　and to every *f·* of the air,— *Gen.* 1 : 30.
　527–22　and every *f·* of the air ;— *Gen.* 2 : 19.
　winged
　g 512– 6　every winged *f·* after his kind :— *Gen.* 1 : 21.

　g 511–20　*f·* that may fly above the earth— *Gen.* 1 : 20.
　512–19　let *f·* multiply in the earth.— *Gen.* 1 : 22.

fowls
　s 125–27　over the fish of the sea and the *f·* of the air.
　f 237–13　"the *f·* of the air,"— *Luke* 8 : 5.
　g 511–29　The *f·*, which fly above the earth

fraction
　s 108–18　not a *f·* more, not a unit less.

fragmentary
　sp 98–28　they are not theoretical and *f·*,
　b 302– 2　Principle is not to be found in *f·* ideas.

fragrance
　ph 175–11　The joy of its presence, its beauty and *f·*,

fragrant
　o 363– 2　jar containing costly and *f·* oil,

frail
　sp 98–15　Beyond the *f·* premises of human beliefs,
　o 346–32　is not this what *f·* mortals are trying to do?
　t 459–15　*f·* mortals, untaught and unrestrained by C. S.,

frailty
　ph 194–18　the *f·* and inadequacy of mortal mind.
　c 266–30　He is above sin or *f·*.
　o 360–27　His angels He chargeth with *f·*.— *see Job* 4 : 18.

frame
　p 415–30　the whole *f·* will sink from sight

franchise
　m 63–20　If the elective *f·* for women will remedy

Franklin
　f 245–19　useful hint, upon which a *F·* might work

Franklin, Benjamin
　an 100–15　Benjamin *F·* was one of the commissioners.

fraternity
　p 389–24　error that there is *f·* between pain and pleasure,

fraternize
　sp 74–21　nor does the insect return to *f·* with or

fratricidal
　g 539– 2　This false sense of existence is *f·*.

fraud
　o 356–26　Does divine Love commit a *f·* on humanity

fraudulent
　f 252–22　deceitful in sentiment, *f·* in purpose,

fraught
　o 346–17　How then can this . . . be "*f·* with falsities

free
　iii– *　the truth shall make you *f·*.— *John* 8 : 32.
　pr 6–10　supposition that . . . we shall be *f·* to repeat
　11–14　leaves the offender *f·* to repeat the offence,
　m 63–32　and own her children *f·* from interference.

free
　sp 74– 4　To be . . . persons must be *f·* from organic
　90–25　sets man *f·* to master the infinite idea.
　an 106– 3　to work against the *f·* course of honesty
　s 114–27　and sets *f·* the imprisoned thought.
　150–22　human view infringes man's *f·* moral agency ;
　ph 171– 8　find himself unfallen, upright, pure, and *f·*,
　176– 8　left the stomach and bowels *f·* to act
　191–16　The human thought must *f·* itself from
　f 206– 6　else it will misguide the judgment and *f·* the
　223–21　Spiritual rationality and *f·* thought accompany
　225– 4　Truth makes man *f·*.
　227–16　God made man *f·*.
　227–17　Paul said, "I was *f·* born."— *Acts* 22 : 28.
　227–18　All men should be *f·*.
　227–19　Love and Truth make *f·*,
　227–25　Citizens of the world, accept the. . .and be *f·* !
　227–27　has bound you, entangled your *f·* limbs,
　244–12　hath made me *f·* from the law of— *Rom.* 8 : 2.
　p 381–24　quite *f·* from some ailment.
　434– 1　can . . . set the captive *f·*.
　442– 8　prisoner rose up regenerated, strong, *f·*.
　t 443–18　leave invalids *f·* to resort to whatever
　448–32　to *f·* another from the fetters of disease.
　453–30　the divine Truth that makes man *f·*.
　r 481– 6　*f·* "to enter into the holiest,"— *Heb.* 10 : 19.
　495–13　sets the captive *f·* physically and morally.
　g 514–11　*F·* and fearless it roams in the forest.
　gl 584–13　that which frets itself *f·* from one belief

freed
　sp 73–23　belief that spirit . . . is *f·* by death,
　73–24　belief . . . that, when it is *f·* from the
　ph 178–24　we are *f·* from the belief of heredity,

freedom (*see also* **freedom's**)
　assert their
　f 228–14　Mortals will some day assert their *f·*
　boundless
　a 22–24　boundless *f·*, and sinless sense,
　breath of
　f 225–21　nor did the breath of *f·* come from the cannon's
　capacity or
　r 475–31　nor . . . engender the capacity or *f·* to sin.
　confers a
　sp 89–23　influence or action of Soul confers a *f·*,
　glorious
　f 248– 1　and glorious *f·* of spiritual harmony.
　heritage of
　f 228–12　when man enters into his heritage of *f·*,
　hope of
　p 368–13　even the hope of *f·* from the bondage
　human
　f 242– 7　towards the joys of Spirit, towards human *f·*
　moral
　m 58–12　There is moral *f·* in Soul.
　right to
　f 227– 5　and mortals are taught their right to *f·*,
　spiritual
　s 118–12　eternally glorified in man's spiritual *f·*.
　p 366– 5　and thus attain the spiritual *f·*
　strength and
　t 454–20　strength and *f·* to speech and action.
　universal
　f 226– 8　sounded the keynote of universal *f·*,
　wild with
　g 552–21　may become wild with *f·*

　f 225–31　ignorant how to obtain their *f·*.
　226–11　and that its *f·* be won,
　236–28　because of their *f·* from wrong
　r 481– 3　God's being is infinity, *f·*, harmony,

freedom's
　f 225– 7　time bears onward *f·* banner.

freely
　sp 89– 8　believing that . . . she talks *f·*.
　g 527– 8　thou mayest *f·* eat :— *Gen.* 2 : 16.
　548– 2　take the water of life *f·*."— *Rev.* 22 : 17.

freer
　s 120–30　When Columbus gave *f·* breath to the globe,

frees
　b 291– 3　suppositions . . . death of the body *f·* from sin,

freezing
　ph 175–26　Damp atmosphere and *f·* snow
　b 329–14　should not tarry in the storm if the body is *f·*,
　r 490–32　will think that he is *f·* when he is warm,

French
　sp 80–22　Even planchette— the *F·* toy which
　an 100–12　In 1784, the *F·* government ordered

frenzy
　f 212–21　In legerdemain and credulous *f·*,

frequency
　m 59–28　the *f·* of divorce shows that the

frequent
ap 566–22   In shade and storm the *f·* night,
frequently
s 153– 1   *f·* attenuated to such a degree that
ph 180–18   Doctors should not . . . as they so *f·* do,
o 358–19   more *f·* cited for our instruction
fresh
an 105–23   to commit *f·* atrocities as opportunity occurs
s 107–12   *f·* pinions are given to faith and understanding,
t 460–24   Science of Mind was a *f·* revelation
freshness
f 246–23   still maintain his vigor, *f·*, and promise.
246–30   into loveliness, *f·*, and continuity,
248– 9   Mind feeds the body with supernal *f·*
fretfulness
m 62–11   their children's *f·* or frivolity,
frets
gl 584–13   that which *f·* itself free from one belief only to
friend
absent
sp 82– 2   We think of an absent *f·* as easily as
best
ph 176–20   while divine Mind is its best *f·*.
better
r 486–17   If. . .then death is not an enemy but a better *f·*
far-off
sp 90–16   In dreams we fly to Europe and meet a far-off *f·*.
of man
a 49–15   the highest instructor and *f·* of man,
of Mortal Man
p 433–32   the spirit of Life and the *f·* of Mortal Man,
of publicans
a 53– 1   and is the "*f·* of publicans and— *Luke* 7 : 34.
our
sp 75–12   "Our *f·* Lazarus sleepeth ;— *John* 11 : 11.
sick
p 430–30   when the prisoner, . . . watched with a sick *f·*.
their
a 53– 7   He rebuked sinners. . .because he was their *f·* ;

pr 8–31   If a *f·* informs us of a fault,
a 28–20   a glutton and a *f·* of the impure,
34– 8   if a *f·* be with us,
34– 9   why need we memorials of that *f·* ?
39–11   causes mortals to regard death as a *f·*,
f 248– 4   One marvels that a *f·* can ever seem less than
p 386–17   mistakenly announcing the death of a *f·*,
friendly
pref ix–25   copies were, however, in *f·* circulation.
p 438–31   to be on *f·* terms with the firm of
friend's
p 386–17   grief that the *f·* real death would bring.
friends
departed
sp 82–19   even if our departed *f·* were near us
few
a 42–13   the desertion of all save a few *f·*,
give to
pref viii–29   give to *f·* the results of her Scriptural study,
her
t 464– 3   Could her *f·* know how little time
his
a 46– 5   Jesus was known to his *f·* by the words, which
o 359– 3   Let any clergyman try to cure his *f·* by
p 436–23   His *f·* struggled hard to rescue the
make
g 552–10   Mortal theories make *f·* of sin,
my
a 21–15   If my *f·* are going to Europe,
21–21   On the contrary, if my *f·* pursue my course,
our
p 386–31   So, when our *f·* pass from our sight
personal
c 266– 6   Would existence without personal *f·* be
prisoner's
p 432–25   One of the prisoner's *f·*, Materia Medica,
professed
p 436–16   professed *f·*, Materia Medica and Physiology,
unpretentious
a 54–23   only a few unpretentious *f·*,

c 266–13   F· will betray and enemies will slander,
friendship
sp 87–26   by *f·* or by any intense feeling
fright
s 151–18   belief says that death has been occasioned by *f·*.
ph 178–14   by the *f·* of his mother.
t 251– 7   F· is so great at certain stages of
frighten
sp 79– 3   is an error that tends to *f·*
p 379–29   The images, held . . . *f·* conscious thought.

frightened
s 154–17   the mother is *f·* and says,
o 352–12   child, who is *f·* at imaginary ghosts
p 371–11   As *f·* children look everywhere for
433–28   to prepare the *f·* sense . . . for *death.*
t 460–15   to the *f·*, false sense of the patient.
frightening
p 439–10   *f·* away Materia Medica,
t 447–18   without *f·* or discouraging the patient
frivolity
m 62–11   their children's fretfulness or *f·*,
frivolous
m 60–22   *f·* amusements, personal adornment,
ph 195–30   to meet a *f·* demand for amusement
front
an 102–17   its aggressive features are coming to the *f·*.
b 301– 3   form, and action of the person in *f·* of the
frost
sp 72–32   As readily can you mingle fire and *f·*
frosts
c 265–19   and nipped by untimely *f·* ;
frown
f 238– 8   To obey . . . is to incur society's *f·* ;
238– 8   but this *f·*, more than flatteries,
frozen
p 373–28   languidly creeps along its *f·* channels,
frugal
t 452–16   Better is the *f·* intellectual repast
fruit
bearing
ph 180–10   seed within itself bearing *f·* after its kind,
bears the
ph 197– 9   bears the *f·* of sin, disease, and death,
bringing forth
g 529– 1   bringing forth *f·* of its own kind,
Cain's
g 541– 3   more nearly resembles . . . than does Cain's *f·*.
541–11   than for the worship expressed by Cain's *f·* ?
forbidden
r 481–12   The forbidden *f·* of knowledge,
g 529– 1   when the forbidden *f·* was bringing forth
good
p 404–19   every tree that brings not forth good *f·*.
t 459–27   tree must be good, which produces good *f·*.
immortal
o 361–29   That which when sown bears immortal *f·*,
known by his
b 299–23   tree is known by his *f·*'"— *Matt.* 12 : 33.
known by its
sp 73–13   belief, which ought to be known by its *f·*,
known by their
an 106–17   demonstrable in Truth and known by their *f·*,
much
b 271– 1   seed of Truth springs up and bears much *f·*.
not much
b 272– 7   else it beareth not much *f·*,
of false knowledge
ph 175–30   Adam, before he ate the *f·* of false knowledge,
of the ground
g 540–25   brought of the *f·* of the ground— *Gen.* 4 : 3.
of the Spirit
an 106–27   the *f·* of the Spirit is love,— *Gal.* 5 : 22.
of the tree
g 529–18   but of the *f·* of the tree which— *Gen.* 3 : 3.
of the trees
g 529–17   We may eat of the *f·* of the trees— *Gen.* 3 : 2.
of the vine
a 18– *   I will not drink of the *f·* of the vine, — *Luke* 22 : 18.
this
ph 165– 2   Evil declared that eating this *f·* would open
yield
g 507–19   tree and herb do not yield *f·* because of
yielding
g 507–13   yielding *f·* after his kind,— *Gen.* 1 : 11.
508–11   and the tree yielding *f·*,— *Gen.* 1 : 12.

p 389–17   the fount and stream, the tree and its *f·*,
g 507–12   the *f·* tree yielding fruit— *Gen.* 1 : 11.
518– 7   the *f·* of a tree yielding seed ;— *Gen.* 1 : 29.
fruitage
o 348–27   the full *f·* of C. S.,
fruit-bearer
g 526–23   Did He create this *f·* of sin
fruitful
g 512–17   Be *f·*, and multiply,— *Gen.* 1 : 22.
517–26   Be *f·*, and multiply,— *Gen.* 1 : 28.
550–28   Amalgamation . . . is seldom *f·*,
fr 600– *   being *f·* in every good work,— *Col.* 1 : 10.

fruition

pr 9–15	before we can enjoy the *f·* of our hope
b 298– 7	Science armed with faith, hope, and *f·*.
298–14	faith, understanding, *f·*, reality.

fruitless

pr 6–28	He said of the *f·* tree,
p 375–17	should be understood and so rendered *f·*.

fruitlessness

a 35– 3	Convinced of the *f·* of their toil

fruits

early

gl 579– 9	surrendering to the creator the early *f·* of

first

g 532– 7	when eating its first *f·* brought death

immediate

g 532–18	produced the immediate *f·* of fear and shame.

immortal

r 494–29	its lap piled high with immortal *f·*.

its

p 426–14	this would be . . . known by its *f·*.

of human faith

pref xi– 6	the *f·* of human faith in matter,

of Love

a 35–24	by bringing forth the *f·* of Love,

of sin

b 299–19	bearing the *f·* of sin, sickness, and death.

of Spirit

p 391–32	and bearing the *f·* of Spirit.

of the Spirit

t 451–18	they bear as of old the *f·* of the Spirit.

present

o 349– 1	If such are the present *f·*, what will the

their

f 204–19	Judging them by their *f·*, they are corrupt.
o 342–28	"By their *f·* ye shall know them"— *Matt.* 7 : 20.
fr 600– *	*by their f· ye shall know them.— Matt.* 7 : 20.

your

r 496–13	Your *f·* will prove what the

a 38–22	the *f·* of other people's sins, not of his own.
f 220–27	The belief that . . . is one of the *f·*
243–30	sin, and death are not the *f·* of Life.

fulfil

m 56– 4	to *f·* all righteousness."— *Matt.* 3 : 15.
f 223– 3	not *f·* the lust of the flesh."— *Gal.* 5 : 16.
233– 7	demands of us only what we can certainly *f·*.
r 474–20	not come to destroy, but to *f·*."— *Matt.* 5 : 17.
483–30	One must *f·* one's mission without timidity

fulfilled

a 41–24	He *f·* his God-mission, and then
55–21	The promises will be *f·*.
s 109–25	Scripture of Isaiah is renewedly *f·* :
p 404–15	can remove this disorder as God's law is *f·*
t 463–20	Truth is here and has *f·* its perfect work.
g 534–12	This prophecy has been *f·*.
ap 569– 7	literally *f·*, when we are conscious of

fulfilling

m 59–11	F· the different demands of their united
p 435–20	"is the *f·* of the law,"— *Rom.* 13 : 10.
r 485–22	by *f·* the spiritual law of being,

fulfils

m 57–32	disappointments it involves or the hopes it *f·*.
s 134–31	A miracle *f·* God's law, but does not violate
b 276– 2	and *f·* these sayings of Scripture,
297–32	A mortal belief *f·* its own conditions.
340–24	ends wars ; *f·* the Scripture,
ap 572–12	Love *f·* the law of C. S.,

full

pref vii– 3	ere cometh the *f·* radiance of a risen day.
viii– 4	To develop the *f·* might of this Science,
x–14	or treat in *f·* detail so infinite a theme.
pr 5–12	*f·* "and running over."— *Luke* 6 : 38.
5–14	Saints and sinners get their *f·* award,
8– 9	*f·* . . . of all uncleanness."— *Matt.* 23 : 27.
a 29–25	with the *f·* recognition that being is Spirit.
31–20	a *f·* understanding of the divine Principle
36–22	*f·* punishment this side of the grave
36–24	bestow on the righteous their *f·* reward.
37– 5	History is *f·* of records of suffering.
39– 6	a *f·* salvation from sin, sickness, and death.
42–17	and gave *f·* evidence of divine Science,
50–19	If his *f·* recognition of eternal Life had
m 59– 2	a *f·* recognition of its enduring obligations
an 105–31	*f·* many a league in the line of light ;
s 122–21	Experience is *f·* of instances of similar
130–20	cannot add to the contents of a vessel already *f·*.
139– 4	the Scriptures are *f·* of accounts of the
ph 182–20	Obedience to material law prevents *f·*
f 201–13	We cannot fill vessels already *f·*,
244–21	when there is no *f·* reflection of the
247– 8	his *f·* set of upper and lower teeth
c 261–19	he was in the *f·* possession of his

full

b 286– 7	gives *f·* faith in Truth,
313– 2	the *f·* and proper translation of the Greek),
o 348–27	the *f·* fruitage of C. S.,
p 395–19	The nurse should be cheerful, . . . *f·* of faith,
406– 6	*f·* salvation from sin, sickness, and death.
t 456–28	contains the *f·* statement of C. S.,
r 493–13	A *f·* answer to the above question
g 507– 8	creation would be *f·* of nameless offspring,
511–17	The changing glow and *f·* effulgence of
536–21	few days, and *f·* of trouble."— *Job* 14 : 1.
542–21	Sin will receive its *f·* penalty,
552–16	few days, and *f·* of trouble."— *Job* 14 : 1.
ap 559–14	to utter the *f·* diapason of secret tones.
565– 4	It is *f·* of lust and hate, loathing the
574– 7	*f·* of the seven last plagues,— *Rev.* 21 : 9.
574–18	the seven angelic vials *f·* of seven plagues,
574–18	has *f·* compensation in the law of Love.
gl 591– 6	Man, . . . the *f·* representation of Mind.
591–19	of whom man is the *f·* and perfect expression ;
598–28	man would be in the *f·* consciousness of

fuller

s 162–27	it requires only a *f·* understanding of the
f 226– 8	a *f·* acknowledgment of the rights of man
o 361–22	to give a clearer and *f·* expression

full-orbed

f 224–21	the harbingers of truth's *f·* appearing.
b 298– 3	and glow *f·* in spiritual understanding.

fully

pref viii– 2	her system has been *f·* tested
a 42–32	must understand more *f·* his Life-principle
45– 6	Our Master *f·* and finally demonstrated
45–32	not sufficiently advanced *f·* to understand
s 132– 3	to heal would *f·* answer the question.
136–24	what the disciples did not *f·* understand?
152– 9	a healing effect, even when not *f·* understood.
f 205–32	When we *f·* understand our relation to the Divine,
227– 2	fetters fall and the rights of man are *f·* known
231–28	impossible, when you *f·* apprehend God
240–27	one must pay *f·* and fairly the
b 284–10	nor be *f·* manifested through corporeality.
288–11	When the . . . effects of C. S. are *f·* apprehended,
326–14	Not partially, but *f·*, the great healer of
339–18	Only those, * . . . can *f·* understand the unreality of evil.
o 343–15	when his teachings are *f·* understood.
344–11	Were it more *f·* understood that Truth heals
p 415–28	Before the thoughts are *f·* at rest,
r 471–16	evidence . . . is *f·* sustained by spiritual sense.
495– 5	hence its healing power is not *f·* demonstrated.
g 556–16	It is made known most *f·* to him who

fulness

b 336–20	neither could God's *f·* be reflected by a single
p 406–24	until we arrive at the *f·* of God's idea,
g 519–20	the stature of the *f·* of Christ"— *Eph.* 4 : 13.
gl 590–12	denial of the *f·* of God's creation ;

fumes

p 407– 3	Puffing the obnoxious *f·* of tobacco,

function

s 148–15	every *f·*, formation, and manifestation.
151–20	Every *f·* of the real man is governed by the

functional

s 125– 3	considered the best condition for . . . *f·* health
149–24	as readily as she has cured purely *f·* disease,
162–26	as surely as it heals what is called *f·*,
p 377–25	organic diseases as readily as *f·* difficulties.

functions

disordered

p 408–18	inflammation of disordered *f·*,

elements and

s 124–32	elements and *f·* of the physical body

entire

p 384–32	entire *f·* and organs of the human system

healthy

p 373–26	disabled organ will resume its healthy *f·*.

my

p 431–30	and perform my *f·* as usual,

natural

p 387–14	perform the natural *f·* of being.
r 478–20	the discharge of the natural *f·* is least noticeable.

of Mind

r 478–23	Matter cannot perform the *f·* of Mind.

of mind

p 388–32	the harmonious *f·* of mind and body,
395–31	cannot kill a man nor affect the *f·* of mind

of the body

p 373–22	Disease is expressed . . . in the *f·* of the body.

vital

p 387–17	and perform the most vital *f·* in society.

fundamental
    m 65– 9 some *f·* error in the marriage state.
    s 113– 9 *f·* propositions of divine metaphysics
    120– 8 arrive at the *f·* facts of being.
    ph 167–29 On this *f·* point, timid conservatism is
    171–31 *f·* error lies in the supposition that
    t 460–10 Yet this most *f·* part of metaphysics
    g 545–13 Such *f·* errors send falsity into

funds
    m 63–31 deposit *f·*, and own her children free from

fungus
    s 160–30 Is man a material *f·* without Mind

fur
    p 431–21 covered with a foul *f·*,
    438–20 said that . . . a garment of foul *f·*
    438–22 this *f·* is a foreign substance,
    438–28 is not an importer or dealer in *f·*,
    438–29 explain how this *f·* is manufactured,

furnace
    m 66–31 *f·* separates the gold from the dross
    s 133–17 in the fiery *f·* and in kings' palaces.
    161– 8 captives, cast into the Babylonian *f·* ;
    f 243– 6 from the fiery *f·*, from the jaws of the lion,

furnish
    pr 6–13 will *f·* more than its equivalent of pain,
    a 51–10 that he might *f·* the proof of immortal life. ·
    s 135–19 "Can God *f·* a table in the— *Psal. 78 :* 19.
    142–10 Truth, alone can *f·* us with absolute evidence.
    ph 189–17 is supposed to *f·* the evidence of
    ap 572–14 *f·* the vision of the Apocalypse,

furnished
    sp 99– 9 Truth has *f·* the key to the kingdom,
    b 317–28 to him Jesus *f·* the proof
    r 472–11 Jesus *f·* proofs of these statements.

furnishes
    m 63–13 C. S. *f·* no precedent for such injustice,
    ph 195–15 Whatever *f·* the semblance of an idea
    195–16 *f·* food for thought.
    f 245–18 This instance of youth preserved *f·*
    b 336–27 The Science of being *f·* the rule of

furnishes
    p 370–10 Homœopathy *f·* the evidence to the
    387–27 The history of Christianity *f·* sublime
    t 461–14 *f·* the eternal interpretation of God and
    ap 571–23 *f·* the mirror in which mortals may see

furnishing
    ph 180–21 Instead of *f·* thought with fear, they should
    p 439– 4 keeps a *f·* store, and advertises

Furred Tongue
    p 438–26 summoned *F· T·* for examination,

further
    an 103– 4 and *f·* defines it as dishonesty
    f 226– 2 *f·* steps towards the banishment of
    b 295–29 It *f·* teaches that when man is
    314– 2 (his *f·* spiritual exaltation),
    338–17 It *f·* suggests the thought of that
    p 441–20 We *f·* recommend that Materia Medica
    ap 576– 8 *f·* describing this holy city,
    576–18 What *f·* indication need we of the

furthermore
    m 64–17 *F·*, the time cometh of which

fury
    f 203–27 The foam and *f·* of illegitimate living
    b 293–21 There is no vapid *f·* of mortal mind

fustian
    s 142–16 tell their story to pride and *f·*.

future
    pref vii–25 *F·* ages must declare what the pioneer has
    a 24–19 in regard to predestination and *f·* punishment.
    sp 84– 6 predicting the *f·* from a groundwork of
    84–13 to know the past, the present, and the *f·*.
    s 150–24 and will be to all others at some *f·* day,
    158–12 The *f·* history of material medicine
    b 306–15 at some uncertain *f·* time and in a manner
    p 374–19 You confess to ignorance of the *f·*
    t 459– 9 Judge not the *f·* advancement of C. S. by the
    g 546– 2 at some *f·* time to be emancipated

future-world
    a 39–20 not that now men must prepare for a *f·*

G

Gabriel
    ap 567– 1 *G·* has the more quiet task
    567– 6 The *G·* of His presence has no contests.

Gad
    gl 586–21 definition of

gain
    pr 11–23 a desire for holiness is requisite in order to *g·*
    12– 4 mere request . . . has no power to *g·*
    13–13 Do we *g·* the omnipotent ear sooner by words
    14– 3 whose ear we would *g·*,
    15–29 *g·* the ear and right hand of omnipotence
    21–13 *g·* a little each day in the right direction,
    m 65–11 To *g·* C. S. and its harmony,
    69– 4 *g·* the sense of health only as
    sp 72– 7 is the *g·* of spiritual life.
    s 156–19 I did so, and she continued to *g·*.
    ph 167–28 impossible to *g·* control over the body in
    f 238–22 Attempts to . . . *g·* dominion over mankind,
    254– 4 *g·* good rapidly and hold their position,
    c 260–15 distrust of one's ability to *g·* the goodness
    264– 8 if they would *g·* the true sense of things.
    264–13 As mortals *g·* more correct views of God
    265– 7 *g·* some proper sense of the infinite,
    266–17 lay down their fleshliness and *g·*
    b 322– 5 we shall *g·* the reality of Life,
    326–13 if we would *g·* the Christ as our only Saviour.
    328–10 they *g·* the true understanding of God
    335–23 we *g·* the eternal unfolding of Life
    o 355– 1 they should *g·* the spiritual meaning of C. S.,
    p 388–28 foolish to stop eating until we *g·*
    t 459– 6 he must *g·* heavenly riches by
    r 486– 7 Even then he must *g·* spiritual understanding
    g 501–10 recompensing human want...with spiritual *g·*.
    ap 560–13 necessity of existence is to *g·* the true idea

gained
    a 23–18 the evidence *g·* from Spirit,
    sp 84– 3 ancient prophets *g·* their foresight from
    91–20 erroneous knowledge *g·* from matter
    92–15 a knowledge *g·* from matter, or evil,
    s 111–32 this system has gradually *g·* ground,
    f 254–10 facts of existence are *g·* step by step,
    c 265–23 *g·* stronger desires for spiritual joy?
    b 269–27 knowledge *g·* through the material senses
    272– 3 spiritual sense of truth must be *g·*
    274– 3 knowledge *g·* from the five senses
    290–19 Perfection is *g·* only by perfection.

gained
    b 299–18 Knowledge *g·* from material sense is
    314– 8 Our Master *g·* the solution of being,
    326–16 purpose and motive to live aright can be *g·*
    o 349–20 this sense must be *g·* by its disciples
    358–21 Is it not because there are few who have *g·*
    p 365–21 such commendation as the Magdalen *g·*
    406–30 normal control is *g·* through divine strength
    t 449– 6 but more of C. S. must be *g·*
    r 474–15 glorious Principle of these marvels is *g·*.
    482– 7 *g·* by substituting the word *God*,
    487– 4 *g·* by walking in the pathway of Truth
    490–20 knowledge *g·* from the so-called material senses
    g 532– 6 *g·* from the five corporeal senses
    536–25 the true idea is *g·* from the immortal side.
    547–25 only by this understanding can truth be *g·*.
    548–22 *g·* the diviner side in C. S.,
    556–13 life everlasting is not to be *g·* by dying.

gaining
    a 47– 5 After *g·* the true idea of their glorified Master,
    ph 198– 7 already developed the disease that is *g·*
    b 324– 8 are not *g·* the true idea of God ;
    327– 2 also by *g·* an affection for good
    327–28 seeking material means for *g·* happiness.

gains
    m 57– 7 the feminine mind *g·* courage and strength
    sp 83–28 man *g·* the divine Principle and explanation
    f 238–24 forsakes popularity and *g·* Christianity.
    c 258–23 in proportion as humanity *g·* the true
    b 294–29 thief believes that he *g·* something by stealing,

gala
    f 252–23 says : . . . my short span of life one *g·* day.

Galatians
    an 106–19 St. Paul in his great epistle to the *G·*,

Galilean Prophet
    o 360–28 the Jews put to death the *G· P·*,
    r 497–18 as demonstrated by the *G· P·*

Galilean Sea
    a 34–32 joyful meeting on the shore of the *G· S·* !

Galilee
    sp 90– 4 on the shores of *G·*,
    s 147–13 and in the valleys of *G·*.

gall
    a 51– 5 This dread added the drop of *g·* to his cup.

gallows
s 134–13 hallowed by the *g·* and the cross.

garden
culture of your
m 61–26 the culture of your *g·* or the raising of stock
of Eden
g 526–27 and put him into the *g·* of Eden,— *Gen.* 2 : 15.
537– 3 forth from the *g·* of Eden,— *Gen.* 3 : 23.
537– 6 at the east of the *g·* of Eden— *Gen.* 3 : 24.

a 47–31 night of gloom and glory in the *g·*,
g 526– 2 in the midst of the *g·*,— *Gen.* 2 : 9.
527– 7 Of every tree of the *g·*— *Gen.* 2 : 16.
529–16 of every tree of the *g·*?— *Gen.* 3 : 1.
529–18 fruit of the trees of the *g·* :— *Gen.* 3 : 2.
529–19 in the midst of the *g·*,— *Gen.* 3 : 3.
532–15 I heard Thy voice in the *g·*,— *Gen.* 3 : 10.

garment
s 142– 8 We must seek the undivided *g·*,
ph 170–27 at least to touch the hem of Truth's *g·*.
197– 4 Parisian name for a novel *g·*.
f 242–28 every part of the Christly *g·* of righteousness.
p 438–20 said that . . . a *g·* of foul fur

garments
c 267–27 "let thy *g·* be always white."— *Eccl.* 9 : 8.
t 452–20 We soil our *g·* with conservatism,
463–15 The new idea, . . . clad in white *g·*.

garnered
g 535– 5 the other to be *g·* into heavenly places.

garrisoned
f 235–11 should be strongly *g·* with virtue.

gas
o 346–26 when you believe that nitrous-oxide *g·* has
p 375– 2 painlessly as *g·* dissipates into the air
399– 8 No gastric *g·* accumulates, . . . apart from

gases
b 293–13 The material so-called *g·* and forces

gash
p 393–23 than the trunk of a tree which you *g·*

gastric
ph 175–24 not so severe upon the *g·* juices.
p 399– 8 No *g·* gas accumulates, . . . apart from

gate
pref ix–18 a willing disciple at the heavenly *g·*,
s 142–14 the poor and the stranger from the *g·*,
t 451–12 for "wide is the *g·*,— *Matt.* 7 : 13.
g 535–16 When will man pass through the open *g·* of C. S.
538– 5 Truth places the cherub wisdom at the *g·* of

gates
s 137–32 and the *g·* of hell— *Matt.* 16 : 18.
146–20 "stranger that is within thy *g·*,"— *Exod.* 20 : 10.
ph 171– 6 man will reopen . . . the *g·* of Paradise
ap 571–28 has opened wide the *g·* of glory,
575–19 "and the *g·* of it shall not be shut— *Rev.* 21 : 25.
575–26 Northward, its *g·* open to the North Star,
577–24 Its *g·* open towards light and glory

gateway
g 537–15 Truth guards the *g·* to harmony.

gather
s 129–24 Can we *g·* peaches from a pine-tree,
b 276–30 Divine Science does not *g·* grapes from
p 370– 4 *g·* the facts of being from the divine Mind.
380–26 Gradually this evidence will *g·* momentum
g 539–24 "Do men *g·* grapes of thorns?"— *Matt.* 7 : 16.

gathered
sp 78–16 Communications *g·* from ignorance are
g 504–23 when *g·* into the focus of ideas,
506–16 *g·* together unto one place,— *Gen.* 1 : 9.
527–16 perception, *g·* from the corporeal senses,

gathering
a 55–16 *g·* beneath its wings the sick and sinning.
t 463–10 Though *g·* new energy, this idea cannot
g 506–23 the *g·* together of the waters— *Gen.* 1 : 10.
535–30 the *g·* together of the waters— *Gen.* 1 : 10.
547–13 the *g·* clouds, the moon and stars,

gathers
b 299–15 whither every real individuality, . . . *g·*.
g 506–18 Spirit, God, *g·* unformed thoughts into

gaudy
an 103–26 whose flimsy and *g·* pretensions,

gave
pr 16–10 then he *g·* that prayer which covers all
a 26–15 Truth, Life, and Love *g·* Jesus authority over
29–18 and *g·* to her ideal the name of Jesus
32–16 and *g·* it to the disciples,— *Matt.* 26 : 26.
32–18 *g·* thanks, and *g·* it to them— *Matt.* 26 : 27.
32–22 yet Jesus prayed and *g·* them bread.
33–16 he *g·* thanks and said,
41–14 proofs of Truth, . . . which Jesus *g·*
42– 4 *g·* no hint of the unchanging love of God.

gave
a 42–17 and *g·* full evidence of divine Science,
44– 5 lonely precincts of the tomb *g·* Jesus a refuge
47– 2 *g·* them a faint conception of the Life
sp 89–29 if life was in the body, and man *g·* it,
s 120–30 When Columbus *g·* freer breath to the globe,
132–10 In other words, he *g·* his benediction to
134–19 the very element, which *g·* it divine force
137–28 the Master *g·* him a spiritual name
ph 176– 9 and *g·* the gospel a chance to be seen
193–11 its death-pallor *g·* place to a natural hue.
194–31 *g·* him a belief of intense pain.
195– 9 *g·* him pain through those very senses,
199–27 His belief that he could do it *g·*
f 210–13 *g·* sight to the blind, hearing to the deaf,
220–24 he *g·* up his abstinence,
242–32 require of Christians the proof which he *g·*,
b 308–22 *g·* him spiritual strength in this Peniel of
309– 4 *g·* him the spiritual sense of being,
325– 8 Jesus *g·* the true idea of being,
p 364–20 such seekers as he *g·* small reward
369–18 never *g·* drugs, never prayed to know if
376–12 should be told that blood never *g·* life
398– 9 Often he *g·* no name to the distemper
431– 5 the prisoner *g·* him drink.
t 456–32 it *g·* the first rules for demonstrating this
r 471–27 and *g·* the spiritual import,
487–11 apprehension of this *g·* sight to the blind
g 528– 4 That Adam *g·* the name and nature of animals,
533– 8 *g·* me of the tree,— *Gen.* 3 : 12.
537–28 and *g·* it to man for a possession,
539–27 The divine origin of Jesus *g·* him
gl 598–11 and *g·* up the ghost ;"— *John* 19 : 30.
598–15 What Jesus *g·* up was indeed air,

gavest
g 533– 8 The woman whom Thou *g·* to be— *Gen.* 3 : 12.
533–16 "The woman, whom Thou *g·* me, is responsible."

gaze
f 248–21 holding it before your *g·* continually.
248–25 first turn our *g·* in the right direction,
c 261–27 Fixing your *g·* on the realities supernal,
264– 9 Where shall the *g·* rest but in the
p 378–14 A man's *g·*, fastened fearlessly on a
420–30 Turn his *g·* from the false evidence of the
t 521–14 turn our *g·* to the spiritual record of creation,

gazing
p 380–15 *G·* at a chained lion, crouched for a spring,

gems
sp 87–20 the sea is ignorant of the *g·* within
f 235–17 adorned with *g·* of scholarly attainment,
247–27 blazons the night with starry *g·*,

gender
b 305–12 *G·* also is a quality, not of God, but
g 508–13 God determines the *g·* of His own ideas.
508–13 *G·* is mental, not material.
508–16 feminine *g·* is not yet expressed in the text.
508–17 *G·* means simply *kind* or *sort*,
508–20 grammars always recognize a neuter *g·*,
508–22 names the female *g·* last in the ascending
511–28 masculine, feminine, or neuter *g·*.

genders
g 516–30 Masculine, feminine, and neuter *g·* are

genera
r 482–18 As woman is but a species of the *g·*,

general
pref x–12 to suit the *g·* drift of thought,
a 32– 4 required to swear allegiance to his *g·*.
m 63–25 the elevation of society in *g·*
sp 83–17 belief that . . . man, is governed in *g·* by
87–11 in the *g·* atmosphere of human mind.
96– 7 interruptions of the *g·* material routine.
s 152–31 Jahr, . . . enumerates the *g·* symptoms,
155– 4 it is the law of a *g·* belief,
155– 8 not yet divorced the drug from the *g·* faith.
155–11 When the *g·* belief endorses the
155–17 erroneous *g·* belief, . . . works against C. S.
c 263–15 He becomes a *g·* mis-creator,
b 306–16 this is the *g·* religious opinion of mankind,
319–10 the *g·* faith in material means
p 394–18 the fallacy of material systems in *g·*,
408– 8 this *g·* craze cannot, . . . shield the
411– 5 as a *g·* rule the body would respond more quickly,
412– 6 the peculiar or *g·* symptoms of the case
t 457–19 C. S. is not an exception to the *g·* rule,
g 548–19 "It is very possible that many *g·* statements
553–21 adopted by *g·* mortal thought
554–29 It is the *g·* belief that the lower animals

General Grant
p 492–18 Discussing his campaign, *G· G·* said :

generalities
s 147–25 taught the *g·* of its divine Principle

generally

a 28–16	nor the work of Jesus was g· understood.
40–29	has come so g· to mean public worship
47–22	world g· loves a lie better than Truth;
s 132–19	and it has not yet been g· accepted.
142– 6	modern religions g· omit all but one of these
164– 9	It is just to say that g· the
ph 181–27	if they are cured, they g· know it
c 267– 8	It is g· conceded that God is Father,
b 270–12	it is g· admitted that this intelligence is
o 341– 5	criticisms are g· based on detached sentences
343–23	Christendom g· demands so much less.
348– 8	it is not g· understood how
349– 2	when this Science is more g· understood
349–25	material terms must be g· employed.
p 429–29	not understood g· by our ethical instructors.
t 446– 9	has g· completely healed such cases.
g 553–16	why are his deductions g· material?

General Progress

p 439–29　awaiting the sentence which G· P· and

generating

m 62– 1　only be permitted for the purpose of g·.

generation

a 29–21	put to silence material law and its order of g·,
50– 3	"Who shall declare his g·?" — Isa. 53 : 8.
m 56– 7	the legal and moral provision for g·
62–16	will do much more for the health of the rising g·
68–31	Proportionately as human g· ceases,
sp 85–25	Jesus knew the g· to be wicked
s 148– 2	"O faithless g·," — Mark 9 : 19.
t 446–13	pours light and healing upon this g·,
g 548–20	general statements . . . about birth and g·,
548–31	besides the ordinary process of g·,
551–22	are brought down from g· to g·?"

generations

ph 174–15	marking out the path for g· yet unborn.
c 260– 9	Through many g· human beliefs will
b 333–19	Throughout all g· both before and after
g 520–16	These are the g· of the heavens — Gen. 2 : 4.
549–14	successive g· do not begin with the birth

generic

c 259– 1	begin to comprehend . . . the g· term man.
r 475–15	g· term for all that reflects God's image
g 516–29	It follows that man is a g· term.
ap 561–22	woman in the Apocalypse symbolizes g· man,

generically

c 267– 6　G· man is one, and specifically man means

generous

s 129–30	The g· liver may object to the
t 450–10	They are sincere, g·, noble,

Genesis

and the Apocalypse

g 546–18　G· and the Apocalypse seem more obscure

beginning with

g 502– 1　second necessity for beginning with G· is

book of

g 502– 9	Spiritually followed, the book of G· is the
521–19	more about creation in the book of G·.
523–17	in the early part of the book of G·.

first chapter of

g 502–14	as given in the first chapter of G·.
505– 3	have no record in the first chapter of G·.
521– 8	(as stated in the first chapter of G·)
523–22	Throughout the first chapter of G·
535–29	In the first chapter of G· we read :
537–10	In the first chapter of G·, evil has no
537–24	recorded in the first chapter of G·.
gl 590–21	not used in the first chapter of G·,

narrative in

s 157–17　(according to the narrative in G·)

order used in

ap 568– 9　The narrative follows the order used in G·.

Science of

g 525–22　In the Science of G· we read

second account in

g 537–20　this second account in G·

second chapter of

g 521–26	second chapter of G· contains a statement of
522–25	latter part of the second chapter of G·,
526–15	is in the . . . second chapter of G·.

spoken of in

ph 180–10　the seed within itself . . . spoken of in G·.

to Revelation

s 139–24　seen from G· to Revelation,

to the Apocalypse

ap 564–24　From G· to the Apocalypse,

g 538–18	in the Elohistic introduction of G·,
ap 564–31	In G·, this allegorical, talking serpent
568–10	In G·, first the true method of creation is
572– 4	Thus we see, . . . in G· and in the Apocalypse,

genial

ap 575–30　southward, to the g· tropics,

genius

g 548–27　endowed by the labors and g· of great men.

Gentile

sp 85–23　Both Jew and G· may have had acute

gentle

g 541–10　the homage bestowed through a g· animal

gentleness

an 106–28	longsuffering, g·, goodness, faith, — Gal. 5 : 22.
gl 592–25	OIL. Consecration; charity; g·;

gently

ph 184–30	Her breath came g·.
193–12	The eyelids closed g· and
f 245–15	youth sat g· on cheek and brow.
r 485–14	Emerge g· from matter into Spirit.
ap 574–30	Then thought g· whispers : "Come hither !

genuine

m 60– 1	if both . . . were g· Christian Scientists.
sp 91–13	his g· being will be understood.
95– 2	only g· Science of reading mortal mind.
95–15	depends upon his g· spirituality.
s 112–26	to establish a g· school of this Science.
b 291– 2	suppositions . . . that happiness can be g· in
294–25	Man's g· selfhood is recognizable only in
p 364–26	by their g· repentance, by their broken hearts,
375–17	g· Christian Scientist is adding to his
r 477–16	the g· and perfect man,
489– 7	not with an artificial limb, but with the g·

genuinely

p 370–29　should naturally and g· change our basis

genus

b 277–16	the order of g· and species is preserved
ap 560–20	botanist must know the g· and species

geology

g 510–19	G· has never explained the earth's formations;
552– 6	Heathen philosophy, modern g·, and

geometric

f 215–11　not subordinate to g· altitudes.

geometrical

b 282– 4　are figured by two g· symbols,

geometry

b 283–30　than we can teach and illustrate g· by

germ

f 246– 7	Man is by no means a material g·
o 361–20	A g· of infinite Truth, . . . is the
g 549–18	simple ovum as the g·, the starting-point,
550– 1	he virtually affirms that the g· of humanity
551–31	resulting g· is doomed to the same routine.

Germany

an 100– 2　brought into notice by Mesmer in G·

germinated

sp 74– 9　The seed which has g· has

germinates

m 66–11	Spiritual development g· not from seed
g 546– 4	Spirit, God, never g·,
549– 4	supposition that life g· in eggs

germinating

f 225–26	always g· in new forms of tyranny,
g 547–14	g· speck of so-called embryonic life

germination

ph 183– 9　g· according to the laws of nature?

gestation

m 62– 3　the period of g· have the sanctity of virginity.

get

pref xi–31	enabled her to g· this institution chartered
pr 5–14	Saints and sinners g· their full award,
7– 2	"G· thee behind me, Satan." — Matt. 16 : 23.
12–31	If . . . only petitioners . . . should g· well.
a 39–25	mortals must g· the true idea and
m 65–21	we g· at last the clear straining of truth,
s 156–22	informed me that she could g· along two days
ph 197– 5	Every one hastens to g· it.
f 231– 2	or the so-called physical senses will g· the
239– 7	and we g· clearer views
239– 9	and we g· better views of humanity.
b 328– 7	mortals g· rid of sin, sickness, and death only
339–28	To g· rid of sin through Science,
p 371–17	before he can g· rid of the illusive sufferings
407–18	and he will g· the better of that desire,
412–19	g· its name, and array your mental plea against
t 447–26	and thus g· the victory over sin
g 553– 7	g· nearer the truth of being,
fr 600– *	Let us g· up early to the vineyards: — Song 7 : 12.

Gethsemane

a 30– 9	This accounts for his struggles in G·
48–11	in holy benediction on the grass of G·,
gl 586–23	definition of

getting

p 406–32	There is no enjoyment in g· drunk,
431–17	g· Mortal Man into close confinement

ghastly
ph 176-10 A g' array of diseases was not paraded
b 272-20 the g' farce of material existence ;

ghost
a 45-25 disciples at first called him a spirit, g', or
o 353-25 grave does not banish the g' of materiality.
353-30 the g', some unreal belief.
p 371-12 children look everywhere for the imaginary g',
g. 587- 1 definition of
598-12 and gave up the g' ;"— John 19 : 30.
598-12 but this word g' is pneuma.

ghostly
sp 86-17 Haunted houses, g' voices,
s 136-20 This g' fancy was repeated by Herod
o 353-13 not wholly outlived the sense of g' beliefs.

ghosts
o 352-13 child, who is frightened at imaginary g'
352-14 Would a mother say . . . "I know that g' are
352-21 by declaring g' to be real, merciless, and
352-23 that g' are not realities,
352-26 should be told not to believe in g',
352-28 terror of g' will depart
352-32 not irrational to tell the truth about g'.
353-27 so long will g' seem to continue.

ghost-stories
p 371- 6 by telling g' in the dark.

giant
f 240- 3 Arctic regions, sunny tropics, g' hills,

gift
sp 88-29 though it is said to be a g'
98- 3 assured . . . in the g' of divine Love.
s 108- 3 "the g' of the grace of God — Eph. 3 : 7.
135-27 nor a special g' from a ritualistic Jehovah ;
b 271-13 was not a supernatural g' to those learners,
g 541- 4 Jealous of his brother's g',
541- 5 instead of making his own g' a higher tribute

Gihon
gl 587- 3 definition of

girl
f 237- 1 A little g', who had occasionally listened to
238-10 Losing her crucifix, the Roman Catholic g' said,

give
pref viii-29 began to write down and g' to friends the
pr 3-19 we try to g' information to this infinite Mind.
9- 1 Do we not rather g' thanks that we
9- 9 though we g' no evidence of the sincerity of
11-28 nor can prayer alone g' us an understanding
16-24 Here let me g' what I understand to be the
17- 4 G' us this day our daily bread ;— Matt. 6 : 11.
17- 5 G' us grace for to-day ;
a 24- 5 willingness to g' up human beliefs
30- 1 could g' a more spiritual idea of life than other
51-12 Jesus could g' his temporal life into his
52-13 foresight of the reception error would g' him.
55-27 "He shall g' you another— John 14 : 16.
m 61- 8 celestial condition would . . . g' higher aims
65- 4 and to g' to human life an inspiration
67-18 notion that animal natures can possibly g' force
sp 81-21 g' to the worms the body called man,
94-21 but one returned to g' God thanks,
99-27 g' everlasting place to the scientific
s 115- 9 difficulty is to g' the right impression,
138-24 more willing . . . than are sinners to g' up the
141-30 G' to it the place in our institutions of learning
143-29 g' to Mind the glory, honor, dominion, and
148-27 When physiology fails to g' health or life by
152- 7 that it may g' hope to the sick
156-16 unwilling to g' up the medicine
156-17 occurred to me to g' her unmedicated pellets
156-20 she would g' up her medicine for one day,
ph 169-27 the action of Truth, . . . can g' harmony.
191- 1 The brain can g' no idea of God's man.
191- 4 As mortals g' up the delusion that
192-21 senses must g' up their false testimony.
f 203-31 does not kill a man in order to g' him eternal
214-25 would spread their table . . . and g' thanks.
216-30 G' up your material belief of mind in matter,
219- 8 No more can we say . . . muscles g' strength,
219- 9 No more can we say . . . nerves g' pain or
223-17 and try to "g' it pause."
249- 2 g' up imperfect models and illusive ideals ;
253- 4 saith : . . . I g' immortality to man,
253- 6 saith : . . . I g' life, without beginning
253- 7 saith : . . . I am supreme and g' all,
c 260- 7 conceptions of mortal, erring thought must g'way
b 268- 5 things which g' impulse to inquiry.
272-17 "G' not that which is holy— Matt. 7 : 6.
283- 2 they g' up the belief that there is
284-17 Can the . . . g' correct testimony
313- 2 to g' the full and proper translation of
330- 1 as mortals g' up error for Truth
o 353-19 We must g' up the spectral at all points.
354-13 opponents of C. S. neither g' nor offer any

give
o 360- 8 replies : . . . mine g' me such personal pleasure
361-21 to g' a clearer and fuller expression
p 396-23 G' them divine and wholesome understanding,
397-28 G' up the belief that mind is,
410- 1 If here we g' no heed to C. S.,
417- 3 G' sick people credit for sometimes knowing
417-31 G' your patients an underlying understanding
438- 5 Behold, I g' unto you power— Luke 10 : 19.
440- 9 were influenced to g' a verdict
441- 8 to g' heavy bonds for good behavior.
442-28 to g' you the kingdom."— Luke 12 : 32.
t 443- * G' instruction to a wise man,— Prov. 9 : 9.
443-18 g' up such cases, and leave invalids free to
453-26 nor g' names to diseases,
454-20 Right motives g' pinions to thought,
464-17 would g' him a hypodermic injection,
r 489-27 no organic construction can g' it hearing
g 510- 7 to g' light upon the earth :— Gen. 1 : 15.
511- 8 to g' light upon the earth,— Gen. 1 : 17.
524-28 Could Spirit . . . g' matter ability to sin and
525-25 if we g' the same heed to the history of
536-27 They g' up their belief in perishable life
539- 6 as if . . . matter can both g' and take away.
ap 568-24 For victory over a single sin, we g' thanks
570-16 G' them a cup of cold water
570-24 Those ready for the blessing . . . will g' thanks.
gl 596-15 illuminations of Science g' us a sense of the
598-16 for never did he g' up Spirit, or Soul.
(see also place)

given
pref x-13 bluntly and honestly g' the text of Truth.
xii-16 next two years of her life should be g' to
pr 9-11 If selfishness has g' place to kindness,
a 49-27 to whom he had g' the highest proofs
50-20 If his full recognition . . . had for a moment g' way
m 56- * nor are g' in marriage,— Matt. 22 : 30.
67- 2 The cup our Father hath g', shall we not drink
69-11 or to be "g' in marriage"— Matt. 22 : 30.
69-27 and are g' in marriage :— Luke 20 : 34.
69-29 nor are g' in marriage."— Luke 20 : 35.
sp 98- 7 no other sign shall be g'.
s 107-13 fresh pinions are g' to faith
108- 4 the grace of God g' unto me by the— Eph. 3 : 7
118-26 definitions of material law, as g'
133-31 Jewish conception of God, . . . has not quite g' place
137-12 rejection of the answer already g'
156- 5 case of dropsy, g' up by the faculty,
ph 175- 5 and less thought is g' to sanitary subjects,
179-32 Descriptions of disease g' by physicians
f 204-23 theories have g' sinners the notion that
b 313-17 the cause g' for the exaltation of Jesus,
328-28 Had it been g' only to his immediate disciples,
o 341-16 demonstrated according to a divine g' rule,
360-22 as g' in the excellent translation of
361-30 hence the many readings g' the Scriptures,
p 382- 5 If half the attention g' to hygiene were g' to
389- 3 it will be g' in behalf of the control of Mind
428-28 more apparent, as material beliefs are g' up
433-15 The case is g' to the jury.
g 502-13 as g' in the first chapter of Genesis.
518- 5 Behold, I have g' you— Gen. 1 : 29.
518-11 I have g' every green herb— Gen. 1 : 30.
534-30 The spiritual idea has g' the understanding
538-26 This account is g', . . . of mortal man,
545-11 Man, . . . was g' dominion over the whole
547- 8 so ascertain if the author has g' you the
ap 571-14 and yet have g' no warning.

Giver
s 112-19 like the great G', are "the same— Heb. 13 : 8.

gives
pref viii- 7 g' sweet concord to sound.
xi-13 as necessarily as darkness g' place to light
pr 6- 6 talents He g' we must improve.
7- 8 g' momentary solemnity and elevation to
7-12 g' occasion for reaction unfavorable to
a 33-22 It g' all for Christ, or Truth.
m 58- 3 Unity of spirit g' new pinions to joy,
sp 80-14 It is mysticism which g' spiritualism its force.
83-19 belittles omnipotent wisdom, and g' to matter
s 128-10 C. S. . . . g' them acuteness and
ph 168- 5 g' preponderance to the opposite.
176-14 human mind g' place to the divine Mind,
183-23 Obedience to Truth g' man power and strength.
183-27 the law which g' sight to the blind,
187- 7 material sense . . . g' them material names,
188-31 Astronomy g' the desired information
192-23 g' you the only power obtainable.
195- 8 All that g' pleasure to our educated senses
f 202-22 God g' man dominion over all the earth.
217-19 When mentality g' rest to the body,
246-11 robs youth and g' ugliness to age.
b 285-21 the better understanding that Science g'

gives

b	286– 7	understanding of Truth *g·* full faith in Truth,
	307–26	and *g·* man dominion over all things.
	316–22	*g·* man dominion over all the earth.
	320–26	*g·* a profound idea of the divine power
	323–25	true idea of God *g·* the true understanding
	339–23	until the finite *g·* place to the infinite.
p	383–15	To the mind equally gross, dirt *g·* no uneasiness.
	387–30	*g·* man faith and understanding
	420–12	divine Love *g·* them all power over
	430– 8	When man *g·* up his belief in death,
	442–23	Christ, Truth, *g·* mortals temporary food
r	467–26	Spirit *g·* the true mental idea.
	482– 1	*g·* the exact meaning in a majority of cases.
g	509–15	This text *g·* the idea of the rarefaction of
	509–18	understanding *g·* gleams of the infinite only,
	516–16	The great rock *g·* shadow and shelter.
	518–13	God *g·* the lesser idea of Himself
	522–12	This second record unmistakably *g·* the
	528–24	Adam— *alias* error— *g·* them names.
gl	586– 7	that which *g·* action to thought.

giveth

g	518–19	Love *g·* to the least spiritual idea

giving

pr	5–18	*g·* us strength according to our day.
a	19– 7	reconciling man to God by *g·* man
	25–23	*g·* the requisite proofs of their own piety.
	36–27	*g·* us only toil, sacrifice, cross-bearing,
m	64– 5	the ready aid her sympathy and
	64–20	no more marrying nor *g·* in marriage,
sp	79–31	G· does not impoverish us in the service
	80– 2	strength is not lessened by *g·* utterance
s	112–28	without *g·* that author proper credit,
	128–17	*g·* mortals access to broader and higher
ph	196–32	It does this by *g·* names to diseases
	198–18	Again, *g·* another direction to faith,
f	206–19	*g·* the mother her child
	210–15	*g·* a better understanding of Soul
	221–24	"*g·* God thanks ;"— *see Eph.* 5: 20.
	234– 7	and *g·* living waters to the thirsty.
c	266– 4	*g·* place to man's higher individuality
b	299–15	By *g·* earnest heed to these spiritual guides
p	365–30	unchristian practitioner is not *g·*
	366– 8	debars him from *g·* drink to the thirsty
	396–29	never *g·* the body life and sensation.
	400–21	*g·* no heed to the body,
	407–12	*g·* strength to the weakness of mortal mind,
	413–24	G· drugs to infants,
	422–16	*g·* more spirituality to consciousness
	424–19	either by *g·* antagonistic advice or
	436–11	G· a cup of cold water in Christ's name,
t	457– 3	borrowed from this book without *g·* it credit,
r	470–15	seem to be real by *g·* reality to the unreal.
g	505–24	*g·* the spiritual proof of the universe
	510–17	*g·* existence and intelligence to the universe.
	527–29	and is man *g·* up his dignity?
	530–18	error . . . *g·* the lie to divine Science
	538–11	The sun, *g·* light and heat to the earth,
gl	579– 6	Bible terms, *g·* their spiritual sense,

glad

sp	75–32	*g·* welcome of those who have gone before.
s	121–11	bird and blossom were *g·*

gladden

s	121–13	goodness and beauty to *g·* the heart ;

gladdens

m	67–16	or sunshine *g·* the troubled sea.

gladly

a	37–19	would *g·* have turned his sacred career into
s	151–16	from which multitudes would *g·* escape.

gladness

b	313– 8	the oil of *g·* above thy fellows.— *Heb.* 1: 9.
	324– 2	G· to leave the false landmarks
p	367–14	the oil of *g·* and the perfume of *gratitude,*

glances

f	247–25	Love . . . *g·* in the warm sunbeam,
g	516–17	The sunlight . . . *g·* into the prison-cell,

glancing

f	220–20	a kitten *g·* into the mirror at itself

gland

f	211–16	the effect seen in the lachrymal *g·*?

glandular

ph	175–14	*g·* inflammation, sneezing, and nasal pangs.

glass

s	126– 7	even as man sees his reflection in a *g·*.
b	295–18	The light and the *g·* never mingle,
	295–18	the *g·* is less opaque than the walls.

gleam

r	471–25	until she caught the first *g·* of
gl	582–11	a *g·* of the infinite idea of the

gleams

s	112–11	opinions may have occasional *g·* of divinity,
	144–10	and afford faint *g·* of God, or Truth.
g	509–18	understanding gives *g·* of the infinite only,
	538– 8	the sword of Truth *g·* afar

glean

c	323– 2	they will not be able to *g·* from C. S. the

glides

f	240–19	towards good or evil as time *g·* on.
g	516–18	The sunlight . . . *g·* into the sick-chamber,

glimpses

f	205–17	we can catch clear *g·* of God only as
b	333–24	caught glorious *g·* of the Messiah,
r	477–27	Indians caught some *g·* of the underlying

glints

g	516–17	The sunlight *g·* from the church-dome,

glistering

c	267–26	"white and *g·*," like the raiment— *Luke* 9: 29.

gloaming

p	371–18	illusive sufferings which throng the *g·*.

gloat

a	36–25	*g·* over their offences to the last

globe

a	52–17	the best man that ever trod the *g·*.
s	120–31	When Columbus gave freer breath to the *g·*,
b	313–24	the most scientific man that ever trod the *g·*.
t	459–31	than any other healer on the *g·*.

globe's

ap	559–10	to the *g·* remotest bound.

globules

s	156–22	she could get along two days without *g·* ;

gloom

a	34–32	His *g·* had passed into glory,
	47–31	During his night of *g·* and glory
ph	174–14	are our guardians in the *g·*.
f	248– 8	instead of lapsing into darkness or *g·*.

gloomy

a	45– 3	stepped forth from his *g·* resting-place,

glories

f	246–16	with bright and imperishable *g·*.
c	258– 2	the *g·* of limitless, incorporeal Life and **Love.**
	264–30	all the *g·* of earth and heaven and man.

glorification

a	43–15	to the *g·* of the man

glorified

a	45–30	and so *g·* the supremacy of Mind
	47– 5	After gaining the true idea of their *g·* Master,
	54– 6	the harmony his *g·* example introduced.
	54–29	If that Godlike and *g·* man were
s	118–12	eternally *g·* in man's spiritual freedom.
ph	200–29	Jesus Christ, and him *g·*.
b	291–11	not fancy that . . . will awaken them to *g·* being
	299–10	they point upward to a new and *g·* trust,
g	516–22	forever reflect, in *g·* quality,

glorious

a	29–15	*g·* perception that God is the only author
	32–32	in the twilight of a *g·* career
s	110–10	brought to light another *g·* proposition,
ph	176–10	seen in its *g·* effects upon the body.
f	202–13	For this *g·* result C. S. lights the torch
	227–24	"*g·* liberty of the children of— *Rom.* 8: 21.
	240– 5	festive flowers, and *g·* heavens,
	248– 1	*g·* freedom of spiritual harmony.
c	264– 5	must finally give place to the *g·* forms
b	288–27	Science reveals the *g·* possibilities of
	308–27	did not loosen his hold upon this *g·* light until
	333–24	caught *g·* glimpses of the Messiah,
o	359–31	spiritual ideals, indestructible and *g·*.
p	382–26	but for the *g·* Principle you teach,
r	473–32	his teachings and their *g·* proofs,
	474–14	until the *g·* Principle of these marvels is gained.
g	521– 7	We leave this brief, *g·* history of
	529– 9	usher in Science and the *g·* fact of creation,
	545–27	so *g·* in its spiritual signification.
ap	568– 7	warfare in Science, and the *g·* results

glory

bliss and

ap	574–15	the spiritual outpouring of bliss and *g·*,

crowned with the

a	45– 4	crowned with the *g·* of a sublime success,

divine

b	323–12	is winged to reach the divine *g·*.
ap	565– 5	loathing the brightness of divine *g·*.

entire

c	262– 7	but it ascribes to Him the entire *g·*.

gates of

ap	571–29	he has opened wide the gates of *g·*,

gloom and

a	47–31	During his night of gloom and *g·*

glory

God's
b 313–11 "the brightness of His [God's] *g*,— *Heb*. 1 : 3.

great
a 33–15 With the great *g* of an everlasting victory

imperishable
f 253– 3 the perfection of being, imperishable *g*,

His
b 313–21 being a brightness from His *g*,— *see Heb*. 1 : 3.

light and
ap 575–10 represents the light and *g* of divine Science.
577–25 Its gates open towards light and *g*

living
a 39–17 was not the threshold . . . into living *g*.

noontide
p 367–23 but radiate and glow into noontide *g*.

of eternal life
a 54–26 and to share the *g* of eternal life.

of eternity
g 502–17 illuminating time with the *g* of eternity.

of infinite Love
g 520– 4 majesty, and *g* of infinite Love fill all space.

of Mind
f 209–14 sense of Mind-power enhances the *g* of Mind.

throne of
a 26– 4 his loving pathway up to the throne of *g*,

type of the
gl 585–18 a type of the *g* which is to come ;

wonder and
g 501–11 that amplification of wonder and *g*

wondrous
a 42–22 the wondrous *g* which God bestowed on

———

pr 17–13 and the power, and the *g*, forever.— *Matt*. 6 : 13.
a 35– 1 His gloom had passed into *g*,
45–16 G· be to God, and peace to the
s 143–30 the *g*, honor, dominion, and power
f 247–14 Immortality, . . . has a *g* of its own,
b 325–12 [be manifested] with him in *g*."— *Col*. 3 : 4.
ap 566– 8 the *g* prepared for them who love God.

glow

sp 89–11 She says, "I am incapable of words that *g*,
b 298– 3 and *g* full-orbed in spiritual understanding.
329– 3 will *g* in all the grandeur of universal goodness.
p 367–23 but radiate and *g* into noontide glory.
g 511–17 The changing *g* and full effulgence of

glowing

g 522–21 God's *g* denunciations of man when not

glutton

a 28–20 saying : He is a *g*
52–31 the hypocrite, called Jesus a *g* and a

gluttony

f 221–32 *g* is a sensual illusion,

gnarled

sp 78– 1 the *g* oak, the ferocious beast,

gnats

s 140–14 straining out *g* and swallowing camels.
f 202– 2 straining out *g* and swallowing camels.
p 366–20 Such so-called Scientists will strain out *g*,

go

pr 6–18 farther we cannot *g*.
11– 4 "G·, and sin no more."— *John* 8 : 11.
11–10 before mortals can "*g*· up higher."— *Luke* 14 : 10.
12–25 Changes in belief may *g* on indefinitely,
13– 5 we often *g* beyond our convictions,
14–21 because I *g* unto my Father,"— *John* 14 : 12.
15–19 and *g* forth with honest hearts
a 20– 7 publicans and the harlots *g*·— *Matt*. 21 : 31.
22–16 *g* not back to error,
25–29 We must *g* and do likewise,
27– 3 "G· your way, and tell John— *Luke* 7 : 22.
37–29 "G· ye into all the world,— *Mark* 16 : 15.
40– 6 "G· thy way for this time ;— *Acts* 24 : 25.
sp 75–13 but I *g*·, that I may awake him— *John* 11 : 11.
79– 9 Science must *g* over the whole ground,
an 105–32 to *g*· in healing from the use of inanimate drugs
s 125–21 The seasons will come and *g*
132– 4 "G· and show John again those— *Matt*. 11 : 4.
138–27 "G· ye into all the world,— *Mark* 16 : 15.
142–17 causes the left to let *g* its grasp on the
ph 180–19 even before they *g*· to work to eradicate
f 202– 9 they would not *g* on from bad to worse,
214–13 They *g*· out as they came in,
235– 1 cannot *g*· forth, like wandering pollen,
240–16 revolutions of the universe of Mind *g*· on
241–31 to *g*· through the eye of a needle,"— *Matt*. 19 : 24.
c 261–13 to *g*· upon the stage and sustain his
b 296–15 they must *g*· out under the blaze of Truth,
308–24 "Let me *g*·, for the day breaketh ;"— *Gen*. 32 : 26.
309–17 If these children should *g*· astray,
312–14 People *g*· into ecstasies over the sense of a
o 342–10 "G· ye into all the world,— *Mark* 16 : 15.
p 406–23 and this growth will *g*· on until

go

p 408–16 Can drugs *g*· of their own accord to the brain
420– 1 nor *g*· from one part to another,
422–18 These changes which *g*· on in mortal mind
t 449– 9 to *g*· through the eye of a— *Matt*. 19 : 24.
451–14 many there be which *g*· in— *Matt*. 7 : 13.
r 478–11 ever seen to *g*· into the house
g 519–14 the divine power and presence which *g*· with it,
535–13 belief . . . must *g*· down before C. S.
547–22 or *g*· down into dust and nothingness.
556–11 only to *g*· out at last forever ;
ap 559–17 "G· and take the little book.— *Rev*. 10 : 8.

goal

m 61–32 If the . . . is requisite to reach this *g*,
f 233–14 until the *g* of goodness is . . . won.
b 324–17 certainly before we can reach the *g* of Spirit,
o 359–19 but when shall we arrive at the *g* which
p 426– 6 when she has the high *g* always before her
ap 560–15 *g* is never reached while we hate our

goblet

s 153– 8 one drop of that attenuation in a *g* of water,

God (see also God's)

acceptable unto
a 34– 4 "holy, acceptable unto G·,"— *Rom*. 12 : 1.
b 325–23 holy, acceptable unto G·,— *Rom*. 12 : 1.

account with
p 405–17 until you have balanced your account with G·.

advising
pr 3– 3 not sufficient to warrant him in advising G·.

affluence of our
s 140–12 but rejoicing in the affluence of our G·.

agent of
s 146–17 his Science, the curative agent of G·, is silenced.

alienate him from
b 304– 1 nothing could alienate him from G·,

all-inclusive
a 52–21 the mighty actuality of all-inclusive G·,

allness of
t 450–22 understanding . . . the allness of G·,
ap 563–18 the nothingness of evil and the allness of G·.

alone with
a 49–16 met his earthly fate alone with G·.
p 424–26 well to be alone with G· and the sick when

and His Christ
ap 561–15 G· and His Christ, bringing harmony to earth.

and His creation
r 472–24 All reality is in G· and His creation,
g 554–20 opposite of G· and His creation
gl 579–16 the opposite of good,— of G· and His creation ;

and His idea
sp 71– 2 nothing is Spirit,— but G· and His idea.
an 103–16 good is the infinite G· and His idea,
s 116– 8 so that G· and His idea may be to us
ph 167–25 but one way— namely, G· and His idea
p 372– 9 all is divine Mind, or G· and His idea,
r 495–15 cling steadfastly to G· and His idea.

and His reflection
b 314– 7 inseparable as G· and His reflection

and His thoughts
s 114–11 noumenon and phenomena, G· and His thoughts.

and mammon
o 346–31 We cannot serve both G· and mammon
t 462–10 dividing his interests between G· and mammon

and man
s 111– 7 Science of G· and man is no more supernatural
f 202– 3 unity which exists between G· and man
205– 6 their false sense concerning G· and man.
232– 3 Many theories relative to G· and man
c 258– 6 material belief in a physical G· and man.
264–13 gain more correct views of G· and man,
b 303–14 or by both G· and man,
333– 1 agreement, between G· and man in His image.
336–28 G· and man are not the same,
336–30 G· and man coexist and are eternal.
338– 3 the only living and true G· and man
o 361–17 even so G· and man, Father and son,
t 454–17 Love for G· and man is the true incentive
461–14 the eternal interpretation of G· and man.
r 470–19 standard of perfection was originally G· and man.
470–32 relations of G· and man, . . . are indestructible
471–16 evidence that G· and man coexist
g 502–26 the eternal verity and unity of G· and man,
545–20 in its false view of G· and man,
546–15 It supposes G· and man to be
ap 561–24 G· and man as the divine Principle and
577– 2 the incorporeal sense of G· and man
gl 581–11 G· and man coexistent and eternal;
589–24 spiritual understanding of G· and man

and men
a 30–10 mediator, or *way-shower*, between G· and men.
b 332–17 mediator between G· and men,— *I Tim*. 2 : 5.

and Satan
p 389–25 pain and pleasure, good and evil, G· and Satan

and Soul
b 335–16 G· and Soul are one,

God

and the real man
r 476– 4   *G·* and the real man are inseparable

angels of
m 56– *   *as the angels of G· in heaven.*— Matt. 22: 30.

anthropomorphic
f 224–14   were ready to hail an anthropomorphic *G·*,
c 257–18   would say that an anthropomorphic *G·*,
b 317– 5   and proclaimed an anthropomorphic *G·*
o 351–19   a personal devil and an anthropomorphic *G·*
g 517– 5   such a phrase as "an anthropomorphic *G·*,"

apart from
sp 91–26   belief . . . something apart from *G·*.
f 228–25   There is no power apart from *G·*.
b 283– 3   belief . . . true existence apart from *G·*.

applied to
s 116–28   If the term personality, as applied to *G·*, means

approval of
a 42–12   endorsed pre-eminently by the approval of *G·*,

at-one-ment with
a 19–22   in the atonement,— in the *at-one-ment* with *G·*,

attraction of
an 102–11   or the attraction of *G·*, divine Mind.

attribute of
b 319–30   to name Love as merely an attribute of *G·* ;

attributes of
r 465–14   attributes of *G·* are justice, mercy, wisdom,

avail themselves of
pr 13– 1   *all* may avail themselves of *G·*

becomes
g 524–10   *G·* becomes "a man of war,"— Exod. 15: 3.

before
m 64– 5   before *G·* and the Father,— Jas. 1: 27.

before our
ap 568–17   before our *G·* day and night.— Rev. 12: 10.

behests of
r 495–29   and follow the behests of *G·*,

belief in
pr 2–20   belief in *G·* as humanly circumscribed,
a 34–22   from spiritual dulness and blind belief in *G·*

beliefs about
s 132–16   retained their materialistic beliefs about *G·*.

belief that
f 204–30   belief that *G·* lives in matter is pantheistic.
o 357–10   relinquish the belief that *G·* makes sickness,

believed in
a 53–14   Mortals believed in *G·* as humanly mighty,

believe in
f 218–19   If you do believe in *G·*,

belongs to
r 490–11   since all power belongs to *G·*, good.

belong to
b 275–15   cause, and effect belong to *G·*.

bestowed
a 42–22   glory which *G·* bestowed on His anointed,

bestows
b 275–19   no good is, but the good *G·* bestows.
g 555–26   when we admit . . . that *G·* bestows the power to
ap 573– 8   that consciousness which *G·* bestows,

blending with
b 316–22   illustrates that blending with *G·*,

blessed them
g 512–11   And *G·* blessed them, saying,— Gen. 1: 22.
517–25   And *G·* blessed them,— Gen. 1: 28.

born of
t 463–18   born of the Spirit, born of *G·*,

bosom of
a 29–27   dwelt forever an idea in the bosom of *G·*,

brings
gl 596– 4   C. S. brings *G·* much nearer to man,

called
pref xi–22   When *G·* called the author to proclaim His
f 204–13   good, an intelligence or Mind called *G·*
b 281–14   The one Ego, the one Mind or Spirit called *G·*,
331–27   constitute the triune Person called *G·*,
g 504– 3   And *G·* called the light Day,— Gen. 1: 5.
506– 8   And *G·* called the firmament,— Gen. 1: 8.
506–22   *G·* called the dry land Earth ;— Gen. 1: 10.
535–29   *G·* called the dry land Earth ;— Gen. 1: 10.
gl 586–10   the divine Principle, commonly called *G·*.

can never destroy
p 425–17   can never destroy *G·*, who is man's Life.

cannot become
g 550– 7   *G·* cannot become finite, and be limited

cannot be tempted
g 527–12   "*G·* cannot be tempted with evil,— Jas. 1: 13.

cannot mistake
t 455–20   but *G·* cannot mistake.

cannot please
g 534–21   in the flesh cannot please *G·*.— Rom. 8: 8.

caught up unto
ap 565– 8   child was caught up unto *G·*,— Rev. 12: 5.
565–27   and to be caught up unto *G·*,

certainly revealed
r 483–20   to Christ Jesus, *G·* certainly revealed the spirit

God

charges
g 533–15   Adam, . . . charges *G·* and woman with

child of
b 289– 1   man's real existence as a child of *G·*
ap 573–18   regarded . . . as the blessed child of *G·*.

children of
  (*see* **children**)

Christian Science
s 140–25   The C. S. *G·* is universal, eternal,

city of our
ap 558– *   *to be praised in the city of our G·,*— Psal. 48: 1.
577–20   This city of our *G·* has no need of sun or

claims
o 344– 1   claims *G·* as the only absolute Life and Soul,
g 512–30   and claims *G·* as their author ;

claims of
a 23–20   and establishes the claims of *G·*.

claim that
gl 594– 9   first audible claim that *G·* was not omnipotent

coexistent with
m 69– 1   not of the earth earthly but coexistent with *G·*,
r 478– 2   for man is coexistent with *G·*.

coexists with
c 266–32   but he coexists with *G·* and the universe.

coexist with
c 267–12   man and the spiritual universe coexist with *G·*.

combines all-power
r 466– 3   Hence *G·* combines all-power or potency,

comes from
sp 84–28   All we correctly know of Spirit comes from *G·*,
r 479– 6   if aught comes from *G·*, it cannot be mortal
ap 558– 9   This angel or message which comes from *G·*,

communion with
a 30– 1   Mary's self-conscious communion with *G·*.

conception of
s 133–29   The Jewish conception of *G·*, as Yawah,
ph 185–19   rests on the conception of *G·* as the only Life,
c 258– 2   mortal, corporeal, or finite conception of *G·*

confides all to
a 23–31   includes. . . understanding and confides all to *G·*.

connection with his
b 292–30   real man's indissoluble connection with his *G·*,

contrary to
b 273– 2   Matter and its claims . . . are contrary to *G·*,

controls man
sp 73–10   *G·* controls man, and

created
s 140–29   In the beginning *G·* created man
b 294–27   *G·* created man.
r 479–18   "In the beginning *G·* created the— Gen. 1: 1.
g 502–22   In the beginning *G·* created the— Gen. 1: 1.
512– 4   And *G·* created great whales,— Gen. 1: 21.
516–24   So *G·* created man in His own— Gen. 1: 27.
543–24   Did man, whom *G·* created with a word,

created all
f 205–12   *G·* created all through Mind,

created by
g 507–23   Mind and the universe created by *G·*.
514–20   individuality created by *G·* is not carnivorous,
545–10   Man, created by *G·*, was given dominion

creates
m 69–22   If the father replies, "*G·* creates man through
b 295– 5   *G·* creates and governs the universe,
g 503–24   *G·* creates neither erring thought, mortal life,
513–26   *G·* creates all forms of reality.
520–23   declaration that *G·* creates all through Mind,
538–19   *G·* creates the heavens, earth, and man.

creations of
c 266– 1   where the creations of *G·* are good,

daughters of
g 503– 5   highest ideas are the sons and daughters of *G·*.
515–22   the sons and daughters of *G·*.

declare that
b 307– 9   It says : . . . I declare that *G·* makes evil minds
318– 6   Scriptures declare that *G·* made all,
331–14   Scriptures also declare that *G·* is Spirit.
g 539–16   Scriptures declare that *G·* condemned this lie

demands
f 254–20   This task *G·* demands us to accept lovingly

demands of
s 130– 1   the demands of *G·* must be met.
ph 182– 5   The demands of *G·* appeal to thought only ;

demonstrating
a 29–23   demonstrating *G·* as the Father of men.

demonstration of
b 270–18   nature of the teaching and demonstration of *G·*,

deny that
o 357–16   to deny that *G·* made man evil

dependence on
c 262– 2   does not lessen man's dependence on *G·*,

derived from
sp 72–24   In Science, individual good derived from *G·*,
g 539–12   nothing which he has not derived from *G·*.

design of
b 271– 5   uniting all periods in the design of *G·*.

God

determines
g 508–13   *G·* determines the gender of His own ideas.

did not express
r 470–27   If . . . a moment when man did not express *G·*,

dishonor
f 228–27   to acknowledge any other power is to dishonor *G·*.

dishonorest thou
o 349– 6   dishonorest thou *G·* ?"— *Rom.* 2 : 23.

disobedience to
p 440–13   disobedience to *G·*, or an act of homicide.

distinct from
f 204–28   never . . . distinct from *G·*, the *all* Mind.

divided the light
g 503–27   *G·* divided the light from the— *Gen.* 1 : 4.

does not cause
f 206–30   *G·* does not cause man to sin, to be sick, or

does not employ
s 143– 5   It is plain that *G·* does not employ drugs

down from
ap 574–14   coming down from *G·*,— *Rev.* 21 : 2.
575– 9   "down from *G·*, out of heaven,"— *Rev.* 21 : 2.

ended His work
g 519–22   *G·* ended His work which He— *Gen.* 2 : 2.

enmity against
s 131–10   carnal mind is enmity against *G·*."— *Rom.* 8 : 7.
g 534–19   carnal mind is enmity against *G·* ;— *Rom.* 8 : 7.

entireness of
b 293–30   universal harmony, the entireness of *G·*,

equipollence of
s 110– 9   The equipollence of *G·* brought to light

equipped by
b 328–15   man's power, when he is equipped by *G·*,

erects
g 523–10   which *G·* erects between the true and false.

eternal
p 415– 4   Mind in every case is the eternal *G·*,

eternal as
g 554– 3   universe, inclusive of man, is as eternal as *G·*,
gl 594–11   claim that . . . was as real and eternal as *G·*,

eternal with
g 516–22   woman as coexistent and eternal with *G·*

even
a 20– 1   for there is one Life,— even *G·*, good.
f 216–32   and have but one Mind, even *G·* ;
r 470– 1   With one Father, even *G·*, the whole family of
g 544–17   All is under the control of the one Mind, even *G·*.

exclusively to
sp 93–25   and applies exclusively to *G·*.

executor for
a 30–17   Not so did Jesus, the new executor for *G·*,

exists
f 215– 6   but being cannot be lost while *G·* exists.
g 544–11   man exists because *G·* exists.

exponent of
a 49– 9   Had they forgotten the great exponent of *G·*?

expresses
c 258–13   *G·* expresses in man the infinite idea

expressions of
g 518–22   All the varied expressions of *G·* reflect

faith in
pr 12– 8   through a blind faith in *G·*.
s 130–21   and to inculcate a grain of faith in *G·*,
f 226–31   but I pressed on through faith in *G·*,
p 368–17   more faith in *G·* than in man,
373– 8   then we must have more faith in *G·*
395–12   and faith in *G·* destroys all faith in sin
410–14   Every trial of our faith in *G·* makes us
426–27   with unflinching faith in *G·*,

fashions
g 516– 9   *G·* fashions all things, after His own

fatherhood of
ap 562– 4   the idea of the fatherhood of *G·*,

Father-Mother
pr 16–27   Our Father-Mother *G·*, all-harmonious,
g 516–23   the infinite Father-Mother *G·*.

fear
b 340– 7   Fear *G·*, and keep His— *Eccl.* 12 : 13.

filled with
r 469–24   where all space is filled with *G·*.

forms
g 509–16   *G·* forms and peoples the universe.

fully apprehend
f 231–28   impossible, when you fully apprehend *G·*

gives man
f 202–22   *G·* gives man dominion over all

gives the lesser
g 518–13   *G·* gives the lesser idea of Himself

gleams of
s 144–10   and afford faint gleams of *G·*, or Truth.

glimpses of
f 205–17   we can catch clear glimpses of *G·* only as

glory be to
a 45–16   Glory be to *G·*, and peace to the

God

governed by
a 42–27   in C. S. the true man is governed by *G·*
ph 180–25   When man is governed by *G·*,
f 215–12   Whatever is governed by *G·*, is never . . . deprived
b 304–15   governed by *G·*, his perfect Principle
318–29   In Science man is governed by *G·*,
p 409–20   The animate should be governed by *G·*
r 495– 2   whenever man is governed by *G·*.

government of
c 258–29   under the government of *G·* in eternal Science,
p 405–20   demonstrates the government of *G·*,

governs all
an 102– 2   *G·* governs all that is real, harmonious, and

governs the universe
an 102–13   since *G·* governs the universe ;

grace of
s 108– 4   grace of *G·* given unto me by the— *Eph.* 3 : 7.

guest of
f 254–32   stranger, thou art the guest of *G·*.

had blessed
b 338–29   notwithstanding *G·* had blessed the earth

harmony and
b 340– 3   make life its own proof of harmony and *G·*.

harmony in
p 417– 2   peace, and harmony in *G·*,

harmony with
s 130–10   reality is in perfect harmony with *G·*,
131– 5   in order to be in harmony with *G·*,

has almighty power
f 202–27   We admit that *G·* has almighty power,

has appointed
ap 560–17   false estimate of anyone whom *G·* has appointed

has built
f 226–14   *G·* has built a higher platform of human rights,

has countless ideas
g 517–18   *G·* has countless ideas, and they all have

has created
o 344– 7   Scriptures say that *G·* has created man in His

has endowed man
an 106– 7   *G·* has endowed man with inalienable rights,

has sentenced
b 322–14   *G·* has sentenced sin to suffer.

has set His signet
r 472– 6   *G·* has set His signet upon Science,

hath said
g 529–19   *G·* hath said, Ye shall not eat of it,— *Gen.* 3 : 3.

have mercy
p 433–25   "May *G·* have mercy on your soul," is the

heals the sick
ap 570–26   When *G·* heals the sick or the sinning,

her fathers'
ap 566–17   Her fathers' *G·* before her moved,

he served
a 52– 4   He served *G·* ; they served mammon.

highway of our
m 61–11   that the highway of our *G·* may be prepared

honor
r 483–27   And C. S. does honor *G·*

honors
r 483–26   if any system honors *G·*, it ought to receive aid,

hope thou in
p 362– *   *Hope thou in G·; for I shall yet*— *Psal.* 42 : 11.

ideal of
a 25–16   Jesus presented the ideal of *G·* better than
o 361– 5   Christ, . . . is the ideal of *G·* now and forever,

idea of
a 29–17   The Virgin-mother conceived this idea of *G·*,
43–15   glorification of the man and of the true idea of *G·*.
54–10   plant themselves in Christ, the true idea of *G·*.
s 132–25   this rejection . . . of the true idea of *G·*,
ph 200–12   man is the idea of *G·*, not formed materially
c 258–12   this reflection is the true idea of *G·*.
262–14   above the mortal to the immortal idea of *G·*.
b 289– 8   A wicked mortal is not the idea of *G·*.
303–29   Spiritual man is the image or idea of *G·*,
316–12   Jesus represented Christ, the true idea of *G·*.
316–24   The spiritual idea of *G·*, as presented by Jesus,
323–24   true idea of *G·* gives the true understanding
324– 9   are not gaining the true idea of *G·* ;
332–20   Christ is the divine idea of *G·*
o 345–32   not the purpose of C.S. to "educate the idea of *G·*,
347–15   as the spiritual or true idea of *G·*,
r 473–14   has presented Christ, the true idea of *G·*,
475–15   He is the compound idea of *G·*,
476–10   and man is the idea of *G·*.
477–12   C. S. reveals man as the idea of *G·*,
482–21   the divine idea of *G·* outside the flesh.
g 503–20   divine Mind presents the idea of *G·* :
524– 9   true idea of *G·* seems almost lost.
ap 561–23   generic man, the spiritual idea of *G·* ;
577–15   the Christ, the spiritual idea of *G·* ;
gl 582–15   conceiving man in the idea of *G·* ;
585–17   EUPHRATES . . . the true idea of *G·* ;

God

ideas of
f 230–11 It would be contrary to our highest ideas of G·
g 510– 3 seek to apprehend the spiritual ideas of G·,
519– 9 ideas of G· in universal being are complete
548–17 true ideas of G·, the spiritual sense of being.
gl 583– 8 some of the ideas of G· beheld as men,
illustrated
g 501–12 and which G· illustrated by light and harmony,
image of
m 67– 1 may be graven with the image of G·.
ph 173–24 image of G·, the real immortal man.
c 259– 6 In divine Science, man is the true image of G·.
259–17 never beheld in man the reflex image of G·.
b 285–12 claim that a mortal is the true image of G·
289– 6 what constitutes man as the image of G·.
300– 8 who cannot be the image of G·.
318–17 so far as he is discordant, he is not the image of G·.
p 437– 4 Man was made in the image of G·,
g 502–10 the history of the untrue image of G·,
516–25 in the image of G· created He him ; — Gen. 1 : 27.
imparts
g 515–23 All that G· imparts moves in accord
imply that
b 331–11 Scriptures imply that G· is All-in-all.
g 537–30 would imply that G· withheld from man
impute to
g 554–17 to impute to G· the creation of whatever is sinful
infinite
an 103–16 The maximum of good is the infinite G·
c 258– 1 the image and likeness of the infinite G·.
b 277–12 and cannot be the outcome of an infinite G·,
287–11 and the *infinite G·* can have no unlikeness.
335–13 invisible and indivisible infinite G·.
340–23 One infinite G·, good, unifies men and nations ;
p 381–19 and have our being in the infinite G·,
r 497– 6 one supreme and infinite G·.
Inspired by
a 51–3 He was inspired by G·, by Truth and Love,
intelligence or
b 307– 8 declares . . . more than one intelligence or G·.
interpret
s 127–27 and is alone able to interpret G· aright.
interprets
r 471–26 that which interprets G· as above mortal sense.
ap 569– 1 clearly interprets G· as divine Principle,
in the hands of
g 521– 9 in the hands of G·, not of man,
invisible
a 55– 3 a deadened sense of the invisible G·,
b 305– 8 the central light of being, the invisible G·.
337–21 man, as the reflection of the invisible G·,
is able
o 359–24 "G· is able to raise you up from sickness ;"
is All
b 339– 7 Since G· is All, there is no room for
p 366–29 knowing, . . . that Life is God and G· is All.
g 532–24 G· is All and He is Mind
is all
s 116–18 They never . . . insist upon the fact that G· is all,
b 302– 9 when G· is all and eternally his.
is All-in-all
s 113–16 G· is All-in-all.
b 331–11 The Scriptures imply that G· is All-in-all.
p 425–20 since Spirit, G·, is All-in-all.
r 468–11 for G· is All-in-all.
g 503–13 Word of God, saith . . . "G· is All-in-all,"
is come
o 361– 8 the Christian's doctrine that G· is come
is divine Life
b 331– 1 G· is divine Life,
is everywhere
r 473– 8 G· is everywhere, and nothing apart from
is Father
c 267– 8 It is generally conceded that G· is Father,
is good
pr 3–18 G· is good, omnipotent, omnipresent,
a 19–28 although G· is good.
s 113–17 G· is good. Good is Mind.
f 243–32 G· is good and the fount of all being,
b 328– 5 G· is good and the only real Life.
p 399– 1 G· is good, and therefore good is
is his Father
m 63–10 G· is his Father, and Life is the law of his being.
is incorporeal
s 116–22 Mortals are corporeal, but G· is incorporeal.
r 465– 9 G· is incorporeal, divine, supreme,
is individual
b 331–18 G· is individual, incorporeal.
336–32 G· is individual and personal in a scientific
is indivisible
b 336–19 G· is indivisible. A portion of God could not
is infinite
pr 17–14 For G· *is infinite, all-power,*
f 223– 7 G· is infinite omnipresent Spirit.

God

is infinite
b 278–10 Spirit, G·, is infinite, all.
312–21 G· is infinite Love, which must be unlimited.
330–11 G· is infinite, the only Life, substance,
r 469–22 when we admit that, although G· is infinite,
471–18 G· is infinite, therefore ever present,
492–25 G· *is infinite ; hence all is Mind.*
is intelligence
pr 2–23 G· is intelligence. Can we inform the infinite
is just
t 445–31 when I remember that G· is just,"
is Love
pr 2–23 G· is Love. Can we ask Him to be more?
6–17 "G· is Love." — I John 4 : 8.
a 42– 1 Jesus' life proved, . . . that G· is Love,
b 275– 8 G· is Love, and therefore He is divine
302–25 G· is Love. He is therefore the divine,
312–16 G· *is Love, and without Love, God, immortality cannot*
ap 569–14 in a sweet and certain sense that G· is Love.
is love
b 320– 1 "G· is love." — I John 4 : 8.
is Mind
f 239–30 Mind sends forth perfection, for G· is Mind.
b 311– 4 G· is Mind : all that Mind, God, is, or
330–22 Mind is not both good and bad, for G· is Mind ;
r 492–25 G· *is Mind, and God is infinite;*
is more
p 425–21 G· is more to a man than his belief,
is natural good
s 119–21 G· is natural good, and is represented only by
is not corporeal
s 116–21 G· is not *corporeal*, but *incorporeal*,
is not influenced
pr 7–23 G· is not influenced by man.
is not man
r 480–19 Man is not God, and G· is not man.
is not moved
pr 2– 8 G· is not moved by the breath of praise
is not separate
pr 6– 5 G· is not separate from the wisdom He bestows.
is "of purer eyes"
f 243–22 G· is "of purer eyes than — Hab. 1 : 13.
o 357– 4 G· is "of purer eyes than — Hab. 1 : 13.
is omnipotent
pr 17– 2 G· *is omnipotent, supreme.*
s 130–12 since you admit that G· is omnipotent ;
p 394–28 Life is God, and that G· is omnipotent.
is One
s 117– 3 whereas G· is *One*, — not one of a series, but
is one
c 267– 5 G· is one. The allness of Deity is His oneness.
gl 587–17 G· is one God, infinite and perfect,
is our Life
s 107–17 in reality G· is our Life,
p 388–24 self-evident, when we learn that G· is our Life.
is our refuge
t 444–11 "G· is our refuge and strength, — Psal. 46 : 1.
is reflected
g 524–23 yet G· is reflected in all His creation.
is revealed
f 241–25 the Horeb height where G· is revealed ;
b 300–31 G· is revealed only in that which
g 511–12 G· is revealed as infinite light.
is seen
b 300–29 G· is seen only in the spiritual universe
is Spirit
s 117– 6 G· is Spirit ; therefore the language of
f 207– 2 Because G· is Spirit, evil becomes
b 331–14 Scriptures also declare that G· is Spirit.
335– 2 There is no evil in Spirit, because G· is Spirit.
is substance
b 301–17 G· is substance and man is the divine image
is the creator
r 470–21 G· is the creator of man,
is the Father
m 64–26 Until it is learned that G· is the Father of all,
is the infinite
f 249–14 G· is the infinite, and infinity never began,
is the lawmaker
p 381–15 G· is the lawmaker,
is the Life
g 550– 5 G· is the Life, or intelligence, which forms
is the light
ap 558–15 for G· "is the light thereof." — Rev. 21 : 23.
is the only Life
b 289– 4 until he learns that G· is the only Life.
324–14 the understanding that G· is the only Life.
r 472– 1 Science teaches man that G· is the only Life,
is the only Mind
b 308– 5 the lesson is learned that G· is the only Mind
339–26 the great fact that G· is the only Mind ;
is the only power
p 419–27 for G· is the only power.

God

is the only Spirit
sp 73–11 G· is the only Spirit.
is the power
a 27– 8 G· is the power in the Messianic work.
is the Principle
s 112–32 G· is the Principle of divine metaphysics.
r 476– 9 G· is the Principle of man,
is to be understood
r 472– 2 G· is to be understood, adored, and
is true
s 113–24 I find that G· is true,
is Truth
b 312–18 yet G· *is* Truth.
Jehovah
g 543–32 the Lord God [Jehovah G·] made— *Gen.* 2: 4.
kingdom of
    (see **kingdom**)
kingdom of our
ap 568–15 and the kingdom of our G·,— *Rev.* 12: 10.
knowledge of
a 48–31 what the true knowledge of G· can do for man.
s 133–31 not quite given place to the true knowledge of G·.
g 540–21 a false sense which hath no knowledge of G·.''
fr 600– * *increasing in the knowledge of G·.*— *Col.* 1: 10.
known to
pr 15–26 hidden from the world, but known to G·.
knows our need
pr 13–15 G· knows our need before we tell Him
Lamb of
s 132–32 Jesus as ''the Lamb of G· ;''— *John* 1: 29.
ap 564–13 speaks of Jesus as the Lamb of G·
gl 590– 9 definition of
law of
    (see **law**)
laws of
s 128– 5 refers only to the laws of G·
ph 168–17 all in consonance with the laws of G·,
leadeth us
pr 17–10 *And G· leadeth us not into temptation,*
leave the field to
p 419– 5 leave the field to G·, Life, Truth, and Love,
less than
f 203–18 to believe . . . in some power less than G·.
b 336–23 else God would . . . become less than G·.
g 543– 1 misconception of Life as something less than G·,
Life as
sp 79– 4 those who are ignorant of Life as G·.
b 310–27 and if Spirit should lose Life as G·,
life in
a 45–19 the revelation and demonstration of life in G·,
b 324–18 the goal of Spirit, or life in G·.
Life is
    (see **Life**)
Life, or
f 249–11 Any other theory of Life, or G·, is delusive
b 283–14 They insist that Life, or G·, is
o 357–30 and, if so, can Life, or G·, dwell in evil
g 543–29 belief . . . would make Life, or G·, mortal.
Life which is
a 47– 3 faint conception of the Life which is G·.
ap 561–20 understanding the Life which is G·.
likeness of
sp 71–19 neither . . . is the image or likeness of G·,
    81–17 Man in the likeness of G·
f 206–26 the spiritual image and likeness of G· ?
    222–23 far from being the image and likeness of G·,
b 285– 9 not man, the image and likeness of G·,
    287–20 not the image and likeness of G· ;''
    292–11 sick, and dying mortal is not the likeness of G·,
    299–15 individuality, image, or likeness of G·,
    303–23 belief . . . material man is the likeness of G·
    315–17 The likeness of G· we lose sight of through
p 414–27 man is the image and likeness of G·,
r 467–15 man is the likeness of G·, pure and eternal,
    475– 9 man is made in the image and likeness of G·.
g 531–32 man . . . in the image and likeness of G·
    548– 6 man in the image and likeness of G·.
gl 591– 6 the spiritual image and likeness of G· ;
likeness to
pr 12–15 man's likeness to G· and of man's unity
p 395– 5 man's immortality and eternal likeness to G·.
Lord our
c 256–12 the Lord our G· is one Lord.''— *Deut.* 6: 4.
love
pr 4–17 Simply asking that we may love G· will never
ph 167–19 you must love G· supremely.
b 326– 9 man cannot love G· supremely . . . while
    340–10 love G· and keep His commandments :
t 444– 5 to them that love G·,''— *Rom.* 8: 28.
ap 566– 9 glory prepared for them who love G·.
love of
a 42– 4 gave no hint of the unchanging love of G·.
b 304–9 from the love of G·.''— *Rom.* 8: 39.

God

lovingly governs
p 412– 1 great fact that G· lovingly governs all,
made
f 231–20 because G· made you superior to it
g 505–13 And G· made the firmament,— *Gen.* 1: 7.
    510–13 And G· made two great lights ;— *Gen.* 1: 16.
    513–22 And G· made the beast of— *Gen.* 1: 25.
    525–20 Everything good or worthy, G· made.
    526– 4 G· made ''every plant— *Gen.* 2: 5.
made all
f 229– 7 G· made all that was made,
b 318– 6 Scriptures declare that G· made all,
made Man
p 434–31 but G· made Man immortal
made man
ph 167–15 If G· made man both good and evil,
f 227–16 G· made man free.
g 516–28 G· made man in His own image,
maintained by
g 531–18 divine order still maintained by G·
maker is
p 428–14 ''whose builder and maker is G·.''— *Heb.* 11: 10.
makes
g 532– 3 G· makes and governs all.
man and
c 258–24 gains the true conception of man and G·.
g 524–26 or is it a lie concerning man and G· ?
manifestation of
b 295–16 manifestation of G· through mortals is as
gl 583–10 CHRIST. The divine manifestation of G·,
man is not
f 250–12 Man is not G·, but like a ray of
r 480–19 Man is not G·, and God is not man.
man nor
g 533–30 ''Neither man nor G· shall father my fault.''
man of
b 314–10 Jews, who sought to kill this man of G·,
man-projected
s 140–23 tribal Jehovah was a man-projected G·,
man to
a 18–13 reconciles man to G·, not God to man ;
    19– 2 Christ's purpose to reconcile man to G·,
    19– 7 Jesus aided in reconciling man to G·
sp 94– 8 and of the relation of man to G·,
s 114–26 It shows the scientific relation of man to G·,
material view of
g 521–27 this material view of G· and the universe,
meaning of
c 261–23 you may learn the meaning of G·,
message from
b 332–10 the divine message from G· to men
Mind is
sp 91–31 nor the medium of evil, for Mind is G·.
b 275–22 that all is Mind, and that Mind is G·,
    310–29 Mind is G·, and God is not seen by
r 469–13 *Answer.*— Mind is G·.
Mind or
p 372– 9 all is divine Mind, or G· and His idea,
r 482–29 on the basis of the one Mind or G·.
misrepresent
g 538–17 the false claims that misrepresent G·,
motherhood of
g 507– 6 the fatherhood and motherhood of G·.
mouth of
p 410–11 proceedeth out of the mouth of G·,''— *Matt.* 4: 4.
named
ph 200–24 the infinite Spirit, named G·.
r 469–11 Life, Truth, and Love,— named G·.
nature and
s 118–31 the law of Love, in which nature and G· are
nature of
a 20–18 even the nature of G· ;
g 537–32 but this is not the nature of G·,
never decreed disease
f 221–19 that G· never decreed disease,
never endowed matter
p 378–26 G· never endowed matter with power to
never made
f 222–26 concluded that G· never made a dyspeptic,
g 540–20 ''G· never made you, and you are a false sense
never slumbers
f 249–21 G· never slumbers, and His likeness
no law of
p 391–13 No law of G· hinders this result.
no part in
a 19–26 Those who cannot . . . have no part in G·.
no relation to
ph 196–17 They have no relation to G· wherewith
nothing except
f 243–29 because they declare nothing except G·.
notions about
o 357–20 wrong notions about G· must have
not originate in
r 472–10 sin, and death, . . . do not originate in G·

God

return thanks to
  pr 3–28 and yet return thanks to *G·* for all blessings,
reveals
  s 127–17 C. S. reveals *G·*, not as the author of sin,
said
  ph 197– 8 *G·* said of the tree of knowledge,
  f 220–29 *G·* said, "Thou shalt not eat of it."— *Gen.* 2 : 17.
  r 475–23 And *G·* said : "Let us make man— *Gen.* 1 : 26.
  g 503–18 And *G·* said, Let there be light :— *Gen.* 1 : 3.
  505– 4 And *G·* said, Let there be a— *Gen.* 1 : 6.
  506–15 And *G·* said, Let the waters— *Gen.* 1 : 9.
  507–11 And *G·* said, Let the earth— *Gen.* 1 : 11.
  509– 9 And *G·* said, Let there be lights— *Gen.* 1 : 14.
  511–19 And *G·* said, Let the waters— *Gen.* 1 : 20.
  513–14 And *G·* said, Let the earth— *Gen.* 1 : 24.
  515–11 And *G·* said, Let us make man— *Gen.* 1 : 26.
  517–25 *G·* said unto them, Be fruitful,— *Gen.* 1 : 28.
  518– 5 And *G·* said, Behold, I have given— *Gen.* 1 : 29.
  525–13 *G·* said, Let us make man after our mind
  529–15 Yea, hath *G·* said, Ye shall not eat— *Gen.* 3 : 1.
saw everything
  g 518–24 And *G·* saw everything that He— *Gen.* 1 : 31.
saw that it
  g 506–24 and *G·* saw that it was good.— *Gen.* 1 : 10.
  508–11 and *G·* saw that it was good.— *Gen.* 1 : 12.
  511–10 and *G·* saw that it was good.— *Gen.* 1 : 18.
  512– 7 and *G·* saw that it was good.— *Gen.* 1 : 21.
  513–24 and *G·* saw that it was good.— *Gen.* 1 : 25.
  515– 2 "And *G·* saw that it was good."— *Gen.* 1 : 25.
saw the light
  g 503–26 And *G·* saw the light,— *Gen.* 1 : 4.
Science is of
  g 551–16 all Science is of *G·*, not of man.
Science of
  s 111– 7 Science of *G·* and man is no more supernatural
  111–10 as the Science of *G·*, Spirit, must,
seek unto their
  sp 70– * *Should not a people seek unto their G·?— Isa.*
           8 : 19.
selects
  t 455–20 *G·* selects for the highest service
sense of
  c 256–25 material sense of *G·* leads to formalism
  b 279–30 starting from a material sense of *G·*,
  312–24 A personal sense of *G·* and of man's
  r 489–30 A wrong sense of *G·*, man, and creation is
  ap 577– 2 incorporeal sense of *G·* and man
  gl 590–24 when the spiritual sense of *G·* and of infinity
  591– 1 a physical sense of *G·* as finite and corporeal.
sentence of
  f 232–24 the sentence of *G·*, which sealed
sent from
  ap 561–31 "There was a man sent from *G·*— *John* 1 : 6.
sentinel of
  a 49–18 faithful sentinel of *G·* at the highest post
separate from
  a 42–20 belief that man has . . . mind separate from *G·*
  s 136– 6 He claimed no . . . life separate from *G·*.
shaped man
  g 525–14 and *G·* shaped man after His mind ;
smile of
  ph 175–10 to say that a rose, the smile of *G·*, can produce
soldier of
  b 309–11 Israel,— a prince of God, or a soldier of *G·*,
Son of
  (see **Son**)
sonship with
  b 315–12 hid from their sense Christ's sonship with *G·*.
sons of
  b 315–20 the liberty of the sons of *G·*.
Soul as
  b 310–14 Science reveals Sóul as *G·*, untouched by sin
Soul, or
  sp 72–11 Soul, or *G·*, is the only truth-giver to man.
  r 468–22 the synonym of Mind, Soul, or *G·*,
Spirit and
  o 345– 1 Spirit and *G·* are often regarded as
Spirit is
  (see **Spirit**)
spirit of
  s 137–20 Christ, the spirit of *G·*, of Truth, Life, and
  r 480– 3 Where the spirit of *G·* is,
  g 503– 8 the spirit of *G·* moved upon the— *Gen.* 1 : 2.
  534–22 the spirit of *G·* dwell in you."— *Rom.* 8 : 9.
Spirit, or
  sp 73–15 If Spirit, or *G·*, communed with mortals
  r 482–11 Soul is properly the synonym of Spirit, or *G·* ;
spiritual
  f 214–21 more than they do a spiritual *G·*.
supernatural
  t 450– 4 belief in a mysterious, supernatural *G·*,
supposes
  g 538–31 supposes *G·* to be the author of sin

God

supremacy of
  s 130–27 claim of Science for the supremacy of *G·*,
sustained by
  f 221–22 in which being is sustained by *G·*,
  g 530– 5 In divine Science, man is sustained by *G·*,
symbol of
  g 517–20 The only proper symbol of *G·* as person is
talked with
  b 308–15 talked with *G·* as consciously as man talks wit
taught of
  t 455–26 if he is taught of *G·* to discern it.
term for
  b 286–17 In the Saxon . . . *good* is the term for *G·*.
thanks
  t 453–21 masquerader in this Science thanks *G·* that
the All-in-all
  s 127– 4 If *G·*, the All-in-all, be the creator of the
the Father-Mother
  b 331–30 *G·* the Father-Mother ; Christ the
the living
  s 137–18 the Son of the living *G·* !"— *Matt.* 16 : 16.
theories concerning
  s 133–23 special theories concerning *G·*,
those who scoff at
  o 358–15 nor of the inventions of those who scoff at *G·*.
thoughts from
  b 298–28 Angels are pure thoughts from *G·*, winged wit
to ignore
  ph 166–17 To ignore *G·* as of little use in sickness is a
to man
  a 18–14 reconciles man to God, not *G·* to man ;
  19– 2 to reconcile man to God, not *G·* to man.
  an 104– 1 true thoughts, passing from *G·* to man.
  s 117–17 As a divine student he unfolded *G·* to man,
  f 206–15 In the scientific relation of *G·* to man,
  b 284–30 Thought passes from *G·* to man,
  332– 2 relation of *G·* to man and the universe.
to suppose that
  pr 6–19 To suppose that *G·* forgives . . . according
  ph 183– 5 To suppose that *G·* constitutes laws of
towards
  f 213–12 and is a tendency towards *G·*, Spirit.
  p 430– 9 he will advance more rapidly towards *G·*,
tributary to
  r 481– 2 is tributary to *G·*, Spirit, and to nothing else.
tri-unity of
  b 340–18 It inculcates the tri-unity of *G·*, Spirit,
true
  f 237–29 the only living and true *G·* can do.
  b 338– 3 brings to light the only living and true *G·*
  p 410– 8 know Thee, the only true *G·*,— *John* 17 : 3.
trust
  a 20–21 to obey the divine order and trust *G·*,
understand
  pr 3–15 to understand *G·* is the work of eternity,
  a 22–29 does not understand *G·*.
  f 209–32 constant capacity to understand *G·*.
  o 352– 2 they did not sufficiently understand *G·*
  t 446–21 To understand *G·* strengthens hope,
  r 486–29 If . . . medium through which to understand *G·*
understanding of
  a 33–30 a new and higher understanding of *G·*
  sp 76–13 When advanced to . . . the understanding
           of *G·*,
  79–13 through the higher understanding of *G·*,
  s 127– 7 a knowledge or understanding of *G·*,
  b 275–26 The true understanding of *G·* is spiritual.
  315– 5 His better understanding of *G·* was a rebuke to
  328–11 they gain the true understanding of *G·*
  p 428–32 the understanding of *G·* as the only Life.
  r 473–23 a better understanding of *G·* . . . is required.
  496–14 prove what the understanding of *G·* brings
  ap 567– 6 prevails through the understanding of *G·*.
  576–25 in proportion to his understanding of *G·*.
  gl 589–24 understanding of *G·* and man appearing.
understanding that
  b 324–14 the understanding that *G·* is the only Life.
  gl 589– 9 the understanding that *G·* is the divine
unity of
  s 132–12 coming from divine Mind, prove the unity of *G·*
  g 502–26 eternal verity and unity of *G·* and man,
unity with
  a 18– 2 exemplification of man's unity with *G·*,
  r 497–15 unfolding man's unity with *G·*
universal
  sp 78–31 These are the effects of one universal *G·*,
unknown
  p 428–16 not "to the unknown *G·*"— *Acts* 17 : 23.
  gl 596– 8 dedicated "to the unknown *G·*."— *Acts* 17 : 23
unknown to
  p 424– 5 Accidents are unknown to *G·*,
unlike
  f 249–16 and includes nothing unlike *G·*.
  c 262–23 and conquering all that is unlike *G·*.

God

unlikeness of
r 470–14   the unlikeness of *G·*, is unreal.

unsustained by
f 212–18   undirected and unsustained by *G·*.

unto
a 20– 2   unto *G·* the things that — *Matt.* 22 : 21.
g 540–18   unto *G·* the things that — *Matt.* 22 : 21.

verities of
a 28– 5   and taught the unseen verities of *G·*,

voice of
f 226– 5   voice of *G·* in behalf of the African slave
b 321–26   became to him the voice of *G·*,

wait on
b 323–10   we pause, — wait on *G·*.

walked with
f 214–14   "walked with *G·*," — *Gen.* 5 : 24.

waymarks of
g 542–24   not to remove the waymarks of *G·*.

we approach
sp 95– 7   We approach *G·*, or Life, in proportion to

what is
r 465– 8   *Question.* — What is *G·*?

whole of
g 517–23   can never reveal the whole of *G·*,

will arrest
an 105–24   *G·* will arrest him.

will bless
pr 13–17   *G·* will bless it, and we shall incur less risk

will heal
pr 12– 3   A mere request that *G·* will heal the sick
r 495– 1   *G·* will heal the sick through man,

will never place
a 31– 2   *G·* will never place it in such hands.

will not punish
o 357– 1   we must admit that *G·* will not punish man for

will of
pr 11–30   habitual desire to know and do the will of *G·*,
gl 597–22   "For this is the will of *G·*." — *I Thess.* 4 : 3.

will overturn
f 223–31   *G·* will overturn, until

will redeem
o 354–21   *G·* will redeem that weakness,

will save us
pr 2–18   A request that *G·* will save us

will smite
p 439–20   *G·* will smite you, O whited walls,

will still guide
t 444– 9   *G·* will still guide them into the right use of

will supply
ap 571–16   Know thyself, and *G·* will supply the wisdom

will sustain
pr 10– 7   *G·* will sustain us under these sorrows.

will turn to
pref x–19   Few invalids will turn to *G·* till all

winds of
f 201–15   Then, when the winds of *G·* blow,

wisdom of
gl 597–21   The might and wisdom of *G·*.

without
r 486–31   "having no hope, and without *G·* — *Eph.* 2 : 12.
g 531–22   or that matter exists without *G·*?

with us
pref xi–16   Immanuel, or "*G·* with us," — *Matt.* 1 : 23.
a 34– 8   Immanuel, or *G· with us*;
s 107– 8   Immanuel, "*G·* with us," — *Matt.* 1 : 23.

Word of
f 231–32   made by Him [the Word of *G·*] ; — *John* 1 : 3.
b 335–11   the Logos, the Æon or Word of *G·*,
g 503–13   Divine Science, the Word of *G·*, saith to the
525–18   all things were made through the Word of *G·*,

worketh with you
a 22–12   to this end *G·* worketh with you.

work of
g 521– 6   All that is made is the work of *G·*,

works
c 263– 8   When mortal man . . . works only as *G·* works,

worship
ap 576–13   no material structure in which to worship *G·*,

worship of
ph 200– 5   the worship of *G·* in Spirit instead of matter,

would reduce
b 335– 5   would reduce *G·* to dependency on matter,

would rob
f 214–23   for mortal illusions would rob *G·*,

yields to
ph 188– 1   only as the mortal, erring mind yields to *G·*,

pref vii–17   Ignorance of *G·* is no longer the stepping-stone
pr 1–12   no loss can occur from trusting *G·* with
2–31   Asking *G·* to *be G·* is a vain repetition.
2–31   *G·* is "the same yesterday, and — *Heb.* 13 : 8.
8–16   If we feel the aspiration, . . . this *G·* accepts ;
9–17   "love the Lord thy *G·* — *Matt.* 22 : 37.
12–16   Prayer to a corporeal *G·* affects the sick like a

God

a 18–14   the divine Principle of Christ is *G·*,
18–15   how can *G·* propitiate Himself?
27–20   doctrine of pantheism, — that *G·*, or Life,
29–16   *G·* is the only author of man.
31–10   He recognized Spirit, *G·*, as the only creator,
31–32   will think that he doeth *G·* service ; — *John* 16 : 2.
36–31   Can *G·* therefore overlook the law of
42– 2   priest and rabbi affirmed *G·* to be
46–17   higher in the understanding of Spirit, *G·*.
49–32   "stricken, smitten of *G·*." — *Isa.* 53 : 4.
50– 8   "My *G·*, why hast Thou forsaken — *Mark* 15 : 34.
50–13   his divine Principle, the *G·* who is Love,
51–17   no more . . . than *G·* could be extinguished.
m 56– *   *What therefore G· hath joined* — *Matt.* 19 : 6.
57–28   unite thought more closely to *G·*,
69–14   to understand that there is but one creator, *G·*,
sp 70– 7   Man is never *G·*,
71– 7   Soul is synonymous with Spirit, *G·*,
72–21   *G·*, good, being ever present, it follows
76– 7   Life will be recognized . . . as *G·*,
78–24   *G·* is not in the medley where matter
81–29   man's immortality depends upon that of *G·*,
89–21   *G·*, is heard when the senses are silent.
91– 6   belief that man is separated from *G·*,
92–27   a belief in something besides *G·*,
93–26   refer only to quality, not to *G·*.
93–27   He is not *G·*, Spirit.
94–21   but one returned to give *G·* thanks,
99– 7   it is *G·* which worketh in you — *Phil.* 2 : 13.
an 103–14   because Mind-science is of *G·*
103–32   Life and being are of *G·*.
s 107– 3   *G·* had been graciously preparing me
107–14   acquaint themselves intelligently with *G·*.
108–22   all real being is in *G·*,
109–17   I knew the Principle . . . to be *G·*,
109–30   whether it be of *G·*, or whether — *John* 7 : 17.
111–12   The Principle of divine metaphysics is *G·* ;
113–18   *G·*, Spirit, being all, nothing is matter.
113–19   Life, *G·*, omnipotent good, deny death, evil,
115–13   *G·* : Divine Principle, Life, Truth, Love,
116–27   *G· is* infinite *Person*, — in the sense of
119–11   other horn of the dilemma and regard *G·* as
119–17   In one sense *G·* is identical with nature,
119–24   it is opposed to the nature of Spirit, *G·*.
120– 5   man coexists with and reflects Soul, *G·*,
124–15   interpreted . . . from its divine Principle, *G·*,
133–24   he made "himself equal with *G·*," — *John* 5 : 18.
133–28   no . . . substance outside of *G·*.
135–19   "Can *G·* furnish a table in the — *Psal.* 78 : 19.
135–20   What cannot *G·* do?
140– 4   That *G·* is a corporeal being, nobody can truly
140–30   would . . . make *G·* in their own human image.
142–28   *G·* being All-in-all, He made medicine ;
142–31   the nature and character of Mind, *G·*.
143– 9   if the sick cannot rely on *G·* for help
148–31   admits *G·* to be the healer of sin but not
149–26   Since *G·*, divine Mind, governs all,
151–20   nothing to do with Life, *G·*,
161– 1   is *G·* the lawgiver?
ph 166–26   only as a last resort, turns to *G·*.
167– 1   Should we implore a corporeal *G·* to heal
177–23   against *G·*, Spirit and Truth.
180–27   with *G·* all things are possible.
181– 1   since Mind, *G·*, is the source
182–30   To admit that . . . is a condition over which *G·*
186–14   it presupposes the absence of *G·*,
191–32   *G·*, sends forth the aroma of Spirit,
192–10   Spirit is not separate from *G·*.
193–27   "It was none other than *G·* and
196–15   beware, not of Rome, Satan, nor of *G·*, but of
f 202–17   with the divine Principle of his being, *G·*,
203– 7   If *G·* were understood instead of being merely
203–15   destroys reliance on aught but *G·*,
203–31   *G·*, divine good, does not kill a man in order to
203–32   *G·* alone is man's life.
203–32   *G·* is at once the centre and
204–24   notion that they can create what *G·* cannot,
205– 1   else *G·* will continue to be hidden
205– 9   error of believing that . . . are creations of *G·*,
205–31   not of Spirit, *G·*, good, but of
206–19   Does *G·* send sickness,
206–21   Is *G·* creating anew what He has already
206–24   nothing is new to *G·*,
206–26   Instead of *G·* sending sickness and death,
207– 8   *G·* is not the creator of an evil mind.
208– 1   error, which affords no proof of *G·*,
208– 7   this seeming power, independent of *G·*,
208–15   absurd to suppose . . . *G·*, produces disease
208–17   John Young . . . writes : "*G·* is the father of
212–22   *G·* alone makes and clothes the lilies
213– 9   *G·*, good, is self-existent and self-expressed,
214–19   finite thoughts of *G·* like the pagan idolater.
215–20   are the suppositional absence of Life, *G·*,
216– 4   What has touched Life, *G·*, to such strange

God

f 218–23   turning in time of need to *G·*,
221–24   "giving *G·* thanks ;"— *see Eph.* 5 : 20.
222–16   consulting the stomach less . . . and *G·* more,
224–32   supposed power, which opposes itself to *G·* ?
227–30   If *G·* had instituted material laws
229– 8   Mind signifies *G·*,— infinity,
229–23   If *G·* causes man to be sick,
230– 9   salvation which comes through *G·*,
230–16   *G·*, good, can no more produce sickness than
231– 4   If *G·* destroys not sin, sickness, and death,
231– 7   What *G·* cannot do, man need not attempt.
231– 8   If *G·* heals not the sick, they are not healed,
231–10   *G·*, Truth, . . . does heal the sick
231–12   If *G·* makes sin, if good produces evil,
231–16   *G·* is not the author of mortal discords.
232– 4   neither make man harmonious nor *G·* lovable.
232– 9   "with *G·* all things are— *Mark* 10 : 27.
238–10   "If *G·* be for us, who can be— *Rom.* 8 : 31.
239– 6   weigh not one jot in the balance of *G·*,
239–18   whom we acknowledge and obey as *G·*.
241–29   signifies that the pure in heart see *G·*
242– 5   "they shall all know Me [*G·*],— *Jer.* 31 : 34.
242–12   no other consciousness of life— than good, *G·*
244–20   If . . . there must be an instant when *G·*
253– 4   saith : . . . all are Mine, for I am *G·*.
253–26   *G·* never requires obedience to a so-called
254–11   When we wait patiently on *G·*
c 255–14   That *G·* is corporeal . . . no man should affirm.
256–16   precise form of *G·* must be of small importance
258–18   no more . . . than we know of *G·*.
259–23   *G·*, Spirit, works spiritually, not materially.
260–14   to discover what *G·* has already done ;
264–18   finding all in *G·*, good,
b 268– *   *I can do no otherwise ; so help me G· !*
269– 9   Human philosophy has made *G·* manlike.
272–29   *G·* is the divine Principle of all
273– 4   physical senses can take no cognizance of *G·*
273–21   *G·* never ordained a material law to annul
273–23   would oppose the supremacy of Spirit, *G·*,
274–26   firm, called matter and mind, *G·* never formed.
275– 4   matter did not originate in *G·*, Spirit,
275– 7   *G·*, Spirit, is All-in-all,
275–11   begin by reckoning *G·* as the divine Principle
275–14   are the Scriptural names for *G·*.
276– 7   all have one Spirit, *G·*,
276–11   is cognizant only of the things of *G·*.
276–17   If *G·* is admitted to be the only Mind
277– 7   As *G·* Himself is good and is Spirit,
279–19   their only idea or intelligence is in *G·*.
280–26   *G·*, the Soul of man and of all existence,
283–20   deem this the manifestation of the one Life, *G·*.
284– 4   If *G·* were limited to man or matter, or if the
284– 5   If *G·* were limited . . . *G·* would be corporeal,
284–21   The physical senses can obtain no proof of *G·*.
284–32   intercommunication is always from *G·* to
285–15   Is *G·* a physical personality ?
285–23   By interpreting *G·* as a corporeal Saviour
285–30   seek to learn, . . . from the divine Principle, *G·*,
286–23   since *G·*, Spirit, is the only cause,
287–11   Did *G·*, Truth, create error ? No !
287–13   *G·* being everywhere and all-inclusive,
298–23   lead up to their divine origin, *G·*,
300– 4   no true appreciation of infinite Principle, *G·*,
300–24   If . . . *G·* would have no representative,
300–25   and matter would be identical with *G·*.
302–21   Soul, or Mind, of the spiritual man is *G·*,
303–25   *G·*, without the image and likeness of Himself,
305–12   Gender also is a quality, not of *G·*, but a
305–14   he reflects the creation of Mind, *G·*,
305–22   deflections of . . . are all unlike Spirit, *G·*.
306– 8   If *G·*, . . . were parted for a moment from
306–19   cannot be separated for an instant from *G·*,
307–13   as much as *G·*, Spirit, who *is* the only Life."
310–10   *G·* is His own infinite Mind, and expresses all.
310–29   Mind is God, and *G·* is not seen by
311– 5   all that Mind, *G·*, is, or hath made,
312–17   without Love, *G·*, immortality cannot appear.
312–21   Mortals believe in a finite personal *G·* ;
313– 7   Therefore *G·*, even thy *G·*, hath— *Heb.* 1 : 9.
319– 9   understanding, sustains man
319–20   Mind controls man and man has no Mind but *G·*.
320–26   "In my flesh shall I see *G·*,"— *Job* 19 : 26.
321–24   *G·* had lessened Moses' fear by this proof in
322–31   by searching find out *G·* ?"— *Job* 11 : 7.
324– 6   for they shall see *G·*."— *Matt.* 5 : 8.
325–18   "hid with Christ in *G·*,"— *Col.* 3 : 3.
330–13   Eye hath neither seen *G·* nor His
330–14   Neither *G·* nor the perfect man can
330–19   *G·* is what the Scriptures declare Him to be,
331– 7   If . . . *G·* would not be reflected but absorbed,
333–27   inseparable from the divine Principle, *G·*.
334– 5   dwells forever in the bosom of the Father, *G·*,
334– 7   Spirit, which is *G·*,
334–31   Spirit being *G·*, there is but one Spirit,

God

b 335– 7   Spirit, *G·*, has created all in and of Himself.
335–26   can produce nothing unlike the eternal . . . *G·*
336–13   He has been forever in the eternal Mind, *G·* ;
336–19   A portion of *G·* could not enter man ;
336–21   else *G·* would be manifestly finite,
336–24   and nothing less can express *G·*.
336–25   *G·*, the divine Principle of man,
337–15   none but the pure in heart can see *G·*,
338–23   the supposed separation of man from *G·*,
339– 8   *G·*, Spirit, alone created all,
339–10   Therefore evil, . . . cannot be the product of *G·*
340–13   all that really exists is in and of *G·*,
340–19   man shall have no other spirit or mind but *G·*,
o 341–10   for they shall see *G·*'"— *Matt.* 5 : 8.
342–17   If . . . Science is not of *G·*, then there is no
345– 5   *G·* cannot be in His unlikeness
347– 6   Nothing really has Life but *G·*,
348–15   Are we . . . imputing too much power to *G·*,
348–18   no faith . . . in any power but *G·*,
349–11   *G·* is not the author of sickness.
356–19   *G·* is as incapable of producing sin, sickness,
356–24   Does *G·* create a material man out of Himself,
357–26   If . . . *G·* is not supreme and infinite.
358– 3   Can a leaden bullet deprive a man of . . . *G·*,
358– 4   If *G·* is at the mercy of matter, then matter is
360–24   mortal man be more just than *G·* ?— *Job* 4 : 17.
361– 2   the Christian believes that Christ is *G·*.
361–12   Jesus Christ is not *G·*, as Jesus himself declared
p 362– *   *health of my countenance and my G·*.— *Psal.* 42:11
366–16   *G·* whom he hath not seen?"— *I John* 4 : 20.
369–19   to know if *G·* were willing that a man should
369–26   psychology, or the Science of Spirit, *G·*,
380–30   to believe that . . . *G·* endows this opposing
381– 1   null and void by the law of Life, *G·*,
384– 6   *G·* never punishes man for doing right,
387–22   supposition . . . that *G·* punishes man for doing
388–15   hypothesis . . . food has power to destroy
            Life, *G·*,
389–18   If *G·* has, . . . instituted laws that food shall
390–22   *G·* is no more the author of sickness than
392– 7   must be cast out to readjust the balance for *G·*
393–13   *G·* has made man capable of this,
394–22   *G·*, against whom mortals should not contend
395–15   Prayers, in which *G·* is not asked to heal
397–21   confidence in *G·* as All,
399–27   *G·*, contains no mortal opinions.
413– 2   *G·*, the only Mind, does not produce pain
414–21   "The Lord He is *G·*— *Deut.* 4 : 35.
421–17   *G·*, Spirit, is all, and that there is none beside
427–22   in ignorance of what *G·* is.
427–22   *G·*, Life, Truth, and Love make man undying.
433–29   to prepare the frightened sense of Life, *G·*,
435– 2   Spirit which is *G·* Himself
435–27   according to the law of Spirit, *G·*.
440–21   Mortal Man has its appeal to Spirit, *G·*,
t 445–14   "hid with Christ in *G·*,"— *Col.* 3 : 3.
450–28   beliefs in . . . intelligence separated from *G·*,
r 465–18   and this one is *G·*, omnipotent, omniscient,
466–28   Science will declare *G·* aright,
467–18   *G·* as not in man but as reflected by man.
469–14   the great truth that *G·*, good, is the *only* Mind,
470–17   *G·*, the Mind of man, never sins
470–19   Has *G·* taken down His own standard,
471– 3   *G·* and all that He creates are perfect
471–21   "Let *G·* be true, but every— *Rom.* 3 : 4.
472–29   until *G·* strips off their disguise
472–30   not true, because they are not of *G·*.
473– 4   Truth, *G·*, is not the father of error.
473–12   and attributes all power to *G·*,
474–18   If . . . *G·* must be their author.
475–19   that which has no separate mind from *G·* ;
475–30   nor can *G·*, by whom man is evolved,
478–16   No, not if *G·* is true and mortal man a liar.
478–27   "But when it pleased *G·*,— *Gal.* 1 : 15.
480– 3   and there is no place where *G·* is not,
480–11   Consciousness, as well as action, . . . is in *G·*,
480–14   Harmonious action proceeds from Spirit, *G·*,
480–18   thus attempting to separate Mind from *G·*.
480–24   *G·* is not its author.
481– 8   never helps mortals to understand Spirit, *G·*.
481–26   If sin is supported, *G·* must uphold it,
482– 7   gained by substituting the word *G·*,
489–20   the medium for sinning against *G·*,
494– 6   *G·*, who needed no help from Jesus' example
g 501– *   *by the name of G· Almighty ;*— *Exod.* 6 : 3.
502–28   The creative Principle . . . is *G·*.
503–28   *G·*, Spirit, dwelling in infinite light and
506–10   *G·*, unites understanding to eternal harmony.
506–18   Spirit, *G·*, gathers unformed thoughts
508– 6   The only intelligence or substance . . . is *G·*,
511– 7   And *G·* set them in the firmament— *Gen.* 1 : 17.
512–30   albeit *G·* is ignorant of the existence of both
514– 5   of which *G·* is the sole creator.

God

g 515–29 Now compare man before the mirror to . . . *G·*.
516–10 Truth in truthfulness, *G·* in goodness,
517–12 not as much . . . for considering *G·* masculine,
517–15 if *G·* is personal, there is but one person,
522– 6 assigns all might and government to *G·*,
523– 5 and finally declares that *G·* knows error
523–25 it is Elohim (*G·*) who creates.
524–27 for *G·* presently curses the ground.
524–29 Is Spirit, *G·*, injected into dust,
525– 1 Does Mind, *G·*, enter matter to become there a
525– 3 animated by the breath of *G·*?
525–29 as devoid of reality as they are of good, *G·*.
526–22 Was evil instituted through *G·*, Love?
527– 1 *G·* could not put Mind into matter nor
527–17 But is it true that *G·*, good, made
528– 3 *G·* has already created man,
528– 7 cannot be . . . in partnership with *G·* ;
528–15 error, credits Truth, *G·*, with inducing
530–14 for *G·* doth know that in the day — *Gen.* 3 : 5.
530–20 saying, . . . I can do what *G·* has not done
531–21 Who dares to say either that *G·* is in matter or
532– 1 Did *G·* at first create one man unaided,
536–11 The illusion of sin is without hope or *G·*.
536–18 starting from matter instead of from *G·*,
539–10 *G·* could never impart an element of evil,
541– 9 Had *G·* more respect for the homage
546– 4 Spirit, *G·*, never germinates, but is
546– 5 If Mind, *G·*, creates error, that error must
546–10 Has *G·* no Science to declare Mind,
551–27 by searching find out *G·*?"— *Job* 11 : 7.
554–16 Error replies, "*G·* made you."
554–25 Jesus never intimated that *G·* made a devil,
555–30 Knowing that *G·* was the Life of man,
557–26 when *G·*, Mind, spake and it was done.
ap 560–25 something new and better of *G·*
573–16 *G·*, the divine Principle of harmony,
575–11 builder and maker of this New Jerusalem is *G·*,
gl 580–14 image and likeness of what *G·* has not created,
582–18 pure consciousness that *G·*, . . . creates man
582–19 *G·* is the only creative power.
583–24 *G·*, who made all that was made
587– 5 definition of
587–19 Goop. *G·* ; Spirit ; omnipotence ;
588–20 I Am. *G·* ; incorporeal and eternal Mind ;
590–19 unless specially coupled with the name *G·*.
591– 4 Spirit, or intelligence, named Elohim, or *G·*.
591–18 the divine Principle, or *G·*,
592–16 Mother. *G·* ; divine and eternal Principle ;
594–20 *G·* ; that only which is perfect,

(*see also* **All, All-in-All, All-loving, All-power, All-
wise, Almighty, Being, Cause, Comforter, creator,
Deity, Ego, Ego-God, Elohim, Esse, Father, Father-
Mother, First Cause, Giver, Godhead, God-power,
God-principle, He, Him, Himself, His, Holy Ghost,
Holy One, Holy Spirit, I, I** AM, **Immanuel,
Justice, King, Life, Life-principle, Light, Logos,
Lord, Love, Maker, Me, Mind, Most High, Mother,
My, One, Person, Principle, Providence, Ruler,
Soul, Spirit, Sun of Righteousness, Supreme
Being, Supreme Lawgiver, Supreme Ruler, Thee,
Thou, Thy, Truth, Us, Wisdom, Wonderful,
Word**)

god

a 103– 3 "the *g·* of this world,"— *II Cor.* 4 : 4.
s 140–31 What is the *g·* of a mortal, but
158– 3 designated Apollo as "the *g·* of medicine."
158– 8 also regarded as . . . "the *g·* of pestilence."
158–13 may correspond with that of its material *g·*,
ph 165– 3 would open man's eyes and make him as a *g·*.
187– 9 attributes to some material *g·* or medicine
g 524– 3 in the Moabitish *g·* Chemosh,
524–11 "a man of war," a tribal *g·*— *Exod.* 15 : 3.
530–21 saying, . . . and have another *g·*.
544–26 man, in this allegory, is neither a lesser *g·* nor
gl 580– 2 the first *g·* of mythology ;
584–22 saith : "I am . . . created by a tribal *g·*

God-bestowed

g 526–19 doctrine . . . evil is as real, hence as *G·*, as

God-created

g 555–12 as if it were as real and *G·* as

God-crowned

b 313– 4 Jesus the *G·* or the divinely royal man,

God-given

ph 165– 4 man's *G·* dominion over the earth.
182–25 denying man's *G·* ability to
f 228–13 his *G·* dominion over the material senses.
p 378–24 Sickness is not a *G·* . . . material power,
381– 2 Ignorant of our *G·* rights,
381–21 will sooner grasp man's *G·* dominion.
387–10 nor . . . trespass upon *G·* powers
393–10 Exercise this *G·* authority.

God-given

r 489–15 can this sense be the *G·* channel to
g 528–24 calling them real and *G·*,
531–14 man will recognize his *G·* dominion

Godhead

c 255–17 true idea of the infinite *G·*.

God-inspired

a 41– 8 The *G·* walk calmly on

Godlike

a 54–29 If that *G·* and glorified man were
ph 200–19 man is . . . upright and *G·*.
f 203–12 the only true spirit is *G·*.
c 262–14 higher views inspire the *G·* man to reach
b 269–10 C. S. makes man *G·*.
333–15 but Christ Jesus better signifies the *G·*.

godliness

a 26–14 the *g·* which animated him.
s 145–21 the mystery which *g·* always presents to
p 413–16 "Cleanliness is next to *g·*,"

God-mission

a 41–24 He fulfilled his *G·*, and then

God-power

s 138– 3 the *G·* which lay behind Peter's confession

God-principle

r 473– 7 The *G·* is omnipresent and omnipotent.

God's

allness
pr 15–18 we must deny sin and plead *G·* allness.
anointed
gl 597– 9 which was ready to . . . crucify *G·* anointed.
appointing
s 131–15 after the manner of *G·* appointing,
b 326– 4 in the way of *G·* appointing,
attributes
b 301– 1 which manifests *G·* attributes and power,
behest
g 533– 2 Had he lost man's rich inheritance and *G·* behest,
being
r 470–24 Man is the expression of *G·* being.
481– 3 *G·* being is infinity, freedom, harmony, and
care
m 66–11 Trials are proofs of *G·* care.
character
f 208–12 the goodness of *G·* character
b 283–22 false belief . . . detracts from *G·* character and
children
m 69– 7 *G·* children already created will be cognized
b 303– 5 Multiplication of *G·* children comes from
t 444–28 Immortals, or *G·* children in divine Science,
r 476–28 speaking of *G·* children, not the children of
command
g 530– 6 the earth, at *G·* command, brings forth
commandments
g 542–25 to advance itself, breaks *G·* commandments.
condemnation
f 232–24 *G·* condemnation of sin, sickness, and
control
s 125– 7 Neither . . . is beyond *G·* control ;
creation
(*see* **creation**)
creative mandate
g 556–19 *G·* creative mandate was,
creatures
g 514–29 All of *G·* creatures, . . . are harmless,
day
g₁ 584– 7 This unfolding is *G·* day,
divine messages
ap 566–29 to the angels, *G·* divine messages,
divine power
b 316–27 prove *G·* divine power by healing the sick,
dominion
g 516–20 reflects *G·* dominion over all the earth.
forgiveness
r 497– 9 We acknowledge *G·* forgiveness of sin in the
fulness
b 336–20 neither could *G·* fulness be reflected by
glory
b 313–10 "the brightness of His [*G·*] glory,— *Heb.* 1 : 3.
government
(*see* **government**)
gracious means
pr 1– 7 *G·* gracious means for accomplishing
healing
s 141–23 they cannot demonstrate *G·* healing power.
idea
b 299–24 Truth never destroys *G·* idea.
o 345–22 incongruity between *G·* idea and poor humanity,
p 406–24 until we arrive at the fulness of *G·* idea,
ap 565–16 *G·* idea will eventually rule all nations

God's

ideas
g 503–16   infinite space is peopled with *G·* ideas,
504–16   The successive appearing of *G·* ideas is
505–28   *G·* ideas reflect the immortal,
511– 4   *G·* ideas "multiply and— *Gen.* 1 : 28.

identities
sp 70–14   The questions are : What are *G·* identities?

image
   (*see* **image**)

infinite ideas
g 511–17   full effulgence of *G·* infinite ideas,

infinite plan
m 69–12   sense of increasing number in *G·* infinite plan.

kingdom
f 202–19   when *G·* kingdom comes on earth ;
b 339–24   *G·* kingdom comes "in earth, as— *Matt.* 6 : 10.

law
   (*see* **law**)

laws
f 236– 7   emolument rather than the dignity of *G·* laws,

light
f 504–12   no place where *G·* light is not seen,

likeness
   (*see* **likeness**)

love
b 326– 8   All nature teaches *G·* love to man,

man
   (*see* **man**)

method
a 40–11   *G·* method of destroying sin.
o 343– 6   Is not finite mind ignorant of *G·* method?

mind
g 525–15   after *G·* mind shaped He him ;

motherhood
ap 562– 6   the spiritual idea of *G·* motherhood.

nature
g 512–14   their natures are allied to *G·* nature ;

omnipotence
a 55–19   when he shall realize *G·* omnipotence

opportunity
c 266–15   "man's extremity is *G·* opportunity."

own image
b 295–12   immortals, created in *G·* own image ;
g 517–22   This ideal is *G·* own image, spiritual and

own likeness
sp 90–24   The admission . . . that man is *G·* own likeness
r 477– 3   the Saviour saw *G·* own likeness,

own way
g 542–19   destroy error in *G·* own way,

pardon
b 291– 4   The suppositions . . . that *G·* pardon is
339– 5   Does not *G·* pardon, destroying any one sin,

perfection
g 522– 7   endows man out of *G·* perfection

power
a 42–15   great demonstrator of *G·* power
an 102–14   but man, reflecting *G·* power, has dominion
o 351– 3   When we lose faith in *G·* power to heal,
t 450–24   heals them both by understanding *G·* power

qualities
gl 597–26   not be confounded with . . . one of *G·* qualities.

reflection
s 126– 6   when man beholds himself *G·* reflection,
r 471–17   Man is, and forever has been, *G·* reflection.
g 527– 4   Man is *G·* reflection, needing no cultivation,

remedy
s 143– 1   Truth is *G·* remedy for error of every kind,

representatives
b 299–12   Angels are *G·* representatives.

requirements
pr 7–14   wholesome perception of *G·* requirements.
t 445– 1   the Scientist must conform to *G·* requirements.

rule
pr 3–10   we have only to avail ourselves of *G·* rule

servant
p 439–26   meanwhile declaring Disease to be *G·* servant

spiritual idea
s 115–15   MAN : *G·* spiritual idea, individual,
b 315–15   *G·* spiritual idea as presented by Christ Jesus.

supremacy
g 521–10   acknowledging now and forever *G·* supremacy,

thoughts
b 286–21   *G·* thoughts are perfect and eternal,
337–25   Eternal things (verities) are *G·* thoughts
gl 581– 4   ANGELS.   *G·* thoughts passing to man ;
583– 2   whose better originals are *G·* thoughts,

unchangeable law
s 135– 8   the Science of *G·* unchangeable law.

universe
b 289–24   *G·* universe is spiritual and immortal.
331–17   Everything in *G·* universe expresses Him.

will
f 202– 4   *G·* will must be universally done.
241– 2   He, who knows *G·* will . . . and obeys

God's

willingness
f 218–18   if you are without faith in *G·* willingness

word
b 332–24   He was appointed to speak *G·* word

work
ph 167–16   What can improve *G·* work?
g 522–29   declares *G·* work to be finished.

wrath
a 23– 6   That *G·* wrath should be vented upon

---

a 20– 3   unto God the things that are *G·*."— *Matt.* 22 : 21
sp 99–29   and to *G·* spiritual, perfect man.
s 117–10   *G·* essential language is spoken of
121–11   glad in *G·* perennial and happy sunshine,
ph 168–18   *G·* spiritual command relating to perfection,
f 249– 5   "male and female" of *G·* creating— *Gen.* 1 : 27.
b 282–29   Whatever indicates . . . *G·* absence, is the
333– 9   Christ expresses *G·* spiritual, eternal nature.
336–31   man is *G·* spiritual offspring.
o 355–28   *G·* immortal keynotes, proved to be such
p 424– 9   the proper sense of *G·* unerring direction
g 515– 6   serpent of *G·* creating is neither subtle nor
522–21   *G·* glowing denunciations of man when not
534– 5   to manifest the deathless man of *G·* creating.
540–18   unto God the things that are *G·*."— *Matt.* 22 : 21
544– 2   a creation so wholly apart from *G·*,
gl 597–28   the movements of *G·* spiritual government,
599– 1   Eternity is *G·* measurement of Soul-filled years

gods

besought the
s 158– 2   pagan priests, who besought the *g·* to heal

false
p 440– 7   before sacrificing mortals to their false *g·*.

Grecian
ph 199–32   When Homer sang of the Grecian *g·*,

heathen
r 485–28   The heathen *g·* of mythology

many
sp 78–26   where spiritism makes many *g·*,
b 280–16   "*g·* many and lords many."— *I Cor.* 8 : 5.
307– 9   It says : "There shall be lords and *g·* many.
335– 1   There are neither spirits many nor *g·* many.
p 388–10   believing in . . . "*g·* many,"— *I Cor.* 8 : 5.
gl 580– 8   "*g·* many and lords many"— *I Cor.* 8 : 5.
591– 2   mythology,— belief in many *g·*,

material
f 237–26   devote themselves . . . to their material *g·*,

no other
a 19–30   "Thou shalt have no other *g·*— *Exod.* 20 : 3.
b 280–19   "Thou shalt have no other *g·*— *Exod.* 20 : 3.
340–15   "Thou shalt have no other *g·*— *Exod.* 20 : 3.
r 467– 4   "Thou shalt have no other *g·*— *Exod.* 20 : 3.
467–13   Having no other *g·*, turning to no other but

other
ph 187– 1   having other *g·* and believing in more than
b 275–28   misleads thought and points to other *g·*,
g 535–12   A belief in other *g·*, other creators,

popular
o 347–23   If C. S. takes away the popular *g·*,

sacrifice to the
gl 595–23   TITHE . . . . A sacrifice to the *g·*.

shall be as
b 280–22   "Ye shall be as *g·*,"— *Gen.* 3 : 5.
307– 5   "Ye shall be as *g·* ;"— *Gen.* 3 : 5.
g 530–16   and ye shall be as *g·*,— *Gen.* 3 : 5.
541–24   "Ye shall be as *g·*."— *Gen.* 3 : 5.
544–21   "Ye shall be as *g·*."— *Gen.* 3 : 5.
gl 587–16   "Ye shall be as *g·*."— *Gen.* 3 : 5.

strange
g 524– 7   went after "strange *g·*."— *Jer.* 5 : 19.

these
g 544–22   these *g·* must be evolved from materiality

sp 93–28   then men would be spirits, *g·*.
an 105–29   "Whom the *g·* would destroy, they first
ph 200– 1   the *g·* became alive in a nation's belief.
b 294–24   represented as divided into intelligent *g·*.
r 466–20   is as improper as the term *g·*.
gl 587– 9   definition of
594–23   supposed intelligences, or *g·* ;

Godward

c 265– 5   Mortals must gravitate *G·*,

goes

pr 2– 5   the desire which *g·* forth hungering after
an 104– 9   "Every great scientific truth *g·* through three
104–13   C. S. *g·* to the bottom of mental action,
122–26   in Science, Life *g·* on unchanged
145– 5   struggle for the recovery of invalids *g·* on,
145–29   warfare between Spirit and the flesh *g·* on.
ph 189–30   *g·* on in an ascending scale by evolution,
f 250–28   Upon this stage of existence *g·* on the dance o
b 268–12   woman *g·* forth to battle with Goliath.
284–31   neither sensation nor report *g·* from

oes

b	300–31	the ray of light which *g·* out from it.
t	447–16	The recuperative action . . . *g·* on naturally.
	462– 9	If the student *g·* away to practise
r	489–11	as consciousness develops, this belief *g·* out,
	491–22	belief *g·* on, whether our eyes are closed or
g	506–13	the dawn of ideas *g·* on,
	556–22	Even so *g·* on the Adam-belief,
ap	562–27	for joy that the birth *g·* on ;

oing

a	21–15	If my friends are *g·* to Europe,
	21–27	He is like a traveller *g·* westward
s	158–28	Matter is *g·* out of medicine ;
b	323–31	or we are listening to it and *g·* up higher.
p	431– 7	sometimes *g·* to sleep immediately after
g	548–15	This is the new birth *g·* on hourly,
gl	587–14	supposititious minds, . . . *g·* in and out

old

a	47–21	greed for *g·* strengthened his ingratitude,
m	66–32	separates the *g·* from the dross
ap	565–22	purifying even the *g·* of human character.

olden

s	121–12	happy sunshine, *g·* with Truth.
t	457–18	no good aspect, either silvern or *g·*.

Golden Rule

a	41–12	cannot forever break the *G· R·* and escape the
t	234–13	on the basis of the *G· R·* ;

Golden Shore

ap	576– 1	to the grand realization of the *G· S·* of Love

Goliath

b	268–13	woman goes forth to battle with *G·*.

one

m	65–32	will become purer when the scum is *g·*.
sp	76– 1	the glad welcome of those who have *g·* before.
	87–24	Do not suppose that any mental concept is *g·*
	87–32	or altogether *g·* from physical sight
s	124– 6	When . . . its foundations are *g·*.
	135–16	when the devil was *g·* out,— *Luke* 11 : 14.
ph	170–31	from which all ills have *g·* forth,
	185– 2	her difficulty in breathing had *g·*,
	190–25	passeth over it, and it is *g·* ;— *Psal.* 103 : 16.
	193–14	said : . . . My suffering is all *g·*."
f	203–20	When the material body has *g·* to ruin,
	212–12	When the nerve is *g·*,
b	305–24	illusion of life that is here to-day and *g·* to-morrow,
p	368–32	the foundation of disease is *g·*,
	377–20	when the belief of the disease had *g·*.
	398–23	the desire for strong drink is *g·*.
	400– 3	once destroyed . . . the fear of disease is *g·*,
	421–19	When the supposed suffering is *g·*
r	476–26	passeth over it, and it is *g·* ;— *Psal.* 103 : 16.

ood

accomplish the

p	394– 8	Knowledge that we can accomplish the *g·*

according to the

gl	584– 6	measures time according to the *g·* that

affection for

b	327– 3	by gaining an affection for *g·*

all

pr	2–10	nor can the infinite do less than bestow all *g·*,
f	232–10	all *g·* is possible to Spirit ;
c	260–13	the possibility of achieving all *g·*,
b	299–14	but guide to the divine Principle of all *g·*,
r	494–14	in every hour, divine Love supplies all *g·*.

all is

g	521– 6	the work of God, and all is *g·*.
ap	577–25	all is *g·*, and nothing can enter that city, which

all that is

gl	594–20	divine Principle ; all that is *g·* ;

already received

pr	3–22	Are we . . . grateful for the *g·* already received?

and beautiful

gl	593– 1	The love of the *g·* and beautiful,

and evil

sp	92–15	the knowledge of *g·* and evil,
an	103–11	in a knowledge of both *g·* and evil,
ph	167–15	If God made man both *g·* and evil,
	186– 9	Spirit and matter, *g·* and evil,
f	211– 4	sickness and health, *g·* and evil,
	216–20	both matter and Spirit, both *g·* and evil.
	220–28	the knowledge of *g·* and evil,"— *Gen.* 2 : 17.
o	269– 4	the supposed coexistence of . . . *g·* and evil
	283–16	They speak of both . . . *g·* and evil as *spirit*.
	287–29	material senses testify to . . . both *g·* and evil.
	307–21	If we regard . . . Mind as both *g·* and evil,
	338– 6	*g·* and evil, both spiritual and material
p	389–25	*g·* and evil, God and Satan.
r	466–10	truth and error, *g·* and evil ;
	481–15	declaring . . . *g·* and evil to be capable of
	481–17	the knowledge of *g·* and evil,"— *Gen.* 2 : 17.
g	526– 2	tree of knowledge of *g·* and evil.— *Gen.* 2 : 9.

and evil

g	527– 8	the knowledge of *g·* and evil,— *Gen.* 2 : 17.
	530–16	as gods, knowing *g·* and evil.— *Gen.* 3 : 5.
	536–31	to know *g·* and evil :— *Gen.* 3 : 22.

and pure

m	63– 6	The beautiful, *g·*, and pure constitute his

another's

g	518–19	seeking his own in another's *g·*.

availability of

f	236–19	availability of *g·* as the remedy for every woe.

capacities for

t	445– 9	Unfold the . . . capacities for *g·* in your pupil.

choose

r	481– 1	How important, then, to choose *g·* as

claims of

ph	167– 8	Our . . . admission of the claims of *g·* or of evil

consecration to

c	262– 2	Consecration to *g·* does not lessen man's

contrary to

b	339– 9	evil, being contrary to *g·*, is unreal,

demands

c	261–32	*G·* demands of man every hour,

demonstrator of

a	49–14	The meek demonstrator of *g·*,

dies not

f	204– 2	It is evil that dies ; *g·* dies not.

disarmed by

b	290–31	until evil is disarmed by *g·*.

discern the

a	22–19	you will discern the *g·* you have done,

divine

f	203–31	God, divine *g·*, does not kill a man

doing

sp	79–31	It dissipates fatigue in doing *g·*.
f	202–32	in the act of doing *g·*,
	203– 3	and check the reward for doing *g·*.
p	387–20	supposition . . . God punishes man for doing *g·*,
	432–16	The Judge asks if by doing *g·* to his neighbor,

eternal

f	213–14	attraction towards infinite and eternal *g·*
b	340–19	have no other spirit or mind but God, eternal *g·*,
ap	561– 3	which works out the ends of eternal *g·*

evil and

   (see **evil**)

gain

f	254– 4	who gain *g·* rapidly and hold their position,

God is

   (see **God**)

God, or

c	261–23	you may learn the meaning of God, or *g·*,
p	380–29	opposite to God, or *g·*,
t	450–22	understanding . . . the allness of God, or *g·*,
r	469–26	admitting that God, or *g·*, is omnipresent
	470– 2	with one Mind and that God, or *g·*,
	470–13	If God, or *g·*, is real, then evil, . . . is unreal.
	480–20	God, or *g·*, never made man capable of sin.
g	533–11	directly or indirectly to God, or *g·*,
gl	592– 4	and therefore the opposite of God, or *g·* ;

grasp on

b	327–10	until his grasp on *g·* grows stronger.

heavenly

c	265–25	The aspiration after heavenly *g·* comes

highest human

ph	182– 9	capable of producing the highest human *g·*

idea of

b	325– 3	He who has the true idea of *g·*
	327–26	the man . . . who has not the true idea of *g·*?
g	546–14	represents error as starting from an idea of *g·*

immortality of

sp	81–30	consequence of the immortality of *g·*,
f	215–28	the superiority and immortality of *g·*,

individual

sp	72–23	In Science, individual *g·* derived from God,

infinite

sp	93–18	not the offspring of infinite *g·*.

in the name of

t	453–23	yet serves evil in the name of *g·*.
ap	563–28	but doing this in the name of *g·*.

invisible

sp	78–31	the invisible *g·* dwelling in eternal Science.

is infinite

p	399– 2	and therefore *g·* is infinite,

is Mind

s	113–17	God is good. *G·* is Mind.

is natural

s	128– 2	*G·* is natural and primitive.

is self-existent

f	213– 9	God, *g·*, is self-existent and self-expressed,

is the term

b	286–16	In the Saxon . . . *g·* is the term for God.

knowledge of

g	526–22	as the knowledge of *g·*.

maximum of

an	103–16	The maximum of *g·* is the infinite God

good

must dominate
t 446–15   G· must dominate in the thoughts of the healer,
natural
s 119–21   God is natural *g*·, and is represented only by
g 501–15   which subserve the end of natural *g*·,
no
s 113–32   no matter in good, and no *g*· in matter.
   144– 2   since no *g*· can come of it?
b 275–19   no *g*· is, but the good God bestows.
no matter in
s 113–32   no matter in *g*·, and no good in matter.
of one's neighbor
p 440–16   than that it is for the *g*· of one's neighbor?
omnipotent
s 113–19   Life, God, omnipotent *g*·, deny death,
opposite of
sp 72–22   evil, the suppositional opposite of *g*·,
r 480–21   It is the opposite of *g*· — that is, evil
gl 579–16   evil ; the opposite of *g*·,
or evil
ph 171–32   the cognizance of *g*· or evil,
f 205–16   error . . . matter can be intelligent for *g*· or evil
   240–18   Mortals move onward towards *g*· or evil
b 340– 1   their imaginary power for *g*· or evil,
over evil
p 406–23   the supremacy of . . . *g*· over evil,
power of
ap 570–31   the power of *g*· resident in divine Mind,
purposes of
an 103–15   working out the purposes of *g*· only.
reality of
f 205–21   the supremacy and reality of *g*·,
b 269– 7   unfold the unity and the reality of *g*·,
r 480–32   evil would vanish before the reality of *g*·.
g 527–19   Has evil the reality of *g*·?
reflections of
b 280– 6   From Love . . . only reflections of *g*· can come.
represents
b 282– 9   The sphere represents *g*·,
resides in the
g 546–18   resides in the *g*· this system accomplishes,
result in
p 435– 9   an act which should result in *g*· to himself
sense of
b 311–13   Evil is destroyed by the sense of *g*·.
spiritual
m 56– 6   for the advancement of spiritual *g*·.
f 243– 3   and demonstration of spiritual *g*·
g 505–21   Spiritual sense is the discernment of spiritual *g*·.
standard of
g 539– 8   What can be the standard of *g*·, of Spirit,
substance of
b 301–19   man . . . in reality has, only the substance of *g*·,
supremacy of
s 130–28   and doubts the supremacy of *g*·,
supreme
p 496–10   living the life that approaches the supreme *g*·?
Truth and
s 114– 6   the divine Mind, or Truth and *g*·.
g 529–27   has neither origin nor support in Truth and *g*·.
universal
sp 76– 8   will be recognized . . . as God, universal *g*· ;
unlike
p 393–13   to resist all that is unlike *g*·.
unlikeness of
f 204–14   evil, is the unlikeness of *g*·.
voicing
b 332–10   Christ is the true idea voicing *g*·,
your
f 254–29   Your *g*· will be evil spoken of.
your influence for
ph 192–22   Your influence for *g*· depends upon the

————

a 20– 1   for there is one Life, — even God, *g*·.
   42–27   true man is governed by God — by *g*·,
   52–21   the mighty actuality of all-inclusive God, *g*·.
m 60– 7   The beautiful in character is also the *g*·,
   61– 4   The *g*· in human affections must
   68–21   it may have caused the *g*· to ponder
sp 72–21   God, *g*·, being ever present, it follows
   76– 9   belief that . . . was ever in a finite form, or *g*·
       in evil,
   77– 2   "I cannot turn at once from *g*· to evil."
   81–29   man's immortality depends upon that of God, *g*·,
   85– 8   enabling one to do *g*·, but not evil.
   93–13   G· never causes evil.
   93–15   G· does not create a mind susceptible of
   95–13   cannot injure others, and must do them *g*·.
an 103–22   belief . . . that evil is as real as *g*·
s 113–20   Disease, sin, evil, death, deny *g*·,
   130–13   *g*· and its sweet concords have all-power.
   130–32   imagine it to be ever-present and *g*· absent?
   134–26   because it is the immutable law of God, *g*·.
ph 167–21   no more . . . than *g*· can coincide with evil.

good

ph 169–24   whatever *g*· they may seem to receive from
   176–13   "sermons in stones, and *g*· in everything."
   186–18   It says : "I am a real entity, overmastering *g*·.
   186–20   It can never destroy one iota of *g*·,
   186–21   Every attempt . . . to destroy *g*· is a failure,
   186–24   If evil is as real as *g*·, evil is also as immortal
   192–23   The *g*· you do and embody gives you
f 201–12   superabundance of being is on the side of God, *g*·
   204–12   The first power is admitted to be *g*·,
   204–32   The error, which says . . . *g*· is in evil,
   205–31   not of Spirit, God, *g*·, but of
   207–11   Evil is not supreme ; *g*· is not helpless ;
   207–16   nor is evil mightier than *g*·.
   216–23   evil would appear to be the master of *g*·,
   230–15   G· is not, cannot be, the author of
   230–17   God, *g*·, can no more produce sickness
   231–12   If God makes sin, if *g*· produces evil,
   234– 9   become more familiar with *g*· than with evil,
   242–12   It is to know no other reality . . . than *g*·
   244–27   He does not pass . . . from evil to *g*·,
   244–27   He does not pass . . . from *g*· to evil.
c 261– 5   the enduring, the *g*·, and the true,
   261–31   should forget our bodies in remembering *g*·
   263–13   producing evil when he would create *g*·,
   263–18   "The *g*· that I would, I do not : — *Rom. 7 : 19*
   264–18   finding all in God, *g*·, and needing no other
   275–19   no good is, but the *g*· God bestows.
b 277– 7   G· cannot result in evil.
   277–21   asserts . . . that *g*· is the origin of evil.
   278– 8   in Truth there is no error, and in *g*· no evil.
   285– 1   cannot be cognizant of *g*· or of evil,
   288–22   Life is God, *g*·, and not evil ;
   293–30   universal harmony, the entireness of God, *g*·,
   304–12   *g*· can never produce evil ;
   309–18   and forget that Life is God, *g*·,
   309–18   *g*· is not in elements which are not spiritual,
   310–27   if Spirit should lose Life as God, *g*·, then
   323– 5   possess no other consciousness but *g*·.
   323–16   *g*· is not understood until demonstrated.
   327–19   hastening to learn that Life is God, *g*·,
   336– 4   G· never enters into evil,
   340–23   One infinite God, *g*·, unifies men and nations
o 343–16   impossibility of *g*· producing evil ;
   348–18   or in any power but God, *g*·.
   356–25   Does evil proceed from *g*·?
p 368–11   fatal beliefs . . . that evil is equal in power to *g*·
   387–19   That man . . . who does the most *g*·.
   404–25   ability to master evil and to love *g*·.
   405–20   demonstrates the government of God, *g*·,
   414–22   "The Lord He is God [*g*·] ; — *Deut. 4 : 35.*
   415– 4   Mind in every case is the eternal God, *g*·.
t 444– 5   "All things work together for *g*· — *Rom. 8 : 28*
   447– 8   ignorant attempts to do *g*·
   448–15   or upon the *g*· you know and *do* not.
   450–19   evil will boast itself above *g*·.
r 469–14   truth that God, *g*·, is the *only* Mind,
   470–17   How can *g*· lapse into evil,
   490–11   since all power belongs to God, *g*·.
g 504– 2   God, . . . is never reflected by aught but the *g*·
   525–29   as devoid of reality as they are of *g*·,
   527–18   But is it true that God, *g*·, made
   532–24   Is Mind capable . . . of evil as well as of *g*·,
   538–17   false claims that misrepresent God, *g*·.
   555–19   error would seek to unite . . . *g*· with evil,
ap 571–16   At all times . . . . overcome evil with *g*·.
gl 579–13   the purpose of Love to create truth in *g*·,
   580– 5   that which is not the image and likeness of *g*·
   587–19   definition of
   594– 6   claim that there is an opposite of Spirit, or *g*·
   594–11   claim that . . . was as real and eternal as God, *g*·

good (adj., adv.)

pref viii–10   and physics teach that both . . . are real and *g*·
   viii–11   the fact is that Spirit is *g*· and real,
   x–24   Its purpose is *g*·, and its practice is
pr 4–12   The habitual struggle to be always *g*·
   9– 4   the falsehood which does no one any *g*·.
   10– 6   If *g*· enough to profit by Jesus' cup
a 19–18   every *g*· thought and deed, will help us
   21– 3   "I have fought a *g*· fight — *II Tim. 4 : 7.*
   28– 9   While respecting all that is *g*· in the Church
   35–32   *g*· man's heaven would be a hell to the sinner
   40–20   If a career so great and *g*· as that of Jesus
   44– 3   *g*· and faithful servant," — *Matt. 25 : 23.*
m 66–26   the other pre-eminently needs *g*· company.
sp 70–11   that there are *g*· and evil spirits, is a mistake
   83– 6   the incredible *g*· and evil elements
   99– 8   to do of His *g*· pleasure" — *Phil. 2 : 13.*
s 110– 7   is pronounced by His wisdom *g*·,
   120–11   indicate that he is in *g*· health?
   131–22   for so it seemed *g*· in Thy sight." — *Luke 10 : 21*
   155–31   If drugs are *g*· things, it is safe to say
   156– 3   and what made them *g*· or bad
   157–17   If drugs are . . . *g*·, then drugs cannot
       poisonous.

good (adj., adv.)

ph	167–32	Substituting *g·* words for a *g·* life,
	169–31	*g·* that a poisonous drug seems to do is evil,
	181–22	are satisfied with *g·* words instead of effects,
	189–13	sins of others should not make *g·* men suffer.
f	206–24	His work was *finished*, . . . and that it was *g·*.
	210–28	appears . . . to make *g·* its claim.
	229–13	declaring Him *g·* in one instance and
	229–23	If God causes man to be sick, sickness must be *g·*,
	229–25	all that He makes is *g·* and will stand forever.
	236–27	that will make them happy and *g·*.
	237–11	theories of parents often choke the *g·* seed
	237–13	snatches away the *g·* seed before it has
	246–21	and limiting all that is *g·* and beautiful,
	252–24	where the *g·* purpose waits!
c	266– 1	where the creations of God are *g·*,
b	269–19	this advantage . . . they are *g·* and eternal.
	270–32	the *g·* soil wherein the seed of Truth
	272– 6	"honest and *g·* heart" — *Luke* 8 : 15.
	277– 8	As God Himself is *g·*
	286–18	all that He made to be *g·*, like Himself,
	286–18	like Himself, — *g·* in Principle and in idea.
	286–20	Therefore the spiritual universe is *g·*,
	294–26	recognizable only in what is *g·* and true.
	309–12	a soldier of God, who had fought a *g·* fight.
	311– 5	all that Mind, God, is, or hath made, is *g·*,
	330–22	Mind is not both *g·* and bad,
	332–28	incarnate in the *g·* and pure Christ Jesus.
	339– 9	God, . . . created all, and called it *g·*.
o	342–27	to disown the Christliness of *g·* works,
	352–31	To accomplish a *g·* result, it is certainly
	356–28	Would any one call it wise and *g·* to
	357–16	deny that God made man evil and made evil *g·*
p	376–14	more . . . immortality in one *g·* motive and act
	383– 5	One says: "I take *g·* care of my body."
	397–19	you will find the ensuing *g·* effects to be
	404–19	every tree that brings not forth *g·* fruit.
	405–18	The *g·* man finally can overcome his fear of
	413– 1	and cannot transmit *g·* or evil intelligence
	413–10	*g·* or bad effects on the health of children.
	431–31	testifies: . . . I am robbed of my *g·* looks.
	435–15	this was a *g·* deed.
	436–12	Laying down his life for a *g·* deed,
	441– 8	to give heavy bonds for *g·* behavior.
	442–15	one "that bringeth *g·* tidings." — *Isa.* 52 : 7.
	442–27	it is your Father's *g·* pleasure — *Luke* 12 : 32.
t	449–24	a *g·* detective of individual character.
	457–17	to mental malpractice, . . . there is no *g·* aspect,
	458– 4	one *g·* and the other evil,
	459–26, 27	The tree must be *g·*, which produces *g·* fruit.
	464–20	hold fast that which is *g·*." — *I Thess.* 5 : 21.
r	472–25	That which He creates is *g·*,
	482– 5	hypothesis that soul is both an evil and a *g·*
	489–32	sometimes *g·* and sometimes bad.
	492–13	statement proved to be *g·* must be
g	503–26	saw the light, that it was *g·*: — *Gen.* 1 : 4.
	506–24	God saw that it was *g·*. — *Gen.* 1 : 10.
	508–12	God saw that it was *g·*. — *Gen.* 1 : 12.
	511–10	God saw that it was *g·*. — *Gen.* 1 : 18.
	512– 7	God saw that it was *g·*. — *Gen.* 1 : 21.
	513–25	God saw that it was *g·*. — *Gen.* 1 : 25.
	515– 3	God saw that it was *g·*." — *Gen.* 1 : 25.
	518–25	and, behold, it was very *g·*. — *Gen.* 1 : 31.
	525–20	Everything *g·* or worthy, God made.
	525–24	"and, behold, it was very *g·*." — *Gen.* 1 : 31.
	526– 1	pleasant to the sight, and *g·* for food; — *Gen.* 2 : 9.
	526–16	God pronounced *g·* all that He created,
	537–13	represented as spiritual, entire, and *g·*.
gl	583–21	divine Principle of all that is real and *g·*;
fr	600–*	*being fruitful in every g· work*, — *Col.* 1 : 10.
		(see also **deeds**)

Good, Dr. Mason

| *s* | 163–13 | Dr. Mason *G·*, a learned Professor in London, |

goodness

affection and
| *a* | 24–28 | lay in the practical affection and *g·* |

and beauty
| *s* | 121–13 | So we have *g·* and beauty to gladden the |

and blessedness
| *pr* | 10–25 | source and means of all *g·* and blessedness, |

and mercy
| *ap* | 578–16 | *g·* and mercy shall follow me — *Psal.* 23 : 6. |

and power
| *g* | 515–23 | reflecting *g·* and power. |

and purity
| *p* | 364– 1 | a man of undoubted *g·* and purity, |

and spirituality
| *b* | 277– 8 | *g·* and spirituality must be immortal. |
| | 277–10 | If *g·* and spirituality are real, |

and virtue
| *m* | 57–13 | the better claims of intellect, *g·*, and virtue. |

another's
| *a* | 21–7 | another's *g·*, suffering, and triumph, |

attains
| *pr* | 2–16 | *G·* attains the demonstration of Truth. |

goodness

beauty and
sp	76–23	possessing unlimited divine beauty and *g·*
b	304– 4	which hide spiritual beauty and *g·*.
g	503–22	immortal forms of beauty and *g·*.

charms of His
| *f* | 247–23 | and reflects the charms of His *g·* |

culture and
| *sp* | 95–12 | reaches this point of moral culture and *g·* |

divine
| *m* | 66–16 | unfolds new views of divine *g·* and love. |

goal of
| *f* | 233–14 | until the goal of *g·* is . . . won. |

great
| *a* | 47–18 | He knew that the great *g·* of that Master |

happiness and
| *f* | 244– 9 | happiness and *g·* would have no |

idea of
| *s* | 119–22 | God . . . is represented only by the idea of *g·*; |

immortality, and
| *g* | 518–20 | Love giveth . . . immortality, and *g·*, |

inspiration of
| *gl* | 581– 5 | inspiration of *g·*, purity, and |

Life and
| *f* | 246–28 | Life and *g·* are immortal. |

of God's character
| *f* | 208–12 | not in accordance with the *g·* of God's character |

omnipotent in
| *p* | 367–31 | Because Truth is omnipotent in *g·*, |

Principle of
| *s* | 147–31 | Science alone reveals the divine Principle of *g.* |

Principle of all
| *pr* | 3– 8 | Shall we ask the divine Principle of all *g·* to |

towards
| *f* | 213–11 | Every step towards *g·* is a departure from |

universal
| *b* | 329– 4 | glow in all the grandeur of universal *g·*. |

without
| *b* | 328– 4 | suppose that they can live without *g·*, |

---

pr	4–24	*g·* will "be evil spoken of," — *Rom.* 14 : 16.
a	53–24	the lifelong sacrifice which *g·* makes for
an	106–28	longsuffering, gentleness, *g·*, — *Gal.* 5 : 22.
s	147–29	A pure affection takes form in *g·*,
ph	196–19	Sin makes its own hell, and *g·* its own heaven.
f	230–17	no more . . . than *g·* can cause evil
	248–29	Let unselfishness, *g·*, mercy,
c	260–15	distrust of one's ability to gain the *g·*
r	465–15	justice, mercy, wisdom, *g·*,
g	516–11	Life is reflected in existence, . . . God in *g·*,

goods

p	399–30	and spoil his *g·*, — *Matt.* 12 : 29.
	400– 7	of his *g·*, — namely, of sin and disease.
	438–24	and smuggles Error's *g·* into market
	439– 1	introducing their *g·* into the market.

good-will

s	150– 8	"on earth peace, *g·* toward men." — *Luke* 2 : 14.
f	226–17	"on earth peace, *g·* toward men." — *Luke* 2 : 14.
p	407–16	even into spiritual power and *g·* to man.

gorgeousness

| *f* | 252–25 | and says: . . . I am enthroned in the *g·* of matter. |

Gospel

John's
| *gl* | 598– 2 | in John's *G·*, the third chapter, |

Luke's
| *p* | 362– 1 | in the seventh chapter of Luke's *G·* |

Mark's
| *s* | 117–11 | in the last chapter of Mark's *G·* |
| *b* | 272–12 | referred to in the last chapter of Mark's *G·*. |

---

pref	xi–22	called the author to proclaim His *G·*
	525–17	In the *G·* of John, it is declared that
ap	561–30	In the first chapter of the Fourth *G·*

gospel

is preached
| *a* | 27– 6 | to the poor the *g·* is preached." — *Luke* 7 : 22. |

law and
| *p* | 441–30 | a verdict contrary to law and *g·*. |

of healing
| *a* | 55– 9 | the *g·* of healing is again preached |

of Love
| *ap* | 577– 4 | His universal family, held in the *g·* of Love. |

preaches the
| *a* | 33–25 | and preaches the *g·* to the poor, |

preaching the
| *a* | 31– 1 | he was found preaching the *g·* to the poor, |
| *o* | 347–16 | preaching the *g·* to the poor, |

preach the
a	18–*	but to preach the *g·*. — *I Cor.* 1 : 17.
	37–30	preach the *g·* to every — *Mark* 16 : 15.
s	138–28	preach the *g·* to every — *Mark* 16 : 15.

gospel
preach the
- o 342–11   and preach the g·,"— *Mark* 16: 15.
- p 418–28   "Preach the g· to every— *Mark* 16: 15.

- s 107– *   *the g· which was preached of me*— *Gal.* 1: 11.
- 132– 8   the poor have the g· preached— *Matt.* 11: 5.
- 150– 7   the coming anew of the g· of
- ph 176– 9   gave the g· a chance to be seen
- b 309–23   and led to deny . . . even as the g· teaches.
- 337–15   can see God, as the g· teaches.
- o 349– 6   We have the g·, however,
- *government* 592–13   Moses. . . . the proof that, without the g·,

gospel-healing
- o 343–31   to press along the line of g·,

Gospels
- sp 79–21   so far as can be learned from the G·,

gossamer
- p 403–20   the g· web of mortal illusion.

gossip
- f 238–28   no time for g· about false law or testimony.

gotten
- r 479– 5   "I have g· a man from the Lord"— *Gen.* 4: 1.
- g 538–24   I have g· a man from the Lord— *Gen.* 4: 1.
- 538–30   "I have g· a man from the Lord,"— *Gen.* 4: 1.

govern
- s 151–31   mortal mind claims to g· every organ
- 154–18   and her own fears g· her child more than
- ph 175–25   Beaumont's . . . did not g· the digestion.
- f 206– 7   It is the province of spiritual sense to g· man.
- 227–30   If God had instituted material laws to g· man,
- 251–15   learn how mankind g· the body,
- 251–17   learn whether they g· the body through a
- 251–19   or g· it from the higher understanding
- p 380–32   Every law of matter . . . supposed to g· man,
- 393–11   and g· its feeling and action.
- 402–22   we rarely remember that we g· our own bodies.
- 409–15   prevents . . . knowing how to g· their bodies.
- 414–12   guide and g· mortal mind
- r 490– 6   Hence it cannot g· man aright.
- 494– 1   and to g· man's entire action?

governed
- pr 14–10   to be absolutely g· by divine Love,
- a 42–26   in C. S. the true man is g· by God
- m 62–27   The higher nature of man is not g· by the lower ;
- sp 83–17   belief that . . . man, is g· in general by
- an 106–10   g· by his Maker, divine Truth and Love.
- s 125–15   g· by Soul, not by material sense.
- 131– 4   our lives must be g· by reality
- 141–16   the Christ-spirit which g· the corporeal Jesus.
- 146– 4   our systems of religion are g· more or less by
- 150–26   The doctrine that man's harmony is g· by
- 151–21   Every function of the real man is g· by the
- 155–14   such a belief is g· by the majority.
- 160–29   only to learn . . . that muscle is not so g·?
- ph 180–25   When man is g· by God, the ever-present
- 184–17   Whatever is g· by a false belief is discordant
- 187–21   is g· by this so-called mind, not by matter.
- 187–23   man in Science is g· by this Mind.
- 195–15   an idea g· by its Principle,
- f 206–13   prayer, g· by Science instead of the senses,
- 215–12   Whatever is g· by God, is never . . . deprived of
- 216–17   If man is g· by the law of divine Mind,
- 226–23   belief that the body g· them, rather than Mind.
- 231–30   Man, g· by his Maker, having no other Mind,
- 240–12   suppose Mind to be g· by matter
- 245–26   for the mental state g· the physical.
- 246–24   Man, g· by immortal Mind, is always
- c 257–10   it is the belief in . . . soul g· by the body
- b 273–18   Man is harmonious when g· by Soul.
- 274–27   g· by the unerring and eternal Mind,
- 302–22   this real man is g· by Soul instead of sense,
- 304–14   The perfect man— g· by God,
- 318–28   The governor is not subjected to the g·.
- 318–29   man is g· by God, divine Principle,
- p 376–21   a mental concept and g· by mortal mind,
- 409–20   The animate should be g· by God alone.
- r 480–16   Consciousness, as well as action, is g· by
- 495– 2   whenever man is g· by God.
- g 536–14   if man should be g· by corporeality
- 536–18   mortal man would be g· by himself.
- 546–11   while matter is g· by
- gl 583– 7   who, . . . are g· by divine Science ;
- 588–15   though they are g· by one Principle.

governing
- sp 71– 8   God, the creative, g·, infinite Principle
- 81–22   the producing, g·, divine Principle lives on,
- s 158–30   and mortal mind, . . . is g· the pellet.
- ph 174– 1   less faith . . . in a supreme g· intelligence.
- f 209– 5   Mind, . . . g· them all, is the central sun
- 231–15   no antagonistic powers . . . g· man through
- b 282–25   mortal thought, always g· itself erroneously.

governing
- b 303– 5   the Principle g· the reflection.
- 308– 5   God is the only Mind g· man,
- p 370– 8   proves that fear is g· the body.
- 377–21   Remove the leading error or g· fear
- 427–24   Immortal Mind, g· all, must be acknowledged
- g 510–30   g· the universe, including man,
- gl 588–12   Mind, g· all existence ;
- 595– 1   Sun. The symbol of Soul g· man,

Government
- p 442– 3   Our statute is spiritual, our G· is divine.

government
by divine Principle
- gl 587–25   reign of Spirit ; g· by divine Principle ;

divine
- f 225– 3   opposed to the divine g·.

false
- sp 94–12   owe their false g· to the misconceptions of

French
- an 100–12   In 1784, the French g· ordered the

God's
- a 36– 8   not in accordance with God's g·,
- m 62–25   but let no mortal interfere with God's g·
- sp 78–27   claimed to be the agents of God's g·.
- s 125–17   Reflecting God's g·, man is self-governed.
- p 393–17   in Science man reflects God's g·.

His
- s 128– 5   His g· of the universe, inclusive of man.
- f 231–24   To fear sin is . . . to doubt His g·
- r 472–10   do not originate in God nor belong to His g·.

might and
- g 522– 6   first record assigns all might and g· to God,

of God
- c 258–29   man, under the g· of God in eternal Science,
- p 405–20   demonstrates the g· of God,

of the body
- ph 167–26   scientific g· of the body must be
- 182–18   Mind's g· of the body must supersede the
- t 462–30   It urges the g· of the body

of the universe
- s 121–32   in the everlasting g· of the universe.
- 128– 5   His g· of the universe, inclusive of man.
- g 539–15   resigned to matter the g· of the universe?

reins of
- p 422–29   Not holding the reins of g· in his own hands,

spiritual
- gl 597–28   the movements of God's spiritual g·,

- an 100–16   reported to the g· as follows :
- c 265– 1   and its g· is divine Science.
- p 378–23   not . . . take the g· into its own hands.
- 438–25   without the inspection of Soul's g· officers.

governments
- p 378–32   usually find displayed in human g·.

Governor
- p 432–11   I am Mortality, G· of the Province of Body,

governor
- b 318–28   The g· is not subjected to the governed.
- r 480–11   origin and g· of all that Science reveals.

Governor Mortality
- p 432–18   and G· M· replies in the affirmative.

governs
- pr 6– 3   Divine Love corrects and g· man.
- a 39–27   and g· the universe harmoniously.
- an 102– 2   God g· all that is real, harmonious, and
- 102–13   since God g· the universe ;
- s 111–28   Mind g· the body, not partially but wholly.
- 149–26   Mind, g· all, not partially but supremely,
- 154–19   more than the child's mind g· itself,
- 160–28   to learn how mortal mind g· muscle,
- 162–12   Mind g· the body, . . . in every instance.
- ph 180–14   Ignorant that the human mind g· the body,
- 188– 8   but afterwards it g· the so-called man.
- f 209– 4   in proportion as ignorance, . . . g· mortals.
- 219–10   No more can we say . . . that matter g·,
- 219–20   Science . . . g· harmoniously.
- 219–24   and yet misunderstand the science that g· it.
- 222–12   availed himself of the fact that Mind g·
- 224– 6   the Science which g· these changes,
- 231–21   God made you superior to it and g· man,
- b 270–11   intelligence, . . . g· the universe ;
- 286–14   divine Principle, Love, creates and g· all
- 295– 5   God creates and g· the universe,
- 304–22   The science of music g· tones.
- 316–21   Spirit creates, constitutes, and g·.
- 324– 9   the body will reflect what g· it,
- p 375–21   a belief that matter g· mortals,
- 377– 3   convince him . . . that thought g· this liability.
- 393–17   in your understanding that the divine Mind g·,
- 412– 2   great fact that God lovingly g· all,
- 418–22   this simple rule of Truth, which g· all reality.
- 420– 4   Spirit not matter, g· man.

governs

p 422–31   he believes that . . . matter— g· the case.
r 496– 5   Mind is reflected by man and g· the entire
g 507–17   Life, . . . g· the multiplication of the
507–24   Infinite Mind creates and g· all,
508– 7   and Love which g· all.
532– 4   No ! God makes and g· all.
539–29   makes and g· man and the universe.

grace

pr   4– 4   prayer of fervent desire for growth in g·,
17– 5   Give us g· for to-day ;
a   27–26   They fell away from g· because they
m   67–23   G· and Truth are potent beyond all other
s 108– 3   "the gift of the g· of God— Eph. 3 : 7.
118–16   the invisible and infinite power and g·.
134–17   doctrines of Christ or the miracles of g·
f 220–25   never to try dietetics for growth in g·,
247–19   Comeliness and g· are independent of matter.
c 263–13   forming deformity when he would outline g·
b 333–22   has come with some measure of power and g·
r 478–29   called me by His g·,— Gal. 1 : 15.
494–15   miracle of g· is no miracle to Love.

graces

p 429– 4   as well as by other g· of Spirit.

gracious

pr   1– 7   God's g· means for accomplishing

graciously

s 107– 4   God had been g· preparing me

gradation

g 511–26   metaphorically present the g· of

gradations

g 551–13   Evolution describes the g· of human belief,

grade

p 363– 7   as was customary with women of her g·.

grades

ph 172– 7   Materialism g· the human species as
g 551–12   through all the lower g· of existence.

gradually

sp   77–25   The departed would g· rise above ignorance
s 109–23   The revelation of Truth . . . came to me g·
111–31   this system has g· gained ground,
p 380–25   G· this evidence will gather momentum
t 460–30   As former beliefs were g· expelled
ap 576–30   Yet the word g· approaches a higher meaning.

grafting

f 201–20   G· holiness upon unholiness,

Graham

ph 170– 8   Did Jesus understand . . . less than G· or Cutter?
f 221– 2   adopted the G· system to cure dyspepsia.

grain

s 130–21   and to inculcate a g· of faith in God,
t 449– 3   A g· of C. S. does wonders for mortals,

grammars

g 508–20   g· always recognize a neuter gender,

grand

sp   75–31   from earth's sleep to the g· verities of Life,
s 116–13   Works on metaphysics leave the g· point
143–26   Mind is the g· creator, and there can be
164–10   generally . . . are g· men and women,
ph 200– 6   illustrated the g· human capacities of being
f 240– 7   Suns and planets teach g· lessons.
240–11   In the order of Science, . . . all is one g· concord.
244– 4   Divine Science reveals these g· facts.
246–25   Man, . . . is always beautiful and g·.
248–28   carve them out in g· and noble lives.
b 328–12   reveals the g· realities of His allness.
o 341– 7   grow in beauty . . . from one g· root,
354–29   I rejoice in the apprehension of this g· verity.
p 384–15   prove to himself, . . . the g· verities of C. S.
t 448–23   accomplish the g· results of Truth and Love,
460–25   she had to impart, while teaching its g· facts,
r 471– 8   senses, afford no indication of the g· facts
490– 1   the g· truths of C. S. dispute this error.
g 511–25   mountains stand for solid and g· ideas.
514–30   A realization of this g· verity was a source of
518–16   The rich in spirit help the poor in one g·
ap 560–13   the g· necessity of existence is to gain the
575–32   g· realization of the Golden Shore of Love

grandest

a   49–19   charged with the g· trust of heaven,
f 213–21   rapture of his g· symphonies was never heard.

grandeur

a   39– 2   met the mockery of his unrecognized g·.
f 244–31   g· and immortality of development,
b 328– 1   the g· and bliss of a spiritual sense,
329– 4   glow in all the g· of universal goodness.
ap 571–30   the sublime g· of divine Science,

granite

pref vii–25   and to cut the rough g·.

Grant, General

r 492–18   Discussing his campaign, General G· said :

grant

pr   2–13   the All-loving does not g· them simply on the
10–31   In this case infinite Love will not g· the request.

granted

pref xii– 1   No charters were g· . . . after 1883,
m   63–23   let us hope it will be g·.
t 453– 4   should be g· that the author understands

grape

fr 600– *   whether the tender g· appear,— Song 7 : 12.

grapes

f 211–20   "the fathers have eaten sour g·,— Ezek. 18 : 2.
b 276–30   Divine Science does not gather g· from thorns
g 539–24   "Do men gather g· of thorns ?"— Matt. 7 : 16.

graphic

a   52–14   Isaiah's g· word concerning the coming

graphically

sp   92–17   The portrayal is still g· accurate,

grapple

a   29– 2   They must g· with sin in themselves and in
f 235–31   love to g· with a new, right idea
ap 569– 4   Every mortal . . . must g· with and overcome

grasp

pr   13–23   and so we cannot g· the wonders wrought
a   28– 7   determination to hold Spirit in the g· of matter
sp   98–16   above the loosening g· of creeds,
s 119–10   to g· the other horn of the dilemma
142–17   and causes the left to let go its g· on the
147–22   enables you to g· the spiritual facts
ph 192– 5   only as we . . . g· the true.
f 209–11   intelligence which holds the winds in its g·.
254–12   mortals g· the ultimate . . . slowly ;
b 275–10   To g· the reality and order of being
281–29   as we g· the facts of Spirit.
327–10   until his g· on good grows stronger.
o 349–20   in order to g· the meaning of this Science.
p 381–21   will sooner g· man's God-given dominion.
g 519–12   is slow to discern and to g· God's creation
ap 573– 2   is unable to g· such a view.

grasped

an 104–27   leaving the case worse than before it was g· by

grass

blade of

sp   70–13   from a blade of g· to a star,
ph 191–21   By its own volition, not a blade of g· springs up,

days are as

ph 190–23   As for man, his days are as g· :— Psal. 103 : 15.
r 476–24   "As for man, his days are as g· :— Psal. 103 : 15.

of Gethsemane

a   48–11   fell in holy benediction on the g· of Gethsemane,

sp   81–18   the g· seemeth to wither and the flower to
ph 190–15   are as the g· springing from the soil
g 507–12   Let the earth bring forth g·,— Gen. 1 : 11.
508– 9   the earth brought forth g·,— Gen. 1 : 12.
516–13   The g· beneath our feet silently exclaims,

grateful

pr   3–22   Are we really g· for the good
9– 2   the author has been most g· for

gratification

a   38–27   living only for pleasure or the g· of the senses,

gratifications

g 536–22   Their narrow limits belittle their g·,

gratify

a   49–12   O, why did they not g· his last human yearning
s 163–26   exhibition of human invention might g·

gratitude

pr   3–25   G· is much more than a verbal expression of
3–26   Action expresses more g· than speech.
4– 8   worthy evidence of our g· for all that he has
4–10   to express loyal and heartfelt g·,
8–15   If we feel the aspiration, humility, g·,
a   26– 2   heart overflows with g· for what he did
m   66–17   Amidst g· for conjugal felicity, it is well to
p 367–15   oil of gladness and the perfume of g·,
gl 595–22   Tithe. Contribution ; tenth part ; homage ; g·.

grave

beyond the

a   46–24   and progressive state beyond the g·.
p 409–30   cannot . . . expect to find beyond the g· a

death and the

a   39–14   Jesus overcame death and the g·
45– 7   in his victory over death and the g·.
49–25   triumph over sin, sickness, death, and the g·.
s 137– 7   victor over sickness, sin, . . . death, and the g·,

grave

from the

b 291–26	No resurrection from the g· awaits Mind
313–30	which by spiritual power he raised from the g·,
317–22	after his resurrection from the g·,
g 509– 6	to their apprehension he rose from the g·,

has no power

b 291–26	for the g· has no power over either.

of affection

m 68– 9	Jealousy is the g· of affection.

robs the

b 275–27	It robs the g· of victory.
323–26	The true idea . . . robs the g· of victory,

this side of the

a 36–23	punishment this side of the g·

a 24–30	enabled their Master to triumph over the g·,
sp 73–26	g· mistake to suppose that matter is
s 138– 1	[hades, the *under-world*, or the g·]
f 244– 8	seen between the cradle and the g·,
b 291– 5	these are g· mistakes.
o 353–25	The g· does not banish the ghost of
p 426–20	either a desire to die or a dread of the g·,
r 496–23	the spiritual law which says to the g·,

grave-clothes

p 367– 2	nor bury the *morale* of C. S. in the g· of its

graven

m 67– 1	may be g· with the image of God.

gravitate

c 265– 5	Mortals must g· Godward,

gravitates

b 323–21	g· towards Soul and away from

gravitation

b 272–23	earthward g· of sensualism and impurity,
g 536–12	If man's spiritual g· and attraction to

gravity

s 149–18	A physician . . . remarked with great g· :

gray

f 245–14	no care-lined face, no wrinkles nor g· hair,
g 513– 9	g· in the sombre hues of twilight ;

great

pr 5– 4	The next and g· step required by wisdom
9–13	we shall never meet this g· duty simply by
16– 1	A g· sacrifice of material things must precede
a 23– 3	One sacrifice, however g·, is insufficient to
24–17	views of atonement will undergo a g· change,
25– 1	complete was the g· proof of Truth and Love.
25–30	else we are not improving the g· blessings
29–10	G· is the reward of self-sacrifice.
33– 7	It was the g· truth of spiritual being,
33–15	With the g· glory of an everlasting victory
36–15	g· moral distance between Christianity and
40–19	If a career so g· and good as that of Jesus
42–15	The resurrection of the g· demonstrator
44– 6	place in which to solve the g· problem of being.
44–32	a g· stone must be rolled from the cave's mouth ;
47–18	He knew that the g· goodness of that Master
48–19	g· demonstrator of Truth and Love was silent
49– 9	Had they forgotten the g· exponent of God?
53–21	g· distance between the individual and Truth.
m 66– 1	immortal Shakespeare, g· poet of humanity :
66–10	Through g· tribulation we enter the
68– 5	shall learn how Spirit, the g· architect,
sp 83–24	Between C. S. and . . . superstition a g· gulf
85–18	events of g· moment were foretold by the
91– 7	Here is the g· point of departure for all true
91–12	the sooner man's g· reality will appear
an 104– 9	"Every g· scientific truth goes through three
106–18	in his g· epistle to the Galatians,
s 109–32	The three g· verities of Spirit,
112–19	which, like the g· Giver,
115– 1	the one g· obstacle to the reception of
115– 9	g· difficulty is to give the right impression,
122– 4	the g· facts of Life, rightly understood,
125–26	dominion over the atmosphere and the g· deep,
126–28	demonstrations of our g· Master
129–13	there will be "g· tribulation— *Matt.* 24 : 21.
133– 6	"I have not found so g· faith,— *Matt.* 8 : 10.
136–22	and the g· work of the Master,
148–32	our g· Master demonstrated that Truth could
149–17	A physician . . . remarked with g· gravity :
151– 8	G· respect is due the motives and
158–14	and endured g· sufferings upon earth.
ph 184–28	always breathed with g· difficulty when the
200–16	The g· truth in the Science of being,
f 207–23	does not proceed from this g· and only cause.
216–19	The g· mistake of mortals is to suppose that
234–29	laid g· stress on the action of the human mind,
242– 6	Denial of the claims of matter is a g· step

great

f 251– 7	Fright is so g· at certain stages of
254–14	demonstrating the g· problem of being,
c 267–10	The g· I AM made all
b 268– 2	brought to light with g· rapidity
274–16	Jesus demonstrated this g· verity.
293–19	g· difference being that electricity is not
309–21	to be brought back through g· tribulation,
326–14	the g· healer of mortal mind is the healer of
328–30	his g· life-work extends through time
329– 9	the g· might of divine Science
o 358–22	g· import to Christianity of those works
p 375–26	g· hopefulness and courage, even when
395– 6	Like the g· Exemplar, the healer should
397–23	familiar with the g· verities of being.
403– 2	The g· difference between voluntary and
417– 9	If you make the sick realize this g· truism,
422– 5	If the reader of this book observes a g· stir
426–21	destroy the g· fear that besets mortal existence.
427–21	The g· difficulty lies in ignorance of
428–11	this is the g· attainment by means of which
428–22	The g· spiritual fact must be brought out
433– 2	with g· solemnity addresses the jury
t 445– 9	Teach the g· possibilities of man
445–27	g· danger in teaching . . . indiscriminately,
448– 4	went out to the g· heart of Love,
454–13	g· truth which strips all disguise from error.
r 469–14	the g· truth that God, good, is the *only* Mind,
494– 5	so g· a work as the Messiah's
g 510–13	And God made two g· lights ;— *Gen.* 1 : 16.
512– 4	And God created g· whales,— *Gen.* 1 : 21.
516–16	The g· rock gives shadow and shelter.
528–22	declaring what g· things error has done.
543–15	The g· verities of existence are never excluded
546–24	g· spiritual facts of being, like rays of light,
547–20	evolution implies that the g· First Cause
548–27	endowed by the labors and genius of g· men.
549–27	even this g· observer mistakes nature,
550–21	If . . . then the g· I AM is a myth.
555–28	Our g· example, Jesus, could restore
ap 558– *	G· is the Lord, and greatly to be— *Psal.* 48 : 1.
560– 6	And there appeared a g· wonder— *Rev.* 12 : 1.
560–11	The g· miracle, to human sense, is divine Love,
560–24	which made him equal to his g· mission.
562–27	g· is the idea, and the travail portentous.
562–30	and behold a g· red dragon,— *Rev.* 12 : 3.
563– 8	The g· red dragon symbolizes a lie,
565– 2	and becomes the g· red dragon, swollen with sin,
566– 4	walking wearily through the g· desert
567–14	And the g· dragon was cast out.— *Rev.* 12 : 9.
568–22	having g· wrath, because he— *Rev.* 12 : 12.
568–28	clearer and nearer to the g· heart of Christ;
570–27	should know the g· benefit which Mind has wrought.
570–28	also know the g· delusion of mortal mind,
574–22	lifted the seer to behold the g· city,
575–24	the city of the g· King."— *Psal.* 48 : 2.
577–19	interprets this g· example and the g· Exemplar
577–30	as recorded by the g· apostle,
gl 580–10	an unreality as opposed to the g· reality
587– 5	GOD. The g· I AM ; the all-knowing, all-seeing,
596– 4	may define Deity as "the g· unknowable ;"
597– 6	The g· Nazarene, as meek as he was mighty,
597–19	spiritual sense unfolds the g· facts of existence.

(*see also* fact, Teacher)

greater

a 25– 4	infinitely g· than can be expressed by
m 61–24	a g· responsibility, a more solemn charge,
63–22	difficulties of g· magnitude,
sp 82–32	hastening to a g· development of power,
95–14	g· or lesser ability of a Christian Scientist
an 104–25	case of the g· error overcoming the lesser.
104–26	g· error thereafter occupies the ground,
s 108–15	the lesser demonstration to prove the g·,
121–24	rule that the g· controls the lesser.
123– 2	will surely destroy the g· error
128–13	is capable of g· endurance,
133– 3	Was John's faith g· than that of the
143–16	takes the lesser to relieve the g·.
163–25	Nowhere is . . . displayed to a g· extent ;
f 211– 6	who shall say whether Truth or error is the g· ?
223–10	Remember that truth is g· than error,
223–11	and we cannot put the g· into the less.
223–11	Soul is Spirit, and Spirit is g· than body.
b 333–30	"My Father is g·"— *John* 14 : 28.
334– 7	not that the Father is g· than Spirit,
334–7,8	but g·, infinitely g·, than the fleshly Jesus,
p 440–15	what g· justification can any deed have,
r 467–18	The g· cannot be in the lesser.
467–20	belief that the g· can be in the lesser
g 508–24	rising from the lesser to the g·,
510–14	the g· light to rule the day,— *Gen.* 1 : 16.
518–14	lesser idea of Himself for a link to the g·,
534–24	will be g· mental opposition to the
ap 560–31	a g· ignorance of the divine Principle

greatest

f 242– 5 the least of them unto the *g*." — *Jer.* 31 : 34.
p 368– 1 The *g* wrong is but a supposititious opposite
376– 6 Just so is it with the *g* sin.

greatly

m 61–29 formation of mortals must *g* improve
p 411– 1 "The thing which I *g* feared— *Job* 3 : 25.
423– 4 for this fear *g* diminishes the
t 456–12 *g* errs, ignorantly or intentionally,
g 535– 6 I will *g* multiply thy sorrow— *Gen.* 3 : 16.
ap 558– * and *g* to be praised— *Psal.* 48 : 1.

Great Spirit

r 477–29 "the smile of the *G· S·*."

Grecian

ph 199–32 When Homer sang of the *G·* gods,

Greece

c 255– 8 cultured scholars in Rome and in *G·*,
b 324–25 Asia Minor, *G·*, and even in imperial Rome.

Greed

p 430–24 *G·* and Ingratitude, constitute the jury.

greed

a 47–21 *g·* for gold strengthened his ingratitude,

Greek

a 23–21 In Hebrew, *G·*, Latin, and English,
s 134– 4 The word *martyr,* from the *G·*,
137–31 [the meaning of the *G·* word *petros,* or *stone*]
b 313– 3 the full and proper translation of the *G·*),
313–13 is, in the *G·* Testament, *character.*
333–14 proper name of our Master in the *G·* was
r 474–12 *marvel* is the simple meaning of the *G·* word
488– 7 The Hebrew and *G·* words
g 517– 5 derived from two *G·* words, signifying
524– 4 seen . . . in the *G·* Aphrodite,
gl 590–17 In the *G·*, the word *kurios* almost always has
594– 1 (*ophis,* in *G·* ; *nacash,* in Hebrew).
598– 1 The *G·* word for *wind* (*pneuma*) is used also

green

pr 5–19 flourish "like a *g·* bay tree ;"— *Psal.* 37 : 35.
ph 190–15 the grass . . . with beautiful *g·* blades,
g 514–13 or rests in "*g·* pastures,— *Psal.* 23 : 2.
518–11 I have given every *g·* herb— *Gen.* 1 : 30.
ap 578– 6 to lie down in *g·* pastures :— *Psal.* 23 : 2.

greet

s 158–24 Evidences of progress . . . *g·* us on every hand.
f 220– 9 violet lifts her blue eye to *g·* the early spring.

grew

f 245–11 she literally *g·* no older.
o 349–21 Out of this condition *g·* the prophecy
g 520–20 herb of the field before it *g·* :— *Gen.* 2 : 5.

grief

a 35– 1 and his disciples' *g·* into repentance.
50–31 real cross, which Jesus bore up the hill of *g·*,
p 363–29 was her *g·* sufficient evidence to warrant the
377– 3 If *g·* causes suffering, convince the
377–15 sudden joy or *g·* has caused what is termed
386–17 occasions the same *g·* that the friend's
386–20 correcting the mistake, heals your *g·*,
386–24 learn at length that there is no cause for *g·*,
386–27 under the influence of the belief of *g·*,
435–13 bringing joy instead of *g·*,

grind

p 380– 7 it will *g·* him to powder."— *Matt.* 21 : 44.

grinding

pr 10–19 to earn a penny by *g·* out a prayer.

groan

c 255– * *g· within ourselves, waiting for— Rom.* 8 : 23.

groaneth

c 255– * *we know that the whole creation g· — Rom.* 8 : 22.

grope

c 263– 9 he will no longer *g·* in the dark

gropes

t 463– 2 The material physician *g·* among phenomena,

groping

s 164– 1 resembles the *g·* of Homer's Cyclops

gross

m 61–15 promising children in the arms of *g·* parents,
sp 75– 9 *g·* materialism is scientifically impossible,
b 272–14 not to impart to dull ears and *g·* hearts the
o 350–18 "This people's heart is waxed *g·*,— *Matt.* 13 : 15.
p 383–14 To the mind equally *g·*, dirt gives no uneasiness.
383–18 impurity and . . . which do not trouble the *g·*,
t 456–17 betrays a *g·* ignorance of the method

grosser

m 61–19 the *g·* traits of their ancestors.
ph 177–13 material body is our *g·* portion ;
b 293– 8 The *g·* substratum is named matter

grossest

ap 565– 9 Led on by the *g·* element of mortal mind,

grossness

b 272–15 which dulness and *g·* could not accept.

ground

and dust
g 537–17 since *g·* and dust stand for nothingness.
cursed is the
g 535–22 cursed is the *g·* for thy sake ;— *Gen.* 3 : 17.
curses the
g 524–27 for God presently curses the *g·*.
dispute the
r 492–16 will dispute the *g·*, until one is acknowledged
drift to the
f 250–30 like snowflakes, and drift to the *g·*.
drops into the
g 520–27 Mortal thought drops into the *g·*,
dust of the
g 524–14 formed man of the dust of the *g·*,— *Gen.* 2 : 7.
face of the
g 521–22 watered the whole face of the *g·*.— *Gen.* 2 : 6.
fell to the
a 47–25 His dark plot fell to the *g·*,
firmer
f 224– 7 shall plant our feet on firmer *g·*.
fruit of the
g 540–25 Cain brought of the fruit of the *g·* — *Gen.* 4 : 3.
gained
s 111–32 this system has gradually gained *g·*,
herbs of the
g 541–13 more spiritual type . . . than the herbs of the *g·*
hold your
p 417–14 hold your *g·* with the unshaken understanding
occupies the
an 104–26 This greater error thereafter occupies the *g·*,
of demonstration
a 28–10 more on the *g·* of demonstration than
till the
ph 183–12 condemnation of man to till the *g·*,
g 520–22 there was not a man to till the *g·*.— *Gen.* 2 : 5.
520–31 never causing man to till the *g·*,
537– 4 to till the *g·* from whence— *Gen.* 3 : 23.
544– 5 and "not a man to till the *g·*."— *Gen.* 2 : 5.
545– 7 condemnation of mortals to till the *g·*
was accursed
b 338–27 Jehovah declared the *g·* was accursed ;
whole
sp 79–10 Science must go over the whole *g·*,
p 421–16 the great fact which covers the whole *g·*,
g 545–16 Error tills the whole *g·* in this material theory,

pr 2–13 does not grant them simply on the *g·* of
ph 180–12 nor take the *g·* that all causation is matter,
b 338– 3 signifying the *red color of the g·,*
338–28 from this *g·*, or matter, sprang Adam,
p 381– 7 on the *g·* that sin has its necessities.
437–29 on the *g·* that unjust usages were not allowed
440– 2 on the *g·* of hygienic disobedience,
g 525–30 And out of the *g·* made the— *Gen.* 2 : 9.
527–21 And out of the *g·* the Lord God— *Gen.* 2 : 19.
535–26 till thou return unto the *g·* ;— *Gen.* 3 : 19.
537–17 Error . . . buries itself in the *g·*,
541–28 crieth unto Me from the *g·*.— *Gen.* 4 : 10.

groundless

o 352–23 should be assured that their fears are *g·*,

grounds

p 392– 9 take antagonistic *g·* against all that is

groundwork

sp 84– 6 from a *g·* of corporeality and human belief.
s 147–19 plant you firmly on the spiritual *g·* of

grovel

g 539–18 to *g·* beneath all the beasts of the field.

grow

pr 7–19 there would *g·* out of ecstatic moments
10– 5 world must *g·* to the spiritual understanding
m 58–15 benevolence should *g·* more diffusive.
sp 77–24 would *g·* beautifully less with every
ph 197–27 will never *g·* robust until
f 251– 4 an abscess should not *g·* more painful
c 265– 6 their affections and aims *g·* spiritual,
b 300–19 (to mortal sight) they *g·* side by side until
318–19 invalids *g·* more spiritual, as the
o 341– 7 Even the Scriptures, which *g·* in beauty
350– 8 his followers must *g·* into that stature
p 387– 1 when we *g·* into the understanding of Life,
390–20 Suffer no claim of sin or of sickness to *g·*
r 496–13 *g·* brighter "unto the perfect day."— *Prov.* 4 : 18.
g 525–31 to *g·* every tree that is pleasant— *Gen.* 2 : 9.
527– 4 to make it beautiful or to cause it to live and *g·*.

growing

a 43–30 the multitudinous errors *g·* from
f 202–25 contradict the practice *g·* out of them.
245– 1 error of thinking that we are *g·* old,
245–23 nor thought of herself as *g·* old.
c 265–17 as if man were a weed *g·* apace

growing

p 396–12 nor encourage . . . the expectation of g· worse
g 533–24 The belief . . . is g· worse at every step,
ap 570– 3 the people will chain, . . . the g· occultism

grown

ph 188– 4 The belief of sin, which has g· terrible
t 455–21 one who has g· into such a fitness for it
g 533–18 According to this belief, the rib . . . has g·
549– 5 after it has g· to maturity,
553–11 to assume that individuals have g· or

grows

pr 5–27 He g· worse who continues in sin because
sp 89–16 tongue g· mute which before was eloquent.
b 327–10 until his grasp on good g· stronger.
p 387–24 but g· stronger because of it.
433–13 As the Judge proceeds, the prisoner g· restless.
r 489– 2 loses its claw, the claw g· again.
g 520–25 the plant g·, not because of seed or soil, but
554–14 as he g· up into another false claim,

growth

and organization
g 548–24 material sense of animal g· and organization,
child's
pref x– 1 may treasure the memorials of a child's g·,
in grace
pr 4– 4 prayer of fervent desire for g· in grace,
f 220–25 never to try dietetics for g· in grace.
in wisdom
p 363–30 repentance, reformation, and g· in wisdom
material
m 68–28 it manifests no material g· from molecule to
of error
ph 188–22 Sickness is a g· of error,
only through
m 62–18 only through g· in the understanding of
probation and
b 291–24 until probation and g· shall effect the
promotes your
c 266–12 to accept what best promotes your g·.
promote the
ph 195–21 promote the g· of mortal mind out of itself,
spiritual
(see **spiritual**)
subject to
s 124–18 represented as subject to g·, maturity, and
this
p 406–23 and this g· will go on until
r 481–17 this g· of material belief,

m 68–14 to your g· and to your influence on other lives.
ph 190–14 Human birth, g·, maturity, and decay
b 291– 9 in the g· of Christian character.
305–28 not subject to birth, g·, maturity, decay.
310–31 neither g·, maturity, nor decay in Soul.
t 463–16 Its beginning will be meek, its g· sturdy,
g 520–26 g· is the eternal mandate of Mind.

grumble

m 59–23 After marriage, it is too late to g·

guarantee

pref vii–18 only g· of obedience is a right apprehension of

guard

pr 10–20 the advance g· of progress has
a 48– 6 held uncomplaining g· over a world
f 225–10 not to let truth pass the g· until
234–10 and g· against false beliefs as watchfully
t 445– 3 to g· against the attacks of the
458–18 to g· "the tree of life."— Gen. 3: 24.

guarded

t 446–29 This must therefore be watched and g· against.
449–21 ought to be understood and g· against.

guardians

ph 174–13 spiritual intuitions . . . are our g· in the gloom.

guarding

g 538– 4 two-edged sword, g· and guiding.

guards

g 526–19 sword which g· it is the type of
537–15 Truth g· the gateway to harmony.

guess

f 245–15 Asked to g· her age, those unacquainted with

guesswork

t 459–28 Guided by divine Truth and not g·,

guest

a 32– 8 ancient custom . . . to pass each g· a cup of
f 254–32 stranger, thou art the g· of God.
p 362– 2 Jesus was once the honored g· of a
363–13 wondering why, . . . the exalted g· did not at once

guest's

p 364–14 wash and anoint his g· feet,

guests

g 538– 6 at the gate . . . to note the proper g·.

guidance

a 25–25 He worked for their g·, that they might
s 148–31 leaves them to the g· of a theology which admits
154–25 and her affections need better g·,
164– 8 said : . . . none can be adopted as a safe g·

guide

s 126–30 I have had no other g· in
f 226–32 trusting Truth, the strong deliverer, to g· me
b 299–13 g· to the divine Principle of all good,
p 414–12 love will . . . g· and govern mortal mind
t 444– 9 God will still g· them into the right use of
r 467–14 the one perfect Mind to g· him,
497– 4 the Bible as our sufficient g· to eternal Life.
ap 566– 6 so shall the spiritual idea g· all right desires
566–18 An awful g·, in smoke and flame,

guided

pr 7–18 If spiritual sense always g· men,
an 106–10 self-governed only when he is g· rightly
f 214– 7 g· into the demonstration of life eternal.
p 429– 8 When walking, we are g· by the eye.
t 459–27 G· by divine Truth and not guesswork,
ap 566– 1 As the children of Israel were g·

guides

a 21–22 we have the same railroad g·,
s 149–28 Whatever g· thought spiritually benefits
f 235–21 They should be wise spiritual g· to
b 299–16 giving earnest heed to these spiritual g·

guideth

c 257–21 g· "Arcturus with his sons."— Job 38 : 32.

guiding

pref vii–10 and shine the g· star of being.
r 489–10 not equal to g· the hand to the mouth ;
g 538– 4 a two-edged sword, guarding and g·.

guillotine

s 161–22 knelt before a statue . . . erected near the g· :

guillotined

p 427–17 same after as before . . . the body g·.

guilt

t 455– 3 mental state of self-condemnation and g·
g 542– 6 error hides behind a lie and excuses g·,
542–10 disposition to excuse g· . . . is punished.
ap 568– 1 Innocence and Truth overcome g· and error.

guilty

s 119–14 thereby making Him g· of maintaining
p 391–19 supposed to say, "I am sick," never plead g·.
391–21 If you say, "I am sick," you plead g·.
405–23 the cumulative effects of a g· conscience.
433–17 "G· of liver-complaint in the first degree."
433–21 g· of benevolence in the first degree,
434– 3 "Delay the execution ; the prisoner is not g·."
436–28 charged the jury, . . . to find the prisoner g·.
442– 7 and there resounded . . . the cry, Not g·.

gulf

a 47–19 placed a g· between Jesus and his betrayer,
sp 74–26 There is no bridge across the g· which
83–24 Between C. S. and . . . superstition a great g·

gushing

p 367– 6 better than hecatombs of g· theories,

gymnast

ph 199–19 The feats of the g· prove

H

habit

pr 2–19 The mere h· of pleading with the divine Mind,
p 383–25 Does his assertion prove the use . . . a salubrious h·,

habitat

p 413–19 Water is not the natural h· of humanity.

habitation

r 477– 6 Man is not a material h· for Soul ;
g 537–11 In the first chapter . . . evil has no local h·
ap 577–12 This spiritual, holy h· has no boundary

habits

m 62– 5 h· of obedience to the moral and spiritual law,
p 404– 7 suffering which his submission to such h· brings,

habitual

pr 4–12 The h· struggle to be always good
11–29 h· desire to know and do the will of God,

hades

s 137–32 [h·, the under-world, or the grave]

hail

f 224–13 were ready to h· an anthropomorphic God,

hair
f 245–14	no care-lined face, no wrinkles nor gray *h·*,
p 363– 5	her long *h·*, which hung loosely

hairs
p 367–16	with those *h·* all numbered by the Father.

half
m 66– 8	We do not *h·* remember this in the sunshine of
f 202– 7	*h·* the faith they bestow upon the so-called
p 382– 5	If *h·* the attention given to hygiene were
383–21	eating or smoking poison for *h·* a century,
418–10	Then, if your fidelity is *h·* equal to the

half-hidden
o 351– 1	sprang from *h·* Israelitish history

half-way
an 103–13	separate from any *h·* impertinent knowledge,
ph 167–23	It is not wise to take a halting and *h·* position
b 274–23	permits no *h·* position in learning its Principle

hallowed
pr 16–28	*H·* be Thy name. — *Matt.* 6 : 9.
s 134–12	were *h·* by the gallows and the cross.
t 462–29	It unfolds the *h·* influences of unselfishness,

hallowing
m 59–14	thus *h·* the union of interests and affections,
r 474–24	Despite the *h·* influence of Truth in the

hallucination
ph 176–24	in cases of hysteria, hypochondria, and *h·*?

hallucinations
o 348– 4	virtually admit the nothingness of *h·*,
gl 594–24	the opposites of God ; errors ; *h·*.

halo
f 248– 3	Its *h·* rests upon its object.

halt
o 343–10	The sick, the *h·*, and the blind look up to C. S.

halting
ph 167–22	It is not wise to take a *h·* and half-way position
f 236–30	While age is *h·* between two opinions

halts
p 415– 7	leaps or *h·* when it contemplates unpleasant

Ham
gl 582–24	CANAAN (the son of *H·*). A sensuous belief ;
587–21	definition of

hamlet
s 149–32	there is hardly a city, village, or *h·*, in which

hammer
ph 199– 2	if . . . could lift the *h·* and strike the anvil,
199– 7	producing such a result on the *h·*.

hammering
ph 199– 3	it might be thought true that *h·* would

hamper
f 234– 2	even as ritualism and creed *h·* spirituality.

hampers
c 260–17	often *h·* the trial of one's wings

hand
at	
pr 12– 5	no power to gain more . . . than is always at *h·*.
ph 174–13	far spent, the day is at *h·*" — *Rom.* 13 : 12.
p 385–20	you sprain the muscles . . . your remedy is at *h·*.
ap 558– *	*for the time is at h·.* — *Rev.* 1 : 3.
every	
s 158–25	Evidences of progress . . . greet us on every *h·*.
fan in	
r 466–27	Science of Christianity comes with fan in *h·*
guiding the	
r 489–10	not equal to guiding the *h·* to the mouth ;
helping	
m 64–10	lends a helping *h·* to some noble woman,
His	
c 256–22	and none can stay His *h·*, or say — *Dan.* 4 : 35.
his	
b 321–21	when Moses first put his *h·* into his bosom
321–23	restored his *h·* to its natural condition
g 537– 1	and now, lest he put forth his *h·*, — *Gen.* 3 : 22.
ap 558– 6	had in his *h·* a little book open : — *Rev.* 10 : 2.
559– 1	had in his *h·* "a little book," — *Rev.* 10 : 2.
moves the	
f 220–32	as directly as the volition or will moves the *h·*.
my	
ph 187–18	We say, "My *h·* hath done it."
of Love	
a 36–27	or that the *h·* of Love is satisfied with
on the other	
m 58–19	on the other *h·*, a wandering desire for
an 103–12	On the other *h·*, Mind-science is wholly
b 301–10	On the other *h·*, the immortal, spiritual man
333– 8	On the other *h·*, Christ is not a name so much as
o 354–12	On the other *h·*, the Christian opponents
p 364–25	On the other *h·*, do they show their regard
t 452–29	On the other *h·*, if you had the inclination
r 493– 1	On the other *h·*, C. S. speedily shows

hand
right	
pr 15–29	gain the ear and right *h·* of omnipotence
a 38–16	right *h·* of the Lord is exalted." — *Psal.* 118 : 16.
41–25	then sat down at the right *h·* of the Father.
s 141– 7	to cut off the right *h·* and pluck out the
142–17	Sensuality palsies the right *h·*, and causes
f 233–16	Already the shadow of His right *h·* rests upon
table and	
sp 80–22	mind-power which moves both table and *h·*.
thine	
p 398–14	"Stretch forth thine *h·*," — *Matt.* 12 : 13.
vanished	
sp 88– 4	the touch of a vanished *h·*,
which beckons	
sp 76– 3	and the *h·* which beckons them,
withered	
p 398–13	To the sufferer with the withered *h·*
s 126–16	The point at issue between C. S. on the one *h·*
160–13	the heart becomes as torpid as the *h·*.
ph 179–27	with homœopathic pellet and powder in *h·*,
187–15	the *h·*, admittedly moved by the will.
f 213–28	as the *h·*, which sweeps over it, is human or

handcuffed
p 436–20	It was Fear who *h·* Mortal Man and would now

handkerchief
p 379–15	inspecting the hue of her blood on a cambric *h·*,

handle
b 321–11	wisdom bade him come back and *h·* the serpent,
321–32	taught them how to *h·* serpents unharmed,
p 402–26	*h·* themselves as they should do.
t 464–18	he could *h·* his own case

handled
b 268– *	*our hands have h·, of the Word* — *I John* 1 : 1.

handles
ph 176–31	Truth *h·* the most malignant contagion

handmaid
a 36– 9	since justice is the *h·* of mercy.

hands
at the	
p 441–23	executed at the *h·* of our sheriff, Progress.
clap their	
f 220–10	The leaves clap their *h·* as nature's untired
cleansed their	
s 133–32	Creeds and rituals have not cleansed their *h·*
enemies'	
a 51–13	give his temporal life into his enemies' *h·* ;
her	
s 159– 6	Her *h·* were held, and she was forced into
his own	
p 422–29	Not holding the reins of government in his own *h·*,
into the	
p 436– 4	After betraying him into the *h·* of your law,
t 459–17	like putting a sharp knife into the *h·* of a
its own	
ph 170–32	which takes divine power into its own *h·*
p 378–24	and take the government into its own *h·*.
join	
s 122–17	sky and tree-tops apparently join *h·*,
lips or	
f 212–26	we say the lips or *h·* must move in order to
my	
s 156– 6	A case of dropsy, . . . fell into my *h·*.
of God	
g 521– 8	in the *h·* of God, not of man,
of ignorance	
b 305– 1	left in the *h·* of ignorance,
on the sick	
a 38–11	they shall lay *h·* on the sick, — *Mark* 16 : 18.
b 328–25	They shall lay *h·* on the sick, — *Mark* 16 : 18.
o 359–27	They shall lay *h·* on the sick, — *Mark* 16 : 18.
p 362– *	*they shall lay h· on the sick,* — *Mark* 16 : 18.
our	
b 268– *	*our h· have handled, of the Word* — *I John* 1 : 1.
shook	
p 442– 9	We noticed, as he shook *h·* with his counsel,
such	
a 31– 3	God will never place it in such *h·*.
Thy	
ph 200–15	dominion over the works of Thy *h·*. — *Psal.* 8 : 6.
use those	
a 44–17	that he might use those *h·* to remove the
without	
t 454– 8	path which leads to the house built without *h·*
a 38–15	Here the word *h·* is used metaphorically,
sp 80–20	that mind, without the aid of *h·*,
an 105– 1	The *h·*, without mortal mind to direct them,
p 432–27	prisoner to escape from the *h·* of justice,

hangs
p 436–10 Upon this statute *h·* all the law

haply
ph 198–20 *h·* causes a vigorous reaction upon itself,

happens
p 397–13 When an accident *h·*, you think
r 486– 4 Suppose one accident *h·* to the eye,

happify
m 57–32 To *h·* existence by constant intercourse with

happiness
all
c 261– 3 Principle of all *h·*, harmony, and immortality.
and existence
o 356–14 to each other's *h·* and existence.
p 407–19 in the scale of health, *h·*, and existence.
r 487– 1 find a higher sense of *h·* and existence.
and goodness
f 244– 8 *h·* and goodness would have no abiding-place
and life
f 232– 5 beliefs we commonly entertain about *h·* and life
b 308–10 looking for *h·* and life in the body,
and success
p 405–11 conspirators against health, *h·*, and success.
circumscribe
m 61– 1 We cannot circumscribe *h·* within the
crush out
p 407–11 they crush out *h·*, health, and manhood.
each other's
m 59– 4 most tender solicitude for each other's *h·*,
o 356–14 to each other's *h·* and existence.
existence and
g 545–17 false view, destructive to existence and *h·*.
fatal to
m 59–26 for deception is fatal to *h·*.
gaining
b 327–28 seeking material means for gaining *h·*.
harmony and
m 60– 3 higher in the scale of harmony and *h·*.
health and
s 152–27 driven to a spiritual source for health and *h·*.
c 261– 8 The effect of mortal mind on health and *h·* is
p 442–12 his countenance beaming with health and *h·*.
health or
p 420–24 at its best, is not promotive of health or *h·*.
his
ph 172– 2 constitutes his *h·* or misery.
p 383–13 emigrant, whose filth does not affect his *h·*,
hope of
m 61–20 What hope of *h·*, . . . can inspire the child who
human
m 65– 2 human *h·* should proceed from man's highest
is spiritual
m 57–18 *H·* is spiritual, born of Truth and Love.
life and
c 262–21 will then drop the false estimate of life and *h·*,
g 536–28 give up their belief in perishable life and *h·*;
man's
b 304–18 Man's *h·* is not, therefore, at the disposal of
of being
m 60–26 not discerning the true *h·* of being,
b 286– 1 relates most nearly to the *h·* of being.
of mortals
p 397– 4 on the morals and the *h·* of mortals,
of wedlock
m 58–21 a poor augury for the *h·* of wedlock.
of your wife
m 59–18 the welfare and *h·* of your wife
or misery
s 122–14 its status of *h·* or misery.
ph 172– 2 constitutes his *h·* or misery.
pursuit of
s 161–13 life, liberty, and the pursuit of *h·*."
still seeking
b 290– 8 still seeking *h·* through a material,
true
m 58–10 true *h·*, strength, and permanence.
60–26 not discerning the true *h·* of being,
b 337– 7 For true *h·*, man must harmonize with his
would be won
b 290–17 *h·* would be won at the moment of dissolution,

---

m 60–30 and *h·* would be more readily attained
61– 5 or *h·* will never be won.
f 250–31 nor will Science admit that *h·* is ever the sport of
b 291– 2 that *h·* can be genuine in the midst of

happy
a 55–17 My weary hope tries to realize that *h·* day,
m 60– 5 a *h·* and permanent companionship.
65–18 powerlessness of vows to make home *h·*,
s 121–12 glad in God's perennial and *h·* sunshine,
ph 195– 4 said that he should never be *h·* elsewhere.
f 236–27 verities that will make them *h·* and good.
b 297– 2 Mortal belief says, "You are *h·* !"

harbingers
f 224–20 the *h·* of truth's full-orbed appearing.

hard
a 23– 8 The atonement is a *h·* problem in theology,
f 225–24 Legally to abolish unpaid servitude . . . was *h·*
p 436–23 His friends struggled *h·* to rescue the prisoner
t 449– 2 your own wrists manacled, it is *h·* to break

hardened
p 404–16 The healthy sinner is the *h·* sinner.

hardier
ph 197–19 that made them *h·* than our trained

hardly
s 149–32 To-day there is *h·* a city, village, or hamlet,

harlots
a 20–̇7 publicans and the *h·* go into the— *Matt.* 21 : 31

harm
an 103–32 In C. S., man can do no *h·*,
ph 180– 3 should be taught to do the body no *h·*
197–32 will *h·* his patients even more than
198– 2 has in belief more power to *h·* man than
f 234–32 and do no more *h·* than one's belief permits.
o 344–14 misrepresentations, which *h·* the sick ;
352–18 *ought* to fear a reality which can *h·* them
p 385–18 you can do without *h·* to yourself.
442–31 mental malpractice cannot *h·* you
t 448–32 foolish deceit, doing one's self the most *h·*.
g 557– 3 moving and playing without *h·*, like a fish.

harmful
p 405–29 pains of sinful sense are less *h·* than its
413– 6 A single requirement, beyond . . . is *h·*.
t 459–21 ignorance is more *h·* than

harmless
sp 97–11 and the blow of the other will become *h·*.
ph 177–32 a few persons believe the potion . . . to be *h·*,
f 243– 4 The divine Love, which made *h·* the
b 280– 6 All things beautiful and *h·* are ideas of Mind.
g 514–28 Paul proved the viper to be *h·*.
514–29 God's creatures, . . . are *h·*,

harmonies
m 60–28 and teach us life's sweeter *h·*.
p 382– 2 matter, opposed to the *h·* of Spirit,
t 452–23 spiritual sense of Truth unfolds its *h·*,

harmonious
a 29–31 immortal evidence that Spirit is *h·*
m 68–31 the unbroken links of eternal, *h·* being
sp 88–14 Ideas are spiritual, *h·*, and eternal.
an 102– 2 God governs all that is real, *h·*, and
s 109–17 I knew the Principle of all *h·* Mind-action to be
114–28 universe, including man, is spiritual, *h·*, and
125– 5 Moral conditions will be found always *h·*
125– 9 and therefore more *h·* in his manifestations
129– 3 its logic is as *h·* as the reasoning of an
130–22 ability of Spirit to make the body *h·*,
151–27 entire being is found *h·* and
157–30 proof that Life is continuous and *h·*.
ph 166–31 man found to be *h·* and immortal.
184–16 man is *h·* and eternal.
198–22 a picture of healthy and *h·* formations.
f 207–29 is *h·* and is the ideal of Truth.
208–28 he makes it *h·* or discordant according to
209–24 man and the universe will be found *h·* and
214–17 being will be understood and found to be *h·*.
216–15 This understanding makes the body *h·* ;
232– 7 Security for the claims of *h·* and eternal being
239–26 If . . . from the divine Mind, action is *h·*.
c 259–30 to the end that they may produce *h·* results.
b 273–17 never made mortals whole, *h·*, and immortal.
273–18 Man is *h·* when governed by Soul.
283– 5 to retard or check its perpetual and *h·* action.
291–15 manifestations of Mind are *h·* and immortal,
296–12 reveals man and Life, *h·*, real, and eternal.
300–16 The inharmonious and . . . never touch the *h·*
302–15 *h·* and immortal man has existed forever,
306–27 is unfolding to mortals the immutable, *h·*,
320–18 man's eternal and *h·* existence as image,
322– 8 before *h·* and immortal man is obtained
335–27 Reality is spiritual, *h·*, immutable.
335–29 Nothing unspiritual can be real, *h·*, or eternal.
336–26 are inseparable, *h·*, and eternal.
o 346–13 we are *h·* only as we cease to
347–30 The *h·* will appear real,
351–25 demonstrating the self-all-inclusiveness of *h·* Truth.
355–12 let the *h·* and true sense of Life
p 376–23 the true facts in regard to *h·* being,
388–31 If mortals think that food disturbs the *h·*
407–23 spiritual, perfect, *h·* in every action.
409–32 Death will not make us *h·* and immortal
412–25 and the fact of *h·* being,
419– 7 His ideas alone are real and *h·*.
420– 2 no metastasis, no stoppage of *h·* action,
420–31 to the *h·* facts of Soul and immortal being.
t 444–28 Immortals, . . . are one *h·* family ;

harmonious
r 472– 8   with that which is h· and eternal.
472–24   God and His creation, h· and eternal.
478–19   That body is most h· in which the
480–13   H· action proceeds from Spirit, God.
488– 1   brings out the enduring and h· phases of things.
495–18   calm trust, that the recognition of life h·
    (see also **man**)

harmoniously
a 39–27   divine Principle . . . governs the universe h·.
s 120–21   reveals man as h· existent in Truth,
f 219–21   includes no rule of discord, but governs h·.
b 310–16   around which circle h· all things in
p 392–26   you will control yourself h·.

harmonize
s 163–29   To h· the contrarieties of medical doctrines
b 337– 8   man must h· with his Principle,

Harmony
ap 576– 2   and the Peaceful Sea of H·.

harmony
all is
b 331–15   Therefore in Spirit all is h·,
r 489–29   Outside the material sense of things, all is h·.
and happiness
m 60– 3   higher in the scale of h· and happiness.
and immortality
sp 76–22   the perfect h· and immortality of Life,
c 261– 3   all happiness, h·, and immortality.
b 280–28   His own individuality, h·, and immortality,
311–24   prevails . . . through h· and immortality.
324– 7   Unless the h· and immortality of man
p 380–25   produces in man health, h·, and immortality.
381–24   The h· and immortality of man
428– 5   resolves . . . into h· and immortality.
r 492–28   is divine, demonstrating h· and immortality.
g 521–12   The h· and immortality of man are intact.
and reward
a 21– 8   that they shall reach his h· and reward.
and Science
b 299–27   hide Truth, health, h·, and Science,
attain
f 251–30   before we can attain h·.
bringing
ap 561–15   God and His Christ, bringing h· to earth.
bring out
p 424– 9   in order to . . . bring out h·.
brings out all
s 132–13   divine Principle which brings out all h·.
chill
p 378–28   or to chill h· with a long and cold night of discord.
confers
p 418–21   Truth is affirmative, and confers h·.
depredations on
r 490– 4   this belief commits depredations on h·.
determines the
ph 167– 9   determines the h· of our existence,
discord or
f 213–28   discoursing either discord or h· according as
disturbed
p 421– 7   human belief in ill-health, or disturbed h·.
divine Principle of
t 445–25   hiding the divine Principle of h·,
ap 573–16   God, the divine Principle of h·,
establish
ph 189– 9   no more deny the power of C. S. to establish h·
eternal
pref vii–12   this daystar . . . lighting the way to eternal h·.
m 62–29   Our false views of life hide eternal h·,
f 242– 1   than for sinful beliefs to enter . . . eternal h·.
b 338– 2   C. S., rightly understood, leads to eternal h·.
r 479–25   light, understanding, and eternal h·,
494– 8   needed no help . . . to preserve the eternal h·
494–23   the Science of man's eternal h· breaks their
g 506–11   God, unites understanding to eternal h·.
548– 8   man has never lost his . . . eternal h·.
gl 598–29   consciousness of his immortality and eternal h·,
facts of
o 356– 7   Discord can never establish the facts of h·.
gateway to
g 537–16   Truth guards the gateway to h·.
haste towards
gl 586–22   GAD (Jacob's son). . . . haste towards h·.
health and
sp 72–31   the communicator of truth, health, and h·
s 146– 9   health and h· have been sacrificed.
p 412–27   normal conditions of health and h·.
heaven-bestowed
f 253–10   your divine rights, and heaven-bestowed h·,
heavenly
ap 560–11   interprets the Principle of heavenly h·.
hour of
sp 96– 4   Love will finally mark the hour of h·,
immutable
b 298– 6   silences for a while the voice of immutable h·,

harmony
in man
b 276–14   H· in man is as real and immortal as in music.
304–20   H· in man is as beautiful as in music,
is the fact
p 412–23   insist that h· is the fact,
is the real
ap 563– 2   h· is the real and discord the unreal.
is the somethingness
b 276–27   H· is the *somethingness* named Truth.
is universal
p 414–22   Even so, h· is universal, and discord is unreal.
keynote of
p 410–30   begins with Christ's keynote of h·,
law of
s 134–22   natural law of h· which overcomes discord,
light and
b 280– 4   the light and h· which are the abode of Spirit,
g 501–12   which God illustrated by light and h·,
503–28   God, Spirit, dwelling in infinite light and h·
loss of
p 408– 2   sickness is loss of h·.
man's
s 150–26   The doctrine that man's h· is governed by
ph 170–10   present . . . the Principle of man's h·.
f 232–22   He referred man's h· to Mind, not to matter,
normal as
p 368–12   beliefs . . . that discord is as normal as h·,
obtained
p 427–12   understood and h· obtained.
of all things
f 215– 2   Nothing can hide from them the h· of all things
of being
pr 6–15   To reach heaven, the h· of being,
sp 79–16   introduces the h· of being.
s 123– 5   could not affect the h· of being as does the
p 400–27   to bring out the h· of being.
423–20   regarding the truth and h· of being as
427–15   Nothing can interfere with the h· of being
g 553– 6   an understanding of the h· of being.
of health
p 400– 9   Mortals obtain the h· of health, only as
of man
p 392–10   the health, holiness, and h· of man,
423–13   and it restores the h· of man.
of Science
sp 81–27   material sense hides the h· of Science,
g 514–29   moving in the h· of Science,
ap 562–15   divine Principle of man in the h· of Science.
of Soul
p 390– 5   never deny the everlasting h· of Soul,
or health
s 159–26   to ascertain how much h·, or health,
origin of
f 217– 5   notion . . . tones are lost in the origin of h·.
peace, and
p 417– 2   find health, peace, and h· in God,
perfect
sp 76–22   the perfect h· and immortality of Life,
s 130–10   reality is in perfect h· with God,
g 511– 1   governing the universe, . . . in perfect h·.
perpetual
p 381–28   abide by the rule of perpetual h·,
perpetuates
sp 85– 8   whatever constitutes and perpetuates h·,
primeval
ap 565–23   stars sang together and all was primeval h·,
produce
r 486–20   yet supposes Mind unable to produce h· !
production of
ph 183–18   action of Truth is the production of h·.
proof of
b 340– 2   make life its own proof of h· and God.
realm of
s 138– 9   a firm foundation in the realm of h·.
received the
a 54– 6   but earth received the h·
recognition of
ap 576–24   man possesses this recognition of h·
recognize
f 228–17   will recognize h· as the spiritual reality
reign of
sp 93–32   the reign of h· in the Science of being.
s 122– 7   the actual reign of h· on earth.
gl 590– 1   The reign of h· in divine Science ;
592–20   the kingdom of heaven, or reign of h·.
represents
ap 560–10   Heaven represents h·,
restores
p 390– 9   the right understanding of Him restores h·
reverse of
t 447–17   When sin or sickness— the reverse of h·
Science and
ph 192–19   this teaching accords with Science and h·.
scientific
r 486–12   will not establish his scientific h·.

Hauser, Kaspar

ph 194–17 The authentic history of Kaspar *H·* is a

have

pref viii–16 On this basis C. S. will *h·* a fair fight.
pr 1– * he shall *h·* whatsoever he saith.— Mark 11 : 23.
 1– * and ye shall *h·* them.— Mark 11 : 24.
 1– * what things ye *h·* need of,— Matt. 6 : 8.
 3– 9 we *h·* only to avail ourselves of
 3–24 avail ourselves of the blessings we *h·*,
 6– 9 supposition that we *h·* nothing to do but
 8–27 than we are willing to *h·* our neighbors see?
 9–24 and material sense and human will *h·* no place.
 14– 6 to *h·*, not mere emotional ecstasy or
 15–12 that man may *h·* audience with Spirit,
a 19–26 Those who cannot . . . *h·* no part in God.
 19–29 "Thou shalt *h·* no other gods— Exod. 20 : 3.
 19–31 Thou shalt *h·* no belief of Life as mortal ;
 21–17 We *h·* separate time-tables to consult,
 21–19 and we *h·* little opportunity to help each other.
 21–21 we *h·* the same railroad guides,
 23–22 faith and the words corresponding thereto *h·*
 26– 7 *h·* the cup of sorrowful effort to drink
 29– 5 If they keep the faith, they will *h·* the crown
 31– 9 *h·* no record of his calling any man by the name
 39– 8 We must *h·* trials and self-denials,
 40– 6 when I *h·* a convenient season
 41–11 hypocrite may *h·* a flowery pathway here, but
 41–22 Jesus foresaw the reception C. S. would *h·*
 45–27 flesh and bones, as ye see me *h·*."— Luke 24 : 39.
 47–29 St. John, of whose death we *h·* no record.
m 61– 4 must *h·* ascendency over the evil
 62– 3 *h·* the sanctity of virginity.
 66–14 higher joys of Spirit, which *h·* no taint of earth.
 69–21 Do you *h·* one God and creator,
sp 70– * them that *h·* familiar spirits,— Isa. 8 : 19.
 75– 5 to *h·* a material investiture,
 76–19 they will *h·* no power over man,
 76–28 those who *h·* the final understanding of Christ
 79–18 bade men *h·* the Mind that was in the Christ.
 79–25 says : . . . You *h·* nervous prostration,
 80– 1 We *h·* strength in proportion to our
 81– 8 *h·* a continued existence after death
 87–30 We *h·* but to close the eyes,
 95–20 even human invention must *h·* its day,
an 101–17 and *h·* nothing in common with either
 102–12 planets *h·* no more power over man than
 105– 5 To say that these tribunals *h·* no
s 107–19 "I *h·* no pleasure in them."— Eccl. 12 : 1.
 112–11 these opinions may *h·* occasional gleams of
 121–13 So we *h·* goodness and beauty to gladden the
 125–26 The mariner will *h·* dominion over the
 127–21 *h·*— as matter— no intelligence, life, nor
 130–14 good and its sweet concords *h·* all-power.
 136–21 That a wicked king . . . should *h·* no
 141–30 Let it *h·* fair representation by the press.
 150–18 science (so-called) of physics would *h·*
 151–19 brain, etc., *h·* nothing to do with Life,
 151–32 we *h·* overwhelming proof.
 153–26 and we *h·* smallpox because others *h·* it ;
 155–32 is it safe to say that the less in quantity you *h·*
 160– 6 for they *h·* no innate power.
ph 167–17 To *h·* one God and avail yourself of the
 169–29 Whatever teaches man to *h·* other laws
 179–20 ailment, which a wild horse might never *h·*.
 181–30 If you *h·* more faith in drugs
 183– 6 discords *h·* no support from nature
 185–13 They *h·* their birth in mortal mind,
 185–18 Such theories *h·* no relationship to C. S.,
 188–13 is like the dream we *h·* in sleep,
 188–25 and you *h·* an abundant or scanty crop
 188–29 physical senses *h·* no immediate evidence of
 190– 1 Next we *h·* the formation of so-called
 192–20 you can *h·* no power opposed to God,
 196–17 They *h·* no relation to God
 200–14 "Thou madest him to *h·* dominion— Psal. 8 : 6.
f 206– 1 we can *h·* no other Mind but His,
 208– 6 and move, and *h·* our being."— Acts 17 : 28.
 211–24 If it is true that nerves *h·* sensation,
 212–16 and the nerves *h·* no sensation.
 212–17 Mortals *h·* a modus of their own,
 216–32 and *h·* but one Mind, even God ;
 219–15 what we do not wish to *h·* manifested.
 219–16 if we would *h·* it strong ;
 220– 3 *h·* continual colds, catarrh, and cough."
 228– 9 we shall *h·* no dangerous inheritances,
 228–29 supposition that sin, . . . and death *h·* power.
 231–17 discords *h·* only a fabulous existence,
 238–10 said, "I *h·* nothing left but Christ."
 238–27 *h·* no time for gossip about false law or
 242–11 to *h·* no other consciousness of life
 244– 9 goodness would *h·* no abiding-place
 247–31 recipe for beauty is to *h·* less illusion
 249– 3 and so let us *h·* one God, one Mind,
 249–19 Organization and time *h·* nothing to do with
 254–18 for we *h·* not the power to
c 255– * *h·* the firstfruits of the Spirit,— Rom. 8 : 23.

have

c 258–21 so-called senses *h·* no cognizance of either
 258–25 Mortals *h·* a very imperfect sense
 264– 2 They *h·* their day before the permanent facts
 264–12 from Him in whom we *h·* our being.
 267–14 they *h·* the same authority for the
b 268– * may *h·* fellowship with— I John 1 : 3.
 269–18 and they *h·* this advantage over the
 270–23 Meekness and charity *h·* divine authority.
 271–27 *h·* the opportunity now, as aforetime,
 276– 6 but all *h·* one Spirit, God,
 278–11 Spirit can *h·* no opposite.
 279–12 they *h·* the advantage of being eternal.
 280–16 Through this error, human belief comes to *h·*
 280–18 "Thou shalt *h·* no other gods— Exod. 20 : 3.
 281–22 *h·* neither Principle nor permanency,
 284– 8 Mind can *h·* no starting-point,
 287– 1 They *h·* neither Principle nor permanence,
 287–11 the infinite God can *h·* no unlikeness.
 289–10 To suppose that sin, lust, . . . *h·* life
 297–25 Human thoughts *h·* their degrees of
 299–32 he would *h·* no eternal Principle
 300–24 If . . . God would *h·* no representative,
 301–22 Thou shalt *h·* one God, one Mind.
 302–29 mortal sense would fain *h·* us so believe.
 307–13 and matter shall seem to *h·* life
 309–26 impossible . . . to *h·* an intelligence separate
 310– 9 else the clay would *h·* power over the potter.
 311–26 *h·* not the reality of substance.
 320– 7 the Scriptures *h·* both a spiritual and
 323–20 to realize their need of what they *h·* not,
 329– 8 you *h·* no right to question the great might
 339–30 never to admit that sin can *h·* intelligence
 340–15 "Thou shalt *h·* no other gods— Exod. 20 : 3.
 340–19 man shall *h·* no other spirit or mind but God,
 340–20 all men shall *h·* one Mind.
o 348–17 I desire to *h·* no faith in evil or
 349– 6 We *h·* the gospel, however,
 358–25 effect Christian Scientists may *h·* on the sick,
 358–28 belief that . . . these healers *h·* wonderful
 358–29 Is it likely that church-members *h·*
 358–32 than they *h·* in their own accredited and
 359– 6 because the patients *h·* more faith in
 359–30 says : "I *h·* spiritual ideals,
 360– 5 replies : . . . I *h·* no mind-ideals except
 360–11 replies : . . . I *h·* no notion of losing my
 360–15 Both you cannot *h·*.
 360–18 If you try to *h·* two models,
 360–18 then you practically *h·* none.
 361–19 and move, and *h·* our being."— Acts 17 : 28.
p 366–13 we *h·* the apostolic warrant for asking :
 368–15 When we come to *h·* more faith in the truth
 368–15 than we *h·* in error,
 369–28 what *h·* they of the advantages of Mind
 371– 5 Disquisitions on disease *h·* a mental effect
 373– 3 then we must *h·* more faith in God
 375–24 muscles *h·* no power to be lost,
 376–30 after admitting that it must *h·* its course.
 381–19 we live, move, and *h·* our being in the infinite
 386– 6 says that you may catch cold and *h·* catarrh ;
 387–15 If printers and authors *h·* the shortest span
 388–25 we *h·* hope in immortality ;
 390–23 You *h·* no law of His to support the
 390–25 you *h·* divine authority for denying
 393–18 *H·* no fear that matter can ache, swell,
 393–20 self-evident that matter can *h·* no pain
 394–30 the sick usually *h·* little faith in it till they
 396–10 Never say . . . how much you *h·* to contend with
 396–21 as if matter could *h·* sensation.
 403–12 both *h·* their origin in the human mind,
 409–27 We *h·* no right to say that life
 413–31 A child may *h·* worms, if you say so,
 415– 5 disease, and death *h·* no foundations in
 417– 6 Never tell the sick that they *h·* more courage than
 423–29 Bones *h·* only the substance of thought which
 425– 1 His parents, . . . *h·* so believed.
 425– 3 You will *h·* humors, just so long as
 425–29 If you *h·* sound and capacious lungs
 429–23 it must also *h·* an ending,
 429–27 *h·* faith in all the sayings of our Master,
 430–31 Although I *h·* the superintendence of
 433–25 "May God *h·* mercy on your soul,"
 438– 4 and let them *h·* dominion.— Gen. 1 : 26.
 440–16 what greater justification can any deed *h·*,
 441–33 We *h·* no trials for sickness before the
t 447– 2 We *h·* no authority in C. S. . . . to attempt to
 448–18 forsaketh them shall *h·* mercy."— Prov. 28 : 13
 454–24 must "*h·* her perfect work."— Jas. 1 : 4.
 454–26 feeling that you *h·* no more to do for them.
 457– 9 never . . . fears to *h·* fairly understood.
 458– 9 that error will finally *h·* the
 459– 7 he will *h·* nothing in common with the
r 466– 6 manifestations of C. S. . . . *h·* one Principle.
 467– 4 "Thou shalt *h·* no other gods— Exod. 20 : 3.
 467– 6 shalt *h·* no intelligence, . . . but that which
 467– 9 all men *h·* one Mind, one God and Father,

have

r	469– 6	it would also *h·* an ending.
	469–20	We can *h·* but one Mind, if that one is infinite.
	469–23	for evil can *h·* no place, where all
	470– 4	*h·* unity of Principle and spiritual power
	470–16	The children of God *h·* but one Mind.
	472–21	and we should *h·* a self-evident absurdity
	475–24	*h·* dominion over the fish— *Gen.* 1 : 26.
	478– 3	What evidence of Soul . . . *h·* you within
	479– 2	the child must *h·* a material, not a
	482– 9	you will *h·* the scientific signification.
	486– 2	and you can *h·* no faith in falsehood
	488– 9	they *h·* more the significance of
	488–22	Nerves *h·* no more sensation, . . . than the
	489–31	Mortal belief would *h·* the material senses
	491–27	may *h·* an attractive personality.
	496– 7	to *h·* one Mind, and to love another as
	496–28	*H·* Christian Scientists any religious creed?
	496–30	They *h·* not, if by that term is meant
	497–26	as we would *h·* them do unto us ;
g	504–21	Here we *h·* the explanation of another
	505– 3	sin, disease, and death *h·* no record in the
	512–10	angels of His presence, which *h·* the holiest
	515–12	*h·* dominion over the fish— *Gen.* 1 : 26.
	515–21	"Let *them* *h·* dominion."— *Gen.* 1 : 26.
	517–11	we *h·* not as much authority for considering
	517–12	as we *h·* for considering Him feminine,
	517–19	they all *h·* one Principle and parentage.
	517–27	and *h·* dominion over the fish— *Gen.* 1 : 28.
	529–23	We *h·* nothing in the animal kingdom which
	529–28	we should *h·* faith to fight all claims of
	530–21	saying, . . . Bow down to me and *h·* another
	531–20	Who will say that . . . animals *h·* a
	536–13	move, and *h·* our being,"— *Acts* 17 : 28.
	538–17	Sin, sickness, and death *h·* no record in the
	538–28	mortal man and sin *h·* a beginning,
	538–29	they must consequently *h·* an end,
	549–10	Creatures of lower forms . . . are supposed to *h·*,
	553–10	*h·* no right to assume that individuals
	555–11	Error would *h·* itself received as mind,
gl	583–23	matter and evil, which *h·* no Principle ;

having

pr	8–24	We confess to *h·* a very wicked heart
	14–30	speak "as one *h·* authority."— *Matt.* 7 : 29.
a	21– 4	This is *h·* our part in the at-one-ment
	23–17	as a pendulum swinging . . . *h·* no fixity.
	24–13	This is *h·* part in the atonement ;
	38–28	*H·* eyes ye see not,
	38–29	and *h·* ears ye hear not ;
m	63–26	a race *h·* higher aims and motives.
sp	71–22	*h·* no scientific basis nor origin,
	89– 5	*H·* more faith in others than in herself,
s	124– 7	*H·* neither moral might, spiritual basis, nor
ph	187– 1	*h·* other gods and believing in more than
f	215–30	*H·* sought man's spiritual state,
	218–26	temptation to believe in matter as . . . *h·*
	221–12	*h·* exhausted the skill of the doctors,
	222–23	*h·* "dominion over the fish— *Gen.* 1 : 26.
	231–30	governed by his Maker, *h·* no other Mind,
	245–11	*H·* no consciousness of time, she literally
b	276– 1	*H·* one God, one Mind, unfolds the
	291–17	man is found *h·* no righteousness of his own,
	319– 7	*H·* faith in the divine Principle of
o	353– 7	*h·* the stronger evidence of Truth
p	366–16	Not *h·* this spiritual affection,
	382– 3	*h·* only human approval for their sanction.
	395– 7	speak to disease as one *h·* authority
t	458–15	*H·* seen so much suffering from quackery,
r	467–13	*h·* no other gods, turning to no other but
	467–15	*h·* that Mind which was also in Christ.
	486–31	"*h·* no hope, and without God— *Eph.* 2 : 12.
g	518–16	all *h·* the same Principle, or Father ;
	522– 8	as *h·* broken away from Deity
	531–32	*h·* dominion over all the earth.
	536– 8	the sea, . . . is represented as *h·* passed away.
	543– 1	*h·* no truth to support it,
ap	562–30	*h·* seven heads and ten horns,— *Rev.* 12 : 3.
	568–22	*h·* great wrath, because he— *Rev.* 12 : 12.
gl	585– 3	"*H·* ears, hear ye not?"— *Mark* 8 : 18.
	586– 5	"*H·* eyes, see ye not?"— *Mark* 8 : 18.

hay

ph	175–14	to fancy that . . . new-mown *h·* can cause

hay-fever

ph	175– 8	cerebro-spinal meningitis, *h·*, and rose-cold?

He

pr	2– 9	more than *H·* has already done,
	2–10	since *H·* is unchanging wisdom and Love.
	2–14	for *H·* already knows all.
	2–25	of anything *H·* does not already
	3– 1	*H·* who is immutably right will do right
	6– 6	is not separate from the wisdom *H·* bestows.
	6– 6	The talents *H·* gives we must improve.
	15– 8	*H·* knows all things and rewards according to
a	26–17	prove what God is and what *H·* does for man.

He

m	67– 3	learn the lessons *H·* teaches?
sp	97–26	"*H·* uttered His voice, the earth— *Psal.* 46 : 6.
s	110– 6	in which all that *H·* has made is pronounced
	142–29	God being All-in-all, *H·* made medicine ;
	157–17	If drugs are part of God's creation, which. . . *H*
	157–18	If *H·* could create drugs intrinsically bad,
	157–20	If *H·* creates drugs at all and designs them
ph	165– *	*H·* sent *His word, and healed*— *Psal.* 107 : 20.
	166–21	*H·* can do all things for us in sickness as
f	206–21	Is God creating anew what *H·* has already
	206–27	*H·* destroys them, and brings to light
	208–13	not . . . that *H·* should make man sick,
	212–23	this *H·* does by means of Mind,
	223–32	"*H·* come whose right it is."— *Ezek.* 21 : 27.
	226–15	and *H·* has built it on diviner claims.
	229–24	all that *H·* makes is good and will stand
	241– 1	"Whom the Lord loveth *H·*— *Heb.* 12 : 6.
	244– 1	*H·* does not produce moral . . . deformity ;
	254–11	When we wait patiently on God . . . *H·* directs
c	256–15	nor can *H·* be understood aright through
	256–19	*H·* who, in the language of Scripture,
	266–16	Thus *H·* teaches mortals to lay down their
b	275– 8	and therefore *H·* is divine Principle.
	286–17	Scriptures declare all that *H·* made to be good,
	286–20	is good, and reflects God as *H·* is.
	287–14	how can *H·* be absent or suggest the absence of
	295– 6	filled with spiritual ideas, which *H·* evolves,
	303–26	*H·* would be without a witness
	305–18	what things soever *H·* doeth,— *John* 5 : 19.
	311– 5	and *H·* made all.
	331– 6	If *H·* dwelt within what *H·* creates,
	331–20	*H·* is all-inclusive, and is reflected by
	331–22	*H·* fills all space,
o	341– *	*H·* that raised up Christ— *Rom.* 8 : 11.
	354–22	out of the mouth of babes *H·* will perfect praise.
	356–20	as incapable of producing sin, . . . as *H·* is of
	357– 2	will not punish man for doing what *H·*
	357–15	how dare we attempt to destroy what *H·* hath
	360–26	*H·* putteth no trust in His— *see Job* 4 : 18.
	360–27	His angels *H·* chargeth with— *see Job* 4 : 18.
p	381–16	*H·* is not the author of barbarous codes.
	389–20	*H·* cannot annul these regulations by an
	390–23	no more the author of sickness than *H·* is of sin.
	414–21	"The Lord is God— *Deut.* 4 : 35.
t	455–24	When *H·* commissions a messenger, it is one who
r	471– 3	all that *H·* creates are perfect and eternal,
	472–25	That which *H·* creates is good,
	472–26	and *H·* makes all that is made.
k	499– *	*H·* that is holy, *H·* that is true,— *Rev.* 3 : 7.
	499– *	*H·* that hath the key of David,— *Rev.* 3 : 7.
	499– *	*H·* that openeth, and no man— *Rev.* 3 : 7.
g	504– 4	and the darkness *H·* called Night.— *Gen.* 1 : 5.
	506–20	even as *H·* opens the petals of a
	506–23	the waters called *H·* Seas :— *Gen.* 1 : 10.
	510–15	*H·* made the stars also.— *Gen.* 1 : 16.
	516–25	in the image of God created *H·* him ;— *Gen.* 1 : 27.
	516–26	male and female created *H·* them,— *Gen.* 1 : 27.
	518–24	saw everything that *H·* had made,— *Gen.* 1 : 31.
	519– 4	How could *H·* be otherwise, since the
	519–23	His work which *H·* had made ;— *Gen.* 2 : 2.
	519–23	*H·* rested on the seventh day— *Gen.* 2 : 2.
	519–24	all His work which *H·* had made.— *Gen.* 2 : 2.
	524–17	that *H·* should now be called Jehovah?
	525–15	after God's mind shaped *H·* him ;
	525–15	and *H·* shaped them male and female.
	525–21	Whatever is valueless or baneful, *H·* did not
	525–23	we read that *H·* saw everything
	525–23	everything which *H·* had made,
	526–16	God pronounced good all that *H·* created,
	526–17	the Scriptures declare that *H·* created all.
	527–13	Did *H·* create this fruit-bearer of sin
	527–13	neither tempteth *H·* any man."— *Jas.* 1 : 13.
	528–11	and *H·* took one of his ribs,— *Gen.* 2 : 21.
	528–13	the rib, . . . made *H·* a woman,— *Gen.* 2 : 22.
	530–12	as able to feed and clothe man as *H·* doth the
	532–24	God is all and *H·* is Mind
	533– 5	And *H·* said, Who told thee— *Gen.* 3 : 11.
	533–11	as if *H·* were the creator of evil.
	535– 6	Unto the woman *H·* said,— *Gen.* 3 : 16.
	535–19	And unto Adam *H·* said,— *Gen.* 3 : 17.
	536– 1	the waters called *H·* Seas."— *Gen.* 1 : 10.
	537– 5	So *H·* drove out the man :— *Gen.* 3 : 24.
	537– 5	and *H·* placed at the east— *Gen.* 3 : 24.
	541– 8	to his offering, *H·* had not respect.— *Gen.* 4 : 5.
	541–27	And *H·* [Jehovah] said,— *Gen.* 4 : 10.
ap	576–13	*H·* must be worshipped in spirit and in love.
gl	579– *	*H·* that is holy, *H·* that is true,— *Rev.* 3 : 7.
	579– *	*H·* that hath the key of David,— *Rev.* 3 : 7.
	579– *	*H·* that openeth, and no man— *Rev.* 3 : 7.
	580–26	supposition . . . creator entered what *H·* created,

head

and heart

f	213–26	Music is the rhythm of *h·* and heart.

and limbs

p	379–27	dry skin, pain in the *h·* and limbs,

head
anointeth my
  ap 578–14   anointeth my *h·* with oil ;— *see Psal.* 23 : 5.
bruises the
  f 216– 8   Truth bruises the *h·* of error
bruise the
  g 534–29   woman, this idea, will bruise the *h·* of lust.
bruise thy
  g 534–11   it shall bruise thy *h·*,— *Gen.* 3 : 15.
crowned
  s 141–18   Its only crowned *h·* is immortal sovereignty.
his
  m 66– 5   Wears yet a precious jewel in his *h·*.
  p 362–14   with his *h·* towards the table
  gl 598–11   "He bowed his *h·*, and— *John* 19 : 30.
hydra
  ap 563– 6   hatred, which lifts its hydra *h·*,
of the corner
  s 139–27   become "the *h·* of the corner."— *Matt.* 21 : 42.
upon her
  ap 560– 8   and upon her *h·* a crown— *Rev.* 12 : 1.
upon his
  ap 558– 4   and a rainbow was upon his *h·*,— *Rev.* 10 : 1.

  s 140–13   of the heart and not of the *h·*.
  ph 191–18   should no longer ask of the *h·*, heart, or
  197–24   With rules of health in the *h·* and
  f 243–16   The *h·*, heart, lungs, and limbs do not
  b 308– 9   the *h·*, heart, stomach, blood, nerves,

headlong
  ph 192–13   It is the *h·* cataract, the devouring flame,
  f 244–28   Such admissions cast us *h·* into darkness and
  r 490– 8   Will— blind, stubborn, and *h·*

heads
  ph 165–17   distressed stomachs and aching *h·*.
  ap 562–30   having seven *h·* and ten horns,— *Rev.* 12 : 3.
  562–31   and seven crowns upon his *h·*.— *Rev.* 12 : 3.
  569–18   not struggling to lift their *h·* above the

headstone
  p 380– 5   Truth is the rock of ages, the *h·* of the corner,

heal
  pref x–21   so little faith in His . . . power to *h·* disease.
  a 38–30   converted, and I might *h·* you.
  44–16   did not require the skill of a surgeon to *h·* the
  sp 87–17   It enables one to *h·* through Mind,
  95– 1   effect of his Mind was always to *h·*
  s 110–26   the power of C. S. to *h·* mortal minds and
  132– 3   this exhibition of the divine power to *h·*
  136– 4   and *h·* both the sick and the sinning.
  146–14   the power of God . . . to *h·* the body.
  148– 1   never spoke of disease . . . as difficult to *h·*.
  148– 2   a case they had failed to *h·*,
  148– 4   requisite power to *h·* was in Mind.
  152– 7   that it may give hope to the sick and *h·* them,
  152–19   supposed this ceremony was intended to *h·* him,
  155–21   in order to *h·* a single case of disease.
  158–10   divine Mind and its efficacy to *h·*.
  ph 168–12   and depend upon them to *h·* you,
  179– 9   and to *h·* by the Truth-power,
  f 202–29   yet we rely on a drug . . . to *h·* disease, as if
  203– 6   shows that matter can neither *h·* nor make sick,
  208–14   not . . . leave man to *h·* himself ;
  218–18   without faith in God's . . . ability to *h·*
  234– 1   Spiritual draughts *h·*,
  b 272– 1   how shall they . . . *h·* multitudes, except
  318– 9   saying that . . . Mind cannot or will not *h·* it.
  318–25   and attempts to *h·* it with matter.
  318–26   If disease is right it is wrong to *h·* it.
  320–27   the divine power to *h·* the ills of the flesh,
  o 350–23   and *h·* them."— *Matt.* 13 : 15.
  351– 3   When we lose faith in God's power to *h·*,
  351– 6   Neither can we *h·* through the help of Spirit, if
  351–10   learned that her own prayers failed to *h·* her
  352– 3   able to demonstrate His power to *h·*,
  355– 8   which evince no spiritual power to *h·*,
  359– 4   Will that faith *h·* them?
  p 365– 8   benign thought of Jesus, . . . would *h·* the sick,
  366– 1   but *h·* he cannot, while his own . . . barrenness
  366–32   If we would *h·* by the Spirit, we must
  380–11   and deny the power of Mind to *h·*.
  382–20   is more difficult to *h·* through Mind than
  395–15   Prayers, in which God is not asked to *h·*
  399–32   How can I *h·* the body,
  410–27   the power to *h·* mentally will
  412–18   To *h·* by argument, find the type of
  420– 5   If students do not readily *h·* themselves,
  t 446–15   destroying his own power to *h·* and his own
  449–17   than it does to *h·* the most difficult case.
  452–24   Expect to *h·* simply by
  459–24   Any attempt to *h·* mortals with erring
  r 473–10   Truth, that comes to *h·* sickness and sin
  482–29   It can *h·* in no other way, since the
  483– 2   how do drugs, hygiene, and animal magnetism *h·*?
  483– 3   It may be affirmed that they do not *h·*,
  483– 6   which nothing but Truth or Mind can *h·*,

heal
  r 483– 8   In order to *h·* by Science, you must
  494–12   Jesus demonstrated the divine power to *h·*
  ap 558–14   When you look it fairly in the face, you can *h·*
  (*see also* **sick**)

healed
  a 20–16   "with his stripes . . . we are *h·*."— *Isa.* 53 : 5.
  sp 78–29   By it the sick are *h·*,
  79–22   never described . . . but he *h·* disease.
  94–21   Of the ten lepers whom Jesus *h·*,
  94–23   to acknowledge the divine Principle which had *h·*
  s 133–12   *h·* of the poisonous stings of vipers.
  139–31   does not follow that the profane . . . cannot be *h·*
  ph 165– *   *He sent His word, and h· them,— Psal.* 107 : 20.
  168–21   He *h·* sickness in defiance of what is called
  169– 7   said to the patient, "You are *h·*,"
  169–26   sick are never really *h·* except by
  185–32   is *h·* only by removing the influence
  193–21   discharge . . . stopped, and the sore was *h·*.
  193–28   God and that woman who *h·* him."
  f 210–17   Jesus *h·* sickness and sin by
  219–24   Those who are *h·* through metaphysical
  230–23   the sick are never really *h·* by drugs,
  230–27   We think that we are *h·* when a disease disappears.
  230–29   never thoroughly *h·* until the liability to be
  231– 9   If God heals not the sick, they are not *h·*,
  o 346– 8   teaches how this . . . is to be saved and *h·*.
  359– 7   I have *h·* infidels whose only objection to this
  p 369–30   No man is physically *h·* in wilful error
  386–12   *h·* disease through the action of Truth
  403–13   can be *h·* only by the divine Mind.
  406– 3   Sin and sickness are both *h·* by the same
  412– 1   in wholly removing the fear, your patient is *h·*.
  416–27   metaphysical method by which they can be *h·*.
  428–30   The author has *h·* hopeless organic disease,
  t 446–10   has generally completely *h·* such cases.
  447–27   The sick are not *h·* merely by declaring
  463–28   The sick are not *h·* by inanimate matter
  r 493–10   Will you . . . show how it is to be *h·*?
  (*see also* **sick**)

healer
and patient
  t 457– 5   for teacher and student, for *h·* and patient,
Christian Science
  p 417–20   To the C. S. *h·*, sickness is a dream
mental
  p 401–31   while the mental *h·* confines himself chiefly
of mortal mind
  b 326–15   *h·* of mortal mind is the healer of the body.
of sin
  s 148–32   admits God to be the *h·* of sin but not of
  f 251–24   the *h·* of sin, disease, death.
of the body
  b 326–15   healer of mortal mind is the *h·* of the body.
of the sick
  s 138– 7   Life, Truth, and Love, . . . was the *h·* of the sick
thoughts of the
  t 446–16   Good must dominate in the thoughts of the *h·*,
would-be
  p 365–27   through the would-be *h·*,

  s 153–15   human faith or the divine Mind is the *h·*
  p 394–32   faith is not the *h·* in such cases.
  395– 6   the *h·* should speak to disease as one
  401– 5   it is not a *h·*, but it engenders disease
  t 459–31   more certain results than any other *h·*
  r 482–31   human, mortal mind so-called is not a *h·*,
  493–15   enables the *h·* to demonstrate and prove

healers
  a 47– 6   became better *h·*, leaning no longer on matter
  s 144–31   whether the ancient inspired *h·* understood the
  146– 2   The ancient Christians were *h·*.
  ph 179– 6   can heal the sick, who are absent from their *h·*,
  180– 6   when he sees his would-be *h·* busy,
  o 358–27   belief that . . . these *h·* have wonderful power,

healeth
  b 276– 3   the Lord that *h·* thee,"— *Exod.* 15 : 26.
  320–28   encourages mortals to hope in Him who *h·*

healing (noun)
adaptation to
  s 116–12   view of C. S. and of its adaptation to *h·*
and teaching
  o 349– 4   ask concerning our *h·* and teaching,
  t 454–18   the true incentive in both *h·* and teaching.
  455–32   the Science of mental *h·* and teaching,
  458–28   through living as well as *h·* and teaching,
applicable to
  t 463–27   There is a law of God applicable to *h·*,
branch of its
  p 402– 2   surgery is the branch of its *h·* which will be
by the prophets
  s 139–25   nor annul the *h·* by the prophets,
cases of
  pref x–16   By thousands of well-authenticated cases of *h·*,

healing

Christian
pref viii–14 shows that Christian *h·* confers the
    ix–15 the Principle and practice of Christian *h·*,
a 40– 4 tendency of Christian *h·* and its Science,
  55– 4 the idea of Christian *h·* enjoined by Jesus ;
  55–26 the spirit and power of Christian *h·*.
s 109–19 cures were produced in primitive Christian *h·*
  134–18 Denial of the possibility of Christian *h·* robs
  144–31 understood the Science of Christian *h·*,
  145–21 If there is any mystery in Christian *h·*, it is the
  147–24 Our Master . . . practised Christian *h·*,
f 238–32 in the demonstration of Christian *h·*,
b 271–29 to learn and to practise Christian *h·*.
o 351–24 the Spirit-rule of Christian *h·*, which
  355–15 conflicting theories regarding Christian *h·*?
t 460–18 If Christian *h·* is abused by mere
g 515– 1 It supports Christian *h·*, and enables

Christian Science
t 456–14 the true conception of C. S. *h·*

demonstrated by
pref ix–23 this Science must be demonstrated by *h·*,
g 547– 2 statement of C. S., if demonstrated by *h·*,

demonstrate the
t 462–13 Whoever would demonstrate the *h·* of C. S.

demonstration of
a 41–17 this demonstration of *h·* was early lost,

divine
  (*see* **divine**)

divine law of
t 445–16 You render the divine law of *h·* obscure and

divine Principle of
pref x–22 The divine Principle of *h·* is proved
s 112–21 thus are the divine Principle of *h·* and
t 458–12 to think of aiding the divine Principle of *h·*

evoke
p 365–13 with which to evoke *h·* from the

gospel of
a 55– 9 the gospel of *h·* is again preached

in his
s 143– 7 would have . . . employed them in his *h·*.

is easier
p 373–12 *H·* is easier than teaching,

is instantaneous
p 411–12 and the *h·* is instantaneous.

Jesus'
s 147– 3 Principle, upon which Jesus' *h·* was based,

light and
t 446–12 through which Mind pours light and *h·*

living and
s 141– 6 Jesus' divine precepts for living and *h·*.

mental
pref x– 4 Various books on mental *h·* have since
s 107– 6 divine Principle of scientific mental *h·*.
t 455–32 the Science of mental *h·* and teaching,
  459–15 Committing the bare process of mental *h·* to

metaphysical
s 150–13 in the metaphysical *h·* of physical disease :
ph 178–29 Ignorant of the . . . basis of metaphysical *h·*,
  178–31 none . . . mingled with metaphysical *h·*.
p 404–18 results from metaphysical *h·*, which
t 455–18 knowledge of C. S., or metaphysical *h·*,
r 484– 7 Does C. S., or metaphysical *h·*, include
  493–16 rule of C. S. or metaphysical *h·*.

methods of
s 143–31 Inferior and unspiritual methods of *h·* may
p 395–13 destroys all faith in . . . material methods of *h·*,

no
ph 169–20 There can be no *h·* except by this Mind,

physical
pref xi– 1 the phenomena of physical *h·* in C. S.
  xi– 9 The physical *h·* of C. S. results now, as in
s 150–12 is not primarily one of physical *h·*.
t 460–10 spiritual, though used for physical *h·*.

power of
b 271–12 the word indicates that the power of *h·* was not
t 452–29 destroys your power of *h·* from the

Principle of
s 157– 4 its one recognized Principle of *h·* is Mind,
o 343– 3 for teaching Truth as the Principle of *h·*,

proof of
ap 569–13 He . . . rejoices in the proof of *h·*,

purpose in
a 51–21 His purpose in *h·* was not alone to restore

recipe for all
p 406– 1 The Bible contains the recipe for all *h·*.

redemption and
s 151– 7 need of something . . . for its redemption and *h·*.

requisite for
t 448–21 spiritual qualifications requisite for *h·*,

rule of
r 496–17 enables you to demonstrate, . . . the rule of *h·*,

Science of
  (*see* **Science**)

Science of all
a 20–32 seek the divine Principle and Science of all *h·*.

---

healing

scientific
s 145–16 Scientific *h·* has this advantage over other
  147–18 demonstration of the rules of scientific *h·*

spiritual
p 367– 1 we must not hide the talent of spiritual *h·*

success in
sp 95–17 but it is important to success in *h·*,
t 448–28 he cannot fail of success in *h·*.

system of
s 132–17 Jesus' system of *h·* received no aid

theology, and
s 138–18 for all Christianity, theology, and *h·*.

true
ph 192–29 Christianity is the basis of true *h·*.

---

pref xii–25 consolation to the sorrowing and *h·* to the sick,
a 38–17 otherwise the *h·* could not have been done
    spiritually.
an 105–32 but to go in *h·* from the use of
s 109–20 but I must know the Science of this *h·*,
  146– 1 first article of faith . . . was *h·*,
  158– 9 to vegetable and mineral drugs for *h·*.
f 232–11 theories . . . make *h·* possible only through
t 445–13 by recourse to material means for *h·*.
r 483– 8 will ultimately supersede all other means in *h·*.

healing (adj.)
pref x– 7 They regard the human mind as a *h·* agent,
pr 12– 2 What is this *h·* prayer?
  12–12 the divine *h·* Principle as manifested in Jesus,
a 24– 9 *h·* currents of Truth are pointed out.
  55– 8 the *h·* Christ and spiritual idea of being.
sp 98–10 it is the *h·* influence of Spirit (not *spirits*)
s 141–14 *h·* effect followed the understanding of the
  147–11 lost none of its divine and *h·* efficacy,
  152– 9 Truth has a *h·* effect, even when not fully
  160– 5 drugs lose their *h·* force,
ph 166– 5 the *h·* effort is made on the wrong side,
  185–21 as a spiritual factor in the *h·* work.
f 217– 6 may inform us that the *h·* work of C. S.
b 285–31 Truth, as the *h·* and saving power.
  312–29 the intelligent and divine *h·* Principle
  329– 2 the *h·* elements of pure Christianity
p 365–16 the *h·* work will be accomplished at one visit,
  398–25 a belief in the *h·* effects of time and
  410–28 until the practitioner's *h·* ability is
t 445–15 there will be no desire for other *h·* methods.
  449–12 registers his *h·* ability and fitness to teach.
  (*see also* **power**)

healing (ppr.)
pref viii–14 by *h·* both disease and sin ;
sp 95–10 for the purpose of *h·* them.
s 147–27 demonstrating this Principle of *h·*
  150– 3 this Christian system of *h·* disease.
f 227–32 by *h·* in direct opposition to them
o 343– 2 Shall I then be smitten for *h·*
  349– 7 annulled material law by *h·* contrary to it.
p 369–15 in order to discover some means of *h·* the
  406– 2 for the *h·* of the nations." — *Rev.* 22 : 2.
  406– 9 demonstrated in the *h·* of mortals,
  419–28 To succeed in *h·*, you must conquer your
  430– 2 Jesus demonstrated this, *h·* the dying and
  (*see also* **sick, sickness**)

healing-power
sp 94–18 His *h·* evoked denial,

heals
s 135–11 same power which *h·* sin *h·* also sickness.
  137–21 Truth, Life, and Love, which *h·* mentally.
  155– 5 law of a general belief, . . . which *h·* ;
  158–11 truth which *h·* both mind and body.
  162–25 C. S. *h·* organic disease as surely as it
  162–26 as surely as it *h·* what is called functional,
ph 167– 3 the infinite divine Principle which *h·*
  179– 7 Immortal Mind *h·* what eye hath not seen ;
f 219–13 whereas divine Mind *h·*.
  231– 8 If God *h·* not the sick, they are not healed,
b 270–30 and that the divine Mind alone *h·*.
  318–23 The Science of Mind . . . *h·* with Truth.
  328– 7 the divine Principle which saves and *h·*,
o 344–11 more fully understood that Truth *h·*
p 375–12 demonstrates that divine Mind *h·*,
  386–20 despatch, correcting the mistake, *h·* your grief,
t 445–23 cast out by the divine Mind which *h·*
  450–23 he *h·* them both by understanding God's power
ap 559–22 sweet at its first taste, when it *h·* you ;
  (*see also* **sick, sickness**)

health

agrees only with
s 162– 3 the metaphysician agrees only with *h·*

and happiness
s 152–27 a spiritual source for *h·* and happiness.
c 261– 8 The effect of mortal mind on *h·* and happiness
p 442–12 his countenance beaming with *h·* and happiness.

health

and harmony
sp 72–31 the communicator of truth, *h·*, and harmony
s 146– 8 *h·* and harmony have been sacrificed.
p 412–26 normal conditions of *h·* and harmony.
and holiness
a 37–25 by the demonstration of . . . *h·* and holiness.
f 236–24 the truths of *h·* and holiness.
241–24 the way to *h·* and holiness.
b 337–30 the rule of *h·* and holiness in C. S.,
and immortality
f 248– 7 ought to ripen into *h·* and immortality,
and manhood
p 407–11 they crush out happiness, *h·*, and manhood.
and morals
p 400– 5 before its influence upon *h·* and morals can
426–24 would raise the standard of *h·* and morals
r 485–16 through better *h·* and morals
and perfection
ph 167–14 the divine source of all *h·* and perfection.
and the human life
t 451–32 tends to blast moral sense, *h·*, and the human life.
and the morals
t 449–29 improves the *h·* and the morals of his student
basis of
s 120–22 Truth, which is the only basis of *h·* ;
basis of all
b 339–25 The basis of all *h·*, sinlessness, and
belief of
p 398–27 and change the belief of disease to a belief of *h·*.
be restored
o 352–28 terror of ghosts will depart and *h·* be restored.
Christianization and
pr 1– 9 the Christianization and *h·* of mankind.
constitutes
b 297– 9 the understanding of what constitutes *h·* ;
destructive to
t 445–26 The human will . . . is destructive to *h·*,
determines
ph 186– 7 thoroughness of this work determines *h·*.
detrimental to
t 446–28 detrimental to *h·* and integrity of thought.
divine Principle of
b 319– 9 faith in the divine Principle of *h·*
essential for
p 374– 2 has decided upon as essential for *h·*.
establish
f 203– 8 this understanding would establish *h·*.
evidence of
a 52– 6 spiritual evidence of *h·*, holiness, and life ;
facts of
b 319– 5 as subserving the facts of *h·*.
p 370–18 The moral and spiritual facts of *h·*,
fatal to
ph 173–30 idols of civilization are far more fatal to *h·*
functional
s 125– 3 for organic and functional *h·*
good
s 120–11 if the . . . indicate that he is in good *h·*?
guides to
f 235–21 wise spiritual guides to *h·* and hope.
harmony of
p 400– 9 Mortals obtain the harmony of *h·*, only as
harmony, or
s 159–26 to ascertain how much harmony, or *h·*,
has been restored
o 348–31 *h·* has been restored, and longevity increased.
his
f 220–23 Finding his *h·* failing, he gave up his
p 383–23 tells you that the weed preserves his *h·*,
his own
t 446–15 destroying his own power to heal and his own *h·*.
invalid's
p 379–23 does not affect the invalid's *h·*,
is normal
s 120–14 in which *h·* is normal and disease is abnormal.
laws of
(*see* laws)
Life and
p 430–11 to shut out the true sense of Life and *h·*.
life and
ph 185–11 to regulate life and *h·*.
p 428–31 and raised the dying to life and *h·*
morals and
b 273–32 cannot be destructive to morals and *h·* when
most
pref viii–15 Christian healing confers the most *h·*
notion that
p 383–32 notion that *h·* depends on inert matter
of children
p 413–11 good or bad effects on the *h·* of children.
of my countenance
p 362– * *Who is the h· of my countenance— Psal. 42 : 11.*
on the side of
ph 168–10 it ought to be enlisted on the side of *h·*.

health

or disease
s 120–27 supposed consciousness of *h·* or disease,
or happiness
p 420–23 is not promotive of *h·* or happiness.
or life
s 148–27 When physiology fails to give *h·* or life by
our
ph 167– 9 our *h·*, our longevity, and our Christianity.
perfect
f 221–15 and he is now in perfect *h·*
permanent
sp 79– 9 such a mental method produces permanent *h·*.
physiology, and
ph 179–21 Treatises on anatomy, physiology, and *h·*,
presence of
p 412–25 Realize the presence of *h·* and the fact of
produces in man
p 380–25 the divine Mind produces in man *h·*,
prolific in
ap 563–21 prolific in *h·*, holiness, and immortality.
relating to
p 381–23 human theories relating to *h·*,
report of
ph 194– 9 Truth sends a report of *h·* over the body.
restore
a 51–22 His purpose . . . was not alone to restore *h·*,
ph 174– 2 The Esquimaux restore *h·* by incantations
restored
sp 79– 5 *h·* restored by changing the patient's thoughts
s 162–18 the author has restored *h·* in cases of
restored to
ph 185– 5 and she . . . was restored to *h·*.
rules of
ph 169–11 faith in rules of *h·* or in drugs begets and
197–24 With rules of *h·* in the head
scale of
p 407–19 ascend a degree in the scale of *h·*,
sense of
m 69– 5 gain the sense of *h·* only as
p 373–23 Establish the scientific sense of *h·*,
sickness and
sp 74–22 infancy and manhood, sickness and *h·*,
f 211– 4 produce sickness and *h·*, good and evil,
229–10 sickness and *h·*, holiness and unholiness,
246– 3 sickness and *h·*, life and death.
sickness to
b 339–23 sickness to *h·*, sin to holiness,
subject of
s 120–17 testimony on the subject of *h·*.
thoughts of
f 208–31 should delineate upon it thoughts of *h·*,
your
ph 168– 9 Your belief militates against your *h·*,

---

m 59–19 salutary in prolonging her *h·* and smiles
62–15 will do much more for the *h·* of the
sp 99–24 the manifestations of which are *h·*, purity,
s 116– 3 spiritual power, love, *h·*, holiness.
120–15 *H·* is not a condition of matter, but of
125– 5 no longer be found indispensable to *h·*.
126–25 the effects of Truth on the *h·*, longevity,
131– 3 Sickness should not seem so real as *h·*.
ph 166–22 can do all things for us in sickness as in *h·*.
166–23 Failing to recover *h·* through adherence to
f 216–24 while *h·* would seem the exception,
221–20 never ordained . . . fasting should be a means
of *h·*.
224–24 the needs of mortals in sickness and in *h·*,
229–24 If God causes man to be sick, . . . *h·*, must be
evil,
230– 5 bring us into *h·*, holiness, and immortality.
230–18 no more . . . than . . . and *h·* occasion disease.
248–30 justice, *h·*, holiness, love
b 299–27 error, may seem to hide Truth, *h·*,
340–22 by which man demonstrates *h·*, holiness, and
p 370– 7 and if *h·* is not made manifest
371–30 strength instead of weakness, and *h·* instead of
380–31 against Himself, against Life, *h·*, harmony.
392–10 opposed to the *h·*, holiness, and harmony of
397– 3 acting beneficially or injuriously on the *h·*,
405–11 against *h·*, happiness, and success.
408– 6 universal insanity of so-called *h·*,
417– 1 find *h·*, peace, and harmony in God,
426– 4 divine power, which steers the body into *h·*.
t 462–31 both in *h·* and in sickness.
g 518–22 expressions of God reflect *h·*,
553– 8 or *h·* will never be universal,
555– 2 and that *h·* attends the absence of

Health-agent
p 436– 4 After betraying him . . . the *H·* disappeared,

health-belief
b 297–10 either a *h·* or a belief in sickness

healthful
 f 254–28 the ever-agitated but *h·* waters of truth,
 o 344– 5 normal, *h·*, and sinless condition of man
health-giving
 s 125– 6 will be found always harmonious and *h·*.
health-illusion
 b 297– 7 It is as necessary for a *h·*, as for an
Health-laws
 p 430–29 testifies thus :— I represent *H·*.
 431–17 these assistants resigned to me, *H·*,
 436– 1 principal witness (the officer of the *H·*)
 439–25 You aided and abetted Fear and *H·*.
 441–21 *H·*, Mesmerism, Hypnotism,
health-laws
 p 413–27 illusions about disease, *h·*, and death,
Health-officer
 p 439–13 the *H·* had Mortal Man in custody,
health-theories
 p 388–18 ambiguous nature of all material *h·*.
healthy
 m 62–22 if we would be wise and *h·*.
 s 161– 1 supple and elastic condition of the *h·* limb,
 162–22 bones have been restored to *h·* conditions.
 162–24 and *h·* organizations have been established
 ph 179–16 You can even educate a *h·* horse so far
 197–22 helped to make them *h·*,
 198–22 a picture of *h·* and harmonious formations.
 f 232–20 never taught that drugs, . . . make a man *h·*,
 b 276–21 is turned into new and *h·* channels,
 p 373–26 disabled organ will resume its *h·* functions.
 376–24 representing man as *h·* instead of diseased,
 377–10 prove that they can be *h·* in all climates,
 404–15 The *h·* sinner is the hardened sinner.
 414–12 truth and love will establish a *h·* state,
 420–18 It imparts a *h·* stimulus to the body,
 431–28 testifies : . . . I have lost my *h·* hue
heap
 b 339–14 *h·* up "wrath against the day of— Rom. 2 : 5.
hear
 pr 2– 2 Do we pray . . . to benefit those who *h·* us,
 a 27– 5 lepers are cleansed, the deaf *h·*,— Luke 7 : 22.
 37–27 *H·* these imperative commands :
 38–29 and having ears ye *h·* not ;
 m 59–20 Husbands, *h·* this and remember
 sp 75–32 the departing may *h·* the glad welcome of
 s 132– 5 things which ye do *h·* and see :— Matt. 11 : 4.
 132– 7 the deaf *h·*, the dead are raised— Matt. 11 : 5.
 f 211–26 If . . . causes the eyes to see and the ears to *h·*,
 213–17 The ear does not really *h·*.
 219–23 We may *h·* a sweet melody, and yet
 220– 1 We *h·* it said : "I exercise daily
 237–24 or to *h·* about the fallacy of matter
 248–19 Do you not *h·* from all mankind of the imperfect
 c 256–12 "*H·*, O Israel : the Lord our God— Deut. 6 : 4.
 b 271–31 "How shall they *h·* without a— Rom. 10 : 14.
 272– 2 how shall they preach, . . . except the people *h·*?
 284–22 nor *h·* it through the ear,
 292–21 because ye cannot *h·* my word.— John 8 : 43.
 340– 7 "Let us *h·* the conclusion of— Eccl. 12 : 13.
 340– 9 Let us *h·* the conclusion of the whole matter :
 o 342–25 It causes the deaf to *h·*, the lame to walk,
 350–21 *h·* with their ears, and should— Matt. 13 : 15.
 354–24 spiritually to *h·* and to speak the new tongue.
 360–22 *H·* the wisdom of Job, as given in the
 p 397–26 when they act, walk, see, *h·*, enjoy,
 r 479–11 Matter cannot see, feel, *h·*,
 479–16 Does that which we call dead ever see, *h·*,
 ap 558–* *they that* h· *the words of this*— Rev. 1 : 3.
 gl 585– 4 "Having ears, *h·* ye not?"— Mark 8 : 18.
heard
 iii–* Oh! Thou hast *h·* my prayer ;
 pr 2– 3 to enlighten the infinite or to be *h·* of men?
 a 27– 4 things ye have seen and *h·* ;— Luke 7 : 22.
 sp 89–21 God, is *h·* when the senses are silent.
 s 117–14 Ear hath not *h·*, nor hath lip spoken,
 ph 175– 7 In old times who ever *h·* of dyspepsia,
 f 213–21 rapture of his grandest symphonies was never *h·*.
 c 255–18 Eye hath not seen Spirit, nor hath ear *h·* His
 262–17 "I have *h·* of Thee by the— Job 42 : 5.
 b 268–* *which we have* h·, *which we*— I John 1 : 1.
 268–* *That which we have seen and* h·— I John 1 : 3.
 308–14 Soul-inspired patriarchs *h·* the voice of Truth,
 o 352– 1 brought down no proof that it was *h·*,
 355–12 discord of every name and nature be *h·* no more,
 p 416–30 have already *h·* too much on that subject.
 424–23 to make yourself *h·* mentally while
 438–27 he disappeared and was never *h·* of more.
 438–29 we have *h·* Materia Medica explain how
 t 459– 3 "eye hath not seen nor ear *h·*."— I Cor. 2 : 9.
 g 532–15 I *h·* Thy voice in the garden,— Gen. 3 : 10.
 ap 559–12 *h·* in the desert and in dark places of fear.
 568–13 And I *h·* a loud voice saying— Rev. 12 : 10.

hearers
 a 54–17 His *h·* understood neither his words nor
 f 235–30 They should so raise their *h·* spiritually,
hearest
 s 134–26 "I knew that Thou *h·* me— John 11 : 42.
hearing
and sight
 r 489–27 no organic construction can give it *h·* and sight
dull of
 o 350–19 their ears are dull of *h·*,— Matt. 13 : 15.
material
 g 526– 9 Belief involves theories of material *h·*,
medium of
 f 214– 3 If the medium of *h·* is wholly spiritual,
of the ear
 ph 192– 7 They come from the *h·* of the ear,
 c 262–17 by the *h·* of the ear :— Job 42 : 5.
sight and
 gl 582–22 physical sense put out of sight and *h·* ;
to the deaf
 ph 183–28 sight to the blind, *h·* to the deaf,
 f 210–13 gave sight to the blind, *h·* to the deaf,
 r 487–11 gave . . . *h·* to the deaf centuries ago,

 p 437–15 Spirit not allowed a *h·* ;
 441–10 plea of False Belief we deem unworthy of a *h·*.
 r 486–23 Sight, *h·* all the spiritual senses of man,
 487– 7 more Christianity in seeing and *h·* spiritually
 489–18 material means for knowing, *h·*, seeing?
hearken
 b 321–28 neither *h·* to the voice of the— Exod. 4 : 8.
hearkened
 g 535–20 thou hast *h·* unto the— Gen. 3 : 17.
hears
 sp 86–30 It feels, *h·*, and sees its own thoughts.
 ph 198– 3 A patient *h·* the doctor's verdict as a
 198– 4 as a criminal *h·* his death-sentence.
 r 467–28 Matter neither sees, *h·*, nor feels.
 485– 5 Science declares that Mind, . . . sees, *h·*, feels,
 gl 591–15 that which mortal mind sees, feels, *h·*,
heart (*see also* **heart's**)
all thy
 pr 9–18 with all thy *h·*, and with all thy— Matt. 22 : 37.
and soul
 s 113– 6 the *h·* and soul of C. S., is Love.
condemns
 t 448– 6 Evil . . . which the *h·* condemns, has no
finds peace
 m 59–15 in which the *h·* finds peace and home.
gladden the
 s 121–13 goodness and beauty to gladden the *h·* ;
good
 b 272– 6 "honest and good *h·*'"— Luke 8 : 15.
head and
 f 213–26 Music is the rhythm of head and *h·*.
his
 pr 1–* *and shall not doubt in his* h·,— Mark 11 : 23.
 a 32–26 to refresh his *h·* with brighter, . . . views.
 sp 89–13 "As he thinketh in his *h·*,— Prov. 23 : 7.
 f 213– 4 "As he thinketh in his *h·*,— Prov. 23 : 7.
 p 383–28 "As he thinketh in his *h·*,— Prov. 23 : 7.
 t 451–16 where his treasure is, there will his *h·* be also.
honest
 pr 8– 3 We never need to despair of an honest *h·* ;
 t 464–24 fall before an honest *h·*.
human
 ph 190–27 When hope rose higher in the human *h·*,
hungering
 r 482–25 to the hungering *h·* in every age.
many a
 c 265–28 brightens the ascending path of many a *h·*.
meek in
 a 33–26 preaches the gospel to the poor, the meek in *h·*.
nearer the
 g 501– 7 are clearer and come nearer the *h·*.
of Christ
 ap 568–28 and nearer to the great *h·* of Christ ;
of divinity
 c 258–31 you can discern the *h·* of divinity,
of Love
 t 448– 4 went out to the great *h·* of Love,
of prayer
 pr 15–10 To enter into the *h·* of prayer,
or lungs
 ph 191–18 no longer ask of the head, *h·*, or lungs :
overflows
 a 26– 1 and the *h·* overflows with gratitude
pierces the
 m 66– 7 a broken reed, which pierces the *h·*.
pure in
 f 241–28 the pure in *h·* see God
 b 324– 6 "Blessed are the pure in *h·* :— Matt. 5 : 8.
 337–15 none but the pure in *h·* can see God,
 o 341– 9 "Blessed are the pure in *h·* :— Matt. 5 : 8.

heart

purpose of the
pr 8–29   learn what is the affection and purpose of the *h*·,
receptive
 a 46–11   It is revealed to the receptive *h*·,
reforms the
 a 19–23   the practical repentance, which reforms the *h*·
rejoicing the
 c 266– 2   are good, "rejoicing the *h*·."— *Psal.* 19 : 8.
struggling
 m 57–28   for Love supports the struggling *h*·
suffering
 p 365–32   poor suffering *h*· needs its rightful nutriment,
take
 ap 573–29   Take *h*·, dear sufferer, for this reality of
this
 pr 8–26   do we not already know more of this *h*·
this people's
 o 350–18   "This people's *h*· is waxed gross,— *Matt.* 13 : 15.
valves of the
 ph 187–13   valves of the *h*·, . . . obey the mandate of
while the
 pr 3–32   While the *h*· is far from divine Truth
whole
 f 219–12   "sick, and the whole *h*· faint ;"— *Isa.* 1 : 5.
wicked
 pr 8–24   We confess to having a very wicked *h*·

 an 100– *   out of the *h*· proceed evil— *Matt.* 15 : 19.
 s 140–12   Religion will then be of the *h*·
   151–19   The blood, *h*·, lungs, brain, etc.,
   160–12   so-called mind quits the body, the *h*· becomes
 ph 172–23   What is man? Brain, *h*·, blood,
   172–32   When we admit that matter (*h*·, blood, brain,
   181–29   there will your *h*· be also."— *Matt.* 6 : 21.
 f 220–31   controls the stomach, bones, lungs, *h*·,
   243–16   The head, *h*·, lungs, and limbs do not inform us
 c 262–26   there will your *h*· be also."— *Matt.* 6 : 21.
 b 308– 9   the admission from the head, *h*·, stomach,
 o 350–22   should understand with their *h*·,— *Matt.* 13 : 15.
 p 415–21   action . . . of the bowels, and of the *h*·.
   425–27   will never believe that *h*· . . . can destroy you.
 t 444–25   and say in thy *h*· :
 g 521–16   engraved on the understanding and *h*·
 gl 587–23   definition of

heartfelt

 pr 4–10   not . . . sufficient to express loyal and *h*·

heart's

 sp 88– 3   the poet Tennyson expressed the *h*· desire,

hearts

broken
 p 364–27   by their broken *h*·, expressed by
chastened
 a 35– 2   *h*· chastened and pride rebuked.
gross
 b 272–14   not to impart to dull ears and gross *h*·
honest
 pr 15–19   go forth with honest *h*· to work and watch
of men
 s 131–25   until the *h*· of men are made ready for it.
our
 s 116– 7   make this Scriptural testimony true in our *h*·,
struggling
 a 45–16   and peace to the struggling *h*· !
their
 a 46– 6   words, which made their *h*· burn within them,
 b 312–16   with scarcely a spark of love in their *h*· ;
 p 363–11   those around him were saying in their *h*·,
union of
 m 64–17   Marriage should signify a union of *h*·.

 f 233–24   including the *h*· which rejected him.

heat

and cold
 p 374–26   *H*· and cold are products of mortal mind.
animal
 p 374–30   Mortal mind produces animal *h*·,
chills and
 p 375– 6   Chills and *h*· are often the form in which
cold and
 s 125–22   cold and *h*·, latitude and longitude.
febrile
 p 379–26   quickened pulse, coated tongue, febrile *h*·,
fervent
 ap 565–21   with the fervent *h*· of Truth and Love,
light and
 ph 189– 5   we still believe that there is solar light and *h*·.
 g 538–11   The sun, giving light and *h*· to the earth,
light or
 g 548– 9   How little light or *h*· reach our earth when
pain or
 p 376–26   impossible for matter to suffer, to feel pain or *h*·,

heat

would pass
 p 375– 1   *H*· would pass from the body as

 ph 184–19   We say man suffers from the effects of cold, *h*·,
 p 375– 5   the separation of *h*· from the body.
   384– 9   though they expose him to fatigue, cold, *h*·,
 gl 586–11   FEAR. *H*· ; inflammation ; anxiety ;

heathen

 pr 13– 9   prayers . . . such as the *h*· use.
 r 466–23   *H*· mythology and Jewish theology have
   485–28   *h*· gods of mythology controlled war
 g 552– 5   *H*· philosophy, modern geology,

Heaven

 g 506– 8   God called the firmament *H*·.— *Gen.* 1 : 8.

heaven

and earth
 sp 91– 2   Have you ever pictured this *h*· and earth,
 s 131–19   O Father, Lord of *h*· and earth,— *Luke* 10 : 21.
 b 334– 6   it illumines *h*· and earth ;
 g 536– 5   *h*· and earth stand for spiritual ideas,
 ap 576–20   John saw *h*· and earth
and eternity
 g 503–10   constitute spiritual harmony,— *h*· and eternity.
army of
 c 256–21   in the army of *h*·, and among the— *Dan.* 4 : 35.
banished from
 s 158–14   Apollo, who was banished from *h*·
created the
 r 479–18   created the *h*· and the earth.— *Gen.* 1 : 1.
 g 502–22   created the *h*· and the earth.— *Gen.* 1 : 1.
declaration from
 ap 573–14   even the declaration from *h*·, supreme harmony,
down from
 a 33– 7   Their bread indeed came down from *h*·.
   35–26   "which cometh down from *h*·,"— *John* 6 : 33.
 ap 558– 3   mighty angel come down from *h*·,— *Rev.* 10 : 1.
   561–12   a bride coming down from *h*·, wedded to the
earth and
 s 121–10   earth and *h*· were bright,
 c 264–30   all the glories of earth and *h*· and man.
 g 518– 3   lord of the belief in earth and *h*·,
earth to
 a 48– 8   turned forever away from earth to *h*·,
firmament of
 g 511–22   in the open firmament of *h*·.— *Gen.* 1 : 20.
   512– 1   above the earth in the open firmament of *h*·,
firmament of the
 g 509–10   lights in the firmament of the *h*·,— *Gen.* 1 : 14.
   510– 7   lights in the firmament of the *h*·,— *Gen.* 1 : 15.
   511– 8   in the firmament of the *h*·,— *Gen.* 1 : 17.
first
 g 536– 3   the first *h*· and the first earth— *Rev.* 21 : 1.
 ap 572–21   the first *h*· and the first earth— *Rev.* 21 : 1.
good man's
 a 35–32   good man's *h*· would be a hell to the sinner.
high
 ap 568–27   sweeter than has ever before reached high *h*·,
his own
 c 266–21   and the saint his own *h*· by doing right.
hosts of
 ap 566–32   He leads the hosts of *h*· against the power of
impress of
 g 511–12   the seal of Deity and has the impress of *h*·,
kingdom of
   (*see* **kingdom**)
new
 sp 91– 1   "a new *h*· and a new earth."— *Rev.* 21 : 1.
 g 536– 2   a new *h*· and a new earth :— *Rev.* 21 : 1.
   556– 8   Then will the new *h*· and new earth appear,
 ap 572–20   a new *h*· and a new earth :— *Rev.* 21 : 1.
   572–25   but he already saw a new *h*· and a new earth.
   572–29   Were this new *h*· and new earth terrestrial
   573–22   by which he could see the new *h*· and new earth,
of Soul
 g 535–16   the open gate of C. S. into the *h*· of Soul,
order of
 s 118–32   the natural order of *h*· comes down to earth.
our Father in
 b 276–20   even as our Father in *h*· is perfect,
out of
 ap 574–14   coming down from God, out of *h*·,"— *Rev.* 21 : 2.
   575– 9   "down from God, out of *h*·,"— *Rev.* 21 : 2.
represents
 ap 560–10   *H*· represents harmony, and divine Science
revealed from
 m 56–13   its spiritual sense was revealed from *h*·,
stars of
 ap 563–24   third part of the stars of *h*·,— *Rev.* 12 : 4.
thy home is
 f 254–32   Pilgrim on earth, thy home is *h*· ;
to reach
 pr 6–15   To reach *h*·, the harmony of being,
war in
 ap 566–25   And there was war in *h*· :— *Rev.* 12 : 7.

heaven
which is in
a 31- 6 your Father, which is in h'."— Matt. 23:9.
37-29 even as your Father which is in h'— Matt. 5:48.
s 137-24 my Father which is in h';"— Matt. 16:17.
c 259-20 even as your Father which is in h'— Matt. 5:48.
267-17 will of my Father which is in h',— Matt. 12:50.
p 372-26 before my Father which is in h'."— Matt. 10:33.
r 485-23 even as the "Father which is in h'—Matt. 5:48.
wonder in
ap 560- 7 appeared a great wonder in h';— Rev. 12:1.
562-30 appeared another wonder in h';— Rev. 12:3.

pr 16-26 Our Father which art in h',— Matt. 6:9.
17- 1 done in earth, as it is in h'.— Matt. 6:10.
17- 2 Enable us to know,— as in h', so on earth,
a 36-26 suddenly pardoned and pushed into h',
49-20 charged with the grandest trust of h',
m 56- * but are as the angels of God in h'.— Matt. 22:30.
57-30 and begins to unfold its wings for h'.
ph 196-19 Sin makes its own hell, and goodness its own h'.
f 242- 9 There is but one way to h', harmony,
c 263-10 cling to earth because he has not tasted h'.
266-26 infinite Mind enthroned is h'.
b 291-13 H' is not a locality, but a divine state
339-25 "in earth, as it is in h'."— Matt. 6:10.
p 372-17 Therefore he will be as the angels in h'.
g 506-16 Let the waters under the h' be— Gen. 1:9.
516-16 arbutus sends her sweet breath to h'.
ap 566-28 neither was...found any more in h'.— Rev. 12:8.
568-14 a loud voice saying in h',— Rev. 12:10.
gl 587-25 definition of
589-15 JERUSALEM. . . . Home, h'.

heaven-bestowed
f 253-10 divine rights, your h' harmony,
ap 574-23 the four equal sides of which were h'

heaven-bestowing
ap 574-24 the four equal sides of which were . . . h'.

heaven-born
pr 16-21 the h' aspiration and spiritual

heavenly
pref ix-18 at the h' gate, waiting for the Mind of Christ.
a 33- 4 partook of the h' manna,
40-25 Our h' Father, divine Love, demands
s 108- 1 Whence came to me this h' conviction,
121- 5 the h' fields were incorrectly explored.
130-25 such as they belong to the h' kingdom.
c 265-25 aspiration after h' good comes
p 365- 2 pillow of the sick and the h' homesick
387-29 bestowed on man by his h' Father,
435- 1 court commended . . . to h' mercy,
t 447- 1 h' law is broken by trespassing upon
459- 6 gain h' riches by forsaking all worldliness.
r 480- 7 and not a trace of h' tints.
s 509-13 Spirit creates no other than h' . . . bodies,
535- 5 the other to be garnered into h' places.
ap 559-19 Mortals, obey the h' evangel.
560-11 interprets the Principle of h' harmony.
576- 3 This h' city, lighted by the Sun of
577-24 their honors within the h' city.
gl 592-25 gentleness ; prayer ; h' inspiration.

heavenly-minded
m 61-12 The offspring of h' parents

heavens
and earth
ap 573- 6 h' and earth to one human consciousness,
573-19 corporeal sense of the h' and earth
and the earth
g 519- 7 Thus the h' and the earth were— Gen. 2:1.
creates the
g 538-19 in which God creates the h', earth, and
earth and the
g 520-18 made the earth and the h',— Gen. 2:4.
543-32 made the earth and the h',"— Gen. 2:4.
glorious
f 240- 5 festive flowers, and glorious h',
in the
t 454- 9 "eternal in the h'."— II Cor. 5:1.
of astronomy
f 235-15 will reach higher than the h' of astronomy ;
rejoice, ye
ap 568-20 Therefore rejoice, ye h',— Rev. 12:12.
spiritual
ap 562-17 lamps in the spiritual h' of the age,

g 520-16 the generations of the h'— Gen. 2:4.

heavenward
an 106- 5 to push vainly against the current running h'.

heavily
t 449- 7 wrong done another reacts most h'

heavy
p 431- 8 going to sleep immediately after a h' meal.
441- 8 to give h' bonds for good behavior,

heavy-laden
f 217-28 for matter cannot be weary and h'.

Hebrew
a 23-21 In H', Greek, Latin, and English,
23-32 The H' verb to believe means also
sp 85-19 events . . . were foretold by the H' prophets.
s 112-31 divine commandment in the H' Decalogue,
161- 8 case of the three young H' captives,
ph 190-21 The H' bard, . . . thus swept his lyre
b 320-14 is quoted as follows, from the original H' :
333- 6 in common with other H' boys and men,
333- 7 the name Joshua, the renowned H' leader.
338-12 The word Adam is from the H' adamah,
r 488- 7 H' and Greek words often translated
g 523-32 the divine sovereign of the H' people,
525-11 in the H', image, similitude ;
540-22 H' allegory, representing error as assuming
gl 590-15 LORD. In the H', this term is sometimes
594- 1 (ophis, in Greek ; nacash, in H').

Hebrew Lawgiver
b 321- 6 The H' L', slow of speech,

Hebrews
s 112-22 characterized in the epistle to the H'.
133-14 attended the successes of the H' ;
b 313- 6 said of him in the first chapter of H' :
r 468-20 as the Scriptures use this word in H' :
ap 575-12 as we read in the book of H' ;

hecatombs
p 367- 6 better than h' of gushing theories,

hedge
g 536-23 h' about their achievements with thorns.

heed
s 159-11 to take no h' of mental conditions
f 232-27 voices of solemn import, but we h' them not.
b 299-16 By giving earnest h' to these spiritual guides
p 400-21 giving no h' to the body,
410- 1 If here we give no h' to C. S.,
t 462-14 abide strictly by its rules, h' every statement,
g 525-25 if we give the same h' to the history of

heeding
f 225-11 Science, h' not the pointed bayonet, marches on.

heedless
p 362- 7 H' of the fact that she was debarred

heel
f 216- 7 Error bites the h' of truth, but cannot kill
g 534-11 and thou shalt bruise his h'.— Gen. 3:15.
534-27 material sense, will bite the h' of the woman,
ap 563-20 untiring watch, that he may bite the h' of truth
564-29 is perpetually close upon the h' of harmony.

height
pref xii-14 in the h' of its prosperity
f 237- 9 h' their little daughter so naturally attained.
241-25 We should strive to reach the Horeb h'
b 304- 7 nor h', nor depth, nor any other— Rom. 8:39.
g 520- 4 h', might, majesty, and glory of infinite Love

heightens
c 262- 3 does not lessen man's dependence on God, but
h' it.

heights
pref viii- 3 to reach the h' of C. S., man must
b 292- 5 Science alone can compass the h' and depths of
325-26 the divine h' of our Lord.
g 514- 8 In humility they climb the h' of holiness.
ap 566-11 moves before them, . . . leading to divine h'.

heir
s 107-10 from every ill "that flesh is h' to."

held
a 48- 6 h' uncomplaining guard over a world
sp 74-11 the error which has h' the belief dissolves
s 155-13 a belief h' by a minority,
159- 6 Her hands were h', and she was forced into
p 379-28 The images, h' in this disturbed mind,
392-14 thought should be h' fast to this ideal.
400- 5 which must be h' in subjection before its
413-32 timorously h' in the beliefs
431-16 Materia Medica h' out the longest,
g 514-26 the control which Love h' over all,
ap 577- 4 His universal family, h' in the gospel of Love.

hell
a 35-32 good man's heaven would be a h' to the sinner.
s 137-32 and the gates of h'— Matt. 16:18.
ph 196-12 both soul and body in h',— Matt. 10:28.
196-19 Sin makes its own h', and goodness its own
c 266-20 The sinner makes his own h' by doing evil,
266-27 beliefs which originate in mortals are h'.
b 330-31 dementia, insanity, inanity, devil, h',
g 542-24 To envy's own h', justice consigns the lie
gl 588- 1 definition of

helmsman
m 67- 7 We ask the h' : "Do you know your

help

divine
p 393– 3 through divine *h·* we can forbid this entrance.
t 453–17 Dishonesty . . . which forfeits divine *h·*.

effectual
p 372–29 acknowledgment . . . is an effectual *h·*.

ever-present
f 218–23 divine Love, who is an ever-present *h·*

finds
pr 12–23 common custom . . . finds *h·* in blind belief,

in time of
s 148–29 to render *h·* in time of physical need.

look for
sp 82–29 do we look for *h·* to the Esquimaux

needed no
r 494– 7 God, who needed no *h·* from Jesus' example

need of
b 308–27 perceiving his error and his need of *h·*,

obtaining
f 218–22 lead only into material ways of obtaining *h·*,

of Spirit
o 351– 6 Neither can we heal through the *h·* of Spirit, if

others'
t 455–14 little or no power for others' *h·*.

present
pr 13– 1 "a very present *h·* in trouble."— *Psal.* 46 : 1.
f 202–28 "a very present *h·* in trouble ;"— *Psal.* 46 : 1.
o 351–13 this spiritual sense was a *present h·*.
t 444–12 a very present *h·* in trouble."— *Psal.* 46 : 1.

receive no
t 444– 1 and they receive no *h·* from them,

should come
pr 12–23 *h·* should come from the enlightened

———

pr 12–28 and not *h·* another who offers the
a 19–18 will *h·* us to understand Jesus' atonement
21–20 little opportunity to *h·* each other.
21–23 if I take up their line of travel, they *h·* me on,
23–27 *h·* thou mine unbelief !"— *Mark* 9 : 24.
sp 81–18 Man . . . cannot *h·* being immortal.
s 143– 9 if the sick cannot rely on God for *h·*
160–31 a material fungus without Mind to *h·* him?
163–23 we cannot *h·* being disgusted with the
ph 196–23 will *h·* to abate sickness and to destroy it.
f 222–11 Food had less power to *h·* or to hurt him
234–13 and *h·* them on the basis of the
b 268– * *I can do no otherwise ; so h· me God!*
p 404–31 neither . . . can *h·* him permanently, even in
r 494– 9 But mortals did need this *h·*,
g 518–15 The rich in spirit *h·* the poor
527–28 asking a prospective sinner to *h·* Him.
ap 570–22 In this age the earth will *h·* the woman ;

helped

a 34–21 It *h·* them to raise themselves and others
ph 197–22 *h·* to make them healthy,
b 323– 7 *h·* onward in the march towards righteousness,
p 375–11 believes that matter, not mind, has *h·* him.
435– 8 in obedience to higher law, *h·* his fellow-man,
ap 570–11 the earth *h·* the woman,— *Rev.* 12 : 16.

helpers

p 365– 5 and preparing their *h·* for the

helpful

ph 180– 7 is somewhat *h·* to them and to himself ;

helping

m 64–10 When a man lends a *h·* hand to
p 394–12 disarms man, prevents him from *h·* himself,
r 494–17 *h·* erring human sense to flee from its

helpless

m 61–19 reproduce in their own *h·* little ones
ph 191–19 Mind is not *h·*.
f 207–11 Evil is not supreme ; good is not *h·* ;
230–14 to suppose Him capable of . . . punishing the *h·*
231–13 If God makes sin, . . . Science and Christianity
   are *h·* ;
o 342–22 raises from the couch of pain the *h·* invalid.
352–19 they may become its *h·* victims,
p 377–28 a fear that Mind is *h·* to defend
420–10 Instruct the sick that they are not *h·* victims,
437–16 the *h·* innocent body tortured,
r 490–14 theories are *h·* to make man harmonious

helplessness

a 23–28 expresses the *h·* of a blind faith ;
f 235–19 Physicians, whom the sick employ in their *h·*,
244–30 pictures age as infancy, as *h·* and
o 341– 3 raising up thousands from *h·* to strength

help meet

g 533–20 Is this an *h· m·* for man?

helps

b 324– 3 *h·* to precipitate the ultimate harmony.
p 374–20 this belief *h·* rather than hinders disease.
r 481– 7 Material sense never *h·* mortals to
g 548–14 Every agony of mortal error *h·* error to destroy

hem

ph 170–26 at least to touch the *h·* of Truth's garment.
ap 569–11 He that touches the *h·* of Christ's robe

hemisphere

sp 74–25 when we are in the opposite *h·*?

hemlock

f 215–28 feared not the *h·* poison.
ap 559–28 because you must share the *h·* cup

hemorrhage

p 425– 9 inflammation, tubercles, *h·*, and

hence

pr 13–27 *H·* men recognize themselves as merely
14–18 *H·* the hope of the promise
a 25–19 *H·* the force of his admonition,
30– 1 *H·* he could give a more spiritual idea
52–10 *H·* the world's hatred of the just and
53– 7 *h·* the cup he drank.
sp 80–32 *h·* that matter is intelligent.
s 131– 7 *H·* the opposition of sensuous man to the
132– 4 *H·* his reply : "Go and show John— *Matt.* 11 : 4.
136–26 *H·* Herod's assertion : "John have I — *Luke* 9 : 9.
143– 2 *H·* the fact that, to-day, as yesterday,
ph 176–29 *H·* decided types of acute disease
198–27 *H·* the importance that doctors be
199– 9 *H·* the great fact that Mind alone enlarges
f 213– 4 *h·* as a man spiritually *understandeth*,
221–20 *H·* semi-starvation is not acceptable
236–17 *H·* the importance of C. S.,
251– 1 *h·* it is not more imperative
c 257–14 *H·* the Father Mind is not the
258– 3 *H·* the unsatisfied human craving
259–26 Vibration is not intelligence ; *h·* it is not a
267–11 *H·* man and the spiritual universe
b 270– 6 *h·* both cannot be real.
270–15 *h·* their foresight of the new dispensation
270–29 *H·* the fact that the human mind alone
271–16 *H·* the universal application of his saying :
273–12 *H·* the enmity between Science and the senses,
273–18 *H·* the importance of understanding the
274–13 *H·* Christianity and the Science which
275–24 *H·* all is in reality the manifestation of Mind.
278–14 *H·*, as we approach Spirit and Truth,
290–12 *H·* Truth comes to destroy this error
292–17 *H·* the so-called life of mortals is
311– 6 *H·* evil is not made and is not real.
316–12 *H·* the warfare between this spiritual idea and
319–23 *H·* the misapprehension of the spiritual meaning
331–24 *H·* all is Spirit and spiritual.
o 343–28 *H·* the mistake which allows words, rather than
346–24 *h·* pain in matter is a false belief,
347– 7 *h·* all is Life, and death has no dominion.
350–27 *H·* its embodiment in the
357–31 Can matter drive Life, Spirit, *h·*, and so defeat
361–30 *h·* the many readings given the Scriptures,
p 374–32 *H·* it is mortal mind, not matter, which says,
392– 1 *h·* it is through divine Mind that you overcome
402–28 *H·* the proof that hypnotism is not scientific ;
t 455– 7 *H·* the necessity of being right yourself
456–32 *H·* it gave the first rules for demonstrating
461–25 error is not true, *h·* it is unreal.
r 466– 3 *H·* God combines all-power or potency,
471–19 *H·* the spirituality of the universe is
473–16 *h·* the duality of Jesus the Christ.
474– 9 *h·* the misinterpretation and consequent
476–10 *H·* man is not mortal nor material.
480–22 *H·*, evil is but an illusion,
481–29 *h·* the immortality of Soul.
486–26 *h·* their permanence.
488–11 *H·* the Scriptures often appear in our
490– 6 *H·* it cannot govern man aright.
492–26 *God is Mind, and God is infinite ; h· all is Mind.*
495– 4 *h·* its healing power is not fully demonstrated.
g 503–15 *H·* the eternal wonder,
525–22 He did not make,— *h·* its unreality.
526–21 doctrine that . . . evil is as real, *h·* as
532–25 there is but one God, *h·* one Mind
533–31 *H·* she is first to abandon the belief in
545–26 *H·* the seeming contradiction
556–28 *h·* the author's experience ;
gl 584–11 Matter has no life, *h·* it has no real existence.
597–25 *h·* it should not be confounded with the term.

henceforth

f 217–13 "*H·* know we no man after the — II Cor.* 5 : 16.

Herald, Boston

an 102–24 following is an extract from the Boston *H·* :

herald

pref vii– 7 the human *h·* of Christ, Truth,
f 226– 6 the voice of the *h·* of this new crusade

heralds

sp 95–26 the light which *h·* Christ's eternal dawn

herb

g 507–12	the *h·* yielding seed,— *Gen.* 1 : 11.
507–19	The tree and *h·* do not yield fruit because of
508–10	*h·* yielding seed after his kind,— *Gen.* 1 : 12.
518– 6	every *h·* bearing seed,— *Gen.* 1 : 29.
518–11	every green *h·* for meat : — *Gen.* 1 : 30.
520–20	*h·* of the field before it grew : — *Gen.* 2 : 5.
535–25	shalt eat the *h·* of the field : — *Gen.* 3 : 18.

herbs

g 541–12	more spiritual type . . . than the *h·* of the
ap 559–28	share the hemlock cup and eat the bitter *h·* ;

herdmen

t 444–26, 27	between my *h·* and thy *h·* ; — *Gen.* 13 : 8.

herds

m 61–27	raising of stock to increase your flocks and *h·*?

here

iii– *	Thou *h·*, and *everywhere.*
pr 16–24	*H·* let me give what I understand to be the
a 35–31	If the sinner's punishment *h·* has been
38–15	*H·* the word *hands* is used metaphorically,
41–11	may have a flowery pathway *h·*, but he cannot
42–29	He was *h·* to enable them to test his
sp 74–10	When *h·* or hereafter the belief of life
77– 1	comes not suddenly *h·* or hereafter.
77– 7	brings its own self-destruction both *h·* and
83–12	*h·* Science takes issue with popular religions.
91– 7	*H·* is the great point of departure for all true
91–22	erroneous postulates should be *h·* considered
s 158– 7	It is *h·* noticeable that Apollo was
ph 168–30	*H·* let a word be noticed which will
187– 6	*H·* you may see how so-called material sense
196–13	*h·* the word *soul* means a false sense
f 216– 5	*H·* theories cease, and Science unveils the
b 268– *	*H·* I *stand. I can do no otherwise,*
285– 4	not alone hereafter . . . but *h·* and now ;
292– 4	*H·* prophecy pauses.
296– 6	Either *h·* or hereafter, suffering or Science
305–23	In the illusion of life that is *h·* to-day and
308–10	is met by the admission . . . "Lo, *h·* I am,
311–11	Sin exists *h·* or hereafter only so long as
320–17	*H·* the original text declares plainly
324–16	must conquer sin, . . . either *h·* or
328–10	until, *h·* or hereafter, they gain the true
338–21	*H· a dam* is not a mere play upon words ;
o 348– 8	*H·* is the difficulty :
361– 2	*H·* C. S. intervenes, explains these
361– 5	now and forever, *h·* and everywhere.
p 364–16	*H·* is suggested a solemn question,
371– 9	Mortals are believed to be *h·* without their
407–11	*H·* C. S. is the sovereign panacea,
409–29	We cannot spend our days *h·* in ignorance
410– 1	If *h·* we give no heed to C. S.,
410–20	*H·* is a definite and inspired proclamation of
427–30	must be mastered by Mind *h·* or hereafter.
430–13	I *h·* present to my readers an allegory
437–20	*H·* the opposing counsel, False Belief,
440–33	*H·* the counsel for the defence closed,
t 463–20	By this we know that Truth is *h·*
r 465– *	*h· a little, and there a little.*— *Isa.* 28 : 10.
g 504–21	*H·* we have the explanation of another
506–25	*H·* the human concept and divine idea seem
520–23	*H·* is the emphatic declaration that
521– 4	*H·* the inspired record closes its narrative
523–14	It may be worth while *h·* to remark that,
527–11	*H·* the metaphor represents God, Love, as
527–26	*H·* the lie represents God as repeating creation,
528–15	*H·* falsity, error, credits Truth, God, with
533–10	*H·* there is an attempt to trace all human
541–22	*H·* the serpentine lie invents new forms.
547– 3	contains the proof of all *h·* said of C. S.
549–20	*H·* these material researches culminate
552– 2	But we cannot stop *h·*.
ap 564–12	the criminal instinct *h·* described.
568–11	*H·*, also, the Revelator
569– 4	Every mortal at some period, *h·* or hereafter,
569–24	*H·* the Scriptures declare that
573– 7	that we can become conscious, *h·* and now, of a
576–22	is within reach of man's consciousness *h·*,
gl 598– 5	*H·* the original word is the same in both cases,

hereafter

a 41– 9	in the *h·* they will reap what they now sow.
sp 73–19	belief that . . . *h·* to rise up as
74–10	When here or *h·* the belief of life
77– 1	comes not suddenly here or *h·*.
77– 7	its own self-destruction both here and *h·*,
ph 168–31	a word . . . which will be better understood *h·*,
b 285– 4	This Science of being obtains not alone *h·*
296– 6	Either here or *h·*, suffering or Science must
311–11	Sin exists here or *h·* only so long as
324–17	we must conquer sin, . . . either here or *h·*,
328–10	until, here or *h·*, they gain the true
p 410– 3	shall not be ready for spiritual Life *h·*.
427–30	must be mastered by Mind here or *h·*.

hereafter

g 534– 2	This *h·* enabled woman to be the
550–14	should appear now, even as it will *h·*.
ap 569– 4	here or *h·*, must grapple with and overcome

hereditary

p 392–18	If you think that consumption is *h·*
412–32	Scientist knows there can be no *h·* disease,
424–28	scrofula and other so-called *h·* diseases,

heredity

ph 178– 8	*H·* is not a law.
178–24	we are freed from the belief of *h·*,
f 228– 7	*H·* is a prolific subject for mortal belief to
p 392–29	whether it be air, exercise, *h·*, contagion,
425–32	the opposite belief in *h·*.

heresies

an 106–23	strife, seditions, *h·*,— *Gal.* 5 : 20.

heretic

o 343–32	is often accounted a *h·*.

heretofore

a 43 –6	*H·* they had only believed ;

heritage

f 228–12	when man enters into his *h·* of freedom,
b 315–19	when we subdue sin and prove man's *h·*,
g 535–17	the *h·* of the first born among men

hero

s 133–30	or only a mighty *h·* and king,

Herod

a 52–15	*H·* and Pilate laid aside old feuds
s 136–20	This ghostly fancy was repeated by *H·*
136–25	But even *H·* doubted if Jesus was
136–28	No wonder *H·* desired to see the new Teacher.
ap 565– 9	*H·* decreed the death of every male child
565–13	and deprive *H·* of his crown.

Herod's

s 136–26	Hence *H·* assertion :

hesitate

f 229– 5	We should *h·* to say that Jehovah sins or

heterodoxy

c 257– 7	theory that Spirit is not . . . is pantheistic *h·*,

hew

pref vii–24	task of the sturdy pioneer to *h·* the tall oak

hewn

pr 6–28	"[It] is *h·* down."— *Matt.* 7 : 19.

hid

s 107– *	*h· in three measures of meal,*— *Matt.* 13 : 33.
117–32	*h·* in three measures of meal,— *Matt.* 13 : 33.
131–20	Thou hast *h·* these things from — *Luke* 10 : 21.
b 315–11	false views of the people *h·* from their sense
325–17	"*h·* with Christ in God,"— *Col.* 3 : 3.
p 367–21	that is set on an hill cannot be *h·*."— *Matt.* 5 : 14.
367–22	that this light be not *h·*, but radiate
t 445–14	"*h·* with Christ in God,"— *Col.* 3 : 3.
g 532–16	I was naked ; and I *h·* myself.— *Gen.* 3 : 10.
ap 560–22	*h·* from view the apostle's character,
560–27	Because it has *h·* from them the true idea

Hiddekel

gl 588– 5	definition of

hidden

pr 15–25	*h·* from the world, but known to God.
a 44–29	while he was *h·* in the sepulchre,
an 102–18	looms of crime, *h·* in the dark recesses
s 118– 8	*h·* in sacred secrecy from the visible world?
f 205– 1	else God will continue to be *h·* from
o 343–12	and Truth will not be forever *h·*
p 376– 9	the most *h·*, undefined, and insidious beliefs.
t 453–20	*H·* sin is spiritual wickedness in high places.
ap 571– 2	expose evil's *h·* mental ways of
576– 5	seems *h·* in the mist of remoteness,

hide

pr 8– 6	their wickedness and then seek to *h·* it.
a 45–14	had failed to *h·* immortal Truth
m 62–29	false views of life *h·* eternal harmony,
sp 95–11	Error . . . cannot *h·* from the law of God.
f 215– 1	Nothing can *h·* from them the harmony of
242–32	We may *h·* spiritual ignorance from the world
b 299–26	Corporeal sense, or error, may seem to *h·* Truth,
304– 4	which *h·* spiritual beauty and goodness.
308– 7	and will *h·* from the demand,
311– 1	clouds of mortal belief, which *h·* the truth of
p 366–32	we must not *h·* the talent of spiritual healing
r 480–32	One must *h·* the other.

hideous

f 248–19	by vicious sculptors and *h·* forms.
g 550–28	not so *h·* and absurd as the supposition that

hides

sp 81–26	inharmony . . . *h·* the harmony of Science,
83–11	such a belief *h·* Truth and builds on error.
ph 183–20	that which *h·* the power of Spirit.
b 295–23	Then, . . . it no longer *h·* the sun.

hides
b 298– 4   As a cloud *h·* the sun it cannot extinguish,
326– 1   A false sense . . . *h·* the divine possibilities,
g 542– 5   Though error *h·* behind a lie
550–19   *h·* the true and spiritual Life,

hiding
b 294–30   the hypocrite that he is *h·* himself.
t 445–25   a lie, *h·* the divine Principle of harmony,
gl 596–28   VEIL. A cover ; concealment ; *h·* ; hypocrisy.

hierarchies
a 24– 5   established by *h·*, and instigated . . . by the

hieroglyphs
f 240– 6   The floral apostles are *h·* of Deity.

high
iii– *   This is Thy *h·* behest :
s 136–22   no *h·* appreciation of divine Science
147–20   This proof lifts you *h·* above the perishing
153–20   administer . . . a *h·* attenuation of truth,
155–15   weighs against the *h·* and mighty truths of
156–10   *h·* attenuation of *Sulphuris.*
ph 168– 3   worldly, who think the standard of C. S. too *h·*
c 258–30   impossible . . . to fall from his *h·* estate.
p 426– 6   the *h·* goal always before her thoughts,
t 448–20   a *h·* sense of the moral . . . qualifications
453–20   Hidden sin is spiritual wickedness in *h·* places.
456– 8   alone entitles them to the *h·* standing which
r 469–25   the *h·* signification of omnipotence,
494–28   its lap piled *h·* with immortal fruits.
g 505–18   "The Lord on *h·* is mightier than — *Psal.* 93 : 4.
ap 563–30   "spiritual wickedness in *h·* places." — *Eph.* 6 : 12.
568–27   sweeter than has ever before reached *h·* heaven,
572– 1   lifts on *h·* only those who have

high-caste
p 362–10   the household of a *h·* Brahman,

higher
pr 6–18   *h·* we cannot look, farther we cannot go.
7–20   a *h·* experience and a better life
11–10   before mortals can "go up *h·*." — *Luke* 14 : 10.
a 18–16   Truth, which reaches no *h·* than itself.
18–17   fountain can rise no *h·* than its source.
43–21   Jesus rose *h·* in demonstration because of the
46–17   rose even *h·* in the understanding of Spirit,
m 57– 6   masculine mind reaches a *h·* tone through
60– 2   Science inevitably lifts one's being *h·*
60–21   education of the *h·* nature is neglected,
60–30   *H·* enjoyments alone can satisfy the
61– 8   and give *h·* aims to ambition.
61–31   If the propagation of a *h·* human species
62–19   understanding of man's *h·* nature.
62–27   *h·* nature of man is not governed by
63–26   a race having *h·* aims and motives.
65–18   will at length demand a *h·* affection.
66–13   Love propagates anew the *h·* joys of Spirit,
sp 97–23   the *h·* Truth lifts her voice, the louder
s 121– 8   Though no *h·* revelation than the horoscope was
128–17   giving mortals access to broader and *h·* realms.
128–25   destroys with the *h·* testimony of Spirit
150–15   attest the reality of the *h·* mission
151– 9   respect is due . . . the *h·* class of physicians.
158–26   letting in matter's *h·* stratum, mortal mind.
158–29   of a *h·* attenuation than the drug,
162–28   understanding . . . to demonstrate the *h·* rule.
ph 167– 3   If we rise no *h·* than blind faith,
169–15   find stronger supports and a *h·* home.
174– 4   Is civilization only a *h·* form of idolatry,
190–27   When hope rose *h·* in the human heart,
197–13   the *h·* will be the standard of living
198– 1   the *h·* stratum of mortal mind has
f 224–22   A *h·* and more practical Christianity,
226– 3   world-wide slavery, found on *h·* planes of
226–14   God has built a *h·* platform of human rights,
233– 2   makes its demands upon us for *h·* proofs
235–13   moral and spiritual culture, which lifts one *h·*.
235–15   will reach *h·* than the heavens of astronomy ;
246– 8   The stream rises no *h·* than its source.
247–17   reflecting those *h·* conceptions of loveliness
251–25   This process of *h·* spiritual understanding
c 255– 7   anciently classified as the *h·* criticism,
256– 2   Advancing to a *h·* plane of action,
258– 5   craving for something better, *h·*, holier,
258–14   rising *h·* and *h·* from a boundless basis.
259– 9   *h·* than their poor thought-models
260–16   and to bring out better and *h·* results,
262–14   clearer, *h·* views inspire the Godlike man
262–24   Starting from a *h·* standpoint, one rises
265–14   confers . . . a *h·* and more permanent peace.
266– 4   giving place to man's *h·* individuality
267–23   Thought is borrowed from a *h·* source
b 270–14   looked for something *h·* than the
290– 5   If . . . they will rise no *h·* spiritually
297–15   and the human consciousness rises *h·*.
297–20   Faith is *h·* and more spiritual than belief.
299–11   point upward to . . . *h·* ideals of life and
307–29   his province is . . . in the *h·* law of Mind.

higher
b 311–23   even the *h·* law of Soul, which prevails
313–14   Using this word in its *h·* meaning,
314–24   The *h·* his demonstration of divine Science
316–18   the Christ-man, rose *h·* to human view
323–32   listening to it and going up *h·*.
o 349–27   does not at once catch the *h·* meaning,
361–27   is the *h·* hope on earth,
p 364– 8   Which was the *h·* tribute to such ineffable
367–28   my hope, namely, the student's *h·* attainments
401–11   to the end of producing a *h·* manifestation.
416–31   away from their bodies to *h·* objects.
419–30   rise into *h·* and holier consciousness.
435– 8   Mortal Man, in obedience to *h·* law, helped
437–10   before the Judge of our *h·* tribunal,
439–27   Our *h·* statutes declare you all,
t 453– 9   and a *h·* basis is thus won ;
455–30   The *h·* your attainment in the Science
458–21   are summoned to give place to *h·* law,
r 473–27   his acts of *h·* importance than his words.
g 502–15   take on *h·* symbols and significations,
509–16   rarefaction of thought as it ascends *h·*.
518–14   the *h·* always protects the lower.
531– 9   represent the *h·* moral sentiments,
541– 5   instead of making his own gift a *h·* tribute
549– 7   give place to *h·* theories and demonstrations.
553– 3   should awaken thought to a *h·* and purer
554–30   are less sickly than those possessing *h·*
ap 571–20   *h·* humanity will unite all interests in the
576–30   the word gradually approaches a *h·* meaning.
gl 581–19   The *h·* false knowledge builds
590–19   Its *h·* signification is Supreme Ruler.
593–10   a new and *h·* idea of immortality,
(*see also* **sense, understanding**)

highest
pr 16– 2   The *h·* prayer . . . is demonstration.
a 43–11   Jesus' last proof was the *h·*,
49–14   the *h·* instructor and friend of man,
49–18   sentinel of God at the *h·* post of power,
49–27   those to whom he had given the *h·* proofs
50–15   in his *h·* demonstration?
52–23   The *h·* earthly representative of God,
54–16   the *h·* proof he could have offered
m 65– 2   should proceed from man's *h·* nature.
67–11   acting up to his *h·* understanding,
68– 8   which hinders our *h·* selfhood.
s 148–12   from the lowest, instead of from the *h·*,
153–11   The *h·* attenuation of homœopathy
163–16   medicine . . . in the *h·* degree uncertain ;
ph 182– 9   capable of producing the *h·* human good?
189–20   instead of from the *h·* mortal thought.
f 230–11   would be contrary to our *h·* ideas of God
c 265– 2   but of the *h·* qualities of Mind.
b 327– 9   Evil is sometimes a man's *h·* conception of
332–29   He expressed the *h·* type of divinity,
p 368– 2   a supposititious opposite of the *h·* right.
t 455–21   God selects for the *h·* service one who
455–23   does not bestow His *h·* trusts upon the unworthy.
456– 2   adverse to its *h·* hope and achievement.
r 471–29   Since then her *h·* creed has been divine Science,
477–15   interwoven with matter's *h·* stratum,
482–19   Jesus was the *h·* human concept of the perfect
g 503– 4   the *h·* ideas are the sons and daughters of God.
514–18   and keep pace with *h·* purpose.
520– 1   *h·* and sweetest rest, . . . is in holy work.
ap 560–15   without a correct sense of its *h·* visible idea,
564–18   except the *h·* degree of human depravity.
gl 589–16   JESUS. The *h·* human corporeal concept of

high-handed
p 437–25   for such *h·* illegality.

highly
b 322– 9   It is *h·* important . . . to turn our thoughts

high-priest
gl 596–13   the stones in the breast-plate of the *h·*

highway
m 61–10   that the *h·* of our God may be prepared

hill
a 50–30   The real cross, which Jesus bore up the *h·*
b 326– 7   must not try to climb the *h·* of Science by
p 367–20   A city that is set on an *h·* — *Matt.* 5 : 14.

hills
s 135– 4   and ye little *h·*, like lambs? — *Psal.* 114 : 6.
147–13   on the *h·* of Judæa and in the valleys of
f 240– 3   Arctic regions, sunny tropics, giant *h·*,
g 514–17   "the cattle upon a thousand *h·*." — *Psal.* 50 : 10.

Him
pref vii–19   apprehension of *H·* whom to know aright
pr 1– *   *before ye ask H·.* — *Matt.* 6 : 8.
1– 3   a spiritual understanding of *H·*,
2–23   God is Love. Can we ask *H·* to be more?
4–18   Simply asking . . . will never make us love *H·* ;
6– 7   Calling on *H·* to forgive our work

Him

pr	8–23	the reward of *H·* who blesses the poor.
	10– 4	leave our real desires to be rewarded by *H·*.
	13–15	God knows our need before we tell *H·*
a	19–27	If living in disobedience to *H·*, we ought
s	119–12	is not only to make *H·* responsible for
	119–13	but to announce *H·* as their source,
	119–14	thereby making *H·* guilty of maintaining
	140– 5	Bible represents *H·* as saying :
	140– 8	we know *H·* as divine Mind,
	140–10	love *H·* understandingly, warring no more
ph	166–18	Instead of thrusting *H·* aside in times of
	166–20	hour of strength in which to acknowledge *H·*,
f	208– 5	"In *H·* we live, and move, and — *Acts* 17 : 28.
	219–28	the honor due to *H·* alone.
	229–13	virtually declaring *H·* good in one instance
	230–12	to suppose *H·* capable of first arranging law
	231–32	"all things were made by *H·* — *John* 1 : 3.
	232– 1	without *H·* was not anything made — *John* 1 : 3.
c	256–22	none can stay His hand, or say unto *H·*, — *Dan.* 4 : 35.
	262– 7	but it ascribes to *H·* the entire glory.
	264–11	act as possessing all power from *H·*
b	272–30	the divine Principle of all that represents *H·*
	273– 2	contrary to God, and cannot emanate from *H·*.
	307–10	It says : . . . I aid *H·*.
	320–28	encourages mortals to hope in *H·* who healeth
	324–12	"acquaint now thyself with *H·*, — *Job* 22 : 21.
	328–12	which destroys human delusions about *H·*
	330–19	God is what the Scriptures declare *H·* to be,
	331–17	Everything in God's universe expresses *H·*.
	336–16	They are the emanations of *H·* who is Life,
o	341– *	*But if the Spirit of H· that raised up — Rom.* 8 : 11.
	348–15	when we ascribe to *H·* almighty Life
	351–21	if not superior to *H·*.
	356–21	is it possible for *H·* to create man subject to
	361–19	"For in *H·* we live, and move, — *Acts* 17 : 28.
p	362– *	*I shall yet praise H·, — Psal.* 42 : 11.
	390– 9	right understanding of *H·* restores harmony.
	397–22	which the Scriptures declare *H·* to be.
	414–22	there is none else beside *H·*." — *Deut.* 4 : 35.
	421–18	and that there is none beside *H·*.
t	444–11	Step by step will those who trust *H·* find
r	473– 9	nothing apart from *H·* is present or has power.
	479–30	"For the invisible things of *H·*, — *Rom.* 1 : 20.
	480–26	"All things were made by *H·* — *John* 1 : 3.
	480–27	without *H·* was not anything made — *John* 1 : 3.
	483–28	does honor God as no other theory honors *H·*,
g	501– *	*made by H· ; and without H· was not — John* 1 : 3.
	501– *	*In H· was life ; — John* 1 : 4.
	503–16	reflecting *H·* in countless spiritual forms.
	504–13	indicate, . . . spiritually clearer views of *H·*,
	515–23	moves in accord with *H·*,
	517–13	as we have for considering *H·* feminine,
	519–17	How shall we declare *H·*, till, in the language of
	525–18	"and without *H· . . . .* was not — *John* 1 : 3.
	527–28	asking a prospective sinner to help *H·*.
gl	581–13	all things are created by *H·*
	596– 5	makes *H·* better known as the All-in-all,
	596– 9	*H·* declare I unto you." — *Acts* 17 : 23.

Himself

a	18–15	how can God propitiate *H·* ?
sp	94– 2	in the image and likeness of *H·*,
b	277– 7	As God *H·* is good and is Spirit,
	286–18	all that He made to be good, like *H·*,
	303–25	without the image and likeness of *H·*,
	335– 7	in and of *H·*.
o	356–24	Does God create a material man out of *H·*,
	357–29	Has the Father "Life in *H·*," — *John* 5 : 26.
p	380–31	against *H·*, against Life, health, harmony.
	395–16	besought to take the patient to *H·*,
	435– 2	Spirit which is God *H·*
t	455–21	one who is spiritually near *H·*.
g	518–13	God gives the lesser idea of *H·*
gl	583–25	could not create an atom . . . the opposite of *H·*.

hinder

a	28–19	did not *h·* men from saying :
s	145– 5	lack of the letter could not *h·* their work ;
f	209–12	Neither philosophy nor skepticism can *h·*
b	326–19	nothing but wrong intention can *h·* your
	326–21	"Who did *h·* you, — *Gal.* 5 : 7.
p	419– 1	A moral question may *h·* the recovery of
t	445– 7	to *h·* the demonstration of C. S.
	448–25	must always *h·* scientific demonstration.

hindered

a	28– 2	*h·* the success of Jesus' mission.
	41–23	but this foreknowledge *h·* him not.

hinders

pr	5– 1	Whatever . . . *h·* man's spiritual growth
m	68– 8	cherish nothing which *h·* our highest
f	205–24	*h·* man's normal drift towards the one Mind,
b	312–26	limits faith and *h·* spiritual understanding.
p	366– 9	*h·* him from reaching his patient's thought,

hinders

p	369– 2	and this *h·* his destroying them.
	374–21	this belief helps rather than *h·* disease.
	391–13	No law of God *h·* this result.
r	483–11	*h·* its approach to the standard in C. S.

Hindoo

p	362– 9	as positively as if she were a *H·* pariah
g	524– 4	in the *H·* Vishnu, in the Greek Aphrodite,

hindrance

f	253–23	without *h·* from the body.
p	372–31	this will be a *h·* to the recovery of the sick

hint

a	42– 4	theology gave no *h·* of the unchanging love of
m	58–25	This is a *h·* that a wife ought not to
sp	94–27	an infidel blasphemer who should *h·* that
ph	194–17	history of Kaspar Hauser is a useful *h·*
f	245–19	useful *h·*, upon which a Franklin might work
p	383–12	A *h·* may be taken from the emigrant,
g	528–30	may be a useful *h·* to the medical faculty.

hints

p	384–18	*h·* of inflammatory rheumatism,

hip

ph	193– 5	physician had just probed the ulcer on the *h·*,

hip-disease

ph	193– 1	confined to his bed six months with *h·*,

Hippocrates

s	158– 8	*H·* turned from image-gods to vegetable
	163– 1	impossible to calculate the mischief which *H·*

hireling

t	464–26, 27	*h·* fleeth, because he is an *h·*, — *John* 10 : 13.

His

pref	x–21	there is so little faith in *H· . . .* power
	xi–22	called the author to proclaim *H·* Gospel
	xi–24	charge to plant and water *H·* vineyard.
pr	3– 2	without being reminded of *H·* province.
	3– 8	Shall we ask the divine Principle . . . to do *H·*
	3–10	in order to receive *H·* blessing,
	5–17	pours the riches of *H·* love into
	6–20	To suppose that God forgives . . . according as *H·*
a	23– 6	vented upon *H·* beloved Son is, . . . unnatural.
	42–22	which God bestowed on *H·* anointed,
	45–12	[seeming] death of *H·* Son, — *Rom.* 5 : 10.
m	56–10	and *H·* kingdom is come as in the vision
sp	97–26	"He uttered *H·* voice, the earth — *Psal.* 46 : 6.
	99– 8	to will and to do of *H·* good — *Phil.* 2 : 13.
s	109–29	"My doctrine is not mine, but *H·* — *John* 7 : 16.
	109–29	If any man will do *H·* will, he — *John* 7 : 17.
	110– 6	pronounced by *H·* wisdom good.
	114–11	noumenon and phenomena, God and *H·* thoughts.
	117– 9	to the Supreme Being or *H·* manifestation ;
	119–10	is to leave the creator out of *H·* own
	128– 5	refers only to the laws of God and to *H·*
	140–29	created man in *H·*, God's, image ;
ph	165– *	*sent H· word, and healed — Psal.* 107 : 20.
	167– 2	out of *H·* personal volition,
	174–11	but the angels of *H·* presence
	183–17	supposed laws which result in . . . are not *H·* laws,
	187– 5	of the all-knowing Mind and of *H·* creations.
	192–18	holds the "wind in *H·* fists ;" — *Prov.* 30 : 4.
f	206– 1	we can have no other Mind but *H·*,
	222–28	had made him one, contrary to *H·* commands.
	224–14	and array *H·* vicegerent with pomp
	230–14	to suppose Him . . . punishing . . . of *H·* volition
	231–24	to doubt *H·* government
	231–25	and distrust *H·* omnipotent care.
	233–16	the shadow of *H·* right hand rests
	242–12	good, God and *H·* reflection,
	244–20	If man . . . God is without *H·* entire
	247–23	reflects the charms of *H·* goodness
	249– 4	producing *H·* own models of excellence.
c	255–18	hath not seen Spirit, nor hath ear heard *H·* voice.
	256–20	"doeth according to *H·* will — *Dan.* 4 : 35.
	256–22	none can stay *H·* hand. — *Dan.* 4 : 35.
	257–12	Mind creates *H·* own likeness in ideas,
	267– 6	The allness of Deity is *H·* oneness.
b	268– *	*and with H· Son Jesus Christ. — I John* 1 : 3.
	270–18	divine Mind, in *H·* more infinite meanings,
	275–16	These are *H·* attributes,
	275–17	No wisdom is wise but *H·* wisdom ;
	280–28	being perpetual in *H·* own individuality,
	300– 4	of *H·* infinite image or reflection, man.
	303–27	without a witness or proof of *H·* own nature.
	306– 9	were parted for a moment from *H·* reflection,
	308– 4	and keeping *H·* commandment ?"
	310–10	God is *H·* own infinite Mind, and expresses all.
	313–10	"the brightness of *H·* [God's] glory, — *Heb.* 1 : 3.
	313–11	the express [expressed] image of *H·* — *Heb.* 1 : 3.
	313–21	being a brightness from *H·* glory, — *see Heb.* 1 : 3.
	313–22	and an image of *H·* being."
	314– 7	inseparable as God and *H·* reflection
	318–30	are controlled and proved by *H·* laws.
	328–13	reveals the grand realities of *H·* allness.

His

  b 331– 6 the creator reflected in *H·* creations.
     331–13 the divine Mind and *H·* ideas.
     332– 5 *H·* tender relationship to *H·* spiritual
     332– 8 "For we are also *H·* offspring."— *Acts* 17 : 28.
     339– 7 there is no room for *H·* unlikeness.
     340– 8 and keep *H·* commandments : — *Eccl.* 12 : 13.
     340–10 love God and keep *H·* commandments :
     340–13 in and of God, and manifests *H·* love.
  o 341– * *by H· Spirit that dwelleth in you.*— *Rom.* 8 : 11.
     345– 5 God cannot be in *H·* unlikeness
     345– 7 When . . . *H·* absoluteness is set forth,
     348–16 I deny *H·* cooperation with evil,
     360–26 in *H·* ministering spirits,— *see Job* 4 : 18.
     360–27 *H·* angels He chargeth with — *see Job* 4 : 18.
  p 373– 5 and be more alive to *H·* promises.
     390–24 no law of *H·* to support the necessity
     419– 6 God and *H·* ideas alone are real and
     439–27 and the righteous executor of *H·* laws.
  t 455–23 All-wise does not bestow *H·* highest trusts upon
  r 466– 1 *H·* reflection is man and the universe.
     470–19 Has God taken away *H·* own standard,
     472– 6 God has set *H·* signet upon Science,
     472–10 nor belong to *H·* government.
     472–10 *H·* law, rightly understood, destroys them.
     478–29 and called me by *H·* grace,— *Gal.* 1 : 15.
     483–29 does this in the way of *H·* appointing,
     497– 6 We acknowledge *H·* Son, one Christ ;
  g 508–13 God determines the gender of *H·* own ideas.
     512–10 These angels of *H·* presence, which have
     513–26 *H·* thoughts are spiritual realities.
     516– 9 fashions all things, after *H·* own likeness.
     517–17 *H·* personality can only be reflected,
     519– 2 from all eternity knoweth *H·* own ideas.
     519– 5 emanation, of *H·* infinite self-containment
     522–31 Does the creator condemn *H·* own creation?
     525–14 and God shaped man after *H·* mind ;
     527–18 to be the tree of death to *H·* own creation?
     529–11 are *H·* eternal children, belonging to
     543–11 They cannot come into *H·* presence,
  op 558– * *the mountain of H· holiness.*— *Psal.* 48 : 1.
     560–17 whom God has appointed to voice *H·* Word.
     561–15 God and *H·* Christ, bringing harmony to earth.
     565– 8 unto God, and to *H·* throne.— *Rev.* 12 : 5.
     567– 6 The Gabriel of *H·* presence has no contests.
     568–15 and the power of *H·* Christ : — *Rev.* 12 : 10.
     572–10 belongs not to *H·* children,
     573–17 ever with men, and they are *H·* people.
     577– 3 as one Father with *H·* universal family,
     578– 9 for *H·* name's sake.— *Psal.* 23 : 3.
  gl 580– 4 opposite of Spirit and *H·* creations ;
     582–19 creates man as *H·* own spiritual idea,
     589–11 and that man is His idea, the child of *H·* care.
     (see also **creation, idea, image, likeness, power, work**)

historian

  g 537–25 the ordinary *h·* interprets it literally.

historic

  a 27–23 only eleven left a desirable *h·* record.
  an 105–19 these words . . . will become *h·* :
  g 523–30 In the *h·* parts of the Old Testament,

history

all
  sp 93–22 The belief . . . has darkened all *h·*.
  f 225–14 The history of our country, like all *h·*,
ancient
  a 43–10 and is now repeating its ancient *h·*.
authentic
  ph 194–17 The authentic *h·* of Kaspar Hauser is a
Bible
  o 342– 9 presumptuously, in the face of Bible *h·*
brief
  ap 565–14 a brief *h·* in the earthly life of our Master ;
central emblem of
  f 238–31 The cross is the central emblem of *h·*.
Christian
  b 328–16 has sadly disappeared from Christian *h·*.
  ap 577–17 the Christ-idea in Christian *h·* ;
eternal
  r 471– 4 remained unchanged in its eternal *h·*.
evil has no
  g 538–21 evil has no *h·*,
false
  g 522– 1 the false *h·* in contradistinction to the true.
glorious
  g 521– 7 We leave this brief, glorious *h·*
has confirmed
  a 54–27 and *h·* has confirmed the prediction.
her
  f 245–16 those unacquainted with her *h·* conjectured
human
  g 528–31 Later in human *h·*, when the forbidden fruit
Israelitish
  o 351– 1 sprang from half-hidden Israelitish *h·*
Jesus'
  a 20– 8 Jesus' *h·* made a new calendar,

---

history

material
  f 204– 4 false conclusions . . . that material *h·* is as real
  g 547–27 The true theory . . . is not in material *h·*
mortal
  r 476–16 from the beginning of mortal *h·*,
natural
  ph 195–17 Through astronomy, natural *h·*, chemistry,
  b 277–13 Natural *h·* presents vegetables and animals
  g 548–26 Natural *h·* is richly endowed by the
     551– 7 In natural *h·*, the bird is not the product of
of Christianity
  p 387–27 The *h·* of Christianity furnishes sublime
of error
  g 521–29 The *h·* of error or matter, if veritable, would
     522–12 unmistakably gives the *h·* of error
     525–26 if we give the same heed to the *h·* of error as
     530–26 The *h·* of error is a dream-narrative.
of Jesus
  b 315–26 The *h·* of Jesus shows him to have been
of man
  g 557–22 Popular theology takes up the *h·* of man as if
of mortality
  g 547–15 In its *h·* of mortality, Darwin's theory of
of our country
  f 225–14 The *h·* of our country, like all history,
of religion
  a 37–10 one stage with another in the *h·* of religion.
of the errors
  an 101– 5 in the *h·* of the errors of the human mind,
religious
  a 36–30 Religious *h·* repeats itself in the
spiritual
  f 204– 5 that material history is as . . . as spiritual *h·* ;
  g 551– 8 In spiritual *h·*, matter is not the progenitor of
teaches
  o 357–17 *H·* teaches that the popular and false notions

  a 37– 5 *H·* is full of records of suffering.
  s 158–12 The future *h·* of material medicine
  f 245– 3 a sketch from the *h·* of an English woman,
  g 501–17 than the *h·* of perpetual evil.
     502– 9 *h·* of the untrue image of God,

History of Four Thousand Years of Medicine

  s 158– 6 according to the "*H· of F· T· Y· of M·*."

hit

  t 457–22 and at the same time *h·* the mark.

hither

  s 129–16 come *h·* to torment us before the— *Matt.* 8 : 29.
  ap 574– 8 Come *h·*, I will show thee the bride,— *Rev.* 21 : 9.
     575– 1 "Come *h·* ! Arise from your false consciousness

hitherto

  sp 79–20 "My Father worketh *h·*,— *John* 5 : 17.
  s 147–22 spiritual facts of being *h·* unattained

hobbled

  c 261–16 he *h·* every day to the theatre,

hold

  pr 8– 7 They *h·* secret fellowship with sin,
  a 27–31 endeavored to *h·* him at the mercy of matter
     28– 6 The determination to *h·* Spirit in the grasp of
     28–12 we cannot *h·* to beliefs outgrown ;
     30–27 to allow Soul to *h·* the control,
  m 63–31 woman should be allowed to . . . *h·* real estate,
  sp 97– 1 those who discern C. S. will *h·* crime in check.
  an 105–12 over which courts *h·* jurisdiction?
  s 127– 3 nor will Christianity lose its *h·* upon her.
     143–20 you conclude that . . . nerves, bones, etc., *h·* the
     158–25 Drug-systems are quitting their *h·* on matter
  ph 177–22 nor can a lie *h·* the preponderance
     181– 6 does it *h·* the issues of life?"
     182–13 "*h·* to the one, and despise the— *Matt.* 6 : 24.
  f 209–18 which constituent masses *h·* to each other,
     226–29 *h·* the children of Israel in bondage.
     231–20 To *h·* yourself superior to sin, because God
     231–25 To *h·* yourself superior to sickness and
     254– 5 who gain good rapidly and *h·* their position,
  c 261– 4 *H·* thought steadfastly to the enduring,
  b 308–27 did not loosen his *h·* upon this glorious light
  p 395–22 mental quackery . . . to *h·* it as something seen
     396– 1 never *h·* in mind the thought of disease,
     405– 6 to *h·* hatred in abeyance with kindness,
     412–15 adequate to unclasp the *h·* and to
     414–25 *H·* these points strongly in view.
     417–14 *h·* your ground with the unshaken understanding
     426–26 *h·* the banner of Christianity aloft
     428–23 We must *h·* forever the consciousness
  t 444–15 to those who *h·* these differing opinions.
     456– 9 high standing which most of them *h·*
     464–20 *h·* fast that which is good."— *I Thess.* 5 : 21.
  r 493–31 to *h·* man forever intact in his perfect state.
     496–15 *H·* perpetually this thought.
  ap 565–12 *h·* sway and deprive Herod of his crown.
  gl 587–12 theories that *h·* mind to be a material sense,

honest
 pref xii–26 she commits these pages to *h·* seekers for Truth.
 pr 8– 3 We never need to despair of an *h·* heart ;
 13– 6 beyond the *h·* standpoint of fervent desire.
 15–19 go forth with *h·* hearts to work and
 a 21–12 If *h·*, he will be in earnest from the start,
 ph 173–22 Phrenology makes man knavish or *h·* according
 197–19 more *h·* than our sleek politicians.
 199–21 devotion of thought to an *h·* achievement
 b 272– 5 only as we are *h·*, unselfish, loving,
 272– 6 an "*h·* and good heart"— *Luke* 8 : 15.
 327–22 Fear of punishment never made man truly *h·*.
 p 372–30 If . . . error prevents the *h·* recognition of
 384– 7 for *h·* labor, or for deeds of kindness,
 418– 7 Plead with an *h·* conviction of truth
 t 446–19 it is imperative to be *h·*,
 458–26 *h·* and consistent in following the leadings of
 464–24 fall before an *h·* heart.
 ap 570– 1 march of mind and of *h·* investigation

honestly
 pref x–12 bluntly and *h·* given the text of Truth.
 pr 8–30 learn what we *h·* are.
 13–16 cherish the desire *h·* and silently
 s 147– 8 and everywhere, when *h·* applied

honesty
 m 64–29 *H·* and virtue ensure the stability of the
 an 106– 4 the free course of *h·* and justice,
 s 115–26 Moral. Humanity, *h·*, affection,
 f 239– 8 Break up cliques, level wealth with *h·*,
 p 405– 8 and to overcome deceit with *h·*.
 t 449–14 in proportion to your *h·* and fidelity,
 453–16 *H·* is spiritual power.

honey
 ap 559–19 shall be in thy mouth sweet as *h·*."— *Rev.* 10 : 9.

Honor
 p 433– 7 his *H·*, Judge Medicine, urges the jury
 434–30 Your *H·*, the lower court has sentenced
 435–28 what jurisdiction had his *H·*, Judge Medicine,
 436–28 His *H·* sentenced Mortal Man to die

honor
 s 143–30 the glory, *h·*, dominion, and power
 ph 183–32 and the one Mind only is entitled to *h·*.
 f 219–28 not rendering to God the *h·* due to Him
 o 348– 1 which we desire neither to *h·* nor to fear.
 352–30 no longer seeming worthy of fear or *h·*.
 r 483–27 And C. S. does *h·* God as no other theory

honored
 a 28–27 because it is *h·* by sects and societies,
 s 118–22 are *h·* with the name of *laws*.
 o 55–18 Christianity is to be *h·* wherever found,
 p 362– 2 Jesus was once the *h·* guest of a certain
 382–18 "more *h·* in the breach than the observance"?

honoring
 ph 184–11 never *h·* erroneous belief with

honors
 a 39– 4 He won eternal *h·*.
 ph 183–30 it *h·* spiritual understanding ;
 t 459– 5 achieves no worldly *h·* except by sacrifice,
 r 483–15 if any system *h·* God, it ought to receive aid,
 483–28 honor God as no other theory *h·* Him,
 ap 577–23 will lay down their *h·* within the

hope
anchor of
 a 41– 1 the anchor of *h·* must be cast beyond the veil
and achievement
 t 456– 2 adverse to its highest *h·* and achievement.
and faith
 pr 9–16 enjoy the fruition of our *h·* and faith.
 a 45–18 from the door of human *h·* and faith,
 gl 581–15 ASHER (Jacob's son). *H·* and faith ;
 584–27 DOVE. . . . purity and peace ; *h·* and faith.
and fear
 b 298–17 *h·* and fear, life and death,
and fruition
 b 298– 7 Science armed with faith, *h·*, and fruition.
and triumph
 p 434–18 solemn eyes, kindling with *h·* and triumph,
buoyant with
 s 109–16 sweet, calm, and buoyant with *h·*,
depressed
 p 420–18 The fact that . . . reassures depressed *h·*.
faith and
 ap 559–31 into the El Dorado of faith and *h·*.
having no
 r 486–31 "having no *h·*, and without God— *Eph.* 2 : 12.
health and
 f 235–21 spiritual guides to health and *h·*.
human
 a 45–18 from the door of human *h·*
 b 319– 7 and misguide human *h·*.
in immortality
 p 388–25 we have *h·* in immortality ;

hope
little
 pr 8– 4 but there is little *h·* for those who come only
my weary
 a 55–17 My weary *h·* tries to realize that happy day,
of forgiveness
 a 22– 3 between sin and the *h·* of forgiveness,
of freedom
 p 368–12 even the *h·* of freedom from the bondage of
of happiness
 m 61–20 What *h·* of happiness, what noble ambition,
of the promise
 pr 14–18 Hence the *h·* of the promise
on earth
 o 361–27 is the higher *h·* on earth,
reason of its
 r 487–23 from which to explain the reason of its *h·*.
rose higher
 ph 190–27 When *h·* rose higher in the human heart,
strengthens
 t 446–21 To understand God strengthens *h·*,
to the sick
 s 152– 7 that it may give *h·* to the sick
turns
 c 263–16 His "touch turns *h·* to dust,
without
 g 536–11 The illusion of sin is without *h·* or God.

 ———

 a 40–13 "While there 's life there 's *h·*,"
 m 63–23 If . . . let us *h·* it will be granted.
 66–19 Amidst conjugal infelicity, it is well to *h·*,
 s 115–27 *h·*, faith, meekness, temperance.
 125–14 changes . . . from fear to *h·*
 f 206–12 exercise of the sentiments— *h·*, faith, love
 253– 9 I *h·*, dear reader, I am leading you into
 253–13 I *h·* that you are conquering this false sense.
 b 298–14 involves intuition, *h·*, faith, understanding,
 298–20 joy is no longer a trembler, nor is *h·* a cheat.
 301–12 reflects the . . . Spirit, which mortals *h·* for.
 320–28 and encourages mortals to *h·* in Him who
 p 362– * *H·* thou in God ; *for I shall yet*— *Psal.* 42 : 11.
 367–28 I long to see the consummation of my *h·*,
 372–21 and *h·* to succeed with contraries?
 394– 8 we can accomplish the good we *h·* for,
 g 531– 9 as if *h·* were ever prophesying thus :

hoped
 b 279– 5 "the *substance* of things *h·* for."— *Heb.* 11 : 1.
 r 468–20 "The substance of things *h·* for,— *Heb.* 11 : 1.

hopeful
 s 149–19 remarked . . . advise our patients to be *h·*
 p 394– 1 It is well to be calm . . . to be *h·* is still better ;

hopefulness
 p 375–26 Consumptive patients always show great *h·*

hopeless
 pref x–18 abandoned as *h·* by regular medical attendants.
 ph 196–25 Many a *h·* case of disease is induced by a
 f 227– 9 and in subjection to *h·* slavery,
 p 375–28 supposed to be in *h·* danger.
 376– 1 presents to mortal thought a *h·* state,
 382–30 more *h·* suffering and despair.
 394–23 Will you tell the sick that their condition is *h·*,
 405– 4 makes any man, . . . a *h·* sufferer.
 428–30 The author has healed *h·* organic disease,

hopelessly
 f 213–24 Beethoven, who was so long *h·* deaf.

hopes
 m 57–32 disappointments it involves or the *h·* it fulfils.
 66–12 not from seed sown in the soil of material *h·*,
 c 265–21 The loss of earthly *h·* and pleasures
 b 299– 9 human belief has buried its fondest earthly *h·*.
 330– 6 she cherished sanguine *h·* that C. S. would
 t 451–16 If our *h·* and affections are spiritual,
 ap 566– 5 through the great desert of human *h·*,

hopeth
 pref xii–23 "*h·* all things, endureth all— *I Cor.* 13 : 7.

hoping
 m 67–14 *H·* and working, one should stick to the wreck,

Horeb
 f 241–25 We should strive to reach the *H·* height

horizon
 m 58–13 Never contract the *h·* of a worthy outlook
 sp 98– 4 beholds in the mental *h·* the signs of

horn
 s 119– 8 To seize the first *h·* of this dilemma
 119–11 while to grasp the other *h·* of the dilemma

horns
 ap 562–31 having seven heads and ten *h·*,— *Rev.* 12 : 3.
 563– 6 showing its *h·* in the many inventions of evil.
 563–11 The ten *h·* of the dragon typify the belief

horoscope
 s 121– 9 Though no higher revelation than the *h·* was

human

belief
r 495–11 life-giving power of Truth acting on h· belief,
g 551–13 describes the gradations of h· belief,
553–24 If consentaneous h· belief agrees upon an
555– 3 h· belief, and not the divine arbitrament,
gl 585–20 h· belief before it accepts sin, sickness,

beliefs
a 24– 5 and willingness to give up h· beliefs
sp 79–11 Spiritualism relies upon h· beliefs
83–32 investigates and touches only h· beliefs.
98–15 Beyond the frail premises of h· beliefs,
s 164–19 caused by a majority of h· beliefs
ph 171– 7 gates of Paradise which h· beliefs have closed,
f 208–19 in the wilderness" of h· beliefs — Matt. 3 : 3.
252– 7 When false h· beliefs learn even a little
c 260– 9 h· beliefs will be attaining diviner
r 471–27 This view rebuked h· beliefs,
478–25 is composed of material h· beliefs
g 505–30 The mortal, erring, and finite are h· beliefs,

birth
ph 190–14 H· birth, growth, maturity, and decay

blood
a 25– 5 by our sense of h· blood.

body
m 62–23 divine Mind, . . . will care for the h· body,
s 125– 3 organic and functional health in the h· body
t 458–13 or of trying to sustain the h· body

bondage
f 227– 8 The law of . . . must end h· bondage,

brutality
a 40–21 apostles of Truth may endure h· brutality

capacities
ph 200– 6 illustrated the grand h· capacities of being
c 258–22 h· capacities are enlarged and perfected

capacity
g 519–11 H· capacity is slow to discern and to grasp

changeableness
s 140–24 wrath, repentance, and h· changeableness.

character
ap 565–22 purifying even the gold of h· character.

codes
f 226–18 H· codes, scholastic theology,

concept
ph 177–14 body is a sensuous, h· concept.
c 259–25 Brain or matter never formed a h· concept.
b 277–26 not divine, — it is a h· concept.
277–31 a h· concept, sometimes beautiful,
o 359–13 you must change the h· concept of life,
r 469– 4 Matter is a h· concept.
482–19 the highest h· concept of the perfect man.
g 506–25 Here the h· concept and divine idea seem
541–12 even the h· concept of Love

conception
a 50–26 that hour was terrible beyond h· conception.
ph 185–14 puts forth a h· conception in the name of
g 505– 7 by which h· conception, material sense,

conceptions
c 255–12 to belittle Deity with h· conceptions.
257–16 material senses and h· conceptions would

concepts
m 62–26 thrusting in the laws of erring, h· concepts
p 426–31 h· concepts named matter, death, disease,
g 516–31 genders are h· concepts.
531–12 exchanging h· concepts for the divine
536– 7 symbol of tempest-tossed h· concepts

conclusions
b 298– 1 the vague realities of h· conclusions.

conjecture
b 298–30 H· conjecture confers upon angels its own.
330–17 left either to h· conjecture or to the

consciousness
pref xi–12 lose their reality in h· consciousness
xi–17 influence ever present in h· consciousness
sp 95–31 lifts h· consciousness into eternal Truth.
b 297–14 and the h· consciousness rises higher.
327–27 Through h· consciousness, convince the mortal
332–11 speaking to the h· consciousness.
o 355–13 take possession of h· consciousness.
r 484–19 the false h· consciousness is educated to feel.
ap 573– 7 heavens and earth to one h· consciousness,

craving
c 258– 4 unsatisfied h· craving for something better,

creatures
b 298–32 making them h· creatures with suggestive

delusions
b 328–11 in the Science which destroys h· delusions

depravity
ap 564–18 the highest degree of h· depravity.

discord
b 306–32 parent of all h· discord was the Adam-dream,

displeasure
ap 571– 9 to tell a man his faults, and so risk h· displeasure

doctrine
b 286– 2 To seek Truth through belief in a h· doctrine

16

human

doctrines
s 117–31 which he defined as h· doctrines.
g 504–25 a thousand years of h· doctrines,
545–14 errors send falsity into all h· doctrines

doubts
pr 13–21 h· doubts and fears which attend such a belief,

duty
g 541–25 it repudiates even the h· duty of man towards

element
a 33–18 When the h· element in him struggled with

error
b 294– 1 the avenues and instruments of h· error,
p 401– 2 Any h· error is its own enemy,
ap 563–10 This dragon stands for the sum total of h· error.

errors
g 533–10 an attempt to trace all h· errors

existence
ph 190–22 with saddening strains on h· existence :
f 205–28 Selfishness tips the beam of h· existence

experience
sp 99–25 must deepen h· experience, until the
g 552–13 H· experience in mortal life, which
ap 572–24 stage in h· experience called death,

experiences
s 108– 7 h· experiences show the falsity of

eye
a 49–16 No h· eye was there to pity, no arm to save.
ph 188–30 The h· eye knows not where the orb of day is,

faculty
b 327–29 Reason is the most active h· faculty.

faith
pref xi– 6 the fruits of h· faith in matter,
pr 12–18 borrows its power from h· faith and belief.
sp 93–19 h· faith may clothe it with angelic vestments,
s 153–14 learned that either h· faith or the
ph 169–22 towards which h· faith or endeavor is directed.

family
an 103– 8 blesses the whole h· family.
ph 196–32 sorrows and diseases among the h· family.
f 202–11 but the whole h· family would be redeemed
234– 5 blesses the h· family with crumbs of comfort
g 532– 3 in order to create the rest of the h· family?

fear
ph 176–17 H· fear of miasma would load with disease
p 412– 3 to advance and destroy the h· fear of sickness.
ap 563– 4 We may well be perplexed at h· fear ;
566– 3 the dark ebbing and flowing tides of h· fear,

footsteps
f 254– 1 h· footsteps leading to perfection are

form
c 255–16 The h· form, or physical finiteness,
b 315–29 Wearing in part a h· form
g 554–31 especially those of the h· form.

forms
pr 4–32 and clothe religion in h· forms.

freedom
f 242– 7 towards h· freedom and the final triumph ove,

generation
m 68–30 Proportionately as h· generation ceases,

good
ph 182– 9 capable of producing the highest h· good?

governments
p 378–32 usually find displayed in h· governments.

happiness
m 65– 1 and h· happiness should proceed from

hate
t 454– 9 H· hate has no legitimate mandate

hatred
b 330– 5 fixedness of mortal illusions, and the h· hatred
ap 571–19 h· hatred cannot reach you.

heart
ph 190–27 When hope rose higher in the h· heart,

herald
pref vii– 6 the Bethlehem babe, the h· herald of

history
g 528–31 Later in h· history, when the

hope
a 45–17 from the door of h· hope and faith,
b 319– 7 and misguide h· hope.

hopes
ap 566– 5 the great desert of h· hopes,

hypotheses
sp 98–12 Creeds, doctrines, and h· hypotheses do not
t 457– 2 Truth uncontaminated by h· hypotheses.
r 481–19 H· hypotheses first assume the reality of

ignorance
pr 13–25 Because of h· ignorance of the
f 252– 4 H· ignorance of Mind and of the

illusion
r 492–23 h· illusion as to sin, sickness, and death

illusions
c 259–23 and forms its offspring after h· illusions.
r 468– 2 and never can be coordinate with h· illusions.

image
s 140–31 and make God in their own h· image.

human

indignation
ap 570– 6   finally be shocked . . . into *h·* indignation ;

invention
  a 44–27   method infinitely above that of *h·* invention.
  sp 95–20   even *h·* invention must have its day,
  s 163–26   perhaps so ample an exhibition of *h·* invention

Jesus
  b 333–32   meant, not that the *h·* Jesus was or is eternal,
  334–20   even before the *h·* Jesus was incarnate to

joys
  m 66–18   well to remember how fleeting are *h·* joys.

justice
  g 542–20   and let *h·* justice pattern the divine.

kind
  m 56– 8   moral provision for generation among *h·* kind.

knowledge
  sp 92–19   an outgrowth of *h·* knowledge
  s 124– 3   Physical science (so-called) is *h·* knowledge,
  124–27   *H·* knowledge calls them forces of matter ;
  ph 197– 7   What a price for *h·* knowledge !
  f 213–30   Before *h·* knowledge dipped to its depths
  g 532– 5   All *h·* knowledge and material sense
  gl 582– 5   *h·* knowledge, or so-called mortal mind,

language
  g 520– 5   *H·* language can repeat only an infinitesimal

law
  a 43–22   *H·* law had condemned him,
  an 105– 8   to admit that the power of *h·* law is restricted
  105–14   and *h·* law rightly estimates crime,

life
  a 51– 3   loss of something more important than *h·* life
  54– 2   Through the magnitude of his *h·* life,
  m 65– 5   and give to *h·* life an inspiration by which
  ph 173–19   measuring . . . *h·* life by material law.
  f 225–32   and on the lowest plane of *h·* life,
  232–21   or that they could destroy *h·* life ;
  p 389–19   laws that food shall support *h·* life,
  t 451–32   to blast moral sense, health, and the *h·* life.

likeness
  b 301– 2   as the *h·* likeness thrown upon the mirror,

limb
  r 489– 6   Then the *h·* limb would be replaced as readily

links
  a 37– 9   Martyrs are the *h·* links which connect

logic
  b 300– 1   *H·* logic is awry when it attempts

man
  r 473–15   Jesus is the *h·* man, and Christ is the divine

memory
  p 378– 3   are reproduced in union by *h·* memory.

mind
  pref x– 7   They regard the *h·* mind as a healing agent,
  xi– 3   only a phase of the action of the *h·* mind,
  pr 12– 6   on the *h·* mind, making it act more powerfully
  m 58– 6   Tones of the *h·* mind may be different,
  65–18   *h·* mind will at length demand a higher
  sp 83– 1   the *h·* mind or the divine Mind which is
  85– 5   This Soul-sense comes to the *h·* mind
  85–10   when you are able to read the *h·* mind
  87–11   in the general atmosphere of *h·* mind.
  87–16   Science enables one to read the *h·* mind,
  an 101– 6   history of the errors of the *h·* mind,
  104–31   Is it not clear that the *h·* mind must
  s 111– 4   the will, or sensuous reason of the *h·* mind,
  114– 4   *h·* mind and evil in contradistinction to
  126–12   *h·* mind never produced a real tone
  128–11   The *h·* mind, imbued with this
  130–16   disabuse the *h·* mind of material beliefs
  143–13   *h·* mind uses one error to medicine another.
  143–15   *h·* mind takes the lesser to relieve the
  150–32   ignorant that the *h·* mind and body are myths.
  151– 5   *h·* mind has an absolute need of something
  151–21   *h·* mind has no power to kill
  151–24   The *h·* mind is opposed to God
  155–22   The *h·* mind acts more powerfully to offset
  157–13   becomes more like the *h·* mind than the
  162–10   stir the *h·* mind to a change of base,
  ph 166– 2   the *h·* mind is all that can produce pain.
  166–15   *h·* mind is inharmonious in itself.
  168–24   I have discerned disease in the *h·* mind,
  173–28   the error which the *h·* mind alone has created.
  174–31   cause of disease obtains in the mortal *h·* mind,
  176–14   mechanism of the *h·* mind gives place to
  176–28   The *h·* mind, not matter, is supposed to feel,
  177– 1   *H·* mind produces what is termed organic
  180–13   Ignorant that the *h·* mind governs the body,
  185–20   excludes the *h·* mind as a spiritual factor
  185–29   material stratum of the *h·* mind,
  186–32   The *h·* mind has been an idolater from the
  187–10   beliefs of the *h·* mind rob and enslave it,
  187–24   The *h·* mind tries to classify action as
  187–29   but the *h·* mind still holds in belief a body,
  187–31   which appears to the *h·* mind to live,
  189– 7   the cruder theories of the *h·* mind,
  f 214–10   is an object-lesson for the *h·* mind.

human

mind
  f 218– 5   If it were not for what the *h·* mind says
  218–13   the *h·* mind is the sinner, disinclined to
  219–17   must obtain in the *h·* mind before it can
  226–11   the fetters . . . be stricken from the *h·* mind
  234–30   laid great stress on the action of the *h·* mind,
  235– 2   cannot go forth, . . . from one *h·* mind to
  251–21   acts upon the so-called *h·* mind
  251–22   leads the *h·* mind to relinquish all error,
  c 264– 1   the fleeting concepts of the *h·* mind.
  b 270–29   the fact that the *h·* mind alone suffers,
  316–10   manifest by its effects upon the *h·* mind
  327– 7   and all the sinful appetites of the *h·* mind.
  o 357–19   have originated in the *h·* mind.
  p 378– 8   Without the so-called *h·* mind, there can be no
  396–31   sickness is formed by the *h·* mind,
  402–20   We say that one *h·* mind can
  403–10   The *h·* mind is employed to remove the
  403–12   both have their origin in the *h·* mind,
  403–27   The *h·* mind determines the nature of
  g 531–10   The *h·* mind will sometime rise above
  ap 559–11   inaudible voice of Truth is, to the *h·* mind,
  573– 9   while to another, the unillumined *h·* mind,
  573–10   what the *h·* mind terms matter

mind-forces
  ph 186– 7   Erring *h·* mind-forces can work only evil

minds
  f 210–15   action of the divine Mind on *h·* minds

misconceptions
  p 428–20   mental might to offset *h·* misconceptions

misery
  ap 574–17   the sum total of *h·* misery, represented by

mother
  b 315–30   being conceived by a *h·* mother,

motives
  f 239–23   the acknowledged seat of *h·* motives.

name
  b 333– 4   Jesus was a *h·* name, which belonged to him

nature
  b 272– 8   swinish element in *h·* nature uproots it.

need
  sp 95– 9   and in that ratio we know all *h·* need
  r 494–11   and always will meet every *h·* need.

needs
  pr 16–11   prayer which covers all *h·* needs.
  t 453–15   know others and minister to *h·* needs.

opinions
  s 112–10   some particular system of *h·* opinions.
  ph 192– 6   *H·* opinions are not spiritual.
  b 280–31   The only excuse for entertaining *h·* opinions
  o 360–12   replies: . . . my old doctrines or *h·* opinions."
  t 447– 6   must not forget that erring *h·* opinions,

origin
  b 305–29   These mortal dreams are of *h·* origin,
  g 553–21   theory . . . to account for *h·* origin,

parent
  a 50– 9   despairing appeal, if made to a *h·* parent,

peace
  c 265–23   Who that has felt the loss of *h·* peace

pen
  s 110–17   No *h·* pen nor tongue taught me the Science

perception
  s 119–28   As astronomy reverses the *h·* perception of
  o 361–30   A *h·* perception of divine Science,
  ap 561–18   reducing to *h·* perception and understanding

personality
  s 138– 7   Truth, and Love, and not a *h·* personality,

philosophy
  sp 99– 2   *H·* philosophy, ethics, and superstition
  s 144– 8   mortal beliefs formulated in *h·* philosophy,
  b 269– 9   *H·* philosophy has made God manlike.
  279–22   Every system of *h·* philosophy, doctrine,

platitudes
  t 446–25   Not *h·* platitudes, but the divine beatitudes

power
  f 225–15   shows *h·* power to be proportionate to its
  g 539–27   gave him more than *h·* power to expound the

presence
  b 325–28   Science which ushered Jesus into *h·* presence,

probation
  a 35–16   its exemplification of *h·* probation,

progress
  ph 170–24   spiritual causation relates to *h·* progress.

propagation
  g 557– 9   *h·* propagation has its suffering because

race
  a 50–18   its mighty blessing for the *h·* race.
  s 111–25   a yearning of the *h·* race for spirituality.
  c 261–32   in remembering good and the *h·* race.
  g 548–25   he would have blessed the *h·* race more
  550– 4   whence cometh Life, . . . to the *h·* race?
  553–25   as the point of emergence for the *h·* race,
  gl 585–25   belief that the *h·* race originated materially

hygiene

surgery, and
a 44–12 all the claims of medicine, surgery, and *h·*.
system of
ph 185– 6 No system of *h·* but C. S. is purely mental.
think about
p 389– 6 The less we know or think about *h·*,

s 138–12 neither . . . by *materia medica*, nor by *h·*,
144– 9 in human philosophy, physiology, *h·*,
145–14 whether faith in drugs, trust in *h·*,
f 222–27 fear, *h·*, physiology, and physics
226–19 material medicine and *h·*, fetter faith
230–23 the sick are never really healed by drugs, *h·*, or
p 382– 5 If half the attention given to *h·* were
r 483– 1 how do drugs, *h·*, and animal magnetism heal?

hygienic

p 370–25 *H·* treatment also loses its efficacy.
378–10 *h·* drilling and drugging, adopted to
382–13 He, who is ignorant of what is termed *h·* law,
382–15 the devotee of supposed *h·* law,
440– 2 on the ground of *h·* disobedience,

hymn

ap 566–20 prayer which concludes the same *h·*,

hypnotic

ph 181–32 Any *h·* power you may exercise will
p 402–31 pleasure or pain of the person under *h·* control
t 446–28 exercise of will brings on a *h·* state,
g 528–16 inducing a sleep or *h·* state in Adam

Hypnotism

p 430–23 Physiology, *H·*, Envy, Greed and
431–14 summoned Physiology, Materia Medica, and *H·*
439–18 the blind *H·*, and the masked Personal Sense,
441–22 *H·*, Oriental Witchcraft, and Esoteric Magic

hypnotism

and electricity
sp 78–26 *h·* and electricity are claimed to be the
called
an 101–30 effect of animal magnetism, recently called *h·*,
is not scientific
p 402–29 Hence the proof that *h·* is not scientific ;
magnetism nor
p 442–16 Neither animal magnetism nor *h·*
magnetism or
an 103–19 animal magnetism or *h·* is the specific term for
t 454– 1 nor . . . practise animal magnetism or *h·*.
gl 584–19 animal magnetism or *h·* ; the lust of the flesh,
mesmerism and
b 322–16 foreshadowed the mesmerism and *h·* of to-day.
mesmerism, or
an 102– 5 mesmerism, or *h·* is a mere negation,
p 402–23 The error, mesmerism— or *h·*, to use the
spiritualism, or
sp 99–19 theosophy, spiritualism, or *h·*,
without
ph 185–23 not only without drugs, but without *h·*,

an 103–24 The malicious form of *h·*
104–18 mesmerism, animal magnetism, *h·*.
s 129–17 Animal magnetism, *h·*, spiritualism,
ph 178–29 attempt to unite with it *h·*,
f 202–29 and yet we rely on a drug or *h·* . . . as if
p 378–19 whereas *h·* and hygienic drilling and
398–28 *h·* changes such ills into new and
r 484– 8 mesmerism, *h·*, theosophy, or spiritualism?

hypnotist

p 375–12 *h·* dispossesses the patient of his

hypnotized

p 431–23 Morbid Secretion *h·* the prisoner

hypnotizer

an 104–22 *h·* employs one error to destroy another.

hypochondria

ph 176–23 cases of hysteria, *h·*, and hallucination?

hypocrisy

folly of
p 426–15 and see the folly of *h·*,
ignorance or
f 243– 3 can never succeed . . . through ignorance or *h·*.

hypocrisy

is fatal
pr 7–32 *H·* is fatal to religion.
lust and
ap 567–28 beast and the false prophets are lust and *h·*.
571–31 outshining sin, sorcery, lust, and *h·*.
never spared
sp 85–28 never spared *h·* the sternest condemnation.
rebuked the
gl 597– 7 rebuked the *h·*, which offered long petitions

f 241–10 Falsehood, envy, *h·*, malice,
b 289–10 sin, lust, hatred, envy, *h·*,
329–21 There is no *h·* in Science.
330–30 *h·*, slander, hate, theft, adultery,
p 365–25 If *h·*, stolidity, inhumanity, or vice
gl 592–28 self-righteousness ; vanity ; *h·*.
596–28 VEIL. A cover ; concealment ; hiding ; *h·*.

hypocrite

pr 8– 2 though it makes the sinner a *h·*.
a 41–10 *h·* may have a flowery pathway here, but
52–31 The bigot, the debauchee, the *h·*,
c 263–12 They make man an involuntary *h·*,
b 294–30 the *h·* that he is hiding himself.

hypocrites

pr 3–30 sharp censure our Master pronounces on *h·*.
7–28 By it we may become involuntary *h·*,
sp 85–21 "O ye *h·* ! ye can discern the— *Matt.* 16 : 3.

hypocritical

a 20– 6 To the ritualistic priest and *h·* Pharisee

hypodermic

p 416– 6 A *h·* injection of morphine is
t 464–17 would give him a *h·* injection,

hypotheses

beliefs and
sp 79–11 Spiritualism relies upon human beliefs and *h·*.
79–13 C. S. removes these beliefs and *h·*
false
s 127–31 false *h·* that matter is its own lawgiver,
human
sp 98–12 Creeds, doctrines, and human *h·* do not
t 457– 2 Truth uncontaminated by human *h·*.
r 481–19 Human *h·* first assume the reality of
material
b 273– 7 Deductions from material *h·* are not scientific.
g 552– 6 geology, and all other material *h·*
materialistic
b 268–10 Materialistic *h·* challenge metaphysics
of mortals
ph 182–15 The *h·* of mortals are antagonistic to
physical
s 111–15 reverses perverted and physical *h·*
speculative
s 126–21 left to the mercy of speculative *h·* ?
vague
s 110–32 No analogy exists between the vague *h·* of
g 549–21 in such vague *h·* as must necessarily

s 121–14 left to the *h·* of material sense
163–23 *h·* obtruded upon us at different times.
r 484–26 thus putting an end to the *h·*
g 504–25 a thousand years of human doctrines, *h·*,
gl 590– 6 human theories, doctrines, *h·* ;

hypothesis

f 209–27 based on the *h·* of material law or
244–16 *h·* that he returns eventually to his
b 270–10 Few deny the *h·* that intelligence,
p 388–12 Admit the common *h·* that food
t 445– 6 No *h·* as to the existence of another power
r 482– 4 *h·* that soul is both an evil and a good
489– 8 *h·* which supposes life to be in matter
g 522–28 based on some *h·* of error,

hypothetical

g 545–18 Outside of C. S. all is vague and *h·*,
551–32 ancient and *h·* question, Which is first,

hysteria

ph 176–23 cases of *h·*, hypochondria, and hallucination?
177– 2 as certainly as it produces *h·*,
f 217–11 even of catalepsy and *h·* ;

I

a 27–13 I [Spirit] will raise it up."— *John* 2 : 19.
27–14 The *I*— the Life, substance, and intelligence of
f 249–21 The *I* is Spirit. God never slumbers,
g 501– * *And I appeared unto Abraham,— Exod.* 6 : 3.
501– * *was I not known to them.— Exod.* 6 : 3.
533– 6 whereof *I* commanded thee— *Gen.* 3 : 11.

g 535–21 of which *I* commanded thee,— *Gen.* 3 : 17.
540– 5 "*I* make peace, and create evil.— *Isa.* 45 : 7.
540– 5 *I* the Lord do all these things ;"— *Isa.* 45 : 7.
gl 588– 9 definition of
588–11 There is but one *I*, or Us,
591–16 MIND. The only *I*, or Us ; the only Spirit,

I AM

f 253– 8 I am the substance of all, because *I A·* THAT *I A·*.
c 256–11 rather than the one ever-present *I A·*.
  256–13 The everlasting *I A·* is not bounded nor
  267–10 The great *I A·* made all
b 290– 1 the everlasting *I A·*, the Being who was and is
  336– 1 Mind is the *I A·*, or infinity.
g 550–21 If . . . then the great *I A·* is a myth.
gl 587– 5 GOD. The great *I A·* ; the all-knowing,
  588–20 definition of

ice

f 241–17 than can moonbeams to melt a river of *i·*.

Icelandic

g 525–11 the term *man* . . . in the *I·*, *mind*.
  525–12 The following translation is from the *I·* :

idea

advanced
b 324– 2 renders thought receptive of the advanced *i·*.
can give no
ph 191– 1 The brain can give no *i·* of God's man.
clearest
g 517–13 Love imparts the clearest *i·* of Deity.
compound
r 468–24 a compound *i·*, reflecting the divine substance
  475–14 He is the compound *i·* of God,
g 507–18 multiplication of the compound *i·* man.
gl 585– 8 to spiritual sense, it is a compound *i·*.
  591– 5 The compound *i·* of infinite Spirit ;
divine
(*see* divine)
divine Mind and
s 109– 6 the only realities are the divine Mind and *i·*.
gives the
g 509–15 This text gives the *i·* of the rarefaction
God's
b 299–24 Truth never destroys God's *i·*.
o 345–22 incongruity between God's *i·* and
p 406–24 until we arrive at the fulness of God's *i·*,
ap 565–16 Christ, God's *i·*, will eventually rule all nations
great is the
ap 562–27 great is the *i·*, and the travail portentous.
highest visible
ap 560–18 without a correct sense of its highest visible *i·*,
His
sp 71– 2 nothing is Spirit, — but God and His *i·*.
an 103–16 good is the infinite God and His *i·*,
s 116– 9 so that God and His *i·* may be to us
ph 167–25 but one way — namely, God and His *i·*
b 284–32 is always from God to His *i·*,
o 344– 3 and man to be His *i·*, — that is, His image.
p 372– 9 divine Mind, or God and His *i·*,
r 495–15 cling steadfastly to God and His *i·*.
gl 589–10 and that man is His *i·*, the child of His care.
identity, or
sp 71– 5 The identity, or *i·*, of all reality continues
image or
c 257– 1 creation is the infinite image or *i·*
b 336– 9 was and is God's image or *i·*,
immaculate
ap 565–18 This immaculate *i·*, represented first by man
immortal
a 55–15 Truth's immortal *i·* is sweeping down the
c 262–14 above the mortal to the immortal *i·* of God.
b 325– 7 of Truth, unfolding its own immortal *i·*.
r 477–17 the immortal *i·* of being, indestructible
impelled the
ap 565–25 but this only impelled the *i·* to rise to the
individual
g 508–23 The intelligent individual *i·*, be it male or
infinite
sp 90–25 sets man free to master the infinite *i·*.
s 112–17 comes one Principle and its infinite *i·*,
c 258–13 God expresses in man the infinite *i·*
  258–19 infinite Principle is reflected by the infinite *i·*
g 508– 4 Mind's infinite *i·*, man and the universe,
ap 577– 3 as the infinite Principle and infinite *i·*,
gl 582–11 gleam of the infinite *i·* of the infinite Principle
is clad
ap 561–26 *i·* is clad with the radiance of spiritual Truth,
lesser
g 518–13 God gives the lesser *i·* of Himself for a
Life's
b 289–12 Life and Life's *i·*, Truth and Truth's idea,
limitless
g 510–19 Love alone can impart the limitless *i·* of
man is
r 475–13 Man is *i·*, the image, of Love ;
mental
r 467–27 Spirit gives the true mental *i·*.
Mind's
r 492–20 All is Mind and Mind's *i·*.
new
b 281–31 cast out or the new *i·* will be spilled,
p 420–17 are ready to become receptive to the new *i·*.
t 463–14 The new *i·*, . . . is clad in white

idea
new-old
ph 191–12 even to the birth of a new-old *i·*,
not in its
r 467–22 leading point . . . that Principle is not in its *i·*.
of Christian healing
a 55– 4 the *i·* of Christian healing enjoined by Jesus ;
of divine power
g 534–15 the *i·* of divine power, which Jesus presented,
of God
(*see* God)
of good
b 325– 3 He who has the true *i·* of good loses all sense of
  327–26 the man . . . who has not the true *i·* of good?
g 546–14 represents error as starting from an *i·* of good
of goodness
s 119–22 is represented only by the *i·* of goodness ;
of immortality
gl 593–10 a new and higher *i·* of immortality,
of Life
b 314–21 he presented to her, . . . the true *i·* of Life
  325– 2 he who perceives the true *i·* of Life
gl 595– 7 the *i·* of Life, substance, and intelligence ;
of Love
b 326–31 He beheld for the first time the true *i·* of Love,
g 534–28 will struggle to destroy the spiritual *i·* of Love ;
of Spirit
a 29–30 Man as the offspring of God, as the *i·* of Spirit,
c 266–28 Man is the *i·* of Spirit ;
of the supremacy
b 324–28 if the *i·* of the supremacy of Spirit,
of Truth
c 263–22 the discovery of some distant *i·* of Truth ;
r 495– 6 If sickness is true or the *i·* of Truth,
g 526–18 stands for the *i·* of Truth,
  543– 6 it is the *i·* of Truth and changes not,
  555–32 Truth fosters the *i·* of Truth,
gl 595– 3 SWORD. The *i·* of Truth ; justice.
or intelligence
b 279–18 their only *i·* or intelligence is in God.
or reflection
r 470–22 *i·* or reflection, man, remains perfect.
gl 581– 8 ARK. Safety ; the *i·*, or reflection, of Truth,
presented
ap 562– 4 Elias presented the *i·* of the fatherhood
presents the
g 503–20 divine Mind presents the *i·* of God :
present the
c 256–29 Finiteness cannot present the *i·* or the vastness
Principle and
c 259–13 includes a perfect Principle and *i·*,
b 285–22 Supreme Being, or divine Principle, and *i·*.
r 471– 1 God and man, divine Principle and *i·*,
  476– 5 inseparable as divine Principle and *i·*.
g 503– 9 The divine Principle and *i·* constitute
Principle and its
r 465–17 Principle and its *i·* is one,
  475– 4 all is Spirit, divine Principle and its *i·*.
g 520– 9 Principle and its *i·*, man, are coexistent
profound
b 320–26 gives a profound *i·* of the divine power to heal
pure
a 50–14 and to himself, Love's pure *i·*.
right
f 235–31 will love to grapple with a new, right *i·*
semblance of an
ph 195–15 Whatever furnishes the semblance of an *i·*
solitary
c 259– 4 nor is he an isolated, solitary *i·*,
Spirit as
sp 76–17 characterized by the divine Spirit as *i·*,
spiritual
(*see* spiritual)
substance of an
c 257–13 the substance of an *i·* is very far from
this
sp 88–19 but this *i·* can never be seen, . . . through th
t 463–10 this *i·* cannot injure its useful
g 534–29 this *i·*, will bruise the head of lust.
ap 562– 7 This *i·* reveals the universe as secondary
thought and
gl 597–17 Spontaneity of thought and *i·* ;
true
a 39–26 mortals must get the true *i·* and
  43–15 true *i·* of God, which Jesus' persecutors had
  47– 5 gaining the true *i·* of their glorified Master,
  54–10 plant themselves in Christ, the true *i·* of God
s 123– 3 The true *i·* and Principle of man will
  132–25 Anticipating this rejection . . . of the true *i·*
  133–15 but when they departed from the true *i·*,
f 205–20 some word or deed which indicates the true
  235–26 Christ Jesus, the true *i·* of spiritual power.
c 255–17 cannot be made the basis of any true *i·* of
  258– 7 insufficiency of this belief to supply the true
  258–12 and this reflection is the true *i·* of God.
b 314–21 he presented to her, . . . the true *i·* of Life a

ideas

those
b 303– 1   the divine Principle of those *i·*.

veritable
sp 88– 9   How are veritable *i·* to be distinguished

---

c 257–12   Mind creates His own likeness in *i·*,
b 274– 9   *I·*, on the contrary, are born of Spirit,

identical

a 21–22   and our mutual interests are *i·* ;
s 119–17   In one sense God is *i·* with nature,
135–25   proves the one to be *i·* with the other.
b 300–25   and matter would be *i·* with God.
333– 6   it is *i·* with the name Joshua,
r 473– 3   though seeming to be real and *i·*.
482–11   out of Science, soul is *i·* with sense,

identified

a 46– 8   The divine Spirit, which *i·* Jesus thus
s 136–13   Who or what is it that is thus *i·* with

identities

sp 70–12   The divine Mind maintains all *i·*,
70–14   What are God's *i·* ?
b 333–31   The one Spirit includes all *i·*.
g 503– 2   the unfolding of spiritual ideas and their *i·*,
505– 9   divine Mind, not matter, creates all *i·*,

identity

all
b 302– 7   conscious infinitude of existence and of all *i·*

conscious
r 475–17   conscious *i·* of being as found in Science,

his
c 265–12   by no means suggests . . . the loss of his *i·*,

man's
f 217– 1   The loss of man's *i·* . . . is impossible ;

of animals
g 550– 6   preserves the individuality and *i·* of animals

or idea
sp 71– 5   *i·*, or idea, of all reality continues forever ;

or power
r 479–28   So evil should be denied *i·* or power,

reality nor
r 473– 2   illusion, possessing neither reality nor *i·*

spiritual
a 51– 8   spiritual *i·* in the likeness of the divine ;
b 287– 8   and maintains man's spiritual *i·*.
287–23   illusion, without spiritual *i·* or foundation,
333–28   referred to this unity of his spiritual *i·* thus :

your own
b 261–26   you will neither lose . . . nor your own *i·*.

---

b 302– 4   The *i·* of the real man is not lost,
r 477–20   *I·* is the reflection of Spirit,

idiocy

an 103–24   The malicious form . . . ultimates in moral *i·*.

idiosyncrasies

t 228– 3   The transmission of disease or of certain *i·*

idleness

f 240–23   If at present content with *i·*, we must

idolater

ph 186–32   The human mind has been an *i·* from the
f 214–19   finite thoughts of God like the pagan *i·*.

idolaters

p 388– 9   *I·*, believing in more than one mind,

idolatry

and mythology
gl 591– 2   From this follow *i·* and mythology,

and ritualism
r 466–25   *i·* and ritualism are the outcome of

dooms
g 535–11   It dooms *i·*.

error of
r 470– 6   existence of . . . was the basic error of *i·*.

form of
ph 174– 4   Is civilization only a higher form of *i·*,

mythology and
gl 594– 3   the first statement of mythology and *i·* ;

pagan
r 469–30   pernicious to divine theology as . . . pagan *i·*.

the first
s 146– 5   The first *i·* was faith in matter.

---

an 106–22   *i·*, *witchcraft*, hatred, variance, — *Gal.* 5 : 20.
s 158– 2   profession of medicine originated in *i·*
b 340–26   annihilates pagan and Christian *i·*,
g 524– 1   *i·* which followed this material mythology
f 592– 7   *i·* ; the subjective states of error ;

idols

ph 173–30   The *i·* of civilization are far more fatal
173–31   than are the *i·* of barbarism.
173–31   The *i·* of civilization call into action less

ignominy

an 105–27   down to the depths of *i·* and death.

ignorance

and false belief
b 304– 3   It is *i·* and false belief, based on

and malice
f 215–31   *i·* and malice of the age would have killed

and sin
b 290–22   Christ, Truth, removes all *i·* and sin.

and superstition
s 120–31   *i·* and superstition chained the limbs of

bigoted
a 48– 2   the staves of bigoted *i·* smote him sorely.

forgetting her
sp 89– 3   Forgetting her *i·* in the belief that

gathered from
sp 78–14   Communications gathered from *i·*

greater
ap 560–31   greater *i·* of the divine Principle

gross
t 456–17   gross *i·* of the method of the Christ-cure.

her comparative
pref ix–30   her comparative *i·* of the stupendous

human
pr 13–25   human *i·* of the divine Principle, Love,
f 252– 4   Human *i·* of Mind and of the

in proportion as
f 209– 3   in proportion as *i·*, *fear*, or

in the hands of
b 305– 1   left in the hands of *i·*, placed at the disposal of

in your
p 439–21   for injuring in your *i·* the unfortunate

malice or
t 459–20   Whether animated by malice or *i·*,

mark of
g 555– 9   The mark of *i·* is on its forehead,

moral
r 483–10   Moral *i·* or sin affects your demonstration,

mortal
ph 188–23   springing from mortal *i·* or fear.
b 280–32   The only excuse . . . is our mortal *i·* of Spirit,

occasioned by
p 373–19   The fear occasioned by *i·* can be cured ;

of mental cause
p 374–24   because of your . . . *i·* of mental cause and effect.

of the cause
p 374–17   *I·* of the cause or approach of disease

of the error
t 446–31   *I·* of the error to be eradicated

of the future
p 374–19   You confess to *i·* of the future

of the laws
s 145–23   *i·* of the laws of eternal and unerring Mind.

of the Science
p 409–29   in *i·* of the Science of Life,

or hypocrisy
f 243– 3   can never succeed . . . through *i·* or hypocrisy.

or malice
t 451–27   arises from *i·* or malice aforethought.

or sin
p 411–21   foundation of all sickness is fear, *i·*, or sin.
r 483–10   Moral *i·* or sin affects your demonstration,

our
p 390– 7   It is our *i·* of God, the divine Principle, which
g 540–12   may think in our *i·* that the Lord hath

popular
p 398– 8   the popular *i·* of spiritual Life-laws.

recompense for
p 409–32   Death will not . . . recompense for *i·*.

rise above
sp 77–26   The departed would gradually rise above *i·*

spiritual
f 243– 1   We may hide spiritual *i·* from the world,

---

pref vii–17   *I·* of God is no longer the stepping-stone to
s 144–25   *I·*, pride, or prejudice closes the door to
ph 175–32   "Where *i·* is bliss, 't is folly to be wise,"
182–28   *i·* of C. S. and its transcendent power.
197–17   It was the *i·* of our forefathers
f 227–11   some public teachers permit an *i·* of
227–11   an *i·* that is the foundation of
251–28   *I·*, like intentional wrong, is not Science.
251–29   *I·* must be seen and corrected before we
b 280–32   *i·* which yields only to the understanding
336– 1   limits would imply and impose *i·*.
p 409–31   a reward for this *i·*.
427–22   difficulty lies in *i·* of what God is.
t 447–12   *I·*, subtlety, or false charity does not
459–21   *i·* is more harmful than wilful
464–24   weapons of bigotry, *i·*, envy, fall before
464–28   Neither dishonesty nor *i·* ever founded,
ap 560–30   *I·* of the divine idea betrays
560–31   *i·* of Truth and Love.
gl 586–11   anxiety ; *i·* ; error ; desire ; caution.

gnorant
 pr 13–28 *i·* of man as God's image or reflection
  13–30 The world of error is *i·* of the world of Truth,
 a 48–28 Pilate was *i·* of the consequences
 sp 79– 4 those who are *i·* of Life as God.
  86–14 may appear to the *i·* to be apparitions ;
  87–20 sea is *i·* of the gems within its caverns,
 an 103–23 It is either *i·* or malicious.
 s 150–32 *i·* that the human mind and body are myths.
  159–30 *I·* of the fact that a man's belief
 ph 166– 4 *I·* of this, or shrinking from its implied
  178–28 *I·* of the methods and the basis of
  180–13 *I·* that the human mind governs the body,
  181–17 *i·* of the baneful effects of magnetism,
  186–28 Mortal mind is *i·* of self,
  187– 4 how *i·* must they be of the all-knowing Mind
  190– 3 matter is a belief, *i·* of itself,
  190– 3 *i·* of what it is supposed to produce.
 f 225–30 *i·* how to obtain their freedom.
 o 343– 6 Is not finite mind *i·* of God's method?
 p 377–30 Without this *i·* human belief, any
  380–19 *i·* of the truth which chains disease.
  381– 2 *I·* of our God-given rights,
  382–13 He, who is *i·* of what is termed hygienic law,
  382–16 to teach the so-called *i·* one.
  393– 5 *i·* of itself, of its own actions,
  393– 6 *i·* that the predisposing, remote, and
  408–31 Mortal mind is *i·* of itself,
  408–32 *i·* of the errors it includes
  422–12 and *i·* that it is a favorable omen,
 t 447– 7 *i·* attempts to do good may
 r 474– 8 To the *i·* age in which it first appears,
  483– 9 must not be *i·* of the moral and spiritual
 g 512–27 *I·* of the origin and operations of mortal mind,
  512–28 that is, *i·* of itself,
  512–30 *i·* of the existence of both
 ap 560–29 *i·* of the divine idea he taught.

ignorantly
 s 116–25 As the words . . . are commonly and *i·*
 p 428–16 whom we "*i·* worship,"— *Acts* 17 : 23.
 t 456–12 greatly errs, *i·* or intentionally,
 gl 596– 9 "Whom therefore ye *i·* worship,— *Acts* 17 : 23.

ignore
 ph 166–16 To *i·* God as of little use in sickness is a mistake.
 b 275– 2 partnership of mind with matter would *i·*

ignores
 s 148–28 it *i·* the divine Spirit as unable or

ill
 sp 79–23 unscientific practitioner says: "You are *i·*.
 s 107–10 delivering the children of men from every *i·*
 f 218– 9 The body is supposed to say, "I am *i·*."
  222–19 and yet he continued *i·* all the while.
  227–31 disobedience to which would have made man *i·*,
  230–30 the liability to be *i·* is removed.
  231– 3 Unless an *i·* is rightly met and fairly overcome
  231– 4 Unless . . . the *i·* is never conquered.
 b 326– 7 find the divine remedy for every *i·*,
 p 430–19 The patient feels *i·*, ruminates, and
 r 467–21 The belief that . . . is an error that works *i·*.

ill-arranged
 m 58– 5 *I·* notes produce discord.

ill-attuned
 m 60–24 An *i·* ear calls discord harmony,

ill-effects
 ph 176–26 can carry its *i·* no farther than

illegal
 p 434–23 His trial was a tragedy, and is morally *i·*.

illegality
 p 437–25 expelling . . . for such high-handed *i·*.

illegitimate
 f 203–27 The foam and fury of *i·* living
 p 390–22 an abiding conviction that it is *i·*,

ill-health
 p 377–28 mistaken belief . . . necessity and power of *i·* ;
  421– 6 true definition of all human belief in *i·*,

illimitable
 s 127– 8 there can be nothing beyond *i·* divinity.

ill-nature
 m 58–29 Wealth may obviate . . . the chance for *i·*

illness
 p 396– 5 Avoid talking *i·* to the patient.
 t 456–21 So long as matter is the basis . . . *i·* cannot

ills
 destroy all
 p 374–16 destroy all *i·* which proceed from mortal mind.
 r 493–18 Mind must be found . . . able to destroy all *i·*.
 fleshly
 f 228–10 and fleshly *i·* will disappear.
 of flesh
 s 155–23 the discords of matter and the *i·* of flesh,
 b 277–20 produces all the *i·* of flesh,

ills
 of the flesh
 ph 191–31 Truth is able to cast out the *i·* of the flesh.
 b 320–27 the divine power to heal the *i·* of the flesh,
 gl 581–16 Asher . . . the *i·* of the flesh rebuked.
 produce the
 m 62–30 and produce the *i·* of which we complain.
 such
 r 398–29 hypnotism changes such *i·* into
  413–30 making it probable at any time that such *i·* may
 these
 p 395–26 to feel these *i·* in physical belief.
  424–29 you must destroy the belief in these *i·*
  425–13 Then these *i·* will disappear.

 ph 170–31 from which all *i·* have gone forth,
 p 405–28 penalties you incur and the *i·* they bring.
 g 552–23 the redeeming power, from the *i·* they occasion,

ill-tempered
 p 395–17 An *i·*, complaining, or deceitful person

illuminated
 a 43– 9 that influx of divine Science which so *i·* the

illuminating
 g 502–16 *i·* time with the glory of eternity.

illumination
 a 29–20 The *i·* of Mary's spiritual sense
 sp 85– 2 It is the *i·* of the spiritual understanding
 t 461–11 Only by the *i·* of the spiritual sense,
 g 510–10 and this *i·* is reflected spiritually by all who
 gl 584– 5 the *i·* of spiritual understanding,
  596–13 believed that the stones . . . had supernatural *i·*,

illuminations
 gl 596–15 The *i·* of Science give us a sense of the

illuminator
 gl 596–15 reveals Spirit, not matter, as the *i·* of all.

illumine
 gl 596–24 divine Life and Love *i·* it,

illumined
 s 110–15 The Scriptures were *i·* ;
 ap 571–29 and *i·* the night of paganism with the sublime

illumines
 b 334– 6 from which it *i·* heaven and earth ;
 t 454–19 inspires, *i·*, designates, and leads the way.
 g 501– 7 Jesus *i·* them, showing the poverty of
  503–14 light of ever-present Love *i·* the universe.

illuming
 c 266–28 *i·* the universe with light.

illusion
 any
 f 217–26 power of Mind over the body or any *i·* of
 ceases to be even an
 sp 97–16 boundary where, . . . it ceases to be even an *i·*,
 death is the
 p 428– 3 Life is real, and death is the *i·*.
 destroying that
 f 245– 2 benefits of destroying that *i·*, are illustrated in
 dream, or
 f 230– 5 the awakening from this mortal dream, or *i·*,
 effect of
 an 101–31 In no instance . . . other than the effect of *i·*.
 effects of
 p 408–12 baneful effects of *i·* on mortal minds
 falsity and
 g 554–28 and is simply a falsity and *i·*.
 forged by the
 f 223– 5 forged by the *i·* that he lives in body
 human
 r 492–23 human *i·* as to sin, sickness, and death
 illustrate its
 p 380–15 physical effects of fear illustrate its *i·*.
 illustrates the
 b 300– 7 The mirage, . . . illustrates the *i·* of
 less
 f 247–31 recipe for beauty is to have less *i·*
 material
 r 484–21 Mesmerism is mortal, material *i·*.
 mental
 p 403– 8 understood that the difficulty is a mental *i·*,
 mortal
 b 289–19 this shows that . . . death is but a mortal *i·*,
  302–16 always beyond and above the mortal *i·*
 p 403–20 sweeps away the gossamer web of mortal *i·*.
 of belief
 r 490–31 Under the mesmeric *i·* of belief,
 of death
 f 251– 8 In the *i·* of death, mortals wake to the
 r 493–28 awakened Lazarus from the dream, *i·*, of death,
 of error
 g 538–16 is significant of the *i·* of error,
 of life
 b 305–23 *i·* of life that is here to-day and gone to-morrow,

illusion

of material sense
- sp 71– 3 simply a belief, an *i·* of material sense.
- s 122–15 another proof of the *i·* of material sense.
- f 227–26 The *i·* of material sense, not divine law,

of mind
- b 311–11 so long as the *i·* of mind in matter remains.

of mortal mind
- ph 168–27 a latent *i·* of mortal mind,
- p 385–32 Any supposed . . . is an *i·* of mortal mind,

of Moses
- b 321–16 The *i·* of Moses lost its power to alarm

of pleasure
- p 398–21 destroy the *i·* of pleasure in intoxication,

of sickness
- b 297– 8 *i·* of sickness, to be instructed out of itself
- r 495–14 When the *i·* of sickness or sin tempts you,

of sin
- g 536–10 The *i·* of sin is without hope or God.

or dream
- r 490–30 oblivion, nothingness, or an *i·* or dream.

or error
- g 556– 1 and not the belief in *i·* or error.

point out the
- t 447–26 remove the mask, point out the *i·*,

prolong the
- sp 77–20 so prolong the *i·* either of a soul inert or

remove the
- p 403–10 is employed to remove the *i·* in one case,

root of the
- b 303–16 Divine Science lays the axe at the root of the *i·*.

sensual
- f 221–32 another lesson,— that gluttony is a sensual *i·*,

springing from
- p 399–24 to make material beliefs, springing from *i·*.

suffer the
- p 381– 5 Be no more willing to suffer the *i·* that

this
- f 217–27 and so destroy this *i·*,
- b 303–18 will eventually destroy this *i·*

- sp 92– 6 From the *i·* implied in this last postulate arises
- 97–13 until matter reaches its mortal zenith in *i·*
- s 129–29 The very name, *i·*, points to nothingness.
- f 244– 3 is not real, but is *i·*, the mirage of error.
- 245–31 decrepitude is . . . but an *i·*.
- b 271– 5 Neither emasculation, *i·*, nor
- 287–22 it is *i·*, without spiritual identity or
- 293–10 This so-called mind and body is the *i·*
- 308–11 but finding only an *i·*,
- o 348– 7 appear to be— what it really is— an *i·*
- p 379–13 his sense of bleeding was an *i·*,
- r 473– 1 inharmony of mortal mind or body is *i·*,
- 480–23 Hence, evil is but an *i·*,
- 493–26 can only seem real and natural in *i·*.
- 494–23 breaks their *i·* with the unbroken reality of
- g 540–12 when the symptoms of evil, *i·*, are aggravated,
- 543–13 an *i·*, against which divine Science is
- gl 582– 3 BELIEVING. . . . Mortal thoughts, *i·*.
- 582– 7 pride ; envy ; fame ; *i·* ; a false belief ;
- 584– 9 DEATH. An *i·*, the lie of life in matter ;
- 586–19 an *i·* ; a belief that matter has sensation.
- 587– 1 An *i·* ; a belief that mind is outlined and limited ;
- 591– 9 another name for mortal mind ; *i·* ;

illusions

destroy all
- b 296– 7 suffering or Science must destroy all *i·*

dispelling the
- b 332–13 dispelling the *i·* of the senses ;

disposal of
- b 305– 1 placed at the disposal of *i·*,

erring
- r 477–13 corporeal senses to be mortal and erring *i·*.

human
- c 259–23 and forms its offspring after human *i·*.
- r 468– 3 never can be coordinate with human *i·*.

laden with
- p 413–26 being laden with *i·* about disease,

leading
- s 129–27 quite as rational are some of the leading *i·*

mere
- g 556–20 In sleep, cause and effect are mere *i·*.

mortal
- f 214–20 for mortal *i·* would rob God, slay man,
- b 289–29 Matter and death are mortal *i·*.
- 330– 4 learned . . . the fixedness of mortal *i·*,

not the creator of
- f 249–13 the creator of ideas is not the creator of *i·*.

of sin
- ap 572–16 the myriad *i·* of sin, sickness, and death.

old
- f 223–17 but more are blinded by their old *i·*,

similar
- s 122–22 Experience is full of instances of similar *i·*,

illusions

stupefying
- sp 95–28 Lulled by stupefying *i·*, the world is asleep

- sp 88– 9 veritable ideas to be distinguished from *i·*
- f 230– 4 But if sickness and sin are *i·*,
- b 283–11 They are not ideas, but *i·*.
- p 368–26 its conditions are *i·*,

illusive
- ph 187–11 to another *i·* personification, named Satan.
- 191–28 The *i·* senses may fancy affinities with
- f 249– 2 give up imperfect models and *i·* ideals ;
- b 293– 4 the least material form of *i·* consciousness,
- o 343–19 *i·* errors— which he could and did destroy.
- p 371–17 the *i·* sufferings which throng the gloaming,
- 383–26 the *i·* physical effect of a false belief,

illustrate
- s 134–16 how can they *i·* the doctrines of Christ
- f 232–21 nor did he *i·* these errors by his practice.
- b 283–30 than we can teach and *i·* geometry by
- p 380–15 physical effects of fear *i·* its illusion.
- ap 575–14 Did not Jesus *i·* the truths he taught

illustrated
- sp 86– 8 His quick apprehension . . . *i·* his spirituality.
- s 123–26 they *i·* an ever-operative divine Principle.
- 154– 9 This fact in metaphysics is *i·* by the
- ph 171–14 Jesus *i·* the divine Principle
- 200– 5 *i·* the grand human capacities of being
- f 245– 2 *i·* in a sketch from the history of
- b 285–12 *i·* by the opposite natures of
- 333–11 the spirituality which is taught, *i·*, and
- o 358–16 uttered and *i·* by the prophets,
- g 501–12 which God *i·* by light and harmony,
- gl 579–12 This patriarch *i·* the purpose of Love to

illustrates
- s 152–20 Such a fact *i·* our theories.
- f 225–14 history of our country, . . . *i·* the might of
- b 300– 6 *i·* the illusion of material man,
- 316–21 Christ *i·* that blending with God,
- 332–32 *i·* the coincidence, or spiritual agreement,
- p 402–24 The error, mesmerism . . . *i·* the fact
- t 445–20 *i·* the unlabored motion of the divine energy
- 454– 5 Truth, which *i·* the impotence of error.
- 461– 6 that part *i·* and proves the entire Principle.
- g 507– 2 In metaphor, the *dry land i·* the
- ap 561–23 *i·* the coincidence of God and man

illustrating
- s 117–17 *i·* and demonstrating Life and Truth

illustration
- s 118– 5 formal applications of the *i·*.
- f 245–29 the primary of that *i·* makes it plain that
- b 315–26 and presented an *i·* of creation.

illustrative
- p 430–13 allegory *i·* of the law of divine Mind

image

and likeness
- pr 3–13 *i·* and likeness of the patient, tender, and true,
- a 19– 3 are not at war with God's *i·* and likeness.
- sp 94– 2 who makes man in the *i·* and likeness of
- 94– 5 implied by . . . "*i·*" and "likeness"— *Gen.* 1 : 26.
- s 151–24 maintains His own *i·* and likeness.
- ph 172–19 man is the *i·* and likeness of Spirit ;
- f 206–26 the spiritual *i·* and likeness of God?
- 216–20 to suppose that man, God's *i·* and likeness,
- 222–23 very far from being the *i·* and likeness of God,
- c 257–32 Finite man cannot be the *i·* and likeness of,
- 258–17 as the true divine *i·* and likeness,
- 265–20 not of a man in God's *i·* and likeness.
- b 281–12 the *i·* and likeness of perfect Mind,
- 285– 8 not man, the *i·* and likeness of God,
- 287–20 It saith, . . . I am not the *i·* and likeness of
- 301–17 man is the divine *i·* and likeness,
- 303–25 God, without the *i·* and likeness of Himself,
- 330–13 neither seen God nor His *i·* and likeness.
- 332–13 yea, the divine *i·* and likeness,
- 340–12 man in His *i·* and likeness,
- p 414–27 man is the *i·* and likeness of God,
- 441–17 forever in the *i·* and likeness of his Maker.
- r 468–14 Spirit is God, and man is His *i·* and likeness.
- 475– 9 man is made in the *i·* and likeness of God.
- 475–16 all that reflects God's *i·* and likeness ;
- 497– 8 and man in God's *i·* and likeness.
- g 519–16 and reach the spiritual *i·* and likeness,
- 531–31 created by Mind in the *i·* and likeness of God
- 544–26 nor the *i·* and likeness of the one God.
- 548– 6 we discover man in the *i·* and likeness of God.
- gl 580– 4 God's man, . . . is His own *i·* and likeness ;
- 580– 5 that which is not the *i·* and likeness of good,
- 580–14 the *i·* and likeness of what God has not
- 584–25 not after the *i·* and likeness of Spirit,
- 591– 6 MAN. . . . the spiritual *i·* and likeness of God ;

divine
- (*see* **divine**)

image

existence as
  b 320–19 harmonious existence as *i·*, idea,

express
  b 313–13 the phrase "express *i·*"— *Heb.* 1 : 3.

expressed
  b 313–11 the express [expressed] *i·* of— *Heb.* 1 : 3.

God's
  pr 13–28 ignorant of man as God's *i·* or reflection
  a 19– 3 are not at war with God's *i·* and likeness.
  s 116– 5 and man as God's *i·* appears.
  120– 6 and reflects Soul, God, for man is God's *i·*.
  140–29 God created man in His, God's, *i·* ;
  f 204–25 notion that they can create . . . in God's *i·*,
  216–20 to suppose that man, God's *i·* and likeness,
  c 265–20 not of a man in God's *i·* and likeness.
  b 284–11 Is God's *i·* or likeness matter,
  305–13 The verity that God's *i·* is not a creator,
  325–15 then shall man be found in God's *i·*.
  336– 9 Immortal man was and is God's *i·* or idea,
  o 346– 3 When man is spoken of as made in God's *i·*,
  p 392–10 harmony of man, God's *i·*.
  r 475–16 term for all that reflects God's *i·* and likeness ;
  476–31 man in God's *i·* is unfallen
  497– 8 and man in God's *i·* and likeness.

God's own
  b 295–12 Mortals are not . . . created in God's own *i·* ;
  g 517–22 This ideal is God's own *i·*, spiritual and infinite.

His
  ph 188– 2 God, immortal Mind, and man is found in His *i·*.
  b 330–13 neither seen God nor His *i·* and
  333– 2 agreement, between God and man in His *i·*.
  340–12 man in His *i·* and likeness.
  o 344– 3 and man to be His idea,— that is, His *i·*.
  345–24 God's man, made in His *i·*,
  r 468–14 Spirit is God, and man is His *i·*
  g 522–23 denunciations of man when not found in His *i·*,

His own
  s 151–24 maintains His own *i·* and likeness.
  o 344– 7 God has created man in His own *i·*
  g 516–24 God created man in His own *i·*,— *Gen.* 1 : 27.
  516–28 that God made man in His own *i·*,
  gl 580– 4 God's man, . . . is His own *i·* and likeness ;

human
  s 140–31 mortals would . . . make God in their own human *i·*.

infinite
  c 257– 1 creation is the infinite *i·* or idea
  b 300– 5 His infinite *i·* or reflection, man.

in Mind
  s 115–17 Idea : An *i·* in Mind ;

in mortal mind
  s 116–19 matter is nothing beyond an *i·* in mortal mind.

inverted
  s 111–17 optics rejects the incidental or inverted *i·*
  111–17 what this inverted *i·* is meant to represent.
  b 301–27 presents an inverted *i·* of Mind and substance
  ap 572–11 materiality is the inverted *i·* of spirituality.
  gl 580–13 Adam. . . . an inverted *i·* of Spirit ;

lost
  c 259–17 The *lost i·* is no image.

man is
  sp 73–10 for man is *i·*.
  b 301–24 while man is "*i·*"— *Gen.* 1 : 27.

mental
  p 416– 4 unless the mental *i·* occasioning the pain

more terrifying
  p 376– 1 *i·* more terrifying than that of most other

no
  c 259–17 The *lost* image is no *i·*.

of disease
  s 154– 7 the fear that creates the *i·* of disease
  p 400–10 Eradicate the *i·* of disease from the

of God
    (see **God**)

of His being
  b 313–22 and an *i·* of His being."— *see Heb.* 1 : 3.

of his Maker
  f 203–15 and so makes man the *i·* of his Maker

of Love
  r 475–13 Man is idea, the *i·*, of Love ;

of mortal thought
  r 479– 7 *i·* of mortal thought, reflected on the retina,

of Spirit
  g 543– 5 The *i·* of Spirit cannot be effaced,

of the beast
  b 327–14 Sin is the *i·* of the beast

of thought
  p 411–23 Disease is an *i·* of thought externalized.

or idea
  c 257– 1 creation is the infinite *i·* or idea
  b 303–28 Spiritual man is the *i·* or idea of God,
  336– 9 Immortal man was and is God's *i·* or idea,

image

or likeness
  sp 71–19 neither . . . is the *i·* or likeness of God,
  b 284–11 Is God's *i·* or likeness matter,
  299–15 whither every . . . *i·*, or likeness of
  g 515–25 mirrored reflection is your own *i·* or likeness.

or reflection
  p 13–28 ignorant of man as God's *i·* or reflection
  f 204–26 without the nature of the *i·* or reflection
  b 300– 5 His infinite *i·* or reflection, man.

our
  p 438– 3 Let us make man in our *i·*,— *Gen.* 1 : 26.
  r 475–23 "Let us make man in our *i·*,— *Gen.* 1 : 26.
  g 515–12 Let us make man in our *i·*,— *Gen.* 1 : 26.

true
  c 259– 6 man is the true *i·* of God.
  b 285–12 claim that a mortal is the true *i·*

untrue
  g 502–10 the history of the untrue *i·* of God,

---

  ph 171–21 the spiritual,— yea, the *i·* of infinite Mind,
  196–28 from the *i·* brought before the mind ;
  200–18 for if man is the *i·*, reflection, of God,
  p 400–25 the *i·* which becomes visible to the senses.
  g 525–10 the primary sense being *i·*, *form;*
  525–11 in the Hebrew *i·*, *similitude;*
  ap 571–25 mirror in which mortals may see their own *i·*.
  gl 584–25 but after its own *i·*."

imaged

  p 379–30 *i·* on the body through the belief that
  411–26 the physical condition is *i·* forth on the body.

image-gods

  s 158– 9 Hippocrates turned from *i·* to

imagery

  b 299– 6 artist's own observation and "chambers of *i·*."

images

and sounds
  sp 86–19 *i·* and sounds evolved involuntarily by

beautiful
  f 248– 9 supplying it with beautiful *i·* of thought
  r 485–26 it cannot outline . . . beautiful *i·*, but it effaces

dark
  p 418–31 dream-shadows, dark *i·* of mortal thought,

efface the
  ph 196–21 efface the *i·* and thoughts of disease,
  p 396–26 so efface the *i·* of sickness from mortal mind.

inverted
  b 305–20 The inverted *i·* presented by the senses,
  g 502– 7 inverted *i·* of the creator and His creation.

its own
  c 259–22 Mortal thought transmits its own *i·*,
  g 511– 2 Mind forms ideas, its own *i·*,

mental
  p 413–28 these actions convey mental *i·* to

of disease
  ph 175– 1 We should prevent the *i·* of disease from
  197– 2 mirror *i·* of disease distinctly in thought.

of this mind
  p 400–24 We see in the body the *i·* of this mind,

of thought
  sp 86–13 Mortals evolve *i·* of thought.
  f 208–29 the *i·* of thought impressed upon it.
  248– 9 supplying it with beautiful *i·* of thought

---

  sp 71–16 *i·*, which mortal mind holds and evolves
  p 379–28 The *i·*, held in this disturbed mind,
  391– 3 Blot out the *i·* of mortal thought
  425–10 *i·* of mortal thought superimposed upon the
  g 511–18 effulgence of God's infinite ideas, *i·*,

imaginary

  sp 90– 6 the *i·* line called the equator
  s 146–19 divests material drugs of their *i·* power,
  ph 178–25 and we disarm sin of its *i·* power
  f 241– 8 as *i·*, whimsical, and unreal as his pleasures.
  b 274–28 Science and . . . destroy the *i·* copartnership,
  340– 1 their *i·* power for good or evil,
  o 352–19 child, who is frightened at *i·* ghosts
  p 371–12 children look everywhere for the *i·* ghost,
  403–19 error is deprived of its *i·* powers
  t 460–14 Sickness is neither *i·* nor unreal,— that is,
  r 479–24 Darkness and chaos are the *i·* opposites of

imagination

  an 101– 3 or to the excitement of the *i·*
  101– 7 experiment upon the power of the *i·*."
  s 163–25 Nowhere is the *i·* displayed to a greater extent ;
  ph 176–11 array of diseases was not paraded before the *i·*.

imagine

  pref xi– 1 Many *i·* that the phenomena of physical healing
  a 21–31 satisfied if he can only *i·* himself drifting
  s 130–31 no longer *i·* evil to be ever-present
  f 203–18 We *i·* that Mind can be imprisoned
  r 494–11 It is not well to *i·* that Jesus

imagined
f 221–25 as he had *i·* he would

imbecility
ph 197–15 the farther mortals will be removed from *i·*

imbibe
r 495–27 Study thoroughly the letter and *i·* the spirit.

imbibes
t 462– 4 any student, who . . . *i·* the spirit of Christ,

imbued
s 128–12 The human mind, *i·* with this
145– 3 So divinely *i·* were they with the spirit of

imitate
a 37–17 and to *i·* his mighty works

imitates
s 121–28 astronomical order *i·* the action of

imitative
f 212–31 the unreal and *i·* movements of mortal belief,

imitators
a 25–28 will never alone make us *i·* of him.

immaculate
s 137– 5 when their *i·* Teacher stood before them,
ap 561–32 prophesied the coming of the *i·* Jesus,
564–15 he, the *i·*, met and conquered sin
565–18 This *i·* idea, represented first by man

immanent
s 150– 5 is widely demonstrated as an *i·*, eternal
f 209–13 *i·* sense of Mind-power enhances the glory of

Immanuel
pref xi–16 They are the sign of *I·*, or
a 34– 7 for demonstration is *I·*, or *God with us;*
s 107– 8 This . . . points to the revelation of *I·*,

immature
b 313–26 To accommodate himself to *i·* ideas of

immediate
s 115–17 IDEA : . . . the *i·* object of understanding.
ph 188–29 physical senses have no *i·* evidence of a sun.
b 328–29 Had it been given only to his *i·* disciples,
330– 7 would meet with *i·* and universal acceptance.
g 501– 5 often seems so smothered by the *i·* context
532–18 produced the *i·* fruits of fear and shame.

immediately
s 154–11 *I·* the symptoms of this disease appeared,
o 348–26 I have never supposed the world would *i·*
p 431– 7 going to sleep *i·* after a heavy meal.
r 486–15 his body was the same *i·* after death as before.
g 553–26 this potent belief will *i·* supersede the
557–23 as if he . . . *i·* fell into mental sin ;

immense
b 322–10 in view of the *i·* work to be accomplished

immensity
c 263–29 thrown into the face of spiritual *i·*,
g 504–13 Truth, Life, and Love fill *i·* and are ever-present.
509–19 as nebulæ indicate the *i·* of space.

immoral
p 363–13 detect the woman's *i·* status
t 452–14 Never breathe an *i·* atmosphere, unless

immortal
and eternal
gl 588–10 incorporeal, unerring, *i·*, and eternal Mind.
and omnipotent
p 407–13 strength from the *i·* and omnipotent Mind,
and perfect
c 260–10 the *i·* and perfect model of God's creation
and spiritual
f 213– 7 *I·* and spiritual facts exist apart from
r 479– 7 it must be *i·* and spiritual.
g 544–23 antipodes of *i·* and spiritual being.
and unerring
f 243–20 Neither *i·* and unerring Mind nor matter,
beautiful and
b 276–14 and presents them as beautiful and *i·*.
being
ph 178–27 spiritual understanding of the status of *i·* being.
190–18 it never merges into *i·* being,
p 420–32 harmonious facts of Soul and *i·* being.
being is
g 554– 6 because being is *i·*, like Deity,
consciousness
b 279–11 tangible and real to *i·* consciousness,
r 486– 9 in order to possess *i·* consciousness.
cravings
s 108– 8 *i·* cravings, "the price of learning love,"
g 501–17 something more native to their *i·* cravings
evidence
a 29–31 *i·* evidence that Spirit is harmonious
existence
g 513–28 not within the range of *i·* existence
fact
b 327– 3 reveals the *i·* fact that neither pleasure nor

immortal
facts
b 279–17 the *i·* facts of being are seen,
p 428–28 the *i·* facts of being are admitted.
forms
g 503–22 *i·* forms of beauty and goodness.
fruit
o 361–29 That which when sown bears *i·* fruit,
fruits
r 494–28 its lap piled high with *i·* fruits.
good deeds are
p 435–12 but good deeds are *i·*, bringing joy
harmonious and
ph 166–32 man found to be harmonious and *i·*.
b 273–17 never made mortals whole, harmonious, and *i·*
291–16 manifestations of Mind are harmonious and *i·*
337–13 makes man harmonious and *i·*,
p 409–32 Death will not make us harmonious and *i·*
harmonious or
r 490–15 are helpless to make man harmonious or *i·*,
idea
a 55–15 Truth's *i·* idea is sweeping down the
c 262–13 above the mortal to the *i·* idea of God.
b 325– 7 Truth, unfolding its own *i·* idea.
r 477–17 *i·* idea of being, indestructible and eternal.
ideas
c 259–26 *I·* ideas, pure, perfect, and enduring,
immutable and
c 261–24 and the nature of the immutable and *i·*.
b 279– 3 the unerring, immutable, and *i·*?
286– 4 not seek the immutable and *i·* through the finite,
g 550–30 the pure and holy, the immutable and *i·*
keynotes
o 355–28 God's *i·* keynotes, proved to be such
law
a 36–20 *i·* law of justice as well as of mercy.
Life
r 496–22 mortal belief, at war with the facts of *i·* Life
life
a 51–11 that he might furnish the proof of *i·* life.
Man
p 434–31 God made Man *i·* and amenable to Spirit
man
(*see* **man**)
man, being
f 209– 1 Man, being *i·*, has a perfect indestructible life
manhood
p 430– 5 *i·* manhood, the Christ ideal,
man is
(*see* **man**)
men and women
f 247–15 *I·* men and women are models of
Mind
(*see* **Mind**)
Mind is
(*see* **Mind**)
Mind-reading
sp 83–26 mortal mind-reading and *i·* Mind-reading.
83–29 Mortal mind-reading and *i·* Mind-reading
modus
f 212–32 would reverse the *i·* modus and action,
nature
c 260–29 it must lose its *i·* nature.
perfect and
f 246– 5 The perfect and *i·* are the eternal likeness of
p 428–23 man *is*, not *shall be*, perfect and *i·*.
Principle
g 554– 4 God, who is its divine *i·* Principle.
proof
r 488–16 C. S. sustains with *i·* proof
real and
b 276–15 Harmony in man is as real and *i·* as in music.
reality
b 311–19 directly opposite to the *i·* reality of being.
Science is
sp 84– 1 Science is *i·* and coordinate neither with the
scribe
ap 571–22 the Revelator, *i·* scribe of Spirit
sense
sp 72– 3 Principle of man speaks through *i·* sense.
f 210–29 *i·* sense includes no evil nor
210–30 *i·* sense has no error of sense,
216–14 to supply the truth of *i·* sense.
sentences
f 225–17 *i·* sentences, breathing the omnipotence of
sentiment
s 161–15 they will do less violence to that *i·* sentiment
Shakespeare
m 66– 1 Thou art right, *i·* Shakespeare,
side
g 536–26 the true idea is gained from the *i·* side.
Soul
b 311–20 So long as we believe . . . that *i·* Soul is in

immortal

Soul is
 b 311– 7   Soul is *i*· because it is Spirit,
 335–20   Because Soul is *i*·, it does not exist in mortality.
 p 381–13   destroyed by the understanding that Soul is *i*·,
 r 468– 6   Because Soul is *i*·, Soul cannot sin,
sovereignty
 s 141–18   Its only crowned head is *i*· sovereignty.
Spirit
 s 124–13   finite sense of things, which *i*· Spirit silences
 p 435– 1   court commended man's *i*· Spirit to
spiritual and
 b 289–24   God's universe is spiritual and *i*·.
 o 353–29   true idea of being is spiritual and *i*·,
 p 409–21   The real man is spiritual and *i*·,
 g 547–30   and adopts the spiritual and *i*·.
testimony
 r 490–25   destroy all material sense with *i*· testimony.
 490–25   This *i*· testimony ushers in the
things
 b 276–22   towards the contemplation of things *i*·
Truth
   (see **Truth**)
truth
 r 493– 8   must yield to Science, to the *i*· truth of
Truth is
 r 466–13   Truth is *i*· ; error is mortal.
 468– 4   If Truth is *i*·, error must be mortal,
wisdom
 g 519– 6   His infinite self-containment and *i*· wisdom

 a 42–28   is therefore not a mortal but an *i*·.
 m 60–10   purity and constancy, both of which are *i*·.
 sp 80– 8   as follows : . . . never will be, an *i*· spirit."
 81–12   A man's assertion that he is *i*· no more proves
 81–18   as revealed in Science cannot help being *i*·.
 s 152– 3   *i*· divine Mind takes away all its supposed
 ph 174–32   its cure comes from the *i*· divine Mind.
 186–25   If evil is as real as good, evil is also as *i*·.
 186–26   If pain is as real as the . . . both must be *i*· ;
 189–22   all the formations of the *i*· divine Mind.
 192– 9   from the mortal instead of from the *i*·.
 192–13   of the mortal mind and not of the *i*·.
 194–15   man, who is *i*· in spiritual understanding,
 f 211–31   these faculties be conceived of as *i*·.
 229– 2   If Mind is not the master of . . . they are *i*·,
 231– 7   seem to this so-called mind to be *i*·.
 244–26   He does not pass . . . from the mortal to the *i*·,
 246–28   Life and goodness are *i*·.
 c 256– 5   thought rises . . . from the mortal to the *i*·.
 258–11   in order to be *i*·.
 263– 5   *I*· spiritual man alone represents the truth of
 b 277– 6   The *i*· never produces the mortal.
 277– 8   goodness and spirituality must be *i*·.
 277–29   Nothing we can say . . . regarding matter is *i*·,
 295–30   teaches that . . . his *i*· soul is resurrected
 296– 6   the mortal is dropped for the *i*·.
 296–10   Nothing sensual or sinful is *i*·.
 297–16   and man found to be *i*·.
 301–10   *i*·, spiritual man is really substantial,
 306– 1   Pharisees, who believed error to be as *i*· as
 310–20   taught . . . that soul may be lost, and yet be *i*·.
 335–28   Reality is spiritual, . . . *i*·, divine, eternal.
 336– 5   nor the *i*· into mortality.
 p 369–20   He understood man, whose Life is God, to be *i*·,
 370– 2   To be *i*·, we must forsake the
 427– 7   can no more die. . .than can Soul, for both are *i*·,
 429–21   If we live after death and are *i*·, we must have
 433–29   sense of Life, God, — which sense must be *i*·,
 r 474–25   must error still be *i*·?
 g 503–20   *I*· and divine Mind presents the idea of God :
 505–28   God's ideas reflect the *i*·, unerring, and
 520–27   the *i*· creating thought is from above,
 530– 2   the *i*·, spiritual law of Truth is
 536–29   material return to dust, and the *i*· is reached.
 gl 581– 9   proved to be as *i*· as its Principle ;

immortality

almightiness and
 r 487–29   reality of Life, its almightiness and *i*·.
and bliss
 a 39–12   out of mortality into *i*· and bliss.
 f 203–12   not a stepping-stone to Life, *i*·, and bliss.
and goodness
 g 518–20   Love giveth . . . might, *i*·, and goodness,
and life
 sp 98–31   way through which *i*· and life are learned
and Love
 gl 597–15   divine Science, — *i*· and Love.
and supremacy
 gl 589–20   showing the *i*· and supremacy of Truth ;
appears
 sp 76–31   overcome, not submitted to, before *i*· appears.
assurances of
 p 387–12   refreshed by the assurances of *i*·,
basis of
 gl 585–12   Elias. Prophecy ; . . . the basis of *i*·.

being and
 f 215– 4   If . . . then being and *i*· would be lost,
bring
 r 492–12   destroy all error, and bring *i*· to light.
brings
 b 305–26   destroys all error and brings *i*· to light.
 336–28   and brings *i*· to light.
brings to light
 sp 72–13   destroys mortality, and brings to light *i*·.
 f 206–28   He destroys them, and brings to light *i*·.
brought to light
 b 335–24   Life as *i*· brought to light.
 gl 582–23   Submergence in Spirit ; *i*· brought to light.
communing with
 sp 78– 8   at the same time . . . communing with *i*· !
earnest of
 b 317–27   for an earnest of *i*·,
entity or
 o 356– 6   sickness, and death do not prove man's entity
       or *i*·.
eternity and
 gl 585– 5   A sphere ; a type of eternity and *i*·,
exempt from age
 f 247–13   *I*·, exempt from age or decay,
existence and
 o 356– 5   affords no evidence of spiritual existence and *i*·.
foundations of
 g 539– 5   sapping the foundations of *i*·,
harmony and
   (see **harmony**)
health and
 f 248– 7   ought to ripen into health and *i*·,
holiness, and
 f 230– 5   will bring us into health, holiness, and *i*·.
 ap 563–22   prolific in health, holiness, and *i*·.
hope in
 p 388–26   we have hope in *i*· ;
idea of
 gl 593–10   a new and higher idea of *i*·,
in deeds
 o 354–10   words of divine Science find their *i*· in deeds,
is not bounded
 b 301–32   *I*· is not bounded by mortality.
life and
 p 376–13   there is more life and *i*· in one good motive
 g 539– 5   as if life and *i*· were something which
man and
 ph 191–24   reveals man and *i*· as based on Spirit.
man's
 sp 81–28   man's *i*· depends upon that of God, good,
 p 395– 4   man's *i*· and eternal likeness to God.
 428–27   The evidence of man's *i*· will become
 gl 589–18   destroying error and bringing to light man's *i*·.
matrix of
 f 250– 5   and suppose. . .mortality to be the matrix of *i*·.
Mind and
 b 318– 3   nothing can efface Mind and *i*·,
 p 369–29   of the advantages of Mind and *i*·?
of development
 f 244–31   everlasting grandeur and *i*· of development,
of good
 sp 81–30   necessary consequence of the *i*· of good.
 f 215–27   he understood the superiority and *i*· of good,
of man
   (see **man**)
of Soul
 b 306– 7   The *i*· of Soul makes man immortal.
 r 481–29   hence the *i*· of Soul.
prelude to
 sp 90–15   some insist that death is the . . . prelude to *i*·.
proof of
 sp 81–16   Life, Love, Truth, is the only proof of *i*·.
 b 306–18   If. . .we are left without a rational proof of *i*·.
purity, and
 gl 581– 6   the inspiration of goodness, purity, and *i*·,
put on
 s 164–27   mortal shall have put on *i*·— *I Cor*. 15 : 54.
 c 262– 5   mortals "put on *i*·."— *I Cor*. 15 : 54.
 r 496–25   mortal shall have put on *i*·,— *I Cor*. 15 : 54.
reality and
 r 486–24   Their reality and *i*· are in Spirit
 488–21   no cognizance of spiritual reality and *i*·.
rejoice in
 a 22–24   whereby we rejoice in *i*·, boundless freedom,
revelation of
 sp 79–15   C. S., . . . in its revelation of *i*·,
Soul or of
 r 478– 3   What evidence of Soul or of *i*·
to man
 f 253– 4   saith : . . . I give *i*· to man, for I am Truth.
towards
 sp 90–27   and opens it wide towards *i*·.

 sp 78–13   why look to them . . . for proofs of *i*·,
 80–11   assertion that . . . are our only proofs of *i*·.

immortality
- *sp* 81–13 would prove *i·* a lie.
- 81–15 Nor . . . when alleged spirits teach *i·*.
- *ph* 186–25 If death is as real as Life, *i·* is a myth.
- *f* 211–28 for their *i·* is not in Spirit ;
- 215–24 mortality is lost, swallowed up in *i·*.
- 230– 1 If sickness is real, it belongs to *i·* ;
- *b* 275–14 *i·*, cause, and effect belong to God.
- 283–32 Are mentality, *i·*, . . . resident in matter?
- 312–17 without Love, God, *i·* cannot appear.
- 339–26 The basis of all health, sinlessness, and *i·*
- *o* 353–15 Time has not yet reached eternity, *i·*,
- *p* 425–22 the more *i·* we possess.
- *r* 476–18 Mortality is finally swallowed up in *i·*.
- 492– 7 Being is holiness, harmony, *i·*.
- 495–23 replace mortality with *i·*, and silence discord
- *g* 518–22 reflect health, holiness, *i·*
- 555–20 error would seek to unite . . . *i·* with mortality,
- *gl* 592–23 the *i·* of all that is spiritual.
- 593– 2 the good and beautiful, and their *i·*.
- 598–28 man would be in the full consciousness of his *i·*

immortality's
- *gl* 580–18 ADAM. . . . *i·* opposite, mortality ;

immortals
- *b* 295–11 Mortals are not like *i·*,
- *t* 444–27 *I·*, or God's children in divine Science,
- *r* 476– 1 Mortals are the counterfeits of *i·*.
- 476–11 *i·*, or the children of God, will appear as the

immovable
- *s* 160–17 when the cords contract and become *i·*?

immunity
- *f* 219–29 Entire *i·* from the belief in sin, suffering,

immutable
- *s* 134–25 because it is the *i·* law of God,
- *f* 210–22 in obedience to the *i·* law of Spirit.
- *c* 261–23 and the nature of the *i·* and immortal.
- *b* 279– 2 or the unerring, *i·*, and immortal?
- 286– 3 not seek the *i·* and immortal through the finite,
- 298– 6 silences for a while the voice of *i·* harmony,
- 300–14 The mutable and imperfect never touch the *i·*
- 306–27 the *i·*, harmonious, divine Principle,
- 335–27 Reality is spiritual, harmonious, *i·*,
- *t* 446–20 victory rests on the side of *i·* right.
- *g* 550–30 the pure and holy, the *i·* and immortal

immutably
- *pr* 3– 1 He who is *i·* right will do right

impair
- *p* 428–18 the Life which mortal sense cannot *i·*

impart
- *f* 253– 5 saith : . . . I include and *i·* all bliss,
- *b* 272–14 not to *i·* to dull ears and gross hearts
- *p* 371–28 Mind can *i·* purity instead of impurity,
- 401– 7 which you *i·* mentally while destroying error,
- *t* 447–18 *i·* . . . the truth and spiritual understanding,
- 452–19 He must live it and love it, or he cannot *i·* it
- 460–25 she had to *i·*, while teaching its grand facts,
- *g* 510–18 Love alone can *i·* the limitless idea of infinite
- 516–11 which *i·* their own peace and permanence.
- 539–11 God could never *i·* an element of evil,
- *ap* 570–24 Those ready for the blessing you *i·* will give

impartation
- *m* 68–29 *i·* of the divine Mind to man and the universe.
- *b* 309– 3 incorporeal *i·* of divine Love to man,

imparted
- *f* 235–15 pure and uplifting thoughts . . . *i·* to pupils,
- *g* 514–19 Tenderness accompanies all the might *i·* by

impartial
- *pr* 13– 2 Love is *i·* and universal in its adaptation
- *m* 63–18 Our laws are not *i·*, to say the least,
- *o* 355–27 Without this . . . no one is capable of *i·* or

imparting
- *sp* 92– 6 but also capable of *i·* the sensations.
- *g* 519–25 *I·* has not impoverished,
- *ap* 567– 2 Gabriel has the more quiet task of *i·* a

imparts
- *sp* 85–32 truth communicates itself but never *i·* error.
- *ph* 194–22 manifests itself . . . by the false sense it *i·*.
- *b* 271–30 spiritual import of the Word *i·* this power.
- 280–29 *i·* and perpetuates these qualities
- *p* 420–18 It *i·* a healthy stimulus to the body,
- *g* 505–16 Spirit *i·* the understanding which uplifts
- 515–23 All that God *i·* moves in
- 517–13 for Love *i·* the clearest idea of Deity.

impassable
- *sp* 83–24 as *i·* as that between Dives and Lazarus.

impatient
- *f* 237–29 *I·* at your explanation,

impede
- *pr* 5–23 Such an error would *i·* true religion.
- *ap* 563–20 seemingly *i·* the offspring of the

impedes
- *pr* 2–21 an error which *i·* spiritual growth.
- *ph* 166– 4 Mind is all that feels, acts, or *i·* action.
- *p* 415– 6 belief quickens or *i·* the action of the system,

impediment
- *ap* 577–10 no *i·* to eternal bliss,

impel
- *ap* 563–31 which would *i·* them to devour each other

impelled
- *p* 415–22 moving quickly or slowly and *i·* or palsied by
- *ap* 565–25 *i·* the idea to rise to the zenith of

impels
- *s* 118– 1 *i·* the inference that the spiritual leaven

imperative
- *a* 37–27 Hear these *i·* commands :
- *m* 56–19 The commandment, . . . is no less *i·* than
- *f* 251– 1 hence it is not more *i·*
- *b* 329–21 Principle is *i·*.
- *t* 446–19 In the Science . . . it is *i·* to be honest,

imperatively
- *ap* 565–17 God's idea, will eventually rule all . . . *i·*,

imperceptible
- *b* 314–24 the spiritual Jesus was *i·* to them.
- 334–10 invisible Christ was *i·* to the so-called

imperfect
- *s* 114–20 must sometimes recur to the old and *i·*,
- *f* 239–30 *I·* mortal mind sends forth its own
- 246– 7 by no means a . . . germ rising from the *i·*
- 248–20 Do you not hear from all mankind of the *i·* model?
- 249– 2 give up *i·* models and illusive ideals ;
- 254–12 *I·* mortals grasp the ultimate . . . slowly ,
- *c* 258–25 Mortals have a very *i·* sense of
- 260– 4 than the sculptor can . . . from an *i·* model,
- *b* 300–14 The mutable and *i·* never touch the
- *o* 360– 7 materiality renders these ideals *i·*
- *p* 409–21 *i·* so-called "children of men"— *Psal.* 14 : 2.
- *r* 477– 7 Soul, being Spirit, is seen in nothing *i·*
- *g* 555–26 aught that can become *i·*
- *gl* 587–18 and cannot become finite and *i·*.

imperfection
- *sp* 72–17 Perfection is not expressed through *i·*.
- *f* 233– 8 In the midst of *i·*,
- 243–32 Perfection does not animate *i·*.
- 248–16 Is it *i·*, joy, sorrow, sin,
- *c* 259–32 from *i·* instead of perfection, one can no more
- *p* 414–29 whereas *i·* is blameworthy, unreal, and
- 424–11 there is no room for *i·* in perfection.

imperfections
- *a* 52– 9 Their *i·* and impurity felt the

imperfectly
- *pref* ix– 9 voices the more definite thought, though still *i·*.
- *b* 304–29 is, must be, *i·* expressed.
- *r* 467–23 We reason *i·* from effect to cause,

imperial
- *b* 324–25 Asia Minor, Greece, and even in *i·* Rome.

imperious
- *sp* 98–18 It is *i·* throughout all ages

imperishable
- *a* 21–11 looks towards the *i·* things of Spirit.
- *f* 246–16 with bright and *i·* glories.
- 253– 3 saith : . . . *i·* glory, — all are Mine,

impersonation
- *ap* 565–13 *i·* of the spiritual idea had a brief history

impertinent
- *an* 103–13 separate from any half-way *i·* knowledge,

impetuous
- *s* 137–26 Before this the *i·* disciple had been called

impetuosity
- *s* 137–16 With his usual *i·*, Simon replied

impious
- *s* 139– 3 which the *i·* sought to destroy.

implacable
- *a* 40–16 the crimes of his *i·* enemies

implant
- *ph* 180–17 Doctors should not *i·* disease in the thoughts

implicit
- *a* 25–26 *I·* faith in the Teacher and all the

implied
- *a* 26–10 The Christ was the Spirit which Jesus *i·* in
- *sp* 92– 7 the illusion *i·* in this last postulate
- 94– 5 includes all that is *i·* by the terms
- *s* 137–14 the narrow opinion *i·* in their citation
- *ph* 166– 5 shrinking from its *i·* responsibility,
- *g* 504–20 not *i·* by material darkness and dawn.

implies
 pr 6– 8 *i·* the vain supposition that we have
 a 20–25 to acknowledge what the spiritual fact *i·*.
 an 102–26 It *i·* the exercise of despotic control,
 s 114–14 the phrase *mortal mind i·* something untrue
 o 359–20 the goal which that word *i·*?
 p 421– 2 insanity *i·* belief in a diseased brain,
 g 507–21 A material world *i·* a mortal mind and
 547–20 Material evolution *i·* that the great

implore
 ph 167– 1 Should we *i·* a corporeal God to heal the

imply
 b 331–11 The Scriptures *i·* that God is All-in-all.
 336– 1 limits would *i·* and impose ignorance.
 g 515–18 does not *i·* more than one God,
 515–19 nor does it *i·* three persons in one.
 537–30 The literal meaning would *i·* that God
 550–22 If Life is God, as the Scriptures *i·*,

implying
 a 31– 7 *i·* that it is they who do the will of
 s 148– 3 *i·* that the requisite power to heal was in Mind.

import
 a 26–24 the precious *i·* of our Master's sinless career
 37–21 take up the more practical *i·* of that career !
 s 118–17 parable may *i·* that these spiritual laws,
 f 232–27 voices of solemn *i·*, but we heed them not.
 b 271–30 spiritual *i·* of the Word imparts this power.
 o 358–22 great *i·* to Christianity of those works
 p 411–18 Scripture seems to *i·* that Jesus
 r 471–27 gave the spiritual *i·*, expressed through
 g 501– 3 chiefly because the spiritual *i·* of the Word,

importance
 a 31–14 He attached no *i·* to dead ceremonies.
 ph 198–27 Hence the *i·* that doctors be Christian Scientists.
 199–18 of less *i·* than a knowledge of the fact.
 f 209–20 are of no real *i·*, when we remember
 236–17 Hence the *i·* of C. S.,
 c 258–17 The precise form of God must be of small *i·*
 b 273–19 Hence the *i·* of understanding the truth of
 r 473–27 making his acts of higher *i·* than his words.

important
 a 42–18 evidence so *i·* to mortals.
 51– 2 the possible loss of something more *i·* than
 sp 95–17 but it is *i·* to success in healing,
 an 101– 6 *i·* experiment upon the power of the
 105–20 no reason why metaphysics is not as *i·*
 b 320–24 The one *i·* interpretation of Scripture is
 322– 9 It is highly *i·*— in view of the
 o 350– 7 in the New Testament, sayings infinitely *i·*,
 p 387–17 it is not because they occupy the most *i·* posts
 404–21 one of the most *i·* points in the theology of
 424–15 equally *i·* in metaphysical practice
 t 462–24 That is the *i·* question.
 466–18 first and last it is the most *i·* to understand.
 r 481– 1 How *i·*, then, to choose good
 482–13 Is it *i·* to understand these explanations
 497– 1 brief exposition of the *i·* points,
 g 508–29 third stage in the order of C. S. is an *i·* one
 548–28 discoveries have brought to light *i·* facts
 553– 2 accompany their descriptions with *i·* observations,
 553–14 or *i·* to their origin and first introduction.''

imported
 p 438–22 a foreign substance, *i·* by False Belief,

importer
 p 438–28 Morbid Secretion is not an *i·* or dealer

impose
 b 336– 1 limits would imply and *i·* ignorance.
 338–24 sin, would *i·* between man and his creator.
 p 381–31 Christ Jesus overruled the error which would *i·*

imposed
 ap 575– 5 physical plagues *i·* by material sense.

imposing
 p 440–34 with benign and *i·* presence,

imposition
 sp 99–26 are seen to be a bald *i·*,

impossibilities
 f 207–17 Science of being repudiates self-evident *i·*,
 245–27 *I·* never occur.
 g 550–32 C. S. repudiates self-evident *i·*,

impossibility
 s 116–31 Mind in a finite form is an absolute *i·*.
 b 273–13 *i·* of attaining perfect understanding till
 284– 8 would seem to spring from . . . but this is an *i·*.
 o 343–16 the *i·* of good producing evil ;
 p 409– 1 Intelligent matter is an *i·*.
 414– 9 *i·* that matter, brain, can control or derange
 t 455–22 renders any abuse of the mission an *i·*.
 r 488–17 the *i·* of any material sense,

impossible
 a 36–21 It is quite as *i·* for sinners to
 39–24 unreal, because *i·* in Science.
 sp 74– 6 would be as *i·* as would be the restoration
 74–20 Such a backward transformation is *i·* in Science.
 75–10 This gross materialism is scientifically *i·*,
 82–26 intercommunion is as *i·* as it would
 83–12 Miracles are *i·* in Science,
 s 120–18 *i·* for aught but Mind to testify truly
 153–16 You say a boil is painful; but that is *i·*,
 162–32 declared that ''it is *i·* to calculate the
 ph 167–27 *i·* to gain control over the body in any other way.
 182–12 It is *i·* to work from two standpoints,
 195–26 *i·* ideals, and specimens of depravity,
 199–25 Had Blondin believed it *i·* to walk the rope
 f 211–23 The transfer of . . . Science renders *i·*.
 217– 2 The loss of man's identity . . . is *i·* ;
 228– 4 would be *i·* if this great fact of being
 231–27 To fear them is *i·*, when you fully apprehend
 c 258–28 *i·* for man, . . . to fall from his high estate.
 b 302– 8 It is *i·* that man should lose aught
 309–24 *i·* for infinite Spirit or Soul to be in
 331–23 He fills all space, and it is *i·* to conceive of
 o 351–30 from a material standpoint, but this was *i·*.
 p 371–22 No *i·* thing do I ask
 376–25 showing that it is *i·* for matter to suffer,
 t 446–17 protracted, dangerous, and *i·* in
 448–22 *i·* for error, evil, and hate to accomplish the
 455–32 the more *i·* it will become for
 r 477–14 shows it to be *i·* that a material body,
 481–27 *i·*, since Truth cannot support error.
 492–30 theory, . . . uniting on some *i·* basis.
 g 506– 1 apportion to themselves a task *i·*
 522–11 Existence, separate . . . Science explains as *i·*.
 550–23 An egg is an *i·* enclosure for Deity.
 551– 2 their reports are unnatural, *i·*, and unreal.
 551–15 material methods are *i·* in divine Science

impostor
 p 441–28 Your attorney, False Belief, is an *i·*,

impotence
 t 454– 5 Truth, which illustrates the *i·* of error.

impotent
 sp 97– 7 the more *i·* error becomes as a belief.
 s 160–18 or has it bidden them to be *i·*?
 g 555–18 Only *i·* error would seek to unite Spirit with

impoverish
 sp 79–21 Giving does not *i·* us in the service
 g 519–26 Imparting . . . can never *i·*, the divine Mind.

impoverished
 m 63–29 the wronged, and perchance *i·*, woman
 g 519–25 Imparting has not *i·*, can never impoverish,

impracticable
 s 163–30 as *i·* as to arrange the fleeting vapors

impress
 p 412–12 you are liable . . . to *i·* it upon the thought.
 t 448–20 to leave . . . the strong *i·* of divine Science,
 g 511–12 the seal of Deity and has the *i·* of heaven,

impressed
 t 208–29 the images of thought *i·* upon it.

impresses
 s 157–28 C. S. *i·* the entire corporeality,
 t 453–28 *i·* more deeply the wrong mind-picture.

impressing
 ph 196–22 *i·* them with forcible descriptions

impression
 s 115–10 great difficulty is to give the right *i·*,
 f 213–16 Sound is a mental *i·* made on mortal belief.
 t 449–22 The first *i·*, made on a mind which
 g 532–31 The first *i·* material man had of himself

impressions
 sp 87–26 The strong *i·* produced on mortal mind
 87–28 can perceive and reproduce these *i·*.
 an 101– 4 and the *i·* made upon the senses ;
 f 214– 1 *i·* from Truth were as distinct as sound,
 214–15 conveys the *i·* of Mind to man,

impressive
 pr 7– 8 Audible prayer is *i·* ;

imprison
 f 251–32 *i·* themselves in what they create.

imprisoned
 s 114–27 and sets free the *i·* thought.
 f 203–19 We imagine that Mind can be *i·*

improper
 s 114–13 involves an *i·* use of the word *mind*.
 r 466–19 The term *souls* or *spirits* is as *i·* as the

improve
 pr 6– 7 The talents He gives we must *i·*.
 m 60–16 Marriage should *i·* the human species,
 61– 7 would *i·* our progeny, diminish crime,

incites
   f 203–12   This thought *i·* to a more exalted worship and
   ap 564– 5   *i·* mortals to kill morally and physically

inclination
   t 452–30   if you had the *i·* or power to

inclinations
   s 121– 3   favorite *i·* of a sensuous philosophy.

incline
   ph 181–31   will *i·* you to the side of matter and error.
   t 450–12   They do not *i·* longingly to error,

inclined
   f 214–19   Mortals are *i·* to fear and to
   o 356–26   by making man *i·* to sin,

include
   s 118–14   *i·* spiritual laws emanating from
   ph 191– 6   will *i·* in that likeness no material element.
   f 253– 5   saith : . . . I *i·* and impart all bliss,
   b 318–32   body does not *i·* soul, but manifests mortality,
   p 418–26   *I·* moral as well as physical belief in your
   r 484– 7   Does C. S., . . . *i·* medication, material hygiene,
   g 544–20   facts of creation, . . . *i·* nothing of the kind.
   552–12   *i·* no member of this dolorous and fatal triad.

included
   pr   5–32   all evil works, error and disease *i·*.
   s 120– 3   never . . . is *i·* in non-intelligence.
   f 209– 1   disease and sin and of other beliefs *i·* in matter.
   227– 3   I saw that the law of mortal belief *i·* all error,
   b 335–17   never *i·* in a limited mind or a
   o 344–20   not *i·* in the commonly accepted systems :
   p 399–28   All that is real is *i·* in this immortal Mind.
   425– 7   take up the leading points *i·*
   429–28   not *i·* in the teachings of the schools,
   r 484– 9   *Answer.*— Not one of them is *i·* in it.
   g 504– 8   not yet *i·* in the record of creation,

includes
   pr   9–19   This command *i·* much,
   a   23–30   *i·* spiritual understanding and confides all
   m   60– 9   the mother-love *i·* purity and constancy,
   sp   94– 5   *i·* all that is implied by the terms
   s 116–12   *i·* vastly more than is at first seen.
   145–31   The theology of C. S. *i·* healing the sick.
   ph 187–23   The divine Mind *i·* all action and volition,
   191–13   spiritual sense of being and of what Life *i·*.
   f 206–29   infinite Mind made all and *i·* all.
   210–30   immortal sense *i·* no evil nor pestilence.
   219–20   Science *i·* no rule of discord,
   249–16   and *i·* nothing unlike Cod.
   c 259–12   *i·* a perfect Principle and idea,
   b 288– 1   necessarily *i·* the correlated statement,
   328–31   and *i·* universal humanity.
   330–32   with all the etceteras that word *i·*.
   333–31   The one Spirit *i·* all identities.
   p 373– 3   physical exemption which Christianity *i·*,
   408–32   ignorant of the errors it *i·* and of their
   430– 1   *i·* all the phenomena of existence.
   r 469– 3   *i·* in itself all substance
   g 507–21   because they reflect the Mind which *i·* all.
   515–16   eternal Elohim *i·* the forever universe.

including
   sp   83–16   The belief that the universe, *i·* man,
   s 114–10   Mind is *one*, *i·* noumenon and phenomena,
   114–28   the universe, *i·* man, is spiritual,
   127– 5   creator of the spiritual universe, *i·* man,
   ph 171–12   Mind's control over the universe, *i·* man,
   f 233–23   *i·* the hearts which rejected him.
   c 256– 8   Father and Mother of the universe, *i·* man.
   b 276–23   Principle of the universe, *i·* harmonious man.
   295– 5   creates and governs the universe, *i·* man.
   330–12   only intelligence of the universe, *i·* man.
   p 415–24   organs of the human system, *i·* brain and
   r 468–23   The spiritual universe, *i·* individual man, is
   475–15   compound idea of God, *i·* all right ideas ;
   g 502–26   unity of God and man, *i·* the universe.
   510–30   governing the universe, *i·* man,
   547–19   theory, . . . to recreate the universe, *i·* man,
   547–26   The true theory of the universe, *i·* man,
   549–19   *i·* those which we call human.
   gl 584–24   to reproduce a mortal universe, *i·* man,

inclusive
   s 128– 6   His government of the universe, *i·* of man.
   g 554– 3   universe, *i·* of man, is as eternal as God,

incompatibility
   m   59–23   too late to grumble over *i·* of disposition.

incompetent
   m   57–15   *i·* to meet the demands of the affections,
   ph 200– 8   Whoever is *i·* to explain Soul
   p 377–29   a fear that Mind is . . . *i·* to control it.

incomprehensible
   b 304–21   thrusting aside his divine Principle as *i·*,
   337–21   is as *i·* to the limited senses as

inconceivable
   p 378–29   power, without the divine permission, is *i·* ;

inconceivably
   p 407– 2   a suffering *i·* terrible to man's self-respect.

incongruity
   o 345–21   Anybody, who is able to perceive the *i·*

inconsistency
   o 354–19   *I·* is shown by words without deeds,
   355– 3   charge of *i·* . . . is met by something practical,

inconsistent
   o 354–27   It is in itself *i·*, a divided kingdom.
   354–32   If the letter of C. S. appears *i·*,
   p 387–21   reading disquisitions on the *i·* supposition

incontrovertible
   ph 200–17   great truth in the Science of being, . . . is *i·* ;

incontrovertibly
   s 109– 4   C. S. reveals *i·* that Mind is All-in-all,

incorporeal
   pr   13–24   the wonders wrought by infinite, *i·* Love,
   13–29   ignorant . . . of man's eternal *i·* existence.
   sp   74–27   such opposite conditions as the . . . *i·*, and the
   84– 4   from a spiritual, *i·* standpoint,
   s 116–21   that God is not *corporeal*, but *i·*,
   116–23   Mortals are corporeal, but God is *i·*.
   c 258– 3   glories of limitless, *i·* Life and Love.
   b 309– 3   *i·* impartation of divine Love to man,
   331–18   God is individual, *i·*.
   332–12   The Christ is *i·*, spiritual,
   335–21   Soul must be *i·* to be Spirit,
   r 465– 9   God is *i·*, divine, supreme,
   g 512– 2   understanding of the *i·* and divine Principle,
   ap 577– 2   yields to the *i·* sense of God and man
   578– 2   the *i·* or spiritual sense of Deity :
   gl 588– 9   *i·*, unerring, immortal, and eternal Mind.
   588–20   I AM. God ; *i·* and eternal Mind ;

incorporeality
   ap 576–19   What further indication need we of the real
   man's *i·*

incorrect
   pref x– 5   most of them *i·* in theory
   sp   73–21   The belief that material bodies . . . is *i·*.
   73–21   Equally *i·* is the belief that spirit is confined
   ph 195–31   *I·* views lower the standard of truth.
   t 452– 4   *I·* reasoning leads to practical error.
   453– 2   to distinguish the correct from the *i·*

incorrectly
   s 121– 6   the heavenly fields were *i·* explored.

incorruption
   s 164–26   shall have put on *i·*,— *I Cor.* 15 : 54.
   r 496–25   shall have put on *i·*,— *I Cor.* 15 : 54.

increase
   pr   13–13   Can the . . . expression of our desires *i·* them?
   m   61–26   raising of stock to *i·* your flocks and herds?
   sp   95–19   We welcome the *i·* of knowledge
   s 145–26   and thus they *i·* the antagonism of
   159–32   ordinary physician is liable to *i·* disease
   f 220–23   adopted a diet of . . . to *i·* his spirituality.
   p 367–26   *i·* the beneficial effects of Christianity.
   397– 9   You cause bodily sufferings and *i·* them by
   t 443– *   *and he will i· in learning.*— *Prov.* 9 : 9.
   r 492–10   will *i·* longevity, will purify and elevate
   g 548– 2   *i·* their numbers naturally and

increased
   pref viii–22   *i·* violence of diseases since the flood.
   s 157–15   power of action is proportionately *i·*
   ph 198– 8   his fear, . . . is *i·* by the physician's words.
   199– 4   The trip-hammer is not *i·* in size by exercise.
   o 348–32   health has been restored, and longevity *i·*.
   r 465– 3   much labor and *i·* spiritual understanding,

increases
   sp   96–29   As . . . spiritual understanding *i·*,
   s 155–26   potency . . . *i·* as the drug disappears.
   p 374–31   or *i·* it to the point of self-destruction,
   404–25   *i·* his ability to master evil
   415–19   thought *i·* or diminishes the secretions,
   420–19   It *i·* or diminishes the action,
   423– 2   belief that he has met his master. . . *i·* his fear;
   t 453–27   such a course *i·* fear, the foundation of
   g 530– 1   *i·* in falsehood and his days become shorter.
   ap 565– 2   when nearing its doom, this evil *i·*

increasing
   m   56–14   moral regulations as will secure *i·* virtue.
   69–12   sense of *i·* number in God's infinite plan.
   f 221– 4   His dyspepsia *i·*, he decided that
   224– 1   Longevity is *i·* and the power of
   o 352–20   instead of *i·* children's fears by
   p 375–19   *i·* his patient's spirituality while restoring him
   g 557–11   C. S. reveals harmony as proportionately *i·*
   fr 600– *   *i· in the knowledge of God.*— *Col.* 1 : 10.

incredible
   sp   83– 6   Science only can explain the *i·* good

incredulous
   ph 169– 8   sometimes to his discomfiture, when he was *i·*.

incubus
  b 322–21   as the startled dreamer who wakens from an *i·*

inculcate
  s 130–21   and to *i·* a grain of faith in God,

inculcates
  s 112–30   it *i·* a breach of that divine commandment
  b 340–17   It *i·* the tri-unity of God, Spirit, Mind ;
  o 345–29   human, material nothingness, which Science *i·*,

incur
  pr 3–29   *i·* the sharp censure our Master pronounces
  13–18   *i·* less risk of overwhelming our real wishes
  m 68–23   salutary causes sometimes *i·* these effects.
  f 238– 7   To obey the Scriptural command. . . . is to *i·*
  b 317– 9   and he will *i·* the hatred of sinners,
  p 384– 9   If man seems to *i·* the penalty through matter,
  405–28   conquered by the moral penalties you *i·*

incurred
  b 322–21   *i·* through the pains of distorted sense.

incurs
  a 40–10   first removing the sin which *i·* the penalty.
  an 106–13   mental trespasser *i·* the divine penalty
  f 241– 3   He, . . . *i·* the hostility of envy ;
  g 542– 1   It *i·* divine displeasure,

indeed
  pr 11–15   if *i·*, he has not already suffered sufficiently
  16–11   There is *i·* some doubt among Bible scholars,
  a 33– 7   Their bread *i·* came down from heaven.
  s 114–17   *I·*, if a better word or phrase could
  140–27   It is *i·* mournfully true that the older Scripture
  145–19   *I·*, its ethical and physical effects
  163–16   except, *i·*, that it has already destroyed more
  163–30   To harmonize the contrarieties . . . is *i·* a task
  f 207– 8   *I·*, evil is not Mind.
  221–13   informed him that death was *i·* his only
  c 257–31   *I·*, the phrase *infinite form* involves a
  b 302–28   *I·*, the body presents no proper likeness of
  o 345–12   It is *i·* no small matter to know one's self ;
  347–32   will then see that error is *i·* the nothingness,
  p 364–30   that they *i·* love much,
  395–32   a moral offence is *i·* the worst of diseases.
  412–14   It is *i·* adequate to unclasp the hold
  415–29   *I·*, the whole frame will sink from
  r 478–31   "neither *i·* can be ;"— *Rom.* 8 : 7.
  g 521–19   *I·* there is, but the continued account is mortal
  534–20   neither *i·* can be.— *Rom.* 8 : 7.
  535–18   Truth is *i·* "the way."— *John* 14 : 6.
  ap 559–21   It will be *i·* sweet at its first taste,
  573–28   This is *i·* a foretaste of absolute C. S.
  575–25   It is *i·* a city of the Spirit,
  gl 598–15   What Jesus gave up was *i·* air,

indefinable
  f 213–10   self-expressed, though *i·* as a whole.

indefinite
  o 348–29   believed for an *i·* time ;

indefinitely
  pr 12–25   Changes in belief may go on *i·*,

Independence, Declaration of
  an 106– 7   C. S. has its Declaration of *I·*.

independence
  ph 175–18   it would have been routed by their *i·*

independent
  pref vii–13   Truth, *i·* of doctrines and time-honored systems
  ph 200–10   Life is, always has been, and ever will be *i·* of
  f 208– 6   What then is this seeming power, *i·* of God,
  247–19   Comeliness and grace are *i·* of matter.
  c 263– 2   believe themselves to be *i·* workers,

independently
  f 218–15   believing that the body can be sick *i·* of
  p 388–11   thought that they could kill the body . . . *i·* of
  409–13   *i·* of this so-called conscious mind,

indestructible
  a 51–14   his spiritual life, *i·* and eternal,
  sp 76–25   constitutes the only veritable, *i·* man,
  s 162–14   The *i·* faculties of Spirit exist
  f 209– 2   Man, being immortal, has a perfect *i·* life.
  214– 4   wholly spiritual, it is normal and *i·*.
  b 316–20   Christ presents the *i·* man,
  325–17   perfect as the Father, *i·* in Life,
  o 359–31   One says : "I have spiritual ideals, *i·*
  p 369–22   and the other to be made *i·*.
  402–12   Man is *i·* and eternal.
  r 471– 1   divine Principle and idea, are *i·*
  477–17   the immortal idea of being, *i·* and eternal.
  g 514–30   God's creatures, . . . are harmless, useful, *i·*.

indexes
  pr 8– 6   Their prayers are *i·* which do not

India
  b 328–18   Our missionaries carry the Bible to *I·*,

Indians
  r 477–26   The *I·* caught some glimpses of the underlying

indicate
  s 120–11   Is a man sick if the material senses *i·* that he
  136–17   this reply may *i·* that some of the people
  ph 183–13   *i·* that obedience to God will remove this
  b 294– 2   These senses *i·* the common human belief,
  332– 1   *i·* the divine Principle of scientific being,
  t 455– 6   Such mental states *i·* weakness
  r 466– 5   varied manifestations of C. S. *i·* Mind,
  g 504–18   words which *i·*, in the absence of solar time,
  509–18   as nebulæ *i·* the immensity of space.
  554–32   This would *i·* that there is less disease
  ap 575–21   This city is wholly spiritual, as its four sides *i·*.

indicated
  pr 16–22   which is *i·* in the Lord's Prayer
  s 121–28   thus *i·*, astronomical order imitates the
  ph 177–19   *i·* matter's properties, qualities, and forms.
  p 364–16   *i·* by one of the needs of this age.

indicates
  sp 94–30   An approximation of this discernment *i·*
  97–27   Scripture *i·* that all matter will disappear
  an 104–14   *i·* the rightness of all divine action,
  s 123–28   The operation of this Principle *i·* the
  141– 1   *i·* the distance between the theological and
  ph 188–18   The smile of the sleeper *i·* the sensation
  f 205–20   in some word or deed which *i·* the true idea,
  b 271–12   the word *i·* that the power of healing was
  282–28   Whatever *i·* the fall of man or the
  332– 4   *i·* His tender relationship to His
  p 437– 6   It *i·* malice aforethought,
  g 510–23   *i·* a supposed formation of matter
  532–11   this *i·* that the divine Spirit, or Father,
  538– 8   *i·* the infinite distance between Truth and
  ap 573–11   *i·* states and stages of consciousness.
  gl 581–13   The ark *i·* temptation overcome
  597–27   *i·* the might of omnipotence

indication
  r 471– 8   afford no *i·* of the grand facts
  ap 576–18   What further *i·* need we of the

indications
  s 144–13   the weaker the *i·* of Soul.
  f 217–10   *i·* of unnatural mental and bodily
  p 422– 7   these *i·* are favorable.

indifference
  m 59–20   more salutary . . . than stolid *i·* or jealousy.
  f 216– 1   his faith in Soul and his *i·* to the body.

indigenous
  b 270–32   but it was *i·* to his spirituality,

indigestion
  ph 165–16   You say that *i·*, fatigue, sleeplessness,
  p 389–28   A case of convulsions, produced by *i·*,

indignation
  ap 570– 7   will finally be shocked . . . into human *i·* ;

indignities
  a 39– 2   Such *i·* as he received, his followers will endure

indirectly
  g 533–11   to trace all human errors . . . *i·* to God,

indiscriminately
  t 445–27   danger in teaching Mind-healing *i·*,

indispensable
  s 125– 4   may no longer be found *i·* to health.
  f 254– 2   human footsteps leading to perfection are *i·*.
  o 359–12   you aver that the material senses are *i·*
  t 462–24   This branch of study is *i·* to the

indissoluble
  b 292–29   man's *i·* connection with his God,
  r 491–15   and find the *i·* spiritual link which

indissolubly
  m 60– 7   welding *i·* the links of affection.
  s 145–20   ethical and physical effects are *i·* connected.

individual (*see also* **individual's**)
  a 18– 5   His mission was both *i·* and collective.
  26– 5   Jesus spares us not one *i·* experience,
  30–19   As the *i·* ideal of Truth, Christ Jesus
  53–21   great distance between the *i·* and Truth.
  m 68–18   I never knew more than one *i·* who
  sp 72–23   In Science, *i·* good derived from God,
  76–16   but he will be an *i·* consciousness,
  88–21   and the *i·* manifests profound adoration.
  99–21   Therefore my contest is not with the *i·*,
  an 102–28   employed, for the *i·* or society."
  s 115–15   MAN : God's spiritual idea, *i·*, perfect,
  117– 2   because an *i·* may be one of a series,
  117– 3   one of many, as an *i·* man, an *i·* horse ;
  155– 4   a general belief, culminating in *i·* faith,
  155– 6   Even when you take away the *i·* confidence in
  155–12   *i·* dissent or faith, . . . is but a belief held by
  ph 173–20   Man is spiritual, *i·*, and eternal ;
  174–24   Then, if an *i·* is sick,
  197–27   until *i·* opinions improve
  f 217– 4   more absurd than to conclude that *i·*

individual

f 229–18	the *i·* who upholds it is mistaken
b 281–16	reality and divinity in *i·* spiritual man
302–32	reproduction by Spirit's *i·* ideas is but
331–18	God is *i·*, incorporeal.
336–32	God is *i·* and personal in a scientific sense,
p 370–20	medical testimony and *i·* experience,
404–14	while its effects still remain on the *i·*,
408– 9	cannot, in a scientific diagnosis, shield the *i·* case
415– 8	when the *i·* looks upon some object which he
427– 5	Man's *i·* being can no more die . . . than can
t 447– 2	man's *i·* right of self-government.
449–24	a good detective of *i·* character.
r 468–23	spiritual universe, including *i·* man, is a
g 508–23	The intelligent *i·* idea, . . . unfolds the
512–13	Their *i·* forms we know not,
ap 577– 6	two *i·* natures in one ;
gl 588–13	unchanged forever in their *i·* characters,

individualism

b 298–29	no matter what their *i·* may be.

individualities

b 303– 8	The minutiæ of lesser *i·*
g 549–16	egg, from which one or more *i·*

individuality

and identity

g 550– 6	forms and preserves the *i·* and identity of

consciousness and

b 336–15	man's consciousness and *i·* are reflections of

divine

b 303– 9	reflect the one divine *i·*

enlarged

c 265–13	confers upon man enlarged *i·*,

eternal

sp 91–19	man's spiritual and eternal *i·*,
b 282– 9	the self-existent and eternal *i·* or Mind ;

false

f 242– 3	mortals put off their material beliefs and false *i·*.

his

c 259– 2	Man . . . cannot lose his *i·*,
b 337– 2	man, reflecting God, cannot lose his *i·* ;
p 375–13	hypnotist dispossesses the patient of his *i·*

His own

b 280–28	God, . . . being perpetual in His own *i·*,

infinite

b 281–15	infinite *i·*, which supplies all form and

man's

b 285– 2	Man's *i·* is not material.

man's higher

c 266– 4	giving place to man's higher *i·* and destiny.

of man

b 317–16	The *i·* of man is no less tangible
r 491–26	Personality is not the *i·* of man.

of Spirit

b 330–15	The *i·* of Spirit, . . . is unknown,

real

b 299–14	whither every real *i·*, image, or

spiritual

(see **spiritual**)

the term

s 117– 1	The term *i·* is also open to objections,
sp 73– 9	both the *i·* and the Science of man,
b 331–23	to conceive of such omnipresence and *i·*
336– 6	The divine Ego, or *i·*, is reflected
g 513–20	existence, and continuity of all *i·* remain
514–19	The *i·* created by God is not carnivorous,

individualized

ph 173– 8	When the supposition, . . . is *i·*,
b 335– 4	The theory, that Spirit . . . to be *i·*,
p 424– 2	child becomes a separate, *i·* mortal mind,
r 477–23	Soul is the . . . intelligence of man, which is *i·*,
g 555–28	the *i·* manifestation of existence,

individualizes

g 513–17	Spirit diversifies, classifies, and *i·*

individually

m 58– 9	constitute *i·* and collectively true happiness,
sp 87– 6	to be *i·* and consciously present.

individual's

pr 11–19	not to annul the divine sentence for an *i·* sin,
s 150–20	and that, too, in spite of the *i·* protest

individuals

m 68– 2	I have named her case to *i·*,
sp 81– 8	spiritualism can only prove that certain *i·*
87– 7	Though *i·* have passed away,
99–18	Those *i·*, who adopt theosophy, spiritualism,
f 236– 9	induce the infuriated attacks on *i·*,
254– 2	I *i·* are consistent who, watching and
t 453–10	but with some *i·* the morbid moral or
462– 1	Some *i·* assimilate truth more readily than
g 549–15	*birth* of new *i·*, or personalities,
553–11	"We have no right to assume that *i·* have
ap 577– 6	as no longer two wedded *i·*,

indivisible

b 335–13	the only substance, the invisible and *i·*,
336–19	God is *i·*.

indolence

an 102–22	they ensnare the age into *i·*,

induce

pr 7–16	to *i·* or encourage Christian sentiment.
s 161–27	would naturally *i·* the very disease
f 220– 6	*i·* sufferers to look in other directions for
236– 8	Do not inferior motives *i·* the
p 370–21	A physical diagnosis . . . tends to *i·* disease.
417–29	Show them how mortal mind seems to *i·* disease

induced

s 121–21	deluded the judgment and *i·* false conclusions.
ph 196–25	Many a hopeless case of disease is *i·* by
p 403– 1	So the sick through their beliefs have *i·*
403– 4	voluntary mesmerism is *i·* consciously
403– 6	self-mesmerism is *i·* unconsciously
411–21	Disease is always *i·* by a false sense
421–21	excitement sometimes *i·* by chemicalization,

induces

p 371–14	Darkness *i·* fear.
374–21	Such a state of mind *i·* sickness.
381– 9	This fear . . . *i·* the physical effects.
392–28	When the condition is present which you say *i·*
413– 4	undue contemplation of physical wants . . . *i·*
425– 2	Mortal mind, not matter, *i·* this conclusion

inducing

p 415–12	They quiet the thought by *i·* stupefaction
g 528–15	falsity, error, credits Truth, God, with *i·*

induction

t 461– 5	C. S. must be accepted at this period by *i·*.

indulge

t 448– 1	to *i·* them, is a moral offence.

indulged

a 23– 1	is not destroyed, but partially *i·*.
ph 175–27	but they never *i·* in the refinement of

indulgence

p 405– 2	*i·* of evil motives and aims

indulging

p 380– 8	*i·* the demands of sin, disease, or death,

industry

ph 175–18	routed by their independence and *i·*.

indwelling

r 478– 7	What basis is there for the theory of *i·* spirit,

inebriate

b 294–28	The *i·* believes that there is pleasure in
322–18	cannot make the *i·* leave his besottedness, until
p 404– 3	If a man is an *i·*, a slave to tobacco,

ineffable

p 364– 8	the higher tribute to such *i·* affection,

inefficacy

f 220– 5	open people's eyes to the *i·* of material hygiene,

ineradicable

p 425– 5	just so long as you believe them . . . *i·*.

inert

sp 77–20	and so prolong the illusion either of a soul *i·*
s 143–29	You lean on the *i·* and unintelligent,
f 253–21	can make no opposition . . . for matter is *i·*,
p 383–32	notion that health depends on *i·* matter
385–32	coming from the body or from *i·* matter
r 484–17	Drugs and *i·* matter are unconscious, mindless.

inertia

b 283– 5	there is no *i·* to retard or check its

inevitable

pr 11–20	sin brings *i·* suffering.
a 40–18	No ; but it was *i·*, for not otherwise could he
ph 189–19	human mortal mind, by an *i·* perversion,
f 216–25	health would seem the exception, death the *i·*,
b 310–26	the annihilation of Spirit would be *i·*.
312–19	Mortals claim that death is *i·* ;
314–32	in supposed accord with the *i·* law of life.

inevitably

m 60– 2	Science *i·* lifts one's being higher
s 120– 9	Then the question *i·* arises :
t 462–12	he will *i·* reap the error he sows.

inexhaustible

c 257–28	*i·* Love, eternal Life, omnipotent Truth.
g 507–29	from the nature of its *i·* source.

infallibility

b 330– 9	*i·* of divine metaphysics will be demonstrated.

infancy

sp 74–21	Darkness and light, *i·* and manhood,
74–23	Who will say that *i·* can utter the ideas of
95–29	the world is asleep in the cradle of *i·*,
f 244–29	Even Shakespeare's poetry pictures age as *i·*,
r 489– 9	In *i·* this belief is not equal to guiding

infant
ph 194–24   was still a mental *i·*, crying and chattering
194–27   An *i·* crying in the night,
194–28   An *i·* crying for the light,
p 371–20   I would not transform the *i·* at once into
412–28   If the case is that of a young child or an *i·*,
413–12   The daily ablutions of an *i·*
413–22   in caring for an *i·* one need not
t 463–17   the C. S. *i·* is born of the Spirit,
g 556–31   plunged his *i·* babe, only a few hours old,

infantile
pref ix– 2   but these jottings were only *i·* lispings
g 554–13   unconscious of his fœtal and *i·* existence ;

infants
p 413–24   Giving drugs to *i·*, noticing every symptom

infected
f 235– 4   Better suffer a doctor *i·* with smallpox to
b 279–23   medicine is more or less *i·* with the

infection
s 153–28   mortal mind, . . . contains and carries the *i·*.
154–16   If a child is exposed to contagion or *i·*,
ph 196–26   not from *i·* nor from contact with material virus,

infelicity
m 66–19   Amidst conjugal *i·*, it is well to hope, pray,

inference
s 118– 1   impels the *i·* that the spiritual leaven
118– 3   an *i·* far above the merely ecclesiastical

inferences
b 274–10   not mere *i·* drawn from material premises.

inferior
s 143–31   *I·* and unspiritual methods of healing
f 236– 8   Do not *i·* motives induce the
b 290–10   still seeking . . . from selfish and *i·* motives.
r 477–24   can never reflect anything *i·* to Spirit.
gl 590–16   has the *i·* sense of master, or ruler.

infers
ph 191–26   *i·* the mortality of the body.
b 282–31   rule of inversion *i·* from error its opposite,
o 347– 8   *i·* that if anything needs to be doctored,

infest
f 234–18   brood of evils which *i·* it would be cleared out.

infidel
sp 94–26   what would be said . . . of an *i·* blasphemer
o 342–22   C. S. awakens the sinner, reclaims the *i·*,
344–28   the physician may perchance be an *i·*

infidelity
m 56–15   *I·* to the marriage covenant is the
65–30   has brought conjugal *i·* to the surface,
s 129–18   pantheism, and *i·* are antagonistic to
f 229– 9   Not far removed from *i·* is the belief
r 494– 5   Is it not a species of *i·* to believe that

infidels
o 359– 7   *i·* whose only objection to this method was,

infinite (noun)
but one
b 334–32   for there can be but one *i·*
gleams of the
g 509–18   understanding gives gleams of the *i·* only,
God is the
f 249–15   God is the *i·*, and infinity never began,
nature of the
b 332– 1   the threefold, essential nature of the *i·*.
never began
f 245–32   The *i·* never began nor will it ever end.
reflection of the
b 313–17   the Son of God, the royal reflection of the *i·* ;
represents the
b 282– 6   The circle represents the *i·*
reveal the
b 292– 6   Science alone can . . . reveal the *i·*.
sustaining
pref vii– 1   To those leaning on the sustaining *i·*,
worship the
b 280–12   belief can neither apprehend nor worship the *i·* ;
yield to the
c 256– 2   The finite must yield to the *i·*.

pr 2– 3   to enlighten the *i·* or to be heard of men?
2– 9   nor can the *i·* do less than bestow all good.
sp 73–32   nor can the finite become the channel of the *i·*.
93–29   belief that the *i·* can be contained in the finite.
94–15   belief that the *i·* is formed after the pattern of
f 208– 4   Material sense . . . has a finite sense of the *i·*.
c 263–26   and attempts to pattern the *i·*
265– 8   and gain some proper sense of the *i·*,
b 281–28   does not put . . . the *i·* into the finite.
284– 4   if the *i·* could be circumscribed within the
284–14   Can the *i·* dwell in the finite
284–15   or know aught unlike the *i·* ?
285–18   for a finite conception of the *i·*
286– 3   is not to understand the *i·*.

infinite (noun)
b 312–28   between matter and Spirit, the finite and the *i·*,
330–16   The individuality of Spirit, or the *i·*,
336– 8   reflected . . . from the infinitesimal to the *i·*.
336–23   Allness is the measure of the *i·*,
339–23   until the finite gives place to the *i·*,
g 502–24   The *i·* has no beginning.
519–15   Mortals can never know the *i·*, until
gl 580–23   supposition . . . that the *i·* enters the finite,

infinite (adj.)
ability
r 494–17   as well as the *i·* ability of Spirit,
All
ap 576– 4   this *i·* All, which to us seems hidden in the
All-in-all
sp 72–24   derived from God, the *i·* All-in-all,
All-power
f 231– 9   no lesser power equals the *i·* All-power ;
being
ph 189–24   we constantly ascend in *i·* being.
blessings
pr 15–30   and they assuredly call down *i·* blessings.
b 325– 8   which results in *i·* blessings to mortals.
calculus
f 209–29   swallowed up in the *i·* calculus of Spirit.
g 520–15   and thought accepts the divine *i·* calculus.
capacities
sp 94–31   union with the *i·* capacities of the one Mind.
f 202–21   and the *i·* capacities of Truth,
character
c 257–28   or Mind would lose its *i·* character as
cycles
b 319–13   Throughout the *i·* cycles of eternal existence,
distance
a 47–16   *i·* distance between Judas and his Master.
g 538– 8   the *i·* distance between Truth and error,
elements
g 512–21   From the *i·* elements of the one Mind
expression
b 336–10   the *i·* expression of infinite Mind,
Father-Mother
g 516–23   reflect, . . . the *i·* Father-Mother
form
c 257–30   It would require an *i·* form to
257–31   phrase *i· form* involves a contradiction
God
   (see **God**)
Godhead
c 255–17   any true idea of the *i·* Godhead.
God is
   (see **God**)
good
sp 93–17   electricity is not the offspring of *i·* good.
idea
   (see **idea**)
ideal
g 517–20   proper symbol . . . is Mind's *i·* ideal.
ideas
g 511–17   full effulgence of God's *i·* ideas,
514– 7   Mind's *i·* ideas run and disport themselves.
image
c 257– 1   creation is the *i·* image or idea
b 300– 4   His *i·* image or reflection, man.
individuality
b 281–15   Mind or Spirit called God, is *i·* individuality,
Life
o 347– 6   God, who is *i·* Life ;
p 381–17   In *i·* Life and Love there is no sickness,
g 518–23   varied expressions of God reflect . . . *i·* Life,
light
g 503–28   God, Spirit, dwelling in *i·* light and harmony
511–12   God is revealed as *i·* light.
Love
   (see **Love**)
manifestation
r 468–10   and its *i·* manifestation,
meanings
b 270–19   demonstration of God, . . . in His more *i·* meanings,
Mind
   (see **Mind**)
One
s 112–16   From the *i·* One in C. S.
Person
s 116–29   then God *is i· Person*,—in the sense of
personality
s 116–28   If the term . . . means *i·* personality,
116–29   in the sense of *i·* personality,
plan
m 69–12   sense of increasing number in God's *i·* plan.
possibilities
a 34–23   into the perception of *i·* possibilities.
power
s 118–15   the invisible and *i·* power and grace.
Principle
   (see **Principle**)

infinite (adj.)

range
c 258–26   and of the *i·* range of his thought.

resources
m 60–29   Soul has *i·* resources with which to bless

self-containment
g 519– 5   the emanation, of His *i·* self-containment

space
g 503–15   *i·* space is peopled with God's ideas,

Spirit
    (*see* **Spirit**)

tasks
b 323– 9   Beholding the *i·* tasks of truth,

Truth
    (*see* **Truth**)

understanding
f 253– 1   He reflects the *i·* understanding,

pref x–14   or treat in full detail so *i·* a theme.
pr 3–19   God is good, omnipotent, omnipresent, *i·*,
   13–23   wonders wrought by *i·*, incorporeal Love,
m 69–25   or do you declare that Spirit is *i·*,
sp 71–30   presupposes Spirit, which is ever *i·*, to be
   76– 7   as neither material nor finite, but as *i·*,
   84–19   To understand that Mind is *i·*,
   93–21   The belief that Spirit is finite as well as *i·*
s 127–13   God, the *i·*, supreme, eternal Mind.
ph 167– 3   the *i·* divine Principle which heals
f 213–13   this attraction towards *i·* and eternal good
c 267– 9   God is Father, eternal, self-created, *i·*.
b 275–16   the *i·* divine Principle, Love.
   278–18   another admission, . . . that Spirit is not *i·*
   280– 3   not products of the *i·*, perfect, and eternal
   280–11   would compress Mind, which is *i·*, beneath a
   281– 3   and learn that Spirit is *i·* and supreme.
   284– 1   not rational to say that Mind is *i·*, but dwells in
   284– 3   or that matter is *i·* and the
   328–32   Its Principle is *i·*, reaching beyond the pale of
   340–12   Divine Love is *i·*.
o 357–26   If . . . God is not supreme and *i·*.
p 367–30   Because Truth is *i·*, error should
   399– 2   and therefore good is *i·*, is All.
r 469– 1   Time is finite; eternity is forever *i·*.
   469–21   We can have but one Mind, if that one is *i·*.
g 505–29   God's ideas reflect the immortal, . . . and *i·*.
   517–22   This ideal is God's own image, spiritual and *i·*.
   550–23   Life is not embryonic, it is *i·*.
ap 567– 7   To *i·*, ever-present Love, all is Love,
gl 587–17   God is one God, *i·* and perfect,
   594–21   omnipresent, omnipotent, *i·*.

infinitely

a 25– 4   *i·* greater than can be expressed by
   44–26   a method *i·* above that of human invention.
b 334– 7   *i·* greater, than the fleshly Jesus,
o 350– 7   in the New Testament, sayings *i·* important,
g 538– 1   *i·* wise and altogether lovely,

infinitesimal

ph 178– 6   not by the *i·* minority of opinions in the
b 336– 7   from the *i·* to the infinite.
g 503– 3   These ideas range from the *i·* to infinity,
   520– 6   can repeat only an *i·* part of what exists.

infinitude

s 112–17   with this *i·* come spiritual rules,
c 258–16   all that exists in the *i·* of Truth.
b 280– 1   In the *i·* of Mind, matter must be unknown.
   302– 6   the conscious *i·* of existence and of all
r 469–21   We bury the sense of *i·*, when we admit
g 508–25   individual idea, . . . unfolds the *i·* of Love.
   511– 6   magnitude, and *i·* of spiritual creation.
   517–24   since there is no limit to *i·*

Infinity

f 253– 2   saith : . . . for I am *I·*.

infinity

all-inclusive
g 514– 5   nothing . . . beyond the range of all-inclusive *i·*,

God's being is
r 481– 3   God's being is *i·*, freedom, harmony,

molecule to
g 507–25   governs all, from the mental molecule to *i·*.

never began
f 249–15   *i·* never began, will never end,

numerals of
g 520–10   The numerals of *i·*, called *seven days*,

reflects
c 258–11   Man reflects *i·*, and this reflection is the

Science reveals
g 519–10   Science reveals *i·* and the fatherhood and

vastness of
c 256–30   cannot present the idea or the vastness of *i·*.

sp 76–32   The recognition of Spirit and of *i·* comes
f 229– 8   Mind signifies God, — *i·*, not finity.
b 336– 2   Mind is the I AM, or *i·*.
r 469–23   when we admit that, . . . , evil has a place in this *i·*,

g 503– 4   from the infinitesimal to *i·*,
   513– 3   and is an attempted infringement on *i·*.
   519–17   What can fathom *i·* !
   544–30   It declares . . . *i·* to enter man's nostrils
   545–15   errors . . . do not accord *i·* to Deity.
gl 581– 3   ALMIGHTY. All-power ; *i·* ; omnipotence.
   585–22   EUPHRATES . . . finity ; the opposite of *i·*.
   590–24   when the spiritual sense of God and of *i·* is

infirmities

a 20–14   Jesus bore our *i·* ; he knew the error of
   53–28   at the time when Jesus felt our *i·*,

infirmity

c 261–18   as oblivious of physical *i·* as if he had
ap 564– 8   This last *i·* of sin will sink its perpetrator

inflamed

a 47–20   this spiritual distance *i·* Judas' envy.
ph 175–28   never indulged in the refinement of *i·*
   195– 1   His eyes were *i·* by the light.
p 385–21   discolored, painful, swollen, and *i·*.
   392–15   If you believe in *i·* and weak nerves,
   393–19   Have no fear that matter can . . . be *i·*
   414–32   Matter cannot be *i·*.
ap 565– 3   swollen with sin, *i·* with war against

inflames

p 405– 2   Hatred *i·* the brutal propensities.

inflammation

and pain
p 375– 3   belief that *i·* and pain must accompany

and swelling
s 153–18   manifests, through *i·* and swelling,

destroy the so-called
p 408–17   Can drugs . . . destroy the so-called *i·* of

glandular
ph 175–14   glandular *i·*, sneezing, and nasal pangs.

never appears
p 415– 9   *I·* never appears in a part which

pain nor
p 393–21   self-evident that matter can have no pain nor *i·*.

prevention of
p 401–32   confines himself . . . to the prevention of *i·*.

relieve
p 415–11   That is why opiates relieve *i·*.

to allay
a 44–13   He took no drugs to allay *i·*.

to reduce
ph 180–31   To reduce *i·*, dissolve a tumor,

will subside
p 421–20   when the fear is destroyed, the *i·* will subside.

p 373–24   The *i·*, . . . or deposit will abate,
   374– 3   Anodynes, . . . never reduce *i·* scientifically,
   414–32   *I·* is fear, an excited state of mortals
   415– 5   *I·* as a mortal belief quickens or impedes the
   416– 2   for the *i·* is not suppressed;
   418–30   tubercles, *i·*, pain, deformed joints,
   425– 9   *i·*, tubercles, hemorrhage, . . . are beliefs,
gl 586–11   FEAR. Heat ; *i·* ; anxiety ;
   593– 7   RED DRAGON. Error ; fear ; *i·* ; sensuality ;

inflammatory

p 378– 9   Without . . . there can be no *i·* nor torpid action
   384–19   followed by . . . hints of *i·* rheumatism,

inflicted

a 51–26   *i·* on the physical Jesus,
p 381–30   a sentence never *i·* by divine authority.

inflictions

p 388– 8   when dire *i·* failed to destroy his body.

influence

baneful
p 400–30   the baneful *i·* of sinful thought on the body.

beneficent
p 394–31   till they feel its beneficent *i·*.

divine
pref xi–17   divine *i·* ever present in human consciousness
f 236–16   or through divine *i·*,

exalting
p 383– 6   the pure and exalting *i·* of the divine Mind

excel the
f 228–31   excel the *i·* of their dead faith and ceremonies.

feel their
sp 86–17   though we can always feel their *i·*.

hallowing
r 474–24   Despite the hallowing *i·* of Truth in the

healing
sp 98–10   for it is the healing *i·* of Spirit

holy
s 146–25   demonstrated through the holy *i·* of Truth

losing its
m 59–30   sacredness of this relationship is losing its *i·*,

manifested the
f 245–24   manifested the *i·* of such a belief.

influence

mental
p 397– 6 We throw the mental *i·* on the

mutual
an 100– 8 as follows : "There exists a mutual *i·* between

of divine Love
ph 180–23 the *i·* of divine Love which casteth out fear.

of his career
a 51– 4 the sublimest *i·* of his career.

of human will
t 451–23 defend himself from the *i·* of human will.

of mortal mind
ph 185–32 A patient under the *i·* of mortal mind

of the belief
p 386–27 laboring under the *i·* of the belief of

of this agent
an 100–10 susceptible to the *i·* of this agent,

or action
sp 89–22 *i·* or action of Soul confers a freedom,

removing the
ph 186– 1 by removing the *i·* on him of this mind,

soporific
p 416–12 when the soporific *i·* of the opium is

stay his
a 43–19 slew him to stay his *i·*

strength and
ph 188– 5 has grown terrible in strength and *i·*,

sun's
ph 189– 3 explanation of the sun's *i·* over the earth.

supporting
p 387–28 supporting *i·* and protecting power

yield to this
p 402–27 If they yield to this *i·*, it is because

your
m 68–14 to your growth and to your *i·* on other lives.
ph 192–21 Your *i·* for good depends upon the
p 424–17 should not act against your *i·*
t 464– 1 it feels your *i·* without seeing you.

ph 168– 6 Whatever *i·* you cast on the side of matter,
199–16 according as they *i·* them through
p 400– 5 before its *i·* upon health and morals can be
402–20 We say that one human mind can *i·*
t 447– 4 to attempt to *i·* the thoughts of others,
456– 1 to *i·* mankind adverse to its highest hope

influenced
pr 7–23 God is not *i·* by man.
p 440– 9 and were *i·* to give a verdict

influences
s 143–18 You admit that mind *i·* the body somewhat,
p 403–30 in proportion to the truth or error which *i·* his
t 462–29 It unfolds the hallowed *i·* of unselfishness,
463– 3 *i·* not embraced in his diagnosis,

influencing
sp 83– 2 human mind or the divine Mind which is *i·* one.

influenza
p 384–17 followed by chills, dry cough, *i·*,

influx
a 43– 9 that *i·* of divine Science which so illuminated
47– 7 The *i·* of light was sudden.

infolds
g 556–10 Mortal belief *i·* the conditions of sin.

inform
pr 2–24 Can we *i·* the infinite Mind
sp 70– 3 corporeal senses cannot *i·* us what is real
ph 183–11 and yet the Scriptures *i·* us that sin,
f 217– 6 Medical schools may *i·* us that the healing
235–18 will degrade the characters it should *i·*
243–17 The head, heart, lungs, and limbs do not *i·* us
c 265–28 The pains of sense quickly *i·* us that
b 276–29 Nature and revelation *i·* us that
327–30 Let that *i·* the sentiments and awaken
p 389– 9 Matter does not *i·* you of bodily derangements ;
r 475– 8 The Scriptures *i·* us that man is made in the

information
pr 3–20 and then we try to give *i·* to
ph 188–32 Astronomy gives the desired *i·*
f 243–18 If this *i·* is conveyed, mortal mind conveys it.
p 385–31 Any supposed *i·*, coming from the body
g 548–21 will be changed with the progress of *i·*."

informed
s 156–21 she *i·* me that she could get along two days
ph 193–19 am *i·* that he went to work in two weeks.
193–24 Since his recovery I have been *i·* that
f 221–13 the doctors, who kindly *i·* him

informer
ap 571–11 Is the *i·* one who sees the foe?

informs
pr 8–31 If a friend *i·* us of a fault,
f 232– 9 Scripture *i·* us that "with God — *Mark* 10 : 27.

infraction
s 134–24 nor because it is an *i·* of divine law,
p 389–23 belief in . . . penalties for their *i·*

infringe
s 144–18 will-power may *i·* the rights of man.
b 319– 6 would *i·* upon spiritual law and

infringement
p 435–22 is no *i·* of law,
g 513– 3 is an attempted *i·* on infinity.

infringes
s 150–22 This human view *i·* man's free moral agency ;

infringing
p 381– 8 When *i·* some supposed law, you say

infuriate
p 378–13 An animal may *i·* another by looking

infuriated
f 236– 8 inferior motives induce the *i·* attacks

ingenuously
f 237– 4 On being questioned about it she answered *i·*,

ingrafted
b 338– 9 proves that error has been *i·* into the premises

Ingratitude
p 430–24 Greed and *I·*, constitute the jury.

ingratitude
pr 4– 1 cannot conceal the *i·* of barren lives.
5–16 *I·* and persecution filled it to the brim ;
a 47–10 The world's *i·* and hatred towards
47–21 The greed for gold strengthened his *i·*,
sp 94–19 His healing-power evoked denial, *i·*,

inhabitant
sp 90–18 the supposed *i·* of that body carries it
b 317–31 so long as the Master remained an *i·* of the earth.

inhabitants
c 256–21 and among the *i·* of the earth ; — *Dan.* 4 : 35.

inhabited
sp 91– 3 *i·* by beings under the control of
r 478– 9 declaration that a house was *i·*, and by a

inhabiters
ap 568–21 Woe to the *i·* of the earth — *Rev.* 12 : 12.

inhabits
b 300–26 theory that soul, spirit, intelligence, *i·*

inhaled
c 261–19 as oblivious . . . . as if he had *i·* chloroform,

inhaling
s 159– 4 protested against *i·* the ether
159–10 not by the ether, but by fear of *i·* it.

inharmonies
f 243–31 They are *i·* which Truth destroys.

inharmonious
s 123– 9 the most absolutely weak and *i·*
ph 166–15 The erring human mind is *i·* in itself.
166–16 From it arises the *i·* body.
f 228– 6 nothing *i·* can enter being, for Life *is* God.
251–30 *I·* beliefs, which rob Mind,
b 300–15 The *i·* and self-destructive never touch the
o 347–30 harmonious will appear real, and the *i·* unreal.
r 472– 9 Sickness, sin, and death, being *i·*,

inharmony
sp 81–26 Though the *i·* resulting from material sense
81–27 *i·* cannot destroy the divine Principle of
ph 183– 5 that God constitutes laws of *i·* is a mistake ;
f 233–32 sickness, which is solely the result of *i·*
b 271–10 Truth, casting out all *i·*.
276–12 The realization that all *i·* is unreal
p 406–25 *I·* of any kind involves weakness
r 473– 1 We learn in C. S. that all *i·* of mortal mind
480–14 *I·* has no Principle ;
480–16 *I·* would make matter the cause
493–24 removes any other sense of moral or mental *i·*.

inherent
s 124–29 declares that they . . . are *i·* in this Mind,
f 225–26 The despotic tendencies, *i·* in mortal mind
b 282–23 There is no *i·* power in matter ;

inheres
s 107–16 false consciousness that life *i·* in the body,

inherit
m 61–12 *i·* more intellect, better balanced minds,
an 106–26 shall not *i·* the kingdom of God. — *Gal.* 5 : 21.
b 321– 4 cannot *i·* the kingdom of God." — *I Cor.* 15 : 50.
g 516–14 "The meek shall *i·* the earth." — *Psal.* 37 : 11.

inheritance
g 533– 2 Had he lost man's rich *i·* and God's behest,

inheritances
f 228– 9 we shall have no dangerous *i·*,

inherited
p 425– 8 Show that it is not *i·* ;
425–32 Discard all notions about . . . . *i·* consumption,

inherits
    m 61–21 child who *i·* propensities that must

inhuman
    p 390–32 employ to defeat the passage of an *i·* law.

inhumanity
    m 64– 2 caused by the selfishness and *i·* of man.
    p 365–25 If hypocrisy, stolidity, *i·*, or vice finds its way

inimical
    p 389–21 cannot . . . be *i·* to existence.

iniquity
    an 106– 3 is to drop . . . into the very mire of *i·*.
    b 313–19 "loved righteousness and hated *i·*."— *Heb.* 1 : 9.
    t 446–30 Covering *i·* will prevent prosperity
       448– 3 Blindness and . . . cling fast to *i·*.
    r 476–17 "conceived in sin and brought forth in *i·*."
       485– 9 because of their uselessness or their *i·*,
    g 540–29 and "shapen in *i·*;"—*Psal.* 51 : 5.
    ap 571– 3 hidden mental ways of accomplishing *i·*.

initiate
    t 457–26 intending thereby to *i·* the cure

injected
    g 524–29 Is Spirit, God, *i·* into dust,

injection
    p 416– 6 A hypodermic *i·* of morphine is
    t 464–17 would give him a hypodermic *i·*,

injunction
    pr 15–23 The Master's *i·* is, that we pray in secret
    a 23–29 whereas the *i·*, "Believe — *Acts* 16 : 31.

injure
    sp 94–32 Jesus could *i·* no one by his Mind-reading.
       95–13 cannot *i·* others, and must do them good.
    t 453–18 You uncover sin, not in order to *i·*,
      463–11 this idea cannot *i·* its useful surroundings
    ap 567–20 claiming . . . either to benefit or to *i·* men

injured
    ph 194–13 it will be so without an *i·* nerve.
    r 488–28 If it were possible for . . . to be *i·*,

injures
    p 403–29 improves or *i·* the case in proportion to

injuries
    p 402–16 You say that accidents, *i·*, and disease kill

injuring
    c 263–14 *i·* those whom he would bless.
    p 397– 6 actually *i·* those whom we mean to bless.
      439–20 God will smite you, O whited walls, for *i·*
    t 449–11 than for you to benefit yourself by *i·* others.

injurious
    s 156– 4 what made them . . . beneficial or *i·*?
    ph 176– 2 was not so *i·* before inquisitive modern
    t 451–28 It is the *i·* action of one mortal mind

injuriously
    sp 94–28 used his incisive power *i·*?
    f 206– 8 acts *i·* both upon the body and through it.
    p 397– 3 acting beneficially or *i·* on the health,

injury
    ph 172–28 But the loss of a limb or *i·* to a tissue
      193–22 ever since the *i·* was received in boyhood.
    b 294–14 saying: . . . *I·* can cripple and matter can kill
    p 397–15 more powerful than . . . to make the *i·* real.
      422–28 doubts as to the ultimate outcome of the *i·*.
    t 464–13 If from an *i·* or from any cause,

injustice
    a 55– 7 did Jesus no more *i·* than the
    m 63–14 C. S. furnishes no precedent for such *i·*,
    p 391–17 *I·* declares the absence of law.

inkling
    s 130–22 an *i·* of the ability of Spirit to make

innate
    s 160– 6 for they have no *i·* power.

innocence
    ap 564–14 the dragon as warring against *i·*.
      567–29 killed by *i·*, the Lamb of Love.
      568– 1 *I·* and Truth overcome guilt and error.
    gl 582–14 BRIDE. Purity and *i·*,
      590–10 self-immolation ; *i·* and purity ;
      594–12 SHEEP. *I·* ; inoffensiveness ;

innocent
    ph 175–29 They were as *i·* as Adam, before he
    p 437–16 the helpless *i·* body tortured,
      439–14 though Mortal Man was *i·*.
      439–24 an offence of which he was *i·*.
      442– 1 Man is adjudged *i·* of transgressing
    t 450– 6 so depraved that they appear to be *i·*.
    ap 564– 7 to charge the *i·* with the crime.

innuendoes
    m 68–22 to hatch their silly *i·* and lies,

innumerable
    r 479–23 the only facts are Spirit and its *i·* creations.

inoculation
    t 449–20 The *i·* of evil human thoughts ought to

inoffensiveness
    gl 594–12 SHEEP. . . . *i·* ; those who follow their leader.

inquire
    p 376–28 Some people, mistaught as to Mind-science, *i·*

inquirer
    g 555– 6 An *i·* once said to the discoverer of C. S. :

inquiries
    p 396– 6 Make no unnecessary *i·* relative to feelings

inquiring
    g 555–17 is like *i·* into the origin of God,

inquiry
    sp 86– 2 Supposing this *i·* to be occasioned by
      86– 6 Repeating his *i·*, he was answered by the
    s 131–31 to John's *i·*, "Art thou he — *Matt.* 11 : 3.
      133– 1 and sent the *i·* to Jesus,
      137– 9 This renewed *i·* meant : Who or what is it
    f 223–15 Many are ready to meet this *i·* with the
    b 268– 6 those lower things which give impulse to *i·*.

inquisitive
    ph 176– 3 not so injurious before *i·* modern Eves took

insane
    ph 193–26 threatened with incarceration in an *i·* asylum
    f 245– 6 she became *i·* and lost all account of time.
    p 408–11 people who are committed to *i·* asylums
      411–11 and the *i·* man was changed
      421– 1 he suffers only as the *i·* suffer,

insanity
dementia or
    p 423–29 as directly . . . as is dementia or *i·*.
implies
    p 421– 2 *i·* implies belief in a diseased brain,
incipient
    m 68–18 was suffering from incipient *i·*,
in curing
    p 414– 8 The arguments to be used in curing *i·* are
sin is
    p 407–29 All sin is *i·* in different degrees.
species of
    p 407–29 There are many species of *i·*.
      408–16 is in itself a mild species of *i·*.
treatment of
    p 414– 4 treatment of *i·* is especially interesting.
universal
    p 408– 6 There is a universal *i·* of so-called health,
would produce
    p 408–23 would produce *i·* as perceptibly as

    b 330–31 dementia, *i·*, inanity, devil,
    p 408–10 from the special name of *i·*.
      408–14 The supposition that we can correct *i·* by

insect
    sp 74–17 caterpillar, transformed into a beautiful *i·*,
      74–18 nor does the *i·* return to fraternize with

insensible
    ph 173–10 is required to be made manifest through the *i·*.

insensibly
    p 383–30 sensibly well when it ought to be *i·* so

inseparable
    sp 70– 9 the Ego and the Father are *i·*.
    ph 184– 7 the penalties it affixes . . . are *i·* from it.
    b 314– 7 proved that he and the Father were *i·*
      333–27 *i·* from the divine Principle, God.
      336–26 are *i·*, harmonious, and eternal.
    p 404–28 require the same method and are *i·* in Truth.
    r 476– 5 God and the real man are *i·*.
      482–20 He was *i·* from Christ, the Messiah,
      491–16 in the divine likeness, *i·* from his creator.
    g 554– 7 being and Deity are *i·*.

inside
    c 258– 9 more than a material form with a mind *i·*,

insidious
    p 376– 9 most hidden, undefined, and *i·* beliefs.

insight
    sp 94–25 this *i·* better enabled him to direct those
    s 128–18 into his native air of *i·* and perspicacity.
    p 363–25 did his *i·* detect this unspoken moral uprising?

insignificance
    b 317– 4 insisted on . . . the *i·* of spirit,

insincere
    pr 3–28 If we are ungrateful for . . . we are *i·*
      8–11 If a man, . . . is impure and therefore *i·*,

insist
    sp 90–14 some *i·* that death is the necessary prelude
    s 116–17 They never . . . *i·* upon the fact that God is all,
      122–31 They *i·* that soul is in body
      131–14 Must C.S. come through . . . as some persons *i·*?
    ph 168–15 Because man-made systems *i·* that man

insist

b 283–13   They *i·* that Life, or God, is one and the
p 409– 3   You may say : . . . why do you *i·* that disease
412–23   Mentally *i·* that harmony is the fact,
413–20   I *i·* on bodily cleanliness within and without.
421–15   I· vehemently on the great fact which

insisted

s 159– 1   her physicians *i·* that it would be unsafe to
b 317– 3   *i·* on the might of matter,

insists

b 307– 3   This pantheistic error, or so-called *serpent, i·*
388– 5   Divine Science *i·* that time will prove all this.

inspecting

p 379–15   invalid, *i·* the hue of her blood

inspection

p 438–25   without the *i·* of Soul's government officers.

inspiration

came through
b 319–22   original language of the Bible came through *i·*,
heavenly
gl 592–26   gentleness ; prayer ; heavenly *i·*.
holy
s 161– 5   Holy *i·* has created states of mind which
little
a 37–32   Why has this Christian demand so little *i·*
p 368–14   has little *i·* to nerve endeavor.
needs
b 319–22   and needs *i·* to be understood.
of a sermon
sp 80– 4   whether for the *i·* of a sermon or for
of goodness
gl 581– 5   the *i·* of goodness, purity, and immortality,
of Love
a 35–27   Our wine the *i·* of Love,
restores
f 242–28   while *i·* restores every part of the
spiritual
gl 596–17   they show the spiritual *i·* of Love and Truth
this
a 34– 2   Then why ascribe this *i·* to a dead rite,

—

a 54–12   the *i·* of Jesus' intense human sacrifice.
m 65– 5   and to give to human life an *i·*
sp 88–27   It is due to *i·* rather than to erudition.
b 281–31   the *i·*, which is to change our standpoint,
gl 589– 5   JACOB. . . . I· ; the revelation of Science,
598–17   WINE. I· ; understanding.
599– 6   ZION. . . . *i·* ; spiritual strength.

inspirational

c 256– 4   from the scholastic to the *i·*,

inspirations

ph 184–30   The *i·* were deep and natural.

inspire

m 61–21   what noble ambition, can *i·* the child
ph 180–21   through the material faith which they *i·*.
c 262–14   These clearer, higher views *i·* the
p 370–27   Quackery likewise fails at length to *i·* the

inspired

a 46– 9   has spoken through the *i·* Word
49– 2   They knew what had *i·* their devotion,
51–23   He was *i·* by God, by Truth and Love,
53–17   not interpret aright the . . . which Jesus *i·*
sp 84–17   to be divinely *i·*,— yea, to reach the
s 107–12   *i·* with a diviner nature and essence :
133–26   who taught as he was *i·* by the Father
139–22   darkening to some extent the *i·* pages.
144–30   whether the ancient *i·* healers understood
b 319–27   wrote down what an *i·* teacher had said.
p 368– 3   The confidence *i·* by Science lies in the fact
410–20   Here is a definite and *i·* proclamation of C. S.
418–21   All metaphysical logic is *i·* by this simple
r 497– 3   we take the *i·* Word of the Bible as our
g 521– 4   Here the *i·* record closes its narrative
537–24   I· writers interpret the Word spiritually,
539–31   *i·* his wisest and least-understood sayings,
547–28   I· thought relinquishes a material,
ap 572– 8   and profound counsel of the *i·* writer.
gl 579– 3   elucidates the meaning of the *i·* writer.

inspires

f 234– 4   Whatever *i·* with wisdom, Truth, or Love
t 454–18   Love *i·*, illumines, designates, and leads the way.
g 547–32   lifts humanity out of disease and death and *i·*

instance

every
s 162–13   not in one instance, but in every *i·*.
familiar
sp 89–12   This familiar *i·* reaffirms the Scriptural word
first
f 234–27   You must control evil thoughts in the first *i·*,
p 403– 7   In the first *i·* it is understood that
g 541–24   It is supposed to say in the first *i·*,

instance

for
b 319–29   for *i·*, to name Love as merely an attribute
no
an 101–29   In no *i·* is the effect of animal magnetism,
g 550–25   no *i·* of one species producing its opposite.
one
s 149– 7   The prescription which succeeds in one *i·*
152–11   in one *i·* and not in another.
160–20   Can . . . nerves rebel against mind in one *i·*
162–13   not in one *i·*, but in every instance.
f 229–13   declaring Him good in one *i·* and
245–27   One *i·* like the foregoing proves it possible
g 549–24   In one *i·* a celebrated naturalist, Agassiz,
this
ph 189– 5   Science (in this *i·* named natural)
f 245–18   This *i·* of youth preserved furnishes a
g 553–17   In this *i·*, it is seen that the maternal

instances

sp 79– 5   Thousands of *i·* could be cited of
s 122–21   Experience is full of *i·* of similar illusions,
b 319–26   misinterpretation of the Word in some *i·* by
p 383–25   Such *i·* only prove the illusive physical effect
386–12   in too many *i·* healed disease . . . not to know
398– 7   These *i·* show the concessions which
408–12   are only so many distinctly defined *i·* of the

instant

f 215–13   never for an *i·* deprived of the light and
244–20   If man flickers out in death . . . there must be an *i·*
b 290–23   The sin and error which possess us at the *i·* of
306–19   cannot be separated for an *i·* from God,
389–32   One *i·* she spoke despairingly of herself.
t 463– 2   among phenomena, which fluctuate every *i·*

instantaneous

p 377–16   has caused what is termed *i·* death.
411–12   and the healing is *i·*.

instantaneously

pr 16–23   spiritual consciousness, which . . . *i·* heals
g 504–24   gathered into the focus of ideas, bring light *i·*,

instead

a 34– 3   *i·* of showing, by casting out error
39–14   Jesus overcame death and the grave *i·* of
40–29   to mean public worship *i·* of daily deeds.
53–22   should weep over the warning, *i·* of
sp 87–14   when really it is first sight *i·* of second,
92–16   gained from matter, or evil, *i·* of
92–28   *i·* of urging the claims of Truth alone.
96–30   will be apprehended mentally *i·* of materially.
s 120–27   *i·* of reversing the testimony of the
121–18   *i·* of the earth from west to east.
129–23   *i·* of accepting only the outward sense of things.
132– 2   *i·* of referring to his doctrine,
146–16   *i·* of to the divine Principle, of the man Jesus ;
148–10   as created corporeally *i·* of spiritually
148–11   *i·* of from the highest, conception of being.
148–26   claims to rule man by material law, *i·* of
150– 5   eternal Science, *i·* of a phenomenal exhibition.
159–24   would learn . . . from matter *i·* of from Mind.
ph 165– 3   I· of so doing, it closed the eyes of mortals
166–18   I· of thrusting Him aside in times of
170– 6   faith in matter *i·* of in Spirit.
180–13   the ground that all causation is matter, *i·* of
180–21   I· of furnishing thought with fear,
181–22   are satisfied with good words *i·* of effects,
189–20   makes all things start from the lowest *i·* of
192– 8   from corporeality *i·* of from Principle,
192– 9   from the mortal *i·* of from the immortal.
195–30   demand for amusement *i·* of for improvement.
196–22   *i·* of impressing them with forcible
197–16   We should master fear, *i·* of cultivating it.
f 202–18   The days of our pilgrimage will multiply *i·* of
202–20   the true way leads to Life *i·* of to death,
203– 7   If God were understood *i·* of being merely believed,
206–14   governed by Science *i·* of the senses,
206–26   I· of God sending sickness and death,
212–15   take away this so-called mind *i·* of a piece of
216–16   bones, brain, etc., servants, *i·* of masters.
218–22   *i·* of turning in time of need to God,
223– 5   illusion that he lives in body *i·* of
223– 6   in matter *i·* of in Spirit.
224– 9   life and peace *i·* of discord and death.
242–32   the proof which he gave, *i·* of mere profession.
244–30   *i·* of assigning to man the everlasting grandeur
248– 7   *i·* of lapsing into darkness or gloom.
253–29   which is the law of Life *i·* of death,
253–30   of harmony *i·* of discord,
253–31   of Spirit *i·* of the flesh.
c 257–18   say that an anthropomorphic God, *i·* of
260– 1   from imperfection *i·* of perfection,
263–30   *i·* of a scientific eternal consciousness
b 274–20   which affirm that . . . are material, *i·* of spiritual.
280–25   *i·* of possessing a sentient material form,

intelligence
God is
pr 2–24   God is *i·*. Can we inform the infinite Mind
governing
ph 174– 1   less faith . . . in a supreme governing *i·*.
idea or
b 279–18   their only idea or *i·* is in God.
is not mute
ph 191–19   *I·* is not mute before non-intelligence.
is omniscience
r 469– 8   *Answer.— I·* is omniscience, omnipresence,
Life and
pr 14–13   Life and *i·* are purely spiritual,
b 310–15   reveals Soul . . . as the central Life and *i·*
r 477–22   Soul is the substance, Life, and *i·* of man,
life and
  (*see* **life**)
Life, or
g 550– 5   God is the Life, or *i·*, which forms and
life or
r 485–32   The notion of any life or *i·* in matter
g 584–29   the absence of substance, life, or *i·*.
Life, substance, and
a 27–15   the Life, substance, and *i·* of the universe
ph 185–20   God as the only Life, substance, and *i·*,
gl 595– 7   the idea of Life, substance, and *i·* ;
life, substance, and
  (*see* **life**)
material
a 48– 1   error of a belief in any possible material *i·*.
g 534–16   mythological material *i·* called *energy*
might of
f 215–13   the light and might of *i·* and Life.
p 378–17   latter occurrence represents . . . the might of *i·*
Mind or
f 204–22   realize only one God, one Mind or *i·*
  216–12   there is but one Mind or *i·*,
g 508–21   The Mind or *i·* of production names the
mockery of
ph 192– 2   a mockery of *i·*, a mimicry of Mind.
more
m 62–20   must not attribute . . . more *i·* to matter,
never passes into
b 336– 2   *I·* never passes into non-intelligence, or matter.
no
pr 12–19   The drug does nothing, because it has no *i·*.
s 127–21   have— as matter—no *i·*, life, nor sensation.
  136– 5   no *i·*, action, nor life separate from God.
p 399– 1   Evil has no power, no *i·*,
r 467– 6   have no *i·*, . . . but that which is spiritual.
g 530–27   The dream has no reality, no *i·*, no mind ;
nor power
t 454–11   evil or matter has neither *i·* nor power,
nor sensation
f 243–23   matter has neither *i·* nor sensation.
nor substance
s 133–27   no life, *i·*, nor substance outside of God.
r 468– 9   no life, truth, *i·*, nor substance in matter.
one
b 307– 8   affirms . . . that there is more than one *i·*
or power
b 339–30   never to admit that sin can have *i·* or power,
or reality
r 469–17   not Truth, but error, without *i·* or reality.
or substance
g 508– 5   The only *i·* or substance of a thought,
rights of
sp 79–27   contending for the rights of *i·*
p 384–31   at length quail before the divine rights of *i·*,
scale of
g 511–27   rising in the scale of *i·*,
separate
b 309–26   impossible . . . an *i·* separate from his Maker.
so-called
b 282–27   Error is the so-called *i·* of mortal mind.
Spirit, or
gl 591– 4   the one Spirit, or *i·*, named Elohim, or God.
spiritual
f 240– 6   all point to Mind, the spiritual *i·*
subjugate
ph 165– 8   to subjugate *i·*, to make mind mortal,
substance, life, and
sp 91–26   belief is, that substance, life, and *i·* are
ap 562–10   its reflected light, substance, life, and *i·*.
  563– 9   belief that substance, life, and *i·* can
substance, or
p 418– 6   error that life, substance, or *i·* can be in matter.
the only
b 330–12   the only *i·* of the universe, including man.
g 508– 5   The only *i·* or substance of a thought,
Truth is the
b 282–26   Truth is the *i·* of immortal Mind.
Truth, or
r 468– 1   Thus we arrive at Truth, or *i·*, which
understanding and
g 557–13   towards enlarged understanding and *i·* ;

intelligence
unerring
g 546–12   is governed by unerring *i·* ?
vibration is not
c 259–26   Vibration is not *i·* ; hence it is not a creator.
which holds
f 209–10   *i·* which holds the winds in its grasp.

m 63– 9   nor does he . . . prior to reaching *i·*.
an 102– 6   neither *i·*, power, nor reality,
s 129–11   a belief in the *i·* of matter,
ph 194–25   with no more *i·* than a babe,
f 204–12   is admitted to be good, an *i·* or Mind called God.
  205–10   matter has neither *i·*, life, nor sensation,
  211–25   If it is true . . . that matter has *i·*,
  250– 4   and suppose . . . unintelligence to act like *i·*,
b 270–10   Few deny the hypothesis that *i·*, apart from
  270–12   and it is generally admitted that this *i·* is
  275–14   All substance, *i·*, wisdom, being,
  276–31   *I·* never produces non-intelligence ;
  277– 2   and therefore cannot spring from *i·*.
  285–14   one is *i·* while the other is non-intelligence.
  300–26   theory that soul, spirit, *i·*, inhabits
  318–30   *I·* does not originate in numbers,
p 378–22   Disease is not an *i·* to dispute the
  413– 1   and cannot transmit good or evil *i·* to man,
  441–25   Supreme Bench decides in favor of *i·*,
r 469– 7   *Question.—* What is *i·* ?
  472–15   supposition that pleasure and pain, that *i·*,
  475–21   possesses no life, *i·*, nor creative power of his own,
  478–15   and is there *i·* in matter?
  478–20   How can *i·* dwell in matter
  480–17   would make matter the cause . . . of *i·*,
  482– 5   hypothesis that soul is both an evil and a good *i·*,
g 511– 3   radiates their borrowed light, *i·*,
  513–19   the *i·*, existence, and continuity of all
  516– 4   The substance, Life, *i·*, Truth, and
  517– 9   man corresponds to creation, to *i·*, and to
  531– 6   error, . . . that non-intelligence becomes *i·*,
ap 567–19   claiming that there is *i·* in matter
gl 580–23   supposition that . . . *i·* passes into non-intelligence,
  583–20   CREATOR. Spirit ; Mind ; *i·* ;
  587– 8   Life ; Truth ; Love ; all substance ; *i·*.
  588–24   definition of
  591– 9   illusion ; *i·*, substance, and life in
intelligences
gl 591– 3   belief in many gods, or material *i·*,
  594–23   evil minds ; supposed *i·*, or gods ;
intelligent
sp 73–27   the reality of *i·* existence,
  80–32   belief . . . that matter is *i·*.
  89–25   Matter is neither *i·* nor creative.
  91–32   fourth erroneous postulate is, that matter is *i·*,
s 156– 1   If drugs possess . . . *i·* curative qualities,
f 205–16   error of believing that matter can be *i·*
  211– 1   If brain, nerves, stomach, are *i·*,
  218–26   Resist the temptation to believe in matter as *i·*,
b 275– 6   matter is neither substantial, living, nor *i·*.
  276– 7   but all have . . . one *i·* source,
  293–19   electricity is not *i·*,
  294–24   matter is represented as divided into *i·* gods.
  307–21   If we regard matter as *i·*,
  312–29   away from the *i·* and divine healing Principle
  332– 2   the *i·* relation of God to man
p 385–32   as if either were *i·*,
  409– 1   *I·* matter is an impossibility.
  412–32   since matter is not *i·* and cannot
r 466–14   Truth is *i·* ; error is non-intelligent.
  487–24   belief that life is . . . *i·* matter is erroneous.
g 508–23   The *i·* individual idea, be it male or female,
  526–12   a belief in *i·* matter.
  531– 1   living, substantial, and *i·*.
  556– 7   destroys forever all belief in *i·* matter.
gl 579–17   a curse ; a belief in *i·* matter,
intelligently
s 107–14   and thoughts acquaint themselves *i·* with God.
intended
a 27– 1   which was *i·* to prove beyond a question
  38– 2   assured that this command was *i·* only for
s 152–18   supposed this ceremony was *i·* to heal him,
b 320–30   as if Job *i·* to declare that even if
r 465–13   They are also *i·* to express the nature,
intending
t 457–26   *i·* thereby to initiate the cure
intense
a 54–13   the inspiration of Jesus' *i·* human sacrifice.
sp 87–27   by friendship or by any *i·* feeling
ph 195– 1   gave him a belief of *i·* pain.
b 329–30   the more *i·* the opposition to spirituality,
intent
p 365–24   the result will correspond with the spiritual *i·*.
g 515– 5   tireless worm, . . . persevering in its *i·*.

intention
    b 326–19 nothing but wrong *i·* can hinder your

intentional
    f 251–28 Ignorance, like *i·* wrong, is not Science.

intentionally
    ph 177–29 as directly as if the poison had been *i·* taken.
    t 456– 1 impossible . . . for you *i·* to influence
    456–13 greatly errs, ignorantly or *i·*,

interchange
    m 58–18 the sweet *i·* of confidence and love ;

interchangeably
    s 127–11 The terms Divine Science, . . . she employs *i·*,

intercommunication
    sp 81– 1 not so much evidence to prove *i·*
    b 284–31 The *i·* is always from God to His idea, man.

intercommunion
    sp 72–30 Not personal *i·* but divine law is the
    82–25 so unlike, that *i·* is as impossible as

intercourse
    m 58– 1 by constant *i·* with those adapted to elevate it,
    sp 72–28 The joy of *i·* becomes the jest of sin, when

interest
    c 261–10 with such absorbed *i·* as to forget it,
    p 436– 6 and in the *i·* of Personal Sense,
    437– 8 to condemn Man in the *i·* of Personal Sense.

interested
    p 430–25 The court-room is filled with *i·* spectators,

interesting
    p 414– 4 treatment of insanity is especially *i·*.

interests
    a 21–22 and our mutual *i·* are identical ;
    m 59–15 thus hallowing the union of *i·* and affections,
    f 236– 5 Sacredly, in the *i·* of humanity, not of sect.
    p 414–18 lest you array the sick against their own *i·*
    t 462–10 dividing his *i·* between God and mammon
    ap 571–20 will unite all *i·* in the one divinity.

interfere
    m 62–24 let no mortal *i·* with God's government
    64–13 wife should not say, "It is never well to *i·*
    f 214–29 Neither age nor accident can *i·* with the
    234– 1 material lotions *i·* with truth,
    p 402–12 material beliefs will not *i·* with spiritual facts.
    427–14 Nothing can *i·* with the harmony of being

interfered
    an 106–12 invaded when the divine order is *i·* with,

interference
    m 63–32 and own her children free from *i·*.

interlaced
    s 114–26 disentangles the *i·* ambiguities of being,

intermixture
    g 552–27 The *i·* of different species,

interpose
    pr 12–27 Does Deity *i·* in behalf of one worshipper,
    t 445– 7 No hypothesis . . . should *i·* a doubt or fear

interpret
    a 53–16 The world could not *i·* aright the
    s 117–20 Human theories are inadequate to *i·* the
    127–27 Science . . . is alone able to *i·* God aright.
    b 272–28 divine Principle of the universe must *i·* the
    o 350–10 enables them to *i·* his spiritual meaning.
    r 467–27 We cannot *i·* Spirit, Mind, through matter.
    g 534– 6 enabled woman to be first to *i·* the Scriptures
    537–24 Inspired writers *i·* the Word spiritually,

interpretation
  meek
    a 54–19 They would not accept his meek *i·* of life
  metaphysical
    gl 579– 5 the metaphysical *i·* of Bible terms,
  of God
    t 461–14 furnishes the eternal *i·* of God and man.
  of Scripture
    b 320– 9 "The spiritual *i·* of Scripture
    320–10 The one important *i·* of Scripture
    g 547– 8 given you the correct *i·* of Scripture.
  scientific
    g 501– 1 Scientific *i·* of the Scriptures
  spiritual
    a 47– 1 even to the spiritual *i·* and discernment
    s 118– 3 Science of Christ and its spiritual *i·*,
    b 320– 9 "The spiritual *i·* of Scripture
    g 502–19 each text is followed by its spiritual *i·*

    b 321– 1 an *i·* which is just the opposite of the true,

interpretations
    c 265– 7 they must near the broader *i·* of being,

interpreted
    sp 83–31 standpoints, from which cause and effect are *i·*.
    s 124–14 universe, like man, is to be *i·* by Science
    126–10 Human belief has sought and *i·* in its own way
    f 210– 2 *i·* by the translation of the spiritual original
    g 511–24 Spiritually *i·*, rocks and mountains stand for
    546–20 cannot possibly be *i·* from a material standpoint.

interpreter
    ph 170–15 The best *i·* of man's needs said :
    g 513–13 until divine Science becomes the *i·*.
    ap 577–21 and divine Mind is its own *i·*.

interpreting
    b 285–23 By *i·* God as a corporeal Saviour

interprets
    r 471–25 that which *i·* God as above mortal sense.
    g 537–25 the ordinary historian *i·* it literally.
    ap 560–10 *i·* the Principle of heavenly harmony.
    569– 1 This rule clearly *i·* God as divine Principle,
    577–18 *i·* this great example and the great Exemplar.

interrupt
    p 362– 5 as if to *i·* the scene of Oriental festivity.

interruptions
    sp 96– 6 there will be *i·* of the general material routine.

intertwined
    g 523–28 become more and more closely *i·*

interval
    a 39–28 and the *i·* before its attainment is
    gl 598–27 would bridge over . . . the *i·* of death,

intervals
    s 153– 9 administered at *i·* of three hours,
    p 431– 7 partaking of food at irregular *i·*,

intervenes
    o 361– 2 Here C. S. *i·*, explains these

interwoven
    r 477–15 though *i·* with matter's highest stratum,

intimate
    p 437– 2 He also testified that he was on *i·* terms with

intimated
    g 554–25 Jesus never *i·* that God made a devil,

intimately
    p 408–25 tarsal joint is less *i·* connected with the
    432– 3 testifies : . . . I am *i·* acquainted with the

intimation
    p 391–21 therefore meet the *i·* with a protest.
    r 471–10 these so-called senses receive no *i·* of

intolerable
    r 491– 2 A delicious perfume will seem *i·*.

intolerance
    sp 94–14 Tyranny, *i·*, and bloodshed,

intoxicating
    s 158–20 to victimize the race with *i·* prescriptions
    t 454– 2 use of tobacco or *i·* drinks is not

intoxication
    b 294–28 inebriate believes that there is pleasure in *i·*.
    p 398–22 destroy the illusion of pleasure in *i·*,

intrinsic
    s 156– 1 If drugs possess *i·* virtues or

intrinsically
    s 157–19 If He could create drugs *i·* bad,

introduced
    pref xii– 5 the United States, where C. S. was first *i·*.
    a 54– 7 divine Science *i·* its glorified example *i·*.
    s 123–16 The term C. S. was *i·* by the author
    t 473–18 the teaching and practice of Christianity,
    gl 590–22 It is *i·* in the second and following chapters.

introduces
    pref vii–22 A book *i·* new thoughts,
    sp 79–15 *i·* the harmony of being.
    s 135– 7 The miracle *i·* no disorder,
    r 474– 5 Whoever *i·* the Science of Christianity
    g 543–32 *i·* the record of a material creation

introducing
    s 152–15 *i·* a thermometer into the patient's mouth.
    p 439– 1 and *i·* their goods into the market.

introduction
    g 538–18 have no record in the Elohistic *i·*
    553–14 or important to their origin and first *i·*."
    gl 582–10 the *i·* of a more spiritual origin ;

intruding
    p 362–10 *i·* upon the household of a high-caste
    391–10 that you can possibly entertain a single *i·*
    393– 2 we admit the *i·* belief, forgetting that

intuition
    b 298–14 involves *i·*, hope, faith, understanding,

intuitions
- *sp* 85– 7 Such *i·* reveal whatever constitutes and
- *ph* 174–12 the angels of His presence — the spiritual *i·*
- *gl* 581– 5 spiritual *i·*, pure and perfect ;

invaded
- *an* 106–12 *i·* when the divine order is interfered with,

invalid
- *s* 139–31 does not follow that the profane or atheistic *i·*
- *ph* 166–24 the despairing *i·* often drops them,
- 180–14 the *i·* may unwittingly add more fear
- *o* 342–23 raises from the couch of pain the helpless *i·*.
- *p* 367– 4 Christian encouragement of an *i·*,
- 376–10 The pallid *i·*, . . . should be told that
- 379–14 Let the despairing *i·*, inspecting the hue of
- *t* 460–22 starts a petty crossfire over every cripple and *i·*,

invalid's
- *ph* 166–26 *i·* faith in the divine Mind is less than in
- *p* 379–23 does not affect the *i·* health,

invalids
- *pref* x–19 Few *i·* will turn to God till
- *s* 145– 8 struggle for the recovery of *i·* goes on,
- *f* 237–23 Some *i·* are unwilling to know the facts
- *b* 318–19 *i·* grow more spiritual, as the
- *p* 377– 6 *I·* flee to tropical climates
- 420–14 This fact of C. S. should be explained to *i·*
- *t* 443–18 leave *i·* free to resort to whatever
- 443–20 such *i·* may learn the value of the

invariable
- *o* 342–17 If . . . then there is no *i·* law,

invention
- *a* 44–27 a method infinitely above that of human *i·*.
- *sp* 95–20 even human *i·* must have its day,
- *s* 163–26 so ample an exhibition of human *i·*
- *ph* 195–20 Observation, *i·*, study, and original thought

inventions
- *ph* 196– 2 Man has "sought out many *i·*," — *Eccl.* 7 : 29.
- *b* 273– 5 Human belief has sought out many *i·*,
- *o* 358–14 nor of the *i·* of those who scoff at God.
- *g* 531–23 Has man sought out other creative *i·*,
- *ap* 563– 6 showing its horns in the many *i·* of evil.

invents
- *g* 541–22 Here the serpentine lie *i·* new forms.

inversion
- *s* 113–27 divine metaphysics . . . proves the rule by *i·*.
- *f* 207–32 The only evidence of this *i·* is
- *b* 282–31 rule of *i·* infers from error its opposite,

invert
- *g* 514– 2 could not . . . *i·* the divine creation,

inverted
- *s* 111–16 rejects the incidental or *i·* image
- 111–17 what this *i·* image is meant to represent.
- *ph* 200–19 he is neither *i·* nor subverted,
- *f* 207–30 Spiritual facts are not *i·* ;
- *c* 267–21 *i·* thoughts and erroneous beliefs
- *b* 285– 9 man's counterfeit, the *i·* likeness,
- 301–27 presents an *i·* image of Mind and substance
- 305–20 The *i·* images presented by the senses,
- *g* 502– 7 *i·* images of the creator and His creation.
- *ap* 572–11 materiality is the *i·* image of spirituality.
- *gl* 580–13 an *i·* image of Spirit ;

inverts
- *g* 507–30 Mortal sense *i·* this appearing
- 512–25 Mortal mind *i·* the true likeness,

investigate
- *an* 100–13 to *i·* Mesmer's theory and to report
- *f* 237–30 unwilling to *i·* the Science of Mind
- *o* 344–25 Why should one refuse to *i·* this method
- *g* 550–10 Of what avail is it to *i·* what is miscalled

investigates
- *sp* 83–32 *i·* and touches only human beliefs.

investigation
- *ap* 570– 1 The march of mind and of honest *i·*

investiture
- *sp* 75– 6 would need . . . to have a material *i·*,

invigorate
- *b* 274– 2 and thus *i·* and sustain existence.

invigorates
- *s* 162– 5 the sunlight of Truth, which *i·* and purifies.

invincible
- *a* 55– 5 but this does not affect the *i·* facts.
- *t* 453– 8 until victory rests on the side of *i·* truth.

inviolate
- *sp* 98–20 remains *i·* for every man to understand and

invisible
- *a* 55– 3 from a deadened sense of the *i·* God,
- *sp* 78–31 the *i·* good dwelling in eternal Science.
- *s* 118–15 the *i·* and infinite power and grace.
- 121–17 The earth's diurnal rotation is *i·*
- *c* 264–15 objects of creation, which before were *i·*,

invisible
- *b* 305– 8 the central light of being, the *i·* God.
- 334–10 The *i·* Christ was imperceptible
- 335–12 substance, the *i·* and indivisible infinite God.
- 337–21 man, as the reflection of the *i·* God,
- 337–24 poor counterfeits of the *i·* universe
- *r* 479–30 "For the *i·* things of Him, — *Rom.* 1 : 20.
- *ap* 573– 4 that which is *i·* to the uninspired thought.

invisibly
- *sp* 80–31 both visibly and *i·*,

invites
- *p* 422–32 This mental state *i·* defeat.

invoke
- *o* 354– 6 Why do they *i·* the divine aid to enable them to
- *g* 542–12 tend to perpetuate sin, *i·* crime,

involuntarily
- *sp* 84– 9 men become seers and prophets *i·*,
- 86–20 images and sounds evolved *i·*
- *p* 371–10 removed as *i·*, not knowing why nor when.
- 376– 2 patient turns *i·* from the contemplation of it,

involuntary
- *pr* 7–28 By it we may become *i·* hypocrites,
- *ph* 187–20 All voluntary, as well as miscalled *i·*, action
- 187–22 There is no *i·* action.
- 187–25 tries to classify action as voluntary and *i·*,
- *c* 263–11 They make man an *i·* hypocrite,
- *p* 402–30 The *i·* pleasure or pain of the person
- 403– 3 difference between voluntary and *i·* mesmerism
- *r* 484–22 the voluntary or *i·* action of error
- 491– 7 Material man is made up of *i·* and voluntary error,

involve
- *sp* 86–19 either *i·* feats by tricksters, or
- *f* 212–28 and possibly that other methods *i·* so-called
- *b* 339– 6 prophesy and *i·* the final destruction of all sin
- *ap* 573–22 *i·* the spiritual idea and consciousness of

involved
- *a* 26–22 Jesus' teaching . . . *i·* such a sacrifice
- *sp* 82–11 because different states of consciousness are *i·*,
- *s* 117–20 the divine Principle *i·* in the miracles
- *r* 484–26 *i·* in all false theories and practices.

involves
- *pr* 9–22 It *i·* the Science of Life,
- *m* 57–32 the disappointments it *i·* or the hopes it fulfils.
- *s* 114–12 *i·* an improper use of the word *mind*.
- *f* 240–30 *i·* unwinding one's snarls,
- *c* 257–31 the phrase *infinite form i·* a contradiction
- *b* 298–13 Spiritual sense, . . . *i·* intuition, hope,
- 301– 8 but his sense of substance *i·* error
- *p* 406–26 Inharmony of any kind *i·* weakness
- 429–27 why you . . . do not demonstrate the facts it *i·*.
- *t* 446–18 A wrong motive *i·* defeat.
- *r* 493–14 full answer to the above question *i·* teaching,
- *g* 526– 9 Belief *i·* theories of material hearing, sight,

involving
- *b* 286–23 temporal thoughts are human, *i·* error,

inward
- *s* 139–14 sectarian bitterness, whenever it flows *i·*.
- *b* 321–25 the *i·* voice became to him the voice of God,

iota
- *ph* 186–20 It can never destroy one *i·* of good.

iris
- *p* 393–27 complex humors, lenses, muscles, the *i·* and

iron
- *ph* 199– 6 muscles are as material as wood and *i·*
- *f* 225– 1 What is it that binds man with *i·* shackles
- *ap* 565– 7 rule all nations with a rod of *i·* :— *Rev.* 12 : 5.

irradiance
- *gl* 584– 1 DAY. The *i·* of Life ; light,

irrational
- *o* 352–31 not *i·* to tell the truth about ghosts.
- *p* 433– 9 urges the jury not . . . to be warped by the *i·*,

irreconcilable
- *a* 19– 6 for Truth and error are *i·*.

irrefutably
- *b* 315–22 to prove *i·* how spiritual Truth destroys

irregular
- *p* 431– 6 partaking of food at *i·* intervals,

irresistible
- *m* 67–15 until an *i·* propulsion precipitates his
- *c* 265–17 senses represent . . . death as *i·*,

irrespective
- *p* 423–19 Mind his basis of operation *i·* of matter

irreverent
- *o* 348–14 Are we *i·* towards sin,

Isaac
- *g* 501– * *appeared unto Abraham, unto I·*, — *Exod.* 6 : 3.

Isaiah
- s 109–25   Scripture of *I·* is renewedly fulfilled :
- g 514–21   the millennial estate pictured by *I·* :
- 540– 5   In *I·* we read: "I make peace, — *Isa.* 45 : 7.

Isaiah's
- a 52–13   *I·* graphic word concerning the

isolated
- c 259– 3   nor is he an *i·*, solitary idea,

Israel
- s 133– 7   so great faith, no, not in *I·*." — *Matt.* 8 : 10.
- 135–18   by limiting the Holy One of *I·*
- f 211–19   It should no longer be said in *I·* that
- 226–29   as of yore, hold the children of *I·* in bondage.
- c 256–12   "Hear, O *I·* : the Lord our God — *Deut.* 6 : 4.
- b 308–30   then his name was changed to *I·*,
- 309–10   He was no longer called Jacob, but *I·*,
- 309–16   were to be called the children of *I·*,
- ap 562–12   The twelve tribes of *I·* with all mortals,
- 566– 1   As the children of *I·* were guided
- 566–15   When *I·*, of the Lord beloved,
- gl 583– 5   definition of

Israelites
- s 133– 8   In Egypt, it was Mind which saved the *I·*
- 133–10   The *I·* looked upon the brazen serpent,
- o 351–27   *I·* centred their thoughts on the material

Israelites
- g 524– 6   It was also found among the *I·*,
- ap 559–29   the *I·* of old at the Paschal meal

Israelitish
- o 351– 1   sprang from half-hidden *I·* history

Issachar
- gl 589– 1   definition of

issue
- m 67–13   the mariner works on and awaits the *i·*.
- sp 83–13   here Science takes *i·* with popular religions.
- s 126–15   point at *i·* between C. S. on the one hand
- r 483–17   has called the world to battle over this *i·*

issued
- pref x– 5   books on mental healing have since been *i·*,
- xii–13   the first periodical *i·* by Christian Scientists.

issues
- sp 92– 4   erroneous . . . that matter holds in itself the *i·*
- ph 181– 6   Can matter . . . hold the *i·* of life?"
- f 216– 5   What has touched Life, God, to such strange *i·* ?
- p 392–32   *i·* of pain or pleasure must come through mind,
- g 526– 6   this statement that life *i·* from matter,

Ivanhoe
- ap 566–14   Rebecca the Jewess in the story of *I·*,

J

Jacob
- s 135– 6   presence of the God of *J·*." — *Psal.* 114 : 7.
- b 308–16   *J·* was *alone*, wrestling with error,
- 308–28   When *J·* was asked, "What is thy name?" — *Gen.* 32 : 27.
- 308–32   Then *J·* questioned his deliverer,
- 309–10   He was no longer called *J·*, but Israel,
- 333–23   Abraham, *J·*, Moses, and the prophets
- g 501– *   unto *Isaac, and unto J·* — *Exod.* 6 : 3.
- gl 589– 4   definition of

Jacob's
- b 309– 7   result of *J·* struggle thus appeared.
- gl 581–15   ASHER (*J·* son). Hope and faith ;
- 582– 4   BENJAMIN (*J·* son). A physical belief as to life,
- 583–26   DAN (*J·* son). Animal magnetism ;
- 586–21   GAD (*J·* son). Science;
- 589– 1   ISSACHAR (*J·* son). A corporeal belief ;
- 590–11   LEVI (*J·* son). A corporeal and sensual belief ;
- 593–12   REUBEN (*J·* son). Corporeality ; sensuality ;

Jahr
- s 152–29   *J·*, from *Aconitum* to *Zincum oxydatum*,
- ph 179–26   The sedulous matron — studying her *J·*

James (*see also* **Apostle James**)
- o 343– 4   *J·* said : "Show me thy faith — *Jas.* 2 : 18.

Japhet
- gl 589– 8   definition of

jar
- p 363– 1   She bore an alabaster *j·* containing costly and
- 363– 4   Breaking the sealed *j·*, she perfumed Jesus' feet

jarring
- b 306–25   Undisturbed amid the *j·* testimony of the

jaws
- f 243– 6   from the fiery furnace, from the *j·* of the lion,

jealous
- g 541– 3   *J·* of his brother's gift, Cain seeks

jealousy
- m 58–16   The narrowness and *j·*, which would
- 59–20   more salutary . . . than stolid indifference or *j·*.
- 64– 8   Pride, envy, or *j·* seems on most occasions
- 68– 9   *J·* is the grave of affection.

Jefferson's
- t 445–29   Recalling *J·* words about slavery,

Jehovah (*see also* **Jehovah's**)
- **appeal to**
  - o 351–32   They might appeal to *J·*, but their prayer
- **called**
  - g 523–20   because Deity therein is always called *J·*,
  - 523–27   the creator is called *J·*, or the Lord.
  - 524–17   that He should now be called *J·* ?
- **corporeal**
  - b 312–15   over the sense of a corporeal *J·*,
- **declared**
  - b 338–27   *J·* declared the ground was accursed ;
- **name of**
  - g 524– 8   the Supreme Being by the national name of *J·*.
  - 524– 9   In that name of *J·*, the
- **prophets of**
  - sp 83– 3   What the prophets of *J·* did,
- **ritualistic**
  - s 135–28   nor a special gift from a ritualistic *J·* ;

Jehovah
- **said**
  - b 320–14   "And *J·* said, My spirit shall not
- **synonymous with**
  - ap 576–27   term Lord, . . . is often synonymous with *J·*,
- **tribal**
  - s 140–23   Jewish tribal *J·* was a man-projected God,
- **went before**
  - gl 595–14   on Aaron's breast when he went before *J·*,

- s 133–29   Jewish conception of God, as Yawah, *J·*,
- f 229– 5   We should hesitate to say that *J·* sins or suffers ;
- g 501– *   by *My name J·* was I not known — *Exod.* 6 : 3.
- 520–18   in the day that the Lord God [*J·*] — *Gen.* 2 : 4.
- 520–20   the Lord God [*J·*] had not caused — *Gen.* 2 : 5.
- 523–31   In the historic parts . . . it is usually *J·*,
- 524–13   the Lord God [*J·*] formed — *Gen.* 2 : 7.
- 525–31   made the Lord God [*J·*] to grow — *Gen.* 2 : 9.
- 526–26   the Lord God [*J·*] took the man, — *Gen.* 2 : 15.
- 527– 6   the Lord God [*J·*] commanded — *Gen.* 2 : 16.
- 527–22   the Lord God [*J·*] formed — *Gen.* 2 : 19.
- 528– 9   And the Lord God [*J·*, Yawah] — *Gen.* 2 : 21.
- 528–12   rib, which the Lord God [*J·*] had — *Gen.* 2 : 22.
- 529–14   which the Lord God [*J·*] had made. — *Gen.* 3 : 1.
- 532–13   And the Lord God [*J·*] called unto — *Gen.* 3 : 9.
- 534– 8   And the Lord God [*J·*] said — *Gen.* 3 : 14.
- 536–30   And the Lord God [*J·*] said, — *Gen.* 3 : 22.
- 537– 3   the Lord God [*J·*] sent him — *Gen.* 3 : 23.
- 538–25   gotten a man from the Lord [*J·*]. — *Gen.* 4 : 1.
- 540–26   an offering unto the Lord [*J·*]. — *Gen.* 4 : 3.
- 541– 6   And the Lord [*J·*] had respect — *Gen.* 4 : 4.
- 541–19   And the Lord [*J·*] said unto — *Gen.* 4 : 9.
- 541–27   And He [*J·*] said, . . . The voice of — *Gen.* 4 : 10.
- 542–14   And the Lord [*J·*] said unto him, — *Gen.* 4 : 15.
- 542–16   And the Lord [*J·*] set a mark — *Gen.* 4 : 15.
- 542–28   from the presence of the Lord [*J·*], — *Gen.* 4 : 16.
- 543–31   day that the Lord God [*J·* God] — *Gen.* 2 : 4.
- gl 590–20   LORD GOD. *J·*.
- (*see also* **Lord God**)

Jehovah's
- b 280–17   Moses declared as *J·* first command of the Ten :

Jehovistic
- g 523–19   The other document is called the *J·*,

jeopardize
- g 542–12   *j·* self-control, and mock divine mercy.

Jeremias
- s 136–16   *J·*, or one of the prophets." — *Matt.* 16 : 14.

Jerusalem
- a 42–12   his brief triumphal entry into *J·*
- gl 589–12   definition of

jest
- sp 72–29   joy of intercourse becomes the *j·* of sin, when

Jesus (*see also* **Jesus'**)
- **acknowledged**
  - a 31– 4   *J·* acknowledged no ties of the flesh.
- **acted boldly**
  - a 18–10   *J·* acted boldly, against the accredited
- **also said**
  - g 554–22   *J·* also said, "Have not I — *John* 6 : 70.
- **answered**
  - b 305–16   "Then answered *J·* and said — *John* 5 : 19.
  - p 364–10   *J·* answered by rebuking self-righteousness

Jesus

appeal of
  a 50–12 The appeal of *J·* was made both to his
approached
  p 362–12 (Mary Magdalene, . . . approached *J·*.
approved
  p 363–20 *J·* approved the answer,
asked
  s 132–26 *J·* asked, "When the Son of man— *Luke* 18: 8.
  p 411–13 once *J·* asked the name of a disease,
beheld
  r 476–32 *J·* beheld in Science the perfect man,
benign thought of
  p 365– 7 benign thought of *J·*, finding utterance
betrayal of
  a 47–24 he plotted the betrayal of *J·*
birth of
  g 539–31 Science of creation, so conspicuous in the birth
    of *J·*,
blood of
  a 25– 6 material blood of *J·* was no more efficacious
bore our infirmities
  a 20–14 *J·* bore our infirmities ; he knew the error
bore our sins
  a 53–25 *J·* bore our sins in his body.
brought to light
  b 292–30 connection with his God, which *J·* brought to
    light.
called himself
  r 482–16 *J·* called himself "the Son of— *Matt.* 9: 6.
called the body
  b 313–29 *J·* called the body, which . . . he raised
came to destroy
  r 474–18 Now *J·* came to destroy sin, sickness, and
career of
  a 30–23 throughout the whole earthly career of *J·*,
cast out evil
  sp 79–17 *J·* cast out evil spirits, or false beliefs.
  ph 185–22 *J·* cast out evil and healed the sick,
command of
  o 342–10 and in defiance of the direct command of *J·*,
commemorated
  a 33–31 that you have commemorated *J·* in his cup?
conspired against
  a 47–10 Judas conspired against *J·*.
corporeal
  s 141–16 Christ-spirit which governed the corporeal *J·*.
  b 334– 3 not that the corporeal *J·* was one with the
    334–14 the eternal Christ and the corporeal *J·*
could restore
  g 555–28 Our great example, *J·*, could restore the
crucifixion of
  a 24–20 Does . . . theology regard the crucifixion of *J·*
  r 497–20 the crucifixion of *J·* and his resurrection
declaration of
  o 361–14 This declaration of *J·*, understood,
declared
  f 234–27 *J·* declared that to look with desire on
defined
  g 554–20 *J·* defined this opposite of God and His
demonstrated
  s 110–25 *J·* demonstrated the power of C. S. to heal
  f 244– 5 On their basis *J·* demonstrated Life,
  b 274–16 *J·* demonstrated this great verity.
    332–19 *J·* demonstrated Christ ;
  p 430– 2 *J·* demonstrated this, healing the dying and
  r 494–11 *J·* demonstrated the divine power to heal
    494–15 *J·* demonstrated the inability of corporeality,
demonstrated by
  f 230–10 divine Principle, Love, as demonstrated by *J·*.
  b 272–31 C. S., as demonstrated by *J·*, alone reveals the
    321–31 the Science of being was demonstrated by *J·*,
demonstrated through
  b 316– 8 Truth, was demonstrated through *J·*
demonstration of
  s 139–25 neither . . . mar the demonstration of *J·*, nor
demonstrations of
  s 122– 9 exposed . . . by the demonstrations of *J·* ;
  f 243– 9 It crowned the demonstrations of *J·* with
disciple of
  b 324–19 Paul was not at first a disciple of *J·*
disciples of
  a 29–13 disciples of *J·* believe him the Son of God."
elicited from
  s 137–22 elicited from *J·* the benediction,
enabled
  a 51–31 which enabled *J·* to heal the sick,
  r 482–22 enabled *J·* to demonstrate his
endured from
  a 36–10 *J·* endured the shame, that he might
enjoined by
  a 55– 4 the idea of Christian healing enjoined by *J·* ;

Jesus

established
  s 136– 1 *J·* established his church and maintained
    138–17 *J·* established in the Christian era
  o 348–11 for *J·* established this foundational fact,
  r 473–26 *J·* established what he said by demonstration.
exaltation of
  b 313–18 the cause given for the exaltation of *J·*,
example of
  g 515– 2 its possessor to emulate the example of *J·*.
experienced
  a 38–21 *J·* experienced few of the pleasures of the
forbade him
  a 48–22 *J·* forbade him, thus rebuking resentment
foresaw
  a 41–22 *J·* foresaw the reception C. S. would have
furnished proofs
  r 472–11 *J·* furnished proofs of these statements.
furnished the proof
  b 317–28 *J·* furnished the proof that he was unchanged
had taught
  a 42–28 *J·* had taught his disciples the Science of this
healed sickness
  f 210–16 *J·* healed sickness and sin by
history of
  b 315–26 history of *J·* shows him to have been more
human
  b 334– 1 not that the human *J·* was or is eternal,
    334–20 before the human *J·* was incarnate
humanity of
  a 25–32 was made manifest in the humanity of *J·*.
illumines
  g 501– 7 *J·* illumines them, showing the poverty of
illustrated
  ph 171–14 *J·* illustrated the divine Principle
immaculate
  ap 562– 1 prophesied the coming of the immaculate *J·*,
inaugurated by
  b 288–14 foreshadowed by the. . .and inaugurated by *J·*,
incarnate
  o 350–28 Hence its embodiment in the incarnate *J·*,
inspired
  a 53–17 could not interpret . . . the discomfort which
    J· inspired
instructed
  b 271– 7 *J·* instructed his disciples whereby to heal the
introduced
  r 473–18 *J·* introduced the teaching and practice of
    Christianity,
justification of
  f 203–11 was really the justification of *J·*,
life of
  b 317– 6 Whosoever lives most the life of *J·*
loved
  f 236–28 *J·* loved little children because of their
manger of
  ap 575–29 followed it to the manger of *J·* ;
manifested in
  pr 12–13 divine healing Principle as manifested in *J·*,
mapped out
  a 38–24 *J·* mapped out the path for others.
marked out
  f 227–23 *J·* marked out the way.
martyrdom of
  gl 597–10 martyrdom of *J·* was the culminating sin of
memory of
  a 33–32 Are all who eat bread . . . in memory of *J·*
mission of
  s 131–26 The mission of *J·* confirmed prophecy,
mother of
  g 534– 3 to be the mother of *J·* and to behold at the
name of
  a 29–18 and gave to her ideal the name of *J·*
never intimated
  g 554–24 *J·* never intimated that God made a devil,
never spoke of
  s 147–32 *J·* never spoke of disease as dangerous
never taught
  f 232–19 *J·* never taught that drugs, food, air,
no terror for
  a 42–23 sin, sickness, and death had no terror for *J·*.
of Nazareth
  a 18– 3 *J·* of Nazareth taught and demonstrated
  b 313–23 *J·* of Nazareth was the most scientific man
    333–16 The advent of *J·* of Nazareth marked
  ap 564–11 the accusations against *J·* of Nazareth
once asked
  sp 86– 1 *J·* once asked, "Who touched— *Luke* 8: 45.
once said
  s 109–28 *J·* once said of his lessons :
    131–18 *J·* once said : "I thank Thee,— *Luke* 10: 21.
  g 530– 7 Knowing this, *J·* once said,
origin of
  g 539–27 The divine origin of *J·* gave him more than
overcame death
  a 39–13 *J·* overcame death and the grave instead of

Jesus

overcome by
  c 264–23   sickness and death were overcome by *J·*,
physical
  a 51–26   vengeance, inflicted on the physical *J·*,
practice of
  a 53–10   Because the divine Principle and practice of *J·*
practised
  s 147–12   since *J·* practised these rules
prayed
  a 32–22   yet *J·* prayed and gave them bread.
    32–25   *J·* prayed ; he withdrew from the
    38–18   *J·* prayed, not for the twelve only,
preached and
  o 344–23   the C. S. which *J·* preached and practised
preached by
  s 141– 3   and the truth preached by *J·*.
prepared by
  p 388–21   If food was prepared by *J·* for his disciples,
presented
  a 25–16   *J·* presented the ideal of God better than
  g 534–15   the idea of divine power, which *J·* presented,
presented by
  b 316–24   spiritual idea of God, as presented by *J·*,
proved
  a 27–10   That Life is God, *J·* proved by his
  ph 168–20   an authority which *J·* proved to be false
  b 314–32   *J·* proved them wrong by his resurrection,
  r 473–29   *J· proved* the Principle, which heals the sick
    486–14   *J·* proved by the prints of the nails, that
purposed
  s 138– 2   *J·* purposed founding his society,
raised up
  o 341– *   *that raised up J· from the dead— Rom.* 8 : 11.
realized
  a 47–32   *J·* realized the utter error of a belief in
reappearing of
  a 45–28   reappearing of *J·* was not the return of a spirit
rebuked
  m 67–31   *J·* rebuked the suffering from any such cause
  p 363–14   *J·* rebuked them with a short story or parable.
  g 509–30   *J·* rebuked the material thought of his
record of
  a 46–27   which closed the earthly record of *J·*,
referred
  b 333–28   *J·* referred to this unity of his
represented
  b 316–12   *J·* represented Christ, the true idea of
reputation of
  a 53– 8   reputation of *J·* was the very opposite of his
restored Lazarus
  ap 75–13   *J·* restored Lazarus by the understanding
rose higher
  a 43–21   *J·* rose higher in demonstration because of
said
  a 20– 7   *J·* said, "The publicans and the— *Matt.* 21 : 31.
    31–25   Referring to the materiality of the age, *J·* said :
    31–29   Again, foreseeing the persecution . . . *J·* said :
    38–10   *J·* said : "These signs shall follow— *Mark* 16 : 17.
  m 69–26   *J·* said, "The children of— *Luke* 20 : 34.
  sp 75–12   *J·* said of Lazarus : "Our friend— *John* 11 : 11.
  s 134–26   *J·* said : "I knew that Thou— *John* 11 : 42.
  ph 196–12   "Fear him which is able to . . . said *J·*.—
      Matt. 10 : 28.
  f 201– 5   *J·* said, "No man can serve two— *Matt.* 6 : 24.
  c 259–19   *J·* said : "Be ye therefore perfect,— *Matt.* 5 : 48.
    267–15   *J·* said : "For whosoever shall— *Matt.* 12 : 50.
  b 272– 8   *J·* said : "Ye do err, nor knowing— *Matt.* 22 : 29.
    292–20   *J·* said : "Why do ye not understand— *John*
      8 : 43
    324–32   *J·* said substantially, "He that— *see John* 11 : 26.
    326– 4   *J·* said, "He that believeth— *John* 14 : 12.
    328–22   knowing that there is no material law, *J·* said :
  o 341– 8   *J·* said, "Blessed are the— *Matt.* 5 : 8.
    357– 7   *J·* said of personified evil, that it was
  p 364–29   as *J·* said of the unwelcome visitor,
    422– 2   Wiser than his persecutors, *J·* said :
    429–31   *J·* said . . . "If a man keep my— *John* 8 : 51.
    442–26   *J·* said, "Fear not,— *Luke* 12 : 32.
  r 476–29   When speaking of God's children, . . . *J·* said,
    494– 2   *J·* said : "Destroy this temple— *John* 2 : 19.
  g 539–23   *J·* said : "Do men gather— *Matt.* 7 : 16.
  ap 564–26   *J·* said, quoting a line from the Psalms,
  gl 580–30   *J·* said of the devil, "He was a— *John* 8 : 44.
    585– 3   *J·* said, referring to spiritual perception,
    586– 5   *J·* said, thinking of the outward vision,
says
  p 410– 4   "This is life eternal," says *J·*,— *John* 17 : 3.
self-same
  b 317–22   self-same *J·* whom they had loved before the
sent a message
  a 27– 1   *J·* sent a message to John the Baptist,
sent forth
  a 27–22   *J·* sent forth seventy students at one time,
    49– 7   Where were the seventy whom *J·* sent forth?

Jesus

spares us not
  a 26– 5   *J·* spares us not one individual experience,
speaks of
  ap 564–13   Revelator speaks of *J·* as the Lamb of God
spiritual
  b 314–24   the spiritual *J·* was imperceptible to them.
spoke
  p 367–18   of which *J·* spoke to his disciples, when he said :
  ap 576–16   as when *J·* spoke of his material body
suffered
  pr 11–18   *J·* suffered for our sins, not to annul the
  a 24–15   the understanding, in which *J·* suffered and
sufferings of
  a 34–11   commemorated the sufferings of *J·*
taught
  a 25–13   *J·* taught the way of Life by demonstration,
    30–32   work out our salvation in the way *J·* taught.
    43–17   final demonstration of the truth which *J·* taught,
    43–28   The Science *J·* taught and lived
  sp 94– 1   *J·* taught but one God, one Spirit,
  s 135–26   Christianity as *J·* taught it was not a creed,
  b 306– 5   *J·* taught them how death was to be overcome
  r 477– 4   *J·* taught that the kingdom of God is intact,
taught by
  a 41–18   The truth taught by *J·*, the elders scoffed at.
teachings of
  b 269–23   on the teachings of *J·*, of his apostles,
    324–24   to follow the example and teachings of *J·*,
the anointed
  b 313– 4   "*J·* the anointed," Jesus the God-crowned
the Christ
  b 313– 2   The term Christ Jesus, or *J·* the Christ
    333–14   name of our Master . . . was *J·* the Christ ;
  r 473–16   hence the duality of *J·* the Christ.
the God-crowned
  b 313– 4   "Jesus the anointed," *J·* the God-crowned
the man
  a 26–13   This Christ, or divinity of the man *J·*,
    29–28   the divine Principle of the man *J·*,
  s 146–17   the divine Principle, of the man *J·* ;
  r 473–24   rather than personality or the man *J·*,
  ap 561–17   coincidence, shown in the man *J·*,
    565–11   in order that the man *J·*, . . . might never
theology of
  s 138–30   It was this theology of *J·* which healed
  p 369– 8   and comprehends the theology of *J·*
the true
  b 314–20   This materialism lost sight of the true *J·* ;
time of
  pr 6–30   magistrate, who lived in the time of *J·*,
title of
  b 333– 9   Christ is . . . the divine title of *J·*.
told Simon
  p 364–19   *J·* told Simon that such seekers as he
took bread
  a 32–15   *J·* took bread, and blessed it— *Matt.* 26 : 26.
vanquished every
  a 45– 1   *J·* vanquished every material obstacle,
walked on the
  b 273–24   *J·* walked on the waves, fed the multitude,
was able
  g 555–30   *J·* was able to present himself unchanged
was known
  a 46– 5   In the walk to Emmaus, *J·* was known to
was the mediator
  b 315–31   *J·* was the mediator between Spirit and the
was the offspring
  a 29–32   *J·* was the offspring of Mary's self-conscious
was "the way"
  a 46–25   *J·* was "the way ;"— *John* 14 : 6.
we adore
  a 26– 1   While we adore *J·*, and the heart overflows
which identified
  a 46– 8   The divine Spirit, which identified *J·* thus
wielded by
  s 142–22   as twisted and wielded by *J·*,
words of
  o 358–19   Why are the words of *J·* more frequently
  g 539– 2   In the words of *J·*, it (evil, devil) is
work of
  a 28–16   nor the work of *J·* was generally understood.

  pr 6–23   *J·* uncovered and rebuked sin before he
    8– 8   such externals are spoken of by *J·* as
    14–19   Hence the hope of the promise *J·* bestows :
    15– 3   So spake *J·*. The closet typifies the
  a 19– 6   *J·* aided in reconciling man to God
    19–29   *J·* urged the commandment,
    24–25   presentation, after death, of the material *J·*,
    26–10   The Christ was the Spirit which *J·* implied
    26–15   Love gave *J·* authority over sin,
    30–12   *J·* would not have been appreciable to
    30–16   Not so did *J·*, the new executor for God,
    31–16   the practical Truth, which makes *J·*
    32–28   The Passover, which *J·* ate with his disciples

Jesus

a	40– 8	adjusts the balance as *J·* adjusted it.
	40–17	Was it just for *J·* to suffer?
	40–20	If a career so great and good as that of *J·*
	41– 2	into the Shekinah into which *J·* has passed
	41–14	The proofs . . . which *J·* gave by casting out
	42–20	This error *J·* met with divine Science
	43– 5	enabled the disciples to understand what *J·*
	44– 5	precincts of the tomb gave *J·* a refuge
	44–21	to sustain *J·* in his proof of man's . . . power?
	44–28	His disciples believed *J·* to be dead
	45–22	They who earliest saw *J·* after the
	46–18	*J·* caused him to examine the nail-prints
	47–19	placed a gulf between *J·* and his betrayer,
	48– 8	*J·* turned forever away from earth
	48–17	*J·* had not one of them,
	49–32	esteemed *J·* as "stricken, smitten of— *Isa.* 53 : 4.
	50–30	real cross, which *J·* bore up the hill
	51– 6	*J·* could have withdrawn himself from his
	51–12	*J·* could give his temporal life
	51–28	*J·* was unselfish.
	52–11	world's hatred of the just and perfect *J·*,
	52–31	the hypocrite, called *J·* a glutton and a
	53– 3	*J·* was no ascetic.
	53–28	at the time when *J·* felt our infirmities,
	55– 6	Christian era did *J·* no more injustice than
m	56– 2	Reading his thoughts, *J·* added :
		the time cometh of which *J·* spake,
sp	75–17	Had *J·* believed that Lazarus had
	79–19	*J·* did his own work by the one Spirit.
	85–15	*J·*, as he once journeyed with his students,
	85–24	*J·* knew the generation to be wicked
	86– 4	*J·* knew, as others did not, that it was not
	86– 9	*J·* possessed more spiritual susceptibility
	93– 2	Remember *J·*, who nearly nineteen centuries ago
	94–21	Of the ten lepers whom *J·* healed,
	94–27	blasphemer who should hint that *J·* used
	94–32	*J·* could injure no one by his Mind-reading.
	95– 5	traduced . . . as they would be to-day if *J·*
s	107– *	*by the revelation of J· Christ.— Gal.* 1 : 12.
	117–21	the miracles (marvels) wrought by *J·*
	117–29	*J·* bade his disciples beware of the leaven of
	123–25	so-called miracles of *J·* did not specially
	132– 1	*J·* returned an affirmative reply,
	132–31	once pointed his disciples to *J·* as
	133– 2	and sent the inquiry to *J·*,
	133– 6	centurion of whose faith *J·* himself declared,
	136– 9	How did *J·* heal the sick?
	136–18	some of the people believed that *J·* was a
	136–25	even Herod doubted if *J·* was controlled by
	136–32	*J·* patiently persisted in teaching and
	137–13	*J·* completely eschewed the narrow opinion
	138–10	*J·* explained his cures, which appeared
	138–15	was the foundation on which *J·* built.
	141–14	*J·* elaborated the fact that the healing effect
	143– 6	else *J·* would have recommended and
	146–28	anterior to the period in which *J·* lived.
	157–21	why did *J·* not employ them
ph	170– 7	Did *J·* understand the economy of man
	170–19	*J·* healed the sick and cast out error,
	200–26	*J·* Christ, and him crucified."— *I Cor.* 2 : 2.
	200–28	*J·* Christ, and him glorified.
f	206–16	as *J·* showed with the loaves and the fishes,
	227–31	*J·* would not have disregarded those laws
	233– 5	by the power of Spirit, as *J·* destroyed them.
c	260– 5	can depict the form and face of *J·*
b	268– *	*and with His Son J· Christ.— I John* 1 : 3.
	271–24	eternal life, not the death of *J·*, is its outcome.
	286–15	was put aside . . . by this original man, *J·*.
	292–31	*J·* showed that a mortal man is not the
	314– 3	*J·* waited until the mortal or fleshly sense
	314–12	When *J·* spoke of reproducing his body,
	315–25	The divine conception of *J·* pointed to
	317– 1	*J·* uttered things which had been
	317–30	To this dull and doubting disciple *J·* remained
	325– 7	*J·* gave the true idea of being, which results in
	325–28	the divine Science which ushered *J·* into
	328–19	can it be said that they explained it . . . as *J·* did,
	329–10	Be thankful that *J·*, . . . did these things,
	332– 9	*J·* was born of Mary.
	332–18	The corporeal man *J·* was human.
	332–23	*J·* was the son of a virgin.
	333– 4	word *Christ* is not properly a synonym for *J·*,
	333– 4	*J·* was a human name, which belonged to
	333–32	By these sayings *J·* meant, not that
	334– 8	greater, infinitely greater, than the fleshly *J·*,
	334–11	*J·* appeared as a bodily existence.
	334–16	material concept, or *J·*, disappeared,
	334–30	a reference to the human sense of *J·* crucified.
o	343–14	*J·* strips all disguise from error, when
	351–17	proof of Christianity, which *J·* required,
	352– 8	To *J·*, not materiality, but spirituality,
	356– 9	*J·* reasoned on this subject practically,
	356–15	*J·* knew, "It is the spirit that— *John* 6 : 63.
	358–17	illustrated by the prophets, by *J·*,
	361–12	*J·* Christ is not God, as *J·* himself declared,

Jesus

p	362– 2	*J·* was once the honored guest of a
	363– 8	Did *J·* spurn the woman?
	365–21	commendation as the Magdalen gained from *J·*,
	369–16	*J·* never asked if disease were acute
	393–25	*J·* declares that "the light of— *Matt.* 6 : 22.
	398– 1	Sometimes *J·* called a disease by name,
	398– 8	concessions which *J·* was willing to make
	410– 9	*J·* Christ, whom Thou hast sent."— *John* 17 : 3.
	411–16	Thereupon *J·* cast out the evil,
	411–18	*J·* caused the evil to be self-seen
r	473–12	*J·* is the name of the man who,
	473–15	*J·* is the human man, and Christ is the divine
	474–21	evils which *J·* lived to destroy
	482–19	*J·* was the highest human concept of the
	493–28	If *J·* awakened Lazarus from the
	494– 9	*J·* pointed the way for them.
g	542– 2	would kill *J·* that it might be rid of
ap	562– 4	the fatherhood of God, which *J·*
	564–14	Since *J·* must have been tempted in all points,
	564–18	*J·* "opened not his mouth."— *Isa.* 53 : 7.
	575–14	Did not *J·* illustrate the truths he taught
gl	589–16	definition of
	598–15	What *J·* gave up was indeed air,

(*see also* **Christ Jesus, Galilean Prophet, Lamb, Master, Nazarene, Prince of Peace, Son, Teacher, Way-shower**)

Jesus'

pref	xi–10	healing of C. S. results now, as in *J·* time,
pr	4–30	enable us to follow *J·* example.
	7– 3	evidence that *J·* reproof was pointed
	10– 6	If good enough to profit by *J·* cup of
	11– 1	*J·* prayer, "Forgive us our debts,"— *Matt.* 6 : 12.
a	19– 8	the divine Principle of *J·* teachings,
	19–19	will help us to understand *J·* atonement
	20– 8	*J·* history made a new calendar,
	24–23	Does spiritualism find *J·* death necessary
	25– 4	The efficacy of *J·* spiritual offering is
	26–21	*J·* teaching and practice of Truth involved
	27–17	*J·* parables explain Life as never mingling with
	27–29	*J·* persecutors made their strongest attack
	28– 2	they only hindered the success of *J·* mission.
	30– 5	*J·* advent in the flesh partook partly of
	33– 1	this supper closed forever *J·* ritualism
	37–16	When will *J·* professed followers learn
	42– 1	*J·* life proved, . . . that God is Love,
	43– 3	The magnitude of *J·* work,
	43–11	*J·* last proof was the highest,
	43–16	*J·* persecutors had mocked and
	45– 7	*J·* deed was for the enlightenment of men
	45–32	*J·* students, not sufficiently advanced
	46–20	*J·* unchanged physical condition after
	47– 2	discernment of *J·* teachings and
	47–14	people were in doubt concerning *J·* teachings.
	48–27	acquiescence with the demands of *J·* enemies.
	50– 7	wrung from *J·* lips the awful cry,
	50–22	Even what they did say,— that *J·* teachings
	54–12	the inspiration of *J·* intense human sacrifice.
m	56– 4	*J·* concessions . . . to material methods
sp	75–22	you can then exercise *J·* spiritual power
s	117–27	feebly transmits *J·* works and words.
	131–29	*J·* works established his claim
	132–16	*J·* system of healing received no aid . . . from
	141– 5	Few understand or adhere to *J·* divine precepts
	142–18	As in *J·* time, so to-day, tyranny and pride
	147– 3	divine Principle, upon which *J·* healing was
f	210– 6	are set forth in *J·* demonstrations,
c	266–24	Mortals must follow *J·* sayings
b	269– 5	*J·* demonstrations sift the chaff from the wheat,
	272–13	*J·* parable of "the sower"— *Mark* 4 : 14.
	312–31	*J·* spiritual origin and his demonstration
	315–21	*J·* spiritual origin and understanding
	317–12	blessed benedictions rest upon *J·* followers :
	324–20	but a persecutor of *J·* followers.
	328–28	*J·* promise is perpetual.
o	343–25	those apostles who were *J·* students,
	360–31	on the very basis of *J·* words and works.
p	363– 4	she perfumed *J·* feet with the oil,
	369–11	All these deeds manifested *J·* control
	382–10	receive a useful rebuke from *J·* precept,
	428– 4	demonstration of the facts of Soul in *J·* way
t	446–22	enthrones faith in Truth, and verifies *J·* word :
r	494– 7	God, who needed no help from *J·* example
	497–13	We acknowledge *J·* atonement
ap	573–32	When you read this, remember *J·* words.
	576–16	Revelator was familiar with *J·* use of this word,
gl	598–10	In the record of *J·* supposed death, we read :

Jew

sp	85–23	Both *J·* and Gentile may have had acute
o	360–30	while to-day, *J·* and Christian can unite in
	360–32	The *J·* believes that the Messiah or Christ
	361– 6	The *J·* who believes in the First Commandment
	361– 7	Thus the *J·* unites with the Christian's doctrine

jewel

m	66– 5	Wears yet a precious *j·* in his head.

Jewess
ap 566–13 Rebecca the *J·* in the story of Ivanhoe,
Jewish
a 32–11 used on convivial occasions and in *J·* rites,
42– 3 *J·* theology gave no hint of the unchanging love
s 133–25 one of the *J·* accusations against him who
133–29 The *J·* conception of God, as Yawah,
140–23 *J·* tribal Jehovah was a man-projected God,
o 350–31 In *J·* worship the Word was materially explained,
r 466–23 Heathen mythology and *J·* theology have
ap 576–28 expresses the *J·* concept, not yet elevated to
gl 596–29 *J·* women wore veils over their faces
Jew's
o 361–11 Thus he virtually unites with the *J·* belief
Jews
a 32– 7. Among the *J·* it was an ancient custom
sp 70– * *Then said the J· unto him,— John* 8 : 52.
s 135–18 danger of repeating the offence of the *J·*
b 314–10 The *J·*, who sought to kill this man of God,
o 352– 7 the *J·* took a diametrically opposite view.
360–28 the *J·* put to death the Galilean Prophet,
Job (*see also* **Job's**)
s 115– 8 *J·* says : "The ear trieth words,— *Job* 34 : 3.
c 262–17 *J·* said : "I have heard of Thee— *Job* 42 : 5.
b 320–30 is continually quoted as if *J·* intended
321– 3 as may be seen by studying the book of *J·*.
o 360–22 Hear the wisdom of *J·*, as given in the
p 411– 1 Said *J·* : "The thing which I greatly— *Job* 3 : 25.
g 552–14 corresponds with that of *J·*, when he says,
Job's
c 262–19 Mortals will echo *J·* thought, when the
John (*see also* **St. John** *and* **Apostle John**)
a 36–12 He was forsaken by all save *J·*,
p 373–17 declare, through the exalted thought of *J·*,
t 459– 3 Paul and *J·* had a clear apprehension that,
g 525–17 In the Gospel of *J·*, it is declared that
ap 561–13 To *J·*, "the bride" and— *Rev.* 21 : 9.
561–16 *J·* saw the human and divine coincidence,
562– 1 *J·* saw in those days the spiritual idea
574–11 carried *J·* away in spirit.
576–19 *J·* saw heaven and earth
John's
gl 598– 2 as in the passage in *J·* Gospel,
John
the Baptist
a 27– 1 Jesus sent a message to *J·* the Baptist,
s 132–28 Did the doctrines of *J·* the Baptist confer
136–15 "Some say that thou art *J·* the Baptist ;— *Matt.* 16 : 14.
ap 558–19 prophetically described by *J·* the Baptist
561–32 *J·* the Baptist prophesied the coming of

---

a 27– 3 "Go your way, and tell *J·*— *Luke* 7 : 22.
27– 7 In other words : Tell *J·* what the
m 56– 2 came to him for baptism, *J·* was astounded.
s 132– 5 "Go and show *J·* again— *Matt.* 11 : 4.
136–19 believed that . . . the spirit of *J·* or of Elias.
136–27 "*J·* have I beheaded :— *Luke* 9 : 9.
John's
s 131–31 In reply to *J·* inquiry,
133– 3 Was *J·* faith greater than that of the
Johnson, Dr. James
s 163– 6 Dr. James *J·*, Surgeon to
join
s 122–17 sky and tree-tops apparently *j·* hands,
joined
m 56– * *What therefore God hath j·— Matt.* 19 : 6.
60–14 what she hath not *j·* together.
joining
b 339–15 He is *j·* in a conspiracy against himself,
joint
s 160–31 Is a stiff *j·* or a contracted muscle
p 408–22 A dislocation of the tarsal *j·* would produce
408–24 the tarsal *j·* is less intimately connected with
joints
s 162–21 ankylosed *j·* have been made supple,
p 402– 6 dislocated *j·*, and spinal vertebræ.
418–30 inflammation, pain, deformed *j·*,
423–13 searches "the *j·* and marrow,"— *Heb.* 4 : 12.
Jona
s 137–28 common names, Simon Bar-jona, or son of *J·* ;
Jordan
s 135– 2 Thou *J·*, that thou wast driven— *Psal.* 114 : 5.
Joseph
r 482–17 Son of man," but not the son of *J·*.— *Matt.* 9 : 6.
gl 589–19 definition of

Joshua
a 29–18 the name of Jesus— that is, *J·*, or Saviour.
s 139– 7 Moses proved the . . . so did *J·*, Elijah, and
b 333– 7 it is identical with the name *J·*,
jot
pref ix– 1 She also began to *j·* down her thoughts
f 239– 6 which weigh not one *j·* in the balance of God,
jottings
pref ix– 2 these *j·* were only infantile lispings
journeyed
sp 85–15 as he once *j·* with his students,
journeying
a 21–16 If . . . we are not *j·* together.
ap 574– 4 adapted to console the weary pilgrim, *j·*
joy (*see also* **joy's**)
affords us
ph 194–31 The light which affords us *j·* gave him a belief of
and sorrow
f 246– 2 *j·* and sorrow, sickness and health,
c 262–22 the false estimate of . . . *j·* and sorrow,
and strength
p 365–31 is not giving to mind or body the *j·* and strength
bringing
p 435–13 but good deeds are immortal, bringing *j·*
is spiritual
c 265–29 quickly inform us . . . that *j·* is spiritual.
life and
g 536–25 material conception of life and *j·*,
light or
g 548–12 Earth has little light or *j·* for mortals before
new pinions to
m 58– 3 Unity of spirit gives new pinions to *j·*,
not the master of
b 304–12 for sorrow is not the master of *j·* ;
of its presence
ph 175–10 The *j·* of its presence, its beauty and fragrance,
or grief
p 377–15 A sudden *j·* or grief has caused
promised
ap 566– 6 and anticipating the promised *j·*,
sinless
sp 76–22 The sinless *j·*,— the perfect harmony
sorrow and
s 125–14 pain and painlessness; sorrow and *j·*,
source of
p 377– 4 affliction is often the source of *j·*,
spiritual
c 265–24 gained stronger desires for spiritual *j·*
sunshine of
m 66– 8 We do not half remember this in the sunshine of *j·*
turned into
pr 14–17 Sorrow is turned into *j·* when the body is
with
a 21–14 at last he finishes his course with *j·*.
o 359–23 In childhood, she often listened with *j·* to

sp 72–28 *j·* of intercourse becomes the jest of sin, when
an 106–27 fruit of the Spirit is love, *j·*,— *Gal.* 5 : 22.
f 248–16 Is it imperfection, *j·*, sorrow, sin, suffering?
b 298–20 *j·* is no longer a trembler, nor is hope a cheat.
304–11 *j·* cannot be turned into sorrow,
324– 3 and *j·* to see them disappear,
ap 562–26 remembering no more her sorrow for *j·* that the
575–23 the *j·* of the whole earth,— *Psal.* 48 : 2.
joyful
pref xii–24 *j·* to bear consolation to the sorrowing
a 34–31 *j·* meeting on the shore of the Galilean Sea !
joyfully
g 521–10 *j·* acknowledging now and forever
joyous
g 514– 6 Mind, *j·* in strength, dwells in the realm of
joy's
m 58– 3 or else *j·* drooping wings trail in dust.
joys
additional
m 58–15 With additional *j·*, benevolence should grow
and its
b 299–11 to higher ideals of life and its *j·*.
and sorrows
gl 587–23 motives, affections, *j·*, and sorrows.
and triumphs
a 41– 4 must come through the *j·* and triumphs of the
and victories
a 39– 9 trials and self-denials, as well as *j·* and victories,
fancied
f 252–28 says : . . . all my fancied *j·* are fatal.
fleeting
f 241– 7 Sin breaks in. . .and carries off their fleeting *j·*.
human
m 66–18 remember how fleeting are human *j·*.
of Soul
p 390–11 pleasures and pains of sense for the *j·* of Soul.

joys
  of Spirit
    m 66–14   Love propagates anew the higher *j·* of Spirit,
    f 242– 7   a great step towards the *j·* of Spirit,
  personal
    c 266–11   even if you cling to a sense of personal *j·*,
  supposed
    g 536–21   Their supposed *j·* are cheats.
  your
    p 397–11   as directly as you enhance your *j·*

Juda
    g 514–10   "the lion of the tribe of *J·*," — *Rev.* 5 : 5.

Judæa
    s 147–13   practised these rules on the hills of *J·*

Judah
    gl 589–23   definition of

Judah's
    ap 566–21   And oh, when stoops on *J·* path

Judaic
    s 140–19   *J·* and other rituals are but types and
    gl 597– 3   *J·* religion consisted mostly of rites and

Judaism
    s 133–19   *J·* was the antithesis of Christianity,
    133–20   *J·* engendered the limited form of

Judas
    a 47–10   *J·* conspired against Jesus.
    47–17   distance between *J·* and his Master.
    48–17   *J·* had the world's weapons.
    c 260– 6   while holding in thought the character of *J·*.
    g 554–21   This he said of *J·*, one of Adam's race.

Judas Iscariot
    a 47–17   *J· I·* knew this.

Judas'
    a 47–20   this spiritual distance inflamed *J·* envy.

Judge (*see also* **Judge's**)
    p 432–16   The *J·* asked if by doing good to his neighbor,
    433–13   As the *J·* proceeds, the prisoner grows restless.
    437– 9   before the *J·* of our higher tribunal,
    442– 4   "Shall not the *J·* of all the earth — *Gen.* 18 : 25.

judge
    an 105– 3   Courts and juries *j·* and sentence mortals
    b 299–21   Ought we not then to *j·* the knowledge
    o 344–18   the Scriptural precept, "*J·* not." — *Matt.* 7 : 1.
    p 391– 5   delivered to the judgment of Truth, Christ, the *j·* will
    391–23   your adversary will deliver you to the *j·*
    391–24   and the *j·* will sentence you.
    404– 1   in order to *j·* the case according to C. S.
    405–12   They will deliver you to the *j·*, the arbiter of
    405–13   The *j·* will deliver you to justice,
    435–30   "Sittest thou to *j·* — *Acts* 23 : 3.
    t 443–12   "*J·* not, that ye be not judged." — *Matt.* 7 : 1.
    444–18   "*j·* righteous judgment," — *John* 7 : 24.
    459– 8   *J·* not the future advancement of C. S. by the
    g 523– 1   might so *j·* from an unintelligent perusal of

judged
    f 239– 9   let worth be *j·* according to wisdom,
    t 443–13   "Judge not, that ye be not *j·*." — *Matt.* 7 : 1.

Judge Justice
    p 437–28   *J· J·* of the Supreme Court of Spirit

Judge Medicine
    p 430–24   and *J· M·* is on the bench.
    433– 2   *J· M·* arises, and with great solemnity
    433– 8   *J· M·*, urges the jury not to allow their
    433–18   *J· M·* then proceeds to pronounce the
    435–28   what jurisdiction had his Honor, *J· M·*,
    435–33   neither shall *J· M·* condemn him ;
    436–26   *J· M·* sat in judgment on the case,

Judge's
    p 433–26   "May God have mercy . . . the *J·* solemn

judges
    b 296–26   Mortal mind *j·* by the testimony of the
    p 434–11   Witnesses, *j·*, and jurors, who were
    439–28   witnesses, jurors, and *j·*, to be offenders,

judging
    s 157– 2   C. S. . . . in *j·* and destroying disease.
    f 204–19   *J·* them by their fruits, they are corrupt.
    t 447– 9   may render you incapable of knowing or *j·*

judgment
  by which
    b 291–30   the *j·* by which mortal man is divested of
  deluded the
    s 121–21   deluded the *j·* and induced false conclusions.
  misguide the
    f 206–1   else it will misguide the *j·*
  mistaken in
    t 455–19   may be mistaken in *j·* and demonstration,
  no final
    b 291–28   No final *j·* awaits mortals,

judgment
  of Truth
    p 391– 5   when thou art delivered to the *j·* of Truth,
  pass
    o 345–17   well enough to pass *j·* upon them.
  righteous
    t 444–18   "judge righteous *j·*," — *John* 7 : 24.
  sat in
    p 436–26   Judge Medicine sat in *j·* on the case,
  their
    p 433– 8   not to allow their *j·* to be warped
    an 106–15   Let this age, which sits in *j·* on C. S.,
    s 128–28   and not upon the *j·* of false sensation.

judgment-day
    b 291–28   the *j·* of wisdom comes hourly

judicial
    p 437–26   was overthrowing the *j·* proceedings of

jugular
    s 122–24   the severance of the *j·* vein

juices
    ph 175–24   was not so severe upon the gastric *j·*.

jungle
    p 378–12   sent it cowering back into the *j·*.

juries
    an 105– 3   Courts and *j·* judge and sentence mortals

jurisdiction
    an 105– 6   To say that these tribunals have no *j·*
    105–12   over which courts hold *j·*?
    f 218–16   believing . . . that the divine Mind has no *j·*,
    p 379– 6   The real *j·* of the world is in Mind,
    435–28   what *j·* had his Honor, Judge Medicine,
    435–31   The only *j·* to which the prisoner can submit

Jurisprudence
    p 437–23   Physiology, Scholastic Theology, and *J·*

jurisprudence
    p 441–32   Our great Teacher of mental *j·* speaks of him

juror
    f 238–25   Society is a foolish *j·*, listening only to

jurors
    p 434–12   Witnesses, judges, and *j·*, who were at the
    437–11   and before its *j·*, the Spiritual Senses,
    439–28   witnesses, *j·*, and judges, to be offenders,
    441–27   personal *j·* in the Court of Error

Jury
    p 442– 5   The *J·* of Spiritual Senses agreed at once

jury
    p 430–24   Greed and Ingratitude, constitute the *j·*.
    433– 3   addresses the *j·* of Mortal Minds.
    433– 8   Judge Medicine, urges the *j·* not to allow
    433–10   The *j·* must regard in such cases only
    433–15   The case is given to the *j·*.
    433–16   and the *j·* returns a verdict of
    436–27   charged the *j·*, twelve Mortal Minds,

just
    a 36–31   in the suffering of the *j·* for the unjust.
    40–17   Was it *j·* for Jesus to suffer?
    47–11   ingratitude and hatred towards that *j·* man
    52–11   the world's hatred of the *j·* and perfect Jesus,
    s 126–23   *j·* as I have discovered them.
    164– 9   It is *j·* to say that generally the
    ph 168–14   through *j·* this false belief.
    193– 4   had *j·* probed the ulcer on the hip,
    193–30   the case, occurred *j·* as I have narrated.
    f 251–12   works out the nothingness of error in *j·* these
    b 321– 1   an interpretation which is *j·* the opposite of
    o 344–17   it would be *j·* to observe the
    348– 9   one disease can be *j·* as much a delusion as another.
    360–24   Shall mortal man be more *j·* than — *Job* 4 : 17.
    p 372–28   a *j·* acknowledgment of Truth
    376– 6   *J·* so is it with the greatest sin.
    391–27   be *j·* to yourself and to others.
    402– 3   However, it is but *j·* to say that
    402–24   illustrates the fact *j·* stated.
    411– 6   *j·* as a person replies more readily when
    425– 3   You will have humors, *j·* so long as
    435–23   no demand, . . . renders it *j·* to punish a man for
    440–30   I appeal to the *j·* and equitable decisions of
    t 443– *   *teach a j· man, and he will* — *Prov.* 9 : 9.
    445–31   when I remember that God is *j·*,"
    453–24   treat sickness mentally *j·* as you would sin,
    r 493–23   *j·* as it removes any other sense of
    497–27   and to be merciful, *j·*, and pure.
    g 522–28   Scripture *j·* preceding declares God's work to

Justice
    p 434–13   before the bar of *J·* and eternal Truth.
    437– 9   in the presence of divine *J·*,
    440–34   the Chief *J·* of the Supreme Court,

justice

and affection
gl 592–13   the union of *j·* and affection,
and love
a 50–10   would impugn the *j·* and love of a father
approves
a 22–31   cancels the debt only when *j·* approves.
avoidance of
g 542–11   avoidance of *j·* and the denial of truth
common
o 357– 1   In common *j·*, we must admit that God
consigns the lie
g 542–24   To envy's own hell, *j·* consigns the lie
defies
an 105– 9   while mortal mind, . . . defies *j·* and is
demands
gl 592–14   *j·* demands penalties under the law.
demonstrating
f 224–23   demonstrating *j·* and meeting the needs of
denying
p 434–32   Denying *j·* to the body, that court
divine
a 105–25   Divine *j·* will manacle him.
f 225–18   breathing the omnipotence of divine *j·*,
b 293–25   The manifestations of evil, which counterfeit divine *j·*,
hands of
p 432–27   hands of *j·*, *alias* nature's so-called law ;
honesty and
an 106– 4   against the free course of honesty and *j·*,
human
g 542–20   let human *j·* pattern the divine.
law and
p 434– 5   Some exclaim, "It is contrary to law and *j·*."
law of
pr 5–10   there is no discount in the law of *j·*
a 36–20   the immortal law of *j·* as well as of mercy.
marks the sinner
g 542–22   *J·* marks the sinner, and teaches mortals
mercy and
g 538– 7   Radiant with mercy and *j·*, the sword of Truth

justice

outraged
p 440–17   Wherefore, then, in the name of outraged *j·*,
requires
a 22–30   *J·* requires reformation of the sinner.
sense of
p 390–14   Let your higher sense of *j·* destroy the false
timid
f 238–29   To reconstruct timid *j·* and place the fact
to Christian Science
s 141–29   Let our pulpits do *j·* to C. S.
to himself
a 18– 7   not only in *j·* to himself, but in mercy to
to Truth
b 280– 9   Finite belief can never do *j·* to Truth
uniform
m 64– 1   Want of uniform *j·* is a crying evil caused by

———

a 36– 9   since *j·* is the handmaid of mercy.
f 238–26   *J·* often comes too late to secure a verdict.
248–29   unselfishness, goodness, mercy, *j·*,
p 391–17   *J·* is the moral signification of law.
405–13   The judge will deliver you to *j·*,
440–11   but no warping of *j·* can render
r 465–14   The attributes of God are *j·*, mercy,
gl 595– 3   SWORD. The idea of Truth ; *j·*.

justifiable
p 440–15   Even penal law holds homicide, . . . to be *j·*.

justification
f 203–10   was really the *j·* of Jesus,
p 436–13   Such acts bear their own *j·*,
440–15   Now what greater *j·* can any deed have,

justified
b 317–10   "wisdom is *j·* of her children."— *Matt.* 11 : 19.
t 456–10   a reputation experimentally *j·* by their

justly
p 435–23   to punish a man for acting *j·*.
436–24   from the penalty they considered *j·* due,

K

Kaspar
ph 194–17   The authentic history of *K·* Hauser
194–24   at the age of seventeen *K·* was still a

keep
pr 4– 5   To *k·* the commandments of our Master
4–11   *k·* my commandments."— *John* 14 : 15.
a 25–20   *k·* my commandments."— *John* 14 : 15.
29– 5   If they *k·* the faith, they will have the crown
m 64– 6   *k·* himself unspotted from the— *Jas.* 1 : 27.
69–20   "Do you *k·* the First Commandment?
sp 70– *   *If a man k· my saying,— John 8 : 51.*
f 217–12   "If a man *k·* my saying,— *John* 8 : 51.
234–17   If mortals would *k·* proper ward over
237–19   *k·* out of the minds of your children
241–21   *k·* my commandments."— *John* 14 : 15.
b 340– 8   and *k·* His commandments :— *Eccl.* 12 : 13.
340–10   love God and *k·* His commandments :
o 360–10   replies : . . . and *k·* Soul well out of sight.
p 371–21   nor would I *k·* the suckling a lifelong babe.
383–19   to *k·* the body in proper condition.
396–26   *K·* distinctly in thought that man is the
413–23   to *k·* it sweet as the new-blown flower.
414–26   *K·* in mind the verity of being,
428– 8   "If a man *k·* my saying,— *John* 8 : 51.
429–31   "If a man *k·* my saying,— *John* 8 : 51.
438– 7   "If a man *k·* my saying,— *John* 8 : 51.
441– 7   but be enjoined to *k·* perpetual silence.
t 458–17   the author desires to *k·* it out of C. S.
r 492–31   theory would *k·* truth and error always at war.
g 514–18   and *k·* pace with highest purpose.
526–28   to dress it and to *k·* it.— *Gen.* 2 : 15.
527– 3   to dress it and *k·* it,— to make it beautiful
537– 7   to *k·* the way of the tree of life.— *Gen.* 3 : 24.
ap 558– *   *k· those things which are written— Rev.* 1 : 3.

keeper
g 541–21   Am I my brother's *k·*?— *Gen.* 4 : 9.

keeping
m 60–31   more secure in our *k·*, if sought in Soul.
ph 189–30   *k·* always in the direct line of matter,
b 308– 4   God, and *k·* His commandment?"
p 413–17   only for the purpose of *k·* the body clean,
g 521– 9   in the *k·* of Spirit, not matter,

keeps
pr 5– 1   *k·* him from demonstrating his power
p 439– 4   He manufactures for it, *k·* a furnishing store,

kept
a 21– 3   I have *k·* the faith,"— *II Tim.* 4 : 7.
m 59–28   so long as its moral obligations are *k·* intact ;

kept
m 62– 2   The fœtus must be *k·* mentally pure
s 109–13   *k·* aloof from society, and devoted time and
f 222–18   he had been *k·* alive, as was believed, only by
237–16   *k·* from discussing or entertaining theories
p 387– 3   Because mortal mind is *k·* active, must it

key
sp 99–10   Truth has furnished the *k·* to the kingdom,
99–10   and with this *k·* C. S. has opened the door of the
ph 171– 6   man will reopen with the *k·* of divine Science
k 499– *   *He that hath the k· of David,— Rev.* 3 : 7.
gl 579– *   *He that hath the k· of David,— Rev.* 3 : 7.

keynote
f 226– 7   sounded the *k·* of universal freedom,
240–13   and you lose the *k·* of being,
p 410–30   begins with Christ's *k·* of harmony,

keynotes
o 355–29   are God's immortal *k·*,

KEY TO THE SCRIPTURES
o 361–32   SCIENCE AND HEALTH WITH *K·* TO THE *S·*.

kid
g 514–23   leopard shall lie down with the *k·* ;— *Isa.* 11 : 6.

kill
a 27–32   endeavored . . . to *k·* him according to certain
51–11   Nothing could *k·* this Life of man.
m 56–20   "Thou shalt not *k·*."— *Exod.* 20 : 13.
s 151–22   The human mind has no power to *k·*
159– 4   protested . . . and said it would *k·* her,
f 203–26   and will continue to *k·* him so long as he sins.
203–31   does not *k·* a man in order to give him
216– 7   Error bites the heel of truth, but cannot *k·* truth.
b 294–14   error, saying : . . . matter can *k·* man."
314–10   The Jews, who sought to *k·* this man of God,
p 388–10   thought that they could *k·* the body with matter,
389–15   and then discuss the certainty that food can *k·*
395–30   The knowledge that brain-lobes cannot *k·*
402–17   You say that accidents, . . . and disease *k·*
t 445– 5   who attempts to *k·* morally and
g 542– 2   incurs divine displeasure, and it would *k·* Jesus
542–17   lest any finding him should *k·* him.— *Gen.* 4 : 15.
ap 564– 6   incites mortals to *k·* morally and

killed
a 42–24   Let men think they had *k·* the body !
f 215–32   would have *k·* the venerable philosopher
b 316–16   belief, . . . that the spiritual idea could be *k·*
ap 567–10   dragon warreth not long, for he is *k·* by
567–29   detected and *k·* by innocence, the Lamb of Love.

killeth

a 31–31 that whosoever *k·* you will think — *John* 16 : 2.

kills

f 203–26 Sin *k·* the sinner and will continue to
r 468– 4 sin is mortality's self, because it *k·* itself.

kind

after his
g 507–13 yielding fruit after his *k·*, — *Gen.* 1 : 11.
508–10 herb yielding seed after his *k·*, — *Gen.* 1 : 12.
508–11 seed was in itself, after his *k·* : — *Gen.* 1 : 12.
512– 7 every winged fowl after his *k·* : — *Gen.* 1 : 21.
513–15 the living creature after his *k·*, — *Gen.* 1 : 24.
513–16 beast of the earth after his *k·* : — *Gen.* 1 : 24.
513–23 beast of the earth after his *k·*, — *Gen.* 1 : 25.
513–24 upon the earth after his *k·* : — *Gen.* 1 : 25.
after its
ph 180–10 seed within itself bearing fruit after its *k·*,
after their
g 512– 6 abundantly, after their *k·*, — *Gen.* 1 : 21.
513–23 and cattle after their *k·*, — *Gen.* 1 : 25.
another
a 23–25 Another *k·* of faith understands divine Love
any
sp 95–11 Error of any *k·* cannot hide from the law of
p 393–20 as the result of a law of any *k·*,
406–26 Inharmony of any *k·* involves
every
a 23–19 Spirit, which rebukes sin of every *k·*
s 143– 1 Truth is God's remedy for error of every *k·*,
323– 4 in the endeavor to forsake error of every *k·*
p 394–26 to conquer discord of every *k·* with harmony,
his own
g 528–26 supposed to become the basis . . . of his own *k·*,
human
m 56– 8 moral provision for generation among human *k·*.
one
a 23–24 One *k·* of faith trusts one's welfare to others.
this
sp 95–16 This *k·* of mind-reading is not clairvoyance,

t 444–14 are advised . . . to be charitable and *k·*,
g 508–17 *Gender* means simply *k·* or *sort*,
528–27 calling them *mankind*, — that is, a *k·* of man.
529– 1 bringing forth fruit of its own *k·*,
544–20 facts of creation, . . . include nothing of the *k·*.

kinder

f 220–14 *k·* than the atmosphere of mortal mind,

kindling

p 434–18 earnest, solemn eyes, *k·* with hope

kindly

s 162–29 I *k·* quote from Dr. Benjamin Rush,
f 221–13 the doctors, who *k·* informed him that
gl 594–14 *k·* affection ; love rebuking error ;

kindness

pr 9–11 If selfishness has given place to *k·*,
p 384– 8 for honest labor, for deeds of *k·*,
405– 6 to hold hatred in abeyance with *k·*,

kindred

m 60– 4 *K·* tastes, motives, and aspirations are

King

ap 575–24 the city of the great *K·*." — *Psal.* 48 : 2.

king

s 133–30 Jehovah, or only a mighty hero and *k·*,
136–21 That a wicked *k·* and debauched husband should
144– 6 Naught is the squire, when the *k·* is nigh ;
b 289–15 the "*k·* of terrors" to be but a — *Job* 18 : 14.
g 514–11 Moral courage is . . . the *k·* of the mental realm.

kingdom

animal
g 529–24 nothing in the animal *k·* which represents
divided
o 354–27 It is in itself inconsistent, a divided *k·*.
p 388–19 "*k·* divided against itself," — *Matt.* 12 : 25.
389–17 and the *k·* divided against itself,
gl 581–17 BABEL. . . . a *k·* divided against itself,
God's
f 202–19 when God's *k·* comes on earth ;
b 339–24 until . . . God's *k·* comes
heavenly
s 130–25 such as they belong to the heavenly *k·*.
His
m 56–10 Until . . . His *k·* is come as in the vision
his
ap 565–15 "of his *k·* there shall be no end," — *Luke* 1 : 33.
key to the
sp 99–10 Truth has furnished the key to the *k·*,
of God
a 18– * *until the k· of God shall come.* — *Luke* 22 : 18.
20– 8 into the *k·* of God before you." — *Matt.* 21 : 31.
an 106–26 shall not inherit the *k·* of God. — *Gal.* 5 : 21.
b 321– 4 cannot inherit the *k·* of God." — *I Cor.* 15 : 50.
p 382–22 receive the *k·* of God as a — *Luke* 18 : 17.
r 476–29 "The *k·* of God is within you ;" — *Luke* 17 : 21.

kingdom

of God
r 477– 4 Jesus taught that the *k·* of God is intact,
ap 573–32 "The *k·* of God is within you." — *Luke* 17 : 21.
576–21 This *k·* of God "is within — *Luke* 17 : 21.
of heaven
sp 93–31 to becloud our apprehension of the *k·* of heaven
s 107– * *k· of heaven is like unto leaven,* — *Matt.* 13 : 33.
110–11 establishment of the *k·* of heaven on earth.
122– 6 and reveal the *k·* of heaven,
ph 174–19 proclaiming the *k·* of heaven on earth.
f 208–22 the reign of Spirit, the *k·* of heaven,
241–32 to enter the *k·* of heaven,
248–30 love — the *k·* of heaven
o 361–26 though least in the *k·* of heaven,
ap 560–14 constitutes the *k·* of heaven in man.
gl 592–19 the *k·* of heaven, or reign of harmony.
of our God
ap 568–15 and the *k·* of our God, — *Rev.* 12 : 10.
of Truth
b 281– 2 we enter into the *k·* of Truth on earth
represent a
s 118–27 represent a *k·* necessarily divided against itself,
that
f 252– 2 that *k·* cannot stand." — *Mark* 3 : 24.
Thy
pr 16–30 Thy *k·* come. — *Matt.* 6 : 10.
16–31 *Thy k· is come ; Thou art ever-present.*

pr 17–12 For thine is the *k·*, — *Matt.* 6 : 13.
a 40–32 but in order to enter into the *k·*,
m 66–10 Through great tribulation we enter the *k·*.
an 102–32 C. S. despoils the *k·* of evil,
f 252– 2 If a *k·* be divided against itself, — *Mark* 3 : 24.
252–25 and says : . . . The world is my *k·*,
p 442–28 to give you the *k·*." — *Luke* 12 : 32.
t 454–10 hate has no legitimate mandate and no *k·*.

Kingdom of Heaven

gl 590– 1 definition of

King of England

s 163– 6 William IV, *K· of E·*,

kings

s 141–12 as *k·* are crowned from a royal dynasty.
141–20 "*k·* and priests unto God." — *Rev.* 1 : 6.

kings'

s 133–18 in the fiery furnace and in *k·* palaces.

kinship

b 319– 2 delusion . . . has no *k·* with the Life supernal.

kitten

f 220–19 like a *k·* glancing into the mirror at itself
220–21 thinking it sees another *k·*.

knavish

ph 173–22 Phrenology makes man *k·* or honest according

knelt

s 161–21 Madame Roland, as she *k·* before a statue of

knew

a 20–10 He *k·* that men can be baptized, . . . and yet be
20–14 he *k·* the error of mortal belief,
47–18 Judas Iscariot *k·* this.
47–18 He *k·* that the great goodness of that Master
47–22 He *k·* that the world generally loves a
49– 2 They *k·* what had inspired their devotion,
51–15 He *k·* that matter had no life
53–25 He *k·* the mortal errors which constitute the
m 68–16 I never *k·* more than one individual who
sp 85–16 Jesus, . . . "*k·* their thoughts," — *Matt.* 12 : 25.
85–24 Jesus *k·* the generation to be wicked and
85–30 The great Teacher *k·* both cause and effect,
85–31 *k·* that truth communicates itself
86– 4 Jesus *k·*, . . . that it was not matter,
s 109–16 I *k·* the Principle . . . to be God,
134–26 "I *k·* that Thou hearest me — *John* 11 : 42.
ph 186–29 If mortal mind *k·* how to be better, it would be
p 213–22 He was a musician beyond what the world *k·*.
221– 1 I *k·* a person who when quite a child
247– 4 A woman of eighty-five, whom I *k·*,
b 270–17 But they *k·* not what would be the
271– 8 He *k·* that the philosophy, Science, and proof of
286–13 He *k·* that the divine Principle, Love, creates
315– 6 He *k·* of but one Mind
315– 7 He *k·* that the Ego was Mind
o 356–15 Jesus *k·*, "It is the spirit — *John* 6 : 63.
357– 3 and *k·* from the outset that man would do.
p 364– 4 one who was soon, though they *k·* it not,
369–21 *k·* that man has not two lives,
374– 8 *k·* nothing about, until it appeared on my body
377–19 author never *k·* a patient who did not
432– 7 testifies : . . . I *k·* the prisoner would commit it,
437– 3 testified that he . . . *k·* Personal Sense to be
437–18 testified . . . that he *k·* Man, and that Man was
g 532–29 body had been naked, and Adam *k·* it not ;
538–23 And Adam *k·* Eve his wife ; — *Gen.* 4 : 1.

knife

t 459–17 like putting a sharp k· into the hands of a

knights

t 457–14 led to a quarrel between two k·

knocking

f 224–24 stands at the door of this age, k· for admission.

knocks

pref vii–14 Truth, . . . k· at the portal of humanity.

know

iii– * Ye shall k· the truth,— *John* 8 : 32.
pref vii–19 Him whom to k· aright is Life eternal.
pr 8–26 do we not already k· more of this heart than
11–22 We k· that a desire for holiness is requisite
11–30 to k· and do the will of God,
17– 2 *Enable us to k·,— as in heaven, so on earth,*
a 19–32 thou shalt not k· evil, for there is one Life,
28– 1 The Pharisees claimed to k· and to teach the
36– 1 They, who k· not purity and affection
m 67– 7 "Do you k· your course?
sp 70– * *Now we k· that thou hast a devil.— John* 8 : 52.
80–20 we already k· that it is mind-power which
84–12 to k· the past, the present, and the future.
84–28 All we correctly k· of Spirit comes from
84–31 we can k· the truth more accurately than the
90–31 At present we k· not what man is,
90–31 certainly shall k· this when man reflects God.
95– 8 in that ratio we k· all human need
s 109–19 I must k· the Science of this healing,
109–30 he shall k· of the doctrine,— *John* 7 : 17.
129– 7 If you wish to k· the spiritual fact,
140– 8 we k· Him as divine Mind,
149–18 "We k· that mind affects the body
151– 9 We k· that if they understood the Science
152– 8 although they k· not how the work is done.
ph 178– 1 though they k· nothing of this particular case
181–27 they generally k· it and are satisfied.
190–26 place thereof shall k· it no more.— *Psal.* 103 : 16.
199–17 To k· whether this development is
200–25 "For I determined not to k·"— *I Cor.* 2 : 2.
200–28 I am determined not to k·
f 217–13 k· we no man after the flesh !"— *II Cor.* 5 : 16.
225– 5 You may k· when first Truth leads by the
231–28 and k· that they are no part of His creation.
237–23 Some invalids are unwilling to k· the facts
238–15 "I k· you not."— *Matt.* 25 : 12.
242– 4 "they shall all k· Me [God],— *Jer.* 31 : 34.
242–10 It is to k· no other reality
253–26 knowing (as you ought to k·)
c 255– * *we k· that the whole creation— Rom.* 8 : 22.
258–16 We k· no more of man as the true
258–17 than we k· of God.
b 284–14 or k· aught unlike the infinite?
291– 5 We k· that all will be changed
317–12 "If the world hate you, ye k· that— *John* 15 : 18.
318– 1 to k· that nothing can efface Mind
323–14 must put into practice what we already k·.
o 342–26 "By their fruits ye shall k· them"— *Matt.* 7 : 20.
345–13 It is indeed no small matter to k· one's self ;
350–10 Then they k· how Truth casts out error
352–14 Would a mother say . . . "I k· that ghosts are
359–14 at length k· yourself spiritually
360– 1 and k· that these ideals are real and eternal
p 365– 1 Did the careless doctor, . . . k· the thorns
365– 4 Oh, did they k· !— this knowledge would
369–19 never gave drugs, never prayed to k· if God
376–20 K· that in Science you cannot
386–15 not to k· that this is so.
387– 2 and k· that there is no death.
389– 6 The less we k· or think about hygiene,
390–22 illegitimate, because you k· that God is
410– 8 that they might k· Thee, the only— *John* 17 : 3.
416–24 The sick k· nothing of the mental process
416–28 tell them only what is best for them to k·.
419–31 k· that disease . . . cannot change forms,
420– 8 to k· that error cannot produce
425–19 and k· that there is nothing to consume,
432– 4 and k· him to be truthful and upright,
438–30 k· Morbid Secretion to be on friendly
t 447–31 but to k· it, he must demonstrate his
448–15 or upon the good you k· and *do* not.
449–13 You should practise well what you k·,
452–18 The teacher must k· the truth himself
453–14 Teach your student that he must k· himself
453–15 before he can k· others
463–19 By this we k· that Truth is here
464– 3 Could her friends k· how little time the author
r 476–27 shall k· it no more."— *Psal.* 103 : 16.
490–17 Our only need is to k· this
492–12 We k· that a statement proved to be good
k 499– * *I k· thy works :— Rev.* 3 : 8.
g 512–13 Their individual forms we k· not,
512–14 we do k· that their natures are allied to God's
519–15 Mortals can never k· the infinite, until
529–29 we k· that they are worthless and unreal.

know

g 530–14 God doth k· that in the day ye eat— *Gen.* 3 : 5.
530–24 saying, . . . I shall k· you, and you will be
536–31 to k· good and evil :— *Gen.* 3 : 22.
540–14 but we ought to k· that God's law
541–20 And he said, I k· not :— *Gen.* 4 : 9.
553–30 before they think or k· aught of their origin,
ap 560–20 The botanist must k· the genus and species
569–10 we k· that the nothingness of error is
570–27 k· the great benefit which Mind has wrought.
570–28 should also k· the great delusion of mortal
571–16 K· thyself, and God will supply the
gl 579– * *I k· thy works :— Rev.* 3 : 8.
fr 600– * *by their fruits ye shall k· them.— Matt.* 7 : 20.

knoweth

pr 1– * *Your Father k· what things ye— Matt.* 6 : 8.
sp 77–15 "k· no man . . . neither the Son,— *Mark* 13 : 32.
f 233–12 How long it must be . . . no man k·,
252–18 says : I am wholly dishonest, and no man k· it.
b 292– 3 of that day and hour, k· no man."— *Matt.* 24 : 36.
g 519– 2 from all eternity k· His own ideas.
ap 568–23 k· that he hath but a short time.— *Rev.* 12 : 12.
569–24 for the devil k· his time is short.

knowing

a 20–21 well k· that to obey the divine order
48–29 k· not that he was hastening the
sp 89– 1 what the unaided medium is incapable of k·
f 201– 3 K· this and k· too that one affection
205– 2 will sin without k· that they are sinning,
210–11 K· that Soul and its attributes were
253–15 K· the falsity of so-called material sense,
253–26 k· (as you ought to know) that God never
b 272– 9 not k· the Scriptures."— *Matt.* 22 : 29.
314–13 k·, as he did, that Mind was the builder,
328–21 k· that there is no material law,
p 363–10 K· what those around him were saying
363–14 k· this, Jesus rebuked them with a short story
366–28 k·, as he does, that Life is God
371–10 not k· why nor when.
409–14 error which prevents mortals from k·
417– 3 sometimes k· more than their doctors.
419– 9 k· that there can be no reaction in Truth.
t 447– 8 incapable of k· or judging accurately the
447–25 by k· that there is none.
448–21 well k· it to be impossible for error,
450–29 K· the claim of animal magnetism,
455–12 and if, k· the remedy, you fail to use
r 489–18 material means for k·, hearing, seeing?
g 509–29 K· the Science of creation,
530– 7 K· this, Jesus once said,
530–16 shall be as gods, k· good and evil.— *Gen.* 3 : 5.
555–30 K· that God was the Life of man,

knowingly

f 253–18 If you believe in and practise wrong k·,

knowledge

according to
pr 7–12 "a zeal . . . not according to k·'"— *Rom.* 10 : 2.
and pleasure
g 532–17 K· and pleasure, evolved through material sense,
belief and
gl 589–12 JERUSALEM. Mortal belief and k·
children in
m 62–17 should be allowed to remain children in k·,
comprised in a
s 127– 7 comprised in a k· or understanding of God,
departments of
ph 197–18 in the departments of k· now broadcast
destitute of any
g 554–10 destitute of any k· of the so-called
554–12 destitute of any k· of its origin
dire effects of
ph 196– 4 from the dire effects of k·.
false
ph 175–30 Adam, before he ate the fruit of false k·,
gl 581–19 The higher false k· builds
fruit of
r 481–12 forbidden fruit of k·, . . . is the testimony of
gained
sp 91–20 destroys the erroneous k· gained from
92–15 a k· gained from matter, or evil, instead of
b 269–27 k· gained through the material senses
274– 3 k· gained from the five senses is only
299–18 K· gained from material sense is
r 490–20 k· gained from the so-called material senses
hath no
g 540–21 a false sense which hath no k· of God."
human
(see **human**)
impertinent
an 103–13 separate from any half-way impertinent k·,
increase of
sp 95–19 We welcome the increase of k· . . . because
judge the
b 299–21 Ought we not then to judge the k·

knowledge

material
(*see* **material**)

materialistic
ph 196– 1 If materialistic *k·* is power, it is not wisdom.

mortal
g 527–17 constitutes evil and mortal *k·*.

obtained
b 296–22 The *k·* obtained from the
r 493– 7 *k·* obtained from physical sense
gl 589–12 Mortal belief and *k·* obtained from

of Christian Science
b 285–28 As mortals reach, through *k·* of C. S.,
t 455–17 receives his *k·* of C. S.,

of error
f 252– 8 A *k·* of error and of its operations must
g 533–26 cross-questioning man as to his *k·* of error,

of evil
g 526–21 erroneous doctrine that the *k·* of evil is as real,
527–14 It is true that a *k·* of evil would
537– 9 A *k·* of evil was never the essence of

of good
g 526–22 as the *k·* of good.

of good and evil
sp 92–14 commending . . . the *k·* of good and evil,
f 220–28 tree of the *k·* of good and evil,"— *Gen.* 2 : 17.
r 481–17 "tree of the *k·* of good and evil,"— *Gen.* 2 : 17.
g 526– 2 the tree of *k·* of good and evil.— *Gen.* 2 : 9.
527– 8 the tree of the *k·* of good and evil,— *Gen.* 2 : 17.

of Love
p 410– 6 the *k·* of Love, Truth, and Life.

of Science
b 286– 6 this is fatal to a *k·* of Science.

of the Science
s 128–14 A *k·* of the Science of being

of this
r 492– 8 It is already proved that a *k·* of this,
g 521– 1 *K·* of this lifts man above the sod,

of Truth
s 128–22 So it is with our *k·* of Truth.

physical
a 46–28 he rose above the physical *k·* of his disciples,

present
p 410– 5 a present *k·* of his Father and of himself,

slight
t 446– 1 teaching his slight *k·* of Mind-power,

so-called
b 312– 2 such so-called *k·* is reversed

this
p 365– 4 this *k·* would do much more
404–24 this *k·* strengthens his moral courage
g 532– 6 Is this *k·* safe, when eating its first fruits

tree of
sp 92–12 a serpent coiled around the tree of *k·*
ph 165– 2 one of the apples from "the tree of *k·*."— *Gen.* 2 : 9.
197– 8 God said of the tree of *k·*, which
f 214–22 like the original "tree of *k·*,"— *Gen.* 2 : 9.
g 526– 2 the tree of *k·* of good and evil.— *Gen.* 2 : 9.
526–20 The "tree of *k·*" stands for the — *Gen.* 2 : 9.
538–14 The "tree of *k·*" typifies — *Gen.* 2 : 9.

true
a 48–31 what the true *k·* of God can do for man.
s 133–31 has not quite given place to the true *k·* of God.
o 358–22 few who have gained a true *k·* of the
r 466– 4 all-science or true *k·*, all-presence.

knowledge

wake to the
f 251– 9 mortals wake to the *k·* of two facts :
———
sp 90–23 This shows what mortal mentality and *k·* are.
an 103–10 a *k·* of both good and evil,
ph 196– 3 not yet found it true that *k·* can
199–19 is of less importance than a *k·* of the fact.
b 279–27 the *k·* that there are not two bases of being,
330–17 a *k·* of it is left either to human conjecture or
p 394– 7 *K·* that we can accomplish the good
395–30 The *k·* that brain-lobes cannot kill
g 519–19 and of the *k·* of the Son of God,— *Eph.* 4 : 13.
gl 590– 4 definition of
592–22 *k·* of the nothingness of material things
595–19 human acts, thoughts, beliefs, opinions, *k·* ;
fr 600– * *increasing in the k· of God.— Col. 1 : 10.*

known

pr 7–26 to whom each need of man is always *k·*
15–26 hidden from the world, but *k·* to God.
a 32– 1 have not *k·* the Father nor me."— *John* 16 : 3.
46– 5 In the walk to Emmaus, Jesus was *k·* to
sp 73–13 belief, which ought to be *k·* by its fruit,
81–31 That somebody, somewhere, must have *k·*
an 106–17 and *k·* by their fruit,
f 227– 2 where . . . the rights of man are fully *k·*
b 284–11 Can Deity be *k·* through the material senses?
284–26 and are *k·* only by the effects
299–22 "the tree is *k·* by his fruit"— *Matt.* 12 : 33.
338–32 revealed in due time, and was *k·* as Christ Jesus.
o 350–25 Divine Truth must be *k·* by its effects
p 367–30 error should be *k·* as nothing.
379–13 Had he *k·* his sense of bleeding was an
398–17 are *k·* to relieve the symptoms of disease.
421– 8 afterwards make *k·* to the patient your motive
426–13 a "tree of life," *k·* by its fruits.— *Rev.* 22 : 2.
439– 2 be it *k·* that False Belief, the counsel for
t 456–31 it was the first book *k·*, containing
464– 3 Why do you not make yourself more widely *k·* ?"
464– 5 in which to make herself outwardly *k·*
g 501– * *by My name Jehovah was I not k·— Exod.* 6 : 3.
556–15 It is made *k·* most fully to him who
gl 596– 5 makes Him better *k·* as the All-in-all,

knows

pr 2–14 for He already *k·* all.
13–15 God *k·* our need before we tell Him
15– 8 He *k·* all things and rewards according to
sp 87–19 The mine *k·* naught of the emeralds within
s 154–30 and says, . . . "Mamma *k·* you are hurt."
ph 180–26 man *k·* that with God all things are possible.
188–30 The human eye *k·* not where the orb of day is,
f 241– 2 He, who *k·* God's will or the demands of
250–10 Ego . . . which never believes, but *k·* ;
b 307–17 Error . . . says : "The Lord *k·* it.
o 345–11 neither *k·* itself nor what it is saying.
p 380–13 defendant *k·* will be turned against himself.
388– 6 only because it *k·* less of material law.
412–31 Scientist *k·* that there can be no hereditary disease,
t 450–24 Scientist *k·* that they are errors of belief,
451–20 *k·* that human will is not C. S.,
r 471– 1 *k·* no lapse from nor return to harmony,
g 523– 5 and finally declares that God *k·* error
557–14 the less a mortal *k·* of sin, disease, and

kurios

gl 590–17 In the Greek, the word *k·* almost always has

L

labor

pr 13–10 If our petitions are sincere, we *l·* for what we
a 21– 5 Christians do not continue to *l·* . . . because of
29– 9 because then our *l·* is more needed.
m 67–26 does not put to silence the *l·* of centuries.
sp 99–22 and shall continue to *l·* and to endure.
f 236– 1 should stimulate clerical *l·* and progress.
242–16 let us *l·* to dissolve with the universal solvent
p 384– 7 for honest *l·*, or for deeds of kindness,
387– 7 we conclude that intellectual *l·*
387–23 cannot suffer as the result of any *l·* of love,
t 457–11 since entering this field of *l·*,
457–20 no excellence without *l·* in a direct line.
r 465– 2 much *l·* and increased spiritual understanding,

labored

t 464–22 has *l·* to expound divine Principle,

laboring

s 130–20 *L·* long to shake the adult's faith in matter
p 386–26 *l·* under the influence of the belief of

laborious

t 464– 5 except through her *l·* publications,

labors

f 238–19 to enter unlawfully into the *l·* of others.
p 385– 3 and other philanthropists engaged in humane *l·*
431– 6 prisoner attended to his daily *l·*,
g 548–26 endowed by the *l·* and genius of great men.

lacerated

a 44–17 bind up the wounded side and *l·* feet,

lachrymal

f 211–15 the effect seen in the *l·* gland?

lack

m 65–16 Beholding the world's *l·* of Christianity
67–25 The *l·* of spiritual power in the
sp 85–20 Our Master rebuked the *l·* of this power
s 140–14 tyrannical and proscriptive from *l·* of love,
145– 5 *l·* of the letter could not hinder their work ;
f 243–14 not so much from *l·* of desire
243–15 as from *l·* of spiritual growth.
b 286–24 temporal thoughts . . . *l·* a divine cause.

lacking

p 365–11 but if the unselfish affections be *l·*,
382– 2 laws of matter, . . . *l·* divine authority
gl 592–14 there is something spiritually *l·*,

lacks
a 19–22 he *l·* the practical repentance, which
s 124– 5 When this human belief *l·* organizations to
p 366–12 The physician who *l·* sympathy for his
366–17 physician *l·* faith in the divine Mind

ladder
f 222– 2 and ascend the *l·* of life.

laden
p 413–26 that mind being *l·* with illusions

laid
pr 8–25 and ask that it may be *l·* bare before us,
a 27–18 He *l·* the axe of Science at the root of
44– 2 before the thorns can be *l·* aside for a crown,
52–15 Herod and Pilate *l·* aside old feuds
sp 92–26 The foundation of evil is *l·* on a belief in
f 234–29 He *l·* great stress on the action of the
237– 8 would have *l·* aside their drugs,
241– 5 *l·* up "where moth and rust doth — Matt. 6 : 19.
b 314–18 the body, which they *l·* in a sepulchre,
315– 6 He knew of but one Mind and *l·* no claim to
o 353–30 from this it follows that whatever is *l·* off is
p 390–17 nor *l·* upon a bed of suffering
409–23 to be *l·* aside for the pure reality.
414– 1 Thus are *l·* the foundations of the belief
t 460– 1 rules . . . as *l·* down in this work,
462–15 and advance from the rudiments *l·* down.

lake
r 477–28 when they called a certain beautiful *l·*

lama
a 51– 1 "*Eloi, Eloi, l· sabachthani ?*"—Mark 15 : 34.

Lamb (see also **Lamb's**)
of God
s 132–32 "the *L·* of God ;"— John 1 : 29.
ap 564–13 The Revelator speaks of Jesus as the *L·* of God
gl 590– 9 definition of
of Love
ap 561–12 bride . . . wedded to the *L·* of Love.
567–30 and killed by innocence, the *L·* of Love.

b 334–21 *L·* slain from the foundation — Rev. 13 : 8.
ap 561–13 the "bride" and "the *L·*"— see Rev. 21 : 14.
567–31 Divine Science shows how the *L·* slays the wolf.
568– 4 evil has tried to slay the *L·* ;
568–18 by the blood of the *L·*,— Rev. 12 : 11.
576–11 and the *L·* are the temple of it.— Rev. 21 : 22.

lamb
a 50– 1 brought as a *l·* to the slaughter,— Isa. 53 : 7.
g 514–22 wolf also shall dwell with the *l·*,— Isa. 11 : 6.
541– 1 A *l·* is a more animate form of existence,
541–11 No ; but the *l·* was a more spiritual type
550–27 nor does a lion bring forth a *l·*.

Lamb's
ap 574– 9 show thee the bride, the *L·* wife.— Rev. 21 : 9.
575– 2 Arise . . . and behold the *L·* wife,
577– 4 The *L·* wife presents the unity of

lambs
s 135– 5 and ye little hills, like *l·* ? — Psal. 114 : 6.

lame
a 27– 4 how that the blind see, the *l·* walk,— Luke 7 : 22.
s 132– 6 and the *l·* walk,— Matt. 11 : 5.
149–22 The logic is *l·*, and facts contradict it.
ph 183–29 voice to the dumb, feet to the *l·*.
f 210–14 hearing to the deaf, feet to the *l·*,
226–25 The *l·* the deaf, the dumb, the blind, the sick,
243–18 dizzy, diseased, consumptive, or *l·*.
c 261–16 This old man was so *l·* that he
o 342–25 causes the deaf to hear, the *l·* to walk,

lameness
f 205– 4 and mortals will . . .stumble with *l·*,

lament
p 386–31 pass from our sight and we *l·*,

lamentation
p 386–32 that *l·* is needless and causeless.

lamps
ap 562–17 *l·* in the spiritual heavens of the age,

Lancet, The
f 245– 4 the London medical magazine called The *L·*.

land
dry
r 491– 1 swimming when he is on dry *l·*.
g 506–17 and let the dry *l·* appear : — Gen. 1 : 9.
506–22 And God called the dry *l·* Earth ; — Gen. 1 : 10.
507– 1 In metaphor, the *dry l·* illustrates
535–30 "And God called the dry *l·* Earth ; — Gen. 1 : 10.
557– 5 how to develop their children properly on dry *l·*.
of bondage
ap 566–16 Out of the *l·* of bondage came,
of Christian Science
f 226–32 the *l·* of C. S., where fetters fall

land
of Nod
g 542–28 and dwelt in the *l·* of Nod.— Gen. 4 : 16.
our
f 226– 1 when African slavery was abolished in our *l·*.
226– 6 was still echoing in our *l·*,
p 404–17 The temperance reform, felt all over our *l·*,

landmarks
b 323– 8 peace, and purity, which are the *l·* of
324– 2 Gladness to leave the false *l·*

landscape
g 516–19 brightens the flower, beautifies the *l·*,

landscape-paintings
sp 86–25 Portraits, *l·*, fac-similes of penmanship,

landscapes
sp 71–14 and you may see *l·*, men, and women.

language
afforded by
t 460–28 through the meagre channel afforded by *l·*
Bible
c 263–17 He might say in Bible *l·* :
p 435–29 To him I might say, in Bible *l·*,
essential
s 117–10 God's essential *l·* is spoken of
human
g 520– 5 Human *l·* can repeat only an infinitesimal part
of Scripture
c 256–20 He who, in the *l·* of Scripture,
of Spirit
s 117– 6 the *l·* of Spirit must be, and is, spiritual.
117–14 nor hath lip spoken, the pure *l·* of Spirit.
of the apostle
g 519–18 till, in the *l·* of the apostle,
of the Master
o 355–10 C. S. says, in the *l·* of the Master,
original
b 319–21 taught in the original *l·* of the Bible
solecism in
s 114–12 Mortal mind is a solecism in *l·*,
strong
pr 6–31 The strong *l·* of our Master confirms this

ph 194–29 And with no *l·* but a cry.
f 210– 3 *l·* which human thought can comprehend.

languages
o 349–15 like all other *l·*, English is inadequate
g 516–31 In one of the ancient *l·* the word for man
525– 8 some of the equivalents . . . in different *l·*.

languidly
p 373–28 *l·* creeps along its frozen channels,

languor
p 373–31 producing the propulsion or the *l·*,

lap
r 494–28 its *l·* piled high with immortal fruits.

lapse
r 470–17 How can good *l·* into evil,
471– 2 knows no *l·* from nor return to harmony,

lapsing
f 248– 7 instead of *l·* into darkness or gloom.
g 540– 3 *l·* into sin, sickness, and death.

large
p 363–16 He described two debtors, one for a *l·* sum and
394– 5 a *l·* majority of doctors depress mental energy,
t 450– 1 There is a *l·* class of thinkers whose bigotry

largely
sp 84–15 to commune more *l·* with the divine Mind,
s 156–32 Homœopathy takes mental symptoms *l·* into
p 439– 5 and advertises *l·* for his employers.

larger
f 248– 6 Men and women of riper years and *l·* lessons

lasciviousness
an 106–21 fornication, uncleanness, *l·*,— Gal. 5 : 19.

lash
f 224–17 modern *l·* is less material than the Roman
239– 2 which endured the *l·* of their predecessors,

last
pr 16–12 whether the *l·* line is not an addition
a 34–29 a contrast between our Lord's *l·* supper and
34–30 his *l·* spiritual breakfast with his disciples
36–25 gloat over their offences to the *l·* moment.
39– 3 endure until Christianity's *l·* triumph.
43–11 Jesus' *l·* proof was the highest,
47–27 desertion of their Master in his *l·* earthly
49–12 O, why did they not gratify his *l·* human
50– 5 *l·* supreme moment of mockery, desertion,
m 63– 1 does not make . . . the superior law of Soul *l·*.
sp 92– 7 From the illusion implied in this *l·* postulate
s 116– 8 *l·* shall be first, and the first *l·*."— Matt. 20 : 16.
117–10 spoken of in the *l·* chapter of Mark's Gospel
153–11 sinking in the *l·* stage of typhoid fever.

last

ph 166–25	and in his extremity and only as a *l·* resort,
177–13	but from first to *l·*, the body is a
184– 7	the penalties it affixes *l·* so long as the
f 207–15	Body is not first and Soul *l·*,
210– 9	"the *l·* enemy that shall be — *I Cor.* 15 : 26.
223–26	but the *l·* trump has not sounded,
249–20	You say, "I dreamed *l·* night."
b 269– 3	From first to *l·* the supposed coexistence
272–11	referred to in the *l·* chapter of Mark's Gospel.
286–13	was put aside from first to *l·*
291– 6	when the *l·* trump shall sound ;
291– 7	this *l·* call of wisdom cannot come till
292– 1	When the *l·* mortal fault is destroyed,
334–26	"I am the first and the *l·* : — *Rev.* 1 : 17.
p 390–17	in payment of the *l·* farthing,
390–18	the *l·* penalty demanded by error.
402– 2	which will be *l·* acknowledged.
405–14	will be manacled until the *l·* farthing is paid,
427–19	"The *l·* enemy that shall be — *I Cor.* 15 : 26.
427–28	Spirit is his *l·* resort, but it should have been
r 466–16	This *l·* statement contains the point you will
466–17	first and *l·* it is the most important to
g 508–22	The Mind . . . names the female gender *l·*
ap 564– 8	This *l·* infirmity of sin will sink its perpetrator
565–19	represented first by man and, . . . *l·* by woman,
572– 3	in both the first and *l·* books of the Bible,
574– 7	full of the seven *l·* plagues, — *Rev.* 21 : 9.
gl 585–24	mortality ; that which does not *l·* forever ;
598–14	common statement, "He breathed his *l·*."

last at —

a 20– 3	He at *l·* paid no homage to
21–14	till at *l·* he finishes his course with joy.
31–20	at *l·* we shall rest, sit down with him, in a
m 65–21	until we get at *l·* the clear straining of truth,
s 125–15	the visible manifestation will at *l·*
ph 166–30	but when Mind at *l·* asserts its mastery
b 295–13	will at *l·* yield to the scientific fact
p 416– 1	At *l·* the agony also vanishes.
431– 8	At *l·* he committed liver-complaint,
g 556–12	only to go out at *l·* forever ;
ap 569–23	comes back to him at *l·* with accelerated force,
569–25	is at *l·* stung to death by his own malice ;
574–22	at *l·* lifted the seer to behold the great city,

lasting

pr 7–10	But does it produce any *l·* benefit?
sp 87–27	The strong impressions . . . are *l·*,
ph 186–29	If we concede . . . discord has as *l·* a claim

lastly

an 104–11	*L·*, they say they have always believed it."

lasts

r 497–12	punished so long as the belief *l·*.

late

m 59–23	After marriage, it is too *l·* to grumble
sp 80– 6	purporting to come from the *l·* Theodore Parker
s 147– 6	*L·* in the nineteenth century I demonstrated
f 238–26	Justice often comes too *l·* to secure a verdict.
b 313–20	in the translation of the *l·* George R. Noyes,
o 360–23	the *l·* Rev. George R. Noyes, D.D.:
g 547– 9	The *l·* Louis Agassiz, by his microscopic

latent

s 128–15	the *l·* abilities and possibilities of man.
ph 168–27	a *l·* illusion of mortal mind,
199–20	*l·* mental fears are subdued by him.
p 376– 4	the *l·* fear and the despair of recovery
377–31	It is *l·* belief in disease,
t 445– 8	Unfold the *l·* energies and capacities
ap 559– 5	upon the sea, — upon elementary, *l·* error,
559–13	stirs their *l·* forces to utter the
gl 597– 8	but cloaked the crime, *l·* in thought,

later

pref ix– 8	*L·*, the tongue voices the more definite
pr 7–32	or mean to ask forgiveness at some *l·* day.
16–13	addition to the prayer by a *l·* copyist ;
a 54– 9	must sooner or *l·* plant themselves in Christ,
55– 7	no more injustice than the *l·* centuries have
f 223– 3	Sooner or *l·* we shall learn that the
240–24	Remember that mankind must sooner or *l·*,
b 296–19	Whether mortals will learn this sooner or *l·*,
o 351– 9	*L·* she learned that her own prayers
p 428–25	sooner or *l·*, . . . we must master sin
t 444– 3	In some way, sooner or *l·*, all must rise
449– 8	Right adjusts the balance sooner or *l·*.
g 528–31	*L·* in human history, when the forbidden fruit

Latin

a 23–21	In Hebrew, Greek, *L·*, and English,
32– 4	the *L·* word for this oath was *sacramentum*,
b 271–11	In *L·* the word rendered *disciple* signifies
r 466– 2	*Omni* is adopted from the *L·* adjective

latitude

s 125–22	cold and heat, *l·* and longitude.

latter

a 53– 2	*l·* accusation was true, but not in their meaning.
sp 81– 4	this *l·* evidence is destroyed by Mind-science.
83– 8	to escape the error of these *l·* days.
83–26	The *l·* is a revelation of divine purpose
85– 5	when the *l·* yields to the divine Mind.
an 103–11	for the *l·* is unreal.
ph 187–17	allows the mental cause of the *l·* action,
f 220–15	leaves catarrh to the *l·*.
237–20	*l·* should be excluded on the same principle as
b 269–10	The first is error ; the *l·* is truth.
276–26	The *l·* destroys the former.
320–31	as if Job intended to declare . . . in the *l·* days
321–29	the voice of the *l·* sign." — *Exod.* 4 : 8.
o 353– 9	How can a Christian, . . . think of the *l·* as real
p 378–16	This *l·* occurrence represents the power of
t 459–22	when the *l·* is distrusted and thwarted
r 491– 8	the *l·* calling itself right.
g 522–25	This *l·* part of the second chapter of
544– 9	in the *l·* Life consisteth not of the things which

laughing

f 237– 5	Bounding off with *l·* eyes, she presently

launch

f 254–27	If you *l·* your bark upon the

launched

s 124–23	thought-force, which *l·* the earth in its orbit

lava

f 252–28	and says : . . . Like bursting *l·*, I expand

law

absence of

p 391–18	Injustice declares the absence of *l·*.

all

p 441– 1	comprehending and defining all *l·* and evidence,

and causation

f 230–12	first arranging *l·* and causation so as to

and gospel

p 441–29	a verdict contrary to *l·* and gospel.

and justice

p 434– 5	"It is contrary to *l·* and justice."

and order

sp 97– 3	They will maintain *l·* and order,

and testimony

p 436–10	Upon this statute hangs all the *l·* and testimony.

breaking the

o 349– 5	"Through breaking the *l·*, — *Rom.* 2 : 23.

broken

pr 11–10	Broken *l·* brings penalty

broken no

p 384–26	conviction abides that you have broken no *l·*,

by our

sp 94–10	by our *l·* he ought to die, — *John* 19 : 7.

civil

m 63–12	Civil *l·* establishes very unfair differences

disregard of

m 64–28	Let not mortals permit a disregard of *l·*

divine

(see divine)

eternal

p 385–11	remember that the eternal *l·* of right,

explains the

p 433– 5	explains the *l·* relating to liver-complaint.

false

f 229–21	false *l·* should be trampled under foot.
238–28	no time for gossip about false *l·* or testimony.

fulfils the

ap 572–12	Love fulfils the *l·* of C. S.,

God's

s 134–31	A miracle fulfils God's *l·*, but does not
ph 168–22	in accordance with God's *l·*,
f 229–26	If the transgression of God's *l·* produces
p 381–28	the rule of perpetual harmony, — God's *l·*.
404–14	remove this disorder as God's *l·* is fulfilled
g 540–14	we ought to know that God's *l·* uncovers

heavenly

t 447– 1	the heavenly *l·* is broken by trespassing upon

higher

b 307–30	province is in . . . the higher *l·* of Mind.
311–23	even the higher *l·* of Soul,
p 435– 8	Mortal Man, in obedience to higher *l·*,
t 458–22	summoned to give place to higher *l·*,

His

r 472–11	His *l·*, rightly understood, destroys them.

human

a 43–22	Human *l·* had condemned him,
an 105– 8	the power of human *l·* is restricted to matter,
105–14	and human *l·* rightly estimates crime,

hygienic

p 382–13	ignorant of what is termed hygienic *l·*,
382–16	the devotee of supposed hygienic *l·*,

immortal

a 36–20	the immortal *l·* of justice as well as of mercy.

inhuman

p 390–32	to defeat the passage of an inhuman *l·*.

law

material
    (see **material***)*

material sense of
  s 118–18   perverted by a perverse material sense of *l·*,

moral
  pr 11– 8   The moral *l·*, which has the right to acquit or
  p 392– 4   broken moral *l·* should be taken into account
    405–14   sentence of the moral *l·* will be executed upon
  gl 592–12   type of moral *l·* and the demonstration

Mosaic
  a 30–14   Rabbi and priest taught the Mosaic *l·*,

natural
  s 119–16   under the name of natural *l·*.
    134–22   natural *l·* of harmony which overcomes discord,

no
  an 106–29   against such there is no *l·*.''— *Gal. 5 : 23.*
  ph 196–17   No *l·* supports them.
  p 390–24   no *l·* of His to support the necessity either of sin
    391–13   No *l·* of God hinders this result.
    441–26   no *l·* outside of divine Mind can punish

no infringement of
  p 435–22   is no infringement of *l·*,

no such
  f 253–28   for no such *l·* exists.

of a general belief
  s 155– 3   it is the *l·* of a general belief,

of annihilation
  f 243–27   Life, and Love are a *l·* of annihilation to

of any kind
  p 393–19   inflamed as the result of a *l·* of any kind,

of being
  ph 186–27   and if so, harmony cannot be the *l·* of being.

of cause
  p 370– 8   This is the *l·* of cause and effect,

of Christ
  ph 182–32   The *l·* of Christ, . . . makes all things possible
  p 434– 6   Others say, ''The *l·* of Christ supersedes

of divine Love
  a 19–10   the law of Spirit, — the *l·* of divine Love.
  p 436–31   obedience to the *l·* of divine Love

of divine Mind
  s 150–21   contrary to the *l·* of divine Mind.
  f 216–17   If man is governed by the *l·* of divine Mind,
  p 430–14   illustrative of the *l·* of divine Mind

of divorce
  b 306–14   and then are separated as by a *l·* of divorce

of God
  pr 14–10   to be in obedience to the *l·* of God,
  sp 95–11   cannot hide from the *l·* of God.
  s 134–25   because it is the immutable *l·* of God,
  f 230–20   Does a *l·* of God produce sickness,
    233– 6   and progress is the *l·* of God,
    252–26   and says : . . . the *l·* of God, may
    253–29   and death is destroyed by the *l·* of God,
  p 372–16   nor disobey the *l·* of God.
    391–13   No *l·* of God hinders this result.
  t 463–27   There is a *l·* of God applicable to healing,
  g 534–30   it is not subject to the *l·* of God, — *Rom. 8 : 7.*

of his being
  m 63–11   and Life is the *l·* of his being.

of immortal Mind
  f 229–21   made void by the *l·* of immortal Mind,

of justice
  pr 5–10   there is no discount in the *l·* of justice
  a 36–20   *l·* of justice as well as of mercy.

of Life
  ph 180– 9   must understand the resuscitating *l·* of **Life.**
  f 253–29   the *l·* of Life instead of death,
  b 311–23   it will become the *l·* of Life to man,
  p 381– 1   rendered null and void by the *l·* of Life,
    436–32   construed . . . as disobedience to the *l·* of Life.

of life
  b 314–32   supposed accord with the inevitable *l·* of life.
  p 387–22   supposition that. . .in obedience to the *l·* of life,

of Love
  a 30–17   the divine *l·* of Love, which blesses
  s 118–30   and violate the *l·* of Love,
  f 203– 2   as though evil could overbear the *l·* of Love,
  p 384– 6   Let us reassure ourselves with the *l·* of Love.
  ap 574–19   full compensation in the *l·* of Love.

of matter
  a 19– 9   redeems man from the *l·* of matter,
    45– 2   Jesus . . . overcame every *l·* of matter,
  s 127–25   not a *l·* of matter, for matter is not a lawgiver.
  ph 184–21   not because a *l·* of matter has been transgressed,
  f 229–29   not of a *l·* of matter nor of
  p 380–32   Every *l·* of matter or the body,
    382–17   Must we not then consider the so-called *l·* of
          matter
    385–26   for having broken a *l·* of matter,

of Mind
  ph 168–23   in accordance with God's law, the *l·* of Mind.
  b 307–30   province is in . . . the higher *l·* of Mind.
  p 423–25   now at work . . . according to the *l·* of Mind,
  r 484–11   supposed laws of matter yield to the *l·* of Mind.

law

of mortal belief
  f 227– 3   the *l·* of mortal belief included all error,
  r 496–21   *l·* of mortal belief, at war with the facts

of mortal mind
  s 124– 4   a *l·* of mortal mind, a blind belief,
    154– 4   Since it is a *l·* of mortal mind that
    154–18   The *l·* of mortal mind and her own fears
  f 208– 9   a *l·* of mortal mind, wrong in every sense,
    229–19   *l·* of mortal mind, conjectural and
  b 289–22   the universal *l·* of mortal mind,
  p 385–26   a *l·* of mortal mind which you have disobeyed.

of righteousness
  a 36–32   Can God . . . overlook the *l·* of righteousness

of sin
  f 242–19   and is the *l·* of sin and death.
    244–12   free from the *l·* of sin and death.''— *Rom. 8 : 2.*

of Sinai
  ph 200– 3   the *l·* of Sinai lifted thought into

of Soul
  m 63– 1   does not make . . . the superior *l·* of Soul last.
  b 311–23   the higher *l·* of Soul, which prevails over
  p 427– 3   Life is the *l·* of Soul,

of Spirit
  a 19–10   the *l·* of Spirit, — the law of divine Love.
  f 207–12   nor . . . the *l·* of Spirit secondary.
    210–22   in obedience to the immutable *l·* of Spirit,
  b 302–23   by the *l·* of Spirit, not by the so-called
  p 435–27   punished, according to the *l·* of Spirit, God.

of the Spirit
  f 244–11   ''The *l·* of the Spirit of life— *Rom. 8 : 2.*

of the spirit
  p 427– 3   even the *l·* of the spirit of Truth,

of this action
  p 422–13   explain to them the *l·* of this action.

of this so-called mind
  ph 184–22   a *l·* of this so-called mind has been disobeyed.

of Truth
  r 482–27   C. S. is the *l·* of Truth, which heals the sick

opposite
  p 389–21   cannot annul these regulations by an opposite *l·*

our
  p 441–15   Our *l·* refuses to recognize Man as sick

penal
  p 440–14   Even penal *l·* holds homicide, under stress of

physical
  ph 184–26   what is termed a fatally broken physical *l·*.

portray
  s 118–28   these definitions portray *l·* as physical,

rabbinical
  p 362– 9   under the stern rules of rabbinical *l·*,

recognize as
  ph 183–20   mortals commonly recognize as *l·* that which

relative to colleges
  pref xi–29   a *l·* relative to colleges having been passed,

signification of
  p 391–17   Justice is the moral signification of *l·*.

so-called
  f 229–19   The so-called *l·* of mortal mind,
  p 382–17   Must we not then consider the so-called *l·* of
    432–27   *alias* nature's so-called *l·* ;
    441– 3   any so-called *l·*, which undertakes to punish

spiritual
    (see **spiritual***)*

supposed
  p 381– 8   When infringing some supposed *l·*, you say

that
  s 134–32   fulfils God's law, but does not violate that *l·*.
  f 230–21   can man put that *l·* under his feet by healing

this
  s 154– 5   this *l·* obtains credit through association,

title of
  ph 184–11   never honoring . . . with the title of *l·*

tyrannical
  s 161–12   put her foot on a proposed tyrannical *l·*,

unchangeable
  s 135– 8   the Science of God's unchangeable *l·*.

vestments of
  p 372–24   parading in the vestments of *l·*.

which gives
  ph 183–27   the *l·* which gives sight to the blind,

which overcomes
  ph 182–20   the *l·* which overcomes material conditions

your
  p 436– 4   betraying him into the hands of your *l·*,
    436–22   must obey your *l·*, fear its consequences,

---

  s 127–32   false hypotheses . . . that *l·* is founded on
    160–32   Is a stiff joint . . . as much a result of *l·*
  ph 178– 8   Heredity is not a *l·*.
    183–14   Truth never . . . devised a *l·* to perpetuate error.
  f 221–19   never ordained a *l·* that fasting should be
    227– 7   *l·* of the divine Mind must end human bondage,
    229–16   mortal belief has constituted itself a *l·*
    233– 6   whose *l·* demands of us only what we can
    245–30   decrepitude is not according to *l·*,

law

b	273–28	the false claims of material sense or *l·*.
o	342–17	then there is no invariable *l·*,
p	369–28	Limited to matter by their own *l·*,
	385–12	though it can never annul the *l·* which
	385–23	You are a *l·* unto yourself.
	387–24	It is a *l·* of so-called mortal mind,
	390–16	process of mortal opinions which you name *l·*,
	393– 8	a *l·* of so-called mortal mind,
	435–11	The *l·* of our Supreme Court decrees
	435–20	"is the fulfilling of the *l·*,"— *Rom.* 13 : 10.
	435–30	to judge . . . after the *l·*,— *Acts* 23 : 3.
	435–31	to be smitten contrary to the *l·* ?"— *Acts* 23 : 3.
	442–30	Christian Scientists, be a *l·* to yourselves
t	458–24	thus becoming a *l·* unto himself.
r	496–21	the strength of sin is the *l·*,"— *I Cor.* 15 : 56.
gl	592–15	demands penalties under the *l·*.

Lawgiver

b	321– 6	The Hebrew *L·*, slow of speech,
p	440–25	In the presence of the Supreme *L·*,

lawgiver

s	119–18	The *l·*, whose lightning palsies . . . is not the
	127–26	for matter is not a *l·*.
	127–32	false hypotheses that matter is its own *l·*,
	161– 2	and is God the *l·* ?
f	250– 3	and suppose . . . matter to be a *l·*,
p	435– 2	Spirit which is God Himself and Man's only *l·* !

lawgivers

ph	184–14	they are spiritual *l·*, enforcing obedience

lawmaker

ph	183– 4	departing from the basis of one God, one *l·*.
p	381–16	God is the *l·*, but He is not the author of

laws

agent of those

p	435–16	for the agent of those *l·* is an outlaw,

disregarded those

f	227–32	Jesus would not have disregarded those *l·*

divine

s	107– 2	the Christ Science or divine *l·* of Life,

eternal

g	542– 7	Truth, through her eternal *l·*, unveils error.

God's

f	236– 7	emolument rather than the dignity of God's *l·*,

His

ph	183–17	supposed laws which result in . . . are not His *l·*,
b	318–30	controlled and proved by His *l·*.
p	439–27	and the righteous executor of His *l·*.

ignorance of the

s	145–23	ignorance of the *l·* of eternal and unerring Mind.

its

p	425–22	the less we acknowledge matter or its *l·*,

material

(*see* **material**)

name of

s	118–23	are honored with the name of *l·*.

of God

s	128– 5	term Science, . . . refers only to the *l·* of God
ph	168–17	all in consonance with the *l·* of God,

of health

s	125–19	theories about *l·* of health to be valueless.
ph	165–12	Obedience to the so-called physical *l·* of health,
	168–11	the material so-called *l·* of health,
	182–27	*l·* of health come from some sad incident,
	184– 1	The so-called *l·* of health are simply
p	369–18	never recommended attention to *l·* of health,
	381–32	transgressions of the physical *l·* of health ;

of nature

ph	182– 6	what are termed *l·* of nature, appertain to
	183–10	its germination according to the *l·* of nature ?
	183–19	*L·* of nature are laws of Spirit ;
p	433– 6	conclusion is, that *l·* of nature render
t	463–25	never enjoined obedience to the *l·* of nature,

of Spirit

ph	183–19	Laws of nature are *l·* of Spirit ;

oppressive

f	227– 4	even as oppressive *l·* are disputed

other

ph	169–29	Whatever teaches man to have other *l·*

our

m	63–18	Our *l·* are not impartial, to say the least,
an	105–16	When our *l·* eventually take cognizance of
p	434– 6	"The law of Christ supersedes *our l·* ;

physical

m	62– 7	master the belief in so-called physical *l·*,
ph	165–12	Obedience to the so-called physical *l·* of. health
p	381–32	transgressions of the physical *l·* of health ;
	442– 2	innocent of transgressing physical *l·*,

reveals the

b	273–20	reveals the *l·* of spiritual existence.

sanitary

ph	175–23	nor referred to sanitary *l·*.

laws

so-called

sp	81–25	despite the so-called *l·* of matter,
ph	168–11	the material so-called *l·* of health,
	171–25	so-called *l·* of matter are nothing but
	177–22	create the so-called *l·* of the flesh,
	182–19	supersede the so-called *l·* of matter.
	183– 2	but the so-called *l·* of matter would render
	184– 1	The so-called *l·* of health are simply
f	207–12	nor are the so-called *l·* of matter
	210–10	his disregard of matter and its so-called *l·*.
	223–24	supplant unscientific means and so-called *l·*.
b	273–16	so-called *l·* of matter and of medical science
	274–16	supersede the so-called *l·* of matter.
	302–24	not by the so-called *l·* of matter.
p	381–12	The so-called *l·* of mortal belief are
	440–12	disobedience to the so-called *l·* of Matter

spiritual

s	118–15	include spiritual *l·* emanating from the
	118–17	may import that these spiritual *l·*, perverted

state

f	224–20	opposition from church, state *l·*, and the press,

subject to

f	244–14	beasts and vegetables,— subject to *l·* of decay.

such

p	442– 3	because there are no such *l·*.

supposed

ph	183–16	The supposed *l·* which result in weariness
f	237–24	the fallacy of matter and its supposed *l·*.
p	382– 1	supposed *l·* of matter, opposed to the
	430–14	and of the supposed *l·* of matter and hygiene,
r	484–10	supposed *l·* of matter yield to the law of

these

sp	83–18	belief that . . . Spirit sets aside these *l·*,
p	440–24	then render obedience to these *l·* punishable

transgress the

p	432–17	transgress the *l·*, and merit punishment,

m	62–25	the *l·* of erring, human concepts.
s	112–18	spiritual rules, *l·*, and their demonstration,
ph	183– 5	To suppose that God constitutes *l·* of
	184– 1	laws of health are simply *l·* of mortal belief.
	184– 3	Truth makes no *l·* to regulate sickness,
	197–11	less that is said of physical structure and *l·*,
f	231–14	but there are no antagonistic powers nor *l·*,
p	384–22	but if you believe in *l·* of matter
	389–19	If God has, . . . instituted *l·* that food shall
	440–23	compel them to enact wicked *l·* of sickness
t	463–26	if by these are meant *l·* of matter,

Laws of Health

p	435–15	If . . . committed by trampling on *L· of H·*,
	435–17	*L· of H·* should be sentenced to die.

lay

pref	vii– 6	in cradled obscurity, *l·* the Bethlehem babe,
a	20–28	"Let us *l·* aside every weight,— *Heb.* 12 : 1.
	24–27	efficacy of the crucifixion *l·* in the
	38–11	they shall *l·* hands on the sick,— *Mark* 16 : 18.
	51– 7	He had power to *l·* down a human sense
	52– 2	His pursuits *l·* far apart from theirs.
s	138– 4	God-power which *l·* behind Peter's confession
	156– 7	and yet, as she *l·* in her bed,
ph	181–15	but that you *l·* no stress on
	193– 8	Mr. Clark *l·* with his eyes fixed
f	239– 3	*l·* it upon those who are in advance of
c	266–17	teaches mortals to *l·* down their fleshliness
b	311–30	as mortals *l·* off a false sense of life,
	328–25	They shall *l·* hands on the sick,— *Mark* 16 : 18
o	359–27	they shall *l·* hands on the sick,— *Mark* 16 : 18.
p	362– *	*they shall l· hands on the sick,— Mark* 16 : 18.
	364– 5	to *l·* down his mortal existence in behalf of
r	491–14	mortals can *l·* off mortality
ap	568–31	by which we *l·* down all for Truth,
	577–23	dynasties will *l·* down their honors

layeth

a	55–23	whosoever *l·* his earthly all on the altar

laying

p	436–12	*L·* down his life for a good deed,
gl	593– 6	PURSE. *L·* up treasures in matter ; error.

lays

sp	75– 1	truth *l·* bare the mistaken assumption
f	216– 9	Spirituality *l·* open siege to materialism.
b	303–16	Divine Science *l·* the axe at the root

Lazarus

sp	75–12	Jesus said of *L·* :
	75–12	"Our friend *L·* sleepeth ; — *John* 11 : 11.
	75–14	Jesus restored *L·* by the understanding that
	75–15	*L·* had never died,
	75–17	Had Jesus believed that *L·* had
	83–25	impassable as that between Dives and *L·*.
s	134–27	and he raised *L·* from the dead,
r	493–28	If Jesus awakened *L·* from the

lead

pr	7–27	it may *l·* us into temptation.
	17– 8	And *l·* us not into temptation, — *Matt.* 6 : 13.
m	64–28	might *l·* to a worse state of society
an	101–25	*l·* to moral and to physical death.
s	116–25	ignorantly employed, they often *l·*, . . . to
	119– 5	such theories *l·* to one of two things.
	158–18	It is pitiful to *l·* men into temptation through
f	201– 5	and take the *l·* in our lives,
	218–21	which *l·* only into material ways
	223–18	"If the blind *l·* the blind, — *Matt.* 15 : 14.
	227–20	but evil and error *l·* into captivity.
b	271–22	it will *l·* you into all truth.
	298–22	Spiritual ideas *l·* up to their divine origin,
	299–13	never *l·* towards sin, or materiality,
g	513– 7	*l·* on to spiritual spheres and exalted beings.
	514–25	And a little child shall *l·* them. — *Isa.* 11 : 6.

leaden

o	358– 2	Can a *l·* bullet deprive a man of Life,

leader

b	333– 7	Joshua, the renowned Hebrew *l·*.
gl	594–13	SHEEP. . . . those who follow their *l·*.

leaders

f	236– 7	emolument . . . which many *l·* seek?

leadeth

pr	17–10	*And God l· us not into temptation,*
s	127–29	the Comforter which *l·* into all truth.
t	451–13	the way, that *l·* to destruction, — *Matt.* 7 : 13.
ap	578– 7	*l·* me beside the still waters. — *Psal.* 23 : 2.
	578– 8	*l·* me in the paths of righteousness — *Psal.* 23 : 3.

leading

s	109– 2	the *l·* factor in Mind-science.
	129–26	quite as rational are some of the *l·* illusions
f	253– 9	I hope, dear reader, I am *l·* you into the
	254– 1	the human footsteps *l·* to perfection
b	332–22	and *l·* into all truth.
p	377–21	Remove the *l·* error or governing fear
	425– 7	take up the *l·* points included
r	467–21	This is a *l·* point in the Science of Soul,
g	536–19	The blind *l·* the blind, both would fall.
	549–25	Agassiz, discovers the pathway *l·* to
ap	566–11	*l·* to divine heights.

leadings

s	110–13	In following these *l·* of scientific revelation,
	151–30	and follow the *l·* of truth.
t	458–27	in following the *l·* of divine Mind.

leads

sp	92–30	*l·* to belief in the superiority of error.
s	120–29	and so *l·* to disease.
	153–13	This discovery *l·* to more light.
ph	167–26	but one way . . . which *l·* to spiritual being.
	191–11	dawns upon human thought, and *l·* it to
f	202–26	true way *l·* to Life instead of to death,
	205–26	*l·* human thought into opposite channels
	207– 7	Error of statement *l·* to error in action.
	225– 5	You may know when first Truth *l·*
	251–22	*l·* the human mind to relinquish all error,
c	256–26	material sense of God *l·* to formalism
b	277–27	error in the premise *l·* to errors in the
	278–24	*l·* to the conclusion that if a man is
	296–23	The knowledge . . . *l·* to sin and death.
	324–14	*l·* to the understanding that God is the
	338– 2	C. S., rightly understood, *l·* to eternal harmony.
o	346–16	and *l·* to the discernment of Truth.
t	452– 4	Incorrect reasoning *l·* to practical error.
	454– 8	*l·* to the house built without hands
	454–19	inspires, illumines, designates, and *l·* the way.
r	472– 5	The way which *l·* to C. S. is straight
g	505–17	uplifts consciousness and *l·* into all truth
ap	561– 4	*l·* to the discernment of the divine idea.
	566–31	He *l·* the hosts of heaven against the

leaf

ph	191–22	By its own volition, . . . not a *l·* unfolds
p	407– 4	a *l·* naturally attractive to no creature except
g	552–25	blending tints of *l·* and flower show the

leaflet

f	240– 8	*l·* turns naturally towards the light.

league

an	105–31	full many a *l·* in the line of light ;
c	255–12	In *l·* with material sense,

leagues

sp	87–10	Though bodies are *l·* apart

lean

m	66– 6	Trials teach mortals not to *l·* on a material
s	143–21	You *l·* on the inert and unintelligent,
f	205– 3	will *l·* on matter instead of Spirit,
b	321–16	this proof was a staff upon which to *l·*.

leaning

pref	vii– 1	To those *l·* on the sustaining infinite,
a	47– 6	*l·* no longer on matter, but on the

leaps

p	415– 7	thought moves quickly or slowly, *l·* or halts

learn

pr	5– 9	till we *l·* that there is no discount in
	8–28	*l·* what is the affection and purpose of the heart,
	8–30	for in this way only can we *l·*
a	37–16	When will Jesus' professed followers *l·* to
m	60–12	From the logic of events we *l·* that
	67– 2	shall we not drink it and *l·* the lessons
	68– 5	Sometime we shall *l·* how Spirit,
sp	71–11	Thus you *l·* that the flower is a product of the
	71–15	Thus you *l·* that these also are
	71–18	From dreams also you *l·* that
	96– 2	unwillingness to *l·* all things rightly,
an	102–30	Mankind must *l·* that evil is not power.
s	129–25	*l·* from discord the concord of being?
	153– 2	Thus we *l·* that it is not the drug which expels
	159–23	The medical schools would *l·* the state of
	160–27	Why then consult anatomy to *l·*
	160–28	if we are only to *l·* from anatomy that
ph	166–20	we should *l·* that He can do all things for us
	171–11	to *l·* how much of a man he is.
	186–15	must *l·* that there is neither power nor
f	207– 9	We must *l·* that evil is the awful deception
	208–20	Let us *l·* of the real and eternal,
	217–25	*l·* the power of Mind over the body
	223– 3	Sooner or later we shall *l·* that the fetters
	228– 8	if we *l·* that nothing is real but the right,
	236–18	from which we *l·* of the one Mind
	236–26	and *l·* more readily to love the simple verities
	239–16	we must *l·* where our affections are placed
	240–22	we must *l·* to loathe it.
	251–15	*l·* how mankind govern the body,
	251–17	We should *l·* whether they govern the
	252– 7	When false human beliefs *l·* even a little of
c	261–22	and you may *l·* the meaning of God,
	264–28	When we *l·* the way in C. S.
b	271–28	to *l·* and to practise Christian healing.
	276–19	When we *l·* in Science how to be perfect
	281– 3	*l·* that Spirit is infinite and supreme.
	281–22	we shall *l·* that sin and mortality are
	285–29	they will seek to *l·*, not from matter, but
	296–19	Whether mortals will *l·* this sooner or later,
	316– 3	mortals may *l·* how to escape from evil.
	322–29	Then we begin to *l·* Life in divine Science.
	327–19	hastening to *l·* that Life is God, good,
	327–32	by degrees he will *l·* the nothingness of
o	353–22	When we *l·* that error is not real,
p	366–31	first *l·* to bind up the broken-hearted.
	368–21	when we *l·* that life and man survive
	379–18	Then let her *l·* the opposite statement of Life
	386–21	you *l·* that your suffering was merely the
	386–23	You will *l·* at length that there is no
	388–23	self-evident, when we *l·* that God is our Life.
	407–17	Let the slave of wrong desire *l·* the
	439–33	they *l·* that Disease was never there,
t	443–26	may *l·* the value of the apostolic precept :
r	472–30	We *l·* in C. S. that all inharmony
	476–21	*L·* this, O mortal, and earnestly seek the
	481–29	we *l·* that it is material sense, not Soul, which sins ;
	496– 1	You will also *l·* that in Science there is no
	496– 5	You will *l·* that in C. S. the first duty is
	496– 9	We all must *l·* that Life is God.
g	557– 4	*l·* how to develop their children properly
gl	579– 1	In C. S. we *l·* that the substitution of

learned

pref	ix–22	*l·* that this Science must be demonstrated
a	46– 3	Jesus' students, . . . *l·* that he had not died.
m	64–26	Until it is *l·* that God is the father of all,
sp	79–21	so far as can be *l·* from the Gospels,
	84–29	is *l·* through Christ and C. S.
	84–31	If this Science has been thoroughly *l·*
	98–31	through which immortality and life are *l·*
s	108–21	I *l·* these truths in divine Science :
	153–14	From it may be *l·* that either
	163– 5	declared himself "sick of it quackery."
	163–13	Dr. Mason Good, a *l·* Professor in London,
ph	194–14	Every theory . . . (as I *l·* in metaphysics)
f	214–14	When it is *l·* that the spiritual sense,
	221–17	He *l·* that suffering and disease were
	222– 4	*l·* that food affects the body only as
	222– 7	He *l·* also that mortal mind makes a
	222–22	He *l·* that a dyspeptic was very far from
	228– 5	if this great fact of being were *l·*,
b	288–32	seem to have *l·* from error,
	308– 5	Until the lesson is *l·* that God is the
	312– 1	How true it is that whatever is *l·* through
	320–10	and in the *l·* article on Noah
	326–28	He *l·* the wrong that he had done
	326–31	and *l·* a lesson in divine Science.
	330– 3	author of this book *l·* the vastness of C. S.,
o	348–11	medical faculty and clergy have not *l·* this,
	351– 9	Later she *l·* that her own prayers
p	383– 1	wrote . . . I was cured when I *l·* my way in C. S."

learned

p 402–13 Sometime it will be *l·* that mortal mind
426–17 When it is *l·* that disease cannot destroy life,
r 467–32 and cannot be *l·* from its opposite, matter.
486– 2 when you have *l·* falsehood's true nature.
g 533–31 already *l·* that corporeal sense is the serpent.
548–13 before Life is spiritually *l·*.
552–29 Thus it is *l·* that matter is a
gl 591–22 divinely natural, but must be *l·* humanly ;

learner

pref x–31 No . . . is requisite in the *l·*,
a 26–20 to show the *l·* the way by practice
s 147– 2 This system enables the *l·* to demonstrate

learners

b 271–13 not a supernatural gift to those *l·*,
t 457–25 Departing from C. S., some *l·* commend diet

learning

sp 88–10 By *l·* the origin of each.
s 108– 9 immortal cravings, "the price of *l·* love,"
141–31 Give to it the place in our institutions of *l·*
156–12 *l·* that her former physician had prescribed
ph 195–23 tangled barbarisms of *l·* which we deplore,
f 235– 9 reference to their morals as to their *l·*
240–31 unwinding one's snarls, and *l·* from experience
b 274–24 permits no half-way position in *l·* its Principle
290–29 and *l·* that his cruel mind died not.
o 349–29 this is equally true of all *l·*,
p 426–15 *l·* the necessity of working out his
427– 8 *l·* that there is no reality in death,
t 443– * *and he will increase in l·.— Prov. 9 : 9.*
452–17 luxury of *l·* with egotism and vice.

learns

b 289– 3 until he *l·* that God is the only Life.
p 425–16 when he *l·* that matter never sustained
g 554–15 he *l·* to say, "I am somebody ;

least

a 19–25 Those who cannot demonstrate, at *l·* in part,
m 63–18 Our laws are not impartial, to say the *l·*,
s 126– 9 Human thought never projected the *l·* portion
164–20 does not in the *l·* disprove C. S. ;
ph 170–26 and at *l·* to touch the hem of Truth's garment.
f 242– 5 *l·* of them unto the greatest."— *Jer.* 31 : 34.
b 290– 4 If . . . not in the *l·* understood before
293– 3 *l·* material form of illusive consciousness,
o 345–29 at *l·* none which are apparent to those who
361–26 though *l·* in the kingdom of heaven,
p 407– 5 Puffing the obnoxious fumes . . . is at *l·* disgusting.
r 473–32 Few, however, . . . understood in the *l·*
478–20 discharge of the natural functions is *l·*
g 518–19 Love giveth to the *l·* spiritual idea

least-understood

g 539–32 inspired his wisest and *l·* sayings,

leave

pr 9–25 Are you willing to *l·* all for Christ,
10– 4 will *l·* our real desires to be rewarded by Him.
a 33–15 He must *l·* them.
34– 1 and *l·* all for the Christ-principle?
m 66–24 than for a wife precipitately to *l·* her husband
66–25 or for a husband to *l·* his wife.
sp 85–29 and not to *l·* the other undone."— *Matt.* 23 : 23.
s 116–13 Works on metaphysics *l·* the grand point
119– 9 to *l·* the creator out of His own universe ;
141– 9 that is, . . . to *l·* all for Christ.
157–27 they *l·* both mind and body worse
ph 189– 2 they are willing to *l·* with astronomy the
192– 6 not Christian Scientists until we *l·* all for
f 208–13 not . . . *l·* man to heal himself ;
b 271–26 Those, who are willing to *l·* their nets
322–18 cannot make the inebriate *l·* his . . . until
324– 1 Willingness . . . to *l·* the old for the new,
324– 2 Gladness to *l·* the false landmarks
o 354– 6 to enable them to *l·* all for Christ,
p 401–28 better for Christian Scientists to *l·* surgery
419– 5 *l·* the field to God, Life, Truth, and Love,
424– 6 we must *l·* the mortal basis of belief
t 443–18 *l·* invalids free to resort to whatever
448–19 Try to *l·* on every student's mind the
g 521– 6 We *l·* this brief, glorious history
543–25 When Spirit made all, did it *l·* aught for

leaven

s 107– * *l·, which a woman took, and hid*— *Matt.* 13 : 33.
117–29 *l·* of the Pharisees and of the Sadducees,
117–32 "*l·*, which a woman took, and hid — *Matt.* 13 : 33.
118– 2 impels the inference that the spiritual *l·*
118–10 this *l·* of Truth is ever at work.
118–23 until the *l·* of Spirit changes the
b 329– 5 A little *l·* leavens the whole lump.
t 449– 3 A little *l·* causes the whole mass to ferment.

leavened

s 107– * *till the whole was l·.— Matt.* 13 : 33.
118– 1 till the whole was *l·*,"— *Matt.* 13 : 33.

leavens

b 329– 5 A little leaven *l·* the whole lump.

leaves

pr 11–14 *l·* the offender free to repeat the offence,
m 66–30 It never *l·* us where it found us.
s 148–30 this ruling of the schools *l·* them to
f 208–16 or that Spirit, . . . *l·* the remedy to matter.
220–10 The *l·* clap their hands at nature's untired
220–15 *l·* catarrh to the latter.
238–23 He who *l·* all for Christ
b 340–28 and *l·* nothing that can sin, suffer,
p 383– 8 when he *l·* it most out of his thought,
406– 2 "The *l·* of the tree were— *Rev.* 22 : 2.
r 492– 1 *l·* mortal man intact in body and thought,

leaving

an 104–27 *l·* the case worse than before it was grasped by
p 395– 7 *l·* Soul to master the false evidences of
415–31 *l·* the pain standing forth as distinctly as
r 478– 6 man has never beheld Spirit or Soul *l·* a body

led

pref vii–11 The Wisemen were *l·* to behold and to follow
viii–26 experiences which *l·* her, in the year 1866, to the
sp 95–23 *L·* by a solitary star amid the darkness,
s 109– 1 and *l·* up to my demonstration of the
f 215–15 We are sometimes *l·* to believe that darkness is
b 309–22 and *l·* to deny material sense,
316–15 which *l·* to the conclusion that the
321– 8 *l·* by wisdom to cast down his rod,
p 433–22 and this has *l·* him into the commission of
t 457–14 In the legend of the shield, which *l·* to a quarrel
ap 565– 9 *L·* on by the grossest element of mortal mind,
566– 3 as they were *l·* through the wilderness,

lees

m 65–23 impurity and error are left among the *l·*.

left

pr 6– 8 work badly done or *l·* undone,
6–30 a certain magistrate, . . . *l·* this record :
a 27–23 but only eleven *l·* a desirable historic record.
27–25 other disciples who have *l·* no name.
55–13 cannot be *l·* out of Christianity,
m 65–22 impurity and error are *l·* among the lees.
sp 74– 5 after having once *l·* it,
74–15 belief of having died and *l·* a material body
s 121–14 man, *l·* to the hypotheses of material sense
126–20 *l·* to the mercy of speculative hypotheses?
142–17 palsies the right hand, and causes the *l·* to
147–26 he *l·* no definite rule for demonstrating
149–10 *l·* without explanation except in C. S.
153– 7 not a single saline property *l·*.
ph 176– 8 *l·* the stomach and bowels free to act
179–17 the wild animal, *l·* to his instincts,
f 216–22 If the decision were *l·* to the corporeal senses,
238–10 said, "I have nothing *l·* but Christ."
251–26 nothing is *l·* which deserves to perish or
c 266– 8 solitary, *l·* without sympathy ;
b 304–26 *L·* to the decisions of material sense,
304–32 *l·* in the hands of ignorance,
306–17 If . . . *l·* without a rational proof of
329–11 Jesus, . . . *l·* his example for us.
330–17 *l·* either to human conjecture or to the
o 344–23 and *l·* to us as his rich legacy.
347–11 there is nothing *l·* to be doctored.
p 389– 2 If this decision be *l·* to C. S.,
436–21 You have *l·* Mortal Man no alternative.
g 520–29 nothing *l·* to be made by a lower power.
ap 558– 7 and his *l·* foot on the earth.— *Rev.* 10 : 2.
559– 6 The angel's *l·* foot was upon the earth ;

legacy

o 344–24 and left to us as his rich *l·*.

legal

pr 11–12 Mere *l·* pardon . . . leaves the offender
m 56– 7 Marriage is the *l·* and moral provision for
an 105–17 and no longer apply *l·* rulings wholly to

legally

f 225–23 *L·* to abolish unpaid servitude in the

legend

t 457–13 In the *l·* of the shield, which led to a quarrel

legendary

g 526–14 in the *l·* Scriptural text

legerdemain

f 212–21 In *l·* and credulous frenzy, mortals believe

Legion

p 411–16 demon, or evil, replied that his name was *L·*.

legislate

p 381–14 mortal mind cannot *l·* the times, periods,

legislation

m 63–26 the achievement of a nobler race for *l·*,

legislator

p 390–31 as a *l·* would employ to defeat the

legislators
  p 440–22 beliefs of your human mental *l·*

legitimate
  s 120–28 confirms that testimony as *l·*
  ph 182– 8 Which, then, are we to accept as *l·* and
  183–17 the *l·* and only possible action of Truth
  184–13 the only *l·* and eternal demands on man,
  f 227–15 Slavery is not the *l·* state of man.
  228–11 The enslavement of man is not *l·*.
  254–10 To stop eating, drinking, . . . is not *l·*.
  p 367– 8 are but so many parodies on *l·* C. S.,
  t 454– 9 Human hate has no *l·* mandate

lending
  an 102–25 a problem not *l·* itself to an easy explanation

lends
  m 64–10 When a man *l·* a helping hand to some noble
  f 209–15 Nearness, . . . *l·* enchantment to this view.

length
  pref ix–31 she came at *l·* to its solution ;
  a 42– 7 Death will be found at *l·* to be a
  m 65–18 will at *l·* demand a higher affection.
  s 134– 6 at *l·* the word *martyr* was narrowed in its
  b 283–25 practically demonstrated in *l·* of days,
  o 359–13 must at *l·* know yourself spiritually
  p 370–27 Quackery likewise fails at *l·* to inspire the
  380– 1 may rest at *l·* on some receptive thought,
  384–30 Sickness, sin, and death must at *l·*
  386–23 learn at *l·* that there is no cause for grief,
  390–10 Truth will at *l·* compel us all to
  431–16 but at *l·* all these assistants resigned to me,

lengthens
  r 487–27 *l·* our days by strengthening our trust

lengthy
  s 111–26 After a *l·* examination of my discovery

lens
  f 214–27 may end the power of light and *l·* !

lenses
  p 393–27 complex humors, *l·*, muscles, the iris

leopard
  g 514–23 *l·* shall lie down with the kid ;—*Isa.* 11 : 6.

lepers
  a 27– 5 *l·* are cleansed, the deaf hear,— *Luke* 7 : 22.
  sp 94–21 Of the ten *l·* whom Jesus healed,
  s 132– 6 *l·* are cleansed, and the deaf hear,— *Matt.* 11 : 5.

leprosy
  b 321–19 scientifically demonstrated that *l·* was a

less
  pref viii–18 Is there *l·* sickness because of these
  pr 2– 9 nor can the infinite do *l·* than bestow all good,
  13–18 *l·* risk of overwhelming our real wishes
  a 25–17 any man whose origin was *l·* spiritual.
  40–16 crimes of his implacable enemies *l·* criminal?
  54– 1 he would have been *l·* sensitive to those beliefs.
  m 56–19 is no *l·* imperative than the
  62–13 Taking *l·* "thought for your— *Matt.* 6 : 25.
  62–14 *l·* thought "for your body— *Matt.* 6 : 25.
  62–21 but *l·* and *l·*, if we would be wise and healthy.
  63–16 why usage should accord woman *l·* rights
  sp 77–24 beautifully *l·* with every advanced stage
  86–21 Seeing is no *l·* a quality of physical
  98–13 much *l·* can they demonstrate it.
  s 108–18 not a fraction more, not a unit *l·*.
  123–31 but not on that account is it *l·* scientific.
  128–14 and requires *l·* repose.
  142– 1 in *l·* time than the old systems,
  146– 5 governed more or *l·* by our systems of medicine.
  155–23 puts *l·* weight into the material or fleshly scale
  155–32 is it safe to say that the *l·* in quantity you have
  161–15 they will do *l·* violence to that
  163–12 there would be *l·* sickness and *l·* mortality."
  ph 166–26 invalid's faith in the divine Mind is *l·* than
  170– 7 Did Jesus understand . . . *l·* than Graham
  173–32 call into action *l·* faith than Buddhism
  175– 4 and *l·* thought is given to sanitary subjects,
  175– 6 there will be better constitutions and *l·* disease.
  175–19 Then people had *l·* time for selfishness,
  176–30 *l·* distinct type and chronic form of disease.
  197–11 The *l·* that is said of physical structure and
  198–23 A patient's belief is more or *l·* moulded
  198–32 or that a *l·* used arm must be weak.
  199–18 of *l·* importance than a knowledge of the fact.
  f 203–18 prone to believe . . . in some power *l·* than
  217–20 the next toil will fatigue you *l·*,
  222–11 Food had *l·* power to help or to hurt him
  222–13 he also had *l·* faith in the so-called pleasures and
  222–14 Taking *l·* thought about what he should eat
  222–15 consulting the stomach *l·* about the
  223–11 we cannot put the greater into the *l·*.
  224–17 The modern lash is *l·* material than the
  244–18 but man was nearer God than *l·* than man.
  247–31 recipe for beauty is to have *l·* illusion
  248– 4 One marvels that a friend can ever seem *l·* than

less
  f 249–28 night-dream has *l·* matter as its accompaniment.
  b 279–23 medicine is more or *l·* infected with the
  295–19 the glass is *l·* opaque than the walls.
  314– 1 and no *l·* material until the ascension
  317–16 no *l·* tangible because it is spiritual
  336–23 else God would . . . become *l·* than God.
  336–24 and nothing *l·* can express God.
  o 343–24 Christendom generally demands so much *l·*.
  344–31 are more fashionable and *l·* spiritual?
  353–14 It still holds them more or *l·*.
  360–10 They require *l·* self-abnegation,
  p 374–24 your steps are *l·* firm because of your fear,
  378– 7 Disease is *l·* than mind, and Mind can control
  378–31 it would manifest *l·* wisdom than
  381–20 Think *l·* of the enactments of mortal mind,
  388– 6 Stolidity, which is a resisting state . . . suffers *l·*,
  388– 6 only because it knows *l·* of material law.
  389– 5 The *l·* we know or think about hygiene,
  389– 6 the *l·* we are predisposed to sickness.
  395–23 It is no *l·* erroneous to believe in the
  397– 8 Suffering is no *l·* a mental condition than
  405–29 The pains of sinful sense are *l·* harmful than
  406–14 Sin and sickness will abate and seem *l·* real
  408–25 tarsal joint is *l·* intimately connected with
  415–15 only render mortal mind temporarily *l·* fearful,
  419–18 Think *l·* of material conditions
  421–21 If a crisis occurs . . . treat the patient *l·* for the
  422–18 causing it to depend *l·* on material evidence.
  425–15 Mortal man will be *l·* mortal, when he
  425–21 and the *l·* we acknowledge matter or its laws,
  426– 5 discoverer of C. S. finds the path *l·* difficult
  t 449–19 baneful effect of evil associates is *l·* seen than
  450–22 Sickness to him is no *l·* a temptation than is sin,
  461–22 to admit that . . . renders your case *l·* curable,
  r 489– 1 The *l·* mind there is manifested in matter
  490–13 mortals are more or *l·* deprived of Truth.
  g 526– 8 Belief is *l·* than understanding.
  542–29 misconception of Life as something *l·* than
  554–29 belief that the lower animals are *l·* sickly
  554–32 there is *l·* disease in proportion as
  555– 1 as the force of mortal mind is *l·* pungent
  556–25 Ontology receives *l·* attention than
  557–14 the *l·* a mortal knows of sin, disease, and
  557–15 the *l·* pain and sorrow are his.

lessen
  a 40–14 Another's suffering cannot *l·* our
  s 155–30 if drugs are an antidote . . . why *l·* the
  c 262– 2 does not *l·* man's dependence on God,
  t 450–20 enlisted to *l·* evil, disease, and death ;

lessened
  sp 80– 2 not *l·* by giving utterance to truth.
  b 321–24 God had *l·* Moses' fear by this proof in

lessening
  p 405–26 If sin is not regretted and is not *l·*,

lesser
  a 40–21 *l·* apostles of Truth may endure
  sp 95–14 The greater or *l·* ability of a
  an 104–26 case of the greater error overcoming the *l·*.
  s 108–14 the *l·* demonstration to prove the greater,
  121–24 rule that the greater controls the *l·*.
  143–15 takes the *l·* to relieve the greater.
  ph 183–23 No reservation is made for any *l·* loyalty.
  f 231– 9 no *l·* power equals the infinite All-power ;
  b 291– 8 till mortals have already yielded to each *l·* call
  303– 8 The minutiæ of *l·* individualities reflect
  r 467–19 The greater cannot be in the *l·*.
  g 508–24 belief that the greater can be in the *l·*
  510–14 rising from the *l·* to the greater,
  518–13 the *l·* light to rule the night :— *Gen.* 1 : 16.
  529–11 God gives the *l·* idea of Himself for
  544–26 belonging to no *l·* parent.
  man, . . . is neither a *l·* god nor the

lesson
  f 207–13 Without this *l·*, we lose sight of the
  221–32 brings with it another *l·*,
  c 266–14 until the *l·* is sufficient to exalt you ;
  b 308– 5 Until the *l·* is learned that God is the
  326–31 and learned a *l·* in divine Science.
  p 363–22 and so brought home the *l·* to all,

lessons
  m 67– 2 and learn the *l·* He teaches?
  s 109–28 Jesus once said of his *l·* :
  f 237–16 should be taught . . . C. S., among their first *l·*,
  240– 7 Suns and planets teach grand *l·*.
  248– 6 Men and women of riper years and larger *l·*
  p 370–28 These *l·* are useful.
  407–17 Let the slave of wrong desire learn the *l·* of

lest
  pref x–29 *l·* their works be reproved.
  a 38–29 *l·* ye should understand and be converted,
  o 350–20 *l·* at any time they should see— *Matt.* 13 : 15.
  p 366–22 The physician must also watch, *l·* he be
  414–18 *l·* you array the sick against their

lest

p 419–17 l· aught unfit for development enter thought.
t 459–10 l· you yourself be condemned for failing to take
g 529–20 neither shall ye touch it, l· ye— *Gen.* 3 : 3.
537– 1 now, l· he put forth his hand,— *Gen.* 3 : 22.
537–31 l· man should improve it and become better ;
542–17 l· any finding him should kill him.— *Gen.* 4 : 15.

let

pr 15–24 and l· our lives attest our sincerity.
16–24 Here l· me give what I understand to be
a 20–27 "L· us lay aside every weight,— *Heb.* 12 : 1.
20–29 l· us run with patience the race— *Heb.* 12 : 1.
20–30 l· us put aside material self
33–20 L· not the flesh, but the Spirit, be represented
42–24 L· men think they had killed the body !
m 56– * l· not man put asunder.— *Matt.* 19 : 6.
62–24 l· no mortal interfere with God's government
63–22 l· us hope it will be granted.
64–27 L· not mortals permit a disregard of law
sp 91– 5 L· us rid ourselves of the belief that man is
an 106–15 L· this age, which sits in judgment on C. S.,
s 141–28 L· our pulpits do justice to C. S.
141–29 L· it have fair representation by the
142–17 causes the left to l· go its grasp on the divine.
144– 3 l· us rely upon Mind, which needs no
ph 168–30 Here l· a word be noticed which will be
f 201–14 L· us disrobe error.
208–20 L· us learn of the real and eternal,
225– 9 and will command their sentinels not to l· truth
239– 8 l· worth be judged according to wisdom,
239–12 L· it be understood that success in error is
239–14 "L· the wicked forsake his way,— *Isa.* 55 : 7.
242–16 l· us labor to dissolve with the universal
246–29 L· us then shape our views of existence into
248–29 L· unselfishness, goodness, mercy,
249– 1 L· us accept Science, relinquish all theories
249– 3 l· us have one God, one Mind,
249– 5 L· the "male and female" of— *Gen.* 1 : 27.
249– 6 L· us feel the divine energy of Spirit,
249– 8 L· us rejoice that we are subject to
c 255– 3 "L· there be light,"— *Gen.* 1 : 3.
267–27 "l· thy garments be always white."— *Eccl.* 9 : 8.
b 276– 8 "L· this Mind be in you, which,— *Phil.* 2 : 5.
302–14 l· us remember that harmonious and
308–24 "L· me go, for the day breaketh ;"— *Gen.* 32 : 26.
327–29 L· that inform the sentiments
340– 6 "L· us hear the conclusion of— *Eccl.* 12 : 13.
340– 9 L· us hear the conclusion of the whole matter :
o 355–10 l· the dead bury their dead."— *Matt.* 8 : 22.
355–11 L· discord of every name and nature be heard no
355–12 l· the harmonious and true sense of Life
359– 3 L· any clergyman try to cure his friends by
p 367–21 L· us watch, work, and pray that this salt
368–32 Once l· the mental physician believe in the
379–14 L· the despairing invalid, inspecting the hue
379–18 l· her learn the opposite statement of Life
381–27 L· us banish sickness as an outlaw,
384– 5 L· us reassure ourselves with the
385–11 L· us remember that the eternal law of right,
390–13 L· your higher sense of justice
394–20 Will you bid a man l· evils overcome him,
407–17 L· the slave of wrong desire learn
407–24 L· the perfect model be present in your
422–22 L· us suppose two parallel cases of
434– 6 Others say, . . . l· us follow Christ."
436–25 but they were compelled to l· him be taken
438– 3 L· us make man in our image,— *Gen.* 1 : 26.
438– 4 and l· them have dominion.— *Gen.* 1 : 26.
441–11 L· what False Belief utters, now and forever,
t 444–16 L· us be faithful in pointing the way
444–18 but l· us also be careful always to
444–25 "L· there be no strife, I pray thee,— *Gen.* 13 : 8.
454–26 L· your loving care and counsel support all
457–30 L· this Principle be applied to the cure of
r 471–20 "L· God be true, but every— *Rom.* 3 : 4.
475–23 "L· us make man in our image,— *Gen.* 1 : 26.
475–24 and l· them have dominion.— *Gen.* 1 : 26.
495–16 L· neither fear nor doubt overshadow your
495–20 L· C. S., instead of corporeal sense,
g 503–18 And God said, L· there be light :— *Gen.* 1 : 3.
505– 4 God said, L· there be a firmament— *Gen.* 1 : 6.
505– 5 and l· it divide the waters from— *Gen.* 1 : 6.
506–15 L· the waters under the heaven— *Gen.* 1 : 9.
506–16 and l· the dry land appear :— *Gen.* 1 : 9.
507–11 L· the earth bring forth grass,— *Gen.* 1 : 11.
509– 9 And God said, L· there be lights— *Gen.* 1 : 14.
509–11 and l· them be for signs, and for— *Gen.* 1 : 14.
510– 6 And l· them be for lights in the— *Gen.* 1 : 15.
511–19 L· the waters bring forth— *Gen.* 1 : 20.
512–18 l· fowl multiply in the earth.— *Gen.* 1 : 22.
513–14 L· the earth bring forth the— *Gen.* 1 : 24.
515–11 L· us make man in our image,— *Gen.* 1 : 26.
515–12 and l· them have dominion— *Gen.* 1 : 26.
515–21 "L· them have dominion."— *Gen.* 1 : 26.
525–13 Icelandic : . . . L· us make man after our mind
542–19 L· Truth uncover and destroy error

let

g 542–20 l· human justice pattern the divine.
548– 2 l· him take the water of life— *Rev.* 22 : 17.
556–19 "L· there be light."— *Gen.* 1 : 3.
fr 600– * L· us get up early to the vineyards :— *Song* 7 : 12.
600– * l· us see if the vine flourish,— *Song* 7 : 12.

lethargy

a 38– 7 when the l· of mortals, produced by

lets

pr 15– 5 l· in Truth, Life, and Love.
p 407–26 spiritualization of thought l· in the light,

letter

absolute
r 483–21 revealed the spirit . . . if not the absolute l·.
and the spirit
b 330– 9 the l· and the spirit bear witness,
lack of the
s 145– 5 the lack of the l· could not hinder their work ;
of Christian Science
o 354–32 If the l· of C. S. appears inconsistent,
of Science
s 113– 3 The l· of Science plentifully reaches humanity
f 243–11 must always accompany the l· of Science
without the spirit
s 145– 6 l·, without the spirit, would have made void

———

s 113– 7 Without this, the l· is but the dead body of
114–22 has to be poured into the old bottles of the l·.
p 367– 3 nor bury the *morale* of C. S. in the . . . l·.
t 451– 8 Students of C. S., who start with its l·
454–31 Remember that the l· and mental argument are
r 495–27 Study thoroughly the l· and imbibe the spirit.

letting

s 158–26 l· in matter's higher stratum, mortal mind.
163– 2 and afterward l· her loose upon sick people."
g 508–29 l· in the light of spiritual understanding.

level

ph 173– 8 is reduced to the l· of error,
f 239– 8 Break up cliques, l· wealth with honesty,
p 369–27 Unscientific methods are finding their dead l·.
g 508– 1 the divine idea seems to fall to the l· of

lever

r 485–32 is like saying that the power is in the l·.

Levi

gl 590–11 definition of

liability

a 40–15 Another's suffering cannot lessen our own l·.
f 230–29 never thoroughly healed until the l·
p 377– 3 and that thought governs this l·.

liable

s 140–24 a man-projected God, l· to wrath, repentance,
159–32 physician is l· to increase disease
f 230–28 though it is l· to reappear ;
248–22 result is that you are l· to follow
b 304–27 l· to be misapprehended and lost in confusion.
p 369– 1 he is l· to admit also the reality of
392–16 If . . . you are l· to an attack from that source.
392–18 l· to the development of that thought
412–11 by naming it audibly, you are l·
419–22 mortal mind is l· to any phase of belief.

liar

he is a
b 292–25 he is a l·, and the father of it."— *John* 8 : 44.
g 554–21 "He is a l·, and the father of it."— *John* 8 : 44.
gl 580–31 he is a l·, and the father of it."— *John* 8 : 44.
it was "a
o 357– 7 it was "a l·, and the father of it."— *John* 8 : 44.

———

s 113–25 "but every [mortal] man a l·."— *Rom.* 3 : 4.
b 296–31 Mortal belief is a l· from the beginning,
o 357– 9 Truth creates neither a lie, . . . nor a l·.
p 441–13 Material Law is a l· who cannot bear witness
441–31 Personal Sense, is recorded . . . as a l·.
r 471–21 but every [material] man a l·."— *Rom.* 3 : 4.
478–17 No, not if God is true and mortal man a l·.

liars

pr 16–19 the first lie and all l·.

liberal

pr 3–21 and for a l· outpouring of benefactions.

liberally

a 54–10 That he might l· pour his dear-bought treasures

liberation

an 103– 9 As in the beginning, however, this l· does not

liberator

f 225–22 Love is the l·.

Liberty

s 161–21 as she knelt before a statue of L·,
161–22 "L·, what crimes are committed in thy name !"
b 299– 3 when he carves his "Statue of L·,"

liberty

and life
p 434–26   conspiracy against the *l·* and life of Man.

and rights
p 435–17   a destroyer of Mortal Man's *l·* and rights.

elements of
f 224–28   Truth brings the elements of *l·*.

glorious
f 227–25   "glorious *l·* of the children of God," —*Rom.* 8 : 21.

set at
pref xi–21   To set at *l·* them that are bruised.— *Luke* 4 : 18.

standard of
f 227–21   C. S. raises the standard of *l·*

s 161–17   life, *l·*, and the pursuit of happiness."
f 227–18   Spirit of the Lord is, there is *l·*."— *II Cor.* 3 : 17.
b 315–19   the *l·* of the sons of God.
p 435–35   *l·* of which he has been unjustly deprived.
r 481– 5   Spirit of the Lord is, there is *l·*."— *II Cor.* 3 : 17.

licentious
s 130– 2   The *l·* disposition is discouraged over its

lie (noun)

charges its
b 307–17   Error charges its *l·* to Truth and says :

claims to be
c 523– 7   the *l·* claims to be truth.

condemned this
g 539–16   Scriptures declare that God condemned this *l·*

consigns the
g 542–25   justice consigns the *l·* which,

destroys itself
b 286–30   error, the *l·*, destroys itself.

destroy this
ap 568– 5   Science is able to destroy this *l·*, called evil.

first
pr 16–19   is but another name for the first *l·*
gl 594– 4   SERPENT . . . the first *l·* of limitation ;

first voluble
g 533–13   the snake-talker utters the first voluble *l·*,

from the beginning
ap 567–26   must be a *l·* from the beginning.

giving the
g 530–12   represents error as . . . giving the *l·* to

hides behind a
g 542– 6   Though error hides behind a *l·*

loves a
a 47–23   world generally loves a *l·* better than Truth ;

maketh a
ap 577–27   "defileth, . . . or maketh a *l·*."— *Rev.* 21 : 27.
gl 588– 4   "worketh . . . or maketh a *l·*."— *Rev.* 21 : 27.

material
ap 565–24   the material *l·* made war upon the

of false belief
p 370– 3   turn from the *l·* of false belief to Truth,

of material sense
b 318–12   We must silence this *l·* of material sense

rejecting a
o 357– 6   not by accepting, but by rejecting a *l·*.

serpentine
g 541–22   Here the serpentine *l·* invents new forms.

speaketh a
b 292–25   When he speaketh a *l·*, he— *John* 8 : 44.

suppositional
an 103–17   Evil is a suppositional *l·*.

symbolizes a
ap 563– 8   The great red dragon symbolizes a *l·*,

turns the
sp 92–21   Uncover error, and it turns the *l·* upon you.

worketh a
t 445–24   human will which maketh and worketh a *l·*,

sp 81–14   than the opposite . . . would prove immortality a *l·*.
ph 177–20   But a *l·*, the opposite of Truth, cannot
177–22   nor can a *l·* hold the preponderance of
b 330–28   manifested by mankind it stands for a *l·*,
o 357– 8   Truth creates neither a *l·*, . . . nor a liar.
t 448– 9   tell the truth concerning the *l·*.
r 480–15   The supposititious parent of evil is a *l·*.
g 524–25   or is it a *l·* concerning man and God?
524–27   It must be a *l·*, for God presently
527–20   Evil is unreal because it is a *l·*,
527–26   the *l·* represents God as repeating creation,
540–24   is to teach mortals never to believe a *l·*.
gl 584– 9   DEATH. An illusion, the *l·* of life in matter ;
584–17   DEVIL. Evil ; a *l·* ; error ;
594– 2   a *l·* ; the opposite of Truth, named error ;

lie (verb)

sp 87–23   the bodies which *l·* buried in its sands :
f 252–19   says : . . . I can cheat, *l·*, commit adultery,
b 291–22   "As the tree falls, so it must *l·*."
o 357– 9   Truth creates neither a lie, a capacity to *l·*, nor
g 514–23   shall *l·* down with the kid ;— *Isa.* 11 : 6.
ap 578– 6   to *l·* down in green pastures :— *Psal.* 23 : 2.

lies

pr 9– 3   The wrong *l·* in unmerited censure,
9– 5   *l·* in the answer to these questions :
m 68–22   to hatch their silly innuendoes and *l·*,
ph 165–19   your remedy *l·* in forgetting the whole thing ;
171–31   fundamental error *l·* in the supposition
f 250–20   To the observer, the body *l·* listless,
o 349–14   The chief difficulty . . . *l·* in this,
349–19   The elucidation of C. S. *l·* in its spiritual sense,
p 368– 3   confidence inspired by Science *l·* in the fact
385– 6   explanation *l·* in the support which they derived
427–22   difficulty *l·* in ignorance of what God is.
r 489–13   Corporeal sense defrauds and *l·* ;
g 514–12   Undisturbed it *l·* in the open field,

lieth
ap 574–16   the city which "*l·* foursquare." —*Rev.* 21 : 16.
575– 8   as one that "*l·* foursquare"— *Rev.* 21 : 16.

Life (*see also* **Life's**)

abideth in
b 325– 5   Such a one abideth in *L·*,

all
s 146–29   It lives through all *L·*,
g 526– 8   namely, that all *L·* is God.

all is
b 331–16   all is *L·*, and there is no death.
o 347– 7   all is *L·*, and death has no dominion.

and goodness
f 246–28   *L·* and goodness are immortal.

and health
p 430–11   shut out the true sense of *L·* and health.

and intelligence
pr 14–12   *L·* and intelligence are purely spiritual,
b 310–15   Soul . . . as the central *L·* and intelligence
r 477–22   Soul is the substance, *L·*, and intelligence of

and its faculties
f 246– 4   *L·* and its faculties are not measured by

and Love
a 22–12   the demand of *L·* and Love,
26–32   working out the harmony of *L·* and Love.
sp 91– 6   obey only the divine Principle, *L·* and Love.
s 108– 5   It was the divine law of *L·* and Love,
c 258– 3   glories of limitless, incorporeal *L·* and Love.
b 323–25   gives the true understanding of *L·* and Love,
o 348–15   when we ascribe to Him almighty *L·* and Love
p 381–17   In infinite *L·* and Love there is no sickness,
430– 9   advance more rapidly towards God, *L·*, and Love.
g 538–12   a figure of divine *L·* and Love,
ap 561–10   Purity was the symbol of *L·* and Love.
gl 589– 7   yield to the spiritual sense of *L·* and Love.
596–23   divine *L·* and Love illumine it,
598–24   the spiritual understanding of *L·* and Love,

and Soul
o 344– 2   God as the only absolute *L·* and Soul,

and substance
b 314–22   the true idea of *L·* and substance.

and the universe
b 306–28   *L·* and the universe, ever present and eternal.

and Truth
s 117–18   illustrating and demonstrating *L·* and Truth
f 216–18   is in submission to everlasting *L·* and Truth
b 279–20   demonstration of eternal *L·* and Truth
304– 1   sweet sense and presence of *L·* and Truth.

as God
sp 79– 4   those who are ignorant of *L·* as God.
b 310–27   if Spirit should lose *L·* as God, good,

as Love
p 391–30   rise to the true consciousness of *L·* as Love,

as permanent
b 306–24   which cognizes *L·* as permanent.

bread of
f 222–10   and feeds thought with the bread of *L·*.

can be understood
p 427–11   before *L·* can be understood and harmony

corresponds to
g 517–10   ideal woman corresponds to *L·* and

demonstrates
b 306– 7   *L·* demonstrates *L·*.
337–18   which demonstrates *L·* in Christ,

divine
(*see* **divine**)

eternal
pref vii–20   Him whom to know aright is *L·* eternal.
a 50–19   If his full recognition of eternal *L·* had
f 203–32   in order to give him eternal *L·*,
c 257–29   inexhaustible Love, eternal *L·*, omnipotent Truth.
258–27   To him belongs eternal *L·*.
259– 3   for he reflects eternal *L·* ;
b 279–20   demonstration of eternal *L·* and
p 380– 4   must be finally conquered by eternal *L·*.
426–27   with unflinching faith in God, in *L·* eternal.
429– 1   omnipotent and eternal *L·*,
r 469– 3   all substance and is *L·* eternal.
497– 4   the Bible as our sufficient guide to eternal *L·*.

Life

eternal
  r 497–22 faith to understand eternal *L·*,
  g 509– 8 the certain sense of eternal *L·*.
  gl 584–15 until every belief . . . yields to eternal *L·*.
    586– 9 FATHER. Eternal *L·* ; the one Mind ;
    588– 8 development of eternal *L·*, Truth, and Love.

everlasting
  f 216–18 his body is in submission to everlasting *L·*
  r 489–12 yields to the reality of everlasting *L·*.

ever-present
  b 312–20 man's eternal Principle is ever-present *L·*.

evidences of
  b 289–17 with the spiritual evidences of *L·* ;

explain
  a 27–17 Jesus' parables explain *L·* as never mingling

God is our
  s 107–17 remembering that in reality God is our *L·*,
  p 388–24 when we learn that God is our *L·*.

God, or
  a 27–21 pantheism,—that God, or *L·*, is in or of matter.
  sp 95– 7 We approach God, or *L·*, in proportion to

goes on unchanged
  s 122–26 in Science, *L·* goes on unchanged

great facts of
  s 122– 4 but the great facts of *L·*, rightly understood,

his
  a 25–10 His true flesh and blood were his *L·* ;

immortal
  r 496–22 at war with the facts of immortal *L·*,

immortality of
  sp 76–23 perfect harmony and immortality of *L·*,

infinite
  o 347– 7 God, who is infinite *L·*,
  p 381–17 In infinite *L·* and Love there is no
  g 518–23 varied expressions of God reflect . . . infinite *L·*,

in Himself
  o 357–29 Has the Father "*L·* in Himself,"—*John* 5 : 26.

intelligence and
  f 215–14 the light and might of intelligence and *L·*.

irradiance of
  gl 584– 1 DAY. The irradiance of *L·* ;

is continuous
  s 157–30 proof that *L·* is continuous and harmonious.

is deathless
  r 487– 3 *L·* is deathless.

is divine Mind
  r 469– 4 *L·* is divine Mind.

is divine Principle
  r 468–26 *Answer.— L·* is divine Principle, Mind, Soul,

is eternal
  f 246–27 *L·* is eternal.

is God
  a 27–10 That *L·* is God, Jesus proved
    51–16 He knew . . . that real *L·* is God ;
  ph 193–32 demonstrated to me that *L·* is God
    200–11 *L·* is God, and man is the idea of God,
  f 228– 6 nothing . . . can enter being, for *L· is* God.
  b 288–21 *L·* is God, good, and not evil ;
    289–32 Because *L·* is God, Life must be eternal,
    309–17 If these children . . . forget that *L·* is God,
    327–19 mortals are hastening to learn that *L·* is God,
  p 366–28 *L·* is God and God is All.
    369–20 He understood man, whose *L·* is God,
    394–28 We should remember that *L·* is God,
  r 487–27 The understanding that *L·* is God, Spirit,
    496– 9 We all must learn that *L·* is God.
  g 526– 8 namely, that all *L·* is God.
    550–21 If *L·* is God, as the Scriptures imply,

is Mind
  b 331– 5 *L·* is Mind, the creator reflected

is not contingent
  p 368–20 *L·* is not contingent on bodily conditions

is not embryonic
  g 550–22 If Life is God, . . . then *L·* is not embryonic,

is not limited
  r 469– 4 *L·* is not limited.

is real
  p 428– 3 *L·* is real, and death is the illusion.

is reflected
  g 516– 9 *L·* is reflected in existence,

is self-sustained
  p 390– 4 We cannot deny that *L·* is self-sustained,

is Spirit
  c 264–16 When we realize that *L·* is Spirit,
  b 310–26 The only *L·* is Spirit,
  p 376–12 that *L·* is Spirit, and that

is the law
  m 63–10 and *L·* is the law of his being.
  p 427– 2 *L·* is the law of Soul, even the law of

is the origin
  r 487– 3 *L·* is the origin and ultimate of man,

is Truth
  r 472– 1 and that this *L·* is Truth and Love ;

Jesus demonstrated
  f 244– 5 On their basis Jesus demonstrated *L·*,

Life

law of
  (*see* **law**)

laws of
  s 107– 2 the Christ Science or divine laws of *L·*,

leads to
  f 202–20 the true way leads to *L·* instead of to death,

life of
  b 320– 2 of the truth of Truth and of the life of *L·*,

Love, and wisdom
  b 283– 6 Mind is the same *L·*, Love, and wisdom

Love, Truth
  sp 81–15 *L·*, Love, Truth, is the only proof of

manifestations of
  g 543–27 reflected in the myriad manifestations of *L·*,

man's
  o 358– 4 that is, of God, who is man's *L·*
  p 425–17 can never destroy God, who is man's *L·*.

Mind and
  b 276–17 admitted to be the only Mind and *L·*,

Mind or
  b 291–26 No resurrection from the grave awaits Mind or *L·*,

misconception of
  g 542–29 The sinful misconception of *L·*

must be eternal
  b 289–32 *L·* must be eternal, self-existent.

newness of
  g 520–13 they will reveal eternity, newness of *L·*,

no matter in
  s 113–31 no matter in *L·*, and no life in matter ;

not the fruits of
  f 243–30 sin, and death are not the fruits of *L·*.

of all
  g 509– 2 Spirit is discerned to be the *L·* of all,

of man
  a 51–11 Nothing could kill this *L·* of man.
  b 304–17 Divine Principle is the *L·* of man.
  p 388–22 does not affect the absolute *L·* of man,
  g 555–30 Knowing that God was the *L·* of man,

one
  a 19–32 thou shalt not know evil, for there is one *L·*,
  f 204– 4 false conclusions that there is more than one *L·*
  b 283–19 deem this the manifestation of the one *L·*,
  r 467–10 one God and Father, one *L·*, Truth, and Love,

or God
  f 249–11 Any other theory of *L·*, or God, is delusive
  b 283–14 They insist that *L·*, or God, is one . . . with
  o 357–30 if so, can *L·*, or God, dwell in evil
  g 543–29 belief . . . would make *L·*, or God, mortal.

or intelligence
  g 550– 5 God is the *L·*, or intelligence, which

or Mind
  sp 91–17 the substance of *L·* or Mind.
  b 282– 3 The real *L·*, or Mind, and its opposite,
    290–10 That *L·* or Mind is finite . . . is false.
  g 509– 3 and the deathless *L·*, or Mind,
    550– 3 If this be so, whence cometh *L·*, or Mind,

or Soul
  b 306–13 If *L·* or Soul and its representative, man,

or Truth
  a 42– 6 It cannot make *L·* or Truth apparent.
  ph 196–16 are not concomitants of *L·* or Truth.

over death
  p 406–22 the supremacy of . . . *L·* over death,

path of
  t 451–12 strive, to enter the narrow path of *L·*,

Principle, or
  b 283–24 The divine Principle, or *L·*, cannot be
  g 507–16 creative power of the divine Principle, or *L·*,

real
  a 51–16 He knew . . . that real *L·* is God ;
  b 282– 3 The real *L·*, or Mind, and its opposite,
    328– 5 God is good and the only real *L·*.

reality of
  sp 72–27 earthly mortal is not the reality of *L·*
  b 322– 5 we shall gain the reality of *L·*,
  o 353–32 nor apprehend the reality of *L·*.
  r 487–29 our trust in the deathless reality of *L·*,

reveals
  f 250–30 Science reveals *L·* as not being at the mercy of

Science of
  (*see* **Science**)

Soul, or
  p 388–25 sin and sickness are not qualities of Soul, or *L·*

Spirit, and
  b 280–23 belief that . . . Spirit, and *L·*, is in finite forms

spirit of
  p 433–31 Ah ! but Christ, Truth, the spirit of *L·*

spiritual
  (*see* **spiritual**)

statement of
  p 379–19 let her learn the opposite statement of *L·*

substance and
  b 286–22 God's thoughts . . . are substance and *L·*.

Life

substance, and intelligence
- *a* 27–14 *L·*, substance, and intelligence of the universe
- *ph* 185–19 God as the only *L·*, substance, and intelligence,
- *gl* 595– 7 the idea of *L·*, substance, and intelligence ;

supernal
- *b* 319– 2 has no kinship with the *L·* supernal.

that is Truth
- *sp* 97–29 demonstrating the *L·* that is Truth,

the only
- *ph* 185–19 God as the only *L·*, substance, and
- *b* 289– 4 until he learns that God is the only *L·*.
- 307–13 as much as God, Spirit, who *is* the only *L·*."
- 310–26 The only *L·* is Spirit,
- 324–15 the understanding that God is the only *L·*.
- 330–11 God is infinite, the only *L·*, substance,
- *p* 428–32 the understanding of God as the only *L·*.
- *r* 472– 1 Science teaches man that God is the only *L·*,

theory of
- *f* 249–11 Any other theory of *L·*, or God, is delusive

true idea of
- *b* 314–22 the true idea of *L·* and substance.
- 325– 2 he who perceives the true idea of *L·*

true sense of
- *o* 355–13 the harmonious and true sense of *L·*
- *p* 430–11 shut out the true sense of *L·* and health.

Truth and
   (*see* **Truth**)

Truth, and Love
- *pr* 3–27 If we are ungrateful for *L·*, Truth, and Love,
- 14–18 controlled by spiritual *L·*, Truth, and Love.
- *a* 50–14 Had *L·*, Truth, and Love forsaken him
- 54–14 proof that *L·*, Truth, and Love heal the sick
- *s* 107– 2 divine laws of *L·*, Truth, and Love,
- 108–23 *L·*, Truth, and Love are all-powerful and
- 138– 6 evident to Peter that divine *L·*, Truth, and Love
- 140– 8 as divine Mind, as *L·*, Truth, and Love.
- 164–24 *L·*, Truth, and Love save from sin,
- *b* 298– 2 *L·*, Truth, and Love are the realities of
- 303–11 Whatever reflects Mind, *L·*, Truth, and Love, is
- 331–26 *L·*, Truth, and Love constitute the triune
- 336–16 emanations of Him who is *L·*, Truth, and Love.
- *p* 419– 5 leave the field to God, *L·*, Truth, and Love,
- 427–22 God, *L·*, Truth, and Love make man undying.
- *r* 467–10 one God and Father, one *L·*, Truth, and Love.
- 469–10 *L·*, Truth, and Love,— named God.
- 474– 1 *L·*, Truth, and Love . . . destroy all error,
- 474–14 If . . . are as real as *L·*, Truth, and Love,
- *g* 502– 7 The creative Principle—*L·*, Truth, and Love
- 505–23 unfolds Mind,—*L·*, Truth, and Love,
- 508– 7 *L·*, Truth, and Love which governs all.
- 510–27 a symbol of Mind, of *L·*, Truth, and Love
- 515–20 the tri-unity of *L·*, Truth, and Love.
- 518–23 reflect . . . infinite *L·*, Truth, and Love.
- 522–29 Does *L·*, Truth, and Love produce death,
- *ap* 577–14 first, the Word of *L·*, Truth, and Love ;
- *gl* 582–29 representatives of *L·*, Truth, and Love.
- 583–22 self-existent *L·*, Truth, and Love ;
- 588– 8 development of eternal *L·*, Truth, and Love.·
- 592–16 eternal Principle ; *L·*, Truth, and Love.
- 593–20 *L·*, Truth, and Love understood and
- 599– 4 reflected animation of *L·*, Truth, and Love.

Truth, . . . and Love
   (*see* **Truth**)

Truth or
- *sp* 91–14 is by no means the destruction of Truth or *L·*.

Truth, . . . or Love
- *f* 207–26 presuppose the absence of Truth, *L·*, or Love.

Truth that is
- *sp* 97–30 the Life that is Truth, and the Truth that is *L·*,

Truth which is
- *a* 35–23 Life which is Truth and the Truth which is *L·*
- *f* 235–23 who understand not the divine Truth which is *L·*

understanding of
   (*see* **understanding**)

unfolding of
- *b* 335–23 can we gain the eternal unfolding of *L·*

unknown to
- *r* 469– 5 Death and finiteness are unknown to *L·*.

vast forever of
- *c* 266–31 into the vast forever of *L·*,

verities of
- *sp* 75–32 when we awake . . . to the grand verities of *L·*,

vesture of
- *f* 242–21 The vesture of *L·* is Truth.

way of
- *a* 25–13 Jesus taught the way of *L·* by demonstration,
- *s* 137–25 Love hath shown thee the way of *L·* !

we apprehend
- *ph* 167– 6 We apprehend *L·* in divine Science

which is God
- *a* 47– 3 a faint conception of the *L·* which is God.
- *ap* 561–19 understanding the *L·* which is God.

which is Truth
- *a* 35–22 as we reach the *L·* which is Truth

19

Life

will be recognized
- *sp* 76– 6 *L·* will be recognized as neither material nor

Word of
- *ap* 577–14 first, the Word of *L·*, Truth, and Love ;

- *pr* 17–14 *L·*, Truth, Love, over all, and All.
- *a* 19–31 Thou shalt have no belief of *L·* as mortal ;
- 44– 9 He proved *L·* to be deathless and Love to be
- *sp* 72– 1 the *L·* of which corporeal sense can take no
- 98–19 Christ's revelation of Truth, of *L·*, and of Love,
- *s* 113–19 *L·*, God, omnipotent good, deny death, evil,
- 113–21 evil, death, deny good, omnipotent God, *L·*.
- 115–13 God : Divine Principle, *L·*, Truth, Love, Soul,
- 124–10 thus limiting *L·* and holding fast to discord
- 151–20 lungs, brain, etc., have nothing to do with *L·*,
- *ph* 172–20 belief that there is Soul in sense or *L·* in matter
- 186–25 If death is as real as *L·*, immortality is a
- 191–13 spiritual sense of being and of what *L·* includes.
- 200– 9 *L·* is, . . . and ever will be independent of
- *f* 203–24 Death is not a stepping-stone to *L·*.
- 206– 2 no other Love, . . . no other sense of *L·*,
- 215–20 are the suppositional absence of *L·*, God,
- 216– 4 What has touched *L·*, God, to such strange
- 231–10 but God, Truth, *L·*, Love, does heal the
- 243–26 *L·* has no partnership with death.
- 249–18 *L·* is, like Christ, "the same—*Heb.* 13 : 8.
- 249–20 Organization and time have nothing to do with
      L·.
- 253– 7 without beginning and without end, for I am *L·*.
- *c* 260–32 If we look to the body for. . .*L·*, we find death ;
- *b* 275–12 Spirit, *L·*, Truth, Love, combine as one,
- 275–18 no life is *L·* but the divine ;
- 286–11 but by me," Christ, *L·*,—*John* 14 : 6.
- 288–24 that *L·* is not subject to death ;
- 289–11 *L·* and Life's idea, . . . never make men sick,
- 289–27 *L·* is not in matter.
- 289–32 not the offspring of flesh, but of Spirit,— of *L·*,
- 290– 1 *L·* is the everlasting I AM,
- 292–10 belief . . . and *L·* be controlled by death.
- 293–16 whose adhesion and cohesion are *L·*,
- 296–12 is what reveals man and *L·*, harmonious,
- 300–32 God is revealed only in that which reflects *L·*,
- 306– 8 If God, who is *L·*, were parted for a moment
- 307–15 is found to be not *L·*, but only a transient,
- 309–29 *L·* is never for a moment extinct.
- 322–29 Then we begin to learn *L·* in divine Science.
- 325–17 perfect as the Father, indestructible in *L·*,
- 330–20 Scriptures declare Him to be,—*L·*, Truth, Love.
- 331– 1 and *L·* is no more confined to
- 332–14 the Way, the Truth, and the *L·*,
- 335–19 Nothing but Spirit, Soul, can evolve *L·*,
- *o* 347– 6 Nothing really has *L·* but God,
- 349–11 neither *L·* nor man dies,
- 357–31 Can matter drive *L·*, Spirit, hence,
- 358– 3 Can a leaden bullet deprive a man of *L·*,
- *p* 378–27 never endowed matter with power to disable *L·*
- 380–31 opposing . . . against *L·*, health, harmony.
- 388–15 hypothesis . . . food has power to destroy *L·*,
- 406–20 Error is opposed to *L·*.
- 407–27 brings . . .*L·* not death, into your consciousness.
- 428–17 the *L·* which mortal sense cannot impair
- 429– 2 this *L·* must be brought to light
- 429–22 if *L·* ever had any beginning, it must also have
- 433–29 to prepare the frightened sense of *L·*,
- *r* 465–10 Spirit, Soul, Principle, *L·*, Truth, Love.
- 468–25 *Question.*— What is *L·*?
- 468–27 *L·* is without beginning and without end.
- 468–29 Eternity, not time, expresses the thought of *L·*,
- 469– 1 *L·* is neither in nor of matter.
- 469– 6 If *L·* ever had a beginning, it would
- 470– 8 assumed . . . the loss of the spiritual presence
      of *L·*
- 486–18 If . . . a better friend than *L·*.
- 492– 5 *L·* cannot be united to its unlikeness,
- 495–19 life harmonious—as *L·* eternally is
- 495–20 belief in, that which *L·* is not.
- *g* 516– 4 The substance, *L·*, intelligence, Truth, and
- 531–25 Which institutes *L·*,— matter or Mind?
- 531–25 Does *L·* begin with Mind or with matter?
- 531–26 Is *L·* sustained by matter or by Spirit?
- 539– 8 the standard of good, of Spirit, of *L·*,
- 544– 6 Mind, . . . the producer, *L·* was self-sustained.
- 544– 9 *L·* consisteth not of the things which
- 544–30 declares . . . so-called mortal life to be *L·*,
- 548–13 before *L·* is spiritually learned.
- 550–20 If *L·* has any starting-point whatsoever,
- *ap* 561–17 of *L·* and its demonstration,
- 569– 1 as *L·*, represented by the Father ;
- *gl* 580–25 false supposition that *L·* is not eternal,
- 584–10 the unreal and untrue ; the opposite of *L·*.
- 584–14 until every belief of life where *L·* is not
- 587– 7 *L·* ; Truth ; Love ; all substance ;
- 590–14 definition of
- 591–17 substance, *L·*, Truth, Love ; the one God ;

life (*see also* **life's**)

Abel's
g 541– 4 Cain seeks Abel's *l·*, instead of making his

action, nor
s 136– 6 claimed no. . .action, nor *l·* separate from God.

and being
an 103–31 *L·* and being are of God.

and brotherhood
g 541–17 ruptures the *l·* and brotherhood of man

and death
sp 92– 4 the issues of *l·* and death,
ph 190–10 thoughts of pain and pleasure, of *l·* and death,
f 211– 4 good and evil, *l·* and death ;
246– 3 sickness and health, *l·* and death.
b 298–17 hope and fear, *l·* and death,
303–21 belief that pain and pleasure, *l·* and death,
r 466– 9 mind and matter, *l·* and death,

and happiness
c 262–21 drop the false estimate of *l·* and happiness,
g 536–28 their belief in perishable *l·* and happiness ;

and health
ph 185–10 discussed . . . to regulate *l·* and health.
p 428–31 and raised the dying to *l·* and health

and immortality
p 376–13 more *l·* and immortality in one good motive
g 539– 5 as if *l·* and immortality were something which

and intelligence
a 52–20 the nothingness of material *l·* and intelligence
sp 71–17 which simulate mind, *l·*, and intelligence.
s 124– 9 seeks to find *l·* and intelligence in matter,
ph 177–17 theory of *l·* and intelligence in matter,
f 209–28 hypothesis of. . .*l·* and intelligence resident in
222–32 the false belief that *l·* and intelligence in
237–26 a belief in the *l·* and intelligence of matter,
b 279–16 belief disappears that *l·* and intelligence are
279–31 seeks . . . *l·* and intelligence in matter.
294–21 the error that *l·* and intelligence are in matter,
307– 1 delusion that *l·* and intelligence proceeded from
319–16 presuppose *l·* and intelligence to exist in
322– 3 changes the standpoints of *l·* and intelligence
r 476– 7 claim . . . that *l·* and intelligence are in
g 522–13 forms, called *l·* and intelligence in matter.
533–23 belief in material *l·* and intelligence
535–11 supposed material foundations of *l·* and intelligence.
gl 584–20 saith : "I am *l·* and intelligence in matter.

and its joys
b 299–11 higher ideals of *l·* and its joys.

and joy
g 536–25 material conception of *l·* and joy,

and light
f 209– 7 the *l·* and light of all its own vast creation ;

and man
p 368–21 we learn that *l·* and man survive this body.

and mind
b 296– 8 destroy all illusions regarding *l·* and mind,
g 556– 5 are supposed to possess *l·* and mind.

and peace
f 224– 9 painless progress, attended by *l·* and peace

and sensation
b 278–12 That matter . . . has *l·* and sensation, is one of
289– 4 belief that *l·* and sensation are in the body
p 396–29 never giving the body *l·* and sensation.

and substance
b 311–18 dream of *l·* and substance as existent in matter,

and truth
c 262–12 efforts to find *l·* and truth in matter

appearance of
ph 187–28 loses all appearance of *l·* or action,

arbiter of
p 369–12 belief . . . that it can be the arbiter of *l·*

belief of
(*see* **belief**)

belief that
(*see* **belief**)

better
pr 7–20 a higher experience and a better *l·*

breath of
g 524–15 into his nostrils the breath of *l·* ;— *Gen.* 2 : 7.

cannot destroy
p 388–21 prepared by Jesus . . . it cannot destroy *l·*.
426–17 learned that disease cannot destroy *l·*,

chart of
a 24– 8 and make the Bible the chart of *l·*,

consciousness of
f 242–12 to have no other consciousness of *l·*

constitutes
b 283–21 false belief as to what really constitutes *l·*

crown of
c 267–30 he shall receive the crown of *l·*,— *Jas.* 1 : 12.

daily
ph 179– 4 and following Christ in the daily *l·*,
b 272–20 and Christianization of daily *l·*,
283–28 We must receive . . . and live it in daily *l·* ;

days of my
ap 578–17 all the days of my *l·* ;— *Psal.* 23 : 6.

life

demonstrated in the
b 333–12 and demonstrated in the *l·* of which

demonstrated the
s 149–13 have not demonstrated the *l·* of Christ,

demonstration of
a 45–19 the revelation and demonstration of *l·* in God,
f 214– 8 guided into the demonstration of *l·* eternal.
b 278–24 contradicts the demonstration of *l·* as Spirit,

department of
t 462–19 as they usually do in every department of *l·*.

earthly
ap 565–14 a brief history in the earthly *l·* of our Master ;

embryonic
g 547–14 the germinating speck of so-called embryonic *l·*
548–29 facts in regard to so-called embryonic *l·*.
ap 561– 6 at a point of so-called embryonic *l·*.

eternal
a 54–26 and to share the glory of eternal *l·*.
f 214– 8 guided into the demonstration of *l·* eternal.
b 271–24 the essence of this Science, and the eternal *l·*,
289– 2 Truth demonstrated is eternal *l·*.
340–22 demonstrates health, holiness, and *l·* eternal.
p 410– 4 "This is *l·* eternal," says Jesus,— *John* 17 : 3.
410– 7 "This is *l·* eternal, that they— *John* 17 : 3.

everlasting
sp 81–11 this fact affords no certainty of everlasting *l·*.
p 410– 5 and then he defines everlasting *l·* as a
g 556–12 *l·* everlasting is not to be gained by dying.

false views of
m 62–29 false views of *l·* hide eternal harmony,

fountain of
ph 190–30 with Thee is the fountain of *l·* ;— *Psal.* 36 : 9.

good
ph 167–32 Substituting good words for a good *l·*,

had no
a 51–16 He knew that matter had no *l·*

happiness and
f 232– 5 beliefs . . . about happiness and *l·*
b 308–11 looking for happiness and *l·* in the body,

health or
s 148–27 When physiology fails to give health or *l·* by this

her
pref xii–16 conviction that the next two years of her *l·*,
p 379–22 her belief that blood is destroying her *l·*.

his
a 45–13 we shall be saved by his *l·*."— *Rom.* 5 : 10.
ph 171–10 probabilities either of his *l·* or of
b 317–17 his *l·* is not at the mercy of matter.
326–27 and his *l·* became more spiritual.
p 436–12 Laying down his *l·* for a good deed,

holiness, and
a 52– 6 spiritual evidence of health, holiness, and *l·* ;
b 340–22 demonstrates health, holiness, and *l·* eternal.

human
(*see* **human**)

human concept of
o 359–13 you must change the human concept of *l·*,

idea of
a 30– 2 he could give a more spiritual idea of *l·*

illusion of
b 305–23 In the illusion of *l·* that is here to-day and

immortal
a 51–11 that he might furnish the proof of immortal *l·*.

immortality and
sp 98–31 through which immortality and *l·* are learned

indestructible
f 209– 2 Man, . . . has a perfect indestructible *l·*.

in God
a 45–19 the revelation and demonstration of *l·* in God,
b 324–18 the goal of Spirit, or *l·* in God.

in Soul
pr 13–32 not cognizant of *l·* in Soul, not in body.

instead of
p 435–13 pleasure instead of pain, and *l·* instead of

intelligence and
ph 171–26 beliefs that intelligence and *l·* are present
171–29 that intelligence and *l·* are spiritual,
b 269–31 Mind, possessing intelligence and *l·*.

interpretation of
a 54–19 would not accept his meek interpretation of *l·*

issues of
sp 92– 4 the issues of *l·* and death,
ph 181– 6 or does it hold the issues of *l·* ?"

its
b 307–14 Its *l·* is found to be not Life, but only a

Jesus'
a 42– 1 Jesus' *l·* proved, divinely and scientifically,

ladder of
f 222– 3 and ascend the ladder of *l·*.

law of
b 314–32 supposed accord with the inevitable law of *l·*.
p 387–22 supposition that. . .in obedience to the law of *l·*,

man's
ph 166–12 believes in his prescription, . . . to save a man's *l·*.
f 203–32 for God alone is man's *l·*.

life

married
m 59– 6 all the years of married *l·*.

material
(*see* **material**)

matter has no
b 275– 1 Matter has no *l·* to lose, and Spirit never dies.
p 426–30 because matter has no *l·* to surrender.
gl 584–11 Matter has no *l·*, hence it has no real

miscalled
s 164–23 materiality miscalled *l·* in the body

misconception of
g 554– 9 following from a misconception of *l·*,

mortal
p 399–22 so-called mortal *l·* is mortal mind,
g 503–25 God creates neither erring thought, mortal *l·*,
544–30 declares . . . so-called mortal *l·* to be Life,
552–13 Human experience in mortal *l·*, which starts

never gave
p 376–12 should be told that blood never gave *l·*

newness of
a 24–12 rise into newness of *l·* with regeneration.
35– 9 rise . . . into newness of *l·* as Spirit.
f 249– 7 bringing us into newness of *l·*
p 426–19 will quicken into newness of *l·*.

no . . . in matter
s 113–31 no matter in Life, and no *l·* in matter ;

nor sensation
s 127–21 as matter — no intelligence, *l·*, nor sensation.
f 205–10 matter has neither intelligence, *l·*, nor sensation,

of Christ Jesus
b 270–31 The *l·* of Christ Jesus was not miraculous,

of Jesus
b 317– 6 Whosoever lives most the *l·* of Jesus

of Life
b 320– 2 of the truth of Truth and of the *l·* of Life,

of Man
p 434–26 conspiracy against the liberty and *l·* of Man.

of man
p 377–29 to defend the *l·* of man
389–14 theories . . . that food sustains the *l·* of man,
402–17 The *l·* of man is Mind.
410–12 showing that Truth is the actual *l·* of man ;
438–17 conspiracy against the rights and *l·* of man.

or existence
b 311–29 all supposed . . . claim to *l·* or existence,

organic
t 450–32 electricity, animal nature, and organic *l·*,

or intelligence
r 485–32 The notion of any *l·* or intelligence in matter
gl 584–28 the absence of substance, *l·*, or intelligence.

or love
c 257–24 Who hath found finite *l·* or love sufficient to

or mind
sp 76– 8 belief that *l·*, or mind, was ever in a finite form,
b 303–17 illusion that *l·*, or mind, is formed by

or soul
sp 70–15 Does *l·* or soul exist in the thing formed?

physical
f 247– 1 The acute belief of physical *l·* comes on at

possesses no
r 475–21 that which possesses no *l·*, . . . of his own,

queen of
t 451– 7 Christianity, . . . must be their queen of *l·*.

reckoning
g 539– 4 Error begins by reckoning *l·* as separate from

recognition of
r 495–18 that the recognition of *l·* harmonious

recognize no
s 133–27 would recognize no *l·*, . . . outside of God.

resurrection and the
a 31–16 "the resurrection and the *l·*" — *John* 11 : 25.
b 292– 7 "the resurrection and the *l·*" — *John* 11 : 25.

seem to have
b 307–13 and matter shall seem to have *l·*

sensation nor
s 108– 7 matter possesses neither sensation nor *l·* ;

sense of
a 51– 7 He had power to lay down a human sense of *l·*
sp 72–14 Mortal belief (the material sense of *l·*)
b 290– 9 instead of through a spiritual sense of *l·*,
308–17 struggling with a mortal sense of *l·*,
311–30 as mortals lay off a false sense of *l·*,
325–32 A false sense of *l·*, substance, and mind
p 376–16 simulated a corporeal sense of *l·*.
g 548– 5 spiritual sense of *l·*, substance, and intelligence.

so-called
b 292–17 so-called *l·* of mortals is dependent on
309–20 such so-called *l·* always ends in death.
o 358– 2 axe, which destroys a tree's so-called *l·*,

soul, and
r 466–25 fallacy that . . . soul, and *l·* can be in matter ;

span of
f 252–23 says : . . . make my short span of *l·* one gala

spirit and in
a 39–22 experience that salvation in spirit and in *l·*.

life

Spirit is the
s 124–25 Spirit is the *l·*, substance, and continuity of

Spirit of
f 244–11 law of the Spirit of *l·* in Christ — *Rom.* 8 : 2.

spiritual
(*see* **spiritual**)

statement of
g 554– 9 Any statement of *l·*, following from a

structural
b 283–18 such as the structural *l·* of the tree

substance, and
gl 591– 9 illusion ; intelligence, substance, and *l·* in

substance, and intelligence
a 43–29 beliefs about *l·*, substance, and intelligence.
f 249–24 dream that *l·*, substance, and intelligence are
b 274–19 which affirm that *l·*, substance, and intelligence
278–30 the opposite of *l·*, substance, and intelligence.
287–24 supposition that *l·*, substance, and intelligence
294– 2 belief, that *l·*, substance, and intelligence
302–17 illusion of any *l·*, substance, and intelligence as
308–17 a mortal sense of *l·*, substance, and intelligence
311–30 a false sense of *l·*, substance, and intelligence.
t 450–27 beliefs in *l·*, substance, and intelligence
450–31 belief of *l·*, substance, and intelligence
g 541–16 belief that *l·*, substance, and intelligence
548– 5 spiritual sense of *l·*, substance, and intelligence.
gl 583– 3 suppositions of *l·*, substance, and intelligence,
585–24 concerning *l·*, substance, and intelligence
586–19 that *l·*, substance, and intelligence are
587– 9 a belief that *l·*, substance, and intelligence
588–18 the belief that *l·*, substance, and intelligence
592– 2 belief that *l·*, substance, and intelligence

substance, . . . and intelligence
sp 91–26 belief is, that substance, *l·*, and intelligence
ap 562–10 light, substance, *l·*, and intelligence.
563– 9 belief that substance, *l·*, and intelligence

substance, and mind
b 325–32 A false sense of *l·*, substance, and mind
gl 582– 4 physical belief as to *l·*, substance, and mind ;

substance, or intelligence
p 418– 6 error that *l·*, substance, or intelligence can

supposes
r 489– 8 hypothesis which supposes *l·* to be in matter

supposititious
b 322–26 belief in the supposititious *l·* of matter,

temporal
a 51–12 Jesus could give his temporal *l·* into
s 122–27 Temporal *l·* is a false sense of existence.

that approaches
r 496–10 Am I living the *l·* that approaches the supreme

thought and in
pr 11–32 It is best expressed in thought and in *l·*.

to suppose that
sp 83–21 contrary to C. S. to suppose that *l·* is either

tree of
p 426–13 this would be a "tree of *l·*," — *Rev.* 22 : 2.
t 458–19 to guard "the tree of *l·*." — *Gen.* 3 : 24.
g 526– 1 tree of *l·* also, in the midst of the — *Gen.* 2 : 9.
526–18 The "tree of *l·*" stands for the — *Gen.* 2 : 9.
527–18 "the tree of *l·*" to be the — *Gen.* 2 : 9.
537– 2 and take also of the tree of *l·*, — *Gen.* 3 : 22.
537– 8 to keep the way of the tree of *l·*. — *Gen.* 3 : 24.
538–13 The "tree of *l·*" is significant of — *Gen.* 2 : 9.

truth, and love
b 284–18 testimony as to spiritual *l·*, truth, and love?

truth, and the
a 26–11 the way, the truth, and the *l·* ;" — *John* 14 : 6.
b 320– 3 the way, the truth, and the *l·*." — *John* 14 : 6.
o 353–11 "the way, the truth, and the *l·*," — *John* 14 : 6.

vegetable
b 309–28 as organic animal or vegetable *l·*,

water of
g 548– 2 take the water of *l·* freely." — *Rev.* 22 : 17.

Word of
b 268– * handled, of the Word of *l·*, — *I John* 1 : 1.

your
m 62–13 "thought for your *l·*, what ye — *Matt.* 6 : 25.
ph 165– * *Take no thought for your l·,* — *Matt.* 6 : 25.
170–16 "Take no thought for your *l·*, — *Matt.* 6 : 25.
f 228–21 "Take no thought for your *l·*," — *Matt.* 6 : 25.
p 365– 8 "Take no thought for your *l·*," — *Matt.* 6 : 25.
g 530– 8 "Take no thought for your *l·*." — *Matt.* 6 : 25.

your own
s 149–14 not demonstrated . . . more in your own *l·*,

a 40–13 If the saying is true, "While there's *l·* there's
48–31 hastening the final demonstration of what *l·* is
m 65–12 *l·* should be more metaphysically regarded.
sp 75– 2 assumption that man . . . comes to *l·* as spirit.
78– 7 belief that we are wearing out *l·* and
89–28 Cain . . . concluded that if *l·* was in the body,
95– 6 "To be spiritually minded is *l·*." — *Rom.* 8 : 6.
s 107–15 false consciousness that *l·* inheres in the body,
122–25 To material sense, . . . takes away *l·* ;
161–17 among which are *l·*, liberty, and the pursuit of

life

ph 165– * *Is not the l· more than meat,— Matt.* 6 : 25.
 191–19 What are man's prospects for l·?
f 205– 7 error of believing that there is l· in matter,
 216–25 would seem the exception, . . . and l· a paradox.
 246–10 The measurement of l· by solar years robs
 247–21 Beauty is a thing of l·, which dwells
 253– 6 saith : . . . I give l·, without beginning
c 261–26 neither lose the solid objects and ends of l· nor
b 275–18 no l· is Life but the divine ;
 283–17 They claim that to be l· which is but the
 289–10 To suppose that sin, lust, hatred, . . . have l·
 289–21 The belief that matter has l· results, . . . in a
 300– 2 correct spiritual conclusions regarding l·
 304– 6 "Neither death, nor l·,— *Rom.* 8 : 38.
 304–14 nor l· result in death.
 306– 3 They would first make l· result in death, and
 318–11 They would put soul into soil, l· into limbo,
 319–'2 The delusion that there is l· in matter has no
 325– 6 l· obtained not of the body
 325– 6 the body incapable of supporting l·,
 325–11 "When Christ, who is our l·, shall·— *Col.* 3 : 4.
 331– 3 If l· were in mortal man or
 340– 2 and make l· its own proof of harmony and God.
p 388–13 hypothesis that food is the nutriment of l·,
 409–27 no right to say that l· depends on matter now,
 428–21 the l· which is spiritual, not material.
t 445–13 l· "hid with Christ in God,"— *Col.* 3 : 3.
r 467– 6 no intelligence, no l·, . . . but that which is
 468– 9 There is no l·, truth, . . . in matter.
 472–15 Error . . . that intelligence, substance, l·,
g 501– * *In Him was l·; and the l· was— John* 1 : 4.
 511–20 the moving creature that hath l·,— *Gen.* 1 : 20.
 518–11 wherein there is l·,— *Gen.* 1 : 30.
 526– 6 this statement that l· issues from matter,
 535–23 eat of it all the days of thy l· :— *Gen.* 3 : 17.
 543–29 The belief that matter supports l·
 549– 4 supposition that l· germinates in eggs
 554–11 any knowledge of the so-called selfhood of l·,
gl 582– 8 error masquerading as the possessor of l·,
 584– 9 DEATH. An illusion, the lie of l· in matter ;
 591–10, 11 illusion; . . . l· resulting in death, and death in l·;
 594– 8 claim that . . . and death are the realities of l·.
 598–26 would bridge over with l· discerned spiritually

life-basis

ph 191– 8 As a material, theoretical l· is found to be a

life-giving

r 495–10 the l· power of Truth acting on human belief,
g 517– 7 The l· quality of Mind is Spirit.
 522–19 represented as the l· principle of the earth.

Life-laws

p 398– 9 the popular ignorance of spiritual L·.

life-link

o 350–28 that l· forming the connection through which

lifelong

a 53–23 mocking the l· sacrifice which goodness makes
p 371–21 nor would I keep the suckling a l· babe.

life-motives

m 58– 8 Unselfish ambition, noble l·, and purity,

life-practice

f 202– 4 must be wrought out in l·,

life-preserving

gl 579–13 l· power of spiritual understanding.

Life-principle

a 42–32 They must understand more fully his L·

Life-problem

pref ix–30 comparative ignorance of the stupendous L·

life-prospects

b 319– 5 To calculate one's l· from a

Life's

b 289–12 Life and L· idea, Truth and Truth's idea,
 337–18 Christ, L· spiritual ideal.
gl 580–16 L· counterfeit, which ultimates in death ;

life's

a 18– 6 He did l· work aright
m 60–28 and teach us l· sweeter harmonies.

life-work

a 48–16 until the consummation of a l·.
f 248–22 The result is that you . . . limit your l·,
b 328–30 The purpose of his great l· extends through

lift

m 67– 6 waves l· themselves into mountains.
ph 199– 2 could l· the hammer and strike the anvil,
p 373– 9 to l· a student out of a chronic sin.
g 515–26 If you l· a weight, your reflection does this also.
ap 569–18 not struggling to l· their heads above the
 574–25 it will l· the sackcloth from your eyes,

lifted

ph 200– 3 l· thought into the song of David.
c 259– 8 l· their lives higher than their poor

lifted

g 513–10 anon the veil is l·, and the scene shifts
ap 574–22 l· the seer to behold the great city,

lifting

p 400–18 By l· thought above error, or disease,
 407–14 l· humanity above itself into purer desires,

lifts

m 60– 2 Science inevitably l· one's being higher
sp 95–31 l· human consciousness into eternal Truth.
 97–24 the higher Truth l· her voice, the louder will
s 114–24 It l· the veil of mystery from Soul and body.
 147–20 This proof l· you high above the
f 220– 9 The violet l· her blue eye to greet the
 235–13 and spiritual culture, which l· one higher.
 252–16 Material sense l· its voice with the arrogance of
g 521– 1 Knowledge of this l· man above the sod,
 547–31 l· humanity out of disease and death
 557–20 and l· the curtain on man as never
ap 563– 5 hatred, which l· its hydra head,
 563–15 The Revelator l· the veil from this
 571–32 and l· on high only those who have

Light

ap 561–31 to bear witness of that L·."— *John* 1 : 8.

light (*see also* **light's**)

above the
ap 558–15 it has for you a l· above the sun,
absence of
f 215–17 only a mortal sense of the absence of l·,
according to their
t 443–11 privileged to work . . . according to their l·,
accustomed to the
t 452– 7 we are accustomed to the l·
all is
sp 72–11 in the place of darkness all is l·,
and darkness
ph 186– 9 l· and darkness, cannot mingle.
b 281– 5 no more commingle than l· and darkness.
r 474–31 for l· and darkness cannot dwell together.
and glory
ap 575– 9 represents the l· and glory of divine Science.
 577–24 Its gates open towards l· and glory
and harmony
b 280– 4 the l· and harmony which are the abode of
g 501–12 which God illustrated by l· and harmony,
 503–28 Spirit, dwelling in infinite l· and harmony
and healing
t 446–12 through which Mind pours l· and healing
and heat
ph 189– 4 we still believe that there is solar l· and heat.
g 538–11 The sun, giving l· and heat to the earth,
and might
f 215–13 the l· and might of intelligence and Life.
t 446–26 the spiritual l· and might which heal the sick.
and the glass
b 295–17 The l· and the glass never mingle,
beauty and
g 516–13 bathes all in beauty and l·.
beholds the
sp 95–26 beholds the l· which heralds Christ's eternal
borrowed
g 511– 2 subdivides and radiates their borrowed l·,
brave
s 144– 7 when dawns the sun's brave l·.
bring
g 504–24 rays of infinite Truth, . . . bring l·
bringing to
f 210–14 thus bringing to l· the scientific action of
gl 589–18 bringing to l· man's immortality.
brings to
sp 72–13 Truth . . . brings to l· immortality.
f 206–27 He destroys them, and brings to l· immortality.
b 293–29 C. S. brings to l· Truth and its supremacy,
 338– 2 brings to l· the only living and true God
bring to
b 300–10 will bring to l· the true reflection of God
brought to
s 110–10 The equipollence of God brought to l·
b 268– 1 brought to l· . . . many useful wonders.
 292–31 connection with his God, which Jesus brought
  to l·.
 335–24 Life as immortality brought to l·.
p 429– 2 this Life must be brought to l· by the
g 505–28 the reality of all things brought to l·.
 548–28 Modern discoveries have brought to l·
gl 582–23 immortality brought to l·.
central
b 305– 7 Man, . . . reflects the central l· of being,
clearer
a 55–12 in a clearer l· than mere words can
clothed in
ap 561–11 the spiritual ideal as a woman clothed in l·,
come not to the
pref x–29 or discerning the truth, come not to the l· lest
darkness and
sp 74–21 Darkness and l·, infancy and manhood,

light

depends upon Mind
p 393–26 certainly means that *l·* depends upon Mind,

destroys darkness
sp 72–10 As *l·* destroys darkness

divine
s 135–32 as must be the case in the cycles of divine *l·*.
t 457– 7 Since the divine *l·* of C. S. first dawned upon

emits
c 262–25 even as *l·* emits *l·* without effort ;

examined in the
c 267–19 examined in the *l·* of divine Science,
b 274–31 examined in the *l·* of divine metaphysics,

from darkness to
t 459– 1 as the flower turns from darkness to *l·*.

give
g 510– 7 to give *l·* upon the earth :— *Gen.* 1 : 15.
  511– 8 to give *l·* upon the earth,— *Gen.* 1 : 17.

gives place to
pref xi–13 as necessarily as darkness gives place to *l·*

glorious
b 308–27 did not loosen his hold upon this glorious *l·*

God "is the
ap 558–16 for God "is the *l·* thereof."— *Rev.* 21 : 23.

God's
g 504–12 no place where God's *l·* is not seen,

God saw the
g 503–26 And God saw the *l·*,— *Gen.* 1 : 4.

greater
g 510–14 the greater *l·* to rule the day,— *Gen.* 1 : 16.

infinite
g 503–28 Spirit, dwelling in infinite *l·* and harmony
  511–13 God is revealed as infinite *l·*.

influx of
a 47– 8 The influx of *l·* was sudden.

instead of
g 528–19 Beginning creation with darkness instead of *l·*,

in the line of
an 105–32 full many a league in the line of *l·* ;

is a symbol
g 510–27 *L·* is a symbol of Mind,

its own
g 510–30 one Mind, and this one shining by its own *l·*

lesser
g 510–14 the lesser *l·* to rule the night :— *Gen.* 1 : 16.

lets in the
p 407–16 This spiritualization of thought lets in the *l·*,

let there be
c 255– 3 "Let there be *l·*,"— *Gen.* 1 : 3.
g 503–18 God said, Let there be *l·* : — *Gen.* 1 : 3.
  556–20 "Let there be *l·*."— *Gen.* 1 : 3.

life and
f 209– 7 life and *l·* of all its own vast creation ;

line of
p 367–29 student's higher attainments in this line of *l·*.

Love is the
ap 577–21 for Love is the *l·* of it,

manifesting the
ap 562–20 and by manifesting the *l·* which shines

more
s 153–13 This discovery leads to more *l·*.

new
a 35–11 in the dawn of a new *l·*

obscured the
ap 560–26 not only obscured the *l·* of the ages, but

obscures
g 504–29 and darkness obscures *l·*.

of men
g 501– * the life was the l· of men.— John* 1 : 4.
ap 561–29 which is "the *l·* of men."— *John* 1 : 4.

of the body
p 393–25 "the *l·* of the body is the eye,"— *Matt.* 6 : 22.

of Truth
b 308–25 the *l·* of Truth and Love dawns upon thee.
p 418–32 which flee before the *l·* of Truth.
g 557–19 rolls back the clouds of error with the *l·* of Truth,

of understanding
t 461–12 Only by . . . can the *l·* of understanding be

or heat
g 548– 9 How little *l·* or heat reach our earth when

or joy
g 548–12 little *l·* or joy for mortals before

pinions of
ph 191–14 transformed by Truth on its pinions of *l·*,

portrayed
ap 561–28 The *l·* portrayed is really neither solar nor

power of
f 214–27 may end the power of *l·* and lens !

ray of
f 250–12 like a ray of *l·* which comes from the sun,
b 300–31 the ray of *l·* which goes out from it.
o 361–17 a ray of *l·* one with the sun,

rays of
g 546–24 like rays of *l·*, shine in the darkness,

reflected
ap 562– 9 the universe borrows its reflected *l·*,

---

light

reflects no
r 479–28 not a color, because it reflects no *l·*.

shining
o 347–20 and is the *l·* shining in darkness,
ap 566–24 A burning and a shining *l·* !

solar
ph 189– 4 we still believe that there is solar *l·* and heat.
g 510–21 There is no Scriptural allusion to solar *l·* until

Spirit is
g 504–28 Spirit is *l·*, and the contradiction of Spirit is

spiritual
b 324–23 but spiritual *l·* soon enabled him to
t 446–26 the spiritual *l·* and might which heal the sick.

this
p 367–22 and that this *l·* be not hid,
g 504–10 This *l·* is not from the sun
ap 577–22 All who are saved must walk in this *l·*.

Thy
ph 190–31 In Thy *l·* shall we see light.— *Psal.* 36 : 9.

towards the
f 240– 9 leaflet turns naturally towards the *l·*.

true
s 117–26 and because of opacity to the true *l·*,
b 276–13 brings . . . into human view in their true *l·*,
o 359–32 in their true *l·* and loveliness,

Truth is the
b 282–32 but Truth is the *l·* which dispels error.

walking in the
t 452– 7 Walking in the *l·*, we are accustomed to the

walk in the
pr 10– 2 and will walk in the *l·* so far as we receive it,
g 510–11 reflected spiritually by all who walk in the *l·*

ye are the
p 367–19 "Ye are the *l·* of the world.— *Matt.* 5 : 14.

---

a 42– 8 comes in darkness and disappears with the *l·*.
sp 74–24 Who will say that . . . darkness can represent *l·*,
an 101–15 and as adapted to throw *l·* on physiological
ph 190–31 In Thy light shall we see *l·*.— *Psal.* 36 : 9.
  194–28 An infant crying for the *l·*,
  194–31 The *l·* which affords us joy gave him a
  195– 2 His eyes were inflamed by the *l·*.
f 215–16 led to believe that darkness is as real as *l·* ;
c 266–29 beatific presence, illuming the universe with *l·*.
b 289– 1 man's real existence . . . comes to *l·*.
  295–16 as *l·* passing through the window-pane.
  305–27 destroys all error and brings immortality to *l·*.
  325–30 When first spoken . . . Truth, like the *l·*,
  336–28 and brings immortality to *l·*.
t 452– 9 are pained by the *l·*.
r 474–32 *L·* extinguishes the darkness,
  479–24 the imaginary opposites of *l·*,
  492–12 and bring immortality to *l·*.
g 502– 6 the *l·* over the dark,
  503–14 the *l·* of ever-present Love illumines
  503–19 and there was *l·*.— *Gen.* 1 : 3.
  503–21 *first*, in *l·* ; *second*, in reflection ;
  503–27 divided the *l·* from the darkness.— *Gen.* 1 : 4.
  504– 3 God called the *l·* Day,— *Gen.* 1 : 5.
  504– 9 though solar beams are not . . . still there is *l·*.
  504–27 Did infinite Mind create matter, and call it *l·* ?
  508–29 letting in the *l·* of spiritual understanding.
  509–17 The *l·* of spiritual understanding gives
  510–10 in whose "*l·* shall we see *l·* ;"— *Psal.* 36 : 9.
  511– 9 to divide the *l·* from the darkness : — *Gen.* 1 : 18.
  513–10 the veil is lifted, and the scene shifts into *l·*.
  539–25 "What communion hath *l·*— *II Cor.* 6 : 14.
ap 578– 1 the *l·* which C. S. throws on the Scriptures
gl 584– 1 *l·*, the spiritual idea of Truth and Love.
  591–23 MORNING. *L·* ; symbol of Truth ;
  596–11 URIM. *L·*.

lighted
ap 576– 3 *l·* by the Sun of Righteousness,

lighting
pref vii–12 *l·* the way to eternal harmony.

lightning
sp 97– 8 According to human belief, the *l·* is fierce
s 119–19 lawgiver, whose *l·* palsies . . . is not the divine
ph 192–15 It is *l·* and hurricane, all that is
f 245–20 coaxed the enamoured *l·* from the clouds.
b 293–22 wind, wave, *l·*, fire, bestial ferocity
p 439–16 his words flashing as *l·* in the

lightnings
b 288–15 The *l·* and thunderbolts of error

lights
f 202–14 *l·* the torch of spiritual understanding.
g 509– 9 Let there be *l·* in the firmament — *Gen.* 1 : 14.
  510– 6 And let them be for *l·*— *Gen.* 1 : 15.
  510–13 And God made two great *l·* ;— *Gen.* 1 : 16.

like
pr 5–19 "*l·* a green bay tree ;"— *Psal.* 37 : 35.
  8– 8 "*l·* unto whited sepulchres — *Matt.* 23 : 27.

like

pr	8–19	audible prayers are *l·* charity in one respect,
	12–16	Prayer to a corporeal God affects the sick *l·* a
a	21–27	He is *l·* a traveller going westward
	22–3	Vibrating *l·* a pendulum between sin and the
	41–6	L· our Master, we must depart from
	53–22	L· Peter, we should weep over the warning,
m	57–13	seasons of renewal *l·* the returning spring.
	61–16	droop and die, *l·* tropical flowers
	63–7	His origin is not, *l·* that of mortals,
	66–4	Which, *l·* the toad, ugly and venomous,
sp	78–2	*l·* the discords of disease, sin, and death,
an	103–27	*l·* silly moths, singe their own wings
	105–22	*l·* an escaped felon
	106–6	L· our nation, C. S. has its Declaration of
	106–24	revellings and such *l·* : — *Gal.* 5 : 21.
s	107–*	*kingdom of heaven is l· unto* — *Matt.* 13 : 33.
	112–19	spiritual rules, . . . which, *l·* the great Giver,
	113–26	*l·* the method in mathematics,
	124–14	The universe, *l·* man, is to be interpreted by
	124–18	the universe, *l·* man, is, and must
	135–4	that ye skipped *l·* rams, — *Psal.* 114 : 6.
	135–5	and ye little hills, *l·* lambs? — *Psal.* 114 : 6.
	154–3	Disease arises, *l·* other mental conditions, from
	156–8	and yet, . . . the patient looked *l·* a barrel.
	157–13	becomes more *l·* the human mind than
	164–7	true, or anything *l·* the truth,
ph	187–32	a body *l·* the one it had before death.
	188–12	is *l·* the dream we have in sleep,
	193–14	and said : "I feel *l·* a new man."
	197–3	*l·* a Parisian name for a novel garment.
f	214–11	The material senses, *l·* Adam, originate in
	214–19	*l·* the pagan idolater.
	214–22	*l·* the original "tree of — *Gen.* 2 : 9.
	218–5	the body, *l·* the inanimate wheel,
	220–19	*l·* a kitten glancing into the mirror
	225–14	The history of our country, *l·* all history,
	235–1	cannot go forth, *l·* wandering pollen,
	237–12	*l·* "the fowls of the air," — *Luke* 8 : 5.
	244–13	is *l·* the beasts and vegetables,
	245–27	One instance *l·* the foregoing
	249–18	*l·* Christ, "the same yesterday, — *Heb.* 13 : 8.
	250–4	suppose. . .unintelligence to act *l·* intelligence,
	250–12	*l·* a ray of light which comes from the sun,
	250–29	chase one another *l·* snowflakes.
	251–28	Ignorance, *l·* intentional wrong, is not
	252–28	and says : . . . L· bursting lava, I expand
c	260–3	and make himself *l·* it,
	263–28	A sensual thought, *l·* an atom of dust
	267–26	robes of Spirit . . . *l·* the raiment of Christ.
b	268–3	With *l·* activity have thought's swift pinions
	268–11	*l·* the shepherd-boy with his sling,
	276–29, 30	inform us that *l·* produces *l·.*
	277–14	*l·* reproducing *l·.*
	286–18	all that He made to be good, *l·* Himself,
	295–11	Mortals are not *l·* immortals, created in
	295–23	Then, *l·* a cloud melting into thin vapor,
	298–21	Spiritual ideas, *l·* numbers and notes,
	305–10	so man, *l·* all things real, reflects God,
	322–28	turn us *l·* tired children to the arms of
	325–30	When first spoken in any age, Truth, *l·* the
o	349–14	*l·* all other languages, English is inadequate
	352–17	Children, *l·* adults, *ought* to fear a
	354–20	which are *l·* clouds without rain.
	359–29	Scientist and an opponent are *l·* two artists.
	360–19	L· a pendulum in a clock, you will be
p	364–22	If Christian Scientists are *l·* Simon, then
	365–18	*l·* dew before the morning sunshine.
	367–11	nor, *l·* the Pharisee, with the arrogance of
	367–13	but *l·* Mary Magdalene, from the summit of
	370–9	cause and effect, or *l·* producing *l·.*
	374–22	*l·* walking in darkness on the edge of a
	383–9	and, *l·* the Apostle Paul, is
	390–2	I should *l·* something more to eat."
	393–1	*l·* a watchman forsaking his post,
	395–6	L· the great Exemplar, the healer should
	398–15	"was restored whole, *l·* as the — *Matt.* 12 : 13.
	421–30	The perversion of Mind-science is *l·*
t	459–17	*l·* putting a sharp knife into the hands of a
r	467–8	The second is *l·* unto it,
	481–5	L· the archpriests of yore, man is
	485–31	*l·* saying that the power is in the lever.
	486–31	in a terrible situation, where he would be *l·*
g	546–24	*l·* rays of light, shine in the darkness,
	551–6	L· produces *l·.*
	554–6	because being is immortal, *l·* Deity,
	555–7	"I *l·* your explanations of truth,
	555–17	*l·* inquiring into the origin of God,
	557–3	moving and playing without harm, *l·* a fish.
ap	571–5	Because people *l·* you better when you
		(*see also* **manner**)

likely

an	102–27	much more *l·* to be abused by its
o	358–29	Is it *l·* that church-members have more
p	409–7	the more prolific it is *l·* to become

likened

p	372–5	*l·*, by Milton to "chaos and old night."
g	514–16	promptness, and perseverance are *l·* to

likeness

after our

p	438–3	in our image, after our *l·* ; — *Gen.* 1 : 26.
r	475–24	in our image, after our *l·* ; — *Gen.* 1 : 26.
g	515–12	in our image, after our *l·* ; — *Gen.* 1 : 26.

divine

b	300–22	man as reflecting the divine *l·.*
o	356–23	man who is made in the divine *l·* ?
r	491–16	establishes man forever in the divine *l·*,

eternal

f	246–6	the eternal *l·* of their Maker.
p	395–5	man's immortality and eternal *l·* to God.

God's

sp	70–8	spiritual man, made in God's *l·*,
ph	191–5	man in God's *l·* will appear,
b	287–21	declare that man was made in God's *l·.*
	336–26	and man in God's *l·*
o	344–9	God's *l·* is not found in matter, sin,
	346–5	the ideal man, reflecting God's *l·.*

God's own

sp	90–24	man is God's own *l·*
r	477–3	the Saviour saw God's own *l·*,

His

pr	4–22	until we awake in His *l·.*
sp	73–7	God, and man is His *l·.*
s	148–24	unity of Spirit and His *l·.*
f	249–22	and His *l·* never dreams.
b	325–16	Then shall man be found, in His *l·*,
	338–3	and man as made in His *l·* ;
o	344–8	in His own image and after His *l·.*
r	495–16	Allow nothing but His *l·* to abide in your
g	516–20	Man, made in His *l·*, possesses and reflects

His own

c	257–12	Mind creates His own *l·* in ideas,
g	516–9	God fashions . . . after His own *l·.*

human

b	301–2	even as the human *l·*

image and

(*see* **image**)

image or

sp	71–19	neither . . . is the image or *l·* of God,
b	284–11	Is God's image or *l·* matter,
	299–15	whither every . . . image, or *l·* of
g	515–25	mirrored reflection is your own image or *l·.*

inverted

b	285–10	man's counterfeit, the inverted *l·*,

inverts the true

g	512–26	Mortal mind inverts the true *l·*,

its own

f	217–1	this Mind forms its own *l·.*

man's

pr	12–14	of man's *l·* to God and of man's

no proper

b	302–28	the body presents no proper *l·* of divinity,

not that

r	475–10	Matter is not that *l·.*

of God

(*see* **God**)

of his Maker

f	252–13	recognized as the true *l·* of his Maker.
b	305–7	Man, in the *l·* of his Maker,

of man's Maker

r	491–10	It is the *l·* of man's Maker.

of Spirit

(*see* **Spirit**)

of the divine

a	51–8	spiritual identity in the *l·* of the divine ;

of this Ego

f	250–11	Spiritual man is the *l·* of this Ego.

our

g	525–14	after our mind and our *l·* ;

personal

b	302–27	not in any bodily or personal *l·* to

that

ph	191–6	will include in that *l·* no material element.

this

b	315–18	and we realize this *l·* only when we
g	515–27	If you speak, the lips of this *l·* move
	544–25	a material personality is not this *l·.*

Thy

ph	190–29	when I awake, with Thy *l·.* — *Psal.* 17 : 15.

true

m	67–29	presents the true *l·* or spiritual ideal.
f	252–13	recognized as the true *l·* of his Maker.
c	259–18	The true *l·* cannot be lost in divine reflection.
p	406–16	all that is unlike the true *l·* disappears.
g	516–8	we shall see this true *l·* and reflection

---

f	253–1	saith : I am Spirit. Man, . . . is my *l·.*

likes

b	322–23	A man who *l·* to do wrong

iveth
ph 170–11 "Whosoever *l·* and believeth— *John* 11 : 26.
b 315– 1 "Whosoever *l·* and believeth— *John* 11 : 26.
334–26 I am he that *l·*, and was dead— *Rev.* 1 : 18.

living
and healing
s 141– 5 divine precepts for *l·* and healing.
economy of
f 222–16 consulting . . . less about the economy of *l·*
faith in
p 368–17 more faith in *l·* than in dying,
illegitimate
f 203–28 foam and fury of illegimate *l·*
in disobedience
a 19–27 If *l·* in disobedience to Him,
in this world
sp 73– 3 calls one person, *l·* in this world, *material*,
material
pr 14–26 the belief and dream of material *l·*,
only for pleasure
a 38–27 *l·* only for pleasure or the gratification of the
standard of
ph 197–14 the higher will be the standard of *l·*
the life
r 496–10 Am I *l·* the life that approaches the

---

pr 9–10 by *l·* consistently with our prayer?
a 31–15 It is the *l·* Christ, the practical Truth,
39–16 was not the threshold . . . into *l·* glory.
sp 74–15 belief of still *l·* in an organic, material body.
74–31 The so-called dead and *l·* cannot commune
75–25 when those *l·* on the earth and
81– 2 between the so-called dead and the *l·*,
an 100– 5 said could be exerted by one *l·* organism
s 137–18 the Son of the *l·* God !"— *Matt.* 16 : 16.
150– 1 *l·* witnesses and monuments to the
ph 180–28 The only way to this *l·* Truth,
f 204– 5 false . . . that material history is as real and *l·*
234– 7 giving *l·* waters to the thirsty.
237–28 the only *l·* and true God can do.
245– 7 Believing that she was still *l·* in the same hour
c 264–24 Spiritual *l·* and blessedness are the only
b 275– 5 Therefore matter is neither substantial, *l·*, nor
308– 3 or art thou in the *l·* faith that
325–22 your bodies a *l·* sacrifice,— *Rom.* 12 : 1.
338– 3 brings to light the only *l·* and true God
o 351–14 It was the *l·*, palpitating presence of
p 388–22 a clear comprehension of the *l·* Spirit.
t 458–28 He must prove, through *l·* as well as
r 477–21 in multifarious forms of the *l·* Principle,
g 502– 2 the *l·* and real prelude of the older Scriptures
512– 5 and every *l·* creature that moveth,— *Gen.* 1 : 21.
513–15 the *l·* creature after his kind,— *Gen.* 1 : 24.
517–28 every *l·* thing that moveth— *Gen.* 1 : 28.
524–15 and man became a *l·* soul.— *Gen.* 2 : 7.
527–24 whatsoever Adam called every *l·*— *Gen.* 2 : 19.
531– 1 it supposes that . . . matter becomes *l·*,

load
ph 176–17 Human fear of miasma would *l·* with disease
loaf
sp 90– 5 from which *l·* or fish could come?
loathe
a 30–28 we shall *l·* sin and rebuke it
f 240–22 we must learn to *l·* it.
loathing
pr 11–17 to make him turn from it with *l·*.
p 407– 1 in becoming a fool or an object of *l·* ;
ap 565– 4 hate, *l·* the brightness of divine glory.
loathsome
m 61–22 or reduce him to a *l·* wreck?
s 158–23 until . . . men and women become *l·* sots.
p 407–19 attractive to no creature except a *l·* worm,
loaves
sp 90– 3 How were the *l·* and fishes multiplied
f 206–17 as Jesus showed with the *l·* and the fishes,
p 367–11 "for the *l·* and fishes,"— *see John* 6 : 26.
lobster
r 489– 2 When the unthinking *l·* loses its claw,
lobster's
r 489– 6 would be replaced as readily as the *l·* claw,
local
g 537–11 In the first chapter . . . evil has no *l·* habitation
localities
p 400–32 in certain *l·* he did not many
locality
sp 79– 1 its symptoms, *l·*, and fatality
b 291–13 Heaven is not a *l·*, but a divine state
p 439–31 send our best detectives to whatever *l·*
location
b 295– 1 that a severed limb is aching in the old *l·*,

lock
sp 99–12 None may pick the *l·* nor enter by some other
locomotion
sp 84–22 not dependent upon . . . bones for *l·*,
lodestar
f 238–32 It is the *l·* in the demonstration of
lodgment
f 235– 3 cannot go forth, . . . finding unsuspected *l·*,
loftiness
pr 8–13 If he reached the *l·* of his prayer,
lofty
g 515– 5 creeping over *l·* summits,
logic
divine
sp 72–22 it follows in divine *l·* that evil,
93–10 Divine *l·* and revelation coincide.
fair
r 490–21 would, by fair *l·*, annihilate man
human
b 300– 1 Human *l·* is awry when it attempts
materialistic
s 120–24 and refutes materialistic *l·*.
metaphysical
p 418–21 All metaphysical *l·* is inspired by this
of events
m 60–12 From the *l·* of events we learn that
66–23 It is better to await the *l·* of events

sp 93–12 otherwise, we may be sure that either our *l·* is
s 128–31 So is it with *l·*.
129– 2 its *l·* is as harmonious as the reasoning of
149–22 The *l·* is lame, and facts contradict it.
b 278–26 *l·* which would prove his annihilation.
logical
b 270– 9 are scientific and *l·* conclusions reached.
279–26 A *l·* and scientific conclusion is reached
logically
o 358–10 coincides with the Scriptures, and sustains *l·*
Logos
s 134–21 The true *L·* is demonstrably C. S.,
b 335–10 the *L·*, the Æon or Word of God,
logos
g 525–19 [the *l·*, or *word*]
London
s 163–13 a learned Professor in *L·*, said :
164– 4 the Royal College of Physicians, *L·*,
f 245– 4 published in the *L·* medical magazine
loneliness
gl 597–16 WILDERNESS. *L·* ; doubt ; darkness.
lonely
a 44– 5 The *l·* precincts of the tomb gave Jesus a
long
pr 4–30 *L·* prayers, superstition, and creeds
9–27 Then why make *l·* prayers about
a 20–12 men can . . . make *l·* prayers, and yet be
sp 87–29 Memory may reproduce voices *l·* ago silent.
s 130–20 Laboring *l·* to shake the adult's faith in matter
163– 8 founded on *l·* observation and reflection,
ph 174–10 and portend a *l·* night to the traveller ;
197– 1 and by printing *l·* descriptions
f 213–24 Beethoven, who was so *l·* hopelessly deaf.
233–10 How *l·* it must be before we arrive at
b 296–20 how *l·* they will suffer the pangs of
o 353–27 so *l·* will ghosts seem to continue.
p 363– 5 wiping them with her *l·* hair,
367–27 I *l·* to see the consummation of my hope,
373– 8 has struggled *l·*, and perhaps in vain,
378–28 to chill harmony with a *l·* and cold night of
431–15 The struggle on their part was *l·*.
r 492–29 The conservative theory, *l·* believed,
ap 567– 9 Against Love, the dragon warreth not *l·*,
gl 597– 7 hypocrisy, which offered *l·* petitions

long so — as
a 39–31 so *l·* as he believes in the pleasures of sin?
m 59–27 so *l·* as its moral obligations are kept intact ;
ph 179–24 so *l·* you read medical works
184– 1 penalties it affixes last so *l·* as the belief
f 203–27 so *l·* as he sins.
b 311–11 Sin exists here or hereafter only so *l·* as the
311–19 So *l·* as we believe that soul can sin
317–30 so *l·* as the Master remained an inhabitant of the
o 348–19 so *l·* as it remains in mortal mind,
353–26 So *l·* as there are supposed limits to Mind,
p 336– 8 so *l·* as mortals declare that
425– 4 so *l·* as you believe them to be safety-valves
t 456–20 So *l·* as matter is the basis of
r 486–20 So *l·* as this error of belief remains,
497–12 the belief in sin is punished so *l·* as the
g 551–25 so *l·* as it bases creation on materiality.

longer
sp 77–17   will be of *l·* or shorter duration
f 237–25   They devote themselves a little *l·* to their
o 346–25   how can he suffer *l·*?

longer no —
pref vii–17   Ignorance of God is no *l·* the stepping-stone
a 47– 4   They no *l·* measured man by material sense.
47– 6   leaning no *l·* on matter,
m 69–10   No *l·* to marry or to be "given in — *Matt.* 22 : 30.
sp 74–18   The caterpillar, . . . is no *l·* a worm,
76–13   can no *l·* commune with matter ;
an 105–17   and no *l·* apply legal rulings wholly to
s 125– 4   may no *l·* be found indispensable to health.
125–28   astronomer will no *l·* look up to the stars,
126– 2   Error will be no *l·* used in stating truth.
130–30   no *l·* think it natural to love sin
130–31   no *l·* imagine evil to be ever-present
140–13   Mankind will no *l·* be tyrannical and
ph 171–13   no *l·* an open question, but is demonstrable
191–17   It should no *l·* ask of the head, heart, or
f 211–19   It should no *l·* be said in Israel that
c 263– 9   he will no *l·* grope in the dark and cling to earth
b 295– 3   nerves which are no *l·* there,
295–23   it no *l·* hides the sun.
298–20   joy is no *l·* a trembler, nor is hope a cheat.
309–10   He was no *l·* called Jacob, but Israel,
o 352–30   no *l·* seeming worthy of fear and honor.
p 416– 8   To him there is no *l·* any pain.
416–23   the body is no *l·* the parent,
442–13   Mortal Man, no *l·* sick and in prison,
t 460–32   shadow of old errors was no *l·* cast upon
ap 573–17   man was no *l·* regarded as a miserable sinner,
577– 5   as no *l·* two wedded individuals,

longest
*p 431–16   Materia Medica held out the *l·*,

longevity
pref viii–21   the reputed *l·* of the Antediluvians,
s 126–25   the effects of Truth on the health, *l·*,
ph 167–10   our health, our *l·*, and our Christianity.
173–31   are far more fatal to health and *l·* than
f 223–32   *L·* is increasing
o 348–32   health has been restored, and *l·* increased.
r 492–10   will increase *l·*, will purify and elevate

longing
pr 4–18   the *l·* to be better and holier,

longingly
t 450–12   They do not incline *l·* to error,

longings
pr 15–17   In the quiet sanctuary of earnest *l·*,

longitude
s 125–22   cold and heat, latitude and *l·*.

longsuffering
an 106–27   *l·*, gentleness, goodness, faith,— *Gal.* 5 : 22.
t 443–21   with all *l·* and doctrine."— *II Tim.* 4 : 2.
ap 566–23   Be Thou, *l·*, slow to wrath,

look
pr 6–18   higher we cannot *l·*,
sp 78–12   Then why *l·* to them
82–29   do we *l·* for help to the Esquimaux
s 125–28   astronomer will no longer *l·* up to the stars,
125–29   he will *l·* out from them upon the universe ;
129–22   We must *l·* deep into realism
154–26   says . . . "You *l·* sick," "You *l·* tired,"
ph 184–31   I then requested her ɪo *l·* at the weather-vane.
f 219–30   we may *l·* for an abatement of these evils ;
220– 6   to *l·* in other directions for cause and cure.
234–28   Jesus declared that to *l·* with desire on
248–27   and *l·* at them continually,
c 260–31   If we *l·* to the body for pleasure, we find pain ;
261– 2   *L·* away from the body into Truth
264– 7   Mortals must *l·* beyond fading, finite forms,
264–10   We must *l·* where we would walk,
o 343–11   the blind *l·* up to C. S. with blessings,
p 371–11   children *l·* everywhere for the imaginary ghost,
429– 8   We *l·* before our feet,
429– 9   we *l·* beyond a single step
433–14   a *l·* of despair and death settles upon it.
434–18   earnest, solemn eyes, . . . *l·* upward.
g 521–13   We should *l·* away from the opposite
549–17   must therefore *l·* upon the simple ovum as
552–18   peck open their shells with C. S., and *l·* outward
ap 558–14   When you *l·* it fairly in the face,

looked
s 133–11   The Israelites *l·* upon the brazen serpent,
156– 8   the patient *l·* like a barrel.
161–30   if . . . philanthropists *l·* as deeply for
ph 184–32   She *l·* and saw that it pointed due east.
b 268– *   *which we have l· upon,— I John* 1 : 1.
270–14   prophets of old *l·* for something higher

looker-on
sp 90–17   The *l·* sees the body in bed,

lookers-on
a 37–15   merit seen and appreciated by *l·*.

looking
pr 5–19   *l·* farther, the Psalmist could see their end,
7–10   *L·* deeply into these things, we find that
b 268– 8   *l·* away from matter to Mind as the cause of
308–10   *l·* for happiness and life in the body,
317–24   To the materialistic Thomas, *l·* for the
p 365– 3   the heavenly homesick *l·* away from earth,
378–11   By *l·* a tiger fearlessly in the eye,
378–13   may infuriate another by *l·* it in the eye,
t 450– 7   while *l·* you blandly in the face,

looks
a 21–11   and *l·* towards the imperishable things of Spirit
p 371–13   *l·* for relief in all ways except the right
379– 5   where the ordinary physician *l·* for causes.
415– 9   *l·* upon some object which he dreads.
431–31   testifies : . . . I am robbed of my good *l·*.
t 451–11   walks in the direction towards which he *l·*,

looms
an 102–18   The *l·* of crime, hidden in the dark recesses

loose
s 163– 2   afterward letting her *l·* upon sick people."
t 459–18   turning him *l·* in the crowded streets of a city

loosed
sp 89– 3   shows that the beliefs of mortal mind are *l·*.

loosely
p 363– 5   which hung *l·* about her shoulders,

loosen
b 308–27   did not *l·* his hold upon this glorious light

loosened
g 552–19   But thought, *l·* from a material basis

loosening
sp 98–16   above the *l·* grasp of creeds,

loquacious
s 153–30   avoid *l·* tattling about disease,

Lord (*see also* **Lord's**)
and Master
m 67–21   our *L·* and Master healed the sick,
b 317–20   Our *L·* and Master presented himself to
arm of the
a 24–11   "the arm of the *L·*" is revealed.— *Isa.* 53 : 1.
beloved
ap 566–15   When Israel, of the *L·* beloved,
cup of our
a 32–11   nor was the wine, used . . . the cup of our *L·*.
fear of the
p 373–15   "The fear of the *L·* is the— *Psal.* 111 : 10.
mind of the
b 291–18   "the mind of the *L·*,"— *Rom.* 11 : 34.
of heaven
s 131–19   O Father, *L·* of heaven and earth,— *Luke* 10 : 21.
of Hosts
ap 568–25   and magnify the *L·* of Hosts.
on high
g 505–18   "The *L·* on high is mightier than— *Psal.* 93 : 4.
presence of the
s 135– 6   at the presence of the *L·*,— *Psal.* 114 : 7.
g 542–28   from the presence of the *L·*— *Gen.* 4 : 16.
present with the
pr 14– 4   "present with the *L·*"— *II Cor.* 5 : 8.
14– 6   "present with the *L·*"— *II Cor.* 5 : 8.
f 216–30   present with the *L·*."— *II Cor.* 5 : 8.
p 383–11   present with the *L·*."— *II Cor.* 5 : 8.
gl 581–26   present with the *L·*."— *II Cor.* 5 : 8.
shall reign
pref vii–20   "the *L·* shall reign forever."— *Exod.* 15 : 18.
Spirit of the
f 227–18   "Where the Spirit of the *L·* is,— *II Cor.* 3 : 17.
r 481– 4   "Where the Spirit of the *L·* is,— *II Cor.* 3 : 17.
thy God
pr 9–17   Dost thou "love the *L·* thy God— *Matt.* 22 : 37.
wait upon the
f 218–27   "They that wait upon the *L·*— *Isa.* 40 : 31.
with our
a 35–10   This spiritual meeting with our *L·*
with the
pr 14– 9   To be "with the *L·*" is to be— *II Cor.* 5 : 8.
g 504–22   "one day is with the *L·* as a— *II Pet.* 3 : 8.
gl 598–21   "One day is with the *L·* as a— *II Pet.* 3 : 8.

pr 10– 3   and that waiting patiently on the *L·*,
a 3–27   "*L·*, I believe ; help thou— *Mark* 9 : 24.
38–16   "The right hand of the *L·* is— *Psal.* 118 : 16.
f 201– *   *Remember, L·, the reproach— Psal.* 89 : 50.
201– *   *enemies have reproached, O L· ;— Psal.* 89 : 51.
241– 1   "Whom the *L·* loveth He— *Heb.* 12 : 6.
c 256–12   the *L·* our God is one *L·*."— *Deut.* 6 : 4.
267–31   which the *L·* hath promised— *Jas.* 1 : 12.
b 276– 3   "I am the *L·* that healeth— *Exod.* 15 : 26.
b 293–26   "The anger of the *L·*."— *Deut.* 29 : 20.
307–17   and says : "The *L·* knows it.

Lord

b	320–12	"And the *L·* said,— *Gen.* 6 : 3.
	325–26	the divine heights of our *L·*.
p	365– 6	than all cries of "*L·, L·* !"
	414–21	"The *L·* He is God— *Deut.* 4 : 35.
r	479– 5	"I have gotten a man from the *L·*'"— *Gen.* 4 : 1.
g	523–27	the creator is called Jehovah, or the *L·*.
	538–25	I have gotten a man from the *L·*— *Gen.* 4 : 1.
	538–31	"I have gotten a man from the *L·*,'"— *Gen.* 4 : 1.
	540– 6	I the *L·* do all these things ;"— *Isa.* 45 : 7.
	540–13	we may think in our ignorance that the *L·* hath
	540–26	an offering unto the *L·*— *Gen.* 4 : 3.
	541– 6	the *L·* [Jehovah] had respect unto— *Gen.* 4 : 4.
	541–19	the *L·* [Jehovah] said unto Cain,— *Gen.* 4 : 9.
	542–14	the *L·* [Jehovah] said unto him,— *Gen.* 4 : 15.
	542–16	the *L·* [Jehovah] set a mark upon— *Gen.* 4 : 15.
ap	558– *	*Great is the L·, and greatly*— *Psal.* 48 : 1.
	576–26	The term *L·*, as used in our version of
gl	590–15	definition of
fr	600– *	*walk worthy of the L·*— *Col.* 1 : 10.

lord

g	518– 2	He is *l·* of the belief in earth and heaven,

Lord God

g	520–18	in the day that the *L· G·*— *Gen.* 2 : 4.
	520–20	the *L· G·* [Jehovah] had not caused— *Gen.* 2 : 5.
	523–20	is always called Jehovah,— or *L· G·*,
	524–13	the *L· G·* [Jehovah] formed man— *Gen.* 2 : 7.
	525–30	out of the ground made the *L· G·*— *Gen.* 2 : 9.
	526–26	the *L· G·* [Jehovah] took the— *Gen.* 2 : 15.
	527– 6	the *L· G·* [Jehovah] commanded— *Gen.* 2 : 16.
	527–21	out of the ground the *L· G·*— *Gen.* 2 : 19.
	528– 9	*L· G·* [Jehovah, Yawah] caused— *Gen.* 2 : 21.
	528–12	and the rib, which the *L· G·*— *Gen.* 2 : 22.
	529–14	the *L· G·* [Jehovah] had made.— *Gen.* 3 : 1.
	532–13	the *L· G·* [Jehovah] called unto— *Gen.* 3 : 9.
	534– 8	the *L· G·* [Jehovah] said— *Gen.* 3 : 14.
	536–30	the *L· G·* [Jehovah] said,— *Gen.* 3 : 22.
	537– 3	therefore the *L· G·* [Jehovah] sent— *Gen.* 3 : 23.
	543–31	"In the day that the *L· G·*— *Gen.* 2 : 4.
ap	576–10	the *L· G·* Almighty and the Lamb— *Rev.* 21 : 22.
gl	590–20	definition of
		(*see also* **Jehovah**)

lordly

s	142–11	If the soft palm, upturned to a *l·* salary,

Lord of Hosts

ap	568–25	we give thanks and magnify the *L· of H·*.

Lord's

a	31–23	show the *L·* death till he come."— *I Cor.* 11 : 26.
	34–29	What a contrast between our *L·* last supper and
	35–15	They celebrate their *L·* victory over death,

lords

b	280–17	"gods many and *l·* many."— *I Cor.* 8 : 5.
	307– 9	It says : "There shall be *l·* and gods many.
gl	580– 8	"gods many and *l·* many"— *I Cor.* 8 : 5.

Lord's Prayer

pr	14–23	The *L· P·* is the prayer of Soul,
	16– 8	which we name after him the *L· P·*.
	16–22	is indicated in the *L· P·*
	16–25	the spiritual sense of the *L· P·* :

lore

a	23–12	Rabbinical *l·* said : "He that taketh
s	134– 1	have not cleansed their hands of rabbinical *l·*.
g	549–14	According to recent *l·*, successive generations

lose

pref	xi–11	before which sin and disease *l·* their reality
m	65–26	must *l·* its present slippery footing,
	69– 5	only as they *l·* the sense of sin and disease.
s	127– 2	she will not therefore *l·* faith in Christianity,
	127– 3	nor will Christianity *l·* its hold upon her.
	160– 5	drugs *l·* their healing force,
ph	176–15	sin, disease and death, will *l·* their foothold.
f	207–14	Without this lesson, we *l·* sight of the
	240–13	and you *l·* the keynote of being,
c	257–28	or Mind would *l·* its infinite character
	259– 2	Man . . . cannot *l·* his individuality,
	260–29	If . . . it must *l·* its immortal nature.
	261–26	will neither *l·* the solid objects and ends of life
b	275– 1	Matter has no life to *l·*, and Spirit never dies.
	278–15	we *l·* the consciousness of matter.
	296–16	must *l·* all satisfaction in error and sin
	302– 8	It is impossible that man should *l·* aught
	304–23	they would *l·* harmony, if time or
	310–27	if Spirit should *l·* Life as God, good,
	311– 9	he can only *l·* a sense material.
	311–28	sin, and mortality *l·* all supposed consciousness
	315–17	The likeness of God we *l·* sight of through sin,
	316– 5	and *l·* sight of mortal selfhood
	336–22	else God would . . . *l·* the deific character,
	337– 2	Therefore man, . . . cannot *l·* his individuality;
	337– 4	as material sensation, . . . mortals do *l·* sight of
	339–32	will never *l·* their imaginary power . . . until
	340– 1	until we *l·* our faith in them
o	344–28	may *l·* ninety-and-nine patients, while

lose

o	351– 2	When we *l·* faith in God's power to heal,
p	367–22	that this salt *l·* not its saltness,
	370–24	a drug may eventually *l·* its supposed
r	469–25	*l·* the high signification of omnipotence,
	472–22	Thus we should continue to *l·* the standard
	477–31	man, divorced from Spirit, would *l·* his entity,
g	524–31	Does Spirit enter dust, and *l·* therein the
	555–23	We *l·* our standard of perfection . . . when

loses

s	148–16	It *l·* Spirit, drops the true tone, and
ph	187–28	*l·* all appearance of life or action,
	197–28	mortal belief *l·* some portion of its error.
f	215–18	darkness *l·* the appearance of reality.
	248– 3	Love never *l·* sight of loveliness
b	325– 2	*l·* his belief in death.
	325– 3	*l·* all sense of evil, and by reason of this is
	327–11	Then he *l·* pleasure in wickedness,
p	369– 5	In proportion as matter *l·* to human sense all
	370–26	Hygienic treatment also *l·* its efficacy.
r	489– 2	When the unthinking lobster *l·* its claw,

losing

m	59–30	sacredness of this relationship is *l·* its
f	238– 9	*L·* her crucifix, the Roman Catholic girl said,
b	309–19	thus *l·* the divine power which heals
	335–22	Only by *l·* the false sense of Soul can we
o	360–11	replies : . . . I have no notion of *l·* my old

loss

no		
pr	1–11	no *l·* can occur from trusting God
of a limb		
ph	172–27	But the *l·* of a limb or injury to a tissue
of control		
p	406–26	a *l·* of control over the body.
of earthly hopes		
c	265–26	The *l·* of earthly hopes and pleasures
of harmony		
p	408– 2	sickness is *l·* of harmony.
of his identity		
c	265–12	by no means suggests . . . the *l·* of his identity,
of human peace		
c	265–23	Who that has felt the *l·* of human peace
of man's identity		
f	217– 1	The *l·* of man's identity . . . is impossible ;
of power		
ph	183–25	Submission to error superinduces *l·* of power.
possible		
a	51– 2	possible *l·* of something more important than
temporary		
b	311–16	belief strays into a sense of temporary *l·*
their		
r	487– 9	of the Mind-faculties than in their *l·*.
your		
p	386–19	You think that your anguish is occasioned by your *l·*.

b	294– 6	If man is both mind and matter, the *l·* of one
r	470– 7	assumed the *l·* of spiritual power,
	470– 7	assumed . . . the *l·* of the spiritual presence
	470– 9	assumed . . . the *l·* of Love as ever present

lost

a	32–20	The true sense is spiritually *l·*, if the
	41–17	this demonstration of healing was early *l·*,
	49– 9	Had they so soon *l·* sight of his mighty works,
sp	78–24	How can the majesty . . . of Spirit be *l·*?
	87– 3	*l·* to the memory of the mind in which
	87–25	The true concept is never *l·*.
s	110–26	But this power was *l·* sight of,
	143– 8	more deplorably *l·* than the sinning, if
	146– 3	Why has this element of Christianity been *l·*?
	147–10	Truth had *l·* none of its . . . efficacy,
	153– 7	The salt had "*l·* his savour ;"— *Matt.* 5 : 13.
	162–23	what is called the *l·* substance of lungs,
ph	166– 7	thus the conscious control over the body is *l·*.
f	208–23	cannot be *l·* nor remain forever unseen.
	211–27	If . . . these faculties must be *l·*,
	214–28	But the real sight or sense is not *l·*.
	215– 4	If Spirit, Soul, could sin or be *l·*,
	215– 5	then being and immortality would be *l·*,
	215– 6	being cannot be *l·* while God exists.
	215–24	Every quality and condition of mortality is *l·*,
	217– 4	more absurd than to conclude that . . . tones are *l·*
	245– 6	and *l·* all account of time.
	247– 3	age regain two of the elements it had *l·*,
c	259–15	If man was once perfect but has now *l·* his
	259–17	The *l·* image is no image.
	259–18	true likeness cannot be *l·* in divine reflection.
b	282– 1	and the inspiration, . . . will be *l·*.
	283–23	*l·* to all who cling to this falsity.
	295–21	that one which has *l·* much materiality
	302– 5	The identity of the real man is not *l·*,
	302–13	and this belief is all that will ever be *l·*.
	303–29	cannot be *l·* nor separated from its divine
	304–28	misapprehended and *l·* in confusion.

lost

b	310–19	human soul which sins and is spiritually *l*,
	310–20	commonly taught . . . that soul may be *l*,
	311– 8	Is man *l* spiritually? No,
	311–13	It is a sense of sin, . . . which is *l*.
	312– 2	must be *l* because such so-called knowledge
	314–19	This materialism *l* sight of the true Jesus ;
	321–16	The illusion of Moses *l* its power to alarm him,
	323–18	the one unused talent decays and is *l*.
	328–17	has been dormant, a *l* element of Christianity.
	331– 8	*l* through a mortal sense, which
o	360– 2	they will find that nothing is *l*,
p	375–24	muscles have no power to be *l*,
	407–21	If delusion says, "I have lost my memory,"
	407–22	No faculty of Mind is *l*.
	410–29	until the . . . healing ability is wholly *l*.
	431–27	testifies : . . . I have *l* my healthy hue
t	455–11	If you are yourself *l* in the belief and fear
r	470–28	If man has *l* perfection,
	470–29	then he has *l* his perfect Principle,
	481–31	it is the sense of sin which is *l*,
	486–24	They cannot be *l*.
	487– 9	*L* they cannot be, while Mind remains.
	489– 5	the senses of Mind are never *l*
	491–24	In sleep, memory and consciousness are *l*
g	524–10	the true idea of God seems almost *l*.
	533– 1	Had he *l* man's rich inheritance and
	536–14	If man's spiritual gravitation . . . should be *l*,
	548– 7	man has never *l* his spiritual estate

Lot

t	444–25	as did Abraham when he parted from *L*,

lotions

f	234– 1	while material *l* interfere with truth,

lots

f	242–24	for my vesture they did cast *l*."— *John* 19 : 24.

loud

ap	568–13	And I heard a *l* voice saying— *Rev.* 12 : 10.

louder

sp	97–24	the *l* will error scream, until its
ap	568–26	A *l* song, sweeter than has ever before

lovable

f	232– 4	neither make man harmonious nor God *l*.

Love (see also Love's)

abide in
b	274–12	The senses of Spirit abide in *L*,

all is
ap	567– 8	all is *L*, and there is no error, no sin,

alone can
g	510–18	*L* alone can impart the limitless idea of

and Truth
a	19– 2	*L* and Truth are not at war with God's image
f	227–19	*L* and Truth make free,
r	470– 3	brotherhood of man would consist of *L* and Truth,
gl	596–17	the spiritual inspiration of *L* and Truth

anointeth
ap	578–14	[*L*] anointeth my head with— *see Psal.* 23 : 5.

armed him with
a	52–23	Mind-healing, or C. S., which armed him with *L*.

chastened by
f	241– 4	he who . . . is chastened by *L*.

chastisements of
b	323– 6	Through the wholesome chastisements of *L*,

crown of
t	451– 6	with the crown of *L* upon her brow,

design of
a	35–30	The design of *L* is to reform the sinner.

destroys hate
b	339– 3	Truth destroys error, and *L* destroys hate.

Divine
p	439–29	sentence which . . . Divine *L* will pronounce.

divine
(see **divine**)

divine Principle is
b	330–21	and divine Principle is *L*,

divine Principle or
pr	12–20	It is a mortal belief, not divine Principle or *L*,

efficacious
r	497–14	evidence of divine, efficacious *L*,

essence of
b	333–26	in the divine nature, the essence of *L*.

eternal
a	19– 1	his own, derived from the eternal *L*.

everlasting
a	23–11	will fall at the feet of everlasting *L*.

ever-present
p	377– 5	should rejoice always in ever-present *L*.
g	501–13	is consonant with ever-present *L*.
	503–14	light of ever-present *L* illumines the
ap	567– 7	To infinite, ever-present *L*, all is Love,

explained by that
g	501–15	explained by that *L* for whose rest the

flood-tides of
f	201–18	to pour in truth through flood-tides of *L*.

Love

fruits of
a	35–24	by bringing forth the fruits of *L*,

fulfils the law
ap	572–12	*L* fulfils the law of C. S.,

giveth
g	518–19	*L* giveth to the least spiritual idea might,

God is
(see **God**)

Golden Shore of
ap	576– 1	realization of the Golden Shore of *L* and

gospel of
ap	577– 4	held in the gospel of *L*.

hand of
a	36–27	or that the hand of *L* is satisfied with

hath shown
s	137–24	*L* hath shown thee the way of Life !

heart of
t	448– 4	went out to the great heart of *L*,

he defined
a	54– 4	Out of the amplitude of his . . . he defined *L*.

held
g	514–26	the control which *L* held over all,

idea of
b	326–31	He beheld for the first time the true idea of *L*
g	534–29	will struggle to destroy the spiritual idea of *L*
gl	590– 9	LAMB OF GOD. The spiritual idea of *L* ;

image, of
r	475–14	Man is idea, the image, of *L* ;

immortality and
gl	597–15	divine Science,— immortality and *L*.

imparts
g	517–13	*L* imparts the clearest idea of Deity.

incorporeal
pr	13–24	wonders wrought by infinite, incorporeal *L*,

inexhaustible
c	257–29	inexhaustible *L*, eternal Life,

infinite
pr	10–30	In this case infinite *L* will not grant the
a	53–15	rather than as divine, infinite *L*.
c	256–25	No form . . . adequate to represent infinite *L*.
b	312–21	God is infinite *L*, which must be
p	366–18	recognition of infinite *L* which alone confers
g	520– 4	majesty, and glory of infinite *L* fill all space.

infinitude of
g	508–25	unfolds the infinitude of *L*.

inspiration of
a	35–28	Our wine the inspiration of *L*,
gl	596–17	the spiritual inspiration of *L* and Truth

inspires
t	454–18	*L* inspires, illumines, designates, and

is enthroned
t	454–10	*L* is enthroned.

is impartial
pr	13– 2	*L* is impartial and universal

is Mind
b	330–21	and *L* is Mind,

is not hasty
a	22–20	*L* is not hasty to deliver us from temptation,

is priestess
t	454–21	*L* is priestess at the altar of Truth.

is reflected
pr	17– 7	And *L* is reflected in love ;

is Spirit
sp	96– 5	spiritualization will follow, for *L* is Spirit.

is the light
ap	577–20	no need of sun or satellite, for *L* is the light

is with me
ap	578–11	for [*L*] is with me ;— *Psal.* 23 : 4.

Lamb of
ap	561–13	wedded to the Lamb of *L*.
	567–30	killed by innocence, the Lamb of *L*.

law of
(see **law**)

leadeth me
ap	578– 7	[*L*] leadeth me beside the still— *Psal.* 23 : 2.
	578– 8	[*L*] leadeth me in the paths of— *Psal.* 23 : 3.

Life and
(see **Life**)

Life, . . . and wisdom
b	283– 6	Mind is the same Life, *L*, and wisdom

Life as
p	391–31	rise to the true consciousness of Life as *L*,

Life, . . . Truth
sp	81–15	Life, *L*, Truth, is the only proof of

Life, Truth, and
(see **Life**)

love of
b	319–31	speak of the love of *L*, meaning by that

maketh
ap	578– 5	[*L*] maketh me to lie down in— *Psal.* 23 : 2.

ministering
ap	567– 3	a sense of the ever-presence of ministering *L*.

misunderstand
pr	6–21	is to misunderstand *L* and to make prayer the

Love

mocking
 g 528–21　mocking *L·* and declaring
motherhood of
 g 519–11　the fatherhood and motherhood of *L·*.
must triumph
 a 43–32　*L·* must triumph over hate.
no fear in
 p 410–18　"There is no fear in *L·*,— *I John* 4 : 18.
no miracle to
 r 494–15　miracle of grace is no miracle to *L·*.
no other
 f 206– 1　no other *L·*, wisdom, or Truth,
not hate
 p 420– 3　*L·* not hate, Spirit not matter, governs man.
not made perfect in
 p 410–20　is not made perfect in *L·*."— *I John* 4 : 18.
omnipresent
 s 119–21　is not the divine ideal of omnipresent *L·*.
opposite of
 gl 580–17　the opposite of *L·*, called hate ;
panoply of
 ap 571–18　Clad in the panoply of *L·*,
partakers of
 pr 4–16　worthiness to be partakers of *L·*.
perfect
 p 373–18　"perfect *L·* casteth out fear."— *I John* 4 : 18.
 406–10　"Perfect *L·* casteth out fear."— *I John* 4 : 18.
 410–18　perfect *L·* casteth out fear.— *I John* 4 : 18.
power of
 f 231–22　is to misunderstand the power of *L·*
prepareth
 ap 578–13　[*L·*] prepareth a table before— *see Psal.* 23 : 5.
propagates
 m 66–13　*L·* propagates anew the higher joys
purpose of
 gl 579–12　the purpose of *L·* to create trust in good,
realm of
 a 20–27　commands sure entrance into the realm of *L·*.
redolent with
 g 516–12　*L·*, redolent with unselfishness,
religion of
 s 138–16　sublime summary points to the religion of *L·*.
removed by
 p 374– 6　Hatred and its effects . . . are removed by *L·*.
restoreth
 ap 578– 8　[*L·*] restoreth my soul— *Psal.* 23 : 3.
Science of
 a 30– 3　and could demonstrate the Science of *L·*
sends forth
 ap 568–29　*L·* sends forth her primal and everlasting strain.
shrine of
 gl 595– 9　superstructure of Truth ; the shrine of *L·* ;
solvent of
 f 242–17　to dissolve with the universal solvent of *L·*
spiritual
 a 33–22　This is the new understanding of spiritual *L·*.
 c 266–11　spiritual *L·* will force you to accept
supports
 m 57–28　for *L·* supports the struggling heart
truer sense of
 a 19– 7　by giving man a truer sense of *L·*,
 19– 9　and this truer sense of *L·* redeems
true sense of
 ap 575– 2　Arise . . . into the true sense of *L·*,
Truth and
 (see **Truth**)
Truth, Life, and
 p 410– 7　the knowledge of *L·*, Truth, and Life.
Truth, Life, and
 (see **Truth**)
Truth, Life, or
 f 207–26　presuppose the absence of Truth, Life, or *L·*.
Truth, or
 f 234– 4　Whatever inspires with wisdom, Truth, or *L·*
universal
 c 266–18　Universal *L·* is the divine way in C. S.
which paints
 f 247–24　It is *L·* which paints the petal
will finally
 sp 96– 4　*L·* will finally mark the hour of harmony,
winged with
 g 512– 9　and also by holy thoughts, winged with *L·*.
wisdom and
 pr 2–11　since He is unchanging wisdom and *L·*.
 a 23– 1　Wisdom and *L·* may require many sacrifices
 c 265–14　discover what belongs to wisdom and *L·*.

---

 pr 13–26　human ignorance of the divine Principle, *L·*,
 15–13　divine Principle, *L·*, which destroys all error.
 17–14　Truth, *L·*, over all, and All.
 a 22–21　*L·* means that we shall be tried and purified.
 26–23　makes us admit its Principle to be *L·*.
 35–14　commune with the divine Principle, *L·*.
 35–20　Our church is built on the divine Principle, *L·*.
 44– 9　He proved . . . *L·* to be the master of hate.

Love

 a 45–21　man and his divine Principle, *L·*,
 50–13　to his divine Principle, the God who is *L·*,
 51–27　aimed at the divine Principle, *L·*,
 sp 98–19　Christ's revelation of Truth, of Life, and of *L·*,
 s 113– 6　the heart and soul of C. S., is *L·*.
 115–13　GOD : Divine Principle, Life, Truth, *L·*, Soul,
 f 225–21　*L·* is the liberator.
 230–10　comes through God, the divine Principle, *L·*,
 231–10　but God, Truth, Life, *L·*, does heal the sick
 243–25　*L·* has no sense of hatred.
 248– 3　*L·* never loses sight of loveliness.
 253– 5　saith : . . . impart all bliss, for I am *L·*.
 c 256– 7　*L·*, the divine Principle, is the Father and
 b 270–13　eternal Mind or divine Principle, *L·*.
 275–12　Spirit, Life, Truth, *L·*, combine as one,
 275–17　the infinite divine Principle, *L·*.
 280– 4　From *L·* and from the light and harmony which
 286–11　Christ, Life, Truth, *L·* ;
 286–14　the divine Principle, *L·*, creates
 293–15　divine Mind, . . . whose attraction is *L·*,
 300–32　that which reflects Life, Truth, *L·*,
 305–25　were it not that *L·*, the divine Principle
 312–16　and without *L·*, God, . . . cannot appear.
 319–29　as, for instance, to name *L·* as merely an
 330–20　Scriptures declare Him to be,— Life, Truth, *L·*.
 331–19　He is divine Principle, *L·*,
 331–27　that is, the triply divine Principle, *L·*.
 332–22　revealing the divine Principle, *L·*.
 335–25　Mind is the divine Principle, *L·*,
 r 465–15　Spirit, Soul, Principle, Life, Truth, *L·*.
 470– 9　assumed . . . the loss of *L·* as ever present
 473–24　God as divine Principle, *L·*,
 477–22　forms of the living Principle, *L·*.
 490–18　the real man's divine Principle, *L·*.
 496–18　based upon its divine Principle, *L·*,
 g 512– 3　the incorporeal and divine Principle, *L·*.
 517–10　woman corresponds to Life and to *L·*.
 520– 9　no more . . . than is his infinite Principle, *L·*.
 524–11　*L·*, the divine Principle to be lived and loved.
 526–23　Was evil instituted through God, *L·* ?
 527–11　Here the metaphor represents God, *L·*, as
 537–32　this is not the nature of God, who is *L·*
 538– 1　*L·* infinitely wise and altogether lovely,
 541–12　the human concept of *L·*
 ap 567– 9　Against *L·*, the dragon warreth not long,
 569– 2　as *L·*, represented by the Mother.
 574–29　The very circumstance, . . . *L·* can make an
 575– 3　*L·* wedded to its own spiritual idea."
 578–18　[the consciousness] of [*L·*] — *Psal.* 23 : 6.
 gl 587– 7　Life ; Truth ; *L·* ; all substance ;
 591–17　divine Principle, substance, Life, Truth, *L·* ;

love (*see also* **love's**)

confidence and
 m 58–18　the sweet interchange of confidence and *l·* ;
disappointed in
 f 245– 5　Disappointed in *l·* in her early years,
emotional
 a 25–27　and all the emotional *l·* we can bestow
enriches
 m 57–23　*L·* enriches the nature, enlarging, purifying,
feminine
 m 64–24　masculine wisdom and feminine *l·*,
for God
 t 454–17　*L·* for God and man is the true incentive
God is
 b 320– 1　"God is *l·*."— *I John* 4 : 8.
God's
 b 326– 9　All nature teaches God's *l·* to man,
goodness and
 m 66–16　unfolds new views of divine goodness and *l·*.
gratitude, and
 pr 8–15　gratitude, and *l·* which our words express,
His
 pr 5–17　God pours the riches of His *l·* into the
 b 340–14　in and of God, and manifests His *l·*.
his
 a 26– 8　in proportion to their demonstration of his *l·*,
labor of
 p 387–24　cannot suffer as the result of any labor of *l·*,
lack of
 s 140–14　tyrannical and proscriptive from lack of *l·*,
life or
 c 257–25　Who hath found finite life or *l·* sufficient
life, truth, and
 b 284–18　testimony as to spiritual life, truth, and *l·* ?
Master's
 s 130–24　our Master's *l·* for little children,
more expansive
 c 265–14　confers upon man . . . a more expansive *l·*,
no
 b 275–18　no *l·* is lovely, . . . but the divine ;
 r 467– 7　no *l·*, but that which is spiritual.
of a father
 a 50–10　would impugn the justice and *l·* of a father

love

of applause
pr 7–15 may embrace too much *l·* of applause
of Christianity
f 235–32 *L·* of Christianity, rather than love of
of God
a 42– 4 gave no hint of the unchanging *l·* of God.
b 304– 9 to separate us from the *l·* of God."— *Rom.* 8 : 39.
of Love
b 319–31 but we can . . . speak of the *l·* of Love,
of popularity
f 236– 1 rather than *l·* of popularity,
of sin
a 36– 6 sufficient suffering, . . . to quench the *l·* of sin.
p 373–14 The fear of disease and the *l·* of sin are the
of the good
gl 593– 1 The *l·* of the good and beautiful,
our
p 410–17 stronger should be our faith and the purer our *l·*.
pinions of
pr 4–31 creeds clip the strong pinions of *l·*,
power and
f 243– 9 with unsurpassed power and *l·*.
precious
a 22– 9 and through Christ's precious *l·* these efforts
rebuking error
gl 594–15 *l·* rebuking error ; reproof of sensualism.
reflected in
pr 17– 7 *And Love is reflected in l·;*
spiritual
c 264–27 comes from an all-absorbing spiritual *l·*.
t 462–30 unselfishness, philanthropy, spiritual *l·*.
truth and
a 50– 4 Who shall decide what truth and *l·* are?
f 215–21 phantoms of error before truth and *l·*.
p 414–11 truth and *l·* will establish a healthy state,
r 473–20 proof of Christianity's truth and *l·* ;
unselfed
pr 1– 4 understanding of Him, an unselfed *l·*.
ph 192–31 thought in line with unselfed *l·*,
variable
g 503–25 mutable truth, nor variable *l·*.

---

pr 4– 5 patience, meekness, *l·*, and good deeds.
an 106–27 the fruit of the Spirit is *l·*, joy,— *Gal.* 5 : 22.
s 108– 9 immortal cravings, "the price of learning *l·*,"
116– 3 spiritual power, *l·*, health, holiness.
f 206–12 exercise of the sentiments— hope, faith, *l·*
248–30 justice, health, holiness, *l·*
b 312–15 with scarcely a spark of *l·* in their hearts ;
p 435–20 in the exercise of a *l·* that
ap 576–14 worshipped in spirit and in *l·*.
gl 586–24, 25 *l·* meeting no response, but still remaining *l·*.

love (verb)

pr 4–11 "If ye *l·* me, keep my— *John* 14 : 15.
4–17 Simply asking that we may *l·* God
4–18 Simply asking . . . will never make us *l·* Him ;
9– 6 Do we *l·* our neighbor better because of
9–17 Dost thou "*l·* the Lord thy God— *Matt.* 22 : 37.
a 25–20 "If ye *l·* me, keep my— *John* 14 : 15.
54–31 would not some, who now profess to *l·* him,
55–18 and *l·* his neighbor as himself.
sp 88–18 To *l·* one's neighbor as one's self, is a
99–22 I *l·* mankind, and shall continue to labor
s 130–31 and no longer think it natural to *l·* sin
138–29 *L·* thy neighbor as thyself !"— *Matt.* 19 : 19.
140–10 and *l·* Him understandingly,
ph 167–19 you must *l·* God supremely.
181–21 If you are too material to *l·* the Science of
f 234–12 We should *l·* our enemies
235–31 will *l·* to grapple with a new, right idea
236–26 and learn more readily to *l·* the simple verities
241–21 "If ye *l·* me, keep my— *John* 14 : 15.
c 267–31 promised to them that *l·* him."— *Jas.* 1 : 12.
b 326– 9 man cannot *l·* God supremely . . . while
340–10 *l·* God and keep His commandments :
340–25 "*L·* thy neighbor as thyself ;"— *Matt.* 19 : 19.
o 359– 2 whom they have seen and have been taught to *l·*
p 363–18 "Which of them will *l·* him most ?"— *Luke* 7 : 42.
364–23 said of them also that they *l·* little.
364–30 that they indeed *l·* much,
366–16 how can he *l·* God whom he— *I John* 4 : 20.
404–25 to master evil and to *l·* good.
t 444– 5 to them that *l·* God,"— *Rom.* 8 : 28.
452–19 He must live it and *l·* it,
r 467– 8 "Thou shalt *l·* thy neighbor as— *Matt.* 22 : 39.
496– 7 to have one Mind, and to *l·* another as
ap 566– 9 up to the glory prepared for them who *l·* God.
572– 6 *L·* one another"— *I John* 3 : 23.

loved

f 236–28 Jesus *l·* little children because of their
b 313–18 he "*l·* righteousness and— *Heb.* 1 : 9.
317–23 self-same Jesus whom they had *l·* before the

loved

p 433–20 Because he has *l·* his neighbor
g 524–12 the divine Principle to be lived and *l·*.
ap 568–19 *l·* not their lives unto the death.— *Rev.* 12 : 11

loveliness

f 246–30 shape our views of existence into *l·*,
247–17 reflecting those higher conceptions of *l·*
247–27 and covers earth with *l·*.
248– 3 Love never loses sight of *l·*.
o 359–32 in their true light and *l·*,

lovely

pr 3–14 the One "altogether *l·* ;"— *Song* 5 : 16.
m 68–17 she was unmarried, a *l·* character,
b 275–18 no love is *l·*, . . . but the divine ;
g 538– 1 Love infinitely wise and altogether *l·*,

lover

m 58–24 Said the peasant bride to her *l·* :
f 245– 8 in the same hour which parted her from her *l·*

lover's

f 245–10 watching for her *l·* coming.

Love's

a 50–14 and to himself, *L·* pure idea.
t 460– 8 on the divine Mind and *L·* essential qualities
g 515– 8 *L·* ideas are subject to the Mind which
ap 578–11, 12 [*L·*] rod and [*L·*] staff— *Psal.* 23 : 4.

love's

m 68–11 and scatters *l·* petals to decay.

loves

a 42– 3 affirmed God to be a . . . who *l·* and hates.
47–23 world generally *l·* a lie better than Truth ;
r 481– 9 Through spiritual sense only, man . . . *l·* Deity.

loveth

f 241– 1 "Whom the Lord *l·* He— *Heb.* 12 : 6.
p 366–14 "He that *l·* not his brother— *I John* 4 : 20.

loving

a 26– 3 treading alone his *l·* pathway
m 57–11 Both sexes should be *l·*, pure, tender, and strong.
f 205–23 the divine law of *l·* our neighbor
c 262–22 and attain the bliss of *l·* unselfishly,
b 272– 5 only as we are honest, unselfish, *l·*, and meek.
326–10 cannot love God supremely . . . while *l·* the
t 454–27 Let your *l·* care and counsel support

loving-kindness

p 366– 2 a priceless sense of the dear Father's *l·*.

lovingly

f 254–20 This task God demands us to accept *l·*
p 412– 1 fact that God *l·* governs all,

low

m 61–10 every mountain of selfishness be brought *l·*,

lower

m 62–27 higher nature . . . is not governed by the *l·* ;
67– 5 ocean is stirred by a storm, then the clouds *l·*,
s 116–30 but not in the *l·* sense.
144– 4 needs no cooperation from *l·* powers,
ph 181– 1 divine Truth more potent than all *l·* remedies.
189–29 in the *l·*, basal portion of the brain,
195–31 Incorrect views *l·* the standard of truth.
f 206– 6 else it will . . . free the *l·* propensities.
247– 8 his full set of upper and *l·* teeth
248–22 are liable to follow those *l·* patterns,
b 268– 5 those *l·* things which give impulse to inquiry.
319–10 *l·* appeal to the general faith in
p 377–21 governing fear of this *l·* so-called mind,
434–30 the *l·* court has sentenced Mortal Man
437–31 ranks above the *l·* Court of Error.
g 518–15 the higher always protects the *l·*.
520–30 nothing left to be made by a *l·* power.
549– 9 Creatures of *l·* forms of organism
551–12 through all the *l·* grades of existence.
554–29 It is the general belief that the *l·* animals are
557– 6 the birth-throes in the *l·* realms of nature,
gl 590–18 almost always has this *l·* sense,

lowering

ph 195–28 Literary commercialism is *l·* the

lowest

s 148–11 and as emerging from the *l·*, instead of
ph 189–20 from the *l·* instead of from the highest
f 225–32 and on the *l·* plane of human life,
c 265– 2 Man is the offspring, not of the *l·*, but of the
p 405– 4 above the *l·* type of manhood,

loyal

pr 4–10 not of itself sufficient to express *l·* and

loyalty

ph 183–23 No reservation is made for any lesser *l·*.

lozenges

ph 175–31 tubercles and troches, lungs and *l·*.

lubricating

ph 199–29 the unscientific might attribute to a *l·* oil.

uke
p 369–14 We never read that L· or Paul made a
uke's Gospel
p 362– 1 in the seventh chapter of L· G·
lled
sp 95–28 L· by stupefying illusions, the world is asleep
t 464–18 when the belief of pain was l·,
minaries
a 37–10 They are earth's l·, which serve to
mp
b 329– 5 A little leaven leavens the whole l·.
nar
ap 561–28 light portrayed is really neither solar nor l·,
ngs
action of the
p 415–21 the action of the l·, of the bowels,
and lozenges
ph 175–31 tubercles and troches, l· and lozenges.
capacious
p 425–29 If you have sound and capacious l·
heart, or
ph 191–18 should no longer ask of the head, heart, or l· :
notions about
p 425–32 Discard all notions about l·, tubercles,
———
s 127–20 nerves, brain, stomach, l·, and so forth,
151–19 The blood, heart, l·, brain, etc.,
159–25 They examine the l·, tongue, and pulse
162–23 what is called the lost substance of l·,
ph 185– 4 changed the action of her belief on the l·,
f 220–31 and controls the stomach, bones, l·, heart,
243–17 The head, heart, l·, and limbs do not inform us
p 370–32 Physicians examine the pulse, tongue, l·,
384–18 congestive symptoms in the l·,
395–25 a tumor, a cancer, or decayed l·,
rking
p 419– 2 L· error, lust, envy, revenge, malice, or
st
and hate
ap 565– 4 It is full of l· and hate,

lust
and hypocrisy
ap 567–27 beast and the . . . are l· and hypocrisy.
571–31 outshining sin, sorcery, l·, and hypocrisy.
head of
g 534–30 this idea, will bruise the head of l·.
of the flesh
f 223– 3 shall not fulfil the l· of the flesh."— Gal. 5 : 16.
gl 584–19 hypnotism ; the l· of the flesh,
paganism and
ph 171– 2 paganism and l· are so sanctioned by
———
f 218–11 and say, "I am malice, l·, appetite,
b 289–10 To suppose that sin, l·, hatred,
330–29 l·, dishonesty, selfishness, envy,
p 404–10 L·, malice, and all sorts of evil are
405– 7 to conquer l· with chastity,
419– 2 Lurking error, l·, envy, revenge,
gl 586–13 Fire. Fear ; remorse ; l· ; hatred ;
588– 1 Hell. Mortal belief ; error ; l· ; remorse ;
589– 3 envy ; hatred ; selfishness ; self-will ; l·.
lusteth
ph 167–20 "flesh l· against the Spirit."— Gal. 5 : 17.
o 347– 1 flesh l· against the Spirit,— Gal. 5 : 17.
lusts
pr 10–28 may consume it upon your l·."— Jas. 4 : 3.
a 18– * the flesh with the affections and l·.— Gal. 5 : 24.
f 234–32 Evil thoughts, l·, and malicious purposes
b 292–22 the l· of your father ye will do.— John 8 : 44.
Luther, Martin
b 268– * quotation from
luxury
t 452–17 Better . . . than the l· of learning with
lying
g 529–21 Whence comes a talking, l· serpent
Lynn
pref xi–27 with only one student in L·, Massachusetts,
s 158–31 A woman in the city of L·, Massachusetts,
159–20 The sequel proved that this L· woman died
ph 192–32 I was called to visit Mr. Clark in L·,
lyre
ph 190–22 thus swept his l· with saddening strains

M

achinations
p 440– 3 the oleaginous m· of the counsel,
achine
p 399–17 It constructs a m·, manages it,
ad
an 105–29 "Whom the gods would destroy, they first make
  m·."
t 462–28 It teaches the control of m· ambition.
ade
pref ix–27 she m· copious notes of Scriptural exposition,
x–13 She has m· no effort to embellish,
pr 4–13 Its motives are m· manifest in the blessings
5–26 belief . . . that man is m· better merely by
a 20– 8 Jesus' history m· a new calendar,
25–31 The divinity of the Christ was m· manifest
27–30 Jesus' persecutors m· their strongest attack
41–32 never m· a disciple who could cast out evils
46– 6 words, which m· their hearts burn
50– 9 This despairing appeal, if m· to a human parent,
50–12 The appeal of Jesus was m· both to his
sp 70– 8 man, m· in God's likeness, reflects God.
72–18 Spirit is not m· manifest through matter,
73–30 The sensual cannot be m· the mouthpiece of
94–11 he m· himself the Son of God."— John 19 : 7.
an 101– 4 the impressions m· upon the senses ;
110– 6 in which all that He has m· is pronounced
s 122–30 mistake . . . that Ptolemy m· regarding the
131–25 until the hearts of men are m· ready for it.
133–24 m· "himself equal with God,"— John 5 : 18.
141–20 m· "kings and priests unto God."— Rev. 1 : 6.
142–29 He m· medicine ; but that medicine was Mind.
145– 6 would have m· void their practice.
146–11 by which material sense is m· the servant
151–23 The divine Mind that m· man maintains His
152–28 Her experiments in homœopathy had m·
154–10 A man was m· to believe that he
156– 3 and what m· them good or bad
162–21 ankylosed joints have been m· supple,
ph 166– 5 the healing effort is m· on the wrong side,
168–26 for the so-called disease m· its appearance
173– 9 is required to be m· manifest through
183–14 Truth never m· error necessary,
183–22 No reservation is m· for any lesser loyalty.
197–18 that m· them hardier than our trained
f 203– 9 m· himself the Son of God,"— John 19 : 7.

made
205–13 and m· all perfect and eternal.
206–12 Omnipotent and infinite Mind m· all
213–16 Sound is a mental impression m· on
218– 2 that which affirms weariness, m· that
219–18 before it can be m· manifest on the body,
221–11 and finally m· up his mind to die,
222–27 concluded that God never m· a dyspeptic,
222–28 physiology, and physics had m· him one,
226–16 These claims are not m· through code or creed,
227–31 disobedience to which would have m· man ill,
229– 7 God made all that was m·,
229–20 is m· void by the law of immortal Mind,
231–32 "all things were m· by Him— John 1 : 3.
232– 1 anything m· that was m·,"— John 1 : 3.
233–27 tests I have m· of the effects of truth
238–17 an experience we have not m· our own,
243– 4 which m· harmless the poisonous viper,
244–12 hath m· me free from the law of— Rom. 8 : 2.
245–21 Years had not m· her old,
c 255–11 Mortal man has m· a covenant with
255–17 cannot be m· the basis of any true idea of
261–18 a signal which m· him as oblivious of
267–10, 11 I am m· all "that was m·."— John 1 : 3.
b 269– 9 Human philosophy has m· God manlike.
273–17 have never m· mortals whole,
286–18 The Scriptures declare all that He m· to be good,
287–21 man was m· in God's likeness.
288–29 m· him the Way-shower, Truth and Life.
294–26 neither self-made nor m· by mortals.
295–25 All that is called mortal thought is m· up of
306–21 m· manifest as matter,
307–18 and says : "The Lord knows it. He has m· man
307–29 material laws which Spirit never m·,
310– 5 m· up of supposititious mortal mind-force ;
311– 5 all that Mind, God, is, or hath m·,
311– 6 and He m· all.
311– 6 Hence evil is not m· and is not real.
313–19 The passage is m· even clearer in the
316– 9 m· manifest by its effects upon the human mind
323–17 shall be m· rulers over many ;
324–21 Paul was m· blind,
327–22 Fear of punishment never m· man truly honest.
335– 9 nothing in Spirit out of which matter could be m·,
335–11, 12 anything m· that was m·."— John 1 : 3.
338– 3 and man as m· in His likeness ;

made

o 344– 6	this claim is m· because the Scriptures say
345–23	to discern the distinction (m· by C. S.)
345–24	between God's man, m· in His image, and the
346– 2	When man is spoken of as m· in God's image,
346–26	when you believe that nitrous-oxide gas has m·
350–24	"The Word was m· flesh."— John 1 : 14.
356–22	man who is m· in the divine likeness
357–15	dare we attempt to destroy what He hath m·,
357–16	to deny that God m· man evil and m· evil good
358–13	C. S. is neither m· up of contradictory
p 369–14	We never read that Luke or Paul m· a
369–22	the other to be m· indestructible.
370– 7	if health is not m· manifest under this regimen,
380–22	years ago the author m· a spiritual discovery,
393–13	God has m· man capable of this,
410–19	He that feareth is not m· perfect— I John 4 : 18.
437– 4	Man was m· in the image of God,
t 449–22	The first impression, m· on a mind which is
450–18	but unless this admission is m·,
472–26	and He makes all that is m·;
r 475– 6	Man is not matter ; he is not m· up of brain,
475– 8	man is m· in the image and likeness of God.
479–32	by the things that are m·."— Rom. 1: 20.
480–20	God, or good, never m· man capable of sin.
480–26	"All things were m· by Him.— John 1 : 3.
480–28	anything m· that was m·."— John 1 : 3.
491– 7	Material man is m· up of involuntary and
493–21	It is fear m· manifest on the body.
g 501– *	All things were m· by Him ; — John 1 : 3.
501– *	anything m· that was m·.— John 1 : 3.
509–23	Mind m· the "plant of the field— Gen. 2 : 5.
510–15	He m· the stars also.— Gen. 1 : 16.
516–20	Man, m· in His likeness, possesses
517–31	Man is not m· to till the soil.
518–25	saw everything that He had m·,— Gen. 1 : 31.
519–23	ended His work which He had m· ; — Gen. 2 : 2.
519–24	all His work which He had m·.— Gen. 2 : 2.
520–18	m· the earth and the heavens,— Gen. 2 : 4.
520–29	there is nothing left to be m· by a lower power.
521– 5	All that is m· is the work of God,
524–18	Mind had m· man, both male and female.
525–18	all things were m· through the Word of God,
525–19, 20	anything m· that was m·."— John 1 : 3.
525–23	He saw everything which He had m·,
525–30	out of the ground m· the Lord God— Gen. 2 : 9.
527–18	But is it true that God, good, m·
528–13	from man, m· He a woman,— Gen. 2 : 22.
529–15	the Lord God [Jehovah] had m·.— Gen. 3 : 1.
530– 3	m· manifest as forever opposed to
537–26	Literally taken, the text is m· to appear
540–20	It saith . . . "God never m· you,
543–25	When Spirit m· all, did it leave aught for
543–32	m· the earth and the heavens,"— Gen. 2 : 4.
545–32	shall all be m· alive."— I Cor. 15 : 22.
553–12	formed under circumstances which m·
554–16	to say, " I am somebody ; but who m· me?"
554–16	Error replies, "God m· you."
554–25	Jesus never intimated that God m· a devil,
556–15	It is m· known most fully to him who
ap 559–15	m· manifest in the destruction of error.
560–23	which m· him equal to his great mission.
565–24	m· war upon the spiritual idea ;
569–22	sin, which one has m· his bosom companion,
gl 583–24	God, who m· all that was m·
	(see also God)

madest

ph 200–14	"Thou m· him to have dominion— Psal. 8: 6.

madly

p 373–27	When the blood rushes m· through the veins

madness

b 327–15	It is a moral m· which rushes forth
p 407–32	because its method of m· is in consonance with

magazine

f 245– 4	the London medical m· called The Lancet.

Magdalen

p 362–15	It was therefore easy for the M· to
364–10	or the contrition of the M·?
365–20	such commendation as the M· gained from

Magi

sp 95–24	M· of old foretold the Messiahship of Truth.

Magic

p 441–23	and Esoteric M· be publicly executed at the

magic

an 101–32	proportional to one's faith in esoteric m·.

magistrate

pr 6–29	It is believed by many that a certain m·,
11– 5	A m· sometimes remits the penalty,

magnet

ap 575–27	the Word, the polar m· of Revelation ;

magnetic

an 100–20	no proof of the existence of the animal m· flui
ph 185–10	which discussed . . . the earth's m· currents

magnetism

animal

an 100– 1	animal m· was first brought into notice
100–18	"In regard to the . . . utility of animal m·,
101–17	not conclusive in favor of the doctrine of anim m·,
101–22	observations of the workings of animal m·
101–26	If animal m· seems to alleviate
101–30	In no instance is the effect of animal m·,
102– 1	Animal m· has no scientific foundation,
102– 5	in Science animal m·, . . . is a mere negation
102–16	The mild forms of animal m· are disappearing
102–21	So secret are the present methods of animal m
103–18	animal m· or hypnotism is the specific term f
104– 3	When C. S. and animal m· are both compr hended,
104–18	necromancy, mesmerism, animal m·,
s 129–17	Animal m·, hypnotism, spiritualism, theosoph
144–18	not . . . C. S., but is sheer animal m·.
ph 178–19	basis of sensation in matter, is animal m· ;
178–25	freed from the belief of . . . animal m· ;
p 442–16	Neither animal m· nor hypnotism enters into
t 450–30	Knowing the claim of animal m·,
454– 1	nor can he practise animal m· or hypnotism.
r 483– 2	how do drugs, hygiene, and animal m· heal?
484–21	Animal m· is the . . . action of error in all its
491– 3	Animal m· thus uncovers material sense,
gl 583–26	Dan (Jacob's son). Animal m· ;
584–19	Devil. Evil ; a lie ; . . . animal m·
593– 8	Red Dragon. . . . animal m· ; envy ; reveng
594– 4	Serpent . . . animal m· ; the first lie of

effects of

ph 181–17	ignorant of the baneful effects of m·,

electricity and

ph 181–10	When . . . you trust in electricity and m·

first record of

g 528–18	This is the first record of m·.

practice of

an 101– 2	observed in the public practice of m·,

magnetizer

an 101–14	promised by Monsieur Berna [the m·]

magnified

s 140–32	What is the god of a mortal, but a mortal m·

magnify

ap 568–24	give thanks and m· the Lord of Hosts.

magnitude

a 43– 3	m· of Jesus' work, his material disappearance
50– 6	an overwhelming sense of the m· of his work,
54– 2	Through the m· of his human life,
m 63–22	without encouraging difficulties of greater m·,
g 511– 6	the sublimity, m·, and infinitude of

magnitudes

f 209–18	the m·, distances, and revolutions of

main

pref ix– 2	to jot down her thoughts on the m· subject,
o 345–30	the m· cause of the carnal mind's antagonism.

mainly

sp 71–22	spiritualism will be found m· erroneous,
s 144– 9	human philosophy, physiology, hygiene, are m
p 412–29	m· through the parent's thought,

maintain

m 59– 7	Mutual compromises will often m· a
sp 81– 9	and m· their affiliation with
97– 3	They will m· law and order,
f 246–23	still m· his vigor, freshness, and promise.
b 270–21	and m· the Science of Spirit.
p 389–19	If God has, as prevalent theories m·,
395– 4	and m· man's immortality
417–10	M· the facts of C. S.,
t 461– 1	I do not m· that anyone can

maintained

s 136– 1	m· his mission on a spiritual foundation
ph 172– 8	How then is the material species m·,
g 531– 3	m· in all the subsequent forms of belief.
531–18	If, . . . why is not this divine order still m·

maintaining

s 119–14	making Him guilty of m· perpetual misrule
b 271– 3	m· its obvious correspondence with

maintains

sp 70–12	The divine Mind m· all identities,
s 151–24	m· His own image and likeness.
b 287– 7	contradicts this postulate and m· man's
329–24	m· the claim of Truth by quenching error.

maintenance

g 553–13	to their m· and reproduction,

ajesty
sp 78–23 the m· and omnipotence of Spirit be lost?
g 520– 4 The depth, breadth, height, might, m·,
ap 564–19 Until the m· of Truth should be demonstrated

ajor
s 128–31 If both the m· and the minor propositions of a

ajority
m 60–19 This, however, in a m· of cases,
s 155–10 and the beliefs which are in the m· rule.
155–14 such a belief is governed by the m·.
164–18 caused by a m· of human beliefs
ph 177–32 but the vast m· of mankind, though they
178– 5 controlled by the m· of opinions,
p 394– 5 m· of doctors depress mental energy,
r 482– 2 gives the exact meaning in a m· of cases.

ake
iii– * the truth shall m· you free.— John 8 : 32.
pref vii– 7 m· plain to benighted understanding the way
vii–22 but it cannot m· them speedily understood.
pr 2– 2 Do we pray to m· ourselves better
4–18 Simply asking . . . will never m· us love Him ;
6–21 is to misunderstand Love and to m· prayer the
9–27 Then why m· long prayers about
11–16 to m· him turn from it with loathing.
a 20–12 men can . . . m· long prayers, and yet be
22– 8 to m· vigorous efforts to save themselves ;
24– 8 and m· the Bible the chart of life,
25–28 will never alone m· us imitators of him.
40–15 Did the martyrdom of Savonarola m·
42– 6 It cannot m· Life or Truth apparent.
50–25 But this saying could not m· it so.
52–18 error and evil again m· common cause against
m 62–32 this does not m· materiality first
65–17 the powerlessness of vows to m· home happy,
sp 92–24 ability to m· nothing of error will be wanting.
an 105–29 "Whom the gods would destroy, they first m·
mad."
s 115– 5 as to m· them comprehensible to any reader,
116– 6 to m· this Scriptural testimony true
119–12 is not only to m· Him responsible for
120–12 matter can m· no conditions for man.
122–10 senses still m· mortal mind tributary
122–29 Our theories m· the same mistake regarding
130–18 denied and cast out to m· place for truth.
130–22 ability of Spirit to m· the body harmonious,
140–30 would . . . m· God in their own human image.
142–23 m· them meet dwelling-places for the
143–32 may try to m· Mind and drugs coalesce,
144– 1 Why should we wish to m· them do so,
148–22 Then theology tries to explain how to m·
152– 6 The author has endeavored to m· this book the
ph 165– 3 would open man's eyes and m· him as a god.
165– 8 is to subjugate intelligence, to m· mind mortal,
189–13 sins of others should not m· good men suffer.
197–22 helped to m· them healthy,
199–15 Mortals develop their own bodies or m·
f 205– 9 shows that matter can neither heal nor m· sick,
206–29 This Mind does not m· mistakes
208–13 not in accordance . . . that He should m· man
sick,
210–28 appears to itself to m· good its claim.
221–31 neither food nor . . . can m· one suffer,
227–19 Love and Truth m· free,
230–19 Does wisdom m· blunders
232– 3 neither m· man harmonious nor God lovable.
232–11 theories . . . m· healing possible only through
232–20 never taught that . . . could m· a man healthy,
232–23 never tried to m· of none effect the sentence
236–27 the simple verities that will m· them happy
240– 8 The stars m· night beautiful,
252–22 says : . . . I mean to m· my short span of life
253–13 no cause (outside of . . . able to m· you sick
253–20 Matter can m· no opposition
c 260– 2 and m· himself like it.
263–11 They m· man an involuntary hypocrite,
b 289–12 Truth and Truth's idea, never m· men sick,
294–13 saying : . . . The stomach can m· a man cross.
303–15 can never m· both these contraries true.
306– 3 They would first m· life result in death,
307– 5 saying, . . . I will m· error as real and
317–32 Nothing but a display of matter could m·
322–18 cannot m· the inebriate leave his . . . until
339–13 the sinner would m· a reality of sin,
339–13 would m· that real which is unreal,
340– 2 and m· life its own proof of harmony
346–29 beliefs must be expelled to m· room for
o 351–18 while we m· a personal devil and
352– 3 to m· harmony the reality
p 371–31 can m· it "every whit whole."— John 7 : 23.
383–23 but does this m· it so?
383–30 pounding the poor body, to m· it sensibly real
391–27 Therefore m· your own terms with sickness,
395–21 It is mental quackery to m· disease a reality
396– 5 M· no unnecessary inquiries relative to

make
p 397–15 more powerful than the accident itself, to m·
398– 8 concessions which Jesus was willing to m·
399–24 there is no mortal mind out of which to m·
402–25 The operator would m· his subjects believe
404–30 envy, dishonesty, fear, . . . m· a man sick,
409–31 Death will not m· us harmonious
413–15 in order to m· it thrive more vigorously
417– 8 If you m· the sick realize this great truism,
417–24 is to m· disease unreal to him.
421– 8 m· known to the patient your motive
424–22 It is not more difficult to m· yourself heard
427–23 God, Life, Truth, and Love m· man undying.
438– 3 Let us m· man in our image,— Gen. 1 : 26.
440– 6 Morbid Secretion is taught how to m·
t 443– 6 those, who m· such a compromise,
444–31 The teacher must m· clear to students
451– 9 will either m· shipwreck of their faith or
464– 2 Why do you not m· yourself more widely
464– 4 in which to m· herself outwardly known
r 474–27 If evil is real, Truth must m· it so ;
475–23 "Let us m· man in our image,— Gen. 1 : 26.
480–16 Inharmony would m· matter the cause
480–22 evil — which seems to m· men capable of
485–12 how to m· sin, disease, and death . . . unreal
489–28 nor m· it the medium of Mind.
490–14 theories are helpless to m· man harmonious
g 515–11 Let us m· man in our image,— Gen. 1 : 26.
525–13 Icelandic : . . . Let us m· man after our mind
525–22 Whatever is valueless or baneful, He did not m·,
527– 3 to m· it beautiful or to cause it to live and grow.
527–15 knowledge of evil would m· man mortal.
533–19 aids man to m· sinners more rapidly than
540– 5 "I m· peace, and create evil.— Isa. 45 : 7.
543–29 would m· Life, or God, mortal.
552–10 Mortal theories m· friends of sin, sickness,
ap 559–18 it shall m· thy belly bitter,— Rev. 10 : 9.
569– 7 I will m· thee ruler over many,"— Matt. 25 : 23.
574–29 Love can m· an angel entertained unawares.
gl 582–26 the error which would m· man mortal
582–26 and would m· mortal mind a slave to the body.

Maker
allegiance to his
f 226–21 man's birthright of sole allegiance to his M·
endowed by his
s 161–16 "Man is endowed by his M· with certain
governed by his
an 106–11 governed by his M·, divine Truth and Love.
f 231–30 Man, governed by his M·, having no other
his
an 102–13 no more power over man than over his M·,
b 309–26 to have an intelligence separate from his M·.
316– 4 being linked by Science to his M·,
o 360–25 more pure than his M· ?— Job 4 : 17.
r 475–22 reflects spiritually all that belongs to his M·.
488–20 cannot be true either of man or of his M·.
g 518– 4 himself subordinate alone to his M·.
531–24 and so changed the method of his M· ?
image of his
f 203–15 and so makes man the image of his M·
likeness of his
f 252–14 recognized as the true likeness of his M·.
b 305– 7 Man, in the likeness of his M·,
p 441–17 in the image and likeness of his M·.
likeness of their
f 246– 6 are the eternal likeness of their M·.
man and his
b 276– 9 Man and his M· are correlated in divine Science,
man's
p 437– 6 This is a foul aspersion on man's M·.
r 491–11 It is the likeness of man's M·.
reflection of his
b 305–28 Because man is the reflection of his M·,
service of our
sp 79–32 does not impoverish us in the service of our M·,
your
p 397–31 will understand yourself and your M· better

maker
p 428–14 "whose builder and m· is God."— Heb. 11 : 10.
ap 575–11 The builder and m· of this New Jerusalem

makes
pref viii–15 confers the most health and m· the best men.
pr 7–22 ventilation of fervent sentiments never m· a
8– 2 though it m· the sinner a hypocrite.
a 26–23 as m· us admit its Principle to be Love.
31–15 living Christ, the practical Truth, which m·
53–24 lifelong sacrifice which goodness m·
sp 78–25 where spiritism m· many gods,
s 114– 8 evidence of the . . . senses, which m· minds many
119–30 and m· body tributary to Mind.
153–23 this so-called mind m· its own pain
ph 183– 1 Truth, m· all things possible to Spirit ;
184– 3 Truth m· no laws to regulate sickness,
189–19 mortal mind, . . . m· all things start from

makes

ph 196–18	Sin m· its own hell, and goodness its own
199–21	m· the achievement possible.
f 201– 8	Truth m· a new creature.
208–27	m· it harmonious or discordant according to
209– 2	mortal belief which m· the body discordant
212–22	God alone m· and clothes the lilies
216–15	This understanding m· the body harmonious ;
216–15	it m· the nerves, bones, . . . servants,
219–11	m· the whole body "sick, — Isa. 1 : 5.
220–26	belief that either fasting or . . . m· men better
222– 8	mortal mind m· a mortal body,
229–25	all that He m· is good and will stand forever.
231–12	If God m· sin, if good produces evil,
233– 1	Every day m· its demands upon us
236–31	youth m· easy and rapid strides towards Truth.
237–22	This m· C. S. early available.
245–29	primary of that illustration m· it plain that
249–29	m· its mundane flights quite ethereal.
251–21	the divine Mind m· perfect,
c 266–20	The sinner m· his own hell by doing evil,
b 270–26	If sin m· sinners, Truth . . . can unmake them.
295– 8	they are obedient to the Mind that m· them.
300– 5	mirage, which m· trees and cities seem to be
307–10	It says : . . . God m· evil minds and evil spirits,
337–12	The truth of being m· man harmonious
o 343– 7	This m· it doubly unfair to impugn and
357–10	the belief that God m· sickness,
p 385–12	law which m· sin its own executioner,
404–32	unless it m· him better mentally,
405– 3	m· any man, . . . a hopeless sufferer.
407– 9	delay m· the struggle more severe.
410–14	Every trial of our faith in God m· us stronger.
415–17	Note how thought m· the face pallid.
426–10	The struggle for Truth m· one strong
t 456–18	Science m· no concessions to persons
458–20	Sin m· deadly thrusts at the Christian Scientist
464–25	Adulterating C. S., m· it void.
r 472–26	He m· all that is made.
486–18	Alas for the blindness of belief, which m·
487–31	This Principle m· whole the diseased,
g 505– 1	Mind m· its own record,
506– 6	and m· Truth final.
520–29	Because Mind m· all, there is
532– 3	God m· and governs all.
539–29	the one Mind which m· and governs man
ap 570–29	when it m· them sick or sinful.
gl 596– 5	m· Him better known as the All-in-all,
	(see also **man**)

maketh

t 445–24	The human will which m· and worketh a lie,
ap 577–27	"defileth, . . . or m· a lie." — Rev. 21 : 27.
578– 6	m· me to lie down in green — Psal. 23 : 2.
gl 588– 4	"worketh abomination or m· a — Rev. 21 : 27.
596–26	m· the valley to bud and blossom as the rose.

making

pr 12– 6	m· it act more powerfully on the body
a 34– 4	by casting out error and m·
m 66–28	m· his Xantippe a discipline for his
s 119–14	thereby m· Him guilty of maintaining
142–12	m· dome and spire tremulous with beauty,
b 298–32	m· them . . . with suggestive feathers ;
321– 7	despaired of m· the people understand
o 342– 4	"m· wise the simple." — Psal. 19 : 7.
348– 6	m· the disease appear to be . . . an illusion
356–26	by m· man inclined to sin, and then
p 375–22	m· certain portions of it motionless.
382–12	m· clean merely the outside of the platter.
410–13	mankind objects to m· this teaching practical.
413–29	m· it probable at any time that
423–18	m· Mind his basis of operation
431–24	took control of his mind, m· him despondent.
r 466–30	m· mankind better physically, morally, and
472– 6	m· it coordinate with all that is real
473–27	m· his acts of higher importance than his
g 520–31	but m· him superior to the soil.
541– 4	instead of m· his own gift a higher tribute
gl 580– 7	m· "gods many and lords many" — I Cor. 8 : 5.

malady

p 398– 6	clear evidence that the m· was not material.
413–32	or any other m·, timorously held in the
t 488– 4	When, . . . you are able to banish a severe m·,

male

f 249– 5	"m· and female" of God's creating — Gen. 1 : 27.
g 508–21	a neuter gender, neither m· nor female.
508–23	The intelligent individual idea, be it m· or
516–25	m· and female created He them. — Gen. 1 : 27.
524–19	Mind had made man, both m· and female.
525–15	and He shaped them m· and female.
528– 3	created man, both m· and female
ap 565–10	Herod decreed the death of every m· child
577– 5	the unity of m· and female

malevolent

o 357–11	on account of this m· triad.

malice

aforethought

p 437– 7	It indicates m· aforethought,
t 451–27	arises from ignorance or m· aforethought.

his own

ap 569–26	at last stung to death by his own m· ;

ignorance and

f 215–32	The ignorance and m· of the age

mortal

t 458–22	Science will ameliorate mortal m·.

or hate

p 419– 2	Lurking error, lust, envy, revenge, m·, or hate

or ignorance

t 459–20	Whether animated by m· or ignorance,

an 104–20	dishonesty, sensuality, falsehood, revenge, m·
f 218–11	and say, "I am m·, lust, appetite,
241–10	Falsehood, envy, hypocrisy, m·, hate,
b 327– 8	What a pitiful sight is m·,
p 404–10	Lust, m·, and all sorts of evil are
t 462–27	selfishness, m·, envy, and hate.

malicious

an 103–23	It is either ignorant or m·.
103–24	The m· form of hypnotism
s 110–21	or by careless or m· students,
f 235– 1	Evil thoughts, lusts, and m· purposes
p 401– 5	cherishing evil passions and m· purposes,
t 446–14	from sinister or m· motives
ap 564– 4	This m· animal instinct,

malign

r 485–11	Why m· C. S. for instructing mortals

malignant

ph 176–31	Truth handles the most m· contagion
p 373– 6	easier to cure the most m· disease than

maligned

a 41–27	good deeds, for which they were m· and stoned

malignity

a 43–12	The m· of brutal persecutors,

malpractice

p 375–15	any mental despotism or m·.
442–31	mental m· cannot harm you
t 451–27	m· arises from ignorance or malice
451–31	mental m· tends to blast moral sense,
457–17	to mental m·, . . . there is no good aspect,

malpractitioner

p 419–25	Never fear the mental m·,

maltreatment

r 474–10	consequent m· which it receives.

mamma

s 154–30	and says, . . . "M· knows you are hurt."
f 237– 5	"M·, my finger is not a bit sore."

mammon

a 52– 4	He served God ; they served m·.
o 346–31	We cannot serve both God and m·
t 462–11	dividing his interests between God and m·

Man (see also **Man's**)

p 434–27	conspiracy against the liberty and life of M·.
434–31	but God made M· immortal
437– 4	testified . . . that he knew M·,
437– 4	and that M· was made in the image of God,
437– 8	a determination to condemn M·
437–14	M· self-destroyed ; . . . Spirit not allowed a
438– 1	certain extracts on the Rights of M·,
438–12	bearing false witness against M·.
441–16	Our law refuses to recognize M· as sick
441–19	Spirit decides in favor of M·
442– 1	There, M· is adjudged innocent of transgressing
r 482–19	he was literally the Son of M·.
	(see also **Mortal Man**)

man (see also **man's**)

action of

f 207–28	spiritual fact, repeated in the action of m·

actuality of

g 502–13	and the spiritual actuality of m·,

affections of a

gl 597– 4	The motives and affections of a m· were

a man's a

ph 172–31	"a man's a m·, for a' that."

and creation

r 489–30	A wrong sense of God, m·, and creation is

and form

g 517– 5	from two Greek words, signifying m· and form

and God

c 258–23	gains the true conception of m· and God.
g 524–25	or is it a lie concerning m· and God?

and his creator

b 338–24	would impose between m· and his creator.

and his Maker

b 276– 9	M· and his Maker are correlated in

Man

and Mind
b 281–20 false conception as to *m·* and Mind.
and the universe
(*see* **universe**)
and woman
a 37–23 privilege of every child, *m·*, and woman,
g 516–21 *M·* and woman as coexistent and eternal with
529–10 that both *m·* and woman proceed from God
gl 588–12 *m·* and woman unchanged forever
another
sp 73– 9 belief that one . . . can control another *m·*,
any
a 25–17 any *m·* whose origin was less spiritual.
31– 9 no record of his calling any *m·* by the name of
s 109–29 If any *m·* will do His will,— *John* 7 : 17.
p 405– 3 any *m·*, who is above the lowest type
g 527–14 neither tempteth He any *m·*.''— *James* 1 : 13.
apart from
b 270–11 Few deny . . . that intelligence, apart from *m·*
appears
r 477–10 *m·* appears to be matter and mind united ;
as created
s 148– 7 Neither . . . has ever described *m·* as created
by Spirit,
as God's image
pr 13–28 ignorant of *m·* as God's image or reflection
s 116– 4 and *m·* as God's image appears.
assigning to
f 244–30 instead of assigning to *m·* the
as the offspring
a 29–30 *M·* as the offspring of God, as the idea of Spirit,
author of
a 29–16 God is the only author of *m·*.
beliefs that
s 164–19 human beliefs that *m·* must die,
belief that
(*see* **belief**)
belief that one
sp 73– 8 belief that one *m·*, as spirit, can control another
believes
ph 171–17 *m·* believes himself to be combined matter and
p 427– 7 If *m·* believes in death now,
benefit to
r 471–22 Are doctrines and creeds a benefit to *m·*?
bestowed on
p 387–29 protecting power bestowed on *m·* by
393–15 ability and power divinely bestowed on *m·*.
better
a 21– 4 because you are a better *m·*.
blesses
sp 78–28 Spirit blesses *m·*,
blind
t 459–18 a blind *m·* or a raging maniac,
brotherhood of
b 340–24 constitutes the brotherhood of *m·* ;
r 467–13 true brotherhood of *m·* will be established.
470– 3 brotherhood of *m·* would consist of Love and
g 541–18 ruptures the life and brotherhood of *m·*
called
sp 81–22 give to the worms the body called *m·*,
ph 190–13 bulk of a body, called *m·*.
f 250–15 and that one is called *m·* ;
calling that
s 148–20 calling that *m·* which is not the counterpart,
can do for
a 48–32 what the true knowledge of God can do for *m·*.
can do no
an 103–32 In C. S., *m·* can do no harm,
can no longer
sp 76–13 When advanced . . . *m·* can no longer commune with
cannot exceed
a 19– 4 *M·* cannot exceed divine Love,
cannot govern
r 490– 6 Hence it cannot govern *m·* aright.
cannot kill a
p 395–30 knowledge that brain-lobes cannot kill a *m·*
cannot lose
c 259– 2 *m·* cannot lose his individuality,
changed the
b 309– 9 This changed the *m·*.
chronicles
g 522– 8 The second record chronicles *m·* as mutable
claims to rule
s 148–26 Physiology . . . claims to rule *m·* by
clothe
g 530–12 to feed and clothe *m·* as He doth the lilies.
coexists with
s 120– 5 *m·* coexists with and reflects Soul, God,
commanded the
g 527– 7 commanded the *m·*, saying,— *Gen.* 2 : 16.
commands
p 405– 5 commands *m·* to master the propensities,
communicate with
sp 78–22 How then can it communicate with *m·* through

man

compare
g 515–28 Now compare *m·* before the mirror to his
compels
p 436–30 which the divine law compels *m·* to commit.
comprehends
r 481– 8 Through spiritual sense only, *m·* comprehends
conceptions of
f 244– 7 to derive all our conceptions of *m·* from
concerning
r 494–25 Which of these two theories concerning *m·*
g 524–25 or is it a lie concerning *m·* and God?
concerning a
sp 89–13 reaffirms the Scriptural word concerning a *m·*,
p 383–28 the Scriptural conclusion concerning a *m·*,
conclusions as to
c 259–32 Deducing one's conclusions as to *m·* from
condition of
o 344– 5 sinless condition of *m·* in divine Science,
confers upon
c 265–12 confers upon *m·* enlarged individuality,
corporeal
b 332–18 The corporeal *m·* Jesus was human.
t 453–19 but in order to bless the corporeal *m·* ;
correct view of
r 477– 3 this correct view of *m·* healed the sick.
create
o 356–21 is it possible for Him to create *m·* subject to
g 522–21 represented as entering matter in order to create *m·*.
528– 6 cannot be true that man was ordered to create *m·* anew
creates
m 69–23 If the father replies, ''God creates *m·* through
gl 582–18 creates *m·* as His own spiritual idea,
creating
b 338–20 was deemed the agent of Deity in creating *m·*,
creator of
r 470–21 God is the creator of *m·*,
cross-questioning
g 533–26 Truth, cross-questioning *m·* as to his
deathless
m 69–16 and of *m·* deathless and perfect
g 534– 5 to manifest the deathless *m·* of God's creating.
defile a
an 100– * *the things which defile a m·.— Matt.* 15 : 20.
define
s 148–13 define *m·* as both physical and mental,
definition of
b 302–14 Continuing our definition of *m·*,
demands on
ph 184–13 legitimate and eternal demands on *m·*,
demonstrates
b 340–22 by which *m·* demonstrates health, holiness, and
p 372–14 When *m·* demonstrates C. S. absolutely,
405–20 Immortal *m·* demonstrates the government
demoralizes the
g 533–14 beguiles the woman and demoralizes the *m·*.
denunciations of
g 522–22 denunciations of *m·* when not found in His image,
deprive a
o 358– 3 Can a leaden bullet deprive a *m·* of Life,
description of
ph 170–28 The description of *m·* as purely physical,
disarms
p 394–11 The admission that . . . disarms *m·*,
divinely royal
b 313– 5 Jesus the God-crowned or the divinely royal *m·*,
divine Principle of (*see also* **Principle of**)
sp 72– 3 divine Principle of *m·* speaks through
ph 191–10 the spiritual and divine Principle of *m·*
f 207–14 perfect Father, or the divine Principle of *m·*.
b 336–25 God, the divine Principle of *m·*,
r 470–22 the divine Principle of *m·* remaining perfect,
481–28 Soul is the divine Principle of *m·*
ap 562–15 the activities of the divine Principle of *m·*
divine Science of
f 242–25 divine Science of *m·* is woven into one web
divorced from
r 477–30 *m·*, divorced from Spirit, would lose his entity
does not pay the
p 387–18 That *m·* does not pay the severest penalty
drove out the
g 537– 5 So He drove out the *m·* :— *Gen.* 3 : 24.
duty of
b 340– 9 for this is the whole duty of *m·*.''— *Eccl.* 12 : 13.
g 541–25 Now it repudiates even the human duty of *m·*
each need of
pr 7–25 to whom each need of *m·* is always known
earth, and
g 538–19 God creates the heavens, earth, and *m·*.
economy of
ph 170– 7 Did Jesus understand the economy of *m·* less than

man

elevating
gl 586–14 affliction purifying and elevating *m·*.

empowers
ph 199–10 empowers *m·* through its mandate,

enables
a 19–24 enables *m·* to do the will of wisdom.

endows
g 522– 7 endows *m·* out of God's perfection and power.

enslavement of
f 228–11 The enslavement of *m·* is not legitimate.

enslaves
f 225– 3 Whatever enslaves *m·* is opposed to

error supposes
b 287– 6 Error supposes *m·* to be both mental and

establishes
r 491–15 establishes *m·* forever in the divine likeness,

eternal
a 29–32 Spirit is harmonious and *m·* eternal.
ph 191– 6 this eternal *m·* will include in that likeness
b 311–31 the spiritual, eternal *m·* is not touched by

every
sp 98–20 for every *m·* to understand and to practise.
s 144–28 every *m·* will be his own physician.

exempts
p 385–13 exempts *m·* from all penalties but those

existence of
p 427–16 Nothing can . . . end the existence of *m·*

exists
g 544–11 *m·* exists because God exists.

expresses in
c 258–13 God expresses in *m·* the infinite idea

false conception of
b 285–17 is a false conception of *m·*.

family of
r 470– 1 the whole family of *m·* would be brethren ;

finite
c 257–32 Finite *m·* cannot be the image and

forever intact
r 493–31 divine Mind to hold *m·* forever intact

formed
b 281–25 a *m·* formed from dust.
g 524–13 Lord God [Jehovah] formed *m·* — *Gen.* 2 : 7.

friend of
a 49–15 the highest instructor and friend of *m·*,

generic
ap 561–22 generic *m·*, the spiritual idea of God ;

generic term
c 259– 1 the generic term *m·*.

gives
ph 183–23 Obedience to Truth gives *m·* power and
f 202–22 God gives *m·* dominion over all the earth.
b 307–26 and gives *m·* dominion over all things.
316–22 which gives *m·* dominion over all the earth.
p 387–30 gives *m·* faith and understanding
430– 7 When *m·* gives up his belief in death,

giving
a 19– 7 by giving *m·* a truer sense of Love,

glorified
a 54–29 If that Godlike and glorified *m·* were

God and
    (*see* **God**)

God controls
sp 73–11 God controls *m·*, and God is the only Spirit.

God created
s 140–29 God created *m·* in His, God's, image ;
b 294–27 God created *m·*.
g 516–24 God created *m·* in His own image, — *Gen.* 1 : 27.

God has created
o 344– 7 God has created *m·* in His own image

God has endowed
an 106– 7 God has endowed *m·* with inalienable rights,

God has made
p 393–13 God has made *m·* capable of this,

God is not
r 480–19 Man is not God, and God is not *m·*.

Godlike
c 262–15 higher views inspire the Godlike *m·* to reach

God made
ph 167–15 If God made *m·* both good and evil,
f 227–16 God made *m·* free.
g 516–28 God made *m·* in His own image,

God's
sp 92–18 a burlesque of God's *m·* — is an outgrowth of
s 148– 8 man as created by Spirit, — as God's *m·*.
148–21 but the counterfeit, not God's *m·*.
151–23 it has no control over God's *m·*.
ph 191– 1 The brain can give no idea of God's *m·*.
b 306–30 God's *m·*, spiritually created, is not material
o 345–24 God's *m·*, made in His image,
r 476– 1 A mortal sinner is not God's *m·*.
gl 580– 3 the first god of mythology ; not God's *m·*,

God to
    (*see* **God**)

good
p 405–18 The good *m·* finally can overcome his fear of

man

good-will to
p 407–16 even into spiritual power and good-will to *m·*

govern
f 206– 7 the province of spiritual sense to govern *m·*.
227–30 If God had instituted material laws to govern *m·*
p 381– 1 law of matter . . . supposed to govern *m·*,

governed by
s 125–15 *m·* governed by Soul, not by material sense.
f 231–30 M·, governed by his Maker, having no other
246–23 M·, governed by immortal Mind, is
b 304–14 The perfect *m·* — governed by God,

governing
f 231–15 no antagonistic powers . . . governing *m·*
b 308– 6 God is the only Mind governing *m·*,
gl 595– 1 SUN.   The symbol of Soul governing *m·*,

governs
pr 6– 3 Divine Love corrects and governs *m·*.
f 222–12 the fact that Mind governs *m·*,
231–21 God made you superior to it and governs *m·*.
p 420– 4 Spirit not matter, governs *m·*.
g 539–29 one Mind which makes and governs *m·*

harmonious
s 148–19 Principle which produces harmonious *m·*,
f 232– 4 neither make *m·* harmonious nor God lovable
b 276–24 the universe, including harmonious *m·*.
337–12 The truth of being makes *m·* harmonious and
r 490–15 theories are helpless to make *m·* harmonious

harmony in
b 276–15 Harmony in *m·* is as real and immortal as in
304–20 Harmony in *m·* is as beautiful as in music,

harmony of
p 392–10 health, holiness, and harmony of *m·*,
423–14 and it restores the harmony of *m·*.

has never lost
g 548– 7 *m·* has never lost his spiritual estate

has "sought out"
ph 196– 2 M· has "sought out many inventions," — *Ec*
7 : 29.

hath not seen
b 325–19 where human sense hath not seen *m·*.

help meet for
g 533–20 Is this an help meet for *m·* ?

higher nature of
m 62–27 higher nature of *m·* is not governed by the

history of
g 557–22 theology takes up the history of *m·* as if

human
r 473–15 Jesus is the human *m·*, and Christ is the divi

ideal
m 69– 9 the real, ideal *m·* appears in proportion as
b 332–31 Into the real and ideal *m·* the
338–30 Adam was not the ideal *m·* for whom
338–31 The ideal *m·* was revealed in due time,
o 346– 4 the ideal *m·*, reflecting God's likeness.
g 517– 8 The ideal *m·* corresponds to creation,

idea of
a 45–21 spiritual idea of *m·* and his divine Principle,
ph 194– 4 coincidence of the spiritual idea of *m·* with

immortal
m 61– 1 can satisfy the cravings of immortal *m·*.
ph 173–25 the image of God, the real immortal *m·*.
190–19 immortal *m·*, spiritual and eternal,
f 202–16 but immortal *m·*, in accord with the
215–25 Mortal man is the antipode of immortal *m·*
b 288–28 glorious possibilities of immortal *m·*,
294–19 immortal *m·*, representing Spirit,
302–15 immortal *m·* has existed forever,
306– 8 The immortality of Soul makes *m·* immortal.
322– 8 before harmonious and immortal *m·* is
336– 9 Immortal *m·* was and is God's image
336–10 immortal *m·* is coexistent and coeternal with
336–17 Immortal *m·* is not and never was material,
p 405–20 Immortal *m·* demonstrates the government
417–19 is not the Science of immortal *m·*.
r 476–20 the facts which belong to immortal *m·*.
485–18 understanding of Life, makes *m·* immortal.
g 538–26 This account is given, not of immortal *m·*,

immortality of
f 215–31 he recognized the immortality of *m·*.
b 292– 9 Mind, the only immortality of *m·*,
324– 7 Unless the harmony and immortality of *m·* a
p 381–25 The harmony and immortality of *m·*
g 507–27 the immortality of *m·* and the universe.
521–12 The harmony and immortality of *m·* are inta

including
sp 83–17 The belief that the universe, including *m·*,
s 114–28 the universe, including *m·*, is spiritual,
127– 5 the spiritual universe, including *m·*,
ph 171–12 control over the universe, including *m·*,
c 256– 8 Father and Mother of the universe, including *m·*
b 295– 5 governs the universe, including *m·*,
330–12 intelligence of the universe, including *m·*.
g 511– 1 governing the universe, including *m·*,
547–19 to recreate the universe, including *m·*.
547–26 true theory of the universe, including *m·*,
gl 584–24 a mortal universe, including *m·*,

an

inclusive of
s 128– 6 government of the universe, inclusive of *m·*.
g 554– 3 the universe, inclusive of *m·*, is as eternal

indestructible
sp 76–26 indestructible *m·*, whose being is spiritual.
b 316–20 Christ presents the indestructible *m·*,

individual
s 117– 3 an individual *m·*, an individual horse ;
r 468–23 universe, including individual *m·*,

individuality of
b 317–16 individuality of *m·* is no less tangible
r 491–26 Personality is not the individuality of *m·*.

in God's image
r 476–31 *m·* in God's image is unfallen and eternal.
497– 7 and *m·* in God's image and likeness.

in God's likeness
ph 191– 5 *m·* in God's likeness will appear,
b 336–25 divine Principle of man, and *m·* in God's likeness

in His image
b 340–11 for this is the whole of *m·* in His image

insane
p 411–17 the insane *m·* was changed and straightway

in Science
ph 187–23 *m·* in Science is governed by this Mind.
f 244–23 *M·* in Science is neither young nor old.

intelligence of
r 477–23 the substance, Life, and intelligence of *m·*,

in the idea
gl 582–14 conceiving *m·* in the idea of God ;

in the image
sp 94– 1 who makes *m·* in the image and likeness of
g 548– 6 *m·* in the image and likeness of God.

in the likeness
sp 81–17 *M·* in the likeness of God as revealed in
b 305– 6 *M·*, in the likeness of his Maker, reflects

in this allegory
g 544–25 *m·*, in this allegory, is neither a lesser god nor

is become
g 536–31 the *m·* is become as one of us,— *Gen. 3 : 22.*
545– 3 the *m·* is become as one of us."— *Gen. 3 : 22.*

is clothed
p 442–24 and *m·* is clothed and fed spiritually.

is coexistent
r 478– 1 for *m·* is coexistent with God.

is deathless
c 266–29 *M·* is deathless, spiritual.

is endowed
s 161–16 "*M·* is endowed by his Maker with certain

is found
sp 97–19 *m·* is found in the likeness of Spirit,
ph 179–10 is won only as *m·* is found, . . . reflecting
188– 2 and *m·* is found in His image.
b 291–16 *m·* is found having no righteousness of his own,

is free
r 481– 5 *m·* is free "to enter into the— *Heb. 10 : 19.*

is God's image
s 120– 5 reflects Soul, God, for *m·* is God's image.

is God's reflection
g 527– 4 *M·* is God's reflection, needing no

is governed
a 42–26 in C. S. the true *m·* is governed by God
s 151–21 Every function of the real *m·* is governed by
ph 180–25 When *m·* is governed by God,
f 216–16 If *m·* is governed by the law of divine Mind,
b 302–22 this real *m·* is governed by Soul
318–29 In Science *m·* is governed by God,
r 495– 1 whenever *m·* is governed by God.

is harmonious
ph 184–16 *m·* is harmonious and eternal.
b 273–18 *M·* is harmonious when governed by Soul.

is His image
r 468–14 Spirit is God, and *m·* is His image and likeness.

is His likeness
sp 73– 7 Spirit is God, and *m·* is His likeness.

is idea
r 475–13 *M·* is idea, the image, of Love ;

is image
sp 73–10 for *m·* is image.
b 301–24 while *m·* is "image" (idea).— *Gen. 1 : 27.*

is immortal
sp 76–20 *m·* is immortal and lives by divine authority.
f 250–15 a mortal is not man, for *m·* is immortal.
250–27 But the spiritual, real *m·* is immortal.
p 426–29 *M·* is immortal, and the body cannot die,
t 461– 3 but I do believe that the real *m·* is immortal
r 478–31 man is not mortal . . . *m·* is immortal.
g 546– 3 mortality of man is a myth, for *m·* is immortal.

is incapable of sin
r 475–28 *M·* is incapable of sin, sickness, and death.

is indestructible
p 402–12 *M·* is indestructible and eternal.

is never God
sp 70– 7 *M·* is never God, but spiritual man, . . . reflects

is never sick
p 393–29 *M·* is never sick, for Mind is not sick and

man

is not absorbed
c 259– 1 *M·* is not absorbed in Deity,

is not God
f 250–12 *M·* is not God, but like a ray of
r 480–19 *M·* is not God, and God is not man.

is not material
r 468–15 Therefore *m·* is not material ;

is not matter
r 475– 6 *Answer.— M·* is not matter ;

is not mortal
r 476–10 Hence *m·* is not mortal nor material.
478–31 *m·* is not mortal, "neither indeed— *Rom. 8 : 7.*

is perfect
r 485–23 in which *m·* is perfect, even as the

is pure
r 477– 5 and that *m·* is pure and holy.

is self-governed
s 125–17 Reflecting God's government, *m·* is self-governed.

is spiritual
sp 93–26 *M·* is spiritual.
ph 173–20 *M·* is spiritual, individual, and eternal ;
b 302– 4 the real *m·* is spiritual and eternal.
p 396–28 that *m·* is spiritual, not material ;
409–20 The real *m·* is spiritual and immortal,
r 475–11 *M·* is spiritual and perfect ;

is subject to
p 429–12 Science declares that *m·* is subject to Mind.

is sustained
g 530– 5 In divine Science, *m·* is sustained by God,

is the expression
r 470–23 *M·* is the expression of God's being.
477–26 *M·* is the expression of Soul.

is the idea
ph 200–11 Life is God, and *m·* is the idea of God,
c 266–27 *M·* is the idea of Spirit ;
r 476–10 and *m·* is the idea of God.

is the image
ph 172–18 *m·* is the image and likeness of Spirit ;
200–18 *m·* is the image, reflection, of God,
p 414–26 *m·* is the image and likeness of God,

is the likeness
f 250–11 Spiritual *m·* is the likeness of this Ego.
r 467–15 *m·* is the likeness of God,
g 544–24 *M·* is the likeness of Spirit,

is the offspring
m 63– 5 *m·* is the offspring of Spirit.
c 265– 1 *M·* is the offspring, not of the lowest, but of
p 396–27 *m·* is the offspring of God, not of man ;

is the reflection
f 249–31 *M·* is the reflection of Soul.
b 305–27 Because *m·* is the reflection of his Maker,
r 475–17 *m·* is the reflection of God, or Mind,

is tributary
f 209– 8 and *m·* is tributary to divine Mind.
r 481– 2 *M·* is tributary to God, Spirit,

just
a 47–11 ingratitude and hatred towards that just *m·*
t 443– * *teach a just m·, and he will— Prov. 9 : 9.*

let not
m 56– * *let not m· put asunder.— Matt. 19 : 6.*

let us make
p 438– 3 Let us make *m·* in our image,— *Gen. 1 : 26.*
r 475–23 "Let us make *m·* in our image,— *Gen. 1 : 26.*
g 515–11 Let us make *m·* in our image,— *Gen. 1 : 26.*
525–13 And God said, Let us make *m·*

life and
p 368–21 life and *m·* survive this body.

Life of
a 51–12 Nothing could kill this Life of *m·*.
b 304–18 Divine Principle is the Life of *m·*.
p 388–23 does not affect the absolute Life of *m·*,
g 555–30 Knowing that God was the Life of *m·*,

life of
(see **life**)

makes
sp 94– 1 makes *m·* in the image and likeness of
ph 173–22 makes *m·* knavish or honest according to
f 203–15 and so makes *m·* the image of his Maker
225– 4 Truth makes *m·* free.
b 269–10 C. S. makes *m·* Godlike.
306– 8 immortality of Soul makes *m·* immortal.
317–19 understanding . . . makes *m·* more real,
o 357–10 belief that God . . . makes *m·* capable of
t 453–30 the divine Truth that makes *m·* free.
r 485–18 understanding of Life, makes *m·* immortal.

making
o 356–26 by making *m·* inclined to sin,

manifested through
f 210–12 forever manifested through *m·*,

many a
ph 197– 6 costs many a *m·* his earthly days of comfort.

material
(see **material**)

matter and
b 294– 8 If . . . matter and *m·* would be one.

man

measured
a 47– 4 They no longer measured *m·* by material sense.
Mind controls
b 319–19 Mind controls *m·* and man has no Mind but God.
Mind of
r 470–17 when God, the Mind of *m·*, never sins
Mind that made
s 151–23 The divine Mind that made *m·* maintains His
Mind to
f 214–16 conveys the impressions of Mind to *m·*,
misnamed
b 294–11 mortal belief, misnamed *m·*, is error,
moral
p 406–17 moral *m·* has no fear that he will commit a murder,
mortal
(see **mortal**)
most scientific
b 313–23 Jesus of Nazareth was the most scientific *m·*
motive-powers of
r 490– 8 Truth and Love as the motive-powers of *m·*.
must be sinless
b 290–26 To be wholly spiritual, *m·* must be sinless,
must find
m 65–27 *m·* must find permanence and peace
must harmonize
b 337– 8 *m·* must harmonize with his Principle,
must live
pref viii– 3 *m·* must live in obedience to its divine
nature of
sp 94– 4 The nature of *m·*, thus understood,
nearer to
gl 596– 5 but C. S. brings God much nearer to *m·*,
never beheld in
c 259–16 then mortals have never beheld in *m·* the
never causing
g 520–31 never causing *m·* to till the ground,
never dies
r 486–10 In reality *m·* never dies.
never punishes
p 384– 7 God never punishes *m·* for doing right,
no
a 31– 5 "Call no *m·* your father upon the—*Matt.* 23 : 9.
sp 77–15 "knoweth no *m·*— *Mark* 13 : 32.
s 140– 6 shall no *m·* see Me, and live."— *Exod.* 33 : 20.
f 201– 5 "No *m·* can serve two masters."— *Matt.* 6 : 24.
217–14 know we no *m·* after the flesh !"— *II Cor.* 5 : 16.
233–12 no *m·* knoweth,— not even "the Son— *Mark* 13 : 32.
252–18 wholly dishonest, and no *m·* knoweth it.
c 255–14 That God is corporeal...no *m·* should affirm.
b 286– 9 "No *m·* cometh unto the— *John* 14 : 6.
292– 4 knoweth no *m·*."— *Matt.* 24 : 36.
p 369–30 No *m·* is physically healed in wilful error
t 458–25 He does violence to no *m·*.
k 499– * openeth, and no *m·* shutteth;— *Rev.* 3 : 7.
499– * shutteth, and no *m·* openeth;— *Rev.* 3 : 7.
499– * an open door, and no *m·* can shut it.— *Rev.* 3 : 8.
gl 579– * openeth, and no *m·* shutteth;— *Rev.* 3 : 7.
579– * shutteth, and no *m·* openeth;— *Rev.* 3 : 7.
579– * an open door, and no *m·* can shut it.— *Rev.* 3 : 8.
no power over
sp 76–20 they will have no power over *m·*,
nor God
g 533–30 as much as to say . . . "Neither *m·* nor God.
not influenced by
pr 7–23 God is not influenced by *m·*.
of God
b 314–10 The Jews, who sought to kill this *m·* of God,
of sorrows
a 42– 9 The "*m·* of sorrows"— *Isa.* 53 : 3.
52–19 The "*m·* of sorrows"— *Isa.* 53 : 3.
old
c 261–15 This old *m·* was so lame that he
origin of
b 325–27 time cometh when the spiritual origin of *m·*,
r 490–24 explanations of the nature and origin of *m·*
g 529– 7 as to the nature and origin of *m·*,
534– 2 the belief in the material origin of *m·*
534– 7 which reveals the spiritual origin of *m·*.
549–32 a belief in the material origin of *m·*,
555–16 Searching for the origin of *m·*, who is the
or matter
b 284– 4 If God were limited to *m·* or matter,
painless to
p 401–13 but should be as painless to *m·* as to a fluid,
passing to
gl 581– 4 ANGELS. God's thoughts passing to *m·* ;
perfect
sp 99–29 and to God's spiritual, perfect *m·*.
c 259–13 perfect God and perfect *m·*,— as the basis
b 304–14 The perfect *m·*— governed by God,
330–14 Neither God nor the perfect *m·* can be
337–16 In proportion to his purity is *m·* perfect ;
r 477– 1 Jesus beheld in Science the perfect *m·*,

man

perfect
r 477– 2 In this perfect *m·* the Saviour saw
477–16 the genuine and perfect *m·*,
482–20 highest human concept of the perfect *m·*.
g 519–20 unto a perfect *m·*,— *Eph.* 4 : 13.
place
r 486–30 blindness, and deafness would place *m·* in
possesses
g 539–11 *m·* possesses nothing which he has not
ap 576–23 In divine Science, *m·* possesses this
possibilities of
s 128–16 latent abilities and possibilities of *m·*
t 445–10 Teach the great possibilities of *m·*
presupposes
b 281– 7 Error presupposes *m·* to be both mind and
r 480–15 and presupposes *m·* to be in matter.
Principle of (see also **divine Principle of**)
s 123– 4 true idea and Principle of *m·* will then appear
r 476–10 God is the Principle of *m·*,
Principle of the
a 29–28 the divine Principle of the *m·* Jesus,
s 146–17 the divine Principle, of the *m·* Jesus ;
problem of
f 216– 7 and solves the problem of *m·*.
produces in
p 380–24 the divine Mind produces in *m·* health,
qualities in
b 280–30 perpetuates these qualities in *m·*,
real
s 151–21 Every function of the real *m·* is governed by
ph 172–24 If the real *m·* is in the material body,
190–20 immortal man, . . . is found to be the real *m*
200–17 the real *m·* was, is, and ever shall be perfect,
f 250–27 But the spiritual, real *m·* is immortal.
b 288–25 the spiritual real *m·* has no birth,
289–19 to the real *m·* and the real universe there is ?
300–11 the real *m·*, or the *new* man
302– 4 the real *m·* is spiritual and eternal.
302– 5 The identity of the real *m·* is not lost,
302–22 this real *m·* is governed by Soul
314–17 To such . . . the real *m·* seemed a spectre,
316– 4 The real *m·* being linked by Science to
316– 6 the real *m·* and his relation to God,
p 409–20 The real *m·* is spiritual and immortal,
409–24 and the new man or real *m·* is put on,
t 461– 3 but I do believe that the real *m·* is immortal
r 475–29 The real *m·* cannot depart from holiness,
476– 4 In divine Science, God and the real *m·* are
476–31 Truth and Love reign in the real *m·*,
g 538–30 the sinless, real *m·* is eternal.
543– 4 it is only mortal man and not the real *m·*,
reconcile
a 19– 2 Christ's purpose to reconcile *m·* to God,
reconciles
a 18–13 atonement of Christ reconciles *m·* to God,
reconciling
a 19– 7 Jesus aided in reconciling *m·* to God
record of
g 531–31 the scientifically Christian record of *m·*
redeems
a 19– 9 redeems *m·* from the law of matter,
reflected by
pr 3–12 The Divine Being must be reflected by *m·*,
b 336–14 Mind can never be in man, but is reflected by *m*
r 467–18 not in man but as reflected by *m·*,
496– 5 omnipotent Mind is reflected by *m·*
reflects
a 18– 2 whereby *m·* reflects divine Truth, Life, and
sp 90–32 certainly shall know this when *m·* reflects God
94– 3 *M·* reflects infinite Truth, Life, and Love.
c 258–11 *M·* reflects infinity,
b 306–19 cannot be separated . . . if *m·* reflects God.
p 393–17 in Science *m·* reflects God's government.
g 525– 4 *M·* reflects God ;
reform the
b 327–25 But how shall we reform the *m·* who
reign over
g 529–31 He begins his reign over *m·* somewhat mildly,
relation of
sp 94– 8 and of the relation of *m·* to God,
s 114–25 It shows the scientific relation of *m·* to God,
representing
p 376–24 representing *m·* as healthy instead of
reveals
s 120–21 reveals *m·* as harmoniously existent
ph 191–24 reveals *m·* and immortality as based on Spirit
b 296–12 reveals *m·* and Life, harmonious, real,
302–19 The Science of being reveals *m·* as perfect,
r 477–11 C. S. reveals *m·* as the idea of God,
righteous
a 37–19 procured the martyrdom of that righteous *m·*
right of a
a 49–31 turned "aside the right of a *m·*— *Lam.* 3 : 35.
rights of
(see **rights**)

man

robs
  ph 169–32 it robs *m·* of reliance on God,
said
  f 239–32 of which the wise *m·* said,
  g 533– 7 And the *m·* said, The woman whom— *Gen.* 3 : 12.
Science of
  sp 73–10 the individuality and the Science of *m·*,
  p 409–25 as mortals realize the Science of *m·*
Science teaches
  r 472– 1 Science teaches *m·* that God is the only Life,
sees his reflection
  s 126– 6 even as *m·* sees his reflection in a glass.
senses of
  b 284–29 the only real senses of *m·* are spiritual.
  r 486–23 all the spiritual senses of *m·*, are eternal.
  488–28 If it were possible for the real senses of *m·* to be
  489–19 Who dares to say that the senses of *m·* can be
sensuous
  s 131– 8 opposition of sensuous *m·* to the Science of Soul
sent from God
  ap 561–30 "There was a *m·* sent from God— *John* 1 : 6.
separated from
  r 477–29 Separated from *m·*, who expresses Soul,
shall recognize
  a 55–17 when *m·* shall recognize the Science of Christ
shaped
  g 525–14 and God shaped *m·* after His mind ;
should be
  g 529– 3 that *m·* should be born of woman,
should be governed
  g 536–14 if *m·* should be governed by corporeality
should lose aught
  b 302– 8 It is impossible that *m·* should lose aught
should renew
  p 426–14 *M·* should renew his energies and
should wish
  b 301–18 *m·* should wish for, and in reality has,
sick
  s 120–10 Is a *m·* sick if the material senses indicate
  152–18 the sick *m·* supposed this ceremony was
  f 208–13 not . . . that He should make *m·* sick,
  b 318–16 Is the sick *m·* sinful above all others? No !
  p 404–30 envy, dishonesty, fear, . . . make a *m·* sick,
signifies that
  b 340–18 it signifies that *m·* shall have no other spirit or
so-called
  ph 188– 8 but afterwards it governs the so-called *m·*.
  gl 580–11 a so-called *m·*, whose origin, substance, and
Son of
  s 132–26 "When the Son of *m·* cometh,— *Luke* 18 : 8.
  136–12 say that I, the Son of *m·*, am ?"— *Matt.* 16 : 13.
  b 334–25 represents the Son of *m·* as saying
  r 482–17 called himself "the Son of *m·*,"— *Matt.* 9 : 6.
son of
  gl 594–17 son of *m·*, the offspring of the flesh.
Soul of
  b 280–27 God, the Soul of *m·* and of all existence,
  307–26 The divine Mind is the Soul of *m·*,
soweth
  p 405–17 "Whatsoever a *m·* soweth,— *Gal.* 6 : 7.
  g 537–13 "Whatsoever a *m·* soweth,— *Gal.* 6 : 7.
spiritual
  (*see* **spiritual**)
spiritualized
  s 141–19 Its only priest is the spiritualized *m·*.
springs solely
  g 543–28 *m·* springs solely from Mind.
standard of
  g 553– 9 or . . . will never become the standard of *m·*.
state of
  s 159–23 medical schools would learn the state of *m·* from
  f 227–16 Slavery is not the legitimate state of *m·*.
status of
  s 120–19 or to exhibit the real status of *m·*.
  r 476–22 earnestly seek the spiritual status of *m·*,
strength to
  m 60–18 a protection to woman, strength to *m·*,
strive with
  b 320–13 shall not always strive with *m·*, — *Gen.* 6 : 3.
strong
  p 399–31 first bind the strong *m·* ?"— *Matt.* 12 : 29.
  400– 4 Mortal mind is "the strong *m·*,"— *Matt.* 12 : 29.
  400– 7 we can despoil "the strong *m·*"— *Matt.* 12 : 29.
such a
  s 139–32 The moral condition of such a *m·* demands
supposition that
  ph 171–31 supposition that *m·* is a material outgrowth
  g 521–13 supposition that *m·* is created materially,
sustain
  an 103–25 The truths of immortal Mind sustain *m·*,
sustains
  b 319– 9 sustains *m·* under all circumstances ;
taken from
  g 528–13 and the rib, . . . taken from *m·*,— *Gen.* 2 : 22.
  529– 4 not woman again taken from *m··*

man

talks with
  b 308–15 as consciously as *m·* talks with *m·*.
tempting
  g 527–12 represents God, Love, as tempting *m·*,
the best
  a 52–16 the best *m·* that ever trod the globe.
the new
  b 300–11 the real man, or the *new m·*
  p 409–24 and the new *m·* or real man is put on,
the old
  ph 172–22 we must "put off the old *m·*."— *Col.* 3 : 9.
  c 262– 8 putting "off the old *m·*— *Col.* 3 : 9.
  b 296– 9 The old *m·* with his deeds must be put off.
  g 519–16 until they throw off the old *m·*
theories of
  a 20– 4 to forms of doctrine or to theories of *m·*,
theory of
  g 545–13 utterly opposed to the theory of *m·*
the term
  g 525– 8 some of the equivalents of the term *m·*
this
  s 148–22 tries to explain how to make this *m·* a Christian.
  b 314–10 The Jews, who sought to kill this *m·* of God,
  g 522–16 to be temporary and this *m·* to be mortal,
this original
  b 286–13 from first to last by this original *m·*, Jesus.
through
  r 495– 1 God will heal the sick through *m·*,
to become
  ph 172–16 in order to become *m··*
  p 432–17 if . . . it is possible for *m·* to become diseased,
translation of
  f 209–22 by the translation of *m·* and the universe
true
  a 42–26 in C. S. the true *m·* is governed by God
true idea of
  b 337–20 The true idea of *m·*, as the reflection of
truth-giver to
  sp 72–12 God, is the only truth-giver to *m·*.
ultimate of
  r 487– 4 Life is the origin and ultimate of *m·*,
understands
  c 265– 3 *M·* understands . . . existence in proportion as
undying
  p 427–23 Truth, and Love make *m·* undying.
unfashion
  r 488–27 otherwise the very worms could unfashion *m·*.
universe and
  gl 585–17 encompassing the universe and *m·* ;
unrighteous
  s 139– 2 unrighteous *m·* his thoughts."— *Isa.* 55 : 7.
  f 239–15 unrighteous *m·* his thoughts."— *Isa.* 55 : 7.
verities of
  r 476–13 as the only and eternal verities of *m·*.
warns
  r 481–13 against which wisdom warns *m·*,
was accounted
  b 316–26 That *m·* was accounted a criminal who
was made
  b 287–21 *m·* was made in God's likeness.
what constitutes
  b 289– 6 the understanding of what constitutes *m·*
whatever teaches
  ph 169–29 Whatever teaches *m·* to have other laws
what is
  r 475– 5 *Question.*— What is *m· ?*
which define
  sp 81–25 which define *m·* as mortal.
wicked
  f 239–11 The wicked *m·* is not the ruler of his
  r 491–26 A wicked *m·* may have an attractive
will not punish
  o 357– 2 must admit that God will not punish *m·* for
will recognize
  g 531–13 Then *m·* will recognize his God-given dominion
will reopen
  ph 171– 5 *m·* will reopen with the key of divine Science
wisdom of
  pr 3– 2 The wisdom of *m·* is not sufficient to warrant
wise
  sp 95–25 Is the wise *m·* of to-day believed, when he
  f 239–32 of which the wise *m·* said,
  t 443– * *Give instruction to a wise m·,*— *Prov.* 9 : 9.
worldly
  a 21–25 worldly *m·* is at the beck and call of error,
would enjoy
  f 246–21 *m·* would enjoy more than
would presuppose
  ph 194–15 would presuppose *m·*, . . . a mortal in
would procreate
  s 140–30 but mortals would procreate *m·*,

----

  pr 3–13 else *m·* is not the image and likeness of the
  5–26 belief that sin is cancelled, and that *m·* is
  8–10 If a *m·*, though apparently fervent

man

pr	15–12	that *m·* may have audience with Spirit,
a	26–13	This Christ, or divinity of the *m·* Jesus,
	26–18	to prove what God is and what He does for *m·*.
	30–16	"Whoso sheddeth man's blood, by *m·* shall his
		— *Gen.* 9 : 6.
	43–15	glorification of the *m·* and of the true idea of
	53– 4	there never lived a *m·* so far removed from
m	59– 8	*M·* should not be required to participate
	64– 2	caused by the selfishness and inhumanity of *m·*.
	64–10	When a *m·* lends a helping hand
	64–21	but *m·* would be as the angels.
	67–28	*M·* delivered from sin, disease, and death
	68–32	and *m·*, not of the earth earthly
	69– 7	while believing that *m·* is a
	69– 8	only as *m·* finds the truth of
	69–22	or is *m·* a creator?"
	69–23	replies, "God creates man through *m·*,"
sp	70– *	*If a m· keep my saying,— John 8 : 51.*
	75– 2	mistaken assumption that *m·* dies as matter
	76–15	Neither will *m·* seem to be corporeal,
	78–28	*m·* cannot "tell whence it— *John* 3 : 8.
	81–23	in the case of *m·* as truly as
	83–28	by which *m·* gains the divine Principle and
	85–13	"Come, see a *m·*, which told me— *John* 4 : 29.
	89–27	*m·* is not the father of *m·*.
	89–29	if . . . *m·* gave it, *m·* had the right to take it
	90–24	admission to one's self that *m·* is God's own
	90–25	sets *m·* free to master the infinite idea.
	90–31	At present we know not what *m·* is,
	91–27	second erroneous postulate is, that *m·*
	92– 1	fourth erroneous postulate is, . . . that *m·* has
	93–27	If *m·* were Spirit, then men would be spirits,
an	102–12	planets have no more power over *m·* than
	102–13	*m·*, reflecting God's power, has dominion
	103– 7	Science, by which *m·* can escape from sin
	106– 9	*M·* is properly self-governed only when
s	107– *	*which was preached of me is not after m·.— Gal. 1 : 11.*
	107– *	*For I neither received it of m·,— Gal. 1 : 12.*
	115–30	*M·* : God's spiritual idea,
	119–31	Thus it is with *m·*, who is but the humble
	120– 3	and that *m·* is included in
	120–12	matter can make no conditions for *m·*.
	121–14	*m·*, left to the hypotheses of material sense
	123– 8	so that *m·* becomes the most absolutely
	124–14	The universe, like *m·*, is to be interpreted by
	124–18	the universe, like *m·*, is, . . . an enigma.
	125– 7	*m·* will be found normal and natural
	125–18	*m·* cannot be controlled by sin or death,
	125–32	mortal belief, wholly inadequate to affect a *m·*
	126– 5	mortality will cease when *m·* beholds
	132–15	thrust the spiritual idea and the *m·* who
	133–23	material system, . . . concerning God, *m·*,
	148–16	Anatomy takes up *m·* at all points materially.
	154–10	A *m·* was made to believe that he occupied
	154–13	and the *m·* died.
	160–30	Is *m·* a material fungus without Mind
ph	166– 3	As a *m·* thinketh, so is he.
	166–31	then is *m·* found to be harmonious
	167–15	If . . . *m·* must remain thus.
	168–15	Because man-made systems insist that *m·*
	171–11	to learn how much of a *m·* he is.
	172– 9	if *m·* passes through what we call death
	172–15	If *m·* was first a material being,
	172–17	If the material body is *m·*, he is a portion of
	172–23	What is *m·*?
	172–25	If . . . you take away a portion of the *m·* when
	173– 1	When we admit that . . . constitutes *m·*, we fail
	173– 4	or determine when *m·* is really *m·*
	173–17	Anatomy declares *m·* to be structural.
	174– 5	form of idolatry, that *m·* should bow down to
	174– 7	capable of doing so much for *m·* as
	174–24	Anatomy admits that mind is somewhere in *m·*,
	180–26	*m·* knows that with God all things are possible.
	183–12	error, first caused the condemnation of *m·*
	184–18	We say *m·* suffers from the effects of
	190–23	As for *m·*, his days are as— *Psal.* 103 : 15.
	193–14	and said : "I feel like a new *m·*,
	193–29	what I saw and did for that *m·*,
	198– 2	has in belief more power to harm *m·*
f	202–31	Common opinion admits that a *m·* may take
	203–31	God, divine good, does not kill a *m·*
	204–27	can never be said that *m·* has a
	206–25	Can there be any birth or death for *m·*,
	206–30	God does not cause *m·* to sin,
	208–13	then leave *m·* to heal himself ;
	209– 1	*M·*, being immortal, has a perfect . . . life.
	209– 9	mortal body or mind is not the *m·*.
	213– 3	Of a *m·* it has been said,
	213– 5	as a *m·* spiritually *understandeth*, so is he
	214–24	mortal illusions would rob God, slay *m·*,
	216– 3	Who shall say that *m·* is alive to-day, but
	216–19	mistake of mortals is to suppose that *m·*,
	217–12	"If a *m·* keep my saying,— *John* 8 : 51.
	225– 1	What is it that binds *m·* with iron shackles

man

f	227–31	disobedience to which would have made *m·* ill,
	228–12	when *m·* enters into his heritage of freedom,
	229–23	If God cause *m·* to be sick, sickness must
	230–20	which must afterwards be rectified by *m·*?
	230–21	can *m·* put that law under his feet
	231– 8	What God cannot do, *m·* need not attempt.
	232–20	never . . . could make a *m·* healthy,
	244– 9	would have no abiding-place in *m·*,
	244–13	*M·* undergoing birth, maturity, and decay
	244–15	If *m·* were dust in his earliest stage of
	244–18	but *m·* was never more nor less than *m·*.
	244–19	If *m·* flickers out in death or
	246– 1	*M·* is not a pendulum, swinging between
	246– 6	*M·* is by no means a material germ
	247– 7	One *m·* at sixty had retained his
	250–13	*m·*, the outcome of God, reflects God.
	250–15	but a mortal is not *m·*,
	250–26	matter has no more sense as a *m·* than
	252–12	*m·* created by and of Spirit,
	252–32	saith : . . . *M·*, whose senses are spiritual, is
	253– 4	saith : . . . I give immortality to *m·*,
c	258– 9	*M·* is more than a material form with
	258–16	We know no more of *m·* as the true divine image
	258–28	impossible for *m·*, under the government of
	259– 6	In divine Science, *m·* is the true image of God.
	259–10	thoughts which presented *m·* as fallen, sick,
	259–15	If *m·* was once perfect but has now lost
	260– 2	true conception or understanding of *m·*,
	261–32	Good demands of *m·* every hour,
	263–11	They make *m·* an involuntary hypocrite,
	264–31	all the glories of earth and heaven and *m·*.
	265–17	as if *m·* were a weed growing apace
	265–20	this is true only of a mortal, not of a *m·*
	267– 6	Generically *m·* is one,
	267– 7	specifically *m·* means all men.
	267–11	Hence *m·* and the spiritual universe
	267–28	"Blessed is the *m·* that— *Jas.* 1 : 12.
b	277–16	not produced by a vegetable nor the *m·* by the
	278–25	leads to the conclusion that if *m·* is material,
	280–26	*m·* has a sensationless body ;
	282–28	Whatever indicates the fall of *m·*
	282–30	Adam-dream, which is neither Mind nor *m·*,
	284–32	is always from God to His idea, *m·*.
	285– 8	It is not *m·*, the image and likeness of God,
	285–16	belief that a material body is *m·*
	287–19	It saith, "I am *m·*, but I am not the image
	289–22	So *m·*, tree, and flower are supposed to die ;
	289–31	*M·* is not the offspring of flesh, but of Spirit,
	291–22	As *m·* falleth asleep, so shall he awake.
	292–28	*m·* would be annihilated, were it not for
	293–12	both strata, . . . are false representatives of *m·*
	294– 6	If *m·* is both mind and matter,
	294– 7	some quality and quantity of the *m·*,
	294–14	saying : . . . stomach can make a *m·* cross.
	294–14	error, saying : . . . matter can kill *m·*."
	294–26	*M·* is neither self-made nor made by mortals.
	295–30	It further teaches that when *m·* is dead,
	296– 1	theorizes that . . . *m·* has a resurrection from
	296– 2	*m·* is the spiritual, eternal reflection of God.
	297–16	and *m·* found to be immortal.
	299–31	If *m·* were solely a creature of the
	300– 5	His infinite image or reflection, *m·*.
	300– 9	So far as the scientific statement as to *m·*
	300–21	of *m·* as reflecting the divine likeness.
	301–17	*m·* is the divine image and likeness,
	301–31	presupposes . . . *m·* to be material
	303–12	statement that *m·* is conceived and evolved
	303–22	belief that . . . holiness and unholiness, mingl
		in *m·*,
	304–30	So *m·*, not understanding the Science of
	305– 3	discordant mortal is no more a *m·* than
	305–10	so *m·*, like all things real, reflects God,
	305–24	In the illusion . . . *m·* would be wholly mortal
	306– 9	parted . . . from His reflection, *m·*,
	306–13	If Life or Soul and its representative, *m·*,
	306–18	But *m·* cannot be separated for an instant from
	307–18	says : "The Lord knows it. He has made *m·* mortal
	307–26	*M·* was not created from a material basis,
	309– 3	incorporeal impartation of divine Love to *m·*,
	309–25	or for *m·* to have an intelligence separate
	311–13	Is *m·* lost spiritually? No,
	311– 8	it will become the law of Life to *m·*,
	312– 8	The senses regard a corpse, not as *m·*,
	312– 9	People say, "*M·* is dead ;"
	319–14	Spirit and matter neither concur in *m·* nor in
	319–20	*m·* has no Mind but God.
	320–22	according to that error *m·* is mortal.
	322–22	A *m·* who likes to do wrong
	322–25	neither a temperate *m·* nor a reliable
	325–14	then shall *m·* be found in God's image.
	325–16	Then shall *m·* be found, in His likeness,
	326– 9	teaches God's love to *m·*, but *m·* cannot
	326–26	Then the *m·* was changed.
	327–22	Fear of punishment never made *m·* truly honest

man

b 332–17 one mediator. . .the *m·* Christ Jesus."— *I Tim.*
　　　2: 5.
336–13 infinite Mind can never be in *m·*,
336–20 A portion of God could not enter *m·* ;
336–21 neither could . . . be reflected by a single *m·*,
336–31 and *m·* is God's spiritual offspring.
337– 2 Therefore *m·*, reflecting God, cannot lose his
337–10 *m·* is in a degree as perfect as
338– 4 belief— that *m·* orginates in matter
338–23 the supposed separation of *m·* from God,
340–28 annuls the curse on *m·*,
o 344– 2 the only absolute Life and Soul, and *m·* to be
345–26 "For if a *m·* think himself to be— *Gal.* 6: 3.
346– 1 such criticism confounds *m·* with Adam.
346– 2 *m·* is spoken of as made in God's image,
347–13 so-called mortal man is not the reality of *m·*.
349–11 neither Life nor *m·* dies,
356–22 *m·* who is made in the divine likeness
357– 2 that He created *m·* capable of doing,
357– 4 knew from the outset that *m·* would do.
357–16 deny that God made *m·* evil
360–25 Shall *m·* be more pure than— *see Job.* 4: 17.
p 363–32 her affection for a *m·* of undoubted goodness
364– 2 the best *m·* that ever trod this planet.
368–17 more faith in God than in *m·*,
369– 6 loses to human sense all entity as *m·*,
369– 6 in that proportion does *m·* become its master.
369–19 were willing that a *m·* should live.
369–20 He understood *m·*, whose Life is God,
369–21 knew that *m·* has not two lives, one to be de-
　　　stroyed
370– 1 *m·* must be better spiritually
371–21 not transform the infant at once into a *m·*,
372– 7 that its sensations can reproduce *m·*,
372–11 belief that matter is the medium of *m·*,
372–11 or that *m·* can enter his own embodied
379–17 Oxford boys, who caused the death of a *m·*,
380–17 a chained lion, . . . should not terrify a *m·*.
383–25 Does his assertion prove . . . *m·* to be the better
384– 9 If *m·* seems to incur the penalty
384–11 *m·* has only to enter his protest against this
387–22 supposition . . . that God punishes *m·* for doing
　　　good,
389–15 discuss the certainty that food can kill *m·*.
394–14 advice to a *m·* who is down in the world,
394–20 Will you bid a *m·* let evils overcome him,
396–27 man is the offspring of God, not of *m·* ;
402–17 You say that accidents, . . . kill *m·*,
403– 7 by his mistake a *m·* is often instructed.
404– 3 If a *m·* is an inebriate, a slave to
407–10 If *m·* is not victorious over the passions,
410–10 "*M·* shall not live by bread *alone*,— *Matt.* 4: 4.
413– 1 cannot transmit good or evil intelligence to *m·*,
425–12 Show . . . that they are not the truth of *m·* ;
425–21 God is more to a *m·* than his belief,
427– 1 If it is true that *m·* lives, this fact can never
427–16 *M·* is the same after as before a
427–17 If *m·* is never to overcome death,
427–27 what material remedy has *m·* when
428– 7 "If a *m·* keep my saying, he shall— *John* 8: 51.
428–22 *m·* is, not *shall be*, perfect
429–19 If *m·* did not exist before the material
429–31 "If a *m·* keep my saying, he shall— *John* 8: 51.
430–18 A *m·* is charged with having committed
435–23 to punish a *m·* for acting justly.
438– 7 If a *m·* keep my saying, he shall— *John* 8: 51.
t 445–32 a *m·*, for the petty consideration of money,
451–14 *M·* walks in the direction towards
458–23 The Christianly scientific *m·* reflects the
459– 2 *M·* then appropriates those things which
r 467–17 God as not in *m·* but as reflected by man.
467–23 Spirit, Soul, is not confined in *m·*,
470–20 and has *m·* fallen?
470–23 divine idea or reflection, *m·*, remains perfect.
470–25 If there ever was a moment when *m·*
470–26 then there was a moment when *m·* did not
470–28 If *m·* has lost perfection, he has lost his
470–30 If *m·* ever existed without this perfect
471–17 *M·* is, and forever has been, God's reflection.
473–12 Jesus is the name of the *m·* who,
473–24 rather than personality or the *m·* Jesus,
475– 8 *m·* is made in the image and likeness of God.
475–30 God, by whom *m·* is evolved,
476– 3 evil, which declares that *m·* begins in dust
476– 9 will cease to claim . . . that this matter is *m·*.
476–24 "As for *m·*, his days are as— *Psal.* 103: 15.
477– 6 *M·* is not a material habitation for Soul ;
477–16 impossible that a material body, . . . should
　　　be *m·*,
477–18 Were it otherwise, *m·* would be annihilated.
478– 5 *m·* has never beheld . . . Soul leaving a body
478–23 Error says, "I am *m·* ;"
479– 5 gotten a *m·* from the Lord"— *Gen.* 4: 1.
480–20 God, or good, never made *m·* capable of sin.
485–20 The belief . . . that *m·* springs from dust

man

r 486–16 If death restores . . . strength to *m·*,
486–27 If this were not so, *m·* would be speedily
488–15 Do the five corporeal senses constitute *m·*?
488–20 cannot be true either of *m·* or of his Maker.
489–16 can this sense be the God-given channel to *m·*
489–17 How can *m·*, reflecting God, be dependent on
490–22 would, by fair logic, annihilate *m·*
490–31 Under the mesmeric illusion of belief, a *m·* will
491–21 another belief, that *m·* dies.
493–24 That *m·* is material, and that
496–14 what the understanding of God brings to *m·*.
497–16 we acknowledge that *m·* is saved through
g 507–18 multiplication of the compound idea *m·*.
507–22 implies a mortal mind and *m·* a creator.
515–21 *M·* is the family name for all ideas,
515–30 and call *m·* the reflection.
516–19 *M·*, made in His likeness, possesses and reflects
516–29 It follows that *m·* is a generic term.
517– 1 word for *m·* is used also as the synonym of
517–31 *M·* is not made to till the soil.
518–17 blessed is that *m·* who seeth his brother's
520– 7 The absolute ideal, *m·*, is no more seen nor
520– 9 Principle and its idea, *m·*, are coexistent
520–22 was not a *m·* to till the ground.— *Gen.* 2: 5.
521– 1 Knowledge of this lifts *m·* above the sod,
521– 9 in the hands of God, not of *m·*,
524–10 "a *m·* of war," a tribal god— *Exod.* 15: 3.
524–15 and *m·* became a living soul.— *Gen.* 2: 7.
524–18 Mind had made *m·*, both male and female.
524–20 become the basis of *m·*?
526–27 Lord God [Jehovah] took the *m·*,— *Gen.* 2: 15.
527–15 a knowledge of evil would make *m·* mortal.
527–29 and is *m·* giving up his dignity?
527–30 Was it requisite for the formation of *m·*
528– 3 God has already created *m·*,
528– 6 cannot be true that *m·* was ordered to
528–14 and brought her unto the *m·*.— *Gen.* 2: 22.
528–27 calling them *mankind*,— that is, a kind of *m·*.
531–22 Has *m·* sought out other creative inventions,
532– 1 Did God at first create one *m·* unaided, . . .
　　　but
532–22 "Where art thou, *m·*?　Is Mind in matter?
533–19 aids *m·* to make sinners more rapidly
535–15 When will *m·* pass through the open gate of
536–16 *m·* would be annihilated.
537–28 and gave it to *m·* for a possession,
537–30 would imply that God withheld from *m·* the
537–31 lest *m·* should improve it
538–24 I have gotten a *m·* from the Lord— *Gen.* 4: 1.
538–31 gotten a *m·* from the Lord,"— *Gen.* 4: 1.
539–13 How then has *m·* a basis for wrong-doing?
543–18 If *m·* is material and originates in an egg,
543–24 Did *m·*, whom God created with a word,
544– 5 "not a *m·* to till the ground."— *Gen.* 2: 5.
544– 9 not of the things which a *m·* eateth.
545–10 *M·*, created by God, was given dominion
545–32 The mortality of *m·* is a myth,
551–16 all Science is of God, not of *m·*.
552–14 "*M·* that is born of a woman is of— *Job* 14: 1.
555–21 and call this sham unity *m·*,
555–21 as if *m·* were the offspring of
557–20 lifts the curtain on *m·* as never born and
ap 560–15 constitutes the kingdom of heaven in *m·*.
561–17 shown in the *m·* Jesus,
565–11 in order that the *m·* Jesus, . . . might never
565–19 represented first by *m·* and, . . . last by woman,
571– 8 to tell a *m·* his faults,
573–17 Thus *m·* was no longer regarded as
gl 582–26 the error which would make *m·* mortal
585–27 belief . . . that *m·* started first from dust,
589–10 *m·* is His idea, the child of His care.
591– 5 definition of
591–18 not that which is *in m·*, but the divine Principle,
591–19 of whom *m·* is the full and perfect expression ;
598–27 and *m·* would be in the full consciousness of

manacle

an 105–25 Divine justice will *m·* him.

manacled

p 405–15 Both will be *m·* until the last farthing is paid,
t 449– 2 With your own wrists *m·*, it is hard to

manacling

p 439–11 was then *m·* the prisoner

manages

p 399–17 It constructs a machine, *m·* it, and then

man child

ap 565– 6 And she brought forth a *m· c·*,— *Rev.* 12: 5.
569–31 which brought forth the *m· c·*.— *Rev.* 12: 13.

mandate

s 160–14 to convey the *m·* of mind to muscle
ph 187–14 valves of the heart, . . . obey the *m·* of
199–11 empowers man through its *m·*,
p 371– 4 yield to the *m·* of immortal Mind.

mankind
　opinion of
　　b 306–17　this is the general religious opinion of *m·*,
　redemption of
　　t 464–12　working for the redemption of *m·*.
　represents
　　g 525– 5　*m·* represents the Adamic race,
　thoughts of
　　sp 94–24　Our Master easily read the thoughts of *m·*,
　to advance
　　m 61–30　must greatly improve to advance *m·*.
　to bless
　　m 60–29　infinite resources with which to bless *m·*,
　to rule
　　p 419–26　who, in attempting to rule *m·*,
　to stir
　　a 38– 1　so little inspiration to stir *m·* to
　weigh down
　　ph 176–18　and weigh down *m·* with superimposed
　will become
　　r 467–11　*M·* will become perfect in proportion as
　will improve
　　p 371–26　*M·* will improve through Science and

　　a 55–21　in what it has done and is doing for *m·*.
　　sp 99–22　I love *m·*, and shall continue
　　s 140–13　*M·* will no longer be tyrannical
　　157–31　*M·* is the better for this spiritual and profound
　　ph 171– 2　*m·* has caught their moral contagion.
　　f 240–24　Remember that *m·* must sooner or later,
　　251–15　learn how *m·* govern the body,
　　b 318–27　and are not adapted to elevate *m·*.
　　330–28　As manifested by *m·* it stands for
　　o 357– 9　If *m·* would relinquish the belief that
　　357–28　if another . . . exists and sways *m·*?
　　p 425–18　When this is . . . understood, *m·* will be more
　　430–11　When will *m·* wake to this great fact
　　t 456– 1　to influence *m·* adverse to its highest
　　r 466–30　making *m·* better physically, morally, and
　　g 525– 8　In the Saxon, *m·*, *a woman, any one ;*
　　528–27　calling them *m·*, — that is, a kind of man.
　　551–11　he adds that *m·* has ascended through
　　ap 571–10　Who is telling *m·* of the foe in ambush?

manlike
　　b 269– 9　Human philosophy has made God *m·*.

manliness
　　ph 172–28　is sometimes the quickener of *m·* ;

manly
　　p 397–30　and you will quickly become more *m·*

man-made
　　a 23– 7　Such a theory is *m·*.
　　38– 8　lethargy of mortals, produced by *m·* doctrines,
　　s 112–13　divine Science which eschews *m·* systems,
　　134–14　*M·* doctrines are waning.
　　ph 165–14　since *m·* material theories took the
　　168–15　Because *m·* systems insist that
　　o 352–25　traditional beliefs, erroneous and *m·*.
　　r 466–26　the outcome of all *m·* beliefs.

man-midwife
　　s 163–10　physician, surgeon, apothecary, *m·*,

manna
　　a 33– 4　partook of the heavenly *m·*,
　　s 133–10　and *m·* fell from the sky.

manner
　after the
　　s 131–15　after the *m·* of God's appointing,
　after this
　　pr 16– 9　"After this *m·* therefore pray ye," — *Matt.* 6 : 9.
　　sp 85–11　able to read the human mind after this *m·*
　all
　　p 418–27　Cast out all *m·* of evil.
　like
　　sp 82–18　In like *m·* it would follow,
　　85–17　In like *m·* he discerned disease
　　ph 189– 8　In like *m·* mortals should no more deny
　　p 398–21　In like *m·* destroy the illusion of
　　t 453– 4　In like *m·* it should be granted
　most effectual
　　pr 11–18　but wipes it out in the most effectual *m·*.
　unknown
　　b 306–16　at some uncertain future time and in a *m·* unknown,

　　f 224–15　this was not the *m·* of truth's appearing.
　　b 274–29　in a *m·* and at a period as yet unknown.

man-projected
　　s 140–23　Jewish tribal Jehovah was a *m·* God,

Man's
　　p 434–16　Mortal *M·* counsel regards the prisoner with
　　435– 2　Spirit which is . . . *M·* only lawgiver !
　　435–17　a destroyer of Mortal *M·* liberty

man's
　　pr 5– 1　hinders *m·* spiritual growth
　　12–14　of *m·* likeness to God
　　12–15　and of *m·* unity with Truth and Love.
　　13–29　*m·* eternal incorporeal existence.
　　14–27　the consciousness of *m·* dominion over the
　　a 18– 1　Atonement is the exemplification of *m·* unity
　　18– 4　and demonstrated *m·* oneness with the
　　30–15　"Whoso sheddeth *m·* blood, — *Gen.* 9 : 6.
　　35–32　good *m·* heaven would be a hell to the sinner.
　　44–21　in his proof of *m·* truly derived power?
　　m 62–19　in the understanding of *m·* higher nature.
　　65– 2　should proceed from *m·* highest nature.
　　65– 5　by which *m·* spiritual and eternal existence
　　69–11　neither closes *m·* continuity nor his sense of
　　sp 81–11　A *m·* assertion that he is immortal
　　81–28　*m·* immortality depends upon that of God,
　　84–23　by which we discern *m·* nature and existence.
　　91–12　the sooner *m·* great reality will appear
　　91–18　aids the discernment of *m·* spiritual and
　　an 106–12　*M·* rights are invaded when the
　　s 110–10　another glorious proposition, — *m·* perfectibility
　　118–12　eternally glorified in *m·* spiritual freedom.
　　150–22　human view infringes *m·* free moral agency ;
　　150–26　The doctrine that *m·* harmony is governed by
　　159–30　Ignorant of the fact that a *m·* belief produces
　　ph 165– 3　Evil declared . . . this fruit would open *m·* eyes
　　165– 4　it closed the eyes of mortals to *m·* God-given
　　166–11　believes in . . . drugs to save a *m·* life.
　　170–10　the Principle of *m·* harmony.
　　170–15　The best interpreter of *m·* needs said :
　　172– 3　Theorizing about *m·* development from
　　172–31　"a *m·* a man, for a' that."
　　175–23　A *m·* belief in those days was not so severe
　　182–25　denying *m·* God-given ability to demonstrate
　　183–21　rightly demands *m·* entire obedience, affection,
　　191–19　no longer ask . . . What are *m·* prospects for
　　f 203–32　for God alone is *m·* life.
　　205–25　hinders *m·* normal drift towards the one Mind,
　　215–30　Having sought *m·* spiritual state,
　　216–28　When you say, "*M·* body is material,"
　　217– 1　The loss of *m·* identity . . . is impossible ;
　　223– 4　the fetters of *m·* finite capacity are forged by
　　226–20　*m·* birthright of sole allegiance to his Maker
　　227– 9　unaware of *m·* inalienable rights
　　231–23　divine Science of being in *m·* relation to God,
　　232–22　He referred *m·* harmony to Mind,
　　c 262– 2　Consecration to good does not lessen *m·* dependence
　　262– 4　*m·* obligations to God,
　　262–28　a false sense of *m·* origin.
　　264–29　and recognize *m·* spiritual being,
　　265–11　by no means suggests *m·* absorption into
　　266– 4　materiality giving place to *m·* higher individuality
　　266–14　"*m·* extremity is God's opportunity."
　　b 285– 2　*M·* individuality is not material.
　　285– 9　*m·* counterfeit, the inverted likeness,
　　287– 8　and maintains *m·* spiritual identity.
　　288–32　*m·* real existence as a child of God
　　290– 3　rule, and demonstration of *m·* being
　　292–29　*m·* indissoluble connection with his God,
　　294–25　*M·* genuine selfhood is recognizable only in
　　295–10　and then recover *m·* original self
　　301–15　spiritual *m·* substantiality transcends
　　302–26　*M·* true consciousness is in the mental,
　　304–18　*M·* happiness is not, therefore, at the
　　312–19　*m·* eternal Principle is ever-present Life.
　　312–25　A personal sense of God and of *m·* capabilities
　　315–19　prove *m·* heritage, the liberty of the
　　320–18　even *m·* eternal and harmonious existence
　　322–14　*m·* wisdom finds no satisfaction in sin,
　　327– 9　Evil is sometimes a *m·* highest conception
　　327–30　the *m·* dormant sense of moral obligation,
　　328–14　This understanding of *m·* power,
　　336–14　*m·* consciousness and individuality are
　　337–22　as is *m·* infinite Principle.
　　338–29　blessed the earth "for *m·* sake." — *Gen.* 8 : 21.
　　o 356– 6　Sin, sickness, and death do not prove *m·* entity
　　358– 4　God, who is *m·* Life
　　p 373–15　are the sources of *m·* enslavement.
　　378–14　A *m·* gaze, fastened fearlessly on a ferocious
　　380–21　and prove *m·* dominion over error.
　　381–21　you will sooner grasp *m·* God-given dominion.
　　381–28　*m·* moral right to annul an unjust sentence,
　　395– 4　*m·* immortality and eternal likeness to God.
　　399–30　enter into a strong *m·* house — *Matt.* 12 : 29.
　　406– 4　The tree is typical of *m·* divine Principle,
　　407– 3　inconceivably terrible to *m·* self-respect.
　　407– 6　*M·* enslavement to the most relentless
　　414–28　*m·* perfection is real and unimpeachable,
　　425–17　can never destroy God, who is *m·* Life.
　　427– 5　*m·* individual being can no more
　　428– 6　*M·* privilege at this supreme moment
　　428–27　evidence of *m·* immortality will become
　　435– 1　commended *m·* immortal Spirit to

man's

p	437– 5	This is a foul aspersion on *m·* Maker.
t	447– 2	trespassing upon *m·* individual right of
	449–11	*M·* moral mercury, rising or falling,
r	486– 6	What is *m·* remedy?
	490–17	the real *m·* divine Principle, Love.
	491– 9	*M·* spiritual individuality is never wrong.
	491–10	It is the likeness of *m·* Maker.
	494– 1	and to govern *m·* entire action
	494–23	until the Science of *m·* eternal harmony
	497–14	unfolding *m·* unity with God
g	530– 7	brings forth food for *m·* use.
	531–15	If, in the beginning, *m·* body originated in
	533– 2	Had he lost *m·* rich inheritance
	536–11	If *m·* spiritual gravitation and attraction
	539–17	God condemned this lie as to *m·* origin
	544–30	infinity to enter *m·* nostrils
	553– 4	higher and purer contemplation of *m·* origin.
ap	562–13	*m·* divine origin and the true idea,
	576–19	of the real *m·* incorporeality
	576–22	is within reach of *m·* consciousness here,
gl	589–18	and bringing to light *m·* immortality.

(*see also* **existence**)

manufactured

p	438–30	heard Materia Medica explain how this fur is *m·*,

manufactures

p	439– 4	He *m·* for it,

manuscript

t	460–29	by her *m·* circulated among the students.

many

pref	xi– 1	*M·* imagine that the phenomena of
pr	6–29	It is believed by *m·* that a certain magistrate,
a	23– 2	Wisdom and Love may require *m·* sacrifices
	27–25	"*M·* are called, but few are— *Matt.* 22 : 14.
	28– 3	Even *m·* of his students stood in his way.
	38–19	not for the twelve only, but for as *m·* as should
	46– 1	did not perform *m·* wonderful works, until
m	65–20	fermentation over this as over *m·* other
sp	71–28	Its spirits are so *m·* corporealities,
	80–13	philanthropy of *m·* Spiritualists,
	80–23	French toy which years ago pleased so *m·*
an	105–31	full *m·* a league in the line of light ;
s	110–30	apprehended by as *m·* as believe on Christ
	111–24	one of *m·* incidents which show that C. S.
	114– 8	evidence . . . which makes minds *m·*
	117– 2	may be one of a series, one of *m·*,
ph	196– 2	Man has "sought out *m·* inventions,"— *Eccl.* 7 : 29.
	196–25	*M·* a hopeless case of disease is induced
	196–31	The press unwittingly sends forth *m·* sorrows
	197– 6	costs *m·* a man his earthly days of comfort.
	197–26	*M·* of the effeminate constitutions of our time
f	205–24	a belief in *m·* ruling minds hinders
	213–27	Mortal mind is the harp of *m·* strings,
	221–10	He passed in *m·* weary years in hunger
	223–15	*M·* are ready to meet this inquiry with
	224–12	sects *m·* but not enough Christianity.
	232– 3	*M·* theories relative to God and man
	236– 7	emolument . . . which *m·* leaders seek?
	246–19	are so *m·* conspiracies against manhood
c	260– 9	Through *m·* generations human beliefs will
	265–28	brightens the ascending path of *m·* a heart.
b	268– 2	has brought to light . . . *m·* useful wonders.
	273– 5	Human belief has sought out *m·* inventions,
	280–17	"gods many and lords *m·*."— *I Cor.* 8 : 5.
	280–20	the opposite error of *m·* minds.
	319–16	are so *m·* ancient and modern mythologies.
	323–18	shall be made rulers over *m·* ;
	335– 1	There are nether spirits nor *m·* nor
o	361–30	hence the *m·* readings given the Scriptures,
p	367– 8	but so *m·* parodies on legitimate C. S.,
	386–12	in too *m·* instances healed disease . . . not to know
	400–32	in certain localities he did not *m·* mighty
	407–29	There are *m·* species of insanity.
	408– 4	nor discovered to be error by *m·*
	408–11	so *m·* distinctly defined instances of the
t	450–16	*m·* are reluctant to acknowledge that they
	451–14	*m·* there be which go in thereat."— *Matt.* 7 : 13.
r	474–14	misunderstood and misused by *m·*, until
	483–29	by doing *m·* wonderful works through the
g	504–17	taking place on so *m·* *evenings* and *mornings*,
	505–19	than the noise of *m·* waters,— *Psal.* 93 : 4.
	517–15	The world believes in *m·* persons ;
	548–19	"It is very possible that *m·* general statements
	557– 8	*m·* animals suffer no pain in multiplying ;
ap	563– 6	showing its horns in the *m·* inventions of evil.
	569– 7	I will make thee ruler over *m·*,— *Matt.* 25 : 23.
	569–26	how *m·* periods of torture it may take
	570–30	*M·* are willing to open the eyes of the people to
gl	580– 8	"gods many and lords *m·*"— *I Cor.* 8 : 5.

(*see also* **gods, years**)

mapped

a	38–25	Jesus *m·* out the path for others.
s	121– 4	Copernicus *m·* out the stellar system,

maps

ph	176–27	no farther than mortal mind *m·* out the way.

mar

s	139–24	could neither . . . *m·* the demonstration of

marble

f	248–12	sculptor turns from the *m·* to his model

march

f	209–12	the *m·* of the Science which
	225– 7	*m·* of time bears onward freedom's banner.
b	323– 7	in the *m·* towards righteousness,
ap	570– 1	The *m·* of mind and of honest investigation

marches

f	225–11	heeding not the pointed bayonet, *m·* on.

mariner

m	67–12	*m·* works on and awaits the issue.
s	125–25	The *m·* will have dominion over the

mark

sp	96– 4	Love will finally *m·* the hour of harmony,
t	446– 8	or it may *m·* the crisis of the disease.
	457–22	and at the same time hit the *m·*.
g	511–18	*m·* the periods of progress.
	542– 9	and sets upon error the *m·* of the beast.
	542–16	[Jehovah] set a *m·* upon Cain,— *Gen.* 4 : 15.
	555– 9	The *m·* of ignorance is on its forehead.

marked

a	46–25	that is, he *m·* the way for all men.
f	227–23	Jesus *m·* out the way.
b	298–31	*m·* with superstitious outlines,
	333–16	*m·* the first century of the Christian era,
p	370–19	very direct and *m·* effects on the body.

market

f	225–19	abolish the whipping-post and slave *m·* ;
p	438–24	and smuggles Error's goods into *m·*
	439– 2	introducing their goods into the *m·*.

marking

s	163– 1	first *m·* Nature with his name,
ph	174–15	*m·* out the path for generations yet unborn.

marks

g	542–22	Justice *m·* the sinner,

Mark's Gospel

s	117–11	in the last chapter of *M· G·*.
b	272–11	referred to in the last chapter of *M· G·*.

marriage

after

m	59–23	After *m·*, it is too late to grumble

cares of

m	58–30	nothing can abolish the cares of *m·*.

given in

m	56– *	nor are given in *m·*,— *Matt.* 22 : 30.
	69–11	marry or to be "given in *m·*"— *Matt.* 22 : 30.
	69–27	and are given in *m·* :— *Luke* 20 : 34.
	69–30	neither marry, nor are given in *m·*."— *Luke* 20 : 35.

giving in

m	64–20	no more marrying nor giving in *m·*,

scientific *morale* of

m	61–30	The scientific *morale* of *m·* is spiritual unity.

should improve

m	60–16	*M·* should improve the human species,

should signify

m	64–17	*M·* should signify a union of hearts.

will become

m	65–31	*m·* will become purer when the scum is gone.

m	56– 7	*M·* is the legal and moral provision for
	56–13	*m·* will continue, subject to such moral
	56–15	Infidelity to the *m·* covenant is the
	57–31	*M·* is unblest or blest, according to
	58–29	the chance for ill-nature in the *m·* relation,
	64–26	Until . . . *m·* will continue.
	64–30	ensure the stability of the *m·* covenant.
	65–10	some fundamental error in the *m·* state.
ap	575– 4	Then cometh the *m·* feast,

married

m	58–31	"She that is *m·* careth— *I Cor.* 7 : 34.
	59– 6	should wait on all the years of *m·* life.

marrow

p	423–13	it searches "the joints and *m·*,"— *Heb.* 4 : 12.

marry

m	56– *	*In the resurrection they neither m·,*— *Matt.* 22 : 30.
	69–10	*m·* or to be "given in marriage"— *Matt.* 22 : 30.
	69–26	"The children of this world *m·*,— *Luke* 20 : 34.
	69–29	neither *m·*, nor are given in— *Luke* 20 : 35.

marrying

m	64–20	in the resurrection . . . no more *m·*

martyr

a	28–22	Remember, thou Christian *m·*, it is enough if
s	134– 4	The word *m·*, from the Greek, means *witness*,
	134– 6	at length the word *m·* was

martyrdom
  a 37–18 procured the *m·* of that righteous man
      40–15 Did the *m·* of Savonarola make the
  gl 597–10 The *m·* of Jesus was the culminating sin

martyrs
  a 37– 6 blood of the *m·* is the seed of the Church.''
    37– 9 *M·* are the human links which
  p 388– 1 The Christian *m·* were prophets of C. S.

marvel
  m 63–16 *m·* why usage should accord woman less rights
  r 474–11 *m·* is the simple meaning of the Greek word
  ap 563– 1 Human sense may well *m·* at discord,

marvellous
  g 540– 1 was the basis of his *m·* demonstrations.

marvels
  s 117–21 the miracles (*m·*) wrought by Jesus
  f 223–28 *M·*, calamities, and sin will much more abound
    248– 4 One *m·* that a friend can ever seem less than
  r 474–11 Christian *m·* . . . will be misunderstood
    474–14 until the glorious Principle of these *m·* is gained.

Mary (*see also* **Mary's**)
  b 314–20 but the faithful *M·* saw him, and he presented
    332– 9 Jesus was born of *M·*.

Mary Magdalene
  p 362–11 (*M· M·*, as she has since been called)
    367–13 nor, like the Pharisee, . . . but like *M· M·*,

Mary's
  a 29–20 The illumination of *M·* spiritual sense
    29–32 *M·* self-conscious communion with God.
    30– 6 partook partly of *M·* earthly condition,
  b 313–18 the exaltation of Jesus, *M·* son,
    332–26 *M·* conception of him was spiritual,

masculine
  m 57– 4 Union of the *m·* and feminine qualities
    57– 5 The *m·* mind reaches a higher tone through
    57– 8 courage and strength through *m·* qualities.
    64–23 in one person *m·* wisdom and feminine love,
  g 511–28 in *m·*, feminine, or neuter gender.
    516–30 *M·*, feminine, and neuter genders are
    517–12 not as much authority for considering God *m·*,
  ap 565–11 the *m·* representative of the spiritual idea,

masculinity
  g 508–18 does not necessarily refer either to *m·* or

mask
  a 30–28 loathe sin and rebuke it under every *m·*.
  t 447–25 remove the *m·*, point out the illusion,

masked
  p 439–18 blind Hypnotism, and the *m·* Personal Sense,

masonry
  t 450– 9 A third class of thinkers build with solid *m·*.

masquerader
  t 453–21 The *m·* in this Science

masquerading
  gl 582– 7 error *m·* as the possessor of life,

mass
  s 118–11 It must destroy the entire *m·* of error,
  t 449– 3 A little leaven causes the whole *m·* to ferment.

Massachusetts
  pref xi–27 in Lynn, *M·*, about the year 1867.
  s 158–31 A woman in the city of Lynn, *M·*,
    161–11 In 1880, *M·* put her foot on a proposed . . . law,

Massachusetts Metaphysical College
  pref xi–28 In 1881, she opened the *M· M· C·* in Boston,

masses
  f 209–18 relations which constituent *m·* hold

Master (*see also* **Master's**)
  dear
    pr 9–30 to tread in the footsteps of our dear *M·*?
    a 34–24 for soon their dear *M·* would rise again in the
  enabled their
    a 24–30 enabled their *M·* to triumph over the grave,
  example of the
    a 37–24 to follow . . . the example of the *M·*
  forbore not
    a 19–12 The *M·* forbore not to speak the whole truth,
  gave him
    s 137–28 but now the *M·* gave him a spiritual name
  glorified
    a 47– 5 After gaining the true idea of their glorified *M·*,
  had taught
    a 34–19 understood better what the *M·* had taught.
  healed the sick
    s 147–24 Our *M·* healed the sick, practised
    f 210–12 the *M·* healed the sick, gave sight to the blind,
  his
    a 47–17 infinite distance between Judas and his *M·*,
    48–22 would have smitten the enemies of his *M·*,
  language of the
    o 355–10 C. S. says, in the language of the *M·*,

Master
  Lord and
    m 67–21 our Lord and *M·* healed the sick,
    b 317–21 Our Lord and *M·* presented himself to
  often refused
    o 350–16 The *M·* often refused to explain his words,
  our
    pr 3–29 censure our *M·* pronounces on hypocrites.
      4– 6 To keep the commandments of our *M·*
      6–31 The strong language of our *M·* confirms this
     16– 7 Our *M·* taught his disciples one brief prayer,
     16– 8 Our *M·* said, ''After this manner— *Matt.* 6 : 9.
    a 19–26 teachings and practice of our *M·*
     25–30 our *M·* worked and suffered to bestow
     26–28 Our *M·* taught no mere theory, doctrine, or
     35–28 the draught our *M·* drank and commended
     39– 1 Meekly our *M·* met the mockery of his
     40–26 all men should follow the example of our *M·*
     41– 6 Like our *M·*, we must depart from
     45– 6 Our *M·* fully and finally demonstrated
    sp 85–20 Our *M·* rebuked the lack of this power
     94–18 our *M·* confirmed his words by his works.
     94–24 Our *M·* easily read the thoughts of mankind,
     94–28 Our *M·* read mortal mind on a scientific basis,
    s 117–15 Our *M·* taught spirituality by similitudes
     138–27 Our *M·* said to every follower:
     147–24 Our *M·* healed the sick, practised
    ph 192–28 following the example of our *M·*
    f 228–20 If we follow the command of our *M·*,
     241–21 Our *M·* said, ''If ye love me,— *John* 14 : 15.
     242–31 show the way our *M·* trod,
     252– 1 our *M·* said, ''If a kingdom be— *Mark* 3 : 24.
    p 271–20 Our *M·* said, ''But the Comforter— *John* 14 : 26.
     272–14 shows the care our *M·* took not to impart to dull
     314– 8 Our *M·* gained the solution of being,
     315– 3 That saying of our *M·*, . . . separated him from
     333–13 The proper name of our *M·* in the Greek
    o 342–27 our *M·* says, ''By their fruits— *Matt.* 7 : 20.
     349– 7 our *M·* annulled material law
     352– 5 Our *M·* declared that his material body
     355–16 according to the commands of our *M·*,
     355–29 proved to be such by our *M·*
    p 382–21 This verifies the saying of our *M·* :
     399–29 Our *M·* asked : ''How can one— *Matt.* 12 : 29.
     400–31 Even our *M·* felt this.
     428– 7 to prove the words of our *M·* :
     429–28 have faith in all the sayings of our *M·*,
    t 463–24 Our *M·* treated error through Mind.
    r 494–30 Our *M·* cast out devils (evils) and healed the
     495– 8 classify sickness and error as our *M·* did,
    g 509– 4 Our *M·* reappeared to his students,
     539–21 this falsity is exposed by our *M·*
    ap 565–15 brief history in the earthly life of our *M·* ;
    gl 598– 8 This shows how our *M·* had constantly to
  our blessed
    ap 571– 8 It requires the spirit of our blessed *M·*
  our great
    s 126–28 teachings and demonstrations of our great *M·*
    149– 1 although our great *M·* demonstrated
  promised by the
    s 123–23 as promised by the *M·*.
    150– 9 This coming, as was promised by the *M·*,
  their
    a 24–30 enabled their *M·* to triumph over the grave,
     33– 9 Their *M·* had explained it all before,
     33–13 their *M·* was about to suffer violence
     47–27 The disciples' desertion of their *M·*
     49– 5 caused the disciples to say to their *M·* :
    s 136–29 apprehended their *M·* better than did others ;
    b 271–28 divine Science, which their *M·* demonstrated
  work of the
    s 136–23 and the great work of the *M·*,

    a 28– 4 If the *M·* had not taken a student
     46–13 *M·* said plainly that physique was not Spirit,
     47–19 He knew that the great goodness of that *M·*
    sp 75–18 the *M·* would have stood on the same plane
    s 137– 8 Yearning to be understood, the *M·* repeated,
    b 286– 9 The *M·* said, ''No man cometh— *John* 14 : 6.
     317–31 so long as the *M·* remained an

master
  as its
    p 419–16 Meet every adverse circumstance as its *m·*.
  Mind is the
    p 393– 9 Mind is the *m·* of the corporeal senses,
  not the
    b 304–12 sorrow is not the *m·* of joy ;
  of a feast
    a 32– 7 an ancient custom for the *m·* of a feast
  of ceremonies
    m 64– 9 on most occasions to be the *m·* of ceremonies.
  of chords
    b 304–25 To be *m·* of chords and discords,
  of death
    b 316–19 thus proved that Truth was the *m·* of death,

master

of hate
a 44– 9 He proved . . . Love to be the *m·* of hate.
of sin
f 229– 1 If Mind is not the *m·* of sin, sickness,
or ruler
gl 590–16 has the inferior sense of *m·*, or ruler.
our
pr 9–23 divine control of Spirit, in which Soul is our *m·*,
their
a 52– 3 their *m·* was matter.
unreal
f 226–23 years of servitude to an unreal *m·*
was Spirit
a 52– 2 His *m·* was Spirit ;

m 62– 6 the child can meet and *m·* the belief in
sp 90–25 sets man free to *m·* the infinite idea.
ph 197–16 We should *m·* fear, instead of cultivating it.
f 216–23 evil would appear to be the *m·* of good,
p 369– 7 in that proportion does man become its *m·*.
392– 1 you *m·* fear and sin through divine Mind ;
392–22 Your decisions will *m·* you,
395– 8 leaving Soul to *m·* the false evidences of
404–25 increases his ability to *m·* evil
405– 5 C. S. commands man to *m·* the propensities,
415–15 till it can *m·* an erroneous belief.
423– 1 The belief that he has met his *m·* in matter
426–20 It will *m·* either a desire to die or a dread of
428–26 through Christ and C. S., we must *m·* sin and death.

mastered
a 44–10 He met and *m·* on the basis of C. S.,
p 427–11 must be met and *m·* by Science,
427–30 The dream of death must be *m·* by Mind

Master's
pr 15–23 The *M·* injunction is, that we pray in secret
a 26–24 precious import of our *M·* sinless career
27–27 never truly understood their *M·* instruction.
28–24 worthy to unloose the sandals of thy *M·* feet !
33– 4 anticipating the hour of their *M·* betrayal,
35– 4 wakened by their *M·* voice,
46– 1 not . . . advanced fully to understand their *M·*
s 130–23 our *M·* love for little children,
139– 2 It was our *M·* theology which the
145–32 Our *M·* first article of faith
f 233–23 To reveal this truth was our *M·* mission
b 317– 8 will drink of his *M·* cup.
334–15 continued until the *M·* ascension,
o 349– 8 We propose to follow the *M·* example.
350– 6 To understand all our *M·* sayings
354–14 proofs that their *M·* religion can
p 363–19 the *M·* question to Simon the Pharisee ;
t 443–12 our motto should be the *M·* counsel,

masters
pr 14– 5 We cannot "serve two *m·*."— *Matt.* 6 : 24.
ph 167–11 We cannot serve two *m·*
f 201– 6 "No man can serve two *m·*." — *Matt.* 6 : 24.
216–16 makes the nerves, . . . servants, instead of *m·*.
228–22 but we shall be *m·* of the body,
p 407– 6 Man's enslavement to the most relentless *m·*
ap 569–12 *m·* his mortal beliefs, animality, and hate,

mastery
ph 166–30 but when Mind at last asserts its *m·*
198– 8 the disease that is gaining the *m·*,
p 406–29 destroyed only by Mind's *m·* of the body.

match
ph 185–15 to *m·* the divine Science of immortal Mind,

material

accompaniments
sp 78–16 Spiritualism with its *m·* accompaniments
b 310– 8 but without *m·* accompaniments.
age
a 36–15 The earthly price of spirituality in a *m·* age
sp 98– 9 Christianity is misinterpreted by a *m·* age,
o 350–17 because it was difficult in a *m·* age to
g 546–23 C. S. is dawning upon a *m·* age.
application
p 421–29 or by employing a single *m·* application
art
a 44–22 a method of surgery beyond *m·* art,
base
p 422–16 and moral chemistry changes the *m·* base
basis
b 268– 6 Belief in a *m·* basis, from which may be deduced
307–27 Man was not created from a *m·* basis,
319– 6 To calculate . . . from a *m·* basis,
o 351– 7 if we plant ourselves on a *m·* basis.
p 402– 9 its corporeal, structural, and *m·* basis,
g 546–14 as starting from an idea of good on a *m·* basis.
547–16 Darwin's theory of evolution from a *m·* basis
552–19 thought, loosened from a *m·* basis

material

being
ph 172–11 in this supposed chain of *m·* being.
172–15 If man was first a *m·* being, he must
belief
a 20–24 *M·* belief is slow to acknowledge what the
ph 192–11 a *m·* belief, a blind miscalled force,
194–16 would presuppose man, . . . a mortal in *m·* belief.
f 216–31 Give up your *m·* belief of mind in matter,
c 258– 6 *m·* belief in a physical God and man.
258– 8 proves the falsity of *m·* belief.
b 286–31 comprised in human *m·* belief,
289–25 spiritual fact and the *m·* belief of things
o 352– 6 a mortal and *m·* belief of flesh and bones,
p 368–23 and the *m·* belief in them disappears
425–24 Correct *m·* belief by spiritual understanding,
r 481–18 this growth of *m·* belief, of which it is said :
g 508– 1 to fail to the level of a human or *m·* belief,
545– 8 should so improve *m·* belief by thought
ap 568– 3 ever since error would establish *m·* belief,
gl 580– 6 not the image and likeness of good, but a *m·* belief,
589–23 JUDAH. A corporeal *m·* belief
593–11 *m·* belief yielding to spiritual understanding.
beliefs
a 19–15 brought to *m·* beliefs not peace, but a
43–29 *m·* beliefs about life, substance, and
sp 88–13 they are mortal *m·* beliefs.
96–15 The breaking up of *m·* beliefs may seem to
s 130–16 would disabuse the human mind of *m·* beliefs
130–17 and these *m·* beliefs must be denied
ph 186– 5 C. S. destroys *m·* beliefs through the
f 242– 2 mortals put off their *m·* beliefs
c 257–17 would translate spiritual ideas into *m·* beliefs,
b 276–25 *M·* beliefs and spiritual understanding
318–18 Weary of their *m·* beliefs,
o 346–29 *M·* beliefs must be expelled to make room for
p 399–24 *m·* beliefs, springing from illusion.
400–11 and abandon their *m·* beliefs.
402–11 *m·* beliefs will not interfere with spiritual
428–27 more apparent, as *m·* beliefs are given up
g 542– 3 *M·* beliefs would slay the spiritual idea
gl 583–16 rousing the dormant understanding from *m·* beliefs
blood
a 25– 6 The *m·* blood of Jesus was no more efficacious
bodies
sp 73–19 The belief that *m·* bodies return to dust,
body
a 53–26 mortal errors which constitute the *m·* body,
sp 72– 4 If a *m·* body . . . were permeated by Spirit,
73–22 confined in a finite, *m·* body,
73–24 when it is freed from the *m·* body,
74–15 belief of having died and left a *m·* body
74–16 belief of still living in an organic, *m·* body.
92– 1 erroneous . . . that man has a *m·* body
ph 172–17 If the *m·* body is man, he is a portion of
172–24 If the real man is in the *m·* body,
177–12 of which the *m·* body is the grosser portion ;
187–27 mortal *m·* body loses all appearance of life
189–15 We call the body *m·* ; but it is as
f 203–20 When the *m·* body has gone to ruin,
208–25 A *m·* body only expresses a
214–20 obey what they consider a *m·* body more than
b 284–31 but neither . . . goes from *m·* body to Mind.
285–16 belief that a *m·* body is man
285–18 finite conception . . . of a *m·* body as the
302– 3 The *m·* body and mind are temporal,
303–17 illusion that life, . . . is in the *m·* body,
o 352– 5 declared that his *m·* body was not spirit,
p 376–18 the so-called *m·* body is a mental concept
399– 4 but if the *m·* body causes disease,
402–18 The *m·* body manifests only what
416–16 The *m·* body, . . . is mortal mind,
r 477–14 shows it be impossible that a *m·* body,
g 550–30 Eden stands for the mortal, *m·* body.
ap 576–17 Jesus spoke of his *m·* body as the temple
bounds
g 550– 8 God cannot . . . be limited within *m·* bounds.
brain
ph 189–16 the *m·* brain which is supposed to
cause
f 211–18 nature of all so-called *m·* cause and effect.
p 416–11 will tell you that the troublesome *m·* cause is
combinations
p 399– 3 You say that certain *m·* combinations
concept
b 297–17 The only fact concerning any *m·* concept is,
334–16 *m·* concept, or Jesus, disappeared,
conception
f 213– 9 apart from this mortal and *m·* conception.
g 536–24 erroneous, *m·* conception of life and joy,
conceptions
sp 87– 1 So is it with all *m·* conceptions.
t 463– 9 detach mortal thought from its *m·* conceptions,

material

concepts
f 239–24 It forms m· concepts and produces
g 556– 4 mortal and m· concepts classified,

condition
sp 74– 4 return to a m· condition, . . . impossible
p 389– 5 every erroneous belief, or m· condition.
410–15 The more difficult seems the m· condition

conditions
a 46–21 his exaltation above all m· conditions ;
49–22 the Christ is not subject to m· conditions,
m 61–32 If . . . then its m· conditions can only be
63– 8 nor does he pass through m· conditions prior to
s 127–32 false . . . that law is founded on m· conditions,
ph 182–21 the law which overcomes m· conditions
f 228– 1 and in defiance of all m· conditions.
p 368–30 destroy the belief in m· conditions.
419–18 Think less of m· conditions and more of
g 553–12 circumstances which made m· conditions

consciousness
ph 196–13 a false sense or m· consciousness.
b 295–26 matter, named *brain*, or m· *consciousness*,

conservatism
p 364–19 sought the Saviour, through m· conservatism

contact
s 154–14 had not caught the cholera by m· contact,

creation
ph 177–15 Scriptural allegory of the m· creation,
g 522–24 in declaring this m· creation false.
544– 1 introduces the record of a m· creation

cross
a 50–32 Not the spear nor the m· cross

darkness
g 504–20 not implied by m· darkness and dawn.

declaration
p 427–31 will waken from its own m· declaration,

definition
gl 579– 2 substitution of the spiritual for the m· definition

dependence
s 152–23 Every m· dependence had failed her

disappearance
a 43– 3 his m· disappearance before their eyes

drugs
s 146–18 truth divests m· drugs of their

earth
c 263–32 the mortal body and m· earth, are the

ecstasy
pr 7–17 Physical sensation, . . . produces m· ecstasy

effect
p 403– 9 believed that the misfortune is a m· effect.

effects
sp 78–22 through electric, m· effects?

element
ph 191– 7 include in that likeness no m· element.

elements
b 284–24 the more subtle and misnamed m· elements
r 475– 7 blood, bones, and other m· elements.
g 551–19 composed of the simplest m· elements,

embryo
r 476– 3 declares that man begins in dust or as a m· embryo.

error
f 252–11 mortal, m· error finally disappears,
b 291–31 is divested of all m· error.
309– 8 He had conquered m· error
315–23 spiritual Truth destroys m· error,

evidence
a 52– 7 m· evidence of sin, sickness, and death.
p 422–18 causing it to depend less on m· evidence.
gl 584–15 Any m· evidence of death is false,

evidences
p 428– 9 false trusts and m· evidences

evolution
g 547–19 M· evolution implies that the

existence
sp 74– 1 between so-called m· existence and spiritual
82–10 they cannot return to m· existence,
99–26 beliefs of m· existence are seen to be a
s 162–16 false beliefs of a so-called m· existence.
b 272–21 the ghastly farce of m· existence ;
282–11 a belief in a . . . temporary m· existence.
282–12 Eternal Mind and temporary m· existence never
o 356– 4 m· existence affords no evidence of
p 371– 9 By . . . nothing is really understood of m· existence.
r 467–26 *a priori* reasoning shows m· existence to be
g 552–32 the origin of mortal and m· existence

expedients
t 443–22 If the sick find these m· expedients

fable
s 129– 8 by reversing the m· fable,

faith
ph 180–20 through the m· faith which they inspire.

fetters
f 249–29 It throws off some m· fetters.

material

flesh
b 321– 1 still clad in m· flesh,

form
c 258– 9 Man is more than a m· form with a mind inside,
b 280–26 instead of possessing a sentient m· form,
293– 3 the least m· form of illusive consciousness,

forms
b 301–31 an unsubstantial dweller in m· forms,

foundations
g 535–10 the supposed m· foundations of life

fungus
s 160–30 Is man a m· fungus without Mind

germ
f 246– 6 Man is by no means a m· germ

god
s 158–13 may correspond with that of its m· god, Apollo,
ph 187– 9 With pagan blindness, it attributes to some m· god

gods
f 237–26 They devote themselves . . . to their m· gods,

growth
m 68–28 it manifests no m· growth from molecule to

habitation
r 477– 6 Man is not a m· habitation for Soul ;

health-theories
p 388–17 ambiguous nature of all m· health-theories.

hearing
g 526– 9 Belief involves theories of m· hearing,

history
f 204– 4 false . . . that m· history is as real
g 547–27 not in m· history but in spiritual development.

hopes
m 66–12 sown in the soil of m· hopes,

hygiene
f 220– 5 the inefficacy of m· hygiene,
222–20 he dropped drugs and m· hygiene,
t 453–31 never recommends m· hygiene,
r 484– 7 medication, m· hygiene, mesmerism,

hypotheses
b 273– 7 Deductions from m· hypotheses are not
g 552– 6 and all other m· hypotheses

illusion
r 484–21 Mesmerism is mortal, m· illusion.

intelligence
a 48– 1 a belief in any possible m· intelligence.
g 534–16 mythological m· intelligence called *energy*

intelligences
gl 591– 3 belief in many gods, or m· intelligences,

investiture
sp 75– 6 to have a m· investiture,

knowledge
a 27–19 axe of Science at the root of m· knowledge,
sp 96–27 As m· knowledge diminishes and
f 214–22 All m· knowledge, like the original
b 317– 2 since m· knowledge usurped the
gl 581–18 Self-destroying error ; . . . m· knowledge.

law
a 29–21 put to silence m· law and its order of
s 118–26 The definitions of m· law, as given by
148–26 claims to rule man by m· law, instead of
ph 168–21 in defiance of what is called m· law,
173–20 measuring . . . human life by m· law.
179–22 sustained by what is termed m· law,
182–19 Obedience to m· law prevents full obedience to
f 209–27 based on the hypothesis of m· law
229–17 This customary belief is misnamed m· law,
253–27 obedience to a so-called m· law,
b 273–21 God never ordained a m· law to annul
273–22 If there were such a m· law,
328–21 and knowing that there is no m· law,
o 349– 7 and our Master annulled m· law
349– 9 We should subordinate m· law to spiritual law.
p 384– 4 depressing thought that we have transgressed a m· law
387–10 nor can so-called m· law trespass
388– 6 only because it knows less of m· law.
g 549–29 great observer . . . allows matter and m· law to

laws
a 27–32 according to certain assumed m· laws.
m 62–31 Because mortals believe in m· laws
sp 83–17 governed in general by m· laws,
s 148– 5 urged no obedience to m· laws,
ph 170–18 If there are m· laws which prevent
f 227–30 If God had instituted m· laws to govern
b 273–26 raised the dead in direct opposition to m· laws.
307–28 m· laws which Spirit never made ;
314–29 depending on doctrines and m· laws
p 389–23 Their belief in m· laws and in
433–23 liver-complaint, which m· laws condemn as
r 484–12 What are termed natural science and m· laws

lie
ap 565–24 the m· lie made war upon the spiritual idea ;

life
pr 6–14 until belief in m· life and sin is destroyed.
a 52–20 understood the nothingness of m· life

material

life
   a 53–29 he had not conquered . . . his sense of *m·* life,
  sp 77–13 required for this dream of *m·* life, . . . to vanish
   b 282– 4 and its opposite, the so-called *m·* life
     283–14 They insist that . . . is one and the same with
          m· life
     288–25 has no birth, no *m·* life, and no death.
   o 354– 2 notion that there can be *m·* life,
   g 531–29 The mythologic theory of *m·* life
     533–23 The belief in *m·* life and intelligence
     543–12 *m·* life, with all its sin, sickness, and
     550–11 to investigate what is miscalled *m·* life,
     552–17 this notion of *m·* life as all-in-all.
     556–23 of which mortal and *m·* life is the dream.

living
  pr 14–25 separate from the belief and dream of *m·* living,

lotions
   f 234– 1 *m·* lotions interfere with truth,

man
   b 283–18 the structural life of the tree and of *m·* man,
     292–19 Explaining the origin of *m·* man
     300– 7 illustrates the illusion of *m·* man,
     301– 7 To himself, . . . *m·* man seems to be substance,
     303–23 belief that . . . *m·* man is the likeness of God
     337–23 The visible universe and *m·* man are the
     338– 9 The mortality of *m·* man proves that error has
   o 356–24 Does God create a *m·* man out of Himself,
   r 471–21 but every [*m·*] man a liar."— *Rom.* 3 : 4.
     491– 7 *M·* man is made up of . . . error,
     491–21 Science reveals *m·* man as never the real
   g 532–12 condemns *m·* man and remands him to dust.
     532–31 first impression *m·* man had of himself was
     540–28 Cain is the type of mortal and *m·* man,
     543– 8 *m·* man is shut out from the presence of
     545– 5 according to the record, *m·* man was

means
  ph 169–17 we should put no faith in *m·* means.
     182–24 using *m·* means, thus working against
   b 319–10 the general faith in *m·* means
     327–28 mistake in seeking *m·* means for
   p 394–24 Are *m·* means the only refuge from fatal
   t 445–12 by recourse to *m·* means for healing.
   r 489–18 How can man, . . . be dependent on *m·* means

medicine
   s 146–13 *M·* medicine substitutes drugs for the power of
     158–12 The future history of *m·* medicine
   f 226–18 scholastic theology, *m·* medicine and
   p 404–30 neither *m·* medicine nor Mind

mentality
  ph 173–11 matter manifests nothing but a *m·* mentality.
     185–30 a mortal consolidation of *m·* mentality
   b 292–27 *m·* mentality, misnamed *mind*,

method
  sp 78–18 needs no *m·* method for the transmission of
   s 145–13 matters not what *m·* method one may
   f 230–24 by drugs, hygiene, or any *m·* method.

methods
   m 56– 5 Jesus' concessions. . . to *m·* methods were for the
   s 145– 9 not between *m·* methods, but between
  ph 170– 4 The discord which calls for *m·* methods
   f 222– 5 mortal mind has its *m·* methods of working,
   b 318–26 *M·* methods are temporary,
   p 395–13 faith in sin and in *m·* methods of healing,
   g 551–14 *m·* methods are impossible in divine Science
  gl 597– 8 petitions for blessings upon *m·* methods,

mind
   c 257– 9 belief in a bodily soul and a *m·* mind,
   g 529–31 Adam, . . . stands for a belief of *m·* mind.

mindlessness
   b 293– 4 the *m·* mindlessness, which forms no link

modes
  ph 170– 5 exercise of faith in *m·* modes,

mortality
   b 293– 1 this unreal *m·* mortality disappears

motion
   s 118–22 modes of *m·* motion are honored with the

myth
   g 523–12 *m·* myth, instead of the reflection of Spirit.

mythology
   g 524– 1 idolatry which followed this *m·* mythology

names
  ph 187– 7 material sense . . . gives them *m·* names,

nature
   g 551–17 "What can there be, of a *m·* nature,

nothingness
   o 345–28 *m·* nothingness, which Science inculcates,

observations
   r 483–24 schools, which wrestle with *m·* observations

obstacle
   a 45– 2 but Jesus vanquished every *m·* obstacle,

offering
   g 540–31 he brings a *m·* offering to God.

organism
   f 211–25 that the *m·* organism causes the

material

organization
  ph 165–10 *m·* organization and non-intelligent matter.
   p 429–19 If man did not exist before the *m·* organization
   g 509– 4 dependent upon no *m·* organization.
     524–20 How then could a *m·* organization become the

origin
   s 127–28 It has a spiritual, and not a *m·* origin.
   g 534– 1 belief in the *m·* origin of man
     549–32 a belief in the *m·* origin of man,

origins
   f 213–31 knowledge dipped . . . into belief in *m·* origins

outgrowth
  ph 171–32 supposition that man is a *m·* outgrowth

pain
   b 307–22 every sin or supposed *m·* pain

pains
   a 39– 23 so-called *m·* pains and material pleasures

perception
   g 527–15 It is plain also that *m·* perception,

person
  pr 14– 2 regard omnipotence as a . . . . *m·* person,

personalities
  sp 79–14 resting . . . not on *m·* personalities,
     84–26 *m·* personalities called spirits,

personality
   b 285– 7 What, then, is the *m·* personality which
     337– 5 *M·* personality is not realism ;
   g 544–25 a *m·* personality is not this likeness.

physician
   t 463– 1 The *m·* physician gropes among phenomena,

pinions
   b 298–27 flying on spiritual, not *m·*, pinions.

plane
   o 349–25 dwelling on a *m·* plane, material terms must be

pleasure
   p 418– 4 destroying all belief in *m·* pleasure or pain.

pleasures
   a 39–23 so-called material pains and *m·* pleasures

premises
   s 164–12 systems based on *m·* premises
   b 274–11 not mere inferences drawn from *m·* premises.

power
   f 249– 8 no mortal nor *m·* power as able to destroy.
   p 378–25 Sickness is not a . . . self-constituted *m·* power,

reasoning
   s 124–11 a blind conclusion from *m·* reasoning.

remedies
  pref viii–17 by doctors using *m·* remedies ;
   t 453–13 effects from the use of *m·* remedies

remedy
   p 427–26 Called to the bed of death, what *m·* remedy

researches
   g 549–20 Here these *m·* researches culminate

resistance
   s 134–10 spiritual power over *m·* resistance.

routine
  sp 96– 7 interruptions of the general *m·* routine.

science
   s 123–30 C. S. differs from *m·* science,

seed
   g 551–29 declares that the *m·* seed must decay in order to

self
   a 20–30 put aside *m·* self and sense,

selfhood
  sp 91–16 Absorbed in *m·* selfhood we discern . . . faintly
     91–18 The denial of *m·* selfhood aids the
   r 476–22 which is outside of all *m·* selfhood.

sensation
  pr 9–20 even the surrender of all merely *m·* sensation,
   f 249–32 He is the direct opposite of *m·* sensation,
   b 303–10 formed by Spirit, not by *m·* sensation.
     337– 3 as *m·* sensation, or a soul in the body,
   r 482–12 identical with sense, with *m·* sensation.

sensations
  sp 73–20 with *m·* sensations and desires,

sense
  pr 7– 7 relinquishment of error deprives *m·* sense of
     9–24 *m·* sense and human will have no place.
     14–23 prayer of Soul, not of *m·* sense.
   a 21–10 He constantly turns away from *m·* sense,
     30–24 between the offspring of Soul and of *m·* sense,
     30–27 If we have triumphed . . . over the errors of *m·*
          sense
     34–27 he would disappear to *m·* sense
     37–12 rarefy the atmosphere of *m·* sense
     41– 6 we must depart from *m·* sense
     44–31 power of Spirit to overrule mortal, *m·* sense.
     47– 4 They no longer measured man by *m·* sense.
   sp 71– 4 a belief, an illusion of *m·* sense.
     72– 4 in other words, mortal or *m·* sense,
     72–14 Mortal belief (the *m·* sense of life)
     75– 9 from the spiritual . . . back into its *m·* sense.
     81–26 inharmony resulting from *m·* sense hides
     85– 4 capacity of Soul, not of *m·* sense.
     92–20 a mere offshoot of *m·* sense.

material
sense

sp	95–30	*M·* sense does not unfold the facts of existence ;
s	108–26	false testimony of false *m·* sense,
	118–18	perverted by a perverse *m·* sense of law,
	121–14	man, left to the hypotheses of *m·* sense
	122–16	another proof of the illusion of *m·* sense.
	122–24	To *m·* sense, the severance of the jugular vein
	123–15	replaces the objects of *m·* sense with
	125–16	man governed by Soul, not by *m·* sense.
	139–20	*m·* sense stole into the divine record,
	146–10	by which *m·* sense is made the servant
ph	187– 6	Here you may see how so-called *m·* sense
	194–30	His case proves *m·* sense to be but a belief
f	202– 8	so-called pains and pleasures of *m·* sense,
	208– 2	*M·* sense defines all things materially,
	215–23	reverses the evidence of *m·* sense.
	225–30	in bondage to *m·* sense, ignorant how to
	227–26	The illusion of *m·* sense, . . . has bound you,
	247–18	loveliness which transcend all *m·* sense.
	252–15	The false evidence of *m·* sense contrasts
	252–16	*M·* sense lifts its voice with the arrogance of
	253–12	erring, mortal, *m·* sense
	253–15	Knowing the falsity of so-called *m·* sense,
c	255– 5	In league with *m·* sense, mortals take
	256– 3	thought rises from the *m·* sense to the spiritual,
	256–25	A finite and *m·* sense of God leads to
	266–22	opposite persecutions of *m·* sense,
b	269–19	advantage over the . . . thoughts of *m·* sense,
	273–28	the false claims of *m·* sense or law.
	279–30	Pantheism, starting from a *m·* sense of God,
	283–17	is but the objective state of *m·* sense,
	288–12	conflict between . . . Science and *m·* sense,
	296– 8	and regenerate *m·* sense and self.
	296–11	The death of a false *m·* sense and of sin,
	297–22	contradicting the testimony of *m·* sense,
	298– 8	What is termed *m·* sense can report only
	298–10	To *m·* sense, the unreal is the real until
	298–15	*M·* sense expresses the belief that mind is
	299–18	Knowledge gained from *m·* sense is
	304– 3	from the false testimony of *m·* sense,
	304–22	based on a *m·* sense of things,
	304–24	If mortals caught harmony through *m·* sense,
	304–27	if time or accident robbed them of *m·* sense.
	305– 2	Left to the decisions of *m·* sense, music is
	309– 5	subjected to *m·* sense which is discord.
	309–22	and rebuked his *m·* sense.
	310–22	led to deny *m·* sense, or mind in matter,
	310–29	belief of the flesh and of *m·* sense which sins.
	310–30	God is not seen by *m·* sense,
	310–32	Spirit, which *m·* sense cannot
	311– 9	These changes are the mutations of *m·* sense,
	311–24	he can only lose a sense *m·*.
	312– 1	law of Soul, which prevails over *m·* sense
	312– 4	whatever is learned through *m·* sense
	312– 5	That which *m·* sense calls intangible,
	318–12	what to *m·* sense seems substance,
	323–22	We must silence this lie of *m·* sense
	330–26	towards Soul and away from *m·* sense,
o	353– 2	a delusion of *m·* sense,
p	396–14	whatever seems real to *m·* sense, is unreal in
	416–18	refutation of the testimony of *m·* sense
	428– 5	has originated from this *m·* sense
t	444–20	resolves the dark visions of *m·* sense into
	447–17	"children of men" in *m·* sense,— *Psal.* 14 : 2.
r	471–15	When sin or sickness . . . seems true to *m·* sense,
	480–12	by evil, by matter, or by *m·* sense,
	481– 7	*M·* sense has its realm apart from Science
	481–30	*M·* sense never helps mortals to understand
	484–25	it is *m·* sense, not Soul, which sins ;
	484–29	Science must triumph over *m·* sense,
	485– 2	is *m·* sense a necessary preliminary
	488–17	*M· sense* is an absurd phrase,
	489–29	the impossibility of any *m·* sense,
	490–24	Outside the *m·* sense of things, all is harmony.
	490–29	destroy all *m·* sense with immortal testimony.
	490–29	the mythical nature of *m·* sense,
	491– 3	Sleep shows *m·* sense as either oblivion,
g	504– 9	Animal magnetism thus uncovers *m·* sense,
	505– 8	*M·* sense is nothing but a supposition of
	510–12	*m·* sense, is separated from Truth,
	513– 8	turn away from a false *m·* sense.
	530– 4	To *m·* sense, this divine universe is dim
	532– 5	forever opposed to mortal, *m·* sense.
	532–17	All human knowledge and *m·* sense
	532–17	pleasure, evolved through *m·* sense,
	534–27	first manifestation of the error of *m·* sense.
	544– 8	The serpent, *m·* sense, will bite the heel of
	548–24	from the *m·* sense of things, not from the
ap	566– 7	*m·* sense of animal growth and organization,
	572– 9	from a *m·* sense of existence to the spiritual,
	575– 5	but whatever is of *m·* sense, or mortal,
	577– 1	plagues imposed by *m·* sense.
gl	580–24	the *m·* sense of personality yields to the
	582–25	supposition that . . . Soul dwells in *m·* sense ;
		the testimony of what is termed *m·* sense ;

material
sense

gl	585– 7	To *m·* sense, earth is matter ;
	585– 9	spiritual evidence opposed to *m·* sense ;
	587–13	theories that hold mind to be a *m·* sense,
	591–27	MORTAL MIND. . . . a suppositional *m·* sense,
	593– 4	disappearance of *m·* sense before the
	597–18	in which a *m·* sense of things disappears,

senses

pr	15–16	close the lips and silence the *m·* senses.
a	32–26	he withdrew from the *m·* senses to refresh
	38–31	He taught that the *m·* senses shut out Truth
	46–29	and the *m·* senses saw him no more.
sp	75– 6	or the *m·* senses could take no cognizance of
	88–15	Beliefs proceed from the so-called *m·* senses,
	91–21	or through what are termed the *m·* senses.
	98–10	which the *m·* senses cannot comprehend,
s	120–10	if the *m·* senses indicate that he
	120–16	nor can the *m·* senses bear reliable testimony
	126–19	beyond the cognizance of the *m·* senses
	144–15	belongs to the so-called *m·* senses,
ph	167–12	nor perceive divine Science with the *m·* senses.
	189– 1	human or *m·* senses yield to the authority of
	200–23	These so-called *m·* senses must yield to
f	214– 6	confined to the evidence before his *m·* senses,
	214–10	The *m·* senses, like Adam, originate in matter
	228–13	his God-given dominion over the *m·* senses.
c	257–15	The *m·* senses and human conceptions would
	262–13	and rise above the testimony of the *m·* senses,
b	268–17	based on the false testimony of the *m·* senses
	269–21	testimony of the *m·* senses is neither
	269–27	knowledge gained through the *m·* senses
	273–10	reverses the false testimony of the *m·* senses,
	274– 9	the evidence of the *m·* senses.
	278– 5	The *m·* senses oppose this,
	278– 6	there are no *m·* senses, for matter has no
	284–16	Can Deity be known through the *m·* senses?
	284–16	Can the *m·* senses, which receive no direct
	287–27	The five *m·* senses testify to truth and error
	288– 5	and the testimony of the *m·* senses,
	294–15	This verdict of the so-called *m·* senses
	296–27	judges by the testimony of the *m·* senses,
	298–13	Spiritual sense, contradicting the *m·* senses,
	299–31	If man were solely a creature of the *m·* senses,
	303–31	evidence before the *m·* senses yielded to
	306–22	not more distinct nor real to the *m·* senses than
	306–26	amid the jarring testimony of the *m·* senses,
	309–14	power of Spirit over the *m·* senses ;
	317–26	the testimony of the *m·* senses and the body,
	318– 9	*m·* senses originate and support all that
	330–15	Neither . . . can be discerned by the *m·* senses
o	359–11	Even though you aver that the *m·* senses are
	359–16	and is not apparent to the *m·* senses,
p	390–13	dispute the testimony of the *m·* senses
	408– 8	throughout the entire round of the *m·* senses,
	412–17	must break the dream of the *m·* senses.
t	461–13	reverses the evidence before the *m·* senses
r	481–10	various contradictions of . . . by the *m·* senses
	489–31	Mortal belief would have the *m·* senses
	490–21	knowledge gained from the so-called *m·* senses
g	505–12	mindless matter nor the so-called *m·* senses.
	525–28	false conclusion of the *m·* senses.
	530–19	and saying, through the *m·* senses :
	543–17	the evidence before the *m·* senses.
	546–16	*m·* senses can take no cognizance of Spirit
	550–32	the *m·* senses must father these absurdities,
	551– 1	*m·* senses and their reports are unnatural,
gl	585–11	spiritual fact of whatever the *m·* senses
	589– 6	*m·* senses yield to the spiritual sense
	592– 8	the subjective states of error ; *m·* senses ;
	596– 2	which is unknown to the *m·* senses.

senses'

s	122– 7	*m·* senses' reversal of the Science of Soul

sensuousness

pr	16–20	Only as we rise above all *m·* sensuousness

sight

a	35–18	when he rose out of *m·* sight.

significance

gl	598– 9	to employ words of *m·* significance

source

c	256–31	A mind originating from a finite or *m·* source
g	552–22	From a *m·* source flows no remedy for sorrow,

species

ph	172– 8	How then is the *m·* species maintained,

spiritualism

sp	77–27	would outgrow their beliefs in *m·* spiritualism.

staff

m	66– 6	teach mortals not to lean on a *m·* staff,

standpoint

o	351–30	thought to worship Spirit from a *m·* standpoint,
t	458– 8	from both a mental and a *m·* standpoint.
g	546–20	cannot . . . be interpreted from a *m·* standpoint.
	551–26	From a *m·* standpoint, "Canst — *Job* 11 : 7.

standpoints

ph	174– 9	rising above *m·* standpoints,

21

material

state
sp 77–19   to prolong the *m·* state
p 411–24   The mental state is called a *m·* state.

stratum
ph 185–28   the *m·* stratum of the human mind,

structure
ph 172–24   Brain, heart, blood, . . . the *m·* structure?
173–21   *m·* structure is mortal.
g 509–21   no more contingent now on time or *m·* structure
ap 576–12   no *m·* structure in which to worship God,

substance
b 278–17   admission that there can be *m·* substance
301–23   seems to himself to be *m·* substance,

substances
f 209–25   *M·* substances or mundane formations,

suffering
p 405–30   Belief in *m·* suffering causes mortals to

superstructure
gl 595– 9   *m·* superstructure, where mortals congregate

suppositions
p 368–18   no *m·* suppositions can prevent us from healing
gl 583– 3   *m·* suppositions of life, substance, and

surface
b 313–24   He plunged beneath the *m·* surface of things,

symbols
a 34–14   his commemoration through *m·* symbols

system
s 133–21   It was a finite and *m·* system,

systems
b 326–12   must forsake the foundation of *m·* systems,
p 394–18   the fallacy of *m·* systems in general,

tangible and
sp 75– 5   would need to be tangible and *m·*,

temple
b 314–16   they thought that he meant their *m·* temple

terms
s 115– 3   the inadequacy of *m·* terms for
115–10   translating *m·* terms back into the original
o 349–17   one is obliged to use *m·* terms
349–25   *m·* terms must be generally employed.

theories
s 125–19   *m·* theories about laws of health
ph 165–14   *m·* theories took the place of
f 213–12   *M·* theories partially paralyze this
b 339–21   so will our *m·* theories yield to spiritual ideas,
o 355–32   Strangely enough, we ask for *m·* theories

theory
s 152–12   Such errors beset every *m·* theory,
c 257–23   the *m·* theory of mind in matter
g 545–16   Error tills the whole ground in this *m·* theory,

things
pr 16– 1   A great sacrifice of *m·* things must precede
a 35– 5   turned away from *m·* things.
s 108– 8   show the falsity of all *m·* things ;
f 247–11   the beauty of *m·* things passes away,
b 331– 3   If life were in mortal man or *m·* things,
335–14   Things *m·* and temporal are insubstantial.
o 356–12   Understanding the nothingness of *m·* things,
g 506–29   finding names for all *m·* things,
510–26   resolving of thoughts into *m·* things.
gl 592–23   knowledge of the nothingness of *m·* things

thought
c 267– 1   Every object in *m·* thought will be destroyed,
o 356– 2   the *m·* thought must become spiritualized
t 460–12   to the *m·* thought all is material,
g 509–30   the *m·* thought of his fellow-countrymen :

universe
f 238– 5   as well as in the *m·* universe.
g 545–12   notion of a *m·* universe is utterly opposed to

unreality
f 228–18   and discord as the *m·* unreality.

view
g 521–25   the opposite error, a *m·* view of creation,
521–27   this *m·* view of God and the universe,

views
b 314–11   showed plainly that their *m·* views were

virus
ph 196–27   not from infection nor from contact with *m·* virus,

ways
f 218–21   lead only into *m·* ways of obtaining help,

world
a 28–17   Not a single . . . part of his nature did the *m·* world
sp 96–12   This *m·* world is even now becoming the arena
b 268– 1   In the *m·* world, thought has brought to light
t 451– 4   to come out from the *m·* world and be separate.
g 507–21   A *m·* world implies a mortal mind

a 24–24   the presentation, after death, of the *m·* Jesus,
m 69–10   as the false and *m·* disappears.
sp 71–27   are alike *m·* and physical.
73– 3   Spiritualism calls one person, . . . *m·*, but
76– 7   Life will be recognized as neither *m·* nor
83–22   contrary to C. S. to suppose that life is either *m·*

material

sp 85–26   seeking the *m·* more than the spiritual.
91–28   erroneous . . . that man is both mental and *m·*
97–17   The more *m·* the belief, the more obvious its
99– 1   not *m·* but scientifically spiritual.
99–13   The ordinary teachings are *m·*
s 132–23   a *m·* and a doctrinal theory.
143–11   matter required a *m·* and human belief
144–11   The more *m·* a belief, the more . . . tenacious
152–29   skeptical as to *m·* curative methods.
155–24   in proportion as it puts less weight into the *m·*
160– 4   When mortals forsake the *m·* for the spiritual
ph 168–11   the *m·* so-called laws of health,
169– 2   change of belief from a *m·* to a spiritual basis.
170–29   description of man as . . . both *m·* and
171–29   intelligence and life are spiritual, never *m·*,
177–18   had the naming of all that was *m·*.
181–21   If you are too *m·* to love the Science of Mind
185–12   as *m·* as the prevailing systems of medicine.
188–16   the dreamer thinks that his body is *m·*
191– 8   a *m·*, theoretical life-basis
199– 5   since muscles are as *m·* as wood and iron
f 206– 8   *M·*, erring, human thought acts injuriously
208–26   only expresses a *m·* and mortal mind.
209– 9   *m·* and mortal body or mind is not the man.
214–15   spiritual sense, and not the *m·*, conveys the
216–28   When you say, "Man's body is *m·*,"
218– 4   the body is as *m·* as the wheel.
224–18   less *m·* than the Roman scourge,
231–15   no antagonistic powers . . . spiritual or *m·*,
233–18   can discern the face of the sky,— the sign *m·*,
246–13   As the . . . *m·*, the transient sense of beauty fades,
249–25   the dream that life, substance, and . . . are *m·*.
254–21   to abandon so fast as practical the *m·*,
c 255–14   That God is corporeal or *m·*, no man should affirm.
258–20   but the *m·* so-called senses have no
263– 5   creations of mortal mind are *m·*.
b 270–29   disease is mental, not *m·*.
273– 3   There is no *m·* truth.
273–29   *m·*, conflicting mortal opinions
274–20   which affirm that life, substance, and. . . are *m·*,
275–25   Our *m·* human theories are destitute of
277–22   the order of *m·* so-called science.
278–25   leads to the conclusion that if man is *m·*,
282–24   all that is *m·* is a *m·*, human, mortal thought,
285– 3   Man's individuality is not *m·*.
286–22   *M·* and temporal thoughts are human,
286–25   temporal and *m·* are not then creations of Spirit.
287– 3   but belong, with all that is *m·* and temporal,
287– 6   Error supposes man to be both mental and *m·*,
289–27   and therefore the *m·* must be untrue.
290– 7   will remain as *m·* as before the transition,
290– 8   still seeking happiness through a *m·*,
290–31   His body is as *m·* as his mind, and *vice versa*.
292–16   The so-called senses of mortals are *m·*.
293–13   The *m·* so-called gases and forces are
295– 9   would transform the spiritual into the *m·*,
301– 8   and therefore is *m·*, temporal.
301–31   presupposes . . . man to be *m·* instead of
306– 2   thought that they could raise . . . from the *m·*.
306–30   God's man, spiritually created, is not *m·*
307–18   says : . . . He has made man mortal and *m·*,
314– 1   no less *m·* until the ascension
314–23   Because of mortals' *m·* and sinful belief,
318–10   all that is *m·*, untrue, selfish, or debased.
322– 4   from a *m·* to a spiritual basis,
326–11   while loving the *m·* or trusting in it
328– 2   a spiritual sense, which silences the *m·*
334–13   the unseen and the seen, the spiritual and *m·*,
336–17   Immortal man is not and never was *m·*,
338– 7   both good and evil, both spiritual and *m·*
338–10   and conclusions of *m·* and mortal humanity.
o 345– 5   the likeness of Spirit cannot be *m·*,
349–30   all learning, even that which is wholly *m·*.
351–27   Israelites centred their thoughts on the *m·*
353–28   Mind is limitless. It never was *m·*.
360– 6   those which are both mental and *m·*.
360–14   which . . . the *m·* or the spiritual?
p 372–13   and then call his bonds *m·*
376–17   If the body is *m·*, it cannot, . . . suffer with
378–20   represented by two *m·* erroneous bases.
385– 8   The spiritual demand, quelling the *m·*,
396–28   man is spiritual, not *m·* ;
397–24   no more *m·* in their waking hours than
398– 7   clear evidence that the malady was not *m·*.
399–18   constructs a machine, . . . and then calls it *m·*.
416–17   this mind is *m·* in sensation,
416–19   even as the body, . . . is *m·*.
427–14   dream that existence can be *m·*.
428–21   the life which is spiritual, not *m·*.
442–23   until the *m·*, transformed with the ideal,
t 458– 5   one spiritual, the other *m·*,
460–12   to the material thought all is *m·*,
463–28   it is a spiritual law instead of *m·*.

material
r 468–15 Therefore man is not *m·* ;
476–11 Hence man is not mortal nor *m·*.
477– 8 is seen in nothing imperfect nor *m·*.
477– 9 Whatever is *m·* is mortal.
478–25 is composed of *m·* human beliefs
479– 2 must have a *m·*, not a spiritual origin.
479– 7 if aught comes from God, it cannot be…*m·* ;
493–24 That man is *m·*, and that matter suffers,
g 504– 7 both spiritual and *m·*
507–30 inverts this appearing and calls ideas *m·*.
508–14 Gender is mental not *m·*.
521–20 but the continued account is mortal and *m·*.
528– 5 is solely mythological and *m·*.
531–11 will sometime rise above all *m·* and
536–29 the mortal and *m·* return to dust,
538– 9 the *m·* and spiritual, — the unreal and the real.
540–30 *M·* in origin and sense,
541–17 belief that life, substance, and . . . can be *m·*
543–18 If man is *m·* and originates in an egg,
544–28 *M·*, erroneous belief reverses
547–21 implies that the great First Cause must become *m·*,
547–28 relinquishes a *m·*, sensual, and mortal theory
550–16 contemplation of existence as *m·* and
553–16 why are his deductions generally *m·* ?
ap 561–20 *m·* and corporeal selfhood disappear,
563– 9 belief that substance, life, and . . . can be *m·*.
572–27 Not through the *m·* visual organs for seeing,
572–29 terrestrial or celestial, *m·* or spiritual?
573– 9 while to another, . . . the vision is *m·*.
gl 586– 3 Spiritual discernment, — not *m·* but mental.
587–10 a belief that . . . are both mental and *m·* ;
588–19 the belief that . . . are both mental and *m·*.

Material Court of Errors
p 440– 1 Your *M· C· of E·*, when it condemned

materialism
and sensualism
m 65–14 in the *m·* and sensualism of the age,
gross
sp 75– 9 This gross *m·* is scientifically impossible,
lion of
g 549–26 and beards the lion of *m·* in its den.
silent
pr 15–11 Lips must be mute and *m·* silent,
wanes
ap 562–21 as the night of *m·* wanes.

pref vii–16 the cold conventionality of *m·*
sp 85–27 His thrusts at *m·* were sharp, but needed.
ph 172– 7 *M·* grades the human species as
f 216– 9 Spirituality lays open siege to *m·*.
b 314–19 This *m·* lost sight of the true Jesus ;
p 416–20 This *m·* of parent and child is only

materialist
a 51–29 caused the selfish *m·* to hate him ;

materialistic
s 120–24 overthrows false evidence, and refutes *m·* logic.
132–16 and retained their *m·* beliefs about God.
ph 183– 3 laws of matter . . . demand obedience to *m·*
183–26 Truth casts out all evils and *m·* methods
187–19 mortal mind, the cause of all *m·* action
190– 8 This embryonic and *m·* human belief
196– 1 If *m·* knowledge is power, it is not wisdom.
198– 9 The *m·* doctor, though humane, is an artist who
b 268– 9 *M·* hypotheses challenge metaphysics to
298–22 and admit no *m·* beliefs.
316–28 casting out evils, spiritualizing *m·* beliefs,
317–24 To the *m·* Thomas, looking for the
g 553–15 Why, then, is the naturalist's basis so *m·*,

materialists
b 314–17 To such *m·*, the real man seemed a spectre,
p 389–22 *M·* contradict their own statements.

materiality
departure from
f 213–11 Every step towards goodness is a departure from *m·*,
destroy
g 545–10 should so improve . . . as to destroy *m·*.
evil and
b 277–11 evil and *m·* are unreal
evolved from
g 544–22 but these gods must be evolved from *m·*
ghost of
o 353–25 The grave does not banish the ghost of *m·*.
ignorance and
sp 77–26 would gradually rise above ignorance and *m·*,
lost much
b 295–21 one which has lost much *m·*
night of
o 354–23 The night of *m·* is far spent,
of the age
a 31–25 Referring to the *m·* of the age, Jesus said :

materiality
opposite of
ph 171– 4 discernment of the spiritual opposite of *m·*,
rule the
s 164–22 rule the *m·* miscalled life
self-imposed
ph 191–17 must free itself from self-imposed *m·*
superior to
t 444– 3 all must rise superior to *m·*,

m 62–32 this does not make *m·* first
sp 86– 9 misconception of it uncovered their *m·*.
ph 169–25 whatever good they may seem to receive from *m·*.
c 266– 4 *m·* giving place to man's higher
b 276–23 away from *m·* to the Principle of the universe,
293–17 Electricity is the sharp surplus of *m·*
299–13 never lead towards self, sin, or *m·*,
o 352– 9 To Jesus, not *m·* but spirituality, was the
360– 6 It is true that *m·* renders these
r 484–28 *Question.*— Is *m·* the concomitant of
g 533–21 *M·*, so obnoxious to God, is already found in
551–26 so long as it bases creation on *m·*.
ap 572–10 *m·* is the inverted image of spirituality.

materialized
b 288–24 Spirit is not, and cannot be, *m·* ;

materializes
pr 4–32 Whatever *m·* worship hinders man's

Material Law
p 441–13 *M· L·* is a liar who cannot bear witness

materially
m 69–14 "Do you teach that Spirit creates *m·*,
sp 78–21 Spirit is not *m·* tangible.
96–30 will be apprehended mentally instead of *m·*.
s 126–12 seems to have reversed it and repeated it *m·* ;
140– 7 Not *m·* but spiritually we know Him
140–17 only as we cease to worship *m·*.
148–16 Anatomy takes up man at all points *m·*.
ph 200–12 not formed *m·* but spiritually,
f 208– 3 Material sense defines all things *m·*,
213– 7 and then classifies it *m·*.
254– 9 To stop eating, drinking, or being clothed *m·*
c 259–24 God, Spirit, works spiritually, not *m·*.
b 303–13 both spiritually and *m·*,
o 350–31 In Jewish worship the Word was *m·* explained
p 401–19 mortal mind only feels and sees *m·*.
r 487– 8 and hearing spiritually than *m·*,
g 521–14 supposition that man is created *m·*,
527–27 but doing so *m·*, not spiritually,
528–20 *m·* rather than spiritually,
531– 5 error, — that mortal man starts *m·*,
557–23 as if he began *m·* right,
gl 585–26 the belief that the human race originated *m·*

materials
p 402–15 constructs . . . with this mind's own mortal *m·*.

Materia Medica
p 430–22 *M· M·*, Anatomy, Physiology,
431–14 the prisoner summoned Physiology, *M· M·*, and
431–15 *M· M·* held out the longest.
432–25 One of the prisoner's friends, *M· M·*,
432–29 changed the purpose of *M· M·*,
436–16 professed friends, *M· M·* and Physiology,
437–22 *M· M·*, Anatomy, Physiology,
438–29 we have heard *M· M·* explain how
439–10 frightening away *M· M·*, who was then
439–12 *M· M·* was a misguided participant in the
439–17 Scholastic Theology, *M· M·*, Physiology,
441–20 We further recommend that *M· M·*

materia medica
a 41–19 No ancient school of philosophy, *m· m·*, or
s 138–12 cast out neither by corporeality, by *m· m·*, nor
149– 5 Is *m· m·* a science or a bundle of . . . theories?

maternal
m 60–10 Therefore *m·* affection lives on
g 553–18 the *m·* egg never brought forth Adam.

mathematical
s 108–13 to multiply with *m·* certainty

mathematically
s 113–13 showing *m·* their exact relation to Truth.

mathematician's
t 453– 1 You do not deny the *m·* right to

mathematics
pr 3– 5 Who would . . . pray the principle of *m·* to
an 105–21 important to medicine as to mechanics or *m·*."
s 113–14 *M·* has not a
113–27 like the method in *m·*, proves the rule by
128–29 The addition of two sums in *m·* must always
ph 195–17 natural history, chemistry, music, *m·*,
f 219– 6 In *m·*, we do not multiply when we
p 422– 1 and then calling the process *m·*.
g 546–31 If *m·* should present a thousand different

matrimony
m 59– 1   *M·* should never be entered into without
65–25   *M·*, . . . must lose its present slippery footing,
matrix
f 250– 5   and suppose . . . mortality to be the *m·* of
matron
ph 179–26   The sedulous *m·* — studying her Jahr
Matter
p 440–12   disobedience to the so-called laws of *M·*
441–19   decrees of the Court of Error in favor of *M·*,
441–20   Spirit decides in favor of Man and against *M·*.
matter (see also matter's)
admit that
    ph 172–32   When we admit that *m·* (heart, blood, brain,
always surrenders
    g 552–30   *m·* always surrenders its claims when the
and death
    b 289–29   *M·* and death are mortal illusions.
and error
    ph 181–31   will incline you to the side of *m·* and error.
    o 347–26   The dream that *m·* and error are something
and evil
    g 583–23   *m·* and evil, which have no Principle ;
and its claims
    b 273– 1   *M·* and its claims of sin, sickness, and death
and its effects
    b 283– 8   *M·* and its effects— sin, sickness, and death
and man
    b 294– 8   If . . . *m·* and man would be one.
and material law
    g 549–29   and allows *m·* and material law to usurp the
and Mind
    b 270– 5   *M·* and Mind are opposites.
    270– 9   but one power, — not two powers, *m·* and Mind,
    293– 5   which forms no link between *m·* and Mind,
and mind
    s 150–19   would have one believe that both *m·* and mind
    b 274–26   The conventional firm, called *m·* and mind,
    274–28   imaginary copartnership, *m·* and mind,
    279–28   not two bases of being, *m·* and mind, but one
    r 477–10   man appears to be *m·* and mind
    491–17   The belief that *m·* and mind are one,
    492–30   theory, . . . there are two factors, *m·* and mind,
and mortality
    a 43–25   in defiance of *m·* and mortality,
    f 215– 9   *m·* and mortality do not reflect the facts of
and mortal mind
    b 293– 6   *M·* and mortal mind are but different strata of
and Spirit
    ph 171–18   believes himself to be combined *m·* and Spirit.
    f 216–20   both *m·* and Spirit, both good and evil.
    b 312–27   *m·* and Spirit, the finite and the infinite,
appertain to
    ph 182– 7   what are termed laws of nature, appertain to *m·*.
approaches its
    p 409– 5   the nearer *m·* approaches its final statement,
ascension above
    a 35–17   his spiritual and final ascension above *m·*,
assigns to
    s 123– 7   reverses the order of Science and assigns to *m·*
assume that
    s 119– 7   they assume that *m·* is the product of Spirit.
atheism of
    gl 580–27   disappeared in the atheism of *m·*.
based on
    ph 191–26   defines mortal man as based on *m·*,
basis of
    ph 195–13   We should forsake the basis of *m·* for
    b 316–30   resting on the basis of *m·*,
belief in
    s 116–17   even to the extinction of all belief in *m·*,
    gl 581–10   understanding of Spirit, destroying belief in *m·*.
belief of life in
    sp 74–10   When . . . the belief of life in *m·* is extinct,
    89–30   This incident shows that the belief of life in *m·*
belief that
    (see belief)
believes that
    p 375–10   believes that *m·*, not mind, has helped him.
believing that
    f 205–15   error of believing that *m·* can be intelligent
body and
    a 42–17   his final triumph over body and *m·*,
body as
    f 214–31   the body as *m·* has no sensation of its own,
called
    sp 80–24   over its substratum, called *m·*.
    b 274–26   The conventional firm, called *m·* and mind,
    b 374–13   state of mortal mind, though it is called *m·*.
calling it
    f 251–31   beliefs, which rob Mind, calling it *m·*,
call upon
    ph 173–28   and so continue to call upon *m·*

matter
can have no pain
    p 393–20   *m·* can have no pain nor inflammation.
can make no
    s 120–11   *m·* can make no conditions for man.
    f 253–19   *M·* can make no opposition to right
can never produce
    b 304–13   *m·* can never produce mind nor
cannot be inflamed
    p 414–32   *M·* cannot be inflamed.
cannot believe
    r 487–16   *M·* cannot believe, and Mind understands.
cannot be sick
    p 372– 1   *M·* cannot be sick, and Mind is immortal.
cannot be weary
    f 217–27   *m·* cannot be weary and heavy-laden.
cannot connect
    r 491–11   *M·* cannot connect mortals with the true
cannot perform
    r 478–22   *M·* cannot perform the functions of Mind.
cannot suffer
    ph 184–20   This is human belief, . . . for *m·* cannot suffer.
cannot take cold
    p 377– 2   mentally convince him that *m·* cannot take cold.
cannot talk
    p 391–20   Since *m·* cannot talk, it must be mortal mind
claims of
    f 242– 6   Denial of the claims of *m·* is a great step
    r 491–14   Spirit, which annuls the claims of *m·*,
concessions to
    a 33– 2   closed forever Jesus' . . . concessions to *m·*.
conclude that
    r 467–25   when we conclude that *m·* is the
condition of
    p 371– 1   to discover the condition of *m·*,
conditions of
    s 162–15   without the conditions of *m·*
consider
    s 119– 9   and consider *m·* as a power
control over
    r 482–23   enabled Jesus to demonstrate his control over *m·*.
create
    b 278– 2   nothing in Spirit out of which to create *m·*.
    g 504–27   Did infinite Mind create *m·*,
creations of
    b 287– 5   creations of *m·* must return to dust.
    g 523– 8   The creations of *m·* arise from a mist
deals with
    p 423–15   The matter-physician deals with *m·*
death and
    r 486–19   conditional upon death and *m·*,
deflections of
    b 305–21   the deflections of *m·* as opposed to
demand of
    g 524–30   Is Spirit, . . . ejected at the demand of *m·*?
dependency on
    b 335– 5   would reduce God to dependency on *m·*,
dependent on
    b 292–18   so-called life of mortals is dependent on *m·*.
    311– 4   carnal mind, dependent on *m·*
devoted to
    gl 582– 6   so-called mortal mind, devoted to *m·* ;
did not originate
    b 275– 4   This shows that *m·* did not originate in God,
direct line of
    ph 189–31   always in the direct line of *m·*,
disappears
    s 156–30   In metaphysics, *m·* disappears from the remedy
    c 264–21   *M·* disappears under the microscope of Spirit.
discords of
    s 155–23   to offset the discords of *m·*
display of
    b 317–32   Nothing but a display of *m·* could make
disregard of
    f 210–10   his disregard of *m·* and its so-called laws.
distinct from
    f 217– 9   Mind to be scientifically distinct from *m·*,
    b 335– 3   Spirit is distinct from *m·*
does not appear
    f 211–11   *m·* does not appear in the spiritual
does not enter
    b 269–12   *m·* does not enter into metaphysical premises
does not express
    f 223– 7   *M·* does not express Spirit.
does not inform
    p 389– 9   *M·* does not inform you of bodily derangements ;
doom of
    b 279– 6   The doom of *m·* establishes the conclusion
dream of
    g 532–28   error began and will end the dream of *m·*.
elsewhere in
    ph 190– 7   neither . . . is found in brain or elsewhere in *m·*
emerge gently from
    r 485–14   Emerge gently from *m·* into Spirit.

matter

enthrones
ph 186–31 it enthrones *m·* as deity.
p 394–12 and enthrones *m·* through error.
error or
b 293–27 self-destruction of error or *m·*
g 521–30 The history of error or *m·*, if veritable, would
evidence of
s 128–26 the so-called evidence of *m·*.
evil and
b 277– 9 Their opposites, evil and *m·*, are mortal error,
evil or
t 454–11 evil or *m·* has neither intelligence nor power,
exalts
s 148–25 Physiology exalts *m·*, dethrones Mind,
examined
b 274–31 *m·*, examined in the light of . . . disappears.
excludes
s 123–13 excludes *m·*, resolves *things* into *thoughts*,
explains away
b 278– 3 Divine Metaphysics explains away *m·*.
faith in
(*see* **faith**)
fallacy of
f 237–24 the fallacy of *m·* and its supposed laws.
false sense of
p 399–26 It is only a false sense of *m·*,
false views of
b 281–29 Our false views of *m·* perish
fettered to
sp 77–21 a so-called mind fettered to *m·*.
flesh and
b 320–22 the belief that man is flesh and *m·*,
forces of
s 124–28 Human knowledge calls them forces of *m·* ;
formation of
g 510–24 indicates a supposed formation of *m·*
form of
sp 73–16 electricity or any other form of *m·*,
s 145–27 the antagonism of one form of *m·*
159–28 how much . . . one form of *m·* is
159–29 allowing another form of *m·*.
gl 598–16 was indeed air, an etherealized form of *m·*,
forms of
s 145–27 towards other forms of *m·* or error,
ph 172–16 through all the forms of *m·*
c 263–32 The fading forms of *m·*,
forsaking
c 265–10 forsaking *m·* for Spirit,
gained from
sp 91–20 erroneous knowledge gained from *m·*
92–15 a knowledge gained from *m·*, or evil,
gives to
sp 83–19 and gives to *m·* the precedence over Spirit.
gorgeousness of
f 252–26 says : . . . enthroned in the gorgeousness of *m·*.
grasp of
a 28– 7 determination to hold Spirit in the grasp of *m·*
ground, or
b 338–28 from this ground, or *m·*, sprang Adam,
had no life
a 51–15 He knew that *m·* had no life
has no
ph 166– 1 for *m·* has no sensation of its own,
f 211–10 and that *m·* has no sensation
250–26 *m·* has no more sense as a man than
b 275– 1 *M·* has no life to lose, and Spirit never dies.
278– 7 no material senses, for *m·* has no mind.
282–16 *m·* has no place in Spirit,
o 346–23 because *m·* has no sensation,
p 368–25 Because *m·* has no consciousness or Ego,
401–13 since *m·* has no sensation
426–30 because *m·* has no life to surrender.
r 485– 3 for *m·* has no sensation.
489– 5 and that *m·* has no sensation.
489–26 because *m·* has no sensation,
gl 584–11 *M·* has no life, hence it has no real existence.
holding that
p 422–26 holding that *m·* forms its own conditions
inanimate
s 157– 7 never shares its rights with inanimate *m·*.
t 463–29 The sick are not healed by inanimate *m·*
included in
f 209– 1 and of other beliefs included in *m·*.
independent of
ph 200–11 and ever will be independent of *m·* ;
f 247–19 Comeliness and grace are independent of *m·*.
inert
p 383–32 notion that health depends on inert *m·*
385–32 from the body or from inert *m·*
r 484–17 Drugs and inert *m·* are unconscious, mindless.
in proportion as
p 369– 5 In proportion as *m·* loses to human sense

matter

instead of
ph 200– 5 the worship of God in Spirit instead of *m·*,
f 223– 5 illusion that he lives . . . in *m·* instead of Spirit.
b 271– 8 to heal the sick through Mind instead of *m·*.
285–26 and resort to *m·* instead of Spirit for the
307–18 out of *m·* instead of Spirit.''
320–19 harmonious existence as image, idea, instead of
m·
p 415–13 resorting to *m·* instead of to Mind.
430– 7 by resting upon Spirit instead of *m·*.
g 536–17 starting from *m·* instead of from God,
544– 6 Mind, instead of *m·*, being the producer,
irrespective of
p 423–19 Mind his basis of operation irrespective of *m·*
is a belief
ph 190– 3 while *m·* is a belief, ignorant of itself,
is an error
b 277–26 *M·* is an error of statement.
is appealed to
p 403–11 but *m·* is appealed to in the other.
is devoid of
r 480– 9 whereas *m·* is devoid of sensation.
is inert
f 253–21 for *m·* is inert, mindless.
is mortal error
r 468–12 Spirit is immortal Truth ; *m·* is mortal error.
is naught
s 109– 2 Mind is All and *m·* is naught
is non-intelligent
f 217–32 *M·* is non-intelligent.
r 478–21 *m·* is non-intelligent and brain-lobes cannot
is not a lawgiver
s 127–25 for *m·* is not a lawgiver.
is nothing
s 116–18 *m·* is nothing beyond an image in mortal mind.
is not intelligent
p 412–32 since *m·* is not intelligent and cannot
is not self-sustaining
p 372–22 *M·* is not self-sustaining.
is not sensible
p 399–26 since *m·* is not sensible.
is not sentient
b 285– 1 *M·* is not sentient
is represented
b 294–24 *m·* is represented as divided into intelligent
g 522–19 *M·* is represented as the life-giving
is temporal
b 277–30 *m·* is temporal and is therefore
is the falsity
s 127–19 It teaches that *m·* is the falsity, not the fact,
is the unreal
r 468–13 *m·* is the unreal and temporal.
is unknown
r 469– 2 What is termed *m·* is unknown to Spirit,
g 503–11 In the universe of Truth, *m·* is unknown.
law of
(*see* **law**)
laws of (*see also* **so-called laws of** *and* **supposed laws of**)
p 384–22 but if you believe in laws of *m·*
t 463–26 if by these are meant laws of *m·*,
less
f 249–28 night-dream has less *m·* as its accompaniment.
limited to
p 369–28 Limited to *m·* by their own law,
man and
b 270–11 intelligence, apart from man and *m·*,
manifest as
b 306–22 forms of mortal thought, made manifest as *m·*,
manifested in
r 489– 1 The less mind there is manifested in *m·*
man is not
r 475– 6 Man is not *m·* ; he is not made up of
man or
b 284– 4 If God were limited to man or *m·*,
medium of
s 140–19 Worshipping through the medium of *m·* is
Mind and
b 269– 4 the supposed coexistence of Mind and *m·*
270– 1 as reasonable as the second, that Mind and *m·*
g 555–22 as if man were the offspring of both Mind and *m·*,
mind and
(*see* **mind**)
Mind is not in
sp 71–20 and that immortal Mind is not in *m·*.
p 381–26 understanding that Mind is not in *m·*.
mindless
s 159–13 as if she were so much mindless *m·*,
g 505–11 apparent only as Mind, never as mindless *m·*
mind nor
sp 71–19 neither mortal mind nor *m·* is the image
ph 188– 1 It is neither mind nor *m·*.
Mind, not
a 54–16 and triumph over death through Mind, not *m·*.
s 128–27 Science relates to Mind, not *m·*.
142–27 then Mind, not *m·*, must have been the first

matter

Mind, not
f 208–25   Mind, not *m·*, is causation.
212–24   this He does by means of Mind, not *m·*.
c 256– 6   Mind, not *m·*, is the creator.
b 280–30   perpetuates these . . . through Mind, not *m·*.
r 485– 5   Mind, not *m·*, sees, hears, feels, speaks.
g 505– 9   divine Mind, not *m·*, creates all identities,
mind, not
an 105–13   Mortal mind, not *m·*, is the criminal
s 153–27   mortal mind, not *m·*, contains and carries the
ph 169–23   It is mortal mind, not *m·*,
176–28   The human mind, not *m·*, is supposed to feel,
p 375– 1   Hence it is mortal mind, not *m·*, which says,
399–22   is mortal mind, not *m·*.
419–14   If disease moves, mind, not *m·*, moves it ;
425– 2   Mortal mind, not *m·*, induces this conclusion
Mind over
a 44–11   the power of Mind over *m·*,
45–31   the supremacy of Mind over *m·*.
s 139– 5   the triumph of Spirit, Mind, over *m·*.
misnamed
p 387–25   a law of so-called mortal mind, misnamed *m·*,
modes of
ph 170– 3   Modes of *m·* form neither a moral nor a
mortality, or
sp 78–10   If . . . in rapport with mortality, or *m·*,
must be unknown
b 280– 1   In the infinitude of Mind, *m·* must be unknown.
must disappear
ap 572–18   seen and acknowledged that *m·* must disappear.
never called
s 143–10   The divine Mind never called *m· medicine*,
never created
b 335– 8   Spirit never created *m·*.
never endowed
p 378–27   God never endowed *m·* with power to
never entered
sp 76–11   Spirit never entered *m·* and was therefore
never formed
c 259–24   Brain or *m·* never formed a human concept.
never produces
b 277– 5   *M·* never produces mind.
never sustained
p 425–16   he learns that *m·* never sustained existence
no
sp 75–11   to infinite Spirit there can be no *m·*.
s 113–30   no *m·* in Mind, and no mind in matter ;
113–31   no *m·* in Life, and no life in matter ;
113–31   no *m·* in good, and no good in matter.
b 278– 7   In Spirit there is no *m·*,
298–29   no *m·* what their individualism may be.
r 475– 3   To infinite Spirit there is no *m·*,
no affinity with
ph 191–30   Mind has no affinity with *m·*, and therefore
no cognizance of
r 479–15   matter can take no cognizance of *m·*.
no good in
s 113–32   no matter in good, and no good in *m·*.
no life in
s 113–31   no matter in Life, and no life in *m·* ;
no mind in
s 113–30   no matter in Mind, and no mind in *m·* :
non-intelligence and
b 282–19   Mind cannot pass into non-intelligence and *m·*,
non-intelligence, or
b 336– 3   never passes into non-intelligence, or *m·*.
non-intelligent
ph 165–11   material organization and non-intelligent *m·*.
c 257–10   the supposed substance of non-intelligent *m·*.
no place in
b 282–17   and Spirit has no place in *m·*.
no sensation in
f 237– 4   "There is no sensation in *m·*."
not a condition of
s 120–15   Health is not a condition of *m·*, but of Mind ;
not expressed in
s 119–18   spiritual and is not expressed in *m·*.
not found in
o 344– 9   God's likeness is not found in *m·*,
nothing is
s 113–18   God, Spirit, being all, nothing is *m·*.
nothingness of
r 480– 2   in C. S., the nothingness of *m·* is recognized.
497–23   and the nothingness of *m·*.
not the father of
c 257–15   the Father Mind is not the father of *m·*.
not through
g 520–24   God creates all through Mind, not through *m·*,
obtains in
p 409– 2   You may say : "But if disease obtains in *m·*,
of fact
r 486–32   as a *m·* of fact, these calamities often
on the side of
ph 168– 7   Whatever influence you cast on the side
of *m·*,

matter

operation of
s 150–29   by the operation of *m·*,
ph 171–20   ejection by the operation of *m·*.
or body
ph 177–10   *M·*, or body, is but a false concept of
order of
g 552–26   order of *m·* to be the order of mortal mind.
or dust
b 338–18   *m·* or dust was deemed the agent of Deity
or error
s 145–27   towards other forms of *m·* or error,
f 206– 3   no consciousness of the existence of *m·* or error.
organic
b 296–12   not the death of organic *m·*,
or Mind
g 531–25   Which institutes Life,— *m·* or Mind?
possesses neither
s 108– 6   *m·* possesses neither sensation nor life ;
predicated of
s 144– 9   mortal beliefs . . . are mainly predicated of *m·*,
property of
g 510–28   and not a vitalizing property of *m·*.
proved that
f 229– 2   already proved that *m·* has not destroyed them,
regarding
b 277–29   Nothing we can say. . . regarding *m·* is immortal,
reliance on
ph 179–29   sowing the seeds of reliance on *m·*,
required
s 143–11   *m·* required a material and human belief
residence in
p 432– 8   messages from my residence in *m·*,
restricted to
an 105– 8   to admit that . . . law is restricted to *m·*,
rises above
s 153–12   the most potent rises above *m·* into mind.
sections of
s 122–11   sections of *m·*, such as brain and nerves,
seed of
g 535– 3   yea, the seed of Spirit and the seed of *m·*,
seems to be
s 123–12   *m·* seems to be, but is not.
senseless
f 202–29   as if senseless *m·* . . . had more power than
sifted through
ph 171–19   believes that Spirit is sifted through *m·*,
slave of
f 221–26   when, still the slave of *m·*, he thought
so-called
sp 97– 6   so-called *m·* resembles its essence, mortal mind,
f 217–23   control which Mind has over so-called *m·*,
c 257– 4   If *m·*, so-called, is substance,
gl 586–17   between Spirit and so-called *m·*.
so-called law of
p 382–18   Must we not then consider the so-called law
of *m·* a
so-called laws of (*see also* **laws of**)
sp 81–25   despite the so-called laws of *m·*,
ph 171–25   The so-called laws of *m·* are nothing but
182–19   must supersede the so-called laws of *m·*.
183– 2   but the so-called laws of *m·* would render
f 207–12   nor are the so-called laws of *m·* primary,
b 273–16   The so-called laws of *m·* and of medical science
274–16   they supersede the so-called laws of *m·*.
302–24   not by the so-called laws of *m·*.
Soul and
f 215– 7   Soul and *m·* are at variance
Spirit and
(*see* **Spirit**)
Spirit or
b 324–11   understanding or belief, Spirit or *m·*.
o 360–17   Either Spirit or *m·* is your model.
standpoints of
sp 77–32   and they return to their old standpoints of *m·*.
striking the ribs of
o 360–20   striking the ribs of *m·*
supposed laws of (*see also* **laws of**)
p 382– 1   he annulled supposed laws of *m·*,
430–14   the supposed laws of *m·* and hygiene,
r 484–10   supposed laws of *m·* yield to the law of Mind.
sympathy with
a 21–25   Being in sympathy with *m·*, the worldly man is
termed
gl 584–23   the opposite of mind, termed *m·*,
594– 6   opposite of Spirit, or good, termed *m·*, or evil ;
terms
ap 573–11   what the human mind terms *m·*
testimony of
p 437–14   the testimony of *m·* respected ;
think of
o 350– 1   They think of *m·* as something
this
r 476– 9   will cease to claim . . . that this *m·* is man.

matter

through

sp 72–18   Spirit is not made manifest through *m·*,
ph 171–19   believes that Spirit is sifted through *m·*,
    173–13   Neither . . . is obtainable through *m·*.
f 232–12   theories . . . healing possible only through *m·*.
p 384–10   If man seems to incur the penalty through *m·*,
    408–19   thus reaching mortal mind through *m·*?
r 467–28   We cannot interpret Spirit, Mind, through *m·*.
g 532–30   demands that *mind* shall see . . . through *m·*,

to suppose that

sp 73–26   It is a grave mistake to suppose that *m·* is
f 208–14   it is absurd to suppose that *m·* can

tributary to

s 122–32   and mind therefore tributary to *m·*.

trusting

s 146– 8   By trusting *m·* to destroy its own discord,

veil of

a 41– 1   must be cast beyond the veil of *m·*

versus Mind

b 319– 3   disease as error, as *m·* *versus* Mind,

was shown

b 321–12   *M·* was shown to be a belief only.

we define

b 278–29   We define *m·* as error, because it is the

what is termed

s 114–29   Science shows that what is termed *m·* is but the
ph 173–11   What is termed *m·* manifests nothing but
    177–21   qualities and effects of what is termed *m·*,
f 210–25   What is termed *m·*, being unintelligent, cannot
p 384– 2   Can matter, or what is termed *m·*, either feel or
    417–11   what is termed *m·* cannot be sick ;
r 469– 2   What is termed *m·* is unknown to Spirit,

where is

f 223– 9   what and where is *m·*?

whole

b 340– 7   the conclusion of the whole *m·* : — *Eccl.* 12 : 13.
    340–10   Let us hear the conclusion of the whole *m·* :

will disappear

sp 97–27   indicates that all *m·* will disappear before the

without mind

s 153–17   for *m·* without mind is not painful.

would be identical

b 300–25   *m·* would be identical with God.

you employ

ph 181–11   for that reason, you employ *m·* rather than

pref viii–11   and *m·* is Spirit's opposite.
pr 14–11   governed by divine Love, — by Spirit, not by *m·*.
    14–14   neither in nor of *m·*,
a 27–15   The I — the Life, . . . is not in *m·*
    27–21   pantheism, — that God, or Life, is in or of *m·*.
    27–31   endeavored to hold him at the mercy of *m·*
    35– 8   sensuousness, or the burial of mind in *m·*,
    41– 3   this advance beyond *m·* must come
    47– 6   leaning no longer on *m·*, but on the
    52– 3   their master was *m·*.
m 62–21   must not attribute more . . . intelligence to *m·*,
    69–25   therefore *m·* is out of the question
sp 71–14   a formation of thought rather than of *m·*.
    73– 9   belief that . . . can control another man, as *m·*,
    75– 2   mistaken assumption that man dies as *m·*
    76–12   and was therefore never raised from *m·*.
    76–14   no longer commune with *m·* ; neither can he
    76–17   characterized by the divine Spirit . . . not *m·*.
    78–25   not in the medley where *m·* cares for me,
    80–25   which convulses its substratum, *m·*.
    80–32   belief . . . that *m·* is intelligent.
    81– 3   as there is to show the sick that *m·* suffers
    86– 5   it was not *m·*, but mortal mind, whose touch
    88–12   Thoughts, proceeding . . . from *m·*,
    89–25   *M·* is neither intelligent nor creative.
    90–10   the thought that there can be substance in *m·*,
    91–32   erroneous postulate is, that *m·* is intelligent,
    92– 3   erroneous postulate is, that *m·* holds
    92– 4   postulate . . . that *m·* is not only capable of
    94– 3   likeness of Himself, . . . not of *m·*.
    97–11   The more destructive *m·* becomes,
    97–12   until *m·* reaches its mortal zenith
    97–19   divine Spirit, supreme in its domain, dominates
           all *m·*,
an 103–20   false belief that mind is in *m·*,
    105–10   Can *m·* commit a crime?
    105–11   Can *m·* be punished?
s 108–26   false material sense, of mind in *m·* ;
    108–28   this same so-called mind names *m·*,
    119– 1   When we endow *m·* with vague
    119– 3   cannot really endow *m·* with what it
    119– 7   presuppose the . . . self-government of *m·*,
    119–12   and regard God as the creator of *m·*,
    120– 3   never understand this while we admit . . . mind
           in *m·*,
    120–26   deduced from supposed sensation in *m·*
    122–13   seats of pain and pleasure, from which *m·*
    124– 9   seeks to find life and intelligence in *m·*.

matter

s 125–31   *m·* will finally be proved nothing more than
    127–21   have — as *m·* — no intelligence, life, nor
    127–31   false hypotheses that *m·* is its own lawgiver,
    129–12   belief in the intelligence of *m·*,
    142–30   It could not have been *m·*,
    148–14   and place mind at the mercy of *m·*
    148–20   deal . . . with *m·*, calling that *man* which
    150–29   doctrine of the superiority of *m·* over Mind,
    157–14   the substratum . . . which we call *m·* ;
    157–23   *M·* is not self-creative,
    158–26   Drug-systems are quitting their hold on *m·*
    158–28   *M·* is going out of medicine ;
    159–13   as if *m·* were the only factor to be consulted
    159–24   medical schools would learn . . . of man from *m·*
159–26, 27   how much . . . health, *m·* is permitting to *m·*,
    161– 5   mortal mind, and not *m·*, burns it.
    161–31   looked as deeply . . . into mind and into *m·*.
    164–23   miscalled life in the body or in *m·*.
ph 166–29   conceded to be with *m·* by most
    170–32   *M·*, which . . . claims to be a creator,
    172– 8   grades the human species as rising from *m·*
    172–18   If the material body is man, he is a portion of *m·*,
    172–20   the belief that there is . . . Life in *m·*
    173–14   *M·* is Spirit's contrary,
    177–17   erroneous theory of . . . intelligence in *m·*,
    178–19   acting from the basis of sensation in *m·*,
    178–24   the belief of heredity, of mind in *m·*
    180–13   the ground that all causation is *m·*,
    181– 3   Before deciding that the body, *m·*, is
    181– 5   Can *m·* speak for itself,
    181– 6   *M·*, which can neither suffer nor enjoy,
    182–22   puts *m·* under the feet of Mind.
    187–22   governed by this so-called mind, not by *m·*.
    188–12   dream of pain and pleasure in *m·*,
    189–27   belief of inanimate, and then of animate *m·*.
    189–31   *m·* is the subjective condition of mortal mind.
    191– 2   *M·* is not the organ of infinite Mind.
    194– 2   Spirit shares not its strength with *m·*
    198– 3   than the substratum, *m·*.
    198–32   If *m·* were the cause of action,
f 203– 5   shows that *m·* can neither heal nor make sick,
    203–21   overtaxed the belief of life in *m·*
    203–23   believe that . . . Soul, escapes from *m·*
    204–30   belief that God lives in *m·* is pantheistic.
    204–31   The error, which says . . . Mind is in *m·*,
    205– 3   mortals . . . will lean on *m·* instead of Spirit,
    205– 8   error of believing that there is life in *m·*,
    205–10   *m·* has neither intelligence, life, nor
    205–31   into the scale, not of Spirit, . . . but of *m·*.
    206–17   Spirit, not *m·*, being the source of supply.
    208–16   and leaves the remedy to *m·*.
    209–28   hypothesis of . . . intelligence resident in *m·*,
    211– 8   sensations of a so-called mortal mind or of *m·*.
    211–24   If it is true . . . that *m·* has intelligence,
    212–14   in the mortal mind, not in *m·*
    214–11   The material senses, . . . originate in *m·*
    214–18   We bow down to *m·*, . . . like the pagan
    216–31   Give up your material belief of mind in *m·*,
    218–25   Resist the temptation to believe in *m·* as
    219– 9   No more can we say . . . that *m·* governs,
    222–14   so-called pleasures and pains of *m·*.
    222–29   for dyspepsia consult *m·* not at all,
    223– 1   belief that life and intelligence are in *m·*,
    229–31   The remedy is Truth, not *m·*,
    232–23   referred man's harmony to Mind, not to *m·*,
    234– 3   If we trust *m·*, we distrust Spirit.
    237–27   belief in the life and intelligence of *m·*,
    239–19   *m·* is then submitting to Spirit.
    240–13   suppose Mind to be governed by *m·*
    243–20   Neither immortal and unerring Mind nor *m·*,
    243–23   *m·* has neither intelligence nor sensation.
    244–19   or springs from *m·* into being,
    244–26   He does not pass from *m·* to Mind,
    248–24   outline and deformity of *m·* models.
    249–12   Mind is not the author of *m·*,
    249–17   Whence then is soulless *m·*?
    250– 3   suppose . . . mind to be in *m·* and *m·* to be a
c 257–10   governed by the body and a mind in *m·*.
    257–23   theory of mind in *m·* to be the antipode of
    261– 1   we find its opposite, *m·*.
    261–21   Detach sense from the body, or *m·*,
    262–12   efforts to find life and truth in *m·*
    262–20   the supposed pain and pleasure of *m·* cease
    262–31   Cause does not exist in *m·*,
    264–17   Life is Spirit, never in nor of *m·*,
    267– 3   start not from *m·* or ephemeral dust.
    267–23   borrowed from a higher source than *m·*,
b 268– 9   looking away from *m·* to Mind as the cause
    269–29   theories I combat are these : (1) that all is *m·* ;
    269–30   theories I combat . . . . (2) that *m·* originates in
    269–32   The first theory, that *m·* is everything,
    270– 3   statements . . . (1) that everything is *m·* ;
    275– 2   A partnership of mind with *m·* would ignore
    275– 5   *m·* is neither substantial, living, nor
    275–29   *m·*, disease, sin, and death,

matter

g	524–22	$M\cdot$ is not the reflection of Spirit,
	524–28	Could Spirit evolve its opposite, $m\cdot$,
	524–28	Could Spirit . . . give $m\cdot$ ability to sin and
	525– 1	Does Mind, God, enter $m\cdot$
	525– 3	the validity of $m\cdot$ is opposed,
	526– 7	statement that life issues from $m\cdot$, contradicts
	526–13	a belief in intelligent $m\cdot$.
	527– 1	God could not put Mind into $m\cdot$
	530–30	supposes . . . that $m\cdot$ precedes mind.
	530–31	*Second*, it supposes that mind enters $m\cdot$,
	531– 1	*Second*, it supposes that . . . $m\cdot$ becomes living,
	531–21	Who dares to say either that God is in $m\cdot$
	531–22	or that $m\cdot$ exists without God?
	531–26	Does Life begin with Mind or with $m\cdot$?
	531–27	Is Life sustained by $m\cdot$ or by Spirit?
	532–22	Is Mind in $m\cdot$?
	539– 6	as if life . . . were something which $m\cdot$ can
	539–10	such as evil, $m\cdot$, error, and death?
	539–15	Has Spirit resigned to $m\cdot$ the government of
	542– 1	belief of life in $m\cdot$ sins at every step.
	543–23	the creations of erroneous thought, not of $m\cdot$.
	543–26	When Spirit made all, did it leave aught for $m\cdot$
	544–10	$M\cdot$ cannot change the eternal fact that
	544–13	In Science, Mind neither produces $m\cdot$ nor
	544–14	nor does $m\cdot$ produce mind.
	544–29	It declares mind to be in and of $m\cdot$,
	544–31	It declares . . . that $m\cdot$ becomes spiritual.
	545–23	They believed in the existence of $m\cdot$,
	546– 2	belief that spirit is now submerged in $m\cdot$,
	546–11	while $m\cdot$ is governed by
	547–18	theory, — that Mind produces its opposite, $m\cdot$,
	547–18	theory, — that Mind . . . endues $m\cdot$ with
	550– 4	$M\cdot$ surely does not possess Mind.
	550– 9	Spirit cannot become $m\cdot$,
	551– 5	If Mind is first, it cannot produce . . . $m\cdot$.
	551– 5	If $m\cdot$ is first, it cannot produce Mind.
	551– 8	$m\cdot$ is not the progenitor of Mind.
	551–23	How can $m\cdot$ originate or transmit mind?
	551–28	All must be Mind, or else all must be $m\cdot$.
	552– 7	hypotheses deal with causation as contingent on $m\cdot$
	552–29	$m\cdot$ is a manifestation of mortal mind,
	554–15	another false claim, that of self-conscious $m\cdot$,
	554–27	mind in $m\cdot$ is the author of itself,
	555–19	error would seek to unite Spirit with $m\cdot$,
	556– 7	destroys forever all belief in intelligent $m\cdot$.
ap	561–27	and $m\cdot$ is put under her feet.
	563–13	by means of an evil mind in $m\cdot$
	564–22	that the false claim of mind in $m\cdot$
	567–20	claiming that there is intelligence in $m\cdot$
gl	579–17	a belief in intelligent $m\cdot$, finiteness,
	580–14	namely, $m\cdot$, sin, sickness, and death ;
	580–18	called self-creative $m\cdot$;
	580–25	results in $m\cdot$, and $m\cdot$ in mortal mind ;
	584– 9	DEATH. An illusion, the lie of life in $m\cdot$;
	584–21	saith : "I am life and intelligence in $m\cdot$.
	585– 7	To material sense, earth is $m\cdot$;
	585–25	belief concerning life, substance, and . . . in $m\cdot$;
	586–19	supposition that life, substance, . . . are in $m\cdot$;
	587–13	theories . . . sense, existing in brain, nerve, $m\cdot$;
	587–14	going in and out of $m\cdot$,
	591– 8	definition of
	591–12	mind originating in $m\cdot$; the opposite of Truth ;
	592– 1	the belief that sensation is in $m\cdot$,
	592– 3	belief that . . . are in and of $m\cdot$;
	593– 6	PURSE. Laying up treasures in $m\cdot$; error.
	595–19	opinions, knowledge, $m\cdot$; error ;
	596–14	reveals Spirit, not $m\cdot$, as the illuminator of all.

matter-physician

s	162– 1	the $m\cdot$ agrees with the disease,
p	423–15	The $m\cdot$ deals with matter

matter's

s	120–26	$m\cdot$ supposed consciousness of health or disease,
	158–26	letting in $m\cdot$ higher stratum,
ph	177–19	These names indicated $m\cdot$ properties,
c	257– 4	then Spirit, $m\cdot$ unlikeness, must be shadow ;
b	293–27	and point to $m\cdot$ opposite,
r	477–15	though interwoven with $m\cdot$ highest stratum,
	479–14	constitutes $m\cdot$ supposed selfhood,

matters

s	145–13	It $m\cdot$ not what material method

maturity

s	124–18	represented as subject to growth, $m\cdot$, and
ph	190–14	Human birth, growth, $m\cdot$, and decay
f	244–13	Man undergoing birth, $m\cdot$, and decay is like the
b	305–28	not subject to birth, growth, $m\cdot$, decay.
	310–31	neither growth, $m\cdot$, nor decay in Soul.
t	463–16	its growth sturdy, and its $m\cdot$ undecaying.
g	549– 5	after it has grown to $m\cdot$,
gl	583– 3	God's thoughts, not in embryo, but in $m\cdot$;

maximum

an	103–15	The $m\cdot$ of good is the infinite God

mazes

sp	82–17	through different $m\cdot$ of consciousness.

Mazzaroth

c	257–20	$M\cdot$ in his season," — *Job* 38 : 32.

Me

a	19–30	no other gods before $m\cdot$," — *Exod.* 20 : 3.
s	140– 6	no man see $M\cdot$, and live." — *Exod.* 33 : 20.
f	242– 5	"they shall all know $M\cdot$ [God], — *Jer.* 31 : 34.
b	280–19	no other gods before $m\cdot$!" — *Exod.* 20 : 3.
r	467– 4	no other gods before $m\cdot$." — *Exod.* 20 : 3.
	467– 4	This $m\cdot$ is Spirit.
g	541–28	crieth unto $M\cdot$ from the ground. — *Gen.* 4 : 10.

meagre

t	460–28	the $m\cdot$ channel afforded by language

meal

a	35–11	is the morning $m\cdot$ which Christian Scientists
sp	90– 4	and that, too, without $m\cdot$ or monad
s	107– *	*and hid in three measures of $m\cdot$,* — *Matt.* 13 : 33.
	118– 1	and hid in three measures of $m\cdot$, — *Matt.* 13 : 33.
	118–19	presented as three measures of $m\cdot$,
	118–25	as yeast changes the chemical properties of $m\cdot$
f	221– 6	partook of but one $m\cdot$ in twenty-four hours.
	221– 7	this $m\cdot$ consisting of only a thin slice of bread
p	431– 8	going to sleep immediately after a heavy $m\cdot$.
ap	559–29	the Israelites of old at the Paschal $m\cdot$

mean

pr	7–31	or $m\cdot$ to ask forgiveness at some later day.
	8–21	does not always $m\cdot$ a desire for it.
a	40–11	which I understand to $m\cdot$ God's method of
	40–29	has come so generally to $m\cdot$ public worship
s	134– 8	so has come always to $m\cdot$ one who
ph	168–32	By chemicalization I $m\cdot$ the process which
f	252–22	says : . . . I $m\cdot$ to make my short span of life
p	397– 7	those whom we $m\cdot$ to bless.
t	457–27	which they $m\cdot$ to complete with Mind,
r	488–13	they $m\cdot$ to enforce the necessity of

meaning

absolute

b	325–15	The absolute $m\cdot$ of the apostolic words

Christian

g	506–27	in the scientifically Christian $m\cdot$ of the text.

deific

r	482– 8	where the deific $m\cdot$ is required.

elucidates the

gl	579– 3	elucidates the $m\cdot$ of the inspired writer.

exact

r	482– 1	gives the exact $m\cdot$ in a majority of cases.

grasp the

o	349–20	in order to grasp the $m\cdot$ of this Science.

her

pref	x–28	who do not understand her $m\cdot$,

higher

b	313–14	Using this word in its higher $m\cdot$,
o	349–27	does not at once catch the higher $m\cdot$,
ap	576–31	the word gradually approaches a higher $m\cdot$.

literal

b	320– 8	both a spiritual and literal $m\cdot$.
g	537–29	The literal $m\cdot$ would imply that God

of God

c	261–22	you may learn the $m\cdot$ of God, or good,

of that passage

f	218–29	The $m\cdot$ of that passage is not perverted by

of that Scripture

o	359–25	she pondered the $m\cdot$ of that Scripture

of the Greek word

s	137–31	[the $m\cdot$ of the Greek word *petros*, or *stone*]

original

o	361–22	fuller expression of its original $m\cdot$.
gl	579– 7	which is also their original $m\cdot$.

profound

ap	575–17	description of the city . . . has a profound $m\cdot$.

scientific

g	534–25	spiritual, scientific $m\cdot$ of the Scriptures

simple

r	474–12	*marvel* is the simple $m\cdot$ of the Greek word

spiritual

(see **spiritual**)

their

a	53– 3	accusation was true, but not in their $m\cdot$.

whole

s	147–16	never believe that you can absorb the whole $m\cdot$ of

---

pr	16–14	does not affect the $m\cdot$ of the prayer itself.
a	39–19	$m\cdot$, not that now men must prepare for a
s	114– 3	$m\cdot$ by this term the flesh opposed to Spirit,
b	319–31	$m\cdot$ by that what the beloved disciple meant
r	482– 3	Human thought has adulterated the $m\cdot$
	488– 8	differ somewhat in $m\cdot$ from that

meanings

b	270–19	in His more infinite $m\cdot$,

means (noun)

any
p 438– 6 nothing shall by any *m·* hurt you. — *Luke* 10 : 19.
by no
a 25–23 by no *m·* relieved others from giving the
sp 91–14 The destruction of error is by no *m·* the
an 104–21 and by no *m·* the mental qualities which heal
f 246– 6 Man is by no *m·* a material germ
c 265–11 by no *m·* suggests man's absorption into
corporeal
t 443– 5 a resort to faith in corporeal *m·*
employ
f 218–21 and employ *m·* which lead only into
eternal
t 444–10 right use of temporary and eternal *m·*.
gracious
pr 1– 7 God's gracious *m·* for accomplishing
material
(*see* material)
mental
p 373–31 when by mental *m·* the circulation is changed,
other
m 67–24 potent beyond all other *m·* and methods.
s 156–26 but employing no other *m·*,
ph 169–22 however much we trust a drug or any other *m·*
t 457–32 without exploiting other *m·*.
r 483– 8 supersede all other *m·* in healing.
rational
m 63–24 A feasible as well as rational *m·* of improvement
some
p 369–15 in order to discover some *m·* of healing it.
source and
pr 10–24 the source and *m·* of all goodness
spiritual
ph 181–13 when you resort to any except spiritual *m·*.
unscientific
f 223–24 supplant unscientific *m·* and so-called laws.
world's
a 48–18 chose not the world's *m·* of defence.

pr 6–11 is the *m·* of destroying sin.
sp 96–32 wicked minds will endeavor to find *m·*
an 100– 6 as a *m·* of alleviating disease.
s 118–14 are *m·* of divine thought,
152–25 the *m·* by which mortals are divinely driven to a
ph 169–26 never . . . except by *m·* of the divine power.
f 212–24 this He does by *m·* of Mind,
221–20 never . . . that fasting should be a *m·* of health.
p 428–11 the great attainment by *m·* of which
ap 558–14 you can heal by its *m·*,
563–12 and that by *m·* of an evil mind in matter

means (verb)

pr 10– 1 Prayer *m·* that we desire to
a 22–21 Love *m·* that we shall be tried and purified.
23–32 Hebrew verb *to believe m·* also *to be firm*
sp 93–24 It *m·* quantity and quality,
s 116–28 If the term . . . *m·* infinite personality,
134– 4 word *martyr*, from the Greek, *m· witness* ;
ph 196–13 here the word *soul m·* a false sense
c 267– 7 and specifically man *m·* all men.
b 301– 6 what C. S. *m·* by the word *reflection*.
p 393–26 he certainly *m·* that light depends upon Mind,
r 466–22 Soul or Spirit *m·* only one Mind,
467– 5 Therefore the command *m·* this :
g 508–17 *Gender m·* simply *kind* or *sort*,
526–29 name Eden, according to Cruden, *m· pleasure*,
545– 7 condemnation of mortals to till the ground *m·*
ap 576–15 The word *temple* also *m· body*.

meant

a 43– 8 this understanding is what is *m·* by the
46–31 By this is *m·*, that by all they had witnessed
s 111–17 what this inverted image is *m·* to represent.
112– 9 By this is *m·* that they adopt
114–16 it is *m·* to designate that which has no
137–10 renewed inquiry *m·* : Who or what is it that
b 314–16 they thought that he *m·* their material
319–32 what the beloved disciple *m·* in one of his
333–32 By these sayings Jesus *m·*, not that the human
p 367–10 This is what is *m·* by seeking Truth,
t 463–26 if by these are *m·* laws of matter,
r 496–30 if by that term is *m·* doctrinal beliefs.

meanwhile

pref xii– 7 *M·* she was pastor of the first
f 214–24 *m·* would spread their table over
p 416–14 unless the belief . . . has *m·* been changed.
439–25 *m·* declaring Disease to be God's servant

measure

of the infinite
b 336–23 Allness is the *m·* of the infinite,
of the stature
g 519–20 unto the *m·* of the stature of the— *Eph.* 4 : 13.
same
pr 12–28 another who offers the same *m·* of prayer

measure

some
m 63–15 civilization mitigates it in some *m·*.
b 333–22 with some *m·* of power and grace
without
a 30– 8 endowed with . . . the divine Spirit, without *m·*.

pr 5–11 The *m·* ye mete
a 28–18 Not a . . . did the material world *m·* aright.
37– 3 "With what *m·* ye mete,— *Matt.* 7 : 2.
ph 165– 6 To *m·* intellectual capacity by the size of
190–12 which presently *m·* mind by the size of a
r 485–30 as much as . . . muscles *m·* strength.

measured

pr 5–12 "shall be *m·* to you again,"— *Luke* 6 : 38.
a 37– 4 shall be *m·* to you again."— *Matt.* 7 : 2.
47– 4 They no longer *m·* man by material sense.
s 142– 4 *m·* Christianity by its power over sickness,
f 246– 4 Life and its faculties are not *m·* by calendars
g 513–11 In the record, time is not yet *m·* by

measurement

f 246–10 *m·* of life by solar years robs youth
gl 598–19 YEAR. A solar *m·* of time ; mortality ;
599– 1 Eternity is God's *m·* of Soul-filled years.

measurements

gl 595–17 TIME. Mortal *m·* ; limits, in which

measures

s 107– * *and hid in three m· of meal,— Matt.* 13 : 33.
117–32 and hid in three *m·* of meal,— *Matt.* 13 : 33.
118–19 presented as three *m·* of meal,
gl 584– 6 *m·* time according to the good that is

measuring

ph 173–18 Physiology . . . *m·* human strength
f 246–20 the error of *m·* and limiting

meat

s 115– 9 as the mouth tasteth *m·*."— *Job* 34 : 3.
ph 165– * *Is not the life more than m·,— Matt.* 6 : 25.
p 362– 4 While they were at *m·*, an unusual incident
g 518– 8 to you it shall be for *m·*.— *Gen.* 1 : 29.
518–11 every green herb for *m·* : — *Gen.* 1 : 30.

Mecca

ph 166– 8 Mohammedan believes in a pilgrimage to *M·*

mechanics

an 105–21 as important to medicine as to *m·*

mechanism

ph 176–13 When the *m·* of the human mind gives place
p 399–16 If Mind is the only actor, how can *m·*

mediator

a 30–10 this enabled him to be the *m·*,
b 315–31 Jesus was the *m·* between Spirit and the flesh,
332–16 "There is one God, and one *m·*— *I Tim.* 2 : 5.

medical

attendants
pref x–18 abandoned as hopeless by regular *m·* attendants.
details
ph 196–23 forcible descriptions and *m·* details,
doctrines
s 163–29 the contrarieties of *m·* doctrines
effect
t 463–30 Such seeming *m·* effect or action is
faculty
an 100–12 French government ordered the *m·* faculty
o 348–10 It is a pity that the *m·* faculty and clergy
g 528–30 may be a useful hint to the *m·* faculty.
magazine
f 245– 4 the London *m·* magazine called The Lancet.
method
ph 179–12 Every *m·* method has its advocates.
mistake
ph 166–13 the doctor's . . . is a *m·* mistake.
p 383–31 another *m·* mistake, resulting from
practice
an 105–30 from ordinary *m·* practice to C. S.
s 112– 2 the most effective curative agent in *m·* practice.
156–12 in the ordinary theories of *m·* practice,
162–31 the famous Philadelphia teacher of *m·* practice.
p 424–12 In *m·* practice objections would be raised if
practitioners
s 164– 9 the cultured class of *m·* practitioners
purposes
pref xi–31 to get this institution chartered for *m·* purposes.
researches
s 152–21 The author's *m·* researches and experiments
results
s 155–18 sustains medicine and produces all *m·* results,
schools
s 159–23 *m·* schools would learn . . . of man from matter
f 217– 6 *M·* schools may inform us that the
t 444–22 If ecclesiastical sects or *m·* schools turn a deaf
science
b 273–16 The so-called laws of matter and of *m·* science
318–23 *M·* science treats disease as though

medical

study
t 443– 3   as to the . . .consistency of systematic *m·* study,
443– 8   While a course of *m·* study is

systems
ph 166–29   by most of the *m·* systems ;

testimony
p 370–23   According to both *m·* testimony and

theories
o 348– 3   *M·* theories virtually admit the
p 382–19   A patient thoroughly booked in *m·* theories

treatment
t 443–16   ordinary physical methods of *m·* treatment,

use
s 157–21   If He creates . . . and designs them for *m·* use,

works
ph 176– 4   modern Eves took up the study of *m·* works
179–24   so long as you read *m·* works

medication

p 398–26   belief in the healing effects of time and *m·*,
r 484– 7   Does C. S., or metaphysical healing, include *m·*,

Medicine

s 118–14   Science, Theology, and *M·* are
142–25   chapter sub-title

Medicine, Royal Academy of

an 101–20   adopted by the Royal Academy of *M·* in Paris.

medicine

claims of
a 44–12   all the claims of *m·*, surgery, and hygiene.

effects of
s 163–15   "The effects of *m·* on the human system are

equip the
s 155– 9   the doctor, and the nurse equip the *m·* with

first
s 142–28   Mind, not matter, must have been the first *m·*.

give up her
s 156–20   said that she would give up her *m·* for one day,

god of
s 158– 4   and designated Apollo as "the god of *m·*."

material
s 146–13   Material *m·* substitutes drugs for
158–12   The future history of material *m·*
f 226–15   scholastic theology, material *m·* and
p 404–30   neither material *m·* nor Mind can

mental
ph 185– 9   discussed "mental *m·*" and "mind-cure,"

Mind or
s 142–26   Which was first, Mind or *m·* ?

of Science
an 104–19   The *m·* of Science is divine Mind ;

potency of the
s 155–26   potency of the *m·* increases as the

practice of
s 161–12   law, restricting the practice of *m·*.

produced by
p 401–21   The only effect produced by *m·* is

profession of
s 158– 1   the profession of *m·* originated in idolatry

reform in
s 151–13   Even this one reform in *m·* would

religion and
m 67–30   Systems of religion and *m·* treat of
s 107–11   Through C. S., religion and *m·* are
t 444–15   towards differing forms of religion and *m·*,

same
p 370–17   but it uses the same *m·* in both cases.

statutes touching
s 161–19   state statutes touching *m·* remind one of

systems of
s 146– 5   are governed more or less by our systems of *m·*.
ph 185–13   as material as the prevailing systems of *m·*.
o 344–27   Why support the popular systems of *m·*,

an 105–20   as important to *m·* as to mechanics or
s 142–29   He made *m·* ; but that *m·* was Mind.
143–11   The divine Mind never called matter *m·*,
143–12   before it could be considered as *m·*.
143–13   human mind uses one error to *m·* another.
149–20   remarked . . . take as little *m·* as possible ;
154–27   says to her child : . . . "You need *m·*."
155–17   general belief, which sustains *m·*
156–16   she was unwilling to give up the *m·*
158–10   This was deemed progress in *m·* ;
158–29   Matter is going out of *m·* ;
ph 187– 9   it attributes to some material god or *m·* an
b 279–23   *m·* is more or less infected with the
p 398–17   sometimes not containing a particle of *m·*,
t 453–29   A Christian Scientist's *m·* is Mind,
460– 9   its *m·* is intellectual and spiritual,

medicines

p 382–29   wrote . . . treatises I had read and the *m·*

---

medium

of evil
sp 91–31   cannot be evil nor the *m·* of evil,

of hearing
f 214– 3   If the *m·* of hearing is wholly spiritual,

of matter
s 140–18   Worshipping through the *m·* of matter is

unaided
sp 89– 1   what the unaided *m·* is incapable of knowing

sp 72–27   nor the *m·* through which truth passes to earth.
s 136–18   some . . . believed that Jesus was a *m·*,
b 284– 3   or that matter is . . . the *m·* of Mind.
p 372–10   belief that matter is the *m·* of man,
r 486–28   If the five corporeal senses were the *m·*
489–20   at one time the *m·* for sinning
489–20   at another the *m·* for obeying
489–28   nor make it the *m·* of Mind.
g 524–21   How could the non-intelligent become the *m·* of

mediumship

sp 81– 6   their belief in *m·* would vanish.

medley

sp 78–24   God is not in the *m·* where

meek

a 33–25   preaches the gospel to the poor, the *m·* in heart.
49–14   The *m·* demonstrator of good,
54–19   would not accept his *m·* interpretation of life
b 272– 5   honest, unselfish, loving, and *m·*.
t 463–15   Its beginning will be *m·*, its growth sturdy,
g 516–14   *m·* shall inherit the earth."— *Psal.* 37 : 11.
533–29   as much as to say in *m·* penitence,
gl 597– 6   great Nazarene, as *m·* as he was mighty,

meekly

a 39– 1   *M·* our Master met the mockery of his
49–26   before whom he had *m·* walked,
o 343–30   Whoever is the first *m·* and conscientiously

meekness

pr 4– 4   in patience, *m·*, love, and good deeds.
a 30–32   In *m·* and might, he was found preaching
an 106–28   faith, *m·*, temperance :— *Gal.* 5 : 22, 23.
s 115–27   compassion, hope, faith, *m·*, temperance.
f 224–26   who cometh in the quiet of *m·*,
b 270–23   *M·* and charity have divine authority.
o 343–22   *m·* and spirituality are the conditions of
p 364–27   expressed by *m·* and human affection,
t 445–13   Teach the *m·* and might of life
gl 596–20   VALLEY.   Depression ; *m·* ; darkness.

meet

pr 9–13   we shall never *m·* this great duty simply by
m 57–15   Beauty, wealth, or fame is incompetent to *m·*
57–23   though it *m·* no return.
62– 6   the child can *m·* and master the belief
sp 90–16   In dreams we fly to Europe and *m·* a
s 122–11   clouds and ocean *m·* and mingle.
142–23   *m·* dwelling-places for the Most High.
ph 195–30   to *m·* a frivolous demand for amusement
f 223–15   Many are ready to *m·* this inquiry with the
c 257–25   to *m·* the demands of human want and woe,
b 268–10   hypotheses challenge metaphysics to *m·* in
327–23   Moral courage is requisite to *m·* the wrong
330– 6   would *m·* with immediate . . . acceptance.
p 378– 6   and *m·* every circumstance with truth.
390–29   *M·* the incipient stages of disease with
391–21   therefore *m·* the intimation with a protest.
404– 4   *m·* and destroy these errors with the truth
412– 5   to *m·* the peculiar or general symptoms
413– 6   to *m·* the simplest needs of the babe
419– 8   *m·* the cause mentally and courageously,
419–16   *M·* every adverse circumstance as its master.
420–25   they can *m·* disease fearlessly, if they only
422–15   As when an acid and alkali *m·* and
t 449–25   Certain minds *m·* only to separate
r 489–14   to *m·* its own demands.
494–10   and always will *m·* every human need.
ap 568– 8   fatal effects of trying to *m·* error with error.

meeting

a 34–32   joyful *m·* on the shore of the Galilean Sea !
35–10   This spiritual *m·* with our Lord
f 224–23   *m·* the needs of mortals in sickness and in health,
c 262– 5   shows the paramount necessity of *m·* them.
gl 586–24   love *m·* no response, but still remaining love.

meets

s 111–24   C. S. *m·* a yearning of the human race

melodies

f 213–25   Mental *m·* and strains of sweetest music

melody

f 219–23   We may hear a sweet *m·*, and yet

melt

f 205–18   or as they *m·* into such thinness that we
241–16   than can moonbeams to *m·* a river of ice.
b 299–29   sunshine of Truth, will *m·* away the shadow

melted

  sp 97–26   uttered His voice, the earth *m·*." — *Psal.* 46 : 6.

melting

  b 295–23   Then, like a cloud *m·* into thin vapor,
  ap 565–22   *m·* and purifying even the gold of . . . character.

melts

  p 442–21   belief *m·* into spiritual understanding,
  r 480–31   As vapor *m·* before the sun,

member

  c 261–15   as actively as the youngest *m·* of the company.
  o 351– 8   The author became a *m·* of the orthodox
  p 416– 1   as if it were a separate bodily *m·*.
  g 552–12   no *m·* of this dolorous and fatal triad.

memorials

  pref x– 1   may treasure the *m·* of a child's growth,
  a 34– 9   if . . . why need we *m·* of that friend?

memory

  a 33–32   who eat bread and drink wine in *m·* of Jesus
  sp 86–28   taken from pictorial thought and *m·*
  87– 3   even when they are lost to the *m·* of the
  87–29   *M·* may reproduce voices long ago silent.
  f 212– 9   Because the *m·* of pain is more vivid
  212–10   than the *m·* of pleasure.
  p 378– 3   reproduced in union by human *m·*.
  407–21   If delusion says, "I have lost my *m·*,"
  r 491–23   In sleep, *m·* and consciousness are

men

all

  a 40–26   all *m·* should follow the example of our Master
  46–26   that is, he marked the way for all *m·*.
  s 130– 4   When all *m·* are bidden to the feast,
  f 227–17   All *m·* should be free.
  c 267– 7   and specifically man means all *m·*.
  b 340–20   and that all *m·* shall have one Mind.
  r 467– 9   understood that all *m·* have one Mind,

always guided

  pr 7–19   If spiritual sense always guided *m·*,

among

  a 24–29   The truth had been lived among *m·* ;
  s 150–10   as a permanent dispensation among *m·* ;
  g 535–17   the heritage of the first born among *m·*

and women

  (*see* **women**)

are assured

  a 38– 1   Because *m·* are assured that this command

bade

  sp 79–18   Apostle Paul bade *m·* have the Mind that was

become seers

  sp 84– 8   When sufficiently advanced . . . *m·* become
           seers

beheld as

  gl 583– 8   some of the ideas of God beheld as *m·*,

best

  pref viii–15   confers the most health and makes the best *m·*.

boys and

  b 333– 6   in common with other Hebrew boys and *m·*,

business

  s 128– 7   From this it follows that business *m·* and

can be baptized

  a 20–10   He knew that *m·* can be baptized, . . . and yet

causes

  t 458–32   Christianity causes *m·* to turn naturally from

children and of

  p 413– 8   the temperature of children and of *m·*,

children of

  (*see* **children**)

delivered

  f 243– 5   which delivered *m·* from the boiling oil,

did not hinder

  a 28–19   Even his . . . purity did not hinder *m·* from

doctrines of

  s 131–24   the ceremonies and doctrines of *m·*,

drowning

  a 22– 8   This causes them, even as drowning *m·*, to

enlightenment of

  a 45– 8   Jesus' deed was for the enlightenment of *m·*

ever with

  ap 573–16   the divine Principle of harmony, is ever with *m·*,

Father of

  a 29–24   demonstrating God as the Father of *m·*.

fortunes of

  s 121– 8   the fate of empires and the fortunes of *m·*.

God and

  a 30–10   or *way-shower*, between God and *m·*.
  b 332–17   mediator between God and *m·*, — *I Tim.* 2 : 5.

good

  ph 189–14   should not make good *m·* suffer.

good-will toward

  s 150– 8   good-will toward *m·*." — *Luke* 2 : 14.
  f 226–17   good-will toward *m·*." — *Luke* 2 : 14.

great

  g 548–27   by the labors and genius of great *m·*.

he allowed

  a 51– 9   but he allowed *m·* to attempt the destruction of

men

heard of

  pr 2– 4   to enlighten the infinite or to be heard of *m·*?

hearts of

  s 131–25   until the hearts of *m·* are made ready for it.

light of

  g 501– *   *and the life was the light of m·.* — *John* 1 : 4.
  ap 561–29   which is *·*"the light of *m·*." — *John* 1 : 4.

men of

  s 148– 9   The former explains the men of *m·*,

morals of

  s 126–26   the health, longevity, and morals of *m·* ;

mortal

  ph 190– 2   afterwards mortal *m·* or mortals,

other

  pr 9– 1   "not as other *m·*"? — *Luke* 18 : 11.
  a 30– 2   more spiritual idea of life than other *m·*,
  r 473–13   Jesus . . . more than all other *m·*,

pitiful to lead

  s 158–18   It is pitiful to lead *m·* into temptation

rejected of

  a 20–16   "Despised and rejected of *m·*," — *Isa.* 53 : 3.
  52–13   "Despised and rejected of *m·*," — *Isa.* 53 : 3.

save

  s 136– 8   he used his divine power to save *m·*

showing

  pr 6–27   showing *m·* how to destroy sin,

status of

  s 118–21   dignified as the natural status of *m·* and things,

unifies

  b 340–23   One infinite God, good, unifies *m·* and nations ;

will teach

  s 139–12   reform in religious faith will teach *m·*

worst passions of

  a 24– 7   instigated sometimes by the worst passions of *m·*

would transfer

  sp 75– 8   Spiritualism would transfer *m·* from the

———

  pr 6– 3   *M·* may pardon, but this divine Principle
  13–27   hence *m·* recognize themselves as merely
  a 39–20   meaning, not that now *m·* must prepare for a
  42–24   Let *m·* think they had killed the body !
  sp 93–27   If man were Spirit, then *m·* would be spirits,
  s 136–12   "Whom do *m·* say that I, — *Matt.* 16 : 13.
  139– 6   Moses proved . . . by what *m·* called miracles ;
  ph 172– 4   and from monkeys into *m·*
  f 202– 6   If *m·* would bring to bear upon the study of
  220–26   belief that either . . . makes *m·* better
  b 285– 4   not alone hereafter in what *m·* call Paradise,
  289–12   Truth and Truth's idea, never make *m·* sick,
  308–32   "power with God and with *m·*." — *Gen.* 32 : 28.
  320–16   forever rule [or be humbled] in *m·*, seeing that
           they
  329–27   If *m·* understood their real spiritual source
  332–10   the divine message from God to *m·*
  o 354–24   Truth will waken *m.* spiritually to hear
  p 372–25   "Whosoever shall deny me before *m·*, — *Matt.*
           10 : 33.
  r 480–22   which seems to make *m·* capable of wrong-doing.
  g 539–23   "Do *m·* gather grapes of — *Matt.* 7 : 16.
  548–16   by which *m·* may entertain angels,
  550– 7   identity of animals as well as of *m·*.
  ap 567–21   either to benefit or to injure *m·*
  573–25   is, and has been, possible to *m·*
  gl 597– 5   if only he appeared unto *m·* to fast.

mend

  p 423– 2   and may not be able to *m·* the bone,

meningitis

  ph 175– 7   cerebro-spinal *m·*, hay-fever, and rose-cold

mental

action

  an 104–13   C. S. goes to the bottom of *m·* action,
  p 401–22   The only effect . . . is dependent upon *m·* action.
  404– 1   physician should be familiar with *m·* action

agencies

  ap 570– 5   certain active yet unseen *m·* agencies

anatomy

  t 462–32   Scientist, through understanding *m·* anatomy,

argument

  t 454–31   the letter and *m·* argument are only

assassin

  p 419–26   the *m·* assassin, who, in attempting to rule
  t 445– 4   attacks of the would-be *m·* assassin,

assassins

  s 164–19   or produced by *m·* assassins,
  t 447–11   save the victims of the *m·* assassins.

attempt

  g 517– 6   *m·* attempt to reduce Deity to corporeality.

call

  sp 86– 8   His quick apprehension of this *m·* call

case

  p 430–17   Suppose a *m·* case to be on trial,

causation

  p 423– 9   Scientist, . . . commences with *m·* causation,

mental

cause
s 157– 2 C. S. deals wholly with the *m* cause
ph 187–16 Anatomy allows the *m* cause of the latter
p 374–24 and ignorance of *m* cause and effect.
chemicalization
m 65–29 The *m* chemicalization, which has
ph 169– 4 occurred through *m* chemicalization,
p 401–18 *M* chemicalization brings . . . to the surface,
t 453– 8 *M* chemicalization follows the explanation of
concept
sp 87–24 Do not suppose that any *m* concept is gone
p 376–19 the so-called material body is a *m* concept
conception
p 403–30 *m* conception and development of disease
condition
ph 181–19 you must improve your *m* condition
p 397– 8 Suffering is no less a *m* condition than
conditions
s 153–29 we shall be more careful of our *m* conditions,
154– 3 Disease arises, like other *m* conditions,
159–11 Is it skilful . . . to take no heed of *m* conditions
conflict
b 288– 4 *m* conflict between the evidence of the
contagion
s 153–28 When this *m* contagion is understood,
crime
an 105–16 take cognizance of *m* crime
despotism
p 375–15 No person is benefited by . . . any *m* despotism
direction
s 160–23 never capable of acting contrary to *m* direction.
disturbance
p 421–12 treat . . . more for the *m* disturbance
effect
p 371– 5 Disquisitions on disease have a *m* effect
element
s 157– 5 whole force of the *m* element is employed
endowments
r 488–25 *m* endowments are not at the mercy of
endurance
p 387– 6 When we reach our limits of *m* endurance,
energy
p 394– 9 majority of doctors depress *m* energy,
environment
sp 87– 8 their *m* environment remains
fears
ph 199–20 latent *m* fears are subdued by him.
fermentation
sp 96–22 This *m* fermentation has begun,
healer
p 401–31 while the *m* healer confines himself chiefly
healing
pref x– 4 Various books on *m* healing
s 107– 6 divine Principle of scientific *m* healing.
t 455–31 the Science of *m* healing and teaching,
459–15 Committing the bare process of *m* healing to
height
f 237– 8 *m* height their little daughter . . . attained.
horizon
sp 98– 4 beholds in the *m* horizon the signs
idea
r 467–27 Spirit gives the true *m* idea.
illusion
p 403– 8 understood that the difficulty is a *m* illusion,
image
p 416– 4 unless the *m* image occasioning the pain
images
p 413–28 these actions convey *m* images to
impression
f 213–16 Sound is a *m* impression
infant
ph 194–24 Kaspar was still a *m* infant,
influence
p 397– 6 *m* influence on the wrong side,
inharmony
r 493–24 removes any other sense of moral or *m* inharmony.
jurisprudence
p 441–31 Our great Teacher of *m* jurisprudence
legislators
p 440–22 human *m* legislators compel them to
malpractice
p 442–30 *m* malpractice cannot harm you
t 451–26 All *m* malpractice arises from ignorance or
451–31 *m* malpractice tends to blast moral sense,
457–17 *m* malpractice, prolific of evil,
malpractitioner
p 419–25 Never fear the *m* malpractitioner,
manifestation
b 303– 2 The reflection, through *m* manifestation,
means
p 373–31 when by *m* means the circulation is changed,
medicine
ph 185– 8 discussed "*m* medicine" and "mind-cure,"

mental

melodies
f 213–24 *M* melodies and strains of sweetest music
method
sp 79– 7 A scientific *m* method is more sanitary than
79– 8 such a *m* method produces permanent
miasma
b 274– 2 Truth and Love antidote this *m* miasma,
microbes
s 164–15 all the *m* microbes of sin
might
p 428–19 We must realize the ability of *m* might
molecule
g 507–24 governs all, from the *m* molecule to infinity.
negation
p 392–12 should always be met with the *m* negation.
opposition
p 390–30 with as powerful *m* opposition as a
g 534–24 There will be greater *m* opposition
origin
p 374–18 is no argument against the *m* origin of
penury
p 366–10 while *m* penury chills his faith and
physical and
s 132–26 salvation from all error, physical and *m*,
148–14 Both . . . define man as both physical and *m*,
physician
p 368–32 Once let the *m* physician believe in the
picture
c 264– 6 when the *m* picture is spiritual and eternal.
plea
p 412–20 and array your *m* plea against the physical.
power
t 455–26 No person can misuse this *m* power, if
powers
an 105–22 Whoever uses his developed *m* powers
s 128– 9 C. S. enhances their endurance and *m* powers,
practice
ph 185–26 Erroneous *m* practice may seem
p 375–15 All unscientific *m* practice is erroneous
395–27 *M* practice, which holds disease as a
410–23 The Science of *m* practice is susceptible of no
410–25 If *m* practice is abused or is
t 447– 5 In *m* practice you must not forget that
process
p 416–24 The sick know nothing of the *m* process
protest
s 160–21 become cramped despite the *m* protest?
p 425–31 be always ready with the *m* protest
quackery
p 395–21 It is *m* quackery to make disease a reality
t 458– 1 *M* quackery rests on the same platform as
qualities
an 104–21 and by no means the *m* qualities which heal
quality
p 365–12 what *m* quality remains, with which to
realm
sp 82–22 the *m* realm in which we dwell.
g 514–11 the king of the *m* realm.
reconstruction
p 401–31 confines himself chiefly to *m* reconstruction
reservoir
ph 180–15 may . . . add more fear to the *m* reservoir
self-knowledge
t 462–20 Anatomy, . . . is *m* self-knowledge,
sign
f 233–19 how much more should ye discern the sign *m*,
signs
ph 169– 4 I have seen the *m* signs, assuring me
sin
g 557–23 as if he . . . fell into *m* sin ;
slavery
f 225–24 abolition of *m* slavery is a more difficult task.
state
(see state)
states
sp 82–25 The *m* states are so unlike,
s 149– 9 the different *m* states of the patient.
t 455– 5 Such *m* states indicate weakness
surgery
p 402– 6 records of the cure, . . . through *m* surgery
swaddling-clothes
c 255– 2 drop off their *m* swaddling-clothes,
symptoms
s 156–32 Homœopathy takes *m* symptoms largely into
trespasser
an 106–13 the *m* trespasser incurs the divine penalty
ways
ap 571– 2 hidden *m* ways of accomplishing iniquity.
work
f 238–27 People with *m* work before them

———

pr 12–32 In divine Science, where prayers are *m*,
sp 91–28 erroneous . . . that man is both *m* and
s 114–23 C. S. explains all cause and effect as *m*,

mental

s 156– 2 these qualities must be *m·*.
ph 169–10 disease has a *m·*, mortal origin,
169–19 origin of all disease as *m·*,
178–12 predisposing cause and the exciting cause are *m·*.
185– 7 No system of hygiene but C. S. is purely *m·*.
f 204– 6 is as conclusively *m·* as
217–10 unnatural *m·* and bodily conditions,
b 270–28 disease is *m·*, not material.
280– 8 and the product must be *m·*.
287– 6 Error supposes man to be both *m·* and material.
302–27 in the *m·*, not in any bodily or personal likeness
o 360– 5 those which are both *m·* and material.
p 375–18 adding to his patient's *m·* and moral power,
376–31 To fear . . . disease, is to paralyze *m·* and
377–26 The cause of all so-called disease is *m·*,
383– 1 The ailment was not bodily, but *m·*,
422–15 so *m·* and moral chemistry changes the
t 458– 7 from both a *m·* and a material standpoint.
g 508–14 Gender is *m·*, not material.
512–23 these are *m·*, both primarily and secondarily.
gl 586– 4 EYES. . . . not material but *m·*.
587–10 a belief that . . . are both *m·* and material ;
588–18 the belief that . . . are both *m·* and material.

mentality

sp 90–22 This shows what mortal *m·* and knowledge are.
an 105–11 Can you separate the *m·* from the body
ph 173–12 manifests nothing but a material *m·*.
185–30 a mortal consolidation of material *m·*
f 217–19 When *m·* gives rest to the body,
b 283–32 Are *m·*, immortality, consciousness,
292–27 material *m·*, misnamed *mind*,
p 375–14 yielding his *m·* to any mental despotism
g 513– 1 both this mortal *m·*, so-called, and its claim,

mentalizes

s 157–11 Homœopathy *m·* a drug with

mentally

m 62– 2 The fœtus must be kept *m·* pure
sp 86–31 Pictures are *m·* formed before the artist can
90–20 Opium and hashish eaters *m·* travel
96–29 will be apprehended *m·* instead of materially.
s 137–21 Christ, the spirit of God, . . . which heals *m·*.
153–20 Now administer *m·* to your patient a high
f 235– 5 than to be treated *m·* by one who does not obey
p 377– 1 *m·* convince him that matter cannot take cold,
391–29 *M·* contradict every complaint from the body,
392–13 must be expressed *m·*, and thought should be
401– 7 which you impart *m·*
404–32 unless it makes him better *m·*,
410–28 If . . . the power to heal *m·* will diminish,
411–22 induced by a false sense *m·* entertained,
412– 4 *M·* and silently plead the case
412–10 You may call the disease by name when you *m·*
412–20 Argue at first *m·*, not audibly, that the patient
412–23 *M·* insist that harmony is the fact,
418– 3 *m·* destroying all belief in material pleasure or
419– 9 meet the cause *m·* and courageously,
424–23 more difficult to make yourself heard *m·* while
425– 6 If the case to be *m·* treated is consumption,
t 447–15 when *m·* sustained by Truth,
453–24 You should treat sickness *m·* just as you would
461–29 you must *m·* unsee the disease ;
464–15 so violent that he could not treat himself *m·*,
464–19 he could handle his own case *m·*.
g 528–29 performed *m·* and without instruments ;

Mental Treatment Illustrated

p 410–22 chapter sub-title

mention

g 526–14 first *m·* of evil is in the legendary

merchandise

pr 12–25 they are the *m·* of human thought
s 130– 5 One has a farm, another has *m·*,

merciful

pr 10–31 Do you ask wisdom to be *m·*
r 497–27 and to be *m·*, just, and pure.

mercifully

o 344–13 would perhaps *m·* withhold their

merciless

o 352–21 declaring ghosts to be real, *m·*, and

mercury

t 449–11 Man's moral *m·*, rising or falling,

mercy
and justice
g 538– 7 Radiant with *m·* and justice,
at the
a 27–31 endeavored to hold him at the *m·* of matter
s 148–14 and place mind at the *m·* of matter
ph 165–10 to place this so-called mind at the *m·* of
f 250–31 not being at the *m·* of death,
b 317–17 his life is not at the *m·* of matter.
o 358– 4 If God is at the *m·* of matter,

mercy
at the
r 481–14 declaring existence to be at the *m·* of death,
488–25 not at the *m·* of organization and
cancels
a 22–30 *M·* cancels the debt only when
divine
b 329–26 The pardon of divine *m·* is the
g 542–13 jeopardize self-control, and mock divine *m·*.
goodness and
ap 578–16 Surely goodness and *m·* shall— *Psal.* 23 : 6.
handmaid of
a 36– 9 since justice is the handmaid of *m·*.
heavenly
p 435– 1 commended man's immortal Spirit to heavenly *m·*,
His
pr 6–20 according as His *m·* is sought or unsought,
left to the
s 126–20 left to the *m·* of speculative hypotheses?
on your soul
p 433–25 "May God have *m·* on your soul,"
recommended to
an 105–10 defies justice and is recommended to *m·*.
p 437–16 Soul a criminal though recommended to *m·* ;
shall have
t 448–19 whoso confesseth . . . shall have *m·*."— *Prov.* 28 : 13.
to mortals
a 18– 7 did life's work aright . . . in *m·* to mortals,

a 36–21 the immortal law of justice as well as of *m·*.
f 248–29 goodness, *m·*, justice, health,
r 465–15 justice, *m·*, wisdom, goodness, and

mere

pr 2–18 The *m·* habit of pleading with
11–12 *M·* legal pardon . . . leaves the offender free
12– 2 A *m·* request that God will heal
13–12 Can the *m·* public expression of our desires
14– 7 is to have, not *m·* emotional ecstasy
a 23–16 Faith, if it be *m·* belief, is as a pendulum
26–28 Our Master taught no *m·* theory, doctrine,
55–12 in a clearer light than *m·* words can possibly do,
sp 92–19 a *m·* offshoot of material sense.
an 102– 6 mesmerism, or hypnotism is a *m·* negation,
ph 195–24 the *m·* dogma, the speculative theory,
f 242–26 *M·* speculation or superstition
242–32 proof which he gave, instead of *m·* profession.
b 274–10 not *m·* inferences drawn from material
330– 2 understanding of being supersedes *m·* belief.
338–21 Here a *dam* is not a *m·* play upon words ;
o 341–11 In C. S. *m·* opinion is valueless.
355– 7 proofs are better than *m·* verbal arguments
p 363–32 there was encouragement in the *m·* fact that
460–19 If Christian healing is abused by *m·* smatterers
r 487–21 *M·* belief is blindness
g 556–20 In sleep, cause and effect are *m·* illusions.

merely

pr 5–26 and that man is made better *m·* by
9–20 even the surrender of all *m·* material sensation,
13–27 hence men recognize themselves as *m·* physical,
16– 3 highest prayer is not one of faith *m·* ;
40–27 and not *m·* worship his personality.
sp 92–30 when it is *m·* the absence of truth,
s 118– 4 far above the *m·* ecclesiastical
135–30 not *m·* in the *name* of Christ, or Truth,
152–17 This he did *m·* to ascertain the temperature of
f 203– 7 If God were understood instead of being *m·* believed,
230–24 These *m·* evade the question.
b 287–26 Matter is neither a thing nor a person, but *m·*
319–29 for instance, to name Love as *m·* an attribute
339–27 must be not *m·* believed, but
p 382–12 beware of making clean *m·* the outside
386–21 your suffering was *m·* the result of your belief.
t 447–22 A sinner is not reformed *m·* by assuring him
447–27 The sick are not healed *m·* by declaring

merges

ph 190–18 it never *m·* into immortal being,

merit

a 37–14 is *m·* seen and appreciated by lookers-on.
p 432–18 transgress the laws, and *m·* punishment,
t 449–23 according to personal *m·* or demerit,

merited

pr 9– 3 has been most grateful for *m·* rebuke.

merits

f 202–12 redeemed through the *m·* of Christ,
o 344–16 rules which disclose its *m·* or demerits,

Mesmer (see also Mesmer's)

an 100– 2 brought into notice by *M·* in Germany in 1775.

mesmeric

r 490–31 Under the *m·* illusion of belief, a man will

Mesmerism
 p 441–22 Health-laws, M·, Hypnotism,
mesmerism
 an 100– 1 M· or animal magnetism was first brought into
 102– 5 animal magnetism, m·, or hypnotism
 102–25 "M· is a problem not lending itself to
 104–18 occultism, necromancy, m·,
 b 322–16 foreshadowed the m· and hypnotism of to-day.
 p 402–22 The error, m· — or hypnotism,
 403– 3 between voluntary and involuntary m·
 403– 4 voluntary m· is induced consciously
 r 484– 7 hygiene, m·, hypnotism, theosophy,
 484–21 M· is mortal, material illusion.
 490–28 Sleep and m· explain the mythical nature of
mesmerist
 sp 87–18 to heal through Mind, but not as a m·.
Mesmer's
 an 100–13 to investigate M· theory
message
 a 27– 1 Jesus sent a m· to John the Baptist,
 b 308–19 when an angel, a m· from Truth and Love,
 332–10 the divine m· from God to men
 p 399–13 both the service and m· of this telegraphy.
 432–28 with a m· from the Board of Health
 439– 7 when a m· came from False Belief,
 ap 558– 9 This angel or m· which comes from God,
 574–10 This ministry of Truth, this m· from
 574–20 the very m·, or swift-winged thought,
messages
 sp 78–19 for the transmission of m·.
 p 432– 7 testifies : . . . I convey m· from my
 ap 566–30 assigns to the angels, God's divine m·,
 567–26 His angels, or m·, are cast out with their
messenger (see also **Eddy, Mrs. Mary Baker**)
 b 309– 2 the m· was not a corporeal being,
Messiah (see also **Messiah's**)
 s 116–15 They never crown the power of Mind as the M·,
 137–19 The M· is what thou hast declared,
 138– 5 lay behind Peter's confession of the true M·.
 b 288–29 The Christ-element in the M·
 309–16 until the M· should rename them.
 333–10 The name is synonymous with M·,
 333–24 caught glorious glimpses of the M·,
 o 360–32 The Jew believes that the M· or Christ
 p 364–22 spiritual purgation which came through the M·.
 r 482–21 He was inseparable from Christ, the M·,
 ap 562– 2 the spiritual idea as the M·,
 gl 594–16 Son. The Son of God, the M· or Christ.
Messiah's
 r 494– 6 to believe that so great a work as the M·
Messiahship
 sp 95–24 the Magi of old foretold the M· of Truth.
 s 131–30 established his claim to the M·.
Messianic
 a 27– 9 God is the power in the M· work.
 s 133– 1 questioned the signs of the M· appearing,
met
 a 39– 1 Meekly our Master m· the mockery of
 42–20 This error Jesus m· with divine Science
 44–10 He m· and mastered on the basis of C. S.,
 49–15 m· his earthly fate alone with God.
 sp 92–23 Until . . . the moral demand will not be m·,
 s 130– 1 the demands of God must be m·.
 ph 168–29 if the error . . . was m· and destroyed by truth.
 193– 3 On entering the house I m· his physician,
 f 231– 3 Unless an ill is rightly m· and fairly overcome
 b 308– 9 by the admission from the head, heart,
 o 355– 4 The charge . . . is m· by something practical,
 p 392–12 should always be m· with the mental negation.
 412–29 it needs to be m· mainly through the
 423– 1 The belief that he has m· his master
 427–10 must be m· and mastered by Science,
 r 483–25 this Science has m· with opposition ;
 494–10 Divine Love always has m·
 ap 564–16 he, . . . m· and conquered sin in every form.
metal
 m 66–32 that the precious m· may be graven with the
metaphor
 g 507– 1 In m·, the dry land illustrates the
 527–11 Here the m· represents God, Love, as
 529–23 enters into the m· only as evil.
 ap 571–22 Through trope and m·, the Revelator,
metaphoric
 ap 575–13 The description is m·.
metaphorical
 g 510–16 The sun is a m· representation of Soul
metaphorically
 a 38–15 is used m·, as in the text,
 g 511–26 Animals and mortals m· present the gradation

metaphors
 b 320– 4 M· abound in the Bible,
 p 389–16 the m· about the fount and stream,
metaphysical
 sp 99– 1 not physical but m·,
 s 111–30 I submitted my m· system of treating disease to
 113–15 not a foot to stand upon which is not purely m·.
 115– 4 inadequacy of material terms for m· statements,
 115– 5 difficulty of so expressing m· ideas
 144–17 is not the m· practice of C. S.
 ph 185– 3 My m· treatment changed the action of
 195–13 m· Science and its divine Principle.
 f 210–17 by one and the same m· process.
 219–25 Those who are healed through m· Science,
 b 268– 8 is slowly yielding to the idea of a m· basis,
 269–12 matter does not enter into m· premises or
 338–26 aside from their m· derivation,
 p 397– 1 By not perceiving vital m· points,
 416–26 m· method by which they can be healed.
 418–21 All m· logic is inspired by this simple rule
 424–15 It is equally important in m· practice
 t 456–22 efficaciously treated by the m· process.
 460– 5 and it underlies all m· practice.
 gl 579– 5 the m· interpretation of Bible terms,
 (see also **healing**)
metaphysically
 m 65–12 should be more m· regarded.
 s 118–18 are m· presented as three measures of meal,
metaphysician
 s 162– 1 but upon different terms than does the m· ;
 162– 2 while the m· agrees only with health
 p 366– 3 In order to cure his patient, the m· must
 423–18 The m·, making Mind his basis of
metaphysics
act against
 s 160– 3 The systems of physics act against m·,
categories of
 b 269–13 The categories of m· rest on
challenge
 b 268–10 Materialistic hypotheses challenge m·
Christian
 s 155–16 the high and mighty truths of Christian m·.
devoid of
 g 549–23 which rely upon physics and are devoid of m·.
divine
 (see **divine**)
fact in
 s 154– 9 This fact in m· is illustrated by the following
of Christian Science
 s 152–22 prepared her thought for the m· of C. S.
Principle of
 p 419–27 the divine Principle of m·,
resolves things
 b 269–14 M· resolves things into thoughts,
scientific
 b 268–15 no substantial aid to scientific m·,
 r 465– 6 to elucidate scientific m·.
understood
 s 159–15 Had these unscientific surgeons understood m·,
works on
 s 116–13 Works on m· leave the grand point untouched.

 an 105–20 "I see no reason why m· is not
 s 156–28 M·, as taught in C. S., is the
 156–29 In m·, matter disappears from the remedy
 ph 194–14 (as I learned in m·)
 b 269–11 M· is above physics,
 t 460–11 Yet this most fundamental part of m· is
 gl 585–18 m· taking the place of physics ;
metastasis
 p 420– 2 There is no m·, no stoppage
mete
 pr 5–11 measure ye m· "shall be measured — Luke 6 : 38.
 a 37– 3 "With what measure ye m·, — Matt. 7 : 2.
method
but one
 s 112– 5 There can, therefore, be but one m·
changed the
 g 531–23 Has man . . . changed the m· of his Maker?
divine
 f 240–29 The divine m· of paying sin's wages
 b 339– 1 destruction of sin is the divine m· of pardon.
 ap 568– 6 the divine m· of warfare in Science,
false
 p 380–11 This false m· is as though the defendant
God's
 a 40–11 God's m· of destroying sin.
 o 343– 6 Is not finite mind ignorant of God's m·?
her
 pref x–28 Only those quarrel with her m· who
ignorance of the
 t 456–17 betrays a gross ignorance of the m·

method

material
sp 78–18 it needs no material *m·* for the transmission of
s 145–13 It matters not what material *m·*
f 230–24 by drugs, hygiene, or any material *m·*.

medical
ph 179–12 Every medical *m·* has its advocates.

mental
sp 79– 7 A scientific mental *m·* is more sanitary than
79– 8 such a mental *m·* produces permanent

metaphysical
p 416–26 metaphysical *m·* by which they can be healed.

my
f 219– 3 My *m·* of treating fatigue applies to all

of demonstrating
t 456–11 *m·* of demonstrating C. S.

of divine Mind
g 551–14 it does not acknowledge the *m·* of divine Mind,

of madness
p 407–31 its *m·* of madness is in consonance with

of surgery
a 44–22 It was a *m·* of surgery beyond material art,

revealed a
a 44–26 revealed a *m·* infinitely above that of

same
sp 85–18 After the same *m·*, events of great moment
p 404–28 Both cures require the same *m·*

sanitary
pref x–25 than that of any other sanitary *m·*.

scientific
t 456– 6 divine Principle and rules of the scientific *m·*

successful
s 154–31 The better and more successful *m·*

that
ph 179–14 creates a demand for that *m·*,

this
s 112– 6 Those who depart from this *m·*
o 344–25 Why should one refuse to investigate this *m·*
359– 8 infidels whose only objection to this *m·* was,

true
ap 568–10 first the true *m·* of creation is set forth

---

s 113–27 metaphysics of C. S., like the *m·* in
ph 179–13 preference of mortal mind for a certain *m·*
r 493–11 The *m·* of C. S. Mind-healing is touched upon
g 553–23 appearance of its *m·* in finite forms

methods

changed their
a 35– 4 they changed their *m·*,

conclusions and
p 397– 5 in our conclusions and *m·*.

curative
s 152–29 skeptical as to material curative *m·*.

different
g 549–10 three different *m·* of reproduction

erroneous
ph 185–28 because erroneous *m·* act on and through

healing
t 445–15 there will be no desire for other healing *m·*.

ignorant of the
ph 178–28 Ignorant of the *m·* and the basis of

material
(*see* **material**)

materialistic
ph 183–26 Truth casts out all evils and materialistic *m·*

means and
m 67–24 potent beyond all other means and *m·*.

nature and
t 451–25 may perceive the nature and *m·* of error
ap 564– 4 with error's own nature and *m·*.

of Mind
f 212–25 all the *m·* of Mind are not understood,

other
s 145–16 has this advantage over other *m·*,
145–25 Other *m·* undertake to oppose error with error,
f 212–28 and possibly that other *m·* involve

pathological
pref xi– 6 explains that all other pathological *m·* are the

physical
t 443–16 ordinary physical *m·* of medical treatment,

present
an 102–21 So secret are the present *m·* of

sanitary
s 133–23 theories concerning God, man, sanitary *m·*,

scientific
f 217–15 That scientific *m·* are superior to others,
o 355– 4 in Christianly scientific *m·* of dealing with sin

studied
ph 174– 3 civilized practitioners by their more studied *m·*.

such
an 106–16 sanction only such *m·* as are demonstrable

these
ph 178–30 but none of these *m·* can be mingled with
o 355– 6 the proof of the utility of these *m·* ;

methods

unscientific
p 369–27 Unscientific *m·* are finding their dead level.

unspiritual
s 143–31 Inferior and unspiritual *m·* of healing

various
o 344–19 There are various *m·* of treating disease,

Methods of Study in Natural History
g 548–29 "*M· of S· in N· H·*,"

miasma
ph 176–17 Human fear of *m·* would load with disease
b 274– 2 Truth and Love antidote this mental *m·*,

Michael
ap 566–26 *M·* and his angels fought — *Rev.* 12 : 7.

Michael's
ap 566–30 *M·* characteristic is spiritual strength.

microbes
s 164–15 and all the mental *m·* of sin

microscope
c 264–21 Matter disappears under the *m·* of Spirit.
ap 561– 5 Agassiz, through his *m·*, saw the sun in an egg

microscopic
g 547– 9 Louis Agassiz, by his *m·* examination of

midnight
sp 95–22 *M·* foretells the dawn.
b 327–16 rushes forth to clamor with *m·* and tempest.
p 365– 6 preparing their helpers for the "*m·* call,"

midst
pr 7–30 and consoling ourselves in the *m·* of
s 122–20 in the *m·* of murky clouds
f 233– 8 In the *m·* of imperfection,
b 291– 2 that happiness can be genuine in the *m·* of
g 505– 5 firmament in the *m·* of the waters, — *Gen.* 1 : 6.
526– 1 in the *m·* of the garden, — *Gen.* 2 : 9.
529–19 in the *m·* of the garden, — *Gen.* 3 : 3.

might

all
b 310– 6 but all *m·* is divine Mind.
g 552– 6 assigns all *m·* and government to God,

and permanence
f 215– 2 and the *m·* and permanence of Truth.

and wisdom
gl 597–21 The *m·* and wisdom of God.

continuity, and
b 325–14 in all its perfection, continuity, and *m·*,

full
pref viii– 5 To develop the full *m·* of this Science,

great
b 329– 9 no right to question the great *m·* of divine

imparted by
g 514–19 accompanies all the *m·* imparted by Spirit.

light and
f 215–13 the light and *m·* of intelligence and Life.
t 446–26 the spiritual light and *m·* which heal the sick.

meekness and
a 30–32 In meekness and *m·*, he was found preaching
t 445–13 Teach the meekness and *m·* of

mental
p 428–20 We must realize the ability of mental *m·*

moral
s 124– 7 Having neither moral *m·*, spiritual basis, nor
t 455– 9 You must utilize the moral *m·* of Mind

no other
b 275– 8 there is no other *m·* nor Mind,

of divine Mind
s 128– 1 the *m·* of divine Mind.

of intelligence
f 215–13 the light and *m·* of intelligence and Life.
p 378–17 the *m·* of intelligence exercised over mortal

of Mind
s 146–14 even the *m·* of Mind
f 225–15 all history, illustrates the *m·* of Mind,
p 391–11 ruled out by the *m·* of Mind,
t 455– 9 You must utilize the moral *m·* of Mind

of omnipotence
gl 597–27 indicates the *m·* of omnipotence

of Truth
pref vii–27 the author's discovery of the *m·* of Truth

spiritual
ph 192–17 Moral and spiritual *m·* belong to Spirit,

---

ph 194– 1 the *m·* of omnipotent Spirit shares not its
b 317– 4 insisted on the *m·* of matter, the force of falsity,
p 367–32 Truth's opposite, has no *m·*.
g 518–20 Love giveth to the least spiritual idea *m·*,
520– 4 The depth, breadth, height, *m·*, majesty, and
544–14 No mortal mind has the *m·* or right or

mightier
f 207–15 nor is evil *m·* than good.
g 505–18 *m·* than the noise of many waters, — *Psal.* 93 : 4.

mightiest
   a 48–12 shall the humblest or *m·* disciple murmur

mightily
   s 155–20 *m·* outweigh the power of popular belief

mighty
   pref xi–14 these *m·* works are not supernatural,
   a 37–17 and to imitate his *m·* works?
      42– 3 rabbi affirmed God to be a *m·* potentate,
      49–10 Had they so soon lost sight of his *m·* works,
      50–17 its *m·* blessing for the human race.
      52–20 the *m·* actuality of all-inclusive God,
      53–14 Mortals believed in God as humanly *m·*,
   s 117–21 his *m·*, crowning, unparalleled, and
     133–30 or only a *m·* hero and king,
     155–16 high and *m·* truths of Christian metaphysics.
   f 201– * *reproach of all the m· people;* — *Psal.* 89 : 50.
     240– 4 winged winds, *m·* billows, verdant vales,
   o 357–27 Can Deity be almighty, if another *m·* and
   p 401– 1 in certain localities he did not many *m·* works
     407– 8 is conquered only by a *m·* struggle.
   g 505–19 yea, than the *m·* waves of the sea." — *Psal.* 93 : 4.
   ap 558– 3 And I saw another *m·* angel — *Rev.* 10 : 1.
     568–25 What shall we say of the *m·* conquest over
     577–22 *M·* potentates and dynasties will
   gl 597– 6 The great Nazarene, as meek as he was *m·*,

migratory
   f 244–25 not a beast, a vegetable, nor a *m·* mind.

mild
   an 102–16 *m·* forms of animal magnetism
   p 408–15 is in itself a *m·* species of insanity.

mildly
   g 530– 1 He begins his reign over man somewhat *m·*,

miles
   sp 87–31 which are thousands of *m·* away

militates
   ph 168– 8 Your belief *m·* against your health,

mill
   p 399–18 A *m·* at work or the action of a water-wheel

millenarianism
   s 111– 2 theosophy, spiritualism, or *m·*

millennial
   g 514–21 the *m·* estate pictured by Isaiah :

millennium
   a 34–17 they will bring in the *m·*.
   p 382– 7 this alone would usher in the *m·*.

million
   a 50–28 a *m·* times sharper than the thorns which

millions
   pr 10– 9 *m·* of vain repetitions will never
   p 379–30 the fever-picture, drawn by *m·* of mortals
   ap 570–14 *M·* of unprejudiced minds — simple seekers

millstones
   an 105–26 His sins will be *m·* about his neck,

Milton
   p 372– 5 likened by *M·* to "chaos and old night."

mimicry
   ph 192– 3 a mockery of intelligence, a *m·* of Mind.
   gl 580– 9 product of nothing as the *m·* of something ;

Mind (*see also* **Mind's**)
  actual
   p 387– 5 dares to say that actual *M·* can be overworked?
  aid of
   ph 182–24 forthwith shut out the aid of *M·*
  all is
   c 257– 2 If Mind is within and without…then all is *M·*,
   b 275–21 that all is *M·*, and that Mind is God,
   p 371– 2 when in fact all is *M·*.
     423– 9 understanding scientifically that all is *M·*,
   t 444–32 teacher must make clear . . . that all is *M·*,
   r 492–16 or that all is *M·*
     492–20 Science says : All is *M·* and Mind's idea.
     492–26 *God is Mind, and . . . hence all is M·*.
   g 509–29 the Science of creation, in which all is *M·*
  all-knowing
   pr 7 –25 It is the all-hearing and all-knowing *M·*,
   ph 187– 4 how ignorant must they be of the all-knowing *M·*
  alone possesses
   r 488–23 *M·* alone possesses all faculties,
  and body
   b 285–13 Spirit and matter, *M·* and body,
  and drugs
   s 143–32 to make *M·* and drugs coalesce,
  and immortality
   b 318– 3 nothing can efface *M·* and immortality,
   p 369–20 the advantages of *M·* and immortality
  and its formations
   f 245–32 *M·* and its formations can never be annihilated.
   p 402–10 when immortal *M·* and its formations will be

Mind
  and matter
   b 269– 3 the supposed coexistence of *M·* and matter
     270– 1 as reasonable as the second, that *M·* and matter
   g 555–22 as if man were the offspring of both *M·* and matter,
  antipode of
   c 257–24 mind in matter to be the antipode of *M·*.
  apparent only as
   g 505–11 the ideas of Spirit apparent only as *M·*,
  appeals to
   s 130– 2 is alarmed by constant appeals to *M·*.
  atmosphere of
   g 512–12 abound in the spiritual atmosphere of *M·*,
  aught besides
   ph 181–26 It is unnecessary to resort to aught besides *M·*
  aught but
   s 120–18 impossible for aught but *M·* to testify truly
  belief that
   b 292– 8 belief that *M·*, the only immortality of man,
  called God
   f 204–13 an intelligence or *M·* called God.
  can control
   p 378– 7 Disease is less than mind, and *M·* can control it.
  can have no
   b 284– 8 *M·* can have no starting-point,
  can impart
   p 371–28 *M·* can impart purity instead of impurity,
  causation is
   p 417–13 all causation is *M·*, acting through
  character of
   s 142–31 departs from the nature and character of *M·*,
  controlled by
   b 303– 4 controlled by *M·*, the Principle
  controlling
   m 63– 3 never . . . better . . . than the controlling *M·*,
  control of
   ph 169–16 If we understood the control of *M·* over body,
   p 380–10 against the control of *M·* over body,
     389– 4 it will be given in behalf of the control of *M·*
     394–11 admission that . . . is beyond the control of *M·*
  controls
   sp 79–28 asserting that *M·* controls body and brain.
   g 557– 6 *M·* controls the birth-throes in the
  created by
   g 531–31 record of man as created by *M·*
  creates
   c 257–12 *M·* creates His own likeness in ideas,
   b 280– 7 *M·* creates and multiplies them,
   g 507–24 Infinite *M·* creates and governs all,
  deific
   b 334–24 but undying in the deific *M·*.
  derived from
   s 143–27 except that which is derived from *M·*.
  divine
   (*see* **divine**)
  divine state of
   b 291–14 a divine state of *M·* in which
  effect of his
   sp 95– 1 effect of his *M·* was always to heal and to save,
  Ego is
   f 216–11 The understanding that the Ego is *M·*,
  Ego was
   b 315– 7 He knew that the Ego was *M·* instead of body
  elements of
   g 507– 3 while *water* symbolizes the elements of *M·*.
  empire of
   p 378–23 not an intelligence to dispute the empire of *M·*.
  energies of
   t 455–13 if, . . . you fail to use the energies of *M·*
  eternal
   s 127–14 the infinite, supreme, eternal *M·*.
   f 247–22 which dwells forever in the eternal *M·*
   b 270–13 this intelligence is the eternal *M·*
     274–28 governed by the unerring and eternal *M·*,
     277– 3 To all that is unlike unerring and eternal *M·*,
     282–12 Eternal *M·* and temporary material
     336–13 He has been forever in the eternal *M·*, God ;
   g 511–13 In the eternal *M·*, no night is there.
     519– 1 Nothing can be novel to eternal *M·*,
     528– 2 all being is the reflection of the eternal *M·*,
     552–31 when the perfect and eternal *M·* is understood.
   gl 588–10 unerring, immortal, and eternal *M·*.
     588–20 God ; incorporeal and eternal *M·* ;
     588–25 self-existent and eternal *M·* ;
  ever-present
   ph 180–26 the ever-present *M·* who understands all things,
  everything is
   b 270– 4 that everything is *M·*.
  evil is not
   f 207– 9 Indeed, evil is not *M·*.
  evolved from
   g 545–13 the theory of man as evolved from *M·*.
  facts of
   b 268–18 as well as on the facts of *M·*.

22

Mind

faculties of
f 215– 6 with all the faculties of *M·* ;

fetterless
sp 84–18 yea, to reach the range of fetterless *M·*.

forms of
b 303– 3 multitudinous forms of *M·* which people the
g 505–10 and they are forms of *M·*,
507–17 reproduces the multitudinous forms of *M·*

from material body to
b 284–31 but neither . . . goes from material body to *M·*.

from matter to
b 268– 9 looking away from matter to *M·*

functions of
r 478–23 Matter cannot perform the functions of *M·*.

give to
s 143–29 then give to *M·* the glory, honor, dominion,

glory of
f 209–14 enhances the glory of *M·*.

God is
f 239–30 Mind sends forth perfection, for God is *M·*.
b 311– 4 God is *M·* : all that Mind, God, is,
330–23 Mind is not both good and bad, for God is *M·* ;
r 492–25 *God is M·, and God is infinite ;*

God, or
o 347– 9 it must be the one God, or *M·*.
r 475–18 man is the reflection of God, or *M·*,

good is
s 113–17 God is good. Good is *M·*.

governed by
r 480–11 Consciousness, . . . is governed by *M·*,

governs man
g 222–12 availed himself of the fact that *M·* governs man,

governs the body
s 111–28 *M·* governs the body, not partially but wholly.
162–12 the fact that *M·* governs the body,

had made man
g 524–18 *M·* had made man, both male and female.

healing through
t 456–30 C. S., or the Science of healing through *M·*.

heals sickness
f 236–10 *M·* heals sickness as well as sin

heal through
sp 87–17 It enables one to heal through *M·*,
p 382–20 more difficult to heal through *M·* than one who

He is
g 532–24 God is All and He is *M·* and there is but one

ideas of
b 280– 7 All things beautiful and harmless are ideas of *M·*.

ignorance of
f 252– 4 Human ignorance of *M·* and of the

image in
s 115–17 IDEA : An image in *M·* ;

imagine that
f 203–19 We imagine that *M·* can be imprisoned in

immortal
sp 71–20 and that immortal *M·* is not in matter.
an 103–25 The truths of immortal *M·* sustain man,
s 145–10 between mortal minds and immortal *M·*.
145–11 immortal *M·* through Christ, Truth, subdues
ph 171–15 illustrated . . . the power of immortal *M·*
177– 9 both must be destroyed by immortal *M·*.
179– 7 Immortal *M·* heals what eye hath not seen ;
185–16 to match the divine Science of immortal *M·*,
188– 2 yields to God, immortal *M·*, and
190– 7 neither a mortal mind nor the immortal *M·*
195–10 whether it is mortal mind or immortal *M·*
200– 7 capacities of being bestowed by immortal *M·*.
f 208–11 It is the very antipode of immortal *M·*,
229–21 made void by the law of immortal *M·*,
246–24 Man, governed by immortal *M·*, is always
248– 8 Immortal *M·* feeds the body with
b 279– 8 never originated in the immortal *M·*,
282–26 Truth is the intelligence of immortal *M·*.
p 371– 4 yield to the mandate of immortal *M·*.
374–15 Through immortal *M·*, or Truth, we can
387– 8 when we realize that immortal *M·* is ever active,
399–15 matter can return no answer to immortal *M·*.
399–28 All that is real is included in this immortal *M·*,
402–10 when immortal *M·* and its formations will be
403–27 all that is unlike the immortal *M·*.
415– 2 Immortal *M·* is the only cause ;
419–21 from immortal *M·*, there is harmony ;
424– 5 Accidents are unknown to God, or immortal *M·*,
427–23 Immortal *M·*, governing all, must be
r 487–20 Truth, flowing from immortal *M·*.
488–30 since they exist in immortal *M·*, not in matter.
g 505– 1 Immortal *M·* makes its own record,
507–23 divine creation declares immortal *M·* and
ap 564–23 its own crime of defying immortal *M·*.
gl 580–25 supposition that . . . immortal *M·* results in
591–14 of which immortal *M·* takes no cognizance ;

impressions of
f 214–16 conveys the impressions of *M·* to man,

indicate
r 466– 5 The varied manifestations of C. S. indicate *M·*,

Mind

infinite
pr 2–24 Can we inform the infinite *M·*
3–20 we try to give information to this infinite *M·*.
s 116–30 infinite *M·* in a finite form is an
151– 4 Infinite *M·* could not possibly create a
ph 171–21 the spiritual,— yea, the image of infinite *M·*,
191– 3 Matter is not the organ of infinite *M·*.
f 206–28 infinite *M·* made all and includes all.
244–22 If. . .there is no full reflection of the infinite *M·*.
c 256–18 What is infinite *M·* or divine Love?
256–32 Infinite *M·* is the creator,
257–27 Infinite *M·* cannot be limited to a finite form,
257–31 an infinite form to contain infinite *M·*.
259– 4 infinite *M·*, the sum of all substance
266–26 Perfect and infinite *M·* enthroned is heaven.
b 284– 8 Infinite *M·* can have no starting-point,
284–13 Can infinite *M·* recognize matter?
310–10 God is His own infinite *M·*, and expresses all.
313–12 image of His person [infinite *M·*]."—*Heb.* 1 : 3.
336–10 even the infinite expression of infinite *M·*,
336–13 infinite *M·* can never be in man,
r 465–10 infinite *M·*, Spirit, Soul, Principle,
468–10 infinite *M·* and its infinite manifestation,
469–10 quality of infinite *M·*, of the triune Principle,
469–15 supposititious opposite of infinite *M·*
g 503– 2 which are embraced in the infinite *M·*
504–27 Did infinite *M·* create matter, and call it *light?*
507–24 Infinite *M·* creates and governs all,
510–19 the limitless idea of infinite *M·*.
544–12 Nothing is new to the infinite *M·*.
554–19 infinite *M·* sets at naught such a mistaken
gl 587–11 the belief that infinite *M·* is in finite forms ;

infinitude of
b 280– 1 In the infinitude of *M·*, matter must be unknown.

instead of
ph 180–13 that all causation is matter, instead of *M·*.
b 271– 8 to heal the sick through *M·* instead of matter.
315– 7 He knew that the Ego was *M·* instead of body
g 544– 6 *M·*, instead of matter, being the producer,

instead of to
p 415–13 resorting to matter instead of to *M·*.

instituted by
g 507– 2 the absolute formations instituted by *M·*,

inverted image of
b 301–28 inverted image of *M·* and substance

is All
s 109– 2 that *M·* is All and matter is naught
g 508– 2 only as the divine *M·* is All and reproduces all

is All-in-all
s 109– 4 reveals incontrovertibly that *M·* is All-in-all,

is first
g 551– 3 If *M·* is first, it cannot produce its opposite

is foremost
s 144– 3 If *M·* is foremost and superior, let us rely

is God
sp 91–31 nor the medium of evil, for *M·* is God.
b 275–21 that all is Mind, and that *M·* is God,
310–29 *M·* is God, and God is not seen by
r 469–13 *M·* is God. The exterminator of

is immortal
s 114–13 As *M·* is immortal, the phrase *mortal mind*
f 210–20 *M·* is immortal, and Truth pierces the error of
p 372– 2 Matter cannot be sick, and *M·* is immortal.
g 551–29 *M·* is immortal ; but error declares that the
gl 584–11 Matter has no life, . . . *M·* is immortal.
591–26 MORTAL MIND. Nothing . . . for *M·* is immortal ;

is infinite
sp 84–19 To understand that *M·* is infinite,
b 284– 1 not rational to say that *M·* is infinite, but dwells in

is Life
g 508– 7 *M·* is Life, Truth, and Love

is limitless
o 353–28 *M·* is limitless. It never was material.

is not in matter
sp 71–19 and that immortal *M·* is not in matter.
p 381–26 the understanding that *M·* is not in matter.

is not mortal
f 211– 9 Is it not provable that *M·* is not *mortal*

is not sick
p 393–29 *M·* is not sick and matter cannot be.

is one
s 114–10 *M·* is *one*, including noumenon and

is Spirit
b 310–30 *M·* is Spirit, which material sense cannot
g 517– 8 The life-giving quality of *M·* is Spirit,

is substance
p 414–24 C. S. declares that *M·* is substance,

is supreme
p 375–24 for *M·* is supreme,

is the I AM
b 336– 1 *M·* is the I AM, or infinity.

Mind

is the master
p 393– 8   *M·* is the master of the corporeal senses,
is the multiplier
g 508– 3   *M·* is the multiplier,
is the same
b 283– 6   *M·* is the same Life, Love, and wisdom
is the Soul
g 508– 6   *M·* is the Soul of all.
is the source
b 283– 4   *M·* is the source of all movement,
joyous in strength
g 514– 6   *M·*, joyous in strength, dwells in
law of
ph 168–23   in accordance with God's law, the law of *M·*.
b 307–30   in spiritual statutes, in the higher law of *M·*.
p 423–26   according to the law of *M·*, which ultimately
r 484–11   supposed laws of matter yield to the law of *M·*.
Life is
b 331– 5   Life is *M·*, the creator reflected
Life or
    (see Life)
light depends upon
p 393–26   he certainly means that light depends upon *M·*,
limitless
c 256–28   A limitless *M·* cannot proceed from
made the plant
g 509–23   *M·* made the "plant of the — Gen. 2: 5.
makes all
g 520–29   Because *M·* makes all, there is
man and
b 281–20   false conception as to man and *M·*.
mandate of
g 520–26   because growth is the eternal mandate of *M·*.
manifestation of
b 275–24   all is in reality the manifestation of *M·*.
manifestations of
b 291–15   all the manifestations of *M·* are harmonious
manifests all
c 258–15   *M·* manifests all that exists
mastered by
p 427–30   The dream of death must be mastered by *M·*
matter and
b 270– 5   Matter and *M·* are opposites.
270– 9   not two powers, matter and *M·*,
293– 6   which forms no link between matter and *M·*,
matter or
g 531–25   Which institutes Life, — matter or *M·*?
matter versus
b 319– 4   disease as error, as matter versus *M·*,
measures time
gl 584– 5   *M·* measures time according to the good
medicine nor
p 404–31   neither material medicine nor *M·* can
methods of
f 212–25   all the methods of *M·* are not understood,
might nor
b 275– 8   there is no other might nor *M·*,
might of
s 146–14   even the might of *M·* — to heal the body.
f 225–15   illustrates the might of *M·*, and shows
p 391–11   ruled out by the might of *M·*,
t 455– 9   You must utilize the moral might of *M·*
mimicry of
ph 192– 3   a mockery of intelligence, a mimicry of *M·*.
no matter in
s 113–30   no matter in *M·*, and no mind in matter ;
no nerve in
s 113–29   no nerve in *M·*, and no mind in nerve ;
no obstacle to
ph 179– 7   since space is no obstacle to *M·*.
no other
f 206– 1   we can have no other *M·* but His,
231–30   governed by his Maker, having no other *M·*,
r 469–19   if mortals claimed no other *M·*
not facts of
b 283–10   They are not facts of *M·*.
not matter
    (see matter)
obedient to
g 544– 4   ideas became productive, obedient to *M·*,
obedient to the
b 295– 7   they are obedient to the *M·* that makes them.
of man
r 470–17   God, the *M·* of man, never sins
omnipotent
ph 170– 1   reliance on God, omnipotent *M·*,
b 275– 3   would ignore omnipresent and omnipotent *M·*.
p 387–30   by his heavenly Father, omnipotent *M·*,
407–14   from the immortal and omnipotent *M·*,
t 443– 7   from entire confidence in omnipotent *M·*
r 496– 4   omnipotent *M·* is reflected by man and governs
gl 590– 3   unerring, eternal, and omnipotent *M·* ;
omnipresence of
sp 94–29   scientific basis, that of the omnipresence of *M·*.

Mind

one
sp 94–32   with the infinite capacities of the one *M·*.
ph 183–31   the one *M·* only is entitled to honor.
187– 2   believing in more than the one *M·*.
191– 5   delusion that there is more than one *M·*,
f 204–22   and realize only one God, one *M·* or intelligence
205–22   When we realize that there is one *M·*,
205–25   hinders man's normal drift towards the one *M·*,
213–32   belief in material origins which discard the one *M·*
216–12   The understanding . . . that there is but one *M·*
216–32   and have but one *M·*, even God ;
236–19   C. S., from which we learn of the one *M·*   .
249– 3   and so let us have one God, one *M·*,
c 267–24   serve as waymarks to the one *M·*,
b 276– 1   Having one God, one *M·*, unfolds the
281–14   The one Ego, the one *M·* or Spirit called God,
301–23   Thou shalt have one God, one *M·*.
314– 9   demonstrating the existence of but one *M·*
315– 6   He knew of but one *M·* and laid no claim to
330–23   there is in reality one *M·* only,
340–20   and that all men shall have one *M·*.
o 357–20   As there is in reality but one God, one *M·*,
p 399–27   The one *M·*, God, contains no mortal opinions
419–25   for there is but one *M·*,
424– 7   and unite with the one *M·*,
r 466–22   Soul or Spirit means only one *M·*,
467–10   all men have one *M·*, one God and Father,
469–18   There can be but one *M·*,
469–20   We can have but one *M·*, if that one is infinite.
470– 2   with one *M·* and that God, or good,
470–12   statement that there is one *M·*
470–16   The children of God have but one *M·*.
482–29   heals the sick on the basis of the one *M·*
496– 3   for there is but one *M·*, and this ever-present
496– 7   to have one *M·*, and to love another as
g 510–20   Science reveals only one *M·*,
512–22   From the infinite elements of the one *M·*
532–25   there is but one God, hence one *M·*
539–29   the one *M·* which makes and governs man
544–16   All is under the control of the one *M·*,
544–18   suggestion of more than the one *M·*, — is in the
gl 580– 6   a material belief, opposed to the one *M·*,
586– 9   FATHER.   Eternal Life ; the one *M·* ;
588–16   All the objects of God's creation reflect one *M·*,
588–17   whatever reflects not this one *M·*, is false
oneness of
f 205–30   Denial of the oneness of *M·*
or intelligence
f 204–22   and realize only one God, one *M·* or intelligence
216–12   there is but one *M·* or intelligence,
g 508–21   The *M·* or intelligence of production
or Life
b 291–26   No resurrection from the grave awaits *M·* or Life,
or medicine
s 142–26   Which was first, *M·* or medicine?
outcome of
g 555–15   error is neither mind nor the outcome of *M·*.
parent
b 336–31   God is the parent *M·*, and man is God's
g 507– 9   wanderers from the parent *M·*,
perfect
f 239–30   The perfect *M·* sends forth perfection,
247–16   models of spiritual sense, drawn by perfect *M·*
b 281–12   the image and likeness of perfect *M·*,
r 467–14   no other but the one perfect *M·*
point to
f 240– 5   all point to *M·*, the spiritual intelligence
pours light
t 446–12   through which *M·* pours light and healing
power of
    (see power)
produces
p 419–20   *M·* produces all action.
g 551– 3   Either *M·* produces, or it is produced.
properties of
s 124–21   cohesion, and attraction are properties of *M·*.
qualities of
c 265– 3   but of the highest qualities of *M·*.
quality of
g 517– 8   The life-giving quality of *M·* is Spirit,
rather than
ph 181–12   for that reason, you employ matter rather than *M·*.
f 226–24   belief that the body governed them, rather than *M·*.
real
sp 91–30   whereas the real *M·* cannot be evil
b 295–28   the exact opposite of real *M·*, or Spirit.
realities of
sp 78– 5   are not the eternal realities of *M·*.
realm of
c 264–10   in the unsearchable realm of *M·*?
g 514– 7   Mind, . . . dwells in the realm of *M·*.

Mind

recognize
b 284–12 Can matter recognize M·?
reflects
b 303–11 Whatever reflects M·, Life, Truth,
reflect the
g 507–20 reflect the M· which includes all.
regulates
p 413– 7 M· regulates the condition of the stomach,
rely upon
s 144– 3 let us rely upon M·, which needs no
remains
r 487–10 Lost they cannot be, while M· remains.
representation of
gl 591– 7 MAN. . . . the full representation of M·.
resorted to
ph 166–28 or he would have resorted to M· first.
restful
s 119–32 the humble servant of the restful M·,
rests on
s 157– 9 rests on M· alone as the curative Principle,
same
f 243–10 same "M· . . . which was also in — Phil. 2 : 5.
Science of
(see **Science**)
senses of
r 489– 4 the senses of M· are never lost
signifies God
f 229– 8 M· signifies God,— infinity, not finity.
solely from
g 543–28 thus it is seen that man springs solely from M·.
Soul, or
b 302–20 the Soul, or M·, of the spiritual man
spake
g 557–26 M·, spake and it was done.
Spirit or
b 331–24 except as infinite Spirit or M·.
subject to
p 429–13 Science declares that man is subject to M·.
subject to the
g 515– 8 are subject to the M· which forms them,
substance is in
c 267– 2 the spiritual idea, whose substance is in M·,
substance or
b 300–29 expresses the divine substance or M· ;
supposed limits to
o 353–26 So long as there are supposed limits to M·,
supremacy of
a 45–30 and so glorified the supremacy of M·
f 209–13 Science which reveals the supremacy of M·.
b 322– 2 cast out evils in proof of the supremacy of M·.
p 401–28 admits the efficacy and supremacy of M·,
sustained by
sp 90– 8 are sustained by M· alone.
symbol of
g 510–27 Light is a symbol of M·,
synonym of
r 468–22 Spirit, the synonym of M·, Soul, or God,
systems of
b 310–17 all things in the systems of M·.
the all
f 204–29 never . . . distinct from God, the all M·.
the only
f 251–23 to find the divine Mind to be the only M·,
b 276–17 If God is admitted to be the only M·
308– 5 God is the only M· governing man,
339–27 the great fact that God is the only M·;
r 469–14 great truth that God, good, is the only M·,
this
sp 84–12 thought which is in rapport with this M·,
s 124–30 are inherent in this M·,
151–27 in this M· the entire being is
ph 169–21 There can be no healing except by this M·.
187–24 man in Science is governed by this M·.
f 206–29 This M· does not make mistakes
216–32 this M· forms its own likeness.
c 257– 1 image or idea emanating from this M·.
b 276– 8 "Let this M· be in you,— Phil. 2 : 5.
277– 3 this M· saith, "Thou shalt surely — Gen. 2 : 17.
339–27 this M· must be not merely believed, but
r 483– 6 this M· must be divine, not human.
g 503–23 this M· creates no element nor symbol of discord
511– 1 This M· forms ideas, . . . subdivides and radiates
519–27 No exhaustion follows the action of this M·,
through (see also **healing through** and **heal through**)
a 54–16 triumph over death through M·, not matter.
sp 98– 8 Body cannot be saved except through M·.
s 126–24 I have demonstrated through M· the effects of
ph 170–15 and reach the body through M·.
f 205–12 God created all through M·,
217–18 When you have once conquered . . . through M·,
b 271– 8 to heal the sick through M· instead of matter.
280–30 perpetuates these qualities . . . through M·,
p 395–23 and then to attempt its cure through M·.
t 463–25 Our Master treated error through M·.
g 520–24 declaration that God creates all through M·,

Mind

transcends all other
r 483– 7 M· transcends all other power, and will
tributary to
s 119–31 and makes body tributary to M·.
truth is
b 293–20 while spiritual truth is M·.
Truth or
r 483– 6 which nothing but Truth or M· can heal,
understands
r 487–16 Matter cannot believe, and M· understands.
unerring
s 145–24 the laws of eternal and unerring M·.
f 243–20 Neither immortal and unerring M· nor
unfathomable
g 520– 3 Unfathomable M· is expressed.
unfolds
g 505–23 Spiritual understanding unfolds M·,
universe of
f 240–16 revolutions of the universe of M· go on
g 513– 7 in the teeming universe of M·
unlimited
b 284– 6 If. . . unlimited M· would seem to spring from
verity of
s 123–11 The verity of M· shows conclusively
waiting for the
pref ix–18 waiting for the M· of Christ.
was first
s 142–26 If M· was first and self-existent, then Mind,
143–27 If M· was first chronologically,
was the builder
b 314–14 knowing, as he did, that M· was the builder,
we begin with
r 467–30 we begin with M·, which must be understood
which saved
s 133– 8 In Egypt, it was M· which saved the Israelite,
would compress
b 280–11 limits all things, and would compress M·,
would lose
c 257–28 or M· would lose its infinite character

———

sp 79–18 bade men have the M· that was in the Christ.
89–18 M· is not necessarily dependent upon
92– 9 M· is not an entity within the cranium
s 115–14 GOD: Divine Principle, Life, . . . M·.
120–15 Health is not a condition of matter, but of M·
127–18 M·, exempt from all evil.
139– 5 triumph of Spirit, M·, over matter.
142–30 but that medicine was M·.
143–26 M· is the grand creator,
148– 4 the requisite power to heal was in M·.
148–25 Physiology exalts matter, dethrones M·,
149– 3 M· as far outweighs drugs in the cure of disease
150–30 doctrine of the superiority of matter over M·,
156–31 M· takes its rightful and supreme place.
157– 5 its one recognized Principle of healing is M·,
159–24 from matter instead of from M·.
160–30 Is man a material fungus without M·
ph 166– 3 M· is all that feels, acts, or impedes action.
166–30 when M· at last asserts its mastery
168– 7 on the side of matter, you take away from M·,
171–26 false beliefs . . . where M· is not.
180–11 deport themselves as if M· were non-existent,
181– 1 since M·, God, is the source and
182–22 puts matter under the feet of M·.
191– 2 It can take no cognizance of M·.
191–19 M· is not helpless.
191–30 M· has no affinity with matter,
191–32 M·, God, sends forth the aroma of Spirit,
199–10 great fact that M· alone enlarges and
f 203– 3 M·— omnipotence — has all-power,
204–31 The error, which says . . . M· is in matter,
209– 5 M·, supreme over all its formations
209–10 The world would collapse without M·,
217– 8 which prove M· to be scientifically distinct
217–23 as you understand the control which M· has
219– 4 M· should be, and is, supreme,
221–22 in which being is sustained by God, M·.
229– 1 If M· is not the master of sin, sickness,
232–22 He referred man's harmony to M·,
240–12 Change this statement, suppose M· to be
240–14 M· is perpetual motion.
244–26 He does not pass from matter to M·,
249–12 M· is not the author of matter,
250– 2 error when we . . . multiply M· into minds
251–31 Inharmonious beliefs, which rob M·,
253– 7 saith : . . . I am supreme and give all, for I am M·.
c 257– 2 If M· is within and without all things,
257–14 the Father M· is not the father of matter.
b 269–30 theories I combat . . . matter originates in M·,
269–31 M·, possessing intelligence and life.
279– 9 Matter is neither created by M· nor
279–10 nor for the manifestation and support of M·.
279–29 but one alone,— M·.
282–10 eternal individuality or M· ;

Mind

b 282–18   *M·* cannot pass into non-intelligence
282–30   which is neither *M·* nor man,
284– 3   or that matter is . . . the medium of *M·.*
285–19   finite conception of . . . body as the seat of *M·*
287–18   nor is error the offshoot of *M·.*
291–25   *M·* never becomes dust.
303–26   would be a nonentity, or *M·* unexpressed.
305–14   though he reflects the creation of *M·,*
307–21   If we regard . . . *M·* as both good and evil,
311– 4   What we term mortal mind . . . is not *M·.*
311– 5   all that *M·,* God, is, or hath made,
315– 9   matter, sin, and evil were not *M·* ;
319–20   man has no *M·* but God.
330–21   divine Principle is Love, and Love is *M·,*
330–22   *M·* is not both good and bad,
335–25   *M·* is the divine Principle, Love,
336– 2   *M·* never enters the finite.
336–12   coexistent and coeternal with that *M·.*
337–11   as perfect as the *M·* that forms him.
340–18   It inculcates the tri-unity of God, Spirit, *M·* ;
p 371–19   is father to the fact that *M·* can do it ;
377–18   mistaken belief . . . that *M·* is helpless
378–23   to dethrone *M·* and take the government
378–26   not a . . . power, which copes astutely with *M·* !
379– 6   The real jurisdiction of the world is in *M·,*
383– 4   a body rendered pure by *M·*
384– 1   on inert matter instead of on *M·.*
394– 9   in the direction which *M·* points out.
399–15   If *M·* is the only actor,
402–18   The life of man is *M·.*
407–22   No faculty of *M·* is lost.
413– 2   *M·,* does not produce pain in matter.
415– 3   *M·* in every case is the eternal God, good.
417–28   control which *M·* holds over the body.
420–22   *M·* is the natural stimulus of the body,
422–30   he believes that something stronger than *M·*
423–19   making *M·* his basis of operation
t 453–24   A Christian Scientist's medicine is *M·,*
457–27   which they mean to complete with *M·,*
457–28   as if the non-intelligent could aid *M·* !
r 467–16   having that *M·* which was also in Christ.
467–27   cannot interpret Spirit, *M·,* through
468–26   Life is divine Principle, *M·,* Soul,
469–12   *Question.* — What is *M·* ?
469–16   evil — is not *M·,* is not Truth, but error,
470–31   If man ever existed without this . . . *M·,*
472–16   Error is neither *M·* nor one of Mind's faculties.
480–18   thus attempting to separate *M·* from God.
483–16   she affixed . . . the name "substance" to *M·.*
485– 4   declares that *M·,* not matter, sees,
486–20   supposes *M·* unable to produce harmony !
489–28   nor make it the medium of *M·.*
493–17   *M·* must be found superior to all the
494– 3   I [*M·*] will raise it up ;" — *John* 2 : 19.
497–25   that *M·* to be in us which was also in Christ
g 513–18   as eternal as the *M·* conceiving them ;
524–11   How could . . . become the medium of *M·,*
525– 1   Does *M·,* God, enter matter
527– 1   God could not put *M·* into matter
531–26   Does Life begin with *M·* or with matter?
532–22   Is *M·* in matter?
532–22   Is *M·* capable of error as well as truth,
544–13   In Science, *M·* neither produces matter
546– 5   If *M·,* God, creates error, that error must
546–11   Has God no Science to declare *M·,*
547–18   theory, — that *M·* produces its opposite,
547–22   implies that . . . must either return to *M·* or
550– 4   Matter surely does not possess *M·.*
551– 6   If matter is first, it cannot produce *M·.*
551– 8   matter is not the progenitor of *M·.*
551–27   All must be *M·,* or else all must be matter.
ap 570–27   the great benefit which *M·* has wrought.
gl 583–20   CREATOR. Spirit ; *M·* ; intelligence ;
587– 7   Principle ; *M·* ; Soul ; Spirit ; Life ;
588–12   but one divine Principle, or *M·,*
591–16   definition of
594–19   SPIRIT. Divine substance ; *M·* ;
597–26   as applied to *M·* or to one of God's qualities.

mind (*see also* mind's)

absent
sp 82– 4   no more difficult to read the absent *m·* than

Æsculapius of
s 152– 6   to make this book the Æsculapius of *m·*

all thy
pr 9–18   all thy soul, and with all thy *m·*'" — *Matt.* 22 : 37.

and body
  (*see* **body**)

and matter
sp 80–31   the common conviction that *m·* and matter
b 281– 7   presupposes man to be both *m·* and matter.
294– 6   If man is both *m·* and matter,
p 397–23   can never treat mortal *m·* and matter separately,
r 466– 9   constituted of *m·* and matter,
492–22   The notion that *m·* and matter commingle

mind

and soul
g 531– 6   error, . . . that *m·* and soul are both right and

another
sp 89– 4   in the belief that another *m·* is speaking

attracting the
ph 169–12   fosters disease by attracting the *m·* to the

belief of
f 216–31   Give up your material belief of *m·* in matter,
p 372– 3   mortal belief of *m·* in matter.

belief that
  (*see* **belief**)

body and
ph 190– 6   producing mortals, both body and *m·* ;
f 250–14   Mortal body and *m·* are one,
b 302– 3   The material body and *m·* are temporal,

body or
f 209– 9   mortal body or *m·* is not the man.

brain is not
p 372– 1   Remember, brain is not *m·.*

burial of
a 35– 8   sensuousness, or the burial of *m·* in matter,

can never produce
b 304–13   matter can never produce *m·* nor

carnal
s 131–10   "The carnal *m·* is enmity against — *Rom.* 8 : 7.
b 311– 3   What we term mortal mind or carnal *m·,*
o 345–29   enrages the carnal *m·* and is the main cause of
p 395–12   overcomes faith in a carnal *m·,*
g 534–19   "The carnal *m·* is enmity against — *Rom.* 8 : 7.

child's
s 154–19   more than the child's *m·* governs itself,

clean
p 383– 3   We need a clean body and a clean *m·,*

corrupt
p 404– 9   A corrupt *m·* is manifested in a corrupt body.

cruel
b 290–30   learning that his cruel *m·* died not.

directing the
p 413–25   and constantly directing the *m·* to such signs,

disturbed
p 379–29   The images, held in this disturbed *m·,*
400–21   by addressing the disturbed *m·,*

doctor's
ph 197–30   The doctor's *m·* reaches that of his patient.

erring
ph 187–27   If you take away this erring *m·,*
188– 1   only as the mortal, erring *m·* yields to God,
f 211–22   The transfer of the thoughts of one erring *m·* to

evil
f 207– 8   God is not the creator of an evil *m·.*
g 533–18   the rib . . . has grown into an evil *m·,*
ap 563–13   belief . . . that by means of an evil *m·* in matter

evil is not
p 398–32   fact remains that evil is not *m·.*

existence or
a 42–19   belief that man has existence or *m·* separate

false claim of
ap 564–22   the false claim of *m·* in matter

feminine
m 57– 7   the feminine *m·* gains courage and strength

finite
c 257–22   Finite *m·* manifests all sorts of errors,
o 343– 6   Is not finite *m·* ignorant of God's method?
gl 580– 7   so-called finite *m·,* producing other minds,

fleshly
pref xi– 8   not of Spirit, but of the fleshly *m·*
f 222– 9   whereas Truth regenerates this fleshly *m·*

functions of
p 395–31   cannot kill a man nor affect the functions of *m·*

God's
g 525–15   after God's *m·* shaped He him ;

His
g 525–14   and God shaped man after His *m·* ;

his
f 221–12   and finally made up his *m·* to die,
b 290–32   His body is as material as his *m·,* and *vice versa.*
p 431–23   hypnotized the prisoner and took control of his *m·,*

his own
s 159–32   liable to increase disease with his own *m·,*

hold
gl 587–12   theories that hold *m·* to be a material sense,

human
  (*see* **human**)

less than
p 378– 7   Disease is less than *m·,* and Mind can control it.

life and
b 282– 4   material life and *m·,* are figured by
296– 8   must destroy all illusions regarding life and *m·,*
g 556– 5   and are supposed to possess life and *m·.*

life, or
sp 76– 9   belief that life, or *m·,* was ever in a finite form,
b 303–17   illusion that life, or *m·,* is formed by or is in

mind

limited
a 36–19 A selfish and limited *m·* may be unjust,
b 335–17 never included in a limited *m·*

mandate of
s 160–15 to convey the mandate of *m·* to muscle

march of
ap 570– 1 The march of *m·* and of honest investigation

masculine
m 57– 5 The masculine *m·* reaches a higher tone

material
c 257– 9 belief in a bodily soul and a material *m·*,
g 529–31 stands for a belief of material *m·*.

matter and
(*see* **matter**)

migratory
f 244–25 not a beast, a vegetable, nor a migratory *m·*.

misnamed
s 108–31 My discovery, that erring, mortal, misnamed *m·*
b 292–27 material mentality, misnamed *m·*,
p 399–25 This misnamed *m·* is not an entity.
r 477–16 matter's highest stratum, misnamed *m·*,

mortal
(*see* **mortal**)

mortal's
b 312–10 the departure of a mortal's *m·*,

must be clean
p 383–19 This shows that the *m·* must be clean

my
p 374– 7 the sick say : "How can my *m·* cause a

negative
s 143–25 not controlled scientifically by a negative *m·*.

no
s 113–30 no nerve in Mind, and no *m·* in nerve ;
113–30 no matter in Mind, and no *m·* in matter ;
b 278– 7 for matter has no *m·*.
g 530–27 The dream has no reality, no intelligence, no *m·* ;

no separate
r 475–19 that which has no separate *m·* from God ;

not matter
(*see* **matter**)

observe
p 419–17 Observe *m·* instead of body, lest aught unfit

of mortals
f 230–31 So-called mortal mind or the *m·* of mortals
231– 6 not destroyed in the *m·* of mortals,
p 423–31 They are only phenomena of the *m·* of mortals.

of the Lord
b 291–18 "the *m·* of the Lord," — *Rom.* 11 : 34.

one
b 276– 6 in which one *m·* is not at war with another,
p 388– 9 Idolaters, believing in more than one *m·*,
r 469–29 belief that there is more than one *m·*
470– 6 existence of more than one *m·* was the basic error
gl 584–21 which saith : . . . There is more than one *m·*,

opposite of
gl 584–23 the opposite of *m·*, termed matter,

or body
p 365–30 is not giving to *m·* or body the joy and strength
r 473– 1 all inharmony of mortal *m·* or body

our
g 525–13 Let us make man after our *m·*

parent's
p 424– 1 is formed first by the parent's *m·*,

popular
s 137–11 so mysterious to the popular *m·*

presently measure
ph 190–12 which presently measure *m·* by the size of a

quality of
b 279– 4 plainly describes faith, a quality of *m·*, as

rebel against
s 160–19 Can muscles, . . . and nerves rebel against *m·*

rights of
t 453–32 He does not trespass on the rights of *m·*

so-called
sp 71–13 the flower is a product of the so-called *m·*,
77–21 a so-called *m·* fettered to matter.
s 108–28 which this same so-called *m·* names *matter*,
122–13 reports to the so-called *m·* its status of
152– 1 But this so-called *m·* is a myth,
153–23 proof that this so-called *m·* makes its own pain
157–14 substratum of this so-called *m·*,
160–12 When this so-called *m·* quits the body,
ph 165– 9 and to place this so-called *m·* at the mercy of
177–11 This so-called *m·* builds its own
178–19 this so-called *m·*, from which comes all evil,
184–23 a law of this so-called *m·* has been disobeyed.
187–21 mortal body is governed by this so-called *m·*,
187–29 and this so-called *m·* then calls itself dead ;
194–20 education constitutes this so-called *m·*,
f 210–23 this so-called *m·* is self-destructive,
211–15 does not this so-called *m·* produce the effect
212–15 take away this so-called *m·* instead of
231– 7 but seem to this so-called *m·* to be immortal.
234–19 We must begin with this so-called *m·*
b 292–14 this so-called *m·* has no cognizance of Spirit.

mind

so-called
b 293– 9 This so-called *m·* and body is the
293–23 and this so-called *m·* is self-destroyed.
p 371– 3 this so-called *m·* must finally yield to
376–21 only what that so-called *m·* expresses.
377–21 governing fear of this lower so-called *m·*,
380–19 produced by a so-called *m·* ignorant of
399–12 so-called *m·* is both the service and message
400– 2 once destroyed in this so-called *m·*,
401– 4 If so-called *m·* is cherishing evil passions
403–26 so-called *m·* produces all that is unlike the
g 512–29 this so-called *m·* puts forth its own qualities,

spirit or
b 340–19 shall have no other spirit or *m·* but God,

state of
s 159–16 would have considered the woman's state of *m·*,
ph 188–15 to be wholly a state of *m·*.
p 374–21 Such a state of *m·* induces sickness.
375–28 This state of *m·* seems anomalous

states of
s 161– 6 Holy inspiration has created states of *m·* which
p 377–12 Through different states of *m·*, the body

student's
t 448–19 Try to leave on every student's *m·* the

substance, and
b 325–32 A false sense of life, substance, and *m·*
gl 580–12 origin, substance, and *m·* are found to be
582– 5 A physical belief as to life, substance, and *m·* .

substance, or
b 301–21 belief that man has any other substance, or *m·*,
o 354– 2 material life, substance, or *m·*

such a
p 383–16 It is the native element of such a *m·*,

supposed
b 281–18 The *m·* supposed to exist in matter
339–29 is to divest sin of any supposed *m·* or reality,

suppose error to be
f 250– 2 and suppose error to be *m·*,

supposes that
g 530–31 *Second*, it supposes that *m·* enters matter,

synonym of
g 517– 2 is used also as the synonym of *m·*.

theoretical
b 295–26 The theoretical *m·* is matter, named *brain*,

theory of
c 257–23 the material theory of *m·* in matter

this
pref x– 8 this *m·* is not a factor in the Principle of C. S.
ph 186– 1 by removing the influence on him of this *m·*,
p 400–24 We see in the body the images of this *m·*,
416–17 this *m·* is material in sensation, even as the

tongue and
sp 89– 7 believing that . . . possesses her tongue and *m·*,

united in a
b 287–28 testify to truth and error as united in a *m·*

unscrupulous
f 235–16 while the debased and unscrupulous *m·*,

wicked
gl 584–22 a wicked *m·*, self-made or created by a

without
s 153–17 matter without *m·* is not painful.
f 217–31 Without *m·*, could the muscles be tired?
p 384– 2 Can matter, . . . act without *m·*?
386– 7 but no such result occurs without *m·* to

your own
p 412– 7 be thoroughly persuaded in your own *m·*

---

m 68–28 no material growth from molecule to *m·*,
sp 71–17 which simulate *m·*, life, and intelligence.
80–19 It should not seem mysterious that *m·*,
87– 3 lost to the memory of the *m·* in which
88– 6 *m·* may even be cognizant of a present flavor
91–29 erroneous postulate is, that *m·* is both evil and
93–15 Good does not create a *m·* susceptible of
s 108–26 false material sense, of *m·* in matter ;
114– 1 Usage classes both evil and good together as *m·* ;
114– 7 unscientific definition of *m·* is based on the
114– 8 and calls *m·* both human and divine.
114–13 involves an improper use of the word *m·*.
120– 2 never . . . that soul is in body or *m·* in matter,
122–31 and *m·* therefore tributary to matter.
143–18 You admit that *m·* influences the body
148–14 Both . . . place *m·* at the mercy of matter
149–18 "We know that *m·* affects the body
149–21 remarked . . . but *m·* can never cure organic
151– 4 but this . . . they represent to be body, not *m·*.
152–11 action as produced by *m·* in one instance
153–13 rises above matter into *m·*.
154–32 more successful method . . . is to say : "Oh,
never *m·* !
161–31 looked as deeply for cause and effect into *m·*
ph 165– 8 to subjugate intelligence, to make *m·* mortal.
174–23 Anatomy admits that *m·* is somewhere in man
174–26 why . . . administer a dose of despair to the *m·* !
174–28 why . . . picture this disease to the *m·*,

mind

ph 178–24	the belief of heredity, of *m·* in matter or
188– 4	It is neither *m·* nor matter.
192– 2	belief that a pulpy substance . . . is *m·*
196–28	from the image brought before the *m·* ;
199– 6	nobody believes that *m·* is producing such a
199– 8	If *m·* does not move them, they are
f 204–14	It cannot therefore be *m·*,
204–28	can never be said that man has a *m·* of his own,
208–18	writes : "God is the father of *m·*,
211– 9	Nerves are not *m·*.
217–30	what is this *me ?* Is it muscle or *m·*?
250– 2	suppose . . . *m·* to be in matter
250–21	and the *m·* seems to be absent.
c 256–30	A *m·* originating from a finite or material
257–10	belief in . . . a *m·* in matter.
258– 9	more than a material form with a *m·* inside,
b 275– 2	partnership of *m·* with matter would ignore
277– 6	Matter never produces *m·*.
279–24	pantheistic belief that there is *m·* in matter ;
283–15	They speak of both Truth and error as *m·*,
293– 9	the more ethereal is called *m·*.
293–10	illusion called a mortal, a *m·* in matter.
302–10	The notion that *m·* is in matter,
307– 7	Evil still affirms itself to be *m·*, and declares
308– 2	dwelling in the belief . . . that evil is *m·*,
309–22	led to deny material sense, or *m·* in matter,
311–11	so long as the illusion of *m·* in matter remains.
311–15	false estimates of . . . *m·* as dwelling in matter,
330–27	Evil is nothing, no thing, *m·*, nor power.
o 345–11	It is sometimes said, . . . that the *m·* which
350–25	effects on the body as well as on the *m·*,
p 375–10	believes that matter, not *m·*, has helped him.
383–14	To the *m·* equally gross, dirt gives no
385–20	*M·* decides whether or not the flesh shall be
388–11	with matter, independently of *m·*.
393– 1	issues of pain or pleasure must come through *m·*,
396– 1	should never hold in *m·* the thought of disease,
401–22	If the *m·* were parted from the body,
408–25	less intimately connected with the *m·*
409– 6	animate error called nerves, brain, *m·*,
409–14	this so-called conscious *m·*,
413–26	that *m·* being laden with illusions about
414–10	impossibility that . . . can control or derange *m·*,
414–26	Keep in *m·* the verity of being,
416– 2	This process shows the pain to be in the *m·*,
429–13	affirms that *m·* is subordinate to the body,
t 449–22	The first impression, made on a *m·* which is
r 489– 1	The less *m·* there is manifested in matter
491–19	sometimes presenting no appearance of *m·*,
g 525–11	in the Icelandic, *m·*.
530–31	supposes . . . that matter precedes *m·*.
531–16	If, . . . *m·* was afterwards put into body
532–30	error demands that *m·* shall see and feel through
544–14	nor does matter produce *m·*.
544–29	It declares *m·* to be in and of matter,
551–24	How can matter originate or transmit *m·*?
554–27	*m·* in matter is the author of itself,
555–12	Error would have itself received as *m·*,
555–14	error is neither *m·* nor the outcome of Mind.
gl 584–18	neither corporeality nor *m·* ;
584–21	which saith : . . . for I am *m·*,
591–11	*m·* originating in matter ; the opposite of Truth ;

Mind-action
s 109–17	I knew the Principle of all harmonious *M·* to be

mind-cure
ph 185– 9	which discussed "mental medicine" and "*m·*,"
185–12	Such theories and such systems of so-called *m·*,

minded
sp 95– 6	"To be spiritually *m·* is life."— *Rom.* 8 : 6.

Mind-faculties
r 487– 9	in the perpetual exercise of the *M·*

mind-force
b 310– 5	Matter is made up of supposititious mortal *m·* ;

mind-forces
ph 186– 7	Erring human *m·* can work only evil

Mind-healing
Christian
sp 98–17	the demonstration of Christian *M·* stands a

Christian Science
pref xi–25	The first school of C. S. *M·*
r 493–11	The method of C. S. *M·* is touched upon in a

Principle of
t 454–15	He, who understands . . . the Principle of *M·*,

problem of
s 109–12	I sought the solution of this problem of *M·*,

Science of
(*see* **Science**)

scientific
o 342– 6	unqualified condemnations of scientific *M·*,

system of
t 460– 6	Our system of *M·* rests on the

Mind-healing
teaching
t 445–27	danger in teaching *M·* indiscriminately,
a 52–22	These were the two cardinal points of *M·*,

mind-ideals
o 360– 5	artist replies : . . . I have no *m·* except those

mindless
s 159–13	as if she were so much *m·* matter,
f 253–21	for matter is inert, *m·*.
r 484–17	Drugs and inert matter are unconscious, *m·*.
g 505–11	apparent only as Mind, never as *m·* matter

mindlessness
b 293– 4	the material *m·*, which forms no link

mind-offering
g 541– 3	more nearly resembles a *m·* than does Cain's

Mind-physician
t 443–17	*M·* should give up such cases,

mind-picture
o 360–13	which *m·* or externalized thought shall be real
t 453–28	and impresses more deeply the wrong *m·*.

Mind-power
f 209–14	immanent sense of *M·* enhances the glory of
t 446– 1	teaching his slight knowledge of *M·*,

mind-power
sp 80–21	it is *m·* which moves both table and hand.

mind-readers
sp 87– 1	*M·* perceive these pictures of thought.
87–27	*m·* can perceive and reproduce these impressions.

Mind-reading
sp 83–26	There is mortal mind-reading and immortal *M·*.
83–29	Mortal mind-reading and immortal *M·*
85– 1	This *M·* is the opposite of clairvoyance.
94–32	Jesus could injure no one by his *M·*.

mind-reading
sp 83–26	There is mortal *m·* and immortal Mind-reading.
83–29	Mortal *m·* and immortal Mind-reading
95–16	This kind of *m·* is not clairvoyance,

Mind-remedy
p 384–19	your *M·* is safe and sure.

Mind's
ph 171–12	*M·* control over the universe, including man,
177– 5	The evidence of divine *M·* healing power
182–18	*M·* government of the body must supersede the
182–26	ability to demonstrate *M·* sacred power.
p 389–11	better results of *M·* opposite evidence.
406–29	destroyed only by *M·* mastery of the body.
r 472–16	Error is neither Mind nor one of *M·* faculties.
492–20	Science says : All is Mind and *M·* idea.
g 508– 4	*M·* infinite idea, man and the universe, is the
509–25	the days and seasons of *M·* creation,
514– 7	*M·* infinite ideas run and
517–20	symbol of God as person is *M·* infinite ideal.

mind's
o 345–30	cause of the carnal *m·* antagonism.
p 402–14	with this *m·* own mortal materials.
429–16	mortal *m·* affirmation is not true.

minds
and bodies
s 110–26	the power of C. S. to heal mortal *m·* and bodies.
f 210–15	action of the divine Mind on human *m·* and bodies
p 408–13	effects of illusion on mortal *m·* and bodies.

better balanced
m 61–13	better balanced *m·*, and sounder constitutions.

carnal
b 315–14	Their carnal *m·* were at enmity with it.

certain
t 449–25	Certain *m·* meet only to separate

discernment of the
sp 82– 7	discernment of the *m·* of Homer and Virgil,

evil
b 307–10	It says : . . . God makes evil *m·*
gl 594–22	evil *m·* ; supposed intelligences, or gods ;

many
s 114– 8	evidence of the . . . senses, which makes *m·* many
b 280–21	the opposite error of many *m·*.

mortal
(*see* **mortal**)

of mortals
ph 175– 3	formulated in the *m·* of mortals.
p 386–13	action of Truth on the *m·* of mortals,

of students
t 453– 7	will be at strife in the *m·* of students, until

of your children
f 237–19	keep out of the *m·* of your children

other
b 323–27	delusion that there are other *m·*,
gl 580– 7	a so-called finite mind, producing other *m·*,

relieve our
p 384– 3	relieve our *m·* from the depressing thought

minds
ruling
f 205–24 a belief in many ruling *m·* hinders
supposititious
gl 587–14 supposititious *m·*, or souls, going in and out
unprejudiced
ap 570–14 Millions of unprejudiced *m·*
which surround
p 424–16 the *m·* which surround your patient should not
wicked
sp 96–31 wicked *m·* will endeavor to find means

f 237–11 often choke the good seed in the *m·* of
250– 2 error when we . . . multiply Mind into *m·*

Mind-science
sp 79–29 *M·* teaches that mortals
81– 5 this latter evidence is destroyed by *M·*.
84–22 is a step towards the *M·*
an 103–12 On the other hand, *M·* is wholly separate from
103–13 because *M·* is of God
s 109– 3 as the leading factor in *M·*.
115– 2 through which the understanding of *M·* comes,
p 376–27 Some people, mistaught as to *M·*,
421–30 perversion of *M·* is like asserting that

Mine
f 253– 3 saith : . . . all are *M·*, for I am God.

mine
sp 87–19 The *m·* knows naught of the emeralds

mineral
s 158– 9 from image-gods to vegetable and *m·* drugs
b 277–15 A *m·* is not produced by a vegetable
g 509–20 So-called *m·*, vegetable, and animal substances

minerals
f 209–16 compounded *m·* or aggregated substances
g 531–19 Who will say that *m·*, vegetables, and animals
543–21 *M·* and vegetables are found, . . . to be the
557– 8 Vegetables, *m·*, and many animals suffer no

mingle
sp 72–32 As readily can you *m·* fire and frost
s 122–18 clouds and ocean meet and *m·*.
144– 1 but the two will not *m·* scientifically.
ph 186–10 light and darkness, cannot *m·*.
f 239–29 Those two opposite sources never *m·* in fount or
b 276–26 beliefs and spiritual understanding never *m·*.
282–21 At no point can these opposites *m·* or unite.
295–18 The light and the glass never *m·*,
300–18 tares and wheat, which never really *m·*,
303–22 belief that . . . holiness and unholiness, *m·*

mingled
ph 178–31 none of these methods can be *m·* with

mingles
ph 191–29 in C. S., Truth never *m·* with error.

mingling
a 27–17 Life as never *m·* with sin and death.
m 58– 9 these constituents of thought, *m·*,
b 269– 4 the supposed . . . *m·* of good and e7il

minister
t 453–15 and *m·* to human needs.

ministering
o 360–26 putteth no trust in His *m·* — *see Job* 4 : 18.
p 440–18 for *m·* to the wants of his fellow-man
ap 567– 2 a sense of the ever-presence of *m·* Love.

ministry
f 236– 4 A special privilege is vested in the *m·*.
ap 574–10 *m·* of Truth, this message from divine Love,

minor
s 128–31 If both the major and the *m·* propositions of a
145–15 or reliance on some other *m·* curative.

minority
s 155–13 is but a belief held by a *m·*,
ph 178– 6 *m·* of opinions in the sick-chamber.

minus
s 164–13 *m·* the unction of divine Science.

minute
p 390– 1 The next *m·* she said, "My food is all digested,

minutely
ph 197– 5 A *m·* described disease costs many a man his

minutes
ph 193–13 In about ten *m·* he opened his eyes and said :
p 389–32 I cured her in a few *m·*.
416– 7 in twenty *m·* the sufferer is quietly asleep.
g 556–32 plunged . . . into the water for several *m·*,
557– 2 the child could remain under water twenty *m·*,

minutiæ
b 303– 8 The *m·* of lesser individualities reflect

miracle
great
ap 560–12 The great *m·*, to human sense, is divine Love,
mystery and
g 501–14 So-called mystery and *m·*, which subserve the
of grace
r 494–15 The *m·* of grace is no miracle to Love.
word rendered
r 474–12 word rendered *m·* in the New Testament

s 134–31 A *m·* fulfils God's law, but does not violate
135– 1 seems more mysterious than the *m·* itself
135– 6 The *m·* introduces no disorder, but unfolds
b 319–17 Mystery, *m·*, sin, and death will disappear
r 494–15 The miracle of grace is no *m·* to Love.
gl 591–21 definition of

miracles
attended the
s 133–13 *m·* attended the successes of the Hebrews ;
called
s 139– 7 Moses proved . . . by what men called *m·* ;
o 343–18 proving by what are wrongly called *m·*,
of grace
s 134–17 the doctrines of Christ or the *m·* of grace
so-called
s 123–25 the so-called *m·* of Jesus did not specially
131–27 explained the so-called *m·* of olden time
f 212–29 say . . . that other methods involve so-called *m·*.

sp 83–12 *M·* are impossible in Science,
s 117–20 Principle involved in the *m·* (marvels)

miraculous
s 128– 3 It is not *m·* to itself.
138–10 cures, which appeared *m·* to outsiders.
b 270–31 The life of Christ Jesus was not *m·*,

mirage
f 244– 3 but is illusion, the *m·* of error.
b 300– 5 The *m·*, which makes trees and cities seem to be

mire
an 106– 3 is to drop . . . into the very *m·* of iniquity,

mirror
ph 197– 2 descriptions which *m·* images of disease
f 220–20 like a kitten glancing into the *m·* at itself
b 301– 2 the *m·*, repeats the color, form, and
301– 4 the person in front of the *m·*.
305– 5 a face reflected in the *m·* is not the original,
g 515–29 Now compare man before the *m·* to his
515–29 Call the *m·* divine Science, and call man the
516– 3 As the reflection of yourself appears in the *m·*,
ap 571–24 *m·* in which mortals may see their own image.

mirrored
b 305– 9 As there is no corporeality in the *m·* form,
g 515–25 Your *m·* reflection is your own image

misapprehended
b 304–27 liable to be *m·* and lost in confusion.

misapprehension
pr 10–23 There is some *m·* of the source and means of
a 51– 3 the possible *m·* of the sublimest influence of
ph 11– 9 is found to be a *m·* of existence,
b 319–23 Hence the *m·* of the spiritual meaning
o 355–23 *m·* both of the divine Principle and practice of

miscalled
s 164–22 the materiality *m·* life in the body
ph 187–20 voluntary, as well as *m· involuntary*, action
192–11 a material belief, a blind *m·* force,
g 550–11 to investigate what is *m·* material life,

mischief
s 154–23 it is believed that exposure . . . wrought the *m·*.
162–32 "it is impossible to calculate the *m·* which
t 459–20 a false practitioner will work *m·*,

mischief-maker
t 460–20 abused . . . it becomes a tedious *m·*.

misconceived
b 281–19 *m·* sense and false conception as to man and

misconception
sp 86– 9 *m·* of it uncovered their materiality.
p 373–29 This is a *m·*.
g 542–29 *m·* of Life as something less than
554– 9 Any statement of life, following from a *m·*

misconceptions
sp 94–13 owe their false government to the *m·* of Deity
p 428–20 the ability of mental might to offset human *m·*
g 512–27 confers animal names and natures upon its own
m·.

misconstrued
a 45–24 after the resurrection . . . *m·* that event.
f 242–22 the facts of being are commonly *m·*,

mis-creator
c 263–15 He becomes a general *m·*,

misdeed
  p 439–12 a misguided participant in the m·
misdirected
  b 274–18 five physical senses are m·,
miserable
  ap 573–17 man was no longer regarded as a m· sinner,
misery
  s 122–14 its status of happiness or m·.
  ph 172– 2 constitutes his happiness or m·.
  b 327–12 way to escape the m· of sin is to cease sinning.
  ap 574–17 sum total of human m·, represented by
misfortune
  p 403– 9 in the second it is believed that the m· is a
misfortunes
  p 394–21 assuring him that all m· are
misguide
  f 206– 5 else it will m· the judgment and
  b 319– 7 would infringe upon spiritual law and m·
misguided
  f 220– 8 Instinct is better than m· reason,
  p 439–12 Materia Medica was a m· participant
misinterpretation
  b 319–25 the m· of the Word in some instances
  r 474–10 hence the m· and consequent maltreatment
misinterpreted
  sp 93–12 otherwise, we may be sure . . . that we have m·
  98– 9 Science of Christianity is m· by a material age,
  g 507–31 m·, the divine idea seems to fall to the level of
misinterprets
  f 240– 2 but human belief m· nature.
misleads
  b 275–27 It destroys the false evidence that m·
misled
  p 397– 5 By not . . . we are m· in our conclusions
misnamed
  s 108–30 erring, mortal, m· mind produces all the
  f 229–17 This customary belief is m· material law,
  b 284–24 Even the more subtile and m· material elements
  292–27 material mentality, m· mind,
  294–11 This mortal belief, m· man, is
  p 387–25 so-called mortal mind, m· matter,
  399–25 This m· mind is not an entity.
  r 477–15 matter's highest stratum, m· mind,
misplaced
  b 319–27 A m· word changes the sense
misrepresent
  o 343– 7 unfair to impugn and m· the facts,
  g 538–17 the false claims that m· God, good
misrepresentation
  o 341–18 m· and denunciation cannot overthrow it.
misrepresentations
  o 344–14 would perhaps mercifully withhold their m·,
misrepresented
  s 110–22 and its ideas may be temporarily abused and m·;
misrule
  s 119–15 maintaining perpetual m· in the form and
mission
  abuse of the
    t 455–22 renders any abuse of the m· an impossibility.
  curative
    a 55–11 that curative m·, which presents the Saviour
  earthly
    a 41–16 completed his earthly m·;
  fulfil one's
    r 483–31 One must fulfil one's m· without timidity
  higher
    s 150–16 to attest the reality of the higher m·
  his
    a 18– 5 His m· was both individual and collective.
    26–16 His m· was to reveal the Science of
    50–28 disbelieving the purpose of his m·,
    s 136– 1 established his church and maintained his m·
  his great
    ap 560–24 which made him equal to his great m·.
  Jesus'
    a 28– 3 they only hindered the success of Jesus' m·.
  of Christ
    r 474–30 The apostle says that the m· of Christ is
  of Christian Science
    s 150–10 but the m· of C. S. now, as in the time of
  of Jesus
    s 131–26 The m· of Jesus confirmed prophecy,
  our Master's
    f 233–23 To reveal this truth was our Master's m·
  reformatory
    s 129–28 in its reformatory m· among mortals.

missionaries
  b 328–17 Our m· carry the Bible to India,
misstated
  g 546–10 Is the divine Principle of creation m·?
misstates
  b 319–28 and m· the Science of the Scriptures,
mist
  b 299–27 as the m· obscures the sun or the mountain ;
  g 521–21 went up a m· from the earth, — Gen. 2 : 6.
  523– 3 the m· of obscurity evolved by error
  523– 8 The creations of matter arise from a m·
  546–12 went up a m· from the earth." — Gen. 2 : 6.
  557–16 When the m· of mortal mind evaporates,
  ap 576– 5 seems hidden in the m· of remoteness,
mistake
  correcting the
    p 386–20 Another despatch, correcting the m·,
  grave
    sp 73–26 It is a grave m· to suppose that matter is
  great
    f 216–19 The great m· of mortals is to suppose that
  his
    b 327–28 convince the mortal of his m· in
    p 403– 6 by his m· a man is often instructed.
  medical
    ph 166–14 the doctor's . . . is a medical m·.
    p 383–31 another medical m· resulting from the
  only a
    sp 92–26 should blush to call that real which is only a m·.
  same
    s 122–29 Our theories make the same m· regarding
  terrible
    b 289–11 To suppose that . . . is a terrible m·.
  this
    ph 179–31 may erelong reap the effect of this m·.
  through
    ph 177–25 If a dose of poison is swallowed through m·,

  a 28–27 to m· the very nature of religion.
  sp 70–11 The supposition that . . . is a m·.
    92–29 The m· of thinking that error can be real,
  ph 166–17 To ignore God as of little use in sickness is a m·.
    183– 5 To suppose that . . . is a m· ;
    197–22 but that is a m·.
  f 249–21 What a m· is that !
  o 343–28 Hence the m· which allows words, rather than
  t 455–20 but God cannot m·.
  r 474– 9 To the ignorant age . . . Science seems to be a m·,
  g 549– 6 shown by divine metaphysics to be a m·,
mistaken
  sp 75– 1 This simple truth lays bare the m· assumption
  f 229–18 individual who upholds it is m· in theory
  p 377–27 a mortal fear, a m· belief or
  t 451–30 either with a m· or a wicked purpose
    455–19 may be m· in judgment and demonstration,
  g 554–19 infinite Mind sets at naught such a m· belief.
mistakenly
  p 386–16 despatch, m· announcing the death of a friend,
mistakes
  does not make
    f 206–29 This Mind does not make m·
  fatal
    m 59–31 fatal m· are undermining its foundations.
  grave
    b 291– 5 these are grave m·.
  manifest
    s 139–17 the manifest m· in the ancient versions ;
  sins or
    pr 11–13 never pardons our sins or m· till they are
  such
    b 294–31 The Science of Mind corrects such m·,
  unconscious
    s 161–29 Such unconscious m· would not occur, if

  s 124– 8 this belief m· effect for cause
    139–22 But m· could neither wholly obscure the
  p 408– 7 universal insanity . . . which m· fable for fact
  g 549–27 even this great observer m· nature,
mistaking
  sp 84– 5 not by . . . m· fact for fiction,
  ph 171–17 M· his origin and nature, man believes
mistaught
  p 376–27 Some people, m· as to Mind-science,
mistiness
  gl 586– 1 EVENING. M· of mortal thought ;
mistrust
  m 68–10 The presence of m·, where confidence is due,
mists
  f 205–17 glimpses of God only as the m· disperse,

misunderstand
  pr 6–21 is to *m·* Love and to make prayer the
  f 219–23 and yet *m·* the science that governs it.
  219–26 may *m·* it, and impute their recovery to
  231–22 To fear sin is to *m·* the power of Love
  ap 560–28 To *m·* Paul, was to be ignorant of the

misunderstood
  a 53–10 divine Principle and practice of Jesus were *m·*.
  r 474–13 will be *m·* and misused by many, until

misuse
  an 106– 1 the criminal *m·* of human will-power,
  p 410–24 The Science . . . is susceptible of no *m·*.
  t 455–26 No person can *m·* this mental power, if

misused
  r 474–13 will be misunderstood and *m·* by many, until

mitigates
  m 63–15 civilization *m·* it in some measure.

mitre
  ap 571–31 He takes away *m·* and sceptre.

mix
  ph 182–16 antagonistic to Science and cannot *m·* with it.

mixture
  f 204–16 supposed *m·* of the first and second

Moabitish
  g 524– 2 in the *M·* god Chemosh,

moaning
  s 154–29 *m·* more childishly than her child,

mock
  b 329–22 You cannot *m·* it by human will.
  g 542–12 jeopardize self-control, and *m·* divine mercy.

mocked
  a 43–16 had *m·* and tried to slay.
  49–28 *m·* him on the cross, saying derisively,

mockery
  a 36–28 and *m·* of our motives
  39– 1 Meekly our Master met the *m·* of
  50– 5 The last supreme moment of *m·*, desertion,
  ph 192– 2 a *m·* of intelligence, a mimicry of Mind.
  192–25 It is a *m·* of strength, which erelong

mocking
  a 53–23 *m·* the lifelong sacrifice which goodness makes
  f 241–12 what a *m·* spectacle is sin !
  g 528–21 simulates the work of Truth, *m·* Love

model
his
  f 248–12 turns from the marble to his *m·*
imperfect
  f 248–20 Do you not hear . . . of the imperfect *m·*?
  c 260– 4 outlines from an imperfect *m·*,
mortal
  f 248–17 Have you accepted the mortal *m·*?
perfect
  c 260–11 the immortal and perfect *m·* of God's creation
  p 407–24 Let the perfect *m·* be present in your thoughts
true
  p 409–26 and seek the true *m·*.
your
  o 360–17 Either Spirit or matter is your *m·*.

  f 236–15 either after a *m·* odious to herself
  248–15 What is the *m·* before mortal mind?

models
  f 235–20 Physicians, . . . should be *m·* of virtue.
  247–16 Immortal men and women are *m·* of
  248–24 angular outline and deformity of matter *m·*.
  248–27 We must form perfect *m·* in thought
  249– 2 give up imperfect *m·* and illusive ideals ;
  249– 4 producing His own *m·* of excellence.
  c 260–20 in order to improve their *m·*.
  o 360–18 If you try to have two *m·*, then you

modern
  s 126–26 nothing in ancient or in *m·* systems on which to
  142– 6 *m·* religions generally omit all but one of
  ph 176– 3 *m·* Eves took up the study of medical works
  f 224–17 The *m·* lash is less material than the
  b 319–17 so many ancient and *m·* mythologies.
  g 548–27 *M·* discoveries have brought to light
  552– 6 Heathen philosophy, *m·* geology,

moderns
  p 411–14 a disease which *m·* would call *dementia*.

modes
  s 118–19 that is, three *m·* of mortal thought.
  118–22 *m·* of material motion are honored
  ph 170– 3 *M·* of matter form neither a moral nor a
  170– 6 exercise of faith in material *m·*,
  p 373–10 Under all *m·* of pathological treatment,
  406– 7 in place of *m·* and forms,

modest
  g 516–15 The *m·* arbutus sends her sweet

modifying
  sp 93–25 The *m·* derivatives of the word *spirit*

modus
  f 212–17 Mortals have a *m·* of their own,
  213– 1 would reverse the immortal *m·* and action,

modus operandi
  g 529– 2 there came a suggestion of change in the *m· o·*,

Mohammedan
  ph 166– 8 *M·* believes in a pilgrimage to Mecca

Mohammedan's
  ph 166–12 The *M·* belief is a religious delusion ;

molar
  f 247– 7 incisors, cuspids, bicuspids, and one *m·*.

mole
  sp 82–26 as impossible as it would be between a *m·* and a

molecule
  m 68–28 no material growth from *m·* to mind,
  g 507–25 from the mental *m·* to infinity.

mollusca
  g 556– 3 Vertebrata, articulata, *m·*, and radiata are

Moloch
  g 524– 3 in the *M·* of the Amorites,

moment
any
  f 252–27 says : . . . may at any *m·* annihilate my peace,
  o 352–19 for at any *m·* they may become
at that
  b 290–24 The sin and error . . . do not cease at that *m·*,
at the
  b 290–17 would be won at the *m·* of dissolution,
during that
  b 306–10 during that *m·* there would be no
for a
  a 50–19 If his full recognition of eternal Life had for a *m·*
  b 306– 9 If God, who is Life, were parted for a *m·* from
  309–30 Life is never for a *m·* extinct.
great
  sp 85–18 events of great *m·* were foretold by the
last
  a 36–25 gloat over their offences to the last *m·*
one
  gl 598–23 One *m·* of divine consciousness,
possible
  sp 75–25 There is one possible *m·*, when those
single
  pr 14–12 Become conscious for a single *m·* that
supreme
  a 50– 5 The last supreme *m·* of mockery,
  p 428– 7 Man's privilege at this supreme *m·* is to prove
when the link
  sp 75–28 *m·* when the link between their opposite beliefs

  sp 75–27 the *m·* previous to the transition,
  r 470–24 If there ever was a *m·* when man
  470–26 then there was a *m·* when man did not

momentary
  pr 7– 8 gives *m·* solemnity and elevation to thought.

momentous
  a 48–25 in the presence of his own *m·* question,
  g 516–27 To emphasize this *m·* thought,

moments
  pr 7–19 there would grow out of ecstatic *m·*
  ph 184–29 I sat silently by her side a few *m·*.
  193–10 In a few *m·* his face changed ;
  f 218–30 applying it literally to *m·* of fatigue,

momentum
  p 380–26 evidence will gather *m·* and clearness,

monad
  sp 90– 4 and that, too, without meal or *m·*

monarch
  s 152– 2 It would wield the sceptre of a *m·*,

money
  t 445–32 for the petty consideration of *m·*,

monkeys
  ph 172– 4 Theorizing . . . from mushrooms to *m·*
  172– 4 and from *m·* into men

monopoly
  s 141–18 no dynasty, no ecclesiastical *m·*.

monotheist
  o 361– 7 The Jew . . . is a *m·* ;
  361–10 The Christian . . . is a *m·*.

monstrous
  g 550–28 Amalgamation is deemed *m·*

month
  a 32–29 ate with his disciples in the *m·* Nisan

monthly
  pref xii–10 Christian Scientist Association, convening *m·* ;

months

ph	168–25	*m·* before the so-called disease made its
	193– 1	confined to his bed six *m·* with hip-disease.
f	212–12	a finger which had been cut off for *m·*.
	237– 7	It might have been *m·* or years before

monuments

s	150– 1	*m·* to the virtue and power of Truth,

mood

p	420–15	when they are in a fit *m·* to receive it,
ap	570– 6	shocked into another extreme mortal *m·*,

moon

g	547–13	the gathering clouds, the *m·* and stars,
ap	560– 7	and the *m·* under her feet, — *Rev. 12 : 1.*
	562– 7	The *m·* is under her feet.

moonbeams

f	241–16	than can *m·* to melt a river of ice.

moon-god

an	103– 5	Sin was the Assyrian *m·*.

moral

pr	11– 6	this may be no *m·* benefit to the criminal,
	11– 8	The *m·* law, which has the right to acquit or
a	22– 5	Vibrating . . . our *m·* progress will be slow.
	36–15	the great *m·* distance between Christianity and
m	56– 7	Marriage is the legal and *m·* provision for
	56–13	subject to such *m·* regulations as will
	58–12	There is *m·* freedom in Soul.
	59–28	so long as its *m·* obligations are kept intact ;
	62– 5	habits of obedience to the *m·* and spiritual law,
sp	92–23	the *m·* demand will not be met,
	95–12	Whoever reaches this point of *m·* culture
	96–21	will vanish in a *m·* chemicalization.
an	101–25	lead to *m·* and to physical death.
	103–24	malicious form of . . . ultimates in *m·* idiocy.
s	115–26	definition of
	118– 6	Did not this parable point a *m·*
	119–13	all disasters, physical and *m·*,
	124– 7	Having neither *m·* might, spiritual basis, nor
	125– 5	*M·* conditions will be found always harmonious
	139–32	The *m·* condition of such a man demands
	140– 3	effectual in the treatment of *m·* ailments.
	150–22	human view infringes man's free *m·* agency ;
ph	170– 3	neither a *m·* nor a spiritual system.
	171– 3	mankind has caught their *m·* contagion.
	171–21	The intellectual, the *m·*, the spiritual,
	192–17	*M·* and spiritual might belong to Spirit,
	197–12	the more . . . said about *m·* and spiritual law,
f	218–31	the *m·* and physical are as one in their results.
	234–29	was to break a *m·* precept.
	235–13	*m·* and spiritual culture, which lifts one higher.
	244– 2	does not produce *m·* or physical deformity ;
c	260–23	evolves bad physical and *m·* conditions.
b	288–10	When the final physical and *m·* effects of C. S.
	320–10	must rest upon both the literal and *m·* ;"
	327–15	It is a *m·* madness which rushes forth to
	327–31	the man's dormant sense of *m·* obligation,
p	363–26	detect this unspoken *m·* uprising?
	366– 4	must first cast *m·* evils out of himself
	370–18	The *m·* and spiritual facts of health,
	373– 1	If we are Christians on all *m·* questions, but
	375–18	adding to his patient's mental and *m·* power,
	381–11	except a *m·* or spiritual law.
	381–29	man's *m·* right to annul an unjust sentence,
	391–17	Justice is the *m·* signification of law.
	392– 4	broken *m·* law should be taken into account
	395–32	a *m·* offence is indeed the worst of diseases.
	405–14	sentence of the *m·* law will be executed
	405–27	hastening on to physical and *m·* doom.
	405–28	conquered by the *m·* penalties you incur
	406–16	*m·* man has no fear that he will commit a murder,
	418–26	Include *m·* as well as physical belief in your
	419– 1	A *m·* question may hinder the recovery of the
	422– 6	*m·* and physical symptoms seem aggravated,
	422–15	so mental and *m·* chemistry changes the
t	447– 3	no *m·* right to attempt to influence the
	448– 2	to indulge them, is a *m·* offence.
	448–20	the *m·* and spiritual qualifications requisite
	449–11	Man's *m·* mercury, rising or falling,
	451–32	malpractice tends to blast *m·* sense,
	453–11	the morbid *m·* or physical symptoms
	455– 8	You must utilize the *m·* might of Mind
	460– 8	Its pharmacy is *m·*, and its medicine is
r	483– 9	you must not be ignorant of the *m·* and
	483–10	*M·* ignorance or sin affects your
	492– 9	will uplift the physical and *m·* standard of
	493–23	any other sense of *m·* or mental inharmony.
g	531– 9	represent the higher *m·* sentiments,
	540–11	In *m·* chemicalization, when the symptoms
gl	592–12	a type of *m·* law and the
		(*see also* **courage**)

morale

m	61–30	The scientific *m·* of marriage is spiritual unity.
p	367– 2	nor bury the *m·* of C. S. in the grave-clothes of
t	456–19	One must abide in the *m·* of truth

morally

f	220–27	better *m·* or physically
p	369–31	any more than he is *m·* saved in or by sin.
	434–23	His trial was a tragedy, and is *m·* illegal.
t	445– 5	who attempts to kill *m·* and physically.
	451–23	He feels *m·* obligated to open the eyes of
	461– 8	taught only by those who are *m·* advanced
r	466–31	better physically, *m·*, and spiritually.
	495–13	and sets the captive free physically and *m·*.
ap	564– 6	incites mortals to kill *m·* and physically
gl	587– 4	acknowledged *m·*, civilly, and socially.

morals

and health

b	273–32	cannot be destructive to *m·* and health when

bad

t	446– 2	perhaps communicating his own bad *m·*,

health and

p	400– 6	its influence upon health and *m·*
	426–25	would raise the standard of health and *m·*
r	485–17	through better health and *m·*

of men

s	126–25	the health, longevity, and *m·* of men ;

sound

pref	x–31	but sound *m·* are most desirable.

f	235– 9	with as direct reference to their *m·* as to
p	397– 4	the *m·* and the happiness of mortals,
t	445–28	thus disregarding the *m·* of the student
	449–29	improves the health and the *m·* of his student

morbid

p	377–22	the *m·* or excited action of any organ.
t	453–10	the *m·* moral or physical symptoms

Morbid Secretion

p	431–22	*M· S·* hypnotized the prisoner
	438–21	foul fur was spread over him by *M· S·*,
	438–28	*M· S·* is not an importer or dealer in fur,
	438–30	we know *M· S·* to be on friendly terms with
	440– 6	*M· S·* is taught how to make sleep befool

more

pref	ix– 8	voices the *m·* definite thought,
	x–24	its practice is safer and *m·* potent
pr	2– 8	*m·* than He has already done,
	2–11	We can do *m·* for ourselves by humble fervent
	2–23	God is Love. Can we ask Him to be *m·* ?
	2–27	Shall we plead for *m·* at the open fount,
	2–28	which is pouring forth *m·* than we accept
	3–24	and thus be fitted to receive *m·*.
	3–25	Gratitude is much *m·* than a verbal expression
	3–26	Action expresses *m·* gratitude than speech.
	4–20	to assimilate *m·* of the divine character,
	6–13	will furnish *m·* than its equivalent of pain,
	6–17	*M·* than this we cannot ask,
	7–21	with *m·* devout self-abnegation and purity.
	8–26	do we not already know *m·* of this heart than
	11– 4	"Go, and sin no *m·*." — *John* 8 : 11.
	12– 4	to gain *m·* of the divine presence
	12– 7	making it act *m·* powerfully on the body
a	25– 7	was no *m·* efficacious to cleanse from sin when
	25–18	he demonstrated *m·* spiritually than
	28–10	one's consecration to Christ is *m·* on the
	28–13	by understanding *m·* of the divine Principle
	29– 8	It bids us work the *m·* earnestly
	29– 9	because then our labor is *m·* needed.
	30– 2	*m·* spiritual idea of life than other men,
	34–18	they became *m·* spiritual
	35–13	to receive *m·* of his reappearing
	37–21	the *m·* practical import of that career !
	38– 4	even *m·* pernicious than the old doctrine of
	41–29	demanded *m·* than they were willing to practise.
	42–32	must understand *m·* fully his Life-principle
	45–12	much *m·*, being reconciled, — *Rom.* 5 : 10.
	46–29	and the material senses saw him no *m·*.
	51– 2	something *m·* important than human life
	51–17	he could no *m·* be separated from his
	54–23	whose religion was something *m·* than a name.
	55– 6	did Jesus no *m·* injustice than
m	57–27	serves to unite thought *m·* closely to God,
	58–15	benevolence should grow *m·* diffusive.
	58–24	" Two eat no *m·* together than they
	59–18	will prove *m·* salutary in prolonging her health
	60–30	happiness would be *m·* readily attained
	60–31	would be *m·* secure in our keeping,
	61–12	inherit *m·* intellect, better balanced minds,
	61–25	a *m·* solemn charge, than the culture of
	62–15	will do much *m·* for the health of the
	62–20	We must not attribute *m·* and *m·* intelligence
	64–20	no *m·* marrying nor giving in marriage,
	65–12	life should be *m·* metaphysically regarded.
	65–27	find permanence and peace in a *m·* spiritual
	68–16	I never knew *m·* than one individual who
sp	76–14	neither can he return to it, any *m·* than
	79– 7	A scientific mental method is *m·* sanitary than
	81–12	no *m·* proves him to be so, than
	82– 3	It is no *m·* difficult to read the absent mind
	83– 9	Nothing is *m·* antagonistic to C. S. than

more

sp 84–15 to commune *m·* largely with the divine Mind,
84–32 we can know the truth *m·* accurately than
85–26 seeking the material *m·* than the spiritual.
86–10 Jesus possessed *m·* spiritual susceptibility
86–22 Then why is it *m·* difficult to see a thought
89–22 We are all capable of *m·* than we do.
96–32 means by which to accomplish *m·* evil ;
97– 5 In reality, the *m·* closely error simulates truth
97– 7 the *m·* impotent error becomes as a belief.
97–11 The *m·* destructive matter becomes,
97–12 the *m·* its nothingness will appear,
97–17 The *m·* material the belief, the *m·* obvious its
an 101– 5 that there is one *m·* fact to be recorded
102–12 The planets have no *m·* power over man than
102–20 weaving webs *m·* complicated and subtle.
102–27 much *m·* likely to be abused by its possessor,
103–22 belief . . . that evil is as real . . . and *m·* powerful.
s 108–18 not a fraction *m·*, not a unit less.
111– 7 Science of God and man is no *m·* supernatural
112– 3 Is there *m·* than one school of C. S.?
116–12 includes vastly *m·* than is at first seen.
125– 9 *m·* harmonious in his manifestations than
125–31 be proved nothing *m·* than a mortal belief,
128–13 becomes *m·* elastic, is capable of greater
134–32 This fact at present seems *m·* mysterious than
138–23 the sick are *m·* willing to part with pain
140– 1 *m·* than it is needed in most cases ;
140– 2 Science is *m·* than usually effectual in
140–11 warring no *m·* over the corporeality,
141– 3 *M·* than profession is requisite for
143– 8 sick are *m·* deplorably lost than the sinning, if
144–11 The *m·* material a belief, the *m·* obstinately
146– 5 are governed *m·* or less by our systems of
149– 4 The *m·* excellent way is divine Science
149–14 Truth, *m·* in your own life,
153–13 This discovery leads to *m·* light.
153–29 *m·* careful of our mental conditions,
154–19 *m·* than the child's mind governs itself,
154–30 moaning *m·* childishly than her child,
154–31 The better and *m·* successful method
155–22 The human mind acts *m·* powerfully to offset
155–24 and *m·* weight into the spiritual scale.
157–13 drug becomes *m·* like the human mind than
160– 9 The motion of the arm is no *m·* dependent
161– 4 *m·* exact than you suppose ;
163–17 has already destroyed *m·* lives than war,
163–27 if it were not *m·* than compensated by the
164–11 they are *m·* scientific than are
ph 165– * *Is not the life m· than meat,— Matt. 6 : 25.*
167–21 can no *m·* unite in action, than
170–23 for *m·* than all others spiritual causation
171–23 No *m·* sympathy exists between the flesh and
172–29 *m·* nobility than the statuesque athlete,
173–30 *m·* fatal to health and longevity than
174– 3 by their *m·* studied methods.
176–12 *m·* "sermons in stones, and good in
176–25 One disease is no *m·* real than another.
180–15 the invalid may unwittingly add *m·* fear
180–32 I have found divine Truth *m·* potent than
181–10 electricity and magnetism *m·* than
187– 1 believing in *m·* than the one Mind.
189– 8 In like manner mortals should no *m·* deny the
190–26 place thereof shall know it no *m·*.— Psal. 103 : 16.
191– 4 delusion that there is *m·* than one Mind,
191– 5 delusion that there is . . . *m·* than one God,
194–25 with no *m·* intelligence than a babe,
197–12 the *m·* that is thought and said about
197–19 *m·* honest than our sleek politicians.
197–32 *m·* than his calomel and morphine,
198– 2 higher stratum of mortal mind has in belief *m·*
198–23 A patient's belief is *m·* or less moulded
f 202–26 Truth should "much *m·* abound."— Rom. 5 : 20.
202–30 as if senseless matter . . . had *m·* power than
203–12 incites to a *m·* exalted worship
203–17 We are prone to believe either in *m·* than
204– 4 false conclusions that there is *m·* than one
207– 2 evil becomes *m·* apparent and obnoxious
212– 9 the memory of pain is *m·* vivid
213–20 Mozart experienced *m·* than he expressed.
213–23 even *m·* strikingly true of Beethoven,
214–21 *m·* than they do a spiritual God.
217– 3 notion of such a possibility is *m·* absurd than
218– 7 rests us *m·* than hours of repose
219– 7 No *m·* can we say in Science that
220–13 procures a summer residence with *m·* ease than
221– 5 decided that his diet should be *m·* rigid,
222–16 consulting the stomach less . . . and God *m·*,
223–16 but *m·* are blinded by their old illusions,
223–29 will much *m·* abound as truth urges
224–22 A higher and *m·* practical Christianity,
225–25 abolition of mental slavery is a *m·* difficult
226– 4 under *m·* subtle and depraving forms.
230–17 God, good, can no *m·* produce sickness than
233–18 much *m·* should ye discern the sign mental,
233–26 is not *m·* unquestionable than the

more

f 234– 9 become *m·* familiar with good than with evil,
234–31 and do no *m·* harm than
236–25 children are *m·* tractable than adults,
236–26 and learn *m·* readily to love the simple verities
237–10 The *m·* stubborn beliefs and theories of
237–27 *m·* for them than they are willing to admit
238– 8 but this frown, *m·* than flatteries,
239–19 becoming nearer, dearer, and *m·* real to us,
241–16 that compilation can do no *m·* for
242–15 Self-love is *m·* opaque than a solid body.
243–13 That those wonders are not *m·* commonly
244–18 man was never *m·* nor less than man.
245–19 a Franklin might work with *m·* certainty
246–22 would enjoy *m·* than threescore years and ten
247–32 to have less illusion and *m·* Soul,
250–22 Is there any *m·* reality in the waking dream
250–26 matter has no *m·* sense as a man than
251– 1 hence it is not *m·* imperative
251– 4 an abscess should not grow *m·* painful
251– 5 neither should a fever become *m·* severe
c 258– 9 Man is *m·* than a material form with a
258–16 know no *m·* of man as the . . . than
260– 1 can no *m·* arrive at the true conception
264–13 As mortals gain *m·* correct views of God and
265–14 a *m·* expansive love,
265–14 a higher and *m·* permanent peace.
267–20 *m·* than is detected upon the surface,
b 270–19 divine Mind, in His *m·* infinite meanings,
279–14 one can no *m·* create the other than
279–23 *m·* or less infected with the pantheistic
281– 4 Spirit and matter no *m·* commingle than
283–29 and unless we so do, we can no *m·* demonstrate
284–24 Even the *m·* subtile and misnamed
287–16 How can there be *m·* than all ?
290–28 He is no *m·* spiritual for believing that
293– 8 the *m·* ethereal is called mind.
294– 9 not *m·* real than the belief that matter
297–20 Faith is higher and *m·* spiritual than belief.
299– 1 It has behind it no *m·* reality than has the
305– 3 discordant mortal is no *m·* a man than
306–22 not *m·* distinct nor real to the
307– 8 declares that there is *m·* than one intelligence
314– 1 and the body no *m·* perfect because of death
314–21 presented to her, *m·* than ever before,
314–26 the *m·* distinctly he uttered the demands
314–28 the *m·* odious he became to sinners
315–27 *m·* spiritual than all other earthly
317–27 *m·* real, *m·* formidable in truth,
317–27 to the testimony of . . . *m·* than to Soul,
318– 4 but for him to . . . was *m·* difficult.
318–19 invalids grow *m·* spiritual,
323–13 In order to apprehend *m·*, we must
324– 8 Unless the . . . are becoming *m·* apparent,
326–11 or trusting in it *m·* than in the spiritual.
326–27 and his life became *m·* spiritual.
327–25 the man who has *m·* animal than moral
329–30 the *m·* intense the opposition to spirituality,
331– 1 Life is no *m·* confined to the forms which
335–20 for Spirit is *m·* than all else.
339–21 has yielded to a *m·* spiritual idea of Deity,
o 344–11 Were it *m·* fully understood that Truth heals
344–30 *m·* fashionable and less spiritual?
349– 2 when this Science is *m·* generally understood
353–14 It still holds them *m·* or less.
354–18 seen in example *m·* than in precept.
355–12 Let discord . . . be heard no *m·*,
356–32 Then there must have been *m·* than one creator
m· than one God.
358–19 *m·* frequently cited for our instruction
360–24 Shall mortal man be *m·* just than— Job 4 : 17
360–25 Shall man be *m·* pure than his— see Job 4 : 17
p 365– 5 much *m·* towards healing the sick
369–31 any *m·* than he is morally saved in or by sin
370–25 and do no *m·* for the patient.
371–15 no *m·* comprehends his real being than
372–19 How, then, in Christianity any *m·* than in C. S.
373– 4 and be *m·* alive to His promises.
373–10 the sick recover *m·* rapidly from disease than
376– 1 an image *m·* terrifying than that of most
376–13 *m·* life and immortality in one good motive
380–28 Nothing is *m·* disheartening than
381– 4 Be no *m·* willing to suffer the illusion that
382–14 *m·* receptive of spiritual power
382–18 "*m·* honored in the breach than the
382–20 is *m·* difficult to heal through Mind than one
382–32 abandoned me to *m·* hopeless suffering
386– 3 any *m·* than it is in the case of sin.
388– 9 Idolaters, believing in *m·* than one mind,
390– 2 and I should like something *m·* to eat."
390–22 God is no *m·* the author of sickness than
393–22 Your body would suffer no *m·* from tension
395–29 may appear in a *m·* alarming form.
397–13 Your thought is *m·* powerful than your words
397–14 *m·* powerful than the accident itself,
397–24 no *m·* material in their waking hours

mortal (adj.)

beings
g 554– 5   nor are there properly any *m·* beings,

belief
pr 12–19   It is a *m·* belief, . . . which causes a drug to be
   a 20–14   he knew the error of *m·* belief,
 sp 72–13   *M·* belief (the material sense of life)
   73–12   attraction of so-called spirit is a *m·* belief,
   88–25   for both arise from *m·* belief.
   s 125–32   proved nothing more than a *m·* belief,
   151–17   *M·* belief says that death has been occasioned
 ph 174–22   *M·* belief is all that enables a drug to cure
   181– 8   but *m·* belief has such a partnership.
   184– 1   laws of health are simply laws of *m·* belief.
   197–28   and *m·* belief loses some portion of its error.
   f 209– 2   the *m·* belief which makes the body discordant
   212–32   unreal and imitative movements of *m·* belief,
   213–16   a mental impression made on *m·* belief.
   227– 3   I saw that the law of *m·* belief included
   228– 7   Heredity is a prolific subject for *m·* belief to
   229–15   *m·* belief has constituted itself a law to bind
   230–26   soothing syrups to . . . satisfy *m·* belief,
   247–12   passes away, fading and fleeting as *m·* belief.
   251– 7   Fright is so great at certain stages of *m·* belief
   c 262–10   by diving into the shallows of *m·* belief.
   b 278–28   and death is a *m·* belief.
   281– 9   rebukes *m·* belief, and asks :
   287–22   Error is false, *m·* belief ; it is illusion,
   289–16   "king of terrors" to be but a *m·* belief, — *Job*
   18 : 14.
   294–11   This *m·* belief, misnamed *man*, is error,
   296–16   *M·* belief must lose all satisfaction in error
   296–31   *M·* belief is a liar from the beginning,
   297– 2   *M·* belief says, "You are happy !"
   297–32   A *m·* belief fulfils its own conditions.
   302–12   that mind is in matter, . . . is a *m·* belief ;
   308– 6   Until the lesson is learned . . . *m·* belief will be
   311– 1   the varying clouds of *m·* belief, which hide them
   311–27   They are only what *m·* belief calls them.
   321–18   was really but a phase of *m·* belief.
   p 372– 3   The mortal body is only an erroneous *m·* belief
   381–12   so-called laws of *m·* belief are destroyed by the
   401–17   is destroying erroneous *m·* belief.
   407–32   in consonance with common *m·* belief.
   415– 5   Inflammation as a *m·* belief quickens or
   428–18   mortal sense cannot impair nor *m·* belief destroy.
   r 478– 8   except the claim of *m·* belief?
   489–31   *M·* belief would have the material senses
   496–21   the law of *m·* belief, at war with the facts
   g 556–10   *M·* belief infolds the conditions of sin.
   556–10   *M·* belief to live again in renewed
  ap 569– 5   the *m·* belief in a power opposed to God.
  gl 588– 1   HELL. *M·* belief ; error ; lust ; remorse ;
   589– 1   JERUSALEM. *M·* belief and knowledge
   589–20   higher sense of Truth rebuking *m·* belief,
   597–20   WILL. The motive-power of error ; *m·* belief ;

beliefs
 sp 84– 2   nor with the conclusions of *m·* beliefs.
   s 144– 8   The various *m·* beliefs formulated in
   f 231–18   *m·* beliefs which divine Truth and Love destroy.
   o 353–31   *M·* beliefs can neither demonstrate
   p 378–18   exercised over *m·* beliefs to destroy them ;
   r 488–18   defines these so-called senses as *m· beliefs,*
  ap 569–12   masters his *m·* beliefs, animality, and hate,
  gl 583– 1   Sensual and *m·* beliefs ;
   594–22   SPIRITS. *M·* beliefs ; corporeality ;

blindness
   p 374–13   *m·* blindness and its sharp consequences

bodies
 sp 92– 8   decomposition of *m·* bodies in what is termed
   o 341– *   *shall also quicken your m· bodies* — *Rom.* 8 : 11.

body
   a 51–10   to attempt the destruction of the *m·* body
   s 108–32   the organism and action of the *m·* body,
   122–11   senses . . . make mortal mind tributary to *m·*
   body,
   151–32   claims to govern every organ of the *m·* body,
 ph 187–21   action of the *m·* body is governed by this
   f 209– 9   material and *m·* body or mind is not the man.
   220–30   forms all conditions of the *m·* body,
   222– 8   also that mortal mind makes a *m·* body,
   250–14   *M·* body and mind are one,
   c 263–32   The fading forms of matter, the *m·* body and
   b 293–11   mortal mind and *m·* body, are false
   305–11   divine Principle, not in a *m·* body.
   311–21   or that immortal Soul is in *m·* body,
   p 372– 2   The *m·* body is only an erroneous mortal belief
   402–14   mortal mind constructs the *m·* body
   403–17   producing on *m·* body the results of

concepts
   c 256–15   nor can He be understood . . . through *m·*
   concepts.

consciousness
 sp 77–22   Even if . . . to *m·* consciousness were possible,
   b 278–14   in a supposititious *m·* consciousness.
   295–13   *m·* consciousness will at last yield to

mortal (adj.)

consolidation
 ph 185–30   a *m·* consolidation of material mentality

deviations
   g 502– 7   the *m·* deviations and inverted images

discord
 sp 98– 3   elevation of existence above *m·* discord
   c 262–27   The foundation of *m·* discord is a false sense

discords
   f 231–16   God is not the author of *m·* discords.

disorder
 ph 184–10   belief which produces a *m·* disorder,

dream
   a 42– 7   found at length to be a *m·* dream,
   f 219– 2   and the *m·* dream will forever cease.
   230– 5   the awakening from this *m·* dream,
   250–25   whatever appears to be . . . is a *m·* dream.
   b 311–17   This state of error is the *m·* dream
   p 418–13   This *m·* dream of sickness, sin, and death

dreams
   b 305–29   These *m·* dreams are of human origin,

elements
   p 374–28   is resolved into its primitive *m·* elements.

error
 sp 96–21   *M·* error will vanish in a moral chemicalization.
   f 204– 5   that *m·* error is as conclusively mental
   b 277– 9   Their opposites, evil and matter, are *m·* error,
   315–15   Their thoughts were filled with *m·* error,
   p 403–18   until *m·* error is deprived of its imaginary
   r 468–12   Spirit is immortal Truth ; matter is *m·* error.
   485–21   *m·* error which Christ, or Truth, destroys
   g 533–15   Adam, *alias m· error,*
   548–13   Every agony of *m·* error helps . . . destroy error,

errors
   a 53–26   He knew the *m·* errors which constitute the

existence
 sp 70– 1   *M·* existence is an enigma.
   s 108–19   apparently near the confines of *m·* existence,
 ph 187– 3   mortals do not comprehend even *m·* existence,
   188–11   *M·* existence is a dream of pain and
   f 250– 6   *M·* existence is a dream ;
   250– 6   *M* existence has no real entity,
   250–23   the waking dream of *m·* existence
   p 364– 5   to lay down his *m·* existence in behalf of
   403–15   *m·* existence is a state of self-deception
   426–21   destroy the great fear that besets *m·* existence.
   g 501– 8   showing the poverty of *m·* existence,

eyes
   b 334–20   before the human Jesus was incarnate to *m·* eyes.

fault
   b 292– 1   When the last *m·* fault is destroyed,

fear
   p 377–26   cause of . . . disease is mental, a *m·* fear,

feelings
  gl 587–23   HEART. *M·* feelings, motives, affections,

flesh
 sp 81–10   their affiliation with *m·* flesh ;

forms
   s 118–20   In all *m·* forms of thought, dust is

history
   r 476–16   They were, from the beginning of *m·* history,

humanity
   b 338–10   conclusions of material and *m·* humanity.

ignorance
 ph 188–22   springing from *m·* ignorance or fear.
   b 280–32   The only excuse . . . is our *m·* ignorance

illusion
   b 289–19   death is but a *m·* illusion,
   302–16   is always beyond and above the *m·* illusion
   p 403–20   sweeps away the gossamer web of *m·* illusion.

illusions
   f 214–23   for *m·* illusions would rob God,
   b 289–29   Matter and death are *m·* illusions.
   330– 4   the fixedness of *m·* illusions,

knowledge
   g 527–17   constitutes evil and *m·* knowledge.

life
   p 399–22   so-called *m·* life is mortal mind,
   g 527– 9   *m·* life, mutable truth, nor variable love.
   544–30   declares . . . so-called *m·* life to be Life,
   552–13   Human experience in *m·* life,

malice
   t 458–22   Science will ameliorate *m·* malice.

man
 sp 92–17   for the common conception of *m·* man
   s 113–24   "but every [*m*] man a liar." — *Rom.* 3 : 4.
 ph 190– 9   human belief called *m·* man
   191–25   Physical sense defines *m·* man as based on
   f 204– 9   (*m·* man) who carries out the delusions of sin,
   204–15   *m·* man, is a supposed mixture of
   208–26   *m·* man possesses this body,
   215–24   *M·* man is the antipode of immortal man
   250–24   whatever appears to be a *m·* man is a
   c 255–11   *M·* man has made a covenant with his eyes
   263– 7   When *m·* man blends his thoughts of
   b 289– 2   *M·* man can never rise . . . until he learns

mortal (adj.)
man

b	291–23	As death findeth *m·* man, so shall he
	291–30	the judgment by which *m·* man is divested of
	292–32	a *m·* man is not the real essence of manhood,
	294–20	*m·* man, representing the error that life and
	296– 5	It is the ripening of *m·* man, through which
	301–23	*M·* man seems to himself to be material
	331– 3	If life were in *m·* man or material things,
o	346– 3	not sinful and sickly *m·* man who is
	347–12	so-called *m·* man is not the reality of man.
	300–24	Shall *m·* man be more just than— *Job* 4 : 17.
p	425–15	*M·* man will be less mortal,
t	459– 4	*m·* man achieves no worldly honors except by
r	476–23	Remember that the Scriptures say of *m·* man:
	477– 1	where sinning *m·* man appears to mortals.
	478–16	No, not if God is true and *m·* man a liar.
	478–30	*M· man* is really a self-contradictory phrase,
	491–32	that this dream . . . may not be *m·* man?
	492– 1	leaves in *m·* man intact in body and thought,
g	508– 1	human or material belief, called *m·* man.
	531– 5	the error,— that *m·* man starts materially,
	536–18	starting from matter . . . *m·* man would be
	538–26	of *m·* man, and of sin which is temporal.
	538–27	As both *m·* man and sin have a beginning,
	540– 3	Spirit creates neither a wicked nor a *m·* man,
	543– 4	but it is only *m·* man and not the real man,
gl	590–12	*m·* man ; denial of the fulness of God's creation;

manhood

g	543–21	thinking that apehood preceded *m·* manhood?

materials

p	402–15	with this mind's own *m·* materials.

measurements

gl	595–17	TIME. *M·* measurements ;

men

ph	190– 2	afterwards *m·* men or mortals,

mentality

sp	90–22	shows what *m·* mentality and knowledge are.
g	513– 1	this *m·* mentality, so-called, and its claim,

mind

a	30–12	appreciable to *m·* mind as "the way."— *John* 14 : 6.
sp	71–16	images, which *m·* mind holds and evolves
	71–18	neither *m·* mind nor matter is the image
	77– 8	*m·* mind creates its own physical conditions.
	78– 4	the changing deflections of *m·* mind ;
	80–24	control of *m·* mind over its substratum,
	80–25	It is *m·* mind which convulses its substratum,
	80–27	*M·* mind produces table-tipping
	83–32	act of reading *m·* mind investigates and
	86– 5	*m·* mind, whose touch called for aid.
	86–20	sounds evolved involuntarily by *m·* mind.
	86–29	*M·* mind sees what it believes
	87–15	it presents primal facts to *m·* mind.
	87–26	strong impressions produced on *m·* mind
	88–13	are offshoots of *m·* mind ;
	89– 3	shows that the beliefs of *m·* mind are loosed.
	90–11	transitions now possible for *m·* mind
	94–28	Our Master read *m·* mind on a scientific basis,
	95– 2	the only Science of reading *m·* mind.
	97– 6	resembles its essence, *m·* mind,
an	102– 8	unreal concept of the so-called *m·* mind
	103– 6	The destruction of the claims of *m·* mind
	103–19	specific term for error, or *m·* mind.
	103–26	they annihilate the fables of *m·* mind,
	103–29	In reality there is no *m·* mind,
	104–32	Is not *m·* mind the murderer?
	105– 1	hands, without *m·* mind to direct them,
	105– 6	jurisdiction over the carnal or *m·* mind,
	105– 8	*m·* mind, evil, which is the real outlaw,
	105–13	*M·* mind, not matter, is the criminal
s	108–10	the only sufferer is *m·* mind,
	108–27	subjective state of *m·* mind which
	114– 3	author calls sick and sinful humanity *m·* mind,
	114–12	*M·* mind is a solecism in language,
	114–14	*m· mind* implies something untrue
	114–31	what is termed by the author *m· mind.*
	116– 4	In the third degree *m·* mind disappears,
	116–19	is nothing beyond an image in *m·* mind.
	122–10	so-called senses still make *m·* mind tributary
	124– 4	a law of *m·* mind, a blind belief,
	125– 1	as *m·* mind changes its beliefs.
	126– 4	*m·* mind will be without form and void,
	138–13	casting out the errors of *m·* mind.
	145–29	*m·* mind must continually weaken its own
	151–31	*m·* mind claims to govern every organ of
	152– 5	and saves *m·* mind from itself.
	153–22	pain cannot exist where there is no *m·* mind
	153–27	*m·* mind, not matter, contains and carries
	154– 4	law of *m·* mind that certain diseases should be
	154–18	law of *m·* mind and her own fears
	157–24	*m·* mind confers the power which the drug
	157–26	Narcotics quiet *m·* mind.
	158–21	*m·* mind acquires an educated appetite
	158–27	letting in matter's higher stratum, *m·* mind.
	158–29	*m·* mind, of a higher attenuation than

mortal (adj.)
mind

s	159–21	from effects produced by *m·* mind,
	160–10	no more dependent upon the direction of *m·* mind,
	160–17	Has *m·* mind ceased speaking to them,
	160–27	to learn how *m·* mind governs muscle,
	161– 4	*m·* mind, and not matter, burns it.
	161–28	if it were not already determined by *m·* mind.
ph	168–27	a latent illusion of *m·* mind,
	168–32	process which *m·* mind and body undergo
	169–23	It is *m·* mind, not matter, which brings
	172–21	obtains in mortals, *alias m·* mind,
	176– 2	action of *m·* mind on the body was not so
	176–19	*M·* mind is the worst foe of the body,
	176–27	no farther than *m·* mind maps out the way.
	177– 8	*M·* mind and body are one.
	177–10	body, is but a false concept of *m·* mind.
	178–\4	it is set down as a poison by *m·* mind.
	178–18	*M·* mind, acting upon the basis of sensation
	179–13	The preference of *m·* mind for a certain method
	180– 2	As *m·* mind is the husbandman of error,
	180–23	correct this turbulent element of *m·* mind
	184–21	*M·* mind alone suffers,
	185–14	They have their birth in *m·* mind,
	185–32	A patient under the influence of *m·* mind
	186–28	*M·* mind is ignorant of self,
	186–29	If *m·* mind knew how to be better,
	187–14	the mandate of *m·* mind
	187–19	What is this *my* but *m·* mind,
	188–24	The soil of disease is *m·* mind,
	189–10	effect of *m·* mind on the body,
	189–15	it is as truly *m·* mind, according to its
	189–19	*m·* mind, by an inevitable perversion,
	189–25	From *m·* mind comes the reproduction of
	189–28	the development of embryonic *m·* mind
	189–32	matter is the subjective condition of *m·* mind.
	190– 2	so-called embryonic *m·* mind,
	190– 6	neither a *m·* mind nor the immortal Mind
	192–12	offspring . . . of the *m·* mind and not of the
	194–12	if *m·* mind says, "I am deaf and blind,"
	194–18	the frailty and inadequacy of *m·* mind.
	194–21	and that, in turn, *m·* mind manifests itself
	195–11	whether it is *m·* mind or immortal Mind
	195–21	promote the growth of *m·* mind out of itself,
	196– 5	The power of *m·* mind over its own body is
	196– 6	Better the suffering which awakens *m·* mind
	196–20	Such books as will rule disease out of *m·* mind,
	198– 2	for the higher stratum of *m·* mind has
	198–13	to prevent disease from forming in *m·* mind
	199– 1	muscles, without volition of *m·* mind,
	199–16	as they influence them through *m·* mind.
f	201–17	The way to extract error from *m·* mind is to
	202–30	senseless matter or erring *m·* mind
	208– 9	a law of *m·* mind, wrong in every sense,
	208–26	only expresses a material and *m·* mind.
	210–19	The expression *m· mind* is really a solecism,
	210–27	It is the so-called *m·* mind which voices this
	211– 8	the sensations of a so-called *m·* mind or
	211–14	seem to obtain in *m·* mind.
	211–16	Without *m·* mind, the tear could not
	212–14	proves sensation to be in the *m·* mind,
	213– 2	Whoever contradicts this *m·* mind supposition
	213– 6	*M·* mind conceives of something as either
	213–27	*M·* mind is the harp of many strings,
	218– 1	*M·* mind does the false talking,
	218–15	independently of *m·* mind
	219–11	Not muscles, nerves, nor bones, but *m·* mind
	220–15	kinder than the atmosphere of *m·* mind,
	220–18	*M·* mind produces its own phenomena,
	220–30	*M·* mind forms all conditions of the
	221–30	without the consent of *m·* mind,
	222– 1	this phantasm of *m·* mind disappears as we
	222– 5	food affects the body only as *m·* mind has its
	222– 8	He learned also that *m·* mind makes a
	225–26	The despotic tendencies, inherent in *m·* mind
	228– 4	or of certain idiosyncrasies of *m·* mind
	229–20	The so-called law of *m·* mind, conjectural and
	229–29	It is the transgression of a belief of *m·* mind,
	230–30	So-called *m·* mind or the mind of mortals
	234–17	If mortals would keep proper ward over *m·* mind,
	236–14	form the embryo of another *m·* mind,
	239–23	*M·* mind is the acknowledged seat of
	239–27	If it comes from erring *m·* mind,
	239–31	Imperfect *m·* mind sends forth its own
	243–19	If this information is conveyed, *m·* mind
	243–21	the inanimate substratum of *m·* mind,
	248–15	What is the model before *m·* mind?
	250–25	Take away the *m·* mind, and matter has no
	250–28	Upon this stage . . . goes on the dance of *m·* mind.
	251– 3	The so-called belief of *m·* mind apparent as
c	260–24	Selfishness and sensualism are educated in *m·* mind
	261– 8	The effect of *m·* mind on health and
	262–32	Cause does not exist in matter, in *m·* mind, or

mortal (adj.)
mind

c	263– 5	The creations of *m·* mind are material.
b	273–31	atmosphere of *m·* mind cannot be
	274– 5	the conception of *m·* mind, the offspring of
	274–19	simply the manifested beliefs of *m·* mind,
	282–27	Error is the so-called intelligence of *m·* mind.
	283– 9	states of *m·* mind which act, react, and
	289–22	results, by the universal law of *m·* mind, in
	292–13	Matter is the primitive belief of *m·* mind,
	292–15	To *m·* mind, matter is substantial,
	292–19	the origin of material man and *m·* mind,
	293– 7	Matter and *m·* mind are but different strata of human belief.
	293–11	*m·* mind and mortal body, are false
	293–21	There is no vapid fury of *m·* mind
	295– 8	*M·* mind would transform the spiritual into the
	295–19	The *m·* mind . . . which has lost much materiality
	296–26	*M·* mind judges by the testimony of the
	305–13	a characteristic of *m·* mind.
	311– 3	What we term *m·* mind or carnal mind,
	321–20	that leprosy was a creation of *m·* mind
	323–23	elevates even *m·* mind to the contemplation of
	326–15	great healer of *m·* mind is the healer of the
	329–29	the error into which *m·* mind is plunged,
	338–16	suggests the thought . . . of *m·* mind in solution.
o	348–19	Is it not well to eliminate from so-called *m·* mind
	348–20	so long as it remains in *m·* mind,
p	370–15	The effect, which *m·* mind produces through
	370–20	since *m·* mind must be the cause of disease
	371– 2	The body is the substratum of *m·* mind,
	372– 5	error in solution, elementary *m·* mind,
	372– 6	One theory about this *m·* mind is, that its
	373–30	*M·* mind is producing the propulsion or the
	374– 1	that standard which *m·* mind has decided upon
	374– 4	whispered into the ear of *m·* mind,
	374– 6	Because *m·* mind seems to be conscious,
	374–12	which is in fact the objective state of *m·* mind,
	374–16	can destroy all ills which proceed from *m·* mind.
	374–26	Heat and cold are products of *m·* mind.
	374–27	The body, when bereft of *m·* mind, at first cools,
	374–30	*M·* mind produces animal heat,
	375– 1	Hence it is *m·* mind, not matter, which says,
	375–23	show *m·* mind that muscles have no power
	376–19	a mental concept and governed by *m·* mind,
	377–13	showing *m·* mind to be the producer of
	379–28	are pictures drawn on the body by a *m·* mind.
	381–14	*m·* mind cannot legislate the times, periods,
	381–20	Think less of the enactments of *m·* mind,
	382–31	*M·* mind needed to be set right.
	384–10	this is but a belief of *m·* mind,
	385–26	it is a law of *m·* mind which you have disobeyed.
	386– 1	an illusion of *m·* mind, — one of its dreams.
	387– 3	Because *m·* mind is kept active, must it
	387–25	It is a law of so-called *m·* mind,
	388– 5	Stolidity, which is a resisting state of *m·* mind,
	389– 8	*m·* mind, which reports food as undigested.
	391– 1	to overthrow the plea of *m·* mind,
	391–20	it must be *m·* mind which speaks ;
	391–23	will deliver you to the judge (*m·* mind),
	391–26	*M·* mind alone sentences itself.
	392–31	Exclude from *m·* mind the offending errors ;
	393– 4	only because *m·* mind is ignorant of itself,
	393– 8	a law of so-called *m·* mind, not of matter.
	393–24	were it not for *m·* mind.
	396–26	so efface the images of sickness from *m·* mind.
	397– 2	not seeing how *m·* mind affects the body,
	397–27	can never treat *m·* mind and matter separately,
	398–23	Appetite and disease reside in *m·* mind, not in
	399– 5	*M·* mind prescribes the drug,
	399– 7	*M·* mind plans the exercise, and puts the
	399–10	mortal thought, *alias m·* mind.
	399–11	*m·* mind sends its despatches over its body,
	399–16	*M·* mind perpetuates its own thought.
	399–20	and continuation of, the primitive *m·* mind.
	399–22	so-called mortal life is *m·* mind,
	399–23	Scientifically speaking, there is no *m·* mind
	400– 1	*m·* mind, which directly controls the body
	400– 4	*M·* mind is "the strong man," — *Matt.* 12 : 29.
	400–17	except what *m·* mind assigns to it.
	400–22	*M·* mind rules all that is mortal.
	400–26	action of so-called *m·* mind must be destroyed
	401–14	*m·* mind only feels and sees materially.
	402– 8	The time approaches when *m·* mind will forsake
	402–13	*m·* mind constructs the mortal body
	402–18	body manifests only what *m·* mind believes,
	403–16	*M·* mind is constantly producing on mortal body
	404–13	If the evil is over in the repentant *m·* mind,
	405– 1	The basic error is *m·* mind.
	405–14	will be executed upon *m·* mind and body.
	407–13	giving strength to the weakness of *m·* mind,
	408–18	thus reaching *m·* mind through matter?
	408–24	were it not that *m·* mind thinks that the
	408–31	*M·* mind is ignorant of itself,
	409– 3	formed by *m·* mind and not by matter?"
	409– 4	*M· mind* and body combine as one,

mortal (adj.)
mind

p	409– 9	Unconscious *m·* mind — *alias* matter,
	409–12	unconscious substratum of *m·* mind,
	409–16	so-called conscious *m·* mind is believed to be
	411–25	Whatever is cherished in *m·* mind
	414–12	love will . . . guide and govern *m·* mind
	415–15	They only render *m·* mind . . . less fearful,
	415–26	instruct *m·* mind with immortal Truth.
	416–16	material body, which you call *me*, is *m·* mind,
	416–21	This materialism . . . is only in *m·* mind,
	417–29	Show them how *m·* mind seems to induce
	419–21	*m·* mind is liable to any phase of belief.
	420–28	If it becomes necessary to startle *m·* mind
	421– 7	Should you thus startle *m·* mind
	421–19	When the supposed suffering is gone from *m·* mind,
	422–19	changes which go on in *m·* mind serve to
	423–28	as directly the action of *m·* mind as
	424– 2	a separate, individualized *m·* mind,
	425– 2	*M·* mind, not matter, induces this conclusion
	425–15	this is but one of the beliefs of *m·* mind.
	426– 2	*m·* mind, when instructed by Truth, yields to
	429–13	*M·* mind affirms that mind is subordinate
	430– 3	*M·* mind must part with error,
	451–28	action of one *m·* mind controlling another
	454–23	to move upon the waters of *m·* mind,
	459–12	Any attempt to heal mortals with erring *m·* mind,
	463–31	action is that of so-called *m·* mind.
r	473– 1	all inharmony of *m·* mind or body is illusion,
	479–13	Take away so-called *m·* mind, which constitutes
	482–30	the human, *m·* mind so-called is not a healer,
	484–13	the objective states of *m·* mind.
	484–15	Physical force and *m·* mind are one.
	487–21	there is in reality no such thing as *m·* mind.
	493–21	Disease is an experience of so-called *m·* mind.
g	505– 2	but *m·* mind, . . . sin, disease, and death have no
	507–21	material world implies a *m·* mind
	511–23	To *m·* mind, the universe is liquid, solid, and
	512–25	*M·* mind inverts the true likeness,
	512–28	Ignorant of the origin . . . of *m·* mind,
	513–27	So-called *m·* mind — being non-existent
	536–24	*M·* mind accepts the erroneous,
	544–14	No *m·* mind has the might or right
	552–26	the order of matter to be the order of *m·* mind,
	552–29	matter is a manifestation of *m·* mind,
	555– 1	as the force of *m·* mind is less pungent
	555– 2	health attends the absence of *m·* mind.
	556–26	*m·* mind must waken to spiritual life
	557–16	When the mist of *m·* mind evaporates,
ap	564–21	before the tribunal of so-called *m·* mind,
	564–32	talking serpent typifies *m·* mind,
	565– 9	Led on by the grossest element of *m·* mind,
	570–28	should also know the great delusion of *m·* mind,
	571–26	the thoughts which he beholds in *m·* mind.
gl	580–25	and matter in *m·* mind ;
	582– 6	human knowledge, or so-called *m·* mind,
	582–10	self-offering ; an improved state of *m·* mind ;
	582–26	and would make *m·* mind a slave to the body
583–26, 27		so-called *m·* mind controlling *m·* mind ;
	586– 2	EVENING. . . . weariness of *m·* mind ;
	591– 9	mortality ; another name for *m·* mind ;
	591–14	that which *m·* mind sees, feels, . . . only in belief
	591–25	definition of
	597–24	Will, as a quality of so-called *m·* mind,
		(*see also* **Mortal Mind**)

mind-force

b	310– 5	made up of supposititious *m·* mind-force ;

mind-reading

sp	83–25	*m·* mind-reading and immortal Mind-reading.
	83–29	*M·* mind-reading and immortal Mind-reading

mind's

p	429–16	*m·* mind's affirmation is not true.

minds

a	50–27	The distrust of *m·* minds, disbelieving the
s	110–26	the power of C. S. to heal *m·* minds and bodies.
	145– 9	between *m·* minds and immortal Mind.
p	408–12	baneful effects of illusion on *m·* minds and
	419–24	in mortals or so-called *m·* minds,
		(*see also* **Mortal Minds**)

model

f	248–17	Have you accepted the *m·* model?

mood

ap	570– 6	shocked into another extreme *m·* mood,

night-dream

f	249–25	*m·* night-dream is sometimes nearer the fact

opinions

b	273–29	conflicting *m·* opinions and beliefs
p	390–15	false process of *m·* opinions which you name law
	399–27	The one Mind, God, contains no *m·* opinions

origin

ph	169–11	disease has a mental, *m·* origin,

passions

gl	597–29	Destruction ; anger ; *m·* passions.

mortal (adj.)
personality
  sp 94–16 *m·* personality, passion, and impulse.
phenomenon
  b 277–30 and is therefore a *m·* phenomenon,
seeming
  ph 190–17 This *m·* seeming is temporal ;
selfhood
  b 316– 5 and lose sight of *m·* selfhood
sense
  sp 72– 6 would disappear to *m·* sense,
  f 210–29 To *m·* sense, sin and suffering are real,
  212– 8 Why need pain, . . . come to this *m·* sense?
  212–31 realities of being, . . . are unseen to *m·* sense ;
  215–16 only a *m·* sense of the absence of light,
  216–13 to destroy the errors of *m·* sense
  c 263–27 a human and *m·* sense of persons and things
  b 301–14 seems to *m·* sense transcendental,
  302–29 *m·* sense would fain have us so believe.
  308–17 struggling with a *m·* sense of life,
  331– 8 *m·* sense, which falsely testifies to
  p 370– 3 we must forsake the *m·* sense of things,
  406–15 scientific period, in which *m·* sense is subdued
  428–18 the Life which *m·* sense cannot impair
  t 459–24 To *m·* sense C. S. seems abstract,
  r 471–26 that which interprets God as above *m·* sense.
  g 507–30 *M·* sense inverts this appearing
  558–10 To *m·* sense Science seems at first obscure,
  gl 596–23 Though the way is dark in *m·* sense,
senses
  b 288–28 unlimited by the *m·* senses.
  p 390– 6 to the *m·* senses, there is seeming discord.
sensuousness
  a 35– 7 to rise somewhat from *m·* sensuousness,
sight
  f 214–26 How transient a sense is *m·* sight,
  b 300–18 though (to *m·* sight) they grow side by side
sinner
  r 475–31 A *m·* sinner is not God's man,
  g 525– 2 to become there a *m·* sinner,
testimony
  b 297–27 no *m·* testimony is founded on the
  297–28 *M·* testimony can be shaken.
  r 494–26 One is the *m·* testimony, changing,
theories
  g 552–10 *M·* theories make friends of sin, sickness, and
theory
  g 547–29 sensual, and *m·* theory of the universe,
thought
  an 102–19 hidden in the dark recesses of *m·* thought,
  103–30 consequently no transference of *m·* thought
  s 118–20 that is, three modes of *m·* thought.
  118–24 changes the whole of *m·* thought.
  125– 8 normal and natural to changed *m·* thought,
  ph 189–18 the evidence of all *m·* thought or things.
  189–21 lowest instead of from the highest *m·* thought.
  189–27 According to *m·* thought, the development of
  198–20 until the elasticity of *m·* thought haply
  c 259–22 *M·* thought transmits its own images,
  263–29 multiplication or self-division of *m·* thought,
  264– 4 The crude creations of *m·* thought must
  b 282–24 is a material, human, *m·* thought,
  295–25 All that is called *m·* thought is made up of
  306–21 The myriad forms of *m·* thought,
  o 349–26 *M·* thought does not at once catch the
  p 375–32 in consumption presents to *m·* thought
  391– 3 Blot out the images of *m·* thought
  399–10 not . . . apart from the action of *m·* thought,
  415–10 in a part which *m·* thought does not reach.
  418–31 dark images of *m·* thought,
  425–10 beliefs, images of *m·* thought
  t 463– 8 detach *m·* thought from its material
  r 479– 9 image of *m·* thought, reflected on the retina,
  g 511–27 the gradation of *m·* thought,
  520–26 *M·* thought drops into the ground,
  553– 6 *M·* thought must obtain a better basis,
  553–21 theory . . . adopted by general *m·* thought
  gl 585–21 a state of *m·* thought, the only error of which
  586– 1 EVENING. Mistiness of *m·* thought ;
  596–24 Life and Love . . . destroy the unrest of *m·* thought,
  598–30 Time is a *m·* thought, the divisor of which
thoughts
  s 164–22 *m·* thoughts in belief rule the materiality
  ph 178–10 connection of past *m·* thoughts with present.
  190–21 Hebrew bard, swayed by *m·* thoughts,
  f 250–29 *M·* thoughts chase one another like snowflakes,
  gl 582– 3 BELIEVING. . . . *M·* thoughts, illusion.
universe
  gl 584–24 thence to reproduce a *m·* universe,
usage
  a 30–11 Had his . . . birth been wholly apart from *m·* usage,
veins
  p 376–15 which ever flowed through *m·* veins

mortal (adj.)
vestures
  c 260–29 If we array thought in *m·* vestures,
view
  b 315–30 (that is, as it seemed to *m·* view),
vision
  b 301–15 man's substantiality transcends *m·* vision
will
  gl 599– 5 Blind enthusiasm ; *m·* will.
zenith
  sp 97–13 until matter reaches its *m·* zenith in illusion

  ——

  a 19–32 Thou shalt have no belief of Life as *m·* ;
  44–31 power of Spirit to overrule *m·*, material sense.
  sp 72– 4 In other words, *m·*, material sense
  78–11 *m·*, sinning, suffering, and dying.
  81–13 the opposite assertion, that he is *m·*,
  81–25 so-called laws of matter, which define man as *m·*.
  88–13 they are *m·* material beliefs.
  93–28 Finite spirit would be *m·*,
  s 108–30 My discovery that erring, *m·*, . . . *mind*
  124–12 This is a *m·*, finite sense of things,
  139–20 these facts show how a *m·* and material sense
  ph 165– 8 to subjugate intelligence, to make mind *m·*,
  173–21 material structure is *m·*.
  174–31 cause of disease obtains in the *m·* human mind,
  184–18 governed by a false belief is discordant and *m·*,
  187–27 *m·* material body loses all appearance of life
  188– 1 only as the *m·*, erring mind yields to God,
  195–22 growth of mortal mind . . . out of all that is *m·*.
  f 210–23 I name it *m·*.
  211–10 Is it not provable that Mind is not *m·*
  213– 8 this *m·* and material conception.
  249– 7 no *m·* nor material power as able to destroy.
  252–11 until the entire *m·*, material error finally
  253–12 erring, *m·*, material sense
  c 256– 5 rises . . . from the *m·* to the immortal.
  258– 1 A *m·*, corporeal, or finite conception of God
  260– 7 The conceptions of *m·*, erring thought
  262–13 above the *m·* to the immortal idea of God.
  265–29 inform us that the pleasures of sense are *m·*
  b 276–16 Discord is unreal and *m·*.
  279– 2 changing, and dying, the mutable and *m·*,
  286– 4 the finite, mutable, and *m·*,
  289–13 never make men sick, sinful, or *m·*.
  292–28 material mentality, . . . is *m·*.
  296– 5 the *m·* is dropped for the immortal.
  298– 8 a *m·* temporary sense of things,
  298–18 never reaches beyond the boundary of the *m·*
  300– 1 and would be mutable and *m·*.
  301– 6 *m·* and material man seems to be substance,
  303–23 belief . . . that *m·*, material man is the
  305–24 man would be wholly *m·*, were it not that
  306–31 God's man, . . . is not material and *m·*.
  307–18 says : . . . He has made man *m·*
  314– 3 Jesus waited until the *m·* or fleshly sense had
  320–23 for according to that error man is *m·*.
  337–13 while error is *m·* and discordant.
  o 347– 5 whatever is *m·* or discordant has no
  352– 6 a *m·* and material belief of flesh and bones,
  p 400–23 Mortal mind rules all that is *m·*.
  403–26 The *m·* so-called mind produces
  409–21 the *m·* and imperfect . . . are counterfeits
  425–15 Mortal man will be less *m·*, when he
  r 466–13 Truth is immortal ; error is *m·*.
  468– 3 If Soul sinned, it would be *m·*.
  468– 5 error must be *m·*, because error is unlike Truth.
  476–11 Hence man is not *m·* nor material.
  477– 9 Whatever is material is *m·*,
  477–13 corporeal senses to be *m·* and erring illusions.
  478–21 this belief is *m·* and far from actual.
  478–25 whatever is *m·* is composed of
  478–31 for man is not *m·*,
  479– 6 it cannot be *m·* and material ;
  481–24 If Soul sins, it must be *m·*.
  484–21 Mesmerism is *m·*, material illusion.
  486–21 So long . . . mortals will continue *m·* in belief
  487–18 believer and belief are one and are *m·*,
  g 505–29 *m·*, erring, and finite are human beliefs,
  521–20 the continued account is *m·* and material.
  522– 8 chronicles man as mutable and *m·*,
  522–16 and this man to be *m·*,
  526–30 Eden stands for the *m·*, material body.
  527–15 a knowledge of evil would make man *m·*.
  530– 4 forever opposed to *m·*, material sense.
  536–28 the *m·* and material return to dust,
  540–28 Cain is the type of *m·* and material man,
  543–30 belief . . . would make Life, or God, *m·*.
  545– 1 Error . . . explains Deity through *m·* and finite
  546– 3 this belief alone is *m·*.
  550–31 originate the impure and *m·*
  552–32 Naturalists describe the origin of *m·* and
  554–18 whatever is sinful and *m·* ;
  556– 3 are *m·* and material concepts
  556–23 *m·* and material life is the dream.

mortal (adj.)

ap 572– 9 whatever is of material sense, or m·,
gl 582–26 the error which would make man m·
587–15 supposititious minds, . . . erring and m· ;

Mortality

p 432–11 says :— I am M·, Governor of the Province of

mortality

and disease
p 395– 9 assert its claims over m· and disease.
claims of
ph 182– 6 the claims of m·, . . . appertain to
condition of
f 215–23 Every quality and condition of m· is lost,
death and
b 295–31 teaches that . . . is resurrected from death and m·.
destroys
sp 72–13 Truth destroys m·, and brings to light
b 323–27 The true idea of God . . . destroys m·.
disappears
b 293– 1 this unreal material m· disappears
g 520–12 These days will appear as m· disappears,
discord and
b 338– 7 belief . . . terminates in discord and m·,
disease, and
g 557–15 the less a mortal knows of sin, disease, and m·,
error and
b 292– 3 the battle of Truth with error and m· ;
error of
f 210–20 Truth pierces the error of m· as a sunbeam
escape from the
b 295–11 in order to escape from the m· of this error.
finiteness, and
gl 580– 1 a belief in intelligent matter, finiteness, and m· ;
history of
g 547–15 In its history of m·, Darwin's theory
infers the
ph 191–26 infers the m· of the body.
is finally
r 476–17 M· is finally swallowed up in immortality.
lay off
r 491–14 that mortals can lay off m·
less
s 163–12 there would be less sickness and less m·."
manifests
b 319– 1 body does not include soul, but manifests m·,
matter and
a 43–26 in defiance of matter and m·,
f 215–10 matter and m· do not reflect the facts of Spirit.
not bounded by
b 301–32 Immortality is not bounded by m·.
opposed to
p 387–12 the assurances of immortality, opposed to m·.
out of
a 39–12 out of m· into immortality and bliss.
phases of
b 311–32 is not touched by these phases of m·.
replace
r 495–23 replace m· with immortality,
sickness, and
b 335–30 Sin, sickness, and m· are the suppositional
sin and
(see **sin**)
will cease
s 126– 5 m· will cease when man beholds

———

sp 78– 9 If the departed are in rapport with m·,
f 241– 6 M· is their doom.
250– 4 and suppose . . . m· to be the matrix of
b 278–31 Matter, with its m·, cannot be substantial
335–21 Soul . . . does not exist in m·.
336– 6 nor the immortal into m·.
338– 8 The m· of material man proves that
p 368–28 Admit the . . . and you admit that m·
r 478– 4 What evidence of Soul . . . have you within m·?
492– 6 Life cannot be united to its unlikeness, m·.
g 545–32 The m· of man is a myth,
554– 5 There is no such thing as m·,
555–20 would seek to unite . . . immortality with m·,
gl 580–19 immortality's opposite, m· ;
581– 7 counteracting all evil, sensuality, and m·.
585–23 m· ; that which does not last forever ;
590– 5 KNOWLEDGE. . . . ; beliefs and opinions ;
591– 8 MATTER. Mythology ; m· ;
591–10 MATTER. . . . life in non-intelligence and m· ;
593–14 sensuality ; delusion ; m· ; error.
595– 4 TARES. M· ; error ; sin ; sickness ;
598–19 A solar measurement of time ; m· ;

mortality's

r 468– 4 sin is m· self, because it kills itself.

mortally

g 517– 6 may be defined as a m· mental attempt to

Mortal Man

p 430–21 M· M· is the defendant.
431–10 Therefore I arrested M· M· in behalf of
431–18 getting M· M· into close confinement
432– 2 Commissioner for M· M·.
432– 5 whereas M· M·, the prisoner at the bar,
432–12 says : . . . Body, in which M· M· resides.
433–11 evidence of Personal Sense against M· M·.
433–20 M· M· has been guilty of benevolence
433–24 M· M· is sentenced to be tortured until
433–32 the spirit of Life and the friend of M· M·,
434–15 the case for M· M· versus Personal Sense
434–23 M· M· has had no proper counsel
434–30 lower court has sentenced M· M· to die,
435– 8 M· M·, in obedience to higher law,
435–25 M· M· can suffer only for his sin.
436– 3 for which M· M· is under sentence of death.
436– 6 as a witness against M· M·
436–12 M· M· should find it again.
436–20 It was Fear who handcuffed M· M·
436–21 You have left M· M· no alternative.
436–29 His Honor sentenced M· M· to die
436–32 Claiming to protect M· M· in right-doing,
437– 1 in which province M· M· resides.
438–10 in which M· M· was reported to reside,
439–13 Health-officer had M· M· in custody,
439–14 though M· M· was innocent.
439–21 unfortunate M· M· who sought your aid
439–25 You betrayed M· M·, meanwhile declaring
440– 2 when it condemned M· M·
440– 9 a verdict delivering M· M· to Death.
440–18 Wherefore, then, . . . do you sentence M· M·
440–20 M· M· has his appeal to Spirit,
440–28 forbidden to enter against M· M· any more
440–31 restore to M· M· the rights of which he
441–14 cannot bear witness against M· M·,
441–14 neither can Fear arrest M· M·
441–26 no law outside of . . . can punish or reward M· M·,
442–13 M· M·, no longer sick and in prison,

Mortal Man's

p 434–16 M· M· counsel regards the prisoner with
435–16 a destroyer of M· M· liberty

Mortal Mind

p 435– 3 Has the body or has M· M· committed a
435– 6 M· M·, which alone is capable of sin

Mortal Minds

p 430–22 M· M·, Materia Medica, Anatomy,
433– 3 addresses the jury of M· M·.
436–28 charged the jury, twelve M· M·, to find the
440– 8 M· M· were deceived by your attorney,
441–29 persuading M· M· to return a verdict

mortal's

b 312–10 the departure of a m· mind,

mortals

all
ap 562–12 The twelve tribes of Israel with all m·,
alone
s 117– 9 m· alone do this.
among
s 129–28 in its reformatory mission among m·.
animals and
g 511–25 Animals and m· metaphorically present
appear to
b 332–24 and to appear to m· in such a form of humanity
apprehension of
p 368– 7 nearer . . . to the apprehension of m·,
are corporeal
s 116–22 M· are corporeal, but God is incorporeal.
are divinely driven
s 152–26 by which m· are divinely driven to a
are egotists
c 263– 1 M· are egotists.
are hastening
b 327–18 but m· are hastening to learn that Life is God,
are inclined
f 214–19 M· are inclined to fear and to
are not like
b 295–11 M· are not like immortals,
are taught
f 227– 4 m· are taught their right to freedom,
are unacquainted
f 215– 8 M· are unacquainted with the reality of
arrive at the
s 120– 8 by this reversal m· arrive at the
g 543–12 until m· arrive at the understanding that
assures
r 489–32 It assures m· that there is real pleasure in
attempt to heal
t 459–12 Any attempt to heal m· with
awaits
b 291–28 No final judgment awaits m·,

mortals

beliefs of
   f 221–18   the self-imposed beliefs of *m·*,
   b 278–13   is one of the false beliefs of *m·*,
believe
   m 62–31   Because *m·* believe in material laws
   f 203–22   then *m·* believe that the deathless Principle,
   212–21   In legerdemain and credulous frenzy, *m·* believe
   b 312–20   *M·* believe in a finite personal God ;
believed
   a 53–13   *M·* believed in God as humanly mighty,
betrays
   r 485– 7   betrays *m·* into sickness, sin, and death.
bind
   f 229–16   a law to bind *m·* to sickness, sin, and death.
birth of
   a 529– 5   were needed to assist the birth of *m·*.
blessings to
   b 325– 9   which results in infinite blessings to *m·*.
blind
   b 337– 4   blind *m·* do lose sight of spiritual
bring to
   pr 11–21   Petitions bring to *m·* only the results of
can never know
   g 519–14   *M·* can never know the infinite, until they
cannot connect
   r 491–11   Matter cannot connect *m·* with the true
claim
   b 312–19   *M·* claim that death is inevitable ;
claimed
   r 469–19   if *m·* claimed no other Mind
cling to
   b 328–10   must therefore cling to *m·* until,
commonly recognize
   ph 183–19   *m·* commonly recognize as law that which
communed with
   sp 73–15   If Spirit, or God, communed with *m·*
condemnation of
   g 545– 7   The condemnation of *m·* to till the ground
congregate
   gl 595– 9   where *m·* congregate for worship.
declare
   p 386– 8   So long as *m·* declare that certain states of the
did need
   r 494– 8   But *m·* did need this help,
does wonders for
   t 449– 4   A grain of C. S. does wonders for *m·*,
drive
   r 487– 1   these calamities often drive *m·* to seek and
encourages
   b 320–28   and encourages *m·* to hope in Him
entreat the divine
   ph 182–22   *M·* entreat the divine Mind to heal
experience
   a 22– 6   Waking to Christ's demand, *m·* experience
eyes of
   ph 165– 4   it closed the eyes of *m·*
formation of
   m 61–29   The formation of *m·* must greatly improve
frail
   o 346–32   is not this what frail *m·* are trying to do?
   t 459–15   frail *m·*, untaught and unrestrained by C. S.,
gives
   p 442–23   Truth, gives *m·* temporary food and clothing
give up
   ph 191– 4   As *m·* give up the delusion that there is
   b 330– 1   in proportion as *m·* give up error
giving
   s 128–17   giving *m·* access to broader and higher realms.
governs
   f 209– 4   as ignorance, . . . or human will governs *m·*.
happiness of
   p 397– 4   on the morals and the happiness of *m·*,
healing of
   p 406– 9   demonstrated in the healing of *m·*,
he taught
   a 20–17   he taught *m·* the opposite of themselves,
He teaches
   c 266–17   He teaches *m·* to lay down their fleshliness
hypotheses of
   ph 182–15   The hypotheses of *m·* are antagonistic to
imperfect
   f 254–12   Imperfect *m·* grasp the ultimate . . . slowly ;
important to
   a 42–18   evidence so important to *m·*.
incites
   ap 564– 5   incites *m·* to kill morally and physically
in mercy to
   a 18– 8   not only in justice to himself, but in mercy to *m·*,
instructing
   r 485–11   Why malign C. S. for instructing *m·*
lethargy of
   a 38– 7   when the lethargy of *m·*, . . . is broken
may learn
   b 316– 2   From him *m·* may learn how to

mortals

may see
   ap 571–24   in which *m·* may see their own image.
may seek
   b 322–32   *M·* may seek the understanding of C. S.,
millions of
   p 379–30   the fever-picture, drawn by millions of *m·*
mind of
   f 230–31   So-called mortal mind or the mind of *m·*
   231– 6   If . . . they are not destroyed in the mind of *m·*,
   p 423–31   They are only phenomena of the mind of *m·*.
minds of
   ph 175– 3   formulated in the minds of *m·*.
   p 386–13   the action of Truth on the minds of *m·*,
mistake of
   f 216–19   The great mistake of *m·* is to suppose
move onward
   f 240–18   *M·* move onward towards good or evil
must change
   c 260–19   *M·* must change their ideals in order to
must emerge
   g 552–16   *M·* must emerge from this notion of
must find
   sp 83– 7   *M·* must find refuge in Truth
must follow
   c 266–24   *M·* must follow Jesus' sayings
must get
   a 39–25   To break this earthly spell, *m·* must get the
must look
   c 264– 7   *M·* must look beyond fading, finite forms,
need
   sp 85–24   but *m·* need spiritual sense.
need not
   sp 79–29   *m·* need "not be weary in— Gal. 6 : 9.
   b 291– 9   *M·* need not fancy that belief in the
need only
   b 316– 5   *m·* need only turn from sin and lose sight of
needs of
   f 224–23   meeting the needs of *m·* in sickness
never helps
   r 481– 7   Material sense never helps *m·* to
obtains in
   ph 172–20   obtains in *m·*, *alias* mortal mind,
obtain the harmony
   p 400– 9   *M·* obtain the harmony of health, only as
offspring of
   gl 592– 6   the belief that man is the offspring of *m·* ;
origin of
   g 548–18   Speaking of the origin of *m·*,
other
   sp 77– 3   Neither do other *m·* . . . at a single bound.
overtakes
   b 290– 5   before what is termed death overtakes *m·*,
prevents
   p 409–14   prevents *m·* from knowing how to govern
progress
   m 68– 2   At present *m·* progress slowly
put off
   f 242– 2   *m·* put off their material beliefs
put on
   c 262– 8   *m·* "put on immortality."— I Cor. 15 : 54.
sacrificing
   p 440– 7   before sacrificing *m·* to their false gods.
senses of
   b 292–16   The so-called senses of *m·* are material.
sentence
   an 105– 3   Courts and juries judge and sentence *m·*
sinful
   f 204–25   notion that they can create . . . sinful *m·*
standard of
   r 492–10   uplift the physical and moral standard of *m·*,
standards of
   f 247–13   form the transient standards of *m·*.
suppose
   b 328– 4   *M·* suppose that they can live without
tabernacled with
   ap 576– 7   while yet he tabernacled with *m·*.
teach
   m 66– 6   Trials teach *m·* not to lean on a material staff,
   g 540–23   is to teach *m·* never to believe a lie.
teaches
   c 266–17   He teaches *m·* to lay down their fleshliness
   g 542–13   teaches *m·* not to remove the waymarks
thoughts of
   f 249–27   than are the thoughts of *m·* when awake.
   b 337–27   Temporal things are the thoughts of *m·*
   r 484–14   conscious and unconscious thoughts of *m·*.
try in vain
   a 37– 6   *M·* try in vain to slay Truth with the
try to believe
   b 312–17   *M·* try to believe without understanding Truth ;
unfolding to
   b 306–27   Science, still enthroned, is unfolding to *m·*
urges upon
   f 223–29   truth urges upon *m·* its resisted claims ;

mortals

victimizes
b 294–16 victimizes *m·*, taught, as they are by physiology
wake
f 251– 9 *m·* wake to the knowledge of two facts :
waken
p 429–17 *M·* waken from the dream of death
will behold
o 347–27 Then *m·* will behold the nothingness of
will disappear
r 476–11 *M·* will disappear, and . . . will appear
will echo
c 262–18 *M·* will echo Job's thought,
will sin
f 205– 2 *m·* will sin without knowing that they are
would procreate
s 140–29 but *m·* would procreate man,

---

pr 11–10 always demands restitution before *m·* can
a 26– 2 gratitude for what he did for *m·*,
39–11 belief that Soul is in the body causes *m·*
39–32 When *m·* once admit that evil confers no
m 63– 7 His origin is not, like that of *m·*,
64–27 Let not *m·* permit a disregard of law
69– 4 *m·* gain the sense of health only as
69– 6 *M·* can never understand God's creation while
sp 72–25 may flow from the departed to *m·* ;
86–13 *M·* evolve images of thought.
99– 4 divine Principle by which *m·* can escape
s 148–30 When *m·* sin, this ruling of the schools
156– 3 what made them good or bad for *m·*,
160– 4 When *m·* forsake the material for the
ph 187– 3 As *m·* do not comprehend even
188–21 are traced upon *m·* by unmistakable signs.
189– 8 *m·* should no more deny the power of C. S. to
190– 2 afterwards mortal men or *m·*,
190– 5 The mortal says . . . seedling is producing *m·*,
190– 7 or elsewhere in matter or in *m·*.
197–14 the farther *m·* will be removed from imbecility
199–15 *M·* develop their own bodies
f 212–17 *M·* have a modus of their own,
227– 8 or *m·* will continue unaware of
228–14 *M·* will some day assert their freedom
234–17 If *m·* would keep proper ward over mortal,
240–19 If *m·* are not progressive,
241–16 can do no more for *m·* than can moonbeams to
249–22 *M·* are the Adam dreamers.
c 255– 1 As *m·* drop off their mental swaddling-clothes,
255–13 *m·* take limited views of all things.
258–25 *M·* have a very imperfect sense of
259– 8 threw upon *m·* the truer reflection of God
259–16 then *m·* have never beheld in man the reflex
260–14 sets *m·* at work to discover what
264–13 As *m·* gain more correct views of God and
265– 5 *M·* must gravitate Godward,
266–27 evil beliefs which originate in *m·* are hell.
267–19 in the light of divine Science, *m·* present
b 270–24 *M·* think wickedly ; consequently they
273–17 have never made *m·* whole, harmonious,
283– 1 As *m·* begin to understand Spirit,
285–27 As *m·* reach, . . . a higher sense,
288–31 destroys what *m·* seem to have learned
291– 8 till *m·* have already yielded to each lesser call
292–17 so-called life of *m·* is dependent on
294–27 neither self-made nor made by *m·*.
295–16 The manifestation of God through *m·* is as
295–29 Brainology teaches that *m·* are created to
296–19 Whether *m·* will learn this sooner or later,
296–32 It says to *m·*, "You are wretched !"
297– 3 belief says, "You are happy !" and *m·* are so ;
297– 5 Human belief says to *m·*, "You are sick !"
301–12 substance, or Spirit, which *m·* hope for.
304–22 If *m·* caught harmony through material sense,
311–30 as *m·* lay off a false sense of life,
325–21 the demands of Truth upon *m·*
328– 7 *m·* get rid of sin, sickness, and death only in
o 357–13 if we theoretically endow *m·* with the
p 371– 9 *M·* are believed to be here without
375–21 a belief that matter governs *m·*,
379– 2 and control the body without the consent of *m·*,
381–15 types of disease, with which *m·* die.
388–31 If *m·* think that food disturbs the
394–22 against whom *m·* should not contend?
397–24 *M·* are no more material in their
405–30 causes *m·* to retreat from their error,
409–25 in proportion as *m·* realize
415– 1 excited state of *m·* which is not normal.
419–23 cannot in reality occur in *m·*
426–18 *m·* are not saved . . . by death,
435–23 If *m·* sin, our Supreme Judge in equity decides
t 444–29 *m·*, or the "children of men"— *Psal.* 14: 2.
458–30 by which *m·* are radically saved from sin and
r 476– 1 *M·* are the counterfeits of immortals.
476–13 *M·* are not fallen children of God.
477– 2 where sinning mortal man appears to *m·*.

mortals

r 486–21 So long . . . *m·* will continue mortal in belief
490–13 *m·* are more or less deprived of Truth.
491–14 It is only by . . . that *m·* can lay off mortality
g 520– 8 no more seen nor comprehended by *m·*, than
536–27 Through toil, struggle, . . . what do *m·* attain?
545– 8 *m·* should so improve material belief
548–12 Earth has little light or joy for *m·* before
551– 9 argues that *m·* spring from eggs
553–29 You may say that *m·* are formed before they
ap 559–19 *M·*, obey the heavenly evangel.
563–31 It is the animal instinct in *m·*,

mortals'

pr 11–21 only the results of *m·* own faith.
b 314–23 Because of *m·* material and sinful belief,

Mosaic Decalogue

r 489–14 it breaks all the commands of the *M· D·*

Mosaic law

a 30–14 Rabbi and priest taught the *M· l·*,

Moses

s 139– 6 *M·* proved the power of Mind by what men called
ph 185–17 strove to emulate the wonders wrought by *M·*.
200– 4 *M·* advanced a nation to the worship of God in
b 280–17 *M·* declared as Jehovah's first command of the
321– 9 When, . . . he saw it become a serpent, *M·* fled
321–16 illusion of *M·* lost its power to alarm him,
321–21 When *M·* first put his hand into his bosom
333–23 Abraham, Jacob, *M·*, and the prophets
gl 592–11 definition of

Moses'

b 321–11 and then *M·* fear departed.
321–25 God had lessened *M·* fear

most

pref viii–15 Christian healing confers the *m·* health
x– 5 *m·* of them incorrect in theory
x–17 These cases for the *m·* part have been
x–31 but sound morals are *m·* desirable.
pr 4– 3 What we *m·* need is the prayer of
9– 2 During many years the author has been *m·* grateful
11–18 but wipes it out in the *m·* effectual manner.
a 43–11 Jesus' last proof was the . . . *m·* convincing,
43–12 the *m·* profitable to his students.
m 59– 3 There should be the *m·* tender solicitude for
64– 8 envy, or jealousy seems on *m·* occasions to
sp 97–21 The broadest facts array the *m·* falsities
s 112– 1 to be the *m·* effective curative agent
123– 9 *m·* absolutely weak and inharmonious creature
140– 1 more than it is needed in *m·* cases ;
141– 8 even the *m·* cherished beliefs and practices,
153–12 the *m·* potent rises above matter into mind.
ph 166–29 by *m·* of the medical systems ;
176–31 Truth handles the *m·* malignant contagion
197–25 and the *m·* digestible food in the stomach,
b 286– 1 relates *m·* nearly to the happiness of being.
295–20 through which Truth appears *m·* vividly
313–23 Jesus of Nazareth was the *m·* scientific man
317– 6 Whosoever lives in the *m·* the life of Jesus
320– 5 The *m·* distinguished theologians in Europe
327–29 Reason is the *m·* active human faculty.
o 355–21 and the *m·* egregious fallacies
p 363–18 "Which of them will love him *m·* ?" — *Luke* 7 : 42.
363–20 "He to whom he forgave *m·*." — *Luke* 7 : 43.
373– 5 easier to cure the *m·* malignant disease than
376– 2 an image more terrifying than that of *m·* other
376– 6 It is the *m·* subtle, and does its work
376– 9 *m·* hidden, undefined, and insidious beliefs.
383– 9 when he leaves it *m·* out of his thought,
387–16 they occupy the *m·* important posts
387–17 and perform the *m·* vital functions in society.
387–19 That man . . . who does the *m·* good.
402– 1 C. S. is always the *m·* skilful surgeon.
403–21 The *m·* Christian state is one of rectitude
404–21 is one of the *m·* important points in the
407– 6 enslavement to the *m·* relentless masters
414– 6 it yields more readily than do *m·* diseases
t 448–31 doing one's self the *m·* harm.
449– 7 reacts *m·* heavily against one's self.
449–18 than it does to heal the *m·* difficult case.
456– 4 is *m·* dangerous quackery.
456– 9 high standing which *m·* of them hold
460–10 this *m·* fundamental part of metaphysics
460–11 is the one *m·* difficult to understand
r 466–17 the point you will *m·* reluctantly admit,
466–18 it is the *m·* important to understand.
478–18 That body is *m·* harmonious in which
495–25 *Question.* — How can I progress *m·* rapidly
g 547–17 is more consistent than *m·* theories.
549–19 the *m·* complicated corporeal structures,
556–16 It is made known *m·* fully to him who
572– 7 is the *m·* simple and profound counsel

Most High
a 49–31 before the face of the *M· H·*,"— *Lam.* 3 : 35.
s 142–24 make them meet dwelling-places for the *M· H·*.
p 436–14 under the protection of the *M· H·*.
gl 541– 5 a higher tribute to the *M· H·*.
gl 596–19 presence and power of the *M· H·*.

mostly
gl 597– 3 The Judaic religion consisted *m·* of rites

mote
t 455–16 the *m·* out of thy brother's eye."— *Matt.* 7 : 5.

moth
f 241– 5 "where *m·* and rust doth— *Matt.* 6 : 19.

Mother
c 256– 8 Father and *M·* of the universe, including man.
g 530–11 recognizing God, the Father and *M·* of all,
ap 569– 3 as Love, represented by the *M·*.
gl 592–16 definition of

mother (*see also* **mother's**)
any
s 154–32 successful method for any *m·* to adopt
r 479– 4 could the Scriptural rejoicing be uttered by any *m·*,
of Jesus
g 534– 3 to be the *m·* of Jesus and to behold at the
saintly
o 359–24 from the lips of her saintly *m·*,
such a
s 154–28 Such a *m·* runs to her little one, who
who is my
a 31– 7 "Who is my *m·*, and who are my— *Matt.* 12 : 48.

s 154–17 the *m·* is frightened and says,
154–24 That *m·* is not a Christian Scientist,
ph 178–14 produced, . . . by the fright of his *m·*.
193–25 and that his *m·* has been threatened with
f 206–19 giving the *m·* her child
236–12 A *m·* is the strongest educator,
c 267–15 the same authority for the appellative *m·*,
267–18 my brother, and sister, and *m·*."— *Matt.* 12 : 50.
b 315–30 being conceived by a human *m·*,
o 352–12 Would a *m·* say to her child,
t 463–19 and can cause the *m·* no more suffering.

motherhood
g 507– 6 the fatherhood and *m·* of God.
519–11 the fatherhood and *m·* of Love.
ap 562– 7 the spiritual idea of God's *m·*.

mother-love
m 60– 9 the *m·* includes purity and constancy,

mother's
m 60– 8 A *m·* affection cannot be weaned from
r 478–28 separated me from my *m·* womb,— *Gal.* 1 : 15.

moths
an 103–27 like silly *m·*, singe their own wings

motion
sp 90– 7 The earth's *m·* and position are sustained
s 118–22 modes of material *m·* are honored with
119–27 to believe that the earth is in *m·*
160– 9 *m·* of the arm is no more dependent upon
f 240–15 Mind is perpetual *m·*.
t 445–20 the unlabored *m·* of the divine energy

motionless
ph 199– 9 If mind does not move them, they are *m·*,
p 375–23 making certain portions of it *m·*.

motions
p 399– 8 and puts the body through certain *m·*.
437–29 overruled their *m·* on the ground that
r 471–10 no intimation of the earth's *m·* or
g 513–12 the *m·* and reflections of deific power

motive
good
p 376–14 more life and immortality in one good *m·*
purpose and
b 326–16 The purpose and *m·* to live aright can be
right
t 452–29 destroys your power of healing from the right *m·*.
453–19 a right *m·* has its reward.
without
ph 188– 7 an embryonic thought without *m·* ;
wrong
t 446–18 A wrong *m·* involves defeat.
your
p 421– 9 afterwards make known to the patient your *m·*

m 58– 2 should be the *m·* of society.
an 104–29 Our courts recognize evidence to prove the *m·*
105–15 reasonably pass sentence, according to the *m·*.

motive-power
gl 597–20 WILL. The *m·* of error ;

motive-powers
r 490– 8 reveals Truth and Love as the *m·* of man.

motives
abuse of the
ap 560–22 Abuse of the *m·* and religion of St. Paul
according to
pr 15– 9 and rewards according to *m·*,
aims and
m 63–27 a race having higher aims and *m·*.
and acts
f 238– 1 *M·* and acts are not rightly valued before
and affections
gl 597– 4 The *m·* and affections of a man
and aims
sp 95– 3 His holy *m·* and aims were traduced
p 405– 3 The indulgence of evil *m·* and aims
t 459– 8 the worldling's affections, *m·*, and aims.
and aspirations
m 60– 4 Kindred tastes, *m·*, and aspirations
and philanthropy
s 151– 8 the *m·* and philanthropy . . . of physicians.
for prayer
pr 2– 1 What are the *m·* for prayer?
for verbal prayer
pr 7–14 *m·* for verbal prayer may embrace too much
human
f 239–23 the acknowledged seat of human *m·*.
inferior
f 236– 8 Do not inferior *m·* induce the infuriated
b 290–10 and from selfish and inferior *m·*.
its
pr 4–13 Its *m·* are made manifest in the blessings
malicious
t 446–14 from sinister or malicious *m·*
our
a 36–29 and mockery of our *m·*
right
t 454–19 Right *m·* give pinions to thought,
selfish
t 447– 7 erring human opinions, conflicting selfish *m·*,
sinful
t 452–28 Acting from sinful *m·* destroys your
true
b 326–20 Working and praying with true *m·*,
wicked
p 404–12 the wicked *m·* which produce them.
wrong
t 451–29 controlling another from wrong *m·*,

a 51–24 The *m·* of his persecutors were pride, envy,
gl 587–23 HEART. Mortal feelings, *m·*, affections,

motto
f 224–29 On its banner is the Soul-inspired *m·*,
t 443–11 our *m·* should be the Master's counsel,
458–15 *Semper paratus* is Truth's *m·*.

mould
pr 4–21 will *m·* and fashion us anew,
f 236–14 Her thoughts . . . unconsciously *m·* it.

moulded
pr 1–13 that they may be *m·* and exalted
ph 198–23 *m·* and formed by his doctor's belief

moulding
f 248–14 *m·* and chiseling thought.

mount
f 236–17 pattern showed to thee in the *m·*."— *Heb.* 8 : 5.
ap 561– 9 beheld the spiritual idea from the *m·* of vision.
575–23 joy of the whole earth, is *m·* Zion,— *Psal.* 48 : 2.

mountain
pr 1– * *whosoever shall say unto this m·,— Mark* 11 : 23.
m 61–10 and every *m·* of selfishness be brought low,
b 299–28 as the mist obscures the sun or the *m·* ;
ap 558– * in the *m·* of His holiness.— *Psal.* 48 : 1.

mountain-peak
p 415–32 standing forth as distinctly as a *m·*,

mountains
m 67– 6 and the waves lift themselves into *m·*.
s 135– 3 Ye *m·*, that ye skipped like— *Psal.* 114 : 6.
p 442–15 feet "beautiful upon the *m·*,"— *Isa.* 52 : 7.
g 511–24 rocks and *m·* stand for solid and grand ideas.

mournful
a 32–30 was a *m·* occasion, a sad supper

mournfully
s 140–27 *m·* true that the older Scripture is reversed.

mouth
cannon's
f 225–21 nor did . . . freedom come from the cannon's *m·*.
cave's
a 45– 1 great stone must be rolled from the cave's *m·* ;
her
ap 570–11 and the earth opened her *m·*,— *Rev.* 12 : 16.

mouth
his
a 48–19   "He opened not his *m·*."— *Isa.* 53 : 7.
    50– 2   so he openeth not his *m·*."— *Isa.* 53 : 7.
ap 564–19   Jesus "*opened not his m·*."— *Isa.* 53 : 7.
   570– 9   serpent cast out of his *m·* water— *Rev.* 12 : 15.
   570–13   the dragon cast out of his *m·*.— *Rev.* 12 : 16.
of God
p 410–11   proceedeth out of the *m·* of God,"— *Matt.* 4 : 4.
patient's
s 152–16   introducing a thermometer into the patient's *m·*.

s 115– 9   as the *m·* tasteth meat."— *Job* 34 : 3.
o 354–22   and out of the *m·* of babes
r 489–10   not equal to guiding the hand to the *m·* ;
ap 559–19   in thy *m·* sweet as honey."— *Rev.* 10 : 9.
   566–13   into the *m·* of Rebecca the Jewess

mouthpiece
sp 73–30   sensual cannot be made the *m·* of the spiritual,

move
sp 80–20   should not seem mysterious that mind, . . . can
an 104–31   clear that the human mind must *m·* the body
s 121–18   the sun seems to *m·* from east to west,
ph 179–28   to *m·* the bowels, or to produce sleep
   199– 8   If mind does not *m·* them,
f 208– 5   "In Him we live, and *m·*, and— *Acts* 17 : 28.
   212–26   we say the lips or hands must *m·* in order to
   240–18   Mortals *m·* onward towards good or evil
o 343–10   "None of these things *m·* me."— *Acts* 20 : 24.
   361–19   "For in Him we live, and *m·*,— *Acts* 17 : 28.
p 381–18   we live, *m·*, and have our being in the
   419–13   has no intelligence with which to *m·* itself
   419–15   therefore be sure that you *m·* it.
t 454–22   Wait patiently for divine Love to *m·* upon the
g 515–27   If you speak, the lips of this likeness *m·*
   536–13   in whom we "live, and *m·*, and— *Acts* 17 : 28.

moved
pr 2– 8   God is not *m·* by the breath of praise
a 20– 4   *m·*, not by spirits but by Spirit.
   51– 3   It was the possible loss . . . which *m·* him,
ph 187–16   as does the hand, admittedly *m·* by the will.
g 503– 8   *m·* upon the face of the waters.— *Gen.* 1 : 2.
ap 566–17   Her fathers' God before her *m·*,

movement
s 119–29   the *m·* of the solar system,
b 283– 4   Mind is the source of all *m·*,

movement-cure
p 383–29   The *m·* — pinching and pounding the

movements
sp 80–26   These *m·* arise from the volition of
   90–10   the *m·* and transitions now possible
f 212–31   whereas the unreal and imitative *m·* of
gl 597–28   the *m·* of God's spiritual government,

moves
sp 80–21   mind-power which *m·* both table and hand.
f 220–32   as directly as the volition or will *m·* the hand.
b 329– 1   As time *m·* on, the healing elements
p 415– 7   because thought *m·* quickly or slowly,
   419–14, 15   If disease *m·* mind, not matter, *m·* it ;
g 515–23   *m·* in accord with Him,
ap 566–10   but *m·* before them, a pillar of cloud by day

moveth
g 512– 5   every living creature that *m·*,— *Gen.* 1 : 21.
   517–29   over every living thing that *m·*— *Gen.* 1 : 28.

moving
p 415–22   The muscles, *m·* quickly or slowly
g 511–30   the *m·* creature that hath life,— *Gen.* 1 : 20.
   514–29   *m·* in the harmony of Science,
   557– 2   *m·* and playing without harm,

Mozart
f 213–20   *M·* experienced more than he expressed.

much
pr 3–25   Gratitude is *m·* more than a verbal expression
   7–15   may embrace too *m·* love of applause
   9–19   This command includes *m·*,
a 28–32   There is too *m·* animal courage in society
   37– 2   sin brings suffering as *m·* to-day as
   45–12   *m·* more, being reconciled,— *Rom.* 5 : 10.
m 62–15   will do *m·* more for the health of the
sp 81– 1   There is not so *m·* evidence to prove
   98–13   *m·* less can they demonstrate it.
an 102–27   *m·* more likely to be abused by its possessor,
s 159–13   as if she were so *m·* mindless matter,
   159–26   to ascertain how *m·* harmony, or health,
   159–27   how *m·* pain or pleasure, action or stagnation,
   160–32   Is a stiff joint . . . as *m·* a result of law
   163–28   humiliating view of so *m·* absurdity,
   164–13   *M·* yet remains to be said and done
ph 169–21   however *m·* we trust a drug
   171–11   to learn how *m·* of a man he is.
   172– 6   nothing in the right direction and very *m·* in

much
ph 174– 7   capable of doing so *m·* for man as
   183– 7   however *m·* is said to the contrary.
f 202–26   Truth should "*m·* more abound."— *Rom.* 5 : 20.
   223–28   calamities, and sin will *m·* more abound
   233–18   *m·* more should ye discern the sign mental,
   235–12   it is not so *m·* academic education,
   243–14   arises not so *m·* from lack of desire as from
   254–15   to *begin* aright and to continue . . . is doing *m·*.
b 271– 1   seed of Truth springs up and bears *m·* fruit.
   272– 7   else it beareth not *m·* fruit,
   295–21   one which has lost *m·* materiality— *m·* error
   307–13   shall seem to have life as *m·* as
   318–19   beliefs, from which comes so *m·* suffering,
   323–28   effects of C. S. are not so *m·* seen as felt.
   333– 8   not a name so *m·* as the divine title of Jesus.
o 343–24   Christendom generally demands so *m·* less.
   348– 9   one disease can be just as *m·* a delusion as
           another.
   348–14   Are we . . . imputing too *m·* power to God,
p 364–30   that they indeed love *m·*.
   364–31   because *m·* is forgiven them.
   373–22   Disease is expressed not so *m·* by the lips as
   394–14   as *m·* so as would be the advice to a man
   396–10   Never say . . . how *m·* you have to
   401– 3   nothing in the right direction and *m·* in
   416–29   they think too *m·* about their ailments,
   416–30   have already heard too *m·* on that subject.
   434– 8   After *m·* debate and opposition,
t 458–16   Having seen so *m·* suffering from quackery,
   464– 6   how *m·* time and toil are still required
r 465– 2   After *m·* labor . . . she revised that treatise
   485–29   controlled war and agriculture as *m·* as
g 510– 2   How *m·* more should we seek to apprehend the
   517–11   not as *m·* authority for considering
   533–29   as *m·* as to say in meek penitence,
ap 559–19   will triumph by *m·* tribulation yield
gl 596– 5   C. S. brings God *m·* nearer to man,

muddy
g 540–10   The *m·* river-bed must be stirred in order to
gl 593–16   *m·*, foaming, and dashing, it is a type of error.

multifarious
r 477–21   in *m·* forms of the living Principle,

multiform
b 331–29   the same in essence, though *m·* in office :

multiplication
pref viii–22   *m·* and increased violence of diseases
c 263–23   a new *m·* or self-division of mortal thought,
   263–27   The *m·* of a human and mortal sense
b 303– 5   *M·* of God's children comes from no power of
g 507–17   and governs the *m·* of the
   512–20   the *m·* of its own pure and perfect ideas.
   549– 2   shows that the *m·* of certain animals

multiplied
a 36–28   *m·* trials, and mockery of our motives
sp 90– 3   How were the loaves and fishes *m·*
s 108–15   the product of three *m·* by three,
ph 165–13   Diseases have *m·*, since
p 421–31   the products of eight *m·* by five,

multiplier
g 508– 3   Mind is the *m·*,

multiplies
f 214–23   All material knowledge, . . . *m·* their pains,
b 280– 7   Mind creates and *m·* them,
g 533–25   and *m·* until the end thereof.

multiply
pr 11– 1   Without punishment, sin would *m·*.
s 108–13   to *m·* with mathematical certainty
f 202–18   The days of our pilgrimage will *m·*
   219– 6   we do not *m·* when we should subtract,
   250– 1   We run into error when we . . . *m·* Mind into
g 511– 4   "*m·* and replenish the earth."— *Gen.* 1 : 28.
   512–18   Be fruitful, and *m·*,— *Gen.* 1 : 22.
   512–19   and let fowl *m·* in the earth.— *Gen.* 1 : 22.
   517–26   Be fruitful, and *m·*,— *Gen.* 1 : 28.
   517–31   causes them to *m·*,— to manifest His power.
   535– 7   I will greatly *m·* thy sorrow— *Gen.* 3 : 16.
   549–11   to *m·* their species sometimes through eggs,

multiplying
g 557– 9   many animals suffer no pain in *m·* ;

multitude
pr 8–20   they "cover the *m·* of sins."— *I Pet.* 4 : 8.
sp 86– 3   "The *m·* throng thee."— *Luke* 8 : 45.
s 163–23   the *m·* of hypotheses obtruded upon us
b 273–25   fed the *m·*, healed the sick,

multitudes
sp 98–24   *m·* consider that what they call *science*
s 151–16   theories, from which *m·* would gladly escape.
b 272– 2   how shall they preach, convert, and heal *m·*,

multitudinous
a 43–30 and the *m·* errors growing from
c 264–14 *m·* objects of creation, . . . will become visible.
b 303– 2 *m·* forms of Mind which people the realm of
g 507–16 reproduces the *m·* forms of Mind

mundane
f 209–25 Material substances or *m·* formations,
249–30 but makes its *m·* flights quite ethereal.

murder
an 105– 2 The hands, without . . . could not commit a *m·*.
f 252–19 says : . . . lie, commit adultery, rob, *m·*,
b 330–31 *m·*, dementia, insanity, inanity,
p 406–17 moral man has no fear that he will commit a *m·*,

murderer
sp 89–31 "a *m·* from the beginning."— *John* 8 : 44.
an 104–32 Is not mortal mind the *m·*?
b 290–27 The *m·*, though slain in the act, does not
292–23 a *m·* from the beginning,— *John* 8 : 44.
p 436– 7 in the interest of Personal Sense, a *m·*.
441–32 "a *m·* from the beginning."— *John* 8 : 44.
g 539– 3 "a *m·* from the beginning."— *John* 8 : 44.
gl 580–30 a *m·* from the beginning,— *John* 8 : 44.

murderers
f 234–12 against the approach of thieves and *m·*.

murders
an 100– * *evil thoughts, m·, adulteries,— Matt.* 15 : 19.
106–23 envyings, *m·*, drunkenness,— *Gal.* 5 : 21.

murky
s 122–20 in the midst of *m·* clouds and drenching rain.

murmur
a 48–12 shall the humblest or mightiest disciple *m·*
p 369–32 It is error even to *m·*
ap 559–22 *m·* not over Truth, if you find its digestion

murmuring
a 40–22 may endure human brutality without *m·*,

muscle
s 160–15 to convey the mandate of mind to *m·*
160–28 to learn how mortal mind governs *m·*,
160–29 only to learn from anatomy that *m·* is not
160–32 Is a stiff joint or a contracted *m·*
ph 165– 7 To measure . . . strength by the exercise of *m·*,
f 217–30 But what is this *me?* Is it *m·* or mind?

muscles
and bones
sp 84–21 not dependent . . . upon *m·* and bones for
relaxes rigid
s 162– 8 dissolves tumors, relaxes rigid *m·*,
sprain the
p 385–19 If you sprain the *m·* or wound the flesh,

———

s 160–19 Can *m·*, bones, blood, and nerves rebel against
160–22 Unless *m·* are self-acting at all times,
160–24 If *m·* can cease to act . . . of their own prefer-ence,
ph 198–29 Because the *m·* of the blacksmith's arm are
199–11 *m·*, without volition of mortal mind,
199– 4 thought . . . hammering would enlarge the *m·*.
199– 5 since *m·* are as material as wood and iron
199– 8 *M·* are not self-acting.
199–28 gave his thought-forces, called *m·*, their
f 217–31 Without mind, could the *m·* be tired?
217–32 Do the *m·* talk,
219– 8 No more can we say . . . that *m·* give strength,
219–11 Not *m·*, nerves, nor bones, but mortal mind
p 375–24 show . . . that *m·* have no power to be lost,
393–27 lenses, *m·*, the iris and pupil,
415–21 The *m·*, moving quickly or slowly
r 485–30 as much as . . . *m·* measure strength.

muscular
s 152–10 Anatomy describes *m·* action as
ph 199–12 Not because of *m·* exercise, but by reason of

muscularity
ph 200– 2 Pagan worship began with *m·*,

mushrooms
ph 172– 3 Theorizing about man's development from *m·*

music
poetry and
p 378– 2 even as poetry and *m·* are reproduced
science of
pref viii– 7 science of *m·* corrects false tones
b 304–22 The science of *m·* governs tones
304–26 the science of *m·* must be understood.
sweetest
f 213–25 Mental melodies and strains of sweetest *m·*
tones of
sp 81–21 silence the tones of *m·*, . . . and yet the

———

a 26–19 A musician demonstrates the beauty of the *m·*
sp 81–24 in the case of numbers and of *m·*,
89–27 Sound is not the originator of *m·*,
ph 195–17 astronomy, natural history, chemistry, *m·*,

music
f 213–26 *M·* is the rhythm of head and heart.
c 255– 6 and discord into the *m·* of the spheres.
b 276–15 Harmony in man is as real . . . as in *m·*.
304–21 Harmony in man is as beautiful as in *m·*,
304–27 Left to the decisions of material sense, *m·* is
304–29 Controlled by belief, . . . *m·* is, must be,
305– 4 no more a *man* than discord is *m·*.

musical
f 217– 4 to conclude that individual *m·* tones are

musician
a 26–19 A *m·* demonstrates the beauty of the music
s 145– 2 caught its sweet tones, as the natural *m·*
f 213–22 He was a *m·* beyond what the world knew.
t 453– 3 You do not . . . disbelieve the *m·*

mustard-seed
ap 575–15 Did not Jesus illustrate . . . by the *m·*

mutable
f 202–15 Outside of this Science all is *m·* ;
b 279– 2 changing, and dying, the *m·* and mortal,
286– 4 through the finite, *m·*, and mortal,
299–32 and would be *m·* and mortal.
300–14 The *m·* and imperfect never touch the
g 503–25 mortal life, *m·* truth, nor variable love.
522– 8 second record chronicles man as *m·* and

mutations
c 261–25 Breaking away from the *m·* of time and sense,
b 310–32 These changes are the *m·* of material

mute
pr 15–11 Lips must be *m·* and materialism silent,
sp 89–16 tongue grows *m·* which before was eloquent.
ph 191–20 Intelligence is not *m·* before non-intelligence.

mutilated
a 37–20 into a *m·* doctrinal platform.

mutter
sp 70– * *wizards that peep and that m· ;— Isa.* 8 : 19.

mutual
a 21–22 our *m·* interests are identical ;
m 59– 4 *m·* attention and approbation should
59– 7 *M·* compromises will often maintain a
59–24 A *m·* understanding should exist
an 100– 8 as follows : "There exists a *m·* influence

My
s 140– 6 "Thou canst not see *M·* face ;— *Exod.* 33 : 20.
g 501– * *but by M· name Jehovah— Exod.* 6 : 3.

my
ph 187–18 What is this *m·* but mortal mind,

myriad
f 247–25 Love which paints the petal with *m·* hues,
b 306–21 The *m·* forms of mortal thought,
p 404– 4 any one of the *m·* forms of sin,
g 543–27 reflected in the *m·* manifestations of Life,
ap 572–16 uncover the *m·* illusions of sin, sickness, and

mysteries
sp 90–29 improve our time in solving the *m·* of being

mysterious
sp 80–19 It should not seem *m·* that mind,
86–14 but they are *m·* only because
s 134–32 This fact at present seems more *m·* than
137–11 so *m·* to the popular mind
t 450– 3 teaches belief in a *m·*, supernatural God,

mystery
dispels
sp 80–15 Science dispels *m·* and explains
unveils the
f 216– 6 Science unveils the *m·* and solves the problem
veil of
s 114–24 It lifts the veil of *m·* from Soul and body.

———

sp 70– 2 Every day is a *m·*.
98–26 *M·* does not enshroud Christ's teachings,
s 145–20 If there is any *m·* in Christian healing,
145–21 *m·* which godliness always presents to the
145–22 the *m·* always arising from ignorance
b 319–17 *M·*, miracle, sin, and death will disappear
g 501–14 So-called *m·* and miracle, which subserve the

mystical
b 334–28 a *m·* statement of the eternity of the Christ,

mysticism
sp 80–14 It is *m·* which gives spiritualism its force.
80–18 from the domain of reason into the realm of *m·*.

mystification
g 523– 9 arise from a mist or false claim, or from *m·*,

myth
s 152– 1 But this so-called mind is a *m·*,
ph 186–25 If death is as real as Life, immortality is a *m·*.
b 281–19 a *m·*, a misconceived sense and false
r 470–31 If . . . then man's existence was a *m·*.

myth
  g 523–12 material *m·*, instead of the reflection of Spirit.
    528– 8 this supposition was a dream, a *m·*.
    530–17 This *m·* represents error as always asserting
    546– 1 The mortality of man is a *m·*,
    550–21 If . . . then the great I AM is a *m·*.

mythical
  c 255– 6 The *m·* human theories of creation,
  r 490–28 the *m·* nature of material sense.

mythologic
  g 531–29 *m·* theory of material life at no point resembles

mythological
  f 249–11 theory of Life, . . . is delusive and *m·*.
  g 528– 5 is solely *m·* and material.
    534–16 *m·* material intelligence called *energy*

mythologies
  b 319–17 are so many ancient and modern *m·*.

mythology
  ancient
  r 469–30 as are ancient *m·* and pagan idolatry.

mythology
  father of
  b 294–23 and human belief in them to be the father of *m*
  god of
  gl 580– 2 nothingness ; the first god of *m·* ;
  gods of
  r 485–28 heathen gods of *m·* controlled war
  heathen
  r 466–23 Heathen *m·* and Jewish theology have

  b 339–20 As the *m·* of pagan Rome has yielded to a
  g 524– 1 idolatry which followed this material *m·*
  gl 587– 9 GODS. *M·* ; a belief that life, substance, and
  591– 2 From this follow idolatry and *m·*,
  591– 8 MATTER. *M·* ; mortality ; another name for
  591–26 *m·* ; error creating other errors ;
  594– 3 the first statement of *m·* and idolatry ;

myths
  s 151– 1 the human mind and body are *m·*.
  b 294–22 show the pleasures and pains of matter to be *m*
  p 441–28 Your personal jurors . . . are *m·*.

N

nabob
  f 220–13 procures . . . with more ease than a *n·*.

nacash
  gl 594– 1 (*ophis*, in Greek ; *n·*, in Hebrew).

nail-prints
  a 46–18 Jesus caused him to examine the *n·* and

nails
  r 486–14 Jesus proved by the prints of the *n·*,

naked
  g 532–16 I was *n·* ; and I hid myself. — *Gen.* 3 : 10.
    532–29 In the allegory the body had been *n·*,
    533– 6 Who told thee that thou wast *n·* ? — *Gen.* 3 : 11.

nakedness
  g 533– 1 first impression . . . was one of *n·* and shame.

name (*see also* **name's**)
  Adam
  b 338–14 Divide the *n·* Adam into two syllables,
  gl 580–21 The *n·* Adam represents the false
  affixed the
  r 483–14 she affixed the *n·* "Science" to Christianity,
  and nature
  o 355–11 Let discord of every *n·* and nature
  r 483–30 through the divine *n·* and nature.
  g 528– 4 That Adam gave the *n·* and nature of animals, is
  announce its
  p 391–26 has no intelligence to . . . announce its *n·*.
  another
  pr 16–19 is but another *n·* for the first lie
  gl 591– 8 MATTER. . . . another *n·* for mortal mind ;
  asked the
  p 411–13 once Jesus asked the *n·* of a disease,
  Christ's
  p 436–11 Giving a cup of cold water in Christ's *n·*,
  coupled with the
  gl 590–19 unless specially coupled with the *n·* God.
  Eden
  g 526–29 *n·* Eden, according to Cruden, means *pleasure*,
  family
  g 515–21 Man is the family *n·* for all ideas,
  gave no
  p 398– 9 Often he gave no *n·* to the distemper he cured.
  get its
  p 412–19 get its *n·*, and array your mental plea
  his
  s 109–26 his *n·* shall be called Wonderful." — *Isa.* 9 : 6.
    163– 2 by first marking Nature with his *n·*,
  b 308–30 then his *n·* was changed to Israel,
  p 411– 7 replies more readily when his *n·* is spoken ;
    411–15 demon, or evil, replied that his *n·* was Legion.
  holy
  s 143–31 everlastingly due its holy *n·*.
  human
  b 333– 5 Jesus was a human *n·*, which belonged to
  in Christ's
  ap 570–17 Give them a cup of cold water in Christ's *n·*,
  in my
  p 362– * *In my n· shall they cast out* — *Mark* 16 : 17.
  in the
  s 135–30 not merely in the *n·* of Christ, or Truth,
  p 438–15 I ask your arrest in the *n·* of Almighty God
    440–17 Wherefore, then, in the *n·* of outraged justice,
  t 453–22 yet serves evil in the *n·* of good.
    456– 3 Teaching or practising in the *n·* of Truth,
  ap 563–28 but doing this in the *n·* of good.

name
  Joshua
  b 333– 7 it is identical with the *n·* Joshua,
  left no
  a 27–25 other disciples who have left no *n·*.
  more than a
  a 54–24 whose religion was something more than a *n·*.
  My
  g 501– * *by My n· Jehovah was I not known* — *Exod.* 6 : 3
  new
  ph 197– 3 A new *n·* for an ailment affects people like a
  b 326–30 in humility he took the new *n·* of Paul.
  of father
  a 31– 9 of his calling any man by the *n·* of *father.*
  of God Almighty
  g 501– * *by the n· of God Almighty ;* — *Exod.* 6 : 3.
  of Jehovah
  g 524– 8 by the national *n·* of Jehovah.
  524– 9 In that *n·* of Jehovah,
  of Jesus
  a 29–18 gave to her ideal the *n·* of Jesus
  of laws
  s 118–22 are honored with the *n·* of *laws.*
  of Science
  s 111–11 some may deny its right to the *n·* of Science.
  ph 185–15 a human conception in the *n·* of Science
  of the disease
  p 396– 9 avoid speaking aloud the *n·* of the disease.
  Parisian
  ph 197– 4 like a Parisian *n·* for a novel garment.
  proper
  b 333–13 The proper *n·* of our Master
  special
  p 408–10 from the special *n·* of insanity.
  spiritual
  s 137–29 but now the Master gave him a spiritual *n·*
  the very
  s 129–28 The very *n·*, *illusion*, points to nothingness.
  Thy
  pr 16–28 Hallowed be Thy *n·*. — *Matt.* 6 : 9.
  thy
  a 49– 6 subject unto us through thy *n·*." — *Luke* 10 : 17.
  s 161–23 "Liberty, what crimes are committed in thy *n·* !"
  b 308–29 "What is thy *n·* ?" — *Gen.* 32 : 27.
    309– 1 "Tell me, I pray thee, *thy n· ;*" — *Gen.* 32 : 29.
  under the
  s 119–15 in the form and under the *n·* of natural law.
  usurping the
  f 204–25 usurping the *n·* without the nature

  pr 16– 8 which we *n·* after him the Lord's Prayer.
  sp 76– 2 *n·* the face that smiles on them
  93–23 Spirit, as a proper noun, is the *n·* of the
  ph 169–10 I *n·* these facts to show that disease has a
    177–20 the opposite of Truth, cannot *n·* the qualities
    186– 8 under whatever *n·* or pretence they are
  f 210–23 I *n·* it mortal.
    228–15 their freedom in the *n·* of Almighty God.
  b 319–29 for instance, to *n·* Love as merely an attribute
    332– 3 Father-Mother is the *n·* for Deity,
    333– 8 Christ is not a *n·* so much as the
    333–10 The *n·* is synonymous with Messiah,
  p 362– 3 a certain Pharisee, by *n·* Simon,
    372–13 and *n·* them divine law.
    390–15 mortal opinions which you *n·* law,
    398– 1 Sometimes Jesus called a disease by *n·*,
    411– 4 If the student silently called the disease by *n·*,
    412–10 You may call the disease by *n·* when you

ame
t 448–30   has any claim to the n·.
449–32   is a Scientist only in n·.
r 473–12   Jesus is the n· of the man who,
483–14   affixed . . . the n· "error" to corporeal sense,
483–15   affixed . . . the n· "substance" to Mind.
g 515–17   The n· Elohim is in the plural,
527–25   that was the n· thereof.— *Gen. 2 : 19.*
537–11   has no local habitation nor n·.
ap 563–19   that old serpent, whose n· is devil
567–19   that old serpent whose n· is devil
gl 581– 1   the n· often conferred upon him

named
m 68–19   I have n· her case to individuals,
an 103–18   As n· in C. S., animal magnetism
s 107– 3   and n· my discovery C. S.
156– 2   Who n· drugs, and what made them good or
ph 187–12   another illusive personification, n· Satan.
189– 5   Science (in this instance n· natural)
200–24   the infinite Spirit, n· God.
b 276–27   the *nothingness* n· error.
276–28   the *somethingness* n· Truth.
293– 8   The grosser substratum is n· matter
295–26   The theoretical mind is matter, n· *brain,*
p 426–31   human concepts n· matter, death, disease,
r 469–11   Life, Truth, and Love,— n· God.
469–28   still believe there is another power, n· *evil.*
471– 6   The unlikeness of Truth,— n· *error,*
471–31   which, . . . she has n· C. S.
g 502–10   untrue image of God, n· a sinful mortal.
533–18   the rib . . . changed into an evil mind, n· *woman,*
gl 591– 4   one Spirit, or intelligence, n· Elohim, or God.
594– 2   the opposite of Truth, n· error ;
594–10   claim . . . that there was another power, n· *evil,*

nameless
b 309– 2   a n·, incorporeal impartation of divine Love
g 507– 9   n· offspring,— wanderers from the parent Mind,
550–10   which ends, . . . in n· nothingness

namely
pr 5– 6   the test of our sincerity,— n·, reformation.
a 53–20   n·, that this shock arises from the great
sp 92–22   fact concerning error— n·, its nothingness
s 157–29   C. S. impresses the entire corporeality,— n·,
ph 167–25   There is but one way— n·,
f 204– 8   n·, Spirit and matter,
204–24   notion . . . can create what God cannot,— n·,
228– 5   n·, that nothing inharmonious can enter being,
b 278–18   requires another admission,— n·,
o 347–19   n·, apostolic, divine healing
355– 5   n·, the proof of the utility of these methods ;
p 367–28   n·, the student's higher attainments
400– 7   his goods, — n·, of sin and disease.
414– 9   n·, the impossibility that matter, brain,
422–30   believes that something . . . n·, matter
431–11   in behalf of the state (n·, the body)
432–13   a statute regarding disease,— n·,
r 472–21   absurdity— n·, *erroneous truth.*
474– 1   and their glorious proofs, — n·,
492– 4   but one fact before the thought, n·,
g 526– 8   n·, that all Life is God.
gl 580–14   n·, matter, sin, sickness, and death ;

name's
ap 578– 9   for his n· sake.— *Psal. 23 : 3.*

names
s 108–28   which this same so-called mind n· *matter,*
137–27   common n·, Simon Bar-jona, or son of Jona ;
ph 177–18   These n· indicated matter's properties,
187– 7   gives them material n·,
197– 1   It does this by giving n· to diseases
b 275–12   and are the Scriptural n· for God.
320– 4   are often expressive of spiritual ideas.
t 453–26   nor give n· to diseases,
g 506–29   finding n· for all material things,
507– 6   Spirit n· and blesses all.
508–22   n· the female gender last
512–26   confers animal n· and natures upon its
528–24   Adam — *alias* error— gives them n·.

naming
ph 177–18   had the n· of all that was material.
o 348– 1   which they chide us for n· nothing
p 412–10   by n· it audibly, you are liable

Napier, Sir Charles
p 378–12   Sir Charles N· sent it cowering back into the

napkin
a 44–18   to remove the n· and winding-sheet,
p 367– 1   under the n· of its form,

narcotics
s 157–26   N· quiet mortal mind, and so relieve the body ;
p 408–15   the use of purgatives and n· is in itself a

narrated
ph 193–31   occurred just as I have n·.

narrating
pref viii–25   n· experiences which led her,

narrative
s 157–17   according to the n· in Genesis
g 502– 4   preponderance of unreality in the entire n·,
507– 1   Adam has not yet appeared in the n·.
521– 4   closes its n· of being
525– 3   In this n·, the validity of matter
528–28   according to this n·, surgery was
530–29   *First,* this n· supposes that
ap 568– 9   The n· follows the order used in Genesis.

narratives
g 501– 6   whereas the New Testament n· are clearer

narrow
a 44–30   demonstrating within the n· tomb
sp 77–30   where the chances . . . for improvement n· into
s 126–31   in "the straight and n· way"— *see Matt. 7 : 14.*
137–13   Jesus completely eschewed the n· opinion
151–28   The straight and n· way is to see and
c 256–14   within the n· limits of physical humanity,
b 324–14   The way is straight and n·,
t 451–12   strive, to enter the n· path of Life,
454–29   tread firmly in the straight and n· way.
r 472– 6   way which leads to C. S. is straight and n·.
g 536–22   Their n· limits belittle their gratifications,

narrowed
s 134– 7   the word *martyr* was n· in its significance

narrowness
m 58–16   n· and jealousy, which would confine
c 256–26   material sense of God leads to formalism and n· ;

nasal
ph 175–15   glandular inflammation, sneezing, and n· pangs.

nation (*see also* **nation's**)
an 106– 6   Like our n·, C. S. has its Declaration of
ph 200– 4   Moses advanced a n· to the worship of God

national
a 41–30   It was enough for them to believe in a n· Deity ;
s 133–13   In n· prosperity, miracles attended the
133–20   limited form of a n· or tribal religion.
g 524– 8   the Supreme Being by the n· name of Jehovah.

nation's
ph 200– 2   the gods became alive in a n· belief.

nations
ph 94–12   The eastern empires and n·
s 133–16   Even in captivity among foreign n·,
b 340–23   One infinite God, good, unifies men and n· ;
p 406– 2   were for the healing of the n·."— *Rev. 22 : 2.*
ap 565– 7   to rule all n· with a rod of iron :— *Rev. 12 : 5.*
565–16   will eventually rule all n· and peoples

native
m 57–12   The attraction between n· qualities
sp 91–11   reduced to its n· nothingness,
s 128–18   It raises the thinker into his n· air of insight
ph 190–16   and return to its n· nothingness.
b 281–24   They are n· nothingness, out of which
p 365–17   will vanish into its n· nothingness
383– 5   It is the n· element of such a mind,
g 501–16   something more n· to their immortal cravings
ap 572– 6   scientifically reduced to its n· nothingness.

Natrum muriaticum
s 153– 5   The author has attenuated *N· m·*

natural
pref xi–15   not supernatural, but supremely n·.
a 32–24   it was n· and beautiful.
44–24   On the contrary, it was a divinely n· act,
s 111– 6   C. S. is n·, but not physical.
118–21   as the n· status of men and things,
118–31   and the n· order of heaven comes down to earth.
119–15   under the name of n· law.
119–21   God is n· good, and is represented only by
125– 8   man will be found normal and n·
126–18   as being both n· and spiritual?
128– 2   Good is n· and primitive.
130–30   no longer think it n· to love sin
131–27   n· demonstrations of the divine power,
134–22   n· law of harmony which overcomes discord,
145– 1   as the n· musician catches the tones of
ph 175– 9   What an abuse of n· beauty to say that a rose,
184–30   The inspirations were deep and n·.
189– 5   Science (in this instance named n·)
193–11   its death-pallor gave place to a n· hue.
193–12   and the breathing became n· ;
195–17   Through astronomy, n· history, chemistry,
f 240– 1   Nature voices n·, spiritual law and
b 272–32   reveals the n·, divine Principle of Science.
274– 8   is not really n· nor scientific, because it
277–13   N· history presents vegetables and animals as
321–23   presently restored his hand to its n· condition
p 387–14   faithfully perform the n· functions of being.
413–12   are no more n· nor necessary than
413–19   Water is not the n· habitat of humanity.

aught
sp 87–19 The mine knows *n·* of the emeralds within
s 109– 2 Mind is All and matter is *n·*
144– 6 *N·* is the squire, when the king is nigh ;
c 262– 6 C. S. takes *n·* from the perfection of God,
p 435–26 For *n·* else can he be punished,
g 554–19 infinite Mind sets at *n·* such a mistaken belief.

auseous
ph 195–25 the speculative theory, the *n·* fiction.

autical
m 67–10 *n·* science is not equal to the Science of Mind.

avigator
s 120–32 chained the limbs of the brave old *n·*,

Nazarene
a 53– 5 so far removed from . . . passions as the *N·*.
54–25 it enabled them to understand the *N·*
f 228–27 The humble *N·* overthrew the supposition that
gl 597– 6 The great *N·*, as meek as he was mighty,

Nazareth
a 18– 3 Jesus of *N·* taught and demonstrated
b 313–23 Jesus of *N·* was the most scientific man
333–16 The advent of Jesus of *N·* marked the
ap 564–11 the accusations against Jesus of *N·*

ear
sp 82– 1 as easy to read distant thoughts as *n·*.
82–19 even if our departed friends were *n·* us
s 108–19 When apparently *n·* the confines of
161–21 a statue . . . erected *n·* the guillotine :
c 265– 6 they must *n·* the broader interpretations
t 455–25 one who is spiritually *n·* Himself.
gl 596– 6 known as the All-in-all, forever *n·*.

earer
pr 2–29 The unspoken desire does bring us *n·* the
sp 96–25 As this consummation draws *n·*,
97–14 The *n·* a false belief approaches truth
s 121–30 thus brought *n·* the spiritual fact,
f 239–19 If divine Love is becoming *n·*,
248–11 which each day brings to a *n·* tomb.
249–26 sometimes *n·* the fact of being than
p 368– 7 *n·* than ever before to the apprehension
409– 5 the *n·* matter approaches its final statement,
g 501– 7 are clearer and come *n·* the heart.
553– 7 get *n·* the truth of being,
ap 559–24 When you approach *n·* and *n·* to this
567– 4 Truth and Love come *n·* in the hour of woe,
568–28 *n·* to the great heart of Christ ;
gl 596– 5 but C. S. brings God much *n·* to man,

earing
ap 565– 1 when *n·* its doom, this evil increases

early
sp 93– 2 Remember Jesus, who *n·* nineteen centuries ago
b 286– 1 what relates most *n·* to the happiness of being.
g 541– 2 more *n·* resembles a mind-offering than

earness
f 209–15 *N·*, not distance, lends enchantment

nebulæ
g 509–18 as *n·* indicate the immensity of space.

necessarily
pref xi–13 as *n·* as darkness gives place to light
sp 89–18 not *n·* dependent upon educational processes.
s 118–27 a kingdom *n·* divided against itself;
b 288– 1 *n·* includes the correlated statement,
312–25 *n·* limits faith and hinders . . . understanding.
g 508–18 and does not *n·* refer either to
549–21 in such vague hypotheses as must *n·* attend
552– 8 as *n·* apparent to the corporeal senses,

necessary
a 24–23 Does spiritualism find Jesus' death *n·* only for
m 60– 4 Kindred tastes, motives, and aspirations are *n·*
sp 81–29 and follows as a *n·* consequence
89–32 If seed is *n·* to produce wheat,
90–14 some insist that death is the *n·* prelude
ph 183–14 Truth never made error *n·*,
194–11 are not *n·* to ensure deafness
b 297– 7 It is as *n·* for a health-illusion, as for
p 413– 5 A single requirement, beyond what is *n·*
413–13 no more natural nor *n·* than would be the
419–31 If it is found *n·* to treat against relapse,
420–28 If it becomes *n·* to startle mortal mind
t 460– 3 "the science of the *n·* constituents and
r 484–29 is material sense a *n·* preliminary
485– 1 *Answer.—* If error is *n·* to define
ap 571– 4 since exposure is *n·* to ensure

necessities
p 381– 7 the ground that sin has its *n·*.

necessity
and power
p 377–27 conviction of the *n·* and power of
assume the
r 481–21 hypotheses . . . assume the *n·* of these evils

necessity
belief in the
f 251–18 belief in the *n·* of sickness and death,
enforce the
r 488–13 when they mean to enforce the *n·* of
finds a
s 160–14 Anatomy finds a *n·* for nerves
for uplifting
p 371–27 *n·* for uplifting the race is father to the fact
learning the
p 426–16 while also learning the *n·* of
obviate the
m 58–32 Wealth may obviate the *n·* for toil
of being right
t 455– 7 Hence the *n·* of being right yourself
of existence
ap 560–13 and the grand *n·* of existence
paramount
c 262– 5 shows the paramount *n·* of meeting them.
remove this
ph 183–13 obedience to God will remove this *n·*.
reveals a
pr 10–12 C. S. reveals a *n·* for overcoming the world,
reveals the
a 36– 5 Divine Science reveals the *n·* of
second
g 502– 1 A second *n·* for beginning with Genesis is that
showing the
pr 7– 4 showing the *n·* for such forcible utterance,
sin's
p 405–19 This is sin's *n·*,— to destroy itself.
supposed
f 253–25 Do not believe in any supposed *n·* for sin,
p 365–10 to rise above the supposed *n·* for

s 116–10 is and must of *n·* be, — all-inclusive.
f 205–14 Where then is the *n·* for recreation or
215– 8 from the very *n·* of their opposite natures.
245–30 nor is it a *n·* of nature,
p 384– 5 and must of *n·* pay the penalty.
388–13 there follows the *n·* for another admission
390–24 You have no law of His to support the *n·*
390–25 you have divine authority for denying that *n·*

neck
an 105–26 His sins will be millstones about his *n·*,

necromancers
ph 185–16 as the *n·* of Egypt strove to emulate the

necromancy
an 104–18 evil, occultism, *n·*, mesmerism,
b 322–15 The *n·* of yesterday foreshadowed the

need (noun)
absolute
s 151– 6 erring, finite, human mind has an absolute *n·* of
brother's
g 518–18 that man who seeth his brother's *n·*
each
pr 7–25 to whom each *n·* of man is always known
has no
ap 577–20 has no *n·* of sun or satellite,
human
sp 95– 9 and in that ratio we know all human *n·*
r 494–11 and always will meet every human *n·*.
little
pr 11–31 Such a desire has little *n·* of audible expression.
our
pr 13–15 God knows our *n·* before we tell Him
p 371–25 we should not deny our *n·* of its spiritual
374–14 show our *n·* of divine metaphysics.
our only
r 490–16 Our only *n·* is to know this and reduce to practice
physical
s 148–29 to render help in time of physical *n·*.
precludes the
r 487–16 this precludes the *n·* of believing.
time of
f 218–22 turning in time of *n·* to God, divine Love,

pr 1– * *knoweth what things ye have n· of,—Matt.* 6:8.
b 308–26 the patriarch, perceiving his error and his *n·*
323–19 awake to realize his *n·* of
t 447– 9 or judging accurately the *n·* of your

need (verb)
pr 4– 3 What we most *n·* is the prayer of fervent desire
pr 8– 3 We never *n·* to despair of an honest heart;
a 34– 8 if a friend be with us, why *n·* we memorials of
39– 7 We *n·* "Christ, and him crucified." *— I Cor.* 2:2.
sp 75– 5 would *n·* to be tangible and material,
79–29 Mind-science teaches that mortals *n·*
85–24 but mortals *n·* spiritual sense.
s 142–18 *n·* to be whipped out of the temple,
149–29 We *n·* to understand the affirmations of
154–25 her affections *n·* better guidance,

need (verb)

s 154–26	says to her child : . . . "You n˙ rest,"
154–27	says to her child : . . . "You n˙ medicine."
158–11	but what we n˙ is the truth
f 212– 8	Why n˙ pain, . . . come to this mortal sense?
231– 8	What God cannot do, man n˙ not attempt.
b 291– 9	Mortals n˙ not fancy that belief in the
316– 5	mortals n˙ only turn from sin and
o 346–10	we n˙ to understand that error
p 383– 3	We n˙ a clean body and a clean mind,
413–22	but in caring for an infant one n˙ not
420– 8	they n˙ only to know that error cannot produce
424–21	still you n˙ the ear of your auditor.
t 454– 1	It n˙ not be added that the use of tobacco
r 494– 9	mortals did n˙ this help, and Jesus pointed the
ap 576–18	What further indication n˙ we of the real

needed

a 29–10	because then our labor is more n˙.
34–23	They n˙ this quickening,
m 67–28	Spiritual, not corporeal, consciousness is n˙.
sp 85–27	His thrusts at materialism were sharp, but n˙.
s 140– 1	more than it is n˙ in most cases ;
142–22	are still n˙ to purge the temples of their
159– 1	a n˙ surgical operation without the ether.
b 291–25	until . . . shall effect the n˙ change.
p 382–32	Mortal mind n˙ to be set right.
411– 9	n˙ the arguments of truth for reminders.
t 448– 9	When n˙ tell the truth concerning the
r 494– 7	God, who n˙ no help from Jesus' example
g 529– 5	It came about, also, that instruments were n˙

needing

ph 171– 9	not n˙ to consult almanacs for the
171–10	not n˙ to study brainology
c 264–18	finding all in God, good, and n˙ no other
g 501–16	when n˙ something more native to their
527– 4	God's reflection, n˙ no cultivation,

needle

an 102–10	The pointing of the n˙ to the pole symbolizes
f 241–32	to go through the eye of a n˙," — Matt. 19 : 24.
t 449–10	to go through the eye of a n˙," — Matt. 19 : 24.

needless

sp 87– 5	It is n˙ for the thought or for the person
p 386–32	that lamentation is n˙ and causeless.

needle-thrusts

r 491– 1	N˙ will not hurt him.

needs

pr 16–11	that prayer which covers all human n˙.
m 66–26	the other pre-eminently n˙ good company.
sp 78–18	If Spirit pervades all space, it n˙ no
78–19	Spirit n˙ no wires nor electricity
s 144– 4	Mind, which n˙ no cooperation from
147–17	The book n˙ to be studied,
ph 170–15	The best interpreter of man's n˙ said :
174–20	Truth is revealed. It n˙ only to be practised.
f 224–23	meeting the n˙ of mortals in sickness
b 319–22	and n˙ inspiration to be understood.
339– 4	n˙ no other form of forgiveness.
o 347– 8	infers that if anything n˙ to be doctored,
p 364–17	indicated by one of the n˙ of this age.
365–32	suffering heart n˙ its rightful nutriment,
412–28	it n˙ to be met mainly through the
413– 6	to meet the simplest n˙ of the babe
417–21	from which the patient n˙ to be awakened.
t 453–15	before he can . . . minister to human n˙.
r 490–12	The Science of Mind n˙ to be understood.

negation

an 102– 6	mesmerism, or hypnotism is a mere n˙,
ph 186–11	Evil is a n˙, because it is the
p 392–12	should always be met with the mental n˙.
418–18	the n˙ must extend to the supposed disease

negative

s 143–24	not controlled scientifically by a n˙ mind.
ph 173–15	to pass through a n˙ condition would be
b 284–20	The answer . . . must forever be in the n˙.
r 491– 8	a n˙ right and a positive wrong,

neglect

a 48– 1	pangs of n˙ and the staves of

neglected

m 60–21	the education of the higher nature is n˙,
p 364–13	what his rich entertainer had n˙ to do,

neighbor

loved his

p 433–20	Because he has loved his n˙ as himself,

love his

a 55–18	and love his n˙ as himself,

love thy

s 138–29	Love thy n˙ as thyself !" — Matt. 19 : 19.
340–25	"Love thy n˙ as thyself ;" — Matt. 19 : 19.
r 467– 8	love thy n˙ as thyself." — Matt. 22 : 39.

one's

sp 88–18	To love one's n˙ as one's self,
p 440–16	than that it is for the good of one's n˙?

neighbor

our

pr 8–27	than we are willing to have our n˙ see?
9– 6	Do we love our n˙ better because of
9–12	we shall regard our n˙ unselfishly,
f 205–23	the divine law of loving our n˙ as
ap 560–16	goal is never reached while we hate our n˙

upright

f 239–12	is not the ruler of his upright n˙.

p 432–16	Judge asks if by doing good to his n˙,

neighbor's

m 64–13	never well to interfere with your n˙ business.'

neither

pr 12–10	n˙ Science nor Truth which acts through
14–13	purely spiritual, — n˙ in nor of matter,
a 28–15	N˙ the origin, the character, nor
54–18	understood n˙ his words nor his works.
m 56– *	In the resurrection they n˙ marry, nor— Mat. 22 : 30.
69–11	n˙ closes man's continuity nor his sense of
69–29	n˙ marry, nor are given in— Luke 20 : 35.
sp 71– 2	It is n˙ person, place, nor thing,
71–18	n˙ mortal mind nor matter is the image
72–25	evil is n˙ communicable nor scientific.
73– 6	n˙ the one nor the other is infinite
76– 7	recognized as n˙ material nor finite,
76–14	n˙ can he return to it, any more than
76–15	N˙ will man seem to be corporeal,
77– 2	N˙ do other mortals . . . at a single bound.
77–16	n˙ the Son, but the Father." — Mark 13 : 32.
79–32	n˙ does withholding enrich us.
80–27	but they are n˙ scientific nor rational.
84– 1	coordinate n˙ with the premises nor
89–25	Matter is n˙ intelligent nor creative.
an 102– 3	His power is n˙ animal nor human.
102– 6	possessing n˙ intelligence, power, nor reality,
s 107– *	n˙ received it of man, n˙ was I— Gal. 1 : 12.
108– 6	matter possesses n˙ sensation nor life ;
110–19	n˙ tongue nor pen can overthrow it.
124– 7	Having n˙ moral might, spiritual basis, nor
125– 6	N˙ organic inaction nor overaction
135–23	but n˙ is unimportant or untrue,
138–11	n˙ by corporeality, by materia medica, nor
139–22	But mistakes could n˙ wholly obscure the
141–24	N˙ can this manifestation of Christ be
148– 7	N˙ anatomy nor theology has ever
153–31	N˙ sympathy nor society should ever
ph 170– 3	Modes of matter form n˙ a moral nor a
173–12	N˙ the substance nor the manifestation
177– 8	N˙ exists without the other,
181– 6	which can n˙ suffer nor enjoy,
186–15	there is n˙ power nor reality in evil.
188– 3	It is n˙ mind nor matter.
190– 6	n˙ a mortal mind nor the immortal Mind
194–23	n˙ sight nor sound could reach him,
200–18	he is n˙ inverted nor subverted,
f 202–17	immortal man, . . . n˙ sins, suffers, nor
203– 6	matter can n˙ heal nor make sick,
205–10	matter has n˙ intelligence, life, nor
209–11	N˙ philosophy nor skepticism can hinder
214–28	N˙ age nor accident can interfere with
221–29	This new-born understanding, that n˙ food nor
225–20	oppression n˙ went down in blood, nor
232– 3	n˙ make man harmonious nor God lovable.
232–32	n˙ place nor opportunity in Science for error
243–20	N˙ immortal and unerring Mind nor
243–23	matter has n˙ intelligence nor sensation.
244–23	Man in Science is n˙ young nor old.
244–24	He has n˙ birth nor death.
251– 5	n˙ should a fever become more severe
c 261–25	n˙ lose the solid objects and ends of life nor
262– 3	N˙ does consecration diminish man's obligations
b 269–21	The testimony . . . is n˙ absolute nor divine.
271– 5	N˙ emasculation, illusion, nor
271–17	" N˙ pray I for these alone,— John 17 : 20.
272–17	n˙ cast ye your pearls before— Matt. 7 : 6.
275– 5	matter is n˙ substantial, living, nor intelligent.
279– 9	Matter is n˙ created by Mind nor
279–13	Spirit and matter can n˙ coexist nor
280–12	Such belief can n˙ apprehend nor
281–22	have n˙ Principle nor permanency,
282–29	which is n˙ Mind nor man,
284–22	They can n˙ see Spirit through the eye nor
284–30	but n˙ sensation nor report goes from
287– 1	They have n˙ Principle nor permanence,
287–17	N˙ understanding nor truth accompanies error,
287–26	Matter is n˙ a thing nor a person,
294–26	Man is n˙ self-made nor
297–17	it is n˙ scientific nor eternal,
304– 5	" N˙ death, nor life,— Rom. 8 : 38.
310–31	n˙ growth, maturity, nor decay in Soul.
319–14	Spirit and matter n˙ concur in man nor in
321–27	n˙ hearken to the voice of the— Exod. 4 : 8.
322–24	n˙ a temperate man nor a

neither

b	327– 4	n˙ pleasure nor pain, appetite nor passion,
	327–20	evil has in reality n˙ place nor power
	330–13	Eye hath n˙ seen God nor His image
	330–14	N˙ God nor the perfect man can be
	335– 1	There are n˙ spirits many nor gods many.
	336–20	n˙ could God's fulness be reflected by a
o	345–11	n˙ knows itself nor what it is saying.
	348– 1	and which we desire n˙ to honor nor to fear.
	349–11	n˙ Life nor man dies,
	351– 5	N˙ can we heal through the help of Spirit, if we
	351–22	such starting-points are n˙ spiritual nor
	353–31	beliefs can n˙ demonstrate Christianity nor
	354–13	opponents of C. S. n˙ give nor offer any proofs
	356–17	n˙ a present nor an eternal copartnership
	357– 8	Truth creates n˙ a lie, a capacity to lie, nor
	358–13	C. S. is n˙ made up of contradictory
p	368–22	N˙ evil, disease, nor death can be
	372–15	He can n˙ sin, suffer, be subject to
	384–26	n˙ rheumatism, consumption, nor
	387– 9	spiritual energies can n˙ wear out nor
	388–30	we shall n˙ eat to live nor live to eat.
	404–30	n˙ material medicine nor Mind
	414–24	matter n˙ feels, suffers, nor enjoys.
	415– 2	disease is n˙ a cause nor an effect.
	419–10	N˙ disease itself, sin, nor fear has the power to
	435–33	n˙ shall Judge Medicine condemn him ;
	441–14	n˙ can Fear arrest Mortal Man
	442–16	N˙ animal magnetism nor hypnotism enters
t	454–11	evil or matter has n˙ intelligence nor power,
	458–25	N˙ is he a false accuser.
	460–14	Sickness is n˙ imaginary nor unreal, — that is,
	464–27	N˙ dishonesty nor ignorance ever
r	466–12	n˙ dwell together nor assimilate.
	467–28	Matter n˙ sees, hears, nor feels.
	469– 1	Life is n˙ in nor of matter.
	472–16	Error is n˙ Mind nor one of Mind's faculties.
	473– 2	illusion, possessing n˙ reality nor identity
	478–31	not mortal, "n˙ indeed can be ;" — Rom. 8 : 7.
	479– 8	Matter is n˙ self-existent nor a product of
	484– 3	When this is accomplished, n˙ pride, prejudice,
	492–32	Victory would perch on n˙ banner.
	495–16	Let n˙ fear nor doubt overshadow your
g	503–24	God creates n˙ erring thought, mortal life,
	508–20	neuter gender, n˙ male nor female.
	515– 6	The serpent of God's creating is n˙ subtle nor
	527–13	n˙ tempteth He any man." — Jas. 1 : 13.
	529–20	n˙ shall ye touch it, lest ye die. — Gen. 3 : 3.
	529–27	has n˙ origin nor support in Truth
	530–28	the dreamer and dream are one, for n˙ is true
	533–30	as much as to say . . . "N˙ man nor God shall
	534–20	not subject to the law of God, n˙— Rom. 8 : 7.
	540– 3	Spirit creates n˙ a wicked nor a mortal man,
	544–13	In Science, Mind n˙ produces matter nor
	544–26	Therefore man, in this allegory, is n˙ a
	551–28	N˙ can produce the other.
	555–10	it n˙ understands nor can be understood.
	555–13	C. S. attributes to error n˙ entity nor power,
	555–14	error is n˙ mind nor the outcome of Mind.
ap	561–28	light portrayed is really n˙ solar nor lunar,
	566–27	n˙ was their place found any more— Rev. 12 : 8.
	570–20	He can n˙ drown your voice with its roar, nor
gl	584–17	error ; n˙ corporeality nor mind ;
	592– 8	that which n˙ exists in Science nor

Nerve

p	432– 2	I am N˙, the State Commissioner for
	436–35	N˙, testified that he was a ruler of Body,
	437–12	I proclaim this witness, N˙, to be destitute of
	438– 8	C. S. proved the witness, N˙, to be a perjurer
	438–11	N˙ was an insubordinate citizen,

nerve

auditory

pr	7–24	The "divine ear" is not an auditory n˙.
ph	194–10	Destruction of the auditory n˙ and

optic

ph	194–11	paralysis of the optic n˙

s	113–29, 30	no n˙ in Mind, and no mind in n˙ ;
ph	171–19	carried on a n˙, exposed to ejection
	194–13	if . . . it will be so without an injured n˙.
f	212– 2	is not communicated through a n˙.
	212–12	When the n˙ is gone, which we say was
p	368–14	has little inspiration to n˙ endeavor,
gl	587–13	theories . . . sense, existing in brain, n˙,

nerves

are unable

p	399–13	N˙ are unable to talk,

blood, and

s	160–19	Can muscles, bones, blood,. and n˙ rebel

brain and

s	122–12	certain sections of matter, such as brain and n˙,
b	290–11	manifested through brain and n˙,

have no sensation

f	212–16	and the n˙ have no sensation.

nerves

olfactory

f	212–20	bring the rose into contact with the olfactory n˙

weak

p	392–15	If you believe in inflamed and weak n˙,

an	100–11	through the substance of the n˙."
s	127–20	n˙, . . . have — as matter — no intelligence, life,
	143–19	you conclude that the stomach, blood, n˙,
	160–14	Anatomy finds a necessity for n˙
f	211– 1	If brain, n˙, stomach, are intelligent,
	211– 8	N˙ are not mind.
	211–24	If it is true that n˙ have sensation,
	211–32	N˙ are not the source of pain or pleasure.
	216–15	it makes the n˙, . . . servants, instead of
	219– 9	No more can we say . . . that n˙ give pain
	219–11	Not muscles, n˙, nor bones, but
b	294–12	error, saying : . . . N˙ feel. Brain thinks and
	295– 2	seeming to be in n˙ which are no longer there,
	308–10	head, heart, stomach, blood, n˙,
p	389– 7	Recollect that it is not the n˙,
	409– 6	animate error called n˙, brain, mind,
r	478–14	Question.— Does brain think, and do n˙ feel,
	480– 8	N˙ are an element of the belief that there is
	485–29	as much as n˙ control sensation
	488–21	N˙ have no more sensation,

nervous

sp	79–26	says : . . . You have n˙ prostration,

net

a	35– 5	and cast their n˙ on the right side.

nets

b	271–26	Those, who are willing to leave their n˙

neuralgia

p	392–17	You will call it n˙, but we call it a belief.

neuter

g	508–20	a n˙ gender, neither male nor female.
	511–28	in masculine, feminine, or n˙ gender.
	516–30	Masculine, feminine, and n˙ genders are

neutralizes

s	157–31	Science both n˙ error and destroys it.

neutralizing

s	162– 6	C. S. acts as an alterative, n˙ error

never

pref	ix–28	notes . . . which have n˙ been published.
	xii–20	she had n˙ read this book throughout
	4–17	Simply asking . . . will n˙ make us love Him ;
	4–27	Audible prayer can n˙ do the works of
	7–22	ventilation of fervent sentiments n˙ makes a
	8– 3	We n˙ need to despair of an honest heart ;
	9–13	we shall n˙ meet this great duty simply by
	10–10	vain repetitions will n˙ pour into prayer the
	11–13	Principle n˙ pardons our sins . . . till they
a	24– 2	Firmness in error will n˙ save from sin,
	25–28	faith in the Teacher . . . will n˙ alone make
	27–17	parables explain Life as n˙ mingling with
	27–27	n˙ truly understood their Master's instruction.
	29–11	though we may n˙ receive it in this world.
	31– 2	God will n˙ place it in such hands.
	36– 2	They, . . . can n˙ find bliss in the
	38–24	his spiritual selfhood, n˙ suffered.
	41–31	belief, . . . n˙ made a disciple who could
	53– 4	n˙ lived a man so far removed from
m	57–16	should n˙ weigh against the better claims
	58–12	N˙ contract the horizon of a worthy outlook
	59– 1	Matrimony should n˙ be entered into without a
	59–27	nuptial vow should n˙ be annulled, so long as
	59–32	Separation n˙ should take place,
	59–32	it n˙ would, if both husband and wife were
	61– 6	or happiness will n˙ be won.
	63– 1	You would n˙ think that flannel was better
	64–12	n˙ well to interfere with your neighbor's
	65–24	transitional stage is n˙ desirable on its own
	66–21	Husbands and wives should n˙ separate if
	66–30	It n˙ leaves us where it found us.
	68–16	I n˙ knew more than one individual who
	69– 6	Mortals can n˙ understand God's creation while
sp	70– *	he shall n˙ see death.— John 8 : 51.
	70– 6	Whatever is false or sinful can n˙ enter
	70– 7	Man is n˙ God,
	71–25	I n˙ could believe in spiritualism.
	72–22	suppositional opposite of good, is n˙ present.
	74–12	n˙ returns to the old condition.
	74–23	different beliefs, which n˙ blend.
	74–29	In C. S. there is n˙ a retrograde step,
	74–30	n˙ a return to positions outgrown.
	75–15	the understanding that Lazarus had n˙ died,
	76–11	Spirit n˙ entered matter
	76–11	and was therefore n˙ raised from
	76–29	Death can n˙ hasten this state of
	79–20	He n˙ described disease,
	80–7, 8	"There n˙ was, and there n˙ will be, an
	80–16	Science n˙ removes phenomena from
	85–27	He n˙ spared hypocrisy the sternest

never

sp 85–31 truth communicates itself but *n·* imparts error.
87–25 The true concept is *n·* lost.
88–19 can *n·* be seen, . . . through the physical senses.
93–13 Good *n·* causes evil,
an 105–24 Whoever uses . . . is *n·* safe.
s 110– 8 I beheld, as *n·* before, the awful unreality
116–14 They *n·* crown the power of Mind as
120– 1 shall *n·* understand this while we admit
126– 8 Human thought *n·* projected the least portion of
126–13 the human mind *n·* produced a real tone
143–10 The divine Mind *n·* called matter *medicine,*
143–22 *n·* discerning how this deprives you of the
147–15 *n·* believe that you can absorb the whole
147–32 Jesus *n·* spoke of disease as dangerous
149–12 and its perfection of operation *n·* vary
149–21 remarked . . . mind can *n·* cure organic
151–18 Fear *n·* stopped being and its action.
154–32 "Oh, *n·* mind ! You 're not hurt,
157– 6 *n·* shares its rights with inanimate matter.
157–20 then they should *n·* be used.
160–23 Unless . . . self-acting at all times, they are *n·*
160–23 *n·* capable of acting contrary to
ph 169–25 the sick are *n·* really healed except by means of
170–11 believeth in me shall *n·* die,"— *John* 11 : 26.
170–20 always in opposition, *n·* in obedience, to
171–29 intelligence and life are spiritual, *n·* material,
175–27 but they *n·* indulged in the refinement of
179–20 epizoötic . . . which a wild horse might *n·* have.
183–14 Truth *n·* made error necessary,
184–10 *n·* honoring erroneous belief with the
185– 4 and she *n·* suffered again from east winds,
186–20 It can *n·* destroy one iota of good.
186–28 ignorant of self, or it could *n·* be self-deceived.
190–18 it *n·* merges into immortal being,
191–29 Truth *n·* mingles with error.
192–26 betrays its weakness and falls, *n·* to rise.
195– 4 that he should *n·* be happy elsewhere.
197–27 will *n·* grow robust until
199–26 he could *n·* have done it.
f 204–18 They can *n·* stand the test of Science.
204–27 in Science it can *n·* be said that man
206–10 Will-power . . . can *n·* heal the sick,
213–21 The rapture of . . . was *n·* heard.
214– 6 he could *n·* have "walked with God,"— *Gen.*
5 : 24.
215–12 Whatever is governed by God, is *n·* . . . deprived
217–13 he shall *n·* see death !"— *John* 8 : 51.
217–18 once conquered . . . that condition *n·* recurs,
218– 6 the body, . . . would *n·* be weary.
219–14 When this is understood, we shall *n·* affirm
220–24 and advised others *n·* to try dietetics for
221–19 God *n·* decreed disease, — *n·* ordained a law that
221–25 he *n·* enjoyed his food as he had
222–27 concluded that God *n·* made a dyspeptic,
228–21 we shall *n·* depend on bodily conditions,
230–23 the sick are *n·* really healed by drugs,
230–28 but we are *n·* thoroughly healed until
231– 4 Unless . . . overcome by Truth, the ill is *n·*
232–19 Jesus *n·* taught that drugs, food,
232–23 and *n·* tried to make of none effect the
234–21 empty it of . . . or sin and sickness will *n·* cease.
236– 3 should emanate from the pulpit, but *n·* be
238–13 To fall away . . . shows that we *n·* understood
239–29 opposite sources *n·* mingle in fount or stream.
243– 1 but we can *n·* succeed . . . through ignorance or
244– 5 Jesus demonstrated Life, *n·* fearing nor
244–18 but man was *n·* more nor less than man.
245–27 Impossibilities *n·* occur.
245–32 The infinite *n·* began nor will it ever end.
246– 1 Mind and its formations can *n·* be annihilated.
246–17 *N·* record ages.
248– 3 Love *n·* loses sight of loveliness.
248–28 look at them continually, or we shall *n·*
249–15 infinity *n·* began, will *n·* end,
249–22 God *n·* slumbers, and His likeness *n·* dreams.
250– 8 Spirit is the Ego which *n·* dreams,
250– 9 Spirit is the Ego . . . which *n·* errs,
250–10 Spirit is the Ego . . . which *n·* believes, but
250–10, 11 the Ego . . . which is *n·* born and *n·* dies.
253–27 God *n·* requires obedience to a so-called
c 258–27, 28 *N·* born and *n·* dying, it were impossible for
259–16 then mortals have *n·* beheld in man the
259–25 Brain or matter *n·* formed a human concept.
264–16 Life is Spirit, *n·* in nor of matter,
b 273–17 The so-called laws of matter . . . have *n·* made
273–21 God *n·* ordained a material law to annul
274–26 firm, called matter and mind, God *n·* formed.
275– 1 Matter has no life to lose, and Spirit *n·* dies.
276–25 beliefs and . . . understanding *n·* mingle.
276–32 Intelligence *n·* produces non-intelligence ;
277– 6 Matter *n·* produces mind.
277– 6 The immortal *n·* produces the mortal.
279– 7 protoplasm *n·* originated in the immortal Mind,
280– 9 Finite belief can *n·* do justice to Truth
282–12 *n·* unite in figure or in fact.

never

b 284– 9 It can *n·* be in bonds, nor be fully
288– 9 Superstition and understanding can *n·*
289– 2 Mortal man can *n·* rise . . . until he learns that
289–12 Truth and Truth's idea, *n·* make men sick,
291–25 Mind *n·* becomes dust.
295–25 The light and the glass *n·* mingle,
298–17 This human belief, . . . *n·* reaches beyond the
299–13 These upward-soaring beings *n·* lead towards
299–24 Truth *n·* destroys God's idea.
300–13 The temporal and unreal *n·* touch the eternal
300–14 The mutable and imperfect *n·* touch the
300–16 The inharmonious and self-destructive *n·* touch
300–18 tares and wheat, which *n·* really mingle,
303–15 All the vanity of the ages can *n·* make
304–13 good can *n·* produce evil ;
304–13 matter can *n·* produce mind nor
307–28 material laws which Spirit *n·* made ;
309–30 Life is *n·* for a moment extinct.
309–30 Therefore it is *n·* structural nor organic,
309–31 Life is . . . *n·* absorbed nor limited by its
311–21 So long as . . . we can *n·* understand the
315– 2 and believeth in me shall *n·* die."— *John* 11 : 26.
325–25 can *n·* reach in this world the divine heights of
327–22 Fear of punishment *n·* made man truly
329–24 its divine Principle *n·* repents,
335– 8 Spirit *n·* created matter.
335–17 *n·* included in a limited mind or a
336– 2 Mind *n·* enters the finite.
336– 3 Intelligence *n·* passes into non-intelligence,
336– 4 Good *n·* enters into evil,
336–13 but infinite Mind can *n·* be in man,
336–17 Immortal man is not and *n·* was material,
339–30 *n·* to admit that sin can have intelligence
339–32 will *n·* lose their imaginary power . . . until
o 348–26 I have *n·* supposed the world would
353–28 Mind is limitless. It *n·* was material.
356– 7 Discord can *n·* establish the facts of harmony.
358–31 whom they have perhaps *n·* seen
p 369–14 We *n·* read that Luke or Paul made a
369–16 Jesus *n·* asked if disease were acute or chronic,
369–17 *n·* recommended attention to laws of health,
369–18 *n·* gave drugs, *n·* prayed to know if
374– 2 Anodynes, counter-irritants, and depletion *n·*
374– 8 "How can my mind cause a disease I *n·*
376–12 blood *n·* gave life and can *n·* take it away,
377–19 The author *n·* knew a patient who did not
378–27 God *n·* endowed matter with power to
381–23 or you will *n·* believe that you
381–25 will *n·* be reached without the understanding
381–29 a sentence *n·* inflicted by divine authority.
384– 6 God *n·* punishes man for doing right,
384–29 evidence before the senses can *n·* overrule.
385–12 though it can *n·* annul the law which
390– 5 *n·* deny the everlasting harmony of Soul,
391–19 When the body is supposed to . . . *n·* plead guilty.
393–29 Man is *n·* sick, for Mind is not sick
396– 1 One should *n·* hold in mind the thought of disease,
396– 6 *N·* startle with a discouraging remark
396–10 *N·* say beforehand how much you have to
396–29 outside of matter, *n·* in it, *n·* giving the
397–27 can *n·* treat mortal mind and matter separately
403–23 *N·* conjure up some new discovery from
409–18 *n·* yields to the weaker, except through fear or
412– 2 governs all, *n·* punishing aught but sin,
415–10 Inflammation *n·* appears in a part which
417– 5 *N·* tell the sick that they have more courage than
419–25 *N·* fear the mental malpractitioner,
425–16 he learns that matter *n·* sustained existence
425–17 can *n·* destroy God, who is man's Life.
425–26 You will *n·* fear again except to offend God,
425–27 will *n·* believe that heart . . . can destroy you
427– 1 can *n·* change in Science to the opposite belief
427– 4 Soul is *n·* without its representative.
427–18 If man is *n·* to overcome death, why do the
428– 8 he shall *n·* see death."— *John* 8 : 51.
429–12 is cold and decays, but it *n·* suffers.
429–32 he shall *n·* see death."— *John* 8 : 51.
434–28 alleged crime *n·* to have been committed.
438– 7 he shall *n·* see death. — *John* 8 : 51.
438–27 he disappeared and was *n·* heard of more.
439–33 they learn that Disease was *n·* there,
t 444–19 and *n·* to condemn rashly.
450– 7 *n·* fail to stab their benefactor in the back.
452–14 *N·* breathe an immoral atmosphere, unless
453–12 I have *n·* witnessed so decided effects from
453–30, 31 *n·* recommends material hygiene, *n·* manipulates
457– 8 has *n·* used this newly discovered power in any
463–25 He *n·* enjoined obedience to the laws of nature
r 466– 5 manifestations of . . . indicate Mind, *n·* matter
467–23 not confined in man, and is *n·* in matter.
468– 2 *n·* can be coordinate with human illusions.
470–18 when God, the Mind of man, *n·* sins
476–14 They *n·* had a perfect state of being,
477–24 can *n·* reflect anything inferior to Spirit.

ever
- r 478– 5   n· beheld Spirit or Soul leaving a body
- 480–20   good, n· made man capable of sin.
- 481– 7   Material sense n· helps mortals to understand
- 481–28   Soul is the divine Principle of man and n·
- 484– 1   will n· be based on a divine Principle . . . until
- 486–11   In reality man n· dies.
- 487– 4   n· attainable through death, but gained by
- 489– 5   found that the senses of Mind are n· lost
- 491–10   spiritual individuality is n· wrong.
- 491–21   reveals material man as n· the real being.
- g 504– 1   is n· reflected by aught but the good.
- 505–11   apparent only as Mind, n· as mindless matter
- 509–28   in man and the universe n· to disappear.
- 510–19   Geology has n· explained the earth's
- 517–23   Even eternity can n· reveal the whole of God,
- 519–15   Mortals can n· know the infinite,
- 519–26   can n· impoverish the divine Mind.
- 520–11   can n· be reckoned according to the calendar
- 520–31   n· causing man to till the ground,
- 533– 3   This had n· been bestowed on Adam.
- 537– 9   was n· the essence of divinity or manhood.
- 539–10   God could n· impart an element of evil,
- 540–20   It saith to the human sense . . . "God n· made
- 540–23   is to teach mortals n· to believe a lie.
- 543–16   verities of existence are n· excluded
- 545– 6   and n· had been divinely conceived.
- 546– 4   Spirit, God, n· germinates, but is
- 548– 7   man has n· lost his spiritual estate
- 550–26   A serpent n· begets a bird,
- 553– 8   or health will n· be universal,
- 553– 8   or . . . harmony will n· become the standard
- 553–18   the maternal egg n· brought forth Adam.
- 554–24   Jesus n· intimated that God made a devil,
- 557–20, 21   as n· born and as n· dying,
- ap 560–15   This goal is n· reached while we hate our
- 560–19   without a correct sense of . . . we can n· understand
- 565–12   might n· hold sway and deprive Herod of his
- 570–18   and n· fear the consequences.
- gl 588–14   as numbers which n· blend with each other,
- 588–25   that which is n· unconscious nor limited.
- 598–16   for n· did he give up Spirit, or Soul.

nevertheless
- s 112–13   n· remain wholly human in their origin

New
- s 139–19   and the three hundred thousand in the N·,

new
- pref vii–22   A book introduces n· thoughts,
- a 20– 9   Jesus' history made a n· calendar,
- 30–17   Jesus, the n· executor for God,
- 33–22   This is the n· understanding of spiritual Love.
- 33–29   which attend a n· and higher understanding
- 35–11   in the dawn of a n· light
- 43–18   opened a n· era for the world.
- m 58– 3   Unity of spirit gives n· pinions to joy,
- 66–15   unfolds n· views of divine goodness
- sp 74– 9   seed which has germinated has a n· form
- 96–17   sin, sickness, and death, which assume n· phases
- 98– 1   persecutions which attend a n· step
- s 108–32   set my thoughts to work in n· channels,
- 109–24   When a n· spiritual idea is borne to earth,
- 112–27   if any so-called n· school claims to be C. S.,
- 114–19   in expressing the n· tongue we must
- 114–20   the n· wine of the Spirit has to be
- 114–32   opposition to everything n·,
- 117–11   spoken of . . . as the n· tongue,
- 134– 9   The n· faith in the Christ, Truth, so roused the
- 136–28   No wonder Herod desired to see the n· Teacher.
- 139–11   but the present n·, yet old, reform
- ph 193–14   and said : "I feel like a n· man.
- 197– 3   A n· name for an ailment affects people
- f 201– 8   Truth makes a n· creature,
- 201– 9   "all things are become n·." — II Cor. 5 : 17.
- 206–24   nothing is n· to God,
- 210– 1   expressed only in "n· tongues ;" — Mark 16 : 17.
- 225–27   always germinating in n· forms of tyranny,
- 226– 7   the voice of the herald of this n· crusade
- 235–31   will love to grapple with a n·, right idea
- 247– 6   Another woman at ninety had n· teeth,
- 251– 8   as to drive belief into n· paths.
- 251–11   they have but passed the portals of a n· belief.
- c 263–21   Whatever seems to be a n· creation, is but
- 263–23   else it is a n· multiplication or self-division
- b 270– 5   their foresight of the n· dispensation
- 272–11   and is the n· tongue referred to in the
- 276–21   is turned into n· and healthy channels,
- 281–27   does not put n· wine into old bottles,
- 281–31   old belief must be cast out or the n· idea will
- 299–10   they point upward to a n· and glorified trust,
- 300–11   real man, or the n· man (as St. Paul has it).
- 324– 1   and to leave the old for the n·,
- 326–30   in humility he took the n· name of Paul.
- o 349–23   shall speak with n· tongues." — Mark 16 : 17.
- 354–25   to hear and to speak the n· tongue.

new
- p 362– *   shall speak with n· tongues ; — Mark 16 : 17.
- 398–20   and produces a n· effect upon the body.
- 398–29   changes such ills into n· and more difficult
- 403–23   Never conjure up some n· discovery from
- 404–22   Arouse the sinner to this n· and true view
- 409–24   and the n· man or real man is put on,
- 420–17   ready to become receptive to the n· idea.
- t 452–11   you should not fear to put on the n·.
- 463– 7   To attend properly the birth of the n· child,
- 463–10   Though gathering n· energy, this idea cannot
- 463–14   The n· idea, conceived and born of Truth
- 463–17   When this n· birth takes place,
- r 492–13   N· thoughts are constantly obtaining the floor.
- g 518–29   Nothing is n· to Spirit.
- 541–22   Here the serpentine lie invents n· forms.
- 544–11   Nothing is n· to the infinite Mind.
- 548–15   This is the n· birth going on hourly,
- 549–15   the birth of n· individuals, or personalities,
- 556–29   existence will be on a n· standpoint.
- ap 560–25   spoken something n· and better of God
- 570–19   What if the old dragon should send forth a n·
- gl 593– 9   a n· and higher idea of immortality,
- (see also **earth, heaven**)

new-blown
- p 413–23   in order to keep it sweet as the n· flower.

new-born
- a 35–31   can unite with this church only as we are n·
- f 221–29   This n· understanding, that neither food nor

New Covenant
- a 33–28   Have you shared the blood of the N· C·,

New Jerusalem
- ap 574–13   "N· J·, coming down from God, — Rev. 21 : 2.
- 575–11   The builder and maker of this N· J· is God,
- 576– 4   this N· J·, this infinite All, which
- gl 592–18   definition of

newly
- pref viii–31   the first steps of a child in the n· discovered
- t 457– 8   she has never used this n· discovered power in

new-mown
- ph 175–14   perfume of clover and the breath of n· hay

newness
- a 24–12   rise into n· of life with regeneration.
- 35– 8   from mortal sensuousness, . . . into n· of life
- f 249– 7   bringing us into n· of life and recognizing
- p 426–19   understanding will quicken into n· of life.
- g 520–13   and they will reveal eternity, n· of Life,

new-old
- ph 191–12   even to the birth of a n· idea,

New Testament
- b 279– 3   A N· T· writer plainly describes faith,
- o 350– 7   our Master's sayings as recorded in the N· T·,
- r 474–13   Greek word rendered miracle in the N· T·
- g 501– 6   whereas the N· T· narratives are clearer
- gl 598– 7   and elsewhere in the N· T·.

next
- pref xii–16   conviction that the n· two years of her life
- pr 5– 4   The n· and great step required by wisdom is
- sp 77– 9   on the n· plane of existence as on this, until
- an 104–11   N·, they say it has been discovered before.
- s 156–29   the n· stately step beyond homœopathy.
- ph 190– 1   N· we have the formation of so-called
- 193–18   The n· day I saw him in the yard.
- f 217–20   The n· toil will fatigue you less,
- b 296–29   and aids in taking the n· step
- o 350– 3   They think of . . . Spirit as n· to nothing,
- p 390– 1   The n· minute she said, "My food is all digested,
- 413–16   "Cleanliness is n· to godliness,"
- 416–25   and n· to nothing of the metaphysical method
- 431–20   The n· witness is called: — I am Coated Tongue.
- 432– 1   The n· witness testifies : — I am Nerve,

Niagara
- sp 76– 3   as one at N·, with eyes open only to that

Niagara's
- ph 199–26   to walk the rope over N· abyss of waters,

nice
- f 252–23   says : . . . What a n· thing is sin !

nigh
- s 144– 6   Naught is the squire, when the king is n· ;

Night
- g 504– 4   and the darkness He called N·. — Gen. 1 : 5.
- gl 592–21   definition of

night
after
- c 261–13   a noted actor was accustomed n· after n·
before his crucifixion
- a 32–29   on the n· before his crucifixion,
blazons the
- f 247–26   blazons the n· with starry gems,
cold
- p 378–28   with a long and cold n· of discord.

night
day and
ap 568–17 before our God day and n·.— Rev. 12 : 10.
every
p 431– 4 watched with the sick every n· in the week.
frequent
ap 566–22 In shade and storm the frequent n·,
is far spent
ph 174–12 "the n· is far spent,— Rom. 13 : 12.
last
f 249–20 You say, "I dreamed last n·."
long
ph 174–10 and portend a long n· to the traveller ;
no
r 475– 2 there is "no n· there."— Rev. 22 : 5.
g 511–13 In the eternal Mind, no n· is there.
ap 575–20 for there shall be no n· there."— Rev. 21 : 25.
gl 584– 7 "there shall be no n· there."— Rev. 22 : 5.
of error
pref vii– 9 across a n· of error should dawn the morning
of gloom
a 47–31 During his n· of gloom and glory
of his arrest
p 436–15 Prior to the n· of his arrest, the prisoner
of materialism
ap 562–20 as the n· of materialism wanes.
of materiality
o 354–23 The n· of materiality is far spent,
of paganism
ap 571–29 and illumined the n· of paganism with the
old
p 372– 6 likened by Milton to "chaos and old n·."
ap 570–21 into the deep waters of chaos and old n·.
over the
g 511– 9 rule over the day and over the n·,— Gen. 1 : 18.
rule the
g 510–15 the lesser light to rule the n· :— Gen. 1 : 16.
traversed the
pref vii– 5 yet it traversed the n·, and came where,
without a star
ap 564– 8 will sink its perpetrator into a n· without a star.

ph 194–27 An infant crying in the n·,
f 240– 8 The stars make n· beautiful,
p 431–22 the n· of the liver-attack.
431–27 since the n· of the liver-attack.
436– 8 on the n· of the alleged offence
438–20 on the n· of the crime
g 509–10 to divide the day from the n· ;— Gen. 1 : 14.
552– 5 hatched from the "egg of n·"
ap 566–11 a pillar of cloud by day and of fire by n·,

night-dream
f 249–25 mortal n· is sometimes nearer the fact
249–27 The n· has less matter as its accompaniment.

Nightingale, Florence
p 385– 2 It is proverbial that Florence N·

nightmare
s 128–24 waking him from a cataleptic n·,

nights
p 430–29 testifies . . . I was present on certain n·

nine
an 101– 8 In 1837, a committee of n· persons was
s 108–16 three multiplied by three, equalling n·,
108–17 must be n· duodecillions,

nineteen
sp 93– 2 Remember Jesus, who nearly n· centuries ago
s 122– 8 n· hundred years ago
f 224–11 In the record of n· centuries, there are
232–17 as it did over n· hundred years ago,
r 495– 3 as surely as it did n· centuries ago.

nineteenth
s 147– 6 Late in the n· century I demonstrated the
ap 560– 2 in connection with the n· century.

ninety
f 247– 6 Another woman at n· had new teeth,

ninety-and-nine
o 344–28 may lose n· patients, while C. S. cures its

nipped
c 265–18 withered by the sun and n· by untimely frosts ;

Nisan
a 32–29 with his disciples in the month N·

nitrous-oxide
o 346–26 when you believe that n· gas has made

No
pref viii–20 A vigorous "N·" is the response

Noah
b 320–11 in the learned article on N·
gl 592–22 definition of

Noah's
gl 587–21 HAM (N· son). Corporeal belief ;
589– 8 JAPHET (N· son). A type of spiritual peace,
594–14 SHEM (N· son). A corporeal mortal ;

nobility
ph 172–29 may present more n· than the

noble
m 58– 8 Unselfish ambition, n· life-motives,
61–20 What hope of happiness, what n· ambition,
64–11 lends a helping hand to some n· woman,
f 248–29 carve them out in grand and n· lives.
t 450–10 They are sincere, generous, n·,

nobler
m 63–25 achievement of a n· race for legislation,
b 326–27 Thought assumed a n· outlook,

nobody
s 140– 4 That God is a corporeal being, n· can truly affirm
ph 199– 6 n· believes that mind is producing such a result

Nod
g 542–28 and dwelt in the land of N·.— Gen. 4 : 16.

noise
g 505–18 than the n· of many waters,— Psal. 93 : 4.

noises
sp 86–18 Haunted houses, ghostly voices, unusual n·,

none
sp 86–24 In reality there is n·.
99–12 N· may pick the lock nor enter by some other
s 147–11 had lost n· of its divine and healing efficacy,
164– 7 said : . . . n· can be adopted as a safe guidance
ph 178–30 n· of these methods can be mingled with
193–27 saying : "It was n· other than God and
f 232–23 never tried to make of n· effect the
250–19 experiencing n· of these dream-sensations.
c 256–22 and n· can stay His hand,— Dan. 4 : 35.
b 269–25 Other foundations there are n·.
291–32 As for spiritual error there is n·.
337–14 C. S. demonstrates that n· but the pure in heart
o 343–10 "N· of these things move me."— Acts 20 : 24.
345–15 n· which are apparent to those who understand
360–18 then you practically have n·.
p 414–22 there is n· else beside Him."— Deut. 4 : 35.
421–17 God, Spirit, is all, and that there is n· beside
t 447–20 by knowing that there is n·.
r 479–29 because it has n· of the divine hues.

nonentity
b 303–26 would be a n·, or Mind unexpressed.
r 477–30 Separated from . . . Spirit would be a n· ;

non-existent
ph 180–12 deport themselves a if Mind were n·,
g 513–27 mortal mind — being n· and consequently

non-intelligence
and matter
b 282–19 Mind cannot pass into n· and matter,
and mortality
gl 591–10 Mythology ; . . . life in n· and mortality ;
before
ph 191–20 Intelligence is not mute before n·.
intelligence and
sp 73–28 Spirit and matter, intelligence and n·,
f 204–17 intelligence and n·, of Spirit and matter.
never produces
b 276–32 Intelligence never produces n· ;
subject to
ph 171–22 infinite Mind,— subject to n· !

s 120– 3 and that man is included in n·.
b 282–21 nor can n· become Soul.
285–14 one is intelligence while the other is n·.
336– 3 Intelligence never passes into n·,
g 531– 5 the error, . . . that n· becomes intelligence,
gl 580–23 supposition . . . intelligence passes into n·,

non-intelligent
ph 165–10 material organization and n· matter.
f 214–12 material senses, . . . are proved n·.
217–32 Matter is n·.
c 257–14 the supposed substance of n· matter.
b 277– 1 but matter is ever n·
277– 5 The n· relapses into its own unreality.
t 457–28 as if the n· could aid Mind !
r 466–15 Truth is intelligent ; error is n·.
478–21 matter is n· and brain-lobes cannot think
g 524–21 How could the n· become the medium of Mind,
531–15 If, . . . man's body originated in n· dust,
550– 1 a circumscribed and n· egg.

non-sense
r 489–30 A wrong sense of God, man, and creation is n·,

noon
f 246–12 Manhood is its eternal n·, undimmed by a

noonday
m 56–17 destruction that wasteth at n·."— Psal. 91 : 6.
f 224–27 as he came of old to the patriarch at n·

noontide
p 367-23 but radiate and glow into n· glory.

normal
s 120-14 health is n· and disease is abnormal.
125-8 n· and natural to changed mortal thought,
f 205-25 hinders man's n· drift towards the one Mind,
212-30 The realities of being, its n· action,
214-4 it is n· and indestructible.
b 307-22 If . . . material pain and pleasure seems n·,
o 344-5 the n·, healthful, and sinless condition of man
p 368-12 beliefs . . . that discord is as n· as harmony,
406-30 n· control is gained through divine strength
412-26 until the . . . corresponds with the n· conditions
415-1 an excited state of mortals which is not n·.

north
ap 575-24 on the sides of the n·,— Psal. 48: 2.

North Star
ap 575-26 Northward, its gates open to the N· S·,

northward
ap 575-26 N·, its gates open to the North Star,

nostrils
sp 88-8 and no scent salutes the n·.
g 524-14 and breathed into his n·— Gen. 2: 7.
544-30 to enter man's n· so that

notables
p 437-22 Various n·— Materia Medica, Anatomy,

note
f 245-8 taking no n· of years,
p 415-17 N· how thought makes the face pallid.
g 515-30 Then n· how true, . . . is the reflection
538-6 to n· the proper guests.
ap 574-19 N· this,— that the very message,

noted
c 261-12 a n· actor was accustomed night after night to

notes
pref ix-27 she made copious n· of Scriptural exposition,
m 58-5 Ill-arranged n· produce discord.
b 298-21 Spiritual ideas, like numbers and n·, start from

noteworthy
b 313-12 n· that the phrase "express image"— Heb. 1: 3.

nothing
amounts to
ph 172-5 amounts to n· in the right direction
and something
a 23-17 swinging between n· and something,
apart from
r 473-9 n· apart from Him is present or has power.
but a display
b 317-31 N· but a display of matter
but a supposition
g 504-30 n· but a supposition of the absence of Spirit.
but false beliefs
ph 171-25 n· but false beliefs that intelligence
but His likeness
r 495-15 Allow n· but His likeness to abide in your
but Spirit
b 335-18 N· but Spirit, Soul, can evolve Life,
but Truth
r 483-5 which n· but Truth or Mind can heal,
can abolish
m 58-29 but n· can abolish the cares of marriage.
can be novel
g 519-1 N· can be novel to eternal Mind,
can change
b 297-1 and n· can change this state, until
can efface
b 318-3 n· can efface Mind and immortality,
can enter
ap 577-26 n· can enter that city, which
can erase
b 290-2 was and is and shall be, whom n· can erase.
can hide
f 215-1 N· can hide from them the harmony of
can interfere
p 427-14 N· can interfere with the harmony of being
can produce
b 335-26 and can produce n· unlike the eternal
can vitiate
p 393-13 n· can vitiate the ability and power
cherish
m 68-7 cherish n· which hinders our highest
could alienate
b 303-32 declared that n· could alienate him from God,
could kill
a 51-11 N· could kill this Life of man.
covered
pr 8-17 "there is n· covered that shall not— Matt. 10: 26.
difficult
t 462-16 There is n· difficult nor toilsome in this task;
drug does
pr 12-19 drug does n·, because it has no intelligence.

nothing
else
f 208-18 writes: "God is the father of mind, and of n· else."
b 331-22 reflected by all that is real . . . and by n· else.
466-20 Soul or Spirit signifies Deity and n· else.
478-26 of material human beliefs and of n· else.
481-2 tributary to God, Spirit, and to n· else.
error is
o 346-10 we need to understand that error is n·,
evil becomes
r 480-4 Where the spirit of God is, . . . evil becomes n·,
evil is
b 330-27 Evil is n·, no thing, mind, nor power.
except God
f 243-29 because they declare n· except God.
imperfect
r 477-7 Spirit, is seen in n· imperfect nor material.
in common
a 101-17 n· in common with either physiology or
t 459-7 n· in common with the worldling's affections.
inharmonious
f 228-5 namely, that n· inharmonious can enter being,
is left
f 251-26 n· is left which deserves to perish
is lost
o 360-2 they will find that n· is lost, and all is won,
is matter
s 113-18 God, Spirit, being all, n· is matter.
is new
f 206-24 His work was finished, n· is new to God,
g 518-29 N· is new to Spirit.
544-11 N· is new to the infinite Mind.
leaves
b 340-29 and leaves n· that can sin, suffer,
less
b 336-24 and n· less can express God.
manifests
ph 173-11 What is termed matter manifests n· but
matter is
s 116-18 matter is n· beyond an image in mortal mind.
naming
o 348-1 which they chide us for naming n·
narrow into
sp 77-31 the chances of . . . narrow into n·
next to
o 350-3 They think of . . . Spirit as next to n·,
p 416-25 next to n· of the metaphysical method
nothingness of
o 346-9 The nothingness of n· is plain;
of the kind
g 544-20 facts of creation, . . . include n· of the kind.
product of
gl 580-9 a product of n· as the mimicry of something;
proved
s 125-31 matter will finally be proved n· more than a
reveals
b 278-2 Science reveals n· in Spirit out of which
short of
t 448-29 n· short of right-doing has any claim to the
ap 572-12 n· short of this divine Principle, . . . can ever
that lives
p 374-29 N· that lives ever dies, and vice versa.
there can be
s 127-8 there can be n· beyond illimitable divinity.
to consume
p 425-19 and know that there is n· to consume,
unlike God
f 249-16 and includes n· unlike God.
unspiritual
b 335-28 N· unspiritual can be real, harmonious,
when it is
b 287-19 Evil calls itself something, when it is n·.

---

pr 6-9 vain supposition that we have n· to do but
m 61-27 N· unworthy of perpetuity should be
sp 71-1 N· is real and eternal, . . . but God and His
71-1 n· is Spirit,— but God and His idea.
83-9 N· is more antagonistic to C. S. than
92-24 the ability to make n· of error
s 126-26 I have found n· in ancient or in modern
151-19 lungs, brain, etc., have n· to do with Life,
ph 174-6 N· save divine power is capable of
178-1 though they know n· of this particular case
186-12 It is n·, because it is the absence of
198-25 the doctor says n· to support his theory.
f 221-3 and drank n· but water.
228-8 if we learn that n· is real but the right,
238-10 Catholic girl said, "I have n· left but Christ."
249-10 Organization and time have n· to do with Life.
b 270-23 It has n· in Christ.
277-29 N· we can say or believe regarding matter is
296-10 N· sensual or sinful is immortal.
305-17 the Son can do n· of himself,— John 5: 19.
326-21 n· but wrong intention can hinder
330-29 n· claiming to be something,

nothing

b 331–12   n· possesses reality . . . except the divine Mind
   335– 8   n· in Spirit out of which matter could be made,
o 345–27   to be something, when he is n·,— Gal. 6: 3.
   347– 6   N· really has Life but God,
   347–10   there is n· left to be doctored.
   353–17   Without perfection, n· is wholly real.
   356–16   the flesh profiteth n·.''— John 6: 63.
p 367–31   error should be known as n·.
   371– 8   By those uninstructed . . . n· is really understood of
   374– 8   never thought of and knew n· about,
   378–14   and both will fight for n·.
   380–19   N· but the power of Truth can prevent the
   380–28   N· is more disheartening than to believe that
   401– 3   it does n· in the right direction
   416–24   sick know n· of the mental process by which
   431–28   testifies : . . . although n· on my part has
   438– 6   n· shall by any means hurt you.— Luke 10: 19.
t 460–23   superficial and cold assertion, ''N· ails you.''
g 514– 3   n· exists beyond the range of
   520–29   n· left to be made by a lower power.
   521–18   will naturally ask if there is n· more about
   529–23   n· in the animal kingdom which
   530–30   supposes that something springs from n·,
   539–12   possesses n· which he has not derived from God.
gl 591–25   N· claiming to be something,

nothingness

aghast at
ap 563– 7   But why should we stand aghast at n·?
and unreality
f 205–21   the n· and unreality of evil.
counterpoise of
p 368– 1   Evil is but the counterpoise of n·.
discord is the
b 276–27   Discord is the n· named error.
dust and
g 547–22   or go down into dust and n·.
elements of
r 479–26   and they are the elements of n·.
exposes his
sp 91–10   because Science exposes his n· ;
its
sp 92–22   the fact concerning error— namely, its n·
   97–12   the more its n· will appear, until
o 346–11   its n· is not saved, but must be demonstrated
learn the
b 327–32   learn the n· of the pleasures of human sense
material
o 345–28   This thought of human, material n·,
nameless
g 550–12   material life, which ends, . . . in nameless n·
native
sp 91–11   the sooner error is reduced to its native n·,
ph 190–17   to wither and return to its native n·.
b 281–24   native n·, out of which error would simulate
p 365–18   the disease will vanish into its native n·
ap 572– 6   scientifically reduced to its native n·.
of error
f 251–12   Truth works out the n· of error
b 287– 3   the n· of error, which simulates the
o 351–24   which proves the n· of error, discord,
ap 569– 9   by which the n· of error is seen ;
   569–10   the n· of error is in proportion to its
gl 596–16   give us a sense of the n· of error,
of evil
b 269– 7   the unreality, the n·, of evil.
   293–30   the entireness of God, good, and the n· of evil.
ap 563–17   the n· of evil and the allness of God.
of hallucinations
o 348– 3   admit the n· of hallucinations,
of matter
r 480– 2   When . . . the n· of matter is recognized.
   497–22   and the n· of matter.
of nothing
o 346– 9   The n· of nothing is plain ;
of sickness
o 347–28   Then mortals will behold the n· of sickness and
phase of
an 102– 2   Its so-called despotism is but a phase of n·.
points to
s 129–29   The very name, illusion, points to n·.
problem of
s 126– 3   The problem of n·, . . . will be solved,
proved its
a 42–21   This error Jesus met . . . and proved its n·.
prove its
t 446–24   Resisting evil, you overcome it and prove its n·.
proves their
o 347–25   destroys these evils, and so proves their n·.
proving their
a 39– 6   He overcame . . . thus proving their n·.
stand for
g 537–18   since ground and dust stand for n·.
teaches the
o 346– 7   It is sometimes said that C. S. teaches the n· of

nothingness

their
sp 96–18   until their n· appears.
t 450–21   will overcome them by understanding their n·
this
o 346– 8   said that C. S. . . . . teaches how this n· is to be saved
understood as
r 480–30   If sin, sickness, and death were understood as n·
understood the
a 52–19   understood the n· of material life
vanish into
o 352–29   The objects of alarm will then vanish into n·,
   b 312– 6   What . . . seems substance, becomes n·,
   338–13   the red color of the ground, dust, n·.
o 347–32   will then see that error is indeed the n·,
   356–11   Understanding the n· of material things,
p 382–28   n· of the so-called pleasures and pains of sense
r 490–30   shows material sense as either oblivion, n·,
g 540– 9   reducing it to its common denominator, n·.
   545–29   ''Dust [n·] thou art,— Gen. 3: 19.
   545–29   unto dust [n·] shalt thou return.''— Gen. 3: 19
ap 567–24   show the dragon to be n·, dust to dust ;
gl 580– 2   ''dust to dust ;'' red sandstone ; n· ;
   584–28   Dust. N· ; the absence of substance,
   592–22   knowledge of the n· of material things

notice

an 100– 2   was first brought into n· by Mesmer in Germany
f 237– 3   She seemed not to n· it.

noticeable

s 158– 7   It is here n· that Apollo was also regarded
r 478–20   discharge of the natural functions is least n·.

noticed

ph 168–30   Here let a word be n· . . . chemicalization.
p 442– 9   We n·, as he shook hands with his counsel,

noticing

p 413–24   n· every symptom of flatulency,

notion

against the
o 354– 1   against the n· that there can be material life,
common
p 383–32   common n· that health depends on inert matter
have no
o 360–11   replies : . . . I have no n· of losing my old
of any life
r 485–32   The n· of any life or intelligence in matter
of chance
p 424– 8   in order to change the n· of chance
that mind
b 302–10   The n· that mind is in matter,
r 492–22   The n· that mind and matter commingle
this
r 492–25   the Science of Mind, which denies this n·.
g 552–17   Mortals must emerge from this n· of
   m 67–18   The n· that animal natures can possibly give
f 204–24   the n· that they can create
   217– 3   n· of such a possibility is more absurd than
b 278– 9   false supposition, the n· that there is
   330–25   The n· that both evil and good are real
g 545–11   n· of a material universe is utterly opposed to

notions

f 251–32   Inharmonious beliefs, . . . deify their own n·,
o 357–17   popular and false n· about the Divine Being
   357–20   wrong n· about God must have
p 425–32   Discard all n· about lungs, tubercles,
gl 597– 2   and in accordance with Pharisaical n·.

notwithstanding

b 338–28   n· God had blessed the earth
p 431– 2   N· . . . the prisoner watched with the sick

noumenon

s 114–10   including n· and phenomena,

noun

sp 93–23   Spirit, as a proper n·, is the name of the

nourishes

pr 5–25   If prayer n· the belief that

novel

ph 197– 4   like a Parisian name for a n· garment.
g 519– 1   Nothing can be n· to eternal Mind,

novels

ph 195–25   N·, remarkable only for their exaggerated

now

pref xi–10   healing of C. S. results n·, as in Jesus' time,
   xi–14   N·, as then, these mighty works are . . . natural
   xi–18   coming n· as was promised aforetime.
a 31–26   ''The hour cometh, and n· is,— John 4: 23.
   33– 9   n· this bread was feeding and sustaining them
   33–12   and n· it comforted themselves.
   39–18   '' N·,'' cried the apostle, ''is the— II Cor. 6: 2
   39–19   n· is the day of salvation,''— II Cor. 6: 2.
   39–20   meaning, not that n· men must prepare for a

ow

a	39–21	but that *n·* is the time in which to experience
	39–22	*N·* is the time for so-called . . . to pass away,
	41–10	in the hereafter they will reap what they *n·* sow.
	43– 7	they had only believed ; *n·* they understood.
	43–10	and is *n·* repeating its ancient history.
	54–30	would not some, who *n·* profess to love him,
	55– 8	*N·* that the gospel of healing is again
	55–25	drinketh of Christ's cup *n·*, and is endued with
m	56– 3	"Suffer it to be so *n·* :— *Matt.* 3 : 15.
	64–29	a worse state of society than *n·* exists.
sp	70– *	*N· we know that thou hast a— John* 8 : 52.
	83– 7	evil elements *n·* coming to the surface.
	90–10	movements and transitions *n·* possible for
	90–13	though *n·* some insist that death is the
	92–10	not . . . with the power of sinning *n·* and forever.
	93– 6	"But the hour cometh, and *n· is,— John* 4 : 23.
	93– 8	"Behold, *n·* is the accepted time :— *II Cor.* 6 : 2.
	93– 8	*n·* is the day of salvation,"— *II Cor.* 6 : 2.
	96–12	This material world is even *n·* becoming the
	98–24	Even *n·* multitudes consider that which they call
an	106–20	''*N·* the works of the flesh are— *Gal.* 5 : 19.
s	123–26	did not . . . belong to a dispensation *n·* ended,
	125– 2	What is *n·* considered the best condition
	136– 9	The question then as *n·* was,
	137–28	but *n·* the Master gave him a spiritual name
	138– 6	It was *n·* evident to Peter
	138–19	under as direct orders *n·*, as they were then,
	141–22	did not then, and do not *n·*, understand
	141–31	Give to it the place . . . *n·* occupied by
	146–31	Divine metaphysics is *n·* reduced to a system,
	150–11	but the mission of C. S. *n·*, as in the time of
	150–12	*N·*, as then, signs and wonders are wrought
	151–15	bondage *n·* enforced by false theories,
	152–25	and she can *n·* understand why,
	153–20	*N·* administer mentally to your patient a
ph	197–18	departments of knowledge *n·* broadcast in the
f	221–15	and he is *n·* in perfect health
	222–20	He dropped drugs and material hygiene,
	250–22	*N·* I ask, Is there any more reality in
c	255– *	*travaileth in pain together until n··— Rom.* 8 : 22.
	259–15	If man . . . has *n·* lost his perfection,
	261– 1	*N·* reverse this action.
	262–18	but *n·* mine eye seeth Thee."— *Job* 42 : 5.
b	271–28	the opportunity *n·*, as aforetime,
	282– 1	*N·*, as of old, Truth casts out evils
	285– 5	This Science of being obtains . . . here and *n·* ;
	324–12	"acquaint *n·* thyself with Him,— *Job* 22 : 21.
	326–17	purpose and motive . . . can be gained *n·*.
o	347–15	true idea of God, comes *n·* as of old,
	361– 5	the ideal of God *n·* and forever,
	361– 9	God is come and is present *n·* and forever.
p	409–28	to say that life depends on matter *n·*, but
	423–25	Both Science and consciousness are *n·* at work
	427– 7	If man believes in death *n·*, he must disbelieve
	434–13	*n·* summoned to appear before the bar of Justice
	436–20	Fear . . . would *n·* punish him.
	440–15	*N·* what greater justification can any deed have,
	441–11	Let what False Belief utters, *n·* and forever,
r	474–18	*N·* Jesus came to destroy sin, sickness, and
	495– 2	Truth casts out error *n·* as surely as
g	509–21	no more contingent *n·* on time or
	515–28	*N·* compare man before the mirror to his
	521–10	joyfully acknowledging *n·* and forever
	521–24	*n·* the opposite error, . . . is to be set forth.
	523– 2	Scriptural account *n·* under comment.
	524–17	that He should *n·* be called Jehovah?
	528–20	error *n·* simulates the work of Truth,
	529–13	*N·* the serpent was more subtle—*Gen.* 3 : 1.

now

g	532–29	but *n·* error demands that *mind* shall
	537– 1	and *n·*, lest he put forth his hand,— *Gen.* 3 : 22.
	541–25	*N·* it repudiates even the human duty of man
	541–29	And *n·* art thou cursed from the— *Gen.* 4 : 11.
	546– 2	belief that spirit is *n·* submerged in matter,
	548–20	many general statements *n·* current,
	550–13	perfection should appear *n·*, even as it will
ap	568–14	*N·* is come salvation, and strength,— *Rev.* 12 : 10.
	568–28	*n·* rises clearer and nearer to the great heart
	573–27	we can become conscious, here and *n·*, of a

nowhere

s	163–24	*N·* is the imagination displayed to a

Noyes, George R.

b	313–21	the late George R. *N·*, D.D. :
o	360–23	Rev. George R. *N·*, D.D. :

nucleus

g	549–16	the formation of the *n·*, or egg,

null

p	381– 1	rendered *n·* and void by the law of Life,
	441– 4	so-called law, which . . . is *n·* and void.

nullify

s	161– 6	able to *n·* the action of the flames,

number

a	38– 3	a select *n·* of followers.
m	69–12	sense of increasing *n·* in God's infinite plan.
sp	81–20	Erase the figures which express *n·*,
r	494–12	to imagine that Jesus . . . only for a select *n·*

numbered

p	367–16	and with those hairs all *n·* by the Father.

numbers

pref	ix–11	she "lisped in *n·*, for the *n·* came."
sp	81–24	as truly as in the case of *n·*
s	111– 8	no more supernatural than is the science of *n·*,
f	233–25	When *n·* have been divided according to
b	298–21	Spiritual ideas, like *n·* and notes, start from
	318–30	as *n·* are controlled and proved by
	318–31	Intelligence does not originate in *n·*,
g	548–32	increase their *n·* naturally and
gl	588–14	*n·* which never blend with each other,

numerals

g	520–10	The *n·* of infinity, called *seven days*,

numeration-table

b	326–18	You have begun at the *n·* of C. S.,

numerous

o	341–17	facts are so absolute and *n·* in support of

nuptial

m	59–27	The *n·* vow should never be annulled,

nurse

s	155– 9	the druggist, the doctor, and the *n·*
p	364–32	the careless doctor, the *n·*, the cook,
	395–18	complaining, . . . person should not be a *n·*.
	395–18	The *n·* should be cheerful, orderly,

nurseries

r	235–10	*N·* of character should be strongly garrisoned

nurtured

t	448– 7	if evil is uncondemned, it is undenied and *n·*.

nutriment

f	222– 6	to believe that proper food supplies *n·*
p	365–32	suffering heart needs its rightful *n·*,
	388–12	hypothesis that food is the *n·* of life,

O

ak

pref	vii–24	task of the sturdy pioneer to hew the tall *o·*
sp	78– 1	the gnarled *o·*, the ferocious beast,

ath

a	32– 4	The Latin word for this *o·* was *sacramentum*,
	32–10	does not commemorate a Roman soldier's *o·*,

bduracy

ap	569–28	must depend upon sin's *o·*.

bedience
and suffering

ap	572– 2	washed their robes white in *o·* and suffering.

demand

ph	183– 3	so-called laws of matter . . . demand *o·* to

demands our

c	256–19	Who is it that demands our *o·*?

devout

pr	4–29	silent prayer, watchfulness, and devout *o·*

enforcing

ph	184–14	enforcing *o·* through divine statutes.

entire

ph	183–21	man's entire *o·*, affection, and strength.

obedience
guarantee of

pref	vii–18	guarantee of *o·* is a right apprehension of

habits of

m	62– 5	habits of *o·* to the moral and spiritual law,

live in

pref	viii– 4	man must live in *o·* to its divine Principle.

patient

f	242–16	In patient *o·* to a patient God,

to divine law

p	440–19	in *o·* to divine law?

to God

a	25–18	By his *o·* to God, he demonstrated
ph	183–13	*o·* to God will remove this necessity.
f	241– 4	he who refuses *o·* to God, is chastened

to higher law

p	435– 8	in *o·* to higher law, helped his fellow-man,

to material law

ph	182–19	*O·* to material law prevents

to nature

ph	176– 8	free to act in *o·* to nature,

obedience
to spiritual law
ph 182–20 prevents full *o·* to spiritual law,
to the law
pr 14–10 is to be in *o·* to the law of God,
p 387–21 supposition that death comes in *o·* to the law of
436–31 construed *o·* to the law of divine Love as
to these laws
p 440–24 and then render *o·* to these laws punishable
to Truth
ph 183–23 *O·* to Truth gives man power and strength.
urged no
s 148– 5 urged no *o·* to material laws,
yielding
ph 184–12 nor yielding *o·* to it.

ph 165–12 *O·* to the so-called physical laws of health
170–21 always in opposition, never in *o·*, to physics.
f 210–22 in *o·* to the immutable law of Spirit,
253–27 never requires *o·* to a so-called material law,
p 436– 9 the divine law, and in *o·* thereto.
t 463–25 He never enjoined *o·* to the laws of nature,

obedient
b 295– 7 *o·* to the Mind that makes them.
g 544– 4 ideas became productive, *o·* to Mind.

obey
a 20–21 to *o·* the divine order and trust God,
m 67–23 commanded even the winds and waves to *o·*
sp 91– 6 and *o·* only the divine Principle, Life and Love.
s 140– 9 We shall *o·* and adore in proportion as we
ph 186– 9 We cannot *o·* both physiology and Spirit,
187–14 The valves of the heart, . . . *o·* the mandate of
f 214–20 to fear and to *o·* what they consider a
235– 5 one who does not *o·* the requirements of
236–21 Children should *o·* their parents ;
238– 6 To *o·* the Scriptural command,
239–18 whom we acknowledge and *o·* as God.
b 307–28 nor bidden to *o·* material laws
326–22 that ye should not *o·* the truth?'' — *Gal.* 5 : 7.
o 354– 4 Why then dc Christians try to *o·* the
p 436–22 must *o·* your law, fear its consequences,
r 496– 6 in C. S. the first duty is to *o·* God,
ap 559–19 Mortals, *o·* the heavenly evangel.

obeyed
s 149–15 because you have not *o·* the rule
b 328–26 It were well had Christendom believed and *o·*,

obeying
a 31–17 *O·* his precious precepts,
f 244– 6 never fearing nor *o·* error in any form.
r 489–21 the medium for *o·* God?

obeys
f 241– 3 He, who . . . *o·* them, incurs the hostility of

object
s 115–18 the immediate *o·* of understanding.
129–30 may *o·* to the author's small estimate of the
f 248– 4 Its halo rests upon its *o·*.
c 267– 1 Every *o·* in material thought will be destroyed,
b 304–11 cannot be deprived of its manifestation, or *o·* ;
p 407– 1 becoming a fool or an *o·* of loathing ;
415– 9 looks upon some *o·* which he dreads.
t 457–10 Her prime *o·*, since entering this field of labor,
g 507– 4 Spirit duly feeds and clothes every *o·*,

objected
o 344– 1 It is *o·* to C. S. that it claims

objectified
b 310– 2 picture is the artist's thought *o·*.

objection
o 359– 8 infidels whose only *o·* to this method was,

objections
s 117– 1 The term *individuality* is also open to *o·*,
p 424–12 In medical practice *o·* would be raised if

objective
b 283–17 the *o·* state of material sense,
287–27 the *o·* supposition of Spirit's opposite.
p 374–12 the *o·* state of mortal mind.
r 484–12 the *o·* states of mortal mind.

object-lesson
f 214–10 an *o·* for the human mind.

objects
all the
gl 588–15 All the *o·* of God's creation reflect one Mind,
and subjects
g 507– 7 *o·* and subjects would be obscure,
and thoughts
b 269–18 the *o·* and thoughts of material sense,
276–13 brings *o·* and thoughts into human view
cognized by
b 311–26 The *o·* cognized by the physical senses
forbidden
f 234–28 to look with desire on forbidden *o·* was to

objects
higher
p 416–31 away from their bodies to higher *o·*.
of alarm
o 352–29 The *o·* of alarm will then vanish into
of creation
c 264–14 *o·* of creation, which before were invisible,
of sense
b 269–15 exchanges the *o·* of sense for the ideas of Soul
g 510– 3 to dwell on the *o·* of sense !
of time
gl 584– 4 The *o·* of time and sense disappear
real
sp 96–29 real *o·* will be apprehended mentally
solid
c 261–26 will neither lose the solid *o·* and ends of life
surrounding
p 415–31 will sink from sight along with surrounding *o·*

sp 79–27 Science *o·* to all this, contending for
86–28 as readily as from *o·* cognizable by the senses.
s 123–14 replaces the *o·* of material sense with
f 239–20 The *o·* we pursue and the spirit we manifest
o 348– 5 and who *o·* to this?
p 410–-13 mankind *o·* to making this teaching practical.
g 506– 2 *O·* utterly unlike the original do not

obligated
t 451–23 He feels morally *o·* to open the eyes of

obligation
b 327–31 the man's dormant sense of moral *o·*,

obligations
m 59– 2 recognition of its enduring *o·* on both sides.
59–28 so long as its moral *o·* are kept intact ;
68–13 Consider its *o·*, its responsibilities,
c 262– 4 Neither does . . . diminish man's *o·* to God,
p 363–17 who were released from their *o·* by

obliged
o 349–17 one is *o·* to use material terms

obliterated
f 231– 1 the cause of disease must be *o·* through Christ
p 426–12 If the belief in death were *o·*,
r 485–10 views of error ought to be *o·* by Truth.

obliterates
b 296–18 until Science *o·* this false testimony.

oblivion
sp 97–25 inarticulate sound is forever silenced in *o·*.
f 214–32 there is no *o·* for Soul and its faculties.
b 310–25 and spiritual death is *o·*.
o 341– 2 strictures on this volume would condemn to *o*
p 382–24 One whom I rescued from seeming spiritual *o*
441–12 now and forever, fall into *o·*,
r 490–30 Sleep shows material sense as either *o·*,
g 556–21 *O·* and dreams, not realities, come with sleep.

oblivious
c 261–18 which made him as *o·* of physical infirmity

obnoxious
f 207– 3 evil becomes more apparent and *o·*
p 407– 3 Puffing the *o·* fumes of tobacco,
g 533–21 Materiality, so *o·* to God,

obscure
s 139–23 mistakes could neither wholly *o·* the
t 445–16 You render the divine law of healing *o·* and
g 507– 8 objects and subjects would be *o·*,
546–18 Genesis and the Apocalypse seem more *o·* tha
ap 558–11 To mortal sense Science seems at first *o·*,

obscured
ap 560–26 not only *o·* the light of the ages, but
gl 586– 2 weariness of mortal mind ; *o·* views ;

obscures
b 299–27 as the mist *o·* the sun or the mountain ;
g 504–29 and darkness *o·* light.

obscurity
pref vii– 6 and came where, in cradled *o·*,
g 523– 3 the mist of *o·* evolved by error

observance
p 382–19 ''more honored in the breach than the *o·*''

observation
s 163– 9 founded on long *o·* and reflection,
ph 195–19 *O·*, invention, study, and original thought
b 299– 5 save in the artist's own *o·*
p 389–29 A case of convulsions, . . . came under my *o·*

observations
an 101–21 The author's own *o·* of the workings of
r 483–24 schools, which wrestle with material *o·* alone,
g 553– 2 accompany their descriptions with important *o*

observe
a 20–12 support the clergy, *o·* the Sabbath,
o 344–17 it would be just to *o·* the
p 419–16 *O·* mind instead of body,

bserved
an 101– 1　the violent effects, which are *o·* in the

bserver
f 250–27　To the *o·*, the body lies listless,
g 549–27　even this great *o·* mistakes nature,

bserves
p 422– 5　If the reader of this book *o·* a great stir

bsolete
sp 90–13　and death will be *o·*,
c 265–22　the error is unreal and *o·*.
b 274–31　This suppositional partnership is already *o·*,
gl 588–22　IN. A term *o·* in Science if used with

bstacle
a 45– 2　Jesus vanquished every material *o·*,
s 115– 1　the one great *o·* to the reception of
ph 179– 6　since space is no *o·* to Mind.
b 338–23　the *o·* which the serpent, sin, would impose
p 424–21　certain that the divine Mind can remove any *o·*,

bstetrics
o 342–30　If . . . teaching or practising pharmacy or *o·*
t 463– 6　the *o·* taught by this Science.
s 529– 6　The first system of suggestive *o·* has changed.

bstinate
p 414– 5　However *o·* the case, it yields more readily

bstinately
s 144–11　the more *o·* tenacious its error ;

bstruction
b 338–15　and it reads, *a dam*, or *o·*.
　338–22　it stands for *o·*, error,

btain
m 69–28　worthy to *o·* that world,— *Luke* 20 : 35.
f 211–14　seem to *o·* in mortal mind.
　219–17　must *o·* in the human mind before it
　225–30　ignorant how to *o·* their freedom.
b 284–21　physical senses can *o·* no proof of God.
p 400– 9　Mortals *o·* the harmony of health, only as
　427–20　shows that we shall *o·* the victory over
g 539–14　Whence does he *o·* the propensity to
　553– 7　Mortal thought must *o·* a better basis,

btainable
ph 173–13　Neither . . . is *o·* through matter.
　192–24　gives you the only power *o·*.

btained
sp 88–30　said to be a gift whose endowment is *o·* from
f 207–32　evidence of this inversion is *o·* from
b 296–22　knowledge *o·* from the corporeal senses
　299–21　to judge the knowledge thus *o·* to be untrue
　322– 8　before harmonious and immortal man is *o·*
　325– 6　life *o·* not of the body incapable of
p 388– 3　they *o·* a victory over the corporeal senses,
　426–12　and the understanding *o·* that
　427–12　before Life can be understood and harmony *o·*.
　434– 8　permission is *o·* for a trial in the Court of Spirit,
r 490–26　which can be *o·* in no other way.
　493– 7　all the knowledge *o·* from
gl 581–20　evidence *o·* from the five corporeal senses,
　589–12　*o·* from the five corporeal senses ;
　590– 4　Evidence *o·* from the five corporeal senses ;
　598–25　This exalted view, *o·* and retained

btaining
f 218–22　lead only into material ways of *o·* help,
r 492–14　New thoughts are constantly *o·* the floor.

btains
s 154– 5　this law *o·* credit through association,
ph 172–20　and the belief that . . . *o·* in mortals,
　174–31　the cause of disease *o·* in the
b 285– 3　Science of being *o·* not alone hereafter
　305–25　the divine Principle that *o·* in divine Science,
p 409– 2　You may say : "But if disease *o·* in matter,
t 448– 5　Evil which *o·* in the bodily senses,

btruded
s 163–24　hypotheses *o·* upon us at different times.

bviate
m 58–28　Wealth may *o·* the necessity for toil

bvious
sp 97–18　The more material the belief, the more *o·* its
b 271– 3　maintaining its *o·* correspondence with

ccasion
pr 7–12　gives *o·* for reaction unfavorable to spiritual
　8–14　there would be no *o·* for comment.
a 32–30　a mournful *o·*, a sad supper
f 212–13　When the nerve is gone, which we say was the *o·*
　230–18　and health *o·* disease.
b 329–17　he should avoid their *o·*.
g 552–24　the redeeming power, from the ills they *o·*,
ap 571–17　and the *o·* for a victory over evil.

ccasional
s 112–11　Although these opinions may have *o·* gleams of
　156– 9　*o·* doses of a high attenuation of *Sulphuris*.
　156–25　and receiving *o·* visits from me,

occasionally
sp 83–18　belief . . . that *o·* Spirit sets aside these laws,
f 237– 1　A little girl, who had *o·* listened to my

occasioned
m 62–12　which the parents themselves have *o·*.
sp 86– 2　Supposing this inquiry to be *o·* by
s 151–17　Mortal belief says that death has been *o·* by
　159– 9　a verdict was returned that death was *o·*,
ph 199–23　failure is *o·* by a too feeble faith.
b 312–12　The belief of that mortal . . . . *o·* his departure ;
p 373–19　The fear *o·* by ignorance can be cured ;
　386–19　You think that your anguish is *o·* by your loss.
　431–29　testifies : . . . nothing on my part has *o·* this

occasioning
p 416– 4　unless the mental image *o·* the pain

occasions
a 32–10　nor was the wine, used on convivial *o·*
m 64– 8　Pride, envy, or jealousy seems on most *o·*
ph 182–32　presuppose that . . . is powerless on some *o·*.
f 252– 5　Human ignorance . . . *o·* the only skepticism
p 386–17　*o·* the same grief that the friend's
　416–14　unless the belief which *o·* the pain has
　430–32　testifies . . . was personally abused on those *o·*.

occultism
an 104–17　evil, *o·*, necromancy, mesmerism,
ap 570– 3　the growing *o·* of this period.

occupancy
c 261– 6　proportionably to their *o·* of your thoughts.

occupied
s 141–31　the place . . . now *o·* by scholastic theology and
　154–10　was made to believe that he *o·* a bed where

occupies
an 104–26　This greater error thereafter *o·* the ground,
p 367–17　A Christian Scientist *o·* the place at this

occupy
a 22–13　"*O·* till I come !"— *Luke* 19 : 13.
m 60–23　Because . . . display, and pride,— *o·* thought.
p 387–19　it is not because they *o·* the most important posts

occupying
f 235–28　Clergymen, *o·* the watchtowers

occur
pr 1–11　no loss can *o·* from trusting God with
sp 77– 9　Death will *o·* on the next plane of
s 161–29　Such unconscious mistakes would not *o·*, if
f 245–27　Impossibilities never *o·*.
p 402–16　no breakage nor dislocation can really *o·*.
　419–23　A relapse cannot in reality *o·* in

occurred
s 156–17　It then *o·* to me to give her
ph 169– 3　Whenever an aggravation of symptoms has *o·*
　193–30　*o·* just as I have narrated.
p 362– 5　an unusual incident *o·*, as if to interrupt

occurrence
p 378–16　This latter *o·* represents the power of

occurs
an 105–23　to commit fresh atrocities as opportunity *o·*
p 386– 7　no such result *o·* without mind to demand it
　421–11　If a crisis *o·* in your treatment, you must

ocean
m 67– 4　When the *o·* is stirred by a storm,
　67–14　on the seething *o·* of sorrow.
sp 90–19　carries it through the air and over the *o·*.
s 122–17　On the eye's retina, . . . clouds and *o·* meet
o 361–17　As a drop of water is one with the *o·*,
ap 559– 9　thought reaches over continent and *o·*

o'clock
ph 193–15　between three and four *o·* in the afternoon

odds
a 22–15　If your endeavors are beset by fearful *o·*,

odious
f 236–15　either after a model *o·* to herself or
b 314–28　the more *o·* he became to sinners

odiousness
p 366–23　a sense of the *o·* of sin

odor
sp 88– 7　cognizant of a present flavor and *o·*,
s 128–20　An *o·* becomes beneficent and agreeable

offence
alleged
p 436– 8　on the night of the alleged *o·*
analyzes the
p 433– 4　He analyzes the *o·*, reviews the testimony,
moral
p 395–32　a moral *o·* is indeed the worst of diseases.
t 448– 2　and yet to indulge them, is a moral *o·*.
of the Jews
s 135–18　danger of repeating the *o·* of the Jews
preliminary
t 449–27　enemies without the preliminary *o·*.

offence

repeat the
  pr 5– 8   Temptation bids us repeat the *o*ʼ,
      6–10   supposition . . . we shall be free to repeat the *o*ʼ.
    11–15   leaves the offender free to repeat the *o*ʼ,

  pr 6–25   "Thou art an *o*ʼ unto me." — *Matt.* 16 : 23.
  p 431– 9   inasmuch as this *o*ʼ is deemed punishable
    435– 7   The body committed no *o*ʼ.
    439–23   an *o*ʼ of which he was innocent.

offences
  a 36–25   gloat over their *o*ʼ to the last moment
  an 105–18   no longer apply legal rulings wholly to physical *o*ʼ,

offend
  p 425–26   You will never fear again except to *o*ʼ God,

offended
  s 132– 9   whosoever shall not be *o*ʼ in me." — *Matt.* 11 : 6.

offender
  pr 11–14   leaves the *o*ʼ free to repeat the offence,

offenders
  p 439–28   *o*ʼ, awaiting the sentence which

offending
  p 392–31   Exclude from mortal mind the *o*ʼ errors ;

offensive
  t 463–13   truth removes properly whatever is *o*ʼ.

offer
  o 354–13   opponents of C. S. neither give nor *o*ʼ any
  ap 566–19   we may also *o*ʼ the prayer which concludes the

offered
  a 54–17   highest proof he could have *o*ʼ of divine Love.
  s 111–19   A prize of one hundred pounds, *o*ʼ in Oxford
  o 355–22   ever *o*ʼ for acceptance,"
  gl 597– 7   rebuked the hypocrisy, which *o*ʼ long petitions

offering
  a 25– 4   The efficacy of Jesus' spiritual *o*ʼ is
  p 406– 5   *o*ʼ full salvation from sin, sickness, and death.
  g 540–24   an *o*ʼ unto the Lord — *Gen.* 4 : 3.
    540–31   he brings a material *o*ʼ to God.
    541– 1   Abel takes his *o*ʼ from the firstlings of the
    541– 7   unto Abel, and to his *o*ʼ : — *Gen.* 4 : 4.
    541– 8   and to his *o*ʼ, He had not respect. — *Gen.* 4 : 5.

offerings
  b 286– 8   is better than all burnt *o*ʼ.

offers
  pr 12–28   another who *o*ʼ the same measure of prayer

office
  b 331–30   the same in essence, though multiform in *o*ʼ :
  p 392–29   then perform your *o*ʼ as porter
    438–12   putting in false claims to *o*ʼ
  gl 595–16   can fit us for the *o*ʼ of spiritual teaching.

officer
  p 432–22   by the *o*ʼ of the Board of Health,
    436– 1   (the *o*ʼ of the Health-laws)

officers
  p 438–25   without the inspection of Soul's government *o*ʼ.

offices
  ap 566–30   assigns to the angels, . . . different *o*ʼ.

offset
  s 111–21   essay calculated to *o*ʼ the tendency of the age
    155–22   to *o*ʼ the discords of matter
  p 428–20   must realize the ability of mental might to *o*ʼ

offshoot
  sp 92–19   a mere *o*ʼ of material sense.
  b 287–18   nor is error the *o*ʼ of Mind.

offshoots
  sp 88–13   are *o*ʼ of mortal mind ;

offspring
Christ's
  gl 583– 9   CHILDREN OF ISRAEL. . . . Christ's *o*ʼ.
fate of their
  ph 176– 5   their own downfall and the fate of their *o*ʼ
forms its
  c 259–23   and forms its *o*ʼ after human illusions.
His
  b 332– 8   "For we are also His *o*ʼ." — *Acts* 17 : 28.
man is the
  m 63– 5   man is the *o*ʼ of Spirit.
  c 265– 1   Man is the *o*ʼ, not of the lowest,
  p 396–27   man is the *o*ʼ of God, not of man ;
  gl 592– 5   the belief that man is the *o*ʼ of mortals ;
nameless
  g 507– 9   creation would be full of nameless *o*ʼ,
not the
  sp 93–17   electricity is not the *o*ʼ of infinite good.
  b 289–31   Man is not the *o*ʼ of flesh, but of Spirit,
of error
  gl 589– 2   A corporeal belief ; the *o*ʼ of error ;

offspring
of God
  a 29–30   Man as the *o*ʼ of God, the idea of Spirit,
  c 267– 3   The *o*ʼ of God start not from matter
  p 396–27   man is the *o*ʼ of God, not of man ;
of mortals
  gl 592– 5   the belief that man is the *o*ʼ of mortals ;
of physical sense
  r 479– 1   If a child is the *o*ʼ of physical sense
of sense
  b 274– 5   the *o*ʼ of sense, not of Soul,
of Soul
  a 30–24   the difference between the *o*ʼ of Soul and
of Spirit
  m 63– 5   man is the *o*ʼ of Spirit.
  g 540– 1   Christ is the *o*ʼ of Spirit,
  gl 583– 6   *o*ʼ of Spirit, who, having wrestled with error,
of spirit
  f 229–11   calls both the *o*ʼ of spirit,
of the flesh
  gl 594–17   The son of man, the *o*ʼ of the flesh.
of will
  ph 192–12   the *o*ʼ of will and not of wisdom,
spiritual
  b 336–31   and man is God's spiritual *o*ʼ.
their
  ph 176– 5   their own downfall and the fate of their *o*ʼ
  f 237–12   in the minds of themselves and their *o*ʼ.
their own
  m 69–17   educate their own *o*ʼ spiritually,

  a 29–32   *o*ʼ of Mary's self-conscious communion with
  m 61–11   The *o*ʼ of heavenly-minded parents
  sp 71–24   It is the *o*ʼ of the physical senses.
  o 350–12   His words were the *o*ʼ of his deeds,
  r 474–22   or the *o*ʼ of the divine will?
  g 555–21   as if man were the *o*ʼ of both
  ap 563–21   and seemingly impede the *o*ʼ of the

oft
  t 444– 4   suffering is *o*ʼ the divine agent in this

often
  pr 13– 5   In public prayer we *o*ʼ go beyond our
  a 31–22   "As *o*ʼ as ye eat this bread, — *I Cor.* 11 : 26.
    53–19   the shock so *o*ʼ produced by the truth,
  m 59– 7   compromises will *o*ʼ maintain a compact
    61–15   *o*ʼ these beautiful children early droop
  s 116–25   they *o*ʼ lead, . . . to confused and erroneous
    121–22   Science shows appearances *o*ʼ to be erroneous,
    122– 1   evidence of the physical senses *o*ʼ reverses
    130–23   author has *o*ʼ remembered our Master's love fo
    134– 5   those who testified for Truth were so *o*ʼ perse
cuted
    136–32   or they would not have questioned him so *o*ʼ.
  ph 166–24   the despairing invalid *o*ʼ drops them,
  f 206–32   There are evil beliefs, *o*ʼ called evil spirits ;
    237–11   beliefs and theories of parents *o*ʼ choke the
    238–19   Truth *o*ʼ remains unsought, until we
    238–26   Justice *o*ʼ comes too late to secure a verdict.
  c 260–16   *o*ʼ hampers the trial of one's wings
  b 320– 4   names are *o*ʼ expressive of spiritual ideas.
  o 343–31   is *o*ʼ accounted a heretic.
    345– 1   Spirit and God are *o*ʼ regarded as
    350–16   The Master *o*ʼ refused to explain his words,
    359–22   In childhood, she *o*ʼ listened with joy to
    359–26   that Scripture she so *o*ʼ quotes :
  p 375– 6   Chills and heat are *o*ʼ the form in which
    377– 4   affliction is *o*ʼ the source of joy,
    378–15   *o*ʼ causes the beast to retreat in terror.
    398– 9   *O*ʼ he gave no name to the distemper he cured
    403– 7   by his mistake a man is *o*ʼ instructed.
    413–19   and *o*ʼ stamp them there,
    422–10   the tremor which Truth *o*ʼ brings to error
  r 486–32   these calamities *o*ʼ drive mortals to seek and
    488– 7   Hebrew and Greek words *o*ʼ translated *belief*
    488–11   Hence the Scriptures *o*ʼ appear . . . to
  g 501– 4   *o*ʼ seems so smothered by the immediate conte:
  ap 576–27   term Lord, . . . is *o*ʼ synonymous with Jehoval
  gl 579– 3   *o*ʼ elucidates the meaning of the
    581– 1   the name *o*ʼ conferred upon him in Scripture,

oftentimes
  p 423– 6   Remember that the unexpressed belief *o*ʼ
  t 446–32   Ignorance of the error to be eradicated *o*ʼ

ofttimes
  t 444–30   are discordant and *o*ʼ false brethren.

oil
boiling
  f 243– 5   which delivered men from the boiling *o*ʼ,
croton
  ph 198–18   the application of caustic or croton *o*ʼ,
fragrant
  p 363– 2   jar containing costly and fragrant *o*ʼ,
lubricating
  ph 199–29   the unscientific might attribute to a lubricating *o*ʼ.

oil
  of gladness
    b 313– 8   *o·* of gladness above thy fellows.— *Heb.* 1 : 9.
    p 367–14 the *o·* of gladness and the perfume of *gratitude,*
  sandal
    p 363– 2   sandal *o·* perhaps, which is in such common
    p 363– 4   she perfumed Jesus' feet with the *o·*,
    363–28   before she anointed them with the *o·*.
    ap 578–14 anointeth my head with *o·* ; — *see Psal.* 23 : 5.
    gl 592–25 definition of

old
  pr 9– 7   Do we pursue the *o·* selfishness, satisfied with
  a 38– 5   the *o·* doctrine of foreordination,
    52–15   Herod and Pilate laid aside *o·* feuds
  m 59–22   a word or deed may renew the *o·* trysting-times.
  sp 74–12 and never returns to the *o·* condition.
    77–31   they return to their *o·* standpoints of matter.
    92–11   In *o·* Scriptural pictures we see a
  s 114–20 must sometimes recur to the *o·* and imperfect,
    114–21   poured into the *o·* bottles of the letter.
    120–32   the limbs of the brave *o·* navigator,
    139–11   but the present new, yet *o·*, reform
    142– 1   in less time than the *o·* systems,
    143–21   you continue in the *o·* routine.
    144–24   the *o·* schools still oppose it.
    149–17   A physician of the *o·* school remarked
    161–30   if this *o·* class of philanthropists looked
  ph 172–22 we must "put off the *o·* man."— *Col.* 3 : 9.
    175– 6   In *o·* times who ever heard of dyspepsia,
  f 201– 8   in whom *o·* things pass away
    212– 4   and the pain seems to be in its *o·* place.
    221–16   without a vestige of the *o·* complaint.
    223–17   but more are blinded by their *o·* illusions,
    244–23   Man in Science is neither young nor *o·*.
    245– 1   error of thinking that we are growing *o·*,
    245–21   Years had not made her *o·*,
    245–23   nor thought of herself as growing *o·*.
  c 261–15 This *o·* man was so lame that he
    262– 7   By putting "off the *o·* man— *Col.* 3 : 9.
  b 281– 7   does not put new wine into *o·* bottles,
    281–30   The *o·* belief must be cast out
    295– 1   belief that a . . . limb is aching in the *o·* location,
    296– 9   The *o·* man with his deeds must be put off.
    324– 1   Willingness . . . to leave the *o·* for the new,
  o 360–11 replies : . . . no notion of losing my *o·* doctrines
  p 372– 6   likened by Milton to "chaos and *o·* night."
  t 452–10 When outgrowing the *o·*, you should not fear
    460–31   until finally the shadow of *o·* errors
  g 519–15 until they throw off the *o·* man
    556–32   his infant babe, only a few hours *o·*,
  ap 563–18 The Revelator sees that *o·* serpent,
    567–15   that *o·* serpent, called the devil,— *Rev.* 12 : 9.
    567–18   that *o·* serpent whose name is devil (evil),
    570–18   What if the *o·* dragon should send forth a
    570–21   the deep waters of chaos and *o·* night.

old of —
  a 33– 5   manna, which of *o·* had fed in the wilderness
    52–17   To-day, as of *o·*, error and evil again
  sp 95–24 Magi of *o·* foretold the Messiahship of Truth.
  s 132–14 The Pharisees of *o·* thrust the spiritual idea and
  f 224–16 Of *o·* the cross was truth's central sign,
    224–27   as he came of *o·* to the patriarch at noonday
  c 255– *   *Thy throne is established of o· : — Psal.* 93 : 2.
  b 270–14 prophets of *o·* looked for something higher
    282– 1   Now, as of *o·*, Truth casts out evils
  o 347–16 true idea of God, comes now as of *o·*,
    360–28   Of *o·*, the Jews put to death the
  t 451–18 and they bear as of *o·* the fruits of the Spirit.
  r 482–24 Angels announced to the Wisemen of *o·*
  ap 559–29 for the Israelites of *o·* at the Paschal meal
    564– 3   As of *o·*, evil still charges the spiritual idea

olden
  s 131–27 explained the so-called miracles of *o·* time

older
  s 140–28 true that the *o·* Scripture is reversed.
  f 245–12 she literally grew no *o·*.
  g 502– 2 living and real prelude of the *o·* Scriptures

old-school
  p 375– 8 The *o·* physician proves this when

Old Testament
  s 139–18 thirty thousand different readings in the *O· T·*,
  g 501– 2 starts with the beginning of the *O· T·*,
    523–30   In the historic parts of the *O· T·*,
    557–26   the first chapter of the *O· T·*,
  ap 576–26 The *O· T·* assigns to the angels,
    576–26   as used in our version of the *O· T·*,

oleaginous
  p 440– 3   *o·* machinations of the counsel,

olfactory
  f 212–20 into contact with the *o·* nerves

ology
  f 223–21 efforts . . . to answer this question by some *o·*

Olympus
  ph 199–32 When Homer sang of the Grecian gods, *O·* was

omen
  p 422–12 and ignorant that it is a favorable *o·*,

omit
  s 142– 6 modern religions generally *o·* all but one of

omitted
  b 340– 6 when the word *duty,* . . . is *o·* :

omni
  r 466– 2 *O·* is adopted from the Latin adjective

omni-action
  gl 587–20 omniscience ; omnipresence ; *o·*.

omnipotence
  divine nature and
    g 525– 1   Does . . . lose therein the divine nature and *o·*?
  escutcheon of
    p 437– 6   It blots the fair escutcheon of *o·*.
  God's
    a 55–19   when he shall realize God's *o·*
  might of
    gl 597–27 That which indicates the might of *o·*
  of divine justice
    f 225–17   breathing the *o·* of divine justice,
  of God
    o 345– 7   When the *o·* of God is preached
    t 445–18   the omnipresence and *o·* of God.
  of Spirit
    sp 78–23 How can the majesty and *o·* of Spirit be lost?
    g 521–30 if veritable, would set aside the *o·* of Spirit ;
  of the divine Mind
    t 459–13 instead of resting on the *o·* of the divine Mind,
  of Truth
    t 454– 4   Teach your students the *o·* of Truth,
  pure sense of
    b 318–15 would efface the pure sense of *o·*.
  signification of
    r 469–25 We lose the high signification of *o·*, when

---

  pr 14– 1   If we are sensibly with the body and regard *o·*
    15–29   gain the ear and right hand of *o·*
  s 109–32 *o·*, omnipresence, omniscience,
  f 203– 4   Mind — *o·*— has all-power,
    228–25   *O·* has all-power,
    249–14   Either there is no *o·*, or *o·* is the only power.
  b 270–21 establish the definition of *o·*, and maintain
    275–22   *o·*, omnipresence, omniscience,
    287–15   or suggest the absence of . . . *o·* ?
  o 357–32 Can matter . . . and so defeat *o·* ?
    358– 2   Is the woodman's axe, . . . superior to *o·* ?
  r 469– 9   omnipresence, omniscience, and *o·*.
  g 521–11 supremacy, *o·*, and omnipresence.
    549–30   to usurp the prerogatives of *o·* ;
  gl 581– 3 ALMIGHTY. All-power ; infinity ; *o·*.
    587–19   GOOD. God ; Spirit ; *o·* ; omniscience ;

omnipotent
  pr 3–18   *o·*, omnipresent, infinite,
    13–13   Do we gain the *o·* ear sooner by words than
    17– 3   *God is o·, supreme.*
  sp 73–17 the Science of *o·*, omnipresent Spirit
    83–19   this belief belittles *o·* wisdom,
  s 113–19 Life, God, *o·* good, deny death, evil, sin,
    113–20   Disease, sin, evil, death, deny good, *o·* God,
    130–12   since you admit that God is *o·* ;
  ph 182–31 is to presuppose that *o·* power is
    186–14   God, the *o·* and omnipresent.
    194– 1   *o·* Spirit shares not its strength with matter
  f 202–30   as if . . . had more power than *o·* Spirit.
    206–28   and infinite Mind made all and includes all.
    231–25   To fear sin is to . . . distrust His *o·* care.
  c 257–29   inexhaustible Love, eternal Life, *o·* Truth.
  o 353–11 *o·* Truth certainly does destroy error.
    358– 5   If God is at the mercy of matter, then matter is *o·*.
  p 367–31   Because Truth is *o·* in goodness,
    394–29   that Life is God, and that God is *o·*.
    412–14   The power of C. S. and divine Love is *o·*.
    429– 1   sin to believe that aught can overpower *o·*
  t 449– 4   the wonders for mortals, so *o·* is Truth,
  r 465–18 this one is God, *o·*, omniscient, and omnipresent
    473– 8   The God-principle is omnipresent and *o·*.
  gl 594– 9 The first audible claim that God was not *o·*
    594–21   everlasting, omnipresent, *o·*,
    (see also **Mind**)

omnipresence
  sp 94–29 a scientific basis, that of the *o·* of Mind.
  s 109–32 omnipotence, *o·*, omniscience,
  b 275–22 omnipotence, *o·*, omniscience,
    287–15   how can He . . . suggest the absence of *o·*
    331–23   to conceive of such *o·* and individuality
  t 445–18 the *o·* and omnipotence of God.
  r 469– 8   Intelligence is omniscience, *o·*,
  g 521–11 supremacy, omnipotence, and *o·*.
  gl 587–19 omniscience ; *o·* ; omni-action.

omnipresent

pr	3–18	omnipotent, o·, infinite,
sp	73–17	the Science of omnipotent, o· Spirit
	78–20	Spirit needs no . . . in order to be o·.
s	119–21	not the divine ideal of o· Love.
ph	186–14	God, the omnipotent and o·.
f	223– 7	God is infinite o· Spirit.
b	275– 2	would ignore o· and omnipotent Mind.
o	361– 7	a monotheist ; he has one o· God.
r	465–18	omnipotent, omniscient, and o·
	469–26	admitting that God, or good, is o·
	473– 8	The God-principle is o· and omnipotent.
gl	594–21	SPIRIT. . . . o·, omnipotent,

omniscience

s	110– 1	omnipotence, omnipresence, o·,
b	275–22	omnipotence, omnipresence, o·,
r	469– 8	Intelligence is o·, omnipresence,
gl	587–19	o· ; omnipresence ; omni-action.

omniscient

r	465–18	omnipotent, o·, and omnipresent

once

a	39–32	o· admit that evil confers no pleasure,
m	65–25	which was o· a fixed fact among us,
sp	74– 5	after having o· left it,
	77– 2	"I cannot turn at o· from good to evil."
	85–15	as he o· journeyed with his students,
	86– 1	o· asked, "Who touched me?"— Luke 8 : 45.
s	109– 9	This proof o· seen, no other conclusion can
	109–28	Jesus o· said of his lessons :
	121–26	the earth revolves about the sun o· a year,
	131– 6	When o· destroyed by divine Science,
	131–18	Jesus o· said : "I thank Thee,— Luke 10 : 21.
	132–31	o· pointed his disciples to Jesus
	152–14	o· apparently cured a case of paralysis
f	217–16	When you have o· conquered a diseased
	220–22	A clergyman o· adopted a diet of
	223–12	If Spirit were o· within the body,
c	259–15	If man was o· perfect but has now lost his
p	362– 2	Jesus was o· the honored guest of a certain
	368–32	O· let the mental physician believe in the
	400– 2	When disease is o· destroyed in this so-called
	411–13	o· Jesus asked the name of a disease,
	432–30	he decided at o· that the prisoner should die.
g	530– 8	Knowing this, Jesus o· said,
	552– 5	was o· an accepted theory.
	555– 6	o· said to the discoverer of C. S. :

once at —

a	27– 8	he will at o· perceive that God is the
f	204– 1	at o· the centre and circumference of being.
	216–12	begins at o· to destroy the errors of
	253–19	can at o· change your course and do right.
o	349–26	Mortal thought does not at o· catch the higher
p	363–13	why, . . . the exalted guest did not at o·
	371–20	I would not transform the infant at o· into
	442– 5	The Jury of Spiritual Senses agreed at o·
ap	560–30	betrays at o· a greater ignorance

One

pr	3–14	the O· "altogether lovely ;"— Song 5 : 16.
	16–29	Adorable O·.
s	112–16	From the infinite O· in C. S. comes
	117– 4	whereas God is O·,
	135–18	danger of . . . limiting the Holy O·.

one (see also one's)

pref	xi–26	started by the author with only o· student
	xii–23	In the spirit of Christ's charity,— as o· who
pr	2–19	as o· pleads with a human being,
	5– 3	Sorrow for wrong-doing is but o· step
	8–19	audible prayers are like charity in o· respect,
	9– 4	the falsehood which does no o· any good.
	10–17	O· of the forms of worship in Thibet
	11– 7	only saves . . . from o· form of punishment.
	12– 8	This, however, is o· belief casting out another.
	12–27	Does Deity interpose in behalf of o· worshipper,
	13– 4	"Ho, every o· that thirsteth,— Isa. 55 : 1.
	14–30	"as o· having authority."— Matt. 7 : 29.
	16– 3	highest prayer is not o· of faith merely ;
	16– 7	taught his disciples o· brief prayer,
	16–19	"the evil one," or o· evil,
a	19–32	thou shalt not know evil, for there is o· Life,
	23– 3	O· sacrifice, however great, is insufficient
	23–12	taketh o· doctrine, firm in faith,
	23–23	O· kind of faith trusts one's welfare to others.
	26– 5	spares us not o· individual experience,
	26–12	"I and my Father are o·."— John 10 : 30.
	27–22	Jesus sent forth seventy students at o· time,
	31– 5	for o· is your Father,— Matt. 23 : 9.
	37– 9	human links which connect o· stage with
	47–28	each o· came to a violent death except St. John,
	48– 4	"Could ye not watch with me o· hour?"— Matt. 26 : 40.
	48–17	Jesus had not o· of them,
	49–13	why did they not gratify . . . with o· sign of

one

m	56–19	is no less imperative than the o·,
	57– 3	without it o· cannot attain the
	64–23	white robed purity will unite in o· person
	66–25	If o· is better than the other,
	67–15	o· should stick to the wreck,
	68–16	I never knew more than o· individual who
	69–14	to understand that there is but o· creator,
sp	72– 1	There is but o· spiritual existence,
	73– 1	In either case, o· does not support the other.
	73– 3	Spiritualism calls o· person, living in this
	73– 6	neither the o· nor the other is infinite
	73– 8	belief that o· man, as spirit, can control
	75–25	There is o· possible moment, when
	75–30	from o· dream to another dream,
	76– 3	as o· at Niagara, with eyes open only to
	78–31	These are the effects of o· universal God,
	82– 2	as easily as we do of o· present.
	82–11	o· person cannot exist in two different
	83– 2	or the divine Mind which is influencing o·.
	85– 8	enabling o· to do good, but not evil.
	86–22	to see a thought than to feel o·?
	87–16	Science enables o· to read the human mind,
	87–17	It enables o· to heal through Mind,
	88–15	so-called material senses, which at o· time
	89–14	If o· believes that he cannot be an orator
	90– 1	if o· animal can originate another,
	90–22	yet their bodies stay in o· place.
	94–21	but o· returned to give God thanks,
	94–32	Jesus could injure no o· by his Mind-reading
	95–17	and is o· of the special characteristics thereof
	96–13	On o· side there will be discord and dismay ;
	97–10	the flight of o· and the blow of the other
an	100– 5	exerted by o· living organism over another,
	100–15	Benjamin Franklin was o· of the
	101– 4	and that there is o· more fact to be
	102– 9	There is but o· real attraction,
	103–22	This belief has not o· quality of Truth.
	104–23	The hypnotizer employs o· error to
s	111–19	A prize of o· hundred pounds, offered
	111–23	o· of many incidents which show that C. S.
	112– 3	Is there more than o· school of C. S.?
	112– 5	can, therefore, be but o· method in its teaching
	113– 1	there can be but o· divine Principle
	114–10	In Science, Mind is o·,
	115– 1	the o· great obstacle to the reception of
	117– 2	an individual may be o· of a series, o· of many,
	117– 4	God is One,— not o· of a series, but o· alone
	118–31	in which nature and God are o·
	119– 5	such theories lead to o· of two things.
	119–17	In o· sense God is identical with nature,
	119–25	In viewing the sunrise, o· finds that it
	125–12	As human thought changes from o· stage to
	126–16	between C. S. on the o· hand and
	128–22	If o· would not quarrel with his fellow-man
	130– 5	O· has a farm, another has merchandise,
	132–10	to any o· who should not deny that
	133–24	was o· of the Jewish accusations
	134– 8	o· who suffers for his convictions.
	135–22	else o· or the other is false and useless ;
	135–25	This proves the o· to be identical with
	136–16	Jeremias, or o· of the prophets."— Matt. 16 : 14
	142– 6	o· of these powers,— the power over sin.
	143–13	the human mind uses o· error to
	145–13	what material method o· may adopt,
	145–26	antagonism of o· form of matter towards
	148–19	the o· wholly, the other primarily
	150–12	not primarily o· of physical healing.
	150–18	physics would have o· believe that
	151– 2	as if there was but o· factor in the case ;
	151– 3	this o· factor they represent to be body,
	151–13	Even this o· reform in medicine would
	152–12	in which o· statement contradicts another
	153– 3	or changes o· of the symptoms of disease.
	153– 8	o· drop of that attenuation in a goblet of water
	154–28	Such a mother runs to her little o·, who
	156–20	that she would give up her medicine for o· day
	157– 4	its o· recognized Principle of healing is Mind,
	159–28	how much . . . o· form of matter is
	161–20	remind o· of the words of the famous
ph	166– 1	Physiology is o· of the apples from
	167–25	There is but o· way — namely,
	170–22	Spiritual causation is the o· question
	176–24	O· disease is no more real than another.
	177– 8	Mortal mind and body are o·.
	180– 8	in Science o· must understand the
	181– 3	Before deciding . . . o· should ask,
	182–10	for o· absolutely destroys the other,
	182–11	and o· or the other must be supreme
	182–13	"hold to the o·, and despise the— Matt. 6 : 24
	183– 4	departing from the basis of . . . o· lawmaker
	186–20	It can never destroy o· iota of good.
	187–32	a body like the o· it had before death.
	188–13	in which every o· recognizes his condition
	195–11	The point for each o· to decide is,
	197– 4	Every o· hastens to get it.

one

one

r	496– 3	no transfer . . . from o· mortal to another,
	497– 5	We acknowledge and adore o· supreme and
	497– 6	We acknowledge His Son, o· Christ ;
g	502–29	There is but o· creator and o· creation.
	504–22	"o· day is with the Lord as a— II Pet. 3 : 8.
	506–16	gathered together unto o· place,— Gen. 1 : 9.
	508–29	an important o· to the human thought,
	510–29	and this o· shining by its own light
	515–19	nor does it imply three persons in o·.
	516–31	In o· of the ancient languages the word
	517–16	but if God is personal, there is but o· person,
	518–16	in o· grand brotherhood,
	522– 4	If o· is true, the other is false,
	523– 1	o· might so judge from an unintelligent perusal
	523–17	O· is called the Elohistic.
	525– 9	In the Saxon, mankind, a woman, any o· ;
	528–11	and He took o· of his ribs,— Gen. 2 : 21.
	530–28	therefore the dreamer and dream are o·,
	532– 1	Did God at first create o· man unaided,
	533– 1	was o· of nakedness and shame.
	535– 4	o· to be burned, the other to be garnered
	536–12	gravitation and attraction to o· Father,
	536–31	the man is become as o· of us,— Gen. 3 : 22.
	537–19	No o· can reasonably doubt that the purpose
	545– 3	the man is become as o· of us."— Gen. 3 : 22.
	545–28	Truth has but o· reply to all error,
	546–32	a thousand different examples of o· rule,
	546–32	the proving of o· example would
	547– 4	If o· of the statements in this book is true,
	547– 5	every o· must be true,
	547– 5	for not o· departs from the stated system
	549–16	from which o· or more individualities
	550–25	no instance of o· species producing its opposite.
	551– 9	O· distinguished naturalist argues that
	553–10	O· of our ablest naturalists has said :
	554–23	and o· of you is a devil?"— John 6 : 70.
	554–24	This he said of Judas, o· of Adam's race.
ap	569–21	sin, which o· has made his bosom companion,
	570– 7	for o· extreme follows another.
	571–11	Is the informer o· who sees the foe?
	571–20	will unite all interests in the o· divinity.
	572– 6	"Love o· another"— I John 3 : 23.
	573– 7	heavens and earth to o· human consciousness,
	574– 6	o· of the seven angels— Rev. 21 : 9.
	575– 8	as o· that "lieth four-square"— Rev. 21 : 16.
	577– 3	as o· Father with His universal family,
	577– 7	two individual natures in o· ;
	577–32	In the following Psalm o· word shows,
gl	580–28	An adversary is o· who opposes,
	580–29	not o· who constructs and sustains reality
	583–28	o· belief preying upon another.
	584–13	frets itself free from o· belief only to be
	588–11	There is but o· I, or Us, but o· divine Principle,
	592– 7	belief that there can be more than o· creator ;
	597–26	as applied to Mind or to o· of God's qualities.
	598– 4	every o· that is born of the Spirit— John 3 : 8.
	598–21	"O· day is with the Lord as a— II Pet. 3 : 8.
	598–23	O· moment of divine consciousness,

(see also **God, instance, Mind, mind, Principle, Spirit**)

oneness

a	18– 4	demonstrated man's o· with the Father,
m	57–10	their true harmony is in spiritual o·.
f	205–29	Denial of the o· of Mind throws our weight into
c	267– 6	The allness of Deity is His o·.
p	424–25	the o· and the allness of divine Love ;
g	515–20	It relates to the o·, the tri-unity of

one's

a	22–26	pinning o· faith . . . to another's vicarious
	23–24	One kind of faith trusts o· welfare to others.
	23–26	work out o· "own salvation,— Phil. 2 : 12.
	28–10	o· consecration to Christ is more on the
m	60– 2	Science inevitably lifts o· being higher
sp	88–18	To love o· neighbor as o· self, is a
	90–24	The admission to o· self that man is
an	101–32	proportional to o· faith in esoteric magic.
ph	194– 8	When o· false belief is corrected,
f	234–32	no more harm than o· belief permits.
	240–30	involves unwinding o· snarls,
	241–23	O· aim, a point beyond faith,
c	259–32	Deducing o· conclusions as to man from
	260–15	but distrust of o· ability to gain
	260–17	often hampers the trial of o· wings
	260–25	by the thoughts ever recurring to o· self,
b	319– 5	To calculate o· life-prospects from a
	322–32	easier to desire Truth than to rid o· self of error.
o	345–13	no small matter to know o· self ;
p	368–24	in the ratio of o· spiritual growth.
	396– 4	both for o· own sake and for that of the patient.
	413– 3	The act of yielding o· thoughts to the
	440–16	that it is for the good of o· neighbor?
t	448–31	doing o· self the most harm.
	449– 8	reacts most heavily against o· self.
r	483–31	One must fulfil o· mission without timidity

ones

m	61–19	may reproduce in their own helpless little o·
sp	76– 1	The o· departing may whisper this vision,
g	501–16	that Love for whose rest the weary o· sigh

one-sided

f	235–12	School-examinations are o· ;

only

pref	vii–18	The o· guarantee of obedience is
	ix– 2	but these jottings were o·
	x–27	O· those quarrel with her method who
	xi– 2	o· a phase of the action of
	xi–26	was started by the author with o·
	xii– 3	hers was the o· College of this
pr	3– 9	we have o· to avail ourselves of
	3–10	In such a case, the o· acceptable prayer
	4– 7	o· worthy evidence of our gratitude
	5–24	o· as it is destroyed by Christ,
	7– 1	The o· civil sentence which he had for
	8– 4	those who come o· spasmodically
	8–30	in this way o· can we learn
	9–22	recognizes o· the divine control
	11– 7	it o· saves the criminal from
	11–21	Petitions bring to mortals o· the
	11–26	that we may walk securely in the o·
	12–30	o· petitioners (per se or by proxy)
	16–20	O· as we rise above all material
a	18– 7	not o· in justice to himself,
	21–31	satisfied if he can o· imagine himself
	22–31	Mercy cancels the debt o· when
	22–32	Wrath which is o· appeased is not
	24–24	o· for the presentation, after death,
	27–22	o· eleven left a desirable historic
	28– 2	but they o· hindered the success of
	29–16	God is the o· author of man.
	30–28	O· in this way can we bless
	31–10	recognized Spirit, God, as the o· creator,
	35–21	o· as we are new-born of Spirit,
	36–27	o· toil, sacrifice, cross-bearing,
	37– 8	error falls o· before the sword of Spirit.
	38– 2	assured that this command was intended o· for
	38–19	prayed, not for the twelve o·, but
	38–27	living o· for pleasure or the gratification of
	40– 9	Science removes the penalty o· by
	43– 6	Heretofore they had o· believed ;
	51–20	but o· through doing the works which
	52–26	speaking not for their day o· but
	54–22	o· a few unpretentious friends,
m	57–12	perpetual o· as it is pure and true,
	62– 1	can o· be permitted for the purpose of
	62–18	become men and women o· through
	69– 5	o· as they lose the sense of sin and disease.
	69– 8	o· as man finds the truth of being.
sp	71– 9	which forms o· reflect.
	72–12	God, is the o· truth-giver to man.
	73–11	and God is the o· Spirit.
	76– 4	with eyes open o· to that wonder,
	76–25	the o· veritable, indestructible man,
	76–27	a perfection discernible o· by those
	80–11	assertion that . . . are our o· proofs of
	81– 8	can o· prove that certain individuals
	81–15	Life, Love, Truth, is the o· proof
	83– 6	Science o· can explain the incredible good
	83–32	investigates and touches o· human beliefs.
	86–15	they are mysterious o· because
	89– 2	This phenomenon o· shows that the
	91– 6	and obey o· the divine Principle,
	92– 5	not o· capable of experiencing pleasure and
	92–26	to call that real which is o· a mistake.
	93–26	refer o· to quality, not to God.
	95– 2	and this is the o· genuine Science of
	98–11	which can o· be spiritually discerned.
	99–14	C. S. teaches o· that which is spiritual
an	103–15	working out the purposes of good o·.
	106–10	Man is properly self-governed o· when
	106–16	sanction o· such methods as
s	108–10	the o· sufferer is mortal mind,
	109– 5	the o· realities are the divine Mind and
	110–14	the Bible was my o· textbook.
	113– 5	but its spirit comes o· in small degrees.
	119–12	is not o· to make Him responsible for
	119–22	represented o· by the idea of goodness ;
	120–22	which is the o· basis of health ;
	126–29	The Bible has been my o· authority.
	128– 4	refers o· to the laws of God
	128–20	becomes beneficent and agreeable o· in
	129–23	o· the outward sense of things.
	133–30	Jehovah, or o· a mighty hero and king,
	137–27	called o· by his common names,
	140–16	We worship spiritually, o· as we
	141–18	Its o· crowned head is immortal
	141–19	Its o· priest is the spiritualized man.
	143– 2	destroys o· what is untrue.
	145–11	o· as immortal Mind . . . subdues the
	150–14	but these signs are o· to demonstrate
	159–14	as if matter were the o· factor

only

p 420–11 for if they will o· accept Truth,
420–25 if they o· realize that divine Love gives
421– 1 o· as the insane suffer,
421– 1 The o· difference is, that insanity
423–30 o· the substance of thought which forms them.
423–31 They are o· phenomena of the mind of
427–29 should have been his first and o· resort.
428–32 understanding of God as the o· Life.
433–11 o· the evidence of Personal Sense
434–27 The o· valid testimony in the case
434–32 and amenable to Spirit o·.
435– 2 God Himself and Man's o· lawgiver !
435–25 Mortal Man can suffer o· for his sin.
435–31 The o· jurisdiction to which
439–23 o· to fasten upon him an offence
440–21 God, who sentences o· for sin.
t 444–14 not o· towards differing forms of religion
445–29 and caring o· for the fees.
449–25 meet o· to separate
449–28 O· virtue is a rebuke to vice.
449–31 is a Scientist o· in name.
451–11 They must not o· seek, but strive,
454–32 o· human auxiliaries to aid in bringing
456– 7 the o· success of the students of
458–29 that Christ's way is the o· one
461– 8 o· by those who are morally advanced
461–11 O· by the illumination of the
462–10 to practise Truth's teachings o· in part,
r 466–22 Soul or Spirit means o· one Mind,
468–22 God, is the o· real substance.
469–14 God, good, is the o· Mind,
470–15 evil can o· seem to be real
471–20 is the o· fact of creation.
472– 1 teaches man that God is the o· Life,
472– 7 o· with that which is harmonious
472–27 Therefore the o· reality of
476–12 the o· and eternal verities of man.
478–26 That o· is real which reflects God.
479–22 the o· facts are Spirit and its
480– 6 o· the darkness of vacuity
481– 8 Through spiritual sense o·,
483– 3 but o· relieve suffering temporarily,
485– 8 o· soon to disappear because of their
489–24 the o· source of evil or error.
490–16 Our o· need is to know this
491–12 o· by acknowledging the supremacy of
493–25 these propositions can o· seem real and
494–12 o· for a select number or for a
g 501–11 which angels could o· whisper
502–25 beginning is employed to signify the o·,
505–11 ideas of Spirit apparent o· as Mind,
508– 2 o· as the divine Mind is All
508– 5 The o· intelligence or substance of a
509–18 gives gleams of the infinite o·,
510–29 Science reveals o· one Mind,
512–24 o· through the spiritual senses.
517–17 His personality can o· be reflected,
517–19 The o· proper symbol of God as
520– 6 can repeat o· an infinitesimal part
529–23 enters into the metaphor o· as evil.
530–22 saying, . . . O· admit that I am real,
538–21 evil is brought into view o· as
540–15 o· that Truth may annihilate all
543– 4 o· mortal man and not the real man,
546–15 o· through the corporeal senses,
547–24 o· by this understanding can truth be
548–11 o· as the clouds of corporeal sense roll away.
554– 1 It can o· be replied, that
555–18 O· impotent error would seek to
556–11 o· to go out at last forever ;
556–31 infant babe, o· a few hours old,
ap 560–26 not o· obscured the light of the ages, but
565–25 this o· impelled the idea to rise to
572– 1 o· those who have washed their robes
gl 582–19 God is the o· creative power.
584–13 o· to be fettered by another,
585–21 the o· error of which is limitation ;
588–21 divine Principle ; the o· Ego.
591–15 hears, tastes, and smells o· in belief.
591–16 Mind. The o· I, or Us ; the o· Spirit,
594–20 that o· which is perfect,
596–17 the o· fit preparation for admission to
597– 5 if o· he appeared unto men to fast.

ontology

s 129–21 abandon pharmaceutics, and take up o·,
t 460– 3 O· is defined as "the science of the
g 556–25 O· receives less attention than physiology.

onward

f 225– 7 bears o· freedom's banner.
240–18 Mortals move o· towards good or evil
b 323– 7 we are helped o· in the march towards
323–10 Then we push o·, until boundless thought

opacity

s 117–25 because of o· to the true light,

opaque

f 242–15 Self-love is more o· than a solid body.
b 295–19 the glass is less o· than the walls.

open

pr 2–27 Shall we plead for more at the o· fount,
10–15 Spiritual attainments o· the door to
13– 3 It is the o· fount which cries,
15– 6 Closed to error, it is o· to Truth,
a 24– 7 o· the way for C. S. to be understood,
sp 76– 4 with eyes o· only to that wonder,
s 117– 1 term individuality is also o· to objections,
ph 165– 3 that eating this fruit would o· man's eyes
171–13 is no longer an o· question,
f 216– 9 Spirituality lays o· siege to materialism.
220– 1 We hear it said : "I exercise daily in the o· air
220– 5 Such admissions ought to o· people's eyes to
224–25 Will you o· or close the door upon this angel
b 326–21 your Father will o· the way.
p 366–30 If we would o· their prison doors
433–32 can o· wide those prison doors
t 444– 2 these very failures may o· their blind eyes.
450–10 o· to the approach and recognition of Truth.
451–24 He feels morally obligated to o· the eyes of
r 491–23 goes on, whether our eyes are closed or o·.
k 499– * I have set before thee an o· door,— Rev. 3 : 8.
g 511–21 in the o· firmament of heaven.— Gen. 1 : 20.
511–29 which fly . . . in the o· firmament of heaven,
514–12 Undisturbed it lies in the o· field,
530–20 and saying, . . . "I can o· your eyes.
535–16 When will man pass through the o· gate of
552–18 They must peck o· their shells with C. S.,
ap 558– 6 had in his hand a little book o· :— Rev. 10 : 2.
559– 1 o· for all to read and understand.
570–30 Many are willing to o· the eyes of the
572–15 o· the seven seals of error with Truth,
575–26 Northward, its gates o· to the North Star,
577–24 Its gates o· towards light and glory
gl 579– * I have set before thee an o· door,— Rev. 3 : 8.

opened

pref xi–28 o· the Massachusetts Metaphysical College
a 43–18 o· a new era for the world.
48–19 "He o· not his mouth."— Isa. 53 : 7.
49– 3 o· the eyes of their understanding,
sp 99–11 o· the door of the human understanding.
ph 193–13 In about ten minutes he o· his eyes
p 434–16 When the case for Mortal Man . . . is o·,
g 530–15 then your eyes shall be o· ;— Gen. 3 : 5.
ap 564–18 Jesus "o· not his mouth."— Isa. 53 : 7.
570–11 and the earth o· her mouth,— Rev. 12 : 16.
571–28 he has o· wide the gates of glory,
gl 597–14 o· the sepulchre with divine Science,

openeth

a 50– * so he o· not his mouth."— Isa. 53 : 7.
k 499– * He that o·, and no man shutteth ;— Rev. 3 : 7.
499– * and shutteth, and no man o· ;— Rev. 3 : 7.
gl 579– * He that o·, and no man shutteth ;— Rev. 3 : 7.
579– * and shutteth, and no man o· ;— Rev. 3 : 7.

opening

ph 187–13 o· and closing for the passage of the blood,
f 221–23 These truths, o· his eyes,
ap 560– 2 In the o· of the sixth seal, typical of

openly

pr 13– 7 secretly yearning and o· striving
13–12 and our Father, . . . will reward us o·
15– 2 shall reward thee o·."— Matt. 6 : 6.

opens

sp 90–26 and o· it wide towards immortality.
ph 174–14 Whoever o· the way in C. S.
p 434–20 and o· the argument for the defence ;
r 495–12 o· the prison doors to such as are bound,
g 506–20 even as He o· the petals of a holy purpose

operate

p 399– 9 not a secretion nor combination can o·, apart
from

operating

ph 185– 9 o· through the power of the

operation
basis of
p 423–19 making Mind his basis of o·
from the
pref xi–10 from the o· of divine Principle,
of matter
s 150–28 by the o· of matter,
ph 171–20 ejection by the o· of matter.
perfection of
s 149–11 The rule and its perfection of o·
performed the
s 159–18 would have performed the o· without ether.

operation

surgical
s 159– 2   to perform a needed surgical o·
ph 198–18   caustic or croton oil, or by a surgical o·.
g 528–17   in order to perform a surgical o· on him

s 123–27   The o· of this Principle indicates
159–22   and not from the disease or the o·.
b 272–24   attest the divine origin and o· of C. S.
o 346–27   the tooth, the o·, and the forceps are unchanged.
g 545–25   they could not apprehend the nature and o· of
557– 1   and repeated this o· daily, until

operations

f 252– 9   A knowledge of error and of its o·
t 464– 7   to establish the stately o· of C. S.,
g 512–27   Ignorant of the origin and o· of mortal mind,
553–23   appearance of its method in finite forms and o·.

operator

p 402–24   The o· would make his subjects believe that

ophis

gl 594– 1   (o·, in Greek ; *nacash*, in Hebrew).

opiates

p 415–11   That is why o· relieve inflammation.
415–13   O· do not remove the pain in any scientific

opinion

s 137–14   Jesus completely eschewed the narrow o·
163– 8   said : "I declare my conscientious o·,
f 202–31   Common o· admits that a man may
b 306–17   and this is the general religious o· of mankind,
o 341–11   In C. S. mere o· is valueless.
342– 3   proof and demonstration, instead of o· and
355–23   an o· wholly due to a misapprehension

opinions

beliefs and
gl 590– 5   mortality ; beliefs and o· ;
differing
t 444–16   to those who hold these differing o·.
false
p 403–18   producing on mortal body the results of false o· ;
human
  (*see* **human**)
individual
ph 197–27   until individual o· improve
majority of
ph 178– 6   controlled by the majority of o·,
minority of
ph 178– 6   minority of o· in the sick-chamber.
mortal
b 273–29   conflicting mortal o· and beliefs
p 390–15   destroy the false process of mortal o·
399–27   The one Mind, God, contains no mortal o·.
persons or
t 456–18   Science makes no concessions to persons or o·.
popular
a 24–18   popular o· in regard to predestination and
such
p 424–18   such o· as may alarm or discourage,
these
s 112–11   these o· may have occasional gleams of
two
f 236–30   While age is halting between two o·
weight of
p 396–20   overwhelming weight of o· on the wrong side,

gl 595–18   thoughts, beliefs, o·, knowledge ;

opium

sp 90–20   O· and hashish eaters mentally travel far
p 406–29   alcoholic drinks, tobacco, tea, coffee, o·,
416–12   when the soporific influence of the o· is

opponent

o 359–29   A Christian Scientist and an o· are like

opponents

a· 18–12   and he refuted all o· with his healing power.
s 134–10   the hatred of the o· of Christianity,
o 344–12   the o· of a demonstrable Science
349–32   of C. S. believe substance to be
354–12   On the other hand, the Christian o· of C. S.
354–30   The o· of divine Science must be charitable,
t 444–24   part from these o· as did Abraham

opportunities

f 238–15   Unimproved o· will rebuke us when we

opportunity

a 21–19   paths have diverged . . . and we have little o· to
an 105–23   to commit fresh atrocities as o· occurs
f 232–32   neither place nor o· in Science for error
c 266–15   for "man's extremity is God's o·."
b 271–27   o· now, as aforetime, to learn and to practise
276–18   ceases to be any o· for sin and death.
g 537–30   would imply that God withheld from man the o·

oppose

s 144–25   the old schools still o· it.
145–25   Other methods undertake to o· error with error,
b 273–22   it would o· the supremacy of Spirit,
278– 6   The material senses o· this, but there are no
r 484–16   Drugs and hygiene o· the supremacy of the

opposed

s 111– 4   sensuous reason of the human mind, to be o· to
114– 4   meaning by this term the flesh o· to Spirit,
119–23   because it is o· to the nature of Spirit, God.
134– 3   truth is still o· with sword and spear.
139–29   theosophy, and agnosticism are o· to C. S.,
151–25   The human mind is o· to God
ph 192–30   you can have no power o· to God,
194–13   Every theory o· to this fact
f 225– 3   Whatever enslaves man is o· to the
b 273–32   when it is o· promptly and persistently by C. S.
305–21   as o· to the Science of spiritual reflection,
338–21   when matter, . . . stood o· to Spirit.
p 382– 1   o· to the harmonies of Spirit,
387–12   assurances of immortality, o· to mortality.
392– 9   o· to the health, holiness, and harmony of
406–20   Error is o· to Life.
g 522–14   It records pantheism, o· to the
525– 3   the validity of matter is o·,
530– 4   forever o· to mortal, material sense.
534–17   called *energy* and o· to Spirit.
545–12   notion of a material universe is utterly o· to
ap 569– 5   overcome the mortal belief in a power o· to
gl 580– 6   a material belief, o· to the one Mind, or Spirit ;
580–10   o· to the great reality of spiritual existence
583– 4   suppositions . . . o· to the Science of being.
585– 9   spiritual evidence o· to material sense ;

opposer

gl 580–15   the o· of Truth, termed error ;

opposes

f 224–32   supposed power, which o· itself to God
o 357–25   If what o· God is real,
gl 580–28   An adversary is one who o·, denies,

opposing

sp 93–16   evil is the o· error and not the truth of
p 380–30   to believe . . . that God endows this o· power
437–20   Here the o· counsel, False Belief,

opposite (noun)

demoralized
p 407–25   instead of its demoralized o·.
direct
f 249–31   He is the direct o· of material sensation,
exact
b 295–27   the exact o· of real Mind, or Spirit.
g 521–28   which is the exact o· of scientific truth
523– 7   presenting the exact o· of Truth,
immortality's
gl 580–19   ADAM. . . . immortality's o·, mortality ;
its
a 40–13   If the saying is true, . . . its o· is also true,
f 229–24   If . . . its o·, health, must be evil,
c 261– 1   we find its o·, matter.
b 282– 3   The real Life, or Mind, and its o·,
282–32   inversion infers from error its o·, Truth ;
r 467–32   cannot be learned from its o·, matter.
g 524–28   Could Spirit evolve its o·, matter,
547–18   Darwin's theory,— that Mind produces its o·,
550–10   nor can Spirit be developed through its o·.
550–26   supplies no instance of one species producing its o·.
551– 4   it cannot produce its o· in quality
just the
b 321– 1   an interpretation which is just the o· of the true,
matter's
b 293–27   and point to matter's o·,
of clairvoyance
sp 85– 2   This Mind-reading is the o· of clairvoyance.
of God
b 282–28   the fall of man or the o· of God
g 554–20   Jesus defined this o· of God and His
gl 591–13   the o· of God ;
592–33   and therefore the o· of God, or good ;
of good
sp 72–22   evil, the suppositional o· of good,
r 480–20   It is the o· of good
gl 579–16   o· of good,— of God and His creation ;
of Himself
gl 583–25   could not create. . . an element the o· of Himself.
of infinity
gl 585–22   limitation ; finity ; the o· of infinity.
of Life
gl 584–10   the unreal and untrue ; the o· of Life.
of life
b 278–29   error, because it is the o· of life,
of Love
gl 580–17   the o· of Love, called hate ;
of materiality
ph 171– 4   the spiritual o· of materiality,

opposite (noun)

of matter
gl 583–23 *o·* of matter and evil, which have no Principle ;

of mind
gl 584–23 the *o·* of mind, termed matter,

of Science
r 471– 6 *o·* of Science, and the evidence before the

of Spirit
b 278–10 the *o·* of Spirit.
o 359–17 that which is the *o·* of Spirit.
gl 580– 4 *o·* of Spirit and His creations ;
  591–12 the *o·* of Spirit ;
  592– 3 the *o·* of Spirit, and therefore the
  594– 5 the first claim that there is an *o·* of Spirit,

of themselves
a 20–18 he taught mortals the *o·* of themselves,

of the real
b 277–25 and the *o·* of the real is not divine,
  337–27 the *o·* of the real or the spiritual

of Truth
s 108–24 the *o·* of Truth, — called error,
ph 177–20 But a lie, the *o·* of Truth, cannot name the
b 307– 4 *serpent*, insists still upon the *o·* of Truth,
g 523– 7 presenting the exact *o·* of Truth,
  545–19 vague and hypothetical, the *o·* of Truth ;
gl 584–18 the *o·* of Truth ; a belief in sin, sickness,
  591–12 the *o·* of Truth ;
  594– 2 a lie ; the *o·* of Truth, named error ;

supposititious
p 368– 2 a supposititious *o·* of the highest right.
r 469–15 the supposititious *o·* of infinite Mind

Truth's
p 367–32 Truth's *o·*, has no might.

very
a 53– 8 reputation of Jesus was the very *o·* of his

pref viii–11 and matter is Spirit's *o·*.
ph 168– 5 gives preponderance to the *o·*.
b 278–11 Spirit can have no *o·*.
  287–27 the objective supposition of Spirit's *o·*.
r 480– 4 the *o·* of the something of Spirit.
g 545–19 yet this *o·*, in its false view of God and man,
gl 590– 7 the *o·* of spiritual Truth and understanding.
  591– 3 as the *o·* of the one Spirit,

opposite (adj.)

sp 74–14 persons in such *o·* dreams
  74–25 when we are in the *o·* hemisphere?
  74–27 the gulf which divides two such *o·* conditions
  75–28 the link between their *o·* beliefs
  81–12 the *o·* assertion, that he is mortal,
  83–30 are distinctly *o·* standpoints,
  88–22 Excite the *o·* development, and he blasphemes.
  92–28 This belief tends to support two *o·* powers,
an 104–17 wrongness of the *o·* so-called action,
s 154–21 prevented through the *o·* understanding.
  161– 9 while an *o·* mental state might produce
ph 171–28 The *o·* truth, that intelligence and life are
  195–10 those very senses, trained in an *o·* direction.
f 205–14 leads human thought into *o·* channels
  207–30 the *o·* discord, which bears no
  213–14 an *o·* attraction towards the finite,
  215– 8 from the very necessity of their *o·* natures.
  239–28 Those two *o·* sources never mingle
  252–31 Spirit, bearing *o·* testimony, saith :
c 266–21 The *o·* persecutions of material sense,
b 280–20 the *o·* error of many minds.
  285–12 the *o·* natures of Spirit and matter,
  286–28 (by the supposition of *o·* qualities)
  300–17 These *o·* qualities are the tares and wheat,
  311–19 is directly *o·* to the immortal reality of being.
  315–11 The *o·* and false views of the people
o 350– 5 C. S. takes exactly the *o·* view.
  352– 8 whereas the Jews took a diametrically *o·* view.
b 379–18 Then let her learn the *o·* statement of Life
  380–29 to believe that there is a power *o·* to God,
  385–30 would produce the *o·* result.
  388–14 another admission in the *o·* direction,
  389–11 by the better results of Mind's *o·* evidence.
  389–20 cannot annul these regulations by an *o·* law
  417–31 how divine Mind can cure by *o·* thoughts.
t 448–24 pursuit of instructions *o·* to absolute C. S.
  457–30 and there must and can be no *o·* rule.
g 521–13 should look away from the *o·* supposition
  521–25 the *o·* error, a material view of creation,
  526– 5 This *o·* declaration, . . . contradicts the
  (*see also* **belief**)

oppositely

a 52– 7 their senses testified *o·*,

opposites

imaginary
r 479–24 the imaginary *o·* of light,

these
b 282–20 At no point can these *o·* mingle or unite.

two
o 356–13 he spoke of flesh and Spirit as the two *o·*,

opposites

unites such
f 229–10 belief which unites such *o·* as

sp 74–22 sickness and health, are *o·*,
  86–11 *O·* come from contrary directions,
ph 191–28 senses may fancy affinities with their *o·* ;
b 270– 5 Matter and Mind are *o·*.
  277– 9 *o·*, evil and matter, are mortal error,
g 539– 9 if they produce their *o·*,
gl 594–23 the *o·* of God ; errors ;

opposition

debate and
p 434– 8 After much debate and *o·*,

direct
f 228– 1 healing in direct *o·* to them
b 273–26 in direct *o·* to material laws.

mental
p 390–30 Meet . . . disease with as powerful mental *o·*
g 534–24 There will be greater mental *o·*

met with
r 483–25 this Science has met with *o·* ;

no
f 253–20 Matter can make no *o·* to

usual
s 114–32 Apart from the usual *o·* to everything new,

s 131– 8 Hence the *o·* of sensuous man to the Science of
ph 170–20 always in *o·*, never in obedience, to physics.
f 224–19 *o·* from church, state laws, and the press,
b 329–30 the more intense the *o·* to spirituality,
p 395– 3 They should plead in *o·* to the testimony of the
r 483–26 it ought to receive aid, not *o·*,
gl 595–25 Ungodliness. *O·* to the divine Principle and

oppressed

p 373–24 and you relieve the *o·* organ.

oppression

f 225–20 but *o·* neither went down in blood, nor
  227–15 cannot fail to foresee the doom of all *o·*.
t 451– 5 must renounce aggression, *o·* and the pride of
gl 589–14 sensuality ; envy ; *o·* ; tyranny.

oppressive

s 151–14 from the awful and *o·* bondage
  161–19 *o·* state statutes touching medicine
f 227– 4 even as *o·* laws are disputed

optic

ph 194–11 and paralysis of the *o·* nerve

optical

s 122–15 The *o·* focus is another proof of the

optics

s 111–16 even as the explanation of *o·* rejects
p 400–24 even as in *o·* we see painted on the retina
ap 572–27 *o·* are inadequate to take in so wonderful a

oracles

sp 78–13 and accept them as *o·* ?

orally

t 460–27 and she had to do this *o·* through the

orator

sp 89–14 If one believes that he cannot be an *o·*

orb

ph 188–30 human eye knows not where the *o·* of day is,
  189–12 when the *o·* of day disappears,

orbit

sp 90– 6 earth's *o·* and the imaginary line called the
s 124–23 launched the earth in its *o·*
g 522– 9 and as revolving in an *o·* of his own.

ordain

s 122–11 so-called senses . . . *o·* certain sections of

ordained

f 221–19 never *o·* a law that fasting should be a means
b 273–21 God never *o·* a material law

ordeal

a 48–14 the exalting *o·* of sin's revenge on its destroyer

order

astronomical
s 121–28 thus indicated, astronomical *o·* imitates the

disorder and
p 402–30 Science cannot produce both disorder and *o·*.

divine
  (*see* **divine**)

follows the
ap 568– 9 The narrative follows the *o·* used in Genesis.

law and
sp 97– 3 They will maintain law and *o·*,

of being
b 275–10 To grasp the reality and *o·* of being

of celestial being
b 337–17 perfection is the *o·* of celestial being

of Christian Science
g 508–28 The third stage in the *o·* of C. S. is

order

of creation
  g 508–22 in the ascending *o·* of creation.

of divine Science
  b 334–18 exist in the eternal *o·* of divine Science,
  336–29 in the *o·* of divine Science, God and man

of generation
  a 29–21 material law and its *o·* of generation,

of genus
  b 277–16 the *o·* of genus and species is preserved

of heaven
  s 118–31 natural *o·* of heaven comes down to earth.

of matter
  g 552–26 the *o·* of matter to be the order of mortal mind.

of mortal mind
  g 552–26 the order of matter to be the *o·* of mortal mind.

of Science
  s 123– 7 which reverses the *o·* of Science
  f 240–10 In the *o·* of Science, in which the Principle is

of this allegory
  g 531– 2 The *o·* of this allegory—the belief that everything

of wisdom
  m 62–28 the *o·* of wisdom would be reversed.

primal
  s 135– 7 but unfolds the primal *o·*,

scientific
  s 123–28 the scientific *o·* and continuity of being.

this
  an 100–14 Under this *o·* a commission was appointed,
  b 277–19 Error relies upon a reversal of this *o·*,

  c 255– 5 changing chaos into *o·* and discord into the
  b 277–22 even the *o·* of material so-called science.
  p 437–21 False Belief, called C. S. to *o·*

order in — that
  a 51–10 in *o·* that he might furnish the proof of
  sp 91–23 in *o·* that the spiritual facts may be
  c 265– 8 in *o·* that sin and mortality may be put off.
  p 428– 9 in *o·* that the spiritual facts of being may
  g 506–21 in *o·* that the purpose may appear.
  ap 564–22 in *o·* that the false claim of
  565–10 in *o·* that the man Jesus, . . . might never

order in — to
  pref xii–21 in *o·* to elucidate her idealism.
  pr 3–10 in *o·* to receive His blessing,
  11–11 in *o·* to compel this progress.
  11–23 in *o·* to gain holiness ;
  15–14 In *o·* to pray aright, we must
  a 26–20 in *o·* to show the learner the way by practice
  40–32 but in *o·* to enter into the kingdom,
  47–24 in *o·* to raise himself in popular estimation.
  52–15 in *o·* to unite in putting to shame and death
  m 58– 7 should be concordant in *o·* to blend properly.
  sp 75– 3 in *o·* to reappear
  78–19 in *o·* to be omnipresent.
  83– 8 in *o·* to escape the error of these latter days.
  an 105– 3 in *o·* to restrain crime,
  s 131– 4 in *o·* to be in harmony with God,
  155–21 in *o·* to heal a single case of disease.
  ph 165–18 in *o·* to remember what has hurt you,
  169–14 in *o·* to avoid it.
  172–16 in *o·* to become man.
  181–26 in *o·* to satisfy the sick
  f 203–31 does not kill a man in *o·* to give him
  212–26 in *o·* to convey thought,
  220– 2 said : . . . in *o·* to overcome a predisposition to
  243–11 in *o·* to confirm and repeat the
  248–13 in *o·* to perfect his conception.
  c 258–11 in *o·* to be immortal.
  260–19 in *o·* to improve their models.
  b 295–10 in *o·* to escape from the mortality of
  295–22 in *o·* to become a better transparency for Truth.
  296–17 in *o·* to part with them.
  323–13 In *o·* to apprehend more,
  o 346–12 in *o·* to prove the somethingness
  349–20 in *o·* to grasp the meaning of this Science.
  361–24 must be correct in *o·* to be Science
  p 366– 3 In *o·* to cure his patient, the metaphysician
  369–15 in *o·* to discover some means of healing it.
  375–13 hypnotist dispossesses . . . in *o·* to control
  377– 6 Invalids flee to tropical climates in *o·* to
  384–12 enter his protest . . . in *o·* to annul it.
  404– 1 in *o·* to judge the case according to C. S.
  413–15 in *o·* to make it thrive more vigorously
  413–23 in *o·* to keep it sweet as the new-blown flower.
  421– 8 in *o·* to remove its beliefs,
  424– 7 in *o·* to change the notion of chance
  t 449– 6 in *o·* to continue in well doing.
  451–22 in *o·* to defend himself from the influence of
  453–18 not in *o·* to injure, but in *o·* to bless
  455– 7 in *o·* to teach this Science of healing.
  455– 9 in *o·* to walk over the waves of error
  r 482–14 Is it important . . . in *o·* to heal the sick?
  483– 8 In *o·* to heal by Science, you must not
  486– 8 in *o·* to possess immortal consciousness.

order in — to
  g 522–21 in *o·* to create man.
  528–16 in *o·* to perform a surgical operation
  532– 2 in *o·* to create the rest of the human family?
  540–10 must be stirred in *o·* to purify the stream.
  551–30 in *o·* to propagate its species,
  ap 560–20 in *o·* to classify it correctly.
  gl 598– 9 in *o·* to unfold spiritual thoughts.

ordered
  an 100–12 In 1784, the French government *o·* the
  g 528– 6 It cannot be true that man was *o·* to

orderly
  p 395–19 The nurse should be cheerful, *o·*,

orders
  s 138–19 under as direct *o·* now, as they were then,

ordinary
  a 24–16 the *o·* theological views of atonement
  sp 99–13 The *o·* teachings are material
  an 105–30 from *o·* medical practice to C. S.
  s 128–11 ability to exceed their *o·* capacity.
  139–29 opposed to C. S., as they are to *o·* religion ;
  156–12 Believing then somewhat in the *o·* theories of
  159–31 the *o·* physician is liable to increase disease
  161–24 *o·* practitioner, examining bodily symptoms,
  p 379– 5 where the *o·* physician looks for causes.
  385– 5 exposures which *o·* people could not endure.
  t 443– 4 under *o·* circumstances a resort to
  443–16 *o·* physical methods of medical treatment,
  r 483–25 the *o·* scientific schools, which wrestle with
  g 537–25 the *o·* historian interprets it literally.
  548–31 besides the *o·* process of generation,

organ
  sp 88–20 Excite the *o·* of veneration or religious faith,
  s 151–31 claims to govern every *o·* of the mortal body,
  ph 191– 2 Matter is not the *o·* of infinite Mind.
  p 373–24 and you relieve the oppressed *o·*.
  373–25 disabled *o·* will resume its healthy functions.
  377–23 the morbid or excited action of any *o·*.

organic
  sp 74– 4 must be free from *o·* bodies ;
  74–16 belief of still living in an *o·*, material body.
  s 125– 3 now considered the best condition for *o·*
  125– 6 Neither *o·* inaction nor overaction is
  126– 1 its supposed *o·* action or supposed existence.
  149–21 remarked. . .mind can never cure *o·* difficulties.''
  149–23 The author has cured what is termed *o·* disease
  160–10 *o·* action and secretion of the viscera.
  162–25 I have restored . . . where disease was *o·*.
  162–25 C. S. heals *o·* disease as surely as
  ph 176–21 Should all cases of *o·* disease be treated by a
  177– 1 Human mind produces what is termed *o·* disease
  180–32 dissolve a tumor, or cure *o·* disease,
  b 296–11 not the death of *o·* matter,
  309–28 *o·* animal or vegetable life,
  309–31 Therefore it is never structural nor *o·*,
  p 377–24 what are termed *o·* diseases
  428–30 author has healed hopeless *o·* disease,
  t 450–32 belief of . . . animal nature, and *o·* life,
  r 489–26 no *o·* construction can give it hearing

organically
  sp 83–22 to suppose that life is . . . *o·* spiritual.

organism
  an 100– 5 which he said could be exerted by one living *o·*
  s 108–31 all the *o·* and action of the mortal body,
  f 211–25 If it is true . . . that the material *o·*
  p 393–28 constituting the visual *o·*.
  g 549– 9 Creatures of lower forms of *o·*
  555– 5 brings the physical *o·* under the yoke of disease.

organization

and decomposition
  r 488–26 not at the mercy of *o·* and decomposition,

and time
  f 249–19 *O·* and time have nothing to do with Life.

growth and
  g 548–24 his material sense of animal growth and *o·*,

material
  ph 165–10 material *o·* and non-intelligent matter.
  p 429–19 If man did not exist before the material *o·*
  g 509– 4 dependent upon no material *o·*.
  524–20 How then could a material *o·* become the basis of

physical
  ph 170–30 in either case dependent upon his physical *o·*,

  p 401–25 Would the drug remove paralysis, affect *o·*,

organizations
  s 124– 5 When this human belief lacks *o·* to support it,
  162–24 and healthy *o·* have been established
  f 239– 5 Take away wealth, fame, and social *o·*,
  g 554–30 less sickly than those possessing higher *o·*,

organs

p 384–32 the entire functions and o· of the
415–23 all the o· of the human system,
ap 572–27 Not through the material visual o· for seeing,
gl 585– 1 Not o· of the so-called corporeal senses,

Orient

ap 575–28 star seen by the Wisemen of the O·,

Oriental

p 362– 6 as if to interrupt the scene of O· festivity.
364–15 a special sign of O· courtesy.

Oriental Witchcraft

p 441–22 Hypnotism, O· W·, and Esoteric Magic

origin

above his
f 246– 8 by no means a material germ rising . . . above his o·.
and birth
a 30–11 Had his o· and birth been wholly apart from
and enlightenment
g 556–17 Did the o· and enlightenment of the race
and facts
r 491–12 the true o· and facts of being,
and governor
r 480–11 God, the o· and governor of all
and operations
g 512–27 Ignorant of the o· and operations of mortal
and ultimate
r 487– 3 Life is the o· and ultimate of man,
basis nor
sp 71–23 having no scientific basis nor o·,
describe the
g 552–32 Naturalists describe the o· of mortal and
divine
(see **divine**)
explaining the
b 292–19 Explaining the o· of material man
has no
o 347– 5 whatever is mortal or discordant has no o·,
his
a 30–11 Had his o· and birth been wholly apart from
m 63– 6 His o· is not, like that of mortals,
ph 171–17 Mistaking his o· and nature, man believes
human
b 305–29 These mortal dreams are of human o·,
g 553–21 to account for human o·,
learning the
sp 88–10 By learning the o· of each.
man's
c 262–28 a false sense of man's o·.
g 539–17 God condemned this lie as to man's o·
553– 4 a higher and purer contemplation of man's o·.
material
s 127–28 It has a spiritual, and not a material o·.
g 534– 1 the belief in the material o· of man
549–32 a belief in the material o· of man,
material in
g 540–30 Material in o· and sense, he brings a
mental
p 374–18 no argument against the mental o· of
mortal
ph 169–11 disease has a mental, mortal o·,
of all disease
ph 169–18 Science not only reveals the o· of all disease
of all things
f 212–30 its normal action, and the o· of all things
of man
(see **man**)
of mortals
g 548–18 Speaking of the o· of mortals,
of sin
gl 590– 7 the o· of sin, sickness, and death ;
or existence
b 287– 1 They are without a real o· or existence.
g 554–12 any knowledge of its o· or existence.
primal
sp 90– 2 how then can we account for their primal o·?
quantity, and
t 462–22 to discover their quality, quantity, and o·.
spiritual
(see **spiritual**)
their
s 112–14 they . . . remain wholly human in their o·
p 403–12 both have their o· in the human mind,
g 553–14 their o· and first introduction."
553–30 before they think or know aught of their o·,
without actual
b 281–23 sin and mortality are without actual o·

a 25–17 any man whose o· was less spiritual.
28–15 Neither the o·, the character, nor the work
f 215–25 in o·, in existence, and in his relation to God.
217– 5 in the o· of harmony.
b 277–21 asserts . . . that good is the o· of evil.
281–10 What is the Ego, whence its o· and what its

origin

g 529–27 and has neither o· nor support in Truth
555–17 is like inquiring into the o· of God,
gl 580–11 a so-called man, whose o·, substance, and mind

original

pr 16–15 the o· properly reads,
a 24– 4 Acquaintance with the o· texts,
sp 74– 7 the restoration to its o· condition
97–20 found in the likeness of Spirit, his o· being.
s 115–11 into the o· spiritual tongue.
ph 195–20 Observation, invention, study, and o· thought
197– 8 But the price does not exceed the o· cost.
f 210– 3 the translation of the spiritual o· into the
214–22 like the o· "tree of knowledge,"— Gen. 2 : 9.
b 277–14 preserving their o· species,
286–13 from first to last by this o· man, Jesus.
295–10 and then recover man's o· self
305– 6 is not the o·, though resembling it.
319–21 taught in the o· language of the Bible
320–14 quoted as follows, from the o· Hebrew :
320–17 Here the o· text declares plainly the
340– 6 the word duty, which is not in the o·,
o 356–31 Was there o· self-creative sin?
361–22 fuller expression of its o· meaning.
g 506– 3 Objects . . . unlike the o· do not reflect that o·.
516– 2 how true, . . . is the reflection to its o·.
552–28 results in a return to the o· species.
gl 579– 6 spiritual sense, which is also their o· meaning.
579–15 Error ; a falsity ; the belief in "o· sin,"
598– 5 Here the o· word is the same in both cases,

originally

an 104–24 If . . . a belief o· caused the sickness,
p 372– 4 What you call matter was o· error
r 470–18 standard of perfection was o· God and man.

originals

gl 583– 2 whose better o· are God's thoughts,

originate

sp 90– 1 or if one animal can o· another,
f 214–11 The material senses, like Adam, o· in matter
c 266–27 The evil beliefs which o· in mortals are hell.
b 275– 4 This shows that matter did not o· in God,
318– 9 senses o· and support all that is material,
318–31 Intelligence does not o· in numbers,
r 472–10 Sickness, sin, and death, . . . do not o· in God
g 543–24 Did man, whom God created . . . o· in an egg?
550–30 supposition that Spirit . . . can o· the impure
551–23 How can matter o· or transmit mind?

originated

s 158– 1 profession of medicine o· in idolatry
b 278–25 if man is material, he o· in matter
279– 7 protoplasm never o· in the immortal Mind,
307– 1 the deep sleep, in which o· the delusion
o 357–18 notions about the Divine Being . . . have o· in
357–21 must have o· in a false supposition,
p 416–18 body, which has o· from this material sense
g 531–15 If, in the beginning, man's body o· in
gl 585–26 belief that the human race o· materially

originates

b 269–30 theories I combat. . .(2) that matter o· in Mind,
338– 4 opposite belief— that man o· in matter
p 377–16 Because a belief o· unseen,
g 543–18 If man is material and o· in an egg,

originating

c 256–30 A mind o· from a finite or material source
p 374–10 explanation of disease as o· in human belief
gl 591–12 mind o· in matter ; the opposite of Truth ;

originator

sp 89–26 Sound is not the o· of music,

originators

c 263– 3 They believe themselves to be . . . o· of

origins

f 213–31 belief in material o· which discard

orthodox

o 351– 8 a member of the o· Congregational Church
358–32 their own accredited and o· pastors,
r 471–23 subscribed to an o· creed in early youth,

ossification

p 423–27 O· or any abnormal condition

other (see also **other's**)

pref x–25 than that of any o· sanitary method.
xi– 6 explains that all o· pathological methods are
pr 9– 1 that we are "not as o· men"— Luke 18 : 11.
11–12 Mere legal pardon (and there is no o·,
a 27– 6 In o· words : Tell John what the
27–24 two or three hundred o· disciples
30– 2 could give a more spiritual idea. . .than o· men,
34– 6 no o· commemoration is requisite,
38–22 the fruits of o· people's sins, not of his own.
46–16 in o· words, rose even higher in the
55– 1 if he entertained any o· sense of being
m 58–19 on the o· hand, a wandering desire for

other

  m 59–14 each partner sustaining the *o·*,
     60–21 and *o·* considerations, — passion,
     65–21 over this as over many *o·* reforms,
     66–25 If one is better than the *o·*,
     66–26 the *o·* pre-eminently needs good company.
     67–23 potent beyond all *o·* means and methods.
     68–14 and to your influence on *o·* lives.
  sp 72–4 in *o·* words, mortal, material sense
     73–2 In either case, one does not support the *o·*,
     73–6 neither the one nor the *o·* is infinite Spirit,
     73–12 Any *o·* control or attraction of so-called spirit
     73–16 electricity or any *o·* form of matter,
     77–3 Neither do *o·* mortals . . . at a single bound.
     85–29 and not to leave the *o·* undone." — *Matt.* 23 : 23.
     96–14 on the *o·* side there will be Science and peace.
     97–10 the flight of one and the blow of the *o·*
     98–7 and no *o·* sign shall be given.
     99–12 None may pick the lock nor enter by some *o·*
  an 101–30 *o·* than the effect of illusion.
     103–12 On the *o·* hand, Mind-science is wholly
  s 109–10 once seen, no *o·* conclusion can be reached.
     112–9 the Spencerian, or some *o·* school.
     119–10 while to grasp the *o·* horn of the dilemma
     126–16 C. S. on the one hand . . . theology on the *o·*
     126–30 I have had no *o·* guide
     129–20 and so are some *o·* systems.
     132–10 In *o·* words, he gave his benediction to
     132–18 from *o·* sanitary or religious systems,
     135–23 else one or the *o·* is false and useless ;
     135–26 proves the one to be identical with the *o·*.
     138–2 In *o·* words, Jesus purposed founding his
     140–19 Judaic and *o·* rituals are but types and
     145–15 or reliance on some *o·* minor curative.
     145–16 has this advantage over *o·* methods,
     145–25 *O·* methods undertake to oppose error with
     145–27 towards *o·* forms of matter or error,
     148–19 the one wholly, the *o·* primarily
     154–3 Disease arises, like *o·* mental conditions,
     156–26 employing no *o·* means, and she was cured.
  ph 167–28 impossible to gain control . . . in any *o·* way.
     169–22 however much we trust a drug or any *o·*
     169–29 Whatever teaches man to have *o·* laws
     169–30 Whatever teaches man to . . . acknowledge *o·*
     177–7 Neither exists without the *o·*,
     182–10 for one absolutely destroys the *o·*,
     182–11 one or the *o·* must be supreme
     182–14 and despise the *o·*." — *Matt.* 6 : 24.
     185–7 *o·* books were in circulation, which
     193–27 for saying : "It was none *o·* than God and
     200–21 in *o·* words the five senses,
  f 201–14 Christian perfection is won on no *o·* basis.
     206–1 we can have no *o·* Mind but His,
     206–1 no *o·* Love, wisdom, or Truth,
     206–2 no *o·* sense of Life,
     207–21 there can be no effect from any *o·* cause,
     208–32 and of *o·* beliefs included in matter.
     212–28 and possibly that *o·* methods involve so-called
     214–30 senses of Soul, and there are no *o·* real senses.
     220–6 to look in *o·* directions for cause and cure.
     228–26 to acknowledge any *o·* power is to dishonor God.
     231–30 governed by his Maker, having no *o·* Mind,
     242–11 It is to know no *o·* reality
     242–11 to have no *o·* consciousness of life
     249–10 Any *o·* theory of Life, or God, is delusive
  c 257–17 infinite Principle, — in *o·* words, divine Love,
     264–18 and needing no *o·* consciousness.
  b 269–25 *O·* foundations there are none.
     269–26 All *o·* systems . . . are reeds shaken by the
     270–6 One is contrary to the *o·*
     270–7 If one is real, the *o·* must be unreal.
     275–7 there is no *o·* might nor Mind,
     275–28 *o·* so-called powers, such as matter,
     279–14 and one can no more create the *o·* than
     281–5 When one appears, the *o·* disappears.
     282–22 and the *o·* a straight line.
     285–14 while the *o·* is non-intelligence.
     286–16 In the Saxon and twenty *o·* tongues
     301–10 On the *o·* hand, the immortal, spiritual man
     301–20 belief that man has any *o·* substance,
     304–8 nor depth, nor any *o·* creature, — *Rom.* 8 : 39.
     310–28 Spirit, which has no *o·* existence,
     315–1 and laid no claim to any *o·*.
     315–27 more spiritual than all *o·* earthly personalities.
     323–5 and to possess no *o·* consciousness but good.
     323–27 the delusion that there are *o·* minds,
     326–8 not try to climb the hill of Science by some *o·*
     327–13 There is no *o·* way.
     331–20 and there is no *o·* self-existence.
     333–6 in common with *o·* Hebrew boys and men,
     333–8 On the *o·* hand, Christ is not a name so much as
     338–1 heals the sick and sinning as no *o·* system can.
     339–4 Being destroyed, seems no *o·*
     340–9 In *o·* words : Let us hear the conclusion of
     340–19 man shall have no *o·* spirit or mind but God,

other

  o 348–25 and that of *o·* persons as well?
     349–15 like all *o·* languages, English is inadequate
     354–12 On the *o·* hand, the Christian opponents of C. S.
     355–16 The *o·*, popular religion, declines to admit
     358–7 If . . . one is true, the *o·* must be false.
     360–4 The *o·* artist replies :
  p 363–28 In the absence of *o·* proofs,
     364–25 On the *o·* hand, do they show their regard for
     369–22 and the *o·* to be made indestructible.
     376–2 more terrifying than that of most *o·* diseases.
     384–26 neither rheumatism, consumption, nor any *o·*
     385–2 Florence Nightingale and *o·* philanthropists
     385–9 energy and endurance surpassing all *o·* aids,
     391–15 Truth, will destroy all *o·* supposed suffering,
     398–15 restored whole, like as the *o·*." — *Matt.* 12 : 13.
     399–31 In *o·* words : How can I heal the body, without
     403–11 but matter is appealed to in the *o·*.
     413–9 views of parents and *o·* persons
     413–32 or any *o·* malady, timorously held in the
     414–9 the same as in *o·* diseases :
     414–14 dementia, hatred, or any *o·* discord.
     421–4 belief that *o·* portions of the body are
     422–25 and a Christian Scientist in the *o·*.
     424–28 scrofula and *o·* so-called hereditary diseases,
     429–3 as well as by *o·* graces of Spirit.
  t 443–19 whatever *o·* systems they fancy will
     444–8 *o·* Scientists, — their brethren upon whom
     444–20 turn to him the *o·* also." — *Matt.* 5 : 39.
     445–15 will be no desire for *o·* healing methods.
     452–29 On the *o·* hand, if you had the inclination
     457–2 *O·* works, which have borrowed from this
     457–6 more . . . than has been accomplished by *o·*
         books.
     457–22 To pursue *o·* vocations and
     457–31 without exploiting *o·* means.
     458–2 on the same platform as all *o·* quackery.
     458–4 one good and the *o·* evil,
     458–5 one spiritual, the *o·* material,
     459–31 than any *o·* healer on the globe.
  r 467–14 turning to no *o·* but the one perfect Mind
     468–30 in proportion as the *o·* is recognized.
     469–19 claimed no *o·* Mind and accepted no *o·*,
     471–19 and there is no *o·* power nor presence.
     473–13 who, more than all *o·* men, has presented
     475–7 blood, bones, and *o·* material elements.
     481–1 One must hide the *o·*.
     482–8 In *o·* cases, use the word *sense*,
     482–30 It can heal in no *o·* way,
     483–7 Mind transcends all *o·* power,
     483–8 supersede all *o·* means in healing.
     483–28 does honor God as no *o·* theory honors Him,
     485–24 If thought yields its dominion to *o·* powers,
     490–27 can be obtained in no *o·* way.
     492–5 In reality there is no *o·* existence,
     493–1 On the *o·* hand, C. S. speedily shows
     493–23 just as it removes any *o·* sense of
     494–27 The *o·* is the eternal and real evidence,
  g 509–13 Spirit creates no *o·* than heavenly . . . bodies,
     522–4 If one is true, the *o·* is false,
     523–18 The *o·* document is called the Jehovistic,
     524–5 and in a thousand *o·* so-called deities.
     531–22 Has man sought out *o·* creative inventions,
     535–5 the *o·* to be garnered into heavenly places.
     535–12 A belief in other gods, *o·* creators,
     535–13 belief in . . . *o·* creations must go down
     536–9 and there is no *o·* consciousness.
     546–19 seem more obscure than *o·* portions of the
     551–28 Neither can produce the *o·*
     552–6 modern geology, and all *o·* material hypotheses
  gl 580–2 a so-called finite mind, producing *o·* minds,
     591–26 mythology ; error creating *o·* errors ;
     598–6 as in *o·* passages in this same chapter
     (*see also* **each, gods**)

other's

  m 59–4 tender solicitude for each *o·* happiness,
  o 356–14 not contributing in any way to each *o·* happiness

others (*see also* **others'**)

  all
    a 25–19 demonstrated more spiritually than all *o·*
   an 106–18 and classify all *o·* as did St. Paul
    s 150–24 and will be to all *o·* at some future day,
   ph 170–23 more than all *o·* spiritual causation relates
    b 318–16 Is the sick man sinful above all *o·*?
  all the
    g 547–1 one example would authenticate all the *o·*.
  beliefs of
    a 53–32 Had he shared the sinful beliefs of *o·*,
  cannot injure
   sp 95–13 cannot injure *o·*, and must do them good.
  doing "unto
    p 435–21 doing "unto *o·* as ye would that they should do
  faith in
   sp 89–6 Having more faith in *o·* than in herself,

others

injuring

t 449–11 than for you to benefit yourself by injuring *o·*.

labors of

f 238–19 to enter unlawfully into the labors of *o·*.

relieved

a 25–23 by no means relieved *o·* from giving the

saved

a 49–29 "He saved *o·* ; himself he cannot — *Matt.* 27 : 42.

say

p 434– 5 *O·* say, "The law of Christ supersedes *our* laws ;

sins of

ph 189–13 sins of *o·* should not make good men suffer.
o 346–15 belief that we suffer from the sins of *o·*.

themselves and

a 34–22 It helped them to raise themselves and *o·*
r 494–32 cast fear . . . out of themselves and *o·*

---

pr 8–17 wise not to try to deceive ourselves or *o·*,
a 23–24 One kind of faith trusts one's welfare to *o·*.
29– 3 must grapple with sin in themselves and in *o·*,
33–12 *breaking* (explaining) it to *o·*,
38–25 Jesus mapped out the path for *o·*.
51–21 the works which he did and taught *o·* to do.
m 69–18 they can educate *o·* spiritually
sp 75–21 When you can waken yourself or *o·*
86– 4 Jesus knew, as *o·* did not, that it was not
99–19 may possess natures above some *o·*
s 136–16 and *o·*, Jeremias, or one of the — *Matt.* 16 : 14.
136–30 apprehended their Master better than did *o·* ;
153–25 We weep because *o·* weep,
153–26 and we have smallpox because *o·* have it ;
f 217–15 That scientific methods are superior to *o·*,
220–24 advised *o·* never to try dietetics for
234–16 thereby robbing both themselves and *o·*.
b 297–26 Some thoughts are better than *o·*.
o 359–31 One says : . . . When *o·* see them as I do,
p 391–28 be just to yourself and to *o·*.
424–23 while *o·* are thinking about your patients
435–10 should result in good to himself as well as to *o·*.
t 447– 5 attempt to influence the thoughts of *o·*,
452–20 live it and love it, or he cannot impart it to *o·*.
453–15 must know himself before he can know *o·*
461–18 if this be requisite to protect *o·*.
462– 2 Some . . . assimilate truth more readily than *o·*,
464– 9 *O·* could not take her place, even if willing
r 497–26 to do unto *o·* as we would have

others'

t 455–14 little or no power for *o·* help.

otherwise

a 38–17 *o·* . . . . could not have been done spiritually.
40–18 for not *o·* could he show us the way
m 59– 8 compact which might *o·* become unbearable.
sp 75–24 you can then . . . but not *o·*.
93–11 If we believe *o·*, we may be sure that
an 102–28 more likely to be abused . . . than *o·* employed,
s 120– 1 though it seems *o·* to finite sense.
134–11 burned, crucified, and *o·* persecuted :
ph 168– 8 Mind, which would *o·* outweigh all else.
b 268– * *Here I stand. I can do no o· ; so help me God !*
o 358–11 *O·* it would not be Science,
p 392–21 unless Science shows you *o·*.
423– 4 either verbally or *o·*,
r 477–18 Were it *o·*, man would be annihilated.
485– 2 If error is necessary to define . . . but not *o·*.
488–26 *o·* the very worms could unfashion man.
491–32 Who can rationally say *o·*,
g 519– 4 How could He be *o·*, since the
525–25 The corporeal senses declare *o·* ;

ought

a 19–27 In disobedience to Him, we *o·* to feel no security,
m 58–26 a wife *o·* not to court vulgar extravagance
68– 6 We *o·* to weary of the fleeting and false
sp 73–13 belief, which *o·* to be known by its fruit,
85–29 "These *o·* ye to have done, — *Matt.* 23 : 23.
94–10 by our law he *o·* to die, — *John* 19 : 7.
s 130–28 *o·* we not, contrariwise, to be astounded
ph 168– 9 when it *o·* to be enlisted on the side of health.
f 220– 4 Such admissions *o·* to open people's eyes
248– 6 *o·* to ripen into health and immortality,
253–26 knowing (as you *o·* to know) that
b 278–32 Which *o·* to be substance to us,
299–20 *O·* we not then to judge the knowledge
o 345–22 *o·* to be able to discern the distinction
348– 5 *O·* we not, then, to approve
352–17 *o·* to fear a reality which can harm them
p 383–30 when it *o·* to be insensibly so
t 449–20 to be understood and guarded against.
r 483–26 it *o·* to receive aid, not opposition,
485–10 views of error *o·* to be obliterated by Truth.
g 540–13 but we *o·* to know that God's law

our

p 438– 3 in *o·* image, after *o·* likeness ; — *Gen.* 1 : 26.
r 475–23, 24 in *o·* image, after *o·* likeness ; — *Gen.* 1 : 26.
g 515–11, 12 in *o·* image, after *o·* likeness ; — *Gen.* 1 : 26.
525–13, 14 Let us make man after *o·* mind and *o·* likeness

outcome

f 250–13 man, the *o·* of God, reflects God.
b 271–25 eternal life, not the death of Jesus, is its *o·*.
277–12 and cannot be the *o·* of an infinite God,
p 422–28 the ultimate *o·* of the injury.
r 466–26 idolatry and ritualism are the *o·* of
g 555–14 error is neither mind nor the *o·* of Mind.
ap 577–16 third, Christianity, which is the *o·* of

outgrow

sp 77–27 Spiritualists would *o·* their beliefs in

outgrowing

t 452–10 *o·* the old, you should not fear to put on the new.

outgrown

a 28–12 In conscience, we cannot hold to beliefs *o·* ;
sp 74–30 never a return to positions *o·*.

outgrowth

pr 12–26 and not the *o·* of divine Science.
sp 92–18 is an *o·* of human knowledge
ph 171–32 supposition that man is a material *o·*
g 519– 5 the spiritual creation was the *o·*,

outlaw

an 105– 9 while mortal mind, evil, which is the real *o·*,
p 381–27 Let us banish sickness as an *o·*,
435–16 for the agent of those laws is an *o·*,

outline

f 247–24 in expression, form, *o·*, and color.
248–23 angular *o·* and deformity of matter models.
c 263–13 forming deformity when he would *o·* grace
r 485–25 it cannot *o·* on the body its own

outlined

ph 196–29 mental state, which is afterwards *o·* on the
gl 587– 1 a belief that mind is *o·* and limited ;
591–20 Deity, which outlines but is not *o·*.

outlines

ph 175– 2 we should efface the *o·* of disease
191–23 not a leaf unfolds its fair *o·*,
198–10 *o·* his thought relative to disease,
c 260– 3 than the sculptor can perfect his *o·* from
b 298–31 marked with superstitious *o·*,
gl 591–20 Deity, which *o·* but is not outlined.

outlived

o 353–13 The age has not wholly *o·* the sense of

outlook

m 58–13 Never contract the horizon of a worthy *o·*
b 326–27 Thought assumed a nobler *o·*,

outpouring

pr 3–21 and for a liberal *o·* of benefactions.
ap 574–14 spiritual *o·* of bliss and glory,

outraged

p 440–17 Wherefore, then, in the name of *o·* justice,

outset

a 21–19 Our paths have diverged at the very *o·*,
c 260–18 and ensures failure at the *o·*.
o 357– 3 and knew from the *o·* that man would do.
g 541–18 ruptures the life . . . of man at the very *o·*.

outshining

ap 571–30 *o·* sin, sorcery, lust, and hypocrisy.

outside

m 58–20 incessant amusement *o·* the home circle
sp 71– 8 *o·* of finite form, which forms only reflect.
71–23 no proof nor power *o·* of human testimony.
89– 9 Destroy her belief in *o·* aid,
s 133–28 no life, intelligence, nor substance *o·* of God.
151– 5 could not possibly create a remedy *o·* of itself,
ph 195– 5 *O·* of dismal darkness and cold silence he
f 202–15 *O·* of this Science all is mutable ;
253–12 (*o·* of erring, mortal, material sense
b 301–26 supposed standpoint *o·* the focal distance of
p 382–12 making clean merely the *o·* of the platter.
396–29 Spirit, *o·* of matter, never in it,
405–32 and to appeal to divine sources *o·* of themselves.
441–26 decides . . . that no law *o·* of divine Mind can
r 476–22 which is *o·* of all material selfhood.
482–21 the divine idea of God *o·* the flesh.
489–28 *O·* the material sense of things, all is harmony.
g 510–16 representation of Soul *o·* the body,
545–17 *O·* of C. S. all is vague and hypothetical,

outsiders

s 138–11 cures, which appeared miraculous to *o·*.
141–21 The *o·* did not then, and do not now,

outstretched

p 365–14 from the o· arm of righteousness?

outward

pref	ix– 3	drinks in the o· world through the eyes
pr	4– 9	O· worship is not of itself sufficient to
s	129–23	instead of accepting only the o· sense of things.
f	254–22	which determines the o· and actual.
g	552–18	peck open their shells with C. S., and look o·
gl	586– 5	Jesus said, thinking of the o· vision,

outwardly

t 464– 5 in which to make herself o· known

outweigh

s	155–20	must mightily o· the power of popular belief
ph	168– 8	which would otherwise o· all else.
p	392– 8	enables truth to o· error.

outweighs

s 149– 3 Mind as far o· drugs in the cure of disease

over

pref	xii– 6	During seven years o· four thousand students
pr	5– 2	from demonstrating his power o· error.
	5–13	will be full "and running o·." — Luke 6 : 38.
	7–31	the recollection that we have prayed o· it
	14–28	man's dominion o· the whole earth.
	17–14	Truth, Love, o· all, and All.
a	24–18	change . . . which has come o· popular opinions
	24–30	enabled their Master to triumph o· the grave,
	25–15	casts out error, and triumphs o· death.
	25–22	Though mortals may control o· sin and
	26–15	Love gave Jesus authority o· sin,
	26–25	his demonstration of power o· death.
	28–14	to heal the sick and to triumph o· sin.
	30–26	If we have triumphed . . . . o· the errors of
	31–22	the divine Principle which triumphs o· death.
	35–15	They celebrate their Lord's victory o· death,
	36–25	gloat o· their offences to the last
	39–16	death was not the threshold o· which he
	42–16	his final triumph o· body and matter,
	43–28	must triumph o· all material beliefs
	43–32	Love must triumph o· hate.
	44– 1	seal the victory o· error and death,
	44–11	the power of Mind o· matter,
	45– 7	in his victory o· death and the grave.
	45–30	glorified the supremacy of Mind o· matter.
	48– 6	held uncomplaining guard o· a world
	49–24	to triumph o· sin, sickness, death,
	53–22	Like Peter, we should weep o· the warning,
	54–15	and triumph o· death through Mind,
m	57–29	until it ceases to sigh o· the world
	59–23	After marriage, it is too late to grumble o·
	61– 5	The good . . . must have ascendency o· the evil
	61– 5	and the spiritual o· the animal,
	65–20	There will ensue a fermentation o· this
	65–20	as o· many other reforms,
sp	76–20	they will have no power o· man,
	79– 9	Science must go o· the whole ground,
	80–24	o· its substratum, called matter.
	83–20	and gives to matter the precedence o· Spirit.
	90–19	through the air and o· the ocean.
an	100– 5	said could be exerted by one . . . . o· another,
	102–12	no more power o· man than o· his Maker,
	102–14	has dominion o· all the earth
	105– 6	To say . . . no jurisdiction o· the carnal or
	105–12	body o· which courts hold jurisdiction?
s	111–13	utilization of the power of Truth o· error ;
	117–18	his power o· the sick and sinning.
	125–26	mariner will have dominion o· the atmosphere
	125–27	o· the fish of the sea and the fowls of the air.
	130– 3	discouraged o· its slight spiritual prospects.
	131–11	superiority of spiritual o· physical power.
	134–30	spiritual power o· material resistance.
	137– 6	the victor o· sickness, sin, disease, death, and
	139– 5	the triumph of Spirit, Mind, o· matter.
	140–11	warring no more o· the corporeality,
	142– 5	its power o· sickness, sin, and death ;
	142– 7	one of these powers, — the power o· sin.
	145–16	this advantage o· other methods,
	150–30	the superiority of matter o· Mind,
	151–23	it has no control o· God's man.
	152–13	one . . . contradicts another o· and o· again.
ph	165–15	man's God-given dominion o· the earth.
	166– 6	thus the conscious control o· the body is lost.
	166–30	its mastery o· sin, disease, and death,
	169– 5	assuring me that danger was o·,
	169–16	If we understood the control of Mind o· body,
	171–12	Mind's control o· the universe,
	175–17	If . . . had tried to tyrannize o· our forefathers,
	182–30	To admit that sickness is a condition o· which
	188–28	When darkness comes o· the earth,
	189– 3	the sun's influence o· the earth.
	190–25	wind passeth o· it, — Psal. 103 : 16.
	196– 5	The power of mortal mind o· its own body
	199–26	to walk the rope o· Niagara's abyss of waters,

ph	200–14	o· the works of Thy hands. — Psal. 8 : 6.
f	202–23	God gives man dominion o· all the earth.
	209– 5	Mind, supreme o· all its formations
	210– 1	superiority of faith by works o· faith in words.
	213–29	as the hand, which sweeps o· it, is human or
	217–23	understand the control which Mind has o· so-called
	222–24	"dominion o· the fish of the sea, — Gen. 1 : 26.
	222–24	o· the fowl of the air, — Gen. 1 : 26.
	222–25	and o· the cattle," — Gen. 1 : 26.
	228–13	his God-given dominion o· the material senses.
	232– 2	can triumph o· sin, sickness, and death.
	232–17	as it did o· nineteen hundred years ago,
	232–18	healing the sick and triumphing o· death.
	234–17	If mortals would keep proper ward o· mortal
	238–22	Attempts to . . . gain dominion o· mankind,
	242– 8	and the final triumph o· the body.
	243– 8	and triumph o· sin and death.
	247–30	shining resplendent and eternal o· age
b	269–18	o· the objects and thoughts of material sense,
	291–27	for the grave has no power o· either.
	307–26	gives man dominion o· all things.
	309–14	the power of Spirit o· the material senses ;
	310– 9	else the clay would have power o· the potter.
	311–24	which prevails o· material sense
	312–14	People go into ecstasies o· the sense of a
	316– 9	to prove the power of Spirit o· the flesh,
	316–23	which gives man dominion o· all the earth.
	322– 5	the control of Soul o· sense,
	323–17	"faithful o· a few things," — Matt. 25 : 21.
	323–18	shall be made rulers o· many ;
o	346–21	If a dream ceases, . . . the terror is o·.
p	369–10	raising the dead, and walking o· the wave.
	369–11	control o· the belief that matter is substance,
	369–32	or to be angry o· sin.
	378–17	represents the power of Truth o· error,
	378–18	might of intelligence . . . . o· mortal beliefs
	379–12	stream of warm water was trickling o· his arm.
	380–10	the control of Mind o· body,
	380–21	and prove man's dominion o· error.
	384–32	the power of Mind o· the entire functions
	388– 3	obtained a victory o· the corporeal senses,
	389– 4	given in behalf of the control of Mind o·
	395– 7	as one having authority o· it,
	395– 9	assert its claims o· mortality and disease.
	396–23	power which their beliefs exercise o· their
	399–11	mortal mind sends its despatches o· its body,
	404–22	If the evil is o· in the repentant mortal mind,
	404–17	The temperance reform, felt all o· our land,
	406–22	the supremacy of Truth o· error,
	406–23	Life o· death, and good o· evil,
	406–27	involves . . . a loss of control o· the body.
	407–10	If man is not victorious o· the passions,
	413–22	need not wash his little body all o· each day
	418–2, 3	the conquest o· sickness, as well as o· sin,
	420–26	gives them all power o· every physical action
	427–21	obtain the victory o· death in proportion as
	438– 5	o· all the power of the enemy :— Luke 10 : 19.
	438–20	a garment of foul fur was spread o·
t	447–26	and thus get the victory o· sin
	450–13	They do not . . . whine o· the demands of
	450–24	by understanding God's power o· them.
	454–30	superiority of spiritual power o· sensuous
	455– 9	in order to walk o· the waves of error
	460–21	it starts a petty crossfire o· every cripple
r	475–24	let them have dominion o· the fish — Gen. 1 : 26.
	475–25	o· the fowl of the air, and o· the cattle, — Gen. 1 : 26.
	475–26	o· all the earth, and o· every creeping — Gen. 1 : 26.
	476–26	the wind passeth o· it, — Psal. 103 : 16.
	482–23	enabled Jesus to demonstrate his control o·
	483–17	Science has called the world to battle o· this
	484–25	Science must triumph o· material sense,
	484–25	and Truth o· error,
g	502– 5	as if reality did not predominate o· unreality,
	502– 6	the light o· the dark,
	502– 6	straight line of Spirit o· the mortal deviations
	511–8, 9	to rule o· the day and o· the night, — Gen. 1 : 18.
	514–26	the control which Love held o· all,
	515– 5	creeping o· lofty summits,
	515–13	dominion o· the fish of the sea, — Gen. 1 : 26.
	515–13	o· the fowl of the air, and o· the cattle, — Gen. 1 : 26.
	515–14	o· all the earth, and o· every creeping — Gen. 1 : 26.
	516–21	reflects God's dominion o· all the earth.
	517–27	dominion o· the fish of the sea, — Gen. 1 : 28.
	517–28	o· the fowl of the air, and o· every — Gen. 1 : 28.
	529–31	He begins his reign o· man somewhat mildly,
	530–18	as always asserting his superiority o·
	531–32	and having dominion o· all the earth.
	533– 2	God's behest, dominion o· all the earth
	535– 9	and he shall rule o· thee. — Gen. 3 : 16.
	545–11	given dominion o· the whole earth.

over

ap 559– 9 reaches o· continent and ocean
 559–23 murmur not o· Truth, if you find its
 568–24 For victory o· a single sin, we give thanks
 568–26 the mighty conquest o· all sin
 569– 6 faithful o· a few things,— *Matt.* 25 : 23.
 569– 7 I will make thee ruler o· many,"— *Matt.* 25 : 23.
 571–18 the occasion for a victory o· evil.
 578–15 my cup runneth o·.— *Psal.* 23 : 5.
gl 593–21 and demonstrated as supreme o· all ;
 596–29 Jewish women wore veils o· their faces
 598–26 would bridge o· . . . the interval of death,
 (*see also* **body**)

overaction

s 125– 7 Neither organic inaction nor o·
p 428– 1 no inaction, diseased action, o·, nor

overbear

f 203– 1 as though evil could o· the law of Love,

overcame

a 39– 4 He o· the world, the flesh, and
 39–14 Jesus o· death and the grave
 45– 2 Jesus . . . o· every law of matter,
b 289–14 Truth, o· and still overcomes death
ap 568–17 o· him by the blood of the Lamb,— *Rev.* 12 : 11.

overcome

a 43–27 The divine must o· the human at every point.
m 61–22 propensities that must either be o· or
sp 76–30 death must be o·, not submitted to,
f 220– 2 said : . . . in order to o· a predisposition to
 231– 3 rightly met and fairly o· by Truth,
 240–26 convinced of the error that is to be o·.
 253–16 to o· the belief in sin, disease, or
c 264–23 sickness and death were o· by Jesus,
b 289– 5 should be o· by the understanding of
 289– 7 Then Spirit will have o· the flesh.
 306– 5 how death was to be o· by spiritual Life,
p 392– 2 through divine Mind that·you o· disease.
 394–21 Will you bid a man let evils o· him,
 405– 8 and to o· deceit with honesty.
 405–18 The good man finally can o· his fear of sin.
 410–16 material condition to be o· by Spirit,
 427–18 If man is never to o· death, why do the
 427–21 in proportion as we o· sin.
t 446–24 Resisting evil, you o· it
 450–20 he will o· them by understanding their
ap 568– 1 Innocence and Truth o· guilt and error.
 569– 4 must grapple with and o· the mortal belief in
 571–15 under all circumstances, o· evil with good.
gl 581–14 temptation o· and followed by exaltation.

overcomes

s 134–22 law of harmony which o· discord,
ph 182–21 the law which o· material conditions
b 289–15 Truth, overcame and still o· death
 315–24 Truth . . . heals sickness, and o· death.
p 395–11 divine Science o· faith in a carnal mind,
 420–17 Truth o· both disease and sin

overcometh

c 267–29 "Blessed is the man that endureth [o·]— *Jas.*
  1 : 12.

overcoming

pr 10–12 C. S. reveals a necessity for o· the world,
a 21– 1 If Truth is o· error in your daily walk
an 104–25 a case of the greater error o· the lesser.
f 233–20 o· the thoughts which produce them,
b 273–27 Science, o· the false claims of
r 497–18 and o· sin and death.

overeaten

p 385–22 You say that you have not slept well or have o·.

over-exertion

p 417–10 there will be no reaction from o·

overflowing

ph 180–16 reservoir already o· with that emotion.

overflows

a 26– 1 the heart o· with gratitude for what he

overlook

a 36–32 Can God therefore o· the law of

overlooked

t 455–29 This strong point in C. S. is not to be o·,

overlying

r 496–18 o·, and encompassing all true being.

overmastering

ph 186–17 It says : "I am a real entity, o· good."

overpower

f 222–26 if eating a bit of animal flesh could o· him.
p 429– 1 It is a sin to believe that aught can o·

overrule

a 44–31 to o· mortal, material sense.
s 128– 1 hypotheses . . . that these are final and o· the
p 384–29 the evidence before the senses can never o·.

overruled

a 43–14 were o· by divine Love
p 381–31 Christ Jesus o· the error which would
 437–28 But Judge Justice . . . o· their motions

overshadow

r 495–17 Let neither fear nor doubt o· your clear sense

overshadowed

a 29–24 o· the pure sense of the Virgin-mother

overshadowing

a 33–16 glory of an everlasting victory o· him,

overtake

ph 174–18 are pursuing and will o· the ages,

overtakes

b 290– 5 before what is termed death o· mortals,

overtaxed

sp 79–24 says : . . . Your brain is o·,
f 203–21 o· the belief of life in matter

overthrew

f 228–27 The humble Nazarene o· the supposition

overthrow

s 110–19 neither tongue nor pen can o· it.
o 342– 1 denunciation cannot o· it.
p 391– 1 to o· the plea of mortal mind,
t 464–28 nor can they o· a scientific system

overthrowing

p 437–26 C. S. was o· the judicial proceedings of a

overthrows

s 120–23 heals the sick, o· false evidence,
 129–12 a belief which Science o·.

overturn

f 223–31 God will o·, until

overwhelmed

p 366–22 physician must also watch, lest he be o·

overwhelming

pr 13–18 o· our real wishes with a torrent of words.
a 47– 8 It was sometimes an o· power
 50– 6 added to an o· sense of the magnitude of
s 151–32 That mortal mind claims . . . we have o· proof.
p 396–19 the o· weight of opinions on the wrong side,

overworked

p 387– 5 Who dares to say that actual Mind can be o·?

ovum

g 547–10 microscopic examination of a vulture's o·,
 549–18 look upon the simple o· as the
 553–20 from Adam's rib, not from a fœtal o·.
 553–24 If . . . human belief agrees upon an o· as

owe

a 18– 4 and for this we o· him endless homage.
sp 94–12 The eastern empires and nations o· their

owing

s 149– 8 o· to the different mental states of the patient.

own

pref ix– 5 as sure of the world's existence as he is of his o·
 xii–11 she was . . . publisher of her o· works ;
pr 3– 8 Shall we ask . . . to do His o· work?
 3–11 enables us to work out our o· salvation.
 7– 4 Still stronger evidence . . . found in his o· words
 11–22 the results of mortals' o· faith.
 12–17 has no efficacy of its o·
a 18–18 could conciliate no nature above his o·,
 22–11 "Work out your o· salvation,"— *Phil.* 2 : 12.
 23–26 work out one's "o· salvation,— *Phil.* 2 : 12.
 24–30 his o· disciples could not admit such
 25–24 the requisite proofs of her o· piety.
 26–11 which Jesus implied in his o· statements :
 37–13 right-doing brings its o· reward ;
 38–23 fruits of other people's sins, not of his o·.
 40–15 Another's suffering cannot lessen our o· liability.
 48–25 in the presence of his o· momentous question,
m 61–19 may reproduce in their o· helpless little ones
 63–30 should be allowed to collect her o· wages,
 63–31 and o· her children free from interference.
 64–22 Then shall Soul rejoice in its o·,
 64–31 Spirit will ultimately claim its o·,
 65–25 is never desirable on its o· account.
 69–17 educate their o· offspring spiritually,
sp 77– 7 Error brings its o· self-destruction
 77– 8 mortal mind creates its o· physical conditions.
 79–19 Jesus did his o· work by the one Spirit.

P

pace
　g 514–18　and keep *p·* with highest purpose.

pacified
　ap 570–24　The waters will be *p·*, and Christ will command

pagan
　s 158– 2　*p·* priests, who besought the gods to heal
　ph 187– 8　With *p·* blindness, it attributes to some
　　200– 2　*P·* worship began with muscularity,
　f 214–19　finite thoughts of God like the *p·* idolater.
　b 339–20　As the mythology of *p·* Rome has yielded to
　　340–26　annihilates *p·* and Christian idolatry,
　r 469–30　ancient mythology and *p·* idolatry.

paganism
　s 140–19　Worshipping through the medium of matter is *p·*.
　ph 171– 1　*p·* and lust are so sanctioned by society
　ap 571–29　illumined the night of *p·* with
　gl 596– 3　*P·* and agnosticism may define Deity as

page
　gl 585–15　ERROR. See . . . *p·* 472.
　　588–26　INTELLIGENCE. . . . *p·* 469.
　　590–14　LIFE. See . . . *p·* 468.
　　593– 3　PRINCIPLE. See . . . *p·* 465.
　　594–18　SOULS. See . . . *p·* 466.
　　594–24　SPIRITS. . . . (See *p·* 466.)
　　594–25　SUBSTANCE. See . . . *p·* 468.

pages
　pref xii–26　she commits these *p·* to honest seekers for
　s 139–22　darkening to some extent the inspired *p·*.
　g 548– 4　and breathes through the sacred *p·* the

paid
　pr 10–21　has *p·* for the privilege of prayer the price of
　a 20– 3　He at last *p·* no homage to forms of doctrine
　p 405–16　will be manacled until the last farthing is *p·*,

pain
absence of
　ph 186–26　If pain is as real as the absence of *p·*, both must
and painlessness
　s 125–13　*p·* and painlessness, sorrow and joy,
and pleasure
　s 122–12　seats of *p·* and pleasure, from which
　ph 181– 7　has no partnership with *p·* and pleasure,
　　188–11　dream of *p·* and pleasure in matter,
　　188–20　*p·* and pleasure, sickness and care,
　　190–10　fills itself with thoughts of *p·* and pleasure,
　f 242–19　the so-called *p·* and pleasure of the senses.
　c 262–19　when the supposed *p·* and pleasure of matter
　b 303–21　The belief that *p·* and pleasure,
　　307–22　supposed material *p·* and pleasure
　p 389–25　between *p·* and pleasure, good and evil,
and sorrow
　g 557–15　the less *p·* and sorrow are his.
any
　p 416– 9　To him there is no longer any *p·*.
belief in
　s 153–19　The boil simply manifests, . . . a belief in *p·*,
　　153–24　its own pain— that is, its own *belief in p·*.
belief of
　f 247–32　to retreat from the belief of *p·* or
　o 346–13　that there is no reality in his belief of *p·*,
　p 416– 3　the belief of *p·* will presently return, unless
　t 464–18　when the belief of *p·* was lulled,
couch of
　o 342–22　raises from the couch of *p·* the helpless invalid.
　p 435–19　Watching beside the couch of *p·*
development of
　p 391–12　can prevent the development of *p·*
does not produce
　p 413– 2　Mind, does not produce *p·* in matter.
end in
　g 536–20　Passions and appetites must end in *p·*.
equivalent of
　pr 6–13　will furnish more than its equivalent of *p·*,
inflammation and
　p 375– 4　the belief that inflammation and *p·* must
instead of
　p 435–13　pleasure instead of *p·*, and life instead of death.
intense
　ph 195– 1　gave him a belief of intense *p·*.
intruding
　p 391–10　a single intruding *p·* which
makes its own
　s 153–24　this so-called mind makes its own *p·*
memory of
　f 212– 9　Because the memory of *p·* is more vivid
no
　m 69–15　the sweet assurance of no parting, no *p·*,
　s 113–28　no *p·* in Truth, and no truth in pain ;
　c 261–11　the body experiences no *p·*.

pain
no
　p 393–21　matter can have no *p·* nor inflammation.
　　421–19　gone from mortal mind, there can be no *p·* ;
　g 557– 9　many animals suffer no *p·* in multiplying ;
no more
　ap 573–31　no more *p·*, and all tears will be wiped away.
no truth in
　s 113–29　no pain in Truth, and no truth in *p·* ;
occasion of
　f 212–13　which we say was the occasion of *p·*,
occasions the
　p 416–14　unless the belief which occasions the *p·* has
or fear
　b 327– 6　the false beliefs of pleasure, *p·*, or fear
or heat
　p 376–26　impossible for matter . . . to feel *p·* or heat,
or pleasure
　s 159–27　*p·* or pleasure, action or stagnation,
　f 211–32　Nerves are not the source of *p·* or pleasure.
　　212– 1　this *p·* or pleasure is not communicated through
　　219– 9　No more can we say . . . that nerves give *p·* or
　　　　　　 pleasure,
　　247–32　to retreat from the belief of *p·* or pleasure
　b 339–31　intelligence or power, *p·* or pleasure.
　p 392–32　issues of *p·* or pleasure must come through mind,
　r 478–17　assertion that there can be *p·* or pleasure in
part with
　s 138–24　sick are more willing to part with *p·* than
pleasure and
　sp 92– 5　experiencing pleasure and *p·*,
　b 298–17　alternating between a sense of pleasure and *p·*,
　r 472–15　Error is a supposition that pleasure and *p·*,
pleasure nor
　b 327– 4　neither pleasure nor *p·*, appetite nor passion,
pleasure or
　　(see **pleasure**)
produce
　ph 166– 2　the human mind is all that can produce *p·*.
quiets
　s 143–17　and quiets *p·* with anodynes.
same
　p 416–13　patient will find himself in the same *p·*, unless
seized with
　t 464–14　seized with *p·* so violent
sensation of
　f 212– 6　If the sensation of *p·* in the limb can return,
sorrow, and
　ap 573–27　a cessation of death, sorrow, and *p·*.
suffer no
　g 557– 9　many animals suffer no *p·* in multiplying ;
travaileth in
　c 255– *　*travaileth in p· together until—* Rom. 8 : 22.
where is the
　p 416–15　Where is the *p·* while the patient sleeps?
without
　f 215– 1　Spirit's senses are without *p·*,

---

　s 153–22　*p·* cannot exist where there is no mortal mind
　ph 186–26　If *p·* is as real as the absence of pain, both must
　　195– 9　gave him *p·* through those very senses,
　f 212– 4　and the *p·* seems to be in its old place.
　　212– 5　has continued in belief to *p·* the owner.
　　212– 8　Why need *p·*, rather than pleasure, come
　　212–13　When . . . the *p·* still remains, it proves
　　219– 1　all disease, *p·*, weakness, . . . will be unknown,
　c 260–31　If we look to the body for pleasure, we find *p·* ;
　b 285– 2　cannot be cognizant . . . of pleasure or of *p·*.
　　308–12　a blending of false claims, false pleasure, *p·*,
　o 346–24　hence *p·* in matter is a false belief,
　　346–25　Do you feel the *p·* of tooth-pulling, when you
　p 379–26　*p·* in the head and limbs,
　　415–14　Opiates do not remove the *p·* in any scientific
　　415–31　leaving the *p·* standing forth as distinctly as
　　416– 2　shows the *p·* to be in the mind,
　　416– 5　mental image occasioning the *p·*
　　418–30　Tumors, ulcers, tubercles, inflammation, *p·*,
　　421–15　belief that this chemicalization produces *p·*

pained
　f 250–16　weary or *p·*, enjoy or suffer, according to
　t 452– 9　eyes accustomed to darkness are *p·* by the light.
　ap 562–23　and *p·* to be delivered.— *Rev.* 12 : 2.

painful
　s 153–16　You say a boil is *p·* ;
　　153–17　for matter without mind is not *p·*.
　f 251– 4　an abscess should not grow more *p·*
　o 346–18　How then . . . "fraught with falsities *p·* to
　p 385–21　discolored, *p·*, swollen, and inflamed.
　r 495–19　can destroy any *p·* sense of, or belief in,

painless
  f 224– 9 There should be p· progress,
  p 401–13 but should be as p· to man as to a fluid,
  414–28 in whom all being is p· and permanent.

painlessly
  p 375– 2 as p· as gas dissipates into the air

painlessness
  s 125–13 pain and p·, sorrow and joy,

pains
  and pleasures
  m 67–30 physical p· and pleasures,
  f 202– 8 so-called p· and pleasures of material sense,
  r 491–28 we dream of the p· and pleasures of matter.
  material
  a 39–23 material p· and material pleasures to pass away.
  multiplies their
  f 214–23 All material knowledge, . . . multiplies their p·,
  of sense
  f 232–28 so-called pleasures and p· of sense pass away
  c 265–28 The p· of sense quickly inform us that
  265–31 The p· of sense are salutary, if they
  p 382–28 the so-called pleasures and p· of sense.
  390–11 to exchange the pleasures and p· of sense for
  of sinful sense
  p 405–29 p· of sinful sense are less harmful than its
  pleasures and
    (see **pleasures**)

  ————

  b 322–22 incurred through the p· of distorted sense.

painted
  p 400–24 we see p· on the retina the image which

painter
  c 260– 4 or the p· can depict the form and face of

painting
  b 310– 1 The artist is not in his p·.

paints
  f 247–24 It is Love which p· the petal with myriad hues,

pairs
  r 466–11 but these contrasting p· of terms

palaces
  s 133–18 in the fiery furnace and in kings' p·.

palate
  sp 88– 7 when no viand touches the p·

pale
  pref vii– 4 So shone the p· star to the prophet-shepherds ;
  a 48– 8 P· in the presence of his own momentous
  b 328–32 reaching beyond the p· of a single period
  p 415–18 causing a p· or flushed cheek.

pallid
  p 376–10 p· invalid, whom you declare to be
  415–17 Note how thought makes the face p·.

palm
  s 142–11 If the soft p·, upturned to a lordly salary,

palms
  a 44–16 to heal the torn p·
  48–15 Truth and Love bestow few p· until

palpable
  o 359–15 p· only to spiritual sense,

palpitating
  o 351–14 the living, p· presence of Christ,

palsied
  p 415–22 impelled or p· by thought,

palsies
  s 119–19 The lawgiver, whose lightning p· . . . is not
  142–16 Sensuality p· the right hand,

palsy
  p 375–21 P· is a belief that matter governs mortals,
  375–25 and you cure the p·.
  r 486–29 then p·, blindness, and deafness would

pampered
  a 41–10 p· hypocrite may have a flowery pathway here,

pamphlet
  pref ix–20 Her first p· on C. S. was copyrighted in 1870 ;

panacea
  s 144–29 Truth will be the universal p·.
  p 407–12 Here C. S. is the sovereign p·,

Pandemonium
  b 269– 1 P·, a house divided against itself.

Pandora box
  ph 170–30 the P· b·, from which all ills have

pang
  a 19–17 Every p· of repentance and suffering,

pangs
  a 48– 1 The p· of neglect and the staves of
  ph 175–15 inflammation, sneezing, and nasal p·.
  b 296–20 and how long they will suffer the p· of

panoply
  ap 571–18 Clad in the p· of Love,

pantheism
  a 27–20 to cut down the false doctrine of p·,
  s 111– 1 agnosticism, p·, theosophy, spiritualism,
  129–11 P· may be defined as a belief in the
  129–18 p·, and infidelity are antagonistic to true
  139–28 Atheism, p·, theosophy, and
  c 257–11 This belief is shallow p·.
  b 279–30 P·, starting from a material sense of
  294– 4 This is p·, and carries within itself the
  335– 6 would . . . establish a basis for p·.
  g 522–14 It records p·, opposed to the

pantheistic
  f 204–30 belief that God lives in matter is p·.
  c 257– 7 theory that Spirit is not the . . . is p·
  b 269– 1 These . . . systems are one and all p·,
  279–23 p· belief that there is mind in matter ;
  307– 3 This p· error, or so-called serpent,

parable
  s 117–31 His p· of the "leaven, which a·— Matt. 13 : 33
  118– 6 Did not this p· point a moral
  118–16 The p· may import that these
  b 272–13 Jesus' p· of "the sower"— Mark 4 : 14.
  o 343–15 By p· and argument he explains the
  p 363–15 Jesus rebuked them with a short story or p·.
  g 539–20 In p· and argument, this falsity is

parables
  a 27–17 Jesus' p· explain Life as never mingling with
  s 117–16 taught spirituality by similitudes and p·.

paraded
  ph 176–11 ghastly array of diseases was not p· before the

parading
  p 372–24 only by falsely p· in the vestments of law.

Paradise
  ph 171– 7 gates of P· which human beliefs have closed,
  b 285– 4 not alone hereafter in what men call P·, but

paradox
  f 216–25 would seem the exception, . . . and life a p·.

parallel
  p 422–22 Let us suppose two p· cases of bone-disease,

paralysis
  s 152–15 once apparently cured a case of p· simply by
  ph 194–10 p· of the optic nerve
  p 401–25 Would the drug remove p·,
  420– 3 no stoppage of harmonious action, no p·.

paralyze
  f 213–13 Material theories partially p· this attraction
  p 375–20 belief that matter . . . can p· the body,
  376–31 is to p· mental and scientific demonstration.

paramount
  s 164–24 the forever fact remains p·
  c 262– 5 shows the p· necessity of meeting them.

paraphernalia
  f 209–26 all the p· of speculative theories,

paraphrased
  g 532–21 Its summons may be thus p· :

parched
  f 221– 9 that he should not wet his p· throat until

pardon
  ask
  pr 6– 9 supposition . . . nothing to do but to ask p·,
  divine
  a 40–11 This is my sense of divine p·,
  God's
  b 291– 4 suppositions . . . that God's p· is aught but
  339– 5 Does not God's p·, destroying any one sin,
  legal
  pr 11–12 Mere legal p· (and there is no other,
  no
  pr 11–17 Truth bestows no p· upon error,
  ready
  a 24–21 chiefly as providing a ready p· for all sinners
  sin and
  f 251–19 sickness and death, sin and p·,
  unmerited
  pr 3–21 We plead for unmerited p·

  ————

  pr 6– 4 Men may p·, but this divine Principle alone
  a 36– 7 would be for Truth to p· error.
  b 285–25 through p· and not through reform,
  329–26 The p· of divine mercy is the
  339– 2 destruction of sin is the divine method of p·.
  p 365–20 enough Christly affection to win his own p·,

pardoned
  a 36–26 suddenly p· and pushed into heaven,
  b 291– 1 suppositions that sin is p· while unforsaken,

pardons
  pr 11–13 never p· our sins or mistakes till

parent (*see also* **parent's**)
pref ix–32 as a *p·* may treasure the memorials of a
a 50– 9 despairing appeal, if made to a human *p·*,
m 69–20 Some day the child will ask his *p·* :
b 306–32 *p·* of all human discord was the
336–31 God is the *p·* Mind, and man is God's
p 416–20 This materialism of *p·* and child is only
416–23 is no longer the *p·*, even in appearance.
r 480–25 The supposititious *p·* of evil is a lie.
g 507– 9 wanderers from the *p·* Mind,
529–12 belonging to no lesser *p·*.
552– 2 is answered, if the egg produces the *p·*.
552– 3 Who or what produces the *p·* of the egg?

parentage
g 517–19 they all have one Principle and *p·*.

parental
m 63–19 person, property, and *p·* claims of the two sexes.

parent's
p 412–29 met mainly through the *p·* thought,
424– 1 formed first by the *p·* mind,

parents
devout
o 351–11 the prayers of her devout *p·*
gross
m 61–15 promising children in the arms of gross *p·*,
heavenly-minded
m 61–12 The offspring of heavenly-minded *p·*
her
f 237– 7 months or years before her *p·* would have
his
p 425– 1 His *p·* or some of his progenitors
obey their
f 236–21 Children should obey their *p·* ;
our first
sp 92–14 in the act of commending to our first *p·*
Puritan
o 359–20 From Puritan *p·*, the discoverer of C. S.
those
m 62–10 those *p·* should not, in after years, complain
views of
p 413– 9 views of *p·* and other persons on these subjects

m 61–18 If perchance they live to become *p·*,
62– 8 If *p·* create in their babes a desire for
62–12 which the *p·* themselves have occasioned.
f 236–23 *P·* should teach their children at the earliest
237–11 stubborn beliefs and theories of *p·*
b 314–11 material views were the *p·* of their
g 557– 3 *P·* should remember this, and learn how to

pariah
p 362–10 as positively as if she were a Hindoo *p·*

Paris
an 100–13 ordered the medical faculty of *P·*
101–20 the Royal Academy of Medicine in *P·*.

Parisian
ph 197– 4 like a *P·* name for a novel garment.

Parker, Theodore
sp 80– 7 purporting to come from the late Theodore *P·*

Parmenter, Judge
an 105–18 these words of Judge *P·* of Boston will become

parodies
p 367– 8 but so many *p·* on legitimate C. S.,

parody
o 343–12 will not be forever hidden by unjust *p·*

part
any
sp 73–26 mistake to suppose that matter is any *p·* of
component
a 28–17 Not a single component *p·* of his nature
early
g 523–16 in the early *p·* of the book of Genesis.
every
f 242–28 restores every *p·* of the Christly garment
p 423–11 reaching to every *p·* of the human system.
from one
p 420– 1 nor go from one *p·* to another,
fundamental
t 460–10 this most fundamental *p·* of metaphysics
having
a 24–13 This is having *p·* in the atonement ;
his
c 261–12 strong impulse of a desire to perform his *p·*,
infinitesimal
g 520– 6 can repeat only an infinitesimal *p·* of what
is proved
t 461– 6 We admit the whole, because a *p·* is proved
latter
g 522–25 This latter *p·* of the second chapter
little
a 19–21 he has little *p·* in the atonement,
most
pref x–17 for the most *p·* have been abandoned

part
no
a 19–26 Those who cannot . . . have no *p·* in God.
m 64–22 in which passion has no *p·*.
f 231–28 and know that they are no *p·* of His creation.
242–27 appropriates no *p·* of the divine vesture,
246–17 Chronological data are no *p·* of the vast forever.
r 468–29 and time is no *p·* of eternity.
of himself
sp 92– 1 which is *p·* of himself.
of the error
r 482–26 Sickness is *p·* of the error which
only in
t 462–10 to practise Truth's teachings only in *p·*,
our
a 21– 5 This is having our *p·* in the at-one-ment
sinner's
a 23– 5 constant self-immolation on the sinner's *p·*.
tenth
gl 595–22 TITHE. Contribution ; tenth *p·* ; homage ;
that
t 461– 6 that *p·* illustrates and proves the entire
their
p 431–15 The struggle on their *p·* was long.
third
ap 563–23 drew the third *p·* of the stars— *Rev.* 12 : 4.
vital
s 113– 5 The vital *p·*, the heart and soul of C. S.,

a 19–25 Those who cannot demonstrate, at least in *p·*,
m 68–12 "until death do us *p·*."
sp 98–23 has not been considered a *p·* of any religion,
s 138–23 the sick are more willing to *p·* with pain than
157–16 If drugs are *p·* of God's creation,
f 230– 2 if true, it is a *p·* of Truth.
b 296–17 in order to *p·* with them.
307–23 a *p·* of God's creation,
315–29 Wearing in *p·* a human form
p 415–10 Inflammation never appears in a *p·* which
430– 3 Mortal mind must *p·* with error,
431–29 testifies : . . . nothing on my *p·* has
439– 8 commanding him to take *p·* in the homicide.
t 444–23 then *p·* from these opponents as did Abraham

partake
a 20–11 can be baptized, *p·* of the Eucharist,
25–11 and they . . . who *p·* of that divine Life.
31–19 we drink of his cup, *p·* of his bread,

partaken
p 385–28 because you have *p·* of salt fish,

partakers
pr 4–16 attest our worthiness to be *p·* of Love.
9–31 that you may be *p·* of his nature?

partakes
b 307–19 Thus error *p·* of its own nature

partaking
p 431– 6 *p·* of food at irregular intervals,
ap 559–25 thus *p·* of the nature, or primal elements,

parted
f 242–23 "They *p·* my raiment— *John* 19 : 24.
245– 7 in the same hour which *p·* her from her lover,
b 306– 8 If God, who is Life, were *p·* for a moment from
p 401–22 If the mind were *p·* from the body,
t 444–24 as did Abraham when he *p·* from Lot,

partially
a 23– 1 is not destroyed, but *p·* indulged.
s 111–29 Mind governs the body, not *p·* but wholly.
149–26 divine Mind, governs all, not *p·* but
f 213–13 Material theories *p·* paralyze
223–26 Peals that should startle . . . are *p·* unheeded ;
b 326–14 Not *p·*, but fully, the great healer of

participant
p 439–12 a misguided *p·* in the misdeed

participate
m 59– 9 Man should not be required to *p·* in

participation
g 544– 3 so wholly apart . . . that Spirit had no *p·* in it.

particle
p 398–17 sometimes not containing a *p·* of medicine,

particular
a 38– 2 only for a *p·* period
s 112–10 some *p·* system of human opinions.
ph 178– 1 though they know nothing of this *p·* case

particularly
g 507– 7 Without natures *p·* defined,

parting
m 69–15 sweet assurance of no *p·*,

partly
a 30– 6 Jesus' advent in the flesh partook *p·* of
b 269–26 systems based wholly or *p·* on
p 373– 7 *p·* because they were willing to be restored,

partner
m 59–14 each *p·* sustaining the other,

partners
p 379– 3 announced as *p·* in the beginning.

partnership
ph 181– 7 Matter, . . . has no *p·* with pain
181– 8 but mortal belief has such a *p·*.
f 243–26 Life has no *p·* with death.
b 274–30 This suppositional *p·* is already obsolete,
275– 2 A *p·* of mind with matter would
p 438–23 who is in *p·* with Error
t 458– 4 doctrine that Science has two principles in *p·*,
g 528– 7 cannot be true that man was . . . in *p·* with God ;

partook
a 30– 5 *p·* partly of Mary's earthly condition,
33– 4 *p·* of the heavenly manna,
34–10 If all who ever *p·* of the sacrament
f 221– 6 *p·* of but one meal in twenty-four hours,

parts
s 123–19 The revelation consists of two *p·* :
g 523–30 In the historic *p·* of the Old Testament,

parturition
g 557– 7 where *p·* is without suffering.

Paschal
ap 559–29 the Israelites of old at the *P·* meal

pass
pr 1– * *which he saith shall come to p·;— Mark* 11 : 23.
a 32– 8 custom . . . to *p·* each guest a cup of wine.
32–13 the cup which he prayed might *p·* from him,
39–16 not the threshold over which he must *p·*
39–24 and material pleasures to *p·* away,
m 63– 8 nor does he *p·* through material conditions
sp 75–30 In the vestibule through which we *p·*
an 105–15 and courts reasonably *p·* sentence.
s 118–10 Ages *p·*, but this leaven of Truth is ever
135–16 "it came to *p·*, when the devil— *Luke* 11 : 14.
164–27 then shall be brought to *p·* the— *I Cor.* 15 : 54.
ph 173–15 For positive Spirit to *p·* through a
188–10 only to *p·* from shame and woe to
f 201– 8 new creature, in whom old things *p·* away
225– 9 command their sentinels not to let truth *p·*
232–28 so-called pleasures and pains of sense *p·* away
244–25 He does not *p·* from matter to Mind,
b 282–19 Mind cannot *p·* into non-intelligence
289–28 Therefore it cannot be said to *p·* out of
321–27 "It shall come to *p·*, if they— *Exod.* 4 : 8.
335– 4 theory, that Spirit . . . must *p·* through it, or
o 345–16 well enough to *p·* judgment upon them.
p 375– 2 Heat would *p·* from the body as painlessly
386–31 So, when our friends *p·* from our sight
401–19 forcing impurities to *p·* away,
r 496–26 then shall be brought to *p·* the— *I Cor.* 15 : 54.
g 535–15 When will man *p·* through the open gate of

passage
another
b 313– 9 With this agrees another *p·* in the same
g 504–21 explanation of another *p·* of Scripture,
defeat the
p 390–31 to defeat the *p·* of an inhuman law.
of the blood
ph 187–13 opening and closing for the *p·* of the blood,
perilous
ap 559–30 prefigured this perilous *p·* out of bondage
Scriptural
b 328–29 the Scriptural *p·* would read *you*, not *they*.
this
b 320–29 whereas this *p·* is continually quoted as if
g 504– 7 are answered in this *p·*,

f 218–29 The meaning of that *p·* is not perverted
b 313–19 The *p·* is made even clearer in the translation
ap 566– 7 in their *p·* from sense to Soul,
gl 598– 2 as in the *p·* in John's Gospel,

passages
gl 598– 7 as in other *p·* in this same chapter

passed
pref xi–30 a law relative to colleges having been *p·*,
a 35– 1 His gloom had *p·* into glory,
41– 2 into which Jesus has *p·* before us ;
sp 87– 8 Though individuals have *p·* away,
s 147–12 even though centuries had *p·* away since Jesus
ph 172–15 he must have *p·* through all the forms of
f 221–10 He *p·* many weary years in hunger
251–11 they have but *p·* the portals of a new belief.
b 307– 2 delusion that life . . . *p·* into matter.
p 396–13 before a crisis is *p·*.
g 536– 3 and the first earth were *p·* away ;— *Rev.* 21 : 1.
536– 8 the sea, . . . is represented as having *p·* away.
556– 9 for the former things will have *p·* away.
ap 572–21 and the first earth were *p·* away ;— *Rev.* 21 : 1.
572–23 The Revelator had not yet *p·* the

passes
sp 72–28 nor the medium through which truth *p·* to
ph 172– 9 if man *p·* through what we call death
195–18 *p·* naturally from effect back to cause.
f 247–11 the beauty of material things *p·* away,
b 284–30 Thought *p·* from God to man,
336– 3 Intelligence never *p·* into non-intelligence,
gl 580–23 supposition that . . . intelligence *p·* into

passeth
ph 190–25 the wind *p·* over it,— *Psal.* 103 : 16.
r 476–26 the wind *p·* over it,— *Psal.* 103 : 16.

passing
sp 97–14 approaches truth without *p·* the boundary
an 104– 1 true thoughts, *p·* from God to man.
f 245–22 she had taken no cognizance of *p·* time
b 295–17 as light *p·* through the window-pane.
gl 581– 4 ANGELS. God's thoughts *p·* to man ;

passion
m 60–22 *p·*, frivolous amusements,
64–22 in which *p·* has no part.
sp 94–16 pattern of mortal personality, *p·*, and impulse.
ph 188– 8 *P·*, depraved appetites, dishonesty,
b 327– 4 neither pleasure nor pain, appetite nor *p·*,
p 407– 7 relentless masters— *p·*, selfishness,
t 445–22 Self-seeking, envy, *p·*, pride, hatred,
r 490– 9 cooperates with appetite and *p·*.
gl 598–18 Error ; fornication ; temptation ; *p·*.

passions
a 24– 6 instigated sometimes by the worst *p·* of men
53– 5 so far removed from appetites and *p·*
s 115–21 Evil beliefs, *p·* and appetites, fear,
f 201– 9 *P·*, selfishness, false appetites, hatred,
p 401– 5 cherishing evil *p·* and malicious purposes,
407–10 If man is not victorious over the *p·*,
g 526–11 The appetites and *p·*, sin, sickness,
536–20 *P·* and appetites must end in pain.
gl 597–30 Destruction ; anger ; mortal *p·*.

Passover
a 32–28 The *P·*, which Jesus ate with his disciples

passport
a 22– 1 he would borrow the *p·* of some

past
pref vii–15 Contentment with the *p·* and the
a 28–25 To suppose that persecution . . . belongs to the *p·*,
sp 84–13 to know the *p·*, the present, and the future.
an 106–25 as I have also told you in time *p·*,— *Gal.* 5 : 21
ph 178–10 connection of *p·* mortal thoughts with present.
f 224– 4 As the crude footprints of the *p·* disappear
240–19 If mortals are not progressive, *p·* failures will

pastor (*see also* **Eddy, Mrs. Mary Baker**)
o 359– 7 more faith in the Scientist than in their *p·* ?

pastors
o 359– 1 their own accredited and orthodox *p·*,

pastures
g 514–13 or rests in "green *p·*,— *Psal.* 23 : 2.
ap 578– 6 to lie down in green *p·* :— *Psal.* 23 : 2.

path
along the
s 129–27 along the *p·* which Science must tread
ascending
c 265–28 brightens the ascending *p·* of many a heart.
Judah's
ap 566–21 And oh, when stoops on Judah's *p·*
narrow
t 451–12 but strive, to enter the narrow *p·* of Life,
our
f 254–12 He directs our *p·*.
true
t 454– 7 and plants the feet in the true *p·*,

a 20–22 traversing anew the *p·* from sin to holiness.
38–25 Jesus mapped out the *p·* for others.
m 66–20 wait patiently on divine wisdom to point out the *p·*.
ph 174–15 marking out the *p·* for generations yet unborn.
p 426– 5 finds the *p·* less difficult when she has
t 454– 8 *p·* which leads to the house built without hands

pathological
pref xi– 6 explains that all other *p·* methods are the
ph 185–24 the reverse of ethical and *p·* Truth-power.
p 373–10 Under all modes of *p·* treatment,
t 464–21 In founding a *p·* system of Christianity,

pathology
s 157–32 this spiritual and profound *p·*.
f 252– 6 regarding the *p·* and theology of C. S.
b 294–16 taught, as they are by physiology and *p·*,

paths

a	21–18	Our *p·* have diverged at the very outset,
	22–25	is not reached through *p·* of flowers nor by
f	224– 5	disappear from the dissolving *p·* of the
	251– 8	as to drive belief into new *p·*.
ap	578– 9	in the *p·* of righteousness— *Psal.* 23 : 3.

pathway

a	26– 3	treading alone his loving *p·*
	41–11	hypocrite may have a flowery *p·* here, but he
r	487– 5	gained by walking in the *p·* of Truth
g	549–25	the *p·* leading to divine Science,

patience

pr	4– 4	expressed in *p·*, meekness, love, and good deeds
	4–25	and *p·* must bring experience.
a	20–29	let us run with *p·* the race— *Heb.* 12 : 1.
	49–11	his divine *p·*, sublime courage,
m	66–27	Socrates considered *p·* salutary under such
p	366– 1	such as peace, *p·* in tribulation, and
	367– 4	pitiful *p·* with his fears
t	454–11	*P·* must "have her perfect work."— *Jas.* 1 : 4.
g	515– 4	*P·* is symbolized by the tireless worm,

patient (*see also* **patient's**)

cholera

s	154–11	a bed where a cholera *p·* had died.
	154–14	no cholera *p·* had been in that bed.

cured a

s	153–10	she has cured a *p·* sinking in the last stage of

cure his

p	366– 3	In order to cure his *p·*, the metaphysician

cure the

p	417–24	the way to cure the *p·* is to make

discouraging the

t	447–18	without frightening or discouraging the *p·*

dispossesses the

p	375–13	the hypnotist dispossesses the *p·* of his

healer and

t	457– 6	for teacher and student, for healer and *p·*,

his

ph	197–30	The doctor's mind reaches that of his *p·*.
p	366– 7	to cast physical evils out of his *p·* ;
	375– 9	when his *p·* says, "I am better,"

needs to be

p	417–21	from which the *p·* needs to be awakened.

physician and

ph	174–29	the thought of both physician and *p·*?
	177–27	even though physician and *p·* are expecting

reaches his

p	365–15	reaches his *p·* through divine Love,

sensitive

p	423– 6	oftentimes affects a sensitive *p·*

strengthens his

p	423–23	strengthens his *p·* with the stimulus of courage

telling the

s	161–25	telling the *p·* that he is sick,

thought of the

p	414–13	mortal mind or the thought of the *p·*,

treat the

s	159–12	and to treat the *p·* as if she were
p	421–12	treat the *p·* less for the disease and more for

while the

p	416–15	Where is the pain while the *p·* sleeps?

will find

p	416–12	the *p·* will find himself in the same pain, unless

your

s	153–20	Now administer mentally to your *p·* a
p	377– 1	If your *p·* believes in taking cold,
	395–26	than it is for your *p·* to feel these ills
	403–25	Never . . . and then acquaint your *p·* with it.
	412– 1	removing the fear, your *p·* is healed.
	419– 8	If your *p·* from any cause suffers a relapse,
	420–29	vehemently tell your *p·* that he must awake.
	424–16	the *minds* which surround your *p·* should not
	424–20	unspoken thoughts resting on your *p·*.

s	149– 9	the different mental states of your *p·*.
	156– 8	the *p·* looked like a barrel.
	156–15	and told the *p·* so ;
ph	169– 6	before the *p·* felt the change ;
	169– 7	and I have said to the *p·*, "You are healed,"
	177–26	swallowed through mistake, and the *p·* dies
	177–32	the potion swallowed by the *p·*
	185–32	A *p·* under the influence of mortal mind
	193– 4	said that the *p·* was dying.
	198– 3	A *p·* hears the doctor's verdict
	198– 5	The *p·* may seem calm under it,
o	342–32	even if their treatment resulted in the death of a *p·*.
p	370–25	and do no more for the *p·*.
	375–10	the *p·* believes that matter, not mind, has
	376– 2	The *p·* turns involuntarily from the
	377–19	The author never knew a *p·* who did not
	382–19	A *p·* thoroughly booked in medical theories
	395–16	besought to take the *p·* to Himself,
	395–28	fastens disease on the *p·*,
	396– 4	for one's own sake and for that of the *p·*.
	396– 5	Avoid talking illness to the *p·*.

patient

p	398–19	faith of the doctor and the *p·*,
	403–32	are not understood by the *p·*,
	412–21	Argue . . . that the *p·* has no disease,
	416– 7	morphine is administered to a *p·*,
	421– 9	afterwards make known to the *p·* your motive
	421–24	sometimes explain the symptoms . . . to the *p·*.
	423– 3	belief should not be communicated to the *p·*,
	424–31	The *p·* may tell you that he
	430–19	The *p·* feels ill, ruminates, and
	430–30	when the prisoner, or *p·*, watched with a
t	453–25	you must not tell the *p·* that he is sick
	460–15	to the frightened, false sense of the *p·*.

patient (adj.)

pr	3–13	likeness of the *p·*, tender, and true,
ph	180– 5	The *p·* sufferer tries to be satisfied when he
f	242–15, 16	In *p·* obedience to a *p·* God,
p	395–19	cheerful, orderly, punctual, *p·*,
	413–21	I am not *p·* with a speck of dirt ;
gl	586–23	GETHSEMANE. *P·* woe ; the human yielding to

patiently

pr	8–31	do we listen *p·* to the rebuke
	10– 3	and that waiting *p·* on the Lord,
m	66–19	wait *p·* on divine wisdom to point out the path.
s	136–32	Jesus *p·* persisted in teaching and
	139–12	*p·* and wisely to stem the
f	254–11	When we wait *p·* on God and seek Truth
c	262–23	the bliss of loving unselfishly, working *p·*,
t	454–22	Wait *p·* for divine Love to move upon

patient's

sp	79– 6	changing the *p·* thoughts regarding death.
s	145–11	victory will be on the *p·* side only as
	152–16	introducing a thermometer into the *p·* mouth.
	152–17	to ascertain the temperature of the *p·* body ;
ph	168–25	and recognized the *p·* fear of it,
	198–23	A *p·* belief is more or less moulded and
	198–26	His thoughts and his *p·* commingle,
f	235–25	the *p·* feet may be planted on the rock
p	365–29	the *p·* spiritual power to resuscitate himself.
	366– 9	hinders him from reaching his *p·* thought,
	375–18	adding to his *p·* mental and
	375–19	increasing his *p·* spirituality
	376–22	destroy the *p·* false belief
	396–11	nor encourage in the *p·* thought the

patients (*see also* **patients'**)

consumptive

p	375–26	Consumptive *p·* always show great hopefulness

fear of

p	411–28	by allaying the fear of *p·*.

his

ph	197–32	will harm his *p·* even more than
p	365–22	and deal with his *p·* compassionately ;

manipulate

ph	181– 9	When you manipulate *p·*, you trust in
	181–14	to declare that you manipulate *p·* but that

ninety-and-nine

o	344–28	may lose ninety-and-nine *p·*, while C. S. cures

our

s	149–19	advise our *p·* to be hopeful

students and

t	456–27	and so do all his students and *p·*.

your

p	414–17	not until your *p·* are prepared for the
	417–27	Explain audibly to your *p·*,
	417–32	Give your *p·* an underlying understanding
	419–29	as well as those of your *p·*,
	424–24	while others are thinking about your *p·*

ph	180–18	in the thoughts of their *p·*,
o	359– 6	Is this because the *p·* have more faith in
	359–10	while they, the *p·*, did not.
p	422–11	*P·*, unfamiliar with the cause of this
t	443–14	If *p·* fail to experience the healing power
	446– 6	If *p·* sometimes seem worse while reading

patients'

p	414–15	To fix truth steadfastly in your *p·* thoughts,

patriarch

f	224–27	as he came of old to the *p·* at noonday?
b	308–26	But the *p·*, perceiving his error and
gl	579–12	This *p·* illustrated the purpose of Love

patriarchs

b	283–26	in length of days, as it was by the *p·*,
	308–14	The Soul-inspired *p·* heard the voice

patron

a	28–21	and Beelzebub is his *p·*.

pattern

sp	94–16	*p·* of mortal personality, passion, and impulse.
f	236–16	*p·* showed to thee in the mount."— *Heb.* 8 : 5.
c	263–25	and attempts to *p·* the infinite.
g	542–20	let human justice *p·* the divine.

patterns

f	248–22	are liable to follow those lower *p·*,

Paul (*see also* **Paul's**)
alludes
 o 342– 1 *P·* alludes to "doubtful disputations."— *Rom.* 14 : 1.
asked
 f 216–25 *P·* asked : . . . "What concord hath— *II Cor.* 6 : 15.
 o 349– 3 As *P·* asked of the unfaithful in ancient days,
 g 539–24 *P·* asked : "What communion hath— *II Cor.* 6 : 14.
said
 sp 93– 9 the day of salvation," said *P·*.— *II Cor.* 6 : 2.
  95– 5 *P·* said, "To be spiritually minded— *Rom.* 8 : 6.
 f 223– 2 *P·* said, "Walk in the Spirit, and ye— *Gal.* 5 : 16.
  227–17 *P·* said, "I was free born."— *Acts* 22 : 28.
 b 304– 5 *P·* said : "Neither death, nor life,— *Rom.* 8 : 38.
saw
 gl 596– 7 *P·* saw in Athens an altar dedicated
says
 a 31–22 what says *P·*? "As often as ye— *I Cor.* 11 : 26.
 b 271–31 *P·* says, "How shall they hear— *Rom.* 10 : 14.
  321– 3 *P·* says, . . . "Flesh and blood cannot— *I Cor.* 15 : 50.
  332–16 *P·* says : "There is one God,— *I Tim.* 2 : 5.
 o 346–32 *P·* says : "The flesh lusteth against— *Gal.* 5 : 17.
 r 479–29 *P·* says : "For the invisible things of Him,— *Rom.* 1 : 20.
 g 534–18 *P·* says . . . "The carnal mind— *Rom.* 8 : 7.
to misunderstand
 ap 560–29 To misunderstand *P·*, was to be ignorant of
was not at first
 b 324–19 *P·* was not at first a disciple of Jesus
writes
 a 45–10 *P·* writes : "For if, when we were— *Rom.* 5 : 10.
 f 244–10 *P·* writes : "The law of the Spirit— *Rom.* 8 : 2.
 b 324–27 *P·* writes, "If Christ [Truth]— *I Cor.* 15 : 14.
  325–10 *P·* writes : "When Christ, who is— *Col.* 3 : 4.
 f 216–29 I say with *P·* : Be "willing rather— *II Cor.* 5 : 8.
 b 324–21 *P·* was made blind,
  325–20 *P·* had a clear sense of the demands of
  326–30 in humility he took the new name of *P·*.
 o 343–26 *P·* who was not one of his students,
 p 369–14 We never read that Luke or *P·* made a
 t 459– 3 *P·* and John had a clear apprehension
 g 514–27 *P·* proved the viper to be harmless.
 ap 563–29 Its sting is spoken of by *P·*,
 (*see also* **St. Paul** *and* **Apostle Paul**)

Paul's
 f 217– 7 *P·* peculiar Christian conversion and
pause
 f 223–18 and try to "give it *p·*."
 b 323–10 Beholding the . . . we *p·*,— wait on God.
pauses
 b 292– 4 Here prophecy *p·*.
 ap 566– 9 Stately Science *p·* not, but moves before them,
pay
 pr 5–10 *p·* "the uttermost farthing."— *Matt.* 5 : 26.
 a 23– 4 insufficient to *p·* the debt of sin.
 f 240–27 one must *p·* fully and fairly
 p 384– 5 and must of necessity *p·* the penalty.
  387– 3 must it *p·* the penalty in a softened brain?
  387–18 That man does not *p·* the severest penalty who
  439– 1 receiving *p·* from them and introducing
paying
 f 240–30 The divine method of *p·* sin's wages
payment
 p 390–17 in *p·* of the last farthing,
peace
and harmony
 p 417– 1 find health, *p·*, and harmony in God,
and permanence
 g 516–11 which impart their own *p·* and permanence.
and purity
 b 323– 8 towards righteousness, *p·*, and purity,
and rest
 gl 586– 2 EVENING. . . . obscured views ; *p·* and rest.
annihilate my
 f 252–27 says : . . . may at any moment annihilate my *p·*,
be at
 b 324–12 "with Him, and be at *p·*."— *Job* 22 : 21.
  329–29 to the spiritual and be at *p·* ;
brightness and
 s 139–11 even when the end has been brightness and *p·* ;
forever at
 f 215– 1 without pain, and they are forever at *p·*.
found no
 ph 195– 6 Outside of dismal darkness . . . he found no *p·*.
heart finds
 m 59–15 in which the heart finds *p·* and home.
human
 c 265–23 Who that has felt the loss of human *p·*
life and
 f 224– 9 life and *p·* instead of discord and death.

peace
make
 g 540– 5 "I make *p·*, and create evil.— *Isa.* 45 : 7.
not
 a 19–15 brought to material beliefs not *p·*, but
on earth
 s 150– 7 "on earth *p·*, good-will toward— *Luke* 2 : 14.
 f 226–17 "on earth *p·*, good-will toward— *Luke* 2 : 14.
permanence and
 m 65–27 man must find permanence and *p·*
perpetual
 m 64–25 spiritual understanding and perpetual *p·*.
purity and
 gl 584–26 purity and *p·* ; hope and faith.
Science and
 sp 96–15 on the other side there will be Science and *p·*.
spiritual
 gl 589– 8 JAPHET . . . A type of spiritual *p·*,
to the struggling
 a 45–16 and *p·* to the struggling hearts !
unspeakable
 c 264–26 and feel the unspeakable *p·* which
 a 28–26 To suppose . . . that Christianity to-day is at *p·*
 an 106–27 fruit of the Spirit is love, joy, *p·*,— *Gal.* 5 : 22.
 s 144–22 says to disease, "*P·*, be still."— *Mark* 4 : 39.
 c 265–15 a higher and more permanent *p·*.
 p 365–32 such as *p·*, patience in tribulation.
 t 449–27 The impure are at *p·* with the impure.
 g 506–12 The calm and exalted thought . . . is at *p·*.
peaceful
 a 40–31 nature of Christianity is *p·* and blessed,
Peaceful Sea
 ap 576– 1 and the *P· S·* of Harmony.
peaches
 s 129–24 Can we gather *p·* from a pine-tree,
peaks
 b 299–30 and reveal the celestial *p·*.
peals
 f 223–25 *P·* that should startle the slumbering thought
pearls
 f 234–14 avoid casting *p·* before those who trample them
 b 272–18 neither cast ye your *p·* before swine."— *Matt.* 7 : 6.
peasant
 m 58–24 Said the *p·* bride to her lover :
peck
 g 552–17 They must *p·* open their shells with C. S.,
peculiar
 f 217– 7 Paul's *p·* Christian conversion and experience,
 p 412– 6 to meet the *p·* or general symptoms
peculiarities
 sp 86–25 *p·* of expression, recollected sentences,
 g 551–20 by which all *p·* of ancestry,
peculiarly
 g 523–31 *p·* the divine sovereign of the Hebrew people,
pedantic
 o 351– 2 *p·* and void of healing power.
pedantry
 p 366–21 they swallow the camels of bigoted *p·*.
peep
 sp 70– * *wizards that p· and that mutter ;*— *Isa.* 8 : 19.
peers
 c 263–24 as when some finite sense *p·* from its cloister
pellet
 s 158–30 and mortal mind, . . . is governing the *p·*.
 ph 179–27 with homœopathic *p·* and powder in hand,
pellets
 s 156–18 to give her unmedicated *p·*
  156–25 in this way, taking the unmedicated *p·*,
pen
 s 110–17 No human *p·* nor tongue taught me the Science
  110–19 neither tongue nor *p·* can overthrow it.
 g 521–17 and the *p·* of an angel.
penal
 p 440–13 Even *p·* law holds homicide,
penalties
 ph 184– 6 the *p·* it affixes last so long as the belief
 p 381–32 would impose *p·* for transgressions of
  385–13 exempts man from all *p·* but those due for
  389–23 Their belief in material laws and in *p·* for
  405–28 conquered by the moral *p·* you incur
  440–11 into crimes, to which you attach *p·* ;
 gl 592–15 justice demands *p·* under the law.
penalty
brings
 pr 11–11 Broken law brings *p·* in order to
divine
 an 106–14 incurs the divine *p·* due this crime.

penalty

due for sin
pr 6– 1 We cannot escape the *p·* due for sin.
a 36– 6 To remit the *p·* due for sin, would be
escape the
pr 6– 1 We cannot escape the *p·* due for sin.
a 41–13 cannot forever . . . escape the *p·* due.
forestalls the
p 385–10 forestalls the *p·* which our beliefs would attach
full
g 542–21 Sin will receive its full *p·*,
incurs the
a 40–10 by first removing the sin which incurs the *p·*.
incur the
p 384– 9 If man seems to incur the *p·* through matter,
is coupled
p 389– 1 the *p·* is coupled with the belief.
last
p 390–18 the last *p·* demanded by error.
not the
p 385–25 Your sufferings are not the *p·* for
pay the
p 384– 5 and must of necessity pay the *p·*.
387– 4 must it pay the *p·* in a softened brain?
remits the
pr 11– 5 A magistrate sometimes remits the *p·*,
removes the
a 40– 9 Science removes the *p·* only by
severest
p 387–18 That man does not pay the severest *p·* who

p 435–24 decides what *p·* is due for the sin,
436–24 to rescue the prisoner from the *p·*

pendulum
a 22– 3 Vibrating like a *p·* between sin and
23–16 Faith, if it be mere belief, is as a *p·*
f 246– 2 Man is not a *p·*, swinging between evil and good,
o 360–19 Like a *p·* in a clock, you will be

penetrate
b 312–24 which cannot *p·* beyond matter.

penetrates
f 210–21 as a sunbeam *p·* the cloud.

Peniel
b 308–23 spiritual strength in this *P·* of divine Science.

penitence
g 533–29 as much as to say in meek *p·*,

penitent
p 364–12 and declaring the absolution of the *p·*.

penmanship
sp 86–25 landscape-paintings, fac-similes of *p·*,

penny
pr 10–19 and stop at the doors to earn a *p·* by

Pentecost, Day of
a 47– 9 overwhelming power as on the Day of *P·*.

Pentecostal Day
a 43– 9 which so illuminated the *P· D·*

penury
p 366–10 mental *p·* chills his faith and understanding.

people (see also people's)
affects
ph 197– 3 A new name for an ailment affects *p·* like a
are taught
o 342–32 The *p·* are taught in such cases to say, Amen.
go into ecstasies
b 312–14 *P·* go into ecstasies over the sense of
Hebrew
g 523–32 the divine sovereign of the Hebrew *p·*,
His
ap 573–17 ever with men, and they are His *p·*.
mighty
f 201– * *reproach of all the mighty p· ; — Psal.* 89 : 50.
of God
s 133–17 wrought wonders for the *p·* of God
b 288–19 a rest to the *p·* of God"— *Heb.* 4 : 9.
ordinary
p 385– 5 exposures which ordinary *p·* could not endure.
say
an 104–10 First, *p·* say it conflicts with the Bible.
b 312– 9 *P·* say, "Man is dead ;"
sick
s 163– 3 and afterward letting her loose upon sick *p·*."
p 417– 3 Give sick *p·* credit for sometimes knowing
so many
sp 80–23 French toy which years ago pleased so many *p·*
some
p 376–27 Some *p·*, mistaught as to Mind-science,
t 450–15 Some *p·* yield slowly to the touch of Truth.
unfortunate
p 408–10 Those unfortunate *p·* who are committed to
views of the
b 315–11 The opposite and false views of the *p·*

people
were in doubt
a 47–14 when the *p·* were in doubt concerning

sp 70– * *Should not a p· seek unto their God ? — Isa.* 8 : 19
79– 2 Warning *p·* against death is an error that
s 136–18 may indicate that some of the *p·* believed
ph 175–19 Then *p·* had less time for selfishness,
f 238–27 *P·* with mental work before them
b 272– 2 how shall they preach, . . . except the *p·* hear
272–16 Reading the thoughts of the *p·*,
303– 3 the multitudinous forms of Mind which *p·* the
321– 7 despaired of making the *p·* understand
o 343–13 from the quickened sense of the *p·*.
ap 570– 2 the hour when the *p·* will chain, with fetters
570–30 Many are willing to open the eyes of the *p·* to
571– 5 Because *p·* like you better when you tell them

peopled
c 264–32 The universe of Spirit is *p·* with
g 503–16 infinite space is *p·* with God's ideas,

people's
a 38–22 the fruits of other *p·* sins, not of his own.
f 220– 5 Such admissions ought to open *p·* eyes
o 350–18 "This *p·* heart is waxed gross,— *Matt.* 13 : 15.

peoples
g 509–17 God forms and *p·* the universe.
ap 565–17 will eventually rule all nations and *p·*

perceive
a 27– 8 he will at once *p·* that God is the power
sp 87– 1 Mind-readers *p·* these pictures of thought.
87–28 mind-readers can *p·* and reproduce these
ph 167–11 nor *p·* divine Science with the material
f 205–18 we *p·* the divine image in some word or
b 322– 6 and we shall *p·* Christianity, or Truth,
332–26 as they could understand as well as *p·*
o 345–21 Anybody, who is able to *p·* the incongruity
p 387– 1 We shall *p·* this to be true
t 451–24 may *p·* the nature and methods of error

perceived
a 29–28 and woman *p·* this spiritual idea,
f 247–20 before they are *p·* humanly.
o 350–32 and the spiritual sense was scarcely *p·*.

perceives
b 325– 1 he who *p·* the true idea of Life

perceiving
a 40– 3 *p·* the scope and tendency of
b 308–26 the patriarch, *p·* his error and
p 397– 1 By not *p·* vital metaphysical points,

percentage
s 155–19 the *p·* of power on the side of this Science

perceptibly
s 156–11 She improved *p·*.
p 408–23 would produce insanity as *p·* as
408–26 and the results would be *p·* different.

perception
clear
p 418– 8 a clear *p·* of the unchanging, unerring,
Enoch's
f 214– 5 If Enoch's *p·* had been confined to the
glorious
a 29–16 the glorious *p·* that God is the only
human
s 119–28 As astronomy reverses the human *p·* of the
o 361–23 A human *p·* of divine Science,
ap 561–19 reducing to human *p·* and understanding
of character
s 128– 9 enlarges their *p·* of character,
spiritual
(see spiritual)
wholesome
pr 7–14 wholesome *p·* of God's requirements.

a 34–23 into the *p·* of infinite possibilities.
f 202–12 the *p·* and acceptance of Truth.
r 488–24 Mind alone possesses . . . *p·*, and
g 527–16 It is plain also that material *p·*,
gl 582– 2 the *p·* of spiritual Truth.

perch
r 492–32 Victory would *p·* on neither banner.

perchance
m 61–17 If *p·* they live to become parents
63–29 wronged, and *p·* impoverished, woman
o 344–27 the physician may *p·* be an infidel

peremptorily
ph 186–21 and only aids in *p·* punishing the evil-doer.

peremptory
b 327–18 the strict demands of C. S. seem *p·* ;

perennial
s 121–12 in God's *p·* and happy sunshine,
c 265–21 The truth of being is *p·*.

perfect (noun)

g 555–25　when we admit that the *p·* is the author of

perfect (verb)

f 248–13　in order to *p·* his conception.
c 260– 3　than the sculptor can *p·* his outlines from
o 354–22　out of the mouth of babes He will *p·* praise.

perfect (adj.)

a 37–28　"Be ye therefore *p·*, — *Matt.* 5 : 48.
　37–29　Father which is in heaven is *p·* !" — *Matt.* 5 : 48.
　52–11　the world's hatred of the just and *p·* Jesus,
m 69–16　deathless and *p·* and eternal.
sp 76–22　the *p·* harmony and immortality of Life,
　85– 9　You will reach the *p·* Science of healing when
s 115–15　God's spiritual idea, individual, *p·*, eternal.
　130–10　reality is in *p·* harmony with God,
ph 176–32　Truth handles . . . contagion with *p·* assurance.
　200–17　the real man was, is, and ever shall be *p·*,
f 205–13　and made all *p·* and eternal.
　207–13　the *p·* Father, or the divine Principle of man.
　209– 1　Man, . . . has a *p·* indestructible life.
　221–15　and he is now in *p·* health
　223– 1　upon what is pure and *p·*.
　239–29　The *p·* Mind sends forth perfection,
　246– 5　*p·* and immortal are the eternal likeness of
　247–16　models of spiritual sense, drawn by *p·* Mind
　248–26　We must form *p·* models in thought
　249– 4　have one God, one Mind, and that one *p·*,
　251–21　understanding that the divine Mind makes *p·*,
　253–32　divine demand, "Be ye therefore *p·*," — *Matt.*
　　　　5 : 48.
c 259–12, 13　includes a *p·* Principle and idea, — *p·* God and
　259–15　If man was once *p·* but has now
　259–20　"Be ye therefore *p·*, — *Matt.* 5 : 48.
　259–21　Father which is in heaven is *p·*." — *Matt.* 5 : 48.
　259–27　Immortal ideas, pure, *p·*, and enduring,
　260– 8　the ideal of all that is *p·* and eternal.
　260–11　the immortal and *p·* model of God's creation
　266–25　*P·* and infinite Mind enthroned is heaven.
b 273–14　impossibility of . . . *p·* understanding till
　276–19　When we learn in Science how to be *p·*
　276–20　even as our Father in heaven is *p·*,
　280– 3　not products of the infinite, *p·*, and eternal *All.*
　281–12　the image and likeness of *p·* Mind,
　286–21　God's thoughts are *p·* and eternal,
　292–12　not the likeness of God, the *p·* and eternal.
　295–14　and the real sense of being, *p·* and
　300–15　The . . . never touch the immutable and *p·*.
　302–19　The Science of being reveals man as *p·*,
　302–20　even as the Father is *p·*,
　304–15　governed by God, his *p·* Principle
　314– 1　and the body no more *p·* because of death
　325–17　*p·* as the Father, indestructible in Life,
　337– 6　it is not the . . . likeness of Spirit, the *p·* God.
　337–11　According to . . . man is in a degree as *p·* as
p 372–19　When man demonstrates C. S. . . . he will be *p·*.
　373–18　"*p·* Love casteth out fear." — *I John* 4 : 18.
　388–29　In that *p·* day of understanding,
　394– 4　is the universal and *p·* remedy.
　406– 9　"*P·* Love casteth out fear." — *I John* 4 : 18.
　407–23　spiritual, *p·*, harmonious in every action.
　407–24　Let the *p·* model be present in your thoughts
　410–18　but *p·* Love casteth out fear. — *I John* 4 : 18.
　410–19　He that feareth is not made *p·* — *I John* 4 : 18.
　428–23　man *is*, not *shall be*, *p·* and immortal.
t 454–21　and form the *p·* concept.
　454–24　Patience must "have her *p·* work." — *Jas.* 1 : 4.
　463–20　is here and has fulfilled its *p·* work.
r 467–11　Mankind will become *p·* in proportion as
　467–14　the one *p·* Mind to guide him,
　470–14　and, the divine Principle of man remaining *p·*,
　470–23　divine idea or reflection, man remains *p·*.
　470–29　If . . . he has lost his *p·* Principle
　470–30　If man ever existed without this *p·* Principle
　471– 4　all that He creates are *p·* and eternal,
　475–11　Man is spiritual and *p·*;
　475–12　and because he is spiritual and *p·*,
　476–14　They never had a *p·* state of being,
　476–32　Jesus beheld in Science the *p·*
　485–23　in which man is *p·*, even as the
　485–24　"Father which is in heaven is *p·*." — *Matt.* 5 : 48.
　494– 1　to hold man forever intact in his *p·* state,
　496–13　brighter "unto the *p·* day." — *Prov.* 4 : 18.
g 511– 1　governing the universe, . . . in *p·* harmony.
　512–21　multiplication of its own pure and *p·* ideas.
　518–28　all must therefore be as the *p·* as the
　518–29　as the divine Principle is *p·*.
　552–31　when the *p·* and eternal Mind is
ap 562–20　which shines "unto the *p·* day" — *Prov.* 4 : 18.
gl 581– 5　spiritual intuitions, pure and *p·* ;
　583–22　that which is *p·* and eternal ;
　587–17　God is one God, infinite and *p·*,
　591–19　of whom man is the full and *p·* expression ;
　594–20　that only which is *p·*, everlasting,
　(*see also* **man**)

perfected

c 258–22　The human capacities are enlarged and *p·*

perfectibility

s 110–10　glorious proposition, — man's *p·*
ap 577–10　no impediment . . . to the *p·* of God's creation

perfection

and power
g 522– 7　endows man out of God's *p·* and power.
appears
o 353–18　until *p·* appears and reality is reached.
celestial
b 320–32　in celestial *p·* before Elohim,
Christian
f 201–18　Christian *p·* is won on no other basis.
divine
r 470–25　If . . . man did not express the divine *p·*,
eternal
g 550–13　its eternal *p·* should appear now,
God requires
f 254– 6　God requires *p·*, but not until the
health and
ph 167–14　the divine source of all health and *p·*.
his
a 52–10　the ever-present rebuke of his *p·* and purity.
f 259–15　If man was once perfect but has now lost his *p·*,
in Spirit
c 264– 1　permanent facts and their *p·* in Spirit
instead of
c 260– 1　from imperfection instead of *p·*,
is gained
b 290–19　*P·* is gained only by
is seen
f 233– 8　*p·* is seen and acknowledged only by degrees.
leading to
f 254– 1　human footsteps leading to *p·*
man's
p 414–28　man's *p·* is real and unimpeachable,
of being
f 253– 2　The beauty of holiness, the *p·* of being,
of Deity
g 546– 7　assumption . . . would dethrone the *p·* of Deity.
of God
c 262– 6　C. S. takes naught from the *p·* of God,
reaches
b 290–27　becomes thus only when he reaches *p·*.
relating to
ph 168–19　denies God's spiritual command relating to *p·*,
rule of
b 336–27　The Science of being furnishes the rule of *p·*,
sends forth
f 239–30　The perfect Mind sends forth *p·*,
spiritual
f 254–13　mortals grasp . . . spiritual *p·* slowly ;
gl 595–21　until . . . disappears and spiritual *p·* appears.
standard of
r 470–18　standard of *p·* was originally God and man.
g 555–24　We lose our standard of *p·* . . . when we
ultimate
sp 97– 4　await the certainty of ultimate *p·*.
underlies
o 353–16　*P·* underlies reality.
work up to
f 233–10　ages must slowly work up to *p·*.

pr 2–26　Do we expect to change *p·*?
sp 72–17　*P·* is not expressed through imperfection.
　76–27　a *p·* discernible only by those who
s 149–11　The rule and its *p·* of operation never vary
f 243–31　*P·* does not animate imperfection.
b 290–20　is gained only by *p·*.
　325–14　When spiritual being is understood in all its *p·*,
　337–17　*p·* is the order of celestial being
o 353–17　Without *p·*, nothing is wholly real.
p 388–28　foolish to stop eating until we gain *p·*
　424–11　since there is no room for imperfection in *p·*.
r 470–28　If man has lost *p·*, then he has lost his
　488–29　Soul could reproduce them in all their *p·* ;
gl 595–11　THUMMIM. *P·* ; the eternal demand of

perfectly

b 269–17　These ideas are *p·* real and tangible to
p 411– 8　the student was not *p·* attuned to

perform

a 46– 1　did not *p·* many wonderful works, until
s 159– 1　to *p·* a needed surgical operation
ph 179– 1　will *p·* the sudden cures of which it is capable ;
c 261–12　the strong impulse of a desire to *p·* his part,
p 387–14　faithfully *p·* the natural functions of being.
　387–17　and *p·* the most vital functions in society.
　392–29　then *p·* your office as porter
　431–30　and *p·* my functions as usual,
r 478–22　Matter cannot *p·* the functions of Mind.
g 528–16　in order to *p·* a surgical operation on him

performed
s 159–18 would have *p·* the operation without ether.
g 528–28 according to . . . surgery was first *p·* mentally

perfume
ph 175–13 profane to fancy that the *p·* of clover
p 367–15 the oil of gladness and the *p·* of *gratitude,*
r 491– 2 A delicious *p·* will seem intolerable.

perfumed
p 363– 4 she *p·* Jesus' feet with the oil,

perfunctory
a 316–13 between this spiritual idea and *p·* religion,

perhaps
s 55– 6 *P·* the early Christian era did Jesus no more
s 163–25 *p·* so ample an exhibition of
ph 178–13 *P·* an adult has a deformity
198–17 by a counter-irritant, — *p·* by a blister,
o 344–13 would *p·* mercifully withhold their
358–30 whom they have *p·* never seen
p 363– 2 sandal oil *p·*, which is in such common use
373– 8 while she has struggled long, and *p·* in vain,
t 446– 1 *p·* communicating his own bad morals,

peril
a 42– 9 was in no *p·* from salary or popularity.

perilous
t 450–27 Who, that has felt the *p·* beliefs
ap 559–30 thus prefigured this *p·* passage

period
at some
ap 569– 3 at some *p·*, here or hereafter,
earliest possible
f 236–24 teach their children at the earliest possible *p·*
limited
r 494–13 a select number or for a limited *p·* of time,
of gestation
m 62– 3 *p·* of gestation have the sanctity of virginity.
particular
a 38– 3 for a particular *p·* and for a select number
remote
f 247– 2 comes on at a remote *p·*,
required
sp 77–13 *p·* required for this dream of material life,
revolutionary
b 268–11 In this revolutionary *p·*, . . . woman goes forth
scientific
p 406–15 as we approach the scientific *p·*, in which
single
b 329– 1 reaching beyond the pale of a single *p·*
that
sp 95– 4 traduced by the sinners of that *p·*,
this
sp 77–16 This *p·* will be of longer or
94–26 but what would be said at this *p·* of an
ph 197–24 Their diet would not cure dyspepsia at this *p·*.
f 219–30 may not be reached at this *p·*,
p 367–17 place at this *p·* of which Jesus
t 461– 5 must be accepted at this *p·* by induction.
g 509– 1 This *p·* corresponds to the resurrection,
ap 570– 3 the growing occultism of this *p·*.
was approaching
a 47–16 A *p·* was approaching which would reveal

s 146–27 far anterior to the *p·* in which Jesus lived.
b 274–30 in a manner and at a *p·* as yet unknown.
306–14 If Life or Soul and . . . man, unite for a *p·*
p 372–23 Matter succeeds for a *p·* only by falsely

periodical
pref xii–13 the first *p·* issued by Christian Scientists.
sp 80– 9 Yet the very *p·* containing this sentence

periods
b 271– 4 uniting all *p·* in the design of God.
p 381–14 the times, *p·*, and types of disease,
g 509–24 The *p·* of spiritual ascension are the
511–18 infinite ideas, images, mark the *p·* of progress.
ap 569–26 but how many *p·* of torture it may take

perish
f 251–27 nothing is left which deserves to *p·*
b 281–29 Our false views of matter *p·*
296–14 so-called pleasures and pains of matter *p·*,
g 542–18 shall *p·* with the sword." — *Matt.* 26 : 52.

perishable
b 274– 7 and symbolizes all that is evil and *p·*.
g 536–28 give up their belief in *p·* life

perishing
s 147–21 the *p·* fossils of theories already antiquated,

perjurer
p 438– 9 proved the witness, Nerve, to be a *p·*.

perjury
p 438–16 *p·*, treason, and conspiracy against the rights

permanence
m 58–11 true happiness, strength, and *p·*.
65–27 find *p·* and peace in a more spiritual adherence
f 215– 3 and the might and *p·* of Truth.
b 287– 2 They have neither Principle nor *p·*,
r 486–26 hence their *p·*.
g 516–12 impart their own peace and *p·*.

permanency
b 281–22 have neither Principle nor *p·*,
293–28 opposite, the strength and *p·* of Spirit.

permanent
m 60– 5 a happy and *p·* companionship.
sp 79– 8 such a mental method produces *p·* health.
s 150– 9 its establishment as a *p·* dispensation
ph 185–27 but the recovery is not *p·*,
f 217–25 scientific and *p·* remedy for fatigue
232– 6 afford no scatheless and *p·* evidence of either.
c 264– 2 the *p·* facts and their perfection in Spirit
265–14 a higher and more *p·* peace.
b 290–18 happiness would be won . . . and be forever *p·*
306–24 spiritual sense, which cognizes Life as *p·*.
p 414–28 in whom all being is painless and *p·*.

permanently
p 404–31 neither . . . can help him *p·*, even in body, unless

permeate
a 37–12 and to *p·* humanity with purer ideals.

permeated
sp 72– 5 *p·* by Spirit, that body would disappear

permission
p 378–29 power, without the divine *p·*, is inconceivable
394–26 Is there no divine *p·* to conquer discord
434– 8 *p·* is obtained for a trial in divine

permit
m 64–27 Let not mortals *p·* a disregard of law
f 227–10 some public teachers *p·* an ignorance of

permits
f 234–32 no more harm than one's belief *p·*.
b 274–23 Divine Science is absolute, and *p·* no

permitted
m 62– 1 only be *p·* for the purpose of generating.
p 441– 6 not *p·* to enter any suits at the bar of Soul,

permitting
s 159–26 how much harmony, or health, matter is *p·*

pernicious
a 38– 4 more *p·* than the old doctrine of
sp 78–14 Communications gathered from . . . are *p·*
p 394–19 their theories are sometimes *p·*,
r 469–29 is as *p·* to divine theology as

peroration
p 433–26 is the Judge's solemn *p·*.

perpetrator
p 403– 5 should and does cause the *p·* to suffer,
ap 564– 8 will sink its *p·* into a night without a star.

perpetual
m 57–12 will be *p·* only as it is pure and true,
64–24 spiritual understanding and *p·* peace.
s 119–14 making Him guilty of maintaining *p·* misrule
f 231–15 governing man through *p·* warfare.
240–15 Mind is *p·* motion.
c 255– 4 the *p·* demand of Truth and Love,
260–27 expectation of *p·* pleasure or pain
b 280–28 *p·* in His own individuality, harmony, and
283– 5 its *p·* and harmonious action.
328–28 Jesus' promise is *p·*.
p 381–28 and abide by the rule of *p·* harmony,
441– 7 but be enjoined to keep *p·* silence,
r 487– 8 the *p·* exercise of the Mind-faculties
g 501–17 than the history of *p·* evil.

perpetually
s 107–15 Feeling so *p·* the false consciousness
r 496–15 Hold *p·* this thought, — that it is the spiritual
ap 564–28 serpent is *p·* close upon the heel of harmony.

perpetuate
ph 183–15 nor devised a law to *p·* error.
196– 8 false pleasures which tend to *p·* this
p 419– 3 hate will *p·* or even create the belief in
g 542–11 and the denial of truth tend to *p·* sin,

perpetuated
a 43–19 *p·* and extended it.
r 466–24 mythology and Jewish theology have *p·* the

perpetuates
pr 2–20 *p·* the belief in God as humanly circumscribed,
sp 85– 7 whatever constitutes and *p·* harmony,
f 235–23 divine Truth which is Life and *p·* being,
b 280–29 and *p·* these qualities in man,
p 399–16 Mortal mind *p·* its own thought.

perpetuating
b 293–16 *p·* the eternal facts
g 531–18 maintained by God in *p·* the species?

Personal Sense

p 439–18 the blind Hypnotism, and the masked *P· S·*,
440–27 I repudiate the false testimony of *P· S·*.
441– 5 He also decided that the plaintiff, *P· S·*,
441–18 Reversing the testimony of *P· S·*
441–30 *P· S·*, is recorded in our Book of books as a liar.

personification

an 103– 3 The Apostle Paul refers to the *p·* of evil as
ph 187–12 another illusive *p·*, named Satan.

personified

o 357– 7 Jesus said of *p·* evil, that it was

persons
and souls
b 280–14 seeks to divide the one Spirit into *p·* and souls.
and things
c 263–27 a human and mortal sense of *p·* and things
certain class of
r 478–10 and by a certain class of *p·*,
few
ph 177–31 In such cases a few *p·* believe the
b 301– 5 Few *p·* comprehend what C. S. means by
many
g 517–15 The world believes in many *p·* ;
nine
an 101– 8 a committee of nine *p·* was appointed,
or things
g 514– 2 could not . . . recreate *p·* or things
other
o 348–25 and that of other *p·* as well?
p 413–10 views of parents and other *p·*
some
s 131–14 Must C. S. come . . . as some *p·* insist?
such
r 478–10 no such *p·* were ever seen to
three
c 256– 9 The theory of three *p·* in one God
g 515–19 nor does it imply three *p·* in one.

———

sp 74– 3 To be on communicable terms with Spirit, *p·*
must
74–14 *p·* in such opposite dreams as the
b 328–20 hundreds of *p·* die there annually from
t 456–18 Science makes no concessions to *p·*
r 483–27 aid, not opposition, from all thinking *p·*.
ap 560–21 As it is with things, so is it with *p·*.

perspicacity

s 128–19 raises the thinker into his native air of . . . *p·*.

perspiration

p 384–17 while in a state of *p·*

persuaded

p 412– 7 be thoroughly *p·* in your own mind

persuading

p 441–28 *p·* Mortal Minds to return a verdict

pertain

o 350– 3 and of the things which *p·* to Spirit

perturbed

p 400–12 Eradicate the image . . . from the *p·* thought
439–16 in the *p·* faces of these worthies,

perusal

s 147–16 by a simple *p·* of this book.
t 446– 5 thorough *p·* of the author's publications
446– 9 Perseverance in the *p·* of the book has generally
g 523– 2 *p·* of the Scriptural account

pervades

sp 78–17 If Spirit *p·* all space,
r 465– 5 Absolute C. S. *p·* its statements,

perverse

s 118–18 perverted by a *p·* material sense of law,

perversion

ph 189–19 The human mortal mind, by an inevitable *p·*,
p 421–30 The *p·* of Mind-science is like

perverted

s 111–14 reverses *p·* and physical hypotheses
118–17 *p·* by a perverse material sense of law,
f 218–30 The meaning of that passage is not *p·* by

pestilence

m 56–16 "the *p·* that walketh in darkness,— *Psal.* 91 : 6.
sp 96–16 may seem to be famine and *p·*,
s 158– 8 the sender of disease, "the god of *p·*."
163–17 war, *p·*, and famine, all combined."
f 210–30 immortal sense includes no evil nor *p·*.

petal

f 247–24 It is Love which paints the *p·* with myriad hues,

petals

m 68–11 and scatters love's *p·* to decay.
g 506–20 even as He opens the *p·* of a holy purpose

Peter

pr 6–25 to *P·* he said, "Thou art an offence—*Matt.* 16 : 23
a 48–21 *P·* would have smitten the enemies of his
53–22 Like *P·*, we should weep over the warning,
s 137–30 thou art *P·*; and upon this rock—*Matt.* 16 : 18.
138– 3 not on the personal *P·* as a mortal, but on
138– 6 It was now evident to *P·* that divine Life,

Peter's

s 138– 4 which lay behind *P·* confession

petition

pr 16–17 our scientific apprehension of the *p·*,

petitioners

pr 12–30 only *p·* (*per se* or by proxy)

petitions

pr 2–12 can do more for ourselves by humble fervent *p·*
11–21 *P·* bring to mortals only the results of
13–10 If our *p·* are sincere, we labor for what we ask
gl 597– 7 hypocrisy, which offered long *p·* for

petros

s 137–31 [the meaning of the Greek word *p·*, or *stone*]

petty

s 130– 1 The *p·* intellect is alarmed by constant
t 445–32 for the *p·* consideration of money,
460–21 it starts a *p·* crossfire over every cripple

phantasm

f 222– 1 and that this *p·* of mortal mind disappears

phantoms

f 215–20 and flee as *p·* of error before truth and love.

Pharaohs

f 226–28 the educational systems of the *P·*, who to-day

Pharisaical

a 18–11 against *P·* creeds and practices,
gl 597– 2 and in accordance with *P·* notions.

Pharisaism

gl 597–11 martyrdom of Jesus was the culminating sin of
P·.

Pharisee

a 20– 6 To the ritualistic priest and hypocritical *P·*
p 362– 3 a certain *P·*, by name Simon,
363–19 the Master's question to Simon the *P·* ;
364– 9 the hospitality of the *P·* or the
367–11 nor, like the *P·*, with the arrogance of rank
gl 592–27 definition of

Pharisees

a 28– 1 The *P·* claimed to know and to teach the
47–13 thirty pieces of silver and the smiles of the *P·*,
52–29 The accusations of the *P·* were
s 117–30 leaven of the *P·* and of the Sadducees,
132–14 *P·* of old thrust the spiritual idea . . . out of
b 305–32 but not so blindly as the *P·*, who
306– 1 *P·* thought that they could raise the spiritual
from
g 539–22 Disputing these points with the *P·*

pharmaceutics

s 129–21 We must abandon *p·*, and take up ontology,

pharmacist

ph 166–10 *p·* believes in the power of his drugs

pharmacist's

ph 166–13 the doctor's and the *p·* is a medical

pharmacy

o 342–30 teaching or practising *p·* or obstetrics
t 460– 8 Its *p·* is moral, and its medicine is intellectual

phase

pref xi– 2 only a *p·* of the action of the human mind,
an 102–31 Its so-called despotism is but a *p·* of
b 321–18 was really but a *p·* of mortal belief.
p 419–22 mortal mind is liable to any *p·* of belief.
427–13 Death is but another *p·* of the dream that

phases

sp 96–18 sin, sickness, and death, which assume new *p·*
f 249–24 Sleep and apathy are *p·* of the dream that
b 311–32 is not touched by these *p·* of mortality.
r 488– 1 enduring and harmonious *p·* of things.

phenomena
extraordinary
sp 80–16 Science . . . explains extraordinary *p·* ;
gropes among
t 463– 2 material physician gropes among *p·*, which
its own
f 220–18 Mortal mind produces its own *p·*,
noumenon and
s 114–10 including noumenon and *p·*,
of existence
p 430– 1 includes all the *p·* of existence.
of improvisation
sp 89–23 which explains the *p·* of improvisation

phenomena

spiritual
sp 88–24   nor are they spiritual *p·*,

pref xi– 1   Many imagine that the *p·* of physical healing
sp 80–17   Science never removes *p·* from the
an 101–11   the *p·* exhibited by a reputed clairvoyant.
p 423–31   They are only *p·* of the mind of mortals.

phenomenal
s 150– 6   eternal Science, instead of a *p·* exhibition.

phenomenon
sp 89– 2   This *p·* only shows that the beliefs of
ph 180–14   the human mind governs the body, its *p·*,
b 277–30   and is therefore a mortal *p·*,
gl 591–22   MIRACLE. . . . a *p·* of Science.

Philadelphia
s 162–31   the famous *P·* teacher of medical practice.

philanthropists
s 161–30   if this old class of *p·* looked as
p 385– 2   Florence Nightingale and other *p·*

philanthropy
sp 80–12   I entertain no doubt of the humanity and *p·*
s 151– 8   *p·* of the higher class of physicians.
t 462–29   hallowed influences of unselfishness, *p·*,

philosopher
f 216– 1   would have killed the venerable *p·*
g 556–14   may absorb the attention of sage and *p·*,

philosophy

heathen
g 552– 6   Heathen *p·*, modern geology, and

his
m 66–29   making his Xantippe a discipline for his *p·*.
f 215–29   faith of his *p·* spurned physical timidity.

human
sp 99– 2   Human *p·*, ethics, and superstition
s 144– 8   beliefs formulated in human *p·*,
b 269– 9   Human *p·* has made God manlike.
279–22   Every system of human *p·*, doctrine, and

school of
a 41–19   No ancient school of *p·*, . . . ever taught

sensuous
s 121– 3   the favorite inclinations of a sensuous *p·*.

f 209–12   Neither *p·* nor skepticism can hinder
b 269– 5   resulted from the *p·* of the serpent.
271– 8   He knew that the *p·*, Science, and proof of
o 347– 4   It is said . . . to verify this wonderful *p·*

Phœnician
g 524– 2   is seen in the *P·* worship of Baal,

phrase

absurd
r 485– 3   *Material sense* is an absurd *p·*,

divine service
a 40–28   It is sad that the *p· divine service* has

"express image"
b 313–12   the *p·* "express image" — *Heb.* 1: 3.

infinite form
c 257–31   *p· infinite form* involves a contradiction

mortal mind
s 114–14   the *p· mortal mind* implies something untrue

Scripture
g 511– 3   and so explains the Scripture *p·*,

self-contradictory
r 478–30   *Mortal man* is really a self-contradictory *p·*,

such a
g 517– 4   word *anthropomorphic*, in such a *p·* as

word or
s 114–18   if a better word or *p·* could be suggested,

pr 16–15   In the *p·*, "Deliver us from evil," — *Matt.* 6: 13.
s 114–15   as the *p·* is used in teaching C. S.,
gl 598–13   the *p·* is equivalent to our common statement,

phraseology
o 354– 7   Why do they use this *p·*, and yet

phrenology
ph 173–22   *P·* makes man knavish or honest according
173–24   physiology, *p·*, do not define the image of God,

physical

action
p 420–26   gives them all power over every *p·* action

affirmation
p 392–11   The *p·* affirmation of disease

ailments
p 421– 3   *p·* ailments (so-called) arise from

belief
p 395–27   to feel these ills in *p·* belief.
418–26   Include moral as well as *p·* belief in your
gl 582– 4   A *p·* belief as to life, substance, and
586–18   FLESH. An error of *p·* belief ;

body
s 124–32   elements and functions of the *p·* body

physical

causation
b 286–12   *P·* causation was put aside

causes
s 111–22   to attribute physical effects to *p·* causes

combination
c 256–24   No form nor *p·* combination is adequate to

condition
a 46–20   Jesus' unchanged *p·* condition after what
b 297–11   change in either . . . affects the *p·* condition.
p 411–25   as the *p·* condition is imaged forth

conditions
sp 77– 8   mortal mind creates its own *p·* conditions.
s 150–27   *p·* conditions all his earthly days,

contact
sp 86– 2   to be occasioned by *p·* contact alone,

death
an 101–25   its effects . . . lead to moral and to *p·* death.

deformity
f 244– 2   He does not produce moral or *p·* deformity ;

diagnosis
s 161–26   according to his *p·* diagnosis,
p 370–20   A *p·* diagnosis of disease . . . tends to induce

disease
s 150–14   in the metaphysical healing of *p·* disease ;

effect
p 383–26   the illusive *p·* effect of a false belief,

effects
s 111–22   tendency of the age to attribute *p·* effects to
145–18   its ethical as well as its *p·* effects.
145–19   its ethical and *p·* effects are indissolubly
p 380–15   The *p·* effects of fear illustrate an
381–10   This fear . . . induces the *p·* effects.

enemies
s 116–16   nor do they carry the day against *p·* enemies,

evils
p 366– 6   to cast *p·* evils out of his patient ;

exemption
p 373– 2   in darkness as to the *p·* exemption which

eye
s 121–17   is invisible to the *p·* eye,

finiteness
c 255–16   The human form, or *p·* finiteness,

force
r 484–15   *P·* force and mortal mind are one.

forms
c 282–32   Cause does not exist . . . in *p·* forms.

healing
pref xi– 1   the phenomena of *p·* healing in C. S.
xi– 9   The *p·* healing of C. S. results now, as in
s 150–12   is not primarily one of *p·* healing.
t 460–10   though used for *p·* healing.

humanity
c 256–14   within the narrow limits of *p·* humanity,

hypotheses
s 111–15   reverses perverted and *p·* hypotheses

infirmity
c 261–18   made him as oblivious of *p·* infirmity

Jesus
a 51–26   inflicted on the *p·* Jesus,

knowledge
a 46–28   he rose above the *p·* knowledge of his disciples,

law
ph 184–25   what is termed a fatally broken *p·* law.

laws
m 62– 7   master the belief in so-called *p·* laws,
ph 165–12   Obedience to the so-called *p·* laws of health
p 381–32   transgressions of the *p·* laws of health ;
442– 2   adjudged innocent of transgressing *p·* laws,

life
f 247– 1   The acute belief of *p·* life comes on at a

limitations
c 256–28   Mind cannot proceed from *p·* limitations.

merely
pr 13–28   men recognize themselves as merely *p·*,

methods
t 443–16   ordinary *p·* methods of medical treatment,

nature
s 117– 7   C. S. attaches no *p·* nature and significance to

need
s 148–29   to render help in time of *p·* need.

offences
an 105–17   legal rulings wholly to *p·* offences,

organism
g 555– 9   which brings the *p·* organism under the

organization
ph 170–30   in either case dependent upon his *p·* organization,

pains
m 67–30   *p·* pains and pleasures,

personality
b 285–15   Is God a *p·* personality?

plagues
ap 575– 5   will destroy forever the *p·* plagues

power
s 131–11   the superiority of spiritual over *p·* power.

physical

proximity
sp 82–15 despite his *p·* proximity, '
realm
p 427–25 acknowledged as supreme in the *p·* realm,
science
s 124– 3 *P·* science (so-called) is human knowledge,
127–23 There is no *p·* science, inasmuch as
144–23 divine Science wars with so-called *p·* science,
sensation
pr 7–17 *P·* sensation, . . . produces material ecstasy
sense
m 60–25 *p·* sense, not discerning the true happiness
64–31 voices of *p·* sense will be forever hushed.
sp 86–21 no less a quality of *p·* sense than feeling.
s 124–17 explained on the basis of *p·* sense
ph 191–25 *P·* sense defines mortal man as based on
b 304–19 not, therefore, at the disposal of *p·* sense.
322–19 until his *p·* sense of pleasure yields to
r 479– 1 If a child is the offspring of *p·* sense
493– 6 All the evidence of *p·* sense and all the
493– 7 knowledge obtained from *p·* sense must yield
493–22 takes away this *p·* sense of discord,
g 531–11 sometime rise above all material and *p·* sense,
gl 582–21 *p·* sense put out of sight and hearing ;
591– 1 through a *p·* sense of God as finite
senses
pr 15– 7 The Father in secret is unseen to the *p·* senses,
a 38–21 few of the pleasures of the *p·* senses,
46–14 proved to the *p·* senses that his body
sp 71–25 It is the offspring of the *p·* senses.
75– 4 in the existence cognized by the *p·* senses,
88–20 nor understood through the *p·* senses.
s 108– 2 antagonistic to the testimony of the *p·* senses
114– 7 is based on the evidence of the *p·* senses,
117–24 Evidence drawn from the five *p·* senses
120– 7 reverses the false testimony of the *p·* senses,
120–21 reversing the testimony of the *p·* senses,
120–28 instead of reversing the testimony of the *p·* senses,
122– 1 The evidence of the *p·* senses often reverses
ph 173– 1 acting through the five *p·* senses
188–28 the *p·* senses have no immediate evidence of
192–20 *p·* senses must give up their false testimony.
f 231– 2 or the so-called *p·* senses will get the victory.
b 273– 3 The *p·* senses can take no cognizance of God
274–17 what we erroneously term the five *p·* senses
284–21 The *p·* senses can obtain no proof of God.
293–32 The five *p·* senses are the avenues and
311–26 The objects cognized by the *p·* senses
327–17 To the *p·* senses, the strict demands of
o 353– 3 The *p·* senses and Science have ever
353– 5 till the testimony of the *p·* senses yields
r 479–16 hear, feel, or use any of the *p·* senses?
sight
sp 87–32 or altogether gone from *p·* sight
structure
ph 197–11 The less that is said of *p·* structure
supports
pref x–20 till all *p·* supports have failed,
symptoms
ph 194– 6 change in . . . changes all the *p·* symptoms,
p 422– 6 and certain moral and *p·* symptoms seem
t 453–11 the morbid moral or *p·* symptoms
testimony
b 295– 4 proof of the unreliability of *p·* testimony.
theories
s 123–13 Divine Science, rising above *p·* theories,
thought-taking
p 365–10 the supposed necessity for *p·* thought-taking
timidity
f 215–29 his philosophy spurned *p·* timidity.
universe
r 484–13 *p·* universe expresses the . . . thoughts of
wants
p 413– 4 the undue contemplation of *p·* wants
weariness
f 217–26 or any illusion of *p·* weariness,
world
s 125– 1 functions of the physical body and of the *p·* world

sp 71–28 are alike material and *p·*.
74–28 and the *p·*, or corporeal.
99– 1 not *p·* but metaphysical,
s 111– 6 C. S. is natural, but not *p·*.
111– 9 departing from the realm of the *p·*,
114–24 explains all cause and effect as mental, not *p·*.
115–21 definition of
118–29 these definitions portray law as *p·*,
119–13 all disasters, *p·* and moral,
132–25 salvation from all error, *p·* and mental,
148–13 define man as both *p·* and mental,
ph 170–28 The description of man as purely *p·*,
f 218–31 the moral and *p·* are as one in their results.
245–26 for the mental state governed by the *p·*.
246–13 As the *p·* and material, the transient sense

physical

c 258– 6 material belief in a *p·* God and man.
260–23 evolves bad *p·* and moral conditions.
b 285–15 Spirit is not *p·*.
288–10 When the final *p·* and moral effects of C. S. ar
290–11 That Life or Mind is finite and *p·* . . . is false
299– 5 which has no *p·* antecedent reality
p 405–27 it is hastening on to *p·* and moral doom.
412–20 and array your mental plea against the *p·*.
r 492– 9 will uplift the *p·* and moral standard

physicality
gl 587–11 a supposition of sentient *p·* ;

physically
a 54–29 If that . . . glorified man were *p·* on earth
s 151–12 to benefit the race *p·* and spiritually,
ph 188–19 produced *p·* by the pleasure of a dream.
f 220–27 better morally or *p·*
b 325–21 demands of Truth upon mortals *p·* and
p 369–30 No man is *p·* healed in wilful error
370– 2 must be better spiritually as well as *p·*.
375–20 while restoring him *p·* through divine Love.
t 445– 5 who attempts to kill morally and *p·*.
r 466–30 making mankind better *p·*, morally, and
495–13 and sets the captive free *p·* and morally.
ap 564– 6 incites mortals to kill morally and *p·*

physician (*see also* **physician's**)

alarm of the
t 446– 8 either arise from the alarm of the *p·*, or
and patient
ph 174–29 the thought of both *p·* and patient
177–26 even though *p·* and patient are expecting
any
p 416– 9 Yet any *p·* — allopathic, homœopathic, botanic
her former
s 156–13 her former *p·* had prescribed these remedies,
his
ph 193– 3 On entering the house I met his *p·*,
193–24 I have been informed that his *p·* claims to
193–30 and what his *p·* said of the case,
f 221– 8 His *p·* also recommended that he
his own
s 144–28 every man will be his own *p·*,
material
t 463– 1 The material *p·* gropes among phenomena,
mental
p 368–32 Once let the mental *p·* believe in the
must understand
p 417–25 To do this, the *p·* must understand
old-school
p 375– 8 The old-school *p·* proves this when
ordinary
s 159–31 the ordinary *p·* is liable to
p 379– 5 where the ordinary *p·* looks for causes.
prescribes
ph 198–19 the *p·* prescribes drugs,
who lacks
p 366–12 The *p·* who lacks sympathy for his

s 149–17 A *p·* of the old school remarked
161–31 *p·* agrees with his "adversary— *Matt.* 5: 25.
163–10 if there were not a single *p·*, surgeon,
ph 193– 4 The *p·* had just probed the ulcer
344–27 when the *p·* may perchance be an infidel
p 366–17 *p·* lacks faith in the divine Mind
366–22 *p·* must also watch, lest he be overwhelmed
403–32 *p·* should be familiar with mental action
417–22 Disease should not appear real to the *p·*,
422– 9 the book will become the *p·*,

physician's
ph 198– 8 is increased by the *p·* words.

physicians

class of
s 151– 9 philanthropy of the higher class of *p·*.
given by
ph 179–32 Descriptions of disease given by *p·*
her
s 158–32 her *p·* insisted that it would be unsafe
159– 5 she was compelled by her *p·* to take it.

ph 180–11 *P·* should not deport themselves as if
235–19 *P·*, . . . should be models of virtue.
235–24 *p·* should be able to teach it.
p 370–32 *P·* examine the pulse, tongue, lungs,

physics

above
b 269–11 Metaphysics is above *p·*,
belief in
s 155–15 universal belief in *p·* weighs against the
disbelief in
p 397–20 in exact proportion to your disbelief in *p·*,
doctrines of
s 132–19 from doctrines of *p·* or of divinity ;
physiology, and
f 222–28 physiology, and *p·* had made him one,

physics
  place of
    gl 585–19   metaphysics taking the place of *p·* ;
  rely upon
    g 549–22   false systems, which rely upon *p·*
  systems of
    s 160– 3   systems of *p·* act against metaphysics,
  theology and
    pref viii– 9   Theology and *p·* teach that both

    s 150–18   science (so-called) of *p·* would have one
    ph 170–21   always in opposition, . . . to *p·*.
physiological
    an 101–15   *p·* and therapeutical questions,
physiologists
    ph 197–19   hardier than our trained *p·*,
Physiology
    p 430–23   Materia Medica, Anatomy, *P·*, Hypnotism,
    431–13   the prisoner summoned *P·*, Materia Medica,
    436–16   professed friends, Materia Medica and *P·*,
    437–22   Materia Medica, Anatomy, *P·*,
    439–18   Scholastic Theology, Materia Medica, *P·*,
physiology
  adherence to
    ph 166–23   through adherence to *p·* and hygiene,
  and health
    ph 179–21   Treatises on anatomy, *p·*, and health,
  and pathology
    b 294–16   taught, as they are by *p·* and pathology,
  and Spirit
    ph 182– 9   We cannot obey both *p·* and Spirit,
  exalts matter
    s 148–25   *P·* exalts matter, dethrones Mind,
  or therapeutics
    an 101–18   nothing in common with either *p·* or therapeu-
             tics."
  theology and
    s 141–32   now occupied by scholastic theoloogy and *p·*,

    s 144– 9   in human philosophy, *p·*, hygiene,
    148–27   When *p·* fails to give health
    ph 165– 1   *P·* is one of the apples from
    173–17   *P·* continues this explanation,
    173–23   *p·*, phrenology, do not define the image of God,
    179–16   can even educate a healthy horse so far in *p·*
    f 222–27   fear, hygiene, *p·*, and physics
    g 556–25   Ontology receives less attention than *p·*.
physique
    a 46–13   Master said plainly that *p·* was not Spirit,
    r 475–14   Man is idea, . . . he is not *p·*.
pick
    sp 99–12   None may *p·* the lock nor enter by some other
pictorial
    sp 86–27   can all be taken from *p·* thought and memory
picture
    sp 87– 6   or for the person holding the transferred *p·*
    ph 174–17   Why . . . *p·* this disease to the mind,
    198–21   a *p·* of healthy and harmonious formations.
    c 264– 6   when the mental *p·* is spiritual and eternal.
    b 305– 5   A *p·* in the camera or a face reflected in the
    310– 1   The *p·* is the artist's thought objectified.
    g 526–25   second biblical account is a *p·* of error
pictured
    sp 91– 2   Have you ever *p·* this heaven and earth,
    g 514–21   the millennial estate *p·* by Isaiah :
pictures
    sp 86–31   *P·* are mentally formed before the
    87– 2   Mind-readers perceive these *p·* of thought.
    92–11   In old Scriptural *p·* we see a serpent
    ph 195–26   remarkable only for their exaggerated *p·*,
    f 244–29   Even Shakespeare's poetry *p·* age as infancy,
    p 379–27   *p·* drawn on the body by a mortal mind.
piece
    f 212–16   this so-called mind instead of a *p·* of the flesh,
pieces
    a 47–12   The traitor's price was thirty *p·* of silver
pierced
    a 50–29   sharper than the thorns which *p·* his flesh.
pierces
    m 66– 7   a broken reed, which *p·* the heart.
    f 210–20   Truth *p·* the error of mortality
piety
    a 25–24   requisite proofs of their own *p·*.
    sp 98–26   connection with faith and *p·*.
Pilate
    a 48–26   *P·* was drawn into acquiescence with the
    48–27   *P·* was ignorant of the consequences of
    52–15   Herod and *P·* laid aside old feuds

Pilate's
    a 49– 1   women at the cross could have answered *P·*
             question.
piled
    r 494–28   its lap *p·* high with immortal fruits.
pilgrim
    a 22– 1   borrow the passport of some wiser *p·*,
    ph 174–15   Whoever opens the way in C. S. is a *p·* and
    f 254–31   *P·* on earth, thy home is heaven ;
    ap 574– 4   adapted to console the weary *p·*,
pilgrimage
    ph 166– 8   Mohammedan believes in a *p·* to Mecca
    f 202–18   The days of our *p·* will multiply
pillar
    ap 566–10   a *p·* of cloud by day and of fire by night,
pillars
    ap 558– 5   and his feet as *p·* of fire :— *Rev.* 10 : 1.
    558–16   Its feet are *p·* of fire, foundations of Truth and
pillow
    p 365– 2   the thorns they plant in the *p·* of the sick
pin
    f 228– 7   subject for mortal belief to *p·* theories upon ;
pinching
    p 383–29   *p·* and pounding the poor body,
pine-tree
    s 129–25   Can we gather peaches from a *p·*,
pinions
    pr 4–31   creeds clip the strong *p·* of love,
    m 58– 3   Unity of spirit gives new *p·* to joy,
    s 107–12   fresh *p·* are given to faith and understanding,
    ph 191–14   transformed by Truth on its *p·* of light,
    b 268– 3   With like activity have thought's swift *p·*
    298–28   flying on spiritual, not material, *p·*.
    t 454–20   Right motives give *p·* to thought,
pinnacle
    t 448–11   casts thee down from the *p·*.
pinning
    a 22–25   *p·* one's faith . . . to another's vicarious effort.
pioneer
    pref vii–24   It is the task of the sturdy *p·* to hew the tall oak
    vii–25   must declare what the *p·* has accomplished.
    a 28–31   await, in some form, every *p·* of truth.
pious
    sp 77– 1   The *p·* Polycarp said : "I cannot turn at once
Pison
    gl 593– 1   definition of
pitiful
    s 158–18   It is *p·* to lead men into temptation through the
    b 327– 8   What a *p·* sight is malice, finding pleasure in
    b 367– 4   *p·* patience with his fears and the removal
pitilessly
    t 446– 3   dealing *p·* with a community unprepared for
pity
    a 49–16   No human eye was there to *p·*, no arm to save.
    o 348–10   It is a *p·* that the medical faculty and clergy
place
  and power
    ph 167–13   cannot successfully usurp the *p·* and power
    t 450–14   nor play the traitor for *p·* and power.
  everlasting
    sp 99–27   everlasting *p·* to the scientific demonstration of
  gave
    ph 193–11   its death-pallor gave *p·* to a natural hue.
  give
    f 209–21   they all must give *p·* to the spiritual fact
    c 264– 4   must finally give *p·* to the glorious forms which
    b 285–19   to give *p·* to a diviner sense of intelligence
    p 428–12   sweep away the false and give *p·* to the true.
    t 458–21   summoned to give *p·* to higher law,
    r 476–19   must disappear to give *p·* to the facts
    g 549– 7   will finally give *p·* to higher theories and
  given
    pr 9–11   If selfishness has given *p·* to kindness,
    s 133–31   not quite given *p·* to the true knowledge of God.
  gives
    pref xi–13   as necessarily as darkness gives *p·* to light
    ph 176–14   of the human mind gives *p·* to
    b 339–23   until the finite gives *p·* to the infinite,
  giving
    c 266– 4   giving *p·* to man's higher individuality
  has no
    b 282–16   matter has no *p·* in Spirit,
    282–17   and Spirit has no *p·* in matter.
  have no
    pr 9–24   material sense and human will have no *p·*.
    r 469–23   for evil can have no *p·*, where
  her
    t 464– 9   Others could not take her *p·*,

place
in its old
 f 212– 4   and the pain seems to be in its old *p*˙.
in our institutions
 s 141–31   Give to it the *p*˙ in our institutions of learning
in which
 a 44– 6   a *p*˙ in which to solve the great problem
is no
 r 480– 3   and there is no *p*˙ where God is not,
 g 504–12   there is no *p*˙ where God's light is not seen,
nor opportunity
 f 232–32   neither *p*˙ nor opportunity in Science for error
nor power
 b 327–20   evil has in reality neither *p*˙ nor power
nor thing
 sp 71– 3   It is neither person, *p*˙, nor thing,
occupies the
 p 367–17   A Christian Scientist occupies the *p*˙ at this
of modes
 p 406– 7   when, in *p*˙ of modes and forms,
of Spirit
 g 522–18   erroneous theory, matter takes the *p*˙ of Spirit.
one
 sp 90–22   yet their bodies stay in one *p*˙.
 g 506–16   gathered together unto one *p*˙,— *Gen.* 1 : 9
same
 b 287–13   fountain send forth at the same *p*˙— *Jas.* 3 : 11.
such a
 p 362– 8   she was debarred from such a *p*˙
supreme
 s 156–32   and Mind takes its rightful and supreme *p*˙.
take
 m 59–32   Separation never should take *p*˙,
takes
 t 463–17   When this new birth takes *p*˙, the C. S. infant
 g 549– 3   takes *p*˙ apart from sexual conditions.
taking
 g 504–17   represented as taking *p*˙ on so many *evenings*
taking the
 gl 585–19   metaphysics taking the *p*˙ of physics ;
their
 ap 566–28   neither was their *p*˙ found— *Rev.* 12 : 8.
thereof
 ph 190–26   the *p*˙ thereof shall know it no more.— *Psal.*
      103 : 16.
 r 476–26   the *p*˙ thereof shall know it no more."— *Psal.*
      103 : 16.
to make
 s 130–19   denied and cast out to make *p*˙ for truth.
took
 ph 193–16   in the afternoon when this took *p*˙.
took the
 ph 165–14   material theories took the *p*˙ of

 a 31– 2   God will never *p*˙ it in such hands.
 sp 72–10   in the *p*˙ of darkness all is light,
 s 148–14   Both . . . *p*˙ mind at the mercy of
 ph 165– 9   to *p*˙ this so-called mind at the mercy of
 167– 5   Soul-existence, in the *p*˙ of sense-existence,
 f 238–29   *p*˙ the fact above the falsehood,
 b 291–19   "In the *p*˙ where the tree falleth,— *Eccl.* 11 : 3.
 r 469–23   when we admit that, . . . evil has a *p*˙ in this
 486–30   would *p*˙ man in a terrible situation,
 ap 565–30   hath a *p*˙ prepared of God.— *Rev.* 12 : 6.
 573–20   in *p*˙ of this false sense was the

placed
 pr 5– 7   *p*˙ under the stress of circumstances.
 a 47–19   *p*˙ a gulf between Jesus and his betrayer,
 f 239–17   we must learn where our affections are *p*˙
 b 305– 1   *p*˙ at the disposal of illusions,
 p 431–22   covered with a foul fur, *p*˙ on me the night of
 g 537– 5   *p*˙ at the east of the garden— *Gen.* 3 : 24.

places
 m 60–26   So physical sense, . . . *p*˙ it on a false basis.
 61–14   If some fortuitous circumstance *p*˙ promising
 t 453–21   spiritual wickedness in high *p*˙.
 g 535– 5   the other to be garnered into heavenly *p*˙.
 537–27   text is made to appear contradictory in some *p*˙,
 538– 5   Truth *p*˙ the cherub wisdom at the gate
 ap 559–12   heard in the desert and in dark *p*˙ of fear.
 563–30   "spiritual wickedness in high *p*˙."— *Eph.* 6 : 12.

plagiarisms
 pref x– 6   and filled with *p*˙ from SCIENCE AND HEALTH.

plague
 p 405–22   better to be exposed to every *p*˙ on earth than

plagues
 s 133– 9   saved the Israelites from belief in the *p*˙.
 ap 574– 7   full of the seven last *p*˙,— *Rev.* 21 : 9.
 574–18   the seven angelic vials full of seven *p*˙,
 575– 5   the physical *p*˙ imposed by material sense.

plain
 pref vii– 7   make *p*˙ to benighted understanding the way
 s 137–13   it is *p*˙ that Jesus completely eschewed the
 143– 5   It is *p*˙ that God does not employ drugs
 f 245–29   *p*˙ that decrepitude is not according to law,
 o 346– 9   The nothingness of nothing is *p*˙ ;
 g 527–15   It is *p*˙ also that material perception,

plainly
 a 46–13   Master said *p*˙ that physique was not Spirit,
 b 279– 3   New Testament writer *p*˙ describes faith,
 314–11   showed *p*˙ that their material views were
 320– 2   Christ *p*˙ declared, "I am the way,— *John* 14 :
 320–17   text declares *p*˙ the spiritual fact of being,
 332–28   which were *p*˙ incarnate in the good and
 p 400–30   Scriptures *p*˙ declare the baneful influence of

plaintiff
 p 380–12   as though the defendant should argue for the *p*
 430–21   Personal Sense is the *p*˙.
 432– 3   acquainted with the *p*˙, Personal Sense,
 433– 1   The testimony for the *p*˙, Personal Sense,
 437– 3   he was on intimate terms with the *p*˙,
 439– 3   the *p*˙, Personal Sense, is a buyer for this firm
 441– 5   He also decided that the *p*˙, Personal Sense,
 441–30   *p*˙, Personal Sense, is recorded in our

plaintive
 a 51– 1   the *p*˙ cry, "*Eloi, Eloi, lama*— *Mark* 15 : 34.

plan
 m 69–13   sense of increasing number in God's infinite *p*
 r 493– 6   solar system as working on a different *p*˙.

planchette
 sp 80–22   Even *p*˙— the French toy which

plane
 sp 75–18   on the same *p*˙ of belief as those who
 77– 9   Death will occur on the next *p*˙ of existence
 f 225–32   on the lowest *p*˙ of human life,
 c 256– 2   Advancing to a higher *p*˙ of action,
 o 349–25   while dwelling on a material *p*˙,
 g 514– 3   recreate persons or things upon its own *p*˙,
 ap 573– 3   The Revelator was on our *p*˙ of existence,

planes
 f 226– 3   found on higher *p*˙ of existence

planet
 p 364– 3   the best man that ever trod this *p*˙.

planetary
 g 504–31   No . . . *p*˙ revolutions form the day of Spirit.

planets
 an 102–12   The *p*˙ have no more power over man than
 f 240– 7   Suns and *p*˙ teach grand lessons.

plank
 t 458– 2   The chief *p*˙ in this platform is the doctrine
 458– 8   Another *p*˙ in the platform is this,

plans
 p 399– 7   Mortal mind *p*˙ the exercise, and puts the

plant
every
 g 520–19   every *p*˙ of the field before it— *Gen.* 2 : 5.
 526– 4   "every *p*˙ of the field before it— *Gen.* 2 : 5.
fibres of a
 r 488–23   no more sensation, . . . than the fibres of a *p*
grows
 g 520–24   the *p*˙ grows, not because of seed or soil,
Mind made the
 g 509–23   Mind made the "*p*˙ of the field— *Gen.* 2 : 5.
species of a
 ap 560–20   the genus and species of a *p*˙

 pref xi–23   the charge to *p*˙ and water His vineyard.
 a 54– 9   All must sooner or later *p*˙ themselves in Christ
 s 147–19   *p*˙ you firmly on the spiritual groundwork of
 f 223– 1   *p*˙ ourselves upon what is pure and perfect.
 224– 6   shall *p*˙ our feet on firmer ground.
 b 269–22   I therefore *p*˙ myself unreservedly on the
 o 351– 6   if we *p*˙ ourselves on a material basis.
 p 365– 2   the thorns they *p*˙ in the pillow of the sick

planted
 s 133–25   him who *p*˙ Christianity on the foundation of
 f 231–31   *p*˙ on the Evangelist's statement that
 235–26   patient's feet may be *p*˙ on the rock

plants
 t 454– 7   and *p*˙ the feet in the true path,

platform
 a 37–20   into a mutilated doctrinal *p*˙.
 an 106– 2   to drop from the *p*˙ of common manhood
 f 226– 2   God has built a higher *p*˙ of human rights,
 b 330– 8   When the following *p*˙ is understood
 t 458– 1   Mental quackery rests on the same *p*˙
 458– 2   The chief plank in this *p*˙ is the doctrine that
 458– 8   Another plank in the *p*˙ is this,

platitudes
 t 446–25   Not human *p*˙, but divine beatitudes,

Platonic
s 112– 8 adherents of the Socratic, the *P·*,

platter
p 382–12 merely the outside of the *p·*.

play
s 155– 2 Presently the child . . . is at *p·*.
b 338–21 Here *a dam* is not a mere *p·* upon words ;
t 450–14 nor *p·* the traitor for place and power.

playing
g 557– 2 moving and *p·* without harm, like a fish.

plea
p 391– 1 to overthrow the *p·* of mortal mind,
412–20 and array your mental *p·* against the physical.
417–17 When you silence the witness against your *p·*,
418–10 half equal to the truth of your *p·*,
430–15 in which the *p·* of C. S. heals the sick.
441–10 The *p·* of False Belief we deem unworthy of a

plead
pr 2–27 Shall we *p·* for more at the open fount,
3–20 We *p·* for unmerited pardon
15–18 we must deny sin and *p·* God's allness.
p 391–19 supposed to say, "I am sick," never *p·* guilty.
391–22 If you say, "I am sick," you *p·* guilty.
395– 3 should *p·* in opposition to the testimony of
412– 4 *p·* the case scientifically for Truth.
418– 7 *P·* with an honest conviction of truth

pleading
pr 2–19 The mere habit of *p·* with the divine Mind,

pleads
pr 2–19 as one *p·* with a human being,

pleas
ph 182–26 *P·* for drugs and laws of health come from

pleasant
m 65–24 fermentation even of fluids is not *p·*.
g 525–31 every tree that is *p·* to the sight,— *Gen. 2 : 9.*
530–23 more *p·* to the eyes than

pleasantest
m 58–32 and this is the *p·* thing to do.

please
m 58–31 how she may *p·* her husband,"— *I Cor. 7 : 34.*
s 160–26 as they *p·* or as disease directs,
g 534–21 in the flesh cannot *p·* God.— *Rom. 8 : 8.*

pleased
sp 80–23 which years ago *p·* so many people
r 478–27 "But when it *p·* God,— *Gal. 1 : 15.*

pleasing
fr 600– * *worthy of the Lord unto all p·,— Col. 1 : 10.*

pleasurable
c 265–32 if they wrench away false *p·* beliefs
g 506–28 Upon Adam devolved the *p·* task of

pleasure
and pain
sp 92– 5 experiencing *p·* and pain,
b 298–17 alternating between a sense of *p·* and pain,
r 472–14 Error is a supposition that *p·* and pain,
beliefs of
b 327– 6 destroy the false beliefs of *p·*, pain, or
confers no
a 40– 1 once admit that evil confers no *p·*,
p 404–23 show him that sin confers no *p·*,
false
b 308–12 false *p·*, pain, sin, sickness, and death."
finding
b 322–23 finding *p·* in it and refraining . . . only through
327– 8 malice, finding *p·* in revenge !
gives
ph 195– 8 All that gives *p·* to our educated senses
good
p 442–28 it is your Father's good *p·*— *Luke 12 : 32.*
have no
s 107–19 must say, "I have no *p·* in them."— *Eccl. 12 : 1.*
His good
sp 99– 9 to will and to do of His good *p·*"— *Phil. 2 : 13.*
illusion of
p 398–22 destroy the illusion of *p·* in intoxication,
instead of
p 435–13 *p·* instead of pain, and life instead of death.
knowledge and
g 532–17 Knowledge and *p·*, evolved through
living only for
a 38–27 living only for *p·* or the gratification of the
loses
b 327–11 Then he loses *p·* in wickedness,
memory of
f 212–10 more vivid than the memory of *p·*.
no abiding
b 327– 2 there is no abiding *p·* in evil,
no real
p 404– 8 there is no real *p·* in false appetites.
404–20 that there is no real *p·* in sin, is one of the

pleasure
nor pain
b 327– 4 neither *p·* nor pain, appetite nor passion,
of a dream
ph 188–19 produced physically by the *p·* of a dream.
or pain
sp 76–24 without a single bodily *p·* or pain,
f 224– 7 Every sensuous *p·* or pain is self-destroyed
c 260–27 the expectation of perpetual *p·* or pain
p 402–30 The involuntary *p·* or pain of the person
418– 4 destroying all belief in material *p·* or pain.
pain and
(*see* **pain**)
pain or
(*see* **pain**)
personal
o 360– 9 replies : . . . mine give me such personal *p·*,
rather than
f 212– 8 Why need pain, rather than *p·*, come to
sense of
b 298–17 alternating between a sense of *p·* and pain,
322–19 until his physical sense of *p·* yields to a
so-called
s 138–24 the sinful, so-called *p·* of the senses.
supposed
pr 6–12 Every supposed *p·* in sin will furnish more than

c 260–31 If we look to the body for *p·*, we find pain ;
b 285– 2 cannot be cognizant . . . of *p·* or of pain.
294–28 The inebriate believes that there is *p·* in
r 490–1 It assures mortals that there is real *p·* in sin ;
g 526–29 The name Eden, according to Cruden, means *p·*.

pleasures
and pains
sp 77–14 embracing its so-called *p·* and pains,
f 222–13 less faith in the so-called *p·* and pains of matter.
232–28 so-called *p·* and pains of sense pass away
b 294–22 the *p·* and pains of matter to be myths,
296–14 so-called *p·* and pains of matter perish,
302–10 and that the so-called *p·* and pains,
308–18 matter with its false *p·* and pains,
p 382–28 nothingness of the so-called *p·* and pains of
390–10 to exchange the *p·* and pains of sense for the
false
ph 196– 7 the false *p·* which tend to perpetuate
b 308–18 matter with its false *p·* and pains,
few of the
a 38–21 Jesus experienced few of the *p·* of the
hopes and
c 265–27 The loss of earthly hopes and *p·*
material
a 39–23 material pains and material *p·* to pass away,
of human sense
b 327–32 the nothingness of the *p·* of human sense
of sense
c 265–29 quickly inform us that the *p·* of sense are
of the table
s 129–31 author's small estimate of the *p·* of the table.
pains and
m 67–31 physical pains and *p·*,
f 202– 8 so-called pains and *p·* of material sense,
r 491–28 awake, we dream of the pains and *p·* of matter.
unreal as his
f 241– 9 sensualist's affections are . . . unreal as his *p·*.

a 21–29 The company is alluring and the *p·* exciting.
39–32 so long as he believes in the *p·* of sin?
p 405–30 pains of sinful sense are less harmful than its *p·*.

pleasure-trip
a 21–28 He is like a traveller going westward for a *p·*.

plentifully
s 113– 4 The letter of Science *p·* reaches humanity

plot
a 47–25 His dark *p·* fell to the ground,

plotted
a 47–23 he *p·* the betrayal of Jesus

pluck
s 141– 7 cut off the right hand and *p·* out the right eye,

plump
ph 175–27 empurpled the *p·* cheeks of our ancestors,

plunged
b 313–24 He *p·* beneath the material surface of things,
329–30 deeper the error into which mortal mind is *p·*,
g 556–31 *p·* his infant babe, . . . into the water

plural
r 466–23 Soul or . . . cannot be rendered in the *p·*.
g 515–17 The name Elohim is in the *p·*,

plurality
g 515–17 this *p·* of Spirit does not imply more than one

pneuma

gl	598– 1	The Greek word for *wind* (*p·*)
	598– 3	"The wind [*p·*] bloweth where—*John* 3 : 8.
	598– 5	is born of the Spirit [*p·*]."—*John* 3 : 8.
	598–12	but this word *ghost* is *p·*.

poet

pref	ix–10	As a certain *p·* says of himself,
m	66– 1	immortal Shakespeare, great *p·* of humanity :
sp	88– 2	which the *p·* Tennyson expressed
ph	176– 1	"Where ignorance is bliss,. . . says the English *p·*,
f	219–21	"The wish," says the *p·*, "is ever father to the
b	332– 7	quoted with approbation from a classic *p·* :

poetry

sp	89–19	It possesses of itself all beauty and *p·*,
f	244–29	Even Shakespeare's *p·* pictures age as
p	378– 2	even as *p·* and music are reproduced in union

point

at every

a	43–27	must overcome the human at every *p·*.

at issue

s	126–15	The *p·* at issue . . . is this :

at no

b	282–20	At no *p·* can these opposites mingle or unite.
g	531–30	theory of material life at no *p·* resembles

at that

g	549–27	At that *p·*, however, even this great observer

beyond faith

f	241–23	One's aim, a *p·* beyond faith, should be

central

t	454–30	the central *p·* of C. S.

contains the

r	466–16	contains the *p·* you will most reluctantly admit,

every

o	358–11	sustains logically . . . every *p·* it presents.

for each one

ph	195–11	The *p·* for each one to decide is,

fundamental

ph	167–29	On this fundamental *p·*, timid conservatism is

grand

s	116–13	Works on metaphysics leave the grand *p·*

great

sp	91– 7	Here is the great *p·* of departure for all true

leading

r	467–21	This is a leading *p·* in the Science of Soul,

of a diamond

g	521–16	the *p·* of a diamond" and the pen of an angel.

of emergence

g	553–25	as the *p·* of emergence for the human race,

of self-destruction

p	374–32	or increases it to the *p·* of self-destruction.

strong

t	455–28	This strong *p·* in C. S. is not to be overlooked,

this

pr	9–27	Do you really desire to attain this *p·*?
sp	95–12	Whoever reaches this *p·* of moral culture
f	206–23	The Scriptures are definite on this *p·*,
	221–14	At this *p·* C. S. saved him,
b	326–17	This *p·* won, you have started as you

this very

a	27–30	made their strongest attack upon this very *p·*.

won a

f	217–19	and you have won a *p·* in Science.

a	30–21	to *p·* out the way of Truth and Life.
m	66–20	wait patiently on divine wisdom to *p·* out the
s	118– 6	Did not this parable *p·* a moral
f	240– 5	all *p·* to Mind, the spiritual intelligence
b	293–27	and *p·* to matter's opposite, the strength and
	299–10	they *p·* upward to a new and glorified trust,
t	447–25	remove the mask, *p·* out the illusion,
ap	561– 6	at a *p·* of so-called embryonic life.
	571– 1	but they are not so willing to *p·* out the evil

pointed

pr	7– 3	Jesus' reproof was *p·* and pungent
a	24– 9	healing currents of Truth are *p·* out.
s	132–31	once *p·* his disciples to Jesus as
ph	184–32	She looked and saw that it *p·* due east.
f	225–11	but Science, heeding not the *p·* bayonet,
b	315–25	The divine conception of Jesus *p·* to this truth
t	462–17	nothing difficult . . . when the way is *p·* out ;
r	494– 9	Jesus *p·* the way for them.

pointedly

a	53– 6	He rebuked sinners *p·* and unflinchingly,

pointing

an	102–10	The *p·* of the needle to the pole symbolizes
t	444–16	Let us be faithful in *p·* the way through Christ,

points

all

s	148–16	Anatomy takes up man at all *p·* materially.
o	353–20	We must give up the spectral at all *p·*.
ap	564–15	Since Jesus must have been tempted in all *p·*,

points

cardinal

a	52–22	These were the two cardinal *p·* of Mind-healing
ap	577–13	but its four cardinal *p·* are :

certain

p	422–27	and renders them fatal at certain *p·*,

doctrinal

o	361– 3	C. S. intervenes, explains these doctrinal *p·*,

hold these

p	414–25	Hold these *p·* strongly in view.

important

p	404–21	one of the most important *p·* in the theology c
r	497– 1	the important *p·*, or religious tenets, of C. S. :

leading

p	425– 7	take up the leading *p·* included

metaphysical

p	397– 1	By not perceiving vital metaphysical *p·*,

two essential

o	349–10	Two essential *p·* of C. S. are,

s	107– 7	apodictical Principle *p·* to the revelation of
	122–20	*p·* to fair weather in the midst of
	129–29	The very name, *illusion*, *p·* to nothingness.
	138–15	His sublime summary *p·* to the religion of Love
ph	170–12	*p·* to the self-sustaining and eternal Truth.
b	275–28	misleads thought and *p·* to other gods,
	277–18	*p·* to the spiritual truth and Science of being.
p	394– 9	to act in the direction which Mind *p·* out.
t	454–15	*p·* out to his student error as well as truth,
g	539–22	Disputing these *p·* with the Pharisees

poison

ph	177–25	If a dose of *p·* is swallowed through mistake,
	177–29	as if the *p·* had been intentionally taken.
	178– 4	set down as a *p·* by mortal mind.
f	215–28	Socrates feared not the hemlock *p·*.
p	383–21	The tobacco-user, eating or smoking *p·*

poisonous

pr	12–21	to be apparently either *p·* or sanative.
s	133–12	healed of the *p·* stings of vipers.
	157–18	If . . . then drugs cannot be *p·*.
ph	169–32	The good that a *p·* drug seems to do is evil,
	178– 3	believe . . . the drug used, to be *p·*,
f	243– 4	divine Love, which made harmless the *p·* viper
g	515– 7	serpent of God's creating is neither . . . nor *p·*

poisons

ph	170– 2	and according to belief, *p·* the human system.

polar

ap	575–27	the Word, the *p·* magnet of Revelation ;

pole

an	102–10	The pointing of the needle to the *p·* symbolize

policy

t	452–23	take no risks in the *p·* of error.

political

m	59–11	nor . . . be expected to understand *p·* economy
b	340–27	civil, criminal, *p·*, and religious codes ;

politicians

ph	197–20	more honest than our sleek *p·*.

pollen

f	235– 1	cannot go forth, like wandering *p·*,

Polycarp

sp	77– 1	pious *P·* said : "I cannot turn at once from

polytheism

c	256–10	suggests *p·*, rather than the one ever-present

pomegranates

fr	600– *	*and the p· bud forth.*—*Song* 7 : 12.

pomp

f	224–14	and array His vicegerent with *p·* and splendor

ponder

m	68–21	it may have caused the good to *p·*
ph	170–25	to *p·* somewhat the supremacy of Spirit,
ap	559–21	Read this book . . . Study it, *p·* it.

pondered

o	359–25	she *p·* the meaning of that Scripture

poor

pr	8–22	If we turn away from the *p·*, we are not
	8–24	the reward of Him who blesses the *p·*.
a	27– 6	to the *p·* the gospel is preached."—*Luke* 7 : 22
	31– 1	he was found preaching the gospel to the *p·*.
	33–25	preaches the gospel to the *p·*, the meek
	34–16	and preach Christ, or Truth, to the *p·*,
m	59–26	a *p·* augury for the happiness of wedlock.
s	132– 8	the *p·* have the gospel preached—*Matt.* 11 : 5.
	142–13	If the . . . turn the *p·* and the stranger from
ph	168– 1	is a *p·* shift for the weak and worldly,
f	247–28	are *p·* substitutes for the charms of being,
c	259– 9	higher than their *p·* thought-models
b	337–23	the *p·* counterfeits of the invisible universe
o	345–22	incongruity between God's idea and *p·* humanity
	347–16	preaching the gospel to the *p·*,

poor

p	364–13	He even said that this *p·* woman had
	365–31	*p·* suffering heart needs its rightful nutriment,
	383–29	pinching and pounding the *p·* body,
g	518–15	The rich in spirit help the *p·*

popular

a	24–18	*p·* opinions in regard to predestination
	47–24	in order to raise himself in *p·* estimation.
m	67–26	the limited demonstration of *p·* Christianity
sp	83–13	and here Science takes issue with *p·* religions.
s	126–16	C. S. on the one hand and *p·* theology on the
	137–11	the work, so mysterious to the *p·* mind?
	141–10	All revelation (such is the *p·* thought !)
	155–21	mightily outweigh the power of *p·* belief
ph	166– 9	*p·* doctor believes in his prescription,
b	291–21	has been transformed into the *p·* proverb,
	316–15	and the blindness of *p·* belief,
o	344–26	Why support the *p·* systems of medicine, when
	347–23	If C. S. takes away the *p·* gods,
	355–17	*p·* religion, declines to admit that
	357–17	*p·* and false notions about the Divine Being
p	398– 8	the *p·* ignorance of spiritual Life-laws.
g	557–22	*P·* theology takes up the history of man as if

popularity

a	42–10	was in no peril from salary or *p·*.
f	236– 1	Love of Christianity, rather than love of *p·*,
	238–24	forsakes *p·* and gains Christianity.

pore

f	224– 3	feels the . . . effect of truth through every *p·*.

portal

pref	vii–15	Truth, . . . knocks at the *p·* of humanity.

portals

f	251–11	they have but passed the *p·* of a new belief.

portend

ph	174–10	and *p·* a long night to the traveller ;

portentous

ap	562–28	great is the idea, and the travail *p·*.

porter

p	392–24	Stand *p·* at the door of thought.
	392–30	then perform your office as *p·*

portion
basal

ph	189–29	in the lower, basal *p·* of the brain,

least

s	126– 9	Human thought never projected the least *p·* of

some

ph	197–28	and mortal belief loses some *p·* of its error.

pref	xii–11	and (for a *p·* of this time) sole editor
ph	172–17	If the material body is man, he is a *p·* of
	172–25	If . . . you take away a *p·* of the man when
	177–13	of which the material body is the grosser *p·* ;
b	336–19	A *p·* of God could not enter man :
p	425–27	will never believe that heart or any *p·* of the

portions

p	375–22	making certain *p·* of it motionless.
	421– 4	belief that other *p·* of the body are
g	531– 8	It is well that the upper *p·* of the
	546–19	seem more obscure than other *p·* of the

portraits

sp	86–25	*P·*, landscape-paintings, fac-similes of

portray

s	118–28	these definitions *p·* law as physical,

portrayal

sp	92–16	The *p·* is still graphically accurate,

portrayed

ap	561–28	The light *p·* is really neither solar nor

portrays

g	522–26	*p·* Spirit as supposedly cooperating

position

sp	90– 8	earth's motion and *p·* are sustained by Mind
ph	167–23	It is not wise to take a halting and half-way *p·*
	182– 3	shows your *p·* as a Christian Scientist.
f	207– 5	This fact proves our *p·*,
	254– 5	who gain good rapidly and hold their *p·*,
b	274–24	no half-way *p·* in learning its Principle
t	448–16	A dishonest *p·* is far from Christianly scientific.

positions

sp	74–30	never a return to *p·* outgrown.

positive

s	109–15	time and energies to discovering a *p·* rule.
	126–13	human mind never . . . sent forth a *p·* sound.
ph	173–13	Spirit is *p·*.
	173–15	For *p·* Spirit to pass through a
r	491– 8	a negative right and a *p·* wrong,

positively

p	362– 9	as *p·* as if she were a Hindoo pariah
	420–12	as *p·* as they can the temptation to sin.

possess

sp	99–19	may *p·* natures above some others
s	119– 4	with what it does not and cannot *p·*,
	138–20	to be Christlike, to *p·* the Christ-spirit,
	156– 1	If drugs *p·* intrinsic virtues
	157–25	confers the power which the drug seems to *p·*.
b	290–23	sin and error which *p·* us at the instant of
	323– 4	and to *p·* no other consciousness but good.
p	425–23	the more immortality we *p·*.
r	486– 9	in order to *p·* immortal consciousness.
g	550– 4	Matter surely does not *p·* Mind.
	556– 5	and are supposed to *p·* life and mind.

possessed

sp	86–10	Jesus *p·* more spiritual susceptibility than
b	313–27	was *p·* only in a limited degree

possesses

sp	89– 7	believing that somebody else *p·* her tongue
	89–19	It *p·* of itself all beauty and poetry,
s	108– 6	matter *p·* neither sensation nor life ;
f	208–27	A mortal man *p·* this body,
	247–20	Being *p·* its qualities before they
b	331–12	nothing *p·* reality nor existence except
r	475–21	*p·* no life, intelligence, nor . . . of his own,
	488–24	Mind alone *p·* all faculties,
g	516–20	*p·* and reflects God's dominion
	539–11	man *p·* nothing which he has not derived from
ap	576–23	In divine Science, man *p·* this recognition

possessing

sp	76–23	*p·* unlimited divine beauty and goodness
an	102– 6	*p·* neither intelligence, power, nor reality,
s	110– 1	Spirit *p·* all power, filling all space,
c	264–11	we must act as *p·* all power from Him
b	269–31	Mind, *p·* intelligence and life.
	280–25	instead of *p·* a sentient material form,
t	443– 7	Mind as really *p·* all power.
r	473– 2	illusion, *p·* neither reality nor identity
g	554–30	less sickly than those *p·* higher organizations,

possession

s	151–11	if they . . . were in *p·* of the enlarged power
c	261–19	though he was in the full *p·* of his so-called
b	291–17	in *p·* of "the mind of the Lord," — *Rom.* 11 : 34.
o	355–13	let the . . . sense of Life and being take *p·*
p	393–11	Take *p·* of your body, and govern its feeling
	402– 4	author has already in her *p·* well-authenticated
	424– 3	takes *p·* of itself and its own thoughts
g	537–28	blessed the earth and gave it to man for a *p·*,

possessor

an	102–28	more likely to be abused by its *p·*, than
g	515– 1	enables its *p·* to emulate the example of Jesus.
gl	582– 7	error masquerading as the *p·* of life,

possibilities
divine

b	326– 1	A false sense of life, . . . hides the divine *p·*,

glorious

b	288–27	Science reveals the glorious *p·* of

infinite

a	34–23	into the perception of infinite *p·*.

of being

f	203–14	Spiritual perception brings out the *p·* of being,

of man

s	128–16	the latent abilities and *p·* of man.
t	445– 9	the great *p·* of man endued with divine Science.

of Spirit

b	316–31	the *p·* of Spirit and its correlative truth.

of thought

sp	90–20	This shows the *p·* of thought.

sp	88–28	the *p·* derived from divine Mind,

possibility

s	134–17	Denial of the *p·* of Christian healing robs
f	217– 3	the notion of such a *p·* is more absurd than
c	260–13	reveals the *p·* of achieving all good,
p	424–30	faith in the *p·* of their transmission.
t	445–11	Teach the dangerous *p·* of dwarfing
ap	574– 2	spiritual consciousness is . . . a present *p·*.

possible

pr	1– 3	all things are *p·* to God,
	13–24	incorporeal Love, to whom all things are *p·*.
a	24–31	could not admit such an event to be *p·*.
	37–22	It is *p·*, — yea, it is the duty and privilege
	45–20	elevated them to *p·* at-one-ment with the
	47–32	a belief in any *p·* material intelligence.
	51– 2	the *p·* loss of something more important than
	51– 3	*p·* misapprehension of the sublimest influence
sp	75–25	There is one *p·* moment, when those living
	77–23	Even if communications . . . were *p·*,
	78–12	even were communication *p·*
	90–11	the movements and transitions now *p·*
	90–12	will be found to be equally *p·* for the body.
s	147–10	where demonstration was humanly *p·*,
	149–21	remarked . . . take as little medicine as *p·* ;
ph	178–16	the divine Mind, to which all things are *p·*,
	180–27	man knows that with God all things are *p·*.

possible

ph 183– 1 Truth, makes all things p· to Spirit ;
183–17 the legitimate and only p· action of Truth
199–22 makes the achievement p·.
f 214– 1 it is p· that the impressions from Truth were
232–10 "with God all things are p·,"— *Mark* 10 : 27.
232–10 all good is p· to Spirit ;
232–12 theories . . . make healing p· only through
236–24 teach their children at the earliest p· period
245–28 proves it p· to be young at seventy-four ;
o 356–21 is it p· for Him to create man subject to
p 365–27 it would, if it were p·, convert into a den of
432–17 The Judge asks if . . . it is p· for man to
t 456–15 and from its p· demonstration.
457–24 To pursue other vocations and . . . is not p·.
r 474–21 Is it p·, then, to believe that the evils
488–27 If it were p· for the real senses of man to
g 548–19 "It is very p· that many general statements
ap 573–25 p· to men in this present state of existence,

possibly

a 55–12 in a clearer light than mere words can p· do,
m 67–18 notion that animal natures can p· give force
s 151– 4 could not p· create a remedy outside of itself,
f 212–28 and p· that other methods involve
p 391– 9 Banish the belief that you can p· entertain a
440– 1 for he could not p· elude their search.
g 546–20 because they cannot p· be interpreted from a

post

a 49–19 faithful sentinel of God at the highest p·
m 67–12 firm at the p· of duty, the mariner works on
p 393– 2 like a watchman forsaking his p·,
t 464–10 She therefore remains unseen at her p·,

post mortem

ph 196–26 induced by a single p· m· examination,

posts

p 387–17 not because they occupy the most important p·

postulate

erroneous
sp 91–25 The first erroneous p· of belief is,
91–27 The second erroneous p· is,
91–29 The third erroneous p· is,
91–32 The fourth erroneous p· is,
92– 3 The fifth erroneous p· is,
last
sp 92– 7 From the illusion implied in this last p· arises
this
b 287– 7 Divine Science contradicts this p·

postulates

sp 91–22 Certain erroneous p· should be here considered
b 288–21 are to be found in the following p· :

potency

s 155–26 p· of the medicine increases as the
158–17 the dignity and p· of divine Mind
b 293–14 whose p· is Truth, whose attraction is Love,
t 462– 7 understanding, p·, enlightenment, and success.
r 466– 3 Hence God combines all-power or p·,

potent

pref x–24 safer and more p· than that of any other
m 67–23 Grace and Truth are p· beyond all other means
s 153–12 and the most p· rises above matter into mind.
ph 180–32 I have found divine Truth more p· than
f 225–18 p· to break despotic fetters
o 351–17 cannot bring out . . . while error seems as p·
g 553–25 this p· belief will immediately supersede the

potentate

a 42– 3 rabbi affirmed God to be a mighty p·,

potentates

ap 577–23 p· and dynasties will lay down their honors

potentially

s 143–28 If Mind was first chronologically, is first p·,

potion

ph 177–31 a few persons believe the p· . . . to be harmless,

potter

ph 173– 7 supposition, that . . . the p· is subject to the
f 243–16 The clay cannot reply to the p·.
b 310– 8 The p· is not in the clay ;
310– 9 else the clay would have power over the p·.

pounding

p 383–29 pinching and p· the poor body,

pounds

s 111–19 A prize of one hundred p·,

pour

pr 10–10 vain repetitions will never p· into prayer the
a 36–10 that he might p· his dear-bought bounty into
54–10 liberally p· his dear-bought treasures into
f 201–17 to p· in truth through flood-tides of Love.

poured

m 57–22 Human affection is not p· forth vainly,
s 114–21 has to be p· into the old bottles of the letter.
ap 574–20 swift-winged thought, which p· forth hatred

pouring

pr 2–27 which is p· forth more than we accept

pours

pr 5–17 God p· the riches of His love into the
t 446–12 p· light and healing upon this generation,

poverty

g 501– 8 showing the p· of mortal existence,

powder

ph 179–27 homœopathic pellet and p· in hand,
p 380– 7 it will grind him to p·."— *Matt.* 21 : 44.

power

ability and
p 393–14 nothing can vitiate the ability and p·
admit that the
an 105– 8 to admit that the p· of human law is
against the
ap 566–32 He leads the hosts of heaven against the p· of
all
s 110– 1 Spirit possessing all p·, filling all space,
157–10 acknowledging that the divine Mind has all p·
c 264–11 we must act as possessing all p· from Him
b 275–23 that is, all p·, all presence, all Science.
p 420–26 divine Love gives them all p· over every
t 443– 8 omnipotent Mind as really possessing all p·.
r 473–12 and attributes all p· to God.
490–11 since all p· belongs to God, good.
g 540–16 all sense of evil and all p· to sin.
all-embracing
an 102–11 symbolizes this all-embracing p·
all other
r 483– 7 Mind transcends all other p·,
almighty
f 202–27 We admit that God has almighty p·,
Almighty's
f 218–20 why do you substitute drugs for the Almighty
p·,
and grace
s 118–16 the invisible and infinite p· and grace.
b 333–22 has come with some measure of p· and grace
and prerogative
s 123– 8 the p· and prerogative of Spirit,
and prestige
f 244–32 of development, p·, and prestige.
and strength
ph 183–24 Obedience to Truth gives man p· and strength
and willingness
r 493–31 the p· and willingness of divine Mind to
animal
gl 597–21 mortal belief ; animal p·.
another
t 445– 6 No hypothesis as to the existence of another p·
r 469–28 still believe there is another p·,
gl 594–10 claim . . . that there was another p·,
any
o 348–18 I desire to have no faith in . . . any p· but
any other
f 228–26 to acknowledge any other p· is to dishonor God
assumed
s 145–30 must continually weaken its own assumed p·.
attributes and
b 301– 1 which manifests God's attributes and p·,
balance of
ph 166–28 The balance of p· is conceded to be with
belief in a
ap 569– 5 mortal belief in a p· opposed to God.
believes in the
ph 166–11 pharmacist believes in the p· of his drugs
bestows the
g 555–26 when we admit . . . that God bestows the p·
borrows its
pr 12–18 borrows its p· from human faith and belief.
Christian
f 233– 2 rather than professions of Christian p·.
coequal in
o 351–21 if we consider Satan as a being coequal in p·
conceding
p 394– 5 By conceding p· to discord,
conscious
p 423–24 with the stimulus of courage and conscious p·
consecrating
p 388– 2 and consecrating p· of divine Truth,
creative
b 302–32 the reflection of the creative p· of
r 475–21 no life, intelligence, nor creative p· of his own
g 507–15 creative p· of the divine Principle, or Life,
gl 582–20 God is the only creative p·.
deific
g 513–12 the motions and reflections of deific p·
514– 1 could not by simulating deific p· invert the
demonstrated the
sp 93– 3 demonstrated the p· of Spirit
s 110–25 Jesus demonstrated the p· of C. S. to heal

power
demonstration of
pr 10–11 in demonstration of p· and "with signs— *Mark*
16 : 20.
a 26–25 and of his demonstration of p· over death.
destroying the
r 473–15 and destroying the p· of death.
destroys your
t 452–28 Acting from sinful motives destroys your p·
destroy your
ph 181–12 You weaken or destroy your p· when you
development of
sp 82–32 hastening to a greater development of p·,
divine
(*see* **divine**)
dominant
ap 559– 4 dominant p· of which was upon the sea,
dominion, and
s 143–30 the glory, honor, dominion, and p·
enlarged
s 151–11 the enlarged p· it confers to benefit the race
entity nor
g 555–14 C. S. attributes to error neither entity nor p·,
erring
ph 192–11 Erring p· is a material belief,
evil is not
an 102–30 Mankind must learn that evil is not p·.
ph 192–24 Evil is not p·.
first
f 204–12 The first p· is admitted to be good,
flexibility and
ph 199–28 gave his . . . muscles, their flexibility and p·
God is the
a 27– 8 God is the p· in the Messianic work.
God's
a 42–16 the great demonstrator of God's p·
an 102– 4 man, reflecting God's p·, has dominion
o 351– 3 When we lose faith in God's p· to heal,
t 450–24 by understanding God's p· over them.
goodness and
g 515–24 reflecting goodness and p·.
has no
pr 12– 4 A mere request . . . has no p· to gain more of
s 151–22 The human mind has no p· to kill
b 291–27 the grave has no p· over either.
p 399– 1 Evil has no p·, no intelligence,
hath no
sp 77–12 "the second death hath no p·."— *Rev.* 20 : 6.
p 290–15 the second death hath no p·."— *Rev.* 20 : 6.
healing
a 18–12 and he refuted all opponents with his healing p·.
31–13 the healing p· of Truth and Love.
38–32 shut out Truth and its healing p·.
55–20 and the healing p· of the divine Love
s 132–29 Did the doctrines . . . confer healing p·
141–23 they cannot demonstrate God's healing p·.
146–26 This healing p· of Truth must have been
150– 4 the healing p· of Truth is widely demonstrated
ph 167–31 Only through . . . can scientific healing p· be
177– 5 The evidence of divine Mind's healing p·
o 351– 2 pedantic and void of healing p·.
355–18 any systematic healing p· since the
p 366–19 infinite Love which alone confers the healing p·.
t 443–14 If patients fail to experience the healing p·
r 495– 4 hence its healing p· is not fully demonstrated.
496–11 demonstrating the healing p· of Truth and
he had
a 51– 7 He had p· to lay down a human sense of life
His
an 102– 3 and His p· is neither animal nor human.
s 108– 4 by the effectual working of His p·."— *Eph.* 3 : 7.
b 283–25 the true sense of His p· is lost to all who
o 352– 2 able to demonstrate His p· to heal,
g 517–31 causes them to multiply,— to manifest His p·.
his
pr 5– 2 and keeps him from demonstrating his p·
s 117–18 his p· over the sick and sinning.
ph 199–30 his p· of putting resolve into action
human
f 225–15 and shows human p· to be proportionate to
g 539–28 gave him more than human p· to expound the
identity or
r 479–28 So evil should be denied identity or p·,
imaginary
s 146–19 divests material drugs of their imaginary p·,
ph 178–25 disarm sin of its imaginary p· in proportion to
b 340– 1 will never lose their imaginary p· . . . until
incisive
sp 94–28 used his incisive p· injuriously?
inclination or
t 452–19 if you had the inclination or p·
intelligence nor
t 454–11 matter has neither intelligence nor p·,
intelligence or
b 339–31 never to admit that sin can have intelligence or
p·,

power
less
f 222–11 Food had less p· to help or to hurt him
less than
f 203–18 prone to believe . . . in some p· less than God.
life-preserving
gl 579–13 life-preserving p· of spiritual understanding.
loss of
ph 183–25 Submission to error superinduces loss of p·.
lost its
b 321–16 The illusion of Moses lost its p· to alarm him,
lower
g 520–30 there is nothing left to be made by a lower p·.
manifestation of
sp 83–14 The scientific manifestation of p· is from the
man's
b 328–14 man's p·, when he is equipped by God,
material
f 249– 8 no mortal nor material p· as able to destroy.
p 378–25 Sickness is not a . . . material p·,
mental
t 455–26 No person can misuse this mental p·, if
moral
p 375–18 adding to his patient's mental and moral p·,
necessity and
p 377–28 conviction of the necessity and p· of
newly discovered
t 457– 9 has never used this newly discovered p· in any
no
sp 76–20 will have no p· over man, for man is immortal
s 143–26 no p· except that which is derived from Mind.
149–24 and with no p· but the divine Mind.
ph 192–20 you can have no p· opposed to God,
f 224–31 No p· can withstand divine Love.
228–25 There is no p· apart from God.
b 303– 6 no p· of propagation in matter,
p 375–24 show mortal mind that muscles have no p·
405–21 government of God, good, in which is no p· to
sin.
t 452– 3 when one understands that evil has in reality no
p·.
455–14 if, . . . you can exercise little or no p· for
no inherent
b 282–23 There is no inherent p· in matter;
no innate
s 160– 6 for they have no innate p·.
no lesser
f 231– 9 no lesser p· equals the infinite All-power;
no more
an 102–12 planets have no more p· over man than
no proof nor
sp 71–23 mainly erroneous, having . . . no proof nor p·
nor presence
r 471–19 there is no other p· nor presence.
nor reality
an 102– 6 possessing neither intelligence, p·, nor reality,
ph 186–16 there is neither p· nor reality in evil.
of action
s 157–14 p· of action is proportionately increased.
of Christian Science
s 110–25 Jesus demonstrated the p· of C. S. to heal
ph 189– 8 the p· of C. S. to establish harmony
b 317– 7 Whosoever . . . declares best the p· of C. S.,
p 412–13 The p· of C. S. and divine Love is omnipotent.
of divine Love
p 411–10 If Spirit or the p· of divine Love bear witness
of divine Principle
f 232–17 again demonstrating the p· of divine Principle,
of God
s 146–13 medicine substitutes drugs for the p· of God
f 224–30 p· of God brings deliverance to the captive.
p 406– 8 the p· of God is understood
of good
ap 570–31 the p· of good resident in divine Mind,
of healing
b 271–12 the p· of healing was not a supernatural gift
t 452–28 Acting from . . . destroys your p· of healing
of His Christ
ap 568–15 and the p· of His Christ :— *Rev.* 12 : 10.
of immortal Mind
ph 171–15 and the p· of immortal Mind
of its own
ap 563–12 the belief that matter has p· of its own,
of light
f 214–27 may end the p· of light and lens !
of Love
f 231–22 To fear sin is to misunderstand the p· of Love
of Mind
a 44–11 the p· of Mind over matter,
s 116–14 They never crown the p· of Mind as the
139– 6 Moses proved the p· of Mind
f 217–25 to learn the p· of Mind over the body
b 321–31 Jesus, who showed his students the p· of Mind
p 380–11 and deny the p· of Mind to heal.

power

of Mind
p 382–27 supporting the *p·* of Mind over the body
384–31 the *p·* of Mind over the entire functions
417– 5 their trust in the *p·* of Mind to sustain the
of pride
gl 589–14 the pride of power and the *p·* of pride ;
of Spirit
a 44–30 *p·* of Spirit to overrule mortal, material sense.
sp 93– 3 demonstrated the *p·* of Spirit
ph 167–18 and avail yourself of the *p·* of Spirit,
183–20 that which hides the *p·* of Spirit.
f 233– 4 the destruction of sin, . . . by the *p·* of Spirit,
b 309–14 the *p·* of Spirit over the material senses ;
316– 8 to prove the *p·* of Spirit over the flesh,
of the divine Mind
s 160– 2 destroying it through the *p·* of the divine Mind.
of their own
g 507–19 not . . . any propagating *p·* of their own,
of Truth
  (*see* **Truth**)
omnipotent
ph 182–31 to presuppose that omnipotent *p·* is powerless
one
b 270– 8 there is but one *p·*, — not two powers,
opposing
p 380–30 to believe . . . that God endows this opposing *p·*
outweigh the
s 155–20 mightily outweigh the *p·* of popular belief
over all the
p 438– 5 over all the *p·* of the enemy :— *Luke* 10 : 19.
over sickness
s 142– 5 by its *p·* over sickness, sin, and death ;
over sin
s 142– 7 generally omit all but . . . the *p·* over sin.
overwhelming
a 47– 9 It was sometimes an overwhelming *p·*
percentage of
s 155–19 the percentage of *p·* on the side of this Science
perfection and
g 522– 7 endows man out of God's perfection and *p·*.
physical
s 131–11 the superiority of spiritual over physical *p·*.
place and
ph 167–13 cannot successfully usurp the place and *p·* of
t 450–14 nor play the traitor for place and *p·*.
place nor
b 327–20 evil has in reality neither place nor *p·*
post of
a 49–19 at the highest post of *p·*,
preponderance of
s 143–20 you conclude that . . . the preponderance of *p·*.
ph 177–23 the preponderance of *p·* in any direction
presence and
g 512– 8 symbolized by strength, presence, and *p·*,
gl 596–18 the presence and *p·* of the Most High.
pride of
t 451– 5 renounce . . . oppression and the pride of *p·*.
gl 589–13 the pride of *p·* and the power of pride ;
propagation and
g 545–24 They believed in . . . its propagation and *p·*.
propensity or
g 539–14 the propensity or *p·* to do evil?
protecting
p 387–28 the supporting influence and protecting *p·*
reality and
p 372–20 How, . . . can we believe in the reality and *p·* of
recuperative
p 394– 7 which is the only real recuperative *p·*.
redeeming
g 552–23 for the redeeming *p·*, . . . is not in egg nor in dust.
sacred
ph 182–26 ability to demonstrate Mind's sacred *p·*.
same
s 135–11 same *p·* which heals sin heals also sickness.
saving
b 285–31 the healing and saving *p·*.
second
f 204–13 so-called second *p·*, evil, is the unlikeness of
secondary
ap 559– 7 a secondary *p·* was exercised upon visible error
seeming
s 122– 3 assigning seeming *p·* to sin, sickness, and death ;
f 208– 6 What then is this seeming *p·*,
t 452– 2 bar the door of his thought against this seeming *p·*,
sensation or
f 218–26 to believe in matter as . . . having sensation or *p·*.
spirit and
a 55–25 the spirit and *p·* of Christian healing.
spiritual
  (*see* **spiritual**)
such a
p 378–29 Such a *p·*, . . . is inconceivable ;
378–30 if such a *p·* could be divinely directed,

power

supply of
ph 199–12 its demand for and supply of *p·*.
supposed
f 224–32 What is this supposed *p·*, which opposes
370–24 a drug may eventually lose its supposed *p·*
the only
ph 186–19 The only *p·* of evil is to destroy itself.
192–24 gives you the only *p·* obtainable.
f 249–14 omnipotence is the only *p·*.
p 419–28 for God is the only *p·*.
third
f 204–15 The third *p·*, mortal man, is a supposed
this
a 25–25 that they might demonstrate this *p·* as he did
sp 85–20 Our Master rebuked the lack of this *p·*
s 110–26 But this *p·* was lost sight of,
151–29 acknowledge this fact, yield to this *p·*,
b 271–30 spiritual import of the Word imparts this *p·*.
to act
gl 582– 8 strength, animation, and *p·* to act.
to demonstrate
f 254–18 not the *p·* to demonstrate what we do not
to heal
pref x–21 so little faith in His disposition and *p·* to heal
s 148– 3 implying that the requisite *p·* to heal was in
o 351– 3 When we lose faith in God's *p·* to heal,
352– 2 able to demonstrate His *p·* to heal,
p 410–27 If . . . the *p·* to heal mentally will diminish,
t 446–15 destroying his own *p·* to heal and his own
transcendent
ph 182–29 ignorance of C. S. and its transcendent *p·*.
truly derived
a 44–21 in his proof of man's truly derived *p·*?
unfolds the
b 276– 1 unfolds the *p·* that heals the sick,
unsurpassed
f 243– 9 with unsurpassed *p·* and love.
wrong
t 452–32 the wrong *p·* would be destroyed.

pr 17–12 Thine is the kingdom, and the *p·*, — *Matt.* 6 : 13
sp 89–20 beauty and poetry, and the *p·* of expressing
92– 9 Mind is not an entity . . . with the *p·* of sinning
an 101– 7 upon the *p·* of the imagination."
s 119– 9 this dilemma and consider matter as a *p·*
157–24 confers the *p·* which the drug seems to
ph 181–32 Any hypnotic *p·* you may exercise will
185–10 discussed . . . "mind-cure," operating through the *p·* of
196– 1 If materialistic knowledge is *p·*,
196– 4 The *p·* of mortal mind over its own body is
196–18 wherewith to establish their *p·*.
206– 2 has in belief more *p·* to harm
f 202–30 as if senseless matter . . . had more *p·* than
206– 4 The *p·* of the human will should be
224– 1 and the *p·* of sin diminishing.
228–29 supposition that sin, . . . and death have *p·*.
253–13 mortal, material sense which is not *p·*
b 296–32 a liar from the beginning, not deserving *p·*.
308–31 "*p·* with God and with men." — *Gen.* 32 : 28.
310– 9 else the clay would have *p·* over the potter.
330–27 Evil is nothing, no thing, mind, nor *p·*.
o 348–15 or imputing too much *p·* to God,
358–28 belief that . . . these healers have wonderful *p·*
p 368–11 fatal beliefs . . . that evil is equal in *p·* to good
376–31 To fear and admit the *p·* of disease, is to
378–27 never endowed matter with *p·* to disable Life
380–29 to believe that there is a *p·* opposite to God,
388–15 another admission . . . that food has *p·*
396–22 At the right time explain to the sick the *p·*
419–11 Neither disease itself, sin, nor fear has the *p·* to
438– 5 Behold, I give unto you *p·* — *Luke* 10 : 19.
r 473–10 nothing apart from Him is present or has *p·*.
485–32 is like saying that the *p·* in the lever.
495–11 a *p·* which opens the prison doors
g 515– 9 the *p·* which changeth the serpent into a staff.
547–19 theory, — that Mind . . . endues matter with *p·*

powerful

an 103–22 false belief . . . that evil is . . . more *p·*.
o 352–21 declaring ghosts to be real, merciless, and *p·*,
390–30 as *p·* mental opposition as a legislator
397–14 Your thought is more *p·* than your words,
397–15 more *p·* than the accident itself,

powerfully

pr 12– 7 making it act more *p·* on the body
s 155–22 The human mind acts more *p·* to offset

powerless

s 152– 3 would wield the sceptre of a monarch, but it is *p·*
160– 8 the inanimate drug becomes *p·*.
ph 182–32 to presuppose that . . . is *p·* on some occasions
f 228–29 He proved them *p·*.
p 375–16 All unscientific mental practice is . . . *p·*,
377–31 is of itself *p·* to produce suffering.
ap 567–23 and so proved to be *p·*.

Powerlessness

m	65–17	the *p·* of vows to make home happy,
r	490–10	From this also comes its *p·*,

Powers

broadcast
m	65–13	broadcast *p·* of evil so conspicuous to-day

divine
f	249– 9	the divine "*p·* that be."— *Rom.* 13 : 1.

God-given
p	387–10	nor . . . trespass upon God-given *p·*

imaginary
p	403–19	deprived of its imaginary *p·* by Truth,

lower
s	144– 4	needs no cooperation from lower *p·*,

mental
an	105–22	Whoever uses his developed mental *p·*
s	128– 9	C. S. enhances their endurance and mental *p·*,

no antagonistic
f	231–14	but there are no antagonistic *p·* nor laws,

not two
b	270– 9	but one power, — not two *p·*,

of this world
f	225– 8	The *p·* of this world will fight,

other
ph	169–30	Whatever teaches man . . . to acknowledge other *p·*
r	485–25	If thought yields its dominion to other *p·*,

so-called
s	144– 5	even if these so-called *p·* are real.
b	275–29	other gods, or other so-called *p·*,

sp	92–28	This belief tends to support two opposite *p·*,
s	142– 7	generally omit all but one of these *p·*,
f	204– 8	false conclusions . . . two *p·*, — namely,
	204–16	the first and second antagonistic *p·*,
o	357–26	If . . . there must be two *p·*,

Practical

pr	11–26	in the only *p·* road to holiness.
a	19–23	the *p·* repentance, which reforms the heart
	24–27	the *p·* affection and goodness
	31–15	It is the living Christ, the *p·* Truth,
	37–21	the more *p·* import of that career !
sp	98–17	a revealed and *p·* Science.
	98–28, 29	*p·* and complete ; and being *p·* and complete,
s	111–31	the broadest *p·* tests.
	147– 8	submitted to the broadest *p·* test,
f	224–22	A higher and more *p·* Christianity,
	254–21	to abandon so fast as *p·* the material,
o	341– 4	from a theoretical to a *p·* Christianity.
	345–19	and this *p·* proof is the only feasible evidence
	351–16	the *p·* proof of Christianity,
	355– 5	is met by something *p·*,
p	410–13	mankind objects to making this teaching *p·*.
t	452– 4	Incorrect reasoning leads to *p·* error.

Practically

s	122– 8	was *p·* exposed nineteen hundred years ago
	146–21	effects *p·* prove its divine origin and efficacy.
	150–24	the *p·* rejected doctrine of the predestination
f	232–11	but our prevalent theories *p·* deny this,
b	283–25	cannot be *p·* demonstrated . . . unless
	328–19	can it be said that they explain it *p·*,
o	356– 9	Jesus reasoned on this subject *p·*,
	360–18	If you try to have two models, then you *p·* have none.

Practice, Christian Science

r	493–13	a previous chapter entitled C. S. *P·*.

Practice

basis of
t	456–21	So long as matter is the basis of *p·*,

by his
f	232–22	nor did he illustrate these errors by his *p·*.

Christian scientific
p	410–29	Christian scientific *p·* begins with

contradict the
p	202–25	beliefs . . . contradict the *p·* growing out of

experience in
t	461–32	spiritual growth and experience in *p·*

guidance in
s	164– 8	none can be adopted as a safe guidance in *p·*."

its
pref	x–24	its *p·* is safer and more potent than that of any

made void their
s	145– 7	would have made void their *p·*.

medical
    (see **medical**)

mental
    (see **mental**)

metaphysical
s	144–17	is not the metaphysical *p·* of C. S.,
p	424–15	It is equally important in metaphysical *p·*
t	460– 5	it underlies all metaphysical *p·*.

practice

of Christian Science
s	144–17	is not the metaphysical *p·* of C. S.,
o	355–24	the divine Principle and *p·* of C. S.
p	442–17	Neither . . . enters into the *p·* of C. S.,

of divine metaphysics
s	111–12	the *p·* of divine metaphysics is the

of magnetism
an	101– 2	observed in the public *p·* of magnetism,

of medicine
s	161–12	law, restricting the *p·* of medicine.

of sin
a	39–31	Who will stop the *p·* of sin so long as

of Truth
a	26–22	Jesus' teaching and *p·* of Truth
p	410–24	does not appear in the *p·* of Truth

Principle and
pref	ix–14	the Principle and *p·* of Christian healing,
a	53–10	the divine Principle and *p·* of Jesus
o	355–24	the divine Principle and *p·* of C. S.

put into
b	323–13	we must put into *p·* what we already know.

reduce to
r	490–17	reduce to *p·* the real man's divine Principle,

right
t	454–17	the wrong as well as the right *p·*.

Science in
s	162–17	Working out the rules of Science in *p·*,

such a
t	452–26	Such a *p·* does not demonstrate the

teaching and
a	26–22	Jesus' teaching and *p·* of Truth
r	473–19	the teaching and *p·* of Christianity,

teachings and
a	19–26	the teachings and *p·* of our Master

theory and
t	456–16	Any dishonesty in your theory and *p·*

theory and in
f	229–19	mistaken in theory and in *p·*.

the student's
p	411– 3	My first discovery in the student's *p·*

without
f	241–18	The error of the ages is preaching without *p·*.

pr	15–22	in so far as we put our desires into *p·*.
	15–28	*P·* not profession, understanding not belief,
a	26–20	to show the learner the way by *p·* as well as
t	458– 7	This theory is supposed to favor *p·* from
ap	561– 3	destroys both faith in evil and the *p·* of

practices

a	18–11	against Pharisaical creeds and *p·*,
s	141– 9	even the most cherished beliefs and *p·*,
r	484–27	involved in all false theories and *p·*.

practise

a	41–30	demanded more than they were willing to *p·*.
sp	98–21	for every man to understand and to *p·*.
an	101–24	its effects upon those who *p·* it,
f	253–18	If you believe in and *p·* wrong knowingly,
b	271–28	to learn and to *p·* Christian healing.
p	365–22	then he is Christian enough to *p·* scientifically
	431–29	testifies : . . . I *p·* daily ablutions
t	446–13	can *p·* on no one from . . . motives without
	449–13	You should *p·* well what you know,
	452–30	the inclination or power to *p·* wrongly
	453–32	nor can he *p·* animal magnetism
	457–26	They even *p·* these, intending
	462– 9	to *p·* Truth's teachings only in part,

practised

a	24– 2	Truth and Love understood and *p·*.
	26–30	which he taught and *p·*.
s	147–12	Jesus *p·* these rules on the hills of Judæa
	147–24	healed the sick, *p·* Christian healing,
ph	174–21	Truth is revealed. It needs only to be *p·*.
f	201– 1	The best sermon ever preached is Truth *p·*
o	344–23	the C. S. which Jesus preached and *p·*
t	451–29	and it is *p·* either with a mistaken or a wicked

practises

t	446–11	Whoever *p·* the Science the author teaches,
	449–30	if the student *p·* what he is taught,

practising

o	342–29	If Christian Scientists were teaching or *p·*
t	456– 3	Teaching or *p·* in the name of Truth,

practitioner

sp	79–23	The unscientific *p·* says : "You are ill.
s	161–24	ordinary *p·*, examining bodily symptoms,
ph	176–22	Should . . . disease be treated by a regular *p·*,
p	365–30	The unchristian *p·* is not giving
	403–28	*p·* improves or injures the case in proportion
t	459–20	a false *p·* will work mischief,

practitioner's

p	410–28	until the *p·* healing ability is

practitioners

praise

praised

pray

prayed

Prayer, the Lord's

prayer
acceptable
audible
child at
consistent
desire is
governed by Science
healing
heart of
highest
Jesus'
loftiness of his
motives for
of faith
of fervent desire
of Soul
of the righteous
of the unrighteous
one brief
our
public
silent

prayer
such
test of all
their
unceasing
understanding of
verbal
wordy

prayerful

prayers
are mental
audible
constant
her own
humble
in which
long
our
their

prayest

praying

praying-machine

preach

preached

a 27– 6 to the poor the gospel is *p·*."— *Luke* 7 : 22.
55– 9 Now that the gospel of healing is again *p·*
s 107– * *the gospel which was p· of me*— *Gal.* 1 : 11.
132– 8 the poor have the gospel *p·* to them.—*Matt.* 11 : 5.
141– 2 and the truth *p·* by Jesus.
f 201– 1 The best sermon ever *p·* is Truth practised
o 344–23 the C. S. which Jesus *p·* and practised
345– 7 When the omnipotence of God is *p·*

preacher

s 132–30 This righteous *p·* once pointed his disciples to
136–26 doubted if Jesus was controlled by the sainted *p·*.
b 271–32 "How shall they hear without a *p·*?— *Rom.* 10 : 14.

preaches

a 33–25 and *p·* the gospel to the poor,

preaching

a 23–14 This *p·* receives a strong rebuke in the
31– 1 In meekness and might, he was found *p·*
f 241–17 The error of the ages is *p·* without practice.
b 324–24 healing the sick and *p·* Christianity
324–28 "If . . . then is our *p·* vain."— *I Cor.* 15 . 14.
o 347–16 *p·* the gospel to the poor, healing the sick,

precede

pr 16– 1 A great sacrifice of material things must *p·*
f 252– 9 must *p·* that understanding of Truth which
g 553– 5 must *p·* an understanding of the harmony of

preceded

g 543–21 thinking that apehood *p·* mortal manhood?

precedence

sp 83–20 and gives to matter the *p·* over Spirit.

precedent

m 63–14 C. S. furnishes no *p·* for such injustice,
sp 72– 7 A condition *p·* to communion with Spirit
an 105– 7 would be to contradict *p·* and to admit
s 138–17 Jesus established in the Christian era the *p·*

precedes

sp 96–11 "The darkest hour *p·* the dawn."
g 530–30 narrative supposes . . . that matter *p·* mind.
553–32 which *p·* the development of that belief.

preceding

g 522–28 for the Scripture just *p·* declares

precept

a 26–21 by practice as well as *p·*.
f 234–29 was to break a moral *p·*.
o 344–17 would be just to observe the Scriptural *p·*,
354–18 is seen in example more than in *p·*.
p 382–10 a useful rebuke from Jesus' *p·*,
t 443–21 may learn the value of the apostolic *p·* :
r 465– * *For p· must be upon p·, p· upon p·;* — *Isa.* 28 : 10.

precepts

a 31–17 Obeying his precious *p·*,
s 141– 5 Jesus' divine *p·* for living and healing.
141– 6 Because his *p·* require the disciple to
b 276– 4 When the divine *p·* are understood,

precincts

a 44– 5 The lonely *p·* of the tomb

precious

a 22– 9 through Christ's *p·* love these efforts are
26–24 *p·* import of our Master's sinless career
31–17 Obeying his *p·* precepts,
m 66– 5 Wears yet a *p·* jewel in his head.
66–32 that the *p·* metal may be graven with the

precipice

p 374–22 walking in darkness on the edge of a *p·*.

precipitate

b 324– 4 helps to *p·* the ultimate harmony.
p 436–19 Fear, the sheriff, to *p·* the result

precipitately

m 66–23 for a wife *p·* to leave her husband

precipitates

m 67–16 *p·* his doom or sunshine gladdens the

precise

c 256–16 *p·* form of God must be of small importance
b 270–17 knew not what would be the *p·* nature of

precisely

a 19–13 declaring *p·* what would destroy sickness,
o 354– 8 when it teaches *p·* this thought

preclude

a 36–16 *p·* C. S. from finding favor with the

precludes

r 487–15 this *p·* the need of believing.

preconceptions

s 129–10 be it in accord with your *p·* or

predecessors

f 239– 2 The sects, which endured the lash of their *p·*,

predestination

a 24–18 in regard to *p·* and future punishment.
s 150–25 the practically rejected doctrine of the *p·* of

predicated

s 144– 9 physiology, hygiene, are mainly *p·* of matter,

predicting

sp 84– 5 *p·* the future from a groundwork of
s 149–27 *p·* disease does not dignify therapeutics.

prediction

a 54–28 and history has confirmed the *p·*.
g 532– 9 the *p·* in the story under consideration.

predisposed

p 389– 6 the less we are *p·* to sickness.

predisposing

ph 178–11 *p·* cause and the exciting cause are mental.
f 230–31 remote, *p·*, and the exciting cause
p 393– 6 *p·*, remote, and exciting cause

predisposition

f 220– 2 in order to overcome a *p·* to take cold ;

predominate

c 262–20 supposed pain and pleasure of matter cease to *p·*,
g 502– 5 as if reality did not *p·* over unreality,

pre-eminently

a 42–11 endorsed *p·* by the approval of God,
m 66–26 the other *p·* needs good company.
an 102–32 *p·* promotes affection and virtue in families
s 123–32 On the contrary, C. S. is *p·* scientific,

preens

c 261–29 and *p·* its wings for a skyward flight.

preferable

an 101–29 Discomfort under error is *p·* to comfort.

preference

s 160–25 If muscles can . . . become rigid of their own *p·*,
ph 179–12 *p·* of mortal mind for a certain method

prefigured

ap 559–29 *p·* this perilous passage out of bondage

prefigures

ap 558–10 This angel . . . *p·* divine Science.

prejudice

s 144–25 Ignorance, pride, or *p·* closes the door to
r 484– 3 neither pride, *p·*, bigotry, nor envy can

preliminary

t 449–26 They are enemies without the *p·* offence.
r 484–29 is material sense a necessary *p·*

prelude

sp 90–14 some insist that death is the necessary *p·* to
g 502– 2 the living and real *p·* of the older Scriptures

premise

s 129– 6 can tolerate no error in *p·* or conclusion.
130–13 from this *p·* it follows that good and its
ph 167–17 an error in the *p·* must appear in the conclusion.
191–26 and from this *p·* infers the
b 277–27 error in the *p·* leads to errors in the conclusion

premises

sp 84– 2 coordinate neither with the *p·* nor
98–15 Beyond the frail *p·* of human beliefs,
s 164–13 human systems based on material *p·*
ph 184– 2 The *p·* being erroneous,
b 269–12 does not enter into metaphysical *p·* or
274–11 not mere inferences drawn from material *p·*.
312–23 theories are based on finite *p·*,
338–10 error has been engrafted into the *p·*

preparation

pref xii–16 given to the *p·* of the revision of
gl 596–18 the only fit *p·* for admission to the presence

preparatory

r 486– 9 Earth's *p·* school must be improved

prepare

a 39–20 not that now men must *p·* for a
f 208–21 and *p·* for the reign of Spirit,
p 433–28 is sent for to *p·* the frightened sense

prepared

m 61–11 that the highway of our God may be *p·*
s 152–22 *p·* her thought for the metaphysics of C. S.
b 322–12 finite belief may be *p·* to relinquish its error.
333–22 to all *p·* to receive Christ, Truth.
p 388–20 If food was *p·* by Jesus for his disciples,
414–17 not until your patients are *p·* for the
ap 565–30 where she hath a place *p·* of God. — *Rev.* 12 : 6.
566– 8 up to the glory *p·* for them who love God.

prepares

o 361–28 until God *p·* the soil for the seed.

prepareth

ap 578–13 [LOVE] *p·* a table before me— *see Psal.* 23 : 5.

preparing

s 107– 4 God had been graciously *p·* me
f 208–20 and *p·* the way of Science.
p 365– 5 and *p·* their helpers for the "midnight call,"

preponderance

s	143–20	you conclude that . . . hold the *p·* of power.
ph	168– 5	removal . . . from either scale gives *p·* to the
	177–22	hold the *p·* of power in any direction
g	502– 4	the *p·* of unreality in the entire narrative,

prerogative

sp	84–11	the *p·* of the ever-present, divine Mind,
s	123– 8	the power and *p·* of Spirit,
f	253–16	your *p·* to overcome the belief in sin,
g	530–10	presuming not on the *p·* of his creator,

prerogatives

g	513– 2	for the claim usurps the deific *p·*
	549–30	to usurp the *p·* of omnipotence.

prescribed

s	148– 4	He *p·* no drugs, urged no obedience to
	156– 8	*p·* the fourth attenuation of *Argentum nitratum*
	156–13	former physician had *p·* these remedies,
p	424–14	to counteract the working of a remedy *p·* by

prescribes

ph	198–19	*p·* drugs, until the elasticity of
p	399– 6	Mortal mind *p·* the drug,

prescription

s	149– 7	The *p·* which succeeds in one instance
	158– 5	He was supposed to have dictated the first *p·*,
ph	166–10	The popular doctor believes in his *p·*,

prescriptions

s	158–21	to victimize the race with intoxicating *p·*
ph	175– 4	When there are fewer *p·*,

presence

all

b	275–23	all power, all *p·*, all Science.

and power

g	512– 8	symbolized by strength, *p·*, and power,
gl	596–18	the *p·* and power of the Most High.

beatific

c	266–28	he reflects the beatific *p·*, illuming the universe

calm in the

p	366–27	Christian Scientist will be calm in the *p·* of

divine

pr	12– 4	no power to gain more of the divine *p·* than

His

ph	174–11	but the angels of His *p·* . . . are our guardians
g	512–10	These angels of His *p·*, which have the
	543–11	They cannot come into His *p·*,
ap	567– 6	The Gabriel of His *p·* has no contests.

human

b	325–28	which ushered Jesus into human *p·*,

imposing

p	441– 1	with benign and imposing *p·*,

joy of its

ph	175–11	The joy of its *p·*, its beauty and fragrance,

of Christ

o	351–14	the living, palpitating *p·* of Christ,

of divine Justice

p	437– 9	in the *p·* of divine Justice,

of God

g	543– 9	shut out from the *p·* of God.

of health

p	412–24	Realize the *p·* of health and

of his

a	50–11	withhold a clear token of his *p·*

of Life

b	304– 1	the sweet sense and *p·* of Life and Truth.
r	470– 8	assumed . . . the loss of the spiritual *p·* of Life

of mine enemies

ap	578–13	in the *p·* of mine enemies :— *Psal* 23 : 5.

of mistrust

m	68– 9	The *p·* of mistrust, where confidence is due,

of the Lord

s	135– 5	at the *p·* of the Lord,— *Psal.* 114 : 7.
g	542–27	went out from the *p·* of the Lord— *Gen.* 4 : 16.

of the reality

b	293– 1	mortality disappears in *p·* of the reality.

power and

g	519–13	the divine power and *p·* which go with it,

power nor

r	471–19	and there is no other power nor *p·*.

reproduce the

sp	75–23	to reproduce the *p·* of those who

a	48–25	Pale in the *p·* of his
s	135– 6	at the *p·* of the God of Jacob."— *Psal.* 114 : 7.
p	432–23	and that my *p·* was required to
	440–25	In the *p·* of the Supreme Lawgiver,

present (noun)

sp	84–13	the past, the *p·*, and the future.
f	224– 5	disappear from the dissolving paths of the *p·*,

present (adj.)

pr	13– 1	"a very *p·* help in trouble."— *Psal.* 46 : 1.
	14– 4	"*p·* with the Lord"— *II Cor.* 5 : 8.
	14– 6	"*p·* with the Lord"— *II Cor.* 5 : 8.
	14–22	and *p·* with Truth and Love.
a	22–16	If . . . you receive no *p·* reward, go not back to

present (adj.)

m	60–20	in a majority of cases, is not its *p·* tendency,
	65– 3	May Christ, Truth, be *p·* at every bridal altar
	65–26	must lose its *p·* slippery footing,
sp	72–23	suppositional opposite of good, is never *p·*.
	82– 3	as easily as we do of one *p·*.
	82– 4	no more difficult . . . than it is to read the *p·*.
	87– 7	to be individually and consciously *p·*.
	88– 6	may even be cognizant of a *p·* flavor
	95– 5	would be to-day if Jesus were personally *p·*.
an	102–21	So secret are the *p·* methods of
s	123–24	The proof, by *p·* demonstration, that the
	139–11	but the *p·* new, yet old, reform
	147– 4	its *p·* application to the cure of disease.
ph	171–26	beliefs that intelligence and life are *p·*
	178–10	connection of past mortal thoughts with *p·*.
	179– 6	absent from their healers, as well as those *p·*,
f	202–28	"a very *p·* help in trouble ;"— *Psal.* 46 : 1.
	216–30	and to be *p·* with the Lord."— *II Cor.* 5 : 8.
	228–17	Dropping their *p·* beliefs, they will recognize
	234–21	The *p·* codes of human systems disappoint the
b	304– 6	things *p·*, nor things to come,— *Rom.* 8 : 38.
o	348–32	If such are the *p·* fruits, what will the
	349– 4	so the rabbis of the *p·* day ask concerning
	351–13	this spiritual sense was a *p·* *help*.
	356–17	neither a *p·* nor an eternal copartnership
	361– 9	God is come and is *p·* now and forever.
p	383–10	*p·* with the Lord."— *II Cor.* 5 : 8.
	388–27	foolish to venture beyond our *p·* understanding
	392–27	When the condition is *p·* which you say induce
	407–25	Let the perfect model be *p·* in your thoughts
	410– 5	a *p·* knowledge of his Father and of himself,
	426–25	far beyond the *p·* elevation,
	430–29	testifies . . . I was *p·* on certain nights when
	432–25	Materia Medica, was *p·* when I arrived,
t	444–12	a very *p·* help in trouble."— *Psal.* 46 : 1.
r	473– 9	nothing apart from Him is *p·* or has power.
ap	560– 5	has reference to *p·* age.
	570– 4	The *p·* apathy as to the tendency of
	573–25	in this *p·* state of existence,
	574– 2	This . . . is therefore a *p·* possibility.
	577–28	The writer's *p·* feeble sense of C. S.
gl	581–26	and to be *p·* with the Lord."— *II Cor.* 5 : 8.

present at—

m	63–24	rational means of improvement at *p·*
	68– 2	At *p·* mortals progress slowly
sp	90–30	At *p·* we know not what man is,
s	134–32	This fact at *p·* seems more mysterious than
f	240–21	If at *p·* satisfied with wrong-doing,
	240–22	If at *p·* content with idleness, we must

present ever —

pref	xi–17	ever *p·* in human consciousness
sp	72–21	God, good, being ever *p·*, it follows
b	300–11	through the realization of God as ever *p·*
	306–28	the universe, ever *p·* and eternal.
r	470– 9	assumed . . . the loss of Love as ever *p·*
	471–18	God is infinite, therefore ever *p·*

present (verb)

pref	xi– 2	*p·* only a phase of the action of the
a	30–17	Not so did Jesus, . . . *p·* the divine law
ph	170– 8	Christian ideas certainly *p·* what human
	172–29	unfortunate cripple may *p·* more nobility tha
c	256–29	Finiteness cannot *p·* the idea or the vastness o
	267–20	*p·* more than is detected upon the surface,
b	325–31	"*P·* your bodies a living sacrifice,— *Rom.* 12 :
o	358–12	and could not *p·* its proofs.
p	430–13	I here *p·* to my readers an allegory
g	511–26	Animals and mortals metaphorically *p·* the
	546–31	If mathematics should *p·* a thousand
	555–31	Jesus was able to *p·* himself unchanged

presentation

a	24–24	only for the *p·*, after death, of

presented

a	25–16	Jesus *p·* the ideal of God better than
	45–29	He *p·* the same body that he had before his
	54–14	he *p·* the proof that Life, Truth, and Love he
s	118–18	*p·* as three measures of meal,
c	259–10	thoughts which *p·* man as fallen,
b	305–20	The inverted images *p·* by the senses,
	314–21	and he *p·* to her, . . . the true idea
	315–16	God's spiritual idea as *p·* by Christ Jesus.
	315–25	and *p·* an illustration of creation.
	316–24	The spiritual idea of God, as *p·* by Jesus,
	317–21	Our Lord and Master *p·* himself to his
o	344–21	only one which should be *p·* to the whole worl
r	473–13	has *p·* Christ, the true idea of God,
g	509– 7	*p·* to them the certain sense of eternal Life.
	521–24	*p·* in the verses already considered,
	529–26	evil, by whatever figure *p·*, contradicts itself
	534–15	idea of divine power, which Jesus *p·*,
ap	560–28	hid from them the true idea which has been *p·*
	562– 3	Elias *p·* the idea of the fatherhood of

presenting
r 491–19   sometimes *p·* no appearance of mind,
g 523– 6   *p·* the exact opposite of Truth,

presently
s 155– 1   *P·* the child forgets all about the accident,
ph 182–13   If we attempt it, we shall *p·*
190–11   so-called senses, which *p·* measure mind by
f 237– 5   Bounding off . . . she *p·* added,
b 321–23   *p·* restored his hand to its natural condition
p 416– 4   the belief of pain will *p·* return, unless
g 524–27   for God *p·* curses the ground.

presents
a 55–11   *p·* the Saviour in a clearer light
m 67–29   *p·* the true likeness or spiritual ideal.
68–27   C. S. *p·* unfoldment, not accretion ;
sp 87–14   for it *p·* primal facts to mortal mind.
s 145–22   mystery which godliness always *p·* to the
b 276–14   and *p·* them as beautiful and immortal.
277–13   Natural history *p·* vegetables and
301–27   *p·* an inverted image of Mind and substance
302–28   body *p·* no proper likeness of divinity,
316–20   Christ *p·* the indestructible man,
o 358–11   and sustains logically . . . every point it *p·*.
358–15   It *p·* the calm and clear verdict of Truth
p 375–32   *p·* to mortal thought a hopeless state,
423–18   according to the evidence which matter *p·*.
g 503–20   Immortal and divine Mind *p·* the idea of God :
ap 577– 5   The Lamb's wife *p·* the unity of

preserve
p 374–19   incapacity to *p·* your own existence,
r 494– 8   needed no help . . . to *p·* the eternal harmony

preserved
f 245–18   This instance of youth *p·* furnishes a
b 277–17   the order of genus and species is *p·*

preserves
p 383–22   tells you that the weed *p·* his health,
g 550– 6   which forms and *p·* the individuality

preserving
b 277–14   as *p·* their original species,

President
(*see* **Eddy, Mrs. Mary Baker**)

press
s 141–30   Let it have fair representation by the *p·*.
ph 196–31   The *p·* unwittingly sends forth many sorrows
f 224–20   opposition from church, state laws, and the *p·*,
o 343–30   to *p·* along the line of gospel-healing,

pressed
f 226–31   but I *p·* on through faith in God,

pressure
t 451– 3   constant *p·* of the apostolic command

prestige
f 244–32   of development, power, and *p·*.

presuming
g 530– 9   *p·* not on the prerogative of his creator,

presumptuously
o 342– 8   He that decries this Science does it *p·*,

presuppose
s 119– 6   They either *p·* the self-evolution and
ph 182–31   is to *p·* that omnipotent power is powerless
194–15   would *p·* man, . . . a mortal in material belief.
f 207–25   which *p·* the absence of Truth,
b 319–15   doctrines and theories which *p·*

presupposes
sp 71–30   Spiritualism therefore *p·* Spirit, . . . to be
ph 186–13   because it *p·* the absence of God,
b 281– 7   Error *p·* man to be both mind and
301–30   This falsity *p·* soul to be
r 480–15   its action is erroneous and *p·* man to be

pretence
ph 186– 8   under whatever name or *p·* they are employed ;
ap 567–25   in his *p·* of being a talker,

pretensions
an 103–22   mortal mind, whose flimsy and gaudy *p·*,
ph 186–19   This falsehood should strip evil of all *p·*.

preternatural
s 134–23   not because this Science is . . . *p·*,

prevail
s 138– 1   shall not *p·* against it."— *Matt.* 16 : 18.
ap 567–10   Truth and Love *p·* against the dragon

prevailed
b 308–31   "as a prince" had he *p·*— *Gen.* 32 : 28.
ap 566–27   dragon fought, . . . and *p·* not ;— *Rev.* 12 : 7, 8.

prevailing
ph 185–13   as material as the *p·* systems of medicine.

prevails
b 311–24   law of Soul, which *p·* over material sense
ap 567– 5   spiritual strength wrestles and *p·*

prevalent
sp 94–13   the misconceptions of Deity there *p·*.
f 232–10   our *p·* theories practically deny this,
283–13   But what say *p·* theories?
p 389–18   as *p·* theories maintain,

prevent
pr 13–21   this will *p·* us from relinquishing the
an 105– 4   to *p·* deeds of violence or to punish them.
ph 170–18   If there are material laws which *p·* disease,
174–32   We should *p·* the images of disease from
198–12   to *p·* disease from forming in mortal mind
f 237–18   To *p·* the experience of error and its sufferings,
b 329–16   Until one is able to *p·* bad results, he should
o 341–14   cannot *p·* that from being scientific which
p 368–18   then no material suppositions can *p·* us from
380–20   Nothing but the power of Truth can *p·* the
391–12   you can *p·* the development of pain
395–31   would *p·* the brain from becoming diseased,
400–14   and you *p·* the development of disease.
412–16   To *p·* disease or to cure it,
424–28   To *p·* or to cure scrofula and other so-called
431–14   summoned. . . . Hypnotism to *p·* his punishment.
436–17   to *p·* his committing liver-complaint,
436–19   result which they were called to *p·*.
t 446–30   Covering iniquity will *p·* prosperity
457–11   to *p·* suffering, not to produce it.

prevented
sp 82–24   Communion . . . would be *p·* by this difference.
s 154–21   the very results which might have been *p·*

preventing
s 147–28   he left no definite rule for . . . *p·* disease.

prevention
p 401–32   reconstruction and to the *p·* of inflammation.

preventive
p 369–23   (that is, the *p·* and curative) arts

prevents
ph 182–19   Obedience to material law *p·* full obedience to
p 372–30   *p·* the honest recognition of benefits received,
394–11   *p·* him from helping himself,
p 409–14   the error which *p·* mortals from

previous
sp 75–27   that is the moment *p·* to the transition,
p 434–12   were at the *p·* Court of Error,
r 493–12   is touched upon in a *p·* chapter
g 526– 3   The *p·* and more scientific record

previously
g 544–19   The facts of creation, as *p·* recorded,

preying
gl 583–28   one belief *p·* upon another.

price
pr 10–21   has paid for . . . prayer the *p·* of persecution.
a 36–15   The earthly *p·* of spirituality in a material age
47–12   The traitor's *p·* was thirty pieces of silver
s 108– 9   "the *p·* of learning love,"
ph 197– 7   What a *p·* for human knowledge !
197– 7   But the *p·* does not exceed the original cost.

priceless
p 366– 1   a *p·* sense of the dear Father's loving-kindness.

pride
and fear
a 31– 1   *P·* and fear are unfit to bear the standard of
and fustian
s 142–16   tell their story to *p·* and fustian.
display, and
m 60–23   personal adornment, display, and *p·*,
humbled the
f 228–30   It should have humbled the *p·* of the priests,
of power
t 451– 5   must renounce . . . oppression and the *p·* of power.
gl 589–13   the *p·* of power and the power of pride ;
of priesthood
b 270–22   The *p·* of priesthood is the prince of this world.
or prejudice
s 144–25   Ignorance, *p·*, or prejudice closes the
power of
gl 589–14   the pride of power and the power of *p·* ;
rebuked
a 35– 2   hearts chastened and *p·* rebuked.
tyranny and
s 142–18   tyranny and *p·* need to be whipped out of the

—————

a 51–25   *p·*, envy, cruelty, and vengeance,
m 64– 8   *P·*, envy, or jealousy seems on most occasions
68– 4   They are slaves to fashion, *p·*, and sense.
s 115–22   *p·*, envy, deceit, hatred, revenge,
p 372–29   If *p·*, superstition, or any error prevents
t 445–22   Self-seeking, envy, passion, *p·*, hatred,
r 484– 3   When this is accomplished, neither *p·*, prejudice,
gl 582– 6   *p·* ; envy ; fame ; illusion ; a false belief ;

priest

a	20– 6	ritualistic *p·* and hypocritical Pharisee
	30–14	Rabbi and *p·* taught the Mosaic law,
	42– 2	*p·* and rabbi affirmed God to be a
s	141–19	Its only *p·* is the spiritualized man.

priestess

t	454–21	Love is *p·* at the altar of Truth.

priesthood

b	270–22	The pride of *p·* is the prince of this world.

priests

a	49–26	*p·* and rabbis, before whom he had
s	141–21	"kings and *p·* unto God." — *Rev.* 1 : 6.
	158– 2	originated in idolatry with pagan *p·*,
f	228–30	It should have humbled the pride of the *p·*,

primal

sp	87–15	it presents *p·* facts to mortal mind.
	90– 2	how then can we account for their *p·* origin?
s	135– 7	unfolds the *p·* order,
f	207–20	There is but one *p·* cause.
r	469– 9	It is the *p·* and eternal quality of
ap	559–26	*p·* elements, of Truth and Love,
	568–30	Love sends forth her *p·* and everlasting strain.

primarily

s	148–19	the one wholly, the other *p·*
	150–12	is not *p·* one of physical healing.
g	512–23	these are mental, both *p·* and secondarily.
	543–19	who shall say that he is not *p·* dust?

primary

f	207–12	nor are the so-called laws of matter *p·*,
	245–29	the *p·* of that illustration makes it plain
g	525–10	the *p·* sense being *image, form ;*

prime

t	457–10	Her *p·* object, since entering this field

primeval

s	110– 4	These eternal verities reveal *p·* existence as
g	553–28	from dust or from the rib of our *p·* father.
ap	565–23	stars sang together and all was *p·* harmony,

primitive

m	63– 9	Spirit is his *p·* and ultimate source of being ;
	64– 9	ruling out *p·* Christianity.
s	109–18	cures were produced in *p·* Christian healing
	128– 2	Good is natural and *p·*.
ph	176– 7	*p·* custom of taking no thought about food
f	214– 3	they came as sound to the *p·* prophets.
	244–17	that he returns eventually to his *p·* condition ;
b	292–13	Matter is the *p·* belief of mortal mind,
o	356–22	create the *p·*, and then punish its derivative?
p	374–28	resolved into its *p·* mortal elements.
	399–20	continuation of, the *p·* mortal mind.

prince

b	270–22	The pride of priesthood is the *p·* of this world.
	308–30	"as a *p·*'" had he prevailed — *Gen.* 32 : 28.
	309–11	Israel, — a *p·* of God, or a soldier of God,

Prince of Peace

a	52–14	concerning the coming *P· of P·*.

principal

p	436– 1	*p·* witness (the officer of the Health-laws)
	436–35	One of the *p·* witnesses, Nerve, testified

Principle

and idea
(*see* **idea**)

and its idea

r	465–17	*P·* and its idea is one,
	475– 4	all is Spirit, divine *P·* and its idea.
g	520– 9	*P·* and its idea, man, are coexistent

and practice

pref	ix–14	the *P·* and practice of Christian healing,
o	355–24	misapprehension both of the divine *P·* and practice

and proof

f	210– 5	*P·* and proof of Christianity are discerned

and rule

r	493–15	prove for himself the *P·* and rule of C. S.

an understood

r	487–30	This faith relies upon an understood *P·*.

apodictical

s	107– 7	This apodictical *P·* points to the revelation of

cause or

c	262–31	Divine Mind is the only cause or *P·* of existence.

contradict its

f	232–14	religions which contradict its *P·* are false.

creative

g	502–27	The creative *P·* — Life, Truth, and Love
	513–21	God who is the divinely creative *P·* thereof.

curative

s	157– 9	rests on Mind alone as the curative *P·*,

deathless

f	203–22	then mortals believe that the deathless *P·*,

demonstrable

g	546–29	it cures on a divine demonstrable *P·*

Principle

divine
(*see* **divine**)

entire

t	461– 7	part illustrates and proves the entire *P·*.

eternal

b	312–20	man's eternal *P·* is ever-present Life.
gl	579–11	faith in the divine Life and in the eternal *P·*
	592–16	divine and eternal *P·* ; Life, Truth, and Love.

factor in the

pref	x– 8	this mind is not a factor in the *P·* of C. S.

fixed

s	128–28	It rests on fixed *P·* and not upon the

glorious

p	382–26	but for the glorious *P·* you teach,
r	474–14	until the glorious *P·* of these marvels is gained.

God is the

s	112–32	God is the *P·* of divine metaphysics.
r	476– 9	God is the *P·* of man, and man is the idea of

good in

b	286–19	like Himself, — good in *P·* and in idea.

governed by its

ph	195–16	semblance of an idea governed by its *P·*,

healing

pr	12–12	the divine healing *P·* as manifested in Jesus,
b	312–29	away from the intelligent and divine healing *P·*

heals the sick

o	354–10	*P·* heals the sick and spiritualizes humanity.

holy

s	124– 8	nor holy *P·* of its own,

immortal

g	554– 4	God, who is its divine immortal *P·*.

infinite

sp	71– 8	the creative, governing, infinite *P·*
c	257–18	anthropomorphic God, instead of infinite *P·*,
	258–19	infinite *P·* is reflected by the infinite idea
b	300– 4	no true appreciation of infinite *P·*,
	302–25	infinite *P·*, called Person or God.
	337–22	as incomprehensible . . . as is man's infinite *P·*.
g	520– 8	no more seen . . . by mortals, than is his infinite *P·*.
	524–11	Did the divine and infinite *P·* become a
ap	577– 3	as the infinite *P·* and infinite idea,
gl	582–11	a gleam of the infinite idea of the infinite *P·* ;

inharmony has no

r	480–15	Inharmony has no *P·* ;

interprets the

ap	560–11	interprets the *P·* of heavenly harmony.

is absolute

b	283–11	*P·* is absolute.

is imperative

b	329–21	*P·* is imperative.

is infinite

b	328–32	Its *P·* is infinite, reaching beyond the

learning its

b	274–24	no half-way position in learning its *P·*

living

r	477–21	in multifarious forms of the living *P·*,

of all

s	109–17	*P·* of all harmonious Mind-action

of all happiness

c	261– 3	Truth and Love, the *P·* of all happiness,

of all science

s	124– 1	being based on Truth, the *P·* of all science.

of being

a	25–19	more spiritually than all others the *P·* of being.

of divine metaphysics

s	111–11	The *P·* of divine metaphysics is God ;
	112–32	God is the *P·* of divine metaphysics.

of healing

s	147–27	demonstrating this *P·* of healing
o	343– 2	teaching Truth as the *P·* of healing,

of man

s	123– 4	the true idea and *P·* of man will then appear.
r	476– 9	God is the *P·* of man, and man is the idea of

of man's harmony

ph	170– 9	the *P·* of man's harmony.

of Mind-healing

t	454–14	understands . . . the *P·* of Mind-healing,

of the cure

f	219–26	not comprehending the *P·* of the cure,

of the universe

b	272–28	divine *P·* of the universe must interpret
	276–23	from materiality to the *P·* of the universe,

one

s	112–17	comes one *P·* and its infinite idea,
t	456–11	affirms that there is more than one *P·*
	457–29	The Scientist's demonstration rests on one *P·*,
r	466– 6	indicate Mind, never matter, and have one *P·*
g	517–19	they all have one *P·* and parentage.
gl	588–15	though they are governed by one *P·*.

or its idea

c	258–21	no cognizance of either *P·* or its idea.

Principle

perfect
c 259–12 includes a perfect *P* and idea,
b 304–15 governed by God, his perfect *P*
r 470–29 his perfect *P*, the divine Mind.
470–30 If man ever existed without this perfect *P*
produced by its
b 304–16 Harmony is produced by its *P*,
proved the
s 149–15 not . . . proved the *P* of divine Science.
r 473–30 Jesus *proved* the *P*, which heals the
recognized
s 157– 4 its one recognized *P* of healing is Mind,
same
p 395–10 The same *P* cures both sin and sickness.
406– 4 Sin and sickness are both healed by the same *P*.
g 518–17 all having the same *P*, or Father;
saving
b 285–24 but not as the saving *P*, or divine Love,
start from
b 298–12 like numbers and notes, start from *P*,
this
s 123–28 The operation of this *P* indicates
141–17 For this *P* there is no dynasty,
147–27 demonstrating this *P* of healing
t 457–30 Let this *P* be applied to the cure of disease
r 487–31 This *P* makes whole the diseased,
ap 559–25 eat the divine body of this *P*,
triune
r 469–10 quality of infinite Mind, of the triune *P*,
unerring
g 522–32 Does the unerring *P* of divine law change
unity of
r 470– 4 and have unity of *P* and spiritual power
views of
f 239– 7 and we get clearer views of *P*.
was rejected
b 316–25 scourged in person, and its *P* was rejected.
without
r 487–22 Mere belief is blindness without *P*

a 26–23 makes us admit its *P* to be Love.
ph 192– 8 from corporeality instead of from *P*,
f 240–10 in which the *P* is above what it reflects,
b 279–31 seeks cause in effect, *P* in its idea,
281–22 and see that . . . have neither *P* nor
287– 2 They have neither *P* nor permanence,
290– 3 If the *P*, rule, and demonstration of
299–32 If . . . he would have no eternal *P*
302– 1 *P* is not to be found in fragmentary ideas.
303– 4 the *P* governing the reflection.
337– 8 man must harmonize with his *P*,
r 465–10 Spirit, Soul, *P*, Life,
465–16 Is there more than one God or *P*?
467–22 *P* is not in its idea.
474– 1 (the *P* of this unacknowledged Science)
492–27 the *P* of this Science is divine,
ap 561– 2 the *P* which works out the ends of
gl 581– 9 proved to be as immortal as its *P*;
583–23 matter and evil, which have no *P*;
587– 6 *P*; Mind; Soul; Spirit; Life; Truth;
593– 3 definition of

principle

pr 3– 5 Who would . . . pray the *p* of mathematics to
f 237–21 excluded on the same *p* as the
g 522–19 represented as the life-giving *p* of the earth.

principles

t 458– 3 doctrine that Science has two *p*

print

pref ix–21 it did not appear in *p* until 1876,

printers

p 387–14 If *p* and authors have the shortest span of

printing

ph 197– 1 by *p* long descriptions which

prints

r 486–14 Jesus proved by the *p* of the nails, that

prior

m 63– 8 nor does he pass through material conditions *p* to
s 125–10 the *p* states which human belief created
ph 178–13 deformity produced *p* to his birth
f 254–17 *p* to the change called death,
c 267–10 must have had children *p* to Adam.
b 310– 4 Did it exist *p* to thought?
p 436–15 *P* to the night of his arrest, the prisoner

priority

ph 178– 9 is not dangerous because of its *p*

prism

ap 558–13 When understood, it is Truth's *p* and praise.

27

prison

f 202–10 until disciplined by the *p* and the scaffold;
p 366–30 If we would open their *p* doors for the sick,
431–12 arrested Mortal Man . . . and cast him into *p*.
433–32 can open wide those *p* doors
441–15 nor can Disease cast him into *p*.
442–14 Mortal Man, no longer sick and in *p*,
r 495–12 opens the *p* doors to such as are bound,

prison-cell

g 516–18 glints from the church-dome, glances into the *p*,

prisoner

assist the
p 432–26 endeavoring to assist the *p* to escape from
attended to
p 431– 5 the *p* attended to his daily labors,
at the bar
p 432– 5 Mortal Man, the *p* at the bar,
434–22 The *p* at the bar has been unjustly sentenced.
grows restless
p 433–13 As the Judge proceeds, the *p* grows restless.
guilty
p 436–28 twelve Mortal Minds, to find the *p* guilty.
hypnotized the
p 431–23 Morbid Secretion hypnotized the *p*
is not guilty
p 434– 3 "Delay the execution; the *p* is not guilty."
is then remanded
p 433–27 The *p* is then remanded to his cell
manacling the
p 439–11 who was then manacling the *p*
regards the
p 434–16 regards the *p* with the utmost tenderness.
rescue the
p 436–24 His friends struggled hard to rescue the *p*
rose up
p 442– 8 Then the *p* rose up regenerated, strong, free.
should die
p 432–30 he decided at once that the *p* should die.
summoned
p 431–13 the *p* summoned Physiology, Materia Medica,
436–15 the *p* summoned two professed friends,
unfortunate
p 434–11 as counsel for the unfortunate *p*.
watched with
p 431– 3 the *p* watched with the sick every night
would commit
p 432– 7 testifies: . . . I knew the *p* would commit it,

p 430–30 the *p*, or patient, watched with a sick friend.
431– 5 the *p* gave him drink.
432–23 who protested that the *p* had abused him,
433–19 solemn sentence of death upon the *p*.
434–28 *p* is not proved "worthy of death, — *Acts* 23:29.
435–32 The only jurisdiction to which the *p* can submit
435–34 I ask that the *p* be restored
436– 7 the *p* on the night of the alleged offence

prisoner's

p 432–25 One of the *p* friends, Materia Medica,

prison-yard

p 434– 4 Consternation fills the *p*.

privations

a 49–10 his mighty works, his toils, *p*, sacrifices,

privilege

pr 10–21 has paid for the *p* of prayer
a 37–23 duty and *p* of every child, man, and woman,
f 236– 3 A special *p* is vested in the ministry.
p 428– 6 Man's *p* at this supreme moment is to prove

privileged

c 263– 2 believe themselves to be . . . *p* originators of
t 443–10 *p* to work out their own salvation

prize

s 111–19 A *p* of one hundred pounds, offered in
t 462–18 self-denial, sincerity, . . . win the *p*,

pro

s 120–25 Any conclusion *p* or *con*,
129– 9 be the fable *p* or *con*, —

probabilities

ph 171– 9 not needing to consult almanacs for the *p*

probable

p 413–29 making it *p* at any time that such ills may

probation

a 35–15 his *p* in the flesh after death,
35–16 its exemplification of human *p*,
b 291–12 salvation rests on progression and *p*,
291–24 until *p* and growth shall effect the

probationary

a 46–24 a *p* and progressive state beyond the grave.

probe

ph 193– 6 He even showed me the *p*,
t 462–26 to *p* the self-inflicted wounds of selfishness,

probed

ph 193– 5 had just *p* the ulcer on the hip,

probing

ph 184– 8 *p* the trouble to the bottom,

problem

in theology
a 23– 8 The atonement is a hard *p·* in theology,
mesmerism is a
an 102–25 "Mesmerism is a *p·* not lending itself to an
of being
a 44– 7 a place in which to solve the great *p·* of being.
f 217–21 you are working out the *p·* of being
254–14 demonstrating the great *p·* of being,
c 262– 1 in which to work out the *p·* of being.
b 273– 6 not one of them can solve the *p·* of being
314–26 The higher his . . . carried the *p·* of being,
g 556–27 before it cares to solve the *p·* of being,
of Euclid
b 329–18 attempts to solve a *p·* of Euclid,
of man
f 216– 6 unveils the mystery and solves the *p·* of man.
of Mind-healing
s 109–12 I sought the solution of this *p·* of Mind-healing,
of nothingness
s 126– 3 The *p·* of nothingness, or "dust to dust,"
rule of the
b 329–19 and denies the rule of the *p·*
to solve the
pr 3– 5 principle of mathematics to solve the *p·*?

proceed

m 65– 2 should *p·* from man's highest nature.
sp 88–15 Beliefs *p·* from the so-called material senses,
88–23 These effects, . . . do not *p·* from Christianity,
an 100– * *out of the heart p· evil thoughts,— Matt.* 15 : 19.
ph 189–22 They *p·* from the divine source ;
f 207–22 does not *p·* from this great and only cause.
c 256–28 a limitless Mind cannot *p·* from
260–22 Sickness, disease, and death *p·* from fear.
o 356–25 Does evil *p·* from good?
p 374–16 can destroy all ills which *p·* from mortal mind.
r 484–18 Certain results, supposed to *p·* from drugs,
g 529–10 both man and woman *p·* from God

proceeded

b 307– 2 the delusion that life and intelligence *p·*

proceedeth

p 410–11 every word that *p·* out of the—*Matt.* 4: 4.

proceeding

sp 88–12 Thoughts, *p·* from the brain or from matter,

proceedings

p 437–26 *p·* of a regularly constituted court.

proceeds

sp 88–31 When eloquence *p·* from the belief that a
s 127–24 all truth *p·* from the divine Mind.
f 239–25 If action *p·* from the divine Mind,
p 419–20 If the action *p·* from Truth,
433–13 As the Judge *p·*, the prisoner grows restless.
433–18 Judge Medicine then *p·* to pronounce the
r 471–28 all that *p·* from the divine Mind.
480–14 Harmonious action *p·* from Spirit, God.
g 543–17 All error *p·* from the evidence before the
gl 583–13 rests upon and *p·* from divine Principle.

process

by this
s 148–28 fails to give health or life by this *p·*,
calling the
p 422– 1 and then calling the *p·* mathematics.
false
p 390–15 false *p·* of mortal opinions which you name law,
is simple
t 459–25 the *p·* is simple and the results are sure if
mental
p 416–24 The sick know nothing of the mental *p·*
metaphysical
f 210–18 by one and the same metaphysical *p·*.
t 456–22 treated by the metaphysical *p·*.
of mental healing
t 459–15 Committing the bare *p·* of mental healing to
of weaning
b 322–30 Without this *p·* of weaning,
ordinary
g 548–31 besides the ordinary *p·* of generation,
reverse the
f 212–15 Reverse the *p·* ; take away this so-called mind
p 397–17 Now reverse the *p·*.
simple
b 321–24 restored his hand . . . by the same simple *p·*.

ph 168–32 By chemicalization I mean the *p·* which
f 251–24 This *p·* of higher spiritual understanding
p 398–31 Then we understand the *p·*.
413–13 the *p·* of taking a fish out of water every day
416– 2 This *p·* shows the pain to be in the mind,
439–10 where the liver-complaint was in *p·*,

processes

sp 89–19 not necessarily dependent upon educational *p·*.

proclaim

pref xi–22 When God called the author to *p·* His Gospel
b 327–24 to meet the wrong and to *p·* the right.
p 437–11 I *p·* this witness, Nerve, to be destitute of

proclaimed

b 317– 5 and *p·* an anthropomorphic God.

proclaiming

ph 174–19 *p·* the kingdom of heaven on earth.

proclaims

g 557–24 revealed religion *p·* the Science of Mind

proclamation

p 410–20 a definite and inspired *p·* of C. S.

procreate

s 140–30 but mortals would *p·* man,

procreation

f 205–14 the necessity for recreation or *p·*?

procured

a 37–18 Those who *p·* the martyrdom of that righteous

procurers

r 481–22 These human verdicts are the *p·* of all discord.

procures

f 220–13 *p·* a summer residence with more ease than

procuring

ph 171–27 the *p·* cause of all sin and disease.
p 411–20 The *p·* cause and foundation of all sickness

prodigal

ap 575–15 taught by the mustard-seed and the *p·*?

produce

pr 7– 9 But does it *p·* any lasting benefit?
m 58– 5 Ill-arranged notes *p·* discord.
62–30 and *p·* the ills of which we complain.
sp 86–11 Opposites . . . *p·* unlike results.
89–32 If seed is necessary to *p·* wheat,
90– 1 and wheat to *p·* flour,
an 102–22 and *p·* the very apathy on the subject which
s 148–23 to *p·* the concord and unity of Spirit
154–20 and they *p·* the very results which
161– 9 might *p·* spontaneous combustion.
ph 166– 2 human mind is all that can *p·* pain.
175–10 to say that a rose, . . . can *p·* suffering !
179–28 to move the bowels, or to *p·* sleep
183– 8 Can the agriculturist, . . . *p·* a crop without
190– 4 ignorant of what it is supposed to *p·*.
f 202–32 Common opinion . . . that this cold may *p·*
211– 4 If . . . *p·* sickness and health, good and evil,
211–15 does not this so-called mind *p·* the effect
212–18 They *p·* a rose through seed and soil,
212–22 mortals believe that unseen spirits *p·* the
230–17 God, good, can no more *p·* sickness than
230–20 Does a law of God *p·* sickness,
233–21 by overcoming the thoughts which *p·* them,
244– 1 He does not *p·* moral or physical deformity ;
c 257– 5 and shadow cannot *p·* substance.
259–30 that they may *p·* harmonious results.
b 304–13 good can never *p·* evil ;
304–13 matter can never *p·* mind nor
335–25 can *p·* nothing unlike the eternal
p 370–19 *p·* very direct and marked effects on the
377–18 watched that it may not *p·* blindly its bad
377–31 is of itself powerless to *p·* suffering.
385–30 opposite belief would *p·* the opposite result.
386– 8 to demand it and *p·* it.
386– 9 mortals declare that . . . *p·* catarrh, fever,
399– 3 You say that certain material combinations *p·*
401–23 could you *p·* any effect upon the brain or body
402–29 Science cannot *p·* both disorder and order.
404–12 the wicked motives which *p·* them.
408–22 would *p·* insanity as perceptibly as
413– 2 Mind, does not *p·* pain in matter.
413–10 *p·* good or bad effects on the
420– 8 cannot *p·* this unnatural reluctance.
t 457–12 to prevent suffering, not to *p·* it.
461–21 because of the different effects they *p·*.
r 486–20 yet supposes Mind unable to *p·* harmony !
g 522–30 Does Life, Truth, and Love *p·* death,
539– 9 if they *p·* their opposites,
544–14 nor does matter *p·* mind.
551– 4 If Mind is first, it cannot *p·* its opposite
551– 5 If matter is first, it cannot *p·* Mind.
551–28 Neither can *p·* the other.

produced

a 38– 7 *p·* by man-made doctrines,
53–19 the shock so often *p·* by the truth,
sp 87–26 The strong impressions *p·* on mortal mind
s 109–18 cures were *p·* in primitive Christian healing
126–13 but the human mind never *p·* a real tone
152–10 Anatomy describes muscular action as *p·* by
159–21 this Lynn woman died from effects *p·* by
164–19 or *p·* by mental assassins,

produced
ph 178–13   p· prior to his birth by the
185– 2   The wind had not p· the difficulty.
188–18   sensation p· physically by the
195– 7   All that he ate, except his black crust, p·
198–31   does not follow that exercise has p· this
199–17   p· consciously or unconsciously,
b 277–15   A mineral is not p· by a vegetable
304–16   Harmony is p· by its Principle,
p 370–11   symptoms, which might be p· by a
371– 6   p· on children by telling ghost-stories
373–20   the effects of fear p· by sin,
380–18   belief of disease p· by a so-called
389–28   A case of convulsions, p· by indigestion,
392–22   Whatever benefit is p· on the body,
401–16   *chemicalization* is the upheaval p· when
401–21   The only effect p· by medicine is
421–22   the alterative effect p· by Truth upon error,
422–23   both similarly p· and attended by the same
g 532–18   p· the immediate fruits of fear and shame.
551– 3   Either Mind produces, or it is p·.

producer
p 377–14   showing mortal mind to be the p· of
g 544– 6   Mind, instead of matter, being the p·,
544–32   Error begins with corporeality as the p·

produces
pr 7–17   p· material ecstasy and emotion.
sp 79– 8   p· permanent health.
80–28   Mortal mind p· table-tipping as certainly as
s 108–31   p· all the organism and action of the
144–19   It p· evil continually, and is not a factor in
148–18   the divine Principle which p· harmonious man,
155– 5   sustains medicine and p· all medical results,
159–30   a man's belief p· disease and all its symptoms,
ph 177– 1   Human mind p· what is termed organic disease
177– 2   as certainly as it p· hysteria,
184– 6   Belief p· the results of belief,
184–10   error of belief which p· a mortal disorder,
f 208–15   absurd to suppose that . . . God, p· disease
220–18   Mortal mind p· its own phenomena,
229–26   If the transgression of God's law p· sickness,
231–12   If God makes sin, if good p· evil,
239–24   It forms material concepts and p· every
b 270–27   If a sense of disease p· suffering
276–29   inform us that like p· like.
276–32   Intelligence never p· non-intelligence ;
277– 6   Matter never p· mind.
277– 6   The immortal never p· the mortal.
277–20   Error . . . asserts that Spirit p· matter
277–20   asserts that . . . matter p· all the
p 370–15   The effect, which mortal mind p· through one
374–30   Mortal mind p· animal heat,
379–23   her belief p· the very results she dreads.
380–24   the divine Mind p· in man health,
386–25   Error, not Truth, p· all the suffering on earth.
390– 8   which p· apparent discord,
398–18   What p· the change?
398–20   and p· a new effect upon the body.
403–26   The mortal so-called mind p· all
408–29   The unconscious thought . . . p· no effect,
419–20   Mind p· all action.
421–15   belief that this chemicalization p· pain
t 459–27   The tree must be good, which p· good fruit.
g 544–16   In Science, Mind neither p· matter nor
547–18   Darwin's theory,— that Mind p· its opposite,
551– 3   Either Mind p·, or it is produced.
551– 6   Like p· like.
552– 1   if the egg p· the parent.
552– 3   Who or what p· the parent of the egg?

producing
sp 81–22   the p·, governing, divine Principle lives on,
ph 182– 8   capable of p· the highest human good
190– 5   The mortal says . . . seedling is p· mortals,
199– 7   nobody believes that mind is p· such a result
f 249– 4   p· His own models of excellence.
c 263–12   p· evil when he would create good,
o 343–16   the impossibility of good p· evil ;
356–19   incapable of p· sin, sickness, and death
p 370– 9   the law of cause and effect, or like p· like.
373–30   Mortal mind is p· the propulsion or the
401–11   to the end of p· a higher manifestation.
403–17   p· on mortal body the results of false opinions ;
415–25   To remove the error p· disorder,
g 550–25   no instance of one species p· its opposite,
gl 580– 7   a so-called finite mind, p· other minds,

product
cannot be the
b 339–10   and cannot be the p· of God.
flower is a
sp 71–12   the flower is a p· of the so-called mind,
not the
g 551– 7   the bird is not the p· of a beast.
of belief
r 490– 3   Will-power is but a p· of belief,

product
of nothing
gl 580– 9   a p· of nothing as the mimicry of something ;
─────
s 108–15   as the p· of three multiplied by three,
119– 7   they assume that matter is the p· of Spirit.
f 219– 7   and then say the p· is correct.
b 280– 8   and the p· must be mental.
r 479– 8   Matter is neither self-existent nor a p· of
g 508– 5   Mind's infinite idea, . . ,. is the p·.

production
ph 183–18   action of Truth is the p· of harmony.
g 508–21   The Mind or intelligence of p·

productive
g 544– 4   In God's creation ideas became p·,

products
b 274–21   These false beliefs and their p· constitute the flesh,
280– 2   elements of discord and decay are not p· of
p 374–26   Heat and cold are p· of mortal mind.
421–31   the p· of eight multiplied by five, and of

profane
s 139–30   the p· or atheistic invalid
ph 175–13   It is p· to fancy that the perfume of clover

profess
a 27–28   Why do those who p· to follow Christ reject the
54–30   would not some, who now p· to love him, reject

professed
a 37–16   When will Jesus' p· followers learn to
p 436–16   the prisoner summoned two p· friends,

profession
pr 15–28   Practice not p·, understanding not belief,
a 28–11   more on the ground of demonstration than of p·.
s 141– 3   More than p· is requisite for
158– 1   the p· of medicine originated in idolatry
f 242–32   the proof which he gave, instead of mere p·.

professional
f 236– 6   Is it not p· reputation and emolument

professions
pr 8–18   P· and audible prayers are like charity
f 233– 2   higher proofs rather than p· of Christian power.

Professor
s 163– 4   Dr. Benjamin Waterhouse, P· in Harvard
163–13   Dr. Mason Good, a learned P· in London,
163–19   P· of the Institutes and Practice of Physic

proficiency
pref x–30   No intellectual p· is requisite in the learner,

profit
pr 10– 6   If good enough to p· by Jesus' cup

profitable
a 43–12   the most p· to his students.

profitably
pref ix–24   before a work on the subject could be p· studied.

profiteth
o 356–16   the flesh p· nothing."— *John* 6 : 63.

profound
sp 88–22   and the individual manifests p· adoration.
s 157–32   better for this spiritual and p· pathology.
b 320–26   a p· idea of the divine power to heal
ap 572– 7   the most simple and p· counsel of the
575–17   description of the city . . . has a p· meaning.

progenitor
g 551– 8   matter is not the p· of Mind.

progenitors
ph 173– 5   progressed farther than his animal p·.
p 425– 1   or some of his p· farther back

progeny
m 61– 8   improve our p·, diminish crime,
g 532–10   Adam and his p· were cursed, not blessed ;
539– 1   the author of sin and sin's p·.

Progress
p 441–24   executed at the hands of our sheriff, P·

progress
civilization and
m 57– 1   the cement of civilization and p·.
consistent with
m 65– 8   If . . . consistent with p·, they will be strong
deemed
s 158–10   This was deemed p·
element of
f 233– 6   This is an element of p·,
evidences of
s 158–24   Evidences of p· and of spiritualization
human
ph 170–24   spiritual causation relates to human p·.
is born
b 296– 4   P· is born of experience.
is the law
f 233– 6   and p· is the law of God,

progress
labor and
 f 236– 2 should stimulate clerical labor and *p·*.
moral
 a 22– 5 Vibrating . . . our moral *p·* will be slow.
not united by
 sp 72–16 tares and the wheat, which are not united by *p·*,
of information
 g 548–21 changed with the *p·* of information."
of truth
 sp 94–17 The *p·* of truth confirms its claims,
our
 f 239–16 To ascertain our *p·*, we must
 p 426– 9 expectation speeds our *p·*.
painless
 f 224– 9 There should be painless *p·*,
periods of
 g 511–18 infinite ideas, images, mark the periods of *p·*.
proof of
 b 324– 5 purification of sense and self is a proof of *p·*.
ready for
 o 353–23 When we learn that . . . we shall be ready for *p·*,
revelation and
 gl 591–24 symbol of Truth ; revelation and *p·*.
some
 pref ix–17 To-day, though rejoicing in some *p·*,
stage of
 g 506–14 forming each successive stage of *p·*.
takes off
 c 256– 1 *P·* takes off human shackles.
this
 pr 11–11 in order to compel this *p·*.
will finally destroy
 r 492–11 Thus *p·* will finally destroy all error,

 pr 10–20 the advance guard of *p·* has
 m 68– 2 At present mortals *p·* slowly
 s 142–15 they . . . shut the door on *p·*.
 r 495–25 How can I *p·* most rapidly in the

progressed
 ph 173– 4 *p·* farther than his animal progenitors.
progressing
 gl 589–23 material belief *p·* and disappearing ;
progression
 b 291–12 Universal salvation rests on *p·* and probation,
progressive
 a 46–24 probationary and *p·* state beyond the grave.
 f 240–19 If mortals are not *p·*,
projected
 s 126– 8 Human thought never *p·* the least portion of
prolific
 ph 180– 1 are both *p·* sources of sickness.
 f 205–11 the *p·* source of all suffering
 228– 7 Heredity is a *p·* subject for mortal belief to
 p 409– 7 the more *p·* it is likely to become in sin and
 t 457–17 mental malpractice, *p·* of evil,
 ap 563–21 *p·* in health, holiness, and immortality.
prolong
 sp 77–19 Of what advantage, . . . to *p·* the material
 77–20 and so *p·* the illusion
prolonged
 s 156–15 aggravation of symptoms from their *p·* use,
 f 212– 6 If the sensation . . . can return, can be *p·*,
prolonging
 m 59–19 in *p·* her health and smiles
promise
 pr 14–19 Hence the hope of the *p·* Jesus bestows :
 f 246–23 and still maintain his vigor, freshness, and *p·*.
 b 328–28 Jesus' *p·* is perpetual.
 o 342–11 the *p·* that his students should cast out evils
 r 497–24 we solemnly *p·* to watch, and pray
 ap 558–12 but a bright *p·* crowns its brow.
 562–20 waiting to be delivered of her sweet *p·*,
promised
 pref xi–18 coming now as was *p·* aforetime,
 an 101–13 *p·* by Monsieur Berna [the magnetizer]
 s 123–22 teachings of the Comforter, as *p·* by the Master.
 150– 8 This coming, as was *p·* by the Master,
 c 267–31 hath *p·* to them that love him."— *Jas.* 1 : 12.
 g 566– 5 and anticipating the *p·* joy,
promises
 a 55–21 The *p·* will be fulfilled.
 p 373– 5 and be more alive to His *p·*.
promising
 m 61–14 places *p·* children in the arms of gross parents,
promote
 m 58–18 will not *p·* the sweet interchange of confidence
 ph 195–21 *p·* the growth of mortal mind out of itself,
 p 410–27 to *p·* right thinking and doing,
promoters
 ph 179–22 are the *p·* of sickness and disease.

promotes
 m 59–17 *p·* the welfare and happiness of your wife
 an 103– 1 *p·* affection and virtue in families
 c 266–12 to accept what best *p·* your growth.
promotive
 p 420–23 is not *p·* of health or happiness.
promptly
 b 273–32 when it is opposed *p·* and persistently by C. S.
promptness
 g 514–15 diligence, *p·*, and perseverance
promulgated
 s 164– 6 therapeutic agents, ever yet *p·*,
prone
 f 203–17 We are *p·* to believe either in more than
pronounce
 p 433–18 Judge Medicine then proceeds to *p·* the
 439–30 the sentence which . . . Divine Love will *p·*.
pronounced
 s 110– 6 is *p·* by His wisdom good.
 157–17 which . . . He *p·* *good,*
 p 436–33 that court *p·* a sentence of death for
 g 526–15 God *p·* good all that He created,
pronounces
 pr 3–29 sharp censure our Master *p·* on hypocrites.
proof
added
 b 295– 3 added *p·* of the unreliability of
affording the
 r 473–20 affording the *p·* of Christianity's truth
affords no
 f 208– 1 error, which affords no *p·* of God,
and demonstration
 o 342– 2 hour has struck when *p·* and demonstration,
another
 s 122–15 The optical focus is another *p·* of the
brings out the
 s 157–30 brings out the *p·* that Life is
contains the
 g 547– 3 contains the *p·* of all here said of C. S.
divine
 f 215–22 With its divine *p·*, Science reverses the
final
 a 45–23 beheld the final *p·* of all that he had taught,
furnished the
 b 317–28 to him Jesus furnished the *p·* that
furnish the
 a 51–11 that he might furnish the *p·* of immortal life.
great
 a 25– 1 the great *p·* of Truth and Love.
hence the
 p 402–28 Hence the *p·* that hypnotism is not scientific ;
highest
 a 54–17 This was the highest *p·* he could have offered
his
 a 26–30 His *p·* of Christianity was no form or
 44–21 in his *p·* of man's truly derived power
immortal
 r 488–17 C. S. sustains with immortal *p·*
is essential
 o 341–11 *P·* is essential to a due estimate of this subject.
Jesus' last
 a 43–11 Jesus' last *p·* was the highest,
no
 sp 71–23 no *p·* nor power outside of human testimony.
 an 100–20 no *p·* of the existence of the animal magnetic
 f 208– 1 error, which affords no *p·* of God,
 b 284–21 physical senses can obtain no *p·* of God.
 o 352– 1 but their prayer brought down no *p·* that
of Christianity
 a 26–30 His *p·* of Christianity was no form or
 s 142– 9 as our first *p·* of Christianity,
 f 210– 5 The Principle and *p·* of Christianity
 b 271– 9 the philosophy, Science, and *p·* of Christianity
 o 351–16 the practical *p·* of Christianity,
of harmony
 b 340– 2 make life its own *p·* of harmony and God.
of healing
 ap 569–13 rejoices in the *p·* of healing,
of immortality
 sp 81–15 Life, Love, Truth, is the only *p·* of immortality.
 b 306–18 a rational *p·* of immortality.
of its utility
 gl 583–14 institution, which affords *p·* of its utility
of progress
 b 324– 5 purification of sense and self is a *p·* of progress.
of the supremacy
 b 322– 2 in *p·* of the supremacy of Mind.
of the utility
 o 355– 5 the *p·* of the utility of these methods ;
once seen
 s 109– 9 *p·* once seen, no other conclusion can be reached.

proof		
	overwhelming	
	s 151–32	we have overwhelming *p·*.
	practical	
	o 345–19	this practical *p·* is the only feasible evidence
	351–16	the practical *p·* of Christianity,
	presented the	
	a 54–14	he presented the *p·* that Life, Truth, and Love
	requisite	
	g 552– 9	even where the *p·* requisite . . . is undiscovered.
	spiritual	
	g 505–24	giving the spiritual *p·* of the universe
	statement and	
	s 113–13	found to agree in statement and *p·*,
	p 380–28	its culmination of scientific statement and *p·*.
	subjected to	
	o 341–16	according to a divine given rule, and subjected to *p·*.
	support of his	
	f 236–10	Christ's teachings in support of his *p·*
	this	
	a 42–29	had taught his disciples the Science of this *p·*.
	s 147–20	This *p·* lifts you high above the
	b 321–15	this *p·* was a staff upon which to lean.
	321–25	God had lessened Moses' fear by this *p·*
	witness or	
	b 303–27	a witness or *p·* of His own nature.
	a 24–25	as a *p·* that spirits can return to earth?
	42–16	the *p·* of his final triumph over body
	m 69– 4	as fixed in divine Science as is the *p·* that
	s 123–24	The *p·*, by present demonstration, that
	153–23	*p·* that this so-called mind makes its own pain
	f 207– 6	every scientific statement . . . has its *p·*.
	242–31	require of Christians the *p·* which he gave,
	g 546–27	The *p·* that the system stated in this book
	gl 592–12	the *p·* that, without the gospel,
proofs		
	any	
	o 354–13	neither give nor offer any *p·* that their
	furnished	
	r 472–12	Jesus furnished *p·* of these statements.
	glorious	
	r 474– 1	his teachings and their glorious *p·*,
	higher	
	f 233– 2	makes its demands upon us for higher *p·*
	highest	
	a 49–28	to whom he had given the highest *p·* of
	of God's care	
	m 66–11	Trials are *p·* of God's care.
	of immortality	
	sp 78–13	why look to them . . . for *p·* of immortality,
	80–11	assertion that. . .are our only *p·* of immortality.
	requisite	
	a 25–24	giving the requisite *p·* of their own piety.
	sublime	
	p 387–27	history of Christianity furnishes sublime *p·*
	these	
	f 233– 3	These *p·* consist solely in the destruction of
	a 41–14	*p·* of Truth, Life, and Love, which Jesus gave
	o 355– 6	*p·* are better than mere verbal arguments
	358–13	Otherwise it . . . could not present its *p·*.
	p 363–29	In the absence of other *p·*,
pro* or *con		
	s 120–25	Any conclusion *p·* or *c·* deduced from
	129– 9	the material fable, be the fable *p·* or *c·*,
propagate		
	g 551–30	in order to *p·* its species,
propagated		
	b 272–27	from which are *p·* the dismal beliefs of
propagates		
	m 66–13	Love *p·* anew the higher joys of Spirit,
propagating		
	g 507–19	not . . . because of any *p·* power of their own,
	531–20	a *p·* property of their own?
propagation		
	m 61–24	Is not the *p·* of the human species a
	61–31	If the *p·* of a higher human species is requisite
	s 142– 3	required for self-establishment and *p·*.
	b 303– 6	from no power of *p·* in matter,
	g 545–23	They believed in the existence of matter, its *p·*
	557– 9	human *p·* has its suffering because it is a
propensities		
	m 61–21	*p·* that must either be overcome or
	an 104–20	falsehood, revenge, malice, are animal *p·*
	f 206– 6	and free the lower *p·*.
	p 405– 2	Hatred inflames the brutal *p·*.
	405– 5	C. S. commands man to master the *p·*,
propensity		
	f 252–21	Animal in *p·* deceitful in sentiment,
	r 490– 5	Human will is an animal *p·*,
	g 539–14	Whence does he obtain the *p·* or power to

proper		
	pr 4– 7	and follow his example, is our *p·* debt to him
	sp 93–23	Spirit, as a *p·* noun, is the name of the
	98–25	what they call *science* has no *p·* connection
	s 112–29	without giving that author *p·* credit,
	ph 179– 1	understanding of C. S. in its *p·* signification
	f 222– 6	one of which is to believe that *p·* food supplies
	234–17	If mortals would keep *p·* ward over mortal
	c 265– 7	and gain some *p·* sense of the infinite,
	b 302–28	body presents no *p·* likeness of divinity,
	313– 3	the full and *p·* translation of the Greek),
	319–30	but we can by special and *p·* capitalization
	333–13	*p·* name of our Master in the Greek was
	p 383–20	to keep the body in *p·* condition.
	424– 8	the *p·* sense of God's unerring direction
	434–24	Mortal Man has no *p·* counsel in the case.
	t 449–28	A *p·* teacher of C. S.
	463–21	To decide quickly as to the *p·* treatment of
	r 482– 6	The *p·* use of the word *soul*
	g 502–12	serves to suggest the *p·* reflection of God
	506–19	gathers unformed thoughts into their *p·* channels,
	517–20	The only *p·* symbol of God as person is
	538– 6	to note the *p·* guests.
	555–24	and set aside the *p·* conception of Deity,
properly		
	pr 16–16	*p·* reads, "Deliver us from the— *Matt.* 6 : 13.
	m 58– 7	should be concordant in order to blend *p·*.
	sp 84–31	If . . . thoroughly learned and *p·* digested,
	an 106– 9	Man is *p·* self-governed only when he
	s 128– 4	The term Science, *p·* understood,
	128–32	conclusion, if *p·* drawn, cannot be false.
	129– 4	a *p·* computed sum in arithmetic.
	130–15	C. S., *p·* understood, would
	b 333– 3	The word *Christ* is not *p·* a synonym for
	t 449–17	to teach this subject *p·* and correctly
	463– 6	To attend *p·* the birth of the new child,
	463–13	truth removes *p·* whatever is offensive.
	r 482–10	Soul is *p·* the synonym of Spirit, or God ;
	g 501– 1	interpretation of the Scriptures *p·* starts with
	554– 5	nor are there *p·* any mortal beings,
	557– 4	how to develop their children *p·* on dry land.
properties		
	s 118–25	as yeast changes the chemical *p·* of meal.
	124–20	cohesion, and attraction are *p·* of Mind.
	ph 177–19	indicated matter's *p·*, qualities, and forms.
property		
	m 63–19	*p·*, and parental claims of the two sexes.
	s 153– 6	until there was not a single saline *p·* left.
	g 510–28	and not a vitalizing *p·* of matter.
	531–20	a propagating *p·* of their own?
prophecy		
	s 118– 6	Did not this parable point a moral with a *p·*,
	131–26	The mission of Jesus confirmed *p·*,
	c 266–16	The author has experienced the foregoing *p·*
	b 292– 4	Here *p·* pauses.
	o 349–21	Out of this condition grew the *p·*
	g 534–12	This *p·* has been fulfilled.
	ap 558– *	*they that hear the words of this p·*,— *Rev.* 1 : 3.
	gl 585– 9	ELIAS. *P·* ; spiritual evidence
prophesied		
	ap 561–32	John the Baptist *p·* the coming of
prophesy		
	b 339– 5	*p·* and involve the final destruction of all sin?
prophesying		
	g 531– 9	as if hope were ever *p·* thus :
prophesyings		
	r 490–19	Despise not *p·*."— *I Thess.* 5 : 20.
Prophet		
	o 360–28	the Jews put to death the Galilean *P·*,
	r 497–18	as demonstrated by the Galilean *P·*
prophet	(see also **prophet's**)	
	a 28–29	trials encountered by *p·*, disciple, and apostle,
	sp 98– 4	*p·* of to-day beholds in the mental horizon
	122–19	The barometer,— that little *p·* of
	p 363–12	they were wondering why, being a *p·*,
	g 540– 6	but the *p·* referred to divine law
	gl 593– 4	definition of
prophetic		
	s 109–25	*p·* Scripture of Isaiah is renewedly fulfilled :
	f 226– 2	*p·* of further steps towards the banishment of
prophetically		
	a 52–25	*p·* said to his disciples,
	ap 558–18	whose flames of Truth were *p·* described by
prophet's		
	a 52–12	*p·* foresight of the reception error would give
prophets		
	ancient	
	sp 84– 3	ancient *p·* gained their foresight from

roud
s 124–24　and said to the p· wave,

rovable
f 211– 9　Is it not p· that Mind is not *mortal*

rove
a　26–17　to p· what God is and what He does for man.
　27– 2　intended to p· beyond a question that the
　49–21　He was to p· that the Christ is not subject to
m　59–18　will p· more salutary in prolonging her
sp　81– 1　There is not so much evidence to p·
　81– 8　on its own theories, spiritualism can only p·
　81–13　than the opposite assertion, . . . would p·
an 104–29　courts recognize evidence to p· the motive
s 108–14　the lesser demonstration to p· the greater,
　132–12　such effects, coming from divine Mind, p· the
　138–25　The Christian can p· this to-day as readily as
　146–22　practically p· its divine origin and efficacy.
ph 199–20　The feats of the gymnast p· that
f 217– 8　p· Mind to be scientifically distinct from
b 278–26　logic which would p· his annihilation.
　315–19　subdue sin and p· man's heritage,
　315–22　to p· irrefutably how spiritual Truth destroys
　316– 8　to p· the power of Spirit over the flesh,
　316–27　could p· God's divine power by healing the
　329–13　We must p· our faith by demonstration.
o 346–12　in order to p· the somethingness
　356– 6　Sin, sickness, and death do not p·
p 368– 6　Divine Science insists that time will p· all this.
　373–31　we p· this to be so when by mental means the
　377– 9　p· that they can be healthy in all climates,
　380–21　and p· man's dominion over error.
　380–24　to p· that the divine Mind produces
　383–24　Does his assertion p· the use of tobacco to be
　383–26　p· the illusive physical effect of a false belief,
　384–14　will p· to himself, by small beginnings,
　400–21　we p· that thought alone creates the suffering.
　428– 7　Man's privilege . . . is to p· the words of
t 446–24　you overcome it and p· its nothingness.
　447–26　get the victory over sin and so p· its unreality.
　458–28　He must p·, through living as well as
　459–14　Any attempt to . . . must p· abortive.
　461–26　To p· . . . the error or unreality of sin,
　461–28　to p· . . . the error or unreality of disease,
　464–19　"p· all things ;— *I Thess.* 5: 21.
r 493–15　and p· for himself the Principle and rule
　496–14　will p· what the understanding of God
g 547– 6　You can p· for yourself, dear reader,

roved
pref　x–16　have p· the worth of her teachings.
　x–22　The divine Principle of healing is p· in the
a　26–25　He p· by his deeds that C. S. destroys sickness,
　27–10　Jesus p· by his reappearance after the
　42– 1　Jesus' life p·, divinely and scientifically,
　42–21　and p· its nothingness.
　44– 9　He p· Life to be deathless
　46–14　he p· to the physical senses
s 109– 9　and thus p· absolute and divine.
　111–32　p· itself, whenever scientifically employed,
　112–24　already been stated and p· to be true,
　125–31　matter will finally be p· nothing more than
　138–26　as readily as it was p· centuries ago.
　139– 6　Moses p· the power of Mind by what men called
　146– 1　and he p· his faith by his works.
　149–15　because you have not obeyed the rule and p·
　159–20　The sequel p· that this Lynn woman
ph 168–21　an authority which Jesus p· to be false
f 214–12　material senses, . . . are p· non-intelligent.
　228–29　He p· them powerless.
　229– 2　p· that matter has not destroyed them,
c 264–23　who p· them to be forms of error.
　267–30　when he is tried, [p· faithful],— *Jas.* 1: 12.
b 300–10　So far as . . . is understood, it can be p·
　307–14　This error has p· itself to be error.
　314– 6　p· that he and the Father were inseparable
　314–32　Jesus p· them wrong by his resurrection,
　316–19　thus p· that Truth was the master of death.
　318–30　as numbers are controlled and p· by
　332–19　he p· that Christ is the divine idea
o 355–29　p· to be such by our Master
p 368–21　p·, when we learn that life and man survive this
　386–30　might afterwards be p· to you.
　394–17　Experience has p· to the author the fallacy of
　402–31　p· to be a belief without a real cause.
　434–29　not p· "worthy of death,— *Acts* 23: 29.
　438– 8　C. S. p· the witness, Nerve, to be a perjurer.
t 461– 6　We admit the whole, because a part is p·
r 473–28　He p· what he taught.
　473–29　Jesus p· the Principle, . . . to be divine.
　486–14　Jesus p· by the prints of the nails, that
　492– 8　It is already p· that a knowledge of this,
　492–13　a statement p· to be good must be correct.
　493–29　p· that the Christ could improve on a false
g 514–27　Paul p· the viper to be harmless.
ap 567–23　and so p· to be powerless.
gl 581– 8　p· to be as immortal as its Principle ;

proverb
b 291–21　has been transformed into the popular p·,

proverbial
ph 179–24　It should not be p·, that so long as
p 385– 1　It is p· that Florence Nightingale

proves
ap　81–12　no more p· him to be so, than
s 108–16　p· conclusively that three times three
　113–27　p· the rule by inversion.
　135–25　This p· the one to be identical with the other.
ph 194–19　p· beyond a doubt that education constitutes
　194–30　p· material sense to be but a belief
f 207– 5　This fact p· our position,
　212–14　it p· sensation to be in the mortal mind,
　245–28　p· it possible to be young at seventy-four ;
c 257–23　p· the material theory of mind in matter to be
　258– 7　The insufficiency of this belief. . .p· the falsity of
b 289–15　p· the "king of terrors" to be but — *Job* 18: 14.
　306–20　Science p· man's existence to be intact.
　329– 6　A little understanding of C. S. p· the truth of
　338– 9　The mortality of material man p· that
o 347–25　and so p· their nothingness.
　351–24　which p· the nothingness of error,
p 370– 8　this p· that fear is governing the body.
　375– 9　The old-school physician p· this when
　416–21　is only in mortal mind, as the dead body p· ;
t 461– 7　illustrates and p· the entire Principle.
g 522– 3　p· the falsity of the second.

provide
s 143– 6　nor p· them for human use ;

Providence
p 424–10　Under divine P· there can be no accidents,

providing
a　24–21　chiefly as p· a ready pardon for all sinners

Province
p 432–11　Governor of the P· of Body,
　438– 9　Instead of being a ruler in the P· of Body,
　439– 6　was absent from the P· of Body,

province
pr　3– 2　without being reminded of His p·.
f 206– 7　the p· of spiritual sense to govern man.
b 307–29　his p· is in spiritual statutes,
p 432–12　In this p· there is a statute regarding
　437– 1　in which p· Mortal Man resides.

proving
a　39– 5　thus p· their nothingness.
s 125–19　p· our material theories . . . to be valueless,
ph 199–23　p· that failure is occasioned by
o 343– 3　and for p· my word by my deed
　343–18　p· by what are wrongly called miracles,
g 546–32　the p· of one example would authenticate

provision
m　56– 7　the legal and moral p· for generation

provoke
t 452–11　Your advancing course may p· envy,

proximity
sp 82–15　dreamer by our side despite his physical p·,

proxy
pr 12–31　petitioners (*per se* or by p·)

prudent
s 131–21　from the wise and p·,— *Luke* 10: 21.

Psalm
ap 577–32　In the following P· one word shows,
　578– 4　chapter sub-title

Psalmist
pr　5–20　the P· could see their end,
s 135– 1　P· sang : "What ailed thee, O thou— *Psal.*
　　　　 114: 5.
ph 200–13　P· said : "Thou madest him to— *Psal.* 8: 6.
b 309– 4　which, to use the word of the P·,
g 505–17　P· saith : "The Lord on high— *Psal.* 93: 4.
ap 575–22　P· saith, "Beautiful for situation,— *Psal.* 48: 2.

Psalms
ap 564–27　quoting a line from the P·,

pseudo-mental
p 389–10　This p· testimony can be destroyed only by

psychology
p 369–25　readily seen, if p·, . . . was understood.

Ptolemaic
s 123– 4　The P· blunder could not affect the

Ptolemy
s 122–30　mistake . . . that P· made regarding the

public
pr 13– 5　In p· prayer we often go beyond our
　13–12　Can the mere p· expression of our desires
a　40–29　has come so generally to mean p· worship
an 101– 2　observed in the p· practice of magnetism,
　227–10　some p· teachers permit an ignorance of

Publican's
t 448– 3 When the P· wail went out to the
publicans
a 20– 7 "The p· and the harlots— *Matt.* 21 : 31.
53– 1 the "friend of p· and sinners."— *Luke* 7 : 34.
publications
p 446– 5 A thorough perusal of the author's p·
464– 6 except through her laborious p·,
publicly
p 441–23 p· executed at the hands of our sheriff,
published
pref ix–28 copious notes . . . which have never been p·.
x– 3 SCIENCE AND HEALTH was p· in 1875.
xii–18 which was p· in 1891.
s 163–20 Dr. Chapman, . . . in a p· essay said :
ph 185– 7 Before this book was p·,
f, 245– 3 p· in the London medical magazine
publisher
(*see* **Eddy, Mrs. Mary Baker**)
Publius Lentulus
a 29–12 There is a tradition that P· L· wrote to
puffing
p 407– 3 P· the obnoxious fumes of tobacco,
pulmonary
m 63– 2 for warding off p· disease
f 203– 1 that this cold may produce fatal p· disease ;
p 392–20 in the form of what is termed p· disease,
pulpit
a 55–10 does not the p· sometimes scorn it?
f 236– 2 Truth should emanate from the p·,
pulpits
s 141–29 Let our p· do justice to C. S.
pulpy
ph 192– 1 belief that a p· substance under the skull is
pulse
s 159–25 They examine the lungs, tongue, and p·
p 370–32 Physicians examine the p·, tongue, lungs,
379–26 The quickened p·, coated tongue,
pulseless
s 113– 8 letter is but the dead body of Science,— p·,
punctual
p 395–19 cheerful, orderly, p·, patient,
pungent
pr 7– 3 Jesus' reproof was pointed and p·
g 555– 1 as the force of mortal mind is less p·
punish
pr 10–32 Do you ask wisdom to be merciful and not to p· sin?
an 105– 4 to prevent deeds of violence or to p· them.
o 356–28 create the primitive, and then p· its derivative?
357– 2 must admit that God will not p· man for
p 435–23 to p· a man for acting justly.
436–21 handcuffed Mortal Man and would now p· him.
441– 4 which undertakes to p· aught but sin,
441–26 no law created of divine Mind can p·
t 447–13 will in time disclose and p· itself.
punishable
p 431–10 this offence is deemed p· with death.
440–24 and then render obedience to these laws p·
punished
a 47–28 The disciples' desertion . . . was p· ;
an 105–11 Can matter be p·?
f 251–27 nothing is left which deserves . . . to be p·.
b 340–29 leaves nothing that can sin, suffer, be p· or
p 432–15 treated as a criminal and p·
435–26 For naught else can he be p·,
436–22 fear its consequences, and be p· for his fear.
r 497–11 But the belief in sin is p· so long as
g 542–10 the disposition to excuse guilt . . . is p·.
punishes
pr 6–19 To suppose that God forgives or p·
p 384– 7 God never p· man for doing right,
387–22 supposition. . .that God p· man for doing good,
punishing
ph 186–22 only aids in peremptorily p· the evil-doer.
f 230–14 and then p· the helpless victims
o 356–27 and then p· him for it?
p 412– 2 never p· aught but sin,
punishment
escape from
a 36– 8 Escape from p· is not in accordance with
fear of
b 327–22 Fear of p· never made man truly honest.
final
ph 188–10 from shame and woe to their final p·.
full
a 36–22 impossible . . . to receive their full p· this side
future
a 24–19 in regard to predestination and future p·.

punishment
its own
g 537–15 Sin is its own p·.
merit
p 432–18 transgress the laws, and merit p·,
one form of
pr 11– 8 only saves the criminal from one form of p·.
prevent his
p 431–14 summoned . . . to prevent his p·.
the sinner's
a 35–31 If the sinner's p· here has been insufficient
without
pr 11– 1 Without p·, sin would multiply.
pupil
b 329–17 To be discouraged, is to resemble a p· in addition
p 393–28 lenses, muscles, the iris and p·,
t 445– 9 capacities for good in your p·.
pupils
pref ix–13 still in circulation among her first p· ;
f 235–15 uplifting thoughts . . . imparted to p·,
pure
a 29–25 the p· sense of the Virgin-mother
44–14 He did not depend upon food or p· air
50–14 and to himself, Love's p· idea.
52– 5 His affections were p· ; theirs were carnal.
54– 3 Out of the amplitude of his p· affection,
m 57–11 Both sexes should be loving, p·,
57–13 will be perpetual only as it is p· and true,
62– 2 The fœtus must be kept mentally p·
63– 6 The beautiful, good, and p· constitute his
64– 4 "P· religion and undefiled—*Jas.* 1 : 27.
s 117–14 the p· language of Spirit.
147–29 A p· affection takes form in goodness,
ph 171– 8 and will find himself unfallen, upright, p·,
f 223– 1 and plant ourselves upon what is p· and perfect
235–14 The p· and uplifting thoughts of the teacher,
241–28 the p· in heart see God
c 259–27 Immortal ideas, p·, perfect, and enduring,
b 298–28 Angels are p· thoughts from God,
318–15 would efface the p· sense of omnipotence.
324– 6 "Blessed are the p· in heart :— *Matt.* 5 : 8.
329– 2 healing elements of p· Christianity will be
332–29 incarnate in the good and p· Christ Jesus.
337–15 none but the p· in heart can see God,
o 341– 9 "Blessed are the p· in heart :— *Matt.* 5 : 8.
360–25 Shall man be more p· than his— *see Job* 4 : 17.
p 383– 4 a body rendered p· by Mind as well as
383– 5 To do this, the p· and exalting influence of th
391–31 as Love,— as all that is p·,
409–23 to be laid aside for the p· reality.
r 467–15 man is the likeness of God, p· and eternal,
477– 5 and that man is p· and holy.
497–27 and to be merciful, just, and p·.
g 508– 1 The seed within itself is the p· thought
512–20 multiplication of its own p· and perfect ideas.
550–29 the p· and holy, the immutable and immortal
ap 567–21 That false claim . . . p· delusion,
571–32 He enthrones p· and undefiled religion,
gl 581– 5 spiritual intuitions, p· and perfect ;
582–17 the p· consciousness that God,
589–21 p· affection blessing its enemies.
purely
pr 14–13 Life and intelligence are p· spiritual,
s 113–15 which is not p· metaphysical,
149–24 as readily as she has cured p· functional disease
ph 170–28 The description of man as p· physical,
185– 6 No system of hygiene but C. S. is p· mental.
g 510– 5 to be holy, thought must be p· spiritual.
purer
a 37–12 and to permeate humanity with p· ideals.
65–31 marriage will become p· when the scum is gone.
f 243–22 "of p· eyes than to behold evil,"— *Hab.* 1 : 13.
b 290–30 His thoughts are no p· until
o 357– 4 "of p· eyes than to behold evil."— *Hab.* 1 : 13.
p 407–15 lifting humanity above itself into p· desires,
410–17 the stronger should be our faith and the p· our
g 553– 4 a higher and p· contemplation of man's origin.
purgation
p 364–21 in return for the spiritual p·
purgatives
p 408–15 supposition that . . . by the use of p· and
purgatory
sp 77–29 Spiritism consigns . . . to a wretched p·,
purge
s 142–22 to p· the temples of their vain traffic
purification
a 35–19 Our baptism is a p· from all error.
b 324– 4 p· of sense and self is a proof of progress.
gl 581–23 BAPTISM. P· by Spirit ;
595–15 holiness and p· of thought and deed,
purified
a 22–22 Love means that we shall be tried and p·.

urifies
s 162– 5 Truth, which invigorates and *p*·.

urify
t 452–15 unless in the attempt to *p*· it.
r 492–10 will *p*· and elevate character.
g 540–10 river-bed must be stirred in order to *p*· the stream.

urifying
m 57–24 enlarging, *p*·, and elevating it.
ap 565–22 *p*· even the gold of human character.
gl 586–14 affliction *p*· and elevating man.

uritan
o 359–20 From *P*· parents, the discoverer of C. S.

urity
and affection
pr 15–27 *p*·, and affection are constant prayers.
a 36– 1 They, who know not *p*· and affection
and constancy
m 60– 9 the mother-love includes *p*· and constancy,
and holiness
s 509–26 in which beauty, sublimity, *p*·, and holiness
and immortality
gl 581– 6 *p*·, and immortality, counteracting all evil,
and innocence
gl 582–14 BRIDE. *P*· and innocence,
and peace
gl 584–26 *p*· and peace ; hope and faith.
and self-immolation
sp 99–24 health, *p*·, and self-immolation,
chastity and
b 272–21 it is chastity and *p*·, in contrast with the
goodness and
p 364– 1 a man of undoubted goodness and *p*·,
his
a 31–19 are baptized with his *p*· ;
b 337–16 In proportion to his *p*· is man perfect ;
impart
p 371–29 Mind can impart *p*· instead of impurity,
innocence and
gl 590–10 self-immolation ; innocence and *p*· ;
peace, and
b 323– 8 peace, and *p*·, which are the landmarks of
perfection and
a 52–10 ever-present rebuke of his perfection and *p*·.
righteousness and
a 28–19 Even his righteousness and *p*· did not
was the symbol
ap 561–10 *P*· was the symbol of Life and Love.
white-robed
m 64–23 white-robed *p*· will unite in one person

pr 7–21 with more devout self-abnegation and *p*·,
m 58– 8 Unselfish ambition, noble life-motives, and *p*·,
s 116– 2 Wisdom, *p*·, spiritual understanding,
f 241–27 the corner-stone of all spiritual building is *p*·.
b 332–27 only *p*· could reflect Truth and Love,

urporting
sp 80– 6 A communication *p*· to come from

urpose
affection and
pr 8–29 the affection and *p*· of the heart,
and motive
b 326–16 *p*· and motive to live aright can be gained
changed the
p 432–29 a message from the Board of Health changed the *p*·
Christ's
a 19– 1 Christ's *p*· to reconcile man to God,
divine
sp 83–27 The latter is a revelation of divine *p*·
fraudulent in
f 252–22 deceitful in sentiment, fraudulent in *p*·,
good
f 252–24 where the good *p*· waits !
highest
g 514–18 and keep pace with highest *p*·.
holy
g 506–20 He opens the petals of a holy *p*·
in healing
a 51–21 *p*· in healing was not alone to restore health,
its
pref x–24 Its *p*· is good, and its practice is safer
not the
o 345–31 not the *p*· of C. S. to "educate the idea of God,
of generating
m 62– 1 can only be permitted for the *p*· of generating.
of healing
sp 95–10 for the *p*· of healing them.
of his mission
a 50–28 disbelieving the *p*· of his mission,
of keeping
p 413–17 only for the *p*· of keeping the body clean,
of Love
gl 579–12 This patriarch illustrated the *p*· of Love

purpose
of this allegory
g 537–19 the *p*· of this allegory — this second account
wicked
t 451–30 either with a mistaken or a wicked *p*·.

b 328–30 *p*· of his great life-work extends through time
g 506–21 in order that the *p* may appear.
540–21 The *p*· of the Hebrew allegory,

purposed
s 138– 2 Jesus *p*· founding his society, . . . on the God-power

purposes
pref xi–31 this institution chartered for medical *p*·.
an 103–15 working out the *p*· of good only.
f 235– 1 Evil thoughts, lusts, and malicious *p*·
p 401– 5 cherishing evil passions and malicious *p*·,

purse
ph 195–29 lowering the . . . standard to accommodate the *p*·
gl 593– 6 definition of

pursue
pr 9– 7 Do we *p*· the old selfishness,
a 21–18 different routes to *p*·,
21–21 On the contrary, if my friends *p*· my course,
f 239–20 The objects we *p*· and the spirit we manifest
t 457–22 To *p*· other vocations

pursues
ap 564–30 the serpent *p*· with hatred the spiritual idea.

pursuing
ph 174–18 are *p*· and will overtake the ages,

pursuit
s 161–18 life, liberty, and the *p*· of happiness."
t 448–24 The reception or *p*· of instructions opposite to

pursuits
a 52– 2 His *p*· lay far apart from theirs.

push
a 106– 4 and to *p*· vainly against the current
b 323–10 Then we *p*· onward,

pushed
a 36–26 suddenly pardoned and *p*· into heaven,

put
pr 3–31 to *p*· the finger on the lips and remember our
15–22 as we *p*· our desires into practice.
a 20–30 that is, let us *p*· aside material self and sense,
29–20 *p*· to silence material law and its order of
31–30 shall *p*· you out of the synagogues ; — *John* 16 : 2.
48–23 He said : "*P*· up thy sword." — *John* 18 : 11.
m 56– * *let not man p· asunder.* — *Matt.* 19 : 6.
60–14 wisdom will ultimately *p*· asunder what
62–15 your body, what ye shall *p*· on," — *Matt.* 6 : 25.
67–26 does not *p*· to silence the labor of
s 151–25 The human mind . . . must be *p*· off,
161–11 In 1880, Massachusetts *p*· her foot on a
164–26 shall have *p*· on incorruption, — *I Cor.* 15 : 54.
164–26 shall have *p*· on immortality, — *I Cor.* 15 : 54.
ph 165– * *your body, what ye shall p· on.* — *Matt.* 6 : 25.
169–17 we should *p*· no faith in material means.
172–22 we must "*p*· off the old man." — *Col.* 3 : 9.
179–27 ready to *p*· you into a sweat,
188– 1 This body is *p*· off only as the
200–15 hast *p*· all things under his feet." — *Psal.* 8 : 6.
f 223–10 and we cannot *p*· the greater into the less.
223–22 Spiritual rationality . . . cannot be *p*· down.
230–21 and can man *p*· that law under his feet
230–25 soothing syrups to *p*· children to sleep,
242– 2 mortals *p*· off their material beliefs
c 262– 8 mortals "*p*· on immortality." — *I Cor.* 15 : 54.
265– 9 in order that sin and mortality may be *p*· off.
b 281–20 When we *p*· off the false sense for the true,
281–27 does not *p*· new wine into old bottles,
286–12 Physical causation was *p*· aside
296– 9 The old man with his deeds must be *p*· off.
307–12 says : . . . I will *p*· spirit into what I call
318–11 They would *p*· soul into soil,
321–21 when Moses first *p*· his hand into his bosom
323–13 we must *p*· into practice what we already know.
o 360–28 the Jews *p*· to death the Galilean Prophet,
p 409–24 This mortal is *p*· on, in proportion as
409–24 and the new man or real man is *p*· on,
425–12 treated as error and *p*· out of thought.
430– 4 Mortal mind . . . must *p*· off itself with its
t 447–24 To *p*· down the claim of sin, you must detect it,
452–11 you should not fear to *p*· on the new.
r 496–24 shall have *p*· on incorruption, — *I Cor.* 15 : 54.
496–25 shall have *p*· on immortality, — *I Cor.* 15 : 54.
g 526–27 *p*· him into the garden of Eden, — *Gen.* 2 : 15.
527– 1 God could not *p*· Mind into matter
531–10 If, . . . mind was afterwards *p*· into body
534– 9 I will *p*· enmity between thee and — *Gen.* 3 : 15.
537– 1 lest he *p*· forth his hand, — *Gen.* 3 : 22.
ap 561–27 and matter is *p*· under her feet.

put

gl 582–21 physical sense *p·* out of sight and hearing ;
584–23 *p·* into the opposite of mind, termed matter,

puts

s 155–23 in proportion as it *p·* less weight into the
ph 182–21 and *p·* matter under the feet of Mind.
185–14 which *p·* forth a human conception
p 399– 7 and *p·* the body through certain motions.
g 512–29 this so-called mind *p·* forth its own qualities,
ap 566–13 description which Sir Walter Scott *p·* into the

putteth

o 360–26 Behold, He *p·* no trust in— *see Job* 4 : 18.

putting

a 52–16 *p·* to shame and death the best man that ever
ph 199–30 his power of *p·* resolve into action
c 262– 7 By *p·* "off the old man with his — *Col.* 3 : 9.
p 438–11 *p·* in false claims to office
t 459–17 like *p·* a sharp knife into the hands of a
r 484–25 thus *p·* an end to the hypotheses

Q

quackery

s 163– 5 declared himself "sick of learned *q·*."
ph 180– 1 and advertisements of *q·* are
p 370–26 *Q·* likewise fails at length to inspire the
395–21 It is mental *q·* to make disease a reality
t 456– 4 is most dangerous *q·*.
458– 1 Mental *q·* rests on the same platform
458– 2 on the same platform as all other *q·*.
458–16 Having seen so much suffering from *q·*,

quail

p 384–30 Sickness, sin, and death must at length *q·*

qualifications

t 448–21 moral and spiritual *q·* requisite for healing,

qualified

pr 10– 8 Until we are thus divinely *q·*

qualities

and effects
ph 177–20 cannot name the *q·* and effects of what is
and forms
ph 177–19 indicated matter's properties, *q·*, and forms.
animal
b 298–26 not . . . evolving animal *q·* in their wings ;
curative
s 156– 1 If drugs possess . . . intelligent curative *q·*,
essential
t 460– 8 on the divine Mind and Love's essential *q·*.
feminine
m 57– 4 Union of the masculine and feminine *q·*
God's
gl 597–26 as applied to Mind or to one of God's *q·*.
its own
g 512–29 this so-called mind puts forth its own *q·*,
masculine
m 57– 8 courage and strength through masculine *q·*.
mental
an 104–21 by no means the mental *q·* which heal the sick.
native
m 57–12 The attraction between native *q·* will be
of Mind
c 265– 2 not of the lowest, but of the highest *q·* of Mind.
opposite
b 286–28 (by the supposition of opposite *q·*)
300–17 These opposite *q·* are the tares and wheat,
possesses its
f 247–20 Being possesses its *q·* before they
these
s 156– 2 these *q·* must be mental.
b 280–29 perpetuates these *q·* in man,
which insure
t 449–15 *q·* which insure success in this Science ;

p 388–25 sin and sickness are not *q·* of Soul,

quality

and quantity
b 294– 7 would take away some *q·* and quantity of
g 512–22 all form, color, *q·*, and quantity,
551– 4 cannot produce its opposite in *q·* and quantity,
character and
sp 71–29 limited and finite in character and *q·*.
discover their
t 462–22 to discover their *q·*, quantity, and
eternal
r 469– 9 It is the primal and eternal *q·* of
every
f 215–23 Every *q·* and condition of mortality is lost,
glorified
g 516–22 forever reflect, in glorified *q·*,
mental
p 365–13 what mental *q·* remains,
nature and
c 262– 9 We cannot fathom the nature and *q·* of
not a single
r 475–20 has not a single *q·* underived from Deity ;
not one
an 103–22 This belief has not one *q·* of Truth.
of God
g 506– 5 Understanding is a *q·* of God,

quality

of Mind
g 517– 8 The life-giving *q·* of Mind is Spirit,
of mind
b 279– 4 plainly describes faith, a *q·* of mind, as
or a quantity
p 388–16 a deficiency or an excess, a *q·* or a quantity.
or condition
f 230– 3 to destroy a *q·* or condition of Truth?
b 299– 4 his conception of an unseen *q·* or condition,
quantity and
sp 93–24 It means quantity and *q·*,
refer only to
sp 93–26 modifying derivatives . . . refer only to *q·*,
third
p 422–15 meet and bring out a third *q·*,

sp 86–21 no less a *q·* of physical sense than feeling.
b 305–12 Gender also is a *q·*, . . . of mortal mind.
o 361–16 that is, one in *q·*, not in quantity.
g 506– 5 a *q·* which separates C. S. from supposition
gl 597–24 Will, as a *q·* of so-called mortal mind,

quantity

sp 93–24 It means *q·* and quality,
s 155–32 is it safe to say that the less in *q·* you have
b 294– 7 would take away some quality and *q·* of
o 361–16 that is, one in quality, not in *q·*.
p 388–16 a deficiency or an excess, a quality or a *q·*.
t 462–22 to discover their quality, *q·*, and
g 512–23 form, color, quality, and *q·*,
551– 4 cannot produce its opposite in quality and *q·*,

quarrel

pref x–27 Only those *q·* with her method who
s 128–23 If one would not *q·* with his fellow-man
t 457–14 In the legend of the shield, which led to a *q·*

queen

t 451– 7 Christianity, . . . must be their *q·* of life.

quelling

p 385– 8 the spiritual demand, *q·* the material,

quench

a 36– 6 sufficient suffering, . . . to *q·* the love of sin.
r 490–19 "*Q·* not the Spirit.— *I Thess.* 5 : 19.

quenched

b 314– 5 spiritual sense had *q·* all earthly yearnings.
r 486– 5 until every corporeal sense is *q·*.

quenching

b 329–25 maintains the claim of Truth by *q·* error.

query

p 364–10 This *q·* Jesus answered by

question

another
g 552– 2 Another *q·* follows : Who or what produces
answered this
p 374–10 The author has answered this *q·*
answer the
s 132– 4 would fully answer the *q·*.
answer this
f 223–20 The efforts of error to answer this *q·* by
arises
pref viii–18 the *q·* arises, Is there less sickness because of
asking no
f 222–31 "asking no *q·* for conscience sake."— *I Cor.* 10 : 25
beyond a
a 27– 2 intended to prove beyond a *q·* that the
evade the
f 230–24 These merely evade the *q·*.
hypothetical
g 551–32 The ancient and hypothetical *q·*,
important
t 462–24 That is the important *q·*.
Master's
p 363–19 the Master's *q·* to Simon the Pharisee ;
momentous
a 48–25 in the presence of his own momentous *q·*,
moral
p 419– 1 A moral *q·* may hinder the recovery of the sick.

R

race

Adam's
g 554–24　This he said of Judas, one of Adam's *r·*.
elevating the
gl 583–15　and is found elevating the *r·*,
human
　(*see* **human**)
nobler
m 63–26　achievement of a nobler *r·* for legislation,
our
ap 571–10　doing right and benefiting our *r·*.
sinning
o 345–25　and the sinning *r·* of Adam.

a 20–29　the *r·* that is set before us ;"— *Heb.* 12 : 1.
　22–17　nor become a sluggard in the *r·*.
m 63–26　a *r·* having higher aims and motives.
s 151–12　enlarged power it confers to benefit the *r·*
　158–20　to victimize the *r·* with intoxicating
p 371–27　The necessity for uplifting the *r·*
g 556–17　Did . . . the enlightenment of the *r·* come from

races

m 56–16　the social scourge of all *r·*,
f 225–29　Men and women of all climes and *r·*
g 551–10　argues that mortals spring from eggs and in *r·*.

radiance

pref vii– 3　ere cometh the full *r·* of a risen day.
f 246–14　the *r·* of Spirit should dawn upon the
　247–15　has a glory of its own,— the *r·* of Soul.
ap 561–26　The spiritual idea is clad with the *r·* of

radiant

s 110– 5　as the *r·* reality of God's creation,
f 246–11　*r·* sun of virtue and truth coexists with being.
g 538– 7　*R·* with mercy and justice, the sword of Truth

radiata

g 556– 3　Vertebrata, articulata, mollusca, and *r·*

radiate

p 367–23　but *r·* and glow into noontide glory.

radiates

g 511– 2　subdivides and *r·* their borrowed light,

radiation

g 556– 6　*r·* of Spirit destroys forever all belief in

radical

a 24–17　a change as *r·* as that which has come over
ph 167–30　Only through *r·* reliance on Truth can
p 398–31　come to the rescue, to work a *r·* cure.
t 452–18　Right is *r·*.

radically

t 458–30　by which mortals are *r·* saved from sin

raging

t 459–18　into the hands of a blind man or a *r·* maniac,

railroad

a 21–21　we have the same *r·* guides,

raiment

ph 165– *　and the body than r·?— Matt.* 6 : 25.
f 242–23　"They parted my *r·* among them,— *John* 19 : 24.
c 267–26　like the *r·* of Christ.
t 461– 2　without food and *r·* ;

rain

s 122–21　in the midst of murky clouds and drenching *r·*.
c 257–31　divine Love,— is the father of the *r·*,
o 354–20　which are like clouds without *r·*,
g 520–21　had not caused it to *r·* upon the— *Gen.* 2 : 5.
　544– 5　There was no *r·* and "not a man to— *Gen.* 2 : 5.

rainbow

ap 558– 4　and a *r·* was upon his head,— *Rev.* 10 : 1.

raindrops

b 288–17　the *r·* of divinity refresh the earth.

raise

a 27–13　I [Spirit] will *r·* it up."— *John* 2 : 19.
　34–21　It helped them to *r·* themselves and others
　47–24　in order to *r·* himself in popular estimation.
　51–31　cast out evil, and *r·* the dead.
s 137– 3　heal the sick, cast out evil, *r·* the dead ;
f 235–29　They should so *r·* their hearers spiritually,
b 306– 2　The Pharisees thought that they could *r·* the
　314–15　and in three days I will *r·* it— *John* 2 : 19.
　329– 8　Because you cannot . . . *r·* the dead,
o 359–24　"God is able to *r·* you up from sickness ;"
p 426–24　would *r·* the standard of health and morals
r 494– 3　I [Mind] will *r·* it up ;"— *John* 2 : 19.

raised

a 27– 5　the deaf hear, the dead are *r·*,— *Luke* 7 : 22.
m 67–21　Lord and Master healed the sick, *r·* the dead,
sp 76–12　and was therefore never *r·* from matter.
s 132– 7　the deaf hear, the dead are *r·* up,— *Matt.* 11 : 5.
　134–27　he *r·* Lazarus from the dead,
b 273–25　healed the sick, and *r·* the dead
　313–30　which by spiritual power he *r·* from the grave,
o 341– *　Him that r· up Jesus from the— Rom.* 8 : 11.

raised

o 341– *　He that r· up Christ from the— Rom.* 8 : 11.
p 373– 7　The author has *r·* up the dying,
　424–12　In medical practice objections would be *r·*
　428–31　and *r·* the dying to life and health

raises

a 33–24　*r·* the dead from trespasses and sins,
s 128–18　It *r·* the thinker into his native air of insight
ph 189– 5　*r·* the human thought above the cruder theori◁
f 227–21　C. S. *r·* the standard of liberty
o 342–22　*r·* from the couch of pain the helpless invalid.

raising

a 43– 1　healing the sick, and *r·* the dead,
m 61–26　the *r·* of stock to increase your flocks and
b 316–29　casting out evils, . . . *r·* the dead,
o 341– 2　*r·* up thousands from helplessness to strength
p 369– 9　*r·* the dead, and walking over the wave.
　430– 3　healing the dying and *r·* the dead.

rallying

f 225–12　but there is a *r·* to truth's standard.

rams

s 135– 4　Ye mountains, that ye skipped like *r·*,— *Psa*◁
　114 : 6.

random

ph 175–16　If a *r·* thought, calling itself dyspepsia,

range

sp 84–17　yea, to reach the *r·* of fetterless Mind.
c 258–26　and of the infinite *r·* of his thought.
g 503– 3　These ideas *r·* from the infinitesimal to
　513–28　not within the *r·* of immortal existence
　514– 4　nothing exists beyond the *r·* of

rank

p 367–12　the arrogance of *r·* and display of scholarship,◁

ranks

p 437–30　*r·* above the lower Court of Error.

ransom

b 276– 4　"I have found a *r·*."— *Job* 33 : 24.

rapid

pref viii–22　*r·* multiplication and increased violence of
f 236–31　youth makes easy and *r·* strides towards Trut▷
g 533–22　the *r·* deterioration of the bone and flesh

rapidity

b 268– 2　thought has brought to light with great *r·*

rapidly

f 222–17　he recovered strength and flesh *r·*.
　254– 4　who gain good *r·* and hold their position,
p 373–11　the sick recover more *r·* from disease than
　430– 8　he will advance more *r·* towards God,
t 457–23　and advance *r·* in the demonstration of
r 495–25　How can I progress most *r·* in the
g 533–19　more *r·* than he can alone.

rapport

sp 78– 9　If the departed are in *r·* with mortality,
　84–12　thought which is in *r·* with this Mind,

rapture

sp 76– 5　forgets all else and breathes aloud his *r·*.
f 213–21　*r·* of his grandest symphonies was never hear◁

rarefaction

g 509–15　*r·* of thought as it ascends higher.

rarefy

a 37–11　and *r·* the atmosphere of material sense

rarely

p 402–21　we *r·* remember that we govern our own bodie◁

rashly

t 444–19　and never to condemn *r·*.

rather

pr 9– 1　Do we not *r·* give thanks that we
a 53–14　as humanly mighty, *r·* than as divine,
sp 71–13　formation of thought *r·* than of matter.
　88–27　It is due to inspiration *r·* than to erudition.
s 111–23　physical causes *r·* than to a final spiritual
　146– 7　faith in drugs the fashion, *r·* than faith in Deity
　164–21　*r·* does it evidence the truth of
ph 181–11　for that reason, you employ matter *r·* than Min◁
f 212– 8　Why need pain, *r·* than pleasure, come
　216–29　"willing *r·* to be absent from the— *II Cor.* 5 : 8
　226–24　belief that the body governed them, *r·* than
　233– 2　higher proofs *r·* than professions
　235–32　Love of Christianity, *r·* than love of popularity
　236– 6　emolument *r·* than the dignity of God's laws,
　246–30　freshness, and continuity, *r·* than into age
c 256–11　suggests polytheism, *r·* than the one
o 343–29　mistake which allows words, *r·* than works,
p 374–20　this belief helps *r·* than hinders disease.
　383–10　"willing *r·* to be absent from the— *II Cor.* 5 : 8
　417– 7　Tell them *r·*, that their strength is in
t 445–26　human will . . . is the cause of disease *r·* than
r 473–24　Love, *r·* than personality or the man Jesus,
　491–31　this dream— *r·* than the dreamer

ather
- *g* 524–11 a tribal god to be worshipped, *r·* than Love,
- 528–20 Beginning . . . materially *r·* than spiritually,
- 554– 6 or, *r·*, being and Deity are inseparable.
- *gl* 581–25 "willing *r·* to be absent from the—*II Cor.* 5:8.

atio
- *sp* 95– 8 and in that *r·* we know all human need
- *p* 368–24 in the *r·* of one's spiritual growth.

ational
- *m* 63–23 A feasible as well as *r·* means of improvement
- *sp* 80–27 but they are neither scientific nor *r·*.
- *s* 129–26 quite as *r·* are some of the leading illusions
- *b* 284– 1 It is not *r·* to say that Mind
- 306–18 If . . . we are left without a *r·* proof of

ationality
- *f* 223–21 Spiritual *r·* and free thought accompany
- *b* 268– 7 from which may be deduced all *r·*,

ationally
- *pref* xi– 5 C. S. *r·* explains that all other
- *r* 491–32 Who can *r·* say otherwise,

ay
- *f* 250–12 like a *r·* of light which comes from the sun,
- *b* 300–31 the *r·* of light which goes out from it.
- *o* 361–17 a *r·* of light one with the sun,

ays
- *g* 504–23 The *r·* of infinite Truth, . . . bring light
- 504–31 No solar *r·* nor planetary revolutions form the
- 546–24 spiritual facts of being, like *r·* of light,

each
- *pref* viii– 3 but to *r·* the heights of C. S.,
- *pr* 4–22 We *r·* the Science of Christianity through
- 6–14 To *r·* heaven, the harmony of being, we must
- 16–21 *r·* the heaven-born aspiration and
- *a* 21– 8 that they shall *r·* his harmony and reward.
- 35–22 as we *r·* the Life which is Truth
- 43–24 Out of *r·* of the barbarity of his enemies,
- 49–23 but is above the *r·* of human wrath,
- *m* 61–32 If . . . is requisite to *r·* this goal,
- *sp* 84–17 to *r·* the range of fetterless Mind.
- 85– 9 You will *r·* the perfect Science of healing when
- *ph* 170–14 demands of Truth . . . the *r·* body through
- 194–23 where neither sight nor sound could *r·* him,
- *f* 234–31 Evil thoughts and aims *r·* no farther
- 235–15 will *r·* higher than the heavens of astronomy ;
- 241–25 We should strive to *r·* the Horeb height
- 246– 7 and endeavoring to *r·* Spirit above his origin.
- *c* 262–15 inspire the Godlike man to *r·* the
- *b* 285–28 As mortals *r·*, . . . a higher sense,
- 323–12 is winged to *r·* the divine glory.
- 324–17 before we can *r·* the goal of Spirit,
- 325–25 can never *r·* in this world the divine heights of
- 326– 6 He, who would *r·* the source and find the
- *p* 363– 1 to come behind the couch and *r·* his feet.
- 387– 5 When we *r·* our limits of
- 415–11 in a part which mortal thought does not *r·*.
- 426– 8 counts her footsteps in endeavoring to *r·* it.
- *r* 473–21 to *r·* his example and to test its
- *g* 519–16 and *r·* the spiritual image and likeness.
- 548– 9 How little light or heat *r·* our earth when
- *ap* 571–19 human hatred cannot *r·* you.
- 576–22 is within *r·* of man's consciousness here,

eached
- *pr* 8–12 If he *r·* the loftiness of his prayer,
- *a* 22–25 is not *r·* through paths of flowers nor
- 29–15 Those instructed in C. S. have *r·* the
- *sp* 77– 6 until the Science of being is *r·*.
- 77–11 until the spiritual understanding of Life is *r·*.
- *s* 108–12 My conclusions were *r·* by allowing the
- 109–10 once seen, no other conclusion can be *r·*.
- *f* 219–30 may not be *r·* at this period,
- 237– 8 or *r·* the mental height
- *b* 270–10 are scientific and logical conclusions *r·*.
- 279–19 Spirit is *r·* only through the understanding
- 279–26 scientific conclusion is *r·* only through the
- *o* 353–15 Time has not yet *r·* eternity,
- 353–19 until perfection appears and reality is *r·*.
- *p* 381–25 will never be *r·* without the understanding
- *r* 484– 2 until its absolute Science is *r·*.
- *g* 536–29 and the immortal is *r·*.
- *ap* 560–15 goal is never *r·* while we hate our neighbor
- 568–27 sweeter than has ever before *r·* high heaven,
- 576– 6 *r·* St. John's vision while yet he

eaches
- *a* 18–16 Truth, which *r·* no higher than itself.
- *m* 57– 5 The masculine mind *r·* a higher tone through
- *sp* 95–12 Whoever *r·* this point of moral culture
- 97–12 until matter *r·* its mortal zenith in illusion
- *s* 113– 4 letter of Science plentifully *r·* humanity
- *ph* 178–32 Whoever *r·* the understanding of C. S.
- 197–30 doctor's mind *r·* that of his patient.
- *b* 290–27 becomes thus only when he *r·* perfection.
- 298–18 never *r·* beyond the boundary of the mortal
- *o* 350–29 through which the real *r·* the unreal,

reaches
- *p* 365–15 If the Scientist *r·* his patient through
- 380–27 until it *r·* its culmination of scientific statement
- 406–12 spiritual perception, . . . *r·* Truth.
- *ap* 559– 9 *r·* over continent and ocean

reaching
- *m* 63– 9 prior to *r·* intelligence.
- *b* 328–32 *r·* beyond the pale of a single period
- *p* 366– 9 hinders him from *r·* his patient's thought,
- 408–18 thus *r·* mortal mind through matter?
- 423–11 *r·* to every part of the human system.
- *g* 543– 2 This error, after *r·* the climax of

react
- *b* 283– 9 act, *r·*, and then come to a stop.

reaction
- *pr* 7–12 gives occasion for *r·* unfavorable to
- *ph* 186– 3 the false stimulus and *r·* of will-power
- 198–21 haply causes a vigorous *r·* upon itself,
- *p* 417– 9 there will be no *r·* from over-exertion
- 419–10 knowing that there can be no *r·* in Truth.
- 428– 2 no death, no inaction, . . . nor *r·*."

reacts
- *t* 449– 7 The wrong done another *r·* most heavily

read
- *pref* xii–21 she had never *r·* this book throughout
- *sp* 82– 1 it is as easy to *r·* distant thoughts as
- 82– 3 It is no more difficult to *r·* the absent mind
- 82– 4 than it is to *r·* the present.
- 82– 5 yet we still *r·* his thought in his verse.
- 84–32 can *r·* the stars or calculate an eclipse.
- 85–10 to *r·* the human mind after this manner
- 85–16 *r·* them scientifically.
- 87–16 Science enables one to *r·* the human mind, but
- 94–24 Our Master easily *r·* the thoughts of mankind,
- 94–28 *r·* mortal mind on a scientific basis,
- *s* 109–13 searched the Scriptures and *r·* little else,
- 121– 7 Chaldean Wisemen *r·* in the stars the fate of
- *ph* 179–24 so long as you *r·* medical works
- *f* 217–12 if we turn to the Scriptures, what do we *r·*?
- 253–11 I hope, . . . that, as you *r·*, you see there is no
- *b* 291–20 So we *r·* in Ecclesiastes.
- 328–30 the Scriptural passage would *r·* *you*, not *they*.
- *p* 369–14 We never *r·* that Luke or Paul made a
- 382–29 The treatises I had *r·*
- 422– 8 Continue to *r·*, and the book will become the
- 437–32 The attorney, C. S., then *r·* from the
- *g* 525–23 In the Science of Genesis we *r·*
- 535–29 In the first chapter of Genesis we *r·*:
- 540– 5 In Isaiah we *r·*: "I make peace,—*Isa.* 45:7.
- *ap* 559– 2 open for all to *r·* and understand.
- 559–20 *R·* this book from beginning to end.
- 572–19 In Revelation xxi. 1 we *r·*:
- 573–32 When you *r·* this, remember Jesus' words,
- 575–11 as we *r·* in the book of Hebrews ;
- *gl* 598– 3 in John's Gospel, the third chapter, where we *r·*:
- 598–11 In the record of Jesus' supposed death, we *r·*:

reader
- *s* 115– 6 to make them comprehensible to any *r·*,
- *f* 253– 9 I hope, dear *r·*, I am leading you into the
- *o* 360–13 Dear *r·*, which mind-picture or
- *p* 422– 5 If the *r·* of this book observes a great stir
- *g* 521–18 *r·* will naturally ask if there is nothing more
- 547– 6 You can prove for yourself, dear *r·*, the Science
- *ap* 574–25 Think of this, dear *r·*, for it will lift the

readers
- *ph* 195–27 specimens of depravity, fill our young *r·* with
- *f* 235– 7 and the *r·* in churches
- *p* 430–13 I here present to my *r·* an allegory

readeth
- *ap* 558– * *Blessed is he that r·, and—Rev.* 1:3.

readily
- *m* 60–30 happiness would be more *r·* attained
- *sp* 72–32 As *r·* can you mingle fire and frost as Spirit and
- 86–28 as *r·* as from objects cognizable by the senses.
- *s* 138–26 as *r·* as it was proved centuries ago.
- 149–23 as *r·* as she has cured purely functional disease,
- *f* 236–26 and learn more *r·* to love the simple verities
- *p* 369–25 as would be *r·* seen, if psychology,
- 377–24 as *r·* as functional difficulties.
- 411– 7 just as a person replies more *r·* when
- 414– 5 yields more *r·* than do most diseases
- 418–16 one disease would be as *r·* destroyed as
- 420– 5 If students do not *r·* heal themselves,
- *t* 462– 2 Some . . . assimilate truth more *r·* than
- *r* 489– 6 as *r·* as the lobster's claw,

reading
- *pr* 16–17 This *r·* strengthens our
- *m* 56– 2 *R·* his thoughts, Jesus added :
- *sp* 83–31 *r·* mortal mind . . . touches only human beliefs.
- 95– 2 the only genuine Science of *r·* mortal mind.
- *f* 235–10 their learning or their correct *r·*.
- *b* 272–16 *R·* the thoughts of the people,

reading

p	387–20	instead of r· disquisitions on the
t	446– 6	If patients sometimes seem worse while r· this
r	481–32	When r· the Scriptures,

readings

s	139–18	different r· in the Old Testament,
o	361–30	hence the many r· given the Scriptures,

readjust

p	392– 7	to r· the balance for God.

reads

pr	16–16	the original properly r·,
sp	80– 7	communication purporting to come from...r·
b	338–15	and it r·, a dam, or obstruction.
o	361–19	Scripture r·: "For in Him we live,—Acts 17 : 28.

ready

pr	8–23	If . . . we are not r· to receive the reward of
a	24–21	chiefly as providing a r· pardon for all sinners
	27–19	r· to cut down the false doctrine of pantheism,
	49–20	was r· to be transformed by the renewing of the
	54– 8	Who is r· to follow his teaching and
m	64–15	r· aid her sympathy and charity would afford.
s	131–16	but the churches seem not r· to receive it,
	131–25	until the hearts of men are made r· for it.
ph	170–24	The age seems r· to approach this subject,
	176–30	are quite as r· to yield to Truth as
	179–27	r· to put you into a sweat,
f	223–15	Many are r· to meet this inquiry with the
	224–13	Centuries ago religionists were r· to hail an
	238– 3	wait till those whom you would benefit are r·
o	347– 2	Who is r· to admit this?
	353–23	When we learn that . . . we shall be r· for
p	410– 2	If . . . we shall not be r· for spiritual Life
	420–16	but are r· to become receptive to the new idea.
	425–30	be always r· with the mental protest
t	458–14	the divine Mind is r· to take the case.
	458–15	Divinity is always r·.
r	494–26	Which of these two . . . are you r· to accept?
ap	563–25	which was r· to be delivered,— Rev. 12 : 4.
	570–23	Those r· for the blessing . . . will give thanks.
gl	597– 9	which was r· to spring into action

reaffirms

sp	89–12	r· the Scriptural word concerning a man,

real

and continuous

p	397–12	by believing them to be r· and continuous.

and eternal

sp	71– 1	Nothing is r· and eternal, . . . but God and
f	208–21	Let us learn of the r· and eternal,
b	289–30	things spiritual are the r· and eternal.
	296–12	reveals man . . . harmonious, r·, and eternal.
	301–13	which constitutes the only r· and eternal entity.
	307– 5	saying, . . . as r· and eternal as Truth.
	331–21	reflected by all that is r· and eternal
o	360– 1	and know that these ideals are r· and eternal
r	468–12	Spirit is the r· and eternal ;
g	538–22	in contradistinction to the r· and eternal.
gl	594–10	claim that . . . was as r· and eternal as God,

and God-given

g	528–23	and calling them r· and God-given,

and good

pref	viii–10	physics teach that both . . . are r· and good,
gl	583–21	divine Principle of all that is r· and good ;

and harmonious

p	419– 7	God and His ideas alone are r· and harmonious.

and ideal

b	332–31	Into the r· and ideal man the

and immortal

b	276–15	Harmony in man is as r· and immortal as in

and tangible

b	269–17	These ideas are perfectly r· and tangible to

and the unreal

o	360–21	swinging between the r· and the unreal.

and unimpeachable

p	414–29	perfection is r· and unimpeachable,

and unreal

g	505–22	demarcation between the r· and unreal.

are styled the

f	213– 1	movements of mortal belief,...are styled the r·.

attraction

an	102– 9	There is but one r· attraction,

being

(see **being**)

cause

p	402–32	a belief without a r· cause.
t	463– 1	and deals with the r· cause of disease.

Christianly scientific

o	353– 1	The Christianly scientific r· is the

cross

a	50–30	The r· cross, . . . was the world's hatred of

desires

pr	6– 4	will leave our r desires to be rewarded by Him.

error is not

f	251– 1	Error is not r·, hence it is not
o	353–23	When we learn that error is not r·,

real

eternal and

b	300–14	temporal and unreal never touch the etern· and r·.
r	494–27	The other is the eternal and r· evidence,

good and

pref	viii–11	whereas the fact is that Spirit is good and r·,

harmony is the

ap	563– 2	harmony is the r· and discord the unreal.

individuality

b	299–14	whither every r· individuality, image,

is eternal

o	353–16	All the r· is eternal.
r	474–16	while all that is r· is eternal.

jurisdiction

p	379– 6	r· jurisdiction of the world is in Mind,

Life

a	51–16	He knew . . . that r· Life is God ;
b	282– 3	The r· Life, or Mind, and its opposite,
	328– 5	God is good and the only r· Life.

Life is

p	428– 3	Life is r·, and death is the illusion.

man

(see **man**)

Mind

sp	91–30	whereas the r· Mind cannot be evil
b	295–27	the exact opposite of r· Mind, or Spirit.

nature

sp	93–18	Whatever contradicts the r· nature of the

objects

sp	96–29	r· objects will be apprehended mentally

opposite of the

b	277–25	the opposite of the r· is not divine,
	337–28	the opposite of the r· or the spiritual and etern·

origin

b	287– 1	They are without a r· origin or existence.

or unreal

g	524–24	Is this addition to His creation r· or unreal?

outlaw

an	105– 9	mortal mind, evil, which is the r· outlaw,

prelude

g	502– 2	living and r· prelude of the older Scriptures

realm of the

b	268– 4	rising towards the realm of the r·,
	277–24	The realm of the r· is Spirit.
	303– 4	which people the realm of the r·
	337–26	as they exist in the spiritual realm of the r·.

Science

s	122– 2	often reverses the r· Science of being,
b	273– 8	They differ from r· Science because they

sense

b	295–14	the r· sense of being, perfect and forever intac·

senses

f	214–30	and there are no other r· senses.
b	284–28	only r· senses of man are spiritual,
r	488–28	If it were possible for the r· senses of man to·

sickness is not

p	394– 2	to understand that sickness is not r·

status

s	120–19	or to exhibit the r· status of man.

substance

r	468–22	Spirit, . . . is the only r· substance.

tangible and

b	279–11	tangible and r· to immortal consciousness,

tone

s	126–13	the human mind never produced a r· tone

Truth is

b	288– 1	The statement that Truth is r·
p	368– 4	the fact that Truth is r· and error is unreal.
r	466–15	Moreover, Truth is r·, and error is unreal.

universe

b	289–19	to the . . . r· universe there is no death-proce·

unreal and the

g	538–10	the material and spiritual, — the unreal an· the r·.

unrealities seem

r	472–28	that unrealities seem r· to human, erring belie·

wishes

pr	13–18	overwhelming our r· wishes with a torrent of

pr	7–29	uttering desires which are not r·
m	61– 2	The senses confer no r· enjoyment.
	69– 9	r·, ideal man appears in proportion as
sp	70– 3	corporeal senses cannot inform us what is r·
	92–25	We should blush to call that r· which
	92–29	mistake of thinking that error can be r·,
an	102– 2	God governs all that is r·,
	103–21	false belief . . . that evil is as r· as good
s	114–17	to designate that which has no r· existence.
	131– 2	error should not seem so r· as truth.
	131– 3	Sickness should not seem so r· as health.
	144– 5	even if these so-called powers are r·.
ph	172–11	Spirit can form no r· link in this supposed
	173–24	the image of God, the r· immortal man.
	176–25	One disease is no more r· than another.
	186–17	It says : "I am a r· entity,

eal

ph 186–24 If evil is as r· as good,
  186–25 If death is as r· as Life,
  186–26 If pain is as r· as the absence of pain,
f 204– 5 false conclusions. . .that material history is as r·
  207–31 the opposite discord, . . . is not r·.
  209–20 are of no r· importance,
  210–29 To mortal sense, sin and suffering are r·,
  214–28 the r· sight or sense is not lost.
  215–15 led to believe that darkness is as r· as light ;
  228– 8 learn that nothing is r· but the right,
  230– 1 If sickness is r·, it belongs to immortality ;
  239–19 If divine Love is becoming . . . more r· to us,
  244– 3 therefore such deformity is not r·, but is illusion,
  250– 7 mortal existence has no r· entity,
b 269–31 I combat . . . that matter . . . is as r· as Mind,
  270– 7 hence both cannot be r·.
  270– 7 If one is r·, the other must be unreal.
  276–10 r· consciousness is cognizant only of
  277–11 If goodness and spirituality are r·,
  278– 9 the notion that there is r· substance-matter,
  286–15 and governs all that is r·.
  287–23 it is illusion, . . . and it has no r· existence.
  288–32 man's r· existence as a child of God
  292–16 To mortal mind, . . . evil is r·.
  292–29 the spiritual r· man's indissoluble
  292–32 mortal man is not the r· essence of manhood,
  294–10 is not more r· than the belief that
  297–13 that disappears which before seemed r·
  298–11 To material sense, the unreal is the r· until
  298–19 When the r· is attained,
  302– 9 that man should lose aught that is r·,
  302–12 The notion that . . . are r·, is a mortal belief ;
  305–10 man, like all things r·, reflects God,
  306–22 not more distinct nor r· to the material senses
  311– 6 evil is not made and is not r·.
  317–19 makes man more r·, more formidable
  317–32 Nothing but . . . could make existence r· to Thomas.
  318–24 treats disease as though disease were r·,
  329–27 If men understood their r· spiritual source to be
  330–25 notion that both evil and good are r·
  335–29 Nothing unspiritual can be r·,
  339–13 would make that r· which is unreal,
o 347–30 The harmonious will appear r·,
  350–29 through which the r· reaches the unreal,
  351–18 while error seems as potent and r· to us as
  352–14 Would a mother say . . . ghosts are r·.
  352–21 by declaring ghosts to be r·, merciless, and
  353– 2 whatever seems r· to material sense, is unreal in
  353– 9 How can a Christian, . . . think of the latter as r·
  353–18 Without perfection, nothing is wholly r·.
  357–25 If what opposes God is r·,
  360– 3 by a right estimate of what is r·."
  360–14 which mind-picture . . . shall be r· to you,
p 368–10 the fatal beliefs that error is as r· as Truth,
  379–32 the belief that . . . discord is as r· as harmony,
  386–18 the same grief that the friend's r· death would
  391–15 r· suffering for your own sins
  394– 6 which is the only r· recuperative power.
  395–24 to believe in the r· existence of a tumor,
  397–16 more powerful than . . . to make the injury r·.
  399–28 All that is r· is included in this
  404– 8 there is no r· pleasure in false appetites.
  404–20 there is no r· pleasure in sin,
  406–14 Sin and sickness will abate and seem less r· as
  417–22 Disease should not appear r· to the physician,
r 470–13 If God, or good, is r·,
  470–15 And evil can only seem to be r· by
  472– 7 making it coordinate with all that is r·
  473– 3 seeming to be r· and identical.
  474–16 If sin, sickness, and death are as r· as
  474–22 r· or the offspring of the divine will?
  474–26 If evil is r·, Truth must make it so ;
  478–26 That only is r· which reflects God.
  480–23 and it has no r· basis.
  490– 1 It assures mortals that there is r· pleasure in
  490–17 the r· man's divine Principle, Love.
  493–25 seem r· and natural in illusion.
  494–21 sin, sickness, and death will seem r·
  494–22 the experiences of the sleeping dream seem r·
g 506– 4 matter, . . . has no r· entity.
  526–21 doctrine that the knowledge of evil is as r·,
  530–22 saying, . . . Only admit that I am r·,
  530–29 for neither is true nor r·.
  555–12 as if it were as r· and God-created as
  556– 1 That which is r·, is sustained by Spirit.
ap 576–19 the r· man's incorporeality
gl 584–11 hence it has no r· existence.

real estate

m 63–31 hold r· e·, deposit funds,

realism

s 129–23 We must look deep into r·
  144–20 and is not a factor in the r· of being.

realism

b 337– 5 Material personality is not r· ;
o 354–27 Its supposed r· has no divine authority,

realities

eternal
sp 78– 5 they are not the eternal r· of Mind.
ghosts are not
o 352–24 ghosts are not r·,
grand
b 328–12 reveals the grand r· of His allness.
of being
f 212–29 The r· of being, its normal action,
  229– 6 but if sin and suffering are r· of being,
c 264–20 Spirit and its formations are the only r· of being.
of divine Science
b 298– 2 the r· of divine Science.
of eternal existence
p 387–19 adhering to the r· of eternal existence,
of Spirit
b 325– 5 is being ushered into the undying r· of Spirit.
spiritual
g 513–27 His thoughts are spiritual r·.
gl 581–12 Science showing that the spiritual r·
supernal
c 261–27 Fixing your gaze on the r· supernal,
the only
s 109– 5 the only r· are the divine Mind and idea.
c 264–20 Spirit and its formations are the only r· of being.
the vague
b 298– 1 the vague r· of human conclusions.

  b 318– 5 Corporeal senses define diseases as r· ;
  g 556–22 Oblivion and dreams, not r·,
  g 594– 8 the first claim that . . . are the r· of life.

reality

admit its
p 395– 2 They admit its r·, whereas they should deny it.
all forms of
g 513–26 God creates all forms of r·.
and fatality
ph 197–32 his belief in its r· and fatality will
and immortality
r 486–24 Their r· and immortality are in Spirit
and in Science
b 293–10 In r· and in Science, both strata,
and power
p 372–20 can we believe in the r· and power of
and Truth
gl 580–29 not one who . . . sustains r· and Truth.
appearance of
f 215–18 darkness loses the appearance of r·.
appears
b 312– 7 as the sense-dream vanishes and r· appears.
assume the
r 481–20 Human hypotheses first assume the r· of
attest the
s 150–15 to attest the r· of the higher mission of
by giving
y 470–15 evil can only seem to be real by giving r· to the
cannot in
p 419–23 A relapse cannot in r· occur in mortals
complete
o 353–16 eternity, immortality, complete r·.
consciousness of
ap 573–23 the spiritual idea and consciousness of r·.
contradictions of
b 335–31 and must be contradictions of r·.
devoid of
g 525–29 as devoid of r· as they are of good,
divine
sp 95–22 succeeded by C. S., by divine r·.
eternal
g 538–14 significant of eternal r· or being.
fleshly
b 317–30 remained a fleshly r·, so long as
governed by
s 131– 4 our lives must be governed by r·
governs all
p 418–27 this simple rule of Truth, which governs all r·.
grasp the
b 275–10 To grasp the r· and order of being in its
great
sp 91–12 the sooner man's great r· will appear
gl 580–10 unreality as opposed to the great r· of
harmony the
o 352– 3 to make harmony the r·
idea, of all
sp 71– 5 idea, of all r· continues forever ;
is in God
r 472–24 All r· is in God and His creation,
is reached
o 353–19 until perfection appears and r· is reached.
is spiritual
b 335–27 R· is spiritual, harmonious, immutable,

reality

make a
- *b* 339–13   the sinner would make a *r·* of sin,

no
- *sp* 71– 2   Evil has no *r·*.
- *f* 207–22   there can be no *r·* in aught which
- *o* 346–22   there is no *r·* in his belief of pain,
- *p* 427– 8   when learning that there is no *r·* in death,
- *t* 447–22   but realize no *r·* in them.
- *g* 530–27   The dream has no *r·*, no intelligence, no mind ;

no other
- *f* 242–11   It is to know no other *r·*

nor existence
- *b* 331–12   nothing possesses *r·* nor existence except

nor identity
- *r* 473– 2   illusion, possessing neither *r·* nor identity

of being
- *b* 297–15   Thus the *r·* of being is attained
-    311–19   opposite to the immortal *r·* of being.
- *p* 418–13   no more the *r·* of being than is sin.
- *r* 493–27   is not the *r·* of being.
- *ap* 573–29   this *r·* of being will surely appear sometime

of existence
- *f* 215– 9   unacquainted with the *r·* of existence,

of good
- *f* 205–20   the supremacy and *r·* of good,
- *b* 269– 7   and unfold the unity and the *r·* of good,
- *r* 480–32   evil would vanish before the *r·* of good.
- *g* 527–19   Has evil the *r·* of good?

of Life
- *sp* 72–27   earthly mortal is not the *r·* of Life
- *b* 322– 5   we shall gain the *r·* of Life,
- *o* 353–32   nor apprehend the *r·* of Life.
- *r* 487–29   our trust in the deathless *r·* of Life,

of man's existence
- *pr* 13–31   blind to the *r·* of man's existence,
- *o* 352– 9   spirituality, was the *r·* of man's existence,

of spiritual Life
- *b* 318–21   yields to the *r·* of spiritual Life.

of substance
- *b* 311–27   not the *r·* of substance.

power, nor
- *an* 102– 7   possessing neither intelligence, power, nor *r·*,
- *ph* 186–16   there is neither power nor *r·* in evil.

presence of the
- *b* 293– 2   mortality disappears in presence of the *r·*.

pure
- *p* 409–23   to be laid aside for the pure *r·*.

radiant
- *s* 110– 5   the radiant *r·* of God's creation,

realm of
- *a* 34–25   would rise again in the spiritual realm of *r·*,

reinstate
- *g* 529– 9   destroy the *dream* of existence, reinstate *r·*,

same
- *ph* 186–22   If we concede the same *r·* to discord as to

seeming
- *p* 394– 3   Truth can destroy its seeming *r·*,

spiritual
- *f* 207–27   The spiritual *r·* is the scientific fact
-    228–18   they will recognize harmony as the spiritual *r·*
- *r* 488–21   senses can take no cognizance of spiritual *r·*

supposed
- *gl* 596–25   and the supposed *r·* of error.

supposition of
- *f* 213– 2   this mortal mind supposition of *r·*

their
- *pref* xi–11   before which sin and disease lose their *r·*
- *o* 352–27   If belief in their *r·* is destroyed,
- *p* 395–26   while you argue against their *r·*,
-    397–10   by admitting their *r·* and continuance,
- *r* 486–24   Their *r·* and immortality are in Spirit
- *g* 546–23   though the darkness, . . . may deny their *r·*.

unbroken
- *r* 494–24   breaks their illusion with the unbroken *r·* of

underlies
- *o* 353–17   Perfection underlies *r·*.

underlying
- *b* 305–15   the underlying *r·* of reflection.
- *r* 477–27   caught some glimpses of the underlying *r·*,

without intelligence or
- *r* 469–17   error, without intelligence or *r·*.

- *sp* 73–27   mistake . . . that matter is any part of the *r·*
-    86–23   In *r·* there is none.
-    97– 5   In *r·*, the more closely error simulates truth
- *an* 103–29   In *r·* there is no *mortal* mind,
- *s* 107–17   remembering that in *r·* God is our Life,
-    130–10   It is unwise to doubt if *r·* is
- *ph* 181–16   In *r·* you manipulate because you
-    184– 5   should not be recognized as *r·*.
- *f* 250–22   Is there any more *r·* in the waking dream
-    252–17   lifts its voice with the arrogance of *r·*
- *b* 275–24   all is in *r·* the manifestation of Mind.
-    281–16   which reflects *r·* and divinity

reality
- *b* 293–26   In *r·*, they show the self-destruction of error
-    298–14   faith, understanding, fruition, *r·*.
-    299– 2   no more *r·* than has the sculptor's thought
-    299– 5   which has no physical antecedent *r·*
-    301–18   man should wish for, and in *r·* has,
-    309–28   error . . . that there can be such a *r·* as
-    327–20   evil has in *r·* neither place nor power
-    330–23   there is in *r·* one Mind only,
-    339–30   divest our self of any supposed mind or *r·*,
- *o* 347–13   so-called mortal man is not the *r·* of man.
-    352–17   Children, like adults, *ought* to fear a *r·* which
-    357–19   As there is in *r·* but one God,
- *p* 369– 1   Once let the mental physician believe in the *r·*
-    369– 1   he is liable to admit also the *r·* of
-    369–14   never . . . made a *r·* of disease
-    381–10   We cannot in *r·* suffer from
-    395–21   It is mental quackery to make disease a *r·*
-    395–28   Mental practice, which holds disease as a *r·*,
-    403–11   In *r·*, both have their origin in the
- *t* 452– 3   evil has in *r·* no power.
- *r* 472–27   Therefore the only *r·* of
-    481– 2   How important, then, to choose good as the *r·*
-    486–10   In *r·* man never dies.
-    487–21   there is in *r·* no such thing as
-    489–11   yields to the *r·* of everlasting Life.
-    492– 4   In *r·* there is no other existence,
- *g* 502– 5   as if *r·* did not predominate over unreality,
-    505–27   the *r·* of all things brought to light.

realization
- *b* 276–12   The *r·* that all inharmony is unreal
-    300–20   through the *r·* of God as ever present
- *g* 514–30   A *r·* of this grand verity was a source of strength
- *ap* 575–32   westward, to the grand *r·* of the

realize
- *a* 55–17   My weary hope tries to *r·* that happy day,
-    55–19   when he shall *r·* God's omnipotence
- *f* 204–21   and *r·* only one God,
-    205–22   When we *r·* that there is one Mind,
- *c* 264–16   When we *r·* that Life is Spirit,
- *b* 315–18   we *r·* this likeness only when we subdue sin
-    323–19   When the sick or the sinning awake to *r·*
- *p* 386– 1   *R·* that the evidence of the senses is not
-    387– 8   when we *r·* that immortal Mind is ever active,
-    409–25   in proportion as mortals *r·* the Science of man
-    412–24   *R·* the presence of health and the fact of
-    417– 9   If you make the sick *r·* this great truism,
-    420–25   if they only *r·* that divine Love gives them
-    428–19   We must *r·* the ability of mental might
- *t* 447–21   but *r·* no reality in them.

realized
- *a* 47–32   Jesus *r·* the utter error of a belief in
- *ph* 167–31   Only through . . . can scientific healing power be *r·*.
-    172–14   yet this can be *r·* only as the
- *p* 392–25   Admitting only such conclusions as you wish *r·*

realizing
- *ph* 194–26   and *r·* Tennyson's description :

really
- *pr* 3–22   Are we *r·* grateful for the good
-    9–26   Do you *r·* desire to attain this point?
- *a* 34–10   *r·* commemorate the sufferings of Jesus
-    39–26   divine Principle of all that *r·* exists
- *m* 64–31   Spirit will . . . claim its own,— all that *r·* is,
- *sp* 87–14   when *r·* it is first sight instead of second,
- *s* 116– 9   divinity *r·* is and must of necessity be,
-    119– 3   for of course we cannot *r·* endow matter with
-    151–26   All that *r·* exists is the divine Mind
- *ph* 169–26   the sick are never *r·* healed except by means of
-    173– 4   or determine when man is *r·* *man*
- *f* 203–10   was *r·* the justification of Jesus,
-    210–19   The expression *mortal mind* is *r·* a solecism,
-    213–17   The ear does not *r·* hear.
-    230–23   the sick are never *r·* healed by drugs,
- *b* 272–24   which *r·* attest the divine origin and
-    272–30   the divine Principle . . . of all that *r·* exists.
-    274– 8   *Natural science,* . . . is not *r·* natural nor
-    275–12   the divine Principle of all that *r·* is.
-    283–21   belief as to what *r·* constitutes life
-    300–18   tares and wheat, which never *r·* mingle,
-    301–10   immortal, spiritual man is *r·* substantial,
-    321–17   was *r·* but a phase of mortal belief.
-    328– 9   These errors are not thus *r·* destroyed,
-    340–13   all that *r·* exists is in and of God,
- *o* 347– 6   Nothing *r·* has Life but God,
-    348– 7   making the disease appear to be— what it *r·* is
- *p* 371– 8   uninstructed in C. S., nothing is *r·* understood
-    402–16   no breakage nor dislocation can *r·* occur.
- *t* 443– 7   omnipotent Mind as *r·* possessing all power.
- *r* 478–30   *Mortal man* is *r·* a self-contradictory phrase,
-    484–18   are *r·* caused by the faith in them which
- *ap* 561–28   is *r·* neither solar nor lunar,

realm

mental
- *sp* 82–22 nor are they in the mental *r* in which we dwell.
- *g* 514–11 the king of the mental *r*.

of God
- *r* 481– 6 into the holiest,''— the *r* of God.— *Heb.* 10 : 19.

of harmony
- *s* 138– 8 a firm foundation in the *r* of harmony.

of Love
- *a* 20–27 It commands sure entrance into the *r* of Love.

of Mind
- *c* 264– 9 in the unsearchable *r* of Mind?
- *g* 514– 7 Mind, . . . dwells in the *r* of Mind.

of mysticism
- *sp* 80–18 never . . . into the *r* of mysticism.

of reality
- *a* 34–25 rise again in the spiritual *r* of reality,

of the physical
- *s* 111– 9 though departing from the *r* of the physical,

of the real
- *b* 268– 4 rising towards the *r* of the real,
- 277–24 The *r* of the real is Spirit.
- 303– 3 which people the *r* of the real
- 337–26 as they exist in the spiritual *r* of the real.

physical
- *p* 427–25 in the physical *r*, so-called, as well as

unsearchable
- *c* 264– 9 in the unsearchable *r* of Mind?

- *r* 480–13 Material sense has its *r* apart from Science
- *gl* 590– 2 *r* of unerring, eternal, and omnipotent Mind ;

realms
- *s* 128–18 giving mortals access to broader and higher *r*.
- *g* 557– 6 the birth-throes in the lower *r* of nature,

realness
- *o* 347– 5 has no origin, existence, nor *r*.

reap
- *a* 41– 9 in the hereafter they will *r* what they now sow.
- *ph* 179–30 may erelong *r* the effect of this mistake.
- *f* 238–18 when we . . . try to *r* the harvest we have not
- *p* 405–18 that shall he also *r*.''— *Gal.* 6 : 7.
- *t* 462–12 he will inevitably *r* the error he sows.
- *g* 537–14 that shall he also *r*.''— *Gal.* 6 : 7.

reapeth
- *f* 210–24 and *r* the whirlwind.

reappear
- *sp* 75– 3 The so-called dead, in order to *r*
- 81–19 seemeth to wither and the flower to fade, they *r*.
- *ph* 189–13 or doubt that the sun will *r*.
- *f* 212– 7 why cannot the limb *r*?
- 230–28 though it is liable to *r* ;
- *p* 436– 5 to *r* however at the trial
- *t* 453–11 but with some individuals . . . constantly *r*.

reappearance
- *a* 27–10 by his *r* after the crucifixion
- 43– 4 his material disappearance . . . and his *r*,
- *sp* 98– 5 *r* of the Christianity which heals the sick

reappeared
- *g* 509– 5 Our Master *r* to his students,

reappearing
- *a* 35–13 to receive more of his *r*
- 45–28 *r* of Jesus was not the return of a spirit.
- 55–22 The time for the *r* of the divine healing
- *s* 132–21 unconscious of the *r* of the spiritual idea,
- *b* 271– 2 chain of scientific being *r* in all ages,

reason

and conscience
- *an* 106– 9 self-government, *r*, and conscience.

and demonstration
- *s* 109–21 divine revelation, *r*, and demonstration.

and revelation
- *s* 110–15 *r* and revelation were reconciled,
- *o* 347–27 must yield to *r* and revelation.

befool
- *p* 440– 6 how to make sleep befool *r*

convince
- *g* 522–23 convince *r* and coincide with revelation

domain of
- *sp* 80–17 from the domain of *r* into the realm of

human
- *s* 117–25 relates solely to human *r* ;
- 117–26 human *r* dimly reflects and
- *ph* 173–26 Human *r* and religion come slowly to the

misguided
- *f* 220– 8 Instinct is better than misguided *r*,

no
- *an* 105–19 "I see no *r* why metaphysics

of its hope
- *r* 487–23 from which to explain the *r* of its hope.

sensuous
- *s* 111– 4 the will, or sensuous *r* of the human mind,

that very
- *p* 376–17 it cannot, for that very *r*, suffer with a fever.

reason

understand the
- *p* 397–18 Declare that you are not hurt and understand the *r*

- *ph* 181–11 for that *r*, you employ matter rather than Mind.
- 199–11 by *r* of its demand for and
- 199–12 by *r* of the blacksmith's faith in
- *b* 325– 4 by *r* of this is being ushered into the
- 327–29 *R* is the most active human faculty.
- *r* 467–23 We *r* imperfectly from effect to cause,
- 494–19 *R*, rightly directed, serves to correct the

reasonable
- *b* 270– 1 quite as *r* as the second,
- 325–23 which is your *r* service.''— *Rom.* 12 : 1.

reasonably
- *an* 105–14 courts *r* pass sentence, according to the motive.
- *g* 537–19 No one can *r* doubt that the

reasoned
- *b* 305–31 The Sadducees *r* falsely
- *o* 356– 9 Jesus *r* on this subject practically,

reasoning
- *s* 124–12 a blind conclusion from material *r*.
- 129– 3 the *r* of an accurately stated syllogism
- *b* 279–26 belief contradicts alike revelation and right *r*.
- *p* 389–15 This false *r* is rebuked in Scripture
- *t* 452– 4 Incorrect *r* leads to practical error.
- *r* 467–25 *a priori* *r* shows material existence to be
- 467–29 *R* from cause to effect
- 492– 3 For right *r* there should be but one fact

reassurance
- *r* 494– 4 and he did this for tired humanity's *r*.

reassure
- *p* 384– 5 Let us *r* ourselves with the law of Love.
- 411–28 Silently *r* them as to their

reassures
- *p* 420–18 The fact that . . . . *r* depressed hope.

Rebecca
- *ap* 566–13 *R* the Jewess in the story of Ivanhoe,

rebel
- *s* 160–19 Can muscles, bones, blood, and nerves *r*

rebellion
- *p* 391– 8 rise in *r* against them.

rebuilt
- *ap* 576–17 as the temple to be temporarily *r*

rebuke

ever-present
- *a* 52–10 ever-present *r* of his perfection and purity.

his
- *pr* 6–31 left this record : "His *r* is fearful."

merited
- *pr* 9– 3 author has been most grateful for merited *r*.

strong
- *a* 23–14 receives a strong *r* in the Scripture,

useful
- *p* 382–10 receive a useful *r* from Jesus' precept,

virtue is a
- *t* 449–28 Only virtue is a *r* to vice.

- *pr* 8–32 do we listen patiently to the *r*
- *a* 30–20 Christ Jesus came to *r* rabbinical error
- 30–28 loathe sin and *r* it under every mask.
- *f* 233–30 is designed to *r* and destroy error.
- 238–16 Unimproved opportunities will *r* us when we
- *b* 315– 5 His better understanding of God was a *r*
- *t* 443–21 "Reprove, *r*, exhort— *II Tim.* 4 : 2.
- 452–13 withhold not the *r* or the explanation which

rebuked
- *pr* 6–23 Jesus uncovered and *r* sin before he cast it out.
- *a* 35– 2 hearts chastened and pride *r*.
- 51–27 Love, which *r* their sensuality.
- 53– 6 He *r* sinners pointedly and unflinchingly,
- *m* 67–31 Jesus *r* the suffering from any such cause
- *sp* 85–20 Our Master *r* the lack of this power
- *s* 121–19 *r* by clearer views of the everlasting facts,
- *b* 309– 5 and *r* his material sense.
- *p* 363–14 Jesus *r* them with a short story
- 389–15 This false reasoning is *r* in Scripture
- 392– 5 be taken into account and the error be *r*.
- *r* 471–27 This view *r* human beliefs,
- *g* 509–30 Jesus *r* the material thought of his
- *gl* 581–16 spiritual compensation ; the ills of the flesh *r*.
- 597– 6 *r* the hypocrisy, which offered long petitions

rebukes
- *a* 23–19 which *r* sin of every kind
- *b* 281– 8 *r* mortal belief, and asks :
- *o* 350–29 Soul *r* sense, and Truth destroys error.
- *ap* 571–27 Thus he *r* the conceit of sin,

rebuking
a	48–22	thus *r·* resentment or animal courage.
ph	174–18	*r·* in their course all error
p	364–11	*r·* self-righteousness and declaring
gl	589–17	*r·* and destroying error,
	589–20	a higher sense of Truth *r·* mortal belief,
	594–15	love *r·* error ; reproof of sensualism.

recall
sp	88– 2	In our day-dreams we can *r·*
s	122–22	which every thinker can *r·* for himself.

recalling
t	445–29	*R·* Jefferson's words about slavery,

Recapitulation
gl	585–15	ERROR. See chapter on *R·*, page 472.
	588–26	INTELLIGENCE, . . . See chapter on *R·*, page 469.
	590–14	LIFE. See chapter on *R·*, page 468.
	593– 3	PRINCIPLE. See chapter on *R·*, page 465.
	594–18	SOULS. See chapter on *R·*, page 466.
	594–25	SUBSTANCE. See chapter on *R·*, page 468.

receding
g	536– 7	human concepts advancing and *r·*,

receive
pr	1– *	*believe that ye r· them, — Mark* 11 : 24.
	3–10	in order to *r·* His blessing,
	3–24	and thus be fitted to *r·* more.
	8–23	If . . . we are not ready to *r·* the reward
	10– 2	walk in the light so far as we *r·* it,
	10–22	Experience teaches us that we do not always *r·*
	10–26	or we should certainly *r·* that for which we ask.
	10–27	"Ye ask, and *r·* not, because — *Jas.* 4 : 3.
	10–30	it is not always best for us to *r·*.
	15–32	Without a fitness for holiness, we cannot *r·*
a	22–15	and you *r·* no present reward,
	22–19	and *r·* according to your deserving.
	29–11	though we may never *r·* it in this world.
	35–12	to *r·* more of his reappearing
	36–22	impossible for sinners to *r·* their
s	131–16	but the churches seem not ready to *r·* it,
	132– 6	the blind *r·* their sight — *Matt.* 11 : 5.
ph	169–25	whatever good they may seem to *r·* from
c	267–30	he shall *r·* the crown of life, — *Jas.* 1 : 12.
b	283–27	*r·* the divine Principle in the understanding,
	284–16	which *r·* no direct evidence of Spirit,
	333–22	to all prepared to *r·* Christ, Truth.
	339–11	sinner can *r·* no encouragement from the
p	382–10	*r·* a useful rebuke from Jesus' precept,
	382–22	"Whosoever shall not *r·* the — *Luke* 18 : 17.
	420–15	when they are in a fit mood to *r·* it,
t	444– 1	and they *r·* no help from them,
	444– 7	If Christian Scientists ever fail to *r·* aid
r	471–10	these so-called senses *r·* no intimation of
	483–26	it ought to *r·* aid, not opposition,
	488– 5	therefore you *r·* the blessing of Truth.
g	542–21	Sin will *r·* its full penalty,

received
pr	3–23	Are we really grateful for the good already *r·* ?
a	39– 2	Such indignities as he *r·*, his followers
	46–30	His students then *r·* the Holy Ghost.
	54– 6	but earth *r·* the harmony
sp	88–30	*r·* from the impulsion of departed spirits.
s	107– *	*For I neither r· it of man, — Gal.* 1 : 12.
	131–18	his own *r·* him not." — *John* 1 : 11.
	132–17	*r·* no aid nor approval from
ph	193–23	since the injury was *r·* in boyhood.
o	342–15	where they should be hospitably *r·*.
	348–31	ethics and temperance have *r·* an impulse,
	359–21	early *r·* her religious education.
p	372–31	prevents the honest recognition of benefits *r·*,
g	555–11	Error would have itself *r·* as mind,
gl	598– 6	yet it has *r·* different translations,

receives
a	23–14	This preaching *r·* a strong rebuke
ph	192–31	*r·* directly the divine power.
t	455–17	The student, who *r·* his knowledge of
r	474–11	consequent maltreatment which it *r·*.
g	556–25	Ontology *r·* less attention than physiology.

receiving
s	156–25	and *r·* occasional visits from me,
p	439– 1	*r·* pay from them

recent
p	402–23	mesmerism — or hypnotism, to use the *r·* term
g	549–13	According to *r·* lore,

recently
an	101–30	animal magnetism, *r·* called hypnotism,

reception
a	41–22	Jesus foresaw the *r·* C. S. would have
	52–12	foresight of the *r·* error would give him.
s	107– 5	for the *r·* of this final revelation of
	115– 1	the one great obstacle to the *r·* of
t	448–23	*r·* or pursuit of instructions opposite to
r	474– 4	The *r·* accorded to Truth in the

receptive
a	34–16	preach Christ, . . . to the poor, — the *r·* thought
	46–11	It is revealed to the *r·* heart,
b	323–20	they will be *r·* of divine Science,
	324– 1	renders thought *r·* of the advanced idea.
p	380– 1	may rest at length on some *r·* thought,
	382–14	is more *r·* of spiritual power
	395–20	nurse should be . . . *r·* to Truth
	420–16	are ready to become *r·* to the new idea.

receptiveness
f	236–29	their freedom from wrong and their *r·* of

recesses
an	102–18	hidden in the dark *r·* of mortal thought,

recipe
f	247–31	*r·* for beauty is to have less illusion
p	406– 1	The Bible contains the *r·* for all healing.

reckoned
g	520–11	can never be *r·* according to the

reckoning
b	275–11	begin by *r·* God as the divine Principle
g	539– 4	Error begins by *r·* life as separate from

reclaims
o	342–21	C. S. awakens the sinner, *r·* the infidel,

reclined
p	362–13	he *r·* on a couch

recognition
full
a	29–25	the full *r·* that being is Spirit.
	50–19	If his full *r·* of eternal Life had
m	59– 2	without a full *r·* of its enduring obligations

honest
p	372–30	the honest *r·* of benefits received,

of being
ap	573–24	such a *r·* of being is, and has been, possible

of divine Science
b	322–10	before this *r·* of divine Science can come

of harmony
ap	576–24	possesses this *r·* of harmony consciously

of infinite Love
p	366–18	and has not that *r·* of infinite Love

of life
r	495–18	the *r·* of life harmonious — as Life eternally is

of Spirit
sp	76–32	*r·* of Spirit and of infinity comes not suddenly
	90–28	understanding and *r·* of Spirit must finally come,
b	287–30	yield to Truth, — to the *r·* of Spirit

of Truth
t	450–11	open to the approach and *r·* of Truth.
ph	173–26	to the *r·* of spiritual facts,

recognizable
b	294–25	Man's genuine selfhood is *r·* only in

recognize
pr	13–27	hence men *r·* themselves as merely physical,
a	55–18	when man shall *r·* the Science of Christ
sp	93– 1	to *r·* Soul as substantial
an	104–29	courts *r·* evidence to prove the motive
s	133–27	*r·* no life, . . . nor substance outside of God.
ph	183–20	mortals commonly *r·* as law that which
f	228–17	they will *r·* harmony as the spiritual reality
c	264–26	evidences, by which we can *r·* true existence
	264–28	When we . . . *r·* man's spiritual being,
b	284–12	Can matter *r·* Mind?
	284–13	Can infinite Mind *r·* matter?
	316– 7	and to *r·* the divine sonship.
p	441–16	Our law refuses to *r·* Man as sick or dying,
t	451–21	and he must *r·* this in order to defend himself
	461–23	while to *r·* your sin, aids in destroying it.
g	508–20	and grammars always *r·* a neuter gender,
	531–14	Then man will *r·* his God-given dominion

recognized
a	31–10	He *r·* Spirit, God, as the only creator,
sp	76– 6	When being is understood, Life will be *r·* as
	90–12	Then being will be *r·* as spiritual,
s	157– 4	because its one *r·* Principle of healing is Mind,
ph	168–24	and *r·* the patient's fear of it,
	184– 5	and should not be *r·* as reality.
f	215–31	he *r·* the immortality of man.
	252–13	and *r·* as the true likeness of his Maker.
b	278– 5	the only substance and consciousness *r·* by
r	468–30	One ceases in proportion as the other is *r·*.
	480– 2	the nothingness of matter is *r·*,
gl	592– 9	nor can be *r·* by the spiritual sense ;

recognizes
pr	9–22	and *r·* only the divine control of Spirit,
ph	188–14	in sleep, in which every one *r·* his
o	361–12	*r·* that Jesus Christ is not God,

recognizing
f	249– 7	*r·* no mortal nor material power as able to
p	379– 7	all causation as vested in divine Mind.
	416– 5	removed by *r·* the truth of being.
g	530–10	*r·* God, the Father and Mother of all, as able

recollect
  b 323–14 We must *r·* that Truth is demonstrable when
  p 389– 7 *R·* that it is not the nerves, not matter,
recollected
  sp 86–26 peculiarities of expression, *r·* sentences,
recollection
  pr 7–30 with the *r·* that we have prayed over it
recommend
  s 157–22 why did Jesus not employ them and *r·*
  p 441–20 We further *r·* that Materia Medica
recommended
  an 105–10 defies justice and is *r·* to mercy.
  s 143– 7 else Jesus would have *r·* and employed
  f 221– 8 His physician also *r·* that he should not
  p 369–17 never *r·* attention to laws of health,
  437–16 though *r·* to mercy ;
recommends
  t 453–30 never *r·* material hygiene, never manipulates.
recompense
  sp 98– 1 spiritual *r·* of the persecuted is assured
  p 409–32 as a *r·* for ignorance.
recompensing
  g 501– 9 *r·* human want and woe with spiritual gain.
reconcile
  a 19– 2 to *r·* man to God, not God to man.
  19– 5 Even Christ cannot *r·* Truth to error,
  s 163–31 to *r·* the fixed and repulsive antipathies
reconciled
  a 45–11 we were *r·* to God by the— *Rom. 5 :* 10.
  45–12 being *r·*, we shall be saved by his— *Rom. 5 :* 10.
  s 110–15 reason and revelation were *r·*,
reconciles
  a 18–13 The atonement of Christ *r·* man to God,
reconciling
  a 19– 6 Jesus aided in *r·* man to God
reconstruct
  f 238–29 To *r·* timid justice and place the
  t 422–19 serve to *r·* the body.
reconstruction
  p 401–32 confines himself chiefly to mental *r·*
record
  according to the
  g 545– 5 for according to the *r·*, material man was
  divine
  s 139–21 and material sense stole into the divine *r·*,
  first
  g 522– 3 The Science of the first *r·* proves the
  522– 5 The first *r·* assigns all might and government to
  528–18 This is the first *r·* of magnetism.
  have no
  a 31– 9 We have no *r·* of his calling any man by the
  47–30 except St. John, of whose death we have no *r·*.
  g 505– 3 have no *r·* in the first chapter of Genesis.
  538–18 have no *r·* in the Elohistic introduction of
     Genesis,
  historic
  a 27–23 but only eleven left a desirable historic *r·*.
  inspired
  g 521– 4 Here the inspired *r·* closes its narrative
  introduces the
  g 544– 1 introduces the *r·* of a material creation
  its own
  g 505– 2 Mind makes its own *r·*,
  of creation
  g 504– 9 are not yet included in the *r·* of creation,
  521–15 turn our gaze to the spiritual *r·* of creation,
  526– 3 scientific *r·* of creation declares that God made
  of Jesus
  a 46–27 ascension, which closed the earthly *r·* of Jesus,
  of man
  g 531–31 the scientifically Christian *r·* of man
  of sin
  g 525–27 the Scriptural *r·* of sin and death
  of spiritual creation
  gl 590–22 the *r·* of spiritual creation.
  second
  g 522– 8 The second *r·* chronicles man as mutable
  522–12 second *r·* unmistakably gives the history of
  this
  pr 6–30 left this *r·* : "His rebuke is fearful."
  g 545–21 The translators of this *r·* of
  ——
  f 224–11 In the *r·* of nineteen centuries,
  246–11 Never *r·* ages.
  g 513–11 In the *r·*, time is not yet measured by
  528– 2 *r·* declares that God has already created
  gl 598–10 In the *r·* of Jesus' supposed death,
recorded
  sp 85–15 It is *r·* that Jesus, as he once journeyed
  an 101– 5 to be *r·* in the history of the errors of
  s 158– 1 It is *r·* that the profession of medicine
  b 272–25 triumphs of C. S. are *r·* in the destruction of error

recorded
  o 350– 6 as *r·* in the New Testament,
  358–17 as is *r·* throughout the Scriptures.
  p 400–32 *r·* that in certain localities he did not
  411–13 *r·* that once Jesus asked the name of
  441–30 *r·* in our Book of books as a liar.
  g 521–29 scientific truth as before *r·*.
  537–23 *r·* in the first chapter of Genesis.
  544–19 The facts of creation, as previously *r·*,
  ap 577–29 as *r·* by the great apostle,
recorder's
  gl 590–25 is disappearing from the *r·* thought,
records
  a 37– 5 History is full of *r·* of suffering.
  s 153–22 said : "Consulting the *r·* of our science,
  p 402– 5 well-authenticated *r·* of the cure,
  437–17 the terrible *r·* of your Court of Error,
  g 522–14 It *r·* pantheism, opposed to the
  525–26 as to the *r·* of truth,
recounting
  s 132– 1 *r·* his works instead of referring to
recourse
  b 329–28 they would struggle for *r·* to the spiritual
  t 445–12 by *r·* to material means for healing.
recover
  pr 12–29 If the sick *r·* because they pray
  a 38–12 and they shall *r·*."— *Mark* 16 : 18.
  s 144–16 Willing the sick to *r·* is not the
  155– 3 When the sick *r·* by the use of drugs, it is
  ph 166–23 Failing to *r·* health through adherence to
  b 295–10 and then *r·* man's original self
  328–25 and they shall *r·*."— *Mark* 16 : 18.
  o 359–28 and they shall *r·*."— *Mark* 16 : 18.
  p 362– * *and they shall r·.*— *Mark* 16 : 18.
  373–10 the sick *r·* more rapidly from disease than
  377–19 never knew a patient who did not *r·* when
recovered
  s 152–19 and he *r·* accordingly.
  f 222–16 he *r·* strength and flesh rapidly.
recovering
  pref xi–20 And *r·* of sight to the blind,— *Luke* 4 : 18.
  s 156–16 to give up the medicine while she was *r·*.
recovery
  facilitate
  p 421–10 showing him that it was to facilitate *r·*.
  impute their
  f 219–27 and impute their *r·* to change of air
  of invalids
  s 145– 8 The struggle for the *r·* of invalids goes on,
  of the sick
  pr 12–22 custom of praying for the *r·* of the sick
  f 218–17 Why pray for the *r·* of the sick, if
  p 372–31 this will be a hindrance to the *r·* of the sick
  419– 1 A moral question may hinder the *r·* of the sick.
  ——
  ph 185–27 but the *r·* is not permanent.
  193–24 Since his *r·* I have been informed that
  p 376– 4 the latent fear and the despair of *r·*
  396– 7 a discouraging remark about *r·*,
recreate
  g 514– 2 and afterwards *r·* persons or things
  547–19 theory, . . . endues matter with power to *r·*
recreation
  f 205–14 Where then is the necessity for *r·* or
rectified
  f 230–20 blunders which must afterwards be *r·* by man?
  240–21 until all wrong work is effaced or *r·*.
  t 460–13 is material, till such thought is *r·* by Spirit.
rectitude
  p 403–21 The most Christian state is one of *r·*
recuperative
  f 252– 4 and of the *r·* energies of Truth
  p 394– 7 is the only real *r·* power.
  t 447–14 The *r·* action of the system,
recur
  s 114–20 must sometimes *r·* to the old and imperfect.
recurring
  c 260–25 by the thoughts ever *r·* to one's self,
recurs
  ph 181–24 the question then *r·*,
  f 217–18 that condition never *r·*,
red
  b 338–13 signifying the *r· color of the ground,*
  ap 562–30 and behold a great *r·* dragon,— *Rev.* 12 : 3.
  563– 8 The great *r·* dragon symbolizes a lie,
  565– 2 and becomes the great *r·* dragon,
  567–21 is pure delusion, the *r·* dragon ;
  gl 580– 1 "dust to dust ;" *r·* sandstone ;
Red Dragon
  gl 593– 7 definition of

redeem

o 354–21 God will r· that weakness,

redeemed

a 26– 8 till all are r· through divine Love.
f 202–11 r· through the merits of Christ,
p 364– 7 they might be r· from sensuality and sin.

redeeming

g 552–23 the r· power, from the ills they occasion,

redeems

a 19– 9 r· man from the law of matter,

redemption

s 151– 7 something beyond itself for its r· and healing.
c 255– * *to wit, the r· of our body.— Rom. 8 : 23.*
t 464–12 working for the r· of mankind.

redolent

g 516–12 Love, r· with unselfishness,

Red Sea

f 226–30 the R· S· and the wilderness ;
ap 566– 2 were guided triumphantly through the R· S·,

reduce

m 61–22 must either be overcome or r· him to a
ph 180–31 To r· inflammation, dissolve a tumor,
b 335– 5 would r· God to dependency on matter,
p 374– 3 counter-irritants, and depletion never r·
r 490–17 r· to practice the real man's divine Principle,
g 517– 7 mental attempt to r· Deity to corporeality.

reduced

sp 91–11 but the sooner error is r· to its
s 146–31 Divine metaphysics is now r· to a system,
ph 173– 8 supposition, . . . Truth is r· to the level of
r 471–30 r· to human apprehension, she has named C. S.
ap 572– 5 scientifically r· to its native nothingness.

reduces

p 398–20 which r· self-inflicted sufferings

reducing

g 540– 8 r· it to its common denominator,
ap 561–18 r· to human perception and

re-echoes

sp 88–26 Eloquence r· the strains of Truth and Love.

reed

m 66– 7 a broken r·, which pierces the heart.

reeds

b 269–27 r· shaken by the wind, not houses built on the

reefs

sp 87–21 of the corals, of its sharp r·, of the tall ships

refer

sp 93–26 r· only to quality, not to God.
r 465–12 They r· to one absolute God.
g 508–18 and does not necessarily r· either to

reference

f 235– 8 as direct r· to their morals as to their learning
b 334–29 a r· to the human sense of Jesus crucified.
ap 560– 4 has r· to the present age.
gl 588–22 if used with r· to Spirit, or Deity.

referred

ph 175–22 nor r· to sanitary laws.
f 232–22 He r· man's harmony to Mind,
b 272–11 r· to in the last chapter of Mark's Gospel.
333–28 Jesus r· to this unity of
o 346– 4 not sinful and sickly mortal man who is r· to,
c 523–32 it is usually Jehovah, . . . who is r· to.
540– 6 r· to divine law as stirring up the belief in

referring

a 31–25 R· to the materiality of the age,
s 132– 2 instead of r· to his doctrine,
gl 585– 3 Jesus said, r· to spiritual perception,
596– 8 R· to it, he said to the Athenians :

refers

an 103– 2 Paul r· to the personification of evil as
s 128– 4 r· only to the laws of God
ph 172–21 to which the apostle r· when he says
b 313–10 passage in the same chapter, which r· to
ap 563–29 Its sting is spoken of by Paul, when he r· to

refined

p 383–18 could not be borne by the r·.

refinement

ph 175–28 but they never indulged in the r· of

reflect

a 52–25 speaking of human ability to r· divine power,
sp 71– 9 outside of finite form, which forms only r·.
91–16 Absorbed in . . . we discern and r· but faintly
f 215–10 matter and mortality do not r· the facts of
240– 6 the spiritual intelligence they r·.
b 303– 8 r· the one divine individuality
324– 9 and the body will r· what governs it,
331– 2 no more confined to the forms which r· it
332–27 only purity could r· Truth and Love,
t 446–25 divine beatitudes, r· the spiritual light
r 477–24 Soul can never r· anything inferior to

reflect

g 505–28 God's ideas r· the immortal, unerring, and
506– 3 Objects utterly unlike the original do not r·.
507–20 they r· the Mind which includes all.
516–22 forever r·, in glorified quality, the
516–28 God made man . . . to r· the divine Spirit.
518–22 the varied expressions of God r· health,
gl 588–16 the objects of God's creation r· one Mind,

reflected

pr 3–12 The Divine Being must be r· by man,
17– 7 *And Love is r· in love ;*
c 258–19 infinite Principle is r· by the infinite idea
b 305– 5 a face r· in the mirror is not the original,
306–10 If . . . there would be no divinity r·.
331– 6 Mind, the creator r· in His creations.
331– 7 God would not be r· but absorbed,
331–21 r· by all that is real and eternal
336– 7 is r· in all spiritual individuality
336–14 but is r· by man.
336–20 neither could God's fulness be r· by a single man
r 467–18 God as not in man but as r· by man.
479– 9 An image of mortal thought, r· on the retina,
496– 4 omnipotent Mind is r·
g 503– 3 embraced in the infinite Mind and forever r·.
504– 1 is never r· by aught but the good.
510–10 r· spiritually by all who walk in the light
516– 5 are r· by His creation ;
516–10 Life is r· in existence, Truth in truthfulness,
517–17 His personality can only be r·, not transmitted
524–23 yet God is r· in all His creation.
543–26 r· in the myriad manifestations of Life,
550–15 Error of thought is r· in error of action.
ap 562– 9 the universe borrows its r· light,
gl 599– 4 The r· animation of Life, Truth, and Love.

reflecting

an 102–14 man, r· God's power, has dominion
s 125–16 R· God's government, man is self-governed.
ph 179–10 not in self-righteousness, but r· the
f 247–17 r· those higher conceptions of loveliness
b 300–21 man as r· the divine likeness.
337– 2 man, r· God, cannot lose his individuality ;
346– 4 the ideal man, r· God's likeness.
r 468–24 r· the divine substance of Spirit.
489–17 How can man, r· God, be dependent on
g 503–16 r· Him in countless spiritual forms.
515–23 r· goodness and power.

reflection

and demonstration
f 241–19 the r· and demonstration of divine Love,
God's
s 126– 6 when man beholds himself God's r·,
r 471–17 Man is, and forever has been, God's r·.
g 527– 4 Man is God's r·, needing no cultivation,
governing the
b 303– 5 the Principle governing the r·.
His
f 242–12 no other reality . . . than good, God and His r·,
b 306– 9 If . . . parted for a moment from His r·,
314– 7 inseparable as God and His r·
r 466– 1 His r· is man and the universe.
idea or
r 470–22 idea or r·, man, remains perfect.
gl 581– 8 ARK. Safety ; the idea, or r·, of Truth,
image or
pr 13–28 ignorant of man as God's image or r·
f 204–26 without the nature of the image or r·
b 300– 5 His infinite image or r·, man.
likeness and
g 516– 8 we shall see this true likeness and r·
mirrored
g 515–25 Your mirrored r· is your own image
observation and
s 163– 9 founded on long observation and r·,
of God
s 121–29 the r· of God, is thus brought nearer the
ph 200–18 if man is the image, r·, of God,
c 259– 8 threw upon mortals the truer r· of God
b 296– 3 man is the spiritual, eternal r· of God.
300–11 will bring to light the true r· of God
333–21 the spiritual idea,—the r· of God,
r 475–18 man is the r· of God, or Mind,
g 502–12 serves to suggest the proper r· of God
516– 3 so you, being spiritual, are the r· of God.
555–16 the origin of man, who is the r· of God,
of his Maker
b 305–27 Because man is the r· of his Maker,
of Soul
f 249–31 Man is the r· of Soul.
of Spirit
b 303– 7 Multiplication . . . is the r· of Spirit.
r 477–20 Identity is the r· of Spirit,
g 506– 4 matter, not being the r· of Spirit,
523–12 instead of the r· of Spirit.
524–23 Matter is not the r· of Spirit,

eflection

of the Ego-God
b 281–11   The Ego-man is the *r·* of the Ego-God ;
of the infinite
b 313–17   the royal *r·* of the infinite ;
or likeness
b 337– 6   it is not the *r·* or likeness of Spirit,
scientific
sp 70– 9   In this scientific *r·* the Ego and the
spiritual
b 305–22   as opposed to the Science of spiritual *r·*,
r 480– 5   If there is no spiritual *r·*, then there remains
the right
b 299–25   which cannot destroy the right *r·*.
this
c 258–12   this *r·* is the true idea of God.
b 301–13   This *r·* seems to mortal sense transcendental,
your
g 515–26   If you lift a weight, your *r·* does this also.

---

s 126– 6   even as man sees his *r·* in a glass.
f 244–21   If . . . there is no full *r·* of the infinite Mind.
c 259–18   true likeness cannot be lost in divine *r·*.
b 301– 6   what C. S. means by the word *r·*.
  302–32   is but the *r·* of the creative power of
  303– 1   The *r·*, through mental manifestation,
  305– 9   the mirrored form, which is but a *r·*,
  305–15   constitutes the underlying reality of *r·*.
  337–20   as the *r·* of the invisible God,
r 477–20   the *r·* in multifarious forms of
g 503–21   *first*, in light ; *second*, in *r·* ;
  515–30   and call man the *r·*.
  516– 1   how true, . . . is the *r·* to its original.
  516– 2   As the *r·* of yourself appears in the mirror,
  528– 2   all being is the *r·* of the eternal Mind,

eflections

b 280– 5   only *r·* of good can come.
  336–15   man's consciousness and individuality are *r·* of
g 513–12   the motions and *r·* of deific power
  517–24   there is no limit to infinitude or to its *r·*.

eflects

a 18– 2   whereby man *r·* divine Truth, Life, and Love.
sp 70– 8   spiritual man, made in God's likeness, *r·* God.
  90–32   we certainly shall know this when man *r·* God.
  94– 3   Man *r·* infinite Truth, Life, and Love.
s 117–26   human reason dimly *r·* and
  120– 5   man coexists with and *r·* Soul, God,
f 240–11   the Principle is above what it *r·*,
  247–22   *r·* the charms of His goodness in expression,
  250–13   man, the outcome of God, *r·* God.
  253– 1   He *r·* the infinite understanding,
c 258–11   Man *r·* infinity, and this reflection is the
  259– 2   for he *r·* eternal Life ;
  266–28   he *r·* the beatific presence,
b 281–11   *r·* reality and divinity in individual . . . man
  286–20   the spiritual universe is good, and *r·* God
  300–28   *r·* and expresses the divine substance
  300–32   God is revealed only in that which *r·* Life,
  301–11   and *r·* the eternal substance, or Spirit,
  301–12   He *r·* the divine, which constitutes the only
  303–10   Whatever *r·* Mind, Life, Truth, and Love,
  305– 7   *r·* the central light of being,
  305–10   man, like all things real, *r·* God,
  305–14   though he *r·* the creation of Mind,
  306–19   cannot be separated . . . from God, if man *r·* God.
p 393–17   in Science man *r·* God's government.
t 458–23   Christianly scientific man *r·* the divine law,
r 475–16   term for all that *r·* God's image and likeness ;
  475–22   but *r·* spiritually all that belongs to his Maker.
  478–27   That only is real which *r·* God.
  479–27   black is not a color, because it *r·* no light.
g 502–29   The universe *r·* God.
  507–15   universe of Spirit *r·* the creative power
  516–20   *r·* God's dominion over all the earth.
  525– 4   Man *r·* God ; *mankind* represents
ap 577– 7   this compounded spiritual individuality *r·*
  588–16   whatever *r·* not this one Mind, is false

eflex

c 259–16   mortals have never beheld in man the *r·* image

eform

pr 5– 3   is but one step towards *r·*
a 19–18   every effort for *r·*, every good thought
  35–30   The design of Love is to *r·* the sinner.
  35–31   If . . . insufficient to *r·* him,
s 139–11   but the present new, yet old, *r·*
  151–13   Even this one *r·* in medicine would
b 285–26   through pardon and not through *r·*,
  327– 1   *R·* comes by understanding that there is no
  327–24   But how shall we *r·* the man who
p 404–17   The temperance *r·*, felt all over our land,
g 537–31   the opportunity to *r·*,

reformation

pref xi–14   as darkness gives place to light and sin to *r·*.
pr 5– 6   the test of our sincerity,— namely, *r·*.
a 22–30   Justice requires *r·* of the sinner.
p 363–30   repentance, *r·*, and growth in wisdom?
  404–15   God's law is fulfilled and *r·* cancels the crime

reformatory

s 129–28   in its *r·* mission among mortals.

reformed

sp 78–30   sorrowing are comforted, and the sinning are *r·*.
o 343–27   healed the sick and *r·* the sinner
  355–31   by the sinners who are *r·*.
p 363–25   Had she repented and *r·*,
t 447–22   A sinner is not *r·* merely by

reforming

p 404–26   Healing the sick and *r·* the sinner

reforms

pr 1– 1   The prayer that *r·* the sinner and heals
  6– 4   this divine Principle alone *r·* the sinner.
a 19–23   the practical repentance, which *r·* the heart
m 65–21   over this as over many other *r·*,
s 139– 9   *R·* have commonly been attended with

refraining

b 322–23   *r·* from it only through fear of

refresh

a 32–26   he withdrew . . . to *r·* his heart with
b 288–17   the raindrops of divinity *r·* the earth.

refreshed

p 387–11   *r·* by the assurances of immortality,

refuge

a 44– 5   gave Jesus a *r·* from his foes,
sp 83– 8   Mortals must find *r·* in Truth in order to
p 394–25   Are material means the only *r·* from fatal
t 444–11   "God is our *r·* and strength,— *Psal.* 46 : 1.

refuse

o 344–25   Why should one *r·* to investigate this method

refused

o 350–16   The Master often *r·* to explain his words,

refuses

f 241– 4   he who *r·* obedience to God, is chastened
p 441–15   Our law *r·* to recognize Man as sick

refutation

p 396–14   *r·* of the testimony of material sense
  396–16   The *r·* becomes arduous, not because

refuted

a 18–12   *r·* all opponents with his healing power.

refutes

s 120–24   and *r·* materialistic logic.

regain

f 247– 3   I have seen age *r·* two of the elements it had
r 486– 7   To die, that he may *r·* these senses?

regained

r 476–15   never had a . . . which may subsequently be *r·*.

regard

pref x– 7   They *r·* the human mind as a healing agent,
pr 9–12   we shall *r·* our neighbor unselfishly,
  14– 1   If we are sensibly with the body and *r·*
a 24–18   in *r·* to predestination and future punishment.
  24–20   Does erudite theology *r·* the crucifixion
  39–11   causes mortals to *r·* death as a friend,
an 100–18   "In *r·* to the existence and utility of
s 119–11   and *r·* God as the creator of
b 307–20   If we *r·* matter as intelligent,
  312– 8   The senses *r·* a corpse, not as man,
p 364–25   do they show their *r·* for Truth, or Christ,
  376–23   true facts in *r·* to harmonious being,
  433–10   jury must *r·* in such cases only the evidence
g 548–28   facts in *r·* to so-called embryonic life.

regarded

m 65–12   life should be more metaphysically *r·*.
an 100– 3   he *r·* this so-called force, which he said could be
s 119–23   evil should be *r·* as unnatural, because
  154– 5   that certain diseases should be *r·* as
  158– 7   Apollo was also *r·* as the sender of disease,
b 313–16   *r·* Christ as the Son of God,
o 345– 1   are often *r·* as synonymous terms ;
p 363– 9   He *r·* her compassionately.
  364– 2   *r·* as the best man that ever trod this planet.
ap 573–17   no longer *r·* as a miserable sinner,

regarding

sp 79– 6   changing the patient's thoughts *r·* death.
s 122–29   the same mistake *r·* Soul and body
  122–30   mistake . . . that Ptolemy made *r·* the
ph 188–32   the desired information *r·* the sun.
f 252– 5   *r·* the pathology and theology of C. S.
b 277–29   Nothing we can say . . . *r·* matter is immortal,
  296– 8   must destroy all illusions *r·* life and mind,
  300– 2   spiritual conclusions *r·* life
o 355–15   conflicting theories *r·* Christian healing?

regarding
p 403–24   Never conjure up some new discovery . . . r·
     disease
423–20   r· the truth and harmony of being
432–13   In this province there is a statute r· disease,
t 461–25   The truth r· error is, that error is not true,

regardless
pr   1– 4   R· of what another may say or think

regards
p 423–16   He r· the ailment as weakened or strengthened
434–16   r· the prisoner with the utmost tenderness.

regenerate
b 296– 8   and r· material sense and self.

regenerated
p 442– 8   Then the prisoner rose up r·, strong, free.

regenerates
pr   4–28   spiritual understanding, which r· ;
f 222– 8   whereas Truth r· this fleshly mind

regeneration
a   24–12   rise into newness of life with r·.
f 242– 2   Through repentance, spiritual baptism, and r·,

regimen
p 370– 6   The body improves under the same r·
370– 7   if health is not made manifest under this r·,

regions
f 240– 2   Arctic r·, sunny tropics, giant hills,

registered
t 457– 1   and r· the revealed Truth

registers
t 449–12   r· his healing ability and fitness to teach.

regret
o 346– 1   I r· that such criticism confounds *man* with

regretted
p 405–26   If sin is not r· and is not lessening, then

regular
pref   x–18   abandoned as hopeless by r· medical
ph 176–22   treated by a r· practitioner,

regularly
p 437–26   proceedings of a r· constituted court.

regulate
ph 184– 3   Truth makes no laws to r· sickness,
185–10   discussed . . . to r· life and health.

regulates
p 413– 7   Mind r· the condition of the stomach,
420–19   It . . . r· the system.

regulations
m   56–14   subject to such moral r· as will
p 389–20   cannot annul these r· by an opposite law

rehearses
ph 188–23   Error r· error.

reign
   and rule
     f 208–22   the r· and rule of universal harmony,
   of discord
     s 122– 2   and so creates a r· of discord,
   of harmony
     sp   93–32   the r· of harmony in the Science of being.
     s 122– 7   the actual r· of harmony on earth.
     gl 590– 1   The r· of harmony in divine Science ;
     592–20   the kingdom of heaven, or r· of harmony.
   of righteousness
     gl 585–19   EUPHRATES . . . the r· of righteousness.
   of Spirit
     f 208–21   the r· of Spirit, the kingdom of heaven,
     gl 587–25   HEAVEN. Harmony ; the r· of Spirit ;
   over man
     g 529–31   He begins his r· over man somewhat mildly,

pref vii–21   "the Lord shall r· forever."— *Exod.* 15 : 18.
f 248–30   kingdom of heaven— r· within us,
b 288–14   will cease, and spiritual harmony r·.
r 476–30   Truth and Love r· in the real man,

reigns
f 205–27   into opposite channels where selfishness r·.
b 318– 4   Mind and immortality, in which Spirit r·
g 536– 8   The divine understanding r·, is *all*,

reins
p 422–29   Not holding the r· of government

reinstate
g 529– 9   r· reality, usher in Science and

reiterate
f 236– 9   who r· Christ's teachings

reject
a   27–28   Why do those who profess to follow Christ r·
54–31   would not some, who now profess to love him,
     r· him?
m   62–31   mortals believe in material laws and r· the
s 148–18   Anatomy and theology r· the divine Principle

rejected
a   20–16   "Despised and r· of men,"— *Isa.* 53 : 3.
52–13   "Despised and r· of men,"— *Isa.* 53 : 3.
s 136–10   His answer to this question the world r·.
139–26   "the stone which the builders r·"— *Matt.* 21 : 42
150–24   as the practically r· doctrine of
f 233–24   including the hearts which r· him.
b 316–25   scourged in person, and its Principle was r·.
o 343–21   It would sometimes seem as if truth were r·
361–27   but it will be r· and reviled until

rejecting
b 280–31   and r· the Science of being
o 357– 6   not by accepting, but by r· a lie.

rejection
a   20–15   [the r· of error]
s 132–24   Anticipating this r· of idealism,
137–11   In his r· of the answer already given

rejects
s 111–16   r· the incidental or inverted image

rejoice
pr   15–25   Christians r· in secret beauty and bounty,
a   22–23   whereby we r· in immortality, ·
m   64–21   Then shall Soul r· in its own,
s 151–13   they would r· with us.
f 249– 8   Let us r· that we are subject to the
o 354–28   I r· in the apprehension of this grand verity.
p 377– 5   that he should r· always in ever-present Love.
g 529–25   should r· that evil, . . . contradicts itself
ap 568–20   Therefore r·, ye heavens,— *Rev.* 12 : 12.

rejoices
pref ix– 4   and r· in the draught.
ap 569–13   r· in the proof of healing,

rejoicing
pref ix–16   To-day, though r· in some progress,
a   29– 6   they will have the crown of r·.
40–22   r· to enter into fellowship with him
s 140–11   but r· in the affluence of our God.
c 266– 2   are good, "r· the heart."— *Psal.* 19 : 8.
o 342–24   and they answer with r·.
r 479– 4   could the Scriptural r· be uttered by any mother,
ap 562–17   These are the stars in the crown of r·.

relapse
p 419– 8   If your patient from any cause suffers a r·,
419–12   Neither . . . has the power to cause disease or
     a r·.
419–23   A r· cannot in reality occur in mortals
419–31   If it is found necessary to treat against r·,

relapses
b 277– 5   non-intelligent r· into its own unreality.

related
s 152–14   It is r· that Sir Humphry Davy once
p 362– 1   r· in the seventh chapter of Luke's Gospel
g 556–31   It is r· that a father plunged his

relates
s 117–24   r· solely to human reason ;
127–15   r· especially to Science as applied to
128–27   Science r· to Mind, not matter.
ph 170–23   spiritual causation r· to human progress.
b 286– 1   what r· most nearly to the happiness of being.
290–14   To the spiritual class, r· the Scripture :
g 515–19   r· to the oneness, the tri-unity of Life, Truth,

relating
s 117– 6   as does the error r· to soul and body,
127–13   stand for everything r· to God,
ph 168–19   God's spiritual command r· to perfection,
p 381–23   human theories r· to health,
433– 5   He . . . explains the law r· to liver-complaint.

relation
   exact
     s 113–13   showing mathematically their exact r· to
   little
     b 297–30   has little r· to the actual or divine.
   marriage
     m   58–29   the chance for ill-nature in the marriage r·,
   of God
     f 206–15   In the scientific r· of God to man,
     b 332– 2   r· of God to man and the universe.
   of man
     sp   94– 7   and of the r· of man to God,
     s 114–25   It shows the scientific r· of man to God,
   seeming
     s 119–30   C. S. reverses the seeming r· of Soul and body
   to God
     ph 196–17   They have no r· to God wherewith to
     f 215–26   in origin, in existence, and in his r· to God
     231–23   the divine Science of being in man's r· to God,
     b 316– 6   to find Christ, the real man and his r· to God,

f 205–32   When we fully understand our r· to the Divine,

elations

m 68–13 its r· to your growth and to your influence
s 123– 1 theory as to the r· of the celestial bodies,
f 209–17 the r· which constituent masses hold
t 460– 4 necessary constituents and r· of all beings,"
r 470–32 The r· of God and man,

elationship

m 59–29 sacredness of this r· is losing its influence,
ph 185–18 Such theories have no r· to C. S.,
b 332– 5 His tender r· to His spiritual creation.

elative

pref xi–30 a law r· to colleges having been passed,
ph 198–10 outlines his thought r· to disease,
f 232– 3 Many theories r· to God and man
233–28 The counter fact r· to any disease
o 355–14 r· value of the two conflicting theories
p 396– 6 Make no unnecessary inquiries r· to feelings

elaxes

s 162– 8 dissolves tumors, r· rigid muscles,

elease

p 431–19 into close confinement until I should r· him.

eleased

p 363–17 who were r· from their obligations

elentless

p 407– 6 Man's enslavement to the most r· masters

eliable

s 120–16 nor can the material senses bear r· testimony
b 322–25 nor a r· religionist

eliance

s 145–14 or r· on some other minor curative.
ph 167–30 Only through radical r· on Truth
170– 1 it robs man of r· on God,
179–29 sowing the seeds of r· on matter,
192– 4 only as we quit our r· upon that which
f 203–14 destroys r· on aught but God,

elief

p 371–13 looks for r· in all ways except the right one.
374– 4 the truth of being, . . . will bring r·.
421–30 material application for its r·.
t 443–19 other systems they fancy will afford r·.

elies

sp 79–11 Spiritualism r· upon human beliefs
b 277–19 Error r· upon a reversal of this order,
t 487–30 This faith r· upon an understood Principle.

elieve

a 18– 9 but not to do it for them nor to r· them of a
s 143–15 takes the lesser to r· the greater.
157–26 quiet mortal mind, and so r· the body ;
p 373–23 and you r· the oppressed organ.
384– 3 We should r· our minds from the
398–17 are known to r· the symptoms of disease.
415–11 That is why opiates r· inflammation.
t 464–16 and the Scientists had failed to r· him,
r 483– 3 but only r· suffering temporarily,

elieved

a 25–23 by no means r· others from giving the
s 156–23 and was r· by taking them.
f 221–23 r· his stomach, and he ate

eligion

and medicine
m 67–30 Systems of r· and medicine treat of
s 107–11 Through C. S., r· and medicine are inspired with
t 444–14 towards differing forms of r· and medicine,
any
sp 98–23 has not been considered a part of any r·,
being and
a 55– 1 any other sense of being and r· than theirs?
Christ's
o 355–17 declines to admit that Christ's r· has
essential
a 27–29 the essential r· he came to establish
fatal to
pr 7–32 Hypocrisy is fatal to r·.
his
s 136– 3 He taught his followers that his r· had a
history of
a 37–10 one stage with another in the history of r·.
Judaic
gl 597– 3 The Judaic r· consisted mostly of rites
motives and
ap 560–22 Abuse of the motives and r· of St. Paul
nature of
a 28–28 is to mistake the very nature of r·.
of Love
s 138–15 His sublime summary points to the r· of Love.
ordinary
s 139–29 opposed to C. S., as they are to ordinary r· ;
perfunctory
b 316–14 this spiritual idea and perfunctory r·,
popular
o 355–17 The other, popular r·, declines to admit that

religion

pure
m 64– 4 "Pure r· and undefiled— *Jas.* 1: 27.
reason and
ph 173–26 Human reason and r· come slowly to the
revealed
g 557–24 revealed r· proclaims the Science of Mind
ritualistic
s 141– 2 the theological and ritualistic r· of the ages
scientific
s 141–27 The adoption of scientific r· and
superficial
gl 597–13 false foundations . . . of superficial r·,
system of
a 26–31 proof of Christianity was no form or system of r·
systems of
m 67–30 Systems of r· and medicine treat of
s 146– 4 Because our systems of r· are governed
their
a 52–30 as self-contradictory as their r·.
o 343–28 and reformed the sinner by their r·.
tribal
s 133–21 the limited form of a national or tribal r·.
true
pr 5–23 Such an error would impede true r·.
m 68– 2 understanding . . . will be the basis of true r·.
undefiled
ap 571–32 He enthrones pure and undefiled r·,

pr 4–32 and clothe r· in human forms.
a 20–26 The truth is the centre of all r·.
54–23 whose r· was something more than a name.
s 140–12 R· will then be of the heart and not of the
146–11 and r· becomes Christlike.
b 326–29 whose r· he had not understood,
351– 1 r· which sprang from half-hidden Israelitish
354–14 proofs that their Master's r· can

religionist

b 322–25 neither a temperate man nor a reliable r·.

religionists

f 224–12 Centuries ago r· were ready to

religions

sp 83–13 and here Science takes issue with popular r·.
s 142– 6 but modern r· generally omit all but one of
f 232–14 r· which contradict its Principle are false.

religious

a 36–30 R· history repeats itself
53–13 above and contrary to the world's r· sense.
sp 88–21 Excite the organ of veneration or r· faith,
s 132–18 other sanitary or r· systems,
133–23 sanitary methods, and a r· cultus.
139–12 the present new, yet old, reform in r· faith
ph 166–12 Mohammedan's belief is a r· delusion ;
c 267– 5 in a r· sense, they have the same authority
b 306–17 this is the general r· opinion of mankind,
340–27 civil, criminal, political, and r· codes ;
o 359–22 early received her r· education.
r 496–28 Have Christian Scientists any r· creed?
497– 1 the important points, or r· tenets, of C. S. :

relinquish

ph 177– 2 it must r· all its errors, sicknesses, and sins.
f 249– 1 r· all theories based on sense-testimony,
251–22 leads the human mind to r· all error,
b 322–13 that finite belief may be prepared to r· its
o 357– 9 If mankind would r· the belief that

relinquished

b 314– 3 had r· the belief of substance-matter,

relinquishes

g 547–28 r· a material, sensual, and mortal theory of

relinquishing

pr 13–21 this will prevent us from r· the

relinquishment

pr 7– 6 r· of error deprives material sense of its
p 426–23 The r· of all faith in death

reluctance

p 420– 9 cannot produce this unnatural r·.

reluctant

t 450–16 many are r· to acknowledge that they

reluctantly

t 466–17 the point you will most r· admit,

rely

s 143– 9 if the sick cannot r· on God for help
144– 3 let us r· upon Mind,
f 202–28 and yet we r· on a drug . . . as if
g 549–22 false systems, which r· upon physics

remain

m 62–17 should be allowed to r· children in knowledge,
s 110–23 the Science and truth therein will forever r·
112–13 they nevertheless r· wholly human
ph 167–15 If God made . . . man must r· thus.
f 208–23 which cannot be lost nor r· forever unseen.

remain

b	290– 7	will *r·* as material as before the transition,
	329–15	nor should he *r·* in the devouring flames.
p	376– 4	fear and the despair of recovery *r·* in thought.
	404–13	while its effects still *r·* on the individual,
	425–30	capacious lungs and want them to *r·* so,
	431– 1	must *r·* silent until called for at this trial,
g	513–20	*r·* in God, who is the divinely creative Principle
	557– 1	until the child could *r·* under water

remained

s	147–28	This rule *r·* to be discovered in C. S.
f	245–10	In this mental state she *r·* young.
b	317–30	*r·* a fleshly reality, so long as
	317–31	so long as the Master *r·* an inhabitant of
r	471– 4	*r·* unchanged in its eternal history.

remaineth

b	288–18	"There *r·* therefore a rest— *Heb. 4 : 9.*

remaining

r	470–22	the divine Principle of man *r·* perfect,
gl	586–24	meeting no response, but still *r·* love.

remains

sp	87– 8	their mental environment *r·* to be discerned,
	98–20	*r·* inviolate for every man to understand and
s	153– 2	to such a degree that not a vestige of it *r·*.
	164–14	Much yet *r·* to be said and done
	164–24	the forever fact *r·* paramount
f	212–13	When the nerve is gone, . . . and the pain still *r·*,
	238–19	Truth often *r·* unsought, until we
b	289–23	the fact *r·*, that God's universe is spiritual
	302– 7	is thereby discerned and *r·* unchanged.
	311–12	so long as the illusion . . . *r·*.
o	348–19	so long as it *r·* in mortal mind,
p	365–13	what mental quality *r·*, with which to
	392– 3	Only while fear or sin *r·* can it bring forth death.
	398–32	fact *r·* that evil is not mind.
t	464–10	She therefore *r·* unseen at her post,
r	470–23	divine idea or reflection, man, *r·* perfect.
	480– 6	then there *r·* only the darkness of vacuity
	481–11	the unseen Truth, which *r·* forever intact.
	486–21	So long as this error of belief *r·*,
	487–10	Lost they cannot be, while Mind *r·*.

remanded

p	433–27	The prisoner is then *r·* to his cell

remands

g	532–12	condemns material man and *r·* him to dust.

remark

p	396– 7	Never startle with a discouraging *r·* about
g	523–14	It may be worth while here to *r·* that,

remarkable

ph	195–25	Novels, *r·* only for their exaggerated
b	313–15	that the author of this *r·* epistle
o	358–20	more frequently cited . . . than are his *r·* works
p	363–22	following it with that *r·* declaration

remarked

s	149–17	A physician of the old school *r·*

remarking

p	438– 1	*r·* that the Bible was better authority than

remedial

an	101–23	convince her that it is not a *r·* agent,

remedies

pref	viii–18	by doctors using material *r·* ;
s	152–32	which demand different *r·* ;
	156–13	her former physician had prescribed these *r·*,
ph	181– 1	more potent than all lower *r·*.
p	398–16	*r·*, sometimes not containing a particle of
	427–27	when all such *r·* have failed?
t	453–13	from the use of material *r·*

remedy

divine

b	326– 7	and find the divine *r·* for every ill,

efficient

p	376–21	the efficient *r·* is to destroy the

for every woe

f	236–19	availability of good as the *r·* for every woe.

God's

s	143– 1	Truth is God's *r·* for error of every kind,

knowing the

t	455–12	if, knowing the *r·*, you fail to use the

man's

r	486– 6	What is man's *r·* ?

material

p	427–26	what material *r·* has man when

of Truth

s	140– 1	demands the *r·* of Truth more than

perfect

p	394– 4	the universal and perfect *r·*.

permanent

f	217–25	The scientific and permanent *r·* for fatigue is

m	63–21	If the elective franchise for women will *r·* the
s	151– 5	could not possibly create a *r·* outside of itself,
	156–30	In metaphysics, matter disappears from the *r·*

remedy

ph	165–19	when your *r·* lies in forgetting the whole thing
	184– 8	The *r·* consists in probing the trouble to the
f	208–16	or that Spirit, . . . leaves the *r·* to matter.
	229–31	The *r·* is Truth, not matter,
	238–20	until we seek this *r·* for human
	248–25	To *r·* this, we must first turn our gaze
p	385–20	your *r·* is at hand.
	423–16	deals with matter as both his foe and his *r·*.
	424–14	to counteract the working of a *r·* prescribed b
t	461–24	and Truth is their *r·*.
g	534–13	unfolded the *r·* for Adam, or error ;
	552–22	From a material source flows no *r·* for

remember

pr	3–32	put the finger on the lips and *r·* our blessings.
a	28–22	*R·*, thou Christian martyr, it is enough if
m	59–21	*r·* how slight a word or deed may
	66– 8	We do not half *r·* this in the sunshine of
	66–17	it is well to *r·* how fleeting are human joys.
	67–20	when we *r·* that through spiritual ascendency
sp	93– 2	*R·* Jesus, who nearly nineteen centuries ago
ph	165–18	in order to *r·* what has hurt you,
f	201– *	*R·, Lord, the reproach of Thy— Psal.* 89 : 50.
	209–20	when we *r·* that they all must give place to
	223– 9	*R·* that truth is greater than error,
	240–24	*R·* that mankind must sooner or later,
b	302–14	let us *r·* that harmonious and immortal man
p	372– 1	*R·*, brain is not mind.
	385–11	Let us *r·* that the eternal law of right,
	394–28	We should *r·* that Life is God,
	402–21	we rarely *r·* that we govern our own bodies.
	414–28	*R·* that man's perfection is real and
	423– 5	*R·* that the unexpressed belief oftentimes
t	445–31	"I tremble, when I *r·* that God is just,"
	454–31	*R·* that the letter and mental argument
r	476–23	*R·* that the Scriptures say of mortal man :
g	557– 3	Parents should *r·* this, and
ap	566–12	If we *r·* the beautiful description
	573–32	When you read this, *r·* Jesus' words,

remembered

s	130–23	author has often *r·* our Master's love for
	146–21	*r·* not, even when its elevating effects

remembering

a	48–10	*R·* the sweat of agony which
s	107–16	yet *r·* that in reality God is our Life,
c	261–31	We should forget our bodies in *r·* good
p	419– 6	*r·* that God and His ideas alone are real
ap	562–25	but *r·* no more her sorrow

remembrance

p	407– 2	but there is a very sharp *r·* of it,

remind

s	161–19	*r·* one of the words of the

reminded

pr	3– 2	without being *r·* of His province.

reminders

p	411–10	and needed the arguments of truth for *r·*.

remit

a	36– 6	To *r·* the penalty due for sin,

remits

pr	11– 5	A magistrate sometimes *r·* the penalty,

remorse

a	47–22	and for a time quieted his *r·*.
gl	586–13	FIRE. Fear ; *r·* ; lust ; hatred ;
	588– 1	HELL. Mortal belief ; error ; lust ; *r·* ;

remote

ph	178– 8	The *r·* cause or belief of disease
f	230–31	the *r·*, predisposing, and the exciting cause
	247– 1	The acute belief of . . . comes on at a *r·* period
p	393– 6	ignorant that the predisposing, *r·*, and

remoteness

ap	576– 5	which to us seems hidden in the mist of *r·*,

remotest

ap	559–10	to the globe's *r·* bound.

removal

ph	168– 4	the *r·* of a single weight from either scale
f	219–19	the destruction of the belief will be the *r·* of
o	358–27	in the *r·* of disease
p	367– 5	pitiful patience with his fears and the *r·*

remove

a	40– 1	*R·* error from thought, and it will not
	44–17	to *r·* the napkin and winding-sheet,
an	101–28	since error cannot *r·* the effects of error.
ph	173–28	to *r·* the error which the human mind alone
	183–13	obedience to God will *r·* this necessity.
p	369–23	but to *r·* the effects of fear
	377–20	*R·* the leading error or governing fear
	377–22	and you *r·* the cause of all disease
	377–23	You also *r·* in this way what are termed
	378– 9	*R·* the error, and you destroy its effects.
	382– 9	to *r·* unhealthy exhalations from the cuticle
	400–20	When we *r·* disease by addressing the

remove
p	401–25	Would the drug r· paralysis,
	403–10	The human mind is employed to r· the
	404–14	you can r· this disorder as
	415–14	Opiates do not r· the pain in any scientific
	415–24	To r· the error producing disorder, you must
	421– 8	in order to r· its beliefs,
	424–21	the divine Mind can r· any obstacle,
t	447–25	r· the mask, point out the illusion,
g	542–23	teaches mortals not to r· the waymarks of God.
ap	569–27	how many periods of torture it may take to r·

removed
pr	1– *	Be thou r·, and be thou cast into— Mark 11 : 23.
a	53– 5	yet there never lived a man so far r· from
ph	197–14	r· from imbecility or disease.
f	229– 9	Not far r· from infidelity is the belief which
	230–30	until the liability to be ill is r·.
o	350– 4	or as very far r· from daily experience.
p	370–12	are r· by using the same drug
	371–10	and to be r· as involuntarily,
	374– 5	Hatred and its effects . . . are r· by Love.
	400– 6	before its influence . . . can be r·.
	416– 5	r· by recognizing the truth of being.
g	557–17	the curse will be r· which says to woman,

removes
a	40– 9	Science r· the penalty only by
sp	79–12	C. S. r· these beliefs and hypotheses
	80–17	Science never r· phenomena from the
b	290–21	Christ, Truth, r· all ignorance and sin.
	323–22	r· thought from the body,
p	370–16	it r· through an opposite belief,
	398–28	blind faith r· bodily ailments for a season,
t	463–13	r· properly whatever is defiling
r	493–23	r· any other sense of moral or mental inharmony.

removing
a	40– 9	only by first r· the sin
ph	186– 1	only by r· the influence on him of this mind,
p	411–32	If you succeed in wholly r· the fear,
	421–14	by r· the belief that this chemicalization

rename
b	309–16	until the Messiah should r· them.

renamed
b	309–21	to be r· in C. S. and led to deny

render
s	148–29	to r· help in time of physical need.
ph	183– 2	but the so-called laws of matter would r·
p	415–14	only r· mortal mind temporarily less fearful,
	433– 6	conclusion is, that laws of nature r·
	440–12	but no warping of justice can r·
	440–24	and then r· obedience to these laws
t	445–15	You r· the divine law of healing obscure
	447– 8	ignorant attempts to do good may r· you

rendered
a	19–30	which may be r· : Thou shalt have no
	20– 1	He r· "unto Cæsar the— Matt. 22 : 21.
s	146– 6	schools have r· faith in drugs the fashion,
b	271–11	In Latin the word r· disciple signifies
	313– 3	may be r· "Jesus the anointed,"
p	375–17	should be understood and so r· fruitless.
	381– 1	is r· null and void by the law of Life,
	383– 4	a body r· pure by Mind as well as
	423–21	has r· himself strong, instead of weak,
r	466–23	and cannot be r· in the plural.
	474–12	meaning of the Greek word r· miracle

rendering
f	219–28	not r· to God the honor due to Him

renders
f	211–23	The transfer of . . . Science r· impossible.
	218–12	What r· both sin and sickness difficult of cure
b	324– 1	r· thought receptive of the advanced idea.
o	360– 6	materiality r· these ideals imperfect
p	422–27	and r· them fatal at certain points,
	435–23	for no demand, human or divine, r· it just
t	455–22	r· any abuse of the mission an impossibility.
	461–22	r· your case less curable,
g	540–17	Science r· "unto Cæsar the— Matt. 22 : 21.

rends
f	226–20	Science r· asunder these fetters,

renew
m	59–21	may r· the old trysting-times.
p	426–14	Man should r· his energies and endeavors,

renewal
m	57–12	bringing sweet seasons of r·
s	137–12	and his r· of the question,
f	241–14	transformation of the body by the r· of Spirit.
gl	582– 9	R· of affections ; self-offering ;

renewed
s	137– 9	This r· inquiry meant :
	162–20	the structure has been r·,
g	556–11	belief dies to live again in r· forms,

renewedly
s	109–25	Scripture of Isaiah is r· fulfilled :

renewing
a	49–20	transformed by the r· of the infinite Spirit.

renounce
t	451– 4	must r· aggression, oppression and the pride of

renowned
b	333– 7	Joshua, the r· Hebrew leader.

rent
f	242–26	one web of consistency without seam or r·.
p	398– 5	spirit [error] cried, and r· him— Mark 9 : 26.
gl	597–11	It r· the veil of the temple.

reopen
ph	171– 6	man will r· with the key of divine Science

reopened
pref	xii–19	as its President, r· the College

repaired
p	439– 9	At this request Death r· to the spot

repast
t	452–16	Better is the frugal intellectual r·

repayment
sp	97–32	Earth has no r· for the persecutions

repeat
pr	5– 8	Temptation bids us r· the offence.
	6–10	supposition . . . we shall be free to r· the offence.
	11–14	leaves the offender free to r· the offence.
f	243–12	in order to confirm and r· the
t	487–12	and it will r· the wonder.
g	520– 6	can r· only an infinitesimal part of what exists.

repeated
s	126–12	seems to have reversed it and r· it materially ;
	134– 1	To-day the cry of bygone ages is r·,
	136–20	This ghostly fancy was r· by Herod
	137– 8	Yearning to be understood, the Master r·,
f	207–28	The spiritual fact, r· in the action of man
	240–20	past failures will be r· until
	243–14	That those wonders are not more commonly r·
r	474– 5	reception accorded to Truth . . . is r·
g	516–27	To emphasize this momentous thought, it is r·
	557– 1	r· this operation daily, until the child

repeating
pref	xi–17	and r· itself, coming now
a	43–10	and is now r· its ancient history.
sp	86– 6	R· his inquiry, he was answered by the
s	135–17	There is to-day danger of r· the offence
t	452–24	simply by r· the author's words,
g	527–26	Here the lie represents God as r· creation,

repeats
a	28–28	Error r· itself.
	36–30	Religious history r· itself in the suffering of
sp	80–10	r· weekly the assertion that
b	301– 2	r· the color, form, and action of the

repel
p	363– 8	Did he r· her adoration?

repelled
t	449–23	which is attracted or r· according to

repent
a	19–21	if the sinner continues to pray and r·,
b	339–18	Only those, who r· of sin and forsake the
g	522–32	Does the . . . Principle of divine law change or r·?

repentance
a	19–17	Every pang of r· and suffering,
	19–23	the practical r·, which reforms the heart
	35– 1	and his disciples' grief into r·,
s	140–24	a man-projected God, liable to wrath, r·,
f	242– 1	Through r·, spiritual baptism, and regeneration,
p	363–30	r·, reformation, and growth in wisdom?
	364–26	by their genuine r·,
	367–15	with . . . perfume of gratitude, with tears of r·
gl	589– 4	A corporeal mortal embracing duplicity, r·,
	598–20	mortality ; space for r·.

repentant
p	404–13	If the evil is over in the r· mortal mind,

repented
p	363–25	Had she r· and reformed,

repents
b	329–24	Always right, its divine Principle never r·,

repetition
pr	2–31	Asking God to be God is a vain r·.
sp	73–13	its fruit,— the r· of evil.
s	157–11	with such r· of thought-attenuations,

repetitions
pr	10– 9	millions of vain r· will never
	13– 9	"vain r·," such as the heathen— Matt. 6 : 7.

replace
p	428–20	r· them with the life which is spiritual,
r	495–23	r· mortality with immortality,

replaced
r	489– 6	would be r· as readily as the lobster's claw,

replaces
s 123–14 and *r·* the objects of material sense with

replenish
g 511– 4 "multiply and *r·* the earth."— *Gen.* 1 : 28.
517–26 multiply, and *r·* the earth,— *Gen.* 1 : 28.

replied
s 136–14 They *r·*, "Some say that thou art— *Matt.* 16 : 14.
137–16 Simon *r·* for his brethren,
p 363–19 Simon *r·*, "He to whom he— *Luke* 7 : 43.
411–15 *r·* that his name was Legion.
g 554– 1 It can only be *r·*, that C. S. reveals

replies
m 69–22 If the father *r·*, "God creates man through man,"
o 360– 4 other artist *r·* : "You wrong my experience.
p 411– 7 *r·* more readily when his name is spoken ;
432–18 and Governor Mortality *r·* in the affirmative.
g 554–16 Error *r·*, "God made you."

repliest
ph 181– 4 "Who art thou that *r·* to Spirit?

reply
a 45–26 His *r·* was : "Spirit hath not— *Luke* 24 : 39.
s 131–31 In *r·* to John's inquiry,
132– 1 Jesus returned an affirmative *r·*,
132– 4 his *r·* : "Go and show John— *Matt.* 11 : 4.
136–17 this *r·* may indicate that some of the people
137–17 and his *r·* set forth a great fact :
f 243–16 The clay cannot *r·* to the potter.
r 489–21 affirmative *r·* would contradict the Scripture,
g 545–28 Truth has but one *r·* to all error,

report
a 24–12 will believe our *r·*, and rise into
an 100–14 to investigate Mesmer's theory and to *r·*
101–12 Their *r·* stated the results as follows :
101–19 This *r·* was adopted by the
s 137–14 in their citation of the common *r·* about him.
ph 193–29 I cannot attest the truth of that *r·*,
194– 9 Truth sends a *r·* of health over the body.
f 211– 2 and *r·* how they feel,
b 284–31 but neither sensation nor *r·* goes from
298– 8 What is termed material sense can *r·* only a
p 432–21 shortly after the *r·* of the crime,

reported
an 100–14 *r·* to the government as follows :
p 438–10 in which Mortal Man was *r·* to reside,
439–31 to whatever locality is *r·* to be haunted by

reports
s 122–13 *r·* to this so-called mind its status
f 218– 9 The *r·* of sickness may form a
218–10 a coalition with the *r·* of sin,
p 389– 8 mortal mind, which *r·* food as undigested.
409–13 belief, that the . . . suffers and *r·* disease
g 551– 2 senses and their *r·* are unnatural,

repose
s 128–14 and requires less *r·*.
f 218– 8 more than hours of *r·* in unconsciousness.

reposed
s 160– 7 Unsupported by the faith *r·* in it,
ph 169–14 The faith *r·* in these things should find

represent
sp 74–24 Who will say . . . that darkness can *r·* light,
s 111–18 what this inverted image is meant to *r·*.
118–27 *r·* a kingdom necessarily divided against
151– 3 but this one factor they *r·* to be body,
c 256–24 No form . . . is adequate to *r·* infinite Love.
265–16 The senses *r·* birth as untimely
b 331–28 They *r·* a trinity in unity,
o 344– 4 this is claimed to *r·* the normal, healthful,
p 415–23 *r·* the action of all the organs of the
430–29 a witness testifies thus :— I *r·* Health-laws.
r 466–11 these contrasting pairs of terms *r·*
g 531– 8 *r·* the higher moral sentiments,

representation
s 141–30 Let it have fair *r·* by the press.
g 510–16 The sun is a metaphorical *r·* of Soul
gl 591– 6 MAN. . . . the full *r·* of Mind.

representative
a 52–24 The highest earthly *r·* of God,
b 300–24 If . . . God would have no *r·*,
306–13 If Life or Soul and its *r·*, man,
p 427– 4 Soul is never without its *r·*.
ap 565–11 the masculine *r·* of the spiritual idea,

representatives
b 293–12 both strata, . . . are false *r·* of man.
299–12 Angels are God's *r·*.
gl 582–28 The spiritual thoughts and *r·* of Life,
583– 5 The *r·* of Soul, not corporeal sense ;

represented
pr 13–26 is *r·* as a corporeal creator ;
a 33–21 Let not the flesh, but the Spirit, be *r·* in me.
s 119–21 is *r·* only by the idea of goodness ;
124–17 *r·* as subject to growth, maturity, and decay,

represented
f 214– 9 Adam, *r·* in the Scriptures as formed from
b 294–24 in which matter is *r·* as divided into
299–19 figuratively *r·* in Scripture as a tree,
316–12 Jesus *r·* Christ, the true idea
p 378–20 is *r·* by two material . . . bases.
g 504–16 is *r·* as taking place on so many *evenings* and
522–19 is *r·* as the life-giving principle of the earth.
522–20 Spirit is *r·* as entering matter
536– 7 the sea, . . . is *r·* as having passed away.
537–12 Creation is there *r·* as spiritual,
537–29 and divine Love, . . . is *r·* as changeable.
ap 561–13 *r·* the correlation of divine Principle and
565–18 immaculate idea, *r·* first by man
569– 1 as Life, *r·* by the Father ;
569– 2 as Truth, *r·* by the Son ;
569– 3 as Love, *r·* by the Mother.
574–17 *r·* by the seven angelic vials

representing
b 294–19 *r·* Spirit, and mortal man,
294–20 *r·* the error that life and intelligence are in
p 376–24 *r·* man as healthy instead of diseased,
g 540–22 *r·* error as assuming a divine character,

represents
sp 92–13 This *r·* the serpent in the act of commending
s 140– 5 The Bible *r·* Him as saying :
ph 177–16 which *r·* the erroneous theory of
c 259– 4 *r·* infinite Mind, the sum of all substance.
263– 6 Immortal spiritual man alone *r·* the
b 272–29 God is the divine Principle of all that *r·* Him
282– 6 The circle *r·* the infinite
282– 7 the straight line *r·* the finite,
282– 9 The sphere *r·* good, the self-existent and
282–10 the straight line *r·* evil,
334–24 The Revelator *r·* the Son of man as
p 378–16 *r·* the power of Truth over error,
g 525– 5 *mankind r·* the Adamic race,
527–11 Here the metaphor *r·* God, Love, as
527–26 Here the lie *r·* God as repeating creation,
529–24 nothing in the animal kingdom which *r·* the
530–17 This myth *r·* error as always asserting its
546–13 *r·* error as starting from an idea of good
ap 560–10 Heaven *r·* harmony, and divine Science.
575– 9 *r·* the light and glory of divine Science.
gl 580– 3 not God's man, who *r·* the one God
580–21 The name Adam *r·* the false supposition

reproach
f 201– * *Remember, Lord, the r· of*— *Psal.* 89 : 50.
201– * *how I do bear in my bosom the r·*— *Psal.* 89 : 50

reproached
f 201– * *wherewith Thine enemies have r·*,— *Psal.* 89 : 51
201– * *wherewith they have r· the*— *Psal.* 89 : 51.

reproduce
m 61–18 may *r·* in their own helpless little ones
sp 75–23 to *r·* the presence of those who
87– 2 They copy or *r·* them, even when
87–28 can perceive and *r·* these impressions.
87–29 Memory may *r·* voices long ago silent.
f 246–32 Acute and chronic beliefs *r·* their own types.
b 306– 4 would . . . resort to death to *r·* spiritual life.
p 372– 7 that its sensations can *r·* man,
r 488–28 Soul could *r·* them in all their perfection ;
g 512–12 and consequently *r·* their own characteristics.
gl 584–24 thence to *r·* a mortal universe,

reproduced
p 378– 2 even as poetry and music are *r·*
413–30 such ills may be *r·* in the very ailments feared

reproduces
ph 198–21 and *r·* a picture of healthy and
g 507–16 which *r·* the multitudinous forms of Mind
508– 3 only as the divine Mind is All and *r·* all

reproducing
f 248–17 Are you *r·* it?
b 277–14 preserving their original species,— like *r·* like.
314–12 When Jesus spoke of *r·* his body,

reproduction
ph 189–25 From mortal mind comes the *r·* of the species,
b 277–14 In *r·*, the order of genus and species
302–31 *r·* by Spirit's individual ideas
g 549–10 three different methods of *r·*
553–13 to their maintenance and *r·*,

reproof
pr 7– 3 that Jesus' *r·* was pointed and pungent
gl 594–15 love rebuking error ; *r·* of sensualism.

reprove
t 443–21 "*R·*, rebuke, exhort— *II Tim.* 4 : 2.

reproved
pref x–30 lest their works be *r·*.

repudiate
p 440–27 *r·* the false testimony of Personal Sense.

repudiated
p 418–18 the belief must be *r·*,

repudiates
f 207–16   r· self-evident impossibilities,
g 541–25   Now it r· even the human duty of
550–32   As C. S. r· self-evident impossibilities,

repulsion
t 449–26   only to separate through simultaneous r·.

repulsive
s 163–32   or to reconcile the fixed and r· antipathies of

reputation
a 53– 8   The r· of Jesus was the very opposite of
f 236– 6   Is it not professional r· and emolument
t 456– 9   a r· experimentally justified by their efforts.

reputed
pref viii–21   the r· longevity of the Antediluvians,
an 101–11   phenomena exhibited by a r· clairvoyant.

request
pr 2–17   A r· that God will save us
10–31   In this case infinite Love will not grant the r·.
12– 2   A mere r· that God will heal the sick
p 439– 8   At this r· Death repaired to the spot

requested
ph 184–31   I then r· her to look at the weather-vane.

requests
pr 9–10   though we give no evidence of the sincerity of our r·

require
a 23– 2   Wisdom and Love may r· many sacrifices
44–15   He did not r· the skill of a surgeon
s 141– 6   Why? Because his precepts r· the disciple to
ph 179–14   and the body then seems to r· such treatment.
f 242–31   and r· of Christians the proof which he gave,
c 257–30   It would r· an infinite form to contain
o 360–10   They r· less self-abnegation,
p 404–27   Both cures r· the same method
420–20   or diminishes . . . as the case may r·,
t 452– 8   Walking in the light, we . . . r· it;
g 501– 6   seems so smothered . . . as to r· explication;
532– 2   Did God at first create . . . but afterwards r·

required
pr 2–18   is not all that is r·.
5– 4   The next and great step r· by wisdom is
a 32– 3   In ancient Rome a soldier was r· to
m 59– 9   Man should not be r· to participate in all the
sp 77– 3   The period r· for this dream of
s 142– 2   r· for self-establishment and propagation.
143–11   matter r· a material and human belief
ph 173– 9   is r· to be made manifest through
f 233–29   The counter fact . . . is r· to cure it.
o 351–17   proof of Christianity, which Jesus r·,
p 432–24   was r· to confirm his testimony.
t 464– 6   and how much time and talent are still r·
r 473–25   a better understanding of God . . . is r·,
482– 8   where the deific meaning is r·.

requirement
p 413– 5   A single r·, beyond what is necessary

requirements
pr 7–14   wholesome perception of God's r·.
s 127–11   according to the r· of the context.
f 235– 6   one who does not obey the r· of
t 445– 1   the Scientist must conform to God's r·.

requires
a 22–30   Justice r· reformation of the sinner.
23– 4   The atonement r· constant self-immolation
m 57–20   but r· all mankind to share it.
sp 97–23   It r· courage to utter truth;
s 128–14   and r· less repose.
162–26   for it r· only a fuller understanding of
ph 198–14   but to do this r· attention.
f 253–27   God never r· obedience to a so-called
254– 6   God r· perfection, but not until
b 278–17   r· another admission, — namely,
t 449–16   it r· a higher understanding to teach this
456–25   A Christian Scientist r· my work
ap 571– 7   It r· the spirit of our blessed Master

requisite
pref x–30   No intellectual proficiency is r· in the learner,
pr 11–23   We know that a desire for holiness is r·
a 25–24   the r· proofs of their own piety.
34– 7   no other commemoration is r·,
m 61–32   If the propagation of a higher human species is r·
s 141– 3   More than profession is r· for
148– 3   implying that the r· power to heal was in Mind.
ph 195–19   Academics of the right sort are r·.
b 327–23   Moral courage is r· to meet the wrong
o 361–31   and the r· revisions of SCIENCE AND HEALTH
p 383– 7   influence of the divine Mind on the body is r·,
t 448–21   spiritual qualifications r· for healing,
461– 8   if this be r· to protect others.
461–32   are r· for a thorough comprehension of C. S.
g 527–30   Was it r· for the formation of man
552– 9   even where the proof r· to sustain this

rescue
p 398–30   come to the r·, to work a radical cure.
436–23   struggled hard to r· the prisoner
439–23   You came to his r·, only to

rescued
p 382–24   r· from seeming spiritual oblivion,

researches
s 152–21   The author's medical r· and experiments
g 548–22   Had the naturalist, through his tireless r·,
549–20   Here these material r· culminate

resemblance
f 207–31   discord, which bears no r· to spirituality,

resemblances
f 239–31   mortal mind sends forth its own r·,

resemble
b 329–17   To be discouraged, is to r· a pupil in

resembles
sp 97– 6   and so-called matter r· its essence,
s 164– 1   r· the groping of Homer's Cyclops
g 531–30   theory of material life at no point r·
541– 2   and more nearly r· a mind-offering

resembling
sp 77–28   a state r· that of blighted buds,
b 305– 5   is not the original, though r· it.

resentment
a 48–22   thus rebuking r· or animal courage.

reservation
ph 183–22   No r· is made for any lesser loyalty.

reservoir
ph 180–15   mental r· already overflowing with that emotion

reside
p 398–23   Appetite and disease r· in mortal mind,
438–10   in which Mortal Man was reported to r·,

residence
f 220–13   and procures a summer r· with more ease than
p 432– 8   testifies: . . . I convey messages from my r· in

resident
f 209–28   hypothesis of . . . intelligence r· in matter,
b 283–32   Are mentality, immortality, . . . r· in matter?
r 482– 5   hypothesis that soul is . . . r· in matter.
ap 570–31   the power of good r· in divine Mind,

resides
p 432–22   says: . . . Body, in which Mortal Man r·.
437– 1   in which province Mortal Man r·.
g 546–28   r· in the good this system accomplishes,

resigned
p 416–22   when the mortal has r· his body
431–17   all these assistants r· to me,
g 539–15   Has Spirit r· to matter the government of

resist
an 101–25   and upon their subjects who do not r· it,
s 128–24   he should not r· Truth, which banishes
f 218–25   R· the temptation to believe in matter as
p 393–12   to r· all that is unlike good.
406–19   R· evil — error of every sort
420–11   they can r· disease and ward it off,

resistance
s 134–30   spiritual power over material r·.
f 224–19   Cold disdain, stubborn r·,
b 317– 8   R· to Truth will haunt his steps,
329–32   Human r· to divine Science weakens

resisted
f 223–29   as truth urges upon mortals its r· claims;

resisting
p 388– 5   which is a r· state of mortal mind,
t 446–24   R· evil, you overcome it

resists
s 126–32   If Christendom r· the author's application of

resolve
pr 7–13   unfavorable to spiritual growth, sober r·,
15–18   We must r· to take up the cross,
ph 199–31   his power of putting r· into action
g 514–17   They carry the baggage of stern r·,

resolved
p 374–28   r· into its primitive mortal elements.

resolves
s 123–14   excludes matter, r· *things* into *thoughts*,
b 269–14   Metaphysics r· things into thoughts,
p 428– 4   r· the dark visions of material sense

resolving
g 510–24   by the r· of fluids into solids,
510–25   suppositional r· of thoughts into

resort
ph 166–25   and only as a last r·, turns to God.
181–12   when you r· to any except spiritual means.
181–25   It is unnecessary to r· to aught besides Mind
b 285–26   and r· to matter instead of Spirit for the
306– 4   They would . . . r· to death to reproduce

resort
p 427–28   Spirit is his last r·, but it should have been his
427–29   it should have been his first and only r·.
t 443– 5   a r· to faith in corporeal means
443–18   and leave invalids free to r· to whatever

resorted
ph 166–27   or he would have r· to Mind first.

resorting
p 415–13   by r· to matter instead of to Mind.

resounded
p 442– 6   r· throughout the vast audience-chamber

resources
m 60–29   Soul has infinite r· with which to bless
p 387–11   nor...trespass upon God-given powers and r·,

respect
pr 8–19   are like charity in one r·,
s 151– 8   Great r· is due the motives and
162–29   With due r· for the faculty,
t 452–12   may provoke envy, but it will also attract r·.
g 541– 6   Lord [Jehovah] had r· unto Abel,— Gen. 4 : 4.
541– 8   but unto Cain, . . . He had not r·.— Gen. 4 : 5.
541– 9   Had God more r· for the homage

respected
p 437–14   the testimony of matter r· ;

respecting
a 28– 9   While r· all that is good in the Church

resplendency
f 252–29   with the r· of consuming fire.

resplendent
f 247–29   shining r· and eternal over age and decay.

respond
p 411– 6   the body would r· more quickly,

responds
sp 89–15   the body r· to this belief,

response
pref viii–20   A vigorous "No" is the r·
a 48– 7   There was no r· to that human yearning,
gl 586–24   love meeting no r·, but still remaining love.

responses
t 461–20   Your r· should differ because of the

responsibilities
m 68–13   Consider its obligations, its r·,

responsibility
a 18– 9   nor to relieve them of a single r·.
m 61–25   a greater r·, a more solemn charge,
ph 166– 5   or shrinking from its implied r·,

responsible
s 119–12   is not only to make Him r· for all disasters,
g 533–17   saying, "The woman, whom Thou gavest me, is r·."

rest
and drink
ap 570–16   are waiting and watching for r· and drink.
at
s 119–27   the earth is in motion and the sun at r·.
p 415–28   Before the thoughts are fully at r·,
create the
g 532– 3   in order to create the r· of the human family?
gives
f 217–20   When mentality gives r· to the body,
peace and
gl 586– 2   EVENING. . . . peace and r·.
sweetest
g 520– 1   The highest and sweetest r·, . . . is in holy work.

a 31–20   and at last we shall r·,
38– 6   doctrine . . . few to be saved, while the r· are
sp 79–24   says : . . . brain is overtaxed, and you must r·.
s 154–26   says . . . "You look tired," "You need r·,"
c 264– 9   Where shall the gaze r·
b 269–13   The categories of metaphysics r· on one basis,
288–19   a r· to the people of God"— Heb. 4 : 9.
317–11   These blessed benedictions r· upon
320– 9   must r· upon both the literal and moral ;"
o 358–24   Sometimes it is said : "R· assured that
p 380– 1   may r· at length on some receptive thought,
383–14   because mind and body r· on the same basis.
387–11   we are able to r· in Truth,
t 460– 1   and r· his demonstration on this sure basis.
g 501–15   Love for whose r· the weary ones sigh

rested
g 519–23   and He r· on the seventh day— Gen. 2 : 2.

restful
s 119–32   is but the humble servant of the r· Mind,

resting
sp 79–14   r· on divine Principle, not on
b 316–30   r· on the basis of matter,
p 424–20   through unspoken thoughts r· on your patient.

resting
p 426–11   r· instead of wearying one.
430– 7   and strengthen its base by r· upon Spirit
t 459–13   instead of r· on the omnipotence of the

resting-place
a 45– 3   and stepped forth from his gloomy r·,

restitution
pr 11– 9   always demands r· before

restless
p 433–13   the prisoner grows r·.

restoration
sp 74– 6   as impossible as would be the r· to its

restore
a 51–22   purpose in healing was not alone to r· health,
ph 174– 2   The Esquimaux r· health by incantations
p 401–25   Would the drug . . . r· will and action
440–31   to r· to Mortal Man the rights of which
g 555–28   Our great example, Jesus, could r· the
gl 585–13   first come and r· all things."— Matt. 17 : 11.

restored
sp 75–14   Jesus r· Lazarus by the understanding
79– 5   health r· by changing the patient's thoughts
s 162–17   the author has r· health in cases of
162–22   carious bones have been r· to healthy conditions.
162–23   I have r· what is called the lost substance of
ph 185– 5   but was r· to health.
b 309– 4   to use the word of the Psalmist, r· his Soul,
321–23   r· his hand to its natural condition
o 348–32   health has been r·, and longevity increased.
352–28   will depart and health be r·.
p 373– 8   partly because they were willing to be r·,
398–14   r· whole, like as the other."— Matt. 12 : 13.
435–34   be r· to the liberty of which

restores
s 124–30   and so r· them to their rightful home
162– 8   r· carious bones to soundness.
f 242–28   while inspiration r· every part of the
p 390– 9   the right understanding of Him r· harmony.
423–13   and it r· the harmony of man.
r 486–16   If death r· sight, sound,

restoreth
ap 578– 8   [LOVE] r· my soul— Psal. 23 : 3.

restoring
o 347–18   r· an essential element of Christianity,
347–20   Science of Christianity which is r· it,
p 375–19   while r· him physically through divine Love.

restrain
an 105– 4   in order to r· crime, to prevent deeds

restricted
an 105– 8   to admit that the power of human law is r· to

restricting
s 161–12   tyrannical law, r· the practice of medicine.

rests
sp 80–30   this belief r· on the common conviction that
s 128–27   It r· on fixed Principle
155–13   dissent or faith, unless it r· on Science, is
157– 8   C. S. exterminates the drug, and r· on Mind
ph 185–18   C. S., which r· on the conception of God as
f 218– 7   The consciousness of Truth r· us more than
233–16   shadow of His right hand r· upon the hour.
248– 3   Its halo r· upon its object.
b 283–12   admits of no error, but r· upon understanding.
291–12   Universal salvation r· on progression and
296–25   it r· upon foundations which time is
p 414–20   Christian Scientists' argument r· on the
t 446–20   for victory r· on the side of immutable right.
453– 7   until victory r· on the side of invincible truth.
457–29   demonstration r· on one Principle,
458– 1   Mental quackery r· on the
460– 6   Mind-healing r· on the apprehension of
r 492–26   On this statement r· the Science of being,
g 514–13   or r· in "green pastures,— Psal. 23 : 2.
519–25   God r· in action.
555–23   Creation r· on a spiritual basis.
gl 583–13   r· upon and proceeds from divine Principle.

result (noun)
affect a
g 553–31   how belief can affect a r· which
favorable
p 423– 5   diminishes the tendency towards a favorable r·.
glorious
f 202–13   For this glorious r· C. S. lights the
good
o 352–31   To accomplish a good r·, it is
of education
ph 176–26   All disease is the r· of education,
of inharmony
f 233–32   sickness, which is solely the r· of inharmony
of sin
pr 6–11   To cause suffering as the r· of sin,
of teaching
o 348–30   but this I do aver, that, as a r· of teaching C. S.

esult (noun)
opposite
  p 385–30 opposite belief would produce the opposite *r·*.
precipitate the
  p 436–19 to precipitate the *r·*
same
  s 128–30 must always bring the same *r·*.
this
  ph 187–11 and then impute this *r·* to another
  198–31 does not follow that . . . produced this *r·*
  p 391–13 No law of God hinders this *r·*.
  t 449–31 and unless this *r·* follows,
watch the
  s 156–18 to give her unmedicated pellets and watch the *r·*,
  p 411–29 Watch the *r·* of this simple rule of C. S.,

  s 160–32 Is a stiff joint . . . as much a *r·* of law as the
  ph 170– 5 the *r·* of the exercise of faith in
  178– 5 the *r·* is controlled by the majority
  199– 7 nobody believes that mind is producing such a *r·*
  f 219–10 and then expect that the *r·* will be harmony.
  248–21 *r·* is that you are liable to follow those
  b 271–14 *r·* of their cultivated spiritual understanding
  309– 7 The *r·* of Jacob's struggle thus appeared.
  328– 6 What is the *r·*?
  o 342– 5 the *r·* of some unqualified condemnations
  p 365–23 *r·* will correspond with the spiritual intent.
  386– 7 no such *r·* occurs without mind to demand it
  386–21 suffering was merely the *r·* of your belief.
  387–23 cannot suffer as the *r·* of any labor of love,
  393–19 as the *r·* of a law of any kind,
  r 485–17 and as the *r·* of spiritual growth.
  485–21 *r·* of the mortal error which Christ, . . . destroys
  486–12 Death is not the *r·* of Truth
  488– 1 The *r·* of our teachings is
  g 505–26 This understanding . . . is not the *r·* of scholarly

esult (verb)
  ph 183–16 The supposed laws which *r·* in weariness
  b 277– 7 good cannot *r·* in evil.
  304–14 can never produce mind nor life *r·* in death.
  306– 3 They would first make life *r·* in death,
  p 384–27 nor any other disease will ever *r·* from
  435– 9 an act which should *r·* in good to himself

esulted
  b 269– 4 have *r·* from the philosophy of the serpent.
  o 342–32 even if their treatment *r·* in the death of

esulting
  sp 81–26 the inharmony *r·* from material sense
  f 204– 9 *r·* in a third person (mortal man)
  p 383–31 another medical mistake, *r·* from
  g 551–31 the *r·* germ is doomed to the same routine.
  gl 591–10 MATTER. . . . life *r·* in death, and death in

esults
are sure
  t 459–25 the *r·* are sure if the Science is understood.
bad
  b 329–16 Until one is able to prevent bad *r·*,
better
  p 389–11 the better *r·* of Mind's opposite evidence.
bodily
  f 245–23 The bodily *r·* of her belief that she was young
  p 392–26 conclusions as you wish realized in bodily *r·*,
certain
  t 459–30 treats disease with more certain *r·* than
  r 484–18 Certain *r·*, supposed to proceed from drugs,
evil
  f 230–13 so as to bring about certain evil *r·*,
favorable
  ph 177–27 are expecting favorable *r·*,
glorious
  ap 568– 7 warfare in Science, and the glorious *r·* of
grand
  t 448–23 the grand *r·* of Truth and Love.
harmonious
  c 259–31 that they may produce harmonious *r·*.
higher
  c 260–16 and to bring out better and higher *r·*,
its
  p 384–13 Through this action of thought and its *r·*
  425– 3 induces this conclusion and its *r·*.
medical
  s 155–18 and produces all medical *r·*,
of belief
  ph 184– 6 Belief produces the *r·* of belief,
of false opinions
  p 403–17 producing on mortal body the *r·* of false opinions ;
of sin
  g 535–14 It unveils the *r·* of sin
produces the very
  p 379–24 produces the very *r·* she dreads.
produce the very
  s 154–20 and they produce the very *r·* which
their
  f 218–31 the moral and physical are as one in their *r·*.
  p 393– 6 ignorant . . . of its own actions, and of their *r·*,

results
unlike
  sp 86–12 Opposites . . . produce unlike *r·*.

  pref viii–29 give to friends the *r·* of her Scriptural study,
  xi– 4 which action in some unexplained way *r·* in
  xi– 9 *r·* now, as in Jesus' time,
  pr 11–21 only the *r·* of mortals' own faith.
  an 101–12 Their report stated the *r·* as follows :
  f 231–12 if truth *r·* in error, then
  b 272–20 the *r·* of the ghastly farce of
  289–21 belief that matter has life *r·*, . . . in a belief in
  325– 8 *r·* in infinite blessings to mortals.
  p 404–17 *r·* from metaphysical healing,
  408–26 and the *r·* would be perceptibly different.
  g 552–28 *r·* in a return to the original species.
  gl 580–25 supposition that . . . Mind *r·* in matter,

resume
  p 373–25 disabled organ will *r·* its healthy functions.
resurrected
  b 295–31 further teaches that . . . his immortal soul is *r·*
resurrection
after his
  a 46–14 after his *r·* he proved to the physical senses
  b 317–22 after his *r·* from the grave,
after the
  a 24–32 After the *r·*, even the unbelieving Thomas
  45–22 They who earliest saw Jesus after the *r·*
and the life
  a 31–16 makes Jesus "the *r·* and the life"—*John* 11 : 25.
  b 292– 7 to us "the *r·* and the life"—*John* 11 : 25.
his
  a 34–20 His *r·* was also their resurrection.
  b 292–31 In his *r·* and ascension, Jesus showed that
  315– 1 Jesus proved them wrong by his *r·*,
  r 497–21 the crucifixion of Jesus and his *r·*
their
  a 34–20 His resurrection was also their *r·*.

  a 42–15 The *r·* of the great demonstrator of God's power
  m 56– * *In the r· they neither marry, nor*—*Matt.* 22 : 30.
  64–19 in the *r·* there should be no more marrying nor
  69–28 and the *r·* from the dead,—*Luke* 20 : 35.
  f 232–32 and the *r·* to spiritual life.
  b 291–25 No *r·* from the grave awaits Mind or Life,
  296– 1 error theorizes . . . man has a *r·* from dust ;
  305–31 Sadducees reasoned falsely about the *r·*,
  g 509– 2 This period corresponds to the *r·*,
  g 593– 9 definition of

resuscitate
  a 44–14 to *r·* wasted energies.
  p 365–29 patient's spiritual power to *r·* himself.
resuscitated
  sp 75–20 and he could not have *r·* it.
resuscitating
  ph 180– 8 one must understand the *r·* law of Life.
retained
  pref xii–18 She *r·* her charter, and as its President,
  s 132–15 *r·* their materialistic beliefs about God.
  f 247– 8 One man at sixty had *r·* his full set of
  gl 598–25 *r·* when the Science of being is understood,
retains
  sp 73–24 belief that . . . spirit *r·* the sensations
retard
  b 283– 5 and there is no inertia to *r·* or check its
retards
  p 415–17 It either *r·* the circulation or quickens it,
retchings
  ph 195– 8 All that he ate, . . . produced violent *r·*.
retina
  s 122–16 On the eye's *r·*, sky and tree-tops apparently
  f 214–27 when a wound on the *r·* may
  p 400–25 in optics we see painted on the *r·* the image
  r 479– 9 An image of mortal thought, reflected on the *r·*,
retracing
  a 20–22 saves *r·* and traversing anew the path
retreat
  f 247–32 to *r·* from the belief of pain or pleasure
  p 378–16 often causes the beast to *r·* in terror.
  405–31 causes mortals to *r·* from their error,
retrograde
  sp 74–29 In C. S. there is never a *r·* step,
  p 442–19 An improved belief cannot *r·*.
retrograding
  g 527–29 Is the Supreme Being *r·*,
retrogression
  a 22– 5 selfishness and sensuality causing constant *r·*,

RETROSPECTION AND INTROSPECTION
  pref viii–24 In the author's work, *R· AND I·*,

return

in
   pr 5– 8 and woe comes in *r·* for what is done.
   a 36–29 in *r·* for our efforts at well doing.
   p 364–21 in *r·* for the spiritual purgation which
   g 518–14 in *r·*, the higher always protects the lower.
meet no
   m 57–23 even though it meet no *r·*.
never a
   sp 74–30 never a *r·* to positions outgrown.
not the
   a 45–28 reappearing of Jesus was not the *r·* of a spirit.
of sight
   f 247– 5 A woman of eighty-five, . . . had a *r·* of sight.
results in a
   g 552–28 results in a *r·* to the original species.
their
   sp 74– 4 and their *r·* to a material condition,

   pr 2– 6 and it does not *r·* unto us void.
       3–28 and yet *r·* thanks to God for all blessings,
   a 24–25 as a proof that spirits can *r·* to earth?
   sp 73– 5 and supposedly will *r·* to earth
      73–19 The belief that material bodies *r·* to dust,
      74–18 nor does the insect *r·* to fraternize with
      76–14 neither can he *r·* to it, any more than
      76–15 any more than a tree can *r·* to its seed.
      77–31 and they *r·* to their old standpoints of matter.
      82–10 they cannot *r·* to material existence,
      89–10 The former limits of her belief *r·*.
   ph 190–16 and *r·* to its native nothingness.
   f 212– 6 If the sensation of pain in the limb can *r·*,
      214–12 originate in matter and *r·* to dust,
   b 278–26 originated in matter and must *r·* to dust,
      284– 9 and can *r·* to no limit.
      287– 5 but creations of matter must *r·* to dust.
   p 399–14 and matter can *r·* no answer to
      416– 4 and the belief of pain will presently *r·*, unless
      441–29 to *r·* a verdict contrary to law and gospel.
   r 471– 2 knows no lapse from nor *r·* to harmony,
   g 535–26 till thou *r·* unto the ground ; — *Gen.* 3 : 19.
      535–28 and unto dust shalt thou *r·*.— *Gen.* 3 : 19.
      536–29 the mortal and material to dust,
      545–30 unto dust [nothingness] shalt thou *r·*." — *Gen.* 3 : 19.
      547–21 and afterwards must either *r·* to Mind or

returned
   sp 94–21 but one *r·* to give God thanks,
   s 132– 1 Jesus *r·* an affirmative reply,
      159– 8 and a verdict was *r·* that

returning
   a 20–17 *r·* blessing for cursing,
   m 57–14 sweet seasons of renewal like the *r·* spring.
   g 522–17 dust *r·* to dust.

returns
   sp 74–12 and never *r·* to the old condition.
   f 244–17 hypothesis that he *r·* eventually to
   b 277– 4 Scripture says that dust *r·* to dust.
      295–32 error theorizes that spirit . . . *r·* to matter,
   p 373–32 and *r·* to that standard which
      433–16 and the jury *r·* a verdict of "Guilty
   g 543– 3 yields to Truth and *r·* to dust ;

Reuben
   gl 593–12 definition of

reveal
   a 26–16 His mission was to *r·* the Science of
      47–16 A period was approaching which would *r·*
   sp 85– 7 Such intuitions *r·* whatever constitutes
   s 110– 4 These eternal verities *r·* primeval existence
      122– 6 and *r·* the kingdom of heaven,
   f 233–22 To *r·* this truth was our Master's mission
      239–21 The objects we pursue . . . *r·* our standpoint,
   b 292– 5 Divine Science alone can . . . *r·* the infinite.
      299–29 and *r·* the celestial peaks.
   r 485– 1 If error is necessary to define or to *r·* Truth,
   g 517–23 Even eternity can never *r·* the whole of God,
      520–13 they will *r·* eternity, newness of Life,

revealed
   pr 8–18 nothing. . .that shall not be *r·*." — *Matt.* 10 : 26.
      14– 8 understanding of Life as *r·* in C. S.
   a 24–11 "the arm of the Lord" is *r·*— *Isa.* 53 : 1.
      44–26 *r·* a method infinitely above that of
      46–10 It is *r·* to the receptive heart,
      46–23 and *r·* unmistakably a . . . progressive state
   m 56–12 its spiritual sense was *r·* from heaven,
   sp 81–17 Man in the likeness of God as *r·* in Science
      98–17 stands a *r·* and practical Science.
   s 131–21 and hast *r·* them unto babes :— *Luke* 10 : 21.
      137–23 for flesh and blood hath not *r·* it — *Matt.* 16 : 17.
   ph 174–20 Truth is *r·*. It needs only to be practised.
   f 241–25 the Horeb height where God is *r·* ;
   b 275–20 Divine metaphysics, as *r·* to spiritual
      300–31 God is *r·* only in that which

revealed
   b 301–15 is *r·* only through divine Science.
      321– 7 what should be *r·* to him.
      322– 9 and his capabilities *r·*.
      338–32 The ideal man was *r·* in due time,
   t 457– 1 and registered the *r·* Truth
   r 483–20 God certainly *r·* the spirit of C. S.,
   g 511–12 God is *r·* as infinite light.
      557–24 *r·* religion proclaims the Science of Mind
   gl 593–23 SEAL. The signet of error *r·* by Truth.
      597–11 It *r·* the false foundations and superstructure

revealing
   pr 14–26 Life divine, *r·* spiritual understanding
   b 332–21 *r·* the divine Principle, Love,

reveals
   pr 10–12 C. S. *r·* a necessity for overcoming the world,
   a 36– 4 Divine Science *r·* the necessity of
   an 104–14 and *r·* the theodicy which indicates the
   s 109– 4 C. S. *r·* incontrovertibly that Mind is All-in-all
      120–21 *r·* man as harmoniously existent in Truth,
      127–16 C. S. *r·* God, not as the author of sin,
      147–30 but Science alone *r·* the divine Principle
   ph 169–18 Science not only *r·* the origin of all disease
      172–12 Science *r·* the eternal chain of existence
      191–24 Science of being *r·* man and immortality as
   f 209–13 Science which *r·* the supremacy of Mind.
      213–17 Divine Science *r·* sound as
      244– 4 Divine Science *r·* these grand facts.
      250–30 Science *r·* Life as not being at the mercy of
   c 260–13 Science *r·* the possibility of achieving
   b 272–32 *r·* the natural, divine Principle of Science.
      273–20 *r·* the laws of spiritual existence.
      278– 1 Science *r·* nothing in Spirit out of which to
      288–27 Science *r·* the glorious possibilities of
      296–12 *r·* man and Life, harmonious, real,
      302–19 The Science of being *r·* man as perfect,
      310–14 So Science *r·* Soul as God,
      327– 3 Science, which *r·* the immortal fact that
      328–12 *r·* the grand realities of His allness.
   r 466–12 represent contraries, as C. S. *r·*,
      467–17 *r·* Spirit, Soul, as not in the body,
      477–11 C. S. *r·* man as the idea of God,
      480–12 the origin and governor of all that Science *r·*.
      483–18 and *r·* the universal harmony.
      490– 7 C. S. *r·* Truth and Love as the
      491–21 Science *r·* material man as never the real being
   g 510–29 Science *r·* only one Mind,
      519–10 Science *r·* infinity and the fatherhood
      534– 7 *r·* the spiritual origin of man.
      554– 1 C. S. *r·* what "eye hath not seen," — *I Cor.* 2 : 9
      557–11 C. S. *r·* harmony as proportionately increasing
   ap 562– 8 This idea *r·* the universe as secondary
      577–23 and the spiritual idea *r·* it.
      577–31 the acme of this Science as the Bible *r·* it.
   gl 596–14 C. S. *r·* Spirit, not matter, as the illuminator

Revelation
   s 139–24 seen from Genesis to *R·*,
   ap 558– 2 the tenth chapter of his book of *R·* :
      559–32 the Apocalypse, or *R·* of St. John,
      572–19 In *R·* xxi. 1 we read :
      574– 5 He writes, in *R·* xxi. 9 :
      575–27 the Word, the polar magnet of *R·* ;
      576– 8 In *R·* xxi. 22, further describing this
      577–29 St. John's *R·* as recorded by the great apostle,

revelation
all
   s 141–10 All *r·* (such is the popular thought !) must
and demonstration
   a 45–18 the *r·* and demonstration of life in God,
and progress
   gl 591–23 MORNING. . . . *r·* and progress.
another
   ap 573–14 another *r·*, even the declaration from heaven,
Bible
   g 537–22 Subsequent Bible *r·* is coordinate with
Christ's
   sp 98–19 Christ's *r·* of Truth, of Life, and of Love,
coincide with
   g 522–24 coincide with *r·* in declaring this
divine
   s 109–21 through divine *r·*, reason, and demonstration.
   ap 561–20 In divine *r·*, . . . the spiritual idea is
final
   s 107– 5 for the reception of this final *r·* of
fresh
   t 460–24 When the Science of Mind was a fresh *r·* to
logic and
   sp 93–10 Divine logic and *r·* coincide.
nature and
   b 276–29 Nature and *r·* inform us that
no higher
   s 121– 9 Though no higher *r·* than the horoscope was
of divine purpose
   sp 83–26 The latter is a *r·* of divine purpose

reward

small
p 364–20 small r· in return for the spiritual purgation
your
a 22–13 Wait for your r·,

pr 13–11 our Father, who seeth in secret, will r·
15– 2 shall r· thee openly.'' — *Matt.* 6 : 6.
a 22–16 If . . . you receive no present r·, go not back
34–26 As the r· for his faithfulness, he would
m 66–30 Sorrow has its r·.
p 409–31 and expect to find beyond the grave a r· for this

rewarded
pr 10– 4 will leave our real desires to be r· by Him.

rewards
pr 15– 8 r· according to motives,
f 203– 5 assigns sure r· to righteousness,

rheumatism
p 384–19 or hints of inflammatory r·,
384–26 neither r·, consumption, nor any other disease
386–10 catarrh, fever, r·, or consumption,

rhythm
f 213–26 Music is the r· of head and heart.
g 510– 4 To discern the r· of Spirit

rib
g 528–12 and the r·, which the Lord God — *Gen.* 2 : 22.
533–17 the r· taken from Adam's side
553–19 Eve was formed from Adam's r·,
553–27 or from the r· of our primeval father.
gl 585–27 first from dust, second from a r·,

ribs
o 360–20 striking the r· of matter
g 528–11 He took one of his r·, and — *Gen.* 2 : 21.

rich
o 344–24 and left to us as his r· legacy.
p 364–13 what his r· entertainer had neglected to do,
g 518–15 The r· in spirit help the poor
533– 2 Had he lost man's r· inheritance

riches
pr 5–17 God pours the r· of His love into the
t 459– 6 so he must gain heavenly r· by

richly
b 312–32 Jesus' spiritual origin . . . r· endowed him
g 501– 9 but r· recompensing human want and woe
548–26 Natural history is r· endowed by the

rid
sp 91– 5 Let us r· ourselves of the belief that man is
f 237–30 would r· them of their complaints,
b 322–32 easier to desire Truth than to r· one's self of
328– 8 r· of sin, sickness, and death only in
339–28 To get r· of sin through Science,
p 371–17 before he can get r· of the illusive sufferings
g 542– 3 that it might be r· of troublesome Truth.

ridiculous
m 68– 3 for fear of being thought r·.

right (noun)
adjusts the
t 449– 8 R· adjusts the balance sooner or later.
and wrong
t 453– 6 R· and wrong, truth and error,
calling itself
r 491– 9 the latter calling itself r·.
conception of
b 327–10 sometimes a man's highest conception of r·,
divine
f 227–26 This is your divine r·.
faith in the
a 29– 7 Christian experience teaches faith in the r·
highest
p 368– 2 a supposititious opposite of the highest r·.
immutable
t 446–20 victory rests on the side of immutable r·.
individual
t 447– 2 man's individual r· of self-government.
is radical
t 452–18 R· is radical.
law of
p 385–11 remember that the eternal law of r·,
man's moral
p 381–29 man's moral r· to annul an unjust sentence,
negative
r 491– 8 a negative r· and a positive wrong,
or wisdom
g 544–15 No mortal mind has the might or r· or wisdom
proclaim the
b 327–24 to meet the wrong and to proclaim the r·.
to acquit
pr 11– 9 moral law, which has the r· to acquit or condemn,
to distinguish
t 453– 1 mathematician's r· to distinguish the
to freedom
f 227– 5 mortals are taught their r· to freedom,

right (noun)
to the name
s 111–10 some may deny its r· to the name of Science.
uncertain sense of
b 326–24 only when his uncertain sense of r· yielded to

pr 3– 1 He who is immutably right will do r·
9–32 Consistent prayer is the desire to do r.
a 49–31 turned ''aside the r· of a man — *Lam.* 3 : 35.
sp 89–29 concluded . . . man had the r· to take it away
f 223–32 until ''He come whose r· it is.'' — *Ezek.* 21 : 27.
228– 9 learn that nothing is real but the r·,
236–29 and their receptiveness of r·.
253–19 can at once change your course and do r·.
c 266–21 and the saint his own heaven by doing r·.
b 329– 8 you have no r· to question the great might of
p 384– 7 God never punishes man for doing r·,
405–25 tends to destroy the ability to do r·.
409–27 We have no r· to say that life depends on
436–34 pronounced a sentence of death for doing r·.
442– 4 ''Shall not the Judge . . . do r·?'' — *Gen.* 18 : 2
t 447– 4 and no moral r· to attempt to
448–29 It is C. S. to do r·,
448–30 To talk the r· and live the wrong is foolish
g 553–11 ''We have no r· to assume that individuals
ap 571–10 for the sake of doing r· and benefiting our race

right (adj., adv.)
pref vii–19 a r· apprehension of Him whom to know arigh
pr 3– 1 He who is immutably r· will do right
a 22– 2 to find and follow the r· road.
35– 5 and cast their net on the r· side.
m 66– 1 Thou art r·, immortal Shakespeare,
s 115–10 The great difficulty is to give the r· impression
141– 7 and pluck out the r· eye,
ph 192–23 the weight you throw into the r· scale.
195–19 Academics of the r· sort are requisite.
f 225–16 proportionate to its embodiment of r· thinking
229–27 If . . . produces sickness, it is r· to be sick ;
234–23 the r· education of human thought.
235–31 will love to grapple with a new, r· idea
253–20 no opposition to r· endeavors
b 271–27 or to cast them on the r· side for Truth,
279–25 contradicts alike revelation and r· reasoning.
299–25 which cannot destroy the r· reflection.
318–24 as though disease were real, therefore r·,
318–25 If disease is r· it is wrong to heal it.
326–25 spiritual sense, which is always r·.
329–23 Always r·, its divine Principle never repents,
360– 3 all is won, by a r· estimate of what is real.''
p 371–14 in all ways except the r· one.
382–32 Mortal mind needed to be set r·.
390– 9 r· understanding of Him restores harmony.
396–22 At the r· time explain to the sick the
410–27 to promote r· thinking and doing,
t 444– 9 into the r· use of temporary and
444–20 smite thee on thy r· cheek, — *Matt.* 5 : 39.
452–25 by r· talking and wrong acting,
452–29 destroys your power of healing from the
            motive.
453–19 and a r· motive has its reward.
454–16 the wrong as well as the r· practice.
454–19 R· motives give pinions to thought,
455– 7 Hence the necessity of being r· yourself
460–17 through r· apprehension of the truth of being.
r 475–15 compound idea of God, including all r· ideas ;
492– 3 For r· reasoning there should be
g 531– 7 error, . . . that mind and soul are both r· and
543–20 May not Darwin be r· in thinking that apehoo
557–23 as if he began materially r·,
ap 558– 7 and he set his r· foot upon the sea, — *Rev.* 10 : 2
559– 3 ''r· foot'' or dominant power — *Rev.* 10 : 2.
566– 6 so shall the spiritual idea guide all r· desires
            (*see also* **direction, hand**)

right-doing
a 37–13 Consciousness of r· brings its own reward ;
p 436–33 Claiming to protect Mortal Man in r·,
t 448–29 nothing short of r· has any claim to the name.

righteous
a 22–27 Whosoever believeth that wrath is r·
36–23 to bestow on the r· their full reward.
37–19 procured the martyrdom of that r· man
41– 4 through the joys and triumphs of the r·
s 132–30 This r· preacher once pointed his disciples to
f 206–13 the prayer of the r·.
231–11 does heal the sick through the prayer of the r·
p 439–26 and the r· executor of His laws.
t 444–18 ''judge r· judgment,'' — *John* 7 : 24.

righteously
f 254–11 and seek Truth r·, He directs our path.

righteousness
and purity
a 28–18 Even his r· and purity did not hinder men from
fulfil all
m 56– 4 it becometh us to fulfil all r·.'' — *Matt.* 3 : 15.

ighteousness

garment of
f 242–29 every part of the Christly garment of *r·.*

hungering after
pr 2– 5 the desire which goes forth hungering after *r·*

law of
a 36–32 Can God therefore overlook the law of *r·*

loved
b 313–18 "loved *r·* and hated iniquity."— *Heb.* 1 : 9.

paths of
ap 578– 9 leadeth me in the paths of *r·*— *Psal.* 23 : 3.

reign of
gl 585–19 Euphrates . . . the reign of *r·.*

a 54– 5 The world acknowledged not his *r·,*
ph 190–28 I will behold Thy face in *r·* :— *Psal.* 17 : 15.
f 203– 5 assigns sure rewards to *r·,*
b 291–17 man is found having no *r·* of his own,
323– 7 helped onward in the march towards *r·,*
p 365–14 from the outstretched arm of *r·*

ighteousness'

a 28–25 To suppose that persecution for *r·* sake

ightful
s 124–30 and so restores them to their *r·* home
156–31 and Mind takes its *r·* and supreme place.
b 281–23 without actual origin or *r·* existence.
p 365–32 The poor suffering heart needs its *r·* nutriment,

ightfully
p 364– 2 *r·* regarded as the best man that ever

ightly
sp 96– 2 unwillingness to learn all things *r·,*
an 105–14 human law *r·* estimates crime,
106–10 self-governed only when he is guided *r·*
s 122– 4 the great facts of Life, *r·* understood,
ph 183–21 *r·* demands man's entire obedience.
f 231– 3 Unless an ill is *r·* met and fairly overcome
238– 1 not *r·* valued before they are understood.
c 262–28 To begin *r·* is to end *r·.*
b 280–25 *R·* understood, . . . man has a sensationless
338– 1 C. S., *r·* understood, leads to eternal harmony.
r 472–11 His law, *r·* understood, destroys them.
494–19 Reason, *r·* directed, serves to correct the
g 502–11 This deflection of being, *r·* viewed,

ightness
an 104–14 which indicates the *r·* of all divine action,

ights

and life
p 438–17 against the *r·* and life of man.

divine
f 253–10 the understanding of your divine *r·,*
p 384–31 before the divine *r·* of intelligence,

God-given
p 381– 2 Ignorant of our God-given *r·,*

human
a 48–29 against human *r·* and divine Love,
s 134–12 and so it came about that human *r·*
f 226–14 God has built a higher platform of human *r·,*

inalienable
an 106– 8 God has endowed man with inalienable *r·,*
s 161–17 certain inalienable *r·,* among which are
f 227– 9 unaware of man's inalienable *r·*

less
m 63–16 marvel why usage should accord woman less *r·*

liberty and
p 435–17 Mortal Man's liberty and *r·.*

man's
an 106–12 Man's *r·* are invaded when the

of humanity
a 54–32 Would they not deny him even the *r·* of humanity,

of intelligence
sp 79–27 contending for the *r·* of intelligence
p 384–31 before the divine *r·* of intelligence,

of man
s 144–19 will-power may infringe the *r·* of man.
f 225–31 *r·* of man were vindicated in a single section
226– 9 a fuller acknowledgment of the *r·* of man
227– 1 and the *r·* of man are fully known and
227–14 Discerning the *r·* of man,

of mind
t 453–32 He does not trespass on the *r·* of mind

of woman
gl 587– 3 The *r·* of woman acknowledged

supposed
o 348–22 defending the supposed *r·* of disease,

m 63–13 unfair differences between the *r·* of the two
s 157– 7 never shares its *r·* with inanimate matter.
p 440–31 the *r·* of which he has been deprived.

ights of Man
p 438– 1 certain extracts on the *R· of M·,*

29

rigid
s 160–24 If muscles can cease to act and become *r·*
162– 8 dissolves tumors, relaxes *r·* muscles,
f 221– 5 decided that his diet should be more *r·,*

ripe
ap 565– 3 the great red dragon, . . . *r·* for destruction

ripen
ph 188– 9 hatred, revenge *r·* into action,
f 248– 6 ought to *r·* into health and immortality,

ripening
b 296– 4 It is the *r·* of mortal man,

riper
sp 97–16 the *r·* it becomes for destruction.
f 248– 5 Men and women of *r·* years and larger lessons

rise
pr 16–20 Only as we *r·* above all material sensuousness
a 18–17 The fountain can *r·* no higher than its source.
24–12 and *r·* into newness of life
34–24 would *r·* again in the spiritual realm of reality,
35– 7 they were enabled to *r·* somewhat from
sp 73–20 belief that material bodies . . . *r·* up as
77–26 The departed would gradually *r·* above
87–30 close the eyes, and forms *r·* before us, which
ph 167– 3 If we *r·* no higher than blind faith,
192–26 betrays its weakness and falls, never to *r·.*
193–17 I told him to *r·,* dress himself, and take supper
f 242–13 and to *r·* superior to the so-called pain and
c 261–28 will *r·* to the spiritual consciousness of being,
262–12 *r·* above the testimony of the material senses,
b 289– 2 can never *r·* from the temporal *débris* of error,
290– 5 will *r·* no higher spiritually in the scale of
p 365– 9 and so enable them to *r·* above the supposed
373–21 you must *r·* above both fear and sin.
390–32 *R·* in the conscious strength of the spirit of
391– 8 *r·* in rebellion against them.
391–30 *r·* to the true consciousness of Life as Love,
393–12 *R·* in the strength of Spirit to resist
394–15 to *r·* above his difficulties.
406–21 We can, and ultimately shall, so *r·*
419–30 *r·* into higher and holier consciousness.
t 444– 3 all must *r·* superior to materiality,
r 493– 3 the sun appears to *r·* and set,
g 531–11 will sometime *r·* above all material
ap 565–25 to *r·* to the zenith of demonstration,

risen
pref vii– 4 ere cometh the full radiance of a *r·* day.
a 53–30 nor had he *r·* to his final demonstration
sp 74– 8 a sprout which has *r·* above the soil.
b 324–27 "If Christ [Truth] be not *r·,*— *I Cor.* 15 : 14.
p 379–14 he would have *r·* above the false belief.
t 448–13 if you have not *r·* above sin yourself,
g 534– 4 and to behold at the sepulchre the *r·* Saviour,

rises
s 153–12 *r·* above matter into mind.
f 246– 8 The stream *r·* no higher than its source.
c 256– 3 thought *r·* from the material sense to the
262–24 Starting from a higher standpoint, one *r·*
b 297–15 and the human consciousness *r·* higher.
t 448–12 *r·* above the evidence of the corporeal senses ;
g 525– 9 in the Welsh, *that which r· up,*
557–12 as the line of creation *r·* towards spiritual man,
ap 568–28 now *r·* clearer and nearer to the great heart of

rising
m 62–16 more for the health of the *r·* generation
s 123–13 Divine Science, *r·* above physical theories,
ph 172– 7 grades the human species as *r·* from
174– 9 *r·* above material standpoints,
f 246– 7 by no means a material germ *r·* from
c 258–14 broadening and *r·* higher and higher from a
b 268– 3 *r·* towards the realm of the real,
p 385– 7 the divine law, *r·* above the human.
t 449–11 Man's moral mercury, *r·* or falling,
g 508–24 *r·* from the lesser to the greater,
511–27 mortal thought, *r·* in the scale of intelligence,

risk
pr 13–18 incur less *r·* of overwhelming our real wishes
s 156–20 for one day, and *r·* the effects.
ap 571– 9 and so *r·* human displeasure for the sake of

risked
s 159–17 and not have *r·* such treatment.

risks
t 452–23 take no *r·* in the policy of error.

rite
a 34– 3 Then why ascribe this inspiration to a dead *r·,*

rites
a 32–11 used on convivial occasions and in Jewish *r·,*
gl 597– 3 consisted mostly of *r·* and ceremonies.

ubbing

p 382– 8 bathing and *r·* to alter the secretions

Rubicon

ph 172–10 if . . . death is the *R·* of spirituality?

udiments

t 462–15 and advance from the *r·* laid down.

uin

f 203–20 When the material body has gone to *r·*,

ule (noun)

and demonstration

b 290– 3 If the Principle, *r·*, and demonstration of

clearly interprets

ap 568–32 *r·* clearly interprets God as divine Principle,

confirm this

ph 199–23 Exceptions only confirm this *r·*, proving that

definite

s 147–26 he left no definite *r·* for demonstrating this

denies the

b 329–19 denies the *r·* of the problem because he fails

fixed

f 233–26 divided according to a fixed *r·*,

furnishes the

b 336–27 Science of being furnishes the *r·* of perfection,

general

p 411– 5 as a general *r·* the body would respond more
t 457–20 C. S. is not an exception to the general *r·*,

given

o 341–16 demonstrated according to a divine given *r·*,

God's

pr 3–10 we have only to avail ourselves of God's *r·*

higher

s 162–28 to demonstrate the higher *r·*.

his

r 473–22 test its unerring Science according to his *r·*,

in Christian Science

ap 568–32 Self-abnegation . . . is a *r·* in C. S.

no opposite

t 457–30 and there must and can be no opposite *r·*.

not obeyed the

s 149–15 because you have not obeyed the *r·*

of Christian Science

p 411–30 the result of this simple *r·* of C. S.,
r 493–16 prove . . . the Principle and *r·* of C. S.

of discord

f 219–20 Science includes no *r·* of discord,

of divine Science

ph 184–24 demonstrated this as a *r·* of divine Science

of healing

r 496–17 to demonstrate, . . . the *r·* of healing,

of health

b 337–29 the *r·* of health and holiness in C. S.,

of inversion

b 282–31 The *r·* of inversion infers from error its

of perpetual harmony

p 381–28 and abide by the *r·* of perpetual harmony,

positive

s 109–15 to discovering a positive *r·*.

proves the

s 113–27 proves the *r·* by inversion.

reign and

r 208–22 the reign and *r·* of universal harmony,

simple

s 121–24 the simple *r·* that the greater controls the lesser.
p 411–30 the result of this simple *r·* of C. S.,
418–22 inspired by this simple *r·* of Truth,

system and

g 547– 6 not one departs from the stated system and *r·*.

---

pr 3– 6 The *r·* is already established,
s 147–28 This *r·* remained to be discovered in C. S.
149–11 The *r·* and its perfection of operation
f 216–24 would appear . . . to be the *r·* of existence,
b 274–24 in learning its Principle and *r·*
t 447–10 the *r·* is, heal the sick when called upon
g 546–32 a thousand different examples of one *r·*.

ule (verb)

s 148–26 and claims to *r·* man by material law,
155–11 and the beliefs which are in the majority *r·*.
164–22 the materiality miscalled life
ph 196–20 Such books as will *r·* disease out of mortal mind,
198–26 and the stronger thoughts *r·* the weaker.
320–15 Jehovah said, My spirit shall not forever *r·*
p 419–26 assassin, who, in attempting to *r·* mankind,
g 510–14 the greater light to *r·* the day,— *Gen.* 1 : 16.
510–14 and the lesser light to *r·* the night :— *Gen.* 1 : 16.
511– 8 to *r·* over the day — *Gen.* 1 : 18.
535– 9 and he shall *r·* over thee. — *Gen.* 3 : 16.
ap 565– 7 who was to *r·* all nations— *Rev.* 12 : 5.
565–16 Christ, God's idea, will eventually *r·* all

ruled

a 55–13 although it is again *r·* out of the synagogue.
p 391–11 *r·* out by the might of Mind,

Ruler

f 203–18 Supreme *R·* or in some power less
gl 590–19 Its higher signification is Supreme *R·*.

ruler

f 239–11 The wicked man is not the *r·* of
p 437– 1 Nerve, testified that he was a *r·* of Body,
438– 9 Instead of being a *r·* in the Province of Body,
ap 569– 7 I will make thee *r·* over many,"— *Matt.* 25 : 23.
gl 590–17 the inferior sense of master, or *r·*.

ruler's

p 398–10 To the synagogue *r·* daughter,

rulers

p 323–17 shall be made *r·* over many ;

rules

divine

s 147– 7 I demonstrated the divine *r·* of C. S.
t 462– 3 any student, who adheres to the divine *r·*

divine Principle and

t 456– 6 Strict adherence to the divine Principle and *r·*

first

t 456–32 it gave the first *r·* for demonstrating this

fixed

s 113– 2 there must be fixed *r·* for the demonstration of

of health

ph 169–11 faith in *r·* of health or in drugs begets
197–24 With *r·* of health in the head

of Science

s 162–17 Working out the *r·* of Science in practice,

sacred

s 147– 4 and the sacred *r·* for its present application

spiritual

s 112–18 and with this infinitude come spiritual *r·*,

stern

p 362– 9 under the stern *r·* of rabbinical law,

these

s 147–12 since Jesus practised these *r·*

---

s 111–13 its *r·* demonstrate its Science.
147–18 the demonstration of the *r·* of
147–31 but Science alone . . . demonstrates its *r·*.
o 344–16 according to the *r·* which disclose its merits or
p 400–23 Mortal mind *r·* all that is mortal.
431– 3 Notwithstanding my *r·* to the contrary,
448–27 ventures not to break its *r·*,
456– 4 but contrary to its spirit or *r·*,
459–32 adhere strictly to the *r·* of divine metaphysics
462–14 must abide strictly by its *r·*,

ruling

m 64– 9 ceremonies, *r·* out primitive Christianity.
s 141–22 did not . . . understand this *r·* of the Christ ;
148–30 this *r·* of the schools leaves them to
f 205–24 whereas a belief in many *r·* minds hinders

rulings

an 105–17 and no longer apply legal *r·* wholly to

ruminates

p 430–19 patient feels ill, *r·*, and the trial commences.

run

a 20–29 and let us *r·* with patience— *Heb.* 12 : 1.
f 218–28 shall *r·*, and not be weary ;— *Isa.* 40 : 31.
250– 1 We *r·* into error when we
254– 3 can "*r·*, and not be weary :— *Isa.* 40 : 31.
g 514– 7 Mind's infinite ideas *r·* and disport themselves.

runneth

ap 578–15 my cup *r·* over. — *Psal.* 23 : 5.

running

pr 5–12 and it will be full "and *r·* over." — *Luke* 6 : 38.
an 106– 5 against the current *r·* heavenward.

runs

s 154–28 Such a mother *r·* to her little one,

ruptures

g 541–17 *r·* the life and brotherhood of man

Rush, Dr. Benjamin

s 162–30 I kindly quote from Dr. Benjamin *R·*,

rush

ph 168–10 When sick . . . you *r·* after drugs,

rushes

b 327–15 *r·* forth to clamor with midnight and tempest.
p 373–27 When the blood *r·* madly through the veins

rust

f 241– 5 moth and *r·* doth corrupt."— *Matt.* 6 : 19.

S

sabachthani
a 51– 1 "*Eloi, Eloi, lama s·?*" — *Mark* 15 : 34.

Sabbath
a 20–12 observe the *S·*, make long prayers, and yet

sackcloth
ap 574–25 for it will lift the *s·* from your eyes,

sacrament
a 32– 6 English word *s·* is derived from it.
32–20 if the *s·* is confined to the use of bread and
34–10 If all who ever partook of the *s·*

sacramentum
a 32– 5 The Latin word for this oath was *s·*,

sacred
a 37–20 would gladly have turned his *s·* career into a
s 118– 8 hidden in *s·* secrecy from the visible world?
147– 4 and the *s·* rules for its present application
ph 182–26 ability to demonstrate Mind's *s·* power.
f 232–26 In the *s·* sanctuary of Truth are voices of
b 328–27 believed and obeyed this *s·* saying.
r 483–13 After the author's *s·* discovery,
g 547–23 The Scriptures are very *s·*.
548– 4 breathes through the *s·* pages the
ap 575– 7 This *s·* city, described in the Apocalypse

sacredly
f 236– 4 *S·*, in the interests of humanity,

sacredness
m 59–29 divorce shows that the *s·* of this relationship is

sacrifice
great
pr 16– 1 A great *s·* of material things
human
a 54–13 the inspiration of Jesus' intense human *s·*.
lifelong
a 53–23 the lifelong *s·* which goodness makes for
living
b 325–22 "Present your bodies a living *s·*, — *Rom.* 12 : 1.
one
a 23– 3 One *s·*, however great, is insufficient to

---

pr 11–24 we shall *s·* everything for it.
a 25– 3 The spiritual essence of blood is *s·*.
26–22 Jesus' teaching . . . involved such a *s·* as
36–28 toil, *s·*, cross-bearing, multiplied trials,
t 459– 5 achieves no worldly honors except by *s·*,
gl 590–10 self-immolation ; innocence and purity ; *s·*.
595–23 A *s·* to the gods.

sacrificed
s 146– 9 health and harmony have been *s·*.

sacrifices
a 23– 2 Wisdom and Love may require many *s·* of self
49–11 his mighty works, his toils, privations, *s·*,

sacrificing
p 440– 7 before *s·* mortals to their false gods.

sacrilegious
o 344– 8 Is it *s·* to assume that God's likeness is

sad
a 32–30 a *s·* supper taken at the close of day,
40–28 It is. *s·* that the phrase *divine service*
ph 182–27 come from some *s·* incident, or else
o 342– 6 the *s·* effects on the sick of denying Truth.

saddening
ph 190–22 thus swept his lyre with *s·* strains

Sadducees
s 117–30 the leaven of the Pharisees and of the *S·*,
b 305–31 The *S·* reasoned falsely about the

sadly
a 42–14 who *s·* followed him to the foot of the cross.
b 328–15 has *s·* disappeared from Christian history.
t 451–10 or be turned *s·* awry.

safe
an 105–24 Whoever uses . . . is never *s·*.
s 155–31 is it *s·* to say that the less in quantity you have
164– 7 none can be adopted as a *s·* guidance
p 376–28 Some people, . . . inquire when it will be *s·* to
384–20 your Mind-remedy is *s·* and sure.
t 463–10 that the birth will be natural and *s·*.
g 514–27 Daniel felt *s·* in the lions' den,
532– 7 Is this knowledge *s·*?

safely
m 67– 8 Can you steer *s·* amid the storm?"
f 201– 7 We cannot build *s·* on false foundations.

safer
pref x–24 its practice is *s·* and more potent

safety
a 39–21 a future-world salvation, or *s·*,
m 67–10 the dauntless seaman is not sure of his *s·* ;
r 494–19 and seek *s·* in divine Science.
gl 581– 8 ARK. *S·* ; the idea, or reflection, of Truth,

safety-valve
pr 6–22 to misunderstand Love and to make prayer the *s·*

safety-valves
p 425– 4 so long as you believe them to be *s·* or

sage
g 556–14 C. S. may absorb the attention of *s·* and

said
pr 4–11 has *s·* : "If ye love me, keep— *John* 14 : 15.
6–24 he *s·* that Satan had bound her,
6–25 he *s·*, "Thou art an offence— *Matt.* 16 : 23.
6–28 He *s·* of the fruitless tree,
8–32 and credit what is *s·*?
11– 4 he *s·*, "Go, and sin no more."— *John* 8 : 11.
16– 9 Our Master *s·*, "After this manner— *Matt.* 6 : 9
a 23–12 Rabbinical lore *s·* : "He that taketh
27–14 It is as if he had *s·* : The I — the Life,
30–14 taught the Mosaic law, which *s·* :
31– 4 He *s·* : "Call no man your father— *Matt.* 23 : 9
32–16 and *s·*, Take, eat ; this is my— *Matt.* 26 : 26.
33–16 and *s·*, "Drink ye all of it."— *Matt.* 26 : 27.
33–19 great Teacher *s·* : "Not my will, — *Luke* 22 : 42
38–28 he *s·* in substance : Having eyes ye see not,
43– 6 understand what Jesus had *s·*,
46–13 Master *s·* plainly that physique was not Spirit
48– 3 *s·* unto them : "Could ye not— *Matt.* 26 : 40.
48–23 He *s·* : "Put up thy sword."— *John* 18 : 11.
50–21 what would his accusers have *s·*?
51–24 in all that he *s·* and did.
52–25 prophetically *s·* to his disciples,
52–32 They *s·* : "He casteth out devils— *Luke* 11 : 15
54–26 He *s·* that those who followed him
m 58–24 *S·* the peasant bride to her lover :
64– 4 when he *s·* : "Pure religion and— *Jas.* 1 : 27.
sp 70– * *Then s· the Jews unto him,— John* 8 : 52.
77– 1 The pious Polycarp *s·* : "I cannot
79–19 He *s·* : "My Father worketh— *John* 5 : 17.
85–12 Samaritan woman *s·* : "Come, see a— *John*
 4 : 29.
85–20 he *s·* : "O ye hypocrites !— *Matt.* 16 : 3.
85–28 He *s·* : "These ought ye to have— *Matt.* 23 : 23
88–29 it is *s·* to be a gift whose endowment is
93– 3 *s·*, "He that believeth on me,— *John* 14 : 12.
93– 5 *s·*, "But the hour cometh,— *John* 4 : 23.
94– 9 *s·* : "Crucify him, crucify him— *John* 19 : 6.
94–26 but what would be *s·* at this period of
an 100– 4 which he *s·* could be exerted by one
104– 9 Agassiz, . . . has wisely *s·* : "Every great
s 109–28 *s·* of his lessons : "My doctrine— *John* 7 : 16.
124–23 and *s·* to the proud wave,
127–14 It may be *s·*, however, that the term C. S.
131–19 Jesus once *s·* : "I thank Thee, — *Luke* 10 : 21.
133– 4 who *s·*, "Is not this the Christ?"— *John* 4 : 29
135–21 It has been *s·*, and truly, that Christianity
136–31 did not comprehend all that he *s·*
138–27 *s·* to every follower : "Go ye into— *Mark* 16 : 15
148– 2 *s·* to them, "O faithless— *Mark* 9 : 19.
156–19 *s·* that she would give up her medicine
159– 4 and *s·* it would kill her,
163– 7 Dr. James Johnson, . . . of England, *s·* :
163–14 Dr. Mason Good, a learned Professor . . . *s·* :
163–21 Dr. Chapman, . . . in a published essay *s·* :
164– 4 Sir John Forbes, M.D., . . . *s·* :
164–14 Much yet remains to be *s·* and done
ph 169– 6 *s·* to the patient, "You are healed,"
170–16 *s·* : "Take no thought for your life, — *Matt*
 6 : 25.
183– 7 however much is *s·* to the contrary.
193– 3 I met his physician, who *s·* that the patient
193– 5 *s·* the bone was carious
193–14 opened his eyes and *s·* : "I feel like a new man
193–30 what his physician *s·* of the case,
195– 4 *s·* that he should never be happy elsewhere.
197–11 The less that is *s·* of physical structure
197–12 the more that is thought and *s·* about moral
200–13 Psalmist *s·* : "Thou madest him to— *Psal.* 8 : 6
200–25 St. Paul *s·* : "For I determined— *I Cor.* 2 : 2.
f 204–27 in Science it can never be *s·* that man
211–19 It should no longer be *s·* in Israel
213– 3 called a deceiver, or is *s·* to be deceived.
213– 4 it has been *s·*, "As he thinketh— *Prov.* 23 : 7.
220– 1 We hear it *s·* : "I exercise daily
238–10 Losing her crucifix, the Roman Catholic girl *s·*
239–32 the wise man *s·*, "All is vanity."— *Eccl.* 1 : 2.

aid

f 241–21	Our Master s·, "If ye love me,— John 14 : 15.
252– 1	our Master s·, "If a kingdom be— Mark 3 : 24.
c 262–17	Job s· : "I have heard of Thee— Job 42 : 5.
b 271–20	Our Master s·,"But the Comforter— John 14 : 26.
272–16	s· : "Give not that which is holy— Matt. 7 : 6.
286– 9	s·, "No man cometh unto the— John 14 : 6.
289–28	Therefore it cannot be s· to pass out of
305–16	"Then answered Jesus and s·— John 5 : 19.
308–23	Then s· the spiritual evangel :
313– 5	as it is s· of him in the first chapter of Hebrews :
314–14	spoke of reproducing his body, . . . and s·,
315– 1	and s· : "Whosoever liveth— John 11 : 26.
319–27	wrote down what an inspired teacher had s·.
320– 1	he s·, "God is love."— I John 4 : 8.
320– 8	In Smith's Bible Dictionary it is s· :
320–12	"And the Lord s·, My spirit shall— Gen. 6 : 3.
320–15	"And Jehovah s·, My spirit shall not forever
321–26	became to him the voice of God, which s· :
325–21	when he s· : "Present your bodies— Rom. 12 : 1.
328–18	can it be s· that they explain it practically,
o 343– 4	James s·, "Show me thy faith— Jas. 2 : 18.
345–10	It is sometimes s·, in criticising C. S.,
346– 6	It is sometimes s· that C. S. teaches the
347– 3	It is s· by one critic, that to verify this
350–18	He s· : "This people's heart is— Matt. 13 : 15.
358–24	Sometimes it is s· : "Rest assured that
p 364–12	He even s· that this poor woman had
364–23	then it must be s· of them also that they
364–29	If so, then it may be s· of them,
367–18	of which Jesus spoke to his disciples, when he s· :
386–26	If a Christian Scientist had s·, while you were
390– 1	she s·, "My food is all digested,
398– 2	as when he s· to the epileptic boy,
398–11	whom they called dead but of whom he s·,
398–12	s·, "Damsel, I say unto thee,— Mark 5 : 41.
398–14	To the sufferer with the withered hand he s·,
411– 1	S· Job : "The thing which I— Job 3 : 25.
438–19	Another witness, equally inadequate, s·
439–19	and s· :— God will smite you, O whited walls,
t 463–32	It has been s· to the author,
r 473–26	Jesus established what he s· by demonstration,
478–27	St. Paul s·, "But when it pleased— Gal. 1 : 15.
481–18	growth of material belief, of which it is s· :
487–25	James s·, "Show me thy faith— Jas. 2 : 18.
492–18	Discussing his campaign, General Grant s· :
494–31	It should be s· of his followers also,
g 529–15	And he s· unto the woman,— Gen. 3 : 1.
529–17	And the woman s· unto the serpent,— Gen. 3 : 2.
529–19	God hath s·, Ye shall not eat of it,— Gen. 3 : 3.
530– 8	s·, "Take no thought for your— Matt. 6 : 25.
530–13	the serpent s· unto the woman,— Gen. 3 : 4.
532–14	and s· unto him, Where art thou?— Gen. 3 : 9.
532–15	And he s·, I heard Thy voice— Gen. 3 : 10.
533– 5	He s·, Who told thee that thou— Gen. 3 : 11.
533– 8	the man s·, The woman whom— Gen. 3 : 12.
534– 8	And the Lord God [Jehovah] s·— Gen. 3 : 14.
535– 6	Unto the woman He s·, I will— Gen. 3 : 16.
535–19	And unto Adam He s·, Because— Gen. 3 : 17.
536–30	And the Lord God [Jehovah] s·,— Gen. 3 : 22.
538–24	and s·, I have gotten a man from— Gen. 4 : 1.
541–19	the Lord [Jehovah] s· unto Cain,— Gen. 4 : 9.
541–20	And he s·, I know not :— Gen. 4 : 9.
541–27	s·, ... The voice of thy brother's— Gen. 4 : 10.
542–14	the Lord [Jehovah] s· unto him,— Gen. 4 : 15.
547– 3	contains the proof of all here s· of C. S.
553–10	One of our ablest naturalists has s· :
554–21	Jesus defined this . . . when he s·,
554–22	s·, "Have not I chosen you— John 6 : 70.
554–24	This he s· of Judas, one of Adam's race.
555– 6	An inquirer once s· to the discoverer of C. S. :
gl 596– 5	Referring to it, he s· to the Athenians :
	(see also God, Jesus, Paul)

aint

c 266–21	and the s· his own heaven by doing right.

ainted

s 136–26	doubted if . . . controlled by the s· preacher.

aintly

o 359–24	from the lips of her s· mother,

aints

pr 5–14	S· and sinners get their full award,

aith

pr 1– *	believe that those things which he s·— Mark 11 : 23.
1– *	he shall have whatsoever he s·— Mark 11 : 23.
f 250– 7	has no real entity, but s· "It is I."
252–31	Spirit, bearing opposite testimony, s· :
b 277– 3	s·, "Thou shalt surely die ;"— Gen. 2 : 17.
287–19	It s·, "I am man, but I am not the image and
k 499– *	These things s· He that is holy,— Rev. 3 : 7.
g 503–13	s· to the darkness upon the face of error,
505–17	Psalmist s· : "The Lord on high— Psal. 93 : 4.
540–19	It s· to the human sense of sin,
ap 575–22	s·, "Beautiful for situation,— Psal. 48 : 2,

saith

gl 579– *	These things s· He that is holy,— Rev. 3 : 7.
580–19	that of which wisdom s·,
584–20	the lust of the flesh, which s· :

sake

a 28–25	persecution for righteousness' s·
f 222–31	no question for conscience s·."— I Cor. 10 : 25.
b 338–29	blessed the earth "for man's s·."— Gen. 8 : 21.
p 396– 4	both for one's own s· and for that of the patient.
g 535–22	cursed is the ground for thy s· ;— Gen. 3 : 17.
ap 571– 9	for the s· of doing right and benefiting our
578– 9	for His name's s·.— Psal. 23 : 3.

salary

a 42– 9	was in no peril from s· or popularity.
s 142–11	If the soft palm, upturned to a lordly s·,

saline

s 153– 6	until there was not a single s· property left.

sallow

p 433–14	His s· face blanches with fear,

sallowness

p 442–10	all s· and debility had disappeared.

Sallow Skin

p 431–26	witness . . . testifies :— I am S· S·.

salt

s 153– 7	The s· had "lost his savour ;"— Matt. 5 : 13.
p 367–19	"Ye are the s· of the earth."— Matt. 5 : 13.
367–21	watch, work, and pray that this s· lose not its
385–28	because you have partaken of s· fish,

saltness

p 367–22	that this salt lose not its s·,

salubrious

p 383–24	Does his assertion prove the use . . . . a s· habit,

salutary

m 59–18	more s· in prolonging her health
66– 9	Sorrow is s·.
66–27	Socrates considered patience s· under such
68–23	s· causes sometimes incur these effects.
c 265–31	The pains of sense are s·, if they
p 414– 6	to the s· action of truth,

salutes

sp 88– 8	and no scent s· the nostrils.

salvation

and strength

ap 568–14	Now is come s·, and strength,— Rev. 12 : 10.

day of

a 39–19	behold, now is the day of s·,"— II Cor. 6 : 2.
sp 93– 8	behold, now is the day of s·,"— II Cor. 6 : 2.

experience that

a 39–22	now is the time in which to experience that s·

from all error

s 132–25	this s· from all error, physical and mental,

full

a 39– 6	a full s· from sin, sickness, and death.
p 406– 6	offering full s· from sin, sickness, and death.

future-world

a 39–20	a future-world s·, or safety,

of us all

a 51–19	consummate example was for the s· of us all,

our

a 30–31	must work out our s· in the way Jesus taught.

own

pr 3–11	enables us to work out our own s·.
a 22–11	"Work out your own s·,"— Phil. 2 : 12.
23–26	how to work out one's "own s·,— Phil. 2 : 12.
sp 99– 6	"Work out your own s·— Phil. 2 : 12.
p 426–16	the necessity of working out his own s·.
442–26	"Work out your own s·— Phil. 2 : 12.
t 443–11	to work out their own s· according to

seek

b 285–25	to seek s· through pardon

Soul and

f 210–16	a better understanding of Soul and s·.

universal

b 291–12	Universal s· rests on progression

way of

pref vii– 8	plain to benighted understanding the way of s·
b 316– 2	he became the way of s· to all who

a 45– 9	and for the s· of the whole world
s 146–15	Scholasticism clings for s· to the person,
150–26	predestination of souls to damnation or s·.
ph 166– 9	believes in a pilgrimage to Mecca for the s· of
f 230– 8	This is the s· which comes through God,
gl 593–20	definition of

Samaritan

sp 85–12	The S· woman said : "Come, see— John 4 : 29,
s 133– 3	that of the S· woman, who said,

same
pr 2–32 "the s· yesterday, and to-day,— *Heb.* 13 : 8.
12–28 another who offers the s· measure of prayer?
a 21–21 we have the s· railroad guides,
45–29 He presented the s· body that he had before his
48–13 when he drinks from the s· cup,
51–15 his spiritual life, . . . was found forever the s·.
sp 75–18 the s· plane of belief as those who
78– 7 belief . . . that at the s· time we are communing with
82–13 and one person cannot . . . at the s· time.
85–18 After the s· method, events of great moment
s 108–28 which this s· so-called mind names *matter*,
112–20 "the s· yesterday, and to-day,— *Heb.* 13 : 8.
122–29 the s· mistake regarding Soul and body
128–30 must always bring the s· result.
135–11 The s· power which heals sin heals also
142–14 they at the s· time shut the door on
ph 186–22 If we concede the s· reality to discord as to
188–20 In the s· way pain and pleasure,
f 210–17 by one and the s· metaphysical process.
229–12 and at the s· time admits that Spirit is God,
237–21 The latter should be excluded on the s· principle
243–10 the s· "Mind . . . which was also— *Phil.* 2 : 5.
245– 7 Believing that she was still living in the s· hour
249–18 "the s· yesterday, and to-day,— *Heb.* 13 : 8.
c 267–14 the s· authority for the appellative mother,
267–17 s· is my brother, and sister,— *Matt.* 12 : 50.
b 283– 6 Mind is the s· Life, Love, and wisdom
283–14 They insist that Life, . . . is one and the s· with
287–13 at the s· place sweet water and— *Jas.* 3 : 11.
313– 9 agrees another passage in the s· chapter,
320–11 learned article on Noah in the s· work,
321–24 restored his hand . . . by the s· simple process.
331–29 the s· in essence, though multiform in office :
336–29 God and man are not the s·,
o 346–31 cannot serve both God and mammon at the s· time;
359– 5 will take the s· cases, and cures will follow.
p 370– 6 s· regimen which spiritualizes the thought ;
370–12 by using the s· drug which might cause the
370–17 but it uses the s· medicine in both cases.
379– 2 If . . . sin can do the s·,
383–14 because mind and body rest on the s· basis.
386–17 occasions the s· grief that the
395–10 The s· Principle cures both sin and sickness.
404–27 are one and the s· thing in C. S.
404–28 Both cures require the s· method
406– 3 Sin and sickness are both healed by the s· Principle.
414– 8 are the s· as in other diseases :
415–19 In the s· way thought increases or
416–13 the patient will find himself in the s· pain,
422–23 and attended by the s· symptoms.
427–16 Man is the s· after as before a bone is broken
t 455–29 the s· fountain cannot send forth both
457–22 One cannot scatter his fire, and at the s· time
458– 1 Mental quackery rests on the s· platform as
458– 9 the s· effect as truth.
r 474–17 If . . . then they must all be from the s· source ;
486–15 was the s· immediately after death as before.
489–22 for the s· fountain sendeth not forth
g 518–16 all having the s· Principle, or Father ;
525–25 if we give the s· heed to the history of error
546– 4 "the s· yesterday, and to-day,— *Heb.* 13 : 8.
551–31 the resulting germ is doomed to the s· routine.
ap 559– 2 Did this s· book contain the revelation of
566–19 the prayer which concludes the s· hymn,
gl 598– 5 Here the original word is the s· in both cases,
598– 7 as in other passages in this s· chapter

Samson
s 124– 4 a blind belief, a S· shorn of his strength.

sanative
pr 12–21 apparently either poisonous or s·.

sanction
an 106–16 Let this age, ... s· only such methods as are
s 146–23 Divine Science derives its s· from the Bible,
p 382– 4 having only human approval for their s·.

sanctioned
s 125–11 which human belief created and s·.
ph 171– 2 paganism and lust are so s· by society

sanctity
m 62– 3 the period of gestation have the s· of virginity.

sanctuary
pr 15– 3 The closet typifies the s· of Spirit,
15–17 In the quiet s· of earnest longings,
f 232–26 In the sacred s· of Truth are voices of

sandal
p 363– 2 costly and fragrant oil,— s· oil perhaps,

sandals
a 28–23 to unloose the s· of thy Master's feet !

sands
sp 87–23 the bodies which lie buried in its s· :

sandstone
gl 580– 1 red s· ; nothingness ;

sang
s 135– 1 s· : "What ailed thee, O thou sea,— *Psal.* 114 :
ph 190–27 When hope rose higher . . . he s· :
199–32 When Homer s· of the Grecian gods,
g 509–23 "the morning stars s· together."— *Job* 38 : 7.
ap 565–23 After the stars s· together and all was

sanguine
b 330– 6 she cherished s· hopes that C. S.

sanitary
pref x–25 than that of any other s· method.
sp 79– 7 A scientific mental method is more s· than
s 132–18 from other s· or religious systems,
133–23 s· methods, and a religious cultus.
ph 175– 5 When . . . less thought is given to s· subject
175–22 nor referred to s· laws.

sapped
o 357–12 the foundations of error would be s·

sapping
g 539– 4 thus s· the foundations of

sat
a 41–25 s· down at the right hand of the Father.
ph 184–29 I s· silently by her side a few moments.
f 245–15 youth s· gently on cheek and brow.
c 261–17 s· aching in his chair till his cue was spoken,
p 436–26 Judge Medicine s· in judgment on the case,

Satan
devil, and
ap 567–15 serpent, called the devil, and S·,— *Rev.* 12 : 9.
God and
p 389–26 good and evil, God and S·.
had bound her
pr 6–24 he said that S· had bound her,
hath bound
r 495– 9 "whom S· hath bound,"— *Luke* 13 : 16.
named
ph 187–12 another illusive personification, named S·.
this view of
gl 581– 1 This view of S· is confirmed by the name

───────

pr 7– 2 "Get thee behind me, S·."— *Matt.* 16 : 23.
ph 196–15 not of Rome, S·, nor of God, but of sin.
o 351–20 if we consider S· as a being coequal in power
ap 566–32 the hosts of heaven against the power of sin, S

satellite
ap 577–20 no need of sun or s·,

satisfaction
b 296–17 must lose all s· in error and sin
322–14 Man's wisdom finds no s· in sin,

satisfactory
pref ix–15 not complete nor s· expositions of Truth.

satisfied
pr 9– 8 Do we pursue the old selfishness, s· with
a 21–30 s· if he can only imagine himself drifting
36–27 or that the hand of Love is s· with
ph 180– 5 The patient sufferer tries to be s· when he
181–22 and are s· with good words instead of effects,
181–28 they generally know it and are s·.
190–29 I shall be s·, when I awake,— *Psal.* 17 : 15.
f 240–21 If at present with wrong-doing,
b 316–30 those dead in trespasses and sins, s· with
g 519– 3 Deity was s· with His work.

satisfy
m 60–32 Higher enjoyments alone can s· the cravings
ph 181–26 in order to s· the sick that you are
f 230–25 soothing syrups to . . . s· mortal belief,
c 257–26 to still the desires, to s· the aspirations?

Saul
b 326–23 S· of Tarsus beheld the way— the Christ, or

save
pr 2–18 A request that God will s· us
12– 1 prayer of faith shall s· the sick,"— *Jas.* 5 : 15.
a 22– 8 to make vigorous efforts to s· themselves ;
23– 2 require many sacrifices of self to s· us from
24– 3 Firmness in error will never s· from sin,
36–12 He was forsaken by all s· John, . . . and a few women
42–13 the desertion of all s· a few friends,
49– 8 Were all conspirators s· eleven?
49–17 No human eye was there to pity, no arm to s·
49–30 himself he cannot s·."— *Matt.* 27 : 42.
sp 95– 1 The effect of his Mind was always to heal and to s·,
s 136– 8 to s· men both bodily and spiritually.
149– 1 could s· from sickness as well as from sin.
164–24 s· from sin, disease, and death.
ph 166–11 believes in the power of his drugs to s·

save

ph	174– 6	Nothing s· divine power is capable of
	196– 4	not yet found it true that knowledge can s·
	200–26	s· Jesus Christ, and him crucified."— *I Cor.* 2 : 2.
	200–28	s· Jesus Christ, and him glorified.
f	226–26	to s· from the slavery of their own beliefs
b	299– 5	s· in the artist's own observation
	314–30	depending on . . . .material laws to s· them
p	377– 6	in order to s· their lives,
	436–17	and thus s· him from arrest.
	439–11	in the attempt to s· him.
t	447–11	and s· the victims of the mental assassins.

saved

a	23–29	and thou shalt be s· !"— *Acts* 16 : 31.
	38– 6	foreordination, — the election of a few to be s·,
	45–12	we shall be s· by his life."— *Rom.* 5 : 10.
	49–29	"He s· others ; himself he cannot — *Matt.* 27 : 42.
sp	98– 8	Body cannot be s· except through Mind.
s	133– 8	In Egypt, it was Mind which s· the Israelites
	164–15	before all mankind is s·
f	221–14	At this point C. S. s· him,
b	328– 3	Then he not only will be s·, but *is* s·.
o	346– 8	then teaches how this . . . is to be s· and healed.
	346–11	its nothingness is not s·,
p	369–31	any more than he is morally s· in or by sin.
	426–18	are not s· from sin or sickness by death,
t	458–30	by which mortals are radically s· from sin
r	497–16	we acknowledge that man is s· through Christ,
ap	577–22	All who are s· must walk in this light.

saves

pr	11– 7	it only s· the criminal from one form of
a	20–22	s· retracing and traversing anew the path
s	143–16	On this basis it s· from starvation by
	152– 5	takes away all its supposed sovereignty, and s·
b	328– 7	divine Principle which s· and heals,

saving

b	285–24	not as the s· Principle, or divine Love,
	285–31	as the healing and s· power.

Saviour

a	29–19	that is, Joshua, or S·.
	55–11	which presents the S· in a clearer light
b	285–23	By interpreting God as a corporeal S·
	317–25	Thomas, looking for the ideal S· in matter
	326–14	if we would gain the Christ as our only S·.
p	364–18	as Simon sought the S·,
r	477– 7	In this perfect man the S· saw
g	534– 4	and to behold at the sepulchre the risen S·,

Savonarola

a	40–15	Did the martyrdom of S· make the

savor

b	269– 1	pantheistic, and s· of Pandemonium,

savour

s	153– 7	The salt had "lost his s· ;"— *Matt.* 5 : 13.

saw

a	24–29	but until they s· that it enabled their Master
	45–22	who earliest s· Jesus after the resurrection
	46– 2	until they s· him after his crucifixion
	46–29	and the material senses s· him no more.
s	137– 2	His students s· this power of Truth heal
ph	184–32	She looked and s· that it pointed due east.
	193–18	The next day I s· him in the yard.
	193–29	what I s· and did for that man,
f	226–22	I s· before me the sick, wearing out years of
	226–29	I s· before me the awful conflict,
	227– 3	I s· that the law of mortal belief
	228–30	when they s· the demonstration of Christianity
	245–12	Some American travellers s· her when she
b	308–21	till he s· its unreality.
	314–20	but the faithful Mary s· him,
	321– 9	he s· it become a serpent,
	321–17	what he apparently s· was really but a
r	477– 3	In this perfect man the Saviour s·
g	503–26	And God s· the light, that it was — *Gen.* 1 : 4.
	506–24	and God s· that it was good.— *Gen.* 1 : 10.
	508–11	and God s· that it was good.— *Gen.* 1 : 12.
	511–10	and God s· that it was good.— *Gen.* 1 : 18.
	512– 7	and God s· that it was good.— *Gen.* 1 : 21.
	513–24	and God s· that it was good.— *Gen.* 1 : 25.
	515– 2	"And God s· .that it was good."— *Gen.* 1 : 25.
	518–24	And God s· everything that He— *Gen.* 1 : 31.
	525–23	He s· everything which He had made,
	536– 2	I s· a new heaven and a new earth :— *Rev.* 21 : 1.
ap	558– 3	And I s· another mighty angel— *Rev.* 10 : 1.
	561– 5	through his microscope, s· the sun in an egg
	561– 7	Because of his more spiritual vision, St. John s·
	561–11	Revelator s· also the spiritual ideal
	561–16	John s· the human and divine coincidence,
	562– 1	John s· in those days the spiritual idea as
	569–29	And when the dragon s· that he— *Rev.* 12 : 13.
	572–20	I s· a new heaven and a new earth :— *Rev.* 21 : 1.
	572–25	but he already s· a new heaven and a new earth.

saw

ap	576–10	And I s· no temple therein :— *Rev.* 21 : 22.
	576–19	John s· heaven and earth
gl	596– 7	Paul s· in Athens an altar dedicated

Saxon

b	286–16	In the S· and twenty other tongues
g	525– 8	In the S·, *mankind, a woman, any one;*

say

pr	1– *	*I s· unto you, That whosoever shall s·* — *Mark* 11 : 23.
	1– *	*I s· unto you, What things soever— Mark* 11 : 24.
	1– 4	Regardless of what another may s·
a	18– *	*I s· unto you, I will not drink of— Luke* 22 : 18.
	21– 2	overcoming error . . . you can finally s·,
	33–30	If not, can you then s· that you
	38–13	was addressing his disciples, yet he did not s·,
	40– 5	Another will s· : Go thy way— *Acts* 24 : 25.
	49– 5	caused the disciples to s· to their Master :
	50–22	Even what they did s·, — that Jesus' teachings
m	63–18	Our laws are not impartial, to s· the least,
	64–12	his wife should not s·,
sp	70– *	*And when they shall s· unto you,— Isa.* 8 : 19.
	70– *	*Verily, verily, I s· unto you,— John* 8 : 51.
	74–23	Who will s· that infancy can utter the
	92–32	Do you s· the time has not yet come
an	104–10	First, people s· it conflicts with the Bible.
	104–11	Next, they s· it has been discovered before.
	104–12	Lastly, they s· they have always believed it."
	105– 5	To s· that these tribunals have no
s	107–18	the prospect of those days in which we must s·,
	120–13	is he well if the senses s· he is sick?
	136–12	"Whom do men s· that I,— *Matt.* 16 : 13.
	136–15	"Some s· that thou art John— *Matt.* 16 : 14.
	137– 9	"But whom s· ye that I am?"— *Matt.* 16 : 15.
	137–29	"And I s· also unto thee,— *Matt.* 16 : 18.
	153–16	You s· a boil is painful ;
	154–32	to s· : "Oh, never mind !
	155–31	is it safe to s· that the less in quantity
	160–16	what does anatomy s· when the cords contract
	161– 3	You s·, "I have burned my finger."
	164– 9	It is just to s· that generally the
ph	165– *	*Therefore I s· unto you,— Matt.* 6 : 25.
	165–16	You s· that indigestion, fatigue,
	175– 9	What an abuse of natural beauty to s·
	184–18	We s· man suffers from the
	187–18	We s·, "My hand hath done it."
f	210–25	matter, being unintelligent, cannot s·,
	211– 5	and who shall s· whether Truth or error
	212–12	When the nerve is gone, which we s· was the
	212–26	we s· the lips or hands must move
	216– 3	Who shall s· that man is alive to-day, but
	216–28	When you s·, "Man's body is material,"
	216–28	I s· with Paul : Be "willing— *II Cor.* 5 : 8.
	217–29	You s·, "Toil fatigues me."
	218– 3	You do not s· a wheel is fatigued ;
	218– 9	The body is supposed to s·, "I am ill."
	218–11	a coalition with the reports of sin, and s·,
	219– 7	and then s· the product is correct.
	219– 8	No more can we s· in Science that
	229– 5	We should hesitate to s· that Jehovah sins
	249–20	You s·, "I dreamed last night."
c	256–22	none can stay His hand, or s· unto— *Dan.* 4 : 35.
	257–17	would s· that an anthropomorphic God,
	263–17	He might s· in Bible language :
b	277–29	Nothing we can s· or believe regarding
	278–21	we s· that Spirit is supreme and all-presence.
	283–13	But what s· prevalent theories?
	284– 1	It is not rational to s· that Mind is infinite, but
	286–29	error must also s·, "I am true."
	305–16	Verily, verily I s· unto you,— *John* 5 : 19.
	312– 9	People s·, "Man is dead ;"
	312–12	yet you s· that matter has caused his death.
	324–31	if . . . you cannot be benefited by what I s·.
	329– 7	proves the truth of all that I s· of it.
o	341– *	*And if I s· the truth,— John* 8 : 46.
	343– 1	people are taught in such cases to s·, Amen.
	343– 9	one might not be able to s· with the apostle,
	352–12	Would a mother s· to her child,
p	374– *	the sick s· : "How can my mind cause a
	381– 8	you s· that there is danger.
	385–22	You s· that you have not slept well
	385–27	You s· or think, because you have partaken of
	387– 4	Who dares to s· that actual Mind can be over-worked?
	391– 5	when thou art delivered . . . the judge will s·,
	391–19	When the body is supposed to s·, "I am sick,"
	391–22	If you s·, "I am sick," you plead guilty.
	392–28	When the condition is present which you s·
	396–10	Never s· beforehand how much you
	398–12	"Damsel, I s· unto thee, arise !"— *Mark* 5 : 41.
	399– 3	You s· that certain material combinations
	402– 3	it is but just to s· that the author has
	402–16	You s· that accidents, injuries, and
	402–20	We s· that one human mind can
	409– 2	You may s· : "But if disease obtains in

say
p 409–10 cannot dictate terms . . . nor s·, "I am sick."
409–27 We have no right to s· that life depends on
413–31 A child may have worms, if you s· so,
434– 5 Others s·, "The law of Christ supersedes
435–29 To him I might s·, in Bible language,
t 444–25 s· in thy heart : "Let there be no— *Gen.* 13 : 8.
447–31 He may s·, as a subterfuge, that evil is unreal,
448– 8 to s· that there is no evil,
450–28 Who, . . . can s· that there is no error of belief?
461–16 should you s·, "I am sick"? No.
r 485–30 To s· that strength is in matter,
489–19 Who dares to s· that the senses of man can
491–29 Who will s·, even though he does not understand C. S.,
491–32 Who can rationally s· otherwise,
g 531–19 Who will s· that minerals, vegetables, and
531–21 Who dares to s· either that God is in matter or
533–29 as much as to s· in meek penitence,
539–19 false to s· that Truth and error commingle
541–23 It is supposed to s· in the first instance,
543–19 who shall s· that he is not primarily dust?
544–21 The serpent is supposed to s·,
548– 1 Spirit and the bride s·, Come !— *Rev.* 22 : 17.
553–29 You may s· that mortals are formed before they
554–15 he learns to s·, "I am somebody ;
554–25 but he did s·, "Ye are of your father,— *John* 8 : 44.
555– 8 but I do not comprehend what you s· about
ap 568–25 What shall we s· of the mighty conquest over
gl 587–15 the serpents of error, which s·,
(*see also* **Scriptures**)

saying
his
b 271–17 Hence the universal application of his s· :
keep my
sp 70– * *If a man keep my s·,— John* 8 : 51.
f 217–13 "If a man keep my s·,— *John* 8 : 51.
p 428– 8 "If a man keep my s·,— *John* 8 : 51.
429–31 "If a man keep my s·,— *John* 8 : 51.
438– 7 If a man keep my s·,— *John* 8 : 51.
of our Master
b 315– 3 That s· of our Master,
p 382–21 This verifies the s· of our Master :
Scriptural
s 131–17 according to the Scriptural s·,
this
a 50–24 But this s· could not make it so.
b 286–29 But by this s· error, the lie, destroys itself.
uncomprehended
a 42–30 to test his still uncomprehended s·,

a 28–19 did not hinder men from s· :
32–18 s·, Drink ye all of it."— *Matt.* 26 : 27.
40–12 If the s· is true, "While there's life there's
49–29 mocked him on the cross, s· derisively,
s 140– 5 The Bible represents Him as s· :
164–28 brought to pass the s·— *I Cor.* 15 : 54.
ph 193–27 threatened with incarceration . . . for s· :
b 294–11 mortal belief, misnamed *man*, is error, s· :
307– 4 insists still upon the opposite of Truth, s·,
318– 7 even while the corporeal senses are s· that
328–27 believed and obeyed this sacred s·.
334–25 Revelator represents the Son of man as s·
o 345–12 neither knows itself nor what it is s·.
p 363–11 Knowing what those around him were s·
385–23 S· this and believing it,
t 453– 5 the author understands what she is s·.
r 485–31 is like s· that the power is in the lever.
496–26 brought to pass the s·— *I Cor.* 15 : 54.
g 512–17 And God blessed them, s·,— *Gen.* 1 : 22.
527– 7 commanded the man, s·,— *Gen.* 2 : 16.
530–19 and s·, through the material senses :
533–16 s·, "The woman, whom Thou gavest me,
535–21 of which I commanded thee, s·,— *Gen.* 3 : 17.
ap 568–13 And I heard a loud voice s·— *Rev.* 12 : 10.
574– 8 s·, Come hither, I will show thee— *Rev.* 21 : 9.

sayings
c 266–24 Mortals must follow Jesus' s·
b 276– 2 fulfils these s· of Scripture,
333–32 By these s· Jesus meant, not that the
o 350– 6 To understand all our Master's s·
350– 7 s· infinitely important,
361–15 conflicts not at all with another of his s· :
p 429–27 have faith in all the s· of our Master,
g 539–32 inspired his wisest and least-understood s·,
554–26 All these s· were to show that

says
pref ix–10 As a certain poet s· of himself,
pr 5–29 An apostle s· that the Son of God [Christ]
12– 1 shall save the sick," s· the Scripture.— *Jas.* 5 : 15.
m 58–32 "She that is married . . . s· the Bible ;— *I Cor.* 7 : 34.
sp 79–23 unscientific practitioner s· : "You are ill.
89–11 She s·, "I am incapable of words that glow,

says
sp 99– 6 "Work out your own . . . s· the apostle,— *Phil.* 2 : 12.
s 113–14 De Quincey s· mathematics has
115– 8 Job s· : "The ear trieth words,— *Job* 34 : 3.
144–21 the divine power which s· to disease,
151–17 Mortal belief s· that death has been
154–17 the mother is frightened and s·,
154–25 That mother . . . who s· to her child :
154–29 s·, moaning more childishly than her **child**,
ph 172–21 to which the apostle refers when he s·
175–32 Where ignorance is bliss, . . . s· the
186–17 It s· : "I am a real entity,
190– 4 The mortal s· that an inanimate
194–12 for if mortal mind s·, "I am deaf
198–25 though the doctor s· nothing to support his
200–27 C. S. s· : I am determined not to
f 204–31 error, which s· that Soul is in body,
218– 5 If it were not for what the human mind s·
219–21 "The wish," s· the poet, "is ever father to the
252–17 with the arrogance of reality and s· :
b 277– 4 the Scripture s· that dust returns to
286–11 Christ s·, "I am the way."— *John* 14 : 6.
288–18 St. Paul s· : "There remaineth— *Heb.* 4 : 9.
291–18 as the Scripture s·.
296–32 It s· to mortals, "You are wretched !"
297– 2 Mortal belief s·, "You are happy !"
297– 5 Human belief s· to mortals, "You are sick !"
307– 8 It s· : "There shall be lords and gods many.
307–17 Error charges its lie to Truth and s· :
332–16 As Paul s· : "There is one God,— *I Tim.* 2 : 5.
o 342–27 our Master s·, "By their fruits— *Matt.* 7 : 20.
345–26 The apostle s· : "For if a man think— *Gal.* 6 : 3.
355– 9 C. S. s·, in the language of the Master,
359–30 One s· : "I have spiritual ideals,
p 375– 1 mortal mind, not matter, which s·, "I die."
375– 9 proves this when his patient s·, "I am better,"
383– 5 One s· : "I take good care of my body."
386– 6 belief s· that you may catch cold
407–21 If delusion s·, "I have lost my memory,"
410– 4 "This is life eternal," s· Jesus,— *John* 17 : 3.
410–18 John s· : "There is no fear in— *I John* 4 : 18.
432–10 Another witness is called . . . and s· :
442–25 St. Paul s·, "Work our your— *Phil.* 2 : 12.
r 474–29 The apostle s· that the mission of Christ
478–23 Error s·, "I am man ;" but this belief is mortal
492–19 Science s· : All is Mind and Mind's idea.
496–23 the spiritual law which s· to the grave,
g 527–12 s· : "God cannot be tempted— *Jas.* 1 : 13.
533–28 She s·, "The serpent beguiled me,— *Gen.* 3 : 13.
548–19 a famous naturalist s· : "It is very possible that
552–14 corresponds with that of Job, when he s·,
557–17 the curse will be removed which s· to woman,
(*see also* **Paul**)

scaffold
f 202–10 until disciplined by the prison and the s· ;

scale
ascending
ph 189–30 goes on in an ascending s· by evolution,
fleshly
s 155–24 puts less weight into the material or fleshly s·
of existence
b 290– 6 no higher spiritually in the s· of existence
of harmony
m 60– 2 in the s· of harmony and happiness.
of health
p 407–19 and ascend a degree in the s· of health,
of intelligence
g 511–27 rising in the s· of intelligence,
right
ph 192–23 the weight you throw into the right s·.
spiritual
s 155–25 and more weight into the spiritual s·.

ph 168– 5 the removal of a single weight from either s·
f 205–30 throws our weight into the s·, not of Spirit,
t 445–17 you weigh the human in the s· with the divine,

scales
ph 168– 4 If the s· are evenly adjusted,

scanty
ph 188–25 an abundant or s· crop of disease, according to

scarcely
b 312–15 though with s· a spark of love in their hearts ;
o 350–32 and the spiritual sense was s· perceived.

scatheless
f 232– 6 afford no s· and permanent evidence

scatter
m 57–26 and s· them to the winds ;
t 457–21 One cannot s· his fire, and at the same time

scatters
m 68–11 and s· love's petals to decay.

scene
  p 362– 5 as if to interrupt the *s·* of Oriental festivity.
  g 513–10 and the *s·* shifts into light.
  ap 572–28 inadequate to take in so wonderful a *s·*.

scent
  sp 88– 7 and no *s·* salutes the nostrils.

sceptre
  s 152– 2 It would wield the *s·* of a monarch,
  ap 571–31 He takes away mitre and *s·*.

scholarly
  s 141–11 the line of *s·* and ecclesiastical descent,
  f 235–17 though adorned with gems of *s·* attainment,
  g 505–27 is not the result of *s·* attainments ;

scholars
  pr 16–12 There is indeed some doubt among Bible *s·*,
  s 128– 7 business men and cultured *s·*
  c 255– 8 cultured *s·* in Rome and in Greece,
  g 523–15 according to the best *s·*, there are

scholarship
  p 367–12 arrogance of rank and display of *s·*,

scholastic
  a 41–19 philosophy, *materia medica*, or *s·* theology
  s 141–32 now occupied by *s·* theology and physiology,
  f 226–18 Human codes, *s·* theology,
  c 256– 4 from the *s·* to the inspirational,
  b 315– 4 the *s·* theology of the rabbis.

scholasticism
  s 146–15 *S·* clings for salvation to the person,

Scholastic Theology
  p 433–28 and *S· T·* is sent for to prepare the
  437–22 Materia Medica, Anatomy, Physiology, *S· T·*,
  439–17 *S· T·*, Materia Medica, Physiology,

school
  ancient
    a 41–19 No ancient *s·* of philosophy, *materia medica*,
  its
    s 112– 7 forfeit their claims to belong to its *s·*,
  new
    s 112–27 Also, if any so-called new *s·* claims to be
  of Christian Science
    pref xi–25 The first *s·* of C. S. Mind-healing
    s 112– 3 Is there more than one *s·* of C. S.?
  of this Science
    s 112–26 to establish a genuine *s·* of this Science.
  of virtue
    m 65– 1 Experience should be the *s·* of virtue,
  old
    s 149–17 A physician of the old *s·* remarked
  preparatory
    r 486–10 Earth's preparatory *s·* must be improved
  some other
    s 112– 9 the Spencerian, or some other *s·*.
  such a
    s 112–29 such a *s·* is erroneous, for it

school-examinations
  f 235–11 *S·* are one-sided ;

schools
  have rendered
    s 146– 6 The *s·* have rendered faith in drugs the fashion,
  medical
    s 159–23 The medical *s·* would learn the state of
    f 217– 6 Medical *s·* may inform us that the
    t 444–22 If ecclesiastical sects or medical *s·* turn a
  old
    s 144–24 the old *s·* still oppose it.
  ruling of the
    s 148–30 When mortals sin, this ruling of the *s·*
  scientific
    r 483–23 the ordinary scientific *s·*, which wrestle with
  teachers of
    f 235– 7 The teachers of *s·* and the readers in churches
    s 141–11 from the *s·* and along the line of
    b 300–27 their thought that . . . is taught by the *s·*.
    p 429–29 not included in the teachings of the *s·*,

Science
  absolute
    a 41–21 demonstrated the divine healing of absolute *S·*.
    sp 72–11 so (in absolute *S·*) Soul, or God, is the only
    r 484– 2 until its absolute *S·* is reached.
  accept
    f 249– 1 Let us accept *S·*, relinquish all theories
  according to
    b 327– 3 an affection for goodness according to *S·*,
  actuality of
    s 130– 9 can demonstrate the actuality of *S·*.
    b 321–12 In this incident was seen the actuality of *S·*.
  adulterated the
    t 457– 4 Other works, . . . have adulterated the *S·*.
  advanced in
    sp 84– 8 When sufficiently advanced in *S·*
  aided by
    p 406–12 aided by *S·*, reaches Truth.

Science
  all
    s 110– 2 filling all space, constituting all *S·*,
    113– 2 one divine Principle of all *S·* ;
    126– 8 All *S·* is divine.
    b 275–23 that is, all power, all presence, all *S·*.
    g 551–16 all *S·* is of God, not of man.
  and art
    g 507–26 divine Principle of all expresses *S·* and art
  and Christianity
    f 231–13 If God makes sin, . . . then *S·* and Christianity
    p 371–26 will improve through *S·* and Christianity.
  and consciousness
    p 423–24 Both *S·* and consciousness are now at work
  and demonstration
    f 243– 2 the *S·* and demonstration of spiritual good
  and harmony
    ph 192–19 and this teaching accords with *S·* and harmony.
  and peace
    sp 96–15 on the other side there will be *S·* and peace.
  and the senses
    b 273–13 Hence the enmity between *S·* and the senses,
  and truth
    s 110–23 the *S·* and truth therein will forever remain
    r 479–22 In the vast forever, in the *S·* and truth of being,
    g 521–23 The *S·* and truth of the divine creation
  and understanding
    b 274–27 *S·* and understanding, . . . destroy the imaginary
  annihilates
    b 330–26 a delusion . . . which *S·* annihilates.
  announced by
    b 298–19 real is attained, which is announced by *S·*,
  antagonistic to
    ph 182–15 hypotheses of mortals are antagonistic to *S·*
  apart from
    r 480–13 Material sense has its realm apart from *S·*
  apprehended in
    p 402–11 will be apprehended in *S·*,
  approaching
    f 223–22 accompany approaching *S·*, and cannot be put
  axe of
    a 27–18 He laid the axe of *S·* at the root of
  basis of
    ph 182–17 those who heal the sick on the basis of *S·*.
  battle-axe of
    p 389–27 falling before the battle-axe of *S·*.
  beheld in
    r 476–32 Jesus beheld in *S·* the perfect man,
  can heal
    ph 179– 5 *S·* can heal the sick, who are absent from
  cannot destroy
    b 298– 7 belief cannot destroy *S·* armed with faith,
  cannot produce
    p 402–29 *S·* cannot produce both disorder and order.
  Christ
    s 107– 1 In the year 1866, I discovered the Christ *S·*
    127–10 The terms . . . Christ *S·* or C. S.,
  Christian
    pref viii– 3 to reach the heights of *C· S·*, man must
    viii–16 On this basis *C· S·* will have a fair fight.
    viii–28 the system that she denominated *C· S·*.
    ix–20 Her first pamphlet on *C· S·* was copyrighted in
    x– 9 is not a factor in the Principle of *C· S·*.
    xi– 2 Many imagine that the phenomena. . . in *C· S·*
    xi– 5 On the contrary, *C· S·* rationally explains that
    xi– 9 The physical healing of *C· S·* results now,
    xi–25 The first school of *C. S.* Mind-healing was
    xii– 5 in the United States, where *C· S·* was first
    pr 10–12 *C· S·* reveals a necessity for overcoming the
    14– 9 understanding of Life as revealed in *C· S·*.
    16–18 *C· S·* teaches us that "the evil one,"
    a 24– 7 open the way for *C· S·* to be understood,
    26–26 *C· S·* destroys sickness, sin, and death.
    26–32 *C· S·*, working out the harmony of Life and
    29–15 Those instructed in *C· S·* have reached the
    36–17 preclude *C· S·* from finding favor with the
    41–22 Jesus foresaw the reception *C· S·* would have
    42–26 in *C· S·* the true man is governed by God
    44–11 He met and mastered on the basis of *C· S·*,
    52–23 two cardinal points of Mind-healing, or *C· S·*,
    m 63–13 *C· S·* furnishes no precedent for such injustice.
    63–17 less rights than does either *C· S·* or civilization.
    65–11 To gain *C· S·* and its harmony,
    68–27 *C· S·* presents unfoldment, not accretion ;
    sp 70– 4 revelations of *C· S·* unlock the treasures of
    71–32 a theory contrary to *C· S·*.
    74–29 In *C· S·* there is never a retrograde step,
    79–12 *C· S·* removes these beliefs and hypotheses
    79–14 *C· S·*, . . . introduces the harmony of being.
    83– 9 Nothing is more antagonistic to *C· S·* than
    83–21 It is contrary to *C· S·* to suppose that
    83–23 Between *C· S·* and all forms of superstition
    84–30 is learned through Christ and *C· S·*
    93–22 In *C· S·*, Spirit, as a proper noun, is the
    95–22 we want that day to be succeeded by *C· S·*,
    97– 1 who discern *C· S·* will hold crime in check.
    97– 9 in *C ·S·* the flight of one and the blow of the

Science
Christian

p 394–30	Not understanding $C \cdot S \cdot$, the sick usually
402– 1	$C \cdot S \cdot$ is always the most skilful surgeon,
404– 2	in order to judge the case according to $C \cdot S \cdot$
404–22	important points in the theology of $C \cdot S \cdot$.
404–27	are one and the same thing in $C \cdot S \cdot$.
405– 5	$C \cdot S \cdot$ commands man to master the
406– 7	Sin will submit to $C \cdot S \cdot$ when, in place of
407–12	Here $C \cdot S \cdot$ is the sovereign panacea,
407–18	slave of wrong desire learn the lessons of $C \cdot S \cdot$.
410– 1	If here we give no heed to $C \cdot S \cdot$,
410–21	definite and inspired proclamation of $C \cdot S \cdot$.
410–25	Selfishness does not appear in . . . $C \cdot S \cdot$.
411–30	Watch the result of this simple rule of $C \cdot S \cdot$,
412–13	The power of $C \cdot S \cdot$ and divine Love is omnipotent.
412–31	silently or audibly on the . . . basis of $C \cdot S \cdot$.
414–16	explain $C \cdot S \cdot$ to them, but not too soon,
414–23	$C \cdot S \cdot$ declares that Mind is substance,
417–11	Maintain the facts of $C \cdot S \cdot$,
417–20	To the $C \cdot S \cdot$ healer, sickness is a dream
418–15	mortal dream . . . should cease through $C \cdot S \cdot$.
420–13	This fact of $C \cdot S \cdot$ should be explained to
422–20	Thus $C \cdot S \cdot$, by the alchemy of Spirit,
424–25	if you understand $C \cdot S \cdot$
426– 5	The discoverer of $C \cdot S \cdot$ finds the
428–26	sooner or later, through Christ and $C \cdot S \cdot$,
430–16	in which the plea of $C \cdot S \cdot$ heals the sick.
433–10	urges the jury not to allow . . . $C \cdot S \cdot$.
434–10	Court of Spirit, where $C \cdot S \cdot$ is allowed to appear
434–19	$C \cdot S \cdot$ turns suddenly to the supreme tribunal,
437–21	False Belief, called $C \cdot S \cdot$ to order for contempt
437–24	rose to the question of expelling $C \cdot S \cdot$ from
437–31	They declared that $C \cdot S \cdot$ was overthrowing
437–32	The attorney, $C \cdot S \cdot$, then read from the
438– 8	Then $C \cdot S \cdot$ proved the witness, Nerve, to be
438–14	$C \cdot S \cdot$ continued : — I ask your arrest
438–18	Then $C \cdot S \cdot$ continued : — Another witness,
439–15	$C \cdot S \cdot$ turned from the abashed witnesses,
441–21	recommend that Materia Medica adopt $C \cdot S \cdot$
442–10	as he shook hands with his counsel, $C \cdot S \cdot$,
442–17	Neither . . . enters into the practice of $C \cdot S \cdot$,
442–29	This truth is $C \cdot S \cdot$.
t 443– 1	When the discoverer of $C \cdot S \cdot$ is consulted
443–15	If patients fail to experience the healing power of $C \cdot S \cdot$,
444–23	medical schools turn a deaf ear to . . . $C \cdot S \cdot$
445– 1	to hinder the demonstration of $C \cdot S \cdot$
445–19	$C \cdot S \cdot$ silences human will,
447– 3	We have no authority in $C \cdot S \cdot$ . . . to attempt
448–12	$C \cdot S \cdot$ rises above the evidence of the
448–25	instructions opposite to absolute $C \cdot S \cdot$ must
448–27	adheres strictly to the teachings of $C \cdot S \cdot$
448–29	It is $C \cdot S \cdot$ to do right, and nothing short of
449– 4	A grain of $C \cdot S \cdot$ does wonders for mortals,
449– 5	but more of $C \cdot S \cdot$ must be gained in order to
449–22	A proper teacher of $C \cdot S \cdot$ improves the
450–11	To teach $C \cdot S \cdot$ to such as these is no task.
451– 8	Students of $C \cdot S \cdot$, who start with its letter
451–21	knows that human will is not $C \cdot S \cdot$,
452–32	if you . . . then should adopt $C \cdot S \cdot$,
454– 3	use of tobacco . . . is not in harmony with $C \cdot S \cdot$.
454–12	is the doctrine of absolute $C \cdot S \cdot$,
454–31	spiritual power . . . is the central point of $C \cdot S \cdot$.
455– 8	The student, who receives his knowledge of $C \cdot S \cdot$,
455–28	This strong point in $C \cdot S \cdot$ is not to be overlooked,
456– 7	the only success of the students of $C \cdot S \cdot$.
456–12	Principle and method of demonstrating $C \cdot S \cdot$
456–14	the true conception of $C \cdot S \cdot$ healing
456–29	SCIENCE AND HEALTH . . . contains the full statement of $C \cdot S \cdot$,
456–32	containing a thorough statement of $C \cdot S \cdot$.
457– 7	Since the divine light of $C \cdot S \cdot$ first dawned
457–19	$C \cdot S \cdot$ is not an exception to the general rule,
457–25	Departing from $C \cdot S \cdot$, some learners commend
458–17	the author desires to keep it out of $C \cdot S \cdot$.
459– 9	Judge not the future advancement of $C \cdot S \cdot$ by
459–16	mortals, untaught and unrestrained by $C \cdot S \cdot$,
459–24	To mortal sense $C \cdot S \cdot$ seems abstract,
461– 4	$C \cdot S \cdot$ must be accepted at this period by
461– 7	$C \cdot S \cdot$ can be taught only by those who
462– 1	requisite for a thorough comprehension of $C \cdot S \cdot$.
462– 4	adheres to the divine rules of $C \cdot S \cdot$
462– 5	can demonstrate $C \cdot S \cdot$, cast out error,
462–14	demonstrate the healing of $C \cdot S \cdot$
462–26	$C \cdot S \cdot$ teaches when and how to probe the
463–17	the $C \cdot S \cdot$ infant is born of the Spirit,
464– 8	establish the stately operations of $C \cdot S \cdot$,
464–25	Adulterating $C \cdot S \cdot$, makes it void.
r 465– 5	Absolute $C \cdot S \cdot$ pervades its statements,
466– 5	The varied manifestations of $C \cdot S \cdot$ indicate
466–12	represent contraries, as $C \cdot S \cdot$ reveals,
471–31	which, . . . she has named $C \cdot S \cdot$.
472– 5	The way which leads to $C \cdot S \cdot$ is straight
473– 1	We learn in $C \cdot S \cdot$ that all inharmony of

Science
Christian

r 473–11	comes to heal sickness and sin through $C \cdot S \cdot$,
475–13	he must be so understood in $C \cdot S \cdot$.
477–11	$C \cdot S \cdot$ reveals man as the idea of God,
480– 1	When the substance of Spirit appears in $C \cdot S \cdot$,
482–10	As used in $C \cdot S \cdot$, Soul is properly the
482–27	$C \cdot S \cdot$ is the law of Truth, which heals the sick
483–12	hinders its approach to the standard in $C \cdot S \cdot$,
483–21	God certainly revealed the spirit of $C \cdot S \cdot$,
483–27	And $C. S.$ does honor God
484– 6	Does $C \cdot S \cdot$, or metaphysical healing, include
485–11	Why malign $C \cdot S \cdot$ for instructing
488–16	$C \cdot S \cdot$ sustains with immortal proof
489–25	$C \cdot S \cdot$ shows them to be false,
490– 2	the grand truths of $C \cdot S \cdot$ dispute this error.
490– 7	$C \cdot S \cdot$ reveals Truth and Love as the
490–16	since he is so already, according to $C \cdot S \cdot$.
491–30	even though he does not understand $C \cdot S \cdot$,
493– 1	$C \cdot S \cdot$ speedily shows Truth to be triumphant.
493–11	$C \cdot S \cdot$ Mind-healing is touched upon in a
493–13	in a previous chapter entitled $C \cdot S \cdot$ Practice.
493–16	prove for himself the Principle and rule of $C \cdot S \cdot$
493–22	$C \cdot S \cdot$ takes away this physical sense
495–20	Let $C \cdot S \cdot$, instead of corporeal sense, support
495–26	How can I progress most rapidly in . . . $C \cdot S \cdot$?
495–29	Adhere to the divine Principle of $C \cdot S \cdot$
496– 6	in $C \cdot S \cdot$ the first duty is to obey God,
497– 2	important points, or religious tenets, of $C \cdot S \cdot$:
g 502–20	according to the teachings of $C \cdot S \cdot$.
505–25	spiritual proof of the universe in $C \cdot S \cdot$.
506– 6	which separates $C \cdot S \cdot$ from supposition
508–28	The third stage in the order of $C \cdot S \cdot$ is
516– 1	Then note how true, according to $C \cdot S \cdot$,
535– 1	has given the understanding a foothold in $C \cdot S \cdot$.
535–14	other creations must go down before $C \cdot S \cdot$.
535–16	through the open gate of $C \cdot S \cdot$
545–18	Outside of $C \cdot S \cdot$ all is vague and
546– 9	Is $C \cdot S \cdot$ contradictory?
546–23	$C \cdot S \cdot$ is dawning upon a material age.
547– 2	A simple statement of $C \cdot S \cdot$, if demonstrated
547– 3	contains the proof of all here said of $C \cdot S \cdot$.
548– 3	$C \cdot S \cdot$ separates error from truth,
548–10	So $C \cdot S \cdot$ can be seen only as the
548–23	gained the diviner side in $C \cdot S \cdot$,
550–31	$C \cdot S \cdot$ repudiates self-evident impossibilities,
552–18	They must peck open their shells with $C \cdot S \cdot$,
554– 1	It can only be replied, that $C \cdot S \cdot$ reveals
555– 7	said to the discoverer of $C \cdot S \cdot$:
555–13	$C \cdot S \cdot$ attributes to error neither entity nor
556–13	$C \cdot S \cdot$ may absorb the attention of sage and
557–10	$C \cdot S \cdot$ reveals harmony as
ap 568–32	Self-abnegation, . . . is a rule in $C \cdot S \cdot$.
572–12	Love fulfils the law of $C \cdot S \cdot$,
573–28	This is indeed a foretaste of absolute $C \cdot S \cdot$.
577–18	fourth, $C \cdot S \cdot$, which to-day and forever
577–28	present feeble sense of $C \cdot S \cdot$.
578– 1	the light which $C \cdot S \cdot$ throws on the Scriptures
gl 579– 1	In $C \cdot S \cdot$ we learn that the substitution of
585–10	$C \cdot S \cdot$, with which can be discerned the
596– 4	$C \cdot S \cdot$ brings God much nearer to man,
596–14	but $C \cdot S \cdot$ reveals Spirit, not matter,
596–26	$C \cdot S \cdot$, contradicting sense, maketh the

Christianity must be
s 135–22	It has been said, . . . Christianity must be $S \cdot$,

claim of
s 130–26	If thought is startled at the strong claim of $S \cdot$

declares
s 124–28	divine $S \cdot$ declares that they belong wholly to
o 347– 4	C. $S \cdot$ declares that whatever is mortal
p 414–23	C. $S \cdot$ declares that Mind is substance,
429–12	$S \cdot$ declares that man is subject to Mind.
r 485– 4	$S \cdot$ declares that Mind, not matter, sees, hears, feels,

demands of
r 483–10	moral and spiritual demands of $S \cdot$

demonstrable
ph 171–13	no longer an open question, but is demonstrable $S \cdot$.
o 344–13	the opponents of a demonstrable $S \cdot$ would

demonstrate its
s 111–14	its rules demonstrate its $S \cdot$.

demonstrates
b 337–14	C. $S \cdot$ demonstrates that none but the pure
339–12	$S \cdot$ demonstrates the unreality of evil,

demonstrate the
a 30– 3	and could demonstrate the $S \cdot$ of Love
t 452–27	Such a practice does not demonstrate the $S \cdot$

demonstration of
b 273–27	His acts were the demonstration of $S \cdot$,

denies all disease
s 120–23	and thus $S \cdot$ denies all disease, heals the sick,

destitute of
b 275–25	human theories are destitute of $S \cdot$.

destroyed through
p 380– 1	is destroyed through $S \cdot$,

Science
dispels
sp 80–15 *S*· dispels mystery and explains
Divine
a 55–29 This Comforter I understand to be Divine *S*·.
s 127– 9 The terms Divine *S*·, Spiritual Science,
divine
pref vii–12 to behold and to follow this daystar of divine *S*·,
pr 12–26 not the outgrowth of divine *S*·.
12–32 In divine *S*·, where prayers are mental,
a 36– 4 Divine *S*· reveals the necessity of
38– 9 is broken by the demands of divine *S*·.
40– 8 Divine *S*· adjusts the balance
42–18 gave full evidence of divine *S*·,
42–21 This error Jesus met with divine *S*·
43– 9 that influx of divine *S*· which
43–23 he was demonstrating divine *S*·.
45– 6 demonstrated divine *S*· in his victory over
46–32 an enlarged understanding of divine *S*·,
53–11 He was at work in divine *S*·.
55–24 layeth his earthly all on the altar of divine *S*·,
m 69– 4 as fixed in divine *S*· as is the proof that
sp 76–19 When divine *S*· is universally understood,
76–29 final understanding of Christ in divine *S*·.
91– 9 difficult for the sinner to accept divine *S*·,
96–26 shaped his course in accordance with divine *S*·
s 108–21 I learned these truths in divine *S*·:
111– 5 divine Mind as expressed through divine *S*·.
112–12 divine *S*· which eschews man-made systems,
114–28 In divine *S*·, the universe, including man, is
121–31 is allied to divine *S*· as displayed in the
123–12 Divine *S*·, rising above physical theories,
123–20 discovery of this divine *S*· of Mind-healing,
124–28 divine *S*· declares that they belong wholly to
130– 7 vain to speak dishonestly of divine *S*·,
131– 6 When once destroyed by divine *S*·,
136–22 no high appreciation of divine *S*·
139–23 could neither wholly obscure the divine *S*· of
142–19 divine *S*· to be welcomed in.
144–23 divine *S*· wars with . . . physical science,
146–23 Divine *S*· derives its sanction from the Bible,
149– 5 more excellent way is divine *S*·
149–16 proved the Principle of divine *S*·.
149–30 to understand the affirmations of divine *S*·,
164–13 minus the unction of divine *S*·.
164–27 put on immortality [divine *S*·],— *I Cor.* 15 : 54.
ph 167– 6 We apprehend Life in divine *S*· only as we
167–11 nor perceive divine *S*· with the material
171– 6 will reopen with the key of divine *S*·
172–12 divine *S*· reveals the eternal chain
184–24 demonstrated this as a rule of divine *S*·
185–15 to match the divine *S*· of immortal Mind,
f 213–17 Divine *S*· reveals sound as communicated
221–28 undisciplined by self-denial and divine *S*·.
226–13 but through Christ's divine *S*·.
226–20 Divine *S*· rends asunder these fetters,
228–16 through the understanding of divine *S*·.
231– 1 obliterated through Christ in divine *S*·,
231–23 divine *S*· of being in man's relation to God,
231–27 is in accordance with divine *S*·.
232– 8 Security . . . is found only in divine *S*·.
235– 6 does not obey the requirements of divine *S*·.
241– 2 knows God's will or the demands of divine *S*·.
242–10 and Christ in divine *S*· shows us this way.
242–25 The divine *S*· of man is woven into
242–30 The finger-posts of divine *S*· show the way
244– 4 Divine *S*· reveals these grand facts.
c 259– 6 In divine *S*·, man is the true image of God.
259–28 through divine *S*·, which corrects error with
265– 1 and its government is divine *S*·.
267–19 examined in the light of divine *S*·,
b 271– 6 Neither . . . exists in divine *S*·.
271–15 divine *S*·, which their Master demonstrated
273– 7 without the divine Principle of divine *S*·.
273–10 Divine *S*· reverses the false testimony
274–23 Divine *S*· is absolute, and permits no
275– 6 The starting-point of divine *S*· is
276–10 Man and his Maker are correlated in divine *S*·,
276–30 Divine *S*· does not gather grapes from thorns
278– 5 the only substance . . . recognized by divine *S*·.
281– 1 yields only to the understanding of divine *S*·,
281– 8 Divine *S*· contradicts the corporeal senses,
281–27 Divine *S*· does not put new wine into old
287– 7 Divine *S*· contradicts this postulate
290–21 until in divine *S*· Christ, Truth, removes
292– 4 Divine *S*· alone can compass the heights
298– 3 Truth, and Love are the realities of divine *S*·.
301–16 and is revealed only through divine *S*·.
303–16 Divine *S*· lays the axe at the root of the
305–26 the divine Principle that obtains in divine *S*·
308–23 in this Peniel of divine *S*·.
314–25 The higher his demonstration of divine *S*·
315– 9 his understanding of this divine *S*· brought
316– 1 demonstrating the way of divine *S*·,
319–21 The divine *S*· taught in the original
321–15 destroyed through understanding divine *S*·,
321–25 by this proof in divine *S*·,

Science
divine
b 322–11 before this recognition of divine *S*· can come
322–30 Then we begin to learn Life in divine *S*·.
323–21 they will be receptive of divine *S*·,
325–27 the divine *S*· which ushered Jesus into
326–32 and learned a lesson in divine *S*·.
329– 9 to question the great might of divine *S*·
329–32 Human resistance to divine *S*· weakens
330–18 or to the revelation of divine *S*·.
331–31 divine *S*· or the Holy Comforter.
331–32 express in divine *S*· the threefold, essential
334–18 exist in the eternal order of divine *S*·,
336–29 in the order of divine *S*·, God and man coexist
337–10 According to divine *S*·, man is in a degree
o 344– 6 sinless condition of man in divine *S*·,
349–14 in conveying the teachings of divine *S*·
353– 3 real to material sense, is unreal in divine *S*·.
354– 9 The words of divine *S*· find their immortality in
354–30 opponents of divine *S*· must be charitable,
361–24 A human perception of divine *S*·,
p 368– 5 Divine *S*· insists that time will prove all this.
371–19 The way in divine *S*· is the only way out of
390–13 dispute the testimony of . . . with divine *S*·.
395–11 When divine *S*· overcomes faith in
411– 9 not perfectly attuned to divine *S*·,
418– 9 unerring, and certain effect of divine *S*·.
t 444–28 Immortals, or God's children in divine *S*·,
445–10 possibilities of man endued with divine *S*·.
448–20 the strong impress of divine *S*·,
460–32 was no longer cast upon divine *S*·.
r 470– 5 which constitute divine *S*·.
470–11 Divine *S*· explains the abstract statement
471–13 The facts of divine *S*· should be admitted,
471–30 her highest creed has been divine *S*·,
476– 4 In divine *S*·, God and the real man are
477–13 Divine *S*· shows it to be impossible that
480–29 This is the eternal verity of divine *S*·.
484–10 In divine *S*·, the supposed laws of matter
484–24 the human antipode of divine *S*·.
494–19 and seek safety in divine *S*·.
g 503–12 Divine *S*·, the Word of God, saith
506–10 Through divine *S*·, Spirit, God, unites
511–11 In divine *S*·, which is the seal of Deity
513–13 until divine *S*· becomes the interpreter.
515–30 Call the mirror divine *S*·,
517–11 In divine *S*·, we have not as much authority for
519–28 according to the apprehension of divine *S*·.
526–19 sword which guards it is the type of divine *S*·.
530– 5 In divine *S*·, man is sustained by God,
530–18 represents error . . . giving the lie to divine *S*·
535–10 Divine *S*· deals its chief blow at the
543– 8 In divine *S*·, the material man is shut out from
543–14 against which divine *S*· is engaged in a
543–22 are found, according to divine *S*·, to be
549–25 the pathway leading to divine *S*·,
551–15 material methods are impossible in divine *S*·
557–19 Divine *S*· rolls back the clouds of error with
ap 558–10 This angel . . . prefigures divine *S*·.
559– 3 contain the revelation of divine *S*·,
559–20 Take divine *S*·.
560–10 divine *S*· interprets the Principle of
562– 3 baptize with the Holy Ghost,— divine *S*·.
564–20 should be demonstrated in divine *S*·,
565–18 will eventually rule . . . with divine *S*·.
567–31 Divine *S*· shows how the Lamb slays the wolf.
569–15 Alas for those who break faith with divine *S*·
571–30 with the sublime grandeur of divine *S*·,
575–10 represents the light and glory of divine *S*·.
575–19 the Word, Christ, Christianity, and divine *S*·;
576–23 In divine *S*·, man possesses this recognition
gl 583– 8 are governed by divine *S*·;
583–18 and the demonstration of divine *S*·,
584–26 DOVE. A symbol of divine *S*·;
585–16 Divine *S*· encompassing the universe and man;
588– 5 Divine *S*· understood and acknowledged.
588– 7 HOLY GHOST.' Divine *S*·;
590– 2 The reign of harmony in divine *S*·;
592–18 NEW JERUSALEM. Divine *S*·;
595–12 the eternal demand of divine *S*·.
597–14 and opened the sepulchre with divine *S*·,
enables one
sp 87–15 *S*· enables one to read the human mind, but not
establishing the
s 135– 8 establishing the *S*· of God's . . . law.
eternal
sp 78–32 the invisible good dwelling in eternal *S*·.
s 150– 5 demonstrated as an immanent, eternal *S*·,
c 258–29 under the government of God in eternal *S*·,
explains
r 470–11 Divine *S*· explains the abstract statement
g 522–10 *S*· explains as impossible.
exposes
sp 91–10 because *S*· exposes his nothingness;
expressed in
ph 178–22 Truth, or the divine Mind, expressed in *S*·.

Science

expressed through
r 471–28 the spiritual import, expressed through S·,

fact in
p 430–12 When will mankind wake to this great fact in S·?
ap 573– 6 Holy Writ sustains the fact in S·, that the

facts of
g 516– 7 subordinate the false . . . to the facts of S·,

founded on
r 487–19 Christian evidence is founded on S·

found in
r 475–17 conscious identity of being as found in S·,

genuine
sp 95– 2 the only genuine S· of reading mortal mind.

governed by
f 206–13 governed by S· instead of the senses,

harmony, and
b 299–27 seem to hide Truth, health, harmony, and S·,

harmony of
sp 81–27 hides the harmony of S·,
g 514–29 moving in the harmony of S·,
ap 562–16 divine Principle of man in the harmony of S·.

has called
r 483–16 S· has called the world to battle over this

has explained
b 334–28 [S· has explained me].''

heal by
r 483– 9 In order to heal by S·, you must not be

hill of
b 326– 8 must not try to climb the hill of S· by

illuminations of
gl 596–15 The illuminations of S· give us a sense of the

impossible in
a 39–25 both are unreal, because impossible in S·.
sp 74–21 backward transformation is impossible in S·.
83–12 Miracles are impossible in S·,
t 446–17 or his demonstration is . . . impossible in S·.

indestructible in
r 471– 1 are indestructible in S· ;

inevitably lifts
m 60– 2 S· inevitably lifts one's being higher in the

inspired by
p 368– 3 The confidence inspired by S· lies in the fact

instructed by
g 552–20 but not yet instructed by S·,

interpreted by
s 124–14 universe, like man, is to be interpreted by S·

is able
ap 568– 4 but S· is able to destroy this lie, called evil.

is divine
s 126– 8 All S· is divine.
r 492–27 the Principle of this S· is divine,

is immortal
sp 84– 1 S· is immortal and coordinate neither with the

knowledge of
b 286– 6 for this is fatal to a knowledge of S·.

knows no lapse
r 471– 1 S· knows no lapse from nor return to harmony,

landmarks of
b 323– 9 which are the landmarks of S·.

letter of
s 113– 4 The letter of S· plentifully reaches humanity
f 243–11 must always accompany the letter of S·

linked by
s 316– 4 The real man being linked by S· to his Maker,

mastered by
p 427–11 must be met and mastered by S·,

medicine of
an 104–19 The medicine of S· is divine Mind ;

metaphysical
ph 195–14 metaphysical S· and its divine Principle.
f 219–25 Those who are healed through metaphysical S·

more
r 487– 8 There is more S· in the perpetual exercise of

must be apprehended
s 110–30 Its S· must be apprehended by as many as

must be Christianity
s 135–22 and S· must be Christianity,

must triumph
r 484–24 S· must triumph over material sense,

Natural
s 111–20 A prize . . . for the best essay on Natural S·,

never change in
p 427– 2 this fact can never change in S· to the

never removes
sp 80–16 S· never removes phenomena from the

no error in
s 131– 3 There is no error in S·,

no hypocrisy in
b 329–21 There is no hypocrisy in S·.

obsolete in
gl 588–22 IN. A term obsolete in S· if

of being
pr 2–15 Prayer cannot change the S· of being,
m 63– 3 if you understood the S· of being.
sp 77– 6 until the S· of being is reached.
81– 6 If Spiritualists understood the S· of being,

Science

of being
sp 84–14 Acquaintance with the S· of being enables
93–32 of the reign of harmony in the S· of being.
s 122– 2 often reverses the real S· of being,
128–15 A knowledge of the S· of being
144–27 When the S· of being is . . . understood,
ph 191–24 The S· of being reveals man and immortality
200–16 The great truth in the S· of being,
f 207–16 The S· of being repudiates self-evident
207–24 belong not to the S· of being.
231–23 divine S· of being in man's relation to God,
249–10 Such is the true S· of being.
b 277–18 points to the spiritual truth and S· of being.
280–31 and rejecting the S· of being
285– 3 This S· of being obtains not alone hereafter
302–19 The S· of being reveals man as perfect,
304–30 man, not understanding the S· of being,
309–24 The S· of being shows it to be impossible
311–21 understand the S· of being.
321–30 the S· of being was demonstrated by Jesus,
331– 8 If . . . the S· of being would be forever lost
336–27 The S· of being furnishes the rule of perfection,
340–21 The divine Principle of . . . bases the S· of being,
o 350–26 before the S· of being can be demonstrated.
p 372– 8 The S· of being, in which all is divine Mind,
406–11 The S· of being unveils the errors of sense,
r 492–27 On this statement rests the S· of being,
g 518– 4 is the S· of being.
gl 583– 4 suppositions . . . opposed to the S· of being.
598–25 retained when the S· of being is understood,

of celestial being
a 26–16 to reveal the S· of celestial being,

of Christ
a 55–18 when man shall recognize the S· of Christ
s 118– 2 spiritual leaven signifies the S· of Christ

of Christianity
pr 4–23 We reach the S· of Christianity
sp 98– 8 The S· of Christianity is misinterpreted by
f 203– 3 In the S· of Christianity, Mind . . . has
b 271–21 When the S· of Christianity appears, it will
o 347–19 it is the S· of Christianity which is restoring it,
351–12 discerned in the S· of Christianity,
s 466–26 S· of Christianity comes with fan in hand
r 473–29 This is the S· of Christianity.
474– 6 Whoever introduces the S· of Christianity

of creation
g 509–29 Knowing the S· of creation,
537–23 coordinate with the S· of creation
539–23 arguing for the S· of creation, Jesus said :
539–30 The S· of creation, so conspicuous in the

of divine Mind
ph 180–28 is found in the S· of divine Mind

of Genesis
g 525–22 In the S· of Genesis we read that

of God
s 111– 7 The S· of God and man is
111– 9 as the S· of God, Spirit, must,

of healing
sp 85– 9 You will reach the perfect S· of healing
ph 167– 4 If . . . the S· of healing is not attained,
t 444–31 make clear to students the S· of healing,
455– 8 in order to teach this S· of healing.
456–29 C. S., or the S· of healing through Mind.
g 547– 7 prove for yourself, . . . the S· of healing,

of Life
pr 9–22 It involves the S· of Life.
m 57– 3 cannot attain the S· of Life.
b 303–20 beatified understanding of the S· of Life.
p 409–29 in ignorance of the S· of Life,
r 489– 3 If the S· of Life were understood,

of man
sp 73–10 the individuality and the S· of man,
f 242–25 The divine S· of man is woven into
p 409–25 as mortals realize the S· of man

of mental healing
t 455–31 in the S· of mental healing and teaching,

of mental practice
p 410–23 The S· of mental practice is

of Mind
m 62–32 Because mortals . . . reject the S· of Mind,
67–11 nautical science is not equal to the S· of Mind.
sp 71–21 When the S· of Mind is understood,
s 157– 6 is employed through the S· of Mind,
ph 181–21 If you are too material to love the S· of Mind
f 202– 7 bring to bear upon the study of the S· of Mind
237–30 unwilling to investigate the S· of Mind
b 269–25 on the testimony of the S· of Mind.
294–31 The S· of Mind corrects such mistakes,
318–22 The S· of Mind denies the error of
p 398–30 The S· of Mind must come to the rescue,
t 460–24 When the S· of Mind was a fresh revelation
r 467–29 in the S· of Mind, we begin with Mind,
473– 4 The S· of Mind disposes of all evil.
481–10 various contradictions of the S· of Mind by the
483–22 Because the S· of Mind seems to bring
490–12 The S· of Mind needs to be understood.

Science

of Mind
r 492–24 must eventually submit to the S· of Mind,
495–31 In the S· of Mind, you will soon ascertain
g 520–30 Spirit acts through the S· of Mind,
549– 1 This discovery is corroborative of the S· of Mind
557–24 revealed religion proclaims the S· of Mind

of Mind-healing
s 120–17 The S· of Mind-healing shows it to be
123–20 discovery of this divine S· of Mind-healing,
147–14 contains the complete S· of Mind-healing,
151–10 if they understood the S· of Mind-healing,
t 446–18 In the S· of Mind-healing, it is imperative
451–20 teacher of the S· of Mind-healing,

of Soul
s 122– 8 material senses' reversal of the S· of Soul
131– 8 opposition of sensuous man to the S· of Soul
r 467– 1 the demands of the S· of Soul?
467–21 This is a leading point in the S· of Soul,

of Spirit
a 31–29 which would attend the S· of Spirit,
b 270–21 and maintain the S· of Spirit.
p 369–26 psychology, or the S· of Spirit, God,

of the Scriptures
s 139–23 the divine S· of the Scriptures seen from
b 319–28 and misstates the S· of the Scriptures,

of this proof
a 42–29 taught his disciples the S· of this proof.

opposite of
r 471– 7 error, — the opposite of S·,

order of
s 123– 7 which reverses the order of S·
f 240–10 In the order of S·, in which the Principle is

phenomenon of
gl 591–22 MIRACLE. . . . a phenomenon of S·.

practical
sp 98–18 stands a revealed and practical S·.

practises the
t 446–11 Whoever practises the S· the author teaches,

prepared in
m 61–1 highway of our God may be prepared in S·.

Principle and
a 20–31 the divine Principle and S· of all healing.

Principle of
sp 81–28 cannot destroy the divine Principle of S·.
s 120–20 the divine Principle of S·, reversing the
b 272–32 reveals the natural, divine Principle of S·.

real
s 122– 2 often reverses the real S· of being,
b 273– 8 They differ from real S· because they

reality and in
b 293–11 In reality and in S·, both strata, . . . are false

removes
a 40– 9 S· removes the penalty only by

renders
g 540–17 S· renders "unto Cæsar the— Matt. 22 : 21.

rends asunder
f 226–20 S· rends asunder these fetters,

revealed in
sp 81–17 the likeness of God as revealed in S·

reveals
pr 10–12 C. S· reveals a necessity for overcoming the
a 36– 4 Divine S· reveals the necessity of
s 109– 4 C. S· reveals incontrovertibly that Mind is
127–16 C. S· reveals God, not as the author of sin,
ph 172–12 divine S· reveals the eternal chain
f 213–17 Divine S· reveals sound as communicated
244– 4 Divine S· reveals these grand facts.
250–30 S· reveals Life as not being at the mercy of
c 260–13 S· reveals the possibility of achieving
b 278– 1 S· reveals nothing in Spirit out of which to
288–27 S· reveals the glorious possibilities of
310–14 So S· reveals Soul as God, untouched by sin
r 466–12 represent contraries, as C. S· reveals,
467–17 S· reveals Spirit, Soul, as not in the body,
477–11 C. S· reveals man as the idea of God,
480–12 origin and governor of all that S· reveals.
490– 7 C. S· reveals Truth and Love as the
491–21 S· reveals material man as never the real
g 510–28 S· reveals only one Mind,
519–10 S· reveals infinity and the fatherhood
557–10 C. S· reveals harmony as
gl 596–14 but C. S· reveals Spirit, not matter,

revelation of
gl 589– 6 Inspiration ; the revelation of S·, in which

reverses
s 120– 7 S· reverses the false testimony of the
f 215–22 S· reverses the evidence of
b 273–10 Divine S· reverses the false testimony
t 461–13 S· reverses the evidence before the material

rules of
s 162–17 Working out the rules of S· in practice,

separates the
f 207–18 S· separates the tares and wheat
b 300–19 S· separates the wheat from the tares,

servant of
s 146–11 material sense is made the servant of S·

Science

shows the cause
a 53–18 S· shows the cause of the

signet upon
r 472– 6 God has set His signet upon S·,

smatterers in
t 460–19 abused by mere smatterers in S·, it becomes a

spirit of
s 145– 4 So . . . imbued were they with the spirit of S·,

Spiritual
s 127– 9 The terms Divine Science, Spiritual S·,

spiritual sense and
b 294–18 destroyed . . . through spiritual sense and S·

stately
ap 566– 9 Stately S· pauses not, but moves before them,

suffering or
b 296– 7 suffering or S· must destroy all illusions

sword of
c 266– 3 Such is the sword of S·, with which

test of
f 204–19 They can never stand the test of S·.

the word
s 127– 1 author's application of the word S·
127– 2 or questions her use of the word S·,
o 341–13 Sneers at the application of the word S·

this
pref viii– 5 To develop the full might of this S·,
ix–22 learned that this S· must be demonstrated
sp 84–30 If this S· has been thoroughly learned
s 112–26 to establish a genuine school of this S·.
131–14 This S· has come already,
134–23 not because this S· is supernatural
147–10 this S· showed that Truth had lost none of
155–20 percentage of power on the side of this S·
162– 9 effect of this S· is to stir the human mind
f 202–15 Outside of this S· all is mutable ;
b 271–24 Sermon on the Mount is the essence of this S·,
285– 3 This S· of being obtains not alone hereafter
311–22 When humanity does understand this S·,
337–31 you ascertain that this S· is demonstrably true,
o 342– 8 He that decries this S· does it presumptuously,
345–20 evidence that one does understand this S·.
349– 1 when this S· is more generally understood?
349–21 in order to grasp the meaning of this S·.
355–26 inability to demonstrate this S·.
t 449–16 qualities which insure success in this S· ;
453–21 The masquerader in this S·
455– 8 in order to teach this S· of healing.
457– 1 gave the first rules for demonstrating this S·,
457–24 advance rapidly in the demonstration of this S·,
461–12 light of understanding be thrown upon this S·,
463– 6 familiar with the obstetrics taught by this S·.
r 467– 3 The first demand of this S· is,
471–32 This S· teaches that God is the only Life,
483–24 this S· has met with opposition ;
492–27 the Principle of this S· is divine,
g 548– 5 In this S·, we discover man in the image and
ap 577–30 for his vision is the acme of this S·

Truth or
g 545– 4 This could not be the utterance of Truth or S·,

truth, or
s 127– 6 entitled to a classification as truth, or S·,

unerring
r 473–21 and to test its unerring S· according to his rule,

unexplained by
s 121–15 man, . . . unexplained by S·, is as the

unfolds the
b 296– 2 whereas S· unfolds the eternal verity,

usher in
g 529– 9 usher in S· and the glorious fact of

warfare in
ap 568– 6 typifies the divine method of warfare in S·,

war with
f 252– 1 They are at war with S·,

which expounds
b 274–13 Christianity and the S· which expounds it

which governs
f 224– 5 the S· which governs these changes,

which reveals
f 209–13 the S· which reveals the supremacy of Mind.

will ameliorate
t 458–22 but S· will ameliorate mortal malice.

will correct
m 60–27 S· will correct the discord, and teach us

will declare
r 466–28 S· will declare God aright,

will destroy
sp 73–29 This error S· will destroy.

will eventually
b 303–18 S· will eventually destroy this illusion

yield to
pref xi– 8 the fleshly mind which must yield to S·.
r 493– 8 must yield to S·, to the immortal truth of all
things.

———

pr 12–10 neither S· nor Truth which acts through
a 37– 1 Does not S· show that sin brings suffering

Science

a 40– 5	tendency of Christian healing and its *S·*,
43–28	*S·* Jesus taught and lived must triumph over
63– 5	In *S·* man is the offspring of Spirit.
68– 6	Spirit, . . . has created men and women in *S·*.
sp 72–23	In *S·*, individual good derived from God,
73–17	the divine order and the *S·* of omnipotent,
79– 9	*S·* must go over the whole ground,
79–27	*S·* objects to all this, contending for the
81–28	In *S·*, man's immortality depends upon that of
83– 6	*S·* only can explain the incredible good
83–12	*S·* takes issue with popular religions.
83–15	since *S·* is an explication of nature.
an 102– 5	in *S·* . . . hypnotism is a mere negation,
103– 7	The destruction of the claims of mortal mind through *S·*,
s 109–20	I must know the *S·* of this healing,
110–18	No human pen nor tongue taught me the *S·*
111–11	may deny its right to the name of *S·*.
113– 7	letter is but the dead body of *S·*,
114–10	In *S·*, Mind is *one*, including noumenon and
114–29	*S·* shows that what is termed *matter* is but
116– 5	*S·* so reverses the evidence before the
118–13	*S·*, Theology, and Medicine are means of
120–13	Yes, he is well in *S·* in which
121–22	*S·* shows appearances often to be erroneous,
122–26	in *S·*, Life goes on unchanged
126–17	Shall *S·* explain cause and effect
127–10	terms . . . Christ Science or C. S., or *S·* alone,
127–16	relates especially to *S·* as applied to
127–26	*S·* is an emanation of divine Mind,
128– 4	term *S·*, properly understood, refers only to
128–27	*S·* relates to Mind, not matter.
129–12	a belief which *S·* overthrows.
129–27	illusions along the path which *S·* must tread
130–11	*S·*, when understood and demonstrated, will
140– 2	and *S·* is more than usually effectual in the
144–14	Human will-power is not *S·*.
144–32	understood the *S·* of Christian healing,
146–17	and his *S·*, the curative agent of God, is
146–20	*S·* is the "stranger that is— *Exod.* 20:10.
146–24	divine origin of *S·* is demonstrated
147–16	the whole meaning of the *S·*
147–30	*S·* alone reveals the divine Principle
149–12	its perfection of operation never vary in *S·*.
155–13	unless it rests on *S·*, is but a belief held by
157–30	*S·* both neutralizes error and destroys it.
ph 169–18	not only reveals the origin of all disease
178–15	based on *S·* or the divine Mind,
180– 8	in *S·* one must understand the resuscitating
185–15	a human conception in the name of *S·*
187–23	man in *S·* is governed by this Mind.
192–19	in *S·* you can have no power opposed to God,
f 204–27	in *S·* it can never be said that man
208–20	and preparing the way of *S·*.
211–23	transfer of the thoughts . . . *S·* renders impossible.
215–16	*S·* affirms darkness to be only a
216– 5	*S·* unveils the mystery and solves the problem
217– 2	through the understanding which *S·* confers
217–19	and you have won a point in *S·*.
219– 8	No more can we say in *S·* that muscles
219–20	*S·* includes no rule of discord.
221–22	equally far from *S·*, in which being is
225–10	*S·*, heeding not the pointed bayonet,
232–32	neither place nor opportunity in *S·* for error
234– 5	be it song, sermon, or *S·*
238– 3	*S·* is working changes in personal character
240–25	either by suffering or by *S·*, to be convinced of
244–25	Man in *S·* is neither young nor old.
250–31	nor will *S·* admit that happiness is ever the
251–28	Ignorance, like intentional wrong, is not *S·*.
c 258–32	to comprehend in *S·* the generic term *man*.
b 271– 9	He knew that the philosophy, *S·*, and proof of
273–29	*S·* shows that material, conflicting
275–10	grasp the reality and order of being in its *S·*,
276–19	When we learn in *S·* how to be perfect
283–26	unless its *S·* be accurately stated.
283–29	unless we so do, we can no more demonstrate *S·*,
285–21	to the better understanding that *S·* gives of the
287–10	In *S·*, Truth is divine,
288–12	the conflict between . . . *S·* and material sense,
296–27	until *S·* obliterates this false testimony.
299–28	*S·*, the sunshine of Truth, will melt away the
305–21	as opposed to the *S·* of spiritual reflection,
306–20	*S·* proves man's existence to be intact.
306–26	*S·*, still enthroned, is unfolding to mortals the
312– 4	the spiritual facts of being in *S·*.
313– 1	entitled him to sonship in *S·*.
318–29	In *S·* man is governed by God, divine Principle,
319– 5	*S·* depicts disease as error,
324–21	When the truth first appeared to him in *S·*,
328–11	in the *S·* which destroys human delusions
329–11	Jesus, who was the true demonstrator of *S·*,
329–12	In *S·* we can use only what we understand.
329–22	*S·* is a divine demand, not a human.
339–29	To get rid of sin through *S·*, is to divest sin of

Science

o 342–16	If . . . *S·* is not of God, then there is no
345–28	material nothingness, which *S·* inculcates,
353– 4	senses and *S·* have ever been antagonistic,
358– 8	Is *S·* thus contradictory?
358–12	Otherwise it would not be *S·*,
361–25	must be correct in order to be *S·*
p 376–29	in *S·* you cannot check a fever after admitting
384–28	In *S·* this is an established fact
388– 4	a victory which *S·* alone can explain.
392–20	unless *S·* shows you otherwise.
393–17	in *S·* man reflects God's government.
402–15	In *S·*, no breakage nor dislocation can
407–22	In *S·*, all being is eternal, spiritual,
417–19	is not the *S·* of immortal man.
417–26	understand the unreality of disease in *S·*.
427–16	Nothing can . . . end the existence of man in *S·*.
t 456–17	*S·* makes no concessions to persons or
458– 3	the doctrine that *S·* has two principles
459–25	the results are sure if the *S·* is understood.
r 474– 2	(the Principle of this unacknowledged *S·*)
474– 9	To the ignorant age . . . *S·* seems to be a mistake,
481–29	In *S·* we learn that it is material sense,
482–11	out of *S·*, soul is identical with sense,
483–14	she affixed the name "*S·*" to Christianity,
492–19	*S·* says: All is Mind and Mind's idea.
494–22	until the *S·* of man's eternal harmony
496– 2	in *S·* there is no transfer of evil suggestions
g 522– 3	The *S·* of the first record proves the
544–13	In *S·*, Mind neither produces matter nor
546–10	Has God no *S·* to declare Mind,
ap 558–11	To mortal sense *S·* seems at first obscure,
572– 8	In *S·* we are children of God ;
gl 581–11	*S·* showing that the spiritual realities
586–21	*S·* ; spiritual being understood ;
592– 8	that which neither exists in *S·* nor

science

all

s 124– 2	being based on Truth, the Principle of all *s·*.

astronomical

s 122–32	Astronomical *s·* has destroyed the false theory
r 493– 4	but astronomical *s·* contradicts this,

material

s 123–30	C. S. differs from material *s·*,

medical

b 273–16	The so-called laws of matter and of medical *s·*
318–23	Medical *s·* treats disease as though

natural

sp 98–22	natural *s·* has not been considered a part of
s 118–27	material law, as given by natural *s·*,
127–30	C. S. eschews what is called natural *s·*,
b 274– 7	*Natural s·*, as it is commonly called, is not
p 429–24	according to the calculations of natural *s·*.
r 471–12	yield assent . . . on the authority of natural *s·*,
478– 5	Even according to the teachings of natural *s·*,
484–12	What are termed natural *s·* and material laws

nautical

m 67–10	nautical *s·* is not equal to the Science of Mind.

of astronomy

r 471–11	earth's motions or of the *s·* of astronomy,

of music

pref viii– 7	even as the *s·* of music corrects false tones
b 304–22	The *s·* of music governs tones.
304–25	To be master of chords . . . the *s·* of music must be

of numbers

s 111– 8	no more supernatural than is the *s·* of numbers,

of real being

s 129–22	ontology,— "the *s·* of real being."

physical

s 124– 3	Physical *s·* (so-called) is human knowledge,
127–23	There is no physical *s·*, inasmuch as all
144–24	divine Science wars with so-called physical *s·*,

so-called

s 124– 3	Physical *s·* (so-called) is human knowledge,
150–18	The *s·* (so-called) of physics
b 277–23	the order of material so-called *s·*.

this

ph 189– 1	yield to the authority of this *s·*,

which they call

sp 98–25	multitudes consider that which they call *s·*

s 149– 6	Is *materia medica* a *s·* or a bundle of
163–22	said : "Consulting the records of our *s·*,
ph 189– 5	*S·* (in this instance named natural)
f 219–24	and yet misunderstand the *s·* that governs it.
t 460– 3	Ontology is defined as "the *s·* of

Science and Health

pref ix–26	Before writing this work, *S· and H·*,
x– 3	first edition of *S· and H·* was published in 1875.
x– 6	filled with plagiarisms from *S· and H·*.
xii–17	the revision of *S· and H·*
s 110–18	the Science contained in this book, *S· and H·* ;
o 361–21	I have revised *S· and H·* only to
361–31	*S· and H·* with Key to the Scriptures.
t 456–25	Scientist requires my work *S· and H·*

scientific

pr	16–17	strengthens our s· apprehension of the
a	23– 8	but its s· explanation is, that
m	61–30	The s· *morale* of marriage is spiritual unity.
	69– 2	The s· fact that man and the universe
sp	70– 8	In this s· reflection the Ego and the Father are
	71–22	having no s· basis nor origin,
	72–26	but evil is neither communicable nor s·.
	76–27	This state of existence is s· and intact,
	79– 2	The act of describing disease . . . is not s·.
	79– 7	A s· mental method is more sanitary than
	80–27	are neither s· nor rational.
	83–13	s· manifestation of power is from the
	94–29	Our Master read mortal mind on a s· basis,
an	102– 1	Animal magnetism has no s· foundation,
	104– 1	s· thoughts are true thoughts,
	104– 9	"Every great s· truth goes through three stages.
s	107– 6	divine Principle of s· mental healing.
	110–13	In following these leadings of s· revelation,
	114–25	It shows the s· relation of man to God,
	123–17	the s· system of divine healing.
	123–28	the s· order and continuity of being.
	123–31	but not on that account is it less s·.
	124– 1	On the contrary, C. S. is pre-eminently s·,
	138– 9	On this spiritually s· basis Jesus explained his
	141–27	The adoption of s· religion and
	145–16	S· healing has this advantage
	147–18	demonstration of the rules of s· healing
	159–11	Is it skilful or s· surgery to take no heed of
	164–11	they are more s· than are false claimants
ph	167–26	The s· government of the body must be
	167–31	Only through . . . can s· healing power be
f	202– 3	The s· unity which exists between
	206–15	In the s· relation of God to man,
	207–27	spiritual reality is the s· fact in all things.
	210–14	thus bringing to light the s· action of
	217–15	That s· methods are superior to others,
	217–24	The s· and permanent remedy for fatigue
	219–31	this s· beginning is in the right direction.
	233–27	the s· tests I have made of the effects of truth
	253–32	The divine demand, . . . is s·,
c	257– 3	and this definition is s·.
	263–30	instead of a s· eternal consciousness of creation.
b	268–15	no substantial aid to s· metaphysics,
	270– 9	Only by . . . are s· and logical conclusions
	273– 8	Deductions from material hypotheses are not s·.
	274– 8	is not really natural nor s·,
	279–26	A logical and s· conclusion is reached
	295–13	will at last yield to the s· fact
	297–18	that it is neither s· nor eternal,
	313–23	the most s· man that ever trod the globe.
	338–26	definition of words, aside from . . . is not s·.
o	341–14	cannot prevent that from being s· which
	342– 6	condemnations of s· Mind-healing,
	342–16	If Christianity is not s·,
	351–23	are neither spiritual nor s·,
	353– 1	The Christianly s· real is the
	355– 3	Christianly s· methods of dealing with sin
p	380–23	s· evidence of which has accumulated
	402–29	Hence the proof that hypnotism is not s· ;
	406–15	as we approach the s· period, in which
	408– 8	this general craze cannot, in a s· diagnosis,
	410–29	Christian s· practice begins with
	411–11	this is the ultimatum, the s· way,
	414–20	rests on the Christianly s· basis of being.
	421–25	It is no more Christianly s· to see disease
t	448–17	A dishonest position is far from Christianly s·.
	456– 6	divine Principle and rules of the s· method
	458–23	Christianly s· man reflects the divine law,
	459–29	the student — the Christian and s· expounder
	464–29	nor can they overthrow a s· system of ethics.
r	465– 5	to elucidate s· metaphysics
	482– 9	and you will have the s· signification.
	483–23	seems to bring into dishonor the ordinary s·
	486–12	belief . . . will not establish his s· harmony.
	496–17	to demonstrate, with s· certainty,
g	501– 1	S· interpretation of the Scriptures
	507–22	The s· divine creation declares
	521–29	which is the exact opposite of s· truth
	523–24	spiritually s· account of creation.
	526– 3	The previous and more s· record of
	534–25	spiritual, s· meaning of the Scriptures
	545–21	The translators of this record of s· creation
	546–28	system stated in this book is Christianly s·
	547–11	conclusions as to the s· theory of creation.
	552–11	whereas the spiritual s· facts of
ap	559– 9	"still, small voice" of s· thought — *I Kings* 19: 12.
	573–13	Accompanying this s· consciousness was
gl	586–15	s· line of demarcation between Truth and
	590–25	when the true s· statements of the Scriptures

(*see also* **being, demonstration, sense, statement**)

scientifically

a	42– 1	Jesus' life proved, divinely and s·, that
sp	75–10	This gross materialism is s· impossible,
	85–16	"knew their thoughts," — read them s·. — *Matt.* 12: 25.

scientifically

sp	95–15	ability . . . to discern thought s·, depends upon
	99– 1	not material but s· spiritual.
an	103–10	does not s· show itself in a knowledge of
s	111–32	and has proved itself, whenever s· employed,
	112–15	these opinions . . . are not s· Christian.
	141–25	until its divine Principle is s· understood.
	143–24	body is not controlled s· by a negative mind.
	144– 1	but the two will not mingle s·.
f	217– 9	which prove Mind to be s· distinct from matter,
b	275–31	Truth, spiritually discerned, is s· understood.
	321–19	It was s· demonstrated that leprosy was
o	343–17	he also s· demonstrates this great fact,
	359–14	at length know yourself spiritually and s·.
p	365–22	then he is Christian enough to practise s·
	374– 3	Anodynes, . . . never reduce inflammation s·,
	399–23	S· speaking, there is no mortal mind
	412– 4	plead the case s· for Truth.
	423– 8	understanding s· that all is Mind,
t	457–12	we cannot s· both cure and cause disease
	458–11	It is anything but s· Christian to
	460–20	Instead of s· effecting a cure, it starts a
	461–26	To prove s· the error or unreality of sin,
	461–28	to prove s· the . . . unreality of disease,
r	490–23	The s· Christian explanations of the nature and
g	522–15	s· Christian views of the universe
	506–26	not so in the s· Christian meaning of the text.
	531–30	at no point resembles the s· Christian record
ap	572– 5	s· reduced to its native nothingness.

Scientific Translation of Immortal Mind

s	115–12	chapter sub-title

Scientific Translation of Mortal Mind

s	115–19	chapter sub-title

Scientist (*see also* Scientist's)

become a

ph	182– 1	will diminish your ability to become a S·,

Christian

m	68–19	and a Christian S· cured her.
sp	95–14	ability of a Christian S· to discern thought
s	154–24	That mother is not a Christian S·, . . . who
ph	176–22	Should . . . the Christian S· try truth only in
	182– 4	shows your position as a Christian S·.
o	358–30	Christian S·, whom they have perhaps never
	359– 9	I as a Christian S· believed in the Holy Spirit,
	359–29	A Christian S· and an opponent are like
p	366–27	the Christian S· will be calm in the presence of
	367–17	A Christian S· occupies the place at this period
	375–11	The Christian S· demonstrates that
	375–18	The genuine Christian S· is adding to
	379– 4	The Christian S· finds only effects, where the
	383– 8	the Christian S· takes the best care of his
	384–20	If you are a Christian S·, such symptoms
	386–26	If a Christian S· had said, while you were
	420– 6	should early call an experienced Christian S·
	422–25	and a Christian S· in the other.
	423– 8	The Christian S·, understanding . . . that all is Mind,
t	450–19	Christian S· has enlisted to lessen evil,
	450–24	Christian S· knows that they are errors
	451–19	Christian S·, . . . knows that human will is not
	453–30	A Christian S· never recommends material
	456–25	A Christian S· requires my work SCIENCE AND HEALTH
	458–20	Sin makes deadly thrusts at the Christian S·
	458–26	The Christian S· wisely shapes his course,
	459–31	The Christian S· should understand and adhere
	462–31	The Christian S·, . . . deals with the real cause
	464–13	If . . . a Christian S· were seized with

must conform

t	445– 1	the S· must conform to God's requirements.

only in name

t	449–31	is a S· only in name.

reaches his patient

p	365–15	If the S· reaches his patient through

o	359– 6	more faith in the S· than in
p	365–19	If the S· has enough Christly affection to
	412–31	S· knows that there can be no hereditary disease,

Scientist's

p	414–19	The Christian S· argument rests on the
t	453–29	A Christian S· medicine is Mind,
	457–28	The S· demonstration rests on one Principle,

Scientists

Christian

pref	xii– 1	No charters were granted to Christian S· for
	xii–13	the first periodical issued by Christian S·.
a	35–11	morning meal which Christian S· commemorate.
m	60– 1	if both . . . were genuine Christian S·.
	69–17	If Christian S· educate their own offspring
ph	192– 4	We are Christian S·, only as we quit our
	192– 6	We are not Christian S· until we leave all for
	198–28	the importance that doctors be Christian S·.
c	267–13	Christian S· understand that, . . . they have
o	342–29	If Christian S· were teaching or
	358–25	it is said : . . . whatever effect Christian S·

Scientists

Christian

p 364–18 Do Christian S· seek Truth as Simon sought
364–22 If Christian S· are like Simon, then it must be
401–28 better for Christian S· to leave surgery
442–30 Christian S·, be a law to yourselves
t 444– 7 If Christian S· ever fail to receive aid from
451– 2 Christian S· must live under the constant
r 483–19 natural Christian S·, the ancient worthies,
496–28 Have Christian S· any religious creed?

---

o 359– 4 Yet S· will take the same cases,
p 366–19 Such so–called S· will strain out gnats,
t 443– 9 severely condemned by some S·,
444– 8 ever fail to receive aid from other S·,
464–15 and the S· had failed to relieve him,

scoff

o 358–14 nor of the inventions of those who s· at God.

scoffed

a 41–28 The truth taught by Jesus, the elders s· at.
r 474– 6 will be s· at and scourged

scoffers

a 49–30 s·, who turned "aside the right— Lam. 3 : 35.

scope

a 40– 4 perceiving the s· and tendency of

scorn

a 55–10 does not the pulpit sometimes s· it?

Scotch

sp 87–13 The S· call such vision "second sight,"

Scott, Sir Walter

ap 566–13 the beautiful description which Sir Walter S·

scourge

a 20–19 s· and the cross awaited the great Teacher.
m 56–15 the social s· of all races,
f 224–18 less material than the Roman s·,

scourged

b 316–25 s· in person, and its Principle was rejected.
r 474– 7 will be scoffed at and s· with worse cords than

scratch

f 212–11 unwitting attempt to s· the end of a finger

scream

sp 97–24 the louder will error s·,

scribe

ap 571–23 immortal s· of Spirit and of a true idealism,

Scriptural

pref viii–29 give to friends the results of her S· study,
ix–27 made copious notes of S· exposition,
sp 89–12 This familiar instance reaffirms the S· word
92–11 In old S· pictures we see a serpent
s 116– 7 as to make this S· testimony true
131–17 according to the S· saying,
ph 177–15 In the S· allegory of the material creation,
f 238– 6 To obey the S· command.
239–14 The watchword of C. S. is S· :
b 275–13 and are the S· names for God.
276– 8 in accordance with the S· command :
328–29 the S· passage would read you, not they.
o 342–20 Shall it be denied that . . . has S· authority?
344–17 it would be just to observe the S· precept,
p 383–27 confirming the S· conclusion concerning a
r 479– 4 With what truth, then, could the S· rejoicing
g 510–21 There is no S· allusion to solar light until
523– 2 the S· account now under comment.
525–26 the S· record of sin and death
526–14 in the legendary S· text
ap 573–23 This is S· authority for concluding that
gl 579– 2 the material definition of a S· word

Scripture

according to

p 423–12 According to S·, it searches

according to the

s 113–23 According to the S·, I find that

another passage of

g 504–22 the explanation of another passage of S·,

declares

p 414–21 S· declares, "The Lord He is God— Deut. 4 : 35.
r 475– 1 S· declares that there is "no night— Rev. 22 : 5.

dictum of

t 444– 6 is the dictum of S·.

fulfils the

b 340–25 fulfils the S·, "Love thy neighbor— Matt. 19 : 19.

informs

f 232– 9 S· informs us that "with God— Mark 10 : 27.

interpretation of

b 320– 9 "The spiritual interpretation of S·
320–24 The one important interpretation of S· is
g 547– 8 has given you the correct interpretation of S·.

is true

f 232–13 theories must be untrue, for the S· is true.

language of

c 256–20 He who, in the language of S·,

Scripture

older

s 140–28 true that the older S· is reversed.

perception of

g 547–31 It is this spiritual perception of S·, which

phrase

g 511– 3 and so explains the S· phrase,

portions of the

g 546–19 seem more obscure than other portions of the S·,

prophetic

s 109–25 prophetic S· of Isaiah is renewedly fulfilled :

rebuked in

p 389–16 This false reasoning is rebuked in S·

rebuke in the

a 23–15 receives a strong rebuke in the S·,

represented in

b 299–19 figuratively represented in S· as a tree,

sayings of

b 276– 2 and fulfils these sayings of S·,

says the

pr 12– 2 shall save the sick," says the S·.— Jas. 5 : 15.

seems to import

p 411–18 The S· seems to import that

significance of the

s 131– 9 and the significance of the S·,
r 481–16 This is the significance of the S·

this

sp 97–26 This S· indicates that all matter will

used in

sp 94– 6 and "likeness" as used in S·.— Gen. 1 : 26.

---

f 241–15 Take away the spiritual signification of S·, and
b 277– 4 the S· says that dust returns to dust.
290–14 To the spiritual class, relates the S· :
291–18 as the S· says.
o 359–25 that S· she so often quotes :
361–18 S· reads : "For in Him we live,— Acts 17 : 28.
r 489–22 affirmative reply would contradict the S·,
g 522–28 for the S· just preceding declares
545–26 Hence the seeming contradiction in that S·,
ap 569– 6 The S·, "Thou hast been faithful— Matt. 25 : 23.
gl 581– 2 the name often conferred upon him in S·,

Scriptures

according to the

o 342–19 a system which works according to the S·

also declare

b 331–14 The S· also declare that God is Spirit.
p 373–16 but the S· also declare,

are definite

f 206–22 The S· are definite on this point,

are very sacred

g 547–23 The S· are very sacred.

aver

r 474–20 S· aver, "I am not come to destroy,— Matt. 5 : 17.

confirms the

m 69–14 unfolds all creation, confirms the S·,

declare

b 286–17 The S· declare all that He made to be good,
287–20 S· declare that man was made in
318– 6 S· declare that God made all,
330–19 God is what the S· declare Him to be,
p 381–18 and the S· declare that we live, move, and
397–21 which the S· declare Him to be.
g 526–19 and the S· declare that He created all.
539–16 S· declare that God condemned this lie
ap 569–24 Here the S· declare that evil is temporal,

imply

b 331–11 The S· imply that God is All-in-all.
g 550–22 If Life is God, as the S· imply,

inform us

ph 183–11 S· inform us that sin, or error, first caused
r 475– 8 S· inform us that man is

interpret

g 534– 6 enabled woman to be first to interpret the S·

KEY TO THE

o 361–32 SCIENCE AND HEALTH WITH KEY TO THE S·.

meaning of the

g 534–25 spiritual, scientific meaning of the S·

not knowing the

b 272– 9 "Ye do err, not knowing the S·."— Matt. 22 : 29.

obey the

o 354– 4 Why then do Christians try to obey the S·

often appear

r 488–11 Hence the S· often appear in our

older

g 502– 2 the living and real prelude of the older S·

plainly declare

p 400–30 The S· plainly declare the baneful influence of

reading the

r 481–32 When reading the S·, the substitution of the

say

pr 6– 1 The S· say, that if we deny Christ,
10–26 The S· say : "Ye ask, and receive not,— Jas. 4 : 3.
f 208– 5 The S· say, "In Him we live,— Acts 17 : 28.
218–27 S· say, "They that wait upon— Isa. 40 : 31.

Scriptures
say
o 344– 6 S· say that God has created man in
357–29 "Life in Himself," as the S· say,— John 5 : 26.
p 410– 9 S· say, "Man shall not live by— Matt. 4 : 4.
427–18 the S· say, "The last enemy that— I Cor. 15 : 26.
r 476–23 Remember that the S· say of mortal man :
Science of the
s 139–23 the divine Science of the S·
b 319–29 and misstates the Science of the S·,
searched the
s 109–12 searched the S· and read little else,
throughout the
o 358–18 as is recorded throughout the S·.
turn to the
f 217–11 yet if we turn to the S·, what do we read?
were illumined
s 110–14 The S· were illumined ;

s 123–21 through a spiritual sense of the S·
139– 4 the S· are full of accounts of the triumph of
f 214– 9 represented in the S· as formed from dust,
b 271– 4 its obvious correspondence with the S·
271–29 The S· contain it.
272–10 The spiritual sense of the S· brings out the
293–25 called in the S·, "The anger of— Deut. 29 : 20.
320– 7 the S· have both a spiritual and literal meaning.
o 341– 6 Even the S·, . . . appear contradictory when
358–10 C. S., understood, coincides with the S·,
361–31 hence the many readings given the S·,
r 468–19 as the S· use this word in Hebrews :
g 501– 1 Scientific interpretation of the S·
ap 578– 1 the light which C. S. throws on the S·
gl 590–26 S· become clouded through a physical sense of

scrofula
p 424–28 To prevent or to cure s· and other so-called

scrofulous
p 424–32 a humor in the blood, a s· diathesis.

scrubbing
p 413–18 without s· the whole surface daily.

sculptor
f 248–12 The s· turns from the marble to his model
c 260– 3 no more . . . than the s· can perfect his outlines from

sculptor's
b 299– 2 s· thought when he carves his

sculptors
f 248–13 We are all s·, working at various forms,
248–19 by vicious s· and hideous forms.

scum
m 65–31 marriage will become purer when the s· is gone.

Sea
a 34–32 joyful meeting on the shore of the Galilean S· !
f 226–30 the Red S· and the wilderness ;
ap 566– 2 were guided triumphantly through the Red S·,
576– 1 and the Peaceful S· of Harmony.

sea
cast into the
pr 1– * and be thou cast into the s·;— Mark 11 : 23.
fish of the
  (see fish)
no more
g 536– 4 and there was no more s·."— Rev. 21 : 1.
ap 572–22 and there was no more s·.— Rev. 21 : 1.
O thou
s 135– 2 "What ailed thee, O thou s·,— Psal. 114 : 5.
surging
ap 569–18 They are in the surging s· of error,
troubled
m 67–17 or sunshine gladdens the troubled s·.
upon the
ap 558– 7 and he set his right foot upon the s·,— Rev. 10 : 2.
559– 5 dominant power of which was upon the s·,
waves of the
g 505–20 the mighty waves of the s·."— Psal. 93 : 4.

sp 87–20 s· is ignorant of the gems within its caverns,
g 536– 6 the s·, . . . is represented as having passed away.
ap 568–23 of the earth and of the s· !— Rev. 12 : 12.

seal
pref xi–29 under the s· of the Commonwealth,
a 44– 1 must s· the victory over error and death,
44– 8 set the s· of eternity on time.
g 511–11 In divine Science, which is the s· of Deity
ap 560– 3 In the opening of the sixth s·,
gl 593–23 definition of

sealed
f 232–24 which s· God's condemnation of sin,
p 363– 4 Breaking the s· jar, she perfumed Jesus' feet

seals
o 354–17 who thereunto have set their s·.
ap 572–15 open the seven s· of error with Truth,

seam
f 242–26 one web of consistency without s· or rent.

seaman
m 67– 9 the dauntless s· is not sure of his safety ;

seances
sp 86–18 apparitions brought out in dark s·

search
s 109–15 The s· was sweet, calm, and buoyant with hope
152–24 in her s· for truth ;
ph 168–11 rush after drugs, s· out the material so-called
p 440– 1 he could not possibly elude their s·.

searched
s 109–12 s· the Scriptures and read little else,

searcher
s 121–16 "a weary s· for a viewless home."
f 234–22 the weary s· after a divine theology,

searches
p 423–12 it s· "the joints and marrow,"— Heb. 4 : 12.

searching
b 322–31 "Canst thou by s· find out God?"— Job 11 : 7.
g 551–27 "Canst thou by s· find out God?"— Job 11 : 7.
555–16 S· for the origin of man, who is the

Seas
g 506–23 the waters called He S· :— Gen. 1 : 10.
536– 1 the waters called He S·."— Gen. 1 : 10.

seas
g 512–18 and fill the waters in the s· ;— Gen. 1 : 22.

season
a 40– 7 when I have a convenient s· I will— Acts 24 : 25.
c 257–20 "forth Mazzaroth in his s·,"— Job 38 : 32.
p 398–28 blind faith removes bodily ailments for a s·,

seasons
m 57–13 bringing sweet s· of renewal like the
s 125–21 The s· will come and go with changes of
g 509–11 let them be for signs, and for s·,— Gen. 1 : 14.
509–25 the days and s· of Mind's creation,

seat
f 239–23 Mortal mind is the acknowledged s· of
b 285–19 finite conception of . . . body as the s· of Mind

seats
s 122–12 as the s· of pain and pleasure,

secluded
t 464– 8 they would understand why she is so s·.

second
sp 77–12 "the s· death hath no power."— Rev. 20 : 6.
87–13 The Scotch call s· vision "s· sight,"
87–14 when really it is first sight instead of s·,
91–27 The s· erroneous postulate is,
s 115–25 S· Degree: Evil beliefs disappearing.
118– 7 foretelling the s· appearing in the flesh
f 204–13 The so-called s· power, evil, is the unlikeness
204–16 mixture of the first and s· antagonistic
234–27 or they will control you in the s·.
b 270– 1 is quite as reasonable as the s·,
290–14 the s· death hath no power."— Rev. 20 : 6.
314– 9 but one Mind without a s· or equal.
p 403– 9 in the s· it is believed that the
433–22 led him into the commission of the s· crime,
t 456–30 S· : Because it was the first book
r 467– 7 The s· is like unto it,
g 502– 1 A s· necessity for beginning with Genesis
503–21 first, in light ; s·, in reflection ;
506– 9 and the morning were the s· day.— Gen. 1 : 8.
521–26 The s· chapter of Genesis contains a
522– 4 proves the falsity of the s·.
522– 7 The s· record chronicles man as mutable
522–12 This s· record unmistakably gives the
522–25 This latter part of the s· chapter of
523–23 and in three verses of the s·,
526–15 first mention of evil is in . . . the s· chapter
526–24 This s· biblical account is a picture of error
530–31 S·, it supposes that mind enters matter,
537–20 this s· account in Genesis
ap 577–14 s·, the Christ, the spiritual idea of God ;
gl 585–27 first from dust, s· from a rib,
590–23 in the s· and following chapters,

secondarily
g 512–24 are mental, both primarily and s·.

secondary
f 207–13 nor . . . the law of Spirit s·.
ap 559– 7 a s· power was exercised upon visible error
562– 8 This idea reveals the universe as s·

secrecy
s 118– 8 hidden in sacred s· from the visible world?

secret
pr 8– 7 They hold s· fellowship with sin,
11–31 our Father, who seeth in s·, will reward us
15– 1 thy Father which is in s· ;— Matt. 6 : 6.
15– 2 thy Father, which seeth in s·,— Matt. 6 : 6.
15– 7 Father in s· is unseen to the physical senses,

secret
  pr 15–23 The Master's injunction is, that we pray in s·
      15–25 Christians rejoice in s· beauty and bounty,
  an 102–20 So s· are the present methods of
   b 317– 1 "s· from the foundation of — *Matt.* 13 : 35.
  ap 559–14 to utter the full diapason of s· tones.

secretion
   s 160–11 the organic action and s· of the viscera.
   p 399– 8 not a s· nor combination can operate, apart from

secretions
   s 162– 7 It changes the s·, expels humors,
      162–19 S· have been changed,
   p 382– 9 Constant bathing and rubbing to alter the s·
      415–20 the s·, the action of the lungs,

secretly
  pr 13– 7 s· yearning and openly striving for the

sect
   f 236– 5 in the interests of humanity, not of s·.

sectarian
   s 139–13 wisely to stem the tide of s· bitterness,

section
   f 225–32 rights of man were vindicated in a single s·

sections
   s 122–11 certain s· of matter, such as brain and

sects
   a 28–27 because it is honored by s· and societies,
   f 224–11 s· many but not enough Christianity.
      239– 2 The s·, which endured the lash of their
   t 444–22 If ecclesiastical s· or medical schools

secure
   m 56–14 such moral regulations as will s·
      60–31 would be more s· in our keeping, if
   f 238–26 Justice often comes too late to s· a verdict.

secured
   t 456– 6 has s· the only success of the students of

securely
  pr 11–26 that we may walk s· in the

security
   a 19–27 in disobedience to Him, we ought to feel no s·,
   f 232– 7 S· for the claims of harmonious and

seditions
  an 106–23 wrath, strife, s·, heresies, — *Gal.* 5 : 20.

sedulous
  ph 179–26 The s· matron — studying her Jahr

see
  pr 5–20 the Psalmist could s· their end,
       8–27 that we are willing to have our neighbor s·?
   a 27– 4 how that the blind s·, — *Luke* 7 : 22.
      38–29 Having eyes ye s· not,
      45–27 as ye s· me have." — *Luke* 24 : 39.
  sp 70– * *he shall never s· death.* — *John* 8 : 51.
      71–10 you may dream that you s· a flower,
      71–14 and you may s· landscapes, men,
      85–12 "Come, see a man, which — *John* 4 : 29.
      86–15 only because it is unusual to s· thoughts,
      86–22 why is it more difficult to s· a thought than
      92–11 In old Scriptural pictures we s· a serpent
  an 105–19 "I s· no reason why metaphysics may not
   s 132– 5 things which ye do hear and s· : — *Matt.* 11 : 4.
      136–28 No wonder Herod desired to s· the new Teacher.
      140– 6 "Thou canst not s· My face ; — *Exod.* 33 : 20.
      140– 6 shall no man s· Me, and live." — *Exod.* 33 : 20.
      151–29 to s· and acknowledge this fact,
      152–25 and can s· the means by which mortals
  ph 173– 2 we fail to s· how anatomy can distinguish
      187– 6 Here you may s· how so-called material sense
      189– 3 If the eyes s· no sun for a week,
      190–31 In Thy light shall we s· light. — *Psal.* 36 : 9.
      211–26 If . . . organism causes the eyes to s·
   f 217–31 he shall never s· death !" — *John* 8 : 51.
      241–29 signifies that the pure in heart s· God
      253–11 I hope, dear reader, . . . that, as you read, you s·
   b 281–21 and s· that sin and mortality have neither
      284–22 They can neither s· Spirit through the eye nor
      320–26 "In my flesh shall I s· God," — *Job* 19 : 26.
      324– 3 and joy to s· them disappear,
      324– 6 for they shall s· God." — *Matt.* 5 : 8.
      325– 1 shall not s· death." — *see John* 11 : 26.
             shall be the pure in heart can s· God,
   o 341– 9 for they shall s· God" — *Matt.* 5 : 8.
      342– 6 one may s· with sorrow the sad effects
      342–26 the lame to walk, and the blind to s·.
      347–31 These critics will then s· that error is indeed
      350–20 lest at any time they should s· — *Matt.* 13 : 15.
      359–31 When others s· them as I do,
   p 367–27 I long to s· the consummation of my hope,
      397–25 when they act, walk, s·, hear, enjoy,
      400–23 We s· in the body the images of this mind,
      400–24 we s· painted on the retina the image which
      421–25 no more Christianly scientific to s· disease than
      421–28 should not build it up by wishing to s· the forms

see
   p 426–15 and s· the folly of hypocrisy,
      428– 8 he shall never s· death." — *John* 8 : 51.
      429–32 he shall never s· death." — *John* 8 : 51.
      438– 7 he shall never s· death. — *John* 8 : 51.
   t 452– 8 we cannot s· in darkness.
      455–15 then shalt thou s· clearly to — *Matt.* 7 : 5.
      457–15 because each of them could s· but one face of it,
      461–27 you must first s· the claim of sin,
   r 478–12 Who can s· a soul in the body?
      479–10 Matter cannot s·, feel, hear, taste,
      479–12 cannot feel itself, s· itself, nor understand itself.
      479–16 Does that which we call dead ever s·, hear,
   g 510–10 "light shall we s· light ;" — *Psal.* 36 : 9.
      516– 7 we shall s· this true likeness and reflection
      527–23 to s· what he would call them : — *Gen.* 2 : 19.
      532–30 error demands that *mind* shall s· . . . through
             matter,
      547–26 was able to s· in the egg the earth's atmosphere,
      548– 6 We s· that man has never lost his
      551–14 nor s· that material methods are impossible in
  ap 571–24 mirror in which mortals may s· their own image.
      572– 3 Thus we s·, in both the first and last books
      573– 4 while yet beholding what the eye cannot s·,
      573–22 by which he could s· the new heaven and
  gl 585–15 ERROR. S· chapter on Recapitulation, page 472.
      586– 6 "Having eyes, s· ye not?" — *Mark* 8 : 18.
      588–26 INTELLIGENCE. . . . S· chapter on Recapitula-
             tion, page 469.
      590–14 LIFE. S· chapter on Recapitulation, page 468.
      593– 3 PRINCIPLE. S· chapter on Recapitulation, page
             465.
      594–18 SOULS. S· chapter on Recapitulation, page 466.
      594–24 SPIRITS. . . . (S· page 466.)
      594–25 SUBSTANCE. S· chapter on Recapitulation,
             page 468.
  fr 600– * *let us s· if the vine flourish,* — *Song* 7 : 12.

seed
  and soil
   f 212–18 They produce a rose through s· and soil,
  bearing
   g 518– 6 every herb bearing s·, — *Gen.* 1 : 29.
  dig up every
  sp 79–10 and dig up every s· of error's sowing.
  good
   f 237–11 theories of parents often choke the good s·
      237–13 snatches away the good s· before it
  is in itself
   g 507–13 whose s· is in itself, — *Gen.* 1 : 11.
      508– 2 But the s· is in itself, even as the
      511– 4 "whose s· is in itself." — *Gen.* 1 : 11.
  material
   g 551–30 declares that the material s· must decay
  of error
   g 535– 2 The seed of Truth and the s· of error,
  of matter
   g 535– 3 the seed of Spirit and the s· of matter,
  of Spirit
   g 535– 3 the s· of Spirit and the seed of matter,
  of the Church
   a 37– 6 blood of the martyrs is the s· of the Church."
  of Truth
   b 271– 1 s· of Truth springs up and bears much fruit.
   g 535– 1 The s· of Truth and the seed of error,
  or soil
   g 520–25 the plant grows, not because of s· or soil, but
  sowing the
  ph 183– 9 without sowing the s·
  sown in the soil
   m 66–12 not from s· sown in the soil of material hopes,
  was in itself
   g 508–11 whose s· was in itself, — *Gen.* 1 : 12.
  within itself
  ph 180– 9 This is the s· within itself
   g 508–14 The s· within itself is the pure thought
  yielding
   g 507–12 the herb yielding s·, — *Gen.* 1 : 11.
      508–10 and herb yielding s· after his kind, — *Gen.* 1 : 12.
      518– 8 the fruit of a tree yielding s· ; — *Gen.* 1 : 29.

  sp 74– 8 The s· which has germinated
      76–15 any more than a tree can return to its s·.
      89–32 If s· is necessary to produce wheat,
   s 125–30 florist will find his flower before its s·.
   b 272– 7 In . . . an "honest and good heart" the s· —
             Luke 8 : 15.
   o 361–28 until God prepares the soil for the s·.
   g 508– 6 substance of a thought, a s·, or a flower
      534–10 between thy s· and her s· ; — *Gen.* 3 : 15.

seedling
  ph 190– 5 mortal says that an inanimate unconscious s· is
seedlings
  ph 188–26 according to the s· of fear.

seeds
- *ph* 179–29   sowing the *s·* of reliance on matter,
- *b* 294– 5   carries within itself the *s·* of all error.

seedtime
- *sp* 96– 9   but summer and winter, *s·* and harvest

seeing
- *a* 54– 6   acknowledged not his righteousness, *s·* it not ;
- *sp* 86–20   *S·* is no less a quality of physical sense
- *b* 320–16   *s·* that they are [or, in their error they are]
- *p* 397– 1   not *s·* how mortal mind affects the body,
- *t* 464– 1   but it feels your influence without *s·* you.
- *r* 487– 7   more Christianity in *s·* and hearing spiritually
- 489–18   material means for knowing, hearing, *s·*?
- *g* 529–27   *S·* this, we should have faith to
- *ap* 572–27   Not through the material visual organs for *s·*,

seek
- *pr* 5–31   and *s·* the destruction of all evil works,
- 8– 5   their wickedness and then *s·* to hide it.
- *a* 20–31   and *s·* the divine Principle and Science
- 34–13   If all who *s·* his commemoration
- *sp* 70– *   *S· unto them that have familiar* — Isa. 8 : 19.
- 70– *   *Should not a people s· unto their* — Isa. 8 : 19.
- *s* 142– 8   We must *s·* the undivided garment,
- *f* 236– 7   reputation . . . which many leaders *s·*?
- 238–20   until we *s·* this remedy for human woe
- 254–11   *s·* Truth righteously, He directs our path.
- *b* 285–25   to *s·* salvation through pardon
- 285–29   they will *s·* to learn, not from matter,
- 286– 1   To *s·* Truth through belief in a human doctrine
- 286– 3   We must not *s·* the immutable . . . through
- 323– 1   Mortals may *s·* the understanding of C. S.,
- *p* 364–18   Do Christian Scientists *s·* Truth
- 409–26   and *s·* the true model.
- *t* 451–11   They must not only *s·*, but strive,
- *r* 476–21   Learn this, O mortal, and earnestly *s·* the
- 487– 1   to *s·* and to find a higher sense of happiness
- 494–19   and *s·* safety in divine Science.
- *g* 510– 2   How much more should we *s·* to apprehend
- 555–19   Only impotent error would *s·* to

seeker
- *pref* x–23   personal experience of any sincere *s·* of Truth.

seekers
- *pref* xii–26   she commits these pages to honest *s·* for Truth.
- *p* 364–20   Jesus told Simon that such *s·* as he
- *ap* 570–14   simple *s·* for Truth, weary wanderers,

seeketh
- *g* 538– 1   "*s·* not her own."— I Cor. 13 : 5.

seeking
- *pr* 10–14   *S·* is not sufficient.
- *sp* 85–25   *s·* the material more than the spiritual.
- *f* 222–29   In *s·* a cure for dyspepsia
- *b* 290– 8   still *s·* happiness through a material, . . . sense
- 327–28   mistake in *s·* material means for
- *p* 367–10   This is what is meant by *s·* Truth, Christ,
- *t* 464–10   at her post, *s·* no self-aggrandizement
- *g* 518–18   *s·* his own in another's good.

seeks
- *s* 124– 9   *s·* to find life and intelligence in matter,
- *b* 279–31   Pantheism, . . . *s·* cause in effect,
- 280–14   it *s·* to divide the one Spirit into persons
- *g* 541– 4   Cain *s·* Abel's life,

seem
- *sp* 76–15   Neither will man *s·* to be corporeal,
- 80–19   It should not *s·* mysterious that mind,
- 96–16   may *s·* to be famine and pestilence,
- *s* 131– 1   Truth should not *s·* so surprising
- 131– 2   error should not *s·* so real as truth.
- 131– 2   Sickness should not *s·* so real as
- 131–16   but the churches *s·* not ready to receive it,
- *ph* 169–25   whatever good they may *s·* to receive from
- 185–26   Erroneous mental practice may *s·*
- 198– 5   may *s·* calm under it, but he is not.
- *f* 211–13   *s·* to obtain in mortal mind.
- 216–24   while health would *s·* the exception,
- 231– 6   but *s·* to this so-called mind to be immortal.
- 248– 4   One marvels that a friend can ever *s·* less than
- *b* 282–21   though they *s·* to touch, goes in a curve
- 284– 6   would *s·* to spring from a limited body ;
- 288–31   what mortals *s·* to have learned
- 299–26   error, may *s·* to hide Truth,
- 300– 6   makes trees and cities *s·* to be where they
- 307–12   matter shall *s·* to have life as much as
- 327–18   the strict demands of C. S. *s·* peremptory ;
- *o* 343–21   It would sometimes *s·* as if
- 353–27   so long will ghosts *s·* to continue.
- *p* 406–14   Sin and sickness will abate and *s·* less real
- 422– 7   If . . . moral and physical symptoms *s·* aggravated,
- *t* 446– 6   If patients sometimes *s·* worse while
- *r* 470–15   can only *s·* to be real by giving reality to the
- 472–28   unrealities *s·* real to human, erring belief,
- 491– 2   A delicious perfume will *s·* intolerable.
- 493–25   *s·* real and natural in illusion.

seem
- *r* 494–21   sin, sickness, and death will *s·* real . . . until
- 494–22   experiences of the sleeping dream *s·* real
- *g* 502– 3   is so brief that it would almost *s·*,
- 506–25   human concept and divine idea *s·* confused b
- 546–18   Genesis and the Apocalypse *s·* more obscure
- 556–17   They *s·* to be something, but are not.

seemed
- *a* 46–20   after what *s·* to be death
- *s* 131–22   so it *s·* good in Thy sight."— Luke 10 : 21.
- *f* 237– 2   She *s·* not to notice it.
- *b* 297–13   that disappears which before *s·* real
- 314–17   To such . . . the real man *s·* a spectre,
- 314–19   and the body, . . . *s·* to be substance.
- 315–29   (that is, as it *s·* to mortal view),
- *g* 547–14   speck of so-called embryonic life *s·* a
- 555–29   which *s·* to vanish in death.

seemeth
- *sp* 81–18   Though the grass *s·* to wither
- *r* 472–19   that which *s·* to be and is not.

seeming
- *a* 45–11   by the [*s·*] death of His Son,— Rom. 5 : 10.
- *an* 101–31   Any *s·* benefit derived from it is
- *s* 119–30   C. S. reverses the *s·* relation of Soul and body
- 122– 3   assigning *s·* power to sin, sickness, and death ;
- 164–18   The *s·* decease, caused by a
- *ph* 167–32   fair *s·* for straightforward character,
- 190–17   This mortal *s·* is temporal ;
- *f* 208– 6   What then is this *s·* power,
- *c* 266– 9   this *s·* vacuum is already filled
- *b* 295– 2   sensation *s·* to be in nerves which
- *o* 352–30   no longer *s·* worthy of fear or honor.
- *p* 368–27   the source of all *s·* sickness.
- 382–24   I rescued from *s·* spiritual oblivion,
- 390– 6   simply because, . . . there is *s·* discord.
- 394– 2   Truth can destroy its *s·* reality,
- *t* 452– 2   bar the door of his thought against this *s·* powe
- 463–30   Such *s·* medical effect or action is
- *r* 473– 2   though *s·* to be real and identical.
- *g* 545–26   the *s·* contradiction in that Scripture,

seemingly
- *s* 147–23   hitherto unattained and *s·* dim.
- *ap* 563–20   *s·* impede the offspring of the spiritual idea,

seems
- *m* 64– 8   Pride, envy, or jealousy *s·* on most occasions
- *an* 101–26   If animal magnetism *s·* to alleviate
- *s* 120– 1   though it *s·* otherwise to finite sense.
- 121–18   and the sun *s·* to move from east to west,
- 123–12   matter *s·* to be, but is not.
- 126–11   and so *s·* to have reversed it
- 134–32   This fact at present *s·* more mysterious than
- 157–24   power which the drug *s·* to possess.
- *ph* 169–32   The good that a poisonous drug *s·* to do is evil
- 170–24   The age *s·* ready to approach this subject,
- 179–14   the body then *s·* to require such treatment.
- *f* 212– 4   and the pain *s·* to be in its old place.
- 250–21   and the mind *s·* to be absent.
- *c* 262–29   Every concept which *s·* to begin with the brain
- 263–21   Whatever *s·* to be a new creation, is but the
- *b* 296–24   When the evidence of . . . *s·* to commingle,
- 301– 7   To himself, mortal and material man *s·* to be
- 301–14   *s·* to mortal sense transcendental,
- 301–23   Mortal man *s·* to himself to be
- 307–22   If . . . material pain and pleasure *s·* normal,
- 312– 6   What to material sense *s·* substance,
- 351–17   while error *s·* as potent and real
- *o* 353– 2   whatever *s·* real to material sense, is unreal i
- *p* 374– 6   Because mortal mind *s·* to be conscious,
- 375–28   This state of mind *s·* anomalous except to the
- 384– 9   If man *s·* to incur the penalty
- 393– 4   The body *s·* to be self-acting,
- 410–15   The more difficult *s·* the material condition
- 411–18   The Scripture *s·* to import that Jesus caused
- 417–29   Show them how mortal mind *s·* to induce
- *t* 447–17   When sin . . . *s·* true to material sense,
- 459–24   To mortal sense C. S. *s·* abstract,
- *r* 474– 9   To the ignorant age . . . Science *s·* to be a mis take,
- 480–15   which *s·* to make men capable of wrong-doing.
- 483–22   Because the Science of Mind *s·* to bring into
- *g* 501– 5   often *s·* so smothered by the immediate contex
- 507–31   divine idea *s·* to fall to the level of
- 524–10   the true idea of God *s·* almost lost.
- *ap* 558–11   To mortal sense Science *s·* at first obscure abstract,
- 576– 5   which to us *s·* hidden in the mist of remoteness

seen
- *a* 27– 4   things ye have *s·* and heard ;— Luke 7 : 22.
- 37–14   but not amid the smoke of battle is merit *s·*
- 46–11   again *s·* casting out evil and healing the sick.
- *sp* 88–19   can never be *s·*, felt, nor understood through
- 99–26   are *s·* to be a bald imposition,
- *an* 104– 5   it will be *s·* why the author of this book
- *s* 109– 6   This great fact is not, however, *s·* to be

seen
s 109- 9 once s·, no other conclusion can be reached.
116-12 includes vastly more than is at first s·.
139-23 s· from Genesis to Revelation.
ph 169- 4 I have s· the mental signs, assuring me that
176- 9 and gave the gospel a chance to be s· in its
179- 8 Immortal Mind heals what eye hath not s· ;
193-19 Since then I have not s· him,
f 211-15 the effect s· in the lachrymal gland?
212-10 I have s· an unwitting attempt to
217-16 is s· by their effects.
233- 8 is s· and acknowledged only by degrees.
244- 8 s· between the cradle and the grave,
247- 3 I have s· age regain two of the elements
251-29 Ignorance must be s· and corrected before we
c 255-18 Eye hath not s· Spirit, nor hath ear heard His
260-11 s· as the only true conception of being.
261- 9 The effect of mortal mind . . . is s· in this :
b 268- * which we have s· with our eyes,— I John 1: 1.
268- * That which we have s· and heard— I John 1: 3.
279-18 the immortal facts of being are s·,
300-29 God is s· only in the spiritual universe
300-30 as the sun is s· in the ray of light
310- 7 and s· in all form, substance, and color,
310-29 God is not s· by material sense,
321- 2 as may be s· by studying the book of Job.
321-12 In this incident was s· the actuality of Science.
323-28 effects of C. S. are not so much s· as felt.
325-19 where human sense hath not s· man.
330-13 Eye hath neither s· God nor His image
o 354-18 dual personality of the unseen and the s·,
358-31 whom they have perhaps never s·
359- 1 orthodox pastors, whom they have s·
p 366-15 his brother whom he hath s·,— I John 4: 20.
366-16 God whom he hath not s·?"— I John 4: 20.
369-22 as would be readily s·, if psychology,
395-22 mental quackery . . . to hold it as something s·
t 449-19 The baneful effect . . . is less s· than felt.
458-15 Having s· so much suffering from quackery,
459- 3 things which "eye hath not s·— I Cor. 2: 9.
r 468-21 the evidence of things not s·."— Heb. 11: 1.
477- 7 Soul, being Spirit, is s· in nothing imperfect
478-10 no such persons were ever s· to go into the
479-31 are clearly s·, being understood by— Rom. 1: 20.
g 504-13 no place where God's light is not s·,
520- 7 is no more s· nor comprehended by mortals,
524- 2 s· in the Phœnician worship of Baal,
543-28 it is s· that man springs solely from Mind.
548-10 So C. S. can be s· only as the
553-18 it is s· that the maternal egg never
554- 2 reveals what "eye hath not s·,"— I Cor. 2: 9.
ap 569-10 by which the nothingness of error is s· ;
571-13 unfaithful stewards who have s· the danger
572-17 Under the supremacy of Spirit, it will be s·
575-28 eastward, to the star s· by the Wisemen

seer
ap 574-22 lifted the s· to behold the great city,
gl 593- 4 PROPHET. A spiritual s· ;

seers
sp 84- 9 men become s· and prophets involuntarily,
b 333-25 which baptized these s· in the divine nature,

sees
sp 86-29 Mortal mind s· what it believes
86-30 as certainly as it believes what it s·.
86-31 It feels, hears, and s· its own thoughts.
90-17 The looker-on s· the body in bed, but the
s 126- 6 as man s· his reflection in a glass.
129-31 The sinner s·, in the system taught in
ph 180- 5 when he s· his would-be healers busy,
198-15 formed before one s· a doctor
f 220-21 thinking it s· another kitten.
b 294- 9 The belief that matter thinks, s·, or feels
p 371-12 so sick humanity s· danger in every direction,
401-14 and mortal mind only feels and s· materially.
t 445-32 whenever she s· a man, for the petty consideration
r 467-27 Matter neither s·, hears, nor feels.
485- 5 Science declares that Mind, not matter, s·,
ap 563-17 but he also s· the nothingness of evil
563-18 The Revelator s· that old serpent,
571-11 Is the informer one who s· the foe?
gl 591-14 that which mortal mind s·, feels, hears, tastes,

seeth
pr 13-11 our Father, who s· in secret, will reward us
15- 1 thy Father, which s· in secret,— Matt. 6: 6.
c 262-18 but now mine eye s· Thee."— Job 42: 5.
b 305-18 what he s· the Father do :— John 5: 19.
g 518-17 man who s· his brother's need and

seething
m 67-14 on the s· ocean of sorrow.

seize
s 119- 8 To s· the first horn of this dilemma

seized
t 464-14 s· with pain so violent

seldom
g 550-28 is deemed monstrous and is s· fruitful,

select
a 38- 3 and for a s· number of followers.
r 494-12 for a s· number or for a limited period

selected
f 235- 8 s· with as direct reference to their morals

selects
t 455-20 God s· for the highest service one who

self
and sense
a 20-30 put aside material s· and sense,
human
f 254-19 But the human s· must be evangelized.
ignorant of
ph 186-28 Mortal mind is ignorant of s·,
mortality's
r 468- 4 sin is mortality's s·, because it
one's
sp 88-18 To love one's neighbor as one's s·,
90-24 The admission to one's s· that man is
c 260-25 by the thoughts ever recurring to one's s·,
b 322-32 easier . . . than to rid one's s· of error.
o 345-15 no small matter to know one's s· ;
t 448-31 doing one's s· the most harm.
449- 8 reacts most heavily against one's s·.
original
b 295-10 and then recover man's original s·
sacrifices of
a 23- 2 and Love may require many sacrifices of s·
sense and
b 296- 9 and regenerate material sense and s·.
324- 5 The purification of sense and s·
sin and
a 38-27 To those buried in the belief of sin and s·,
sin, or materiality
b 299-13 never lead towards s·, sin, or materiality,
spiritual
b 334-17 while the spiritual s·, or Christ,

self-abnegation
pr 7-21 with more devout s· and purity.
f 203-13 a more exalted worship and s·.
c 266-18 This is done through s·.
o 360-10 They require less s·,
ap 568-30 S·, . . . is a rule in C. S.

self-acting
s 160-22 Unless muscles are s· at all times,
ph 199- 8 Muscles are not s·.
p 393- 4 The body seems to be s·, only because

self-aggrandizement
t 464-10 remains unseen at her post, seeking no s·

self-assertive
ph 186-17 Evil is s·.
f 204-23 False and s· theories have

self-cognizant
r 479-11 It is not s·,— cannot feel itself,

self-completeness
c 264-17 this understanding will expand into s·,

self-condemnation
t 455- 3 A mental state of s· and

self-conscious
a 29-32 Mary's s· communion with God.
g 554-14 another false claim, that of s· matter,

self-constituted
p 378-25 Sickness is not a God-given, nor a s· material

self-containment
g 519- 5 His infinite s· and immortal wisdom

self-contradictory
a 52-29 as s· as their religion.
p 388-18 They are s· and self-destructive,
r 478-30 Mortal man is really a s· phrase,
g 552-21 may become wild with freedom and so be s·.

self-control
g 542-10 invoke crime, jeopardize s·,

self-correction
f 218-14 human mind is the sinner, disinclined to s·,

self-created
c 267- 8 God is Father, eternal, s·, infinite.

self-creative
s 157-23 Matter is not s·, for it is unintelligent.
b 278-18 another admission, ... that matter is s·,
o 356-31 Was there original s· sin?
357-18 if another mighty and s· cause exists
gl 580-18 usurper of Spirit's creation, called s· matter ;

self-deceived
ph 186-29 or it could never be s·.
p 376- 7 and does its work almost s·.

self-deception
  p 403–15   mortal existence is a state of *s·*
self-defence
  t 446– 3   a community unprepared for *s·*.
self-denial
  f 221–28   undisciplined by *s·* and divine Science.
  t 462–17   *s·*, sincerity, Christianity, and persistence
self-denials
  a 39– 8   We must have trials and *s·*,
self-destroyed
  f 224– 8   pain is *s·* through suffering.
  b 293–23   and this so-called mind is *s·*.
  o 346–21   If a dream ceases, it is *s·*,
  p 368– 8   still clearer as error is *s·*.
  437–14   Man *s·* ; the testimony of matter respected ;
  r 476– 6   Error, urged to its final limits, is *s·*.
self-destroying
  gl 581–17   BABEL.   *S·* error ;
self-destruction
  element of
  b 310–24   Sin is the element of *s·*,
  elements of
  r 481–25   Sin has the elements of *s·*.
  no element of
  b 311– 8   which has no element of *s·*.
  of all error
  b 303–19   through the *s·* of all error
  of error
  b 293–26   In reality, they show the *s·* of error
  point of
  p 374–32   or increases it to the point of *s·*.
  suffering and
  gl 588– 2   suffering and *s·* ; self-imposed agony ;

  sp 77– 7   Error brings its own *s·*
  f 251– 2   as it hastens towards *s·*.
self-destructive
  f 210–13   this so-called mind is *s·*,
  b 300–16   The inharmonious and *s·* never touch the
  p 388–18   They are self-contradictory and *s·*,
self-directing
  s 160–26   If muscles can cease to act . . . they must be *s·*.
self-division
  c 263–23   a new multiplication or *s·* of mortal thought,
  p 424– 1   by the parent's mind, through *s·*.
  g 548–32   also increase their numbers . . . by *s·*.''
  549–13   and sometimes through *s·*.
self-establishment
  s 142– 2   have required for *s·* and propagation.
self-evident
  s 113–10   the four following, to me, *s·* propositions.
  f 207–16   Science of being repudiates *s·* impossibilities,
  b 309–27   It is a *s·* error to suppose that there can be
  o 346–13   It is *s·* that we are harmonious only as we
  p 388–23   and this becomes *s·*, when we learn that
  393–20   when it is *s·* that matter can have no pain
  t 457–13   cannot . . . both cure and cause disease is *s·*.
  r 470–12   by the following *s·* proposition :
  472–21   and we should have a *s·* absurdity
  g 550–32   As C. S. repudiates *s·* impossibilities,
self-evidently
  g 539–21   exposed by our Master as *s·* wrong.
self-evolution
  s 119– 6   They either presuppose the *s·* . . . of matter,
self-existence
  b 331–20   and there is no other *s·*.
self-existent
  s 142–27   If Mind was first and *s·*,
  f 213– 9   God, good, is *s·* and self-expressed,
  b 278–19   admission . . . that matter is self-creative, *s·*,
  282– 9   The sphere represents good, the *s·*
  290– 1   Because Life is God, Life must be eternal, *s·*.
  300–17   The . . . never touch the harmonious and *s·*.
  r 479– 8   Matter is neither *s·* nor a product of Spirit.
  g 555–17   God, the *s·* and eternal.
  gl 583–21   *s·* Life, Truth, and Love ;
  588–24   Substance ; *s·* and eternal Mind ;
self-expressed
  f 213–10   God, good, is self-existent and *s·*,
self-forgetfulness
  pr 15–26   *S·*, purity, and affection are constant prayers.
self-governed
  an 106– 9   Man is properly *s·* only when he
  s 125–17   Reflecting God's government, man is *s·*.
self-government
  an 106– 8   among which are *s·*, reason, and conscience.
  s 119– 6   They either presuppose the . . . *s·* of matter,
  f 236–22   blighting the buddings of *s·*.
  t 447– 2   trespassing upon man's individual right of *s·*.

selfhood
  a 38–24   Christ, his spiritual *s·*, never suffered.
  m 68– 8   cherish nothing which hinders our highest *s·*.
  sp 91–16   Absorbed in material *s·* we discern . . . faintly
  91–18   The denial of material *s·* aids the
  b 294–25   Man's genuine *s·* is recognizable only in
  316– 6   and lose sight of mortal *s·*
  r 476–22   outside of all material *s·*.
  479–14   which constitutes matter's supposed *s·*,
  g 538– 3   Truth . . . does, drive error out of all *s·*.
  554–11   destitute of any knowledge of the so-called *s·*
  ap 561–20   material and corporeal *s·* disappear,
self-immolation
  pr 1– 6   watching, and working, combined with *s·*,
  a 23– 5   The atonement requires constant *s·*
  sp 99–24   health, purity, and *s·*,
  gl 590– 9   LAMB OF GOD. The spiritual idea of Love ; *s·*
self-imposed
  ph 191–16   must free itself from *s·* materiality
  f 221–17   suffering and disease were the *s·* beliefs of
  gl 588– 3   suffering and self-destruction ; *s·* agony ;
self-inflicted
  p 398–20   which reduces *s·* sufferings
  t 462–26   to probe the *s·* wounds of selfishness,
selfish
  a 36–19   A *s·* and limited mind may be unjust,
  51–29   and caused the *s·* materialist to hate him ;
  m 58–13   the *s·* exaction of all another's time
  s 109–16   buoyant with hope, not *s·* nor depressing.
  ph 192–15   all that is *s·*, wicked, dishonest, and impure.
  b 290–10   and from *s·* and inferior motives.
  318–10   all that is material, untrue, *s·*, or debased.
  t 447– 7   erring human opinions, conflicting *s·* motives,
selfishness
  and impurity
  m 60–12   *s·* and impurity alone are fleeting,
  and sensualism
  c 260–24   *S·* and sensualism are educated in
  and sensuality
  a 22– 4   *s·* and sensuality causing constant retrogression,
  and sin
  ph 176–14   *s·* and sin, disease and death, will lose their
  mountain of
  m 61–10   and every mountain of *s·* be brought low,
  old
  pr 9– 7   Do we pursue the old *s·*, satisfied with
  tips the beam
  f 205–28   *S·* tips the beam of human existence towards

  pr 9–11   If *s·* has given place to kindness,
  m 64– 2   caused by the *s·* and inhumanity of man.
  ph 175–19   Then people had less time for *s·*, coddling, and
  f 201– 9   Passions, *s·*, false appetites, hatred,
  205–27   into opposite channels where *s·* reigns.
  b 330–30   dishonesty, *s·*, envy, hypocrisy,
  p 407– 7   passion, *s·*, envy, hatred,
  410–24   *S·* does not appear in the practice of
  t 462–27   the self-inflicted wounds of *s·*,
  gl 589– 2   hatred ; *s·* ; self-will ; lust.
self-justification
  pr 8– 1   may afford a quiet sense of *s·*,
  s 115–22   depraved will, *s·*, pride, envy,
  f 242–18   self-will, *s·*, and self-love,
self-knowledge
  t 462–20   Anatomy, . . . is mental *s·*,
self-love
  f 242–15   *S·* is more opaque than a solid body.
  242–18   self-will, self-justification, and *s·*,
self-made
  b 282–11   a belief in a *s·* and temporary
  294–26   Man is neither *s·* nor made by mortals.
  gl 584–22   saith : . . . a wicked mind, *s·* or
self-mesmerism
  p 403– 5   while *s·* is induced unconsciously
self-offering
  gl 579– 8   ABEL. Watchfulness ; *s·* ;
  582– 9   Renewal of affections ; *s·* ;
self-reliant
  a 23–30   demands *s·* trustworthiness,
self-respect
  p 407– 3   inconceivably terrible to man's *s·*.
self-righteousness
  ph 179–10   not in *s·*, but reflecting the divine
  p 364–11   This query Jesus answered by rebuking *s·*
  t 448– 2   Blindness and *s·* cling fast to
  gl 592–27   PHARISEE. Corporeal and sensuous belief ; *s·*
self-sacrifice
  a 29–10   Great is the reward of *s·*,
self-same
  b 317–22   as the *s·* Jesus whom they had loved

self-satisfied
  pr 7–21 A *s·* ventilation of fervent sentiments
self-seeking
  t 445–21 S·, envy, passion, pride,
self-seen
  p 411–19 Jesus caused the evil to be *s·*
self-sentence
  p 378– 6 will enable you to commute this *s·*,
self-sustained
  p 390– 4 We cannot deny that Life is *s·*,
  g 544– 7 Mind, . . . being the producer, Life was *s·*.
self-sustaining
  ph 170–12 points to the *s·* and eternal Truth.
  p 372–22 Matter is not *s·*.
self-will
  f 242–18 the adamant of error,— *s·*,
  gl 589– 2 envy ; hatred ; selfishness ; *s·* ; lust.
semblance
  ph 195–15 Whatever furnishes the *s·* of an idea
semi-god
  c 263–16 mis-creator, who believes he is a *s·*.
semi-metaphysical
  b 268–14 *s·* systems afford no substantial aid
  268–18 These *s·* systems are one and all
semi-starvation
  f 221–20 Hence *s·* is not acceptable to wisdom,
semper paratus
  t 458–15 S· p· is Truth's motto.
send
  f 206–19 Does God *s·* sickness,
  b 287–12 "Doth a fountain *s·* forth— *Jas.* 3: 11.
  p 439–31 We *s·* our best detectives to
  t 455–29 same fountain cannot *s·* forth both
  g 545–14 errors *s·* falsity into all human doctrines
  ap 570–19 What if the old dragon should *s·* forth a
sender
  s 158– 7 Apollo was also regarded as the *s·* of disease,
sendeth
  r 489–22 *s·* not forth sweet waters and bitter.
sending
  f 206–26 Instead of God *s·* sickness and death,
sends
  ph 191–32 Mind, God, *s·* forth the aroma of Spirit,
  194– 9 Truth *s·* a report of health over the body.
  196–31 The press unwittingly *s·* forth many sorrows
  f 239–30 The perfect Mind *s·* forth perfection,
  239–31 Imperfect mortal mind *s·* forth its own
  p 399–11 mortal mind *s·* its despatches over its body,
  g 516–15 arbutus *s·* her sweet breath to heaven.
  ap 568–29 Love *s·* forth her primal and everlasting strain.
sensation
  basis of
    ph 178–18 acting from the basis of *s·* in matter,
  belief that
    gl 592– 1 *alias* the belief that *s·* is in matter,
  changes
    r 491– 5 Change the belief, and the *s·* changes.
  devoid of
    r 480– 9 whereas matter is devoid of *s·*.
  disappears
    r 491– 6 Destroy the belief, and the *s·* disappears.
  false
    s 128–28 and not upon the judgment of false *s·*.
  has no
    ph 166– 1 matter has no *s·* of its own,
    f 211–10 Is it not provable . . . that matter has no *s·*?
    214–31 the body as matter has no *s·* of its own,
    o 346–23 because matter has no *s·*,
    p 401–14 since matter has no *s·*
    r 485– 4 for matter has no *s·*.
    489– 5 and that matter has no *s·*,
    489–26 because matter has no *s·*,
  intelligence and
    b 294–14 error, saying : "Matter has intelligence and *s·*.
  life and
    b 278–12 That matter . . . has life and *s·*, is one of the
    289– 4 The belief that life and *s·* are in the body
    p 396–30 never giving the body life and *s·*.
  life, nor
    s 127–22 have— as matter— no intelligence, life, nor *s·*.
    f 205–11 matter has neither intelligence, life, nor *s·*,
  material
    (see **material***)*
  material in
    p 416–17 and this mind is material in *s·*,
  no
    f 212–16 and the nerves have no *s·*.
    237– 4 "There is no *s·* in matter."
    b 284–30 neither *s·* nor report goes from material body

sensation
  nor life
    s 108– 6 matter possesses neither *s·* nor life ;
  of pain
    f 212– 6 If the *s·* of pain in the limb can return,
  of sickness
    f 211–13 The *s·* of sickness and the impulse to sin
  physical
    pr 7–17 Physical *s·*, . . . produces material ecstasy
  supposed
    s 120–25 deduced from supposed *s·* in matter
  world of
    pr 13–31 the world of *s·* is not cognizant of
    ————
    sp 81– 4 as there is to show the sick that matter . . . has *s·*;
    ph 168–28 the *s·* would not appear if
    188–18 The smile of the sleeper indicates the *s·*
    f 211–24 If it is true that nerves have *s·*,
    212–14 it proves *s·* to be in the mortal mind,
    218–26 to believe in matter as . . . having *s·* or power.
    243–24 matter has neither intelligence nor *s·*.
    b 295– 2 the *s·* seeming to be in nerves
    318–22 denies the error of *s·* in matter,
    p 370–30 change our basis from *s·* to C. S.,
    396–25 as if matter could have *s·*.
    408–30 that condition of the body which we call *s·*
    r 480– 8 belief that there is *s·* in matter,
    485–29 as much as nerves control *s·*
    488–22 Nerves have no more *s·*, . . . than the
    gl 586–20 a belief that matter has *s·*.
    591–11 *s·* in the sensationless ;
sensationless
  f 250–20 the body lies listless, undisturbed, and *s·*,
  b 280–26 man has a *s·* body ;
  gl 591–11 MATTER. . . . sensation in the *s·* ;
  592– 1 matter, which is *s·* ;
sensations
  sp 73–20 with material *s·* and desires,
  73–24 belief that . . . spirit retains the *s·*
  92– 6 but also capable of imparting these *s·*.
  f 211– 7 The *s·* of the body must either be the
  211– 7 the *s·* of a so-called mortal mind or of
  p 372– 7 theory . . . that its *s·* can reproduce man,
sense
  allegorical
    ap 575–16 Taken in its allegorical *s·*,
  and Soul
    f 240–31 how to divide between *s·* and Soul.
  anthropomorphic
    b 337– 1 but not in any anthropomorphic *s·*.
  captives [of
    pref xi–19 deliverance to the captives [of *s·*],— *Luke* 4: 18.
  certain
    g 509– 7 presented to them the certain *s·* of eternal Life.
    ap 569–14 in a sweet and certain *s·* that God is Love.
  changes the
    b 319–28 A misplaced word changes the *s·*
  clear
    b 325–20 Paul had clear *s·* of the demands of Truth
    r 495–17 your clear *s·* and calm trust,
  common
    p 365–12 and common *s·* and common humanity are
  contradicting
    gl 596–26 C. S., contradicting *s·*, maketh the valley to bud
  corporeal
    pref viii– 5 the discords of corporeal *s·* must yield to the
    m 56–11 where the corporeal *s·* of creation was cast out,
    sp 72– 2 of which corporeal *s·* can take no cognizance.
    77– 5 continues to be a belief of corporeal *s·* until the
    ph 167– 7 only as we live above corporeal *s·*
    b 299–26 *s·*, or error, may seem to hide Truth,
    p 376–16 simulated a corporeal *s·* of life.
    r 483–15 the name "error" to corporeal *s·*,
    486– 5 until every corporeal *s·* is quenched.
    489–13 Corporeal *s·* defrauds and lies ;
    493– 2 To corporeal *s·*, the sun appears to rise and set,
    494–20 serves to correct the errors of corporeal *s·* ;
    495–21 Let C. S., instead of corporeal *s·*,
    g 533–31 learned that corporeal *s·* is the serpent.
    548–11 only as the clouds of corporeal *s·* roll away.
    ap 573–19 Because St. John's corporeal *s·* of the
    578– 2 substituting for the corporeal *s·*, the
    gl 583– 6 The representatives of Soul, not corporeal *s·* ;
  correct
    ap 560–18 without a correct *s·* of its highest visible idea,
  deadened
    a 55– 2 from a deadened *s·* of the invisible God,
  detach
    c 261–21 Detach *s·* from the body, or matter,
  distorted
    b 322–22 incurred through the pains of distorted *s·*.
  divine
    g 505–24 the divine *s·*, giving the spiritual proof
    ap 577– 1 human sense of Deity yields to the divine *s·*,

sense

diviner
b 285–20 to give place to a diviner *s·* of
p 369– 7 He enters into a diviner *s·* of the facts,
ap 563– 2 while, to a diviner *s·*, harmony is the real

dormant
b 327–31 awaken the man's dormant *s·* of

enraptured
f 246–15 should dawn upon the enraptured *s·*

erroneous
p 396–25 with which to combat their erroneous *s·*,

errors of
f 240–27 In trying to undo the errors of *s·*
b 273–14 till the errors of *s·* are eliminated.
p 406–11 The Science of being unveils the errors of *s·*,

every
f 208– 9 a law of mortal mind, wrong in every *s·*,

false
s 108–26 this false *s·* evolves, in belief, a
   122–27 Temporal life is a false *s·* of existence.
ph 172–14 as the false *s·* of being disappears.
   194–22 by the false *s·* it imparts.
   196–13 here the word *soul* means a false *s·*
f 205– 5 their false *s·* concerning God and man.
   213–31 dipped to its depths into a false *s·* of things,
   253–14 I hope that you are conquering this false *s·*.
c 262–27 a false *s·* of man's origin.
b 281–21 When we put off the false *s·* for the true,
   307–15 a transient, false *s·* of an existence which
   311–30 as mortals lay off a false *s·* of life,
   319– 1 manifests mortality, a false *s·* of soul.
   325–32 A false *s·* of life, substance, and mind
   335–23 Only by losing the false *s·* of Soul can we
p 399–26 It is only a false *s·* of matter,
   411–22 induced by a false *s·* mentally entertained,
t 460–15 to the frightened, false *s·* of the patient.
r 485– 6 the false *s·*, which ever betrays mortals into
   493–30 the Christ could improve on a false *s·*.
g 539– 1 This false *s·* of existence is fratricidal.
   540–21 a false *s·* which hath no knowledge of God.''
   545–22 translators of this . . . entertained a false *s·* of
ap 573–20 and in place of this false *s·* was the

falsities of
sp 78– 4 They are the falsities of *s·*,

finite
s 120– 1 though it seems otherwise to finite *s·*.
   124–12 This is a mortal, finite *s·* of things,
f 208– 3 and has a finite *s·* of the infinite.
c 263–24 as when some finite *s·* peers from its cloister
b 280–13 its finite *s·* of the divisibility of Soul
   300– 3 Finite *s·* has no true appreciation of

fleshly
b 314– 3 waited until the mortal or fleshly *s·* had

for soul
r 482– 1 substitution of the word *s·* for *soul*

high
t 448–20 a high *s·* of the moral and

higher
b 285–29 As mortals reach, . . . a higher *s·*,
   322–20 physical sense of pleasure yields to a higher *s·*.
p 390–14 Let your higher *s·* of justice destroy the
r 487– 1 to seek and to find a higher *s·* of happiness
gl 589–19 higher *s·* of Truth rebuking mortal belief,

human
   (*see* **human**)

identical with
r 482–12 out of Science, soul is identical with *s·*,

immanent
f 209–14 immanent *s·* of Mind-power enhances the glory
        of

immortal
sp 72– 3 Principle of man speaks through immortal *s·*.
f 210–30 immortal *s·* includes no evil nor pestilence.
   210–31 immortal *s·* has no error of sense,
   216–14 to supply the truth of immortal *s·*.

imparting a
ap 567– 2 imparting a *s·* of the ever-presence of

imperfect
c 258–25 Mortals have a very imperfect *s·* of the

incorporeal
ap 577– 2 yields to the incorporeal *s·* of God and man

inferior
gl 590–16 which has the inferior *s·* of master, or ruler.

instead of
b 302–23 this real man is governed by Soul instead of *s·*,

literal
a 32–24 This would have been foolish in a literal *s·*;

lower
s 116–30 but not in the lower *s·*.
gl 590–18 word *kurios* almost always has this lower *s·*,

material
   (*see* **material**)

misconceived
b 281–19 is a myth, a misconceived *s·*.

moral
t 451–32 tends to blast moral *s·*, health, and

sense

mortal
   (*see* **mortal**)

must be immortal
p 433–29 sense of Life, God, — which *s·* must be immortal,

my
a 40–10 This is my *s·* of divine pardon,

no
f 210–31 it has no *s·* of error ; therefore it is
   243–26 Love has no *s·* of hatred.

no error of
f 210–31 immortal sense has no error of *s·*,

no more
f 250–26 matter has no more *s·* as a man than

objects of
b 269–15 exchanges the objects of *s·* for the ideas of
g 510– 4 than to dwell on the objects of *s·* !

of being
   (*see* **being**)

of Christian Science
ap 577–28 The writer's present feeble *s·* of C. S.

of disease
b 270–27 If a *s·* of disease produces suffering
p 421–26 If you would destroy the *s·* of disease,

of ease
b 270–28 and a *s·* of ease antidotes suffering,

of error
f 210–31 it has no *s·* of error ; therefore it is
g 520–13 in which all *s·* of error forever disappears

of evil
b 325– 3 He who . . . loses all *s·* of evil,
g 540–15 that Truth may annihilate all *s·* of evil

offspring of
b 274– 5 the offspring of *s·*, not of Soul, Spirit,

of good
b 311–13 Evil is destroyed by the *s·* of good.

of health
m 69– 4 mortals gain the *s·* of health only as
p 373–23 Establish the scientific *s·* of health,

of infinitude
r 469–21 we bury the *s·* of infinitude, when we admit

of Life
f 206– 2 no other *s·* of Life, and no consciousness of the
o 355–12 let the harmonious and true *s·* of Life
p 430–11 shut out the true *s·* of Life and health.
   433–29 *s·* of Life, God, — which sense must be

of life
   (*see* **life**)

of material life
a 53–29 beliefs of the flesh or his *s·* of material life,

of personal joys
c 266–11 even if you cling to a *s·* of personal joys,

of pleasure
b 298–16 alternating between a *s·* of pleasure and pain,
   322–19 until his physical *s·* of pleasure yields to a

of sin
m 69– 5 only as they lose the *s·* of sin and disease.
b 311–12 It is a *s·* of sin, and not a sinful soul,
r 481–31 it is the *s·* of sin which is lost, and not

of Soul
b 335–23 Only by losing the false *s·* of Soul can we
gl 582–15 a *s·* of Soul, which has spiritual bliss

of soul
b 319– 1 manifests mortality, a false *s·* of soul.
r 493–26 Any *s·* of soul in matter is not the

of substance
b 301– 7 but his *s·* of substance involves error

one
s 119–17 In one *s·* God is identical with nature,

our
a 25– 5 expressed by our *s·* of human blood.

outward
s 129–24 instead of accepting only the outward *s·*

overwhelming
a 50– 6 overwhelming *s·* of the magnitude of his work,

painful
r 495–19 can destroy any painful *s·* of, or belief in, that

pains of
   (*see* **pains**)

personal
m 61– 2 within the limits of personal *s·*.
b 312–24 A personal *s·* of God and of

physical
   (*see* **physical**)

priceless
p 366– 1 priceless *s·* of the dear Father's loving-kindness.

primary
g 525–10 the primary *s·* being *image, form,*

proper
c 265– 8 gain some proper *s·* of the infinite,
   424– 8 the proper *s·* of God's unerring direction

pure
a 29–25 overshadowed the pure *s·* of the Virgin-mother
b 318–15 would efface the pure *s·* of omnipotence.

purification of
b 324– 5 The purification of *s·* and self is a proof of

ense

quickened
o 343–13   from the quickened *s·* of the people.

quiet
pr 8– 1   A wordy prayer may afford a quiet *s·* of

real
b 295–14   the real *s·* of being, perfect and

rebukes
o 350–29   Soul rebukes *s·*, and Truth destroys error.

religious
a 53–13   contrary to the world's religious *s·*.
c 267–14   in a religious *s·*, they have the same authority

scientific
m 69–19   not conflict with the scientific *s·* of
c 265–10   This scientific *s·* of being, forsaking matter
b 272–10   brings out the scientific *s·*,
337– 1   in a scientific *s·*, but not in any anthropomorphic
p 373–23   Establish the scientific *s·* of health,
415–14   Opiates do not remove . . . in any scientific *s·*.

self and
a 20–31   put aside material self and *s·*, and seek the

sight and
sp 87–32   gone from physical sight and *s·*,

sight or
f 214–28   But the real sight or *s·* is not lost.

sin and
g 530–22   saying, . . . that sin and *s·* are more pleasant
gl 583– 7   who, having wrestled with error, sin, and *s·*,

sinful
pr 15– 4   the door of which shuts out sinful *s·*
16– 6   Truth that is sinless and the falsity of sinful *s·*.
a 23– 9   suffering is an error of sinful *s·*
p 405–29   pains of sinful *s·* are less harmful than

sinless
a 22–24   immortality, boundless freedom, and sinless *s·*,

sinning
sp 96– 1   Humanity advances slowly out of sinning *s·*

spiritual
(*see* **spiritual**)

suffering
sp 77–21   or of a sinning, suffering *s·*,
ap 574–28   which your suffering *s·* deems wrathful

sweet
b 304– 1   the sweet *s·* and presence of Life and Truth.

temporary
b 298– 9   a mortal temporary *s·* of things.

this
b 272– 4   This *s·* is assimilated only as we are honest,
298–11   until this *s·* is corrected by C. S.
o 349–19   this *s·* must be gained by its disciples
489–15   How then can this *s·* be the God-given channel

time and
c 261–25   the mutations of time and *s·*,
gl 584– 2   The objects of time and *s·* disappear in the

to Soul
a 48– 9   from earth to heaven, from *s·* to Soul.
c 266– 1   and transplant the affections from *s·* to Soul,
ap 566– 7   in their passage from *s·* to Soul,

transient
f 246–14   the transient *s·* of beauty fades,

true
a 32–20   The true *s·* is spiritually lost, if the
s 108–29   thereby shutting out the true *s·* of Spirit.
c 264– 8   if they would gain the true *s·* of things.
b 283–23   the true *s·* of His power is lost to all who
o 355–12   let the harmonious and true *s·* of Life
p 430–11   shut out the true *s·* of Life and health.
g 534– 7   to interpret the Scriptures in their true *s·*,
550–12   The true *s·* of being and its eternal perfection
ap 575– 2   Arise . . . into the true *s·* of Love,

truer
a 19– 7   by giving man a truer *s·* of Love,
19– 9   and this truer *s·* of Love redeems

uncertain
b 326–24   only when his uncertain *s·* of right yielded to

want of
r 489–30   A wrong sense . . . is *non-sense*, want of *s·*.

woes of
f 248–10   and destroying the woes of *s·*

wrong
r 489–29   A wrong *s·* of God, man, and creation is

m 68– 4   They are slaves to fashion, pride, and *s·*.
69–12   nor his *s·* of increasing number
an 102– 7   in *s·* it is an unreal concept of the
s 116–29   in the *s·* of infinite personality, but not
ph 172–30   belief that there is Soul in *s·* or Life in matter
175–12   and dissuade any *s·* of fear or fever.
f 214–26   How transient a *s·* is mortal sight,
c 265–29   inform us that the pleasures of *s·* are mortal
b 311–11   false estimates of soul as dwelling in *s·*
311–16   belief strays into a *s·* of temporary loss
312–14   the *s·* of a corporeal Jehovah,
315–12   hid from their *s·* Christ's sonship
322– 6   the reality of Life, the control of Soul over *s·*,
o 353–13   not wholly outlived the *s·* of ghostly beliefs.

sense
p 362– *   *Why art thou cast down, O my soul* [*s·*]? — *Psal.* 42 : 11.
366–23   a *s·* of the odiousness of sin
379–13   Had he known his *s·* of bleeding was an
r 482– 8   use the word *s·*, and you will have the scientific
493–23   it removes any other *s·* of moral or mental
g 540–31   Material in origin and *s·*, he brings a
ap 572–26   Through what *s·* came this vision to St. John?
gl 596–16   a *s·* of the nothingness of error,

sense-dream
b 312– 6   as the *s·* vanishes and reality appears.

sense-existence
ph 167– 5   Soul-existence, in the place of *s·*,

senseless
f 202–29   as if *s·* matter . . . had more power than

senses

are silent
sp 89–21   Spirit, God, is heard when the *s·* are silent.

are spiritual
f 252–32   Man, whose *s·* are spiritual, is

bodily
a 50–20   before the evidence of the bodily *s·*,
ph 172– 1   which he has through the bodily *s·*,
t 448– 5   Evil which obtains in the bodily *s·*,

cognizable by the
sp 86–29   as readily as from objects cognizable by the *s·*.

corporeal
sp 70– 2   corporeal *s·* cannot inform us what is real
85–24   Jew and Gentile may have had acute corporeal *s·*,
s 131– 7   the false evidence before the corporeal *s·*
144–13   the manifestations of the corporeal *s·*,
f 216–22   If the decision were left to the corporeal *s·*,
b 281– 8   Divine Science contradicts the corporeal *s·*,
296–22   knowledge obtained from the corporeal *s·*
318– 5   Corporeal *s·* define diseases as realities ;
318– 7   even while the corporeal *s·* are saying that
334–23   according to the testimony of the corporeal *s·*,
p 388– 4   obtained a victory over the corporeal *s·*,
393– 9   Mind is the master of the corporeal *s·*,
395– 9   master the false evidences of the corporeal *s·*
417–18   The evidence before the corporeal *s·*
t 448–13   rises above the evidence of the corporeal *s·* ;
r 471– 8   the evidence before the five corporeal *s·*
477–10   To the five corporeal *s·*, man appears to be
477–12   declares the corporeal *s·* to be mortal and
486–28   If the five corporeal *s·* were the medium
488–14   Do the five corporeal *s·* constitute man?
488–20   corporeal *s·* can take no cognizance of
489–24   The corporeal *s·* are the only source of evil
493–18   the beliefs of the five corporeal *s·*,
g 516– 7   the false testimony of the corporeal *s·*
525–24   The corporeal *s·* declare otherwise ;
527–16   gathered from the corporeal *s·*,
531–28   corporeal *s·* can take no cognizance of Spirit.
532– 6   must be gained from the five corporeal *s·*.
532–21   calling out to the corporeal *s·*.
543– 9   five corporeal *s·* cannot take cognizance of
546–16   manifested only through the corporeal *s·*,
552– 8   necessarily apparent to the corporeal *s·*,
557–14   but in the line of the corporeal *s·*,
gl 581–20   evidence obtained from the five corporeal *s·*,
585– 1   Not organs of the so-called corporeal *s·*,
589–13   knowledge obtained from the five corporeal *s·* ;
590– 5   Evidence obtained from the five corporeal *s·* ;

deceitful
p 395– 4   the testimony of the deceitful *s·*,

educated
ph 195– 8   All that gives pleasure to our educated *s·*

enslaving
f 227– 6   claims of the enslaving *s·* must be denied

erring
pr 15–10   door of the erring *s·* must be closed.

evidence of the
a 18–11   against the accredited evidence of the *s·*,
p 386– 2   evidence of the *s·* is not to be accepted
420–31   Turn his gaze from the false evidence of the *s·*

evidence to the
p 370–10   furnishes the evidence to the *s·*,

five
ph 200–22   in other words the five *s·*,
b 274– 4   knowledge gained from the five *s·*
g 526–10   material hearing, sight, . . . termed the five *s·*
532–31   through matter, the five *s·*.

his
a 52– 5   His *s·* drank in the spiritual evidence of

human
s 116– 6   evidence before the corporeal human *s·*,
t 461–10   from the standpoint of the human *s·*.

illusions of the
b 332–13   dispelling the illusions of the *s·* ;

illusive
ph 191–28   The illusive *s·* may fancy affinities with

senses
  limited
    b 337–21 incomprehensible to the limited *s·*
  material
    (*see* **material**)
  mortal
    b 288–28 unlimited by the mortal *s·*.
    p 390– 6 to the mortal *s·*, there is seeming discord.
  of man
    b 284–28 the only real *s·* of man are spiritual,
    r 486–23 all the spiritual *s·* of man, are eternal.
    488–28 If it were possible for the real *s·* of man to be
    489–19 Who dares to say that the *s·* of man can be
  of Mind
    r 489– 4 the *s·* of Mind are never lost
  of Soul
    f 213–18 communicated through the *s·* of Soul
    214–29 Neither . . . can interfere with the *s·* of Soul,
  of Spirit
    b 274–12 The *s·* of Spirit abide in Love,
  personal
    b 334–11 imperceptible to the so-called personal *s·*,
  physical
    (*see* **physical**)
  real
    f 214–30 and there are no other real *s·*.
    b 284–28 the only real *s·* of man are spiritual,
    r 488–28 If it were possible for the real *s·* of man to be
  represent
    c 265–16 The *s·* represent birth as untimely
  Science and the
    b 273–13 Hence the enmity between Science and the *s·*,
  so-called
    s 122–10 these so-called *s·* still make mortal
    ph 190–11 arranges itself into five so-called *s·*,
    c 258–20 material so-called *s·* have no cognizance
    261–20 he was in the full possession of his so-called *s·*.
    b 292–16 The so-called *s·* of mortals are material.
    r 471– 9 these so-called *s·* receive no intimation of
    488–18 defines these so-called *s·* as *mortal beliefs*,
  Spirit's
    f 214–32 Spirit's *s·* are without pain,
  spiritual
    b 288– 5 between the evidence of the spiritual *s·* and
    r 486–23 all the spiritual *s·* of man, are eternal.
    g 512–25 discerned only through the spiritual *s·*.
  testimony of the
    s 122–20 denying the testimony of the *s·*,
  these
    b 284–26 are beyond the cognizance of these *s·*,
    294– 2 These *s·* indicate the common human belief,
    r 486– 7 To die, that he may regain these *s·*?
  those very
    ph 195– 9 gave him pain through those very *s·*,
  unseen to the
    f 234–30 action of the human mind, unseen to the *s·*.
  visible to the
    p 400–26 image which becomes visible to the *s·*.

    a 38–28 living only for . . . the gratification of the *s·*,
    52– 7 their *s·* testified oppositely, and absorbed the
    m 61– 2 The *s·* confer no real enjoyment.
    an 101– 4 the impressions made upon the *s·*;
    s 119–26 contradicts the evidence before the *s·*
    120–13 is he well if the *s·* say he is sick?
    138–25 the sinful, so-called pleasure of the *s·*.
    f 206–14 governed by Science instead of the *s·*,
    242–14 so-called pain and pleasure of the *s·*.
    b 289–18 what appears to the *s·* to be death is but
    305–20 inverted images presented by the *s·*,
    312– 8 The *s·* regard a corpse, not as man,
    p 382–25 oblivion, in which the *s·* had engulfed him,
    384–29 all the evidence before the *s·* can never

senses'
    s 122– 7 The material *s·* reversal of the
sense-testimony
    f 249– 2 relinquish all theories based on *s·*,
sensible
    s 109– 7 not, . . . seen to be supported by *s·* evidence,
    ph 173– 9 the *s·* is required to be made manifest through
    p 399–27 since matter is not *s·*.
sensibly
    pr 14– 1 If we are *s·* with the body and regard
    p 383–30 pounding the poor body, to make it *s·* well
sensitive
    a 54– 1 he would have been less *s·* to those beliefs.
    p 423– 6 oftentimes affects a *s·* patient more
    g 555– 1 mortal mind is less pungent or *s·*,
sensual
    a 20–13 men can be baptized, . . . and yet be *s·* and
    sp 73–30 The *s·* cannot be made the mouthpiece of
    f 221–32 another lesson,— that gluttony is a *s·* illusion,
    226–26 the sick, the *s·*, the sinner, I wished to save
    241– 5 *S·* treasures are laid up "where moth —*Matt.* 6:19.

sensual
    f 254–16 During the *s·* ages, absolute C. S. may not
    c 263–28 A *s·* thought, like an atom of dust
    b 296–10 Nothing *s·* or sinful is immortal.
    g 547–28 *s·*, and mortal theory of the universe,
    gl 583– 1 *S·* and mortal beliefs;
    590–11 A corporeal and *s·* belief; mortal man;
sensualism
    a 36–16 distance between Christianity and *s·*
    m 65–14 in the materialism and *s·* of the age,
    c 260–22 *S·* evolves bad physical and moral conditions.
    260–24 Selfishness and *s·* are educated in
    b 272–23 earthward gravitation of *s·* and impurity,
    337– 6 *S·* is not bliss, but bondage.
    gl 589– 5 mortal embracing duplicity, repentance, *s·*.
    594–15 love rebuking error; reproof of *s·*.
sensualist's
    f 241– 8 The *s·* affections are as imaginary, whimsical,
sensuality
  all
    f 201–10 false appetites, hatred, fear, all *s·*,
  and sin
    p 364– 7 might be redeemed from *s·* and sin.
  arising from
    sp 94–20 betrayal, arising from *s·*.
  palsies
    s 142–16 *S·* palsies the right hand, and causes the left to
  rebuked their
    a 51–27 divine Principle, Love, which rebuked their *s·*.
  selfishness and
    a 22– 4 selfishness and *s·* causing constant retrogression,
  sin and
    sp 82–31 In a world of sin and *s·* hastening to

    sp 71–25 There is no *s·* in Spirit.
    92–19 an outgrowth of human knowledge or *s·*,
    an 104–20 dishonesty, *s·*, falsehood, revenge,
    gl 581– 6 counteracting all evil, *s·*, and mortality.
    587–21 HAM (Noah's son). Corporeal belief; *s·*;
    589–14 *s·*; envy; oppression; tyranny.
    593– 7 Error; fear; inflammation; *s·*;
    593–12 REUBEN (Jacob's son). Corporeality; *s·*;
sensuous
    s 111– 3 the will, or *s·* reason of the human mind,
    121– 3 inclinations of a *s·* philosophy.
    131– 8 Hence the opposition of *s·* man
    ph 177–14 the body is a *s·*, human concept.
    f 203–19 imprisoned in a *s·* body.
    224– 7 *s·* pleasure or pain is self-destroyed
    o 353– 1 scientific real is the *s·* unreal.
    t 454–30 superiority of spiritual power over *s·*
    gl 582–24 CANAAN (the son of Ham). A *s·* belief;
    592–27 PHARISEE. Corporeal and *s·* belief;
sensuousness
    pr 16–20 Only as we rise above all material *s·* and
    a 35– 8 enabled to rise somewhat from mortal *s·*,
    51–29 His spirituality separated him from *s·*,
sent
    a 18– * *For Christ s· me not to baptize,— I Cor.* 1:17.
    27– 1 Jesus *s·* a message to John the Baptist,
    27–22 Jesus *s·* forth seventy students at one time,
    49– 7 Where were the seventy whom Jesus *s·* forth?
    s 109–29 not mine, but His that *s·* me.—*John* 7:16.
    126–13 nor *s·* forth a positive sound.
    133– 1 and *s·* the inquiry to Jesus,
    ph 165– * *He s· His word, and healed them,— Psal.* 107:20.
    b 272– 1 except they be *s·*?"— *Rom.* 10:15.
    272– 1 If *s·*, how shall they preach, . . . except the
    p 378–12 *s·* it cowering back into the jungle.
    410– 9 Jesus Christ, whom Thou hast *s·*."—*John* 17:3.
    433–28 and Scholastic Theology is *s·* for
    g 537– 3 *s·* him forth from the garden— *Gen.* 3:23.
    ap 561–30 "There was a man *s·* from God—*John* 1:6.
sentence
  awaiting the
    p 439–29 awaiting the *s·* which General Progress
  civil
    pr 7– 1 The only civil *s·* which he had for error
  divine
    pr 11–19 not to annul the divine *s·*
  of death
    p 433–19 proceeds to pronounce the solemn *s·* of death
    436– 3 for which Mortal Man is under *s·* of death.
    436–33 that court pronounced a *s·* of death for
  of God
    f 232–23 never tried to make of none effect the *s·* of God,
  this
    sp 80– 9 the very periodical containing this *s·*
  unjust
    p 381–29 man's moral right to annul an unjust *s·*,

    an 105– 3 Courts and juries judge and *s·* mortals

sentence

an	105–15	courts reasonably pass s·, according to the mo-
		tive.
p	378– 4	Unwittingly you s· yourself to suffer.
	381–29	a s· never inflicted by divine authority.
	391–24	and the judge will s· you.
	405–13	s· of the moral law will be executed
	440–17	Wherefore, then, . . . do you s· Mortal Man

sentenced

b	322–15	since God has s· sin to suffer.
p	433–24	For this crime Mortal Man is s·
	434–22	The prisoner at the bar has been unjustly s·.
	434–30	the lower court has s· Mortal Man to die,
	435–17	Laws of Health should be s· to die.
	436–28	His Honor s· Mortal Man to die

sentences

sp	86–26	peculiarities of expression, recollected s·,
f	225–17	A few immortal s·, . . . have been potent
o	341– 5	are generally based on detached s·
p	391–26	Mortal mind alone s· itself.
	440–21	God, who s· only for sin.

sentient

b	280–25	instead of possessing a s· material form,
	285– 1	Matter is not s· and cannot
r	487–23	The belief that life is s· and intelligent
g	528– 1	Was it requisite . . . that dust should become s·,
gl	587–11	a supposition of s· physicality ;

sentiment

pr	7–16	to induce or encourage Christian s·.
s	161–15	that immortal s· of the Declaration,
ph	176– 1	and there is truth in his s·.
f	252–21	Animal in propensity, deceitful in s·,
p	408–21	a supposed effect on intelligence and s·.

sentiments

pr	7–22	A self-satisfied ventilation of fervent s·
ph	195–28	with wrong tastes and s·.
f	206–12	exercise of the s· — hope, faith, love
b	327–30	Let that inform the s· and awaken the
g	531– 9	represent the higher moral s·,

sentinel

a	49–18	faithful s· of God at the highest post of

sentinels

f	225– 9	and will command their s· not to let truth pass

separate

pr	6– 5	God is not s· from the wisdom He bestows
	14–25	Entirely s· from the belief and dream of
a	21–17	We have s· time-tables to consult,
	42–19	belief that man has existence or mind s· from
m	66–21	Husbands and wives should never s· if
sp	74–32	in s· states of existence, or consciousness.
an	103–12	Mind-science is wholly s· from
	105–11	Can you s· the mentality from the body
s	136– 6	no intelligence, action, nor life s· from God.
ph	192–10	Spirit is not s· from God.
f	204– 7	false conclusions . . . that there are two s·,
	238– 7	and be ye s·,"— II Cor. 6 : 17.
b	304– 8	to s· us from the love of God."— Rom. 8 : 39.
	309–26	impossible . . . for man to have an intelligence s·
p	415–32	as if it were a s· bodily member.
	424– 2	becomes a s·, individualized mortal mind,
t	449–25	only to s· through simultaneous repulsion.
	451– 4	to come out from the material world and be s·.
r	466–27	to s· the chaff from the wheat.
	475–19	that which has no s· mind from God ;
	480–18	thus attempting to s· Mind from God.
	491–25	apparently with their own s· embodiment.
g	522–10	Existence, or . . . Science explains as impossible.
	535– 4	the wheat and tares which time will s·,
	539– 4	Error begins by reckoning life as s· from Spirit,

separated

a	51–17	therefore he could no more be s· from his
	51–28	His spirituality s· him from sensuousness,
sp	72–16	which are not united by progress, but s·.
	91– 5	the belief that man is s· from God,
b	303–29	nor s· from its divine Principle.
	306–14	and then are s· as by a law of divorce
	306–18	cannot be s· for an instant from God,
	315– 4	s· him from the scholastic theology of the
o	341– 5	or clauses s· from their context.
t	450–28	beliefs in . . . intelligence s· from God,
r	477–29	S· from man, who expresses Soul,
	478–28	God, who s· me from— Gal. 1 : 15.
p	505– 8	material sense, is s· from Truth,
ap	562–12	s· by belief from man's divine origin

separately

m	58–25	"Two eat no more together than they eat s·."
p	397–27	can never treat mortal mind and matter s·,

separates

m	66–31	furnace s· the gold from the dross
f	207–18	Science s· the tares and wheat in time of
b	300–20	Science s· the wheat from the tares,

separates

t	456–13	s· himself from the true conception of
g	506– 6	a quality which s· C. S. from supposition
	548– 3	C. S. s· error from truth,

separation

m	59–31	S· never should take place,
b	338–23	even the supposed s· of man from God,
p	375– 4	belief that . . . pain must accompany the s·

separator

gl	586– 7	FAN. S· of fable from fact ;

sepulchre

a	44– 8	His three days' work in the s·
	44–29	while he was hidden in the s·,
	45–15	failed to hide immortal Truth and Love in a s·.
b	299– 8	appearing at the door of some s·,
	314–18	the body, which they laid in a s·,
g	534– 4	and to behold at the s· the risen Saviour,
gl	597–14	opened the s· with divine Science,

sepulchres

pr	8– 9	"like unto whited s·— Matt. 23 : 27.

sequel

s	159–20	The s· proved that this Lynn woman

series

s	117– 2	because an individual may be one of a s·,
	117– 4	God is One,— not one of a s·, but

seriously

s	132–32	yet afterwards he s· questioned the signs of the

sermon

sp	80– 4	whether for the inspiration of a s· or
f	201– 1	best s· ever preached is Truth practised
	234– 5	be it song, s·, or Science

Sermon on the Mount

ph	174–17	The thunder of Sinai and the S· on the M·
b	271–23	The S· on the M· is the essence of

sermons

ph	176–12	"s· in stones, and good in everything."
o	345– 8	Christian s· will heal the sick.

serpent

argument of the

b	280–21	The argument of the s· in the allegory,

beguiled me

g	533–28	She says,"The s· beguiled me,— Gen. 3 : 13.

brazen

s	133–11	looked upon the brazen s·,

changeth the

g	515– 9	power which changeth the s· into a staff.

coiled around

sp	92–11	a s· coiled around the tree of knowledge

enters

g	529–22	s· enters into the metaphor only as

fable of the

g	544–19	first suggestion . . . is in the fable of the s·.

handle the

b	321–11	wisdom bade him come back and handle the s·,

is perpetually

ap	564–28	The s· is perpetually close upon the

is supposed

g	544–21	The s· is supposed to say,

lying

g	529–21	Whence comes a talking, lying s·

represents the

sp	92–13	This represents the s· in the act of

so-called

b	307– 3	This pantheistic error, or so-called s·,

strangle the

ap	569–16	and fail to strangle the s· of sin

talking

g	529–25	the species described,— a talking s·,
ap	564–31	allegorical, talking s· typifies mortal mind,

testimony of the

g	538–15	The testimony of the s· is significant of

typified by a

ap	564–26	are typified by a s·, or animal subtlety.

b	269– 5	resulted from the philosophy of the s·.
	321– 9	he saw it become a s·,
	321–13	s·, evil, under wisdom's bidding, was destroyed
	338–24	the obstacle which the s·, sin, would impose
g	515– 5	The s· of God's creating is neither subtle nor
	529–13	Now the s· was more subtle— Gen. 3 : 1.
	529–17	And the woman said unto the s·,— Gen. 3 : 2.
	530–13	the s· said unto the woman,— Gen. 3 : 4.
	533–31	learned that corporeal sense is the s·.
	534– 9	[Jehovah] said unto the s·,— Gen. 3 : 14.
	534–27	The s·, material sense, will bite the heel
	539–18	by condemning its symbol, the s·,
	550–26	A s· never begets a bird,
ap	563–18	that old s·, whose name is devil or evil,
	564–30	the s· pursues with hatred the
	567–15	that old s·, called the devil, — Rev. 12 : 9.
	567–18	that old s· whose name is devil (evil),
	570– 8	s· cast out of his mouth water-- Rev. 12 : 15.
gl	594– 1	definition of

serpent-bites

b 328–20   hundreds . . . die there annually from *s·*

serpentine

g 541–22   Here the *s·* lie invents new forms.
ap 563–27   The *s·* form stands for subtlety,

serpents

b 322– 1   taught them how to handle *s·* unharmed,
   328–23   they shall take up *s·*,— *Mark* 16 : 18.
p 362– *   *they shall take up s·;*— *Mark* 16 : 18.
gl 587–15   the *s·* of error, which say,

servant

a 44– 3   good and faithful *s·*,"— *Matt.* 25 : 23.
s 119–32   is but the humble *s·* of the restful Mind,
   146–11   by which material sense is made the *s·* of
p 404– 4   or the special *s·* of any one of the
   439–26   declaring Disease to be God's *s·*

servants

f 201– *   *the reproach of Thy s·;*— *Psal.* 89 : 50.
   216–16   it makes the nerves, . . . *s·*,

serve

pr 14– 5   We cannot "*s·* two masters."— *Matt.* 6 : 24.
a 37–11   *s·* to cleanse and rarefy the atmosphere of
ph 167–11   We cannot *s·* two masters
f 201– 5   "No man can *s·* two masters."— *Matt.* 6 : 24.
c 267–24   by reversal, errors *s·* as waymarks to the
o 346–30   We cannot *s·* both God and mammon
p 422–19   changes . . . in mortal mind to reconstruct

served

a 52– 4   He *s·* God ; they *s·* mammon.
r 497–21   his resurrection *s·* to uplift faith

serves

m 57–27   *s·* to unite thought more closely to God,
b 325–25   begotten of the beliefs of the flesh and *s·* them,
t 453–22   yet *s·* evil in the name of good.
r 494–20   *s·* to correct the errors of corporeal sense ;
g 502–11   *s·* to suggest the proper reflection of God

service

a 31–32   will think that he doeth God *s·* ; — *John* 16 : 2.
   40–28   It is sad that the phrase *divine s·* has
sp 79–32   Giving does not impoverish us in the *s·* of our
b 325–24   which is your reasonable *s·*."— *Rom.* 12 : 1.
p 399–12   this so-called mind is both the *s·* and message
   436–12   Giving a cup of cold water . . . is a Christian *s·*.
t 455–21   God selects for the highest *s·* one who

servitude

f 225–23   Legally to abolish unpaid *s·* in the
   226–22   wearing out years of *s·* to an unreal master

sessions

an 101–10   which tested during several *s·* the phenomena

set

pref xi–21   To *s·* at liberty them that are— *Luke* 4 : 18.
a 19–14   although his teaching *s·* households at variance,
   20–30   the race that is *s·* before us ;"— *Heb.* 12 : 1.
   44– 8   His three days' work in the sepulchre *s·* the
s 108–32   *s·* my thoughts to work in new channels,
   126–22   I have *s·* forth C. S. and its application to
   137–17   his reply *s·* forth a great fact :
   141– 8   to *s·* aside even the most cherished beliefs
ph 178– 4   it is *s·* down as a poison by mortal mind.
f 210– 6   are *s·* forth in Jesus' demonstrations,
   211–20   children's teeth are *s·* on edge."— *Ezek.* 18 : 2.
   222–30   and eat what is *s·* before you,
   247– 8   retained his full *s·* of upper and lower teeth
b 326– 9   and *s·* his whole affections on spiritual things,
o 345– 8   When . . . His absoluteness is *s·* forth,
   354–17   who thereunto have *s·* their seals.
p 367–20   A city that is *s·* on an hill— *Matt.* 5 : 14.
   382–32   Mortal mind needed to be *s·* right.
   434– 1   can open wide those prison doors and *s·* the
r 472– 6   God has *s·* his signet upon Science,
   493– 3   the sun appears to rise and *s·*,
k 499– *   *I have s· before thee an open door,*— *Rev.* 3 : 8.
g 511– 7   And God *s·* them in the firmament— *Gen.* 1 : 17.
   521–26   a material view of creation, is to be *s·* forth.
   521–30   if veritable, would *s·* aside the omnipotence of
   542–16   *s·* a mark upon Cain, lest any— *Gen.* 4 : 15.
   555–24   and *s·* aside the proper conception of Deity,
ap 558– 7   he *s·* his right foot upon the sea,— *Rev.* 10 : 2.
   568–10   first the true method of creation is *s·* forth
gl 579– *   *I have s· before thee an open door,*— *Rev.* 3 : 8.

sets

sp 83–18   belief that . . . Spirit *s·* aside these laws,
   90–25   *s·* man free to master the infinite idea.
s 114–27   and *s·* free the imprisoned thought.
c 260–14   *s·* mortals at work to discover what
r 495–13   *s·* the captive free physically and morally.
g 542– 8   and *s·* upon error the mark of the beast.
   554–19   infinite Mind *s·* at naught such a mistaken

settle

b 288– 7   will *s·* all questions through faith in

settles

o 361– 4   cancels the disagreement, and *s·* the question.
p 433–15   a look of despair and death *s·* upon it.

seven

pref xii– 6   During *s·* years over four thousand students
p 421–32   of eight multiplied by five, and of *s·* by ten,
g 520–10   The numerals of infinity, called *s· days*,
ap 559–13   It arouses the "*s·* thunders"— *Rev.* 10 : 3.
   562–30   having *s·* heads and ten horns,— *Rev.* 12 : 3.
   562–31   and *s·* crowns upon his heads.— *Rev.* 12 : 3.
   572–15   open the *s·* seals of error with Truth,
   574– 6   one of the *s·* angels which had— *Rev.* 21 : 9.
   574– 7   the *s·* vials full of the *s·* last— *Rev.* 21 : 9.
   574–18   the *s·* angelic vials full of *s·* plagues,

sevenfold

g 542–16   vengeance shall be taken on him *s·*.— *Gen.* 4 : 15

seventeen

ph 194–24   at the age of *s·* Kaspar was still a

seventh

a 21–30   he turns east on the *s·*,
p 362– 1   in the *s·* chapter of Luke's Gospel
g 519–22   on the *s·* day God ended His work— *Gen.* 2 : 2
   519–23   and He rested on the *s·* day— *Gen.* 2 : 2.

seventy

a 27–22   Jesus sent forth *s·* students at one time,
   49– 7   Where were the *s·* whom Jesus sent forth?
o 342–13   He bade the *s·* disciples, as well as the twelve,

seventy-four

f 245–13   saw her when she was *s·*,
   245–28   proves it possible to be young at *s·* ;

several

an 101–10   which tested during *s·* sessions the phenomen
ph 193– 6   said the bone was carious for *s·* inches.
g 556–32   plunged . . . into the water for *s·* minutes,

severance

m 57–26   this *s·* of fleshly ties serves to
s 122–24   To material sense, the *s·* of the jugular vein

severe

ph 175–23   was not so *s·* upon the gastric juices.
f 251– 5   neither should a fever become more *s·*
p 407– 9   Every hour of delay makes the struggle more *s·*
r 488– 4   When, . . . you are able to banish a *s·* malady

severed

b 295– 1   The belief that a *s·* limb is aching

severely

f 238–21   because we suffer *s·* from error.
t 443– 9   at times *s·* condemned by some

severest

s 162–19   in their *s·* forms.
p 387–18   That man does not pay the *s·* penalty who

sex

g 551–21   peculiarities of ancestry, belonging to either *s·*

sexes

m 57–10   Both *s·* should be loving, pure, tender, and
   63–13   differences between the rights of the two *s·*.
   63–20   property, and parental claims of the two *s·*.
   65–10   The union of the *s·* suffers fearful discord.
b 340–28   equalizes the *s·* ; annuls the curse on man,
g 532– 2   the union of the two *s·*

sexual

g 549– 3   takes place apart from *s·* conditions.

sexuality

g 508–19   The word is not confined to *s·*,

shackles

f 225– 2   What is it that binds man with iron *s·*
c 256– 1   Progress takes off human *s·*.

shade

ap 566–22   In *s·* and storm the frequent night,

shadow

and shelter
g 516–16   The great rock gives *s·* and shelter.
beneath the
a 36–14   in silent woe beneath the *s·* of his cross.
of death
ap 578–10   valley of the *s·* of death,— *Psal.* 23 : 4.
gl 596–21   valley of the *s·* of death,— *Psal.* 23 : 4.
within the
s 108–20   within the *s·* of the death-valley,

f 233–16   Already the *s·* of His right hand
c 257– 5   If . . . then Spirit, matter's unlikeness, must
         be *s·* ;
   257– 5   and *s·* cannot produce substance.
b 299–29   sunshine of Truth, will melt away the *s·*
   331– 3   no more . . . than substance is in its *s·*.
o 351–29   To them . . . Spirit was *s·*.
t 460–31   the *s·* of old errors was no longer cast upon

shadows
  a 32–32 with *s·* fast falling around ;
  s 140–20 are but types and *s·* of true worship.
  b 310–11 Day may decline and *s·* fall,
shake
  s 130–20 Laboring long to *s·* the adult's faith in matter
shaken
  o 269–28 reeds *s·* by the wind, not houses built on the
  297–28 Mortal testimony can be *s·*.
Shakespeare
  m 66– 1 Thou art right, immortal *S·*,
Shakespeare's
  f 244–29 Even *S·* poetry pictures age as infancy,
shallow
  s 110–20 This book may be distorted by *s·* criticism
  c 257–11 This belief is *s·* pantheism.
shallows
  c 262–10 diving into the *s·* of mortal belief.
sham
  g 555–21 and call this *s·* unity *man,*
shame
  a 36–10 Jesus endured the *s·*,
  52–16 in order to unite in putting to *s·* and death
  ph 188–10 from *s·* and woe to their final punishment.
  g 532–18 produced the immediate fruits of fear and *s·*.
  533– 1 was one of nakedness and *s·*.
shape
  f 246–29 Let us then *s·* our views of existence
  p 400–14 before it has taken tangible *s·* in
shaped
  sp 96–26 *s·* his course in accordance with divine Science
  g 525–14 and God *s·* man after His mind ;
  525–15 after God's mind *s·* He him ;
  525–15 and He *s·* them male and female.
shapen
  g 540–29 and "*s·* in iniquity ;"— *Psal.* 51 : 5.
shapes
  t 458–26 The Christian Scientist wisely *s·* his course,
share
  a 54–25 and to *s·* the glory of eternal life.
  m 57–21 but requires all mankind to *s·* it.
  ap 559–28 because you must *s·* the hemlock cup
shared
  a 33–28 Have you *s·* the blood of the New Covenant,
  53–32 Had he *s·* the sinful beliefs of others,
shares
  s 157– 6 never *s·* its rights with inanimate matter.
  ph 194– 1 *s·* not its strength with matter
sharp
  pr 3–29 *s·* censure our Master pronounces on hypocrites.
  sp 85–27 His thrusts at materialism were *s·*, but needed.
  87–21 of the corals, of its *s·* reefs, of the tall ships
  b 293–17 Electricity is the *s·* surplus of materiality
  322–26 The *s·* experiences of belief in the
  p 374–14 This mortal blindness and its *s·* consequences
  407– 1 but there is a very *s·* remembrance of it,
  t 459–17 is like putting a *s·* knife into the hands of
sharper
  a 50–29 *s·* than the thorns which pierced his flesh.
shearers
  a 50– 2 as a sheep before her *s·* is dumb,— *Isa.* 53 : 7.
shed
  a 25– 7 *s·* upon "the accursed tree,"— *see Gal.* 3 : 13.
  30–16 by man shall his blood be *s·*."— *Gen.* 9 : 6.
  p 379–14 when not a drop of his blood was *s·*.
sheddeth
  a 30–15 "Whoso *s·* man's blood,— *Gen.* 9 : 6.
sheep
  a 50– 1 as a *s·* before her shearers is dumb,— *Isa.* 53 : 7.
  t 464–27 and careth not for the *s·*."— *John* 10 : 13.
  gl 594–12 definition of
sheep's
  an 104– 6 and belied by wolves in *s·* clothing.
  ap 567–29 These wolves in *s·* clothing are detected
sheer
  s 144–18 but is *s·* animal magnetism.
Shekinah
  a 41– 2 into the *S·* into which Jesus has passed
shells
  g 552–18 They must peck open their *s·* with C. S.,
shelter
  g 516–16 The great rock gives shadow and *s·*.
Shem
  gl 594–14 definition of
shepherd
  pref vii– 2 The wakeful *s·* beholds the first
  ap 578– 5 [DIVINE LOVE] is my *s·* ;— *Psal.* 23 : 1.

shepherd-boy
  b 268–11 like the *s·* with his sling,
sheriff
  p 436–18 But they brought with them Fear, the *s·*,
  441–23 executed at the hands of our *s·*, Progress.
shield
  p 408– 9 cannot, in a scientific diagnosis, *s·* the
  418– 1 to *s·* them from the baneful effects of
  t 457–14 In the legend of the *s·*, which led to a quarrel
shift
  ph 168– 1 a poor *s·* for the weak and worldly,
shifts
  g 513–10 and the scene *s·* into light.
shine
  pref vii–10 and *s·* the guiding star of being.
  f 252–29 and *s·* with the resplendency of
  g 518–20 immortality, and goodness, which *s·* through
  546–24 like rays of light, *s·* in the darkness,
shines
  g 518–21 as the blossom *s·* through the bud.
  ap 562–20 *s·* "unto the perfect day"— *Prov.* 4 : 18.
shineth
  b 325–31 like the light, "*s·* in darkness,— *John* 1 : 5.
shining
  f 247–29 *s·* resplendent and eternal over age and decay
  o 347–21 and is the light *s·* in darkness,
  g 510–29 and this one *s·* by its own light
  ap 566–24 A burning and a *s·* light !
ships
  sp 87–21 the tall *s·* that float on its bosom,
shipwreck
  t 451–10 will either make *s·* of their faith or
shock
  a 53–19 the *s·* so often produced by the truth,
  53–20 this *s·* arises from the great distance between
  p 421– 9 make known . . . your motive for this *s·*,
shocked
  ap 570– 6 *s·* into another extreme mortal mood,
shockingly
  o 360– 9 replies : . . . they are not so *s·* transcendental.
shone
  pref vii– 4 So *s·* the pale star to the prophet-shepherds ;
shook
  p 442– 9 We noticed, as he *s·* hands with his counsel,
shore
  a 34–32 joyful meeting on the *s·* of the Galilean Sea !
  35– 6 Discerning Christ, Truth, anew on the *s·* of
  f 203–29 should disappear on the *s·* of time ;
shores
  sp 90– 3 loaves and fishes multiplied on the *s·* of
shorn
  a 50–17 that hour would be *s·* of its mighty blessing
  s 124– 4 a Samson *s·* of his strength.
short
  f 249–29 It falls *s·* of the skies, but
  252–22 says : . . . my *s·* span of life one gala day.
  o 352–26 In *s·*, children should be told not to
  p 363–15 Jesus rebuked them with a *s·* story or parable.
  t 448–29 nothing *s·* of right-doing has any claim to
  ap 568–23 that he hath but a *s·* time.— *Rev.* 12 : 12.
  569–24 for the devil knoweth his time is *s·*.
  572–13 nothing *s·* of this divine Principle, understood
shortened
  s 162–20 *s·* limbs have been elongated,
shorter
  sp 77–17 will be of longer or *s·* duration
  g 530– 2 increases in falsehood and his days become *s·*.
shortest
  p 387–15 If printers and authors have the *s·* span of
shortly
  p 432–21 testifies : . . . I was called for, *s·* after the
shoulders
  p 363– 6 which hung loosely about her *s·*,
show
  pref ix–29 These efforts *s·* . . . the degrees by which
  a 18– 8 to *s·* them how to do theirs,
  26–20 to *s·* the learner the way by practice as well as
  31–23 *s·* the Lord's death till he come."— *I Cor.* 11 : 26.
  37– 1 Does not Science *s·* that sin brings suffering
  40–18 not otherwise could he *s·* us the way
  42–25 Afterwards he would *s·* it to them unchanged.
  m 65–14 *s·* themselves in the materialism and
  sp 81– 3 as there is to the sick that matter
  an 103–10 does not scientifically *s·* itself in a knowledge
  s 108– 7 human experiences *s·* the falsity of
  111–24 incidents which *s·* that C. S. meets a
  132– 4 "Go and *s·* John again those— *Matt.* 11 : 4.
  139–20 *s·* how a mortal and material sense stole into

show
ph 169–10	to *s·* that disease has a mental, mortal origin,
f 210– 7	set forth in Jesus' demonstrations, which *s·*
239–21	and *s·* what we are winning.
242–30	The finger-posts of divine Science *s·* the way
b 293–26	they *s·* the self-destruction of error
294–21	*s·* the pleasures and pains of matter to be myths,
313–30	To *s·* that the substance of himself was Spirit
316– 9	to *s·* that Truth is made manifest by its effects
o 343– 4	"S· me thy faith without thy — *Jas.* 2 : 18.
343– 5	I will *s·* thee my faith by my — *Jas.* 2 : 18.
348–20	will *s·* itself in forms of sin, sickness, and
p 364–25	do they *s·* their regard for Truth, or Christ,
374–14	*s·* our need of divine metaphysics.
375–23	*s·* mortal mind that muscles have no power
375–26	Consumptive patients always *s·* great hopeful-ness
398– 7	These instances *s·* the concessions which
404–23	*s·* him that sin confers no pleasure,
417–29	*S·* them how mortal mind seems to induce
418– 2	*S·* them that the conquest over sickness,
425– 8	*S·* that it is not inherited ;
438–21	while the facts in the case *s·* that this fur
443– 4	to *s·* them that under ordinary circumstances
t 451–31	*S·* your student that mental malpractice
r 487–25	"S· me thy faith without thy — *Jas.* 2 : 18.
487–26	I will *s·* thee my faith by my — *Jas.* 2 : 18.
493– 9	Will you explain sickness and *s·* how
g 552–25	blending tints of leaf and flower *s·* the
554–27	All these sayings were to *s·* that
ap 562–18	which *s·* the workings of the spiritual idea
567–24	*s·* the dragon to be nothingness,
574– 8	I will *s·* thee the bride, — *Rev.* 21 : 9.
gl 596–16	they *s·* the spiritual inspiration of Love

showed
s 138–11	He *s·* that diseases were cast out
147–10	*s·* that Truth had lost none of its
ph 193– 6	He even *s·* me the probe,
f 206–16	as Jesus *s·* with the loaves and the fishes,
236–17	the pattern *s·* to thee — *Heb.* 8 : 5.
b 292–31	In his resurrection and ascension, Jesus *s·*
314–10	*s·* plainly that their material views were
321–31	Jesus, who *s·* his students the power of Mind
gl 579–13	and *s·* the life-preserving power of

showing
pr 6–27	came teaching and *s·* men how to destroy sin,
7– 4	*s·* the necessity for such forcible utterance,
a 30–23	*s·* the difference between the offspring of Soul
34– 3	instead of *s·*, by casting out error
s 113–13	*s·* mathematically their exact relation
p 363–32	mere fact that she was *s·* her affection
376–25	*s·* that it is impossible for matter to suffer,
377–13	*s·* mortal mind to be the producer of
382–27	*s·* me the nothingness of the so-called
410–11	*s·* that Truth is the actual life of man ;
421– 9	*s·* him that it was to facilitate recovery.
r 476–31	*s·* that man in God's image is unfallen
g 501– 8	*s·* the poverty of mortal existence,
ap 563– 6	*s·* its horns in the many inventions of evil.
gl 581–11	Science *s·* that the spiritual realities
589–20	*s·* the immortality and supremacy of Truth ;

shown
s 137–25	Love hath *s·* thee the way of Life !
b 321–13	Matter was *s·* to be a belief only.
o 354–19	Inconsistency is *s·* by words without deeds,
g 535–14	the results of sin as *s·* in sickness and
549– 6	*s·* by divine metaphysics to be a mistake,
ap 561–16	*s·* in the man Jesus,

shows
pref viii–14	*s·* that Christian healing confers the
a 32–11	The cup *s·* forth his bitter experience,
53–19	Science *s·* the cause of the shock
m 59–29	the frequency of divorce *s·* that the
sp 88–27	*s·* the possibilities derived from divine Mind,
89– 2	*s·* that the beliefs of mortal mind are loosed.
89–30	*s·* that the belief of life in matter was
90–19	This *s·* the possibilities of thought.
90–22	*s·* what mortal mentality and knowledge are.
s 111–17	*s·* what this inverted image is meant to
114–25	*s·* the scientific relation of man to God,
114–29	*s·* that what is termed *matter* is but the
120–18	*s·* it to be impossible for aught but Mind to
121–22	*s·* appearances often to be erroneous,
123–11	*s·* conclusively how it is that matter seems
ph 182– 3	*s·* your position as a Christian Scientist.
196–12	*s·* that here the word *soul* means a
f 203– 5	*s·* that matter can neither heal
209–32	*s·* the superiority of faith by works
211–17	*s·* the nature of all so-called material cause
225–15	*s·* human power to be proportionate to its
238–12	To fall away from Truth . . . *s·* that
242–10	Christ in divine Science *s·* us this way.
c 262– 4	*s·* the paramount necessity of meeting them.
b 272–13	Jesus' parable of "the sower" *s·* — *Mark* 4 : 14.
273–29	Science *s·* that material, conflicting

shows
b 275– 3	This *s·* that matter did not originate in God,
275–21	*s·* clearly that all is Mind, and that Mind is
289–18	*s·* that what appears to the senses to be death
309–24	The Science of being *s·* it to be impossible
315–27	The history of Jesus *s·* him to have been
p 383–19	This *s·* that the mind must be clean
392–20	unless Science *s·* you otherwise.
394–31	This *s·* that faith is not the healer in such cases.
399–21	this deadness *s·* that so-called mortal life is
416– 2	This process *s·* the pain to be in the mind,
427–20	*s·* that we shall obtain the victory
434–27	*s·* the alleged crime never to have been
r 467–26	*s·* material existence to be enigmatical.
477–14	Divine Science *s·* it to be impossible
488– 4	the cure *s·* that you understand this
489–25	C. S. *s·* them to be false,
490–29	Sleep *s·* material sense as either
491– 4	uncovers material sense, and *s·* it to be a
493– 1	C. S. speedily *s·* Truth to be triumphant.
g 504–12	This also *s·* that there is no place where
533–12	The allegory *s·* that the snake-talker utters the
540– 2	*s·* that Spirit creates neither a wicked nor a
549– 2	for this discovery *s·* that the
ap 567–31	*s·* how the Lamb slays the wolf.
573–10	This *s·* unmistakably that what the
577–32	one word *s·*, though faintly, the light which C. S.
gl 598– 8	This *s·* how our Master had constantly

shrank
g 532–19	error *s·* abashed from the divine voice

shrieks
m 67– 5	*s·* through the tightened shrouds,

shrine
gl 595– 8	TEMPLE. . . . the *s·* of Love ;

shrinking
ph 166– 4	*s·* from its implied responsibility,

shrouds
m 67– 5	shrieks through the tightened *s·*,

shut
pr 14–32	when thou hast *s·* thy door, pray — *Matt.* 6 : 6.
15–15	enter into the closet and *s·* the door.
a 38–31	the material senses *s·* out Truth
s 142–14	they at the same time *s·* the door on progress.
ph 182–23	and forthwith *s·* out the aid of Mind
p 392–30	*s·* out these unhealthy thoughts and fears.
430–10	tends to *s·* out the true sense of Life and
k 499– *	*open door, and no man can s· it.* — *Rev.* 3 : 8.
g 543– 8	the material man is *s·* out from the
ap 575–19	"and the gates of it shall not be *s·* — *Rev.* 21 : 25.
gl 579– *	*open door, and no man can s· it.* — *Rev.* 3 : 8.

shuts
pr 15– 4	the door of which *s·* out sinful sense
sp 90–26	This conviction *s·* the door on death,
s 132–21	blind belief *s·* the door upon it,

shutteth
k 499– *	*openeth, and no man s· ;* — *Rev.* 3 : 7.
499– *	*s·, and no man openeth ;* — *Rev.* 3 : 7.
gl 579– *	*openeth, and no man s· ;* — *Rev.* 3 : 7.
579– *	*s·, and no man openeth ;* — *Rev.* 3 : 7.

shutting
s 108–28	thereby *s·* out the true sense of Spirit.

sick (noun)
affects the
pr 12–16	Prayer to a corporeal God affects the *s·* like a

and sinning
pr 7– 6	he cast out devils and healed the *s·* and sinning.
a 55–16	beneath its wings the *s·* and sinning.
s 117–19	by his power over the *s·* and sinning.
132–22	condemns the cure of the *s·* and sinning
141–13	In healing the *s·* and sinning, Jesus elaborated
b 271–16	by healing the *s·* and sinning,
309–20	divine power which heals the *s·* and sinning,
337–32	heals the *s·* and sinning as no other system can.

and the sinning
a 54–15	Truth, and Love heal the *s·* and the sinning,
sp 95–10	to discern the thought of the *s·* and the sinning
s 136– 5	and heal both the *s·* and the sinning,
138–31	which healed the *s·* and the sinning.
r 473–14	healing the *s·* and the sinning
ap 562–19	by healing the *s·* and the sinning,

are healed
sp 78–29	the *s·* are healed, the sorrowing are comforted,

are terrified
p 366–25	The *s·* are terrified by their sick beliefs,

brings to the
ph 169–24	mortal mind, not matter, which brings to the *s·*

cure of the
s 132–22	and condemns the cure of the *s·* and sinning
b 285–27	and resort to matter . . . for the cure of the *s·*.

effects on the
o 342– 7	the sad effects on the *s·* of denying Truth.

evidenced by the
o 355–30	and evidenced by the *s·* who are cured

sick (noun)

explain to the
p 396–22   At the right time explain to the s· the power

healed the
pr   7– 6   when he cast out devils and healed the s·
a   49– 4   healed the s·, cast out evil,
m   67–21   our Lord and Master healed the s·,
sp   85–18   he discerned disease and healed the s·.
s   134–28   healed the s·, walked on the water.
138–31   theology of Jesus which healed the s·
147–24   Our Master healed the s·,
ph 170–20   Jesus healed the s· and cast out error,
185–22   healed the s·, not only without drugs, but
f 210–12   the Master healed the s·, gave sight to the
b 273–25   Jesus . . . healed the s·, and raised the dead
o 343–27   healed the s· and reformed the sinner
351–15   Christ, Truth, which healed the s·.
r 477– 4   this correct view of man healed the s·.
494–30   cast out devils (evils) and healed the s·.

healer of the
s 138– 8   Life, Truth, and . . . was the healer of the s·

healing the
a   33– 8   healing the s· and casting out error.
35–25   casting out error and healing the s·.
41–15   by casting out error and healing the s·,
43– 1   healing the s·, and raising the dead,
46–12   again seen casting out evil and healing the s·.
sp   97–32   work of casting out error and healing the s·
s 109– 5   is demonstrated by healing the s·
111–27   and its demonstration in healing the s·,
135–29   divine Love casting out error and healing the s·,
136–14   with casting out evils and healing the s·?
141–13   In healing the s· and sinning, Jesus
145–31   The theology of C. S. includes healing the s·.
ph 182– 2   The act of healing the s· through divine Mind
f 210– 8   by his healing the s·, casting out evils,
232–18   by healing the s· and triumphing over death.
b 271–16   demonstrated by healing the s· and sinning.
316–28   prove God's divine power by healing the s·,
324–24   healing the s· and preaching Christianity
332–14   healing the s· and casting out evils,
o 347–17   preaching the gospel to the poor, healing the s·,
p 365– 5   would do much more towards healing the s·
368–19   no . . . can prevent us from healing the s·
369– 9   as demonstrated in healing the s·,
390–26   denying that necessity and healing the s·.
403–23   this is best adapted for healing the s·.
404–26   Healing the s· and reforming the sinner are
t 445–21   divine energy in healing the s·.
455– 5   unsuitable conditions for healing the s·.
r 473–14   healing the s· and the sinning
497–18   demonstrated . . . in healing the s·
ap 562–19   by healing the s· and the sinning,
gl 583– 9   casting out error and healing the s·;
583–19   casting out devils, or error, and healing the s·.

healing to the
pref xii–25   and is joyful to bear . . . healing to the s·,

heals the
pr   1– 2   reforms the sinner and heals the s·
14–29   understanding casts out error and heals the s·,
16–23   and which instantaneously heals the s·.
a   25–15   how this divine Principle heals the s·,
33–24   It blesses its enemies, heals the s·,
sp   98– 6   Christianity which heals the s·
s 120–23   thus Science denies all disease, heals the s·,
135–13   when Truth heals the s·, it casts out evils,
135–15   casts out the evil called disease, it heals the s·.
139– 1   It is his theology . . . which heals the s·
143– 4   Christ casts out evils and heals the s·.
ph 180–28   way to this living Truth, which heals the s·,
f 206–14   prayer, governed by Science . . . heals the s·,
230– 8   which casts out error and heals the s·.
b 275–23   It casts out error and heals the s·.
276– 2   unfolds the power that heals the s·,
282– 2   Truth casts out evils and heals the s·.
309–20   thus losing the divine power which heals the s·
337–32   heals the s· and sinning as no other system can.
o 350–11   Truth casts out error and heals the s·.
354–10   heals the s· and spiritualizes humanity.
355–16   according to the commands of our Master, heals the s·.
p 430–16   in which the plea of C. S. heals the s·.
t 452–27   by which divine Mind heals the s·.
455– 2   heals the s· and the sinner.
r 472– 4   Truth casts out . . . error and heals the s·.
473–30   heals the s· and casts out error,
482–28   heals the s· on the basis of the one Mind
483–18   heals the s·, destroys error, and
ap 570–26   When God heals the s· or the sinning,

heal the
pr   12– 3   A mere request that God will heal the s·
a   28–14   enabled to heal the s· and to triumph over sin.
34–15   take up the cross, heal the s·, cast out evils,
37–31   "Heal the s·!"— Matt. 10: 8.
41–32   cast out evils and heal the s·.
51–31   enabled Jesus to heal the s·, cast out evil,

sick (noun)

heal the
54–15   proof that Life, Truth, and Love heal the s·
an 104–22   by no means the mental qualities which heal the s·.
s 136–10   How did Jesus heal the s·?
137– 2   students saw this power of Truth heal the s·,
138–21   to heal the s· as well as the sinning.
138–29   Heal the s·!— Matt. 10: 8.
158– 3   priests, who besought the gods to heal the s·
ph 167– 1   Should we implore a corporeal God to heal the s·?
179– 5   Science can heal the s·, who are absent
182–17   to those who heal the s· on the basis of Science.
182–23   Mortals entreat the divine Mind to heal the s·,
f 206–11   It can never heal the s·, for it is the
231–11   does heal the s· through the prayer of
243– 7   can heal the s· in every age
b 271– 5   instructed his disciples whereby to heal the s·
322– 1   taught them how to . . . heal the s·
o 342–12   students should cast out evils and heal the s·.
342–14   He bade the seventy disciples, . . . heal the s·
345– 6   cannot . . . work through drugs to heal the s·
345– 9   Christian sermons will heal the s·.
345–18   One who understands C. S. can heal the s·
351– 5   When we lose faith . . . we cannot heal the s·.
354–14   nor offer any proofs that . . . can heal the s·.
365– 9   would heal the s·, and so enable them
p 397–23   To heal the s·, one must be familiar with
418–11   Then, . . . you will heal the s·.
418–25   by the spirit of . . . you will heal the s·.
t 446–27   spiritual light and might which heal the s·.
447–10   heal the s· when called upon for aid,
462– 6   cast out error, heal the s·,
r 482–14   Is it important . . . in order to heal the s·?
494–32   out of themselves and others and heal the s·.
495– 1   God will heal the s· through man,

hope to the
s 152– 7   that it may give hope to the s· and heal them,

instruct the
p 420–10   Instruct the s· that they are not helpless

lay hands on the
a   38–11   they shall lay hands on the s·,— Mark 16: 18.
b 328–25   They shall lay hands on the s·,— Mark 16: 18.
o 359–27   they shall lay hands on the s·,— Mark 16: 18.
p 362– *   they shall lay hands on the s·,— Mark 16: 18.

prayer for the
pr   12– 6   The beneficial effect of such prayer for the s·

recover
pr   12–29   If the s· recover because they pray
s 155– 3   When the s· recover by the use of drugs, it is
p 373–10   the s· recover more rapidly from disease than

recovery of the
pr   12–23   custom of praying for the recovery of the s·
f 218–17   Why pray for the recovery of the s·, if you
p 372–32   will be a hindrance to the recovery of the s·
419– 1   moral question may hinder the recovery of the s·.

save the
pr   12– 1   prayer of faith shall save the s·,"— Jas. 5: 15.

show the
sp   81– 3   as there is to show the s· that matter

treat the
s 151– 2   they sometimes treat the s· as if there was

willing the
s 144–16   Willing the s· to recover is not the

---

s 138–23   the s· are more willing to part with pain than
143– 8   s· are more deplorably lost than the sinning, if
143– 9   if the s· cannot rely on God for help
158–21   with intoxicating prescriptions for the s·,
ph 169–25   But the s· are never really healed except by
181–26   in order to satisfy the s· that you are
185–27   may seem for a time to benefit the s·,
f 226–22   I saw before me the s·, wearing out years of
226–25   The lame, the deaf, the dumb, the blind, the s·,
230–23   According to Holy Writ, the s· are never really
231– 8   If God heals not the s·, they are not healed,
233–28   tests . . . of the effects of truth upon the s·.
235–19   Physicians, whom the s· employ in their
b 323–19   When the s· or the sinning awake to realize their
o 343–10   The s·, the halt, and the blind look up to C. S.
344–14   misrepresentations, which harm the s·;
358–25   effect Christian Scientists may have on the s·,
358–26   rousing within the s· a belief
p 365– 2   the thorns they plant in the pillow of the s·
366–30   If we would open their prison doors for the s·,
370–28   fails at length to inspire the credulity of the s·,
374– 7   the s· say: "How can my mind cause a disease
394–23   Will you tell the s· that their condition is
394–30   the s· usually have little faith in it till they
394–32   The s· unconsciously argue for suffering,
395–17   Prayers, in which . . . do not benefit the s·.
403– 1   So the s· through their beliefs have induced
414–18   lest you array the s· against their own interests
416–24   The s· know nothing of the mental process

sick (noun)

p 417– 6	Never tell the s· that they have more courage than
417– 8	If you make the s· realize this great truism,
420–24	Tell the s· that they can meet disease fearlessly,
424–26	it is well to be alone with God and the s· when
431– 3	the prisoner watched with the s· every night
t 443–22	If the s· find these . . . unsatisfactory,
447–27	The s· are not healed merely by declaring
458– 6	simultaneously at work on the s·.
463–28	The s· are not healed by inanimate matter
r 495– 9	when he spoke of the s·,

sick (adj.)

pr 6–24	Of a s· woman he said that Satan had bound
sp 86– 7	he was answered by the faith of a s· woman.
s 114– 2	calls s· and sinful humanity mortal mind,
120–13	And is he well if the senses say he is s·?
154–17	is frightened and says, "My child will be s·."
154–26	says to her child: "You look s·,"
161–25	telling the patient that he is s·,
163– 2	afterward letting her loose upon s· people."
163– 5	declared himself "s· of learned quackery."
ph 168–10	When s· (according to belief) you rush after
168–16	man-made systems insist that man becomes s·
174–25	if an individual is s·, why treat the body alone
179–25	so long as you read medical works you will be s·.
199–15	develop their own bodies or make them s·,
f 203– 6	matter can neither heal nor make s·,
206–31	God does not cause man to sin, to be s·, or to
210–26	cannot say, "I suffer, I die, I am s·,
218–15	believing that the body can be s·
219–12	"s·, and the whole heart faint;"— Isa. 1:5.
229–23	If God causes man to be s·, sickness must be
229–27	If . . . produces sickness, it is right to be s·;
253–13	no cause (outside of . . . able to make you s·
c 259–10	thoughts which presented man as fallen, s·
260–20, 21	A s· body is evolved from s· thoughts.
b 270–26	They think sickly thoughts, and so become s·.
270–30	human mind alone suffers, is s·,
289–13	Truth and Truth's idea, never make men s·,
292–11	s·, and dying mortal is not the likeness of
297– 6	Human belief says to mortals, "You are s·!"
o 352–13	and s· in consequence of the fear:
p 366–25	The sick are terrified by their s· beliefs,
371–12	s· humanity sees danger in every direction,
372– 1	Matter cannot be s·, and Mind is immortal.
376–26	impossible for matter . . . to be thirsty or s·.
381– 5	to suffer the illusion that you are s·
391– 9	When the body is supposed to say, "I am s·,"
391–22	If you say, "I am s·," you plead guilty.
393–29	Man is never s·, for Mind is not s·
406–25	no more fear that we shall be s· and
408– 5	nor discovered . . . by many who are s·.
409–10	cannot dictate terms . . . nor say, "I am s·."
417– 3	Give s· people credit for sometimes knowing
417–12	Spirit is God, and therefore cannot be s·;
417–13	what is termed matter cannot be s·;
430–30	prisoner, or patient, watched with a s· friend.
431– 4	When the s· mortal was thirsty,
441–16	refuses to recognize Man as s· or dying,
442–13	Mortal Man, no longer s· and in prison,
t 453–26	you must not tell the patient that he is s·
461–16	If you believe that you are s·, should you say,
461–17	should you say, "I am s·"? No,
461–22	to admit that you are s·, renders your case
ap 570–29	delusion of mortal mind, when it makes them s·
	(see also man)

sick-bed

p 433–27	The prisoner is then remanded to his cell (s·),

sick-chamber

ph 178– 7	infinitesimal minority of opinions in the s·.
g 516–18	glances into the prison-cell, glides into the s·,

sickly

ph 175–20	selfishness, coddling, and s· after-dinner talk.
b 270–25	They think s· thoughts, and so become sick.
o 346– 3	it is not sinful and s· mortal man who
g 554–30	belief that the lower animals are less s· than

sickness

abate

ph 196–24	will help to abate s· and to destroy it.

and care

ph 188–20	s· and care, are traced upon mortals by

and death

f 206–27	Instead of God sending s· and death,
231–26	To hold yourself superior to s· and death
251–19	a belief in the necessity of s· and death,
c 264–22	s· and death were overcome by Jesus,
p 386–22	Thus it is with all sorrow, s·, and death.
430– 9	Belief in s· and death, as certainly as
g 535–15	the results of sin as shown in s· and death.

and disease

ph 179–23	are the promoters of s· and disease.

and error

r 495– 8	Then classify s· and error as our Master did,

sickness

and health

sp 74–22	infancy and manhood, s· and health,
f 211– 4	s· and health, good and evil, life and death;
229–10	s· and health, holiness and unholiness,⌋
246– 3	joy and sorrow, s· and health,

and mortality

b 335–29	Sin, s·, and mortality are the suppositional

and sin

s 142– 1	it will eradicate s· and sin in less time than
146–25	influence of Truth in healing s· and sin.
ph 171–15	healing s· and sin and destroying the
f 210–17	Jesus healed s· and sin by one and the same
230– 4	But if s· and sin are illusions,
o 347–28	will behold the nothingness of s· and sin,
p 368–13	freedom from the bondage of s· and sin
380– 4	S· and sin fall by their own weight.
391– 4	mortal thought and its beliefs in s· and sin.
426–32	matter, death, disease, s·, and sin
r 473–11	the ideal Truth, that comes to heal s· and sin

associates

p 377–32	associates s· with certain circumstances

banish

p 381–27	Let us banish s· as an outlaw, and abide by

belief in

(see **belief**)

belief of

f 229–30	which causes the belief of s·.

calm in

p 393–32	It is well to be calm in s·;

cast out

s 138–22	easier for Christianity to cast out s· than sin,

caused the

an 104–25	and a belief originally caused the s·,

conquest over

p 418– 2	the conquest over s·, as well as over sin,

disease, and death

c 260–21	S·, disease, and death proceed from fear.

efficient in

f 233–31	Why should truth not be efficient in s·,

every sort of

p 408– 1	Every sort of s· is error,

explain

r 493– 9	explain s· and show how it is to be healed?

fear of

p 412– 4	to advance and destroy the human fear of s·.

foundation of all

p 411–20	foundation of all s· is fear, ignorance, or sin.

fountain of

p 391–32	Fear is the fountain of s·,

has been combated

pref viii–16	S· has been combated for centuries by doctors

has not checked

ph 165–13	Obedience to . . . has not checked s·.

healing

s 146–25	influence of Truth in healing s·
ph 171–15	by healing s· and sin
f 230–22	put that law under his feet by healing s·?
241–20	healing s· and destroying sin.
b 316–11	healing s· and destroying sin.
r 473–22	healing s·, sin, and death,

heals

pr 16– 4	Such prayer heals s·, and must destroy sin
an 104–23	If he heals s· through a belief,
f 236–10	Mind heals s· as well as sin
b 315–24	heals s·, and overcomes death.
t 446– 6	perusal of the author's publications heals s·.

heals also

s 135–11	same power which heals sin heals also s·.

health and in

t 462–31	government of the body both in health and in s·,

he healed

ph 168–21	He healed s· in defiance of what is called

illusion of

b 297– 8	illusion of s·, to be instructed out of itself
r 495–14	When the illusion of s· or sin tempts you,

images of

p 396–26	efface the images of s· from

induces

p 374–21	Such a state of mind induces s·.

is a belief

r 493–18	S· is a belief, which must be annihilated

is a dream

p 417–20	To the C. S. healer, s· is a dream

is formed

p 396–31	understand that s· is formed by the human

is not real

p 394– 1	to understand that s· is not real

less

pref viii–19	Is there less s· because of these practitioners?
s 163–12	there would be less s· and less mortality."

no trials for

p 441–33	We have no trials for s· before the tribunal of

or of sin

o 353– 9	either in the form of s· or of sin?

produces

f 229–26	If the transgression of God's law produces s·,

sickness

reports of
f 218–10 The reports of *s·* may form a coalition with

save from
s 149– 1 Truth could save from *s·* as well as from sin.

seeming
p 368–27 are the source of all seeming *s·*.

sensation of
f 211–13 sensation of *s·* and the impulse to sin

sin and
    (see **sin**)

sin, and death
a 19–13 what would destroy *s·*, sin, and death,
26–26 C. S. destroys *s·*, sin, and death.
s 142– 5 by its power over *s·*, sin, and death;
ph 184– 3 makes no laws to regulate *s·*, sin, and death,
196–15 *S·*, sin, and death are not concomitants of
f 227– 2 Escape from the bondage of *s·*, sin, and death !"
229–16 to bind mortals to *s·*, sin, and death.
243–30 *S·*, sin, and death are not the fruits of Life.
c 257– 8 which ultimates in *s·*, sin, and death ;
b 290–13 error and its effects,— *s·*, sin, and death.
297–32 *S·*, sin, and death are the vague
337–29 Subject *s·*, sin, and death to the rule of
o 356–10 controlled *s·*, sin, and death on the basis of
357–10 the belief that God makes *s·*, sin, and death,
p 384–30 *S·*, sin, and death must at length quail before
393– 9 and can conquer *s·*, sin, and death.
418–14 This mortal dream of *s·*, sin, and death
r 472– 9 *S·*, sin, and death, being inharmonious,
473–22 healing *s·*, sin, and death,
481–20 hypotheses first assume . . . *s·*, sin, and death,
485– 7 betrays mortals into *s·*, sin, and death.

sin, . . . and death
    (see **sin**)

sin, nor death
p 381–17 In infinite Life . . . there is no *s·*, sin, nor death,

sin, . . . nor death
ap 567– 8 there is no error, no sin, *s·*, nor death.

sin or
f 253–21 right endeavors against sin or *s·*,
p 390–24 either of sin or *s·*,
426–18 not saved from sin or *s·* by death,
t 447–16 When sin or *s·* . . . seems true

sin, or death
t 463–22 manifested in forms of *s·*, sin, or death

sin, . . . or death
r 472–27 the only reality of sin, *s·*, or death is the
gl 585–20 before it accepts sin, *s·*, or death ;

sources of
ph 180– 1 are both prolific sources of *s·*.

struggling with
p 394–13 To those struggling with *s·*, such admissions are

subject of
ph 169–13 by attracting the mind to the subject of *s·*,

terms with
p 391–27 Therefore make your own terms with *s·*,

thoughts about
f 237–18 theories or thoughts about *s·*.

treat
t 453–24 You should treat *s·* mentally just as you

victor over
s 137– 6 the victor over *s·*, sin, disease, death,

worse than
p 408– 3 sin is worse than *s·*,

—

a 49–24 to triumph over sin, *s·*, death, and the grave.
s 108–25 opposite of Truth,—called error, sin, *s·*, disease,
115–23 revenge, sin, *s·*, disease, death.
131– 2 *S·* should not seem so real as
148–32 admits God to be the healer of sin but not of *s·*,
ph 166–17 To ignore God as of little use in *s·* is a mistake.
166–21 He can do all things for us in *s·* in health.
182–30 To admit that *s·* is a condition over which God
188–22 *S·* is a growth of error, springing from
f 206–19 Does God send *s·*,
207–23 Sin, *s·*, disease, and death belong not to the
208–31 delineate upon it thoughts of health, not of *s·*.
216–23 and *s·* to be the rule of
224–23 meeting the needs of mortals in *s·* and in health,
229–23 If God causes man to be sick, *s·* must be good,
230– 1 If *s·* is real, it belongs to immortality ;
230–17 God, good, can no more produce *s·* than
230–20 Does a law of God produce *s·*,
239–28 it is discordant and ends in sin, *s·*, death.
251–13 *S·*, as well as sin, is an error
b 297– 7 manifests itself on the body as *s·*.
339–23 *s·* to health, sin to holiness,
o 349–12 God is not the author of *s·*.
359–24 "God is able to raise you up from *s·* ;"
p 378–24 *S·* is not a God-given, nor a
386– 3 not to be accepted in the case of *s·*,
389– 7 the less we are predisposed to *s·*.
390–20 Suffer no claim of sin or of *s·* to grow
390–23 is no more the author of *s·* than He is of sin.

sickness
p 408– 1 *s·* is loss of harmony.
408– 3 *s·* is not . . . discovered to be error
412–24 *s·* is a temporal dream.
418–12 *s·* is no more the reality of being than is sin.
440–23 compel them to enact wicked laws of *s·*
442–20 Christ changes a belief of sin or of *s·* into a
t 447–28 by declaring there is no *s·*,
450–22 *S·* to him is no less a temptation than is sin,
460–14 *S·* is neither imaginary nor unreal,— that is,
460–15 *S·* is more than fancy ;
r 482–26 *S·* is part of the error which Truth casts out.
495– 6 If *s·* is true or the idea of Truth,
495– 7 If . . . you cannot destroy *s·*,
ap 569–16 and fail to strangle . . . sin as well as of *s·* !
gl 588– 2 hatred ; revenge ; sin ; *s·* ; death ;
592– 9 MORTAL MIND. . . . sin ; *s·* ; death.
595– 5 TARES. Mortality ; error ; sin ; *s·* ;

sicknesses
ph 177– 3 relinquish all its errors, *s·*, and sins.

sick-room
p 390–16 and then you will not be confined to a *s·*

side

Adam's
g 533–18 the rib taken from Adam's *s·*

by her
ph 184–29 I sat silently by her *s·* a few moments.

by our
sp 82–14 with the dreamer by our *s·*

diviner
g 548–23 gained the diviner *s·* in C. S.,

of error
f 205–29 tips the beam . . . towards the *s·* of error,

of God
f 201–11 superabundance of being is on the *s·* of God,

of health
ph 168–10 when it ought to be enlisted on the *s·* of health.

of immutable right
t 446–20 victory rests on the *s·* of immutable right.

of invincible truth
t 453– 7 victory rests on the *s·* of invincible truth.

of matter
ph 168– 6 Whatever influence you cast on the *s·* of matter,
181–31 this faith will incline you to the *s·* of matter

of Personal Sense
p 434–25 has been on the *s·* of Personal Sense,

one
sp 96–13 On one *s·* there will be discord and dismay ;
f 238–25 listening only to one *s·* of the case.

on which
f 216–10 On which *s·* are we fighting?

other
sp 96–14 on the other *s·* there will be Science and peace.

right
a 35– 6 and cast their net on the right *s·*.
b 271–27 or to cast them on the right *s·* for Truth,

side by
b 300–19 (to mortal sight) they grow side by *s·* until the

this
a 36–23 this *s·* of the grave

wounded
a 44–16 bind up the wounded *s·* and lacerated feet,

wrong
ph 166– 6 healing effort is made on the wrong *s·*,
p 396–20 weight of opinions on the wrong *s·*,
397– 6 mental influence on the wrong *s·*,

—

s 145–11 victory will be on the patient's *s·* only as
155–20 percentage of power on the *s·* of this Science
g 536–26 the true idea is gained from the immortal *s·*.

sides
m 59– 3 its enduring obligations on both *s·*.
b 307–11 It says : . . . Truth shall change *s·*
t 457–16 both *s·* were beautiful according to their
ap 574–23 the four equal *s·* of which were heaven-bestowed
575–18 The four *s·* of our city are the
575–21 This city is wholly spiritual, as its four *s·*
575–23 mount Zion, on the *s·* of the north,— *Psal.* 48 : 2.

siege
f 216– 9 Spirituality lays open *s·* to materialism.

sieve
sp 72–19 Error is not a convenient *s·* through which

sift
b 269– 6 Jesus' demonstrations *s·* the chaff from the

sifted
ph 171–19 believes that Spirit is *s·* through matter,

sigh
m 57–29 until it ceases to *s·* over the world
g 501–16 that Love for whose rest the weary ones *s·*

sight

and teeth
f 247– 4   I have seen age regain . . . *s·* and teeth.
first
sp 87–14   when really it is first *s·* instead of second,
good in Thy
s 131–22   for so it seemed good in Thy *s·*." — *Luke* 10 : 21.
hearing and
r 489–27   no organic construction can give it hearing and *s·*
lose
f 207–13   Without this lesson, we lose *s·* of the
b 315–17   The likeness of God we lose *s·* of through sin,
316– 5   and lose *s·* of mortal selfhood
337– 4   mortals do lose *s·* of spiritual individuality.
lost
a 49–10   Had they so soon lost *s·* of his mighty works,
s 110–27   But this power was lost *s·* of,
b 314–19   This materialism lost *s·* of the true Jesus ;
material
a 35–18   when he rose out of material *s·*.
mortal
f 214–26   How transient a sense is mortal *s·*,
b 300–19   though (to mortal *s·*) they grow side by side
never loses
f 248– 3   Love never loses *s·* of loveliness.
or sense
f 214–28   But the real *s·* or sense is not lost.
out of
ph 174–24   though out of *s·*.
o 360–11   replies : . . . and keep Soul well out of *s·*.
gl 582–22   physical sense put out of *s·* and hearing ;
pass from our
p 386–31   So, when our friends pass from our *s·*
physical
sp 87–32   or altogether gone from physical *s·*
pitiful
b 327– 8   What a pitiful *s·* is malice,
pleasant to the
g 525–31   every tree that is pleasant to the *s·*, — *Gen.* 2 : 9.
receive their
s 132– 6   the blind receive their *s·* — *Matt.* 11 : 5.
recovering of
pref xi–20   And recovering of *s·* to the blind, — *Luke* 4 : 18.
restores
r 486–10   If death restores *s·*, sound, and strength
return of
f 247– 5   A woman of eighty-five, . . . had a return of *s·*.
second
sp 87–13   The Scotch call such vision "second *s·*,"
sink from
p 415–30   Indeed, the whole frame will sink from *s·*
sound or
sp 84–21   not dependent upon the ear and eye for sound or *s·*
to the blind
ph 183–28   the law which gives *s·* to the blind,
f 210–13   healed the sick, gave *s·* to the blind,
r 487–11   apprehension of this gave *s·* to the blind

ph 194–23   where neither *s·* nor sound could reach him,
r 486–23   S·, hearing, all the spiritual senses of man,
g 526–10   theories of material hearing, *s·*, touch, taste,

sightless
ph 193– 9   Mr. Clark lay with his eyes fixed and *s·*,

sign
pref xi–16   They are the *s·* of Immanuel,
a 49–13   with one *s·* of fidelity?
sp 98– 7   and no other *s·* shall be given.
f 224–17   Of old the cross was truth's central *s·*,
233–18   discern the face of the sky, — the *s·* material,
233–19   much more should ye discern the *s·* mental,
b 321–28   to the voice of the first *s·*, — *Exod.* 4 : 8.
321–29   the voice of the latter *s·*." — *Exod.* 4 : 8.
p 364–15   a special *s·* of Oriental courtesy.

signal
c 261–17   a *s·* which made him as oblivious of
g 553–22   the *s·* for the appearance of its method

signet
r 472– 6   God has set his *s·* upon Science,
494–28   eternal and real evidence, bearing Truth's *s·*,
gl 593–23   SEAL. The *s·* of error revealed by Truth.

significance
s 117– 8   C. S. attaches no physical nature and *s·* to the
118–13   In their spiritual *s·*, Science, Theology,
131– 9   and the *s·* of the Scripture,
134– 7   the word *martyr* was narrowed in its *s·*
r 481–16   This is the *s·* of the Scripture concerning this
488– 9   they have more the *s·* of faith,
gl 598– 9   to employ words of material *s·*

significant
g 538–13   *s·* of eternal reality or being.
538–16   The testimony of the serpent is *s·* of the
ap 571–25   In *s·* figures he depicts the thoughts

signification
a 32–24   in its spiritual *s·*, it was natural and beautiful.
ph 179– 1   the understanding of C. S. in its proper *s·*
f 241–14   Take away the spiritual *s·* of Scripture, and
p 391–17   Justice is the moral *s·* of law.
r 469–25   We lose the high *s·* of omnipotence, when
482– 9   and you will have the scientific *s·*.
g 545–27   Scripture, which is so glorious in its spiritual *s·*
gl 590–19   Its higher *s·* is Supreme Ruler.

significations
g 502–15   crude forms . . . take on higher symbols and *s·*.

signifies
s 118– 2   spiritual leaven *s·* the Science of Christ
f 229– 8   Mind *s·* God, — infinity,
241–28   *s·* that the pure in heart see God
b 271–11   the word rendered *disciple s·* student ;
333–14   but Christ Jesus better *s·* the Godlike.
340–18   it *s·* that man shall have no other
r 466–20   Soul or Spirit *s·* Deity and nothing else.

signify
m 64–17   Marriage should *s·* a union of hearts.
g 502–25   word *beginning* is employed to *s·* the *only*,

signifying
b 338–13   *s·* the *red color of the ground, dust*,
r 466– 2   is adopted from the Latin adjective *s· all.*
g 517– 5   two Greek words, *s· man* and *form*,

signs

and for seasons
g 509–11   let them be for *s·*, and for seasons, — *Gen.* 1 : 14
and wonders
s 139– 8   Christian era was ushered in with *s·* and wonders.
150–13   Now, as then, *s·* and wonders are wrought
characteristic
s 152–32   the general symptoms, the characteristic *s·*,
following
pr 10–11   and "with *s·* following." — *Mark* 16 : 20.
s 110–29   with "*s·* following." — *Mark* 16 : 20.
117–12   attained through "*s·* following." — *Mark* 16 : 20
mental
ph 169– 5   I have seen the mental *s·*, assuring me
of Christ's coming
o 347–14   would behold the *s·* of Christ's coming.
of these times
sp 98– 5   in the mental horizon the *s·* of these times,
of the times
sp 85–22   not discern the *s·* of the times?" — *Matt.* 16 : 3
g 510– 1   not discern the *s·* of the times?" — *Matt.* 16 : 3
questioned the
s 133– 1   questioned the *s·* of the Messianic appearing,
such
p 413–26   constantly directing the mind to such *s·*,
these
a 38–10   "These *s·* shall follow them — *Mark* 16 : 17.
38–13   he did not say, "These *s·* shall follow *you*,"
52–28   "These *s·* shall follow them — *Mark* 16 : 17.
s 150–14   but these *s·* are only to demonstrate its
b 328–22   "These *s·* shall follow them — *Mark* 16 : 17.
o 359–26   these *s·* shall follow them — *Mark* 16 : 17.
p 362– *   *these s· shall follow them* — *Mark* 16 : 17.
unmistakable
ph 188–21   traced upon mortals by unmistakable *s·*.
unquestionable
f 232–30   unquestionable *s·* of the burial of error

silence
pr 15–16   close the lips and *s·* the material senses.
a 29–21   put to *s·* material law
m 67–26   does not put to *s·* the labor of centuries.
sp 81–20   *s·* the tones of music, give to the worms the
ph 195– 5   Outside of dismal darkness and cold *s·*
b 318–12   We must *s·* this lie of material sense
p 417–16   When you *s·* the witness against your plea,
441– 7   but be enjoined to keep perpetual *s·*,
r 495–23   and *s·* discord with harmony.

silenced
sp 97–25   until its inarticulate sound is forever *s·*
s 146–18   and his Science, the curative agent of God, is *s·*.

silences
s 124–13   finite sense . . . which immortal Spirit *s·*
b 298– 5   so false belief *s·* for a while the voice of
328– 2   *s·* the material or corporeal.
t 445–19   C. S. *s·* human will,

silent
pr 4–28   *s·* prayer, watchfulness, and devout obedience
15–11   Lips must be mute and materialism *s·*,
a 33– 3   His followers, sorrowful and *s·*,
36–14   in *s·* woe beneath the shadow of his cross.
48–20   great demonstrator of Truth and Love was *s·*
sp 87–29   Memory may reproduce voices long ago *s·*.
89–21   God, is heard when the senses are *s·*.
p 367–25   through *s·* utterances and divine anointing
431– 1   testifies . . . I was told that I must remain *s·*
438–13   Personal Sense, by this time *s·*,

silently
- pr 13–17   If we cherish the desire honestly and s·
- a 35–13   s· to commune with the divine Principle, Love.
- ph 184–29   I sat s· by her side a few moments.
- p 376–22   by both s· and audibly arguing
- 411– 4   If the student s· called the disease by name,
- 411–28   S· reassure them as to their exemption
- 412– 4   Mentally and s· plead the case
- 412–29   s· or audibly on the aforesaid basis of C. S.
- g 516–14   The grass beneath our feet s· exclaims,

silly
- m 68–22   to hatch their s· innuendos and lies,
- an 103–27   flimsy and gaudy pretensions, like s· moths,

silver
- a 47–12   The traitor's price was thirty pieces of s·

silvern
- t 457–18   no good aspect, either s· or golden.

similar
- s 122–22   Experience is full of instances of s· illusions,
- p 371– 5   s· to that produced on children by telling

similarly
- b 282–15   S·, matter has no place in Spirit,
- p 422–23   cases of bone-disease, both s· produced

similitude
- g 525–11   in the Hebrew, *image, s·* ;

similitudes
- s 117–15   taught spirituality by s· and parables.

Simon (the disciple)
- s 137–16   S· replied for his brethren,
- p 362– 4   though he was quite unlike S· the disciple.

Simon Bar-jona
- s 137–22   "Blessed art thou, S· B· :— *Matt.* 16 : 17.
- 137–27   his common names, S· B·, or son of Jona ;

Simon (the Pharisee)
- p 362– 3   guest of a certain Pharisee, by name S·,
- 363–19   the Master's question to S· the Pharisee ;
- 363–19   S· replied, "He to whom he forgave— *Luke* 7 : 43.
- 364–18   as S· sought the Saviour,
- 364–20   Jesus told S· that such seekers as he
- 364–22   If Christian Scientists are like S·,

simple
- sp 75– 1   This s· truth lays bare the mistaken assumption
- s 121–23   the s· rule that the greater controls the lesser.
- 147–16   a s· perusal of this book.
- ph 197–21   We are told that the s· food our forefathers ate
- f 236–26   and learn more readily to love the s· verities
- b 321–24   restored his hand . . . by the same s· process.
- o 342– 4   "making wise the s·."— *Psal.* 19 : 7.
- p 411–30   Watch the result of this s· rule of C. S.,
- 418–21   this s· rule of Truth, which governs all reality.
- 429– 5   with the more s· demonstrations of control,
- t 459–25   C. S. seems abstract, but the process is s·
- r 474–11   *marvel* is the s· meaning of the Greek word
- g 547– 1   A s· statement of C. S., if demonstrated by
- 549–18   look upon the s· ovum as the germ,
- ap 570–14   s· seekers for Truth,
- 572– 7   the most s· and profound counsel of the

simplest
- p 413– 6   to meet the s· needs of the babe
- g 551–19   composed of the s· material elements,

simply
- pr 2–13   does not grant them s· on the ground of
- 4–17   S· asking that we may love God
- 9–14   we shall never meet this great duty s· by
- a 36– 3   s· through translation into another sphere.
- sp 71– 3   s· a belief, an illusion of material sense.
- s 152–15   s· by introducing a thermometer into the
- 153–17   The boil s· manifests, through inflammation
- ph 184– 1   are s· laws of mortal belief.
- b 274–18   s· the manifested beliefs of mortal mind,
- 312– 8   The senses regard a corpse, . . . s· as matter.
- p 375–30   s· because it is a stage of fear so excessive
- 390– 5   s· because, . . . there is seeming discord.
- 398–12   he s· said, "Damsel, I say unto— *Mark* 5 : 41.
- t 452–24   s· by repeating the author's words,
- g 508–17   *Gender* means s· *kind* or *sort*,
- 554–28   and is s· a falsity and illusion.

simulate
- sp 71–17   which s· mind, life, and intelligence.
- b 281–25   out of which error would s· creation

simulated
- p 376–15   and s· a corporeal sense of life.

simulates
- sp 97– 5   In reality, the more closely error s· truth
- b 287– 4   error, which s· the creations of Truth.
- g 528–20   error now s· the work of Truth,

simulating
- g 514– 1   could not by s· deific power invert the

simultaneous
- t 449–25   only to separate through s· repulsion.

simultaneously
- t 458– 6   s· at work on the sick.

sin (*see also* **sin's**)

above
- c 266–30   He is above s· or frailty.

all
- a 30–20   error and all s·, sickness, and death,
- ph 171–29   the procuring cause of all s· and
- b 311– 9   All s· is of the flesh.
- 323–26   takes away all s· and the delusion that there are
- 339– 6   and involve the final destruction of all s·?
- p 407–29   All s· is insanity in different degrees.
- ap 568–26   the mighty conquest over all s·?
- 569–27   periods of torture it may take to remove all s·,

and death
- pr 16– 5   heals sickness, and must destroy s· and death.
- a 19–10   the law of matter, s·, and death
- 27–18   Life as never mingling with s· and death.
- f 242–19   and is the law of s· and death.
- 243– 8   and triumph over s· and death.
- 244–12   free from the law of s· and death."— *Rom.* 8 : 2.
- 253–28   belief in s· and death is destroyed by the
- b 276–18   ceases to be any opportunity for s· and death.
- 296–23   The knowledge . . . leads to s· and death.
- 310–15   reveals Soul as God, untouched by s· and death,
- 318–14   brought the belief of s· and death
- 319–18   s·, and death will disappear when it
- p 422–20   Thus C. S., . . . destroys s· and death.
- 428–26   we must master s· and death.
- r 497–19   and overcoming s· and death.
- g 525–27   the Scriptural record of s· and death favors the
- 552–23   From . . . flows no remedy for sorrow, s·, and death,

and disease
- pref xi–11   before which s· and disease lose their reality
- a 25–22   demonstrating his control over s· and disease,
- m 69– 5   only as they lose the sense of s· and disease.
- ph 171–28   the procuring cause of all s· and disease.
- f 234–25   S· and disease must be thought before
- o 355– 4   scientific methods of dealing with s· and disease
- 355– 9   As for s· and disease, C. S. says,
- p 366–28   calm in the presence of both s· and disease,
- 400– 8   of his goods,— namely, of s· and disease.

and error
- b 290–23   s· and error which possess us at the instant of

and evil
- b 315– 8   He knew . . . that matter, s·, and evil were not

and mortality
- an 103– 7   escape from s· and mortality,
- c 265– 8   in order that s· and mortality may be put off.
- b 281–21   s· and mortality have neither Principle nor
- 281–23   s· and mortality are without actual origin
- 311–28   Matter, s·, and mortality lose all supposed

and pardon
- f 251–19   sickness and death, s· and pardon,

and sense
- g 530–22   saying, . . . that s· and sense are more pleasant
- gl 583– 7   who, having wrestled with error, s·, and sense,

and sensuality
- sp 82–31   In a world of s· and sensuality

and sickness
- f 218–12   What renders both s· and sickness difficult of
- 233–20   compass the destruction of s· and sickness
- 234–20   and empty it of s· and sickness,
- 234–20   or s· and sickness will never cease.
- 239– 1   by which s· and sickness are destroyed.
- b 314–30   to save them from s· and sickness,
- o 347–29   s· and sickness will disappear from
- p 388–24   s· and sickness are not qualities of Soul,
- 395–10   The same Principle cures both s· and sickness.
- 401–18   brings s· and sickness to the surface,
- 406– 3   S· and sickness . . . healed by the same Principle.
- 406–13   S· and sickness will abate and seem less real
- t 458–30   radically saved from s· and sickness.
- 461–23   Both s· and sickness are error,

and sorrow
- f 215–19   So s· and sorrow, disease and death, are the

and suffering
- a 23–10   s· and suffering will fall at the feet of
- f 210–29   To mortal sense, s· and suffering are real,
- 229– 6   but if s· and suffering are realities of being,
- p 435– 7   which alone is capable of s· and suffering.

and the hope
- a 22– 3   Vibrating like a pendulum between s· and the hope of

and the sinner
- p 393–31   the s· and the sinner, the disease and its cause.

any one
- b 339– 5   Does not God's pardon, destroying any one s·,

atonement for
- a 19–19   to understand Jesus' atonement for s·

sin

audible
ap 559– 8 exercised upon visible error and audible *s*.
aught but
p 441– 4 which undertakes to punish aught but *s*,
belief called
a 37– 1 which destroys the belief called *s*
belief in
(*see* **belief**)
belief of
(*see* **belief**)
brought death
p 426–28 *S*. brought death, and death will disappear with
calamities, and
f 223–28 calamities, and *s*. will much more abound
ceases
p 391–16 will cease in proportion as the *s*. ceases.
chronic
p 373– 9 to lift a student out of a chronic *s*.
claim of
t 447–24 To put down the claim of *s*, you must detect it,
461–27 first see the claim of *s*, and then destroy it.
cleanse from
a 25– 7 no more efficacious to cleanse from *s*. when
conceit of
ap 571–27 Thus he rebukes the conceit of *s*,
conceived in
r 476–16 "conceived in *s*. and brought forth in iniquity."
g 540–29 mortal and material man, conceived in *s*
conditions of
g 556–10 Mortal belief infolds the conditions of *s*.
confers no pleasure
p 404–23 show him that *s*. confers no pleasure,
conquered
ap 564–16 met and conquered *s*. in every form.
continues in
pr 5–27 He grows worse who continues in *s*. because he
culminating
gl 597–11 martyrdom of Jesus was the culminating *s*. of
cure of
s 149– 4 in the cure of disease as in the cure of *s*.
debt of
a 23– 4 is insufficient to pay the debt of *s*.
deny
pr 15–18 we must deny *s*. and plead God's allness.
destroying
pr 6–12 To cause suffering, . . . is the means of destroying *s*.
a 40–12 God's method of destroying *s*.
f 241–21 healing sickness and destroying *s*.
b 316–11 healing sickness and destroying *s*.
332–15 Life, . . . destroying *s*, disease, and death.
ap 565–26 destroying *s*, sickness, and death,
destruction of
(*see* **destruction**)
disappearance of
p 426–29 will disappear with the disappearance of *s*.
disarm
ph 178–25 and we disarm *s*. of its imaginary power
disease and
pref viii–13 by healing both disease and *s* ;
f 208–32 banish all thoughts of disease and *s*
p 420–18 Truth overcomes both disease and *s*
r 485–27 foreign agents, called disease and *s*.
disease, and death
pr 17–11 *but delivereth us from s*, *disease, and death.*
a 24– 3 error will never save from *s*, disease, and death.
m 67–28 Man delivered from *s*, disease, and death
sp 99–27 *s*, disease, and death give everlasting place
s 164–25 save from *s*, disease, and death.
ph 166–30 its mastery over *s*, disease, and death,
197– 9 bears the fruit of *s*, disease, and death,
f 248–31 *s*, disease, and death will diminish
b 301–24 *s*, disease, and death arise from the
317–20 to conquer *s*, disease, and death.
332–15 Life, . . . destroying *s*, disease, and death.
o 348–27 or that *s*, disease, and death would not be
p 395–13 *s*, disease, and death will disappear.
415– 4 *S*, disease, and death have no foundations in
442–22 and *s*, disease, and death disappear.
r 485–12 make *s*, disease, and death appear . . . unreal
g 505– 2 *s*, disease, and death have no record in the
disease, . . . and death
sp 78– 2 like the discords of disease, *s*, and death,
b 275–29 such as matter, disease, *s*, and death,
p 412–15 and to destroy disease, *s*, and death.
disease or
b 323–24 something better than disease or *s*.
p 402–19 whether it be a broken bone, disease, or *s*.
t 455–11 lost in the belief and fear of disease or *s*,
disease, or death
f 253–16 to overcome the belief in *s*, disease, or death.
253–25 supposed necessity for *s*, disease, or death,
p 380– 9 the demands of *s*, disease, or death,
divest
b 339–29 to divest *s*. of any supposed mind or reality,

sin

effects of
gl 588– 3 self-imposed agony ; effects of *s*. ;
error and
b 296–17 lose all satisfaction in error and *s*
every
b 307–21 every *s*. or supposed material pain and
expiate their
ap 569–21 They must eventually expiate their *s*
fear and
p 373–21 you must rise above both fear and *s*.
392– 1 you master fear and *s*. through divine
fear of
p 405–19 man finally can overcome his fear of *s*.
fellowship with
pr 8– 8 They hold secret fellowship with *s*,
fettered by
t 448–32 Fettered by *s*. yourself, it is difficult to
forgiveness of
r 497– 9 We acknowledge God's forgiveness of *s*. in the
forms of
p 404– 4 servant of any one of the myriad forms of *s*,
forsake
b 290–28 The murderer, . . . does not thereby forsake *s*
fruit-bearer of
g 526–23 Did He create this fruit-bearer of *s*
grapple with
a 29– 3 They must grapple with *s*
greatest
p 376– 6 Just so is it with the greatest *s*.
has the elements
r 481–24 *S*. has the elements of self-destruction.
healer of
s 148–32 a theology which admits God to be the healer of *s*
f 251–24 the healer of *s*, disease, death.
heals
s 135–11 same power which heals *s*. heals also sickness.
hidden
t 453–20 Hidden *s*. is spiritual wickedness in high places
if without
p 385–16 all untoward conditions, *if without s*,
ignorance and
b 290–22 Christ, Truth, removes all ignorance and *s*.
ignorance or
p 411–21 foundation of . . . is fear, ignorance, or *s*.
r 483–11 Moral ignorance or *s*. affects your
illusion of
g 536–11 The illusion of *s*. is without hope or God.
infirmity of
ap 564– 8 This last infirmity of *s*. will
is destroyed
pr 6–14 until belief in material life and *s*. is destroyed.
is not there
b 291–16 immortal, because *s*. is not there
is the image
b 327–13 *S*. is the image of the beast
is unsustained
c 264–21 *S*. is unsustained by Truth,
jest of
sp 72–29 joy of intercourse becomes the jest of *s*, when
love of
a 36– 6 sufficient suffering, . . . to quench the love of *s*
p 373–14 The fear of disease and the love of *s*. are the
mental
g 557–24 but immediately fell into mental *s*. ;
microbes of
s 164–15 and all the mental microbes of *s*
midst of
pr 7–30 in the midst of *s*
b 291– 3 suppositions that . . . in the midst of *s*,
misery of
b 327–13 The way to escape the misery of *s*
no
t 447–24 not reformed merely by assuring him . . . there
is no *s*.
r 472–23 *Question.* — Is there no *s*. ?
ap 567– 8 no error, no *s*, sickness, nor death.
no claim of
p 390–20 Suffer no claim of *s*. or of sickness to grow
no real pleasure in
p 404–20 conviction, that there is no real pleasure in *s*,
no satisfaction in
b 322–14 Man's wisdom finds no satisfaction in *s*,
odiousness of
p 366–23 by a sense of the odiousness of *s*
or death
s 125–18 man cannot be controlled by *s*. or death,
or disease
p 396–17 not because the testimony of *s*. or disease is true.
or error
ph 183–11 *s*, or error, first caused the condemnation of
or materiality
b 289–19 never lead towards self, *s*, or materiality,
or sickness
f 253–21 right endeavors against *s*. or sickness,
p 390–24 either of *s*. or sickness,

sin

pr	5–22	not to be used as a confessional to cancel s'.
	5–23	S' is forgiven only as it is destroyed
	5–25	If prayer nourishes the belief that s' is
	6– 1	We cannot escape the penalty due for s'.
	6–12	Every supposed pleasure in s' will
	6–19	To suppose that God . . . punishes s' according
	10–32	to be merciful and not to punish s'?
	11–20	divine sentence for an individual's s',
	11–20	s' brings inevitable suffering.
	16–21	Only as we rise above all . . . s', can we
a	20–28	s' which doth so easily beset us,— Heb. 12 : 1.
	30–28	we shall loathe s' and rebuke it
	36– 7	To remit the penalty due for s', would be
	39–32	so long as he believes in the pleasures of s'?
	40–14	While there's s' there's doom.
sp	99– 4	by which mortals can escape from s' ;
	99– 5	to escape from s', is what the Bible demands.
an	103– 5	S' was the Assyrian moon-god.
s	108–24	that the opposite of Truth,— called error, s',
	113–19	God, omnipotent good, deny death, evil, s',
	113–20	Disease, s', evil, death, deny good,
	115–23	hatred, revenge, s', sickness, disease,
	137– 6	the victor over sickness, s', disease,
	138–23	easier . . . to cast out sickness than s',
	149– 2	save from sickness as well as from s',
ph	188–26	S' and the fear of disease must be
	196– 8	S' alone brings death,
	196– 9	s' is the only element of destruction.
	196–15	not of Rome, Satan, nor of God, but of s'.
	196–18	S' makes its own hell,
f	201–20	supposing that s' can be forgiven when
	203–26	S' kills the sinner and will continue to
	207–23	S', sickness, disease, and death belong not to
	218–24	Treat a belief in sickness as you would s',
	219– 1	sorrow, s', death, will be unknown,
	223–30	but the awful daring of s' destroys s',
	224– 1	the power of s' diminishing,
	231–18	If God makes s', if good produces evil,
	231–20	To hold yourself superior to s',
	236–11	Mind heals sickness as well as s'
	239–28	it is discordant and ends in s', sickness,
	241– 6	S' breaks in upon them, and carries off their
	241–12	what a mocking spectacle is s' !
	248–16	Is it imperfection, joy, sorrow, s', suffering?
	251–13	Sickness, as well as s', is an error that
	252–23	and says : . . . What a nice thing is s' !
	252–24	and says : . . . How s' succeeds, where the
b	270–26	If s' makes sinners, Truth . . . can unmake them.
	289– 9	To suppose that s', lust, hatred,
	291– 1	The suppositions that s' is pardoned while
	291– 3	that the so-called death of the body frees from s',
	296–11	The death of a false material sense and of s',
	310–24	S' is the element of self-destruction.
	310–25	If there was s' in Soul,
	311–10	S' exists here or hereafter only so long as
	315–17	likeness of God we lose sight of through s',
	316– 5	mortals need only turn from s'
	322–15	God has sentenced s' to suffer.
	335–29	S', sickness, and mortality are the suppositional
	338–24	the obstacle which the serpent, s', would impose
	339– 4	Being destroyed, s' needs no other form of
	339–13	for the sinner would make a reality of s',
	339–28	To get rid of s' through Science, is to
	339–30	never to admit that s' can have intelligence
o	341– *	Which of you convinceth me of s'?— John 8 : 46.
	348–14	Are we irreverent towards s', . . . when we
	353– 2	S', disease, whatever seems real to
	354–26	S' should become unreal to every one.
	356–31	Was there original self-creative s'?
p	369–31	any more than he is morally saved in or by s'.
	369–32	to murmur or to be angry over s'.
	373–11	more rapidly . . . than does the sinner from his s'.
	379– 2	If . . . s' can do the same,
	381– 7	on the ground that s' has its necessities.
	385–12	the law which makes s' its own executioner,
	386– 4	any more than it is in the case of s'.
	390–23	no more the author of sickness than He is of s'.
	392– 3	Only while fear or s' remains can it bring forth
	395–12	faith in God destroys all faith in s'
	405–26	If s' is not regretted and is not lessening,
	407–30	S' is spared from this classification, only because
	408– 3	s' is worse than sickness,
	409– 7	the more prolific it is likely to become in s'
	412– 2	never punishing aught but s',
	418– 3	the conquest over sickness, as well as over s',
	418–13	is no more the reality of being than is s'.
	419–11	Neither disease itself, s', nor fear
	435–25	decides what penalty is due for the s',
	435–26	and Mortal Man can suffer only for his s'.
	440–21	God, who sentences only for s'.
t	445– 3	to defend themselves against s',
	445–12	by s', or by recourse to material means
	450–23	Sickness to him is no less a temptation than is s',
	453–25	treat sickness . . . as you would s', except that
	458–20	S' makes deadly thrusts at the

sin

r	468– 3	for s' is mortality's self,
	468– 7	s' is not the eternal verity of being.
	480–20	good, never made man capable of s'.
	481–25	If s' is supported, God must uphold it,
	490– 1	assures mortals that there is real pleasure in s'
	496–20	"The sting of death is s' ;— I Cor. 15 : 56.
	496–20	the strength of s' is the law,"— I Cor. 15 : 56.
g	537–14	S' is its own punishment.
	538–27	and of s' which is temporal.
	538–28	both mortal man and s' have a beginning,
	539– 1	supposes God to be the author of s'
	542– 8	Truth causes s' to betray itself,
	542–11	and the denial of truth tend to perpetuate s',
	557–14	the less a mortal knows of s', disease, and
ap	566–32	leads the hosts . . . against the power of s',
	569–21	s', which one has made his bosom companion,
	592– 4	s' is to be . . . reduced to its native nothingness.
gl	588– 2	HELL. . . . revenge ; s' ; sickness ; death ;
	592– 9	MORTAL MIND. . . . s' ; sickness ; death.
	595– 5	TARES. Mortality ; error ; s' ; sickness ;
	595–24	UNCLEANLINESS. Impure thoughts ; error ; s' ;

sin (verb)

pr	11– 4	"Go, and s' no more."— John 8 : 11.
a	19–21	if the sinner continues to . . . s' and be sorry,
	37– 3	They who s' must suffer.
s	148–30	When mortals s', this ruling of the schools
f	205– 2	and mortals will s' without knowing
	206–31	God does not cause man to s', to be sick, or to
	211–13	sensation of sickness and the impulse to s'
	215– 4	If Spirit, Soul, could s' or be lost, then being
b	310–21	If Soul could s', Spirit, Soul, would be flesh
	311–20	So long as we believe that soul can s'
	340–29	and leaves nothing that can s', suffer,
o	356–26	by making man inclined to s',
p	372–15	He can neither s', suffer, be subject to
	405–21	good, in which is no power to s'.
	420–13	as positively as they can the temptation to s',
	435–24	If mortals s', our Supreme Judge in equity
r	468– 6	Because Soul is immortal, Soul cannot s',
	475–31	the capacity or freedom to s'.
g	524–29	Could Spirit . . . give matter ability to s'
	540–16	all sense of evil and all power to s',
	555–27	when we admit . . . God bestows the power to s',

Sinai

ph	174–17	The thunder of S' and the Sermon on the Mount
	200– 3	the law of S' lifted thought into the

since

pref	vii–27	S' the author's discovery of the
	viii–23	increased violence of diseases s' the flood.
	x– 5	books on mental healing have s' been issued,
pr	2–10	s' He is unchanging wisdom and Love.
	4–10	s' he has said : "If ye love me,— John 14 : 15.
	9–29	s' you do not care to tread in the footsteps of our
a	34–28	change which has s' been called the ascension.
	36– 9	s' justice is the handmaid of mercy.
m	68–22	s' salutary causes sometimes incur these
sp	75–10	s' to infinite Spirit there can be no matter.
	83–15	s' Science is an explication of nature.
an	101–27	s' error cannot remove the effects of error.
	102–13	s' God governs the universe ;
s	111–31	S' then this system has gradually gained
	129–14	s' the beginning of the world ;"— Matt. 24 : 21.
	130–12	s' you admit that God is omnipotent ;
	144– 2	s' no good can come of it?
	147–12	s' Jesus practised these rules
	149–26	S' God, divine Mind, governs all,
	154– 4	S' it is a law of mortal mind that certain
ph	165–13	s' man-made material theories took the place
	179– 6	s' space is no obstacle to Mind.
	181– 1	S' Mind, God, is the source and condition of all
	186–30	S' it must believe in something besides itself,
	193–19	S' then I have not seen him, but am informed
	193–22	ever s' the injury was received in boyhood.
	193–24	S' his recovery I have been informed that
	199– 5	s' muscles are as material as wood and iron
f	219– 4	s' Mind should be, and is, supreme,
	250–24	s' whatever appears to be a mortal man
c	267–20	s' inverted thoughts and erroneous beliefs
b	286–23	s' God, Spirit, is the only cause,
	299–22	s' "the tree is known by his— Matt. 12 : 33.
	317– 2	s' material knowledge usurped the throne of
	322–14	s' God has sentenced sin to suffer.
	339– 7	S' God is All, there is no room for
o	355–18	systematic healing power s' the first century.
p	362–12	Mary Magdalene, as she has s' been called
	364– 1	who has s' been rightfully regarded as
	370–20	s' mortal mind must be the cause of disease
	391–19	S' matter cannot talk, it must be mortal mind
	399–26	s' matter is not sensible.
	401–13	s' matter has no sensation
	412–32	s' matter is not intelligent
	417–23	s' it is demonstrable that the way to cure
	424–11	s' there is no room for imperfection in
	425–19	s' Spirit, God, is All-in-all.

since

p 427– 9	s· the truth of being is deathless.
431–27	s· the night of the liver-attack.
t 457– 7	S· the divine light of C. S. first dawned upon
457–10	s· entering this field of labor,
r 471–29	S· then her highest creed has been
481–27	s· Truth cannot support error.
482–15	s· Christ is "the way"— John 14 : 6.
482–30	s· the human, mortal mind so-called is not
488–30	s· they exist in immortal Mind, not in matter.
490–11	s· all power belongs to God, good.
490–15	s· he is so already, according to C. S.
492– 5	s· Life cannot be united to its unlikeness,
494–13	s· to all mankind and in every hour,
g 504–13	s· Truth, Life, and Love fill immensity
514– 3	s· nothing exists beyond the range of
517–23	s· there is no limit to infinitude
519– 4	s· the spiritual creation was the outgrowth,
531–27	s· flesh wars against Spirit
534–26	s· the Christian era began.
537–17	s· ground and dust stand for nothingness.
543– 5	s· it is the idea of Truth and changes not,
ap 560– 3	typical of six thousand years s· Adam,
564–14	S· Jesus must have been tempted in all points,
568– 2	Ever s· the foundation of the world,
568– 2	ever s· error would establish material belief,
571– 4	s· exposure is necessary to ensure the
gl 592–14	s· justice demands penalties

sincere

pref x–23	personal experience of any s· seeker of Truth.
pr 13–10	If our petitions are s·, we labor for what
13–15	Even if prayer is s·, God knows our need
t 450– 9	They are s·, generous, noble, and

sincerity

pr 5– 5	the test of our s·,— namely, reformation.
9– 9	no evidence of the s· of our requests
15–24	and let our lives attest our s·.
t 462–17	self-denial, s·, Christianity, and persistence

sinew

b 308–20	smote the s·, or strength, of his error,

sinews

ph 173–19	measuring human strength by bones and s·,

sin-filled

a 54–11	empty or s· human storehouses,

sinful

pr 15– 4	the door of which shuts out s· sense
16– 6	and the falsity of s· sense.
a 20–13	can be baptized, . . . and yet be sensual and s·.
23– 9	suffering is an error of s· sense
53–32	Had he shared the s· beliefs of others,
sp 70– 5	Whatever is false or s· can never enter
s 114– 2	author calls sick and s· humanity mortal mind,
138–24	the s·, so-called pleasure of the senses.
f 204–25	notion that they can create . . . s· mortals
237–20	either s· or diseased thoughts.
241–32	than for s· beliefs to enter the kingdom
253–14	to make you sick or s· ;
b 289–13	never make men sick, s·, or mortal.
292–10	A s·, sick, and dying mortal is not the
296–10	Nothing sensual or s· is immortal.
311–12	It is a sense of sin, and not a s· soul,
314–23	Because of mortals' material and s· belief,
318–16	Is the sick man s· above all others?
327– 7	and all the s· appetites of the human mind.
o 346– 3	it is not s· and sickly mortal man who
p 366–26	sinners should be affrighted by their s· beliefs ;
381– 6	than you are to yield to a s· temptation
400–31	the baneful influence of s· thought on the body.
405–29	pains of s· sense are less harmful than
t 452–28	Acting from s· motives destroys your power of
r 481–32	the sense of sin which is lost, and not a s· soul.
g 502–10	untrue image of God, named a s· mortal.
542–29	The s· misconception of Life as
554–18	the creation of whatever is s· and mortal ;
ap 570–29	when it makes them sick or s·.

singe

an 103–27	s· their own wings and fall into dust.

single

pr 14–12	Become conscious for a s· moment that
a 18– 9	nor to relieve them of a s· responsibility.
28–16	Not a s· component part of his nature
sp 76–24	without a s· bodily pleasure or pain,
77– 4	Neither . . . from error to truth at a s· bound.
s 153– 6	until there was not a s· saline property left.
155–21	in order to heal a s· case of disease.
163– 9	if there were not a s· physician, surgeon,
ph 168– 4	the removal of a s· weight from either scale
196–25	induced by a s· post mortem examination,
f 225–31	rights of man were vindicated in a s· section
b 290– 2	on account of that s· experience,
329– 1	reaching beyond the pale of a s· period
336–21	neither could . . . be reflected by a s· man,
p 391–10	that you can possibly entertain a s· intruding

single

p 413– 5	A s· requirement, beyond what is necessary
421–29	or by employing a s· material application
429– 9	we look beyond a s· step in the line of
t 463–12	spiritual idea has not a s· element of error,
r 475–20	has not a s· quality underived from Deity ;
g 524–18	With a s· command, Mind had made man,
ap 568–24	For victory over a s· sin, we give thanks

sings

f 220–11	The snowbird s· and soars amid the blasts ;

sinister

t 446–13	from s· or malicious motives

sink

p 415–30	the whole frame will s· from sight
ap 564– 8	s· its perpetrator into a night without a star.
570–21	nor again s· the world into the deep waters of

sinking

s 153–10	patient s· in the last stage of typhoid fever.
p 385– 4	have been able to undergo without s·

sinless

pr 16– 6	Truth that is s· and the falsity of sinful sense.
a 22–24	boundless freedom, and s· sense,
26–24	precious import of our Master's s· career
sp 76–22	The s· joy,— the perfect harmony and
b 288–22	Soul is s·, not to be found in the body ;
290–26	To be wholly spiritual, man must be s·,
304–15	The perfect man . . . is s· and eternal.
o 344– 5	normal, healthful, and s· condition of man
g 538–29	while the s·, real man is eternal.

sinlessness

b 339–25	basis of all health, s·, and immortality

sinned

b 310–23	If Soul s·, Soul would die.
p 435– 3	Who or what has s·?
r 468– 3	If Soul s·, it would be mortal,

sinner (see also **sinner's**)

a hypocrite

pr 8– 2	though it makes the s· a hypocrite.

arouse the

p 404–22	Arouse the s· to this new and true view of sin,

awakens the

o 342–21	C. S. awakens the s·,

is afraid

t 447–30	A s· is afraid to cast the first stone.

is a suicide

f 203–25	The so-called s· is a suicide.

miserable

ap 573–18	no longer regarded as a miserable s·,

mortal

r 475–31	A mortal s· is not God's man.
g 525– 2	to become there a mortal s·,

prospective

g 527–28	lie . . . asking a prospective s· to help Him.

reformed the

o 343–27	healed the sick and reformed the s·

reforming the

p 404–26	Healing the sick and reforming the s·

reforms the

pr 1– 1	The prayer that reforms the s·
6– 5	divine Principle alone reforms the s·.

reform the

a 35–30	The design of Love is to reform the s·.

sin and the

p 393–31	the sin and the s·, the disease and its cause.

sin kills the

f 203–26	Sin kills the s· and will continue to kill him

such a

s 136–24	for how could such a s· comprehend

---

a 19–20	but if the s· continues to pray and repent,
22–33	Justice requires reformation of the s·.
36– 1	good man's heaven would be a hell to the s·
sp 73– 4	another, who has died to-day a s·
91– 9	difficult for the s· to accept divine Science,
s 129–31	The s· sees, in the system taught in this
f 218–14	the human mind is the s·,
226–26	the sick, the sensual, the s·, I wished to save
c 266–20	The s· makes his own hell.
b 339–11	A s· can receive no encouragement from
339–12	for the s· would make a reality of sin,
p 373–11	sick recover more rapidly . . . than does the s·
404–16	The healthy s· is the hardened s·.
t 447–22	A s· is not reformed merely by
447–23	not . . . by assuring him that he cannot be a s·
455– 2	Love, which heals the sick and the s·.
g 542–23	Justice marks the s·,

sinner's

a 23– 5	constant self-immolation on the s· part.
35–31	If the s· punishment here has been

sinners

all

a 24–21	chiefly as providing a ready pardon for all s·
p 364– 6	in behalf of all s·,

sinners
counted among
pr 9–26 and so be counted among *s*·?
flourish
pr 5–18 *S*· flourish "like a green bay tree ;" — *Psal.* 37 : 35.
hatred of
b 317–10 and he will incur the hatred of *s*·, till
he rebuked
a 53– 6 He rebuked *s*· pointedly and unflinchingly,
saints and
pr 5–14 Saints and *s*· get their full award,
traduced by the
sp 95– 4 were traduced by the *s*· of that period,

———

a 36–22 It is quite as impossible for *s*· to receive their
53– 2 the "friend of publicans and *s*·." — *Luke* 7 : 34.
s 138–24 than are *s*· to give up the sinful,
f 204–23 theories have given *s*· the notion that
b 270–26 If sin makes *s*·, Truth . . . can unmake them.
314–28 the more odious he became to *s*·
o 355–30 and by the *s*· who are reformed.
p 366–26 *s*· should be affrighted by their sinful beliefs ;
g 533–19 who aids man to make *s*·

sinneth
p 435–12 decrees that whosoever *s*· shall die ;

sinning
sp 72–26 A *s*·, earthly mortal is not the reality of
76–18 Suffering, *s*·, dying beliefs are unreal.
77–20 the illusion . . . of a *s*·, suffering sense,
78–11 must still be mortal, *s*·, suffering,
78–30 and the *s*· are reformed.
92–10 with the power of *s*· now and forever.
96– 1 Humanity advances slowly out of *s*· sense
s 138–22 to heal the sick as well as the *s*·.
143– 9 sick are more deplorably lost than the *s*·, if
143–10 if the sick cannot rely on God . . . and the *s*· can.
f 205– 3 will sin without knowing that they are *s*·,
c 259–11 presented man as fallen, sick, *s*·, and dying.
b 323–19 When the sick or the *s*· awake to realize
327–13 way to escape the misery of sin is to cease *s*·.
o 345–24 between God's man, . . . and the *s*· race of
r 477– 1 where *s*· mortal man appears to mortals.
489–20 the medium for *s*· against God,
ap 570–26 When God heals the sick or the *s*·,
(*see also* **sick**)

sin's
a 48–14 exalting ordeal of *s*· revenge on its destroyer
f 240–30 The divine method of paying *s*· wages
p 405–19 This is *s*· necessity, — to destroy itself.
g 539– 1 the author of sin and *s*· progeny.
ap 569–28 must depend upon *s*· obduracy.

sins
bore our
a 53–25 Jesus bore our *s*· in his body.
covereth his
t 448–17 "He that covereth his *s*· shall not — *Prov.* 28 : 13.
experimental
f 230–16 cannot be, the author of experimental *s*·.
his
an 105–25 His *s*· will be millstones about his neck,
multitude of
pr 8–20 they "cover the multitude of *s*·." — *I Pet* 4 : 8.
of others
ph 189–13 *s*· of others should not make good men suffer.
o 346–15 belief that we suffer from the *s*· of others.
of the world
s 150–16 Christ-power to take away the *s*· of the world.
b 334–18 taking away the *s*· of the world,
other people's
a 38–23 the fruits of other people's *s*·, not of his own.
our
pr 11–13 never pardons our *s*· or mistakes till
11–19 Jesus suffered for our *s*·,
sicknesses, and
ph 177– 3 relinquish all its errors, sicknesses, and *s*·.
thy
p 363–23 "Thy *s*· are forgiven." — *Luke* 7 : 48.
trespasses and
a 33–25 raises the dead from trespasses and *s*·,
b 316–30 those dead in trespasses and *s*·,
your own
p 391–14 It is error to suffer for aught but your own *s*·.
391–16 and real suffering for your own *s*· will

———

f 202–17 but immortal man, . . . neither *s*·, suffers, nor
203–27 so long as he *s*·.
229– 5 We should hesitate to say that Jehovah *s*· or
b 285– 8 material personality which suffers, *s*·, and
294–13 saying : . . . Nerves feel. Brain thinks and *s*·.
310–19 taught that there is a human soul which *s*·
310–23 It is the belief . . . of material sense which *s*·.
r 470–18 God, the Mind of man, never *s*·
481–24 If Soul *s*·, it must be mortal.

sins
r 481–28 Soul is the divine Principle of man and never *s*·,
481–30 it is material sense, not Soul, which *s*· ;
g 542– 1 The belief of life in matter *s*· at every step.

sister
s 159– 3 After the autopsy, her *s*· testified that the
161–13 If her *s*· States follow this example
c 267–15 as for that of brother and *s*·.
267–17 my brother, and *s*·, and mother." — *Matt.* 12 : 50.

sit
a 31–20 *s*· down with him, in a full understanding of

sits
an 106–15 Let this age, which *s*· in judgment on C. S.,

sittest
p 435–29 "*S*· thou to judge — *Acts* 23 : 3.

situation
b 296–30 and in understanding the *s*· in C. S.
297– 4 and no circumstance can alter the *s*·, until the
p 403–14 You command the *s*· if you understand that
r 486–30 would place man in a terrible *s*·,
ap 575–22 Psalmist saith, "Beautiful for *s*·, — *Psal.* 48 : 2.

six
a 21–30 After following the sun for *s*· days,
ph 193– 1 confined to his bed *s*· months with
ap 560– 3 typical of *s*· thousand years since Adam,

sixth
g 518–26 and the morning were the *s*· day. — *Gen.* 1 : 31.
ap 560– 3 In the opening of the *s*· seal,

sixty
f 247– 7 One man at *s*· had retained

size
ph 165– 6 To measure intellectual capacity by the *s*· of
190–12 by the *s*· of a brain and the bulk of a body,
199– 4 trip-hammer is not increased in *s*· by exercise.

skeptical
s 152–28 experiments in homœopathy had made her *s*·

skepticism
f 209–12 Neither philosophy nor *s*· can hinder the
252– 5 occasions the only *s*· regarding the pathology

sketch
pref viii–25 a biographical *s*·, narrating experiences
f 245– 3 a *s*· from the history of an English woman,

sketches
ph 198–11 fills in his delineations with *s*· from

skies
f 249–29 It falls short of the *s*·, but makes its
ap 575–30 with the Southern Cross in the *s*·,

skilful
s 159–11 Is it *s*· or scientific surgery to take no
p 402– 1 C. S. is always the most *s*· surgeon,

skill
a 44–15 He did not require the *s*· of a surgeon
s 142–12 architectural *s*·, making dome and spire
f 221–12 having exhausted the *s*· of the doctors,

skin
p 379–26 dry *s*·, pain in the head and limbs,

skipped
s 135– 4 mountains, that ye *s*· like rams, — *Psal.* 114 : 6.

skull
ph 192– 2 The belief that a pulpy substance under the *s*·
b 280–11 would compress Mind, . . . beneath a *s*· bone.
281–19 The mind supposed to exist . . . beneath a *s*· bone
p 397–29 belief that mind is, . . . within the *s*·,

sky
sp 85–21 discern the face of the *s*· ; — *Matt.* 16 : 3.
s 122–16 *s*· and tree-tops apparently join hands,
133–10 and manna fell from the *s*·.
f 233–17 Ye who can discern the face of the *s*·,
g 510– 1 discern the face of the *s*· ; — *Matt.* 16 : 3.

skyward
c 261–30 and preens its wings for a *s*· flight.

slain
b 290–27 The murderer, though *s*· in the act,
334–21 This was "the Lamb *s*· from the — *Rev.* 13 : 8.
334–22 *s*·, that is, according to the testimony of the

slander
c 266–13 Friends will betray and enemies will *s*·,
b 330–30 hypocrisy, *s*·, hate, theft, adultery,

slaughter
a 50– 1 brought as a lamb to the *s*·, — *Isa.* 53 : 7.

slave
f 221–26 when, still the *s*· of matter, he thought
225–19 and abolish the whipping-post and *s*· market ;
226– 5 The voice of God in behalf of the African *s*·
p 404– 3 If a man is an inebriate, a *s*· to tobacco,
407–17 Let the *s*· of wrong desire learn the
gl 582–27 and would make mortal mind a *s*· to the body.

slavery

African
f 226– 1   when African s· was abolished in our land.
hopeless
f 227–10   and in subjection to hopeless s·,
mental
f 225–24   abolition of mental s· is a more difficult task.
world-wide
f 226– 3   banishment of a world-wide s·,

f 224–29   the Soul-inspired motto, "S· is abolished."
226–26   to save from the s· of their own beliefs
227–15   S· is not the legitimate state of man.
p 381– 4   the bias of education enforces this s·.
t 445–30   Recalling Jefferson's words about s·,
gl 587–22   Corporeal belief; sensuality; s·; tyranny.

slaves

m 68– 4   They are s· to fashion, pride, and sense.

slay

a 37– 7   Mortals try in vain to s· Truth
43–16   had mocked and tried to s·.
f 214–24   mortal illusions would rob God, s· man,
g 542– 4   Material beliefs would s· the spiritual idea
ap 568– 3   evil has tried to s· the Lamb;

slayeth

g 542–15   Therefore whosoever s· Cain.— Gen. 4: 15.

slays

ap 567–31   Science shows how the Lamb s· the wolf.

sleek

ph 197–20   more honest than our s· politicians.

sleep

and apathy
f 249–24   S· and apathy are phases of the
and mesmerism
r 490–28   S· and mesmerism explain the mythical nature
deep
b 307– 1   the Adam-dream, the deep s·,
g 528–10   a deep s· to fall upon Adam,— Gen. 2: 21.
556–18   the deep s· which fell upon Adam?
dreamy
sp 88– 1   and this not in dreamy s·.
earth's
sp 75–31   when we awake from earth's s· to the
is darkness
g 556–18   S· is darkness, but God's creative mandate

sp 75–13   that I may awake him out of s·."— John 11: 11.
82–13   In s· we do not communicate with the
ph 179–28   to move the bowels, or to produce s·
188–13   is like the dream we have in s·,
f 230–25   They are soothing syrups to put children to s·,
250–17   according to the dream he entertains in s·.
p 431– 7   going to s· immediately after a heavy meal.
440– 6   is taught how to make s· befool reason
r 490–29   S· shows material sense as either
491–23   In s·, memory and consciousness are lost from
g 505– 2   mortal mind, s·, dreams, sin,
528–16   inducing a s· or hypnotic state in Adam
556–20   In s·, cause and effect are mere illusions.
556–22   and dreams, not realities, come with s·.

sleeper

ph 188–18   The smile of the s· indicates the

sleepeth

sp 75–12   "Our friend Lazarus s·;— John 11: 11.
p 398–12   "she is not dead, but s·,"— Luke 8: 52.

sleeping

ph 188–15   In both the waking and the s· dream,
f 250–23   any more reality in . . . than in the s· dream?
r 494–22   experiences of the s· dream seem real

sleeplessness

ph 165–16   You say that indigestion, fatigue, s·, cause

sleeps

p 416–15   Where is the pain while the patient s·?

slept

a 48– 3   His students s·.
p 385–22   You say that you have not s· well
g 528–10   sleep to fall upon Adam, and he s·:— Gen. 2: 21.

slew

a 43–19   Those who s· him to stay his influence
g 541–15   against Abel his brother, and s· him.— Gen. 4: 8.

slice

f 221– 7   only a thin s· of bread without water.

slight

m 59–21   and remember how s· a word or deed
s 130– 3   discouraged over its s· spiritual prospects.
t 446– 1   teaching his s· knowledge of Mind-power,

slime

b 279– 7   s·, or protoplasm never originated in

sling

b 268–12   like the shepherd-boy with his s·,

slippery

m 65–26   must lose its present s· footing,

slough

ph 168–13   already brought yourself into the s· of disease

slow

a 20–24   Material belief is s· to acknowledge what the
22– 6   Vibrating . . . our moral progress will be s·.
ph 174–10   The footsteps of thought, . . . are s·,
b 321– 6   The Hebrew Lawgiver, s· of speech,
g 519–12   Human capacity is s· to discern and to grasp
ap 566–23   Be Thou, longsuffering, s· to wrath,

slowly

a 39–28   This thought is apprehended s·,
m 68– 2   At present mortals progress s·
sp 96– 1   Humanity advances s· out of sinning sense
ph 173–26   Human reason and religion come s· to the
f 233– 9   The ages must s· work up to perfection.
254– 5   or attain s· and yield not to discouragement.
254–13   mortals grasp the ultimate . . . s·;
b 268– 7   is s· yielding to the idea of a
p 415– 7   because thought moves quickly or s·,
415–22   The muscles, moving quickly or s·
t 450–15   Some people yield s· to the touch of Truth.

sluggard

a 22–17   nor become a s· in the race.

slumbering

f 223–25   Peals that should startle the s· thought

slumbers

f 249–22   God never s·, and His likeness never

small

s 113– 5   but its spirit comes only in s· degrees.
129–30   the author's s· estimate of the pleasures of
c 256–17   precise form of God must be of s· importance
b 323–29   "still, s· voice" of Truth— I Kings 19: 12.
o 345–13   It is indeed no s· matter to know one's self;
p 364–20   such seekers as he gave s· reward
367–25   through a "still, s· voice,"— I Kings 19: 12.
384–14   will prove to himself, by s· beginnings,
r 492– 8   a knowledge of this, even in s· degree,
g 547–15   speck of so-called embryonic life seemed a s· sun.
ap 559– 8   The "still, s· voice" of— I Kings 19: 12.

smaller

p 363–16   one for a large sum and one for a s·,

smallpox

s 153–26   and we have s· because others have it;
f 235– 4   Better suffer a doctor infected with s· to
p 390–29   whether it is cancer, consumption, or s·.

smatterers

t 460–19   If Christian healing is abused by mere s·

smell

sp 71–11   that you see a flower,— that you touch and s·
f 212–20   and bring the rose . . . that they may s· it.
b 284–23   nor can they feel, taste, or s· Spirit.
r 479–11   cannot see, feel, hear, taste, nor s·.
g 526–10   material hearing, sight, touch, taste, and s·,

smells

gl 591–15   sees, feels, hears, tastes, and s· only in belief.

smile

ph 175–10   to say that a rose, the s· of God, can produce
188–18   The s· of the sleeper indicates the
r 477–28   "the s· of the Great Spirit."

smiles

a 47–13   thirty pieces of silver and the s· of the
m 59–19   in prolonging her health and s·
sp 76– 2   name the face that s· on them

smite

p 439–20   God will s· you, O whited walls,
t 444–20   "Whosoever shall s· thee on thy— Matt. 5: 39.
444–21   Fear not that he will s· thee again

Smith's Bible Dictionary

b 320– 8   In S· B· D· it is said:

smitten

a 48–21   Peter would have s· the enemies of
49–32   "stricken, s· of God."— Isa. 53: 4.
o 343– 2   Shall I then be s· for healing
p 435–31   and commandest . . . to be s·— Acts 23: 3.

smoke

a 22–18   When the s· of battle clears away,
37–14   but not amid the s· of battle is merit seen
ap 566–23   An awful guide, in s· and flame,

smoking

p 383–21   The tobacco-user, eating or s· poison

smooth

gl 593–15   When s· and unobstructed, it typifies the

smooth-tongued

f 252–30   says: . . . and I elude detection by s· villainy.

smote

a 48– 2   bigoted ignorance s· him sorely.
b 308–20   and s· the sinew, or strength, of his error,

smothered
g 501– 5 seems so *s·* by the immediate context

smuggles
p 438–24 and *s·* Error's goods into market

snake-talker
g 533–13 the *s·* utters the first voluble lie,

snarls
s 240–30 involves unwinding one's *s·*,

snatches
f 237–13 *s·* away the good seed before it has sprouted.

sneers
o 341–12 *S·* at the application of the word *Science* to

sneezing
ph 175–15 glandular inflammation, *s·*, and nasal pangs.

sniffs
ph 179–18 the wild animal, . . . *s·* the wind with delight.

snow
sp 82–30 to the Esquimaux in their *s·* huts?
ph 175–26 Damp atmosphere and freezing *s·*
b 321–22 white as *s·* with the dread disease,

snowbird
f 220–11 The *s·* sings and soars amid the blasts ;

snowflakes
f 250–29 Mortal thoughts chase one another like *s·*,

snows
m 61–17 like tropical flowers born amid Alpine *s·*.

soaring
g 512– 1 *s·* beyond and above corporeality

soars
f 220–11 The snowbird sings and *s·* amid the blasts ;

sober
pr 7–13 unfavorable to spiritual growth, *s·* resolve,
b 324–13 Be watchful, *s·*, and vigilant.

so-called
a 39–23 the time for *s·* material . . . to pass away,
m 62– 6 and master the belief in *s·* physical laws,
sp 72– 9 *S· spirits* are but corporeal communicators.
73–12 Any other control or attraction of *s·* spirit
73–32 between *s·* material existence and
77–14 embracing its *s·* pleasures and pains,
77–21 a *s·* mind fettered by matter.
88–15 Beliefs proceed from the *s·* material senses,
97– 6 and *s·* matter resembles its essence,
an 100– 4 he regarded this *s·* force,
102– 7 an unreal concept of the *s·* mortal mind.
102–30 Its *s·* despotism is but a phase of
104–17 wrongness of the opposite *s·* action,
s 123–16 Also, if any *s·* new school claims to be C. S.,
123–24 The proof, . . . that the *s·* miracles of Jesus
124– 3 Physical science (*s·*) is human knowledge,
128–26 forever destroys . . . the *s·* evidence of matter.
131–27 the *s·* miracles of olden time
138–24 the sinful, *s·* pleasure of the senses.
144– 5 even if these *s·* powers are real.
144–15 belongs to the *s·* material senses,
144–23 divine Science wars with *s·* physical science,
150–18 The science (*s·*) of physics would
162–16 false beliefs of a *s·* material existence.
ph 165–12 Obedience to the *s·* physical laws of health
168–25 before the *s·* disease made its appearance
185–11 and such systems of *s·* mind-cure,
187– 6 Here you may see how a *s·* material sense
188– 8 but afterwards it governs the *s·* man.
190– 1 formation of *s·* embryonic mortal mind,
200–21 the *s·* human soul or spirit,
200–23 These *s·* material senses must yield to
f 202– 7 the *s·* pains and pleasures of material sense,
203–25 The *s·* sinner is a suicide.
204–13 The *s·* second power, evil, is the unlikeness
210–26 It is the *s·* mortal mind which voices this
211– 8 sensations of a *s·* mortal mind
211–17 the nature of all *s·* material cause and effect.
212–29 possibly that other methods involve *s·* miracles.
217–23 control which Mind has over *s·* matter,
222–13 he also had less faith in the *s·* pleasures
229–19 The *s·* law of mortal mind,
230–30 *S·* mortal mind or the mind of mortals
231– 2 or the *s·* physical senses will get the victory.
232–28 the *s·* pleasures and pains of sense
242–13 rise superior to the *s·* pain and pleasure of the
251– 2 The *s·* belief of mortal mind
251–21 acts upon the *s·* human mind
253–15 the falsity of *s·* material sense,
253–27 never requires obedience to a *s·* material law,
c 257– 4 If matter, *s·*, is substance,
258–20 material *s·* senses have no cognizance of
b 275–28 other gods, or other *s·* powers,
277–23 the order of material *s·* science.
282– 3 and its opposite, the *s·* material life
282–27 Error is the *s·* intelligence of mortal mind.
283–14 with material life *s·*.

so-called
291– 3 that the *s·* death of the body
b 292–17 *s·* life of mortals is dependent on
293–13 The material *s·* gases and forces are
294–15 This verdict of the *s·* material senses
296–14 *s·* pleasures and pains of matter perish,
302–10 and that the *s·* pleasures and pains,
307– 3 This pantheistic error, or *s· serpent*,
309–29 such *s·* life always ends in death.
312– 2 such *s·* knowledge is reversed
334–11 imperceptible to the *s·* personal senses,
o 347–12 the *s·* mortal man is not the reality of man.
348–19 well to eliminate from *s·* mortal mind
356– 4 *S·* material existence affords no
358– 1 axe, which destroys a tree's *s·* life,
p 366–19 Such *s·* Scientists will strain out gnats,
376–18 *s·* material body is a mental concept
377–26 cause of all *s·* disease is mental,
378– 8 Without the *s·* human mind,
379–22 The *s·* vital current does not affect the
382–16 to teach the *s·* ignorant one.
382–17 Must we not then consider the *s·* law of
382–28 nothingness of the *s·* pleasures and
387–10 nor can *s·* material law trespass
387–24 It is a law of *s·* mortal mind,
393– 8 a law of *s·* mortal mind,
399–11 *S·* mortal mind sends its despatches
399–22 *s·* mortal life is mortal mind,
399–32 without beginning with *s·* mortal mind,
400–26 The action of *s·* mortal mind
408– 6 universal insanity of *s·* health,
408–17 *s·* inflammation of disordered functions,
409–13 independently of this *s·* conscious mind,
409–16 *s·* conscious mortal mind is believed
409–22 *s·* "children of men" — *Psal.* 14: 2.
419–24 in mortals or *s·* mortal minds,
421– 3 while physical ailments (*s·*) arise from
423–32 The *s·* substance of bone is formed first
424–28 scrofula and other *s·* hereditary diseases,
427–25 in the physical realm, *s·*, as well as in the
432–27 the hands of justice, *alias* nature's *s·* law ;
441– 3 any *s·* law, which undertakes to punish
t 463–30 action is that of *s·* mortal mind.
r 479–13 Take away *s·* mortal mind,
482–30 mortal mind *s·* is not a healer,
490–20 knowledge gained from the *s·* material senses
492– 2 the *s·* dreamer is unconscious?
493–21 Disease is an experience of *s·* mortal mind.
g 501–13 *S·* mystery and miracle,
505–12 mindless matter nor the *s·* material senses.
509–20 *S·* mineral, vegetable, and
513– 1 mortal mentality, *s·*, and its claim,
513–27 *S·* mortal mind — being non-existent
524– 5 and in a thousand other *s·* deities.
540–14 uncovers *s·* sin and its effects,
544–29 declares . . . *s·* mortal life to be Life,
547–14 germinating speck of *s·* embryonic life
548–28 important facts in regard to *s·* embryonic life.
554–11 destitute of any knowledge of the *s·* selfhood
ap 561– 6 at a point of *s·* embryonic life.
564–21 before the tribunal of *s·* mortal mind,
gl 580– 7 a *s·* finite mind, producing other minds,
580–11 a *s·* man, whose origin, substance, and mind
582– 5 human knowledge, or *s·* mortal mind,
583–26 *s·* mortal mind controlling mortal mind ;
585– 1 Not organs of the *s·* corporeal senses,
586–17 between Spirit and *s·* matter.
589– 6 in which the *s·* material senses yield to
597–24 Will, as a quality of *s·* mortal mind,
(*see also* **dead, laws, mind, senses**)

social
m 56–15 the *s·* scourge of all races,
f 239– 5 wealth, fame, and *s·* organizations,
b 340–27 whatever is wrong in *s·*, civil, criminal,

socially
gl 587– 4 acknowledged morally, civilly, and *s·*.

societies
a 28–27 because it is honored by sects and *s·*,

society
aloof from
s 109–13 kept aloof from *s·*,
elevation of
m 63–25 the elevation of *s·* in general
founding his
s 138– 2 Jesus purposed founding his *s·*,
human
ap 575–31 which binds human *s·* into solemn union ;
motive of
m 58– 2 To happify existence . . . should be the motive of *s·*.
sanctioned by
ph 171– 2 paganism and lust are so sanctioned by *s·*
state of
m 64–28 a worse state of *s·* than now exists.

society

sympathy nor
s 153–32 Neither sympathy nor s· should ever

a 28–32 There is too much animal courage in s·
m 57– 2 Without it there is no stability in s·,
an 102–29 employed, for the individual or s·.''
f 238–22 Attempts to conciliate s· and so
238–25 S· is a foolish juror,
p 362– 8 debarred from such a place and such s·,
387–18 and perform the most vital functions in s·.

society's
f 238– 7 is to incur s· frown ;

Socrates
m 66–27 S· considered patience salutary
f 215–28 S· feared not the hemlock poison.

Socratic
s 112– 8 adherents of the S·, the Platonic,

sod
g 521– 2 Knowledge of this lifts man above the s·,

soever
pr 1– * *What things s· ye desire— Mark* 11 : 24.
b 305–18 for what things s· He doeth,— *John* 5 : 19.

soft
s 142–11 If the s· palm, upturned to a lordly salary,

softened
p 387– 4 must it pay the penalty in a s· brain?

soft-winged
ap 574–26 and you will behold the s· dove

soil

barren
g 537–16 Error tills its own barren s·
good
b 270–32 the good s· wherein the seed of Truth
of disease
ph 188–24 The s· of disease is mortal mind,
seed and
f 212–19 They produce a rose through seed and s·,
seed or
g 520–25 plant grows, not because of seed or s·,
sown in the
m 66–12 not from seed sown in the s· of material hopes,
till the
g 518– 1 Man is not made to till the s·.

—

sp 74– 8 a sprout which has risen above the s·.
ph 190–15 as the grass springing from the s·
b 272– 6 s· of an ''honest and good heart''— *Luke* 8 : 15.
318–11 They would put soul into s·, life into limbo,
o 361–28 until God prepares the s· for the seed.
t 452–20 We s· our garments with conservatism,
g 521– 1 making him superior to the s·.

solar
s 119–29 perception of the movement of the s· system,
121–25 so far as our s· system is concerned,
122–30 mistake . . . regarding the s· system.
ph 189– 4 we still believe that there is s· light and heat.
f 246–10 The measurement of life by s· years
r 493– 5 and explains the s· system as
g 504– 8 though s· beams are not yet included in the
504–18 words which indicate, in the absence of s· time,
504–31 No s· rays nor planetary revolutions form the
510–21 There is no Scriptural allusion to s· light until
513–11 not yet measured by s· revolutions.
ap 561–28 light portrayed is really neither s· nor lunar,
gl 598–19 YEAR. A s· measurement of time ;
599– 1 the divisor of which is the s· year.

soldier
a 32– 3 In ancient Rome a s· was required to
b 309–11 a prince of God, or a s· of God,

soldier's
a 32– 9 does not commemorate a Roman s· oath,

sole
pref viii–30 for the Bible was her s· teacher ;
xii–11 s· editor and publisher of the C. S. Journal,
f 226–21 man's birthright of s· allegiance to his Maker
p 370–14 faith in the drug is the s· factor in the cure.
g 514– 6 of which God is the s· creator.

solecism
s 114–12 Mortal mind is a s· in language,
f 210–19 The expression *mortal mind* is really a s·,

solely
s 117–25 relates s· to human reason ;
157– 4 succeeds where homœopathy fails, s· because
f 220–16 engendered s· by human theories.
233– 3 proofs consist s· in the destruction of
233–31 sickness, which is s· the result of inharmony
b 299–31 If man were s· a creature of the
p 396–18 but s· on account of the tenacity of belief
g 528– 5 s· mythological and material.
543–28 it is seen that man springs s· from Mind.

solemn
m 61–25 more s· charge, than the culture of your garden
f 232–26 In the sacred sanctuary . . . are voices of s·
p 364–16 Here is suggested a s· question,
433–18 proceeds to pronounce the s· sentence
433–26 the Judge's s· peroration.
434–18 earnest, s· eyes, kindling with hope
ap 575–32 binds human society into s· union ;

solemnity
pr 7– 9 it gives momentary s· and elevation to
p 433– 2 and with great s· addresses the jury

solemnly
r 497–24 we s· promise to watch, and pray

solicitude
m 59– 4 There should be the most tender s·

solid
f 213– 7 conceives of something as either liquid or s·,
242–15 Self-love is more opaque than a s· body.
c 261–26 will neither lose the s· objects and ends of
t 450– 9 A third class of thinkers build with s· masonry.
460–16 Sickness is more than fancy ; it is s· conviction.
g 511–23 To mortal mind, the universe is liquid, s·, and
511–25 and mountains stand for s· and grand ideas.

solids
g 510–24 by the resolving of fluids into s·,

solitary
sp 95–23 Led by a s· star amid the darkness,
c 259– 3 nor is he an isolated, s· idea,
266– 8 Then the time will come when you will be s·,

solution
pref ix–32 degrees by which she came at length to its s· ;
pr 3– 7 and it is our task to work out the s·.
s 109–11 I sought the s· of this problem
b 314– 8 Our Master gained the s· of being,
338–17 of something fluid, of mortal mind in s·.
p 372– 4 matter was originally error in s·,

solve
pr 3– 5 to s· the problem?
a 44– 6 a place in which to s· the great problem
b 273– 6 not one of them can s· the problem of being
329–18 attempts to s· a problem of Euclid,
g 556–27 before it cares to s· the problem of being,

solved
s 126– 4 The problem of nothingness, . . . will be s·,

solvent
f 242–17 with the universal s· of Love

solves
f 216– 6 Science unveils the mystery and s· the problem

solving
sp 90–29 we may as well improve our time in s· the

sombre
g 513– 9 gray in the s· hues of twilight ;

some
pref ix–17 To-day, though rejoicing in s· progress,
xi– 3 which action in s· unexplained way
pr 3– 7 or mean to ask forgiveness at s· later day.
10–23 There is s· misapprehension of the
16–11 s· doubt among Bible scholars, whether
a 22– 1 would borrow the passport of s· wiser pilgrim,
28–30 await, in s· form, every pioneer of truth.
37–24 to follow in s· degree
54–30 would not s·, who now profess to love
m 61–14 If s· fortuitous circumstance
63–15 civilization mitigates it in s· measure.
64–11 when a man lends a helping hand to s·
65– 9 s· fundamental error in the marriage state.
69–15 S· day the child will ask his parent :
sp 90–14 s· insist that death is the necessary prelude
99–12 None may pick the lock nor enter by s· other
99–19 may possess natures above s· others
s 111–10 s· may deny its right to the name of
112– 8 the Spencerian, or s· other school.
112–10 s· particular system of human opinions.
129–19 and so are s· other systems.
129–26 of s· of the leading illusions along the path
131–14 through the . . . churches as s· persons insist?
136–14 ''S· say that thou art John— *Matt.* 16 : 14.
136–15 s·, Elias ; and others, Jeremias,— *Matt.* 16 : 14.
136–18 may indicate that s· of the people believed
139–21 darkening to s· extent the inspired pages.
145–15 or reliance on s· other minor curative.
150–24 and will be to all others at s· future day,
ph 182–27 come from s· sad incident, or else
182–32 presuppose that . . . is powerless on s· occasions
187– 9 it attributes to s· material god or medicine
197–28 mortal belief loses s· portion of its error.
f 203–18 or in s· power less than God.
205–19 we perceive the divine image in s· word
223–20 to answer this question by s· *ology*
225–12 There is always s· tumult,
227–10 s· public teachers permit an ignorance of

some

f 228–14	Mortals will *s·* day assert their freedom
237–23	*S·* invalids are unwilling to know the facts
245–12	*S·* American travellers saw her when she was
249–28	It throws off *s·* material fetters.
c 263–22	the discovery of *s·* distant idea of Truth ;
263–24	as when *s·* finite sense peers from its cloister
265– 7	and gain *s·* proper sense of the infinite,
b 294– 7	would take away *s·* quality and
297–25	*S·* thoughts are better than others.
299– 8	appearing at the door of *s·* sepulchre,
306–15	at *s·* uncertain future time
319–26	misinterpretation of the Word in *s·* instances
326– 8	must not try to climb . . . by *s·* other road.
333–21	with *s·* measure of power and grace
o 342– 5	In the result of *s·* unqualified condemnations
353–30	whatever is laid off is . . . *s·* unreal belief.
354– 3	"utter falsities and absurdities," as *s·* aver?
358–30	in *s·* Christian Scientist, whom they
p 369–15	in order to discover *s·* means of healing it.
376–27	*S·* people, mistaught as to Mind-science,
380– 1	may rest at length on *s·* receptive thought,
381– 5	or that *s·* disease is developing
381– 8	When infringing *s·* supposed law,
381–24	quite free from *s·* ailment.
403–23	Never conjure up *s·* new discovery from
412–12	liable under *s·* circumstances to impress it
415– 9	looks upon *s·* object which he dreads.
425– 1	or *s·* of his progenitors farther back
434– 4	*S·* exclaim, "It is contrary to law
t 443– 9	severely condemned by *s·* Scientists,
444– 2	In *s·* way, sooner or later,
450–15	*S·* people yield slowly to the touch of Truth.
453–10	but with *s·* individuals the morbid moral or
457–25	Departing from C. S., *s·* learners commend diet
462– 1	*S·* individuals assimilate truth more readily
r 477–27	The Indians caught *s·* glimpses of the
492–30	uniting on *s·* impossible basis.
g 522–27	is based on *s·* hypothesis of error,
525– 7	*s·* of the equivalents of the term *man*
537–27	is made to appear contradictory in *s·* places,
546– 2	at *s·* future time to be
ap 569– 3	Every mortal at *s·* period, here or hereafter,
570– 3	will chain, with fetters of *s·* sort,
573–30	will surely appear sometime and in *s·* way.
gl 583– 8	*s·* of the ideas of God beheld as men,

somebody

sp 81–31	That *s·*, somewhere, must have known the
89– 7	believing that *s·* else possesses her tongue
g 554–15	he learns to say, "I am *s·* ;

something

absence of

ph 186–12	It is nothing, because it is the absence of *s·*.

belief in

sp 92–27	laid on a belief in *s·* besides God.

calls itself

b 287–18	Evil calls itself *s·*, when it is nothing.

claiming to be

b 330–29	nothing claiming to be *s·*,
gl 591–25	MORTAL MIND. Nothing claiming to be *s·*,

conceives of

f 213– 6	Mortal mind conceives of *s·* as

gains

b 294–29	The thief believes that he gains *s·* by stealing,

looked for

b 270–14	looked for *s·* higher than the

mimicry of

gl 580– 9	product of nothing as the mimicry of *s·* ;

needing

g 501–16	when needing *s·* more native to their

need of

s 151– 6	an absolute need of *s·* beyond itself

new

ap 560–25	Persecution of all who have spoken *s·* new and

nothing and

a 23–17	swinging between nothing and *s·*.

possible loss of

a 51– 2	the possible loss of *s·* more important than

practical

o 355– 4	The charge . . . is met by *s·* practical,

prayed for

pr 9– 8	having prayed for *s·* better,

seen and felt

p 395–22	to hold it as *s·* seen and felt

supposes that

g 530–30	supposes that *s·* springs from nothing,

---

a 54–23	whose religion was *s·* more than a name.
sp 91–26	postulate of belief . . . *s·* apart from God.
s 114–14	the phrase *mortal mind* implies *s·* untrue
ph 181–26	to satisfy the sick that you are doing *s·*
186–30	Since it must believe in *s·* besides itself,
f 220–19	and then charges them to *s·* else,
c 258– 4	human craving for *s·* better,
263– 3	even privileged originators of *s·* which

something

b 323–23	contemplation of *s·* better than disease or sin.
338–16	suggests the thought of *s·* fluid,
o 345–27	if a man think himself to be *s·*,— *Gal.* 6 : 3.
347–26	The dream that matter and error are *s·*
350– 1	They think of matter as *s·*
p 390– 2	and I should like *s·* more to eat."
391–25	has no intelligence to declare itself *s·*
422–30	he believes that *s·* stronger than Mind
r 480– 4	the opposite of the *s·* of Spirit.
492–15	theories— that matter is *s·*, or that
g 539– 6	as if life and immortality were *s·* which
542–29	misconception of Life as *s·* less than God,
556–21	They seem to be *s·*, but are not.
gl 592–14	there is *s·* spiritually lacking,

somethingness

b 276–27	Harmony is the *s·* named Truth.
o 346–12	in order to prove the *s·*— yea, the allness
353–21	not continue to admit the *s·* of superstition,

sometime

m 68– 4	*S·* we shall learn how Spirit,
p 402–13	*S·* it will be learned that mortal mind
g 531–10	The human mind will *s·* rise above
ap 573–30	will surely appear *s·* and in some way.

sometimes

pr 11– 5	A magistrate *s·* remits the penalty,
a 24– 6	*s·* by the worst passions of men),
47– 8	It was *s·* an overwhelming power
55–10	does not the pulpit *s·* scorn it?
m 64–14	A wife is *s·* debarred
68–23	salutary causes *s·* incur these effects.
s 114–20	we must *s·* recur to the old and
143–13	*S·* the human mind uses one error
151– 1	To be sure, they *s·* treat the sick as if
ph 169– 7	*s·* to his discomfiture,
172–28	is *s·* the quickener of manliness ;
f 212– 3	A tooth which has been extracted *s·* aches again
215–15	We are *s·* led to believe that darkness is as
249–26	mortal night-dream is *s·* nearer the fact
c 264– 5	the glorious forms which we *s·* behold in the
b 277–31	*s·* beautiful, always erroneous.
327– 9	Evil is *s·* a man's highest conception of
o 343–21	It would *s·* seem as if truth were
345–10	It is *s·* said, in criticising C. S.,
346– 6	It is *s·* said that C. S. teaches the
358–24	*S·* it is said : "Rest assured that
p 376– 8	diseases deemed dangerous *s·* come from
383–22	*s·* tells you that the weed preserves his health,
394–19	their theories are *s·* pernicious,
398– 1	*S·* Jesus called a disease by name,
398–16	remedies, *s·* not containing a
417– 3	Give sick people credit for *s·* knowing
421–21	Calm the excitement *s·* induced by
421–23	*s·* explain the symptoms and their cause
431– 7	*s·* going to sleep immediately after a
t 446– 6	If patients *s·* seem worse while
461–17	you should tell your belief *s·*,
r 489–31, 32	would have the material senses *s·* good and *s·* bad.
491–18	*s·* presenting no appearance of mind,
g 549–11, 12	*s·* through eggs, *s·* through buds,
549–13	and *s·* through self-division.
gl 590–15	this term is *s·* employed as a title,

somewhat

a 35– 7	they were enabled to rise *s·* from
s 128–14	escapes *s·* from itself, and requires less repose.
143–18	You admit that mind influences the body *s·*,
149–18	remarked . . . mind affects the body *s·*,
156–11	Believing then *s·* in the ordinary theories
ph 170–25	to ponder *s·* the supremacy of
180– 7	his faith in their efforts is *s·* helpful
r 488– 8	differ *s·* in meaning from
g 529–31	He begins his reign over man *s·* mildly,

somewhere

sp 81–31	That somebody, *s·*, must have known the
ph 174–23	Anatomy admits that mind is *s·* in man,

Son

His

a 45–12	by the [seeming] death of His *S·*,— *Rom.* 5 : 10.
r 497– 6	We acknowledge His *S·*, one Christ ;

His beloved

a 23– 6	vented upon His beloved *S·*,

of God

pr 5–29	An apostle says that the *S·* of God [Christ]
a 29–14	disciples of Jesus believe him the *S·* of God."
sp 94–11	he made himself the *S·* of God."— *John* 19 : 7
f 203–10	"He made himself the *S·* of God,"— *John* 19 : 7.
226– 9	rights of man as a *S·* of God,
b 313–16	regarded Christ as the *S·* of God,
o 361–13	Jesus Christ is not God, . . . but is the *S·* of God.
g 519–19	of the knowledge of the *S·* of God,— *Eph.* 4 : 13.
gl 594–16	The *S·* of God, the Messiah or Christ.

of Man

r 482–19	he was literally the *S·* of Man.

Son

of man
s 132–26   "When the *S·* of man cometh, — *Luke* 18 : 8.
136–12   that I, the *S·* of man, am?" — *Matt.* 16 : 13.
b 334–25   Revelator represents the *S·* of man as saying
r 482–17   called himself "the *S·* of man," — *Matt.* 9 : 6.

of the living God
s 137–18   Christ, the *S·* of the living God !" — *Matt.* 16 : 16.

sp 77–16   neither the *S·*, but the Father." — *Mark* 13 : 32.
f 233–13   not even "the *S·* but the Father ;" — *Mark* 13 : 32.
b 268– *   *and with his S· Jesus Christ.* — *I John* 1 : 3.
305–17   the *S·* can do nothing of himself, — *John* 5 : 19.
305–19   these also doeth the *S·* likewise." — *John* 5 : 19.
313–10   another passage . . . which refers to the *S·* as
337– 9   the *S·* must be in accord with the Father,
g 534–12   The *S·* of the Virgin-mother unfolded the
ap 569– 2   as Truth, represented by the *S·* ;
gl 594–16   definition of

son

Jacob's
gl 581–15   ASHER (Jacob's *s·*). Hope and faith ;
582– 4   BENJAMIN (Jacob's *s·*). A physical belief as to
583–26   DAN (Jacob's *s·*). Animal magnetism ;
586–21   GAD (Jacob's *s·*). Science ;
589– 1   ISSACHAR (Jacob's *s·*). A corporeal belief ;
590–11   LEVI (Jacob's *s·*). A corporeal and sensual belief ;
593–12   REUBEN (Jacob's *s·*). Corporeality ;

Mary's
b 313–18   the exaltation of Jesus, Mary's *s·*,

Noah's
gl 587–21   HAM (Noah's *s·*). Corporeal belief ;
589– 8   JAPHET (Noah's *s·*). A type of spiritual peace,
594–14   SHEM (Noah's *s·*). A corporeal mortal ;

of a virgin
b 313– 1   He was the *s·* of a virgin.
332–23   Jesus was the *s·* of a virgin.

of Ham
gl 582–24   CANAAN (the *s·* of Ham). A sensuous belief ;

of Jona
s 137–27   Simon Bar-jona, or *s·* of Jona ;

of man
gl 594–17   The *s·* of man, the offspring of the flesh.

a 50–12   to sustain and bless so faithful a *s·*.
o 361–18   Father and *s·*, are one in being.
r 482–17   but not the *s·* of Joseph.
gl 594–17   "*S·* of a year."

song

ph 200– 4   lifted thought into the *s·* of David.
f 234– 5   be it *s·*, sermon, or Science
ap 568–26   A louder *s·*, sweeter than has ever before

Son of God
(see Son)

Son of man
(see Son)

Son of the living God
(see Son)

sons

c 257–21   guideth "Arcturus with his *s·*." — *Job* 38 : 32.
b 315–20   the liberty of the *s·* of God.
g 503– 4   highest ideas are the *s·* and daughters of God.
515–22   all ideas, — the *s·* and daughters of God.

sonship

b 312–32   and entitled him to *s·* in Science.
315–12   hid from their sense Christ's *s·* with God.
316– 7   and to recognize the divine *s·*.
331–31   Christ the spiritual idea of *s·* ;

soon

a 34–24   for *s·* their dear Master would rise again
49– 9   Had they so *s·* lost sight of his mighty works,
s 153–21   and it will *s·* cure the boil.
b 324–23   spiritual light *s·* enabled him to follow the
p 364– 4   manifested towards one who was *s·*,
414–16   explain C. S. to them, but not too *s·*,
417–27   as *s·* as they can bear it,
424– 1   *S·* the child becomes a separate, . . . mortal mind,
r 485– 8   only *s·* to disappear because of their uselessness
495–31   *s·* ascertain that error cannot destroy error.
g 534– 4   *s·* to manifest the deathless man of
ap 563–26   to devour her child as *s·* as it — *Rev.* 12 : 4.

sooner

pr 13–14   Do we gain the omnipotent ear *s·* by words than
a 54– 9   must *s·* or later plant themselves in Christ,
sp 91–10   the *s·* error is reduced to its native nothingness,
91–12   the *s·* man's great reality will appear
f 223– 3   *S·* or later we shall learn that the fetters
240–24   Remember that mankind must *s·* or later,
b 296–15   Whether mortals will learn this *s·* or
p 381–21   and you will *s·* grasp man's God-given dominion.
428–25   *s·* or later, . . . we must master sin

sooner

p 429– 6   and the *s·* we begin the better.
t 444– 3   *s·* or later, all must rise superior to
449– 8   Right adjusts the balance *s·* or later.

soonest

pref x–26   The unbiased Christian thought is *s·* touched by

soothe

p 398–26   will *s·* fear and change the belief of disease to

soothing

f 230–25   They are *s·* syrups to put children to sleep,

soporific

p 416–12   when the *s·* influence of the opium is

sorcery

ap 571–30   outshining sin, *s·*, lust, and hypocrisy.

sore

ph 193–21   discharge from the *s·* stopped,
193–21   and the *s·* was healed.
f 237– 6   "Mamma, my finger is not a bit *s·*."
p 398– 5   rent him *s·* and came out of him, — *Mark* 9 : 26.

sorely

a 48– 2   the staves of bigoted ignorance smote him *s·*.

sorrow

and death
f 203–30   waves of sin, *s·*, and death beat in vain.

and joy
s 125–13   pain and painlessness, *s·* and joy,

and pain
ap 573–27   cessation of death, *s·*, and pain.

cup of
a 33–14   and drain to the dregs his cup of *s·*.

has its
m 66–30   *S·* has its reward.

her
ap 562–26   but remembering no more her *s·*

is salutary
m 66– 9   *S·* is salutary.

is turned
pr 14–16   *S·* is turned into joy when the

joy and
f 246– 3   swinging between evil and good, joy and *s·*,
c 262–22   false estimate . . . of joy and *s·*,

multiply thy
g 535– 7   will greatly multiply thy *s·* — *Gen.* 3 : 16.

ocean of
m 67–14   on the seething ocean of *s·*.

pain and
g 557–16   the less pain and *s·* are his.

sin and
f 215–19   So sin and *s·*, disease and death,

with
o 342– 6   one may see with *s·* the sad effects

your
p 386–27   "Your *s·* is without cause,"

pr 5– 3   *S·* for wrong-doing is but one step
f 219– 1   weakness, weariness, *s·*, sin, death,
248–16   Is it imperfection, joy, *s·*, sin, suffering?
b 304–12   joy cannot be turned into *s·*,
304–12   *s·* is not the master of joy ;
p 386–22   Thus it is with all *s·*, sickness, and death.
g 535– 7   in *s·* thou shalt bring forth — *Gen.* 3 : 16.
535–23   in *s·* shalt thou eat of it — *Gen.* 3 : 17.
536–26   Through toil, struggle, and *s·*,
552–22   From a material source flows no remedy for *s·*,
557–18   "In *s·* thou shalt bring forth — *Gen.* 3 : 16.

sorrowful

a 26– 7   all have the cup of *s·* effort to drink
33– 3   His followers, *s·* and silent,

sorrowing

pref xii–25   is joyful to bear consolation to the *s·*
sp 78–29   the sick are healed, the *s·* are comforted,

sorrows

pr 10– 7   to profit by Jesus' cup of earthly *s·*,
10– 7   God will sustain us under these *s·*.
a 41– 5   as well as through their *s·* and afflictions.
42– 9   "man of *s·*" was in no peril from — *Isa.* 53 : 3.
52–19   "man of *s·*" best understood the — *Isa.* 53 : 3.
ph 196–31   The press unwittingly sends forth many *s·*
gl 587–24   motives, affections, joys, and *s·*.

sorry

a 19–21   continues to pray and repent, sin and be *s·*,

sort

ph 195–19   Academics of the right *s·* are requisite.
f 233– 1   nor opportunity in Science for error of any *s·*.
p 406–19   Resist evil — error of every *s·*
408– 1   Every *s·* of sickness is error,
t 451–25   nature and methods of error of every *s·*,
g 508–17   *Gender* means simply *kind* or *s·*,
ap 570– 3   will chain, with fetters of some *s·*,

sorts

   c 257–22 Finite mind manifests all *s·* of errors,
   p 404–10 Lust, malice, and all *s·* of evil
      419– 4 Errors of all *s·* tend in this direction.

sots

   s 158–23 and men and women become loathsome *s·*.

sought

   pr 6–20 according as His mercy is *s·* or unsought,
   m 60–31 more secure in our keeping, if *s·* in Soul.
   s 109–11 I *s·* the solution of this problem
    126–10 has *s·* and interpreted in its own way
    139– 3 theology which the impious *s·* to destroy.
   ph 196– 2 Man has "*s·* out many inventions,"— *Eccl.* 7 : 29.
   f 215–30 Having *s·* man's spiritual state,
   b 273– 5 Human belief has *s·* out many inventions,
    314–10 The Jews, who *s·* to kill this man of God,
    329– 3 they will be *s·* and taught,
   p 364–18 as Simon *s·* the Saviour,
    439–21 the unfortunate Mortal Man who *s·* your aid
   g 531–22 Has man *s·* out other creative

Soul (*see also* **Soul's**)

  action of
   sp 89–23 The influence or action of *S·* confers a freedom,
  allness of
   r 497–22 even the allness of *S·*, Spirit,
  and body
   s 114–24 It lifts the veil of mystery from *S·* and body.
    119–30 reverses the seeming relation of *S·* and body
    122–29 the same mistake regarding *S·* and body
  and its attributes
   f 210–11 Knowing that *S·* and its attributes were
  and matter
   f 215– 7 *S·* and matter are at variance
  and Spirit
   b 335–16 *S·* and Spirit being one,
  and substance
   b 280–13 sense of the divisibility of *S·* and substance,
  as God
   b 310–14 Science reveals *S·* as God, untouched by
  atmosphere of
   gl 587–27 spirituality ; bliss ; the atmosphere of *S·*.
  bar of
   p 441– 6 not permitted to enter any suits at the bar of *S·*,
  belief that
   a 39–10 belief that *S·* is in the body causes mortals to
  body and
   r 477–19 *Question.*— What are body and *S·* ?
  body instead of by
   g 536–16 governed . . . by body instead of by *S·*,
  body instead of in
   f 223– 5 the illusion that he lives in body instead of in *S·*,
  cannot sin
   r 468– 6 Because Soul is immortal, *S·* cannot sin,
  capacity of
   sp 85– 4 which demonstrates the capacity of *S·*,
  changeth not
   b 310–18 *S·* changeth not.
  could reproduce
   r 488–28 *S·* could reproduce them in all their perfection ;
  explain
   ph 200– 8 Whoever is incompetent to explain *S·*
  expresses
   r 477–30 Separated from man, who expresses *S·*,
  facts of
   p 420–32 harmonious facts of *S·* and immortal being.
    428– 4 A demonstration of the facts of *S·*
  faith in
   f 216– 1 his faith in *S·* and his indifference to the body.
  false sense of
   b 335–23 Only by losing the false sense of *S·* can we
  freedom in
   m 58–12 There is moral freedom in *S·*.
  from sense to
   a 48– 9 from earth to heaven, from sense to *S·*,
   c 266– 1 and transplant the affections from sense to *S·*,
   ap 566– 7 in their passage from sense to *S·*,
  God and
   b 335–16 God and *S·* are one,
  governed by
   s 125–16 man governed by *S·*, not by material sense.
   b 273–18 Man is harmonious when governed by *S·*.
    302–22 this real man is governed by *S·*
  gravitates towards
   b 323–21 divine Science, which gravitates towards *S·*
  harmony of
   p 390– 5 never deny the everlasting harmony of *S·*,
  has infinite
   m 60–29 *S·* has infinite resources with which to bless
  heaven of
   g 535–16 into the heaven of *S·*, into the heritage of the
  ideas of
   b 269–16 exchanges the objects of sense for the ideas of *S·*.
  immortal
   b 311–20 or that immortal *S·* is in mortal body,

Soul

  immortality of
   b 306– 7 immortality of *S·* makes man immortal.
   r 481–29 hence the immortality of *S·*.
  indications of
   s 144–13 the weaker the indications of *S·*.
  intelligence, or
   r 480–17 would make . . . the effect of intelligence, or *S·*,
  is immortal
   b 311– 7 *S·* is immortal because it is Spirit,
    335–20 *S·* is immortal, it does not exist in mortality.
   p 381–13 by the understandng that *S·* is immortal,
   r 468– 6 Because *S·* is immortal, Soul cannot sin,
  is not in matter
   b 300–23 therefore *S·* is not in matter.
  is sinless
   b 288–22 *S·* is sinless, not to be found in the body ;
  is Spirit
   f 223–11 *S·* is Spirit, and Spirit is greater than body.
   p 396–28 *S·* is Spirit, outside of matter,
  is supreme
   gl 590– 3 the atmosphere of Spirit, where *S·* is supreme.
  is synonymous
   sp 71– 7 *S·* is synonymous with Spirit, God,
  joys of
   p 390–11 pleasures and pains of sense for the joys of *S·*.
  law of
   m 63– 1 does not make . . . the superior law of *S·* last.
   b 311–24 even the higher law of *S·*,
   p 427– 3 Life is the law of *S·*,
  Life and
   o 344– 2 it claims God as the only absolute Life and *S·*,
  life in
   pr 13–32 is not cognizant of life in *S·*, not in body.
  Life or
   b 306–13 If Life or *S·* and its representative, man,
  Mind is the
   b 307–25 divine Mind is the *S·* of man,
   g 508– 7 Mind is the *S·* of all.
  more
   f 247–32 to have less illusion and more *S·*,
  no oblivion for
   f 214–32 there is no oblivion for *S·* and its faculties.
  not qualities of
   p 388–25 Because sin and sickness are not qualities of *S·*,
  offspring of
   a 30–24 the difference between the offspring of *S·* and of
  of man
   b 280–27 God, the *S·* of man and of all existence,
    307–25 divine Mind is the *S·* of man,
  or God
   sp 72–11 *S·*, or God, is the only truth-giver to man.
   r 468–22 the synonym of Mind, *S·*, or God,
  or Mind
   b 302–20 *S·*, or Mind, of the spiritual man is God,
  or Spirit
   s 120– 4 *S·*, or Spirit, is God, unchangeable and
   r 466–20 *S·* or Spirit signifies Deity and nothing else.
    466–21 *S·* or Spirit means only one Mind,
  over sense
   b 322– 5 the control of *S·* over sense,
  prayer of
   pr 14–23 The Lord's Prayer is the prayer of *S·*,
  radiance of
   f 247–15 has a glory of its own,— the radiance of *S·*.
  rebukes sense
   o 350–29 *S·* rebukes sense, and Truth destroys error.
  recognize
   sp 93– 1 to recognize *S·* as substantial and able to
  reflection of
   f 249–31 Man is the reflection of *S·*.
  reflects
   s 120– 5 and man coexists with and reflects *S·*, God,
  rejoice in
   m 64–21 Then shall *S·* rejoice in its own,
  representation of
   g 510–16 The sun is a metaphorical representation of *S·*
  representatives of
   gl 583– 5 representatives of *S·*, not corporeal sense ;
  restored his
   b 309– 4 to use the word of the Psalmist, *restored* his *S·*,
  Science of
   s 122– 8 material senses' reversal of the Science of *S·*
    131– 9 opposition of sensuous man to the Science of *S·*
   r 467– 2 the demands of the Science of *S·* ?
    467–21 This is a leading point in the Science of *S·*,
  sense and
   f 240–32 how to divide between sense and *S·*.
  sense of
   gl 582–15 a sense of *S·*, which has spiritual bliss
  Spirit or
   b 309–25 impossible for infinite Spirit or *S·* to be in a
    330–12 the only Life, substance, Spirit, or *S·*,
   r 478– 6 has never beheld Spirit or *S·* leaving a body
   gl 598–16 for never did he give up Spirit, or *S·*.

Soul

symbol of
g 595– 1 SUN. The symbol of *S·* governing man,
the senses of
f 213–18 as communicated through the senses of *S·*
214–29 Neither . . . can interfere with the senses of *S·*,
understanding of
f 210–16 a better understanding of *S·* and salvation.

---

pr 7–17 Physical sensation, not *S·*, produces material
9–23 control of Spirit, in which *S·* is our master,
a 30–27 to allow *S·* to hold the control,
m 60–31 more secure in our keeping, if sought in *S·*.
sp 70–15 What are God's identities? What is *S·*?
s 115–14 Life, Truth, Love, *S·*, Spirit, Mind.
ph 172–20 the belief that there is *S·* in sense
f 203–23 believe that the deathless Principle, or *S·*,
204–31 The error, which says that *S·* is in body,
207–15 Body is not first and *S·* last,
215– 4 If Spirit, *S·*, could sin or be lost,
240–10 to be governed by matter or *S·* in body,
250– 1 We run into error when we divide *S·* into souls,
b 274– 6 the offspring of sense, not of *S·*, Spirit,
280–23 the belief that *S·* is in body,
281–28 Divine Science does not put . . . *S·* into matter,
282–20 nor can non-intelligence become *S·*.
300–23 Spirit is God, *S·* ;
302– 1 *S·* is not compassed by finiteness.
310–21 If *S·* could sin, Spirit, *S·*, would be flesh
310–23 If *S·* sinned, *S·* would die.
310–25 If there was sin in *S·*.
310–32 neither growth, maturity, nor decay in *S·*.
317–27 and to the testimony of . . . more than to *S·*,
335–19 Nothing but Spirit, *S·*, can evolve Life,
335–21 *S·* must be incorporeal to be Spirit,
o 359–15 evidence of the existence of Spirit, *S·*,
360–10 replies : . . . and keep *S·* well out of sight.
p 395– 7 leaving *S·* to master the false evidences of the
427– 4 *S·* is never without its representative.
427– 6 can no more die . . . than can *S·*,
437–15 *S·* a criminal though recommended to
r 465–10 God is . . . Mind, Spirit, *S·*,
467–17 Science reveals Spirit, *S·*, as not in the body,
467–22 Spirit, *S·*, is not confined in man,
468– 3 If *S·* sinned, it would be mortal,
468–26 Life is divine Principle, Mind, *S·*, Spirit.
477– 6 Man is not a material habitation for *S·* ;
477– 7 *S·*, being Spirit, is seen in nothing imperfect
477–22 *S·* is the substance, Life, and
477–24 *S·* can never reflect anything inferior
477–26 Man is the expression of *S·*.
478– 3 What evidence of *S·* or of immortality
479– 2 offspring of physical sense and not of *S·*,
481–24 If *S·* sins, it must be mortal.
481–28 *S·* is the divine Principle of man
481–30 it is material sense, not *S·*, which sins ;
482–10 *S·* is properly the synonym of Spirit,
490– 5 Human will is . . . not a faculty of *S·*.
gl 580–24 supposition that . . . *S·* dwells in material
587– 7 Principle ; Mind ; *S·* ; Spirit ; Life ; Truth ;
588– 9 I, or EGO. Divine Principle ; Spirit ; *S·* ;
591–16 the only Spirit, *S·*, divine Principle, substance,

soul

absence of
b 311–16 sense of temporary loss or absence of *s·*,
and body
s 123– 6 the error relating to *s·* and body,
ph 196–11 able to destroy both *s·* and body.— *Matt.* 10 : 28.
b 338– 6 belief . . . that he is both *s·* and body,
and life
r 466–25 fallacy that intelligence, *s·*, and life can be in
believe that
b 311–10 So long as we believe that *s·* can sin
bodily
c 257– 9 a bodily *s·* and a material mind,
false estimates of
b 311–14 Through false estimates of *s·* as dwelling in
false sense of
b 319– 1 manifests mortality, a false sense of *s·*.
his
ph 166– 9 pilgrimage to Mecca for the salvation of his *s·*.
human
ph 200–21 the so-called human *s·* or spirit,
b 310–19 are commonly taught that there is a human *s·*
hypothesis that
r 482– 4 hypothesis that *s·* is both an evil and a good
is identical
r 482–11 out of Science, *s·* is identical with sense,
is willing
f 235–24 Then when the *s·* is willing
life or
sp 70–15 Does life or *s·* exist in the thing formed?
living
g 524–15 and man became a living *s·*.— *Gen.* 2 : 7.
mind and
g 531– 6 error, . . . that mind and *s·* are both right and

soul

no finite
r 466–21 There is no finite *s·* nor spirit.
not a sinful
b 311–12 It is a sense of sin, and not a sinful *s·*,
r 481–32 sense of sin which is lost, and not a sinful *s·*.
of Christianity
s 140–17 Spiritual devoutness is the *s·* of Christianity.
of Christian Science
s 113– 6 the heart and *s·* of C. S., is Love.
sense for
r 482– 1 substitution of the word *sense* for *s·*
sense of
r 493–26 Any sense of *s·* in matter is not the
theory that
b 300–26 theory that *s·*, spirit, intelligence,
the word
ph 196–13 here the word *s·* means a false sense
r 482– 4 has adulterated the meaning of the word *s·*
482– 6 The proper use of the word *s·* can always
with all thy
pr 9–18 and with all thy *s·*,— *Matt.* 22 : 37.
your
p 433–26 "May God have mercy on your *s·*,"

---

sp 77–20 and so prolong the illusion either of a *s·* inert
s 120– 2 never . . . while we admit that *s·* is in body
122–31 They insist that *s·* is in body
c 257– 9 belief in . . . a *s·* governed by the body
b 295–30 teaches that . . . immortal *s·* is resurrected from
301–30 This falsity presupposes *s·* to be an
310–20 taught . . . that *s·* may be lost, and yet be
318–11 They would put *s·* into soil,
318–32 The body does not include *s·*, but
337– 3 as material sensation, or a *s·* in the body,
p 362– * *Why art thou cast down, O my s·—* *Psal.* 42 : 11.
r 476– 7 will cease to claim that *s·* is in body,
478–12 Who can see a *s·* in the body?
485–19 belief that life can be in matter or *s·* in body,
ap 578– 8 [LOVE] restoreth my *s·*— *Psal.* 23 : 3.

Soul-created
b 306–23 not more distinct . . . than are the *S·* forms

Soul-existence
ph 167– 5 *S·*, in the place of sense-existence,

Soul-filled
gl 599– 1 Eternity is God's measurement of *S·* years.

Soul-inspired
f 224–29 On its banner is the *S·* motto,
b 308–14 The *S·* patriarchs heard the voice of Truth,

soulless
f 249–16 Whence then is *s·* matter?

Soul's
p 438–25 without the inspection of *S·* government officers.

souls
s 150–25 doctrine of the predestination of *s·*
f 250– 1 We run into error when we divide Soul into *s·*,
b 280–15 seeks to divide . . . into persons and *s·*.
r 466– 7 *Question.—* What are spirits and *s·*?
466–19 The term *s·* or *spirits* is as improper as the
gl 587–14 suppositious minds, or *s·*,
594–18 definition of

Soul-sense
sp 85– 4 This *S·* comes to the human mind when the

sound
pref viii– 8 and gives sweet concord to *s·*.
x–31 but *s·* morals are most desirable.
sp 84–21 not dependent upon the ear and eye for *s·* or
88– 5 And the *s·* of a voice that is still.
89–26 *S·* is not the originator of music,
97–25 until its inarticulate *s·* is forever silenced
s 126–14 nor sent forth a positive *s·*.
ph 194–23 where neither sight nor *s·* could reach him,
195– 6 Every *s·* convulsed him with anguish.
f 212–28 that the undulations of the air convey *s·*,
213–16 *S·* is a mental impression
213–18 reveals *s·* as communicated through the
213–26 Mental melodies . . . supersede conscious *s·*.
214– 2 impressions from Truth were as distinct as *s·*,
214– 2 and that they came as *s·* to the
b 291– 7 when the last trump shall *s·* ;
292– 2 then the final trump will *s·*
p 425–29 If you have *s·* and capacious lungs
r 486–16 If death restores sight, *s·*, and strength

sounded
f 223–27 but the last trump has not *s·*,
226– 7 *s·* the keynote of universal freedom,

sounder
m 61–13 better balanced minds, and *s·* constitutions.

soundness
s 162– 9 restores carious bones to *s·*.

sounds
sp 86–20 or they are images and *s·* evolved

special		
	sp 95–18	and is one of the s· characteristics thereof.
	s 133–22	carried out in s· theories concerning God,
	135–27	nor a s· gift from a ritualistic Jehovah ;
	ph 178– 2	they know nothing of this . . . s· person,
	f 236– 3	A s· privilege is vested in the ministry.
	b 319–30	but we can by s· and proper capitalization
	p 364–14	a s· sign of Oriental courtesy.
	404– 3	a slave to tobacco, or the s· servant of
	408– 9	from the s· name of insanity.
	ap 560– 1	has a s· suggestiveness in connection with
specially		
	s 123–25	did not s· belong to a dispensation now ended,
	gl 590–18	unless s· coupled with the name God.
species		
different		
	g 552–27	The intermixture of different s·,
floral		
	m 68–24	perpetuation of the floral s· by bud or
genus and		
	b 277–17	the order of genus and s· is preserved
	ap 560–20	The botanist must know the genus and s·
human		
	(see **human***)*	
many		
	p 407–29	There are many s· of insanity.
material		
	ph 172– 8	How then is the material s· maintained,
mild		
	p 408–15	is in itself a mild s· of insanity.
original		
	b 277–14	as preserving their original s·,
	g 552–28	results in a return to the original s·.
their		
	g 549–11	to multiply their s· sometimes through eggs,
	ph 189–26	From . . . comes the reproduction of the s·,
	r 482–18	As woman is but a s· of the genera,
	494– 5	Is it not a s· of infidelity to believe that
	g 529–24	the s· described, — a talking serpent,
	531–19	maintained by God in perpetuating the s·?
	550–25	no instance of one s· producing its opposite.
	551–30	in order to propagate its s·,
specific		
	an 103–19	animal magnetism or hypnotism is the s· term
specifically		
	c 267– 7	s· man means all men.
specified		
	pr 11– 2	s· also the terms of forgiveness.
specimen		
	p 388–17	a s· of the ambiguous nature of
specimens		
	ph 195–26	impossible ideals, and s· of depravity,
speck		
	p 413–21	I am not patient with a s· of dirt ;
	g 547–14	germinating s· of so-called embryonic life
spectacle		
	f 241–12	what a mocking s· is sin !
spectators		
	p 430–24	court-room is filled with interested s·,
spectral		
	o 353–20	We must give up the s· at all points.
spectre		
	a 45–25	called him a spirit, ghost, or s·,
	b 314–17	To such . . . the real man seemed a s·,
speculation		
	f 242–26	s· or superstition appropriates no part of
speculative		
	s 126–20	left to the mercy of s· hypotheses?
	149– 6	or a bundle of s· human theories?
	ph 195–24	the s· theory, the nauseous fiction.
	f 209–26	and all the paraphernalia of s· theories,
	229–20	law of mortal mind, conjectural and s·,
speech		
	pr 3–26	Action expresses more gratitude than s·.
	15– 9	according to motives, not according to s·.
	b 292–20	"Why do ye not understand my s·? — *John* 8 : 43.
	321– 6	The Hebrew Lawgiver, slow of s·,
	t 454–21	strength and freedom to s· and action.
speeches		
	p 367– 7	gushing theories, stereotyped borrowed s·,
speechless		
	a 26– 4	in s· agony exploring the way for us,
speedily		
	pref vii–23	but it cannot make them s· understood.
	r 486–15	If this were not so, man would be s· annihilated.
	493– 1	C. S. s· shows Truth to be triumphant.
speeds		
	p 426– 9	expectation s· our progress.

spell		
	a 39–25	To break this earthly s·, mortals must
Spencerian		
	s 112– 8	the Platonic, the S·, or some other school.
spend		
	p 409–29	We cannot s· our days here in ignorance of
spent		
	ph 174–13	"the night is far s·, — *Rom.* 13 : 12.
	o 354–23	The night of materiality is far s·,
sphere		
	a 36– 4	simply through translation into another s·.
	f 240–15	Its symbol is the s·.
	c 265–13	enlarged individuality, a wider s· of thought
	b 282– 5	a circle or s· and a straight line.
	282– 8	The s· represents good, the self-existent
	283–31	or a straight line a s·.
	gl 585– 5	A s· ; a type of eternity and immortality,
spheres		
	m 59–12	the different demands of their united s·,
	c 255– 6	changing . . . discord into the music of the s·.
	g 513– 7	lead on to spiritual s· and exalted beings.
spike		
	ph 193– 2	caused by a fall upon a wooden s·
spilled		
	b 281–31	or the new idea will be s·,
spinal		
	p 402– 7	dislocated joints, and s· vertebræ.
spire		
	s 142–12	making dome and s· tremulous with beauty,
Spirit *(see also* **Spirit's***)*		
ability of		
	s 130–22	the ability of S· to make the body harmonious,
	r 494–17	as well as the infinite ability of S·,
abode of		
	b 280– 5	light and harmony which are the abode of S·,
acts		
	g 520–30	S· acts through the Science of Mind,
alchemy of		
	p 422–20	C. S., by the alchemy of S·,
all is		
	b 331–25	Hence all is S· and spiritual.
	r 475– 3	all is S·, divine Principle and its idea.
amenable to		
	p 434–32	immortal and amenable to S· only.
and flesh		
	f 254– 7	until the battle between S· and flesh is fought
	b 288– 6	this warfare between the S· and flesh
	g 530–25	Thus S· and flesh war.
and God		
	o 345– 1	S· and God are often regarded as
and its formations		
	c 264–20	S· and its formations are the only
and matter		
	pref viii– 9	physics teach that both S· and matter are real
	sp 73– 1	As readily can you mingle . . . as S· and matter.
	73–27	mistake to suppose . . . that S· and matter,
	ph 167–24	with S· and matter, Truth and error.
	186– 9	S· and matter, good and evil,
	f 204– 9	namely, S· and matter,
	204–17	a supposed mixture . . . of S· and matter.
	211– 3	S· and matter, Truth and error,
	b 279–13	S· and matter can neither coexist nor cooperate,
	281– 4	S· and matter no more commingle than
	285–13	the opposite natures of S· and matter,
	296–23	When the evidence of S· and matter,
	319–14	S· and matter neither concur in man nor in
	p 372–21	Truth and error, S· and matter,
and the bride		
	g 548– 1	"The S· and the bride say, Come! — *Rev.* 22 : 17.
and the flesh		
	s 145–28	warfare between S· and the flesh goes on.
	b 315–31	the mediator between S· and the flesh,
and Truth		
	ph 177–23	against God, S· and Truth.
	b 278–15	Hence, as we approach S· and Truth,
and understanding		
	r 486–25	reality and . . . are in S· and understanding,
antipode of		
	sp 72–19	matter, the antipode of S·.
antipodes of		
	b 335–30	the suppositional antipodes of S·,
appeal to		
	p 440–21	Mortal Man has his appeal to S·, God,
aroma of		
	ph 191–32	Mind, God, sends forth the aroma of S·,
atmosphere of		
	sp 70– 6	can never enter the atmosphere of S·.
	gl 590– 3	the atmosphere of S·, where Soul is supreme.
audience-chamber of		
	p 442– 7	the vast audience-chamber of S·
audience with		
	pr 15–12	that man may have audience with S·,

32

Spirit

baptism of
f 241–27   The baptism of *S·*, washing the body of all the

bar of
p 440– 5   arraigns before the supreme bar of *S·*

based on
ph 191–25   reveals man and immortality as based on *S·*.

being is
a 29–26   with the full recognition that being is *S·*.

belief that
sp 93–21   The belief that *S·* is finite as well as infinite

belong to
ph 192–17   Moral and spiritual might belong to *S·*,

blesses
sp 78–28   *S·* blesses man,
g 512–20   *S·* blesses the multiplication of

born of
b 274–10   Ideas, on the contrary, are born of *S·*,

born of the
t 463–18   the C. S. infant is born of the *S·*,
gl 598– 4   every one that is born of the *S·*

cognizance of
g 543–10   corporeal senses cannot take cognizance of *S·*.

communion with
sp 72– 7   condition precedent to communion with *S·*

contradiction of
g 504–28   and the contradiction of *S·* is matter,

control of
pr 9–23   recognizes only the divine control of *S·*,

Court of
p 434– 9   a trial in the Court of *S·*,
437–10   our higher tribunal, the Supreme Court of *S·*,
437–18   I ask that the Supreme Court of *S·* reverse this
437–28   the Supreme Court of *S·* overruled their

created by
s 148– 8   described man as created by *S·*,

creates
m 69–24   "Do you teach that *S·* creates materially,
b 316–20   the indestructible man, whom *S·* creates,
g 509–13   *S·* creates no other than heavenly or
540– 2   *S·* creates neither a wicked nor a mortal man,

creations of
b 287– 4   All creations of *S·* are eternal ;

day of
g 505– 1   No...planetary revolutions form the day of *S·*.

demonstration of
pr 14– 5   in the demonstration of *S·*.

depend on
ph 181–18   not sufficiently spiritual to depend on *S·*.

diversifies
g 513–17   *S·* diversifies, classifies, and

divine
(see **divine**)

divorced from
r 477–31   man, divorced from *S·*, would lose his

duly feeds
g 507– 3   *S·* duly feeds and clothes every object,

echo of
s 126–11   interpreted in its own way the echo of *S·*,

energy of
f 249– 6   Let us feel the divine energy of *S·*,

evolved from
m 69– 3   man and the universe are evolved from *S·*,

existence of
o 359–15   The evidence of the existence of *S·*,

expression of
r 484–30   to the understanding and expression of *S·*?

facts of
f 215–10   matter and mortality do not reflect the facts of *S·*.
b 281–30   as we grasp the facts of *S·*.

faculties of
s 162–14   The indestructible faculties of *S·*

faith in
p 368–16   more faith in *S·* than in matter,

flesh and
(see **flesh**)

flesh opposed to
s 114– 4   meaning by this term the flesh opposed to *S·*,

formed by
b 303–10   formed by *S·*, not by material sensation.

forsakes
g 549–28   mistakes nature, forsakes *S·*

foundation of
s 133–26   planted Christianity on the foundation of *S·*,

from body to
p 405–31   to flee from body to *S·*,

from matter into
r 485–14   Emerge gently from matter into *S·*.

from matter to
p 370–31   from error to Truth, from matter to *S·*.
t 459– 1   turn naturally from matter to *S·*,

fruit of the
an 106–27   But the fruit of the *S·* is love,— *Gal.* 5 : 22.

fruits of
p 391–32   and bearing the fruits of *S·*.

Spirit

fruits of the
t 451–18   they bear as of old the fruits of the *S·*.

gained from
a 23–19   the evidence gained from *S·*,

gives the true
r 467–26   *S·* gives the true mental idea.

goal of
b 324–18   certainly before we can reach the goal of *S·*,

God is
s 117– 6   God is *S·* ; therefore the language of
f 207– 2   Because God is *S·*, evil becomes
b 331–14   Scriptures also declare that God is *S·*.
335– 2   There is no evil in Spirit, because God is *S·*.

God, or
gl 580–13   the antipode of God, or *S·* ;

graces of
p 429– 4   as well as by other graces of *S·*.

harmonies of
p 382– 2   opposed to the harmonies of *S·*,

hath not flesh
a 45–27   "*S·* hath not flesh and bones,— *Luke* 24 : 39.

hath not seen
c 255–18   Eye hath not seen *S·*, nor hath ear heard Hi voice.

heal by the
p 366–32   If we would heal by the *S·*, we must

help of
o 351– 6   Neither can we heal through the help of *S·*, if

he recognized
a 31–10   He recognized *S·*, God, as the only creator,

Holy
o 359– 9   I as a Christian Scientist believed in the Holy *S·*

idea of
a 29–30   Man as the offspring of God, as the idea of *S·*,
c 266–28   Man is the idea of *S·* ;

ideas of
g 505–11   the ideas of *S·* apparent only as Mind,

if man were
sp 93–27   If man were *S·*, then men would be spirits,

ignorance of
b 280–32   only excuse . . . is our mortal ignorance of *S·*

image of
g 543– 5   The image of *S·* cannot be effaced,

immortal
s 124–13   which immortal *S·* silences forever.
p 435– 1   commended man's immortal *S·* to heavenly

imparted by
g 514–19   accompanies all the might imparted by *S·*.

imparts
g 505–16   *S·* imparts the understanding which uplifts

individuality of
b 330–16   The individuality of *S·*, . . . is unknown,

infinite
a 49–21   by the renewing of the infinite *S·*.
sp 73– 7   neither the one nor . . . is infinite *S·*,
75–10   to infinite *S·* there can be no matter.
ph 200–20   suppositional antipode of divine infinite *S·*,
200–24   material senses must yield to the infinite *S·*,
b 280–23   belief . . . that infinite *S·*, and Life, is in
295–12   but infinite *S·* being all,
301–27   supposed standpoint outside . . . of infinite *S·*
309–25   impossible for infinite *S·* or Soul to be in a
319–12   yield to the all-might of infinite *S·*.
331–24   except as infinite *S·* or Mind.
r 475– 3   To infinite *S·* there is no matter,
g 527– 2   God could not put . . . infinite *S·* into
gl 591– 5   MAN. The compound idea of infinite *S·*;

infinite calculus of
f 209–30   swallowed up in the infinite calculus of *S·*.

influence of
sp 98–10   for it is the healing influence of *S·*

instead of
f 205– 3   will lean on matter instead of *S·*,
b 285–27   and resort to matter instead of *S·*
307–19   out of matter instead of *S·*."
310–22   Spirit, Soul, would be flesh instead of *S·*.
p 430– 7   by resting upon *S·* instead of matter.

instead of by
g 536–17   Created by flesh instead of by *S·*,

inverted image of
gl 580–13   an inverted image of *S·* ;

is all
f 223– 8   If *S·* is *all* and is everywhere,
p 421–17   God, *S·*, is all, and that there is none beside Him.

is all-knowing
r 487–15   *S·* is all-knowing ;

is eternal
b 335–18   *S·* is eternal, divine.

is God
sp 73– 7   *S·* is God, and man is His likeness.
s 120– 4   *S·*, is God, unchangeable and eternal ;
ph 192–10   Spirit is not separate from God. *S· is* God.
f 229–12   and at the same time admits that *S·* is God,
b 300–23   *S·* is God, Soul ;

pirit

is God
p 417–11   *S·* is God, and therefore cannot be sick ;
r 468–13   *S·* is God, and man is His image and

is good
pref viii–11   the fact is that *S·* is good

is greater
f 223–11   Soul is Spirit, and *S·* is greater than body.

is harmonious
a 29–31   the immortal evidence that *S·* is harmonious

is immortal Truth
r 468–11   *S·* is immortal Truth ;

is infinite
m 69–25   or do you declare that *S·* is infinite ?
b 281– 3   and learn that *S·* is infinite and supreme.

is light
g 504–28   *S·* is light, and the contradiction of

is more
b 335–19   for *S·* is more than all else.

is not finite
b 335–22   for *S·* is not finite.

is not physical
b 285–15   *S·* is not physical.

is reached
b 279–19   *S·* is reached only through the understanding

is represented
g 522–20   *S·* is represented as entering matter

is substantial
b 278–32   if *S·* is substantial and eternal.

is supreme
b 278–21   *S·* is supreme and all-presence.

is symbolized
g 512– 8   *S·* is symbolized by strength, presence, and

is the Ego
f 250– 7   *S·* is the Ego which never dreams,

is the life
s 124–25   *S·* is the life, substance, and continuity

is the real
r 468–12   *S·* is the real and eternal ;

it loses
s 148–16   It loses *S·*, drops the true tone,

joys of
m 66–14   Love propagates anew the higher joys of *S·*,
f 242– 7   a great step towards the joys of *S·*,

language of
s 117– 6   the language of *S·* must be, and is, spiritual.
117–15   the pure language of *S·*.

law of
    (*see* **law**)

laws of
ph 183–19   Laws of nature are laws of *S·* ;

learn how
m 68– 5   we shall learn how *S·*, the great architect,

leaven of
s 118–23   until the leaven of *S·* changes the

life as
a 35– 9   into newness of life as *S·*.
b 278–24   contradicts the demonstration of life as *S·*,

Life is
c 264–16   When we realize that Life is *S·*,
b 310–26   The only Life is *S·*,
p 376–13   should be told . . . that Life is *S·*,

likeness of
sp 97–20   man is found in the likeness of *S·*.
ph 172–19   man is the image and likeness of *S·* :
b 337– 6   it is not the reflection or likeness of *S·*,
o 345– 4   the likeness of *S·* cannot be material,
r 475–10   The likeness of *S·* cannot be so unlike
g 522–23   in His image, the likeness of *S·*,
544–24   Man is the likeness of *S·*,
gl 584–25   not after the image and likeness of *S·*,

lives in
t 461– 4   and that he lives in *S·*, not matter.

living
p 388–29   a clear comprehension of the living *S·*.

Love is
sp 96– 5   spiritualization will follow, for Love is *S·*.

made all
g 543–25   When *S·* made all, did it leave aught

matter and
ph 171–18   believes himself to be combined matter and *S·*.
f 216–20   both matter and *S·*, both good and evil.
b 312–27   matter and *S·*, the finite and the infinite,

microscope of
c 264–21   Matter disappears under the microscope of *S·*.

Mind is
b 310–30   Mind is *S·*, which material sense cannot discern.
g 517– 8   The life-giving quality of Mind is *S·*,

Mind or
b 281–14   The one Ego, the one Mind or *S·* called God,
295–28   the exact opposite of real Mind, or *S·*,
gl 580– 6   belief, opposed to the one Mind, or *S·* ;

nature of
s 119–24   it is opposed to the nature of *S·*, God.

needs no wires
sp 78–19   *S·* needs no wires nor electricity

Spirit

never dies
b 275– 1   Matter has no life to lose, and *S·* never dies.

never entered
sp 76–11   understood that *S·* never entered matter

new-born of
a 35–22   only as we are new-born of *S·*,

new wine of the
s 114–21   and the new wine of the *S·* has to be

no cognizance of
b 292–14   this so-called mind has no cognizance of *S·*.
g 531–29   corporeal senses can take no cognizance of *S·*.
546–17   material senses can take no cognizance of *S·*

no evil in
f 207– 1   for there is no evil in *S·*.
b 335– 2   There is no evil in *S·*, because God is Spirit.

no sensuality in
sp 71–25   There is no sensuality in *S·*.

not the reflection of
g 524–23   Matter is not the reflection of *S·*,

not the vestibule of
o 356– 8   Matter is not the vestibule of *S·*.

offspring of
m 63– 5   man is the offspring of *S·*.
g 540– 2   Christ is the offspring of *S·*,
gl 583– 6   offspring of *S·*, who, having wrestled with

of life
f 244–11   "The law of the *S·* of life— *Rom.* 8 : 2.

of the Lord
f 227–18   "Where the *S·* of the Lord is,— *II Cor.* 3 : 17.
r 481– 4   "Where the *S·* of the Lord is,— *II Cor.* 3 : 17.

omnipotence of
sp 78–24   How can the . . . omnipotence of *S·* be lost ?
g 522– 1   would set aside the omnipotence of *S·* ;

omnipotent
ph 194– 1   omnipotent *S·* shares not its strength with
f 202–30   as if . . . had more power than omnipotent *S·*.

omnipresent
sp 73–18   omnipresent *S·* would be destroyed.
f 223– 8   God is infinite omnipresent *S·*.

one
sp 70– 7   There is but one *S·*.
79–19   Jesus did his own work by the one *S·*.
84–10   controlled not by demons, . . . but by the
     one *S·*.
94– 1   Jesus taught but one God, one *S·*,
b 275–30   superior or contrary to the one *S·*.
276– 7   all have one *S·*, God,
280–14   it seeks to divide the one *S·* into persons
333–30   The one *S·* includes all identities.
334–31   but one *S·*, for there can be but one infinite
gl 591– 3   as the opposite of the one *S·*, or intelligence,

operation of
g 545–25   the nature and operation of *S·*.

opposed to
b 338– 3   stood opposed to *S·*.
g 534–17   called *energy* and opposed to *S·*.

opposite of
    (*see* **opposite**)

or Deity
gl 588–23   if used with reference to *S·*, or Deity.

or God
sp 73–15   If *S·*, or God, communed with mortals
r 482–11   Soul . . . the synonym of *S·*, or God ;

or matter
b 324–11   whether it be Truth or error, . . . *S·* or matter.
o 360–17   Either *S·* or matter is your model.

or Soul
b 309–25   impossible for infinite *S·* or Soul to be in
330–11   the only Life, substance, *S·*, or Soul,
r 478– 5   never beheld *S·* or Soul leaving a body
gl 598–16   for never did he give up *S·*, or Soul.

overcome by
p 410–16   the material condition to be overcome by *S·*,

perfection in
c 264– 3   and their perfection in *S·* appear.

permanency of
b 293–28   the strength and permanency of *S·*.

permeated by
sp 72– 5   If a material body . . . were permeated by *S·*,

pertain to
o 350– 3   and of the things which pertain to *S·*

physiology and
ph 182–10   We cannot obey both physiology and *S·*,

physique was not
a 46–13   Master said plainly that physique was not *S·*,

place of
g 522–18   In this . . . theory, matter takes the place of *S·*.

plurality of
g 515–18   this plurality of *S·* does not imply more than one

positive
ph 173–15   For positive *S·* to pass through a

possibilities of
b 316–31   the possibilities of *S·* and its correlative truth.

power of
    (*see* **power**)

Spirit

prerogative of
s 123– 8   the power and prerogative of *S*·,
proceeds from
r 480–14   Harmonious action proceeds from *S*·, God.
purification by
gl 581–23   BAPTISM.   Purification by *S*· ;
quench not the
r 490–19   "Quench not the *S*·.— *I Thess.* 5 : 19.
radiance of
f 246–15   the radiance of *S*· should dawn upon the
radiation of
g 556– 6   radiation of *S*· destroys forever all belief in
realities of
b 325– 5   ushered into the undying realities of *S*·.
recognition of
sp 76–32   The recognition of *S*· and of infinity comes
    90–28   The understanding and recognition of *S*· must
b 287–30   to the recognition of *S*· and of the
rectified by
t 460–13   till such thought is rectified by *S*·.
reflection of
    (see **reflection**)
reign of
f 208–22   and prepare for the reign of *S*·,
gl 587–25   HEAVEN.   Harmony ; the reign of *S*· ;
renewal of
f 241–14   transformation of the body by the renewal of *S*·.
representing
b 294–20   between immortal man, representing *S*·, and
reveals
r 467–14   Science reveals *S*·, Soul, as not in
gl 596–14   C. S. reveals *S*·, not matter, as the
rhythm of
g 510– 4   To discern the rhythm of *S*· and to be holy,
robes of
c 267–26   robes of *S*· are "white and— *Luke* 9 : 29.
sanctuary of
pr 15– 4   closet typifies the sanctuary of *S*·,
Science of
a 31–29   which would attend the Science of *S*·,
b 270–21   and maintain the Science of *S*·.
p 369–26   psychology, or the Science of *S*·, God,
scribe of
ap 571–23   the Revelator, immortal scribe of *S*·
seed of
g 535– 3   yea, the seed of *S*· and the seed of matter,
seek to unite
g 555–19   error would seek to unite *S*· with matter,
senses of
b 274–12   The senses of *S*· abide in Love,
Soul and
b 335–16   Soul and *S*· being one,
Soul is
f 223–11   Soul is *S*·, and Spirit is greater than body.
p 396–28   Soul is *S*·, outside of matter,
Soul or
r 466–20   Soul or *S*· signifies Deity and nothing else.
    466–22   Soul or *S*· means only one Mind,
straight line of
g 502– 6   the straight line of *S*· over the
strength of
p 393–12   Rise in the strength of *S*· to resist
submergence in
gl 581–24   BAPTISM. . . . submergence in *S*·.
    582–22   BURIAL. . . . Submergence in *S*· ;
submitting to
f 239–20   matter is then submitting to *S*·.
substance of
b 301–19   the substance of *S*·, not matter.
r 468–24   reflecting the divine substance of *S*·.
    480– 1   When the substance of *S*· appears
substance, or
b 301–11   reflects the eternal substance, or *S*·,
substantiality of
b 318– 2   to conceive of the substantiality of *S*·
supposition that
ph 173– 6   supposition, that *S*· is within what it
g 550–29   supposition that *S*· . . . can originate the
supremacy of
    (see **supremacy**)
sustained by
p 417– 1   their being is sustained by *S*·,
g 556– 2   That which is real, is sustained by *S*·.
sword of
a 37– 8   error falls only before the sword of *S*·.
symbolizes
ap 561–25   The Revelator symbolizes *S*· by the sun.
synonym of
r 482–11   Soul is properly the synonym of *S*·,
synonymous with
sp 71– 7   Soul is synonymous with *S*·,
testimony of
s 128–26   destroys with the higher testimony of *S*·
f 252–16   contrasts strikingly with the testimony of *S*·.

Spirit

the only
sp 73–11   God is the only *S*·.
gl 591–16   the only *S*·, Soul, divine Principle,
things of
a 21–12   looks towards the imperishable things of *S*·.
o 349–24   Speaking of the things of *S*·
tributary to
ap 562– 8   reveals the universe as . . . tributary to *S*·,
triumph of
s 139– 5   accounts of the triumph of *S*·, Mind,
true sense of
s 108–29   thereby shutting out the true sense of *S*·.
unction of
pr 10–10   the unction of *S*· in demonstration of power
understand
b 283– 1   As mortals begin to understand *S*·,
r 481– 8   sense never helps mortals to understand *S*·,
understanding of
a 46–17   rose even higher in the understanding of *S*·,
ph 186– 6   through the understanding of *S*·,
b 309– 8   the understanding of *S*· and of spiritual power.
gl 581–10   the understanding of *S*·, destroying belief
unity of
s 148–24   to produce the concord and unity of *S*·
universe of
c 264–32   The universe of *S*· is peopled with
g 507–15   The universe of *S*· reflects the creative power
unknown to
r 469– 2   What is termed matter is unknown to *S*·,
unlike
b 305–22   The inverted images . . . are all unlike *S*·,
    307–11   shall change sides and be unlike *S*·.
r 475–11   likeness of Spirit cannot be so unlike *S*·.
unlikeness of
b 277–24   The unlikeness of *S*· is matter,
validity of
g 525– 4   not the validity of *S*·
verities of
s 109–32   The three great verities of *S*·,
warreth against
ph 200–22   the flesh that warreth against *S*·.
warring against
gl 584–12   The flesh, warring against *S*· ;
wars against
b 274–22   and the flesh wars against *S*·.
g 531–28   since flesh wars against *S*·
will form
p 425–25   and *S*· will form you anew.
will ultimately
m 64–30   *S*· will ultimately claim its own,
world of
pref viii–32   in the newly discovered world of *S*·.
worship
o 351–30   They thought to worship *S*· from a material
would be finite
f 223–12   If . . . . *S*· would be finite,

---

pref xi– 7   the workings, not of *S*·, but of the fleshly mind
pr 14–11   governed by divine Love,— by *S*·, not by
a 20– 5   as he was moved, not by spirits but by *S*·.
    26–10   The Christ was the *S*· which Jesus implied
    27–13   I [*S*·] will raise it up."— *John* 2 : 19.
    28– 6   determination to hold *S*· in the grasp of
    33–21   Let not the flesh, but the *S*·, be represented
    52– 3   His master was *S*· ; their master was matter.
m 63– 9   *S*· is his primitive and ultimate source
sp 71– 1   nothing is *S*·,— but God and His idea.
    71– 6   but *S*·, or the divine Principle of all,
    71–10   Spiritualism therefore presupposes *S*·, . . . to
    72–18   *S*· is not made manifest through matter,
    74– 3   To be on communicable terms with *S*·,
    78–17   If *S*· pervades all space, it needs no
    78–21   *S*· is not materially tangible.
    83–18   belief . . . that occasionally *S*· sets aside these
    83–20   gives to matter the precedence over *S*·.
    84–28   All we correctly know of *S*· comes from God,
    89–20   *S*·, God, is heard when the senses are silent.
    92–16   from matter, or evil, instead of from *S*·.
    93–22   *S*·, as a proper noun, is the name of the
    93–27   He is not God, *S*·.
    94– 2   image and likeness of Himself,— of *S*·,
an 102– 9   but one real attraction, that of *S*·.
s 110– 1   *S*· possessing all power, filling all space,
    111–10   as the Science of God, *S*·, must,
    113–18   God, *S*·, being all, nothing is matter.
    115–14   Life, Truth, Love, Soul, *S*·, Mind.
    119– 8   they assume that matter is the product of *S*·.
    146–19   and clothes *S*· with supremacy.
ph 167–20   "flesh lusteth against the *S*·."— *Gal.* 5 : 17.
    170– 6   faith in matter instead of in *S*·.
    171–18   believes that *S*· is sifted through matter,
    172–10   *S*· can form no real link in this
    173–13   nor the manifestation of *S*· is obtainable through
    173–13   *S*· is positive.
    173–14   Spirit's contrary, the absence of *S*·.

Spirit
ph 181– 5 "Who art thou that repliest to S·?
   183– 1 Truth, makes all things possible to S· ;
   183– 2 so-called laws of matter would render S·
   192– 9 S· is not separate from God. Spirit *is* God.
   200– 5 advanced . . . to the worship of God in S·
 f 205–31 into the scale, not of S·, . . . but of matter.
   206–17 S·, not matter, being the source of supply.
   207– 1 but these evils are not S·,
   208– 2 which affords no proof of God, S·,
   208–15 to suppose that . . . S·, God, produces disease
   209–22 translation of man and the universe back into
           S·.
   211–28 for their immortality is not in S·,
   213–12 and is a tendency towards God, S·.
   215– 4 If S·, Soul, could sin or be lost,
   223– 2 "Walk in the S·, and ye shall not — *Gal.* 5 : 16.
   223– 6 in matter instead of in S·.
   223– 7 Matter does not express S·.
   223–12 If S· were once within the body,
   223–13 and therefore could not be S·.
   232–10 all good is possible to S· ;
   234– 3 If we trust matter, we distrust S·.
   246– 8 endeavoring to reach S·
   249–21 The I is S·,
   252–12 man created by and of S·,
252–31, 32 S·, bearing opposite testimony, saith : I am S·.
   253–30 the law of . . . S· instead of the flesh.
 c 255– * *have the firstfruits of the S·,* — *Rom.* 8 : 23.
   257– 4 If matter, so-called, is substance, then S·,
   257– 6 The theory that S· is not the only substance
   259–23 God, S·, works spiritually, not materially.
   260–32 If we look to the body . . . for S·, we find
   265–11 forsaking matter for S·, by no means suggests
   267– 4 They are in and of S·, divine Mind,
 b 274– 6 the offspring of sense, not of Soul, S·,
   275– 4 shows that matter did not originate in God, S·,
   275– 7 S·, is All-in-all, and that there is no other might
   275–12 S·, Life, Truth, Love, combine as one,
   277– 8 As God Himself is good and is S·,
   277–20 Error . . . asserts that S· produces matter
   277–24 The realm of the real is S·.
   278– 1 Is S· the source or creator of matter?
   278– 2 nothing in S· out of which to create matter.
   278– 4 S· is the only substance and consciousness
   278– 7 In S· there is no matter,
   278–10 S·, God, is infinite, all.
   278–11 S· can have no opposite.
   278–18 another admission, — namely, that S· is not
   281–12 the image and likeness of perfect Mind, S·,
   282–16 matter has no place in S·,
   282–16 and S· has no place in matter.
   284–17 which receive no direct evidence of S·,
   284–22 They can neither see S· through the eye nor
   284–23 nor can they feel, taste, or smell S·.
   286–23 since God, S·, is the only cause, they lack a
   286–25 The temporal . . . are not then creations of S·.
   288–19 people of God" (of S·). — *Heb.* 4 : 9.
   288–23 S· is not, and cannot be, materialized ;
   289– 7 Then S· will have overcome the flesh.
   289–29 S· and all things spiritual are the real
   289–31 Man is not the offspring of flesh, but of S·,
   294– 4 human belief, . . . a unison of matter with S·.
   300–24 If S· were in matter,
   302–28 not in any bodily . . . likeness to S·.
   307–13 as much as God, S·, who *is* the only Life."
   307–28 material laws which S· never made ;
   310–21 If Soul could sin, S·, Soul, would be flesh
   310–26 the annihilation of S· would be inevitable.
   310–27 if S· should lose Life as God, good, then S·,
   311– 7 Soul is immortal because it is S·,
   313–31 To show that the substance of himself was S·
   317–25 looking . . . in matter instead of in S·
   318– 4 Mind and immortality, in which S· reigns
   330–20 S· is divine Principle,
   331–15 Therefore in S· all is harmony,
   334– 7 not that the Father is greater than S·,
   334–31 S· being God, there is but one Spirit,
   335– 3 The theory, that S· is distinct from matter but
   335– 7 S·, God, has created all in and of Himself.
   335– 8 S· never created matter.
   335– 9 nothing in S· out of which matter could be
   335–12 S· is the only substance,
   335–19 Nothing but S·, Soul, can evolve Life,
   335–22 Soul must be incorporeal to be S·,
   339– 8 God, S·, alone created all,
   340–18 It inculcates the tri-unity of God, S·, Mind ;
 o 344–32 the word S· is so commonly applied to Deity,
   347– 1 flesh lusteth against the S·, — *Gal.* 5 : 17.
   347– 1 and the S· against the flesh." — *Gal.* 5 : 17.
   349–32 In C. S., substance is understood to be S·,
   351–29 To them . . . S· was shadow.
   356–24 Does God create a material man out of Himself,
           S·?
   357–31 Can matter drive Life, S·, hence,
 p 411–10 If S· . . . bear witness to the truth,

Spirit
 p 420– 4 S·, not matter, governs man.
   425–19 since S·, God, is All-in-all.
   427–27 S· is his last resort, but it should have
   435– 1 S· which is God Himself
   437–15 S· not allowed a hearing ;
   441–19 S· decides in favor of Man
 r 465–10 S·, Soul, Principle, Life, Truth, Love.
   467– 4 This *me* is S·,
   467–22 S·, Soul, is not confined in man,
   467–25 when we conclude that matter is the effect of S· ;
   467–27 We cannot interpret S·, Mind, through matter.
   468–21 S·, the synonym of Mind, Soul, or God,
   468–26 Life is divine Principle, Mind, Soul, S·.
   477– 7 Soul, being S·, is seen in nothing imperfect
   477–25 can never reflect anything inferior to S·.
   477–30 S· would be a nonentity ;
   479– 8 neither self-existent nor a product of S·.
   479–22 the only facts are S· and its
   480– 5 the opposite of the something of S·.
   481– 2 Man is tributary to God, S·,
   485–16 come naturally into S· through better health
   487–27 The understanding that Life is God, S·,
   497–22 even the allness of Soul, S·,
 g 503–28 God, S·, dwelling in infinite light and
   504–31 nothing but a supposition of the absence of S·.
   506–10 S·, God, unites understanding to
   506–18 S·, God, gathers unformed thoughts into their
   507– 6 S·' names and blesses all.
   509– 2 when S· is discerned to be the Life of all,
   518–27 divine Principle, or S·, comprehends and
   518–29 Nothing is new to S·.
   521– 9 in the keeping of S·, not matter,
   522–26 S· as supposedly cooperating with matter
   524–28 Could S· evolve its opposite, matter,
   524–29 Is S·, God, injected into dust,
   524–31 Does S· enter dust, and lose therein the
   531–27 Is Life sustained by matter or by S· ?
   534–22 not in the flesh, but in the S·, — *Rom.* 8 : 9.
   539– 4 begins by reckoning life as separate from S·,
   539– 8 What can be the standard of good, of S·,
   539–14 Has S· resigned to matter the government
   544– 2 S· had no participation in it.
   546– 4 S·, God, never germinates,
   550– 9 S· cannot become matter,
   550– 9 nor can S· be developed through its opposite.
 ap 575–25 It is indeed a city of the S·,
 gl 583–20 CREATOR. S· ; Mind ; intelligence ;
   586–17 between S· and so-called matter.
   587– 7 Principle ; Mind ; Soul ; S· ;
   587–19 GOOD. God ; S· ; omnipotence ; omniscience ;
   588– 9 I, or EGO. Divine Principle ; S· ; Soul ;
   594–19 definition of

spirit
and in life
 a 39–22 to experience that salvation in s· and in life.
and in truth
 a 31–27 the Father in s· and in truth." — *John* 4 : 23.
 sp 93– 7 the Father in s· and in truth." — *John* 4 : 23.
 s 140–21 the Father in s· and in truth." — *John* 4 : 23.
and power
 a 55–25 with the s· and power of Christian healing.
bear witness
 b 330– 9 and the letter and the s· bear witness,
belief that
 sp 73–22 the belief that s· is confined in a
chills the
 c 256–26 it chills the s· of Christianity.
deaf
 p 398– 2 "Thou dumb and deaf s·, I charge — *Mark* 9 : 25.
departed
 sp 88–32 belief that a departed s· is speaking,
finite
 sp 93–28 Finite s· would be mortal,
no other
 b 340–19 shall have no other s· or mind but God,
of Christ
 t 462– 4 and imbibes the s· of Christ,
offspring of
 f 229–11 calls both the offspring of s·,
of God
 s 137–20 the s· of God, of Truth, Life, and Love,
 r 480– 3 Where the s· of God is,
 g 503– 8 And the s· of God moved — *Gen.* 1 : 2.
   534–22 if so be that the s· of God — *Rom.* 8 : 9.
of Life
 p 433–31 Ah ! but Christ, Truth, the s· of Life
of Science
 s 145– 4 So . . . imbued were they with the s· of Science,
of the Christ
 s 131–23 As aforetime, the s· of the Christ,
of Truth
 p 391– 1 in the conscious strength of the s· of Truth
   418–24 and especially by the s· of Truth and Love
   427– 3 law of Soul, even the law of the s· of Truth,
 t 455– 1 into accord with the s· of Truth and Love,

spirit

requires the
ap 571– 8   It requires the *s·* of our blessed Master
revealed the
r 483–21   God certainly revealed the *s·* of C. S.,
rich in
g 518–15   The rich in *s·* help the poor
so-called
sp 73–12   Any other control or attraction of so-called *s·*
soul nor
r 466–21   There is no finite soul nor *s·*.
soul or
ph 200–21   the so-called human soul or *s·*,
supposition that
gl 587– 2   a supposition that *s·* is finite.
unity of
m 58– 3   Unity of *s·* gives new pinions to joy,
was not
o 352– 6   declared that his material body was not *s·*,
without the
s 145– 6   and that letter, without the *s·*, would have
t 451– 9   and think to succeed without the *s·*,
worshipped in
ap 576–14   He must be worshipped in *s·* and in love.

pref xii–23   In the *s·* of Christ's charity,
a 45–25   Even his disciples at first called him a *s·*,
45–28   reappearing of Jesus was not the return of a *s·*.
sp 73– 5   but another, . . . it terms a *s·*.
73– 8   The belief that one man, as *s·*, can control
73–24   belief that . . . *s·* retains the sensations
75– 2   assumption that man . . . comes to life as *s·*.
80– 8   as follows: "There never was, . . . an immortal *s·*."
93–26   The modifying derivatives of the word *s·*
s 113– 5   but its *s·* comes only in small degrees.
136–19   believed that Jesus was . . . controlled by the *s·* of
f 203–12   the only true *s·* is Godlike.
239–21   The objects we pursue and the *s·* we manifest
b 283–16   They speak of both . . . good and evil as *s·*.
295–32   Thus error theorizes that *s·* is born of matter
300–26   The theory that soul, *s·*, . . . inhabits matter
307–12   It says : . . . I will put *s·* into what I call
317– 5   insisted on . . . the insignificance of *s·*,
320–12   My *s·* shall not always strive— *Gen. 6.: 3.*
320–15   My *s·* shall not forever rule [or be humbled]
341– *   *But if the s· of Him— Rom. 8: 11.*
341– *   *by His s· that dwelleth— Rom. 8: 11.*
356–15   "It is the *s·* that quickeneth ;— *John 6: 63.*
p 398– 4   *s·* [error] cried, and rent him— *Mark 9: 26.*
t 456– 4   contrary to its *s·* or rules,
r 478– 7   the theory of indwelling *s·*,
495–28   Study . . . the letter and imbibe the *s·*.
g 546– 1   false belief that *s·* is now submerged in
ap 573–11   what the human mind terms matter and *s·*
574–11   carried John away in *s·*.
gl 598– 2   word for *wind (pneuma)* is used also for *s·*,

spirit-communications
sp 80–10   repeats weekly the assertion that *s·* are

spiritism
sp 77–28   *S·* consigns the so-called dead to a state
78–25   where *s·* makes many gods,

Spirit-rule
o 351–23   they cannot work out the *S·* of Christian

Spirit's
pref viii–11   and matter is *S·* opposite.
sp 71– 6   is not *in S·* formations.
ph 173–14   Matter is *S·* contrary,
173–16   would be *S·* destruction.
f 214–32   *S·* senses are without pain,
b 287–27   the objective supposition of *S·* opposite.
302–31   reproduction by *S·* individual ideas
g 525– 4   not the validity of Spirit or *S·* creations.
gl 580–18   the usurper of *S·* creation,

spirits (see also spirits')
alleged
sp 81–14   Nor is the case improved when alleged *s·* teach
and electricity
sp 80–29   believes that . . . emanates from *s·* and electricity.
departed
sp 88–31   said to be . . . from the impulsion of departed *s·*.
evil
sp 70–11   supposition . . . that there are good and evil *s·*,
79–17   Jesus cast out evil *s·*, or false beliefs.
f 206–32   There are evil beliefs, often called evil *s·* ;
b 307–10   It says : . . . God makes evil minds and evil *s·*,
familiar
sp 70– *   *them that have familiar s·,— Isa. 8: 19.*
ministering
o 360–26   in His ministering *s·,— see Job 4: 18.*
not by
a 20– 5   moved, not by *s·* but by Spirit.

spirits
so-called
sp 72– 9   So-called *s·* are but corporeal communicators.
unseen
f 212–22   mortals believe that unseen *s·* produce the

a 24–25   as a proof that *s·* can return to earth?
sp 70–10   supposition that corporeal beings are *s·*,
71–28   Its *s·* are so many corporealities,
77–22   Even if communications from *s·* to
84–10   controlled not by demons, *s·*, or demigods,
84–26   material personalities called *s·*,
88–17   and at another are called *s·*.
93–28   If man were Spirit, then men would be *s·*,
98–10   the healing influence of Spirit (not *s·*)
b 335– 1   There are neither *s·* many nor gods many.
r 466– 7   *Question.—* What are *s·* and souls?
466–19   The term *souls* or *s·* is as improper as the
gl 594–22   definition of

Spiritual
s 127– 9   The terms Divine Science, *S·* Science,

spiritual
actuality
g 502–13   and the *s·* actuality of man,
adherence
m 65–28   find . . . peace in a more *s·* adherence.
advancement
p 429–10   in the line of *s·* advancement.
affection
p 366–17   Not having this *s·* affection,
agreement
b 333– 1   *s·* agreement, between God and man in His
and eternal
(*see* **eternal**)
apprehension
o 349–28   is educated up to *s·* apprehension.
g 506–12   calm and exalted thought or *s·* apprehension
ascendency
m 67–20   remember that through *s·* ascendency
ascension
g 509–25   The periods of *s·* ascension are the
atmosphere
g 512–11   abound in the *s·* atmosphere of Mind,
attainments
pr 10–15   *S·* attainments open the door to a
baptism
f 242– 1   repentance, *s·* baptism, and regeneration,
barrenness
p 366– 7   while his own *s·* barrenness debars him from
basis
s 124– 7   Having neither moral might, *s·* basis, nor
160– 5   forsake the material for the *s·* basis
ph 169– 2   change of belief from a material to a *s·* basis.
b 322– 4   standpoints . . . from a material to a *s·* basis
g 555–23   Creation rests on a *s·* basis.
beauty
b 304– 4   which hide *s·* beauty and goodness.
being
a 33– 8   It was the great truth of *s·* being,
33–13   For this truth of *s·* being,
sp 76–12   *s·* being and the understanding of God,
ph 167–26   but one way . . . which leads to *s·* being.
c 264–29   and recognize man's *s·* being,
b 325–13   When *s·* being is understood in all its
g 544–23   the very antipodes of immortal and *s·* being.
gl 586–21   Science ; *s·* being understood ;
being is
sp 76–26   indestructible man, whose being is *s·*.
beings
c 264–32   universe of Spirit is peopled with *s·* beings,
birth
t 463–11   in the travail of *s·* birth.
blessings
a 53–17   *s·* blessings which might flow from
g 512–15   *s·* blessings, thus typified, are the
bliss
gl 582–15   a sense of Soul, which has *s·* bliss
bodies
sp 73–20   belief that . . . rise up as *s·* bodies
breakfast
a 34–30   his last *s·* breakfast with his disciples
building
f 241–26   the corner-stone of all *s·* building is purity.
capacity
ph 179– 8   the *s·* capacity to apprehend thought
causation
ph 170–22   *S·* causation is the one question to be
170–23   *s·* causation relates to human progress.
cause
s 111–23   rather than to a final *s·* cause,
b 268– 4   to the *s·* cause of those lower things
313–25   and found the *s·* cause.
class
b 290–13   To the *s·* class, relates the Scripture :

piritual

clear-sightedness
b 316–14   *s·* clear-sightedness and the blindness of

command
ph 168–19   God's *s·* command relating to perfection,

communion
a 35–25   Our Eucharist is *s·* communion with the

compensation
gl 581–15   Hope and faith ; *s·* compensation ;

conceptions
o 349–16   to the expression of *s·* conceptions

conclusions
b 300– 2   when it attempts to draw correct *s·* conclusions

condition
t 460–27   from her own *s·* condition,

consciousness
pr 16–21   heaven-born aspiration and *s·* consciousness,
c 261–28   you will rise to the *s·* consciousness of being,
b 269–17   real and tangible to *s·* consciousness,
ap 574– 1   This *s·* consciousness is therefore a
     577–19   In this divinely united *s·* consciousness,

creation
m 56– 8   Until the *s·* creation is discerned intact,
f 208– 2   which affords no proof . . . of the *s·* creation.
b 287–31   recognition of Spirit and of the *s·* creation.
     332– 5   His tender relationship to His *s·* creation.
g 507– 5   as it appears in the line of *s·* creation,
     511– 6   magnitude, and infinitude of *s·* creation.
     519– 4   since the *s·* creation was the outgrowth,
     521– 7   this brief, glorious history of *s·* creation
     534– 2   Hence she is first . . . to discern *s·* creation.
gl 590–22   the record of *s·* creation.

culture
f 235–13   a moral and *s·* culture, which lifts one higher.

death
b 310–24   and *s·* death is oblivion.

demand
p 385– 7   The *s·* demand, quelling the material,

demands
r 483– 9   must not be ignorant of the moral and *s·* demands

development
m 66–11   *S·* development germinates not from
g 547–27   not in material history but in *s·* development.

devoutness
s 140–17   *S·* devoutness is the soul of Christianity.

discernment
gl 586– 3   EYES. *S·* discernment,

discovery
p 380–22   Many years ago the author made a *s·* discovery,

distance
a 47–20   this *s·* distance inflamed Judas' envy.

draughts
f 234– 1   *S·* draughts heal,

dulness
a 34–22   to raise themselves and others from *s·* dulness

energies
p 387– 9   *s·* energies can neither wear out nor

era
m 65–16   struggling against the advancing *s·* era.

essence
a 25– 3   The *s·* essence of blood is sacrifice.

estate
g 548– 7   man has never lost his *s·* estate

evangel
b 308–24   Then said the *s·* evangel :

evidence
a 52– 6   His senses drank in the *s·* evidence of
b 297–21   *s·* evidence, contradicting the testimony of
gl 585– 9   *s·* evidence opposed to material sense ;

evidences
b 289–17   destroys with the *s·* evidences of Life ;

evolution
s 135– 9   *S·* evolution alone is worthy of the

exaltation
b 314– 2   (his further *s·* exaltation),

existence
sp 72– 1   There is but one *s·* existence,
f 222– 2   as we better apprehend our *s·* existence
c 265– 3   Man understands *s·* existence in proportion as
b 273–20   which reveals the laws of *s·* existence.
     315–13   They could not discern his *s·* existence.
o 356– 5   affords no evidence of *s·* existence
r 492– 4   fact before the thought, namely, *s·* existence.
g 540– 2   *s·* existence shows that Spirit
gl 580–10   the great reality of *s·* existence and creation ;
     593–10   higher idea of immortality, or *s·* existence ;

fact
a 20–25   to acknowledge what the *s·* fact implies.
s 121–30   thus brought nearer the *s·* fact,
     129– 7   If you wish to know the *s·* fact,
f 207–28   The *s·* fact, repeated in the action of man
     209–21   they all must give place to the *s·* fact
b 289–25   The *s·* fact and the material belief
     320–18   declares plainly the *s·* fact of being,
o 356– 3   before the *s·* fact is attained.

spiritual

fact
p 428–22   The great *s·* fact must be brought out
gl 585–11   C. S., with which can be discerned the *s·* fact

factor
ph 185–20   excludes the human mind as a *s·* factor

facts
sp 91–23   that the *s·* facts may be better apprehended.
s 130–17   beliefs which war against *s·* facts ;
     147–22   enables you to grasp the *s·* facts of being
ph 173–27   to the recognition of *s·* facts,
f 207–30   *S·* facts are not inverted ;
     213– 8   Immortal and *s·* facts exist apart from
     254– 9   before the *s·* facts of existence are gained
b 312– 3   is reversed by the *s·* facts of being
p 370–18   The moral and *s·* facts of health,
     402–12   material beliefs will not interfere with *s·* facts.
     428–10   that the *s·* facts of being may appear,
g 546–24   The great *s·* facts of being,
ap 574–12   till he became conscious of the *s·* facts of being
gl 584–16   for it contradicts the *s·* facts of being.
     592–18   the *s·* facts and harmony of the universe ;

forces
b 293–14   counterfeits of the *s·* forces of divine Mind,

forms
g 503–17   reflecting Him in countless *s·* forms.

foundation
s 136– 2   maintained his mission on a *s·* foundation
gl 593–18   ROCK. *S·* foundation ; Truth.
     599– 6   ZION. *S·* foundation and superstructure ;

freedom
s 118–12   eternally glorified in man's *s·* freedom.
p 366– 5   and thus attain the *s·* freedom which

gain
g 501–10   richly recompensing human want and woe with
            s· gain.

God
f 214–21   more than they do a *s·* God.

good
m 56– 6   for the advancement of *s·* good.
f 243– 2   the Science and demonstration of *s·* good
g 505–20   Spiritual sense is the discernment of *s·* good.

government
gl 597–28   the movements of God's *s·* government,

gravitation
g 536–11   If man's *s·* gravitation and attraction to

groundwork
s 147–19   will plant you firmly on the *s·* groundwork

growth
pr 2–21   an error which impedes *s·* growth.
     5– 1   hinders man's *s·* growth
     7–13   reaction unfavorable to *s·* growth,
sp 91– 8   great point of departure for all true *s·* growth.
     94–30   indicates *s·* growth and union with the
f 243–15   arises . . . from lack of *s·* growth.
c 260–28   this education is at the expense of *s·* growth.
p 368–24   disappears in the ratio of one's *s·* growth.
t 461–31   Systematic teaching and the student's *s·* growth
r 485–17   and as the result of *s·* growth.

guides
f 235–20   They should be wise *s·* guides
b 299–16   giving earnest heed to these *s·* guides

happiness is
m 57–18   Happiness is *s·*, born of Truth and Love.

harmony
f 248– 2   glorious freedom of *s·* harmony.
b 288–14   will cease, and *s·* harmony reign.
g 503– 9   divine Principle and idea constitute *s·* harmony,
     521– 3   conscious *s·* harmony and eternal being.

healing
p 367– 1   must not hide the talent of *s·* healing

heavens
ap 562–17   They are the lamps in the *s·* heavens of the age,

history
f 204– 5   that material history is as real . . . as *s·* history ;
g 551– 7   In *s·* history, matter is not the

idea
a 29–28   and woman perceived this *s·* idea,
     30– 2   Hence he could give a more *s·* idea of life
     38–26   the Christ, the *s·* idea of divine Love.
     45–20   possible at-one-ment with the *s·* idea of man
     55– 8   the healing Christ and *s·* idea of being.
s 109–24   When a new *s·* idea is borne to earth,
     115–15   MAN : God's *s·* idea.
     132–14   The Pharisees of old thrust the *s·* idea
     132–21   unconscious of the reappearing of the *s·* idea,
ph 194– 4   coincidence of the *s·* idea of man with the
f 233–21   and by understanding the *s·* idea
c 267– 2   the *s·* idea, whose substance is in Mind,
b 315–15   God's *s·* idea as presented by Christ Jesus.
     316–13   Hence the warfare between this *s·* idea and
     316–16   conclusion that the *s·* idea could be killed
     316–24   The *s·* idea of God, as presented by Jesus,
     331–30   Christ the *s·* idea of sonship ;
     333–20   the Christ, as the *s·* idea,— the reflection

spiritual

idea

b	334– 4	the *s·* idea, Christ, dwells forever in the
	339–21	has yielded to a more *s·* idea of Deity,
o	361– 4	Christ, as the true *s·* idea, is the ideal of God
t	463–12	A *s·* idea has not a single element of
r	496–15	it is the *s·* idea, the Holy Ghost and Christ,
g	518–19	Love giveth to the least *s·* idea might,
	534–28	will struggle to destroy the *s·* idea of Love ;
	534–30	*s·* idea has given the understanding a foothold
	542– 4	Material beliefs would slay the *s·* idea
	546–17	can take no cognizance of Spirit or the *s·* idea.
ap	561– 9	The Revelator beheld the *s·* idea
	561–14	the correlation of divine Principle and *s·* idea,
	561–21	and the *s·* idea is understood.
	561–23	generic man, the *s·* idea of God ;
	561–26	The *s·* idea is clad with the radiance of
	562– 1	John saw in those days the *s·* idea
	562– 6	*s·* idea of God's motherhood.
	562–11	The *s·* idea is crowned with twelve stars.
	562–18	which show the workings of the *s·* idea
	562–24	the *s·* idea is typified by a woman
	563–21	seemingly impede the offspring of the *s·* idea,
	564– 3	evil still charges the *s·* idea with
	564–20	*s·* idea was arraigned before the tribunal of
	564–30	pursues with hatred the *s·* idea.
	565–12	the masculine representative of the *s·* idea,
	565–14	The impersonation of the *s·* idea
	565–24	the material lie made war upon the *s·* idea ;
	566– 6	so shall the *s·* idea guide all right desires
	567–22	cast out by Christ, Truth, the *s·* idea,
	570–22	the *s·* idea will be understood.
	573–23	which involve the *s·* idea and consciousness
	575– 3	Love wedded to its own *s·* idea.''
	576–22	and the *s·* idea reveals it.
	577–15	second, the Christ, the *s·* idea of God ;
gl	582–19	creates man as His own *s·* idea,
	584– 1	light, the *s·* idea of Truth and Love.
	590– 9	LAMB OF GOD. The *s·* idea of Love ;
	595–26	the divine Principle and its *s·* idea.

ideal

m	67–29	presents the true likeness or *s·* ideal.
b	337–18	demonstrates Life in Christ, Life's *s·* ideal.
ap	561–11	saw also the *s·* ideal as a woman

ideals

o	359–30	One says : ''I have *s·* ideals,

ideas

s	123–15	replaces the objects of . . . sense with *s·* ideas.
c	257–16	would translate *s·* ideas into material beliefs,
b	295– 6	The universe is filled with *s·* ideas,
	298–20	*S·* ideas, like numbers and notes,
	298–22	*S·* ideas lead up to their divine origin, God,
	320– 5	and names are often expressive of *s·* ideas.
	339–22	so will our material theories yield to *s·* ideas,
o	349–18	in dealing with *s·* ideas.
	361–22	*S·* ideas unfold as we advance.
t	460–26	she had to impart, . . . the hue of *s·* ideas
g	503– 1	consists of the unfolding of *s·* ideas
	504–11	but it is the revelation of Truth and of *s·* ideas.
	510– 2	seek to apprehend the *s·* ideas of God,
	536– 5	heaven and earth stand for *s·* ideas,
gl	583–17	to the apprehension of *s·* ideas

identity

a	51– 8	his *s·* identity in the likeness of the divine ;
b	287– 8	Divine Science . . . maintains man's *s·* identity.
	287–22	it is illusion, without *s·* identity
	333–28	this unity of his *s·* identity

ignorance

f	243– 1	We may hide *s·* ignorance from the world,

image

f	206–25	the *s·* image and likeness of God
g	519–16	until they . . . reach the *s·* image and likeness.
gl	591– 5	the *s·* image and likeness of God ;

immensity

c	263–29	thrown into the face of *s·* immensity,

import

b	271–30	The *s·* import of the Word imparts this power.
r	471–27	gave the *s·* import, expressed through
g	501– 3	chiefly because the *s·* import of the Word,

individuality

c	258–20	the infinite idea and *s·* individuality,
b	317–18	The understanding of his *s·* individuality
	336– 7	is reflected in all *s·* individuality
	337– 4	lose sight of *s·* individuality.
r	491– 9	Man's *s·* individuality is never wrong.
ap	577– 7	this compounded *s·* individuality reflects

inspiration

gl	596–17	they show the *s·* inspiration of Love and Truth

intelligence

f	240– 5	Mind, the *s·* intelligence they reflect.

intent

p	365–23	the result will correspond with the *s·* intent.

interpretation

a	47– 1	even to the *s·* interpretation and discernment of
s	118– 3	and its *s·* interpretation,

spiritual

interpretation

b	320– 9	''The *s·* interpretation of Scripture
g	502–19	each text is followed by its *s·* interpretation

intuitions

ph	174–11	the angels of His presence— the *s·* intuitions
gl	581– 4	*s·* intuitions, pure and perfect ;

Jesus

b	314–24	the *s·* Jesus was imperceptible to them.

joy

c	265–24	has not gained stronger desires for *s·* joy?

law

a	43–25	he was acting under *s·* law
	43–26	and that *s·* law sustained him.
m	62– 5	form habits of obedience to the moral and *s·* law
ph	182–20	prevents full obedience to *s·* law,
	183–27	casts out all evils . . . with the actual *s·* law,
	197–13	and the more . . . about moral and *s·* law,
f	208–11	of immortal Mind, of Truth, and of *s·* law.
	240– 1	Nature voices natural, *s·* law
b	273–21	never ordained a material law to annul the *s* law.
	319– 7	would infringe upon *s·* law
	328–21	Understanding *s·* law . . . Jesus said :
o	349– 9	should subordinate material law to *s·* law.
p	381–12	except a moral or *s·* law.
	417–14	causation is Mind, acting through *s·* law.
t	463–28	and it is a *s·* law instead of material.
r	471– 3	but holds the divine order or *s·* law,
	485–22	by fulfilling the *s·* law of being,
	496–22	the *s·* law which says to the grave,
g	530– 3	*s·* law of Truth is made manifest

lawgivers

ph	184–14	and they are *s·* lawgivers,

laws

s	118–14	which include *s·* laws emanating from the
	118–17	may import that these *s·* laws, perverted

leaven

s	118– 2	the *s·* leaven signifies the Science of Christ

less

a	25–17	any man whose origin was less *s·*.

Life

pr	14–17	controlled by *s·* Life, Truth, and Love.
a	51–17	could no more be separated from his *s·* Life
f	241–29	see God and are approaching *s·* Life
b	306– 6	how death was to be overcome by *s·* Life,
	318–21	yields to the reality of *s·* Life.
p	410– 2	shall not be ready for *s·* Life hereafter.
g	530–23	saying, . . . more pleasant to the eyes than *s·* Life
	550–19	hides the true and *s·* Life,
ap	561–28	The light portrayed is . . . *s·* Life,

life

a	51–14	his *s·* life, indestructible and eternal,
sp	72– 8	the gain of *s·* life.
	74– 1	*s·* life which is not subject to death.
	82– 9	If *s·* life has been won by the departed,
f	232–31	and the resurrection to *s·* life.
b	284–18	testimony as to *s·* life, truth, and love?
	306– 4	would . . . resort to death to reproduce *s·* life
p	430– 1	That statement is not confined to *s·* life,
g	556–26	Because mortal mind must waken to *s·* life

Life-laws

p	398– 9	the popular ignorance of *s·* Life-laws.

light

b	324–22	but *s·* light soon enabled him to follow the
t	446–26	reflect the *s·* light and might which heal

link

r	491–15	and find the indissoluble *s·* link

living

c	264–24	*S·* living and blessedness are the only

Love

a	33–22	This is the new understanding of *s·* Love.
c	266–11	*s·* Love will force you to accept what best

love

c	264–27	comes from an all-absorbing *s·* love.
t	462–29	unselfishness, philanthropy, *s·* love.

man

sp	70– 7	*s·* man, made in God's likeness, reflects God.
f	250–11	*S·* man is the likeness of this Ego.
c	258–25	a very imperfect sense of the *s·* man
	263– 5	Immortal *s·* man alone represents the
b	281–17	in individual *s·* man and things.
	300–30	the spiritual universe and *s·* man,
	301–10	immortal, *s·* man is really substantial,
	302–21	Mind, of the *s·* man is God,
	303–28	*S·* man is the image or idea of God,
	314– 7	God and His reflection or *s·* man.
	337–24	the invisible universe and *s·* man.
g	557–12	as the line of creation rises towards *s·* man,

meaning

s	117–11	the *s·* meaning of which is attained through
	138–32	his theology . . . and the *s·* meaning of this
b	319–24	misapprehension of the *s·* meaning of
o	350–10	enables them to interpret his *s·* meaning.
	355– 1	they should gain the *s·* meaning of

spiritual

means
ph 181–13   when you resort to any except s· means.
meeting
a 35–10   This s· meeting with our Lord
might
ph 192–17   Moral and s· might belong to Spirit,
name
s 137–28   but now the Master gave him a s· name
nature
g 512–24   Their s· nature is discerned only through the
oblivion
p 382–24   rescued from seeming s· oblivion,
offering
a 25– 4   The efficacy of Jesus' s· offering is
offspring
b 336–31   man is God's s· offspring.
oneness
m 57–10   and their true harmony is in s· oneness.
opposite
ph 171– 4   Through discernment of the s· opposite
origin
b 312–31   Jesus' s· origin and his demonstration of
315–21   Jesus' s· origin and understanding
325–27   The time cometh when the s· origin of man,
r 479– 2   must have a material, not a s· origin.
g 519–14   demonstrating its s· origin.
534– 7   which reveals the s· origin of man.
gl 582–10   the introduction of a more s· origin ;
original
f 210– 3   the translation of the s· original into the
outpouring
ap 574–14   the s· outpouring of bliss and glory,
peace
gl 589– 8   JAPHET (Noah's son). A type of s· peace,
perception
f 203–13   S· perception brings out the possibilities of
p 406–12   s· perception, aided by Science, reaches Truth.
g 531–12   exchanging it for s· perception,
547–31   It is this s· perception of Scripture,
gl 585– 3   Jesus said, referring to s· perception,
perfection
f 254–12   grasp the ultimate of s· perfection slowly ;
gl 595–21   mortal disappears and s· perfection appears.
phenomena
sp 88–24   nor are they s· phenomena,
power
a 38–17   It expresses s· power.
53–31   his final demonstration of s· power.
m 67–25   The lack of s· power in the
sp 75–22   Jesus' s· power to reproduce the presence of
s 116– 3   s· power, love, health, holiness.
119– 1   When we endow matter with vague s· power,
134–30   believing in the superiority of s· power
146–10   barren of the vitality of s· power,
f 235–26   Christ Jesus, the true idea of s· power.
b 309– 9   the understanding of Spirit and of s· power.
313–27   to immature ideas of s· power,
313–29   the body, which by s· power he raised
o 355– 8   prayers which evince no s· power to heal.
p 365–29   patient's s· power to resuscitate himself.
382–14   receptive of s· power and of faith in one God,
407–15   even into s· power and good-will to man.
t 453–16   Honesty is s· power.
454–29   The superiority of s· power over sensuous
r 470– 4   unity of Principle and s· power
470– 7   error assumed the loss of s· power,
presence
r 470– 8   the s· presence of Life as infinite Truth
proof
g 505–24   giving the s· proof of the universe
prospects
s 130– 3   discouraged over its slight s· prospects.
purgation
p 364–21   small reward in return for the s· purgation
qualifications
t 448–21   s· qualifications requisite for healing,
rationality
f 223–21   S· rationality and free thought accompany
realities
g 513–27   His thoughts are s· realities.
gl 581–12   s· realities of all things are created by Him
reality
f 207–27   The s· reality is the scientific fact
228–18   will recognize harmony as the s· reality
r 488–21   senses can take no cognizance of s· reality
realm
a 34–25   would rise again in the s· realm of reality,
b 337–26   as they exist in the s· realm of the real.
recompense
sp 98– 1   the s· recompense of the persecuted
record
g 521–14   turn our gaze to the s· record of creation,
reflection
b 305–21   as opposed to the Science of s· reflection,
r 480– 5   If there is no s· reflection, then there remains

spiritual

rules
s 112–18   s· rules, laws, and their demonstration,
scale
s 155–25   and more weight into the s· scale.
seer
gl 593– 4   PROPHET. A s· seer ;
self
b 334–17   while the s· self, or Christ,
selfhood
a 38–24   his s· selfhood, never suffered.
sense
pref viii– 6   must yield to the harmony of s· sense,
pr 7–18   If s· sense always guided men,
16–24   the s· sense of the Lord's Prayer :
a 29–20   The illumination of Mary's s· sense
41– 7   from material sense into the s· sense of
m 56–12   and its s· sense was revealed from heaven,
sp 72–15   and immortal Truth (the s· sense)
75– 8   would transfer men from the s· sense of
85–24   but mortals need s· sense.
95–31   s· sense lifts human consciousness into
s 122–25   to s· sense and in Science, Life goes on
123–21   through a s· sense of the Scriptures
ph 191–12   the s· sense of being and of what Life includes
f 206– 7   the province of s· sense to govern man.
209–31   S· sense is a conscious, constant capacity to
210– 6   are discerned by s· sense.
214–11   When it is learned that the s· sense,
247–16   Immortal men and women are models of s· sense,
c 258–31   Through s· sense you can discern the
b 272– 3   The s· sense of truth must be gained
272– 9   The s· sense of the Scriptures brings out the
290– 9   instead of through a s· sense of life,
294–18   destroyed by Truth through s· sense
296–15   s· sense, and the actuality of being.
298– 9   s· sense can bear witness only to Truth.
298–13   S· sense, contradicting the material senses,
298–23   and to the s· sense of being.
303–31   before the material senses yielded to s· sense,
306–24   s· sense, which cognizes Life as permanent.
309– 5   gave him the s· sense of being
314– 4   s· sense had quenched all earthly yearnings.
315–17   which beclouds the s· sense of Truth ;
318–13   silence this lie . . . with the truth of s· sense.
326–25   yielded to a s· sense, which is always right.
328– 1   the grandeur and bliss of a s· sense,
o 349–19   The elucidation of C. S. lies in its s· sense,
350–32   and the s· sense was scarcely perceived.
351–12   when the s· sense of the creed was discerned
351–13   this s· sense was a present help.
359–16   Soul, is palpable only to s· sense,
t 452–22   the s· sense of Truth unfolds its harmonies,
461–11   Only by the illumination of the s· sense,
r 471–17   is fully sustained by s· sense,
481– 8   Through s· sense only, man comprehends
486– 8   gain spiritual understanding and s· sense
490–26   ushers in the s· sense of being.
g 505–20   S· sense is the discernment of spiritual good.
548– 4   s· sense of life, substance, and intelligence.
548–17   the true ideas of God, the s· sense of being.
ap 573–21   and in place of this . . . was the s· sense,
578– 3   the incorporeal or s· sense of Deity :
578– 8   restoreth my soul [s· sense] :— Psal. 23 : 3.
gl 579– 6   s· sense, which is also their original meaning.
585– 7   to s· sense, it is a compound idea.
589– 7   yield to the s· sense of Life and Love.
590–24   when the s· sense of God and of infinity is
592– 9   nor can be recognized by the s· sense ;
596– 1   That which s· sense alone comprehends,
597–18   s· sense unfolds the great facts of existence.
senses
b 288– 4   between the evidence of the s· senses and
r 486–23   all the s· senses of man,
g 512–25   is discerned only through the s· senses.
significance
s 118–13   In their s· significance, Science, Theology,
signification
a 32–24   in its s· signification, it was natural
f 241–14   Take away the s· signification of Scripture, and
g 545–27   which is so glorious in its s· signification.
source
s 152–26   divinely driven to a s· source for health
b 329–27   If men understood their real s· source
spheres
g 513– 7   lead on to s· spheres and exalted beings.
state
f 215–30   Having sought man's s· state,
status
r 476–21   and earnestly seek the s· status of man,
statutes
b 307–29   his province is in s· statutes,
steps
g 513– 6   Advancing s· steps in the teeming universe

spiritual

strength

b 308–22	s· strength in this Peniel of divine Science.
ap 566–31	Michael's characteristic is s· strength.
567– 5	s· strength wrestles and prevails
571–28	With his s· strength, he has opened wide the
gl 599– 7	inspiration ; s· strength.

susceptibility

sp 86–10	Jesus possessed more s· susceptibility than

system

ph 170– 4	form neither a moral nor a s· system.

teaching

ap 575–13	S· teaching must always be by symbols.
gl 595–16	can fit us for the office of s· teaching.

teachings

b 272–15	the s· teachings which dulness and

things

b 326–10	and set his whole affections on s· things,
335–13	Things s· and eternal are substantial.

thoughts

c 259–29	and demands s· thoughts, divine concepts,
gl 582–28	The s· thoughts and representatives of
598–10	to unfold s· thoughts.

tongue

s 115–11	back into the original s· tongue.

transfiguration

ap 576–29	through s· transfiguration.

Truth

sp 96–20	all discord will be swallowed up in s· Truth.
b 273– 4	can take no cognizance of God and s· Truth.
315–23	how s· Truth destroys material error,
o 350–17	in a material age to apprehend s· Truth.
ap 561–27	idea is clad with the radiance of s· Truth,
gl 582– 2	BELIEVING. . . . the perception of s· Truth.
590– 8	the opposite of s· Truth and understanding.
593– 5	before the conscious facts of s· Truth.

truth

ph 165–14	theories took the place of s· truth.
b 277–18	This points to the s· truth
293–20	while s· truth is Mind.
311–16	loss or absence of soul, s· truth.

type

g 541–11	the lamb was a more s· type of
gl 582–12	a s· type ; that which comforts, consoles,

ultimate

r 485–15	Think not to thwart the s· ultimate of

understanding

pr 1– 3	a s· understanding of Him, an unselfed love.
4–27	can never do the works of s· understanding,
10– 5	must grow to the s· understanding of prayer.
14–26	Life divine, revealing s· understanding
16– 2	must precede this advanced s· understanding.
a 23–18	Faith, advanced to s· understanding,
23–30	which includes s· understanding and
m 64–24	s· understanding and perpetual peace.
sp 77–10	until the s· understanding of Life is
83–27	through s· understanding, by which man
85– 3	It is the illumination of the s· understanding
96– 1	advances slowly . . . into s· understanding ;
96–24	but s· understanding is changeless.
96–28	and s· understanding increases,
s 115– 2	SPIRITUAL. Wisdom, purity, s· understanding,
128–12	imbued with this s· understanding
ph 178–26	in proportion to our s· understanding of
183–30	C. S. . . . honors s· understanding ;
194–15	man, who is immortal in s· understanding,
f 202–14	lights the torch of s· understanding.
211–12	matter does not appear in the s· understanding
213–19	senses of Soul—through s· understanding.
226–19	fetter faith and s· understanding.
251–25	process of higher s· understanding
b 271–14	the result of his cultivated s· understanding
274–14	are based on s· understanding,
275–20	metaphysics, as revealed to s· understanding,
276–25	beliefs and s· understanding never mingle.
286– 7	s· understanding is better than all burnt
297–29	and faith becomes s· understanding.
298– 4	and glow full-orbed in s· understanding.
312–26	limits faith and hinders s· understanding.
o 346–30	expelled to make room for s· understanding.
355–28	demonstration and s· understanding are
p 402–28	better instructed by s· understanding.
403–21	Christian state is one of . . . s· understanding,
425–25	Correct material belief by s· understanding,
442–21	then belief melts into s· understanding,
t 445–11	dwarfing the s· understanding
447–19	impart . . . the truth and s· understanding,
462– 7	his store of s· understanding, potency,
r 465– 3	much labor and increased s· understanding,
486– 8	must gain s· understanding and spiritual sense
497–10	s· understanding that casts out evil
g 505– 7	S· understanding, . . . is the firmament.
505–22	S· understanding unfolds Mind,
509– 1	letting in the light of s· understanding.
509–17	The light of s· understanding gives gleams of
512–16	states of faith and s· understanding.

spiritual

understanding

gl 579–14	the life-preserving power of s· understanding.
582–17	BRIDEGROOM. S· understanding ;
584– 5	in the illumination of s· understanding,
585– 2	EARS. . . . s· understanding.
586–15	FIRMAMENT. S· understanding ;
589–24	the s· understanding of God and man
593–11	material belief yielding to s· understanding.
598–23	the s· understanding of Life and Love,

unfoldment

p 371–25	our need of its s· unfoldment.

unity

m 61–31	The scientific *morale* of marriage is s· unity.

universe

s 127– 5	creator of the s· universe, including man,
c 267–11	man and the s· universe coexist
b 286– 9	the s· universe is good, and reflects God
300–30	God is seen only in the s· universe
r 468–23	s· universe, including individual man,

views

a 32–27	refresh his heart with brighter, with s· views.

vision

f 215–11	S· vision is not subordinate to
ap 561– 7	Because of his more s· vision,

wickedness

t 453–20	Hidden sin is s· wickedness in high places.
ap 563–30	"s· wickedness in high places."— *Eph.* 6 : 12.

pr 14–13	Life and intelligence are purely s·,
a 34–19	they became more s· and understood better
35–17	his s· and final ascension above matter,
m 61– 5	and the s· over the animal,
65– 5	s· and eternal existence may be discerned.
67–27	S·, . . . consciousness is needed.
69– 3	evolved from Spirit, and so are s·,
sp 73–31	cannot be made the mouthpiece of the s·,
74–27	the s·, or incorporeal, and the physical,
78–10	If . . . they are not s·, but must still be mortal,
83–22	to suppose that life is . . . organically s·.
84– 4	foresight from a s·, incorporeal standpoint,
85–26	seeking the material more than the s·.
88–14	Ideas are s·, harmonious, and eternal.
90–13	Then being will be recognized as s·,
93–26	Man is s·.
99– 2	not material but scientifically s·.
99–13	ordinary teachings are material and not s·.
99–14	C. S. teaches only that which is s·
99–29	of divine Spirit and to God's s·, perfect man.
s 114–28	the universe, including man, is s·,
116– 2	definition of
117– 7	the language of Spirit must be, and is, s·.
118–29	portray law as physical, not s·.
119–18	this nature is s· and is not expressed in matter
126–18	as being both natural and s·?
127–28	It has a s·, and not a material origin.
131–11	the superiority of s· over physical power.
148–26	to rule man by material law, instead of s·.
157–32	better for this s· and profound pathology.
ph 170–14	The demands of Truth are s·,
170–29	The description of man as . . . material and s·,
171–21	The intellectual, the moral, the s·,
171–29	intelligence and life are s·, never material,
172–13	eternal chain of existence as . . . wholly s· ;
173–20	Man is s·, individual, and eternal ;
181–18	are not sufficiently s· to depend on Spirit.
191– 9	the s· and divine Principle of man dawns
192– 7	Human opinions are not s·.
f 214– 4	If the medium of hearing is wholly s·,
231–14	no antagonistic powers nor laws, s· or
250–27	But the s·, real man is immortal.
252–32	Man, whose senses are s·,
254–22	and to work out the s· which determines
c 256– 4	rises from the material sense to the s·,
263– 8	blends his thoughts of existence with the s·
265– 6	their affections and aims grow s·,
265–30	and that joy is s·.
266–29	Man is deathless, s·.
b 274–20	affirm that . . . are material, instead of s·.
275–26	The true understanding of God is s·.
284–29	the only real senses of man are s·,
288–25	the s· real man has no birth,
289–24	God's universe is s· and immortal.
289–26	but the s· is true, and therefore
289–30	Spirit and all things s· are the real and
290–25	To be wholly s·, man must be sinless,
290–29	no more s· for believing that his body died
291–32	As for s· error there is none.
292–29	s· real man's indissoluble connection with
295– 9	Mortal mind would transform the s· into the material,
296– 2	man is the s·, eternal reflection of God.
297–20	Faith is higher and more s· than belief.
298–27	flying on s·, not material, pinions.
299–24	Truth is s·, eternal substance, which cannot
301–14	the s· man's substantiality transcends

spiritual
  b 301–21 is not s˙ and breaks the First Commandment,
  301–32 presupposes . . . man to be material instead of s˙.
  306– 2 thought that they could raise the s˙ from
  309–19 not in elements which are not s˙,
  311–10 All sin is of the flesh. It cannot be s˙.
  311–31 But the s˙, eternal man is not touched by
  315–27 more s˙ than all other earthly personalities.
  317–17 is no less tangible because it is s˙
  318–30 invalids grow more s˙, as the error
  320– 7 Scriptures have both a s˙ and literal meaning.
  320–25 important interpretation of Scripture is the s˙.
  326–11 or trusting in it more than in the s˙.
  326–27 and his life became more s˙.
  329–28 they would struggle for recourse to the s˙
  331–25 Hence all is Spirit and s˙.
  332–12 The Christ is incorporeal, s˙,
  332–27 Mary's conception of him was s˙,
  333– 9 Christ expresses God's s˙, eternal nature.
  334–13 the unseen and the seen, the s˙ and material,
  335–27 Reality is s˙, harmonious, immutable,
  336–14 The s˙ man's consciousness and
  338– 6 both good and evil, both s˙ and material
  o 344–31 are more fashionable and less s˙?
  347–14 Christ, as the s˙ or true idea of God,
  351–22 such starting-points are neither s˙ nor scientific,
  351–28 in their attempted worship of the s˙.
  352–10 to the rabbis the s˙ was the intangible
  353–29 The true idea of being is s˙ and immortal,
  360–14 which . . . the material or the s˙?
  p 368–23 Neither evil, disease, nor death can be s˙,
  396–28 man is s˙, not material;
  407–23 In Science, all being is eternal, s˙, perfect,
  409–21 real man is s˙ and immortal,
  419–19 less of material conditions and more of s˙.
  425–18 mankind will be more s˙
  427–25 physical realm, so-called, as well as in the s˙.
  428–21 to replace them with the life which is s˙,
  442– 3 Our statute is s˙,
  451–17 If our hopes and affections are s˙,
  453–13 as from the use of s˙.
  458– 5 one s˙, the other material,
  460– 9 and its medicine is intellectual and s˙,
  r 467– 7 no truth, no love, but that which is s˙.
  468–15 man is not material ; he is s˙.
  475–11 Man is s˙ and perfect ;
  475–12 and because he is s˙ and perfect,
  477– 7 he is himself s˙.
  479– 7 it must be immortal and s˙.
  g 503–21 third, in s˙ and immortal forms
  504– 7 as to the divine creation being both s˙ and
  510– 5 to be holy, thought must be purely s˙.
  516– 3 so you, being s˙, are the reflection of God.
  517–22 This ideal is God's own image, s˙ and infinite.
  534–24 opposition to the s˙, scientific meaning
  537–12 Creation is there represented as s˙, entire,
  538– 9 distance . . . between the material and s˙,
  544– 1 record of a material creation which followed
        the s˙,
  544– 8 the material sense of things, not from the s˙,
  544–31 declares . . . that matter becomes s˙.
  547–29 and adopts the s˙ and immortal.
  552–11 whereas the s˙ scientific facts
  ap 566– 8 from a material sense of existence to the s˙,
  573– 1 terrestrial or celestial, material or s˙?
  573– 8 the heavens and earth to one . . . are s˙,
  575–21 This city is wholly s˙, as its four sides indicate.
  577–12 This s˙, holy habitation has no boundary
  gl 579– 2 substitution of the s˙ for the material
  592–24 and of the immortality of all that is s˙.

spiritualism
belief of
  sp 84–24 destroys the belief of s˙ at its very inception,
has no basis
  sp 84–26 s˙ has no basis upon which to build.
material
  sp 77–27 would outgrow their beliefs in material s˙.
relies upon
  sp 79–11 S˙ relies upon human beliefs and hypotheses.
structure of
  sp 71–27 basis and structure of s˙ are alike material and
will be found
  sp 71–21 s˙ will be found mainly erroneous,
would transfer
  sp 75– 8 S˙ would transfer men from the

  a 24–23 Does s˙ find Jesus' death necessary only for the
  sp 71–26 I never could believe in s˙.
  71–29 S˙ therefore presupposes Spirit, which is
  73– 3 S˙ calls one person, living in this world, *material*,
  78–16 S˙ . . . would destroy the supremacy of Spirit.
  80–14 It is mysticism which gives s˙ its force.
  81– 7 on its own theories, s˙ can only
  99–18 Those individuals, who adopt theosophy, s˙,
  s 111– 1 agnosticism, pantheism, theosophy, s˙,

spiritualism
  s 129–17 hypnotism, s˙, theosophy, agnosticism,
  ph 178–30 may attempt to unite with it hypnotism, s˙,
  r 484– 8 hypnotism, theosophy, or s˙?
Spiritualists
  sp 77–26 and S˙ would outgrow their beliefs
  80–13 humanity and philanthropy of many S˙,
  81– 5 If S˙ understood the Science of being,
spirituality
alludes to the
  b 333–11 alludes to the s˙ which is taught,
concomitant of
  r 484–28 Is materiality the concomitant of s˙,
essence of
  b 293–18 counterfeits the true essence of s˙
genuine
  sp 95–15 depends upon his genuine s˙.
giving more
  p 422–17 giving more s˙ to consciousness
goodness and
  b 277– 8 goodness and s˙ must be immortal.
  277–10 If goodness and s˙ are real,
hamper
  f 234– 2 even as ritualism and creed hamper s˙.
his
  a 51–28 His s˙ separated him from sensuousness,
  sp 86– 8 His quick apprehension . . . illustrated his s˙.
  f 220–23 a diet of bread and water to increase his s˙.
  b 270–32 but it was indigenous to his s˙,
  o 356–10 on the basis of his s˙.
his patient's
  p 375–19 increasing his patient's s˙ while restoring
in proportion to our
  sp 95– 7 approach God, or Life, in proportion to our s˙,
lays open siege
  f 216– 9 S˙ lays open siege to materialism.
Master taught
  s 117–15 Our Master taught s˙ by similitudes
meekness and
  o 343–22 meekness and s˙ are the conditions of
no resemblance to
  f 207–31 which bears no resemblance to s˙,
of the universe
  r 471–19 the s˙ of the universe is the only fact of
opposition to
  b 329–31 the more intense the opposition to s˙,
price of
  a 36–15 The earthly price of s˙ in a material age
reception of that
  s 115– 1 obstacle to the reception of that s˙,
Rubicon of
  ph 172–10 and death is the Rubicon of s˙?
this
  a 51–30 this s˙ which enabled Jesus to heal the sick,
true
  sp 99–23 The calm, strong currents of true s˙,
war against
  ap 565– 3 inflamed with war against s˙,
wars against
  f 242–19 which wars against s˙
yield to
  f 201–10 fear, all sensuality, yield to s˙,

  s 111–25 meets a yearning of the human race for s˙.
  c 266–17 lay down their fleshliness and gain s˙.
  b 313–27 s˙ was possessed only in a limited degree
  o 352– 9 but s˙, was the reality of man's existence,
  ap 572–11 materiality is the inverted image of s˙.
  gl 587–26 s˙ ; bliss ; the atmosphere of Soul.
spiritualization
  sp 96– 4 s˙ will follow, for Love is Spirit.
  96–10 until the final s˙ of all things.
  s 158–24 Evidences of progress and of s˙ greet us
  f 211–29 through dematerialization and s˙ of thought
  b 272–19 It is the s˙ of thought and Christianization of
  p 382– 6 and to the s˙ of thought,
  407–26 This s˙ of thought lets in the light,
  gl 593– 9 RESURRECTION. S˙ of thought ;
spiritualized
  s 141–19 Its only priest is the s˙ man.
  o 356– 2 the material thought must become s˙
spiritualizes
  o 354–11 heals the sick and s˙ humanity.
  p 370– 6 the same regimen which s˙ the thought ;
spiritualizing
  b 316–28 s˙ materialistic beliefs,
spiritually
  a 21– 9 If the disciple is advancing s˙,
  25–18 he demonstrated more s˙ than all others
  32–20 The true sense is s˙ lost,
  38–18 otherwise the healing could not have been done
        s˙.
  m 68–32 the unbroken links . . . will be s˙ discerned ;

spiritually

m	69–13	S· to understand that there is but one creator,
	69–18	educate their own offspring s·,
	69–18	they can educate others s·
sp	95– 6	"To be s· minded is life."— Rom. 8 : 6.
	98–11	which can only be s· discerned.
s	110–27	and must again be s· discerned, taught,
	110–31	and s· understand Truth.
	114– 6	s· unscientific definition of mind is based on
	136– 8	divine power to save men both bodily and s·.
	137– 4	was not s· discerned, even by them, until
	138– 9	On this s· scientific basis Jesus explained his
	140– 7	Not materially but s· we know Him
	140–16	We worship s·, only as we
	148–10	as created corporeally instead of s·
	149–28	Whatever guides thought s· benefits
s	151–12	to benefit the race physically and s·,
ph	200–12	the idea of God, not formed materially but s·,
f	207– 3	proportionately as we advance s·,
	213– 5	as a man s· understandeth, so is he in truth.
	235–30	They should so raise their hearers s·,
c	256– 6	All things are created s·.
	259–24	God, Spirit, works s·, not materially.
b	275–31	Truth, s· discerned, is . . . understood.
	290– 5	they will rise no higher s·
	303–11	is s· conceived and brought forth ;
	303–13	both s· and materially,
	306–30	God's man, s· created, is not material and
	310–19	which sins and is s· lost,
	311– 8	Is man lost s·? No,
	319– 8	s· understanding God, sustains man
	325–21	demands of Truth upon mortals physically and s·,
o	354–24	s· to hear and to speak the new tongue.
	359–14	must at length know yourself s·
p	370– 1	must be better s· as well as physically.
	442–25	and man is clothed and fed s·.
t	455–25	it is one who is s· near Himself.
	461– 9	morally advanced and s· endowed,
	462–20	Anatomy, when conceived of s·, is
r	466–31	better physically, morally, and s·.
	475–22	reflects s· all that belongs to his Maker.
	487– 7	more Christianity in seeing and hearing s· than
g	502– 9	S· followed, the book of Genesis is the
	504–19	s· clearer views of Him,
	510–11	reflected s· by all who walk in the light
	511–24	S· interpreted, rocks and mountains stand for
	523–24	the s· scientific account of creation,
	527–27	but doing so materially, not s·,
	528–20	Beginning . . . materially rather than s·,
	537–25	Inspired writers interpret the Word s·,
	545– 9	by thought tending s· upward
	547–24	Our aim must be to have them understood s·,
	548–13	little light or joy . . . before Life is s· learned.
gl	585–26	materially instead of s·,
	592–14	without . . . there is something s· lacking,
	598–27	would bridge over with life discerned s·

Spiritual Senses

p	437–11	and before its jurors, the S· S·,
	442– 5	The Jury of S· S· agreed at once upon a verdict,

Spiritward

b	307–24	and so weighs against our course S·.

spite

s	150–20	and that, too, in s· of the individual's protest

splendor

f	224–15	and array His vicegerent with pomp and s· ;

spoil

p	399–30	and s· his goods, except he first — Matt. 12 : 29.

spoke

s	147–32	Jesus never s· of disease as dangerous
b	314–12	When Jesus s· of reproducing his body,
o	356–12	he s· of flesh and Spirit as the two opposites,
	360–29	for the truth he s· and demonstrated,
p	367–18	of which Jesus s· to his disciples.
	389–32	One instant she s· despairingly of herself.
r	495– 9	when he s· of the sick,
ap	576–16	as when Jesus s· of his material body as the

spoken

pr	4–25	goodness will "be evil s· of,"— Rom. 14 : 16.
	8– 8	such externals are s· of by Jesus as
a	46– 9	has s· through the inspired Word
s	117–10	God's essential language is s· of
	117–14	Ear hath not heard, nor hath lip s·, the
ph	180–10	bearing fruit after its kind, s· of in Genesis.
f	254–29	Your good will be evil s· of
c	261–17	sat aching in his chair till his cue was s·,
b	325–30	When first s· in any age, Truth, like the
o	346– 2	When man is s· of as made in God's image,
p	411– 7	replies more readily when his name is s· ;
ap	560–25	Persecution of all who have s· something new
	563–29	Its sting is s· of by Paul, when he

spontaneity

gl	597–16	S· of thought and idea ;

spontaneous

s	161– 9	might produce s· combustion.

spontaneously

c	262–24	from a higher standpoint, one rises s·,

sport

f	250–32	nor . . . admit that happiness is ever the s· of

spot

m	58–21	Home is the dearest s· on earth,
p	439– 9	At this request Death repaired to the s·
	439–32	but on visiting the s·, they learn

sprain

p	385–19	If you s· the muscles or wound the flesh,

sprang

c	255– 7	s· from cultured scholars in Rome
b	338–28	and from this ground, or matter, s· Adam,
o	351– 1	which s· from half-hidden Israelitish history

spray

ph	191–22	not a s· buds within the vale,

spread

f	214–24	would s· their table with cannibal tidbits
p	438–20	a garment of foul fur was s· over him

spring

m	57–14	seasons of renewal like the returning s·.
f	220–10	violet lifts her blue eye to greet the early s·.
b	277– 1	and therefore cannot s· from intelligence.
	284– 7	would seem to s· from a limited body ;
p	380–16	Gazing at a chained lion, crouched for a s·,
g	551– 9	argues that mortals s· from eggs
gl	597– 9	which was ready to s· into action

springing

ph	188–22	s· from mortal ignorance or fear.
	190–15	are as the grass s· from the soil
p	399–24	material beliefs, s· from illusion.

springs

ph	191–21	By its own volition, not a blade of grass s· up,
f	244–19	or s· from matter into being,
b	271– 1	seed of Truth s· up and bears much fruit.
r	485–20	belief . . . that man s· from dust
g	530–30	supposes that something s· from nothing,
	581– 3	belief that everything s· from dust
	543–28	thus it is seen that man s· solely from Mind.

sprout

sp	74– 8	the acorn, already absorbed into a s·

sprouted

f	237–14	the good seed before it has s·.

sprung

ph	185–12	systems of so-called mind-cure, which have s· up.

spurn

p	363– 8	Did Jesus s· the woman?

spurned

f	215–29	his philosophy s· physical timidity.

square

ap	575–26	a city of the Spirit, fair, royal, and s·.

squire

s	144– 6	Naught is the s·, when the king is nigh ;

stab

t	450– 8	they never fail to s· their benefactor

stability

m	57– 2	Without it there is no s· in society,
	64–29	the s· of the marriage covenant.

staff

m	66– 6	teach mortals not to lean on a material s·,
b	321–15	this proof was a s· upon which to lean.
g	515–10	changeth the serpent into a s·.
ap	578–12	[LOVE'S] rod and [LOVE'S] s·— Psal. 23 : 4.

stage

each successive

m	66–15	Each successive s· of experience unfolds new
g	506–14	forming each successive s· of progress.

last

s	153–11	sinking in the last s· of typhoid fever.

of existence

sp	77–24	less with every advanced s· of existence.
f	244–15	If man were dust in his earliest s· of existence,
	250–28	Upon this s· of existence goes on the

of fear

p	375–31	a s· of fear so excessive that it amounts to

one

a	37– 9	human links which connect one s· with another
s	125–12	As human thought changes from one s· to

third

g	508–28	The third s· in the order of C. S.

transitional

m	65–24	An unsettled, transitional s· is never
ap	572–24	had not yet passed the transitional s·

c	261–13	to go upon the s· and sustain his

stages
  an 104–10   scientific truth goes through three *s*.
  f 251– 7   Fright is so great at certain *s* of
  p 390–29   Meet the incipient *s* of disease with
  391– 8   the incipient or advanced *s* of disease,
  405– 9   Choke these errors in their early *s*,
  g 550–19   decay, and dissolution as its component *s*
  ap 573–11   indicate states and *s* of consciousness.

stagnation
  s 159–28   pain or pleasure, action or *s*,

stake
  a 37– 7   to slay Truth with the steel or the *s*,

stammeringly
  pref ix– 7   *s* attempts to convey his feeling.

stamp
  p 413–29   and often *s* them there,

stand
  pr 3– 4   Who would *s* before a blackboard, and pray the
  s 113–15   has not a foot to *s* upon which is not
  127–13   These synonymous terms *s* for
  f 204–19   They can never *s* the test of Science.
  229–21   all that He makes is good and will *s* forever.
  252– 3   that kingdom cannot *s*.” — *Mark* 3 : 24.
  b 268– *   *Here I s*.   *I can do no otherwise;*
  320–32   *s* in celestial perfection before Elohim,
  p 392–24   *S* porter at the door of thought.
  431–25   Another witness takes the *s* and testifies :
  432–20   Another witness takes the *s* and testifies :
  r 493– 3   appears to rise and set, and the earth to *s* still ;
  g 511–24   rocks and mountains *s* for solid . . . ideas.
  536– 5   heaven and earth *s* for spiritual ideas,
  537–17   since ground and dust *s* for nothingness.
  ap 563– 7   why should we *s* aghast at nothingness?
  gl 581–18   divided against itself, which cannot *s* ;

standard
  His own
  r 470–19   Has God taken down His own *s*,
  in Christian Science
  r 483–12   and hinders its approach to the *s* in C. S.
  intellectual
  ph 195–29   lowering the intellectual *s* to accommodate the
  moral
  r 492– 9   will uplift the physical and moral *s* of mortals,
  of Christian Science
  ph 168– 2   worldly, who think the *s* of C. S. too high
  of good
  g 539– 8   What can be the *s* of good, of Spirit,
  of man
  g 553– 9   become the *s* of man.
  of perfection
  r 470–18   The *s* of perfection was originally God and man.
  g 555–23   We lose our *s* of perfection . . . when we
  of Truth
  a 31– 2   are unfit to bear the *s* of Truth,
  f 235–29   should uplift the *s* of Truth.
  472–22   Thus we should continue to lose the *s* of Truth.
  of truth
  ph 195–31   Incorrect views lower the *s* of truth.
  our
  g 550–20   and causes our *s* to trail in the dust.
  555–23   We lose our *s* of perfection . . . when we
  raises the
  f 227–21   C. S. raises the *s* of liberty
  raise the
  p 426–24   would raise the *s* of health and morals
  truth’s
  f 225–13   but there is a rallying to truth’s *s*.

  ph 197–13   the higher will be the *s* of living
  p 373–32   circulation is changed, and returns to that *s*

standards
  f 247–13   form the transient *s* of mortals.

standing
  s 108–20   *s* already within the shadow of the
  p 415–31   leaving the pain *s* forth as distinctly as a
  440–25   *s* at the bar of Truth,
  t 456– 8   the high *s* which most of them hold
  ap 561– 8   an “angel *s* in the sun.”— *Rev.* 19 : 17.

standpoint
  higher
  c 262–24   Starting from a higher *s*,
  honest
  pr 13– 6   beyond the honest *s* of fervent desire.
  human
  g 520– 1   sweetest rest, even from a human *s*, is in
  incorporeal
  sp 84– 4   from a spiritual, incorporeal *s*,
  material
  o 351–31   to worship Spirit from a material *s*,
  t 458– 8   from both a mental and a material *s*.
  g 546–20   cannot . . . be interpreted from a material *s*.
  551–26   From a material *s*, “Canst thou— *Job* 11 : 7.

standpoint
  new
  g 556–29   existence will be on a new *s*.
  of error
  g 545–24   From that *s* of error, they could not apprehend
  our
  f 239–21   reveal our *s*, and show what we
  b 281–32   the inspiration, which is to change our *s*,
  supposed
  b 301–26   from a supposed *s* outside the
  your
  p 412– 2   that God lovingly governs all, . . . is your *s*,

  t 461–10   from the *s* of the human senses.

standpoints
  sp 77–31   and they return to their old *s* of matter.
  83–30   are distinctly opposite *s*,
  ph 174– 9   rising above material *s*,
  182–12   It is impossible to work from two *s*.
  b 322– 3   changes the *s* of life and intelligence

stands
  sp 98–17   *s* a revealed and practical Science.
  f 224–24   practical Christianity, . . . *s* at the door of this
  b 330–28   manifested by mankind it *s* for a lie,
  338–22   it *s* for obstruction, error,
  g 526–18   *s* for the idea of Truth,
  526–20   “tree of knowledge” *s* for the — *Gen.* 2 : 9.
  526–30   In this text Eden *s* for the mortal, . . . body.
  529–30   Adam, . . . *s* for a belief of material mind.
  ap 563–10   This dragon *s* for the sum total of human error.
  563–27   The serpentine form *s* for subtlety,

star
  pref vii– 4   So shone the pale *s* to the prophet-shepherds ;
  vii–10   and shine the guiding *s* of being.
  sp 70–13   from a blade of grass to a *s*,
  95–23   Led by a solitary *s* amid the darkness,
  s 121–16   is as the wandering comet or the desolate *s*
  144– 7   Withdraws the *s*, when dawns the
  ap 564– 9   into a night without a *s*.
  575–28   eastward, to the *s* seen by the Wisemen

stared
  s 121– 1   and starvation *s* him in the face ;

starry
  f 247–27   blazons the night with *s* gems,

stars
  moon and
  g 547–13   the gathering clouds, the moon and *s*,
  morning
  g 509–22   “the morning *s* sang together.”— *Job* 38 : 7.
  of heaven
  ap 563–24   the third part of the *s* of heaven,— *Rev.* 12 : 4.
  twelve
  ap 560– 9   a crown of twelve *s*.— *Rev.* 12 : 1.
  562–11   The spiritual idea is crowned with twelve *s*.

  sp 85– 1   read the *s* or calculate an eclipse.
  s 121– 7   The Chaldean Wisemen read in the *s*
  125–28   astronomer will no longer look up to the *s*,
  f 240– 8   The *s* make night beautiful,
  g 510–15   He made the *s* also.— *Gen.* 1 : 16.
  ap 562–16   These are the *s* in the crown of rejoicing.
  565–23   After the *s* sang together

start
  a 21–13   If honest, he will be in earnest from the *s*,
  ph 189–20   mortal mind, . . . makes all things *s* from the
  c 267– 3   offspring of God *s* not from matter
  b 298–21   Spiritual ideas, . . . *s* from Principle,
  t 451– 8   Students of C. S., who *s* with its letter

started
  pref xi–26   *s* by the author with only one student
  b 326–17   This point won, you have *s* as you should.
  gl 585–27   the belief . . . that man *s* first from dust,

starting
  c 262–24   *S* from a higher standpoint, one rises
  b 279–30   Pantheism, *s* from a material sense of
  g 536–17   *s* from matter instead of from God,
  546–14   represents error as *s* from an idea of good

starting-point
  b 275– 6   of divine Science is that God, Spirit, is
  284– 8   Mind can have no *s*,
  g 549–18   the simple ovum as the germ, the *s*,
  550–20   If Life has any *s* whatsoever,

starting-points
  o 351–20   and while we make . . . our *s*,
  351–22   such *s* are neither spiritual nor scientific,

startle
  f 223–25   Peals that should *s* the slumbering thought
  p 396– 7   Never *s* with a discouraging remark
  420–28   If it becomes necessary to *s* mortal mind
  421– 7   Should you thus *s* mortal mind

startled
s 130–26 If thought is *s·* at the strong claim of Science
b 322–21 as the *s·* dreamer who wakens from an incubus

startling
a 50–15 This was a *s·* question.

starts
ph 191–23 not a flower *s·* from its cloistered cell.
f 211–14 When a tear *s·*, does not this so-called mind
t 460–21 it *s·* a petty crossfire over every cripple and
g 501– 2 *s·* with the beginning of the Old Testament,
531– 5 error,— that mortal man *s·* materially,
552–13 mortal life, which *s·* from an egg,

starvation
s 120–32 and *s·* stared him in the face;
143–16 On this basis it saves from *s·* by theft,
f 221–11 in hunger and weakness, almost in *s·*,

state
Christian
p 403–21 The most Christian *s·* is one of rectitude
chrysalis
b 297–21 It is a chrysalis *s·* of human thought,
excited
p 415– 1 an excited *s·* of mortals which is not normal.
healthy
p 414–12 truth and love will establish a healthy *s·*,
hopeless
p 376– 1 presents to mortal thought a hopeless *s·*,
hypnotic
t 446–28 exercise of will brings on a hypnotic *s·*,
g 528–16 inducing a sleep or hypnotic *s·* in Adam
improved
gl 582–10 an improved *s·* of mortal mind ;
marriage
m 65–10 some fundamental error in the marriage *s·*.
material
sp 77–19 to prolong the material *s·*
p 411–24 The mental state is called a material *s·*.
mental
s 161– 9 while an opposite mental *s·* might produce
ph 196–29 it is a mental *s·*, which is afterwards outlined
f 245–10 In this mental *s·* she remained young.
245–26 for the mental *s·* governed the physical.
p 375– 7 Change the mental *s·*, and the
375–30 This mental *s·* is not understood,
377–17 the mental *s·* should be continually watched
411–24 The mental *s·* is called a material state.
422–32 This mental *s·* invites defeat.
t 455– 3 A mental *s·* of self-condemnation and guilt
objective
b 283–17 is but the objective *s·* of material sense,
p 374–12 is in fact the objective *s·* of mortal mind,
of being
r 476–14 They never had a perfect *s·* of being,
of consciousness
sp 82–21 their *s·* of consciousness must be different from
of error
b 311–17 This *s·* of error is the mortal dream of life
of existence
sp 74– 9 a new form and *s·* of existence.
76–26 This *s·* of existence is scientific and intact,
76–29 Death can never hasten this *s·* of existence,
82–19 if . . . in as conscious a *s·* of existence as
ap 573–26 possible to men in this present *s·* of existence,
of her blood
p 379–20 not dying on account of the *s·* of her blood,
of man
s 159–23 medical schools would learn the *s·* of man from
f 227–16 Slavery is not the legitimate *s·* of man.
of Mind
b 291–14 not a locality, but a divine *s·* of Mind
of mind
s 159–16 considered the woman's *s·* of mind,
ph 188–14 to be wholly a *s·* of mind.
p 374–21 Such a *s·* of mind induces sickness.
375–28 This *s·* of mind seems anomalous
of mortal thought
gl 585–21 a *s·* of mortal thought, the only error of which
of perspiration
p 384–16 If exposure . . . while in a *s·* of perspiration
of self-deception
p 403–15 mortal existence is a *s·* of self-deception
of things
g 522–15 this *s·* of things is declared to be temporary
perfect
r 476–14 They never had a perfect *s·* of being,
494– 1 to hold man forever intact in his perfect *s·*,
progressive
a 46–24 a probationary and progressive *s·*
resembling
sp 77–28 a *s·* resembling that of blighted buds,
resisting
p 388– 5 Stolidity, which is a resisting *s·* of
spiritual
f 215–31 Having sought man's spiritual *s·*,

state
subjective
s 108–27 a subjective *s·* of mortal mind
114–30 subjective *s·* of what is termed by the
ap 573–21 the subjective *s·* by which he could see the
their
sp 82–21 their *s·* of consciousness must be different from
82–22 We are not in their *s·*, nor are they in the
worse
m 64–28 a worse *s·* of society than now exists.

pref ix–14 but they are feeble attempts to *s·* the
s 161–19 The oppressive *s·* statutes touching medicine
f 224–20 opposition from church, *s·* laws, and the press,
b 297– 1 nothing can change this *s·*, until the
p 431–11 arrested Mortal Man in behalf of the *s·*

State Commissioner
p 432– 2 I am Nerve, the *S· C·* for

stated
an 101–12 Their report *s·* the results as follows :
s 112–24 which departs from what has already been *s·*
129– 3 the reasoning of an accurately *s·* syllogism
b 283–27 unless its Science be accurately *s·*.
o 347– 9 Had he *s·* his syllogism correctly,
p 402–24 illustrates the fact just *s·*,
g 521– 8 (as *s·* in the first chapter of Genesis)
546–27 The proof that the system *s·* in this book
547– 5 not one departs from the *s·* system and

stately
s 156–29 Metaphysics, . . . is the next *s·* step beyond
t 464– 7 to establish the *s·* operations of C. S.,
ap 566– 9 *S·* Science pauses not, but moves before them

statement
abstract
r 470–11 Divine Science explains the abstract *s·*
agree in
s 113–12 found to agree in *s·* and proof,
any
g 554– 8 Any *s·* of life, following from a
change this
f 240–12 Change this *s·*, suppose Mind to be
common
gl 598–14 is equivalent to our common *s·*,
contains a
g 521–27 contains a *s·* of this material view
contradicts this
r 485– 6 Whatever contradicts this *s·* is the false sense,
correlated
b 288– 2 the correlated *s·*, that *error*, . . . *is unreal.*
demonstrate his
t 447–32 to know it, he must demonstrate his *s·*.
doubt the
p 429–26 This is why you doubt the *s·*
error of
f 207– 6 Error of *s·* leads to error in action.
b 277–26 Matter is an error of *s·*.
Evangelist's
f 231–31 planted on the Evangelist's *s·* that
every
b 277–28 in every *s·* into which it enters.
t 462–14 abide strictly by its rules, heed every *s·*,
g 527–20 a lie,— false in every *s·*.
exact
s 161– 4 This is an exact *s·*,
final
p 409– 5 the nearer matter approaches its final *s·*,
first
g 544–17 The first *s·* about evil,
gl 594– 3 the first *s·* of mythology and idolatry ;
mystical
b 334–28 a mystical *s·* of the eternity of the Christ,
of Christian Science
t 456–29 contains the full *s·* of C. S.,
456–31 first book known, containing a . . . *s·* of C. S.
g 547– 1 A simple *s·* of C. S., if demonstrated
one
152–13 theory, in which one *s·* contradicts another
opposite
p 379–18 Then let her learn the opposite *s·*
scientific
a 27–12 in strict accordance with his scientific *s·* :
sp 94– 7 Christian and scientific *s·* of personality
f 207– 5 every scientific *s·* in Christianity has its proof.
b 300– 9 So far as the scientific *s·* as to man
p 380–27 culmination of scientific *s·* and proof.
r 468– 8 What is the scientific *s·* of being?
that
p 429–32 That *s·* is not confined to spiritual life,
this
b 302–18 This *s·* is based on fact, not fable.
r 492–26 On this *s·* rests the Science of being,
g 526– 6 this *s·* that life issues from matter,

statement

this last
r 466–16 This last *s·* contains the

b 287–32 The *s·* that *Truth is real*
303–12 but the *s·* that man is conceived and
o 355–20 The *s·* that the teachings of C. S.
r 492–13 a *s·* proved to be good
g 521–28 a *s·* which is the exact opposite of

statements

following
b 270– 2 One only of the following *s·* can be true :
general
g 548–19 "It is very possible that many general *s·*
his own
a 26–11 which Jesus implied in his own *s·* :
metaphysical
s 115– 4 material terms for metaphysical *s·*,
scientific
gl 590–26 when the true scientific *s·* of the
these
r 472–12 Jesus furnished proofs of these *s·*.
two
o 358– 6 If two *s·* directly contradict each other

o 345–15 in this volume . . . there are no contradictory *s·*,
p 389–22 Materialists contradict their own *s·*.
r 465– 5 Absolute C. S. pervades its *s·*,
q 547– 4 If one of the *s·* in this book is true,

States

s 161–13 If her sister *S·* follow this example

states

certain
p 386– 9 mortals declare that certain *s·* of the
different
sp 82–11 different *s·* of consciousness are involved,
82–12 cannot exist in two different *s·* . . . at the same time.
p 377–12 Through different *s·* of mind,
mental
sp 82–25 The mental *s·* are so unlike,
s 149– 9 the different mental *s·* of the patient.
t 455– 6 Such mental *s·* indicate weakness
objective
r 484–13 the objective *s·* of mortal mind.
of mind
s 161– 6 Holy inspiration has created *s·* of mind which
p 377–12 Through different *s·* of mind,
prior
s 125–10 the prior *s·* which human belief created
separate
sp 74–32 for they are in separate *s·* of existence,
subjective
g 512–16 subjective, *s·* of faith and
gl 592– 7 idolatry ; the subjective *s·* of error ;
these
s 149– 9 These *s·* are not comprehended,

b 283– 9 *s·* of mortal mind which act, react, and then
ap 573–11 indicates *s·* and stages of consciousness.

stating

s 126– 2 Error will be no longer used in *s·* truth.

Statue

b 299– 3 when he carves his "*S·* of Liberty,"

statue

s 161–21 knelt before a *s·* of Liberty,

statuesque

ph 172–30 may present more nobility than the *s·* athlete,

stature

o 350– 8 grow into that *s·* of manhood in Christ Jesus
g 519–20 unto the measure of the *s·* of — *Eph. 4 : 13.*

status

s 118–21 dignified as the natural *s·* of men
120–19 or to exhibit the real *s·* of man.
122–13 its *s·* of happiness or misery.
ph 178–26 the *s·* of immortal being.
p 363–14 detect the woman's immoral *s·*
r 476–22 and earnestly seek the spiritual *s·* of man,

statute

p 432–12 In this province there is a *s·* regarding
436–10 Upon this *s·* hangs all the law and
441–13 According to our *s·*, Material Law is a
442– 3 Our *s·* is spiritual,

statute-book

p 437–33 read from the supreme *s·*, the Bible,
441– 2 explained from his *s·*, the Bible,

statutes

s 161–19 oppressive state *s·* touching medicine
ph 184–29 enforcing obedience through divine *s·*.
b 307–29 his province is in spiritual *s·*,
p 439–27 Our higher *s·* declare you all,
440–27 and in accordance with the divine *s·*,

staves

a 48– 2 *s·* of bigoted ignorance smote him sorely.

stay

a 43–19 Those who slew him to *s·* his influence
sp 90–21 yet their bodies *s·* in one place.
c 256–22 and none can *s·* His hand, — *Dan. 4 : 35.*

steadfastly

c 261– 4 Hold thought *s·* to the enduring,
p 414–15 To fix truth *s·* in your patients' thoughts,
r 495–15 cling *s·* to God and His idea.
495–30 abiding *s·* in wisdom, Truth, and Love.

steal

s 112–31 "Thou shalt not *s·*." — *Exod. 20 : 15.*
f 241–10 hate, . . . *s·* away the treasures of Truth.

stealing

b 294–29 The thief believes that he gains something by *s·*,

steel

a 37– 7 Mortals try in vain to slay Truth with the *s·*

steer

m 67– 8 Can you *s·* safely amid the storm?"

steers

p 426– 3 divine power, which *s·* the body into health.

stellar

s 121– 4 Copernicus mapped out the *s·* system,
g 509–14 *s·* universe is no more celestial than our earth.

stem

s 139–13 to *s·* the tide of sectarian bitterness,

step

advancing
s 134– 2 At every advancing *s·*, truth is still opposed
easiest
pr 5– 4 and the very easiest *s·*.
every
f 213–11 Every *s·* towards goodness is a departure from
g 533–24 The belief . . . is growing worse at every *s·*,
542– 1 The belief of life in matter sins at every *s·*.
first
t 459–11 failing to take the first *s·*.
463–23 the first *s·* towards destroying error.
great
pr 5– 4 The next and great *s·* required by wisdom
f 242– 6 Denial of the claims of matter is a great *s·*
in advance
s 158–27 Homœopathy, a *s·* in advance of allopathy,
new
sp 98– 1 persecutions which attend a new *s·*
next
b 296–29 and aids in taking the next *s·*
one
pr 5– 3 Sorrow for wrong-doing is but one *s·*
b 296–28 An improved belief is one *s·* out of error,
retrograde
sp 74–29 In C. S. there is never a retrograde *s·*,
single
p 429– 9 we look beyond a single *s·*
stately
s 156–29 the next stately *s·* beyond homœopathy.
step by
f 254–10 facts of existence are gained step by *s·*,
t 444–11 Step by *s·* will those who trust Him find

sp 84–22 a *s·* towards the Mind-science by which

stepped

a 45– 3 and *s·* forth from his gloomy resting-place,

stepping-stone

pref vii–17 Ignorance of God is no longer the *s·* to faith.
a 39–11 causes mortals to regard death . . . as a *s·*
f 203–24 Death is not a *s·* to Life,

steps

pref viii–31 were crude, — the first *s·* of a child
f 226– 2 That was only prophetic of further *s·*
b 317– 9 Resistance to Truth will haunt his *s·*,
p 374–23 your *s·* are less firm because of your fear,
t 459– 9 Judge not . . . by the *s·* already taken,
g 513– 6 Advancing spiritual *s·* in the teeming universe

stereotyped

s 144–26 to whatever is not *s·*.
s 367– 6 gushing theories, *s·* borrowed speeches,

stern

p 362– 8 under the *s·* rules of rabbinical law,
433– 7 In compliance with a *s·* duty, his Honor,
g 514–17 They carry the baggage of *s·* resolve,

sterner

s 121– 1 but *s·* still would have been his fate, if

sternest

sp 85–28 He never spared hypocrisy the *s·* condemnation.

stewards

ap 571–13 and designate those as unfaithful *s·*

store
p 439– 4 He manufactures for it, keeps a furnishing s·,
t 462– 6 his s· of spiritual understanding,

storehouses
a 54–12 into empty or sin-filled human s·,

storm
m 67– 4 When the ocean is stirred by a s·,
67– 8 Can you steer safely amid the s·?"
s 122–19 that little prophet of s· and sunshine,
b 329–14 One should not tarry in the s· if the
ap 566–22 In shade and s· the frequent night,

storms
f 254–28 you will encounter s·.

story
s 142–16 In vain do the manger and the cross tell their
s· to
p 363–15 Jesus rebuked them with a short s· or parable.
g 532– 9 the prediction in the s· under consideration.
ap 566–14 Sir Walter Scott . . . in the s· of Ivanhoe,

St. Paul (*see also* **Paul**)
a 20–27 St. P· wrote, "Let us lay aside— *Heb.* 12 : 1.
an 106–18 and classify all others as did St. P·
s 108– 3 According to St. P·, it was "the gift of— *Eph.*
3 : 7.
151–25 must be put off, as St. P· declares.
ph 200–25 St. P· said : "For I determined— *I Cor.* 2 : 2.
b 288–18 St. P· says : "There remaineth— *Heb.* 4 : 9.
300–12 the real man, or the *new* man (as St. P· has it).
p 442–25 St. P· says, "Work out your— *Phil.* 2 : 12.
r 478–27 St. P· said, "But when it pleased— *Gal.* 1 : 15.
ap 560–22 Abuse of the motives and religion of St. P·

straight
s 126–30 "the s· and narrow way"— *see Matt.* 7 : 14.
151–28 The s· and narrow way is to see and
b 282– 5 a circle or sphere and a s· line.
282– 7 the s· line represents the finite,
282–10 the s· line represents evil,
282–14 A s· line finds no abiding-place in a curve,
282–15 a curve finds no adjustment to a s· line.
282–22 and the other a s· line.
283–30 by calling a curve a s· line
283–31 or a s· line a sphere.
324–13 The way is s· and narrow, which leads to the
t 454–20 tread firmly in the s· and narrow way.
r 472– 5 The way which leads to C. S. is s· and narrow.
g 502– 6 the s· line of Spirit over the mortal deviations

straightforward
ph 168– 1 fair seeming for s· character,

straightway
sp 99– 7 he s· adds : "for it is God which— *Phil.* 2 : 13.
s 133–11 and s· believed that they were healed
b 308–29 he s· answered ; and then his name was changed
p 411–17 man was changed and s· became whole.

strain
p 366–20 Such so-called Scientists will s· out gnats,
ap 568–30 Love sends forth her primal and everlasting s·.

strained
sp 72–20 not a . . . through which truth can be s·

straining
m 65–21 until we get at last the clear s· truth,
s 140–14 s· out gnats and swallowing camels.
f 202– 2 foolish as s· out gnats and swallowing camels.

strains
sp 88–26 Eloquence re-echoes the s· of Truth and Love.
ph 190–22 thus swept his lyre with saddening s·
f 213–25 Mental melodies and s· of sweetest music

strange
f 216– 5 What has touched Life, God, to such s· issues?
p 362– 6 A "s· woman" came in.— *Prov.* 23 : 27.
g 524– 7 constantly went after "s· gods."— *Jer.* 5 : 19.

strangely
o 355–32 S· enough, we ask for material theories

stranger
s 142–13 the poor and the s· from the gate,
146–20 the "s· that is within thy— *Exod.* 20 : 10.
ph 174–15 a pilgrim and s·, marking out the path for
f 254–32 s·, thou art the guest of God.

strangers
g 507–10 s· in a tangled wilderness.

strangle
ap 569–15 and fail to s· the serpent of sin

strangled
f 236– 3 but never be s· there.

strata
b 293– 7 are but different s· of human belief.
293–11 both s·, mortal mind and mortal body,

stratum
s 158–26 so letting in matter's higher s·, mortal mind.
ph 185–29 the material s· of the human mind,
198– 1 for the higher s· of mortal mind has
r 477–15 though interwoven with matter's highest s·,

strays
b 311–15 belief s· into a sense of temporary loss

stream
f 239–29 opposite sources never mingle in fount or s·.
246– 8 The s· rises no higher than its source.
p 379–11 only a s· of warm water was trickling over
389–17 the metaphors about the fount and s·,
g 540–11 in order to purify the s·.

streams
s 133– 9 In the wilderness, s· flowed from the rock,

streets
pr 10–18 to carry a praying-machine through the s·,
t 459–19 turning him loose in the crowded s· of a city.

strength
affection, and
ph 183–22 man's entire obedience, affection, and s·.
and freedom
t 454–20 s· and freedom to speech and action.
and influence
ph 188– 5 has grown terrible in s· and influence,
and permanence
m 58–10 true happiness, s·, and permanence.
and permanency
b 293–28 the s· and permanency of Spirit.
conscious
p 390–32 Rise in the conscious s· of the spirit of Truth
courage and
m 57– 8 feminine mind gains courage and s·
divine
p 406–31 normal control is gained through divine s·
giving
p 407–12 giving s· to the weakness of mortal mind,
giving us
pr 5–18 giving us s· according to our day.
helplessness to
o 341– 3 raising up thousands from helplessness to s·
hour of
ph 166–20 Instead of . . . waiting for the hour of s·
human
ph 173–19 measuring human s· by bones and sinews,
in proportion
sp 80– 1 We have s· in proportion to our
instead of
p 371–29 s· instead of weakness,
t 455– 6 indicate weakness instead of s·.
joy and
p 365–31 not giving to mind or body the joy and s· of
joyous in
g 514– 6 Mind, joyous in s·, dwells in the realm of Mind.
measure
r 485–30 as much as . . . muscles measure s·.
mockery of
ph 192–25 It is a mockery of s·, which erelong betrays its
nutriment and
f 222– 7 nutriment and s· to the human system.
of Spirit
p 393–12 Rise in the s· of Spirit
or weakness
p 377–14 the producer of s· or weakness.
our
sp 80– 2 our s· is not lessened by giving
power and
ph 183–24 Obedience to Truth gives man power and s·.
recovered
f 222–17 he recovered s· and flesh rapidly.
refuge and
t 444–12 "God is our refuge and s·,— *Psal.* 46 : 1.
salvation, and
ap 568–14 Now is come salvation, and s·,— *Rev.* 12 : 10.
shares not its
ph 194– 2 Spirit shares not its s· with matter
shorn of his
s 124– 5 a blind belief, a Samson shorn of his s·.
sound, and
r 486–16 If death restores sight, sound, and s· to man,
source of
g 514–31 a source of s· to the ancient worthies.
spiritual
(*see* **spiritual**)
symbolized by
g 512– 8 Spirit is symbolized by s·, presence, and
their
p 417– 7 their s· is in proportion to their courage.
to man
m 60–17 a protection to woman, s· to man,

———

ph 165– 7 To measure . . . s· by the exercise of muscle,
f 219– 8 No more can we say . . . that muscles give s·,
b 308–21 and smote the sinew, or s·, of his error,

strength

p	380–30	this opposing power with s' to
	407–13	s' from the immortal and omnipotent Mind,
	417– 7	Never . . . that they have more courage than s'.
r	485–31	To say that s' is in matter,
	488– 3	When, on the s' of these instructions,
	496–20	the s' of sin is the law," — I Cor. 15 : 56.
gl	582– 8	s', animation, and power to act.

strengthen

p	430– 6	should enlarge its borders and s' its base

strengthened

a	47–21	greed for gold s' his ingratitude,
sp	79–25	says : . . . body is weak, and it must be s'.
p	423–17	He regards the ailment as weakened or s'

strengthening

r	487–28	s' our trust in the deathless reality of Life,

strengthens

pr	16–17	This reading s' our scientific apprehension
p	404–24	and this knowledge s' his moral courage
	423–23	and he proportionately s' his patient with
t	446–21	To understand God s' hope,
g	547–10	s' the thinker's conclusions as to the

stress

pr	5– 7	placed under the s' of circumstances.
ph	181–15	but that you lay no s' on manipulation.
f	234–29	He laid great s' on the action of the
p	440–14	under s' of circumstances, to be justifiable.

stretch

p	393–23	or the electric wire which you s',
	398–14	"S' forth thine hand," — Matt. 12 : 13.

stricken

a	49–32	"s', smitten of God." — Isa. 53 : 4.
f	226–10	demanding that the fetters . . . be s' from the

strict

a	27–11	in s' accordance with his scientific statement :
b	327–11	the s' demands of C. S. seem peremptory ;
t	456– 5	S' adherence to the divine Principle and rules

strictest

f	222–18	only by the s' adherence to

strictly

t	448–26	If the student adheres s' to the teachings of
	459–32	should understand and adhere s' to the
	462–14	must abide s' by its rules,

strictures

o	341– 1	s' on this volume would condemn to oblivion

strides

f	236–31	youth makes easy and rapid s' towards Truth.

strife

an	106–23	wrath, s', seditions, heresies, — Gal. 5 : 20.
t	254–14	but to begin aright and to continue the s'
b	323– 3	This s' consists in the endeavor to forsake error
t	444–25	"Let there be no s', — Gen. 13 : 8.
	453– 6	will be at s' in the minds of students,

strike

ph	199– 2	lift the hammer and s' the anvil,

striking

o	360–20	s' the ribs of matter

strikingly

f	213–23	This was even more s' true of Beethoven,
	252–15	contrasts s' with the testimony of Spirit.

strings

f	213–27	Mortal mind is the harp of many s',

strip

ph	186–18	This falsehood should s' evil of all pretensions.
f	254–26	What is there to s' off error's disguise?

stripes

a	20–15	and "with his s' — Isa. 53 : 5.

stripped

f	241–11	S' of its coverings,

strips

o	343–14	Jesus s' all disguise from error,
t	454–13	the great truth which s' all disguise from error.
r	472–29	until God s' off their disguise.

strive

f	241–25	We should s' to reach the Horeb height
b	320–13	My spirit shall not always s' — Gen. 6 : 3.
t	451–11	They must not only seek, but s', to enter

striving

pr	4–20	s' to assimilate more of the divine character,
	10–14	It is s' that enables us to enter.
	13– 7	If we are not secretly yearning and openly s'
a	21– 9	he is s' to enter in.
b	309–13	through earnest s' followed his demonstration
	323– 3	will not be able . . . without s' for them.

strong

pr	4–31	clip the s' pinions of love,
	6–31	The s' language of our Master confirms this
a	23–14	This preaching receives a s' rebuke
m	57–11	Both sexes will be loving, pure, tender, and s'
	65– 8	they will be s' and enduring.
sp	87–26	The s' impressions produced on mortal mind
	99–23	The calm, s' currents of true spirituality,
s	130–26	If thought is startled at the s' claim of
	134–15	They have not waxed s' in times of trouble.
	142–20	The s' cords of scientific demonstration,
	158–22	acquires an educated appetite for s' drink,
f	219–16	if we would have it s' ;
	226–32	trusting Truth, the s' deliverer, to guide me
	235– 3	if virtue and truth build a s' defence.
c	261–11	Under the s' impulse of a desire to
p	377–13	suddenly weak or abnormally s',
	398–22	and the desire for s' drink is gone.
	399–29	enter into a s' man's house— Matt. 12 : 29.
	399–31	first bind the s' man?" — Matt. 12 : 29.
	400– 4	Mortal mind is "the s' man," — Matt. 12 : 29.
	400– 7	we can despoil "the s' man" — Matt. 12 : 29.
	423–21	has rendered himself s', instead of weak,
	426–10	The struggle for Truth makes one s'
	442– 8	prisoner rose up regenerated, s', free,
t	448–19	the s' impress of divine Science,
	455–28	This s' point in C. S. is
ap	567– 4	when s' faith or spiritual strength wrestles

stronger

pr	7– 2	Still s' evidence that Jesus' reproof was
an	104–28	worse than before it was grasped by the s' error.
s	144–12	the s' are the manifestations of the
ph	169–15	should find s' supports and a higher home.
	198–26	and the s' thoughts rule the weaker.
	199–14	his arm becomes s'.
c	265–24	gained s' desires for spiritual joy
b	327–10	until his grasp on good grows s'.
o	353– 7	having the s' evidence of Truth
p	387–24	but grows s' because of it.
	409–18	the s' never yields to the weaker, except
	410–14	Every trial of our faith in God makes us s'.
	410–16	the s' should be our faith and the purer our
	422–30	he believes that something s' than

strongest

a	27–30	made their s' attack upon this very point.
f	236–12	A mother is the s' educator,

strongly

s	116–20	C. S. s' emphasizes the thought that
ph	198–30	muscles of the blacksmith's arm are s'
f	235–11	should be s' garrisoned with virtue.
p	414–25	Hold these points s' in view.
	423– 7	more s' than the expressed thought.

strove

ph	185–16	s' to emulate the wonders wrought by Moses.

struck

o	342– 2	The hour has s' when proof and

structural

ph	173–17	Anatomy declares man to be s'.
b	283–18	such as the s' life of the tree
	309–30	Therefore it is never s' nor organic,
p	402– 9	forsake its corporeal, s', and material basis,

structure

sp	71–27	The basis and s' of spiritualism are
s	162–20	the s' has been renewed,
ph	172–24	Brain, heart, blood, . . . the material s'?
	173–21	material s' is mortal.
	197–11	The less that is said of physical s'
f	228–22	bodily conditions, s', or economy,
g	509–21	no more contingent now on time or material s'
ap	576–12	no material s' in which to worship God,
gl	581–22	the more certain is the downfall of its s'.
	583–12	Church. The s' of Truth and Love ;

structures

g	549–19	the most complicated corporeal s',

struggle

earthly

a	47–28	desertion of their Master in his last earthly s'

final

b	268–14	In this final s' for supremacy,

for Truth

p	426–10	s' for Truth makes one strong

habitual

pr	4–12	The habitual s' to be always good

Jacob's

b	309– 7	The result of Jacob's s' thus appeared.

mighty

p	407– 8	is conquered only by a mighty s'.

---

s	145– 8	The s' for the recovery of invalids goes on,
b	329–28	they would s' for recourse to the spiritual
p	407– 9	Every hour of delay makes the s' more severe.
	431–15	The s' on their part was long.

truggle
t 450–16	Few yield without a *s·*,
g 534–28	will *s·* to destroy the spiritual idea of Love ;
536–26	Through toil, *s·*, and sorrow,

truggled
a 33–18	When the human element in him *s·* with the
p 373– 8	*s·* long, and perhaps in vain, to
436–23	His friends *s·* hard to rescue the prisoner

truggles
a 30– 8	This accounts for his *s·* in Gethsemane
p 439–22	in his *s·* against liver-complaint

truggling
a 45–16	and peace to the *s·* hearts !
48– 5	waiting and *s·* in voiceless agony,
m 57–28	for Love supports the *s·* heart
64–11	some noble woman, *s·* alone with adversity,
65–15	*s·* against the advancing spiritual era.
b 308–16	*s·* with a mortal sense of life,
p 394–13	To those *s·* with sickness,
ap 569–18	not *s·* to lift their heads above the

trychnine
ph 178– 3	the *s·*, or whatever the drug used,

tubborn
f 224–19	Cold disdain, *s·* resistance,
237–10	*s·* beliefs and theories of parents
r 490– 8	Will — blind, *s·*, and headlong

tubbornness
gl 593–19	Rock. . . . Coldness and *s·*.

tudent (*see also* **student's**)
adheres
t 448–26	If the *s·* adheres strictly to the teachings of

any
t 462– 3	any *s·*, who adheres to the divine rules of C. S.

divine
s 117–16	As a divine *s·* he unfolded God to man,

his
t 449–30	improves the health and the morals of his *s·*
454–15	points out to his *s·* error as well as truth,

lift a
p 373– 9	to lift a *s·* out of a chronic sin.

morals of the
t 445–28	thus disregarding the morals of the *s·*

one
pref xi–26	started by the author with only one *s·*

show your
t 451–31	Show your *s·* that mental malpractice

signifies
b 271–11	the word rendered *disciple* signifies *s·* ;

success of the
p 372–32	will be a hindrance to the . . . success of the *s·*.

teacher and
t 457– 5	has done more for teacher and *s·*,
463– 5	Teacher and *s·* should also be familiar with

teach your
t 453–14	Teach your *s·* that he must know himself

will prove
p 384–14	the *s·* will prove to himself, by

a 28– 5	If the Master had not taken a *s·*
p 411– 4	If the *s·* silently called the
411– 8	because the *s·* was not perfectly attuned to
t 449–30	if the *s·* practises what he is taught,
455–17	The *s·*, who receives his knowledge of C. S.,
459–28	the *theologus* (that is, the *s·*
462– 9	If the *s·* goes away to practise

student's
p 367–28	namely, the *s·* higher attainments
411– 3	My first discovery in the *s·* practice
t 448–19	Try to leave on every *s·* mind
461–31	*s·* spiritual growth and experience

students
are advised
t 444–13	*S·* are advised by the author

do not dismiss
t 454–25	Do not dismiss *s·* at the close of a

English
p 379– 9	on whom certain English *s·* experimented,

four thousand
pref xii– 6	over four thousand *s·* were taught

her
pref x–16	she and her *s·* have proved the worth of
p 402– 5	records of the cure, by herself and her *s·*

his
a 28– 3	Even many of his *s·* stood in his way.
43–12	the most profitable to his *s·*.
46–30	His *s·* then received the Holy Ghost.
48– 2	His *s·* slept.
sp 85–34	Jesus, as he once journeyed with his *s·*,
s 136–11	He appealed to his *s·* :
137– 1	His *s·* saw this power of Truth heal
146– 1	first article of faith propounded to his *s·*
147–26	and taught the generalities . . . to his *s·* ;
148– 1	When his *s·* brought to him a case

students
his
b 321–31	Jesus, who showed his *s·* the power of Mind
o 342–12	the promise that his *s·* should cast out evils
343–26	Paul who was not one of his *s·*,
t 445– 2	teacher must thoroughly fit his *s·*
451–24	obligated to open the eyes of his *s·*
456–26	and so do all his *s·* and patients.
r 473–31	Few, however, except his *s·* understood
g 509– 5	Our Master reappeared to his *s·*,

Jesus'
a 45–32	Jesus' *s·*, not sufficiently advanced
o 343–25	those apostles who were Jesus' *s·*,

malicious
s 110–21	or by careless or malicious *s·*,

minds of
t 453– 7	will be at strife in the minds of *s·*,

of Christian Science
t 451– 8	*S·* of C. S., who start with its letter
456– 7	secured the only success of the *s·* of C. S.

seventy
a 27–22	Jesus sent forth seventy *s·* at one time,

your
t 454– 4	Teach your *s·* the omnipotence of Truth,
454–28	until your *s·* tread firmly in the

p 420– 5	If *s·* do not readily heal themselves,
t 444–31	The teacher must make clear to *s·* the
460–29	by her manuscript circulated among the *s·*.

studied
pref ix–24	before a work on the subject could be profitably *s·*.
s 147–17	The book needs to be *s·*,
ph 174– 3	practitioners by their more *s·* methods.

study
branch of
t 462–24	This branch of *s·* is indispensable to the

careful
ph 196–12	A careful *s·* of this text shows that

classic
sp 82– 6	What is classic *s·*, but discernment of the

medical
t 443– 4	consistency of systematic medical *s·*,
443– 8	While a course of medical *s·* is

Scriptural
pref viii–29	give to friends the results of her Scriptural *s·*,

sp 89–15	believes that he cannot be an orator without *s·*
ph 171–10	not needing to *s·* brainology to learn
176– 4	modern Eves took up the *s·* of medical works
195–20	Observation, invention, *s·*, and
f 202– 6	If men would bring to bear upon the *s·* of
p 382– 6	given to the *s·* of C. S. and to the
r 495–27	*S·* thoroughly the letter and imbibe the spirit.
ap 559–21	*S·* it, ponder it.

studying
ph 179–26	The sedulous matron — *s·* her Jahr
b 321– 2	as may be seen by *s·* the book of Job.

stumble
f 205– 3	*s·* with lameness, drop with drunkenness,
t 463– 4	and so he may *s·* and fall in the darkness.

stung
ap 569–26	is at last *s·* to death by his own malice ;

stupefaction
p 415–12	They quiet the thought by inducing *s·*

stupefying
sp 95–28	Lulled by *s·* illusions, the world is asleep

stupendous
pref ix–30	comparative ignorance of the *s·* Life-problem

stupid
m 58–27	not to court vulgar extravagance or *s·* ease,
s 158–16	cataplasms, and whiskey are *s·* substitutes

sturdy
pref vii–23	the task of the *s·* pioneer to hew the tall oak
t 463–16	Its beginning will be meek, its growth *s·*,

styled
f 213– 1	movements of mortal belief, . . . are *s·* the real.

subdivides
g 511– 2	*s·* and radiates their borrowed light,

subdue
b 315–19	we realize this likeness only when we *s·* sin
p 421–13	and *s·* the symptoms by removing the
g 517–27	replenish the earth, and *s·* it ; — *Gen.* 1 : 28.

subdued
ph 199–20	latent mental fears are *s·* by him.
p 406–15	period, in which mortal sense is *s·*

subdues
s 145–12	Truth, *s·* the human belief in disease.

subduing
s 142– 2	the old systems, devised for *s·* them,

subject

main
pref ix– 2 began to jot down her thoughts on the main *s·*,
of sickness
ph 169–13 by attracting the mind to the *s·* of sickness,
prolific
f 228– 7 Heredity is a prolific *s·* for mortal belief to
that
p 416–30 have already heard too much on that *s·*.
this
pr 1– 5 what another may say or think on this *s·*,
ph 170–25 The age seems ready to approach this *s·*,
b 297– 4 until the belief on this *s·* changes.
o 341–12 Proof is essential to a due estimate of this *s·*.
356– 9 Jesus reasoned on this *s·* practically,
p 373– 4 we must have more faith in God on this *s·*
t 449–17 requires a higher understanding to teach this *s·*
work on the
pref ix–23 before a work on the *s·* could

---

a 49– 5 "Even the devils are *s·* unto us— *Luke* 10 : 17.
49–22 the Christ is not *s·* to material conditions,
m 56–13 *s·* to such moral regulations as will
sp 74– 2 spiritual life which is not *s·* to death.
an 102–23 produce the very apathy on the *s·* which
s 120–16 nor . . . bear reliable testimony on the *s·*
124–17 represented as *s·* to growth, maturity, and
150–19 believe that both . . . are *s·* to disease,
ph 171–22 infinite Mind,— *s·* to non-intelligence !
173– 7 supposition, that . . . the potter is *s·* to the clay,
200–13 and not *s·* to decay and dust.
f 244–14 *s·* to laws of decay.
249– 9 Let us rejoice that we are *s·* to the
b 288–24 Life is not *s·* to death ;
297–18 but *s·* to change and dissolution.
305–28 not *s·* to birth, growth, maturity, decay.
331– 4 it would be *s·* to their limitations
337–29 *S·* sickness, sin, and death to the rule of
o 356–22 How then is it possible for Him to create man *s·* to
361–25 must be correct . . . and *s·* to demonstration.
p 372–15 He can neither . . . be *s·* to matter, nor
429–12 Science declares that man is *s·* to Mind,
r 486–22 mortal in belief and *s·* to chance and change.
g 515– 8 ideas are *s·* to the Mind which forms them,
534–19 for it is not *s·* to the law of God, — *Rom.* 8 : 7.

subjected

b 305– 2 *s·* to material sense which is discord.
318–28 The governor is not *s·* to the governed.
o 341– 8 appear contradictory when *s·* to such usage.
341–16 according to a divine given rule, and *s·* to proof.

subjection

f 227– 9 and in *s·* to hopeless slavery,
240–29 is finally brought into *s·* to Truth.
p 400– 5 which must be held in *s·* before its influence
g 518– 1 His birthright is dominion, not *s·*.

subjective

s 108–27 a *s·* state of mortal mind which
114–30 what is termed *matter* is but the *s·* state of
ph 189–31 for matter is the *s·* condition of mortal mind.
g 512–16 externalized, yet *s·*, states of faith and
ap 573–21 the *s·* state by which he could see the
gl 592– 7 the *s·* states of error ; material senses ;

subjects

a 55– 3 *s·* to unchristian comment and usage
an 101–24 upon those who practise it, and upon their *s·*
ph 175– 5 and less thought is given to sanitary *s·*,
p 402–25 The operator would make his *s·* believe
413–10 views of parents and other persons on these *s·*
t 446–32 oftentimes *s·* you to its abuse.
g 507– 8 objects and *s·* would be obscure,

subjugate

ph 165– 8 to *s·* intelligence, to make mind mortal,

sublime

a 45– 4 crowned with the glory of a *s·* success,
49–11 sacrifices, his divine patience, *s·* courage,
s 138–15 His *s·* summary points to the religion of Love.
c 256–17 the *s·* question, What is infinite Mind
p 387–27 history of Christianity furnishes *s·* proofs
ap 571–30 the *s·* grandeur of divine Science,

sublimest

a 51– 4 the *s·* influence of his career.

sublimity

g 509–26 in which beauty, *s·*, purity, and holiness
511– 5 the *s·*, magnitude, and infinitude

submerged

g 546– 2 false belief that spirit is now *s·* in

submergence

gl 581–22 Purification by Spirit ; *s·* in Spirit.
582–22 *S·* in Spirit ; immortality brought to light.

submission

a 32–13 he bowed in holy *s·* to the divine decree.
s 157–27 both mind and body worse for this *s·*.
159– 6 and she was forced into *s·*.
ph 183–24 *S·* to error superinduces loss of power.
f 216–17 his body is in *s·* to everlasting Life and
p 391– 1 Instead of blind and calm *s·* to
404– 7 suffering which his *s·* to such habits brings,
gl 597– 1 in token of reverence and *s·*

submissive

b 314–30 *s·* to death as being in supposed accord with

submit

p 381– 2 Ignorant of . . . we *s·* to unjust decrees,
406– 7 Sin will *s·* to C. S.
435–32 only jurisdiction to which the prisoner can *s·*
r 492–24 must eventually *s·* to the Science of Mind,

submitted

sp 76–30 death must be overcome, not *s·* to,
s 111–29 I *s·* my metaphysical system of
147– 7 were *s·* to the broadest practical test,

submitting

f 239–20 matter is then *s·* to Spirit.

subordinate

s 125–17 When *s·* to the divine Spirit,
f 215–11 Spiritual vision is not *s·* to
o 349– 9 We should *s·* material law to spiritual law.
p 429–14 affirms that mind is *s·* to the body,
g 516– 6 when we *s·* the false testimony
518– 3 himself *s·* alone to his Maker.

subordination

f 206– 5 should be exercised only in *s·* to Truth ;

subscribed

r 471–23 The author *s·* to an orthodox creed

subscribes

f 225–10 until it *s·* to their systems ;

subsequent

o 356–30 Does *s·* follow its antecedent ?
g 531– 4 maintained in all the *s·* forms of belief.
537–22 *S·* Bible revelation is coordinate with the

subsequently

f 206–30 does not make mistakes and *s·* correct them.
r 476–15 which may *s·* be regained.
g 549–17 from which one or more individualities *s·*

subserve

g 501–14 which *s·* the end of natural good,

subserving

b 319– 4 error reversed as *s·* the facts

subside

p 421–20 when the fear is destroyed, the inflammatio
will *s·*.

subsides

p 384–25 When the fear *s·* and the conviction

substance

all
c 259– 5 for he represents . . . the sum of all *s·*.
b 275–14 All *s·*, intelligence, wisdom, being,
r 469– 3 Spirit, which includes in itself all *s·*
gl 587– 7 Truth ; Love ; all *s·* ; intelligence.
and color
b 310– 7 seen in all form, *s·*, and color,
and continuity
s 124–25 Spirit is the life, *s·*, and continuity
and creator
c 257– 7 theory that Spirit is not the only *s·* and creato
and Life
b 286–21 God's thoughts . . . are *s·* and Life.
and life
gl 591– 9 intelligence, *s·*, and life
and mind
b 325–32 A false sense of life, *s·*, and mind
gl 580–12 *s·*, and mind are found to be the
any other
b 301–21 The belief that man has any other *s·*,
are not
sp 90– 7 The earth's orbit and . . . are not *s·*.
cannot produce
c 257– 6 and shadow cannot produce *s·*.
divine
b 300–29 universe reflects and expresses the divine *s·*
r 468–24 reflecting the divine *s·* of Spirit.
gl 594–19 SPIRIT. Divine *s·* ; Mind ;
eternal
b 299–25 Truth is spiritual, eternal *s·*,
301–11 and reflects the eternal *s·*, or Spirit,
foreign
p 438–22 the facts . . . show that this fur is a foreign *s·*
God is
b 301–17 As God is *s·* and man is the
intelligence, nor
s 133–28 no life, intelligence, nor *s·* outside of God.
r 468– 9 no life, truth, intelligence, nor *s·* in matter.

substance

intelligence or
g 508– 5 The only intelligence or *s·* of a thought,
is in Mind
c 267– 2 the spiritual idea, whose *s·* is in Mind,
Life and
b 314–22 presented to her, . . . the true idea of Life and *s·*.
life and
b 311–18 dream of life and *s·* as existent in matter,
life, and intelligence
sp 91–25 postulate . . . that *s·*, life, and intelligence are
ap 562– 9 reflected light, *s·*, life, and intelligence.
563– 9 belief that *s·*, life, and intelligence can be
Life, . . . and intelligence
a 27–14 Life, *s·*, and intelligence of the universe
ph 185–19 God as the only Life, *s·*, and intelligence,
gl 595– 7 the idea of Life, *s·*, and intelligence ;
life, . . . and intelligence
(see life*)*
life, . . . and mind
gl 582– 5 belief as to life, *s·*, and mind ;
life, or
gl 584–28 the absence of *s·*, life, or intelligence.
material
b 278–17 The admission that there can be material *s·*
301–23 seems to himself to be material *s·*,
Mind and
b 301–28 presents an inverted image of Mind and *s·*
Mind is
p 414–24 C. S. declares that Mind is *s·*,
of all
f 253– 8 the *s·* of all, because I AM THAT I AM.
of all devotion
f 241–19 *s·* of all devotion is the reflection and
of an idea
c 257–12 the *s·* of an idea is very far from
of good
b 301–19 and in reality has, only the *s·* of good,
of Life
sp 91–17 the *s·* of Life or Mind.
of Spirit
b 301–19 and in reality has, . . . the *s·* of Spirit,
r 468–24 reflecting the divine *s·* of Spirit.
480– 1 When the *s·* of Spirit appears in C. S.,
of things
b 279– 4 "the *s·* of things hoped for." — *Heb.* 11 : 1.
r 468–20 "The *s·* of things hoped for, — *Heb.* 11 : 1.
of thought
p 423–30 Bones have only the *s·* of thought
or intelligence
p 418– 6 error that life, *s·*, or intelligence can be in
or mind
o 354– 2 material life, *s·*, or mind
pulpy
ph 192– 2 The belief that a pulpy *s·* under the skull
real
r 468–22 Soul, or God, is the only real *s·*.
reality of
b 311–27 have not the reality of *s·*.
seemed to be
b 314–19 and the body, . . . seemed to be *s·*.
seems
b 312– 6 What to material sense seems *s·*,
seems to be
b 301– 7 To himself, . . . material man seems to be *s·*,
sense of
b 301– 8 his sense of *s·* involves error
so-called
p 423–32 The so-called *s·* of bone is
Soul and
b 280–14 finite sense of the divisibility of Soul and *s·*,
supposed
c 257–13 the supposed *s·* of non-intelligent matter.
the only
c 257– 7 theory that Spirit is not the only *s·*
b 278– 4 Spirit is the only *s·* and consciousness
335–12 Spirit is the only *s·*,

a 38–28 he said in *s·* : Having eyes ye see not,
sp 90– 9 the thought that there can be *s·* in matter,
an 100–11 through the *s·* of the nerves."
s 162–23 what is called the lost *s·* of lungs,
ph 173–15 Neither the *s·* nor the manifestation
c 257– 4 If matter, so-called, is *s·*,
b 279– 1 Which ought to be *s·* to us,
312– 5 is found to be *s·*.
313–31 To show that the *s·* of himself was Spirit
330–11 God is infinite, the only Life, *s·*, Spirit,
331– 2 no more . . . than *s·* is in its shadow.
o 349–31 In C. S., *s·* is understood to be Spirit,
350– 1 opponents of C. S. believe *s·* to be matter.
351–29 To them matter was *s·*,
369–11 the belief that matter is *s·*,
r 467– 6 no *s·*, no truth, no love, but that which
468–16 *Question.* — What is *s·*?

substance

r 468–17 *S·* is that which is eternal
468–19 Truth, Life, and Love are *s·*,
472–15 that intelligence, *s·*, life,
477–22 Soul is the *s·*, Life, and
483–15 she affixed . . . the name "*s·*" to Mind.
g 516– 4 The *s·*, Life, intelligence, Truth, and
gl 588–24 *S·* ; self-existent and eternal Mind ;
591–17 divine Principle, *s·*, Life, Truth, Love ;
594–25 definition of

substance-matter

sp 88–16 at one time are supposed to be *s·*
b 278– 9 the notion that there is real *s·*,
314– 4 relinquished the belief of *s·*,

substances

f 209–16 compounded minerals or aggregated *s·*
209–25 Material *s·* or mundane formations,
g 509–20 So-called mineral, vegetable, and animal *s·*

substantial

sp 93– 1 as *s·* and able to control the body
b 268–15 semi-metaphysical systems afford no *s·* aid
275– 5 matter is neither *s·*, living, nor
278–12 That matter is *s·* or has life and
278–31, 32 cannot be *s·* if Spirit is *s·*
292–15 To mortal mind, matter is *s·*,
301–11 immortal, spiritual man is really *s·*,
335–14 Things spiritual and eternal are *s·*.
g 531– 1 living, *s·*, and intelligent.

substantiality

b 301–15 spiritual man's *s·* transcends mortal vision
318– 2 but for him to conceive of the *s·* of Spirit

substantially

b 324–32 said *s·*, "He that believeth — *see John* 11 : 26.
p 436–27 *s·* charged the jury, twelve Mortal Minds,

substitute

f 218–19 why do you *s·* drugs for the

substitutes

s 146–13 Material medicine *s·* drugs for the
158–16 Drugs, cataplasms, and whiskey are stupid *s·*
f 247–28 embellishments of the person are poor *s·*

substituting

ph 167–32 *S·* good words for a good life,
t 462–11 and *s·* his own views for Truth,
r 482– 7 can always be gained by *s·* the word *God*,
ap 578– 2 by *s·* for the corporeal sense, the incorporeal

substitution

r 481–32 *s·* of the word *sense* for *soul*
gl 579– 1 the *s·* of the spiritual for the material

substratum

corporeal
p 408–28 in the corporeal *s·* of brain
grosser
b 293– 8 The grosser *s·* is named matter
inanimate
f 243–21 the inanimate *s·* of mortal mind,
its
sp 80–24 control of mortal mind over its *s·*,
80–25 mortal mind which convulses its *s·*,
unconscious
p 409–11 the unconscious *s·* of mortal mind,
409–17 superior to its unconscious *s·*, matter,

s 157–13 more like the human mind than the *s·* of
ph 198– 3 more power . . . than the *s·*, matter.
p 371– 2 body is the *s·* of mortal mind,

subterfuge

t 447–31 He may say, as a *s·*, that evil is unreal,

subtile

b 284–24 the more *s·* and misnamed material elements

subtle

an 102–20 weaving webs more complicated and *s·*.
f 226– 4 under more *s·* and depraving forms.
p 376– 6 It is the most *s·*,
t 451–26 especially any *s·* degree of evil,
g 515– 6 serpent of God's creating is neither *s·* nor
529–13 Now the serpent was more *s·* — *Gen.* 3 : 1.
ap 564–32 "more *s·* than any beast of the — *Gen.* 3 : 1.

subtlety

t 447–12 Ignorance, *s·*, or false charity does not
ap 563–27 The serpentine form stands for *s·*,
564–26 are typified by a serpent, or animal *s·*.
gl 593– 8 sensuality ; *s·* ; animal magnetism;
594– 2 *S·* ; a lie ; the opposite of Truth,

subtract

f 219– 7 we do not multiply when we should *s·*,

subverted

ph 200–19 he is neither inverted nor *s·*,

succeed

s 149–12   If you fail to s· in any case,
f 243– 2   but we can never s· . . . through ignorance
p 372–21   and hope to s· with contraries?
411–32   If you s· in wholly removing the fear,
419–28   To s· in healing, you must conquer your
t 451– 9   and think to s· without the spirit,

succeeded

sp 95–21   and we want that day to be s· by C. S.,
p 431–17   s· in getting Mortal Man into

succeeding

f 246–25   Each s· year unfolds wisdom,

succeeds

s 149– 7   The prescription which s· in one instance
157– 3   It s· where homœopathy fails,
f 252–24   says : . . . How sin s·,
p 372–23   Matter s· for a period only by falsely parading

success

crowned with
a 22–10   these efforts are crowned with s·.
enlightenment, and
t 462– 8   potency, enlightenment, and s·.
happiness, and
p 405–11   conspirators against health, happiness, and s·.
in error is defeat
f 239–12   s· in error is defeat in Truth.
in healing
sp 95–17   but it is important to s· in healing,
t 448–28   he cannot fail of s· in healing.
insure
t 449–15   qualities which insure s· in this Science ;
of Jesus' mission
a 28– 2   they only hindered the s· of Jesus' mission.
of the student
p 372–32   recovery of the sick and the s· of the student.
of the students
t 456– 7   has secured the only s· of the students
sublime
a 45– 4   crowned with the glory of a sublime s·,
unequalled
s 134–20   and unequalled s· in the first century.

successes

s 133–13   miracles attended the s· of the Hebrews ;

successful

s 154–31   The better and more s· method
p 369– 3   unfitted for the s· treatment of disease.

successfully

pr 1– 8   whatever has been s· done for the
ph 167–13   Drugs and hygiene cannot s· usurp the

successive

m 66–14   Each s· stage of experience
g 504–16   The s· appearing of God's ideas
506–14   forming each s· stage of progress.
549–14   s· generations do not begin with the

such

pref xii– 2   for s· institutions after 1883,
pr 3–30   In s· a case, the only acceptable prayer is to
5–23   S· an error would impede true religion,
7– 4   showing the necessity for s· forcible utterance,
8– 8   s· externals are spoken of by Jesus
11–31   S· a desire has little need of
12– 6   The beneficial effect of s· prayer for the sick is
13– 9   s· as the heathen use.
13–22   doubts and fears which attend s· a belief,
15–21   S· prayer is answered, in so far as we
16– 4   S· prayer heals sickness,
a 23– 7   S· a theory is man-made.
24–31   could not admit s· an event to be possible.
26–22   involved s· a sacrifice as makes us admit
31– 3   and God will never place it in s· hands.
39– 2   S· indignities as he received,
43–30   errors growing from s· beliefs.
53–18   which might flow from s· discomfort.
m 56–13   s· moral regulations as will secure increasing
62– 4   education of children should be s· as to
63–14   C. S. furnishes no precedent for s· injustice,
66–28   salutary under s· circumstances,
67–32   rebuked the suffering from any s· cause
sp 74–14   persons in s· opposite dreams
74–19   S· a backward transformation is impossible
74–27   two s· opposite conditions as the
77–23   s· communications would grow beautifully less
79– 8   s· a mental method produces permanent
83–10   for s· a belief hides Truth
85– 7   S· intuitions reveal whatever constitutes
87–13   Scotch call s· vision "second sight,"
an 106–16   sanction only s· methods as are
106–24   revellings and s· like — Gal. 5 : 21.
106–26   they which do s· things — Gal. 5 : 21.
106–29   against s· there is no law." — Gal. 5 : 23.
s 112–29   s· a school is erroneous, for it
119– 5   s· theories lead to one of two things.
122–11   s· as brain and nerves,

such

s 129–14   tribulation s· as was not since — Matt. 24 : 21.
130–24   s· as they belong to the heavenly kingdom.
132–11   s· effects, coming from divine Mind,
136–23   for how could s· a sinner comprehend
139–32   The moral condition of s· a man demands
141–10   All revelation (s· is the popular thought !)
146– 9   S· systems are barren of the vitality of
152–11   S· errors beset every material theory,
152–19   S· a fact illustrates our theories.
153– 1   is frequently attenuated to s· a degree
154–28   S· a mother runs to her little one,
155–14   s· a belief is governed by the majority.
157–11   s· repetition of thought-attenuations,
159–17   and not have risked s· treatment.
161–29   S· unconscious mistakes would not occur, if
ph 177–31   In s· cases a few persons believe the
179–15   body then seems to require s· treatment.
181– 8   but mortal belief has s· a partnership.
185–11   S· theories and s· systems of so-called
185–17   S· theories have no relationship to C. S.,
196–20   S· books as will rule disease out of
199– 7   producing s· a result on the hammer.
f 204–18   S· theories are evidently erroneous.
204–32   must unsay it and cease from s· utterances ;
205–18   or as they melt into s· thinness that
207–17   s· as the amalgamation of Truth and error
208–18   S· an utterance is "the voice of — Matt. 3 : 3.
216– 4   What has touched Life, God, to s· strange issues?
217– 3   and the notion of s· a possibility is
220– 4   S· admissions ought to open people's eyes
229–10   the belief which unites s· opposites
243–22   Neither . . . can carry on s· telegraphy ;
244– 2   therefore s· deformity is not real,
244–27   S· admissions cast us headlong
245–24   manifested the influence of s· a belief.
249–10   S· is the true Science of being.
253–28   for no s· law exists.
c 261– 9   with s· absorbed interest as to forget it,
266– 2   S· is the sword of Science,
b 273–22   If there were s· a material law, it would
275–29   s· as matter, disease, sin, and death,
280–11   S· belief can neither apprehend nor
283–18   s· as the structural life of the tree
290–14   "On s· the second death hath no — Rev. 20 : 6.
294–31   The Science of Mind corrects s· mistakes,
309–28   to suppose that there can be s· a reality as
309–29   s· so-called life always ends in death.
312– 2   s· so-called knowledge is reversed
314–16   To s· materialists, the real man seemed a
320–20   however transcendental s· a thought
325– 5   S· a one abideth in Life,
331–23   s· omnipresence and individuality
332–24   in s· a form of humanity as they
o 341– 8   when subjected to s· usage.
343– 1   are taught in s· cases to say, Amen.
343–29   to follow s· examples !
346– 1   s· criticism confounds man with Adam.
348–32   If s· are the present fruits,
351–22   Because s· starting-points are neither
352–27   because there are no s· things.
355–29   proved to be s· by our Master
358– 5   S· doctrines are "confusion
360– 8   for mine give me s· personal pleasure,
p 362– 8   debarred from s· a place and s· society,
363– 3   sandal oil perhaps, which is in s· common use
364– 8   tribute to s· ineffable affection,
364–20   Jesus told Simon that s· seekers as he
365– 7   finding utterance in s· words as
365–20   s· commendation as the Magdalen gained
365–32   s· as peace, patience in tribulation,
366–19   S· so-called Scientists will strain out gnats,
374–21   S· a state of mind induces sickness.
378–29   S· a power, . . . is inconceivable ;
378–30   and if s· a power could be divinely directed,
383–15   It is the native element of s· a mind,
383–25   S· instances only prove the illusive
384–20   s· symptoms are not apt to follow
386– 7   no s· result occurs without mind
392–25   Admitting only s· conclusions as you
394–13   s· admissions are discouraging,
394–32   faith is not the healer in s· cases.
398–29   changes s· ills into new and more difficult
404– 7   suffering which his submission to s· habits
413–25   directing the mind to s· signs,
413–30   probable at any time that s· ills may
422–13   If s· be the case, explain to them the
424–18   s· opinions as may alarm or discourage,
427–27   when all s· remedies have failed
433–10   The jury must regard in s· cases only the
436–13   S· acts bear their own justification,
437–24   for s· high-handed illegality.
442– 2   because there are no s· law.
t 443– 6   those, who make s· a compromise,
443–18   give up s· cases, and leave invalids free
443–20   s· invalids may learn the value of

such

t 446–10	has generally completely healed *s·* cases.
448– 8	Under *s·* circumstances, to say that there is no
450–12	To teach C. S. to *s·* as these is no task.
452–26	*S·* a practice does not demonstrate the
453–26	for *s·* a course increases fear,
455– 5	*S·* mental states indicate weakness
455–21	one who has grown into *s·* a fitness for it
460–13	till *s·* thought is rectified by Spirit.
463–30	*S·* seeming medical effect or action is that of
r 478– 1	But there is, there can be, no *s·* division,
478–10	when no *s·* persons were ever seen to go into
487–21	there is in reality no *s·* thing as *mortal* mind.
495–12	opens the prison doors to *s·* as are bound,
g 504–26	vague conjectures emit no *s·* effulgence.
517– 4	in *s·* a phrase as "an anthropomorphic God,"
539– 9	*s·* as evil, matter, error, and death?
545–13	*S·* fundamental errors send falsity into
549–21	culminate in *s·* vague hypotheses
554– 4	There is no *s·* thing as mortality,
554–19	Mind sets at naught *s·* a mistaken belief.
ap 573– 2	is unable to grasp *s·* a view.
573–24	*s·* a recognition of being is, . . . possible

suckling

p 371–21	nor would I keep the *s·* a lifelong babe.

sudden

a 47– 8	The influx of light was *s·*.
ph 179– 1	the *s·* cures of which it is capable ;
f 218–24	in sickness . . . with *s·* dismissal.
p 377–15	A *s·* joy or grief has caused what is termed

suddenly

pr 14–16	you will find yourself *s·* well.
a 36–26	*s·* pardoned and pushed into heaven,
sp 77– 1	recognition of Spirit and of infinity comes not *s·*
p 377–15	becomes *s·* weak or abnormally strong,
434–19	Then C. S. turns *s·* to the supreme tribunal,
438–13	Turning *s·* to Personal Sense,

suffer

a 33–14	their Master was about to *s·* violence
37– 3	They who sin must *s·*.
40–17	Was it just for Jesus to *s·*?
m 56– 3	"*S·* it to be so now :"— Matt. 3 : 15.
s 108–11	for the divine Mind cannot *s·*.
ph 176–28	human mind, . . . is supposed to feel, *s·*, enjoy.
181– 7	which can neither *s·* nor enjoy,
184–21	for matter cannot *s·*.
189–14	sins of others should not make good men *s·*.
f 210–26	matter, being unintelligent, cannot say, "I *s·*,
212– 1	We *s·* or enjoy in our dreams,
221–31	neither food nor . . . can make one *s·*,
235– 4	Better *s·* a doctor infected with smallpox to
237–31	they hug false beliefs and *s·* the delusive
238–21	because we *s·* severely from error.
250–16	weary or pained, enjoy or *s·*, according to
b 295–29	teaches that mortals are created to *s·* and die.
296–20	will *s·* the pangs of destruction,
322–15	since God has sentenced sin to *s·*.
340–29	leaves nothing that can sin, *s·*, be punished or
o 346–14	belief that we *s·* from the sins of others.
346–24	how can he *s·* longer?
p 372–15	He can neither sin, *s·*, be subject to
376–18	it cannot, for that very reason, *s·* with a fever.
376–25	showing that it is impossible for matter to *s·*,
378– 4	Unwittingly you sentence yourself to *s·*.
381– 4	Be no more willing to *s·* the illusion that you
381–10	cannot in reality *s·* from breaking anything except
385–24	will *s·* in proportion to your belief and fear.
387–23	one cannot *s·* as the result of any labor of love,
390–20	*S·* no claim of sin or of sickness to grow
391–13	It is error to *s·* for aught but your own sins.
392–32	then the body cannot *s·* from them.
393–21	Your body would *s·* no more from tension
397–26	walk, see, hear, enjoy, or *s·*
403– 5	should and does cause the perpetrator to *s·*,
414–10	impossibility that matter, brain, . . . can *s·*
421– 1	he suffers only as the insane *s·*,
435–25	and Mortal Man can *s·* only for his sin.
g 524–29	Could Spirit . . . give matter ability to sin and *s·*?
557– 8	many animals *s·* no pain in multiplying ;
gl 582–16	has spiritual bliss and enjoys but cannot *s·*.

suffered

pr 11–16	if indeed, he has not already *s·* sufficiently
11–18	Jesus *s·* for our sins,
a 24–15	in which Jesus *s·* and triumphed.
25–30	worked and *s·* to bestow upon us.
38–24	his spiritual selfhood, never *s·*.
46–31	by all they had witnessed and *s·*,
s 156–23	but on the third day she again *s·*,
ph 185– 4	and she never *s·* again from east winds,

sufferer

s 108–10	the truism that the only *s·* is mortal mind.
ph 180– 5	The patient *s·* tries to be satisfied when he sees
o 346–22	When a *s·* is convinced that there is no

sufferer

p 377– 4	convince the *s·* that affliction is often the
398–13	To the *s·* with the withered hand
405– 4	makes any man, . . . a hopeless *s·*.
416– 7	and in twenty minutes the *s·* is quietly asleep.
t 464–16	the *s·* could call a surgeon,
ap 573–29	Take heart, dear *s·*, for this reality

sufferers

f 220– 6	and induce *s·* to look in other directions

suffering

all the

p 386–25	Error, not Truth, produces all the *s·* on earth.

and death

f 219–29	the belief in sin, *s·*, and death

and despair

p 382–30	to more hopeless *s·* and despair.

and disease

f 221–17	He learned that *s·* and disease were the

and triumph

a 21– 7	another's goodness, *s·*, and triumph,

another's

a 40–14	Another's *s·* cannot lessen our own liability.

antidotes

b 270–28	and a sense of ease antidotes *s·*,

bed of

p 390–17	nor laid upon a bed of *s·*

bodily

p 387–32	not only from temptation, but from bodily *s·*.

capable of

o 357–11	belief that God . . . makes man capable of *s·*

cause

p 414–11	that matter, . . . can suffer or cause *s·* ;

cause of all

f 230–32	predisposing, and the exciting cause of all *s·*,

causes

p 377– 3	If grief causes *s·*, convince the

climax of

g 543– 2	This error, after reaching the climax of *s·*,

creates the

p 400–22	we prove that thought alone creates the *s·*.

delusion of

ph 184–25	by destroying the delusion of *s·*

dream of

p 420–29	to break its dream of *s·*,

evil and

sp 72–29	when evil and *s·* are communicable.

experience

a 22– 7	Waking to Christ's demand, mortals experience *s·*.

from quackery

t 458–16	Having seen so much *s·* from quackery,

human

a 22–28	or that divinity is appeased by human *s·*,
f 227–13	of continued bondage and of human *s·*

inevitable

pr 11–20	sin brings inevitable *s·*.

is an error

a 23– 9	*s·* is an error of sinful sense

material

p 405–30	Belief in material *s·* causes mortals to

no more

t 463–19	and can cause the mother no more *s·*.

obedience and

ap 572– 2	washed their robes white in obedience and *s·*.

of the just

a 36–30	the *s·* of the just for the unjust.

or Science

b 296– 6	Either here or hereafter, *s·* or Science

prevent

t 457–11	Her prime object, . . . has been to prevent *s·*,

produces

b 270–27	If a sense of disease produces *s·*

real

p 391–15	and real *s·* for your own sins will

rebuked the

m 67–31	Jesus rebuked the *s·* from any such cause

records of

a 37– 5	History is full of records of *s·*.

relieve

r 483– 3	they do not heal, but only relieve *s·* temporarily,

repentance and

a 19–17	Every pang of repentance and *s·*,

sin and

a 23–10	and that eventually both sin and *s·* will
f 210–29	To mortal sense, sin and *s·* are real,
229– 6	but if sin and *s·* are realities of being,
p 435– 7	which alone is capable of sin and *s·*.

sin brings

a 37– 2	sin brings *s·* as much to-day as yesterday

source of all

f 205–12	the prolific source of all *s·*

sufficient

a 36– 5	sufficient *s·*, . . . to quench the love of sin.

supposed

p 391–15	Truth, will destroy all other supposed *s·*,
421–18	When the supposed *s·* is gone from

suffering

through
pr 5–21 the destruction of sin through s'.
f 224– 8 is self-destroyed through s'.
ap 569–21 eventually expiate their sin through s'.

to cause
pr 6–11 To cause s' as the result of sin,

weakness and
p 406–26 Inharmony . . . involves weakness and s',

which awakens
ph 196– 6 Better the s' which awakens mortal mind

without
f 221–24 and he ate without s',
p 385–17 can be experienced without s'.
g 557– 7 where parturition is without s'.

your
p 386–21 you learn that your s' was merely the

---

pr 14–15 If s' from a belief in sickness,
m 68–18 was s' from incipient insanity,
sp 76–18 S', sinning, dying beliefs are unreal.
77–21 or of a sinning, s' sense,
78–11 must still be mortal, sinning, s', and dying.
ph 175–10 to say that a rose, . . . can produce s' !
188–16 thinks that . . . the s' is in that body.
193–14 My s' is all gone."
f 240–11 must sooner or later, either by s' or by Science,
248–16 Is it imperfection, joy, sorrow, sin, s'?
b 318–19 beliefs, from which comes so much s',
o 348–22 while complaining of the s' disease brings,
p 365–31 The poor s' heart needs its
377–31 is of itself powerless to produce s'.
379–21 but is s' from her belief that blood is
389–30 was then s' from a complication of symptoms
395– 1 The sick unconsciously argue for s',
397– 8 S' is no less a mental condition than
404– 6 s' which his submission to such habits brings,
407– 2 a s' inconceivably terrible to
t 444– 4 s' is oft the divine agent in this elevation.
g 557–10 has its s' because it is a false belief.
ap 574–28 which your s' sense deems wrathful
gl 588– 2 death ; s' and self-destruction ;

sufferings

bodily
p 397– 9 You cause bodily s' and increase them by

error and its
f 237–19 To prevent the experience of error and its s',

great
s 158–14 and endured great s' upon earth.

his
a 38–22 his s' were the fruits of other people's sins,

illusive
p 371–17 before he can get rid of the illusive s'

of Jesus
a 34–11 had really commemorated the s' of Jesus

self-inflicted
p 398–20 which reduces self-inflicted s'

your
p 385–25 Your s' are not the penalty for

suffers

m 65–11 The union of the sexes s' fearful discord.
sp 81– 3 to show the sick that matter s'
s 134– 8 one who s' for his convictions.
ph 168–16 sick and useless, s' and dies,
184–18 We say man s' from the effects of
184–21 Mortal mind alone s',
187–25 and s' from the attempt.
f 202–17 but immortal man, . . . neither sins, s', nor
229– 5 should hesitate to say that Jehovah sins or s' ;
b 270–30 Hence the fact that the human mind alone s',
285– 7 the material personality which s',
294–10 that matter enjoys and s'.
p 388– 5 s' less, only because it knows less of
396–21 all teaching that the body s',
409–12 belief, that . . . the body, s' and reports disease
414–25 matter neither feels, s', nor enjoys.
419– 8 If your patient from any cause s' a relapse,
420–32 Tell him that he s' only as the insane suffer,
429–12 is cold and decays, but it never s'.
r 493–25 That man is material, and that matter s',

sufficient

pr 3– 3 is not s' to warrant him in advising God.
4– 9 Outward worship is not of itself s' to
10–14 Seeking is not s'.
a 29– 1 and not s' moral courage.
36– 5 reveals the necessity of s' suffering,
c 257–25 Who hath found finite life or love s'
266–14 until the lesson is s' to exalt you ;
p 363–29 was her grief s' evidence to warrant the
t 454–14 He, who understands in a s' degree the Principle
r 488– 2 result of our teachings is their s' confirmation.
497– 4 the Bible as our s' guide to eternal Life.

sufficiently

pr 11–16 if indeed, he has not already suffered s'
a 30–26 If we have triumphed s' over the errors
45–32 Jesus' students, not s' advanced
sp 84– 7 When s' advanced in Science
ph 181–18 or are not s' spiritual to depend on Spirit.
o 352– 1 because they did not s' understand God
p 387– 7 we conclude that . . . has been carried s' far ;

suggest

b 287–15 how can He be absent or s' the absence of
g 502–12 serves to s' the proper reflection of God

suggested

a 114–18 if a better word or phrase could be s',
p 364–16 Here is s' a solemn question,

suggestion

g 529– 2 a s' of change in the *modus operandi*,
544–18 the first s' of more than the one Mind,

suggestions

p 433– 9 warped by the irrational, unchristian s'
r 496– 2 in Science there is no transfer of evil s'

suggestive

b 298–32 making them human creatures with s' feathers ;
g 529– 6 The first system of s' obstetrics has changed.

suggestiveness

ap 560– 1 a special s' in connection with the

suggests

c 256–10 s' polytheism, rather than the one
265–11 by no means s' man's absorption
b 338–16 This s' the thought of something fluid,
338–17 It further s' the thought of

suicide

a 43–13 the treason and s' of his betrayer,
f 203–25 The so-called sinner is a s'.

suit

pref x–11 to s' the general drift of thought,
t 450– 2 twist every fact to s' themselves.

suits

p 440–29 forbidden to enter . . . any more s'
441– 6 not permitted to enter any s' at the bar of

Sulphuris

s 156–10 occasional doses of a high attenuation of *S'*.

sum

s 129– 4 a properly computed s' in arithmetic.
c 259– 4 he represents infinite Mind, the s' of all
p 363–16 one for a large s' and one for a smaller,
422– 1 and that their combined s' is
ap 563–10 dragon stands for the s' total of human error.
574–17 the s' total of human misery,

summarize

p 363–24 Why did he thus s' her debt to

summarized

s 113–10 propositions of divine metaphysics are s' in the

summary

s 138–15 His sublime s' points to the religion of Love.

summed

gl 595–18 limits, in which are s' up all human acts,

summer

sp 96– 8 s' and winter, seedtime and harvest
f 220–13 procures a s' residence with more ease than
r 492–19 fight it out on this line, if it takes all s'."

summit

p 367–13 from the s' of devout consecration,
g 549–31 He absolutely drops from his s',

summits

g 515– 5 creeping over lofty s',

summoned

o 342– 3 are s' to the support of Christianity,
p 431–13 the prisoner s' Physiology,
434–13 s' to appear before the bar of Justice
436–15 the prisoner s' two professed friends,
438–26 Court of Truth s' Furred Tongue
t 458–21 as ritualism and creed are s' to give place to

summons

g 532–21 Its s' may be thus paraphrased :

sums

s 128–29 The addition of two s' in mathematics

sun (*see also* sun's)

appears to rise
r 493– 2 To corporeal sense, the s' appears to rise and set,

a small
g 547–15 germinating speck . . . seemed a small s'.

at rest
s 119–27 the earth is in motion and the s' at rest.

central
f 209– 6 is the central s' of its own systems

clothed with the
ap 560– 7 a woman clothed with the s',— *Rev.* 12 : 1.

sun

declining
f 246–13   undimmed by a declining *s·*.
following the
a 21–29   After following the *s·* for six days,
hides the
b 298– 4   As a cloud hides the *s·* it cannot extinguish,
melts before the
r 480–31   As vapor melts before the *s·*,
obscures the
b 299–28   as the mist obscures the *s·* or the mountain ;
of virtue
f 246–11   The radiant *s·* of virtue and truth
or satellite
ap 577–20   has no need of *s·* or satellite,
seems to move
s 121–18   and the *s·* seems to move from east to west,
standing in the
ap 561– 8   an "angel standing in the *s·*."— *Rev.* 19 : 17.

    s 121–24   The *s·* is the central stillness,
    121–26   earth revolves about the *s·* once a year,
   ph 188–29   senses have no immediate evidence of a *s·*.
    188–32   desired information regarding the *s·*.
    189– 3   If the eyes see no *s·* for a week,
    189–12   or doubt that the *s·* will reappear.
   f 250–13   like a ray of light which comes from the *s·*,
   c 265–18   or a flower withered by the *s·*
   b 295–24   it no longer hides the *s·*.
    300–30   the *s·* is seen in the ray of light which
    310–12   The *s·* is not affected by the revolution of the
   o 310–17   a ray of light one with the *s·*,
   g 504–10   This light is not from the *s·*
    510–16   The *s·* is a metaphorical representation of
    538–11   The *s·*, giving light and heat to the earth,
   ap 558– 5   his face was as it were the *s·*,— *Rev.* 10 : 1.
    558–15   it has for you a light above the *s·*,
    561– 5   Agassiz, . . . saw the *s·* in an egg
    561–26   The Revelator symbolizes Spirit by the *s·*.
   gl 595– 1   definition of

sunbeam

   f 210–21   as a *s·* penetrates the cloud.
    247–25   glances in the warm *s·*,

sundered

   sp 75–29   the moment when the link . . . is being *s·*.

sunlight

   s 162– 4   C. S. brings to the body the *s·* of Truth,
   ph 189–11   the existence of the *s·*
   g 516–17   *s·* glints from the church-dome,

sunny

   f 240– 3   Arctic regions, *s·* tropics, giant hills,

Sun of Righteousness

   ap 576– 3   lighted by the *S· of R·*,

sunrise

   s 119–25   In viewing the *s·*, one finds that it

sun's

   s 144– 7   when dawns the *s·* brave light.
   ph 189– 3   the *s·* influence over the earth.
   g 548–10   when clouds cover the *s·* face !

suns

   f 240– 7   *S·* and planets teach grand lessons.

sunshine

   m 66– 8   in the *s·* of joy and prosperity.
    67–16   or *s·* gladdens the troubled sea.
   s 121–12   in God's perennial and happy *s·*,
    122–19   that little prophet of storm and *s·*,
   b 299–28   *s·* of Truth, will melt away the shadow
   p 365–18   like dew before the morning *s·*.

superabundance

   f 201–11   *s·* of being is on the side of God, good.

superficial

   t 460–22   the *s·* and cold assertion, "Nothing ails you."
    461– 9   for it is not *s·*, nor is it
   gl 597–12   the false foundations . . . of *s·* religion,

superimposed

   ph 176–18   with *s·* and conjectural evils.
   p 425–10   images of mortal thought *s·* upon the body ;

superinduced

   sp 89–15   without study or a *s·* condition,

superinduces

   ph 183–24   Submission to error *s·* loss of power.

superintendence

   p 430–31   Although I have the *s·* of human affairs,

superior

   m 63– 1   and the *s·* law of Soul last.
   s 144– 3   If Mind is foremost and *s·*,
   f 217–15   That scientific methods are *s·* to others,
    231–20   To hold yourself *s·* to sin,
    231–21   because God made you *s·* to it
    231–25   To hold yourself *s·* to sickness and death
    242–13   and to rise *s·* to the so-called pain and

superior

   b 275–29   *s·* or contrary to the one Spirit.
   o 351–21   if not *s·* to Him.
    358– 2   Is the woodman's axe, . . . *s·* to omnipotence?
   p 368–11   beliefs . . . that evil is equal . . . if not *s·*,
    409–17   conscious mortal mind is believed to be *s·* to
    423–20   as *s·* to error and discord,
   t 444– 3   all must rise *s·* to materiality,
   r 493–17   Mind must be found *s·* to all the beliefs of the
   g 521– 1   but making him *s·* to the soil.

superiority

   sp 92–31   leads to belief in the *s·* of error.
   s 131–11   the *s·* of spiritual over physical power.
    134–29   *s·* of spiritual power over material resistance.
    143–23   deprives you of the available *s·* of
    150–29   even the doctrine of the *s·* of matter over
   f 209–32   It shows the *s·* of faith by works
    215–27   understood the *s·* and immortality of good,
   t 454–29   The *s·* of spiritual power over sensuous
   g 530–17   as always asserting its *s·*

supernal

   f 248– 8   feeds the body with *s·* freshness
   c 261–27   Fixing your gaze on the realities *s·*,
   b 319– 2   has no kinship with the Life *s·*.

supernatural

   pref xi–15   these mighty works are not *s·*,
   a 44–20   Could it be called *s·* for the God of nature to
    44–23   but it was not a *s·* act.
   sp 83–15   is not *s·*, since Science is an explication
   s 111– 7   no more *s·* than is the science of numbers,
    126–20   Or shall all that . . . be called *s·*,
    134–23   not because this Science is *s·* or preternatural,
   b 271–13   was not a *s·* gift to those learners,
   t 450– 3   teaches belief in a mysterious, *s·* God,
   gl 596–13   believed that the stones...had *s·* illumination,

supersede

   ph 182–18   must *s·* the so-called laws of matter.
   f 213–25   strains of sweetest music *s·* conscious sound.
   b 274–15   and they *s·* the so-called laws of matter.
   r 483– 7   will ultimately *s·* all other means in healing.
   g 553–26   this potent belief will immediately *s·* the

superseded

   f 227– 7   must be denied and *s·*.

supersedes

   b 330– 2   understanding of being *s·* mere belief.
   p 434– 6   law of Christ *s·* our laws ; let us follow Christ."

superstition

   pr 4–31   Long prayers, *s·*, and creeds
   sp 83–23   Between C. S. and all forms of *s·*
    99– 2   Human philosophy, ethics, and *s·* afford no
   s 120–31   ignorance and *s·* chained the limbs
    149–30   dismiss *s·*, and demonstrate truth
   f 237–12   *S·*, . . . snatches away the good seed
    242–27   Mere speculation or *s·* appropriates no part of
   b 288– 9   *S·* and understanding can never combine.
   o 353–21   not continue to admit the somethingness of *s·*,
   p 372–29   If pride, *s·*, or any error prevents
   g 553–26   ancient *s·* about the creation from dust
   gl 597–13   tore from bigotry and *s·* their coverings,

superstitious

   b 298–31   forms of thought, marked with *s·* outlines,

superstructure

   ph 177–12   so-called mind builds its own *s·*,
   gl 595– 8   *s·* of Truth ; the shrine of Love ;
    595– 9   a material *s·*, where mortals congregate
    599– 6   Zion.   Spiritual foundation and *s·* ;

superstructures

   gl 597–12   false foundations and *s·* of

supper

   a 32–30   a sad *s·* taken at the close of day,
    33– 1   and this *s·* closed forever Jesus' ritualism
    34–29   contrast between our Lord's last *s·* and
   ph 198–17   I told him to rise, dress himself, and take *s·*

supplant

   f 223–23   *s·* unscientific means and so-called laws.
   r 495–22   understanding will *s·* error with Truth,

supple

   s 160–32   the *s·* and elastic condition of the healthy limb,
    162–21   ankylosed joints have been made *s·*,

supplied

   pr 7–26   and by whom it will be *s·*.

supplies

   m 58–27   because another *s·* her wants.
   f 222– 6   to believe that proper food *s·* nutriment
   b 281–15   *s·* all form and comeliness
   p 385– 8   *s·* energy and endurance surpassing all other
   r 494–14   and in every hour, divine Love *s·* all good.
   g 550–25   Embryology *s·* no instance of

supplieth

   g 518–18   seeth his brother's need and *s·* it,

supply

ph 199–11	by reason of its demand for and *s·* of power.
f 206–18	Spirit, not matter, being the source of *s·*.
216–13	to *s·* the truth of immortal sense.
c 258– 7	insufficiency of this belief to *s·* the true idea
ap 571–16	Know thyself, and God will *s·* the wisdom

supplying

f 248– 9	*s·* it with beautiful images of thought

support

basis and

f 229– 4	but is their basis and *s·*.

discords have no

ph 183– 6	discords have no *s·* from nature or

manifestation and

b 279–10	nor for the manifestation and *s·* of Mind.

of bodily endurance

sp 80– 5	or for the *s·* of bodily endurance.

of Christian Science

o 341–17	so absolute and numerous in *s·* of C. S.,

of his proof

f 236– 9	in *s·* of his proof by example that the divine

origin nor

g 529–27	and has neither origin nor *s·* in Truth

summoned to the

o 342– 4	are summoned to the *s·* of Christianity,

theories in

o 355–32	material theories in *s·* of

which they derived

p 385– 6	explanation lies in the *s·* which they derived from

a 20–11	partake of the Eucharist, *s·* the clergy,
40– 5	The advanced thinker . . . will *s·* them.
sp 73– 1	one does not *s·* the other.
92–27	This belief tends to *s·* two opposite powers,
s 124– 6	When this . . . lacks organizations to *s·* it,
124–21	and *s·* the equipoise of that thought-force,
ph 198–25	says nothing to *s·* his theory.
f 204– 3	All forms of error *s·* the false conclusions
b 318–10	The material senses originate and *s·*
o 344–26	Why *s·* the popular systems of
p 389–19	If God has, . . . instituted laws that food shall *s·*
390–24	You have no law of His to *s·* the
417– 4	Always *s·* their trust in the power of Mind
417–32	an underlying understanding to *s·* them
t 454–27	*s·* all their feeble footsteps, until
455–10	and *s·* your claims by demonstration.
r 481–27	since Truth cannot *s·* error.
495–21	Let C. S., . . . *s·* your understanding
g 543– 1	having no truth to *s·* it,

supported

s 109– 7	is not, . . . *s·* by sensible evidence, until
r 471–14	the evidence . . . is not *s·* by evil,
481–26	If sin is *s·*, God must uphold it,

supporting

b 325– 6	not of the body incapable of *s·* life,
p 382–27	*s·* the power of Mind over the body
387–28	sublime proofs of the *s·* influence and

supports

pref x–20	till all physical *s·* have failed,
m 57–28	for Love *s·* the struggling heart
ph 169–15	should find stronger *s·* and a higher home.
196–17	No law *s·* them.
p 372–22	Its false *s·* fail one after another.
g 511– 5	The divine Mind *s·* the sublimity,
515– 1	It *s·* Christian healing, and
543–29	The belief that matter *s·* life
gl 582–13	that which comforts, consoles, and *s·*.

suppose

pr 6–19	To *s·* that God forgives or punishes sin according
a 28–24	To *s·* that persecution for righteousness' sake
36–24	It is useless to *s·* that the wicked can
sp 73–26	It is a grave mistake to *s·* that matter is
83–21	It is contrary to C. S. to *s·* that life
87–24	Do not *s·* that any mental concept is
s 161– 4	more exact than you *s·* ;
ph 183– 4	To *s·* that God constitutes laws of
f 208–14	it is absurd to *s·* that matter can
216–19	The great mistake of mortals is to *s·* that man
230–12	to *s·* Him capable of first arranging law and
240–12	*s·* Mind to be governed by matter
f 250– 2	and *s·* error to be mind,
b 289– 9	To *s·* that sin, lust, hatred, envy, hypocrisy,
309–27	It is a self-evident error to *s·* that
328– 4	Mortals *s·* that they can live without goodness,
p 422–22	Let us *s·* two parallel cases of bone-disease,
430–17	*S·* a mental case to be on trial,
r 486– 4	*S·* one accident happens to the eye,

supposed

pr 6–12	Every *s·* pleasure in sin
sp 81–32	deceased person, *s·* to be the communicator,
88–16	at one time are *s·* to be substance-matter
90–17	but the *s·* inhabitant of that body

supposed

s 120–25	deduced from *s·* sensation in matter
120–26	or from matter's *s·* consciousness of
126– 1	its *s·* organic action or *s·* existence.
152– 4	takes away all its *s·* sovereignty,
152–18	sick man *s·* this ceremony was intended to
158– 4	was *s·* to have dictated the first prescription,
ph 172–11	Spirit can form no real link in this *s·* chain
176–28	The human mind, not matter, is *s·* to feel,
189–17	brain which is *s·* to furnish the evidence
190– 4	ignorant of what it is *s·* to produce.
f 204–15	The third power, mortal man, is a *s·* mixture
218– 9	The body is *s·* to say, "I am ill."
224–32	What is this *s·* power, which opposes
245–13	and *s·* her to be a young woman.
253–25	Do not believe in any *s·* necessity for sin,
c 257–13	the *s·* substance of non-intelligent matter.
262–19	when the *s·* pain and pleasure of matter
b 269– 3	the *s·* coexistence of Mind and matter
281–18	The mind *s·* to exist in matter
289–23	So man, tree, and flower are *s·* to die ;
301–26	*s·* standpoint outside the focal distance of
307–22	every sin or *s·* material pain and
311–29	Matter, sin, and mortality lose all *s·*
314–31	in *s·* accord with the inevitable law of life.
338–22	even the *s·* separation of man from
339–29	is to divest sin of any *s·* mind or reality,
o 348–21	defending the *s·* rights of disease,
348–26	I have never *s·* the world would immediately
353–26	So long as there are *s·* limits to Mind,
354–27	Its *s·* realism has no divine authority,
p 365– 9	*s·* necessity for physical thought-taking
370–24	a drug may eventually lose its *s·* power
375–27	even when they are *s·* to be in hopeless danger.
380–32	Every law of matter or the body, *s·* to govern
381– 8	When infringing some *s·* law,
382–15	the devotee of *s·* hygienic law,
385–31	Any *s·* information, coming from the body
389–10	Matter does not . . . it is *s·* to do so.
391–15	will destroy all other *s·* suffering,
391–18	When the body is *s·* to say,
408–21	a *s·* effect on intelligence and
418–19	negation must extend to the *s·* disease
421–18	When the *s·* suffering is gone from
t 458– 7	This theory is *s·* to favor
r 470– 5	*s·* existence of more than one mind
479–14	constitutes matter's *s·* selfhood,
484–18	Certain results, *s·* to proceed from
g 510–23	indicates a *s·* formation of matter
528–25	Afterwards he is *s·* to become the basis of
535–10	*s·* material foundations of life and intelligence.
536–21	Their *s·* joys are cheats.
541–23	It is *s·* to say in the first instance,
544–21	The serpent is *s·* to say,
549– 9	are *s·* to have, as classes, three different
556– 4	classified, and are *s·* to possess life and mind.
gl 594–23	evil minds ; *s·* intelligences, or gods ;
596–25	fear of death, and the *s·* reality of error.
598–10	In the record of Jesus' *s·* death, we read :
	(*see also* **laws**)

supposedly

sp 73– 4	and *s·* will return to earth to-morrow,
g 522–26	portrays Spirit as *s·* cooperating with matter

supposes

b 287– 6	Error *s·* man to be both mental and material.
r 486–20	yet *s·* Mind unable to produce harmony !
489– 8	hypothesis which *s·* life to be in matter
g 530–29	*s·* that something springs from nothing,
530–31	it *s·* that mind enters matter,
538–31	*s·* God to be the author of sin
546–15	*s·* God and man to be manifested only through

supposing

sp 86– 1	*S·* this inquiry to be occasioned by
f 201–20	*s·* that sin can be forgiven when it

supposition

error is a

r 472–14	Error is a *s·* that pleasure and pain,

false

b 278– 9	It is a false *s·*, the notion that there is
o 357–21	must have originated in a false *s·*,
gl 580–21	the false *s·* that Life is not eternal,

inconsistent

p 387–21	inconsistent *s·* that death comes in obedience to

no

g 503–11	No *s·* of error enters there.

objective

b 287–27	objective *s·* of Spirit's opposite.

of opposite qualities

b 286–28	(by the *s·* of opposite qualities)

of reality

f 213– 2	contradicts this mortal mind *s·* of reality

opposite

g 521–13	We should look away from the opposite *s·*

overthrew the

f 228–28	The humble Nazarene overthrew the *s·*

supposition
that man is
ph 171–31   the *s·* that man is a material outgrowth
that Spirit is
ph 173– 6   the *s·*, that Spirit is within what it creates
that spirit is
gl 587– 2   a *s·* that spirit is finite.
vain
pr   6– 8   the vain *s·* that we have nothing to do but

sp   70–10   The *s·* that corporeal beings are spirits,
b 287–24   The *s·* that life, substance, and intelligence
p 408–14   The *s·* that we can correct insanity by
g 504–30   a *s·* of the absence of Spirit.
  506– 6   a quality which separates C. S. from *s·*
  528– 7   this *s·* was a dream, a myth.
  549– 4   The *s·* that life germinates in eggs
  550–29   not so hideous and absurd as the *s·* that Spirit
gl 586–18   a *s·* that life, substance, and intelligence
  587–10   a *s·* of sentient physicality ;

suppositional
sp   72–22   evil, the *s·* opposite of good,
an 103–17   Evil is a *s·* lie.
ph 185–31   material mentality and its *s·* activities.
  200–20   The *s·* antipode of divine infinite Spirit,
f 208– 1   *s·* error, which affords no proof of God,
  215–19   the *s·* absence of Life, God,
b 274–30   This *s·* partnership is already obsolete,
  288– 3   The *s·* warfare between truth and error
  335–30   the *s·* antipodes of Spirit,
r 472– 3   Truth casts out *s·* error and heals
g 510–25   analogous to the *s·* resolving of thoughts
  533–25   but error has its *s·* day
gl 591–27   a *s·* material sense, *alias* the belief that

suppositions
b 277–22   These *s·* contradict even the order of
  291– 1   *s·* that sin is pardoned while unforsaken,
p 368–18   no material *s·* can prevent us from
gl 583– 3   material *s·* of life, substance, and intelligence,

suppositious
b 278–14   in a *s·* mortal consciousness.
  310– 5   Matter is made up of *s·* mortal mind-force ;
  322–26   belief in the *s·* life of matter,
p 368– 2   a *s·* opposite of the highest right.
r 469–15   the *s·* opposite of infinite Mind
  480–24   The *s·* parent of evil is a lie.
gl 587–13   *s·* minds, or souls, going in and out of matter,

suppress
ph 197–31   The doctor should *s·* his fear of disease,

suppressed
p 416– 3   for the inflammation is not *s·* ;

suppurates
p 251– 4   should not grow more painful before it *s·*,

supremacy
absolute
p 423–26   which ultimately asserts its absolute *s·*.
and reality
f 205–20   the *s·* and reality of good,
God's
g 521–10   God's *s·*, omnipotence, and omnipresence.
its
b 293–29   C. S. brings to light Truth and its *s·*,
of divine Mind
p 400–10   acknowledge the *s·* of divine Mind,
of divine Spirit
g 522–15   opposed to the *s·* of divine Spirit ;
of God
s 130–27   strong claim of Science for the *s·* of God,
of good
s 130–27   and doubts the *s·* of good,
of Mind
a   45–30   glorified the *s·* of Mind over matter.
f 209–13   the Science which reveals the *s·* of Mind.
b 322– 2   cast out evils in proof of the *s·* of Mind.
p 401–27   admits the efficacy and *s·* of Mind,
of Spirit
a   44– 3   and the *s·* of Spirit be demonstrated.
sp   78–17   would destroy the *s·* of Spirit.
  97–28   will disappear before the *s·* of Spirit.
s 138–14   The *s·* of Spirit was the foundation on which
ph 170–26   to ponder somewhat the *s·* of Spirit,
b 273–23   it would oppose the *s·* of Spirit, God,
  324–28   if the idea of the *s·* of Spirit,
p 391– 2   matter, arrayed against the *s·* of Spirit.
r 491–13   It is only by acknowledging the *s·* of Spirit,
ap 572–17   Under the *s·* of Spirit, it will be seen
of the divine Mind
r 484–16   Drugs and...oppose the *s·* of the divine Mind.
of Truth
p 406–22   the *s·* of Truth over error,
ap 569– 8   when we are conscious of the *s·* of Truth,
gl 589–21   showing the immortality and *s·* of Truth ;

supremacy
struggle for
b 268–14   In this final struggle for *s·*,

s 146–19   and clothes Spirit with *s·*.

supreme
pr   17– 3   *Enable us to know, ... God is omnipotent, s·.*
a   50– 5   The last *s·* moment of mockery, desertion,
sp   91– 3   by beings under the control of *s·* wisdom?
  97–18   until divine Spirit, *s·* in its domain,
s 127–14   God, the infinite, *s·*, eternal Mind.
  156–31   and Mind takes its rightful and *s·* place.
ph 174– 1   in a *s·* governing intelligence.
  182–11   one or the other must be *s·*
f 201– 4   knowing too that one affection would be *s·*
  207–11   Evil is not *s·* ; good is not helpless ;
  209– 5   Mind, *s·* over all its formations
  219– 4   Mind should be, and is, *s·*, absolute, and final.
  253– 7   saith : . . . I am *s·* and give all, for I am Mind.
b 278–21   and yet we say that Spirit is *s·*
  281– 4   and learn that Spirit is infinite and *s·*.
o 357–26   If . . . and God is not *s·*
p 375–25   no power to be lost, for Mind is *s·*,
  427–24   acknowledged as *s·* in the physical realm,
  428– 6   Man's privilege at this *s·* moment
  434–20   Then C. S. turns suddenly to the *s·* tribunal.
  437–33   read from the *s·* statute-book, the Bible,
  440– 5   whom Truth arraigns before the *s·* bar of
r 465– 9   God is incorporeal, divine, *s·*,
  496–10   the life that approaches the *s·* good?
  497– 5   one *s·* and infinite God.
ap 573–14   the declaration from heaven, *s·* harmony,
gl 590– 3   atmosphere of Spirit, where Soul is *s·*,
  593–21   understood and demonstrated as *s·* over all ;

Supreme Being
  93–23   Spirit, as a proper noun, is the name of the *S· B·*.
s 117– 8   the *S· B·* or His manifestation ;
  127–18   as divine Principle, *S· B·*, Mind,
f 202–24   Our beliefs about a *S· B·* contradict
b 285–22   the *S· B·*, or divine Principle, and idea.
g 523–18   the *S· B·* is therein called Elohim.
  524– 7   They called the *S· B·* by the national name of
  527–29   Is the *S· B·* retrograding,

Supreme Bench
p 440–20   cannot trample upon the decree of the *S· B·*.
  441–25   *S· B·* decides in favor of intelligence,

Supreme Court
p 435–11   The law of our *S· C·* decrees that whosoever
  436– 7   Your *S· C·* must find the prisoner on the night of
  437–10   the Judge of our higher tribunal, the *S· C·*
  437–17   I ask that the *S· C·* of Spirit reverse this
  437–28   Judge Justice of the *S· C·* of Spirit
  440–34   the Chief Justice of the *S· C·*,

Supreme Judge
p 435–24   If mortals sin, our *S· J·* in equity decides

Supreme Lawgiver
p 440–25   In the presence of the *S· L·*,

supremely
pref xi–15   not supernatural, but *s·* natural.
s 149–27   divine Mind, governs all, not partially but *s·*,
ph 167–19   you must love God *s·*.
b 326– 9   cannot love God *s·*...while loving the material

Supreme Ruler
f 203–17   prone to believe either in more than one *S· R·*
gl 590–19   Its higher signification is *S· R·*.

sure
pref ix– 5   He is as *s·* of the world's existence as he is
a   20–26   It commands *s·* entrance into the realm of Love.
m   67–10   dauntless seaman is not *s·* of his safety ;
sp   93–11   otherwise, we may be *s·* that either our logic is
s 151– 1   To be *s·*, they sometimes treat the sick as if
f 203– 4   assigns *s·* rewards to righteousness,
p 384–20   your Mind-remedy is safe and *s·*.
  419–15   therefore be *s·* that you move it off.
t 459–25   the results are *s·* if the Science is understood.
  460– 2   and rest his demonstration on this *s·* basis.
g 553–22   that theory is *s·* to become the signal for the

surely
s 123– 2   will *s·* destroy the greater error
  162–26   as *s·* as it heals what is called functional,
ph 197–10   thou shalt *s·* die.''— *Gen.* 2 : 17.
b 277– 3   ''Thou shalt *s·* die ;''— *Gen.* 2 : 17.
o 354–14   *S·* it is not enough to cleave to
r 481–19   thou shalt *s·* die.'' — *Gen.* 2 : 17.
  495– 3   as *s·* as it did nineteen centuries ago.
g 527–10   thou shalt *s·* die.— *Gen.* 2 : 17.
  530–14   Ye shall not *s·* die.— *Gen.* 3 : 4.
  532– 9   thou shalt *s·* die,''— *Gen.* 2 : 17.
  550– 4   Matter *s·* does not possess Mind.
ap 573–30   will *s·* appear sometime and in some way.
  578–16   *S·* goodness and mercy shall— *Psal.* 23 : 6.
gl 580–20   ''Thou shalt *s·* die.''— *Gen.* 2 : 17.

surface

m 65–30	has brought conjugal infidelity to the s·,
sp 83– 7	elements now coming to the s·.
f 254–24	If you venture upon the quiet s· of error
c 267–20	more than is detected upon the s·,
b 313–25	He plunged beneath the material s·
p 401–19	brings sin and sickness to the s·,
413–19	without scrubbing the whole s· daily.
g 540– 8	when bringing it to the s· and

Surgeon

s 163– 6	Dr. James Johnson, S· to William IV,

surgeon

a 44–15	He did not require the skill of a s·
s 163–10	physician, s·, apothecary, man-midwife,
ph 172–26	If . . . the s· destroys manhood,
p 401–30	leave . . . to the fingers of a s·,
402– 1	C. S. is always the most skilful s·,
422–24	A s· is employed in one case,
422–25	The s·, holding that matter forms its
t 464–16	the sufferer could call a s·,

surgeons

s 159–15	Had these unscientific s· understood

surgery

a 44–12	the claims of medicine, s·, and hygiene.
44–22	It was a method of s· beyond material art,
s 159–11	Is it skilful or scientific s· to take no heed of
p 401–29	to leave s· and the adjustment of
402– 2	but s· is the branch of its healing which
402– 6	the cure, . . . through mental s· alone,
g 528–28	s· was first performed mentally

surgical

s 159– 2	to perform a needed s· operation
ph 198–18	perhaps by a blister,…or by a s· operation.
g 528–17	in order to perform a s· operation on him

surging

ap 569–17	They are in the s· sea of error,

surpassing

p 385– 9	energy and endurance s· all other aids,

surplus

b 293–17	Electricity is the sharp s· of materiality

surprised

ap 559–27	do not be s· nor discontented

surprising

s 131– 1	Truth should not seem so s· and
136–23	That a wicked king . . . was not s· ;

surrender

pr 9–19	s· of all merely material sensation,
p 426–30	because matter has no life to s·.

surrendering

gl 579– 8	s· to the creator the early fruits of

surrenders

g 552–30	and that matter always s· its claims

surround

p 424–16	the minds which s· your patient should not

surrounding

s 128–21	its escape into the s· atmosphere.
p 415–31	will sink from sight along with s· objects,

surroundings

p 383–16	symbolized, and not chafed, by its s· ;
t 463–11	cannot injure its useful s·

survive

p 368–21	when we learn that life and man s· this body.

susceptibility

sp 86–10	possessed more spiritual s· than the disciples.

susceptible

sp 93–15	Good does not create a mind s· of
an 100–10	as follows : . . . Animal bodies are s· to the
p 410–23	Science of mental practice is s· of no misuse.

sustain

pr 10– 7	God will s· us under these sorrows.
a 44–21	to s· Jesus in his proof of
50–11	to s· and bless so faithful a son.
an 103–25	The truths of immortal Mind s· man,
ph 198– 6	His fortitude may s· him,
c 261–14	and s· his appointed task,
b 274– 2	and thus invigorate and s· existence.
o 357– 5	We s· Truth, . . . by rejecting a lie.
p 417– 5	the power of Mind to s· the body.
t 458–12	or of trying to s· the human body
r 481–25	It cannot s· itself.
g 552– 9	even where the proof requisite to s· this

sustained

a 43–26	and that spiritual law s· him.
sp 90– 8	earth's motion and position are s· by Mind
ph 179–21	s· by what is termed material law,
f 221–22	in which being is s· by God,
p 416–32	Teach them that their being is s· by Spirit,
425–16	learns that matter never s· existence
t 447–15	when mentally s· by Truth,

sustained

r 471–16	is fully s· by spiritual sense.
g 530– 5	In divine Science, man is s· by God,
531–26	Is Life s· by matter or by Spirit?
556– 1	That which is real, is s· by Spirit.

sustaining

pref vii– 1	To those leaning on the s· infinite,
a 33–10	now this bread was feeding and s· them.
m 59–14	each partner s· the other,
g 538–12	enlightening and s· the universe.

sustains

s 155–17	erroneous general belief, which s· medicine
b 319– 9	s· man under all circumstances ;
o 358–10	and s· logically and demonstratively
p 389–13	theories first admit that food s· the life of
r 488–16	C. S. s· with immortal proof
ap 569– 8	This testimony of Holy Writ s· the fact
gl 580–29	not one who constructs and s· reality

swaddling-clothes

c 255– 2	As mortals drop off their mental s·,

swallow

p 366–20	while they s· the camels of bigoted pedantry.

swallowed

sp 96–20	all discord will be s· up in spiritual Truth.
s 164–28	Death is s· up in victory"— I Cor. 15 : 54.
ph 177–25	If a dose of poison is s· through mistake,
177–31	a few persons believe the potion s· by the
f 209–29	s· up in the infinite calculus of Spirit.
215–24	s· up in immortality.
r 476–17	Mortality is finally s· up in immortality.
496–27	Death is s· up in victory."— I Cor. 15 : 54.
ap 570–12	and s· up the flood— Rev. 12 : 16.

swallowing

s 140–15	straining out gnats and s· camels.
f 202– 2	straining out gnats and s· camels.

sway

ap 565–12	that the man Jesus, . . . might never hold s·

swayed

ph 190–21	The Hebrew bard, s· by mortal thoughts,

sways

o 357–28	if another . . . cause exists and s· mankind?

swear

a 32– 3	was required to s· allegiance to his general.

sweat

a 48–10	the s· of agony which fell in holy benediction
ph 179–28	ready to put you into a s·,
b 327–14	to be effaced by the s· of agony.
g 535–26	in the s· of thy face shalt thou— Gen. 3 : 19.

sweep

p 428–11	we shall s· away the false

sweeping

a 55–15	Truth's immortal idea is s· down the centuries,

sweeps

f 213–29	as the hand, which s· over it, is human or divine.
p 403–20	s· away the gossamer web of mortal illusion.

sweet

pref viii– 7	and gives s· concord to sound.
m 57–13	bringing s· seasons of renewal
58–18	the s· interchange of confidence and love ;
59–13	should blend in s· confidence and cheer,
66– 3	S· are the uses of adversity ;
69–15	brings the s· assurance of no parting,
s 109–15	The search was s·, calm, and buoyant with hope,
130–14	good and its s· concords have all-power.
145– 1	whether they caught its s· tones, as the
ph 174–28	rolling it under the tongue as a s· morsel
f 219–23	We may hear a s· melody, and yet
b 287–13	same place s· water and bitter?"— Jas. 3 : 11.
304– 1	the s· sense and presence of Life and Truth.
p 413–23	in order to keep it s· as the new-blown flower.
t 455–30	cannot send forth both s· waters and bitter.
r 489–23	sendeth not forth s· waters and bitter.
g 516–15	The modest arbutus sends her s· breath to
ap 559–19	shall be in thy mouth s· as honey."— Rev. 10 : 9.
559–22	s· at its first taste, when it heals you ;
562–25	waiting to be delivered of her s· promise,
569–13	in a s· and certain sense that God is Love.

sweeter

m 60–28	and teach us life's s· harmonies.
ap 568–26	s· than has ever before reached high heaven,

sweetest

f 213–25	Mental melodies and strains of s· music
g 520– 1	s· rest, even from a human standpoint,

swell

p 393–19	Have no fear that matter can ache, s·,

swelling

s 153–18	through inflammation and s·,

swept

ph 190–22	thus s· his lyre with saddening strains

swerved
   a 20–20 Yet he s· not, well knowing that to obey
swift
   sp 97– 9 and the electric current s·,
   b 268– 3 With like activity have thought's s· pinions
   p 434– 1 S· on the wings of divine Love,
swift-winged
   ap 574–20 the very message, or s· thought,
swimming
   r 491– 1 and that he is s· when he is on dry land.
swine
   b 272–18 neither cast ye your pearls before s·."—*Matt.* 7 : 6.
swinging
   a 23–16 pendulum s· between nothing and something,
   f 246– 2 is not a pendulum, s· between evil and good,
   o 360–20 s· between the real and the unreal.
swinish
   b 272– 8 s· element in human nature uproots it.
swollen
   p 385–21 discolored, painful, s·, and inflamed.
   ap 565– 2 the great red dragon, s· with sin,
sword
  and spear
   s 134– 3 truth is still opposed with s· and spear.
  flaming
   g 537– 6 Cherubims, and a flaming s·—*Gen.* 3 : 24.
  of Science
   c 266– 2 Such is the s· of Science,
  of Spirit
   a 37– 8 but error falls only before the s· of Spirit.
  of Truth
   t 458–17 The two-edged s· of Truth must turn
   g 538– 7 the s· of Truth gleams afar and indicates
  put up thy
   a 48–24 He said : "Put up thy s·."—*John* 18 : 11.
  two-edged
   t 458–17 The two-edged s· of Truth must turn
   g 538– 4 Truth is a two-edged s·, guarding and
  which guards
   g 526–18 the s· which guards it is the type of

   a 19–16 to material beliefs not peace, but a s·.
   g 542–18 "They that take the s·—*Matt.* 26 : 52.
   542–19 shall perish with the s·."—*Matt.* 26 : 52.
   gl 595– 3 definition of
syllables
   b 338–14 Divide the name Adam into two s·,
syllogism
   s 128–32 the major and the minor propositions of a s·
   129– 3 the reasoning of an accurately stated s·
   o 347– 9 Had he stated his s· correctly,
symbol
  condemning its
   g 539–17 by condemning its s·, the serpent, to grovel
  of God
   g 517–20 The only proper s· of God as person
  of Life
   ap 561–10 Purity was the s· of Life and Love.
  of Mind
   g 510–27 Light is a s· of Mind, of Life, Truth, and
  of Soul
   gl 595– 1 Sun.   The s· of Soul governing man,
  of Truth
   gl 591–23 Morning.   Light ; s· of Truth ;

   f 240–15 Its s· is the sphere.
   g 503–23 creates no element nor s· of discord and decay.
   536– 6 as a s· of tempest-tossed human concepts
   gl 584–26 Dove.   A s· of divine Science ;
symbolized
   p 383–16 s·, and not chafed, by its surroundings ;
   g 512– 8 Spirit is s· by strength, presence, and
   515– 4 Patience is s· by the tireless worm,
symbolizes
   an 102–10 The pointing of the needle to the pole s· this
   b 274– 6 and s· all that is evil and perishable.
   g 507– 3 while *water* s· the elements of Mind.
   ap 561–22 woman in the Apocalypse s· generic
   561–25 The Revelator s· Spirit by the sun.
   563– 8 The great red dragon s· a lie,
symbols
   a 34–14 If all who seek . . . through material s·
   b 280– 2 S· and elements of discord and decay are
   282– 5 are figured by two geometrical s·,
   g 502–15 take on higher s· and significations,
   ap 575–14 Spiritual teaching must always be by s·.
symmetrical
   s 160–25 If muscles can . . . be deformed or s·,
sympathetically
   p 365– 1 s· know the thorns they plant in the

sympathies
   m 59–12 their s· should blend in sweet confidence
sympathy
   a 21–25 Being in s· with matter,
   m 64–15 the ready aid her s· and charity would afford.
   s 153–32 Neither s· nor society should ever tempt us to
   ph 171–23 No more s· exists between the flesh and
   f 211–21 S· with error should disappear.
   254–25 and are in s· with error,
   c 266– 8 solitary, left without s· ;
   p 366–12 The physician who lacks s· for his
symphonies
   f 213–21 rapture of his grandest s· was never heard.
symptom
   p 413–24 noticing every s· of flatulency,
symptoms
  aggravation of
   s 156–14 to fear an aggravation of s· from
   ph 169– 3 Whenever an aggravation of s· has occurred
  alleviates the
   p 411–31 it alleviates the s· of every disease.
  all its
   s 159–31 belief produces disease and all its s·,
  approaching
   p 390–27 approaching s· of chronic or acute disease,
  bodily
   s 161–24 ordinary practitioner, examining bodily s·,
  certain
   p 396– 8 nor draw attention to certain s·
  complication of
   p 389–31 complication of s· connected with this belief.
  congestive
   p 384–18 congestive s· in the lungs, or hints of
  disease or its
   p 419–32 disease or its s· cannot change forms,
  general
   s 152–31 the general s·, the characteristic signs,
   p 412– 6 to meet the peculiar or general s· of the case
  mental
   s 156–32 Homœopathy takes mental s· largely into
  of disease
   s 153– 3 or changes one of the s· of disease.
   p 390–12 When the first s· of disease appear,
   398–17 are known to relieve the s· of disease.
  of evil
   p 540–11 when the s· of evil, illusion, are aggravated,
  of this disease
   s 154–12 Immediately the s· of this disease appeared,
  physical
   ph 194– 6 changes all the physical s·,
   p 422– 7 and certain moral and physical s· seem
   t 453–11 morbid moral or physical s·
  same
   p 422–23 and attended by the same s·.
  subdue the
   p 421–14 subdue the s· by removing the belief that
  such
   p 384–21 such s· are not apt to follow exposure ;
  type and
   p 418–20 and to whatever decides its type and s·.

   sp 79– 1 The act of describing disease— its s·,
   p 370–11 s·, which might be produced by
   370–13 drug which might cause the s·.
   421–23 and sometimes explain the s· and their cause
synagogue
   a 55–14 although it is again ruled out of the s·.
   p 398–10 To the s· ruler's daughter, whom they
synagogues
   a 31–30 "They shall put you out of the s· ;—*John* 16 : 2.
   s 132–15 thrust . . . the man who lived it out of their s·,
synonym
   b 333– 3 word *Christ* is not properly a s· for Jesus,
   r 468–21 Spirit, the s· of Mind, Soul, or God,
   482–10 Soul is properly the s· of Spirit,
   g 517– 1 word for *man* is used also as the s· of
   529–30 Adam, the s· for error,
synonymous
   sp 71– 7 Soul is s· with Spirit, God,
   s 127–12 These s· terms stand for
   b 333–10 The name is s· with Messiah,
   o 345– 1 Spirit and God are often regarded as s· terms ;
   r 465–11 *Question.*— Are these terms s·?
   ap 576–27 The term Lord, . . . is often s· with Jehovah,
syrups
   f 230–25 They are soothing s· to put children to sleep,
system
  action of the
   p 378– 9 no inflammatory nor torpid action of the s·.
   415– 6 quickens or impedes the action of the s·,
   t 447–15 The recuperative action of the s·,
  and rule
   g 547– 5 not one departs from the stated s· and rule.

system
any
r 483–25 but if any *s·* honors God,
Christian
s 150– 3 this Christian *s·* of healing disease.
developing in the
p 381– 6 or that some disease is developing in the *s·*,
discovery of the
pref viii–27 led her, . . . to the discovery of the *s·*
entire
p 371–31 Truth is an alterative in the entire *s·*,
every
b 279–22 Every *s·* of human philosophy, doctrine,
false
sp 99–21 not with the individual, but with the false *s·*.
first
g 529– 6 The first *s·* of suggestive obstetrics has
Graham
f 221– 2 adopted the Graham *s·* to cure dyspepsia.
her
pref viii– 1 her *s·* has been fully tested
human
(*see* human)
Jesus'
s 132–17 Jesus' *s·* of healing received no aid nor
material
s 133–22 It was a finite and material *s·*,
metaphysical
s 111–30 my metaphysical *s·* of treating disease
no other
b 338– 1 heals the sick and sinning as no other *s·* can.
of ceremonies
s 135–27 was not a creed, nor a *s·* of ceremonies,
of hygiene
ph 185– 6 No *s·* of hygiene but C. S. is purely mental.
of Mind-healing
t 460– 5 Our *s·* of Mind-healing rests on the
of religion
a 26–31 Christianity was no form or *s·* of religion
particular
s 112–10 some particular *s·* of human opinions.
pathological
t 464–21 In founding a pathological *s·* of Christianity,
reduced to a
s 146–31 Divine metaphysics is now reduced to a *s·*,
regulates the
p 420–19 and regulates the *s·*.
scientific
s 123–17 the scientific *s·* of divine healing.
t 464–29 a scientific *s·* of ethics.
solar
s 119–29 the movement of the solar *s·*,
121–25 so far as our solar *s·* is concerned,
122–30 mistake . . . regarding the solar *s·*.
r 493– 5 science . . . explains the solar *s·*
spiritual
ph 170– 4 neither a moral nor a spiritual *s·*.
stellar
s 121– 4 Copernicus mapped out the stellar *s·*,
stimulates the
p 394– 9 stimulates the *s·* to act in the direction which
this
s 111–31 Since then this *s·* has gradually gained ground,
147– 1 This *s·* enables the learner to demonstrate
g 546–28 resides in the good this *s·* accomplishes,

system
whole
p 422– 6 a great stir throughout his whole *s·*,
s 129–32 The sinner sees, in the *s·* taught in this
o 342–18 Shall it be denied that a *s·* which
g 546–27 The proof that the *s·* stated in this book
systematic
s 164– 5 "No *s·* or theoretical classification of
o 355–18 any *s·* healing power since the
t 443– 3 consistency of *s·* medical study,
461–31 *S·* teaching and the student's spiritual growth
systems
accepted
o 344–20 not included in the commonly accepted *s·* ;
educational
f 226–28 and from the educational *s·* of the Pharaohs,
false
g 549–22 false *s·*, which rely upon physics
human
s 164–12 But all human *s·* based on
ph 170–12 not only contradicts human *s·*, but
f 234–22 present codes of human *s·* disappoint
man-made
s 112–13 divine Science which eschews man-made *s·*,
ph 168–15 Because man-made *s·* insist that man
material
b 326–12 forsake the foundation of material *s·*,
p 394–18 fallacy of material *s·* in general,
medical
ph 166–29 conceded . . . by most of the medical *s·* ;
modern
s 126–27 nothing in ancient or in modern *s·* on which to
of ideas
f 209– 6 the central sun of its own *s·* of ideas,
of medicine
s 146– 5 governed more or less by our *s·* of medicine.
ph 185–13 as material as the prevailing *s·* of medicine.
o 344–26 Why support the popular *s·* of medicine,
of Mind
b 310–16 all things in the *s·* of Mind.
of physics
s 160– 3 *s·* of physics act against metaphysics,
of religion
m 67–30 *S·* of religion and medicine treat of
s 146– 4 Because our *s·* of religion are
old
s 142– 1 in less time than the old *s·*, . . . have required
other
s 129–20 and so are some other *s·*.
b 269–26 All other *s·* — systems based wholly or partly on
t 443–19 whatever other *s·* they fancy will afford relief.
religious
s 132–18 from other sanitary or religious *s·*,
semi-metaphysical
b 268–15 semi-metaphysical *s·* afford no substantial
269– 1 semi-metaphysical *s·* are one and all
such
s 146– 9 Such *s·* are barren of the vitality of
ph 185–11 Such theories and such *s·* of so-called mind-cure,
time-honored
pref vii–14 independent of doctrines and time-honored *s·*,
their
f 225–10 until it subscribes to their *s·* ;

b 269–26 *s·* based wholly or partly on knowledge gained
270–15 higher than the *s·* of their times ;

T

tabernacled
ap 576– 6 while yet he *t·* with mortals.
table
sp 80–20 not seem mysterious that mind, . . . can move a *t·*,
80–21 mind-power which moves both *t·* and hand.
s 129–31 small estimate of the pleasures of the *t·*.
135–19 "Can God furnish a *t·* in the— *Psal.* 78 : 19.
f 214–24 would spread their *t·* with cannibal tidbits
234– 6 with crumbs of comfort from Christ's *t·*,
p 362–14 on a couch with his head towards the *t·*
ap 578–13 prepareth a *t·* before me in the— *see Psal.* 23 : 5.
table-salt
s 153– 6 *Natrum muriaticum* (common *t·*)
table-setting
sp 80–28 table-tipping as certainly as *t·*,
tablet
f 227–29 and defaced the *t·* of your being.
table-tipping
sp 80–28 Mortal mind produces *t·* as certainly as

tail
ap 563–23 his *t·* drew the third part of the— *Rev.* 12 : 4.
taint
m 66–14 joys of Spirit, which have no *t·* of earth.
take
pr 1–13 before they *t·* form in words
15–19 We must resolve to *t·* up the cross,
a 21–23 if I *t·* up their line of travel,
29– 1 Christians must *t·* up arms against error
32–17 *T·*, eat ; this is my body.— *Matt.* 26 : 26.
34– 1 *t·* his cross, and leave all
34–14 *t·* up the cross, heal the sick,
37–21 May the Christians of to-day *t·* up the more
m 59–32 Separation never should *t·* place,
68–12 Be not in haste to *t·* the vow
sp 72– 2 of which corporeal sense can *t·* no cognizance.
75– 6 material senses could *t·* no cognizance of the
89–29 concluded . . . man had the right to *t·* it away.
an 105–16 When our laws eventually *t·* cognizance of
s 129–21 abandon pharmaceutics, and *t·* up ontology,
149–20 remarked . . . *t·* as little medicine as possible ;
150–16 to *t·* away the sins of the world.

take

s 155– 6	t· away the individual confidence in the drug,
159– 5	compelled by her physicians to t· it.
159–11	Is it skilful or scientific surgery to t· no heed
ph 165– *	T· *no thought for your life,— Matt.* 6 : 25.
167–22	not wise to t· a halting and half-way position
168– 7	you t· away from Mind,
170–16	"T· no thought for your life,— *Matt.* 6 : 25.
172–25	If . . . you t· away a portion of the man when
179–16	he will t· cold without his blanket,
180–12	nor t· the ground that all causation
187–27	If you t· away this erring mind,
191– 1	It can t· no cognizance of Mind.
193–17	I told him to rise, dress himself, and t· supper
f 201– 5	would be supreme in us and t· the lead in our
202–31	Common opinion admits that a man may t· cold
212–15	t· away this so-called mind instead of a piece of
220– 2	We hear it said : . . . I t· cold baths, in order to
220– 3	to overcome a predisposition to t· cold ;
228–20	"T· no thought for your life,"— *Matt.* 6 : 25.
239– 5	T· away wealth, fame, and social
241–14	T· away the spiritual signification of Scripture,
250–25	T· away the mortal mind, and matter has no
254–30	T· it up and bear it, for through it you win
c 255–13	mortals t· limited views of all things.
b 273– 3	The physical senses can t· no cognizance of God
294– 7	would t· away some quality and quantity of
328–23	they shall t· up serpents,— *Mark* 16 : 18.
o 355–10	true sense of Life and being t· possession
359– 5	will t· the same cases, and cures will follow.
p 362– *	*they shall t· up serpents ;— Mark* 16 : 18.
365– 8	"T· no thought for your life,"— *Matt.* 6 : 25.
376–12	never gave life and can never t· it away,
377– 2	convince him that matter cannot t· cold,
378–23	and t· the government into its own hands.
382–11	"T· no thought . . . for the— *Luke* 12 : 22.
383– 5	One says : "I t· good care of my body."
392– 9	is to t· antagonistic grounds against all that
392–23	will master you, whichever direction they t·.
393–10	T· possession of your body, and govern its
395–16	but is besought to t· the patient to Himself,
425– 6	t· up the leading points included
439– 8	commanding him to t· part in the homicide.
t 452–23	t· no risks in the policy of error.
458–14	the divine Mind is ready to t· the case.
459–11	for failing to t· the first step.
464– 9	could not t· her place, even if willing so to do.
r 479–13	T· away so-called mortal mind, which constitutes
479–15	matter can t· no cognizance of matter.
488–20	The corporeal senses can t· no cognizance of
497– 3	As adherents of Truth, we t· the inspired
g 502– 3	the crude forms of human thought t·
530– 8	"T· no thought for your life,— *Matt.* 6 : 25.
531–28	corporeal senses can t· no cognizance of Spirit.
537– 1	lest he put forth his hand, and t·— *Gen.* 3 : 22.
539– 6	as if . . . matter can both give and t· away.
542–18	"They that t· the sword— *Matt.* 26 : 52.
543–10	corporeal senses cannot t· cognizance of Spirit.
546–17	material senses can t· no cognizance of Spirit
548– 2	let him t· the water of life freely."— *Rev.* 22 : 17.
ap 559–15	"Go and t· the little book.— *Rev.* 10 : 8.
559–17	T· it, and eat it up ;— *Rev.* 10 : 9.
559–20	T· divine Science.
569–27	but how many periods of torture it may t·
572–28	are inadequate to t· in so wonderful a scene.
573–29	T· heart, dear sufferer, for this reality

taken

pr 9–15	There is a cross to be t· up before we
a 28– 4	If the Master had not t· a student
32–30	a sad supper t· at the close of day,—
sp 86–27	can all be t· from pictorial thought and
ph 177–30	as if the poison had been intentionally t·.
195– 3	he asked to be t· back to his dungeon,
f 245–22	she had t· no cognizance of passing time
p 371–14	adult must be t· out of his darkness,
382–30	the medicines I had t· only abandoned me to
383–12	A hint may be t· from the emigrant,
392– 5	broken moral law should be t· into account
400–13	before it has t· tangible shape in
420–23	erroneous belief, t· at its best, is not
436–25	compelled to let him be t· into custody,
t 459–10	Judge not . . . by the steps already t·,
r 470–19	Has God t· down His own standard,
g 528–13	and the rib, . . . t· from man,— *Gen.* 2 : 22.
529– 4	not woman again t· from man.
533–17	According to this belief, the rib t· from
535–27	for out of it wast thou t· :— *Gen.* 3 : 19.
537– 4	the ground from whence he was t·.— *Gen.* 3 : 23.
537–26	Literally (t·, the text is made to
542–18	vengeance shall be t· on him— *Gen.* 4 : 15.
ap 575–16	T· in its allegorical sense,

takes

sp 83–13	here Science t· issue with popular religions.
s 122–25	To . . . sense, the severance of the jugular vein t·

takes

s 143–15	t· the lesser to relieve the greater.
147–29	A pure affection t· form in goodness,
148–15	Anatomy t· up man at all points materially.
152– 4	Mind t· away all its supposed sovereignty,
156–31	Mind t· its rightful and supreme place.
156–32	Homœopathy t· mental symptoms largely into
ph 170–32	which t· divine power into its own hands
c 256– 1	Progress t· off human shackles.
262– 6	C. S. t· naught from the perfection of
b 323–26	t· away all sin and the delusion that
o 347–23	If C. S. t· away the popular gods,
350– 5	C. S. t· exactly the opposite view.
p 383– 8	t· the best care of his body when he
424– 3	t· possession of itself and its own thoughts
429– 7	The final demonstration t· time
431–25	Another witness t· the stand and testifies :
432–20	Another witness t· the stand and testifies :
t 463–17	When this new birth t· place,
r 492–19	if it t· all summer."
493–22	t· away this physical sense of discord,
g 522–18	In this erroneous theory, matter t· the
541– 1	Abel t· his offering from the firstlings of the
549– 3	t· place apart from sexual conditions.
557–22	Popular theology t· up the history of man
ap 571–31	He t· away mitre and sceptre.
574– 3	The Revelator also t· in another view,
gl 591–14	that of which immortal Mind t· no cognizance ;

taketh

a 23–12	"He that t· one doctrine, firm in faith,
s 131–23	which t· away the ceremonies and doctrines

taking

m 62–13	T· less "thought for your life,— *Matt.* 6 : 25.
s 156–21	was relieved by t· them.
156–24	t· the unmedicated pellets,
ph 175– 1	prevent the images of disease from t· form
176– 7	primitive custom of t· no thought about food
179– 3	this can be done only by t· up the cross
f 206–20	and then t· it away by death?
222–14	T· less thought about what he should eat
245– 8	t· no note of years,
b 296–29	and aids in t· the next step
334–18	t· away the sins of the world,
p 377– 1	If your patient believes in t· cold,
413–13	t· a fish out of water every day
g 504–17	t· place on so many *evenings* and *mornings,*
511–27	t· form in masculine, feminine, or
gl 585–18	metaphysics t· the place of physics ;

talent

b 323–18	but the one unused t· decays and is lost.
p 366–32	we must not hide the t· of spiritual healing

talents

pr 6– 6	The t· He gives we must improve.

talk

ph 175–20	coddling, and sickly after-dinner t·.
f 211– 1	if they t· to us, tell us their condition,
217–32	Do the muscles t·, or do you t· for them?
p 391–20	Since matter cannnot t·, it must be mortal mind
399–14	Nerves are unable to t·,
t 448–30	To t· the right and live the wrong is foolish

talked

a 45–13	Three days after his bodily burial he t· with
m 62– 9	fed, rocked, tossed, or t· to,
b 308–15	heard the voice of Truth, and t· with God
ap 574– 7	t· with me, saying, Come hither,— *Rev.* 21 : 9.

talker

ap 567–25	and therefore, in his pretence of being a t·,

talking

f 218– 1	Mortal mind does the false t·,
p 396– 5	Avoid t· illness to the patient.
t 452–25	by right t· and wrong acting,
g 529–21	Whence comes a t·, lying serpent
529–25	the species described,— a t· serpent,
ap 564–31	this allegorical, t· serpent typifies

talks

sp 89– 8	believing that . . . she t· freely.
b 308–15	as consciously as man t· with man.

tall

pref vii–24	task of the sturdy pioneer to hew the t· oak
sp 87–21	of the t· ships that float on its bosom,

tangible

sp 75– 5	would need to be t· and material,
78–21	Spirit is not materially t·.
b 269–17	These ideas are perfectly real and t·
279–11	Ideas are t· and real to
317–16	is no less t· because it is spiritual
p 400–13	before it has taken t· shape in

tangled

ph 195–23	It is the t· barbarisms of learning which
g 507–10	strangers in a t· wilderness.

tapping
s 156– 6 *T·* had been employed,

tares
sp 72–15 the *t·* and the wheat, which are not united
f 207–19 separates the *t·* and wheat in time of harvest.
b 300–17 These opposite qualities are the *t·* and wheat,
300–20 Science separates the wheat from the *t·*,
g 535– 4 the wheat and *t·* which time will separate,
gl 595– 5 definition of

tarry
b 299–16 they *t·* with us, and we entertain
329–14 One should not *t·* in the storm if the body is

tarsal
p 408–22 A dislocation of the *t·* joint would produce
408–24 mortal mind thinks that the *t·* joint is

Tarsus
b 326–23 Saul of *T·* beheld the way— the Christ,

task
appointed
c 261–14 go upon the stage and sustain his appointed *t·*,
difficult
f 225–25 abolition of mental slavery is a more difficult *t·*.
no
b 318– 1 For him to believe in matter was no *t·*,
t 450–12 To teach C. S. to such as these is no *t·*.
not a difficult
p 396–15 is not a difficult *t·* in view of the conceded
our
pr 3– 7 and it is our *t·* to work out the solution.
pleasurable
g 506–28 Upon Adam devolved the pleasurable *t·* of
quiet
ap 567– 1 Gabriel has the more quiet *t·* of
this
f 254–20 This *t·* God demands us to accept lovingly
p 400–15 This *t·* becomes easy, if you understand that
t 462–16 There is nothing difficult nor toilsome in this *t·*,

pref vii–23 It is the *t·* of the sturdy pioneer to hew the
s 163–30 is indeed a *t·* as impracticable as to arrange
t 452– 2 a *t·* not difficult, when one understands
g 506– 1 apportion to themselves a *t·* impossible

tasks
b 323– 9 Beholding the infinite *t·* of truth,

taste
b 284–23 nor can they feel, *t·*, or smell Spirit.
r 479–11 Matter cannot see, feel, hear, *t·*,
g 526–10 material hearing, sight, touch, *t·*, and smell,
ap 559–22 It will be indeed sweet at its first *t·*,

tasted
c 263–10 and cling to earth because he has not *t·* heaven.

tastes
m 60– 4 Kindred *t·*, motives, and aspirations are
ph 195–27 fill our young readers with wrong *t·* and
gl 591–15 feels, hears, *t·*, and smells only in belief.

tasteth
s 115– 9 as the mouth *t·* meat.''— Job 34 : 3.

tatters
f 201–16 we shall not hug our *t·* close about us.

tattling
s 153–30 and we shall avoid loquacious *t·*

taught
pref xii– 7 were *t·* by the author in this College.
pr 16– 7 Our Master *t·* his disciples one brief prayer,
a 18– 3 Jesus of Nazareth *t·* and demonstrated man's
20–17 he *t·* mortals the opposite of themselves,
25–13 Jesus *t·* the way of Life by demonstration,
26–28 Our Master *t·* no mere theory, doctrine,
26–30 the divine Principle of all real being which he *t·*
28– 5 and *t·* the unseen verities of God,
30–14 Rabbi and priest *t·* the Mosaic law,
30–32 must work out our salvation in the way Jesus *t·*.
31–12 he *t·* his followers the healing power
34–20 understood better what the Master had *t·*.
38–31 He *t·* that the material senses shut out Truth
41–20 ever *t·* or demonstrated the divine healing
41–28 The truth *t·* by Jesus, the elders scoffed at.
42–28 Jesus had *t·* his disciples the Science of this
43–17 final demonstration of the truth which Jesus *t·*,
43–28 The Science Jesus *t·* and lived must triumph
45–23 and beheld the final proof of all that he had *t·*,
46– 4 the truthfulness of all that he had *t·*.
51–21 the works which he did and *t·* others to do.
m 64– 3 in the direction *t·* by the Apostle James,
sp 94– 1 Jesus *t·* but one God, one Spirit,
s 107– * neither was I *t·* it,— Gal. 1 : 12.
110–18 No human pen nor tongue *t·* me the Science
110–28 spiritually discerned, *t·*, and demonstrated
117–15 Our Master *t·* spirituality by similitudes
129–32 The sinner sees, in the system *t·* in this book,
133–26 who *t·* as he was inspired by the Father
135–26 Christianity as Jesus *t·* it was not a creed,

taught
s 136– 2 He *t·* his followers that his religion
147–25 and *t·* the generalities of its divine Principle
156–28 Metaphysics, as *t·* in C. S., is the next
ph 180– 3 it should be *t·* to do the body no harm
180–29 as *t·* and demonstrated by Christ Jesus.
195– 2 After the babbling boy had been *t·* to speak
f 227– 5 and mortals are *t·* their right to freedom,
232–19 Jesus never *t·* that drugs,
237–15 should be *t·* the Truth-cure,
b 294–16 *t·*, as they are by physiology and pathology,
300–27 is *t·* by the schools.
306– 5 Jesus *t·* them how death was to be overcome
310–18 We are commonly *t·* that there is a
319–21 *t·* in the original language of the Bible
321–32 *t·* them how to handle serpents unharmed,
329– 3 they will be sought and *t·*,
333–11 which is *t·*, illustrated, and demonstrated
o 343– 1 The people are *t·* in such cases to say, Amen.
359– 1 whom they have seen and have been *t·* to love
p 379–19 the opposite statement of Life as *t·* in C. S.,
440– 6 is *t·* how to make sleep befool reason
t 449–30 if the student practises what he is *t·*,
455–26 if he is *t·* of God to discern it.
461– 8 C. S. can be *t·* only by those who are
463– 6 familiar with the obstetrics *t·* by this Science.
r 473–28 He proved what he *t·*.
477– 4 Jesus *t·* that the kingdom of God is intact,
ap 560–30 was to be ignorant of the divine idea he *t·*.
575–15 Did not Jesus illustrate the truths he *t·*

tea
sp 80– 3 A cup of coffee or *t·* is not the equal of truth,
p 406–29 alcoholic drinks, tobacco, *t·*, coffee, opium,

teach
pref viii– 9 Theology and physics *t·* that both Spirit and
a 28– 1 The Pharisees claimed to know and to *t·* the
m 60–27 and *t·* us life's sweeter harmonies.
66– 6 Trials *t·* mortals not to lean on a material
69–23 the child may ask, ''Do you *t·* that
sp 81–15 when alleged spirits *t·* immortality.
s 139–12 will *t·* men patiently and wisely to stem the
f 235–24 physicians should be able to *t·* it.
236–23 Parents should *t·* their children at the earliest
240– 7 Suns and planets *t·* grand lessons.
b 271–21 shall *t·* you all things.''— John 14 : 26.
283–29 than we can *t·* and illustrate geometry by
p 382–16 than is the devotee . . . who comes to *t·* the
382–26 but for the glorious Principle you *t·*,
416–32 *T·* them that their being is sustained by Spirit,
t 443– * *t·* a just man, and he will—* Prov. 9 : 9.
445– 9 *T·* the great possibilities of man endued with
445–10 *T·* the dangerous possibility of
445–13 *T·* the meekness and might of life
449–13 registers his healing ability and fitness to *t·*.
449–16 to *t·* this subject properly and correctly
450–11 To *t·* C. S. to such as these is no task.
453–14 *T·* your student that he must know himself
454– 4 *T·* your students the omnipotence of Truth,
455– 8 in order to *t·* this Science of healing.
g 540–23 is to *t·* mortals never to believe a lie.

Teacher
faith in the
a 25–27 faith in the *T·* and all the emotional love
great
a 20–20 the scourge and the cross awaited the great *T·*.
25–23 the great *T·* by no means relieved others from
33–19 our great *T·* said : ''Not my will,— Luke 22 : 42.
m 56– 1 When our great *T·* came to him for baptism,
sp 85–30 The great *T·* knew both cause and effect,
p 441–31 Our great *T·* of mental jurisprudence
immaculate
s 137– 5 when their immaculate *T·* stood before them,
new
s 136–28 No wonder Herod desired to see the new *T·*.

teacher
and student
t 457– 5 this book has done more for *t·* and student,
463– 5 *T·* and student should also be familiar with
human
t 455–18 student, who receives . . . from a human *t·*,
inspired
b 319–27 wrote down what an inspired *t·* had said.
of Christian Science
t 449–28 A proper *t·* of C. S. improves the health and
sole
pref viii–30 for the Bible was her sole *t·* ;
thoughts of the
f 235–14 The pure and uplifting thoughts of the *t·*,

s 162–31 the famous Philadelphia *t·* of medical practice.
t 444–31 The *t·* must make clear to students the
445– 2 *t·* must thoroughly fit his students
449–31 the *t·* is a Scientist only in name.
451–19 every conscientious *t·* of the Science of
452–18 The *t·* must know the truth himself.

teachers

f	227–10	some public *t·* permit an ignorance of
	235– 7	The *t·* of schools and the

teaches

pr	10–22	Experience *t·* us that we do not always
	16–18	C. S. *t·* us that "the evil one,"
a	26–20	demonstrates the beauty of the music he *t·*
	29– 7	Christian experience *t·* faith in the right
m	67– 3	and learn the lessons He *t·*?
sp	79–29	Mind-science *t·* that mortals
	99–14	C. S. *t·* only that which is spiritual
s	127–19	It *t·* that matter is the falsity,
ph	169–29	Whatever *t·* man to have other laws
f	241–13	Bible *t·* transformation of the body by the
c	266–16	Thus He *t·* mortals to lay down their
b	295–28	Brainology *t·* that mortals are created to suffer
	295–30	It further *t·* that when man is dead,
	309–23	led to deny material sense, . . . as the gospel *t·*.
	326– 8	All nature *t·* God's love to man,
	337–16	pure in heart can see God, as the gospel *t·*.
o	346– 6	It is sometimes said that C. S. *t·*
	346– 7	and then *t·* how this nothingness is to be
	354– 8	it *t·* precisely this thought
	357–17	History *t·* that the popular and
t	446–11	Whoever practises the Science the author *t·*,
	450– 3	Their creed *t·* belief in a mysterious,
	462–26	The anatomy of C. S. *t·* when and how to probe
	462–28	It *t·* the control of mad ambition.
r	472– 1	This Science *t·* man that God is the only Life,
g	542–23	*t·* mortals not to remove the waymarks of God.

teaching

and demonstration

b	270–18	nature of the *t·* and demonstration of God,

and practice

a	26–21	Jesus' *t·* and practice of Truth involved
r	473–19	Jesus introduced the *t·* and practice of

became clearer

t	460–31	the *t·* became clearer, until finally

contradicts the

g	526– 7	contradicts the *t·* of the first chapter,

easier than

p	373–12	Healing is easier than *t·*, if the

healing and

o	349– 5	ask concerning our healing and *t·*,
t	454–18	the true incentive in both healing and *t·*.
	455–32	in the Science of mental healing and *t·*,
	458–29	through living as well as healing and *t·*,

his

a	19–14	although his *t·* set households at variance,
	54– 8	Who is ready to follow his *t·*

in its

s	112– 5	can, therefore, be but one method in its *t·*.

involves

r	493–14	full answer to the above question involves *t·*,

or practising

o	342–29	If Christian Scientists were *t·* or practising
t	456– 3	*T·* or practising in the name of Truth,

spiritual

ap	575–13	Spiritual *t·* must always be by symbols.
gl	595–16	alone can fit us for the office of spiritual *t·*.

systematic

t	461–31	Systematic *t·* and the student's spiritual

this

a	38– 4	This *t·* is even more pernicious
ph	192–18	this *t·* accords with Science and harmony.
p	371–24	because this *t·* is in advance of the age,
	410–13	mankind objects to making this *t·* practical.
r	488– 5	the cure shows that you understand this *t·*,

pr	6–26	He came *t·* and showing men how to
s	114–16	as the phrase is used in *t·* C. S.,
	137– 1	*t·* and demonstrating the truth of being.
ph	172–30	*t·* us by his very deprivations, that
o	343– 2	for *t·* Truth as the Principle of healing,
	348–30	this I do aver, that, as a result of *t·* C. S.,
p	373–12	if the *t·* is faithfully done.
	396–20	all *t·* that the body suffers,
t	445–24	danger in *t·* Mind-healing indiscriminately,
	446– 1	*t·* his slight knowledge of Mind-power,
	460–25	while *t·* its grand facts,

teachings

and demonstrations

a	47– 2	discernment of Jesus' *t·* and demonstrations,
s	126–27	except the *t·* and demonstrations of

and practice

a	19–25	of the *t·* and practice of our Master

Christ's

sp	98–27	Mystery does not enshroud Christ's *t·*,
f	236– 9	individuals, who reiterate Christ's *t·*

her

pref	x–17	have proved the worth of her *t·*.

his

o	343–14	when his *t·* are fully understood.
r	473–32	his *t·* and their glorious proofs,

34

teachings

Jesus'

a	19– 8	the divine Principle of Jesus' *t·*,
	47– 2	discernment of Jesus' *t·* and demonstrations,
	47–15	the people were in doubt concerning Jesus' *t·*.
	50–22	Even what they did say, — that Jesus' *t·* were

of Christian Science

o	355–20	The statement that the *t·* of C. S.
t	444–23	medical schools turn a deaf ear to the *t·* of C. S.,
	448–26	adheres strictly to the *t·* of C. S.
g	502–19	according to the *t·* of C. S.

of divine Science

o	349–13	in conveying the *t·* of divine Science

of Jesus

b	269–23	plant myself unreservedly on the *t·* of Jesus,
	324–23	to follow the example and *t·* of Jesus,

of natural science

r	478– 4	Even according to the *t·* of natural science,

of the Comforter

s	123–22	and through the *t·* of the Comforter,

of the schools

p	429–29	not included in the *t·* of the schools,

ordinary

sp	99–13	The ordinary *t·* are material

result of our

r	488– 2	result of our *t·* is their sufficient confirmation.

spiritual

b	272–15	the spiritual *t·* which dulness and

Truth's

t	462– 9	goes away to practise Truth's *t·* only in part,

tear

f	211–14	When a *t·* starts, does not this so-called mind
	211–16	Without mortal mind, the *t·* could not appear;

tears (noun)

p	363–27	She bathed his feet with her *t·*
	367–15	with *t·* of repentance and with
ap	573–31	no more pain, and all *t·* will be wiped away.

tears (verb)

b	273–11	thus *t·* away the foundations of error.

teaspoonful

s	153– 9	and a *t·* of the water administered at

tedious

t	460–20	it becomes a *t·* mischief-maker.

teeming

g	513– 6	in the *t·* universe of Mind

teeth

f	211–20	children's *t·* are set on edge." — *Ezek.* 18 : 2.
	247– 4	two of the elements that had lost, sight and *t·*.
	247– 6	Another woman at ninety had new *t·*,
	247– 8	his full set of upper and lower *t·*

telegraphy

f	243–22	Neither . . . can carry on such *t·*;
p	399–13	both the service and message of this *t·*.

tell

pr	13–15	God knows our need before we *t·* Him
a	27– 3	*t·* John what things ye have seen — *Luke* 7 : 22.
	27– 7	*T·* John what the demonstration of divine
sp	78–28	cannot "*t·* whence it cometh." — *John* 3 : 8.
	89– 1	who can *t·* what the unaided medium
an	106–24	of the which I *t·* you before, — *Gal.* 5 : 21.
s	142–15	In vain do the manger and the cross *t·* their
ph	174–12	the spiritual intuitions that *t·* us when
f	211– 2	if they talk to us, *t·* us their condition,
b	308–32	"*T·* me, I pray thee, *thy* name;" — *Gen.* 32 : 29.
o	341– *	*And because I t· you the truth,* — *John* 8 : 45.
	352–32	not irrational to *t·* the truth about ghosts.
p	394–23	Will you *t·* the sick that their condition is
	416–10	will *t·* you that the troublesome material cause
	416–27	*t·* them only what is best for them to know.
	417– 6	Never *t·* the sick that they have more courage than
	417– 7	*T·* them rather, that their strength is
	420–24	*T·* the sick that they can meet disease
	420–29	vehemently *t·* your patient that he must awake.
	420–32	*T·* that he suffers only as the insane suffer,
	424–31	The patient may *t·* you that he has a humor in
t	448– 9	When needed *t·* the truth concerning
	453–25	you must not *t·* the patient that he is sick
	461–17	you should *t·* your belief sometimes,
ap	571– 6	people like you better when you *t·* them their
	571– 7	than when you *t·* them their vices.
	571– 8	to *t·* a man his faults, and so risk

telling

s	161–25	examining bodily symptoms, *t·* the patient that
p	371– 2	by *t·* ghost-stories in the dark.
ap	571–10	Who is *t·* mankind of the foe in ambush?

tells

sp	91– 1	*t·* us of "a new heaven — *Rev.* 21 : 1.
p	383–22	sometimes *t·* you that the weed preserves his

temperance

an 106–28   goodness, faith, meekness, *t·* :— *Gal.* 5 : 22, 23.
s 115–27   compassion, hope, faith, meekness, *t·*.
o 348–31   ethics and *t·* have received an impulse,
p 404–17   The *t·* reform, felt all over our land,

temperate

b 322–25   is neither a *t·* man nor a reliable religionist.

temperature

s 152–17   to ascertain the *t·* of the patient's body ;
p 413– 8   the *t·* of children and of men,

temperatures

p 386– 5   Expose the body to certain *t·*,

tempest

s 134–28   stilled the *t·*, healed the sick,
b 327–16   to clamor with midnight and *t·*.

tempest's

ph 192–14   the devouring flame, the *t·* breath.

tempest-tossed

g 536– 6   as a symbol of *t·* human concepts

temple

also means body
  ap 576–14   The word *t·* also means *body.*
destroy this
  a 27–12   "Destroy this *t·*— *John* 2 : 19.
  b 314–14   "Destroy this *t·*,— *John* 2 : 19.
  r 494– 2   "Destroy this *t·*— *John* 2 : 19.
material
  b 314–16   their material *t·* instead of his body.
no
  ap 576–10   And I saw no *t·* therein :— *Rev.* 21 : 22.
  576–12   There was no *t·*,— that is, no material
  576–20   with "no *t·* [body] therein"— *Rev.* 21 : 22.
of Christian Science
  b 288–20   The chief stones in the *t·* of C. S.
of the Holy Ghost
  p 365–13   *t·* of the Holy Ghost,— the patient's spiritual
or body
  p 428–13   Thus we may establish in truth the *t·*, or body,
veil of the
  gl 597–11   It rent the veil of the *t·*.

  s 142–19   need to be whipped out of the *t·*,
  ap 576–11   and the Lamb are the *t·* of it.— *Rev.* 21 : 22.
  576–17   spoke of his material body as the *t·*
  gl 595– 7   definition of

temples

s 142–22   to purge the *t·* of their vain traffic

temporal

a 51–12   Jesus could give his *t·* life into his
s 122–27   *T·* life is a false sense of existence.
ph 190–17   This mortal seeming is *t·* ;
b 274– 4   knowledge gained from the five senses is only *t·*,
  277–30   for matter is *t·* and is therefore a
  286–22   Material and *t·* thoughts are human,
  286–25   The *t·* and material are not then creations of
  287– 3   but belong, with all that is material and *t·*,
  289– 2   the *t· débris* of error, belief in sin,
  300–13   The *t·* and unreal never touch the
  301– 9   involves error and therefore is material, *t·*.
  302– 3   The material body and mind are *t·*,
  335–14   Things material and *t·* are insubstantial.
  336– 5   never . . . the eternal into the *t·*,
  337–26   *T·* things are the thoughts of mortals
o 360–16   This ideal is either *t·* or eternal.
p 412–24   and that sickness is a *t·* dream.
r 468–13   matter is the unreal and *t·*.
g 538–27   This account is . . . of sin which is *t·*.
ap 569–25   Scriptures declare that evil is *t·*,

temporarily

s 110–22   and its ideas may be *t·* abused
p 397–29   the belief that mind is, even *t·*, compressed
  415–15   They only render mortal mind *t·* less fearful,
r 483– 3   they do not heal, but only relieve suffering *t·*,
ap 576–17   the temple to be *t·* rebuilt

temporary

f 213–15   towards the finite, *t·*, and discordant.
b 282–11   a belief in a . . . *t·* material existence
  282–12   Eternal Mind and *t·* material existence
  298– 9   a mortal *t·* sense of things,
  311–16   a sense of *t·* loss or absence of soul,
  318–26   Material methods are *t·*,
p 442–23   Christ, Truth, gives mortals *t·* food
t 444–10   right use of *t·* and eternal means.
g 522–16   this state of things is declared to be *t·*

tempt

s 153–32   Neither sympathy nor society should ever *t·*
s 529–21   Whence comes a talking, lying serpent to *t·*

temptation

bids us repeat
  pr 5– 7   *T·* bids us repeat the offence,
deliver us from
  a 22–21   Love is not hasty to deliver us from *t·*,

temptation

may lead us into
  pr 7–27   danger . . . that it may lead us into *t·*.
not into
  pr 17– 8   And lead us not into *t·*,— *Matt.* 6 : 13.
  17–10   *And God leadeth us not into t·,*
resist the
  f 218–25   Resist the *t·* to believe in
sinful
  p 381– 6   than you are to yield to a sinful *t·*
to sin
  p 420–13   as positively as they can the *t·* to sin.

  a 42–22   *t·*, sin, sickness, and death had no terror
  s 158–19   It is pitiful to lead men into *t·*
  c 267–29   the man that endureth . . . *t·* :— *Jas.* 1 : 12
  p 387–31   not only from *t·*, but from bodily suffering.
  441– 8   to keep perpetual silence, and in case of *t·*,
  t 450–22   Sickness to him is no less a *t·* than is sin.
  gl 581–13   The ark indicates *t·* overcome
  598–18   Error ; fornication ; *t·* ; passion.

tempted

p 393–31   false belief is both the tempter and the *t·*,
g 527–13   "God cannot be *t·* with evil,— *Jas.* 1 : 13.
ap 564–15   Since Jesus must have been *t·* in all points,

tempter

p 393–30   false belief is both the *t·* and the tempted,

tempteth

g 527–13   neither *t·* He any man."— *Jas.* 1 : 13.

tempting

g 527–11   represents God, Love, as *t·* man,

tempts

r 495–14   When the illusion of sickness or sin *t·* you,

Ten

b 280–18   declared as Jehovah's first command of the *T·* :
ap 563–13   belief that . . . the *T·* Commandments can be

ten

sp 94–20   Of the *t·* lepers whom Jesus healed,
ph 193–13   In about *t·* minutes he opened his eyes
f 246–22   would enjoy more than threescore years and *t·*
p 421–32   of eight multiplied by five, and of seven by *t·*,
ap 562–31   having seven heads and *t·* horns,— *Rev.* 12 : 3.
  563–11   The *t·* horns of the dragon typify the

tenacious

s 144–12   the more obstinately *t·* its error ;

tenaciously

o 348–21   Instead of *t·* defending the supposed

tenacity

sp 77–18   according to the *t·* of error.
b 296–21   depends upon the *t·* of error.
p 396–18   on account of the *t·* of belief in its truth,

tend

ph 196– 8   false pleasures which *t·* to perpetuate this
p 419– 4   Errors of all sorts *t·* in this direction.
g 542–11   avoidance of justice and the denial of truth *t·* to

tendencies

f 225–25   despotic *t·*, inherent in mortal mind
b 272–22   in contrast with the downward *t·* and

tendency

a 40– 4   devout Christian, perceiving the scope and *t·* of
m 60–20   is not its present *t·*, and why?
sp 78–15   gathered from ignorance are pernicious in *t·*.
s 111–21   an essay calculated to offset the *t·* of the·
  112–14   wholly human in their origin and *t·*
f 213–12   and is a *t·* towards God, Spirit.
p 423– 5   the *t·* towards a favorable result.
ap 570– 4   The present apathy as to the *t·* of

tender

pr 3–14   is not the image and likeness of the patient, *t·*,
m 57–11   should be loving, pure, *t·*, and strong.
  59– 3   There should be the most *t·* solicitude for
  59–17   *T·* words and unselfish care in what
b 332– 5   His *t·* relationship to His spiritual creation.
p 367– 3   The *t·* word and Christian encouragement of
fr 600– *   *whether the t· grape appear,*— *Song* 7 : 12.

tenderly

g 507– 5   *t·* expressing the fatherhood and

tenderness

p 434–17   regards the prisoner with the utmost *t·*.
g 514–18   *T·* accompanies all the might imparted by

tending

g 545– 9   by thought *t·* spiritually upward

tends

pr 2–16   but it *t·* to bring us into harmony
sp 79– 3   *t·* to frighten into death those who are ignorant
  92–27   This belief *t·* to support two opposite powers,
  93–30   This belief *t·* to becloud our apprehension of
p 370–21   physical diagnosis . . . . *t·* to induce disease.
  405–25   *t·* to destroy the ability to do right.

tends
p 430–10 t' to shut out the true sense of Life
t 443– 6 t' to deter those, who make such a
451–31 t' to blast moral sense, health, and

tenets
r 497– 1 important points, or religious t', of C. S. :

Tennyson
sp 88– 2 the poet T' expressed the heart's desire,

Tennyson's
ph 194–26 and realizing T' description :

tenor
p 427–20 The t' of the Word shows that we shall obtain

tension
p 393–22 Your body would suffer no more from t'

tentative
p 422–32 His treatment is therefore t'.

tenth
ap 558– 1 in the t' chapter of his book of Revelation :
gl 595–22 TITHE. Contribution ; t' part ; homage ;

term
class
t 454–25 at the close of a class t',
double
gl 590–21 This double t' is not used in the first chapter
for God
b 286–16 In the Saxon . . . good is the t' for God.
generic
c 259– 1 to comprehend in Science the generic t' man.
r 475–15 the generic t' for all that reflects God's
g 516–30 It follows that man is a generic t'.
gods
r 466–19 is as improper as the t' gods.
Lord
ap 576–26 The t' Lord, as used in our version
man
g 525– 7 some of the equivalents of the t' man
obsolete
gl 588–22 A t' obsolete in Science if used with
recent
p 402–23 mesmerism— or hypnotism, to use the recent t'
souls
r 466–19 The t' souls or spirits is as improper as
specific
an 103–19 the specific t' for error, or mortal mind.
this
s 114– 4 meaning by this t' the flesh opposed to Spirit,
gl 590–15 this t' is sometimes employed as a title,

s 116–27 If the t' personality, as applied to God,
117– 1 The t' individuality is also open to objections,
123–16 The t' C. S. was introduced by the author
127–15 the t' C. S. relates especially to
128– 4 The t' Science, properly understood,
b 274–11 what we erroneously t' the five physical senses
278–28 All that we t' sin, sickness, and death
311– 3 What we t' mortal mind or
313– 1 The t' Christ Jesus, or Jesus the Christ
p 401–16 What I t' chemicalization is the upheaval
r 496–30 if by that t' is meant doctrinal beliefs.
gl 597–25 the t' as applied to Mind or to one of God's

termed
sp 91–20 or through what are t' the material senses.
92– 8 decomposition of mortal bodies in what is t' death.
s 114–29 what is t' matter is but the subjective state
114–30 of what is t' by the author mortal mind.
149–23 has cured what is t' organic disease
ph 173–11 What is t' matter manifests nothing but
177– 1 produces what is t' organic disease
177–21 qualities and effects of what is t' matter,
179–22 sustained by what is t' material law,
182– 6 what are t' laws of nature, appertain to matter.
184–25 what is t' a fatally broken physical law.
188– 3 What is t' disease does not exist.
f 210–15 What is t' matter, being unintelligent,
b 290– 4 before what is t' death overtakes mortals,
298– 8 What is t' material sense can report only a
p 377–16 caused what is t' instantaneous death.
377–24 what are t' organic diseases as readily as
382–13 He, who is ignorant of what is t' hygienic law,
384– 1 Can matter, or what is t' matter, either feel or
392–20 in the form of what is t' pulmonary disease,
409–12 substratum of mortal mind, t' the body,
417–12 what is t' matter cannot be sick ;
r 469– 2 What is t' matter is unknown to Spirit,
484–11 What are t' natural science and material laws
g 526–10 material hearing, sight, . . . t' the five senses.
gl 580–16 the opposer of Truth, t' error ;
582–25 the testimony of what is t' material sense ;
584–23 the opposite of mind, t' matter,
594– 6 opposite of Spirit, or good, t' matter, or evil ;
595–20 continues after, what is t' death, until

terminates
b 338– 7 t' in discord and mortality,

terms
Bible
gl 579– 5 the metaphysical interpretation of Bible t',
communicable
sp 74– 3 To be on communicable t' with Spirit,
contradiction of
c 257–32 infinite form involves a contradiction of t'.
dictate
p 409–10 cannot dictate t' to consciousness
dictate its
f 228–23 dictate its t', and form and control it with
different
s 161–32 different t' than does the metaphysician ;
friendly
p 438–31 to be on friendly t' with the firm of
implied by the
sp 94– 5 includes all that is implied by the t'
intimate
p 437– 2 he was on intimate t' with the plaintiff,
material
s 115– 3 the inadequacy of material t'
115–10 when translating material t' back into
o 349–17 one is obliged to use material t'
349–25 material t' must be generally employed.
of forgiveness
pr 11– 2 specified also the t' of forgiveness.
pairs of
r 466– 1 but these contrasting pairs of t'
synonymous
s 127–13 These synonymous t' stand for
o 345– 2 are often regarded as synonymous t' ;
r 465–11 Question.— Are these t' synonymous?
your own
p 391–27 Therefore make your own t' with sickness,

sp 73– 5 but another, . . . it t' a spirit
s 127– 9 The t' Divine Science, Spiritual Science,
ap 573–10 what the human mind t' matter

terrestrial
s 123– 3 the greater error as to our t' bodies.
ap 572–29 Were this new heaven and new earth t' or

terrible
a 50–26 The burden of that hour was t'
s 156– 6 It was a t' case.
ph 188– 5 belief of sin, which has grown t' in strength
b 289–11 To suppose that . . . is a t' mistake.
p 407– 2 inconceivably t' to man's self-respect.
437–17 the t' records of your Court of Error,
r 486–30 would place man in a t' situation,

terrified
p 366–25 The sick are t' by their sick beliefs,

terrify
p 380–17 Gazing at a chained lion, . . . should not t' a

terrifying
p 376– 1 more t' than that of most other diseases.

terror
a 42–23 sin, sickness, and death had no t' for Jesus.
o 346–21 If a dream ceases, . . . the t' is over.
352–28 t' of ghosts will depart
p 378–16 often causes the beast to retreat in t'.

terrors
b 289–15 proves the "king of t'" to be but a— Job. 18 : 14.

test
pr 5– 5 the t' of our sincerity,— namely, reformation.
9– 5 The t' of all prayer lies in the answer to
a 42–30 to t' his still uncomprehended saying,
s 147– 8 submitted to the broadest practical t',
f 204–19 They can never stand the t' of Science.
o 344–15 until the enemies of C. S. t' its efficacy
r 473–21 and to t' its unerring Science according to his
493–30 Who dares to doubt this consummate t'

Testament (see also Old and New Testament)
b 313–14 is, in the Greek T', character.

tested
pref viii– 2 her system has been fully t'
an 101–10 which t' during several sessions the

testified
a 52– 7 their senses t' oppositely,
s 134– 5 those who t' for Truth were so often persecuted
159– 3 her sister t' that the deceased protested
p 388– 7 Apostle John t' to the divine basis of C. S.,
436–35 t' that he was a ruler of Body,
437– 2 He also t' that he was on intimate terms with
439– 6 Death t' that he was absent from the

testifies
b 331– 9 falsely t' to a beginning and an
p 430–28 being called for, a witness t' thus :
431–25 Another witness takes the stand and t' :
432– 1 The next witness t' :
432–20 Another witness takes the stand and t' :

testify
s 120–19 impossible for aught but Mind to *t·* truly
b 287–28 five material senses *t·* to truth and error
p 431– 2 would be allowed to *t·* in the case.

testimony
according to the
 b 334–22 according to the *t·* of the corporeal senses,
all the
 p 434–24 All the *t·* has been on the side of
confirm his
 p 432–24 my presence was required to confirm his *t·*.
confirms that
 s 120–28 confirms that *t·* as legitimate
correct
 b 284–17 Can the material . . . give correct *t·*
denying the
 s 122–19 denying the *t·* of the senses,
dispute the
 p 390–13 dispute the *t·* of the material senses
false
 s 108–25 is the false *t·* of false material sense,
 120– 7 Science reverses the false *t·* of the
 121–21 false *t·* of the eye deluded the
 ph 192–21 senses must give up their false *t·*.
 b 268–17 based on the false *t·* of the material
 273–10 Divine Science reverses the false *t·*
 294–17 taught, . . . to revere false *t·*,
 296–28 until Science obliterates this false *t·*.
 301–25 arise from the false *t·* of material sense,
 p 440–27 repudiate the false *t·* of Personal Sense.
 g 516– 6 when we subordinate the false *t·* of
for the plaintiff
 p 433– 1 The *t·* for the plaintiff, Personal Sense,
human
 sp 71–24 no proof nor power outside of human *t·*.
immortal
 r 490–25 destroy all material sense with immortal *t·*.
 490–25 This immortal *t·* ushers in the
jarring
 b 306–25 Undisturbed amid the jarring *t·* of the
law and
 p 436–10 Upon this statute hangs all the law and *t·*.
law or
 f 238–28 no time for gossip about false law or *t·*.
medical
 p 370–23 According to both medical *t·* and
mortal
 b 297–27 no mortal *t·* is founded on the
 297–28 Mortal *t·* can be shaken.
 r 494–26 One is the mortal *t·*, changing,
of error
 r 481–17 the *t·* of error, declaring existence to be
of material sense
 b 297–22 contradicting the *t·* of material sense,
 301–25 arise from the false *t·* of material sense,
 p 396–14 refutation of the *t·* of material sense
of matter
 p 437–14 the *t·* of matter respected ;
of sin
 p 396–17 not because the *t·* of sin or disease is true,
of Spirit
 s 128–25 forever destroys with the higher *t·* of Spirit
 f 252–16 contrasts strikingly with the *t·* of Spirit.
of the Science
 b 269–24 and on the *t·* of the Science of Mind.
of the serpent
 g 538–15 The *t·* of the serpent is significant of the
opposite
 f 252–31 Spirit, bearing opposite *t·*, saith :
opposition to the
 p 395– 3 in opposition to the *t·* of the deceitful senses,
physical
 b 295– 4 proof of the unreliability of physical *t·*.
pseudo-mental
 p 389–10 This pseudo-mental *t·* can be destroyed
reversing the
 s 120–20 reversing the *t·* of the physical senses,
 120–27 instead of reversing the *t·* of the physical
 p 441–18 Reversing the *t·* of Personal Sense
reviews the
 p 433– 4 He analyzes the offence, reviews the *t·*,
rise above the
 c 262–12 rise above the *t·* of the material senses,
Scriptural
 s 116– 7 as to make this Scriptural *t·* true
their
 ap 568–18 by the word of their *t·* ;— *Rev.* 12 : 11.
this
 b 297– 6 this *t·* manifests itself on the body
 p 396–16 the conceded falsity of this *t·*.
 ap 573– 5 This *t·* of Holy Writ sustains the
valid
 p 434–27 The only valid *t·* in the case shows

 sp 70– 2 *t·* of the corporeal senses cannot inform us
 s 108– 2 a conviction antagonistic to the *t·* of

testimony
s 120–16 nor can the material senses bear reliable *t·*
b 269–21 *t·* of the material senses is neither
 288– 5 and the *t·* of the material senses,
 296–26 Mortal mind judges by the *t·* of the
 317–25 the *t·* of the material senses
o 353– 5 till the *t·* of the physical senses yields
r 488–19 *beliefs,* the *t·* of which cannot be true
gl 582–25 the *t·* of what is termed material sense ;

tests
s 111–31 to the broadest practical *t·*.
f 233–27 not more unquestionable than the scientific *t·*

text
each
 g 502–18 each *t·* is followed by its
familiar
 b 320–11 in the same work, the familiar *t·*, Genesis vi. 3.
favorite
 b 340–16 The First Commandment is my favorite *t·*.
of Truth
 pref x–13 but has bluntly and honestly given the *t·* of Truth.
original
 b 320–17 original *t·* declares plainly the spiritual fact
this
 ph 196–12 A careful study of this *t·* shows that
 b 291–20 This *t·* has been transformed into the
 340– 4 This *t·* in the book of Ecclesiastes
 g 509–15 This *t·* gives the idea of the rarefaction
 526–30 In this *t·* Eden stands for the mortal,
 ap 574–16 The beauty of this *t·* is, that the sum total of

 a 38–15 in the *t·*, "The right hand of— *Psal.* 118 : 16.
 ph 170–10 The *t·*, "Whosoever liveth and— *John* 11 : 26.
 b 320–25 the *t·*, "In my flesh shall I— *Job* 19 : 26.
 g 506–27 in the scientifically Christian meaning of the *t·*
 508–17 feminine gender is not yet expressed in the *t·*.
 526–15 in the legendary Scriptural *t·*
 537–26 the *t·* is made to appear contradictory
 543–31 The *t·* "In the day that the Lord— *Gen.* 2 : 4.

textbook
s 110–14 the Bible was my only *t·*.
t 456–26 Science and Health for his *t·*,

textbooks
ph 198–11 fills in his delineations with sketches from *t·*.

texts
a 24– 4 Acquaintance with the original *t·*,

thank
s 131–19 "I *t·* Thee, O Father,— *Luke* 10 : 21.

thankful
b 329–10 *t·* that Jesus, who was the true demonstrator of

thanks
expression of
 pr 3–26 more than a verbal expression of *t·*.
gave
 a 32–18 he took the cup, and gave *t·*,— *Matt.* 26 : 27.
 33–16 he gave *t·* and said,
give
 pr 9– 1 Do we not rather give *t·* that we
 f 214–25 with cannibal tidbits and give *t·*.
 ap 568–24 For victory over a single sin, we give *t·*
 570–24 Those ready for the blessing you impart will
     give *t·*.
to God
 pr 3–28 and yet return *t·* to God for all blessings,

 sp 94–22 but one returned to give God *t·*,
 f 221–24 "giving God *t·* ;"— *see Eph.* 5 : 20.
 t 453–21 masquerader in this Science *t·* God that there is

theatre
c 261–16 so lame that he hobbled every day to the *t·*,

Thee
s 131–19 "I thank *T·*, O Father,— *Luke* 10 : 21.
ph 190–30 For with *T·* is the fountain of life ;— *Psal.* 36 : 9.
c 262–17 "I have heard of *T·* by the— *Job* 42 : 5.
 262–18 but now mine eye seeth *T·*."— *Job* 42 : 5.
p 410– 8 that they might know *T·*,— *John* 17 : 3.

theft
s 143–17 it saves from starvation by *t·*,
b 330–30 hypocrisy, slander, hate, *t·*, adultery,

thefts
an 100– * *t·, false witness, blasphemies :*— *Matt.* 15 : 19.

The Lancet
f 245– 4 medical magazine called *T·. L·*.

theme
pref x–15 or treat in full detail so infinite a *t·*.

theodicy
an 104–14 and reveals the *t·* which indicates

theogony
ph 170– 3 Truth is not the basis of *t·*.

theologians
b 320– 6 The most distinguished *t·* in Europe

theological
a 24–16   the ordinary *t·* views of atonement
s 141– 1   indicates the distance between the *t·* and
theologus
t 459–28   the *t·* (that is, the student
Theology
s 118–13   Science, *T·*, and Medicine are means of
131–12   chapter sub-title
theology
anatomy and
s 148–13   anatomy and *t·* define man as
148–17   Anatomy and *t·* reject the divine Principle
anatomy nor
s 148– 7   Neither anatomy nor *t·* has ever described
and healing
s 138–18   precedent for all Christianity, *t·*, and healing.
and physics
pref viii– 9   *T·* and physics teach that both
divine
f 234–23   the weary searcher after a divine *t·*,
r 469–29   is as pernicious to divine *t·* as are
erudite
a 24–20   Does erudite *t·* regard the crucifixion of
guidance of a
s 148–31   leaves them to the guidance of a *t·* which
his
s 138–31   It is his *t·* in this book and the
Jewish
a 42– 3   The Jewish *t·* gave no hint of the
r 466–24   Heathen mythology and Jewish *t·* have
of Christian Science
s 145–31   The *t·* of C. S. includes healing
f 252– 6   regarding the pathology and *t·* of C. S.
p 404–21   most important points in the *t·* of C. S.
of Jesus
s 138–30   It was this *t·* of Jesus which healed
p 369– 8   and comprehends the *t·* of Jesus
our Master's
s 139– 3   It was our Master's *t·* which the impious ·
popular
s 126–16   C. S. on the one hand and popular *t·* on the
g 557–22   Popular *t·* takes up the history of man
problem in
a 23– 8   The atonement is a hard problem in *t·*,
scholastic
a 41–19   philosophy, *materia medica*, or scholastic *t·*
s 141–32   now occupied by scholastic *t·* and physiology,
f 226–18   scholastic *t·*, material medicine
b 315– 4   the scholastic *t·* of the rabbis.
tries to explain
s 148–21   Then *t·* tries to explain how to make this

s 138–32   spiritual meaning of this *t·*,

theoretical
sp 98–27   and they are not *t·* and fragmentary,
s 164– 5   "No systematic or *t·* classification of
ph 191– 8   As a material, *t·* life-basis is found to be a
b 295–26   The *t·* mind is matter, named *brain*, or
o 341– 4   from a *t·* to a practical Christianity.

theoretically
pr 3–18   We admit *t·* that God is good, . . . and then
o 357–13   but if we *t·* endow mortals with the

theories
are sometimes pernicious
p 394–18   that their *t·* are sometimes pernicious,
cease
f 216– 5   Here *t·* cease, and Science unveils the mystery
common
o 342–30   according to the common *t·*,
conflicting
o 355–14   the relative value of the two conflicting *t·*
contradictory
r 492–15   These two contradictory *t·* . . . will dispute
cruder
ph 189– 6   raises the human thought above the cruder *t·*
dietetic
p 389–13   Our dietetic *t·* first admit that food
doctrines and
b 319–15   The varied doctrines and *t·* which
false
s 151–15   false *t·*, from which multitudes would gladly
r 484–26   involved in all false *t·* and practices.
fossils of
s 147–21   perishing fossils of *t·* already antiquated,
gushing
p 367– 6   better than hecatombs of gushing *t·*,
higher
g 549– 7   give place to higher *t·* and demonstrations.
human
(see **human***)*
its own
sp 81– 7   At the very best and on its own *t·*, spiritualism
many
f 232– 3   Many *t·* relative to God and man

theories
material
(see **material***)*
medical
o 348– 3   Medical *t·* virtually admit the nothingness of
p 382–20   A patient thoroughly booked in medical *t·*
mortal
g 552–10   Mortal *t·* make friends of sin,
most
g 547–17   is more consistent than most *t·*.
of man
a 20– 4   to forms of doctrine or to *t·* of man,
of parents
f 237–10   The more stubborn beliefs and *t·* of parents
ordinary
s 156–12   Believing then somewhat in the ordinary *t·*
or thoughts
f 237–17   discussing or entertaining *t·* or thoughts
our
s 119– 2   that is, when we do so in our *t·*,
122–29   Our *t·* make the same mistake regarding
152–20   Such a fact illustrates our *t·*.
b 312–23   Our *t·* are based on finite premises,
physical
s 123–13   Divine Science, rising above physical *t·*,
prevalent
f 232–11   but our prevalent *t·* practically deny this,
b 283–13   But what say prevalent *t·*?
p 389–18   If God has, as prevalent *t·* maintain,
relinquish all
f 249– 1   Let us accept Science, relinquish all *t·*
self-assertive
f 204–23   False and self-assertive *t·* have given
special
s 133–22   carried out in special *t·* concerning God,
speculative
f 209–27   the paraphernalia of speculative *t·*,
such
s 119– 5   such *t·* lead to one of two things.
ph 185–11   Such *t·* and such systems of so-called mind-cure,
185–17   Such *t·* have no relationship to C. S.,
f 204–18   Such *t·* are evidently erroneous.
these
f 232–12   These *t·* must be untrue,
two
r 494–25   Which of these two *t·* concerning
various
b 339–32   Our various *t·* will never lose their imaginary
gl 587–12   the various *t·* that hold mind to be a

f 228– 7   prolific subject for mortal belief to pin *t·* upon ;
b 269–29   The *t·* I combat are these :
g 526– 9   Belief involves *t·* of material hearing,

theorizes
b 295–31   error *t·* that spirit is born of matter

theorizing
ph 172– 3   *T·* about man's development from

theory
accepted
g 552– 5   was once an accepted *t·*.
any other
f 249–10   Any other *t·* of Life, or God, is delusive
confirms my
p 370–14   This confirms my *t·* that faith in the drug
conservative
r 492–29   The conservative *t·*, long believed, is
contrary to Christian Science
sp 71–31   a *t·* contrary to C. S.
Darwin's
g 547–15   Darwin's *t·* of evolution from a material basis
547–17   Darwin's *t·*,— that Mind produces its opposite,
doctrinal
s 132–24   on any but a material and a doctrinal *t·*.
erroneous
ph 177–16   erroneous *t·* of life and intelligence in matter,
g 522–18   In this erroneous *t·*, matter takes the place
every
ph 194–13   Every *t·* opposed to this fact
false
s 123– 1   false *t·* as to the relations of the celestial
first
b 269–32   The first *t·*, that matter is everything,
incorrect in
pref x– 5   incorrect in *t·* and filled with plagiarisms
material
s 152–12   Such errors beset every material *t·*,
c 257–23   the material *t·* of mind in matter
g 545–16   Error tills the whole ground in this material *t·*,
mere
a 26–28   Our Master taught no mere *t·*, doctrine, or
Mesmer's
an 100–13   to investigate Mesmer's *t·* and to report
mistaken in
f 229–19   mistaken in *t·* and in practice.

theory

mortal
g 547–29 sensual, and mortal *t·* of the universe,
mythologic
g 531–29 The mythologic *t·* of material life
no other
r 483–28 does honor God as no other *t·* honors Him,
of Christian Science
s 112–23 Any *t·* of C. S., which departs from
one
p 372– 6 One *t·* about this mortal mind is,
opposed to the
g 545–12 opposed to the *t·* of man as evolved from
scientific
g 547–11 conclusions as to the scientific *t·* of creation.
speculative
ph 195–24 the speculative *t·*, the nauseous fiction.
such a
a 23– 7 Such a *t·* is man-made.
support his
ph 198–25 though the doctor says nothing to support his *t·*.
this
b 300–27 This *t·* is unscientific.
t 458– 7 This *t·* is supposed to favor practice from
r 492–31 This *t·* would keep truth and error always at war.
true
g 547–25 The true *t·* of the universe, including man,
whatever
g 553–20 Whatever *t·* may be adopted by
your
t 456–16 Any dishonesty in your *t·* and practice

c 256– 9 The *t·* of three persons in one God
257– 6 The *t·* that Spirit is not the only substance
b 300–26 The *t·* that soul, spirit, intelligence,
335– 2 The *t·*, that Spirit is distinct from matter
r 478– 7 What basis is there for the *t·* of
g 553–22 that *t·* is sure to become the signal for

theosophy
sp 99–18 Those individuals, who adopt *t·*,
s 111– 1 hypotheses of agnosticism, pantheism, *t·*,
129–17 spiritualism, *t·*, . . . are antagonistic to
139–28 *t·*, and agnosticism are opposed to C. S.,
r 484– 8 mesmerism, hypnotism, *t·*, or spiritualism?

therapeutic
s 164– 6 "No . . . classification of diseases or of *t·* agents,
p 369–23 The prophylactic and *t·* . . . arts

therapeutical
an 101–1 physiological and *t·* questions,

therapeutics
an 101–18 nothing in common with either physiology or *t·*."
s 149–27 predicting disease does not dignify *t·*.

thereafter
an 104–26 This greater error *t·* occupies the ground,
f 221– 6 *t·* he partook of but one meal in

thereat
t 451–14 many there be which go in *t·*."— *Matt.* 7 : 13.

thereby
s 108–28 *t·* shutting out the true sense of Spirit.
119–14 *t·* making Him guilty of maintaining
f 234–15 *t·* robbing both themselves and others.
b 290–28 The murderer, . . . does not *t·* forsake sin.
302– 7 is *t·* discerned and remains unchanged.
308–22 and Truth, being *t·* understood,
p 397– 6 *t·* actually injuring those whom we
t 457–26 intending *t·* to initiate the cure which they
g 528–17 and *t·* create woman.
gl 583–18 *t·* casting our devils, or error,

therefore
pr 1– * *T· I say unto you,— Mark* 11 : 24.
8–11 and *t·* insincere, what must be the comment
16– 9 "After this manner *t·* pray ye,"— *Matt.* 6 : 9.
a 19– 1 It was *t·* Christ's purpose to reconcile man to
31–11 the only creator, and *t·* as the Father of all.
36–32 Can God *t·* overlook the law
37–28 "Be ye *t·* perfect, even as— *Matt.* 5 : 48.
39–15 To him, *t·*, death was not the threshold
42–27 and is *t·* not a mortal but an immortal.
51–16 *t·* he could no more be separated from
m 56– * *What t· God hath joined— Matt.* 19 : 6.
57–19 It is unselfish ; *t·* it cannot exist alone,
60–10 *T·* maternal affection lives on
69–25 *t·* matter is out of the question
sp 71–30 Spiritualism *t·* presupposes Spirit, . . . to be
76–11 Spirit never entered matter and was *t·*
99–20 *T·* my contest is not with the individual,
an 103– 1 virtue in families and *t·* in the community.
s 112– 4 can, *t·*, be but one method in its teaching.
114– 2 *t·*, to be understood, the author
114–15 implies something untrue and *t·* unreal ;
116–18 *t·* that matter is nothing beyond an image in
117– 6 *t·* the language of Spirit must be,
118–29 *T·* they contradict the divine decrees

therefore
s 120–19 *T·* the divine Principle of Science, reversing
122–31 and mind *t·* tributary to matter.
125– 9 *t·* more harmonious in his manifestations
127– 2 she will not *t·* lose faith in Christianity,
127–24 *T·* truth is not human, and is not a law of matter,
130– 6 and *t·* they cannot accept.
141–22 *t·* they cannot demonstrate God's healing
ph 164–10 *t·* they are more scientific than are
165– * *T· I say unto you,— Matt.* 6 : 25.
191–31 *t·* Truth is able to cast out the ills of the
f 204–14 It cannot *t·* be mind, though so called.
207–20 *T·* there can be no effect from any other cause,
210–31 *t·* it is without a destructive element.
223–13 and *t·* could not be Spirit.
231–17 *T·* we accept the conclusion that
244– 2 *t·* such deformity is not real,
253–32 "Be ye *t·* perfect,"— *Matt.* 5 : 48.
c 259–19 "Be ye *t·* perfect,— *Matt.* 5 : 48.
267–22 Even in this world, *t·*,
b 269–22 I *t·* plant myself unreservedly on the
275– 5 *T·* matter is neither substantial, living, nor
275– 8 and *t·* He is divine Principle.
277– 1 and *t·* cannot spring from intelligence.
277–21 and *t·* that good is the origin of
277–30 for matter is temporal and is *t·* a
279– 8 and is *t·* not eternal.
286–19 *T·* the spiritual universe is good,
288–18 "There remaineth *t·* a rest— *Heb.* 4 : 9.
289–26 and *t·* the material must be untrue.
289–28 *T·* it cannot be said to pass out of matter.
292–28 *T·* man would be annihilated,
300–23 *t·* Soul is not in matter.
300–29 *t·* God is seen only in the spiritual
301– 8 involves error and *t·* is material,
302–25 He is *t·* the divine, infinite Principle,
304–18 Man's happiness is not, *t·*, at the disposal of
309–30 *T·* it is never structural nor organic,
313– 7 *T·* God, even thy God,— *Heb.* 1 : 9.
318–24 as though disease were real, *t·* right,
324–11 *T·* "acquaint now thyself with— *Job* 22 : 21.
328– 9 and must *t·* cling to mortals until,
330–23 *t·* there is in reality one Mind only,
331–15 *T·* in Spirit all is harmony, and there can be
334– 2 and *t·* antedated Abraham ;
334–32 and *t·* one God.
337– 1 *T·* man, reflecting God, cannot lose his
339– 9 *T·* evil, being contrary to good,
340–12 *T·* all that really exists is in and of God,
p 362–15 It was *t·* easy for the Magdalen to
368–28 that mortality (and *t·* disease) has a
372–16 *T·* he will be as the angels in heaven.
376–21 *T·* the efficient remedy is to destroy the
391–21 *t·* meet the intimation with a protest.
391–26 *T·* make your own terms with sickness,
399– 1 and *t·* good is infinite, is All.
400– 3 and *t·* the disease is thoroughly cured.
415– 2 *t·* disease is neither a cause nor an effect.
417–12 Spirit is God, and *t·* cannot be sick ;
419–15 *t·* be sure that you move it off.
422–31 His treatment is *t·* tentative.
431–10 *T·* I arrested Mortal Man in behalf of
t 446–29 This must *t·* be watched and guarded against.
447– 9 *T·* the rule is, heal the sick when called upon
450–10 and are *t·* open to the approach and
460–17 It is *t·* to be dealt with through
464–10 She *t·* remains unseen at her post,
r 467– 5 *T·* the command means this :
468–14 *T·* man is not material ; he is spiritual.
471–18 God is infinite, *t·* ever present,
472–26 *T·* the only reality of sin, sickness, or death
475–18 reflection of God, or Mind, and *t·* is eternal ;
488– 5 *t·* you receive the blessing of Truth.
488–25 *T·* mental endowments are not at the mercy of
g 506– 3 *T·* matter, not being the reflection of Spirit,
518–28 and all must *t·* be as perfect as the
530–27 *t·* the dreamer and dream are one,
537– 2 *t·* the Lord God [Jehovah] sent— *Gen.* 3 : 23.
542–15 *T·* whosoever slayeth Cain,— *Gen.* 4 : 15.
544–25 *T·* man, in this allegory, is neither a
549–17 we must *t·* look upon the simple ovum as
ap 567–25 and *t·*, in his pretence of being a talker,
568–19 *T·* rejoice, ye heavens,— *Rev.* 12 : 12.
574– 2 This spiritual consciousness is *t·* a
gl 592– 3 and *t·* the opposite of God, or good;
592– 5 belief that life has a beginning and *t·*
596– 9 "Whom *t·* ye ignorantly worship,— *Acts* 17 : 23.

therein
s 110–23 the Science and truth *t·* will forever remain
p 382–23 shall in no wise enter *t·*."— *Luke* 18 : 17.
g 523–18 the Supreme Being is *t·* called Elohim.
523–19 Deity *t·* is always called Jehovah.
524–31 Does Spirit enter dust, and lose *t·* the
ap 558– * *those things which are written t· : — Rev.* 1 : 3.
576–10 And I saw no temple *t·* : — *Rev.* 21 : 22.
576–20 with "no temple [body] *t·*"— *Rev.* 21 : 22.

thereof

sp 95–18   one of the special characteristics *t*.
ph 190–26 place *t*· shall know it no more.— *Psal.* 103 : 16.
   197–10 "In the day that thou eatest *t*·— *Gen.* 2 : 17.
f 246–28 find this out, and begin the demonstration *t*·.
r 476–26 place *t*· shall know it no more."— *Psal.* 103 : 16.
   481–19 "In the day that thou eatest *t*·— *Gen.* 2 : 17.
g 513–21 God, who is the divinely creative Principle *t*·.
   527–10 in the day that thou eatest *t*·— *Gen.* 2 : 17.
   527–25 that was the name *t*·.— *Gen.* 2 : 19.
   528–12 closed up the flesh instead *t*· ;— *Gen.* 2 : 21.
   530–15 in the day ye eat *t*·,— *Gen.* 3 : 5.
   532– 8 "In the day that thou eatest *t*·— *Gen.* 2 : 17.
   533–25 and multiplies until the end *t*·.
   540–27 his flock, and of the fat *t*·.— *Gen.* 4 : 4.
ap 558–16 for God "is the light *t*·."— *Rev.* 21 : 23.
gl 592–12 a type of moral law and the demonstration *t*· ;

thereto

a 23–22 *faith* and the words corresponding *t*·
p 436–10 the divine law, and in obedience *t*·.

thereunto

o 354–17 who *t*· have set their seals.

thereupon

p 411–16 *T*· Jesus cast out the evil,
   436–26 *T*· Judge Medicine sat in judgment on the case,

thermometer

s 152–16 introducing a *t*· into the patient's mouth.

Thibet

pr 10–17 One of the forms of worship in *T*·

thief

b 294–29 *t*· believes that he gains something by stealing,

thieves

f 234–11 against the approach of *t*· and murderers.
p 365–28 convert into a den of *t*· the temple

thin

f 221– 7 only a *t*· slice of bread without water.
b 295–23 like a cloud melting into *t*· vapor,

Thine

pr 17–12 For *T*· is the kingdom, and the— *Matt.* 6 : 13.
a 33–20 "Not my will, but *T*·, be done !"— *Luke* 22 : 42.
f 201– * *T*· enemies have reproached,— *Psal.* 89 : 51.
   201– * the footsteps of *T*· anointed.— *Psal.* 89 : 51.

thing

creeping

r 475–26 and over every creeping *t*·— *Gen.* 1 : 26.
g 513–15 cattle, and creeping *t*·,— *Gen.* 1 : 24.
   515–15 and over every creeping *t*·— *Gen.* 1 : 26.

deadly

b 328–24 and if they drink any deadly *t*·,— *Mark* 16 : 18.
p 362– * and if they drink any deadly *t*·,— *Mark* 16 : 18.

every living

g 517–28 and over every living *t*·— *Gen.* 1 : 28.

no

b 330–27 Evil is nothing, no *t*·, mind, nor power.
g 554– 8 Error is always error.   It is *no t*·.

no impossible

p 371–22 No impossible *t*· do I ask when urging the

nor a person

b 287–26 Matter is neither a *t*· nor a person,

no such

r 487–21 there is in reality no such *t*· as *mortal* mind.
g 554– 4 There is no such *t*· as mortality,

of life

f 247–21 Beauty is a *t*· of life, which dwells forever

place, nor

sp 71– 3 It is neither person, place, nor *t*·,

pleasantest

m 59– 1 and this is the pleasantest *t*· to do.

same

p 404–27 are one and the same *t*· in C. S.

whole

ph 166– 1 your remedy lies in forgetting the whole *t*· ;

sp 70–15 Does life or soul exist in the *t*· formed?
f 252–23 says : . . . . What a nice *t*· is sin !
o 350– 2 as something and almost the only *t*·,
p 411– 1 "The *t*· which I greatly feared— *Job* 3 : 25.

things

all

pref xii–24 "hopeth all *t*·, endureth all *t*·,"— *I Cor.* 13 : 7.
pr 1– 2 faith that all *t*· are possible to God,
   13–24 Love, to whom all *t*· are possible.
   15– 8 but He knows all *t*·
sp 83–29 the divine Principle and explanation of all *t*·.
   85–13 told me all *t*· that ever I did :— *John* 4 : 29.
   96– 2 unwillingness to learn all *t*· rightly,
   96–11 until the final spiritualization of all *t*·.
s 124–26 life, substance, and continuity of all *t*·.
ph 166–21 He can do all *t*· for us in sickness
   178–16 divine Mind, to which all *t*· are possible,
   180–26 ever-present Mind who understands all *t*·,
   180–27 man knows that with God all *t*· are possible.

things

all

ph 183– 1 makes all *t*· possible to Spirit ;
   189–20 makes all *t*· start from the lowest instead of
   200–15 hast put all *t*· under his feet."— *Psal.* 8 : 6.
f 201– 9 and "all *t*· are become new."— *II Cor.* 5 : 17.
   207–27 spiritual reality is the scientific fact in all *t*·.
   208– 3 Material sense defines all *t*· materially,
   212–30 its normal action, and the origin of all *t*·
   215– 2 Nothing can hide from them the harmony of
          all *t*·
   231–31 "all *t*· were made by Him— *John* 1 : 3.
   232– 9 "with God all *t*· are possible,"— *Mark* 10 : 27.
   250– 8 which never dreams, but understands all *t*· ;
c 255–14 mortals take limited views of all *t*·.
   256– 6 All *t*· are created spiritually.
   257– 2 If Mind is within and without all *t*·,
b 271–21 shall teach you all *t*·."— *John* 14 : 26.
   280– 6 All *t*· beautiful and harmless are ideas of Mind.
   280–10 Finite belief limits all *t*·, and would compress
   289–30 Spirit and all *t*· spiritual are the real
   305–10 so man, like all *t*· real, reflects God,
   307–26 and gives man dominion over all *t*·.
   310–16 around which circle harmoniously all *t*·
   318–12 and doom all *t*· to decay.
o 353–18 All *t*· will continue to disappear, until
p 387–26 which causes all *t*· discordant.
t 444– 5 "All *t*· work together for good— *Rom.* 8 : 28.
   464–19 "prove all *t*· ;— *I Thess.* 5 : 21.
r 480–26 "All *t*· were made by Him— *John* 1 : 3.
   485–15 Think not to thwart the spiritual ultimate of
          all *t*·,
   493– 8 to the immortal truth of all *t*·.
g 501– * *All t*· *were made by Him ;*— *John* 1 : 3.
   505–27 it is the reality of all *t*·
   516– 9 God fashions all *t*·, after His own likeness.
   519– 2 eternal Mind, the author of all *t*·,
   525–17 all *t*· were made through the Word of God,
gl 581–12 the spiritual realities of all *t*· are
   585–13 shall first come and restore all *t*·."— *Matt.* 17 : 11.
   597–29 spiritual government, encompassing all *t*·.

animated

an 100– 9 the celestial bodies, the earth, and animated *t*·.

belief of

b 289–25 The spiritual fact and the material belief of *t*·

eternal

b 337–25 Eternal *t*· (verities) are God's thoughts

evidence of

r 468–21 the evidence of *t*· not seen."— *Heb.* 11 : 1.

false sense of

f 213–31 dipped to its depths into a false sense of *t*·,

few

b 323–17 "faithful over a few *t*·,"— *Matt.* 25 : 21.
ap 569– 7 faithful over a few *t*·,— *Matt.* 25 : 23.

finite sense of

s 124–12 This is a mortal, finite sense of *t*·,

forgetting those

o 353–24 "forgetting those *t*· which— *Phil.* 3 : 13.

former

g 556– 9 for the former *t*· will have passed away.

good

s 155–31 If drugs are good *t*·, is it safe to say

great

g 528–22 and declaring what great *t*· error has done.

human sense of

sp 99–16 the human sense of *t*· errs

immortal

b 276–22 towards the contemplation of *t*· immortal

imperishable

a 21–11 looks towards the imperishable *t*· of Spirit.

invisible

r 479–30 "For the invisible *t*· of Him,— *Rom.* 1 : 20.

lower

b 268– 5 to the spiritual cause of those lower *t*·

man and

b 281–17 reflects reality and divinity in . . . man and *t*·.

material

(*see* **material**)

material sense of

b 304– 4 based on a material sense of *t*·,
r 489–29 Outside the material sense of *t*·, all is harmony.
g 544– 8 arise from the material sense of *t*·,
gl 597–18 in which a material sense of *t*· disappears,

men and

s 118–21 as the natural status of men and *t*·,

mortal sense of

p 370– 3 we must forsake the mortal sense of *t*·,

no such

o 352–27 because there are no such *t*·.

of God

b 276–11 is cognizant only of the *t*· of God.

of Spirit

a 21–11 looks towards the imperishable *t*· of Spirit.
o 349–24 Speaking of the *t*· of Spirit

old

f 201– 8 a new creature, in whom old *t*· pass away

things

persons and
c 263–28 mortal sense of persons and *t·* is not creation.
persons or
g 514– 3 could not . . . recreate persons or *t·*
phases of
r 488– 1 enduring and harmonious phases of *t·*.
present
b 304– 6 nor *t·* present, nor things to come,— *Rom.* 8 : 38.
resolves
s 123–14 excludes matter, resolves *t·* into *thoughts*,
b 269–15 Metaphysics resolves *t·* into thoughts,
spiritual
b 289–30 Spirit and all *t·* spiritual are the real
326–10 and set his whole affections on spiritual *t·*,
335–13 *T·* spiritual and eternal are substantial.
state of
g 572–15 this state of *t·* is declared to be temporary
substance of
b 279– 4 "the *substance* of *t·* hoped for."— *Heb.* 11 : 1.
r 468–20 "The substance of *t·* hoped for,— *Heb.* 11 : 1.
such
an 106–26 they which do such *t·*— *Gal.* 5 : 21.
surface of
b 313–25 He plunged beneath the material surface of *t·*,
temporal
b 337–26 Temporal *t·* are the thoughts of mortals
temporary sense of
b 298– 9 a mortal temporary sense of *t·*,
these
pr 7–11 Looking deeply into these *t·*, we find
a 31–32 and these *t·* will they do unto you,— *John* 16 : 3.
s 131–20 hast hid these *t·* from the wise— *Luke* 10 : 21.
ph 169–15 The faith reposed in these *t·* should
b 329–11 Be thankful that Jesus, . . . did these *t·*,
o 343–10 "None of these *t·* move me."— *Acts* 20 : 24.
k 499– * *These t· saith He that is holy,— Rev.* 3 : 7.
g 540– 6 I the Lord do all these *t· ;"— Isa.* 45 : 7.
gl 579– * *These t· saith He that is holy,— Rev.* 3 : 7.
those
pr 1– * *shall believe that those t· which— Mark* 11 : 23.
s 132– 5 those *t·* which ye do hear and see :— *Matt.* 11 : 4.
t 459– 2 Man then appropriates those *t·* which
ap 558– * *keep those t· which are written— Rev.* 1 : 3.
to come
b 304– 7 nor things present, nor *t·* to come,— *Rom.* 8 : 38.
true sense of
c 264– 8 if they would gain the true sense of *t·*.
unpleasant
p 415– 8 when it contemplates unpleasant *t·*,
uttered
b 317– 1 Jesus uttered *t·* which had been
which pertain
o 350– 2 and of the *t·* which pertain to Spirit

pr 1– * *What t· soever ye desire— Mark* 11 : 24.
1– * *knoweth what t· ye have need of,— Matt.* 6 : 8.
a 20– 1 the *t·* which are Cæsar's ;— *Matt.* 22 : 21.
20– 2 the *t·* that are God's."— *Matt.* 22 : 21.
27– 3 what *t·* ye have seen and heard ;— *Luke* 7 : 22.
an 100– * *the t· which defile a man.— Matt.* 15 : 20.
s 119– 5 such theories lead to one of two *t·*.
129–24 accepting only the outward sense of *t·*.
ph 189–18 evidence of all mortal thought or *t·*.
b 305–18 for what *t·* soever He doeth,— *John* 5 : 19.
r 479–32 by the *t·* that are made."— *Rom.* 1 : 20.
g 540–17 the *t·* which are Cæsar's ;— *Matt.* 22 : 21.
540–18 the *t·* that are God's."— *Matt.* 22 : 21.
544– 9 consisteth not of the *t·* which a man eateth.
ap 560–21 As it is with *t·*, so is it with persons.

think

pr 1– 5 Regardless of what another may say or *t·*
a 31–31 whosoever killeth you will *t·*— *John* 16 : 2.
42–24 Let men *t·* they had killed the body !
48–13 and *t·*, or even wish, to escape the
m 63– 1 You would never *t·* that flannel was better for
sp 82– 2 We *t·* of an absent friend as easily as we
87–25 because you do not *t·* of it.
s 130–30 no longer *t·* it natural to love sin and
155– 1 You 're not hurt, so don't *t·* you are."
ph 168– 2 who *t·* the standard of C. S. too high for them.
f 230–27 We *t·* that we are healed when a disease
b 270–24 Mortals *t·* wickedly ; consequently they
270–25 They *t·* sickly thoughts, and so become sick.
297– 1 and they *t·* they are so ;
o 345–26 if a man *t·* himself to be something,— *Gal.* 6 : 3.
350– 1 They *t·* of matter as something
353– 8 How can a Christian, . . . *t·* of the latter as real
p 379–16 *t·* of the experiment of those Oxford boys,
381–20 *T·* less of the enactments of mortal mind,
385–27 You say or *t·*, because you have partaken of
386–18 You *t·* that your anguish is occasioned by your loss.
388–31 If mortals *t·* that food disturbs the
389– 6 The less we know or *t·* about hygiene,

think

p 392–17 If you *t·* that consumption is hereditary
397–13 When an accident happens, you *t·*
412– 8 concerning the truth which you *t·* or speak,
416–29 they *t·* too much about their ailments,
419–18 *T·* less of material conditions
429–18 unseen by those who *t·* that they bury the body.
t 443–15 and *t·* they can be benefited by
449– 9 *T·* it "easier for a camel— *Matt.* 19 : 24
451– 9 and *t·* to succeed without the spirit,
458–11 to *t·* of aiding the divine Principle of healing
r 478–14 *Question.*— Does brain *t·*, and do nerves feel,
478–22 and brain-lobes cannot *t·*
485–14 *T·* not to thwart the spiritual ultimate
490–32 will *t·* that he is freezing when he is warm,
g 540–12 we may *t·* in our ignorance that the
553–30 before they *t·* or know aught of their origin,
ap 574–25 *T·* of this, dear reader, for it will lift the

thinker

a 40– 3 The advanced *t·* and devout Christian,
s 122–20 which every *t·* can recall for himself.
128–18 It raises the *t·* into his native air of insight

thinker's

g 547–10 strengthens the *t·* conclusions

thinkers

pref vii–13 The time for *t·* has come.
p 387–13 Our *t·* do not die early because they
t 450– 1 There is a large class of *t·* whose bigotry
450– 9 A third class of *t·* build with solid masonry.

thinketh

sp 89–13 "As he *t·* in his heart,— *Prov.* 23 : 7.
ph 166– 3 As a man *t·*, so is he.
f 213– 4 "As he *t·* in his heart,— *Prov.* 23 : 7.
p 383–28 "As he *t·* in his heart,— *Prov.* 23 : 7.

thinking

a 22– 1 *t·* . . . to find and follow the right road.
sp 92–29 The mistake of *t·* that error can be real,
f 220–20 and *t·* it sees another kitten.
225–16 proportionate to its embodiment of right *t·*.
245– 1 The error of *t·* that we are growing old,
p 420–27 to promote right *t·* and doing,
424–23 while others are *t·* about your patients
r 483–26 it ought to receive aid, . . . from all *t·* persons.
g 543–20 May not Darwin be right in *t·* that
gl 586– 5 Jesus said, *t·* of the outward vision,

thinks

s 154–28 who *t·* she has hurt her face by falling on the
ph 188–16 the dreamer *t·* that his body is material
b 294– 9 The belief that matter *t·*, sees, or feels
294–13 saying : . . . Nerves feel. Brain *t·* and sins.
322–17 The drunkard *t·* he enjoys drunkenness,
p 408–24 were it not that mortal mind *t·* that the

thinness

f 205–18 or as they melt into such *t·* that we

third

sp 91–29 The *t·* erroneous postulate is,
s 116– 1 *T·* Degree : Understanding.
116– 4 In the *t·* degree mortal mind disappears,
156–23 but on the *t·* day she again suffered,
f 204– 9 Spirit and matter,— resulting in a *t·* person
204–15 The *t·* power, mortal man, is
p 422–15 meet and bring out a *t·* quality,
t 450– 8 A *t·* class of thinkers build with solid masonry.
457– 4 *T· :* Because this book has done more for
g 503–21 *t·*, in spiritual and immortal forms of beauty
508–27 and the morning were the *t·* day.— *Gen.* 1 : 13.
508–28 The *t·* stage in the order of C. S.
509– 6 he rose from the grave,— on the *t·* day of his
ap 563–23 And his tail drew the *t·* part— *Rev.* 12 : 4.
577–15 *t·*, Christianity, which is the outcome of the
gl 585–28 second from a rib, and *t·* from an egg.
598– 2 John's Gospel, the *t·* chapter, where we read :

thirsteth

pr 13– 4 "Ho, every one that *t·*,— *Isa.* 55 : 1.

thirsty

f 234– 8 and giving living waters to the *t·*.
p 366– 8 debars him from giving drink to the *t·*
376–26 to feel pain or heat, to be *t·* or sick.
385–29 must be *t·*, and you are *t·* accordingly,
431– 4 When the sick mortal was *t·*,

thirty

a 47 –12 The traitor's price was *t·* pieces of silver
s 139–18 the *t·* thousand different readings in the

thistles

b 276–31 not . . . grapes from thorns nor figs from *t·*.
g 535–24 thorns also and *t·* shall it— *Gen.* 3 : 18.

thitherward

a 21–26 and will be attracted *t·*.

Thomas
  a 24–32 unbelieving *T·* was forced to acknowledge
    46–18 To convince *T·* of this, Jesus caused him to
  b 317–24 To the materialistic *T·*, looking for
    318– 1 Nothing but . . . could make existence real to *T·*.

thorns
  a 44– 1 before the *t·* can be laid aside for
    50–29 was a million times sharper than the *t·*
  b 276–31 Divine Science does not gather grapes from *t·*
  p 365– 1 the *t·* they plant in the pillow of the sick
  g 535–23 *t·* also and thistles shall it — *Gen.* 3 : 18.
    536–23 and hedge about their achievements with *t·*.
    539–24 "Do men gather grapes of *t·* ?" — *Matt.* 7 : 16.

thorough
  t 446– 5 A *t·* perusal of the author's publications
    456–31 containing a *t·* statement of C. S.
    461–32 requisite for a *t·* comprehension of C. S.

thoroughly
  sp 84–30 If this Science has been *t·* learned
  f 230–29 we are never *t·* healed until
  p 382–19 A patient *t·* booked in medical theories
    400– 3 and therefore the disease is *t·* cured.
    412– 7 be *t·* persuaded in your own mind
  t 445– 2 teacher must *t·* fit his students
  r 467– 9 It should be *t·* understood that
    495–27 Study *t·* the letter and imbibe the spirit.

thoroughness
  ph 186– 6 and the *t·* of this work determines health.

Thou
    iii– * Oh! *T·* hast heard my prayer ;
    iii– * *T·* here, and *everywhere.*
  pr 16–31 Thy kingdom is come; *T·* art ever-present.
  a 50– 8 why hast *T·* forsaken me?" — *Mark* 15 : 34.
  s 125–24 "As a vesture shalt *T·* change — *Psal.* 102 : 26.
    131–20 *T·* hast hid these things from the — *Luke* 10 : 21.
    134–26 "I knew that *T·* hearest me — *John* 11 : 42.
  ph 200–13 "*T·* madest him to have dominion — *Psal.* 8 : 6.
    200–15 *T·* hast put all things under his — *Psal.* 8 : 6.
  c 255– * *T·* art from everlasting. — *Psal.* 93 : 2.
    256–23 or say unto Him, What doest *T·* ?" — *Dan.* 4 : 35.
  p 410– 9 Jesus Christ, whom *T·* hast sent." — *John* 17 : 3.
  g 533– 8 The woman whom *T·* gavest — *Gen.* 3 : 12.
    533–16 woman, whom *T·* gavest me, is responsible."
  ap 566–23 Be *T·*, longsuffering, slow to wrath,

thought (*see also* thought's)
accepts
  g 520–14 and *t·* accepts the divine infinite calculus.
action of
  p 384–13 Through this action of *t·* and its results
aid in bringing
  t 455– 1 auxiliaries to aid in bringing *t·* into accord
and action
  c 265–13 a wider sphere of *t·* and action,
and deed
  a 19–18 every effort for reform, every good *t·* and deed,
  gl 595–15 purification of *t·* and deed,
and demonstration
  c 259–14 as the basis of *t·* and demonstration.
appeal to
  ph 182– 5 The demands of God appeal to *t·* only ;
apprehend
  ph 179– 9 the spiritual capacity to apprehend *t·*
array
  c 260–29 If we array *t·* in mortal vestures,
artist's
  b 310– 2 picture is the artist's *t·* objectified.
ascending
  g 509– 7 on the third day of his ascending *t·*,
assumed
  b 326–26 *T·* assumed a nobler outlook,
atmosphere of
  s 128–17 It extends the atmosphere of *t·*,
awaken
  g 553– 3 should awaken *t·* to a higher and purer
benign
  p 365– 7 The benign *t·* of Jesus,
body and
  r 492– 2 leaves mortal man intact in body and *t·*,
boundless
  b 323–11 until boundless *t·* walks enraptured,
channel of
  gl 593–14 RIVER. Channel of *t·*.
chiseling
  f 248–15 moulding and chiseling *t·*.
Christian
  pref x–26 unbiased Christian *t·* is soonest touched by
Christian Science
  b 340– 5 conveys the C. S. *t·*,
conscious
  p 379–29 The images, held in . . . mind, frighten conscious *t·*.
    400–14 before it has taken tangible shape in conscious *t·*,
consecration of
  pr 3–16 absolute consecration of *t·*, energy, and

thought
constituents of
  m 58– 9 these constituents of *t·*, mingling,
convey
  f 212–27 in order to convey *t·*,
creating
  g 520–28 but the immortal creating *t·* is from above,
definite
  pref ix– 9 the tongue voices the more definite *t·*,
delineates
  b 310– 3 belief fancies that it delineates *t·* on matter,
depressing
  p 384– 3 relieve our minds from the depressing *t·*
deserted by
  p 429–11 The corpse, deserted by *t·*, is cold
discern the
  sp 95– 9 are able to discern the *t·* of the sick and the
divest
  p 428– 9 To divest *t·* of false trusts
divine
  s 118–14 Theology, and Medicine are means of divine *t·*,
  g 514–15 transmission from the divine *t·* to the
door of
  p 392–24 Stand porter at the door of *t·*.
drift of
  pref x–12 to suit the general drift of *t·*,
efface from
  p 396– 3 efface from *t·* all forms and
elevation to
  pr 7– 9 momentary solemnity and elevation to *t·*.
embodied
  p 372–11 belief . . . that man can enter his own embodied *t·*,
embryonic
  ph 188– 7 an embryonic *t·* without motive ;
emphasizes the
  s 116–20 C. S. strongly emphasizes the *t·* that
encompass
  g 551–25 Darkness and doubt encompass *t·*,
erring
  c 260– 7 The conceptions of mortal, erring *t·*
  g 503–24 God creates neither erring *t·*, mortal life,
erroneous
  g 543–23 to be the creations of erroneous *t·*,
error of
  g 550–15 Error of *t·* is reflected in error of action.
exalted
  p 373–17 through the exalted *t·* of John,
  g 506–12 exalted *t·* or spiritual apprehension
expands
  c 255– 2 *t·* expands into expression.
expressed
  p 423– 7 more strongly than the expressed *t·*.
expressed in
  pr 11–32 It is best expressed in *t·* and in life.
expresses the
  r 468–28 Eternity, not time, expresses the *t·* of Life,
externalized
  o 360–13 which mind-picture or externalized *t·*
father to the
  f 219–22 "is ever father to the *t·*."
feeds
  f 222– 9 and feeds *t·* with the bread of Life.
food for
  ph 195–16 furnishes food for *t·*.
footsteps of
  ph 174– 9 The footsteps of *t·*, rising above
formation of
  sp 71–13 a formation of *t·* rather than of matter.
forms of
  s 118–20 In all mortal forms of *t·*, dust is dignified
  ph 187– 7 material sense creates its own forms of *t·*,
  b 298–31 confers upon angels its own forms of *t·*,
free
  f 223–21 Spiritual rationality and free *t·* accompany
gently whispers
  ap 574–30 Then *t·* gently whispers : "Come hither !
gives action to
  gl 586– 8 that which gives action to *t·*.
guides
  s 149–28 Whatever guides *t·* spiritually benefits
her
  s 152–22 and experiments had prepared her *t·*
  ph 185– 1 but her *t·* of it had
  t 460–30 beliefs were gradually expelled from her *t·*,
his
  sp 82– 5 we still read his *t·* in his verse.
  ph 186– 2 by emptying his *t·* of the false stimulus
    198–10 outlines his *t·* relative to disease,
  c 258–26 and of the infinite range of his *t·*.
  p 383– 9 when he leaves it most out of his *t·*,
  t 452– 1 how to bar the door of his *t·*
hold
  c 261– 4 Hold *t·* steadfastly to the enduring,
human
  (*see* human)

thought

image of
p 411–23 an image of *t·* externalized.
images of
sp 86–13 Mortals evolve images of *t·*.
f 208–29 according to the images of *t·* impressed upon it.
248–10 supplying it with beautiful images of *t·*
imprisoned
s 114–27 and sets free the imprisoned *t·*.
increases or diminishes
p 415–19 *t·* increases or diminishes the
inspired
g 547–28 Inspired *t·* relinquishes a material, . . . theory
integrity of
t 446–29 detrimental to health and integrity of *t·*.
is borrowed
c 267–22 *T·* is borrowed from a higher source
its own
p 399–17 Mortal mind perpetuates its own *t·*.
Job's
c 262–19 Mortals will echo Job's *t·*,
latent in
gl 597– 8 but cloaked the crime, latent in *t·*,
less
m 62–13 Taking less "*t·* for your life,— *Matt.* 6 : 25.
62–14 less *t·* "for your body— *Matt.* 6 : 25.
ph 175– 4 and less *t·* is given to sanitary subjects,
f 222–14 Taking less *t·* about what he should eat
lifted
ph 200– 3 lifted *t·* into the song of David.
lifting
p 400–18 By lifting *t·* above error, or disease,
material
c 267– 1 Every object in material *t·* will be destroyed,
o 356– 2 the material *t·* must become spiritualized
460–12 for to the material *t·* all is material,
g 509–30 Jesus rebuked the material *t·* of his
misleads
b 275–28 misleads *t·* and points to other gods,
models in
f 248–27 We must form perfect models in *t·*
momentous
g 516–27 To emphasize this momentous *t·*,
mortal
(*see* **mortal**)
note how
p 415–17 Note how *t·* makes the face pallid.
occupy
m 60–23 and other considerations, . . . occupy *t·*.
of disease
ph 198–14 *t·* of disease is formed before one
p 396– 2 One should never hold in mind the *t·* of disease,
of the age
s 146–32 and adapted to the *t·* of the age
of the patient
p 414–13 mortal mind or the *t·* of the patient,
original
ph 195–20 invention, study, and original *t·* are
palsied by
p 415–23 quickly or slowly and impelled or palsied by *t·*,
parent's
p 412–29 met mainly through the parent's *t·*,
patient's
p 366– 9 hinders him from reaching his patient's *t·*,
396–12 nor encourage in the patient's *t·* the
perturbed
p 400–13 Eradicate the image . . . from the perturbed *t·*
pictorial
sp 86–27 can all be taken from pictorial *t·*
pictures of
sp 87– 2 Mind-readers perceive these pictures of *t·*.
pinions to
t 454–20 Right motives give pinions to *t·*,
popular
s 141–10 All revelation (such is the popular *t·* !)
possibilities of
sp 90–20 This shows the possibilities of *t·*.
prior to
b 310– 4 Did it exist prior to *t·* ?
pure
g 508–15 seed within itself is the pure *t·*
put out of
p 425–13 treated as error and put out of *t·*.
quiet the
p 415–12 They quiet the *t·* by inducing stupefaction
random
ph 175–16 If a random *t·*, calling itself dyspepsia,
rarefaction of
g 509–16 gives the idea of the rarefaction of *t·*
receptive
a 34–16 to the poor,— the receptive *t·*,
p 380– 1 may rest at length on some receptive *t·*,
recorder's
gl 590–25 disappearing from the recorder's *t·*,
remain in
p 376– 5 fear and the despair of recovery remain in *t·*.

thought

remove error from
a 40– 2 Remove error from *t·*, and it will not appear
removes
b 323–22 removes *t·* from the body,
rises
c 256– 3 *t·* rises from the material sense to the spiritual,
scientific
ap 559– 9 scientific *t·* reaches over continent and ocean
sculptor's
b 299– 2 no more reality than has the sculptor's *t·*
sensual
c 263–28 A sensual *t·*, like an atom of dust
sinful
p 400–31 the baneful influence of sinful *t·* on the body.
slumbering
f 223–25 Peals that should startle the slumbering *t·*
spiritualization of
f 211–30 dematerialization and spiritualization of *t·*
b 272–19 It is the spiritualization of *t·* and
p 382– 7 and to the spiritualization of *t·*,
407–26 This spiritualization of *t·* lets in the light,
gl 593– 9 RESURRECTION. Spiritualization of *t·* ;
spiritualizes the
p 370– 6 regimen which spiritualizes the *t·* ;
spontaneity of
gl 597–17 Spontaneity of *t·* and idea ;
substance of
p 423–30 Bones have only the substance of *t·*
substance of a
g 508– 5 The only intelligence or substance of a *t·*,
such
t 460–13 till such *t·* is rectified by Spirit.
such a
b 320–20 (however transcendental such a *t·* appears),
suggests the
b 338–16 This suggests the *t·* of something fluid,
338–17 It further suggests the *t·* of that
swift-winged
ap 574–20 the very message, or swift-winged *t·*,
take no
ph 165– * *Take no t· for your life,— Matt.* 6 : 25.
170–16 "Take no *t·* for your life,— *Matt.* 6 : 25.
f 228–21 "Take no *t·* for your life,"— *Matt.* 6 : 25.
p 365– 8 "Take no *t·* for your life,"— *Matt.* 6 : 25.
382–11 "Take no *t·* . . . for the body."— *Luke* 12 : 22.
g 530– 8 "Take no *t·* for your life,— *Matt.* 6 : 25.
taking form in
ph 175– 1 prevent the images . . . from taking form in *t·*,
taking no
ph 176– 7 custom of taking no *t·* about food
that
p 392–19 liable to the development of that *t·*
this
a 39–27 This *t·* is apprehended slowly,
f 203–12 This *t·* incites to a more exalted worship
o 345–28 This *t·* of human, material nothingness,
354– 9 when it teaches precisely this *t·* ?
p 388–32 the food or this *t·* must be dispensed with,
r 496–15 Hold perpetually this *t·*,— that it is the
to discern
sp 95–15 to discern *t·* scientifically, depends upon
unconscious
p 408–28 unconscious *t·* in the corporeal substratum
uninspired
ap 573– 5 that which is invisible to the uninspired *t·*.
uplift the
ph 175–12 its beauty and fragrance, should uplift the *t·*,
whispered into
p 370–19 spiritual facts of health, whispered into *t·*,
will waken
p 427–30 *T·* will waken from its own material
wrong
t 452– 5 The wrong *t·* should be arrested before it
your
f 208–30 You embrace your body in your *t·*,
b 324–30 if the idea . . . come not to your *t·*,
p 397–14 Your *t·* is more powerful than your words,
r 495–16 nothing but His likeness to abide in your *t·*.

m 57–27 serves to unite *t·* more closely to God,
sp 84–12 *t·* which is in rapport with this Mind,
86–22 Then why is it more difficult to see a *t·* than
87– 5 It is needless for the *t·* or for the person
90– 9 Divest yourself of the *t·* that there can be
s 130–26 If *t·* is startled at the strong claim of
ph 174–29 and holding it before the *t·* of both
180–22 Instead of furnishing *t·* with fear,
195–18 *t·* passes naturally from effect back to cause.
197– 2 which mirror images of disease distinctly in *t·*.
199–21 The devotion of *t·* to an honest achievement
c 260– 5 while holding in *t·* the character of Judas.
b 268– 5 In the material world, *t·* has brought to light
276–21 *t·* is turned into new and healthy channels,
284–30 *T·* passes from God to man,
310– 6 *T·* will finally be understood and seen

thought
   b 324– 1 renders *t·* receptive of the advanced idea.
   o 349–27 as *t·* is educated up to spiritual apprehension.
   p 377– 2 and that *t·* governs this liability.
     390–21 Suffer no claim . . . to grow upon the *t·*.
     392–14 *t·* should be held fast to this ideal.
     396–27 Keep distinctly in *t·* that man is the
     400–21 *t·* alone creates the suffering.
     412–13 you are liable . . . to impress it upon the *t·*.
     414–19 by troubling and perplexing their *t·*.
     415– 7 *t·* moves quickly or slowly,
     419–18 lest aught unfit for development enter *t·*.
     422–16 changes the material base of *t·*,
   t 445–18 or limit in any direction of *t·*
   r 485–24 If *t·* yields its dominion to other powers,
     492– 4 should be but one fact before the *t·*,
   g 510– 5 to be holy, *t·* must be purely spiritual.
     545– 9 by *t·* tending spiritually upward
     552–19 *t·*, loosened from a material basis

thought (verb)
   m 68– 3 for fear of being *t·* ridiculous.
   sp 75–23 those who have *t·* they died,
   ph 197–12 and the more that is *t·* and said about
     199– 3 might be *t·* true that hammering would
   f 221–26 he *t·* of the flesh-pots of Egypt,
     234–25 Sin and disease must be *t·* before they
     245–22 nor *t·* of herself as growing old.
   b 306– 1 Pharisees *t·* that they could raise the spiritual
     314–15 they *t·* that he meant their material temple
   o 351–30 They *t·* to worship Spirit from a
     374– 8 I never *t·* of and knew nothing about,
     388–10 *t·* that they could kill the body with matter,
   r 478– 8 What would be *t·* of the declaration that

thought-attenuations
   s 157–12 with such repetition of *t·*,

thought-force
   s 124–22 support the equipoise of that *t·*,

thought-forces
   ph 199–26 His belief . . . gave his *t·*, called muscles,

thought-germs
   s 164–16 mental microbes of sin and all diseased *t·*

thought-models
   c 259– 9 higher than their poor *t·* would allow,

thought's
   b 268– 3 With like activity have *t·* swift pinions

thoughts
  about sickness
    f 237–17 entertaining theories or *t·* about sickness.
  all
    f 208–32 You should banish all *t·* of disease and sin
    g 513–18 classifies, and individualizes all *t·*,
  budding
    p 413–29 mental images to children's budding *t·*,
  centred their
    o 351–27 The Israelites centred their *t·* on the
  depicts the
    ap 571–26 depicts the *t·* which he beholds in mortal mind.
  direct those
    sp 94–25 better enabled him to direct those *t·* aright ;
  diseased
    f 237–20 keep out . . . either sinful or diseased *t·*.
  disease in the
    ph 180–17 should not implant disease in the *t·*
  dissection of
    t 462–21 and consists in the dissection of *t·*
  distant
    sp 82– 1 it is as easy to read distant *t·* as near.
  ever recurring
    c 260–25 by the *t·* ever recurring to one's self,
  evil
    an 100– * *out of the heart proceed evil t·*,— *Matt.* 15 : 19.
    f 234–26 must control evil *t·* in the first instance,
    234–31 Evil *t·* and aims reach no farther
    234–32 Evil *t·*, lusts, and malicious purposes
  exalted
    b 299– 7 My angels are exalted *t·*, appearing at the
  finite
    f 214–18 and entertain finite *t·* of God
  God's
    b 286–21 God's *t·* are perfect and eternal,
    337–25 Eternal things (verities) are God's *t·*
    gl 581– 4 ANGELS. God's *t·* passing to man ;
    583– 2 whose better originals are God's *t·*,
  her
    pref ix– 1 She also began to jot down her *t·*
    f 236–13 Her *t·* form the embryo of another
    p 426– 7 the high goal always before her *t·*,
  His
    s 114–11 noumenon and phenomena, God and His *t·*.
    g 513–26 His *t·* are spiritual realities.

thoughts
  his
    m 56– 2 Reading his *t·*, Jesus added :
    s 139– 2 the unrighteous man his *t·*."— *Isa.* 55 : 7.
    ph 198–25 His *t·* and his patient's commingle,
    239–15 and the unrighteous man his *t·*."— *Isa.* 55 : 7.
    c 263– 7 blends his *t·* of existence with the
    b 290–30 His *t·* are no purer until evil is disarmed by
  his own
    p 366–24 by the unveiling of sin in his own *t·*.
  holy
    g 512– 9 and also by holy *t·*, winged with Love.
  human
    b 297–24 Human *t·* have their degrees of comparison.
    t 449–20 The inoculation of evil human *t·*
  impure
    gl 595–24 UNCLEANLINESS. Impure *t·* ; error ; sin ; dirt.
  influence the
    t 447– 4 to attempt to influence the *t·* of others,
  inverted
    c 267–21 inverted *t·* and erroneous beliefs
  its own
    sp 86–31 It feels, hears, and sees its own *t·*.
    p 424– 3 takes possession of itself and its own *t·*
  knew their
    sp 85–16 Jesus, . . . "knew their *t·*,"— *Matt.* 12 : 25.
  mortal
    (*see* **mortal**)
  my
    s 108–32 set my *t·* to work in new channels,
  new
    pref vii–22 A book introduces new *t·*,
    r 492–14 New *t·* are constantly obtaining the floor.
  objects and
    b 269–19 the objects and *t·* of material sense,
    276–13 brings objects and *t·* into human view
  of disease
    ph 196–21 so efface the images and *t·* of disease,
    f 208–32 You should banish all *t·* of disease and sin
  of health
    f 208–31 should delineate upon it *t·* of health,
  of mankind
    sp 94–24 Our Master easily read the *t·* of mankind,
  of mortals
    f 249–27 than are the *t·* of mortals when awake.
    b 337–27 Temporal things are the *t·* of mortals
    r 484–14 the conscious and unconscious *t·* of mortals.
  of pain
    ph 190– 9 fills itself with *t·* of pain and pleasure,
  of the healer
    t 446–16 Good must dominate in the *t·* of the healer,
  opposite
    p 417–31 and how divine Mind can cure by opposite *t·*.
  our
    b 322–11 to turn our *t·* towards divine Principle,
  overcoming the
    f 233–20 by overcoming the *t·* which produce them,
  patient's
    sp 79– 6 by changing the patient's *t·* regarding death.
  patients'
    p 414–15 To fix truth steadfastly in your patients' *t·*,
  pure
    b 298–28 Angels are pure *t·* from God, winged with
  reading the
    b 272–16 Reading the *t·* of the people,
  resolving of
    g 510–25 suppositional resolving of *t·* into
  scientific
    an 104– 1 for scientific *t·* are true thoughts,
  sick
    c 260–21 A sick body is evolved from sick *t·*.
  sickly
    b 270–25 They think sickly *t·*,
  some
    b 297–25 Some *t·* are better than others.
  spiritual
    c 259–29 and demands spiritual *t·*,
    gl 582–28 The spiritual *t·* and representatives of
    598–10 to unfold spiritual *t·*.
  stronger
    ph 198–26 and the stronger *t·* rule the weaker.
  temporal
    b 286–22 Material and temporal *t·* are human,
  these
    g 506–19 and unfolds these *t·*, even as
  things into
    s 123–14 excludes matter, resolves *things* into *t·*,
    b 269–15 Metaphysics resolves things into *t·*,
  time and
    m 58–14 selfish exaction of all another's time and *t·*.
  transfer of the
    f 211–22 transfer of the *t·* of one erring mind
  transitory
    b 286–27 Transitory *t·* are the antipodes of
  true
    an 104– 1 scientific thoughts are true *t·*,

thoughts

turn their
p 416–31   Turn their *t·* away from their bodies

unformed
g 506–18   God, gathers unformed *t·* into their

unhealthy
p 392–30   and shut out these unhealthy *t·*

unspoken
pr   1–10   *T·* unspoken are not unknown to the
p 424–19   unspoken *t·* resting on your patient.

uplifting
f 235–14   The pure and uplifting *t·* of the teacher,

yielding one's
p 413– 3   The act of yielding one's *t·* to the

your
c 261– 7   proportionably to their occupancy of your *t·*.
p 407–25   Let the perfect model be present in your *t·*

pr 13–14   sooner by words than by *t·*?
sp 86–16   only because it is unusual to see *t·*,
88–11   *T·*, proceeding from the brain
s 107–13   *t·* acquaint themselves intelligently with God.
c 259–10   *t·* which presented man as fallen,
b 315–14   Their *t·* were filled with mortal error,
p 415–28   Before the *t·* are fully at rest,
t 462–23   Are *t·* divine or human?
gl 595–18   *t·*, beliefs, opinions, knowledge ; matter ;

thought-taking
p 365–10   supposed necessity for physical *t·*

thousand
pref xii– 6   During seven years over four *t·* students
s 139–18   thirty *t·* different readings in the Old
139–19   and the three hundred *t·* in the New,
g 504–22   is with the Lord as a *t·* years."— *II Pet.* 3 : 8.
504–25   whereas a *t·* years of human doctrines,
514–16   "the cattle upon a *t·* hills."— *Psal.* 50 : 10.
524– 5   and in a *t·* other so-called deities.
546–31   a *t·* different examples of one rule,
ap 560– 3   typical of six *t·* years since Adam,
gl 598–21   is with the Lord as a *t·* years."— *II Pet.* 3 : 8.

thousands
pref x–15   By *t·* of well-authenticated cases of healing,
sp 79– 5   *T·* of instances could be cited of health restored
87–31   which are *t·* of miles away
o 341– 2   raising up *t·* from helplessness to strength

threatened
ph 193–26   *t·* with incarceration in an insane asylum

three
a 27–13   in *t·* days I [Spirit] will raise— *John* 2 : 19.
27–24   credits him with two or *t·* hundred other
41–18   about *t·* centuries after the crucifixion.
44– 7   His *t·* days' work in the sepulchre
45–13   *T·* days after his bodily burial he talked with
an 104–10   scientific truth goes through *t·* stages.
s 107– *   *and hid in t· measures of meal,— Matt.* 13 : 33.
108–15, 16   the product of *t·* multiplied by *t·*,
108–16, 17   *t·* times *t·* duodecillions must be
109–11   For *t·* years after my discovery, I sought
109–32   The *t·* great verities of Spirit,
117–32   and hid in *t·* measures of meal,— *Matt.* 13 : 33.
118–19   presented as *t·* measures of meal,
118–19   that is, *t·* modes of mortal thought.
139–19   and the *t·* hundred thousand in the New,
153–10   administered at intervals of *t·* hours,
161– 7   the *t·* young Hebrew captives, cast into the
ph 193–15   It was between *t·* and four o'clock
f 221– 9   until *t·* hours after eating.
c 256– 9   The theory of *t·* persons in one God
b 314–15   in *t·* days I will raise it up,"— *John* 2 : 19.
331–28   a trinity in unity, *t·* in one,
331–32   These *t·* express in divine Science
p 438–15   on *t·* distinct charges of crime, to wit :
r 494– 3   and in *t·* days I [Mind] will— *John* 2 : 19.
g 515–19   nor does it imply *t·* persons in one.
523–22   and in *t·* verses of the second,
549–10   *t·* different methods of reproduction

threefold
b 331–32   the *t·*, essential nature of the infinite.

threescore
f 246–22   would enjoy more than *t·* years and ten

threshold
a 39–16   To him, therefore, death was not the *t·*

threw
c 259– 8   *t·* upon mortals the truer reflection of God

thrive
p 413–15   in order to make it *t·* more vigorously

throat
f 221– 9   that he should not wet his parched *t·*

throne
a 26– 3   pathway up to the *t·* of glory,
c 255– *   *Thy t· is established of old :— Psal.* 93 : 2.
b 317– 3   the *t·* of the creative divine Principle,
ap 565– 8   caught up unto God, and to His *t·*.— *Rev.* 12 : 5.

throng
sp 86– 3   "The multitude *t·* thee."— *Luke* 8 : 45.
p 371–18   the illusive sufferings which *t·* the gloaming.

throughout
pref xii–21   she had never read this book *t·*
a 30–22   *t·* the whole earthly career of Jesus,
55–23   reappearing of the divine healing is *t·* all time ;
sp 98–18   It is imperious *t·* all ages
s 146–29   and extends *t·* all space.
b 277–17   *t·* the entire round of nature.
319–13   *T·* the infinite cycles of eternal existence,
324–25   *t·* Asia Minor, Greece, and even in
333–19   *T·* all generations both before and after the
o 358–17   as is recorded *t·* the Scriptures.
p 408– 7   *t·* the entire round of the material senses,
422– 5   a great stir *t·* his whole system,
442– 6   *t·* the vast audience-chamber of Spirit
g 507–26   expresses Science and art *t·* His creation,
523–22   *T·* the first chapter of Genesis
526–25   This second . . . is a picture of error *t·*.

throw
m 65–30   will assuredly *t·* off this evil,
an 101–15   to *t·* light on physiological and
ph 192–22   the weight you *t·* into the right scale.
p 397– 5   We *t·* the mental influence on the
g 519–15   until they *t·* off the old man and reach the

thrown
c 263–29   *t·* into the face of spiritual immensity,
b 301– 2   as the human likeness *t·* upon the mirror,
o 360–19   Like a pendulum . . . you will be *t·* back and
t 461–12   light of understanding be *t·* upon this Science,

throws
f 205–30   *t·* our weight into the scale, . . . of matter.
249–28   It *t·* off some material fetters.
ap 578– 1   the light which C. S. *t·* on the Scriptures

thrust
s 132–14   The Pharisees of old *t·* the spiritual idea
150–28   and that he is then *t·* out of

thrusting
m 62–25   by *t·* in the laws of erring, human concepts.
ph 166–18   Instead of *t·* Him aside in times of
b 304–31   *t·* aside his divine Principle as

thrusts
sp 85–27   His *t·* at materialism were sharp, but needed.
t 458–20   Sin makes deadly *t·* at the Christian Scientist

Thummim
gl 595–11   definition of
595–13   The Urim and *T·*, which were

thunder
ph 174–17   The *t·* of Sinai and the Sermon on the Mount

thunderbolts
b 288–15   lightnings and *t·* of error may burst and flash

thunders
ap 559–13   It arouses the "seven *t·*" of evil,— *Rev.* 10 : 3.

thwart
r 485–15   Think not to *t·* the spiritual ultimate

thwarted
t 459–22   distrusted and *t·* in its incipiency.

Thy
iii– *   This is *T·* high behest :
pr 16–28   Hallowed be *T·* name— *Matt.* 6 : 9.
16–30   *T·* kingdom come.— *Matt.* 6 : 10.
16–31   *T· kingdom is come ;*
17– 1   *T·* will be done in earth,— *Matt.* 6 : 10.
s 131–22   so it seemed good in *T·* sight."— *Luke* 10 : 21.
ph 190–28   As for me, I will behold *T·* face— *Psal.* 17 : 15.
190–29   when I awake, with *T·* likeness.— *Psal.* 17 : 15.
190–31   In *T·* light shall we see light.— *Psal.* 36 : 9.
200–14   over the works of *T·* hands.— *Psal.* 8 : 6.
f 201– *   *the reproach of T· servants ;— Psal.* 89 : 50.
c 255– *   *T· throne is established— Psal.* 93 : 2.
g 532–15   I heard *T·* voice in the garden,— *Gen.* 3 : 10.

tidbits
f 214–25   would spread their table with cannibal *t·*

tide
s 125–22   with changes of time and *t·*, cold and heat,
139–13   wisely to stem the *t·* of sectarian bitterness,

tides
ap 566– 2   the dark ebbing and flowing *t·* of human fear,

tidings
p 442–15   as of one "that bringeth good *t·*."— *Isa.* 52 : 7.

ties
a 31– 4   Jesus acknowledged no *t·* of the flesh.
m 57–27   but this severance of fleshly *t·*

tiger
p 378–11   By looking a *t·* fearlessly in the eye,

tightened
m 67– 5   the wind shrieks through the *t·* shrouds,

till

ph 183–12	the condemnation of man to *t·* the ground,
g 518– 1	Man is not made to *t·* the soil.
520–22	was not a man to *t·* the ground.— *Gen.* 2 : 5.
520–31	never causing man to *t·* the ground,
537– 4	to *t·* the ground from whence he— *Gen.* 3 : 23.
544– 5	"not a man to *t·* the ground."— *Gen.* 2 : 5.
545– 7	The condemnation of mortals to *t·* the ground

tills

g 537–16	Error *t·* its own barren soil
545–15	Error *t·* the whole ground in this material

time

accepted

a 39–18	"*Now*," . . . "is the accepted *t·* ;— *II Cor.* 6 : 2.
sp 93– 8	*now* is the accepted *t·* ;— *II Cor.* 6 : 2.

all

a 38–14	in all *t·* to come.
52–26	not for their day only but for all *t·* :
55–23	divine healing is throughout all *t·* ;
b 317–14	not only in all *t·*, but in *all ways*

all account of

f 245– 6	she became insane and lost all account of *t·*.

and energies

s 109–14	and devoted *t·* and energies to discovering a

and eternity

b 285– 5	the great fact of being for *t·* and eternity.

and medication

p 398–26	belief in the healing effects of *t·* and medication,

and tide

s 125–21	will come and go with changes of *t·* and tide,

and toil

t 464– 6	and how much *t·* and toil are still required

another

a 38–18	another *t·* Jesus prayed, not for the twelve only,

another's

m 58–14	the selfish exaction of all another's *t·* and

any

o 350–20	lest at any *t·* they should see— *Matt.* 13 : 15.
p 413–30	making it probable at any *t·* that such ills

approaches

p 402– 8	The *t·* approaches when mortal mind will

at one

a 27–22	Jesus sent forth seventy students at one *t·*,
sp 88–16	at one *t·* are supposed to be substance-matter
r 489–19	at one *t·* the medium for
491–18	that matter is awake at one *t·* and

at the

a 53–27	but at the *t·* when Jesus felt our infirmities,
p 431–13	At the *t·* of the arrest the prisoner

barriers of

c 266–31	He does not cross the barriers of *t·*

before the

s 129–16	to torment us before the *t·* ?"— *Matt.* 8 : 29.

calendar of

g 520–11	according to the calendar of *t·*.

cometh

a 31–31	yea, the *t·* cometh, that— *John* 16 : 2.
m 64–18	the *t·* cometh of which Jesus spake,
b 325–26	The *t·* cometh when the spiritual origin of man,

extends through

b 328–31	his great life-work extends through *t·*

first

b 326–31	He beheld for the first *t·* the true idea

for thinkers

pref vii–13	The *t·* for thinkers has come.

future

b 306–15	at some uncertain future *t·*
g 546– 2	at some future *t·* to be emancipated from it,

glides on

f 240–18	Mortals move onward . . . as *t·* glides on.

has come

b 285–17	The *t·* has come for a finite . . . to give place

help in

s 148–29	to render help in *t·* of physical need.

his

a 47–14	He chose his *t·*, when the people were in doubt
ap 569–24	for the devil knoweth his *t·* is short.

illuminating

g 502–17	illuminating *t·* with the glory of eternity.

indefinite

o 348–29	believed for an indefinite *t·* ;

is at hand

ap 558– *	*for the t· is at hand.— Rev.* 1 : 3.

is finite

r 468–30	*T·* is finite ; eternity is forever

is not distant

a 24–15	The *t·* is not distant when the

Jesus'

pref xi–10	results now, as in Jesus' *t·*,
s 142–18	As in Jesus' *t·*, so to-day, tyranny and pride

less

s 142– 1	in less *t·* than the old systems,
ph 175–19	Then people had less *t·* for selfishness,

little

t 464– 4	Could her friends know how little *t·* the author

time

march of

f 225– 7	march of *t·* bears onward freedom's

measurement of

gl 598–19	YEAR. A solar measurement of *t·* ;

measures

gl 584– 6	measures *t·* according to the good that is

moves on

b 329– 1	As *t·* moves on, the healing elements of

mutations of

c 261–25	Breaking away from the mutations of *t·*

no

f 238–28	no *t·* for gossip about false law or testimony.

objects of

gl 584– 4	The objects of *t·* and sense disappear

of harvest

f 207–19	separates the tares and wheat in *t·* of harvest.

of Jesus

pr 6–30	a certain magistrate, who lived in the *t·* of Jesus,

of need

f 218–22	turning in *t·* of need to God, divine Love,

olden

s 131–27	explained the so-called miracles of olden *t·*

or accident

b 304–24	if *t·* or accident robbed them of

organization and

f 249–19	Organization and *t·* have nothing to do with Life.

our

sp 90–29	may as well improve our *t·* in solving the
ph 197–27	the effeminate constitutions of our *t·*

passing

f 245–22	she had taken no cognizance of passing *t·*

past

an 106–25	as I have also told you in *t·* past,— *Gal.* 5 : 21.

period of

r 494–13	or for a limited period of *t·*,

question of

f 242– 4	It is only a question of *t·* when

right

p 396–22	At the right *t·* explain to the sick the

same

sp 78– 8	and that at the same *t·* we are
82–13	different states of consciousness at the same *t·*.
s 142–14	they at the same *t·* shut the door on
f 229–12	and at the same *t·* admits that Spirit is
o 346–31	cannot serve both God and mammon at the same *t·* ;
t 457–22	One cannot scatter his fire, and at the same *t·*

shore of

a 35– 7	Discerning Christ, . . . anew on the shore of *t·*,
f 203–29	should disappear on the shore of *t·* ;

short

ap 568–23	he hath but a short *t·*.— *Rev.* 12 : 12.

solar

g 504–19	words which indicate, in the absence of solar *t·*,

takes

p 429– 7	The final demonstration takes *t·*

their

a 41–31	but that belief, from their *t·* to ours,

this

pref xii–11	and (for a portion of this *t·*) sole editor
a 40– 6	"Go thy way for this *t·* ;— *Acts* 24 : 25.
p 431– 5	During all this *t·* the prisoner attended to his
438–13	Personal Sense, by this *t·* silent,

will come

c 266– 7	the *t·* will come when you will be solitary,

will prove

p 368– 6	Divine Science insists that *t·* will prove all this.

will separate

g 535– 4	the wheat and tares which *t·* will separate,

work of

f 238–30	place the fact above the falsehood, is the work of *t·*.

---

pref ix–31	her comparative ignorance . . . up to that *t·*,
a 39–21	now is the *t·* in which to experience that
39–23	Now is the *t·* for so-called
44– 8	set the seal of eternity on *t·*.
47–21	and for a *t·* quieted his remorse.
55–22	The *t·* for the reappearing of the
sp 92–32	Do you say the *t·* has not yet come
s 150–11	now, as in the *t·* of its earlier demonstration,
ph 185–26	may seem for a *t·* to benefit the sick,
f 245–11	Having no consciousness of *t·*,
b 296–25	foundations which *t·* is wearing away.
338–32	The ideal man was revealed in due *t·*,
o 353–14	*T·* has not yet reached eternity
p 377– 8	Then is the *t·* to cure them through C. S.,
t 447–13	evil will in *t·* disclose and punish itself.
r 468–28	Eternity, not *t·*, expresses the thought of *Life,*
468–29	and *t·* is no part of eternity.
470–27	and consequently a *t·* when Deity was
g 509–21	are no more contingent now on *t·* or
510–21	until *t·* has been already divided into

time
 g 513–11 *t·* is not yet measured by solar revolutions,
 gl 595–17 definition of
  598–30 *T·* is a mortal thought,

time-honored
 pref vii–14 independent of doctrines and *t·* systems,
 b 326–13 the foundation of material systems, however *t·*,

times
 all
 s 160–22 Unless muscles are self-acting at all *t·*,
 b 273–30 beliefs emit the effects of error at all *t·*,
 ap 571–15 At all *t·* and under all circumstances,
 a million
 a 50–29 a million *t·* sharper than the thorns
 different
 s 163–24 hypotheses obtruded upon us at different *t·*.
 of persecution
 a 29– 9 work the more earnestly in *t·* of persecution,
 f 238–12 To fall away from Truth in *t·* of persecution,
 of trouble
 s 134–15 They have not waxed strong in *t·* of trouble.
 old
 ph 175– 6 In old *t·* who ever heard of dyspepsia,
 signs of the
 sp 85–22 discern the signs of the *t·* ?" — *Matt.* 16 : 3.
 g 510– 1 discern the signs of the *t·* ?" — *Matt.* 16 : 3.
 signs of these
 sp 98– 5 in the mental horizon the signs of these *t·*,
 their
 b 270–15 higher than the systems of their *t·* ;
 three
 s 108–16 three *t·* three duodecillions must be

 ph 166–18 Instead of thrusting Him aside in *t·* of
 p 381–14 mortal mind cannot legislate the *t·*, periods,
 t 443– 8 at *t·* severely condemned by some Scientists,

time-tables
 a 21–17 We have separate *t·* to consult,
 f 246–18 *T·* of birth and death are

timid
 ph 167–29 On this fundamental point, *t·* conservatism is
 f 238–29 To reconstruct *t·* justice and place the fact

timidity
 f 215–30 his philosophy spurned physical *t·*.
 o 352–22 thus watering the very roots of childish *t·*,
 r 483–31 One must fulfil one's mission without *t·*

timorously
 p 413–32 or any other malady, *t·* held in the beliefs

tints
 r 480– 7 and not a trace of heavenly *t·*,
 g 552–25 The blending *t·* of leaf and flower

tips
 f 205–28 Selfishness *t·* the beam of human existence

tired
 s 154–26 says . . . "You look sick," "You look *t·*,"
 f 217–30 Which is *t·* and so speaks?
  217–31 Without mind, could the muscles be *t·*?
 b 322–28 turn us like *t·* children to the arms of
 r 494– 4 and he did this for *t·* humanity's reassurance.

tireless
 g 515– 4 Patience is symbolized by the *t·* worm,
  548–22 Had the naturalist, through his *t·* researches,

tissue
 ph 172–28 But the loss of a limb or injury to a *t·*

tithe
 gl 595–22 definition of

title
 ph 184–11 never honoring erroneous belief with the *t·* of
 b 333– 9 not a name so much as the divine *t·* of
 gl 590–4 this term is sometimes employed as a *t·*,

toad
 m 66– 4 Which, like the *t·*, ugly and venomous,

tobacco
 p 383–24 Does his assertion prove the use of *t·* to be
  404– 3 If a man is an inebriate, a slave to *t·*,
  406–28 depraved appetite for alcoholic drinks, *t·*,
  407– 3 Puffing the obnoxious fumes of *t·*,
 t 454– 2 the use of *t·* or intoxicating drinks

tobacco-user
 p 383–21 The *t·*, eating or smoking poison

to-day
 alive
 f 216– 3 Who shall say that man is alive *t·*, but may
 and forever
 pr 2–32 yesterday, and *t·*, and forever ;" — *Heb.* 13 : 8.
 s 112–20 yesterday, and *t·*, and forever ;" — *Heb.* 13 : 8.
 f 249–18 yesterday, and *t·*, and forever." — *Heb.* 13 : 8.
 b 283– 7 "yesterday, and *t·*, and forever." — *Heb.* 13 : 8.
 g 546– 5 yesterday, and *t·*, and forever." — *Heb.* 13 : 8.
 ap 577–18 which *t·* and forever interprets this great

to-day
 Christianity
 a 28–26 and that Christianity *t·* is at peace with
 Christians of
 a 37–21 May the Christians of *t·* take up the
 conspicuous
 m 65–13 broadcast powers of evil so conspicuous *t·*
 grace for
 pr 17– 5 *Give us grace for t·* ;
 prophet of
 sp 98– 4 The prophet of *t·* beholds in the mental horizon
 repeated
 f 243–14 are not more commonly repeated *t·*,
 r 474– 5 reception accorded to Truth . . . is repeated *t·*.
 wise man of
 sp 95–25 Is the wise man of *t·* believed, when he

 pref vii– 1 To those . . . *t·* is big with blessings.
  ix–16 *T·*, though rejoicing in some progress,
 a 37– 2 sin brings suffering as much *t·* as yesterday
  52–17 *T·*, as of old, error and evil again make
  54–30 glorified man were physically on earth *t·*,
  55– 3 *t·* subjects to unchristian comment
 sp 73– 4 but another, who has died *t·*
  95– 5 as they would be *t·* if Jesus were
 s 113– 4 plentifully reaches humanity *t·*,
  132–20 *T·*, as of yore, unconscious of the reappearing
  134– 1 *T·* the cry of bygone ages is repeated,
  135–17 There is *t·* danger of repeating
  138–25 The Christian can prove this *t·* as readily as
  142–18 As in Jesus' time, so *t·*, tyranny and pride
  143– 2 *t·*, as yesterday, Christ casts out evils
  144–30 It is a question *t·*, whether the ancient
  149–31 *T·* there is hardly a city, village, or hamlet, in
  150– 4 *T·* the healing power of Truth is widely
 f 224–17 cross was truth's central sign, and it is *t·*.
  226–28 the Pharaohs, who *t·*, as of yore,
  254–21 demands us to accept lovingly *t·*,
 b 305–23 illusion of life that is here *t·* and gone to-morrow,
  322–17 foreshadowed the . . . hypnotism of *t·*.
 o 360–30 while *t·*, Jew and Christian can unite in

together
 a 21–16 we are not journeying *t·*.
 m 56– * *What therefore God hath joined t·*, — *Matt.* 19 : 6.
  58–25 "Two eat no more *t·* than they eat separately.
  60–15 put asunder what she hath not joined *t·*.
 sp 73–29 mistake to suppose that . . . can commune *t·*.
  74–31 so-called dead and living cannot commune *t·*,
  75–26 can commune *t·*, and that is the moment
 s 114– 1 classes both evil and good *t·* as *mind* ;
 f 215– 5 *t·* with all the faculties of Mind ;
 c 255– * *travaileth in pain t· until now.* — *Rom.* 8 : 22.
 b 306–15 to be brought *t·* again
 t 444– 5 "All things work *t·* for good — *Rom.* 8 : 28.
 r 466–12 neither dwell *t·* nor assimilate.
  474–32 for light and darkness cannot dwell *t·*.
 g 506–16 be gathered *t·* unto one place, — *Gen.* 1 : 9.
  506–23 the gathering *t·* of the waters — *Gen.* 1 : 10.
  509–23 "the morning stars sang *t·*, — *Job* 38 : 7.
  514–24 young lion, and the fatling *t·* ; — *Isa.* 11 : 6.
  535–30 the gathering *t·* of the waters — *Gen.* 1 : 10.
 ap 565–23 After the stars sang *t·*

toil
 a 35– 3 the fruitlessness of their *t·* in the dark
  36–28 *t·*, sacrifice, cross-bearing, multiplied trials,
 m 58–28 Wealth may obviate the necessity for *t·*
 f 217–20 the next *t·* will fatigue you less,
  217–29 You say, " *T·* fatigues me."
 p 385–15 Constant *t·*, deprivations, exposures,
 t 464– 6 and how much time and *t·* are still required
 g 536–26 Through *t·*, struggle, and sorrow,

toils
 a 49–10 his *t·*, privations, sacrifices, his divine patience,

toilsome
 t 462–16 There is nothing difficult or *t·* in this task,

token
 a 50–11 who could withhold a clear *t·* of his presence
 gl 596–29 in *t·* of reverence and submission

told
 sp 85–13 *t·* me all things that ever I did : — *John* 4 : 29.
 an 106–25 as I have also *t·* you in time past, — *Gal.* 5 : 21.
 s 156–15 and *t·* the patient so ;
 ph 193–17 I *t·* him to rise, dress himself,
  197–21 *t·* that the simple food our forefathers ate
 o 352–26 children directly to *t·* not to believe in ghosts,
 p 364–20 Jesus *t·* Simon that such seekers as he
  376–11 should be *t·* that blood never gave life
  430–32 I was *t·* that I must remain silent until
 g 533– 5 Who *t·* thee that thou wast naked? — *Gen.* 3 : 11.

tolerate
 s 129– 5 and can *t·* no error in premise or conclusion.

tomb

 a 44– 5 the *t·* gave Jesus a refuge from his foes,
  44–30 demonstrating within the narrow *t·* the
 f 248–11 which each day brings to a nearer *t·*.

to-morrow

 sp 73– 5 supposedly will return to earth *t·*,
 f 216– 4 alive to-day, but may be dead *t·* ?
 b 305–24 illusion of life that is here to-day and gone *t·*,

tone

 m 57– 6 The masculine mind reaches a higher *t·*
 s 126–13 the human mind never produced a real *t·*
  148–11 It loses Spirit, drops the true *t·*, and

tones

 pref viii– 7 even as the science of music corrects false *t·*
 m 58– 5 *T·* of the human mind may be different,
 sp 81–21 silence the *t·* of music, . . . and yet the
 s 145– 1 or whether they caught its sweet *t·*,
  145– 2 musician catches the *t·* of harmony,
 f 217– 4 to conclude that individual musical *t·*
 b 304–22 The science of music governs *t·*.
 ap 559–14 to utter the full diapason of secret *t·*.

Tongue

 p 431–21 The next witness is called :— I am Coated *T·*.

tongue

and pulse
 s 159–25 They examine the lungs, *t·*, and pulse
coated
 p 379–26 coated *t·*, febrile heat, dry skin,
grows mute
 sp 89–16 the *t·* grows mute which before was eloquent.
new
 s 114–19 in expressing the new *t·* we must sometimes
  117–11 the new *t·*, the spiritual meaning of which
 b 272–11 and is the new *t·* referred to in the
 o 354–25 to hear and to speak the new *t·*.
nor pen
 s 110–19 neither *t·* nor pen can overthrow it.
pen nor
 s 110–17 No human pen nor *t·* taught me the Science
possesses her
 sp 89– 7 believing that somebody else possesses her *t·*
spiritual
 s 115–11 back into the original spiritual *t·*.
under the
 ph 174–28 rolling it under the *t·* as a sweet morsel
voices
 pref ix– 8 the *t·* voices the more definite thought,

 p 370–32 Physicians examine the pulse, *t·*, lungs,

tongues

 f 210– 2 expressed only in "new *t·* ;"— *Mark* 16: 17.
 b 286–16 In the Saxon and twenty other *t·*
 o 349–23 "They shall speak with new *t·*'"— *Mark* 16: 17.
 p 362– * *they shall speak with new* t· *;*— *Mark* 16: 17.

tonic

 p 420–21 better than any drug, alterative, or *t·*.

took

 a 32–15 Jesus *t·* bread, and blessed it— *Matt.* 26 : 26.
  32–17 he *t·* the cup, and gave thanks,— *Matt.* 26 : 27.
  44–13 He *t·* no drugs to allay inflammation.
 s 107– * *leaven, which a woman* t·,— *Matt.* 13 : 33.
  117–32 "leaven, which a woman *t·*,— *Matt.* 13 : 33.
 ph 165–14 *t·* the place of spiritual truth.
  176– 3 Eves *t·* up the study of medical works
  193–16 in the afternoon when this *t·* place.
 b 272–14 shows the care our Master *t·*
  326–30 and in humility he *t·* the new name of Paul.
 o 352– 7 the Jews *t·* a diametrically opposite view.
 p 431–23 hypnotized the prisoner and *t·* control of
 g 526–26 *t·* the man, and put him into the— *Gen.* 2 : 15.
  528–11 *t·* one of his ribs, and closed up— *Gen.* 2 : 21.

tooth

 f 212– 2 A *t·* which has been extracted
 o 346–27 the *t·*, the operation, and the forceps

tooth-pulling

 o 346–25 Do you feel the pain of *t·*, when you

torch

 f 202–14 lights the *t·* of spiritual understanding.

tore

 gl 597–13 *t·* from bigotry and superstition their coverings,

torment

 s 129–16 to *t·* us before the time?"— *Matt.* 8 : 29.
 b 327–12 and it becomes his *t·*.
 ap 574–21 which poured forth hatred and *t·*,

torn

 a 44–16 to heal the *t·* palms and bind up the

torpid

 s 160–12 the heart becomes as *t·* as the hand.
 p 378– 9 Without . . . there can be no inflammatory nor *t·*

torrent

 pr 13–19 overwhelming our real wishes with a *t·* of words.

torture

 a 50– 5 moment of mockery, desertion, *t·*,
 ap 569–27 but how many periods of *t·* it may take

tortured

 p 433–25 sentenced to be *t·* until he is dead.
  437–16 the helpless innocent body *t·*,

tossed

 m 62– 9 fed, rocked, *t·*, or talked to,

total

 ap 563–10 dragon stands for the sum *t·* of human error.
  574–17 that the sum *t·* of human misery,

totters

 p 389–26 This belief *t·* to its falling

touch

 sp 71–11 that you *t·* and smell it.
  86– 5 mortal mind, whose *t·* called for aid.
  88– 4 the *t·* of a vanished hand,
 ph 170–26 and at least to *t·* the hem of Truth's garment.
 f 252–26 says : . . . But a *t·*, an accident, the law of God,
 c 263–16 His "*t·* turns hope to dust,
 b 282–21 Even though they seem to *t·*,
  300–13 temporal and unreal never *t·* the eternal and
  300–14 mutable and imperfect never *t·* the immutable
  300–16 inharmonious and self-destructive never *t·* the
 t 450–15 Some people yield slowly to the *t·* of Truth.
 g 526–10 material hearing, sight, *t·*, taste, and smell,
  529–20 neither shall ye *t·* it, lest ye die.— *Gen.* 3 : 3.

touched

 pref x–26 unbiased Christian thought is soonest *t·*
 sp 86– 1 Jesus once asked, "Who *t·* me?"— *Luke* 8 : 45.
 f 216– 4 What has *t·* Life, God, to such strange issues?
 b 311–31 But the spiritual, eternal man is not *t·*
 r 493–12 is *t·* upon in a previous chapter

touches

 sp 83–32 investigates and *t·* only human beliefs.
  88– 7 when no viand *t·* the palate
 ap 569–11 He that *t·* the hem of Christ's robe

touching

 s 161–19 The oppressive state statutes *t·* medicine

toward

 s 150– 8 peace, good-will *t·* men."— *Luke* 2 : 14.
 f 226–17 peace, good-will *t·* men."— *Luke* 2 : 14.

towards

 pr 5– 3 one step *t·* reform and the very easiest step.
 a 21–11 looks *t·* the imperishable things of Spirit.
  47–11 The world's ingratitude and hatred *t·*
 sp 84–22 is a step *t·* the Mind-science by which
  90–27 and opens it wide *t·* immortality.
 s 145–27 *t·* other forms of matter or error,
 ph 169–22 or any other means *t·* which
 f 205–25 hinders man's normal drift *t·* the one Mind,
  205–28, 29 *t·* the side of error, not *t·* Truth.
  213–11 Every step *t·* goodness is a departure from
  213–12 and is a tendency *t·* God, Spirit.
  213–13 this attraction *t·* infinite and eternal good
  213–14 by an opposite attraction *t·* the finite,
  226– 2 further steps *t·* the banishment of a
  236–31 youth makes easy and rapid strides *t·* Truth.
  240– 9 and the leaflet turns naturally *t·* the light.
  240–18 Mortals move onward *t·* good or evil
  242– 6 *t·* the joys of Spirit,
  242– 7 *t·* human freedom and the final
  251– 2 as it hastens *t·* self-destruction.
 b 268– 4 rising *t·* the realm of the real,
  276–22 *t·* the contemplation of things immortal
  299–13 never lead *t·* self, sin, or materiality,
  322–12 turn our thoughts *t·* divine Principle,
  323– 7 helped onward in the march *t·* righteousness,
  323–21 gravitates *t·* Soul and away from
 o 348–14 Are we irreverent *t·* sin, or
 p 362–14 with his head *t·* the table
  364– 4 and it was manifested *t·* one who was
  365– 5 would do much more *t·* healing the sick
  423– 5 diminishes the tendency *t·* a favorable result.
  430– 9 he will advance more rapidly *t·* God,
 t 444–14 not only *t·* differing forms of religion and
  451–15 walks in the direction *t·* which he looks,
  463–23 is the first step *t·* destroying error.
 g 541–25 even the human duty of man *t·* his brother.
  557–12 as the line of creation rises *t·* spiritual man,
  557–12 *t·* enlarged understanding and intelligence ;
 ap 577–24 Its gates open *t·* light and glory
 gl 586–22 spiritual being understood ; haste *t·* harmony.

town

 o 342–14 heal the sick in any *t·* where they should

toy

 sp 80–22 Even planchette— the French *t·* which

trace

 r 480– 6 and not a *t·* of heavenly tints.
 g 533–10 an attempt to *t·* all human errors

traceable
 g 523–29 after which the distinction is not definitely *t·*.
traced
 ph 188–21 are *t·* upon mortals by unmistakable signs.
tracing
 ph 189–23 in *t·* them, we constantly ascend
tractable
 f 236–25 Children are more *t·* than adults,
tradition
 a 27–23 *T·* credits him with two or three hundred
 29–12 There is a *t·* that Publius Lentulus wrote
traditional
 o 352–24 *t·* beliefs, erroneous and man-made.
traditions
 o 354–16 derived from the *t·* of the elders
traduced
 sp 95– 3 His holy motives and aims were *t·* by
traffic
 s 142–23 to purge the temples of their vain *t·*
tragedy
 b 317–23 whom they had loved before the *t·* on Calvary.
 p 434–23 His trial was a *t·*, and is morally illegal.
trail
 m 58– 4 or else joy's drooping wings *t·* in dust.
 g 550–20 and causes our standard to *t·* in the dust.
train
 g 526–12 sickness, and death, follow in the *t·* of this error
trained
 ph 195– 9 those very senses, *t·* in an opposite direction.
 197–19 hardier than our *t·* physiologists,
traitor
 a 47–26 fell to the ground, and the *t·* fell with it.
 t 450–14 nor play the *t·* for place and power.
traitor's
 a 47–12 The *t·* price was thirty pieces of silver
traits
 m 61–19 the grosser *t·* of their ancestors.
trample
 f 234–14 pearls before those who *t·* them
 p 440–19 You cannot *t·* upon the decree of the
trampled
 f 229–22 false law should be *t·* under foot.
tramples
 p 419–27 *t·* upon the divine Principle
trampling
 p 435–15 If liver-complaint was committed by *t·* on
transcend
 f 247–18 which *t·* all material sense.
transcendent
 ph 182–28 from ignorance of C. S. and its *t·* power.
transcendental
 b 301–14 This reflection seems to mortal sense *t·*,
 320–20 (however *t·* such a thought appears),
 o 360– 9 replies : . . . they are not so shockingly *t·*.
transcends
 b 301–15 the spiritual man's substantiality *t·*
 r 483– 7 Mind *t·* all other power,
transfer
 sp 75– 8 Spiritualism would *t·* men from the
 f 211–22 The *t·* of the thoughts of one erring mind
 r 496– 2 there is no *t·* of evil suggestions
transference
 an 103–30 and consequently no *t·* of
transferred
 sp 87– 6 or for the person holding the *t·* picture
transfiguration
 ap 576–22 to deific apprehension through spiritual *t·*.
transform
 b 295– 8 Mortal mind would *t·* the spiritual
 p 371–20 I would not *t·* the infant at once into a man,
 401–10 truth of being must *t·* the error
transformation
 sp 74–20 Such a backward *t·* is impossible in Science.
 f 241–13 *t·* of the body by the renewal of Spirit.
transformed
 a 49–20 *t·* by the renewing of the infinite Spirit.
 sp 74–17 The caterpillar *t·* into a beautiful insect,
 ph 191–14 Thus the whole earth will be *t·* by Truth
 b 291–21 has been *t·* into the popular proverb,
 308–28 until his nature was *t·*.
 p 440–10 Good deeds are *t·* into crimes,
 442–24 until the material, *t·* with the ideal,
transgress
 p 432–17 *t·* the laws, and merit punishment,

transgressed
 ph 184–22 not because a law of matter has been *t·*,
 p 384– 4 the depressing thought that we have *t·* a
 384–23 and their fatal effects when *t·*,
transgressing
 p 442– 2 adjudged innocent of *t·* physical laws,
transgression
 f 229–26 If the *t·* of God's law produces
 229–29 It is the *t·* of a belief of mortal mind,
transgressions
 p 381–32 for *t·* of the physical laws of health ;
transient
 f 214–26 How *t·* a sense is mortal sight, when a
 246–14 As the . . . material, the *t·* sense of beauty fades,
 247–13 form the *t·* standards of mortals.
 b 307–15 but only a *t·*, false sense of an existence
transition
 sp 75–27 and that is the moment previous to the *t·*,
 b 290– 8 but will remain as material as before the *t·*,
transitional
 m 65–24 *t·* stage is never desirable on its own account.
 ap 572–23 The Revelator had not yet passed the *t·*
transitions
 sp 90–10 *t·* now possible for mortal mind
transitory
 b 286–27 *T·* thoughts are the antipodes of
translate
 c 257–16 would *t·* spiritual ideas into material beliefs,
translated
 r 488– 7 Hebrew and Greek words often *t·* belief
 gl 598–12 It might be *t·* wind or air,
translates
 g 523–21 as our common version *t·* it.
translating
 s 115–10 when *t·* material terms back into the
translation
 a 36– 3 simply through *t·* into another sphere.
 f 209–22 by the *t·* of man and the universe back into
 210– 2 the *t·* of the spiritual original into the
 b 313– 3 (to give the full and proper *t·* of the Greek),
 313–20 is made even clearer in the *t·* of the
 o 360–22 as given in the excellent *t·* of the
 g 525–12 The following *t·* is from the Icelandic :
translations
 gl 598– 6 yet it has received different *t·*,
translator
 g 506–26 seem confused by the *t·*,
translators
 g 545–21 *t·* of this record of scientific creation
transmission
 sp 78–18 needs no material method for the *t·* of
 f 228– 3 The *t·* of disease or of
 p 424–30 belief . . . in the possibility of their *t·*.
 g 514–14 In the figurative *t·* from the divine thought
transmit
 p 413– 1 cannot *t·* good or evil intelligence
 g 551–23 How can matter originate or *t·* mind?
transmits
 s 117–27 dimly reflects and feebly *t·* Jesus' works
 c 259–22 Mortal thought *t·* its own images,
transmitted
 m 61–28 Nothing unworthy . . . should be *t·* to children.
 sp 87– 9 to be discerned, described, and *t·*.
 c 259–27 *t·* by the divine Mind through divine Science,
 g 517–18 His personality can only be reflected, not *t·*.
 551–18 *t·* through these bodies called eggs,
transparency
 b 295–22 in order to become a better *t·* for Truth.
transparent
 g 546–21 To the author, they are *t·*,
transplant
 c 265–32 and *t·* the affections from sense to Soul,
travail
 t 463–11 in the *t·* of spiritual birth.
 ap 562–24 the spiritual idea is typified by a woman in *t·*,
 562–28 for great is the idea, and the *t·* portentous.
travaileth
 c 255– * *t· in pain together until now.— Rom. 8 : 22.*
travailing
 ap 562–22 she being with child cried, *t· — Rev. 12 : 2.*
travel
 a 21–23 or, if I take up their line of *t·*,
 sp 90–21 hashish eaters mentally *t·* far and
traveller
 a 21–27 He is like a *t·* going westward for a
 ph 174–10 and portend a long night to the *t·* ;

travellers
f 245–12 Some American *t·* saw her when she was

traversed
pref vii– 5 yet it *t·* the night, and came where,

traversing
a 20–22 *t·* anew the path from sin to holiness.

tread
pr 9–29 since you do not care to *t·* in the footsteps of
s 124–26 We *t·* on forces.
129–27 along the path which Science must *t·* in its
t 454–28 until your students *t·* firmly in the straight and

treading
a 26– 2 *t·* alone his loving pathway up to the throne

treason
a 43–13 the *t·* and suicide of his betrayer,
p 438–16 perjury, *t·*, and conspiracy against the rights

treasure
pref x– 1 may *t·* the memorials of a child's growth,
ph 181–29 "Where your *t·* is, there will— *Matt.* 6 : 21.
c 262–26 "where your *t·* is, there will— *Matt.* 6 : 21.
t 451–15 where his *t·* is, there will his heart be also.

treasures
a 54–11 That he might liberally pour his dear-bought *t·*
sp 70– 4 revelations of C. S. unlock the *t·* of Truth.
f 241– 5 Sensual *t·* are laid up "where moth— *Matt.* 6 : 19.
241–11 hate, revenge, . . . steal away the *t·* of Truth.
c 265– 4 as his *t·* of Truth and Love are enlarged.
gl 593– 6 Purse. Laying up *t·* in matter ; error.

treat
pref x–14 or *t·* in full detail so infinite a theme.
m 67–30 Systems of religion and medicine *t·* of
s 151– 1 To be sure, they sometimes *t·* the sick as if
159–12 and to *t·* the patient as if she were
ph 174–25 if an individual is sick, why *t·* the body alone
f 218–24 *T·* a belief in sickness as you would sin,
o 345–32 or *t·* it for disease,"
346–19 We *t·* error through the understanding of
p 397–27 can never *t·* mortal mind and matter separately,
412– 6 symptoms of the case you *t·*,
419–31 If it is found necessary to *t·* against relapse,
421–11 you must *t·* the patient less for the
t 453–24 You should *t·* sickness mentally just as you
464–15 so violent that he could not *t·* himself

treated
sp 79–26 says : . . . and must be *t·* for it."
ph 176–21 Should all cases of organic disease be *t·* by a
f 235– 5 than to be *t·* mentally by one who does not obey
p 425– 6 If the case to be mentally *t·* is consumption,
425–12 *t·* as error and put out of thought.
432–14 *t·* as a criminal and punished with death.
t 456–22 cannot be efficaciously *t·* by the
463–24 Our Master *t·* error through Mind.

treating
s 111–30 my metaphysical system of *t·* disease
161–25 *t·* the case according to his physical diagnosis,
f 219– 3 My method of *t·* fatigue applies to
o 344–19 There are various methods of *t·* disease,
344–26 to investigate this method of *t·* disease?
348– 4 even while *t·* them as disease ;
p 424–27 well to be alone . . . when *t·* disease.

treatise
r 465– 4 she revised that *t·* for this volume in 1875.

treatises
ph 179–21 *T·* on anatomy, physiology, and health,
p 382–29 wrote . . . The *t·* I had read

treatment
begin your
p 411–27 Always begin your *t·* by allaying the fear
his
p 422–31 His *t·* is therefore tentative.
hygienic
p 370–26 Hygienic *t·* also loses its efficacy.
medical
t 443–17 certain ordinary physical methods of medical *t·*,
mental
p 410–22 chapter sub-title
metaphysical
ph 185– 3 My metaphysical *t·* changed the action of
occurs in your
p 421–11 If a crisis occurs in your *t·*, you must
of disease
pref viii– 1 the *t·* of disease as well as of sin,
s 126–23 and its application to the *t·* of disease
157–22 and recommend them for the *t·* of disease?
p 369– 4 unfitted for the successful *t·* of disease.
of insanity
p 414– 4 *t·* of insanity is especially interesting.
of moral ailments
s 140– 3 effectual in the *t·* of moral ailments.
pathological
p 373–10 Under all modes of pathological *t·*,

treatment
proper
t 463–21 To decide quickly as to the proper *t·* of error
such
s 159–17 and not have risked such *t·*.
ph 179–15 the body then seems to require such *t·*.
their
o 342–32 even if their *t·* resulted in the death of
treats
b 318–23 Medical science *t·* disease as though
t 459–30 *t·* disease with more certain results than

tree (*see also* **tree's**)
accursed
a 25– 8 shed upon "the accursed *t·*,"— *see Gal.* 3 : 13.
and flower
b 289–22 So man, *t·*, and flower are supposed to die ;
and herb
g 507–19 The *t·* and herb do not yield fruit because of
and its fruit
p 389–17 the fount and stream, the *t·* and its fruit,
every
p 404–18 cuts down every *t·* that brings not forth
g 518– 7 and every *t·*, in the which is the— *Gen.* 1 : 29.
525–31 every *t·* that is pleasant to the— *Gen.* 2 : 9.
527– 7 Of every *t·* of the garden— *Gen.* 2 : 16.
529–16 Ye shall not eat of every *t·* — *Gen.* 3 : 1.
falleth
b 291–19 "In the place where the *t·* falleth,— *Eccl.* 11 : 3
fruitless
pr 6–28 He said of the fruitless *t·*,
fruit of the
g 529–18 but of the fruit of the *t·* which is— *Gen.* 3 : 3.
is known
b 299–22 "the *t·* is known by his fruit"— *Matt.* 12 : 33.
is typical
p 406– 4 The *t·* is typical of man's divine Principle,
leaves of the
p 406– 2 leaves of the *t·* were for the— *Rev.* 22 : 2.
life of the
b 283–18 such as the structural life of the *t·*
of death
g 527–18 the *t·* of death to His own creation?
of knowledge
(*see* **knowledge**)
of life
(*see* **life**)
trunk of a
p 393–22 the trunk of a *t·* which you gash
yielding fruit
g 507–12 the fruit *t·* yielding fruit— *Gen.* 1 : 11.
508–10 the *t·* yielding fruit, whose seed— *Gen.* 1 : 12.
yielding seed
g 518– 7 the fruit of a *t·* yielding seed ;— *Gen.* 1 : 29.

pr 5–19 flourish "like a green bay *t·* ;"— *Psal.* 37 : 35.
sp 76–15 any more than a *t·* can return to its seed.
89–25 The *t·* is not the author of itself.
f 220–28 "the *t·* of the knowledge of— *Gen.* 2 : 17.
250–27 no more sense as a man than it has as a *t·*.
b 291–21 "As the *t·* falls, so it must lie."
299–19 figuratively represented in Scripture as a *t·*,
t 459–26 The *t·* must be good, which produces good fruit.
r 481–16 this "*t·* of the knowledge of— *Gen.* 2 : 17.
g 527– 8 the *t·* of the knowledge of— *Gen.* 2 : 17.
533– 6 Hast thou eaten of the *t·*,— *Gen.* 3 : 11.
533– 9 she gave me of the *t·*,— *Gen.* 3 : 12.
535–21 and hast eaten of the *t·* — *Gen.* 3 : 17.

tree's
o 358– 1 which destroys a *t·* so-called life,

trees
b 300– 6 The mirage, which makes *t·* and cities seem
g 529–18 the fruit of the *t·* of the garden :— *Gen.* 3 : 2.

tree-tops
s 122–16 sky and *t·* apparently join hands,

tremble
s 107–17 we may well *t·* in the prospect of
135– 5 *T·*, thou earth, at the presence— *Psal.* 114 : 7.
t 445–30 "I *t·*, when I remember that God is just,"

trembler
b 298–20 joy is no longer a *t·*, nor is hope a cheat.

tremblers
f 235–21 To the *t·* on the brink of death,

trembles
t 445–31 the author *t·* whenever she

trembling
a 23–26 with fear and *t·*."— *Phil.* 2 : 12.
sp 99– 6 with fear and *t·*,"— *Phil.* 2 : 12.
p 442–26 with fear and *t·* :"— *Phil.* 2 : 12.

tremor
p 422– 9 will become the physician, allaying the *t·*

tremulous
s 142–12 making dome and spire *t·* with beauty,

trespass
p 387–10 nor . . . *t·* upon God-given powers and re-sources,
t 453–32 He does not *t·* on the rights of mind
trespasser
an 106–13 the mental *t·* incurs the divine penalty
trespasses
a 33–24 raises the dead from *t·* and sins,
b 316–29 those dead in *t·* and sins,
trespassing
t 447– 1 The heavenly law is broken by *t·* upon
triad
s 122– 5 facts of Life, . . . defeat this *t·* of errors,
o 356–22 How then . . . subject to this *t·* of errors,
357–11 on account of this malevolent *t·*,
g 552–12 include no member of this dolorous and fatal *t·*.
trial
brought to
s 159– 7 The case was brought to *t·*.
commences
p 430–20 The patient feels ill, . . . and the *t·* commences.
hampers the
c 260–17 often hampers the *t·* of one's wings
in the Court
p 434– 9 permission is obtained for a *t·* in the Court of Spirit,
of our faith
p 410–14 Every *t·* of our faith in God makes us stronger.

p 430–17 Suppose a mental case to be on *t·*,
431– 1 must remain silent until called for at this *t·*,
434–23 His *t·* was a tragedy, and is morally illegal.
436– 5 to reappear however at the *t·*
trials
a 28–29 The *t·* encountered by prophet, disciple,
36–28 toil, sacrifice, cross-bearing, multiplied *t·*,
39– 8 We must have *t·* and self-denials,
m 66– 6 *T·* teach mortals not to lean on a
66–10 *T·* are proofs of God's care.
p 441–33 We have no *t·* for sickness before the
tribal
s 133–21 limited form of a national or *t·* religion.
140–23 The Jewish *t·* Jehovah was a man-projected God,
g 524–11 God becomes . . . a *t·* god to be worshipped,
gl 584–22 self-made or created by a *t·* god
tribe
g 514–10 "the lion of the *t·* of Juda,"— *Rev.* 5 : 5.
tribes
ap 562–12 The twelve *t·* of Israel with all mortals,
tribulation
m 66–10 Through great *t·* we enter the kingdom.
s 129–13 there will be "great *t·*— *Matt.* 24 : 21.
b 309–21 to be brought back through great *t·*,
p 366– 1 such as peace, patience in *t·*,
ap 562–14 will through much *t·* yield to the
tribunal
p 434–20 C. S. turns suddenly to the supreme *t·*,
437–10 before the Judge of our higher *t·*,
441–33 before the *t·* of divine Spirit.
ap 564–21 before the *t·* of so-called mortal mind,
tribunals
an 105– 5 To say that these *t·* have no jurisdiction
tributary
s 119–31 and makes body *t·* to Mind.
122–10 make mortal mind *t·* to mortal body,
122–31 They insist . . . mind therefore *t·* to matter.
f 209– 8 and man is *t·* to divine Mind.
r 481– 2 Man is *t·* to God, Spirit, and to nothing else.
ap 562– 8 reveals the universe as secondary and *t·* to
tribute
p 364– 8 Which was the higher *t·*
g 541– 5 instead of making his own gift a higher *t·*
trickling
p 379–12 only a stream of warm water was *t·* over his arm.
tricksters
sp 86–19 either involve feats by *t·*, or
tried
a 22–21 Love means that we shall be *t·* and purified.
43–16 persecutors had mocked and *t·* to slay.
ph 175–17 had *t·* to tyrannize over our forefathers,
f 232–23 and never *t·* to make of none effect the
c 267–29 for when he is *t·*,— *Jas.* 1 : 12.
p 430–17 as cases are *t·* in court.
436–25 taken into custody, *t·*, and condemned.
440–29 to be *t·* at the Court of Material Error.
r 471–24 and *t·* to adhere to it until she
ap 568– 3 evil has *t·* to slay the Lamb ;

tries
a 55–17 My weary hope *t·* to realize that happy day,
s 148–22 Then theology *t·* to explain how to make
ph 180– 5 The patient sufferer *t·* to be satisfied
187–24 The human mind *t·* to classify action as
t 443– 4 she *t·* to show them that under ordinary
trieth
s 115– 8 Job says : "The ear *t·* words,— *Job* 34 : 3.
Trinity
c 256–10 (that is, a personal *T·* or Tri-unity)
trinity
b 331–28 They represent a *t·* in unity,
trip-hammer
ph 199– 4 The *t·* is not increased in size by exercise.
triply
b 331–27 that is, the *t·* divine Principle, Love.
triumph
hope and
p 434–18 solemn eyes, kindling with hope and *t·*,
last
a 39– 4 until Christianity's last *t·*.
Master's
a 46– 1 fully to understand their Master's *t·*,
of Spirit
s 139– 5 are full of accounts of the *t·* of Spirit,
of truth
f 223–31 and foreshadows the *t·* of truth.
over body
a 42–16 his final *t·* over body and matter,
over the body
f 242– 8 and the final *t·* over the body.
suffering, and
a 21– 7 another's goodness, suffering, and *t·*,
ultimate
t 446–31 and the ultimate *t·* of any cause.

a 24–30 it enabled their Master to *t·* over the grave,
28–14 are enabled to heal the sick and to *t·* over sin.
43–28 must *t·* over all material beliefs
43–32 Love must *t·* over hate.
49–24 to *t·* over sin, sickness, death,
54–15 and *t·* over death through Mind, not matter.
f 232– 2 can *t·* over sin, sickness, and death.
243– 7 and *t·* over sin and death.
r 484–24 Science must *t·* over material sense,
triumphal
a 40–23 through the *t·* arch of Truth and Love.
42–12 his brief *t·* entry into Jerusalem
triumphant
s 117–22 and *t·* exit from the flesh.
r 493– 2 speedily shows Truth to be *t·*.
triumphantly
ap 566– 1 were guided *t·* through the Red Sea,
triumphed
a 24–15 in which Jesus suffered and *t·*.
30–26 If we have *t·* sufficiently over the errors
triumphing
f 232–18 by healing the sick and *t·* over death.
triumphs
a 25–15 casts out error, and *t·* over death.
31–21 the divine Principle which *t·* over death.
39–30 attended with doubts and defeats as well as *t·*.
41– 4 the joys and *t·* of the righteous
b 272–25 The *t·* of C. S. are recorded in the destruction of
triune
b 331–26 Life, Truth, and Love constitute the *t·* Person
r 469–10 quality of infinite Mind, of the *t·* Principle,
Tri-unity
c 256–10 (that is, a personal Trinity or *T·*)
tri-unity
b 340–17 It inculcates the *t·* of God, Spirit, Mind ;
g 515–20 It relates to the . . . *t·* of Life, Truth, and Love.
troches
ph 175–31 tubercles and *t·*, lungs and lozenges.
trod
a 52–17 the best man that ever *t·* the globe.
f 242–31 show the way our Master *t·*,
c 263–17 the dust we all have *t·*."
b 313–24 most scientific man that ever *t·* the globe.
p 364– 2 the best man that ever *t·* this planet.
trope
ap 571–22 Through *t·* and metaphor, the Revelator,
tropical
m 61–16 like *t·* flowers born amid Alpine snows.
p 377– 6 Invalids flee to *t·* climates
tropics
f 240– 3 Arctic regions, sunny *t·*, giant hills,
ap 575–30 southward, to the genial *t·*,

trouble

pr	13– 1	"a very present help in t." — *Psal.* 46 : 1.
s	134–15	They have not waxed strong in times of t.
ph	166–19	thrusting Him aside in times of bodily t,
	184– 8	remedy consists in probing the t to the bottom,
f	202–28	"a very present help in t ;" — *Psal.* 46 : 1.
p	383–18	which do not t the gross,
t	444–12	a very present help in t." — *Psal.* 46 : 1.
g	536–21	"of few days, and full of t." — *Job.* 14 : 1.
	552–16	of few days, and full of t." — *Job* 14 : 1.

troubled

m	67–17	or sunshine gladdens the t sea.

troublesome

p	416–10	will tell you that the t material cause
g	542– 3	that it might be rid of t Truth.

troubling

p	414–18	by t and perplexing their thought.

true

pr	3–14	likeness of the patient, tender, and t,
	5–23	Such an error would impede t religion.
a	25–10	His t flesh and blood were his Life ;
	31–26	the t worshippers shall — *John* 4 : 23.
	40–12	If the saying is t, "While there 's life there 's
	40–13	its opposite is also t, While there 's sin there 's
	42–26	in C. S. the t man is governed by God
	48–31	and of what the t knowledge of God can do
	53– 2	The latter accusation was t, but not in
m	57–10	their t harmony is in spiritual oneness.
	57–13	perpetual only as it is pure and t,
	58–10	t happiness, strength, and permanence.
	60–25	not discerning the t happiness of being,
	68– 2	understanding . . . will be the basis of t religion.
sp	87–25	The t concept is never lost.
	91– 7	point of departure for all t spiritual growth.
	93– 6	when the t worshippers shall — *John* 4 : 23.
	99–23	The calm, strong currents of t spirituality,
an	104– 1	for scientific thoughts are t thoughts,
s	112–24	has already been stated and proved to be t,
	113–22	Which of the denials in proposition four is t ?
	113–23	Both are not, cannot be, t.
	113–24	According to the Scripture, I find that God is t,
	116– 7	to make this Scriptural testimony t in our
	117–26	and because of opacity to the t light,
	126– 9	never projected the least portion of t being.
	129–18	are antagonistic to t being and fatal to its
	133–31	given place to the t knowledge of God.
	134–21	The t Logos is demonstrably C. S.,
	138– 4	behind Peter's confession of the t Messiah.
	140–20	rituals are but types and shadows of t worship.
	140–20	"The t worshippers shall worship — *John* 4 : 23.
	140–28	mournfully t that the older Scripture
	148–17	It loses Spirit, drops the t tone,
	164– 6	"No . . . classification of diseases . . . is t,
ph	192– 5	quit our reliance upon . . . and grasp the t.
	192–29	Christianity is the basis of t healing.
	196– 3	but he has not yet found it t that knowledge
	199– 3	it might be thought t that hammering would
f	202–20	for the t way leads to Life instead of to death,
	203–11	to the Christian the only t spirit is Godlike.
	203–24	but this is not t.
	211–11	Is it not equally t that matter does not
	211–24	If it is t that nerves have sensation,
	213–23	This was even more strikingly t of Beethoven,
	213–32	discard the one Mind and t source of being,
	230– 1	if t, it is a part of Truth.
	231–21	To hold yourself superior to sin, . . . is t wisdom.
	232–13	theories must be untrue, for the Scripture is t.
	237–29	the only living and t God can do.
	249–10	Such is the t Science of being.
c	258–17	as the t divine image and likeness,
	259– 6	In divine Science, man is the t image of God.
	261– 5	the enduring, the good, and the t,
	264–26	by which we can recognize t existence
	265–19	but this is t only of a mortal, not of a man
b	270– 3	One only of the following statements can be t :
	275–18	no truth is t, . . . but the divine;
	275–26	t understanding of God is spiritual.
	276–13	into human view in their t light,
	281–21	When we put off the false sense for the t,
	283– 2	belief that there is any t existence apart from
	285–12	claim that a mortal is the t image of
	286–29	error must also say, "I am t."
	289–26	but the spiritual is t,
	293–18	counterfeits the t essence of spirituality
	294–26	recognizable only in what is good and t.
	300– 3	Finite sense has no t appreciation of
	300–10	will bring to light the t reflection of God
	302–26	Man's t consciousness is in the mental,
	303–16	can never make both these contraries t,
	312– 1	How t it is that whatever is learned through
	314–20	This materialism lost sight of the t Jesus ;
	321– 2	which is just the opposite of the t,
	323–25	the t understanding of Life and Love,
	326–20	Working and praying with t motives,
	328–10	they gain the t understanding of God

true

b	329–10	Jesus, who was the t demonstrator of
	337– 7	For t happiness, man must harmonize with
	337–32	this Science is demonstrably t, for it heals
	338– 3	brings to light the only living and t God
o	349–29	this is equally t of all learning,
	353– 9	How can a Christian, . . . think of the latter as real or t,
	358– 7	If . . . one is t, the other must be false.
	358–21	a t knowledge of the great import
	359–18	T Christianity is to be honored wherever
	359–32	in their t light and loveliness,
	360– 6	It is t that materiality renders these
	361– 4	Christ, as the t spiritual idea, is the ideal of
p	376–23	audibly arguing the t facts
	387– 1	We shall perceive this to be t when we
	391–30	rise to the t consciousness of Life as Love,
	396–18	not because the testimony of sin or disease is t,
	402–17	but this is not t.
	404–23	Arouse the sinner to this new and t view of sin,
	409–26	and seek the t model.
	410– 8	might know Thee, the only t God, — *John* 17 : 3.
	419– 4	Your t course is to destroy the foe,
	421– 6	a word which conveys the t definition of
	427– 1	If it is t that man lives, this fact can never
	428–12	sweep away the false and give place to the t.
	429–16	mortal mind's affirmation is not t.
	439–11	T, Materia Medica was a misguided
	442–18	but the reverse of error is t.
t	447–17	When sin or sickness . . . seems t to material
	454– 7	and plants the feet in the t path,
	454–17	Love for God and man is the t incentive
	461–25	error is not t, hence it is unreal.
r	466– 4	all-science or t knowledge, all-presence.
	467–12	the t brotherhood of man will be
	467–27	Spirit gives the t mental idea.
	471–21	"Let God be t, but every— *Rom.* 3 : 4.
	472–20	If error were t, its truth would be error,
	472–30	They are not t, because they are not of God.
	474–26	Truth spares all that is t.
	478–16	No, not if God is t and mortal man a liar.
	486– 3	when you have learned falsehood's t nature.
	488–19	testimony of which cannot be t either of man or
	491–11	the t origin and facts of being,
	495– 6	If sickness is t or the idea of Truth,
	496–19	overlying, and encompassing all t being.
k	499– *	*He that is holy, He that is t,* — *Rev.* 3 : 7.
g	506– 2	distinguishing between the false and the t.
	512–25	Mortal mind inverts the t likeness.
	516– 1	Then note how t, according to C. S.
	522– 2	false history in contradistinction to the t.
	522– 4	If one is t, the other is false,
	523–10	which God erects between the t and false.
	527–14	It is t that a knowledge of evil would
	527–17	But is it t that God, good,
	528– 6	It cannot be t that man was ordered to
	530–29	dreamer and dream are one, for neither is t
	547– 4	If one of the statements in this book is t,
	547– 5	every one must be t,
	547–25	The t theory of the universe, including man,
	548–16	may entertain angels, the t ideas of God,
	550–19	hides the t and spiritual Life, and causes our
ap	568–10	first the t method of creation is set forth
	568–12	first exhibits the t warfare and then the false.
	571–23	immortal scribe of Spirit and of a t idealism,
gl	579– *	*He that is holy, He that is t,* — *Rev.* 3 : 7.
	590–25	t scientific statements of the Scriptures
		(*see also* **conception, idea, likeness, sense**)

truer

a	19– 7	by giving man a t sense of Love,
	19– 8	and this t sense of Love redeems
c	259– 8	threw upon mortals the t reflection of God

truest

s	132–29	with the t conception of the Christ?

truism

s	108– 9	the t that the only sufferer is mortal mind,
p	417– 9	make the sick realize this great t,

truly

a	25–10	and they t eat his flesh and drink his blood,
	27–12	never t understood their Master's instruction.
	34– 1	willing t to drink his cup,
	44–21	in his proof of man's t derived power
sp	81–23	in the case of man as t as in the case of
	94– 6	The t Christian and scientific statement of
s	112–12	borrowed from that t divine Science which
	120–19	impossible for aught but Mind to testify t
	130–24	and understood how t such as they belong to
	135–21	It has been said, and t, that Christianity
	140– 4	That God is a corporeal being, nobody can t
ph	189–15	it is as t mortal mind, according to its degree,
b	268– *	*and t our fellowship is with*— *I John* 1 : 3.
	327–22	Fear of punishment never made man t honest.
gl	585–13	"Elias t shall first come— *Matt.* 17 : 11.

trump
  f 223–27   but the last *t·* has not sounded, or this would
  b 291– 7   when the last *t·* shall sound ;
     292– 2   then the final *t·* will sound which will end the

trumpet-word
  p 427–32   to catch this *t·* of Truth,

trunk
  p 393–22   the *t·* of a tree which you gash

trust
  calm
    r 495–18   your clear sense and calm *t·*,
  doubting
    t 455– 4   or a faltering and doubting *t·* in Truth
  glorified
    b 299–11   they point upward to a new and glorified *t·*,
  grandest
    a 49–19   charged with the grandest *t·* of heaven,
  in good
    gl 579–13   the purpose of Love to create *t·* in good,
  in hygiene
    s 145–14   whether faith in drugs, *t·* in hygiene,
  our
    r 487–28   lengthens our days by strengthening our *t·*
  support their
    p 417– 4   Always support their *t·* in the power of Mind

    a 20–21   to obey the divine order and *t·* God, saves
  ph 169–21   however much we *t·* a drug
    181– 9   When you manipulate patients, you *t·* in
    181–23   if you adhere to error and are afraid to *t·*
  f 234– 3   If we *t·* matter, we distrust Spirit.
  o 359– 2   have seen and have been taught to love and to *t·*
    360–26   Behold, He putteth no *t·* in His— *see Job* 4 : 18.
  t 444–11   Step by step will those who *t·* Him
  r 488–10   faith, understanding, *t·*, constancy,

trustfulness
  a 23–23   these two definitions, *t·* and *trustworthiness.*

trusting
  pr 1–12   and no loss can occur from *t·* God
  s 146– 8   By *t·* matter to destroy its own discord,
  f 226–31   *t·* Truth, the strong deliverer,
  b 326–11   or *t·* in it more than in the spiritual.

trusts
  a 23–24   One kind of faith *t·* one's welfare to others.
  p 428– 9   To divest thought of false *t·*
  t 455–24   does not bestow His highest *t·* upon the

trustworthiness
  pr 15–30   *T·* is the foundation of enlightened faith.
  a 23–23   these two definitions, *trustfulness* and *t·.*
    23–30   demands self-reliant *t·*, which includes

Truth (*see also* **Truth's**)
  accept
    p 420–11   for if they will only accept *T·*,
  acceptance of
    f 202–13   the perception and acceptance of *T·.*
  acknowledgment of
    p 372–28   a just acknowledgment of *T·*
  action of
    ph 169–27   Only the action of *T·*, Life, and Love can
    183–18   legitimate and only possible action of *T·*
    p 386–13   through the action of *T·* on the minds of
  adherents of
    r 497– 3   As adherents of *T·*, we take the inspired Word
  affluence of
    a 54– 4   With the affluence of *T·*, he vanquished error.
  afraid to trust
    ph 181–23   if you adhere to error and are afraid to trust *T·*,
  all
    pr 11–31   will bring us into all *T·.*
  all is
    r 475– 2   To Truth there is no error,— all is *T·.*
  allness— of
    o 346–13   the somethingness— yea, the allness— of *T·.*
  all of
    r 495– 4   All of *T·* is not understood ;
  altar of
    t 454–22   Love is priestess at the altar of *T·.*
  and error
    a 19– 6   for *T·* and error are irreconcilable.
    ph 167–24   with Spirit and matter, *T·* and error.
    f 207–18   such as the amalgamation of *T·* and error
    211– 3   Spirit and matter, *T·* and error,
    b 283–15   They speak of both *T·* and error as *mind,*
    287– 9   *T·* and error are unlike.
    296–24   When the evidence of . . . *T·* and error, seems
    315–32   Spirit and the flesh, between *T·* and error.
    p 372–20   can we believe in . . . both *T·* and error,
    g 538– 9   the infinite distance between *T·* and error,
    539–19   It is false to say that *T·* and error commingle
    gl 586–16   line of demarcation between *T·* and error,
  and good
    s 114– 6   the divine Mind, or *T·* and good.
    g 529–27   neither origin nor support in *T·* and good.

Truth
  and Life
    pr 5–24   as it is destroyed by Christ,— *T·* and Life.
    a 30–21   to point out the way of *T·* and Life.
    37–25   by the demonstration of *T·* and Life,
    43–32   *T·* and Life must seal the victory over error and
    b 274–13   and they demonstrate *T·* and Life.
    288–30   made him the Way-shower, *T·* and Life.
    p 410– 7   the knowledge of Love, *T·*, and Life.
  and Love
    pr 4– 1   While the heart is far from divine *T·* and Love,
    12–15   man's unity with *T·* and Love.
    14–22   and present with *T·* and Love.
    15–20   to work and watch for wisdom, *T·*, and Love.
    a 21– 5   our part in the at-one-ment with *T·* and Love.
    24– 1   *T·* and Love understood and practised.
    25– 2   the great proof of *T·* and Love.
    28– 7   is the persecutor of *T·* and Love.
    31–13   the healing power of *T·* and Love.
    36– 3   in the blessed company of *T·* and Love
    40–24   through the triumphal arch of *T·* and Love,
    45–15   failed to hide immortal *T·* and Love in a
    48–14   *T·* and Love bestow few palms until the
    48–20   The great demonstrator of *T·* and Love
    50–31   the world's hatred of *T·* and Love,
    51–24   He was inspired by God, by *T·* and Love,
    m 57–19   Happiness is spiritual, born of *T·* and Love.
    sp 88–26   Eloquence re-echoes the strains of *T·* and Love.
    95– 8   our fidelity to *T·* and Love ;
    an 106–11   governed by his Maker, divine *T·* and Love
    ph 192–27   We walk in the footsteps of *T·* and Love
    f 216–18   submission to everlasting Life and *T·* and Love,
    231–19   beliefs which divine *T·* and Love destroy.
    c 255– 4   the perpetual demand of *T·* and Love,
    261– 2   Look away from the body into *T·* and Love,
    265– 4   as his treasures of *T·* and Love are enlarged.
    b 270–26   *T·* and Love alone can unmake them.
    274– 1   *T·* and Love antidote this mental miasma,
    279–20   demonstration of eternal Life and *T·* and Love.
    298–29   pure thoughts . . . winged with *T·* and Love,
    308–20   a message from *T·* and Love, appeared to him
    308–25   the light of *T·* and Love dawns upon thee.
    314–28   demands of its divine Principle, *T·* and Love,
    332–27   only purity could reflect *T·* and Love,
    p 394–27   to conquer discord . . . with *T·* and Love
    395–20   nurse should be . . . receptive to *T·* and Love.
    417–15   unshaken understanding of *T·* and Love,
    418–24   and especially by the spirit of *T·* and Love
    t 445–20   quiets fear with *T·* and Love,
    448–23   the grand results of *T·* and Love.
    455– 1   into accord with the spirit of *T·* and Love,
    463–14   conceived and born of *T·* and Love,
    r 472– 2   and that this Life is *T·* and Love ;
    476–30   that is, *T·* and Love reign in the real man,
    490– 7   C. S. reveals *T·* and Love as the
    495–30   abiding steadfastly in wisdom, *T·*, and Love.
    496–12   the healing power of *T·* and Love
    g 510– 9   *T·* and Love enlighten the understanding,
    516– 4   substance, Life, intelligence, *T·*, and Love,
    540–30   he is not the type of *T·* and Love.
    ap 558–17   pillars of fire, foundations of *T·* and Love.
    559–26   the nature, or primal elements, of *T·* and Love,
    561– 1   ignorance of *T·* and Love.
    561– 1   The understanding of *T·* and Love,
    565–21   with the fervent heat of *T·* and Love,
    567– 3   *T·* and Love come nearer in the hour of woe,
    567–10   *T·* and Love prevail against the dragon
    gl 583–12   CHURCH. The structure of *T·* and Love ;
    584– 2   light, the spiritual idea of *T·* and Love.
  apostles of
    a 40–21   apostles of *T·* may endure human brutality
  appearing of
    f 230– 7   the advanced appearing of *T·*,
  arraigns
    p 440– 4   *T·* arraigns before the supreme bar of Spirit
  arrive at
    r 468– 1   Thus we arrive at *T·*, or intelligence,
  ashamed before
    g 532–19   Ashamed before *T·*, error shrank abashed
  bar of
    p 437– 8   At the bar of *T·*, in the presence of
    437–30   unjust usages were not allowed at the bar of *T·*,
    440–26   standing at the bar of *T·*,
  based on
    s 124– 1   based on *T·*, the Principle of all science.
  battle of
    b 292– 2   will end the battle of *T·* with error
  belief in
    b 297–26   belief in *T·* is better than a belief in error,
  blaze of
    b 296–15   and they must go out under the blaze of *T·*,
  blessing of
    r 488– 6   receive the blessing of *T·.*
  capacities of
    f 202–22   and the infinite capacities of *T·*,

Truth

casts out
s 135–13   when $T\cdot$ casts out the evil called disease,
ph 183–26 $T\cdot$ casts out all evils
b 282– 1   Now, as of old, $T\cdot$ casts out evils
o 350–11   Then they know how $T\cdot$ casts out error
r 482–26   Sickness is part of the error which $T\cdot$ casts out.
495– 2 $T\cdot$ casts out error now as surely as
celestial
c 267–25   in which all error disappears in celestial $T\cdot$.
Christ is
a 18–16   Christ is $T\cdot$, which reaches
Christ, or
(see **Christ**)
claim of
b 329–25   maintains the claim of $T\cdot$ by quenching error.
claims of
sp 92–28   instead of urging the claims of $T\cdot$ alone.
comes
b 290–12   Hence $T\cdot$ comes to destroy this error
condition of
f 230– 3   to destroy a quality or condition of $T\cdot$?
consciousness of
f 218– 7   The consciousness of $T\cdot$ rests us
contradiction of
r 472–17   Error is the contradiction of $T\cdot$.
controls error
s 145–17   this advantage . . . that in it $T\cdot$ controls error.
counterfeits of
c 267–22   erroneous beliefs must be counterfeits of $T\cdot$.
course of
gl 593–16   unobstructed, it typifies the course of $T\cdot$;
coward before
p 368– 5   Error is a coward before $T\cdot$.
creations of
b 287– 4   which simulates the creations of $T\cdot$.
creative
g 549–29   Spirit as the divine origin of creative $T\cdot$,
currents of
a 24– 9   the buoys and healing currents of $T\cdot$
decapitates error
c 266– 3   Science, with which $T\cdot$ decapitates error,
defeat in
f 239–13   success in error is defeat in $T\cdot$.
demands of
ph 170–14   The demands of $T\cdot$ are spiritual,
b 325–20   Paul had a clear sense of the demands of $T\cdot$
t 450–13   They do not . . . whine over the demands of $T\cdot$,
demonstrable
r 487–20   founded on Science or demonstrable $T\cdot$,
demonstrable in
an 106–17   such methods as are demonstrable in $T\cdot$
demonstrated
b 289– 1 $T\cdot$ demonstrated is eternal life.
ap 559–15   Then is the power of $T\cdot$ demonstrated,
demonstrates
b 294–31   for $T\cdot$ demonstrates the falsity of error.
demonstration of
pr 2–17   Goodness attains the demonstration of $T\cdot$.
a 37–25   by the demonstration of $T\cdot$ and Life,
s 135–31   in demonstration of $T\cdot$, as must be the case
t 445–12   understanding and demonstration of $T\cdot$
denial of
p 372–27   In C. S., a denial of $T\cdot$ is fatal,
denying
o 342– 7   the sad effects on the sick of denying $T\cdot$.
deprived of
r 490–14   mortals are more or less deprived of $T\cdot$.
destroyed by
b 294–18   destroyed by $T\cdot$ through spiritual sense
338– 8   the error which must be destroyed by $T\cdot$.
destroys
a 23–10   an error of sinful sense which $T\cdot$ destroys,
sp 72–12 $T\cdot$ destroys mortality,
s 143– 1   and $T\cdot$ destroys only what is untrue.
f 243–31   They are inharmonies which $T\cdot$ destroys.
b 288–31   The eternal $T\cdot$ destroys what mortals seem
289–16   a mortal belief, or error, which $T\cdot$ destroys
p 420– 1   nor go from one part to another, for $T\cdot$ destroys
r 474–31 $T\cdot$ destroys falsity and error,
destroys error
b 339– 2 $T\cdot$ destroys error, and Love destroys hate.
o 350–30   Soul rebukes sense, and $T\cdot$ destroys error.
discernment of
o 346–16   and leads to the discernment of $T\cdot$.
dispensation of
b 270–16   the new dispensation of $T\cdot$.
divine
(see **divine**)
does not distribute
p 408–20 $T\cdot$ does not distribute drugs through the blood,
does the work
t 456–22 $T\cdot$ does the work, and you must both
drawn from
o 360– 2   real and eternal because drawn from $T\cdot$,

Truth

easier to desire
b 322–32   It is easier to desire $T\cdot$ than to
effects of
s 126–25   the effects of $T\cdot$ on the health, longevity,
p 386–14   corresponding effects of $T\cdot$ on the body,
energies of
ph 186– 4   and filling it with the divine energies of $T\cdot$.
f 252– 5   and of the recuperative energies of $T\cdot$
error and
o 356–13   as the two opposites,— as error and $T\cdot$,
356–18   nor an eternal copartnership between error and $T\cdot$,
error, credits
g 528–15   error, credits $T\cdot$, God, with inducing a
error, not
p 386–25   Error, not $T\cdot$, produces all the suffering
r 474–27   error, not $T\cdot$, is the author of the unreal,
eternal
sp 95–32   lifts human consciousness into eternal $T\cdot$.
ph 170–13   points to the self-sustaining and eternal $T\cdot$.
178–21   must finally yield to the eternal $T\cdot$,
c 255– 1   Eternal $T\cdot$ is changing the universe.
b 288–31   The eternal $T\cdot$ destroys what mortals seem
p 434–14   the bar of Justice and eternal $T\cdot$.
evasion of
t 448–10   Evasion of $T\cdot$ cripples integrity,
everlasting
b 286–28   are the antipodes of everlasting $T\cdot$,
evidence of
o 353– 8   having the stronger evidence of $T\cdot$
existent in
s 120–22   reveals man as harmoniously existent in $T\cdot$,
explanation of
t 453– 9   chemicalization follows the explanation of $T\cdot$,
expositions of
pref ix–16   not complete nor satisfactory expositions of $T\cdot$.
faith in
b 286– 7   gives full faith in $T\cdot$,
t 446–21   strengthens hope, enthrones faith in $T\cdot$,
find refuge in
sp 83– 8   Mortals must find refuge in $T\cdot$
flames of
ap 558–18   flames of $T\cdot$ were prophetically described
followers of
a 33– 6   the persecuted followers of $T\cdot$.
footsteps of
ph 192–27   We walk in the footsteps of $T\cdot$ and Love
f 241–24   the footsteps of $T\cdot$, the way to health
for teaching
o 343– 2   smitten for healing and for teaching $T\cdot$
fosters the idea
g 555–32 $T\cdot$ fosters the idea of Truth,
from error to
p 370–31   from error to $T\cdot$, from matter to Spirit.
God is
b 312–19   yet God *is* $T\cdot$.
God, or
s 130–27   the supremacy of God, or $T\cdot$,
144–10   afford faint gleams of God, or $T\cdot$.
golden with
s 121–12   happy sunshine, golden with $T\cdot$.
grace and
m 67–23   Grace and $T\cdot$ are potent beyond all other
harmonious
o 351–26   the all-inclusiveness of harmonious $T\cdot$.
has come
a 34– 5   instead of showing, . . . that $T\cdot$ has come to the
has no beginning
b 307–25 $T\cdot$ has no beginning.
hatred of
b 330– 5   and the human hatred of $T\cdot$,
heals
s 135–13   when $T\cdot$ heals the sick, it casts out evils,
o 344–11   Were it more fully understood that $T\cdot$ heals
heals with
b 318–23   Science of Mind . . . heals with $T\cdot$.
higher sense of
gl 589–19   higher sense of $T\cdot$ rebuking mortal belief,
ideal
r 473–10   Christ is the ideal $T\cdot$, that comes to heal
ideal of
a 30–19   As the individual ideal of $T\cdot$, Christ Jesus
f 207–29   is harmonious and is the ideal of $T\cdot$.
idea of
(see **idea**)
ideas of
g 543–26   Ideas of $T\cdot$ alone are reflected in the
immortal
a 45–15   had failed to hide immortal $T\cdot$ and Love in a
sp 72–14   and immortal $T\cdot$ (the spiritual sense)
f 204– 7   conclusively mental as immortal $T\cdot$;
o 357–22   in a false supposition, not in immortal $T\cdot$,
p 401–17   when immortal $T\cdot$ is destroying erroneous

Truth

immortal
p 415–26   instruct mortal mind with immortal *T·*.
r 468–12   Spirit is immortal *T·*;
g 548–15   and so aids the apprehension of immortal *T·*.
impressions from
f 214– 1   impressions from *T·* were as distinct as sound,
incarnation of
g 501–10   The incarnation of *T·*, that amplification of
infinite
sp 94– 3   Man reflects infinite *T·*, Life, and Love.
o 361–26   A germ of infinite *T·*, . . . is the
p 367–24   The infinite *T·* of the Christ-cure has come
r 470– 8   spiritual presence of Life as infinite *T·*
g 504–23   The rays of infinite *T·*, when gathered into
infinitude of
c 258–16   all that exists in the infinitude of *T·*.
influence of
s 146–25   through the holy influence of *T·*
r 474–24   Despite the hallowing influence of *T·*
innocence and
ap 568– 1   Innocence and *T·* overcome guilt and error.
inseparable in
p 404–28   Both cures . . . are inseparable in *T·*.
instructed by
p 426– 3   mortal mind, when instructed by *T·*, yields
intelligence, and to
g 517– 9   corresponds to creation, to intelligence, and to *T·*.
is able
ph 191–31   *T·* is able to cast out the ills of the flesh.
is affirmative
p 418–20   *T·* is affirmative, and confers harmony.
is an alterative
p 371–30   *T·* is an alterative in the entire system,
is a revelation
s 117–27   *T·* is a revelation.
is demonstrable
b 323–15   We must recollect that *T·* is demonstrable
is divine
b 287–10   In Science, *T·* is divine,
is ever truthful
s 129– 5   *T·* is ever truthful, and can tolerate no error
is God's remedy
s 142–31   *T·* is God's remedy for error of every kind,
is immortal
r 466–13   *T·* is immortal ; error is mortal.
468– 4   If *T·* is immortal, error must be mortal,
is infinite
p 367–30   Because *T·* is infinite, error should be known as
is intelligent
r 466–14   *T·* is intelligent ;
is limitless
r 466–13   *T·* is limitless ; error is limited.
is made manifest
b 316– 9   to show that *T·* is made manifest by its effects
is omnipotent
p 367–31   Because *T·* is omnipotent in goodness,
is overcoming
a 21– 1   If *T·* is overcoming error in your daily walk
is real
b 288– 1   The statement that *T· is real*
p 368– 4   *T·* is real and error is unreal.
r 466–15   *T·* is real, and error is unreal.
is the intelligence
b 282–26   *T·* is the intelligence of immortal Mind.
is their remedy
t 461–24   and *T·* is their remedy.
is the light
b 282–32   but *T·* is the light which dispels error.
is the rock
p 380– 5   *T·* is the rock of ages, the headstone of the
its opposite
b 282–32   infers from error its opposite, *T·* ;
judgment of
p 391– 5   delivered to the judgment of *T·*,
kingdom of
b 281– 3   into the kingdom of *T·* on earth
knowledge of
s 128–22   So it is with our knowledge of *T·*.
law of
r 482–28   C. S. is the law of *T·*, which heals the sick
g 530– 3   spiritual law of *T·* is made manifest
leaven of
s 118–10   but this leaven of *T·* is ever at work.
Life and
s 117–18   illustrating and demonstrating Life and *T·*
f 216–18   is in submission to everlasting Life and *T·*
b 279–20   demonstration of eternal Life and *T·*
304– 2   sweet sense and presence of Life and *T·*.
Life, and Love
pr 15– 5   but lets in *T·*, Life, and Love.
a 18– 2   whereby man reflects divine *T·*, Life, and Love.
26–14   *T·*, Life, and Love gave Jesus authority
41–14   proofs of *T·*, Life, and Love, which Jesus gave
49–23   able, through *T·*, Life, and Love, to triumph

Truth

Life, and Love
sp 94– 3   Man reflects infinite *T·*, Life, and Love.
s 137–20   *T·*, Life, and Love, which heals mentally.
ph 169–27   Only the action of *T·*, Life, and Love can
184–12   *T·*, Life, and Love are the only legitimate
f 243–27   *T·*, Life, and Love are a law of annihilation to
p 435–32   jurisdiction . . . of *T·*, Life, and Love.
r 468–18   *T·*, Life, and Love are substance,
497–17   *T·*, Life, and Love as demonstrated
g 504–13   since *T·*, Life, and Love fill immensity
gl 595– 2   symbol of Soul . . . of *T·*, Life, and Love.
Life, . . . and Love
  (*see* **Life**)
Life, Love
sp 81–15   Life, Love, *T·*, is the only proof of
Life or
a 42– 6   It cannot make Life or *T·* apparent.
ph 196–16   are not concomitants of Life or *T·*.
Life, or Love
f 207–25   presuppose the absence of *T·*, Life, or Love.
Life that is
sp 97–30   demonstrating the Life that is *T·*,
Life which is
a 35–23   as we reach the Life which is *T·*
lifts her voice
sp 97–23   for the higher *T·* lifts her voice,
light of
p 418–32   which flee before the light of *T·*.
g 557–20   rolls back the clouds of error with the light of *T·*,
lispings of
pref ix– 3   were only infantile lispings of *T·*.
Love and
a 19– 3   Love and *T·* are not at war with God's image
f 227–19   Love and *T·* make free,
r 470– 3   brotherhood of man would consist of Love and *T·*,
gl 596–17   the spiritual inspiration of Love and *T·*
majesty of
ap 564–19   Until the majesty of *T·* should be demonstrated
may annihilate
g 540–15   that *T·* may annihilate all sense of evil
Messiahship of
sp 95–25   Magi of old foretold the Messiahship of *T·*.
might of
pref vii–27   author's discovery of the might of *T·*
ministry of
ap 574–10   This ministry of *T·*, this message from
murmur not over
ap 559–23   but murmur not over *T·*, if you find
name of
t 456– 3   Teaching or practising in the name of *T·*,
never mingles
ph 191–29   in C. S., *T·* never mingles with error.
no pain in
s 113–28   There is no pain in *T·*, and no truth in pain ;
no reaction in
p 419–10   knowing that there can be no reaction in *T·*.
not resist
s 128–24   he should not resist *T·*, which banishes
not the result of
r 486–12   Death is not the result of *T·*
not towards
f 205–29   towards the side of error, not towards *T·*.
obedience to
ph 183–23   Obedience to *T·* gives man power
obliterated by
r 485–10   views of error ought to be obliterated by *T·*.
omnipotence of
t 454– 4   Teach your students the omnipotence of *T·*,
omnipotent
c 257–29   inexhaustible Love, eternal Life, omnipotent *T·*.
o 353–11   omnipotent *T·* certainly does destroy error.
opposer of
gl 580–15   the opposer of *T·*, termed error ;
opposite of
  (*see* **opposite**)
or error
f 211– 5   and who shall say whether *T·* or error
b 324–10   whether it be *T·* or error,
or Life
sp 91–14   is by no means the destruction of *T·* or Life,
or Love
f 234– 4   Whatever inspires with wisdom, *T·*, or Love
or Mind
r 483– 5   which nothing but *T·* or Mind can heal,
overcome by
f 231– 4   rightly met and fairly overcome by *T·*,
overcomes
p 420–17   *T·* overcomes both disease and sin
pathway of
r 487– 5   gained by walking in the pathway of *T·*
permanence of
f 215– 3   and the might and permanence of *T·*,

Truth

pierces the error
   f 210–20 and *T·* pierces the error of mortality

places
   g 538– 5 *T·* places the cherub wisdom at the gate

potency is
   b 293–15 whose potency is *T·*, whose attraction is Love,

power of
   a 20–19 and when error felt the power of *T·*,
      31–13 the healing power of *T·* and Love.
      40–19 show us the way and the power of *T·*.
   s 111–13 utilization of the power of *T·* over error ;
    137– 2 His students saw this power of *T·*
    146–26 This healing power of *T·* must
    150– 2 monuments to the virtue and power of *T·*,
    150– 4 To-day the healing power of *T·* is
   p 378–17 represents the power of *T·* over error,
    380–20 Nothing but the power of *T·* can prevent the
    412–16 the power of *T·*, . . . must break the dream
   r 495–11 in the life-giving power of *T·* acting on
    496–12 the healing power of *T·* and Love
   ap 559–15 Then is the power of *T·* demonstrated,

practical
   a 31–15 It is the living Christ, the practical *T·*,

practice of
   a 26–22 Jesus' teaching and practice of *T·*
   p 410–25 does not appear in the practice of *T·*

practised
   f 201– 1 best sermon ever preached is *T·* practised

proceeds from
   p 419–21 If the action proceeds from *T·*,

produced by
   p 421–23 the alterative effect produced by *T·*

protests of
   pr 12–14 deep and conscientious protests of *T·*,

reality and
   gl 580–30 not one who . . . sustains reality and *T·*.

recognition of
   t 450–11 open to the approach and recognition of *T·*.

reflection, of
   gl 581– 8 ARK. Safety ; the idea, or reflection, of *T·*,

regard for
   p 364–26 do they show their regard for *T·*, or Christ,

regenerates
   f 222– 8 whereas *T·* regenerates this fleshly mind

relation to
   s 113–14 showing . . . their exact relation to *T·*.

reliance on
   ph 167–31 Only through radical reliance on *T·*

remedy of
   s 140– 1 demands the remedy of *T·* more than

resistance to
   b 317– 9 Resistance to *T·* will haunt his steps,

rest in
   p 387–11 we are able to rest in *T·*, refreshed by the

reveal
   r 485– 2 If error is necessary to define or to reveal *T·*,

revealed
   t 457– 1 and registered the revealed *T·*

revealed by
   gl 593–23 SEAL. The signet of error revealed by *T·*.

revelation of
   a 29–23 brought forth her child by the revelation of *T·*,
   sp 98–19 Christ's revelation of *T·*, of Life, and of Love,
   s 109–22 The revelation of *T·* in the understanding
   g 504–11 it is the revelation of *T·* and of spiritual ideas.

rule of
   p 418–22 simple rule of *T·*, which governs all reality.

sanctuary of
   f 232–26 In the sacred sanctuary of *T·* are voices of

seed of
   b 271– 1 seed of *T·* springs up and bears much fruit.
   g 535– 1 The seed of *T·* and the seed of error,

seek
   f 254–11 When we wait patiently on God and seek *T·*
   b 286– 2 To seek *T·* through belief in a human doctrine
   p 364–18 Do Christian Scientists seek *T·* as Simon sought

seeker of
   pref x–23 personal experience of any sincere seeker of *T·*.

seekers for
   pref xii–26 commits these pages to honest seekers for *T·*.
   ap 570–15 simple seekers for *T·*, weary wanderers,

seeking
   p 367–10 This is what is meant by seeking *T·*, Christ,

sends a report
   ph 194– 9 *T·* sends a report of health over the body.

separated from
   p 505– 8 material sense, is separated from *T·*,

somethingness named
   b 276–28 Harmony is the *somethingness* named *T·*.

Spirit and
   ph 177–24 nor can a lie . . . against God, Spirit and *T·*.
   b 278–15 as we approach Spirit and *T·*, we lose the

spirit of
   p 391– 1 in the conscious strength of the spirit of *T·*
    418–24 especially by the spirit of *T·* and Love

Truth

spirit of
   p 427– 4 even the law of the spirit of *T·*,
   t 455– 1 into accord with the spirit of *T·* and Love,

spiritual
   (*see* **spiritual**)

spiritual sense of
   b 315–18 which beclouds the spiritual sense of *T·* ;
   t 452–22 When the spiritual sense of *T·* unfolds its

standard of
   a 31– 2 are unfit to bear the standard of *T·*,
   f 235–29 should uplift the standard of *T·*.
   r 472–22 should continue to lose the standard of *T·*.

strength of
   p 365–31 not giving . . . the joy and strength of *T·*.

struggle for
   p 426–10 The struggle for *T·* makes one strong

subjection to
   f 240–29 is finally brought into subjection to *T·*.

subordination to
   f 206– 5 exercised only in subordination to *T·* ;

sunlight of
   s 162– 5 C. S. brings to the body the sunlight of *T·*,

sunshine of
   b 299–28 the sunshine of *T·*, will melt away the

superstructure of
   gl 595– 8 superstructure of *T·* ; the shrine of Love ;

supremacy of
   p 406–22 to avail ourselves . . . of the supremacy of *T·*
   ap 569– 9 when we are conscious of the supremacy of *T·*,
   gl 589–21 the immortality and supremacy of *T·* ;

sustained by
   t 447–15 when mentally sustained by *T·*,

sword of
   t 458–18 two-edged sword of *T·* must turn in every
   g 538– 7 the sword of *T·* gleams afar

symbol of
   gl 591–23 MORNING. Light ; symbol of *T·* ;

testified for
   s 134– 5 who testified for *T·* were so often persecuted

text of
   pref x–13 but has bluntly and honestly given the text of *T·*.

that is Life
   sp 97–30 again demonstrating . . . the *T·* that is Life,

the ever-present
   b 297–23 *T·*, the ever-present, is becoming understood.

this living
   ph 180–28 The only way to this living *T·*,

touched by
   pref x–26 unbiased Christian thought is soonest touched by *T·*,

touch of
   t 450–15 Some people yield slowly to the touch of *T·*.

transformed by
   ph 191–14 transformed by *T·* on its pinions of light,

transparency for
   b 295–22 in order to become a better transparency for *T·*.

treasures of
   sp 70– 5 revelations of C. S. unlock the treasures of *T·*.
   f 241–11 hate, revenge, . . . steal away the treasures of *T·*.
   c 265– 4 as his treasures of *T·* and Love are enlarged.

trumpet-word of
   p 427–32 to catch this trumpet-word of *T·*,

trusting
   f 226–32 trusting *T·*, the strong deliverer, to guide me

truth of
   b 320– 2 Likewise we can speak of the truth of *T·*

unalterable
   pr 11–28 Prayer cannot change the unalterable *T·*,

unbelief" in
   p 401– 1 "because of their unbelief" in *T·*.— *Matt.* 13 : 58.

understand
   s 110–31 believe on Christ and . . . understand *T·*.

understanding of
   (*see* **understanding**)

universe of
   g 503–10 In the universe of *T·*, matter is unknown.

unknown to
   ph 184– 4 for these are unknown to *T·*

unlike
   r 468– 6 because error is unlike *T·*.

unlikeness of
   r 471– 6 The unlikeness of *T·*,— named *error,*

unseen
   r 481–11 do not change the unseen *T·*,

unsustained by
   c 264–22 Sin is unsustained by *T·*,

utterance of
   g 545– 4 This could not be the utterance of *T·* or Science,

verdict of
   o 358–15 It presents the calm and clear verdict of *T·*

voice of
   (*see* **voice**)

Truth

what is
pref viii–12   The question, What is *T·*, is answered by
  a   48–26   question, "What is *T·*,"— *John* 18 : 38.
  f 223–14   The question, "What is *T·*,"— *John* 18 : 38.
wisdom, or
  f 206– 2   no other Love, wisdom, or *T·*,
words of
  o 342–24   It speaks to the dumb the words of *T·*,
work of
  g 528–21   error now simulates the work of *T·*,
world of
  pr   13–30   The world of error is ignorant of the world of *T·*,
yields to
  b 329–31   opposition to spirituality, till error yields to *T·*.
  g 543– 3   This error, . . . yields to *T·* and returns to dust ;
yield to
  s 152– 2   and must by its own consent yield to *T·*.
  ph 176–30   are quite as ready to yield to *T·* as the
  b 287–30   Their false evidence will finally yield to *T·*,

pref vii– 7   the human herald of Christ, *T·*,
  vii–13   *T·*, . . . knocks at the portal of humanity.
pr   9–25   Are you willing to leave all for Christ, for *T·*,
  11–17   *T·* bestows no pardon upon error,
  12–10   neither Science nor *T·* which acts through
  15– 6   Closed to error, it is open to *T·*,
  16– 5   between *T·* that is sinless and the
  17–14   *all Life, T·, Love, over all,*
  18–18   *T·*, could conciliate no nature above his own,
  a 19– 5   Even Christ cannot reconcile *T·* to error,
  30–24   between the offspring . . . of *T·* and of error.
  34– 6   If Christ, *T·*, has come to us in demonstration,
  35– 6   Discerning Christ, *T·*, anew on the shore of
  35–12   They bow before Christ, *T·*,
  35–23   the Life which is Truth and the *T·* which is Life
  35–27   Our bread, . . . from heaven," is *T·*.— *John* 6 : 33.
  36– 7   would be for *T·* to pardon error.
  37– 7   Mortals try in vain to slay *T·*
  38–31   He taught that the material senses shut out *T·*
  47–23   the world generally loves a lie better than *T·* ;
  53–21   distance between the individual and *T·*
  m 65– 3   May Christ, *T·*, be present at every bridal altar
  sp 83–11   belief hides *T·* and builds on error.
  99– 9   *T·* has furnished the key to the kingdom,
  an 103–23   This belief has not one quality of *T·*.
  s 115–13   GOD : Divine Principle, Life, *T·*, Love,
  118– 8   second appearing in the flesh of the Christ, *T·*,
  126–31   straight and narrow way" of *T·*.— *see Matt.* 7 : 14.
  129–15   "Art thou [*T·*] come hither to— *Matt.* 8 : 29.
  130–32   *T·* should not seem so surprising . . . as error,
  134– 9   The new faith in the Christ, *T·*, so roused the
  142– 9   for Christ, *T·*, alone can furnish
  144–20   *T·*, and not corporeal will, is the divine power
  144–24   even as *T·* wars with error,
  144–28   *T·* will be the universal panacea.
  145–12   *T·*, subdues the human belief in disease.
  147–10   *T·* has lost none of its divine and
  149– 1   *T·* could save from sickness as well as from
  149–14   have not demonstrated the life of Christ, *T·*,
  152– 8   *T·* has a healing effect, even when
  162– 7   neutralizing error with *T·*.
  ph 170– 2   *T·* is not the basis of theogony,
  171– 5   through Christ, *T·*, man will reopen
  173– 8   supposition, . . . *T·* is reduced to the level of
  174–20   *T·* is revealed.
  176–31   *T·* handles the most malignant contagion
  181–10   in electricity and magnetism more than in *T·*,
  181–30   If you have more faith in drugs than in *T·*,
  182– 3   casting out error with *T·*, shows your position
  183–14   *T·* never made error necessary,
  184– 3   *T·* makes no laws to regulate sickness,
  f 201– 7   *T·* makes a new creature,
  202–26   *T·* should "much more abound."— *Rom.* 5 : 20.
  208–11   antipode of immortal Mind, of *T·*,
  216– 8   *T·* bruises the head of error
  224–28   *T·* brings the elements of liberty.
  225– 3   *T·* makes man free.
  225– 5   You may know when first *T·* leads
  228–24   and form and control it with *T·*.
  229–31   The remedy is *T·*, not matter,
  230– 2   if true, it is a part of *T·*.
  231–10   but God, *T·*, Life, Love, does heal
  236–32   makes easy and rapid strides towards *T·*.
  238–12   To fall away from *T·* in times of persecution,
  238–13   shows that we never understood *T·*.
  238–19   *T·* often remains unsought, until we
  242–21   The vesture of Life is *T·*.
  243–25   *T·* has no consciousness of error.
  251–11   *T·* works out the nothingness of error
  251–13   an error that Christ, *T·*, alone can destroy.
  253– 5   saith : . . . I give immortality to man, for I am *T·*.
  c 260–32   If we look to the body . . . for *T·*, we find error ;
  b 271– 9   in *T·*, casting out all inharmony.
  271–27   to cast them on the right side for *T·*,

Truth

  b 272– 4   must be gained before *T·* can be understood.
  275–12   Spirit, Life, *T·*, Love, combine as one,
  275–31   *T·*, spiritually discerned, is scientifically
  278– 8   even as in *T·* there is no error,
  279–15   no more . . . than *T·* can create error, or
  280– 9   Finite belief can never do justice to *T·*
  282–17   *T·* has no home in error,
  282–18   and error has no foothold in *T·*.
  285–31   Christ, *T·*, as the healing and saving power.
  286–11   Christ, Life, *T·*, Love ;
  287– 9   We call the absence of *T·*, *error.*
  287–11   Did God, *T·*, create error?
  287–32   *T·* cannot be contaminated by error.
  289–12   Life and Life's idea, *T·* and Truth's idea,
  290–21   Christ, *T·*, removes all ignorance and sin.
  292– 7   *T·* will be to us "the resurrection— *John* 11 : 25.
  293–29   C. S. brings to light *T·* and its supremacy,
  295–20   through which *T·* appears most vividly
  298–10   spiritual sense can bear witness only to *T·*.
  299–24   *T·* never destroys God's idea.
  299–24   *T·* is spiritual, eternal substance,
  299–26   error, may seem to hide *T·*,
  300–32   in that which reflects Life, *T·*, Love,
  304–19   *T·* is not contaminated by error.
  306– 1   who believed error to be as immortal as *T·*.
  307– 6   as real and eternal as *T·*.
  307–11   It says : . . . *T·* shall change sides
  307–17   Error charges its lie to *T·*
  308–22   *T·*, being thereby understood, gave him
  312–18   Mortals try to believe without understanding *T·* ;
  316– 7   Christ, *T·*, was demonstrated through
  316–19   thus proved that *T·* was the master of death.
  322– 7   Christianity, or *T·*, in its divine Principle.
  324–27   "If Christ [*T·*] be not risen,— *I Cor.* 15 : 14.
  325– 7   *T·*, unfolding its own immortal idea.
  325–18   with *T·* in divine Love,
  325–30   When first spoken in any age, *T·*,
  326– 3   If we wish to follow Christ, *T·*,
  330– 1   as mortals give up error for *T·*
  330–20   Scriptures declare Him to be,— Life, *T·*, Love.
  332–14   the Way, the *T·*, and the Life,
  333–23   to all prepared to receive Christ, *T·*.
  o 341–10   for they shall see God" [*T·*].— *Matt.* 5 : 8.
  343–12   and *T·* will not be forever hidden
  346–20   because *T·* is error's antidote.
  347–24   it is Christ, *T·*, who destroys these evils,
  351–14   presence of Christ, *T·*, which healed the sick.
  351–18   while error seems as potent and real to us as *T·*,
  354– 7   to enable them to leave all for Christ, *T·* ?
  354–24   and with the dawn *T·* will waken men
  357– 5   We sustain *T·*, . . . by rejecting a lie.
  357– 8   *T·* creates neither a lie, a capacity to lie,
  p 368–10   fatal beliefs that error is as real as *T·*,
  370– 4   turn from the lie of false belief to *T·*,
  374–15   Through immortal Mind, or *T·*,
  380– 4   *T·* is always the victor.
  390– 9   *T·* will at length compel us all
  394– 2   *T·* can destroy its seeming reality,
  403–19   deprived of its imaginary powers by *T·*,
  406–12   and spiritual perception, . . . reaches *T·*.
  410–12   showing that *T·* is the actual life of man ;
  412– 5   plead the case scientifically for *T·*.
  415– 5   disease, and death have no foundations in *T·*.
  420– 3   *T·* not error, Love not hate,
  422–10   the tremor which *T·* often brings to error
  433–31   Ah ! but Christ, *T·*, the spirit of Life
  442–22   Christ, *T·*, gives mortals temporary food and
  t 449– 5   does wonders for mortals, so omnipotent is *T·*,
  450–25   errors of belief, which *T·* can and will destroy.
  451– 1   the errors which *T·* must and will annihilate
  455– 4   or a faltering and doubting trust in *T·*
  462–12   and substituting his own views for *T·*,
  463–19   *T·* is here and has fulfilled its perfect work.
  r 465–10   Spirit, Soul, Principle, Life, *T·*, Love.
  469–17   evil— is not Mind, is not *T·*,
  473– 4   *T·*, God, is not the father of error.
  474– 4   The reception accorded to *T·* in the
  474–25   *T·* spares all that is true.
  474–26   If evil is real, *T·* must make it so ;
  475– 2   To *T·* there is no error,— all is Truth.
  481–27   impossible, since *T·* cannot support error.
  484–25   and *T·* over error,
  493– 2   C. S. speedily shows *T·* to be triumphant.
  495–23   this understanding will supplant error with *T·*,
  g 506– 7   and makes *T·* final.
  516–10   Life is reflected in existence, *T·* in truthfulness,
  524–22   How could . . . error be the enunciator of *T·* ?
  530–24   saying, . . . more to be desired than *T·*,
  533–26   *T·*, cross-questioning man as to his
  535–17   *T·* is indeed "the way."— *John* 14 : 6.
  537–15   *T·* guards the gateway to harmony.
  538– 3   *T·* should, and does, drive error out of
  538– 4   *T·* is a two-edged sword,
  539– 9   the standard of good, of Spirit, of Life, or of *T·*,

Truth

g 542– 3 that it might be rid of troublesome *T·*.
542– 7 *T·*, through her eternal laws, unveils error.
542– 8 *T·* causes sin to betray itself,
542–19 Let *T·* uncover and destroy error in
545–27 *T·* has but one reply to all error,
545–31 even so in Christ [*T·*] — *I Cor.* 15 : 22.
555–27 or that *T·* confers the ability to
ap 567–22 cast out by Christ, *T·*, the spiritual idea,
568–31 by which we lay down all for *T·*, or Christ,
569– 2 as *T·*, represented by the Son ;
572–16 open the seven seals of error with *T·*,
gl 587– 7 Mind ; Soul ; Spirit ; Life ; *T·* ; Love ;
591–17 divine Principle, substance, Life, *T·*, Love ;
593–18 Rock. Spiritual foundation ; *T·*.

truth

about ghosts
o 352–32 not irrational to tell the *t·* about ghosts.
absence of
sp 92–30 when it is merely the absence of *t·*,
ph 186–11 because it is the absence of *t·*.
action of
p 414– 7 yields . . . to the salutary action of *t·*,
all
s 127–23 all *t·* proceeds from the divine Mind.
127–29 the Comforter which leadeth into all *t·*.
b 271–22 it will lead you into all *t·*.
332–22 and leading into all *t·*.
g 505–17 the understanding which . . . leads into all *t·*.
and error
b 287–28 five material senses testify to *t·* and error
288– 3 suppositional warfare between *t·* and error
288–11 the conflict between *t·* and error
p 368– 6 Both *t·* and error have come nearer than
t 453– 6 *t·* and error, will be at strife
r 466– 9 life and death, *t·* and error,
492–31 would keep *t·* and error always at war.
and harmony
p 423–20 regarding the *t·* and harmony of being
and love
a 50– 4 Who shall decide what *t·* and love are?
f 215–21 phantoms of error before *t·* and love ;
p 414–11 *t·* and love will establish a healthy state,
r 473–20 proof of Christianity's *t·* and love ;
and the life
a 26–11 the way, the *t·*, and the life ;" — *John* 14 : 6.
b 320– 3 the way, the *t·*, and the life." — *John* 14 : 6.
o 353–11 "the way, the *t·*, and the life," — *John* 14 : 6.
apprehension of the
sp 80– 2 in proportion to our apprehension of the *t·*,
t 460–18 right apprehension of the *t·* of being.
approaches
sp 97–14 The nearer a false belief approaches *t·*
arbiter of
p 405–12 the arbiter of *t·* against error.
arguments of
p 411– 9 and needed the arguments of *t·* for reminders.
assimilate
t 462– 2 Some individuals assimilate *t·* more readily
attenuation of
s 153–21 a high attenuation of *t·*,
beauty, as well as
f 247–10 Beauty, as well as *t·*, is eternal ;
belief in its
p 396–19 on account of the tenacity of belief in its *t·*,
bites the heel of
f 216– 7 Error bites the heel of *t·*,
bite the heel of
ap 563–20 that he may bite the heel of *t·*
communicates itself
sp 85–31 *t·* communicates itself but never imparts error.
concerning the
p 412– 8 persuaded in your own mind concerning the *t·*
conviction of
p 418– 7 Plead with an honest conviction of *t·*
correlative
b 316–32 the possibilities of Spirit and its correlative *t·*.
demonstrate
s 149–31 dismiss superstition, and demonstrate *t·*
denial of
g 542–11 avoidance of justice and the denial of *t·*
denying the
a 53–23 instead of denying the *t·*
destroyed by
ph 168–29 if the error . . . was met and destroyed by *t·*.
b 297–12 Erroneous belief is destroyed by *t·*.
discerning the
pref x–29 or discerning the *t·*, come not to the light
effect of
f 224– 2 world feels the alterative effect of *t·*
effects of
f 233–28 tests I have made of the effects of *t·*
enables
p 392– 8 enables *t·* to outweigh error.
erroneous
r 472–21 absurdity — namely, *erroneous t·*.

truth

error simulates
sp 97– 5 the more closely error simulates *t·*
establish in
p 428–13 Thus we may establish in *t·* the temple,
eternal
b 303–14 statement . . . contradicts this eternal *t·*.
explanations of
g 555– 7 said . . . "I like your explanations of *t·*,
exponents of
a 52–18 common cause against the exponents of *t·*.
first appeared
b 324–20 When the *t·* first appeared to him in Science,
formidable in
b 317–19 makes man . . . more formidable in *t·*,
giving utterance to
sp 80– 3 is not lessened by giving utterance to *t·*.
great
a 33– 7 It was the great *t·* of spiritual being,
ph 200–16 The great *t·* in the Science of being,
t 454–13 the great *t·* which strips all disguise from error.
r 469–14 exterminator of error is the great *t·* that
health, and harmony
sp 72–31 the communicator of *t·*, health, and harmony
ignorant of the
p 380–19 a so-called mind ignorant of the *t·*
immortal
r 493– 8 to the immortal *t·* of all things.
infinite tasks of
b 323–10 Beholding the infinite tasks of *t·*,
in his sentiment
ph 176– 1 and there is *t·* in his sentiment.
intelligence and
p 437–12 to be destitute of intelligence and *t·*
interfere with
f 234– 2 material lotions interfere with *t·*,
invincible
t 453– 8 until victory rests on the side of invincible *t·*.
is greater
f 223– 9 Remember that *t·* is greater than error,
is not human
s 127–24 Therefore *t·* is not human,
know the
sp 84–32 we can know the *t·* more accurately than the
t 452–18 teacher must know the *t·* himself.
leadings of
s 151–30 and follow the leadings of *t·*.
life and
c 262–12 reverse . . . our efforts to find life and *t·* in
life, . . . and love
b 284–18 testimony as to spiritual life, *t·*, and love?
***morale* of**
t 456–19 One must abide in the *morale* of *t·*
mutable
g 503–25 mortal life, mutable *t·*, nor variable love.
no
s 113–29 no pain in Truth, and no *t·* in pain ;
b 275–18 no *t·* is true, . . . but the divine ;
292–24 because there is no *t·* in him. — *John* 8 : 44.
r 467– 7 no *t·*, no love, but that which is spiritual.
g 543– 1 having no *t·* to support it,
not the
p 425–11 that they are not the *t·* of man ;
not the equal of
sp 80– 4 A cup of coffee or tea is not the equal of *t·*,
obey the
b 326–22 that ye should not obey the *t·* ?" — *Gal.* 5 : 7.
of being
m 68– 1 *t·* of being will be the basis of
69– 8 as man finds the *t·* of being.
sp 84– 8 to be in harmony with the *t·* of being,
s 137– 1 teaching and demonstrating the *t·* of being.
ph 184–20 This is human belief, not the *t·* of being,
f 214–14 still the error, not the *t·* of being.
218–32 When we wake to the *t·* of being,
c 265–21 The *t·* of being is perennial,
b 273–19 importance of understanding the *t·* of being,
311– 1 clouds . . . which hide the *t·* of being,
337–11 The *t·* of being makes man harmonious
p 368–15 to have more faith in the *t·* of being
374– 3 the *t·* of being, whispered into the ear of
401– 7 If faith in the *t·* of being, . . . causes
401–10 *t·* of being must transform the error
403–16 mortal existence is . . . not the *t·* of being.
404– 5 destroy these errors with the *t·* of being,
416– 5 removed by recognizing the *t·* of being.
418– 5 Stick to the *t·* of being
423–10 mental causation, the *t·* of being,
427– 9 since the *t·* of being is deathless.
t 460–18 right apprehension of the *t·* of being.
r 479–22 in the Science and *t·* of being,
g 538–20 Until that which contradicts the *t·* of being
553– 7 obtain a better basis, get nearer the *t·* of being,
of Christian Science
s 110–16 afterwards the *t·* of C. S. was demonstrated.

truth

of creation
sp 93–16 and not the *t·* of creation.
c 263– 6 spiritual man alone represents the *t·* of creation.
of spiritual sense
b 318–13 silence this lie . . . with the *t·* of spiritual sense.
of that report
ph 193–28 I cannot attest the *t·* of that report,
of Truth
b 320– 2 we can speak of the *t·* of Truth
of your plea
p 418–10 half equal to the *t·* of your plea,
opposite
ph 171–28 The opposite *t·*, . . . destroys sin, sickness, and
or error
p 403–29 in proportion to the *t·* or error which
or Science
s 127– 6 entitled to a classification as *t·*, or Science,
pioneer of
a 28–31 await, in some form, every pioneer of *t·*.
pour in
f 201–18 pour in *t·* through flood-tides of Love.
preached by
s 141– 2 and the *t·* preached by Jesus.
progress of
sp 94–17 The progress of *t·* confirms its claims,
proves the
b 329– 6 proves the *t·* of all that I say of it.
records of
g 525–26 as to the records of *t·*,
regarding error
t 461–24 *t·* regarding error is, that error is not true,
Science and
s 110–23 the Science and *t·* therein will
r 479–22 in the Science and *t·* of being,
g 521–23 The Science and *t·* of the divine creation
scientific
an 104– 9 scientific *t·* goes through three stages.
g 521–29 the exact opposite of scientific *t·*
search for
s 152–24 in her search for *t·* ;
should emanate
f 236– 2 *T·* should emanate from the pulpit,
simple
sp 75– 1 This simple *t·* lays bare the
speak the
p 418–29 Speak the *t·* to every form of error.
spirit and in
a 31–28 in spirit and in *t·*."— *John* 4 : 23.
sp 93– 7 in spirit and in *t·*."— *John* 4 : 23.
s 140–22 in spirit and in *t·*."— *John* 4 : 23.
spiritual
ph 165–15 theories took the place of spiritual *t·*.
b 277–18 This points to the spiritual *t·*
293–20 while spiritual *t·* is Mind.
311–17 loss or absence of soul, spiritual *t·*.
spirituality or
b 293–18 the true essence of spirituality or *t·*,
spiritual sense of
b 272– 3 spiritual sense of *t·* must be gained
standard of
ph 195–32 Incorrect views lower the standard of *t·*.
stating
s 126– 2 Error will be no longer used in stating *t·*.
supply the
f 216–14 to supply the *t·* of immortal sense.
that disease
f 229–31 the *t·* that disease is *unreal.*
to utter
sp 97–23 It requires courage to utter *t·* ;
triumph of
f 223–31 and foreshadows the triumph of *t·*.
understanding and
g 544–29 belief reverses understanding and *t·*.
understanding nor
b 287–17 Neither understanding nor *t·* accompanies
utterance of
f 233–30 utterance of *t·* is designed to rebuke
virtue and
f 235– 3 if virtue and *t·* build a strong defence.
246–11 The radiant sun of virtue and *t·*
waters of
f 254–28 the ever-agitated but healthful waters of *t·*,
which heals
s 158–11 *t·* which heals both mind and body.
whole
a 19–12 The Master forbore not to speak the whole *t·*,
would be error
r 472–20 If error were true, its *t·* would be error,

iii– * Ye shall know the *t·*,— *John* 8 : 32.
iii– * the *t·* shall make you free.— *John* 8 : 32.
a 20–25 The *t·* is the centre of all religion.
24–29 The *t·* had been lived among men ;
33–13 For this *t·* of spiritual being,
41–28 *t·* taught by Jesus, the elders scoffed at.

truth

a 43–17 demonstration of the *t·* which Jesus taught,
53–20 the shock so often produced by the *t·*,
m 65–22 until we get at last the clear straining of *t·*,
sp 72–20 not a . . . sieve through which *t·* can be strained.
72–28 nor the medium through which *t·* passes to
77– 3 accomplish the change from error to *t·*
s 130–19 to make place for *t·*.
131– 2 error should not seem so real as *t·*.
134– 2 *t·* is still opposed with sword and spear.
146–18 *t·* divests material drugs of their
164– 7 true, or anything like the *t·*,
164–21 rather does it evidence the *t·* of
ph 176–23 and the Christian Scientist try *t·* only in
f 203–16 the image of his Maker in deed and in *t·*.
213– 5 as a man . . . *understandeth*, so is he in *t·*.
216– 8 Error . . . cannot kill *t·*.
223–29 as *t·* urges upon mortals its
225– 9 command their sentinels not to let *t·* pass
231–12 if *t·* results in error,
233–23 To reveal this *t·* was our Master's
233–31 Why should *t·* not be efficient
251–22 acts upon the so-called human mind through *t·*,
c 259–20 which corrects error with *t·*
b 269–11 The first is error ; the latter is *t·*.
273– 3 There is no *material t·*.
292–24 and abode not in the *t·*,— *John* 8 : 44.
315–25 conception of Jesus pointed to this *t·*
o 341– * *And because I tell you the t·*,— *John* 8 : 45.
341– * *And if I say the t·*,— *John* 8 : 46.
341– 2 the *t·*, which is raising up thousands
342–17 If . . . *t·* becomes an accident.
343–21 It would sometimes seem as if *t·* were
360–29 put to death . . . for the *t·* he spoke
p 368– 8 and *t·* will become still clearer
378– 6 and meet every circumstance with *t·*.
400–19 and contending persistently for *t·*,
411–11 If Spirit . . . bear witness to the *t·*,
414–15 To fix *t·* steadfastly in your
442–17 in which *t·* cannot be reversed,
442–28 This *t·* is C. S.
t 447–19 impart . . . the *t·* and spiritual understanding,
448– 9 tell the *t·* concerning the lie.
454–16 points out . . . error as well as *t·*,
458–10 the same effect as *t·*.
463–13 this *t·* removes properly whatever is
r 468– 9 no life, *t·*, intelligence, nor substance in
479– 3 With what *t·*, then, could the Scriptural
482–16 the *t·* casting out all error.
g 523– 7 the lie claims to be *t·*.
524–25 Is it the *t·*, or is it a lie
530–18 error . . . asserting its superiority over *t·*,
532–23 Is Mind capable of error as well as of *t·*,
547–25 only by this understanding can *t·* be gained.
548– 3 C. S. separates error from *t·*,
555–12 as if it were as real and God-created as *t·*;

Truth-cure
f 237–15 Children should be taught the *T·*,
truthful
s 129– 5 Truth is ever *t·*, and can tolerate no error
p 418–23 By the *t·* arguments you employ,
432– 4 and know him to be *t·* and upright,
437– 3 testified that he. . .knew Personal Sense to be *t·* ;
truthfulness
a 46– 4 This convinced them of the *t·* of
g 516–10 Truth in *t·*, God in goodness,
truth-giver
sp 72–12 Soul, or God, is the only *t·* to man.
Truth-power
ph 179– 9 and to heal by the *T·*,
185–24 reverse of ethical and pathological *T·*.
Truth's
a 55–15 *T·* immortal idea is sweeping down the
ph 170–27 to touch the hem of *T·* garment.
b 288– 2 error, *T· unlikeness, is unreal.*
289–12 Life and Life's idea, Truth and *T·* idea,
p 367–32 *T·* opposite, has no might.
t 458–15 *Semper paratus*, is *T·* motto.
462– 9 to practise *T·* teachings only in part,
r 494–28 eternal and real evidence, bearing *T·* signet,
ap 558–13 When understood, it is *T·* prism and praise.
truth's
f 224–16 this was not the manner of *t·* appearing.
224–16 Of old the cross was *t·* central sign,
224–21 the harbingers of *t·* full-orbed appearing.
225–12 there is a rallying to *t·*
truths
an 103–25 The *t·* of immortal Mind sustain man,
s 108–21 I learned these *t·* in divine Science :
111– 2 and the demonstrable *t·* of C. S. ;
155–16 high and mighty *t·* of Christian metaphysics.
f 221–23 These *t·*, opening his eyes,
236–24 the *t·* of health and holiness.

truths
- *o* 356– 1   in support of spiritual and eternal *t*·,
- *r* 490– 1   the grand *t*· of C. S. dispute this error.
- *ap* 575–15   Did not Jesus illustrate the *t*· he taught

try
- *pr* 3–19   and then we *t*· to give information to this
- 8–16   wise not to *t*· to deceive ourselves or others,
- *a* 37– 6   Mortals *t*· in vain to slay Truth with the steel
- *s* 143–32   may *t*· to make Mind and drugs coalesce,
- *ph* 176–22   and the Christian Scientist *t*· truth only in
- 180–22   they should *t*· to correct this turbulent element
- *f* 220–25   never to *t*· dietetics for growth in grace.
- 223–17   and *t*· to "give it pause."
- 238–17   will rebuke us when we . . . *t*· to reap the
- *b* 312–17   Mortals *t*· to believe without understanding
- 326– 7   must not *t*· to climb the hill of Science by
- *o* 354– 4   Why then do Christians *t*· to obey the
- 359– 3   Let any clergyman *t*· to cure his friends by
- 360–18   If you *t*· to have two models, then you
- *p* 394–15   that he should not *t*· to rise above his
- *t* 448–19   *T*· to leave on every student's mind the
- *r* 495– 7   and it would be absurd to *t*·.

trying
- *s* 156–21   After *t*· this, she informed me that she could
- 161–27   the very disease he is *t*· to cure,
- *f* 240–27   In *t*· to undo the errors of sense one must
- *o* 346–32   is not this what frail mortals are *t*· to do?
- *t* 458–12   or of *t*· to sustain the human body
- *ap* 568– 8   of *t*· to meet error with error.

trysting-times
- *m* 59–22   a word or deed may renew the old *t*·.

tubercles
- *ph* 175–30   *t*· and troches, lungs and lozenges.
- *p* 418–30   Tumors, ulcers, *t*·, inflammation,
- 425– 9   *t*·, hemorrhage, and decomposition are beliefs,
- 425–32   Discard all notions about lungs, *t*·,

tubes
- *ph* 175–28   never indulged in . . . inflamed bronchial *t*·.

tumor
- *ph* 180–31   To reduce inflammation, dissolve a *t*·,
- *p* 395–24   erroneous to believe in the real existence of a *t*·,

tumors
- *s* 162– 8   dissolves *t*·, relaxes rigid muscles,
- *p* 418–29   *T*·, ulcers, tubercles, inflammation,

tumult
- *f* 225–12   There is always some *t*·,
- *b* 288–16   the *t*· dies away in the distance.

turbulent
- *ph* 180–22   to correct this *t*· element of mortal mind

turn
- *pref* x–19   Few invalids will *t*· to God till
- *pr* 8–22   If we *t*· away from the poor,
- 11–16   to make him *t*· from it with loathing.
- *a* 40– 1   evil confers no pleasure, they *t*· from it.
- *m* 61–18   live to become parents in their *t*·,
- 65– 4   at every bridal altar to *t*· the water into wine
- *sp* 77– 2   Polycarp said : "I cannot *t*· at once
- *s* 142–13   If the . . . *t*· the poor and the stranger from
- *ph* 190– 9   belief . . . in *t*· fills itself with thoughts of
- 194–20   in *t*·, mortal mind manifests itself in the body
- *f* 217–11   if we *t*· to the Scriptures, what do we read?
- 239– 3   in their *t*· lay it upon those who
- 248–25   must first *t*· our gaze in the right direction,
- *b* 316– 5   mortals need only *t*· from sin
- 322–11   to *t*· our thoughts towards
- 322–28   *t*· us like tired children to the arms of divine
- *p* 370– 3   *t*· from the lie of false belief to Truth,
- 416–30   *T*· their thoughts away from their bodies
- 420–30   *T*· his gaze from the false evidence of the
- *t* 444–20   *t*· to him the other also."— *Matt.* 5 : 39.
- 444–22   If ecclesiastical sects . . . *t*· a deaf ear to the
- 458–18   sword of Truth must *t*· in every direction
- 458–32   Christianity causes men to *t*· naturally from
- *g* 510–11   and *t*· away from a false material sense.
- 521–14   *t*· our gaze to the spiritual record of creation,

turned
- *pr* 14–17   Sorrow is *t*· into joy when the body
- *a* 35– 4   *t*· away from material things,
- 37–19   would gladly have *t*· his sacred career into a
- 48– 8   forever away from earth to heaven,
- 49–30   *t*· "aside the right of a man — *Lam.* 3 : 35.
- *s* 158– 8   Hippocrates *t*· from image-gods to vegetable
- *b* 276–21   is *t*· into new and healthy channels,
- 301–28   with everything *t*· upside down.
- 304–11   joy cannot be *t*· into sorrow,
- 310–12   when the earth has again *t*· upon its axis.
- *p* 380–14   knows will be *t*· against himself.
- 439–15   C. S. *t*· from the abashed witnesses,
- *t* 451–10   or be *t*· sadly awry.
- *g* 537– 7   flaming sword which *t*· every way, — *Gen.* 3 : 24.

turning
- *s* 121–27   besides *t*· daily on its own axis.
- *f* 218–22   instead of *t*· in time of need to God,
- *b* 323–30   We are either *t*· away from this utterance, or
- *p* 438–13   *T*· suddenly to Personal Sense,
- *t* 459–18   *t*· him loose in the crowded streets
- *r* 467–14   Having no other gods, *t*· to no other but the

turns
- *a* 21–10   He constantly *t*· away from material sense,
- 21–30   he *t*· east on the seventh, satisfied if he
- *sp* 92–21   Uncover error, and it *t*· the lie upon you.
- *ph* 166–25   and only as a last resort, *t*· to God.
- *f* 240– 8   the leaflet *t*· naturally towards the light.
- 248–12   The sculptor *t*· from the marble to his model
- *c* 261– 9   If one *t*· away from the body with such
- 263–16   His "touch *t*· hope to dust,
- *b* 312–28   and so *t*· away from the intelligent
- 322–20   he *t*· from his cups, as the startled dreamer
- *p* 376– 2   The patient *t*· involuntarily from the
- 431–27   dry, hot, and chilled by *t*·
- 434–19   Then C. S. *t*· suddenly to the supreme tribunal,
- *t* 459– 1   as the flower *t*· from darkness to light.

twelfth
- *ap* 559–32   The *t*· chapter of the Apocalypse, . . . has a
- 568– 5   The *t*· chapter of the Apocalypse typifies

twelve
- *a* 38–19   not for the *t*· only, but for as many
- *o* 342–13   He bade the seventy disciples, as well as the *t*·,
- *p* 436–27   charged the jury, *t*· Mortal Minds,
- *g* 523–29   closely intertwined to the end of chapter *t*·,
- 554–23   "Have not I chosen you *t*·, — *John* 6 : 70.
- *ap* 560– 8   upon her head a crown of *t*· stars. — *Rev.* 12 : 1.
- 562–11   The spiritual idea is crowned with *t*· stars.
- 562–12   The *t*· tribes of Israel with all mortals,

twenty
- *f* 245–17   conjectured that she must be under *t*·.
- *b* 286–16   In the Saxon and *t*· other tongues
- *p* 416– 7   in *t*· minutes the sufferer is quietly asleep.
- *g* 557– 2   child could remain under water *t*· minutes,

twenty-four
- *f* 221– 6   partook of but one meal in *t*· hours,

twilight
- *a* 32–31   in the *t*· of a glorious career
- *g* 513– 9   gray in the sombre hues of *t*· ;

twinkling
- *b* 291– 6   "in the *t*· of an eye," — *I Cor.* 15 : 52.

twist
- *t* 450– 2   *t*· every fact to suit themselves.

twisted
- *s* 142–21   as *t*· and wielded by Jesus,

two
- *pref* viii–20   deducible from *t*· connate facts,
- xii–16   conviction that the next *t*· years of her life
- *pr* 14– 5   We cannot "serve *t*· masters." — *Matt.* 6 : 24.
- *a* 23–22   definitions, *trustfulness* and *trustworthiness*.
- 27–24   *t*· or three hundred other disciples
- 52–22   These were the *t*· cardinal points of
- *m* 58–24   "*T*· eat no more together than they
- 63–13   differences between the rights of the *t*· sexes.
- 63–20   property, and parental claims of the *t*· sexes.
- *sp* 74–27   gulf which divides *t*· such opposite conditions
- 82–12   cannot exist in *t*· different states of
- 92–28   belief tends to support *t*· opposite powers,
- *s* 119– 5   for such theories lead to one of *t*· things.
- 123–19   The revelation consists of *t*· parts:
- 128–29   The addition of *t*· sums in mathematics
- 143–14   Driven to choose between *t*· difficulties,
- 143–32   but the *t*· will not mingle scientifically.
- 156–22   could get along *t*· days without globules ;
- *ph* 167–11   We cannot serve *t*· masters
- 182–12   It is impossible to work from *t*· standpoints.
- 193–20   informed that he went to work in *t*· weeks.
- *f* 201– 6   "No man can serve *t*· masters." — *Matt.* 6 : 24.
- 204– 7   and that there are *t*· separate, antagonistic
- 204– 8   antagonistic entities and beings, *t*· powers,
- 236–30   While age is halting between *t*· opinions
- 239–28   Those *t*· opposite sources never mingle
- 247– 3   *t*· of the elements it had lost, sight and teeth.
- 251– 9   mortals wake to the knowledge of *t*· facts:
- *b* 270– 8   not *t*· powers, matter and Mind,
- 278–20   From this it would follow that there are *t*·
- 279–27   knowledge that there are not *t*· bases of being,
- 282– 4   are figured by *t*· geometrical symbols,
- 338–14   Divide the name Adam into *t*· syllables,
- *o* 349–10   *T*· essential points of C. S. are,
- 355–14   *t*· conflicting theories regarding Christian
- 356– 1   when the *t*· are so antagonistic that
- 356–13   he spoke of flesh and Spirit as the *t*· opposites,
- 357–25   If what opposes God is real, there must be *t*·
- 358– 6   If *t*· statements directly contradict each other
- 359–29   A Christian Scientist and an opponent are like *t*·
- 360–18   If you try to have *t*· models, then you
- *p* 363–15   He described *t*· debtors, one for a large sum

U

unbroken
m 68–31 the u· links of eternal, harmonious being
r 494–24 breaks their illusion with the u· reality of

unceasing
pr 4–12 struggle to be always good is u· prayer.

uncertain
s 163–16 are in the highest degree u· ;
b 306–15 at some u· future time
326–24 only when his u· sense of right yielded
o 352–11 the spiritual was the intangible and u·,

unchangeable
s 120– 4 Soul, or Spirit, is God, u· and eternal ;
135– 8 establishing the Science of God's u· law.

unchanged
a 42–25 Afterwards he would show it to them u·.
46–20 Jesus' u· physical condition after what seemed
s 122–26 Life goes on u· and being is eternal.
b 302– 8 is thereby discerned and remains u·.
317–29 proof that he was u· by the crucifixion.
o 346–28 the operation, and the forceps are u·.
r 471– 4 remained u· in its eternal history.
g 555–31 Jesus was able to present himself u·
gl 588–12 man and woman u· forever in their

unchanging
pr 2–10 since He is u· wisdom and Love.
a 42– 4 gave no hint of the u· love of God.
f 248– 1 the u· calm and glorious freedom of
p 418– 8 the u·, unerring, and certain effect of

unchristian
a 55– 3 u· comment and usage
p 365–30 u· practitioner is not giving to mind or body
433– 9 warped by the irrational, u· suggestions

unclasp
p 412–14 adequate to u· the hold and to destroy

uncleanliness
p 383–17 impurity and u·, which do not trouble the gross,
gl 595–24 definition of

uncleanness
pr 8– 9 sepulchres. . . full . . . of all u·."— Matt. 23 : 27.
an 106–21 fornication, u·, lasciviousness,— Gal. 5 : 19.

uncoffined
p 441–12 "unknelled, u·, and unknown."

uncomplaining
a 48– 6 held u· guard over a world

uncomprehended
a 42–30 to test his still u· saying,

uncondemned
t 448– 7 but if evil is u·, it is undenied

unconfined
b 323–12 conception u· is winged to reach the divine

unconscious
sp 82–15 because both of us are either u· or
s 132–20 u· of the reappearing of the spiritual idea,
161–29 Such u· mistakes would not occur, if
ph 188– 5 is an u· error in the beginning,
190– 5 The mortal says that an inanimate u· seedling
o 346–26 believe that nitrous-oxide gas has made you u·
p 408–28 The u· thought in the corporeal substratum
409– 9 U· mortal mind — alias matter,
409–11 belief, that the u· substratum of mortal mind,
409–17 believed to be superior to its u· substratum,
r 484–14 conscious and u· thoughts of mortals.
484–17 Drugs and inert matter are u·, mindless.
492– 2 although the so-called dreamer is u·.
g 554–13 The mortal is u· of his fœtal and
gl 588–25 that which is never u· nor limited.

unconsciously
ph 199–18 is produced consciously or u·,
f 236–14 Her thoughts . . . u· mould it,
p 395– 1 The sick u· argue for suffering,
403– 6 self-mesmerism is induced u·

unconsciousness
f 218– 8 rests us more than hours of repose in u·.
p 427– 6 can no more die nor disappear in u· than

uncontaminated
t 457– 1 Truth u· by human hypotheses.

uncover
sp 92–21 U· error, and it turns the lie upon you.
t 453–18 You u· sin, not in order to injure, but
g 542–19 Let Truth u· and destroy error
ap 564–23 might u· its own crime of defying
572–16 u· the myriad illusions of sin, sickness, and

uncovered
pr 6–23 Jesus u· and rebuked sin
sp 86– 9 misconception of it u· their materiality.

uncovers
r 491– 3 Animal magnetism thus u· material sense,
g 540–14 u· so-called sin and its effects,

unction
pr 10–10 will never pour into prayer the u· of Spirit
s 164–13 minus the u· of divine Science.

undecaying
t 463–16 its growth sturdy, and its maturity u·.

undefiled
m 64– 4 "Pure religion and u·— Jas. 1 : 27.
ap 571–32 He enthrones pure and u· religion,

undefined
p 376– 9 the most hidden, u·, and insidious beliefs.

undenied
t 448– 7 but if evil is uncondemned, it is u·

under
pref xi–29 u· the seal of the Commonwealth,
pr 5– 7 placed u· the stress of circumstances.
10– 7 God will sustain us u· these sorrows.
a 30–28 loathe sin and rebuke it u· every mask.
43–25 he was acting u· spiritual law
m 60–11 affection lives on u· whatever difficulties.
66–27 considered patience salutary u· such
sp 91– 3 inhabited by beings u· the control of
97–22 for they bring error from u· cover.
an 100–14 U· this order a commission was appointed,
101–28 Discomfort u· error is preferable to
s 119–15 u· the name of natural law.
138–19 Christians are u· as direct orders now,
147– 9 applied u· circumstances where
ph 174–28 rolling it u· the tongue as a
182–22 puts matter u· the feet of Mind.
185–32 A patient u· the influence of mortal mind
186– 8 u· whatever name or pretence
192– 2 a pulpy substance u· the skull
198– 5 The patient may seem calm u· it, but
200–15 all things u· his feet."— Psal. 8 : 6.
f 226– 4 u· more subtle and depraving forms.
229–22 should be trampled u·
230–21 can man put that law u· his feet
234–15 trample them u· foot,
245–17 conjectured that she must be u· twenty.
c 258–28 man, u· the government of God
261–10 U· the strong impulse of a desire to
264–21 Matter disappears u· the microscope of
b 296–15 must go out u· the blaze of Truth,
319– 9 sustains man u· all circumstances ;
321–13 The serpent, evil, u· wisdom's bidding,
p 362– 8 especially u· the stern rules of
367– 1 u· the napkin of its form,
370– 5 The body improves u· the same regimen
370– 7 made manifest u· this regimen,
373– 9 U· all modes of . . . treatment,
386–27 u· the influence of the belief of grief,
389–29 came u· my observation.
402–31 the person u· hypnotic control
412–11 you are liable u· some circumstances
424–10 U· divine Providence there can be no
436– 3 for which Mortal Man is u· sentence
436–14 u· the protection of the Most High.
440–14 u· stress of circumstances,
t 443–14 u· ordinary circumstances a resort to
448– 7 U· such circumstances, to say that
451– 2 Christian Scientists must live u· the
463– 3 u· influences not embraced in his
r 490–31 U· the mesmeric illusion of belief,
g 505–14 waters which were u· the— Gen. 1 : 7.
506–15 Let the waters u· the— Gen. 1 : 9.
523– 2 the Scriptural account now u· comment.
532– 9 prediction in the story u· consideration.
544–16 u· the control of the one Mind,
553–12 been formed u· circumstances which
555– 5 physical organism u· the yoke of disease.
557– 2 could remain u· water twenty minutes,
ap 560– 8 the moon u· her feet,— Rev. 12 : 1.
561–27 matter is put u· her feet.
562– 7 The moon is u· her feet.
571–15 At all times and u· all circumstances,
572–17 U· the supremacy of Spirit, it will
gl 592–15 justice demands penalties u· the law.

undergo
a 24–17 views of atonement will u· a great change,
ph 169– 1 the process which mortal mind and body u·
p 385– 4 have been able to u· without sinking

undergoing
f 244–13 Man u· birth, maturity, and decay

underived
r 475–20 has not a single quality u· from Deity ;

underlies
o 353–17 Perfection u· reality.
t 460– 4 and it u· all metaphysical practice.

underlying
b 305–15 constitutes the u· reality of reflection.
p 417–32 Give your patients an u· understanding to
r 477–27 caught some glimpses of the u· reality,
496–18 u·, overlying, and encompassing all true being.

undermined
s 121- 2 if his discovery had u· the
undermining
  m 59-31 fatal mistakes are u· its foundations.
understand
  pref x-28 Only those . . . who do not u·
  pr 3-15 but to u· God is the work of eternity,
    6-15 we must u· the divine Principle of being.
    16-24 Here let me give what I u· to be the
  a 19-19 will help us to u· Jesus' atonement
    22-29 Whosoever believeth that'. . . does not u· God.
    25-14 may u· how this divine Principle heals
    25-26 and u· its divine Principle.
    38-29 lest ye should u· and be converted,
    40-11 divine pardon, which I u· to mean
    42-32 They must u· more fully his Life-principle
    43- 2 even as they did u· it after his
    43- 5 enabled the disciples to u·
    45-32 not sufficiently advanced fully to u·
    54-25 it enabled them to u· the Nazarene
    55-29 This Comforter I u· to be Divine Science.
  m 59-11 nor . . . be expected to u· political economy.
    69- 6 Mortals can never u· God's creation while
    69-13 Spiritually to u· that there is but one creator,
  sp 84-19 To u· that Mind is infinite,
    98-20 remains inviolate for every man to u·
  s 110-31 and spiritually u· Truth.
    120- 1 But we shall never u· this while we
    136-25 what the disciples did not fully u·
    141- 4 Few u· or adhere to Jesus' divine precepts
    141-22 did not then, and do not now, u· this
    149-29 We need to u· the affirmations of
    152-25 and she can now u· why,
  ph 167- 2 or should we u· the infinite divine Principle
    170- 7 Did Jesus u· the economy of man less than
    174-30 We should u· that the cause of disease
    180- 8 must u· the resuscitating law of Life.
  f 204-20 When will the ages u· the Ego,
    205-32 When we fully u· our relation to the Divine,
    209-31 a conscious, constant capacity to u· God.
    217-22 and in proportion as you u· the
    224- 5 we shall better u· the Science
    235-22 To the tremblers . . . who u· not the
    254-19 not the power to demonstrate what we do not u·.
  c 264-29 we shall behold and u· God's creation,
    267-13 Christian Scientists u· that, . . . they have the
  b 271-18 which shall believe on me [u· me] — John 17 : 20.
    283- 1 As mortals begin to u· Spirit,
    285-32 It is essential to u·, instead of believe,
    286- 2 is not to u· the infinite.
    292-20 "Why do ye not u· my speech?— John 8 : 43.
    311-21 So long as . . . we can never u· the Science of
    311-22 When humanity does u· this Science,
    321- 7 despaired of making the people u· what should
    329-12 In Science we can use only what we u·.
    332-25 in such a form of humanity as they could u·
    339-18 Only those, . . . can fully u· the unreality of evil.
  o 345-16 none which are apparent to those who u·
    345-20 evidence that one does u· this Science.
    346-10 we need to u· that error is nothing,
    350- 6 To u· all our Master's sayings as recorded
    350-21 and should u· with their heart, — Matt. 13 : 15.
    352- 2 because they did not sufficiently u· God
    352-18 which can harm them and which they do not u·,
  p 379-20 will u· that she is not dying on account of
    381-22 You must u· your way out of human theories
    394- 1 to u· that sickness is not real
    396-30 u· that sickness is formed by the human mind,
    397-18 Declare that you are not hurt and u· the reason
    397-31 will u· yourself and your Maker
    398-31 Then we u· the process.
    400-16 if you u· that every disease is an error,
    403-14 You command the situation if you u· that
    417-25 u· the unreality of disease in Science.
    424-24 if you u· it?
    429-25 Do you u· it? No!
  t 444-17 pointing the way through Christ, as we u· it,
    446-20 To u· God strengthens hope, enthrones faith
    456-23 must both u· and abide by the divine Principle
    459-32 should u· and adhere strictly to the rules
    460-11 the one most difficult to u· and demonstrate,
    464- 8 they would u· why she is so secluded.
  r 466-18 it is the most important to u·.
    479-13 cannot feel itself, see itself, nor u· itself.
    481- 7 Material sense never helps mortals to u·
    482-13 Is it important to u· these explanations
    486-29 If . . . the medium through which to u· God,
    488- 5 the cure shows that you u· this teaching,
    491-30 even though he does not u· C. S.,
    497-21 faith to u· eternal Life.
  g 523-23 in what we u· to be the spiritually scientific
    546-30 demonstrable Principle which all may u·.
  ap 559- 2 open for all to read and u·.
    560-19 without . . . we can never u· the divine

understandeth
  f 213- 5 as a man spiritually u·, so is he in truth.
understanding (noun)
and affections
  pr 5-17 riches of His love into the u· and affections,
and belief
  b 288-12 between truth and error, u· and belief,
and demonstration
  b 279-19 through the u· and demonstration of
and expression
  r 484-30 to the u· and expression of Spirit?
and heart
  g 521-16 should be engraved on the u· and heart
and intelligence
  g 557-13 towards enlarged u· and intelligence;
and recognition
  sp 90-27 The u· and recognition of Spirit
and truth
  g 544-28 belief reverses u· and truth.
arrive at the
  g 543-12 until mortals arrive at the u· that
beatified
  b 303-20 beatified u· of the Science of Life.
belief without
  sp 83-10 a blind belief without u·,
  r 472-18 Error is a belief without u·.
benighted
  pref. vii- 8 would make plain to benighted u·
better
  f 210-16 a better u· of Soul and salvation.
  b 285-21 to the better u· that Science gives of the
    315- 5 His better u· of God was a rebuke to them.
  r 473-23 a better u· of God as divine Principle,
Christlike
  c 259-11 The Christlike u· of scientific being
demonstration and
  pr 14- 8 the actual demonstration and u·
destroyed by the
  p 381-13 laws of mortal belief are destroyed by the u·
divine
  g 536- 8 The divine u· reigns, is all,
divine strength and
  p 406-31 gained through divine strength and u·.
dormant
  gl 583-16 rousing the dormant u· from material beliefs
enlightened
  pr 12-24 help should come from the enlightened u·.
enlighten the
  g 510- 9 Truth and Love enlighten the u·,
eyes of their
  a 49- 3 winged their faith, opened the eyes of their u·,
faith and
  s 107-13 fresh pinions are given to faith and u·,
  b 312-27 It divides faith and u· between matter and
  p 366-10 mental penury chills his faith and u·.
    387-30 gives man faith and u· whereby to
final
  sp 76-28 the final u· of Christ in divine Science.
firm in your
  p 393-16 Be firm in your u· that the divine Mind
flowing from the
  gl 589- 9 flowing from the u· that God is the
followed the
  s 141-15 followed the u· of the divine Principle
full
  a 31-21 in a full u· of the divine Principle
fuller
  s 162-27 requires only a fuller u· of the divine Principle
gate of
  g 538- 6 places the cherub wisdom at the gate of u·
growth in the
  m 62-19 growth in the u· of man's higher nature.
higher
  pr 10-16 to a higher u· of the divine Life.
  a 33-29 which attend a new and higher u· of God?
  sp 79-13 through the higher u· of God,
  f 251-20 or govern it from the higher u·
  t 449-16 but it requires a higher u· to teach this
highest
  m 67-11 Yet, acting up to his highest u·,
his
  b 315- 9 his u· of this divine Science
human
  pr 12-11 nor is it the human u· of the divine
  sp 99-11 C. S. has opened the door of the human u·.
imparts the
  g 505-16 Spirit imparts the u· which uplifts
infinite
  f 253- 1 He reflects the infinite u·,
instead of
  b 304-29 Controlled by belief, instead of u·,
leads to the
  b 324-14 leads to the u· that God is the only Life.

understanding (noun)

light of
t 461–12 light of *u·* be thrown upon this Science,
mutual
m 59–24 A mutual *u·* should exist before this union
necessity of
r 488–13 when they mean to enforce the necessity of *u·*.
new
a 33–22 This is the new *u·* of spiritual Love.
new-born
f 221–29 This new-born *u·*, that neither food nor
nor truth
b 287–17 Neither *u·* nor truth accompanies error,
object of
s 115–18 the immediate object of *u·*.
of being
b 330– 1 *u·* of being supersedes mere belief.
r 495–21 Let C. S., . . . support your *u·* of being,
of Christian Science
ph 178–23 In proportion to our *u·* of C. S.,
178–32 Whoever reaches the *u·* of C. S.
181–20 till you finally attain the *u·* of C. S.
b 323– 1 Mortals may seek the *u·* of C. S.,
329– 5 A little *u·* of C. S. proves the truth of
r 495–26 How can I progress most rapidly in the *u·* of C. S.?
of divine Love
b 288– 7 through faith in and the *u·* of divine Love.
of divine metaphysics
ph 192–28 our Master in the *u·* of divine metaphysics.
of divine Science
a 46–32 roused to an enlarged *u·* of divine Science,
f 228–16 through the *u·* of divine Science.
b 281– 1 yields only to the *u·* of divine Science,
of God
  (*see* **God**)
of Life
pr 14– 8 *u·* of Life as revealed in C. S.
sp 77–10 until the spiritual *u·* of Life is reached.
b 323–25 God gives the true *u·* of Life and Love,
p 387– 1 when we grow into the *u·* of Life,
r 485–18 the *u·* of Life, makes man immortal.
of man
c 260– 2 the true conception or *u·* of man,
of Mind-science
s 115– 2 through which the *u·* of Mind-science comes,
of Spirit
a 46–17 rose even higher in the *u·* of Spirit,
ph 186– 6 through the *u·* of Spirit,
b 309– 8 the *u·* of Spirit and of spiritual power.
gl 581– 9 the *u·* of Spirit, destroying belief in matter.
of Truth
pr 11–28 nor can prayer alone give us an *u·* of Truth ;
f 252–10 that *u·* which destroys error,
b 286– 6 The *u·* of Truth gives full faith in
o 346–19 We treat error through the *u·* of Truth,
p 417–15 the unshaken *u·* of Truth and Love,
ap 561– 1 The *u·* of Truth and Love,
opposite
s 154–21 prevented through the opposite *u·*.
or belief
b 324–11 whether it be Truth or error, *u·* or belief,
perception and
ap 561–19 reducing to human perception and *u·* the Life
perfect
b 273–14 impossibility of attaining perfect *u·* till
perfect day of
p 388–29 In that perfect day of *u·*, we shall
precede an
g 553– 5 clearer consciousness must precede an *u·* of
present
p 388–27 foolish to venture beyond our present *u·*,
rests upon
b 283–12 It admits of no error, but rests upon *u·*.
right
p 390– 9 the right *u·* of Him restores harmony.
Science and
b 274–27 Science and *u·*, governed by the
Spirit and
r 486–25 reality and immortality are in Spirit and *u·*,
spiritual
  (*see* **spiritual**)
superstition and
b 288– 9 Superstition and *u·* can never combine.
that Life is God
r 487–27 The *u·* that Life is God, Spirit,
this
pr 14–28 This *u·* casts out error and heals
a 43– 7 this *u·* is what is meant by the descent of the
f 203– 8 this *u·* would establish health.
216–14 This *u·* makes the body harmonious ;
c 264–17 this *u·* will expand into self-completeness,
328–14 This *u·* of man's power, when he
o 355–26 Without this *u·*, no one is capable of
p 394– 3 this *u·* is the universal and perfect remedy.
426–19 this *u·* will quicken into newness of life.

understanding (noun)

this
r 495–22 and this *u·* will supplant error with Truth,
g 505–26 This *u·* is not intellectual,
547–24 only by this *u·* can truth be gained.
through the
f 217– 2 through the *u·* which Science confers
228–16 through the *u·* of divine Science.
b 279–19 through the *u·* and demonstration of
o 346–19 We treat error through the *u·* of Truth,
Truth and
gl 590– 8 the opposite of spiritual Truth and *u·*.
Truth in the
s 109–22 The revelation of Truth in the *u·*
underlying
p 417–32 Give your patients an underlying *u·* to support
wholesome
p 396–24 Give them divine and wholesome *u·*,
without the
p 381–26 without the *u·* that Mind is not in matter.
yield to
ap 96–23 until all errors of belief yield to *u·*.

———

pr 15–28 Practice not profession, *u·* not belief,
a 24–14 the *u·*, in which Jesus suffered and triumphed.
34– 5 showing, . . . that Truth has come to the *u·*
44–25 divinity brought to humanity the *u·* of
m 68– 1 epoch approaches when the *u·* of the truth
sp 75–14 restored Lazarus by the *u·* that
s 116– 1 *Third Degree: U·*.
125–14 from fear to hope and from faith to *u·*,
f 216–11 The *u·* that the Ego is Mind,
223–16 the assurance which comes of *u·*;
253– 9 into the *u·* of your divine rights,
b 281– 2 the *u·* by which we enter into the
283–27 receive the divine Principle in the *u·*,
289– 5 by the *u·* of what constitutes man
297– 9 into the *u·* of what constitutes health ;
298–14 intuition, hope, faith, *u·*, fruition,
315–21 Jesus' spiritual origin and *u·* enabled him
317–18 The *u·* of his spiritual individuality
322– 3 When *u·* changes the standpoints of life
p 378– 5 The *u·* of this will enable you to
426–12 and the *u·* obtained that there is no death,
429– 2 by the *u·* that there is no death,
t 454– 5 The *u·*, even in a degree, of the
r 479–24 imaginary opposites of light, *u·*, and
488–10 *u·*, trust, constancy, firmness.
489–17 channel to man of divine blessings or *u·*
g 505–21 *U·* is the line of demarcation between
506– 5 *U·* is a quality of God,
506–10 God, unites *u·* to eternal harmony.
512– 2 the *u·* of the incorporeal and divine
523– 9 and not from the firmament, or *u·*,
526– 9 Belief is less than *u·*.
534–30 The spiritual idea has given the *u·* a foothold
535– 2 The seed . . . of belief and of *u·*,
gl 598–17 WINE. Inspiration ; *u·*.

understanding (ppr.)

a 28–12 by *u·* more of the divine Principle
f 233–21 by *u·* the spiritual idea which corrects and
c 259–19 *U·* this, Jesus said :
b 270– 8 Only by *u·* that there is but one power,
273–19 importance of *u·* the truth of being,
296–29 and in *u·* the situation in C. S.
304– 5 *U·* this, Paul said :
304–30 So man, not *u·* the Science of
312–18 Mortals try to believe without *u·* Truth ;
319– 8 spiritually *u·* God, sustains man
321–14 was destroyed through *u·* divine Science,
327– 1 Reform comes by *u·* that there is no
328– 6 *U·* little about the divine Principle
328–20 *U·* spiritual law and knowing that
o 356–11 *U·* the nothingness of material things,
p 394–29 Not *u·* C. S., the sick usually
423– 8 *u·* scientifically that all is Mind,
t 450–21 will overcome them by *u·* their nothingness
450–23 by *u·* God's power over them.
462–32 through *u·* mental anatomy,
g 514–26 *U·* the control which Love held over all,

understandingly

s 140–10 love Him *u·*, warring no more over {

understands

a 23–25 Another kind of faith *u·* divine Love
ph 180–26 the ever-present Mind who *u·* all things,
f 250– 8 which never dreams, but *u·* all things ;
c 265– 3 Man *u·* spiritual existence in proportion
o 345–17 One who *u·* C. S. can heal the sick
t 452– 2 when one *u·* that evil has in reality no power.
453– 5 The author *u·* what she is saying.
454–14 He, who *u·* in a sufficient degree
r 487–17 Matter cannot believe, and Mind *u·*.
g 555–10 for it neither *u·* nor can be understood.
556–16 to him who *u·* best the divine Life.

understood

pref vii–23 but it cannot make them speedily *u·*.
a 24– 2 applies to Truth and Love *u·* and practised.
  24– 8 open the way for C. S. to be *u·*,
  27–27 they never truly *u·* their Master's instruction.
  28–16 nor the work of Jesus was generally *u·*,
  34–19 and *u·* better what the Master had taught.
  41–23 reception C. S. would have before it was *u·*,
  43– 7 they had only believed ; now they *u·*.
  52–19 best *u·* the nothingness of material life
  54–18 hearers *u·* neither his words nor his works.
m 56– 9 discerned intact, is apprehended and *u·*,
  63– 3 if you *u·* the Science of being.
sp 71–21 When the Science of Mind is *u·*,
  76– 6 When being is *u·*, Life will be recognized as
  76–10 will be *u·* that Spirit never entered matter
  76–19 When divine Science is universally *u·*,
  81– 5 If Spiritualists *u·* the Science of being,
  88–19 nor *u·* through the physical senses.
  91–13 and his genuine being will be *u·*.
  94– 4 The nature of man, thus *u·*, includes
s 114– 2 therefore, to be *u·*, the author
  122– 4 but the great facts of Life, rightly *u·*,
  124–15 and then it can be *u·* ;
  128– 4 The term Science, properly *u·*,
  130–11 Science, when *u·* and demonstrated,
  130–15 C. S., properly *u·*, would disabuse the
  130–24 and *u·* how truly such as they belong to
  131–29 demonstrations which were not *u·*.
  137– 8 Yearning to be *u·*, the Master repeated,
  141–26 until its divine Principle is scientifically *u·*.
  144–27 When the Science of being is universally *u·*,
  144–31 *u·* the Science of Christian healing,
  151– 9 if they *u·* the Science of Mind-healing,
  152– 9 has a healing effect, even when not fully *u·*.
  153–29 When this mental contagion is *u·*,
  159–15 Had these unscientific surgeons *u·*
ph 168–31 a word . . . which will be better *u·* hereafter,
  169–16 If we *u·* the control of Mind over body,
  196– 5 The power of . . . is little *u·*.
f 203– 7 If God were *u·* instead of being merely
  205– 9 When will it be *u·* that matter has neither
  212–25 Because all the methods of Mind are not *u·*,
  214–16 being will be *u·* and found to be harmonious.
  215–27 Because he *u·* the superiority and
  219–14 When this is *u·*, we shall never
  238– 2 are not rightly valued before they are *u·*.
  238–13 shows that we never *u·* Truth.
  239–12 Let it be *u·* that success in error is defeat
  252–13 *u·* and recognized as the true likeness
c 256–15 nor can He be *u·* aright through
b 272– 4 must be gained before Truth can be *u·*.
  275–31 spiritually discerned, is scientifically *u·*.
  276– 5 When the divine precepts are *u·*,
  280–25 Rightly *u·*, . . . man has a sensationless body ;
  290– 4 If . . . not in the least *u·*
  297–24 Truth, the ever-present, is becoming *u·*.
  300– 9 So far as the scientific statement as to man is *u·*,
  304–26 the science of music must be *u·*.
  308–22 Truth, being thereby *u·*, gave him
  310– 7 Thought will finally be *u·* and seen
  319–19 when it becomes fairly *u·* that the
  319–23 and needs inspiration to be *u·*.
  323–15 Truth is demonstrable when *u·*,
  323–16 and that good is not *u·* until demonstrated.
  325–13 When spiritual being is *u·* in all its perfection,
  325–28 will be *u·* and demonstrated.
  326–29 Christians, whose religion he had not *u·*,
  329–27 If men *u·* their real spiritual source
  330– 8 When the following platform is *u·*
  334–27 liveth, and was dead [not *u·*] ;— *Rev.* 1 : 18.
  338– 1 C. S., rightly *u·*, leads to
  339–28 not merely believed, but it must be *u·*.
o 343–15 when his teachings are fully *u·*.
  344–11 Were it more fully *u·* that Truth heals
  345– 3 thus they are uniformly used and *u·* in C. S.
  348– 8 it is not generally *u·* how
  349– 2 when this Science is more generally *u·*
  349–31 In C. S., substance is *u·* to be Spirit,
  350–13 both of which must be *u·*.
  358– 9 C. S., *u·* coincides with the Scriptures,
  361–14 This declaration of Jesus, *u·*, conflicts not
  361–30 enriches mankind only when it is *u·*,
p 369–20 He *u·* man, whose Life is God, to be immortal,
  369–26 readily seen, if psychology, . . . was *u·*.
  371– 8 By . . . nothing is really *u·* of material
  375–16 should be *u·* and so rendered fruitless.
  375–30 This mental state is not *u·*, simply because
  386–24 divine wisdom will then be *u·*.
  386–29 you would not have *u·* him,
  403– 7 In the first instance it is *u·* that the
  403–31 are not *u·* by the patient,
  406– 8 power of God is *u·* and demonstrated
  425–18 When this is *u·*, mankind will be
  427–11 before Life can be *u·* and harmony obtained.
  429–29 not *u·* generally by our ethical instructors.

understood

t 449–21 ought to be *u·* and guarded against.
  457–10 never . . . fears to have fairly *u·*.
  459–26 the results are sure if the Science is *u·*.
r 467– 9 should be . . . *u·* that all men have one Mind
  467–30 *u·* through the idea which expresses it
  472– 2 God is to be *u·*, adored, and demonstrated;
  472–11 His law, rightly *u·*, destroys them.
  473–31 Few, however, except his students *u·*
  475–12 he must be so *u·* in C. S.
  479–31 being *u·* by the things that— *Rom.* 1 : 20.
  480–30 If sin, sickness, and death were *u·* as nothingness
  487–30 This faith relies upon an *u·* Principle.
  489– 3 If the Science of Life were *u·*,
  490–12 The Science of Mind needs to be *u·*.
  490–13 Until it is *u·*, mortals are more or less
  495– 4 All of Truth is not *u·* ;
g 547–24 Our aim must be to have them *u·* spiritually,
  552–31 perfect and eternal Mind is *u·*.
  555–11 it neither understands nor can be *u·*.
ap 558–13 When *u·*, it is Truth's prism and praise.
  561–21 and the spiritual idea is *u·*.
  570–23 the spiritual idea will be *u·*.
  572–13 this divine Principle, *u·* and demonstrated,
gl 586–21 spiritual being *u·* ; haste towards harmony.
  588– 5 Divine Science *u·* and acknowledged.
  593–20 Life, Truth, and Love *u·* and demonstrated
  598–26 when the Science of being is *u·*,

undertake

s 145–25 Other methods *u·* to oppose error with error,
ph 200– 9 not to *u·* the explanation of body.

undertakes

ph 198–16 and before the doctor *u·* to dispel it
p 441– 3 which *u·* to punish aught but sin,

under-world

s 137–32 [*hades*, the *u·*, or the *grave*]

undigested

p 389– 8 mortal mind, which reports food as *u·*.

undimmed

f 246–12 Manhood is its eternal noon, *u·* by a declining

undirected

f 212–17 Mortals have a modus of their own, *u·* and

undisciplined

f 221–27 *u·* by self-denial and divine Science.

undiscovered

g 552– 9 proof requisite to sustain this assumption is *u·*.

undisturbed

f 250–20 To the observer, the body lies listless, *u·*,
b 306–25 *U·* amid the jarring testimony of the
g 514–12 *U·* it lies in the open field,

undivided

s 142– 8 We must seek the *u·* garment,

undo

f 240–27 In trying to *u·* the errors of sense

undone

pr 6– 8 work badly done or left *u·*,
sp 85–30 and not to leave the other *u·*."— *Matt.* 23 : 23.

undoubted

p 364– 1 a man of *u·* goodness and purity,

undue

p 413– 3 *u·* contemplation of physical wants

undulations

f 212–27 that the *u·* of the air convey sound,

undying

b 325– 5 being ushered into the *u·* realities of Spirit.
  334–23 but *u·* in the deific Mind.
p 427–23 God, Life, Truth, and Love make man *u·*.

unearth

p 434–26 and we shall *u·* this foul conspiracy

uneasiness

p 383–15 To the mind equally gross, dirt gives no *u·*.

uneducated

sp 89–11 She says, . . . I am *u·*."

unequalled

s 134–20 its astonishing and *u·* success in the first

unerring

sp 99–15 C. S. is *u·* and Divine ;
s 145–23 ignorance of the laws of eternal and *u·* Mind.
f 243–20 Neither immortal and *u·* Mind nor matter,
b 274–27 governed by the *u·* and eternal Mind,
  277– 2 To all that is unlike *u·* and eternal Mind,
  279– 2 the *u·*, immutable, and immortal
p 418– 8 *u·*, and certain effect of divine Science.
  424– 9 the proper sense of God's *u·* direction
r 468– 2 which evolves its own *u·* idea
  473–21 and to test its *u·* Science according to his rule,
  484– 2 on a divine Principle and so found to be *u·*,
g 505–29 God's ideas reflect the immortal, *u·*, and
  522–31 Does the *u·* Principle of divine law change

unerring
  g 546–11   is governed by *u·* intelligence?
  gl 588–10   incorporeal, *u·*, immortal and eternal Mind.
  590– 2   realm of *u·*, eternal, and omnipotent Mind ;

unexplained
  pref xi– 3   which action in some *u·* way results in the
  s 121–14   the hypotheses of material sense *u·* by Science,

unexpressed
  b 303–26   would be a nonentity, or Mind *u·*.
  306–11   The Ego would be *u·*,
  p 423– 6   Remember that the *u·* belief oftentimes
  r 470–27   consequently a time when Deity was *u·*

unfair
  m 63–12   Civil law establishes very *u·* differences
  o 343– 7   This makes it doubly *u·* to impugn and

unfaithful
  o 349– 3   As Paul asked of the *u·* in ancient days,
  ap 571–13   *u·* stewards who have seen the danger

unfaithfulness
  gl 599– 7   Emptiness ; *u·* ; desolation.

unfallen
  ph 171– 8   and will find himself *u·*, upright, pure,
  r 476–32   man in God's image is *u·* and eternal.

unfamiliar
  b 314–18   seemed a spectre, unseen and *u·*,
  p 422–11   Patients, *u·* with the cause of this commotion

unfashion
  r 488–27   otherwise the very worms could *u·* man.

unfathomable
  g 520– 3   *U·* Mind is expressed.

unfavorable
  pr 7–13   reaction *u·* to spiritual growth,
  p 396– 9   nor draw attention to certain symptoms as *u·*,

unfeigned
  p 364– 3   Her reverence was *u·*,

unfit
  a 31– 1   Pride and fear are *u·* to bear the standard of
  p 419–17   lest aught *u·* for development enter

unfitted
  p 369– 3   Thus he is *u·* for the successful

unflinching
  p 426–27   with *u·* faith in God, in Life eternal.

unflinchingly
  a 53– 6   He rebuked sinners pointedly and *u·*,

unfold
  m 57–29   and begins to *u·* its wings for heaven.
  sp 95–30   Material sense does not *u·* the facts of existence ;
  b 269– 6   and *u·* the unity and the reality of good,
  276– 5   they *u·* the foundation of fellowship,
  o 361–23   Spiritual ideas *u·* as we advance.
  t 445– 8   *U·* the latent energies and capacities
  gl 598– 9   to employ words . . . to *u·* spiritual thoughts.

unfolded
  s 117–17   As a divine student he *u·* God to man,
  f 205–23   law of loving our neighbor as ourselves is *u·* ;
  g 534–13   *u·* the remedy for Adam, or error ;
  gl 584– 6   according to the good that is *u·*.

unfolding
  s 108– 5   *u·* to me the demonstrable fact that
  b 306–26   Science, still enthroned, is *u·* to mortals
  306–28   is *u·* Life and the universe,
  325– 7   *u·* its own immortal idea.
  335–23   gain the eternal *u·* of Life
  r 497–14   *u·* man's unity with God
  g 503– 1   consists of the *u·* of spiritual ideas
  gl 584– 7   This *u·* is God's day,

unfoldment
  m 68–27   C. S. presents *u·*, not accretion ;
  p 371–25   our need of its spiritual *u·*.

unfolds
  m 66–15   Each successive stage of experience *u·* new
  69–14   *u·* all creation, confirms the Scriptures,
  s 135– 7   introduces no disorder, but *u·* the primal order,
  ph 191–12   not a leaf *u·* its fair outlines,
  f 246–25   Each succeeding year *u·* wisdom,
  b 276– 1   *u·* the power that heals the sick,
  296– 2   whereas Science *u·* the eternal verity,
  t 452–22   When the spiritual sense of Truth *u·*
  462–21   It *u·* the hallowed influences of unselfishness,
  g 505–22   Spiritual understanding *u·* Mind,
  506–19   Spirit, . . . *u·* these thoughts,
  508–24   *u·* the infinitude of Love.
  gl 597–19   spiritual sense *u·* the great facts of existence.

unformed
  g 506–18   Spirit, God, gathers *u·* thoughts into their

unforsaken
  b 291– 1   suppositions that sin is pardoned while *u·*,

---

unfortunate
  ph 172–29   the *u·* cripple may present more nobility than
  p 408–10   Those *u·* people who are committed to
  434–11   to appear as counsel for the *u·* prisoner.
  439–21   the *u·* Mortal Man who sought your aid
  t 450– 5   Another class, still more *u·*, are so depraved

ungodliness
  gl 595–25   definition of

ungodly
  s 145–22   mystery which godliness always presents to
       the *u·*,

ungrateful
  pr 3–27   If we are *u·* for Life, Truth, and Love,

unharmed
  b 322– 1   and taught them how to handle serpents *u·*,

unhealthy
  p 382– 9   or to remove *u·* exhalations
  392–22   If you decide that climate or atmosphere is *u·*,
  392–30   shut out these *u·* thoughts and fears.

unheeded
  f 223–26   Peals that should startle . . . are partially *u·* ;

unholiness
  f 201–20   Grafting holiness upon *u·*,
  229–11   sickness and health, holiness and *u·*,
  b 303–22   life and death, holiness and *u·*,

unifies
  b 340–23   One infinite God, good, *u·* men and nations ;

uniform
  m 64– 1   Want of *u·* justice is a crying evil

uniformly
  o 345– 2   thus they are *u·* used and understood in C. S.

unillumined
  ap 573– 9   while to another, the *u·* human mind,

unimpeachable
  p 414–29   man's perfection is real and *u·*,

unimportant
  s 135–23   but neither is *u·* or untrue,
  r 485– 7   If the *u·* and evil appear, only soon to

unimproved
  f 238–15   *U·* opportunities will rebuke us when we

uninspired
  b 319–26   misinterpretation of the Word . . . by *u·* writers,
  ap 573– 5   that which is invisible to the *u·* thought.

uninstructed
  p 371– 7   By those *u·* in C. S., nothing is really

unintelligence
  f 250– 4   and suppose . . . *u·* to act like intelligence,

unintelligent
  s 143–22   You lean on the inert and *u·*, never discerning
  157–23   Matter is not self-creative, for it is *u·*.
  f 210–25   What is termed matter, being *u·*, cannot say,
  g 523– 1   Yet one might so judge from an *u·* perusal of

uninterrupted
  ph 172–13   reveals the eternal chain of existence as *u·*

union
  hallowing the
  m 59–14   hallowing the *u·* of interests and affections,
  of hearts
  m 64–17   Marriage should signify a *u·* of hearts.
  solemn
  ap 575–32   which binds human society into solemn *u·* ;

---

  m 57– 4   *U·* of the masculine and feminine qualities
  59–25   should exist before this *u·* and continue
  65–10   The *u·* of the sexes suffers fearful discord.
  sp 94–31   *u·* with the infinite capacities of the one Mind.
  p 378– 3   are reproduced in *u·* by human memory.
  g 532– 2   the *u·* of the two sexes in order to
  gl 592–13   the *u·* of justice and affection,

unison
  b 294– 3   human belief, . . . a *u·* of matter with Spirit.

unit
  s 108–18   not a fraction more, not a *u·* less.

unite
  a 35–21   We can *u·* with this church only as we
  52–15   in order to *u·* in putting to shame and death
  m 57–27   *u·* thought more closely to God,
  64–23   will *u·* in one person masculine wisdom and
  ph 167–21   can no more *u·* in action, than
  178–29   you may attempt to *u·* with it hypnotism,
  b 282–12   never *u·* in figure or in fact.
  282–21   At no point can these opposites mingle or *u·*.
  306–13   If Life or Soul and . . . man, *u·* for a
  o 360–30   Jew and Christian can *u·* in doctrine
  p 424– 7   and *u·* with the one Mind, in order to
  g 555–19   error would seek to *u·* Spirit with matter,
  ap 571–20   will *u·* all interests in the one divinity.

united

m 59–12 different demands of their *u·* spheres,
sp 72–16 which are not *u·* by progress, but separated.
b 287–28 material senses testify to truth and error as *u·*
r 477–10 man appears to be matter and mind *u·* ;
492– 5 since Life cannot be *u·* to its unlikeness,
ap 577– 9 In this divinely *u·* spiritual consciousness,

United States

pref xii– 4 which had been established in the *U· S·*,
f 225–23 Legally to abolish unpaid servitude in the *U· S·*

unites

f 229–10 the belief which *u·* such opposites as
o 361– 8 Thus the Jew *u·* with the Christian's doctrine
361–11 he virtually *u·* with the Jew's belief in one God,
g 506–10 God, *u·* understanding to eternal harmony.

uniting

b 271– 4 *u·* all periods in the design of God.
f 492–30 *u·* on some impossible basis.

unity

man's
pr 12–15 and of man's *u·* with Truth and Love.
a 18– 1 the exemplification of man's *u·* with God,
r 497–14 unfolding man's *u·* with God
of God
s 132–12 such effects, . . . prove the *u·* of God,
g 502–26 the eternal verity and *u·* of God and man,
of Principle
r 470– 4 and have *u·* of Principle and spiritual power
of Spirit
s 148–24 the concord and *u·* of Spirit and His likeness.
of spirit
m 58– 2 *U·* of spirit gives new pinions to joy,
of the faith
g 519–18 "we all come in the *u·* of the faith, — *Eph.* 4 : 13.
presents the
ap 577– 5 The Lamb's wife presents the *u·* of
scientific
f 202– 3 scientific *u·* which exists between God and man
sham
g 555–21 error would . . . call this sham *u· man,*
spiritual
m 61–31 The scientific *morale* of marriage is spiritual *u·*.
this
b 333–28 Jesus referred to this *u·* of
trinity in
b 331–28 They represent a trinity in *u·*,
unfold the
b 269– 7 and unfold the *u·* and the reality of good,

universal

pr 13– 2 Love is impartial and *u·* in its adaptation
a 42– 5 The *u·* belief in death is of no advantage.
sp 76– 8 but as infinite, — as God, *u·* good ;
78–31 These are the effects of one *u·* God,
84–16 events which concern the *u·* welfare,
s 140–25 The C. S. God is *u·*, eternal, divine Love,
144–29 and Truth will be the *u·* panacea.
155–15 The *u·* belief in physics weighs against
f 208–23 the reign and rule of *u·* harmony,
226– 7 sounded the keynote of *u·* freedom,
229–15 By *u·* consent, mortal belief has
242–17 to dissolve with the *u·* solvent of Love
c 266–18 *U·* Love is the divine way in C. S.
b 271–16 Hence the *u·* application of his saying :
289–21 results, by the *u·* law of mortal mind, in a
291–12 *U·* salvation rests on progression and
293–29 Truth and its supremacy, *u·* harmony,
328–31 extends through time and includes *u·* humanity.
329– 4 in all the grandeur of *u·* goodness.
330– 7 would meet with immediate and *u·* acceptance.
331–19 divine Principle, Love, the *u·* cause,
p 394– 3 the *u·* and perfect remedy.
408– 6 There is a *u·* insanity of so-called health,
414–23 Even so, harmony is *u·*, and discord is unreal.
r 470–10 Love as ever present and *u·*
477– 5 taught that the kingdom of God is intact, *u·*,
483–18 and reveals the *u·* harmony.
g 519– 9 the ideas of God in *u·* being are complete
553– 8 nearer the truth . . . or health will never be *u·*,
577– 3 as one Father with His *u·* family,

universally

sp 76–19 When divine Science is *u·* understood,
s 144–27 When the Science of being is *u·* understood,
f 202– 5 and God's will must be *u·* done.

universe

and man
gl 585–17 Divine Science encompassing the *u·* and man ;
changing the
c 255– 1 Eternal Truth is changing the *u·*.
constructing the
g 522–27 supposedly . . . in constructing the *u·*,
control over the
ph 171–12 Mind's control over the *u·*, including man,
divine
g 513– 8 To material sense, this divine *u·* is dim

universe

God and the
c 266–32 but he coexists with God and the *u·*.
g 521–28 this material view of God and the *u·*,
God's
b 289–24 God's *u·* is spiritual and immortal.
331–17 Everything in God's *u·* expresses Him.
governing the
g 510–30 governing the *u·*, including man,
government of the
s 121–32 in the everlasting government of the *u·*.
128– 5 His government of the *u·*, inclusive of man.
g 539–15 resigned to matter the government of the *u·* ?
governs the
a 39–27 and governs the *u·* harmoniously.
an 102–13 since God governs the *u·* ;
b 270–11 intelligence, . . . governs the *u·* ;
295– 5 God creates and governs the *u·*, including man.
harmony of the
gl 592–19 the spiritual facts and harmony of the *u·* ;
His own
s 119–10 to leave the creator out of His own *u·* ;
illumines the
g 503–15 light of ever-present Love illumines the *u·*.
illuming the
c 266–29 the beatific presence, illuming the *u·* with light.
intelligence of the
a 27–15 the Life, substance, and intelligence of the *u·*
b 330–12 the only intelligence of the *u·*,
invisible
b 337–24 the invisible *u·* and spiritual man.
is filled
b 295– 6 The *u·* is filled with spiritual ideas,
Life and the
b 306–28 Life and the *u·*, ever-present and eternal.
man and the
m 68–30 an impartation . . . to man and the *u·*.
69– 2 man and the *u·* are evolved from Spirit,
f 209–22 translation of man and the *u·* back into Spirit.
209–23 man and the *u·* will be found harmonious
b 332– 3 relation of God to man and the *u·*.
r 466– 1 His reflection is man and the *u·*.
g 507–28 immortality of man and the *u·*.
508– 4 man and the *u·*, is the product.
509–27 appear in man and the *u·* never to disappear.
539–30 makes and governs man and the *u·*.
material
f 238– 5 in personal character as well as in the material *u·*.
g 545–12 notion of a material *u·* is utterly opposed to
Mind and the
g 507–23 Mind and the *u·* created by God.
mortal
gl 584–24 thence to reproduce a mortal *u·*,
of Mind
f 240–16 rotations and revolutions of the *u·* of Mind
g 513– 6 spiritual steps in the teeming *u·* of Mind
of Spirit
c 264–32 *u·* of Spirit is peopled with spiritual beings,
g 507–15 The *u·* of Spirit reflects the creative power of
of Truth
g 503–10 In the *u·* of Truth, matter is unknown.
peoples the
g 509–17 God forms and peoples the *u·*.
physical
r 484–13 The physical *u·* expresses the conscious and
Principle of the
b 272–28 The divine Principle of the *u·* must
276–23 Principle of the *u·*, including . . . man.
real
b 289–19 for to the real man and the real *u·*
recreate the
g 547–19 to recreate the *u·*, including man.
reflects
b 300–28 The *u·* reflects and expresses the divine
g 502–28 The *u·* reflects God.
reveals the
ap 562– 8 This idea reveals the *u·* as secondary
spiritual
(see **spiritual**)
stellar
g 509–14 but the stellar *u·* is no more celestial than
sustaining the
g 538–13 enlightening and sustaining the *u·*.
theory of the
g 547–26 The true theory of the *u·*, including man, is
547–29 sensual, and mortal theory of the *u·*,
views of the
g 502–16 Christian views of the *u·* appear,
visible
b 337–22 The visible *u·* and material man are the
whole
f 207–29 repeated in the action of man and the whole *u·*,

sp 83–16 The belief that the *u·*, including man,
s 114–28 the *u·*, including man, is spiritual,

universe
  s 121–29   the *u*·, the reflection of God,
    123–10   the most . . . inharmonious creature in the *u*·.
    124–14   The *u*·, like man, is to be interpreted by
    124–18   the *u*·, like man, is, and must continue to be, an
    125–29   will look out from them upon the *u*· ;
  c 256– 8   Father and Mother of the *u*·, including man.
  b 272–29   must interpret the *u*·.
    319–14   neither concur in man nor in the *u*·.
  r 471–20   the spirituality of the *u*· is the only fact
    496– 5   and governs the entire *u*·.
  g 502–27   unity of God and man, including the *u*·.
    505–24   giving the spiritual proof of the *u*·
    510–18   giving existence and intelligence to the *u*·.
    511–23   To mortal mind, the *u*· is liquid, solid, and
    515–16   eternal Elohim includes the forever *u*·.
    554– 3   the *u*·, inclusive of man, is as eternal as God,
  ap 562– 9   from which the *u*· borrows its

University of Pennsylvania
  s 163–20   Dr. Chapman, Professor . . . in the *U*· *of P*·,

unjust
  a 36–19   A selfish and limited mind may be *u*·,
    36–31   in the suffering of the just for the *u*·.
  o 343–12   will not be forever hidden by *u*· parody
  p 381– 2   Ignorant of . . . we submit to *u*· decrees,
    381–29   man's moral right to annul an *u*· sentence,
    437–29   *u*· usages were not allowed at the bar of Truth,
    440–22   The false and *u*· beliefs of your

unjustly
  an 104– 6   *u*· persecuted and belied by wolves in
  p 434–22   prisoner at the bar has been *u*· sentenced.
    435–35   the liberty of which he has been *u*· deprived.

unknelled
  p 441–12   "*u*·, uncoffined, and unknown."

unknowable
  gl 596– 4   may define Deity as "the great *u*· ;"

unknown
  pr 1–10   Thoughts unspoken are not *u*· to the
    12– 9   a belief in the *u*· casting out a belief in
  a 53–12   His words and works were *u*· to the world
  ph 184– 4   for these are *u*· to Truth
  f 219– 2   sorrow, sin, death, will be *u*·,
  b 274–30   in a manner and at a period as yet *u*·.
    280– 1   In . . . Mind, matter must be *u*·.
    306–16   and in a manner *u*·,
    330–16   The individuality of Spirit, . . . is *u*·,
  p 424– 5   Accidents are *u*· to God,
    428–15   not "to the *u*· God"— *Acts* 17 : 23.
    441–12   "unknelled, uncoffined, and *u*·."
  r 469– 2   What is termed matter is *u*· to Spirit,
    469– 5   Death and finiteness are *u*· to Life.
    469–20   if mortals claimed no other . . . sin would be *u*·.
  g 503–11   In the universe of Truth, matter is *u*·.
  gl 596– 1   definition of
    596– 2   and which is *u*· to the material senses.
    596– 7   dedicated "to the *u*· God."— *Acts* 17 : 23.
    598–29   where sin, sickness, and death are *u*·.

unlabored
  t 445–20   illustrates the *u*· motion of the divine energy

unlawfully
  f 238–19   to enter *u*· into the labors of others.

unless
  s 155–12   dissent or faith, *u*· it rests on Science,
    160–22   *U*· muscles are self-acting at all times,
  f 231– 3   *U*· an ill is rightly met and fairly overcome
  b 283–26   *u*· its Science be accurately stated.
    283–28   *u*· we so do, we can no more demonstrate
    324– 7   *U*· the harmony and immortality of man are
  o 350–13   *U*· the works are comprehended
  p 379–29   *U*· the fever-picture, drawn by
    392–20   *u*· Science shows you otherwise.
    394–23   *u*· it can be aided by a drug
    404–32   *u*· it makes him better mentally,
    416– 4   *u*· the mental image occasioning the pain
    416–13   *u*· the belief which occasions the pain has
  t 449–31   and *u*· this result follows,
    450–17   but *u*· this admission is made,
    452–15   Never breathe an immoral atmosphere, *u*·
  gl 590–18   *u*· specially coupled with the name God.

unlike
  sp 82–25   The mental states are so *u*·,
    86–12   and produce *u*· results.
  f 243–28   a law of annihilation to everything *u*·
    249–16   and includes nothing *u*· God.
  c 262–23   and conquering all that is *u*· God.
  b 277– 2   To all that is *u*· unerring and eternal Mind,
    284–14   or know aught *u*· the infinite?
    287–10   Truth and error are *u*·.
    305–22   the deflections of matter . . . are all *u*· Spirit,
    307–11   shall change sides and be *u*· Spirit.
    335–26   and can produce nothing *u*· the eternal
  p 362– 3   though he was quite *u*· Simon the disciple.
    393–12   to resist all that is *u*· good.

unlike
  p 403–26   so-called mind produces all that is *u*· the
    406–16   all that is *u*· the true likeness disappears.
  r 468– 5   because error is *u*· Truth.
    475–11   The likeness of Spirit cannot be so *u*· Spirit.
  g 506– 2   Objects utterly *u*· the original do not

unlikeness
  f 204–14   evil, is the *u*· of good.
  c 257– 5   then Spirit, matter's *u*·, must be
  b 277–24   The *u*· of Spirit is matter,
    285–10   the *u*· called sin, sickness, and death.
    287–11   the *infinite* God can have no *u*·.
    288– 2   *error, Truth's u*·, *is unreal.*
    339– 8   there is no room for His *u*·.
  o 345– 6   God cannot be in His *u*·
  r 470– 9   infinite Truth without an *u*·,
    470–14   *u*· of God, is unreal.
    471– 6   The *u*· of Truth,— named *error*,
    492– 6   Life cannot be united to its *u*·,

unlimited
  a 36–19   *u*· and divine Mind is the immortal law
  sp 76–23   possessing *u*· divine beauty and goodness
  b 284– 6   and *u*· Mind would seem to spring from a
    288–28   *u*· by the mortal senses.
    312–22   God is infinite Love, which must be *u*·.
    336– 4   never . . . the *u*· into the limited,

unlock
  sp 70– 4   revelations of C. S. *u*· the treasures of

unloose
  a 28–23   if thou art found worthy to *u*· the sandals of

unloosed
  ap 564–22   *u*· in order that the false claim

unmake
  b 270–27   If sin makes sinners, Truth . . . can *u*· them.

unmanly
  ph 176– 4   and *u*· Adams attributed their own downfall

unmarried
  m 68–17   she was *u*·, a lovely character,

unmasked
  f 205– 9   When will the error . . . be *u*·?

unmedicated
  s 156–17   to give her *u*· pellets
    156–25   She went on in this way, taking the *u*· pellets,

unmerited
  pr 3–21   We plead for *u*· pardon
    9– 3   The wrong lies in *u*· censure,

unmistakable
  ph 188–21   are traced upon mortals by *u*· signs.

unmistakably
  a 46–23   and revealed *u*· a probationary
  g 522–12   This second record *u*· gives the
  ap 573–10   This shows *u*· that what the human mind

unnatural
  a 23– 7   divinely *u*·. Such a theory is man-made.
  sp 78– 3   discords of disease, sin, and death,— are *u*·.
  s 119–23   while evil should be regarded as *u*·,
    130–31   no longer think it . . . *u*· to forsake it,
    131– 1   should not seem so surprising and *u*· as error,
  f 217–10   *u*· mental and bodily conditions,
  b 304–21   and discord is *u*·, unreal.
  p 420– 9   cannot produce this *u*· reluctance.
  g 551– 2   material senses and their reports are *u*·,

unnecessary
  ph 181–25   It is *u*· to resort to aught besides Mind
  b 274– 3   *U*· knowledge gained from the
  p 396– 5   Make no *u*· inquiries relative to feelings

unobstructed
  gl 593–15   When smooth and *u*·, it typifies the

unpaid
  f 225–23   Legally to abolish *u*· servitude in the

unparalleled
  s 117–22   his mighty, crowning, *u*·, and

unpleasant
  p 415– 8   when it contemplates *u*· things,

unprejudiced
  ap 570–14   Millions of *u*· minds— simple seekers

unprepared
  t 446– 3   with a community *u*· for self-defence.

unpretentious
  a 54–22   There adhered to him only a few *u*· friends,

unqualified
  o 342– 5   In the result of some *u*· condemnations

unquestionable
  f 232–29   *u*· signs of the burial of error
    233–26   is not more *u*· than the scientific tests

unreal

and the real
g 538–10 the material and spiritual,— the *u·* and the real.

and untrue
gl 584– 9 the *u·* and untrue ; the opposite of Life.

author of the
r 474–28 error, not Truth, is the author of the *u·*,

both are
a 39–24 both are *u·*, because impossible in Science.

concept
an 102– 7 it is an *u·* concept of the so-called

discord is
b 276–16 Discord is *u·* and mortal.
p 414–23 harmony is universal, and discord is *u·*.

discord the
ap 563– 2 harmony is the real and discord the *u·*.

disease is
f 229–32 the truth that disease is *u·*.

error is
c 265–21 the error is *u·* and obsolete.
b 288– 2 correlated statement, that *error, . . . is u·*.
p 368– 4 Truth is real and error is *u·*.
r 466–16 Moreover, Truth is real, and error is *u·*.
472–18 Error is *u·* because untrue.

evil is
t 447–31 He may say, as a subterfuge, that evil is *u·*,
g 527–19 Evil is *u·* because it is a lie,

forsake the
b 339–18 repent of sin and forsake the *u·*,

in divine Science
o 353– 2 real to material sense, is *u·* in divine Science.

inharmony is
b 276–12 The realization that all inharmony is *u·*

master
f 226–23 years of servitude to an *u·* master

matter is the
r 468–13 matter is the *u·* and temporal.

real and
g 505–22 line of demarcation between the real and *u·*.

real and the
o 360–21 swinging between the real and the *u·*.

real or
g 524–24 Is this addition to His creation real or *u·*?

sensuous
o 353– 1 scientific real is the sensuous *u·*.

temporal and
b 300–13 temporal and *u·* never touch the eternal and

vanishes
r 474–28 the *u·* vanishes, while all that is real is eternal.

---

sp 76–18 Suffering, sinning, dying beliefs are *u·*.
an 103–11 for the latter is *u·*.
s 114–15 implies something untrue and therefore *u·* ;
ph 186–13 It is *u·*, because it presupposes the
f 212–31 *u·* and imitative movements of mortal belief,
241– 9 as imaginary, whimsical, and *u·* as his
b 270– 7 If one is real, the other must be *u·*.
277–11 evil and materiality are *u·*
293– 1 this *u·* material mortality disappears
298–11 To material sense, the *u·* is the real
298–18 the boundary of the mortal or the *u·*.
304–21 and discord is unnatural, *u·*.
337–27 Temporal things . . . are the *u·*,
339–10 evil, being contrary to good, is *u·*,
339–14 would make that real which is *u·*,
o 347–31 and the inharmonious *u·*.
350–29 through which the real reaches the *u·*,
352–11 the intangible and uncertain, if not the *u·*.
353–30 the ghost, some *u·* belief.
354–26 Sin should become *u·* to every one.
p 408–31 sensation in matter is *u·*.
414–80 whereas imperfection is blameworthy, *u·*,
417–24 to cure the patient is to make disease *u·*
t 460–14 Sickness is neither imaginary nor *u·*,— that is,
461–25 error is not true, hence it is *u·*.
r 470–14 then evil, the unlikeness of God, is *u·*.
470–16 seem to be real by giving reality to the *u·*.
480–13 has its realm apart from Science in the *u·*.
485–13 sin, disease, and death appear more and more *u·*
494–27 mortal testimony, changing, dying, *u·*.
497–11 casts out evil as *u·*.
g 529–29 we know that they are worthless and *u·*.
538–22 and evil is brought into view only as the *u·*
551– 2 their reports are unnatural, impossible, and *u·*.

unrealities

r 472–28 *u·* seem real to human, erring belief,

unreality

awful
s 110– 9 I beheld, as never before, the awful *u·* called
b 339–16 against his own awakening to the awful *u·*

deception and
f 207–10 evil is the awful deception and *u·* of existence.

discord the
o 352– 4 and discord the *u·*.

unreality

material
f 228–19 and discord as the material *u·*.

of disease
p 417–25 must understand the *u·* of disease in Science.
t 461–28 the error or *u·* of disease,

of evil
f 205–21 the nothingness and *u·* of evil.
b 339–12 Science demonstrates the *u·* of evil,
339–19 fully understand the *u·* of evil.

of sin
t 461–26 To prove scientifically the error or *u·* of sin,

prove its
t 447–27 get the victory over sin and so prove its *u·*.

relapses into its own
b 277– 5 The non-intelligent relapses into its own *u·*.

saw its
b 308–21 till he saw its *u·* ;

typifies
g 538–15 "tree of knowledge" typifies *u·*.— *Gen.* 2 : 9.

---

b 269– 7 the *u·*, the nothingness, of evil.
285–11 The *u·* of the claim that a mortal
g 502– 4 preponderance of *u·* in the entire narrative,
502– 5 as if reality did not predominate over *u·*,
525–22 valueless or baneful, . . . hence its *u·*.
gl 580–10 an *u·* as opposed to the great reality of

unreasonable

sp 78– 6 How *u·* is the belief that we are

unrecognized

a 39– 1 met the mockery of his *u·* grandeur.

unreliability

b 295– 3 proof of the *u·* of physical testimony.

unremoved

p 416–11 will tell you that the . . . material cause is *u·*

unrequited

a 49–11 sublime courage, and *u·* affection

unreservedly

b 269–22 I therefore plant myself *u·* on the

unrest

gl 596–24 illumine it, destroy the *u·* of mortal thought,

unrestrained

t 459–16 untaught and *u·* by C. S.,

unrighteous

s 139– 2 the *u·* man his thoughts."— *Isa.* 55 : 7.
f 206–11 for it is the prayer of the *u·* ;
239–15 the *u·* man his thoughts."— *Isa.* 55 : 7.
b 290–20 They who are *u·* shall be *u·* still,

unsafe

s 159– 1 her physicians insisted that it would be *u·*

unsatisfactory

t 444– 1 If the sick find these material expedients *u·*,

unsatisfied

c 258– 4 Hence the *u·* human craving for

unsay

f 204–32 must *u·* it and cease from such utterances ;

unscientific

sp 79–23 The *u·* practitioner says : "You are ill.
s 114– 6 The spiritually *u·* definition of mind
159–15 Had these *u·* surgeons understood metaphysics,
ph 199–29 the *u·* might attribute to a lubricating oil.
f 223–23 and supplant *u·* means and so-called laws.
b 300–28 This theory is *u·*,
375–15 All *u·* mental practice is erroneous
p 369–27 *U·* methods are finding their dead level.

unscrupulous

f 235–16 while the debased and *u·* mind,

unsearchable

c 264– 9 Where . . . but in the *u·* realm of Mind?

unsee

t 461–29 you must mentally *u·* the disease ;

unseen

pr 15– 7 The Father in secret is *u·* to the physical
a 28– 5 taught the *u·* verities of God,
ph 189–11 though the cause be *u·*,
f 208–24 cannot be lost nor remain forever *u·*.
212–22 mortals believe that *u·* spirits produce the
212–30 origin of all things are *u·* to mortal sense ;
234–30 action of the human mind, *u·* to the senses.
b 299– 4 which embodies his conception of an *u·* quality
314–17 seemed a spectre, *u·* and unfamiliar,
334–13 This dual personality of the *u·* and the seen,
p 377–17 Because a belief originates *u·*,
429–17 bodies *u·* by those who think that they bury the body.
t 464–10 She therefore remains *u·* at her post,
r 481–11 contradictions . . . do not change the *u·* Truth,
ap 570– 5 certain active yet *u·* mental agencies

upright

ph 171– 8   and will find himself unfallen, *u·*, pure,
200–19   neither inverted nor subverted, but *u·* and
f 239–11   is not the ruler of his *u·* neighbor.
p 432– 4   and know him to be truthful and *u·*,

uprising

p 363–26   did his insight detect this unspoken moral *u·*?

uproot

m 57–25   may *u·* the flowers of affection,
ph 180– 3   and to *u·* its false sowing.

uprooted

ph 188–27   disease must be *u·* and cast out.

uproots

b 272– 8   the swinish element in human nature *u·* it.

upsets

sp 73– 9   The belief . . . *u·* both the individuality and

upside

b 301–28   with everything turned *u·* down.

upturned

s 142–11   If the soft palm, *u·* to a lordly salary,

upward

ph 172– 8   as rising from matter *u·*.
b 299–10   they point *u·* to a new and glorified trust,
p 434–18   earnest, solemn eyes, . . . look *u·*.
g 545– 9   by thought tending spiritually *u·*
552–19   open their shells . . . and look outward and *u·*.

upward-soaring

b 299–12   These *u·* beings never lead towards self,

urged

a 19–29   Jesus *u·* the commandment,
s 148– 5   He prescribed no drugs, *u·* no obedience to
r-476– 6   *u·* to its final limits, is self-destroyed.
g 552–27   *u·* to its utmost limits, results in a return to

urges

f 223–29   as truth *u·* upon mortals its resisted claims ;
b 280–22   *u·* through every avenue the belief that
p 433– 8   Judge Medicine, *u·* the jury not to allow
t 462–30   It *u·* the government of the body

urging

sp 92–28   instead of *u·* the claims of Truth alone.
p 371–22   No impossible thing do I ask when *u·* the

Urim

gl 595–13   The *U·* and Thummim, which were to be
596–11   definition of

Us

gl 588–11   but one I, or *U·*, but one divine Principle,
591–16   MIND. The only I, or *U·* ; the only Spirit,

usage

a 30–12   wholly apart from mortal *u·*,
55– 4   to unchristian comment and *u·*
m 63–16   marvel why *u·* should accord woman less
s 114– 1   *U·* classes both evil and good together
o 341– 8   appear contradictory when subjected to such *u·*.

usages

p 437–29   on the ground that unjust *u·* were not allowed

use

common
p 363– 3   which is in such common *u·* in the East.
human
s 143– 6   nor provide them for human *u·* ;
its
s 144–15   and its *u·* is to be condemned.
Jesus'
ap 576–16   was familiar with Jesus' *u·* of this word,
little
ph 166–17   To ignore God as of little *u·* in sickness is a
man's
g 530– 7   brings forth food for man's *u·*.
medical
s 157–21   If He . . . designs them for medical *u·*,
of drugs
sp 79– 8   is more sanitary than the *u·* of drugs,
s 155– 3   When the sick recover by the *u·* of drugs,
of inanimate drugs
an 105–32   from the *u·* of inanimate drugs to the
of material remedies
t 453–12   never . . . from the *u·* of material remedies
of purgatives
p 408–14   by the *u·* of purgatives and narcotics
of the word
s 114–13   involves an improper *u·* of the word *mind.*
127– 1   or questions her *u·* of the word
r 482– 7   The proper *u·* of the word *soul* can always
of tobacco
p 383–24   Does his assertion prove the *u·* of tobacco
t 454– 2   the *u·* of tobacco or intoxicating drinks
prolonged
s 156–15   from their prolonged *u·*,

use

right
t 444–10   guide them into the right *u·* of
———
pr 13–10   such as the heathen *u·*.
a 32–21   confined to the *u·* of bread and wine.
44–17   that he might *u·* those hands to remove the
b 309– 4   which, to *u·* the word of the Psalmist,
329–12   we can *u·* only what we understand.
o 349–17   one is obliged to *u·* material terms
354– 7   Why do they *u·* this phraseology, and yet
p 402–23   or hypnotism, to *u·* the recent term
t 453–13   as from the *u·* of spiritual.
455–12   if, knowing the remedy, you fail to *u·* the
463–26   nor did he *u·* drugs.
r 468–19   as the Scriptures *u·* this word in Hebrews :
479–16   or *u·* any of the physical senses?
482– 8   In other cases, *u·* the word *sense,*

used

pr 5–22   Prayer is not to be *u·* as a confessional
a 32–10   nor was the wine, *u·* on convivial occasions
38–15   Here the word *hands* is *u·* metaphorically,
sp 94– 6   implied by the terms . . . as *u·* in Scripture.
94–27   blasphemer who should hint that Jesus *u·* his
s 114–16   and as the phrase is *u·* in teaching C. S.,
114–19   if . . . could be suggested, it would be *u·* ;
126– 2   Error will be no longer *u·* in stating truth.
136– 7   he *u·* his divine power to save men
157–20   then they should never be *u·*.
ph 178– 3   the strychnine, or whatever the drug *u·*,
198–32   or that a less *u·* arm must be weak.
f 236– 4   How shall it be *u·*?
b 333– 4   though it is commonly so *u·*.
o 345– 2   thus they are uniformly *u·* and understood in
p 380–30   with strength to be *u·* against
410–26   If mental practice is abused or is *u·*
414– 8   The arguments to be *u·* in curing insanity
418–17   if arguments are *u·* to destroy it,
t 457– 8   has never *u·* this newly discovered power in
460– 9   though *u·* for physical healing.
r 482– 9   As *u·* in C. S., Soul is properly the
g 517– 1   word for *man* is *u·* also as the synonym of *mind.*
ap 568– 9   The narrative follows the order *u·* in Genesis.
576–26   as *u·* in our version of the Old Testament,
gl 588–22   obsolete in Science if *u·* with reference to Spirit,
590–21   This double term is not *u·* in the first chapter of
598– 1   word for *wind (pneuma)* is *u·* also for *spirit,*

useful

pref x–10   A few books, however, . . . are *u·*.
ph 194–17   history of Kaspar Hauser is a *u·* hint
f 245–18   instance of youth preserved furnishes a *u·* hint,
b 268– 2   has brought to light . . . many *u·* wonders.
p 370–29   These lessons are *u·*.
382–10   receive a *u·* rebuke from Jesus' precept,
t 463–11   this idea cannot injure its *u·*
g 514–30   All of God's creatures, . . . are harmless, *u·*,
528–30   may be a *u·* hint to the medical faculty.

useless

a 36–24   It is *u·* to suppose that the wicked can
s 135–23   else one or the other is false and *u·* ;
ph 168–16   systems insist that man becomes sick and *u·*,
p 382–31   Adherence to hygiene was *u·*.

uselessness

r 485– 9   because of their *u·* or their iniquity,

uses

m 66– 3   Sweet are the *u·* of adversity ;
an 105–22   Whoever *u·* his developed mental powers like
s 112–28   and yet *u·* another author's discoveries
143–13   the human mind *u·* one error to
p 370–17   but it *u·* the same medicine in both cases.

usher

p 382– 7   this alone would *u·* in the millennium.
g 529– 9   *u·* in Science and the glorious fact of creation,

ushered

s 139– 8   The Christian era was *u·* in with signs and
b 325– 4   *u·* into the undying realities of Spirit.
325–28   which *u·* Jesus into human presence,

ushers

r 490–25   immortal testimony *u·* in the

using

pref viii–17   by doctors *u·* material remedies ;
ph 182–24   and forthwith shut out the aid of Mind by *u·*
b 313–14   *U·* this word in its higher meaning,
p 370–12   *u·* the same drug which might cause the

usual

s 114–32   the *u·* opposition to everything new,
137–16   With his *u·* impetuosity, Simon replied
p 431–30   and perform my functions as *u·*,

usually

s 140– 2   Science is more than *u·* effectual in
p 378–31   we *u·* find displayed in human governments.
394–30   the sick *u·* have little faith in it till they

usually

t 461–21   U· to admit that you are sick,
462–18   as they u· do in every department
g 523–31   it is u· Jehovah, . . . who is referred to.

usurp

ph 167–13   cannot successfully u· the place and power of
g 549–30   to u· the prerogatives of omnipotence.

usurped

b 317– 3   since material knowledge u· the throne of

usurper

gl 580–17   the u· of Spirit's creation,

usurping

f 204–25   thus u· the name without the nature

usurps

g 513– 2   for the claim u· the deific prerogatives
541–23   At first it u· divine power.

utility

an 100–18   "In regard to the existence and u· of
o 355– 6   the proof of the u· of these methods ;
gl 583–15   that institution, which affords proof of its u·

utilization

s 111–12   u· of the power of Truth over error ;

utilize

t 455– 8   You must u· the moral might of Mind

utmost

f 240–28   must pay fully and fairly the u· farthing,
p 434–17   regards the prisoner with the u· tenderness.
r 486–10   preparatory school must be improved to the u·.
g 540– 8   stirring up the belief in evil to its u·,
552–27   intermixture . . . urged to its u· limits,

utter

pr 14–14   and the body will then u· no complaints.
a 47–32   Jesus realized the u· error of a belief in
sp 74–23   Who will say that infancy can u· the ideas of
97–23   It requires courage to u· truth ;

utter

o 354– 2   "u· falsities and absurdities,"
t 450– 6   They u· a falsehood, while
ap 559–14   to u· the full diapason of secret tones.

utterance

pr 7– 5   showing the necessity for such forcible u·,
sp 80– 3   is not lessened by giving u· to truth.
s 127–29   It is a divine u·,— the Comforter
f 208–18   Such an u· is "the voice of— Matt. 3 : 3.
233–29   The u· of truth is designed to rebuke
b 323–31   We are either turning away from this u·,
p 365– 7   The benign thought of Jesus, finding u·
g 545– 4   This could not be the u· of Truth or Science,

utterances

f 205– 1   must unsay it and cease from such u· ;
p 367–25   through silent u· and divine anointing

uttered

sp 97–26   u· His voice, the earth melted."— Psal. 46 : 6.
b 314–27   the more distinctly he u· the demands of
317– 1   Jesus u· things which had been
o 358–16   u· and illustrated by the prophets,
r 479– 4   could the Scriptural rejoicing be u· by any

uttering

pr 7–28   u· desires which are not real
sp 89– 2   is incapable of knowing or u·
b 323–30   "still, small voice" of Truth u·— I Kings 19 : 12.

utterly

s 129–10   your preconceptions or u· contrary to them.
g 506– 2   Objects u· unlike the original do not
545–12   is u· opposed to the theory of

uttermost

pr 5–11   we must pay "the u· farthing."— Matt. 5 : 26.

utters

b 307–20   partakes of its own nature and u· its own falsi- ties.
p 441–11   Let what False Belief u·, now and forever,
g 533–13   the snake-talker u· the first voluble lie,

V

vacuity

r 480– 6   then there remains only the darkness of v·

vacuum

c 266– 9   this seeming v· is already filled with

vacuums

o 346–17   There are no v·.

vague

s 110–32   No analogy exists between the v· hypotheses
119– 1   When we endow matter with v· spiritual power,
b 298– 1   the v· realities of human conclusions.
g 504–26   hypotheses, and v· conjectures emit no such
545–18   Outside of C. S. all is v· and hypothetical,
549–21   in such v· hypotheses as must necessarily

vain

pr 2–31   Asking God to be God is a v· repetition.
6– 8   implies the v· supposition that we
10– 9   millions of v· repetitions will never
13– 9   "v· repetitions," such as the— Matt. 6 : 7.
a 37– 7   Mortals try in v· to slay Truth with the steel
s 130– 7   v· to speak dishonestly of divine Science,
142–15   In v· do the manger and the cross tell their
142–23   to purge the temples of their v· traffic
f 203–30   waves of sin, sorrow, and death beat in v·.
223–21   efforts of error to answer . . . by some ology are v·.
b 324–28   then is our preaching v·."— I Cor. 15 : 14.
p 373– 9   has struggled long, and perhaps in v·, to lift a

vainly

m 57–22   Human affection is not poured forth v·,
an 106– 4   and to push v· against the current

vale

ph 191–22   not a spray buds within the v·,

vales

f 240– 4   mighty billows, verdant v·, festive flowers,

valid

p 434–27   The only v· testimony in the case shows

validity

r 491– 4   without actual foundation or v·.
g 525– 3   the v· of matter is opposed,
525– 4   not the v· of Spirit or Spirit's creations.

valley

m 61– 9   Every v· of sin must be exalted,
ap 578–10   the v· of the shadow of death,— Psal. 23 : 4.
gl 592–20   definition of
596–21   the v· of the shadow of death,— Psal. 23 : 4.
596–26   maketh the v· to bud and blossom as the rose.

valleys

s 147–13   and in the v· of Galilee.

value

o 355–14   What is the relative v· of the two
t 443–20   may learn the v· of the apostolic precept :
gl 597– 5   were of little v·, if only he

valued

f 238– 1   are not rightly v· before they are understood.

valueless

s 125–20   theories about laws of health to be v·.
o 341–11   In C. S. mere opinion is v·.
g 525–21   Whatever is v· or baneful, He did not make,

values

pref ix–32   but she v· them as a parent may

valves

ph 187–13   The v· of the heart, opening and closing

vanish

sp 77–14   period required for this dream . . . to v· from
81– 6   their belief in mediumship would v·.
96–21   error will v· in a moral chemicalization.
f 209–29   will ultimately v·, swallowed up in the
o 352–29   objects of alarm will then v· into nothingness,
355– 2   and then the ambiguity will v·.
p 365–17   will v· into its native nothingness
415–29   the limbs will v· from consciousness.
r 480–32   evil would v· before the reality of good.
g 555–29   which seemed to v· in death.

vanished

sp 88– 4   the touch of a v· hand,
ap 573–20   the heavens and earth had v·,

vanishes

f 250–18   When that dream v·, the mortal finds
b 312– 7   as the sense-dream v· and reality appears.
p 416– 1   At last the agony also v·.
r 474–28   the unreal v·, while all that is real is eternal.

vanity

s 163–27   might gratify our v·, if it were not
f 239–32   the wise man said, "All is v·."— Eccl. 1 : 2.
b 303–15   All the v· of the ages can never make
gl 592–28   self-righteousness ; v· ; hypocrisy.

vanquished

a 45– 2   Jesus v· every material obstacle,
54– 4   With the affluence of Truth, he v· error.

vapid

b 293–21   There is no v· fury of mortal mind

vapor

b 295–23   Then, like a cloud melting into thin v·,
r 480–31   As v· melts before the sun,

vapors

s 163–31   to arrange the fleeting v· around us,

variable
g 503–25   mortal life, mutable truth, nor *v·* love.

variance
a 19–14   his teaching set households at *v·*,
an 106–22   hatred, *v·*, emulations, wrath, strife, — *Gal.* 5 : 20.
f 215– 7   Soul and matter are at *v·*

varied
b 319–15   The *v·* doctrines and theories which
r 466– 4   The *v·* manifestations of C. S. indicate Mind,
g 518–21   *v·* expressions of God reflect health,

various
pref x– 4   V· books on mental healing have since
s 144– 8   The *v·* mortal beliefs formulated in
f 248–14   We are all sculptors, working at *v·* forms,
b 339–32   Our *v·* theories will never
o 344–19   There are *v·* methods of treating disease,
p 379–25   Fevers are errors of *v·* types.
437–21   V· notables— Materia Medica, Anatomy,
r 481– 9   The *v·* contradictions of the Science of Mind
g 553– 1   in the *v·* forms of embryology,
gl 587–12   the *v·* theories that hold mind to be

vary
s 149–12   its perfection of operation never *v·* in Science.
p 412– 5   You may *v·* the arguments to meet the

varying
b 311– 1   the *v·* clouds of mortal belief, which hide

vast
ph 177–32   but the *v·* majority of mankind,
f 209– 7   the life and light of all its own *v·* creation ;
246–18   Chronological data are no part of the *v·* forever.
c 266–31   into the *v·* forever of Life,
p 442– 6   throughout the *v·* audience-chamber of Spirit
r 479–21   In the *v·* forever, in the Science and truth of

vastly
s 116–12   includes *v·* more than is at first seen.

vastness
c 256–29   Finiteness cannot present the idea or the *v·* of
b 330– 3   learned the *v·* of C. S.,

vegetable
s 158– 9   from image-gods to *v·* and mineral drugs
f 244–24   He is not a beast, a *v·*, nor a migratory mind.
b 277–15   A mineral is not produced by a *v·*
309–28   error to suppose that there can be . . . *v·* life,
g 509–20   So-called mineral, *v·*, and animal substances

vegetables
f 221– 3   he ate only bread and *v·*,
244–14   like the beasts and *v·*, — subject to
b 277–13   Natural history presents *v·* and animals
g 531–19   Who will say that minerals, *v·*, and animals
543–22   Minerals and *v·* are found, according to
557– 7   V·, minerals, and many animals

vegetarianism
s 155–28   V·, homœopathy, and hydropathy

vehemently
p 420–29   *v·* tell your patient that he must awake.
421–15   Insist *v·* on the great fact

veil
a 41– 1   must be cast beyond the *v·* of matter
s 114–24   It lifts the *v·* of mystery from Soul and body.
g 513–10   but anon the *v·* is lifted, and the scene shifts
ap 563–15   Revelator lifts the *v·* from this embodiment of
gl 596–28   definition of
597–11   It rent the *v·* of the temple.

veils
gl 596–29   Jewish women wore *v·* over their faces

vein
s 122–24   the severance of the jugular *v·*

veins
a 25– 9   than when it was flowing in his *v·*
p 373–27   When the blood rushes madly through the *v·*
376–15   all the blood, which ever flowed through mortal *v·*

venerable
f 215–32   would have killed the *v·* philosopher

veneration
sp 88–20   Excite the organ of *v·* or religious faith,

vengeance
a 51–25   pride, envy, cruelty, and *v·*,
g 542–15   *v·* shall be taken on him — *Gen.* 4 : 15.

venomous
m 66– 4   Which, like the toad, ugly and *v·*,

vented
a 23– 6   That God's wrath should be *v·* upon His

ventilation
pr 7–22   A self-satisfied *v·* of fervent sentiments

venture
f 254–24   If you *v·* upon the quiet surface of error
p 388–26   foolish to *v·* beyond our present understanding,

ventures
t 448–27   and *v·* not to break its rules,

verb
a 23–32   The Hebrew *v· to believe* means also *to be firm*
r 488– 9   from that conveyed by the English *v· believe;*

verbal
pr 3–25   Gratitude is much more than a *v·* expression
7–15   The motives for *v·* prayer may embrace
o 355– 7   and proofs are better than mere *v·* arguments

verbally
p 423– 3   either *v·* or otherwise,

verdant
f 240– 4   winged winds, mighty billows, *v·* vales,

verdict
s 159– 8   and a *v·* was returned that
ph 198– 4   A patient hears the doctor's *v·* as a
f 238–26   Justice often comes too late to secure a *v·*.
b 294–15   This *v·* of the so-called material senses
o 358–15   It presents the calm and clear *v·* of Truth
p 433–16   and the jury returns a *v·* of "Guilty of
440– 9   to give a *v·* delivering Mortal Man to Death.
441–29   to return a *v·* contrary to law and gospel.
442– 6   Spiritual Senses agreed at once upon a *v·*,

verdicts
r 481–22   human *v·* are the procurers of all discord.

verifies
p 382–21   This *v·* the saying of our Master :
t 446–22   enthrones faith in Truth, and *v·* Jesus' word :

verify
o 347– 3   It is said by one critic, that to *v·* this

verily
pr 1– *   *v·* I say unto you, — *Mark* 11 : 23.
sp 70– *   V·, *v·*, I say unto you, — *John* 8 : 51.
b 305–17   V·, *v·* I say unto you, — *John* 5 : 19.

veritable
sp 76–25   constitutes the only *v·*, indestructible man,
88– 9   How are *v·* ideas to be distinguished from
g 521–30   The history of error or matter, if *v·*, would

verities
eternal
s 110– 4   These eternal *v·* reveal primeval existence as
r 476–13   as the only and eternal *v·* of man.
grand
sp 75–31   from earth's sleep to the grand *v·* of Life,
p 384–15   will prove to himself, . . . the grand *v·* of C. S.
great
s 109–32   The three great *v·* of Spirit,
p 397–24   one must be familiar with the great *v·* of
g 543–15   The great *v·* of existence are never
simple
f 236–26   the simple *v·* that will make them happy
unseen
a 28– 5   and taught the unseen *v·* of God,

———

b 337–25   Eternal things (*v·*) are God's thoughts

verity
s 123–11   The *v·* of Mind shows conclusively
f 252–12   and the eternal *v·*, man created by
b 274–17   Jesus demonstrated this great *v·*.
296– 2   whereas Science unfolds the eternal *v·*,
305–13   The *v·* that God's image is not a creator
339–32   You conquer error by denying its *v·*.
o 354–29   I rejoice in the apprehension of this grand *v·*.
p 414–26   Keep in mind the *v·* of being,
r 468– 7   for sin is not the eternal *v·* of being.
480–29   This is the eternal *v·* of divine Science.
g 502–25   the eternal *v·* and unity of God and man,
514–31   A realization of this grand *v·* was a

verse
sp 82– 6   yet we still read his thought in his *v·*.
ph 200– 1   through his *v·* the gods became alive in a
g 523–26   From the fourth *v·* of chapter two

verses
g 521–24   presented in the *v·* already considered,
523–23   and in three *v·* of the second,

version
r 488–12   often appear in our common *v·*
g 523–21   Lord God, as our common *v·* translates it.
ap 576–26   as used in our *v·* of the Old Testament,

versions
s 139–17   manifest mistakes in the ancient *v·* ;

versus
b 319– 3   disease as error, as matter *v·* Mind,
p 434–15   the case for Mortal Man *v·* Personal Sense

vertebræ
p 402– 7   dislocated joints, and spinal *v·*.

vertebrata
g 556– 3   V·, articulata, mollusca, and radiata are

very

pr	5– 4	one step towards reform and the *v·* easiest step.
	8–24	We confess to having a *v·* wicked heart
	13– 1	"a *v·* present help in trouble."— *Psal.* 46 : 1.
a	21–19	Our paths have diverged at the *v·* outset,
	27–30	made their strongest attack upon this *v·* point.
	28–28	is to mistake the *v·* nature of religion.
	53– 8	The reputation of Jesus was the *v·* opposite of
m	63–12	Civil law establishes *v·* unfair differences
sp	80– 9	Yet the *v·* periodical containing this sentence
	81– 7	At the *v·* best and on its own theories,
	84–25	destroys the belief of spiritualism at its *v·*
	89–28	Cain *v·* naturally concluded that if
an	102–22	produce the *v·* apathy on the subject which
	106– 3	is to drop . . . into the *v·* mire of iniquity,
s	129–28	The *v·* name, *illusion*, points to nothingness.
	134–18	robs Christianity of the *v·* element, which
	154–20	and they produce the *v·* results which
	161–27	would naturally induce the *v·* disease
ph	172– 6	nothing in the right direction and *v·* much in
	172–31	teaching us by his *v·* deprivations,
	195– 9	gave him pain through those *v·* senses,
f	202–28	"a *v·* present help in trouble ;"— *Psal.* 46 : 1.
	208–10	It is the *v·* antipode of immortal Mind,
	215– 8	from the *v·* necessity of their opposite
	222–22	He learned that a dyspeptic was *v·* far from
c	257–13	or *v·* far from being the supposed substance of
	258–25	Mortals have a *v·* imperfect sense of
	266–23	would deceive the *v·* elect.
b	270– 6	in its *v·* nature and essence ;
o	350– 3	or as *v·* far removed from daily experience.
	352–22	thus watering the *v·* roots of childish timidity,
	360–31	on the *v·* basis of Jesus' words and works.
p	370–19	*v·* direct and marked effects on the body.
	376–17	it cannot, for that *v·* reason, suffer with a fever.
	379–24	her belief produces the *v·* results she dreads.
	407– 1	but there is a *v·* sharp remembrance of it,
	413– 4	induces those *v·* conditions.
	413–30	may be reproduced in the *v·* ailments feared.
	436–29	sentenced Mortal Man to die for the *v·* deeds
t	444– 2	*v·* failures may open their blind eyes.
	444–12	a *v·* present help in trouble."— *Psal.* 46 : 1.
r	488–26	otherwise the *v·* worms could unfashion man.
g	518–25	and, behold, it was *v·* good.— *Gen.* 1 : 31.
	525–24	"and, behold, it was *v·* good."— *Gen.* 1 : 31.
	541–18	ruptures the . . . brotherhood of man at the *v·*
	544–23	*v·* antipodes of immortal and spiritual being.
	547–23	The Scriptures are *v·* sacred.
	548–19	"It is *v·* possible that many general statements
ap	574–20	the *v·* message, or swift-winged thought,
	574–27	The *v·* circumstance, which your

vessel

s	130–20	cannot add to the contents of a *v·* already full.

vessels

f	201–13	We cannot fill *v·* already full.

vested

f	236– 3	A special privilege is *v·* in the ministry.
p	379– 7	recognizing all causation as *v·* in divine Mind.

vestibule

sp	75–29	In the *v·* through which we pass
o	356– 8	Matter is not the *v·* of Spirit.
gl	597–17	the *v·* in which a material sense of things

vestige

s	153– 1	that not a *v·* of it remains.
f	221–15	without a *v·* of the old complaint.

vestments

sp	93–20	human faith may clothe it with angelic *v·*,
p	372–24	parading in the *v·* of law.

vesture

s	125–24	"As a *v·* shalt Thou— *Psal.* 102 : 26.
f	242–21	The *v·* of Life is Truth.
	242–24	and for my *v·* they did cast lots."— *John* 19 : 24.
	242–27	appropriates no part of the divine *v·*,

vestures

c	260–29	If we array thought in mortal *v·*,

vials

ap	574– 7	which had the seven *v·* full of the— *Rev.* 21 : 9.
	574–18	the seven angelic *v·* full of seven plagues,

viand

sp	88– 7	when no *v·* touches the palate

vibrating

a	22– 3	*V·* like a pendulum between sin and the

vibration

c	259–25	*V·* is not intelligence : hence it is not a creator.

vicarious

a	22–26	pinning one's faith . . . to another's *v·* effort.

vice

pr	11–16	suffered sufficiently from *v·* to make him
m	60–17	became a barrier against *v·*,
p	365–25	hypocrisy, stolidity, inhumanity, or *v·*
t	449–28	Only virtue is a rebuke to *v·*.
	452–17	the luxury of learning with egotism and *v·*.

vicegerent

f	224–14	and array His *v·* with pomp and splendor ;

vices

ap	571– 7	than when you tell them their *v·*.

vice versa

pr	15– 6	Closed to error, it is open to Truth, and *v· v·*.
s	160– 4	physics act against metaphysics, and *v· v·*.
ph	182– 1	will diminish your ability to become a Scientist, and *v· v·*.
b	279–15	no more. . .than Truth can create error, or *v· v·*.
	290–32	His body is as material as his mind, and *v· v·*.
p	374–30	Nothing that lives ever dies, and *v· v·*.

vicious

f	248–18	by *v·* sculptors and hideous forms?

victimize

s	158–20	to *v·* the race with intoxicating

victimizes

b	294–15	verdict of the so-called material senses *v·*

victims

f	230–14	and then punishing the helpless *v·*
o	352–19	at any moment they may become its helpless *v·* ;
p	420–10	that they are not helpless *v·*,
	447–11	and save the *v·* of the mental assassins.

victor

s	137– 6	the *v·* over sickness, sin, disease, death, and the
p	380– 4	Truth is always the *v·*.
	412– 9	and you will be the *v·*.
r	492–17	until one is acknowledged to be the *v·*.

victories

a	39– 9	trials and self-denials, as well as joys and *v·*,

victorious

p	407–10	If man is not *v·* over the

victory

everlasting

a	33–16	With the great glory of an everlasting *v·*
	45– 5	a sublime success, an everlasting *v·*.

get the

f	231– 2	so-called physical senses will get the *v·*.

obtained a

p	388– 3	obtained a *v·* over the corporeal senses,

over a single sin

ap	568–24	For *v·* over a single sin, we give thanks

over death

a	35–15	They celebrate their Lord's *v·* over death,
	45– 7	in his *v·* over death and the grave.
p	427–20	obtain the *v·* over death in proportion as

over evil

ap	571–17	the wisdom and the occasion for a *v·* over evil.

over sin

t	447–26	get the *v·* over sin and so prove its unreality.

seal the

a	44– 1	must seal the *v·* over error and death,

s	145–10	*v·* will be on the patient's side only as
	164–29	Death is swallowed up in *v·*"— *I Cor.* 15 : 54.
f	254– 8	until the battle . . . is fought and the *v·* won.
b	275–27	It robs the grave of *v·*.
	323–26	robs the grave of *v·*, takes away all sin
p	388– 4	a *v·* which Science alone can explain.
t	446–19	for *v·* rests on the side of immutable right.
	453– 7	until *v·* rests on the side of invincible truth.
r	492–32	*V·* would perch on neither banner.
	496–24	"Where is thy *v·*?"— *I Cor.* 15 : 55.
	496–27	Death is swallowed up in *v·*."— *I Cor.* 15 : 54.

view

another

ap	574– 3	The Revelator also takes in another *v·*,

brought into

g	538–21	is brought into *v·* only as the unreal

correct

s	116–11	A correct *v·* of C. S. and of its adaptation to
r	477– 3	and this correct *v·* of man healed the sick.

exalted

gl	598–25	This exalted *v·*, obtained and retained when

false

g	545–17	a false *v·*, destructive to existence
	545–19	in its false *v·* of God and man,

hid from

ap	560–23	hid from *v·* the apostle's character,

human

s	150–22	human *v·* infringes man's free moral agency ;
b	276–30	brings objects and thoughts into human *v·*
	316–18	rose higher to human *v·* because of the

humiliating

s	163–28	more than compensated by the humiliating *v·*

material

g	521–25	a material *v·* of creation,
	521–27	this material *v·* of God and the universe,

mortal

b	315–30	(that is, as it seemed to mortal *v·*),

view

of sin
p 404–23 Arouse the sinner to this new and true *v·* of sin,
opposite
o 350– 5 C. S. takes exactly the opposite *v·*.
352– 8 the Jews took a diametrically opposite *v·*.
strongly in
p 414–26 Hold these points strongly in *v·*.
such a
ap 573– 2 is unable to grasp such a *v·*.
this
f 209–15 Nearness, . . . lends enchantment to this *v·*.
p 408– 2 This *v·* is not altered by the fact that
r 471–27 This *v·* rebuked human beliefs,
gl 581– 1 This *v·* of Satan is confirmed by the name

b 322– 9 in *v·* of the immense work to be accomplished
p 396–15 in *v·* of the conceded falsity of

viewed
g 502–11 This deflection of being, rightly *v·*,

viewing
s 119–25 In *v·* the sunrise, one finds that it

viewless
s 121–16 "a weary searcher for a *v·* home."

views

accurate
c 255– 9 afforded no foundation for accurate *v·* of
better
f 239– 9 and we get better *v·* of humanity.
clearer
s 121–20 rebuked by clearer *v·* of the everlasting facts,
f 239– 7 and we get clearer *v·*
g 504–19 spiritually clearer *v·* of Him,
correct
c 264–13 As mortals gain more correct *v·* of God and
false
m 62–29 Our false *v·* of life hide eternal harmony,
b 281–29 Our false *v·* of matter perish
315–11 The opposite and false *v·* of the people
higher
c 262–14 These clearer, higher *v·* inspire the
his own
t 462–11 and substituting his own *v·* for Truth,
incorrect
ph 195–31 Incorrect *v·* lower the standard of truth.
limited
c 255–13 mortals take limited *v·* of all things.
material
b 314–11 showed plainly that their material *v·* were
new
m 66–15 unfolds new *v·* of divine goodness and love.
obscured
gl 586– 2 weariness of mortal mind ; obscured *v·* ;
of error
r 485–10 *v·* of error ought to be obliterated by Truth.
of parents
p 413– 9 *v·* of parents and other persons
of the universe
g 502–16 scientifically Christian *v·* of the universe
shape our
f 246–29 Let us then shape our *v·* of existence into
spiritual
a 32–27 refresh his heart with brighter, with spiritual *v·*.
theological
a 24–16 the ordinary theological *v·* of atonement

sp 80–14 but I cannot coincide with their *v·*.
g 504–19 *v·* which are not implied by

vigilant
b 324–13 Be watchful, sober, and *v·*.

vigor
f 246–23 still maintain his *v·*, freshness, and promise.

vigorous
pref viii–19 A *v·* "No" is the response
a 22– 8 to make *v·* efforts to save themselves ;
s 130–29 astounded at the *v·* claims of evil
ph 198–21 haply causes a *v·* reaction upon itself,

vigorously
p 413–15 in order to make it thrive more *v·*

village
s 149–32 there is hardly a city, *v·*, or hamlet, in which

villainy
f 252–20 says : . . . elude detection by smooth-tongued *v·*.

vindicated
f 225–31 The rights of man were *v·* in a single section

vine
a 18– * *not drink of the fruit of the v·, — Luke* 22 : 18.
fr 600– * *let us see if the v· flourish, — Song* 7 : 12.

vineyard
pref xi–24 also the charge to plant and water His *v·*.

vineyards
fr 600– * *Let us get up early to the v· : — Song* 7 : 12.

violate
s 118–30 and *v·* the law of Love, in which
134–31 A miracle fulfils God's law, but does not *v·* that

violence
pref viii–22 increased *v·* of diseases since the flood.
a 33–14 their Master was about to suffer *v·*
an 105– 4 to prevent deeds of *v·* or to punish them.
s 161–15 less *v·* to that immortal sentiment
t 458–25 He does *v·* to no man.

violent
a 47–28 each one came to a *v·* death except St. John,
an 101– 1 that the *v·* effects, which are observed
ph 195– 7 All . . . except his black crust, produced *v·*
t 464–14 seized with pain so *v·*

violet
f 220– 9 The *v·* lifts her blue eye to greet the

viper
f 243– 5 made harmless the poisonous *v·*,
g 514–28 Paul proved the *v·* to be harmless.

vipers
s 133–12 healed of the poisonous stings of *v·*.

Virgil
sp 82– 7 discernment of the minds of Homer and *V·*,

virgin
b 313– 1 He was the son of a *v·*.
332–23 Jesus was the son of a *v·*.

virginity
m 62– 3 period of gestation have the sanctity of *v·*.

Virgin-mother
a 29–17 The *V·* conceived this idea of God,
29–25 overshadowed the pure sense of the *V·*
g 534–12 The Son of the *V·* unfolded the remedy

virtually
f 229–12 *v·* declaring Him good in one instance
o 348– 3 Medical theories *v·* admit the
361–11 Thus he *v·* unites with the Jew's belief
p 380– 9 we *v·* contend against the control of
g 549–32 for he *v·* affirms that the germ of humanity

virtue

affection and
an 103– 1 promotes affection and *v·* in families
and power
s 150– 1 monuments to the *v·* and power of Truth,
and truth
f 235– 3 if *v·* and truth build a strong defence.
246–11 radiant sun of *v·* and truth coexists with being.
contentment and
t 452–16 intellectual repast with contentment and *v·*,
garrisoned with
f 235–11 should be strongly garrisoned with *v·*.
goodness, and
m 57–18 the better claims of intellect, goodness, and *v·*.
honesty and
m 64–29 Honesty and *v·* ensure the stability of the
increasing
m 56–14 moral regulations as will secure increasing *v·*.
is a rebuke
t 449–28 Only *v·* is a rebuke to vice.
models of
f 235–20 Physicians, . . . should be models of *v·*.
school of
m 65– 1 Experience should be the school of *v·*,

virtues
s 156– 1 If drugs possess intrinsic *v·*
ap 571– 6 like you better when you tell them their *v·*

virus
ph 196–27 not from infection nor from contact with material *v·*,

viscera
s 160–11 the organic action and secretion of the *v·*.
p 415–24 all the organs . . . including brain and *v·*.

Vishnu
g 524– 4 in the Hindoo *V·*, in the Greek Aphrodite,

visible
s 118– 8 hidden in a sacred secrecy from the *v·* world
125–15 the *v·* manifestation will at last be
c 264–15 multitudinous objects . . . will become *v·*.
b 337–22 The *v·* universe and material man are the
p 400–25 the image which becomes *v·* to the senses.
r 478–12 nor were they even *v·* through the windows?
ap 559– 6 the source of all error's *v·* forms?
559– 8 exercised upon *v·* error and audible sin.
560–18 without a correct sense of its highest *v·* idea,

visibly
sp 80–31 both *v·* and invisibly,

vision
mortal
b 301–15 man's substantiality transcends mortal *v·*

vision
  mount of
    ap 561– 9 beheld the spiritual idea from the mount of *v*·.
  of St. John
    o 357–24 the *v*· of St. John in the Apocalypse.
  of the Apocalypse
    m 56–10 as in the *v*· of the Apocalypse,
    ap 572–14 can ever furnish the *v*· of the Apocalypse,
  outward
    gl 586– 5 Jesus said, thinking of the outward *v*·,
  spiritual
    f 215–11 Spiritual *v*· is not subordinate to
    ap 561– 7 Because of his more spiritual *v*·,
  St. John's
    g 536– 5 In St. John's *v*·, heaven and earth stand for
    ap 576– 6 reached St. John's *v*· while yet he
  such
    sp 87–13 The Scotch call such *v*· "second sight,"
  whisper this
    sp 76– 2 The ones departing may whisper this *v*·,

    ap 572–26 Through what sense came this *v*· to St. John?
    573– 9 while to another, . . . the *v*· is material.
    577–30 his *v*· is the acme of this Science
visions
    p 428– 5 resolves the dark *v*· of material sense
visit
    m 64– 5 To *v*· the fatherless and widows— *Jas.* 1 : 27.
    ph 192–32 I was called to *v*· Mr. Clark in Lynn,
    p 365–17 healing work will be accomplished at one *v*·,
visitant
    f 224–26 open or close the door upon this angel *v*·,
visitants
    b 298–27 celestial *v*·, flying on spiritual, . . . pinions.
visiting
    p 439–32 but on *v*· the spot, they learn that
visitor
    p 364–30 as Jesus said of the unwelcome *v*·,
    365– 1 the nurse, the cook, and the brusque-business *v*·
visits
    s 156–25 and receiving occasional *v*· from me,
visual
    p 393–28 constituting the *v*· organism.
    ap 572–27 Not through the material *v*· organs for seeing,
vital
    a 54–24 It was so *v*·, that it enabled them to
    s 113– 5 The *v*· part, the heart and soul of C. S.,
    b 293– 3 Electricity is not a *v*· fluid,
    p 379–22 The so-called *v*· current does not affect the
    387–17 and perform the most *v*· functions in society.
    397– 1 By not perceiving *v*· metaphysical points,
vitality
    sp 98–30 they are not deprived of their essential *v*·.
    s 146–10 barren of the *v*· of spiritual power,
vitalizing
    g 510–28 and not a *v*· property of matter.
vitiate
    p 393–14 and nothing can *v*· the ability and power
vivid
    f 212– 9 Because the memory of pain is more *v*·
vividly
    b 295–20 through which Truth appears most *v*·
vocations
    t 457–23 To pursue other *v*· and
voice
  divine
    g 532–20 error shrank abashed from the divine *v*·
  from harmony
    ap 559–16 Then will a *v*· from harmony cry :
  His
    sp 97–26 "He uttered His *v*·,— *Psal.* 46 : 6.
    c 255–18 Eye hath not seen Spirit, nor hath ear heard
                His *v*·.
  inward
    b 321–26 the inward *v*· became to him the
  lifts her
    sp 97–24 for the higher Truth lifts her *v*·,
  lifts its
    f 252–16 Material sense lifts its *v*· with the arrogance of
  loud
    ap 568–13 And I heard a loud *v*·— *Rev.* 12 : 10.
  Master's
    a 35– 4 and wakened by their Master's *v*·,
  of God
    f 226– 5 The *v*· of God in behalf of the African slave
    b 321–26 became to him the *v*· of God, which said :
  of one
    f 208–19 "the *v*· of one crying in the — *Matt.* 3 : 3.
  of the first sign
    b 321–28 to the *v*· of the first sign,— *Exod.* 4 : 8.

voice
  of the herald
    f 226– 6 the *v*· of the herald of this new crusade
  of the latter sign
    b 321–29 the *v*· of the latter sign."— *Exod.* 4 : 8.
  of thy wife
    g 535–20 hearkened unto the *v*· of thy wife,— *Gen.* 3 : 17.
  of Truth
    b 307–31 the *v*· of Truth still calls :
    308–14 Soul-inspired patriarchs heard the *v*· of Truth,
    323–29 the "still, small *v*·" of Truth— *I Kings* 19 : 12.
    t 456–27 Because it is the *v*· of Truth to this age,
    ap 559–10 inaudible *v*· of Truth is, to the human mind,
  still, small
    b 323–29 the "still, small *v*·" of Truth— *I Kings* 19 : 12.
    p 367–25 through a "still, small *v*·,"— *I Kings* 19 : 12.
    ap 559– 8 "still, small *v*·" of scientific— *I Kings* 19 : 12.
  Thy
    g 532–15 I heard Thy *v*· in the garden,— *Gen.* 3 : 10.
  to the dumb
    ph 183–28 hearing to the deaf, *v*· to the dumb,
  your
    ap 570–20 He can neither drown your *v*· with its roar,

    sp 88– 5 And the sound of a *v*· that is still.
    b 298– 6 silences for a while the *v*· of immutable
    g 541–28 The *v*· of thy brother's blood— *Gen.* 4 : 10.
    ap 560–17 whom God has appointed to *v*· His Word.
voiceless
    a 48– 5 waiting and struggling in *v*· agony,
voices
    pref ix– 8 the tongue *v*· the more definite thought,
    m 64–31 and the *v*· of physical sense will be forever
                hushed.
    sp 86–17 Haunted houses, ghostly *v*·, unusual noises,
    87–29 may reproduce *v*· long ago silent.
    f 210–27 so-called mortal mind which *v*· this
    232–26 In the sacred sanctuary of Truth are *v*· of
    240– 1 Nature *v*· natural, spiritual law and
voicing
    b 332–10 Christ is the true idea *v*· good,
void
    pr   2– 7 and it does not return unto us *v*·.
    s 126– 5 mortal mind will be without form and *v*·,
    145– 6 would have made *v*· their practice.
    f 229–20 made *v*· by the law of immortal Mind,
    o 351– 2 was pedantic and *v*· of healing power.
    p 381– 1 is rendered null and *v*· by the law of Life,
    441– 4 so-called law, which . . . is null and *v*·.
    t 445–16 You render the divine law . . . obscure and *v*·,
    464–25 Adulterating C. S., makes it *v*·.
    r 479–19 earth was without form, and *v*· ;— *Gen.* 1 : 2.
    g 503– 6 earth was without form, and *v*· ;— *Gen.* 1 : 2.
volcanic
    g 504–10 not from the sun nor from *v*· flames,
volition
    sp 80–26 These movements arise from the *v*· of
    ph 167– 2 to heal the sick out of His personal *v*·,
    187–23 The divine Mind includes all action and *v*·,
    191–21 By its own *v*·, not a blade of grass
    199– 1 without *v*· of mortal mind,
    f 220–32 as directly as the *v*· or will moves the hand.
    230–14 to suppose Him . . . punishing . . . of His *v*·
voluble
    g 533–13 the snake-talker utters the first *v*· lie,
volume
    s 147–14 Although this *v*· contains the complete Science
    o 341– 1 The strictures on this *v*· would condemn
    345–14 but in this *v*· of mine there are no
    r 465– 4 she revised that treatise for this *v*· in 1875.
voluntarily
    p 402–25 his subjects believe that they cannot act *v*·
voluntary
    ph 187–20 *v*·, as well as miscalled *involuntary*, action
    187–25 tries to classify action as *v*· and
    p 403– 2 great difference between *v*· and involuntary
    403– 3 *v*· mesmerism is induced consciously
    r 484–22 the *v*· or involuntary action of error
    491– 7 made up of involuntary and *v*· error,
vote
    s 139–15 The decisions by *v*· of Church Councils
vow
    m 59–27 The nuptial *v*· should never be annulled,
    68–12 Be not in haste to take the *v*·
vows
    m 65–17 the powerlessness of *v*· to make home happy,
vulgar
    m 58–26 a wife ought not to court *v*· extravagance
vulture's
    g 547–10 microscopic examination of a *v*· ovum,

W

wages
m	63–30	woman should be allowed to collect her own w˙,
f	240–30	The divine method of paying sin's w˙

wail
t	448–3	When the Publican's w˙ went out to the

wait
a	22–13	W˙ for your reward,
m	59–5	should w˙ on all the years of married life.
	66–19	w˙ patiently on divine wisdom to point out the
f	218–27	"They that w˙ upon the Lord — Isa. 40 : 31.
	238–2	well to w˙ till those whom you would benefit
	254–10	When we w˙ patiently on God and seek Truth
b	323–10	we pause, — w˙ on God.
t	454–22	W˙ patiently for divine Love to move upon the

waited
b	314–3	w˙ until the mortal or fleshly sense had

waiting
pref	ix–18	at the heavenly gate, w˙ for the Mind of Christ.
pr	10–3	and that w˙ patiently on the Lord,
a	48–5	w˙ and struggling in voiceless agony,
ph	166–19	w˙ for the hour of strength in which
c	255–*	w˙ for the adoption, to wit, — Rom. 8 : 23.
ap	562–25	w˙ to be delivered of her sweet promise,
	570–15	w˙ and watching for rest and drink.

waits
f	252–24	where the good purpose w˙ !

wake
f	218–32	When we w˙ to the truth of being,
	251–9	mortals w˙ to the knowledge of two facts :
p	430–11	When will mankind w˙ to this great fact in

wakeful
pref	vii–2	The w˙ shepherd beholds the

waken
sp	75–21	When you can w˙ yourself or others out of
o	354–24	Truth will w˙ men spiritually
p	427–31	Thought will w˙ from its own material
	429–11	Mortals w˙ from the dream of death
g	556–26	Because mortal mind must w˙ to spiritual life

wakened
a	35–3	w˙ by their Master's voice, they changed

wakens
b	322–21	as the startled dreamer who w˙ from an

waking
a	22–6	W˙ to Christ's demand, mortals experience
s	128–23	for w˙ him from a cataleptic nightmare,
ph	188–15	In both the w˙ and the sleeping dream,
f	250–22	the w˙ dream of mortal existence
p	397–25	Mortals are no more material in their w˙
	418–30	w˙ dream-shadows, dark images of

walk
pr	10–1	desire to w˙ and will w˙ in the light
	11–26	that we may w˙ securely in the only
a	21–1	If Truth is overcoming error in your daily w˙
	27–4	the blind see, the lame w˙, — Luke 7 : 22.
	41–8	The God-inspired w˙ calmly on
	46–5	In the w˙ to Emmaus, Jesus was known to
s	132–6	the blind receive their sight and the lame w˙, — Matt. 11 : 5.
ph	192–27	We w˙ in the footsteps of Truth and Love
	199–25	Had Blondin believed it impossible to w˙ the
f	218–28	they shall w˙, and not faint." — Isa. 40 : 31.
	223–2	Paul said, "W˙ in the Spirit, — Gal. 5 : 16.
	248–26	in the right direction, and then w˙ that way.
	254–4	w˙, and not faint," — Isa. 40 : 31.
c	264–10	We must look where we would w˙,
b	329–7	Because you cannot w˙ on the water
o	342–25	It causes the deaf to hear, the lame to w˙,
p	397–25	when they act, w˙, see, hear, enjoy,
t	455–9	in order to w˙ over the waves of error
g	510–11	reflected spiritually by all who w˙ in the light
ap	577–22	All who are saved must w˙ in this light.
	578–10	though I w˙ through the valley — Psal. 23 : 4.
gl	596–21	"Though I w˙ through the valley — Psal. 23 : 4.
fr	600–*	That ye might w˙ worthy — Col. 1 : 10.

walked
a	49–27	rabbis, before whom he had meekly w˙,
s	134–28	healed the sick, w˙ on the water.
f	214–6	he could never have "w˙ with God," — Gen. 5 : 24.
b	273–24	Jesus w˙ on the waves, fed the multitude,
p	442–14	no longer sick and in prison, w˙ forth,

walketh
m	56–16	pestilence that w˙ in darkness, — Psal. 91 : 6.

walking
c	261–14	w˙ about as actively as the youngest member
p	369–10	raising the dead, and w˙ over the wave.
	374–22	w˙ in darkness on the edge of a precipice.

walking
p	429–7	When w˙, we are guided by the eye.
t	452–7	W˙ in the light, we are accustomed to the
r	487–4	gained by w˙ in the pathway of Truth
ap	566–4	w˙ wearily through the great desert of

walks
b	323–11	until boundless thought w˙ enraptured,
t	451–14	w˙ in the direction towards which he looks,

walls
a	44–32	There were rock-ribbed w˙ in the way,
m	58–17	would confine . . . forever within four w˙,
b	295–19	the glass is less opaque than the w˙.
p	439–20	God will smite you, O whited w˙,

wander
r	491–24	and they w˙ whither they will

wanderers
g	507–9	nameless offspring, — w˙ from the parent Mind,
ap	570–15	weary w˙, athirst in the desert

wandering
m	58–19	a w˙ desire for incessant amusement
sp	82–16	w˙ . . . through different mazes of consciousness.
	82–28	When w˙ in Australia, do we look for
s	121–15	is as the w˙ comet or the desolate star
f	235–1	cannot go forth, like w˙ pollen,

wanes
ap	562–21	as the night of materialism w˙.

waning
s	134–14	Man-made doctrines are w˙.

want
m	64–1	W˙ of uniform justice is a crying evil
sp	95–21	and we w˙ that day to be succeeded by C. S.,
	96–16	w˙ and woe, sin, sickness, and death,
c	257–26	to meet the demands of human w˙ and woe,
p	425–29	capacious lungs and w˙ them to remain so,
r	489–30	A wrong sense . . . is non-sense, w˙ of sense.
g	501–9	richly recompensing human w˙ and woe
ap	578–5	I shall not w˙. — Psal. 23 : 1.

wanting
pref	viii–2	and has not been found w˙ ;
sp	92–25	Until . . . ability to make nothing of error will be w˙.

wants
m	58–28	because another supplies her w˙.
p	413–4	the undue contemplation of physical w˙
	440–18	ministering to the w˙ of his fellow-man

war
always at
r	492–32	would keep truth and error always at w˙.

and agriculture
r	485–28	gods of mythology controlled w˙ and agriculture

inflamed with
ap	565–3	inflamed with w˙ against spirituality,

in heaven
ap	566–25	And there was w˙ in heaven : — Rev. 12 : 7.

made
ap	565–24	material lie made w˙ upon the spiritual idea ;

man of
g	524–10	God becomes "a man of w˙," — Exod. 15 : 3.

not at
a	19–3	Love and Truth are not at w˙ with
b	276–6	in which one mind is not at w˙ with another,

will cease
r	467–12	as this fact becomes apparent, w˙ will cease

with Science
f	252–1	They are at w˙ with Science,

with the facts
r	496–21	the law of mortal belief, at w˙ with the facts of

s	130–16	beliefs which w˙ against spiritual facts ;
	163–17	w˙, pestilence, and famine, all combined."
o	354–5	and w˙ against "the world, the flesh, and the
g	530–5	Thus Spirit and flesh w˙.
ap	567–11	the dragon cannot w˙ with them.

ward
f	234–17	If mortals would keep proper w˙ over
p	420–12	they can resist disease and w˙ it off,

warding
m	63–2	for w˙ off pulmonary disease

warfare
human
f	226–12	freedom be won, not through human w˙,

in Science
ap	568–6	typifies the divine method of w˙ in Science,

warfare
of extermination
 g 543–14 is engaged in a *w·* of extermination.
our
 ap 568–31 we lay down all for Truth, or Christ, in our *w·*
perpetual
 f 231–16 governing man through perpetual *w·*.
suppositional
 b 288– 3 The suppositional *w·* between truth and error
this
 a 29– 4 and continue this *w·* until they have
 b 288– 6 this *w·* between the Spirit and flesh
 g 534–14 the Apostle Paul explains this *w·* between
 ap 568– 7 the glorious results of this *w·*.
true
 ap 568–12 first exhibits the true *w·* and then the false.
with the flesh
 b 324–15 It is a *w·* with the flesh, in which we must

 s 145–28 the *w·* between Spirit and the flesh goes on.
 b 316–13 Hence the *w·* between this spiritual idea and

warm
 f 247–25 glances in the *w·* sunbeam, arches the cloud
 p 379–12 a stream of *w·* water was trickling over his arm.
 r 190–32 will think that he is freezing when he is *w·*,

warn
 m 65– 9 Divorces should *w·* the age of some

warned
 o 358–31 against whom they have been *w·*,

warning
 a 53–22 Like Peter, we should weep over the *w·*,
 sp 79– 2 *W·* people against death is an error
 ph 196–14 The command was a *w·* to beware,
 f 238–14 the *w·*, "I know you not."— *Matt.* 25 : 12.
 ap 571–14 have seen the danger and yet have given no *w·*.

warns
 r 481–13 against which wisdom *w·* man,

warped
 p 433– 9 not to allow their judgment to be *w·* by

warping
 p 440–11 but no *w·* of justice can render

warrant
 pr 3– 3 is not sufficient to *w·* him in advising God.
 p 363–29 was her grief sufficient evidence to *w·* the
 366–14 we have the apostolic *w·* for asking :

warreth
 ph 200–22 the flesh that *w·* against Spirit.
 ap 567– 9 Against Love, the dragon *w·* not long,

warring
 s 140–10 *w·* no more over the corporeality,
 b 278–20 *w·* forever with each other ;
 ap 564–14 the dragon as *w·* against innocence.
 gl 584–12 The flesh, *w·* against Spirit ;

wars
 s 144–23 Science *w·* with so-called physical science,
 144–24 even as Truth *w·* with error,
 f 242–19 which *w·* against spirituality
 b 274–22 and the flesh *w·* against Spirit.
 340–24 ends *w·* ; fulfils the Scripture,
 g 531–28 since flesh *w·* against Truth
 ap 567– 1 He leads the hosts . . . and fights the holy *w·*.

wash
 p 364–14 *w·* and anoint his guest's feet,
 413–22 need not *w·* his little body all over each day
 t 452–21 and afterwards we must *w·* them clean.
 r 484– 4 neither . . . can *w·* away its foundation,

washed
 p 383– 4 rendered pure by Mind as well as *w·* by water.
 ap 572– 1 *w·* their robes white in obedience and

washing
 f 241–27 *w·* the body of all the impurities of flesh,
 p 413–17 *w·* should be only for the purpose of

wasted
 a 44–14 to resuscitate *w·* energies.

wasteth
 m 56–17 destruction that *w·* at noonday."— *Psal.* 91 : 6.

wasting
 p 376–10 whom you declare to be *w·* away

watch
 pr 15–20 to work and *w·* for wisdom, Truth, and Love.
 a 48– 4 not *w·* with me one hour?"— *Matt.* 26 : 40.
 48– 5 Could they not *w·* with him who,
 s 156–18 to give her unmedicated pellets and *w·* the
 p 366–22 The physician must also *w·*, lest he be
 367–21 Let us *w·*, work, and pray that this
 411–29 *W·* the result of this simple rule
 r 497–24 we solemnly promise to *w·*, and pray
 ap 563–19 holding untiring *w·*, that he may bite the heel

watched
 p 377–18 the mental state should be continually *w·*
 430–30 the prisoner, or patient, *w·* with a sick friend.
 431– 3 *w·* with the sick every night in the week.
 t 446–29 This must therefore be *w·* and guarded against.

watchful
 b 324–13 Be *w·*, sober, and vigilant.

watchfully
 f 234–10 as *w·* as we bar our doors against the

watchfulness
 pr 4–19 expressed in daily *w·* and in striving
 4–29 silent prayer, *w·*, and devout obedience
 gl 579– 8 ABEL. *W·* ; self-offering ;

watching
 pr 1– 6 Prayer, *w·*, and working, combined with
 f 245– 9 she stood daily before the window *w·*
 254– 2 Individuals are consistent who, *w·*
 p 435–19 *W·* beside the couch of pain
 t 464–11 praying, *w·*, and working for
 ap 570–16 waiting and *w·* for rest and drink.

watchman
 p 393– 1 like a *w·* forsaking his post,

watchtowers
 f 235–28 Clergymen, occupying the *w·* of the world,

watchword
 f 239–13 The *w·* of C. S. is Scriptural :

water
as a flood
 ap 570– 9 out of his mouth *w·* as a flood,— *Rev.* 12 : 15.
bread and
 f 220–22 once adopted a diet of bread and *w·*
cold
 p 436–11 Giving a cup of cold *w·* in Christ's name,
 ap 570–17 Give them a cup of cold *w·* in Christ's name,
goblet of
 s 153– 9 one drop of that attenuation in a goblet of *w·*,
nothing but
 f 221– 4 and drank nothing but *w·*.
of life
 g 548– 2 take the *w·* of life freely."— *Rev.* 22 : 17.
out of
 p 413–14 taking a fish out of *w·* every day
sweet
 b 287–13 at the same place sweet *w·* and— *Jas.* 3 : 11.
symbolizes
 g 507– 3 while *w·* symbolizes the elements of
turn the
 m 65– 4 be present . . . to turn the *w·* into wine
under
 g 557– 2 child could remain under *w·* twenty minutes,
walked on the
 s 134–28 healed the sick, walked on the *w·*,
warm
 p 379–12 stream of warm *w·* was trickling over his arm.
washed by
 p 383– 4 rendered pure by Mind as well as washed by *w·*.
without
 f 221– 8 only a thin slice of bread without *w·*.

 pref xi–24 also the charge to plant and *w·* His vineyard.
 s 153– 9 a teaspoonful of the *w·* administered
 b 321–32 by changing *w·* into wine,
 329– 8 Because you cannot walk on the *w·*
 o 361–16 As a drop of *w·* is one with the ocean,
 p 413–19 *W·* is not the natural habitat of humanity.
 g 556–32 plunged . . . into the *w·* for several minutes,

watered
 g 521–22 *w·* the whole face of the ground.— *Gen.* 2 : 6.

Waterhouse, Dr. Benjamin
 s 163– 4 Dr. Benjamin *W·*, Professor in Harvard

watering
 o 352–21 thus *w·* the very roots of childish timidity,

waters
abyss of
 ph 199–26 to walk the rope over Niagara's abyss of *w·*,
come ye to the
 pr 13– 4 come ye to the *w·*."— *Isa.* 55 : 1.
deep
 ap 570–21 the deep *w·* of chaos and old night.
disturb the
 f 254–25 what is there to disturb the *w·*?
divided the
 g 505–14 and divided the *w·* which were— *Gen.* 1 : 7.
divide the
 g 505– 5 and let it divide the *w·* from— *Gen.* 1 : 6.
face of the
 g 503– 8 moved upon the face of the *w·*.— *Gen.* 1 : 2.
fill the
 g 512–18 and fill the *w·* in the seas ;— *Gen.* 1 : 22.
healthful
 f 254–28 the ever-agitated but healthful *w·* of truth,

waters

living
f 234– 7 and giving living *w·* to the thirsty.

many
g 505–19 than the noise of many *w·,—Psal.* 93 : 4.

midst of the
g 505– 5 in the midst of the *w·,—Gen.* 1 : 6.

move upon the
t 454–23 for divine Love to move upon the *w·*

still
g 514–14 beside the still *w·."—Psal.* 23 : 2.
ap 578– 7 beside the still *w·.—Psal.* 23 : 2.

sweet
t 455–30 cannot send forth both sweet *w·* and bitter.
r 489–23 sendeth not forth sweet *w·* and bitter.

upon the
m 68–21 when casting my bread upon the *w·,*

will be pacified
ap 570–24 The *w·* will be pacified,

---

g 505– 6 divide the waters from the *w·.—Gen.* 1 : 6.
505–14 from the *w·* which were above the—*Gen.* 1 : 7.
506–15 And God said, Let the *w·—Gen.* 1 : 9.
506–23 gathering together of the *w·—Gen.* 1 : 10.
511–19 And God said, Let the *w·—Gen.* 1 : 20.
512– 5 which the *w·* brought forth—*Gen.* 1 : 21.
536– 1 gathering together of the *w·—Gen.* 1 : 10.

water-wheel
p 399–19 A mill at work or the action of a *w·*

wave
s 124–24 and said to the proud *w·,*
b 293–22 wind, *w·,* lightning, fire, bestial ferocity
p 369–10 raising the dead, and walking over the *w·.*
ap 569–19 to lift their heads above the drowning *w·.*
570–25 and Christ will command the *w·.*

waves
m 67– 6 and the *w·* lift themselves into mountains.
67–22 and commanded even the winds and *w·*
f 203–29 the *w·* of sin, sorrow, and death beat in vain.
b 273–25 Jesus walked on the *w·,* fed the multitude,
t 455– 9 in order to walk over the *w·* of error
g 505–19 than the mighty *w·* of the sea."—*Psal.* 93 : 4.

waxed
s 134–14 They have not *w·* strong in times of trouble.
o 350–18 "This people's heart is *w·* gross,—*Matt.* 13 : 15.

Way
b 332–14 the *W·,* the Truth, and the Life,

way

all the
ap 574– 4 journeying "uphill all the *w·.*"

beheld the
b 326–23 Saul of Tarsus beheld the *w·—* the Christ,

broad is the
t 451–13 broad is the *w·,* that leadeth to—*Matt.* 7 : 13.

Christ's
t 458–29 Christ's *w·* is the only one by which mortals

divine
c 266–19 Universal Love is the divine *w·* in C. S.

every
g 537– 7 sword which turned every *w·,—Gen.* 3 : 24.

exploring the
a 26– 4 in speechless agony exploring the *w·* for us,

finds its
p 365–26 finds its *w·* into the chambers of disease

forsake his
s 139– 1 the wicked to "forsake his *w·,—Isa.* 55 : 7.
f 239–14 the wicked forsake his *w·,—Isa.* 55 : 7.

give
c 260– 8 erring thought must give *w·* to the ideal

given
a 50–20 had for a moment given *w·* before the

God's own
g 542–20 Let Truth . . . destroy error in God's own *w·,*

go thy
a 40– 6 "Go thy *w·* for this time ;—*Acts* 24 : 25.

go your
a 27– 3 "Go your *w·,* and tell John—*Luke* 7 : 22.

in any
o 356–14 not contributing in any *w·* to each other's
p 410–26 or is used in any *w·* except to

in some
t 444– 2 In some *w·,* sooner or later, all must rise
ap 573–30 will surely appear sometime and in some *w·.*

in the
a 30–31 work out our salvation in the *w·* Jesus taught.
37–27 do they follow him in the *w·* that he
44–32 There were rock-ribbed walls in the *w·,*
b 326– 4 it must be in the *w·* of God's appointing,
p 390–19 whiles thou art in the *w·* with—*Matt.* 5 : 25.
r 483–28 and it does this in the *w·* of His appointing,

in the same
ph 188–20 In the same *w·* pain and pleasure,
p 415–19 In the same *w·* thought increases or

way

is dark
gl 596–23 Though the *w·* is dark in mortal sense,

is pointed out
t 462–16 when the *w·* is pointed out ;

is straight
b 324–13 The *w·* is straight and narrow,

its own
s 126–10 has sought and interpreted in its own *w·*

Jesus'
p 428– 4 demonstration of the facts of Soul in Jesus' *w·*

keep the
g 537– 7 to keep the *w·* of the tree of life.—*Gen.* 3 : 24.

leads the
t 454–19 inspires, illumines, designates, and leads the *w·.*

learned my
p 383– 1 was cured when I learned my *w·* in C. S."

learn the
c 264–28 When we learn the *w·* in C. S.

lighting the
pref vii–12 lighting the *w·* to eternal harmony.

maps out the
ph 176–27 no farther than mortal mind maps out the *w·.*

marked out the
f 227–24 Jesus marked out the *w·.*

marked the
a 46–25 that is, he marked the *w·* for all men.

more excellent
s 149– 4 The more excellent *w·* is divine Science

my
s 109–20 and I won my *w·* to absolute conclusions

narrow
s 126–31 "the straight and narrow *w·"—see Matt.* 7 : 14.
151–28 The straight and narrow *w·* is to see and
t 454–29 tread firmly in the straight and narrow *w·.*

no other
b 327–13 There is no other *w·.*
r 482–30 It can heal in no other *w·,*
490–27 can be obtained in no other *w·.*

of divine Science
b 316– 1 demonstrating the *w·* of divine Science,

of error
g 536–10 The *w·* of error is awful to contemplate.

of Life
a 25–13 Jesus taught the *w·* of Life by demonstration,
s 137–25 Love hath shown thee the *w·* of Life !

of salvation
pref vii– 8 would make plain . . . the *w·* of salvation
b 316– 1 he became the *w·* of salvation to all who

one
ph 167–25 There is but one *w·—* namely, God and His idea
f 242– 9 There is but one *w·* to heaven, harmony,

only
ph 180–27 The only *w·* to this living Truth,
p 371–19 the only *w·* out of this condition.

opens the
ph 174–14 Whoever opens the *w·* in C. S. is a pilgrim

open the
a 24– 7 open the *w·* for C. S. to be understood,
b 326–21 your Father will open the *w·.*

other
ph 167–28 impossible to gain control . . . in any other *w·.*

pointed the
r 494– 9 and Jesus pointed the *w·* for them.

pointing the
t 444–17 Let us be faithful in pointing the *w·*

point out the
a 30–21 to point out the *w·* of Truth and Life.

preparing the
f 208–20 and preparing the *w·* of Science.

scientific
p 411–12 this is the ultimatum, the scientific *w·,*

show us the
f 242–30 The finger-posts of divine Science show the *w·*

show us the
a 40–18 for not otherwise could he show us the *w·*

stood in his
a 28– 4 Even many of his students stood in his *w·.*

this
pr 8–29 for in this *w·* only can we learn
a 30–29 Only in this *w·* can we bless our enemies,
s 156–24 She went on in this *w·,* taking the
f 242–10 and Christ in divine Science shows us this *w·.*
p 377–24 You also remove in this *w·* what are termed
391–11 and in this *w·* you can prevent the
402–21 and in this *w·* affect the body,
t 446– 2 and in this *w·* dealing pitilessly with a

through Christ
ph 171– 5 even the *w·* through Christ, Truth,

to cure
p 417–23 since it is demonstrable that the *w·* to cure the

to escape
b 327–12 The *w·* to escape the misery of sin is to cease

to extract
f 201–17 The *w·* to extract error from mortal mind is to

way
to health
  f 241–24   the *w·* to health and holiness.
true
  f 202–20   the true *w·* leads to Life instead of to death,
unexplained
  pref xi– 4   which action in some unexplained *w·* results in
walk that
  f 248–26   in the right direction, and then walk that *w·*.
which leads
  r 472– 5   *w·* which leads to C. S. is straight and narrow.
will grow
  r 496–12   the *w·* will grow brighter
winding its
  ap 563–28   winding its *w·* amidst all evil,
your
  p 381–22   understand your *w·* out of human theories

  a 26–11   "I am the *w·*, the truth,— *John* 14 : 6.
     26–20   in order to show the learner the *w·*
     30–13   to mortal mind as "the *w·*."— *John* 14 : 6.
     39–15   He was "the *w·*."— *John* 14 : 6.
  a 46–25   Jesus was "the *w·* ;"— *John* 14 : 6.
  sp 98–31   The *w·* through which immortality and life
  b 286–11   "I am the *w·*."— *John* 14 : 6.
     320– 3   "I am the *w·*,— *John* 14 : 6.
  o 353–10   Christ is "the *w·*,— *John* 14 : 6.
  p 371–18   The *w·* in divine Science is the only way out of
  r 482–15   since Christ is "the *w·*"— *John* 14 : 6.
  g 535–18   Truth is indeed "the *w·*."— *John* 14 : 6.

waymarks
  c 267–24   by reversal, errors serve as *w·* to
  g 542–24   not to remove the *w·* of God.

ways
  a 37–17   learn to emulate him in *all* his *w·*
  f 218–21   lead only into material *w·* of obtaining help,
     251–12   Truth works . . . in just these *w·*.
  b 317–14   not only in all time, but in *all w·* and
  p 371–13   looks for relief in all *w·* except the right one.
  ap 571– 2   hidden mental *w·* of accomplishing iniquity.

Way-shower and **way-shower**
  a 30–10   enabled him to be the mediator, or *w·*,
  b 288–30   made him the *W·*, Truth and Life.
  r 497–15   unity with God through Christ Jesus the *W·* ;

wayside
  a 55–10   gospel of healing is again preached by the *w·*,

weak
  sp 79–25   says : . . . Your body is *w·*,
  s 123– 9   becomes the most absolutely *w·* and
  ph 168– 1   a poor shift for the *w·* and worldly,
     198–32   or that a less used arm must be *w·*.
  f 219–16   We shall not call the body *w·*, if we
     235–25   when the soul is willing and the flesh *w·*,
  p 377–13   becomes suddenly *w·* or abnormally strong,
     392–15   If you believe in inflamed and *w·* nerves,
     423–22   has rendered himself strong, instead of *w·*,
     426–10   struggle for Truth makes one strong instead
         of *w·*,

weaken
  s 145–30   must continually *w·* its own assumed power.
  ph 181–12   You *w·* or destroy your power

weakened
  p 423–16   He regards the ailment as *w·* or strengthened
  g 517– 2   This definition has been *w·* by

weakens
  b 329–32   Human resistance to divine Science *w·*

weaker
  s 144–13   the *w·* the indications of Soul.
  ph 198–27   and the stronger thoughts rule the *w·*.
  p 409–18   the stronger never yields to the *w·*, except

weakness
betrays its
  ph 192–25   which erelong betrays its *w·*
human
  t 453–17   Dishonesty is human *w·*, which forfeits
indicate
  t 455– 6   Such mental states indicate *w·* instead of
involves
  p 406–26   Inharmony of any kind involves *w·*
strength or
  p 377–14   the producer of strength or *w·*.
worldly
  f 238–23   Attempts to . . . arise from worldly *w·*.

  ph 176– 6   to the *w·* of their wives.
  f 219– 1   all disease, pain, *w·*, weariness, sorrow,
     221–11   passed many weary years in hunger and *w·*,
  o 354–22   God will redeem that *w·*,
  p 371–29   strength instead of *w·*,
     407–13   giving strength to the *w·* of mortal mind,

wealth
  m 57–15   Beauty, *w·*, or fame is incompetent
     58–28   *W·* may obviate the necessity for toil
  f 239– 5   Take away *w·*, fame, and
     239– 8   Break up cliques, level *w·* with honesty,

weaned
  m 60– 8   mother's affection cannot be *w·* from her child,

weaning
  b 322–30   Without this process of *w·*,

weapons
  a 48–17   Judas had the world's *w·*.
  t 464–23   The *w·* of bigotry, ignorance, envy,

wear
  f 254–31   for through it you win and *w·* the crown.
  p 387– 9   spiritual energies can neither *w·* out nor

wearily
  ap 566– 4   walking *w·* through the great desert of

weariness
  ph 183–16   *w·* and disease are not His laws,
  f 217–26   or any illusion of physical *w·*,
     218– 2   that which affirms *w·*, made that *w·*,
     219– 1   all disease, pain, weakness, *w·*, sorrow,
  gl 586– 1   *w·* of mortal mind ; obscured views ;

wearing
  sp 78– 6   the belief that we are *w·* out life
  f 226–22   *w·* out years of servitude to an
  b 296–26   foundations which time is *w·* away.
     315–29   *W·* in part a human form

wears
  m 66– 5   *W·* yet a precious jewel in his head.

weary
  a 22–14   "be not *w·* in well doing."— *II Thess.* 3 : 13.
     55–17   My *w·* hope tries to realize that happy day,
  m 68– 6   We ought to *w·* of the fleeting and false
  sp 79–29   need "not be *w·* in well doing."— *Gal.* 6 : 9.
  s 121–16   "a *w·* searcher for a viewless home."
  f 217–27   for matter cannot be *w·* and heavy-laden.
     218– 8   the body, . . . would never be *w·*.
     218–28   shall run, and not be *w·* ;— *Isa.* 40 : 31.
     221–10   He passed many *w·* years in hunger
     234–22   human systems disappoint the *w·* searcher
     250–16   A mortal may be *w·* or pained, enjoy or suffer,
     254– 3   "run, and not be *w·* ;— *Isa.* 40 : 31.
  b 318–18   *W·* of their material beliefs,
  g 501–16   that Love for whose rest the *w·* ones sigh
  ap 570–15   *w·* wanderers, athirst in the desert
     574– 4   adapted to console the *w·* pilgrim,

wearying
  p 426–11   instead of weak, resting instead of *w·* one.

weather
  s 122–20   points to fair *w·* in the midst of murky clouds
  ph 171–10   either of his life or of the *w·*,
  p 384–27   neither . . . will ever result from exposure to
         the *w·*.

weather-vane
  ph 184–31   I then requested her to look at the *w·*.

weaving
  an 102–19   *w·* webs more complicated and subtle.

web
  f 242–25   The divine Science of man is woven into one *w·*
  p 403–20   the gossamer *w·* of mortal illusion.

webs
  an 102–20   weaving *w·* more complicated and subtle.

Webster
  s 115–18   definition from

wedded
  ap 561–12   *w·* to the Lamb of Love.
     575– 3   Love *w·* to its own spiritual idea."
     577– 6   as no longer two *w·* individuals,

wedlock
  m 58–21   a poor augury for the happiness of *w·*.

weed
  c 265–17   as if man were a *w·* growing apace
  p 383–22   sometimes tells you that the *w·* preserves his

week
  ph 189– 4   If the eyes see no sun for a *w·*,
  p 431– 4   watched with the sick every night in the *w·*.

weekly
  sp 80–10   repeats *w·* the assertion that

weeks
  ph 193–20   am informed that he went to work in two *w·*.

weep
  a 53–22   Like Peter, we should *w·* over the warning,
  s 153–25   We *w·* because others *w·*, we yawn because

weigh
  m 57–16   should never *w·* against the better claims of
  ph 176–18   and *w·* down mankind with superimposed
  f 239– 6   which *w·* not one jot in the balance of God,
  t 445–16   when you *w·* the human in the scale with

weighing
  an 105–26   *w·* him down to the depths of ignominy

weighs
  s 155–15   The universal belief in physics *w·* against
  b 307–23   and so *w·* against our course Spiritward.

weight
  a 20–28   "Let us lay aside every *w·*,— *Heb.* 12 : 1.
  s 155–24   in proportion as it puts less *w·* into
  155–24   and more *w·* into the spiritual scale.
  ph 168– 5   removal of a single *w·* from either scale
  192–22   the *w·* you throw into the right scale.
  f 205–30   Denial of the oneness of Mind throws our *w·*
  p 380– 5   Sickness and sin fall by their own *w·*.
  396–20   and the overwhelming *w·* of opinions
  515–26   If you lift a *w·*, your reflection does this also.

welcome
  sp 75–32   the departing may hear the glad *w·*
  95–19   We *w·* the increase of knowledge

welcomed
  s 142–20   humility and divine Science to be *w·* in.

welding
  m 60– 7   *w·* indissolubly the links of affection.

welfare
  a 23–24   One kind of faith trusts one's *w·* to others.
  m 59–18   promotes the *w·* and happiness of your wife
  sp 84–16   foretell events which concern the universal *w·*,

well
  pref viii– 1   in the treatment of disease as *w·* as of sin,
  pr 12–31   If . . . only petitioners . . . should get *w·*.
  14–16   you will find yourself suddenly *w·*.
  a 20–21   Yet he swerved not, *w·* knowing that
  22–14   "be not weary in *w·* doing."— *II Thess.* 3 : 13.
  26–21   by practice as *w·* as precept.
  36–21   law of justice as *w·* as of mercy.
  36–29   in return for our efforts at *w·* doing.
  39– 8   trials and self-denials, as *w·* as joys and
  39–29   attended with doubts and defeats as *w·* as triumphs.
  41– 5   as *w·* as through their sorrows and afflictions.
  44– 3   "*W·* done, good and faithful— *Matt.* 25 : 23.
  m 63–23   A feasible as *w·* as rational means of
  64–12   "It is never *w·* to interfere with your
  66–17   it is *w·* to remember how fleeting are
  66–19   it is *w·* to hope, pray, and wait patiently
  sp 79–30   need "not be weary in *w·* doing."— *Gal.* 6 : 9.
  90–29   we may as *w·* improve our time in solving the
  93–21   belief that Spirit is finite as *w·* as infinite
  an 104–30   to prove the motive as *w·* as the commission of
  s 107–17   we may *w·* tremble in the prospect of
  120–12   And is he *w·* if the senses say he is sick?
  120–13   Yes, he is *w·* in Science in which health is
  138–21   and to heal the sick as *w·* as the sinning.
  145–13   its ethical as *w·* as its physical effects.
  149– 2   could save from sickness as *w·* as from sin.
  152– 6   Æsculapius of mind as *w·* as of body,
  ph 179– 6   as *w·* as those present,
  187–20   as *w·* as miscalled *involuntary*, action
  f 210–24   cannot say, . . . I am sick, or I am *w·*."
  222–21   he dropped drugs and . . . hygiene, and was *w·*.
  236–11   Mind heals sickness as *w·* as sin
  238– 2   *w·* to wait till those whom you would benefit
  238– 5   as *w·* as in the material universe.
  247–10   Beauty, as *w·* as truth, is eternal ;
  251–13   Sickness, as *w·* as sin, is an error
  b 268–18   as *w·* as on the facts of Mind.
  322–27   as *w·* as our disappointments and ceaseless
  328–26   It were *w·* had Christendom believed
  332–26   as they could understand as *w·* as perceive.
  o 342–13   He bade the seventy disciples, as *w·* as the
  343–26   as *w·* as Paul who was not one of his students,
  345–16   who understand its propositions *w·* enough to
  348–18   Is it not *w·* to eliminate from so-called mortal
  348–23   would it not be *w·* to abandon the defence,
  348–25   improved and that of other persons as *w·*
  350–25   its effects on the body as *w·* as on the
  360–10   They . . . keep Soul *w·* out of sight.
  p 370– 1   better spiritually as *w·* as physically.
  377–22   remove the cause of all disease as *w·* as
  377–32   as *w·* as the fear of disease,
  383– 4   rendered pure by Mind as *w·* as washed by
  383–30   pounding the poor body, to make it sensibly *w·*
  385–22   You say that you have not slept *w·*
  393–32   It is *w·* to be calm in sickness ;
  397– 3   as *w·* as on the morals and the happiness of
  418– 3   the conquest over sickness, as *w·* as over sin,
  418–26   Include moral as *w·* as physical belief
  419–26   as *w·* as those of your patients,
  424–26   it is *w·* to be alone with God and the

well *(continued)*
  p 427–25   physical realm, so-called, as *w·* as in the
  429– 3   as *w·* as by other graces of Spirit.
  435– 9   result in good to himself as *w·* as to others.
  t 448–21   *w·* knowing it to be impossible for error,
  449– 6   in order to continue in *w·* doing.
  449–13   You should practise *w·* what you know,
  454–16   points out to his student error as *w·* as truth,
  454–16   the wrong as *w·* as the right practice.
  458–28   through living as *w·* as healing and
  r 480–10   Consciousness, as *w·* as action,
  480–17   would make matter the cause as *w·* as
  483–32   to be *w·* done, the work must be done unselfishly.
  494–11   It is not *w·* to imagine that Jesus
  494–16   as *w·* as the infinite ability of Spirit,
  g 531– 8   It is *w·* that the upper portions of the brain
  532–23   Is Mind capable of error as *w·* as of truth,
  532–23   Is Mind capable . . . of evil as *w·* as of good,
  550– 7   identity of animals as *w·* as of men.
  ap 563– 1   Human sense may *w·* marvel at discord,
  563– 3   We may *w·* be astonished at sin,
  563– 4   We may *w·* be perplexed at human fear ;
  569–16   the serpent of sin as *w·* as of sickness !

well-authenticated
  pref x–15   By thousands of *w·* cases of healing,
  p 402– 4   already in her possession *w·* records

Welsh
  g 525– 9   in the *W·*, *that which rises up,*

went
  a 25– 9   as he *w·* daily about his Father's business.
  41–26   still *w·* about doing good deeds,
  s 156–24   She *w·* on in this way, taking the
  ph 193– 8   The doctor *w·* out.
  193– 9   I *w·* to his bedside.
  193–20   am informed that he *w·* to work in two weeks.
  f 225–20   oppression neither *w·* down in blood, nor
  p 377– 7   they come back no better than when they *w·*
  t 448– 4   When the Publican's wail *w·* out to the
  g 521–21   there *w·* up a mist from the earth,— *Gen.* 2 : 6.
  524– 7   *w·* after "strange gods."— *Jer.* 5 : 19.
  542–27   Cain *w·* out from the presence of— *Gen.* 4 : 16.
  546–12   "There *w·* up a mist— *Gen.* 2 : 6.
  gl 595–14   on Aaron's breast when he *w·* before Jehovah,

west
  s 121–18   sun seems to move from east to *w·*,
  121–19   instead of the earth from *w·* to east.

westward
  a 21–27   like a traveller going *w·*
  ap 575–32   *w·*, to the grand realization of the

wet
  f 220–12   he has no catarrh from *w·* feet,
  221– 9   should not *w·* his parched throat until

whales
  g 512– 4   And God created great *w·*,— *Gen.* 1 : 21.

whatever
  pr 1– 8   *w·* has been successfully done for the
  4–32   *W·* materializes worship hinders
  8–20   Praying for humility with *w·* fervency of
  m 60–11   maternal affection lives on under *w·*
  sp 70– 5   *W·* is false or sinful can never enter
  85– 7   *w·* constitutes and perpetuates harmony,
  93–18   *W·* contradicts the real nature of the
  s 144–26   pride, or prejudice closes the door to *w·*
  149–28   *W·* guides thought spiritually benefits
  ph 168– 6   *W·* influence you cast on the side of matter,
  169–24   *w·* good they may seem to receive from
  169–29   *W·* teaches man to have other laws
  178– 3   arsenic, the strychnine, or *w·* the drug used,
  184–17   *W·* is governed by a false belief
  186– 8   under *w·* name or pretence they are employed ;
  192–30   *W·* holds human thought in line with
  195–15   *W·* furnishes the semblance of an idea
  f 206–16   we find that *w·* blesses one blessses all,
  215–12   *W·* is governed by God, is never
  225– 2   *W·* enslaves man is opposed to
  234– 4   *W·* inspires with wisdom, Truth, or
  250–24   *w·* appears to be a mortal man is a
  c 263–21   *W·* seems to be a new creation, is but
  b 282–28   *W·* indicates the fall of man
  303–10   *W·* reflects Mind, Life, Truth, and **Love**,
  312– 1   *w·* is learned through material sense
  340–26   *w·* is wrong in social, civil, criminal,
  o 347– 4   C. S. declares that *w·* is mortal
  353– 2   *w·* seems real to material sense,
  353–30   from this it follows that *w·* is laid off
  358–24   it is said : "Rest assured that *w·* effect
  p 385–17   *W·* it is your duty to do, you can do
  392–12   *W·* benefit is produced on the
  411–24   *W·* is cherished in mortal mind as the
  418–16   *W·* the belief is, if arguments are used
  418–19   and to *w·* decides its type and symptoms.
  439–31   *w·* locality is reported to be haunted by Disease,
  t 443–19   *w·* other systems they fancy will afford relief.

37

whatever

t 463–13   truth removes properly *w·* is offensive.
r 477– 9   *W·* is material is mortal.
478–25   From beginning to end, *w·* is mortal is
485– 5   *W·* contradicts this statement is the
g 525–21   *W·* is valueless or baneful, He did not make,
529–26   evil, by *w·* figure presented,
553–20   *W·* theory may be adopted by
554–18   the creation of *w·* is sinful and mortal ;
ap 572– 9   but *w·* is of material sense, or mortal,
gl 583–12   *w·* rests upon and proceeds from
585–11   *w·* the material senses behold ;
588–16   *w·* reflects not this one Mind,

whatsoever

pr   1– *   he shall have *w·* he saith. — *Mark* 11 : 23.
p 405–17   "*W·* a man soweth, — *Gal.* 6 : 7.
g 527–24   and *w·* Adam called every living — *Gen.* 2 : 19.
537–13   "*W·* a man soweth, — *Gal.* 6 : 7.
550–21   If Life has any starting-point *w·*,

wheat

sp 72–15   tares and the *w·*, which are not united
89–32   If seed is necessary to produce *w·*,
89–32   and *w·* to produce flour,
r 207–19   separates the tares and *w·* in time of harvest.
b 269– 6   Jesus' demonstrations sift the chaff from the *w·*,
300–18   These opposite qualities are the tares and *w·*,
300–20   Science separates the *w·* from the tares,
r 466–28   to separate the chaff from the *w·*.
g 535– 3   the *w·* and tares which time will separate,

wheel

f 218– 3   You do not say a *w·* is fatigued ;
218– 4   yet the body is as material as the *w·*.
218– 6   the body, like the inanimate *w·*,

whence

sp 78–28   cannot "tell *w·* it cometh." — *John* 3 : 8.
s 108– 1   *W·* came to me this heavenly conviction,
f 225– 1   *W·* cometh it?
229– 6   *w·* did they emanate?
249–16   *W·* then is soulless matter?
b 281–10   *w·* its origin and what its destiny?
g 529–21   *W·* comes a talking, lying serpent
537– 4   the ground from *w·* he was taken. — *Gen.* 3 : 23.
539–13   *W·* does he obtain the propensity or power
550– 3   If this be so, *w·* cometh Life, or Mind,

whenever

s 111–32   proved itself, *w·* scientifically employed,
139–13   stem the tide . . . *w·* it flows inward.
ph 169– 3   *W·* an aggravation of symptoms has
t 445–30   *w·* she sees a man, for the petty consideration
r 495– 1   *w·* man is governed by God.
g 542– 4   *w·* and wherever it appears.

whereas

pref viii–10   *w·* the fact is that Spirit is good and real,
x– 8   *w·* this mind is not a factor in the
pr 12–23   *w·* help should come from the enlightened
a 23–28   *w·* the injunction, "Believe— *Acts* 16 : 31.
42– 2   *w·* priest and rabbi affirmed God to be a
44–29   *w·* he was alive, demonstrating within the
sp 91–30   *w·* the real Mind cannot be evil
s 117– 3   *w·* God is One,
ph 179–17   *w·* the wild animal, left to his instincts,
f 205–24   *w·* a belief in many ruling minds
211–28   *w·* the fact is that only through
212–31   *w·* the unreal and imitative movements
219–12   *w·* divine Mind heals.
222– 8   *w·* Truth regenerates this fleshly mind
b 287–20   *w·* the Scriptures declare that
296– 1   *w·* Science unfolds the eternal verity,
298– 9   *w·* spiritual sense can bear witness only to
319–10   *w·* the lower appeal to the general faith in
320–29   *w·* this passage is continually quoted as if
334–11   *w·* Jesus appeared as a bodily existence.
338– 4   *w·* the opposite belief — that man
o 352– 7   *w·* the Jews took a diametrically opposite view.
p 378–18   *w·* hypnotism and hygienic drilling
395– 2   They admit its reality, *w·* they should deny it.
414–29   *w·* imperfection is blameworthy,
432– 4   *w·* Mortal Man, the prisoner at the bar,
t 461–28   *W·*, to prove scientifically the error
r 480– 9   *w·* matter is devoid of sensation.
g 501– 6   *w·* the New Testament narratives are clearer
504–24   *w·* a thousand years of human doctrines,
552–11   *w·* the spiritual scientific facts of existence
557–24   *w·* revealed religion proclaims the Science or

whereby

a 18– 2   *w·* man reflects divine Truth, Life, and
22–23   *w·* we rejoice in immortality,
44–24   *w·* divinity brought to humanity the
b 271– 7   *w·* to heal the sick through Mind
p 387–31   faith and understanding *w·* to defend himself,

wherefore

p 440–16   *W·*, then, in the name of outraged justice,
fr 600– *   *W· by their fruits* — *Matt.* 7 : 20.

wherein

b 270–32   the good soil *w·* the seed of Truth
g 518–10   *w·* there is life, — *Gen.* 1 : 30.

whereof

g 533– 6   Hast thou eaten of the tree, *w·* — *Gen.* 3 : 11.

wherever

sp 94–14   intolerance, and bloodshed, *w·* found,
o 359–18   True Christianity is to be honored *w·*
g 542– 5   would slay . . . whenever and *w·* it appears.

wherewith

ph 196–18   They have no relation to God *w·* to establish
f 201– *   *w· Thine enemies have reproached,* — *Psal.* 89 : 51.
201– *   *w· they have reproached the* — *Psal.* 89 : 51.

whether

pr 16–12   *w·* the last line is not an
sp 80– 4   *w·* for the inspiration of a sermon or
83– 1   *w·* it is the human mind or
s 109–30   *w·* it be of God, — *John* 7 : 17.
109–31   *w·* I speak of myself." — *John* 7 : 17.
144–30   *w·* the ancient inspired healers
145– 1   *w·* they caught its sweet tones,
145–14   *w·* faith in drugs, trust in hygiene,
ph 195–11   *w·* it is mortal mind or
199–17   To know *w·* this development is produced
f 211– 5   *w·* Truth or error is the greater?
251–16   *w·* through faith in hygiene, in drugs, or
251–17   We should learn *w·* they govern the
b 296–19   *W·* mortals will learn this sooner or later,
324–10   *w·* it be Truth or error,
p 385–20   Mind decides *w·* or not the
390–28   *w·* it is cancer, consumption, or
392–28   *w·* it be air, exercise, heredity,
402–19   *w·* it be a broken bone, disease, or sin.
414–13   *w·* it is called dementia, hatred, or
t 459–17   *W·* animated by malice or
463–22   *w·* error is manifested in forms of
r 491–22   *w·* our eyes are closed or open.
fr 600– *   *w· the tender grape appear,* — *Song* 7 : 12.

whichever

p 392–23   Your decisions will master you, *w·* direction

whimsical

f 241– 9   as imaginary, *w·*, and unreal as his pleasures.

whine

t 450–13   They do not . . . *w·* over the demands of Truth,

whipped

s 142–19   tyranny and pride need to be *w·* out of the

whipping-post

f 225–19   abolish the *w·* and slave market ;

whirlwind

f 210–24   and reapeth the *w·*.

whiskey

s 158–16   cataplasms, and *w·* are stupid substitutes

whisper

sp 76– 1   The ones departing may *w·* this vision,
r 482–24   and angels *w·* it, through faith, to the
g 501–12   glory which angels could only *w·*

whispered

p 370–18   spiritual facts of health, *w·* into thought,
374– 4   truth of being, *w·* into the ear of

whispers

ap 574–30   Then thought gently *w·* : "Come hither !

whit

p 370– 1   To be every *w·* whole, man must be
371–31   can make it "every *w·* whole." — *John* 7 : 23.

white

c 267–26   are "*w·* and glistering," — *Luke* 9 : 29.
267–28   "let thy garments be always *w·*." — *Eccl.* 9 : 8.
b 299– 9   With *w·* fingers they point upward to a
321–22   *w·* as snow with the dread disease,
t 463–15   The new idea, . . . is clad in *w·* garments.
ap 572– 1   washed their robes *w·* in obedience

whited

pr   8– 9   "like unto *w·* sepulchres — *Matt.* 23 : 27.
p 439–20   God will smite you, O *w·* walls,

white-robed

m 64–23   Then *w·* purity will unite in one person

whither

b 299–14   *w·* every real individuality, image, or
r 491–24   and they wander *w·* they will

whoever

sp 95–12   *W·* reaches this point of moral culture
an 105–22   *W·* uses his developed mental powers
ph 174–14   *W·* opens the way in C. S.
178–32   *W·* reaches the understanding of C. S.
200– 8   *W·* is incompetent to explain Soul
f 213– 1   *W·* contradicts this mortal mind supposition

whoever

o 343–30	*W·* is the first meekly and conscientiously to
t 446–11	*W·* practises the Science the author teaches,
456–10	*W·* affirms that there is more than one
462–13	*W·* would demonstrate the healing of C. S.
r 474– 5	*W·* introduces the Science of Christianity

whole

pr 14–28	man's dominion over the *w·* earth.
a 19–12	The Master forbore not to speak the *w·* truth,
30–22	throughout the *w·* earthly career of Jesus,
45– 9	for the salvation of the *w·* world from sin,
sp 79– 9	Science must go over the *w·* ground,
an 103– 8	blesses the *w·* human family.
s 107– *	*measures of meal, till the w· was*— *Matt.* 13 : 33.
118– 1	measures of meal, till the *w·* was— *Matt.* 13 : 33.
118–24	changes the *w·* of mortal thought,
142– 8	must seek the undivided garment, the *w·* Christ,
147–15	never . . . can absorb the *w·* meaning of
157– 5	the *w·* force of the mental element is
ph 166– 1	remedy lies in forgetting the *w·* thing ;
191–13	Thus the *w·* earth will be transformed by
f 202–11	but the *w·* human family would be redeemed
207–29	in the action of man and the *w·* universe,
213–10	self-expressed, though indefinable as a *w·*.
219–12	makes the *w·* body "sick,— *Isa.* 1 : 5.
219–12	and the *w·* heart faint ;"— *Isa.* 1 : 5.
c 255– *	*the w· creation groaneth*— *Rom.* 8 : 22.
b 273–17	never made mortals *w·*, harmonious, and
326–10	and set his *w·* affections on spiritual things,
329– 5	A little leaven leavens the *w·* lump.
340– 7	the conclusion of the *w·* matter :— *Eccl.* 12 : 13.
340– 8	for this is the *w·* duty of man."— *Eccl.* 12 : 13.
340–10	Let us hear the conclusion of the *w·* matter :
340–11	for this is the *w·* of man in His image
o 344–22	should be presented to the *w·* world,
p 370– 1	To be every *w·*, man must be better
371–32	can make it "every whit *w·*."— *John* 7 : 23.
391– 6	"Thou art *w·* !"— *see John* 5 : 14.
398–15	*w·*, like as the other."— *Matt.* 12 : 13.
411–18	was changed and straightway became *w·*.
413–19	without scrubbing the *w·* surface daily.
415–30	the *w·* frame will sink from sight
421–16	the great fact which covers the *w·* ground,
422– 6	a great stir throughout his *w·* system,
t 449– 3	A little leaven causes the *w·* mass to ferment.
461– 9	We admit the *w·*, because a part is proved
r 470– 1	the *w·* family of man would be brethren ;
487–31	This Principle makes *w·* the diseased,
g 517–23	Even eternity can never reveal the *w·* of God,
521–22	watered the *w·* face of the ground.— *Gen.* 2 : 6.
545–11	was given dominion over the *w·* earth.
545–16	Error tills the *w·* ground in this
ap 567–16	which deceiveth the *w·* world :— *Rev.* 12 : 9.
575–23	the joy of the *w·* earth,— *Psal.* 48 : 2.

wholeness

r 465–14	the nature, essence, and *w·* of Deity.

wholesome

pr 7–14	*w·* perception of God's requirements.
b 323– 6	Through the *w·* chastisements of Love,
p 396–24	Give them divine and *w·* understanding,

wholly

a 30–11	Had his origin and birth been *w·* apart from
sp 96– 6	Before error is *w·* destroyed,
an 103–12	Mind-science is *w·* separate from any
105–17	no longer apply legal rulings *w·* to
s 111–29	Mind governs the body, not partially but *w·*.
112–14	*w·* human in their origin and tendency
124–29	they belong *w·* to divine Mind,
125–32	mortal belief, *w·* inadequate to affect a man
139–23	But mistakes could neither *w·* obscure the
148–19	and deal— the one *w·*, the other primarily
157– 2	C. S. deals *w·* with the mental cause
ph 172–13	as uninterrupted and *w·* spiritual ;
188–14	recognizes his condition to be *w·* a state of
f 214– 3	If the medium of hearing is *w·* spiritual,
252–18	says : I am *w·* dishonest,
b 269–26	systems based *w·* or partly on
290–25	To be *w·* spiritual, man must be sinless,
305–24	man would be *w·* mortal, were it not that
o 349–30	all learning, even that which is *w·* material.
353–13	The age has not *w·* outlived the sense of
353–17	Without perfection, nothing is *w·* real.
355–23	an opinion *w·* due to a misapprehension
p 410–29	until the practitioner's healing ability is *w·* lost.
413–31	If you succeed in *w·* removing the fear,
g 544– 2	a creation so *w·* apart from God's,
ap 575–21	This city is *w·* spiritual,

whomsoever

p 380– 6	"but on *w·* it shall fall,— *Matt.* 21 : 44.

whoso

a 30–15	"*W·* sheddeth man's blood,— *Gen.* 9 : 6.
t 448–18	but *w·* confesseth and— *Prov.* 28 : 13.

whosoever

pr 1– *	*w· shall say unto this mountain,*— *Mark* 11 : 23.
a 22–27	*W·* believeth that wrath is righteous
31–31	*w·* killeth you will think that he— *John* 16 : 2.
55–23	and *w·* layeth his earthly all on the altar of
s 132– 9	*w·* shall not be offended in me."— *Matt.* 11 : 6.
ph 170–10	"*W·* liveth and believeth in me— *John* 11 : 26.
c 267–16	*w·* shall do the will of my Father— *Matt.* 12 : 50.
b 315– 1	"*W·* liveth and believeth in me— *John* 11 : 26.
317– 6	*W·* lives most the life of Jesus in this
p 372–25	"*W·* shall deny me before men,— *Matt.* 10 : 33.
382–22	"*W·* shall not receive me— *Luke* 18 : 17.
435–11	our Supreme Court decrees that *w· sinneth*
t 444–19	"*W·* shall smite thee on thy— *Matt.* 5 : 39.
g 542–15	Therefore *w·* slayeth Cain,— *Gen.* 4 : 15.
548– 1	and *w·* will, let him take the— *Rev.* 22 : 17.

wicked

pr 4–24	but in this *w·* world goodness will
8–24	We confess to having a very *w·* heart
a 36–25	to suppose that the *w·* can gloat over their
sp 85–25	Jesus knew the generation to be *w·*
96–31	During this final conflict, *w·* minds will
an 104–32	must move the body to a *w·* act?
s 136–21	That a *w·* king and debauched husband should
139– 1	causes the *w·* to "forsake his way,— *Isa.* 55 : 7.
ph 192–16	all that is selfish, *w·*, dishonest,
f 239–11	The *w·* man is not the ruler of his
239–14	"Let the *w·* forsake his way,— *Isa.* 55 : 7.
b 270–25	consequently they are *w·*,
289– 8	A *w·* mortal is not the idea of God.
314–12	were the parents of their *w·* deeds.
p 404–11	destroying the *w·* motives which produce them.
440–23	compel them to enact *w·* laws
t 451–30	either with a mistaken or a *w·* purpose.
r 491–26	A *w·* man may have an attractive
g 540– 3	Spirit creates neither a *w·* nor a mortal man,
gl 584–22	saith : . . . I am mind,— a *w·* mind, self-made

wickedly

b 270–24	Mortals think *w·* ; consequently they

wickedness

pr 8– 5	face to face with their *w·*
b 327–11	Then he loses pleasure in *w·*,
t 453–20	Hidden sin is spiritual *w·* in high places.
459–21	is more harmful than wilful *w·*,
ap 563–30	"spiritual *w·* in high places."— *Eph.* 6 : 12.
569–11	nothingness of error is in proportion to its *w·*.

wicked one

r 476– 2	They are the children of the *w· o·*,

wide

sp 90–27	shuts the door on death, and opens it *w·* towards
p 433–32	can open *w·* those prison doors and set the
t 451–12	"*w·* is the gate, and broad is the— *Matt.* 7 : 13.
ap 571–28	he has opened *w·* the gates of glory,

widely

s 150– 4	healing power of Truth is *w·* demonstrated
t 464– 2	Why do you not make yourself more *w·* known?"

wider

c 265–13	a *w·* sphere of thought and action,

widows

m 64– 6	To visit the fatherless and *w·*— *Jas.* 1 : 27.

wield

s 152– 2	It would *w·* the sceptre of a monarch,

wielded

s 142–21	as twisted and *w·* by Jesus,

wife (*see also* wife's)

deserts his

m 63–28	If a dissolute husband deserts his *w·*,

husband and

m 60– 1	it never would, if both husband and *w·* were

Lamb's

ap 574– 9	the bride, the Lamb's *w·*.— *Rev.* 21 : 9.
575– 3	behold the Lamb's *w·*,— Love wedded to its
577– 5	The Lamb's *w·* presents the unity of

your

m 59–18	the welfare and happiness of your *w·*

m 58–17	a *w·* or a husband forever within four walls,
58–26	a *w·* ought not to court vulgar extravagance
64–12	his *w·* should not say, "It is never well to
64–13	A *w·* is sometimes debarred by a
66–23	for a *w·* precipitately to leave her husband
66–25	or for a husband to leave his *w·*.
g 535–20	unto the voice of thy *w·*,— *Gen.* 3 : 17.
538–23	And Adam knew Eve his *w·* ;— *Gen.* 4 : 1.

wild

ph 179–17	whereas the *w·* animal, left to his instincts,
179–19	ailment, which a *w·* horse might never have.
g 552–20	may become *w·* with freedom

wilderness
a	33– 5	manna, which of old had fed in the *w·*
s	133– 9	In the *w·*, streams flowed from the rock,
	135–19	furnish a table in the *w·*?"— *Psal.* 78 : 19.
	158–19	the byways of this *w·* world,
f	208–19	voice of one crying in the *w·*'"— *Matt.* 3 : 3.
	226–20	the awful conflict, the Red Sea and the *w·* ;
g	507–10	strangers in a tangled *w·*.
ap	565–29	And the woman fled into the *w·*,— *Rev.* 12 : 6.
	566– 4	as they were led through the *w·*,
gl	597–16	definition of

wilful
p	369–30	No man is physically healed in *w·* error
t	459–21	is more harmful than *w·* wickedness,

will
and action
p	401–26	Would the drug . . . restore *w·* and action

corporeal
s	144–21	Truth, and not corporeal *w·*, is the divine power

depraved
s	115–22	depraved *w·*, self-justification, pride,

divine
a	28– 2	claimed to know and to teach the divine *w·*,
r	474–23	or the offspring of the divine *w·*?

exercise of
t	446–27	The exercise of *w·* brings on a

God's
f	202– 4	and God's *w·* must be universally done.
	241– 2	He, who knows God's *w·* or the demands of

His
s	109–29	If any man will do His *w·*,— *John* 7 : 17.
c	256–20	"doeth according to His *w·*— *Dan.* 4 : 35.

human
(*see* **human**)

mortal
gl	599– 5	ZEAL. . . . Blind enthusiasm ; mortal *w·*.

not my
a	33–19	"Not my *w·*, but Thine, be done !"— *Luke* 22 : 42.

offspring of
ph	192–12	the offspring of *w·* and not of wisdom,

of God
pr	11–30	habitual desire to know and do the *w·* of God,
gl	597–22	"For this is the *w·* of God."— *I Thess.* 4 : 3.

of his Father
a	31– 8	they who do the *w·* of his Father.

of my Father
c	267–16	shall do the *w·* of my Father— *Matt.* 12 : 50.

of the Father
ph	168–20	He did the *w·* of the Father.

of wisdom
a	19–24	and enables man to do the *w·* of wisdom.

Thy
pr	17– 1	Thy *w·* be done in earth,— *Matt.* 6 : 10.

volition or
f	220–32	as directly as the volition or *w·* moves the
sp	99– 8	to *w·* and to do of His good pleasure"— *Phil.* 2 : 13.
s	111– 3	the *w·*, or sensuous reason of the human mind,
ph	187–16	the hand, admittedly moved by the *w·*.
r	490– 8	*W·*— blind, stubborn, and headlong
gl	597–20	definition of
	597–24	*W·*, as a quality of so-called mortal mind, is a

William IV
s	163– 6	*W·* IV, King of England,

willing
pref	ix–17	a *w·* disciple at the heavenly gate,
pr	8–27	than we are *w·* to have our neighbor see?
	9–25	Are you *w·* to leave all for Christ, for Truth,
	10– 9	Until we are . . . *w·* to drink his cup,
	11–25	We must be *w·* to do this, that we may
a	24–22	and are *w·* to be forgiven?
	33–32	*w·* truly to drink his cup, take his cross,
	41–29	more than they were *w·* to practise.
s	138–23	the sick are more *w·* to part with pain than
	144–16	*W·* the sick to recover is not the
ph	189– 2	*w·* to leave with astronomy the explanation of
f	216–29	"*w·* rather to be absent from the— *II Cor.* 5 : 8.
	235–25	when the soul is *w·* and the flesh weak,
	237–28	more . . . than they are *w·* to admit
b	271–26	Those, who are *w·* to leave their nets
p	369–19	were *w·* that a man should live.
	373– 7	partly because they were *w·* to be restored,
	381– 4	Be no more *w·* to suffer the illusion that you
	383–10	"*w·* rather to be absent from the— *II Cor.* 5 : 8.
	398– 8	the concessions which Jesus was *w·* to make
t	464– 3	could not take her place, even if *w·* so to do.
ap	570–30	Many are *w·* to open the eyes of the people
	571– 1	not so *w·* to point out the evil in human thought,
gl	581–25	"*w·* rather to be absent from the— *II Cor.* 5 : 8.

willingness
a	24– 4	and *w·* to give up human beliefs
f	218–18	if you are without faith in God's *w·*
b	323–32	*W·* to become as a little child
r	493–31	this consummate test of the power and *w·* of

will-power
an	103–31	no transference of mortal thought and *w·*.
	106– 1	to the criminal misuse of human *w·*,
s	144–14	Human *w·* is not Science.
	144–18	Human *w·* may infringe the rights of man.
ph	186– 3	the false stimulus and reaction of *w·*
f	206–10	*W·* is capable of all evil.
	251–16	in hygiene, in drugs, or in *w·*.
r	490– 3	*W·* is but a product of belief,

win
f	254–31	for through it you *w·* and wear the crown.
p	365–20	enough Christly affection to *w·* his own pardon,
	417–16	hold your ground . . . and you will *w·*.
t	462–18	Christianity, and persistence alone *w·* the

wind
holds the
ph	192–18	holds the "*w·* in His fists ;"— *Prov.* 30 : 4.

shrieks
m	67– 5	the *w·* shrieks through the tightened shrouds,

sniffs the
ph	179–18	left to his instincts, sniffs the *w·* with delight.

soweth the
f	210–24	soweth the *w·* and reapeth the
ph	184–28	when the *w·* was from the east.
	184–32	*w·* had not changed, but her thought of it had
	185– 2	The *w·* had not produced the difficulty.
	190–25	For the *w·* passeth over it,— *Psal.* 103 : 16.
b	269–28	are reeds shaken by the *w·*,
	293–22	*w·*, wave, lightning, fire, bestial ferocity
r	476–25	For the *w·* passeth over it,— *Psal.* 103 : 16.
gl	597–27	definition of
	598– 1	Greek word for *w·* (*pneuma*) is used also for
	598– 3	*w·* [*pneuma*] bloweth where it — *John* 3 : 8.
	598–13	It might be translated *w·* or *air*,

winding
ap	563–27	*w·* its way amidst all evil,

winding-sheet
a	44–18	to remove the napkin and *w·*,

window
f	245– 9	she stood daily before the *w·* watching for

window-pane
b	295–19	is as light passing through the *w·*.

windows
r	478–12	nor were they even visible through the *w·*?

winds
m	57–26	may uproot . . . and scatter them to the *w·* ;
	67–22	even the *w·* and waves to obey him.
ph	185– 5	and she never suffered again from east *w·*,
f	201–15	Then, when the *w·* of God blow,
	209–11	which holds the *w·* in its grasp.
	240– 3	giant hills, winged *w·*, mighty billows,

wine
bread and
a	32–21	confined to the use of bread and *w·*.

cup of
a	32– 8	to pass each guest a cup of *w·*.

new
s	114–21	the new *w·* of the Spirit has to be poured into
b	281–27	does not put new *w·* into old bottles,

our
a	35–27	Our *w·* the inspiration of Love,
a	32–10	the *w·*, used on convivial occasions
	33–32	Are all who eat bread and drink *w·* in memory of
m	65– 4	at every bridal altar to turn the water into *w·*
b	321–32	by changing water into *w·*,
gl	598–17	definition of

wine-bibber
a	52–32	the hypocrite, called Jesus a glutton and a *w·*.

winged
a	49– 3	inspired their devotion, *w·* their faith,
f	240– 3	giant hills, *w·* winds, mighty billows,
b	298–29	pure thoughts from God, *w·* with Truth and
	323–12	and conception unconfined is *w·* to reach the
g	512– 6	and every *w·* fowl after his kind :— *Gen.* 1 : 21.
	512– 9	and also by holy thoughts, *w·* with Love.

wings
drooping
m	58– 4	or else joy's drooping *w·* trail in dust.

its
a	55–16	gathering beneath its *w·* the sick and sinning.
m	57–29	and begins to unfold its *w·* for heaven.
c	261–29	and preens its *w·* for a skyward flight.

one's
c	260–17	often hampers the trial of one's *w·*

their
b	298–26	evolving animal qualities in their *w·* ;

their own
an	103–27	singe their own *w·* and fall into dust.
p	434– 1	Swift on the *w·* of divine Love, there comes

winning
   f 239–22   and show what we are *w*.
winter
   sp 96– 8   summer and *w*, seedtime and harvest
wintry
   m 57–24   The *w* blasts of earth may uproot the flowers of
wiped
   ap 573–31   no more pain, and all tears will be *w* away.
wipes
   pr 11–18   but *w* it out in the most effectual manner.
wiping
   p 363– 5   *w* them with her long hair, which hung loosely
wire
   p 393–23   or the electric *w* which you stretch,
wires
   sp 78–19   Spirit needs no *w* nor electricity in order to
wisdom (*see also* **wisdom's**)
   according to
     f 239– 9   let worth be judged according to *w*,
   and Love
     pr 2–11   since He is unchanging *w* and Love.
     a 23– 1   *W* and Love may require many sacrifices
     c 265–26   before we discover what belongs to *w* and Love.
   bade him
     b 321–10   but *w* bade him come back and handle the
   beginning of
     p 373–16   is the beginning of *w*," — *Psal.* 111 : 10.
   bridal chamber of
     f 238–14   From out the bridal chamber of *w* there will
   decrees of
     f 229–28   should not if we could, annul the decrees of *w*.
   divine
     m 66–20   wait patiently on divine *w* to point out the
     p 386–24   and divine *w* will then be understood.
   growth in
     p 363–31   repentance, reformation, and growth in *w*
   He bestows
     pr 6– 5   God is not separate from the *w* He bestows.
   His
     s 110– 6   is pronounced by His *w* good.
     b 275–18   No wisdom is wise but His *w* ;
   immortal
     g 519– 6   His infinite self-containment and immortal *w* ?
   inspires with
     f 234– 4   Whatever inspires with *w*, Truth, or Love
   is justified
     b 317–10   "*w* is justified of her children." — *Matt.* 11 : 19.
   judgment-day of
     b 291–29   the judgment-day of *w* comes hourly
   last call of
     b 291– 7   but this last call of *w* cannot come till
   led by
     b 321– 8   When, led by *w* to cast down his rod,
   less
     p 378–31   it would manifest less *w* than
   Life, Love, and
     b 283– 6   Mind is the same Life, Love, and *w*
   Man's
     b 322–14   Man's *w* finds no satisfaction in sin,
   masculine
     m 64–23   masculine *w* and feminine love,
   of God
     gl 597–21   The might and *w* of God.
   of Job
     o 360–22   Hear the *w* of Job, as given in the
   of man
     pr 3– 2   The *w* of man is not sufficient to
   of the creator
     b 273–24   and impugn the *w* of the creator.
   omnipotent
     sp 83–19   this belief belittles omnipotent *w*,
   or Truth
     f 206– 2   no other Love, *w*, or Truth,
   required by
     pr 5– 5   The next and great step required by *w*
   saith
     gl 580–19   that of which *w* saith,
   supply the
     ap 571–17   Know thyself, and God will supply the *w* and
   supreme
     sp 91– 4   under the control of supreme *w* ?
   true
     f 231–21   To hold yourself superior to sin, . . . is true *w*.
   Truth, and Love
     pr 15–20   to work and watch for *w*, Truth, and Love.
     r 495–30   abiding steadfastly in *w*, Truth, and Love.
   unchanging
     pr 2–11   since He is unchanging *w* and Love.
   warns man
     r 481–13   against which *w* warns man,
   will of
     a 19–24   and enables man to do the will of *w*.

wisdom
   work of
     sp 83– 5   claimed that they could equal the work of *w*.
     pr 10–31   Do you ask *w* to be merciful and not to punish
     m 60–13   *w* will ultimately put asunder what she
     62–28   the order of *w* would be reversed.
     s 116– 2   *W*, purity, spiritual understanding,
     ph 192–12   the offspring of will and not of *w*,
     196– 1   If materialistic knowledge is power, it is not *w*.
     f 221–21   semi-starvation is not acceptable to *w*,
     230–19   Does *w* make blunders
     246–25   unfolds *w*, beauty, and holiness.
     b 275–14   All substance, intelligence, *w*, being,
     275–17   No *w* is wise but His wisdom ;
     p 384–11   a belief of mortal mind, not an enactment of *w*,
     r 465–15   justice, mercy, *w*, goodness, and so on.
     g 538– 5   the cherub *w* at the gate of understanding
     544–15   the might or right or *w*
wisdom's
   b 321–14   evil, under *w* bidding, was destroyed
wise
   pr 8–16   and it is *w* not to try to deceive ourselves
   m 62–21   if we would be *w* and healthy.
   sp 82–32   it is *w* earnestly to consider whether it is the
   95–25   Is the *w* man of to-day believed,
   s 131–20   hast hid these things from the *w* — *Luke* 10 : 21.
   ph 167–22   It is not *w* to take a halting and half-way
   175–32   "Where ignorance is bliss, 't is folly to be *w*,"
   200– 8   would be *w* not to undertake the
   f 231–26   To hold yourself superior to . . . is equally *w*,
   235–20   They should be *w* spiritual guides
   239–32   the *w* man said, "All is vanity." — *Eccl.* 1 : 2.
   b 275–17   No wisdom is *w* but His wisdom ;
   o 342– 4   "making *w* the simple." — *Psal.* 19 : 7.
   353–22   we must yield up all belief in it and be *w*.
   356–28   Would any one call it *w* and good to
   p 382–23   shall in no *w* enter therein." — *Luke* 18 : 17.
   413– 9   The *w* or unwise views of parents
   429– 9   and if we are *w*, we look beyond a
   t 443– *   *Give instruction to a w man*, — *Prov.* 9 : 9.
   g 515– 7   a *w* idea, charming in its adroitness,
   538– 1   infinitely *w* and altogether lovely,
   ap 571–12   If so, listen and be *w*.
wisely
   an 104– 9   the celebrated naturalist and author, has *w* said:
   s 139–12   will teach men patiently and *w* to
   t 458–26   The Christian Scientist *w* shapes his course,
Wisemen
   pref vii–10   The *W* were led to behold and to follow
   s 121– 7   The Chaldean *W* read in the stars the fate
   r 482–23   Angels announced to the *W* of old
   ap 575–28   the star seen by the *W* of the Orient,
wiser
   a 22– 1   would borrow the passport of some *w* pilgrim,
   p 422– 2   *W* than his persecutors, Jesus said :
   t 443– *   *and he will be yet w* : — *Prov.* 9 : 9.
wisest
   g 539–31   inspired his *w* and least-understood sayings,
wish
   a 48–13   and think, or even *w*, to escape the exalting
   s 129– 7   If you *w* to know the spiritual fact,
   144– 1   Why should we *w* to make them do so,
   f 219–15   what we do not *w* to have manifested.
   219–21   "The *w*," . . . "is ever father to the thought."
   238–18   *w* to enter unlawfully into the labors of others.
   b 301–18   man should *w* for, and in reality has,
   326– 3   If we *w* to follow Christ, Truth, it must be
   p 392–25   only such conclusions as you *w* realized
wished
   f 226–26   I *w* to save from the slavery of their
wishes
   pr 13–19   less risk of overwhelming our real *w*
wishing
   p 421–28   *w* to see the forms it assumes
wit
   c 255– *   *to w, the redemption of our* — *Rom.* 8 : 23.
   p 438–16   three distinct charges of crime, to *w* :
Witchcraft
   p 441–22   Mesmerism, Hypnotism, Oriental *W*,
witchcraft
   an 106–22   idolatry, *w*, hatred, variance, — *Gal.* 5 : 20.
withdraw
   s 124–26   *W* them, and creation must collapse.
withdrawn
   a 51– 6   Jesus could have *w* himself
withdraws
   s 144– 7   *W* the star, when dawns the
withdrew
   a 32–25   he *w* from the material senses

wither
sp 81–19 Though the grass seemeth to w·
ph 190–16 to w· and return to its native nothingness.

withered
c 265–18 or a flower w· by the sun
p 398–13 To the sufferer with the w· hand

withers
m 68–10 mistrust, . . . w· the flowers of Eden

withheld
b 309– 1 but this appellation was w·,
g 537–30 would imply that God w· from man the

withhold
a 50–10 who could w· a clear token of his presence
o 344–15 mercifully w· their misrepresentations,
t 452–13 w· not the rebuke or the explanation

withholding
sp 79–32 neither does w· enrich us.

within
a 44–30 demonstrating w· the narrow tomb
46– 6 made their hearts burn w· them,
m 58–17 would confine . . . forever w· four walls,
61– 1 cannot circumscribe happiness w· the
sp 87–19 the emeralds w· its rocks ;
87–20 the gems w· its caverns,
92– 9 Mind is not an entity w· the cranium
s 108–20 w· the shadow of the death-valley,
146–20 that is w· thy gates,"— Exod. 20 : 10.
ph 173– 6 supposition, that Spirit is w· what it
180– 9 This is the seed w· itself
191–22 not a spray buds w· the vale,
f 223–12 If Spirit were once w· the body,
248–31 Let unselfishness, . . . reign w· us,
c 255– * groan w· ourselves,— Rom. 8 : 23.
256–14 nor compressed w· the narrow limits
257– 2 If Mind is w· and without all things,
b 284– 5 if the infinite could be . . . w· the finite,
294– 5 carries w· itself the seeds of all error.
331– 6 If He dwelt w· what He creates,
o 358–26 through rousing w· the sick a
p 362– * disquieted w· me ?— Psal. 42 : 11.
397–29 compressed w· the skull,
413–20 bodily cleanliness w· and without.
436– 9 w· the limits of the divine law,
r 476–29 kingdom of God is w· you ;"— Luke 17 : 21.
478– 4 What evidence of Soul . . . w· mortality?
g 508–14 The seed w· itself is the pure
513–28 consequently not w· the range of
550– 8 and be limited w· material bounds.
ap 574– 1 kingdom of God is w· you."— Luke 17 : 21.
576–21 "is w· you,"— Luke 17 : 21.
576–21 is w· reach of man's consciousness
577–24 honors w· the heavenly city.
577–25 Its gates open towards light . . . w· and

without
pr 3– 1 w· being reminded of His province.
11– 1 W· punishment, sin would multiply.
15–21 We must "pray w· ceasing."— I Thess. 5 : 17.
15–31 W· a fitness for holiness, we cannot
a 22–26 pinning one's faith w· works to
23–15 "Faith w· works is dead."— Jas. 2 : 26.
30– 7 the divine Spirit, w· measure.
40–22 endure human brutality w· murmuring,
m 57– 2 W· it there is no stability in society,
57– 2 w· it one cannot attain the
59– 2 w· a full recognition of its
63–21 w· encouraging difficulties
sp 76–24 w· a single bodily pleasure or pain,
80–19 w· the aid of hands,
83–10 a blind belief w· understanding,
84–25 w· the concession of material personalities
89–14 w· study or a superinduced condition,
90– 4 and that, too, w· meal or monad
93–20 Whatever contradicts . . . is w· foundation.
97–14 w· passing the boundary where,
an 105– 1 w· mortal mind to direct them,
s 112–28 w· giving that author proper credit,
113– 6 W· this, the letter is but the
117– 4 one alone and w· an equal.
126– 4 mortal mind will be w· form and
145– 2 w· being able to explain them.
145– 6 letter, w· the spirit, would have
149–10 left w· explanation except in C. S.
153–17 matter w· mind is not painful.
156–22 could get along two days w· globules ;
159– 2 surgical operation w· the ether.
159–19 performed the operation w· ether.
160–30 Is man a material fungus w· Mind
162–14 w· the conditions of matter
162–15 w· the false beliefs of a so-called
ph 177– 8 Neither exists w· the other,
179–17 will take cold w· his blanket,
183– 9 produce a crop w· sowing the seed
185–22, 23 not only w· drugs, but w· hypnotism,

without
ph 188– 7 an embryonic thought w· motive ;
194–13 it will be so w· an injured nerve.
199– 1 w· volition of mortal mind,
f 204–26 usurping the name w· the nature
205– 2 w· knowing that they are sinning,
207–13 W· this lesson, we lose sight of
209–10 w· Mind, w· the intelligence which holds the
210–32 it is w· a destructive element.
211–16 W· mortal mind, the tear could not
214–32 Spirit's senses are w· pain,
217–31 W· mind, could the muscles be tired?
218–17 w· faith in God's willingness
221– 8 a thin slice of bread w· water.
221–15 w· a vestige of the old complaint.
221–24 and he ate w· suffering,
221–30 w· the consent of mortal mind,
230– 3 Would you attempt with drugs, or w·,
231–32 w· Him was not anything made— John 1 : 3.
241–17 error of the ages is preaching w· practice.
242–26 one web of consistency w· seam
244–20 w· His entire manifestation,
247– 8 w· a decaying cavity.
253– 6 without beginning and w· end,
253–23 w· hindrance from the body.
c 257– 2 If Mind is within and w· all things,
262–25 even as light emits light w· effort ;
266– 6 Would existence w· personal friends be
266– 8 solitary, left w· sympathy ;
b 271–31 "How shall they hear w· a— Rom. 10 : 14.
273– 6 w· the divine Principle of
281–23 sin and mortality are w· actual origin
287– 1 are w· a real origin or existence.
287–22 w· spiritual identity or
291–13 is unattainable w· them.
303–25 w· the image and likeness of
303–27 w· a witness or proof of His
306–17 w· a rational proof of immortality.
310– 8 w· material accompaniments.
312–16 w· Love, . . . immortality cannot appear.
312–18 w· understanding Truth ;
314– 9 one Mind w· a second or equal.
322–30 W· this process of weaning,
323– 3 w· striving for them.
328– 4 that they can live w· goodness,
335–10 w· the Logos, the Æon
o 343– 4 thy faith w· thy works,— Jas. 2 : 18.
343– 8 w· this cross-bearing,
353–17 W· perfection, nothing is wholly real.
354–19 shown by words w· deeds,
354–20 are like clouds w· rain.
355–26 W· this understanding, no one
p 371– 9 believed to be here w· their consent
377–29 W· this ignorant human belief,
378– 8 W· the so-called human mind,
378–29 w· the divine permission,
379– 1 w· the consent of mortals,
381–26 will never be reached w· the
384– 2 Can matter, . . . act w· mind?
385– 4 undergo w· sinking fatigues and
385–16 if w· sin, can be experienced w·
385–18 can do w· harm to yourself.
386– 7 w· mind to demand it
386–28 "Your sorrow is w· cause,"
399–20 W· this force the body is
400–28 W· divine control there is discord,
402–32 a belief w· a real cause.
413–18 w· scrubbing the whole surface daily.
413–20 bodily cleanliness within and w·.
427– 4 never w· its representative.
438–24 w· the inspection of
t 446–14 w· destroying his own power to heal
447–18 w· frightening or discouraging
449–26 w· the preliminary offence.
450–16 Few yield w· a struggle,
451– 9 and think to succeed w· the spirit,
454– 8 leads to the house built w· hands
457– 3 w· giving it credit,
457–20 there is no excellence w· labor in a
457–31 w· exploiting other means.
461– 2 w· food and raiment ;
464– 1 feels your influence w· seeing you.
r 468–27 Life is without beginning and w· end.
469–17 error, w· intelligence or reality.
470– 8 infinite Truth w· an unlikeness,
470–28 unexpressed— that is, w· entity.
470–30 If man ever existed w· this perfect
472–18 Error is a belief w· understanding.
479–19 w· form, and void ; — Gen. 1 : 2.
480–27 and w· Him was not— John 1 : 3.
483–31 w· timidity or dissimulation,
486– 1 is w· foundation in fact,
486–31 w· God in the world ;"— Eph. 2 : 12.
487–22 belief is blindness w· Principle
487–25 "Show me thy faith w·"— Jas. 2 : 18.
491– 4 a belief w· actual foundation

without

g 501– * *and w· Him was not— John* 1 : 3.
503– 6 *w·* form, and void ;— *Gen.* 1 : 2.
507– 7 *W·* natures particularly defined,
525–18 "and *w·* Him . . . was not— *John* 1 : 3.
528–29 performed mentally and *w·* instruments ;
531–22 or that matter exists *w·* God?
536–11 The illusion of sin is *w·* hope
557– 2 moving and playing *w·* harm,
557– 7 where parturition is *w·* suffering.
ap 560–18 *w·* a correct sense of its highest
564– 9 into a night *w·* a star.
564–28 hated me *w·* a cause."— *John* 15 : 25.
577–25 both within and *w·*,
gl 592–13 the proof that, *w·* the gospel,
(see also **beginning**)

withstand

f 224–31 No power can *w·* divine Love.

witness

another
p 431–25 Another *w·* takes the stand and testifies :
432– 9 Another *w·* is called for by the
432–20 Another *w·* takes the stand and testifies :
438–19 Another *w·*, equally inadequate, said

bear
b 298–10 spiritual sense can bear *w·* only to Truth.
330– 9 and the letter and the spirit bear *w·*,
411–11 bear *w·* to the truth,
441–14 Material Law is a liar who cannot bear *w·*
ap 561–31 to bear *w·* of that Light."— *John* 1 : 8.

false
an 100– * thefts, false *w·*, blasphemies :— *Matt.* 15 : 19.
p 437–13 Nerve, . . . to be a false *w·*.
438–12 and bearing false *w·* against Man.

next
p 431–20 The next *w·* is called :
432– 1 The next *w·* testifies :

principal
p 436– 1 The principal *w·* (the officer of the

proved the
p 438– 8 proved the *w·*, Nerve, to be a perjurer.

silence the
p 417–16 When you silence the *w·* against your plea,

testifies
p 430–28 a *w·* testifies thus :— I represent Health-laws.

without a
b 303–27 would be without a *w·* or proof of

a 54–13 In *w·* of his divine commission, he presented
s 134– 4 word *martyr*, from the Greek, means *w·* ;
o 348–27 would immediately *w·* the full fruitage of
p 432– 6 *w·* to the crime of liver-complaint.
436– 5 to reappear however at the trial as a *w·* against
437–11 I proclaim this *w·*, Nerve, to be destitute of
g 514–20 as *w·* the millennial estate pictured by

witnessed

a 46–31 that by all they had *w·* and suffered,
t 453–12 I have never *w·* so decided effects from

witnesses

s 122– 6 contradict their false *w·*, and reveal the
150– 1 *w·* and monuments to the virtue and power of
p 434–11 *W·*, judges, and jurors, who were at the
436–35 One of the principal *w·*, Nerve, testified
439–15 C. S. turned from the abashed *w·*,
439–28 *w·*, jurors, and judges, to be offenders,

wives

m 66–21 Husbands and *w·* should never separate if
ph 176– 6 attributed . . . to the weakness of their *w·*.

wizards

sp 70– * *w·* that peep and that mutter;— *Isa.* 8 : 19.

woe

comes
pr 5– 8 and *w·* comes in return for what is done.

every
f 236–20 good as the remedy for every *w·*.

hour of
ap 567– 4 Truth and Love come nearer in the hour of *w·*,

human
f 238–20 until we seek this remedy for human *w·*

patient
gl 586–23 GETHSEMANE. Patient *w·* ; the human yielding

shame and
ph 188–10 from shame and *w·* to their final punishment.

silent
a 36–14 a few women who bowed in silent *w·* beneath the

want and
sp 96–17 want and *w·*, sin, sickness, and death,
c 257–26 to meet the demands of human want and *w·*,
g 501– 9 but richly recompensing human want and *w·*

ap 568–20 *W·* to the inhabiters of the earth— *Rev.* 12 : 12.

woes
f 248–10 and destroying the *w·* of sense
b 322–28 as well as our disappointments and ceaseless *w·*,

wolf

g 514–22 *w·* also shall dwell with the lamb,— *Isa.* 11 : 6.
ap 567–31 shows how the Lamb slays the *w·*.

wolves

an 104– 6 and belied by *w·* in sheep's clothing.
ap 567–28 These *w·* in sheep's clothing are detected

woman (see also woman's)

accord
m 63–16 a marvel why usage should accord *w·* less

adulterous
pr 11– 3 When forgiving the adulterous *w·* he said,

another
f 247– 5 Another *w·* at ninety had new teeth,

beguiles the
g 533–14 beguiles the *w·* and demoralizes the man.

born of
g 529– 3 that man should be born of *w·*,

born of a
a 30– 5 Born of a *w·*, Jesus' advent in the flesh
g 552–15 "Man that is born of a *w·*"— *Job* 14 : 1.

clothed in light
ap 561–11 as a *w·* clothed in light,

clothed with
ap 560– 7 a *w·* clothed with the sun,— *Rev.* 12 : 1.

create
g 528–14 and thereby create *w·*.

creation of
g 528–26 supposed . . . basis of the creation of *w·*

enabled
g 534– 3 This hereafter enabled *w·* to be the
534– 6 This enabled *w·* to be first to interpret the

English
f 245– 3 sketch from the history of an English *w·*,

fled
ap 565–29 the *w·* fled into the wilderness,— *Rev.* 12 : 6.

God and
g 533–15 *mortal error*, charges God and *w·* with his own

goes forth
b 268–12 *w·* goes forth to battle with Goliath.

helped the
ap 570–11 And the earth helped the *w·*,— *Rev.* 12 : 16.

help the
ap 570–22 In this age the earth will help the *w·* ;

ideal
g 517–10 The ideal *w·* corresponds to Life and to Love.

impoverished
m 63–29 the wronged, and perchance impoverished, *w·*

man and
a 37–23 duty and privilege of every child, man, and *w·*
g 516–21 Man and *w·* as coexistent and eternal
529–10 both man and *w·* proceed from God
gl 588–12 man and *w·* unchanged forever in their

noble
m 64–11 lends a helping hand to some noble *w·*,

perceived
a 29–28 and *w·* perceived this spiritual idea,

persecuted the
ap 569–30 he persecuted the *w·* which— *Rev.* 12 : 13.

protection to
m 60–17 a barrier against vice, a protection to *w·*,

rights of
gl 587– 3 The rights of *w·* acknowledged morally,

Samaritan
sp 85–12 The Samaritan *w·* said :
s 133– 4 than that of the Samaritan *w·*, who said,

sick
pr 6–24 Of a sick *w·* he said that Satan had
sp 86– 7 he was answered by the faith of a sick *w·*.

stood before the
ap 563–25 and the dragon stood before the *w·*— *Rev.* 12 : 4.

strange
p 362– 6 A "strange *w·*'" came in.— *Prov.* 23 : 27.

that
ph 193–27 "It was none other than God and that *w·*

this
p 362–11 this *w·* (Mary Magdalene,. . . approached Jesus.
364–28 do they show their regard . . . as did this *w·*?

this poor
p 364–13 He even said that this poor *w·* had

young
f 245–13 and supposed her to be a young *w·*.

m 59–10 nor should *w·* be expected to
s 107– * *leaven, which a w· took, and hid— Matt.* 13 : 33.
117–32 "leaven, which a *w·* took, and hid— *Matt.* 13 : 33.
158–31 A *w·* in the city of Lynn,
159–20 sequel proved that this Lynn *w·*
ph 184–27 A *w·*, whom I cured of consumption,
f 247– 4 A *w·* of eighty-five, whom I knew,
p 363– 8 Did Jesus spurn the *w·*?
363–22 that remarkable declaration to the *w·*,
389–29 In her belief the *w·* had chronic liver-complaint,

woman

r 482–18	As w· is but a species of the genera,
g 525– 9	In the Saxon, *mankind, a w·, any one*;
528–13	and the rib, . . . made He a w·,— *Gen.* 2 : 22.
529– 3	not w· again taken from man.
529–15	And he said unto the w·,— *Gen.* 3 : 1.
529–17	And the w· said unto the serpent,— *Gen.* 3 : 2.
530–13	And the serpent said unto the w·,— *Gen.* 3 : 4.
533– 8	The w· whom Thou gavest — *Gen.* 3 : 12.
533–16	"The w·, whom Thou gavest me, is responsible."
533–19	has grown into an evil mind, named w·,
533–27	finds w· the first to confess her fault.
534–10	enmity between thee and the w·,— *Gen.* 3 : 15.
534–28	material sense, will bite the heel of the w·,
534–29	and the w·, this idea, will bruise the head of
535– 6	Unto the w· He said,— *Gen.* 3 : 16.
557–17	the curse will be removed which says to w·,
·ap 561–22	The w· in the Apocalypse symbolizes
562– 6	w·, typifying the spiritual idea of
562–24	spiritual idea is typified by a w· in travail,
565–19	represented first by man and, . . . last by w·,
570– 9	water as a flood, after the w·,— *Rev.* 12 : 15.

womanhood

f 246–20	conspiracies against manhood and w·.

womanly

p 397–30	will quickly become more manly or w·.

woman's

s 159–16	would have considered the w· state of mind,
p 363–13	detect the w· immoral status

womb

r 478–28	separated me from my mother's w·,— *Gal.* 1 : 15.

women

at the cross

a 49– 1	The w· at the cross could have answered

few

a 36–13	a few w· who bowed in silent woe

franchise for

m 63–21	If the elective franchise for w· will remedy

Jewish

gl 596–29	The Jewish w· wore veils over their faces

men and

m 62–18	should become men and w· only through
68– 6	has created men and w· in Science.
sp 71–15	and you may see landscapes, men, and w·.
s 158–22	and men and w· become loathsome sots.
164–10	generally . . . are grand men and w·,
f 225–29	Men and w· of all climes and races
247–15	Immortal men and w· are models of
248– 5	Men and w· of riper years and larger lessons

p 363– 6	as was customary with w· of her grade.

won

a 39– 4	He w· eternal honors.
m 61– 6	or happiness will never be w·.
sp 82– 9	If spiritual life has been w· by the departed,
s 109–20	and I w· my way to absolute conclusions
ph 179– 9	w· only as man is found, not in
f 201–19	Christian perfection is w· on no other basis.
217–19	and you have w· a point in Science.
226–11	and that its freedom be w·,
233–15	until the goal . . . is assiduously earned and w·.
254– 8	is fought and the victory w·.
b 290–17	happiness would be w· at the
326–17	This point w·, you have started as you should.
o 360– 3	nothing is lost, and all is w·,
t 448– 4	it w· his humble desire.
453–10	and a higher basis is thus w· ;

wonder

sp 76– 4	with eyes open only to that w·,
80–29	and believes that this w· emanates from
s 136–28	No w· Herod desired to see the new Teacher.
r 487–12	centuries ago, and it will repeat the w·.
g 501–11	that amplification of w· and glory
503–15	Hence the eternal w·,
ap 560– 6	And there appeared a great w·— *Rev.* 12 : 1.
562–29	And there appeared another w·— *Rev.* 12 : 3.

Wonderful

s 109–27	and his name shall be called W·."— *Isa.* 9 : 6.

wonderful

a 46– 2	did not perform many w· works, until
s 137– 3	but the ultimate of this w· work was not
o 347– 3	to verify this w· philosophy
358–28	a belief that . . . these healers have w· power,
r 483–29	by doing many w· works through the
ap 572–28	are inadequate to take in so w· a scene.

wondering

p 363–12	they were w· why, being a prophet,

wonders

pr 13–23	the w· wrought by infinite, incorporeal Love,
sp 90–21	hashish eaters mentally travel far and work w·,
s 133–17	the divine Principle wrought w· for the
139– 9	was ushered in with signs and w·.

wonders

s 150–13	Now, as then, signs and w· are wrought in the
ph 185–17	strove to emulate the w· wrought by Moses.
f 243–13	That those w· are not more commonly repeated
b 268– 2	has brought to light . . . many useful w·.
t 449– 4	A grain of C. S. does w· for mortals,

wondrous

a 42–21	the w· glory which God bestowed on His

wood

ph 199– 6	since muscles are as material as w· and iron

wooden

ph 193– 2	caused by a fall upon a w· spike

woodman's

o 358– 1	Is the w· axe, which destroys a

Word

His

ap 560–17	whom God has appointed to voice His W·.

inspired

a 46– 9	has spoken through the inspired W·
r 497– 3	As adherents of Truth, we take the inspired W·

interpret the

g 537–25	Inspired writers interpret the W· spiritually,

of God

f 231–32	made by Him [the W· of God] ;— *John* 1 : 3.
b 335–11	the Logos, the Æon or W· of God,
g 503–12	the W· of God, saith to the darkness upon the
525–18	were made through the W· of God,

of Life

ap 577–14	first, the W· of Life, Truth, and Love ;

of life

b 268– *	*have handled, of the W· of life,*— *I John* 1 : 1.

spiritual import of the

b 271–30	spiritual import of the W· imparts this power.
g 501– 4	chiefly because the spiritual import of the W·,

tenor of the

p 427–20	The tenor of the W· shows that we shall

the divine

r 480–27	made by Him [the divine W·] ;— *John* 1 : 3.

was made flesh

o 350–24	"The W· was made flesh."— *John* 1 : 14.

b 319–25	and the misinterpretation of the W·
o 350–31	the W· was materially explained,
ap 575–18	the W·, Christ, Christianity, and divine Science ;
575–27	the W·, the polar magnet of Revelation ;

word

accepted his

b 316– 2	salvation to all who accepted his w·.

Adam

b 338–12	The w· *Adam* is from the Hebrew *adamah*,

anthropomorphic

g 517– 3	The w· *anthropomorphic*, in such a phrase as

cannot hear my

b 292–21	because ye cannot hear my w·.— *John* 8 : 43.

Christ

b 333– 3	The w· *Christ* is not properly a synonym for

created with a

g 543–24	Did man, whom God created with a w·,

duty

b 340– 5	when the w· *duty*, which is not in the original,

English

a 32– 5	our English w· *sacrament* is derived from it.

every

p 410–11	every w· that proceedeth out of— *Matt.* 4 : 4.

for man

g 517– 1	w· for *man* is used also as the synonym of *mind*.

God

r 482– 7	gained by substituting the w· *God*,

God's

b 332–24	appointed to speak God's w· and to

graphic

a 52–14	Isaiah's graphic w· concerning the coming

Greek

s 137–31	[the meaning of the Greek w· *petros*, or *stone*]
r 474–12	the Greek w· rendered *miracle* in the
gl 598– 1	The Greek w· for *wind* (*pneuma*) is used also

hands

a 38–15	Here the w· *hands* is used metaphorically,

indicates

b 271–12	and the w· indicates that the power of healing

Jesus'

t 446–22	enthrones faith in Truth, and verifies Jesus' w· :

kurios

gl 590–17	In the Greek, the w· *kurios* almost always has

Latin

a 32– 4	The Latin w· for this oath was *sacramentum*,

logos, or

g 525–19	without Him [the *logos*, or w·]— *John* 1 : 3.

martyr

s 134– 4	w· *martyr*, from the Greek, means *witness*;
134– 6	w· *martyr* was narrowed in its significance

misplaced

b 319–28	A misplaced w· changes the sense

word

or deed
m 59–21   remember how slight a *w·* or deed may renew
f 205–19   perceive the divine image in some *w·* or deed

original
gl 598– 5   Here the original *w·* is the same in both cases

or phrase
s 114–18   if a better *w·* or phrase could be suggested,

proving my
o 343– 3   for proving my *w·* by my deed

reflection
b 301– 6   what C. S. means by the *w·* reflection.

rendered
b 271–11   the *w·* rendered *disciple* signifies student ;

Science
s 127– 1   author's application of the *w·* Science
127– 2   or questions her use of the *w·* Science,
o 341–13   the application of the *w·* Science to Christianity

Scriptural
sp 89–13   reaffirms the Scriptural *w·* concerning a man,
gl 579– 3   the material definition of a Scriptural *w·*

sense
r 482– 1   substitution of the *w· sense* for *soul* gives the
482– 8   In other cases, use the *w· sense,*

sent His
ph 165– *   *He sent His w·, and healed them,* — *Psal.* 107 : 20.

soul
ph 196–13   shows that here the *w· soul* means a false sense
r 482– 4   has adulterated the meaning of the *w· soul*
482– 6   The proper use of the *w· soul* can always

Spirit
o 344–32   the *w· Spirit* is so commonly applied to Deity,

spirit
sp 93–25   The modifying derivatives of the *w· spirit*

temple
ap 576–14   The *w· temple* also means *body.*

tender
p 367– 3   The tender *w·* and Christian encouragement

this
b 313–14   Using this *w·* in its higher meaning, we may
r 468–19   as the Scriptures use this *w·* in Hebrews :
g 502–24   This *w· beginning* is employed to signify
ap 576–16   was familiar with Jesus' use of this *w·*,
gl 598–12   but this *w· ghost* is *pneuma.*

through his
p 364– 6   that through his *w·* and works they might

through their
a 38–20   believe "through their *w·*." — *John* 17 : 20.
b 271–19   believe . . . through their *w·*." — *John* 17 : 20.

---

s 114–13   involves an improper use of the *w· mind.*
124–11   In a *w·* human belief is a blind conclusion
ph 168–30   Here let a *w·* be noticed which will be
b 309– 4   which, to use the *w·* of the Psalmist,
330–32   with all the etceteras that *w·* includes.
o 359–19   the goal which that *w·* implies
p 421– 5   Derangement, or *disarrangement,* is a *w·* which
g 508–19   The *w·* is not confined to sexuality,
ap 568–18   and by the *w·* of their testimony ; — *Rev.* 12 : 11.
576–30   the *w·* gradually approaches a higher meaning.
577–32   In the following Psalm one *w·* shows,

words

about slavery
t 445–30   Recalling Jefferson's *w·* about slavery,

apostolic
b 325–16   The absolute meaning of the apostolic *w·*

are blind
o 350–14   Unless the works are comprehended . . . the *w·* are blind.

audible
pr 4–15   which, even if not acknowledged in audible *w·*,

definition of
b 338–25   The dissection and definition of *w·*,

ear trieth
s 115– 8   "The ear trieth *w·*, as the — *Job* 34 : 3.

employ
gl 598– 9   to employ *w·* of material significance

faith in
f 210– 1   superiority of faith by works over faith in *w·*.

few
pref ix– 6   He finds a few *w·*, and with these he
ph 195– 3   taught to speak a few *w·*,

good
ph 167–32   Substituting good *w·* for a good life,
181–22   satisfied with good *w·* instead of effects,

Greek
r 488– 7   The Hebrew and Greek *w·* often translated
g 517– 5   two Greek *w·*, signifying *man* and *form,*

his
a 53–11   His *w·* and works were unknown to the
54–18   understood neither his *w·* nor his works.
sp 94–18   our Master confirmed his *w·* by his works.
o 350–12   His *w·* were the offspring of his deeds,
350–14   Unless the works are comprehended which his *w·*
350–16   The Master often refused to explain his *w·*,

words

his
p 439–16   his *w·* flashing as lightning in the
r 473–28   his acts of higher importance than his *w·*.

his own
pr 7– 4   stronger evidence . . . is found in his own *w·*,

in other
a 27– 6   In other *w·* : "Tell John what the demonstration
46–16   in other *w·*, rose even higher in the
sp 72– 4   in other *w·*, mortal, material sense
s 132–10   In other *w·*, he gave his benediction to
138– 2   In other *w·*, Jesus purposed founding his
200–21   in other *w·* the five senses,
c 257–18   in other *w·*, divine Love, — is the father of the
b 340– 9   In other *w·* : Let us hear the conclusion of the
p 399–31   In other *w·* : How can I heal the body, without

Jesus'
b 360–32   the very basis of Jesus' *w·* and
ap 573–32   When you read this, remember Jesus' *w·*,

mere
a 55–12   clearer light than mere *w·* can possibly do,

of divine Science
o 354– 9   The *w·* of divine Science find their immortality

of Jesus
b 358–19   Why are the *w·* of Jesus more frequently
g 539– 2   In the *w·* of Jesus, it (evil, devil)

of our Master
p 428– 7   is to prove the *w·* of our Master :

of St. John
a 55–27   *w·* of St. John : "He shall give — *John* 14 : 16.

of this prophecy
ap 558– *   *that hear the w· of this prophecy,* — *Rev.* 1 : 3.

of Truth
o 342–23   It speaks to the dumb the *w·* of Truth,

our
pr 8–15   gratitude, and love which our *w·* express,
a 30–30   though they may not so construe our *w·*.
o 354–20   If our *w·* fail to express our deeds,

physician's
ph 198– 8   is increased by the physician's *w·*.

tender
m 59–17   Tender *w·* and unselfish care in what

the author's
t 452–24   simply by repeating the author's *w·*,

these
an 105–18   these *w·* of Judge Parmenter of Boston
s 137–29   gave him a spiritual name in these *w·* :
o 359–23   she often listened with joy to these *w·*,

torrent of
pr 13–19   overwhelming our real wishes with a torrent of *w·*.

which indicate
g 504–18   *w·* which indicate, in the absence of solar

without deeds
o 354–19   Inconsistency is shown by *w·* without deeds,

works and
s 117–27   feebly transmits Jesus' works and *w·*.

your
p 397–14   Your thought is more powerful than your *w·*,

---

pr 1–13   take form in *w·* and in deeds.
13–14   Do we gain the omnipotent ear sooner by *w·*
a 23–22   *faith* and the *w·* corresponding thereto
46– 6   by the *w·*, which made their hearts burn
sp 89–11   incapable of *w·* that glow,
s 116–24   As the *w· person* and *personal* are commonly
161–20   the *w·* of the famous Madame Roland
b 332– 6   in *w·* which he quoted with approbation
338–22   Here *a dam* is not a mere play upon *w·* ;
o 343–29   Hence the mistake which allows *w·*, rather than
p 365– 8   finding utterance in such *w·* as
ap 567–23   The *w·* "cast unto the earth" — *Rev.* 12 : 13.

wordy
pr 8– 1   A *w·* prayer may afford a quiet sense of

wore
gl 596–29   The Jewish women *w·* veils over their faces

work (noun)

apostolic
sp 97–31   the apostolic *w·* of casting out error and

author's
pref viii–24   In the author's *w·*, RETROSPECTION AND

ever at
s 118–10   but this leaven of Truth is ever at *w·*.

God's
ph 167–16   What can improve God's *w·*?
g 522–29   Scripture . . . declares God's *w·* to be finished.

healing
ph 185–21   as a spiritual factor in the healing *w·*.
f 217– 6   may inform us that the healing *w·* of C. S.
p 365–16   the healing *w·* will be accomplished

His
pr 3– 9   His *w·* is done, and we have only to
f 206–23   declaring that His *w·* was *finished,*
g 519– 3   Deity was satisfied with His *w·*.

work (noun)

His

g 519–23   God ended His w·— *Gen.* 2 : 2.
519–24   all His w· which He had made.— *Gen.* 2 : 2.

His own

pr 3– 9   Shall we ask the divine . . . to do His own w·?

his own

sp 79–19   Jesus did his own w· by the one Spirit.

holy

g 520– 2   highest and sweetest rest, . . . is in holy w·.

immense

b 322–10   in view of the immense w· to be accomplished

Jesus'

a 43– 3   The magnitude of Jesus' w·,

life's

a 18– 6   He did life's w· aright

magnitude of his

a 50– 7   overwhelming sense of the magnitude of his w·,

mental

f 238–27   People with mental w· before them

Messianic

a 27– 9   God is the power in the Messianic w·.

my

t 456–25   my w· Science and Health for his textbook,

of eternity

pr 3–15   to understand God is the w· of eternity,

of God

g 521– 6   All that is made is the w· of God,

of the Master

s 136–22   and the great w· of the Master,

of time

f 238–30   To reconstruct timid justice. . . is the w· of time.

of Truth

g 528–21   error now simulates the w· of Truth,

of wisdom

sp 83– 5   claimed that they could equal the w· of wisdom.

on the subject

pref ix–23   before a w· on the subject could be

our

pr 6– 7   Calling on Him to forgive our w·

perfect

t 454–24   must "have her perfect w·."— *Jas.* 1 : 4.
463–20   Truth . . . has fulfilled its perfect w·.

same

b 320–11   in the same w·, the familiar text, Genesis vi. 3,

so great a

r 494– 6   so great a w· as the Messiah's

their

a 47– 7   but on the divine Principle of their w·.
s 145– 5   the lack of the letter could not hinder their w· ;

this

pref ix–26   Before writing this w·, Science and Health,
ph 186– 6   thoroughness of this w· determines health.
o 355–21   statement that the teachings of C. S. in this w·
t 460– 1   divine metaphysics as laid down in this w·,

three days'

a 44– 7   His three days' w· in the sepulchre

Truth does the

t 456–23   Truth does the w·, and you must both understand and

wonderful

s 137– 3   but the ultimate of this wonderful w·

wrong

f 240–20   until all wrong w· is effaced or rectified.

your

f 248–18   Then you are haunted in your w· by

a 28–15   Neither the origin, the character, nor the w·
53–11   He was at w· in divine Science.
s 137–10   Who or what is it that is able to do the w·,
152– 8   although they know not how the w· is done.
160– 1   should address himself to the w· of
c 260–14   and sets mortals at w· to discover
p 376– 7   and does its w· almost self-deceived.
399–18   A mill at w· or the action of a water-wheel
423–25   are now at w· in the economy of being
t 458– 6   simultaneously at w· on the sick.
r 483–32   the w· must be done unselfishly.
fr 600– *   *being fruitful in every good w·,*— *Col.* 1 : 10.

work (verb)

pr 3– 7   it is our task to w· out the solution.
3–11   enables us to w· out our own salvation.
15–20   to w· and watch for wisdom, Truth, and Love.
a 22–11   "W· out your own salvation,"— *Phil.* 2 : 12.
23–26   w· out one's "own salvation,— *Phil.* 2 : 12.
29– 3   It bids us w· the more earnestly in times of
30–31   w· out our salvation in the way Jesus taught.
sp 79–20   worketh hitherto, and I w·."— *John* 5 : 17.
90–21   mentally travel far and w· wonders,
99– 5   "W· out your own salvation."— *Phil.* 2 : 12.
an 106– 3   to w· against the free course of honesty
s 108–32   set my thoughts to w· in new channels,
ph 167–23   or to expect to w· equally with
180–20   even before they go to w· to eradicate the
182–12   It is impossible to w· from two standpoints.
186– 7   Erring human mind-forces can w· only evil

work (verb)

ph 193–20   informed that he went to w· in two weeks.
f 233–10   The ages must slowly w· up to perfection.
245–19   a useful hint, upon which a Franklin might w·
254–22   and to w· out the spiritual which determines
c 262– 1   in which to w· out the problem of being.
o 345– 6   and w· through drugs to heal the sick?
351–23   they cannot w· out the Spirit-rule of
p 367–21   watch, w·, and pray that this salt lose not
398–31   must come to the rescue, to w· a radical cure.
442–25   "W· out your own salvation— *Phil.* 2 : 12.
t 443–10   privileged to w· out their own salvation
444– 5   "All things w· together for good— *Rom.* 8 : 28.
459–20   false practitioner will w· mischief,

worked

a 25–24   He w· for their guidance,
25–30   our Master w· and suffered to bestow

workers

c 263– 2   They believe themselves to be independent w·,

worketh

a 22–12   for to this end God w· with you.
sp 79–20   "My Father w· hitherto,— *John* 5 : 17.
99– 8   "for it is God which w· in you— *Phil.* 2 : 13.
t 445–24   The human will which maketh and w· a lie,
gl 588– 4   that which "w· abomination— *Rev.* 21 : 27.

working

pr 1– 6   Prayer, watching, and w·, combined with
a 26–32   w· out the harmony of Life and Love.
m 67–14   Hoping and w·, one should stick to the wreck,
an 103–15   w· out the purposes of good only.
s 108– 4   by the effectual w· of His power."— *Eph.* 3 : 7.
162–16   W· out the rules of Science in practice,
ph 182–24   thus w· against themselves and their prayers
f 217–21   for you are w· out the problem of being
222– 5   has its material methods of w·,
238– 4   Science is w· changes in personal character
248–14   We are all sculptors, w· at various forms,
c 262–23   the bliss of loving unselfishly, w· patiently,
b 326–20   W· and praying with true motives,
p 424–13   to counteract the w· of a remedy
426–16   the necessity of w· out his own salvation.
t 464–11   w· for the redemption of mankind.
r 493– 5   solar system as w· on a different plan.
gl 583–27   error, w· out the designs of error ;

workings

pref xi– 7   in the w·, not of Spirit, but of the
an 101–21   The author's own observations of the w· of
ap 562–18   which show the w· of the spiritual idea

works (noun)

by his

sp 94–18   our Master confirmed his words by his w·.
s 146– 2   and he proved his faith by his w·,

by my

o 343– 5   will show thee my faith by my w·."— *Jas.* 2 : 18.
r 487–26   will show thee my faith by my w·."— *Jas.* 2 : 18.

doing the

a 51–20   but only through doing the w· which he did

evil

pr 5–32   and seek the destruction of all evil w·,

faith by

f 209–32   It shows the superiority of faith by w·

faith without

a 23–15   "Faith without w· is dead."— *Jas.* 2 : 26.

good

o 342–27   to disown the Christliness of good w·,

her own

pref xii–11   publisher of her own w· ;

his

a 54–18   understood neither his words nor his w·.

Jesus'

s 117–27   feebly transmits Jesus' w· and words.
131–29   Jesus' w· established his claim

medical

ph 176– 4   took up the study of medical w·
179–24   so long as you read medical w·

mighty

pref xi–14   these mighty w· are not supernatural,
a 37–17   in *all* his ways and to imitate his mighty w·?
49–10   Had they so soon lost sight of his mighty w·,
p 401– 1   in certain localities he did not many mighty w·

of the devil

pr 5–30   "destroy the w· of the devil."— *I John* 3 : 8.
r 474–30   "destroy the w· of the devil."— *I John* 3 : 8.

of the flesh

an 106–20   "Now the w· of the flesh are— *Gal.* 5 : 19.

of Thy hands

ph 200–14   dominion over the w· of Thy hands.— *Psal.* 8 : 6.

on metaphysics

s 116–13   W· on metaphysics leave the grand point untouched.

other

t 457– 2   Other w·, which have borrowed from this book

rather than

o 343–29   mistake which allows words, rather than w·,

works (noun)

recounting his
s 132– 1 recounting his *w·* instead of referring to his

remarkable
o 358–20 than are his remarkable *w·*?

that I do
pr 14–20 the *w·* that I do shall he do also ; — *John* 14 : 12.
a 42–31 the *w·* that I do shall he do also." — *John* 14 : 12.
52–27 the *w·* that I do shall he do also;" — *John* 14 : 12.
sp 93– 4 the *w·* that I do shall he do also," — *John* 14 : 12.
b 326– 5 the *w·* that I do shall he do also." — *John* 14 : 12.

their
pref x–30 lest their *w·* be reproved.

without
a 22–26 nor by pinning one's faith without *w·*

without thy
o 343– 4 thy faith without thy *w·*, — *Jas.* 2 : 18.
r 487–26 thy faith without thy *w·*, — *Jas.* 2 : 18.

wonderful
a 46– 2 did not perform many wonderful *w·*, until
r 483–29 by doing many wonderful *w·* through the

word and
p 364– 2 that through his word and *w·* they might

words and
a 53–12 His words and *w·* were unknown to the
o 360–32 on the very basis of Jesus' words and *w·*.

pr 4–27 Audible prayer can never do the *w·* of
o 350–13 Unless the *w·* are comprehended which
358–23 great import to Christianity of those *w·*
k 499– * I know thy *w·* : — *Rev.* 3 : 8.
gl 579– * I know thy *w·* : — *Rev.* 3 : 8.

works (verb)

m 67–12 the mariner *w·* on and awaits the issue.
s 155–18 general belief, . . . *w·* against C. S. ;
f 251–12 Truth *w·* out the nothingness of error
c 259–23 God, Spirit, *w·* spiritually, not materially.
263– 8 and *w·* only as God *w·*,
o 342–19 which *w·* according to the Scriptures
p 401– 2 its own enemy, and *w·* against itself ;
r 467–21 The belief that . . . is an error that *w·* ill.
ap 561– 2 *w·* out the ends of eternal good

world (*see also* **world's**)

acknowledged not
a 54– 5 The *w·* acknowledged not his righteousness,

all the
a 37–29 "Go ye into all the *w·*, and preach—*Mark* 16 : 15.
s 138–28 "Go ye into all the *w·*, and preach—*Mark* 16 : 15.
o 342–10 "Go ye into all the *w·*, and preach—*Mark* 16 : 15.

beginning of the
s 129–15 not since the beginning of the *w·* ;"—*Matt.* 24 : 21.

believes in
g 517–15 The *w·* believes in many persons ;

citizens of the
f 227–24 Citizens of the *w·*, accept the

convulses the
f 223–14 The question, . . . convulses the *w·*.

could not
a 53–16 The *w·* could not interpret aright the

creation of the
r 479–31 from the creation of the *w·*, — *Rom.* 1 : 20.

describe the
pref ix– 6 yet he cannot describe the *w·*.

end of the
t 446–23 even unto the end of the *w·*." — *Matt.* 28 : 20.

feels the
f 224– 2 for the *w·* feels the alterative effect of truth

flooding the
s 150–31 The hosts of Æsculapius are flooding the *w·*

foundation of the
b 317– 2 from the foundation of the *w·*," — *Matt.* 13 : 35.
334–22 from the foundation of the *w·*," — *Rev.* 13 : 8.
ap 568– 2 Ever since the foundation of the *w·*,

from the
pr 15–26 hidden from the *w·*, but known to God.
m 64– 7 unspotted from the *w·*." — *Jas.* 1 : 27.
f 243– 1 We may hide spiritual ignorance from the *w·*,

guard over
a 48– 6 held uncomplaining guard over a *w·*

homage of the
a 42–10 Though entitled to the homage of the *w·*

is asleep
sp 95–28 the *w·* is asleep in the cradle of infancy,

is benefited by
t 463–32 said to the author, "The *w·* is benefited by

light of the
p 367–20 "Ye are the light of the *w·*. — *Matt.* 5 : 14.

material
(*see* **material**)

must grow
pr 10– 5 *w·* must grow to the spiritual understanding of

new era for the
a 43–19 opened a new era for the *w·*.

newly discovered
pref viii–32 in the newly discovered *w·* of Spirit.

world

of error
pr 13–30 *w·* of error is ignorant of the world of Truth,

of sensation
pr 13–31 *w·* of sensation is not cognizant of

of sin
sp 82–31 In a *w·* of sin and sensuality

of Truth
pr 13–30 world of error is ignorant of the *w·* of Truth,

outward
pref ix– 3 A child drinks in the outward *w·*

overcame the
a 39– 5 He overcame the *w·*, the flesh, and

overcoming the
pr 10–13 overcoming the *w·*, the flesh, and evil,

physical
s 125– 1 of the physical body and of the physical *w·*

revolutionized the
a 34–13 they would have revolutionized the *w·*.

sigh over the
m 57–29 until it ceases to sigh over the *w·*

sink the
ap 570–21 nor again sink the *w·* into the deep waters

sins of the
s 150–17 to take away the sins of the *w·*.
b 334–19 taking away the sins of the *w·*,

this
pr 5–15 full award, but not always in this *w·*.
a 29–11 though we may never receive it in this *w·*.
36–23 impossible . . . for this *w·* to bestow
m 69–26 "The children of this *w·* marry, — *Luke* 20 : 34.
sp 73– 3 one person, living in this *w·*,
an 103– 4 "the god of this *w·*," — *II Cor.* 4 : 4.
f 225– 8 The powers of this *w·* will fight,
c 267–27 Even in this *w·*, therefore,
b 270–22 The pride of priesthood is the prince of this *w·*.
325–25 can never reach in this *w·* the divine heights of

to battle
r 483–16 Science has called the *w·* to battle over this

unknown to the
a 53–12 His words and works were unknown to the *w·*

visible
s 118– 9 hidden in sacred secrecy from the visible *w·*

was not worthy
a 28–30 "of whom the *w·* was not worthy," — *Heb.* 11 : 38.

whole
a 45– 9 for the salvation of the whole *w·* from sin,
o 344–22 one which should be presented to the whole *w·*,
ap 567–16 which deceiveth the whole *w·* : — *Rev.* 12 : 9.

wicked
pr 4–24 but in this wicked *w·* goodness will

with the
a 28–26 Christianity to-day is at peace with the *w·*

a 47–22 the *w·* generally loves a lie better than Truth ;
m 69–28 worthy to obtain that *w·*, — *Luke* 20 : 35.
s 136–10 His answer to this question the *w·* rejected.
158–20 the byways of this wilderness *w·*,
f 209–10 The *w·* would collapse without Mind,
213–12 He was a musician beyond what the *w·* knew.
235–28 occupying the watchtowers of the *w·*,
248–20 The *w·* is holding it before your gaze
252–24 says : . . . The *w·* is my kingdom.
b 317–12 "If the *w·* hate you, ye know that— *John* 15 : 18.
o 348–26 never supposed the *w·* would immediately
354– 5 against "the *w·*, the flesh, and the devil"?
p 379– 6 The real jurisdiction of the *w·* is in Mind,
394–15 advice to a man who is down in the *w·*,
r 486–32 and without God in the *w·* ;" — *Eph.* 2 : 12.

worldliness
t 459– 6 gain heavenly riches by forsaking all *w·*.

worldling's
t 459– 8 nothing in common with the *w·* affections,

worldly
a 21–25 the *w·* man is at the beck and call of error,
s 142–23 purge the temples of their vain traffic in *w·*
ph 168– 2 is a poor shift for the weak and *w·*,
f 238–23 arise from *w·* weakness.
t 459– 5 achieves no *w·* honors except by sacrifice,

worldly-minded
a 36–17 preclude C. S. from finding favor with the *w·*.

world's
pref ix– 5 He is as sure of the *w·* existence as he is of his
own ;
a 47–10 The *w·* ingratitude and hatred towards
48–17 Judas had the *w·* weapons.
48–18 and chose not the *w·* means of defence.
50–31 the *w·* hatred of Truth and Love.
52–10 the *w·* hatred of the just and perfect Jesus,
53–13 and contrary to the *w·* religious sense.
m 65–16 Beholding the *w·* lack of Christianity

world-wide
f 226– 3 the banishment of a *w·* slavery,

writers

b 319–26	uninspired w·, who only wrote
g 537–24	Inspired w· interpret the Word spiritually,

writes

a 45–10	Paul w·: "For if, when we— Rom. 5: 10.
f 208–17	John Young of Edinburgh w·:
244–11	Paul w·: "The law of the— Rom. 8: 2.
o 324–27	Paul w·, "If Christ [Truth]— I Cor. 15: 14.
325–10	Paul w·: "When Christ, who is— Col. 3: 4.
ap 558–1	St. John w·, in the tenth chapter of his
574–5	He w·, in Revelation xxi. 9:
576–9	Revelation xxi. 22, . . . the beloved Disciple w·:

writing

pref ix–26	Before w· this work, SCIENCE AND HEALTH,

written

s 164–28	Certain essays w· at that early date
	the saying that is w·,— I Cor. 15: 54.
f 242–23	for it is w·: "They parted my— John 19: 24.
r 496–27	the saying that is w·,— I Cor. 15: 54.
g 536–2	In the Apocalypse it is w·:
ap 558–*	those things which are w· therein:— Rev. 1: 3.
561–30	it is w·, "There was a man sent— John 1: 6.

wrong

disbelief in the

a 29–8	and disbelief in the w·.

done another

t 449–27	The w· done another reacts most heavily

freedom from

f 236–29	because of their freedom from w·

greatest

p 368–1	The greatest w· is but a supposititious

intentional

f 251–28	Ignorance, like intentional w·, is not

learned the

b 326–28	He learned the w· that he had done

meet the

b 327–23	Moral courage is requisite to meet the w·

positive

r 491–8	a negative right and a positive w·,

practise

t 253–18	If you believe in and practise w· knowingly,

right and

t 453–6	Right and w·, truth and error,
g 531–7	error, . . . that mind and soul are both right and w·.

self-evidently

g 539–22	exposed by our Master as self-evidently w·.

pr 9–3	The w· lies in unmerited censure,
ph 166–6	the healing effort is made on the w· side,
172–6	and very much in the w·.
184–3	the conclusions are w·.
195–27	Novels, . . . fill our young readers with w·
f 208–9	a law of mortal mind, w· in every sense,
240–20	until all w· work is effaced
253–23	you can alter this w· belief and action
b 314–32	Jesus proved them w· by his resurrection,
318–26	If disease is right it is w· to heal it.
322–23	A man who likes to do w·
326–19	nothing but w· intention can hinder your

wrong

b 340–26	whatever is w· in social, civil, criminal,
o 357–20	w· notions about God must have
360–4	replies: "You w· my experience.
p 396–20	weight of opinions on the w· side,
397–6	mental influence on the w· side,
401–4	nothing in the right . . . and much in the w·.
407–17	Let the slave of w· desire learn the
t 446–18	A w· motive involves defeat.
448–31	To talk the right and live the w·
451–29	controlling another from w· motives,
452–5	The w· thought should be arrested
452–25	by right talking and w· acting,
452–32	the w· power would be destroyed.
453–28	impresses more deeply the w· mind-picture.
454–16	the w· as well as the right practice.
r 489–29	A w· sense of God, man, and creation
491–10	spiritual individuality is never w·.

wrong-doer

p 404–6	by exhibiting to the w· the suffering which
gl 597–24	Will, as a quality of so-called mortal mind, is a w·;

wrong-doing

pr 5–3	Sorrow for w· is but one step towards
6–22	the safety-valve for w·.
f 240–22	If at present satisfied with w·,
p 385–14	from all penalties but those due for w·.
405–24	The abiding consciousness of w· tends to
r 480–22	which seems to make men capable of w·,
g 539–13	How then has man a basis for w·?

wronged

m 63–29	the w·, and perchance impoverished, woman

wrongly

o 343–18	proving by what are w· called miracles,
t 452–31	the inclination or power to practise w·

wrongness

an 104–16	and the consequent w· of the opposite

wrote

a 20–27	St. Paul w·, "Let us lay aside— Heb. 12: 1.
29–12	w· to the authorities at Rome:
sp 82–5	Chaucer w· centuries ago, yet we still read his
an 106–19	in his great epistle to the Galatians, when he w·
b 319–26	who only w· down what an inspired
p 382–25	One whom I rescued . . . w· to me:

wrought

pr 13–23	and so we cannot grasp the wonders w· by
a 39–6	He w· a full salvation from sin, sickness, and
s 117–21	in the miracles (marvels) w· by Jesus
132–23	if it is w· on any but a material and
133–16	w· wonders for the people of God
150–13	Now, as then, signs and wonders are w·
154–22	believed that exposure . . . w· the mischief.
ph 185–17	strove to emulate the wonders w· by Moses.
f 202–4	must be w· out in life-practice,
g 540–13	may think . . . that the Lord hath w· an evil;
ap 570–27	know the great benefit which Mind has w·.

wrung

a 50–7	w· from Jesus' lips the awful cry,
50–32	w· from his faithful lips the plaintive cry,

X, Y

Xantippe

m 66–28	making his X· a discipline for his

yard

ph 193–19	The next day I saw him in the y·.

Yawah

s 133–29	The Jewish conception, of God, as Y·,
g 528–9	And the Lord God [Jehovah, Y·]— Gen. 2: 21.

yawn

s 153–25, 26	we y· because they y·,

yea

a 31–30	y·, the time cometh, that— John 16: 2.
37–22	It is possible,— y·, it is the duty and privilege
sp 84–17	y·, to reach the range of fetterless Mind.
98–22	For centuries— y·, always— natural science
s 128–25	y·, forever destroys with the higher testimony
ph 171–22	the spiritual,— y·, the image of infinite Mind,
b 301–1	y·, which manifests God's attributes
332–12	y·, the divine image and likeness,
o 346–12	to prove the somethingness— y·, the allness
p 366–10	y·, while mental penury chills his faith
g 505–19	y·, than the mighty waves of— Psal. 93: 4.
509–27	purity, and holiness— y·, the divine nature
529–15	Y·, hath God said, Ye shall not— Gen. 3: 1.
535–2	y·, the seed of Spirit and the seed of matter,
ap 578–10	Y·, though I walk through the— Psal. 23: 4.

year

pref viii–26	experiences which led her, in the y· 1866,
xi–27	was started by the author . . . about the y· 1867.
s 107–1	In the y· 1866, I discovered the Christ Science
121–26	earth revolves about the sun once a y·,
f 246–25	Each succeeding y· unfolds wisdom,
gl 594–17	"Son of a y·."
598–19	definition of
599–1	mortal thought, the divisor of which is the solar y·.

yearning

pr 13–7	If we are not secretly y· and openly striving
a 48–7	There was no response to that human y·,
49–13	O, why did they not gratify his last human y·
s 111–25	C. S. meets a y· of the human race
137–8	Y· to be understood, the Master repeated,

yearnings

b 314–5	had quenched all earthly y·.

years

all the

m 59–5	should wait on all the y· of married life.

days, and

g 509–12	and for days, and y·.— Gen. 1: 14.

during the

pref ix–28	This was during the y· 1867 and 1868.

early

f 245–5	Disappointed in love in her early y·,
o 351–9	became a member . . . in early y·.

years

few
f 206–20   for the brief space of a few y·
in after
m 62–10   those parents should not, in after y·, complain
many
pr 9– 2   During many y· the author has been most grateful
s 107– 5   graciously preparing me during many y· for the
f 221– 2   For many y·, he ate only bread and
222–17   For many y· he had been kept alive,
p 380–22   Many y· ago the author made a . . . discovery,
months or
f 237– 7   It might have been months or y· before
nineteen hundred
s 122– 9   exposed nineteen hundred y· ago
f 232–18   as it did over nineteen hundred y· ago,
of servitude
f 226–22   wearing out y· of servitude to an
riper
f 248– 6   Men and women of riper y· and larger lessons
seven
pref xii– 6   During seven y· over four thousand students
six thousand
ap 560– 3   typical of six thousand y· since Adam,
solar
f 246–10   The measurement of life by solar y· robs youth
Soul-filled
gl 599– 2   Eternity is God's measurement of Soul-filled y·.
thousand
g 504–23   with the Lord as a thousand y·." — II Pet. 3 : 8.
504–25   whereas a thousand y· of human doctrines,
gl 598–21   with the Lord as a thousand y·." — II Pet. 3 : 8.
three
s 109–11   For three y· after my discovery, I sought
threescore
f 246–22   would enjoy more than threescore y· and ten
two
pref xii–16   conviction that the next two y· of her life
weary
f 221–10   He passed many weary y· in hunger and

sp 80–23   French toy which y· ago pleased so many people
f 245– 8   taking no note of y·, she stood daily
245–21   Y· had not made her old,
b 333–18   without beginning of y· or end of days.

yeast
s 118–24   as y· changes the chemical properties of meal.

yesterday
pr 2–32   "the same y·, and to-day, — Heb. 13 : 8.
a 37– 2   brings suffering as much to-day as y·
s 112–20   "the same y·, and to-day, — Heb. 13 : 8.
143– 3   to-day, as y·, Christ casts out evils
f 249–18   "the same y·, and to-day, — Heb. 13 : 8.
b 283– 7   "y·, and to-day, and forever." — Heb. 13 : 8.
322–15   The necromancy of y· foreshadowed the
g 546– 5   "the same y·, and to-day, — Heb. 13 : 8.

yet
pref vii– 5   y· it traversed the night, and came
ix– 5   y· he cannot describe the world.
pr 3–28   y· return thanks to God for all blessings,
a 20–12   and y· be sensual and sinful.
20–20   Y· he swerved not, well knowing that
26– 5   y· Jesus spares us not one individual
32–22   y· Jesus prayed and gave them bread.
38–13   addressing his disciples, y· he did not say,
53– 4   y· there never lived a man so far removed
m 66– 5   Wears y· a precious jewel in his head.
67–11   Y·, acting up to his highest understanding,
sp 80– 9   Y· the very periodical containing this
81– 4   y· this latter evidence is destroyed by
81–22   and y· the producing, governing, divine
82– 5   y· we still read his thought in his verse.
83– 3   y· artifice and delusion claimed
87–23   y· these are all there.
90–21   y· their bodies stay in one place.
92–32   Do you say the time has not y· come
97– 9   the electric current swift, y· in C. S.
99– 4   y· to escape from sin, is what the
s 107–16   y· remembering that in reality
112–28   y· uses another author's discoveries
122–10   y· these so-called senses still make
129–26   Y· quite as rational are some of the
132–19   has not y· been generally accepted.
132–32   y· afterwards he seriously questioned
139–11   but the present new, y· old, reform
153– 7   and y·, with one drop of that attenuation
155– 7   have not y· divorced the drug from the
156– 7   and y·, as she lay in her bed,
164– 6   or of therapeutic agents, ever y· promulgated,
164–14   Much y· remains to be said
ph 165– *   nor y· for your body, — Matt. 6 : 25.
172–13   y· this can be realized only as
174–16   the path for generations y· unborn.
183–11   and y· the Scriptures inform us that

yet
ph 190– 6   and y· neither a mortal mind nor the
196– 3   has not y· found it true that knowledge can
f 202–28   and y· we rely on a drug . . . as if
217–11   y· if we turn to the Scriptures,
218– 3   y· the body is as material as the wheel.
219–23   and y· misunderstand the science that
220– 3   said : . . . and y· I have continual colds,
222–19   and y· he continued ill
b 274–30   at a period as y· unknown.
278–21   and y· we say that Spirit is supreme
310–20   and y· be immortal.
312–12   y· you say that matter has caused his death.
312–16   y· God is Love,
312–18   y· God is Truth.
320–31   y· in the latter days he should stand
346–27   Y·, in your concept, the tooth,
o 353–15   Time has not y· reached eternity,
354– 8   and y· deny C. S., when it teaches
359– 4   Y· Scientists will take the same cases,
360– 7   y· I would not exchange mine for
361– 1   Jew believes that . . . Christ has not y· come ;
p 362– *   I shall y· praise Him, — Psal. 42 : 11.
416– 9   Y· any physician . . . will tell you
423– 2   y· this belief should not be
t 443– *   and he will be y· wiser : — Prov. 9 : 9.
448– 1   and y· to indulge them, is a moral offense.
453–22   y· serves evil in the name of good.
460–10   Y· this most fundamental part of
r 474–19   y· the Scriptures aver,
486–19   and y· supposes Mind unable to
g 504– 8   though solar beams are not y· included
506–29   Adam has not y· appeared in the narrative.
508–16   The feminine gender is not y· expressed in
512–15   the externalized, y· subjective, states
513–11   time is not y· measured by solar revolutions,
523– 1   Y· one might so judge from an
524–23   y· God is reflected in all His creation.
545–19   y· this opposite, in its false view
552–20   but not y· instructed by Science,
ap 570– 5   certain active y· unseen mental agencies
571–14   and y· have given no warning.
572–23   The Revelator had not y· passed the
573– 3   while y· beholding what the
576– 6   while y· he tabernacled with mortals.
576–28   not y· elevated to deific apprehension
576–30   Y· the word gradually approaches a
gl 598– 6   y· it has received different translations,

yield
pref viii– 6   must y· to the harmony of spiritual sense,
xi– 8   the fleshly mind which must y· to Science.
sp 96–23   until all errors of belief y· to understanding.
s 151–29   y· to this power, and follow the leadings of
152– 1   and must by its own consent y· to Truth.
162–11   it may y· to the harmony of the divine Mind.
ph 176–30   are quite as ready to y· to Truth as
178–21   must finally y· to the eternal Truth,
189– 1   human or material senses y· to the authority of
200–23   material senses must y· to the infinite Spirit,
f 201–10   fear, all sensuality, y· to spirituality,
254– 6   or attain slowly and y· not to discouragement.
c 256– 2   The finite must y· to the infinite.
b 287–30   Their false evidence will finally y· to Truth,
295–13   will at last y· to the scientific fact
319–11   must y· to the all-might of
339–22   so will our material theories y· to spiritual
o 347–27   must y· to reason and revelation.
353–21   we must y· up all belief in it and be wise.
p 371– 3   this so-called mind must finally y· to
381– 6   than you are to y· to a sinful temptation
402–26   If they y· to this influence, it is because
t 450–15   Some people y· slowly to the touch of Truth.
450–16   Few y· without a struggle,
r 471–11   y· assent to astronomical propositions
484–10   supposed laws of matter y· to the law of Mind.
493– 7   All the evidence of physical sense . . . must y·
g 507–19   tree and herb do not y· fruit because of
ap 562–14   y· to the activities of the divine Principle
gl 589– 6   y· to the spiritual sense of Life and Love.

yielded
b 291– 8   cannot come till mortals have already y· to
303–31   When the evidence before the material senses y·
326–24   only when his uncertain sense of right y·
339–20   As the mythology of pagan Rome has y· to a
t 450–17   reluctant to acknowledge that they have y· ;

yielding
a 39–14   overcame death and the grave instead of y·
ph 184–11   nor y· obedience to it.
b 268– 7   Belief in a material basis, . . . is slowly y· to the
p 375–14   No person is benefited by y· his mentality to
413– 3   The act of y· one's thoughts to
g 507–12   the herb y· seed, — Gen. 1 : 11.
507–12   and the fruit tree y· fruit — Gen. 1 : 11.
508–10   herb y· seed after his kind, — Gen. 1 : 12.
508–10   and the tree y· fruit, — Gen. 1 : 12.

yielding

g 518– 8 the fruit of a tree y· seed ;— *Gen.* 1 : 29.
gl 586–23 the human y· to the divine ;
593–11 material belief y· to spiritual understanding.

yields

sp 85– 5 when the latter y· to the divine Mind.
ph 188– 1 only as the mortal, erring mind y· to God,
b 281– 1 ignorance which y· only to the understanding
318–21 y· to the reality of spiritual Life.
322–19 his physical sense of pleasure y· to a higher
329–31 till error y· to Truth.
o 353– 6 till the testimony of the physical senses y·
p 409–18 the stronger never y· to the weaker, except
414– 5 it y· more readily than do most diseases
426– 3 when instructed by Truth, y· to divine power,
r 485–24 If thought y· its dominion to other powers,
489–11 y· to the reality of everlasting Life.
g 543– 3 This error, . . . y· to Truth and returns to dust ;
ap 576–31 human sense of Deity y· to the divine sense,
577– 1 y· to the incorporeal sense of God and man
gl 584–15 until every belief . . . y· to eternal Life.

yoke

g 555– 5 the physical organism under the y· of disease.

yore

s 132–20 To-day, as of y·, unconscious of the reappearing
f 226–29 the Pharaohs, who to-day, as of y·,
r 481– 5 Like the archpriests of y·, man is free

you

gl 599– 3 definition of

young

s 161– 8 the Bible case of the three y· Hebrew captives,
ph 191–11 "where the y· child was,"— *Matt.* 2 : 9.
195–27 Novels, . . . fill our y· readers with wrong
f 244–23 Man in Science is neither y· nor old.
245–10 In this mental state she remained y·.
245–13 and supposed her to be a y· woman.
245–24 The bodily results of her belief that she was y·
245–25 She could not age while believing herself y·,
245–28 proves it possible to be y· at seventy-four ;
p 412–28 If the case is that of a y· child
g 514–24 And the calf and the y· lion,— *Isa.* 11 : 6.

Young, John

f 208–17 John Y· of Edinburgh writes :

youngest

c 261–15 as actively as the y· member of the company.

youth

f 236–31 y· makes easy and rapid strides towards Truth.
245–15 y· sat gently on cheek and brow.
245–18 This instance of y· preserved furnishes a
246–10 robs y· and gives ugliness to age.
r 471–24 subscribed to an orthodox creed in early y·,

Z

zeal

pr 7–11 "a z· . . . not according to— *Rom.* 10 : 2.
b 280–20 But behold the z· of belief to establish
gl 599– 4 definition of

zenith

sp 97–13 until matter reaches its mortal z· in illusion
ap 565–25 to rise to the z· of demonstration,

zigzag

a 21–32 By-and-by, ashamed of his z· course,

Zincum oxydatum

s 152–30 Jahr, from *Aconitum* to Z· o·,

Zion

ap 575–23 joy of the whole earth, is mount Z·,— *Psal.* 48 : 2.
gl 599– 6 definition of

yielding

yields

yoke

yore

zeal

zenith

son

young

Young, John

youngest

youth

Z

Zuingas

Zuingle or Zwingli

Zion

APPENDIX A

COMPREHENSIVE INDEX
TO THE MARGINAL HEADINGS
IN
SCIENCE AND HEALTH
WITH KEY TO THE SCRIPTURES

COMPREHENSIVE INDEX
TO THE MARGINAL HEADINGS

IN

SCIENCE AND HEALTH

WITH KEY TO THE SCRIPTURES

Beginning, scientific, 219.
Begin rightly, 382.
Beguiling first lie, the, 533.
Behest of the cross, 20.
Being, and seeming, 123.
  deflection of, 502.
  figures of, 282.
  indestructible, 325.
  is immortal, 553.
  man's genuine, 91.
  real, never lost, 215.
Belief an autocrat, 297.
  and climate, 386.
  and firm trust, 488.
  and practice, 202.
  and understanding, 183.
  and understanding, our, 203.
  change of, 194.
  faith higher than, 297.
  in death, a, 42.
  in many gods, 280.
  in physics, 155.
  laws of human, 184.
  on the wrong side, 168.
  physical science a blind, 124.
  suicidal, a, 39.
  understanding *versus*, 487.
Beliefs and fears, conquer, 419.
  illusive, 383.
  material, 485.
Benefactor, death no, 409.
Beneficence, trustworthy, 15.
Benefit of philanthropy, 385.
Benefits of metaphysics, 380.
  recognition of, 372.
Benevolence hindered, 64.
Be not afraid, 410.
Better basis than embryology, 553.
Biblical basis, 126.
  facts, scientific and, 358.
  foundations, 269.
Biological inventions, 531.
Birth and death, mortal, 265.
  and death unreal, 206.
  the immortal, 191.
Birthright, immortal, 479.
  of man, 518.
Blessing of Christ, 65.
Blessings from pain, 265.
Blight of avarice, 445.
Blind belief, physical science a, 124.
  force, human power a, 192.
Blissful ignorance, 382.
Blood, mind circulates, 373.
  true flesh and, 25.
Blunders and blunderers, 149.
  philosophical, 250.
Bodily presence, 14.
  resurrection, the, 314.
Body, a clean mind and, 383.
  material, never God's idea, 477.
  mind governs, 377.
  sensationless, 280.
  Soul greater than, 223.
  Soul not confined in, 467.
  the, death and, 187.
Bondage, higher law ends, 227.
  house of, 226.
Bone-healing by surgery, 422.
Book, effect of this, 422.
Both words and works, 350.
Brain, medicine and, 401.

Brain not intelligent, 372.
Brain-disease, Mind heals, 387.
Brain-lobes, drugs and, 408.
Brainology a myth, 295.
Breakfast, the last, 34.
Bridgeless division, 74.
Bright outlook, a, 323.
Brotherhood, assistance in, 518.
  repudiated, 541.
  universal, 276.
Bruising sin's head, 534.
Buried secrets, 87.
Business, Master's, 52.

C

Calmness, source of, 366.
Camera, Mind's true, 264.
Cancellation of human sin, 5.
Career, Jesus' sinless, 19.
Careful guidance, 429.
Carnality, the error of, 131.
Case, a mental court, 430.
Cast out, moral evils to be, 366.
Causation considered, 170.
  mental, 114.
  not in matter, 552.
Cause, Mind the only, 262.
  one primal, 207.
  supreme, one, 278.
  the universal, 331.
Causes of sickness, 165.
Celestial evidence, 471.
Central intelligence, the, 310.
Centre for affections, 60.
Certain contradictions, 118.
Certainty of results, 459.
Chalice sacrificial, the, 9.
Challenge, materialistic, 268.
Change demanded, a, 141.
  of belief, 194.
  requisite, of our ideals, 260.
Changed mentality, 168.
Changes, corporeal, 125.
  radical, 24.
Chaos and darkness, 479.
Character, and reputation, 53.
Charge of the Chief Justice, 441.
Charity to those opposed, 444.
Charlatanism, mental, 458.
Chicanery impossible, 456.
Chief Justice, charge of the, 441.
  stones in the temple, the, 288.
Childless, divinity not, 306.
Childlike receptivity, 323.
Children and adults, 130.
  teaching, 237.
Children's ailments, 154.
  tractability, 236.
Cholera, imaginary, 154.
Choose ye to-day, 360.
Chord and discord, 58.
Christ, blessing of, 65.
  eternity of the, 334.
  fellowship with, 34.
  Jesus, 332.
  Messiah or, 333.
  rejected, 132.
  the great physician, 442.
  the ideal Truth, 473.
  treatment, the, 369.
Christ's demonstration, 26.

Christ's mission, 233.
  reappearance, 95.
Christ-element, the, 288.
Christ-mission, the, 136.
Christ-power, absence of, 134.
Christian history, 387.
  pleading, 418.
  standard, 426.
  warfare, 29, 354.
Christian Science as old as God, 146.
  discovered, 107.
  mission of, 107.
Christian's privilege, the, 556.
Christianity, and Science, 127.
  essential element of, 347.
  scientific, 342.
  still rejected, 97.
  the unity of Science and, 135.
Christly warning, 571.
Churchly neglect, 131.
City foursquare, the, 575.
  of our God, the, 577.
Claim, false, or mist, 523.
Claims, false, annihilated, 450.
  two, omitted, 142.
Clairvoyance, magnetism, 101.
Classes, three, of neophytes, 450.
Classified, diseases not to be, 176.
Clay replying to the potter, 429.
Cleanliness, ablutions for, 413.
Clean mind and body, a, 383.
Cleansing the mind, 234.
  upheaval, 540.
Clergymen's duty, 235.
Climate and belief, 386.
  harmless, 377.
Climax of suffering, 543.
Closed question, a, 171.
Clouds dissolving, the, 548.
Coalescence, impossible, 143.
Coalition of sin and sickness, 218.
Combinations, corporeal, 399.
Comfort, crumbs of, 234.
Comforter, Holy Ghost or, 332.
Commands of Jesus, 342.
  two chief, 467.
Compassion requisite, 365.
Complete emulation, 37.
Completeness, the divine, 275.
Conception, erroneous, 538.
  immaculate, 315.
  spiritual, 29.
Conceptions, misleading, 28.
Concepts, insidious, 376.
Concessions, no dishonest, 456.
Conclusions, personal, 101.
Concord, spiritual, 60.
Condition of progress, 496.
Conditions, mental, to be heeded, 159.
  of criticism, 355.
  opposing, 74.
Confidence, and self-reliance, 23.
  personal, 358.
Confirmation by healing, 488.
  in a parable, 399.
Confirmatory tests, 111.
Conflict, the great, 288.
  with purity, the, 565.
Conflicting standpoints, 83.
Conforming to explicit rules, 445.
Confusion, ancient, 389.
  confounded, 268.

Conquer beliefs and fears, 419.
Conscious development, our, 554.
Consciousness, spiritualized, 14.
Consecration, intelligent, 428.
　required, 325.
Conservative antagonism, 144.
Consistency, scientific, 354.
Consolation, vials of wrath and, 574.
Conspiracy, the traitor's, 47.
Conspirators, mental, 405.
Construction, organic, valueless, 489.
Consume, nothing to, 425.
Contact, mental, 86.
Contagion, source of, 153.
Contention, misdirected, 380.
Contest, arena of, 96.
Continuity of existence, 429.
　of interest, 454.
　of thoughts, 513.
Contradict error, 391.
Contradicting first creation, 526.
Contradictions, certain, 118.
　not found, 345.
Contrasted testimony, 538.
Contrasts, unspiritual, 272.
Contumely, cruel, 49.
Conversion of Saul, 326.
Convincing evidence, 43.
Copartnership impossible, 356.
Coping with difficulties, 423.
Corporeal changes, 125.
　combinations, 399.
　ignorance, 13.
　penalties, 384.
Corporeality and Spirit, 46.
　no divine, 256.
Corrective, scientific, 423.
Counsel for defence, 434.
Counterfeit, and real, 368.
　creation's, 527.
　forces, the, 293.
　the human, 285.
Courage, moral, 327.
Course, zigzag, 21.
Court case, a mental, 430.
Cramping systems, 226.
Cravings, morbid, 406.
Creation, ever-appearing, 507.
　first, contradicting, 526.
　God's, intact, 68.
　inadequate theories of, 255.
　no baneful, 525.
　no material, 256.
　no new, 263.
　perfect, 205.
　perfection of, 519.
　reversed, 524.
Creation's counterfeit, 527.
Creator, Life the, 331.
Creators, two infinite, absurd, 357.
Creatures of God useful, 514.
Creditor, parable of the, 363.
Crimes, mental, 105.
Crisis, how to treat a, 421.
Criticism, conditions of, 355.
Cross and crown, the, 254.
　behest of the, 20.
Crown, and cross, the, 254.
Crucifixion, purpose of, 24.
Cruel contumely, 49.
　desertion, 42.
Crumbs of comfort, 234.

Crusade, liberty's, 226.
Cry of despair, a, 50.
Cumulative repentance, 405.
Cup of Jesus, the, 317.
Curative, error not, 143.
Cure for palsy, 375.
　of infants, the, 412.
　of insanity, 414.
Currents, Life's healing, 24.
Curse, murder brings its, 542.
　removed, the, 557.

D

Danger from audible prayer, 7.
Dangerous knowledge, 459.
　resemblances, 97.
　shoals avoided, 196.
Darkest hours of all, the, 96.
Darkness, and light, 215.
　and chaos, 479.
　egotistic, 452.
　light shining in, 108.
　scattered, 511.
　Spirit versus, 504.
Dawning of spiritual facts, 546.
Day of judgment, 291.
　tests in our, 149.
Dead, raising the, 75.
Deadness in sin, 316.
Death, a belief in, 42.
　and birth unreal, 206.
　and the body, 187.
　an error, 486.
　but an illusion, 289.
　illusion of, 251.
　mortal birth and, 265.
　no advantage, 290.
　no, nor inaction, 427.
　no benefactor, 409.
　outdone, 42.
　second, 77.
　thought regarding, 79.
　triumph over, 496.
Decalogue disregarded, 489.
Decapitation of error, 266.
Decision, important, 105.
　the important, 181.
　unhesitating, 463.
Deeds, not words but, 181.
Deep-reaching interrogations, 550.
Defamatory accusations, 52.
Defence, counsel for, 434.
　indispensable, 452.
Defensive weapons, 48.
Deference to material law, 549.
Definite rule discovered, a, 147.
Definition of man, 302.
　of mortal mind, 114.
Definitions of man, 525.
　the deific, 330.
Deflection of being, 502.
Deflections, unnatural, 78.
Deformity and perfection, 244.
Degrees, advancing, 158.
　of development, 172.
Deific definitions, the, 330.
　naturalism, the, 44.
　supremacy, the, 330.
Deity, divine sense of, 576.
　finite views of, 255.
　nearness of, 573.

Deity, tribal, Jehovah a, 524.
　unchangeable, 2.
Deliverance not vicarious, 22.
Deluded invalids, 237.
Delusion, all disease a, 348.
Delusions, mortal, 90.
　pagan and medical, 166.
Demands, affection's, 57.
　peremptory, 327.
Demonstrable evidence, 108.
Demonstration, Christ's, 26.
　lost and found, the, 110.
Denial, and ingratitude, 94.
　of immortality, a, 80.
Denials of divine power, 232.
Derivatives of spirit, 93.
Desertion, cruel, 42.
Desire for holiness, 11.
Despair, a cry of, 50.
Despatch, erroneous, 386.
Despotism, mental, 103.
Destroy all ills, Mind can, 374.
Destruction, final, of error, 328.
　of all evil, 231, 495.
Dethroned, mortal mind, 152.
Development, degrees of, 172.
　our conscious, 554.
　progressive, 64.
Devotion, veritable, 4.
Diabolism destroyed, 5.
Diagnosis of matter, 371.
Dictation of error, 409.
Diet and digestion, 389.
　and dyspepsia, 197.
Differences, irreconcilable, 356.
Differing duties, 59.
Difficulties, coping with, 423.
Digestion, and diet, 389.
Dilemma, unescapable, 119.
Disappearance, mortal mind's, 251.
Disciples, doubting, 136.
　example of the, 343.
　recreant, 27.
　studious, 271.
Discipline, and help, 57.
Discontent, inspiring, 53.
　with life, 107.
Discord, chord and, 58.
　sickness as, 318.
Discovery, a higher, 380.
　spiritual, 260.
Discrimination, unfair, 63.
Disease, a delusion, all, 348.
　a dream, 188.
　avoid talking, 396.
　depicted, 198.
　far more docile than iniquity, 373.
　foreseen, 168.
　images of, effacing, 396.
　mental, 151.
　neutralized, 422.
　no real, 393.
　powerless, 378.
　to be made unreal, 417.
　treatment of, 390.
Disease-production, 403.
Diseases, naming, 411.
　not to be classified, 176.
　novel, 175.
Dishonest concessions, no, 456.
Disregard of matter, Jesus', 210.
Distinct documents, 523.

Guidance, spiritual, 566.
Guilt, and weakness, 455.

H

Habit, power of, 194.
Half-way success, 167.
Harm done by physicians, 198.
Harmonious functions, 478.
life-work, 202.
Harmony from Spirit, 480.
natural, 304.
spiritual, 503.
ultimate, 390.
Hate, impotence of, 454.
Head and heart, music, rhythm of, 213.
bruising sin's, 534.
Healer, Mind the only, 169.
mortal mind not a, 401.
Healers, ancient, 145.
Healing, confirmation by, 488.
early lost, 41.
genuine, 367.
in sin, no, 370.
omitted, 354.
primary, 31.
proof given in, 547.
speedy, 365.
the leaves of, 406.
the true, 230.
true, transcendent, 483.
was lost, how, 146.
Health and good, hospitality to, 234.
and immortality, basis of, 339.
and the senses, 120.
from reliance on spirituality, 166.
purity, and beauty, Mind imparts, 371.
Healthful explanation, 396.
theology, 138.
Heart, and head, music, rhythm of, 213.
searching the, 8.
Hearts, receptive, 570.
Heathen, gods of the, 524.
Heaven, treasure in, 451.
Heaven's sentinel, 49.
Heaven-bestowed prerogative, 253.
Heavenly supplies, 33.
Heavenward, our footsteps, 426.
Hebrew theology, 315.
Help and discipline, 57.
and hindrance, 28.
Truth a present, 351.
Helpful encouragement, 417.
Heralds of Science, 223.
Heredity, no fleshly, 228.
Hidden agents, 102.
ways of iniquity, 570.
Higher discovery, a, 380.
hope, 531.
law ends bondage, 227.
standard for mortals, 197.
statutes, 307.
Hindrance, and help, 28.
Hip-disease, Mind cures, 193.
Historic illustrations, 120.
History, Christian, 387.
Holiness, desire for, 11.
Holy Ghost or Comforter, 332.
Holy struggle, the, 33.

Homer and Moses, 200.
Homœopathic attenuations, 152.
Homœopathy, the modus of, 157.
Honest toil has no penalty, 385.
Honesty, and knowledge, 453.
Hope, higher, 531.
Hopeful outlook, the, 330.
Horses mistaught, 179.
Hospitality, penitence or, 364.
to health and good, 234.
Hours, the darkest, of all, 96.
House of bondage, 226.
How healing was lost, 146.
to treat a crisis, 421.
Human belief, laws of, 184.
counterfeit, the, 285.
the divine and, contrasted, 118.
egotism, 263.
falsities, 212.
frailty, 190.
power a blind force, 192.
reconciliation, 18.
reflection, 305.
reproduction, 189.
rights, no trespass on, 447.
stature, 190.
Humanity, and divinity, 561.
right views of, 239.
Humility, and gratitude, 367.
Hygiene excessive, 382.
ineffectual, 220.
Hypnotic surgery, 528.
Hypnotism, and Jesus, 185.
Science versus, 375.
Hypocrisy condemned, 85.
Hypotheses, fallacious, 79.
Hypothetical reversal, 522.

I

Idea, God's, the ideal man, 346.
material body never God's, 477.
Mind's, faultless, 503.
spiritual, crowned, 562.
spiritual, revealed, 562.
the divine Principle and, 333.
the true new, 281.
true, of man, 337.
Ideal man and woman, 516.
man, God's idea the, 346.
Ideals, requisite change of our, 260.
Ideas and identities, 502.
illusions not, 88.
inverted images and, 301.
multiplication of pure, 512.
spiritual, apprehended, 510.
Identities, and ideas, 502.
Identity, imperishable, 476.
not lost, 172, 302.
of man, immutable, 261.
personal, 216.
real and unreal, 70.
Idolatrous illusions, 214.
Idolatry, ignorant, 186.
Ignorance, blissful, 382.
corporeal, 13.
excuses for, 130.
of our rights, 381.
prophetic, 270.
spiritual, 251.
the sign of error, 555.
Ignorant idolatry, 186.

Ills, Mind can destroy all, 374.
Mind destroys all, 493.
Illusion, death but an, 289.
of death, 251.
sleep an, 490.
trance speaking, 88.
Illusions about nerves, 392.
idolatrous, 214.
not ideas, 88.
Illusive, beliefs, 383.
dreams, 249.
Illustration of Science, optical, 111.
Illustrations, historic, 120.
Image, divine, 115.
God and His, 281.
of the beast, 327.
perceiving the divine, 205.
the divine, not lost, 259.
Images, inverted, 305.
inverted, and ideas, 301.
of disease, effacing, 396.
of thought, 86.
Imaginary cholera, 154.
Imagination, mischievous, 460.
power of, 379.
Imitation of Jesus, 329.
Immaculate conception, 315.
Immaterial pleasure, 76.
Immortal achieval, 41.
being is, 553.
birth, the, 191.
birthright, 479.
man, 292.
memory, 407.
Mind's manifestations, 81.
models, 259.
sentences, 225.
Immortality, a denial of, 80.
basis of health and, 339.
no proof of, 81.
the present, 428.
Immortals, mortals are not, 476.
mortals unlike, 295.
Immutable identity of man, 261.
Imperfect terminology, 114.
Imperishable identity, 476.
Important decision, 105.
decision, the, 181.
Impossibilities, evident, 207.
Impossible coalescence, 143.
intercommunion, 82.
partnership, 274.
tritheism, 256.
Impotence of hate, 454.
Improvisation, scientific, 89.
Inaction, no death nor, 427.
Inadequacy, philological, 115.
Inadequate theories of creation, 255.
Incentive, love the, 454.
Inception, material, 544.
Incisive questions, 33.
Incorrect theories, 73.
Independent mentality, 397.
Indestructible being, 325.
life of man, 402.
relationship, 470.
Indispensable defence, 452.
Individual experience, 26.
permanency, 258.
Individualization, 173.
Indivisibility of the infinite, 336.
Induction, proof by, 461.

Inebriate, saving the, 322.
Inexhaustible divine Love, 257, 494.
Infants, the cure of, 412.
Infinite, indivisibility of the, 336.
　one Spirit, the, 70.
　physique impossible, 258.
　Spirit, 335.
Infinitude of God, the, 267.
　true sense of, 469.
Infinity measureless, 519.
Infinity's reflection, 258.
Ingratitude and denial, 94.
　prayerful, 3.
　students', 49.
Inharmonious travellers, 21.
Inheritance heeded, 62.
Iniquity, disease far more docile than, 373.
　hidden ways of, 570.
　overcome, 446.
Injustice to the Saviour, 54.
Inoculation of thought, 449.
Insanity and agamogenesis, 68.
　cure of, 414.
　sin a form of, 407.
Insensibility to Spirit, our physical, 284.
Insidious concepts, 376.
Insight, divine, 363.
　spiritual, 95.
Insistence requisite, 412.
Inspiration of sacrifice, 54.
Inspired interpretation, 537.
Inspiring discontent, 53.
Instructions, author's early, 460.
Instruments of error, 294.
Integrity assured, 455.
Intelligence and substance, Spirit the only, 204.
　the central, 310.
Intelligent, brain not, 372.
　consecration, 428.
Intemperance, footsteps to, 158.
Intentions respected, 151.
Intercommunion, impossible, 82.
Interest, continuity of, 454.
Interior meaning, 320.
Interpretation, inspired, 537.
　right, 124.
　spiritual, 46, 501.
Interrogations, deep-reaching, 550.
Intolerance, and society, 238.
Introspection, unscientific, 319
Intuition, value of, 85.
Invalid's outlook, the, 180.
Invalids, deluded, 237.
Inventions, biological, 531.
Inversion, truth by, 129.
Inversions, metaphysical, 113.
Inverted images, 305.
　images and ideas, 301.
Investigations, earliest, 100.
Investiture, unscientific, 75.
Invocation, effectual, 15.
Irreconcilable differences, 356.
Israel the new name, 309.

J

Jacob, wrestling of, 308.
Jehovah a tribal deity, 524.
　or Elohim, 523.

Jesus and hypnotism, 185.
　as mediator, 316.
　commands of, 342.
　followers of, 495.
　imitation of, 329.
　in the tomb, 44.
　new era in, 138.
　not God, 473.
　not understood, 473.
　sonship of, 482.
　the cup of, 317.
　the miracles of, 117.
　the Scientist, 313.
　the way-shower, 30.
Jesus' disregard of matter, 210.
　own practice, 148.
　sad repast, 32.
　sinless career, 19.
　teaching belittled, 38.
Jesus Christ, the prayer of, 16.
Jewish traditions, 306.
Job, on the resurrection, 320.
John's misgivings, 132.
John the Baptist, and the Messiah, 131.
Joy, and travail, 562.
Jubilee, pæan of, 568.
Judaism antipathetic, 133.
Judge Medicine charges the jury, 433.
Judgment, day of, 291.
　on error, 535.
Jurisdiction of Mind, 379.
Jury, Judge Medicine charges the, 433.
Justice and recompense, 537.
　and substitution, 23.
Juvenile ailments, 413.

K

Key to the kingdom, 99.
Kingdom, key to the, 99.
　within, the, 476.
Knowledge and honesty, 453.
　and Truth, 299.
　dangerous, 459.
　false source of, 159.
　material, illusive, 274.
　of good and evil, 92.
　useful, 195.

L

Lack of originality, a, 126.
Language inadequate, 349.
　spiritual, 117.
Last breakfast, the, 34.
Latent fear diagnosed, 375.
　fear subdued, 199.
　power, 378.
Law and gospel, 349.
　fulfilment of the, 572.
　God's, destroys evil, 472.
　higher, ends bondage, 227.
　material, deference to, 549.
　no material, 182.
　self-constituted, 229.
　spiritual, the only law, 273.
　superior, of Soul, 62.
Lawful wonders, 135.
Laws of human belief, 184.
　of matter, no, 381.
　of nature spiritual, 183.

Learning, priestly, 133.
Leaven of Truth, 117.
Leaves of healing, the, 406.
Leprosy healed, 321.
Lesson, to-day's, 560.
Lessons, failure's, 443.
　some, from nature, 240.
Liberation of mental powers, 103.
Liberty, standard of, 227.
Liberty's crusade, 226.
Lie, the beguiling first, 533.
Life, abiding in, 325.
　all-inclusive, 430.
　and action, source of all, 283.
　discontent with, 107.
　eternal and present, 410.
　eternity of, 468.
　independent of matter, 368.
　never structural, 309.
　not contingent on matter, 427.
　of man, indestructible, 402.
　only in Spirit, 222.
　possibilities of, 489.
　real, is God, 76.
　spiritual sense of, 122.
　the creator, 331.
　true, eternal, 246.
Life's healing currents, 24.
Life-link, the divine, 350.
Life-power indestructible, 51.
Life-work, harmonious, 202.
Light and darkness, 215.
　preceding the sun, 504.
　rising to the, 509.
　shining in darkness, 108.
Like curing like, 370.
　evolving like, 276.
Likeness, reflected, 515.
Limitless Mind, 256.
Lines, new, of thought, 108.
Living temple, 27.
Loftiest adoration, 16.
Logic and revelation, 93.
　scientific, and mathematics, 128.
Loss, and selfishness, 142.
Love, and aspiration, 8.
　and man coexistent, 520.
　casteth out fear, 410.
　divine, inexhaustible, 257, 494.
　frees from fear, 373.
　impartial and universal, 12.
　imparts beauty, 516.
　man inseparable from, 304.
　the incentive, 454.
Love's endowment, 248.
Loveliness, the divine, 247.
Loving God supremely, 326.
Loyalty, divided, 462.
Lungs re-formed, the, 425.

M

Magnetism, animal, destroyed, 178.
　animal, error, 484.
　clairvoyance, 101.
Main purpose, the, 150.
Maladies, naming, 398.
Malicious barbarity, 564.
Malpractice, exclusion of, 446.
Man, Adam not ideal, 338.
　a mortal not, 200.
　and Love, coexistent, 520.

Man, birthright of, 518.
  definition of, 302.
  definitions of, 525.
  eternal, recognized, 252.
  God sustains, 388.
  God's, discerned, 259.
  governed by Mind, 151.
  ideal, and woman, 516.
  ideal, God's idea the, 346.
  immortal, 292.
  immutable identity of, 261.
  indestructible life of, 402.
  inseparable from Love, 304.
  inseparable from Spirit, 477.
  linked with Spirit, 491.
  mortal, a mis-creator, 263.
  Mortal, sentenced, 433.
  never less than man, 244.
  not evolved, 244.
  not structural, 165, 173.
  of anatomy and of theology, the,
    148.
  old and new, 300.
  reflects God, 246.
  reflects the perfect God, 337.
  scientific, 94.
  springs from Mind, 543.
  true government of, 420.
  true idea of, 337.
  unfallen, 475.
  wickedness is not, 289.
Man's entity, 369.
  entity spiritual, 303.
  genuine being, 91.
  present possibilities, 572.
Manhood, the real, 336.
Manifestations, Mind's, immortal, 81.
Manipulation unscientific, 181.
Mankind redeemed, 466.
Man-made theories, 312.
Marriage temporal, 56.
Martyrs inevitable, 37.
  testimony of, 134.
Marvels and reformations, 139.
Master's business, 52.
Masters, and servants, 216.
  serving two, 346.
  the two, 167.
Materia medica, and mythology, 158.
Material, and spiritual, 540.
  basis, no truth from a, 546.
  beliefs, 485.
  creation, no, 256.
  body never God's idea, 477.
  error, 277.
  inception, 544.
  knowledge illusive, 274.
  law, deference to, 549.
  law, no, 182.
  man as a dream, 491.
  misconceptions, 285.
  mortality, 279.
  personality, 544.
  pleasures, 38.
  recognition impossible, 284.
  skepticism, 317.
Materialistic challenge, 268.
Materialists, opposition of, 314.
Materiality, evanescent, 472.
Mathematics and scientific logic, 128.
  the spiritual, 3.
Matter and animate error, 408.

Matter, causation not in, 552.
  diagnosis of, 371.
  impotent, 358.
  is not inflamed, 415.
  is not substance, 257.
  Jesus' disregard of, 210.
  life independent of, 368.
  life not contingent on, 427.
  mindless, 210.
  Mind over, 160, 198.
  modes of, 169.
  no laws of, 381.
  no pain in, 393.
  not, but Mind, 384.
  not medicine, 369.
  sensationless, 211.
  versus matter, 145.
  versus Spirit, 171.
Matter's supposed selfhood, 479.
Meaning, interior, 320.
  spiritual, 354.
Mechanism, automatic, 399.
Mediator, Jesus as, 316.
Medica, materia, and mythology, 158.
Medical and pagan delusions, 166.
  errors, 174.
  works objectionable, 179.
Medicine and brain, 401.
  Judge, charges the jury, 433.
  matter not, 369.
  study of, 443.
  the author's experiments in, 152.
Mediumship, no, 73.
Members, severed, 295.
Memory, immortal, 407.
Mendacity of error, 554.
Mental and physical oneness, 177.
  causation, 114.
  charlatanism, 458.
  conditions to be heeded, 159.
  conspirators, 405.
  contact, 86.
  court case, a, 430.
  crimes, 105.
  despotism, 103.
  elements, 57.
  emancipation, 224.
  environment, 87.
  midwifery, 528.
  narcotics, 230.
  powers, liberation of, 103.
  preparation, 493.
  propagation, 303.
  quackery, 395.
  sculpture, 248.
  strength, 399.
  telegraphy, 243.
  tillage, 545.
Mentality, changed, 168.
  independent, 397.
  opposing, 424.
Mercy without partiality, 6.
Mere negation, 102.
Mesmerism, the evil of, 402.
Messenger, true estimate of God's,
    560.
Messengers, our angelic, 299.
Messiah, John the Baptist, and the,
    131.
  or Christ, 333.
Metaphysical inversions, 113.
  treatment, 453.

Metaphysics, benefits of, 380.
  challenges physics, 161.
  divine, 269.
Method, the one divine, 344.
Methods, mindless, 484.
  misleading, 397.
  mistaken, 79.
  of reproduction, 548.
  rejected, 143.
  right, 106.
Midwifery, mental, 528.
Millennial glory, 34, 96.
Mind, all faculties from, 488.
  anatomy and, 160.
  and body, a clean, 383.
  and stomach, 221.
  can destroy all ills, 374.
  circulates blood, 373.
  cleansing the, 234.
  creative, the, 62.
  cures hip-disease, 193.
  destroys all ills, 493.
  God the only, 319.
  governs body, 377.
  growth is from, 520.
  heals brain-disease, 387.
  imparts purity, health, and
    beauty, 371.
  is substance, 90.
  jurisdiction of, 379.
  limitless, 256.
  man governed by, 151.
  man springs from, 543.
  mortal, action of, 187.
  mortal, controlled, 400.
  mortal, definition of, 114.
  mortal, dethroned, 152.
  mortal, not a healer, 401.
  never limited, 284.
  never weary, 218.
  not matter, but, 384.
  not mortal, 210.
  one and all, 492.
  over matter, 160, 198.
  parent, God the, 336.
  removes scrofula, 424.
  sickness from mortal, 229.
  sinlessness of, Soul, 467.
  the one divine, 335.
  the only cause, 262.
  the only healer, 169.
  unbounded, the, 84.
Mind's idea faultless, 503.
  manifestations immortal, 81.
  mortal, disappearance, 251.
  pure thought, 508.
  true camera, 264.
Mind-cure, a so-called, 185.
Mind-faculties, exercise of, 487.
Mindless methods, 484.
Mind-methods, no miracles in, 212.
Mind-science, no perversion of, 421.
Miracles, ancient and modern, 243.
  basis of, 134.
  in Mind-methods, no, 212.
  of Jesus, the, 117.
  proof from, 343.
  rejected, 474.
Misbeliefs, pulmonary, 175.
Mischievous imagination, 460.
Misconceptions, material, 285.
Mis-creator, mortal man a, 263.

Pain, origin of, 153.
 unreality of, 261.
Painful prospect, 31.
Palsy, cure for, 375.
Panacea, universal, 407.
Pangs caused by the press, 197.
Panoply of wisdom, the, 458.
Pantheistic tendencies, 279.
Parable, confirmation in a, 399.
 of the creditor, 363.
Paradise regained, 171.
Pardon and amendment, 6.
 divine, 339.
Parentage, author's, 359.
Parent Mind, God the, 336.
Partiality, mercy without, 6.
Partnership, impossible, 274.
Path to perfection, purity the, 337.
Pathway, narrow, 324.
Patience and final perfection, 254.
 is wisdom, 66.
Patient, awaken the, 420.
 waiting, 238.
Patients, absent, 179.
Paul's enlightenment, 324.
 experience, 217.
Peculiarities, transmitted, 551.
Penalties, corporeal, 384.
Penalty, and sin, 40.
 honest toil has no, 385.
 remission of, 11.
Penitence or hospitality, 364.
Pentecostal power, 47.
Pentecost repeated, 43.
Perceiving the divine image, 205.
Perception, Scriptural, 548.
Peremptory demands, 327.
Perennial beauty, 121.
Perfect example, 20.
 God, man reflects the, 337.
 models, 248.
Perfection, and deformity, 244.
 final, and patience, 254.
 gained slowly, 233.
 of creation, 519.
 of divine government, 104.
 purity the path to, 337.
 requisite, 276.
 the divine standard of, 470.
Perfunctory prayers, 10.
Permanency, individual, 258.
Permanent affection, 60.
 obligation, 59.
 sensibility, 486.
Perpetual motion, 240.
 youth, 245.
Persecution harmful, 560.
 prolonged, 28.
Persistence of species, 552.
Personal conclusions, 101.
 confidence, 358.
 experience, 343.
 identity, 216.
Personality, divine, 116, 517.
 material, 544.
Pertinent proposal, 111.
Perusal and practice, 147.
Perversion of Mind-science no, 421.
Petitions, efficacious, 4.
Phenomena explained, 86.
 scientific, 72.
 the reflex, 220.

Philanthropy, benefit of, 385.
Philological inadequacy, 115.
Philosophical blunders, 250.
Physical affinity, no, 191.
 falsities, 80.
 insensibility to Spirit, our, 284.
 oneness, mental and, 177.
 science a blind belief, 124.
 science, no, 127.
Physician, Christ the great, 442.
 old-school, 149.
 the true, 366.
Physicians, harm done by, 198.
Physicians' privilege, 235.
Physics, belief in, 155.
 metaphysics challenges, 161.
Physiology deficient, 148.
 or Spirit, 182.
 unscientific, 170.
 versus ontology, 556.
Physique, infinite, impossible, 258.
Pilate's question, 48.
Pillory, the real, 50.
Pleading, Christian, 418.
 unspoken, 411.
Pleasure, immaterial, 76.
 mythical, 294.
Pleasures, material, 38.
Plurality, Elohistic, 515.
Poison defined mentally, 177.
Poor post-mortem evidence, 81.
Position, strong, 344.
Positive reassurance, 420.
Possibilities, man's present, 572.
 of Life, 489.
Post-mortem evidence, poor, 81.
Postulates, erroneous, 91.
Potency, transient, of drugs, 370.
Potter, clay replying to the, 429.
Power, divine, denials of, 232.
 error's, imaginary, 403.
 human, a blind force, 192.
 latent, 378.
 mental, the misuse of, 105.
 of habit, 194.
 of imagination, 379.
 opposing, 92.
 Pentecostal, 47.
 spiritual, 67.
 the one real, 192.
Powerless promises, 65.
Powers, mental, liberation of, 103
Practical arguments, 355.
 preaching, 201.
 religion, 9.
 Science, 128.
 success, 162.
Practice, and perusal, 147.
 and Principle, 113.
 belief and, 202.
 Jesus' own, 148.
 proof in, 26.
Prayer, audible, danger from, 7.
 for the sick, 12.
 of Jesus Christ, the, 16.
Prayerful ingratitude, 3.
Prayers, perfunctory, 10.
Praying, audible, 7.
Preaching, practical, 201.
Precedence, question of, 142.
Prediction of a naturalist, 548.
 Saviour's, 52.

Premises, fatal, 351.
Preparation, mental, 493.
Prerogative, heaven-bestowed, 253.
Presence, beatific, 266.
 bodily, 14.
Present immortality, the, 428.
 Life eternal and, 410.
 salvation, 39.
Press, pangs caused by the, 197.
Pride, priestly, humbled, 228.
Priestly learning, 133.
 pride humbled, 228.
Primitive error, 292.
Principle and practice, 113.
 of all, God the, 272.
 the divine, and idea, 333.
 unchanging, 112.
Privilege, physicians', 235.
 the age's, 93.
 the Christian's, 556.
Probation, and salvation, 291.
Processes, the three, 549.
Producer, the real, 551.
Profession, more than, required,
 141.
 and proof, 233.
Progeny cursed, 532.
Progress and purgatory, 77.
 condition of, 496.
 demanded, 240.
Progressive development, 64.
Promise perpetual, 328.
Promises, powerless, 65.
Proof, and profession, 233.
 by induction, 461.
 from miracles, 343.
 given in healing, 547.
 in practice, 26.
 of immortality, no, 81.
Proofs, spiritual, of existence, 264.
Propensities inherited, 61.
Propensity, will-power an animal,
 490.
Propagation, divine, 507.
 mental, 303.
Proper self-government, 106.
 stimulus, 420.
Prophetic ignorance, 270.
Proposal, pertinent, 111.
Propositions, reversible, 113.
Prospect, painful, 31.
Prostration, unnecessary, 390.
Providence, divine, 530.
Psychical, and Ptolemaic error, 123.
Ptolemaic and psychical error,
 123.
Public exaggerations, 13.
Pulmonary misbeliefs, 175.
Pure ideas, multiplication of, 512.
 religion enthroned, 571.
Purgation, scientific, 296.
Purgatory, and progress, 77.
Purification, future, 290.
Purity, health, and beauty, Mind
 imparts, 371.
 of science, 457.
 the conflict with, 565.
 the path to perfection, 337.
Purity's rebuke, 52.
Purpose, final, 36.
 of crucifixion, 24.
 the main, 150.

Spiritual reflection, 479.
refreshment, 32.
sanctuary, 15.
sense of life, 122.
spheres, 513.
structure, 283.
subdivision, 510.
sunlight, 561.
synonyms, 468.
tangibility, 279.
thoughts, 286.
translation, 209.
universe, 116.
wedlock, 574.
Spiritualism, ancient, 136.
Spirituality, health from reliance on, 166.
of Scripture, 272.
Spiritualized consciousness, 14.
Stages of existence, 550.
Standard, Christian, 426.
God's, 2.
higher, for mortals, 197.
of liberty, 227.
of perfection, the divine, 470.
only one, 539.
Standpoint, erroneous, 545.
revealed, 239.
Standpoints changed, 322.
conflicting, 83.
Starting-point, Spirit the, 275.
Starvation and dyspepsia, 221.
Stately advance, a, 156.
Stature, human, 190.
Statutes, higher, 307.
Steadfast and calm trust, 495.
Stimulus, false, 186.
proper, 420.
Sting of the serpent, the, 563.
Stomach, and mind, 221.
Stone rolled away, the, 45.
Stones, the chief, in the temple, 288.
Storm, weathering the, 67.
Story of error, the, 521.
Strength, divine, 79.
mental, 399.
of Spirit, the, 393.
refuge and, 444.
Strong position, 344.
Structure, spiritual, 283.
Struggle and victory, the, 145.
the holy, 33.
Students' ingratitude, 49.
Studious disciples, 271.
Study, divine, 202.
of medicine, 443.
Subdivision, spiritual, 510.
Sublime summary, 138.
Subordination of evil, 207.
Substance, and intelligence, Spirit the only, 204.
is Spirit, 278.
matter is not, 257.
Mind is, 90.
spiritual, 350.
the only, 335.
thought seen as, 310.
versus supposition, 278.
Substitution, and justice, 23.
Success, half-way, 167.
practical, 162.

Success, veritable, 372.
Suffering, climax of, 543.
expiation by, 569.
inevitable, 40.
sin destroyed through, 196.
uses of, 322.
vicarious, 36.
Suggestion, a useful, 58.
first evil, 544.
Suicide and sin, 203.
Summary, sublime, 138.
Summit of aspiration, 9.
Sun and Soul, the, 119.
light preceding the, 504.
Sunlight, spiritual, 561.
Superiority, so-called, 409.
to sickness and sin, 231.
Superior law of Soul, 62.
Supernal, espousals, 561.
Superstition obsolete, 353.
Supplies, heavenly, 33.
Supply, and need, 323.
Supported by facts, 341.
Supposed selfhood, matter's, 479.
Supposition, substance *versus*, 278.
Supremacy, one, 357.
the deific, 330.
Sure reward of righteousness, 203.
Surgery, bone-healing by, 422.
hypnotic, 528.
skilful, 401.
Sustenance spiritual, 388.
Symbols, opposite, 282.
seraphic, 512.
Synonyms, divine, 115, 275.
spiritual, 468.
System, reduction to, 147.
Systems, cramping, 226.

T

Talking disease, avoid, 396.
Tangibility, spiritual, 279.
Tares and wheat, the, 300.
Teachers, obligations of, 451.
testimony of medical, 162.
Teachers' functions, 235.
Teaching children, 237.
Jesus', belittled, 38.
Teeth, and eyes, renewed, 247.
Telegraphy, mental, 243.
Temperance reform, 404.
Temperature is mental, 374.
Temptation from God, no, 527.
Temple cleansed, 142.
living, 27.
the chief stones in the, 288.
Tendencies, pantheistic, 279.
Tendency, animal, 563.
Terminology, imperfect, 114.
Terms adopted by the author, 483.
scientific, 127.
Testament, New, basis, 271.
Testimony, false, refuted, 396.
mixed, 296.
of martyrs, 134.
of medical teachers, 162.
of sense, 252.
of Soul, 253.
of the senses, 122.
opposing, 122.
reversal of, 120.

Test of experience, the, 471.
Tests, confirmatory, 111.
in our day, 149.
Theology, Hebrew, 315.
healthful, 138.
the man of anatomy and of, 148.
Theories, antagonistic, 129.
helpless, 490.
incorrect, 73.
man-made, 312.
of creation, inadequate, 255.
rejected, 269.
unscientific, 204.
weakness of material, 356.
Theory, true, of the universe, 547.
Things of God are beautiful, the, 280.
thoughts are, 261.
This volume indispensable, 456.
Thorns and flowers, the, 41.
Thought, all activity from, 152.
all nativity in, 553.
eradicate error from, 400.
evil, depletes, 416.
exalted, 506.
formation from, 423.
images of, 86.
inoculation of, 449.
Mind's pure, 508.
new lines of, 108.
qualities of, 514.
rarefaction of, 509.
regarding death, 79.
rise of, 174.
seen as substance, 310.
sickness as only, 208.
Truth calms the, 415.
Thought-angels, 298.
Thought-forms, 306.
Thoughts are things, 261.
continuity of, 513.
God's, are spiritual realities, 514.
reading, 82.
sinful, embryonic, 188.
spiritual, 286.
unfolding of, 506.
Thought-transference, 103.
Three classes of neophytes, 450.
processes, the, 549.
Tide, the time and, 125.
Ties, fleshly, temporal, 31.
Tillage, mental, 545.
Time and tide, the, 125.
To-day, choose ye, 360.
To-day's lesson, 560.
Toil, honest, has no penalty, 385.
Tomb, Jesus in the, 44.
Touchstone of Science, 450.
Tractability, children's, 236.
Traditions, Jewish, 306.
Traitor's conspiracy, the, 47.
Trance speaking illusion, 88.
Transient potency of drugs, 370.
Transitional qualities, 115.
Transition and reform, 65.
Translation, spiritual, 209.
Translations, scientific, 485.
Transmitted peculiarities, 551.
Travail and joy, 562.
Travellers, inharmonious, 21.
Treasure in heaven, 451.
Treatment, metaphysical, 453.

APPENDIX B

LIST OF THE SCRIPTURAL QUOTATIONS

IN

SCIENCE AND HEALTH

WITH KEY TO THE SCRIPTURES

LIST OF THE SCRIPTURAL QUOTATIONS

IN

SCIENCE AND HEALTH

WITH KEY TO THE SCRIPTURES

OLD TESTAMENT

Genesis

1: 1 In the beginning God created the heaven and the earth.— *g* 502–22.

1: 1, 2 "In the beginning God created the heaven and the earth. And the earth was without form, and void ; and darkness was upon the face of the deep."— *r* 479–18.

1: 2 And the earth was without form, and void ; and darkness was upon the face of the deep. And the spirit of God moved upon the face of the waters. — *g* 503–6.

1: 2 "darkness…upon the face of the deep,"— *b* 338–18.

1: 3 And God said, Let there be light : and there was light.— *g* 503–18.

1: 3 "Let there be light,"— *c* 255–3 ; *g* 556–19.

1: 4 And God saw the light, that it was good : and God divided the light from the darkness.— *g* 503–26.

1: 5 And God called the light Day, and the darkness He called Night. And the evening and the morning were the first day.— *g* 504–3.

1: 5 "And the evening and the morning were the first day."— *gl* 584–3.

1: 6 And God said, Let there be a firmament in the midst of the waters, and let it divide the waters from the waters.— *g* 505–4.

1: 7 And God made the firmament, and divided the waters which were under the firmament from the waters which were above the firmament : and it was so.— *g* 505–13.

1: 8 And God called the firmament Heaven. And the evening and the morning were the second day.— *g* 506–8.

1: 9 And God said, Let the waters under the heaven be gathered together unto one place, and let the dry land appear : and it was so.— *g* 506–15.

1: 10 And God called the dry land Earth ; and the gathering together of the waters called He Seas : and God saw that it was good.— *g* 506–22.

1: 10 "And God called the dry land Earth ; and the gathering together of the waters called He Seas." — *g* 535–29.

1: 11 And God said, Let the earth bring forth grass, the herb yielding seed, and the fruit tree yielding fruit after his kind, whose seed is in itself, upon the earth : and it was so.— *g* 507–11.

1: 11 "whose seed is in itself."— *g* 511–3.

1: 12 And the earth brought forth grass, and herb yielding seed after his kind, and the tree yielding fruit, whose seed was in itself, after his kind : and God saw that it was good.— *g* 508–9.

1: 13 And the evening and the morning were the third day.— *g* 508–26.

1: 14 And God said, Let there be lights in the firmament of the heaven, to divide the day from the night ; and let them be for signs, and for seasons, and for days, and years.— *g* 509–9.

1: 15 And let them be for lights in the firmament of the heaven, to give light upon the earth : and it was so.— *g* 509–7.

1: 16 And God made two great lights ; the greater light to rule the day, and the lesser light to rule the night : He made the stars also.— *g* 510–13.

1: 17, 18 And God set them in the firmament of the heaven, to give light upon the earth, and to rule over the day and over the night, and to divide the light from the darkness : and God saw that it was good. — *g* 511–7.

Genesis

1: 19 And the evening and the morning were the fourth day.— *g* 511–15.

1: 20 And God said, Let the waters bring forth abundantly the moving creature that hath life, and fowl that may fly above the earth in the open firmament of heaven.— *g* 511–19.

1: 21 And God created great whales, and every living creature that moveth, which the waters brought forth abundantly, after their kind, and every winged fowl after his kind : and God saw that it was good.— *g* 512–4.

1: 22 And God blessed them, saying, Be fruitful, and multiply, and fill the waters in the seas ; and let fowl multiply in the earth.— *g* 512–17.

1: 23 And the evening and the morning were the fifth day. — *g* 513–4.

1: 24 And God said, Let the earth bring forth the living creature after his kind, cattle, and creeping thing, and beast of the earth after his kind : and it was so.— *g* 513–14.

1: 25 And God made the beast of the earth after his kind, and cattle after their kind, and everything that creepeth upon the earth after his kind : and God saw that it was good.— *g* 513–22.

1: 25 "And God saw that it was good."— *g* 515–2.

1: 26 And God said, Let us make man in our image, after our likeness ; and let them have dominion over the fish of the sea, and over the fowl of the air, and over the cattle, and over all the earth, and over every creeping thing that creepeth upon the earth. — *r* 475–23 ; *g* 515–11.

1: 26 Let us make man in our image, after our likeness ; and let them have dominion.— *p* 438–3.

1: 26 "image" "likeness"— *sp* 94–5, 6.

1: 26 "Let *them* have dominion."— *g* 515–21.

1: 26 "dominion…over the fish of the sea, and over the fowl of the air, and over the cattle,"— *f* 222–23.

1: 27 So God created man in His own image, in the image of God created He him ; male and female created He them.— *g* 516–24.

1: 27 "image"— *b* 301–24.

1: 27 "male and female"— *f* 249–5.

1: 28 And God blessed them, and God said unto them, Be fruitful, and multiply, and replenish the earth, and subdue it ; and have dominion over the fish of the sea, and over the fowl of the air, and over every living thing that moveth upon the earth.— *g* 517–25.

1: 28 "multiply and replenish the earth."— *g* 511–4.

1: 29, 30 And God said, Behold, I have given you every herb bearing seed, which is upon the face of all the earth, and every tree, in the which is the fruit of a tree yielding seed ; to you it shall be for meat. And to every beast of the earth, and to every fowl of the air, and to everything that creepeth upon the earth, wherein there is life, I have given every green herb for meat : and it was so.— *g* 518–5.

1: 31 And God saw everything that He had made, and, behold, it was very good. And the evening and the morning were the sixth day.— *g* 518–24.

1: 31 "and, behold, it was very good."— *g* 525–24.

2: 1 Thus the heavens and the earth were finished, and all the host of them.— *p* 519–7.

2: 2 And on the seventh day God ended His work which He had made ; and He rested on the seventh day from all His work which He had made.— *g* 519–22.

Genesis

2 : 4   "In the day that the Lord God [Jehovah God] made the earth and the heavens," — *g* 543–31.

2 : 4, 5   These are the generations of the heavens and of the earth when they were created, in the day that the Lord God [Jehovah] made the earth and the heavens, and every plant of the field before it was in the earth, and every herb of the field before it grew : for the Lord God [Jehovah] had not caused it to rain upon the earth, and there was not a man to till the ground. — *g* 520–16.

2 : 5   "plant of the field before it was in the earth." — *g* 509–23.

2 : 5   "every plant of the field before it was in the earth." — *g* 526–4.

2 : 5   "not a man to till the ground." — *g* 544–5.

2 : 6   But there went up a mist from the earth, and watered the whole face of the ground. — *g* 521–21.

2 : 6   "There went up a mist from the earth." — *g* 546–12.

2 : 7   And the Lord God [Jehovah] formed man of the dust of the ground, and breathed into his nostrils the breath of life ; and man became a living soul. — *g* 524–13.

2 : 9   And out of the ground made the Lord God [Jehovah] to grow every tree that is pleasant to the sight, and good for food ; the tree of life also, in the midst of the garden, and the tree of knowledge of good and evil. — *g* 525–30.

2 : 9   "the tree of life" — *g* 527–18.

2 : 9   "tree of life," — *p* 426–13 ; *g* 526–17 ; 538–13.

2 : 9   "the tree of knowledge." — *ph* 165–1.

2 : 9   "tree of knowledge," — *f* 214–22 ; *g* 526–19 ; 538–14.

2 : 15   And the Lord God [Jehovah] took the man, and put him into the garden of Eden, to dress it and to keep it. — *g* 526–26.

2 : 16, 17   And the Lord God [Jehovah] commanded the man, saying, Of every tree of the garden thou mayest freely eat : but of the tree of the knowledge of good and evil, thou shalt not eat of it : for in the day that thou eatest thereof thou shalt surely die. — *g* 527–6.

2 : 17   "the tree of the knowledge of good and evil," — *f* 220–27.

2 : 17   "tree of the knowledge of good and evil," — *r* 481–16.

2 : 17   "Thou shalt not eat of it." — *f* 220–29.

2 : 17   "In the day that thou eatest thereof thou shalt surely die." — *ph* 197–9 ; *r* 481–18 ; *g* 532–8.

2 : 17   "Thou shalt surely die ;" — *b* 277–3 ; *gl* 580–20.

2 : 19   And out of the ground the Lord God [Jehovah] formed every beast of the field, and every fowl of the air ; and brought them unto Adam to see what he would call them : and whatsoever Adam called every living creature, that was the name thereof. — *g* 527–21.

2 : 21, 22   And the Lord God [Jehovah, Yawah] caused a deep sleep to fall upon Adam, and he slept: and He took one of his ribs, and closed up the flesh instead thereof ; and the rib, which the Lord God [Jehovah] had taken from man, made He a woman, and brought her unto the man. — *g* 528–9.

3 : 1–3   Now the serpent was more subtle than any beast of the field which the Lord God [Jehovah] had made. And he said unto the woman, Yea, hath God said, Ye shall not eat of every tree of the garden? And the woman said unto the serpent, We may eat of the fruit of the trees of the garden : but of the fruit of the tree which is in the midst of the garden, God hath said, Ye shall not eat of it, neither shall ye touch it, lest ye die. — *g* 529–13.

3 : 1   "more subtle than any beast of the field." — *ap* 564–32.

3 : 4, 5   And the serpent said unto the woman, Ye shall not surely die : for God doth know that in the day ye eat thereof, then your eyes shall be opened ; and ye shall be as gods, knowing good and evil. — *g* 530–13.

3 : 5   "Ye shall be as gods." — *b* 280–21 ; 307–5 ; *g* 541–24 ; 544–21 ; *gl* 587–15.

3 : 9, 10   And the Lord God [Jehovah] called unto Adam, and said unto him, Where art thou? And he said, I heard Thy voice in the garden, and I was afraid, because I was naked ; and I hid myself. — *g* 532–13.

3 : 9   "Adam, where art thou?" — *ph* 181–24 ; *b* 308–8.

3 : 9   "Where art thou?" — *b* 308–7.

3 : 11, 12   And He said, Who told thee that thou wast naked? Hast thou eaten of the tree, whereof I commanded thee that thou shouldst not eat? And the man said, The woman whom Thou gavest to be with me, she gave me of the tree, and I did eat. — *g* 533–5.

3 : 13   "The serpent beguiled me, and I did eat ;" — *g* 533–28.

3 : 14, 15   And the Lord God [Jehovah] said unto the serpent, . . . I will put enmity between thee and the woman, and between thy seed and her seed ; it shall bruise thy head, and thou shalt bruise his heel. — *g* 534–8.

3 : 16   Unto the woman He said, I will greatly multiply thy

Genesis

sorrow and thy conception : in sorrow thou shalt bring forth children ; and thy desire shall be to thy husband, and he shall rule over thee. — *g* 535–6.

3 : 16   "In sorrow thou shalt bring forth children." — *g* 557–18.

3 : 17–19   And unto Adam He said, Because thou hast hearkened unto the voice of thy wife, and hast eaten of the tree of which I commanded thee, saying, Thou shalt not eat of it : cursed is the ground for thy sake ; in sorrow shalt thou eat of it all the days of thy life : thorns also and thistles shall it bring forth to thee ; and thou shalt eat the herb of the field : in the sweat of thy face shalt thou eat bread, till thou return unto the ground ; for out of it wast thou taken : for dust thou art, and unto dust shalt thou return. — *g* 535–19.

3 : 19   "Dust [nothingness] thou art, and unto dust [nothingness] shalt thou return." — *g* 545–29.

3 : 22–24   And the Lord God [Jehovah] said, Behold, the man is become as one of us, to know good and evil : and now, lest he put forth his hand, and take also of the tree of life, and eat, and live forever ; therefore the Lord God [Jehovah] sent him forth from the garden of Eden, to till the ground from whence he was taken. So He drove out the man : and He placed at the east of the garden of Eden Cherubims, and a flaming sword which turned every way, to keep the way of the tree of life. — *g* 536–30.

3 : 22   "Behold, the man is become as one of us." — *g* 545–3.

3 : 24   "the tree of life." — *t* 458–18.

4 : 1   And Adam knew Eve his wife ; and she conceived, and bare Cain, and said, I have gotten a man from the Lord [Jehovah]. — *g* 538–23.

4 : 1   "I have gotten a man from the Lord," — *r* 479–4 ; *g* 538–30.

4 : 3, 4   Cain brought of the fruit of the ground an offering unto the Lord [Jehovah]. And Abel, he also brought of the firstlings of his flock, and of the fat thereof. — *g* 540–25.

4 : 4, 5   And the Lord [Jehovah] had respect unto Abel, and to his offering : but unto Cain, and to his offering, He had not respect. — *g* 541–6.

4 : 8   Cain rose up against Abel his brother, and slew him. — *g* 541–14.

4 : 9   And the Lord [Jehovah] said unto Cain, Where is Abel thy brother? And he said, I know not : Am I my brother's keeper? — *g* 541–19.

4 : 10, 11   And He [Jehovah] said, . . . The voice of thy brother's blood crieth unto Me from the ground. And now art thou cursed from the earth. — *g* 541–27.

4 : 15   And the Lord [Jehovah] said unto him, Therefore whosoever slayeth Cain, vengeance shall be taken on him sevenfold. And the Lord [Jehovah] set a mark upon Cain, lest any finding him should kill him. — *g* 542–14.

4 : 16   And Cain went out from the presence of the Lord [Jehovah], and dwelt in the land of Nod. — *g* 542–27.

5 : 24   "walked with God," — *f* 214–6.

6 : 3   "And the Lord said, My spirit shall not always strive with man, for that he also is flesh," — *b* 320–12.

8 : 21   "for man's sake." — *b* 338–29.

9 : 6   "Whoso sheddeth man's blood, by man shall his blood be shed." — *a* 30–15.

13 : 8   "Let there be no strife, I pray thee, between me and thee, and between my herdmen and thy herdmen ; for we be brethren." — *t* 444–25.

18 : 25   "Shall not the Judge of all the earth do right?" — *t* 442–4.

32 : 26   "Let me go, for the day breaketh ;" — *b* 308–24.

32 : 27   "What is thy name?" — *b* 308–29.

32 : 28   "as a prince" — *b* 308–30.

32 : 28   "power with God and with men." — *b* 308–31.

32 : 29   "Tell me, I pray thee, *thy* name ;" — *b* 308–32.

Exodus

4 : 8   "It shall come to pass, if they will not believe thee, neither hearken to the voice of the first sign, that they will believe the voice of the latter sign." — *b* 321–27.

6 : 3   *And I appeared unto Abraham, unto Isaac, and unto Jacob by the name of God Almighty ; but by My name Jehovah was I not known to them.* — *g* 501–*.

15 : 3   "a man of war," — *g* 524–10.

15 : 18   "the Lord shall reign forever." — *pref* vii–20.

15 : 26   "I am the Lord that healeth thee," — *b* 276–2.

20 : 3   "Thou shalt have no other gods before me." — *a* 19–29 ; *b* 280–18 ; 340–15 ; *r* 467–3.

20 : 10   "stranger that is within thy gates," — *s* 146–20.

20 : 13   "Thou shalt not kill." — *m* 56–19.

20 : 14   "Thou shalt not commit adultery," — *m* 56–18.

20 : 15   "Thou shalt not steal." — *s* 112–31.

33 : 20   "Thou canst not see My face ; for there shall no man see Me, and live." — *s* 140–5.

Deuteronomy

4: 35   "The Lord He is God [good] ; there is none else beside Him." — *p* 414–21.

6: 4   "Hear, O Israel : the Lord our God is one Lord." — *c* 256–12.

29: 20   "The anger of the Lord." — *b* 293–25.

I Kings

19: 12   "still, small voice" — *b* 323–29 ; *p* 367–25 ; *ap* 559–8.

Job

3: 25   "The thing which I greatly feared is come upon me." — *p* 411–1.

4: 17, 18   Shall mortal man be more just than God?
Shall man be more pure than his Maker?
Behold, He putteth no trust in His ministering spirits,
And His angels He chargeth with frailty. — *o* 360–24.
(The above reference is from the translation of the late Rev. George R. Noyes, D.D.)

11: 7   "Canst thou by searching find out God?" — *b* 322–31 ; *g* 551–26.

14: 1   "Man that is born of a woman is of few days, and full of trouble." — *g* 552–14.

14: 1   "of few days, and full of trouble." — *g* 536–21.

18: 14   "king of terrors" — *b* 289–15.

19: 26   "In my flesh shall I see God," — *b* 320–25.

22: 21   "acquaint now thyself with Him, and be at peace." — *b* 324–12.

33: 24   "I have found a ransom." — *b* 276–3.

34: 3   "The ear trieth words, as the mouth tasteth meat." — *s* 115–8.

38: 7   "the morning stars sang together." — *g* 509–22.

38: 28   "who hath begotten the drops of dew," — *c* 257–19.

38: 32   "forth Mazzaroth in his season," — *c* 257–20.

38: 32   "Arcturus with his sons." — *c* 257–21.

42: 5   "I have heard of Thee by the hearing of the ear : but now mine eye seeth Thee." — *c* 262–17.

Psalms

8: 6   "Thou madest him to have dominion over the works of Thy hands. Thou hast put all things under his feet." — *ph* 200–13.

14: 2   "children of men," — *s* 148–9 ; *p* 409–22 ; *t* 444–29.

17: 15   As for me, I will behold Thy face in righteousness : I shall be satisfied, when I awake, with Thy likeness. — *ph* 190–28.

19: 7   "making wise the simple." — *o* 342–4.

19: 8   "rejoicing the heart." — *c* 266–2.

23: 1–6   [DIVINE LOVE] is my shepherd ; I shall not want.
[LOVE] maketh me to lie down in green pastures : [LOVE] leadeth me beside the still waters.
[LOVE] restoreth my soul [spiritual sense] : [LOVE] leadeth me in the paths of righteousness for His name's sake.
Yea, though I walk through the valley of the shadow of death, I will fear no evil : for [LOVE] is with me ; [LOVE'S] rod and [LOVE'S] staff they comfort me.
[LOVE] prepareth a table before me in the presence of mine enemies : [LOVE] anointeth my head with oil ; my cup runneth over.
Surely goodness and mercy shall follow me all the days of my life ; and I will dwell in the house [the consciousness] of [LOVE] for ever. — *ap* 578–5.

23: 2   "green pastures, . . . beside the still waters." — *g* 514–13.

23: 4   "Though I walk through the valley of the shadow of death, I will fear no evil." — *gl* 596–21.

29: 2   "the beauty of holiness," — *s* 135–12.

36: 9   For with Thee is the fountain of life ; In Thy light shall we see light. — *ph* 190–30.

36: 9   "light shall we see light ;" — *g* 510–10.

37: 11   "The meek shall inherit the earth." — *g* 516–14.

37: 35   "like a green bay tree ;" — *pr* 5–19.

42: 11   *Why art thou cast down, O my soul [sense] ? And why art thou disquieted within me? Hope thou in God ; for I shall yet praise Him, Who is the health of my countenance and my God.* — *p* 362–*.

46: 1   "God is our refuge and strength, a very present help in trouble." — *t* 444–11.

46: 1   "a very present help in trouble." — *pr* 13–1 ; *f* 202–27.

46: 6   "He uttered His voice, the earth melted." — *sp* 97–26.

48: 1   *Great is the Lord, and greatly to be praised in the city of our God, in the mountain of His holiness.* — *ap* 558–*.

48: 2   "Beautiful for situation, the joy of the whole earth, is mount Zion, on the sides of the north, the city of the great King." — *ap* 575–22.

50: 10   "the cattle upon a thousand hills." — *g* 514–16.

51: 5   "shapen in iniquity ;" — *g* 540–29.

78: 19   "Can God furnish a table in the wilderness?" — *s* 135–19.

89: 50, 51   *Remember, Lord, the reproach of Thy servants ; how I do bear in my bosom the reproach of all the mighty people ; wherewith Thine enemies*

Psalms

have reproached, O Lord ; wherewith they have reproached the footsteps of Thine anointed. — *f* 201–*.

91: 6   "the pestilence that walketh in darkness, . . . the destruction that wasteth at noonday." — *m* 56–16.

93: 2   *Thy throne is established of old ; Thou art from everlasting.* — *c* 255–*.

93: 4   "The Lord on high is mightier than the noise of many waters, yea, than the mighty waves of the sea." — *s* 505–18.

102: 26   "As a vesture shalt Thou change them and they shall be changed." — *s* 125–24.

103: 15, 16   "As for man, his days are as grass : as a flower of the field, so he flourisheth. For the wind passeth over it, and it is gone ; and the place thereof shall know it no more." — *ph* 190–23 ; *r* 476–24.

107: 20   *He sent His word, and healed them, and delivered them from their destructions.* — *ph* 165–*.

111: 10   "The fear of the Lord is the beginning of wisdom," — *p* 373–15.

114: 5–7   "What ailed thee, O thou sea, that thou fleddest? Thou Jordan, that thou wast driven back ? Ye mountains, that ye skipped like rams, and ye little hills, like lambs? Tremble, thou earth, at the presence of the Lord, at the presence of the God of Jacob." — *s* 135–1.

118: 16   "The right hand of the Lord is exalted." — *a* 38–16.

146: 10   "the Lord shall reign forever." — *pref* vii–20.

Proverbs

4: 18   "unto the perfect day." — *r* 496–13 ; *ap* 562–20.

9: 9   *Give instruction to a wise man, and he will be yet wiser : teach a just man, and he will increase in learning.* — *t* 443–*.

23: 7   "As he thinketh in his heart, so is he." — *sp* 89–13 ; *f* 213–4 ; *p* 383–28.

23: 27   "strange woman" — *p* 362–6.

28: 13   "He that covereth his sins shall not prosper : but whoso confesseth and forsaketh them shall have mercy." — *t* 448–17.

30: 4   "wind in His fists ;" — *ph* 192–18.

Ecclesiastes

1: 2   "All is vanity." — *f* 239–32.

7: 29   "sought out many inventions," — *ph* 196–2.

9: 8   "let thy garments be always white." — *c* 267–27.

11: 3   "In the place where the tree falleth, there it shall be." — *b* 291–19.

12: 1   "I have no pleasure in them." — *s* 107–18.

12: 13   "Let us hear the conclusion of the whole matter : Fear God, and keep His commandments : for this is the whole duty of man." — *b* 340–6.

Song of Solomon

5: 16   "altogether lovely ;" — *pr* 3–14.

7: 12   *Let us get up early to the vineyards : let us see if the vine flourish, whether the tender grape appear, and the pomegranates bud forth.* — *fr* 600–*.

Isaiah

1: 5   "sick, and the whole heart faint ;" — *f* 219–12.

8: 19   *And when they shall say unto you, Seek unto them that have familiar spirits, And unto wizards that peep and that mutter; Should not a people seek unto their God?* — *sp* 70–*.

9: 6   "Unto us a child is born, . . . and his name shall be called Wonderful." — *s* 109–26.

11: 6   The wolf also shall dwell with the lamb, And the leopard shall lie down with the kid ; And the calf and the young lion, and the fatling together ; And a little child shall lead them. — *g* 514–22.

28: 10   *For precept must be upon precept, precept upon precept; line upon line, line upon line ; here a little, and there a little.* — *r* 465–*.

40: 31   "They that wait upon the Lord . . . shall run, and not be weary ; and they shall walk, and not faint." — *f* 218–27.

40: 31   "run, and not be weary ; . . . walk, and not faint," — *f* 254–3.

45: 7   "I make peace, and create evil. I the Lord do all these things ;" — *g* 540–5.

52: 7   "beautiful upon the mountains," — *p* 442–14.

52: 7   "that bringeth good tidings." — *p* 442–15.

53: 1   "the arm of the Lord" — *a* 24–11.

53: 3   "Despised and rejected of men," — *a* 20–16 ; *52*–13.

53: 3   "man of sorrows" — *a* 42–9 ; *52*–19.

53: 4   "stricken, smitten of God." — *a* 49–32.

53: 5   "with his stripes [the rejection of error] we are healed." — *a* 20–15.

53: 7   "He opened not his mouth." — *a* 48–19.

53: 7   *opened not his mouth.* — *ap* 564–18.

53: 7   "He is brought as a lamb to the slaughter, and as a sheep before her shearers is dumb, so he openeth not his mouth." — *a* 50–3.

53: 8   "Who shall declare his generation ?" — *a* 50–3.

55: 1   "Ho, every one that thirsteth, come ye to the waters." — *pr* 13–3.

Isaiah

55: 7 "Let the wicked forsake his way, and the unrighteous man his thoughts."—f 239–14.
55: 7 "forsake his way, and the unrighteous man his thoughts."—s 139–1.

Jeremiah

5: 19 "strange gods."—g 524–7.
17: 1 "with the point of a diamond"—g 521–16
31: 34 "they shall all know Me [God], from the least of them unto the greatest."—f 242–4.

Lamentations

3: 35 "aside the right of a man before the face of the Most High,"—a 49–31.

Ezekiel

18: 2 "the fathers have eaten sour grapes, and the children's teeth are set on edge."—f 211–19.
21: 27 "He come whose right it is."—f 223–32.

Daniel

4: 35 "doeth according to His will in the army of heaven, and among the inhabitants of the earth ; and none can stay His hand, or say unto Him, What doest Thou?"—c 256–20.
7: 9 "the Ancient of days."—s 146–28.

Habakkuk

1: 13 "of purer eyes than to behold evil,"—f 243–22 ; o 357–4.

NEW TESTAMENT

Matthew

1: 23 "God with us,"—pref xi–16 ; s 107–8.
2: 9 "where the young child was,"—ph 191–11.
3: 3 "the voice of one crying in the wilderness"—f 208–19.
3: 15 "Suffer it to be so now : for thus it becometh us to fulfil all righteousness."—m 56–3.
4: 4 "Man shall not live by bread alone, but by every word that proceedeth out of the mouth of God,"—p 410–10.
5: 8 "Blessed are the pure in heart : for they shall see God."—b 324–5; o 341–9.
5: 13 "Ye are the salt of the earth."—b 367–18.
5: 13 "lost his savour ;"—s 153–7.
5: 14 "Ye are the light of the world. A city that is set on an hill cannot be hid."—b 367–19.
5: 17 "I am not come to destroy, but to fulfil."—r 474–20.
5: 25 "Agree with thine adversary quickly, whiles thou art in the way with him."—p 390–18.
5: 25 "adversary quickly,"—s 161–32.
5: 26 "the uttermost farthing."—pr 5–11.
5: 38 "An eye for an eye,"—a 30–15.
5: 39 "Whosoever shall smite thee on thy right cheek, turn to him the other also."—t 444–19.
5: 48 "Be ye therefore perfect, even as your Father which is in heaven is perfect !"—a 37–28 ; c 259–19.
5: 48 "Be ye therefore perfect,"—f 253–32.
5: 48 "Father which is in heaven is perfect."—r 485–23.
6: 6 "When thou prayest, enter into thy closet, and, when thou hast shut thy door, pray to thy Father which is in secret ; and thy Father, which seeth in secret, shall reward thee openly."—pr 14–31.
6: 7 "vain repetitions,"—pr 13–9.
6: 8 Your Father knoweth what things ye have need of, before ye ask Him.—pr 1–*.
6: 9 "After this manner therefore pray ye,"—pr 16–9.
6: 9 Our Father which art in heaven, Hallowed be Thy name.—pr 16–26.
6: 10 Thy kingdom come.—pr 16–30.
6: 10 Thy will be done in earth, as it is in heaven.—pr 17–1.
6: 10 "in earth, as it is in heaven."—b 339–24.
6: 11 Give us this day our daily bread ;—pr 17–4.
6: 12 And forgive us our debts, as we forgive our debtors.—pr 17–6.
6: 12 "Forgive us our debts,"—pr 11–2.
6: 13 And lead us not into temptation, but deliver us from evil ;—pr 17–8.
6: 13 For Thine is the kingdom, and the power, and the glory, forever.—pr 17–12.
6: 13 "Deliver us from evil,"—pr 16–15.
6: 19 "where moth and rust doth corrupt."—f 241–5.
6: 21 "Where your treasure is, there will your heart be also."—ph 181–29 ; c 262–25.
6: 22 "the light of the body is the eye,"—p 393–25.
6: 24 "No man can serve two masters."—f 201–5.
6: 24 "serve two masters."—pr 14–5.
6: 24 "hold to the one, and despise the other."—ph 182–13.
6: 25 Therefore I say unto you, Take no thought for your life, what ye shall eat, or what ye shall drink ; nor yet for your body, what ye shall put on. Is not the life more than meat, and the body than raiment ?—ph 165–*.
6: 25 "thought for your life, what ye shall eat, or what ye shall drink" ;—m 62–13.
6: 25 "for your body what ye shall put on,"—m 62–14.
6: 25 "Take no thought for your life, what ye shall eat, or what ye shall drink."—ph 170–16 ; g 530–8.
6: 25 "Take no thought for your life,"—f 228–20 ; p 365–8.
7: 1 "Judge not."—o 344–18.
7: 1 "Judge not, that ye be not judged."—t 443–12.
7: 2 "With what measure ye mete, it shall be measured to you again."—a 37–3.
7: 5 "First cast out the beam out of thine own eye ; and then shalt thou see clearly to cast out the mote out of thy brother's eye."—t 455–14.
7: 6 "Give not that which is holy unto the dogs, neither cast ye your pearls before swine."—b 272–17.

Matthew

7: 13 "wide is the gate, and broad is the way, that leadeth to destruction, and many there be which go in thereat."—t 451–12.
7: 16 "Do men gather grapes of thorns?"—g 539–23.
7: 19 "[It] is hewn down."—pr 6–28.
7: 20 Wherefore by their fruits ye shall know them.—fr 600–*.
7: 20 "By their fruits ye shall know them"—o 342–27.
7: 29 "as one having authority."—pr 14–30.
8: 10 "I have not found so great faith, no, not in Israel."—s 133–6.
8: 22 "Follow me ; and let the dead bury their dead."—o 355–10.
8: 29 "Art thou [Truth] come hither to torment us before the time?"—s 129–15.
9: 6 "the Son of man,"—r 482–16.
10: 8 Heal the sick!—a 37–30 ; s 138–29.
10: 26 "there is nothing covered that shall not be revealed."—pr 8–17.
10: 28 "Fear him which is able to destroy both soul and body in hell,"—ph 196–11.
10: 33 "Whosoever shall deny me before men, him will I also deny before my Father which is in heaven."—p 372–25.
11: 3 "Art thou he that should come?"—s 131–31 ; 133–2.
11: 4–6 "Go and show John again those things which ye do hear and see : the blind receive their sight and the lame walk, the lepers are cleansed, and the deaf hear, the dead are raised up, and the poor have the gospel preached to them. And blessed is he, whosoever shall not be offended in me."—s 132–4.
11: 19 "friend of publicans and sinners."—a 53–1.
11: 19 "wisdom is justified of her children."—b 317–10.
12: 13 "Stretch forth thine hand,"—p 398–14.
12: 13 "was restored whole, like as the other."—p 398–14.
12: 25 "knew their thoughts,"—sp 85–16.
12: 25 "kingdom divided against itself,"—p 388–19.
12: 25 "brought to desolation."—p 388–20.
12: 27 "If I by Beelzebub cast out devils, by whom do your children cast them out?"—p 422–2.
12: 29 "How can one enter into a strong man's house and spoil his goods, except he first bind the strong man?"—p 399–29.
12: 29 "the strong man,"—p 400–4 ; 400–7.
12: 33 "the tree is known by its fruit"—b 299–22.
12: 48 "Who is my mother, and who are my brethren,"—a 31–6.
12: 50 "For whosoever shall do the will of my Father which is in heaven, the same is my brother, and sister, and mother."—c 267–16.
13: 15 "This people's heart is waxed gross, and their ears are dull of hearing, and their eyes they have closed ; lest at any time they should see with their eyes, and hear with their ears, and should understand with their heart, and should be converted, and I should heal them."—o 350–18.
13: 33 The kingdom of heaven is like unto leaven, which a woman took, and hid in three measures of meal, till the whole was leavened.—s 107–*.
13: 33 "leaven, which a woman took, and hid in three measures of meal, till the whole was leavened,"—s 117–32.
13: 35 "secret from the foundation of the world,"—b 317–1.
13: 58 "because of their unbelief"—p 401–1.
15: 14 "If the blind lead the blind, both shall fall into the ditch."—f 223–18.
15: 19, 20 For out of the heart proceed evil thoughts, murders, adulteries, fornications, thefts, false witness, blasphemies : these are the things which defile a man.—an 100–*.
16: 3 "O ye hypocrites ! ye can discern the face of the sky ; but can ye not discern the signs of the times?"—sp 85–21.
16: 3 "Ye can discern the face of the sky ; but can ye not discern the signs of the times?"—g 509–31.
16: 13 "Whom do men say that I, the Son of man, am?"—s 136–11.
16: 14 "Some say that thou art John the Baptist ; some,

Matthew

Elias; and others, Jeremias, or one of the prophets." — s 136–14.
16 : 15 "But whom say ye that I am?" — s 137–9.
16 : 16 "Thou art the Christ, the Son of the living God !" —
s 137–17.
16 : 17 "Blessed art thou, Simon Bar-jona : for flesh and
blood hath not revealed it unto thee, but my
Father which is in heaven ;" — s 137–22.
16 : 18 "And I say also unto thee, That thou art Peter ; and
upon this rock [the meaning of the Greek word
petros, or stone] I will build my church ; and the
gates of hell [hades, the under-world, or the grave]
shall not prevail against it." — s 137–29.
16 : 23 "Get thee behind me, Satan." — pr 7–2.
16 : 23 "Thou art an offence unto me." — pr 6–25.
17 : 11 "Elias truly shall first come and restore all things."
— gl 585–13.
19 : 6 What therefore God hath joined together, let not
man put asunder. — m 56–*.
19 : 19 "Love thy neighbor as thyself ;" — s 138–29 ; b 340–25.
19 : 24 "easier for a camel to go through the eye of a
needle," — f 241–31 ; t 449–9.
20 : 16 "The last shall be first, and the first last," — s 116–8.
21 : 31 "The publicans and the harlots go into the kingdom
of God before you." — a 20–7.
21 : 42 "the stone which the builders rejected" — s 139–26.
21 : 42 "the head of the corner." — s 139–27.
21 : 44 "but on whomsoever it shall fall, it will grind him
to powder." — p 380–6.
22 : 14 "Many are called, but few are chosen." — a 27–25.
22 : 21 "unto Cæsar the things which are Cæsar's ; and
unto God the things that are God's." — a 20–1 ;
g 540–17.
22 : 29 "Ye do err, not knowing the Scriptures." — b 272–9.
22 : 30 In the resurrection they neither marry, nor are
given in marriage, but are as the angels of God
in heaven. — m 56–*.
22 : 30 "given in marriage" — m 69–11.
22 : 37 "love the Lord thy God with all thy heart, and with
all thy soul, and with all thy mind" — pr 9–17.
22 : 39 "Thou shalt love thy neighbor as thyself." — r 467–8.
23 : 9 "Call no man your father upon the earth : for one is
your Father, which is in heaven." — a 31–4.
23 : 23 "These ought ye to have done, and not to leave the
other undone." — sp 85–29.
23 : 27 "like unto whited sepulchres . . . full . . . of all
uncleanness." — pr 8–8.
24 : 21 "great tribulation such as was not since the beginning of the world ;" — s 129–13.
24 : 36 "but of that day and hour, knoweth no man." —
b 292–3.
25 : 12 "I know you not." — f 238–15.
25 : 21 "faithful over a few things," — b 323–17.
25 : 23 "Well done, good and faithful servant," — a 44–3.
25 : 23 "Thou hast been faithful over a few things, I will
make thee ruler over many," — ap 569–6.
26 : 26, 27 "As they were eating, Jesus took bread, and blessed
it and brake it, and gave it to the disciples, and
said, Take, eat ; this is my body. And he took the
cup, and gave thanks, and gave it to them saying,
Drink ye all of it." — a 32–15.
26 : 27 "Drink ye all of it." — a 33–17.
26 : 40 "Could ye not watch with me one hour?" — a 48–3.
26 : 52 "They that take the sword shall perish with the
sword." — g 542–18.
27 : 42 "He saved others ; himself he cannot save." — a 49–
29.
27 : 46 "My God, why hast thou forsaken me?" — a 50–8.
28 : 20 "Lo, I am with you alway, even unto the end of the
world." — t 446–22.
28 : 20 "Lo, I am with you alway," — b 317–13.

Mark

3 : 24 "If a kingdom be divided against itself, that kingdom cannot stand." — f 252–2.
4 : 14 "the sower" — b 272–13.
4 : 39 "Peace, be still." — s 144–22.
5 : 41 "Damsel, I say unto thee, arise !" — p 398–12.
6 : 50 "Be not afraid !" — p 410–30.
8 : 18 "Having eyes, see ye not?" — gl 586–5.
8 : 18 "Having ears, hear ye not?" — gl 585–3.
9 : 19 "O faithless generation," — s 148–2.
9 : 24 "Lord, I believe ; help thou mine unbelief !" — a 23–
27.
9 : 25 "Thou dumb and deaf spirit, I charge thee, come
out of him, and enter no more into him." —
p 398–2.
9 : 26 "the spirit [error] cried, and rent him sore and
came out of him, and he was as one dead," —
p 398–4.
10 : 27 "with God all things are possible," — f 232–9.
11 : 23, 24 For verily I say unto you, That whosoever shall say
unto this mountain, Be thou removed, and be thou
cast into the sea ; and shall not doubt in his heart,
but shall believe that those things which he saith

Mark

shall come to pass ; he shall have whatsoever he
saith. Therefore I say unto you, What things soever ye desire when ye pray, believe that ye receive them, and ye shall have them. — pr 1–*.
12 : 30 "love the Lord thy God with all thy heart, and with
all thy soul, and with all thy mind" — pr 9–17.
13 : 32 "knoweth no man . . . neither the Son, but the
Father." — sp 77–15.
13 : 32 "the Son but the Father ;" — f 233–12.
15 : 34 "Eloi, Eloi, lama sabachthani ?" — a 51–1.
15 : 34 "My God, why hast Thou forsaken me?" — a 50–8.
16 : 15 "Go ye into all the world, and preach the gospel to
every creature !" — a 37–29 ; s 138–27.
16 : 15 "Go ye into all the world, and preach the gospel," —
o 342–10.
16 : 15 "Preach the gospel to every creature." — p 418–27.
16 : 17, 18 And these signs shall follow them that believe : In
my name shall they cast out devils : they shall
speak with new tongues ; they shall take up serpents ; and if they drink any deadly thing, it shall
not hurt them ; they shall lay hands on the sick,
and they shall recover. — p 362–*.
16 : 17, 18 "These signs shall follow them that believe , . . .
they shall take up serpents, and if they drink any
deadly thing, it shall not hurt them. They shall
lay hands on the sick, and they shall recover." —
b 328–22.
16 : 17, 18 "These signs shall follow them that believe ; . . .
they shall lay hands on the sick, and they shall
recover." — a 38–10 ; o 359–26.
16 : 17 "These signs shall follow them that believe." — a 52–
28.
16 : 17 "them that believe" — a 38–14.
16 : 17 "They shall speak with new tongues." — o 349–22.
16 : 17 "new tongues ;" — f 210–1.
16 : 20 "with signs following." — pr 10–11.
16 : 20 "signs following." — s 110–29 ; 117–12.

Luke

1 : 33 "of his kingdom there shall be no end," — ap 565–15.
2 : 14 "on earth peace, good-will toward men." — s 150–7 ;
f 226–17.
2 : 49 "Father's business." — a 52–1.
4 : 18 To preach deliverance to the captives [of sense],
And recovering of sight to the blind,
To set at liberty them that are bruised. — pref xi–19.
6 : 38 "shall be measured to you again," — pr 5–11.
6 : 38 "and running over." — pr 5–12.
7 : 22 "Go your way, and tell John what things ye have
seen and heard ; how that the blind see, the lame
walk, the lepers are cleansed, the deaf hear, the
dead are raised, to the poor the gospel is preached."
— a 27–3.
7 : 34 "friend of publicans and sinners." — a 53–1.
7 : 42 "Which of them will love him most?" — p 363–18.
7 : 43 "He to whom he forgave most." — p 363–20.
7 : 48 "Thy sins are forgiven." — p 363–23.
8 : 5 "the fowls of the air," — f 237–12.
8 : 15 "honest and good heart" — b 272–6.
8 : 45 "Who touched me?" — sp 86–1.
8 : 45 "The multitude throng thee." — sp 86–3.
8 : 52 "she is not dead, but sleepeth," — p 398–11.
9 : 9 "John have I beheaded : but who is this?" — s 136–27.
9 : 29 "white and glistering," — c 267–26.
10 : 17 "Even the devils are subject unto us through thy
name." — a 49–5.
10 : 19 Behold, I give unto you power . . . over all the
power of the enemy : and nothing shall by any
means hurt you. — p 438–5.
10 : 21 "I thank Thee, O Father, Lord of heaven and earth,
that Thou hast hid these things from the wise and
prudent, and hast revealed them unto babes : even
so, Father, for so it seemed good in Thy sight." —
s 131–19.
11 : 14 "it came to pass, when the devil was gone out. the
dumb spake." — s 135–16.
11 : 15 "He casteth out devils through Beelzebub," — a 52–32.
12 : 22 "Take no thought . . . for the body." — p 382–11.
12 : 32 "Fear not, little flock ; for it is your Father's good
pleasure to give you the kingdom." — p 442–27.
13 : 16 "whom Satan hath bound," — r 495–9.
14 : 10 "go up higher." — pr 11–10.
17 : 21 "The kingdom of God is within you ;" — r 476–29 ;
ap 573–32.
17 : 21 "is within you," — ap 576–21.
18 : 8 "When the Son of man cometh, shall he find faith
on the earth?" — s 132–26.
18 : 11 "not as other men" — pr 9–1.
18 : 17 "Whosoever shall not receive the kingdom of God
as a little child, shall in no wise enter therein."
— p 382–22.
19 : 13 "Occupy till I come !" — a 22–13.
20 : 34, 35 "The children of this world marry, and are given
in marriage : But they which shall be accounted
worthy to obtain that world, and the resurrection

Luke

from the dead, neither marry, nor are given in marriage." — *m* 69–26.

20 : 35   "given in marriage" — *m* 69–11.

22 : 18   *For I say unto you, I will not drink of the fruit of the vine, until the kingdom of God shall come.* — *a* 18–*.

22 : 42   "Not my will, but Thine, be done !" — *a* 33–19.

24 : 39   "Spirit hath not flesh and bones, as ye see me have." — *a* 45–27.

24 : 39   "flesh and bones." — *b* 313–30.

John

1 : 3   *All things were made by Him ; and without Him was not anything made that was made.* — *f* 231–31 ; *r* 480–*.

1 : 3   "and without Him [the *logos*, or *word*] was not anything made that was made." — *g* 525–18.

1 : 3   "was not anything made that was made." — *b* 335–11.

1 : 3   "that was made." — *c* 267–11.

1 : 4   *In Him was life ; and the life was the light of men.* — *g* 501–*.

1 : 4   "the light of men." — *ap* 561–29.

1 : 5   "shineth in darkness, and the darkness comprehended it not." — *b* 325–31.

1 : 6, 8   "There was a man sent from God . . . to bear witness to that Light." — *ap* 561–30.

1 : 11   "He came unto his own, and his own received him not." — *s* 131–17.

1 : 14   "The Word was made flesh." — *o* 350–24.

1 : 29   "the Lamb of God ;" — *s* 132–31.

2 : 19   "Destroy this temple, and in three days I will raise it up." — *a* 27–12 ; *b* 314–14 ; *r* 494–2.

3 : 8   "The wind [*pneuma*] bloweth where it listeth. . . . So is every one that is born of the Spirit [*pneuma*]." — *gl* 598–3.

3 : 8   "tell whence it cometh." — *sp* 78–28.

4 : 23   "The hour cometh, and now is, when the true worshippers shall worship the Father in spirit and in truth." — *a* 31–26 ; *g* 93–5.

4 : 23   "The true worshippers shall worship the Father in spirit and in truth." — *s* 140–20.

4 : 29   "Come, see a man, which told me all things that ever I did : is not this the Christ ?" — *sp* 85–12.

4 : 29   "Is not this the Christ ?" — *s* 133–4.

5 : 14   "Thou art whole !" — *p* 391–5.

5 : 17   "My Father worketh hitherto, and I work." — *sp* 79–19.

5 : 18   "himself equal with God," — *s* 133–24.

5 : 19   "Then answered Jesus and said unto them : Verily, verily I say unto you, the Son can do nothing of himself, but what he seeth the Father do : for what things soever He doeth, these also doeth the Son likewise." — *b* 305–15.

5 : 26   "Life in Himself," — *o* 357–29.

6 : 33 }
6 : 50 }   "which cometh down from heaven," — *a* 35–26.

6 : 63   "It is the spirit that quickeneth ; the flesh profiteth nothing." — *o* 356–15.

6 : 70   "Have not I chosen you twelve, and one of you is a devil." — *g* 554–22.

7 : 16, 17   "My doctrine is not mine, but His that sent me. If any man will do His will, he shall know of the doctrine, whether it be of God, or whether I speak of myself." — *s* 109–28.

7 : 23   "every whit whole." — *p* 371–31.

7 : 24   "judge righteous judgment," — *t* 444–18.

8 : 11   "Go, and sin no more." — *pr* 11–4.

8 : 32   Ye shall know the truth, and the truth shall make you free. — iii–*.

8 : 43, 44   "Why do ye not understand my speech? Even because ye cannot hear my word. Ye are of your father, the devil [evil], and the lusts of your father ye will do. He was a murderer from the beginning, and abode not in the truth, because there is no truth in him. When he speaketh a lie, he speaketh of his own : for he is a liar, and the father of it." — *b* 292–20.

8 : 44   "He was a murderer from the beginning, . . . he is a liar and the father of it." — *ap* 580–30.

8 : 44   "a murderer from the beginning." — *sp* 89–31 ; *p* 441–32 ; *g* 539–3.

8 : 44   "Ye are of your father, the devil." — *g* 554–25.

8 : 44   "He is a liar, and the father of it." — *g* 554–21.

8 : 44   "a liar, and the father of it." — *o* 357–7.

8 : 45, 46   *And because I tell you the truth, ye believe me not. Which of you convinceth me of sin ? And if I say the truth, why do ye not believe me ?* — *o* 341–*.

8 : 51, 52   *Verily, verily, I say unto you, If a man keep my saying, he shall never see death. Then said the Jews unto him, Now we know that thou hast a devil.* — *sp* 70–*.

8 : 51   "If a man keep my saying, he shall never see death !" — *f* 217–12 ; *p* 428–7 ; 429–31 ; 438–7.

8 : 58   "Before Abraham was, I am ;" — *b* 333–29.

John

10 : 13   "The hireling fleeth, because he is an hireling, and careth not for the sheep." — *t* 464–26.

10 : 30   "I and my Father are one." — *a* 26–12 ; *b* 315–3 ; 333–29 ; *o* 361–15.

11 : 11   "Our friend Lazarus sleepeth ; but I go, that I may awake him out of sleep." — *sp* 75–12.

11 : 25   "the resurrection and the life" — *a* 31–16 ; *b* 292–7.

11 : 26   "Whosoever liveth and believeth in me shall never die," — *ph* 170–10 ; *b* 315–1 ; (*see also b* 324–32).

11 : 42   "I knew that Thou hearest me always ;" — *s* 134–26.

12 : 38   "the arm of the Lord" — *a* 24–11.

14 : 6   "I am the way, the truth, and the life." — 26–11 ; *b* 320–3.

14 : 6   "the way, the truth, and the life," — *o* 353–10.

14 : 6   "I am the way." — *b* 286–11.

14 : 6   "the way." — *a* 30–13 ; 39–15 ; 46–25 ; *r* 482–15 ; *g* 535–18.

14 : 6   "No man cometh unto the Father [the divine Principle of being] but by me," — *b* 286–9.

14 : 12   "He that believeth on me, the works that I do shall he do also ; . . . because I go unto my Father," — *pr* 14–19.

14 : 12   "He that believeth on me, the works that I do shall he do also." — *a* 42–30 ; 52–27 ; *sp* 93–4 ; *b* 326–4.

14 : 15   "If ye love me, keep my commandments." — *pr* 4–11 ; *a* 25–20 ; *f* 241–21.

14 : 16   "He shall give you another Comforter, that he may abide with you *forever*." — *a* 55–27.

14 : 26   "But the Comforter . . . shall teach you all things." — *c* 271–20.

14 : 28   "My Father is greater than I." — *b* 333–30.

15 : 18   "If the world hate you, ye know that it hated me before it hated you ;" — *b* 317–12.

15 : 25   "They hated me without a cause." — *ap* 564–27.

16 : 2, 3   "They shall put you out of the synagogues ; yea, the time cometh, that whosoever killeth you will think that he doeth God service ; and these things will they do unto you, because they have not known the Father nor me." — *a* 31–30.

17 : 3   "This is life eternal, that they might know Thee, the only true God, and Jesus Christ, whom Thou hast sent." — *p* 410–7.

17 : 3   "This is life eternal," — *p* 410–4.

17 : 20   "Neither pray I for these alone, but for them also which shall believe on me [understand me] through their word." — *b* 271–17.

17 : 20   "through their word." — *a* 38–20.

18 : 11   "Put up thy sword." — *a* 48–23.

18 : 38   "What is Truth," — *a* 48–26 ; *f* 223–14.

19 : 6, 7   "Crucify him, crucify him . . . by our law he ought to die, because he made himself the Son of God." — *sp* 94–9.

19 : 6   "Crucify him !" — *s* 134–2.

19 : 7   "He made himself the Son of God," — *f* 203–9.

19 : 24   "They parted my raiment among them, and for my vesture they did cast lots." — *f* 242–23.

19 : 30   "He bowed his head, and gave up the ghost ;" — *gl* 598–11.

Acts

16 : 31   "Believe . . . and thou shalt be saved !" — *a* 23–29.

17 : 23   "to the unknown God" — *p* 428–15 ; *gl* 596–7.

17 : 23   "Whom therefore ye ignorantly worship, Him declare I unto you." — *gl* 596–8.

17 : 23   "ignorantly worship," — *p* 428–16.

17 : 28   "For in Him we live, and move, and have our being." — *o* 361–19 ; *f* 208–5.

17 : 28   "live, and move, and have our being," — *g* 536–13.

17 : 28   "For we are also His offspring." — *b* 332–8.

20 : 24   "None of these things move me." — *o* 343–10.

22 : 28   "I was free born." — *f* 227–17.

23 : 3   "Sittest thou to judge . . . after the law, and commandest . . . to be smitten contrary to the law?" — *p* 435–29.

23 : 29   "worthy of death, or of bonds." — *p* 434–29.

24 : 25   "Go thy way for this time ; when I have a convenient season I will call for thee." — *a* 40–6.

26 : 31   "worthy of death, or of bonds." — *p* 434–29.

Romans

1 : 20   "For the invisible things of Him, from the creation of the world, are clearly seen, being understood by the things that are made." — *r* 479–30.

2 : 5   "wrath against the day of wrath." — *b* 339–14.

2 : 23   "Through breaking the law, dishonorest thou God?" — *o* 349–5.

3 : 4   "Let God be true, but every [material] man a liar." — *r* 471–20.

3 : 4   "but every [mortal] man a liar." — *s* 113–24.

5 : 10   "For if, when we were enemies, we were reconciled to God by the [seeming] death of His Son, much more, being reconciled, we shall be saved by his life." — *a* 45–10.

5 : 20   "much more abound." — *f* 202–26.

7 : 19   "The good that I would, I do not : but the evil which I would not, *that I do.*" — *c* 263–17.

Romans

8: 2 "The law of the Spirit of life in Christ Jesus hath made me free from the law of sin and death."— *f* 244–11.

8: 6 "To be spiritually minded is life."— *sp* 95–6.

8: 7– 9 "The carnal mind is enmity against God ; for it is not subject to the law of God, neither indeed can be. So then they that are in the flesh cannot please God. But ye are not in the flesh, but in the Spirit, if so be that the spirit of God dwell in you."— *g* 534–18.

8: 7 "The carnal mind is enmity against God."— *s* 131–9.

8: 7 "neither indeed can be ;"— *r* 478–31.

8: 11 *But if the spirit of Him that raised up Jesus from the dead dwell in you, He that raised up Christ from the dead shall also quicken your mortal bodies by His spirit that dwelleth in you.— o* 341–*.

8: 21 "glorious liberty of the children of God,"— *f* 227–24.

8: 22, 23 *For we know that the whole creation groaneth and travaileth in pain together until now. And not only they, but ourselves also, which have the firstfruits of the Spirit, even we ourselves groan within ourselves, waiting for the adoption, to wit, the redemption of our body.— c* 255–*.

8: 28 "All things work together for good to them that love God,"— *t* 444–4.

8: 31 "If God be for us, who can be against us?"— *f* 238– 10.

8: 38, 39 "Neither death, nor life, . . . nor things present, nor things to come, nor height, nor depth, nor any other creature, shall be able to separate us from the love of God."— *b* 304–5.

10: 2 "a zeal . . . not according to knowledge"— *pr* 7– 11.

10: 14, 15 "How shall they hear without a preacher? and how shall they preach, except they be sent?"— *c* 271– 31.

11: 34 "the mind of the Lord,"— *b* 291–18.

12: 1 "Present your bodies a living sacrifice, holy, acceptable unto God, which is your reasonable service."— *b* 325–21.

12: 1 "holy, acceptable unto God,"— *a* 34–4.

13: 1 "powers that be."— *f* 249–9.

13: 10 "is the fulfilling of the law,"— *p* 388–10.

13: 12 "the night is far spent, the day is at hand"— *ph* 174–12.

14: 1 "doubtful disputations."— *o* 342–1.

14: 16 "be evil spoken of,"— *pr* 4–25.

I Corinthians

1: 17 *For Christ sent me not to baptize, but to preach the gospel.— a* 18–*.

2: 2 "For I determined not to know anything among you, save Jesus Christ, and him crucified."— *ph* 200–25.

2: 2 "Christ, and him crucified."— *a* 39–7.

2: 9 "eye hath not seen nor ear heard."— *t* 459–2.

2: 9 "eye hath not seen,"— *g* 554–1.

7: 34 "She that is married careth. . .how she may please her husband,"— *m* 58–31.

8: 5 "gods many and lords many."— *b* 280–16 ; *gl* 580–8.

8: 5 "gods many,"— *p* 388–10.

10: 25 "asking no question for conscience sake."— *f* 222–30.

11: 26 "As often as ye eat this bread, and drink this cup, ye do show the Lord's death till he come."— *a* 31–22.

13: 5 "seeketh not her own."— *g* 538–1.

13: 7 "hopeth all things, endureth all things,"— *pref* xii–22.

15: 14 "If Christ [Truth] be not risen, then is our preaching vain."— *b* 324–27.

15: 22 "As in Adam [error] all die, even so in Christ [Truth] shall all be made alive."— *g* 545–31.

15: 26 "The last enemy that shall be destroyed is death"— *p* 427–19.

15: 26 "the last enemy that shall be destroyed,"— *f* 210–9.

15: 50 "Flesh and blood cannot inherit the kingdom of God."— *b* 321–4.

15: 52 "in the twinkling of an eye,"— *b* 291–6.

15: 54 "when this corruptible shall have put on incorruption, and this mortal shall have put on immortality, then shall be brought to pass the saying that is written, Death is swallowed up in victory." — *s* 164–25 ; *r* 496–24.

15: 54 "put on immortality."— *c* 262–8.

15: 55 "Where is thy victory?"— *r* 496–23.

15: 56 "The sting of death is sin ; and the strength of sin is the law,"— *r* 496–20.

II Corinthians

3: 17 "Where the Spirit of the Lord is, there is liberty." — *f* 227–18 ; *r* 481–4.

4: 4 "the god of this world,"— *an* 103–3.

5: 1 "eternal in the heavens."— *t* 454–9.

5: 8 "willing rather to be absent from the body, and to be present with the Lord."— *f* 216–29 ; *p* 383–10 ; *gl* 581–25.

II Corinthians

5: 8 "absent from the body"— *pr* 14–3.

5: 8 "present with the Lord"— *pr* 14–4, 6.

5: 8 "with the Lord"— *pr* 14–9.

5: 16 "Henceforth know we no man after the flesh !"— *f* 217–31.

5: 17 "all things are become new."— *f* 201–9.

6: 2 "Behold, *now* is the accepted time ; behold, *now* is the day of salvation,"— *sp* 93–7.

6: 2 "*Now*," cried the apostle, "is the accepted time ; behold, *now* is the day of salvation,"— *a* 39–18.

6: 14 "What communion hath light with darkness?— *g* 539–24.

6: 15 And what concord hath Christ with Belial?"— *f* 216– 26 ; *g* 539–25.

6: 17 "Come out from among them, and be ye separate," — *f* 238–6.

Galatians

1: 11, 12 *But I certify you, brethren, that the gospel which was preached of me is not after man. For I neither received it of man, neither was I taught it, but by the revelation of Jesus Christ.— s* 107–*.

1: 15, 16 "But when it pleased God, who separated me from my mother's womb, and called me by His grace, . . . I conferred not with flesh and blood."— *r* 478–27.

5: 7 "Who did hinder you, that ye should not obey the truth?"— *b* 326–21.

5: 16 "Walk in the Spirit, and ye shall not fulfil the lust of the flesh."— *f* 223–2.

5: 17 "The flesh lusteth against the Spirit, and the Spirit against the flesh."— *o* 347–1.

5: 17 "flesh lusteth against the Spirit."— *ph* 167–20.

5: 19 "Now the works of the flesh are manifest, which are these ; Adultery, fornication, uncleanness, lasciviousness,— *an* 106–20.

5: 20, 21 idolatry, *witchcraft*, hatred, variance, emulations, wrath, strife, seditions, heresies, envyings, murders, drunkenness, revellings and such like : of the which I tell you before, as I have also told you in time past, that they which do such things shall not inherit the kingdom of God.— *an* 106–22.

5: 22, 23 But the fruit of the Spirit is love, joy, peace, longsuffering, gentleness, goodness, faith, meekness, temperance : against such there is no law."— *an* 106–26.

5: 24 *And they that are Christ's have crucified the flesh with the affections and lusts.— a* 18–*.

6: 3 "For if a man think himself to be something, when he is nothing, he deceiveth himself."— *o* 345–26.

6: 7 "Whatsoever a man soweth, that shall he also reap." *p* 405–17 ; *g* 537–13.

6: 9 "not be weary in well doing."— *sp* 79–29.

Ephesians

2: 12 "having no hope, and without God in the world ;" — *r* 486–31.

3: 7 "the gift of the grace of God given unto me by the effectual working of His power."— *s* 108–3.

4: 13 "we all come in the unity of the faith, and of the knowledge of the Son of God, unto a perfect man, unto the measure of the stature of the fulness of Christ"— *g* 519–18.

6: 12 "spiritual wickedness in high places."— *ap* 563–30.

Philippians

2: 5 "Let this Mind be in you, which was also in Christ Jesus."— *b* 276–8.

2: 5 "Mind . . . which was also in Christ Jesus"— *f* 243–10.

2: 12 "Work out your own salvation with fear and trembling,"— *sp* 99–5 ; *p* 442–25.

2: 12 "Work out your own salvation,"— *a* 22–11.

2: 12 "own salvation, with fear and trembling,"— *a* 23–26.

2: 13 "for it is God which worketh in you both to will and to do of His good pleasure."— *sp* 99–7.

3: 13 "forgetting those things which are behind."— *o* 353–23.

Colossians

1: 10 *That ye might walk worthy of the Lord unto all pleasing, being fruitful in every good work, and increasing in the knowledge of God.— fr* 600–*.

3: 3 "hid with Christ in God,"— *b* 325–17 ; *t* 445–14.

3: 4 "When Christ, who is our life, shall appear [be manifested], then shall ye also appear [be manifested] with him in glory."— *b* 325–10.

3: 9 "put off the old man."— *ph* 172–22.

3: 9 "off the old man with his deeds,"— *c* 262–7.

I Thessalonians

4: 3 "For this is the will of God."— *gl* 597–22.

5: 17 "pray without ceasing."— *pr* 15–21.

5: 19, 20 "Quench not the Spirit. Despise not prophesyings."— *r* 490–19.

5: 21 "prove all things ; [and] hold fast that which is good."— *t* 464–19.

II Thessalonians
3 : 13   "be not weary in well doing." — a 22–14.

I Timothy
2 : 5   "There is one God, and one mediator between God and men, the man Christ Jesus." — b 332–16.

II Timothy
2 : 12   "he also will deny us." — pr 6–2.

4 : 2   "Reprove, rebuke, exhort with all longsuffering and doctrine." — t 443–21.

4 : 7   "I have fought a good fight . . . I have kept the faith," — a 21–2.

Hebrews
1 : 3   "the brightness of His [God's] glory, and the express [expressed] image of His person [infinite Mind]." — b 313–10.

1 : 3   "Who, being a brightness from His glory, and an image of His being." — b 313–21.
     (The above reference is from the translation of the late Rev. George R. Noyes, D.D.)

1 : 3   "express image" — b 313–12.

1 : 9   "loved righteousness and hated iniquity." — b 313–18.

1 : 9   Therefore God, even thy God, hath anointed thee With the oil of gladness above thy fellows. — b 313–7.

4 : 9   "There remaineth therefore a rest to the people of God." — b 288–18.

4 : 12   "the joints and marrow," — p 423–13.

8 : 5   "according to the pattern showed to thee in the mount." — f 236–16.

10 : 19   "to enter into the holiest," — r 481–6.

11 : 1   "The substance of things hoped for, the evidence of things not seen." — r 468–20.

11 : 1   "the substance of things hoped for." — b 279–4.

11 : 10   "a city which hath foundations." — ap 575–12.

11 : 10   "whose builder and maker is God." — p 428–13.

11 : 38   "of whom the world was not worthy," — a 28–30.

12 : 1   "Let us lay aside every weight, and the sin which doth so easily beset us, and let us run with patience the race that is set before us ;" — a 20–27.

12 : 6   "Whom the Lord loveth He chasteneth." — f 241–1.

13 : 2   "angels unawares." — b 299–17.

13 : 8   "the same yesterday, and to-day, and forever ;" — pr 2–32 ; s 112–19 ; f 249–18 ; b 283–7 ; g 546–4.

James
1 : 4   "have her perfect work." — t 454–24.

1 : 12   "Blessed is the man that endureth [overcometh] temptation : for when he is tried, [proved faithful], he shall receive the crown of life, which the Lord hath promised to them that love him." — c 267–28.

1 : 13   "God cannot be tempted with evil, neither tempteth He any man." — g 527–21.

1 : 27   "Pure religion and undefiled before God and the Father, is this, To visit the fatherless and widows in their affliction, and to keep himself unspotted from the world." — m 64–4.

2 : 18   "Show me thy faith without thy works, and I will show thee my faith by my works." — o 343–4 ; r 487–25.

2 : 26   "Faith without works is dead." — a 23–15.

3 : 11   "Doth a fountain send forth at the same place sweet water and bitter ?" — b 287–12.

4 : 3   "Ye ask, and receive not, because ye ask amiss, that ye may consume it upon your lusts." — pr 10–27.

4 : 3   "ye ask amiss." — pr 10–32.

5 : 15   "The prayer of faith shall save the sick," — pr 12–1.

I Peter
4 : 8   "cover the multitude of sins." — pr 8–19.

5 : 8   "adversary." — gl 581–2.

II Peter
3 : 8   "one day is with the Lord as a thousand years." — g 504–22 ; gl 598–21.

I John
1 : 1, 3   That which was from the beginning, which we have heard, which we have seen with our eyes, which we have looked upon, and our hands have handled, of the Word of life, . . . That which we have seen and heard declare we unto you, that ye also may have fellowship with us: and truly our fellowship is with the Father, and with His Son Jesus Christ. — b 268–*.

3 : 8   "destroy the works of the devil." — pr 5–30 ; r 474–30.

3 : 23   "Love one another" — ap 572–6.

4 : 8   "God is love." — pr 6–17 ; b 320–1.

4 : 18   "There is no fear in Love, but perfect Love casteth out fear. . . . He that feareth is not made perfect in Love." — p 410–18.

4 : 18   "perfect Love casteth out fear." — p 373–18 ; 406–9.

4 : 20   "He that loveth not his brother whom he hath seen, how can he love God whom he hath not seen ?" — p 366–14.

Revelation
1 : 3   Blessed is he that readeth, and they that hear the words of this prophecy, and keep those things which are written therein : for the time is at hand. — ap 558–*.

1 : 6   "kings and priests unto God." — s 141–20.

1 : 17, 18   "I am the first and the last : I am he that liveth, and was dead [not understood] ; and, behold, I am alive for evermore, — b 334–25.

3 : 7, 8   These things saith He that is holy, He that is true, He that hath the key of David, He that openeth, and no man shutteth ; and shutteth, and no man openeth ; I know thy works : behold, I have set before thee an open door, and no man can shut it. — k 499–* ; gl 579–*.

5 : 5   "the lion of the tribe of Juda," — g 514–10.

10 : 1, 2   And I saw another mighty angel come down from heaven, clothed with a cloud : and a rainbow was upon his head, and his face was as it were the sun, and his feet as pillars of fire : and he had in his hand a little book open : and he set his right foot upon the sea, and his left foot on the earth. — ap 558–3.

10 : 2   "a little book," — ap 559–1.

10 : 2   "right foot" — ap 559–3.

10 : 3   "as when a lion roareth."   ap 559–11.

10 : 3   "seven thunders" — ap 559–13.

10 : 8, 9   "Go and take the little book. . . . Take it, and eat it up ; and it shall make thy belly bitter, but it shall be in thy mouth sweet as honey." — ap 559–17.

12 : 1   And there appeared a great wonder in heaven ; a woman clothed with the sun, and the moon under her feet, and upon her head a crown of twelve stars. — ap 560–6.

12 : 2   And she being with child cried, travailing in birth, and pained to be delivered. — ap 562–22.

12 : 3   And there appeared another wonder in heaven ; and behold a great red dragon, having seven heads and ten horns, and seven crowns upon his heads. — ap 562–29.

12 : 4   And his tail drew the third part of the stars of heaven, and did cast them to the earth : and the dragon stood before the woman which was ready to be delivered, for to devour her child as soon as it was born. — ap 563–23.

12 : 5   And she brought forth a man child, who was to rule all nations with a rod of iron : and her child was caught up unto God, and to His throne. — ap 565–6.

12 : 6   And the woman fled into the wilderness, where she hath a place prepared of God. — ap 565–29.

12 : 7, 8   And there was war in heaven : Michael and his angels fought against the dragon ; and the dragon fought, and his angels, and prevailed not ; neither was their place found any more in heaven. — ap 566–25.

12 : 9   And the great dragon was cast out, that old serpent, called the devil, and Satan, which deceiveth the whole world : he was cast out into the earth, and his angels were cast out with him. — ap 567–14.

12 : 10–12   And I heard a loud voice saying in heaven, Now is come salvation, and strength, and the kingdom of our God, and the power of His Christ : for the accuser of our brethren is cast down, which accused them before our God day and night. And they overcame him by the blood of the Lamb, and by the word of their testimony ; and they loved not their lives unto the death. Therefore rejoice, ye heavens, and ye that dwell in them. Woe to the inhabiters of the earth and of the sea ! for the devil is come down unto you, having great wrath, because he knoweth that he hath but a short time. — ap 568–13.

12 : 13   And when the dragon saw that he was cast unto the earth, he persecuted the woman which brought forth the man child. — ap 569–29.

12 : 13   "cast unto the earth" — ap 567–23.

12 : 15, 16   And the serpent cast out of his mouth water as a flood, after the woman, that he might cause her to be carried away of the flood. And the earth helped the woman, and the earth opened her mouth, and swallowed up the flood which the dragon cast out of his mouth. — ap 570–8.

13 : 8   "the Lamb slain from the foundation of the world," — b 334–21.

19 : 17   "angel standing in the sun." — ap 561–8.

20 : 6   "On such the second death hath no power." — b 290–14.

20 : 6   "the second death hath no power." — sp 77–12.

21 : 1   "And I saw a new heaven and a new earth : for the first heaven and the first earth were passed away ; and there was no more sea." — g 536–2 ; ap 572–20.

21 : 1   "a new heaven and a new earth." — sp 91–1.

21 : 2   New Jerusalem, coming down from God, out of heaven," — ap 574–13.

Revelation

21 : 2   "down from God, out of heaven,"— *ap* 575–8.

21 : 9   And there came unto me one of the seven angels which had the seven vials full of the seven last plagues, and talked with me, saying, Come hither, I will show thee the bride, the Lamb's wife.— *ap* 574–6.

21 : 9   "the bride"— *ap* 561–13.

21 : 14 "the Lamb"— *ap* 561–13.

21 : 16 "lieth foursquare."— *ap* 574–16 ; 575–8.

21 : 22 And I saw no temple therein : for the Lord God Almighty and the Lamb are the temple of it.— *ap* 576–10.

21 : 22 "no temple [body] therein"— *ap* 576–20.

Revelation

21 : 23 "is the light thereof."— *ap* 558–15.

21 : 25 "and the gates of it shall not be shut at all by day : for there shall be no night there."— *ap* 575–19.

21 : 27 "defileth, . . . or maketh a lie."— *ap* 577–26.

21 : 27 "worketh abomination or maketh a lie."— *gl* 588–4.

22 : 2   "tree of life,"— *p* 426–13.

22 : 2   "The leaves of the tree were for the healing of the nations."— *p* 406–1.

22 : 5   "there shall be no night there."— *gl* 584–7.

22 : 5   "no night there."— *r* 475–1.

22 : 17 "The Spirit and the bride say, Come ! . . . and whosoever will, let him take the water of life freely."— *g* 548–1.

THE · PLIMPTON · PRESS · NORWOOD · MASS · U · S · A